LAW FLIX

At the end of most chapters you can find a reference to a Hollywood film, one that could be used to study and understand the concepts presented in the chapter. For example, what better film for understanding insurance law than Billy Wilder's *Double Indemnity*? And you can find a clip on insurable interest in West's Digital Video Library (**http://wdvl.westbuslaw.com**). Or you can assign the students the enviable task of watching the movie and determining the insurance law issues. Or, for contract formation you can watch another clip from *Midnight Run* and witness the great Robert DeNiro playing a bounty hunter who is trying to negotiate a binding contract with a bailbondsman. There is offer, counteroffer, statute of frauds, and good fun all in a short clip to get the students involved and thinking.

Midnight Run (1988) (R)

Is the contract Robert DeNiro has for bringing in Charles Grodin, an embezzler, legal? Discuss the issues of consideration and ethics as the bail bondsman puts another bounty hunter on the case and DeNiro flees from law enforcement agents in order to collect his fee. And finally, discuss the legality of DeNiro's acceptance of money from Grodin and his release of Grodin at the end of the movie.

For movie clips that illustrate business law concepts, see LawFlix at **http://wdvl.westbuslaw.com.**

BUSINESS LAW

PRINCIPLES FOR TODAY'S COMMERCIAL ENVIRONMENT

SECOND EDITION

DAVID P. TWOMEY

Professor of Law
Carroll School of Management
Boston College
Member of the Massachusetts and Florida Bars

MARIANNE MOODY JENNINGS

Professor of Legal and Ethical Studies
W. P. Carey School of Business
Arizona State University
Member of the Arizona Bar

Australia · Brazil · Canada · Mexico · Singapore · Spain · United Kingdom · United States

Business Law: Principles for Today's Commercial Environment, 2e
David P. Twomey, Marianne Moody Jennings

VP/Editorial Director:
Jack W. Calhoun

Publisher:
Rob Dewey

Acquisitions Editor:
Steven H. Silverstein, Esq.

Senior Developmental Editor:
Bob Sandman

Executive Marketing Manager:
Lisa L. Lysne

Content Project Manager:
Colleen A. Farmer

Technology Project Manager:
Pam Wallace

Manufacturing Coordinator:
Charlene Taylor

Production House:
LEAP Publishing Services, Inc.

Compositor:
ICC Macmillan Inc.

Printer:
Quebecor World
Versailles, KY

Art Director:
Michelle Kunkler

Internal Designer:
Design Matters
Nick and Diane Gliebe

Cover Designer:
Design Matters
Nick and Diane Gliebe

Cover Images:
© Jeremy Walker/The Image Bank/Getty Images

Part Opener Image:
© DC Productions/Getty Images, Inc.

Chapter Opener Image:
© Akira Kaede/Getty Images, Inc.

Printed in the United States of America
1 2 3 4 5 11 10 09 08 07

Student Edition ISBN 13:
978-0-324-30394-0
Student Edition ISBN 10:
0-324-30394-7

Library of Congress Control Number:
2006940534

For more information about our products, contact us at:

Thomson Learning
Academic Resource Center
1-800-423-0563

Thomson Higher Education
5191 Natorp Boulevard
Mason, Ohio 45040
USA

BRIEF CONTENTS

CONTENTS

PART 6

AGENCY AND EMPLOYMENT

PREFACE

Regardless of the day of the week, newspapers and magazines constantly carry stories about law and business together. The former chairwoman of the Hewlett-Packard (HP) board admitted that the board hired private investigators to obtain the phone records of HP board members because she felt there was a "snitch" among them. The private investigators used "pretexting," the act of pretending to be the directors themselves to get the records. HP is under state and federal investigation, executives were subpoenaed by Congress, and some were indicted. BP, the international energy company, is dealing with a burst pipeline and the damage to Alaska, an accident that followed years of warning about corrosion in BP pipes near Prudhoe Bay, Alaska. Fannie Mae, the federal mortgage company, was forced to remove its CEO and make a $7 billion restatement on its financials after auditors uncovered earnings manipulation. And all of these events are years after we saw the financial collapses of Enron, WorldCom, HealthSouth, and too many others.

Why, we even lost Martha Stewart to a five-month prison sentence for her lies to prosecutors about how she managed to sell her shares of ImClone stock just before the company announced some problems with its new key drug. Martha Stewart has done much for our homes and cooking, but her case can teach us much more about obstruction of justice, regulatory consent decrees, jury *voir dire* and selection, appellate courts, and reversible error. Martha Stewart's legal difficulties presented a richness of legal issues each step of the way. What happened when she sold those shares? Did she indeed violate the law? Was it insider trading? What are the shareholders' rights? What about the creditors?

And there are so many other companies, here in the United States and around the world. Did Tyco, Adelphia, and Parmalat company officers intentionally overstate earnings? If so, are they criminally liable? And who is responsible for crimes committed by companies? As major corporations have continued to experience criminal, legal, and ethical difficulties, we can see how important it is for business managers to understand the law and the foundations of ethics. When a manager has a void in knowledge on law and ethics, running a company can be tricky business. Microsoft Corporation learned the intricacies of federal antitrust laws while its charges of monopolization were tried in federal court. Wall Street analysts learned that internal e-mails are discoverable and admissible as evidence. And when those e-mails to co-workers and friends are inconsistent with public statements those analysts made about companies and the value of their stocks, there is more than embarrassment. The analysts' companies learned through nearly one billion dollars in fines that hard lesson about e-mails and the law.

When an entrepreneur is struggling with the decision of whether to incorporate or create an LLC, or the shareholders of Disney are grappling with issues about their rights when their CEO makes a bad decision, the law is there. No business or manager can hope to succeed without an understanding of the laws and legal environment of business. Students in business must be prepared with both knowledge of the law and the skill of applying it in the business setting. We learn principles and application through interaction with examples and by working our way through dilemmas, issues, and problems. This edition of *Business Law: Principles for Today's Commercial Environment* enhances the learning process while still providing a detailed and rigorous case approach.

Features of the Text

The features of this text make the business and law connection easily understood and offer students clarity for grasping the often challenging complexities of law. The features are summarized in the following sections, which offer an overview of this edition.

Sports and Entertainment Law—New!

New to this edition is a feature that is sure to engage students. Using pop culture, the book teaches students about law and ethics. Kate Moss lost an endorsement contract after a video surfaced in which she was shown to be using cocaine. Can contracts be terminated because of public behavior? Who won't learn what obstruction of justice is if they learn it through Martha Stewart's conduct? Was the clause in John Lennon's will, one that said anyone who contested the will lost his or her inheritance, valid? And what about baseball fans who lease space on rooftops to watch baseball games in stadiums across the way? And all without paying? What are their rights? What are the rights of the teams and stadium owners? And what happens when the yacht company that sold Tiger Woods his yacht uses Tiger's names in its ads and without his permission? Students have the chance to explore the law through these examples of sports figures' and entertainers' brushes with the law.

Law Flix—New!

At the end of most chapters you can find a reference to a Hollywood film, one that could be used to study and understand the concepts presented in the chapter. For example, what better film for understanding insurance law than Billy Wilder's *Double Indemnity?* And you can find a clip on insurable interest from that film in West's Digital Video Library (http://wdvl.westbuslaw.com). Or you can assign to students the enviable task of watching the movie and determining the insurance law issues. Or, for contract formation, you can watch another clip from *Midnight Run* and witness the great Robert DeNiro playing a bounty hunter who is trying to negotiate a binding contract with a bailbondsman. There is offer, counteroffer, statute of frauds, and good fun all in a short clip to get the students involved and thinking.

Clarity

The writing style has been evolving, and once again, we have changed those passages that fell victim to the passive voice. The writing is clear and lively. The examples are student-friendly, and the discussions of law are grounded in the book's strong connection to business. The principles of law are taught in the language and examples of business. Students can relate to the examples, which provide memorable illustrations of complex but critical legal concepts.

CPA Helps

As always, the text provides coverage for all the legal topics covered on the CPA exam. This edition reflects the content changes to the law and business regulation portions of the recently revised CPA exam. For example, there is less detail on personal property and bailments and trusts. Business organizations, now a substantial portion of the exam, remain a focus of eight chapters with up-to-date coverage of Sarbanes-Oxley and its impact on business forms and disclosures. This edition continues to feature sample CPA exam questions at the end of those chapters that include legal areas covered on the exam. Answers for the odd-numbered CPA exam questions in each of the appropriate chapters are given in the Instructor's Manual along with explanations for the answers. This edition of the book also continues to use a CPA highlight icon to alert students to those areas that are particularly critical in preparing for the law portion of the CPA exam.

Innovative Chapters

This text features, for example, a chapter on cyberlaw (Chapter 11). Updated for this edition, this chapter provides students with a look at how the Internet and new technology have resulted in new interpretations of existing laws as well as new laws to govern unique issues of commerce involving these new tools. Bloggers and spammers beware, for the law has caught up with you. The chapter has been shortened because so much of the cyberlaw material is now mainstream in other topic areas. But provides a nice introductory tool for instructors who want to show how much the law affects this new generation of Internet-savvy students.

Cases at the Core

Specially selected cases appear in abundance in this text. Most chapters include three to five cases, many of them recent. Landmark decisions also appear. To highlight the charm and induce the student's recall of the principles of the cases, one line appears above each case. There can be a humorous introduction, a play on words, or a simple memorable description of the parties or facts of the case. The one-line introduction is intriguing for students and makes the strong cases even more memorable.

E-Commerce and Cyberlaw

Beyond the cyberlaw chapter (11), this feature covers e-mail privacy, Internet taxes, identity theft, contract formation on the Internet, e-commerce employment rules, electronic signatures, and more. Chapter 8, the criminal law chapter, also includes great detail on the new and evolving computer crimes. Chapter 10, the intellectual property chapter, features a section on Protection of Computer Software and Mask Works, covering copyright and patent protection of computer programs, restrictive licensing, semiconductor chip protection, and more.

Thinking Things Through

This feature is designed to help students apply the law they have learned from the chapter and cases to a hypothetical or another case that varies slightly from the examples in the reading. With these problems built into the reading, students have the chance to really think through what they have just read and studied with regard to the law presented in that chapter. This feature can be used to promote classroom discussion or as an assignment for analysis. For example, in Chapter 11, students can walk through a series of examples on whether an Internet service provider must disclose a customer's name to the courts when the customer's posting on a blog or chat room has created potential legal liability.

Major Regulatory Reforms: USA Patriot Act and Sarbanes-Oxley

Businesses have been affected dramatically not only by new laws at the federal level but also by complex and intricate new federal regulatory schemes. Sarbanes-Oxley affects everything from corporate governance to the Federal Sentencing Guidelines to accountants' liability. The USA Patriot Act has an impact on searches, funds transfers, and issues of citizenship for employers. These dramatic new pieces of legislation enjoy coverage throughout this edition.

Ethical Focus

In addition to Chapter 3, which is devoted exclusively to the current issues in business ethics, each chapter continues to provide students with an ethical dilemma related to that particular area of law. The Ethics & the Law feature presents problems in each area of law. Students will be able to analyze ethical issues and problems that are very real and very challenging for anyone in business—for example, the issues involved in the Berkeley graduate school applicants who lied about their work experience in order to be admitted to the MBA program, the cast members of Friends and their salaries, the bankruptcies of musicians from TLC to George Michael, and the issues surrounding steroid use by professional baseball players.

Weekly Updates

Users of this text have the opportunity to catch up on new cases, business events, and changing laws and regulations with the weekly updates prepared by co-author Marianne Jennings. These updates carry information on law and business practice, which is often just days old and allows students to stay up to date. Instructors can use the cases, examples, and questions from the weekly updates for quizzes, class discussion, or exam questions. The weekly updates provide a never-ending resource for new and enhancing materials for lectures, discussions, assignments, and group work. Available to instructors and students, the weekly updates on the law are at **www.thomsonedu.com/westbuslaw/twomey**.

Critical Thinking

This text addresses the mandate on critical thinking by the American Assembly of Collegiate Schools of Business (AACSB). The Thinking Things Through feature asks students to analyze a problem that requires application of the law and examination of slight changes in factual patterns from examples in the text and the cases. For example, in the negotiable instruments chapters, students can look at a sample instrument in one problem and apply the requirements for negotiability to determine whether the instrument is indeed negotiable. In the Ethics & the Law feature, students must connect ethical thought with law and public policy and walk through the logic of application and results. End-of-chapter problems are, for the most part, real cases that summarize fact patterns and ask the students to find the applicable laws in the chapter and determine applicability and results. The fact patterns in the chapter problems are detailed and realistic and offer students the chance to test their mastery of the chapter concepts.

For Additional Help in Teaching and Learning

For more detailed information about any of the following ancillaries, contact your local Thomson Learning/West Legal Studies sales representative or visit the *Business Law: Principles for Today's Commercial Environment* Web site at **www.thomsonedu.com/westbuslaw/twomey**.

Student Study Guide (ISBN: 0-324-63986-4) Students may purchase a study guide that includes chapter outlines, general rules, study hints, and review and application exercises. Solutions to all study guide case problems are also included.

Instructor's Resource CD (IRCD) (ISBN: 0-324-63819-1) The IRCD contains the Instructor's Manual in Microsoft Word files. This manual provides instructor insights, chapter outlines, and teaching strategies for each chapter. Discussion points are provided for Thinking Things Through and Ethics & the Law vignettes. Also included are answers to CPA questions. The Instructor's Manual is prepared by Marianne Jennings, one of the textbook authors. In addition, the IRCD includes the ExamView testing software files, the test bank in Microsoft Word files, and the Microsoft PowerPoint lecture slides.

ExamView Testing Software—Computerized Testing Software This testing software contains all of the questions in the printed test bank. This program is an easy-to-use test creation software compatible with Microsoft Windows. Instructors can add or edit questions, instructions, and answers; they can select questions by previewing them on the screen, selecting them randomly, or selecting them by number. Instructors can also create and administer quizzes online, whether over the Internet, a local area network (LAN), or a wide area network (WAN). The ExamView testing software is available on the Instructor's Resource CD.

Test Bank (ISBN: 0-324-63984-8) Thousands of true/false, multiple-choice, and case questions are available. The test bank may be obtained in hard copy or in electronic format.

Microsoft PowerPoint® Lecture Review Slides PowerPoint slides are available for use by instructors for enhancing their lectures. Download these slides at **www.thomsonedu.com/westbuslaw/twomey**. The PowerPoint slides are also available on the IRCD.

West's Digital Video Library Featuring 60+ segments on the most important topics in Business Law, West's Digital Video Library helps students make the connection between their textbook and the business world. Access to West's Digital Video Library is free when bundled with a new text. New to this edition are LawFlix, twelve scenes from Hollywood movies with instructor materials for each film clip. The accompanying instructor materials were written by co-author Marianne Jennings and include elements such as goals for the clips, questions for students (with answers for the instructor), background on the film and the scene, and fascinating trivia about the film, its actors, and its history. For more information about West's Digital Video Library, visit **http://wdvl.westbuslaw.com**

West Legal Studies in Business Resource Center This Web site offers a unique, rich, and robust online resource for instructors and students. The address **http://www.thomsonedu.com/westbuslaw** provides customer service and product information, links to all text-supporting Web sites, and other cutting-edge resources such as **NewsEdge** and **Court Case Updates**.

Thomson Custom Solutions Whether you need print, digital, or hybrid course materials, Thomson Custom Solutions can help you create your perfect learning solution. Draw from Thomson's extensive library of texts and collections, add or create your own original work, and create customized media and technology to match your learning and course objectives. Our editorial team will work with you through each step, allowing you to concentrate on the most important thing—your students. Learn more about all our services at **www.thomsoncustom.com**.

CaseNet CaseNet is Thomson's legal and business case collection featuring selections from the West Legal Studies in Business case database and other prestigious partners. Using TextChoice, you can search, preview, arrange cases, and add your original material or legal cases from your state to create the perfect case resource for your course. To start building your casebook, visit CaseNet at **www.textchoice.com/casenet** or contact your local Thomson Learning/West Legal Studies sales representative.

ACKNOWLEDGMENTS

The development and revision of a textbook represent teamwork in its highest form. We thank the innumerable instructors, students, attorneys, and managers who have added to the quality of this textbook through its many editions. In particular, we thank the following reviewers who provided their honest and valuable commentary to this text:

Christen Adels
Geneva College

Robert A. Arnold
Thomas More College

Todd Barnet
Pace University

Marie F. Benjamin
Valencia Community College

Kenneth V. Bevan
Valencia Community College

David A. Clough
Naugatuck Valley Community College

Lawrence J. Danks
Camden County College

James G. Etheredge
Troy University

Edward J. Gac
University of Colorado

Teresa R. Gillespie
Northwest University

Heidi Helgren
Delta College

Lawrence A. Joel
Bergen Community College

Bruce F. Johnson
College of the Desert

Jeff W. Meverden
Fox Valley Technical College

Neal Orkin
Drexel University

William B. Read
Husson College

Richard J. Riley
Samford University

Samuel L. Schrager
University of Connecticut

Richard L. Still
Mississippi State University

Mike Teel
Samford University

We also thank the instructors who have reviewed previous editions of this text:

Dean Alexander
Miami-Dade Community College

Hazel L. Baer
Lehigh Carbon Community College

John T. Ballantine
University of Colorado

Robert Boeke
Delta College

Greg Cermigiano
Widener University

Anne Cohen
University of Massachusetts

Thomas S. Collins
Loras College

Darrell Dies
Illinois State University

De Vee E. Dykstra
University of South Dakota

Adam Epstein
University of Tennessee

Phillip Evans
Kutztown University of Pennsylvania

Deborah Lynn Bundy Ferry
Marquette University

Darrel Ford
University of Central Oklahoma

David Grigg
Pfeiffer University

Ronald Groeber
Ball State University

Thomas E. Guild
University of Central Oklahoma

Florence Elliot Howard
Stephen F. Austin University

Richard Hurley
Francis Marion University

Michael A. Katz
Delaware State University

Thomas E. Knothe
Viterbo University

Ruth Kraft
Audrey Cohen College

Claire La Roche
Longwood College

Susan D. Looney
Mohave Community College

Roy J. Millender, Jr.
Westmont College

Steven Murray
Community College of Rhode Island

Ann Olazábal
University of Miami

Ronald Picker
St. Mary's of the Woods College

Francis Polk
Ocean County College

Robert Prentice
University of Texas at Austin

Linda Reppert
Marymount University

Gary Sambol
Rutgers University School of Business

Lester Smith
Eastern New Mexico University

Lisa M. Storm
Hartnell College

Michael Sugameli
Oakland University

Cathy L. Taylor
Park University and Webster University

Bob Vicars
Bluefield State University

James Welch
Kentucky Wesleyan College

We extend our thanks to our families for their support and patience as we work our long hours to ensure that each edition is better than the last.

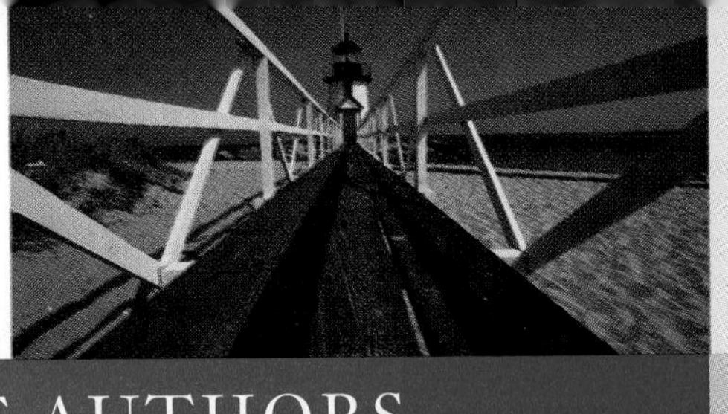

ABOUT THE AUTHORS

David P. Twomey graduated from Boston College, earned his MBA at the University of Massachusetts at Amherst, and after two years of business experience, entered Boston College Law School, where he earned his Juris Doctor degree.

While a law student, he began his teaching career serving as a Lecturer in Finance and Marketing at Simmons College in Boston. He joined the faculty of the Boston College Carroll School of Management in 1968 as an assistant professor and was promoted to the rank of professor in 1978. Professor Twomey has received numerous teaching and service awards at Boston College. He has written 31 editions of books and numerous articles on labor, employment, and business law topics. He has a special interest in curriculum development, serving four terms as chairman of his school's Education Policy Committee. As chairman of the Business Law Department for over a decade, he serves as a spokesperson for a strong legal and ethical component in both the undergraduate and graduate curriculum.

Professor Twomey is a nationally known labor arbitrator, having been selected by the parties as arbitrator in numerous disputes throughout the country in the private and public sectors. In the context of impending nationwide railroad and airline strikes, his service includes appointments by Presidents Reagan, George Bush, Clinton, and George W. Bush to eight Presidential Emergency Boards, whose recommendations served as the basis for the resolution of these labor disputes. Professor Twomey is a member of the National Academy of Arbitrators. He is also a member of the Massachusetts, Florida, and federal Bars.

Professor *Marianne Jennings* is a member of the Department of Management in the W. P. Carey School of Business at Arizona State University and is a professor of legal and ethical studies in business. She served as director of the Joan and David Lincoln Center for Applied Ethics from 1995 to 1999. In 2006, she was appointed faculty director for the W. P. Carey Executive MBA Program. She has done consulting work for law firms, businesses and professional groups including AES, AICPA, Boeing, Dial Corporation, Edward Jones, Mattel, Motorola, CFA Institute, Southern California Edison, the Institute of Internal Auditors, AIMR, DuPont, Blue Cross Blue Shield, Hy-Vee Foods, IBM, Bell Helicopter, Amgen, Raytheon, and VIAD.

The fifth edition of her textbook *Case Studies in Business Ethics* was published in February 2005. The eighth edition of her textbook *Business: Its Legal, Ethical and Global Environment* is in production for 2007 release. Her book *A Business Tale: A Story of Ethics, Choices, Success, and a Very Large Rabbit*, a fable about business ethics, was chosen by Library Journal in 2004 as its business book of the year. *A Business Tale* was also a finalist for two other literary awards for 2004. In 2000, her book on corporate governance was published by the New York Times MBA Pocket Series. Her book on long-term success, *Building a Business Through Good Times and Bad: Lessons from Fifteen Companies, Each With a Century of Dividends*, was published in October 2002 and has been used by Booz, Allen, Hamilton for its work on business longevity. Her latest book, *The Seven Signs of Ethical Collapse*, was published by St. Martin's Press in July 2006 and was named one of the best business books for 2006 by *Library Journal.*

Her weekly columns are syndicated around the country, and her work has appeared in the *Wall Street Journal, the Chicago Tribune, the New York Times, Washington Post,* and the *Reader's Digest.* A collection of her essays, *Nobody Fixes Real Carrot Sticks Anymore,* first published in 1994 is still being published. She has been a commentator on business issues on *All Things Considered* for National Public Radio.

She has served on four boards of directors, including Arizona Public Service (1987–2000), Zealous Capital Corporation, and the Center for Children with Chronic Illness and Disability at the University of Minnesota. She was appointed to the board of advisors for the Institute of Nuclear Power Operators in 2004 and has served on the board of trustees for Think Arizona, a public policy think tank. She has appeared on CNBC, CBS This Morning, the Today Show, and CBS Evening News.

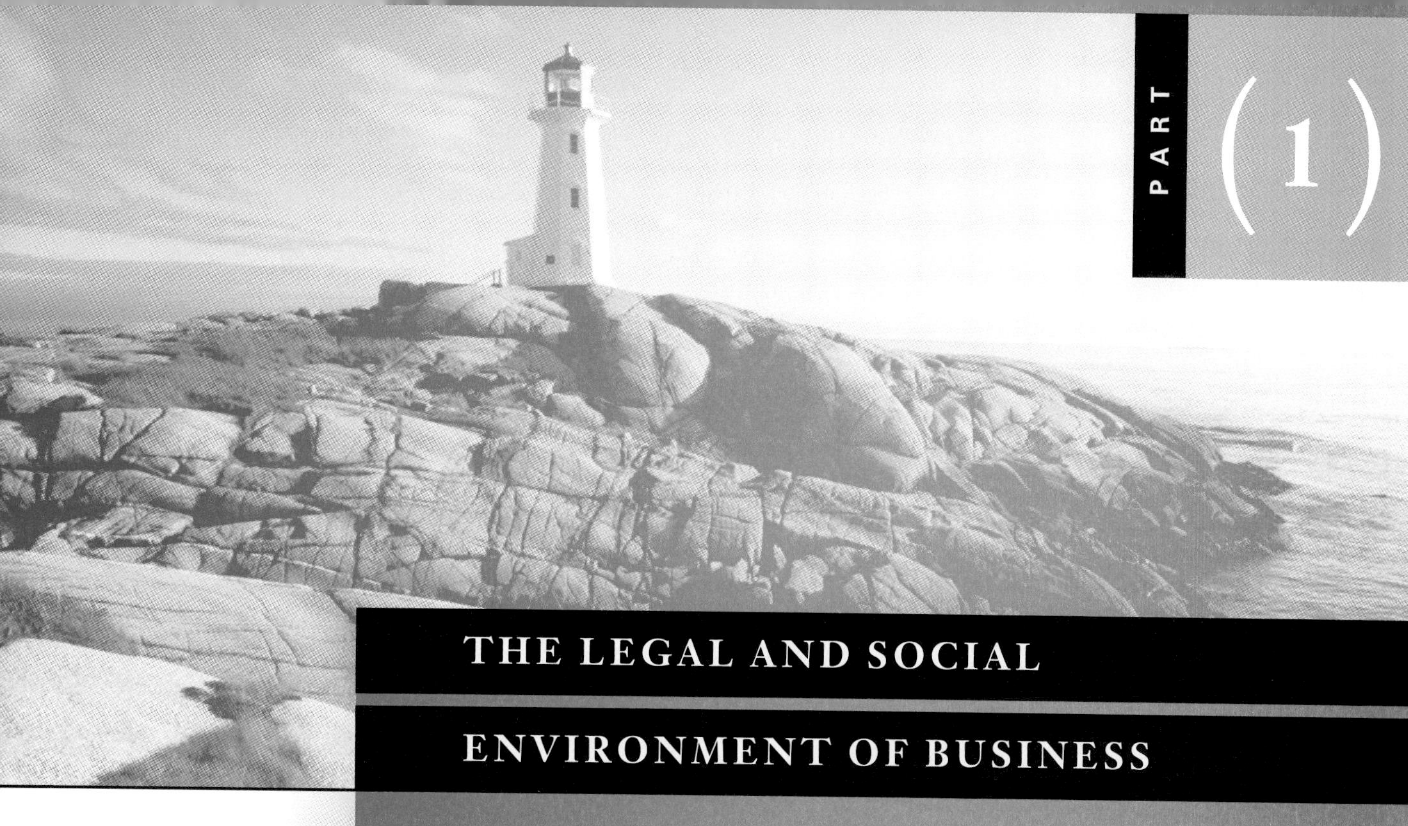

PART (1)

THE LEGAL AND SOCIAL ENVIRONMENT OF BUSINESS

THE NATURE AND SOURCES OF LAW

CHAPTER (1)

LEARNING OBJECTIVES

After studying this chapter, you should be able to

LO.1 Discuss the nature of law

LO.2 Define legal rights and give examples

LO.3 Explain how rights and duties relate

LO.4 Discuss the right to privacy and the protections it provides, including issues in Internet use

LO.5 List the sources of law and give examples from each level

LO.6 Describe uniform laws and their purposes

LO.7 Give the classifications of law

Why have law? If you have ever been stuck in a traffic jam or jostled in a crowd leaving a stadium, you have observed the need for order to keep those involved moving in an efficient and safe manner. The interruptions and damages from Internet viruses demonstrate the need for rules and order in this era of new technology. When our interactions are not orderly, whether at our concerts or through our e-mail, all of us and our rights are affected. The order or pattern of rules that society uses to govern the conduct of individuals and their relationships is called **law**. Law keeps society running smoothly and efficiently.

A. Nature of Law and Legal Rights

Law consists of the body of principles that govern conduct and that can be enforced in courts or by administrative agencies. The law could also be described as a collection or bundle of rights.

1. Legal Rights

A **right** is a legal capacity to require another person to perform or refrain from performing an act. Our rights flow from the U.S. Constitution, state constitutions, federal and state statutes, and ordinances at the local levels, including cities, counties, and boroughs. Within these sources of rights are also duties. A **duty** is an obligation of law imposed on a person to perform or refrain from performing a certain act.

Duties and rights coexist. No right exists in one person without a corresponding duty resting on some other person or persons. For example, if the terms of a lease provide that the premises will remain in a condition of good repair so that the tenant can live there comfortably, the landlord has a corresponding duty to provide a dwelling that has hot and cold running water.

2. Individual Rights

The U.S. Constitution gives individuals certain rights. Those rights include the right to freedom of speech, the right to due process or the right to have a hearing before any freedom is taken away, and the right to vote. There are also duties that accompany individual rights, such as the duty to speak in a way that does not cause harm to others. For example, individuals are free to express their opinions about the government or its officials, but they would not be permitted to yell "Fire!" in a crowded theater and cause unnecessary harm to others. The rights given in the U.S. Constitution are rights that cannot be taken away or violated by any statutes, ordinances, or court decisions. These rights provide a framework for the structure of government and other laws.

3. The Right of Privacy

One very important individual legal right is the right of privacy, which has has two components. The first is the right to be secure against unreasonable searches and seizures by the government. The Fourth Amendment of the U.S. Constitution guarantees this portion of the **right of privacy**. A police officer, for example, may not search your home unless the officer has a reasonable suspicion (which is generally established through a warrant) that your home contains evidence of a crime, such as illegal drugs. If your home or business is searched unlawfully, any items obtained during that unlawful search could be excluded as evidence in a criminal trial because of the Fourth Amendment's exclusionary rule. **For Example,** in the murder trial of O.J. Simpson, Judge Lance Ito excluded some of the evidence the police had obtained from inside Mr. Simpson's Ford Bronco, which was parked on the street outside his home. Judge Ito ruled that the officers should have first obtained a warrant for the locked vehicle, which was not going to be taken anywhere because Mr. Simpson was out of town at that time.

A second aspect of the right of privacy protects individuals against intrusions by others. Your private life is not subject to public scrutiny when you are a private citizen. This right is provided in many state constitutions and exists through interpretation at the federal level in the landmark case of *Roe v Wade*,[1] in which the U.S. Supreme Court established a right of privacy that gives women the right to choose whether to have an abortion.

These two components of the right to privacy have many interpretations. These interpretations are often found in statutes that afford privacy rights with respect to certain types of conduct. **For Example,** a

[1] 410 US 113 (1973).

WILSON V LAYNE, 526 U.S. 603 (1999)

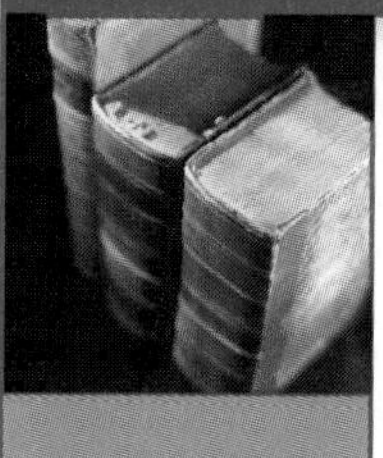

WHEN WARRANTS ARE INVOLVED, NO BRIEF PHOTOGRAPHS

In early 1992, the Attorney General of the United States approved "Operation Gunsmoke," a special national fugitive apprehension program in which United States Marshals worked with state and local police to apprehend dangerous criminals.

In the early morning hours of April 16, 1992, a Gunsmoke team of Deputy United States Marshals and Montgomery County Maryland Police officers executed warrants that had been issued against Dominic Wilson, who was wanted for robbery, theft, and assault and who had a "use caution" warning posted on law enforcement files and records. The team was accompanied by a reporter and a photographer from the *Washington Post*, who had been invited by the Marshals to accompany them as part of a Marshals Service ride-along policy.

At around 6:45 A.M., the officers (Respondents), with media representatives in tow, entered the dwelling noted in the warrant. They were unaware that the residence in the warrant and the one that they entered was actually the home of Dominic's parents, Charles and Geraldine Wilson (Petitioners). Charles and Geraldine were still in bed when they heard the officers enter the home. Charles Wilson, dressed only in a pair of briefs, ran into the living room to investigate. Discovering at least five men in street clothes with guns in his living room, he angrily demanded that they state their business, and repeatedly cursed the officers. Believing him to be an angry Dominic Wilson, the officers quickly subdued him on the floor. Geraldine Wilson next entered the living room to investigate, wearing only a nightgown. She observed her husband being restrained by the armed officers. The officers learned that Dominic Wilson was not in the house, and they departed. During the time that the officers were in the home, the *Washington Post* photographer took numerous pictures. The print reporter was also apparently in the living room observing the confrontation between the police and Charles Wilson. The reporters were not involved in the execution of the arrest warrant. The *Washington Post* never published its photographs of the incident.

The Wilsons filed suit against the officers for invasion of their privacy and violation of their Fourth Amendment rights. The district court found that the officers could be held liable. The Court of Appeals reversed and found that the officers had immunity despite the presence of the photographer because the law on reporters and warrants was not clear at the time these officers used reporters. The U.S. Supreme Court granted *certiorari* because of several conflicting decisions on the issue of cameras and reporters present during arrests and warrant executions.

Judicial Opinion

REHNQUIST, Chief Justice . . . In 1604, an English court made the now-famous observation that "the house of every one is to him as his castle and fortress, as well for his defence against injury and violence, as for his repose." In his Commentaries on the Laws of England, William Blackstone noted that "the law of England has so particular and tender a regard to the immunity of a man's house, that it stiles it his castle, and will never suffer it to be violated with impunity: agreeing herein with the sentiments of ancient Rome . . . . For this reason no doors can in general be broken open to execute any civil process; though, in criminal causes, the public safety supersedes the private."

The Fourth Amendment embodies this centuries-old principle of respect for the privacy of the home: "The right of the people to be secure in their persons, houses, papers, and effects, against unreasonable searches and seizures, shall not be violated, and no Warrants shall issue, but upon probable cause, supported by Oath or affirmation, and particularly describing the place to be searched, and the persons or things to be seized."

Our decisions have applied these basic principles of the Fourth Amendment to situations, like the one in this case, in which police enter a home under the authority of an arrest warrant in order to take into custody the suspect named in the warrant. We decided that "an arrest warrant founded on probable cause implicitly carries with it the limited authority to enter a dwelling in which the suspect lives when there is reason to believe the suspect is within."

Here, of course, the officers had such a warrant, and they were undoubtedly entitled to enter the Wilson home in order to execute the arrest warrant for Dominic Wilson. But it does not necessarily follow that they were entitled to bring a newspaper reporter and a photographer with them. In *Horton v California*, 496 US 128, 140, 110 S.Ct. 2301, 110 L.Ed.2d 112 (1990), we held "[i]f the scope of the search exceeds that permitted by the terms of a validly issued warrant or the character of the relevant exception from the warrant requirement, the subsequent seizure is unconstitutional without more." While this does not mean that every police action while inside a home must be explicitly authorized by the text of the warrant, the Fourth Amendment does require that police actions in execution of a warrant be related to the objectives of the authorized intrusion. . . Certainly the presence of reporters inside the home was not related to the objectives of the authorized intrusion. Respondents concede that the reporters did not engage in the execution of the warrant, and did not assist the police in their task. The reporters therefore were not present for any reason related to the justification for police entry into the home—the apprehension of Dominic Wilson.

This is not a case in which the presence of the third parties directly aided in the execution of the warrant. Where the police enter a home under the authority of a warrant to search for stolen property, the presence of third parties for the purpose of identifying the stolen property has long been approved by this Court and our common-law tradition.

Respondents argue that the presence of the *Washington Post* reporters in the Wilsons' home nonetheless served a number of legitimate law enforcement purposes. They first assert that officers should be able to exercise reasonable discretion about when it would "further their law enforcement mission to permit members of the news media to accompany them in executing a warrant." But this claim ignores the importance of the right of residential privacy at the core of the Fourth Amendment. It may well be that media ride-alongs further the law enforcement objectives of the police in a general sense, but that is not the same as furthering the purposes of the search. Were such generalized "law enforcement objectives" themselves sufficient to trump the Fourth Amendment, the protections guaranteed by that Amendment's text would be significantly watered down.

Respondents next argue that the presence of third parties could serve the law enforcement purpose of publicizing the government's efforts to combat crime, and facilitate accurate reporting on law enforcement activities. There is certainly language in our opinions interpreting the First Amendment which points to the importance of "the press" in informing the general public about the administration of criminal justice. No one could gainsay the truth of these observations, or the importance of the First Amendment in protecting press freedom from abridgment by the government. But the Fourth Amendment also protects a very important right, and in the present case it is in terms of that right that the media ride-alongs must be judged.

Surely the possibility of good public relations for the police is simply not enough, standing alone, to justify the ride-along intrusion into a private home. And even the need for accurate reporting on police issues in general bears no direct relation to the constitutional justification for the police intrusion into a home in order to execute a felony arrest warrant.

Finally, respondents argue that the presence of third parties could serve in some situations to minimize police abuses and protect suspects, and also to protect the safety of the officers. While it might be reasonable for police officers to themselves videotape home entries as part of a "quality control" effort to ensure that the rights of homeowners are being respected, or even to preserve evidence. The Washington Post reporters in the Wilsons' home were working on a story for their own purposes. They were not present for the purpose of protecting the officers, much less the Wilsons. A private photographer was acting for private purposes, as evidenced in part by the fact that the newspaper and not the police retained the photographs. Thus, although the presence of third parties during the execution of a warrant may in some circumstances be constitutionally permissible, the presence of these third parties was not.

The reasons advanced by respondents, taken in their entirety, fall short of justifying the presence of media inside a home. We hold that it is a violation of the Fourth Amendment for police to bring members of the media or other third parties into a home during the execution of a warrant when the presence of the third parties in the home was not in aid of the execution of the warrant.

Questions

1. How long has the right to privacy in one's home been a judicial issue?
2. What arguments do law enforcement officials make to justify including third parties in arrests and service of warrants?
3. Does the Court find that the arguments justify the presence of the reporters?
4. What if the Humane Society brought along reporters when it was investigating a private home for possible animal abuse? Would this action be a breach of privacy?

SPORTS & ENTERTAINMENT LAW

On March 17, 2005, former and current major league baseball players, Commissioner Bud Selig, and the parents of young baseball players who had taken their own lives after taking steroids testified before the U.S. House of Representatives Government Reform Committee. The House held the hearings to determine whether government regulation of baseball is necessary.

The committee issued subpoenas to seven current or former major league players: Jose Canseco, Jason Giambi, Mark McGwire, Rafael Palmeiro, Curt Schilling, Sammy Sosa, and Frank Thomas. Subpoenas were also issued to four baseball officials. Only Jose Canseco, Don Fehr, and Rob Manfred had already agreed to appear voluntarily, according to a release by the committee chair.*

Committee Chair Tom Davis made an opening statement with the following excerpts:

Fourteen years ago, anabolic steroids were added to the Controlled Substance Act as a Schedule III drug, making it illegal to possess or sell them without a valid prescription. Today, however, evidence strongly suggests that steroid use among teenagers–especially aspiring athletes–is a large and growing problem.

The Centers for Disease Control and Prevention tells us that more than 500,000 high school students have tried steroids, nearly triple the number just ten years ago. A second national survey, conducted in 2004 by the National Institute on Drug Abuse and the University of Michigan, found that over 40 percent of 12th graders described steroids as "fairly easy" or "very easy" to get, and the perception among high school students that steroids are harmful has dropped from 71 percent in 1992 to 56 percent in 2004.

This is but a snapshot of the startling data we face. Today we take the committee's first steps toward understanding how we got here, and how we begin turning those numbers around. Down the road, we need to look at whether and how Congress should exercise its legislative powers to further restrict the use and distribution of these substances.

Our specific purpose today is to consider MLB's recently negotiated drug policy; how the testing policy will be implemented; how it will effectively address the use of prohibited drugs by players; and, most importantly, the larger societal and public health ramifications of steroid use.

In February of this year, former MLB All-Star Jose Canseco released a book that not only alleges steroid use by well known MLB players, but also discusses the prevalence of steroids in baseball during his 17-year career. After hearing Commissioner Bud Selig's public statements that MLB would not launch an investigation into Mr. Canseco's allegations, my Ranking Member Henry Waxman wrote me asking for a Committee hearing to, quote, "find out what really happened and to get to the bottom of this growing scandal." End quote. Furthermore, today's hearing will not be the end of our inquiry. Far from it. Nor will Major League Baseball be our sole or even primary focus. We're in the first inning of what could be an extra inning ballgame.

Ultimately, it is MLB, the union, and team executives that will determine the strength of the game's testing policy. Ultimately, it is MLB and the union that will or will not determine accountability and punishment. Ultimately, it is MLB and the union that can remove the cloud over baseball, and maybe save some lives in the process.

Oh, somewhere in this favored land the sun is shining bright;
The band is playing somewhere, and somewhere hearts are light;
And somewhere men are laughing, and somewhere children shout;
*But there is no joy in Mudville—until the truth comes out.***

*http://www.commondreams.org/news2005/0309-22.htm.

**http://reform.house.gov/GovReform/Hearings/EventSingle.aspx?EventID=1637.

SPORTS & ENTERTAINMENT LAW

continued

Following are excerpts from the players' and former players' testimony:

Jose Canseco, whose book alleges that he, Sammy Sosa, and Mark McGwire, all used steroids, testified:

*It was as acceptable in the late '80s and the mid-'90s as a cup of coffee.****

Mark McGwire, now retired, and a record holder, stated during the hearing:

Asking me, or any other player, to answer questions about who took steroids in front of television cameras, will not solve this problem. If a player answers 'no,' he simply will not be believed. If he answers 'yes,' he risks public scorn and endless government investigations. My lawyers have advised me that I cannot answer these questions without jeopardizing my friends, my family, or myself. I intend to follow their advice.[†]

Give a list of all the laws, rights, and duties you can find in this information.

[***] **http://reform.house.gov/GovReform/Hearings/EventSingle.aspx?EventID=1637**.

[†] **http://reform.house.gov/GovReform/Hearings/EventSingle.aspx?EventID=1637**. Click on Mark McGwire.

federal statute provides a right of privacy to bank customers that prevents their banks from giving out information about their accounts except to law enforcement agencies conducting investigations. Some laws protect the rights of students. **For Example,** the Family Educational Rights and Privacy Act of 1974 (FERPA, also known as the *Buckley Amendment*) prevents colleges and universities from disclosing students' grades to third parties without the students' permission. From your credit information to your Social Security number, you have great privacy protections.

4. Privacy and Technology

Technology creates new situations that may require the application of new rules of law. Technology has changed the way we interact with each other, and new rules of law have developed to protect our rights. Today, business is conducted by computers, wire transfers of funds, e-mail, electronic data interchange (EDI) order placements, and the Internet. We still expect that our communication is private. However, technology also affords others the ability to eavesdrop on conversations and intercept electronic messages. The law has stepped in to reestablish that the right of privacy still exists even in these technologically nonprivate circumstances. Some laws now make it a crime and a breach of privacy to engage in such interceptions of communications.[2] (See Chapter 11.)

B. Sources of Law

Several layers of law are enacted at different levels of government to provide the framework for business and personal rights and duties. At the base of this framework of laws is constitutional law. Constitutional law is the branch of law that is based on the constitution for a particular level of government. A **constitution** is a body of principles that establishes the structure of a government and the relationship of that government to the people who are governed. A constitution is generally a combination of the written document and the practices and customs that develop with the passage of time and the emergence of new problems. In each state, two constitutions are in force: the state constitution and the federal Constitution.

Statutory law includes legislative acts. Both Congress and the state legislatures enact statutory law. Examples of congressional legislative enactments include the Securities Act of 1933 (Chapter 46), the Sherman Antitrust Act (Chapter 5), the bankruptcy laws (Chapter 35), and consumer credit protection provisions (Chapter 33). At the state level, statutes govern the creation of corporations, probate

[2] *State v Christensen*, 79 P3d 12 (CA Wash 2003).

of wills, and the transfer of title to property. In addition to the state legislatures and the U.S. Congress, all cities, counties, and other governmental subdivisions have some power to adopt ordinances within their sphere of operation. Examples of the types of laws found at this level of government include traffic laws, zoning laws, and pet and bicycle licensing laws.

Administrative regulations are rules promulgated by state and federal administrative agencies, such as the Securities and Exchange Commission and the National Labor Relations Board. These regulations generally have the force of statutes.

Even individuals and businesses create their own laws, or **private law**. Private law consists of the rules and regulations parties agree to as part of their contractual relationships. **For Example,** landlords develop rules for tenants on everything from parking to laundry room use. Employers develop rules for employees on everything from proper computer use to posting pictures and information on bulletin boards located within the company walls. Homeowner associations have rules on everything from your landscaping to the color of your house paint.

Law also includes principles that are expressed for the first time in court decisions. This form of law is called **case law**. When a court decides a new question or problem, its decision becomes a **precedent**, which stands as the law in future cases that involve that particular problem.

Using precedent and following decisions in similar cases is the doctrine of ***stare decisis***. However, the rule of *stare decisis* is not cast in stone. Judges have some flexibility. When a court finds an earlier decision to be incorrect, it overrules that decision. **For Example,** in 1954, the U.S. Supreme Court departed from the rule of *stare decisis* in *Brown v Board of Education.*[3] In that case, the Court decided that it was incorrect in 1896 when it held in *Plessy v Ferguson*[4] that separate facilities for blacks were equal to facilities for whites.

Court decisions do not always deal with new problems or make new rules. In many cases, courts apply rules as they have been for many years, even centuries. These time-honored rules of the community are called the **common law**. Statutes sometimes repeal or redeclare the common law rules. Many statutes depend on the common law for definitions of the terms in the statutes.

Law also includes treaties made by the United States and proclamations and executive orders of the president of the United States or of other public officials.

C. Uniform State Laws

To facilitate the national nature of business and transactions, the National Conference of Commissioners on Uniform State Laws (NCCUSL), composed of representatives from every state, has drafted statutes on various subjects for adoption by the states. The best example of such laws is the Uniform Commercial Code (UCC).[5] (See Chapters 23–31, 34.) The UCC regulates the sale and leasing of goods; commercial paper, such as checks; funds transfers; secured transactions in personal property; banking; and letters of credit. Having the same principles of law on contracts for the sale of goods and other commercial transactions in most of the 50 states makes doing business easier and less expensive. Other examples of uniform laws across the states include the Model Business Corporations Act (Chapter 44), the Uniform Partnership Act (Chapter 42), and the Uniform Residential Landlord Tenant Act (Chapter 51). The Uniform Computer Information Transactions Act (UCITA) as well as the Uniform Electronic Transactions Act (UETA) are new technology statutes that have been adopted or are under consideration for passage by the states. These two uniform laws and versions of them take contract law from the traditional paper era to the paperless computer age.

D. Classifications of Law

Law is classified in many ways. **Substantive law** creates, defines, and regulates rights and liabilities.

[3] 349 US 294 (1954).

[4] 163 US 537 (1895).

[5] The UCC has been adopted in every state, except that Louisiana has not adopted Article 2, Sales. Guam, the Virgin Islands, and the District of Columbia have also adopted the UCC. The NCCUSL has adopted amendments to Article 8, Investment Securities (1977 and 1994), and Article 9, Secured Transactions (1999, and as amended 2001). There have been new articles of the UCC: Article 2A, Leases, and Article 4A, Funds Transfers. The United Nations Convention on Contracts for the International Sale of Goods (CISG) has been adopted as the means for achieving uniformity in sale-of-goods contracts on an international level. Provisions of CISG were strongly influenced by Article 2 of the UCC.

WARNING CUSTOMERS NOT TO TAKE YOUR MEDICATIONS

Johnson & Johnson has adopted a new policy on direct-to-consumer advertisements for prescription drugs as well as for its over-the-counter drugs. The new policy will have doctors disclose all of the risks to patients who are interested in taking the medication. For example, in an ad for J&J's Ortho Evra birth control patch, the doctor explains that the patch does contain hormones and that smokers have higher risks for strokes and blood clots if they choose to use it. In another ad, the company's director of marketing warns customers about the dangers of taking too much Tylenol and concludes by saying she would rather customers not take Tylenol at all than take too much Tylenol.

Johnson & Johnson CEO William Weldon announced the new policy in the following way:

> *If our industry is to retain the important right to talk directly to consumers, each of our companies in its own way must work to make DTC [direct to consumer] what it very definitely can be—a way to educate and counsel consumers in improving their health.*

Spending on DTC ads increased by 27 percent in 2004, for a total of $4.44 billion. Some in the industry say consumers will be frightened away. However, a J&J spokesperson said, "If a woman sees the Evra ad and she is a smoker (the ad discloses a higher risk of the drug for smokers), then quite frankly, she should be scared away. We're better off when they're not on the product." DTC advertising is under review by regulators following the withdrawal of popular DTC products such as Celebrex, Vioxx, and others from the market following consumer deaths and illnesses attributed to use of the drug when other conditions (such as heart problems) cautioned against their use.

Who regulates advertising? What types of laws cover advertising? Why would a company voluntarily disclose more information in ads than the government requires? What do you think of the statement by the J&J spokesperson who says everyone is better off if some consumers are frightened away by the ads? Why would a company deliberately advertise so as to keep consumers away from its products?

Source: Scott Hensley, "In Switch, J&J Gives Straight Talk on Drug Risks in New Ads," *Wall Street Journal*, March 21, 2005, B1, B6.

E-COMMERCE AND CYBERLAW

EMPLOYERS, E-MAIL, AND PRIVACY

Courts have taken the position that e-mail accounts of employees that are created through their employers are not private and that any messages and information in the employees' e-mail are the property of the employer and can be reviewed. Courts also permit, during the course of litigation, discovery of employee e-mail messages when the employer is named in a lawsuit. All e-mail messages can be retrieved and read for information relevant to the litigation. A recent survey revealed that 50 percent of executive-level managers review their employees' e-mail. Two Nissan Motor Corporation employees were fired after their managers warned them not to use company e-mail for personal messages. The managers were monitoring all of their employees' e-mails.

E-COMMERCE AND CYBERLAW

continued

The Principal Financial Group has the following policy in its employee handbook:

The corporation's electronic mail system is business property and is to be used for business purposes. The corporation reserves the right to monitor all electronic messages.

Michelle Murphy, a former customer service representative at Principal, was fired when her supervisor discovered she had used the company e-mail system to forward jokes, such as "A Few Good Reasons Cookie Dough Is Better Than Men" and "Top 10 Reasons Why Trick-or-Treating Is Better Than Sex."

Would you have fired Ms. Murphy? Why or why not? Should employees have any workplace protections for their e-mail? What problems would be created if the employer were denied the right to review employees' e-mail? What problems arise when managers are given access to employee e-mail?

Procedural law specifies the steps that must be followed in enforcing those rights and liabilities. For example, the laws that grant employees protection against discrimination are substantive laws. The regulations of the Equal Employment Opportunity Commission (EEOC) for bringing suits against or investigations of employers for discrimination charges are procedural laws. The laws that prohibit computer theft are substantive laws. The prosecution of someone for computer theft follows procedural laws. Law may also be classified in terms of its origin from Roman (or civil) law, from English common law based on customs and usages of the community,[6] or from the law merchant. Law may be classified according to subject matter, such as the law of contracts, the law of real estate, or the law of wills.

LAWFLIX

And Justice for All (1979) (R)

An excellent film that gives an overview of the judicial system in Maryland. Rights, precedent, and the role of lawyers are all topics for satire and analysis in the movie.

For movie clips that illustrate business law concepts, see LawFlix at **http://wdvl.westbuslaw.com.**

Law is at times classified in terms of principles of law and principles of equity. The early English courts were very limited as to the kinds of cases they could handle. Persons who could not obtain relief in those courts would petition the king to grant them special relief according to principles of **equity** and justice. In the course of time, these special cases developed certain rules that are called *principles of equity*. In general, the rules of equity apply when the remedies provided at law cannot provide adequate relief in the form of monetary damages. At one time, the United States had separate law courts and equity courts. Except in a few states, these courts have been combined so that one court applies principles of both law and equity. A party may ask for both legal and equitable remedies in a single court.[7] **For Example,** suppose a homeowner contracts to sell his home to a buyer. If the homeowner then refuses to go through with the contract, the buyer has the legal remedy of recovering damages. The rules of equity go further, when appropriate, and could require the owner to actually transfer the ownership of the house to the buyer. Such remedies require a court order for specific conduct, known as *specific performance*. Equitable remedies may also be available in certain contract breaches (see Chapters 2 and 20).

[6] For example, in *Welsh v Boy Scouts of America*, 510 US 1012 (1993), the Court relied on the age-old maxim, "A man's home is his castle," in its decision, and in *BMW of North America, Inc. v Gore*, 517 US 559 (1996), Justice Antonin Scalia, in his dissenting opinion, wrote, "One expects the court to conclude, 'To thine own self be true.'"

[7] *Actuant Corp. v Huffman*, 2005 WL 39661 (D Or).

Summary

Law consists of the pattern of rules established by society to govern conduct and relationships. These rules can be expressed as constitutional provisions, statutes, administrative regulations, and case decisions. Law can be classified as substantive or procedural, and it can be described in terms of its historical origins, by the subject to which it relates, or in terms of law or equity.

Law provides rights and imposes duties. One such right is the right of privacy, which affords protection against unreasonable searches of our property and intrusion into or disclosure of our private affairs.

The sources of law include constitutions, federal and state statutes, administrative regulations, ordinances, and uniform laws generally codified by the states in their statutes. The courts are also a source of law through their adherence to case precedent under the doctrine of *stare decisis* and through their development of time-honored principles called the common law.

Questions and Case Problems

1. Give an example of how law protects privacy.
2. The Family Educational Rights and Privacy Act (FERPA) protects students' rights to keep their academic records private. What duties are imposed and upon whom because of this protection of rights? Discuss the relationship between rights and duties.
3. List the sources of law.
4. What is the difference between common law and statutory law?
5. Classify the following laws as substantive or procedural:

   a. A law that requires public schools to hold a hearing before a student is expelled
   b. A law that establishes a maximum interest rate for credit transactions of 24 percent
   c. A law that provides employee leave for the birth or adoption of a child for up to 12 weeks
   d. A law that requires the county assessor to send four notices of taxes due and owing before a lien can be filed (attached) to the property

6. What do uniform laws accomplish? Why do states adopt them? Give an example of a uniform law.
7. Cindy Nathan is a student at West University. While she was at her 9:00 A.M. anthropology class, campus security entered her dorm room and searched all areas, including her closet and drawers. When Cindy returned to her room and discovered what had happened, she complained to the dorm's senior resident. The senior resident said that this was the university's property and that Cindy had no right of privacy. Do you agree with the senior resident's statement? Is there a right of privacy in a dorm room?
8. Professor Lucas Phelps sent the following e-mail to Professor Marlin Jones: "I recently read the opinion piece you wrote for the *Sacramento Bee* on affirmative action. Your opinion is incorrect, your reasoning and analysis are poor, and I am embarrassed that you are a member of the faculty here at Cal State Yolinda." Professor Jones forwarded the note from Professor Phelps to the provost of the university and asked that Professor Phelps be disciplined for using the university e-mail system for harassment purposes. Professor Phelps objected when the provost contacted him: "He had no right to send that e-mail to you. That was private correspondence. And you have no right of access to my e-mail. I have privacy rights." Do you agree with Professor Phelps? Was there a breach of privacy?
9. Under what circumstances would a court disregard precedent?
10. What is the difference between a statute and an administrative regulation?
11. What is the difference between a remedy in equity and other forms of judicial remedies?
12. Give examples of the areas covered by federal laws. Give examples of areas covered by city ordinances. What are the limitations on these two sources of laws? What could the laws at these two levels not do?
13. What is the principle of *stare decisis?*
14. List some purposes of law that you were able to spot in reading this chapter.
15. During the 2001 baseball season, San Francisco Giants player Barry Bonds hit 73 home runs, a new record that broke the one set by Mark McGwire in 2000 (72 home runs). When Mr. Bonds hit his record-breaking home run, the ball went into the so-called cheap seats. Alex Popov was sitting in those seats and had brought along his baseball glove for purposes of catching any hits that might come into the stands. Everyone sitting in the area agreed that Mr. Popov's glove touched Bonds's home-run ball. Videotape also shows Mr. Popov's glove on the ball. However, the ball dropped and, following a melee among the cheap-seat fans, Patrick Hayashi ended up with Bonds's home-run ball. Mr. Popov filed suit for the ball, claiming it is his property. Such baseballs can be very valuable. The baseball from Mr. McGwire's record-breaking home run in 2000 sold for $3 million. List those areas of law that will apply as the case is tried and the owner of the baseball is determined.

THE COURT SYSTEM AND DISPUTE RESOLUTION

CHAPTER (2)

LEARNING OBJECTIVES

After studying this chapter, you should be able to

LO.1 Explain the federal and state court systems

LO.2 Define the types of jurisdiction courts can have and how these are different

LO.3 Give the names of the parties and persons involved in a lawsuit

LO.4 List the initial steps in a lawsuit and explain how pleadings are used

LO.5 Describe the actual steps in a trial

LO.6 Explain how a party who prevails in court collects the judgment

LO.7 List the forms of alternative dispute resolution and distinguish among them

Despite carefully negotiated and well-written contracts and high safety standards in the workplace or in product design and production, businesses can still encounter disputes that may result in a lawsuit. **For Example,** you could hire the brightest and most expensive lawyer in town to prepare a contract with another party and believe the final agreement is "bulletproof." However, even a bulletproof contract does not guarantee performance by the other party, and a lawsuit for damages may be necessary.

Parties in a dispute either go to court to seek resolution or resolve the situation through alternative means. This chapter covers the structure of the court system and the litigation process as well as alternative means used to resolve disputes outside the court system.

A. The Court System

A **court** is a tribunal established by government to hear and decide matters brought before it, provide remedies when a wrong has been committed, and prevent possible wrongs from happening. A court could award to a business party money damages for a breach of contract following a trial, but it could also issue an injunction to halt patent infringement. **For Example,** in 2006, a court threatened to issue an injunction to shut down operation of the Blackberry wireless e-mail device system unless and until Research in Motion, Ltd. (RIM), the Blackberry service provider, compensated NTP, Inc., the company that had won its patent infringement case against RIM for the technology in the Blackberry device.[1]

1. The Types of Courts

Every type of court is given the authority to decide certain types or classes of cases. The power to hear cases is called **jurisdiction**. One form of jurisdiction, **subject matter jurisdiction**, covers the type of proceedings that the court holds. A court with **original jurisdiction** is the trial court or the court with the authority to conduct the first proceedings in the case. **For Example,** a court of original jurisdiction would be one where the witnesses actually testify, the documents are admitted into evidence, and the jury, in the case of a jury trial, is present to hear all the evidence and to make a decision.

Other types of subject matter jurisdiction are applicable to courts. A court with **general jurisdiction** has broad authority over different types of cases. The authority of a court with general jurisdiction can extend to both general civil and criminal cases. When a general jurisdiction trial court hears criminal cases, it conducts the trials of those charged with crimes. When a general trial court exercises its civil jurisdiction, it uses its authority to hear civil disputes, such as breach of contract cases and disputes about leases between landlords and tenants.

A court with **limited** or **special jurisdiction** has the authority to hear only particular kinds of cases. **For Example,** many states have courts that can hear only disputes in which the damages are $10,000 or less. Many types of courts have special jurisdiction, including juvenile courts, probate courts, and domestic relations courts. States vary in the names they give these courts, but all are courts of special or limited jurisdiction because they have very narrow authority for their subject matter jurisdiction. In the federal system, courts with limited or special jurisdiction include bankruptcy courts and the U.S. Tax Court.

A court with **appellate jurisdiction** reviews the work of a lower court. **For Example,** a trial court may issue a judgment that a defendant in a breach of contract suit should pay $500,000 in damages. That defendant could appeal the decision to an appellate court and seek review of the decision itself or even the amount of the damages.[2] An **appeal** is a review of the trial and decision of the lower court. An appellate court does not hear witnesses or take testimony. An appellate court, usually a panel of three judges, simply reviews the transcript and evidence from the lower court and determines whether there has been **reversible error**. A reversible error is a mistake in applying the law or a mistake in admitting evidence that affected the outcome of the case. An appellate court can **affirm** or **reverse** a lower court decision or **remand** that decision for another trial or additional hearings.

2. The Federal Court System

The federal court system consists of three levels of courts. Figure 2-1 illustrates federal court structure.

[1] RIM eventually settled the suit with NTP by agreeing to pay $612.5 million.

[2] A case that is sent back for a redetermination of damages is remanded for what is known as *remittur*.

YATES V STATE, 171 SW 3D 215 (TEX APP 2005)

LAW AND ORDER ON TV AND IN THE COURT

Andrea Pia Yates (Appellant) and Russell Yates were married on April 17, 1993. Their first child, Noah, was born in February 1994; their second child, John, was born in December 1995; and their third child, Paul, was born in September 1997. During this time, the Yates family moved from place to place living in a recreational vehicle. In 1998, they moved from the recreational vehicle to a converted bus and continued to live in a trailer park. At one point, appellant told her husband she felt depressed and overwhelmed, and he suggested that she talk to her mother and a friend.

In February 1999, a fourth child, Luke, was born. On June 18, 1999, Andrea suffered severe depression and tried to commit suicide by taking an overdose of an antidepressant that had been prescribed for her father. She was admitted to the psychiatric unit of Methodist Hospital. After her release six days later, she began seeing a psychiatrist as an outpatient. On July 20, 1999, her husband found Andrea in the bathroom, holding a knife to her neck. She was admitted to Spring Shadows Glen Hospital where a physician classified her among the five sickest patients she had ever seen. When she was discharged, her treating physician warned Mr. Yates that having another baby could result in a severe psychotic episode. Following her release in August 1999, the Yates family moved from the converted bus to a house and Yates began home-schooling Noah. In November 2000, Andrea had her fifth child, Mary. Several months later her father died and Andrea experienced another depression and resulting hospitalization. Upon her discharge, her treating physician recommended that someone stay with her at all times and that she not be left alone with her children.

During April 2001, Mr. Yates' mother came to the house each day to help. Andrea's mother-in-law described Andrea as almost catatonic, unresponsive, trembling, and scratching her head until she created bald spots. She did not eat. On May 3, Andrea filled a bathtub with water, but could not give a good reason for doing so. When asked, she said, "I might need it." She was readmitted to the hospital for ten days from May 4 until May 14.

On June 20, 2001, at 9:48 A.M., appellant called 9-1-1 and told the operator that she needed a police officer to come to her home. She also called Yates at his work and told him that he needed to come home, but would not say why. As Yates was leaving, he called her and asked if anyone was hurt, and she said that the kids were hurt. He asked, "Which ones?" She responded, "All of them."

Within minutes of the 9-1-1 call, several police officers arrived at the Yates' home. They discovered four dead children, soaking wet and covered with a sheet, lying on appellant's bed. The fifth child, Noah, was still in the bathtub, floating face down.

Mrs. Yates was charged with capital murder and entered a plea of "not guilty by reason of insanity."

At trial, ten psychiatrists and two psychologists testified regarding Andrea's mental illness. The tenth psychiatrist, Dr. Park Dietz, who interviewed Yates and was the State's sole mental-health expert in the case, testified that Yates, although psychotic on June 20, knew that what she did was wrong. Dr. Dietz reasoned that because Yates indicated that her thoughts were coming from Satan, she must have known they were wrong; that if she believed she was saving the children, she would have shared her plan with others rather than hide it as she did; that if she really believed that Satan was going to harm the children, she would have called the police or a pastor or would have sent the children away; and that she covered the bodies out of guilt or shame.

On cross-examination, Yates's counsel asked Dr. Dietz about his consulting work with the television show *Law & Order,* which Yates was known to watch. The testimony was as follows:

Q. Now, you are, are you not, a consultant on the television program known as *Law & Order?*
A. Two of them.
Q. Okay. Did either one of those deal with postpartum depression or women's mental health?
A. As a matter of fact, there was a show of a woman with postpartum depression who drowned her children in the bathtub and was found insane and it was aired shortly before the crime occurred.

The second mention of *Law & Order* came during Dr. Lucy Puryear's testimony. Dr. Puryear, a defense expert witness, was cross-examined by the State regarding her evaluation of appellant. The State specifically asked about her failure to inquire into whether or not Yates had seen *Law & Order.* Dr. Puryear testified as follows:

Q. You know she watched *Law & Order* a lot; right?
A. I didn't know. No.
Q. Did you know that in the weeks before June 20th, there was a *Law & Order* episode where a woman killed her children by drowning them in a bathtub, was defended on the basis of whether she was sane or insane under the law, and the diagnosis was postpartum depression and in the program the person was found insane, not guilty by reason of insanity? Did you know that?
A. No.
Q. If you had known that and had known that Andrea Yates was subject to these delusions, not that she was the subject of a delusion of reference, but that she regularly watched *Law & Order* and may have seen that episode, would you have changed the way you went about interviewing her, would you have interviewed whether she got the idea somehow she could do this and not suffer hell or prison?
A. I certainly wouldn't have asked her that question. No.
Q. Would you have—you didn't have to ask her that question, but you could have explored that?
A. If I had known she watched that show, I would have ask[ed] her about it, yes.

In his final argument at the guilt-innocence phase of the trial, appellant's attorney referred to Dr. Dietz's testimony by stating, "Or maybe even we heard some evidence that she saw some show on TV and knew she could drown her children and get away with it."

The prosecutor, in his final argument, made the following reference to Dietz's testimony about the *Law & Order* episode:

She gets very depressed and goes into Devereux. And at times she says these thoughts came to her during that month. These thoughts came to her, and she watches Law & Order regularly, she sees this program. There is a way out. She tells that to Dr. Dietz. A way out.

The jury returned a guilty verdict. Mrs. Yates's counsel discovered that Dr. Dietz had given false testimony. The producer of *Law & Order* spoke to counsel by telephone and said he could not recall such an episode. An attorney representing the producer, after talking to Dr. Dietz and researching the shows, verified to counsel that there was no show with a plot as outlined by Dr. Dietz. Dr. Dietz acknowledged that he had made an error in his testimony. Mrs. Yates appealed the guilty verdict on the grounds that the testimony about the show constituted reversible error.

Judicial Opinion

NUCHIA, Justice. . . The State recognizes that the State's knowing use of perjured testimony that is likely to materially affect the judgment violates the Due Process Clause of the Fourteenth Amendment of the United States Constitution. The State argues that it did not know that the testimony was false, did not use the false information, and the information was not material. We agree that this case does not involve the State's knowing use of perjured testimony. At the hearing on appellant's motion for mistrial, appellant did not complain that there had been prosecutorial misconduct. Rather, appellant stated, [M]ake no mistake, the issue is not whether or not the State was aware and we have no reason to believe the State was aware that such a program did not exist. The issue is that the defense of insanity was rebutted by the testimony of Dr. Dietz relative to an act of premeditation, that is a planned and/or a deceptive act on Mrs. Yates' part, that is something that would give her an idea, a way out of these particular allegations. And that was relayed to this jury and we believe that the jury relied upon the presentation of Dr. Dietz as well as the cross-examination by [the State's attorney] of Dr. Puryear relative to this particular issue.

It is uncontested that the testimony of Dr. Dietz regarding his consultation on a *Law & Order* television show having a plot remarkably similar to the acts committed by appellant was untrue and that there was no *Law & Order* television show with such a plot. However, the State asserts that it is "very questionable whether it can be said that the trial prosecutors used Dr. Dietz' testimony on cross-examination, especially in light of the fact that it played absolutely no role in the development of Dr. Dietz' conclusion that the appellant knew that her conduct was wrong. . . ."

The record reflects that the State used Dr. Dietz's testimony twice. First, the State used the testimony to cross-examine Dr. Puryear, who had seen appellant for several months while appellant was in the county jail, asking Dr. Puryear whether she knew that appellant watched *Law & Order* and whether she knew that there was an episode with a plot line mirroring appellant's acts. In so doing, the State repeated those facts that were common to appellant's acts and the referenced episode, thus emphasizing those facts already stated by Dr. Dietz. Second, the State connected the dots in its final argument by juxtaposing appellant's depression, her dark thoughts, watching *Law & Order* and seeing "a way out." Thus, the State used Dr. Dietz's false testimony to suggest to the jury that appellant patterned her actions after that *Law & Order* episode. We emphasize that the State's use of Dr. Dietz's false testimony was not prosecutorial misconduct. Rather, it served to give weight to that testimony.

The State argues that Dr. Dietz's testimony regarding the *Law & Order* episode was not material. The State asserts that "there is no reasonable likelihood" that the testimony "could have affected the judgment of the jury," but does not make any argument to support such a conclusory statement. We conclude that the testimony, combined with the State's cross-examination of Dr. Puryear and closing argument, was material. The materiality of the testimony is further evidenced by the fact that appellant's attorney felt compelled to address it in his own closing argument.

The State also asserts that Dr. Dietz did not suggest that appellant used the plot of the show to plan killing her children. Although it is true that Dr. Dietz did not make such a suggestion, the State did in its closing argument.

Five mental health experts testified that appellant did not know right from wrong or that she thought what she did was right. Dr. Dietz was the only mental health expert who testified that appellant knew right from wrong. Therefore, his testimony was critical to establish the State's case. Although the record does not show that Dr. Dietz intentionally lied in his testimony, his false testimony undoubtedly gave greater weight to his opinion.

We conclude that there is a reasonable likelihood that Dr. Dietz's false testimony could have affected the judgment of the jury. We further conclude that Dr. Dietz's false testimony affected the substantial rights of appellant. We reverse the trial court's judgment and remand the cause for further proceedings.[3]

Questions

1. What was Mrs. Yates' family and mental health history?
2. What was the significance of the *Law & Order* show testimony?
3. Why does the appellate court find that the false testimony about the *Law & Order* segment was reversible error?

(a) Federal District Courts

The **federal district courts** are the general trial courts of the federal system. They are courts of original jurisdiction that hear both civil and criminal matters. Criminal cases in federal district courts are those in which the defendant is charged with a violation of federal law (the U.S. Code). In addition to the criminal cases, the types of civil cases that can be brought in federal district courts include (1) civil suits in which the United States is a party, (2) cases between citizens of different states that involve damages of $75,000 or more, and (3) cases that arise under the U.S. Constitution or federal laws and treaties.

Federal district courts are organized within each of the states. There are 94 federal districts (each state has at least one federal district and there are 89 federal districts in the United States with the

[3]Mrs. Yates was found to be criminally insane in her 2006 retrial and is now institutionalized.

FIGURE 2-1 The Federal Court System

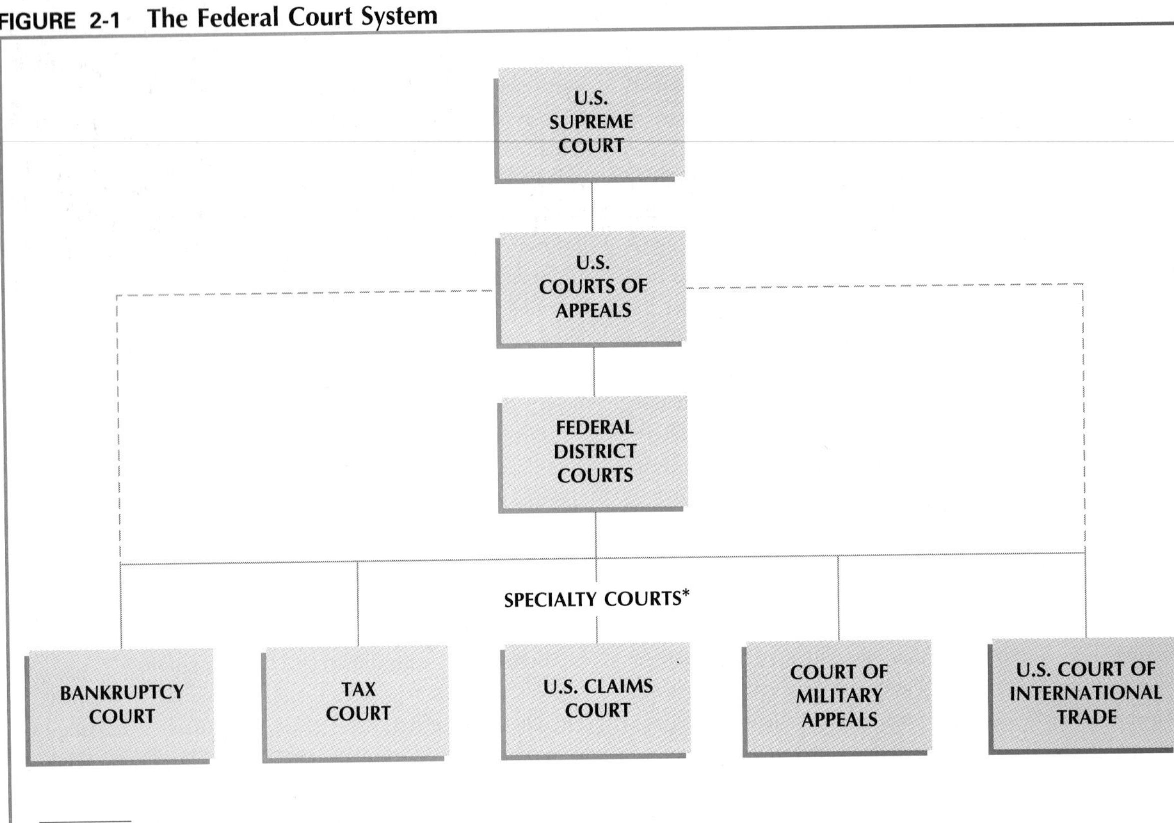

*Appeals often go directly to U.S. Courts of Appeals.

remaining courts found in Puerto Rico, Guam, etc.) Judges and courtrooms are assigned according to the caseload in that geographic area of the state.[4] Some states, such as New York and California, have several federal districts because of the population base and the resulting caseload. Figure 2-2 shows the geographic structure of the federal court system, including the appellate circuits.

The federal system has additional trial courts with limited jurisdiction, differing from the general jurisdiction of the federal district courts. These courts include, for example, the federal bankruptcy courts, Indian tribal courts, Tax Court, Court of Federal Claims, Court of Veterans Appeals, and the Court of International Trade.

(b) U.S. Courts of Appeals

The final decision in a federal district court is not necessarily the end of a case because it is a court of original jurisdiction, and its decisions can be appealed to a court with appellate jurisdiction. In the federal court system, the federal districts are grouped together geographically into 12 judicial circuits, including one for the District of Columbia. Additionally, a thirteenth federal circuit, called the *Federal Circuit*, hears certain types of appeals from all of the circuits, including specialty cases such as patent appeals. Each circuit has an appellate court called the U.S. Court of Appeals, and the judges for these courts review the decisions of the federal district courts. Generally, a panel of three judges reviews the cases. However, some decisions, called ***en banc*** decisions, are made by the circuit's full panel of judges. **For Example,** in 2003, the Ninth Circuit heard an appeal on a father's right to challenge the requirement that his daughter recite the Pledge of Allegiance in the public school she attended. The contentious case had so many issues that the Ninth

[4] For complete information about the courts and the number of judgeships, go to 28 USC §§ 81-144 and 28 USC §133.

FIGURE 2-2 The Thirteen Federal Judicial Circuits

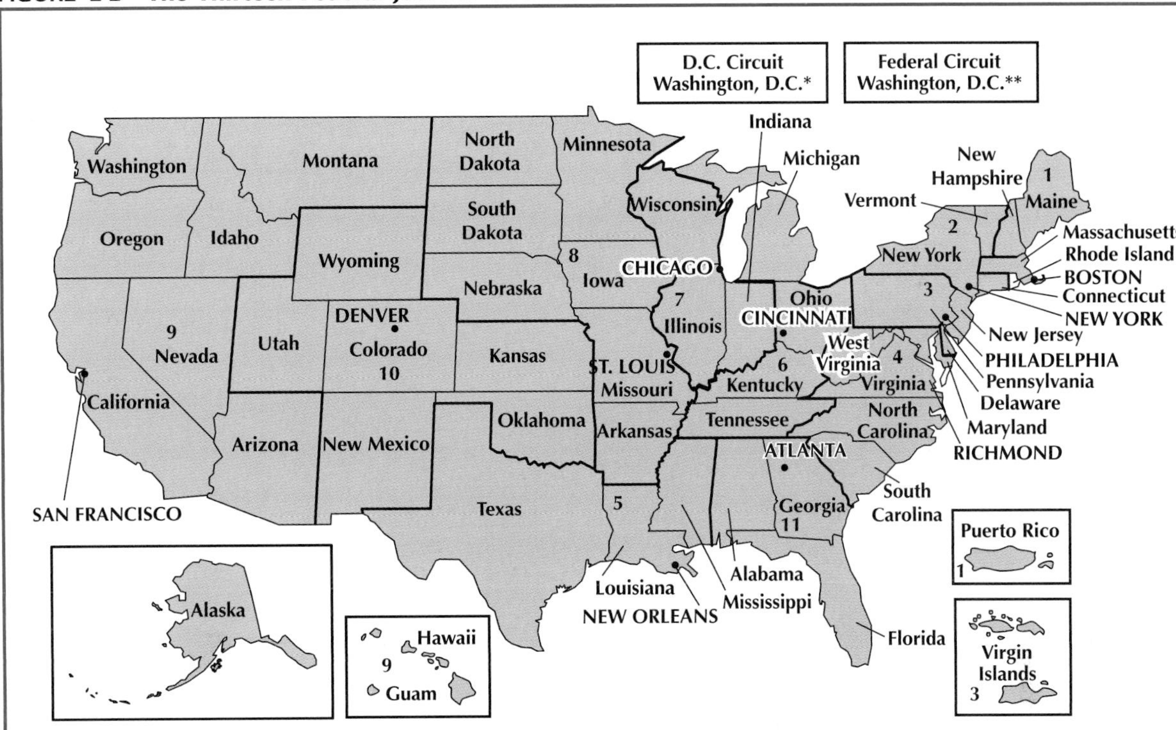

*A sizable portion of the caseload of the D.C. Circuit comes from the federal administrative agencies and offices located in Washington, D.C., such as the Securities and Exchange Commission, the National Labor Relations Board, the Federal Trade Commission, the Secretary of the Treasury, and the Labor Department, as well as appeals from the U.S. District Court of the District of Columbia.

**Rather than being defined by geography like the regional courts of appeals, the Federal Circuit is defined by subject matter, having jurisdiction over such matters as patent infringement cases, appeals from the Court of Federal Claims and the Court of International Trade, and appeals from administrative rulings regarding subject matter such as unfair import practices and tariff schedule disputes.

Circuit issued three opinions and on the third opinion the case was heard *en banc.*[5]

(c) U.S. Supreme Court

The final court in the federal system is the U.S. Supreme Court. The U.S. Supreme Court has appellate jurisdiction over cases that are appealed from the federal courts of appeals as well as from state supreme courts when a constitutional issue is involved in the case or a state court has reversed a federal court ruling. The U.S. Supreme Court does not hear all cases from the federal courts of appeals but has a process called granting a **writ of *certiorari,*** which is a preliminary review of those cases appealed to decide whether a case will be heard or allowed to stand as ruled on by the lower courts.[6]

[5] *Newdow v U.S. Congress*, 292 F3d 597, 602 (CA 9 2002) (*Newdow I*); *Newdow v U.S. Congress*, 313 F3d 500, 502 (CA 9 2002) (*Newdow II*); and *Newdow v U.S. Congress*, 328 F3d 466, 468 (CA 9 2003) (*Newdow III*). The U.S. Supreme Court eventually heard the case. *Elkgrove Unified School District v Newdow*, 542 US 1 (2004). Another *en banc* hearing occurred at the Ninth Circuit over the issues in the California gubernatorial recall election. The three-judge panel held that the voting methods in California violated the rights of voters and therefore placed a stay on the election. However, the Ninth Circuit then heard the case *en banc* and reversed the decision of the original three-judge panel. The recall election then proceeded.

[6] For example, the Supreme Court refused to grant *certiorari* in a Fifth Circuit case on law school admissions at the University of Texas. However, it granted *certiorari* in a later case involving law school admissions at the University of Michigan. *Gratz v Bollinger*, 539 US 244 (2003).

FIGURE 2-3 Sample State Court System

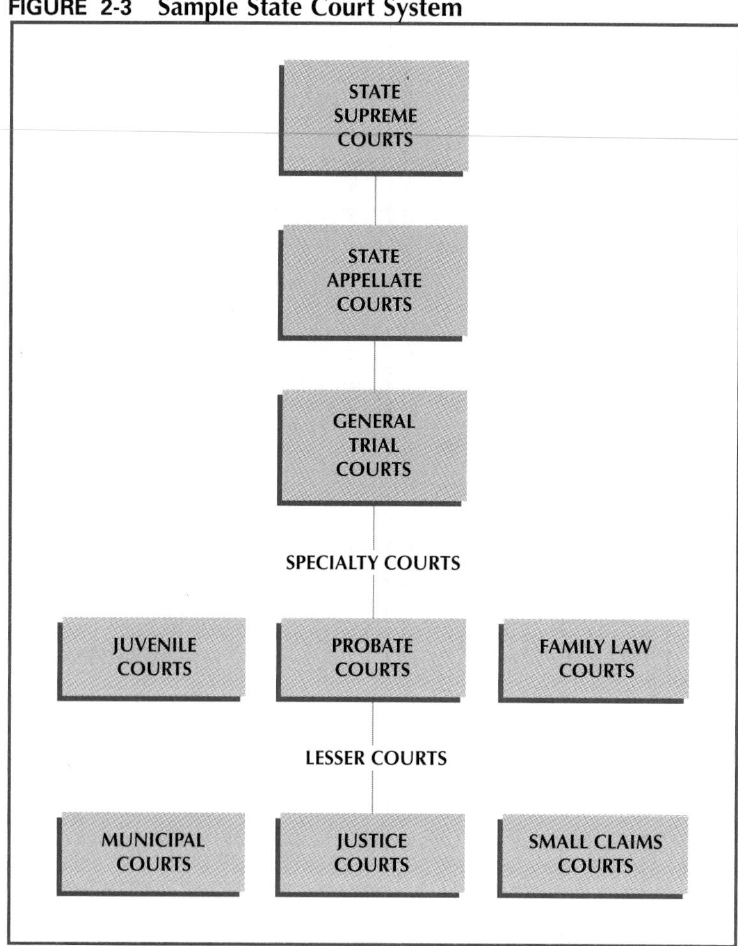

The U.S. Supreme Court is the only court expressly created in the U.S. Constitution. All other courts in the federal system were created by Congress pursuant to the Constitution's language allowing such a system if Congress found it necessary. The Constitution also makes the U.S. Supreme Court a court of original jurisdiction. The U.S. Supreme Court serves as the trial court for cases involving ambassadors, public ministers, or consuls and for cases in which two states are involved in a lawsuit. **For Example,** the U.S. Supreme Court has served for a number of years as the trial court for a Colorado River water rights case in which California, Nevada, and Arizona are parties.

3. State Court Systems

(a) General Trial Courts

Most states have trial courts of general jurisdiction that may be called superior courts, circuit courts, or county courts. These courts of general and original jurisdiction usually hear both criminal and civil cases. Cases that do not meet the jurisdictional requirements for the federal district courts would be tried in these courts. Figure 2-3 illustrates a sample state court system.

(b) Specialty Courts

Most states also have courts with limited jurisdiction, sometimes referred to as *specialty courts*. **For Example,** most states have juvenile courts, or courts with limited jurisdiction over criminal matters that involve defendants who are under the age of 18. Other specialty courts or lesser courts in state systems are probate and family law courts.

(c) City, Municipal, and Justice Courts

Cities and counties may also have lesser courts with limited jurisdiction, which may be referred to as *municipal courts* or *justice courts*. These courts generally handle civil matters in which the claim made in the suit is an amount below a certain level, such as $5,000 or $10,000. These courts may also handle misdemeanor types of offenses, such as traffic violations or violations of noise ordinances, and the trials for them.

(d) Small Claims Courts

Most states also have **small claims courts** at the county or city level. These are courts of limited jurisdiction where parties with small amounts in dispute may come to have a third party, such as a justice of the peace or city judge, review their disputes and determine how they should be resolved. A true small claims court is one in which the parties are not permitted to be represented by counsel. Rather, the parties present their cases to the judge in an informal manner without the strict procedural rules that apply in courts of general jurisdiction. Small claims courts provide a faster and inexpensive means for resolving a dispute that does not involve a large amount of claimed damages.

(e) State Appellate Courts

Most states also have intermediate-level courts similar to the federal courts of appeals. They are courts with appellate jurisdiction that review the decisions of lower courts in that state. Decisions of the general trial courts in a state would be appealed to these courts.

(f) State Supreme Courts

The highest court in most states is generally known as the *state supreme court*, but a few states, such as New York, may call their highest court the *court of appeals*; Maine and Massachusetts, for example, call their highest court the *supreme judicial court*. State supreme courts primarily have appellate jurisdiction, but some states' courts do have original jurisdiction, such as in Arizona, where counties in litigation have their trial at the supreme court level. Most state supreme courts do not hear all cases appealed. These courts also have a screening process. They are required to hear some cases, such as criminal cases in which the defendant has received the death penalty. A decision of a state supreme court is final except in those circumstances in which a federal law or treaty or the U.S. Constitution is involved. Cases with these federal subject matter issues can then be appealed to the U.S. Supreme Court.

B. Court Procedure

Once a party decides to use the court system for resolution of a dispute, that party enters a world with specific rules, procedures, and terms that must be used to have a case proceed.

4. Participants in the Court System

The **plaintiff** is the party that initiates the proceedings in a court of original jurisdiction. In a criminal case in which charges are brought, the party initiating the proceedings would be called the **prosecutor**. The party against whom the civil or criminal proceedings are brought is the **defendant**. A **judge** is the primary officer of the court and is either an elected or an appointed official who presides over the matters brought before the court. Attorneys or lawyers are trained individuals selected by the plaintiff and the defendant as their representatives in the matter for purposes of presenting their cases.

A **jury** is a body of citizens sworn by a court to reach a verdict on the basis of the case presented to them. Jurors are chosen for service based on lists compiled from voter registration and driver's license records.

5. Which Law Applies—Conflicts of Law

When a lawsuit is brought, there is not just the question of where a case will be tried but also of what law will be applied in determining the rights of the parties. The principle that determines when a court applies the law of its own state—the law of the forum—or some foreign law is called *conflict of laws*. Because there are 50 state court systems and a federal court system, as well as a high degree of interstate activity, conflicts of law questions arise frequently.

Some general rules apply. For example, the law of the state in which the court is located governs the case on procedural issues and rules of evidence. In contract litigation, the court applies the law of the state in which the contract was made for determining issues of formation. Matters relating to the performance of the contract, excuse or liability for nonperformance, and the measure of damages for nonperformance are generally governed by the law of the state where the contract is to be performed. Similar considerations apply to the interpretation of international contracts. **For Example,** a California court will apply Swiss law to a contract made in Switzerland that is to be performed in that country.

However, it is becoming more common in cases of contracts with interstate aspects for the parties to specify their choice of law in their contract. In the absence of a law-selecting provision in the contract, there is a growing acceptance of the rule that a contract should be governed by the law of the state that has the most significant contacts with the transaction.

For Example, assume the buyer's place of business and the seller's plant are located in Nebraska, and the buyer is purchasing goods from the seller to resell to Nebraska customers. Many courts will hold that this is a contract governed by the law of Nebraska in all respects. In determining which state has the most significant contacts, the court considers the place of contracting, negotiating, and performing; the location of the subject matter of the contract; and the domicile (residence), states of incorporation, and principal place of business of the parties.

6. Initial Steps in a Lawsuit

The following steps in a lawsuit generally apply in cases brought in courts of original jurisdiction. Not every step applies in every case, but understanding the terminology of litigation is important for businesspeople.

(a) Commencement of a Lawsuit

A lawsuit begins with the filing of a **complaint.** The complaint generally contains a description of the conduct complained of by the plaintiff and a request for damages, such as a monetary amount. **For Example,** a plaintiff in a contract suit would describe the contract, when it was entered into, and when the defendant stopped performance on the contract. A copy of the contract would be attached to the complaint.

(b) Service of Process

Once the plaintiff has filed the complaint with the clerk of the court that has jurisdiction over the case, the plaintiff has the responsibility of notifying the defendant that the lawsuit has been filed. The defendant must be served with **process.** Process, often called a *writ, notice*, or *summons*, is delivered to the defendant and includes a copy of the complaint and notification that the defendant must appear and respond to the allegations in the complaint.

(c) The Defendant's Response and the Pleadings

After the defendant is served with process in the case, the defendant is required to make some response or to **answer** the complaint within the time provided under the court's rules. In answering the plaintiff's complaint, the defendant has several options. For example, the defendant could make a **motion to dismiss**, which is a request to the court to dismiss the lawsuit on the grounds that, even if everything the plaintiff said in the complaint were true, there is still no right of recovery. A motion to dismiss is also called a **demurrer**.

A defendant could also respond and deny the allegations. **For Example,** in a contract lawsuit, the defendant-seller could say he did not breach the contract but stopped shipment of the goods because the plaintiff-buyer did not pay for the goods in advance as the contract required. A defendant could also **counterclaim** in the answer, which is asking the court for damages as a result of the underlying dispute. **For Example,** the defendant-seller in the contract lawsuit might ask for damages for the plaintiff-buyer's failure to pay as the contract required.

All documents filed in this initial phase of the case are referred to as the **pleadings**. The pleadings, when accepted following the defendant's objections and the plaintiff's corrections, are a statement of the case and the basis for recovery if all the facts alleged can be proved.

(d) Discovery

The Federal Rules of Civil Procedure and similar rules in all states permit one party to obtain from the adverse party information about all witnesses, documents, and any other items relevant to the case. **Discovery** requires each side to name its potential witnesses and to provide each side the chance to question those witnesses in advance of the trial. Each party also has the opportunity to examine, inspect, and photograph books, records, buildings, and machines. Even examining the physical or mental condition of a party is part of discovery when it has relevance in the case. The scope of discovery is extremely broad because the rules permit any questions that are likely to lead to admissible evidence.

(1) Deposition. A **deposition** is the testimony of a witness taken under oath outside the courtroom; it is transcribed by a court reporter. Each party is permitted to question the witness. If a party or a witness gives testimony at the trial that is inconsistent with her deposition testimony, the prior inconsistent testimony can be used to **impeach** the witness's credibility at trial.

Depositions can be taken either for discovery purposes or to preserve the testimony of a witness who will not be available during the trial. Some states now permit depositions to be videotaped. A videotape is a more effective way of presenting deposition testimony than reading that testimony at trial from a reporter's transcript because jurors can see the witness and the witness's demeanor and hear the words as they were spoken, complete with inflection.[7]

(2) Other Forms of Discovery. Other forms of discovery include written **interrogatories** (questions) and written **requests for production of documents**. These discovery requests can be very time consuming to the answering party and often lead to pretrial legal disputes between the parties and their attorneys as a result of the legal expenses involved.

(e) Motion for Summary Judgment

If no issue of material fact in the case is disputed, either party can file a **motion for summary judgment**. Using affidavits or deposition testimony obtained in discovery, the party can establish that there are no factual issues and that the case can be decided as an issue of law by a judge. For example, suppose that the parties can agree that they entered into a life insurance contract but dispute whether the policy applies when there is a suicide. The facts are not in dispute; the law on payment of insurance proceeds in the event that a suicide is in dispute. Such a case is one that is appropriate for summary judgment.

(f) Designation of Expert Witnesses

In some cases, such as those involving medical malpractice, the parties may want to designate an expert witness. An **expert witness** is a witness who has some special expertise, such as an economist who gives expert opinion on the value of future lost income or a physician who testifies whether a doctor followed protocol in treating a patient. There are rules for naming expert witnesses as well as for admitting into evidence any studies or documents of the expert.[8] The purpose of these rules is to avoid the problem of what has been called *junk science*, or the admission of experts' testimony and research that has not been properly conducted or reviewed by peers.

7. The Trial

(a) Selecting a Jury

Jurors drawn for service are questioned by the judge and lawyers to determine whether they are biased or have any preformed judgments about the parties in the case. Jury selection is called ***voir dire* examination.** **For Example,** in the trial of Martha Stewart, the multimedia home and garden diva, it took a great deal of time for the lawyers to question the potential jurors about their prior knowledge concerning the case, which had received nationwide attention and much media coverage. Lawyers have the opportunity to remove jurors who know parties in the case or who indicate they have already formed opinions about guilt or innocence. The attorneys question the potential jurors to determine if a juror should be *challenged for cause* (e.g., when the prospective juror states he is employed by the plaintiff's company). Challenges for cause are unlimited, but each side can also exercise six to eight peremptory challenges.[9] A peremptory challenge is an arbitrary challenge that may be used to strike (remove) a juror except for racial reasons.

(b) Opening Statements

After the jury is called, the opposing attorneys make their **opening statements** to the jury. An opening statement, as one lawyer has explained, makes a puzzle frame for the case so jurors can follow the witnesses and place the pieces of the case—the various forms of evidence—within the frame.

(c) The Presentation of Evidence

Following the opening statements, the plaintiff then begins to present his case with witnesses and other evidence. A judge rules on the **admissibility** of evidence. Evidence can consist of documents, testimony, and even physical evidence.

In the case of testimony, the attorney for the plaintiff conducts **direct examination** of his witnesses during his case, and the defense attorney then **cross-examines** the plaintiff's witnesses. The plaintiff's

[7] At the civil trial of O. J. Simpson for the wrongful death of Nicole Brown Simpson and Ronald Goldman, Daniel Petrocelli used a videotape of Mr. Simpson's deposition very effectively in impeaching Mr. Simpson's testimony at trial. Daniel Petrocelli, *Triumph of Justice: The Final Judgment on the Simpson Saga* (New York: Crown, 1998).

[8] *Daubert v Merrell Dow Pharmaceuticals, Inc.*, 509 US 579 (1993).

[9] The number of peremptory challenges varies from state to state and may also vary within a particular state depending on the type of case. For example, in Arizona, peremptory challenges are unlimited in capital cases.

ETHICS & THE LAW

On July 9, 1999, a Los Angeles jury awarded Patricia Anderson, her four children, and her friend Jo Tigner $107 million in actual damages and $4.8 billion in punitive damages from General Motors (GM) in a lawsuit the five brought against GM because they were trapped and burned in their Chevrolet Malibu when it exploded on impact following a rear-end collision.

Jury foreman Coleman Thorton, explaining the magnitude of the jury verdict, said, "GM has no regard for the people in their cars, and they should be held responsible for it." Richard Shapiro, an attorney for GM, said, "We're very disappointed. This was a very sympathetic case. The people who were injured were innocent in this matter. They were the victims of a drunk driver."

The accident, which occurred on Christmas Eve 1993, was the result of a drunk driver's striking the Anderson's Malibu at 70 mph. The driver's blood alcohol level was 0.20, but the defense lawyers noted they were not permitted to disclose to the jury that the driver of the auto that struck the Malibu was drunk.

During the discovery process, lawyers for the Andersons uncovered a 1973 internal "value analysis" memo written by a low-level engineer, Edward C. Ivey, analyzing the potential cost to GM of "post-collision fuel-tank fires." Mr. Ivey used a figure of $200,000 for the cost of a fatality and noted that there are 500 fatalities per year in GM auto fuel fire accidents. The memo also stated that his analysis must be read in the context of "it is really impossible to put a value on human life."* Mr. Ivey wrote that the cost of these explosions to GM would be $2.40 per car.

Lawyers uncovered another memo related to the Ivey memo. An in-house lawyer discovered the Ivey memo in 1981 and wrote:

*Obviously, Ivey is not an individual whom we would ever, in any conceivable situation, want identified to the plaintiffs in a post-collision fuel-fed fire case, and the documents he generated are undoubtedly some of the potentially most harmful and most damaging were they ever to be produced.***

In the initial cases brought against GM, the company's defense was that the engineer's thinking was his own and did not reflect company policy. However, when the 1981 lawyer's commentary was found as part of discovery in a Florida case in 1998, GM lost that line of defense. In the Florida case in which a 13-year-old boy was burned to death in a 1983 Oldsmobile Cutlass station wagon, the jury awarded his family $33 million.

The two documents have become the center of each case. Judge Ernest G. Williams of Los Angeles Superior Court, who upheld the verdict in the $4.8 billion Los Angeles case but reduced the damages, wrote in his opinion:

The court finds that clear and convincing evidence demonstrated that defendants' fuel tank was placed behind the axle of the automobiles of the make and model here in order to maximize profits to the disregard of public safety.

On appeal, the California appellate court reduced the verdict amount to $1.2 billion.***

Discuss the ethical issues involved with Mr. Ivey's memo and the lawyer's conduct in 1981.

*Milo Geyelin, "How an Internal Memo Written 26 Years Ago Is Costing GM Dearly," *Wall Street Journal*, September 29, 1999, A1.

** *Id.* at A6.

*** *Id.*

attorney can then ask questions again of his witnesses in what is called **redirect examination**. Finally, the defendant may question the plaintiff's witnesses again in **recross-examination**. This procedure is followed with all of the plaintiff's witnesses, and then the defendant presents her case after the plaintiff's case concludes. During the defendant's case, the lawyer for the defendant conducts direct examination of the defendant's witnesses, and the plaintiff's lawyer can then cross-examine the defendant's witnesses.

THINKING THINGS THROUGH

WHY DO WE REQUIRE SWORN TESTIMONY?

There is a difference between what people say in conversation and even what company executives say in speeches and reports and what they are willing to say under oath. The taking of the oath often means that different information and recollections will emerge. The oath is symbolic and carries the penalty of criminal prosecution for perjury if the testimony given is false.

The *Wall Street Journal* has reported that the testimony of executives in the Microsoft antitrust trial and their statements regarding their business relationships outside the courtroom are quite different. For example, the following quotations indicate some discrepancies. Eric Benhamou, the CEO of Palm, Inc., said:

We believe that the handheld opportunity remains wide open. . . . Unlike the PC industry, there is no monopoly of silicon, there is no monopoly of software.

However, at the Microsoft trial, another officer of Palm, Michael Mace, offered the following testimony:

We believe that there is a very substantial risk that Microsoft could manipulate its products and its standards in order to exclude Palm from the marketplace in the future.

Likewise, Microsoft has taken different positions inside and outside the courtroom. For example, an attorney for Microsoft, in grilling a witness for a competitor, stated that Microsoft had "zero deployments of its interactive TV middleware products connected to cable systems in the United States; isn't that correct, sir?" However, Microsoft's marketing materials provide as follows:

*Microsoft's multiple deployments around the world now including Charter-show Microsoft TV is ready to deploy now and set the standard for what TV can be.**

For more information on the Microsoft antitrust cases, go to **http://www.usdoj.gov** or **http://www.microsoft.com**.

*Rebecca Buckman, and Nicholas Kulish, "Microsoft Trial Prompts an Outbreak of Doublespeak," *Wall Street Journal*, April 15, 2002, B1, B3.

(d) Motion for a Directed Verdict

A motion for a **directed verdict** asks the court to grant a verdict because even if all the evidence that has been presented by each side were true, there is either no basis for recovery or no defense to recovery. For example, in some states, the defendant can make a motion for a directed verdict after the plaintiff's case is concluded. The defendant's motion argues that even if the plaintiff's case were 100 percent true, there is no basis in law for recovery. It is also possible for either side to move for a directed verdict after both sides have presented their cases. The defendant is arguing the same position as stated earlier, that there is no basis for recovery even assuming all facts to be true. The plaintiff is arguing that even if everything the defendant presented was 100 percent true, there was nothing in the defense case that challenged the plaintiff's right to recovery.

(e) Summation

After the witnesses for both parties have been examined and all the evidence has been presented, each attorney makes another address to the jury. These statements are called **summations** or *closing arguments;* they summarize the case and suggest that a particular verdict be returned by the jury.

(f) Motion for Mistrial

During the course of a trial, when necessary to avoid great injustice, the trial court may declare that there has been a **mistrial**. The declaration of a mistrial terminates the trial and requires that it start over with a new jury. A mistrial can be declared for jury or attorney misconduct. **For Example,** if a juror were caught fraternizing with one of the lawyers in the case, objectivity would be compromised and the court would most likely declare a mistrial.

(g) Jury Instructions and Verdict

After the summation by the attorneys, the court gives the jurors **instructions** on the appropriate law to apply to the facts they find to be true or untrue. The jury then deliberates and renders its verdict. After the jury renders a verdict, the court enters a judgment conforming to the verdict. If the jury is deadlocked and unable to reach a verdict, the case is reset for a new trial at some future date.

(h) Motion for New Trial; Motion for Judgment N.O.V.

A court may grant a judgment *non obstante veredicto* or a **judgment n.o.v.** (notwithstanding the verdict) if the verdict is clearly wrong as a matter of law. The court can set aside the verdict and enter a judgment in favor of the other party. Perhaps one of the most famous judgments n.o.v. occurred in Boston in 1997 when a judge reversed the murder conviction of nanny Louise Woodward, who was charged with the murder of one of her young charges.

8. Posttrial Procedures

(a) Recovery of Costs/Attorney Fees

Generally, the prevailing party is awarded costs. Costs include filing fees, service-of-process fees, witness fees, deposition transcript costs, and jury fees. Costs do not include compensation spent by a party for preparing the case or being present at trial, including the time lost from work because of the case and the fee paid to the attorney, although lost wages from an injury are generally part of damages.

Attorney fees may be recovered by a party who prevails if a statute permits the recovery of attorney fees or if the complaint involves a claim for breach of contract and the contract contains a clause providing for recovery of attorney fees.

(b) Execution of Judgment

After a judgment for the amount of damages plus costs has been entered or all appeals or appeal rights have ended, the losing party should comply with the judgment of the court. If not, the winning party may then take steps to execute, or carry out, the judgment. The **execution** is accomplished by the seizure and sale of the losing party's assets by the sheriff according to a writ of execution or a writ of possession.

Garnishment is a common method of satisfying a judgment. When the judgment debtor is an employee, the appropriate judicial authority in the state garnishes (by written notice to the employer) a portion of the employee's wages on a regular basis until the judgment is paid.

C. Alternative Dispute Resolution (ADR)

Parties can use means other than litigation to resolve disagreements or disputes. The discussion of the details of litigation shows its time and money costs and should encourage those with disputes to pursue alternative methods for resolving them. Those methods, which include arbitration, mediation, and several other forms of resolution, are enjoying increasing popularity. Figure 2-4 provides an overall view of dispute resolution procedures.

9. Arbitration

In **arbitration**, a dispute is settled by one or more arbitrators (disinterested persons selected by the parties to the dispute). Arbitration enables the parties to present the facts before trained experts familiar with the industry practices that may affect the nature and outcome of the dispute. Arbitration first reached extensive use in the field of commercial contracts and is encouraged as a means of avoiding expensive litigation and easing the workload of courts.[10]

A number of states have adopted the Uniform Arbitration Act.[11] Under this act and similar statutes, the parties to a contract may agree in advance that all disputes arising under it will be submitted to arbitration. In some instances, the contract will name the arbitrators for the duration of the contract.

[10] *Hart v McChristian*, 42 SW2d 552 (Ark 2001). Arbitration has existed in the United States since 1920 when New York passed an arbitration statute. For a look at the history of arbitration, see Charles L. Knapp, "Taking Contracts Private: The Quiet Revolution in Contract Law," 71 *Fordham L. Rev.* 761 (2002).

[11] On August 3, 2000, the National Conference of Commissioners on Uniform State Laws unanimously passed major revisions to the Uniform Arbitration Act (UAA). These revisions were the first major changes in 45 years to the UAA, which is the basis of arbitration law in 49 states, although not all states have adopted it in its entirety. Thirty-five states and the District of Columbia have adopted the 1955 version. Only 8 states have adopted the UAA 2000 revisions. Christopher Benne, *et al.*, State Legislative Update, 2 *Journal of Dispute Resolution* 4A (2005).

FIGURE 2-4 Dispute Resolution Procedures

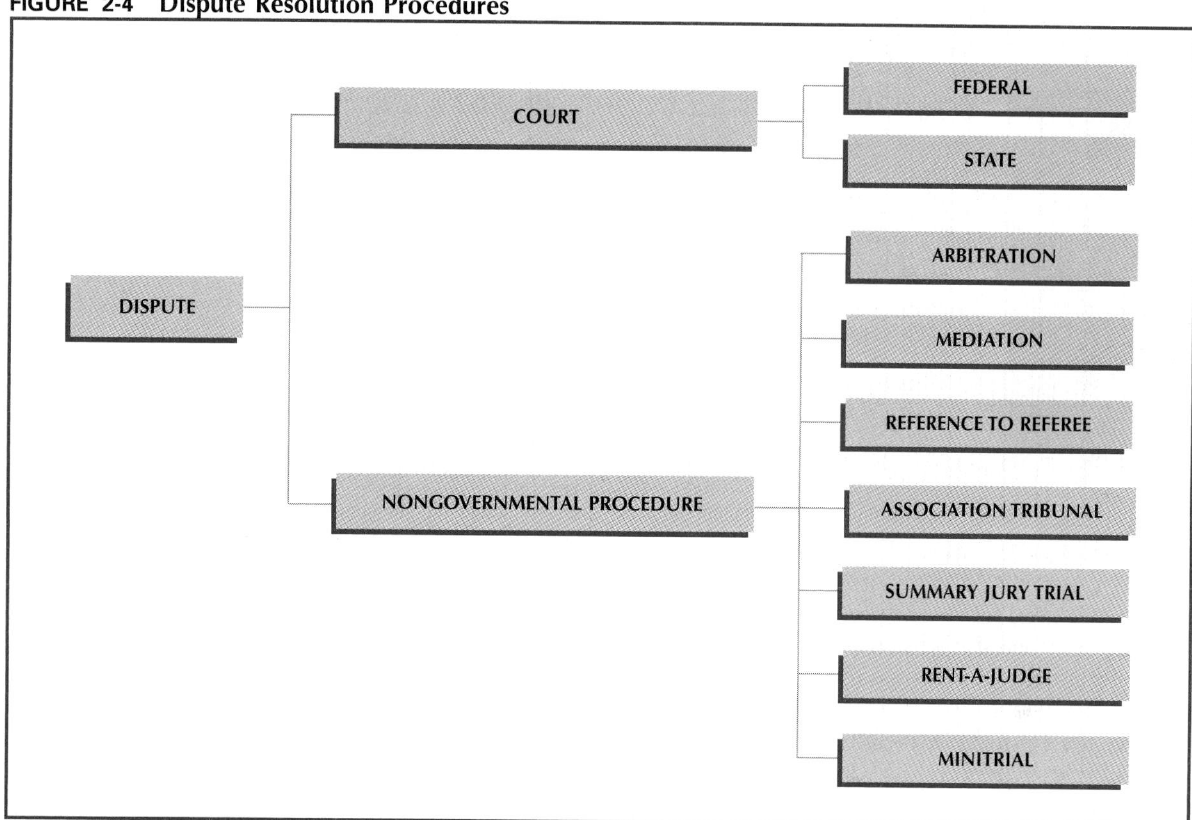

The uniform act requires a written agreement to arbitrate.[12]

The Federal Arbitration Act[13] provides that an arbitration clause in a contract relating to an interstate transaction is valid, irrevocable, and enforceable. When a contract subject to the Federal Arbitration Act provides for the arbitration of disputes, the parties are bound to arbitrate in accordance with the federal statute even if the agreement to arbitrate would not be binding under state law.

(a) Mandatory Arbitration

In contrast with statutes that merely regulate arbitration when it is selected voluntarily by the parties, some statutes require that certain kinds of disputes be submitted to arbitration. In some states, by rule or statute, the arbitration of small claims is required.

(b) Scope of Arbitration

When arbitration is required by statute, the terms of the statute will define the scope of the arbitration. When the parties have voluntarily agreed to arbitrate, their agreement will control the scope of the dispute. In such a case, questions may arise as to what disputes are covered. Because arbitration is now favored, any doubt as to its scope will be decided in favor of arbitration by the arbitrator.[14]

(c) Finality of Arbitration

Most parties provide, within their arbitration agreements, that the decision of the arbitrator will be final. Such a clause is binding on the parties, even when the decision seems to be wrong, and can be set aside only if there is clear proof of fraud, arbitrary conduct, or a significant procedural error.[15]

[12] *Anderson v Federated Mutual Ins. Co.*, 465 NW2d 68 (Minn App 1991).

[13] 9 USC § 114 *et. seq.*

[14] *First Options v Kaplan*, 514 US 938 (1995). See also *Engel v Refco, Inc.*, 746 NYS 2d 826 (2002), in which the court noted that parties can agree to an arbitration clause through conduct.

[15] *Trans Chemical Ltd. v China Nat. Machinery Import & Export*, 161 F3d 314 (5th Cir 1998); *Crim v Pepperidge Farm, Inc.*, 32 F Supp 2d 326 (D Md 1999).

E-COMMERCE AND CYBERLAW

SPEED OF LIGHT INJUNCTIONS: REMEDIES AND THE INTERNET

Because e-commerce moves quickly, legal wrongs in cyberspace can very rapidly cause irreparable damage. For example, suppose that a Web site is selling gray market goods. The trademark holder who relies on courts and an injunction will find the goods sold over the Internet before the court can rule. As a result, many judges, when facing a petition for an injunction for a cyberspace company, encourage the parties to discuss and resolve the issue because just a hearing for a preliminary injunction will take too much time. As one court notes, "technology can outdistance" us very quickly.*

* *Sun Microsystems, Inc. v Microsoft Corp.*, 188 F3d 1115 (9th Cir 1999).

In contrast, when arbitration is mandatory under statute or rule, it is generally provided that the losing party may appeal from such arbitration to a court.[16] The appeal proceeds just as though there had never been any prior arbitration. This new court proceeding is called a **trial *de novo*** and is necessary to preserve the constitutional right to a jury trial. As a practical matter, however, relatively few appeals are taken from arbitration decisions.

10. Mediation

In **mediation**, a neutral person acts as a messenger between opposing sides of a dispute, carrying to each side the latest settlement offer made by the other. The mediator has no authority to make a decision, although in some cases the mediator may make suggestions that might ultimately be accepted by the disputing parties.

The use of mediation has the advantage of keeping discussions going when the disputing parties have developed such fixed attitudes or personal animosity that direct discussion between them has become impossible.

11. MedArb

In this new form of alternative dispute resolution (ADR), the arbitrator is also empowered to act as a mediator. Beyond just hearing a case, the arbitrator acts as a messenger for the parties on unresolved issues.

12. Reference to a Third Person

Many types of transactions provide for **reference to a third person**, in which a third person or a committee makes an out-of-court determination of the rights of persons. **For Example,** employees and an employer may have agreed as a term of the employment contract that claims of employees under retirement plans will be decided by a designated board or committee. In a sales contract, the seller and buyer can select a third person to determine the price to be paid for goods. Construction contracts often include a provision that any disputes shall be referred to the architect in charge of the construction and that the architect's decision will be final.

Ordinarily, with these types of clauses, the parties agree that the decision of such a third person or board is final and there will be no judicial appeal or review. These referrals often eliminate the disputes or pursuit of remedies. **For Example,** fire insurance policies commonly provide that if the parties cannot agree on the amount of the loss, each will appoint an appraiser, the two appraisers will appoint a third appraiser, and the three will determine the amount of the loss the insurer is required to pay. These appraisers must be independent and impartial.

13. Association Tribunals

Many disputes never reach the courts because both parties to a dispute belong to a group or an association, and the **association tribunal** created by the

[16] *Porreco v Red Top RV Center*, 216 Cal App 3d 113, 264 Cal Rptr 609 (1989). See *Business Law Today* 8 (March/April 1999), which is an entire issue devoted to ADR issues and advantages.

group or association disposes of the matter. A dispute between members of a labor union, a stockbrokers' exchange, or a church may be heard by some board or committee within the association or group. Courts review the actions of such tribunals to determine that a fair and proper procedure was followed, but generally they go no further. Courts do not examine the facts of the case to see if the association tribunal reached the same conclusion that the court could have reached.

Trade associations commonly require their members to employ out-of-court methods of dispute settlement. **For Example,** the National Association of Home Builders requires its member builders to employ arbitration. The National Automobile Dealers Association provides for panels to determine warranty claims of customers. The decision of such panels is final as to the builder or dealer, but the consumer can still bring a regular lawsuit after losing before the panel. Members of an association must use the association tribunal, which means they cannot bypass the association tribunal and go directly to a law court.[17]

14. Summary Jury Trial

A **summary jury trial** is, in effect, a dry run or mock trial in which the lawyers present their claims before a jury of six persons. The object is to get the reaction of a sample jury. No evidence is presented before this jury, and it bases its opinion solely on what the lawyers state. The determination of the jury has no binding effect, but it has value in that it gives the lawyers some idea of what a jury might think if there were an actual trial. This type of ADR has special value when the heart of a case is whether something is reasonable under all circumstances. When the lawyers and their clients see how the sample jury reacts, they may moderate their positions and reach a settlement.

15. Rent-a-Judge

Under the **rent-a-judge plan**, the parties hire a judge to hear the case. In many states, the parties voluntarily choose the judge as a "referee," and the judge acts under a statute authorizing the appointment of referees. Under such a statute, the referee hears all evidence just as though there were a regular trial, and the rented judge's determination is binding on the parties unless reversed on appeal if such an appeal (like a court trial) is permitted under the parties' agreement. In some jurisdictions, special provision is made for the parties to agree that the decision of the judge selected as referee will be final.

16. Minitrial

When only part of a case is disputed, the parties may stay within the framework of a lawsuit but agree that only the disputed issues will be taken to trial and submitted to a jury. When there is no real dispute over the liability of the defendant but the parties disagree as to the damages, the issue of damages alone may be submitted to the jury. This shortened trial is often called a **minitrial**.

A minitrial may also consist of the parties agreeing to submit their case to a particular person, frequently a retired judge, to listen to the evidence on just the disputed issues and decide the case. The agreement of the parties for the minitrial may specify whether this decision will be binding on the parties. As a practical matter, the evaluation of a case by a neutral person often brings the opposing parties together to reach a settlement.

17. Judicial Triage

The court systems, experiencing heavy caseloads, now practice **judicial triage**. Judges examine cases from a timeliness perspective. For example, in asbestos cases, judges are now evaluating plaintiffs on the basis of "how sick they are" and expediting trials for those plaintiffs who are the most ill from the alleged effects of asbestos that are the subject of their suits. The trials of those who do not have medical documentation of current illness are postponed and placed on the inactive docket until the court can get to them or until the plaintiffs become sick. Using triage, one judge has been able to bring to trial 40 percent of all asbestos cases brought since 1992.[18]

18. Contract Provisions

The parties' contract may pave the way for the settlement of future disputes by containing clauses requiring the parties to use one of the procedures already described. In addition, contracts may provide that no action may be taken until after the expiration of a specified cooling-off period. Contracts may also

[17] *Canady v Meharry Medical College*, 811 SW2d 902 (Tenn App 1991).

[18] Susan Warren, "Swamped Courts Practice Plaintiff Triage," *Wall Street Journal*, January 27, 2003, B1, B3.

specify that the parties should continue in the performance of their contract even though a dispute between them still exists.

19. Disposition of Complaints and Ombudsmen

In contrast with the traditional and alternative procedures for resolving disputes are the procedures aimed at removing the grounds for a complaint before it develops into a dispute that requires resolution. **For Example,** the complaint department in a department store is often be able to iron out a difficulty before the customer and the store are locked in an adversarial position that could end in a lawsuit. Grievance committee procedures are often effective in bringing about an adjustment or resolution. A statute may designate a government official to examine complaints. Such an official is often called an **ombudsman**. The few federal statutes that have required such an officer have not given the ombudsman any judicial power. Typically, the ombudsman is limited to receiving complaints, supervising the administration of the system, and making recommendations for improvements.

Class Action (1991) (R)

Here is a good movie to illustrate discovery and the ethics of withholding documents in production of evidence/paperwork.

For movie clips that illustrate business law concepts, see LawFlix at **http://wdvl.westbuslaw.com.**

Summary

Courts have been created to hear and resolve legal disputes. A court's specific power is defined by its jurisdiction. Courts of original jurisdiction are trial courts, and courts that review the decisions of trial courts are appellate courts. Trial courts may have general jurisdiction to hear a wide range of civil and criminal matters, or they may be courts of limited jurisdiction—such as a probate court or the Tax Court—with the subject matter of their cases restricted to certain areas.

The courts in the United States are organized into two different systems: the state and federal court systems. There are three levels of courts, for the most part, in each system, with trial courts, appellate courts, and a supreme court in each. The federal courts are federal district courts, federal courts of appeals, and the U.S. Supreme Court. In the states, there may be specialized courts, such as municipal, justice, and small claims courts, for trial courts. Within the courts of original jurisdiction, there are rules for procedures in all matters brought before them. A civil case begins with the filing of a complaint by a plaintiff, which is then answered by a defendant. The parties may be represented by their attorneys. Discovery is the pretrial process used by the parties to find out the evidence in the case. The parties can use depositions, interrogatories, and document requests to uncover relevant information.

The case is managed by a judge and may be tried to a jury selected through the process of *voir dire*, with the parties permitted to challenge jurors on the basis of cause or through the use of their peremptory challenges. The trial begins following discovery and involves opening statements and the presentation of evidence, including the direct examination and cross-examination of witnesses. Once a judgment is entered, the party who has won can collect the judgment through garnishment and a writ of execution.

Alternatives to litigation for dispute resolution are available, including arbitration, mediation, MedArb, reference to a third party, association tribunals, summary jury trials, rent-a-judge plans, minitrials, and the use of ombudsmen. Court dockets are relieved and cases consolidated using judicial triage, a process in which courts hear the cases involving the most serious medical issues and health conditions first. Triage is a blending of the judicial and alternative dispute resolution mechanisms.

Questions and Case Problems

1. List the steps in a lawsuit. Begin with the filing of the complaint, and explain the points at which there can be a final determination of the parties' rights in the case.
2. Distinguish between mandatory and voluntary arbitration.

3. What is the difference between mediation and arbitration?
4. Ralph Dewey has been charged with a violation of the Electronic Espionage Act, a federal statute that prohibits the transfer, by computer or disk or other electronic means, of a company's proprietary data and information. Ralph is curious. What type of court has jurisdiction? Can you determine which court?
5. Jerry Lewinsky was called for jury duty. When *voir dire* began, Jerry realized that the case involved his supervisor at work. Can Jerry remain as a juror on the case? Why or why not?
6. Carolyn, Elwood, and Isabella are involved in a real estate development. The development is a failure, and Carolyn, Elwood, and Isabella want to have their rights determined. They could bring a lawsuit, but they are afraid the case is so complicated that a judge and jury not familiar with the problems of real estate development would not reach a proper result. What can they do?
7. Larketta Randolph purchased a mobile home from Better Cents Home Builders, Inc., in Opelika, Alabama. She financed her purchase through Green Tree Financial Corporation. Ms. Randolph signed a standard form Manufactured Home Retail Installment Contract and Security Agreement that required her to buy Vendor's Single Interest insurance, which protects the seller against the costs of repossession in the event of default. The agreement also provided that all disputes arising from, or relating to, the contract, whether arising under case law or statutory law, would be resolved by binding arbitration. Larketta has a dispute with Green Tree over an additional $15 in finance charges she claims were not disclosed in the contract. She and other Green Tree customers file a class action suit to recover the fees. Green Tree has moved to dismiss the suit because Larketta had not submitted the issue to arbitration. Larketta protests, "But I want the right to go to court!" Does she have that right? What are the rights of parties under a contract with an arbitration clause? [*Green Tree Financial Corp. v Randolph*, 531 US 79]
8. Esmeralda sued Adolphus. She lost the lawsuit because the judge made a wrong decision. What can Esmeralda do now? Explain her options.
9. Indicate whether the following courts are courts of original, general, limited, or appellate jurisdiction:

   a. Small claims court
   b. Federal bankruptcy court
   c. Federal district court
   d. U.S. Supreme Court
   e. Municipal court
   f. Probate court
   g. Federal court of appeals

10. John purchased a computer from Gateway, Inc. He noted upon starting it up that he had to agree to a number of provisions in the contract of purchase in order to continue his initial installation. The program indicated that if he did not wish to agree to the terms, he could return the computer to Gateway at Gateway's expense. One of the provisions requires that any disputes arising under the agreement be submitted to binding arbitration. John wonders if such a clause is valid. "What if I have statutory rights and protections in court?" Advise John on his rights under the Gateway agreement.
11. Mostek Corp., a Texas corporation, made a contract to sell computer-related products to North American Foreign Trading Corp., a New York corporation. North American used its own purchase order form, on which appeared the statement that any dispute arising out of an order would be submitted to arbitration, as provided in the terms set forth on the back of the order. Acting on the purchase order, Mostek delivered almost all of the goods but failed to deliver the final installment. North American then demanded that the matter be arbitrated. Mostek refused to do so. Was arbitration required? [*Application of Mostek Corp.*, 120 App Div 2d 383, 502 NYS2d 181]
12. Ceasar Wright was a longshoreman in Charleston, South Carolina, and a member of the International Longshoremen's Association (AFL-CIO). Wright used the union hiring hall. The collective bargaining agreement (CBA) of Wright's union provides for arbitration of all grievances. Another clause of the CBA states: "It is the intention and purpose of all parties here to that no provision or part of this Agreement shall be violative of any Federal or State Law."

    On February 18, 1992, while Wright was working for Stevens Shipping and Terminal Company (Stevens), he injured his right heel and back. He sought permanent compensation from Stevens and settled his claims for $250,000 and another $10,000 in attorney fees. Wright was also awarded Social Security disability benefits.

    In January 1995, Wright, whose doctor had approved his return to work, returned to the hiring hall and asked to be referred for work. Wright did work between January 2 and January 11, 1995, but when the companies realized Wright had been certified as permanently disabled, they deemed him not qualified for longshore work under the CBA and refused to allow him to work for them.

    Wright did not file a grievance under the union agreement but instead hired a lawyer and proceeded with a claim under the Americans with Disabilities Act. The district court dismissed the case because Wright had failed to pursue the grievance procedure provided by the CBA. Must Wright pursue the dispute procedure first, or can he go right to court based on his federal rights under the Americans with Disabilities Act? [*Wright v Universal Maritime Service Corp.*, 525 US 70]

13. Winona Ryder was arrested for shoplifting from Saks Fifth Avenue in California. One of the members of the jury panel for her trial was Peter Guber, a Hollywood executive in charge of the production of three films in which Ms. Ryder starred, including *Bram Stoker's Dracula*, *The Age of Innocence*, and *Little Women*. If you were the prosecuting attorney in the case, how could you discover such information about this potential juror, and what are your options for excluding him from selection? [Rick Lyman, "For the Ryder Trial, a Hollywood Script," *New York Times*, November 3, 2002, SL-1]
14. What is the difference between the role of a trial court and the role of an appellate court? What functions do they perform, and how do they perform them?
15. Martha Simms is the plaintiff in a contract suit she has brought against Floral Supply, Inc., for its failure to deliver the green sponge Martha needed in building the floral designs she sells to exclusive home decorators. Martha had to obtain the sponge from another supplier and was late on seven deliveries. One of Martha's customers has been called by Martha's lawyer as a witness and is now on the witness stand, testifying about Martha's late performance and the penalty she charged. The lawyer for Floral Supply knows that Martha's customer frequently waives penalties for good suppliers. How can Floral Supply's lawyer get that information before the jury?

BUSINESS ETHICS, SOCIAL FORCES, AND THE LAW

CHAPTER (3)

LEARNING OBJECTIVES

After studying this chapter, you should be able to

LO.1 Describe the role of ethics in business and law

LO.2 List the methods for recognizing ethical dilemmas

LO.3 Explain the questions to address in resolving ethical dilemmas

LO.4 Understand the importance of ethics in e-commerce

Each day businesspeople work together on contracts and projects. Their completion of the work is partially the result of the laws that protect contract rights. Much of what businesspeople do, however, is simply a matter of their word. Executives arrive at a 9:00 A.M. meeting because they promised they would be there. An employee meets a deadline for an ad display board because she said she would. Business transactions are completed through a combination of the values of the parties and the laws that reflect those values and the importance of one's word in business. Over time, the rules that govern business, from written laws to unwritten expressions of value, have evolved to provide a framework of operation that ensures good faith in our dealings with each other.

This chapter takes you behind the rules of law to examine the objectives in establishing rules for business conduct. Both social forces and business needs contribute to the standards that govern businesses and their operations.

A. What Is Business Ethics?

Some people have said that the term *business ethics* is an oxymoron, that the word *business* and the word *ethics* contradict each other. **Ethics** is a branch of philosophy dealing with values that relate to the nature of human conduct and values associated with that conduct. Conduct and values in business operations become more complex because individuals are working together to maximize profit. Balancing the goal of profits with the values of individuals and society is the focus of **business ethics**. Some economists make the point that insider trading on the stock market is an efficient way to run that market. To an economist, inside information allows those with the best information to make the most money. This quantitative view ignores the issues of fairness: What about those who trade stock who do not have access to that information? Is the philosophy fair to them? What will happen to the stock market if investors perceive there is not a level playing field? In the U.S. Supreme Court decision *United States v O'Hagan*[1] on insider trading, Justice Ruth Ginsburg noted, "Investors likely wouldn't invest in a market where trading based on misappropriated nonpublic information is unchecked." The field of business ethics deals with the balance between society's values and the need for businesses to remain profitable.

[1] 521 US 657 (1997).

1. The Law as the Standard for Business Ethics

Moral standards come from different sources. Philosophers debate the origin of moral standards as well as which of those standards should be applied. One set of moral standards is simply what codified or **positive law** requires. The test of whether an act is legal is a common moral standard used frequently in business. Codified law, or law created by governmental authority, is used as the standard for ethical behavior. Absent illegality, all behavior is ethical under this simple standard. The phrase "AS IS," when communicated conspicuously on a contract or electronic message (see Chapter 25 for further discussion), means by law that there are no warranties for the goods being sold. **For Example,** if a buyer purchases a used car and the phrase "AS IS" is in the contract, the seller has no legal obligation, in most states, if the transmission falls apart the day after the buyer's purchase. Following a positive law standard, the seller who refuses to repair the transmission has acted ethically. However, the issue of fairness still arises. We know there was no legal obligation to fix the transmission, but was it fair that the car fell apart the day after it was purchased?

2. The Notion of Universal Standards for Business Ethics

Another view of ethics holds that standards exist universally and cannot be changed or modified by law. In many cases, individuals believe the universal standards stem from religious beliefs. In some countries today, the standards for business are still determined by religious tenets. Proponents of **natural law** maintain that higher standards of behavior than those required by positive law must be followed even if those higher standards run contrary to codified law. In the early nineteenth century when slavery was legally permissible in the United States, a positive law standard would sanction such ownership as legal. However, such deprivation of a person's rights violates the natural law principle of individual freedom and would be unethical. Accordingly, **civil disobedience** occurs when natural law proponents violate positive law.

Former Supreme Court Justice Sandra Day O'Connor, who was second in her class at Stanford Law School (the late Chief Justice William Rehnquist was first), was offered a job as a receptionist for a law firm while her male classmates were hired as attorneys. At that time, no law prohibited discrimination against women, so law firms' hiring practices, using only a positive law standard, were ethical. However, if the natural law standard of equality is applied, the refusal to hire Sandra O'Connor as a lawyer, a position for which she was qualified, was discriminatory conduct and unethical.

3. The Standard of Situational Business Ethics or Moral Relativism

Situational ethics or **moral relativism** is a flexible standard of ethics that permits an examination of circumstances and motivation before attaching the label of right or wrong to conduct. The classic example of moral relativism: Would it be unethical to steal a loaf of bread to feed a starving child? A question a Florida court faced was whether to go forward with the prosecution for arson of a man who set fire to an abandoned property in his neighborhood that was used as a crack-cocaine house. In both cases, the law has been broken. The first crime is theft, and the second crime is arson. Neither person, either the bread thief or the arsonist, denied committing the crime. The issue in both cases is not whether the crime was committed but whether the motivation and circumstances excuse the actions and eliminate the punishment. An employee embezzles money from her employer because she is a single parent trying to make ends meet. Was her conduct unethical? The conduct is illegal, but moral relativism would consider the employee's personal circumstances in determining whether it is ethical.

THINKING THINGS THROUGH

CORRUPT CLIMATES: GOOD OR BAD FOR BUSINESS?

As you examine the following list of countries, those in the column labeled "Least Corrupt" (countries in which government officials are least likely to accept bribes) and those in the column marked "Most Corrupt" (countries in which government officials are most likely to accept bribes), can you comment on the business climates in them?

Least Corrupt (Least Likely to Accept Bribes)

- Iceland
- Finland
- New Zealand
- Denmark
- Singapore
- Sweden
- Switzerland
- Norway
- Australia
- Austria
- Netherlands
- United Kingdom
- Luxembourg
- Canada
- Hong Kong
- Germany
- USA
- France
- Belgium
- Ireland
- Chile
- Japan
- Spain

Most Corrupt (Most Likely to Accept Bribes)

- Chad
- Bangladesh
- Turkmenistan
- Myanmar
- Haiti
- Nigeria
- Equatorial Guinea
- Cote 'd Ivoire
- Angola
- Tajikistan
- Sudan
- Somalia
- Paraguay
- Pakistan
- Kenya
- Congo
- Uzbekistan
- Liberia
- Iraq

*From 2005 Transparency International annual survey, **http://www.transparency.org.**

FIGURE 3-1 Guidelines for Analyzing a Contemplated Action

1. DEFINE THE PROBLEM FROM THE DECISION MAKER'S POINT OF VIEW.
2. IDENTIFY WHO COULD BE INJURED BY THE CONTEMPLATED ACTION.
3. DEFINE THE PROBLEM FROM THE OPPOSING POINT OF VIEW.
4. WOULD YOU (AS THE DECISION MAKER) BE WILLING TO TELL YOUR FAMILY, YOUR SUPERVISOR, YOUR CEO, AND THE BOARD OF DIRECTORS ABOUT THE PLANNED ACTION?
5. WOULD YOU BE WILLING TO GO BEFORE A COMMUNITY MEETING, A CONGRESSIONAL HEARING, OR A PUBLIC FORUM TO DESCRIBE THE ACTION?
6. WITH FULL CONSIDERATION OF THE FACTS AND ALTERNATIVES, REACH A DECISION ABOUT WHETHER THE CONTEMPLATED ACTION SHOULD BE TAKEN.

Businesses use moral relativism standards frequently in their international operations. Bribery is illegal in the United States, but, as many businesses argue, it is an accepted method of doing business in other countries.[2] The standard of moral relativism is used to allow behavior in international business transactions that would be a violation of the law in the United States. For example, Google and other Internet service providers have agreed to do business in China despite the restrictions the Chinese government places on the use of the Internet and the content of search engines. Such restrictions in the United States would be an unconstitutional violation of our First Amendment. In China, however, government control of information is legal. Google and others testified before Congress that some entry, however restricted, was better for the Chinese people than no access at all. Their decision weighed the conflicting values and concluded that they would use the standard of honoring the law of China despite the censorship.

4. The Business Stakeholder Standard of Behavior

Businesses have different constituencies, referred to as **stakeholders**, often with conflicting goals for the business. Shareholders, for example, may share economists' view that earnings, and hence dividends, should be maximized. Members of the community where a business is located are also stakeholders in the business and have an interest in preserving jobs. The employees of the business itself are stakeholders and certainly wish to retain their jobs. A **downsizing**, or reduction in workforce, would offer the shareholders of the company a boost in earnings and share price. That same reduction, however, would affect the local economy and community in a negative way. Balancing the interests of these stakeholders is a standard used in resolving ethical dilemmas in business. Figure 3-1 lists the areas of concern that should be examined as businesses analyze an ethical dilemma.

As Figure 3-1 indicates, stakeholder analysis requires the decision maker to view a problem from different perspectives in the light of day. **Stakeholder analysis** requires measurement of the impact of a decision on various groups but also requires that public disclosure of that decision be defensible. The questions are helpful and provide insight in a variety of situations and ethical dilemmas. The employee who is about to leave the office for half a day without taking vacation time could ask: Could I tell my family or my supervisor that I have done this? A company faced with the temptation of price fixing: Could I describe before a congressional committee what I am about to do?

In other situations, a business is not facing questions of dishonesty or unfair competition. In many ethical dilemmas, a business faces the question of taking voluntary action or simply complying with the law. Some experts maintain that the shareholders' interest is paramount in resolving these conflicts among stakeholders. Others maintain that a business must assume some responsibility for social issues and their resolution. Economist Milton Friedman

[2] The United States, Mexico, Korea, and most of the countries in the European Union have joined together and signed a resolution denouncing bribery, specifically noting that its practice is neither legally nor culturally accepted in their nations.

ETHICS & THE LAW

ETHICS AND SOCIAL RESPONSIBILITY

Ben & Jerry's Homemade, Inc., is a Vermont-based ice-cream company founded by Ben Cohen and Jerry Greenfield, who began the company with the goal of social contribution. A portion of all proceeds from the sale of their ice cream is donated to charity.* The company issues strong position statements on social issues.

Following some slowing in market growth and reduction in profits, Cohen and Greenfield retired as officers of the company (although they remained majority shareholders and, therefore, in control of the board)** and hired Robert Holland as CEO. After Holland had been CEO for a year, a Japanese supplier approached him and offered to distribute Ben & Jerry's ice cream in Japan. Holland turned down the offer because the Japanese company had no history of involvement in social issues and explained, "The only clear reason to take the opportunity was to make money."

Do you agree with Holland's decision? What approach do Ben & Jerry's and Holland take with respect to their stakeholders? Is it troublesome that the company had not turned around financially when the offer was declined? Holland added that the only growth opportunities are in international markets. Is Ben & Jerry's passing up business? Is this a good or bad practice for a company? Holland left the company shortly after the decision on the Japanese opportunity had been made. How do you view Holland's position on business ethics and social responsibility? Is it best to find a company with values consistent with your own? How would you be able to tell the values of a company?

*Ben & Jerry's gave 7.5 percent of its pretax income to charity.

**Ben & Jerry's Homemade, Inc., has been sold and is now part of an international conglomerate, Unilever, Inc.

expresses his views on resolving the conflicts among stakeholders as follows:

A corporate executive's responsibility is to make as much money for the shareholders as possible, as long as he operates within the rules of the game. When an executive decides to take action for reasons of social responsibility, he is taking money from someone else—from the stockholders, in the form of lower dividends; from the employees, in the form of lower wages; or from the consumer, in the form of higher prices. The responsibility of the corporate executive is to fulfill the terms of his contract. If he can't do that in good conscience, then he should quit his job and find another way to do good. He has the right to promote what he regards as desirable moral objectives only with his own money.[3]

In direct opposition to the Friedman view is the social responsibility view of Anita Roddick, CEO of Body Shop International. She has stated that she does not care about earning money because the sole reason for a business to exist is to solve social problems. In between these two views are compromise positions in which businesses exist primarily to benefit the shareholders but do take opportunities to solve social problems. Many businesses today have created flextime, job sharing, and telecommuting as work options for their employees to accommodate family needs. These options are a response to larger societal issues surrounding children and their care but may also serve as a way to retain a quality workforce that is more productive without the worry of poor child care arrangements. The law currently does not require businesses to furnish such options, but the businesses offer the programs voluntarily as a means of addressing a social issue.

Between the Friedman and Roddick views on business ethics and social responsibility are businesses with varying views on the role of business in society. Among these businesses are very profitable firms that are also involved in their communities through employees' volunteer work and companies' charitable donations. For example, Bill Gates, the CEO of Microsoft who is ranked as the richest man

[3] "Interview: Milton Friedman," *Playboy*, February 1973. © 1973 *Playboy*.

THE "BAWDY" MAGAZINES AT WAL-MART

Wal-Mart stores have banned three men's magazines—*Maxim, Stuff,* and *FHM*—from sales in its stores. The magazines feature scantily clothed women and "bawdy humor."

The banned products are parts of an ongoing series of decisions Wal-Mart has made about carrying products. Wal-Mart has long banned the sales of certain CDs in its stores. Last year it banned the sales of certain video games as well. Because it is the largest seller of CDs and DVDs, producers offer sanitized versions of these materials for sale at Wal-Mart.*

Why do you think Wal-Mart makes the voluntary decision to not sell certain products? Some argue that the First Amendment is violated with these bans on sales. Refer to Chapter 4 and evaluate whether they have a point.

*David Carr and Constance L. Hays, "3 Racy Men's Magazine Are Banned by Wal-Mart," *New York Times*, May 6, 2003, C1, C3.

in the United States, in 2003 pledged $3 billion for fighting AIDS and providing childhood vaccine programs around the world. He has also used his foundation to provide scholarships for minorities. One different view on the social responsibility of business comes from Warren Buffett, the second richest man in the United States, according to the *Forbes* ranking, and the CEO of Berkshire Hathaway, a company with shares selling for more than $60,000 each. Mr. Buffett's view is that Berkshire Hathaway should not try to determine the best charitable or social causes. The shareholders, not he, should make decisions about corporate profits and their use and do so on an individual, not company, level. Mr. Buffett pledged his personal wealth to the Gates Foundation in 2006. In 2004, the average amount for corporate charitable giving was 1.3 percent of pretax income or an average of $31.79 million per Fortune 100 company. In addition, 81 percent of these companies have volunteer programs that provide help from employees to their communities.

B. Why Is Business Ethics Important?

Regardless of a firm's views on social responsibility issues, the notions of compliance with the law and fairness in business transactions and operations are universal concerns. Values represent an important part of business success. Business ethics is important for more than the simple justification that "it's the right thing to do." This section covers the significance of ethics in business success.

5. The Importance of Trust

Capitalism succeeds because of trust. Investors provide capital for a business because they believe the business will use it and return it with earnings. Customers are willing to purchase products and services from businesses because they believe the businesses will honor their commitments to deliver quality and then stand behind their product or service. Businesses are willing to purchase equipment and hire employees on the assumption that investors will continue to honor their commitment to furnish the necessary funds and will not withdraw their promises or funds. Business investment, growth, and sales are a circle of trust. Although courts provide remedies for breaches of agreements, no economy could grow if it were based solely on positive law and court-mandated performance. It is the reliance on promises, not the reliance on litigation, that produces good business relationships. In economics, the concept of rational expectations of investors and consumers plays a role in economic growth and performance. The assumption every investor makes is that her initial investment will earn a return. An assumption that employees make is that, absent problems with their performance, their employment will continue. Those assumptions encourage investment by investors and spending by

E-COMMERCE AND CYBERLAW

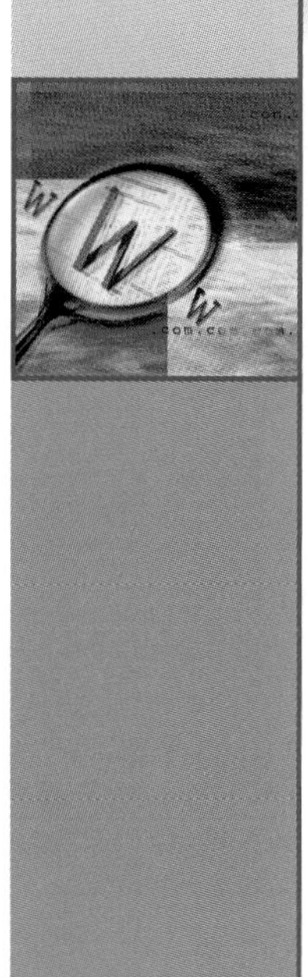

USING TECHNOLOGY TO CHANGE THE ETHICAL CULTURE OF A COMPANY

Companies are using technology to help them with the requirements of new ethics programs that must be part of their operations since the SOX legislation (the post-Enron changes on corporate governance and operations; see Chapters 8, 46, and 47). In addition to codes of ethics, companies must have the programs and technology for making sure that employees are complying with their codes and for reporting any violations they witness.

For example, Columbia HCA paid one of the largest fines in government history for Medicare fraud. To prevent such activity in the future and to comply with SOX requirements, HCA has now implemented the following for its 430 firms and 2.5 million employees:

- An anonymous hotline that now receives 100,000 calls every year
- A response to every call within 24 hours
- Documentation of what is found within the 24 hours
- Procedures by which callers can check on the status of their report and issue (even those who do not give their names can follow up with an identification number they are given for their complaint; about 30 percent report anonymously)
- A hotline staff who check employees' computers and e-mails for information and cull them to investigate charges and issues reported over the hotline*

*"Cops, Inc," *Forbes*, March 17, 2003, p. 68.

employees. Their assumptions demonstrate trust in the relationship and in the underlying economic system.

As economists have had the opportunity to watch nations with new forms of government enter the international markets, they have documented distinctions in growth rates. In those countries where government officials control market access through individual payments to them, the business climate is stalled, and growth lags behind that found in free-market nations.

Following the financial collapse of many companies during the period from 2001 through 2002, Congress passed legislation known as *Sarbanes-Oxley* (covered in more detail in Chapters 8 and 46). SOX, as it is known, however, includes many provisions that apply to companies' ethics programs. For example, all publicly traded companies must have some form of anonymous method for employees to report issues with protection from retaliation. In carrying out the intent of SOX, publicly traded companies now have ethics officers and ethics programs to set the right tone and atmosphere for an ethical culture.

6. Business Ethics and Financial Performance

Studies centering on a business's commitment to values and its financial performance suggest that those with the strongest value systems survive and do so successfully. According to the book *Built to Last* by James C. Collins and Jerry I. Porras,[4] an in-depth look at companies with long-term growth and profits produced a common thread: the companies' commitment to values. All firms studied had focused on high standards for product quality, employee welfare, and customer service.

[4] *Harper Business* (1994).

A study of companies that had paid dividends for 100 years without interruption revealed the same pattern of values.[5] Companies that had survived two world wars and a depression without missing a dividend remained committed to their customers and employees with standards of fairness and honesty. Recent studies in finance and accounting indicate that if investors want the greatest return on their investments over a 30-year period then they should invest in those companies that are the most candid in their disclosures about where the company stands and the risks it faces. For example, a company that indicates in its annual report that a major contract is at risk is being forthright and will perform over a 30-year period because it is facing its problems and coming up with strategies for coping. A company that boasts that it has met earnings to the penny for 47 quarters in a row, as HealthSouth did in the last year before it collapsed financially and many of its executives entered guilty pleas to fraud, is one to avoid.[6]

An examination of companies involved in an ethical breach demonstrates the impact of poor value choices on financial performance. A study of the impact of breaches of the law by companies showed that for five years after their regulatory or legal misstep, these companies were still struggling to recover the financial performances they had achieved prior to their legal difficulties.[7]

After Enron announced that it would restate its income because it had been spinning off its debt obligations into off-the-book-entities, its price per share dropped from $83 on January 14, 2001, to $0.67 on January 14, 2002.[8] By the time former Enron CEO Jeffrey Skilling and its former chairman, Kenneth Lay, were convicted of multiple federal felonies, Enron stock was trading at $0.15 per share, a figure that was up four cents from the preverdict value of $0.11. After WorldCom revealed that it had capitalized ordinary expenses, it had to reduce its earnings by $11 billion. The chief financial officer at WorldCom, Scott Sullivan, entered a guilty plea and testified against his boss, former CEO Bernie Ebbers. Mr. Ebbers was convicted of multiple federal felonies and sentenced to 25 years in prison, and other employees of both companies have been indicted, with many resulting guilty pleas and convictions. The accounting firm for both companies, Arthur Andersen, was convicted of obstruction of justice, a conviction that was later reversed but still destroyed the firm's reputation and resulted in its physical liquidation. Columbia Health Care's share price dropped 58 percent and it experienced a 93 percent drop in earnings after it was charged with overbilling for Medicare reimbursements. Its share price dropped from $40 to $18. The nation's largest hospital chain has had to spin off 100 hospitals and has paid record fines to settle the charges.[9]

Insurance broker Marsh & McLennan paid $850 million to former clients to settle price-fixing charges brought by New York Attorney General Eliot Spitzer. The 134-year-old company saw a drop in both its earnings (64 percent) and its share price (40 percent).[10] The financial crunch resulted in 3,000 employees losing their jobs. AIG, the insurance giant, paid $1.64 billion, the largest penalty ever by a U.S. company, to settle charges that it smoothed its earnings over time. The fine came after the company was forced to reduce its reported earnings by $1.3 billion.[11] The company also issued an apology as part of the settlement, "Providing incorrect information to the investing public and regulators was wrong and is against the values of our current leadership and employees."[12] Its $73 share price dropped to $50 before the financial reporting allegations were settled.

[5] Louis Grossman and Marianne Jennings, *Building and Growing a Business: The Story of 15 Extraordinary Companies Each with 100 Years of Consistent Dividends* (Greenwood, 2003).

[6] Stephen Taub, "Link Found Between Candor, Share Prices," *CFO.com*, June 24, 2004.

[7] Melinda S. Baucus and David A. Baucus, "Paying the Piper: An Empirical Examination of Longer-Term Financial Consequences of Illegal Corporate Behavior," 40 *Academic Management Journal* 129 (1997).

[8] From stock price chart, **http://www.enron.com.**

[9] Lucette Lagnado, "Columbia/HCA Warns of Profit Decline," *Wall Street Journal*, September 10, 1987, A3.

[10] Ian McDonald, "After Spitzer Probe, Marsh CEO Tries Corporate Triage," *Wall Street Journal*, A1, A5.

[11] Ian McDonald and Liam Pleven, "AIG Reaches Accord with Regulators, Stock Rises But May Still Be a Bargain," *Wall Street Journal*, February 10, 2006, C1, C4.

[12] Gretchen Morgenson, "AIG Apologizes and Agrees to $1.64 Billion Settlement," *New York Times*, February 10, 2006, C1, C5.

ETHICS & THE LAW

ETHICS IN GOVERNMENT EMPLOYMENT

The state of Arizona mandates emissions testing for cars before drivers can obtain updated registrations. The state hires a contractor to conduct the emissions tests in the various emissions-testing facilities around the state. In October 1999, the Arizona attorney general announced the arrest of 13 workers at one of the emissions-testing facilities for allegedly taking payoffs of between $50 to $200 from car owners to pass their cars on the emissions tests when those cars fell below emissions standards and would not have been registered. Nearly half of the staff at the emissions facility were arrested.

Why is it a crime for someone working in a government-sponsored facility to accept a payment for a desired outcome? Do the payoffs to the workers really harm anyone?

Asbestos liability bankrupted Johns-Manville when documentation showed that the company's executives knew about the lethal effect of asbestos on the lungs but took no action to warn buyers and users of the product. Bausch & Lomb, Fannie Mae, Krispy Kreme, Leslie Fay, Nortel, Phar-Mor, Cendant, Refco, Sunbeam, Xerox, and even General Electric all experienced financial fallout after accounting irregularities carried out by company officers assisted by many employees resulted in earnings restatements when proper accounting rules were applied. Martha Stewart, once a billionaire, was convicted of federal crimes, including obstruction of justice, related to her conduct after she sold her ImClone stock one day prior to the company's announcement that the FDA was not yet approving the company's drug for the market. ImClone is a bio-tech company that was headed by Ms. Stewart's friend, former CEO Sam Waksal, who entered a plea regarding his activities related to the sales of his shares in advance of the FDA announcement and is now serving time in prison. As a result, Ms. Stewart's own company, Omnimedia, International, which was not involved in the ImClone share trading and did not face any charges of earnings misstatements, still experienced a dramatic drop in earnings and stock prices because of the concerns about Ms. Stewart and shareholder concerns about their ability to trust her. Bankruptcy and/or free falls in the worth of shares are the fates that await firms that make poor ethical choices.

7. The Importance of a Good Reputation

Richard Teerlink, the CEO of Harley-Davidson, once said, "A reputation, good or bad, is tough to shake.[13] A breach of ethics is costly to a firm not only in the financial sense of drops in earnings and possible fines. A breach of ethics also often carries with it a lasting memory that affects the business and its sales for years to come. **For Example,** following Sears, Roebuck's settlement with the California Consumer Affairs Department of fraud charges involving the operation of its auto centers, Montgomery Ward Auto Centers enjoyed an increase in business.[14] Customers were concerned about taking their cars to Sears because of the scandal surrounding the nationally reported charges of unnecessary repairs. Because business declined, Sears was forced to close some of its auto centers.

When an ethical breach occurs, businesses lose that component of trust important to customers' decisions to buy and invest. **For Example,** Beech-Nut, the baby food company, has an outstanding product line and offers quality at a good price. Yet it has not regained its former market share as a result of the federal charges it faced in 1986.[15] Its apple juice tasted good, but it was a chemical concoction containing no apple juice despite advertising claims to the contrary. Even though no one was harmed, the customers' view of Beech-Nut changed. Trust

13 David K. Wright, *The Harley-Davidson Motor Co.: An Official Ninety-Year History* (Motorbook International, 1993).

14 "Sears Fires Head of Its Auto Unit," *Wall Street Journal*, December 21, 1992, B6.

15 Chris Welles, "What Led Beech-Nut Down the Road to Disgrace," *Business Week*, February 22, 1988, 128.

ETHICS & THE LAW

ETHICS & SOCIAL RESPONSIBILITY

Aaron Feuerstein is the owner of Malden Mills, a textile plant in Methuen, Massachusetts. Feuerstein's grandfather founded the company in 1906 as a swimsuit and sweater manufacturer. Feuerstein changed the direction of traditional garment manufacturing when he switched the factory to produce Polartec, a revolutionary fabric made from recycled plastic bottles. The fabric is used in skiing and hiking clothing because of its unique qualities: warm, lightweight, and easy to dry and dye. L.L. Bean, Patagonia, and Eddie Bauer are all on Malden Mills' customer list, which has generated $425 million in sales each year.

On December 11, 1995, the Malden Mills factory was almost completely destroyed by a fire started by a boiler that exploded. Feuerstein held a meeting with his employees several days later and guaranteed their pay for 30 days and their health benefits for 90 days. Malden Mills had 3,000 employees and an annual payroll of $65 million.

Feuerstein gave all of his employees three months' pay and had all but 20 percent working full-time again by March 1996. By midsummer 1996, Malden Mills was back at full production. One employee said, "Another person would have taken the insurance money and walked away. I might have done that."* Feuerstein described his role as follows:

*The fundamental difference is that I consider our workers an asset, not an expense. I have a responsibility to the worker, both blue-collar and white-collar. I have an equal responsibility to the community. It would have been unconscionable to put 3,000 people on the streets and deliver a death blow to the cities of Lawrence and Methuen. Maybe on paper our company is worth less to Wall Street, but I can tell you it's worth more. We're doing fine.***

Was it right for Feuerstein to keep his promise to employees? Did he really have a promise to keep? Does it matter that Malden Mills was not a publicly held company? In 2002, Malden Mills entered Chapter 11 bankruptcy. It emerged from bankruptcy under new ownership with Feuerstein asked to stay on as CEO. He has been working to raise the money to buy his company back. Do you think Feuerstein behaved too ethically to be financially successful?

* Steve Wulf, "The Glow from a Fire," *Time*, January 8, 1996, 49.
** *Id.*

disappeared, and so did a good portion of the company's market share. Two decades later, the company continues to struggle to overcome that one-time breach in ethics.

8. Business Ethics and Business Regulation: Public Policy, Law, and Ethics

When business behavior results in complaints from employees, investors, or customers, laws or regulations are often used to change the behavior. **For Example,** the bankruptcy of Orange County and the large losses experienced by Procter & Gamble and Gibson Greetings resulting from their heavy investments in high-risk financial instruments[16] motivated the Securities and Exchange Commission (SEC) (see Chapter 46) to promulgate regulations about disclosures in financial statements on high-risk investments known as *derivatives.* The collapse of Refco and other hedge funds now has the attention of regulators focused on these financial instruments

[16] Susan Antilla, "P & G Sees Charge on Derivatives," *New York Times*, April 13, 1994, C1, C16; Matt Murray and Paulette Thomas, "After the Fall: Fingers Point and Heads Roll," *Wall Street Journal*, December 23, 1994, B1, B4; Del Jones, "County Seeks Bankruptcy Protection," *USA Today*, December 7, 1994, IC, 2C.

ETHICS & THE LAW

ETHICS, TRUST, AND ANALYSTS

The cover of *Fortune* magazine from May 14, 2001, featured a picture of Wall Street financial analyst Mary Meeker and the words, "Can we ever trust again?"* The inside story focused on the relationship of underwriters, analysts, and brokerage houses with the companies whose stocks they were touting and selling. They had continued to pump the virtues of stock shares they knew had overinflated prices. When the market bubble burst, the losses to shareholders were catastrophic. The analysts, underwriters, and brokers had not violated the law. Those in the financial markets had too much at stake to be honest with investors.

During 2002, new stories about analysts emerged, such as that of Jack Grubman, the analyst for Salomon Smith Barney (SSB) who continued to tout WorldCom stock even as it was headed downward and into financial ruin.** The father of twins, Jack Grubman wanted to see them admitted to one of Manhattan's most prestigious preschools—the 92nd Street Y. Mr. Grubman wrote a memo to Sanford Weill, the chairman of Citigroup, that contained the following language:

On another matter, as I alluded to you the other day, we are going through the ridiculous but necessary process of pre-school applications in Manhattan. For someone who grew up in a household with a father making $8,000 a year and for someone who attended public schools, I do find this process a bit strange, but there are no bounds for what you do for your children.

Anything, anything you could do Sandy would be greatly appreciated. As I mentioned, I will keep you posted on the progress with AT&T which I think is going well.

Thank you.

Citigroup pledged $1 million to the school at about the same time Grubman's children were admitted. Mr. Weill, Mr. Grubman's CEO at SSB, asked Mr. Grubman to "take a fresh look" at AT&T, a major corporate client of Citigroup. Mr. Weill served on the board of AT&T, and AT&T's CEO, C. Michael Armstrong, served as a Citigroup director. Mr. Weill was courting Armstrong's vote for the ouster of his co-chairman at Citigroup, John Reed. A follow-up e-mail from Mr. Grubman to Carol Cutler, another New York analyst, connected the dots:

I used Sandy to get my kids in the 92nd Street Y pre-school (which is harder than Harvard) and Sandy needed Armstrong's vote on our board to nuke Reed in showdown. Once the coast was clear for both of us (ie Sandy clear victor and my kids confirmed) I went back to my normal self on AT&T.

At the same time as all the other movements, Mr. Grubman upgraded AT&T from a "hold" to a "strong buy." After Mr. Reed was ousted, Mr. Grubman downgraded AT&T again. Mr. Grubman said that he sent the e-mail "in an effort to inflate my professional importance." In another e-mail, Mr. Grubman wrote, "I have always viewed [AT&T] as a business deal between me and Sandy."

The *Fortune* headline on June 10, 2002, read, "In search of THE LAST HONEST ANALYST."***

Were there conflicts of interest in this situation? Do you think any laws were violated? How do you think such problems in the market will be fixed? What types of rules do you think will result? Why?

*"Can We Ever Trust Again?" *Fortune*, May 14, 2000 (cover).

**Charles Gasparino, "Ghosts of E-Mails Continue to Haunt Wall Street," *Wall Street Journal*, November 18, 2002, C1, C13.

***"In search of THE LAST HONEST ANALYST," *Fortune*, June 10, 2002 (cover).

FIGURE 3-2 The Endless Cycle of Societal Interaction

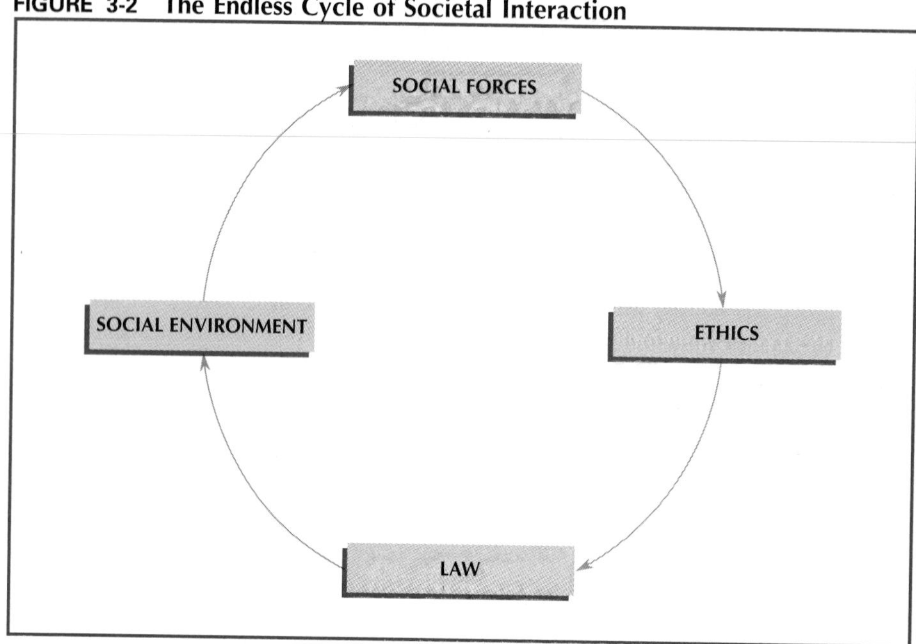

and the relatively regulation-free environment in which they are run. The Federal Reserve stepped in to regulate virtually all aspects of credit transactions, focusing on the disclosure of the actual costs of credit to ensure full information for borrowers.

Confusion among consumers about car leasing and its true costs and the fees applicable at the end of the lease terms caused the Federal Reserve to expand its regulation of credit to car leases. Figure 3-2 depicts the relationships among ethics, the social forces of customers and investors, and the laws that are passed to remedy the problems raised as part of the social forces movement.

From the nutrition facts that appear on food packages to the type of pump at the gas station, government regulation of business activity is evident. Congress begins its legislative role and administrative agencies begin their process of regulation (see Chapter 6) when congressional hearings and studies reveal abuses and problems within an industry or throughout business. Legislation and regulation are responses to activities of businesses that are perfectly legal but raise questions of fairness that cause customer and investor protests.

Antidiscrimination laws were passed when evidence established that many companies had policies that required, for example, pregnant employees to stop working. Hotels at one time had policies that permitted minorities to work in kitchens and perform housekeeping tasks but did not permit them to hold "guest-contact" positions. These policies did not violate any laws at the time. However, employees justifiably raised concerns about the fairness or the ethics of such policies, and legislation was passed, in large part because of the unwillingness of business to change its practices to remedy employees' concerns. Businesses that act voluntarily on the basis of value choices often avoid the costs and the sometimes arbitrariness of legislation and regulation. Voluntary change by businesses is less costly and is considered less intrusive. Regulation costs are substantial, and regulation is extensive.

Businesses that respond to social forces and the movements of the cycle of societal interaction gain a competitive advantage. Businesses that act irresponsibly and disregard society's views and desire for change speed the transition from value choice to enforceable law. Businesses should watch the cycle of social forces and follow trends there to understand the values attached to certain activities and responses. These values motivate change either in the form of voluntary business activity or legislation. All values that precipitate change have one of several basic underlying goals. These underlying goals, discussed in the following sections, offer signals about the pattern of social change.

(a) Protection of the State

A number of laws exist today because of the underlying goal or value of protection of the state. Laws that condemn treason are examples of laws passed to preserve the government of the state. Another less dramatic set of laws offering protection to the state are the tax codes, which provide authority for collecting taxes for the operation of government facilities and enforcement agencies. The U.S Patriot Act and airport security regulations are also examples of government programs and regulations created with the protection and security of the state as the goal.

(b) Protection of the Person

A second social force is protection of the person. From the earliest times, laws have been developed to protect the individual from being injured or killed. Criminal laws are devoted to protection of individuals and their properties. In addition, civil suits permit private remedies for wrongful acts toward people and their property. Over time, the protection of personal rights has expanded to include the rights of privacy and the protection of individuals from defamation. Contract rights are protected from interference by others. Laws continue to evolve to protect the reputations, privacy, and mental and physical well-being of individuals.

Individual rights have been the values at the core of legislation and regulation relating to governmental assistance programs, public schools, service on a jury, and access to public facilities. The antidiscrimination laws that affect nearly all businesses are grounded in the value of protection of the individual. Labor laws and regulations exist to protect the individual rights of workers.

(c) Protection of Public Health, Safety, and Morals

Food-labeling regulations are an example of laws grounded in the value of protecting the safety and health of individuals. Food and restaurant inspections, mandatory inoculation, speed limits on roadways, mandatory smoke detectors and sprinkler systems in hotels, and prohibitions on the sale of alcohol to minors are all examples of laws based on the value of safety for the public. Zoning laws that prohibit the operation of adult bookstores and movie theaters near schools and churches are examples of laws based on moral values.

(d) Protection of Property: Its Use and Title

Someone who steals another's automobile is a thief and is punished by law with fines and/or imprisonment. A zoning law that prohibits the operation of a steel mill in a residential area also provides protection for property. A civil suit brought to recover royalties lost because of another's infringement of one's copyrighted materials is based on federal laws that afford protection for property rights in nontangible or intellectual property (see Chapter 10). Laws afford protection of title for all forms of property. The deed recorded in the land record is the legal mechanism for protecting the owner's title. The copyright on a software program or a song protects the creator's rights in that intellectual property. The title documents issued by a department of motor vehicles afford protection of title for the owner of a vehicle.

Those who have title to property are generally free to use the property in any manner they see fit. However, even ownership has restrictions imposed by law. A landowner cannot engage in activities on his property that damage another's land or interfere with another's use of land. A business may operate a factory on its real property, but if the factory creates a great deal of noise, adjoining landowners may successfully establish it as a nuisance (see Chapter 49) that interferes with their use and enjoyment of their land. The law affords remedies for such a nuisance that might include an injunction, or court order, limiting the hours of the factory's operation so that neighbors have the opportunity to sleep.

If that factory releases chemicals into the river flowing nearby, others' rights and use of their land are affected. Environmental laws (see Chapter 50) have been passed that regulate the use of property. Those environmental laws evolved through social activism after landowners and residents located near factories and other operations with harmful emissions became concerned about the impact on the value of their properties as well as the impact on their health and safety. Environmental laws thus emerged as regulation of land use in response to concerns about legal, but harmful, emissions by companies.

(e) Protection of Personal Rights

The desire for individual freedom to practice religion and freedom from political domination gave rise to the colonization of the United States and, eventually, the American Revolution. The desire for freedom from economic domination resulted in the free enterprise philosophy that exists in the United States today. Individual freedoms and personal rights continue as a focus of value discussions followed by legislation if those individual rights are violated.

Economic freedoms and the free enterprise system were in jeopardy at the end of the nineteenth century as large conglomerates began to dominate certain markets and inhibit the ability of individuals to compete. Repressive activities in the marketplace by some companies led to federal regulation in the form of antitrust laws. These laws were passed in response to social concerns about economic freedom and individual opportunities within the economy (see Chapter 5). For example, Microsoft's 90 percent domination of the operating systems market led to extensive antitrust litigation against the company that was eventually settled.

(f) Enforcement of Individual Intent

When someone has voluntarily entered into a transaction, that person has a responsibility to carry forward the promises made. Principles of honesty and honoring commitments are the ethical values at the heart of the parties' conduct in carrying out contracts. If, however, the parties do not keep their promises, the law does enforce transactions through sets of rules governing requirements for them. **For Example,** if a person provides by will for the distribution of property at death, the law will generally allow the property to pass to the persons intended by the deceased owner. The law will also carry out the intentions of the parties to a business transaction.

Laws exist to honor the intent of parties because not all commitments are fulfilled voluntarily. The law may impose requirements that a transaction or agreement be in writing to ensure that the intent of the parties is adequately documented and fulfilled (see Chapter 17). The law may also place restrictions on honoring intentions. A contract to commit a murder may be evidenced by intent and fully documented in writing. However, the intent of the parties will not be honored because of the social values manifested in the protection of individuals and individuals' rights and safety.

(g) Protection from Exploitation, Fraud, and Oppression

Many laws have evolved because businesses took advantage of another group. The law has given some groups or individuals protection because of excesses by businesses in dealing with them. Minors, or persons under legal age (see Chapter 14), are given special protections under contract laws that permit them to disaffirm their contracts so they are not disadvantaged by excessive commitments without the benefit of the wisdom of age and with the oppressive presence of an adult party.

The federal laws on disclosure with respect to the sales of securities and shareholder relations (see Chapters 45 and 46) were developed following the 1929 stock market crash when many investors lost all they had because of the lack of candor and information by the businesses in which they were investing.

Food manufacturers have exclusive control over the canning and processing of their products. The opportunity for taking advantage of customers who do not generally have access to the factories and plants is great. The contents of canned products are not visible to consumers before they make their purchases. Because of excesses and exploitations by food processors, there are both federal and state regulations of food processing and food labeling. Adulterating or poisoning food products carries criminal penalties. Misrepresenting the contents in food packages may constitute a federal felony.

(h) Furtherance of Trade

Some laws are the result of social forces seeking to simplify business and trade. Installment sales and credit transactions, and their accompanying laws and regulations, have made additional capital available for businesses and provided consumers with alternatives to cash purchases. The laws on checks, drafts, and notes have created instruments used to facilitate trade. The Board of Governors of the Federal Reserve System's oversight of federal banks and interest rates has mitigated the harmful effects of alternating economic periods of depression and inflation.

(i) Protection of Creditors and Rehabilitation of Debtors

Society seeks to protect the rights of creditors and to protect them from dishonest or fraudulent acts of debtors. Initially, the laws that make contracts binding and enforceable protect creditors. Statutes that make it a fraud for a debtor to conceal property from a creditor also protect creditors. To meet the social demands for facilitation of trade, credit transactions were authorized. With that authorization, however, came the demand for the creditor's assurance of repayment by the debtor. Mortgages, security interests, and surety relationships (see Chapters 32, 34, and 49) are mechanisms created by law to provide creditors the legal mechanisms for collecting their obligations.

When collection techniques became excessive and exploitative, new laws on debtors' rights were enacted. Debtors' prisons were abolished. Congress mandated disclosure requirements for credit

ETHICS & THE LAW

ETHICS AND LYING TO GET AHEAD

A study by an executive search firm revealed that 25 percent of all the résumés they reviewed contained inaccurate information about the individual's educational background or past employment. The types of inaccuracies included listing attendance at and the receipt of a degree from a university that the applicant never attended and misrepresenting responsibilities at previous jobs (e.g., a sales manager referring to himself on his résumé as "director of marketing").*

Another study by Rutgers University concluded, based on surveys conducted of students, that 75 percent of all students in master of business administration (MBA) programs lied or cheated to get into their graduate programs. Examples of their misconduct included cheating in undergraduate school, falsifying letters of reference, and having someone else take the Graduate Management Admission Test (GMAT) for them.**

Ronald L. Zarrella, the CEO of Bausch & Lomb, admitted that he had included false information in his résumé, which stated that he had an MBA from New York University (NYU). He had attended NYU and taken graduate courses in business at night while he was working for Bristol-Myers, but he never completed the degree program. The information from the résumé had been included in Bausch & Lomb press releases since 1982. In addition, Credit Suisse First Boston released a statement indicating that information on Mr. Zarrella regarding his serving on its subsidiary's board, First USA, was inaccurate. He had instead served on the board of US First, a nonprofit organization that supported students entering the sciences and engineering fields.

The news about this false information resulted in a drop of $1.01 in the price of Bausch & Lomb's shares from $31.48. Mr. Zarrella said he would not resign, and the Board issued a statement expressing confidence in him. Mr. Zarrella had been hired as CEO just 11 months before this incident. Bausch & Lomb had hired Heidrick & Struggles to conduct its CEO search at that time, and the company had not checked Mr. Zarrella's background because he came in as a candidate through a board member's recommendation, not through the search firm.***

Why do people lie about their backgrounds and qualifications? Is anyone really hurt by this individual misconduct? Why is it important that the information on résumés and applications for graduate school be accurate?

*Dan Barry, "Cheating Hearts and Lying Resumes," *New York Times*, December 14, 1997, WK1, WK4.

**Carol Innerst, "Colleges Are Stepping Up the War Against Cheaters," *Washington Times*, November 6–12, 1995, 25.

***Leslie Wayne, "Bausch & Lomb Executive Admits to Falsified Resume," *New York Times*, October 20, 2002, C1; William M. Bulkeley, "Bausch & Lomb Now Says CEO Has No M.B.A.," *Wall Street Journal*, October 21, 2002, A10.

contracts. The Fair Debt Collections Practices Act (see Chapter 33) limited collection techniques. The remedy of bankruptcy was afforded debtors under federal law to provide them an opportunity to begin a new economic life when their existing debts reached an excessive level and could no longer be paid in a timely fashion (see Chapter 35).

(j) Stability and Flexibility

Stability is particularly important in business transactions. When you buy a house, for example, you want to know not only what the exact meaning of the transaction is under today's law but also that the transaction will have the same meaning in the future.

Because of the desire for stability, courts will ordinarily follow former decisions unless there is a strong reason to depart from them. Similarly, when no former case bears on the point involved, a court will try to reach a decision that is a logical extension of some former decision or that follows a former decision by analogy rather than strike out on a new path to reach a decision unrelated to the past.

If stability were always required, the cause of justice would often be defeated. The reason that originally existed for a rule of law may have ceased to exist. Also, a rule may later appear unjust because it reflects a concept of justice that is outmoded or obsolete. The policies surrounding adoption of children and the rights of natural versus adoptive parents have continued to evolve because of changing attitudes about these relationships and new technology that permits laboratory creation and insemination.

The typical modern statute, particularly in the area of business regulation, often contains an escape clause by which a person can "escape" from the operation of the statute under certain circumstances. **For Example,** a rent control law may impose a rent ceiling, that is, a maximum rent a landlord can charge a tenant. The same law may also authorize a higher charge when special circumstances make it just and fair to allow such an exception. For example, the landlord may have made expensive repairs to the property or taxes on the property may have increased substantially.

Protection of the person is frequently the controlling factor in determining whether a court should adhere to the common law, thereby furthering stability, or whether it should change the law, thereby furthering flexibility.

C. How to Recognize and Resolve Ethical Dilemmas

Business managers find themselves in circumstances in which they are unclear about right and wrong and are confused about how to resolve the dilemmas they face. A recent survey showed that 98 percent of all Fortune 500 companies have codes of ethics designed to help their employees recognize and resolve ethical dilemmas. Nearly 75 percent of those firms provide their employees some form of training in ethics.[17] Almost 80 percent of companies now have an ethics officer. These codes of ethics provide employees information about categories of behavior that constitute ethical breaches. Regardless of the industry, the type of business, or the size of the company, certain universal categories can help managers recognize ethical dilemmas. Figure 3-3 provides a list of those categories.

FIGURE 3-3 Categories of Ethical Behavior

1. INTEGRITY AND TRUTHFULNESS
2. PROMISE KEEPING
3. LOYALTY—AVOIDING CONFLICTS OF INTEREST
4. FAIRNESS
5. DOING NO HARM
6. MAINTAINING CONFIDENTIALITY

[17] Survey of the Society for Human Resource Management and Ethics Resource Center (2005).

9. Categories of Ethical Behavior

(a) Integrity and Truthfulness

Mark Twain once wrote, "Always tell the truth. That way you don't have to remember anything." As discussed earlier, trust is a key component of business relationships and of the free enterprise system. Trust begins with the belief that honesty is at the heart of relationships. Many contract remedies in law are based on the failure of the parties to be truthful with each other. If you purchase a home that has been certified as termite free but you discover termites in the home shortly after you move in, someone has not been truthful. If you also discover that two termite inspections were conducted and that the first one, which revealed there were termites, was concealed from you, your trust in both the sellers and their exterminators is diminished.

An assurance that a seller has the expertise to handle your project is important in building that relationship. If you discover later that the seller lacks the expertise, you are harmed by the delay and possible poor work that has been done. When the prospectus for a stock offering fails to provide full information about the company's obsolete inventory, investors are not given the full truth and are harmed when they invest without complete disclosure. Investors become skeptical when offerings do not carry with them a very basic level of honesty in their disclosures. Honesty is necessary for the wheels of commerce to turn.

Integrity is the adherence to one's values and principles despite the costs and consequences. **For Example,** an executive contracted with a variety of companies to sell his hard-to-find computer components. When he was approached by one of his largest customers to break a contract with a small customer, the executive refused. The customer assured the executive it would be his last order with the company if he did not get more components. Despite facing the threat of losing a multimillion-dollar

SPORTS & ENTERTAINMENT LAW

HIRING PROSECUTORS TO POLICE CORPORATE ETHICS

Ethics officers at companies now have unprecedented power. They have full access to speak to all employees and direct lines to boards and CEOs. For example, Patrick J. Gnazzo is the new ethics officer at Computer Associates (CA), a company whose former CEO has entered a guilty plea to federal fraud charges for cooking the books. At a speech at the company retreat in Las Vegas, Gnazzo told the 1,200 staff members there, "What happens at CA World can make us great. Don't lie, don't cheat, don't steal."*

To avoid criminal prosecution, the CA board agreed to accept Gnazzo, the former chief trial attorney for the U.S. Navy, as its chief compliance officer. Former prosecutors are now becoming ethics officers at companies that have experienced legal or ethical difficulties:

- Richard C. Breeden, former SEC chairman, is outside monitor at KPMG and at Hollinger.
- Eric R. Dinallo, formerly with Eliot Spitzer at the NY Attorney general's office, is chief compliance officer at Morgan Stanley.
- Beth L. Golden, also from Spitzer's office, is chief compliance officer at Bear Stearns.
- Mari B. Maloney, formerly with NASD and the Manhattan district attorney's office, is chief compliance officer at AIG.
- Frederick B. Lacey, former federal judge, will serve as independent monitor at Bristol-Myers Squibb.

The new ethics officer differs from those in the past who tended to come from human resources and public relations. They have direct access to boards and CEOs and also have an edge in knowing how to question employees to obtain information that will lead to halting unacceptable activities.

*Joseph Weber, "The New Ethics Enforcers," *Business Week*, February 13, 2006, 76–77.

ETHICS & THE LAW

LYING TO GET INTO A TOP SCHOOL

The University of California at Berkeley has implemented a new step in its admission process. The Haas School of Business has begun running background checks on students who have applied to determine whether the information in their applications is correct. The Wharton School implemented a similar procedure and charges applicants a $35 fee for these background checks.

Of the 100 students admitted to Berkeley in the fall of 2003, 5 students were found to have offered false information on their admissions applications. The most common type of false information was the job titles they held, and the second most common type was their number of years of work experience. Haas admissions officers indicated that had the students not lied, they otherwise met the GMAT score and GPA standards for admission to Haas.

What risk do the students take in lying on their applications? What are the long-term consequences?

Source: "Cheaters Don't Make the Grade at Berkeley Business School," **http://www.azcentral.com**, March 14, 2003, AP wire reports.

customer, the executive fulfilled his promises to the small purchasers. The executive kept his word on all of his contracts and demonstrated integrity.

(b) Promise Keeping

If we examine the types of things we do in a day, we would find that most of them are based on promises. We promise to deliver goods either with or without a contract. We promise to pay the dentist for our dental work. We promise to provide someone with a ride. Keeping those promises, regardless of whether there is a legal obligation to do so, is a key component of being an ethical person and practicing ethical business. Keeping promises is also evidence of integrity.

The issue of employee downsizing is debated with the underlying question of whether the downsized employees had a promise from their company of continued employment. As stakeholder analysis is reviewed, the ethical issue surrounding the question is whether there are promises to others who are at risk. Weren't shareholders promised a return on their investment? Weren't suppliers promised payment? In many circumstances, the question is not *whether* a promise will be kept but rather *which* promise will be kept. The strategic issue is whether businesses should make commitments and promises in circumstances that create a very thin margin of profit and perhaps even thinner margin for error. Over the long term, the importance of a company's keeping its promises to all stakeholders translates into its reputation.

(c) Loyalty—Avoiding Conflicts of Interest

An employee who works for a company owes allegiance to that company. Conduct that compromises that loyalty is a **conflict of interest. For Example,** suppose that your sister operates her own catering business. Your company is seeking a caterer for its monthly management meetings. You are responsible for these meetings and could hire your sister to furnish the lunches for the meetings. Your sister would have a substantial contract, and your problems with meal logistics would be solved. Nearly all companies have a provision in their codes of ethics covering this situation. An employee cannot hire a relative, friend, or even her own company without special permission because it is a conflict of interest. Your loyalty to your sister conflicts with the loyalty to your employer, which requires you to make the best decision at the best price.

A conflict of interest arises when a purchasing agent accepts gifts from suppliers, vendors, or manufacturers' representatives. The purchasing agent has introduced into the buy-sell relationship an element of *quid pro quo*, or the supplier's expectation that the gift will bring about a return from the agent in the form of a contract. Some companies have zero tolerance for conflicts and establish a complete prohibition on employees accepting any gifts from

SPORTS & ENTERTAINMENT LAW

OPRAH WAS DUPED

Oprah Winfrey named James Frey's autobiographical book, *A Million Little Pieces,* to her television book club. The impact of the book's inclusion in the Oprah Book Club was the sale of 10 million copies, making it the fastest-selling book in the club's history. The book allegedly addressed Mr. Frey's addictions and recovery. However, on January 8, 2006, the Web site The Smoking Gun found significant and multiple discrepancies between Frey's accounts of his life experiences in the book and what really happened. For example, Frey wrote that he spent 87 days in prison. In reality, he spent 3 hours. When the discrepancies initially emerged, Ms. Winfrey defended Mr. Frey, saying the book was the "essential truth" about his life. She also called the controversy "much ado about nothing."

The public reaction was different, and Ms. Winfrey had Mr. Frey on her show, or, as some critics labeled it, "had him into the woodshed." Ms. Winfrey told Mr. Frey, "I feel really duped. You betrayed millions of readers. Why would you lie?"

In the week following his Oprah appearance, Mr. Frey sold 50,000 copies of *A Million Little Pieces,* but the publisher for his next book canceled his contract. Was there truthfulness? Mr. Frey said the book was a "creative novel memoir" that had not been intended to be autobiographical. Does this clarification help? Were Mr. Frey's actions ethical? Evaluate Ms. Winfrey's initial response.

Source: Carol Memmot, "Oprah grills 'Pieces' author, apologizes," *USA Today,* January 26, 2006, p. 1D.

suppliers and manufacturers. **For Example,** Wal-Mart buyers are not permitted to accept even a cup of coffee from potential merchandise suppliers, and Amgen's buyers can go out to dinner with a supplier only if Amgen pays.

(d) Fairness

In business transactions in which the buyer was not told about the crack in the engine block or the dry well on the property, a typical response is, "That's not fair. I wouldn't have bought it if I'd known." A question often posed to the buyer in response is "Wouldn't you have done the same thing?" We feel differently about such situations, depending on whether we are the victims of unfairness or whether we hold the superior knowledge in the transaction. The ethical standard of fairness requires both sides to ask these questions: "How would I want to be treated? Would this information make a difference to me?" Imposing our own standards and expectations on our own behavior in business transactions produces fairness in business.

(e) Doing No Harm

Imagine selling a product that your company's internal research shows presents significant health dangers to its users. Selling the product without disclosure of the information is unfair. There is the additional ethical breach of physical harm to your customers and users. Ford designed and sold its Pinto with a fundamental flaw in the placement of the car's gas tank. Rear-end collisions in which a Pinto was involved resulted, even at very low speeds, in fires that engulfed the car so quickly that occupants could not always escape from it. An internal memo from engineers at Ford revealed that employees had considered doing an analysis of the risk of the tanks versus the cost of redesign but never did. The late Peter Drucker's advice on ethics for businesses is *primum non nocere*, or "above all, do no harm." Such a rule might have helped Ford.

(f) Maintaining Confidentiality

Often the success of a business depends on the information or technology that it holds. If the competitive edge that comes from the business's peculiar niche or knowledge is lost through disclosure, so are its profits. Employees not only owe a duty of loyalty to their employers, but they also owe an obligation of confidentiality. Employees should not use, either personally or through a competitor, information they have obtained through their

ETHICS & THE LAW

CONFLICTS AND COMBAT

Richard N. Perle served as chairman of the Defense Policy Board, a position appointed by the Secretary of Defense, Donald H. Rumsfield. Mr. Perle was hired by Global Crossing, a telecommunications company in Chapter 11 bankruptcy, to work with the Defense Department because the Department opposed the sale of Global Crossing to Hutchison Whampoa and Singapore Technology, two foreign companies. Mr. Perle earned $725,000 for his work, $600,000 of which depended on the Defense Department's approval of the sale. The Defense Department opposed the sale because it used the Global Crossing fiber-optics network for its telecommunications needs and the sale would put that network under Chinese control.

Mr. Perle filed an affidavit in the review process for the FBI and Defense Department (whose approvals were required) that contained the following language:

*As the chairman of the Defense Policy Board, I have a unique perspective on and intimate knowledge of the national defense and security issues that will be raised be the CFUIS review process that is not and could not be available to the other CFIUS professionals.**

When asked about his dual role, Mr. Perle said,

*I've abided by the rules. The question, I think, is have I recommended anything to the secretary or discussed this with the secretary, and I haven't. The alternative is if you are on the board, you can't have any action before the Defense Department. That isn't the rule. If that were the rule, I'd have to make a choice between being on an unpaid advisory board and my business.***

What ethical issue exists in Mr. Perle's conduct?

*CFUIS is the Committee on Foreign Investment in the United States and consists of representatives from the Defense Department and other agencies. CFUIS has the authority to block foreign acquisitions.

**Stephen Labaton, "Pentagon Adviser Is Also Advising Global Crossing," *New York Times*, March 21, 2003, C1, C2.

ETHICS & THE LAW

ETHICS AND INCENDIARY DEVICES

Dateline NBC, a television news magazine program that airs several nights a week, presented a segment on General Motors (GM) and the safety of GM's trucks with sidesaddle gas tanks. *Dateline* producers staged and taped an accident with a GM truck that showed a gas tank explosion and subsequent fire that engulfed the pickup truck. The tape was shown on *Dateline.* Disclosures of several crew members later revealed that explosive devices had been used to create the scene for the cameras, but the use of those devices was not disclosed during the *Dateline* piece.*

Was it fair to use the explosive devices? Was it fair to use the explosive devices and not disclose that to the audience? Was the program fair to GM?

Note: *Dateline* later read an on-air apology for using the tape.

*Elizabeth Jensen, "Some Journalists Join GM in Criticizing NBC's Treatment of Truck Crash Story," *Wall Street Journal*, February 10, 1993, B1, B8.

PIGGYBACKING ON WIRELESS NETWORKS

A new issue that has evolved because of technology could require legal steps to stop it. People are "piggybacking" or tapping onto their neighbors' wireless Internet connection. The original subscriber pays a monthly fee for the service, but without security, people located in the area are able to tap into the wireless network, which bogs down the speed of the service. Once limited to geeks and hackers, the practice is now common among the ordinary folk who just want free Internet service.

One college student said, "I don't think it's stealing. I always find people out there who aren't protecting their connection, so I just feel free to go ahead and use it."* According to a recent survey, only about 30 percent of the 4,500 wireless networks onto which the surveyors logged were encrypted.

An apartment dweller said she leaves her connection wide open because "I'm sticking it to the man. I open up my network, leave it wide open for anyone to jump on." One of the users of another's wireless network said, "I feel sort of bad about it, but I do it anyway. It just seems harmless." She said that if she gets caught, "I'm a grandmother. They're not going to yell at an old lady. I'll just play the dumb card."

Some neighbors offer to pay those with wireless service in exchange for their occasional use rather than paying a wireless company for full-blown service. However, the original subscribers do not really want to run their own Internet service.

Do you think we need new legislation to cover this activity? What do you think of the users' statements? Is their conduct legal? Is it ethical?

*Michael Marriott, "Hey Neighbor, Stop Piggybacking on My Wireless," *New York Times*, March 5, 2006, A1, A23.

employer's work or research. Providing customer lists or leads is a breach of employees' obligation of confidentiality.

In addition, managers have responsibilities regarding their employees' privacy. Performance evaluations of individual employees are private and should never be disclosed or revealed, even in one-on-one conversations outside the lines of authority and the workplace.

10. Resolving Ethical Dilemmas

Recognizing an ethical dilemma is perhaps the easiest part of business ethics. Resolution of that dilemma is more difficult. The earlier section on stakeholders offers one model for resolution of ethical dilemmas (see Figure 3-1). Other models have been developed to provide managers analytical methods for resolving dilemmas in a timely fashion.

(a) Blanchard and Peale Three-Part Test

Dr. Kenneth Blanchard, author of books on the *One-Minute Manager*, and the late Dr. Norman Vincent Peale developed a model for evaluating ethical breaches that is widely used among Fortune 500 companies.[18] To evaluate situations, ask the following three questions: Is it legal? Is it balanced? How does it make me feel?

In answering the questions on legality, a manager should look to positive law both within and outside the company. If the proposed conduct would violate antitrust laws, the manager's analysis can stop there. If the proposed conduct would violate company policy, the manager's analysis can stop. In the field of business ethics, there is little room for civil disobedience. Compliance with the law is a critical component of a successful ethics policy in any company.

[18] Kenneth Blanchard and Norman Vincent Peale, *The Power of Ethical Management* (New York:William Morrow, 1986).

ETHICS & THE LAW

BRIBERY, ETHICS, AND OLYMPICS

Salt Lake City, Utah, had been a contender as a potential site for the Winter Olympics for 30 years when the choice to locate the 2002 games was being made. Each time, the city, famous for its extensive ski resorts and powder snow, lost to other cities around the world. When city and state officials and representatives from business made their bid for Salt Lake for the 2002 Winter Olympics, they were determined to win. During the course of the International Olympic Committee's decision-making process, some members of the Salt Lake City Olympic Committee gave benefits to members of the International Olympic Committee. Those benefits included everything from entertainment to medical care and college educations for family members of International Olympic Committee members.

When all of the perks were revealed, members of the International Olympic Committee, as well as the Salt Lake City Olympic Committee, resigned. Some Olympic sponsors withdrew.*

How could the Blanchard and Peale test have helped those involved in courting the International Olympic Committee? Does it matter that those types of benefits and perks are expected in the cultures of some of the International Olympic Committee members?

*Ira Berkow, "Greed Knows Few Bounds in Olympics," *New York Times*, February 10, 1999, C23.

The second question on balance forces the manager to examine the ethical value of fairness. Perhaps the decision to downsize must be made, but couldn't the company offer the employees a severance package and outplacement assistance to ease the transition?

The final question of the Blanchard and Peale model is conscience based. Although some managers may employ any tactics to maximize profits, this final question forces a manager to examine the physical impact of a decision: Does it cause sleeplessness or appetite changes? Personalizing business choices often helps managers to see the potential harm that comes from poor ethical choices.

(b) The Front-Page-of-the-Newspaper Test

This simple but effective model for ethical evaluation helps a manager visualize the public disclosure of proposed conduct. When he temporarily took over as the leader of Salomon Brothers after its bond-trading controversy, Warren Buffett described the newspaper test as follows:

Contemplating any business act, an employee should ask himself whether he would be willing to see it immediately described by an informed and critical reporter on the front page of his local paper, there to be read by his spouse, children, and friends. At Salomon, we simply want no part of any activities that pass legal tests but that we, as citizens, would find offensive.[19]

(c) Laura Nash Model

In her work, business ethicist Laura Nash has developed a series of questions to help businesspeople reach the right decision in ethical dilemmas. These are her questions: Have you defined the problem accurately? How would you define the problem if you stood on the other side of the fence? How did this situation occur in the first place? What is your intention in making this decision? How does the intention compare with the probable results? Whom could your decision or action injure? Can you discuss your decision with the affected parties? Are you confident that your position will be as valid over a long period of time as it seems now? Could you discuss your decision with your supervisor, coworkers, officers, board, friends, and family?

The Nash model requires an examination of the dilemma from all perspectives. Defining the problem and how the problem arose provides the business assistance in avoiding the dilemma again. **For Example,** suppose that a supervisor is asked to provide a reference

[19]Janet Lowe, *Warren Buffett Speaks: Wit and Wisdom from the World's Greatest Investor* (New York:Wiley, 1997).

ETHICS & THE LAW

BURGER KING, COKE, AND NUMBERS

Coca-Cola has admitted that it paid a consultant $10,000 to drive up the demand for its Frozen Coke beverage being test-marketed in Burger Kings in the Richmond, Virginia, area. The consultant used the money to make donations to Boys and Girls Clubs. The clubs then provided meal coupons to the children in exchange for them doing their homework. The impressive demand that resulted from the Richmond area test market led Burger King to invest $65 million to put the machines in restaurants around the country, However, the demand was not what it had been falsely alleged to be, and the result is that, following a six-week investigation by a law firm hired by the Coca-Cola board, Coca-Cola admitted that the marketing studies were inflated.

The board investigation followed an allegation in a lawsuit filed by a former employee, Matthew Whitley. Whitley was terminated following his questioning of an expense claim by the consultant and his resulting investigation that produced an internal memo describing the consultant's work on driving up the demand. Coca-Cola also issued an earnings restatement of $9 million based on an investigation of those allegations. The *Wall Street Journal* was following the Whitley lawsuit when the underlying issues emerged, and it reported the marketing scheme.* Coca-Cola settled with Burger King by paying $21 million.

Was this conduct ethical? Was it fraud? What does Mr. Whitley's termination say about the company? Does he have protection? Why do you think the marketing managers decided to involve the consultant and report the false demand? What effect does this incident have on Burger King's relationship with Coke? How do you think the story played on the front page of the *Wall Street Journal?***

*Chad Terhune, "Coke Employees Acted Improperly in Marketing Test," *Wall Street Journal*, June 18, 2003, A3, A6; Sherri Day, "Coke Confirms Product Test Was Rigged," *New York Times*, June 18, 2003, C1, C10.

**Marianne Jennings, one of the authors of this text, has done consulting work for Coca-Cola since this incident. Why is this disclosure important?

for a friend who works for her. The supervisor is hesitant because the friend has not been a very good employee. The ethical dilemma the manager believes she faces is whether to lie or tell the truth about the employee. The real ethical dilemma is why the supervisor never provided evaluation or feedback indicating the friend's poor performance. Avoiding the problem in the future is possible through candid evaluations. Resolving the problem requires that the supervisor talk to her friend now about the issue of performance and the problem with serving as a reference.

One final aspect of the Nash model that businesspeople find helpful is a question that asks for a perspective on an issue from family and friends. The problem of groupthink in business situations is very real. As businesspeople sit together in a room and discuss an ethical dilemma, they can persuade each other to think the same way. The power of consensus can overwhelm each person's concerns and values. There is a certain fear in bringing up a different point of view in a business meeting. Proper perspective is often lost as the discussion centers around numbers. Therefore, bringing in the views of an outsider is often helpful. For example, when McNeil, the manufacturer of Tylenol, faced the cyanide poisonings from contaminated capsules sold in the Chicago area, it had to make a decision about the existing Tylenol inventory. It was clear to both insiders and outsiders that the poison had not been put in the capsules at McNeil but after delivery to the stores. Despite the huge numbers involved in the recall and the destruction of inventory, the McNeil managers made the decision easily because they viewed the risk to their own families, that is, from the outside. From this standpoint, the issue became a question of human life, not of numbers.[20]

[20] "Brief History of Johnson & Johnson" (company pamphlet, 1992).

(d) *Wall Street Journal* Model

The *Wall Street Journal* presented a simple, three-prong test for resolving ethical dilemmas known as the three-C model: (1) Will this conduct be in compliance with the law? (2) What contribution does this decision make to the shareholders? To the community? To the employees? (3) What are the consequences of this decision? This model requires an examination of the impact of a choice, which then produces a different perspective on a course of conduct. **For Example,** Sears paid $475 million in fines and penalties for its unauthorized collection of debts from debtors who were in bankruptcy or had debts discharged in bankruptcy. Such collection beyond what the law allows did not comply with the law.[21] The contribution to the company was more collections and hence more cash, but the consequences were the large fine and the damage to Sears' reputation for putting its interests above the law and above the interests of other creditors who conducted themselves within the limits of the bankruptcy law. Sears may have resented the fact that debtors had not paid, but the company was not justified in taking the law into its own hands or profiting at the expense of other creditors.

Breaking Away (1979) (PG)

In this story about "cutters" (a nickname for natives of Bloomington, Indiana), a recent high school graduate trains to be a first-class bike rider. He idolizes the Italian world racing team and enters an Indiana race to have the opportunity to compete with them. He does well in the race and manages to catch up and keep pace with the Italian team. As he rides alongside his idols, one of the members of the Italian team places a tire pump in his spoke. His bike crashes, he loses the race and is injured. He becomes disillusioned. Is this experience like business? Do unethical tactics get you ahead? Do nice guys finish last? Are there sanctions for unethical conduct?

For movie clips that illustrate business law concepts, see LawFlix at **http://wdvl.westbuslaw.com.**

[21] Leslie Kaufman, "Sears Settles Suit on Raising of Its Credit Card Rates," *New York Times*, March 11, 1999, C2.

Summary

Business ethics is the application of values and standards to business conduct and decisions. These values originate in various sources from positive (codified) law to natural law to stakeholder values. Business ethics is important because trust is a critical component of good business relationships and free enterprise. A business with values will enjoy the additional competitive advantage of a good reputation and, over the long term, better earnings. When businesses make decisions that violate basic ethical standards, they set into motion social forces and cause the area of abuse to be regulated, resulting in additional costs and restrictions for business. Voluntary value choices by businesses position them for a competitive advantage.

The categories of ethical values in business are truthfulness and integrity, promise keeping, loyalty and avoiding conflicts of interest, fairness, doing no harm, and maintaining confidentiality.

Resolution of ethical dilemmas is possible through the use of various models that require a businessperson to examine the impact of a decision before it is made. These models include stakeholder analysis, the Blanchard and Peale test, the front-page-of-the-newspaper test, the Laura Nash model, and the *Wall Street Journal* model.

Questions and Case Problems

1. Marty Mankamyer, the president of the United States Olympic Committee (USOC), resigned in early February 2003 following reports in *The Denver Post* that indicated she had demanded a commission from a fellow real estate broker in the Colorado Springs area, the home of the USOC, who had sold property to Lloyd Ward, the CEO of the USOC. Mr. Ward had purchased a 1.3-acre lot in Colorado Springs for $475,000 and had paid the listing broker, Brigette Ruskin, a commission. Ms. Mankamyer allegedly demanded a portion of the commission from

Ms. Ruskin, and Ms. Ruskin sent her a check. Ms. Mankamyer had shown Mr. Ward and his wife properties in the area when they were being considered for the job and when he was considering taking the job. However, Mrs. Ward indicated that Ms. Mankamyer did not identify herself as a real estate agent and that she assumed that Ms. Mankamyer was showing the properties as a "goodwill gesture."[22] What conflicts of interest do you see here?

2. Ann Elkin, who works for Brill Co., has been sent out to conduct two customer evaluations, which have gone much more quickly than Ann anticipated. Her supervisor does not expect Ann back until after lunch. It is now 10:30 A.M., and Ann would like to run some personal errands and then go to lunch before returning to work at 1:00 P.M. Should Ann take the time? Would you? Why or why not? Be sure to consider the categories of ethical values and apply one or two models before reaching your conclusion.

3. Fred Sanguine is a New York City produce broker. Ned Santini is a 19-year-old college student who works for Sanguine from 4:00 A.M. until 7:00 A.M. each weekday before he attends classes at Pace University. Fred has instructed Ned on the proper packing of produce as follows: "Look, put the bad and small cherries at the bottom. Do the same with the strawberries and blueberries. Put the best fruit on top and hide the bad stuff at the bottom. This way I get top dollar on all that I sell." Ned is uncomfortable about the instructions, but, as he explains to his roommate, "It's not me doing it. I'm just following orders. Besides, I need the job." Should Ned just follow instructions? Is the manner in which the fruit is packed unethical? Would you do it? Why or why not? Is anyone really harmed by the practice?

4. Alan Gellen is the facilities manager for the city of Milwaukee and makes all final decisions on purchasing items such as chairs, lights, and other supplies and materials. Alan also makes the final decisions for the award of contracts to food vendors at event sites. Grand Beef Franks has submitted a bid to be one of the city's vendors. Alan went to school with Grand Beef's owner, Steve Grand, who phones Alan and explains that Grand Beef owns a condominium in Maui that Alan could use. Steve's offer to Alan is: "All it would cost you for a vacation is your airfare. The condo is fully stocked with food. Just let me know." Should Alan take the offer? Would you? Be sure to determine which category of ethical values this situation involves and to apply several models as you resolve the question of whether Alan should accept the invitation.

5. Television network CNBC and other television networks have been working to develop policies for their business correspondents and guests on their business shows because of a practice known as *pump-and-dump*, the practice of a Wall Street professional or network business correspondent appearing on television to tout a particular stock as being a good buy. Often, unbeknown to the viewing audience, the guest or correspondent promoting the stock has a large holding in it and, after the television show runs and the stock price creeps up, sells his or her interest at a higher price than would have been possible before the show on which the person raved about the stock. What category of ethical issue exists here? If you were a network executive, what would you do to remedy the problem? Could the government regulate such practices? What kind of regulation could it impose?

6. Adam Smith wrote the following in *The Theory of Moral Sentiments:*

> *In the practice of the other virtues, our conduct should rather be directed by a certain idea of propriety, by a certain taste for a particular tenor of conduct, than by any regard to a precise maxim or rule; and we should consider the end and foundation of the rule, more than the rule itself.*[23]

Do you think Adam Smith adhered to positive law as his ethical standard? Was he a moral relativist? Does his quote match stakeholder analysis? What would his ethical posture be on violating the law?

7. A new phenomenon for admissions to MBA programs is hiring consultants to help applicants hone their applications. About 20 percent of those who apply to the top MBA programs have hired consultants at a cost of $150 to $200 per hour to help them say and do the right things to be admitted. The total cost for most who use a consultant is $5,000. The consultants help with personal essays and applications. One admissions officer points out that one function of the consultant is to draw out and emphasize skills that the applicant may not see as important. For example, playing the piano is looked upon favorably because it shows discipline and focus. However, admissions committees are becoming adept at spotting the applications via consultant because, as the faculty describe it, these essays and applications have a certain "sameness" to them. The Fuqua School at North Carolina suggests that students simply call the admissions office and get comparable advice for free. Is it ethical to use an admissions consultant? When would you cross a line in using the consultant on the essay?

8. Marv Albert, the longtime NBC sportscaster famous for his "Yes!" commentary, was charged with violations of several Virginia statutes, including criminal assault,

[22] Richard Sandomir, "U.S. Olympic Chief Resigns in a Furor Over Ethics Issues," *New York Times*, February 5, 2003, A1, C17; Bill Briggs, "Realtor Waving Red Flag," **http://www.denverpost.com**, February 4, 2003.

[23] Adam Smith, *The Theory of Moral Sentiments* (Arlington House, 1969; originally published in 1769).

battery, and sodomy, for his alleged conduct with a woman in a hotel room. Initially, Albert went to trial on the case and denied that the charges were true. During the trial, another woman testified that Albert had engaged in similar behavior with her. Following plea negotiations, Albert entered a guilty plea the next day. NBC then fired him under a provision in his contract that prohibited employees from making false statements. Albert had assured his superiors at NBC that the charges were baseless. Do you agree with NBC's decision to fire Albert? Was his personal behavior relevant for his job performance? Do you agree that lying to your employer should result in automatic termination? Albert is back as a network commentator. Does his reinstatement mean that moral issues and private conduct are irrelevant in business decisions?

9. In 1997, the Federal Trade Commission (FTC) issued a cease-and-desist order against Toys "R" Us. The order required Toys "R" Us to stop what the FTC calls its "blacklisting" practices. The FTC ruled that Toys "R" Us had forced large toy manufacturers, such as Mattel and Hasbro, to withhold their products from such discount warehouse stores as Sam's Club and Costco. Toys "R" Us allegedly threatened not to carry these companies' products if they were also sold at the discount warehouse chains. Mattel's Barbie doll is one toy that Toys "R" Us carried that the discount warehouses were not permitted to carry. Costco CEO James Sinegal said, "You could fill Madison Square Garden with the people who don't want to sell to us." Are these types of sales agreements ethical? Is it fair for Toys "R" Us to insist on these arrangements? How do you think these arrangements would affect price?
10. The president and athletic director at the University of California at Los Angeles (UCLA) fired the school's basketball coach because an expense form he had submitted for reimbursement had the names of two students he said had joined him for a recruiting dinner. The students had not been to the dinner. The coach was stunned because he had been at UCLA for eight years and had established a winning program. He said, "And to throw it all away on a meal?" Do you agree with the coach's assessment? Was it too harsh to fire him for one inaccurate expense form? Did the coach commit an ethical breach?
11. A new trend is emerging in health insurance: premium increases based on claims. It is common practice in the auto insurance industry, for example, for insurers to revisit your premium each year and adjust it based on factors such as your driving record or number of accidents. However, health insurers have generally evaluated their insured's health only once, at the outset, when issuing a policy. The reevaluation of health and premiums was a practice that ended in the 1950s because the insurers feared regulators would impose limitations on premiums. At least one health insurer, however, has begun to evaluate the health of its insureds annually and to adjust policy premiums accordingly. Even without examination of insureds, some insurers have increased the insureds' premiums based simply on the nature of their claims for the year and the possibility that more claims will arise. Those who are healthy are in favor of this annual review. Perceiving themselves as the equivalent of good drivers, they want to pay less when they stay healthy. The health discount is, in their minds, the equivalent of the safe driver discount. However, those who are less healthy argue that people buy insurance so it will be there when they need it, and the coverage should apply without regard to claims. Consider the ethical issues in this type of pricing for health insurance.
12. David A. Vise, a Putlitzer Prize winner and a reporter for the *Washington Post*, wrote the book *The Bureau and the Mole.* When the book hit the market, Mr. Vise purchased 20,000 copies via Barnes & Noble.com, taking advantage of both free shipping offered by the publisher and a discounted initial price. Mr. Vise's book had already hit the *New York Times'* bestseller list in the week before the purchases. He used the books he purchased to conduct online sales of autographed copies of the books, and then returned 17,500 books and asked for his money back. However, that return of 17,500 books represented more books than a publisher generally runs for a book. Mr. Vise said that he did not intend to manipulate the market or profit from the transactions. He said his only intent was to "increase awareness of *The Bureau and the Mole.*" Mr. Vise's editor offered to pay Barnes & Noble for any expenses it incurred. Was it ethical to do what Mr. Vise did? Was he within his rights to return the books? What are his remedies? Does Barnes & Noble have any rights?
13. Suzy Wetlaufer, editor of the *Harvard Business Review*, interviewed former General Electric CEO Jack Welch for a piece in the business magazine. In December 2001, she asked that the piece be withdrawn because her objectivity might have been compromised. Those at the magazine did another interview and published that interview in the February issue of the magazine. Editorial director of the magazine, Walter Kiechel, who supervised Ms. Wetlaufer, acknowledged as true a report in the *Wall Street Journal* about an alleged affair between Ms. Wetlaufer and Mr. Welch and that Mr. Welch's wife had called to protest the article's objectivity. Mr. Welch refused to confirm or deny an affair with Ms. Wetlaufer, who was divorced. Some staff members asked that Ms. Wetlaufer resign from her $277,000-per-year job, but she refused. Their objections were that she compromised her journalistic integrity. Mr. Kiechel, on the other hand, noted that she did "the right thing in raising

her concerns."[24] About six weeks later, Ms. Wetlaufer did resign from her position as editor, announcing that she would be spending time with her four children. Do you think there was a conflict of interest because of the affair between Welch and Wetlaufer?[25] Note: Mr. Welch and Ms. Wetlaufer have married and have written a book together. They now write a semiweekly column for *Busienss Week* magazine.

14. Piper High School in Piper, Kansas, a town located about 20 miles west of Kansas City, experienced national attention because of questions about students and their term papers for a botany class. Christine Pelton, a high school science teacher, had warned students in her sophomore class not to use papers posted on the Internet for their projects. When their projects were turned in, Ms. Pelton noticed that the writing in some of the papers was well above the students' usual quality and ability. She found that 28 of her 118 students had taken substantial portions of their papers from the Internet. She gave these students a zero grade on their term paper projects with the result that many of the students were going to fail the course for that semester. The students' parents protested, and the school board ordered Ms. Pelton to raise the grades. She resigned in protest. She received a substantial number of job offers from around the country following her resignation. Nearly half of the high school faculty as well as its principal announced their plans to resign at the end of the year. Several of the parents pointed to the fact that there was no explanation in the Piper High School handbook on plagiarism. They also said that the students were unclear about what could be used, when they had to reword, and when quotations marks were necessary. The annual Rutgers University survey on academic cheating has revealed that 15 percent of college papers turned in for grades are completely copied from the Internet. Do you think such copying is unethical? Why do we worry about such conduct? Isn't this conduct just a function of the Internet? Isn't it accepted behavior?
15. Pharmaceutical companies, faced with the uphill battle of getting doctors to take a look at their new products, have created complex systems and programs for enticing doctors to come, sit, and absorb information about the new products. Following is a list of the various type of benefits and gifts that drug companies have given doctors over the past few years to entice them to consider prescribing their new offerings:

- An event called "Why Cook?" in which doctors were given the chance to review drug studies and product information at a restaurant as their meals were being prepared—they could leave as soon as their meals were ready, and they were treated to appetizers and drinks as they waited
- Events at Christmas tree lots where doctors can come and review materials and pick up a free Christmas tree
- Flowers sent to doctors' offices on Valentine's Day with materials attached
- Manicures as they study materials on new drugs
- Pedicures as they study materials on new drugs
- Free car washes during which they study materials
- Free books with materials enclosed
- Free CDs with materials attached
- Bottles of wine with materials attached
- Events at Barnes & Noble where doctors can browse and pick out a book for themselves for free as long as they also take some materials on a new drug

Some doctors say that they can enjoy dinner on a drug company as often as five times per week. The American Medical Association (AMA) frowns on the "dine-and-dash" format because its rules provide that dinners are acceptable only as long as the doctors sit and learn something from a featured speaker. The AMA also limits gifts to those of a "minimal value" that should be related to their patients, such as note pads and pens with the new drug's name imprinted on them. The chairman of the AMA Committee on Ethics says the following about gifts, "There are doctors who say, 'I always do what's best for my patients, and these gifts and dinners and trips do not influence me.' They are wrong."[26] In which category of ethical issues do these gifts fall? Do you think doctors act ethically in accepting gifts, meals, and favors? The Food and Drug Administration recently issued rules about such favors and perks. Why?

[24] Del Jones, "Editor Linked with Welch Finds Job at Risk," *USA Today*, March 5, 2002, 3B.
[25] Ms. Wetlaufer and Mr. Welch were engaged to be married after Mr. Welch divorced Jane Welch.
[26] Chris Adams, "Doctors on the Run Can 'Dine 'n' Dash' in Style in New Orleans," *Wall Street Journal*, May 14, 2001, A1, A6.

THE CONSTITUTION AS THE FOUNDATION OF THE LEGAL ENVIRONMENT

CHAPTER (4)

A. The U.S. Constitution and the Federal System
   1. What a Constitution Is
   2. The Branches of Government

B. The U.S. Constitution and the States
   3. Delegated and Shared Powers
   4. Other Powers
   5. Federal Supremacy

C. Interpreting and Amending the Constitution
   6. Conflicting Theories
   7. Amending the Constitution
   8. The Living Constitution

D. Federal Powers
   9. The Power to Regulate Commerce
   10. The Financial Powers

E. Constitutional Limitations on Government
   11. Due Process
   12. Equal Protection of the Law
   13. Privileges and Immunities
   14. Protection of the Person
   15. The Bill of Rights and Businesses as Persons

LEARNING OBJECTIVES

After studying this chapter, you should be able to

LO.1 Describe the system of government created by the U.S. Constitution

LO.2 List the branches and levels of government and describe their relationship to each other

LO.3 Explain how the U.S. Constitution adapts to change

LO.4 List and describe three significant federal powers

LO.5 Discuss two significant constitutional limitations on governmental power

This chapter introduces you to the powers of government and to the protections that you have for your rights. The Constitution of the United States sets forth not only the structure and powers of government but also the limitations on those powers. This Constitution, together with the constitutions of each of the states, forms the foundation of our legal environment.

A. The U.S. Constitution and the Federal System

By establishing a central government to coexist with the governments of the individual states, the U.S. Constitution created a federal system. In a **federal system,** a central government has power to address national concerns, while the individual states retain the power to handle local concerns.

1. What a Constitution Is

A **constitution** is the written document that establishes the structure of the government and its relationship to the people. The U.S. Constitution was adopted in 1789 by the 13 colonies that had won their independence from King George.[1]

2. The Branches of Government

The U.S. Constitution establishes a **tripartite** (three-part) government: a **legislative branch** (Congress) to make the laws, an **executive branch** (the president) to execute or enforce the laws, and a **judicial branch** (courts) to interpret the laws. The national legislature or Congress is a **bicameral** (two-house) body consisting of the Senate and the House of Representatives. Members of the Senate are popularly elected for a term of six years. Members of the House of Representatives are popularly elected for a term of two years. The president is elected by an electoral college whose membership is popularly elected. The president serves for a term of four years and is eligible for reelection for a second term. Judges of the United States are appointed by the president with the approval of the Senate and serve for life, subject to removal only by impeachment because of misconduct. (See Chapter 2 for a discussion of the federal court system.)

B. The U.S. Constitution and the States

The Constitution created certain powers within the national government that would have been exercised by the individual states, which are given their powers by the people of the state. Figure 4-1 illustrates the delegation of powers. Likewise, the states, as the power-granting authorities, reserved certain powers for themselves.

3. Delegated and Shared Powers

(a) Delegated Powers

The powers given by the states to the national government are described as *delegated powers.* Some of these **delegated powers** are given exclusively to the national government. For example, the national government alone may declare war or establish a currency.

(b) Shared Powers

The powers delegated to the national government that may still be exercised by the states are **shared powers.** **For Example,** the grant of power to the national government to impose taxes did not destroy the state power to tax. Some of the shared powers may be exercised by the states only so long as there is no federal exercise.

For Example, a state's law on appliance safety may apply until Congress adopts a federal appliance safety law. In other cases, a state may provide regulation along with, but subject to the supremacy of, federal law. **For Example,** regulation of the use of navigable waterways within a state is an example of joint state and federal regulation.

4. Other Powers

(a) State Police Power

The states possess the power to adopt laws to protect the general welfare, health, safety, and morals of the people. This authority is called the **police power.** **For Example,** states may require that businesses be licensed with state agencies to protect persons dealing with the business. State exercise of the police power may not unreasonably interfere with federal powers.

[1] To examine the U.S. Constitution, go to **http://www.constitution.org** and click on "Founding Documents" or refer to Appendix 2.

FIGURE 4-1 Governments of the United States

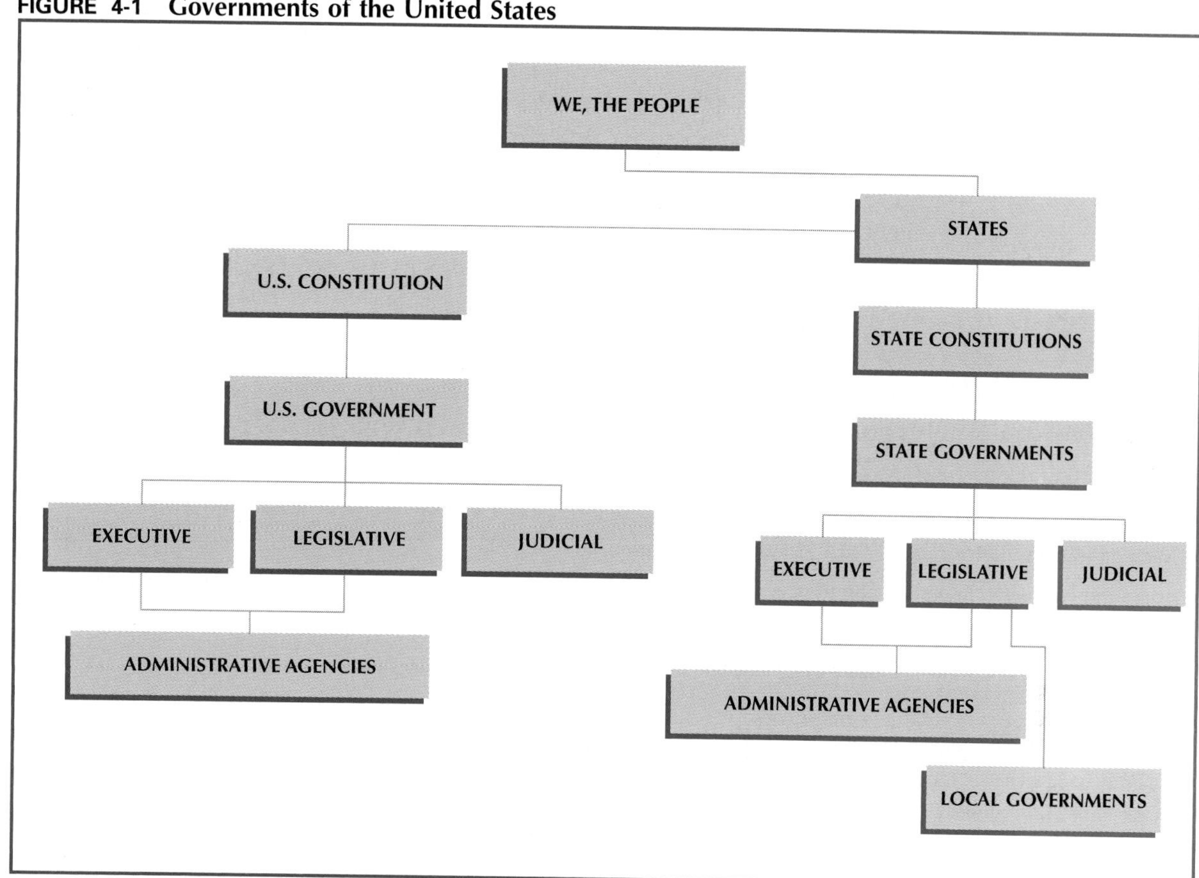

(b) Prohibited Powers

The Constitution also prohibits both states and the federal government from doing certain things. **For Example,** neither states nor the national government may adopt ***ex post facto*** **laws,** which make criminal an act that has already been committed but was not criminal when it was committed. Laws that increase the penalty for an act already committed above the penalty in force when the act was committed are also *ex post facto* laws.

5. Federal Supremacy

Federal law bars or preempts conflicting state regulation when a federal law regulates that particular subject. Federal law also preempts state action when congressional intent to regulate exclusively can be inferred from the details of congressional regulation. **Preemption** means that the federal regulatory scheme is controlling.

(a) Express Federal Regulation

The Constitution and statutes passed by Congress are the supreme law of the land. They cancel out any conflicting state law.[2] When a direct conflict exists between federal and state statutes, it is clear that federal law prevails.

In some cases, however, no obvious conflict occurs because the federal statute covers only part of the subject matter. In such cases, the question becomes whether a state law can regulate the areas not regulated by Congress or whether the partial regulation made by Congress preempts, or takes over, the field so as to preclude state legislation.

(b) Silence of Congress

In some situations, the silence of Congress in failing to cover a particular subject area indicates that Congress does not want any law on the matter. However, when national uniformity is essential,

[2] U.S. Const., Art VI, cl 2. *Michigan Canners and Freezers' Ass'n, Inc. v Agricultural Marketing and Bargaining Board*, 467 US 461 (1984).

MID-CON FREIGHT SYSTEMS, INC. V MICHIGAN PUBLIC SERVICE COMMISSION, 545 US 440 (2005)

TRUCK BINGO: A CONSTITUTIONAL ISSUE

Federal law requires most interstate truckers to obtain a permit (Federal Permit) that reflects compliance with certain federal requirements. The 1965 version of the law authorized states to require proof that a truck operator had such a permit. By 1991, 39 states demanded such proof, requiring a $10 per truck registration fee (state registration) and giving each trucker a stamp to affix to a multistate "bingo card" carried in the vehicle. Finding this scheme inefficient and burdensome, Congress created the current Single State Registration System (SSRS), 49 U.S.C. § 14504(b), which allows a trucking company to fill out one set of forms in one state (base state), thereby registering its Federal Permit in every participating state through which its trucks travel. The base state can demand proof of the Federal Permit, proof of insurance, the name of an agent to receive service of process, and a fee equal to the sum of the individual state fees. The SSRS prohibits a state from imposing any additional "state registration requirement." Michigan Comp. Laws Ann. § 478.2(2) (MCL) imposes an annual $100 fee on each Michigan license-plated truck operating entirely in interstate commerce. The American Truckers Association (ATA) and interstate trucking companies (petitioners) that are subject to the Michigan law sought to have it invalidated, but the Michigan Court of Claims refused. The State Court of Appeals affirmed. The truckers appealed to the U.S. Supreme Court.

Judicial Opinion

BREYER, Justice... The SSRS statute specifies that a State may not impose any additional "registration requirement." It states specifically, in the statutory sentence at issue here, that when a State Registration requirement imposes further obligations, "the part in excess is an unreasonable burden." It adds that a State may not require "decals, stamps, cab cards, or any other means of registering... specific vehicles." And it provides that the "charging or collection of any fee under this section that is not in accordance with the fee system established [in this provision] shall be deemed to be a burden on interstate commerce." At the same time, the statute makes clear that a State that complies with the SSRS system need not fear Commerce Clause attack, for it says that a state requirement that an interstate truck "must register with the State" is "not an unreasonable burden on transportation," provided that "the State registration is completed" in accordance with the SSRS statute.

The Court of Appeals wrote that the $100 fee is a "regulatory fee"—a "fee imposed for the administration" of the State's Motor Carrier Act and for enforcement of Michigan "safety regulations." As such, it falls outside the scope of the term "registration requirement" as used in the federal SSRS statute. We granted their petition for certiorari and consolidated the case with *American Trucking Assns., Inc. v. Michigan Pub. Serv. Comm'n*, — U.S. —, 125 S. Ct. 2419, 162 L.Ed.2d 407, 2005 WL 1421164 (2005), a case in which interstate truckers sought review of a separate Michigan fee.

The first legal question before us concerns the meaning of the federal statutory words "State registration requirement." They appear in a subsection that reads in relevant part as follows:

"The requirement of a State that a motor carrier, providing [interstate transportation] in that State, must register with the State is not an unreasonable burden on transportation... when the State registration is completed under standards of the Secretary [of Transportation] under subsection (c). When a State registration requirement imposes obligations in excess of the standards of the Secretary, the part in excess is an unreasonable burden."

Petitioners ask us to give these words a broad interpretation, sweeping within their ambit every state requirement involving some form of individualized registration that affects an interstate motor carrier. The United States argues for a somewhat narrower interpretation, submitting that the words apply to "state registration requirements that are imposed on interstate carriers by reason of their operation in interstate commerce." In our view, however, the language, read in context, is yet more narrow.

Reference to text, historical context, and purpose discloses that the words "State registration requirement" do not apply to every State Registration requirement that happens to cover interstate carriers, nor to every such requirement specifically focused on a trucking operation's interstate character. Rather, they apply only to those state requirements that concern SSRS registration—that is, registration with a State of evidence that a carrier possesses a Federal Permit, registration of proof of insurance, or registration of the name of an agent "for service of process." Thus, the federal provision pre-empts only those state requirements that (1) concern the subject matter of the SSRS and (2) are "in excess" of the requirements that the SSRS imposes in respect to that subject matter.

When Congress created the new SSRS, it did not indicate (in the text, structure, or divinable purpose of the new provision) that the pre-emptive scope of the new scheme would be any broader than that of the old. The relevant differences between the SSRS and the "bingo card" regime were that: (1) one State, rather than many, would collect the relevant filings; (2) one State, rather than many, would collect the relevant fees; and (3) these fees, limited to the same amount as before, would relate to filing of proof of insurance rather than to filing of the Federal Permit. These modifications merely sought more efficient, not greater, federal regulation. And while the new regulations implementing the SSRS do not explicitly exempt unrelated state requirements from the statute's pre-emptive reach, neither they nor the rulemaking that produced them suggest any change to pre-existing practice in this respect.

Finally, we have found nothing in the statute's basic purposes or objectives—improving the efficiency of the "bingo card" system and simplifying a uniform scheme for providing States with certain vital information—that either requires a broader reading of the statutory term, or that impliedly pre-empts other, non-SSRS-related state rules. That is, we can find no indication that Congress sought to use this narrowly focused statute to forbid state fee or registration obligations that have nothing to do with basic SSRS (or earlier "bingo card") objectives—say, for example, a State Registration requirement related to compliance by interstate carriers with rules governing the introduction of foreign pests into the jurisdiction, or with a State's version of the Amber Alert system, or with size, weight, and safety standards.

The second legal question involves the Michigan statute imposing the $100 fee on Michigan-plated trucks operating entirely in interstate commerce. Do the requirements set forth in that statute concern the SSRS statute's subject matter? We think that they do not.

For one thing, the Michigan statute imposing the $100 fee makes no reference to evidence of a Federal Permit, to any insurance requirement, or to an agent for receiving service of process. Nor, as far as we can tell, do any state rules related to the $100 fee require the filing of information about these matters.

For another thing, Michigan law imposed a separate fee on interstate motor carriers with trucks license plated in Michigan before the SSRS existed and before Michigan began to participate in the "bingo card" system. Hence such a fee does not represent an effort somehow to circumvent the limitations imposed in connection with federal laws governing State Registration of Federal Permits.

Finally, Michigan rules provide that a Michigan-plated interstate truck choosing Michigan as its SSRS base State can apparently comply with Michigan's SSRS requirements even if it does not comply with Michigan's $100 fee requirement. The owner of that truck can fill out Michigan form RS-1, thereby providing Michigan with evidence that it has a Federal Permit. It can also fill out form RS-2, on which it indicates the total SSRS fees it owes to all participating States whose borders the truck will cross. Upon submission of the two forms and payment of the fees, Michigan apparently will give the owner form RS-3, an SSRS receipt, a copy of which the owner can place in the vehicle of the truck, thereby complying with Michigan's (and all other participating States') SSRS-related "State registration requirements." If that owner fails to pay Michigan's $100 fee for that truck, the owner will not receive a state fee decal. But that owner will have violated only Michigan's $100 fee statute here at issue. Petitioners have provided us with nothing that suggests the owner will have violated any other provision of Michigan law. And they have not demonstrated that Michigan law in practice holds hostage a truck owner's SSRS compliance until the owner pays [the] $100 fee.

For these reasons, we conclude that 49 U.S.C. § 14504(b) does not pre-empt Michigan's $100 fee. The judgment of the Michigan Court of Appeals is affirmed.

Questions

1. What was the "bingo card" system?
2. What did Congress hope to accomplish with the SRSS?
3. What is the difference between Michigan's requirements and what is covered under the SRSS?

the silence of Congress generally means that the subject has been preempted for practical reasons by Congress and that no state law on the subject may be adopted. The *Mid-Con Freight Systems, Inc. v Michigan Public Service Commission* case deals with an issue of preemption.

(c) Effect of Federal Deregulation

The fact that the federal government removes the regulations from a regulated industry does not automatically give the states the power to regulate that industry. If under the silence-of-Congress doctrine the states cannot regulate, they are still barred from regulating after deregulation. **For Example,** deregulation cannot be considered authorization for state regulation.[3]

C. Interpreting and Amending the Constitution

The Constitution as it is interpreted today has changed greatly from the Constitution as originally written. The change has been brought about by interpretation, amendment, and practice.

6. Conflicting Theories

Shortly after the Constitution was adopted, conflict arose over whether it was to be interpreted strictly, so as to give the federal government the least power possible, or broadly, so as to give the federal government the greatest power that the words would permit. These two views may be called the *bedrock view* and the *living-document view*, respectively.

In the **bedrock view,** or strict constructionist or originalist view, the purpose of a constitution is to state certain fundamental principles for all time. In the **living-document view,** a constitution is merely a statement of goals and objectives and is intended to grow and change with time.

Whether the Constitution is to be liberally interpreted under the living-document view or narrowly interpreted under the bedrock view has a direct effect on the Constitution. For the last century, the Supreme Court has followed the living-document view. This view has resulted in strengthening the power of the federal government, permitting the rise of administrative agencies, and expanding the protection of human rights.

One view is not selected to the exclusion of the other. As contradictory as these two views sound, the Constitution remains durable. We do not want a set of New Year's resolutions that will soon be forgotten. At the same time, we know that the world changes, and therefore, we do not want a constitution that will hold us tied in a straitjacket of the past.

In terms of social forces that make the law, we are torn between our desire for stability and our desire for flexibility. We want a constitution that is stable. At the same time, we want one that is flexible.

7. Amending the Constitution

The U.S. Constitution has been amended in three ways: (1) expressly, (2) by interpretation, and (3) by practice. Figure 4-2 illustrates these three methods of amendment.

(a) Constitutional Method of Amending

Article V of the Constitution gives the procedure to be followed for amending the Constitution.

FIGURE 4-2 Amending the U.S. Constitution

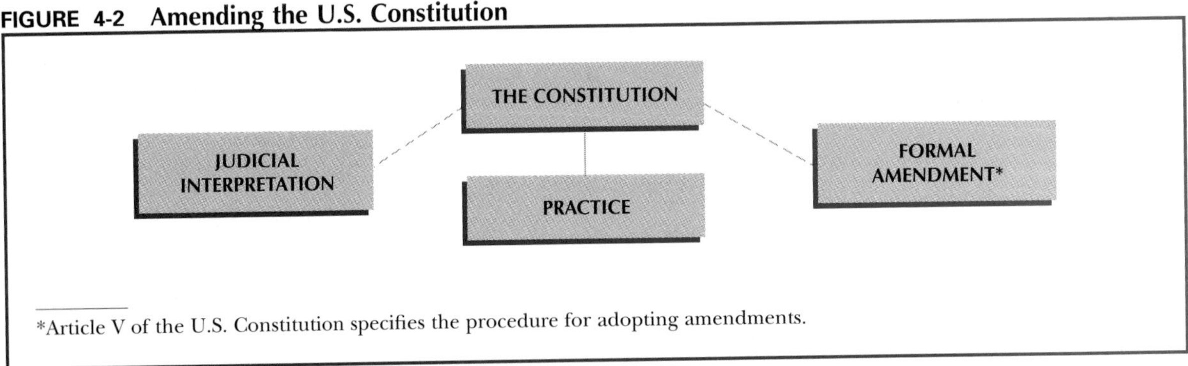

*Article V of the U.S. Constitution specifies the procedure for adopting amendments.

[3] *New York v Trans World Airlines,* 556 NYS2d 803 (1990).

Relatively few changes have been made to the Constitution by this formal process, although thousands of proposals have been made. Since the time of its adoption, there have been only 27 amendments to the Constitution.

(b) Amendment by Judicial Interpretation

The U.S. Supreme Court has made the greatest changes to the written Constitution by interpreting it. Generally, interpretation is used to apply the Constitution to a new situation that could not have been foreseen when the written Constitution was adopted.

(c) Amendment by Practice

In practice, the letter of the Constitution is not always followed. Departure from the written Constitution began as early as 1793 when George Washington refused to make treaties as required by the Constitution, by and with the consent of the Senate. Washington began the practice of the president's negotiating a treaty with a foreign country and then submitting it to the Senate for approval. This practice has been followed since that time. Similarly, the electoral college was originally intended to exercise independent judgment in selecting the president, but it now automatically elects the official candidate of the party that elected the majority of the members of the electoral college.

8. The Living Constitution

The Constitution that has developed in the manner described in the preceding section is radically different from the Constitution that was written on paper. The living Constitution has the following characteristics.

(a) Strong Government

One of the characteristics of the new Constitution is strong government. Business enterprises can now be regulated and the economy controlled.

(b) Strong President

Instead of being merely an officer who carries out the laws, the president has become the political leader of a party, exerting a strong influence on the lawmaking process. If the president's political party is in control of both houses of Congress, the president acts as the leader of the lawmaking process.

(c) Eclipse of the States

Under constitutional interpretations, all levels of government have powers that they never possessed before, but the center of gravity has shifted from the states to the nation. When the Constitution was adopted in 1789, the federal government was to have only the very limited powers specified in Article I, Section 8, of the Constitution. Whatever regulation of business was permissible was to be imposed by the states. Today, the great bulk of the regulation of business is adopted by the federal government through Congress or its administrative agencies. As the U.S. economy moved from the local community stage to the nationwide stage, the individual states were unable to provide effective regulation of business. It was inevitable that regulation would migrate to the central government.

(d) Administrative Agencies

These units of government were virtually unheard of in 1789, and the Constitution made no mention of them. The vast powers of the new Constitution are exercised to a very large degree by administrative agencies. They are in effect a fourth branch of the government, not provided for in the written Constitution. More importantly, the administrative agencies are the ones that come in contact with the majority of businesspersons and citizens. The agencies are the government for most people.

In other words, the legislatures, the courts, or the executive officers do not directly exercise the vast power of government to regulate business. Rather, agencies exercise this power. The members and heads of the agencies, boards, or commissions are not elected by the voters (see Chapter 6). They are appointed by the president and, at certain levels of appointment in the agency, must be approved by Congress.

D. Federal Powers

The federal government possesses powers necessary to administer matters of national concern.

9. The Power to Regulate Commerce

The desire to protect commerce from restrictions and barriers set up by the individual states was a prime factor leading to the adoption of the Constitution of 1789. To protect commerce, Congress was given Article I, Section 8, Clause 3—now known as the **commerce clause**—the power "[t]o regulate commerce with foreign nations, and among the several states, and with the Indian tribes"[4]

Until 1937, the Supreme Court held that this provision gave Congress the power to control or regulate only that commerce crossing a state line, such as an interstate railway train or an interstate telegraph message.

(a) The Commerce Power Becomes a General Welfare Power

In 1937, the Supreme Court began expanding the concept of interstate commerce. By 1946, the power to regulate interstate commerce had become very broad. By that year, the power had expanded to the point that it gave authority to Congress to adopt regulatory laws that were "as broad as the economic needs of the nation."[5] By virtue of this broad interpretation, Congress can regulate manufacturing, agriculture, mining, stock exchanges, insurance, loan sharking, monopolies, and conspiracies in restraint of trade. The far reach of the interstate commerce power is seen in the Freedom of Access to Clinic Entrances Act,[6] which prohibits obstruction of entrances to clinics.[7]

The case that was the beginning point in the transition of the commerce clause was *NLRB v Jones & Laughlin Steel*, 301 US 1 (1937). The "affectation" doctrine expanded the authority of the federal government under the commerce clause. At that time, the Court concluded, "If it is interstate commerce that feels the pinch, it does not matter how local the squeeze."

(b) The Commerce Clause Today

Today, judicial review of the commerce clause typically finds some connection between the legislation and congressional authority. However, in the past five years, the U.S. Supreme Court has found some areas Congress may not regulate and has placed some limitations on the commerce clause. These constraints on the commerce clause focus on the nature of the underlying activity being regulated. So long as the federal regulation relates to economic/commercial activity, it is constitutional. If, however, the underlying activity is not economic and has only an economic impact, the Supreme Court has imposed restrictions on congressional authority under the commerce clause. The *U.S. v Morrison* case is the most recent Supreme Court decision on the commerce clause.

(c) The Commerce Power as a Limitation on States

The federal power to regulate commerce not only gives Congress the power to act but also prevents states from acting in any way that interferes with federal regulation or burdens interstate commerce. **For Example,** if the federal government establishes safety device regulations for interstate carriers, a state cannot require different devices.

States may not use their tax power for the purpose of discriminating against interstate commerce, because such commerce is within the protection of the national government. **For Example,** a state cannot impose a higher tax on goods imported from another state than it imposes on the same kind of goods produced in its own territory.

State regulations designed to advance local interests may conflict with the commerce clause. Such regulations are invalid. A state cannot refuse to allow an interstate waste collector to conduct business within the state on the ground that the state already has enough waste collectors. The *Granholm v Heald* case deals with an issue of state power.

10. The Financial Powers

The financial powers of the federal government include the powers to tax and to borrow, spend, and coin money.

(a) The Taxing Power

The federal Constitution provides that "Congress shall have power [t]o lay and collect taxes, duties, imposts and excises, to pay the debts and provide for the common defence and general welfare of the United States."[8] Subject to the express and implied limitations arising from the Constitution, the states

[4] For more details on the actual language in the U.S. Constitution, go to **http://www.constitution.org** and click on "Founding Documents" or refer to Appendix 2.

[5] *American Power & Light Co. v Securities and Exchange Commission*, 329 US 90 (1946).

[6] 18 USC § 248.

[7] The act is constitutional. *United States v Wilson*, 73 F3d 675 (7th Cir 1995), *cert denied*, 519 US 806 (1996).

[8] U.S. Const., Art 1, § 8, cl 1. To read more of the U.S. Constitution, refer to Appendix 2 or go to **http://www.constitution.org** and click on "Founding Documents."

U.S. V MORRISON, 529 US 598 (2000)

THE COMMERCE CLAUSE MEETS VIOLENCE

Christy Brzonkala filed a suit under the federal Violence Against Women Act (VAWA) after she was raped by two of her fellow students at the Virginia Polytechnic Institute. The VAWA gives women who are the victims of violence a civil rights action against their assailants. The district court dismissed the suit because it found Congress lacked authority under the Commerce Clause for the VAWA. The court of appeals reversed. Because a lower court invalidated a federal statute, the Supreme Court granted *certiorari.*

Judicial Opinion

REHNQUIST, Chief Justice... [we] consider the constitutionality of 42 U.S.C. § 13981, which provides a federal civil remedy for the victims of gender-motivated violence.

Section 13981 was part of the Violence Against Women Act of 1994. It states that "[a]ll persons within the United States shall have the right to be free from crimes of violence motivated by gender."

Every law enacted by Congress must be based on one or more of its powers enumerated in the Constitution. Due respect for the decisions of a coordinate branch of Government demands that we invalidate a congressional enactment only upon a plain showing that Congress has exceeded its constitutional bounds. With this presumption of constitutionality in mind, we turn to the question whether § 13981 falls within Congress' power under Article I, § 8, of the Constitution. Brzonkala and the United States rely upon the third clause of the Article, which gives Congress power "[t]o regulate Commerce with foreign Nations, and among the several States, and with the Indian Tribes."

As we discussed at length in *U.S. v Lopez,* 514 US 549 (1995), our interpretation of the Commerce Clause has changed as our Nation has developed. We need not repeat that detailed review of the Commerce Clause's history here; it suffices to say that, in the years since *NLRB v. Jones & Laughlin Steel Corp.,* 301 U.S. 1, 57 S.Ct. 615, 81 L.Ed. 893 (1937), Congress has had considerably greater latitude in regulating conduct and transactions under the Commerce Clause than our previous case law permitted.

Both petitioners and Justice SOUTER's dissent downplay the role that the economic nature of the regulated activity plays in our Commerce Clause analysis. But a fair reading of *Lopez* shows that the noneconomic, criminal nature of the conduct at issue was central to our decision in that case. The possession of a gun in a local school zone is in no sense an economic activity that might, through repetition elsewhere, substantially affect any sort of interstate commerce. "[U]nlike the earlier cases to come before the Court here neither the actors nor their conduct has a commercial character, and neither the purposes nor the design of the statute has an evident commercial nexus. The statute makes the simple possession of a gun within 1,000 feet of the grounds of the school a criminal offense. In a sense any conduct in this interdependent world of ours has an ultimate commercial origin or consequence, but we have not yet said the commerce power may reach so far." *Lopez*'s review of Commerce Clause case law demonstrates that in those cases where we have sustained federal regulation of intrastate activity based upon the activity's substantial effects on interstate commerce, the activity in question has been some sort of economic endeavor.

Finally, our decision in *Lopez* rested in part on the fact that the link between gun possession and a substantial effect on interstate commerce was attenuated. The United States argued that the possession of guns may lead to violent crime, and that violent crime "can be expected to affect the functioning of the national economy." The Government also argued that the presence of guns at schools poses a threat to the educational process, which in turn threatens to produce a less efficient and productive workforce, which will negatively affect national productivity and thus interstate commerce.

We rejected these "costs of crime" and "national productivity" arguments because they would permit Congress to "regulate not only all violent crime, but all activities that might lead to violent crime, regardless of how tenuously they relate to interstate commerce." We noted that, under this but-for reasoning: "Congress could regulate any activity that it found was related to the economic productivity of individual citizens: family law (including marriage, divorce, and child custody), for example. Gender-motivated crimes of violence are not, in any sense of the phrase, economic activity. While we need not adopt a categorical rule against aggregating the effects of any noneconomic activity in order to decide these cases, thus far in our Nation's history our cases have upheld

Commerce Clause regulation of intrastate activity only where that activity is economic in nature.

The reasoning that petitioners advance seeks to follow the but-for causal chain from the initial occurrence of violent crime (the suppression of which has always been the prime object of the States' police power) to every attenuated effect upon interstate commerce. If accepted, petitioners' reasoning would allow Congress to regulate any crime as long as the nationwide, aggregated impact of that crime has substantial effects on employment, production, transit, or consumption.

We accordingly reject the argument that Congress may regulate noneconomic, violent criminal conduct based solely on that conduct's aggregate effect on interstate commerce. The Constitution requires a distinction between what is truly national and what is truly local. In recognizing this fact we preserve one of the few principles that has been consistent since the Clause was adopted. The regulation and punishment of intrastate violence that is not directed at the instrumentalities, channels, or goods involved in interstate commerce has always been the province of the States. Affirmed.

Justice SOUTER, with whom Justice STEVENS, Justice GINSBURG, and Justice BREYER join, dissenting. Congress has the power to legislate with regard to activity that, in the aggregate, has a substantial effect on interstate commerce. The fact of such a substantial effect is not an issue for the courts in the first instance, but for the Congress, whose institutional capacity for gathering evidence and taking testimony far exceeds ours. By passing legislation, Congress indicates its conclusion, whether explicitly or not, that facts support its exercise of the commerce power. The business of the courts is to review the congressional assessment, not for soundness but simply for the rationality of concluding that a jurisdictional basis exists in fact.

One obvious difference from *United States v Lopez*, 514 U.S. 549, 115 S.Ct. 1624, 131 L.Ed.2d 626 (1995), is the mountain of data assembled by Congress, here showing the effects of violence against women on interstate commerce. Passage of the Act in 1994 was preceded by four years of hearings, which included testimony from physicians and law professors; from survivors of rape and domestic violence; and from representatives of state law enforcement and private business.

All of this convinces me that today's ebb of the commerce power rests on error, and at the same time leads me to doubt that the majority's view will prove to be enduring law.

Questions

1. What does the Violence Against Women Act do?
2. What did Congress do to establish the connection of VAWA to commerce?
3. What does the majority opinion say is the test for the constitutionality of federal regulation under the Commerce Clause?
4. What does the dissenting opinion say the test for the constitutionality of federal regulation under the Commerce Clause should be?

may impose such taxes as they desire and as their own individual constitutions and statutes permit. In addition to express constitutional limitations, both national and local taxes are subject to the unwritten limitation that they be imposed for a public purpose. Taxes must also be apportioned. A business cannot be taxed for all of its revenues in all 50 states. There must be apportionment of taxes, and there must be sufficient connection with the state. The *Quill v North Dakota* case deals with an issue of state taxation of an interstate company.

(b) The Spending Power

The federal government may use tax money and borrowed money "to pay the debts and provide for the common defence and general welfare of the United States."[9]

(c) The Banking Power

The federal Constitution is liberally interpreted to authorize the U.S. government to create banks and to regulate banks created under state laws. The Federal Reserve System is responsible for this regulatory oversight of banks.

E. Constitutional Limitations on Government

The constitutional limitations discussed in the following sections afford protections of rights for both persons and businesses.

[9] U.S. Const., Art 1, § 8, cl 1. See **http://www.constitution.org** or Appendix 2.

GRANHOLM V HEALD, 544 US 460 (2005)

WHINING ABOUT WINE

Like many other states, Michigan and New York regulate the sale and importation of alcoholic beverages, including wine, through a three-tier distribution system. Separate licenses are required for producers, wholesalers, and retailers. Both the regulations and statutory frameworks in New York and Michigan prohibit out-of-state wine producers from selling their wines directly to consumers there. In-state wineries can sell directly to consumers. The impact of the prohibition on the out-of-state wine producers is that they are required to pay wholesaler fees and cannot compete with in-state wine producers on direct-to-consumer sales. The direct-to-consumer sales avenue has been a means for small wineries to compete. Also, technological improvements, in particular the ability of wineries to sell wine over the Internet, have helped make direct shipments an attractive sales channel.

Several wine producers filed suit in their federal districts challenging these laws that prohibit direct shipment. The district court granted summary judgment for the state of Michigan. The Sixth Circuit Court of Appeals reversed on the grounds that the out-of-state restrictions violated the commerce clause. The state of Michigan appealed. In the New York case, the district court found the out-of-state restrictions violative of the Commerce Clause and Second Circuit Court of Appeals reversed and upheld the New York statute as constitutional. The out-of-state wine producers appealed, and the Supreme Court agreed to hear the cases to resolve the conflict in the circuits.

Judicial Opinion

KENNEDY, Justice... We consolidated these cases and granted certiorari on the following question: "'Does a State's regulatory scheme that permits in-state wineries directly to ship alcohol to consumers but restricts the ability of out-of-state wineries to do so violate the ... Commerce Clause...?'"

Time and again this Court has held that, in all but the narrowest circumstances, state laws violate the Commerce Clause if they mandate "differential treatment of in-state and out-of-state economic interests that benefits the former and burdens the latter." This rule is essential to the foundations of the Union. The mere fact of nonresidence should not foreclose a producer in one State from access to markets in other States. States may not enact laws that burden out-of-state producers or shippers simply to give a competitive advantage to in-state businesses. This mandate "reflect[s] a central concern of the Framers that was an immediate reason for calling the Constitutional Convention: the conviction that in order to succeed, the new Union would have to avoid the tendencies toward economic Balkanization that had plagued relations among the Colonies and later among the States under the Articles of Confederation."

The rule prohibiting state discrimination against interstate commerce follows also from the principle that States should not be compelled to negotiate with each other regarding favored or disfavored status for their own citizens. States do not need, and may not attempt, to negotiate with other States regarding their mutual economic interests. Rivalries among the States are thus kept to a minimum, and a proliferation of trade zones is prevented.

Laws of the type at issue in the instant cases contradict these principles. They deprive citizens of their right to have access to the markets of other States on equal terms. State laws that protect local wineries have led to the enactment of statutes under which some States condition the right of out-of-state wineries to make direct wine sales to in-state consumers on a reciprocal right in the shipping State. The current patchwork of laws—with some States banning direct shipments altogether, others doing so only for out-of-state wines, and still others requiring reciprocity—is essentially the product of an ongoing, low-level trade war. Allowing States to discriminate against out-of-state wine "invite [s] a multiplication of preferential trade areas destructive of the very purpose of the commerce clause."

The discriminatory character of the Michigan system is obvious. Michigan allows in-state wineries to ship directly to consumers, subject only to a licensing requirement. Out-of-state wineries, whether licensed or not, face a complete ban on direct shipment. The differential treatment requires all out-of-state wine, but not all in-state wine, to pass through an in-state wholesaler and retailer before reaching consumers. These two extra layers of overhead increase the cost of out-of-state wines to Michigan consumers. The cost differential, and in some cases the inability to secure a wholesaler for small shipments, can effectively bar small wineries from the Michigan market.

The New York regulatory scheme differs from Michigan's in that it does not ban direct shipments altogether. Out-of-state wineries are instead required to establish a distribution operation in New York in order to gain the privilege of direct shipment.

The New York scheme grants in-state wineries access to the State's consumers on preferential terms. The suggestion of a limited exception for direct shipment from out-of-state wineries does nothing to eliminate the discriminatory nature of New York's regulations. In-state producers, with the applicable licenses, can ship directly to consumers from their wineries. Out-of-state wineries must open a branch office and warehouse in New York, additional steps that drive up the cost of their wine. For most wineries, the expense of establishing a bricks-and-mortar distribution operation in 1 State, let alone all 50, is prohibitive. It comes as no surprise that not a single out-of-state winery has availed itself of New York's direct-shipping privilege. We have "viewed with particular suspicion state statutes requiring business operations to be performed in the home State that could more efficiently be performed elsewhere." *Pike v. Bruce Church, Inc.* 397 U.S. 137, 145, 90 S.Ct. 844, 25 L.Ed.2d 174 (1970). New York's in-state presence requirement runs contrary to our admonition that States cannot require an out-of-state firm "to become a resident in order to compete on equal terms."

We have no difficulty concluding that New York, like Michigan, discriminates against interstate commerce through its direct-shipping laws.

Affirmed as to judgment of the Sixth Circuit Court of Appeals; reversed and remanded as to judgment of the Second Circuit Court of Appeals.

NOTE: There was a strong dissent in the case that indicated that because of the 21st Amendment the federal government (and the court) could not be involved in state liquor regulation and that the Commerce Clause could not be applied to these state laws on liquor sales.

Questions

1. What do the Michigan and New York statutes require?
2. Why did the U.S. Supreme Court grant *certiorari* in the cases? Why do you think the court heard and decided the two cases together?
3. What is the economic impact of the statutes on wineries, both in- and out-of-state? On wholesalers? On consumers?

11. Due Process

The power of government is limited by both the Fifth and Fourteenth Amendments to the Constitution. Those amendments respectively prohibit the national government and state governments from depriving any person "of life, liberty, or property without due process of law."[10]

(a) When Due Process Rights Arise

As a result of liberal interpretation of the Constitution, the **due process clause** now provides a guarantee of

THINKING THINGS THROUGH

The $100 Michigan trucking fee noted earlier in the *American Trucking Association* case had an additional constitutional issue that was litigated at the same time as the question on preemption. This fee applied only to vehicles that engage in ***intrastate*** commercial operations—that is, on trucks that undertake point-to-point hauls between Michigan cities. The American Truckers Association (ATA) and others challenged the fee as an undue burden on interstate commerce. The trial court found for the state of Michigan, the court of appeals affirmed, and the Michigan Supreme Court refused to hear an appeal. The ATA and others appealed to the U.S. Supreme Court. What do you think the U.S. Supreme Court did with this commerce clause issue? Is the Michigan fee an unconstitutional burden on interstate commerce? [AMERICAN TRUCKING ASSOCIATION, INC. AND USF HOLLAND, INC. V MICHIGAN PUBLIC SERVICE COMMISSION 545 US 249 (2005)]

[10] For more information on the language of the Fifth and Fourteenth Amendments, see the U.S. Constitution in Appendix 2 or go to **http://www.constitution.org**.

QUILL V NORTH DAKOTA, 504 US 298 (1992)

A QUILL IN YOUR STATE MEANS TAXES IN THE COFFER

Quill is a Delaware corporation with offices and warehouses in Illinois, California, and Georgia. None of its employees works or lives in North Dakota, and it owns no property in North Dakota.

Quill sells office equipment and supplies; it solicits business through catalogs and flyers, advertisements in national periodicals, and telephone calls. Its annual national sales exceed $200 million, of which almost $1 million are made to about three thousand customers in North Dakota. The sixth largest vendor of office supplies in the state, it delivers all of its merchandise to its North Dakota customers by mail or common carriers from out-of-state locations.

As a corollary to its sales tax, North Dakota imposes a use tax upon property purchased for storage, use, or consumption within the state. North Dakota requires every "retailer maintaining a place of business in" the state to collect the tax from the consumer and remit it to the state. In 1987, North Dakota amended its statutory definition of the term "retailer" to include "every person who engages in regular or systematic solicitation of a consumer market in th[e] state." State regulations in turn define "regular or systematic solicitation" to mean three or more advertisements within a 12-month period. Thus, since 1987, mail-order companies that engage in such solicitation have been subject to the tax even if they maintain no property or personnel in North Dakota.

Quill has taken the position that North Dakota does not have the power to compel it to collect a use tax from its North Dakota customers. Consequently, the state, through its tax commissioner, filed this action to require Quill to pay taxes (as well as interest and penalties) on all such sales made after July 1, 1987. The trial court ruled in Quill's favor.

The North Dakota Supreme Court reversed, and Quill appealed.

Judicial Opinion

STEVENS, J. . . . This case, like *National Bellas Hess, Inc. v Department of Revenue of Ill.*, 386 U.S. 753, 87 S.Ct. 1389, 18 L.Ed.2d 505 (1967), involves a State's attempt to require an out-of-state mail-order house that has neither outlets nor sales representatives in the State to collect and pay a use tax on goods purchased for use within the State. In *Bellas Hess* we held that a similar Illinois statute violated the Due Process Clause of the Fourteenth Amendment and created an unconstitutional burden on interstate commerce. In particular, we ruled that a "seller whose only connection with customers in the State is by common carrier or the United States mail" lacked the requisite minimum contacts with the State.

In this case the Supreme Court of North Dakota declined to follow *Bellas Hess* because "the tremendous social, economic, commercial, and legal innovations" of the past quarter-century have rendered its holding "obsole[te]."

As in a number of other cases involving the application of state taxing statutes to out-of-state sellers, our holding in *Bellas Hess* relied on both the Due Process Clause and the Commerce Clause.

The Due Process Clause "requires some definite link, some minimum connection, between a state and the person, property or transaction it seeks to tax," and that the "income attributed to the State for tax purposes must be rationally related to 'values connected with the taxing State.'" Prior to *Bellas Hess*, we had held that that requirement was satisfied in a variety of circumstances involving use taxes. For example, the presence of sales personnel in the State, or the maintenance of local retail stores in the State, justified the exercise of that power because the seller's local activities were "plainly accorded the protection and services of the taxing State." We expressly declined to obliterate the "sharp distinction . . . between mail order sellers with retail outlets, solicitors, or property within a State, and those who do no more than communicate with customers in the State by mail or common carrier as a part of a general interstate business."

Our due process jurisprudence has evolved substantially in the 25 years since *Bellas Hess*, particularly in the area of judicial jurisdiction. Building on the seminal case of *International Shoe Co. v. Washington*, 326 U.S. 310, 66 S.Ct. 154, 90 L.Ed. 95 (1945), we have framed the relevant inquiry as whether a defendant had minimum contacts with the jurisdiction "such that the maintenance of the suit does not offend 'traditional notions of fair play and substantial justice.'"

Applying these principles, we have held that if a foreign corporation purposefully avails itself of the benefits of an economic market in the forum State, it may subject itself to the State's ***in personam*** jurisdiction even if it has no physical presence in the State.

Comparable reasoning justifies the imposition of the collection duty on a mail-order house that is engaged in continuous and widespread solicitation of business within a State. In "modern commercial life" it matters little that such solicitation is accomplished by a deluge of catalogs rather than a phalanx of drummers: the requirements of due process are met irrespective of a corporation's lack of physical presence in the taxing State. Thus, to the extent that our decisions have indicated that the Due Process Clause requires physical presence in a State for the imposition of duty to collect a use tax, we overrule those holdings as superseded by developments in the law of due process.

In this case, there is no question that Quill has purposefully directed its activities at North Dakota residents, that the magnitude of those contacts are more than sufficient for due process purposes, and that the use tax is related to the benefits Quill receives from access to the State. We therefore agree with the North Dakota Supreme Court's conclusion that the Due Process Clause does not bar enforcement of that State's use tax against Quill.

[Affirmed]

Questions

1. Did Quill Corporation own any property in North Dakota? Were any Quill offices or personnel located in North Dakota?
2. How did Quill come to have customers in North Dakota?
3. Will Quill be subject to North Dakota's use tax?
4. Is there a jurisdictional difference between pamphlets being present in a state and the presence of salespeople in that state?

protection against the loss of property or rights without the chance to be heard. These amendments also guarantee that all citizens are given the same protections. **For Example,** the Supreme Court has extended the due process clause to protect the record or standing of a student.[11] A student cannot lose credit in a course or be suspended or expelled without some form of a hearing.

Due process of law does not bar the regulation of business because any regulation that would have sufficient support to pass a legislature or Congress would have sufficient claim to validity to be debatable. The fact that many would deem a law unsound, unwise, hazardous, or un-American does not in itself make the law invalid under the due process clause. There is, however, a remedy through legislative change, not individual accommodation. The laws apply to all equally, and the chance to be heard is during the legislative process.

Because the due process concept is a limitation on governmental action, it does not apply to transactions between private persons or to private employment or other nonpublic situations. In some cases, however, statutes, such as the federal Civil Rights Act and those addressing consumer protection, apply due process concepts to private transactions.

Speeding up due process has required the use of **quasi-judicial proceedings.** In these types of proceedings, the parties need not go through the complex, lengthy, and formal procedures of a trial (described in Chapter 2). Rather, these proceedings have a hearing officer or administrative law judge (see Chapter 6) who conducts an informal hearing in which the rules of evidence and procedure are relaxed.

For Example, a student taking a grade grievance beyond a faculty member's decision will generally have his case heard by a panel of faculty and students as established by college or university rules. An employer appealing its unemployment tax rate will have the appeal heard by an administrative law judge.

(b) What Constitutes Due Process?

Due process does not require a trial on every issue of rights. Shortcut procedures, such as grade grievance panels, have resulted as a compromise for providing the right to be heard along with a legitimate desire to be expeditious in resolving these issues.

[11] That is, a student cannot be expelled without a chance to have his or her side of the story reviewed.

E-COMMERCE AND CYBERLAW

INTERNET AND INTERSTATE

Collection of sales tax from Internet stores has been a stickler of an issue for businesses, state revenue officials, and the U.S. Supreme Court. All three were grappling with how to collect, what to collect, and whether anybody had any authority to collect. Internet sales represent a large, untapped source of revenue. A study from the Center for Business and Economic Research at the University of Tennessee estimates the lost tax revenue from untaxed Internet sales as $21 billion by 2008.

The merchants involved fell into several different legal groups in terms of their theories on whether tax was owed and if they paid it:

1. Those stores with physical presences in states (Wal-Mart and J.C. Penney) that just collected sales tax as if they were collecting it in a store in that state where the Internet purchaser was located.
2. Those stores without a physical presence (Amazon) that did collect taxes, particularly in those states known for taking a hard-line approach.
3. Those stores without a physical presence that do not collect taxes and maintain t-hat it is unconstitutional to do so. Indeed, the U.S. Supreme Court held in 1992 that any tax rate with so many permutations that it becomes difficult for the retailer to administer is an undue burden on interstate commerce.
4. Those stores with or without a physical presence that have collected taxes but held them until everyone could figure out the legal status of the companies.

Wal-Mart, Target, and Office Depot settled an Internet sales tax case with Illinois for $2.4 million in sales taxes for 2003.

However, representatives from 18 states have formed the Architects of the Streamlined Sales Tax Project with the goal of finding a uniform and simple means for taxing Internet sales. Some states are reluctant to join because this group proposes giving the sales tax revenue to the state and local body where the purchaser is, not where the sale originates. Some of the states, such as Nevada, would lose a substantial amount of revenue if sales tax did not apply at the point of origin of the sale (e.g., the warehouse; Nevada, for example, is loaded with warehouses because of its no-inventory-tax policy).

As of October 1, 2006, eighteen states implemented a computer program that determines the average tax for the state and its localities and adds that on to the Internet purchase. The officials in the states are offering amnesty to merchants who sign up for the program. That is, if they owe taxes for past transactions, they are not liable if they go with the new program. Internet merchants have one year to sign up for the new rates and the amnesty. In addition to this incentive, Internet retailers who use the program are also immune from penalties for mistakes and miscalculations.

What are the constitutional issues in this taxation question?

Robery Guy Matthews, "Some States Push to Collect Sales Tax from Internet Stores," *Wall Street Journal*, Sept. 30, 2005, B1–B4.

12. Equal Protection of the Law

The Constitution prohibits the states and the national government from denying any person the equal protection of the law.[12] This guarantee prohibits a government from treating one person differently from another when there is no reasonable ground for classifying them differently.

(a) Reasonable Classification

Whether a classification is reasonable depends on whether the nature of the classification bears a

[12] U.S. Constitution, Fourteenth Amendment as to the states; modern interpretation of due process clause of the Fifth Amendment as to national government. Congress adopted the Civil Rights Act to implement the concept of equal protection.

reasonable relation to the wrong to be remedied or to the object to be attained by the law. In determining the constitutionality of classifications, the courts have been guided generally by historical treatment and logic. The judicial trend is to permit the classification to stand as long as there is a rational basis for the distinction made.[13] Whether a rational basis exists is determined by answering whether the lawmaking body has been arbitrary or capricious.

The equal protection clause provides broad protections and is the basis of many of the U.S. Supreme Court's most complicated decisions. **For Example,** during the 2000 presidential election, the U.S. Supreme Court faced an issue of equal protection with regard to the challenge then-vice president and presidential candidate Al Gore made to the undervotes in Florida's ballots. However, then-presidential candidate George W. Bush argued that counting the undervotes in some counties and not in others and applying different standards for counting or not counting the infamous dimpled chads, hanging chads, and other undervotes was unconstitutional because it deprived other Florida voters of equal protection because each vote is intended to count equally and the recounts occuring in only some counties and using varying standards resulted in those counties being given greater weight in Florida's presidential election. The U.S. Supreme Court agreed in a 7–2 decision that the recounts were unconstitutional on equal protection grounds.[14] However, the ultimate decision in the case was based on a 5–4 vote because the justices could not agree on a remedy for the unconstitutional recounts.

(b) Improper Classification

Laws that make distinctions in the regulation of business, the right to work, and the right to use or enjoy property on the basis of race, national origin, or religion are invalid. Also invalid are laws that impose restrictions on some, but not all, persons without any justification for the distinction.[15] A state statute taxing out-of-state insurance companies at a higher rate than in-state insurance companies violates the equal protection clause.[16]

13. Privileges and Immunities

The federal Constitution declares that "[t]he citizens of each state shall be entitled to all privileges and immunities of citizens in the several states."[17] The so-called **privileges and immunities clause** means that a person going into another state is entitled to make contracts, own property, and engage in business to the same extent as the citizens of that state. **For Example,** a state cannot bar someone who comes from another state from engaging in local business or from obtaining a hunting or fishing license merely because the person is not a resident of that state. Likewise, a law that requires an attorney to be a resident of the state in order to practice is unconstitutional as a violation of this provision.[18]

14. Protection of the Person

The Constitution does not contain any express provision protecting "persons" from governmental action. Persons are expressly protected by the Constitution with respect to particular matters, such as freedom of speech, ownership of property, right to a jury trial, and so on. There is, however, no general provision declaring that the government shall not impair rights of persons. The Constitution does not mention the phrase "unalienable right" that was part of the Declaration of Independence.[19]

The Bill of Rights, the first 10 amendments to the Constitution, do provide protections for freedom of speech, jury trials, and freedom of religion and

[13] *Urton v Hudson*, 101 Or App 147, 790 P2d 12 (1990).

[14] *Bush v Gore*, 531 US 98 (2000).

[15] *Associated Industries of Missouri v Lohman*, 511 US 641 (1994).

[16] *Metropolitan Life Ins. Co. v Ward*, 470 US 869 (1985).

[17] U.S. Const., Art IV, § 2, cl 1. See **http://www.constitution.org** and click on "Founding Documents" to access more language of the Constitution, or see Appendix 2.

[18] *Barnard v Thorstenn*, 489 US 546 (1989).

[19] The term *unalienable right* is employed in reference to natural right, fundamental right, or basic right. Apart from the question of scope of coverage, the adjective *unalienable* emphasizes the fact that the people still possess the right rather than having surrendered or subordinated it to the will of society. The word *alien* is the term of the old common law for transferring title or ownership. Today, we would say *transfer* and, instead of saying unalienable rights, would say *nontransferable* rights. Unalienable rights of the people were therefore rights that the people not only possessed but also could not give up even if they wanted to. Thus, these rights are still owned by everyone. It is important to note that the Declaration of Independence actually uses the word "unalienable" when describing the rights eventually placed in the Constitution as Amendments I–X, the Bill of Rights, not "inalienable."

association. It is within the Bill of Rights that the protections against unlawful searches and seizures as well as due process are found.

In addition, during the last six decades, the Supreme Court has been interpreting the rights in these amendments and has been finding constitutional protection for a wide array of rights of the person that are not expressly protected by the Constitution. Examples are the right of privacy, the right to marry the person one chooses,[20] protection from unreasonable zoning, protection of parental control, protection from discrimination because of poverty, and protection from gender discrimination.[21]

15. The Bill of Rights and Businesses as Persons

The first 10 amendments to the U.S. Constitution (the Bill of Rights) provide protections for both individuals and corporations. **For Example,** the Fourth Amendment (see Chapter 8) provides protections against unreasonable searches. Individuals enjoy that protection in their homes, and corporations enjoy that protection with their files, offices, and business records.

Businesses also enjoy freedom of speech protections under the First Amendment. The First Amendment provides that "Congress shall make no law . . . abridging the freedom of speech . . . "[22]

The U.S. Supreme Court has clarified the free speech rights of business through classification of the types of business speech. One form of business or commercial speech is advertising. This form of speech in which businesses tout their products is subject to regulation and restriction on form, content, and placement, and such regulation has been deemed constitutional. (See Chapter 25 and 33 for more information on the regulation of advertising.) However, there are other forms of commercial speech. Businesses do have the right to participate in political processes such as creating political action committees and supporting or opposing ballot initiatives. Businesses often take positions and launch campaigns on ballot initiatives that will affect the taxes they will be required to pay. The *First National Bank of Boston v Bellotti* case deals with an issue of corporate speech.

FIRST NATIONAL BANK OF BOSTON V BELLOTTI, 435 US 765 (1978)

BANKS ARE PEOPLE TOO: FIRST AMENDMENT POLITICAL SPEECH

Massachusetts had passed a statute that prohibited businesses and banks from making contributions or expenditures "for the purpose of . . . influencing or affecting the vote on any question submitted to the voters, other than one materially affecting any of the property, business or assets of the corporation." The statute also provided that "no question submitted to the voters solely concerning the taxation of the income, property or transactions of individuals shall be deemed materially to affect the property, business or assets of the corporation." The statute carried a fine of up to $50,000 for the corporation and $10,000 and/or one year imprisonment for corporate officers.

First National Bank and other banks and corporations (appellants) wanted to spend money to publicize their views on an upcoming ballot proposition that would permit the legislature the right to impose a graduated tax on individual income. Frances X. Bellotti, the attorney general for Massachusetts (appellee), told First National and the others that

[20] *Akron v Akron Center for Reproductive Health, Inc.*, 462 US 416 (1983); but see *Colorado v Hill, cert granted*, 527 US 1068 (2000). For more on commercial speech and expression, see *Greater New Orleans Broadcasting Association, Inc., v U.S.* 527 US 173(1999).

[21] In some cases, the courts have given the due process and equal protection clauses a liberal interpretation in order to find a protection of the person, thereby making up for the fact that there is no express constitutional guarantee of protection of the person. *Davis v Passman* 442 US 228 (1979) (due process); *Orr v Orr*, 440 US 268 (1979) (equal protection).

[22] To read the full language of the First Amendment, go to Appendix 2 or **http://www.constitution.org** and click on "Founding Documents."

he intended to enforce the statute against them. First National and the others brought suit to have the statute declared unconstitutional and First National appealed.

Judicial Opinion

POWELL, J. . . . "There is practically universal agreement that a major purpose of [the First] Amendment was to protect the free discussion of governmental affairs." If the speakers here were not corporations, no one would suggest that the State could silence their proposed speech. It is the type of speech indispensable to decision-making in a democracy, and this is no less true because the speech comes from a corporation rather than an individual. The inherent worth of the speech in terms of its capacity for informing the public does not depend upon the identity of its source, whether corporation, association, union, or individual.

The court below nevertheless held the corporate speech is protected by the First Amendment only when it pertains directly to the corporation's interests. In deciding whether this novel and restrictive gloss on the First Amendment comports with the Constitution and the precedents of this Court, we need not survey the outer boundaries of the Amendment's protection of corporate speech, or address the abstract question whether corporations have the full measure of rights that individuals enjoy under the First Amendment. The question in this case, simply put, is whether the corporate identity of the speaker deprives this proposed speech of what otherwise would be its clear entitlement to protection.

Freedom of speech and the other freedoms encompassed by the First Amendment always have been viewed as fundamental components of the liberty safeguarded by the Due Process Clause, and the Court has not identified a separate source for the right when it has been asserted by corporations.

In the realm of protected speech, the legislature is constitutionally disqualified from dictating the subjects about which persons may speak and the speakers who may address a public issue. If a legislature may direct business corporations to "stick to business," it may also limit other corporations—religious, charitable, or civic—to their respective "business" when addressing the public. Such power in government to channel the expression of views is unacceptable under the First Amendment. Especially where, as here, the legislature's suppression of speech suggests an attempt to give one side of a debatable public question an advantage in expressing its views to people, the First Amendment is plainly offended. Yet the State contends that its action is necessitated by governmental interests of the highest order. We next consider these asserted interests.

Appellee ... advances two principal justifications for the prohibition of corporate speech. The first is the State's interest in sustaining the active role of the individual citizen in the electoral process and thereby preventing diminution of the citizen's confidence in government. The second is the interest in protecting the rights of shareholders whose views differ from those expressed by management on behalf of the corporation.

Preserving the integrity of the electoral process, preventing corruption and "sustaining the active, alert responsibility of the individual citizen in a democracy for the wise conduct of government" are interests of the highest importance. Preservation of the individual citizen's confidence in government is equally important.

To be sure, corporate advertising may influence the outcome of the vote; this would be its purpose. But the fact that advocacy may persuade the electorate is hardly a reason to suppress it: The Constitution "protects expression which is eloquent no less than that which in unconvincing." We noted only recently that "the concept that government may restrict speech of some elements of our society in order to enhance the relative voice of others is wholly foreign to the First Amendment. . . ." Moreover, the people in our democracy are entrusted with the responsibility for judging and evaluating the relative merits of conflicting arguments. They may consider, in making their judgment, the source and credibility of the advocate. But if there be any danger that the people cannot evaluate the information and arguments advanced by appellants, it is a danger contemplated by the Framers of the First Amendment. . . .

The statute is said to ... prevent the use of corporate resources in furtherance of views with which some shareholders may disagree. This purpose is belied, however, by the provisions of the statute, which are both under- and over-inclusive.

The under-inclusiveness of the statute is self-evident. Corporate expenditures with respect to a referendum are prohibited, while corporate activity with respect to the passage or defeat of legislation is permitted, even though corporations may engage in lobbying more often than they take positions on ballot questions submitted to voters.

The over-inclusiveness of the statute is demonstrated by the fact that [it] would prohibit a corporation from supporting or opposing a referendum even if its shareholders unanimously authorized the contribution or expenditure.

Assuming, arguendo, that protection of shareholders is a "compelling" interest under the circumstances of this case, we find "no substantially relevant correlation between the governmental interest asserted and the State's effort" to prohibit appellants from speaking.

[Reversed]

Case Questions

1. What did the Massachusetts statute regulate?
2. What justification did Massachusetts offer for the statute? What were its concerns in passing the statute?
3. Why does the Court discuss under-inclusiveness and over-inclusiveness?
4. How does the Court respond to the fact that corporate speech might be more persuasive?
5. Is the statute constitutional?

THINKING THINGS THROUGH

SWEATING IT OUT ON FREE SPEECH

A third form of commercial speech has emerged through *Nike v Kasky.* In 1996, Nike was inundated with allegations about its labor practices in shoe factories around the world. Nike responded to the negative reports and allegations with a series of releases, advertisements, and op-ed pieces in newspapers around the country. In addition, Nike commissioned a report from a former Atlanta mayor and U.S. ambassador, Andrew Young, on the condition of its factories around the world. Young issued a report in 1997 that reflected favorably on Nike and its labor practices.

New York Times columnist Bob Herbert wrote two columns that were sharply critical of Nike's conditions in plants throughout Asia. The columns compared CEO Philip Knight's compensation with the $2.20 per day wages of Nike workers in Indonesia.

After the columns appeared, CEO Knight wrote a letter to the editor in response to them. In that letter, he wrote, "Nike has paid, on average, double the minimum wage as defined in countries where its products are produced under contract. History shows that the best way out of poverty for such countries is through exports of light manufactured goods that provide the base for more skilled production."*

Marc Kasky filed suit against Nike in California, alleging that the op-ed pieces and letters in response to negative op-ed pieces about Nike violated the False Advertising Act of California. The act permits state agencies to take action to fine corporate violators of the act as well as to obtain remedies such as injunctions to halt the ads.

Nike challenged the suit on the grounds that such an interpretation and application of the advertising regulation violated its rights of free speech. The lower court agreed with Kasky and held that the advertising statute applied to Nike's defense of its labor practices, even on the op-ed pages of newspapers. The California Supreme Court, 45 P.3d 243 (Cal. 2002), ruled that Nike could be subject to regulatory sanctions for false advertising. Nike appealed to the U.S. Supreme Court.

The Supreme Court did not reach the heart of the case—the commercial speech and First Amendment issues. Rather, the Court held that the case was not ripe for resolution because no action had been taken against Nike and because there had been no factual determinations with regard to the content of Nike's responses. There was, according to the Court, no final judgment in the case, and so it was not ripe for decision. The case was, therefore, remanded.

There is no substantive ruling from the case on commercial speech, but the Court's decision still constitutes precedent for appellate cases. An appellate court does not decide an issue in a case until the lower courts have made their

THINKING THINGS THROUGH

continued

factual determinations and a final decision. However, following the U.S. Supreme Court remand, Nike settled the case so that another similar case will be required before we have a definitive resolution to the questions surrounding this third form of commercial speech.

Read the *Nike v Kasky* opinion at **http://www.supremecourtus.gov/opinions/02pdf/02-575.pdf.** The opinion, however, is only one sentence: "The writ of certiorari is dismissed as improvidently granted." 539 US 654 (2003).

[*]Roger Parloff "Can We Talk?" *Fortune*, September 2, 2002, 102–110.

LAWFLIX

The Candidate (1972) (PG)

The movie depicts an idealist running for office who finds himself caught in the political process of fundraising, image-building, and winning. A number of scenes with speeches, fundraising, and principles in conflict provide excellent discussion issues with respect to government structure, the First Amendment, and campaign contributions.

For movie clips that illustrate business law concepts, see LawFlix at **http://wdvl.westbuslaw.com.**

Summary

The U.S. Constitution created the structure of our national government and gave it certain powers. It also placed limitations on those powers. It created a federal system with a tripartite division of government and a bicameral national legislature.

The national government possesses some governmental powers exclusively, while both the states and the federal government share other powers. In areas of conflict, federal law is supreme.

The U.S. Constitution is not a detailed document. It takes its meaning from the way it is interpreted. In recent years, liberal interpretation has expanded the powers of the federal government. Among the powers of the federal government that directly affect business are the power to regulate commerce; the power to tax and to borrow, spend, and coin money; and the power to own and operate businesses. Among the limitations on government that are most important to business are the requirement of due process and the requirement of equal protection of the law.

The due process requirement stipulates that no person shall be deprived of life, liberty, or property without due process of law. This requirement applies to both the federal government and the state governments but does not apply to private transactions.

The equal protection concept of the U.S. Constitution prohibits both the federal government and the state governments from treating one person differently from another unless there is a legitimate reason for doing so and unless the basis of classification is reasonable.

Questions and Case Problems

1. J.C. Penney, a retail merchandiser, has its principal place of business in Plano, Texas. It operates retail stores in all 50 states, including 10 stores in Massachusetts, and a direct mail catalog business. In connection with its catalog business, each year Penney issued three major seasonal catalogs, as well as various small sale or specialty

catalogs, that described and illustrated merchandise available for purchase by mail order. The planning, artwork, design, and layout for these catalogs were completed and paid for outside of Massachusetts, primarily in Texas, and Penney contracted with independent printing companies located outside Massachusetts to produce the catalogs. The three major catalogs were generally printed in Indiana, while the specialty catalogs were printed in South Carolina and Wisconsin. Penney supplied the printers with paper, shipping wrappers, and address labels for the catalogs; the printers supplied the ink, binding materials, and labor. None of these materials was purchased in Massachusetts. Printed catalogs, with address labels and postage affixed, were transported by a common carrier from the printer to a U.S. Postal Service office located outside Massachusetts, where they were sent to Massachusetts addressees via third- or fourth-class mail. Any undeliverable catalogs were returned to Penney's distribution center in Connecticut.

The catalogs advertised a broader range of merchandise than was available for purchase in Penney's retail stores. The purpose for mailing these catalogs, free of charge, to residents of, among other places, Massachusetts, was to solicit mail-order purchases from current and potential customers. Purchases of catalog merchandise were made by telephoning or returning an order form to Penney at a location outside Massachusetts, and the merchandise was shipped to customers from a Connecticut distribution center. The Massachusetts Department of Revenue audited Penney's in 1995 and assessed a use tax, penalty, and interest on the catalogs that had been shipped into Massachusetts. The use tax is imposed in those circumstances "in which tangible personal property is sold inside or outside the Commonwealth for storage, use, or other consumption within the Commonwealth." The position of the department was that there was a tax due of $314,674.62 on the catalogs that were used by Penney's Massachusetts customers. Penney said such a tax was unconstitutional in that it had no control or contact with the catalogs in the state. Can the state impose the tax? [*Commissioner of Revenue v J.C. Penney Co., Inc.*, 730 NE2d 266 (Mass)]

2. Wolens and others are participants in American Airlines' frequent flyer program, AAdvantage. AAdvantage members earn mileage credits when they fly on American. The members can exchange those credits for flight tickets or class-of-service upgrades. Wolens complained that AAdvantage program modifications, instituted by American in 1988, devalued credits that AAdvantage members had already earned. The examples Wolens gave were American's imposition of capacity controls (limiting the number of seats per flight available to AAdvantage members) and blackout dates (restrictions on dates AAdvantage members could use their credits). Wolens brought suit alleging that these changes and cutbacks violated the Illinois Consumer Fraud and Deceptive Business Practices Act. American Airlines challenged the suit on the grounds that the regulation of airlines was preempted by the Airline Deregulation Act (ADA) of 1978, which deregulated domestic air transportation but also included the following clause on preemption: "[N]o State . . . shall enact or enforce any law, rule, regulation, standard, or other provision having the force and effect of law relating to rates, routes, or services of any air carrier . . ." [49 USC App § 1305(a)] The Illinois Supreme Court found that the rules on the frequent flyer program were only tangentially related to rates, routes, and services and required American Airlines to defend the suit. American Airlines appealed. Is American Airlines correct? Is state regulation preempted here? [*American Airlines, Inc. v Wolens*, 513 US 219]

3. The state of Arizona passed a regulation that required that cantaloupes grown within the state be packed in in-state facilities before shipment. California companies with Arizona farms were thus required to build packing facilities in Arizona in order to ship their harvest. Is the Arizona law constitutional? [*Pike v Bruce Church, Inc.*, 397 US 137]

4. The University of Wisconsin requires all of its students to pay, as part of their tuition, a student activity fee. Those fees are used to support campus clubs and activities. Some students who objected to the philosophies and activities of some of the student clubs filed suit to have the fees halted. What constitutional basis do you think they could use for the suit? [*Board of Regents of Wisconsin System v Southworth*, 529 US 217]

5. The Crafts' home was supplied with gas by the city gas company. Because of some misunderstanding, the gas company believed that the Crafts were delinquent in paying their gas bill. The gas company had an informal complaint procedure for discussing such matters, but the Crafts had never been informed that such a procedure was available. The gas company notified the Crafts that they were delinquent and that the company was shutting off the gas. The Crafts brought an action to enjoin the gas company from doing so on the theory that a termination without any hearing was a denial of due process. The lower courts held that the interest of the Crafts in receiving gas was not a property interest protected by the due process clause and that the procedures the gas company followed satisfied the requirements of due process. The Crafts appealed. Were they correct in contending that they had been denied due process of law]? Why or why not? [*Memphis Light, Gas and Water Division v Craft*, 436 US 1]

6. Alexis Geier was injured in an accident while driving a 1987 Honda Accord that did not have passive safety restraints. When her Honda Accord was manufactured, the

U.S. Department of Transportation required passive safety restraints on some, but not all, vehicles. Geier and her parents filed suit against Honda for its negligence in not equipping the Honda Accord with a driver's side airbag. Geier alleged that because Honda knew of the safety standard but did not voluntarily comply with it (it was not required to do so under the federal regulations), it was negligent under state negligence standards for liability and should be held liable. The district court granted Honda summary judgment based on Honda's argument that safety requirements for cars were set exclusively by the federal government. The court of appeals affirmed, and Geier appealed. What would be the effect of a decision that requires a car company to comply with state-by-state standards of negligence? Would a state court finding of negligence be a constitutional exercise of state power? Should the U.S. Supreme Court affirm or reverse the summary judgment for Honda? [*Geier v American Honda Motor Co.*, 529 US 1913]

7. Montana imposed a severance tax on every ton of coal mined within the state. The tax varied depending on the value of the coal and the cost of production. It could be as high as 30 percent of the price at which the coal was sold. Montana mine operators and some out-of-state customers claimed that this tax was unconstitutional as an improper burden on interstate commerce. Decide. [*Commonwealth Edison Co. v Montana*, 453 US 609]

8. Ollie's Barbecue is a family-owned restaurant in Birmingham, Alabama, specializing in barbecued meats and homemade pies, with a seating capacity of 220 customers. It is located on a state highway 11 blocks from an interstate highway and a somewhat greater distance from railroad and bus stations. The restaurant caters to a family and white-collar trade, with a take-out service for "Negroes." (Note: This term is used by the Court in its opinion in the case.) In the 12 months preceding the passage of the Civil Rights Act, the restaurant purchased locally approximately $150,000 worth of food, $69,683 or 46 percent of which was meat that it bought from a local supplier who had procured it from outside the state. Ollie's has refused to serve Negroes in its dining accommodations since opening in 1927, and since July 2, 1964, it has been operating in violation of the Civil Rights Act. A lower court concluded that if it were required to serve Negroes, it would lose a substantial amount of business. The lower court found that the Civil Rights Act did not apply because Ollie's was not involved in "interstate commerce." Will the commerce clause permit application of the Civil Rights Act to Ollie's? [*Katzenbach v McClung*, 379 US 294]

9. Heald was the executor of the estate of a deceased person who had lived in Washington, D.C. Heald refused to pay federal tax owed by the estate on the ground that the tax had been imposed by an act of Congress, and because residents of the District of Columbia had no vote in Congress, the tax law was adopted without their representation. Not only did District residents have no voice in the adoption of the tax laws, but also the proceeds from taxes collected in the District were paid into the general treasury of the United States and were not maintained as a separate District of Columbia fund. Heald objected that the tax law was void as contrary to the Constitution because it amounted to taxation without representation. Evaluate Heald's argument. [*Heald v District of Columbia*, 259 US 114]

10. Ellis was employed by the city of Lakewood. By the terms of his contract, he could be discharged only for cause. After working for six years, he was told that he was going to be discharged because of his inability to generate safety and self-insurance programs, because of his failure to win the confidence of employees, and because of his poor attendance. He was not informed of the facts in support of these conclusions and was given the option to resign. He claimed that he was entitled to a hearing. Is he entitled to one? Why or why not? [*Ellis v City of Lakewood*, 789 P2d 449 (Colo App)]

11. The Federal Food Stamp Act provided for the distribution of food stamps to needy households. In 1971, section 3(e) of the statute was amended to define households as limited to groups whose members were all related to each other. This was done because of congressional dislike for the lifestyles of unrelated hippies who were living together in hippie communes. Moreno and others applied for food stamps but were refused them because the relationship requirement was not satisfied. An action was brought to have the relationship requirement declared unconstitutional. Is it constitutional? Discuss why or why not. [*USDA v Moreno*, 413 US 528]

12. New Hampshire adopted a tax law that in effect taxed the income of nonresidents working in New Hampshire only. Austin, a nonresident who worked in New Hampshire, claimed that the tax law was invalid. Was he correct? Explain. [*Austin v New Hampshire*, 420 US 656]

13. Arkansas is primarily a rural state, and in many areas there, it is not feasible to employ cable television. Arkansas imposes a tax on sales and services, and cable television service was added to the list of taxed enterprises. No tax, however, was imposed on satellite television service. The cable companies claimed there was a denial of equal protection by taxing them but not satellite transmission of television. Are they correct? Why or why not? [*Medlock v Leathers*, 842 SW2d 428 (Ark)]

14. Following a boom in cruise ship construction, the ships are now looking for ports at which they can dock in order to begin voyages, most of which begin in the United States. With so many new ships, the companies are trying to establish connections with cities that are not ordinarily considered cruise ship docks. The companies pursue these alternatives because the traditional docking cities of New York, Seattle, Miami, Los Angeles, and Houston

have become crowded with cruise ship traffic. The following issues have arisen:

- Some ports are just not large enough for the larger cruise ships.
- Without proper scheduling and departures, cruise ships often end up waiting in the harbor for three to eight hours; as a result, ports such as Tampa, a nontraditional cruise ship port, are experiencing traffic jams of ships waiting to dock.
- The presence of the large boats and the resulting number of tourists cause overwhelming flooding of the often-quaint alternative ports such as Charleston, South Carolina. Charleston residents worry that tourists from the cruise ships flooding their city will result in irreversible destruction of the town's preserved landmarks and quaint looks.
- Rising water levels in ports such as New Orleans mean that the tall ships cannot clear power lines and have to be redirected to ports nearby that are not prepared, as when New Orleans had to redirect a 2,974-passenger cruise ship to Gulfport, Mississippi.
- The ships do bring passengers with tourist dollars to spend and additional work for harbor pilots and service industries.
- The port facilities are not adequate to handle all of the boats, the passengers, and even the ships' fueling needs.

Most cruise ship lines are incorporated outside of the United States, and they do not pay federal income taxes and are certainly not subject to state income taxes even though the bulk of their passengers comes from the United States.[23]

Can the ships be taxed to cover the harbor expenses? Can they be required by states and cities to pay docking fees, or are they internationally exempt companies?

15. A federal statute prohibited granting federal funds to libraries that did not control access to pornographic Internet sites on library computers so that children did not gain access and were not exposed to such sites as they used the public facilities. The American Library Association challenged the prohibition as a violation of First Amendment rights.

    Are free speech rights violated with the funding regulation? [**www.supremecourtus.gov/opinions/02pdf/02-361.pdf**, slip op. 1; *U.S. v American Library Association*, 539 US 194; lower court decision at 201 F Supp 2d 401]

[23] Nicole Harris "Big Cruise Ships Cause Traffic Jams in Ports," *Wall Street Journal*, August 20, 2003, B1–B6.

GOVERNMENT REGULATION OF COMPETITION AND PRICES

CHAPTER (5)

LEARNING OBJECTIVES

After studying this chapter, you should be able to

LO.1 State the extent to which government can regulate business

LO.2 Explain what laws protect free enterprise from unfair competition and from unfair restraints

LO.3 Define *price discrimination* and explain when it is prohibited

LO.4 Discuss the Sherman Antitrust Act, what it prohibits, and when it applies

The government can regulate not just businesses but also business competition and prices. Antitrust legislation and a regulatory scheme help to ensure that businesses compete fairly.

A. Power to Regulate Business

The federal government may regulate any phase of business that is necessary to advance the nation's economic needs.[1] Under the police power, states may regulate all aspects of business so long as they do not impose an unreasonable burden on interstate commerce or any activity of the federal government. (See Chapter 4 for a discussion of the protections and limits of the commerce clause.) Local governments may also exercise this power to the extent each state permits.

1. Regulation, Free Enterprise, and Deregulation

Milton Friedman, the Nobel economist, has written that government regulation of business interferes with the free enterprise system. Under a true free enterprise system, there would not be any regulation of airline safety, safety of food and drugs for human consumption, prices, and so on, for the free market would put those protections in place through demand. Sometimes, however, the demand response, or market reaction, to problems or services is not rapid enough to prevent harm, and government regulation steps in to stop abuses. For example, the FTC stepped in to curb the tactics and practices of telemarketers when the number of consumer complaints increased dramatically without any industry self-regulation.

There has been some deregulation in certain industries. For many years, for example, the banking and savings industry was heavily regulated, but beginning in 1978, various acts were adopted to deregulate this industry.[2] The deregulation did not proceed as well as anticipated, and the 1980s witnessed the collapse of major financial institutions attributed to lax oversight. As a result, Congress adopted bank-regulating laws and reforms toward the end of the 1980s. The broadest regulation was the Financial Institutions Reform, Recovery, and Enforcement Act of 1989 (FIRREA),[3] which regulates savings and loan associations and similar organizations to ensure their financial stability.

More recently, the collapse of companies such as Enron, WorldCom, HealthSouth, Adelphia, and others revealed that more oversight was necessary with regard to audit practice by CPAs as well as financial reporting by publicly traded companies. As a result, Congress passed extensive and detailed legislation regulating both accountants and financial reporting with the Sarbanes-Oxley Act and the mandated Securities and Exchange Commission (SEC) regulations that implement its provisions. (See Chapters 8 and 47 for more details on Sarbanes-Oxley.)

2. Regulation of Production, Distribution, and Financing

To protect the public from harm, the government may prohibit false advertising and labeling, and establish health and purity standards for cosmetics, foods, and drugs. Licenses may be required to be able to deal in certain goods, and these licenses may be revoked for improper conduct or violations of statutes and regulations.[4] The government may also regulate markets themselves: the quantity of a product that may be produced or grown and the price at which the finished product may be sold. For example, agricultural products markets and commodities have significant government constraints. Government may also engage in competition with private enterprises or own and operate an industry. **For Example,** the U.S. Postal Service competes directly with UPS and FedEx for the delivery of packages as well as for overnight delivery services.

The financing of business is directly affected by the national government, which creates a national currency and maintains the Federal Reserve banking system. State and other national laws may also affect financing by regulating financing contracts and documents, such as bills of lading and commercial paper.

[1] *American Power & Light Co. v SEC*, 329 US 90 (1946).

[2] See, for example, the Depository Institutions Deregulation and Monetary Control Act of 1980, 12 USC § 1735. *Sweeney v Savings First Mortgage, LLC*, 878 A2d 1037 (CA Md 2006).

[3] Act of October 9, 1989, PL 101-73, 103 Stat 183, codified at various sections of titles 12 and 15 of USC.

[4] *Ganter v Dept. of Insurance*, 620 So 2d 202 (CA Fla 1993).

3. Regulation of Unfair Competition

Each of the states and the federal government have statutes and regulations that prohibit unfair methods of competition. Unfair competition is controlled by both statutes and administrative agencies and regulations.

Congress has enacted the Federal Trade Commission Act,[5] which made all "unfair methods of competition... and unfair or deceptive acts or practices"[6] unlawful and created the Federal Trade Commission (FTC) to administer the act. The FTC has taken enforcement steps against refusals to sell, boycotts, market restrictions, disparagment of competitors' products, and unlawful methods of billing and collection. The FTC regulates false and misleading advertising and controls even the statements on packaged foods to ensure that the nutritional content of the food described on the label is accurate **For Example,** Beech-Nut Baby Food Company paid significant fines in the late 1980s for representing its baby apple juice to actually contain apple juice. The product was made from a very good-tasting chemical concoction, but it had no apple juice. Such misrepresentation on the label was a violation of Section 5 of the Federal Trade Commission Act that prohibits unfair methods of competition. Business missteps, from false advertising to boycotts, constitute unfair methods of competition prohibited under the FTC Act.[7]

B. Regulation of Markets and Competition

4. Regulation of Prices

Governments, both national and state, may regulate prices. Price regulation may be delegated to an administrative officer or agency. Prices in various forms are regulated, including not only what a buyer pays for goods purchased from a store (through controls on price fixing—see discussion that follows) but also through limits on interest rates and rent controls.

(a) Prohibition on Price Fixing

Agreements among competitors, as well as "every contract, combination ... or conspiracy," to fix prices violate Section 1 of the Sherman Act.[8] Known as *horizontal price-fixing,* any agreements to charge an agreed-upon price or to set maximum or minimum prices between or among competitors are *per se*—in, through, or by themselves—a violation of the Sherman Act. An agreement among real estate brokers to never charge below a 6 percent commission is price-fixing.[9] **For Example,** in 2001, Christie's and Sotheby's auction houses settled an antitrust lawsuit for charging the same commissions for many years.[10]

THINKING THINGS THROUGH

ANTITRUST VIOLATIONS AND CORPORATE DEFENDANTS

Alfred Taubman, the former chairman of Sotheby's Auction House, was sentenced to one year and one day in federal prison and fined $7.5 million for his role in a price-fixing scheme between Sotheby's and Christie's. The government case said that the scheme resulted in damages of $100 million to those who used the services of the auction houses. The sentence of one year and one day allowed Mr.Taubman to take advantage of the federal early release provisions for good behavior. Mr. Taubman was released from the medical facility federal prison two months early for good behavior and served the remainder of his sentence at a half-way house.

5 15 USC § 41*et seq.*

6 To review the Federal Trade Commission Act, go to **http://www.ftc.gov**.

7 In many states, such a seller would also be guilty of committing a deceptive trade practice or violating a consumer protection statute.

8 To view the full language of Section 1 of the Sherman Act, see 15 USC § 1.

9 *McClain v Real Estate Board of New Orleans, Inc.*, 441 US 942 (1980).

10 Carol Vogel and Ralph Blumenthall, "Ex-Chairman of Sotheby's Gets a Year and a Day for Price-Fixing," *New York Times*, April 12, 2002, A26.

THINKING THINGS THROUGH

continued

The two auction houses have settled class-action lawsuits brought by more than 100,000 customers for a total of $512 million. Mr. Taubman paid $156 million of Sotheby's share of the class-action suit. Sotheby's paid a $45 million fine. Mr. Taubman also paid $30 million as his portion of a stockholder suit brought against the company.

Judge George Daniels said that Mr.Taubman had "neither acknowledged responsibility nor shown any remorse" and that "[p]rice-fixing is a crime whether it's committed in the grocery story or the halls of a great auction house."* Diana D. Brooks, the former CEO of Sotheby's, was sentenced to six months of house arrest. She cooperated with the federal government in the prosecution of the case against her former boss. Her testimony indicated that she was simply following the directions of her boss. Of Ms. Brooks, Judge Daniels said, "You substituted shame for fame."**

Do you think the judge held the corporation responsible through fines? Does the imprisonment and house arrest of the chairman and CEO bring personal accountability and responsibility to the conduct of corporations?

* Carol Vogel and Ralph Blumenthall, "Ex-Chairman of Sotheby's Gets a Year and a Day for Price-Fixing," *New York Times*, April 23, 2002, A26.

** *Id.*

(b) Prohibited Price Discrimination

The **Clayton Act** and the **Robinson-Patman Act** prohibit price discrimination.[11] **Price discrimination** occurs when a seller charges different prices to different buyers for "commodities of like grade and quality," with the result being reduced competition or a tendency to create a monopoly.[12]

Price discrimination prohibits charging different prices to buyers as related to marginal costs. That is, volume discounts are permissible because the marginal costs are different on the larger volume of goods. However, the Robinson-Patman Act makes it illegal to charge different prices to buyers when the marginal costs of the seller for those goods are the same. Any added incentives or bonuses are also considered part of price.

For Example, offering one buyer free advertising while not offering it to another as an incentive to buy would be a violation of the Robinson-Patman Act. The Clayton Act makes both the giving and the receiving of any illegal price discrimination a crime.

State statutes frequently prohibit favoring one competitor by giving a secret discount when the effect is to harm the competition.[13] A state may prohibit either selling below cost to harm competitors or selling to one customer at a secret price that is lower than the price charged other customers when there is no economic justification for the lower price. Some state statutes specifically permit sellers to set prices so that they can match competitive prices, but not to undercut a competitor's prices.[14] The issue of state antitrust regulation and wide variations in state laws and decisions prompted the creation of the Antitrust Modernization Commission, a group likely to recommend changes in laws and judicial review standards at both the state and federal levels.[15]

11 15 USC §§ 1, 2, 3, 7, 8.

12 15 USC § 13a. To read the full Clayton Act, go to **http://www.usdoj.gov** or **http://www.justice.gov** and plug in "Clayton Act" in a site search.

13 *Eddins v Redstone*, 35 Cal Rptr 3d 863 (2006).

14 *Home Oil Company, Inc. v Sams East, Inc.* 252 F Supp 1302 (MD Ala 2003).

15 21st Century Department of Justice Appropriations Authorization Act, Pub. L. No. 107-273, 116 Stat. 1758 (2002), available at **http://amc.gov/pdf/statute/amc_act.pdf**.

(c) Permitted Price Discrimination

Price discrimination is expressly permitted when it can be justified on the basis of (1) a difference in grade, quality, or quantity; (2) the cost of transportation involved in performing the contract; (3) a good-faith effort to meet competition; (4) differences in methods or quantities; (5) deterioration of goods; or (6) a close-out sale of a particular line of goods. The Robinson-Patman Act[16] reaffirms the right of a seller to select customers and refuse to deal with anyone. The refusal, however, must be in good faith, not for the purpose of restraining trade. The *Utah Pie Co. v Continental Baking Co.* case deals with an issue of price discrimination.

5. Prevention of Monopolies and Combinations

Monopolies and combinations that restrain trade are prohibited under the federal antitrust laws.

(a) The Sherman Act

The **Sherman Antitrust Act** includes two very short sections that control anticompetitive behavior. They provide:

> *[§ 1] Every contract, combination in the form of trust or otherwise, or conspiracy, in restraint of trade or commerce among the several states, or with foreign nations, is declared to be illegal.*

UTAH PIE CO. V CONTINENTAL BAKING CO., 386 US 685 (1967)

GETTING A PIECE OF THE PIE MARKET

Utah Pie Company (petitioner) is a Utah corporation that for 30 years has been baking pies in its plant in Salt Lake City and selling them in Utah and surrounding states. It entered the frozen pie business in 1957 and was immediately successful with its new line of frozen dessert pies—apple, cherry, boysenberry, peach, pumpkin, and mince.

Continental Baking Company, Pet Milk, and Carnation (respondents), based in California, sell pies in Utah primarily on a delivered-price basis.

The major competitive weapon in the Utah pie market was price. Between 1958 and 1961, there was a deteriorating price structure for pies in the Utah market. Utah Pie was selling pies for $4.15 per dozen at the beginning of the period; at the time it filed suit for price discrimination, it was selling the same pies for $2.75 per dozen. Continental's price went from $5.00 per dozen in 1958 to $2.85 at the time suit was filed. Pet's prices went from $4.92 per dozen to $3.46, and Carnation's from $4.82 per dozen to $3.30.

Utah Pie filed suit, charging price discrimination by respondents based on allegations outlined in the opinion that follows. The district court found for Utah Pie. The court of appeals reversed, and Utah Pie appealed.

Judicial Opinion

WHITE, J. . . . We deal first with petitioner's case against the Pet Milk Company. . . . Pet's initial emphasis was on quality, but in the face of competition from regional and local companies and in an expanding market where price proved to be a crucial factor, Pet was forced to take steps to reduce the price of its pies to the ultimate consumer. These developments had consequences in the Salt Lake City market which are the substance of petitioner's case against Pet.

First, Pet successfully concluded an arrangement with Safeway, which is one of the three largest customers for frozen pies in the Salt Lake market, whereby it would sell frozen pies to Safeway under the latter's own "Bel-air" label at a price significantly lower than it was selling its comparable "Pet-Ritz" brand in the same Salt Lake market and elsewhere. . . .

Second, it introduced a 20-ounce economy pie under the "Swiss Miss" label and began selling the new pie in the Salt Lake market in August 1960 at prices ranging from $3.25 to $3.30 for the remainder of the period. This pie was at times sold at a lower price in the Salt Lake City market than it was sold in other markets.

Third, Pet became more competitive with respect to the prices for its "Pet-Ritz" proprietary label. . . . According to the Court of Appeals, in seven of the 44 months Pet's

[16] 15 USC §§ 13, 21.

prices in Salt Lake were lower than prices charged in the California markets. This was true although selling in Salt Lake involved a 30- to 35-cent freight cost.

The burden of proving cost justification was on Pet and, in our view, reasonable men could have found that Pet's lower priced "Bel-air" sales to Safeway were not cost justified in their entirety.

The Court of Appeals almost entirely ignored other evidence which provides material support of the jury's conclusion that Pet's behavior satisfied the statutory test regarding competitive injury. This evidence bore on the issue of Pet's predatory intent to injure Utah Pie. As an initial matter, the jury could have concluded that Pet's discriminatory pricing was aimed at Utah Pie; Pet's own management, as early as 1959, identified Utah Pie as an "unfavorable factor," one which "d[u]g holes in our operation" and posed a constant "check" on Pet's performance in the Salt Lake City market. Moreover, Pet candidly admitted that during the period when it was establishing its relationship with Safeway, it sent into Utah Pie's plant an industrial spy to seek information that would be of use to Pet in convincing Safeway that Utah Pie was not worthy of its customers.... Finally, Pet does not deny that the evidence showed it suffered substantial losses on its frozen pie sales during the greater part of time involved in this suit, and there was evidence from which the jury could have concluded that the losses Pet sustained in Salt Lake City were greater than those incurred elsewhere. It would not have been an irrational step if the jury concluded that there was a relationship between the price and the losses.

It seems clear to us that the jury heard adequate evidence from which it could have concluded that Pet had engaged in predatory tactics in waging competitive warfare in the Salt Lake City market. Coupled with the incidence of price discrimination attributable to Pet, the evidence as a whole established, rather than negated, the reasonable possibility that Pet's behavior produced a lessening of competition proscribed by the Act.

Petitioner's case against Continental is not complicated. Continental was a substantial factor in the market in 1957. But its sales of frozen 22-ounce dessert pies, sold under the "Morton" brand, amounted to only 1.3 percent of the market in 1958, 2.9 percent in 1959, and 1.8 percent in 1960. Its problems were primarily that of cost and in turn that of price, the controlling factor in the market. In late 1960 it worked out a co-packing arrangement in California by which fruit would be processed directly from the trees into the finished pies without large intermediate packing, storing, and shipping expenses. Having improved its position, it attempted to increase its share of the Salt Lake City market by utilizing a local broker and offering short-term price concessions in varying amounts. Its efforts for seven months were not spectacularly successful. Then in June 1961, it took the steps which are the heart of petitioner's complaint against it. Effective for the last two weeks of June it offered its 22-ounce frozen apple pies in the Utah area at $2.85 per dozen. It was then selling the same pies at substantially higher prices in other markets. The Salt Lake City price was less than its direct cost plus an allocation for overhead.... Utah's response was immediate. It reduced its price on all of its apple pies to $2.75 per dozen.... Continental's total sales of frozen pies increased from 3,350 dozen in 1960 to 18,800 dozen in 1961. Its market share increased from 1.8 percent in 1960 to 8.3 percent in 1961. The Court of Appeals concluded that Continental's conduct had had only minimal effect, that it had not injured or weakened Utah Pies as a competitor, that it had not substantially lessened competition and that there was no reasonable possibility that it would do so in the future.

Even if the impact on Utah Pie as a competitor was negligible, there remain the consequences to others in the market who had to compete not only with Continental's 22-ounce pie at $2.85 but with Utah's even lower price of $2.75 per dozen for both its proprietary and controlled labels.... The evidence was that there were nine other sellers in 1960 who sold 23,473 dozen pies, 12.7 percent of the total market. In 1961 there were eight other sellers who sold less than the year before—18,565 dozen or 8.2 percent of the total—although the total market had expanded from 184,569 dozen to 226,908 dozen. We think there was sufficient evidence from which the jury could find a violation of § 2(a) by Continental.

Section 2(a) does not forbid price competition which will probably injure or lessen competition by eliminating competitors, discouraging entry into the market or enhancing the market shares of the dominant sellers. But Congress has established some ground rules for the game. Sellers may not sell like goods to different purchasers at different prices if the result may be to injure competition to either the sellers' or the buyers' market unless such discriminations are justified as permitted by the Act. In this case there was some evidence of predatory intent with respect to each of these respondents. There was also other evidence upon which the jury could rationally find the requisite injury to competition. The frozen pie market in Salt Lake City was highly competitive. At times Utah Pie was a leader in moving the general level of prices down, and at other times each of the respondents also bore responsibility for the downward pressure on the price structure. We believe that the Act reaches price discrimination that erodes competition as much as it does price discrimination that is intended to have immediate destructive impact. In this case, the evidence shows a drastically declining price structure which the jury could rationally attribute to continued or sporadic price discrimination.

[Reversed]

Questions

1. Describe the competitors in the Utah Pie frozen pie market.
2. Is it significant that the national competitors were selling their pies at different prices in Utah?
3. Does it matter that the size of the pie market (i.e., number of pies sold) increased during the period examined?

[§ 2] Every person who shall monopolize or attempt to monopolize, or combine or conspire with any other person or persons to monopolize any part of the trade or commerce among the several states, or with foreign nations, shall be deemed guilty of a felony.[17]

The Sherman Act applies not only to buying and selling activities but also to manufacturing and production activities. Section 1 of the Sherman Act applies to agreements, conduct, or conspiracies to restrain trade, which can consist of price-fixing, tying, and monopolization. Section 2 prohibits monopolizing or attempting to monopolize by companies or individuals.

(b) Monopolization

To determine whether a firm has engaged in monopolization or attempts to monopolize, the courts determine whether the firm has **market power,** which is the ability to control price and exclude competitors. Market power is defined by looking at both the geographic and product markets. **For Example,** a cereal manufacturer may have 65 percent of the nationwide market for its Crispy Clowns cereal (the product market), but it may have only 10 percent of the Albany, New York, market because of a local competitor, Crunchy Characters. Crispy Clowns may have market power nationally, but in Albany, it would not reach monopoly levels.

Having a large percentage of a market is not necessarily a monopoly. The Sherman Act requires that the monopoly position be gained because of a superior product or consumer preference, not because the company has engaged in purposeful conduct to exclude competitors by other means, such as preventing a competitor from purchasing a factory. The *U.S. v Microsoft* case deals with an issue of monopolization.

U.S. V MICROSOFT, 253 F3D 34 (CA DC 2001)

PERFORMING AN ILLEGAL OPERATION

Microsoft Corporation, a company based in Washington and doing business in all 50 states and around the world, is the leading supplier of operating systems for personal computers (PCs). Although Microsoft licenses its software programs directly to consumers, the largest part of its sales consists of licensing the products to manufacturers of personal computers.

Microsoft was concerned about its strategic position with respect to the Internet, a global electronic network consisting of smaller interconnected networks, which allows millions of computers to exchange information over telephone wires, dedicated data cables, and wireless links.

The United States Justice Department had an ongoing inquiry into the market shares and practices of Microsoft. The concerns of the Justice Department included:

1. Microsoft's position in the market as a monopolist (90 percent market share for operating systems).

[17] 15 USC § 1. Read the full Sherman Antitrust Act at **http://www.usdoj.gov** or **http://www.justice.gov**. Plug in "Sherman Act" in a site search and you will be directed to all of the federal antitrust statutes. Free competition has been advanced by the Omnibus Trade and Competitiveness Act of 1988, 19 USC § 2901 *et seq.*

2. Microsoft's barriers to entry for other operating systems and Web browsers. Microsoft has refused to sell its software operating system to computer companies that installed Microsoft's competitive browser, Netscape, which was gaining popularity as Microsoft's Explorer struggled.
3. Microsoft's efforts to inhibit the efforts of Netscape with its browser by first trying to acquire Netscape and then working to "cut off [its] air supply" by retarding Sun Corporation's development and implementation of the Java program. When Microsoft altered the portions of Sun's Java program that allowed it to work without Windows, Sun notified Microsoft that such was a violation of its licensing agreement. Microsoft's response was, "Sue us." Sun sued Microsoft one week before the Justice Department brought its suit against Microsoft. Sun's suit then ran parallel with the Justice Department's.

In issuing a three-part opinion, Judge Thomas Penfield Jackson of the district court found that Microsoft had violated the antitrust laws and ordered a remedy of breaking up the company. Microsoft appealed the decision.

Judicial Opinion

PER CURIAM . . .

A. Monopoly Power

While merely possessing monopoly power is not itself an antitrust violation, it is a necessary element of a monopolization charge. The Supreme Court defines monopoly power as "the power to control prices or exclude competition." Because such direct proof is only rarely available, courts more typically examine market structure in search of circumstantial evidence of monopoly power.

1. Market Structure

a. Market definition

In this case, the District Court defined the market as "the licensing of all Intel-compatible PC operating systems worldwide," finding that there are "currently no products—and . . . there are not likely to be any in the near future—that a significant percentage of computer users worldwide could substitute for [these operating systems] without incurring substantial costs." Calling this market definition "far too narrow," Microsoft argues that the District Court improperly excluded three types of products: non-Intel compatible operating systems (primarily Apple's Macintosh operating system, Mac OS), operating systems for non-PC devices (such as handheld computers and portal websites), and "middleware" products, which are not operating systems at all.

The District Court found that consumers would not switch from Windows to Mac OS in response to a substantial price increase because of the costs of acquiring the new hardware needed to run Mac OS (an Apple computer and peripherals) and compatible software applications, as well as because of the effort involved in learning the new system and transferring files to its format.

Microsoft's challenge to the District Court's exclusion of non-PC based competitors, such as information appliances (handheld devices, etc.) and portal websites suffers from [this] defect: the company fails to challenge the District Court's key factual findings. In particular, the District Court found that because information appliances fall far short of performing all of the functions of a PC, most consumers will buy them only as a supplement to their PCs.

Having thus properly defined the relevant market, the District Court found that Windows accounts for a greater than 95% share. The court also found that even if Mac OS were included, Microsoft's share would exceed 80%. Microsoft challenges neither finding, nor does it argue that such a market share is not predominant.

Having sustained the District Court's conclusion that circumstantial evidence proves that Microsoft possesses monopoly power, we turn to Microsoft's alternative argument that it does not behave like a monopolist.

Even if we were to require direct proof, moreover, Microsoft's behavior may well be sufficient to show the existence of monopoly power.

More telling, the District Court found that some aspects of Microsoft's behavior are difficult to explain unless Windows is a monopoly product. For instance, according to the District Court, the company set the price of Windows without considering rivals' prices, something a firm without a monopoly would have been unable to do.

B. Anticompetitive Conduct

1. Licenses Issued to Original Equipment Manufacturers

[T]he District Court condemned the license provisions prohibiting the OEMs from: (1) removing any desktop icons, folders, or "Start" menu entries; (2) altering the initial boot sequence; and (3) otherwise altering the appearance of the Windows desktop.

The District Court concluded that the first license restriction—the prohibition upon the removal of desktop icons, folders, and Start menu entries—thwarts the distribution of a rival browser by preventing OEMs from removing visible means of user access to IE [Internet Explorer]. The OEMs cannot practically install a second browser in addition to IE, the court found, in part because "[p]re-installing more than one product in a given category . . . can significantly increase an OEM's [Original Equipment Manufacturers] support costs, for the redundancy can lead to confusion among novice users." That is, a certain number of novice computer users, seeing two browser icons, will wonder which to use when and will call the OEM's support line. Support calls are extremely expensive and, in the highly competitive original equipment market, firms have a strong incentive to minimize costs.

The second license provision at issue prohibits OEMs from modifying the initial boot sequence—the process that occurs the first time a consumer turns on the computer. Prior to the imposition of that restriction, "among the programs that many OEMs inserted into the boot sequence were Internet sign-up procedures that encouraged users to choose from a list of IAPs [Internet Access Providers]." Microsoft's prohibition on any alteration of the boot sequence thus prevents OEMs from using that process to promote the services of IAPs, many of which used Navigator rather than IE in their Internet access software. (Upon learning of OEM practices including boot sequence modification, Microsoft's Chairman, Bill Gates, wrote: "Apparently a lot of OEMs are bundling non-Microsoft browsers and coming up with offerings together with [IAPs] that get displayed on their machines in a FAR more prominent way than MSN or our Internet browser."). Because this prohibition has a substantial effect in protecting Microsoft's market power, and does so through a means other than competition on the merits, it is anticompetitive.

2. Microsoft's justifications for the license restrictions

Microsoft argues that the license restrictions are legally justified because, in imposing them, Microsoft is simply "exercising its rights as the holder of valid copyrights." Microsoft's primary copyright argument borders upon the frivolous. The company claims an absolute and unfettered right to use its intellectual property as it wishes: "[I]f intellectual property rights have been lawfully acquired," it says, then "their subsequent exercise cannot give rise to antitrust liability." That is no more correct than the proposition that use of one's personal property, such as a baseball bat, cannot give rise to tort liability. As the Federal Circuit succinctly stated: "Intellectual property rights do not confer a privilege to violate the antitrust laws."

* * * *

4. Dealings with Internet Content Providers, Independent Software Vendors, and Apple Computer

In dozens of "First Wave" agreements signed between the fall of 1997 and the spring of 1998, Microsoft has promised to give preferential support, in the form of early Windows 98 and Windows NT betas, other technical information, and the right to use certain Microsoft seals of approval, to important ISVs [Internet Software Vendors] that agree to certain conditions. One of these conditions is that the ISVs use Internet Explorer as the default browsing software for any software they develop with a hypertext-based user interface.

[T]he effect of these deals is to "ensure that many of the most popular Web-centric applications will rely on browsing technologies found only in Windows," and that Microsoft's deals with ISVs therefore "increase the likelihood that the millions of consumers using [applications designed by ISVs that entered into agreements with Microsoft] will use Internet Explorer rather than Navigator."

When Microsoft entered into the First Wave agreements, there were 40 million new users of the Internet. Because, by keeping rival browsers from gaining widespread distribution (and potentially attracting the attention of developers away from the APIs in Windows), the deals have a substantial effect in preserving Microsoft's monopoly, we hold that plaintiffs have made a prima facie showing that the deals have an anticompetitive effect.

In May 1995 Netscape agreed with Sun to distribute a copy of the Java [a product of Sun Microsystems] runtime environment with every copy of Navigator, and "Navigator quickly became the principal vehicle by which Sun placed copies of its Java runtime environment on the PC systems of Windows users." Microsoft, too, agreed to promote the Java technologies—or so it seemed. For at the same time, Microsoft took steps "to maximize the difficulty with which applications written in Java could be ported from Windows to other platforms, and vice versa." Specifically, the District Court found that Microsoft took four steps to exclude Java from developing as a viable cross-platform threat: (a) designing a JVM incompatible with the one developed by Sun; (b) entering into contracts, the so-called "First Wave Agreements," requiring major ISVs to promote Microsoft's JVM exclusively; (c) deceiving Java developers about the Windows-specific nature of the tools it distributed to them; and (d) coercing Intel to stop aiding Sun in improving the Java technologies.

When specifically accused by a *PC Week* reporter of fragmenting Java standards so as to prevent cross-platform uses, Microsoft denied the accusation and indicated it was only "adding rich platform support" to what remained a crossplatform implementation. An e-mail message internal to Microsoft, written shortly after the conversation with the reporter, shows otherwise:

[O]k, i just did a followup call.... [The reporter] liked that i kept pointing customers to w3c standards [(commonly observed internet protocols)].... [but] he accused us of being schizo with this vs. our java approach, i said he misunderstood [-] that [with Java] we are merely trying to add rich platform support to an interop layer.... this plays well.... at this point its [sic] not good to create MORE noise around our win32 java classes. instead we should just quietly grow j++ [(Microsoft's development tools)] share and assume that people will take more advantage of our classes without ever realizing they are building win32-only java apps.

Microsoft's ultimate objective was to thwart Java's threat to Microsoft's monopoly in the market for operating systems. One Microsoft document, for example, states as a strategic goal: "Kill cross-platform Java by grow[ing] the polluted Java market."

* * * *

The District Court's remedies-phase proceedings are a different matter. It is a cardinal principle of our system of justice that factual disputes must be heard in open court and resolved through trial-like evidentiary proceedings. Any other course would be contrary "to the spirit which imbues our judicial tribunals prohibiting decision without hearing."

This rule is no less applicable in antitrust cases. Despite plaintiffs' protestations, there can be no serious doubt that the parties disputed a number of facts during the remedies phase. In two separate offers of proof, Microsoft identified 23 witnesses who, had they been permitted to testify, would have challenged a wide range of plaintiffs' factual representations, including the feasibility of dividing Microsoft, the likely impact on consumers, and the effect of divestiture on shareholders.

The reason the court declined to conduct an evidentiary hearing was not because of the absence of disputed facts, but because it believed that those disputes could be resolved only through "actual experience," not further proceedings. But a prediction about future events is not, as a prediction, any less a factual issue. Indeed, the Supreme Court has acknowledged that drafting an antitrust decree by necessity "involves predictions and assumptions concerning future economic and business events." Trial courts are not excused from their obligation to resolve such matters through evidentiary hearings simply because they consider the bedrock procedures of our justice system to be "of little use."

In sum, we vacate the District Court's remedies decree for three reasons. First, the District Court failed to hold an evidentiary hearing despite the presence of remedies-specific factual disputes. Second, the court did not provide adequate reasons for its decreed remedies. Finally, we have drastically altered the scope of Microsoft's liability, and it is for the District Court in the first instance to determine the propriety of a specific remedy for the limited ground of liability which we have upheld.

The judgment of the District Court is affirmed in part, reversed in part, remanded in part. We vacate in full the Final Judgment embodying the remedial order, and remand the case to the District Court for reassignment to a different trial judge for further proceedings consistent with this opinion.

Case Questions

1. What is the relevant market? What does Microsoft say the relevant market is?
2. What intellectual property argument does Microsoft make as a defense to the antitrust charges?
3. What error did the trial judge make with respect to the remedies?

THINKING THINGS THROUGH

MICROSOFT SETTLES UP

A federal district court* approved the Justice Department's settlement of the Microsoft antitrust litigation following the decision by the appellate court that had found a violation of the Sherman Act. The terms of the settlement are as follows:

- Microsoft can add any type of capabilities to its Windows operating system.

*"Ruling Stings but Doesn't Really Hurt Microsoft," *New York Times*, November 2, 2002, B5.

THINKING THINGS THROUGH

continued

- Microsoft cannot impose restrictions on PC manufacturers that limit their ability to install non-Microsoft software on their computers.
- Microsoft cannot retaliate against PC manufacturers for installing non-Microsoft software on their computers.
- Microsoft must offer the same sale terms for Windows to all PC manufacturers, and those terms and conditions must be posted on a Web site for easy access.
- Microsoft must provide the information software rivals need in order to have their programs work successfully with Windows.
- Microsoft cannot punish or retaliate against software manufacturers that develop competing software.
- Microsoft will appoint an internal compliance officer.
- All Microsoft officers and the board must sign off that they have read the provisions of the settlement.
- These conditions are in effect for five years.

Explain how these requirements help eliminate the antitrust violations discussed in the case and how each will work to restore competition.

E-COMMERCE AND CYBERLAW

E-MAIL'S REVELATIONS

E-mail is redefining the way cases are tried. In the U.S. Justice Department's case against Microsoft, a lawyer commented, "The Government does not need to put Mr. Gates on the stand because we have his e-mail and memoranda."

The lawyer's comment reflects the tendency of e-mail to speak for itself. Witnesses can shrug and assert they cannot remember, but an e-mail from them is always available for recollection purposes as well as admission as evidence. At Microsoft, e-mail supplanted the telephone as the primary means of communication, and the government was able to tap into the entire e-mail system. There were 30 million pages of e-mail used as evidence in the Microsoft trial.

E-mail provides what is known as a *contemporaneous record of events* and has the added bonus that, for whatever psychological reason, those communicating with e-mail tend to be more frank and informal than they would be in a memo. E-mail can also contradict a witness's testimony and serve to undermine credibility. For example, when asked whether he recalled discussions with a subordinate about whether Microsoft should offer to invest in Netscape, Mr. Gates responded in his deposition, "I didn't see that as something that made sense." But Mr. Gates's e-mail included an urging to his subordinates to consider a Netscape alliance: "We could even pay them money as part of the deal, buying a piece of them or something."

E-mail is discoverable, admissible as evidence, and definitely not private. Employees should follow the admonition of one executive whose e-mail was used to fuel a million-dollar settlement by his company with a former employee, "If you wouldn't want anyone to read it, don't send it in e-mail."

The impact of e-mail in the Microsoft antitrust case on companies and their e-mail policies was widespread. For example,

E-COMMERCE AND CYBERLAW

continued

Amazon.com launched a companywide program called "Sweep and Keep," under which employees were instructed to purge e-mail messages no longer needed for conducting business. Amazon.com offered employees who purged their e-mail immediately free lattes in the company cafeteria. The company had a two-part program. The first portion included instructions on document retention and deletion. The second part of the program was on document creation and included the following warning for employees: "Quite simply put, there are some communications that should not be expressed in written form. Sorry, no lattes this time."

The American Management Association has reported that a 5 percent increase occurred in the number of companies monitoring their employees' e-mail, from 15 percent to 20 percent, during 1998. In 2005, employees around the country reported that they are now holding back on their e-mail communications and being careful about their choice of words.

Source: Adapted from Marianne M. Jennings, *Business: Its Legal, Ethical and Global Environment*, 6th ed. (Cincinnati, OH: West Legal Studies in Business, 2003), ch. 17, 674.

STATE OIL V KHAN, 522 US 3 (1997)

FILL IT UP: THE PRICE IS RIGHT AND FIXED

Barkat U. Khan and his corporation (respondents) entered into an agreement with State Oil (petitioner) to lease and operate a gas station and convenience store owned by State Oil. The agreement provided that Khan would obtain the gasoline supply for the station from State Oil at a price equal to a suggested retail price set by State Oil, less a margin of 3.25 cents per gallon. Khan could charge any price he wanted, but if he charged more than State Oil's suggested retail price, the excess went to State Oil. Khan could sell the gasoline for less than State Oil's suggested retail price, but the difference would come out of his allowed margin.

After a year, Khan fell behind on his lease payments and State Oil gave notice of and began proceedings for eviction. The court had Khan removed and appointed a receiver for operation of the station. The receiver operated the gas station without the price constraints and received an overall profit margin above the 3.25 cents imposed on Khan.

Khan filed suit, alleging that the State Oil agreement was a violation of Section 1 of the Sherman Act because State Oil was controlling price. The district court held that there was no *per se* violation and that Khan had failed to demonstrate antitrust injury. The Court of Appeals reversed and State Oil appealed.

Judicial Opinion

O'CONNOR, J.... Under § 1 of the Sherman Act, 26 Stat. 209, as amended, 15 U.S.C. § 1, "[e]very contract, combination..., or conspiracy, in restraint of trade" is illegal. In *Albrecht v. Herald Co.*, 390 U.S. 145, 88 S. Ct. 869, 19 L.Ed.2d 998 (1968), this Court held that vertical maximum price fixing is a per se violation of that statute. In this case, we are asked to reconsider that decision in light of subsequent decisions of this Court. We conclude that *Albrecht* should be overruled.

Although the Sherman Act, by its terms, prohibits every agreement "in restraint of trade," this Court has long recognized that Congress intended to outlaw only unreasonable restraints.

As a consequence, most antitrust claims are analyzed under a "rule of reason," according to which the finder of fact must decide whether the questioned practice imposes an unreasonable restraint on competition, taking into account a variety of factors, including specific information about the relevant business, its condition before and after the restraint was imposed, and the restraint's history, nature, and effect.

Some types of restraints, however, have such predictable and pernicious anticompetitive effect, and such limited potential for procompetitive benefit, that they are deemed unlawful per se.

Thus, we have expressed reluctance to adopt per se rules with regard to "restraints imposed in the context of business relationships where the economic impact of certain practices is not immediately obvious."

[I]n *United States v Arnold, Schwinn & Co.*, 388 U.S. 365, 87 S.Ct. 1856, 18 L. Ed. 2d 1249 (1967), the Court reconsidered the status of exclusive dealer territories and held that, upon the transfer of title to goods to a distributor, a supplier's imposition of territorial restrictions on the distributor was "so obviously destructive of competition" as to constitute a per se violation of the Sherman Act. In *Schwinn*, the Court acknowledged that some vertical restrictions, such as the conferral of territorial rights or franchises, could have procompetitive benefits by allowing smaller enterprises to compete, and that such restrictions might avert vertical integration in the distribution process. The Court drew the line, however, at permitting manufacturers to control product marketing once dominion over the goods had passed to dealers.

Albrecht, decided the following Term, involved a newspaper publisher who had granted exclusive territories to independent carriers subject to their adherence to a maximum price on resale of the newspapers to the public. Influenced by its decisions in *Socony-Vacuum*, *Kiefer-Stewart*, and *Schwinn*, the Court concluded that it was per se unlawful for the publisher to fix the maximum resale price of its newspapers. The Court acknowledged that "[m]aximum and minimum price fixing may have different consequences in many situations," but nonetheless condemned maximum price fixing for "substituting the perhaps erroneous judgment of a seller for the forces of the competitive market."

Nine years later, in *Continental T.V., Inc. v GTE Sylvania Inc.*, 433 U.S. 36, 97 S.Ct. 2549, 53 L.Ed.2d 568 (1977), the Court overruled *Schwinn*, thereby rejecting application of a per se rule in the context of vertical non-price restrictions. The Court acknowledged the principle of *stare decisis*, but explained that the need for clarification in the law justified reconsideration of *Schwinn:*

> *"Since its announcement, Schwinn has been the subject of continuing controversy and confusion, both in the scholarly journals and in the federal courts. The great weight of scholarly opinion has been critical of the decision, and a number of the federal courts confronted with analogous vertical restrictions have sought to limit its reach."*

Thus, our reconsideration of *Albrecht's* continuing validity is informed by several of our decisions, as well as a considerable body of scholarship discussing the effects of vertical restraints. Our analysis is also guided by our general view that the primary purpose of the antitrust laws is to protect interbrand competition. "Low prices," we have explained, benefit consumers regardless of how those prices are set, and so long as they are above predatory levels, they do not threaten competition." Our interpretation of the Sherman Act also incorporates the notion that condemnation of practices resulting in lower prices to consumers is "especially costly" because "cutting prices in order to increase business often is the very essence of competition."

So informed, we find it difficult to maintain that vertically-imposed maximum prices could harm consumers or competition to the extent necessary to justify their per se invalidation. As Chief Judge Posner wrote for the Court of Appeals in this case:

> *"As for maximum resale price fixing, unless the supplier is a monopsonist he cannot squeeze his dealers' margins below a competitive level; the attempt to do so would just drive the dealers into the arms of a competing supplier. A supplier might, however, fix a maximum resale price in order to prevent his dealers from exploiting a monopoly position. . . . [S]uppose that State Oil, perhaps to encourage . . . dealer services . . . has spaced its dealers sufficiently far apart to limit competition among them (or even given each of them an exclusive territory); and suppose further that Union 76 is a sufficiently distinctive and popular brand to give the dealers in it at least a modicum of monopoly power. Then State Oil might want to place a ceiling on the dealers' resale prices in order to prevent them from exploiting that monopoly power fully. It would do this not out of disinterested malice, but in its commercial self-interest. The higher the price at which gasoline is resold, the smaller the volume sold, and so the lower the profit to the supplier if the higher profit per gallon at the higher price is being snared by the dealer."*

Further, although vertical maximum price fixing might limit the viability of inefficient dealers, that consequence is not necessarily harmful to competition and consumers.

After reconsidering *Albrecht*'s rationale and the substantial criticism the decision has received, however, we conclude that there is insufficient economic justification for per se invalidation of vertical maximum price fixing. That is so not only because it is difficult to accept the assumptions underlying *Albrecht*, but also because *Albrecht* has little or no relevance to ongoing enforcement of the Sherman Act.

We approach the reconsideration of decisions of this Court with the utmost caution. *Stare decisis* reflects "a policy judgment that 'in most matters it is more important that the applicable rule of law be settled than that it be settled right.' "

But "[*s*]*tare decisis* is not an inexorable command." In the area of antitrust law, there is a competing interest, well-represented in this Court's decisions, in recognizing and adapting to changed circumstances and the lessons of accumulated experience. Thus, the general presumption that legislative changes should be left to Congress has less force with respect to the Sherman Act in light of the accepted view that Congress "expected the courts to give shape to the statute's broad mandate by drawing on common-law tradition."

In overruling *Albrecht*, we of course do not hold that all vertical maximum price fixing is per se lawful. Instead, vertical maximum price fixing, like the majority of commercial arrangements subject to the antitrust laws, should be evaluated under the rule of reason. In our view, rule-of-reason analysis will effectively identify those situations in which vertical maximum price fixing amounts to anticompetitive conduct.

There remains the question whether respondents are entitled to recover damages based on State Oil's conduct. Although the Court of Appeals noted that "the district judge was right to conclude that if the rule of reason is applicable, Khan loses," its consideration of this case was necessarily premised on *Albrecht*'s per se rule. Under the circumstances, the matter should be reviewed by the Court of Appeals in the first instance. We therefore vacate the judgment of the Court of Appeals and remand the case for further proceedings consistent with this opinion.

[Remanded.]

Questions

1. What were the price requirements for Khan's lease?
2. What happened when someone else took over Khan's station?
3. What does the court discuss about long-standing precedent and *stare decisis?*

ETHICS & THE LAW

MARSH MCLENNAN

Marsh-McLennan (MMC) is best known as the world's largest insurance broker with 43,000 employees in its global operations.* In 2004, its revenues were $2 billion more than those of its closest competitor, Aon Corporation.** MMC was a market performer with revenues of $6.9 billion in 2003, up from $5.9 billion in 2002, and $5.2 billion in 2001.*** MMC had a different way of achieving growth.

As a broker of the company it represents, MMC should have been obtaining competing bids. However, MMC developed a "pay-to-play" format for obtaining bids that allowed the insurers and MMC to profit. MMC received not only its commissions but also payments from insurers in exchange for renewals, or bonuses paid to MMC when its corporate customers renewed their policies. To be sure (1) that the policies were renewed and (2) that the renewal bonus was a given, MMC had all of its insurers agree to roll over on renewals. For example, if Insurer A was up for renewal, Insurers B and C would submit fake and higher bids that MMC would then take to the corporate client and, of course, recommend renewal at the lower rate. In some cases, MMC did not even have official bids from the competing insurers. MMC sent bids forward that had not even been signed by the insurers who were playing along to receive the same treatment when their renewals came

*Monica Langley and Ianthe Jeanne Dugan, "How a Top Marsh Employee Turned the Tables on Insurers," *Wall Street Journal*, October 23, 2004, A1, A9. Some put the number of employees at 60,000. Gretchen Morgenson, "Who Loses the Most at Marsh? Its Workers," *New York Times*, October 24, 2004, 3–1 (Sunday Business 1) and 9.

**Monica Langley and Theo Francis, "Insurers Reel From Bust of a 'Cartel,' " *Wall Street Journal*, October 18, 2004, A1, A14.

****Id.*

ETHICS & THE LAW

continued

along. There was no competitive bidding and the payments inflated the prices. Once MCC implemented the "pay-to-play system," its insurance revenue became 67.1% of its revenue.[†] Commissions from these arrangements represented one-half of MMC's 2003 income of $1.5 billion.[††]

One of the companies to complain about MMC's practices was Munich RE. One of its e-mails to an MMC executive (whose name was blacked out) wrote, "I am not some Goody Two Shoes who believes that truth is absolute, but I do feel I have a pretty strict ethical code about being truthful and honest. This idea of 'throwing the quote' by quoting artificially high numbers in some predetermined arrangement for us to lose is repugnant to me, not so much because I hate to lose, but because it is basically dishonest. And I basically agree with the comments of others that it comes awfully close to collusion and price-fixing."

New York Attorney General Eliot Spitzer filed suit against MMC for antitrust violations.[‡] Without admitting or denying guilt, MMC settled the case with Mr. Spitzer by agreeing to drop the commission system and pay $850 million to its clients as a means of compensating for what might have been overcharges. MMC also agreed to hire a new CEO. The value of MMC's shares dropped almost 50 percent within 10 days following the mid-October Spitzer announcement of his suit against the company.[‡‡] About 3,000 jobs were cut in early November 2004.[‡‡‡]

What antitrust violations are part of "cartel" behavior? MMC's new CEO fired several senior executives despite the fact that there was no evidence that they had broken the law. When asked why he would fire them, Michael G. Cherkasky, a former district attorney in New York, said, "Freedom from criminal culpability is not our standard for executive leadership."[#] Is he employing a standard of ethics for his executives? What standard is it? What do the loss-of-income figures teach us about shortcuts on making money?

[†] Monica Langley and Ianthe Jeanne Dugan, "How a Top Marsh Employee Turned the Tables on Insurers," *Wall Street Journal*, October 23, 2004, A1, A9.

[††] *Id.*

[‡] Thor Valdmanis, "Marsh & McLennan lops off 3,000 jobs," *USA Today*, November 10, 2004, 1B.

[‡‡] "The Chatter," *New York Times*, November 14, 2004, BU2.

[‡‡‡] "The Chatter," *New York Times*, November 14, 2004, BU2.

[#] Ian McDonald, "After Spitzer Probe, Marsh CEO Tries Corporate Triage," *Wall Street Journal*, August 29, 2005, p. A1.

(c) Price-Fixing

The Sherman Act prohibits, as discussed previously, competitors agreeing to set prices. Price-fixing can involve competitors: agreeing to not sell below a certain price, agreeing on commission rates, agreeing on credit terms, or exchanging cost information. Price is treated as a sensitive element of competition, and discussion among competitors has also been deemed to be an attempt to monopolize. The *State Oil v Khan* case deals with the issue of price controls.

(d) Tying

It is a violation of the Sherman Act to force "tying" sales on buyers. **Tying** occurs when the seller makes a buyer who wants to purchase one product buy an additional product that he or she does not want.

The essential characteristic of a tying arrangement that violates Section 1 of the Sherman Act is the use of control over the tying product within the relevant market to compel the buyer to purchase the tied article that either is not wanted or could be purchased

SPORTS & ENTERTAINMENT LAW

CELEBRITY ISSUES AND ANTITRUST

Public Interest Corporation (PIC) owned and operated television station WTMV-TV in Lakeland, Florida. MCA Television Ltd. (MCA) owns and licenses syndicated television programs. In 1990, the two companies entered into a licensing contract for several first-run television shows. With respect to all but one of these shows, MCA exchanged the licenses on a "barter" basis for advertising time on WTMV. However, MCA conditioned this exchange on PIC's agreeing to license the remaining show, *Harry and the Hendersons,* for cash as well as for barter. *Harry and the Hendersons* was what some in the industry would call a "dog," a show that was not very good that attempted to capitalize on a hit movie. PIC agreed to this arrangement, although it did not want *Harry and the Hendersons.* The shows that PIC did want were *List of a Lifetime, List of a Lifetime II, Magnum P.I.,* and 17 other miscellaneous features.

The relationship between the parties was strained over nonpayment, poor ratings performance of *Harry,* and other issues. When litigation resulted, PIC alleged that it had been subjected to an illegal tying arrangement. PIC requested damages for MCA's violation of the Sherman Act. What violation do you think occurred?

Source: Adapted from *MCA Television Ltd. v Public Interest Corp.,* 171 F3d 1265 (CA 11 1998).

elsewhere on better terms. **For Example,** in the Microsoft antitrust case, Microsoft is accused of requiring the purchase and use of its browser as a condition for purchasing its software. The Sherman Act also prohibits professional persons, such as doctors, from using a peer review proceeding to pressure another professional who competes with them in private practice and refuses to become a member of a clinic formed by them.

(e) Business Combinations

The Sherman Antitrust Act does not prohibit bigness. However, Section 7 of the Clayton Act provides that "no corporation ... shall acquire the whole or any part of the assets of another corporation ... where in any line of commerce in any section of the country, the effect of such acquisition may be substantially to lessen competition, or to tend to create a monopoly." If the Clayton Act is violated through ownership or control of competing enterprises, a court may order the violating defendant to dispose of such interests by issuing a decree called a **divestiture order.**[18]

(1) Premerger Notification. When large-size enterprises plan to merge, they must give written notice to the FTC and to the head of the Antitrust Division of the Department of Justice. This advance notice gives the department the opportunity to block the merger and thus avoid the loss that would occur if the enterprises merged and were then required to separate.[19] **For Example,** Time Warner was required to notify the Justice Department and seek approval for its merger with AOL, which the Justice Department eventually gave. However, when WorldCom proposed its merger with Sprint, the Justice Department refused approval because it believed this would reduce competition in telecommunications too much.[20]

(2) Takeover Laws. Antitrust laws usually focus on whether the combination or agreement is fair to society or to a particular class, such as consumers. Some legislation aims to protect the various parties directly involved in combining different enterprises. Concern arises that one enterprise may in effect be raiding another enterprise. Congress and four-fifths of

18 *California v American Stores Co.,* 492 US 1301 (1989).

19 Antitrust Improvement Act of 1976, PL 94-435, § 201, PL 94-435, 90 Stat 1383, 15 USC § 1311 *et seq.*

20 Rebecca Blumenstein and Jared Sandberg, "WorldCom CEO Quits Amid Probe of Firm's Finances," *Wall Street Journal,* April 30, 2002, A1, A9.

the states have adopted **takeover laws,** which seek to guard against unfairness in such situations. State laws apply only to corporations chartered in their state.

C. Power to Protect Business

In addition to controlling business combinations, the federal government protects others. By statute or decision, associations of exporters, marine insurance associations, farmers' cooperatives, and labor unions are exempt from the Sherman Act with respect to agreements between their members. Certain pooling and revenue-dividing agreements between carriers are exempt from the antitrust law when approved by the appropriate federal agency. The Newspaper Preservation Act of 1970 grants an antitrust exemption to operating agreements entered into by newspapers to prevent financial collapse. The Soft Drink Interbrand Competition Act[21] grants the soft drink industry an exemption when it is shown that, in fact, substantial competition exists in spite of the agreements.

The general approach of the U.S. Supreme Court has been that these types of agreements should not be automatically, or *per se*, condemned as a restraint of interstate commerce merely because they create the power or potential to monopolize interstate commerce. It is only when the restraint imposed is unreasonable that the practice is unlawful. The court applies the rule of reason in certain cases because the practice may not always harm competition.

6. Remedies for Anticompetitive Behavior

(a) Criminal Penalties

A violation of either section of the Sherman Act is punishable by fine or imprisonment or both at the discretion of the court. The maximum fine for a corporation is $10 million. A natural person can be fined a maximum of $350,000 or imprisoned for a maximum term of three years or both.

(b) Civil Remedies

In addition to these criminal penalties, the law provides for an injunction to stop the unlawful practices and permits suing the wrongdoers for damages.

(1) Individual Damage Suit. Any person or enterprise harmed may bring a separate action for **treble damages** (three times the damages actually sustained).

(2) Class-Action Damage Suit by State Attorney General. When the effect of an antitrust violation is to raise prices, the attorney general of a state may bring a class-action suit to recover damages on behalf of those who have paid the higher prices. This action is called a *parens patriae* action on the theory that the state is suing as the parent of its people.

ANTITRUST (2001) (R)

This movie is based on Bill Gates and Microsoft.

For movie clips that illustrate business law concepts, see LawFlix at **http://wdvl.westbuslaw.com.**

[21] Act of July 9, 1980, PL 96-308, 94 Stat 939, 15 USC § 3501 *et seq.*

Summary

Regulation by government has occurred primarily to protect one group from the improper conduct of another group. The police power is the basis for government regulation. Regulation is passed when the free enterprise system fails to control abuses as with the recent passage of SOX. Unfair methods of competition are prohibited.

Prices have been regulated both by prohibiting setting the exact price or a maximum price and discrimination in pricing. Price discrimination between buyers is prohibited when the effect of such discrimination could tend to create a monopoly or lessen competition. Price discrimination occurs when the prices charged different buyers are different despite the same marginal costs.

The Sherman Antitrust Act prohibits conspiracies in restraint of trade and the monopolization of trade. The Clayton Act prohibits mergers or the acquisition of the assets of another corporation when this conduct would tend to lessen competition or create a monopoly. The Justice Department requires premerger notification for proposed mergers. Violation of the federal antitrust statutes subjects the wrongdoer to criminal prosecution and possible civil liability that can include treble damages.

Questions and Case Problems

1. American Crystal Sugar Co. was one of several refiners of beet sugar in northern California, and it distributed its product in interstate commerce. American Crystal and the other refiners had a monopoly on the seed supply and were the only practical market for the beets. In 1939, all of the refiners began using identical form contracts that computed the price paid to the sugar beet growers using a "factor" common to all the refiners. As a result, all refiners paid the same price for beets of the same quality. Though there was no hard evidence of an illegal agreement, the growers brought suit under the Sherman Act against the refiners, alleging that they conspired to fix a single uniform price among themselves to hold down the cost of the beets. The growers sued for the treble damages available under the Sherman Act. Can they recover? [*Mandeville Island Farms v American Crystal Sugar Co.*, 334 US 219]
2. A Wisconsin statute prohibits "the secret payment or allowance of rebates, refunds, commissions, or unearned discounts" to some customers without allowing them to all customers on the same conditions when such practices injure or tend to injure competition or a competitor. Kolbe generally gave dealers a 50 percent discount, but it gave Stock Lumber Co. a discount of 54 percent. Other dealers were not informed of this or of the conditions that had to be satisfied to obtain the same discount. Kolbe gave Jauquet, another lumber dealer, only a 50 percent discount and, when asked, expressly stated that it did not give any other dealer a higher discount. When Jauquet learned of the higher discount given to Stock, it brought suit against Kolbe for violation of the Wisconsin statute. Did Kolbe violate the statute? [*Jauquet Lumber Co., Inc. v Kolbe & Kolbe Millwork, Inc.*, 476 NW2d 305 (Wis App)]
3. The major record companies settled an antitrust suit brought by 40 state attorneys general against them for alleged price-fixing in the sale of CDs. The record companies agreed to pay $67.4 million to consumers who purchased CDs during the period from 1995 to 2000. The consent decree stipulated that the record companies had required retailers that accepted subsidies from record companies for advertising CDs not to advertise CDs for sale at a price agreed upon in advance. The record companies said that the policy helped keep independent retailers in business because they could not afford to price at Wal-Mart levels. Wal-Mart always advertised CDs for sale at a price below the floor agreed to by the subsidized independent retailers and the record companies. The record companies did not admit any wrongdoing and, in addition to agreeing to the $67.4 million, also agreed to provide 5.5 million CDs to libraries, schools, and nonprofit organizations (worth $75.7 million).[22] What antitrust violation were the attorneys general alleging? Is a minimum price a violation of antitrust laws?
4. The Three Tenors (Luciano Pavarotti, Placido Domingo, and Jose Carreras) make a record of their live performances together once every four years. The first two CDs and videos in the series, made by Time Warner, sold millions, with both becoming two of the highest-volume opera recordings in history. However, by the third performance and CD and video, the public demand was not as great, and Time Warner believed the first two releases would cannibalize the sales for the third. As a result, all parties involved in the sales of these CDs and tapes had to agree not to discount the first two performance tapes so that the third would have an opportunity to sell. The Federal Trade Commission (FTC) stumbled across the information on the pricing program when its staff members located a memo on the marketing plan and advertising constraints as it was reviewing documents for the proposed Time Warner/EMI Music merger proposal, a merger that fell through after European officials balked at the idea. The FTC pursued the case, and Time Warner settled the charges by agreeing not to restrain competition or set prices in the future. Is establishing a minimum price a violation of the Sherman Act? Is restricting advertising a violation of the Sherman Act?
5. Hines Cosmetic Co. sold beauty preparations nationally to beauty shops at a standard or fixed-price schedule. Some of the shops were also supplied with a free demonstrator and free advertising materials. The shops that were not supplied with them claimed that giving the free services and materials constituted unlawful price discrimination. Hines replied that there was no price discrimination because it charged everyone the same. What it was giving free was merely a promotional campaign that was not intended to discriminate against those who were not given anything free. Was Hines guilty of unlawful price discrimination? Explain.
6. Moore ran a bakery in Santa Rosa, New Mexico. His business was wholly intrastate. Meads Fine Bread Co., his competitor, engaged in an interstate business. Meads cut the price of bread in half in Santa Rosa but made no price cut in any other place in New Mexico or in any other state. This price-cutting drove Moore out of business. Moore then sued Meads for damages for violating the Clayton and Robinson-Patman Acts. Meads claimed that the price-cutting was purely intrastate and, therefore, did not constitute a violation of federal statutes. Was Meads correct? Why or why not? [*Moore v Meads Fine Bread Co.*, 348 US 115]

22 Claudia Deutsch, "Suit Settled over Pricing of Recordings at Big Chains," *New York Times*, October 1, 2002, C1, C10; David Lieberman, "States Settle CD Price-fixing Case," *USA Today*, October 1, 2002, 3B.

7. A&P Grocery Stores decided to sell its own brand of canned milk (referred to as *private label* milk). A&P asked its longtime supplier, Borden, to submit an offer to produce the private label milk. Bowman Dairy also submitted a bid, which was lower than Borden's. A&P's Chicago buyer then contacted Borden and said, "I have a bid in my pocket. You people are so far out of line it is not even funny. You are not even in the ballpark." The Borden representative asked for more details but was told only that a $50,000 improvement in Borden's bid "would not be a drop in the bucket." A&P was one of Borden's largest customers in the Chicago area. Furthermore, Borden had just invested more than $5 million in a new dairy facility in Illinois. The loss of the A&P account would result in underutilization of the plant. Borden lowered its bid by more than $400,000. The Federal Trade Commission charged Borden with price discrimination, but Borden maintained it was simply meeting the competition. Did Borden violate the Robinson-Patman Act? Does it matter that the milk was a private label milk, not its normal trade name Borden milk? [*Great Atlantic & Pacific Tea Co., Inc. v FTC*, 440 US 69]
8. James Owen was the general manager of Obron Atlantic Corp., a manufacturer of powdered brass, which is finely flaked metal used in metallic paints, brakes, and explosives. Trained as a chemist, Owen earned his MBA at night school while he worked in Obron's labs during the day. In 1985, he was promoted from the lab to management. During a business trip in 1986, a fellow executive from Obron's German operations, Bruno Dachlauer, told Owen that a price increase for the company's products would be coming in the fall. Dachlauer added that details of the price increase would have to be worked out with Obron's two main competitors based in the United States. Owen reminded Dachlauer that such an agreement about price was against the law in the United States, to which Dachlauer allegedly responded, "There are laws against speeding, too." Owen complied with the fall price increases but admitted that he began "cheating" by lowering those prices to win customers. He was then threatened by competitors. Following the threats, Owen went to the Antitrust Division of the Justice Department and explained his situation. The FBI wired Owen for his meetings. One taped conversation between him and his supervisor, Carl Eckart, was used in a price-fixing case filed in Ohio. The conversation is as follows:

   Owen: *Carl, can we go over this one more time?*
   Eckart: *You (expletive) dummy. One more time. On fine powders, 30 cents. Coarse powders, 15 cents.*
   Owen: *Are you sure Rink will go along with it?*
   Eckart: *Of course.*

   In the course of a year, Owen taped more than 100 conversations involving internal and external meetings for the FBI and the Justice Department. Owen's activities were not revealed until the Justice Department served Obron with a subpoena for its sales records. Officers and directors of Obron and its competitors were indicted, and some entered guilty pleas. Owen, whose marriage of 32 years ended in 1993, said that his undercover work took a tremendous toll on him and his family. He said of his conduct, "I could see people being hurt, customers being cheated. My concern shifted to protecting the customer. Maybe that's not the fiduciary role of the general manager." Was what Owen did in recording the conversations ethical? Was it honest? What do you think of Owen's view of focusing on the customers' rights? Is his duty to his company even when the conduct is illegal?
9. Dr. Edwin G. Hyde, a board-certified anesthesiologist, applied for permission to practice at East Jefferson Hospital in Louisiana. An approval was recommended for his hiring, but the hospital's board denied him employment on grounds that the hospital had a contract with Roux & Associates for Roux to provide all anesthesiological services required by the hospital's patients. Dr. Hyde filed suit for violation of antitrust laws. Had the hospital done anything illegal? [*Jefferson Parish Hosp. Dist. No. 2 v Hyde*, 466 US 2]
10. BRG of Georgia, Inc. (BRG), and Harcourt Brace Jovanovich Legal and Professional Publications (HJB) are the nation's two largest providers of bar review materials and lectures. HJB began offering a Georgia bar review course on a limited basis in 1976 and was in direct, and often intense, competition with BRG from 1977 to 1979 when the companies were the two main providers of bar review courses in Georgia. In early 1980, they entered into an agreement that gave BRG an exclusive license to market HJB's materials in Georgia and to use its trade name "Bar/Bri." The parties agreed that HJB would not compete with BRG in Georgia and that BRG would not compete with HJB outside of Georgia. Under the agreement, HJB received $100 per student enrolled by BRG and 40 percent of all revenues over $350. Immediately after the 1980 agreement, the price of BRG's course was increased from $150 to more than $400. Is their conduct illegal under federal antitrust laws? [*Palmer v BRG of Georgia, Inc.*, 498 US 46 (1990)]
11. Favorite Foods Corp. sold its food to stores and distributors. It established a quantity discount scale that was publicly published and made available to all buyers. The top of the scale gave the highest discount to buyers purchasing more than 100 freight cars of food in a calendar year. Only two buyers, both national food chains, purchased in such quantities, and therefore, they alone received the greatest discount. Favorite Foods was prosecuted for price discrimination in violation of the Clayton Act. Was it guilty?
12. Run America, Inc., manufactures running shoes. Its shoe is consistently rated poorly by *Run Run Run* magazine in

its annual shoe review. The number one shoe in *Run Run Run*'s review is the Cheetah, a shoe that Run America has learned is manufactured by the parent company of the magazine. Is this conduct a violation of the antitrust laws? Do you think it is ethical to run the shoe review without disclosing ownership?

13. The Quickie brand wheelchair is the most popular customized wheelchair on the market. Its market share is 90 percent. Other manufacturers produce special-use wheelchairs that fold, that are made of mesh and lighter frames, and that are easily transportable. These manufacturers do not compete with Quickie on customized chairs. One manufacturer of the alternative wheelchairs has stated, "Look, it's an expensive market to be in, that Quickie market. We prefer the alternative chairs without the headaches of customizations." Another has said, "It is such a drain on cash flow in that market because insurers take so long to pay. We produce chairs that buyers purchase with their own money, not through insurers. Our sales are just like any other product." Quickie entered the market nearly 40 years ago and is known for its quality and attention to detail. Buying a Quickie custom chair, however, takes time, and the revenue stream from sales is slow but steady because of the time required to produce custom wheelchairs. Has Quickie violated the federal antitrust laws with its 90 percent market share? Discuss.

14. Gardner-Denver is the largest manufacturer of ratchet wrenches and their replacement parts in the United States. Gardner-Denver had two different lists of prices for its wrenches and parts. Its blue list had parts that, if purchased in quantities of five or more, were available for substantially less than its white list prices. Did Gardner-Denver engage in price discrimination with its two price lists? [*D. E. Rogers Assoc., Inc. v Gardner-Denver Co.*, 718 F2d 1431 (6th Cir)]

15. The Aspen ski area consisted of four mountain areas. Aspen Highlands, which owned three of those areas, and Aspen Skiing, which owned the fourth, had cooperated for years in issuing a joint, multiple-day, all-area ski ticket. After repeatedly and unsuccessfully demanding an increased share of the proceeds, Aspen Highlands canceled the joint ticket. Aspen Skiing, concerned that skiers would bypass its mountain without some joint offering, tried a variety of increasingly desperate measures to recreate the joint ticket, even to the point of in effect offering to buy Aspen Highland's tickets at retail price. Aspen Highlands refused even that. Aspen Skiing brought suit under the Sherman Act, alleging that the refusal to cooperate was a move by Aspen Highlands to eliminate all competition in the area by freezing it out of business. Is there an antitrust claim here in the refusal to cooperate? What statute and violation do you think Aspen Skiing alleged? What dangers do you see in finding the failure to cooperate to be an antitrust violation? [*Aspen Skiing Co. v Aspen Highlands Skiing Corp.*, 472 US 585 (1985)]

ADMINISTRATIVE AGENCIES

CHAPTER (6)

LEARNING OBJECTIVES

After studying this chapter, you should be able to

LO.1 Describe the nature and purpose of administrative agencies

LO.2 Discuss the rights of access to administrative agencies and their records and processes

LO.3 Explain the legislative or rule-making function of administrative agencies

LO.4 Discuss agencies' authority to obtain business records

LO.5 Explain when an administrative agency's decision may be reviewed and reversed by a court

LO.6 Describe the rule on exhaustion of administrative remedies

Late in the nineteenth century, a new type of governmental structure began to develop to meet the highly specialized needs of government regulation of business: the administrative agency. The administrative agency is now typically the instrument through which government makes and carries out its regulations.

A. Nature of the Administrative Agency

An **administrative agency** is a government body charged with administering and implementing legislation. An agency may be a department, independent establishment, commission, administration, authority, board, or bureau. Agencies exist on the federal and state levels. One example of a federal agency is the Federal Trade Commission (FTC), whose structure is shown in Figure 6-1.

1. Purpose of Administrative Agencies

Federal administrative agencies are created to carry out general policies specified by Congress. Federal agencies include the Securities Exchange Commission (SEC), the Consumer Product Safety Commission (CPSC), and the Food and Drug Administration (FDA). The law governing these agencies is known as **administrative law.**

State administrative agencies also exist and may have jurisdiction over areas of law affecting business, such as workers' compensation claims, real estate licensing, and unemployment compensation.

2. Uniqueness of Administrative Agencies

The federal government and state governments alike are divided into three branches: executive, legislative, and judicial. Many offices in these branches are filled by persons who are elected. In contrast, members of administrative agencies are ordinarily appointed (in the case of federal agencies, by the president of the United States with the consent of the Senate).

In the tripartite structure, the judicial branch reviews actions of the executive and legislative branches to ensure that they have not exceeded their constitutional powers. However, the major governmental agencies combine legislative, executive, and judicial powers (see Figure 6-2). These agencies make the rules, conduct inspections to see that the rules have been or are being obeyed, and sit in judgment to determine whether there have been violations of their rules. Because agencies have broad powers, they are subject to strict procedural rules as well as disclosure requirements (discussed in the following section).

FIGURE 6-1 Structure of the Federal Trade Commission

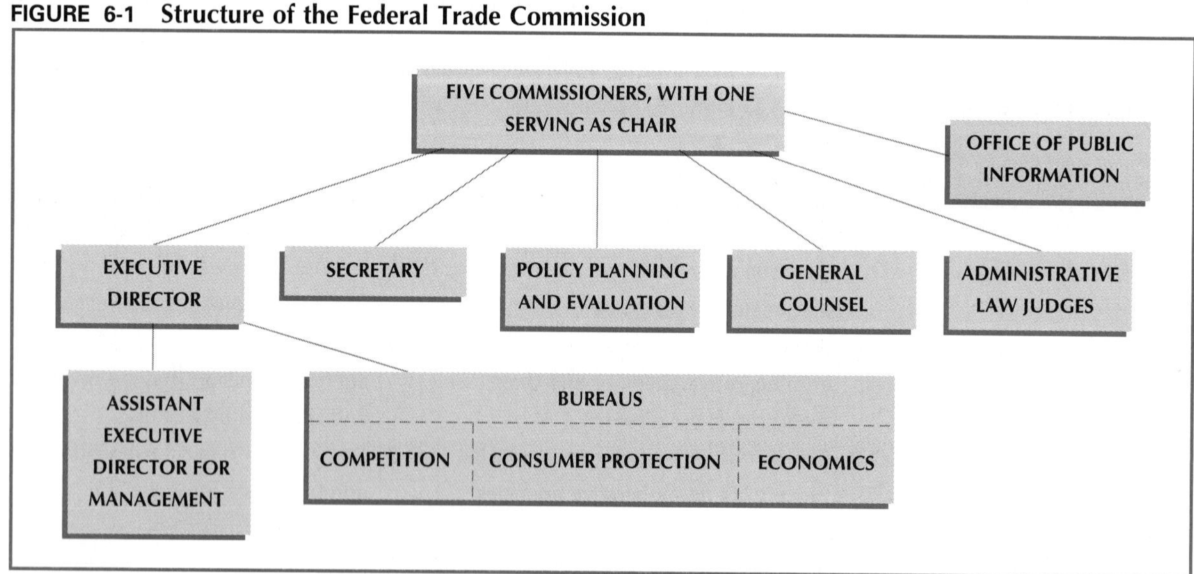

FIGURE 6-2 The Administrative Chain of Command

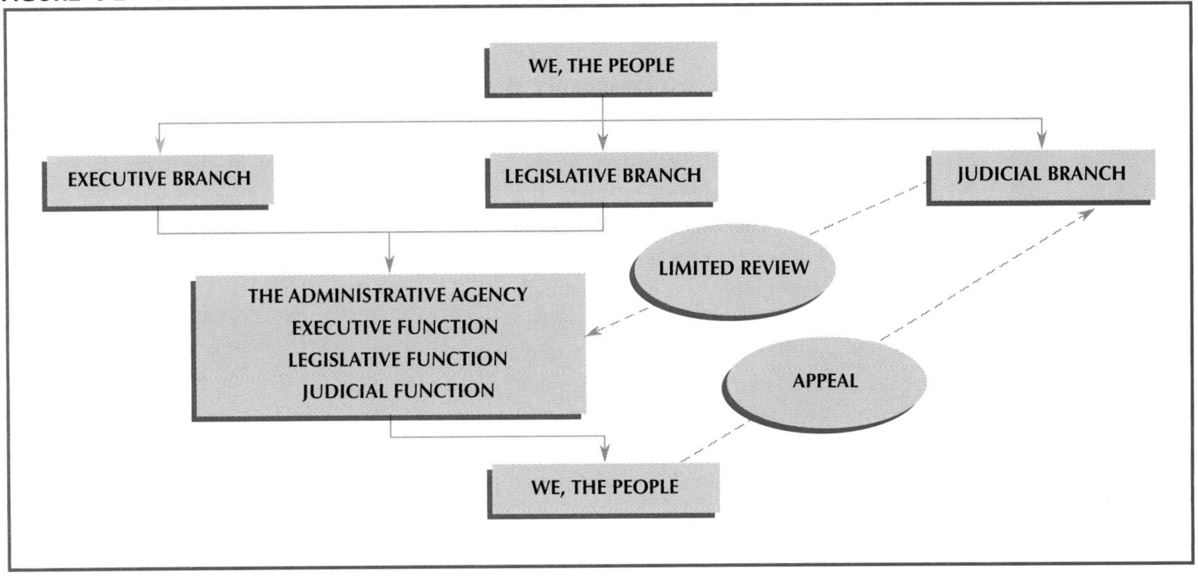

3. Open Operation of Administrative Agencies

The public has ready access to the activity of administrative agencies. That access comes in three ways: (1) open records, (2) open meetings, and (3) public announcement of agency guidelines. The actions and activities of most federal agencies that are not otherwise regulated are controlled by the **Administrative Procedure Act** (APA).[1] Many states have adopted statutes with provisions similar to those of the APA.

(a) Open Records

The **Freedom of Information Act**[2] (FOIA) provides that information contained in records of federal administrative agencies is available to citizens on proper request. The primary purpose of this statute is "to ensure that government activities be opened to the sharp eye of public scrutiny."[3] To ensure that members of the public understand how to obtain records, the FOIA provides, "Each agency shall . . . publish in the *Federal Register* for the guidance of the public . . . the methods whereby the public may obtain information, make submittals or requests, or obtain decisions.[4] There are exceptions to this right of public scrutiny. They prevent individuals and companies from obtaining information that is not necessary to their legitimate interests and might harm the person or company whose information is being sought.[5] State statutes typically exempt from disclosure any information that would constitute an invasion of the privacy of others. However, freedom of information acts are broadly construed, and unless an exemption is clearly given, the information in question is subject to public inspection. Moreover, the person claiming that there is an exemption that prohibits disclosure has the burden of proving that the exemption applies to the particular request made. Exemptions include commercial or financial information not ordinarily made public by the person or company that supplies the information to the agency as part of the agency's enforcement role.[6]

The FOIA 's primary purpose is to subject agency action to public scrutiny. Its provisions are liberally interpreted, and agencies must make good-faith efforts to comply with its terms.

[1] *Administrative Procedures Act* 5 USC § 550 *et seq.*

[2] 5 USC § 552 *et seq.* The Electronic Freedom of Information Act Amendments of 1996 extend the public availability of information to electronically stored data.

[3] *Brady-Lunny v Massey*, 185 F Supp 2d 928 (CD Ill 2002).

[4] 5 USC § 552(a)(1)(a).

[5] Additional protection is provided by the Privacy Act of 1974, 5 USC § 552a(b); *Pilon v U.S. Department of Justice*, 73 F3d 1111 (DC Cir 1996).

[6] *Sun-Sentinel Company v U.S. Dept. of Homeland Security*, 431 F Supp 2d 1258 (SD Fla 2006).

THINKING THINGS THROUGH

ALLOW ME TO MAKE A COMMENT (PUBLIC)

The SEC began in May 2005 to publish its comments on companies' securities filings. Prior to this action, the SEC released the comments only in response to FOIA requests. The comments are very revealing, showing what the SEC accountants and staff members believe are important issues in company securities filings. For example, in a Brookstone, Inc., proxy statement filed in 2005 that included approval of a merger, the SEC issued a letter with 52 comments. One example was just a request for additional information:

19. Please provide an organizational chart that shows how the ownership of Brookstone, Inc., will be structured after completion of the merger including the members of Brookstone management who will retain an indirect interest in Brookstone and the owners of Brookstone Holdings Corp.

RESPONSE: Additional disclosure has been included in the Proxy Statement at page 11.

Brookstone added an organizational chart to its proxy.

Another request asked for more information on a possible delay in the meeting for the merger approval:

Adjournment or Postponement of the Annual Meeting (Proposal No. 2), page 102

52. Please provide more details about the circumstances under which you would postpone the meeting and for how long.

And the company offered the following response:

RESPONSE: The disclosure in the Proxy Statement has been revised in response to the Staff's comment. Please see page 109.

Not only will investors benefit from being able to read of the SEC's concerns, but also other companies will be able to make adjustments to their own decisions and reporting so that the SEC does not raise the same flags with each company. Many believe the comments will have the effect of developing a "case law" for financial reporting.

Explain how the release of these comments and the companies' responses will be helpful to businesses. Explain how they might cause some difficulties.

(b) Open Meetings

Under the Sunshine Act of 1976,[7] called the **open meeting law,** the federal government requires most meetings of major administrative agencies to be open to the public. The Sunshine Act[8] applies to those meetings involving "deliberations" of the agency or those that "result in the joint conduct or disposition of official agency business." The object of this statute is to enable the public to know what actions agencies are taking and to prevent administrative misconduct by having open meetings and public scrutiny. Many states also have enacted sunshine laws.

(c) Public Announcement of Agency Guidelines

To inform the public of the way administrative agencies operate, the APA, with certain exceptions, requires that each federal agency publish the rules, principles, and procedures that it follows.[9]

[7] The Government in the Sunshine Act can be found at 5 USC § 552b.

[8] 5 USC § 552b(a)(2).

[9] APA codified at 5 USC § 552. See Section 5(c) of this chapter for a description of the *Federal Register*, the publication in which these agency rules, principles, and procedures are printed.

B. Legislative Power of the Agency

An administrative agency has the power to make laws and does so by promulgating regulations with public input.

4. Agency's Regulations as Law

An agency may adopt regulations within the scope of its authority. The power of an agency to carry out a congressional program "necessarily requires the formulation of policy and the making of rules to fill any gap left by Congress."[10] If the regulation is not authorized by the law creating the agency, anyone affected by it can challenge the regulation on the basis that the agency has exceeded its authority. [See Section 11(d), "Beyond the Jurisdiction of the Agency."]

An administrative agency cannot act beyond the scope of the authority in the statute that created it or assigned a responsibility to it.[11] However, the authority of an agency is not limited to the technology in existence at the time the agency was created or assigned jurisdiction for enforcement of laws. The sphere in which an agency may act expands with new scientific developments.[12]

When an agency's proposed regulation deals with a policy question that is not specifically addressed by statute, the agency that was created or given the discretion to administer the statute may establish new policies covering such issues. This power is granted regardless of whether the lawmaker intentionally left such matters to the agency's discretion or merely did not foresee the problem. In either case, the matter is one to be determined within the agency's discretion, and courts defer to agencies' policy decisions.[13] For example, the FCC has authority to deal with cell phones and cell phone providers even though when the agency was created, there were only the traditional types of land-line telephones.

Today, regulations adopted by an agency may interpret or clarify the law. In effect, many regulations have the feel of legislation. Courts have come to recognize the authority of an agency even though the lawmaker creating the agency did nothing more than state the goal or objective to be attained by the agency. The modern approach is to regard the administrative agency as holding all powers necessary to effectively perform the duties entrusted to it. When the agency establishes a rational basis for its rule, courts accept the rule and do not substitute their own judgment.[14]

Legislatures have met the judicial standard for approval with various types of agencies created for different purposes such as licensing to protect the public, prohibiting unfair methods of competition, or administering the registration of autos andother vehicles. The purposes in these types of statutes

E-COMMERCE AND CYBERLAW

COMPLYING WITH REGULATIONS ONLINE

Federal agencies have been adapting to online business. For example, the IRS offers electronic filing of income tax returns. The SEC permits electronic submission of various forms and reports due from companies. Corporations are using the Web to telecast their discussions with analysts to comply with SEC rules on uniform disclosure of all company information to all investors in the same time frame. All federal agencies are accepting e-mail comments on proposed rules as valid public comments during the public comment periods for proposed rules.

10 *Virginia v Browner*, 80 F3d 869 (4th Cir 1996).

11 *Home Depot U.S.A. v Contractors' State License Board*, 49 Cal Rptr 302 (1996).

12 *United States v Midwest Video Corp.*, 406 US 649 (1972) (sustaining a commission regulation that provided that "no CATV system having 3,500 or more subscribers shall carry the signal of any television broadcast station unless the system also operates to a significant extent as a local outlet by cablecasting and has available facilities for local production and presentation of programs other than automated services").

13 *Chevron, U.S.A., Inc. v National Resources Defense Council, Inc.*, 467 US 837 (1984).

14 *Covad Communications Co. v FCC*, 430 F 3d 528 (DC Cir 2006).

include the typical public safety and welfare areas such as ensuring competence and integrity of professionals through the licensing process or ensuring that there are free markets that allow open competition.[15]

5. Agency Adoption of Regulations

(a) Congressional Enabling Act

Before an agency can begin rulemaking proceedings, it must be given jurisdiction by congressional enactment in the form of a statute. For example, Congress has enacted broad statutes governing discrimination in employment practices and has given authority to the Equal Employment Opportunity Commission (EEOC) to establish definitions, rules, and guidelines for compliance with those laws. Sometimes an existing agency is assigned the responsibility for new legislation implementation and enforcement. **For Example,** the Department of Labor has been assigned the responsibility to handle the whistle-blower protection provisions of Sarbanes-Oxley that provide protection against retaliation and/or termination to those who report financial chicanery at their companies. The Department of Labor has been in existence for almost a century, but it was assigned a new responsibility and given new jurisdiction by Congress.

(b) Agency Research of the Problem

After jurisdiction is established, the agency has the responsibility to research the issues and various avenues of regulation for implementing the statutory framework. As the agency does so, it determines the cost and benefit of the problems, issues, and solutions. The study may be done by the agency itself, or it may be completed by someone hired by the agency. **For Example,** before red lights were required equipment in the rear windows of all cars, the Department of Transportation developed a study using taxicabs with the red lights in the rear windows and found that the accident rate for rear-end collisions with taxicabs was reduced dramatically. The study provided justification for the need for regulation as well as the type of regulation itself. The *Motor Vehicles Manufacturers Ass'n v State Farm* case deals with an issue of research on withdrawal of a proposed regulation.

ETHICS & THE LAW

FLUSH WITH REGULATION: HOW MANY GALLONS AND WHERE

The Energy Policy Act of 1992 requires that toilets installed after the act took effect (1994) use only 1.6 gallons of water rather than the nearly century-old standard of 3.5 gallons. As of 2000, about one-fourth of the nation's toilets were the 1.6-gallon types. The EPA mandated that permits be conditioned on the use of the 1.6-gallon toilets and that inspection approvals be denied if anything but a 1.6-gallon toilet had been installed.

As homeowners have remodeled and replaced older toilets, they have learned that the 3.5-gallon toilets are no longer sold in the United States. However, just across the U.S./Canadian border near Detroit, Canadian hardware stores are doing a land-office business selling 3.5-gallon tanks to U.S. citizens.

Those who are remodeling, and even some who are building new homes, provide for 1.6-gallon toilets in their plans and generally install $100 1.6-gallon toilets from Home Depot in order to pass inspection. They then purchase a standard fixture Canadian toilet for anywhere from $500 to $1,000 because of the high demand, and install it. Plumbing stores all over Canada report that sales are brisk. In a survey conducted in May 2000, the Canadian plumbing store owners said that they sell, on average, one toilet per day to U.S. citizens either via direct sale or shipment.

Do the citizens break any laws by what they do? Is what they do ethical? How could the regulation be challenged? What foundation in administrative law might be used?

[15] All of these are examples of the general legislative authority given to agencies. Agencies are given generic commands of law and then create the law's specifics.

MOTOR VEHICLES MANUFACTURERS ASS'N V STATE FARM MUTUAL INSURANCE CO., 463 US 29 (1983)

SEATS BELTS AND AIR BAGS AND RULES, OH MY!

The Department of Transportation (DOT), charged with the enforcement of the National Traffic and Motor Vehicle Safety Act of 1966 and the task of reducing auto accidents, passed Standard 208 in 1967. Standard 208 is the seat belt requirement for motor vehicles, and its original form simply required that all cars be equipped with seat belts. It soon became clear to the DOT that people did not use the belts, so the department began a study of passive restraint systems, which do not require any action on the part of the occupant other than operating the vehicle. The two types considered were automatic seat belts and air bags. Studies showed that these devices could prevent approximately 12,000 deaths a year and over 100,000 serious injuries.

In 1972, after many hearings and comments, the DOT passed a regulation requiring some type of passive restraint system on all vehicles manufactured after 1975. The regulation allowed an ignition interlock system, which requires car occupants to have their seat belts fastened before a car could be started. Congress, however, revoked the requirement of the ignition interlock because of public outcry.

Because of changes in directors of the DOT and the unfavorable economic climate in the auto industry, the requirements for passive restraints were postponed. In 1981, the department proposed a rescission of the passive restraint rule. After receiving written comments and holding public hearing, the agency concluded there was no longer a basis for reliably predicting that passive restraints increased safety levels or decreased accidents. Further, the agency found it would cost $1 billion to implement the rule, and they were unwilling to impose such substantial costs on auto manufacturers.

State Farm filed suit on the rescission of the rule on the basis that it was arbitrary and capricious. The court of appeals held the rescission was, in fact, arbitrary and capricious. Auto manufacturers appealed.

Judicial Opinion

WHITE, J. . . . The ultimate question before us is whether NHTSA's (National Highway Traffic Safety Administration) rescission of the passive restraint requirement of Standard 208 was arbitrary and capricious. We conclude, as did the Court of Appeals, that it was.

The first and most obvious reason for finding the rescission arbitrary and capricious is that NHTSA apparently gave no consideration whatsoever to modifying the standard to require that airbag technology be utilized. Standard 208 sought to achieve automatic crash protection by requiring automobile manufacturers to install either of two passive restraint devices: airbags or automatic seatbelts. There was no suggestion in the long rulemaking process that led to Standard 208 that if only one of these options were feasible, no passive restraint standard should be promulgated. Indeed, the agency's original proposed standard contemplated the installation of inflatable restraints in all cars. Automatic belts were added as a means of complying with the standard because they were believed to be as effective as airbags in achieving the goal of occupant crash protection.

The agency has now determined that the detachable automatic belts will not attain anticipated safety benefits because so many individuals will detach the mechanism. Even if this conclusion were acceptable in its entirety, standing alone it would not justify any more than an amendment of Standard 208 to disallow compliance by means of the only technology which will not provide effective passenger protection. It does not cast doubt on the need for a passive restraint standard or upon the efficacy of airbag technology. In its most recent rulemaking, the agency again acknowledged the life-saving potential of the airbag. Given the effectiveness ascribed to airbag technology by the agency, the mandate of the Safety Act to achieve traffic safety would suggest that the logical response to the faults of detachable seatbelts would be to require the installation of airbags. At the very least this alternative way of achieving objectives of the Act should have been addressed and adequate reasons given for its abandonment. But the agency not only did not require compliance through airbags, it did not even consider the possibility in its 1981 rulemaking. Not one sentence of its rulemaking statement discusses the airbags-only option. We have frequently reiterated that an agency must cogently explain why it had exercised its discretion in a given manner.

For nearly a decade, the automobile industry waged the regulatory equivalent of war against the airbag and lost—the inflatable restraint was proven sufficiently effective. Now the automobile industry has decided to employ a seatbelt system which will not meet the safety objectives of Standard 208. This hardly constitutes cause to revoke the standard itself. Indeed the Motor Vehicle Safety Act was necessary because the industry was not sufficiently responsive to safety concerns. The Act intended that safety standards not depend on current technology and would be "technology-forcing" in the sense of inducing the development of superior safety design.

It is not infrequent that the available data does not settle a regulatory issue and the agency must then exercise its judgment in moving from the facts and probabilities on the record to a policy conclusion. Recognizing that policy making in a complex society must account for uncertainty, however, does not imply that it is sufficient for an agency to merely recite the terms "substantial uncertainty" as a justification for its actions. The agency must explain the evidence which is available, and must offer a "rational connection between the facts found and the choice made."

In this case, the agency's explanation for rescission of the passive restraint requirement is not sufficient to enable us to conclude that the rescission was the product of reasoned decision making. We start with the accepted ground that if used, seatbelts unquestionably would save many thousands of lives and would prevent tens of thousands of crippling injuries. Unlike recent regulations we have reviewed, the safety benefits of wearing seatbelts are not in doubt and it is not challenged that were those benefits to accrue, the monetary costs of implementing the standard would be easily justified.

Since 20 to 50 percent of motorists currently wear seatbelts on some occasions, there would seem to be grounds to believe that seatbelt use by occasional users will be substantially increased by the detachable passive belts. Whether this is the case is a matter for the agency to decide, but it must bring its expertise to bear on the question.

An agency's view of what is in the public interest may change, either with or without a change in circumstances. But an agency changing its course must supply a reasoned analysis. We do not accept all of the reasoning of the Court of Appeals but we do conclude that the agency has failed to supply the requisite "reasoned analysis" in this case. Accordingly, we remand the matter to the NHTSA for further consideration consistent with this opinion.

[Affirmed]

Questions

1. Why does the DOT want to withdraw the regulation?
2. What does the DOT need to withdraw the regulation?
3. Will the regulation go into effect?

THINKING THINGS THROUGH

COST-BENEFIT ANALYSIS AND FEDERAL REGULATION

Following a Supreme Court decision on the issue in 1983, the Department of Transportation (DOT) promulgated auto safety regulations that required automobile manufacturers to equip all vehicles with some form of passive restraint. The most popular was the air bag. The DOT had attempted to hold off on regulation until further information could be obtained about the efficacy and risks of air bags. General Motors warned in 1979 that if an air bag were inflated while a child was sitting in the front passenger side of the vehicle, the effect would be severe injury or death. In 1984, Lee Iacocca, then CEO of Chrysler, wrote: "Air bags are one of those areas where the solution may actually be worse than the problem."* Insurers and consumer groups dismissed the claims as reflecting self-interest because of the costs mandatory passive restraints would impose on automobile manufacturers.

*James R. Heal, and Jayne O'Donnell, "Deadly Air Bags," *USA Today*, July 8, 1996, 1B, 2B.

THINKING THINGS THROUGH

continued

In 1996, the DOT revealed that 23 people had been killed by air bags; 22 were children between the ages of one week and nine years. A mother of one of those killed by an air bag said, "It's wrong for it to be in cars." In 1998, the DOT mandated disclosure stickers in all cars about the dangers of placing infants and children in passenger seats where there is an air bag:

WARNING: Children may be killed or injured by passenger air bag. The back seat is the safest place for children 12 and under.

Data released by the National Highway Traffic Safety Administration show that the complaints about airbags increased as more were installed in cars. So little was known about the technology and so many consumers were unfamiliar with them that the NHSTA began a decade of grappling with consumer complaints about the safety device. In 1990, only 200 air bag complaints were filed. In 2001, there were 3,000 with 2001 being the peak year. The NHSTA began changing the requirements and manufacturers made technological changes. By 2003, the number of complaints had dropped to just 800 and there was only one airbag death, down from a previous high of 57. The types of complaints about the air bags were:

- Not being able to find the horn on the steering wheel because of the thickness the air bag brings
- Air bags inflating when there has not been a crash
- Air bags not inflating when there has been a crash
- Air bags' degree of inflation harming smaller passengers**

There have been 112 recalls of air bags in autos since 1990, and those recalls affected 6.2 million cars.

By 2003, air bags changed the dynamic of safety quite dramatically because at that point the bags carried sensors to determine the size of the individual and, therefore, how much to inflate. The air bags, however, remain at the standard of not inflating unless something hits the vehicle at a speed above 12 miles per hour.

Did the regulation move too quickly? What was the purpose of the regulation? Should more studies have been done before the airbags were mandated? Is cost-benefit analysis a good approach to making decisions on rules? You can visit the National Highway Traffic Safety Administration at **http://www.nhtsa.gov.**

**Jayne O'Donnell, "Air Bag Gripes Rise; New Rules May Complicate Matters," *USA Today*, April 9, 2002, 1B.

(c) Proposed Regulations

Following a study, the agency proposes regulations, which must be published. To provide publicity for all regulations, the **Federal Register Act**[16] provides that proposed administrative regulation be published in the ***Federal Register***. This is a government publication published five days a week that lists all administrative regulations, all presidential proclamations and executive orders, and other documents and classes of documents that the president or Congress directs to be published.

The Federal Register Act provides that printing an administrative regulation in the *Federal Register* is public notice of the contents of the regulation to persons subject to it or affected by it, but in addition, the Regulatory Flexibility Act,[17] passed during the Reagan administration, requires that all proposed rules be published in the trade journals of those trades that will be affected by the proposed rules. **For Example,** any changes in federal regulations on real property closings and escrows have to be published in real estate broker trade magazines. In

16 44 USC § 1505 *et seq.*

17 5 USC § 601 *et seq.*

addition to the public notice of the proposed rule, the agency must also include a "regulatory flexibility analysis" that "shall describe the impact of the proposed rule on small entities."[18] The goal of this portion of the APA was to be certain that small businesses were aware of proposed regulatory rules and their cost impact. The *San Diego Air Sports Center, Inc. v FAA* case deals with an issue of notice of regulatory changes.

(d) Public Comment Period

Following the publication of the proposed rules, the public has the opportunity to provide input on the proposed rules. Called the *public comment period*, this time must last at least 30 days (with certain emergency exceptions) and can consist simply of letters written by those affected that are filed with the agency or of hearings conducted by the agency in Washington, D.C., or at specified locations around

SAN DIEGO AIR SPORTS CENTER, INC. V FAA, 887 F2D 966 (9TH CIR 1989)

GET OFF OF MY CLOUD, ER, PARACHUTE

San Diego Air Sports (SDAS) Center operates a sports parachuting business in Otay Mesa, California. SDAS offers training to beginning parachutists and facilitates recreational jumping for experienced parachutists. It indicates that the majority of SDAS jumps occur at altitudes in excess of 5,800 feet. The jump zone used by SDAS overlaps the San Diego Traffic Control Area (TCA). Although the aircraft carrying the parachutists normally operate outside the TCA, the parachutists themselves are dropped through it. Thus, each jump must be approved by the air traffic controllers. In July 1987, an air traffic controller in San Diego filed an Unsatisfactory Condition Report complaining of the strain that parachuting was putting on the controllers and raising safety concerns. The report led to a staff study of parachute jumping within the San Diego TCA. In October 1987, representatives of the San Diego Terminal Radar Approach Control (TRACON) facility met with SDAS operators. In December 1987, the San Diego TRACON sent to SDAS a draft letter of agreement outlining agreed-upon procedures and coordination requirements. Nonetheless, the San Diego TRACON conducted another study between January 14, 1988, and February 11, 1988; and about two months after the draft letter was sent, the San Diego TRACON withdrew it.

SDAS states that the air traffic manager of the San Diego TRACON assured SDAS that it would be invited to attend all meetings on parachuting in the San Diego TCA. However, SDAS was not informed of or invited to any meetings.

In March 1988, the Federal Aviation Agency (FAA) sent a letter to SDAS informing SDAS that "[e]ffective immediately parachute jumping within or into the San Diego TCA in the Otay Reservoir Jump Zone will not be authorized." The FAA stated that the letter was final and appealable.

SDAS challenged the letter in federal court on grounds that it constituted rulemaking without compliance with required Administrative Procedure Act (APA) procedures.

Judicial Opinion

BEEZER, C. J. . . . The Federal Aviation Act requires that rules affecting the use of navigable airspace be issued in accordance with the Administrative Procedure Act (APA). The "principal purpose" of section 553 of the APA is "to provide that the legislative functions of administrative agencies shall so far as possible be exercised only upon public participation." Section 553 of the APA requires agencies to adhere to three steps when promulgating rules: Notice of the proposed rule, opportunity to comment, and an explanation of the rule ultimately adopted. These three requirements have been referred to as "the statutory *minima*" imposed by Congress.

Not every decision made by administrative agencies requires citizen participation. The APA lists four instances when the statutory *minima* do not apply: When the agency is promulgating (1) interpretive rules, (2) general statements of policy, or (3) rules of agency organization,

[18] 5 USC § 603(a).

procedure, or practice, or (4) when the requirement of notice and participation are impractical or contrary to public interest.

Congress was concerned that the exceptions to section 553, though necessary, might be used too broadly. The Senate noted that the courts have a "duty . . . to prevent avoidance of the requirements of the [Act] by any manner or form of indirection." We have stated that "[t]he exceptions to section 553 will be 'narrowly construed and only reluctantly countenanced.'"

The FAA letter does not come within either of the first two exceptions. The letter creates an immediate, substantive rule, i.e., that no parachuting will be allowed in the San Diego TCA.

The FAA argues that parachuting created an emergency to which it responded in the letter at issue. It is further argued that a response to an immediate emergency is covered by the fourth exception. This argument is not persuasive. The only accident known to the FAA occurred two years before it issued its letter. Furthermore, the FAA itself claims to have extensively studied the situation before issuing the letter. The FAA does not explain why public participation as required by the APA could not be included in its study.

Finally, the FAA argues that the letter is not a rule at all; rather, the FAA characterizes the letter as an order to which the requirements set forth in section 553 of the APA does [sic] not apply. We find this argument somewhat mystifying, as there are equally stringent participation requirements for orders. Furthermore, the FAA is wrong; the letter is a rule.

A time-honored principle of administrative law is that the label an agency puts on its actions "is not necessarily conclusive." Equally true, however, is the fact that agencies can issue rules through adjudication (the process by which orders are normally issued) and orders through rulemaking.

In this case no record was kept of the "process" that resulted in the FAA letter; we can only scrutinize the letter itself. The letter clearly promulgates a rule. It states that *all* parachuting by any party will be prohibited in the San Diego TCA from the time it is issued. This comports with this court's statement that "[s]ubstantive rules are those which effect a change in existing law or policy."

The Federal Aviation Act requires that rules affecting the use of navigable airspace be issued in accordance with the APA, In issuing this substantive rule, the FAA failed to do so. A substantive rule is invalid if the issuing agency fails to comply with the APA. Therefore, the petition for review is granted.

Questions

1. Was the letter a form of regulation?
2. Did the agency skirt procedure?
3. Was SDAS deprived of due process by the letter?

ETHICS & THE LAW

ETHICS AND GOVERNMENT REGULATION

Rowena Fullinwider is the founder of Rowena's, Inc., which makes Rowena Fullinwider's Wonderful Almond Pound Cake and other products, such as lemon curd and carrot jam. The specialty gourmet food manufacturer specializes in high-calorie and, often, high-fat treats. When the Nutrition Labeling and Education Act requiring disclosure of food products' nutrients and contents went into effect in 1995, compliance with the new federal mandates for Rowena's 30 products cost $100,000 for redesigning the labels, testing the products for verification of ingredients, and printing and production.

Rowena's, like many other specialty food manufacturers, has very narrow profit margins, ranging from 0.5 percent to 5 percent. It employs 16 people and has $1 million in annual sales. At the top end of its profit margin, Rowena's has a net profit of $50,000.

Fullinwider expresses her concerns with the labeling act as follows: "I am not going to put new products out. In the gourmet industry, we are always improving our recipes. I want to

ETHICS & THE LAW

continued

make improvements, but I can't afford to if I'm all bound up by regulations."

Do you believe the federal food labeling act was necessary? Why or why not? Do you think Rowena's was guilty of deception in the sale of its products? Should food manufacturers voluntarily have disclosed the content of their products? Why would they resist? Is it possible that the label requirements will put some companies out of business? Is it desirable to have regulations that eliminate businesses? What could Rowena have done differently to change the content of the new regulations?

the country. An emergency exemption for the 30-day comment period was made when airport security measures and processes were changed following the September 11, 2001, attacks on the World Trade Center and the Pentagon that used domestic, commercial airliners.

(e) Options after Public Comment

After receiving the public input on the proposed rule, an agency can decide to pass, or promulgate, the rule. The agency can also decide to withdraw the rule. **For Example,** the EEOC had proposed rules on handling religious discrimination in the workplace. The proposed rules, which would have required employers to police those wearing a cross or other religious symbol, met with so much public and employer protest that they were withdrawn. Finally, the agency can decide to modify the rule based on comments and then promulgate or, if the modifications are extensive or material, modify and put the proposed rule back out for public comment again. A diagram of the rule-making process can be found in Figure 6-3.

C. Executive Power of the Agency

The modern administrative agency has the power to execute the law and to bring proceedings against violators.

6. Enforcement or Execution of the Law

An agency has the power to investigate, to require persons to appear as witnesses, to require witnesses to produce relevant papers and records, and to bring proceedings against those who violate the law. In this connection, the phrase *the law* embraces regulations adopted by an agency as well as statutes and court decisions.

An agency may investigate to determine whether any violation of the law or of its rules generally has occurred. An agency may also investigate to determine whether additional rules need to be adopted, to ascertain the facts with respect to a particular suspected or alleged violation, and to see whether the defendant in a proceeding before it is complying with its final order. An agency may issue subpoenas to obtain information reasonably required by its investigation.[19]

7. Constitutional Limitations on Administrative Investigation

Although administrative agencies have broad enforcement authority, they remain subject to the constitutional protections afforded individuals and businesses.

(a) Inspection of Premises

In general, a person has the same protection against unreasonable searches and seizures by an administrative officer as by a police officer. In contrast, when the danger of concealment is great, a warrantless search can be made of the premises of a highly regulated business, such as one selling liquor or firearms. Likewise, when violation of the law is dangerous to health and safety, the law may authorize inspection of the workplace without advance notice or a search warrant when such a requirement could defeat the purpose of the inspection.

[19] *EEOC v Sidley, Austen, Brown and Wood,* 35 F 3d 696 (CA 7 2002).

FIGURE 6-3 Steps in Agency Rulemaking

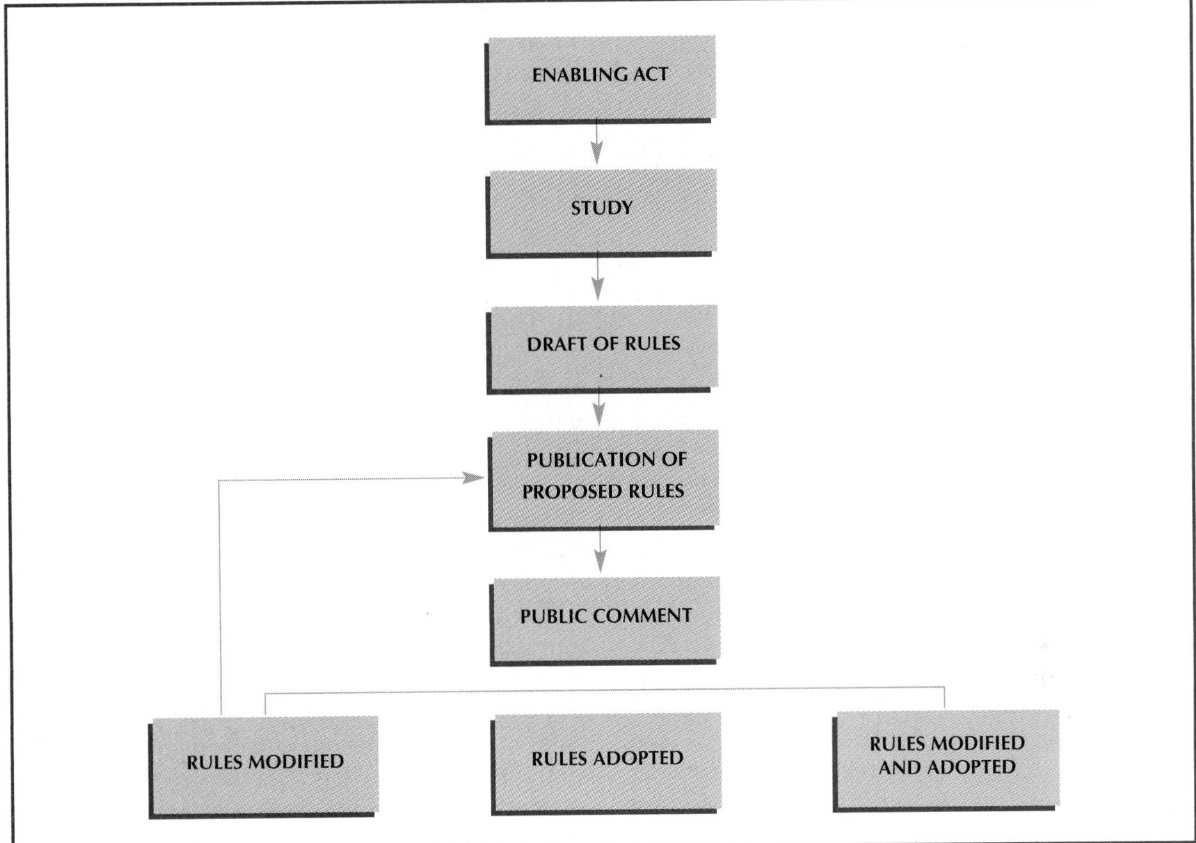

(b) Aerial Inspection

A search warrant is never required when the subject matter can be seen from a public place. **For Example,** when a police officer walking on a public sidewalk can look through an open window and see illegal weapons, a search warrant is not required to enter the premises and seize the weapons. Using airplanes and helicopters, law enforcement officers can see from the air; an agency, too, can gather information in this manner.[20]

(c) Production of Papers

For the most part, the constitutional guarantee against unreasonable searches and seizures does not afford much protection for papers and records being investigated by an agency. **For Example,** a subpoena to testify or to produce records cannot be opposed on the ground that it is a search and seizure. The constitutional protection is limited to cases of actual physical search and seizure rather than obtaining information by compulsion. Employers must turn over to the Occupational Health and Safety Administration (OSHA) their records on workplace injuries and lost workdays.

The protection afforded by the guarantee against self-incrimination is likewise narrow. It cannot be invoked when a corporate employee or officer in control of corporate records is compelled to produce those records even though he or she would be incriminated by them.[21] The privilege against self-incrimination cannot be invoked if records required to be kept by law are involved.

(d) Compliance Verification

To ensure that a particular person or business is obeying the law, including an agency's regulations

20 *Dow Chemical Co. v United States,* 476 US 1819 (1986).

21 *Braswell v United States,* 487 US 99 (1988).

and orders, the administrative agency may require proof of compliance. At times, the question of compliance may be directly determined by an agency investigation, involving an examination either of a building or plant or of witnesses and documents. An agency may require the regulated person or enterprise to file reports in a specified form.[22]

D. Judicial Power of the Agency

Once the investigation of an agency reveals a potential violation of the law, an agency assumes its third role of judicial arbiter to conduct hearings on violations.

8. The Agency as a Specialized Court

An agency, although not a court by law, may be given power to sit as a court and to determine whether any violations of the law or of agency regulations have occurred. The National Labor Relations Board (NLRB) determines whether a prohibited labor practice has been committed. The Federal Trade Commission (FTC) acts as a court to determine whether someone has engaged in unfair competition.

(a) Beginning Enforcement—Preliminary Steps

Either a private individual or company or an agency may file a written complaint alleging some violation of law or regulation that is within the agency's jurisdiction. This complaint is then served on the company or individual named in the complaint, who then has the opportunity to file an answer to the allegations. There may be other phases of pleading between the parties and the agency, but eventually, the matter comes before the agency to be heard. After a hearing, the agency makes a decision and enters an order either dismissing the complaint or directing remedies or resolutions.

(b) The Administrative Hearing

To satisfy the requirements of due process, an agency handling a complaint must generally give notice and hold a hearing at which all persons affected may be present. A significant difference between an agency hearing and a court hearing is that there is no right of trial by jury before an agency. **For Example,** a workers' compensation board may decide a claim without any jury. Similarly, a case in which an employer protests the unemployment tax rate assigned to her company by a state agency has no right to a jury trial. The lack of a jury does not deny due process (see Chapter 4). An administrative law judge (ALJ) hears the complaint and has the authority to swear witnesses, take testimony, make evidentiary rulings, and make a decision to recommend to the agency heads for action.

An agency hearing is ordinarily not subject to the rules of evidence. Another difference between an administrative hearing and a judicial determination is that an agency may be authorized to make an initial

ETHICS & THE LAW

THE OTHER CIA

Corporate integrity agreements are forms of or parts of consent decrees entered into between federal agencies and corporations after charges have been settled. Corporate integrity agreements (CIAs) are common between health care providers, medical device manufacturers, and similar organizations and companies and the U.S. Department of Health and Human Services. CIAs generally require the company or organization to provide additional ethics training, enhance compliance program development, and step up audits to ensure that the same or similar problems do not arise again.

If the company or organization violates the CIA, which is a form of civil probation, the government can take additional steps. The usual step for a second violation during the CIA is to banish the company or organization from

[22] *United States v Morton Salt Co.*, 338 US 632 (1950).

ETHICS & THE LAW

continued

all federal programs, whether as a provider or a beneficiary of Medicare, Medicaid, and any Veteran's Administration program. The loss of such large customers can be devastating for the company or organization. These additional penalties are envisioned and discussed as part of the CIA.

However, the CIA has emerged as an issue in private litigation. For example, suppose that a pharmaceutical company is subject to a CIA for five years because it failed to alert the FDA to side effects of one of its drugs. The government could impose a fine and a CIA. What would happen if the company failed to notify the government of another side effect problem during the CIA's five-year period? What right would a patient who is harmed by the side effects have to use the CIA against the company to recover punitive damages?. The courts must determine how these government settlements and CIAs can be used in civil litigation.

Should the agencies cover all of these issues in the CIA or wait for the courts to determine the outcome? Should agency officials warn companies entering into CIAs of these potential minefields?

determination without holding a hearing. If its conclusion is challenged, the agency then holds a hearing. A court, on the other hand, must have a trial before it makes a judgment. This difference has important practical consequences because the party objecting to the agency's initial determination has the burden of proof and the cost of going forward. The result is that fewer persons go to the trouble of seeking such a hearing, which reduces the number of hearings and the amount of litigation in which an agency becomes involved. The government saves money and time with this abbreviated process.

When an administrative action involves only the individuals directly affected rather than a class of persons or the community in general, the agency must have some form of hearing before it makes a decision. The Supreme Court has held that because a civil service employee may be removed only for cause, it is a denial of due process for a statute to authorize an agency to remove the employee without a hearing.[23] Just giving the employee the right to appeal such action is not sufficient. Because the employee has a significant interest in continued employment, there must be some form of hearing prior to removing the employee to determine that there were not errors in the administrative action.

(c) Streamlined Procedure: Consent Decrees

Informal settlements or **consent decrees** are practical devices to cut across the procedures already outlined. In many instances, an alleged wrongdoer informally notified that a complaint has been made is willing to change. An agency's informing an alleged wrongdoer of the charge before filing any formal complaint is sound public relations, as well as expeditious policy. A matter that has already gone into the formal hearing stage may also be terminated by agreement, and a stipulation or consent decree may be filed setting forth the terms of the agreement. The Administrative Dispute Resolution Act of 1990 encourages the streamlining of the regulatory process and authorizes federal agencies to use alternative means of dispute resolution.[24]

(d) Form of Administrative Decision

When an administrative agency makes a decision, it usually files an opinion that sets forth the findings of facts and reasons on which the decision is based. In some instances, a statute expressly requires this type of opinion, but an agency should always file one so that the parties and the court (in the event of an appeal) will understand the agency's action and reasoning.[25]

[23] *Cleveland Board of Education v Loudermill*, 470 US 532 (1985).

[24] 5 USC § 571 *et. seq.*

[25] *Jordan v Civil Service Bd., Charlotte*, 570 SE 2d 912 (CA NC 2002).

9. Punishment and Enforcement Powers of Agencies

(a) Penalty

Within the last few decades, agencies have increasingly been given the power to impose a penalty and to issue orders that are binding on a regulated party unless an appeal is taken to a court, which reverses the administrative decision. As an illustration of the power to impose penalties, the Occupational Safety and Health Act of 1970 provides for the assessment of civil penalties against employers who fail to end dangerous working conditions when ordered to do so by the administrative agency created by that statute.[26]

(b) Cease and Desist Order

Environmental protection statutes adopted by states commonly give a state agency the power to assess a penalty for violating environmental protection regulations. As an illustration of the issuance of binding orders, the FTC can issue a **cease-and-desist order** to stop a practice that it decides is improper. This order to stop is binding unless reversed on an appeal. **For Example,** the FTC can order a company to stop making claims in ads that have been determined by that agency to be deceptive.

10. Exhaustion of Administrative Remedies

All parties interacting with an agency must follow the procedure specified by the law. No appeal to a court is possible until the agency has acted on the party's matter before it. As a matter of policy, parties are required to exhaust administrative remedies before they may go into court or take an appeal.

As long as an agency is acting within the scope of its authority or jurisdiction, a party cannot appeal before the agency has made a final decision. The fact that the complaining party does not want the agency to decide the matter or is afraid that the agency will reach a wrong decision is not grounds for bypassing the agency by going to court before the agency has acted.

Exceptions to the **exhaustion-of-administrative-remedies** requirement are (1) available remedies that provide no genuine opportunity for adequate relief; (2) irreparable injury that could occur if immediate judicial relief is not provided; (3) an appeal to the administrative agency that would be useless; or (4) a substantial constitutional question that the plaintiff has raised.

11. Appeal from Administrative Action and Finality of Administrative Determination

The statute creating the modern administrative agency generally provides that an appeal may be taken from the administrative decision to a particular court. The statute may provide the basis for an appeal. However, judicial precedent holds that courts may review administrative agency decisions on the bases covered in the following sections.

(a) Procedural Issues

If the procedure that an agency is to follow is specified by law, a decision of the agency that was made without following that procedure will be set aside and the matter sent back to the agency to proceed according to the required law.[27] An agency's actions, whether enforcement or rule promulgation, can be set aside if the agency has not followed the procedures required for rulemaking or, in the case of enforcement, the due process rights of the charged business or individual. The *Mainstream Marketing Services, Inc. v FTC* case deals with an issue of agency authority.

(b) Substantive Law or Fact Issues

When the question that an agency decides is a question of law, the court on appeal will reverse the agency if the court disagrees with the legal interpretation.[28] This concept is being eroded to some extent by technical aspects of regulation. Courts now accept an agency's interpretation of a statute that involves a technical matter. Courts now tend to accept the agency's interpretation so long as it was reasonable even though it was not the only interpretation that could have been made.

In contrast with an agency's decision on matters of law, a controversy may turn on a question of fact or a mixed question of law and fact. In such cases, a court accepts an agency's conclusion if it is supported by substantial evidence. This means that the court must examine the entire record of the proceedings before

[26] 29 USC § 651 *et seq.*

[27] *Tingler v State Board of Cosmetology*, 814 SW2d 683 (Mo App 1991).

[28] *In re Minnesota Joint Underwriting Ass'n*, 408 NW2d 599 (Minn App 1987).

MAINSTREAM MARKETING SERVICES, INC. V F.T.C., 358 F3D 1228 (10TH CIR 2004) CERT DENIED 543 US 812 (2004)

I'LL CALL YOU—MAYBE DURING DINNER: THE FCC AND THE NATIONAL DO-NOT-CALL LIST REGULATION

Many different organizations, including businesses, charities, religious groups, and political parties, generate revenue by calling individuals in their homes and soliciting sales and donations. This practice, known as telemarketing, has grown into an industry that generates $275 billion dollars annually and employs roughly 5.4 million persons in the United States.

The FTC issued the rulemaking for the do-not-call list under the authority of the Telephone Consumer Protection Act of 1991 (TCPA), which granted the FCC the authority to promulgate rules creating a procedure to protect telephone subscribers from receiving unwanted telemarketing calls. In 1994, Congress enacted the Telemarketing Act, which granted the FTC the authority to promulgate rules prohibiting "deceptive or abusive telemarketing practices." Congress specifically found that consumers were being increasingly victimized by telemarketing fraud and other abuses, and it required the FTC in promulgating its rules to (1) define "deceptive telemarketing acts or practices," (2) prohibit abusive patterns of unsolicited telephone calls, (3) restrict the hours of the day when telemarketing calls may be placed, and (4) require telemarketers to promptly disclose to call recipients the nature of their call.

Under the Implementation Act and the TCPA, the FCC announced its intention to adopt rules similar to the FTC's, enforcing the do-not-call list. On July 25, 2003, the FCC promulgated rules mirroring the FTC's amended rules and adding entities subject to the do-not-call restrictions to include those beyond the reach of the FTC's jurisdiction, such as banks, insurance companies, and common carriers.

Mainstream Marketing and TMG, independent telemarketing companies based in Colorado, brought suit challenging the authority of the Federal Trade Commission (FTC) to create a national do-not-call list that allows consumers to opt out, with certain exceptions, from receiving these telemarketing calls, alleging that the do-not-call list violates the First Amendment and the APA. The District Court for Colorado held that FTC's do-not-call rules were unconstitutional on First Amendment grounds, and the District Court for the Western District of Oklahoma held that FTC lacked statutory authority to enact its do-not-call rules. The two appeals by the FCC and FTC were consolidated in the Tenth Circuit.

Judicial Opinion

EBEL, C. J.. . . The national do-not-call registry is the product of a regulatory effort dating back to 1991 aimed at protecting the privacy rights of consumers and curbing the risk of telemarketing abuse. In the Telephone Consumer Protection Act of 1991 ("TCPA")—under which the FCC enacted its do-not-call rules—Congress found that for many consumers telemarketing sales calls constitute an intrusive invasion of privacy. Moreover, the TCPA's legislative history cited statistical data indicating that "most unwanted telephone solicitations are commercial in nature" and that "unwanted commercial calls are a far bigger problem than unsolicited calls from political or charitable organizations." TCPA therefore authorized the FCC to establish a national database of consumers who object to receiving "telephone solicitations," which the act defined as commercial sales calls.

Furthermore, in the Telemarketing and Consumer Fraud and Abuse Prevention Act of 1994 ("Telemarketing Act")—under which the FTC enacted its do-not-call rules—Congress found that consumers lose an estimated $40 billion each year due to telemarketing fraud. Therefore, Congress authorized the FTC to prohibit sales calls that a reasonable consumer would consider coercive or abusive of his or her right to privacy.

The national do-not-call registry's telemarketing restrictions apply only to commercial speech. Like most commercial speech regulations, the do-not-call rules draw a line between commercial and non-commercial speech on the basis of content. In reviewing commercial speech regulations, we apply the *Central Hudson* test. *Central Hudson Gas & Elec. Corp. v. Pub. Serv.* Comm'n of N.Y., 447 U.S. 557, 566, 100 S.Ct. 2343, 65 L.Ed.2d 341 (1980).

Central Hudson established a three-part test governing First Amendment challenges to regulations restricting non-misleading commercial speech that relates to lawful activity. First, the government must assert a substantial interest to be achieved by the regulation. Second, the regulation must directly advance that governmental interest, meaning that it must do more than provide "only ineffective or remote support for the government's purpose." Third, although the regulation need not be the least restrictive measure available, it must be narrowly tailored not to restrict more speech than necessary.

A. Governmental Interests

The government asserts that the do-not-call regulations are justified by its interests in 1) protecting the privacy of individuals in their homes, and 2) protecting consumers against the risk of fraudulent and abusive solicitation. Both of these justifications are undisputedly substantial governmental interests.

B. Reasonable Fit

A reasonable fit exists between the do-not-call rules and the government's privacy and consumer protection interests if the regulation directly advances those interests and is narrowly tailored. In this context, the "narrowly tailored" standard does not require that the government's response to protect substantial interests be the least restrictive measure available. All that is required is a proportional response.

The individuals on the do-not-call list have declared that they do not wish to receive unsolicited commercial telemarketing calls, whereas those who do want to continue receiving such calls will not register.

Additionally, the FTC has found that commercial callers are more likely than non-commercial callers to engage in deceptive and abusive practices. Specifically, the FTC concluded that in charitable and political calls, a significant purpose of the call is to sell a cause, not merely to receive a donation, and that non-commercial callers thus have stronger incentives not to alienate the people they call or to engage in abusive and deceptive practices.

In sum, the do-not-call list directly advances the government's interests—reducing intrusions upon consumer privacy and the risk of fraud or abuse—by restricting a substantial number (and also a substantial percentage) of the calls that cause these problems.

2. Narrow Tailoring

Although the least restrictive means test is not the test to be used in the commercial speech context, commercial speech regulations do at least have to be "narrowly tailored" and provide a "reasonable fit" between the problem and the solution. Whether or not there are "numerous and obvious less-burdensome alternatives" is a relevant consideration in our narrow tailoring analysis.

We hold that the national do-not-call registry is narrowly tailored because it does not over-regulate protected speech; rather, it restricts only calls that are targeted at unwilling recipients. The do-not-call registry prohibits only telemarketing calls aimed at consumers who have affirmatively indicated that they do not want to receive such calls and for whom such calls would constitute an invasion of privacy.

The idea that an opt-in regulation is less restrictive than a direct prohibition of speech applies not only to traditional door-to-door solicitation, but also to regulations seeking to protect the privacy of the home from unwanted intrusions via telephone, television, or the Internet.

For the reasons discussed above, the government has asserted substantial interests to be served by the do-not-call registry (privacy and consumer protection), the do-not-call registry will directly advance those interests by banning a substantial amount of unwanted telemarketing calls, and the regulation is narrowly tailored because its opt-in feature ensures that it does not restrict any speech directed at a willing listener. In other words, the do-not-call registry bears a reasonable fit with the purposes the government sought to advance. Therefore, it is consistent with the limits the First Amendment imposes on laws restricting commercial speech.

The judgments below in [both] cases are REVERSED.

Questions

1. List the arguments that the telemarketers make to challenge the national do-not-call list.
2. What does the court do with each of the arguments and why?
3. What lessons on business practices do you see with the passage of the rules on the national do-not-call list?

the administrative agency to determine if there was substantial evidence to support the administrative findings. So long as reasonable minds could have reached the same conclusion as the agency after considering all of the evidence as a whole, the court must sustain the agency's findings of fact.[29]

A court will not reverse an agency's decision merely because the court would have made a different decision based on the same facts.[30] Because most disputes before an agency are based on questions of fact, the net result is that the agency's decision will be final in most cases.

Courts must give administrative agencies the freedom to do the work delegated to them and should not intervene unless the agency action is clearly unreasonable or arbitrary (see below). The agency action is presumed proper, and a person seeking reversal of the agency action has the burden to prove a basis for reversal.[31]

(c) Beyond the Jurisdiction of the Agency

When the question is whether an administrative action is in harmony with the policy of the statute creating the agency, an appellate court will sustain the administrative action if substantial evidence supports it. The *Mainstream Marketing Services, Inc. v FTC* case deals with an issue of agency authority.

(d) Arbitrary and Capricious

When an agency changes its prior decisions and customary actions, it must give its reasons. In the absence of such an explanation, a reviewing court cannot tell whether the agency changed its interpretation of the law for a valid reason or has made a mistake. The absence of an explanation condemns the agency action as arbitrary and requires reversal.[32]

The greatest limitation on court review of administrative action is the rule that a decision involving discretion will not be reversed in the absence of an error of law or a clear abuse of, or the arbitrary or capricious exercise of, discretion. The courts reason that because agency members were appointed on the basis of expert ability, it would be absurd for the court, which is unqualified technically to make a decision in the matter, to step in and determine whether the agency made the proper choice. Courts will not do so unless the agency has clearly acted wrongly, arbitrarily, or capriciously. As a practical matter, an agency's action is rarely found to be arbitrary or capricious. As long as an agency has followed proper procedure, the fact that the court disagrees with the agency's conclusion does not make that conclusion arbitrary or capricious. In areas in which economic or technical matters are involved, it is generally sufficient that the agency had a reasonable basis for its decision. A court will not attempt to second-guess the agency about complex criteria with which an administrative agency is intimately familiar. The judicial attitude is that for protection from laws and regulations that are unwise, improvident, or out of harmony with a particular school of thought, the people must resort to the ballot box, not to the court.

The fact that other agencies or trade associations disagree with the view of an agency does not make the latter's decision improper. There was much disagreement on the do-not-call list rules, but the court found that the FTC and FCC acted reasonably.[33]

Because of limited funding and staff, an agency must exercise discretion in deciding which cases it should handle. Ordinarily, a court will not reverse an agency's decision to do nothing about a particular complaint.[34] That is, the courts will not override an agency's decision to do nothing. Exceptions include acting arbitrarily in those enforcement actions as when an agency refuses to act in circumstances in which action is warranted and necessary.

12. Liability of the Agency

The decision of an agency may cause substantial loss to a business by increasing its operating costs or by making a decision that later is shown to be harmful to the economy. An agency is not liable for such loss when it has acted in good faith in the exercise of discretionary powers. An administrator who wrongly denies a person the benefit of a government program is not personally liable to that person.

[29] *Wilmer-Hutchins Independent School District v Brown*, 912 SW2d 848 (Tex App 1995).

[30] *In re Smith*, 121 P 3d 150 (Wyo 2005). An appellate court cannot review the evidence to determine the credibility of witnesses who testified before the administrative agency. *Hammann v City of Omaha*, 17 NW2d 323 (Neb 1987).

[31] *Reaux v Louisiana State Board of Medical Examiners*, 689 So 2d 718 (La App 1997).

[32] *Lorillard Tobacco Co. v Roth*, 786 NE 2d 7 (CA NY 2003).

[33] *Mainstream Marketing Services, Inc. v FTC*, 358 F 3d 1228 (10th Cir 2004).

[34] *Heckler v Chaney*, 470 US 821 (1985).

Summary

The administrative agency is unique because it combines the three functions that are kept separate under our traditional governmental system: legislative, executive, and judicial. By virtue of legislative power, an agency adopts regulations that have the force of law, although agency members are not elected by those subject to the regulations. By virtue of the executive power, an agency carries out and enforces the regulations, makes investigations, and requires the production of documents. By virtue of the judicial power, an agency acts as a court to determine whether a violation of any regulation has occurred. To some extent, an agency is restricted by constitutional limitations in inspecting premises and requiring the production of papers. These limitations, however, have a very narrow application in agency actions. When an agency acts as a judge, a jury trial is not required, nor must ordinary courtroom procedures be followed. Typically, an agency gives notice to the person claimed to be acting improperly, and a hearing is then held before the agency. When the agency has determined that there has been a violation, it may order that the violation stop. Under some statutes, the agency may go further and impose a penalty on the violator.

An appeal to a court may be taken from any decision of an agency by a person harmed by the decision. Only a person with a legally recognized interest can appeal from the agency ruling. No appeal can be made until every step available before the agency has been taken; that is, the administrative remedy must first be exhausted. An agency's actions can be reversed by a court if the agency exceeded its authority, the decision is not based in law or fact, the decision is arbitrary and capricious, or, finally, the agency violated procedural steps.

Protection from secret government is provided by Sunshine laws that afford the right to know what most administrative agency records contain; by the requirement that most agency meetings be open to the public; by the invitation to the public to take part in rulemaking; and by publicity given, through publication in the *Federal Register* and trade publications, to the guidelines followed by the agency and the regulations it has adopted.

Questions and Case Problems

1. Following the events of September 11, 2001, in which four airplanes crashed as a result of the presence of terrorists on those flights, the FAA concluded that it needed to implement new procedures for airports and flights. The new procedures for security and flights took effect when the airports reopened five days later. Why did the FAA not need to go through the promulgation and public comment processes and time periods to have the new rules take effect?

2. Reserve Mining Co. obtained a permit from the Minnesota Pollution Control Agency to dump wastewater into the nearby Beaver River. The permit specified that no more than 1 million fibers per liter could be discharged in the company's wastewater. The agency did not make or file any explanation as to how or why that maximum was selected. Normally, the wastewater that the company generated was kept in a tailings dam with a discharge in the river necessary only in an emergency. Because of a sudden economic downturn, the company foresaw the need to dispose of wastewater in the river and discovered that the discharge it would have to make would likely be between 10 to 15 times the amount of fiber allowed by the permit. Reserve Mining appealed the maximum limitation imposed by the agency. How could Reserve Mining challenge the 1-million-fibers standard? [*Reserve Mining Co. v Minnesota Pollution Control Agency*, 364 NW2d 411 (Minn App)]

3. The Tacoma-Pierce County Health Department conducted an investigation into the quality of care provided by ambulance service providers in its jurisdiction. On the basis of that investigation, the department issued a set of temporary rules and regulations that established minimum requirements for equipment, drugs, and service availability for ambulance service providers in Pierce County. The *Tacoma News* wanted to publish an article on the matter and sought discovery of everything that had led to the adoption of the regulations, including all details of the investigation made by the health department. The health department objected to disclosing the names of the persons who had volunteered information on which the department had based its action and the names of the ambulance companies. Were the names subject to a Freedom of Information Act (FOIA) request? [*Tacoma News, Inc. v Tacoma-Pierce County Health Dept.*, 778 P2d 1066 (Wash App)]

4. Congress adopted a law to provide insurance to protect wheat farmers. The agency in charge of the program adopted regulations to govern applications for this insurance. These regulations were published in the *Federal Register*. Merrill applied for insurance, but his application did not comply with the regulations. He claimed that he was not bound by the regulations because he never knew they had been adopted. Is he bound by the regulations? [*Federal Crop Ins. Corp. v Merrill*, 332 US 380]

5. Santa Monica adopted a rent control ordinance authorizing the Rent Control Board to set the amount of rents that could be charged. At a hearing before it, the board determined that McHugh was charging his tenants a rent higher than the maximum allowed. McHugh claimed

that the action of the board was improper because there was no jury trial. Is McHugh correct? Why or why not? [*McHugh v Santa Monica Rent Control Board*, 49 Cal 3d 348, 777 P2d 91]

6. New York City's charter authorized the New York City Board of Health to adopt a health code that it declared to have the force and effect of law. The board adopted a code that provided for the fluoridation of the public water supply. A suit was brought to enjoin the carrying out of this program on the grounds that it was unconstitutional and that money could not be spent to carry out such a program in the absence of a statute authorizing the expenditure. It was also claimed that the fluoridation program was unconstitutional because there were other means of reducing tooth decay; fluoridation was discriminatory by benefiting only children; it unlawfully imposed medication on children without their consent; and fluoridation was or may be dangerous to health. Was the code's provision valid? [*Paduano v City of New York*, 257 NYS2d 531]
7. What is the *Federal Register?* What role does it play in rulemaking?
8. The Consumer Product Safety Commission is reconsidering a rule it first proposed in 1997 that would require child-resistant caps on household products, including cosmetics. When the rule was first proposed in 1997, it was resisted by the cosmetics industry and abandoned. However, in May 2001, a 16-month-old baby died after drinking baby oil from a bottle with a pull-tab cap.

   The proposed rule would cover products such as baby oil and suntan lotion and any products containing hydrocarbons such as cleansers and spot removers. The danger, according to the commission, is simply the inhalation for children, not necessarily the actual ingestion of the products. Five children have died from inhaling such fumes since 1993, and 6,400 children under the age of 5 were brought into emergency rooms and/or hospitalized for treatment after breathing in hydrocarbons. There is no medical treatment for the inhalation of hydrocarbons.

   Several companies in the suntan oil/lotion industry have supported the new regulations. The head of a consumer group has said, "We know these products cause death and injury. That is all we need to know."[35]

   What process must the CPSC follow to promulgate the rules? What do you think of the consumer group head's statement? Will that statement alone justify the rulemaking?
9. The *Federal Register* contained the following provision from the Environmental Protection Agency on January 14, 2002:

   We, the U.S. Fish and Wildlife Service (Service), announce the re-opening of the comment period on the proposed listing of Lomatium cookii *(Cook's lomatium) and* Limnanthes floccosa ssp. grandiflora *(large-flowered wooly meadowfoam) as endangered species under the Endangered Species Act of 1973, as amended (Act). We are re-opening the comment period to provide the public an opportunity to review additional information on the status, abundance, and distribution of these plants, and to request additional information and comments from the public regarding the proposed rule. Comments previously submitted need not be resubmitted as they will be incorporated into the public record as part of this extended comment period; all comments will be fully considered in the final rule.*

   DATES: We will accept public comments until March 15, 2002.

   What was the EPA doing and why? What could those who had concerns do at that point?
10. Macon County Landfill Corp. applied for permission to expand the boundaries of its landfill. Tate and others opposed the application. After a number of hearings, the appropriate agency granted the requested permission to expand. Tate appealed and claimed that the agency had made a wrong decision on the basis of the evidence presented. Will the court determine whether the correct decision was made? [*Tate v Illinois Pollution Control Board*, 188 Ill App 3d 994, 544 NE2d 1176]
11. The planning commissioner and a real estate developer planned to meet to discuss rezoning certain land that would permit the real estate developer to construct certain buildings not allowed under the then-existing zoning law. A homeowners association claimed it had the right to be present at the meeting. This claim was objected to on the theory that the state's Open Meetings Act applied only to meetings of specified government units and did not extend to a meeting between one of them and an outsider. Was this objection valid?
12. The Michigan Freedom of Information Act declares that it is the state's policy to give all persons full information about the actions of the government and that "the people shall be informed so that they may participate in the democratic process." The union of clerical workers at Michigan State University requested the trustees of the university to give them the names and addresses of persons making monetary donations to the university. Michigan State objected because the disclosure of addresses was a violation of the right of privacy. Decide. [*Clerical-Technical Union of Michigan State University v Board of Trustees of Michigan State University*, 475 NW2d 373 (Mich)]
13. The Department of Health and Human Services has proposed new guidelines for the interpretation of federal statutes on gifts, incentives, and other benefits bestowed on physicians by pharmaceutical

[35] Julian E. Barnes, "Safety Caps Are Considered for Cosmetics," *New York Times*, October 10, 2001, C1, C8.

companies. The areas on which the interpretation focused follow:

- Paying doctors to act as consultants or market researchers for prescription drugs
- Paying pharmacies fees to switch patients to new drugs
- Providing grants, scholarships, and anything more than nominal gifts to physicians for time, information sessions, and so on, on new drugs[36]

The Office of Inspector General is handling the new rules interpretation and has established a public comment period of 60 days. Explain the purpose of the public comment period. What ethical issues do the regulations attempt to address?

14. A state law authorized the state's insurance commissioner to impose a fine and suspend the license of any insurance agent selling "unnecessary or excessive" insurance. The insurance commissioner fined Eloise, a licensed agent, $600 and suspended her license for three months for selling "unnecessary and excessive" insurance. She objected to this action on the ground that the statute under which the commissioner acted did not have any definitive meaning and the agency did not have the authority to define the term "unnecessary or excessive." Decide whether the agency had authority.
15. The Endangered Species Act (ESA) charges the National Marine Fisheries Service (a federal agency) with the duty to "ensure" that any proposed action by the Council does not "jeopardize" any threatened or endangered species. The Steller sea lion is on the list of endangered species. The agency developed a North Pacific marine fishery plan that permitted significant harvest of fish by commercial fisheries in the area. Greenpeace, an environmental group, challenged the agency on the grounds that the plan was not based on a sufficient number of biological studies on the impact of the allowed fishing on the Steller sea lion. Greenpeace's biologic opinion concluded that the fishery plan would reduce the level of food for the sea lions by about 40% to 60%, if the juvenile fish were not counted in that figure. Greenpeace's expert maintained that counting juvenile fish was misleading because they were not capable of reproducing and the government agency's figure was, as a result, much lower at 22%. What would Greenpeace need to show to be successful in challenging the agency's fishery plan? [*Greenpeace, American Oceans Campaign v National Marine Fisheries Service*, 237 F Supp 2d 1181 (W.D.Wash)]

[36] See 67 *Federal Register* 62057, October 3, 2002. Go to **http://www.oig.hhs.gov**. See also Robert Pear, "U.S. Warning to Drug Makers Over Payments," *New York Times*, October 1, 2002, A1, A23; Julie Appleby, "Feds Warn Drugmakers: Gifts to Doctors May Be Illegal," *USA Today*, October 2, 2002, 1A.

THE LEGAL ENVIRONMENT OF INTERNATIONAL TRADE

CHAPTER (7)

LEARNING OBJECTIVES

After studying this chapter, you should be able to

LO.1 Identify seven major international organizations, conferences, and treaties

LO.2 Describe the forms of business organizations that exist for doing business abroad

LO.3 Identify conduct outside the United States to which the U.S. antitrust laws will apply

LO.4 Differentiate between secrecy laws and blocking laws in regard to SEC enforcement of U.S. securities laws

LO.5 List and explain the laws that provide protection against unfair competition from foreign goods

LO.6 List and explain the laws that provide economic relief for those adversely affected by import competition

LO.7 List and explain the laws enacted to increase the foreign sales of U.S. firms

The success or failure of the U.S. firms doing business in foreign countries may well depend on accurate information about the laws and customs of the host countries. In their domestic operations, U.S. business firms compete against imports from other nations. Such imported goods include Canadian lumber, Mexican machinery, Japanese automobiles, German steel, French wine, Chinese textiles, and Chilean copper. To compete effectively, U.S. firms should learn about the business practices of foreign firms. They should be alert to unfair trade practices that will put U.S. firms at a disadvantage. Such practices may include the violation of U.S. antitrust and antidumping laws or violation of international trade agreements. Individuals from all over the world participate in the U.S. securities markets. Special problems exist in the regulation and enforcement of U.S. securities laws involving financial institutions of countries with secrecy laws.

A. General Principles

Nations enter into treaties and conferences to further international trade. The business world has developed certain forms of organizations for conducting that trade.

1. The Legal Background

Because of the complexity and ever-changing character of the legal environment of international trade, this section will focus on certain underlying elements.

(a) What Law Applies

When there is a sale of goods within the United States, one law typically applies to the transaction. Some variation may be introduced when the transaction is between parties in different states, but for the most part, the law governing the transaction is the U.S. law of contracts and the Uniform Commercial Code (UCC). In contrast, when an international contract is made, it is necessary to determine whether it is the law of the seller's country or the law of the importer's country that will govern. The parties to an international contract often resolve that question themselves as part of their contract, setting forth which country's law will govern should a dispute arise. Such a provision is called a **choice-of-law clause**. **For Example,** U.S. investors Irmgard and Mitchell Lipcon provided capital to underwriters at Lloyd's of London and signed choice-of-law clauses in their investment agreements binding them to proceed in England under English law should disputes arise. When the Lipcons realized that their investments were exposed to massive liabilities for asbestos and pollution insurance claims, they sued in U.S. district court in Florida for alleged U.S. securities acts violations. However, their complaints were dismissed based on the choice-of-law clauses in their contracts. The U.S. court of appeals stated that the Lipcons must "honor their bargains" and attempt to vindicate their claims in English courts under English law.[1]

The major trading countries of the world have entered into a number of treaties. When their citizens deal with each other and their respective rights are not controlled in their contract, their rights and liabilities are determined by looking at the treaty. These treaties are discussed in Section 7 of this chapter, including the United Nations Convention on Contracts for the International Sale of Goods (CISG), which deals with certain aspects of the formation and performance of international commercial contracts for the sale of goods.

(b) The Arbitration Alternative

Traditional litigation may be considered too time consuming, expensive, and divisive to the relationships of the parties to an international venture. The parties, therefore, may agree to arbitrate any contractual disputes that may arise according to dispute resolution procedures set forth in the contract.

Pitfalls exist for U.S. companies arbitrating disputes in foreign lands. **For Example,** were a U.S. company to agree to arbitrate a contractual dispute with a Chinese organization in China, it would find that the arbitrator must be Chinese. Also, under Chinese law, only Chinese lawyers can present an arbitration case, even if one party is a U.S. company. Because of situations like this, it is common for parties to international ventures to agree to arbitrate their disputes in neutral countries.

An arbitration agreement gives the parties more control over the decision-making process. The parties can require that the arbitrator have the technical, language, and legal qualifications to best understand their dispute. While procedures exist for the prearbitration exchange of documents, full "discovery"

[1] *Lipcon v Underwriters at Lloyd's, London,* 148 F2d 1285, 1299 (11th Cir 1998).

is ordinarily not allowed. The decision of the arbitrator is final and binding on the parties with very limited judicial review possible.

(c) Conflicting Ideologies

Law, for all people and at all times, is the result of the desire of the lawmaker to achieve certain goals. These are the social forces that make the law. In the eyes of the lawmaker, the attainment of these goals is proper and therefore ethical. This does not mean that we all can agree on what the international law should be because different people have different ideas as to what is right. This affects our views as to ownership, trade, and dealings with foreign merchants. **For Example,** a very large part of the world does not share the U.S. dislike of trusts. Other countries do not have our antitrust laws; therefore, their merchants can form a trust to create greater bargaining power in dealing with U.S. and other foreign merchants.

(d) Financing International Trade

There is no international currency. This creates problems as to what currency to use and how to make payment in international transactions. Centuries ago, buyers used precious metals, jewels, or furs in payment. Today, the parties to an international transaction agree in their sales contract on the currency to be used to pay for the goods. They commonly require that the buyer furnish the seller a **letter of credit,** which is a commercial device used to guarantee payment to a seller in an international transaction. By this, an issuer, typically a bank, agrees to pay the drafts drawn against the buyer for the purchase price. In trading with merchants in some countries, the foreign country itself will promise that the seller will be paid.

2. International Trade Organizations, Conferences, and Treaties

A large number of organizations exist that affect the multinational markets for goods, services, and investments. A survey of major international organizations, conferences, and treaties follows.

(a) GATT and WTO

The *General Agreement on Tariffs and Trade* 1994 (GATT 1994) is a multilateral treaty subscribed to by 126 member governments, including the United States.[2] It consists of the original 1947 GATT, numerous multilateral agreements negotiated since 1947, the Uruguay Round Agreements, and the agreement establishing the *World Trade Organization* (WTO). On January 1, 1995, the WTO took over responsibility for policing the objectives of the former GATT organization. Since 1947 and the end of the World War II era, the goal of the GATT has been to liberalize world trade and make it secure for furthering economic growth and human development. The current round of WTO negotiations began in Doha, Qatar, in 2001. As the talks continued in Cancun in 2003, the developed countries and developing countries divided on key issues such as agricultural subsidies. The Doha Round continues in an effort to meet the WTO's objectives of liberalizing world trade.

The GATT is based on the fundamental principles of (1) trade without discrimination and (2) protection through tariffs. The principle of trade without discrimination is embodied in its **most-favored-nation clause**. In treaties between countries, a most-favored-nation clause is one whereby any privilege subsequently granted to a third country in relation to a given treaty subject is extended to the other party to the treaty. In the application and administration of import and export duties and charges under the GATT most-favored-nation clause, all member countries grant each other equal treatment. Thus, no country gives special trading advantages to another. All member countries are equal and share the benefits of any moves toward lower trade barriers. Exceptions to this basic rule are allowed in certain special circumstances involving regional trading arrangements, such as the European Union (EU) and the North American Free Trade Agreement (NAFTA). Special preferences are also granted to developing countries. The second basic principle is protection for domestic industry, which should be extended essentially through a tariff, not through other commercial measures. The aim of this rule is to make the extent of protection clear and to make competition possible.

[2] Russia has applied to join the GATT and is in the final phase of accession to the World Trade Organization. However, to attain this goal, it is widely accepted that Russia will have to provide meaningful market access to member countries in goods and services and have a solid legal and administrative framework that will guarantee the implementation of contractual commitments.

The WTO provides a **Dispute Settlement Body (DSB)** to enable member countries to resolve trade disputes rather than engage in unilateral trade sanctions or a trade war. The DSB appoints panels to hear disputes concerning allegations of GATT agreement violations, and it adopts (or rejects) the panels' decisions. If a GATT agreement violation is found and not removed by the offending country, trade sanctions authorized by a panel may be imposed on that country in an amount equal to the economic injury caused by the violation.

(b) CISG

The *United Nations Convention on Contracts for the International Sale of Goods* (CISG or convention) sets forth uniform rules to govern international sales contracts. National law, however, is sometimes required to fill gaps in areas not covered by the CISG. The CISG became effective on January 1, 1988, between the United States and the 60 other nations that had approved it.[3] The provisions of the CISG have been strongly influenced by Article 2 of the UCC.

However, as set forth in Chapter 23 on sales, several distinct differences exist between the convention and the UCC. Excluded from the coverage of the convention under Article 2 are the sale of goods for personal, family, or household uses and the sale of watercraft, aircraft, natural gas, or electricity; letters of credit; and auctions and securities.[4] The CISG is often viewed by foreign entities as a neutral body of law, the utilization of which can be a positive factor in successfully concluding negotiations of a contract. The parties to an international commercial contract may opt out of the convention. However, absent an express "opt-out provision," the CISG is controlling and preempts all state actions.

(c) UNCTAD

The *United Nations Conference on Trade and Development* (UNCTAD) represents the interests of the less developed countries. Its prime objective is the achievement of an international redistribution of income through trade. Through UNCTAD pressure, the developed countries agreed to a system of preferences, with quota limits, for manufactured imports from the developing countries.

(d) EU

The *European Economic Community* (EEC) was established in 1958 by the Treaty of Rome to remove trade and economic barriers between member countries and to unify their economic policies. It changed its name and became the *European Union* (EU) after the Treaty of Maastricht was ratified on November 1, 1993. The Treaty of Rome containing the governing principles of this regional trading group was signed by the original six nations of Belgium, France, West Germany, Italy, Luxembourg, and the Netherlands. Membership expanded by the entry of Denmark, Ireland, and Great Britain in 1973; Greece in 1981; Spain and Portugal in 1986; and Austria, Sweden, and Finland in 1995. Ten countries joined the EU in 2004: Cyprus, the Czech Republic, Estonia, Hungary, Latvia, Lithuania, Malta, Poland, Slovakia, and Slovenia. Bulgaria, Romania, Croatia, and Turkey expect to join in the coming years.

Four main institutions make up the formal structure of the EU. The first, the European Council, consists of the heads of state of the member countries. The council sets broad policy guidelines for the EU. The second, the European Commission, implements decisions of the council and initiates actions against individuals, companies, or member states that violate EU law. The third, the European Parliament, has an advisory legislative role with limited veto powers. The fourth, the European Court of Justice (ECJ) and the lower Court of First Instance make up the judicial arm of the EU. The courts of member states may refer cases involving questions on the EU treaty to these courts.

The Single European Act eliminated internal barriers to the free movement of goods, persons, services, and capital between EU countries. The Treaty on European Union, signed in Maastricht, Netherlands (the Maastricht Treaty), amended the Treaty of Rome with a focus on monetary and political union. It set goals for the EU of (1) single monetary and fiscal policies, (2) common foreign and security policies, and (3) cooperation in justice and home affairs.

[3] 52 Fed Reg 6262 (1987). As of October 2006, the contracting nations were Argentina, Australia, Austria, Belarus, Belgium, Bosnia and Herzegovina, Bulgaria, Byelorussian Republic, Canada, Chile, China, Cuba, Czech Republic, Denmark, Ecuador, Egypt, Estonia, Finland, France, Georgia, Germany, Greece, Guinea, Hungary, Iraq, Israel, Italy, Latavia, Lesotho, Lithuania, Luxembourg, Mexico, Moldavia, Mongolia, the Netherlands, New Zealand, Norway, Peru, Poland, Romania, Russian Federation, Singapore, Slovakia, Slovenia, Spain, Sweden, Switzerland, Syria, Uganda, Ukraine, United States, Uruguay, Uzbekistan, Venezuela, Yugoslavia, and Zambia. Ratification proceedings are presently under way in other countries.

[4] CISG art. 2(a)–(f).

E-COMMERCE AND CYBERLAW

GLOBAL FACILITATION OF ELECTRONIC CONTRACTS AND TRANSACTIONS

Under the Electronic Signatures in Global and National Commerce Act of 2000 (E-Sign), the Secretary of Commerce is directed to promote the use of electronic signatures on an international basis by (1) removing paper-based obstacles to electronic transactions by adopting relevant principles from the Model Law on Electronic Commerce adopted in 1996 by the UN Commission on International Trade Law; (2) permitting parties to a transaction to choose their own appropriate authentication technologies; and (3) permitting these parties to prove in court or other proceedings that their authentication approaches and their transactions are valid.

(e) NAFTA

The *North American Free Trade Agreement* (NAFTA) is an agreement between Mexico, Canada, and the United States, effective January 1, 1994, that included Mexico in the arrangements previously initiated under the United States–Canada Free Trade Agreement of 1989. NAFTA eliminates all tariffs among the three countries over a 15-year period. Side agreements exist to prevent the exploitation of Mexico's lower environmental and labor standards.

Products are qualified for NAFTA tariff preferences only if they originate in one or more of the three member countries. Documentation is required in a NAFTA *Certificate of Origin*, except for certain "low-value" items for which the statement of North American origin is recorded on an invoice. NAFTA ensures nondiscriminatory and open markets for a wide range of services and lowers barriers to U.S. investments in both Canada and Mexico. Although NAFTA does not create a common labor market, as does the European Union, the agreement provides temporary access for businesspersons across borders.

The *DaimlerChrysler* decision is an example of the interrelationship of the manufacturing and assembly process between the U.S. and Mexico and the tariff preferences when the finished goods are shipped back to the U.S. for sale.

DAIMLERCHRYSLER CORP. V U.S., 361 F3D 1378 (FED CIR 2004)

A REASON TO ASSEMBLE CARS IN MEXICO?

DaimlerChrysler assembles trucks in Mexico utilizing sheet metal components manufactured in the United States. The sheet metal is subject to painting in Mexico, consisting of primer coats followed by a color-treated coat and a clear coat, referred to as the *top coats*. After the assembly is completed, the trucks are shipped to and sold in the United States. The U.S. Customs Service believes the top coats are subject to duty payments. DaimlerChrysler asserts that the entire painting process is duty free. Subheading 9802.00.80 of the Harmonized Tariff Schedule of the U.S. (HTSUS) provides duty-free treatment for:

> *Articles . . . assembled abroad in whole or in part of fabricated components, the product of the United States, which (a) were exported in condition ready for assembly without further fabrication, (b) have not lost their physical identity in such articles by change in form, shape or otherwise, and (c) have not been advanced in value or improved in condition abroad except by being assembled and except by operations incidental to the assembly process such as cleaning, lubricating and* ***painting****. (emphasis added by the court)*

From a judgment by the Court of International Trade in favor of the United States, DaimlerChrysler appealed.

Judicial Opinion

PROST, C. J.... [T]he United States Supreme Court addressed the application and interpretation of HTSUS 9802.00.80 in *Haggar I*.... In answering that question in the affirmative, the Court specifically considered HTSUS 9802.00.80 and noted that it established two different categories of operations incidental to assembly—one specific and unambiguous and the other general and ambiguous. "The statute under which respondent claims an exemption gives direction not only by stating a general policy (to grant the partial exemption where only assembly and incidental operations were abroad) but also by determining some specifics of the policy (finding that painting, for example, is incidental to assembly)." *Haggar I*, 526 U.S. at 393...

On appeal, DaimlerChrysler primarily argues that the Supreme Court's analysis in *Haggar I* provides that painting, without limitation, is an operation incidental to assembly. By using the term "painting" generally to describe a category of incidental operations, DaimlerChrysler argues, Congress unambiguously intended to include all painting, regardless of purpose. Because Customs' regulation regarding painting therefore conflicts with the clear statutory language, DaimlerChrysler continues, the Court of International Trade erred as a matter of law in applying this regulation so as to deny DaimlerChrysler a partial duty exemption...

The government counters that the statute cannot be read to cover all painting, only painting incidental to assembly. It argues that DaimlerChrysler reads too much into the Supreme Court's statements regarding painting in *Haggar I*, which are simply dicta....

We agree with DaimlerChrysler that the Supreme Court in *Haggar I* determined generally that painting is incidental to the assembly process. In order to qualify for the duty exemption, subheading 9802.00.80 requires that articles not be "advanced in value or improved in condition abroad except by being assembled and except by operations incidental to the assembly process such as cleaning, lubricating and *painting*." HTSUS 9802.00.80 (emphasis added). For purposes of interpreting subheading 9802.00.80, the Court in *Haggar I* found that it established both an unambiguous category and an ambiguous category of operations incidental to assembly. As noted, subheading 9802.00.80 "determin[es] some specifics of the policy (finding that *painting*, for example, *is incidental to assembly*)." *Haggar I*, 526 U.S. at 393, 119 S.Ct. 1392 (emphases added). Moreover, the Court concluded that subheading 9802.00.80 is "ambiguous in that the agency must use its discretion to determine how best to implement the policy *in those cases not covered by the statute's specific terms.*" *Id.* (emphasis added)....

... Because subheading 9802.00.80 unambiguously covers painting operations broadly, DaimlerChrysler's entire painting process, including the application of the tops coats, qualifies for the partial duty exemption....

[Reversed]

Case Questions

1. What is the question at issue in this case?
2. How did the Court of Appeals decide the case?
3. Discuss the advantages and disadvantages regarding the U.S. economy and employment issues regarding USTSUS 9802.00.80.

(f) Regional Trading Groups of Developing Countries

In recent years, numerous trading arrangements between groups of developing countries have been established.

(g) IMF—World Bank

The *International Monetary Fund* (IMF) was created after World War II by a group of nations meeting in Bretton Woods, New Hampshire. The Articles of Agreement of the IMF state that its purpose is "to facilitate the expansion and balanced growth of international trade" and to "shorten the duration and lessen the disequilibrium in the international balance of payments of members." The IMF helps to achieve such purposes by administering a complex lending system. A country can borrow money from other IMF members or from the IMF by means of **special drawing rights (SDRs)** sufficient to permit that country to maintain the stability of its currency's relationship to other world currencies. The Bretton Woods conference also set up the *International Bank for Reconstruction and Development* (World Bank) to facilitate the lending of money by capital surplus countries—such as the United States—to countries needing economic help and wanting foreign investments after World War II.

(h) OPEC

The *Organization of Petroleum Exporting Countries* (OPEC) is a producer cartel or combination. One of its main goals was to raise the taxes and royalties earned from crude oil production. Another major goal was to take control over production and exploration from the major oil companies. Its early success in attaining these goals led other nations that export raw materials to form similar cartels. **For Example,** copper and bauxite-producing nations have formed cartels.

3. Forms of Business Organizations

The decision to participate in international business transactions and the extent of that participation depend on the financial position of the individual firm, production and marketing factors, and tax and legal considerations. There are a number of forms of business organizations for doing business abroad.

(a) Export Sales

A direct sale to customers in a foreign country is an **export sale.** A U.S. firm engaged in export selling is not present in the foreign country in such an arrangement. The export is subject to a tariff by the foreign country, but the exporting firm is not subject to local taxation by the importing country.

(b) Agency Requirements

A U.S. manufacturer may decide to make a limited entry into international business by appointing an agent to represent it in a foreign market. An **agent** is a person or firm with authority to make contracts on behalf of another—the **principal**. The agent will receive commission income for sales made on behalf of the U.S. principal. The appointment of a foreign agent commonly constitutes "doing business" in that country and subjects the U.S. firm to local taxation.

(c) Foreign Distributorships

A **distributor** takes title to goods and bears the financial and commercial risks for the subsequent sale. To avoid making a major financial investment, a U.S. firm may decide to appoint a foreign distributor. A U.S. firm may also appoint a foreign distributor to avoid managing a foreign operation with its complicated local business, legal, and labor conditions. Care is required in designing an exclusive distributorship for an EU country lest it would violate EU antitrust laws.

(d) Licensing

U.S. firms may select licensing as a means of doing business in other countries. **Licensing** involves the transfer of technology rights in a product so that it may be produced by a different business organization in a foreign country in exchange for royalties and other payments as agreed. The technology being licensed may fall within the internationally recognized categories of patents, trademarks, and "know-how" (trade secrets and unpatented manufacturing processes outside the public domain). These intellectual property rights, which are legally protectable, may be licensed separately or incorporated into a single, comprehensive licensing contract. **Franchising,** which involves granting permission to use a trademark, trade name, or copyright under specified conditions, is a form of licensing that is now very common in international business.

(e) Wholly Owned Subsidiaries

A firm seeking to maintain control over its own operations, including the protection of its own technological expertise, may choose to do business abroad through a wholly owned subsidiary. In Europe the most common choice of foreign business organization, similar to the U.S. corporate form of business organization, is called the *societé anonyme* (S.A.). In German-speaking countries, this form is called *Aktiengesellschaft* (A.G.). Small and medium-sized companies in Europe now utilize a newly created form of business organization called the limited liability company (*Gesellschaft mit beschränkter Haftung,* or "GmbH" in Germany; *Società a responsabilità limitata,* or "S.r.l." in Spain). It is less complicated to form but is restrictive for accessing public capital markets.

A corporation doing business in more than one country poses many taxation problems for the governments in those countries where the firm does business. The United States has established tax treaties with many countries granting corporations relief from double taxation. Credit is normally given by the United States to U.S. corporations for taxes paid to foreign governments.

There is a potential for tax evasion by U.S. corporations from their selling goods to their overseas subsidiaries. Corporations could sell goods at less than the fair market value to avoid a U.S. tax on the full profit for such sales. By allowing the foreign subsidiaries located in countries with lower tax rates to make higher profits, a company as a whole would minimize its taxes. Section 482 of the Internal Revenue Code (IRC), however, allows the Internal Revenue Service (IRS) to reallocate the income between the parent and its foreign subsidiary. The parent corporation is insulated from such a reallocation if it can show, based on independent transactions with unrelated parties, that its charges were at arm's length.[5]

(f) Joint Ventures

A U.S. manufacturer and a foreign entity may form a **joint venture,** whereby the two firms agree to perform different functions for a common result. The responsibilities and liabilities of such operations are governed by contract. **For Example,** Hughes Aircraft Co. formed a joint venture with two Japanese firms, C. Itoh & Co. and Mitsui, and successfully bid on a telecommunications space satellite system for the Japanese government.

China has two forms of joint ventures: a *contract joint venture,* which allows the parties to operate as separate entities governed by a contract, and an *equity joint venture* whereby each party owns a portion of the business. Such an arrangement is governed by the Chinese Foreign Equity Joint Venture Law. This law requires a Chinese limited liability company to be formed and requires the foreign participant to contribute at least 25 percent of the firm's capital.

B. Governmental Regulation

Nations regulate trade to protect the economic interests of their citizens or to protect themselves in international relations and transactions.

4. Export Regulations

For reasons of national security, foreign policy, or short supply of certain domestic products, the United States controls the export of goods and technology. The Export Administration Act[6] imposes export controls on goods and technical data from the United States. Since April 2002, the Bureau of Industry and Security (BIS) of the Department of Commerce has issued Export Administration Regulations to enforce export controls.

Export Administration Regulations effective in 1996 simplify the process and enhance export trade by U.S. citizens.[7] The new regulations eliminate the former system of general and validated licenses under which every export required a license. Under the 1996 *Simplification Regulations,* no license is required unless the regulations affirmatively require a license. However, when no license is required, the exporter must fill out a Shipper's Export Declaration and attach it to the bill of lading for shipment with the goods being exported.

(a) Determining If a License Is Needed

To determine whether a product requires a BIS export license, the exporter should review the Commerce Control List (CCL) to see whether the product to be exported is listed. Listed products have Export Control Classification Numbers (ECCNs) that conform to those used by the EU. If a product is on the list, the ECCN code will provide the reason for control, such as national security, missile technology, nuclear nonproliferation, chemical and/or biological weapons, antiterrorism, crime control, short supply, or UN sanctions.[8] The exporter should then consult the Commerce Country Chart to determine whether a license is needed to send the product to its proposed destination. **For Example,** domestic crude petroleum products and western red cedar are on the Commerce Control List because of the "short supply" of these products. As a result, they are controlled to all destinations, and no reference to the Commerce Country Chart is necessary.

(b) Sanctions

Export licenses are required for the export of certain high-technology and military products. **For Example,** a company intending to ship "maraging 350 steel" to a user in Pakistan would find by checking the CCL and the ECCN code for the product that such steel is used in making high-technology products and has nuclear applications. Thus, an export license would be required. Because Pakistan is a nonsignatory nation of the Nuclear Non-Proliferation Treaty, the

[5] *Bausch & Lomb Inc. v Commissioner,* 933 F2d 1084 (2d Cir 1991).

[6] The Export Administration Act of 1979 expired in August 1994 and was extended by Executive Orders signed by Presidents Clinton and G. W. Bush. The EAA is now extended annually by presidential notice published in the *Federal Register.*

[7] Simplification of Export Regulations, 61 Fed Reg 12,714 (1996).

[8] *Id.*

Department of Commerce would be expected to deny a license application for the use of this steel in a nuclear plant. However, a license to export this steel for the manufacture of high-speed turbines or compressors might be approved. The prospective purchaser must complete a "Statement of Ultimate Consignee and Purchaser" form with the application for an export license. The prospective purchaser must identify the "end use" for the steel and indicate where the purchaser is located and the location in Pakistan where a U.S. embassy official can make an on-site inspection of the product's use. Falsification of the information in the license application process is a criminal offense. Thus, if the exporter of maraging 350 steel asserted that it was to be used in manufacturing high-speed turbines when in fact the exporter knew it was being purchased for use in a nuclear facility, the exporter would be guilty of a criminal offense.[9]

Civil charges may also be brought against U.S. manufacturers who fail to obtain an export license for foreign sales of civilian items that contain any components that have military applications under the Arms Control Export Act. **For Example,** between 2000 and 2003, Boeing Co. shipped overseas 94 commercial jets that carried a gyrochip used as a backup system in determining a plane's orientation in the air. This 2-ounce chip that costs less than $2,000 also has military applications and can be used to stabilize and steer guided missiles. Boeing is asserted to have made false statements on shipping documents to get around the export restrictions. Boeing argued that the State Department is without legal authority to regulate its civilian rather than military items. However, Boeing agreed to pay a $15 million fine for the violations.[10]

(c) Expert Assistance

The Department of Commerce's Exporter Assistance Staff provides assistance to exporters needing help in determining whether an export license is needed.[11] Licensed foreign-**freight forwarders** are in the business of handling the exporting of goods to foreign destinations. They are experts on U.S. Department of Commerce export license requirements. Licensed foreign-freight forwarders can attend to all of the essential arrangements required to transport a shipment of goods from the exporter's warehouse to the overseas buyer's specified port and inland destination. They are well versed in all aspects of ocean, air, and inland transportation as well as banking, marine insurance, and other services relating to exporting.

5. Protection of Intellectual Property Rights

U.S. laws protect **intellectual property rights,** which consist of trademarks, copyrights, and patents.

(a) Counterfeit Goods

The importation of counterfeit compact discs, tapes, computer software, and movies into the United States violates U.S. copyright laws. Importing goods, such as athletic shoes, jeans, or watches, bearing counterfeits of U.S. companies' registered trademarks violates the Lanham Act. Importing machines or devices that infringe on U.S. patents violates U.S. patent laws. A full range of remedies is available to U.S. firms under U.S. laws. Possible remedies include injunctive relief, seizure and destruction of counterfeit goods that are found in the United States, damages, and attorney fees. U.S. firms injured by counterfeit trademarks may recover triple damages from the counterfeiters.[12]

Intellectual property rights are also protected by international treaties, such as the Berne Convention, which protects copyrights; the Patent Cooperation Treaty, and the Madrid System of International Registration of Marks (the Madrid Protocol), a treaty providing for the international registration of marks applicable to more than 60 signatory countries, including the United States as of November 2003.[13]

(b) Gray Market Goods

A U.S. trademark holder may license a foreign business to use its trademark overseas. If a third party

[9] See *United States v Perez*, 871 F2d 310 (3d Cir 1989), on the criminal application of the Export Administration Regulations to an individual who stated a false end use for maraging 350 steel on his export application to ship this steel to Pakistan.

[10] Associated Press, "Boeing to Pay $15 Million Fine for Export of Military Technology," *The Boston Globe*, April 10, 2006, E3.

[11] Exporter Assistance Staff, U.S. Department of Commerce, Washington, DC 20230.

[12] 15 USC § 1117(b); *Nintendo of America v NTDEC*, 822 F Supp 1462 (D Ariz 1993).

[13] The Agreement on Trade-Related Aspects of Intellectual Property (TRIPS) is a WTO agreement that requires WTO members to adhere to certain treaties and guidelines in respecting copyright, trademark, and patent rights. Enforcement of such rights, however, varies, depending on national law.

imports these foreign-made goods into the United States to compete against the U.S. manufacturer's goods, the foreign-made goods are called **gray market goods**. The Tariff Act of 1930 prevents importation of foreign-made goods bearing a U.S. registered trademark owned by a U.S. firm unless the U.S. trademark owner gives written consent.[14] The Lanham Act may also be used to exclude gray market goods.[15]

A gray market situation also arises when foreign products made by affiliates of U.S. companies have trademarks identical to U.S. trademarks but the foreign products are physically different from the U.S. products.

In the *Lever Brothers* case, the U.S. trademark holder sought to exclude the importation of the foreign-made goods by third parties.

6. Antitrust

Antitrust laws exist in the United States to protect the U.S. consumer by ensuring the benefits of competitive products from foreign competitors as well as domestic competitors. Competitors' agreements designed to raise the price of imports or to exclude imports from our domestic markets in exchange for not competing in other countries are restraints of trade in violation of our antitrust laws.[16]

Antitrust laws also exist to protect U.S. export and investment opportunities against privately imposed restrictions, whereby a group of competitors seeks to exclude another competitor from a particular foreign market. Antitrust laws exist in other countries where U.S. firms compete. These laws are usually directed not at breaking up cartels to further competition but at regulating them in the national interest.

LEVER BROTHERS CO. V U.S., 796 F SUPP 1 (DC 1992)

BARRING IMPORTED SOAP!

Lever Brothers (Lever U.S.) manufactures a soap under the trademark Shield and a dishwashing liquid under the trademark Sunlight for sale in the United States. A British affiliate, Lever U.K., also makes products using the marks Shield and Sunlight. As a result of different preferences of U.S. and British consumers, the products of each country differ physically. Third parties imported the British products into the United States. Lever U.S. sought an injunction against the U.S. Customs Service, contending that Section 42 of the Lanham Act requires the Customs Service to bar these foreign products. The U.S. Customs Service contended that the products should be allowed to enter the United States under its affiliate exception.

Judicial Opinion

GREENE, D. J. ... Plaintiff, Lever U.S., is a wholly owned subsidiary of Unilever U.S., Inc., which in turn is wholly owned by Unilever N.V. A British company, Lever U.K., manufactures Shield and Sunlight, and holds the trademark for those words in the United Kingdom. Lever U.K. is a subsidiary of Unilever PLC. The two corporate parents, Unilever N.V. and Unilever PLC, are not under common ownership but are affiliated with one another and are under common control....

The Shield logos on the American and the British versions of the soap are virtually identical. The American product, however, is designed to produce more lather and contains an anti-bacteria agent absent from the British version. The two soaps are also perfumed and colored differently.

The two versions of Sunlight dishwashing detergent have similar lettering but the packaging is different. The detergents themselves are also quite different. The British product is designed for water with a mineral content higher than is generally found in the United States. It therefore does not perform as well as the American Sunlight in the "soft-water" typical of this country. Thus the trademarks of the American and British versions of the two products are identical but the products are physically different.

[14] 19 USC § 1526(1). The Copyright Act of 1976 may also apply to gray market goods. One provision of this act gives the copyright holder exclusive right to distribute copies of the copyrighted work. Still another section states that once a copyright owner sells an authorized copy of the work, subsequent owners may do what they like with it. The gray market issue occurs when U.S. manufacturers sell their products overseas at deep discounts, and other firms reimport the products back to the United States for resale. The Supreme Court held that a copyrighted label on the products would not protect a U.S. manufacturer's claim of unauthorized importation because the copyright owner's rights cease upon the original sale to the overseas buyer. *Quality King v L'Anza Research*, 118 S Ct 1125 (1998).

[15] *Bourdeau Bros. v International Trade Commission*, 444 F3d 1314 (Fed Cir 2006).

[16] *United States v Nippon Paper Industries Co. Ltd.*, 64 F Supp 2d 173 (1999).

Third parties have imported the British versions of the products into the United States without the consent of Lever U.S. or Lever U.K. The outward similarities and substantive differences of the American and British products created confusion and dissatisfaction on the part of American consumers who purchased the British products in the belief that they were purchasing the American version or not realizing that there were two different products under the same name.

This case focuses on interpretation of section 42 of the Lanham Act which states that:

no article of imported merchandise which shall copy or simulate the name of . . . any domestic manufacturer, . . . or which shall copy or simulate a trademark registered in accordance with the provisions of this chapter or shall bear a name or mark calculated to induce the public to believe that the article is manufactured in the United States, . . . shall be admitted to entry at any customhouse of the United States. . . .
15 U.S.C. § 1124 (1982) (emphasis added).

Lever U.S. argues that where a foreign company produces goods that bear the same trademark as a U.S. markholder but that are materially, physically different, the foreign product copies or simulates the domestic trademark within the meaning of section 42 even where the foreign manufacturer is affiliated with the domestic markholder. Defendants argue that a markholder cannot infringe, i.e., "copy or simulate," its own trademark, and that therefore the affiliation of Lever U.S. with Lever U.K. makes all the difference, placing this case outside the scope of section 42.

The Customs Service has permitted the British versions of the two products to enter the United States under its affiliate exception. Under the Customs Service regulation, foreign goods that bear a trademark identical to one owned and recorded by a United States corporation will not be seized by Customs, notwithstanding section 42 of the statute, if "the foreign and domestic trademark or trade name owners are parent and subsidiary companies or are otherwise subject to common ownership or control." 19 C.F.R. 133 (c) (2) (1988).

The Court of Appeals has come to the tentative conclusion that the Lanham Act bars "foreign goods bearing a trademark identical to a valid U.S. trademark but which are physically different, regardless of the trademarks' genuine character abroad or affiliation between the producing firms." *Lever Bros. Co. v. United States* . . . 877 F.2d at 111. However, as indicated, the appellate court remanded the case for consideration of the legislative history and the administrative practice.

Legislative History

The Court of Appeals regarded its reading of the language of section 42 as being "the natural, virtually inevitable" interpretation. . . . It is well established that where the statute is clear on its face and the legislative intent is expressed in "reasonably plain terms" by the text, the statutory language controls. . . .

Representative Fritz G. Lanham, the sponsor of the Act, explained that one purpose of the statute was "to protect the public so that it may be confident that, in purchasing a product bearing a particular trademark, which it favorably knows, it will get the product which it asks for and wants to get." H. R. Rep. No. 219 at 2, 79th Cong., 1st Sess. (February 26, 1945) U.S. Code Cong. Serv. 1946, p.1274. In this case, the outward similarities and physical differences between the British and American versions of Shield and Sunlight have already created consumer confusion and dissatisfaction, and they would be likely to do so again in the future. As the House Report on the Lanham Act stated, "Trademarks encourage the maintenance of quality by securing to the producer the benefit of the good reputation which excellence creates." H. R. No. 219 at 3, 1946 U.S. Code Cong. Serv. at 1274, 1275. Thus, the legislative goals of trademark law generally and of the Lanham Act specifically are served by the barring of goods such as those of the British company. . . .

Neither the legislative history of the statute nor the administrative practice of the Customs Service clearly contradicts the plain meaning of section 42. The Court therefore concludes that section 42 of the Lanham Act prohibits the importation of foreign goods that bear a trademark identical to a valid United States trademark but which are physically different, regardless of the validity of the foreign trademark or the existence of an affiliation between the U.S. and foreign markholders.

Plaintiff's motion for summary judgment will be granted and defendants' motion will be denied. . . .

[Judgment for Lever U.S.]

Questions

1. Why did Lever U.S. want to exclude the two British products?
2. What was the contention of the U.S. Customs Service?
3. Are the legislative goals of the Lanham Act, as expressed by Representative Lanham, served by barring the British soap products?

(a) Jurisdiction

In U.S. courts, the U.S. antitrust laws have a broad extraterritorial reach. Our antitrust laws must be reconciled with the rights of other interested countries as embodied in international law.

(1) The Effects Doctrine. Judge Learned Hand's decision in *United States v Alcoa*[17] established the **effects doctrine.** Under this doctrine, U.S. courts assume jurisdiction and apply the antitrust laws to conduct outside of the United States where the activity of the business firms outside the United States has a direct and substantial effect on U.S. commerce. This basic rule has been modified to require that the effect on U.S. commerce also be foreseeable.

(2) The Jurisdictional Rule of Reason. The jurisdictional rule of reason applies when conduct taking place outside the United States affects U.S. commerce but a foreign state also has a significant interest in regulating the conduct in question. The **jurisdictional rule of reason** balances the vital interests, including laws and policies, of the United States with those of the foreign country involved. This rule of reason is based on **comity,** a principle of international law, that means that the laws of all nations deserve the respect legitimately demanded by equal participants in international affairs.

(b) Defenses

Three defenses are commonly raised to the extraterritorial application of U.S. antitrust laws. These defenses are also commonly raised to attack jurisdiction in other legal actions involving international law.

(1) Act-of-State Doctrine. By the **act-of-state doctrine,** every sovereign state is bound to respect the independence of every other sovereign state, and the courts of one country will not sit in judgment of another government's acts done within its own territory.[18] The act-of-state doctrine is based on the judiciary's concern over its possible interference with the conduct of foreign relations. Such matters are considered to be political, not judicial, questions.

(2) The Sovereign Compliance Doctrine. The **sovereign compliance doctrine** allows a defendant to raise as an affirmative defense to an antitrust action the fact that the defendant's actions were compelled by a foreign state. To establish this defense, compulsion by the foreign government is required. The Japanese government uses informal and formal contacts within an industry to establish a consensus on a desired course of action. Such governmental action is not a defense for a U.S. firm, however, because the activity in question is not compulsory.

(3) The Sovereign Immunity Doctrine. The **sovereign immunity doctrine** states that a foreign sovereign generally cannot be sued unless an exception to the Foreign Sovereign Immunities Act of 1976 applies.[19] The most important exception covers the commercial conduct of a foreign state.[20] **For Example,** receivers for various insurance companies brought suit against the Vatican City State, contending that the Vatican's conduct fell within the commercial activity exception to the FSIA. Martin Frankel had engaged in a massive insurance fraud scheme, using front organizations to acquire and loot several insurance agencies. Masquerading as "David Rose," a philanthropist, he met Monsignor Emilio Cologiovani and convinced him to create a Vatican-affiliated entity, the St. Francis of Assisi Foundation (SFAF), which was used as part of Frankel's scam. The Court of Appeals held, however, that Cologiovani, acting with only apparent authority of the state, could not trigger the commercial activity doctrine.[21]

(c) Legislation

In response to business uncertainty as to when the antitrust laws apply to international transactions, Congress passed the Foreign Trade Antitrust Improvements Act of 1982. This act, in essence, codified the effects doctrine. The act requires a

[17] 148 F2d 416 (2d Cir 1945).

[18] *Underhill v Hernandez,* 108 US 250, 252 (1897).

[19] See *Verlinden B.V. v Central Bank of Nigeria,* 461 US 574 (1983).

[20] See *Dole Food Co. v Patrickson,* 123 S Ct 1655 (2003), for a limited discussion of when a foreign state can assert a defense of sovereign immunity under the Foreign Sovereign Immunities Act of 1976 (FSIA). The FSIA allows certain foreign-state commercial entities not entitled to sovereign immunity to have the merits of a case heard in federal court. The U.S. Supreme Court held in the *Dole Food* case that a foreign state must itself own a majority of the shares of a corporation if the corporation is to be deemed an instrumentality of the state under the FSIA, and the instrumentality status is determined at the time of the filing of the complaint.

[21] *Dale v Cologiovani,* 443 F3d 425 (5th Cir 2006).

direct, substantial, and reasonably foreseeable effect on U.S. domestic commerce or exports by U.S. residents before business conduct abroad may come within the purview of U.S. antitrust laws.[22]

(d) Foreign Antitrust Laws

Attitudes in different countries vary toward cartels and business combinations. Because of this, antitrust laws vary in content and application. **For Example,** Japan has stressed consumer protection against such practices as price-fixing and false advertising. However, with regard to mergers, stock ownership, and agreements among companies to control production, Japanese law is much less restrictive than U.S. law.

Europe is a major market for U.S. products, services, and investments. U.S. firms doing business in Europe are subject to the competition laws of the EU.[23] The Treaty of Rome uses the term *competition* rather than *antitrust*. Articles 85 and 86 of the Treaty of Rome set forth the basic regulation on business behavior in the EU.[24] Article 85(1) expressly prohibits agreements and concerted practices that

1. even indirectly fix prices of purchases or sales or fix any other trading conditions;
2. limit or control production, markets, technical development, or investment;
3. share markets or sources of supply;
4. apply unequal terms to parties furnishing equivalent considerations, thereby placing one at a competitive disadvantage; or
5. make a contract's formation depend on the acceptance of certain additional obligations that, according to commercial usage, have no connection with the subject of such contracts.

Article 85(3) allows for an individual exemption if the agreement meets certain conditions, such as improving the production or distribution of goods, promoting technical or economic progress, and reserving to consumers a fair share of the resulting economic benefits.

Article 86 provides that it is unlawful for one or more enterprises having a dominant market position within at least a substantial part of the EU to take improper advantage of such a position if trade between the member states may be affected.

7. Securities Regulation in an International Environment

Illegal conduct in the U.S. securities markets, whether this conduct is initiated in the United States or abroad, threatens the vital economic interests of the United States. Investigation and litigation concerning possible violations of the U.S. securities laws often have an extraterritorial effect. Conflicts with the laws of foreign countries may occur.

(a) Jurisdiction

U.S. district courts have jurisdiction over violations of the antifraud provisions of the Securities Exchange Act of 1934 when losses occur from sales to Americans living in the United States.[25] U.S. district courts also have jurisdiction when losses occur to Americans living abroad if the acts occurred in the United States. The antifraud provisions do not apply, however, to losses from sales of securities to foreigners outside the United States unless acts within the United States caused the losses.

(b) Impact of Foreign Secrecy Laws in SEC Enforcement

Secrecy laws are confidentiality laws applied to home-country banks. These laws prohibit the disclosure of business records or the identity of bank customers. **Blocking laws** prohibit the disclosure, copying, inspection, or removal of documents located in the enacting country in compliance with orders from foreign authorities. These laws impede, and sometimes foreclose, the SEC's ability to police its securities markets properly.

The *Banca Della Suizzera* case demonstrates how the SEC, in certain circumstances, can obtain discovery from foreign financial institutions in spite of secrecy laws.

22 PL 97-290, 96 Stat 1233, 15 USC § 6(a).

23 The European Commission is the executive branch of the EU government and performs most of the EU's regulatory work. The Competition Commission oversees antitrust and mergers for the European Commission. New merger regulations took effect on May 1, 2004. The regulations require the Competition Commission to review proposed mergers and prohibit those mergers when the effects may "significantly impede effective competition" (called the *SIEC test*). The U.S. test prohibits mergers when the effect "may substantially lessen competition. . . ." 15 USC § 18 (2005). The wording of the EU and U.S. tests is relatively similar.

24 See *Osakeyhtio v EEC Commission*, 1988 Common Mkt Rep (CCH) ¶ 14,491 for discussion of the extraterritorial reach of the European Commission.

25 *Kauthar Sdn Bhd v Sternberg*, 149 F3d 659 (7th Cir 1998).

SEC V BANCA DELLA SUIZZERA ITALIANA, 92 FRD 111 (SDNY 1981)

THE LONG REACH OF THE SEC

Banca Della Suizzera Italiana (BSI) is a Swiss bank with an office in the United States. BSI purchased certain call options and common stock of St. Joe Minerals Corporation (St. Joe), a New York corporation. This purchase was made immediately prior to the announcement on March 11, 1981, of a cash tender offer by Joseph Seagram & Sons, Inc., for all St. Joe common stock at $45 per share. On March 10, 1981, when BSI acted, the stock traded at approximately $30 per share. On March 11, 1981, the stock moved sharply higher in price. BSI instructed its broker to close out the purchases of the options and sell most of the shares of stock, resulting in an overnight profit of $2 million. The SEC noticed the undue activity in the options market, initiated suit against BSI, and obtained a temporary restraining order. The restraining order froze the proceeds in BSI's bank account at a New York bank. The SEC, through the Departments of State and Justice, and the Swiss government sought without success to learn the identity of BSI's customers involved in the transactions. The SEC believed that the customers had used inside information in violation of the Securities Exchange Act of 1934. The SEC filed a motion to compel disclosure. BSI, a Swiss bank, contended that it might be subject to criminal liability under Swiss penal and banking laws if it disclosed the requested information.

Judicial Opinion

POLLACK, D. J. . . . BSI claims that it may be subject to criminal liability under Swiss penal and banking law if it discloses the requested information. However, this Court finds the factors in § 40 of the Restatement of Foreign Relations* to tip decisively in favor of the SEC. Moreover, it holds BSI to be "in the position of one who deliberately courted legal impediments . . . and who thus cannot now be heard to assert its good faith after this expectation was realized." BSI acted in bad faith. It made deliberate use of Swiss nondisclosure law to evade in a commercial transaction for profit to it, the strictures of American securities law against insider trading. . . .

The first of the § 40 factors is the vital national interest of each of the States. The strength of the United States' interest in enforcing its securities laws to ensure the integrity of its financial markets cannot seriously be doubted. That interest is being continually thwarted by the use of foreign bank accounts. Congress, in enacting legislation on bank record-keeping, expressed its concern over the problem over a decade ago. . . .

The Swiss government, on the other hand, though made expressly aware of the litigation, has expressed no opposition. In response to BSI's lawyers' inquiries, the incumbent Swiss Federal Attorney General . . . said only that a foreign court could not change the rule that disclosure required the consent of the one who imparted the secret and that BSI might thus be subject to prosecution. The Swiss government did not "confiscate" the Bank records to prevent violations of its law. . . . NEITHER THE UNITED STATES NOR THE SWISS GOVERNMENT has suggested that discovery be halted. . . .

The Court of Appeals in *United States v. National City Bank*, 396 F.2d 897 (2d Cir 1968), found the fact that the governments concerned had not intervened of great importance. It observed that "when foreign governments, including Germany, have considered their vital national interests threatened, they have not hesitated to make known their objections . . . to the issuing court." It is true that BSI may be subject to fines and its officers to imprisonment under Swiss law. However, this Court notes that there is some flexibility in the application of that law. Not only may the particular bank involved obtain waivers from its customers to avoid prosecution, but Article 34 of the Swiss Penal Code contains a "State of Necessity" exception that relieves a person of criminal liability for acts committed to protect one's own good, including one's fortune, from an immediate danger if one is not responsible for the danger and one cannot be expected to give up one's good.

Of course, given BSI's active part in the insider trading transactions alleged here, the Swiss government might well conclude—as this Court has—that BSI is responsible for the conflict it is in and that therefore the "State of Necessity" exception should not apply. However, that is certainly no cause for this Court to withhold its sanctions since the dilemma would be a result of BSI's bad faith. A party's good or bad faith is an important factor to consider, and this court finds that BSI, which deposited the proceeds of these transactions in an American bank account in its name and which certainly profited in some measure from the challenged activity, undertook such transactions fully expecting to use foreign law to shield it from the reach of our laws. Such "deliberate courting" of foreign legal impediments will not be countenanced. . . .

It would be a travesty of justice to permit a foreign company to invade American markets, violate American laws if they were indeed violated, withdraw profits and resist accountability for itself and its principals for the illegality by claiming their anonymity under foreign law. . . .

. . . BSI is directed to complete its answers to all of the demands in the SEC's First Interrogatories, pertaining to St. Joe.

[So ordered]

[*Authors' Note:* Faced with the judge's opinion and the possibility of substantial fines, BSI obtained a waiver of the secrecy laws from its customer and produced the requested information.]

Questions

1. What are the dominant factors considered by a court when deciding whether to issue a subpoena or discovery order to a foreign bank in a secrecy jurisdiction?
2. Did the court find that the Swiss interest in bank secrecy outweighed the U.S. interest?
3. Did BSI act in good faith?
4. Did the court give significant weight to BSI's potential liability under Swiss law?

* § 40 reads as follows:

§ 40. Limitations on Exercise of Enforcement Jurisdiction. Where two states have jurisdiction to prescribe and enforce rules of law and the rules they may prescribe require inconsistent conduct upon the part of a person, each state is required by international law to consider, in good faith, moderating the exercise of its enforcement jurisdiction, in the light of such factors as

(a) vital national interests of each of the states,
(b) the extent and the nature of the hardship that inconsistent enforcement actions would impose upon the person,
(c) the extent to which the required conduct is to take place in the territory of the other state,
(d) the nationality of the person, and
(e) the extent to which enforcement by action of either state can reasonably be expected to achieve compliance with the rule prescribed by that state.

The SEC is not limited to litigation when a securities law enforcement investigation runs into secrecy or blocking laws. For example, the SEC may rely on the 1977 Treaty of Mutual Assistance in Criminal Matters between the United States and Switzerland.[26] Although this treaty has served to deter the use of Swiss secrecy laws to conceal fraud in the United States, its benefits for securities enforcement have been limited. It applies only where there is a dual criminality—that is, the conduct involved constitutes a criminal offense under the laws of both the United States and Switzerland.

8. Barriers to Trade

The most common barrier to the free movement of goods across borders is a tariff. A wide range of nontariff barriers also restricts the free movement of goods, services, and investments. Government export controls used as elements of foreign policy have proven to be a major barrier to trade with certain countries.

(a) Tariff Barriers

A **tariff** is an import or export duty or tax placed on goods as they move into or out of a country. It is the most common method used by countries to restrict foreign imports. The tariff raises the total cost, and thus the price, of an imported product in the domestic market. Thus, the price of a domestically produced product not subject to the tariff is more advantageous.

The U.S. Customs Service imposes tariffs on imported goods at the port of entry. The merchandise is classified under a tariff schedule, which lists each type of merchandise and the corresponding duty rate (or percentage). The Customs Service also determines the "computed value" of the imported goods under very precise statutory

[26] 27 UST 2021.

formulas.[27] The total amount of the duty is calculated by applying the duty percentage to the computed value figure.[28]

In the *Sabritas* case, an importer challenged the Custom Service's classification of imported taco shells and potato chips.

(b) Nontariff Barriers

Nontariff barriers consist of a wide range of restrictions that inhibit the free movement of goods between countries. An import quota, such as a limitation on the number of automobiles that can be imported into one country from another, is such a

SABRITAS V UNITED STATES, 998 F SUPP 1123 (CIT 1998)

CUSTOMS CRUNCH!

Frito-Lay, Inc., owns a Mexican affiliate, Sabritas, S.A. de C.V., and it imports taco shells and *Munchos* potato crisps from Mexico to the United States. The U.S. Customs Service classified these products as "other bakers' wares" under Section 1905.90.90 of the Tariff Schedule subject to a 10 percent duty rate. Frito-Lay contends before the Court of International Trade that the import of taco shells is properly classified as "bread," which carries duty-free status. And, it contends that *Munchos* are properly classified as potato chips and entitled to duty-free treatment.

Judicial Opinion

TSOUCALAS, S. J. ... The issue of whether an imported article has been classified under an appropriate tariff provision entails a two-step process: (1) ascertaining the proper meaning of specific terms in the tariff provision; and (2) determining whether the article comes within the description of such terms as properly construed. *Sports Graphics, Inc. v. United States*, 24 F.3d 1390, 1391 (Fed.Cir.1994. ...

... to determine the common meaning of a tariff term, the Court may utilize standard dictionaries and scientific authorities, as well as its own understanding of the term. The Court may also consider the testimony of credible witnesses as an aid in its understanding, although such testimony is not dispositive.

1. Taco Shells

Frito-Lay contends its taco shells are not properly classified as other bakers' wares because they are more specifically provided for as bread or, alternatively, as "biscuits and similar baked products" under ... 1905.90.10. Customs disagrees with plaintiff, alleging, mostly through testimonial evidence, that the frying of taco shells necessarily removes them from classification as either bread or biscuits and similar baked products. ...

An *eo nomine* provision, such as 1905.90.10, includes all forms of the named article, in this case bread. As bread is not specifically defined in the [tariff provision] or in the relevant legislative history, it is necessary for the Court to determine, as a matter of law, the common and commercial meaning of the term bread to decide whether Frito-Lay's taco shells can be classified as such.

Customs maintains that Frito-Lay bases its contention on an intermediate article, the tortilla, and argues that frying baked tortillas substantially transforms them into a different article of commerce such that they are removed from the realm of bread. Indeed, Customs' expert, food scientist Dr. Nicholas Pintauro, defined bread in the following narrow manner:

Bread is a product that is formulated with a cereal grain that's in a flour form, with other ingredients such as shortening, salt, baking powder or a leavening agent and it is prepared as a dough and that dough has to be treated, which we call kneading so that you could develop the protein that's in the cereal portion of that dough so that the protein is in the form that would encapsulate the gas that's generated by the leavening agent so that you get a rise out of the dough and then at the proper time, in the form of a loaf, that dough is baked.

[27] See Tariff Act of 1930, as amended, 19 USC § 1401a(e).

[28] It is common for importers to utilize customs brokers who research the tariff schedules to see whether a product fits unambiguously under one of the Customs Service's classifications. A broker will also research the classifications given to similar products. It may find that a fax switch may be classified as "other telephonic switching apparatus" at a tariff rate of 8.5 percent or "other telegraphic switching apparatus" with a tariff of 4.7 percent. Obviously, the importer desires to pay the lower rate, and the broker with the assistance of counsel will make a recommendation to the Customs Service for the lower rate, and Customs will make a ruling. The decisions of the Customs Service are published in the *Customs Bulletin*, the official weekly publication of the Customs Service. See *Command Communications v Fritz Cos.*, 36 P3d 182 (Colo App 2001).

Tr. 164-65. Dr. Pintauro's definition necessarily precludes any unleavened or fried products from falling within the common and commercial meaning of bread. Nothing could be further from the truth. . . .

First, **Sharon T. Herbst,** *Barron's Cooking Guide: Food Lover's Companion* 49 (1990) (emphasis added), recognizes that a bread may be fried, as it defines bread as a "staple . . . made from flour, water (or other liquid) and usually a LEAVENER [that] can be baked . . . fried or steamed." The Court also deems it exceptionally significant that two recognized bread treatises devote entire chapters to fried breads. *See* **Judith Jones,** *The Book of Bread* (1982) & **Dolores Casela,** *A World of Breads* (1966).

To contend that the common and commercial meaning of bread is limited to baked leavened (or even unleavened) products ignores the reality that flat, fried, usually ethnic breads exist in the United States market and are generally accepted as forms of bread. As Dr. Pintauro noted on cross-examination, "ethnic bread is bread. Period." Tr. 236; *see also* Tr. 132 (testimony that tortillas, of which hard taco shells are a type, are consumed throughout the United States, but primarily in the south and southwest); *Atwood-Stone Co. v. United States* 5 Ct. Cust.App. 472, 474 (CCPA 1914) ("The term 'bread' . . . is broad enough to cover all articles of food made from the flour or meal of grain, whether it will 'raise' or not"). The taco shells at issue, in particular, are not only found in obscure Mexican restaurants, but also on grocery store shelves and in the world's largest Mexican food chain, Taco Bell, which operates outlets across the United States. Tr. 45–46; 132–33.

Contrary to Customs' argument, therefore, the Court finds that the hard, flat, corn-based taco shells at issue are not "bread of de minimis commercial significance" or an "ancient or obscure product" but, rather, articles that are commonly and commercially known as bread in the United States. . . .

2. Munchos

Frito-Lay contends its *Munchos* should be classified under . . . A2005.20.20 because they are fabricated, as opposed to natural, potato chips, and so, are a type of potato chips. . . .

In opposition, Customs contends *Munchos* are not prepared or preserved potatoes, and so, cannot be classified under . . . A2005, Customs further points to several physical characteristics that differentiate *Munchos* from natural potato chips, including bulk density, color, texture and flavor. Finally, Customs claims that the process of producing *Munchos*, as well as the ingredient composition and merchandising of *Munchos*, differ greatly from those of potato chips. . . .

Potato chips are consistently defined in food and non-food related sources as snack articles produced from thin slices of whole potatoes that are fried. For instance, *Webster's Third New International Dictionary* at 1774, defines a potato chip as "a thin slice of raw white potato fried crisp in deep fat.". . .

Munchos are composed of several ingredients, including dehydrated potato flakes, corn meal and potato starch, while potato chips are produced entirely from sliced raw whole potatoes. . . .

The physical characteristics of *Munchos* in their final form also set them apart from conventional, natural potato chips. . . .

Upon consideration of the proffered testimonial and documentary evidence and based on the Court's *in camera* inspection of the subject potato crisps, the Court agrees with [Customs] that Munchos are not a form of potato chips and are, therefore, removed from the scope of the . . . provision for potato chips.

Conclusion

Consequently, the Court concludes that Customs properly classified plaintiff's import *Munchos* potato crisps under 1905.90.90. The court also concludes that plaintiff's import taco shells are properly classified as bread under 1905.90.10 and orders Customs to reliquidate these items accordingly.

Questions

1. Summarize the matter before the court.
2. What decisional process does the court follow in determining whether an imported article is properly classified under the appropriate tariff provision by the Customs Service?
3. Compare Frito-Lay's *Munchos* to its Lay's Potato Chips and Pringles potato chips. Review the ingredients of each product and the merchandising of each product. Should all of these products be subject to the same tax treatment by the Customs Service?

barrier. More subtle nontariff barriers exist in all countries. **For Example,** Japan's complex customs procedures resulted in the restriction of the sale of U.S.-made aluminum baseball bats in Japan. The customs procedures required the individual uncrating and "destruction testing" of bats at the ports of entry. Government subsidies are also nontariff barriers to trade.

One U.S. law—the Turtle Law—prohibits the importation of shrimp from countries that allow the harvesting of shrimp with commercial fishing technology that could adversely affect endangered sea turtles. **For Example,** two U.S. importers sought an exemption from the embargo, representing that their Brazilian supply of shrimp was caught in the wild by vessels using turtle excluder devices (TEDs). Because Brazil had failed to comply with the U.S. Turtle Law by requiring TEDs on its commercial shrimp fleet, even though it had seven years to do so, the exemption was not granted.[29]

(c) Export Controls as Instruments of Foreign Policy

U.S. export controls have been used as instruments of foreign policy in recent years. **For Example,** the United States has sought to deny goods and technology of strategic or military importance to unfriendly nations. The United States has also denied goods such as grain, technology, and machine parts, to certain countries to protest or to punish activities considered violative of human rights or world peace.

9. Relief Mechanisms for Economic Injury Caused by Foreign Trade

Certain U.S. industries may suffer severe economic injury because of foreign competition. U.S. law provides protection against unfair competition from foreigners' goods and provides economic relief for U.S. industries, communities, firms, and workers adversely affected by import competition. U.S. law also provides certain indirect relief for U.S. exporters and producers who encounter unfair foreign import restrictions.

(a) Antidumping Laws and Export Subsidies

Selling goods in another country at less than their fair value is called **dumping**. The dumping of foreign goods in the United States is prohibited under the Tariff Act of 1930, as amended including the antidumping laws contained in the Uraguay Round Agreement Act of 1994.[30] Proceedings in antidumping cases are conducted by two federal agencies, which separately examine two distinct components. The International Trade Administration (ITA) of the Department of Commerce investigates whether specified foreign goods are being sold in the United States at less than fair value (LTFV). The International Trade Commission (ITC) conducts proceedings to determine if there is an injury to a domestic industry as a result of such sales. Findings of both LTFV sales and injury must be present before remedial action is taken. Remedial action might include the addition of duties to reflect the difference between the fair value of the goods and the price being charged in the United States. ITA and ITC decisions may be appealed to the Court of International Trade. Decisions of this court are reviewable by the U.S. Court of Appeals for the Federal Circuit and then the U.S. Supreme Court.

A settlement of the matter may be reached through a suspension agreement, whereby prices are revised to eliminate any LTFV sales and other corrective measures are taken.

The 1979 act also applies to subsidy practices by foreign countries. If subsidized goods are sold in the United States at less than their fair value, the goods may be subject to a countervailing duty.

Canada and Mexico may appeal countervailing duty assessments by the United States to an arbitration panel established under NAFTA. The NAFTA panel, however, can determine only whether the U.S. determinations were made in accordance with U.S. law. An appeal can also be made by member states to the WTO Dispute Settlement Body, which can determine whether the United States breached its obligations under the WTO.

A dispute between the United States and Canada over government subsidies to the Canadian softwood lumber industry and the dumping of softwood lumber products on the U.S. market at less than fair value is outlined in Figure 7-1.

(b) Relief from Import Injuries

Title II of the Trade Act of 1974[31] provides relief for U.S. industries, communities, firms, and workers when any one or more of them are substantially adversely affected by import competition. The Department of

[29] *Earth Island Institute v Christopher*, 948 F Supp 1062 (Ct Int'l Trade 1996). See *Turtle Island Restoration Network v Evans*, 284 F3d 1282 (Fed Cir 2002), on the continuing litigation on this topic and the clash between statutory enforcement and political and diplomatic considerations.

[30] 19 USC § 1675b (2000). See *Allegheny Ludlum Corp. v United States*, 287 F3d 1365 (Fed Cir 2002).

[31] PL 93-618, 88 Stat 1978, 19 USC §§ 2251, 2298.

FIGURE 7-1 Countervailing Duty and Antidumping Proceedings

Phase 1: International Trade Administration (ITA)

Date	Event
April 2, 2001	Following the expiration of a softwood lumber agreement in 2001, the U.S. lumber industry files a countervailing duty petition alleging Canadian government subsidies and an antidumping petition to the ITA.
April–July 2001	ITA investigates whether lumber exports from Canada are subsidized and whether they are being sold at less than fair value (LTFV).
August 9, 2001	ITA issues its preliminary determination that Canadian softwood lumber exports to the U.S. are subsidized at 19.31%.
April 25, 2002	ITA issues its final subsidy determinations in both the antidumping (AD) and countervailing duty (CVD) cases. The final subsidy rate is set at 18.79% and the average dumping rate is set at 8.43% for a combined CVD/AD rate of 27.22%.
	Phase 2: International Trade Commission (ITC)
May 16, 2001	ITC issues preliminary determination that subsidies pose a threat to U.S. industry.
May 2, 2002	ITC determines that U.S. lumber firms are suffering injury due to dumping and subsidies.
May 22, 2002	U.S. Customs begins collecting duties on Canadian softwood lumber imports.
	Phase 3: Dispute Settlement Procedures Progress through NAFTA, the WTO, and the U.S. Court of International Trade
August 13, 2003	NAFTA panel rules that Canadian lumber industry is subsidized but the 18.79% tariff is too high. It orders a review by U.S. Commerce Department (ITA).
January 10, 2005	Proceedings initiated in the U.S. Court of International Trade challenging the CVD/AD duties.
August 10, 2005	NAFTA panel dismisses U.S. claims that Canadian softwood exports are subsidized. U.S. disagrees.
March 2006	A NAFTA panel again rules in Canada's favor. At this point, the total duties collected by the U.S. Customs Service is $5.2 billion.
April 2006	A WTO appellate body rejects Canada's request to overturn the ITC's May 22, 2002, rulings.
	Phase 4: Resolution by a Negotiated Agreement
April 26, 2006	The trade representatives for both the United States and Canada reach agreement on a seven-year pact to end the dispute. The United States will return 80% of the $5 billion in tariffs it has collected. Canada-sourced lumber will be kept at its current 34% share of the U.S. softwood market, and Canada will collect an export tax on softwood lumber if the price drops below $355 per a thousand board feet.

Commerce, the secretary of labor, and the president have roles in determining eligibility. The relief provided may be temporary import relief through the imposition of a duty or quota on the foreign goods. Workers, if eligible, may obtain readjustment allowances, job training, job search allowances, or unemployment compensation.

For Example, trade adjustment assistance, including unemployment compensation and training and relocation allowances, was provided for former employees of Johnson Controls Battery Group plants in Garland, Texas; Bennington, Vermont; and Owosso, Michigan; because surveys of the customers of those plants by the Department of Labor indicated that increased imports of aftermarket batteries, the products produced at these closed plants, caused the shutdowns. Former workers of the closed Louisville battery plant were not provided assistance because this plant produced new car batteries, and the work was shifted to another Johnson Controls plant in the United States.[32]

(c) Retaliation and Relief against Foreign Unfair Trade Restrictions

U.S. exporters of agricultural or manufactured goods or of services may encounter unreasonable, unjustifiable, or discriminatory foreign import restrictions. At the same time, producers from the foreign country involved may be benefiting from trade agreement concessions that allow producers from that country access to U.S. markets. Prior trade acts and the Omnibus Trade and Competitiveness Act of 1988[33]contain broad authority to retaliate against "unreasonable," "unjustifiable," or "discriminatory" acts by a foreign country. The authority to retaliate is commonly referred to as "Section 301 authority." The fear or actuality of the economic sting of Section 301 retaliation often leads offending foreign countries to open their markets to imports. Thus, indirect relief is provided to domestic producers and exporters adversely affected by foreign unfair trade practices.

Enforcement of the act is entrusted to the U.S. trade representative (USTR), who is appointed by the president. Under the 1988 act, mandatory retaliatory action is required if the USTR determines that (1) rights of the United States under a trade agreement are being denied or (2) actions or policies of a foreign country are unjustifiable and a burden or restrict U.S. commerce. The overall thrust of the trade provisions of the 1988 act is to open markets and liberalize trade.

10. Expropriation

A major concern of U.S. businesses that do business abroad is the risk of expropriation of assets by a host government. Firms involved in the extraction of natural resources, banking, communications, or defense-related industries are particularly susceptible to nationalization. Multinational corporations commonly have a staff of full-time political scientists and former Foreign Service officers studying the countries relevant to their operations to monitor and calculate risks of expropriation. Takeovers of U.S.-owned businesses by foreign countries may be motivated by a short-term domestic political advantage or the desire to demonstrate political clout in world politics. Takeovers may also be motivated by long-term considerations associated with planned development of the country's economy.

Treaty commitments, or provisions in other international agreements between the United States and the host country, may serve to narrow expropriation uncertainties. Treaties commonly contain provisions whereby property will not be expropriated except for public benefit and with the prompt payment of just compensation.

One practical way to mitigate the risk of investment loss as a result of foreign expropriation is to purchase insurance through private companies, such as Lloyd's of London. Commercial insurance is also available against such risks as host governments' arbitrary recall of letters of credit and commercial losses resulting from embargoes.

The Overseas Private Investment Corporation (OPIC) is a U.S. agency under the policy control of the secretary of state. OPIC supports private investments in less developed, friendly countries. OPIC also offers asset protection insurance against risk of loss to plant and equipment as well as loss of deposits in overseas bank accounts to companies that qualify on the basis of the involvement of a "substantial U.S. interest."

[32] 20 F Supp 2d 1288 (Ct Int'l Trade 1998). See also *Former Employees of Merrill Corp. v U.S.*, 387 F Supp 2d 1336 (Ct Int'l Trade 2005).
[33] PL 100-418, 102 Stat 1346, 15 USC § 4727.

11. Government-Assisted Export Programs

The U.S. government has taken legislative action to increase the foreign sales of U.S. firms.

(a) Export Trading Company Act

The Export Trading Company Act (ETCA) of 1982[34] is designed to stimulate and promote additional U.S. exports. The ETCA promotes the formation of U.S.-based export trading companies and allows banks to invest in these export trading companies. The ETCA also clarifies applicable antitrust restrictions and provides a limited exception from antitrust liability.

(b) Foreign Sales Corporations

The Foreign Sales Corporation Act of 1984, Title VIII of the Tax Reform Act of 1984,[35] provides export incentives for U.S. firms that form foreign sales corporations (FSCs). To qualify for the tax incentives provided under the 1984 act, an FSC subsidiary of a U.S. firm must be organized under the laws of a U.S. possession (such as the Virgin Islands or Guam, but not Puerto Rico) or under the laws of a foreign country with an income tax treaty with the United States containing an exchange-of-information program. The FSC must satisfy certain other organizational requirements to be eligible for the tax incentives provided by the law.

(c) United States Export-Import Bank (EXIMBANK)

EXIMBANK is wholly owned by the U.S. government. Its primary purpose is to facilitate U.S. exports by making direct loans in the form of dollar credits to foreign importers for the purchase of U.S. goods and services. Payments are then made directly to the U.S. exporter of goods and services. Such loans are made when private financial sources are unwilling to assume the political and economic risks that exist in the country in question. Loans are also made by EXIMBANK to enable U.S. suppliers of goods and services to compete for major foreign contracts with foreign firms that have government-subsidized export financing.

(d) Other Programs

As stated previously, OPIC provides expropriation insurance for U.S. private investments in friendly, less developed countries. The Commodity Credit Corporation (CCC) provides financing for agricultural exports. In addition, the Small Business Administration has an export loan program.

12. The Foreign Corrupt Practices Act

There are restrictions on U.S. firms doing business abroad that disallow payments to foreign government officials for getting business from their governments. The Foreign Corrupt Practices Act of 1977 requires strict accounting standards and internal control procedures to prevent the hiding of improper payments to foreign officials. The act prohibits any offers, payments, or gifts to foreign officials—or third parties who might have influence with foreign officials—to influence a decision on behalf of the firm making the payment. It provides for sanctions of up to $1 million against the company and fines and imprisonment for the employees involved. Moreover, the individuals involved may be responsible for damages as a result of civil actions brought by competitors under federal and state antiracketeering acts.[36]

The act does not apply to payments made to low-level officials for expediting the performance of routine government services.

The In-Laws (1979) (PG)

Review the segment in the film in which money is paid by a dictator for the sale of U.S. currency plates. The dictator's plan is to create worldwide inflation. List the various laws and conventions Peter Falk and Alan Arkin violate through their sale of the plates.

For movie clips that illustrate business law concepts, see LawFlix at **http://wdvl.westbuslaw.com.**

34 PL 97-290, 96 Stat 1233, 15 USC § 4001.

35 Title VIII of the Tax Reform Act of 1984, PL 98-369, 98 Stat 678. See IRC §§ 921–927.

36 PL 95-213, 94 Stat 1494, 15 USC § 78a nt.

Summary

The General Agreement on Tariffs and Trade, a multilateral treaty subscribed to by the United States and most of the industrialized countries of the world, is based on the principle of trade without discrimination. The United Nations Convention on Contracts for the International Sale of Goods provides uniform rules for international sales contracts between parties in contracting nations. The European Union is a regional trading group that includes most of western Europe. The North American Free Trade Agreement involves Mexico, Canada, and the United States and eliminates all tariffs between the three countries over a 15-year period.

U.S. firms may choose to do business abroad by making export sales or contracting with a foreign distributor to take title to their goods and sell them abroad. U.S. firms may also license their technology or trademarks for foreign use. An agency arrangement or the organization of a foreign subsidiary may be required to participate effectively in foreign markets. This results in subjecting the U.S. firm to taxation in the host country. However, tax treaties commonly eliminate double taxation. The Export Administration Act is the principal statute imposing export controls on goods and technical data.

In choosing the form for doing business abroad, U.S. firms must be careful not to violate the antitrust laws of host countries. Anticompetitive foreign transactions may have an adverse impact on competition in U.S. domestic markets. U.S. antitrust laws have a broad extraterritorial reach. U.S. courts apply a "jurisdictional rule of reason," weighing the interests of the United States against the interests of the foreign country involved in making a decision on whether to hear a case. Illegal conduct may occur in U.S. securities markets. U.S. enforcement efforts sometimes run into foreign countries' secrecy and blocking laws that hinder effective enforcement.

Antidumping laws offer relief for domestic firms threatened by unfair foreign competition. In addition, economic programs exist to assist industries, communities, and workers injured by import competition. Programs also exist to increase the foreign sales of U.S. firms.

Questions and Case Problems

1. How does the most-favored-nation clause of the GATT work to foster the principle of trade without discrimination?
2. How does the selling of subsidized foreign goods in the United States adversely affect free trade?
3. PepsiCo has registered its PEPSI trademarks in the U.S. Patent and Trademark Office. PEPSI products are bottled and distributed in the United States by PepsiCo and by authorized bottlers pursuant to Exclusive Bottling Appointment agreements, which authorize local bottlers to bottle and distribute PEPSI products in their respective territories. Similarly, PepsiCo has appointed local bottlers to bottle and distribute PEPSI products in Mexico within particular territories. Pacific Produce, Ltd., has been engaged in the sale and distribution within the United States and Nevada of PEPSI products that were manufactured and bottled in Mexico and intended for sale in Mexico ("Mexican product"). The Mexican product sold by Pacific Products in the United States has certain material differences from domestic PEPSI products sold by PepsiCo: (1) it contains inferior paper labels that improperly report nutritional information; (2) it does not comply with the labeling standards followed by PepsiCo in the United States; (3) it is sold in channels of trade different from PepsiCo's authorized distribution channels without "drink by" notice dates on the Mexican product and monitoring on the Mexican product for proper shipment and storage conditions; and (4) it conflicts with the bottle return policies of PepsiCo. The Mexican product with its "Marca Reg" and Spanish language bottle caps is well received by consumers in Pacific Produce distribution channels. Classify the goods being sold by Pacific Produce. State the applicable law governing a dispute between PepsiCo and Pacific Produce. How would you decide this case? [*PepsiCo, Inc. v Pacific Produce, Ltd.*, 2001 US Dist LEXIS 12085]
4. Ronald Sadler, a California resident, owned a helicopter distribution company in West Germany, Delta Avia. This company distributed U.S.-made Hughes civilian helicopters in western Europe. Sadler's German firm purchased 85 helicopters from Hughes Aircraft Co. After export licenses were obtained in reliance on the purchaser's written assurance that the goods would not be disposed of contrary to the export license, the helicopters were exported to Germany for resale in western Europe. Thereafter, Delta Avia exported them to North Korea, which was a country subject to a trade embargo by the United States. The helicopters were converted to military use. Sadler was charged with violating the Export Administration Regulations. In Sadler's defense, it was contended that the U.S. regulations have no effect on what occurs in the resale of civilian helicopters in another sovereign country. Decide.
5. Mirage Investments Corp. (MIC) planned a tender offer for the shares of Gulf States International Corp. (GSIC). Archer, an officer of MIC, placed purchase orders for GSIC stock through the New York office of the Bahamian Bank (BB) prior to the announcement of the

tender offer, making a $300,000 profit when the tender offer was made public. The Bahamas is a secrecy jurisdiction. The bank informed the SEC that under its law, it could not disclose the name of the person for whom it purchased the stock. What, if anything, may the SEC do to discover whether the federal securities laws have been violated?

6. United Overseas, Ltd. (UOL), is a U.K. firm that purchases and sells manufacturers' closeouts in Europe and the Middle East. UOL's representative, Jay Knox, used stationery listing a UOL office in New York to solicit business from Revlon, Inc., in New York. On April 1, 1992, UOL faxed a purchase order from its headquarters in England to Revlon's New York offices for the purchase of $4 million worth of shampoo. The purchase order on its face listed six conditions, none of which referred to a forum selection clause. When Revlon was not paid for the shampoo it shipped, it sued UOL in New York for breach of contract. UOL moved to dismiss the complaint because of a forum selection clause, which it stated was on the reverse side of the purchase order and provided that "the parties hereby agree to submit to the jurisdiction of the English Courts disputes arising out of the contract." The evidence did not show that the reverse side of the purchase order had been faxed with the April 1992 order. Should the court dismiss the complaint based on the "forum selection clause"? Read Chapter 32 on letters of credit and advise Revlon how to avoid similar litigation in the future. [*Revlon, Inc. v United Overseas, Ltd.*, 1994 WL 9657 (SDNY)]

7. Reebok manufactures and sells fashionable athletic shoes in the United States and abroad. It owns the federally registered Reebok trademark and has registered this trademark in Mexico as well. Nathan Betech is a Mexican citizen residing in San Diego, California, with business offices there. Reebok believed that Betech was in the business of selling counterfeit Reebok shoes in Mexican border towns, such as Tijuana, Mexico. It sought an injunction in a federal district court in California ordering Betech to cease his counterfeiting activity and to refrain from destroying certain documents. It also asked the court to freeze Betech's assets pending the outcome of a Lanham Act lawsuit. Betech contended that a U.S. district court has no jurisdiction or authority to enter the injunction for the activities allegedly occurring in Mexico. Decide. [*Reebok Int'l, Ltd. v Marnatech Enterprises, Inc.*, 970 F2d 552 (9th Cir)]

8. Assume that before the formation of the European Union, the lowest-cost source of supply for a certain product consumed in France was the United States. Explain the basis by which, after the EU was formed, higher-cost German producers could have replaced the U.S. producers as the source of supply.

9. A complaint was filed with the U.S. Commerce Department's ITA by U.S. telephone manufacturers AT&T, Comidial Corp., and Eagle Telephones, Inc., alleging that 12 Asian manufacturers of small business telephones, including the Japanese firms Hitachi, NEC, and Toshiba and the Taiwanese firm Sun Moon Star Corp., were dumping their small business phones in the U.S. market at prices that were from 6 percent to 283 percent less than those in their home markets. The U.S. manufacturers showed that the domestic industry's market share had dropped from 54 percent in 1985 to 33 percent in 1989. They asserted that it was doubtful if the domestic industry could survive the dumping. Later, in a hearing before the ITC, the Japanese and Taiwanese respondents contended that their domestic industry was basically sound and that the U.S. firms simply had to become more efficient to meet worldwide competition. They contended that the United States was using the procedures before the ITA and ITC as a nontariff barrier to imports. How should the ITC decide the case? [*American Telephone and Telegraph Co. v Hitachi*, 6 ITC 1511]

10. Campbell Soup Co. imports tomato paste from a wholly owned Mexican subsidiary, Sinalopasta, S.A. de C.V. It deducted $416,324 from the computed value of goods shipped to the United States, which was the cost of transportation of the finished tomato paste from Sinalopasta's loading dock in Mexico to the U.S. border. The deduction thus lowered the computed value of the goods and the amount of duty to be paid the U.S. government by Campbell Soup Co. United States Customs questioned this treatment of freight costs. Tariff Act § 140a(e)(1)(B) requires that profits and general expenses be included in calculating the computed value of goods, which in part quantify the value of the merchandise in the country of production. Is Campbell's position correct? [*Campbell Soup Co., Inc. v United States*, 107 F3d 1556 (Fed Cir)]

11. Roland Staemphfli was employed as the chief financial officer of Honeywell Bull, S.A. (HB), a Swiss computer company operating exclusively in Switzerland. Staemphfli purportedly arranged financing for HB in Switzerland through the issuance of promissory notes. He had the assistance of Fidenas, a Bahamian company dealing in commercial paper. Unknown to Fidenas, the HB notes were fraudulent. The notes were prepared and forged by Staemphfli, who lost all of the proceeds in a speculative investment and was convicted of criminal fraud. HB denied responsibility for the fraudulently issued notes when they came due. Fidenas's business deteriorated because of its involvement with the HB notes. It sued HB and others in the United States for violations of U.S. securities laws. HB defended, arguing that the U.S. court did not have jurisdiction over the transactions in question. Decide. [*Fidenas v Honeywell Bull, S.A.*, 606 F2d 5 (2d Cir)]

12. Marc Rich & Co., A.G., a Swiss commodities trading corporation, refused to comply with a grand jury

subpoena requesting certain business records maintained in Switzerland and relating to crude oil transactions and possible violations of U.S. income tax laws. Marc Rich contended that a U.S. court has no authority to require a foreign corporation to deliver to a U.S. court documents located abroad. The court disagreed and imposed fines, froze assets, and threatened to close a Marc Rich wholly owned subsidiary that did business in the state of New York. The fines amounted to $50,000 for each day the company failed to comply with the court's order. Marc Rich appealed. Decide. [*Marc Rich v United States*, 707 F2d 633 (2d Cir)]

13. U.S. Steel Corp. formed Orinoco Mining Co., a wholly owned corporation, to mine large deposits of iron ore that U.S. Steel had discovered in Venezuela. Orinoco, which was incorporated in Delaware, was subject to Venezuela's maximum tax of 50 percent on net income. Orinoco was also subject to U.S. income tax, but the U.S. foreign tax credit offset this amount. U.S. Steel purchased the ore from Orinoco in Venezuela. U.S. Steel formed Navios, Inc., a wholly owned subsidiary, to transport the ore. Navios, a Liberian corporation, was subject to a 2.5 percent Venezuelan excise tax and was exempt from U.S. income tax. Although U.S. Steel was Navios's primary customer, it charged other customers the same price it charged U.S. Steel. U.S. Steel's investment in Navios was $50,000. In seven years, Navios accumulated nearly $80 million in cash but had not paid any dividends to U.S. Steel. The IRS used IRC § 482 to allocate $52 million of Navios's income to U.S. Steel. U.S. Steel challenged this action, contending Navios's charges to U.S. Steel were at arm's length and the same it charged other customers. Decide. [*United States Steel Corp. v Commissioner*, 617 F2d 942 (2d Cir)]

14. National Computers, Inc., a U.S. firm, entered into a joint venture with a Chinese computer manufacturing organization, TEC. A dispute arose over payments due the U.S. firm under the joint venture agreement with TEC. The agreement called for disputes to be arbitrated in China, with the arbitrator being chosen from a panel of arbitrators maintained by the Beijing arbitration institution, Cietac. What advantages and disadvantages exist for the U.S. firm under this arbitration arrangement? Advise the U.S. firm on negotiating future arbitration agreements with Chinese businesses.

15. Sensor, a Netherlands business organization wholly owned by Geosource, Inc., of Houston, Texas, made a contract with C.E.P. to deliver 2,400 strings of geophones to Rotterdam by September 20, 1982. The ultimate destination was identified as the USSR. Thereafter, in June 1982, the president of the United States prohibited shipment to the USSR of equipment manufactured in foreign countries under license from U.S. firms. The president had a foreign policy objective of retaliating for the imposition of martial law in Poland, and he was acting under regulations issued under the Export Administration Act of 1979. Sensor, in July and August of 1982, notified C.E.P. that as a subsidiary of a U.S. corporation, it had to respect the president's embargo. C.E.P. filed suit in a district court of the Netherlands asking that Sensor be ordered to deliver the geophones. Decide. [*Compagnie Européenne des Pétroles v Sensor Nederland*, 22 ILM 66]

CRIMES

CHAPTER (8)

LEARNING OBJECTIVES

After studying this chapter, you should be able to

LO.1 Discuss the nature and classification of crimes

LO.2 Describe the basis of criminal liability

LO.3 Identify who is responsible for criminal acts

LO.4 Explain the penalties for crimes and the sentencing for corporate crimes

LO.5 List examples of white-collar crimes and their elements

LO.6 Describe the common law crimes

LO.7 Discuss crimes related to computers

LO.8 Describe the rights of businesses charged with crimes and the constitutional protections afforded them

Society sets certain standards of conduct and punishes a breach of those standards as a crime. This chapter introduces the means by which government protects people and businesses from prohibited conduct.

A. General Principles

Detailed criminal codes and statutes define crimes and specify their punishment. These vary from state to state but still show the imprint of a common law background through similar elements and structure.

1. Nature and Classification of Crimes

A **crime** is conduct that is prohibited and punished by a government. Crimes are classified as *common law* or *statutory* according to their origin. Offenses punishable by less than one year in prison are called **misdemeanors.** More serious crimes are called **felonies,** including serious business crimes such as bribery and embezzlement, which are punishable by confinement in prison for more than one year. Misdemeanors include weighing goods with uninspected scales or operating without a sales tax license. An act may be a felony in one state and a misdemeanor in another.[1]

2. Basis of Criminal Liability

A crime generally consists of two elements: (1) a mental state and (2) an act or omission. Harm may occur as a result of a crime, but harm is not an essential element of a crime.

(a) Mental State

Mental state does not require an awareness or knowledge of guilt. In most crimes, it is sufficient that the defendant voluntarily committed the act that is criminal regardless of motive or intent. An act may be a crime even though the actor has no knowledge

[1] Some states further define crimes by seriousness with different degrees of a crime, such as first-degree murder, second-degree murder, and so on. Misdemeanors may be differentiated by giving special names to minor misdemeanors.

that a law is being broken. Actions that are in themselves crimes are not made innocent by the claim that the defendant was exercising a constitutional right. **For Example,** freedom of speech does not give the right to send threatening letters.

(b) Act or Omission.

Specific statutes define the conduct that, when coupled with sufficient mental state, constitutes a crime. **For Example,** writing a check knowing you do not have the funds available is conduct that is a crime.

U.S. V QUATTRONE, 443 F3D 153 (2ND CIR. 2006)

OH, YOU MEAN *THOSE* E-MAILS! WHO KNEW?

FACTS: In 2000, former investment banker Frank Quattrone was head of the technology division of Credit Suisse First Boston Corporation (CSFB), earning about $120 million per year. He managed 400 technology investment bankers from the firm's Palo Alto, California, office. Quattrone and members of the Tech Group did the underwriting of the Tech Group's initial public offerings (IPOs). The investigation and prosecution of Quattrone arose out of investigations of IPO allocation practices of CSFB and other investment banking firms. The investigations focused on allegations that allocations in forthcoming "hot issues (IPOs)" were awarded in advance to favored clients.

The National Association of Securities Dealers (NASD), the Securities and Exchange Commission (SEC), and a grand jury impaneled in the Southern District of New York conducted the investigations in the fall of 2000. As a result of the SEC investigation, CSFB agreed to pay $10 million dollars to the SEC.

A timeline of critical events and actions follows.

October 18, 2000

The SEC issued subpoenas in connection with the investigation. Quattrone never saw the SEC's subpoena or earlier document requests.

October 2000

Quattrone received several e-mails from LCD seeking documents. One e-mail informed him and four other CSFB employees of the need to produce documents that went to the heart of the IPO process, including documents that bankers working under Quattrone in the Tech Group would hold.

November 21, 2000

The grand jury in New York issued subpoenas to CSFB and eight CSFB officers.

December 3, 2000

Quattrone learned that the grand jury had joined the IPO investigation.

December 4, 2000, 3:20 P.M

Richard Char, a banker in the Tech Group, circulated the draft of an e-mail (the "Char Email") to Quattrone, his two principal deputies in the Tech Group, and a Tech Group lawyer:

> *With the recent tumble in stock prices, and many deals now trading below issue price, I understand the securities litigation bar is mounting an all out assault on broken tech IPOs.*
>
> *In the spirit of the end of the year (and the slow down in corporate finance work) you may want to send around a memo to all corporate finance bankers (and their assistants) reminding them of the CSFB document retention policy and suggesting that before they leave for the holidays, they should catch up on file cleanup.*
>
> *Today, it's administrative housekeeping. In January, it could be improper destruction of evidence.*

Quattrone immediately responded, scolding Char that he "shouldn't make jokes like that on email!"

December 4, 2000, 5:13 P.M

Char sent the e-mail to all Tech Group bankers:

Subject: Time to clean up those files....

With the recent tumble in stock prices, and many deals now trading below issue price, the securities litigation bar is expected to [sic] an all out assault on broken tech IPOs.

In the spirit of the end of the year (and the slow down in corporate finance work), we want to remind you of the CSFB document retention policy [the policy was reproduced here].

Note that if a lawsuit is instituted, our normal document retention policy is suspended and any cleaning of files is prohibited under the CSFB guidelines (since it constitutes the destruction of evidence). We strongly suggest that before you leave for the holidays, you should catch up on file cleanup.

December 4, 2000, before leaving the office

After receiving the Char Email, Quattrone began drafting a reply directed to the Tech Group (the "Endorsement Email"). He managed to write only "having been a key witness in a securities litigation case in south texas (miniscribe)" before the draft Endorsement Email was saved to a computer folder housing e-mail drafts.

December 5, 2000, 1:47 P.M. Eastern Standard Time

Brodsky telephoned Quattrone and informed him that he should retain a lawyer because it was likely that he would be called before the grand jury or the SEC as a witness. Brodsky also told Quattrone that someone had leaked the investigations of CSFB's allocation practices to the *Wall Street Journal.*

December 5, 2000, 6:28 P.M.

Quattrone then transmitted his completed Endorsement Email:

having been a key witness in a securities litigation case in south texas (miniscribe) i strongly advise you to follow these procedures.

Quattrone placed the day-old Char Email below his

As a result of the Quattrone e-mail (called the endorsement e-mail), at least some Tech Group bankers began or continued "cleaning" their files.

December 6, 2000

LCD took steps to countermand the Char and Quattrone endorsement e-mail. It sent an e-mail informing Tech Group bankers not to destroy documents:

Yesterday Frank [Quattrone] and Richard [Char] reminded everyone to edit their files to comply with our Document Retention Policy. However, due to a routine regulatory inquiry, we must stop the editing process for public offerings until further notice.

December 7, 2000

Brodsky contacted Quattrone by phone and told him that Quattrone's Endorsement Email was "a pretty serious problem for the bank and for him."

Quattrone was indicted for obstruction of justice and witness tampering in connection with the investigations. He was also charged with U.S.C. §§ 1512 & 2 for knowingly and corruptly persuading or endeavoring to persuade others to withhold or destroy documents with intent to interfere with the proceedings.

Quattrone testified that although he was aware of the SEC and grand jury investigations into IPO allocations, he believed that the investigations related only to hedge funds that paid large commissions to get IPO allocations. He also testified that he did not intend to obstruct any SEC or grand jury investigation and did not intend to influence others to destroy documents that had been called for by a grand jury or SEC subpoena. Rather than thinking about the investigations when he sent the Endorsement Email, Quattrone testified that he was concerned about getting home to meet family commitments. He further testified that he never knew that the SEC had issued a subpoena and that while he was aware that there was a grand jury subpoena, he never read it or had its contents described to him.

The jury was unable to reach a verdict in Quattrone's first trial. The second jury found him guilty on all counts. The district court imposed a sentence of 18 months' imprisonment and concurrent two-year terms of supervised release for each count and fines and assessments totaling $90,300.00. Quattrone appealed both the verdict and the sentence.

Judicial Opinion

WESLEY, Circuit Judge . . . In order to convict for obstruction of justice under the omnibus clause of section 1503, the government must establish (1) that there is a pending judicial or grand jury proceeding constituting the administration of justice, (2) that the defendant knew or had notice of the proceeding, and (3) that the defendant acted with the wrongful intent or improper purpose to influence the judicial or grand jury proceeding, whether or not the defendant is successful in doing so—that is, "that the defendant corruptly intended to impede the administration of that judicial proceeding."

A rational trier of fact could conclude beyond a reasonable doubt that Quattrone knew that his conduct would obstruct the grand jury's investigation because there was a logical relationship between his knowing conduct—sending the Endorsement Email while aware of the grand jury subpoena's call for documents relating to the IPO allocation process that were in the possession of Tech Group bankers—and the effect it was likely to have—destruction of documents that otherwise would have been produced. The evidence clearly indicates Quattrone knew of the parallel investigations of CSFB's IPO allocation practices and that the Tech Group was involved in allocation decisions. Combined with the threat that the investigations posed to Quattrone, the jury could infer that Quattrone was aware that his conduct was likely to affect the grand jury investigation.

There was also sufficient evidence from which the jury could conclude beyond a reasonable doubt that when he sent his Endorsement Email, Quattrone acted with corrupt intent, i.e. the "wrongful" or "immoral" intent to obstruct the grand jury's administration of justice.

Evidence also established Quattrone's opportunity to obstruct and acts aimed at that end. On December 4, 2000, Quattrone received the Char Email, began to respond, but then stopped. The next day, before sending his Endorsement Email, Quattrone learned from Brodsky about the potentially damning leak of the investigations and the ominous threat that Quattrone might now be a target. Quattrone then sent his Endorsement Email that evening, promoting the Char Email while employing an exculpatory reason for endorsing the destruction of subpoenaed documents. The proximity in time between additional negative information from Brodsky and the Endorsement Email, along with Quattrone's awareness that the subpoena called for documents Quattrone knew to be in possession of the Tech Group bankers, provided legally sufficient evidence from which a jury could conclude that Quattrone acted with corrupt intent to obstruct by seeking the destruction of relevant documents.

The government asserts that the jury could not have found Quattrone acted corruptly unless it concluded that Quattrone "believed that his actions would obstruct justice by causing documents responsive to the subpoenas to be destroyed." The government presents a forceful and thoughtful argument. However, that argument overlooks a glaring deficiency in the court's charge. When the court finally explained to the jury how to apply the law to the facts, it eviscerated the nexus requirement. It removed the defendant's specific knowledge of the investigatory proceedings and the subpoenas/document requests from the obstruction equation. It left a bare-bones strict liability crime. Given the court's instruction for the nexus determination, all that need be proven was that an investigation had called for certain documents and that the defendant had ordered the destruction of those documents. Although wrongful intent, corrupt intent, and the nexus requirement were correctly defined, the charge, as a whole, relieved the jury of having to make those findings in assessing criminal liability.

Quattrone's theory of the case relied on several innocent explanations for his conduct and each has some basis in the record. Among these, Quattrone testified that he had no wrongful intent and that he was not aware that the investigations were focusing on IPO-allocation issues germane to Tech Group activity. While the government did offer proof that Quattrone knew that the grand jury and the SEC sought Tech IPO-allocation related documents, we cannot say that the proof convinces us beyond a reasonable doubt that the error was harmless. That conclusion finds strong support in the deficiency of the court's charge. Under the charge, the jury was allowed to convict Quattrone of obstruction regardless of whether he intended such. Quattrone's defense of lack of knowledge of the specific focus of the investigation of Tech Group IPO activities was eliminated from the jury's consideration. Accordingly, the judgment of conviction with regard to Counts 1 and 2 must be vacated and the case remanded for retrial.

Questions

1. What e-mails do you find support Mr. Quattrone's claims that he did not know that the investigations related to the documents in his unit?
2. What e-mails and conduct do you find that contradict Mr. Quattrone's story and show intent?
3. Is this case one of a technicality? What do you learn of the significance of criminal intent from the case?

3. Responsibility for Criminal Acts

In some cases, persons who did not necessarily commit the criminal act itself are still held criminally responsible for acts committed by others.

(a) Corporate Liability

Corporations are held responsible for the acts of their employees. A corporation may also be held liable for crimes based on the failure of its employees to act. In the past decade, some of the nation's largest corporations have paid fines for crimes based on employees' failure to take action or for the actions they did take. **For Example, AIG,** the world's largest insurer, paid the largest fine in corporate history in the United States, $1.6 billion, for its questionable accounting practices and alleged sham insurance contracts undertaken for the purpose of boosting its earnings.[2]

(b) Officers and Agents of Corporations

One of the main differences between nonbusiness and business crimes is that more people in a company can be convicted for the same business crime. For nonbusiness crimes, only those who are actually involved in the act itself can be convicted of the crime. For business crimes, however, managers of firms whose employees commit criminal acts can be held liable if the managers authorized the conduct of the employees or knew about their conduct and did nothing or failed to act reasonably in their supervisory positions to prevent the employees from engaging in criminal conduct.

(c) Penalty for Crime: Forfeiture

When a defendant is convicted of a crime, the court may also declare that the defendant's rights in any property used or gained from a crime (an instrument of that crime) be confiscated. Some types of instruments of the crime are automatically forfeited, such as the tools of a crime. **For Example,** engraved plates can be used only to make counterfeit money or are the subject of an illegal sale, so the government can confiscate them. Confiscation is, in effect, an increased penalty for the defendant's crime.

Forfeiture is not limited to property that can be used only for crime. An automobile that is used to carry illegal merchandise may itself be seized by the government even though it is obvious that the automobile could also be put to a lawful use.

(d) Penalties for Business and White-Collar Crimes

As they existed at common law, most criminal penalties were created with "natural" persons in mind, as opposed to "artificial" or corporate persons. A $100,000 fine may be significant to an individual but to a corporation with $3 billion in assets and hundreds of millions in income, such a fine could be viewed as simply a relatively minimal cost of doing business.

Over the years criminal penalties have been reformed to address this need to have corporate penalties act as deterrents. Rather than using fixed-amount fines, statutes and courts apply a percentage of revenue penalties. **For Example,** a bad decision on a product line would cost a company 10 percent to

[2] www.sec.gov.

UNITED STATES V PARK, 421 US 658 (1975)

RATS IN THE WAREHOUSE AND A CEO WITH A FINE

Acme Markets, Inc., was a national food retail chain headquartered in Philadelphia, Pennsylvania. At the time of the government action, John R. Park [respondent] was president of Acme, which employed 36,000 people and operated 16 warehouses.

In 1970, the Food and Drug Administration (FDA) forwarded a letter to Mr. Park describing, in detail, problems with rodent infestation in Acme's Philadelphia warehouse facility. In December 1971, the FDA found the same types of conditions in Acme's Baltimore warehouse facility. In January 1972, the FDA's chief of compliance for its Baltimore office wrote to Mr. Park about the inspection. The letter included the following language:

> *We note with much concern that the old and new warehouse areas used for food storage were actively and extensively inhabited by live rodents. Of even more concern was the observation that such reprehensible conditions obviously existed for a prolonged period of time without any detection, or were completely ignored.*
>
> *We trust this letter will serve to direct your attention to the seriousness of the problem and formally advise you of the urgent need to initiate whatever measures are necessary to prevent recurrence and ensure compliance with the law.*

After Mr. Park received the letter, he met with the vice president for legal affairs for Acme and was assured that he was "investigating the situation immediately and would be taking corrective action."

When the FDA inspected the Baltimore warehouse in March 1972, there was some improvement in the facility, but there was still rodent infestation. Acme and Park were both charged with violations of the Federal Food, Drug, and Cosmetic Act. Acme pleaded guilty. Mr. Park was convicted and fined $500; he appealed based on error in the judge's instruction, given as follows:

> *The individual is or could be liable under the statute, even if he did not consciously do wrong. However, the fact that the Defendant is president and is a chief executive officer of the Acme Markets does not require a finding of guilt. Though he need not have personally participated in the situation, he must have had a responsible relationship to the issue. The issue is, in this case, whether the Defendant, John R. Park, by virtue of his position in the company, had a position of authority and responsibility in the situation out of which these charges arose.*

The court of appeals reversed Mr. Park's conviction, and the government appealed.

Judicial Opinion

BURGER, C. J.... Central to the Court's conclusion [in *United States v Dotterweich*], 320 U.S. 277 (1943), that individuals other than proprietors are subject to the criminal provisions of the Act was the reality that "the only way in which a corporation can act is through the individuals who act on its behalf."

At the same time, however, the Court was aware of the concern... that literal enforcement "might operate too harshly by sweeping within its condemnation any person however remotely entangled in the proscribed shipment." A limiting principle, in the form of "settled doctrines of criminal law" defining those who "are responsible for the commission of a misdemeanor," was available. In this context, the Court concluded, those doctrines dictated that the offense was committed "by all who have... a responsible share in the furtherance of the transaction which the statute outlaws."

The Act does not, as we observed in *Dotterweich*, make criminal liability turn on "awareness of some wrongdoing" or "conscious fraud." The duty imposed by Congress on responsible corporate agents is, we emphasize, one that requires the highest standard of foresight and vigilance, but the Act, in its criminal aspect, does not require that which is objectively impossible. The theory upon which responsible corporate agents are held criminally accountable for "causing" violations of the Act permits a claim that a defendant was "powerless" to prevent or correct the violation to "be raised defensively at a trial on the merits." *U.S. v Wiesenfield Warehouse Co.*, 376 U.S. 86 (1964). If such a claim is made, the defendant has the burden of coming forward with evidence, but this does not alter the Government's ultimate burden of proving beyond a reasonable doubt the defendant's guilt, including his power, in light of the duty imposed by the Act, to prevent or correct the prohibited condition.

Turning to the jury charge in this case, it is of course arguable that isolated parts can be read as intimating that a finding of guilt could be predicated solely on respondent's corporate position.... Viewed as a whole, the charge did not permit the jury to find guilt solely on the basis of respondent's position in the corporation; rather, it fairly advised the jury that to find guilt it must find respondent "had a responsible relation to the situation," and "by virtue of his position . . . had authority and responsibility" to deal with the situation. The situation referred to could only be "foods . . . held in unsanitary conditions in a warehouse with the result that it consisted, in part, of filth or . . . may have been contaminated with filth."

Park testified in his defense that he had employed a system in which he relied upon his subordinates, and that he was ultimately responsible for this system. He testified further that he had found these subordinates to be "dependable" and had "great confidence" in them.

[The rebuttal] evidence was not offered to show that respondent had a propensity to commit criminal acts, that the crime charged had been committed; its purpose was to demonstrate that respondent was on notice that he could not rely on his system of delegation to subordinates to prevent or correct unsanitary conditions at Acme's warehouses, and that he must have been aware of the deficiencies of this system before the Baltimore violations were discovered. The evidence was therefore relevant since it served to rebut Park's defense that he had justifiably relied upon subordinates to handle sanitation matters.

[Reversed]

Questions

1. How long had Mr. Park known about the rats in the warehouse?
2. Does it matter that a subordinate did not respond?
3. Do officers need to be certain their subordinates are reliable in order to avoid criminal liability?

20 percent of its earnings. A criminal penalty could be imposed in the same percentage fashion with the idea that the company simply made a bad legal decision that should be reflected in earnings. A company that fixed prices might face a criminal fine of 20 percent of the profits it made from the price-fixing.

Another change in penalties for business and white collar crimes has been the requirement for mandatory prison sentences for officers and directors who are convicted of crimes committed as they led their corporations. The human element of the corporation is then punished for the crimes that the business committed. The U.S. Sentencing Commission, established by Congress in 1984, has developed both federal sentencing guidelines and a carrot-and-stick approach to fighting business crime. If the managers of a company are involved and working to prevent criminal misconduct in the company and a crime occurs, the guidelines permit sentence reductions for the managers' efforts. If the managers do not adequately supervise conduct and do not encourage compliance with the law, the guidelines require judges to impose harsher sentences and fines. The guidelines, referred to as the **Federal Sentencing Guidelines or the U.S. Sentencing Guidelines,** apply to federal crimes such as securities fraud, antitrust violations, racketeering, theft (embezzlement), Medicare fraud, and other business crimes. The sentencing guidelines permit a judge to place a guilty company on probation, with the length of the probation controlled by whether the company had prevention programs in place.

Following the collapse of companies such as Enron, WorldCom, and Adelphia, the U.S. Sentencing Commission (USSC) piloted the passage of the 2001 Economic Crime Package: Consolidation, Clarification, and Certainty. The 2001 package amends the Sentencing Guidelines. The Economic Crime Package consists of several major parts, including (1) consolidation of fraud, theft, and other financial crimes into one table for purposes of sentencing and (2) a revised, common loss table to determine losses. In addition to the statutory clarification on the types of financial crimes, the

THINKING THINGS THROUGH

EMPLOYEES SHREDDING—EMPLOYER LIABLE?

As the financial problems of the infamous energy company Enron grew, its audit firm, Arthur Andersen, became concerned that some of Enron's accounting and financial statements were doubtful. On October 16, 2001, Enron would not change the numbers in an earnings release in response to Andersen's concerns. Nancy Temple, legal counsel for Arthur Andersen, wrote an e-mail to David Duncan, the audit partner for the Enron account in Houston, about a release that Andersen was going to issue regarding Enron's accounting.

Later that same day, Temple also sent an e-mail to a member of Andersen's internal team of accounting experts and attached a copy of the company's document policy. On October 20, the Enron crisis-response team held a conference call, during which Temple instructed everyone to "[m]ake sure to follow the [document] policy." On October 23, 2001, Enron CEO Ken Lay declined to answer questions during a call with analysts because of "potential lawsuits, as well as the SEC inquiry." After the call, Duncan met with other Andersen partners on the Enron engagement team and told everyone to comply with the document policy. Following the meeting, Andersen employees began destroying documents related to Enron.

On October 30, 2001, the SEC opened a formal investigation and sent Enron a letter that requested accounting documents.

Throughout this time period, the document destruction continued despite reservations by some of Andersen's managers. On November 8, 2001, Enron announced that it would issue a comprehensive restatement of its earnings and assets. Also on November 8, the SEC served Enron and Andersen with subpoeanas for records. On November 9, Duncan's secretary sent an e-mail that stated: "Per Dave—No more shredding. . . . We have been officially served for our documents." Enron filed for bankruptcy less than a month later. Duncan was fired and later pleaded guilty to witness tampering. *

Applying the *Park* case, who is criminally liable for the document shredding? The employees who actually did it? The managers who ordered it to begin? The company itself? [Arthur Andersen LLP v U.S., 544 US 696 (2005)]

*Duncan withdrew his plea following the appeal and U.S. Supreme Court ruling in this case.

amendments also required the USSC to reform its guidelines according to the legislation. The guidelines, amended in November 2003 to address the increased corporate and white-collar criminal penalties enacted under Sarbanes-Oxley (SOX), consider the seriousness of the offense, the company's history of violations, its cooperation in the investigation, the effectiveness of its compliance program (often called an *ethics program*), and the role of senior management in the wrongdoing. Corporate managers found to have masterminded any criminal activity must be sentenced to prison time.[3] Figure 8-1 is a summary of the current penalties for federal crimes.

(e) Sarbanes-Oxley Reforms to Criminal Penalties

Part of SOX, passed by Congress following the collapses of Enron and WorldCom corporations, was the **White-Collar Crime Penalty Enhancement Act of 2002.**[4] This act increases penalties substantially. **For Example,** the penalties for mail and wire fraud are increased from a maximum of five years to a maximum of 20 years. Penalties for violation of pension laws increased from one year to 10 years and the fines increased from $5,000 to $100,000.[5] The U.S. Sentencing Commission has amended its

[3] Mary Kreiner Ramirez, "Just in Crime: Guiding Economic Crime Reform after the Sarbanes-Oxley Act of 2002," *34 Loyola University of Chicago Law Journal* 359, 387 (2003).

[4] 18 USC § 1314 *et seq.*

[5] 18 USC §§ 1341 and 1343; 29 USC § 1131.

FIGURE 8-1 Penalties for Federal Crimes

Company/Person	Issue	Status
Andrew Fastow, former CFO of Enron (2004)	Multimillion-dollar earnings from serving as principal in SPEs of Enron created to keep debts off the company books; significant sales of shares during the time frame preceding company collapse	Resigned as CFO; appeared before Congress and took the Fifth Amendment; entered guilty plea to securities and wire fraud; sentence of 10 years
Bernie Ebbers (2005) Former CEO, WorldCom	Fraud	Convicted; sentenced to 25 years
Computer Associates (2004)	Criminal investigation pending on securities fraud and obstruction following $2.2 billion restatement in sales	Pending investigations; former CEO entered guilty plea to felony charges
Enron (2001)	Earnings overstated through mark-to-market accounting; off-the-book/special-purpose entities (SPEs) carried significant amounts of Enron debt not reflected in the financial statements; significant offshore SPEs (881 of 3,000 SPEs were offshore, primarily in Cayman Islands)	Company in bankruptcy (touted as the largest bankruptcy in U.S. history); shareholder litigation pending; Congressional hearings held; CFO Andrew Fastow and others entered guilty pleas; *see* Lea Fastow, Kenneth Lay, and Jeffrey Skilling
HealthSouth (2003)	$2.7 billion accounting fraud; overstatement of revenues	16 former executives indicted; 5 guilty please; *see* Richard Scrushy
KPMG (2006)	Tax shelter fraud	Settled by paying a penalty of $456 million fine in lieu of indictment; 16 former partners and employees under indictment
L. Dennis Kozlowski, former CEO of Tyco (2003)	Accused of improper use of company funds	Indicted in New York for failure to pay sales tax on transactions in fine art; hung jury on charges of looting Tyco; convicted on retrial with 25-year sentence
Marsh McLennan (2005)	Price-fixing	Paid $850 million in restitution to end investigation of its brokerage practices
Martha Stewart, CEO of Martha Stewart Living, Omnimedia, Inc., and close friend of Dr. Waksal (2003)	Sold 5,000 shares of ImClone one day before public announcement of negative FDA action on Erbitux	Indicted and convicted, along with her broker at Merrill Lynch, of making false statements and conspiracy; served sentence and currently on probation
Parmalat (based in Italy) (2004)	Accounting fraud–fake $5 billion account in Bank of America via forged documents	Company entered bankruptcy; top executives charged or entered guilty pleas; trials began in 2006
Xerox (2003)	Improper booking of revenues ($6.4 billion)	Had settled charges with SEC in April 2003 for $10 million; inquiry expanded to KPMG (settled)

guidelines to reflect the higher penalties and, as noted earlier, to group all types of financial crimes into the same treatment and results in terms of the sentence required and the formulas for determination of the number of years and the fine.[6]

In 2005, the U.S. Supreme Court imposed some restrictions on the sentencing process under the guidelines. In *U.S. v Booker*, 543 US 220 (2005), the court held that when judges are determining sentences for defendants under the guidelines any facts, other than the defendant's prior conviction, must be established by a jury beyond a reasonable doubt. In the case, Booker had been convicted of possession of 50 grams of crack cocaine. The sentencing judge considered additional evidence in the sentencing hearing that Booker had 566 additional grams of crack that was not used as evidence at the trial. The result was that Booker was not eligible under the sentencing guidelines for a lesser sentence of 21 years and 10 months and the judge imposed a sentence of 30 years. The Supreme Court reversed the sentencing portion of the case, remanded the case for resentencing and held that if the judge was going to consider additional facts that affected the length of sentence, such as the additional crack, those additional facts must be proved in the same way as the crime—before a jury and beyond a reasonable doubt. The impact of the *Booker* case has been widespread with many defendants now in the process of being resentenced, including many of the business executives convicted and sentenced as a result of the Enron-era scandals.

4. Indemnification of Crime Victims

Penalties are paid to the government. Typically, the victim of a crime does not benefit from the criminal prosecution and conviction of the wrongdoer, although courts can order that restitution be paid to victims.

Several states have adopted statutes providing a limited degree of indemnification to victims of crime to compensate them for the harm or loss sustained.[7] Under some criminal victim indemnification statutes, dependents of a deceased victim are entitled to recover the amount of support they were deprived of by the victim's death. The Victims of Crime Act of 1984 creates a federal Crime Victims Fund. Using the fines paid into the federal courts as well as other monies, the federal government makes grants to the states to assist them in financing programs to provide assistance for victims of crime.[8] The Victim and Witness Protection Act of 1982 authorizes the sentencing judge in a federal district court to order, in certain cases, that the defendant make restitution (restoration) to the victim or pay the victim the amount of medical expenses or loss of income caused by the crime.[9]

(a) Action for Damages

The criminal prosecution of a wrongdoer is not undertaken primarily for the financial benefit of the victim of the crime, but the victim is typically entitled to bring a civil action for damages against the wrongdoer for the harm sustained. Statutes creating business crimes often give the victim the right to sue for damages. **For Example,** a company or individual violating federal antitrust laws is liable to the victim for three times the damages actually sustained.

(b) Indemnification of Unjustly Convicted

If an innocent person is convicted of a crime, the state legislature typically pays the person damages to compensate for the wrong that has been done. In some states, this right to indemnity is expressly established by statute, as in the case of the New York Unjust Conviction and Imprisonment Act. The fact that a person has been imprisoned while awaiting trial and is then acquitted does not entitle that person to compensation under such a statute because an acquittal does not mean that the person was found innocent. It means only that the government was not able to prove guilt beyond a reasonable doubt.[10]

[6] 18 USCA § 1348 (West Supp. 2003).

[7] A 1973 Uniform Crime Victims Reparations Act was adopted in Kansas, Louisiana, Montana, North Dakota, Ohio, and Utah. This act has been superseded by the Uniform Victims of Crime Act of 1992 adopted only in Montana, with variations.

[8] 18 USC § 1401 *et seq.*

[9] 18 USC § 3579, as amended by 18 USC § 18.18; see *Hughey v United States,* 495 US 411 (1990). Some states likewise provide for payment into a special fund. *Ex parte* Lewis, 556 So 2d 370 (Ala 1989). In 2002, Congress passed another victims' compensation statute, with this one providing relief and assistance to the victims of terrorist attacks in the United States. 42 USCA § 10603b.

[10] *People v Neff,* 731 NY S2d 269 (2001).

B. White-Collar Crimes

White-collar crime is generally considered business crime, the type committed without physical threats or acts.

5. Conspiracies

Prior to the commission of an intended crime, a person may engage in conduct that is itself a crime, such as a conspiracy. A **conspiracy** is an agreement between two or more persons to commit an unlawful act or to use unlawful means to achieve an otherwise lawful result. The crime is the agreement itself; generally, it is immaterial that nothing is done to carry out the agreement, although some conspiracy statutes do require that some act is done to carry out the agreement before the crime of conspiracy is committed.

6. Crimes Related to Production, Competition, and Marketing

(a) Improper Use of Interstate Commerce

The shipment of improper goods or the transmission of improper information in interstate commerce constitutes a crime under various federal statutes. It is a federal crime to use interstate commerce as part of a scheme to defraud, blackmail, or extort. Shipping adulterated or mislabeled foods, drugs, or cosmetics is also a federal crime.

The Communications Act of 1934, as amended, makes it a crime to manufacture or sell devices knowing their primary use is to unscramble satellite telecasts without having paid for the right to do so.[11]

(b) Securities Crimes

To protect the investing public, both state and federal laws have regulated the issuance and public sale of stocks and bonds. Between 1933 and 1940, Congress adopted seven such regulatory statutes. These statutes and the crimes associated with sales of securities are covered in Chapter 46.

7. Money Laundering

The federal government has adopted a Money Laundering Control Act (MLCA).[12] The act prohibits the knowing and willful participation in a financial transaction involving unlawful proceeds when the transaction is designed to conceal or disguise the source of the funds. The so-called *USA Patriot Act* that was passed on October 26, 2001, less than two months after the destruction of the World Trade Center and the damage to the Pentagon on September 11, 2001, includes a substantial number of changes and amendments to the Money Laundering Control Act and the Bank Secrecy Act (BSA).[13] Both statutes have been used as means to control bribery, tax evasion, and money laundering. Their changes and amendments were designed to curb the funding of terrorist activities in the United States.

Prior to the September 11, 2001 reforms, these two statutes applied only to financial institutions. The Patriot Act expands the coverage of the law to anyone involved in financial transactions, which includes securities brokers; travel agents; those who close real estate transactions; insurance companies; loan or finance companies; casinos; currency exchanges; check-cashing firms; auto, plane, and boat dealers; and branches and agencies of foreign banks located in the United States. The amendments make even small businesses subject to the requirements of disclosure under MLCA and BSA, such as reporting cash transactions in excess of $10,000.

In addition, the types of accounts covered have been expanded. The accounts covered are not only securities accounts but also money market accounts. Furthermore, banks must designate one person who will be responsible for following through on information furnished to the bank by law enforcement agencies on suspicious transactions and activities as well as individuals. Following the receipt of this information from the federal government, the bank's designated official is required to implement new policies to prevent the transactions noted or investigate internally for transactions of any individuals reported.

The Patriot Act also expands the scope of the more detailed regulations from large financial institutions to smaller ones. Prior to the changes, most small banks assumed that they were exempt from the more detailed reporting and record-keeping requirements. With the changes, no bank is exempt unless it applies for such an exemption from the U.S. Treasury Department.

[11] 47 USC § 705(d)(1), (e)(4), 47 USC § 605 (d)(1), (e)(4); *United States v Harrell*, 983 F2d 36 (5th Cir 1993); but see *DIRECTV, Inc. v Robson*, 420 F3d 532 (5th Cir. 2005).

[12] 18 USC §§ 1956–1957 (2000). *U.S. v Prince*, 214 F3d 740 (6th Cir 2000).

[13] 31 USC § 531(h).

The businesses subject to these laws have developed anti–money-laundering programs. To enjoy reduced sentencing benefits under the Federal Sentencing Guidelines, businesses must have such a program in place. These programs must include a "Know Your Customer" training segment that teaches employees how to spot suspicious customers and transactions.

8. Racketeering

Congress passed the **Racketeer Influenced and Corrupt Organizations (RICO) Act**[14] in 1970 as part of the Organized Crime Control Act. The law was designed primarily to prevent individuals involved in organized crime from investing money obtained through racketeering in legitimate businesses. However, the broad language of the act, coupled with a provision that allows individuals and businesses to sue for treble damages, has resulted in an increasing number of lawsuits against ordinary businesspersons not associated with organized crime.

(a) Criminal and Civil Applications

RICO authorizes criminal and civil actions against persons who use any income derived from racketeering activity to invest in, control, or conduct an enterprise through a pattern of *racketeering activity.*[15] In criminal and civil actions under RICO, a pattern of racketeering activity must be established by proving that at least two acts of racketeering activity—so-called *predicate acts*—have been committed within 10 years.[16] Conviction under RICO's criminal provisions may result in a $25,000 fine and up to 20 years' imprisonment as well as forfeiture of the property involved. A successful civil plaintiff may recover three times the actual damages suffered and attorney fees.[17]

(b) Expanding Usage

Civil RICO actions have been successful against business entities, such as accounting firms, labor unions, insurance companies, commercial banks, and stock brokerage firms. However, under the Private Securities Litigation Reform Act of 1995, securities fraud is eliminated as a **predicate act,** or a qualifying underlying offense, for private RICO actions, absent a prior criminal conviction.[18]

9. Bribery

Bribery is the act of giving money, property, or any benefit to a particular person to influence that person's judgment in favor of the giver. At common law, the crime was limited to doing such acts to influence a public official.

The giving and the receiving of a bribe constitute separate crimes. In addition, the act of trying to obtain a bribe may be a crime of solicitation of bribery in some states, while in other states bribery is broadly defined to include solicitation of bribes.

10. Commercial Bribery

Commercial bribery is a form of bribery in which an agent for another is paid or given something of value in order to make a decision on behalf of his or her principal that benefits the party paying the agent. **For Example,** a napkin supplier who pays a restaurant agent $500 in exchange for that agent's decision to award the restaurant's napkin contract to that supplier has engaged in commercial bribery. Connecticut's commercial bribery statute is a good example. It provides:

> *A person is guilty of commercial bribery when he confers, or agrees to confer, any benefit upon any employee, agent or fiduciary without the*

[14] 18 USC §§ 1961–1968.

[15] § 1961. Definitions
(1) "Racketeering activity" means any act or threat involving murder, kidnapping, gambling, arson, robbery, bribery, extortion, dealing in obscene matter, dealing in a controlled substance or listed chemical, or sports bribery; counterfeiting; theft from interstate shipment; embezzlement from pension and welfare funds; extortionate credit transactions; fraud; wire fraud; mail fraud; procurement of citizenship or nationalization unlawfully; reproduction of naturalization or citizenship papers; obstruction of justice; tampering with a witness, victim, or an informant; retaliating against a witness, victim, or an informant; false statement in application and use of passport; forgery or false use of passport; fraud and misuse of visas, permits and other documents; racketeering; unlawful welfare fund payments; laundering of monetary instruments; use of interstate commerce facilities in the commission of murder-for-hire; sexual exploitation of children; interstate transportation of stolen motor vehicles; interstate transportation of stolen property; trafficking in counterfeit labels of phonorecords, computer programs or computer program documentation, or packaging and copies of motion pictures or other audiovisual works; criminal infringement of a copyright; trafficking in contraband cigarettes; and white slave traffic.

[16] Brian Slocum, "RICO and the Legislative Supremacy Approach to Federal Criminal Lawmaking," 31 *Loyola Univ. Chicago Law Journal* 639 (2000).

[17] 18 USC § 1963.

[18] 15 USC § 78(a), (n)–(t).

consent of the latter's employer or principal, with intent to influence his conduct in relation to his employer's or principal's affairs.[19]

11. Extortion and Blackmail

Extortion and *blackmail* are crimes in which money is exchanged for either specific actions or restraint in taking action.

(a) Extortion

When a public officer, acting under the apparent authority of his or her office, makes an illegal demand, the officer has committed the crime of **extortion.** **For Example,** if a health inspector threatens to close down a restaurant on a false charge of violating the sanitation laws unless the restaurant pays the inspector a sum of money, the inspector has committed extortion. (If the restaurant voluntarily offers the inspector the money to prevent the restaurant from being shut down because of actual violations of the sanitation laws, the crime committed would be bribery.) Modern statutes tend to ignore the public officer aspect of the common law and expand extortion to include obtaining anything of value by threat, which might be, for example, loan sharking. In a number of states, statutes extend the extortion concept to include making terrorist threats.[20]

(b) Blackmail

In jurisdictions where extortion is limited to the conduct of public officials, a nonofficial commits **blackmail** by making demands that would be extortion if made by a public official. Ordinarily, blackmail is the act of threatening someone with publicity about a matter that would damage the victim's personal or business reputation.

12. Corrupt Influence

In harmony with changing concepts of right and wrong, society has increasingly outlawed certain practices on the ground that they exert a corrupting influence on business transactions.

(a) Improper Political Influence

To protect against the improper influencing of political or governmental action, various acts have been classified as crimes. **For Example,** it is a crime for the holder of a government office to be financially interested in, or to receive money from, an enterprise that is seeking to do business with the government. Such conflicts of interest are likely to produce a result that is harmful to the public. Likewise, lobbyists and foreign agents must register in Washington, D.C.,[21] and must adhere to statutes regulating the giving and receiving of contributions for political campaigns. Violation of these regulatory statutes is a crime.

(b) Foreign Corrupt Practices Act

The **Foreign Corrupt Practices Act (FCPA)** is a federal criminal statute that applies to businesses whose principal offices are in the United States; it is an antibribery and anticorruption statute covering these companies' international operations.[22] The FCPA prohibits making, authorizing, or promising payments or gifts of money or anything of value with the intent to corrupt. This prohibition applies to payments or gifts designed to influence official acts of foreign officials, parties, party officials, candidates for office, nongovernmental organizations (NGOs), or any person who transmits the gift or money to these types of persons.

The FCPA does not prohibit **grease** or **facilitation payments.** These are payments made only to get officials to perform their normal duties or to perform them in a timely manner. Facilitation payments are those made to (1) secure a permit or a license, (2) obtain paper processing, (3) secure police protection, (4) provide phone, water, or power services, or (5) obtain any other similar action.

13. Counterfeiting

Counterfeiting is making, with fraudulent intent, a document or coin that appears to be genuine but is not because the person making it did not have the authority to make it. It is a federal crime to make, to

[19] CGSA § 53a-160 (2002). Other examples of commercial bribery statues can be found at Minn Stat Ann § 6-9.86 (Minnesota 2001); NH Rev Stat § 638:8 (New Hampshire 2001); Alaska Stat 11.45.670 (Alaska 2001); and Ala Code § 13A-11-120 (Alabama 2001). Mississippi prohibits commercial bribery as well as sports bribery, which is paying the agent of a sports team in order to influence the outcome of a sporting event. Miss Code Ann § 97-9-10 (2001).

[20] *Pennsylvania v Bunting*, 426 A2d 130 (Pa 1981).

[21] Foreign Agents Registration Act, 22 USC § 611 *et seq.*, as amended.

[22] 15 USC § 78dd-1 *et seq.*

ETHICS & THE LAW

WHY REGULATE BRIBES?

In 1999, a scandal involving the International Olympic Committee (IOC) erupted when it was discovered that members of the Salt Lake City Olympic Committee had given extensive gifts to members of the IOC to win the 2002 Winter Olympics for Salt Lake City. The gifts included everything from college tuition to medical care to entertainment. The attitude at the time toward the Salt Lake City revelations was, "It's always been done this way," or "Everybody does this," or "It doesn't really hurt anyone."

Why should criminal indictments be brought against the U.S. citizens who bribed IOC members?* Why do we care?

*The criminal charges against two members of the Salt Lake City Olympic Committee were dismissed by the court but were reinstated by the Tenth Circuit. *U.S. v Welch*, 327 F3d 1081 (10th Cir. 2003). The federal charges were conspiracy to commit commercial bribery in violation of the Utah statute prohibiting such.

possess with intent to transfer, or to transfer counterfeit coins, bank notes, or obligations or other securities of the United States. Legislation has also been adopted to prohibit the passing of counterfeit foreign securities or counterfeit notes of foreign banks. Various states also have statutes prohibiting the making and passing of counterfeit coins and bank notes. These statutes often provide, as does the federal statute, a punishment for the mutilation of bank notes or the lightening (of the weight) or mutilation of coins.

14. Forgery

Forgery consists of the fraudulent making or material altering of an instrument, such as a check, that attempts to create or changes a legal liability of another person.[23] The instrument must have the appearance of legal efficacy to constitute forgery.

Ordinarily, **forgery** consists of signing another's name with intent to defraud, but it may also consist of making an entire instrument or altering an existing one. It may result from signing a fictitious name or the offender's own name with the intent to defraud. When the nonowner of a credit card signs the owner's name on a credit card invoice without the owner's permission, this act is a forgery.

The issuing or delivery of a forged instrument to another person constitutes the crime of **uttering** a forged instrument. The elements of the crime are (1) the offering of a forged instrument with a representation by words or acts that it is true and genuine, (2) the knowledge that it is false, forged, or counterfeit, and (3) the intent to defraud.[24] Any sending of a forged check through the channels of commerce or of bank collection constitutes an uttering of a forged instrument. The act of depositing a forged check into the forger's bank account by depositing it in an automatic teller machine constitutes uttering within the meaning of a forgery statute.[25]

15. Perjury

Perjury consists of knowingly giving false testimony in a judicial proceeding after having been sworn to tell the truth. Knowingly making false answers on any form filed with a government typically constitutes perjury or is subjected to the same punishment as perjury. In some jurisdictions, the false answers given in a situation other than in court or the litigation process is called the crime of *false swearing*.

16. False Claims and Pretenses

Many statutes make it a crime to submit false claims or to obtain goods by false pretenses.

(a) False Claims

Some statutes provide that making a false claim to an insurance company, a government office, or a relief agency is a crime. The federal false statement statute

23 A bank withdrawal slip or a charge slip may be a forged written instrument. See *State v Daniels*, 23 P3d 1125 (CA Wash 2001).

24 *Id.*

25 *Wisconsin v Tolliver*, 440 NW2d 571 (Wis App 1989).

makes it a crime to knowingly and willfully make a false material statement about any matter within the jurisdiction of any department or agency of the United States. It is a crime for a contractor to make a false claim against the United States for payment for work that was never performed. Other statutes indirectly regulate the matter by declaring that signing a false written claim constitutes perjury or is subject to the same punishment as perjury.[26]

(b) Obtaining Goods by False Pretenses

Almost all states have statutes that forbid obtaining money or goods under false pretenses.[27] These statutes vary in detail and scope. Sometimes they are directed against a particular form of deception, such as using a bad check. An intent to defraud is an essential element of obtaining property by false pretenses.[28]

Examples of false pretense include delivering a check knowing that there is insufficient money in the bank account to cover the check.[29] False representations as to future profits in a business are also forms of false pretenses.

Failing to perform on a contract is not a false pretense crime unless the contract had been entered into with the intent of not performing it.[30]

(c) Unauthorized Use of Automated Teller Machine

Obtaining money from an automated teller machine (ATM) by the unauthorized use of the depositor's ATM card is a federal crime.

(d) False Information Submitted to Banks

Knowingly making false statements in a loan application to a federally insured bank is a federal crime.[31] It is also a crime for a landowner to put a false value on land transferred to a bank as security for a loan.[32]

17. Bad Checks

The use of a bad check is commonly made a crime by statute. In the absence of a bad check statute, the use of a bad check could generally be prosecuted under a false pretenses statute.

Under a bad check statute, it is a crime to use or pass a check with the intent to defraud with the knowledge that there are insufficient funds in the bank to pay the check when it is presented for payment. Knowledge that the bad check will not be paid when presented to the bank is an essential element of the crime. The bad check statutes typically provide that if the check is not made good within a specified number of days after payment by the bank is refused, it is presumed that the defendant acted with the intent to defraud.[33] For more information on checks, see Chapter 28.

18. Credit Card Crimes

It is a crime to steal a credit card and, in some states, to possess the credit card of another person without that person's consent. Using a credit card without the permission of the card owner is the crime of obtaining goods or services by false pretenses or with the intent to defraud. Likewise, a person who continues to use a credit card with the knowledge that it has been canceled is guilty of the crime of obtaining goods by false pretenses.

When, without permission, someone signs the name of the card owner for the credit card transaction, she has committed the crime of forgery.

The Credit Card Fraud Act of 1984[34] makes it a federal crime to obtain anything of value in excess of $1,000 in a year by means of a counterfeit credit card, to make or sell such cards, or to possess more than 15 counterfeit cards at one time.

[26] The Federal False Claims Act is violated only when the false claim is submitted with knowledge of its falsity. *See U.S. ex rel. Foundation Aiding the Elderly v Horizon West*, 265 F3d 1011 (9th Cir 2001).

[27] *Mass. v Cheromcka*, 850 NE2d 1088 (Mass App 2006).

[28] *State v Moore*, 97 Conn App 2006 WL 2370553 243, (Conn App).

[29] *U.S. v Tudeme*, 457 F3d 577 (Fed App 2006).

[30] *Jacobs v State*, 2006 WL 2069423 (Tex App).

[31] 18 USC § 1014. See *United States v Autorino*, 381 F3d 48 (2nd Cir 2004).

[32] *United States v Faulkner*, 17 F3d 745 (5th Cir 1994).

[33] *U.S. v Smith*, 2003 WL 2145660 (CA 10).

[34] 18 USC § 1029.

19. Embezzlement

Embezzlement is the fraudulent conversion of another's property or money by a person to whom it has been entrusted.[35] Employees who take their employer's property or funds for personal use have committed the crime of embezzlement. An agent employee commits embezzlement when he receives and keeps payments from third persons—payments the agent should have turned over to the principal. **For Example,** when an insured gives money to an insurance agent to pay the insurance company but the insurance agent uses the money to pay premiums on the policies of other persons, the agent is guilty of embezzlement. Generally, the fact that the defendant intends to return the property or money embezzled or does in fact do so is no defense.

Today, every jurisdiction has not only a general embezzlement statute but also various statutes applicable to particular situations. **For Example,** statutes cover embezzlement by government officials and employees.

20. Obstruction of Justice: Sarbanes-Oxley

Another of the provisions of the Sarbanes-Oxley Act of 2002 clarifies what constitutes obstruction of justice and increases the penalties for such an act. The new section makes it a felony for anyone, including company employees, auditors, attorneys, and consultants,

> *to alter, destroy, mutilate, conceal, cover up, falsify or make a false entry with the "intent to impede, obstruct, or influence the investigation or proper administration of any matter within the jurisdiction of any department or agency of the United States."*[36]

The statute goes on to address audit records specifically and requires auditors to retain their work papers related to a client's audit for at least five years. Any destruction of documents prior to that time constitutes a felony and carries a penalty of up to

SPORTS & ENTERTAINMENT LAW

MARTHA STEWART AND OBSTRUCTION

Martha Stewart, the legendary domestic doyenne, had purchased shares in ImClone, a company headed by her friend, Dr. Sam Waksal. In early December 2001, the Food and Drug Administration (FDA) indicated to scientists and others at ImClone that its approval to sell its promising anti-cancer drug, Erbitux, would not be forthcoming. The company did not release this negative information. Waksal and his family, however, spent most of the month of December selling their shares of ImClone to avoid the losses they would experience when the information about the lack of approval for Erbitux was released. He was later sentenced to seven years in prison for selling his shares and forging documents that were necessary for such extensive sales by a corporate insider.

Peter Bacanovic was a Merrill Lynch broker whose clients included Stewart and Waksal. During the last week of December 2001 and the first week of January 2002, Bacanovic was vacationing in Florida. Douglas Faneuil, a Merrill Lynch client associate in his mid-twenties who had been working as Bacanovic's assistant for about six months, was responsible for covering Bacanovic's desk when he was away. Between 9 and 10 A.M. on December 27, 2001, Faneuil received several phone calls on Bacanovic's line from Sam Waksal's daughters. They wanted to sell their ImClone shares.

Faneuil kept Bacanovic apprised of the details of the calls from the Waksal family by telephone. In the midst of one of their conversations, Faneuil heard Bacanovic say suddenly, "Oh, my God, get Martha [Stewart] on the phone."

Shortly thereafter, Stewart—who was en route to Mexico for a vacation with her friend Mariana Pasternak—called Bacanovic's office. Stewart asked Faneuil for a price quote and

[35] *State v Weaver*, 607 SE2d 599 (NC 2005).

[36] 18 USC § 1519. The newly defined and expanded crime of obstruction carries an unspecified fine and a sentence of up to 20 years.

SPORTS & ENTERTAINMENT LAW

continued

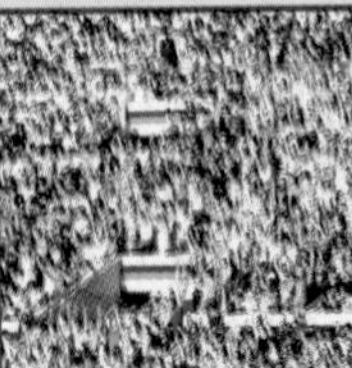

directed him to sell all of the ImClone shares that remained in her portfolio.

Stewart's ImClone sell order was executed at an average price of $58.43 per share, yielding proceeds of approximately $230,000. Pursuant to Stewart's instructions, Faneuil sent an e-mail to her personal account confirming the trade. Ms. Stewart was able to avoid a $40,000 loss by selling on December 27 as opposed to December 28 when the information became public.

When SEC and Justice Department officials confronted Stewart about the timing of her sale of ImClone stock, which did not violate any securities or criminal laws because she sold the stock based on others' sale of their shares, she was not forthright.

- On January 31, 2002, Stewart asked Ann Armstrong (her assistant) to show her the messages, including the entry for the December 27 message from Bacanovic. Upon reading the message, Stewart took the computer mouse from Armstrong and deleted and typed over a portion of the text so that what had initially read, "Peter Bacanovic thinks Imclone is going to start trading downward" was revised to read, "Peter Bacanovic re imclone [sic]." Immediately thereafter, Stewart told Armstrong to restore the message to the original, and Armstrong did so.
- On February 4, 2002, Stewart met at the offices of the U.S. Attorney with two SEC enforcement attorneys, an Assistant United States Attorney and an FBI agent, all of whom were investigating the December 27 ImClone trading. She produced a log showing the notation of this decision (a stop-loss order), but the government was able to show through scientific lab analysis that the date on the log had been altered from its original to reflect her contention and limited date and sale.

The government also uncovered the following:

- Discussions between and among the three about the "story" they would tell
- Faneuil's receipt of New York Knicks tickets given in exchange for remaining on the same page with the story of Stewart and Baconovic

A jury convicted Stewart of obstruction of justice.

List the mistakes Martha Stewart made in handling the government inquiry about her ImClone stock sales. What types of conduct described here would constitute obstruction of justice? If there is no underlying crime, can someone be convicted of obstruction of justice? Discuss the ethical issues in the series of actions Ms. Stewart took. **[U.S. v Stewart, 443 F3d 273 (2nd Cir NY 2006)]**

10 years. The statute is a direct response to the reversed federal case brought against Arthur Andersen, the audit firm for the collapsed Enron Corporation.

21. Corporate Fraud: Sarbanes-Oxley

SOX also created a new form of mail and wire fraud. Ordinary, mail or wire fraud consists of the use of the mail or telephones for purposes of defrauding someone of money and/or property. However, the SOX form of mail or wire fraud is based on new requirements imposed on corporate officers to certify their financial statements when they are issued. If a corporate officer fails to comply with all requirements for financial statement certification or certifies financial statements that contain false material information, the officer and company have committed corporate fraud with penalties that range from fines of $1,000,000 and/or 10 years to $5,000,000 and/or 20 years for willful violation of the certification requirements.

22. The Common Law Crimes

In contrast to white-collar crimes, *common law crimes* are crimes that involve the use of force or the threat of force or cause injury to persons or damage to property. The following sections discuss crimes of force and crimes against property that affect businesses.

(a) Larceny

Larceny is the wrongful or fraudulent taking of the personal property of another by any person with fraudulent intent. Shoplifting is a common form of larceny. In many states, shoplifting is made a separate crime.

Although the term *larceny* is broadly used in everyday speech, not every unlawful taking is a larceny. At common law, a defendant who took property of another with the intent to return it was not guilty of larceny. The common law has been changed in some states so that a person who borrows a car for a joyride is guilty of larceny, theft, or some other statutory offense. In some states, all forms of larceny and robbery are consolidated into a statutory crime of theft. At common law, there was no crime known as theft.

(b) Robbery

Robbery is the taking of personal property from the presence of the victim by use of force or fear. Most states have aggravated forms of robbery, such as robbery with a deadly weapon. Snatching a necklace from the neck of the victim involves sufficient force to constitute robbery. When the unlawful taking is not by force or fear, as when the victim does not know that the property is being taken, the offense is larceny, but it cannot be robbery.

Some statutes may be aimed at a particular kind of robbery. **For Example,** carjacking is a federal crime under the Anti-Car Theft Act of 1992.[37]

(c) Burglary

At common law, *burglary* was the breaking and entering during the night into the dwelling house of another with the intent to commit a felony. Inserting the automatic teller card of another, without their knowledge or permission, into an automatic teller machine set in the wall of the bank may constitute an entry into the bank for the purpose of committing burglary.[38] Some states word their burglary statutes, however, so that there is no burglary in this automatic teller case. This act would be covered by other criminal statutes.

Modern statutes have eliminated many of the elements of the common law definition so that under some statutes it is now immaterial when or whether there was an entry to commit a felony. The elements of breaking and entering are frequently omitted. Under some statutes, the offense is aggravated and the penalty is increased, depending on the place where the offense was committed, such as a bank building, freight car, or warehouse. Related statutory offenses, such as the crime of possessing burglars' tools, have been created.

(d) Arson

At common law, *arson* was the willful and malicious burning of another's dwelling. The law was originally designed to protect human life, although arson has been committed just with the burning of the building even if no one is actually hurt. In most states, arson is a felony, so if someone is killed in the resulting fire, the offense is considered a felony-murder. Under the felony-murder rule, homicide, however unintended, occurring in the commission of a felony is automatically classified as murder.

Virtually every state has created a special offense of burning to defraud an insurer. Such burning is not arson when an insured burns his own house in order to collect insurance money.

(e) Riots and Civil Disorders

Damage to property in the course of a riot or civil disorder is ordinarily covered by other types of crimes such as the crime of larceny or arson. In addition, the act of assembling as a riotous mob and engaging in civil disorders is generally some form of crime in itself under either common law concepts of disturbing the peace or modern antiriot statutes, even without destruction or theft of property.

A statute may make it a crime to riot or to incite to riot. However, a statute relating to inciting must be carefully drawn to avoid infringing on constitutionally protected free speech.

[37] 18 USC § 2119. See *United States v Hutchinson*, 75 F3d 626 (11th Cir 1996).

[38] *California v Ravenscroft*, 243 Cal Rptr 827 (Ct App 1988).

C. Criminal Law and the Computer

In some situations, ordinary crimes cover computer crimes situations. In other situations, new criminal law statutes are required.

23. What Is a Computer Crime?

The term **computer crime** is frequently used even though it has no established definition. Generally, the phrase is used to refer to a crime that can be committed only by a person having some knowledge of the operation of a computer. Just as stealing an automobile requires knowledge of how to operate and drive a car, so the typical computer crime requires the knowledge of how the computer works.

Because the more serious and costly wrongs relating to computers do not fit into the ordinary definitions of crime, there are now computer-specific criminal statutes: Computer crimes can be committed against the computer, using the computer, or through the computer.

24. The Computer as Victim

A traditional crime may be committed by stealing or intentionally damaging a computer.

(a) Theft of Hardware

When a computer itself is stolen, the ordinary law relating to theft crimes should apply. Theft of a computer is subject to the same law as the theft of a typewriter or a desk.

(b) Theft of Software

When a thief takes software, whether in the form of a program written on paper or a program on a disk or tape, a situation that does not fit into the common law definition of larceny arises. Larceny at common law was confined to the taking of tangible property. At common law, the value of stolen software would be determined by the value of the tangible substance on which the program was recorded. Under a traditional concept of property, which would ignore the value of the intangible program, theft of software would be only petty larceny. Now, however, virtually every state has amended its definition of larceny or theft to make stealing software a crime. In some states, the unauthorized taking of information may constitute a crime under a trade secrets protection statute.

(c) Intentional Damage

The computer may be the "victim" of a crime when it is intentionally destroyed or harmed. In the most elementary form of damage, the computer could be harmed if it was smashed with an ax or destroyed in an explosion or a fire. In such cases, the purpose of the intentional damage is to cause the computer's owner the financial loss of the computer and the destruction of the information that is stored in it.

Intentional damage can result from more subtle means. Gaining access to the computer and then erasing or altering the data is also the crime of intentional damage. Likewise, interfering with the air conditioning so that damage to the computer results or the computer malfunctions would also be covered under intentional damage statutes. The wrongdoer also may intentionally plant a bug or virus in the software, causing the program to malfunction or to give incorrect output. Such damage may be the work of an angry employee or a former employee, or it may be the work of a competitor.

In earlier years, the crime of malicious destruction of, or damage to, property was used to prosecute computer crimes.[39] Again, lawmakers have filled the gap between the technological environment and the law. Many states have adopted statutes that now make it a crime to damage software or computer-stored information.

25. Unauthorized Use of Computers

In contrast to conduct intended to harm a computer or its rightful user or to acquire secret information, the least serious of the computer crimes is the unlawful use of a computer belonging to someone else. In some states, however, the unlawful use of a computer is not a crime. Recent statutes have widely regulated this computer crime.

26. Computer Raiding

Taking information from a computer without the consent of the owner of the information is a crime. Whether this is done by instructing the computer to make a printout of stored information or by

[39] The crime of maliciously damaging or destroying property is ordinarily a misdemeanor and, as such, is subject only to a relatively small fine or short imprisonment.

E-COMMERCE AND CYBERLAW

THEY TOOK ME: IDENTITY THEFT

Identity theft is an increasing problem with the Internet. Criminals are invading e-commerce Web sites and acquiring personal information about customers. They then use these customers' credit and credit cards to make purchases. Such criminals have acquired, in some cases, as many as 70 credit cards using other people's names and identities.

In 1998, the total number of identity thefts was 11,000; in 1997, it was only 7,868. In 2002, the FBI broke up one identity theft ring that had stolen funds and credit card access from more than 30,000 Americans. In 2004, the FBI had 150,000 victims of identity theft.

Identity thieves begin by obtaining a person's name, address, date of birth, and Social Security number. They then use the information to get fake driver's licenses, which they use to obtain credit cards. With these tools, they can live someone else's life.

Do you think e-commerce sites should be held responsible for lack of sufficient security to prevent identity theft?

tapping into its data bank by some electronic means is not important. In many instances, taking information from the computer constitutes the crime of stealing trade secrets. In some states, taking information is known as the crime of "computer trespass."[40]

Both Congress and state legislatures have adopted statutes that declare it a crime to make any unauthorized use of a computer or to gain unauthorized access to a computer or the information stored in its database in order to cause harm to the computer or its rightful user.[41]

27. Diverted Delivery by Computer

In many industries, a computer controls the delivery of goods. The person in charge of that computer or someone unlawfully gaining access to it may cause the computer to direct delivery to an improper place. That is, instead of shipping goods to the customers to whom they should go, the wrongdoer diverts the goods to a different place, where the wrongdoer or a confederate receives them.

In precomputer days, written orders were sent from the sales department to the shipping department. The shipping department then sent the ordered goods to the proper places. If the person in the sales department or the person in the shipping department was dishonest, either one could divert the goods from the proper destination. Today, instructing the computer to give false directions can cause this fraudulent diversion of goods. Basically, the crime has not changed. The computer is merely the new instrument by which the old crime is committed. This old crime has taken on a new social significance because of the amazingly large dollar value of the thefts. In one case, several hundred loaded freight cars disappeared. In another case, a loaded oil tanker was diverted to unload into a fleet of tank trucks operated by an accomplice of the computer operator.

The crime of diverted delivery is not limited to goods. Diverted delivery can involve transferring money from a proper account to a wrong account. Computers can divert millions of dollars in a single criminal act. Statutes or courts may impose more severe penalties in these cases because of the huge dollar values involved.

28. Economic Espionage by Computer

The **Economic Espionage Act (EEA)** is a federal law[42] passed in response to several cases in which

[40] *Washington v Riley*, 846 P2d 1365 (Wash 1993).

[41] The Counterfeit Access Device and Computer Fraud Act of 1984, 18 USC § 1030 *et seq.;* Computer Fraud and Abuse Act of 1986, as amended in 1999, 18 USC § 1001; Electronic Communications Privacy Act of 1986, Act of 1986, 18 USC § 2510; Computer Fraud Act of 1987, 15 USC §§ 272, 278, 40 USC § 759; National Information Infrastructure Protection Act, 18 USC § 1030 (protecting confidentiality and integrity on the Internet).

[42] 18 USC § 1831.

ETHICS & THE LAW

ETHICS AND COMPETITION

In a long-running case that involved international competition, General Motors and Volkswagen AG battled in courts and in newspapers over the departure of several GM employees for Volkswagen and allegedly taking proprietary information about GM's supply chain management system in Europe.* The case resulted in the passage of the Economic Espionage Act (EEA) in the United States, which makes it a crime to download or in any way, electronically or otherwise, take proprietary information from one company to give or sell to another company.

Why is it an ethical issue for an employee to take information that she memorized about her former employer? What risks do you see in hiring someone who offers to bring proprietary information to you? What precautions could companies take to prevent employees from taking proprietary information to competitors?

* "Judge Sets Michigan Venue for GM Suit against VW," *Wall Street Journal*, October 18, 1996, B5.

high-level executives took downloaded proprietary information from their computers to their new employers. The EEA makes it a felony to steal, appropriate, or take a trade secret as well as to copy, duplicate, sketch, draw, photograph, download, upload, alter, destroy, replicate, transmit, deliver, send, mail, or communicate a trade secret. The penalties for EEA violations are up to $500,000 and 15 years in prison for individuals and $10 million for organizations. When employees take new positions with another company, their former employers are permitted to check the departing employees' computer e-mails and hard drives to determine whether the employees have engaged in computer espionage.

29. Electronic Fund Transfer Crimes

The Electronic Fund Transfers Act (EFTA) [43] makes it a crime to use any counterfeit, stolen, or fraudulently obtained card, code, or other device to obtain money or goods in excess of a specified amount through an electronic fund transfer system. The EFTA also makes it a crime to ship in interstate commerce devices or goods so obtained or to knowingly receive goods that have been obtained by means of the fraudulent use of the transfer system.

30. Circumventing Copyright Protection Devices via Computer

The Digital Millennium Copyright Act (DMCA)[44] makes it a federal offense to circumvent or create programs to circumvent encryption devices that copyright holders place on copyrighted material to prevent unauthorized copying. **For Example,** circumventing the encryption devices on software, CDs, or DVDs is a violation of the DMCA.

Dmitry Sklyarov, a Russian computer programmer, was the first person to be charged with a violation of the DMCA. Mr. Sklyarov was arrested in early 2002 at a computer show after giving a speech in Las Vegas at the Defcon convention on his product that he developed to permit the circumvention of security devices on copyrighted materials. His program unlocks password-protected e-books and PDF files. He gave his speech and was returned to Russia in exchange for his agreement to testify in a case that will determine the constitutionality of DMCA.

31. Spamming

More states are addressing the use of computers to send unsolicited e-mails. Nevada was the first state to regulate spam and California, Washington, and Virginia followed shortly after. Criminal regulation began with very narrowly tailored statutes such as

[43] 15 USC § 1693(n).

[44] 17 USC § (1998).

one in Washington that made it a crime to send an e-mail with a misleading title line.[45] The specific criminal statutes on spamming are evolving, and Virginia became the first state to pass a criminal anti-spamming law. The statute prohibits sending "unsolicited bulk electronic mail" or spam and makes the offense a felony based on the level of activity.[46] Spamming becomes a felony if the volume of spam exceeds 10,000 in 24 hours or 100,000 in 30 days or 1 million in one year. Thirty-six states now have some form of spamming regulation. The penalties range from fines to imprisonment.

D. Criminal Procedure Rights for Businesses

Business criminals are treated the same procedurally as other criminals. They have the same rights under the criminal justice system. The U.S. Constitution guarantees the protection of individual rights within the criminal justice system.

32. Fourth Amendment Rights for Businesses

(a) Search and Seizure: Warrants

The **Fourth Amendment** to the U.S. Constitution provides that "the right of the people to be secure in their persons, houses, papers, and effects, against unreasonable searches and seizures, shall not be violated." This amendment protects individual privacy by preventing unreasonable searches and seizures. Before a government agency can seize the property of individuals or businesses, it must obtain a valid **search warrant** issued by a judge or magistrate, based on probable cause, or an exception to this warrant requirement must apply. In other words, there must be good reason to believe that instruments or other evidence of a crime are present at the business location to be searched. The Fourth Amendment applies equally to individuals and corporations. In an unauthorized search, a corporation's property is given the same protection. If an improper search is conducted, evidence obtained during the course of that search may be inadmissible in the criminal proceedings for the resulting criminal charges.

(b) Exceptions to the Warrant Requirement

Exceptions to the warrant requirement are emergencies, such as a burning building, and the "plain-view" exception, which allows law enforcement officials to take any property that anyone can see, for no privacy rights are violated when items and property are left in the open for members of the public to see. **For Example,** you have an expectation of privacy in the garbage in your garbage can when it is in your house. However, once you move that garbage can onto the public sidewalk for pickup, you no longer have the expectation of privacy because you have left your garbage out in plain view of the public.

DOW CHEMICAL CO. V UNITED STATES, 476 US 1819 (1986)

LOW-FLYING AIRCRAFT BEARING FEDERAL AGENTS WITH CAMERAS

Dow Chemical (petitioner) operates a two thousand-acre chemical plant at Midland, Michigan. The facility, with numerous buildings, conduits, and pipes, is visible from the air. Dow has maintained ground security at the facility and has investigated flyovers by other, unauthorized aircraft. However, none of the buildings or manufacturing equipment is concealed.

In 1978, the Environmental Protection Agency (EPA) conducted an inspection of Dow. EPA requested a second inspection, but Dow denied the request. The EPA then employed a commercial aerial photographer to take photos of the plant from 12,000, 3,000, and 1,200 feet. The EPA had no warrant, but the plane was always within navigable air space when the photos were taken.

[45] Saul Hansell, "Total Up the Bill for Spam," *New York Times*, July 28, 2003, C1, C4.
[46] *Ibid.*

When Dow became aware of the EPA photographer, it brought suit in federal district court and challenged the action as a violation of its Fourth Amendment rights. The district court found that the EPA had violated Dow's rights and issued an injunction prohibiting the further use of the aircraft. The court of appeals reversed and Dow appealed.

Judicial Opinion

BURGER, Chief Justice. . . . The photographs at issue in this case are essentially like those used in map-making. Any person with an airplane and an aerial camera could readily duplicate them. In common with much else, the technology of photography has changed in this century. These developments have enhanced industrial processes, and indeed all areas of life; they have also enhanced enforcement techniques. Whether they may be employed by competitors to penetrate trade secrets is not a question presented in this case. Governments do not generally seek to appropriate trade secrets of the private sector, and the right to be free of appropriation of trade secrets is protected by law.

That such photography might be barred by state law with regard to competitors, however, is irrelevant to the questions presented here. State tort law governing unfair competition does not define the limits of the Fourth Amendment. The Government is seeking these photographs in order to regulate, not compete with, Dow.

Dow claims first the EPA has no authority to use aerial photography to implement its statutory authority of "site inspection" under the Clean Air Act.

Congress has vested in EPA certain investigatory and enforcement authority, without spelling out precisely how this authority was to be exercised in all the myriad circumstances that might arise in monitoring matters relating to clean air and water standards.

Regulatory or enforcement authority generally carries with it all the modes of inquiry and investigation traditionally employed or useful to execute the authority granted. Environmental standards cannot be enforced only in libraries and laboratories, helpful as those institutions may be.

The EPA, as a regulatory and enforcement agency, needs no explicit statutory provisions to employ methods of observation commonly available to the public at large; we hold that the use of aerial photography is within the EPA's statutory authority.

Dissenting Opinion

POWELL, MARSHALL, BRENNAN, and BLACKMUN, Justices . . . The Fourth Amendment protects private citizens from arbitrary surveillance by their Government. Today, in the context of administrative aerial photography of commercial premises, the Court retreats from that standard. It holds that the photography was not a Fourth Amendment "search" because it was not accompanied by a physical trespass and because the equipment used was not the most highly sophisticated form of technology available to the Government. Under this holding the existence of an asserted privacy interest apparently will be decided solely by reference to the manner of surveillance used to intrude on that interest. Such an inquiry will not protect Fourth Amendment rights, but rather will permit their gradual decay as technology advances.

EPA's aerial photography penetrated into a private commercial enclave, an area in which society has recognized that privacy interests may legitimately be claimed. The photographs captured highly confidential information that Dow had taken reasonable and objective steps to preserve as private.

Questions

1. Of what significance is the fact that Dow's plant could be seen from the air?
2. Did the EPA need a warrant for taking its aerial photographs?
3. What objections does the dissent raise to the decision?

Another exception allows officers to enter when they are needed to give aid because of an ongoing criminal act. For example, officers who are able to see a fight through the windows of a house and that some are injured can enter to render help. Another exception would be that the person who lives in the property to be searched has given permission for the search.

(c) Business Records and Searches

In many business crimes, the records that prove a crime was committed are not in the hands of the person who committed that crime. Accountants, attorneys, and other third parties may have the business records in their possession. In addition to the Fourth Amendment issues involved in seizing these records (a warrant is still required), there may be protections for the business defendants. The next section covers those protections.

(d) Protections for Privileged Records and Documents

All states recognize an attorney-client privilege, which means that an individual's conversations with her lawyer and the notes of those conversations are not subject to seizure unless the privilege is waived. In many of the prosecutions of companies, the Justice Department has asked companies to waive the attorney/client privilege so that it can have access to information that is then used to find other companies that may have participated in criminal activity. Some states recognize an accountant-client privilege and other privileges, such as those between priest and parishioner or doctor and patient. A privileged relationship is one in which the records and notes resulting from the contact between individuals cannot be seized even with a warrant (with some exceptions).

33. Fifth Amendment Self-Incrimination Rights for Businesses

(a) Self-Incrimination

The words "I take the Fifth" are used to invoke the constitutional protections against self-incrimination provided under the **Fifth Amendment** that prevents compelling a person to be a witness against himself. **For Example,** Charles Keating, the former CEO of a California savings and loan who was tried for fraud and other business crimes, invoked the Fifth Amendment 80 times in his testimony before Congress on the failure of his Lincoln Savings and Loan.[47] Ken Lay, former CEO and chairman of

GEORGIA V RANDOLPH, 2006 WL 707380 (2006)

A MAN'S HOME IS HIS CASTLE, AND HIS WIFE CAN'T TURN HIM IN

FACTS: Scott Randolph (Respondent) (defendant) and his wife, Janet, separated in late May 2001, when she left their Americus, Georgia home and went to stay with her parents in Canada, taking their son and some belongings. In July, she returned to the Americus house with the child. No one is sure whether she had returned to reconcile or whether she had come to gather her remaining possessions.

On July 6, 2001, Mrs. Randolph complained to the police that after a domestic dispute her husband took their son away, and when officers reached the house she told them that her husband was a cocaine user whose habit had caused financial troubles. She mentioned the marital problems and said that she and their son had only recently returned after a stay of several weeks with her parents. Shortly after the police arrived, Scott Randolph returned and explained that he had removed the child to a neighbor's house out of concern that his wife might take the boy out of the country again; he denied cocaine use, and countered that it was in fact his wife who abused drugs and alcohol.

One of the officers, Sergeant Murray, went with Janet Randolph to reclaim the child, and when they returned she not only renewed her complaints about her husband's drug use, but also volunteered that there were "'items of drug evidence'" in the house. Sergeant Murray asked Scott Randolph for permission to search the house, which he unequivocally refused.

The sergeant turned to Janet Randolph for consent to search, which she readily gave. She led the officer upstairs to a bedroom that she identified as Scott's, where the sergeant noticed a section of a drinking straw with a powdery residue he suspected was cocaine. He then left the house to get an evidence bag from his car and to call the district attorney's office, which instructed him to stop the search and apply for a warrant. When Sergeant Murray returned to the house, Janet Randolph withdrew her consent. The police took the straw to the police station, along with the

[47] Keating's convictions were reversed in 1999.

Randolphs. After getting a search warrant, they returned to the house and seized further evidence of drug use, on the basis of which Scott Randolph was indicted for possession of cocaine.

Mr. Randolph moved to suppress the evidence, as products of a warrantless search of his house unauthorized by his wife's consent over his express refusal. The trial court denied the motion, ruling that Janet Randolph had common authority to consent to the search.

The Court of Appeals of Georgia reversed, and the Georgia Supreme Court sustained the reversal. The state of Georgia appealed and the U.S. Supreme Court granted *certiorari.*

Judicial Opinion

SOUTER, Justice... To the Fourth Amendment rule ordinarily prohibiting the warrantless entry of a person's house as unreasonable per se, one "jealously and carefully drawn" exception recognizes the validity of searches with the voluntary consent of an individual possessing authority. None of our co-occupant consent-to-search cases, however, has presented the further fact of a second occupant physically present and refusing permission to search, and later moving to suppress evidence so obtained.

[S]hared tenancy is understood to include an "assumption of risk," on which police officers are entitled to rely, and although some group living together might make an exceptional arrangement that no one could admit a guest without the agreement of all, the chance of such an eccentric scheme is too remote to expect visitors to investigate a particular household's rules before accepting an invitation to come in. So, *Matlock* relied on what was usual and placed no burden on the police to eliminate the possibility of atypical arrangements, in the absence of reason to doubt that the regular scheme was in place.

The want of any recognized superior authority among disagreeing tenants is also reflected in the law's response when the disagreements cannot be resolved. The law does not ask who has the better side of the conflict; it simply provides a right to any co-tenant, even the most unreasonable, to obtain a decree partitioning the property and terminating the relationship. And while a decree of partition is not the answer to disagreement among rental tenants, this situation resembles co-ownership in lacking the benefit of any understanding that one or the other rental co-tenant has a superior claim to control the use of the quarters they occupy together. In sum, there is no common understanding that one co-tenant generally has a right or authority to prevail over the express wishes of another, whether the issue is the color of the curtains or invitations to outsiders.

Since we hold to the "centuries-old principle of respect for the privacy of the home," "it is beyond dispute that the home is entitled to special protection as the center of the private lives of our people." We have, after all, lived our whole national history with an understanding of "the ancient adage that a man's home is his castle [to the point that t]he poorest man may in his cottage bid defiance to all the forces of the Crown."

Disputed permission is thus no match for this central value of the Fourth Amendment, and the State's other countervailing claims do not add up to outweigh it. Yes, we recognize the consenting tenant's interest as a citizen in bringing criminal activity to light. And we understand a co-tenant's legitimate self-interest in siding with the police to deflect suspicion raised by sharing quarters with a criminal.

Nor should this established policy of Fourth Amendment law be undermined by the principal dissent's claim that it shields spousal abusers and other violent co-tenants who will refuse to allow the police to enter a dwelling when their victims ask the police for help. It is not that the dissent exaggerates violence in the home; we recognize that domestic abuse is a serious problem in the United States. But this case has no bearing on the capacity of the police to protect domestic victims. The dissent's argument rests on the failure to distinguish two different issues: when the police may enter without committing a trespass, and when the police may enter to search for evidence. No question has been raised, or reasonably could be, about the authority of the police to enter a dwelling to protect a resident from domestic violence; so long as they have good reason to believe such a threat exists, it would be silly to suggest that the police would commit a tort by entering, say, to give a complaining tenant the opportunity to collect belongings and get out safely, or to determine whether violence (or threat of violence) has just occurred or is about to (or soon will) occur, however much a spouse or other co-tenant objected. Thus, the question whether the police might lawfully enter over objection in order to provide any protection that might be reasonable is easily answered yes.

This case invites a straightforward application of the rule that a physically present inhabitant's express refusal of consent to a police search is dispositive as to him, regardless of the consent of a fellow occupant. Scott Randolph's refusal is clear, and nothing in the record justifies the search on grounds independent of Janet Randolph's consent. The State does not argue that she gave any indication to the police of a need for protection inside the house that might have justified entry into the portion of the premises where the police found the powdery straw (which, if lawfully seized, could have been used when attempting to establish probable cause for the warrant issued later).

The judgment of the Supreme Court of Georgia is therefore affirmed.

Dissenting Opinion

Chief Justice ROBERTS, with whom Justice SCALIA joins, dissenting.

The Court creates constitutional law by surmising what is typical when a social guest encounters an entirely atypical situation. The rule the majority fashions does not implement the high office of the Fourth Amendment to protect privacy, but instead provides protection on a random and happenstance basis, protecting, for example, a co-occupant who happens to be at the front door when the other occupant consents to a search, but not one napping or watching television in the next room. And the cost of affording such random protection is great, as demonstrated by the recurring cases in which abused spouses seek to authorize police entry into a home they share with a nonconsenting abuser.

The correct approach to the question presented is clearly mapped out in our precedents: The Fourth Amendment protects privacy. If an individual shares information, papers, or places with another, he assumes the risk that the other person will in turn share access to that information or those papers or places with the government. And just as an individual who has shared illegal plans or incriminating documents with another cannot interpose an objection when that other person turns the information over to the government, just because the individual happens to be present at the time, so too someone who shares a place with another cannot interpose an objection when that person decides to grant access to the police, simply because the objecting individual happens to be present.

A warrantless search is reasonable if police obtain the voluntary consent of a person authorized to give it. Co-occupants have "assumed the risk that one of their number might permit [a] common area to be searched." Just as Mrs. Randolph could walk upstairs, come down, and turn her husband's cocaine straw over to the police, she can consent to police entry and search of what is, after all, her home, too.

The majority's assumption about voluntary accommodation simply leads to the common stalemate of two gentlemen insisting that the other enter a room first.

The fact is that a wide variety of differing social situations can readily be imagined, giving rise to quite different social expectations. A relative or good friend of one of two feuding roommates might well enter the apartment over the objection of the other roommate. The reason the invitee appeared at the door also affects expectations: A guest who came to celebrate an occupant's birthday, or one who had traveled some distance for a particular reason, might not readily turn away simply because of a roommate's objection. The nature of the place itself is also pertinent: Invitees may react one way if the feuding roommates share one room, differently if there are common areas from which the objecting roommate could readily be expected to absent himself. Altering the numbers might well change the social expectations: Invitees might enter if two of three co-occupants encourage them to do so, over one dissenter.

The possible scenarios are limitless, and slight variations in the fact pattern yield vastly different expectations about whether the invitee might be expected to enter or to go away. Such shifting expectations are not a promising foundation on which to ground a constitutional rule, particularly because the majority has no support for its basic assumption—that an invited guest encountering two disagreeing co-occupants would flee—beyond a hunch about how people would typically act in an atypical situation.

If two friends share a locker and one keeps contraband inside, he might trust that his friend will not let others look inside. But by sharing private space, privacy has "already been frustrated" with respect to the lockermate. If two roommates share a computer and one keeps pirated software on a shared drive, he might assume that his roommate will not inform the government. But that person has given up his privacy with respect to his roommate by saving the software on their shared computer.

The same analysis applies to the question whether our privacy can be compromised by those with whom we share common living space. If a person keeps contraband in common areas of his home, he runs the risk that his co-occupants will deliver the contraband to the police.

In this sense, the risk assumed by a joint occupant is comparable to the risk assumed by one who reveals private information to another. If a person has incriminating information, he can keep it private in the face of a request from police to share it, because he has that right under the Fifth Amendment. If a person occupies a house with incriminating information in it, he can keep that information private in the face of a request from police to search the house, because he has that right under the Fourth Amendment. But if he shares the information—or the house—with another, that other can grant access to the police in each instance.

Questions

1. What factors in the case caused such strong opinions by the majority and dissenting judges?
2. What role did the issue of property law play in the decision and opinions?
3. Why did the issue of domestic violence come up in the opinion?

Enron, took the Fifth Amendment before Congress when asked to testify as did Bernie Ebbers, former CEO of WorldCom. Richard Grasso, the former chairman of the New York Stock Exchange took the Fifth Amendment when he was questioned about his compensation package while he headed the NYSE. However, both Lay and Ebbers took the witness stand in their own trials. They were not required to, but hoped to help their cases. The Fifth Amendment protection applies only to individuals; corporations are not given Fifth Amendment protection. A corporation cannot prevent the disclosure of its books and records on the grounds of self-incrimination. The officers and employees of a corporation can assert the Fifth Amendment, but the records of the corporation belong to the corporation, not to them, so they cannot use the Fifth Amendment to prevent the disclosure of the records.

(b) Miranda Rights

The famous ***Miranda* warnings** come from a case interpreting the extent of Fifth Amendment rights. In *Miranda v Arizona*,[48] the U.S. Supreme Court ruled that certain warnings must be given to persons who face custodial interrogation for the purposes of possible criminal proceedings. The warnings consist of an explanation to individuals that they have the right to remain silent; that if they do speak, anything they say can be used against them; that they have the right to have an attorney present; and that if they cannot afford an attorney, one will be provided for them. Failure to give the *Miranda* warnings means that any statements, including a confession, obtained while the individual was being interrogated cannot be used as evidence against that individual. The prosecution will have to rely on evidence other than the statements made in violation of *Miranda*, if such evidence exists.

34. Due Process Rights for Businesses

Also included in the Fifth Amendment is the language of due process. **Due process** is the right to be heard, question witnesses, and present evidence before any criminal conviction can occur. Due process in criminal cases consists of an initial appearance at which the charges and the defendant's rights are outlined; a preliminary hearing or grand jury proceeding in which the evidence is determined to be sufficient to warrant a trial; an arraignment for entering a plea and setting a trial date when the defendant pleads innocent; a period of discovery for obtaining evidence; and a trial at which witnesses for the prosecution can be cross-examined and evidence presented to refute the charges. In addition to these procedural steps, the **Sixth Amendment** guarantees that the entire process will be completed in a timely fashion because this amendment guarantees a speedy trial.

LAWFLIX

Twelve Angry Men (1957)(G)

This film offers a look at the jury process and whether the evidence is sufficient to label the conduct a crime.

For movie clips that illustrate business law concepts, see LawFlix at **http://wdvl.westbuslaw.com.**

[48] 384 US 436 (1966).

Summary

When a person does not live up to the standards set by law, society may regard this person's conduct as so dangerous to the government, to other people, or to property that society will prosecute the person for the misconduct. This punishable conduct, called *crime*, may be common law or statutory in origin. Crimes are classified as *felonies*, which generally carry greater sentences and more long-term consequences, and *misdemeanors*.

Employers and corporations may be criminally responsible for their acts and the acts of their employees. The federal sentencing guidelines impose mandatory sentences for federal crimes and allow judges to consider whether the fact that a business promotes compliance with the law is a reason to reduce a sentence.

White-collar crimes include those relating to financial fraud. Sarbanes-Oxley reforms increased the penalties for financial fraud and added fraudulent financial statement certification as a crime. Other white-collar crimes include bribery, extortion, blackmail, and corrupt influence in politics and in business. Also included as white-collar crimes are counterfeiting, forgery, perjury, making false claims against the government, obtaining goods or money by false pretenses, using bad checks, false financial reporting, and embezzlement. The common law crimes include those that involve injury to person and/or property, such as arson and murder.

Statutes have expanded the area of criminal law to meet situations in which computers are involved. Both federal and state statutes make the unauthorized taking of information from a computer a crime. The diversion of deliveries of goods and the transfer of funds, the theft of software, and the raiding of computers are made crimes to some extent by the federal Computer Access Device and Computer Fraud and Abuse Act of 1984 and the Electronic Fund Transfers Act of 1978. Newer federal statutes that apply to computers are the Economic Espionage Act, which prohibits downloading or copying information via computer to give to a competitor, and the Digital Millennium Copyright Act that prohibits circumventing or designing programs to circumvent encryption devices.

Criminal procedure is dictated by the Fourth, Fifth, and Sixth amendments. The Fourth Amendment protects against unreasonable searches, the Fifth Amendment protects against self-incrimination and provides due process, and the Sixth Amendment guarantees a speedy trial.

Questions and Case Problems

1. Bernard Flinn operated a business known as Harvey Investment Co., Inc./High Risk Loans. Flinn worked as a loan broker, matching those who came to him with lenders willing to loan them money given their credit history and the amount involved. From 1982 through 1985, Flinn found loans for five people. Indiana requires that persons engaged in the business of brokering loans obtain a license from the state. Flinn was prosecuted for brokering loans without having a license. He raised the defense that he did not know that a license was required and that, accordingly, he lacked the criminal intent to broker loans without having a license. Does Flinn have a good defense? [*Flinn v Indiana*, 563 NE2d 536 (Ind)]
2. H. J., Inc., and other customers of Northwestern Bell Corp. alleged that Northwestern Bell had furnished cash and tickets for air travel, plays, and sporting events and had offered employment to members of the Minnesota Public Utilities Commission in exchange for favorable treatment in rate cases before the commission. A Minnesota statute makes it a felony to bribe public officials. H. J. and other customers brought suit against Northwestern for violating the criminal bribery statute. Can the customers bring a criminal action? [*H. J., Inc. v Northwestern Bell Corp.*, 420 NW 2d 673 (Minn App)]
3. Baker and others entered a Wal-Mart store shortly after 3:00 A.M. by cutting through the metal door with an acetylene torch. They had moved some of the merchandise in the store to the rear door, but the police arrived before the merchandise could be taken from the store. Baker was prosecuted for larceny. He raised the defense that he was not guilty of larceny because no merchandise had ever left the store. Is there enough intent and action for a crime? [*Tennessee v Baker*, 751 SW2d 154 (Tenn App)]
4. Gail drove her automobile after having had dinner and several drinks. She fell asleep at the wheel and ran over and killed a pedestrian. Prosecuted for manslaughter, she raised the defense that she did not intend to hurt anyone and because of the drinks did not know what she was doing. Was this a valid defense?
5. Clarence Conrad Bolton was in his early 90s in December 1989 when conservatorship proceedings were commenced in which Joyce Van Buren sought to be appointed his guardian and conservator. While the proceedings were pending and before the appointment could be completed, Bolton gave Souter two checks totaling $2,200 in an attempt to hide money from others and to establish an emergency fund. Souter cashed both checks and deposited $2,200 in an account she had opened at a Hutchinson bank. A few days after entrusting the money to Souter, Bolton asked for $500 "to test her out to see if she was honest about it." Souter delivered $500 to Bolton

as he requested. Later, at Bolton's request, Souter cashed another check for $300, which Bolton gave Souter to help with the purchase of a car. When Bolton asked Souter to return more of his money, Souter refused, contending she was not indebted to him. Souter said that she deposited only $1,000 of Bolton's money in the account and that the $1,200 deposit shown on the bank statement came from her separate funds. She claimed she gave $800 to Bolton, which left $200 she claimed Bolton gave to her to buy a car and car insurance.

The bank's records indicate that between late December 1989 and June 1, 1990, Souter wrote checks on the account payable to her children, Reno County, State Farm, KPL Gas Service, and others. On June 2, 1990, Souter deposited $1,172 of her income tax return into the account, and by October 1990, the balance was under $10. The account was closed in overdraft status in March 1991. The state prosecuted Souter for embezzlement. She says you cannot embezzle money that was given to you. Is she right? [*Bolton v Souter*, 872 P2d 758 (Kan)]

6. Dr. Doyle E. Campbell, an ophthalmologist, established his practice in southern Ohio in 1971. Many of Dr. Campbell's patients are elderly people who qualify for federal Medicare benefits and state Medicaid benefits. Under the existing financing system, a doctor who treats a Medicare patient is required to submit a "Medicare Health Insurance Claim Form" (HCFA Form 1500). The doctor is required to certify that "the services shown on this form were medically indicated and necessary for the health of the patient and were personally rendered by me or were rendered incident to my professional service by my employees." Claims Dr. Campbell submitted for his elderly patients ranged from $900 to $950, of which $530 to $680 were covered by the Medicare program. The government alleged that Dr. Campbell billed Medicare for several treatments that were either not performed or not necessary. Dr. Campbell was charged with fraud for the paperwork he submitted. Has he committed a crime? [*United States v Campbell*, 845 F2d 1374 (6th Cir)]

7. In the late 1980s, Life Energy Resources, Ltd. (LER), a New York corporation, was a multilevel marketing network. LER's marketing plan provided that members of the general public could purchase its products only through an official LER distributor or by becoming LER distributors themselves. Each potential distributor had to be sponsored by an existing distributor and was required to sign a distributorship agreement with LER stating that he or she would not make medical claims or use unofficial literature or marketing aids to promote LER products.

   Ballistrea and his partner Michael Ricotta were at the top of the LER distribution network. Two products sold by LER were the REM SuperPro Frequency Generator (REM) and the Lifemax Miracle Cream (Miracle Cream). The REM, which sold for $1,350 to distributors, was a small box powered by electricity that ran currents through the feet and body of the user.

   Ballistrea and Ricotta distributed literature and audiotapes to many potential downstream distributors and customers—some of whom were undercover government agents—touting the REM and the Miracle Cream. Other literature claimed that the Miracle Cream could alleviate the discomforts of premenstrual syndrome and reverse the effects of osteoporosis. The Food and Drug Administration charged Ballistrea and Ricotta with violating federal law for making medical claims concerning LER products. Their defense is that they never sold any of the products. They simply earned commissions as part of the marketing scheme and could not be held criminally liable on the charges. Are they correct? [*United States v Ballistrea*, 101 F3d 827 (2d Cir)]

8. Thomas Iverson was a founder of CH2O, Inc., and served as the company's president and chairman of the board. CH2O ships blended chemicals to its customers in drums. CH2O asked its customers to return the drums so that it could reuse them. Although customers returned the drums, they often did not clean them sufficiently, and the drums still contained chemical residue. Before CH2O could reuse the drums, it had to remove that residue. To do so, CH2O instituted a drum-cleaning operation, which in turn generated wastewater.

   Beginning in about 1985, Iverson personally discharged the wastewater and ordered employees of CH2O to discharge the wastewater. In April 1992, Iverson bought a warehouse in Olympia. After the purchase, CH2O restarted its drum-cleaning operation at the warehouse and disposed of its wastewater through the sewer. CH2O obtained neither a permit nor permission to make these discharges. The drum-cleaning operation continued until the summer of 1995, when CH2O learned that it was under investigation for discharging pollutants into the sewer.

   A few months before CH2O restarted its drum-cleaning operation, Iverson had announced his "official" retirement from CH2O. However, he continued to receive money from CH2O, to conduct business at the company's facilities, and to give orders to employees. CH2O continued to list him as the president in documents that it filed with the state, and the employee who was responsible for running the day-to-day aspects of the drum-cleaning operation testified that he reported to Iverson.

   The federal government has charged CH2O and Iverson with criminal violations of the Clean Water Act. Iverson says he is not responsible because he had retired. Can he be held criminally liable for a violation of the Clean Water Act through the drum-cleaning operations? [*United States. v Iverson*, 162 F3d 1015 (9th Cir)]

9. James Durham runs an art gallery. He has several paintings from unknown artists that he has listed for sale. The

paintings always sell at his weekly auction for $20,000 to $50,000 above what James believes them to be worth. James learns that the bidders at the auctions are employed by an olive distributor located near the shipping yards of the city. What concerns should Durham have about the art, the bidders and the large purchase prices?

10. Jennings operated a courier service to collect and deliver money. The contract with his customers allowed him a day or so to deliver the money that had been collected. Instead of holding collections until delivered, Jennings made short-term investments with the money. He always made deliveries to the customers on time, but because he kept the profit from the investments for himself, Jennings was prosecuted for embezzlement. Was he guilty? [*New York v Jennings*, 504 NE2d 1079 (NY)]
11. Chaussee sold franchises to a number of persons authorizing them to sell a product that did not exist. He was prosecuted under the Colorado Organized Crime Control Act on the ground that he was guilty of a pattern of racketeering. His defense was that there was no pattern because there was only one scheme. Was he guilty?
12. Grabert ran Beck's, an amusement center in Louisiana. He held a license for video gambling machines. Louisiana makes it illegal to allow a minor to play a video gambling machine. A mother came into Grabert's center carrying her 23-month-old baby in her arms. She sat at the video poker machine with her child on her lap and proceeded to play. State troopers witnessed the baby pushing the buttons on the machine at least three times. The Department of Public Safety and Corrections revoked Grabert's video gaming license because a minor had been allowed to play the machines, and Grabert sought judicial review. The trial court reversed, and the department appealed. Has Grabert committed the crime of allowing a minor to engage in gaming? Is this the crime of allowing a minor to gamble? [*Grabert v Department of Public Safety & Corrections*, 680 So 2d 764 (La App) *cert. denied; Grabert v State Through Dept. of Public Safety and Corrections*, 685 So 2d 126 (La)]
13. The Banco Central administered a humanitarian plan for the government of Ecuador. Fernando Banderas and his wife presented false claims that the bank paid. After the fraud was discovered, the bank sued Banderas and his wife for damages for fraud and treble damages under the Florida version of RICO. Banderas and his wife asserted that they were not liable for RICO damages because there was no proof that they were related to organized crime and because the wrong they had committed was merely ordinary fraud. They had not used any racketeering methods. Is involvement with organized crime a requirement for liability under RICO? [*Banderas v Banco Central del Ecuador*, 461 So 2d 265 (Fla App)]
14. Kravitz owned 100 percent of the stock of American Health Programs, Inc. (AHP). To obtain the Philadelphia Fraternal Order of Police as a customer for AHP, Kravitz paid money bribes to persons who he thought were officers of that organization but who in fact were federal undercover agents. He was prosecuted for violating RICO. He was convicted, and the court ordered the forfeiture of all of Kravitz's shares of AHP stock. Can a forfeiture be ordered? [*United States v Kravitz*, 738 F2d 102 (3d Cir)]
15. Howell made long-distance telephone calls through the telephone company's computer-controlled switching system to solicit funding for a nonexistent business enterprise. What crimes did Howell commit? [*New Mexico v Howell*, 895 P2d 232 (NM App)]

TORTS

CHAPTER (9)

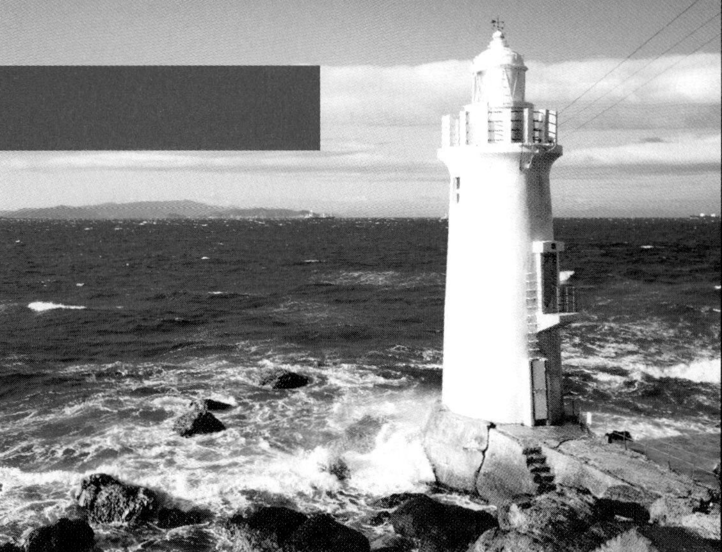

LEARNING OBJECTIVES

After studying this chapter, you should be able to

LO.1 Define torts and distinguish them from crimes

LO.2 List the types of torts

LO.3 Provide examples of intentional torts and the elements of each

LO.4 Discuss the elements of negligence

LO.5 Explain the defenses to negligence

LO.6 Explain concerns about levels of tort liability and possible reforms

The law of torts permits individuals and companies to recover from other individuals and companies for wrongs committed against them. Tort law provides rights and remedies for conduct that meets the elements required to establish that a wrong has occurred.

A. General Principles

Civil, or noncriminal, wrongs that are not breaches of contract are governed by tort law. This chapter covers the types of civil wrongs that constitute torts and the remedies available for those wrongs.

1. What Is a Tort?

Tort comes from the Latin term *tortus*, which means "crooked, dubious, twisted." Torts are actions that are not straight but are crooked, or civil, wrongs. A tort is an interference with someone's person or property. **For Example,** entering someone's house without his or her permission is an interference and constitutes the tort of trespass. Causing someone's character to be questioned is a wrong against the person and is the tort of defamation. The law provides protection against these harms in the form of remedies awarded after the wrongs are committed. These remedies are civil remedies for the acts of interference by others.

2. Tort and Crime Distinguished

A *crime* is a wrong that arises from a violation of a public duty, whereas a *tort* is a wrong that arises from a violation of a private duty. A crime is a wrong of such a serious nature that the appropriate level of government steps in to prosecute and punish the wrongdoer to deter others from engaging in the same type of conduct. However, whenever the act that is committed as a crime causes harm to an identifiable person, that person may recover from the wrongdoer for monetary damages to compensate for the harm. For the person who experiences the direct harm, the act is called a *tort;* for the government, the same act is called a *crime*.

When the same act is both a crime and a tort, the government may prosecute the wrongdoer for a violation of criminal law, and the individual who experiences the direct harm may recover damages. **For Example,** O. J. Simpson was charged by the state of California with the murder of his ex-wife, Nicole Brown Simpson, and her friend Ron Goldman. A criminal trial was held in which O. J. Simpson was acquitted. Simpson was subsequently sued civilly by the families of Nicole Simpson and Ron Goldman for the tort of wrongful death. The jury in the civil case found Simpson civilly liable and the court ordered him to pay nearly $20 million in damages plus interest. Only $382,000 of this judgment has actually been paid to the families.

3. Types of Torts

There are three types of torts: intentional torts, negligence, and strict liability. **Intentional torts** are those that occur when wrongdoers engage in intentional conduct. **For Example,** striking another person in a fight is an intentional act and would be the tort of battery and possibly also the crime of battery. Your arm striking another person's nose in a fast-moving crowd of people at a rock concert is not a tort or crime because your arm was pushed unintentionally by the force of the crowd. If you stretched out your arms in that crowd or began to swing your arms about and struck another person, you would be behaving carelessly in a crowd of people; and, although you may not have committed an intentional tort, it is possible that your careless conduct constitutes the tort of **negligence**. Careless actions, or actions taken without thinking through their consequences, constitute negligence. The harm to the other person's nose may not have been intended, but there is liability for these accidental harms under negligence. **For Example,** if you run a red light, hit another car, and injure its driver, you did not intend the result. However, your careless behavior of disregarding a traffic signal resulted in the injury, and you would have liability for your negligence to that driver.

Strict liability is another type of tort that imposes liability without regard to whether there was any intent to harm or any negligence occurred. Strict liability is imposed without regard to fault. Strict or absolute liability is imposed because the activity involved is so dangerous that there must be full accountability. Nonetheless, the activity is necessary and cannot be prohibited. The compromise is to allow the activity but ensure that its dangers and resulting damages are fully covered through the imposition of full liability for all injuries that result. **For Example,** contractors often need to use dynamite to take a roadway through a mountainside or demolish a building that has become a hazard. When the dynamite is used, noise, debris, and possibly dangerous pieces of earth and building will descend on others' land and possibly on people. In most states, contractors are held strictly liable for the resulting damage from the use of dynamite. The activity is necessary and not illegal, but those who use dynamite must be prepared to compensate those who are injured as a result.

Other areas in which there is strict liability for activity include the storage of flammable materials and crop dusting. The federal government and the states have pure food laws that impose absolute liability on manufacturers who fail to meet the statutory standards for their products. Another area of strict liability is *product liability*, which is covered in Chapter 25.

B. Intentional Torts

4. Assault

An *assault* is intentional conduct that threatens a person with a well-founded fear of imminent harm coupled with the present ability to carry out the threat of harm. **For Example,** the angry assertion "I'm going to kick your butt" along with aggressive movement in the direction of the victim with the intent to carry out the threat is an assault, even though a third person intervenes to stop the intended action. Mere words, however, although insulting, are ordinarily insufficient to constitute an assault.

5. Battery

A *battery* is the intentional, wrongful touching of another person without that person's consent. Thus, a threat to use force is an assault, and the actual use of force is the battery. The single action of striking an individual can be both a crime and a tort. A lawsuit for the tort of battery provides a plaintiff with the opportunity to recover damages resulting from the battery. The plaintiff must prove damages, however.

6. False Imprisonment

False imprisonment is the intentional detention of a person without that person's consent.[1] The detention need not be for any specified period of time, for any detention against one's will is false imprisonment. False imprisonment is often called the *shopkeeper's tort* because so much liability has been imposed on store owners for their unreasonable detention of customers suspected of shoplifting. Requiring a customer to sit in the manager's office or not allowing a customer to leave the store can constitute the tort of false imprisonment. Shop owners do, however, need the opportunity to investigate possible thefts in their stores. As a result, all states have some form of privilege or protection for store owners called a *shopkeeper's privilege*.

The **shopkeeper's privilege** permits the store owner to detain a suspected shoplifter based on reasonable suspicion for a reasonable time without resulting liability for false imprisonment to the accused customer.[2] The privilege applies even if the store owner was wrong about the customer being a shoplifter, so long as the store owner acted based on reasonable suspicions and treated the accused shoplifter in a reasonable manner. These privilege statutes do not protect the store owner from liability for unnecessary physical force or for invasion of privacy.

7. Intentional Infliction of Emotional Distress

The **intentional infliction of emotional distress** is a tort involving conduct that goes beyond all bounds of decency and produces mental anguish in the harmed individual. This tort requires proof of outrageous conduct and resulting emotional distress in the victim. The types of conduct for which this tort is used for recovery include outrageous collection methods employed by debt collection agencies. **For Example,** if a collection agent constantly called a debtor while he was hospitalized following heart surgery, such conduct would rise to the level of outrageous conduct beyond all standards of decency. Such a collection effort would constitute the tort of intentional infliction of emotional distress.

8. Invasion of Privacy

The right of privacy is the right to be free of unreasonable intrusion into one's private affairs. The tort of **invasion of privacy** actually consists of three different torts: (1) intrusion into the plaintiff's private affairs (for example, planting a microphone in an office or home); (2) public disclosure of private facts (for example, disclosing private financial information, such as a business posting returned checks from

[1] *Forgie-Buccioni v Hannaford Bros. Inc.*, 413 F3d 175 (1st Cir 2005).

[2] *Limited Stores, Inc. v Wilson-Robinson*, 876 SW2d 248 (Ark 1994); see also *Wal-Mart Stores, Inc. v Binns*,15 SW3d 320 (Ark 2000).

customers near its cash register in a public display); and (3) appropriation of another's name, likeness, or image for commercial advantage. This form of invasion of privacy is generally referred to as the *right of publicity.* The elements of this tort are (1) appropriation of the plaintiff's name or likeness for the value associated with it, and not in an incidental manner or for a newsworthy purpose, (2) identification of the plaintiff in the publication, and (3) an advantage or benefit to the defendant. The right of publicity is designed to protect the commercial interest of celebrities in their identities. **For Example,** popular and critically acclaimed rock and roll musician Don Henley, the founder and member of the band The Eagles, successfully sued a department store chain that ran an international newspaper advertisement for its Henley shirt, which stated in large letters as the focus of the ad "This is Don's henley." The ad (1) used the value associated with the famous name Don Henley to get consumers to read it, (2) the plaintiff was identifiable in the ad, and (3) the ad was created with the belief that use of the words "Don's henley" would help sell the product.[3]

9. Defamation

Defamation is an untrue statement by one party about another to a third party. **Slander** is oral or spoken defamation, and **libel** is written (and in some cases broadcast) defamation. The elements for defamation are (1) a statement about a person's reputation, honesty, or integrity that is untrue; (2) publication (which is accomplished when a third party hears or reads the defamatory statement); (3) a statement that is directed at a particular person; and (4) damages that result from the statement.

For Example, a false statement by the owner of a business that the former manager was fired for stealing when he was not would be defamation, and the former manager's damages could be his inability to find another position because of the statement's impact on his reputation.

In cases in which the victim is a public figure, such as a Hollywood celebrity or a professional sports player, another element is required, the element of malice, which means that what was said or written was done with the knowledge that the information was false or with reckless disregard for whether it was true or false.

The defenses to defamation include the truth. If the statement is true, even if it is harmful to the victim, it is not the tort of defamation.

Some statements are privileged, and this privilege provides a full or partial defense to the tort of defamation. **For Example,** members of Congress enjoy an **absolute privilege** when they are speaking on the floor of the Senate or the House because public policy requires a free dialogue on the issues pending in a legislative body. The same absolute privilege applies to witnesses in court proceedings to encourage witnesses with information to come forward and testify.

The media enjoy a **qualified privilege** for stories that turn out to be false. Their qualified privilege is a defense to defamation so long as the information was released without malice and a retraction or correction is made when the matter is brought to their attention.

A *qualified privilege* to make a defamatory statement in the workplace exists when the statement is made to protect the interests of the private employer on a work-related matter, especially when reporting actual or suspected wrongdoing. **For Example,** Neda Lewis was fired from her job at Carson Oil Company for allegedly stealing toilet paper. The employee in charge of supplies noticed toilet paper was regularly missing from the ladies room, and one evening from a 3rd floor window overlooking the parking lot, she observed that the plaintiff's bag contained two rolls of toilet paper. She reported the matter to the executive secretary, who reported it to both the president and the CEO of the firm, who decided to fire her. Two other employees were also informed. The employer was able to successfully raise the defense of a qualified privilege to Ms. Lewis' defamation action for "false accusations of theft" since all of the employees involved were participants in the investigation and termination of the employee.[4]

A new statutory privilege has been evolving over the past few years with respect to letters of recommendation and references given by employers for employees who are applying for jobs at other companies. Most companies, because of concerns about liability for defamation, will only confirm that a former employee did work at their firm and will provide the time period during which the person was employed. However, many employees who had

[3] *Henley v Dillard Department Stores,* 46 F Supp 2d 587 (ND Tex 1999).
[4] *Lewis v Carson Oil Co.,* 127 P3d 1207 (Or App 2006).

E-COMMERCE AND CYBERLAW

Many companies are working to resolve a defamation issue facilitated by the Internet. The defamation of a company occurs because a disgruntled employee posts false information in a chat room about a company's earnings or an investor who wishes to affect the value of a particular stock for exercising call and put options likewise posts negative information in a chat room. For example, Mark S. Jakob was dealing in call options in Emulex stock in mid-August. His prediction that Emulex stock would take a dive was wrong; the stock in fact increased in value with a resulting loss of $100,000 for Jacob. To cover his losses, the 23-year-old sent an e-mail press release to an Internet wire service. The fake press release indicated that the CEO of Emulex would resign because earnings had been overstated.* The news release was then distributed to various Web sites.

The overall loss to shareholders when the market opened in reaction to Jakob's fake news release was $2.5 billion as the share price plummeted. However, Jakob made $240,000 by selling short in the stock. He was arrested for securities fraud and wire fraud.

Visit some investor chat rooms:

http://www.vault.com

http://www.greedyassociates.com

In addition to securities issues (see Chapter 46), there is the issue of defamation and the resulting damage to the company because of false statements posted on the Internet. The Internet is a rapid source of information and misinformation.

Following the Emulex fiasco, the FBI and other law enforcement officials counseled investors to "Know thy source" and always question information posted on Internet chat rooms.

*Alex Berenson, "Man Charged in Stock Fraud Based on Fake News," *New York Times*, September 1, 2000, C1, C2.

histories that should have been revealed for safety reasons have been hired because no negative information was released. About one-third of the states now have statutes that provide employers a qualified privilege with respect to references and recommendations. So long as the employer acts in good faith in providing information, there is no liability for defamation to the former employee as a result of the information provided.

The *Randi v Muroc Joint Unified School District* involves a liability issue for less-than-complete disclosure in references.

RANDI V MUROC JOINT UNIFIED SCHOOL DISTRICT, 929 P2D 582 (CAL 1997)

PUTTING IN AN EXAGGERATED GOOD WORD

Randi W. (plaintiff) is a 13-year-old minor who attended the Livingston Middle School where Robert Gadams served as vice principal. On February 1, 1992, while Randi was in Gadam's office. Gadams molested and sexually touched Randi.

Gadams's last place of employment (1990–1991) before Livingston was Muroc Unified School District, where disciplinary actions were taken against him for sexual harassment. When allegations of "sexual touching" of female students were made, Gadams was forced to resign from Muroc. Nonetheless, Gary Rice and David Malcolm, officials at Muroc, provided a letter of recommendation for Gadams that described him as "an upbeat, enthusiastic administrator who relates well to the students," and who was responsible "in large part," for making Boron Junior High School (located in Muroc) "a safe, orderly and clean environment for students and staff." The letter concluded that they recommended Gadams "for an assistant principalship or equivalent position without reservation."

All of the letters provided by previous administrators of Gadams were sent in on forms that included a disclosure that the information provided "will be sent to prospective employers."

Through her guardian, Randi W. filed suit against the districts, alleging that her injuries from Gadams's sexual touching were proximately caused by their failure to provide full and accurate information about Gadams to the placement service. The trial court dismissed the case, and the Court of Appeals reversed. The districts appealed.

Judicial Opinion

CHIN, Assoc. J.... Although ordinarily a duty of care analysis is unnecessary in determining liability for intentional misrepresentation or fraud, here we consider liability to *a third person* injured as a result of the alleged fraud, an extension of ordinary tort liability based on fraud. [We] consider whether plaintiff has sufficiently pleaded that defendants owed her a *duty of care*, that they breached that duty by making *misrepresentations* or, giving *false information*, and that Livingston's *reasonable reliance* on their statements *proximately caused* plaintiff's injury.

Did defendants owe plaintiff a duty of care? In defendants' view, absent some special relationship between the parties, or some specific and known threat of harm to plaintiff, defendants had no duty of care toward her, and no obligation to disclose in their letters any facts regarding the charges against Gadams.

[N]o California case has yet held that one who intentionally or negligently provides false information to another owes a duty of care *to a third person* who did not receive the information and who has no special relationship with the provider. Accordingly, the issue before us is one of first impression.

In this state, the general rule is that all persons have a duty to use ordinary care to prevent others from being injured as the result of their conduct.

The major (considerations) are the foreseeability of harm to the plaintiff, the degree of certainty that the plaintiff suffered injury, the closeness of the connection between the defendant's conduct and the injury suffered, the moral blame attached to the defendant's conduct, the policy of preventing future harm, the extent of the burden to the defendant and consequences to the community of imposing a duty to exercise, care with resulting liability for breach, and the availability, cost, and prevalence of insurance for the risk involved.

[W]e first examine whether plaintiff's injuries were a *foreseeable* result of defendants' representations regarding Gadams's qualifications and character, coupled with their failure to disclose to the Fresno Pacific College placement office information regarding charges or complaints of Gadams's sexual misconduct. Could defendants reasonably have foreseen that the representations and omissions in their reference letters would result in physical injury to someone? Although the chain of causation leading from defendants' statements and omissions to Gadams's alleged assault on plaintiff is somewhat attenuated, we think the assault was reasonably foreseeable. Based on the facts alleged in the complaint, defendants could foresee that Livingston's officers would read and rely on defendants' letters in deciding to hire Gadams. Likewise, defendants could foresee that, had they not unqualifiedly recommended Gadams, Livingston would not have hired him. And, finally, defendants could foresee that Gadams, after being hired by Livingston, might molest or injure a Livingston student such as the plaintiff. As the plaintiffs complaint alleges, her injury was a "direct and proximate result" of defendants' fraud and misrepresentations.

As for public policy, the law certainly recognizes a *policy of preventing future harm* of the kind alleged here. One of society's highest priorities is to protect children from sexual or physical abuse.

Defendants urge that *competing social or economic policies* may disfavor the imposition of liability for misrepresentation or nondisclosure in employment references. They observe that a rule imposing liability in these situations could greatly inhibit the preparation and distribution of reference letters, to the general detriment of employers and employees alike.

Defendants argue that a rule imposing tort liability on writers of recommendation letters could have one very predictable consequence: employers would seldom write such letters, even in praise of exceptionally qualified employees.

In defendants' view, rather than prepare a recommendation letter stating all "material" facts, positive and negative, an employer would be better advised to decline to write a reference letter or, at most, merely to confirm the former employee's position, salary, and dates of employment. According to defendants apart from the former employer's difficulty in deciding how much "negative" information to divulge an employer who disclosed more than minimal employment data would risk a defamation, breach of privacy, or wrongful interference suit from a rejected job seeker.

We agree with the Court of Appeal's reliance analysis. Under the Restatement provisions, plaintiff need only allege that her injury resulted from action that the *recipient* of defendants' misrepresentations took in reliance on them. In a case involving false or fraudulent letters of recommendation sent to prospective employers regarding a potentially dangerous employee, it would be unusual for *the person ultimately injured* by the employee actually to "rely" on such letters, much less even be aware of them.

Based on the facts alleged in the complaint, plaintiff's injury foreseeably and proximately resulted from Livingston's decision to hire Gadams in reliance on defendant's unqualified recommendation of him.

The judgment of the Court of Appeal is affirmed as to counts three and four (negligent misrepresentation and fraud).

[Affirmed in part, reversed in part]

Questions

1. What information was not included in the letters of recommendation? Do you consider that information relevant?
2. What issues do you see in holding writers of recommendation letters and former employers liable for their failure to disclose information?
3. How would you draft a letter of recommendation in light of this case?

10. Product Disparagement

Although the comparison of products and services is healthy for competition, false statements about another's products constitute a form of slander called **slander of title** or libel called **trade libel**; collectively, these are known as **product disparagement**, which occurs when someone makes false statements about another business, its products, or its abilities.[5] The elements of product disparagement are (1) a false statement about a particular business product or about its service in terms of honesty, reputation, ability, or integrity; (2) communication of the statement to a third party; and (3) damages.

11. Wrongful Interference with Contracts

The tort of **contract interference** or (tortious interference with contracts) occurs when parties are not allowed the freedom to contract without interference from third parties. While the elements required to establish the tort of contract interference are complex, a basic definition is that the law affords a remedy when a third party intentionally causes another to break a contract already in existence. **For Example,** Nikke Finke, a newspaper reporter who had a contract with the *New York Post* to write stories about the entertainment industry for the *Post's* business section, wrote two articles about a lawsuit involving a literary agent and the Walt Disney Company over merchandising rights to the Winnie-the-Pooh characters. Finke reported that the trial court sanctioned Disney for engaging in "misuse of the discovery process" and acting in "bad faith" and ordered Disney to pay fees and costs of $90,000. Disney's president, Robert Iger, sent a letter to the *Post's* editor-in-chief, Col Allan, calling Finke's reporting an "absolute distortion" of the record and "absolutely false." Approximately two weeks after the Pooh articles were published, the *Post* fired Finke; her editor told her she was being fired for the Pooh articles. She sued Disney on numerous tort theories, including interference with her contract with the *Post*. Disney sought to have the complaint dismissed, a motion which was denied by the court. The court of appeals concluded that Finke demonstrated a reasonable probability of proving that Iger's allegations that she made false statements in her article were themselves false; and it concluded that a jury could find Disney liable for intentional interference with contractual relations based on circumstantial evidence and negligent interference with contractual relations because it was reasonably foreseeable to Disney that the nature of its accusations against

[5] *Sannerud v Brantz*, 879 P2d 341 (Wyo 1994). See *Suzuki Motor Corp. v Consumers Union*, 230 F3d 1110 (9th Cir 2003), *cert denied* 2003 WL 22005685 (US), for an example of the complexity of a product disparagement action.

Finke would result in her termination from employment.[6]

12. Trespass

A **trespass** is an unauthorized action with respect to land or personal property. A *trespass to land* is any unpermitted entry below, on, across, or above the land of another. **For Example,** Joyce Ameral's home abutts the mid-way point of the 240-yard, par-4 ninth hole of the public Middlebrook Country Club. Balls sliced and hooked by golfers have damaged her windows and screens, dented her car, and made her deck too dangerous for daytime use. Her landscapers are forced to wear hard hats when cutting her lawn. In her lawsuit against the country club owner, the court ruled that the projection of golf balls onto Ameral's property constituted a continuing trespass and it enjoined the trespass.[7]

A *trespass to personal property* is the invasion of personal property without the permission of the owner. **For Example,** the use of someone's car without that person's permission is a trespass to personal property.

C. Negligence

The widest range of tort liability today arises in the field of negligence. Accidents happen! Property is damaged, and/or injuries result. The fact that an individual suffers an injury does not necessarily mean that the individual will be able to recover damages for the injury. **For Example,** Rhonda Nichols was shopping in the outdoor garden center at a Lowe's Home Center when a "wild bird" flew into the back of her head, causing injuries. Her negligence lawsuit against Lowe's was dismissed because the owner did not have a duty to protect her from a wild bird attack because it was not reasonably foreseeable.[8] Jane Costa was passively watching a Boston Red Sox baseball game at Fenway Park when a foul ball struck her in the face, causing severe and permanent injuries. Her negligence lawsuit against the Boston Red Sox was unsuccessful because it was held that the owners had no duty to warn Ms. Costa of the obvious danger of foul balls being hit into the stands.[9] Although cases involving injury to spectators at baseball games in other jurisdictions have turned on other tort doctrines, injured fans, like Ms. Costa, are left to bear the costs of their injuries. Only when an injured person can demonstrate the following four elements of negligence is a right to recover established: (1) a duty, (2) breach of duty, (3) causation, and (4) damages. Several defenses may be raised in a negligence lawsuit.

13. Elements of Negligence

(a) Duty to Exercise Reasonable Care

The first element of negligence is a *duty*. There is a general duty of care imposed to act as a reasonably prudent person would in similar circumstances. **For Example,** Gustavo Guzman worked for a subcontractor as a chicken catcher at various poultry farms where a Tyson Foods employee, Brian Jones, operated a forklift and worked with the catchers setting up cages to collect birds for processing at a Tyson plant. Contrary to Tyson's instructions "never to allow catchers to move behind the forklift or otherwise out of sight," Brian moved his forklift and struck Guzman, who suffered a serious spinal injury. A general contractor, Tyson Foods, owes a duty to exercise reasonable care to a subcontractor's employee, Gustavo Guzman.[10]

Professionals have a duty to perform their jobs at the level of a reasonable professional. For a professional such as an accountant, doctor, lawyer, dentist, or architect to avoid liability for **malpractice,** the professional must perform his or her skill in the same manner as, and at the level of, other professionals in the same field.

Those who own real property have a duty of care to keep their property in a condition that does not create hazards for guests. Businesses have a duty to inspect and repair their property so that their customers are not injured by hazards, such as spills on the floor or uneven walking areas. When customer safety is a concern, businesses have a duty to provide adequate security, such as security patrols in mall parking lots.

[6] *Finke v The Walt Disney Co.*, 2 Cal Rptr 3d 436 (Cal App 2003).

[7] *Ameral v Pray*, 831 NE2d 915 (Mass App 2005).

[8] *Nichols v Lowe's Home Center, Inc.*, 407 F Supp 2d 979 (SD Ill 2006).

[9] *Costa v Boston Red Sox Baseball Club*, 809 NE2d 1090 (Mass App 2004).

[10] *Tyson Foods Inc. v Guzman*, 116 SW3d 233 (Tex App 2003).

(b) Breach of Duty

The second element of negligence is the breach of duty imposed by statute or by the application of the reasonable person standard. The defendant's conduct is evaluated against what a reasonable person would have done under the circumstances. That is, when there is sufficient proof to raise a jury question, the jury decides whether the defendant breached the duty to the injured person from a reasonable person's perspective.[11] **For Example,** the jury in Guzman's lawsuit against Tyson Foods (the *Tyson* case), after weighing all of the facts and circumstances, determined that Tyson's employee's operation of the forklift constituted a breach of Tyson's duty of care to Guzman.

(c) Causation

A third element of negligence is *causation*, the element that connects the duty and the breach of duty to the injuries to the plaintiff. **For Example,** in Guzman's lawsuit, the forklift operator's careless conduct was the cause in fact of this worker's injuries. A "but for" test for causation is used. *But for* Tyson employee Brian Jones' negligent conduct in moving the forklift under the circumstances surrounding the accident, Guzman would not have been injured.

Once the cause in fact is established, the plaintiff must establish *proximate cause*. That is, it must establish that the harm suffered by the injured person was a foreseeable consequence of the defendant's negligent actions. Foreseeability requires only the general danger to be foreseeable. In the *Tyson* case, the court determined that while there was some evidence that a jury could possibly infer that Tyson could not foresee an accident similar to the one involving Guzman, the evidence was legally sufficient to support the jury's finding that Tyson's negligence was foreseeable and the cause in fact of Guzman's injuries.

The landmark *Palsgraf v Long Island Rail Road Co.* case established a limitation on liability for unforeseeable or unusual consequences following a negligent act.

(d) Damages

The plaintiff in a personal injury negligence lawsuit must establish the actual losses caused by the defendant's breach of duty of care and is entitled to be made whole for all losses. The successful plaintiff is entitled to compensation for (1) past and future pain and suffering (mental anguish), (2) past and future physical impairment, (3) past and future medical care, and (4) past and future loss of earning capacity. Life and work life expectancy are critical factors to consider in assessing damage involving permanent disabilities with loss of earning capacity. Expert witnesses are utilized at trial to present evidence based on worklife tables and present value tables to deal with these economic issues. The jury considers all of the evidence in the context of the elements necessary to prove negligence and all defenses raised, and it renders a verdict. **For Example,** in the *Tyson* case, the defendant presented evidence and argued that Gustavo Guzman was himself negligent regarding the accident. The jury found that both parties were negligent and attributed 80 percent of the fault to Tyson and 20 percent to Guzman (this is called *comparative negligence* and is discussed in the following section). The jury awarded Guzman $931,870.51 in damages ($425,000.00 for past physical pain and mental anguish, $150,000.00 for future physical pain and mental anguish, $10,000.00 for past physical impairment, $10,000.00 for future physical impairment, $51,870.51 for past medical care, $5,000.00 for future medical care, $70,000.00 for past lost earning capacity, and $210,000.00 for future lost earning capacity). After deducting 20 percent of the total jury award for Guzman's own negligence, the trial court's final judgment awarded Guzman $745,496.41.

In some situations, the independent actions of two defendants occur to cause harm. **For Example,** Penny Shipler was rendered a quadriplegic as a result of a Chevrolet S-10 Blazer rollover accident. She sued the driver Kenneth Long for negligence and General Motors for negligent design of the Blazer's roof. She was awarded $18.5 million in damages. Because two causes provided a single indivisible injury, the two defendants were held jointly and severally liable.[12] Under *joint and several liability*, each defendant may be held liable to pay the entire judgment. However, should one defendant pay the entire judgment, that party may sue the other for "contribution" for its proportionate share.

[11] A breach of duty may be established by the very nature of the harm to the plaintiff. The doctrine of *res ipsa loquitur* ("the event speaks for itself") provides a rebuttable presumption that the defendant was negligent when a defendant owes a duty to the plaintiff, the nature of the harm caused the plaintiff is such that it ordinarily does not happen in the absence of negligence, and the instrument causing the injury was in the defendant's exclusive control. An example of the doctrine is a lawsuit against a surgeon after a surgical device is discovered in a former patient months after the surgery by another physician seeking the cause of the patient's continuing pain subsequent to the operation.

[12] *Shipler v General Motors Corp.*, 710 NW2d 807 (Neb 2006).

PALSGRAF V LONG ISLAND RY. CO., 162 NE 99 (NY 1928)

THE SCALES TIPPED ON CAUSATION

Helen Palsgraf (plaintiff) had purchased a ticket to travel to Rockaway Beach on the Long Island Railway (defendant). While she was standing on a platform at the defendant's station waiting for the train, another train stopped at the station. Two men ran to catch the train, which began moving as they were running. One of the men made in onto the train without difficulty but the other man who was carrying a package, was unsteady as he tried to jump aboard. Employees of the defendant helped pull the man in and push him onto the train car, but in the process the package was dropped. The package contained fireworks, and when it was dropped, it exploded. The vibrations from the explosion caused some scales (located at the end of the platform on which Palsgraf was standing) to fall. As they fell, they hit Palsgraf, who was injured. Palsgraf filed suit against the railroad for negligence.

Judicial Opinion

CARDOZO, C. J.... The conduct of the defendant's guard, if a wrong in its relation to the holder of the package, was not a wrong in its relation to the plaintiff, standing far away. Nothing in the situation gave notice that the falling package had in it the potency of peril to persons thus removed. Negligence is not actionable unless it involves the invasion of a legally protected interest, the violation of a right. "Proof of negligence in the air, so to speak, will not do." The plaintiff, as she stood upon the platform of the station, might claim to be protected against intentional invasion of her bodily security. Such invasion is not charged. She might claim to be protected against unintentional invasion by conduct involving in the thought of reasonable men an unreasonable hazard that such invasion would ensue. These, from the point of view of the law, were the bounds of her immunity, with perhaps some rare exceptions, survivals for the most part of ancient forms of liability, where conduct is held to be at the peril of the actor. If no hazard was apparent to the eye of ordinary vigilance, an act innocent and harmless, at least to outward seeming, with reference to her, did not take to itself the quality of a tort because it happened to be a wrong, though apparently not one involving the risk of bodily insecurity, with reference to some one else.

A different conclusion will involve us, and swiftly too, in a maze of contradictions. A guard stumbles over a package which has been left upon a platform. It seems to be a bundle of newspapers. It turns out to be a can of dynamite. To the eye of ordinary vigilance, the bundle is abandoned waste, which may be kicked or trod on with impunity. Is a passenger at the other end of the platform protected by the law against the unsuspected hazard concealed beneath the waste? If not, is the result to be any different, so far as the distant passenger is concerned, when the guard stumbles over a valise which a truckman or a porter has left upon the walk? The passenger far away, if the victim of a wrong at all, has a cause of action, not derivative, but original and primary. His claim to be protected against invasion of his bodily security is neither greater nor less because the act resulting in the invasion is a wrong to another far removed. In this case, the rights that are said to have been violated, the interests said to have been invaded, are not even of the same order. The man was not injured in his person or even put in danger. The purpose of the act, as well as its effect, was to make his person safe. If there was a wrong to him at all, which may very well be doubted, it was a wrong to a property interest only, the safety of his package. Out of this wrong to property, which threatened injury to nothing else, there has passed, we are told, to the plaintiff by derivation or succession a right of action for the invasion of an interest of another order, the right to bodily security. The diversity of interests emphasizes the futility of the effort to build the plaintiff's right upon the basis of a wrong to some one else. The gain is one of emphasis, for a like result would follow if the interests were the same. Even then, the orbit of the danger as disclosed to the eye of reasonable vigilance would be the orbit of the duty. One who jostles one's neighbor in a crowd does not invade the rights of others standing at the outer fringe when the unintended contact casts a bomb upon the ground. The wrongdoer as to them is the man who carries the bomb, not the one who explodes it without suspicion of the danger. Life will have to be made over, and human nature transformed, before prevision so extravagant can be accepted as the norm of conduct, the customary standard to which behavior must conform.

The risk reasonably to be perceived defines the duty to be obeyed, and risk imports relation; it is risk to another or to others within the range of apprehension. Here, by concession, there was nothing in the situation to suggest to the most cautious mind that the parcel wrapped in newspaper would spread wreckage through the station. If the guard had thrown it down knowingly and willfully, he would not have threatened the plaintiff's safety, so far as appearances could warn him. His conduct would not have involved, even then, an unreasonable probability of invasion of her bodily security. Liability can be no greater where the act is inadvertent.

Dissenting Opinion

ANDREWS, J.... The proposition is this: Every one owes to the world at large the duty of refraining from those acts that may unreasonably threaten the safety of others. Such an act occurs. Not only is the wronged to whom harm might reasonably be expected to result, but he also who is in fact injured, even if he be outside what would generally be thought the danger zone.

As we have said, we cannot trace the effect of an act to the end, if end there is. Again, however, we may trace it part of the way. An overturned lantern may burn all Chicago. We may follow the fire from the shed to the last building. We rightly say the fire started by the lantern caused its destruction. A cause, but not the proximate cause. What we do mean by the word "proximate" is that, because of convenience, of public policy of a rough sense of justice, the law arbitrarily declines to trace a series of events beyond a certain point. This is not logic. It is practical politics.

The act upon which defendant's liability rests is knocking an apparently harmless package onto the platform. The act was negligent. For its proximate consequences the defendant is liable. If its contents were broken, to the owner; if it fell upon and crushed a passenger's foot, then to him; if it exploded and injured one in the immediate vicinity, to him. Mrs. Palsgraf was standing some distance away. How far cannot be told from the record—apparently 25 to 30 feet, perhaps less. Except for the explosion, she would not have been injured.... The only intervening cause was that, instead of blowing her to the ground, the concussion smashed the weighing machine which in turn fell upon her. There was no remoteness in time, little in space. And surely, given such an explosion as here, it needed no great foresight to predict that the natural result would be to injure one on the platform at no greater distance from its scene than was the plaintiff. Just how no one might be able to predict. Whether by flying fragments, by broken glass, by wreckage of machines or structures no one could say. But injury in some form was most probable.

Under these circumstances I cannot say as a matter of law that the plaintiff's injuries were not the proximate result of the negligence.

Questions

1. Do you think helping someone onto a moving train is a breach of duty? Do reasonable people do this?
2. Was Mrs. Palsgraf's injury foreseeable?
3. What is the court choosing to limit?

In some cases in which the breach of duty was shocking, plaintiffs may be awarded *punitive damages*. However, punitive (also called *exemplary*) damages are ordinarily applied when the defendant's tortious conduct is attended by circumstances of fraud, malice, or willful or wanton conduct.[13]

14. Defenses to Negligence

(a) Contributory Negligence

A plaintiff who is also negligent gives the defendant the opportunity to raise the defense of **contributory negligence,** which the defendant establishes by utilizing the elements of negligence previously discussed, including the plaintiff's duty to exercise reasonable care for his or her own safety, the breach of that duty, causation, and harm. Under common law, the defense of contributory negligence, if established, is a complete bar to recovery of damages from the defendant.

The *Hardesty* case involves the application of the contributory negligence defense.

[13] See *Eden Electrical, Ltd. v Amana Co.*, 370 F3d 824 (8th Cir 2004); and *University of Colorado v American Cyanamid Co.*, 342 F3d 1298 (Fed Cir 2003).

HARDESTY V AMERICAN SEATING CO., 194 F SUPP 2D 447 (D MD 2002)

KEEP YOUR EYE ON THE BALL IN SPORTS: KEEP YOUR EYE ON THE 300-POUND BOXES IN TRUCKING

Lawrence Hardesty is an over-the-road tractor-trailer truck driver who picked up a load of stadium seating equipment for the NFL stadium under construction in Baltimore. The equipment was packaged in large corrugated cardboard boxes weighing several hundred pounds. The shipper, American Seating Co., loaded the trailer while Hardesty remained in the cab of his truck doing "paperwork" and napping. Considerable open space existed between the boxes and the rear door of the trailer. The evidence showed that Hardesty failed to properly examine the load bars used to secure the boxes from movement during transit. When Hardesty arrived at the Baltimore destination, he opened the rear trailer door and boxes at the end of the trailer fell out and injured him. Hardesty brought a personal injury negligence action against the shipper. American Seating Co. responded that Hardesty was contributorily negligent, thus barring his negligence claim.

Judicial Opinion

DAVIS, D. J.... Under Maryland tort law, a negligence claim requires a showing of the following four elements: "(1) a duty owed to the plaintiff by the defendant; (2) a breach of that duty by the defendant; (3) a legally cognizable causal relationship between the breach of duty and the harm suffered; and (4) damages suffered by the plaintiff." Although the question "whether there is adequate proof of the required elements needed to succeed in a negligence action is [generally] a question of fact to be determined by the fact finder,... *the existence of a legal duty is a question of law to be decided by the court.*" Contributory negligence, "that degree of reasonable and ordinary care that a plaintiff fails to undertake in the face of an appreciable risk which cooperates with the defendant's negligence in bringing about the plaintiff's harm," is a complete bar to recovery....

As a matter of law, Plaintiff's claim is barred by his own contributory negligence....

Questions

1. How does the court define contributory negligence?
2. Is contributory negligence a complete bar to Hardesty's recovery of damages for his injuries in this case?
3. If Maryland applied a "comparative negligence" defense, as set forth in the following section of the text, rather than contributory negligence, would a more fair or just result have been reached in this case?

The contributory negligence defense has given way to the defense of comparative negligence in most states.

(b) Comparative Negligence

Because contributory negligence produced harsh results with no recovery of damages for an injured plaintiff, most states have adopted a fairer approach to handling situations in which both the plaintiff and the defendant are negligent; it is called *comparative negligence*. Comparative negligence is a defense that permits a negligent plaintiff to recover some damages but only in proportion to the defendant's degree of fault.[14] **For Example,** in the *Tyson* case, both the defendant and the plaintiff were found to be negligent. The jury attributed 80 percent of the fault for the plaintiff's injury to Tyson and 20 percent of the fault to the plaintiff, Guzman. While Guzman's total damages were $931,870, they were reduced by 20 percent, and the final judgment awarded Guzman was $745,496.

Some comparative negligence states refuse to allow the plaintiff to recover damages if the plaintiff's fault was more than 50 percent of the cause of the harm.[15]

(c) Assumption of the Risk

The assumption of the risk defense has two categories. *Express assumption of the risk* involves a written

[14] *City of Chicago v M/V Morgan*, 375 F3d 563 (7th Cir 2004).

[15] *Davenport v Cotton Hope Plantation*, 482 SE2d 569 (SC App 1997).

exculpatory agreement under which a plaintiff acknowledges the risks involved in certain activities and releases the defendant from prospective liability for personal injuries sustained as a result of the defendant's negligent conduct. Examples include ski lift tickets, whitewater rafting contracts, permission for high school cheerleading activities, and parking lot claim checks. In most jurisdictions these agreements are enforceable as written. However, in some jurisdictions they may be considered unenforceable because they violate public policy. **For Example,** Gregory Hanks sued the Powder Ridge Ski Resort for negligence regarding serious injuries he sustained while snowtubing at the defendant's facility. He had signed a release which explicitly provided that the snowtuber: *["fully] assume[s] all risks associated with [s]nowtubing,* even if due to the NEGLIGENCE" of the defendants [emphasis in original]. The Supreme Court of Connecticut found that the release was unenforceable because it violated the public policy by shifting the risk of negligence to the weaker bargainer.[16]

Implied primary assumption of the risk arises when a plaintiff has impliedly consented, often in advance of any negligence by the defendant, to relieve a defendant of a duty to the plaintiff regarding specific known and appreciated risks. It is a subjective standard, one specific to the plaintiff and his or her situation. **For Example,** baseball mom Delinda Taylor took her two boys to a Seattle Mariners baseball game and was injured during the pregame warm-up when a ball thrown by José Mesa got past Freddie Garcia, striking Taylor in the face and causing serious injuries. The defendant baseball team successfully raised the affirmative defense of implied primary assumption of the risk by showing that Mrs. Taylor had full subjective understanding of the specific risk of getting hit by a thrown baseball, and she voluntarily chose to encounter that risk.[17]

A number of states have either abolished the defense of assumption of the risk, reclassifying the defense as comparative negligence so as not to completely bar a plaintiff's recovery of damages, or have eliminated the use of the assumption of the risk terminology and handle cases under the duty, breach of duty, causation, and harm elements of negligence previously discussed.[18]

(d) Immunity

Governments are generally immune from tort liability.[19] This rule has been eroded by decisions and in some instances by statutes, such as the Federal Tort Claims Act. Subject to certain exceptions, this act permits the recovery of damages from the United States for property damage, personal injury, or death action claims arising from the negligent act or omission of any employee of the United States under such circumstances that the United States, if a private person, would be liable to the claimant in accordance with the law of the place where the act or omission occurred. A rapidly growing number of states have abolished governmental immunity, although many still recognize it.

Until the early 1900s, charities were immune from tort liability, and children and parents and spouses could not sue each other. These immunities are fast disappearing. **For Example,** if a father's negligent driving of his car causes injuries to his minor child passenger, the child may recover from the father for his injuries.[20]

D. Strict Liability

The final form of tort liability is known as *strict liability*. When the standards of strict liability apply, very few defenses are available. Strict liability was developed to provide guaranteed protection for those who are injured by conduct the law deems both serious and inexcusable.

15. What is Strict Liability?

Strict liability is an absolute standard of liability imposed by the law in circumstances the courts or legislatures have determined require a high degree of protection. When strict liability is imposed, the result is that the company or person who has caused injury or damages by the conduct will be required to compensate

[16] *Hanks v Powder Ridge,* 885 A2d 734 (Conn 2005).

[17] *Taylor v Baseball Club of Seattle,* 130 P3d 835 (Wash App 2006).

[18] See, for example, *Costa v The Boston Red Sox Baseball Club,* 809 NE2d 1090 (Mass App 2004), where the court cites state precedent that "... the abolishment of assumption of the risk as an affirmative defense did not alter the plaintiff's burden ... to prove the defendant owed [the plaintiff] a duty of care ... and thus left intact the open and obvious damages rule, which operates to negate the existence of a duty to care."

[19] *Kirby v Macon County,* 892 SW2d 403 (Tenn 1994).

[20] *Cates v Cates,*588 NE2d 330 (Ill App 1992); see also *Doe v McKay,*700 NE2d 1018 (Ill 1998).

SPORTS & ENTERTAINMENT LAW

Charles "Booby" Clark played football for the Cincinnati Bengals as a running back on offense. Dale Hackbart played defensive free safety for the Denver Broncos. As a consequence of an interception by the Broncos, Hackbart became an offensive player, threw a block, and was watching the play with one knee on the ground when Clark "acting out of anger and frustration, but without a specific intent to injure," stepped forward and struck a blow to the back of Hackbart's head and neck, causing a serious neck fracture. Is relief precluded for injuries occurring during a professional football game? The answer is no. While proof of mere negligence is insufficient to establish liability during such an athletic contest, liability must instead be premised on heightened proof of reckless or intentional conduct on the part of the defendant. In the *Hackbart* case, the court determined that if the evidence established that the injury was the result of acts of Clark that were in reckless disregard of Hackbart's safety, Hackbart is entitled to damages.* Why didn't Hackbart pursue recovery under negligence law, contending that Clark had a general duty of care to act as a reasonably prudent person would in similar circumstances? Because football and other contact sports contain within the rules of the games inherent *unreasonable* risks of harm, a negligence theory is not applicable. What contact sports do you believe qualify under this "sports exception" doctrine for which proof of negligence is insufficient to establish liability for injuries sustained during the athletic contest?

PGA golfer Walter Mallin sued PGA golfer John Paesani for injuries that Mallin sustained while competing in a PGA golf tournament when Paesani drove a golf ball that struck Mallin in the head on his right temple. Paesani contends that the "sports exception" doctrine applies and the negligence case must be dismissed. How would you decide this case?**

* *Hackbart v Cincinnati Bengals, Inc.*, 601 F2d 516 (10th Cir 1979).
** *Mallin v Paesani*, 892 A2d 1043 (Conn Super, 2005).

THINKING THINGS THROUGH

TORTS AND PUBLIC POLICY

Over a decade ago, a jury awarded 81-year-old Stella Liebeck nearly $3 million because she was burned after she spilled a cup of McDonald's coffee on her lap. Based on these limited facts, a national discussion ensued about a need for tort reform, and to this day "Stella Awards" are given on Web sites for apparently frivolous or excessive lawsuits. Consider the following additional facts and the actual damages awarded Stella Liebeck. Decide whether her recovery was just.

- McDonald's coffee was brewed at 195 to 205 degrees.
- McDonald's quality assurance manager "was aware of the risk [of burns] . . . and had no plans to turn down the heat."
- Mrs. Liebeck spent seven days in the hospital with third degree burns and had skin grafts. Gruesome photos of burns of the inner thighs, groin, and buttocks were entered as evidence.
- Compensatory damages were $200,000, which were reduced to $160,000 because Mrs. Liebeck was determined to be 20 percent at fault.

THINKING THINGS THROUGH

continued

- The jury awarded $2.7 million in punitive damages. The trial court judge reduced this amount to $480,000.
- The total recovery at the trial court for Mrs. Liebeck was $640,000. Both parties appealed, and a settlement was reached at what is believed to be close to the $640,000 figure.

Tort remedies have evolved because of public policy incentives for the protection of individuals from physical, mental, and economic damage. Tort remedies provide economic motivation for individuals and businesses to avoid conduct that could harm others.

The amount of the compensation and the circumstances in which compensation for torts should be paid are issues that courts, juries, and legislatures review. Many legislatures have examined and continue to review the standards for tort liability and damages.

The U.S. Supreme Court devoted three decisions over a recent seven-year period dealing with excessive punitive damages in civil litigation, and it has set "guideposts" to be used by courts in assessing punitive damages.* In *State Farm Mutual Automobile Insurance Co. v Campbell*, compensatory damages for the plaintiffs at the trial court level were $1 million, and punitive damages, based in part on evidence that State Farm's nationwide policy was to underpay claims regardless of merit to enhance profits, were assessed at $145 million. The Supreme Court concluded that the facts of *Campbell* would likely justify a punitive damages award only at or near the amount of compensatory damages. Thus, even those who act very badly as State Farm Insurance did have a constitutionally protected right under the Due Process Clause of the Fourteenth Amendment to have civil law damages assessed in accordance with the Supreme Court's guideposts.

***BMW of North America v Gore*, 517 US 559 (1996); *Cooper Industries v Leatherman Tool Group, Inc.*, 532 US 424 (2001); and *State Farm Insurance v Campbell*, 538 US 408 (2003).

for those damages in an absolute sense. Few, if any, defenses apply in a situation in which the law imposes a strict liability standard. **For Example,** as noted earlier in the chapter, engaging in ultrahazardous activities, such as using dynamite to excavate a site for new construction, results in strict liability for the contractor performing the demolition. Any damages resulting from the explosion are the responsibility of that contractor, so the contractor is strictly liable.

16. Imposing Strict Liability

Strict liability arises in a number of different circumstances, but the most common are in those situations in which a statutory duty is imposed and in product liability. For example at both the state and federal levels, there are requirements for the use, transportation, and sale of radioactive materials, as well as the disposal of biomedical materials and tools. Any violation of these rules and regulations would result in strict liability for the company or person in violation.

Product liability, while more fully covered in Chapter 25, is another example of strict liability. A product that is defective through its design, manufacture, or instructions and that injures someone results in strict liability for the manufacturer.

LAWFLIX

Class Action (1991) (R)

This movie depicts the magnitude of damages and recovery when multiple injuries occur. The film provides insights on tort reform and the ethics of lawyers. You can learn about the magnitude of discovery and evidence.

For movie clips that illustrate business law concepts, see LawFlix at **http://wdvl.westbuslaw.com.**

Summary

A *tort* is a civil wrong that affords recovery for damages that result. The three forms of torts are intentional torts, negligence, and strict liability. A tort differs from a crime in the nature of its remedy. Fines and imprisonment result from criminal violations, whereas money damages are paid to those who are damaged by conduct that constitutes a tort. An action may be both a crime and a tort, but the tort remedy is civil in nature.

Selected intentional torts are false imprisonment, defamation, product disparagement, contract interference or tortious interference, and trespass. False imprisonment is the detention of another without his or her permission. False imprisonment is often called the *shopkeeper's tort* because store owners detain suspected shoplifters. Many states provide a privilege to store owners if they detain shoplifting suspects based on reasonable cause and in a reasonable manner. Defamation is slander (oral) or libel (written) and consists of false statements about another that damage the person's reputation or integrity. Truth is an absolute defense to defamation, and there are some privileges that protect against defamation, such as those for witnesses at trial and for members of Congress during debates on the floor. There is a developing privilege for employers when they give references for former employees. Invasion of privacy is intrusion into private affairs; public disclosure of private facts; or appropriation of someone's name, image, or likeness for commercial purposes.

To establish the tort of negligence, one must show that there has been a breach of duty in the form of a violation of a statute or professional competency standards or of behavior that does not rise to the level of that of a reasonable person. That breach of duty must have caused the foreseeable injuries to the plaintiff, and the plaintiff must be able to quantify the damages that resulted. Possible defenses to negligence include contributory negligence, comparative negligence, and assumption of risk.

Strict liability is absolute liability with few defenses.

Questions and Case Problems

1. Christensen Shipyards built a 155-foot yacht for Tiger Woods at its Vancouver, Washington, facilities. It used Tiger's name and photographs relating to the building of the yacht in promotional materials for the shipyard without seeking his permission. Was this a right to publicity tort because Tiger could assert that his name and photos were used to attract attention to the shipyard to obtain commercial advantage? Did the shipyard have a First Amendment right to present the truthful facts regarding their building of the yacht and the owner's identity as promotional materials? Does the fact that the yacht was named *Privacy* have an impact on this case? Would it make a difference as to the outcome of this case if the contract for building the yacht had a clause prohibiting the use of Tiger's name or photo without his permission?
2. ESPN held its Action Sports and Music Awards ceremony in April, at which celebrities in the fields of extreme sports and popular music such as rap and heavy metal converged. Well-known musicians Ben Harper and James Hetfield were there, as were popular rappers Busta Rhymes and LL Cool J. Famed motorcycle stuntman Evel Knievel, who is commonly thought of as the "father of extreme sports," and his wife Krystal were photographed. The photograph depicted Evel, who was wearing a motorcycle jacket and rose-tinted sunglasses, with his right arm around Krystal and his left arm around another young woman. ESPN published the photograph on its "extreme sports" Web site with a caption that read "Evel Knievel proves that you're never too old to be a pimp." The Knievels brought suit against ESPN, contending that the photograph and caption were defamatory because they accused Evel of soliciting prostitution and implied that Krystal was a prostitute. ESPN contends that the caption was a figurative and slang usage and was not defamatory as a matter of law. Decide. [*Knievel v ESPN*, 393 F3d 1068 (9th Cir)]
3. While snowboarding down a slope at Mammoth Mountain Ski Area (Mammoth), 17-year-old David Graham was engaged in a snowball fight with his 14-year-old brother. As he was "preparing to throw a snowball" at his brother, David slammed into Liam Madigan, who was working as a ski school instructor for Mammoth, and injured him. Madigan sued Graham for damages for reckless and dangerous behavior. The defense contended that the claim was barred under the doctrine of assumption of the risk, applicable in the state, arising from the risk inherent in the sport that allows for vigorous participation and frees a participant from a legal duty to act with due care. Decide. [*Mammoth Mountain Ski Area v Graham*, 38 Cal Rptr 3d 422 (Cal App)]
4. James Lee Boyter, a cement truck driver for Concrete Specialties of America, collided head-on with Robin Langley as she drove on a curved portion of a two-lane road. Langley testified that Boyter hit her head-on as he came around the curve because he was in her lane and hence driving on the wrong side of the road. A witness testified that Langley was driving at an excessive rate of speed before Boyter's truck struck her car between the

left front fender and the door. Langley filed suit against Boyter and Concrete Specialties. They defended on the grounds that Langley was contributorily negligent. What happens if there is contributory negligence on the part of Langley? Do you think she was contributorily negligent? [*Langley v Boyter*, 325 SE2d 550 (SC)]

5. JoKatherine Page and her 14-year-old son Jason were robbed at their bank's ATM at 9:30 P.M. one evening by a group of four thugs. The thieves took $300, struck Mrs. Page in the face with a gun, and ran. Mrs. Page and her son filed suit against the bank for its failure to provide adequate security. Should the bank be held liable? [*Page v American National Bank & Trust Co.*, 850 SW2d 133 (Tenn)]
6. A Barberton Glass Co. truck was transporting large sheets of glass down the highway. Elliot Schultz was driving his automobile some distance behind the truck. Because of the negligent way that the sheets of glass were fastened in the truck, a large sheet fell off the truck, shattered on the highway, and then bounced up and broke the windshield of Shultz's car. He was not injured but suffered great emotional shock. He sued Barberton to recover damages for this shock. Barberton denied liability on the grounds that Schultz had not sustained any physical injury at the time or as the result of the shock. Should he be able to recover? [*Schultz v Barberton Glass Co.*, 447 NE2d 109 (Ohio)]
7. Mallinckrodt produces nuclear and radioactive medical pharmaceuticals and supplies. Maryland Heights Leasing, an adjoining business owner, claimed that low-level radiation emissions from Mallinckrodt damaged its property and caused a loss in earnings. What remedy should Maryland Heights have? What torts are involved here? [*Maryland Heights Leasing, Inc. v Mallinckrodt, Inc.*, 706 SW2d 218 (Mo App)]
8. An owner abandoned his van in an alley in Chicago. In spite of repeated complaints to the police, the van was allowed to remain in the alley. After several months, it was stripped of most of the parts that could be removed. Jamin Ortiz, age 11, was walking down the alley when the van's gas tank exploded. The flames from the explosion set fire to Jamin's clothing, and he was severely burned. Jamin and his family brought suit brought against the city of Chicago to recover damages for his injuries. Could the city be held responsible for injuries caused by property owned by someone else? Why or why not? [*Ortiz v Chicago*, 398 NE2d 1007 (Ill App)]
9. Carrigan, a district manager of Simples Time Recorder Co., was investigating complaints of mismanagement of the company's Jackson office. He called the home of Hooks, the secretary of that office, who expressed the opinion that part of the trouble was caused by the theft of parts and equipment by McCall, another employee. McCall was later discharged and sued Hooks for slander. Was she liable? [*Hooks v McCall*, 272 So 2d 925 (Miss)]
10. Defendant no. 1 parked his truck in the street near the bottom of a ditch on a dark, foggy night. Iron pipes carried in the truck projected nine feet beyond the truck in back. Neither the truck nor the pipes carried any warning light or flag, in violation of both a city ordinance and a state statute. Defendant no. 2 was a taxicab owner whose taxicab was negligently driven at an excessive speed. Defendant no. 2 ran into the pipes, thereby killing the passenger in the taxicab. The plaintiff brought an action for the passenger's death against both defendants. Defendant no. 1 claimed he was not liable because it was Defendant no. 2's negligence that had caused the harm. Was this defense valid? [*Bumbardner v Allison*, 78 SE2d 752 (NC)]
11. A customer was shopping at the handbag counter of the defendant's store. She did not make any purchase and left the store. When she was a few feet away from the store, a store employee tapped her lightly on the shoulder to attract her attention and asked her if she had made any purchases. When she inquired why, he asked, "What about that bag in your hand?" The customer said that it belonged to her, and she opened it to show by its contents that it was not a new bag. The employee gave the customer a "real dirty look" and went back into the store without saying a word. The customer then sued the store for false imprisonment. Was the store liable? [*Abner v W.T. Grant Co.*, 139 SE2d 408 (Ga App)]
12. Hegyes was driving her car when it was negligently struck by a Unjian Enterprises truck. She was injured, and an implant was placed in her body to counteract the injuries. She sued Unjian, and the case was settled. Two years later Hegyes became pregnant. The growing fetus pressed against the implant, making it necessary for her doctor to deliver the child 51 days prematurely by Cesarean section. Because of its premature birth, the child had a breathing handicap. Suit was brought against Unjian Enterprises for the harm sustained by the child. Was the defendant liable? [*Hegyes v Unjian Enterprises, Inc.*, 286 Cal Rptr 85 (Cal App)]
13. Kendra Knight took part in a friendly game of touch football. She had played before and was familiar with football. Michael Jewett was on her team. In the course of play, Michael bumped into Kendra and knocked her to the ground. He stepped on her hand, causing injury to a little finger that later required its amputation. She sued Michael for damages. He defended on the ground that she had assumed the risk. Kendra claimed that assumption of risk could not be raised as a defense because the state legislature had adopted the standard of comparative negligence. What happens if contributory negligence applies? What happens if the defense of comparative negligence applies?
14. A passenger on a cruise ship was injured by a rope thrown while the ship was docking. The passenger was sitting on a lounge chair on the third deck when she was struck by

the weighted end of a rope thrown by an employee of Port Everglades, where the boat was docking. These ropes, or heaving lines, were being thrown from the dock to the second deck, and the passenger was injured by a line that was thrown too high.

The trial court granted the cruise line's motion for directed verdict on the ground there was no evidence that the cruise line knew or should have known of the danger. The cruise line contended that it had no notice that this "freak accident" could occur. What is the duty of a cruise ship line to its passengers? Is there liability here? Does it matter that an employee of the port city, not the cruise lines, caused the injury? Should the passenger be able to recover? Why or why not? [*Kalendareva v Discovery Cruise Line Partnership*, 798 So 2d 804 (Fla App)]

15. Blaylock was a voluntary psychiatric outpatient treated by Dr. Burglass, who became aware that Blaylock was violence prone. Blaylock told Dr. Burglass that he intended to do serious harm to Wayne Boynton, Jr., and shortly thereafter he killed Wayne. Wayne's parents then sued Dr. Burglass on grounds that he was liable for the death of their son because he failed to give warning or to notify the police of Blaylock's threat and nature. Was a duty breached here? Should Dr. Burglass be held liable? [*Boynton v Burglass*, 590 So 2d 446 (Fla App)]

INTELLECTUAL PROPERTY RIGHTS AND THE INTERNET

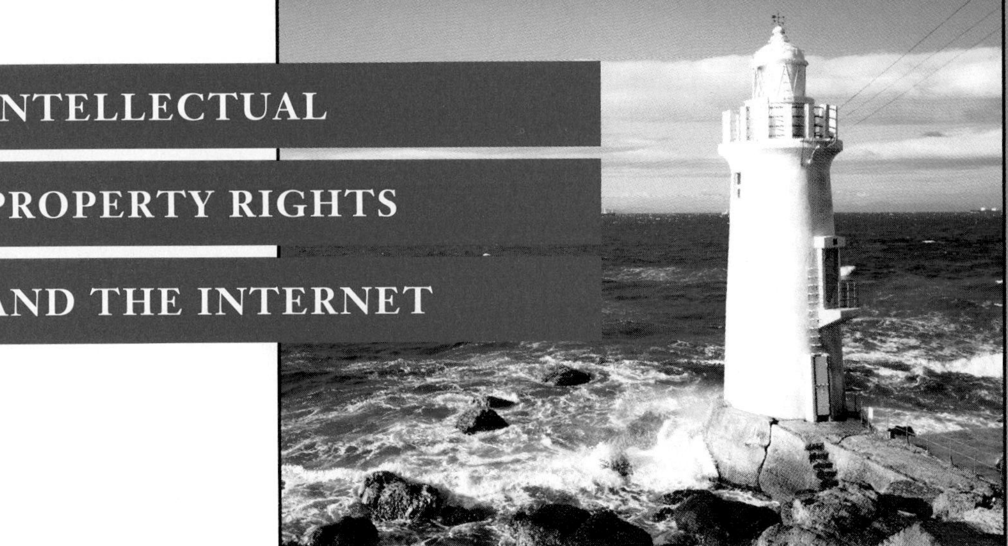

CHAPTER (10)

LEARNING OBJECTIVES

After studying this chapter, you should be able to

LO.1 Explain how to obtain a copyright, a patent, and a trademark

LO.2 Identify the rights obtained by owners of copyrights, patents, and trademarks

LO.3 State the duration of the protection afforded owners of copyrights, trademarks, and patents

LO.4 Set forth the remedies available to owners for infringement of intellectual property rights

LO.5 List and explain the extent of protection provided by federal laws for owners of software and mask works

Intellectual property comes in many forms: the writing by an author or the software developed by an employee, the new product or process developed by an inventor, the company name Hewlett-Packard, and the secret formula used to make Coca-Cola. Federal law provides rights to owners of these works, products, company names, and secret formulas that are called *copyrights*, *patents*, *trademarks*, and *trade secrets*. State laws provide protection for trade secrets. These basic legal principles are also applicable in an Internet and e-commerce context. This chapter discusses the federal and state laws governing intellectual property rights and their Internet context.

A. Trademarks and Service Marks

The Lanham Act, a federal law, grants a producer the exclusive right to register a trademark and prevent competitors from using that mark. This law helps assure a producer that it, not an imitating competitor, will reap the financial, reputation-related rewards of a desirable product.

1. Introduction

A mark is any word, name, symbol, device, or combination of these used to identify a product or service.[1] If the mark identifies a product, such as an automobile or soap, it is called a **trademark.** If it identifies a service, such as a restaurant or dry cleaner, it is called a **service mark.**

The owner of a mark may obtain protection from others using it by registering the mark in accordance with federal law.[2] To be registered, a mark must distinguish the goods or services of the applicant from those of others. Under the federal statute, a register, called the Principal Register, is maintained for recording such marks. Inclusion on the Principal Register grants the registrant the exclusive right to use the mark. Challenges may be made to the registrant's right within five years of registration, but after five years, the right of the registrant is incontestable.

An advance registration of a mark may be made not more than three years before its actual use by filing an application certifying a bona fide "intent-to-use." Fees must be paid at six-month intervals from the filing of the application until actual use begins.

[1] 15 USC § 1127.

[2] *Lanham Act*, 15 USC §§ 1050–1127.

2. Registrable Marks

Marks that are coined, completely fanciful, or arbitrary are capable of registration on the Principal Register. The mark Exxon, for example, was coined by the owner. The name Kodak is also a creation of the owner of this trademark and has no other meaning in English, but it serves to distinguish the goods of its owner from all others.

A suggestive term may also be registered. Such a term suggests rather than describes some characteristics of the goods to which it applies and requires the consumer to exercise some imagination to reach a conclusion about the nature of the goods. **For Example,** as a trademark for refrigerators, Penguin would be suggestive of the product's superior cooling and freezing features. As a trademark for paperback books, however, Penguin is arbitrary and fanciful.

Ordinarily, descriptive terms, surnames, and geographic terms are not registrable on the Principal Register.[3] A descriptive term identifies a characteristic or quality of an article or service, such as color, odor, function, or use. **For Example,** America Online, Inc. (AOL) sued its Internet competitor AT&T for trademark infringement over the use of the words "You Have Mail!" by AT&T, relating to e-mail service. AOL's displaying the words "You Have Mail" and playing a recording "You've got mail" when a subscriber in fact has e-mail are words used in their common meaning and are thus a functional use and may not be appropriated as exclusive trademark property.[4] Boston Beer was denied trademark protection because it was a geographic term.[5]

An exception is made, however, when a descriptive or geographic term or a surname has acquired a *secondary meaning;* such a mark is registrable. A term or terms that have a primary meaning of their own acquire a secondary meaning when, through long use in connection with a particular product, they have come to be known by the public as identifying the particular product and its origin. **For Example,** the geographic term *Philadelphia* has acquired a secondary meaning when applied to cream cheese. It is widely accepted by the public as denoting a particular brand rather than any cream cheese made in Philadelphia. Factors considered by a court in determining whether a trademark has acquired secondary meaning are the amount and manner of advertising, volume of sales, length and manner of use, direct consumer testimony, and consumer surveys.

With a limited number of colors available for use by competitors, along with possible shade confusion, courts had held for some 90 years that color alone could not function as a trademark. The U.S. Supreme Court has overturned this legal rule, and now if a color serves as a symbol that distinguishes a firm's goods and identifies their source without serving any other significant function, it may, sometimes at least, meet the basic legal requirements for use as a trademark.[6] **For Example,** Owens-Corning Fiberglass Corp. has been allowed to register the color pink as a trademark for its fiberglass insulation products.

Generic terms—that is, terms that designate a kind or class of goods, such as *soap, shirts, cola* or *rosé wine*—are never registrable.

Generic terms also apply to service marks. **For Example,** Robert Donchez was the first licensed beer vendor hired by the Colorado Rockies baseball team for its inaugural season. He was referred to as "Bob the Beerman." He authored a book about his first season vending beer titled in part "... A Season with Bob the Beerman"; and he obtained a service mark for the "Bob the Beerman" character under state law. Coors Brewing Co. began an advertising campaign for its Coors Light product using many different actors and actresses portraying beer vendors interacting with the crowd in amusing ways. Some of the vendors called themselves "the beerman" or "Hey, beerman." Bob Donchez's lawsuit against Coors and the ad agency under the Lanham Act was unsuccessful because the word *beerman* is an unprotected generic term.

In the *Harley-Davidson* case, the motorcycle manufacturer sought to appropriate the word *hog* as its trademark, and a local motorcycle shop sought to parody Harley's logo to promote his own products and services.

[3] A Supplemental Register exists for recording such marks. This recording does not give the registrant any protection, but it provides a source to which other persons designing a mark can go to make sure they are not duplicating an existing mark.

[4] *America Online, Inc. v AT&T Corporation,* 243 F3d 812 (4th Cir 2001).

[5] *Boston Beer Co. v Slesar Bros. Brewing Co.,* 9 F3d 125 (1st Cir 1994).

[6] *Qualitex Co. v Jacobson Products Co.,* Inc., 514 US 159 (1995).

HARLEY-DAVIDSON, INC. V GROTTANELLI, 164 F3D 987 (2D CIR 1999)

NO HOGGING GENERIC TERMS

Harley-Davidson obtained a judgment against Ronald Grottanelli in the U.S. District for the Western District of New York for infringement of its bar-and-shield trademark, and the court enjoined his future use of that mark. The judgment also enjoined Grottanelli from using the word "hog" in reference to some of his products and services. Both parties appealed.

Judicial Opinion

NEWMAN, J. . . .

1. The Word "Hog" Applied to Motorcycles

Public use of the word "hog." In the late 1960s and early 1970s, the word "hog" was used by motorcycle enthusiasts to refer to motorcycles generally and to large motorcycles in particular. The word was used that way in the press at least as early as 1965, and frequently thereafter, prior to the 1980s when Harley first attempted to make trademark use of the term. Several dictionaries include a definition of "hog" as a motorcycle, especially a large one. The October 1975 issue of *Street Chopper* contained an article entitled "Honda Hog," indicating that the word "hog" was generic as to motorcycles and needed a tradename adjective.

Beginning around the early 1970s and into the early 1980s, motorcyclists increasingly came to use the word "hog" when referring to Harley-Davidson motorcycles. However, for several years, as Harley-Davidson's Manager of Trademark Enforcement acknowledged, the company attempted to disassociate itself from the word "hog." The Magistrate judge drew the reasonable inference that the company wished to distance itself from the connection between "hog" as applied to motorcycles and unsavory elements of the population, such as Hell's Angels, who were among those applying the term to Harley-Davidson motorcycles.

Harley-Davidson's use of the word "hog." In 1981, Harley-Davidson's new owners recognized that the term "hog" had financial value and began using the term in connection with its merchandise, accessories, advertising, and promotions. In 1983, it formed the Harley Owners' Group, pointedly using the acronym "H.O.G." In 1987, it registered the acronym in conjunction with various logos. It subsequently registered the mark "HOG" for motorcycles. That registration lists Harley-Davidson's first use as occurring in 1990.

Grottanelli's use of the word "hog." Grottanelli opened a motorcycle repair shop under the name "The Hog Farm" in 1969. Since that time his shop has been located at various sites in western New York. At some point after 1981, Grottanelli also began using the word "hog" in connection with events and merchandise. He has sponsored an event alternatively known as "Hog Holidays" and "Hog Farm Holidays," and sold products such as "Hog Wash" engine degreaser and a "Hog Trivia" board game.

2. The Bar-and-Shield Logo

Harley-Davidson's use of the logo. Since approximately 1909, Harley-Davidson has used variations of its bar-and-shield logo—a shield traversed across the middle by a horizontal bar. The words "Motor" and "Cycles" (or sometimes "Company") appear at the chief and base of the shield, respectively, and the name "Harley-Davidson" appears on the horizontal bar. Variations of the bar-and-shield logo were registered with the United States Patent and Trademark Office in 1982 and thereafter.

Grottanelli's use of the logo. By 1979, Grottanelli had begun using variants of Harley-Davidson's bar-and-shield logo. His 1979 advertisements include a hand-drawn copy of the bar-and-shield logo, with the name "Harley-Davidson" displayed on the horizontal bar. Since 1982, in response to letters of protest from Harley-Davidson, Grottanelli has replaced the words "Harley-Davidson" on the horizontal bar of his logo with the words "American-Made." He has also placed a banner at the bottom of his logo with the words "UNAUTHORIZED DEALER." In 1986, Grottanelli began using his current log, which adds an eagle's wings behind the shield. This addition was apparently patterned after Harley-Davidson's bicentennial logo design mark, which included an eagle above the shield. Grottanelli's 1986 version of his logo also features a drawing of a pig wearing sunglasses. Grottanelli acknowledged at trial that his bar-and-shield logo is his version of Harley-Davidson's logo and that his version is "supposed to be similar, but confusing . . . [t]o a Harley-Davidson bar and shield." . . .

Discussion

1. USE OF THE WORD "HOG"

. . . No manufacturer can take out of the language a word, even a slang term, that has generic meaning as to a category of products and appropriate it for its own trademark use. . . .

...In this case, one dictionary cites a generic use of "hog" to mean a large motorcycle as early as 1967, long before Harley's first trademark use of the word, and the recent dictionary editions continuing to define the word to mean a large motorcycle indicate that the word has not lost its generic meaning. We have observed that newspaper and magazine use of a word in a generic sense is "a strong indication of the general public's perception" that the word is generic. In this case, media use of "hog" to mean a large motorcycle began as early as 1935 and continued thereafter.

However, rather than recognize that the word "hog," originally generic as applied to motorcyles, cannot subsequently be appropriated for trademark use, the Magistrate Judge upheld Harley-Davidson's anti-dilution claim on the ground that its "HOG" mark has become a strong trademark. This was error. Even the presumption of validity arising from federal registration, *see Reese Publishing Co. v Hampton International Communications, Inc.*, 620 F.2d 7, 11 [205 USPQ 585] (2d Cir. 1980), cannot protect a mark that is shown on strong evidence to be generic as to the relevant category of products prior to the proprietor's trademark use and registration....

...Harley-Davidson suggests...that it is entitled to trademark use of "HOG" as applied to motorcycles because a substantial segment of the relevant consumers began to use the term specifically to refer to Harley-Davidson motorcycles before the company made trademark use of the term. Some decisions have invoked this principle to accord a company priority as to its subsequent trademark use of a term. *See National Cable Television Ass'n, Inc. v American Cinema Editors, Inc.*, 937 F.2d 1572 [19 USPQ2d 1424] (Fed. Cir. 1991) (mark "ACE"); *Volkswagenwerk AG v Hoffman*, 489 F. Supp. 678 [209 USPQ 398] (D.S.C. 1980) (mark "BUG"). Whether or not we would agree with these decisions, they present a significantly different situation. Neither "ACE" nor "BUG" was a generic term in the language as applied, respectively, to a category of film editors or a category of automobiles prior to the public's use of the terms to refer to the American Cinema Editors and Volkswagen cars. By contrast, "hog" was a generic term in the language as applied to large motorcycles before the public (or at least some segments of it) began using the word to refer to Harley-Davidson motorcycles. The public has no more right than a manufacturer to withdraw from the language a generic term, already applicable to the relevant category of products, and accord it trademark significance, at least as long as the term retains some generic meaning.

For all of these reasons, Harley-Davidson may not prohibit Grottanelli from using "hog" to identify his motorcycle products and services. Like any other manufacturer with a product identified by a word that is generic, Harley-Davidson will have to rely on all or a portion of its tradename (or other protectable marks) to identify its brand of motorcycles, *e.g.*, "Harley Hogs."

II. BAR-AND-SHIELD LOGO

Parody defense. Grottanelli admits that his use of his bar-and-shield logo "purposefully suggests an association with Harley," but argues that his use is a protectable parody. We have accorded considerable leeway to parodists whose expressive works aim their parodic commentary at a trademark or a trademarked product, *see, e.g., Cliffs Notes, Inc. v Bantam Doubleday Dell Publishing Group, Inc.*, 886 F.2d 490, 493–95 (2d Cir. 1989), *cf. Rogers, v Grimaldi*, 875 F.2d 994, 998 (2d Cir. 1989), but have not hesitated to prevent a manufacturer from using an alleged parody of a competitor's mark to sell a competing product, *see Deere & Co. v MTD Products, Inc.*, 41 F.3d 39 (2d Cir. 1994) (applying New York's anti-dilution statute). Grottanelli uses his bar-and-shield logo on the signage of his business, in his newsletter, and on T-shirts. The signage on his business is, in effect, trademark use for a competing service, since, Harley-Davidson offers motorcycle repair services through its authorized dealers, and Grottanelli's placement of his bar-and-shield logo on his newsletter and T-shirts promotes his repair and parts business. In this context, parodic use is sharply limited. *See Deere*, 41 F.3d at 45 (citing *Wendy's International, Inc. v Big Bite, Inc.*, 576 F. Supp. 816 (S.D. Ohio 1983)).

In light of our ruling, we need not consider, with respect to Grottanelli's use of the term "hog," his defense of laches or both parties' challenge to the geographic scope of the injunction.

...Grottanelli's mark makes no comment on Harley's mark; it simply uses it somewhat humorously to promote his own products and services, which is not a permitted trademark parody use....

Disclaimer defense. Grottanelli gains no protection by coyly adding to his version of the bar-and-shield logo the wording "UNAUTHORIZED DEALER." We have alluded to commentary questioning the capacity of brief negating words like "not" or "no" in disclaimers adequately to avoid confusion.

...Whatever the worth of such disclaimers in other contexts, the use of the prefix "UN" before "AUTHORIZED DEALER" provides Grottanelli with no defense when used on signage designed to attract speeding motorcyclists. *See* Restatement (Third) of Unfair Competition § 21 cmt. c (noting that "[a]lthough in theory *prominent* disclaimer of association with the prior user can reduce or eliminate confusion, the courts have ordinarily found the use of disclaimers insufficient to avoid liability for infringement") [emphasis added]. . . .

For all of these reasons, Grottanelli was properly enjoined from using his current bar-and-shield logo and any mark that so resembles Harley-Davidson's trademarked logo as to be likely to cause confusion.

Conclusion

The judgment of the District Court is affirmed to the extent it enjoined Grottanelli's use of his bar-and-shield logo and reversed to the extent that it enjoined his use of the word "hog.". . .

[Judgment affirmed]

Questions

1. If a term is classified as generic, may a manufacturer enforce trademark usage of that term if it shows that a substantial segment of the relevant consumer population believes the term refers to the products of that manufacturer?
2. Did the court accept Grottanelli's parody defense?
3. Did Grottanelli's disclaimer that he was an unauthorized dealer enable him to avoid liability for infringement of Harley's bar-and-shield logo?

3. International Registration

Under the Madrid System of International Registration of Marks (the Madrid Protocol), the United States became a party to a treaty providing for the international registration of marks in November 2003. Now U.S. companies that sell products and provide services in foreign countries may register their marks and obtain protection for them in more than 60 signatory countries by filing a single application in English for each mark with the U.S. Patent and Trademark Office.[7] Before the mark can be the subject of an international application, it must have already been registered or applied for with the U.S. Patent and Trademark Office (PTO). A change in ownership of a mark can be accomplished by a single filing. Renewal is required every 10 years by paying a single renewal fee.

4. Trade Dress Protection

Firms invest significant resources to develop and promote the appearance of their products and the packages in which these products are sold so that they are clearly recognizable by consumers.

Trade dress involves a product's total image and, in the case of consumer goods, includes the overall packaging look in which each product is sold.

When a competitor adopts a confusingly similar trade dress, it dilutes the first user's investment and goodwill and deceives consumers, hindering their ability to distinguish between competing brands. The law of trade dress protection was initially settled by the U.S. Supreme Court in 1992,[8] and courts have subsequently become more receptive to claims of trade dress infringement under Section 43(a) of the Lanham Act. To prevail, a plaintiff must prove that its trade dress is distinctive and nonfunctional and the defendant's trade dress is confusingly similar to the plaintiff's.[9] Thus, a competitor who copied the Marlboro cigarettes package for its Gunsmoke brand of cigarettes was found to have infringed the trade dress of the Marlboro brand.[10] Trade dress protection under the Lanham Act is the same as that provided a qualified unregistered trademark and does not provide all of the protection available to the holder of a registered trademark.

5. Limited Lanham Act Protection of Product Design

Trade dress originally included only the packaging and "dressing" of a product, but in recent years, federal courts of appeals' decisions have expanded trade dress to encompass the design of a product itself. Some manufacturers have been successful in

[7] Signatory countries include most U.S. trading partners with the exception of Canada and Mexico.

[8] *Two Pesos, Inc. v Taco Cabana, Inc.*, 505 US 763 (1992).

[9] *Clicks Billiards v Sixshooters, Inc.*, 251 F3d 1252 (9th Cir 2001); and *Woodland Furniture, LLC v Larsen*, 124 P3d, 1016 (Idaho 2005).

[10] *Philip Morris, Inc. v Star Tobacco Corp.*, 879 F Supp 379 (SDNY 1995).

asserting Section 43(a) Lanham Act protection against "knockoffs"—that is, copies of their furniture designs, sweater designs, and notebook designs. In this context, Samara Brothers, Inc., discovered that Wal-Mart Stores, Inc., had contacted a supplier to manufacture children's outfits based on photographs of Samara garments, and Wal-Mart was selling these so-called knockoffs. Samara sued Wal-Mart, claiming infringement of unregistered trade dress under Section 43(a) of the Lanham Act. The matter progressed to the U.S. Supreme Court, which considered whether a product's design can be distinctive and, therefore, protectable under Section 43(a) of the Lanham Act. The Court set aside the trial court's decision in favor of Samara Brothers and concluded that a product's design is not inherently distinctive and can meet only the "distinctiveness" element required in a Section 43(a) case by a showing of secondary meaning. That is, the manufacturer must show that the design has come to be known by the public as identifying the product in question and its origin. The matter was remanded for further proceeding consistent with the Court's decision.[11]

It is clear from the Supreme Court's *Wal-Mart Stores, Inc. v Samara Bros, Inc.* decision that ordinarily only famous designers whose works are widely recognized by the public by their designs alone, such as certain Tommy Hilfiger and Ralph Lauren garments, Dooney & Bourke handbags, and Movado watches, will be able to successfully pursue Section 43(a) trade dress protection for their designs against knockoff versions of their works sold under Wal-Mart or other private labels. Of course, if a manufacturer's design is copied along with the manufacturer's labels or logo, the makers and sellers of these counterfeit goods are always in clear violation of the Lanham Act. As discussed later, design patents also have limited applicability and protect new and nonobvious ornamental features of a product.

6. Injunction against Improper Use of Mark

A person who has the right to use a mark may obtain a court order prohibiting a competitor from imitating or duplicating the mark. The basic question in such litigation is whether the general public is likely to be confused by the mark of the defendant and to believe wrongly that it identifies the plaintiff.[12] If there is this danger of confusion, the court will enjoin the defendant from using the particular mark.

The *Australian Gold* case deals with initial interest confusion.

AUSTRALIAN GOLD, INC. V HATFIELD, 436 F3D 1228 (10th Cir 2006)

BUT ... WHAT'S WRONG WITH DIVERTING TRAFFIC?

ETS Inc. manufactures "Australian Gold," "Caribbean Gold," and "Swedish Beauty" indoor tanning products (ETS-products), which are used in some sixty percent of the 25,000 tanning salons in the U.S. ETS contracts with independent distributors to sell its products, who in turn may only sell the products to tanning salons. Its contracts with the distributors prohibit them from selling products over the Internet or to the general public. The Hatfields used fictitious names to purchase products from ETS-authorized distributors and used up to seven Web sites to sell ETS products to the general public, using ETS's trademarks on their Web sites and in the metatags of the Web sites. The Hatfields thus used the goodwill associated with the ETS trademarks to divert traffic to their Web sites where consumers could be lured to buy lotions from ETS's competition. ETS sued for trademark infringement and other theories of relief. From a judgment for ETS for over $3.7 million and injunctive relief, the Hatfields appealed.

[11] *Wal-Mart Stores, Inc. v Samara Bros, Inc.*, 529 US 205 (2000).

[12] *Resource Lenders, Inc. v Source Solutions, Inc.*, 404 F Supp2d 1232 (ED Cal 2005).

Judicial Opinion

EBEL, C. J. . . . "The unauthorized use of 'any reproduction, counterfeit, copy, or colorable imitation' of a registered trademark in a way that 'is likely to cause confusion' in the the marketplace concerning the source of the different products constitutes trademark infringement under the Lanham Act." *Universal Money Ctrs., Inc. v AT & T Co.*, 22 F.3d 1527, 1529 (10th Cir. 1994). The party alleging infringement has the burden of proving likelihood of confusion. *See Universal Money Ctrs.*, 22 F.3d at 1530. Ordinarily, to prevail on a trademark infringement claim, a plaintiff must demonstrate that a defendant's use of the trademark is likely to cause consumers to believe either that the plaintiff is the source of the defendant's products or services (direct confusion), or alternatively, that the defendant is the source of the plaintiff's products or services (reverse confusion). *See id.*

In this case, we recognize another variant of potential confusion: "initial interest confusion." Initial interest confusion results when a consumer seeks a particular trademark holder's product and instead is lured to the product of a competitor by the competitor's use of the same or a similar mark. *See* Buckman, 183 A.L.R. Fed. 553. Even though the consumer eventually may realize that the product is not the one originally sought, he or she may stay with the competitor. *Id.* In that way, the competitor has captured the trademark holder's potential visitors or customers. *Id.*

Even if the consumer eventually becames aware of the source's actual identity, or where no actual sale results, there is nonetheless damage to the trademark. This damage can manifest itself in three ways: (1) the original diversion of the prospective customer's interest to a source that he or she erroneously believes is authorized; (2) the potential consequent effect of that diversion on the customer's ultimate decision whether to purchase caused by an erroneous impression that two sources of a product may be associated; and (3) the initial credibility that the would-be buyer may accord to the infringer's products—customer consideration that otherwise may be unwarranted and that may be built on the strength of the protected mark, reputation and goodwill. *See BigStar Entm't, Inc. v Next Big Star, Inc.*, 105 F.Supp.2d 185 (S.D.N.Y. 2000).

The federal courts, though not using the phrase "initial interest confusion," have acknowledged the potential for such confusion for decades. Initial interest confusion in the Internet context derives from the unauthorized use of trademarks to divert Internet traffic, thereby capitalizing on a trademark holder's goodwill. *See Nissan Motor Co. v Nissan Computer Corp.*, 378 F.3d 1002, 1018 (9th Cir. 2004) (holding that initial interest confusion occurs when a defendant uses a plaintiff's trademark in a way calculated to capture a consumer's attention and divert the consumer to the defendant's own Web site); *Brookfield Commc'ns, Inc. v W. Coast Entm't Corp.*, 174 F.3d 1036, 1061–65 (9th) (holding that the defendant's use of a trademark in a Web site's metatags allowed the defendant to benefit improperly from the goodwill associated with the mark); *Promatek Indus., Ltd. v Equitrac*, 300 F.3d 808, 814 (7th Cir. 2002) (affirming the grant of a preliminary injunction preventing the defendant from using the plaintiff's trademark as a metatag in the defendant's Web site); . . . .

Defendants used Plaintiffs' trademarks on Defendants' Web sites. Defendants also placed Plaintiffs' trademarks in the metatags of Defendants' Web sites. Further, Defendants paid Overture.com to list Defendants in a preferred position whenever a computer user searched for Plaintiffs' trademarks. All of these actions were attempts to divert traffic to Defendants' Web sites. While viewing Defendants' Web sites, consumers had the opportunity to purchase [ETS] Products, but also to purchase lotions from Plaintiffs' competitors. Moreover, defendants continued to use the trademarks to divert Internet traffic to their Web sites even when they were not selling [ETS] Products. Thus, Defendants used the goodwill associated with Plaintiffs' trademarks in such a way that consumers might be lured to the lotions from Plaintiffs' competitors. This is a violation of the Lanham Act.

We evaluate plaintiffs' claim for initial interest confusion according to the six-prong test we announced in *Sally Beauty Co. v Beautyco, Inc.*, 304 F.3d 964 (10th Cir. 2002). We look at (1) the degree of similarity between the marks; (2) the intent of the alleged infringer in adopting the mark; (3) evidence of actual confusion; (4) similarity of products and manner of marketing; (5) the degree of care likely to be exercised by purchasers; and (6) the strength or weakness of the marks. *Id.* at 972. No one factor is dispositive, and likelihood of confusion is a question of fact. *Id.* at 972.

In this case, the degree of similarity of the marks weighed heavily in favor of Plaintiffs, since the trademarked terms were identical to the terms used by Defendants. The intent of the infringer in adopting the mark also weighed in favor of Plaintiffs. Here the Hatfields deliberately used the trademarks to drive Internet traffic to their own Web sites, where they sold both [ETS] Products and lotions from Plaintiffs' competitors.

Moreover, the similarity of products and manner of marketing weighed in favor of Plaintiffs. The trademarked terms were tanning-related, just like the products offered on Defendants' Web site were. Further, the degree of care likely to be exercised in purchasing Products weighed in favor of Plaintiffs because Plaintiffs' low-cost products were subject to impulse purchases. *See id.* at 975.

Finally, the strength of the trademarks weighed in favor of Plaintiffs. Approximately fifty to sixty percent of the tanning salons in the United States carry Plaintiffs' trademarked Products. The substantial volume of sales of Products, both through Defendants' Web sites and through traditional salons, speaks to the strength of the trademarks.

However, Plaintiffs did not offer any direct evidence of actual confusion, so that factor weighs in favor of Defendants. Moreover, Defendants attempted to prevent actual confusion by placing disclaimers on their Web sites—though because these disclaimers do not tie particular trademarks to particular holders, the disclaimers are inadequate.*[1] More importantly, "a defendant's Web site disclaimer, proclaiming its real source and disavowing any connection with its competitor, cannot prevent the damage of initial interest confusion, which will already have been done by the misdirection of consumers looking for the plaintiff's Web sites." *Buckman,* 183 A.L.R. Fed. 553. In any event, even if this one factor does weigh in favor of Defendants, one factor alone is not dispositive of the likelihood of confusion. *See Sally Beauty Co.,* 304 F.3d at 972.

Because the evidence at trial on likelihood of confusion did not point only in favor of Defendants, the district court did not err in denying Defendants' motion for judgment as a matter of law....

[Judgment affirmed]

Questions

1. What is "initial interest confusion" under trademark law?
2. Explain how "initial interest confusion" resulted in a trademark infringement in an Internet use context.
3. The Hatfields placed disclaimers on their Web sites saying that they did not represent any manufacturers of any products displayed on their Web sites. Was this defense valid?

*A disclaimer on one of Defendants' Web sites provides:
COPYRIGHT © 2001 DiscountTanningLotion
All other copyrights and trademarks are the property of their respective owners. DiscountTanningLotion and it's [sic] affiliated salons are independent distributors. DiscountTanningLotion and it's [sic] affiliates are not associated with and do not represent any manufacturer or any distributor of any products displayed on it's [sic] Web sites. We are a licensed salon promoting & advising on professional products for personal consumers.

In some cases, the fact that the products of the plaintiff and the defendant did not compete in the same market was held to entitle the defendant to use a mark that would have been prohibited as confusingly similar if the defendant manufactured the same product as the plaintiff. **For Example,** it has been held that Cadillac, as applied to boats, is not confusingly similar to Cadillac as applied to automobiles; therefore, its use cannot be enjoined.[13]

7. Abandonment of Exclusive Right to Mark

An owner who has an exclusive right to use a mark may lose that right. If other persons are permitted to use the mark, it loses its exclusive character and is said to pass into the English language and become generic. Examples of formerly enforceable marks that have made this transition into the general language are *aspirin, thermos, cellophane,* and *shredded wheat.* Nonuse for three consecutive years is prima facie evidence of abandonment.[14]

8. Prevention of Dilution of Famous Marks

The Federal Trademark Dilution Act of 1995 (FTDA)[15] provides a cause of action against the "commercial use" of another's famous mark or trade name when it results in a "dilution of the distinctive quality of the mark." The act protects against discordant uses, such as Du Pont shoes, Buick aspirin, and Kodak pianos. Unlike an ordinary trademark infringement action, a dilution action applies in the absence of competition and likelihood of confusion. However, when the trademarks at issue in a trademark

[13] *General Motors Corp. v Cadillac Marine and Boat Co.,* 140 USPQ (BNA) 447 (1964). See also *Amstar Corp. v Domino's Pizza, Inc.,* 615 F2d 252 (5th Cir 1980), where the mark Domino as applied to pizza was held not to be confusingly similar to Domino as applied to sugar.

[14] *Doeblers' Pennsylvania Hybrids Inc. v Doebler,* 442 F3d 812 (3rd Cir 2006).

[15] PL 104-98, 109 Stat 985, 15 USC § 125(c)(1).

dilution case are not identical, the famous mark must show actual dilution—actual injury to the economic value of the famous mark—rather than a presumption of harm arising from a subjective "likelihood of dilution" standard, to obtain injunctive and other relief.

The FTDA exempts "fair use" of a mark in comparative advertising as well as uses in news reporting and commentary.

9. Internet Domain Names and Trademark Rights

An *Internet domain name* is a unique address by which an Internet resource can be identified and found by a Web browser accessing the Internet. Examples of commercial Internet domain names are "Amazon.com," "Priceline.com," and the publisher of this book, "westbuslaw.com." These domain names match the names of their respective businesses, and these domain names are also trademarks.

Any unused domain name can be registered on a first-come, first-served basis for a rather modest fee, so long as the name differs from a previously registered name by at least one character. With such quick and inexpensive registration and with the addition of new registrars and new global suffixes such as ".biz," ".info," ".name," and ".pro" to relieve ".com" overcrowding, there exists an ever-increasing chance of intentional and unintentional trademark infringement.

(a) Cybersquatters

Cybersquatters are individuals who register and set up domain names on the Internet that are identical, or confusingly similar, to existing trademarks that belong to others or are the personal names of famous persons. The cybersquatter hopes to sell or "ransom" the domain name to the trademark owner or the famous individual. The Federal Trademark Dilution Act has been used against cybersquatters.

For Example, Toeppen registered the domain name "panavision.com" with Network Solutions, Inc. Toeppen demanded $13,000 from Panavision to discontinue use, and Panavision sued Toeppen under the Federal Trademark Dilution Act. The court held that Toeppen diluted Panavision's famous mark by preventing it from identifying and distinguishing its goods on the Internet.[16]

Because the extent of the legal remedies available to trademark owners or famous individuals who have been victims of cybersquatters have not always been certain, Congress passed the Federal Anti-cybersquatting Consumer Protection Act (ACPA)[17] in 1999 to prohibit the practice of cybersquatting and cyberpiracy and to provide clear and certain remedies. Remedies include (1) injunctive relief preventing the use of the name, (2) forfeiture of the domain name, and (3) attorney fees and costs. In addition, trademark owners may obtain damages and profits that cybersquatters made from the use of the name.

A safe harbor exists under the ACPA for defendants who both "believed and had reasonable grounds to believe that the use of the domain name was fair use or otherwise lawful."[18] A defendant who acts even partially in bad faith in registering a domain name is not entitled to the shelter of the safe harbor provision. **For Example,** Howard Goldberg, the president of Artco, is an operator of Web sites that sell women's lingerie and other merchandise. He registered a domain name http://www.victoriassecrets.net to divert consumers to his Web sites to try to sell them his goods. The court rejected his ACPA safe harbor defense that he intended in good faith to have customers compare his company's products with those of Victoria's Secret. The fact that Victoria's Secret is a distinctive or famous mark deserving of the highest degree of trademark protection, coupled with the fact that the defendant added a mere *s* to that mark and gave false contact information when he requested the domain name, indicates that he and his company acted in bad faith and intended to profit from the famous mark.[19]

(b) Dispute Avoidance

To avoid the expense of trademark litigation, it is prudent to determine whether the Internet domain name selected for your new business is an existing registered trademark or an existing domain name owned by another. Commercial firms provide comprehensive trademark searches for less than $500. Determining whether a domain name is owned by

[16] *Panavision v Toeppen*, 945 F Supp 1296 (CD Cal 1996).

[17] Pub L 106, 113 Stat 1536, 15 USC § 1051.

[18] 15 USC § 1125(d)(1)(B)(ii).

[19] *Victoria's Secret Stores v Artco*, 194 F Supp2d 204 (SD Ohio 2002).

E-COMMERCE AND CYBERLAW

Metatags describe the contents of a Web site using keywords. Some search engines search metatags to identify Web sites related to a search. In *Playboy Enterprises, Inc.* (PEI) *v Welles,** PEI sued "Playmate of the year 1981" Terri Welles for using that and other phrases involving PEI's trademarks on her Internet Web site metatags. Some search engines that use their own summaries of Web sites, or that search the entire text of sites, would be likely to identify Welles's site as relevant to a search for "Playboy" or "Playmate," thus allowing Welles to trade on PEI's marks, PEI asserted. Remembering that the purpose of a trademark is not to provide a windfall monopoly to the mark owner but to prevent confusion over the source of products or services, the court applied a three-factor test for normative use to this case: (1) the product or service must be one not readily identifiable without the use of the mark, (2) only so much of the mark may be used as reasonably necessary to identify the product or service, and (3) the user must not suggest sponsorship or endorsement by the trademark holder.

Welles had no practical way of describing herself without using the trademark terms. The court stated, "We can hardly expect someone searching for Welles's site...to describe Welles without referring to Playboy—as the nude model selected by Mr. Hefner's organization."

The court stated that there is no descriptive substitute for the trademarks used in Welles's metatags, and to preclude their use would inhibit the free flow of information on the Internet, which is not a goal of trademark law. Moreover, the metatag use was reasonable use to identify her products and services and did not suggest sponsorship, thus satisfying the second and third elements of the court's test.

* *Playboy Enterprises, Inc. v Welles*, 279 F3d 796 (9th Cir 2002).

another may be done online at http://www.internic.net/whois.html.

The Internet Corporation for Assigned Names and Numbers (ICANN) provides fast-track arbitration procedures to protect trademark owners from conflicting online domain names under the auspices of the World Intellectual Property Organization (WIPO). **For Example,** Victoria's Secret stores arbitrated the "victoriassecrets.net" domain name held by Howard Goldberg's company, and the arbitration panel transferred the ownership of the name to Victoria's Secret stores. Victoria's Secret stores subsequently brought an action against Goldberg and Artco for damages and injunctive relief under trademark law and the ACPA.

Registrants who lose use of a domain name in a WIPO arbitration proceeding may bring suit in federal court under Article III of the ACPA to require return of the domain name.[20]

B. Copyrights

A **copyright** is the exclusive right given by federal statute to the creator of a literary or an artistic work to use, reproduce, and display the work. Under the international treaty called the *Berne Convention*, copyright of the works of all U.S. authors is protected automatically in all Berne Convention nations that have agreed under the treaty to treat nationals of other member countries like their own nationals.

A copyright prevents not the copying of an idea but only the copying of the way the idea is expressed.[21] That is, the copyright is violated when there is a duplication of the words, pictures, or other form of expression of the creator but not when there is just use of the idea those words, pictures, or other formats express.

The Copyright Act does not apply extraterritorially. However, if the infringement is completed in

[20] *Sallen v Corinthians Licencimenos LTDA*, 273 F3d 14 (1st Cir 2001).
[21] *Attia v New York Hospital*, 201 F3d 50 (2d Cir 2000).

the United States and the copied work is then disseminated overseas, there is liability under the act for the resulting extraterritorial damages. **For Example,** the Los Angeles News Service (LANS), an independent news organization, produced two copyrighted videotapes of the beating of Reginald Denny during the Los Angeles riots of April 1992, and LANS licensed them to NBC for use on the *Today Show* in New York. Visnews taped the works and transmitted them by satellite to Reuters in London, which provided copies to its overseas subscribers. The infringement by Visnews occurred in New York, and Visnews was liable for the extraterritorial damages that resulted from the overseas dissemination of the work.[22]

It is a violation of U.S. copyright law for satellite carriers to capture signals of network stations in the United States and transmit them abroad. **For Example,** Prime Time's satellite retransmission of copyrighted NFL football games to satellite dish owners in Canada was held to be a violation of U.S. copyright law, notwithstanding testimony of PrimeTime's CEO that a law firm in Washington, D.C., told him that U.S. law did not pertain to distributing product in Canada. The NFL was awarded $2,557,500 in statutory damages.[23]

10. Duration of Copyright

Article 1, Section 8, of the U.S. Constitution empowered Congress to

> *promote the Progress of Science and useful Arts, by securing for limited times to Authors and Inventors the exclusive Right to their respective Writings and Discoveries.*

The first U.S. copyright statute was enacted soon after in 1790 and provided protection for any "book, map or chart" for 14 years, with a privilege to renew for an additional 14 years. In 1831, the initial 14-year term was extended to 28 years, with a privilege for an additional 14 years. Under the 1909 Copyright Act, the protection period was for 28 years, with a right of renewal for an additional 28 years.

The Copyright Act of 1976 set the duration of a copyright at the life of the creator of the work plus 50 years. Under the Sonny Bono Copyright Term Extension Act of 1998, the duration has been extended to the life of the creator plus 70 years.[24] If a work is a "work made for hire"—that is, a business pays an individual to create the work—the business employing the creator registers the copyright. Under the 1998 Extension Act, such a copyright has been extended by 20 years and now runs for 120 years from creation or 95 years from publication of the work, whichever period is shorter. After a copyright has expired, the work is in the public domain and may be used by anyone without cost.[25]

11. Copyright Notice

Prior to March 1, 1989, the author of an original work secured a copyright by placing a copyright notice on the work, consisting of the word *copyright* or the symbol ©, the year of first publication, and the name or pseudonym of the author. The author was also required to register the copyright with the Copyright Office. Under the Berne Convention Implementation Act of 1988,[26] a law that adjusts U.S. copyright law to conform to the Berne Convention, it is no longer mandatory that works published after March 1, 1989, contain a notice of copyright. However, placing a notice of copyright on published works is strongly recommended. This notice prevents an infringer from claiming innocent infringement of the work, which would reduce the amount of damages owed. To bring a copyright infringement suit for a work of U.S. origin, the owner must have submitted two copies of the work to the Copyright Office in Washington, D.C., for registration.

12. What Is Copyrightable?

Copyrights protect literary, musical, dramatic, and artistic work. Protected are books and periodicals; musical and dramatic compositions; choreographic works; maps; works of art, such as paintings, sculptures, and photographs; motion pictures and other

[22] *Los Angeles News Service v Reuters*, 149 F3d 987 (9th Cir 1998).

[23] *National Football League v PrimeTime 24 Joint Venture*, 131 F Supp2d 458 (SDNY 2001).

[24] PL 105-298, 112 Stat 2827, 17 USC § 302(b).

[25] Without the Sonny Bono Extension Act of 1998, the copyright on Mickey Mouse, created by Walt Disney Co. in 1928, was set to expire in 2003 and enter the public domain. Pluto, Goofy, and Donald Duck would have followed soon after.

[26] PL 100-568, 102 Stat 2854, 17 USC § 101 *et seq.*

audiovisual works; sound recordings; architectural works; and computer programs.

The work must be original, independently created by the author, and possess at least some minimal degree of creativity.[27] **For Example,** William Darden, a Web page designer, challenged the Copyright Office's denial of a copyright registration for a series of existing maps with some changes in the nature of shading, coloring, or font. A court found that the Copyright Office acted within its discretion when it denied Darden's registration with the finding by the examiner from the Visual Arts Section that the maps were "representations of the preexisting census maps in which the creative spark is utterly lacking or so trivial as to be virtually nonexistent."[28]

13. Copyright Ownership and the Internet

Businesses today commonly use offsite programming services to create copyrightable software, with the delivery of code over the Internet. As set forth previously, when a business pays an employee to create a copyrightable work, it is a "work for hire" and the business employing the creator owns and may register the copyright. On the other hand, if a freelancer is employed offsite to create software for a fixed fee without a contract setting forth the ownership of the work, the freelancer owns the work product and the company utilizing the freelancer has a license to use the work product but does not have ownership of it. To avoid disputes about ownership of custom software, a written contract that addresses these ownership and license questions is necessary.

14. Rights of Copyright Holders

A copyright holder has the exclusive right to (1) reproduce the work; (2) prepare derivative works, such as a script from the original work; (3) distribute copies of recordings of the work; (4) publicly perform the work, in the case of plays and motion pictures; and (5) publicly display the work, in the case of paintings, sculptures, and photographs.

The copyright owner may assign or license some of the rights listed and will receive royalty payments as part of the agreement. The copyright law also ensures royalty payments. **For Example,** Jessie Riviera is a songwriter whose songs are sung at public performances and are recorded by performers on records, tapes, and CDs. Jessie is entitled to royalties from the public performance of her works. Such royalties are collected by two performing rights societies, the American Society of Composers, Authors, and Publishers (ASCAP) and Broadcast Music, Inc. (BMI), who act on behalf of the copyright holders. Jessie is also entitled to so-called mechanical royalties that refer to the royalty stream derived from "mechanically" reproduced records, tapes, and CDs. The principal payers of mechanical royalties are record companies, and the rates are set by the Copyright Royalty Tribunal.[29]

In addition to rights under the copyright law and international treaties, federal and state laws prohibit record and tape piracy.

15. Limitation on Exclusive Character of Copyright

A limitation on the exclusive rights of copyright owners exists under the principle of *fair use*, which allows limited use of copyrighted material in connection with criticism, news reporting, teaching, and research. Four important factors to consider when judging whether the use made in a particular case is fair use include

1. the purpose and character of the use, including whether such use is of a commercial nature or is for nonprofit educational purposes[30];
2. the nature of the copyrighted work;
3. the amount and substantiality of the portion used in relation to the copyrighted work as a whole; and
4. the effect of the use on the potential market for or value of the copyrighted work.

[27] *Feist Publications Inc. v Rural Telephone Services Co.*, 499 US 340 (1991).

[28] *Darden v Peters*, 402 F Supp2d 638 (ED NC 2005).

[29] The statutory mechanical rates are 9.1 cents or 1.75 cents per minute, whichever is greater. See **http://www.copyright.gov/carp/m200a.html.**

[30] In *Princeton University Press v Michigan Document Services, Inc.*, 99 F3d 1381 (6th Cir 1996), a commercial copyshop reproduced "coursepacks" and sold them to students attending the University of Michigan. The court refused to consider the "use" as one for nonprofit educational purposes because the use challenged was that of the copyshop, a for-profit corporation that had decided to duplicate copyrighted material for sale to maximize its profits and give itself a competitive edge over other copyshops by declining to pay the royalties requested by the holders of the copyrights.

In *American Geophysical Union v Texaco, Inc.*, the court applied the four statutory standards to determine whether the defendant's photocopying of scientific journal articles was fair use.

First Amendment privileges of freedom of speech and the press are preserved through the doctrine of *fair use*, which allows for use of portions of another's copyrighted work for matters such as comment and

AMERICAN GEOPHYSICAL UNION V TEXACO, INC., 60 F3D 913 (2D CIR 1995)

FAIR USE OR NOT FAIR USE—THAT IS THE QUESTION

The American Geophysical Union and 82 other publishers of scientific and technical journals brought a class-action lawsuit against Texaco claiming that Texaco's unauthorized photocopying of articles from their journals constituted a copyright infringement. Texaco's defense was that the copying was fair use under Section 107 of the Copyright Act of 1976. To avoid extensive discovery, the parties agreed to focus on one randomly selected Texaco scientist, Dr. Donald Chickering, who had photocopies of eight articles from the *Journal of Catalysis* in his files. The trial court judge held that the copying of the eight articles did not constitute fair use, and Texaco appealed.

Judicial Opinion

NEWMAN, C. J.... Burdens of Proof and Standard of Review

Fair use serves as an affirmative defense to a claim of copyright infringement, and thus the party claiming that its secondary use of the original copyrighted work constitutes a fair use typically carries the burden of proof as to all issues in the dispute. Moreover, since fair use is a "mixed question of law and fact," *Harper & Row*, 471 U.S. at 560, 105 S.Ct. at 2230, we review the District Court's conclusions on this issue *de novo*, though we accept its subsidiary findings of fact unless clearly erroneous, see *Twin Peaks*, 996 F.2d at 1374....

First Factor: Purpose and Character of Use

The first factor listed in section 107 is "the purpose and character of the use, including whether such use is of a commercial nature or is for nonprofit educational purposes." Especially pertinent to an assessment of the first fair use factor are the precise circumstances under which copies of the eight *Catalysis* articles were made. After noticing six of these articles when the original copy of the journal issue containing each of them was circulated to him, Chickering had them photocopied, at least initially, for the same basic purpose that one would normally seek to obtain the original—to have it available on his shelf for ready reference if and when he needed to look at it. The library circulated one copy and invited all the researchers to make their own photocopies. It is a reasonable inference that the library staff wanted each journal issue moved around the building quickly and returned to the library so that it would be available for others to look at. Making copies enabled all researchers who might one day be interested in examining the contents of an article in the issue to have the article readily available in their own offices. In Chickering's own words, the copies of the articles were made for "my personal convenience," since it is "far more convenient to have access in my office to a photocopy of an article than to have to go to the library each time I wanted to refer to it." Affidavit of Donald Chickering at 11 (submitted as direct trial testimony) [hereinafter *Chickering testimony*]. Significantly, Chickering did not even have occasion to use five of the photocopied articles at all, further revealing that the photocopies of the eight *Catalysis* articles were primarily made just for "future retrieval and reference." *Id.*...

The photocopying of these eight *Catalysis* articles may be characterized as "archival"—*i.e.*, done for the primary purpose of providing numerous Texaco scientists (for whom Chickering served as an example) each with his or her own personal copy of each article without Texaco's having to purchase another original journal....

On balance, we agree with the District Court that the first factor favors the publishers; primarily because the dominant purpose of the use is a systematic institutional policy of multiplying the available number of copies of pertinent copyrighted articles by circulating the journals among employed scientists for them to make copies, thereby serving the same purpose for which additional subscriptions are normally sold, or, as will be discussed, for which photocopying licenses may be obtained.

Second Factor: Nature of Copyrighted Work

The second statutory fair use factor is "the nature of the copyrighted work." In assessing this factor, the District Court noted that the articles in *Catalysis* "are created for publication with the purpose and intention of benefiting from the protection of the copyright law," and that copyright protection "is vitally necessary to the dissemination of scientific articles of the sort that are at issue." 802 F.Supp. at 16. Nevertheless, the Court ultimately concluded that this factor favored Texaco because the photocopied articles were essentially factual in nature and the "scope of fair use is greater with respect to factual than nonfactual works."...

Ultimately...the manifestly factual character of the eight articles precludes us from considering the articles as "within the core of the copyright's protective purposes," *Campbell,* 114 S.Ct. at 1175; see also *Harper & Row*, 471 U.S. at 563, 105 S.Ct. at 2232 ("The law generally recognizes a greater need to disseminate factual works than works of fiction or fantasy."). Thus, in agreement with the District Court, we conclude that the second factor favors Texaco.

Third Factor: Amount and Substantiability of Portion Used

The third statutory fair use factor is "the amount and substantiality of the portion used in relation to the copyrighted work as a whole." The District Court concluded that this factor clearly favors the publishers because Texaco copied the eight articles from *Catalysis* in their entirety. . . .

Despite Texaco's claims that we consider its amount of copying "minuscule" in relation to the entirety of *Catalysis,* we conclude, as did the District Court, that Texaco has copied entire works. Though this conclusion does not preclude a finding of fair use, it militates against such a finding, see *Sony*, 464 U.S. at 449–50, 104 S.Ct. at 792–93, and weights the third factor in favor of the publishers. . . .

Fourth Factor: Effect Upon Potential Market or Value

The fourth statutory fair use factor is "the effect of the use upon the potential market for or value of the copyrighted work." Assessing this factor, the District Court detailed the range of procedures Texaco could use to obtain authorized copies of the articles that it photocopied and found that "whatever combination of procedure Texaco used, the publishers' revenues would grow significantly." The Court concluded that the publishers "powerfully demonstrated entitlement to prevail as to the fourth factor," since they had shown "a substantial harm to the value of their copyrights" as the consequence of Texaco's copying. See *id.* at 18–21.

Prior to *Campbell,* the Supreme Court had characterized the fourth factor as "the single most important element of fair use," *Harper & Row*, 471 U.S. at 566, 105 S.Ct. at 2233. However, *Campbell's* discussion of the fourth factor conspicuously omits this phrasing. Apparently abandoning the idea that any factor enjoys primacy, *Campbell* instructs that '[a]ll [four factors] are to be explored, and the results weighed together, in light of the purposes of copyright.' 114 S.Ct. at 1171. . . .

Primarily because of lost licensing revenue, and to a minor extent because of lost subscription revenue, we agree with the District Court that "the publishers have demonstrated a substantial harm to the value of their copyrights through [Texco's] copying," 802 F.Supp. at 21, and thus conclude that the fourth statutory factor favors the publishers.

Aggregate Assessment

We conclude that three of the four statutory factors, including the important first and the fourth factors, favor the publishers. . . . We therefore agree with the District Court's conclusion that Texaco's photocopying of eight particular articles from the *Journal of Catalysis* was not fair use.

Though we recognize the force of many observations made in Judge Jacob's dissenting opinion, we are not dissuaded by his dire predictions that our ruling in this case "has ended fair-use photocopying with respect to a large population of journals," 60 F.3d at 938–39, or, to the extent that the transactional licensing scheme is used, "would seem to require that an intellectual property lawyer be posted at each copy machine," *id.* at 937–38. Our ruling does not consider photocopying for personal use by an individual. Our ruling is confined to the institutional, systematic, archival multiplication of copies revealed by the record—the precise copying that the parties stipulated should be the basis for the District Court's decision now on appeal and for which licenses are in fact available. And the claim that lawyers need to be stationed at copy machines is belied by the ease with which music royalties have been collected and distributed for performances at thousands of cabarets, without the attendance of intellectual property lawyers in any capacity other than as customers. . . .

[Affirmed]

Questions

1. Assess Texaco's position that the purpose and character of its use of the eight articles were for the legitimate reason of use in Dr. Chickering's research and they were not photocopied for resale.
2. Is the "market-effect" factor the single most important element of fair use?
3. Do you believe that the result of this decision will lead to the dire consequences of the posting of intellectual property lawyers at every copy machine, trying to enforce licensing schemes?

criticism. Parodies and caricatures are the most penetrating forms of criticism and are protected under the fair use doctrine. Moreover, while injunctive relief is appropriate in the vast majority of copyright infringement cases because the infringements are simply piracy, in the case of parodies and caricatures where there are reasonable contentions of fair use, preliminary injunctions to prevent publication are inappropriate. The copyright owner can be adequately protected by an award of damages should infringement be found. **For Example,** Suntrust Bank, the trustee of a trust that holds the copyright to Margaret Mitchell's *Gone with the Wind,* one of the all-time best-selling books in the world, obtained a preliminary injunction preventing Houghton Mifflin Co. from publishing Alice Randall's *The Wind Done Gone.* The Randall book is an irreverent parody that turns old ideas upside down. The Court of Appeals set aside the injunction of the federal district court because Houghton Mifflin had a viable fair use defense.[31]

16. Secondary Liability for Infringement

An entity that distributes a device with the object of promoting its use to infringe copyrights as shown by clear expression or other active steps taken to foster the resulting acts of infringement is liable for these acts of infringement by third parties, regardless of the device's lawful uses. **For Example,** Grokster, Ltd., and StreamCast Networks, Inc., distributed free software products that allow all computer users to share electronic files through peer-to-peer networks, so called because users' computers communicate directly with each other, not through central servers. When these firms distributed their free software, each clearly voiced the objective that the recipients use the software to download copyrighted works. These firms derived profits from selling advertising space and streaming ads to the software users. Liability for infringement was established under the secondary liability doctrines of contributory or vicarious infringement.[32]

17. Digital Millennium Copyright Act

The Digital Millennium Copyright Act of 1998 (DMCA)[33] was enacted to curb the pirating of software and other copyrighted works, such as books, films, videos, and recordings, by creating civil and criminal penalties for anyone who circumvents encryption software. The law also prohibits the manufacture, import, sale, or distribution of circumvention devices.

Title II of the DMCA provides a "safe harbor" for Internet Service Providers (ISP) from liability for direct, vicarious, and contributory infringement of copyrights provided the ISP (1) does not have actual knowledge of the infringing activity or expeditiously removed access to the problematic material upon obtaining knowledge of infringing activity, (2) does not receive financial benefit directly attributable to the infringing activity, and (3) responded expeditiously upon notification of the claimed infringement.

C. Patents

Under Article 1, Section 8, of the U.S. Constitution, the founding fathers of our country empowered

[31] *Suntrust Bank v Houghton Mifflin Co.*, 268 F3d 1257 (11th Cir 2001).

[32] *Metro-Goldwyn-Mayer Studios, Inc. v Grokster, Ltd.*, 125 SCt 2764 (2005).

[33] 17 USC § 1201.

Congress to promote the progress of science by securing for limited times to inventors the exclusive rights to their discoveries. Federal patent laws established under Article 1, Section 8, protect inventors just as authors are protected under copyright law authorized by the same section of the U.S. Constitution.

18. Types, Duration, and Notice

There are three types of patents, the rights to which may be obtained by proper filing with the Patent and Trademark Office (PTO) in Washington, D.C. The types and duration of patents are as follows.

(a) Utility Patents

Utility or *functional patents* grant inventors of any new and useful process, machine, manufacture, or composition of matter or any new and useful improvement of such devices the right to obtain a patent.[34] Prior to 1995, these utility patents had a life of 17 years from the date of grant. Under the Uruguay Round Trade Agreement Act, effective June 8, 1995, the duration of U.S. utility patents was changed from 17 years from the date of grant to 20 years from the date of filing to be consistent with the patent law of General Agreement on Tariffs and Trade (GATT) member states.

(b) Design Patents

A second kind of patent exists under U.S. patent law that protects new and nonobvious ornamental features that appear in connection with an article of manufacture.[35] These patents are called *design patents* and have a duration of 14 years. Design patents have limited applicability, for they must not only be new and have nonobvious ornamental features but also be nonfunctional. Thus, when the "pillow shape" design of Nabisco Shredded Wheat was found to be functional, the design patent was held invalid, as the cereal's shape was not capable of design patent protection.[36]

(c) Plant Patents

A third type of patent, called a *plant patent,* protects the inventors of asexually reproduced new varieties of plants. The duration is 20 years from the date of filing, the same duration applied to utility patents.

(d) Notice

The owner of a patent is required to mark the patented item or device using the word *patent* and must list the patent number on the device to recover damages from an infringer of the patent.

19. Patentability and Exclusive Rights

To be patentable, an invention must be something that is new and not obvious to a person of ordinary skill and knowledge in the art or technology to which the invention is related. Whether an invention is new and not obvious in its field may lead to highly technical proceedings before a patent examiner, the PTO's Board of Patent Appeals, or the U.S. Court of Appeals for the Federal Circuit (CAFC). **For Example,** Thomas Devel's application for a patent on complementary DNA (cDNA) molecules encoding proteins that stimulated cell division was rejected by a patent examiner as "obvious" and affirmed by the PTO's Board of Patent Appeals. However, after a full hearing before the CAFC, which focused on the state of research in the field as applied to the patent application, Devel's patent claims were determined to be "not invalid because of obviousness."[37]

Once approved by the Patent and Trademark Office, a patent is presumed valid. However, a defendant in a patent infringement lawsuit may assert a patent's invalidity as a defense to an infringement claim by showing the invention as a whole would have been obvious to a person of ordinary skill in the art when the invention was patented. This showing is called *prior art.* **For Example,** Ron Rogers invented and patented a tree-trimming device that is essentially a chain saw releasably mounted on the end of a telescoping pole. Rogers sued Desa International, Inc. (DIA), for patent infringement after DIA introduced the Remington Pole Saw, a chain saw releasably mounted on the end of a telescoping pole. DIA provided evidence of prior art, citing four preexisting patents dealing with "trimming tools on extension poles" that correlated with Rogers's patent. The court nullified Rogers's patent because it concluded the DIA had met its heavy burden of proof that releasably mounting a lightweight chain saw on the end of a

[34] 35 USC § 101.

[35] 35 USC § 173.

[36] *Kellogg Co. v National Biscuit Co.*, 305 US 111 (1938).

[37] *In re Devel*, 51 F3d 1552 (Fed Cir 1995). See also *Rhenalu v Alcoa*, 224 F Supp2d 773 (D Del 2002).

telescoping pole assembly to trim trees would be obvious to a person of ordinary skill in the art.[38]

The invention itself is what is patented. Thus, new and useful ideas and scientific principles by themselves cannot be patented. There must be an actual physical implementation of the idea or principle in the form of a process, machine, composition of matter, or device.

Under the Supreme Court's "doctrine of equivalents," infringers may not avoid liability for patent infringement by substituting insubstantial differences for some of the elements of the patented product or process. The test for infringement requires an essential inquiry: Does the accused product or process contain elements identical or equivalent to each claimed element of the patented invention?[39]

The patent owner has the exclusive right to make, use, sell, or import into the United States the product or process that uses the patented invention. It is a violation of U.S. patent law to make, use, sell, offer to sell, or import any patented invention within the United States without authority from the patent owner.

20. Patentable Business Methods

Business method patents are proper subjects for patents. A pure business method patent consists basically of a series of steps related to performing a business process. For example, Patent No. 6,846,131 sets forth a legitimate method of doing business setting out steps for Producing Revenue from Gypsum-Based Refuse Sites. So-called junk patents have also been issued as business method patents. For example, Patent No. 4,022,227 Method of Concealing Baldness contains a series of steps for combing one's hair amounting to what is best known as a *comb-over*. Business methods are often in the form of software programs and encompass e-commerce applications.

Competitors of business method patent holders often challenge such patents by attempting to show prior art—that the process was clearly obvious to people in the industry in question. **For Example,** Barnesandnoble.com Inc., attempted to defend a patent infringement lawsuit brought by Amazon.com on the basis that Amazon.com's One Click method for placing a purchase order over the Internet was not new to a person of ordinary skill in this technology, arguing it was just like prior "shopping cart" models of online purchasing. While the trial court initially issued a preliminary injunction prohibiting Barnes & Noble from using the one-click process, the Federal Circuit Court of Appeals reversed the trial court, holding that a substantial question of patent validity existed.[40] Thereafter, the parties settled the case.

With ever-evolving advancements being developed in information technology and telecommunications, a small patented component needed for a new product that a manufacturer seeks to bring to market may lead the patent holder to seek an excessive licensing fee from the manufacturer. An industry has developed that exists not to produce and sell innovative patented products but to charge others for the use of the patented technology inventories owned.

Business method patents as a classification permit the owner under the Patent Act to exclude others "from making, using, offering for sale or selling the invention."[41]

In *MercExchange, LLC v eBay*, the U.S. Supreme Court dealt with the question of whether the patent

EBAY INC. V MERCEXCHANGE, LLC, 126 SCT 1837 (2006)

"SQUEEZE PLAY" AVERTED

eBay and its subsidiary half.com operate popular Internet Web sites that allow private sellers to list goods they wish to sell at either an auction or a fixed price (its "Buy it Now" feature). MercExchange, LLC. sought to license its business method patent to eBay, but no agreement was reached. In MercExchange's subsequent patent infringement suit, a jury found that its patent was valid, that eBay had infringed the patent, and $29.5 million in damages were appropriate. However, the District Court denied MercExchange's motion for permanent injunctions against patent infringement absent

38 *Rogers v Desa International, Inc.*, 166 F Supp2d 1202 (ED Mich 2001).

39 *Warner-Jenkinson Co. v Hilton-Davis Chemical Co.*, 117 S Ct 1040 (1997).

40 *Amazon.com, Inc., v Barnesandnoble.com Inc.*, 239 F3d 1343, 1358-1359 (Fed Cir 2001).

41 35 USC § 154(a)(1).

exceptional circumstances. MercExchange appealed. The Federal Circuit Court of Appeals, reversed, and the U.S. Supreme Court granted certiorari.

Judicial Opinion

THOMAS, A.J . . . According to well-established principles of equity, a plaintiff seeking a permanent injunction must satisfy a four-factor test before a court may grant such relief. A plaintiff must demonstrate: (1) that it has suffered an irreparable injury; (2) that remedies available at law, such as monetary damages, are inadequate to compensate for that injury; (3) that, considering the balance of hardships between the plaintiff and defendant, a remedy in equity is warranted; and (4) that the public interest would not be disserved by a permanent injunction. . . . The decision to grant or deny permanent injunctive relief is an act of equitable discretion by the district court, reviewable on appeal for abuse of discretion.

These familiar principles apply with equal force to disputes arising under the Patent Act. . . . To be sure, the Patent Act also declares that "patents shall have the attributes of personal property," § 261, including "the right to exclude others from making, using, offering for sale, or selling the invention," § 154(a)(1). According to the Court of Appeals, this statutory right to exclude alone justifies its general rule in favor of permanent injunctive relief. But the creation of a right is distinct from the provision of remedies for violations of that right. Indeed, the Patent Act itself indicates that patents shall have the attributes of personal property "[s]ubject to the provisions of this title," 35 U.S.C. § 261, including, presumably, the provision that injunctive relief "may" issue only "in accordance with the principles of equity," § 283. . . .

Because we conclude that neither court below correctly applied the traditional four-factor framework that governs the award of injunctive relief, we vacate the judgment of the Court of Appeals, so that the District Court may apply that framework in the first instance. In doing so, we take no position on whether permanent injunctive relief should or should not issue in this particular case, or indeed in any number of other disputes arising under the Patent Act. . . .

[Reversed and Remanded]

Chief Justice Roberts, with whom Justice Scalia and Justice Ginsburg join, concurring. I agree with the Court's holding that "the decision whether to grant or deny injunctive relief rests within the equitable discretion of the district courts, and that such discretion must be exercised consistent with traditional principles of equity, in patent disputes no less than in other cases governed by such standards," *ante*, at 1841, and I join the opinion of the Court. That opinion rightly rests on the proposition that "a major departure from the long tradition of equity practice should not be lightly implied." . . .

Justice Kennedy, with whom Justice Stevens, Justice Souter, and Justice Breyer join, concurring. . . . To the extent earlier cases establish a pattern of granting an injunction against patent infringers almost as a matter of course, this pattern simply illustrates the result of the four-factor test in the contexts then prevalent. The lesson of the historical practice, therefore, is most helpful and instructive when the circumstances of a case bear substantial parallels to litigation the courts have confronted before.

In cases now arising trial courts should bear in mind that in many instances the nature of the patent being enforced and the economic function of the patent holder present considerations quite unlike earlier cases. An industry has developed in which firms use patents not as a basis for producing and selling goods but, instead, primarily for obtaining licensing fees. See FTC, To Promote Innovation: The Proper Balance of Competition and Patent Law and Policy, ch. 3, pp. 38–39 (Oct. 2003). For these firms, an injunction, and the potentially serious sanctions arising from its violation, can be employed as a bargaining tool to charge exorbitant fees to companies that seek to buy licenses to practice the patent. When the patented invention is but a small component of the product the companies seek to produce and the threat of an injunction is employed simply for undue leverage in negotiations, legal damages may well be sufficient to compensate for the infringement and an injunction may not serve the public interest. In addition injunctive relief may have different consequences for the burgeoning number of patents over business methods, which were not of much economic and legal significance in earlier times. The potential vagueness and suspect validity of some of these patents may affect the calculus under the four-factor test. . . .

Questions

1. What classification of patent is involved in this decision?
2. Did eBay win on the issue before the Supreme Court? Explain.
3. Summarize the position set forth in Justice Kennedy's concurring opinion.

holder had the right to obtain permanent injunctive relief stopping a business entity from "using" the patented technology in addition to obtaining damages for the patent violation. The threat of a court order is used to seek high and often unreasonable licensing fees. Major technology companies contended that trial courts should consider multiple factors in deciding whether to issue a permanent injunction.

Believing that many business method patents are obvious to persons of ordinary skill in their respective fields and have a chilling effect on consumer and public interests, a number of organizations have filed multiple reexamination requests with the PTO to invalidate these patents.[42] For example, Merc Exchange's patent at issue in the *eBay* case is being challenged in proceedings before the PTO.

D. Secret Business Information

A business may have developed information that is not generally known but that cannot be protected under federal law, or a business may want to avoid the disclosure required to obtain a patent or copyright protection of computer software. As long as such information is kept secret, it will be protected under state law relating to trade secrets.[43]

21. Trade Secrets

A **trade secret** may consist of any formula, device, or compilation of information that is used in one's business and is of such a nature that it provides an advantage over competitors who do not have the information. It may be a formula for a chemical compound; a process of manufacturing, treating, or preserving materials; or, to a limited extent, certain confidential customer lists.[44]

Courts will not protect customer lists if customer identities are readily ascertainable from industry or public sources or if products or services are sold to a wide group of purchasers based on their individual needs.[45]

22. Loss of Protection

When secret business information is made public, it loses the protection it had while secret. This loss of protection occurs when the information is made known without any restrictions. In contrast, there is no loss of protection when secret information is shared or communicated for a special purpose and the person receiving the information knows that it is not to be made known to others.

When a product or process is unprotected by a patent or a copyright and is sold in significant numbers to the public, whose members are free to resell to whomever they choose, competitors are free to reverse engineer (start with the known product and work backward to discover the process) or copy the article. **For Example,** Crosby Yacht Co., a boatbuilder on Cape Cod, developed a hull design that is not patented. Maine Boatbuilders, Inc. (MBI), purchased one of Crosby's boats and copied the hull by creating a mold from the boat it purchased. MBI is free to build and sell boats utilizing the copied hull.

23. Defensive Measures

Employers seek to avoid the expense of trade secret litigation by limiting disclosure of trade secrets to employees with a "need to know." Employers also have employees sign nondisclosure agreements, and they conduct exit interviews when employees with confidential information leave, reminding the employees of the employer's intent to enforce the nondisclosure agreement. In addition, employers have adopted industrial security plans to protect their unique knowledge from "outsiders," who may engage in theft, trespass, wiretapping, or other forms of commercial espionage.

24. Criminal Sanctions

Under the federal Industrial Espionage Act of 1996,[46] knowingly stealing, soliciting, or obtaining trade

[42] See Electronic Frontier Foundation, Patent Busting Project at **www.eff.org/patent/wanted** (June 1, 2006).

[43] The Uniform Trade Secrets Act was officially amended in 1985. It is now in force in Alabama, Alaska, Arizona, Arkansas, California, Colorado, Connecticut, Delaware, Florida, Georgia, Hawaii, Idaho, Illinois, Indiana, Iowa, Kansas, Kentucky, Louisiana, Maine, Minnesota, Mississippi, Montana, Nebraska, Nevada, New Hampshire, New Mexico, North Dakota, Ohio, Oklahoma, Oregon, Rhode Island, South Carolina, South Dakota, Utah, Vermont, Virginia, Washington, West Virginia, and Wisconsin. Trade secrets are protected in all states either under the uniform act or common law and under both criminal and civil statutes.

[44] Restatement (Second) of Torts § 757 cmt b. See *Home Pride Foods, Inc. v Johnson*, 634 NW2d 774 (Neb 2001).

[45] *Xpert Automation Systems Corp. v Vibromatic Co.*, 569 NE2d 351 (Ind App 1990).

[46] PL 104–294, 18 USC § 1831 *et seq.* (1996).

secrets by copying, downloading, or uploading via electronic means or otherwise with the intention that it will benefit a foreign government or agent is a crime. This act also applies to the stealing or purchasing of trade secrets by U.S. companies or individuals who intend to convert trade secrets to the economic benefit of anyone other than the owner. The definition of trade secret is closely modeled on the Uniform Trade Secrets Act and includes all forms and types of financial, business, scientific, technical, economic, and engineering information. The law requires the owner to have taken "reasonable and proper" measures to keep the information secret. Offenders are subject to fines of up to $500,000 or twice the value of the proprietary information involved, whichever is greater, and imprisonment for up to 15 years.

Corporations may be fined up to $10,000,000 or twice the value of the secret involved, whichever is greater. In addition, the offender's property is subject to forfeiture to the U.S. government, and import-export sanctions may be imposed.

E. Protection of Computer Software and Mask Works

Computer programs, chip designs, and mask works are protected from infringement with varying degrees of success by federal statutes, restrictive licensing, and trade secrecy.

CPA 25. Copyright Protection of Computer Programs

Under the Computer Software Copyright Act of 1980,[47] a written program is given the same protection as any other copyrighted material regardless of whether the program is written in source code (ordinary language) or object code (machine language). **For Example,** Franklin Computer Corp. copied certain operating-system computer programs that had been copyrighted by Apple Computer, Inc. When Apple sued Franklin for copyright infringement, Franklin argued that the object code on which its programs had relied was an uncopyrightable "method of operation." The Third Circuit held that computer programs, whether in source code or in object code embedded on ROM chips, are protected under the act.[48]

In determining whether there is a copyright violation under the Computer Software Copyright Act, courts will examine the two programs in question to compare their structure, flow, sequence, and organization. Moreover, the courts in their infringement analysis look to see whether the most *significant* steps of the program are similar rather than whether most of the program's steps are similar. To illustrate a copyright violation, substantial similarity in the structure of two computer programs for dental laboratory record-keeping was found even though the programs were dissimilar in a number of respects because five particularly important subroutines within both programs performed almost identically."[49]

The protection afforded software by the copyright law is not entirely satisfactory to software developers because of the distinction made by the copyright law of protecting expressions but not ideas. Also, Section 102(b) of the 1980 Computer Software Copyright Act does not provide protection for "methods of operation." A court has allowed a competitor to copy the identical menu tree of a copyrighted spreadsheet program because it was a noncopyrightable method of operation.[50]

As set forth previously, the Digital Millennium Copyright Act of 1998 was enacted to curb the pirating of a wide range of works, including software.

CPA 26. Patent Protection of Programs

Patents have been granted for computer programs; for example, a method of using a computer to carry out translations from one language to another has been held patentable.

The disadvantage of patenting a program is that the program is placed in the public records and may thus be examined by anyone. This practice poses a potential danger that the program will be copied. To detect patent violators and bring legal action is difficult and costly.[51]

47 Act of December 12, 1980, PL 96–517, 94 Stat 3015, 17 USC §§ 101, 117.

48 *Apple Computer Inc. v Franklin Computer Corp.*, 714 F2d 1240 (3d Cir 1983).

49 *Whelen Associates v Jaslow Dental Laboratory*, 797 F2d 1222 (3d Cir 1986).

50 *Lotus Development Corp. v Borland International Inc.*, 49 F3d 807 (1st Cir 1995), aff'd, 116 S Ct 804 (1996).

51 *The PTO has adopted guidelines for the examination of computer-related inventions*, 61 CFR §§ 7478–7502.

FIGURE 10-1 Summary Comparison of Intellectual Property Rights

TYPE OF INTELLECTUAL PROPERTY	TRADEMARKS	COPYRIGHTS	PATENTS	TRADE SECRETS
PROTECTION	WORDS, NAMES, SYMBOLS, OR DEVICES USED TO IDENTIFY A PRODUCT OR SERVICE	ORIGINAL CREATIVE WORKS OF AUTHORSHIP, SUCH AS WRITINGS, MOVIES, RECORDS, AND COMPUTER SOFTWARE	UTILITY, DESIGN, AND PLANT PATENTS	ADVANTAGEOUS FORMULAS, DEVICES, OR COMPILATION OF INFORMATION
APPLICABLE STANDARD	IDENTIFIES AND DISTINGUISHES A PRODUCT OR SERVICE	ORIGINAL CREATIVE WORKS IN WRITING OR IN ANOTHER FORMAT	NEW AND NONOBVIOUS, ADVANCED IN THE ART	NOT READILY ASCERTAINABLE, NOT DISCLOSED TO THE PUBLIC
WHERE TO APPLY	PATENT AND TRADEMARK OFFICE	REGISTER OF COPYRIGHTS	PATENT AND TRADEMARK OFFICE	NO PUBLIC REGISTRATION NECESSARY
DURATION	INDEFINITE SO LONG AS IT CONTINUES TO BE USED	LIFE OF AUTHOR PLUS 70 YEARS, OR 95 YEARS FROM PUBLICATION FOR "WORKS FOR HIRE"	UTILITY AND PLANT PATENTS, 20 YEARS FROM DATE OF APPLICATION; DESIGN PATENTS, 14 YEARS	INDEFINITE SO LONG AS SECRET IS NOT DISCLOSED TO PUBLIC

CPA 27. Trade Secrets

While primary protection for computer software is found in the Computer Software Copyright Act, industry also uses trade secret law to protect computer programs. When software containing trade secrets is unlawfully appropriated by a former employee, the employee is guilty of trade secret theft.[52]

28. Restrictive Licensing

To retain greater control over proprietary software, it is common for the creator of the software to license its use to others rather than selling it to them. Such licensing agreements typically include restrictions on the use of the software by the licensee and give the licensor greater protection than that provided by copyright law. These restrictions commonly prohibit

[52] The National Conference of Commissioners on Uniform State Laws (NCCUSL) has promulgated a new uniform law, the Uniform Computer Information Transactions Act (UCITA), to govern contracts involving the sale, licensing, maintenance, and support of computer software and books in digital form. This uniform act had been identified as Article 2B and was part of the comprehensive revisions to Article 2 of the Uniform Commercial Code. The act is supported by software publishers and opposed by software developers and buyers. The act can be obtained from the NCCUSL at **http://www.nccusl.org.** Information for and against the UCITA can be found at **http://www.ucitaonline.com.** The act has been adopted by Maryland and Virginia.

the licensee from providing, in any manner whatsoever, the software to third persons or subjecting the software to reverse engineering.[53]

29. Semiconductor Chip Protection

The Semiconductor Chip Protection Act (SCPA) of 1984[54] created a new form of industrial intellectual property by protecting mask works and the semiconductor chip products in which they are embodied against chip piracy. A **mask work** refers to the specific form of expression embodied in chip design, including the stencils used in manufacturing semiconductor chip products. A **semiconductor chip product** is a product placed on a piece of semiconductor material in accordance with a predetermined pattern that is intended to perform electronic circuitry functions. These chips operate microwave ovens, televisions, computers, robots, x-ray machines, and countless other devices. This definition of semiconductor chip products includes such products as analog chips, logic function chips like microprocessors, and memory chips like RAMS and ROMs.

(a) Duration and Qualifications for Protection

The SCPA provides the owner of a mask work fixed in semiconductor chip products the exclusive right for 10 years to reproduce and distribute the products in the United States and to import them into the United States. These rights fully apply to works first commercially exploited after November 8, 1984, the date of the law's enactment. However, the protection of the act applies only to those works that, when considered as a whole, are not commonplace, staple, or familiar in the semiconductor industry.

(b) Application Procedure

The owner of a mask work subject to protection under the SCPA must file an application for a certificate of registration with the Register of Copyrights within two years of the date of the work's first commercial exploitation. Failure to do so within this period will result in forfeiture of all rights under the act. Questions concerning the validity of the work are to be resolved through litigation or arbitration.

ETHICS & THE LAW

Not long ago, the dance song "Macarena" hit the pop music scene and charts in the United States. The line-type dance inspired by the song also is called the Macarena. At camps around the country, the song was played, and children were taught the dance.

The American Society of Composers, Authors, and Publishers (ASCAP) is the organization that serves as a clearinghouse for fee payments for use of copyrighted materials belonging to its members. ASCAP sent a letter to the directors of camps and nonprofit organizations sponsoring camps (Girl Scouts, Boy Scouts, Camp Fire Girls, American Cancer Association, and so forth) warning them that licensed songs should not be used without paying ASCAP the licensing fees and that violators would be pursued. ASCAP's prices for songs are, for example, $591 for the camp season for "Edelweiss" (from *The Sound of Music*) or "This Land Is Your Land."

Some of the nonprofit-sponsored camps charge only $44 per week per camper. The directors could not afford the fees, and the camps eliminated their oldies from their dances and dance classes. ASCAP declined to offer discounted licensing fees for the camps.

Why did ASCAP work so diligently to protect its rights? What ethical and social responsibility issues do you see with respect to the nonprofit camps? Some of these camps are summer retreats for children who suffer from cancer, AIDS, and other terminal illnesses. Does this information change your feelings about ASCAP's fees? What would you do if you were an ASCAP member and owned the rights to a song a camp wished to use?

[53] See *Fonar Corp. v Domenick*, 105 F3d 99 (2d Cir 1997).

[54] PL 98-620, 98 Stat 3347, 17 USC § 901.

(c) Limitation on Exclusive Rights

Under the SCPA's reverse engineering exemption, competitors may not only study mask works but may also use the results of that study to design their own semiconductor chip products embodying their own original masks even if the masks are substantially similar (but not substantially identical) so long as their products are the result of substantial study and analysis, not merely the result of plagiarism.

Innocent infringers are not liable for infringements occurring before notice of protection is given them and are liable for reasonable royalties on each unit distributed after notice has been given them. However, the continued purchasing of infringing semiconductors after notice has been given can result in penalties of up to $250,000.

(d) Remedies

The SCPA provides that an infringer will be liable for actual damages and will forfeit its profits to the owner. As an alternative, the owner may elect to receive statutory damages of up to $250,000 as determined by a court. The court may also order destruction or other disposition of the products and equipment used to make the products. **For Example,** Altera Corporation manufactures programmable logic devices. It was successful in the lawsuit against its competitor Clear Logic, Inc., which works from a different business model. Altera was successful in its lawsuit against Clear Logic under the SCPA, asserting that Clear Logic had copied the layout design of its registered mask works. It also was successful in its claim that Clear Logic induced breach of software licenses with Altera customers. Damages were assessed at $36 million.[55]

LAWFLIX

The Jerk (1979) (R)

Steve Martin invents a special handle for eyeglasses that is mass marketed by a businessman who gives him a percentage of the royalties from sales. Should Martin be paid?

For movie clips that illustrate business law concepts, see LawFlix at **http://wdvl.westbuslaw.com.**

[55] *Altera Corp. v Clear Logic Inc.*, 424 F3d 1079 (9th Cir 2005).

Summary

Property rights in trademarks, copyrights, and patents are acquired as provided primarily in federal statutes. A trademark or service mark is any word, symbol, design, or combination of these used to identify a product (in the case of a trademark) or a service (in the case of a service mark). Terms will fall into one of four categories: (1) generic, (2) descriptive, (3) suggestive, or (4) arbitrary or fanciful. Generic terms are never registrable. However, if a descriptive term has acquired a secondary meaning, it is registrable. Suggestive and arbitrary marks are registrable as well. If there is likelihood of confusion, a court will enjoin the second user from using a particular registered mark.

A copyright is the exclusive right given by federal statute to the creator of a literary or an artistic work to use, reproduce, or display the work for the life of the creator and 70 years after the creator's death.

A patent gives the inventor an exclusive right for 20 years from the date of application to make, use, and sell an invention that is new and useful but not obvious to those in the business to which the invention is related. Trade secrets that give an owner an advantage over competitors are protected under state law for an unlimited period so long as they are not made public.

Protection of computer programs and the design of computer chips and mask works is commonly obtained, subject to certain limitations, by complying with federal statutes, by using the law of trade secrets, and by requiring restrictive licensing agreements. Many so pursue all of these means to protect their in their programs.

Questions and Case Problems

1. China is a signatory country to the Madrid Protocol on the international registration of trademarks. Starbucks opened its first café in China in 1999 and has added outlets in numerous locations including Shanghai and at the Great Wall and the imperial palace in Beijing. Xingbake Café Corp. Ltd. has imitated the designs of Starbuck's cafés in its business coffee café locations in Shanghai. *Xing* (pronounced "Shing") means star, and *bake,* or "bak kuh" is pronounced like "bucks." Does the Seattle, Washington, Starbucks Corporation have standing to bring suit in China against Xingbake Café Corp. Ltd? If so, on what theory? Decide. (*Boston Globe*, January 3, 2006, 1)
2. Cable News Network with its principal place of business in Atlanta, Georgia, is the owner of the trademark CNN in connection with providing news and information services to people worldwide through cable and satellite television networks, Web sites, and news services. Its services are also available worldwide on the Internet at the domain name CNN.com. Maya Online Broadband Network (Maya HK) is a Chinese company. It registered the domain name CNNEWS.com with Network Solutions, Inc. The CNNews.com Web site was designed to provide news and information to Chinese-speaking individuals worldwide, making significant use of the terms *CNNews* and *CNNews.com* as brand names and logos that the Atlanta company contends resembles its logos. Maya HK has admitted that CNNews in fact stands for China Network News abbreviated as CNN. The Atlanta company notified Maya HK of its legal rights to the CNN mark before the Chinese company registered the CNNews.com domain name. Does the federal Anticybersquatting Consumer Protection Act apply to this case? If so, does a "safe harbor" exist under the ACPA for Maya HK in that most people who access its Web site in China have never heard of CNN? Decide. [*Cable News Network v CNN News.com*, 177 F Supp 2d 506 (ED Va)]
3. Banion manufacturers semiconductor chips. He wants to obtain protection for his mask works under federal law, particularly so that competitors will be prohibited from reverse engineering these works. Advise Banion of his legal options, if any, to accomplish his objective.
4. Jim and Eric work for Audio Visual Services (AVS) at Cramer University in Casper, Wyoming. For "expenses" of $5 and the provision of a blank tape, Jim and Eric used AVS facilities after hours to make tapes of Pearl Jam's CD *Vitology* for 25 friends or friends of friends from school. When Mrs. Mullen, who is in charge of AVS, discovered this and confronted them, Jim, a classics major, defended their actions, telling her, "It's *de minimus*... I mean, who cares?" Explain to Jim and Eric the legal and ethical ramifications of their actions.
5. Sullivan sold t-shirts with the name *Boston Marathon* and the year of the race imprinted on them. The Boston Athletic Association (BAA) sponsors and administers the Boston Marathon and has used the name *Boston Marathon* since 1917. The BAA registered the name *Boston Marathon* on the Principal Register. In 1986, the BAA entered into an exclusive license with Image, Inc., to use its service mark on shirts and other apparel. Thereafter, when Sullivan continued to sell shirts imprinted with the name *Boston Marathon,* the BAA sought an injunction. Sullivan's defense was that the general public was not being misled into thinking that his shirts were officially sponsored by the BAA. Without this confusion of source, he contended, no injunction should be issued. Decide. [*Boston Athletic Ass'n v Sullivan*, 867 F2d 22 (1st Cir)]
6. The University of Georgia Athletic Association (UGAA) brought suit against beer wholesaler Bill Laite for marketing Battlin' Bulldog Beer. The UGAA claimed that the cans infringed its symbol for its athletic teams. The symbol, which depicted an English Bulldog wearing a sweater with a G and the word BULLDOGS on it, had been registered as a service mark. Soon after the beer appeared on the market, the university received telephone calls from friends of the university who were concerned that Battlin' Bulldog Beer was not the sort of product that should in any way be related to the University of Georgia. The university's suit was based on the theory of false designation of origin in violation of the Lanham Act. Laite contended that there was no likelihood of confusion because his bulldog was different from the university's and his cans bore the disclaimer "Not associated with the University of Georgia." Decide. [*University of Georgia Athletic Ass'n v Laite*, 756 F2d 1535 (11th Cir)]
7. Twentieth Century Fox (Fox) owned and distributed the successful motion picture *The Commitments.* The film tells the story of a group of young Irish men and women who form a soul music band. In the film, the leader of the band, Jimmy, tries to teach the band members what it takes to be successful soul music performers. Toward that end, Jimmy shows the band members a videotape of James Brown's energetic performance of the song

ıease, Please, Please." This performance came from Brown's appearance in 1965 on a television program called the *TAMI Show*. Portions of the 1965 performance are shown in *The Commitments* in seven separate "cuts" for a total of 27 seconds. Sometimes the cuts are in the background of a scene, and sometimes they occupy the entire screen. Brown's name is not mentioned at all during these relatively brief cuts. His name is mentioned only once later in the film, when Jimmy urges the band members to abandon their current musical interests and tune in to the great soul performers, including James Brown: "Listen, from now on I don't want you listening to Guns & Roses and The Soup Dragons. I want you on a strict diet of soul. James Brown for the growls, Otis Redding for the moans, Smokey Robinson for the whines, and Aretha for the whole lot put together." Would it be fair use under U.S. copyright law for Fox to use just 27 seconds of James Brown cuts in the film without formally obtaining permission to use the cuts? Advise Fox as to what, if anything, would be necessary to protect it from a lawsuit. [See *Brown v Twentieth Century Fox Film Corp.*, 799 F Supp 166 (DDC)]

8. Sony Corporation manufactures videocassette recorders (VCRs) to tape television shows for later home viewing (time-shifting). Sony sold them under the trade name Betamax through retail establishments throughout the country. Universal City Studios and Walt Disney Productions owned the copyrights on some of the television programs that were broadcast on public airwaves. Universal and Disney brought an action against Sony and certain large retailers, contending that VCR consumers had recorded some of their copyrighted works that had been shown on commercially sponsored television and thereby infringed the copyrights. These plaintiffs sought damages and an injunction against the manufacture and marketing of VCRs. Sony contended that the noncommercial, home-use recording of material broadcast over public airwaves for later viewing was a fair use of copyrighted works. Decide. [*Sony Corp. v Universal Studios*, 464 US 417]
9. The menu commands on the Lotus 1-2-3 spreadsheet program enable users to perform accounting functions by using such commands as "Copy," "Print," and "Quit." Borland International, Inc., released its Quattro spreadsheet, a program superior to Lotus 1-2-3 that did, however, use an identical copy of the entire Lotus 1-2-3 menu tree but did not copy any of Lotus's computer code. Lotus believed that its copyright in Lotus 1-2-3 had been violated. Borland insisted that the Lotus menu command was not copyrightable because it is a method of operation foreclosed from protection under Section 102(b) of the Copyright Act of 1976. Decide. [*Lotus Development Corp. v Borland International, Inc.*, 49 F3d 807 (1st Cir), aff'd, 116 S Ct 904]
10. Diehr devised a computerized process for curing rubber that was based on a well-known mathematical formula related to the cure time, and he devised numerous other steps in his synthetic rubber-curing process. The patent examiner determined that because abstract ideas, the laws of nature, and mathematical formulas are not patentable subject matter, the process in this case (based on a known mathematical formula) was also not patentable. Diehr contended that all of the steps in his rubber-curing process were new and not obvious to the art of rubber curing. He contended also that he did not seek an exclusive patent on the mathematical formula, except for its use in the rubber-curing process. Decide. [*Diamond v Diehr*, 450 US 175]
11. Aries Information Systems, Inc., develops and markets computer software specifically designed to meet the financial accounting and reporting requirements of such public bodies as school districts and county governments. One of Aries's principal products is the POBAS III accounting program. Pacific Management Systems Corporation was organized by Scott Dahmer, John Laugan, and Roman Rowan for marketing a financial accounting and budgeting system known as FAMIS. Dahmer, Laugan, and Rowan were Aries employees before, during, and shortly after they organized Pacific. As employees, they each gained access to Aries's software materials (including the POBAS III system) and had information about Aries's existing and prospective clients. Proprietary notices appeared on every client contract, source code list, and magnetic tape. Dahmer, Laugan, and Rowan signed an Employee Confidential Information Agreement after beginning employment with Aries. While still employees of Aries, they submitted a bid on behalf of Pacific to Rock County and were awarded the contract. Pacific's FAMIS software system is substantially identical to Aries's proprietary POBAS III system. Aries sued Pacific to recover damages for misappropriation of its trade secrets. Pacific's defense was that no "secrets" were misappropriated because many employees knew the information in question. Decide. [*Aries Information Systems, Inc. v Pacific Management Systems Corp.*, 366 NW2d 366 (Minn App)]
12. The plaintiff, Herbert Rosenthal Jewelry Corporation, and the defendant, Kalpakian, manufactured jewelry. The plaintiff obtained a copyright registration of a jeweled pin in the shape of a bee. Kalpakian made a similar pin. Rosenthal sued Kalpakian for infringement of copyright registration. Kalpakian raised the defense that he was only copying the idea, not the way the idea was expressed. Was he liable for infringement of the plaintiff's copyright? [*Herbert Rosenthal Jewelry Corp. v Kalpakian*, 446 F2d 738 (9th Cir)]
13. Mineral Deposits, Ltd. (MD, Ltd.), an Australian company, manufactures the Reichert Spiral, a device used

for recovering gold particles from sand and gravel. The spiral was patented in Australia, and MD, Ltd., had applied for a patent in the United States. Theodore Zigan contacted MD, Ltd., stating he was interested in purchasing up to 200 devices for use in his gravel pit. MD, Ltd., agreed to lend Zigan a spiral for testing its efficiency. Zigan made molds of the spiral's components and proceeded to manufacture 170 copies of the device. When MD, Ltd., found out that copies were being made, it demanded the return of the spiral. MD, Ltd., also sought lost profits for the 170 spirals manufactured by Zigan. Recovery was sought on a theory of misappropriation of trade secrets. Zigan offered to pay for the spiral lent him by MD, Ltd. He argued that trade secret protection was lost by the public sale of the spiral. What ethical values are involved? Was Zigan's conduct a violation of trade secret law? [*Mineral Deposits, Ltd. v Zigan*, 773 P2d 609 (Colo App)]

14. Village Voice Media, owners of the famous *Village Voice* newspaper in New York City, sent a letter to *The Cape Cod Voice*, a year-old publication located in Orleans, Massachusetts, objecting to the use of the word *Voice* in the title of its publication. It warned that the Cape Cod publication could cause "confusion as to the source affiliation with the famous Village Voice marks." The publisher of *The Cape Cod Voice* responded that "small places have a right to their own voices." The use of the word *Voice* is thus in dispute between these parties. Would you classify it as generic, descriptive, suggestive, arbitrary, or fanciful? How would you resolve this controversy? [*Cape Cod Times* Business Section, Amy Zipkin, *The New York Times*, October 16, 2004, G-1].

CPA Questions

1. Multicomp Company wishes to protect software it has developed. It is concerned about others copying this software and taking away some of its profits. Which of the following is true concerning the current state of the law?
   a. Computer software is generally copyrightable.
   b. To receive protection, the software must have a conspicuous copyright notice.
   c. Software in human readable source code is copyrightable but machine language object code is not.
   d. Software can be copyrighted for a period not to exceed 20 years.

2. Which of the following is not correct concerning computer software purchased by Gultch Company from Softtouch Company? Softtouch originally created this software.
   a. Gultch can make backup copies in case of machine failure.
   b. Softtouch can typically copyright its software for at least 75 years.
   c. If the software consists of compiled computer databases, it cannot be copyrighted.
   d. Computer programs are generally copyrightable.

3. Using his computer, Professor Bell makes 15 copies to distribute to his accounting class of a database in some software he has purchased for his personal research. The creator of this software is claiming copyright. Which of the following is correct?
   a. This is an infringement of copyright, since he bought the software for personal use.
   b. This is not an infringement of copyright, since databases cannot be copyrighted.
   c. This is not an infringement of copyright because the copies were made using a computer.
   d. This is not an infringement of copyright because of the fair use doctrine.

4. Intellectual property rights included in software may be protected under which of the following?
   a. Patent law
   b. Copyright law
   c. Both of the above
   d. None of the above

CYBERLAW

CHAPTER

(11)

LEARNING OBJECTIVES

After studying this chapter, you should be able to

LO.1 Identify the legal and ethical issues of the new technologies in business

LO.2 Discuss the various areas of law that apply to business issues in cyberspace and the use of the new technologies

LO.3 Explain how the flexibility of the law allows for the resolution of new issues and problems in business

A. Introduction to Cyberlaw

1. What Is Cyberlaw?

Figures from 2005 conclude that 331,473,276 people in North America use the Internet on a regular basis, a whopping 68.1 percent of the population. In Europe, the number of regular users is 807,289,020 or 35.9 percent of the population.[1] About 80 percent of managers and professionals use a computer at work each day. About 55 percent of all U.S. workers use a computer at work, with two of every five (40 percent) workers using e-mail daily.[2] They also use their computers for communicating, contracting, and doing research. The World Wide Web has enabled businesses to move goods and services through commerce at lightning speed. In many ways, the changes in technology and resulting changes in business practices have occurred at speeds that have not permitted the law to keep pace with them. As a result, this new world of business has caused some distress among managers, law professors, and students as they wonder, "Are there laws that cover this new way of doing business?"

The answer to the question is both yes and no. Although certainly some new laws govern aspects of using and operating systems in the new economy and cyberspace, a body of law and precedent—the same body of law and precedent that has seen businesses through many economic and technological revolutions—remains. This same body of law and its characteristics are again a resource for resolving the new economy's legal issues. Examining how the law applies to the new technology provides further evidence of the law's stability, innovation, and flexibility. (See Chapter 1 for more discussion of the characteristics of law.) The rise of the Internet and its pervasive use in business is not the first time the law has had to change to keep pace with technological revolutions. For example, the new clarity of satellite pictures and observation techniques such as thermal scanning have raised new issues concerning searches and the requirements for warrants. The law adjusts and survives through a balancing of the interests at stake as issues arise from the use of new technologies.

Even though the law that is applied to resolve the problems of the new technologies and the new economy is often referred to as **cyberlaw,** you need not fear that you will be required to learn a whole new body of law. There have been and will continue to be changes in the law to accommodate new ways of doing business, but there has also been and will continue to be reliance on the fundamental principles that underlie our laws and the rights they protect. This chapter simply examines the issues and concerns in cyberspace and covers their resolution through a brief overview of new and existing laws. Although other chapters provide more details on these rights and protections, this chapter provides a framework for both the challenges of legal issues in **cyberspace** as well as discussion of the valuable nature of a legal system that can adjust to and absorb the changes business brings about.

2. What Are the Issues in Cyberlaw?

While no new body of law called *cyberlaw* exists, there are new issues in the use of cyberspace in business that require resolution by new statutes, by judicial decisions, or by reliance on existing laws and case precedent. The legal issues of cyberspace can be broken down into six areas: **tort** issues, contract issues, intellectual property issues, criminal law issues, constitutional restraints and protections, and securities law issues. Within each of these six areas of existing law are a number of new legal issues that have arisen because of the nature of cyberspace and the conduct of business there. That various cyberlaw issues can be grouped into traditional areas of law demonstrates the not-so-new nature of cyberlaw in the new economy. The following sections in this chapter include discussions of these six main areas and the new issues that technology has raised for resolution.

B. Tort Issues in Cyberspace

The tort issues in cyberlaw are privacy, appropriation, and defamation.

3. Privacy Issues in Cyberlaw

(a) E-Mail and Privacy

E-mail use in the workplace is a nearly universal practice. Employees use e-mails for contract, customer, supplier, and shareholder communications. However, studies show that 86 percent of employees use their

[1] See **www.internetworldstats.com**, with additional data from Nielsen and the International Telecommunications Union.

[2] "Internet Use at Work," Bureau of Labor Statistics, **www.bls.gov**.

GARRITY V JOHN HANCOCK MUTUAL LIFE INSURANCE COMPANY, 2002 WL 974676 (D MASS)

THE JOKE'S ON THE EMPLOYEE: E-MAIL CONTENT CAN GET YOU FIRED

Nancy Garrity ("Mrs. Garrity") and Joanne Clark ("Ms. Clark") (plaintiffs) were employees of John Hancock Mutual Life Insurance Company ("John Hancock") (defendant) for twelve and two years, respectively. Mrs. Garrity and Ms. Clark received, on their office computers, sexually explicit e-mails from Internet joke sites and other third parties, including Mrs. Garrity's husband, Arthur Garrity, which they then sent to coworkers. Examples included "The Top Ten Reasons Cookie Dough Is Better Than Men."

A fellow employee complained after receiving one such e-mail. Hancock investigated Mrs. Garrity's and Ms. Clark's e-mail folders, as well as the folders of those with whom they e-mailed on a regular basis. Based upon the information gleaned from this investigation, Hancock determined that Mrs. Garrity and Ms. Clark had violated its e-mail policy, which stated:

Messages that are defamatory, abusive, obscene, profane, sexually oriented, threatening or racially offensive are prohibited.

The inappropriate use of E-mail is in violation of company policy and may be subject [sic] to disciplinary action, up to and including termination of employment.

All information stored, transmitted, received, or contained in the company's E-mail systems is the property of John Hancock. It is not company policy to intentionally inspect E-mail usage. However, there may be business or legal situations that necessitate company review of E-mail messages and other documents.

[C]ompany management reserves the right to access all E-mail files.

Hancock periodically sent reminders, but it also provided information on how to keep e-mails private through password usage for the files.

Hancock fired both women, and the women filed suit for invasion of privacy as well as wrongful termination.

Judicial Opinion

ZOBEL, District Judge . . . Plaintiffs' opposition states that "[i]t is uncontested . . . that Ms. Garrity, Mr. Garrity and Ms. Clarke believed that the personal e-mail correspondence they sent and received was private." While that may be true, the relevant inquiry is whether the expectation of privacy was reasonable. Any reasonable expectation on the part of plaintiffs is belied by the record and plaintiffs' own statements. According to deposition testimony, Mrs. Garrity and Ms. Clark assumed that the recipients of their messages might forward them to others. Likewise, Mr. Garrity testified that the e-mails he sent to his wife would eventually be sent to third parties. Although there is a dearth of case law on privacy issues with regard to office email, *Smyth v Pillsbury Co.*, 914 F.Supp. 97 (E.D.Pa.1996) is instructive here. In Smyth, the court held that even in the absence of a company e-mail policy, plaintiffs would not have had a reasonable expectation of privacy in their work e-mail:

Once plaintiff communicated the alleged unprofessional comments to a second person (his supervisor) over an e-mail system which was apparently utilized by the entire company, any reasonable expectation of privacy was lost. Significantly, the defendant did not require plaintiff, as in the case of urinalysis or personal property search to disclose any personal information about himself. Rather, plaintiff voluntarily communicated the alleged unprofessional comments over the company e-mail system. We find no privacy interests in such communications.

Even if plaintiffs had a reasonable expectation of privacy in their work e-mail, defendant's legitimate business interest in protecting its employees from harassment in the workplace would likely trump plaintiffs' privacy interests. Both Title VII of the Civil Rights Act of 1964 and

M.G.L. c. 151B require employers to take affirmative steps to maintain a workplace free of harassment and to investigate and take prompt and effective remedial action when potentially harassing conduct is discovered. Therefore, once defendant received a complaint about the plaintiffs' sexually explicit e-mails, it was required by law to commence an investigation.

Plaintiffs allege, in their Complaint, that defendant's termination of their employment constitutes a violation of the "public policy of the Commonwealth of Massachusetts, which guarantees to every citizen the right to be free from unreasonable, substantial or serious inferences with their privacy, ..." This argument is not only duplicative of the privacy and wire tap claims dismissed above, but it is misplaced. A common law public policy claim cannot lie in a wrongful discharge case where the plaintiff has an available state statutory claim.

The last count asserts that two Hancock supervisors defamed plaintiffs by telling former co-workers, and Hancock employees in other departments, that plaintiffs were terminated for sending and receiving "sexually lewd, harassing [and] defamatory" and "sexually explicit" e-mails. Even if the statements made by defendant met the required elements of a defamation claim, defendant is entitled to a conditional privilege which insulates it from liability for these statements. The privilege "protects an employer's statements of opinion and facts, and statements that an employer reasonably believes to be true." It also extends to "information which may turn out not to be true concerning an employee when the publication is reasonably necessary to serve the employer's legitimate interest in the fitness of an employee to perform his or her job." In order to defeat the employer's conditional privilege, the employee bears the burden of proving that the employer abused the privilege by recklessly publishing the defamatory facts. Plaintiffs have not done so here. Rather, plaintiffs simply state that "[n]o legitimate business purpose was served by disseminating these statements among such a large group of employees." To the contrary, all Hancock employees are subject to its e-mail policy. Therefore, defendant had an obvious legitimate business purpose, as to all employees, if it so chose—to warn them and thereby prevent any recurrence of the events that led to this law suit. Accordingly, defendant's motion for summary judgment is allowed. Judgment may be entered for defendant.

Questions

1. Give the legal protections the plaintiffs offer that they say prevent their termination.
2. What privilege does the court say John Hancock held in disclosing the dismissal?
3. Why is the employer right to monitor employee e-mails important?

company e-mail systems to communicate with their families, and 38 percent of employees indicate that they have used company e-mail systems to send messages that served political purposes. Finally, 30 percent of employees indicate that they have used e-mail to send racist, pornographic, sexist, or otherwise discriminatory messages.[3]

Courts are forced to balance interests when they deal with questions of privacy of such e-mail communication. For example, employers are held responsible for the content of e-mail that serves to create an atmosphere of harassment. (See Chapter 40 for more information on sexual harassment.) If employers are held accountable for the content of e-mail, as they are in cases of harassment and in other forms of discrimination, some means of controlling the content of those e-mails is important. In some cases, employees' e-mails have resulted in convictions or settlements. For example, in 2004, New York's attorney general and federal regulators reached a settlement with the major Wall Street investment houses for the inconsistent stock evaluations of their employees that were found in their e-mails. The employees offered favorable evaluations of companies in their public statements but referred to the companies as "dogs" in their e-mail communications with each other and colleagues. In 2005, Marsh & McLennan, an international insurance broker, settled its price-fixing case with New York's attorney general after e-mails that showed employees were concerned about possible antitrust violations emerged. Monitoring the content of employee e-mails is important for keeping companies out of legal difficulties. However, employees may believe they have an expectation of privacy in their e-mails, even when those e-mails are sent from work.

[3] W. Michael Hoffman, Laura P. Hartman, and Mark Rowe, "You've Got Mail . . . And the Boss Knows: A Survey by the Center for Business Ethics of Companies' Email and Internet Monitoring," 108 *Business and Society* 285 (2003). See also **http://www.elronsoftware.com** for more information on employee use of e-mail.

There were some efforts initially to apply existing law to ensure e-mail privacy. The Electronic Communications Privacy Act of 1986 (ECPA) prohibits the interception of "live" communications, as when someone uses a listening device to intercept a telephone conversation. However, e-mail is stored information, and the question of this act's application for resolving the privacy issue is doubtful.[4]

The tort of **invasion of privacy,** or intrusion into private affairs, has application to this cyberspace communication. The tort of intrusion into private affairs or public disclosure of private facts requires not just the act of revelation of private information but that the information revealed is presumed to be private and entitled to privacy protection.

(b) Web Site Information and Privacy

A second privacy issue in cyberlaw is the use of information that Web sites have gleaned from their users. **For Example,** if you use an airline's Web site to book your travel arrangements, that Web site has a profile of your travel habits. The airline knows how frequently you travel and where you travel. That type of targeted customer information is something other Web sites and retailers are willing to pay dearly for because they know their product is being considered by those most likely to purchase it. If you use Amazon.com to buy books, that Web site has relevant information about the types of books you read, your interests, and even some indications about your income level based on your spending habits. When you log on to a Web site, do you expect that private information about you will be gathered and sold to others for purposes of marketing goods and services to you?

Even though this issue of privacy may seem new and peculiar to cyberspace, it is, in fact, a rather old issue that has long been a concern of credit card companies. These companies' use and sale of information about their customers are restricted. Customers must be given the right to refuse such use of their names and other information for sale as part of lists for target marketing. Some state attorneys general are utilizing these credit card privacy rights to enforce privacy rights against Web site owners who sell information about their users. The Federal Trade Commission (FTC) has begun to take positions that are identical to its stances on other types of commerce issues. **For Example,** if catalog companies are required to provide notice to customers about delays in shipment of goods to customers, Internet companies must comply with the same notification rules.

THINKING THINGS THROUGH

THE BOSS IS WATCHING AND READING YOUR E-MAILS

Discuss whether employees would have the right of privacy in the following e-mail situations:

1. E-mail sent in a company in which there is no warning given about the lack of privacy in e-mails. *Smyth v Pillsbury*, 914 F Supp 97 (ED Pa 1996).
2. An e-mail sent to coworkers from home using the employee's AOL account.
3. An e-mail sent from a laptop while the employee is traveling for the company.
4. An e-mail sent to a coworker over a company Internet system in a company in which the employer has promised privacy in e-mail. *Commonwealth v Proetto*, 771 A2d 823 (Pa Super Ct 2001).
5. Employer monitoring of the e-mails of any employee when those e-mails were stored in a file folder marked "Personal." *McLaren v Microsoft Corp.*, 1999 WL 339015 (Tex App–Dallas 1999).
6. Employees using company e-mail for union organization purposes. *Pratt & Whitney*, NLRB Gen. Couns. Ad v. Mem. Cases 12-CA-18446, 12-CA-18722, 12-CS-18863 (February 23, 1998).

[4] "Every circuit court to have considered the matter has held that an 'intercept' under the ECPA must occur contemporaneously with transmission." See *Fraser v Nationwide Mut. Ins. Co.*, 352 F3d 107, 113 (3d Cir 2003).

ETHICS & THE LAW

EMPLOYER TIPS ON MONITORING EMPLOYEES

Because the law on Internet and e-mail privacy is evolving, taking the initiative not only can avoid future legal problems but also can help employees feel comfortable about company policies and their own e-mail and Internet use. A lawyer for businesses interested in solving the issues of technology, the workplace, and cyberspace provided the following tips.

Ten Commandments for Avoiding Workplace Exposure

1. Publish policies regarding employee use of e-mail, the Internet, and any employer-issued hardware or software.
2. Have employees sign off on the policy each year.
3. Tell employees that the company will monitor e-mail, Internet use, and any other use of employer-issued computers. Be sure to cover all new technology, such as Palm Pilots, Blackberries, and two-way text messaging systems.
4. Create a style guide for writing business e-mails.
5. Train all employees on how to write appropriate business e-mails.
6. Develop a document/e-mail retention policy.
7. Tell employees you will cooperate with law enforcement officials and turn over any evidence of illegal activities.
8. Enforce all policies in an even-handed manner.
9. Keep current on new technology in the marketplace and how it can be used and monitored.
10. Reevaluate all technology-related policies annually.*

About 88 percent of employers tell their employees about the privacy limitations of using the company e-mail system, and about 92 percent of companies engage in monitoring of employees' e-mails.** However, the lack of notice does not mean that the employee has an expectation of privacy. If the employee is using the employer's e-mail system, any messages sent or received on that system are subject to employer review.

Many corporations have monitoring firms that keep track of employee use of Web sites, and the reports of these electronic consultants are then used to confront employees about everything from breach of company rules to efficient use of time at work. Recent surveys indicate that 92 percent of companies monitor their employees' Web site access.*** Of these companies, 91 percent disclose to their employees that they are monitoring their Web site use. Disclosure is again key in allowing employer monitoring of employee Web site use.

*Frank C. Morris, Jr., "The Electronic Platform: Email and Other Privacy Issues in the Workplace," 20 *Computer & Internet Law* (no. 8) 1–20.

"2001 Survey on Privacy, Technology and Internet Use in the Workplace," **http://www.marketingpower.com.

***Hoffman, Hartman, and Rowe, "You've Got Mail . . . And the Boss Knows." See also **http://www.elronsoftware.com** for more information on employee use of e-mail.

In 2002 the FTC reached a settlement with Microsoft over its practice of collecting data through its Passport Service.[5] The FTC found that the payment Microsoft had consumers use that assured them of privacy was actually being used by the company for data gathering on the consumers. As part of the settlement, Microsoft must submit to 20 years of annual privacy audits.[6]

p., FTC No. 012 3240, Complaint at 1-2 (2002) [hereinafter Passport Complaint], available at **http://www.ftc.gov/.**
DoubleClick, Inc., Privacy Litig., 154 F Supp 2d 497, 500 (SDNY 2001), in which the court dismissed a similar privacy nformation from consumer Web browsing.

SONY MUSIC ENTERTAINMENT INC. V DOES 1-40, 326 F SUPP 2D 556 (SDNY 2004)

THE RATFINK ISP: TELLING WHO'S DOING THE DOWNLOADING

Sony and others (Plaintiffs) own the copyrights and exclusive licenses to the various sound recordings. Forty Does (defendants), without permission, used "Fast Track," an online media distribution system—or "peer to peer" ("P2P") file copying network—to download hundreds or thousands of copyrighted sound recordings. Sony was able to identify Cablevision as the Internet service provider ("ISP") to which the Does subscribed. Sony did so by using a publicly available database to trace the Internet Protocol ("IP") address for each Doe. An ISP can identify the computer from which the alleged infringement occurred and the name and address of the subscriber controlling the computer when it is provided with a user's IP address and the date and time of the allegedly infringing activity.

As a condition of providing its Internet service, Cablevision requires its subscribers to agree to its "Terms of Service" under which "[t]ransmission or distribution of any material in violation of any applicable law or regulation is prohibited. This includes, without limitation, material protected by copyright, trademark, trade secret or other intellectual property right used without proper authorization."

On January 26, 2004, the court issued an order granting Sony the right to serve a subpoena upon Cablevision to obtain the identity of each Doe by requesting the name, address, telephone number, email address, and Media Access Control address for each defendant.

On February 2, 2004, amici curiae Electronic Frontier Foundation, Public Citizen, and the American Civil Liberties Union ("amici") submitted a letter to the court objecting to the grant of the subpoena. The court affirmed its order for a subpoena.

Cablevision sent notice to all affected subscribers. Cablevision's letter stated,

> *Unless we hear from you, or your attorney, in writing by February 20, 2004 that you have filed the appropriate papers with the U.S. District Court for the Southern District of New York to have the subpoena set aside, we will disclose your subscriber information to the plaintiffs, as required by the enclosed subpoena.*

On February 20, 2004, Cablevision received a letter from one of the subscriber's attorney stating that he represented one of Cablevision's subscribers and that he "would expect that Cablevision will make every effort to quash the subpoena or otherwise limit the scope of the requested discovery so . . . as not to infringe on [his] client's privacy rights."

On February 23, 2004, Cablevision complied with the subpoena and provided relevant identifying information for about thirty-six Does. The Does filed a motion to quash the subpoena.

Judicial Opinion

CHIN, District Judge . . . Jane Doe moves to quash the subpoena.

A. The First Amendment

Defendants' motions raise two First Amendment issues: (1) whether a person who uses the Internet to download or distribute copyrighted music without permission is engaging in the exercise of speech; and (2) if so, whether such a person's identity is protected from disclosure by the First Amendment.

The Supreme Court has recognized that the First Amendment protects anonymous speech. It is well-settled that the First Amendment's protection extends to the Internet. Courts have recognized the Internet as a valuable forum for robust exchange and debate. The Internet is a particularly effective forum for the dissemination of anonymous speech. Anonymous speech, like speech from identifiable sources, does not have absolute protection. The First Amendment for example, does not protect copyright infringement, and the Supreme Court, accordingly, has rejected First Amendment challenges to copyright infringement actions. Parties may not use the First Amendment to encroach upon the intellectual property rights of others.

Against the backdrop of First Amendment protection for anonymous speech, courts have held that civil subpoenas seeking information regarding anonymous individuals raise First Amendment concerns. For example, in *NAACP v Alabama ex rel. Patterson*, 357 U.S. 449, 462, 78 S.Ct. 1163, 2 L.Ed.2d 1488 (1958), the Supreme Court held that a discovery order requiring the NAACP to disclose its membership list interfered with the First Amendment's freedom of assembly. Similarly, in *NLRB v Midland Daily News*, 151 F.3d 472, 475 (6th Cir.1998), the Sixth Circuit declined on First Amendment grounds to enforce a subpoena duces tecum issued by the National Labor Relations Board seeking to require a newspaper publisher to disclose the identity of an anonymous advertiser.

As a threshold matter, I address whether the use of P2P file copying networks to download, distribute, or make available for distribution copyrighted sound recordings, without permission, is an exercise of speech. I conclude that this conduct qualifies as speech, but only to a degree.

In contrast to many cases involving First Amendment rights on the Internet, a person who engages in P2P file sharing is not engaging in true expression. Such an individual is not seeking to communicate a thought or convey an idea. Instead, the individual's real purpose is to obtain music for free.

Arguably, however, a file sharer is making a statement by downloading and making available to others copyrighted music without charge and without license to do so. Alternatively, the file sharer may be expressing himself or herself through the music selected and made available to others. Although this is not "political expression" entitled to the "broadest protection" of the First Amendment, the file sharer's speech is still entitled to "some level of First Amendment protection."

I conclude, accordingly, that the use of P2P file copying networks to download, distribute, or make sound recordings available qualifies as speech entitled to First Amendment protection. That protection, however, is limited, and is subject to other considerations.

Plaintiffs have alleged ownership of the copyrights or exclusive rights of copyrighted sound recordings at issue in this case sufficiently to satisfy the first element of copyright infringement. Plaintiffs have attached to the complaint a partial list of the sound recordings the rights to which defendants have allegedly infringed. Each of the copyrighted recordings on the list is the subject of a valid Certificate of Copyright Registration issued by the Register of Copyrights to one of the record company plaintiffs. Plaintiffs also allege that among the exclusive rights granted to each plaintiff under the Copyright Act are the exclusive rights to reproduce and distribute to the public the copyrighted recordings. Defendants have failed to refute in any way plaintiffs' allegations of ownership.

Plaintiffs have submitted supporting evidence listing the copyrighted songs downloaded or distributed by defendants using P2P systems. The lists also specify the date and time at which defendants' allegedly infringing activity occurred and the IP address assigned to each defendant at the time. Moreover, the use of P2P systems to download and distribute copyrighted music has been held to constitute copyright infringement. Accordingly, plaintiffs have sufficiently pled copyright infringement to establish a prima facie claim.

Plaintiffs' discovery request is also sufficiently specific to establish a reasonable likelihood that the discovery request would lead to identifying information that would make possible service upon particular defendants who could be sued in federal court. Plaintiffs seek identifying information about particular Cablevision subscribers, based on the specific times and dates when they downloaded specific copyrighted and licensed songs. Such information will enable plaintiffs to serve process on defendants.

Plaintiffs have also established that they lack other means to obtain the subpoenaed information by specifying in their ex parte application for expedited discovery and papers in opposition to Jane Doe's motion to quash the steps they have taken to locate the Doe defendants. These include using a publicly available database to trace the IP address for each defendant, based on the times of infringement.

Plaintiff have also demonstrated that the subpoenaed information is centrally needed for plaintiffs to advance their copyright infringement claims. Ascertaining the identities and residences of the Doe defendants is critical to plaintiffs' ability to pursue litigation, for without this information, plaintiffs will be unable to serve process.

Plaintiffs are also entitled to discovery in light of defendants' minimal expectation of privacy . . . [t]he Terms of Service state that "Cablevision has the right . . . to disclose any information as necessary to satisfy any law, regulation or other governmental request." Accordingly, defendants have little expectation of privacy in downloading and distributing copyrighted songs without permission.

In sum, defendants' First Amendment right to remain anonymous must give way to plaintiffs' right to use the judicial process to pursue what appear to be meritorious copyright infringement claims.

For the reasons set forth above, defendants' motions to quash the subpoena are denied and the arguments raised by amici are rejected.

(c) Freedom of Speech, Screen Names, and Privacy

Another privacy issue that has arisen is whether plaintiffs in suits for defamation can successfully subpoena Internet Service Providers (ISPs) to obtain the identity of individuals who post statements in chat rooms and across the Internet. The issue has been in litigation a number of times in various states with different results. Music companies' actions against individuals who download music but do not pay for their songs requires the discovery of the identity of those who are doing the downloading. Can the music companies require the ISPs to disclose the names of their customers for purposes of preventing copyright infringement? There are now clear standards for determining disclosure of identity.

E-COMMERCE AND CYBERLAW

BLOGGING, ETHICS, AND CYBER LAW

By the end of 2005, there were approximately 27 million U.S. adults who had created a blog or web-based diary.* That means 6% of the U.S. population are bloggers. Employers have begun using Google for more than the ego trip. Rather than plugging their own names into the search engine to see the number of hits and what is said about them, they are plugging in the names of job applicants as a way to uncover information that the job interview and other sources cannot reveal. Employers realize that they have online access as a way to obtain information for job screening and hiring decisions. For example, MySpace.com has proven to be a gold mine for employers in learning more about job applicants.

Employers are also using Google and other internet sources to track employee work excuses. One company's human resources official was on the phone with the company employment lawyer seeking to determine what action could be taken against an employee who was absent frequently but who claimed he was absent to care for his ill grandmother. While they were talking, the lawyer Googled the employee's name and found that he was being arraigned in federal court.

Schools, employment counselors, and lawyers are offering the following warnings about the dangers of Google:

1. Nothing is private on the Internet. People can see everything.
2. Be careful what you blog.
3. Protect your identity when in chat rooms.
4. Assume that everything you write and post will be seen.
5. You can clean up your name on Google using several services, but having no hits at all can lead to suspicions.
6. Think before you write, blog, post, or do anything on the Internet.

Source: Michelle Conlin, "You Are What You Post," *Business Week*, March 27, 2006, 52–53.

*Rainie, "The State of Blogging," Pew Internet and American Life Project Nov. 2005, available at **http://www.pewinternet.org/pdfs/PIP_blogging_data.pdf.** and **www.technorati.com.**

(d) Cookies and Privacy

Technology has permitted companies to plant "cookies" on the computers of those who are using certain Internet sites. With those "cookies" in place, the Web site owner has a way to track the computer owner's activity. At least one court has held that a Web site operator's placing cookies on a user's computer is a violation of an unauthorized access statute that would provide the computer owner a right of action for that breach of the statute and privacy (see discussion of criminal law in Section 8 for more information on unauthorized access).[7]

(e) Statutory Protections for Privacy in Cyberspace

Several federal laws and some state laws provide privacy protections, although somewhat limited, for Internet users. The Privacy Act of 1974 controls the use of information gathered about consumers, but it applies only to government-collected data such as information gathered by the Social Security Administration or the Internal Revenue Service. Furthermore, there are exceptions for the agencies for "routine use."[8] Some segments of the Computer Fraud and Abuse Act (CFAA) and the ECPA provide privacy protection for certain types of communications, such as financial information and its use and transfer.[9] These privacy laws are not general protections but address specific issues. For example, the Children's Online Privacy Protection Act (COPPA) targets online informational privacy but applies only to Web sites that collect information from children.[10]

Numerous state laws on privacy exist; the problem comes in enforcing those laws against Web site sponsors who have no presence in the state. (See the discussion of long-arm jurisdiction over these Internet players in Section 12, Due Process Issues in Cyberspace.)

4. Appropriation in Cyberspace

The tort of **appropriation** involves taking an image, likeness, or name for purposes of commercial advantage. A business cannot use someone's name or likeness for advertising or endorsement without permission. The use of that name or image in cyberspace does not change the nature of the protection that this form of the privacy tort provides. **For Example,** a screen saver program that uses a likeness of Richard, the million-dollar winner on the CBS television program *Survivor*, without his permission has violated his privacy rights. The use of his likeness for the Conniver screen saver program with the *Survivor* logo was appropriation. The method of appropriation may be different, but the elements are the same. Appropriation in cyberspace is still the tort of appropriation.

5. Defamation in Cyberspace

The elements of **defamation** remain the same in cyberspace. (See Chapter 9 for more details.) You must show that someone said or wrote something

ETHICS & THE LAW

The following are Web sites that post information about the performance of companies:

http://www.lfilmpro.com
http://www.vault.com
http://www.greedyassociates.com

Are those who sponsor these Web sites and those who post information there responsible for the postings? If the information is incorrect, are they liable for defamation? What if there is a disclaimer about the information they have posted there?

[7] *In re Intuit Privacy Litigation*, 138 F Supp 2d 1272 (CD Cal 2001); see also *In re Toys R Us, Inc., Privacy Litig.*, 2001 WL 34517252 (ND Cal), in which the court reached a different conclusion.

[8] 5 USC § 552a (2000).

[9] 18 USC § 1030 and 18 USC §§ 2510–2520, 2701 (1997).

[10] 15 USC §§ 6501–6506.

false that portrayed you in a bad light and that the statement, written or oral, was published, heard, or read by others. That the defamation occurs in a chat room does not change the application of tort law. However, the pervasive nature of the Internet could increase the damages for defamation because of the large number of people who obtain the information quickly, and damage can be done rapidly. **For Example,** Mark S. Jakob, a securities trader who had lost $100,000 in August 2000 with poor trades in Emulex, Inc., stock options, decided to correct his declining earnings trend by posting a false press release on the Internet that Emulex's earnings were overstated and that its CEO would resign. The news release was distributed to various Web sites. The overall loss in the value of Emulex stock was $2.5 billion before trading was stopped and the false nature of the press release revealed. As a result of this action, Jakob made $240,000 through a short position.[11] The tort of defamation would permit the investors to recover their losses.

C. Contract Issues in Cyberspace

6. Formation of Contracts in Cyberspace

Formation of a **contract** in cyberspace is simply the result of the desire for speed and better communication in business. If you wanted to form a contract with a New York seller 20 years ago and you were in Los Angeles, you drafted a proposal and mailed it to the seller. The back-and-forth negotiations took time through the mail. Then overnight delivery service arrived to speed up your cross-country negotiations. Next came faxes and their instantaneous exchanges of terms and negotiations. When there was speed, however, businesses wanted to reduce the amount of paperwork involved in transactions. They also recognized the flaws in the paper system: Had the letter arrived? Did the fax get through? Was it legible? Paperless contracts were born with the availability of electronic digital interchange (EDI), and companies using EDI have set and followed contract formation guidelines for almost 20 years. EDI is simply the electronic exchange of business forms. Contracts are formed using purchase orders and invoices submitted via computer.[12]

Even EDI had its flaws, however, in requiring the comparison of forms and numbers and verification of the interchange. With the Internet, e-mail, and the ability to attach documents, cyberspace has provided business yet another method for forming contracts.

Despite this new way of doing business with the instantaneous response to new term proposals, basic contract issues exist in cyberspace contracts that are no different from the contract issues that existed when the law merchant first began to work at finding uniform ways of doing business. Contract issues that continue to dominate discussions in cyberlaw are these: When is a contract formed? What are the contract terms?

The same laws that apply when contracts are formed in a business office govern the formation of contracts in cyberspace. Was there an offer and acceptance, and when did those two requirements come together? Some issues that arise in contract formation in the new economy are, for example, whether a contract is formed when someone downloads a program from the Internet. The person may have paid for the program by credit card and simply downloaded it on the computer. Does the click of the mouse accepting the program mean that all terms of the contract have been accepted? How does the seller of the program make sure that the buyer is aware of all terms in the contract that governs the sale of the program? Can the click of the mouse constitute a signature for the purposes of contracting?

Several new laws currently govern the formation of contracts. (See Chapters 12–17 for more information on the formation of contracts in cyberspace.) The Electronic Signatures in Global and National Commerce Act (called **E-sign**) is a federal law that recognizes digital signatures as authentic for purposes of contract formation. Even though E-sign recognizes the validity of electronic signatures, states are responsible for passing laws regulating the authenticity and security of signatures.

States have responded to the need for legislation on contract formation and authentication with the Uniform Electronic Transactions Act (UETA) and the Uniform Computer Information Transaction

[11] Alex Berenson, "Man Charged in Stock Fraud Based on Fake News," *New York Times*, September 1, 2000, C1, C2.

[12] L. J. Kutten, Bernard D. Reams, and Allen E. Strehler, *Electronic Contracting Law* (Clark Boardman, 1991).

Act (UCITA). UETA is a uniform law that 46 states plus the District of Columbia have adopted;[13] two states have adopted UCITA.[14] (See also Chapter 23 for more information on the formation of sales contracts in cyberspace.)

7. Misrepresentation and Fraud in Cyberspace

The FBI reported in 2000 that its number one source of **fraud** complaints is the Internet. Its Internet Fraud Computer Center receives 1,000 complaints per day, and the FBI has forwarded 4,000 cases to local authorities for prosecution. The average loss per fraud complaint is $800.[15] In 2005, the FBI received 228,400 complaints of Internet fraud. One of the Internet fraud cases sent forward for prosecution was the sale of kidneys for transplantation. The amount spent on computer security is expected to go from $13.5 billion in 2003 to $20 billion in 2004.[16]

The types of **misrepresentation** and fraud on the Internet range from promises of delivery not fulfilled to promises of performance not met. The majority of the fraud complaints relate to Internet auctions. These issues are not new legal issues; only the form of misrepresentation or fraud has changed. **For Example,** seven retailers signed a consent decree with the FTC, which requires them to pay fines totaling $1.5 million to settle a complaint against them for late delivery of Christmas merchandise ordered over the Web. Macys.com, Toysrus.com, and CDNOW all signed the consent decree that was based on the FTC mail-and-telephone rule requiring retailers to let customers know when they do not have a product or that there will be a delay in the shipment. The existing notification rule was simply applied to Internet transactions.

In marketing **search engines,** some companies have misrepresented the capabilities of their products or have failed to disclose the methods they use to give preference to certain links and their order of listing when the search engine is used. The remedy for such misrepresentations and fraud on the Internet is the same as the remedy in situations with paper contracts. Misrepresentation and fraud are defenses to formation and entitle the party who was misled or defrauded to rescind the agreement and/or collect money damages.

In addition to contract remedies available for misrepresenting the nature of the search engine product and capabilities, a small group of search engine companies has proposed a code of ethics for search engine firms. Headed by Mike Adams, founder and owner of WebSeed.com, the rules are called "Search Engine Promotion Code of Ethics." Adams says that his industry needs reform and gave the following example of Dotsubmit.com, a former company that claimed it would submit its clients' Web sites to 10,000 search engines. Other problems include the lack of limitations on the number of pages from any domain, which means there is so much space used that consumers have difficulty finding what they are looking for.

Key provisions of the search engine code of ethics include the following:

- Search engine optimization services shall not impose undue bandwidth burdens on search engines.
- Services shall abide by each search engine's page-submission guidelines and will not attempt to subvert them.
- No service shall say it can submit pages to more search engines than actually exist.
- No service shall engage in keyword repetition, page repetition, invisible hypertext markup language tags, or the use of robot pages.

D. Intellectual Property Issues in Cyberspace

Intellectual property rights have not changed simply because the Internet has facilitated the ability to copy everything from trademarks to songs with great ease. As noted in Chapter 10, intellectual property rights are protected for the sake of innovation. As in the other areas of law discussed to this point, the Internet simply presents new challenges for interpretation of copyright law. The ease of posting items to the internet and the ability to copy them quickly does not change the rights of copyright ownership. As with all other reproductions of work,

[13] Forty-six jurisdictions have adopted UETA. The states that have not adopted it are Georgia, Illinois, New York, and Washington.

[14] Maryland Commercial Law §§ 22-101 to 22-816, and Virginia Code §§ 59.1-501.1 to 59.1-509.2. Both laws can be found online: **http://www.uetaonline.com** and **http://www.ucitaonline.com.**

[15] Noelle Know, "Online Auctions Top List of Internet Fraud," *USA Today*, August 29, 2000, 1A.

[16] Arleene Weintraub and Jim Kerstetter, "Cyber Alert: Portrait of an Ex-Hacker," *Business Week*, June 9, 2003, 118.

permission to reproduce copyrighted work, either using a copy machine or the Internet, is required.[17]

Perhaps no case has brought to a head the discussion of intellectual property rights and their application to cyberspace than that of Napster. Shawn Fanning and Sean Parker, two college students who were then 19 and 20 years old, respectively, founded this company. Napster developed a software program that enabled users to download music files over the Internet at no cost.

The Napster litigation, as with that of other similar companies and programs, such as Grokster, has been either settled or fully litigated with arrangements for music companies to charge fees for access to music and then pay those fees to the copyright holders.

The Recording Industry Association of America (RIAA) has undertaken an aggressive litigation strategy against music downloaders. The first wave of lawsuits consisted of suits against 261 people who were considered the most active "file sharers" of music files. The lawsuits were accompanied by an offer of amnesty for downloaders who turned themselves in prior to having a suit filed against them.

Penalties for copyright infringement range from $750 to $150,000 per incident. In the past, the RIAA has settled the suits for an average of $3,000. However, four university students operating campus-wide file-sharing operations paid between $12,000 and $17,500 in July 2003.

The RIAA estimates that 11 million home computers actively share music files in one month. KaZaA is the most frequently used system, carrying 7.2 million computers. WinMX has 2.3 million homes, and the remaining systems all have fewer than 1 million users. A survey showed that 67 percent of downloaders did not care whether the music they were downloading was copyrighted.[18]

The legal issue in the music cases, as with all other Internet infringement cases, is one that has existed since the copyright laws were first passed: What is fair use of another's intellectual property? Related to this same question is the new technology practice of linking Web sites. Is it **fair use** or **infringement** to provide a link on a Web site to another Web site for copyrighted materials there? The Digital Millennium Copyright Act (DMCA)[19] was enacted as an amendment to federal copyright laws and makes clear that linking to a copyrighted site can constitute an infringement. **For Example,** in *Sega Enterprises, Ltd v MAPHIA*, 857 F Supp 679 (ND Cal 1994), the court held that the creator of a bulletin board that permitted the free downloading of computer games was in violation of the federal copyright laws.

Even when Web sites are not linked, is it fair use to reproduce without permission an article printed on one Web site that is free on another Web site? The universal access of the Web raises interesting questions about fair use. However, existing laws on copyrights and infringement provide the foundation for resolving issues presented for the first time because of new technology. The DMCA[20] makes it a federal offense to circumvent or create programs to circumvent encryption devices placed in copyrighted material to prevent unauthorized copying. **For Example,** circumventing the encryption devices on software or DVDs violates the DMCA.

Another issue that has resulted because of the universal access and availability of the Internet is that of disputes over names for Internet sites. In October 1999, the Internet Corporation for Assigned Names and Numbers (ICANN) approved the Uniform Domain Name Dispute Resolution Policy (UDRP). Prior to this policy, Network Solutions Inc. (NSI) had followed a policy of allowing trademark holders to halt the use of trademarked names for Web sites until the issue of ownership was resolved.

Under UDRP, the parties go through arbitration, and the current user continues to use the name until the matter is resolved. The UDRP also does not require a registration for a complainant to bring proceedings—the party can bring the action without registration and can base a complaint on a Web site's name being deceptively similar.

The first decision under UDRP was issued in January 2000 and granted the rights to the domain name of worldwidewrestlingfederation.com to the

[17] See *Lowry's Reports, Inc. v Legg Mason, Inc.*, 271 F Supp 2d 737 (D Md 2003) in which the employer was found liable for copyright infringement by its employees who posted subscription e-mail of financial newsletter on employer's intranet using employer's equipment and on company time, even though employees violated employer's policy not to do so.

[18] Amy Harmon, "261 Lawsuits Filed on Music Sharing," *New York Times*, September 9, 2003, A1, C6; Nick Wingfield, "The High Cost of Sharing," *Wall Street Journal*, September 9, 2003, B1, B8.

[19] 17 USC § 1201 *et seq.*

[20] *Id.*

Worldwide Wrestling Federation (WWF). Since then, 591 UDRP proceedings have commenced with 120 decisions.

In addition to the use of this international registration system, existing U.S. laws can help protect the identity and property of businesses. **For Example,** the Federal Trademark Dilution Act permits a company whose name is harmed or diluted through its use by another to bring suit for injunctions and damages. Also, the FTC's rules on trademark protection are equally applicable to the Internet.

E. Criminal Law Issues in Cyberspace

8. Nature and Types of Cyberspace Crimes

The FBI has labeled **cybercrime** "epidemic."[21] More than 25 percent of the Fortune 500 companies have fallen victim to computer crime.[22] A summer 2006 computer virus affected web cams on computers. As one expert put it, computer viruses cost the United States more than the total cost of the war in Afghanistan. One virus, known as the "Love Letter" virus, cost U.S. businesses $10 billion.[23] In 1999, one man was able to perpetrate a fraud of $45 million by simply making credit card charges to various credit cards from around the world with information he had gleaned by searching Web sites with consumer information.[24]

Computer crime is simply a more conventional crime carried out through the use of a computer. In other words, using someone else's credit card is fraud, whether you steal the credit card and hand it to the clerk or you use the card number through a transaction on the Web. Some crimes, however, owe their existence to the Internet. **For Example,** rerouting users from the domain they were trying to access to a pornographic Web site does not fit the elements of any particular common law crime, but it is a wrongful use of a computer and its systems. Likewise, using a computer to ensure that your call to a radio station will be answered before other callers' calls is wrong and an unlawful trespass into the radio station's system, but no common law crime covers it. Special computer crime statutes must be developed to deal with the use of computers to carry out new forms of fraud and unfair advantage.[25] Computers can be tools of the crime (**identity theft**), targets of crime (hacking into a system of another), or incidental to a crime (as when they are used for money laundering). Several new crimes have arisen as technology has evolved that are variations of the theft statutes. *Phishing* refers to sending e-mails that appear to be from banks and other account sources to get consumers to respond with their private financial information. *Pharming* is the term for a new tool that redirects consumers to another Web site (even when they have correctly entered the right address) so the redirected site can obtain financial information from the consumers.

Finally, the *evil twins phenomenon* consists of wireless networks that lure consumers to the networks by appearing to be legitimate Wi-Fi networks available in locations such as Starbucks, airports, and hotels. The Wi-Fi networks seem to be original and legitimate. However, they are simply created by hackers as the evil twin of the good Wi-Fi sites. The evil twin manipulators/hackers are just seeking financial information and passwords. Evil twins have also been known to infect computers with viruses.

The Internet has been used to transport pornography across state lines and to children; to facilitate contacts with children by pedophiles; to harass employees via e-mail; to stalk victims; to make threats of harm or death; to commit fraud; to facilitate bets and other means of illegal gambling; to commit industrial and economic espionage; to extort money; to sell controlled substances without authorization; to pirate software; to vandalize, trespass, and steal; to shut down companies and services; and even to facilitate terrorism.

In all of these forms of conduct, either an underlying criminal statute addresses the conduct (such as prohibitions on bribery, money laundering, and gambling) or computer-specific statutes have been passed to place a criminal sanction on such computer use. The statutes covering criminal laws specifically applicable to computer crime were

[21] **http://www.emergency.com**

[22] **http://www.jaring.my**

[23] **http://www.computereconomics.com**

[24] **http://www.computerworld.com/news/1999/**

[25] *United States v Peterson*, 98 F3d 502 (9th Cir 1996).

THINKING THINGS THROUGH

FREE-RIDERS AND PIGGYBACKING

A new issue that has evolved because of technology could require legal steps. Neighbors are *piggybacking* or tapping into their neighbors' wireless Internet connection. The original subscriber pays a monthly fee for the service but, without security, people in the area are able to tap into the wireless network and bog down the speed of the service. Once limited to geeks and hackers, the practice is now common among ordinary folk who just want free Internet service.

One college student said, "I don't think it's stealing. I always find people out there who aren't protecting their connection, so I just feel free to go ahead and use it."* According to a recent survey, only about 30 percent of the 4,500 wireless networks onto which the surveyors logged were encrypted.

An apartment dweller said she leaves her connection wide open because, "I'm sticking it to the man. I open up my network, leave it wide open for anyone to jump on." One of the users of another's wireless network said, "I feel sort of bad about it, but I do it anyway. It just seems harmless." She said that if she gets caught, "I'm a grandmother. They're not going to yell at an old lady. I'll just play the dumb card."

Some neighbors offer to pay those with wireless service in exchange for their occasional use rather than paying a wireless company for full-blown service. However, the original subscribers do not really want to run their own Internet service.

What possible crimes could be committed here? Do you think we need new legislation to cover this activity? What do you think of the users' statements?

*Michael Marriott, "Hey Neighbor, Stop Piggybacking on My Wireless," *New York Times*, March 5, 2006, A1, A23.

covered in Chapter 8 and include the Computer Fraud and Abuse Act[26] and the Economic Espionage Act (EEA).[27] Although the means of committing the crime can be different, the government is still required to prove that criminal intent existed and that the conduct committed using a computer meets the definition in the statute.

The same issue that has arisen with identifying music downloaders applies to criminal violations. Can the federal and state governments require ISPs and search engines to provide information to identify users or even to identify who is looking up what on the Internet? Google has objected to demands from the federal government that it release information about who is requesting what types of information, particularly when the information is related to child pornography. This question leads to issues related to the constitutional rights in criminal procedures for violations of laws related to Internet use and abuse.

9. Criminal Procedure and Rights in Cyberspace

Another issue that arises because of cyberspace relates to **warrants.** Can government law enforcement authorities obtain access to computer information for the purposes of investigating a crime? The Fourth Amendment applies not only to searches of offices and homes but also to searches of computers. Indeed, when a warrant specifies that the officers search computers and files, at least one court has ordered that the warrant be specific as to whether it includes home and/or office computers and files.[28] The protection against unlawful searches and seizures has not changed; only the objects being

[26] 18 USC § 1030 (2002).

[27] 18 USC § 1831 *et seq.* (2002).

[28] *United States v Hunter*, 13 F Supp 2d 574 (D Vt 1998).

THINKING THINGS THROUGH

COLLEGE CAMPUSES AND CYBERSPACE

Colleges and universities continue to work to help students understand that what they post on the Web is not private information and can often have unintended consequences. The following examples resulted in student disciplinary proceedings:

- Several students at The Ohio State University boasted on Facebook (a networking/socializing site) that they had stormed the field after Ohio State beat Penn State and had taken part in what erupted into a riot. Law enforcement officials were able to trace the students through the university system, and 50 Ohio State students were referred to the office of judicial affairs.
- Students at the University of Mississippi stated on an open site that they wanted to have sex with a professor.
- A student at Fisher College threatened to take steps to silence a campus police officer.

Another problem with the open sites is that the students are posting personal information with which stalkers and others can access them. These nefarious individuals can then easily obtain students' cell phone numbers, addresses, whereabouts, and other information.

The most popular college site, Facebook, indicates that students spend an average of 17 minutes per day on the site. A great deal of information can be conveyed during that time period. Students do so without thinking through the possibility that outsiders with bad intentions could be seeking and using information about them that is posted there.

As a result of the increased activity levels on Web sites and related problems, many colleges and universities are offering sessions on Internet security and safety to their entering students. Helping students understand issues of privacy and risk is a critical part of orientation.

What legal and ethical issues do you see in the types of comments that students make on these sites and in the sites themselves? Why and how can the colleges and universities obtain information from these sites without a warrant?

Source: For more information, see Brock Read, "THINK Before You Share," *Chronicle of Higher Education*, January 20, 2006, A38–A40.

searched have become more sophisticated, and a warrant can include them as well, so long as it specifies the extent of the computer and file search. Just as in the case of the employer access and the music downloaders, the question for the courts is whether Internet users who are identified only by their screen names have an expectation of privacy.

F. Constitutional Restraints and Protections in Cyberspace

The constitutional issues that have arisen as a result of the new technology cover everything from the First Amendment to the commerce clause and involve issues ranging from pornography to taxation to Fourth Amendment searches.

10. First Amendment Rights in Cyberspace

The Internet is a method of communication. Some speech on the Internet is commercial, but other forms of speech involve communications relating to voting and ballot initiatives. Speech on the Internet enjoys constitutional protection, but the Internet has also facilitated the transport of pornography with great ease because photos can be sent from computer to computer. The presence of pornography on the Internet and the ease of access that children have to that material have presented challenges for regulation. The Child Pornography Prevention Act[29] made it a crime to knowingly sell, possess, or distribute child pornography on the Web. However, the U.S. Supreme Court ruled that the statute was void for both vagueness and violating First Amendment rights.[30]

11. Commerce Clause Issues in Cyberspace

The commerce clause has also come into play with the Internet because of the desire of both the states and the federal government to tax the transactions taking place via the Internet. The U.S. Constitution requires that there be some "nexus" between the taxing authority and the business paying the tax (see Chapter 4 for more information on constitutional issues in taxation), and many questions arise about the constitutionality of taxing Internet sales because of the lack of "bricks and mortar" in these businesses. Some Internet retailers are located in one state and have no contact, physically, with any other states. Their only contact is through the computers of their customers, who may be located in all 50 states. Is it constitutional for Colorado to tax a New Jersey company operating out of a small office in Trenton? Although the nature of business has changed, the constitutional tests remain the same; and courts will simply apply the standards of fairness and allocation that they have relied on in other eras as businesses grew in reach even though their physical locations did not change.

The Internet Tax Freedom Act (ITFA)[31] has been renewed. The ITFA provides that states and local governments cannot tax Internet access. Contrary to popular belief, ITFA does not suspend sales taxes on transactions over the Internet. However, the same constitutional standards that apply to sales via catalog and phone to residents of other states also apply to the taxation of sales over the Internet. To tax such sales, the seller must have some physical presence in the state or a pattern of distribution and doing business there. **For Example,** Nordstrom might not have stores located in a particular state, but it would be required to collect sales taxes from sales to residents of that state if it had warehouse facilities in that state. Refer to Chapter 3 for a full discussion of the Internet and sales tax.

12. Due Process Issues in Cyberspace

Related to the nexus doctrine and taxation of Internet sales is the issue of whether an Internet business site with few physical facilities and no real presence in other states can be required to travel to the states where its customers are to litigate cases brought by those customers. The notion of long-arm jurisdiction (see Chapter 4) becomes even more critical because of the Internet. When does a company have a sufficient presence in a state that requires it to defend a lawsuit in that state? The answer is the same as the answer for the presence of a "bricks and mortar" business. Is requiring the Internet retailer to come to a state to defend a lawsuit fair, or does it offend notions of justice and fair play? Is reaching out to customers in a state through the Internet sufficient to require the Internet company to come to that state and defend lawsuits brought by those customers, or should the customers be required to travel to the state where the Internet company is located?

G. Securities Law Issues in Cyberspace

The Internet has facilitated access to the capital markets. The existence of computers have led to *day traders*, investors who have online second-by-second financial information about companies as well as the ability to track trades in order to buy and sell stock. However, this universal access means an increase in the players in the market, and those players have often used tactics not entirely within the boundaries of the existing legal framework or the level playing field so important in the stock markets.

One practice that has begun is **pump-and-dump** through which a trader buys a certain stock and then posts information on the Web to increase interest in it, which drives up its price. When the price has climbed to a sufficiently high level, the trader sells it and walks away with the profits earned by the hype she created on the Web. The tactic is new and the

[29] 18 USC § 2252 *et seq.* (2002).

[30] *United States v Hilton*, 167 F3d 61 (1st Cir 1999), *cert denied*, 528 US 844 (1999); *United States v Acheson*, 195 F3d 645 (11th Cir 1999); and *Free Speech Coalition v Reno*, 220 F3d 1113 (9th Cir 1999), *cert granted as Ashcroft v Free Speech Coalition*, 535 US 234 (2002).

[31] Pub. L. No. 105-277, originally enacted on October 21, 1998, and renewed on November 16, 2001.

response time faster, but the practice of pump-and-dump is nothing more than securities fraud. The trader is spreading false information and then trading on that information to personal advantage.

So pervasive is the practice of pump-and-dump that 15-year-old Jonathan Lebed successfully employed it to turn his $8,000 in savings into $800,000 in stock gains. He became the first minor ever prosecuted by the Securities and Exchange Commission (SEC) for securities fraud. His penalty was to repay the gains that he made.[32]

Existing securities laws also cover other issues that have emerged with cyberspace companies. **For Example,** America Online entered into a consent decree with the SEC for its accounting practices in which the company predicted sales on the basis of advertising expenses. The SEC found the model for predicting sales untested and misleading. The advertising methods and the company and its technology were all new, but the same securities principles and laws applied: The financial projections must be based on adequate information.[33]

32 Gretchen Morgenson, "S.E.C. Says Teenager Had After-School Hobby: Online Stock Fraud," *New York Times*, September 21, 2000, A1, C10.

33 Floyd Norris, "AOL Pays a Fine to Settle a Charge That It Inflated Profits," *New York Times*, May 16, 2000, C6.

Summary

The term *cyberlaw* seems to indicate a new body of law that exists or is being created to manage all of the legal issues of the cybereconomy, cyberspace, and cybertechnology. Even though some new criminal statutes have been enacted to address specific types of computer crimes, the law, with its great flexibility, has been able to easily adapt to address many of the legal issues that affect the new economy in cyberspace.

Six existing areas of law apply to cyberspace: tort issues, contract issues, intellectual property issues, criminal violations, constitutional restraints and protections, and securities law issues.

In tort law, the issues that arise on the Internet relate to privacy and defamation. In contracts, the issues center around formation and signatures, as well as the need for diligence in handling fraud and misrepresentation in the course of formation of contracts. Infringement and fair use are the key topics of intellectual property law that arise through the Internet. Although some peculiar issues such as linking Web sites and copyrighted materials or the types of domain names that may be used exist, the laws to address these new ways of possible infringement of others' intellectual property rights are in place. Criminal violations remain centered around the crimes of trespass and theft. Computers are either used to commit crimes or become the object of crimes, and both old criminal statutes and new ones protect property from harm, even on the Internet. The Constitution still applies to questions of jurisdiction and taxation. The standards of fairness still apply, and courts simply face the issue of whether a company is present because the Internet is available in every state and country. Finally, securities fraud is securities fraud whether committed face-to-face, by paper, by phone, or by chat room.

Questions and Case Problems

1. In the midst of the litigation surrounding its program for downloading music, Napster, Inc., discovered that a company was selling t-shirts with its logo on them. Can Napster do anything to prevent the use of its logo? Is the use of the logo for t-shirts any different from the use of songs for purposes of downloading for individual listening?
2. The *New York Times* discovered that 24 of the employees in its payroll processing center were sending "inappropriate and offensive e-mail in violation of corporate policy." Do the employees have any right to privacy with regard to the jokes they send over their e-mail accounts at work? Applying what you have learned about the nature of cyberlaw, determine whether, under existing sexual harassment laws, a company could be held liable for harassment via e-mails.
3. Daniel Dagesse suffered serious injuries when he slipped and fell in his hotel room at the Aruba Marriott Resort (the Plant Hotel). He sued Plant Hotel N.V., the limited liability company that owns the resort; Oranjestad Property Management N.V., Plant Hotel's parent company; Marriott Aruba N.V., the company that manages the resort; and Marriott International, Inc., a corporation that was the agent and management company for Plant Hotel and Oranjestad. Elaine Dagesse, Daniel's wife, also filed suit against the same companies alleging loss of consortium. The Dagesses filed suit in federal district court in New Hampshire, seeking to have the companies

come and defend the lawsuit there. The companies filed a motion to dismiss on the grounds that they had no physical presence in the state of New Hampshire. The Dagesses contended that all of the companies operated an interactive Web site to which they went and through which they made their reservations as they sat in their home in New Hampshire, and that this Web site resulted in New Hampshire's jurisdiction over the companies. Were they correct? [*Dagesse v Plant Hotel N.V.*, 113 F Supp 2d 211 (D NH)]

4. List the areas of law that apply in cyberspace and explain why they are still applicable even though the nature of commerce has changed.
5. On July 24, 2002, the Recording Industry Association of America (RIAA) served its first subpoena to obtain the identity of a Verizon subscriber alleged to have made more than 600 copyrighted songs available for downloading over the Internet through peer-to-peer file transfer software provided by KaZaA. Verizon claimed that because RIAA's subpoena related to material transmitted over Verizon's network—rather than stored on it—it fell outside the scope of the subpoena power. Should the subpoena be quashed as Verizon requests, or should it be honored? [*In re Verizon Internet Services, Inc.*, 257 F Supp 2d 244 (DDC)]
6. Glenayre Electronics announced to its employees that it could inspect the laptops it furnished for its employees to use. An employee challenged the inspection of his laptop as a violation of his privacy. Could the company search the laptops? [*Muick v Glenayre Electronics*, 280 F3d 741 (7th Cir)]
7. A state university provided a written notice to employees that their computers could be monitored and added a splash screen with the same notice that appears on the computers each time employees start their computers. Has the university done enough to allow monitoring without invading employee privacy? Would it make any difference if the employees had a password for their e-mail access and computer access? What about state public records law? Would employee e-mails be subject to public disclosure because the e-mails would be considered public record? [*U.S. v Angevine*, 281 F3d 1130 (10th Cir)]
8. APTC, a publicly traded corporation, filed a complaint, captioned "*Anonymous Publicly Traded Company v John Does 1 through 5*," asserting that the John Doe defendants, whose identities and residences were unknown, "made defamatory and disparaging material misrepresentations" about APTC in Internet chat rooms. APTC asserted its belief that the John Doe defendants were current and/or former employees who breached their fiduciary duties and contractual obligations by publishing "confidential material insider information" about APTC on the Internet. Although it did not specify what harm would be incurred by identifying itself, APTC contended that it had to proceed anonymously "because disclosure of its true company name will cause it irreparable harm." APTC wanted the court to issue subpoenas to the ISP to determine the identity of the John Does. How do you think the court will decide on the issue of the John Does' identity? [*America Online, Inc. v Anonymous Publicly Traded Co.*, 542 SE2d 377 (Va)]
9. In response to legal cases in which companies have had their internal e-mails used to their disadvantage, several companies have developed programs that automatically destroy e-mails once they have been opened and read on the other end. Is it legal and ethical to destroy e-mails on a regular basis such as this? To visit an e-mail destruction site, go to **http://www.authentica.com** or **http://www.qvtech.com.**
10. Scott McNealy, the founder of Sun MicroSystems, made the following statement in response to questions about privacy and the Internet: "You have zero privacy, anyway. . . . Get over it."[34] Evaluate his statement and its implications for cyberlaw and ethics in cyberspace transactions.
11. Immunomedics, Inc., has discovered sensitive information about its technology posted on various Web sites and chat rooms. The information is so proprietary that it could have come only from company employees, all of whom have signed agreements not to disclose such information. Those who posted the information used screen names, and Immunomedics has asked the court to issue a subpoena to the ISP so that it can determine the identity of those posting the information and recover for breach of contract and trade secret infringement. Should the court issue the subpoena? [*Immunomedics, Inc. v Does 1–10*, 2001 WL 770389 (NJ Super)]
12. Jane Doe filed a complaint against Richard Lee Russell and America Online (AOL) to recover for alleged emotional injuries suffered by her son, John Doe. Doe claimed that in 1994, Russell lured John Doe, who was then 11 years old, and two other minor males to engage in sexual activity with each other and with Russell. She asserted that Russell photographed and videotaped these acts and used AOL's chat rooms to market the photographs and videotapes and to sell a videotape. Doe did not allege that Russell transmitted photographs or images of her son via the AOL service. In her six-count complaint, Doe claimed that AOL violated criminal statutes and that AOL was negligent *per se* in distributing an advertisement offering "a visual depiction of sexual conduct involving [John Doe]" and by allowing Russell

[34] Polly Sprenger, "Sun on Privacy: 'Get Over It,'" *Wired News*, January 26, 1999, at **http://www.wired.com/news/politics/0,1283,17538,00.html**.

to sell or arrange to sell child pornography, thus aiding in the sale and distribution of child pornography, including obscene images of John Doe. Does Mrs. Doe have a cause of action? What laws discussed in this chapter apply? [*Doe v America Online, Inc.*, 783 So 2d 1010 (Fla)]

13. Customers of a chat room are using the chat room, Maphia, for access to each other and to transfer Sega games to each other. They are able to avoid paying the $19 to $60 the games cost for purchase in the stores. The users say they are simply transferring files and that there is no crime. The chat room says it cannot stop customers from interacting. Do you think there are any civil or criminal law violations in their conduct? [*Sega Enterprises, Ltd. v Maphia*, 857 F Supp 679 (ND Cal)]

14. The police intercepted a telephone call that one of its informants placed from the police station where he was working with officers. All of the informant's phone calls were being monitored with his consent. The informant called the defendant at his home. Based on the content of that conversation, officers were able to obtain a warrant that permitted them to search the luggage of the defendant who was arriving in Miami from an overseas trip. The defendant's luggage contained cocaine. When the defendant was charged with possession of drugs, he challenged the warrant because it was based on an invasion of privacy of his phone conversation with the informant. The informant did not realize that this particular conversation was being monitored. Is there an expectation of privacy in phone conversations at the police station? Is there an expectation of privacy by the defendant for phone calls in his home? The police argue they were allowed to intercept the calls because the technology was available and because one side had consented. Was the warrant valid? [*Commonwealth v Rekasie*, 778 A2d 624 (Pa)]

15. On October 21, 1999, Amazon.com (Amazon) brought suit against Barnesandnoble.com (BN) alleging infringement of its patent for its one-click order system. Amazon's patent is directed to a method and system for "single-action" ordering of items in a client/server environment such as the Internet. The patent describes a method and system in which a consumer can complete a purchase order for an item via an electronic network using only a "single action," such as the click of a computer mouse button on the client computer system. Amazon developed the patent to cope with what it considered to be frustrations presented by what is known as the "shopping cart model" purchase system for electronic commerce. BN alleges that there is nothing unique about the system that warrants a patent and that its ordering system and that of other dot.com retailers is simply a convenience, not a patentable idea. What laws will the courts apply to this intellectual property dispute for Internet merchants? Are the laws the same for patents on devices and products? [*Amazon.com, Inc. v Barnesandnoble.com*, 239 F3d 1343 (Fed Cir)]

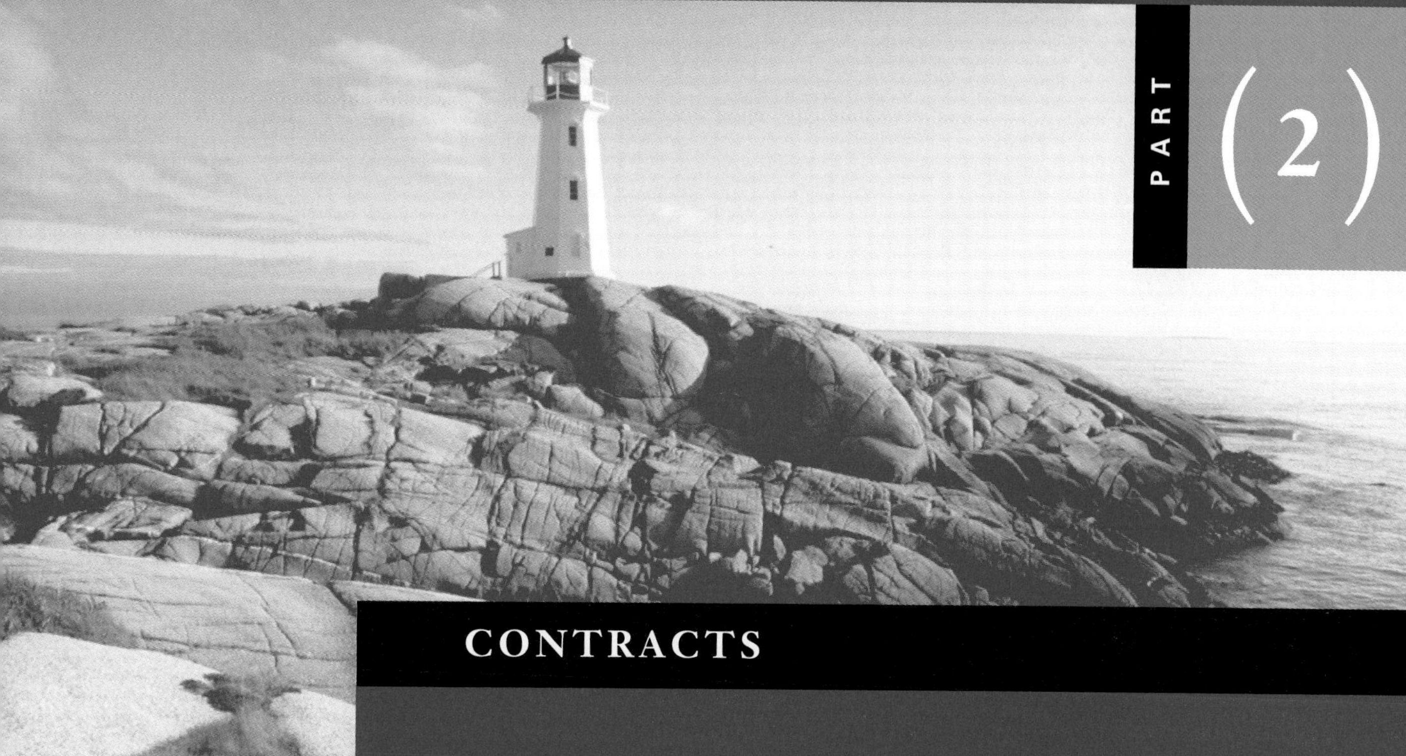

PART (2)

CONTRACTS

NATURE AND CLASSES OF CONTRACTS: CONTRACTING ON THE INTERNET

CHAPTER (12)

LEARNING OBJECTIVES

After studying this chapter, you should be able to

LO.1 List the essential elements of a contract

LO.2 Describe the way in which a contract arises

LO.3 State how contracts are classified

LO.4 Differentiate contracts from agreements that are not contracts

LO.5 Differentiate formal contracts from simple contracts

LO.6 Differentiate express contracts from implied contracts

LO.7 Differentiate contractual liability from quasi-contractual liability

Practically every business transaction affecting people involves a contract.

A. Nature of Contracts

This introductory chapter will familiarize you with the terminology needed to work with contract law. In addition, the chapter introduces quasi contracts, which are not true contracts but obligations imposed by law.

1. Definition of a Contract

A **contract** is a legally binding agreement.[1] By one definition, "a contract is a promise or a set of promises for the breach of which the law gives a remedy, or the performance of which the law in some way recognizes as a duty."[2] Contracts arise out of agreements, so a contract may be defined as an agreement creating an obligation.

The substance of the definition of a contract is that by mutual agreement or assent, the parties create enforceable duties or obligations. That is, each party is legally bound to do or to refrain from doing certain acts.

2. Elements of a Contract

The elements of a contract are (1) an agreement (2) between competent parties (3) based on the genuine assent of the parties that is (4) supported by consideration, (5) made for a lawful objective, and (6) in the form required by law, if any. These elements will be considered in the chapters that follow.

3. Subject Matter of Contracts

The subject matter of a contract may relate to the performance of personal services, such as contracts of employment to work developing computer software or to play professional football. A contract may provide for the transfer of ownership of property, such as a house (real property) or an automobile (personal property), from one person to another.

4. Parties to a Contract

The person who makes a promise is the **promisor,** and the person to whom the promise is made is the **promisee**. If the promise is binding, it imposes on the promisor a duty or obligation, and the promisor may be called the **obligor.** The promisee who can claim the benefit of the obligation is called the **obligee.** The parties to a contract are said to stand in **privity** with each other, and the relationship between them is termed **privity of contract.** **For Example,** when the state of North Carolina and the architectural firm of O'Brien/Atkins Associates executed a contract for the construction of a new building at the University of North Carolina, Chapel Hill, these parties were in privity of contract. However, a building contractor, RPR & Associates, who worked on the project did not have standing to sue on the contract between the architect and the state because the contractor was not in privity of contract.[3]

In written contracts, parties may be referred to by name. More often, however, they are given special names that better identify each party. For example, consider a contract by which one person agrees that another may occupy a house upon the payment of money. The parties to this contract are called *landlord* and *tenant*, or *lessor* and *lessee*, and the contract between them is known as a *lease*. Parties to other types of contracts also have distinctive names, such as *vendor* and *vendee* for the parties to a sales contract, *shipper* and *carrier* for the parties to a transportation contract, and *insurer* and *insured* for the parties to an insurance policy.

A party to a contract may be an individual, a partnership, a limited liability company, a corporation, or a government.[4] One or more persons may be on each side of a contract. Some contracts are three-sided, as in a credit card transaction, which involves the company issuing the card, the holder of the card,

[1] The Uniform Commercial Code defines *contract* as "the total legal obligation which results from the parties' agreement as affected by [the UCC] and any other applicable rules of law." UCC § 1–201(11).

[2] Restatement (Second) of Contracts § 1.

[3] *RPR & Associates v O'Brien/Atkins Associates, P.A.*, 24 F Supp 2d 515 (MDNC 1998). See also *Roof Techs Int. Inc. v State*, 57 P3d 538 (Kan App 2002), where a layer of litigation was avoided regarding lawsuits involving the renovation of the Farrell Library at Kansas State University. The state was the only party in privity of contract with the architectural firm and would thus have to bring claims against the architectural firm on behalf of all of the contractors. Two subcontractors, the general contractor, and the owner of the library, the state of Kansas, used a settlement and liquidation agreement assigning all of the state's claims against the architect to the general contractor.

[4] See *Purina Mills, LLC v Less*, 295 F Supp 2d 1017 (ND Iowa 2003) in which the pig-seller plaintiff, which converted from a corporation to a limited liability company (LLC) while the contract was in effect, was a proper party in interest and could maintain a contract action against defendant buyers.

and the business furnishing goods and services on the basis of the credit card.

If a contract is written, the persons who are the parties and who are bound by it can ordinarily be determined by reading what the document says and seeing how it is signed. A contract binds only the parties to the contract. It cannot impose a duty on a person who is not a party to it. Ordinarily, only a party to a contract has any rights against another party to the contract.[5] In some cases, third persons have rights on a contract as third-party beneficiaries or assignees. A person cannot be bound, however, by the terms of a contract to which that person is not a party.[6]

5. How a Contract Arises

A contract is based on an agreement. An agreement arises when one person, the **offeror,** makes an offer and the person to whom the offer is made, the **offeree,** accepts. There must be both an offer and an acceptance. If either is lacking, there is no contract.

6. Intent to Make a Binding Agreement

Because a contract is based on the consent of the parties and is a legally binding agreement, it follows that the parties must have an intent to enter into an agreement that is binding. Sometimes the parties are in agreement, but their agreement does not produce a contract. Sometimes there is merely a preliminary agreement, but the parties never actually make a contract, or there is merely an agreement as to future plans or intentions without any contractual obligation to carry out those plans or intentions.

7. Freedom of Contract

In the absence of some ground for declaring a contract void or voidable, parties may make such contracts as they choose. The law does not require parties to be fair, or kind, or reasonable, or to share gains or losses equitably.

B. Classes of Contracts

Contracts may be classified according to their form, the way in which they were created, their binding character, and the extent to which they have been performed.

8. Formal and Informal Contracts

Contracts can be classified as formal or informal.

(a) Formal Contracts

Formal contracts are enforced because the formality with which they are executed is considered sufficient to signify that the parties intend to be bound by their terms. Formal contracts include (1) **contracts under seal** where a person's signature or a corporation's name is followed by a scroll, the word *seal,* or the letters *L.S.*;[7] (2) contracts of record, which are obligations that have been entered before a court of record, sometimes called a **recognizance;** and (3) negotiable instruments.

(b) Informal Contracts

All contracts other than formal contracts are called **informal** (or simple) **contracts** without regard to whether they are oral or written. These contracts are enforceable, not because of the form of the transaction but because they represent agreement of the parties.

9. Express and Implied Contracts

Simple contracts may be classified as express *contracts* or *implied contracts* according to the way they are created.

(a) Express Contracts

An **express contract** is one in which the terms of the agreement of the parties are manifested by their words, whether spoken or written.

(b) Implied Contracts

An **implied contract** (or, as sometimes stated, a *contract implied in fact*) is one in which the agreement is shown not by words, written or spoken, but by the acts and conduct of the parties.[8] Such a contract arises when (1) a person renders services under circumstances indicating that payment for them is expected and (2) the other person, knowing such circumstances, accepts the benefit of those services. **For Example,** when a building owner requests a

[5] *Hooper v Yakima County,* 904 P2d 1193 (Wash App 1995).

[6] *Walsh v Telesector Resources Group, Inc.,* 662 NE2d 1043 (Mass App 1996).

[7] Some authorities explain *L.S.* as an abbreviation for *locus sigilium* (place for the seal).

[8] *Janusauskas v Fichman,* 793 A2d 1109 (Conn App 2002).

FIGURE 12-1 Contractual Liability

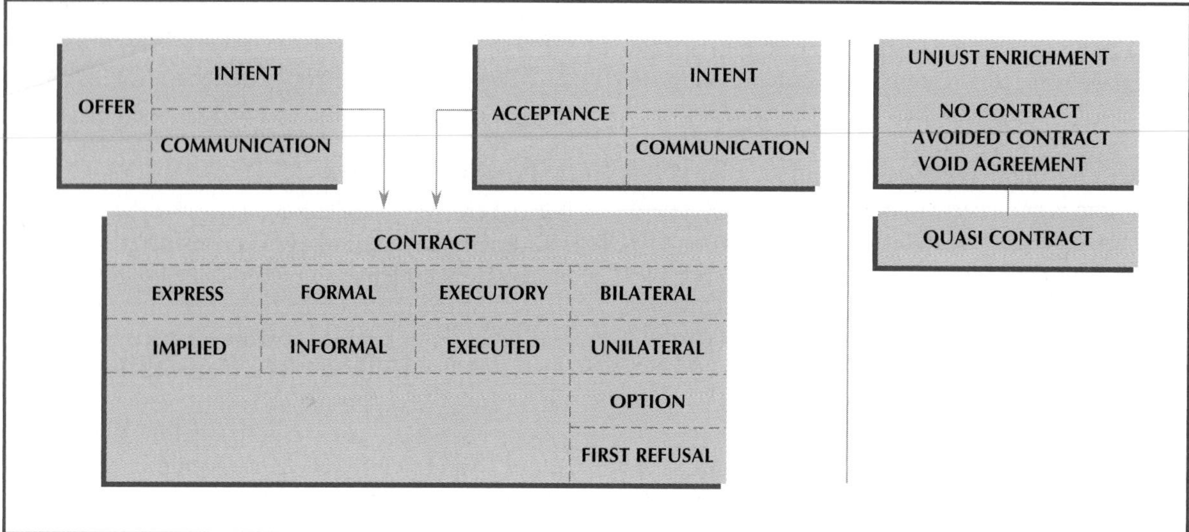

professional roofer to make emergency repairs to the roof of a building, an obligation arises to pay the reasonable value of such services, although no agreement has been made about compensation.

An implied contract cannot arise when there is an existing express contract on the same subject.[9] However, the existence of a written contract does not bar recovery on an implied contract for extra work that was not covered by the contract.

10. Valid and Voidable Contracts and Void Agreements

Contracts may be classified in terms of enforceability or validity.

(a) Valid Contracts

A **valid contract** is an agreement that is binding and enforceable.

(b) Voidable Contracts

A **voidable contract** is an agreement that is otherwise binding and enforceable, but because of the circumstances surrounding its execution or the lack of capacity of one of the parties, it may be rejected at the option of one of the parties. **For Example,** a person who has been forced to sign an agreement that that person would not have voluntarily signed may, in some instances, avoid the contract.

(c) Void Agreements

A **void agreement** is without legal effect. An agreement that contemplates the performance of an act prohibited by law is usually incapable of enforcement; hence it is void. Likewise, it cannot be made binding by later approval or ratification.

11. Executed and Executory Contracts

Contracts may be classified as *executed contracts* and *executory contracts* according to the extent to which they have been performed.

(a) Executed Contracts

An **executed contract** is one that has been completely performed. In other words, an executed contract is one under which nothing remains to be done by either party.[10] A contract may be executed immediately, as in the case of a cash sale, or it may be executed or performed in the future.

(b) Executory Contracts

In an **executory contract,** something remains to be done by one or both parties.[11] **For Example,** on July 10, Mark agreed to sell to Chris his Pearl drum set for $600, the terms being $200 upon delivery on July 14, with $200 to be paid on July 21, and the final

[9] *Pepsi-Cola Bottling Co. of Pittsburgh, Inc., v PepsiCo, Inc.*, 431 F3d 1241 (10th Cir 2000).
[10] *Marsh v Rheinecker*, 641 NE2d 1256 (Ill App 1994).
[11] *DiGeneraro v Rubbermaid, Inc.*, 214 F Supp 2d 1354 (SD Fla 2002).

FIGURE 12-2 Contract

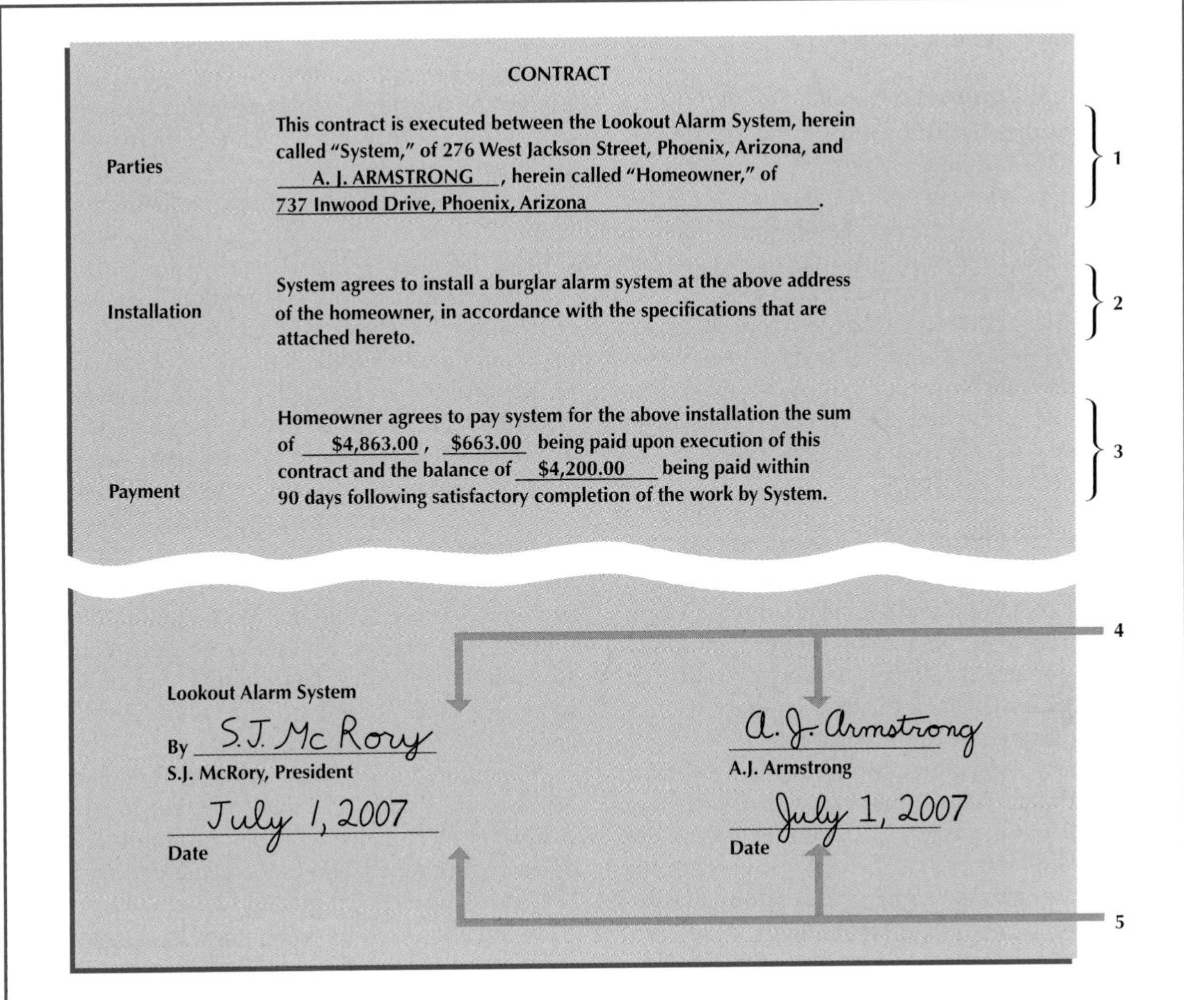
CONTRACT

Parties — This contract is executed between the Lookout Alarm System, herein called "System," of 276 West Jackson Street, Phoenix, Arizona, and A. J. ARMSTRONG, herein called "Homeowner," of 737 Inwood Drive, Phoenix, Arizona. 1

Installation — System agrees to install a burglar alarm system at the above address of the homeowner, in accordance with the specifications that are attached hereto. 2

Payment — Homeowner agrees to pay system for the above installation the sum of $4,863.00, $663.00 being paid upon execution of this contract and the balance of $4,200.00 being paid within 90 days following satisfactory completion of the work by System. 3

4

Lookout Alarm System

By S.J. McRory
S.J. McRory, President

July 1, 2007
Date

A.J. Armstrong
A.J. Armstrong

July 1, 2007
Date

5

Note that this contract includes the following important information: (1) the name and address of each party, (2) the promise or consideration of the seller, (3) the promise or consideration of the buyer, (4) the signature of the two parties, and (5) the date.

$200 being due July 28. Prior to the July 14 delivery of the drums to Chris, the contract was entirely executory. After the delivery by Mark, the contract was executed as to Mark and executory as to Chris until the final payment was received on July 28.

12. Bilateral and Unilateral Contracts

In making an offer, the offeror is in effect extending a promise to do something, such as pay a sum of money, if the offeree will do what the offeror requests. Contracts are classified as *bilateral* or *unilateral*. Some bilateral contracts look ahead to the making of a later contract. Depending on their terms, these are called *option contracts* or *first-refusal contracts*.

(a) Bilateral Contract

If the offeror extends a promise and asks for a promise in return and if the offeree accepts the offer by making the promise, the contract is called a **bilateral contract**. One promise is given in exchange for another, and each party is bound by the obligation. **For Example,** when the house painter offers to paint the owner's house for

$3,700 and the owner promises to pay $3,700 for the job, there is an exchange of promises, and the agreement gives rise to a bilateral contract.

(b) Unilateral Contract

In contrast with a bilateral contract, the offeror may promise to do something or to pay a certain amount of money only when the offeree does an act.[12] **For Example,** suppose the Tyler family posts notices throughout the community offering to pay a $100 reward for the safe return of their lost golden retriever puppy, Henry. A contract is formed when the finder, Billy Sullivan, returns the puppy to the Tylers. It is a **unilateral contract** because only one party, the Tylers, made a promise, and the Tylers were obligated to perform only when the contract was formed by Billy's action of returning the puppy.

(c) Option and First-Refusal Contracts

The parties may make a contract that gives a right to one of them to enter into a second contract at a later date. If one party has an absolute right to enter into the later contract, the initial contract is called an **option contract**. Thus, a bilateral contract may be made today giving one of the parties the right to buy the other party's house for a specified amount. This is an option contract because the party with the privilege has the freedom of choice, or option, to buy or not buy. If the option is exercised, the other party to the contract must follow the terms of the option and enter into the second contract. If the option is never exercised, no second contract ever arises, and the offer protected by the option contract merely expires.

In contrast with an option contract, a contract may merely give a **right of first refusal**. This imposes only the duty to make the first offer to the party having the right of first refusal.

13. Quasi Contracts

In some cases, a court will impose an obligation even though there is no contract.[13] Such an obligation is called a **quasi contract**, which is an obligation imposed by law.

(a) Prevention of Unjust Enrichment

A quasi contract is not a true contract reflecting all of the elements of a contract set forth previously in this chapter. The court is not seeking to enforce the intentions of the parties contained in an agreement. Rather, when a person or enterprise receives a benefit from another, even in the absence of a promise to pay for the benefit, a court may impose an obligation to pay for the reasonable value of that benefit, to avoid *unjust enrichment*.

A successful claim for unjust enrichment usually requires (1) a benefit conferred on the defendant, (2) the defendant's knowledge of the benefit, and (3) a finding that it would be unjust for the defendant to retain the benefit without payment. The burden of proof is on the plaintiff to prove all of the elements of the claim. **For Example,** Hiram College sued Nicholas Courtad for $6,000 plus interest for tuition and other expenses. Because no evidence of a written contract was produced, the court considered it an unjust enrichment claim by the college. Courtad had attended classes for a few weeks and had not paid his tuition due to a problem with his financial aid package. Because he did not receive any credit hours toward a degree, which is the ultimate benefit of attending college, the court found that he did not receive a benefit and that a finding of unjust enrichment was not appropriate.[14]

Sometimes a contract may be unenforceable because of a failure to set forth the contract in writing in compliance with the statute of frauds. In other circumstances, no enforceable contract exists because of a lack of definite and certain terms. Yet in both situations, one party may have performed services for the benefit of the other party and the court will require payment of the reasonable value of services to avoid the unjust enrichment of the party receiving the services without paying for them. These damages are sometimes referred to as *restitution damages*. Some courts refer to this situation as an action or recovery in *quantum meruit* (as much as he or she deserved).

For Example, Arya Group, Inc. (Arya), sued the entertainer Cher for unjust enrichment. In June 1996, Cher negotiated an oral agreement with Arya to design and construct a house on her Malibu property for $4,217,529. The parties' oral agreement was set forth in a written contract with an August 1997 date and was delivered to Cher in October 1997. She never signed it. However, between June

[12] See *Young v Virginia Birth-Related Neurological Injury Compensation Program*, 620 SE2d 131 (Va App 2005).
[13] *Thayer v Dial Industrial Sales, Inc.*, 85 F Supp 2d 263 (SDNY 2000).
[14] *Hiram College v Courtad*, 834 NE2d 432 (Ohio App 2005).

1996 and November 1997, Arya performed and received payment for a number of services discharged under the unsigned contract. In August 1997, Cher requested Arya to meet with a home designer named Bussell who had previously worked with Cher on a Florida project, and Arya showed Bussell the plans and designs for the Malibu property and introduced her to his subcontractors. In November 1997, Cher terminated her agreement with Arya without paying the balance then due, as asserted by Arya, of $415,169.41. Arya claims that Cher and Bussell misappropriated the plans and designs Arya had prepared. Cher and the other defendants demurred to Arya's unjust enrichment complaint, pointing out that construction contracts must be evidenced in a writing signed by both parties under state law in order to be enforceable in a court of law. The appeals court determined that Arya's noncompliance with the state law requiring a signed written contract did not absolutely foreclose Arya from seeking damages for unjust enrichment if he could prove the assertions in the complaint that Cher was a sophisticated homeowner with previous involvement in residential construction, who had legal representation in negotiating the agreement with Arya, and Cher would be unjustly enriched if she were not required to compensate Arya for the reasonable value of the work already performed.[15]

A situation may arise over the mistaken conferrence of a benefit. **For Example,** Nantucket Island has a few approved colors for houses in its historic district. Using the approved gray color, Martin Kane and his crew began painting Sheldon Adams's house in the historic district as the result of a mistaken address. Adams observed the initiation of the work from his office across the street but did nothing to stop the painters. At the end of the day when the work was done, Adams refused to pay for the work, saying, "I signed no contract and never approved this work." The law deems it inequitable that Adams should have received the benefit of this work, having observed the benefit being conferred and knowing that the painters expected payment. Adams would be unjustly enriched if he were allowed to retain the benefit without payment for the reasonable value of the work. If Adams did not have knowledge that the work was being done and thus that payment was expected, quasi-contractual liability would not be imposed.

The mistake that benefits the defendant may be the mistake of a third party.

(b) Extent of Recovery

When recovery is allowed in quasi contract, the plaintiff recovers the reasonable value of the benefit conferred on the defendant,[16] or the fair and reasonable[17] value of the work performed, depending on the jurisdiction. Thus, the plaintiff cannot recover lost profits or other kinds of damages that would be recovered in a suit for breach of a contract.

For Example, Peabody New England, Inc., is in the business of constructing waste system facilities for cities and towns. A facility that Peabody contracted to build for the town of Marshfield was not completed on time. The project's completion date was delayed in part by the contractor's mismanagement. The town also contributed to the delays. The court refused to allow Peabody to recover under the terms of the contract because Peabody did not live up to the contract's terms. However, the court did allow limited damages to Peabody for the reasonable value of the services rendered, an amount that was less than the contract price and did not include lost profits and "overhead" expenses.[18]

THINKING THINGS THROUGH

TWELVE YEARS OF LITIGATION

Brown University accepted the bid of Marshall Contractors, Inc. (Marshall), to build the Pizzitola Sports Facility on its Providence, Rhode Island, campus. The parties intended to execute a formal written contract. Brown decided to pay $7,157,051 for the project, but Marshall sought additional payment for items it deemed extras and not contemplated in its bid. Because the

[15] *Arya Group, Inc. v Cher*, 91 Cal Rptr 2d 815 (Cal App 2d 2000). See also *Fischer v Flax*, 816 A2d 1 (2003).

[16] *Ramsey v Ellis*, 484 NW2d 331 (Wis 1992).

[17] *ADP Marshall, Inc. v Brown University*, 784 A2d 309 (RI 2001).

[18] *Peabody New England, Inc. v Town of Marshfield*, 689 NE2d 774 (Mass 1998).

THINKING THINGS THROUGH

continued

parties were unable to agree on the scope of the project as compared to the price Brown was willing to pay, they never executed the formal written contract. Nevertheless, in the context of this disagreement over terms and price, construction began in May 1987. When the parties could not resolve their disagreements as the project neared completion in January 1989, Marshall sued Brown University, seeking to recover the costs for what it deemed "changes." Brown asserted that an implied-in-fact contract existed for all work at the $7,157,051 figure because the contractor went ahead with the project knowing the money Brown would pay. The litigation ended up in the Supreme Court of Rhode Island, and in 1997, the court concluded that no express or implied-in-fact contract had ever been reached by the parties concerning the scope of the project and what costs were to be included in the price stipulated by Brown. The case was remanded to the trial court for a new trial. After a trial on the theories of *quantum meruit* and unjust enrichment, a jury awarded Marshall $1.2 million dollars, which was some $3.1 million less than Marshall sought. Brown University appealed, and on November 21, 2001, the Supreme Court of Rhode Island affirmed the jury verdict for the contractor, determining that the proper measure of damages on unjust enrichment and *quantum meruit* theories was "the reasonable value of the work done."*

In May 1987 when the parties could not reach agreement enabling the execution of a formal written contract, thinking things through at that point in time should have exposed the potential for significant economic uncertainties to both parties in actually starting the building process under such circumstances. In the spring of 1987 when all parties were unable to reach agreement, mediation or expedited arbitration by construction experts may well have resolved the controversy and yielded an amicable written contract with little or no delay to the project. Instead, the unsettled cost issues during the building process could have had an adverse impact on the "job chemistry" between the contractor and the owner, which may have adversely affected the progress and quality of the job. The 12 years of litigation that, with its economic and human resource costs, yielded just $1.2 million for the contractor was a no-win result for both sides. A primary rule for all managers in projects of this scope is to make sure the written contracts are executed before performance begins! Relying on "implied-in-fact" or quasi-contract legal theories is simply a poor management practice.

* *ADP Marshall, Inc. v Brown University*, 784 A2d 309 (RI 2001).

C. Contracting on the Internet

Doing business online for consumers is very similar to doing business through a catalog purchase or by phone. Before placing an order, a buyer is commonly concerned about the reputation of the seller. The basic purchasing principle of *caveat emptor* still applies: buyer beware! The Internet provides valuable tools to allow a buyer to research the reputation of the seller and its products. Online evaluations of companies and their products can be found at Web sites, such as Consumer Reports **(http://www.consumerreports.org)**, Consumer Digest **(http://www.consumersdigest.com)**, or the Better Business Bureau **(http://www.bbb.org)**. E-consumers may have access to categorized histories of comments by other e-consumers, such as Planet Feedback ratings at **http://planetfeedback.com.**

The intellectual property principles set forth in Chapter 10—as well as the contractual principles, the law of sales, and privacy laws you are about to study—all apply to e-commerce transactions. When you are purchasing an item online, you must carefully read all of the terms and conditions set forth on the seller's Web site when assessing whether to make a contemplated purchase. The proposed terms may require that any disputes be litigated in a distant state or be resolved through arbitration with restricted remedies, or there may be an unsatisfactory return policy, warranty limitations, or limitation of liability. Generally, the Web site terms become the contract of the parties and are legally enforceable.

The laws you have studied that prevent deceptive advertising by brick and mortar businesses also apply to Internet sites.[19] If an in-state site is engaging in false advertising, you may be able to exercise consumer protection rights through your state's attorney general's office, or you may find some therapeutic relief by reporting the misconduct to the Internet Scambusters site (**http://www.scambusters.com**).

From a seller's perspective, it is exceedingly helpful to have as much information as possible on your potential customers' buying habits. Federal law prohibits the collection of personal information from children without parental consent, and some states restrict the unauthorized collection of personal information. European Union countries have strict laws protecting the privacy of consumers. Sellers intending to collect personal information should obtain the consent of their customers, make certain that children are excluded, and make sure that the information is stored in a secure environment.

Advanced encryption technology has made the use of credit card payments through the Internet very safe. No computer system connected to the Internet is totally secure however. In the worst case scenario, credit card issuers will not charge a user for more that the first $50 of unauthorized activity.

As opposed to business-to-consumer and consumer-to-consumer e-commerce, B2B is business-to-business e-commerce.

At the turn of the century, B2B online commerce was perceived as a potentially enormous marketplace that would enable businesses to better manage inventories, save costs, and create new revenue streams. However, the efficiencies and profit margins did not materialize as many venture capitalists and dot-com investors had expected. E-marketplaces tended to oversimplify inherently complex interactions. With pricing, delivery, and payment issues to be resolved, "clicking" often turned out to be less flexible than phoning. Today, ChemConnect is an example of a successful Internet-based exchange for chemicals and plastics. It has succeeded in simulating a physical marketplace, having created online "trading rooms" where buyers and sellers can negotiate in private. B2B online commerce today also consists of manufacturers and various suppliers entering into Trading Partner Agreements setting forth the terms, conditions, and methods for the conducting of business electronically.

State and local governments and the federal government provide a large market for the procurement of goods, services, and information. B2G is business-to-government e-commerce.

Internet contracts involve the same types of issues that are addressed in contracts offline but with certain technology-related nuances. The parties to the e-contracts must still negotiate their obligations in clear and unambiguous language, including such terms as quantity, quality, and price as well as warranties, indemnification responsibilities, limitations on liability, and termination procedures. The federal Electronic Signatures in Global and National Commerce Act (E-Sign) and the Uniform Electronic Transactions Act (UETA) mandate parity between paper and electronic contracts. The basic legal rules that govern contracts offline are the very same rules that govern online contracts. Boxes identifying special Internet e-commerce topics are strategically placed throughout these chapters.

Paper Moon (1973) (PG)

In this movie for which Tatum O'Neal was given an Oscar, the ongoing issue between Annie and her alleged father is her recoupment of the money she says he promised. Discuss the contract issues (voidable [minor], formation, unilateral vs. bilateral, express, informal, etc.).

For movie clips that illustrate business law concepts, see LawFlix at **http://wdvl.westbuslaw.com.**

[19] See *MADCAP I, LLC v McNamee*, 702 NW2d 16 (Wis App 2005) in which the court found genuine issues of material fact as to whether a business Web site falsely represented the size and nature of its business to induce the public to purchase products and services described on its Web site in violation of the state's fraudulent representations statute.

Summary

A contract is a binding agreement between two or more parties. A contract arises when an offer is accepted with contractual intent (the intent to make a binding agreement).

Contracts may be classified in a number of ways according to form, the way in which they were created, validity, and obligations. With respect to form, a contract may be either informal or formal, such as those under seal or those appearing on the records of courts. Contracts may be classified by the way they were created as those that are expressed by words—written or oral—and those that are implied or deduced from conduct. The question of validity requires distinguishing between contracts that are valid, those that are voidable, and those that are not contracts at all but are merely void agreements. Contracts can be distinguished on the basis of the obligations created as executed contracts, in which everything has been performed, and executory contracts, in which something remains to be done. The bilateral contract is formed by exchanging a promise for a promise, so each party has the obligation of thereafter rendering the promised performance. In the unilateral contract, which is the doing of an act in exchange for a promise, no further performance is required of the offeree who performed the act.

In certain situations, the law regards it as unjust for a person to receive a benefit and not pay for it. In such a case, the law of quasi contracts allows the performing person to recover the reasonable value of the benefit conferred on the benefited person even though no contract between them requires any payment. Unjust enrichment, which a quasi contract is designed to prevent, sometimes arises when there was never any contract between the persons involved or when there was a contract, but for some reason it was avoided or held to be merely a void agreement.

Questions and Case Problems

1. What is a contract?
2. Fourteen applicants for a city of Providence, Rhode Island, police academy training class each received from the city a letter stating that it was a "conditional offer of employment" subject to successful completion of medical and psychological exams. The fourteen applicants passed the medical and psychological exams. However, these applicants were replaced by others after the city changed the selection criteria. Can you identify an offer and acceptance in this case? Can you make out a bilateral or unilateral contract? [*Ardito et al. v City of Providence*, 213 F Supp 2d 358 (D RI)]
3. Compare an implied contract with a quasi contract.
4. The Jordan Keys law firm represented the Greater Southeast Community Hospital of Washington, D.C., in a medical malpractice suit against the hospital. The hospital was self-insured for the first $1,000,000 of liability and the St. Paul Insurance Co. provided excess coverage up to $4,000,000. The law firm was owed $67,000 for its work on the malpractice suit when the hospital went into bankruptcy. The bankruptcy court ordered the law firm to release its files on the case to St. Paul to defend under the excess coverage insurance, and the Jordan Keys firm sued St. Paul for its legal fees of $67,000 expended prior to the bankruptcy under an "implied-in-fact contract" because the insurance company would have the benefit of all of its work. Decide. [*Jordan Keys v St. Paul Fire*, 870 A2d 58 (DC)]
5. Beck was the general manager of Chilkoot Lumber Co. Haines sold fuel to the company. To persuade Haines to sell on credit, Beck signed a paper by which he promised to pay any debt the lumber company owed Haines. He signed this paper with his name followed by "general manager." Haines later sued Beck on this promise, and Beck raised the defense that the addition of "general manager" showed that Beck, who was signing on behalf of Chilkoot, was not personally liable and did not intend to be bound by the paper. Was Beck liable on the paper? [*Beck v Haines Terminal and Highway Co.*, 843 P2d 1229 (Alaska)]
6. *A* made a contract to construct a house for *B*. Subsequently, *B* sued *A* for breach of contract. *A* raised the defense that the contract was not binding because it was not sealed. Is this a valid defense? [*Cooper v G. E. Construction Co.*, 158 SE2d 305 (Ga App)]
7. Edward Johnson III, the CEO and principal owner of the world's largest mutual fund company, Fidelity Investments, Inc., was a longtime tennis buddy of Richard Larson. In 1995, Johnson asked Larson, who had construction experience, to supervise the construction of a house on Long Pond, Mount Desert Island, Maine. Although they had no written contract, Larson agreed to take on the project for $6,700 per month plus lodging. At the end of the project in 1997, Johnson made a $175,000 cash payment to Larson, and he made arrangements for Larson to live rent-free on another Johnson property in the area called Pray's Meadow in exchange for looking after Johnson's extensive property interests in Maine. In the late summer of 1999, Johnson initiated a new project on the Long Pond property. Johnson had discussions with Larson about doing this project, but Larson asked to be paid his former rate, and Johnson balked because he had already hired a project manager. According to Johnson, at a later date he again asked Larson to take on

the "shop project" as a favor and in consideration of continued rent-free use of the Pray's Meadow home. Johnson stated that Larson agreed to do the job "pro bono" in exchange for the use of the house, and Johnson acknowledged that he told Larson he would "take care" of Larson at the end of the project, which could mean as much or as little as Johnson determined. Larson stated that Johnson told him that he would "take care of" Larson if he would do the project and told him to "trust the Great Oracle" (meaning Johnson, the highly successful businessperson). Larson sought payment in March 2000 and asked Johnson for "something on account" in April. Johnson offered Larson a loan. In August during a tennis match, Larson again asked Johnson to pay him. Johnson became incensed, and through an employee, he ended Larson's participation in the project and asked him to vacate Pray's Meadow. Larson complied and filed suit for payment for work performed at the rate of $6,700 per month. Did Larson have an express contract with Johnson? What legal theory or theories could Larson utilize in his lawsuit? How would you decide this case if you believed Larson's version of the facts? How would you decide the case if you believed Johnson's version of the facts? [*Larson v Johnson*, 2002 U.S. Dist. LEXIS 1953. See *Bangor Daily News*, March 8, 2002, 1]

8. While Clara Novak was sick, her daughter Janie helped her in many ways. Clara died, and Janie then claimed that she was entitled to be paid for the services she had rendered her mother. This claim was opposed by three brothers and sisters who also rendered services to the mother. They claimed that Janie was barred because of the presumption that services rendered between family members are gratuitous. Janie claimed that this presumption was not applicable because she had not lived with her mother but had her own house. Was Janie correct? [*In re Estate of Novak*, 398 NW2d 653 (Minn App)]

9. Dozier and his wife, daughter, and grandson lived in the house Dozier owned. At the request of the daughter and grandson, Paschall made some improvements to the house. Dozier did not authorize these, but he knew that the improvements were being made and did not object to them. Paschall sued Dozier for the reasonable value of the improvements, but Dozier argued that he had not made any contract for such improvements. Was he obligated to pay for such improvements?

10. When Harriet went away for the summer, Landry, a house painter, painted her house. He had a contract to paint a neighbor's house but painted Harriet's house by mistake. When Harriet returned from vacation, Landry billed her for $3,100, which was a fair price for the work. She refused to pay. Landry claimed that she had a quasi-contractual liability for that amount. Was he correct?

11. Margrethe and Charles Pyeatte, a married couple, agreed that she would work so that he could go to law school and that when he finished, she would go back to school for her master's degree. After Charles was admitted to the bar and before Margrethe went back to school, the two were divorced. She sued Charles, claiming that she was entitled to quasi-contractual recovery of the money that she had paid for Charles's support and law school tuition. He denied liability. Was she entitled to recover for the money she spent for Charles's maintenance and law school tuition? [*Pyeatte v Pyeatte*, 661 P2d 196 (Ariz App)]

12. Carriage Way was a real estate development of approximately 80 houses and 132 apartments. The property owners were members of the Carriage Way Property Owners Association. Each year, the association would take care of certain open neighboring areas, including a nearby lake, that were used by the property owners. The board of directors of the association would make an assessment or charge against the property owners to cover the cost of this work. The property owners paid these assessments for a number of years and then refused to pay any more. In spite of this refusal, the association continued to take care of the areas in question. The association then sued the property owners and claimed that they were liable for the benefit that had been conferred on them. Were the owners liable? [*Board of Directors of Carriage Way Property Owners Ass'n v Western National Bank*, 487 NE2d 974 (Ill App)]

13. Lombard insured his car, and when it was damaged, the insurer sent the car to General Auto Service for repairs. The insurance company went bankrupt and did not pay the repair bill. General Auto Service then sued Lombard for the bill because he had benefited from the repair work. Was he liable?

14. When a college student complained about a particular course, the vice president of the college asked the teacher to prepare a detailed report about the course. The teacher did and then demanded additional compensation for the time spent in preparing the report. He claimed that the college was liable to provide compensation on an implied contract. Was he correct? [*Zadrozny v City Colleges of Chicago*, 581 NE2d 44 (Ill App)]

15. Smith made a contract to sell automatic rifles to a foreign country. Because the sale of such weapons to that country was illegal under an act of Congress, the U.S. government prosecuted Smith for making the contract. He raised the defense that because the contract was illegal, it was void and there is no binding obligation when a contract is void; therefore, no contract for which he could be prosecuted existed. Was he correct?

CPA Questions

1. Kay, an art collector, promised Hammer, an art student, that if Hammer could obtain certain rare artifacts within two weeks, Kay would pay for Hammer's postgraduate education. At considerable effort and expense, Hammer obtained the specified artifacts within the two-week period. When Hammer requested payment, Kay refused. Kay claimed that there was no consideration for the promise. Hammer would prevail against Kay based on
   a. Unilateral contract
   b. Unjust enrichment
   c. Public policy
   d. Quasi contract

FORMATION OF CONTRACTS: OFFER AND ACCEPTANCE

CHAPTER (13)

LEARNING OBJECTIVES

After studying this chapter, you should be able to

LO.1 Decide whether a statement is an offer or an invitation to negotiate

LO.2 Decide whether an agreement is too indefinite to be enforced

LO.3 Describe the exceptions that the law makes to the requirement of definiteness

LO.4 List all of the ways an offer is terminated

LO.5 Compare offers, firm offers, and option contracts

LO.6 Define what constitutes the acceptance of an offer

A *contract* consists of enforceable obligations that have been voluntarily assumed. Thus, one of the essential elements of a contract is an agreement. This chapter explains how the basic agreement arises, when there is a contract, and how there can be merely unsuccessful negotiations without a resulting contract.

A. Requirements of an Offer

An **offer** expresses the willingness of the offeror to enter into a contractual agreement regarding a particular subject. It is a promise that is conditional upon an act, a forbearance (a refraining from doing something one has a legal right to do), or a return promise.

CPA 1. Contractual Intention

To make an offer, the offeror must appear to intend to create a binding obligation. Whether this intent exists is determined by objective standards.[1] This intent may be shown by conduct.

For Example, when one party signs a written contract and sends it to the other party, such action is an offer to enter into a contract on the terms of the writing.

There is no contract when a social invitation is made or when an offer is made in obvious jest or excitement. A reasonable person would not regard such an offer as indicating a willingness to enter into a binding agreement.

(a) Invitation to Negotiate

The first statement made by one of two persons is not necessarily an offer. In many instances, there may be a preliminary discussion or an invitation by one party to the other to negotiate or to make an offer. Thus, an inquiry by a school as to whether a teacher wished to continue the following year was merely a survey or invitation to negotiate and was not an offer that could be accepted. Therefore, the teacher's affirmative response did not create a contract.

Ordinarily, a seller sending out circulars or catalogs listing prices is not regarded as making an offer to sell at those prices. The seller is merely indicating a willingness to consider an offer made by a buyer on those terms. The reason for this rule is, in part, the practical consideration that because a seller does not have an unlimited supply of any commodity, the seller cannot possibly intend to make a contract with everyone who sees the circular. The same principle is applied to merchandise that is displayed with price tags in stores or store windows and to most advertisements. An advertisement in a newspaper is ordinarily considered an invitation to negotiate and is not an offer that can be accepted by a reader of the paper.[2] However, some court decisions have construed advertisements as offers that called for an act on the part of the customer thereby forming a unilateral contract, such as the advertisement of a reward for the return of lost property.

Quotations of prices, even when sent on request, are likewise not offers unless the parties have had previous dealings or unless a trade custom exists that would give the recipient of the quotation reason to believe that an offer was being made. Whether a price quotation is to be treated as an offer or merely an invitation to negotiate is a question of the intent of the party giving the quotation.[3]

(b) Agreement to Make a Contract at a Future Date

No contract arises when the parties merely agree that at a future date they will consider making a contract or will make a contract on terms to be agreed on at that time.[4] In such a case, neither party is under any obligation until the future contract is made. No binding contract to renew a contract when it expires is created by a provision in the original contract that, when it expires, the parties intend to "negotiate in good faith to renew this agreement for an additional year upon terms and conditions to be negotiated."

2. Definiteness

An offer, and the resulting contract, must be definite and certain.[5] If an offer is indefinite or vague or if an essential provision is lacking,[6] no contract arises

[1] *Glass Service Co. v State Farm Mutual Automobile Ins. Co.*, 530 NW2d 867 (Minn App 1995).

[2] *Pico v Cutter Dodge, Inc.*, 98 Hawaii 309 (2002).

[3] Statutes prohibiting false or misleading advertising may require adherence to advertised prices.

[4] *Ellis v Taylor*, 49 SE2d 487 (SC 1994).

[5] *Graziano v Grant*, 744 A2d 156 (NJ Super AD 1999).

[6] *Peace v Doming Holdings Inc.*, 554 SE2d 314 (Ga App 2001).

from an attempt to accept it. The reason is that courts cannot tell what the parties are to do. Thus, an offer to conduct a business for as long as it is profitable is too vague to be a valid offer. The acceptance of such an offer does not result in a contract that can be enforced. Statements by a bank that it was "with" the debtors and would "support" them in their proposed business venture were too vague to be regarded as a promise by the bank to make necessary loans to the debtors.

The fact that minor, ministerial, and nonessential terms are left for future determination does not make an agreement too vague to be a contract.[7]

In the *McCarthy* case, the court was faced with the question of whether a legally enforceable contract had been made where the parties expressed their intent to execute a subsequent purchase and sale agreement.

McCARTHY V TOBIN, 706 NE2D 629 (MASS 1999)

OFFER TO PURCHASE IS CONTROLLING LEGAL DOCUMENT

John McCarthy Jr. brought an action for specific performance against Ann Tobin claiming that the parties created a binding contract when they signed an offer to purchase (OTP) form on August 9, 1995. Robert DiMinico and his wife intervened because they thereafter agreed to purchase the property in question from Ms. Tobin. The trial court granted summary judgment for Tobin and the DiMinicos, which was vacated by the Appeals Court. The Supreme Judicial Court granted further appellate review.

Judicial Opinion

ABRAMS, J. . . . The facts, which are undisputed, are as follows. On August 9, 1995, McCarthy executed an offer to purchase real estate on a pre-printed form generated by the Greater Boston Real Estate Board. The OTP contained, among other provisions, a description of the property, the price to be paid, deposit requirements, limited title requirements, and the time and place for closing. The OTP also included several provisions that are the basis of this dispute. The OTP required that the parties "shall, on or before 5 P.M. August 16, 1995, execute the applicable Standard Form Purchase and Sale Agreement recommended by the Greater Boston Real Estate Board . . . which, when executed, shall be the agreement between the parties hereto." . . . Finally, an unnumbered paragraph immediately above the signature line states: "NOTICE: This is a legal document that creates binding obligations. If not understood, consult an attorney." Tobin signed the OTP on August 11, 1995.

On August 16, 1995, sometime after 5 P.M., Tobin's lawyer sent a first draft of the purchase and sale agreement by facsimile transmission to McCarthy's lawyer. On August 21, McCarthy's lawyer sent a letter by facsimile transmission containing his comments and proposing several changes to Tobin's lawyer. The changes laid out the requirements for good title; imposed on Tobin the risk of casualty to the premises before sale; solicited indemnification, for title insurance purposes, regarding mechanics' liens, parties in possession, and hazardous materials; and sought an acknowledgment that the premises' systems were operational. The next day, the two lawyers discussed the proposed revisions. They did not discuss an extension of the deadline for signing the purchase and sale agreement, and Tobin's lawyer did not object to the fact that the deadline had already passed. On August 23, Tobin's lawyer sent a second draft of the agreement to McCarthy's lawyer. On August 25, a Friday, McCarthy's lawyer informed Tobin's lawyer that the agreement was acceptable, McCarthy would sign it, and it would be delivered the following Monday. On Saturday, August 26, McCarthy signed the purchase and sale agreement. On the same day, Tobin accepted the DiMinicos' offer to purchase the property.

On August 28, McCarthy delivered the executed agreement and a deposit to Tobin's broker. The next day, Tobin's lawyer told McCarthy's lawyer that the agreement was late and that Tobin had already accepted the DiMinicos' offer. In September, 1995, Tobin and the DiMinicos executed a purchase and sale agreement. Before the deal closed,

[7] *Hsu v Vet-A-Mix, Inc.*, 479 NW2d 336 (Iowa App 1991). But see *Ocean Atlantic Development Corp v Aurora Christian Schools, Inc.*, 322 F3d 983 (7th Cir 2003), where letter offers to purchase (OTP) real estate were signed by both parties, but the offers conditioned the purchase and sale of each property upon the subsequent execution of a purchase and sale agreement. The court held that the parties thus left themselves room to walk away from the deal under Illinois law, and the OTPs were not enforced.

McCarthy filed this action for specific performance and damages.

1. *Firm offer*: The primary issue is whether the OTP executed by McCarthy and Tobin was a binding contract. Tobin and the DiMinicos argue that it was not because of the provision requiring the execution of a purchase and sale agreement. McCarthy urges that he and Tobin intended to be bound by the OTP and that execution of the purchase and sale agreement was merely a formality.

McCarthy argues that the OTP adequately described the property to be sold and the price to be paid. The remaining terms covered by the purchase and sale agreement were subsidiary matters which did not preclude the formation of a binding contract. We agree.

The controlling fact is the intention of the parties.... Tobin argues that language contemplating the execution of a final written agreement gives rise to a strong inference that she and McCarthy have not agreed to all material aspects of a transaction and thus that they do not intend to be bound. ...

Although the provisions of the purchase and sale agreement can be the subject of negotiation, "norms exist for their customary resolution."...

The interveners argue that McCarthy departed from the customary resolution of any open issues, and therefore manifested his intent not to be bound, by requesting several additions to the purchase and sale agreement. We agree with the Appeals Court, however, that McCarthy's revisions were "ministerial and nonessential terms of the bargain." ...

The inference that the OTP was binding is bolstered by the notice printed on the form. McCarthy and Tobin were alerted to the fact that the OTP "create[d] binding obligations." The question is what those obligations were. The DiMinicos argue that the OTP merely obligated the parties to negotiate the purchase and sale agreement in good faith. We disagree. The OTP employs familiar contractual language. It states that McCarthy "hereby offer[s] to buy" the property, and Tobin's signature indicates that "[t]his Offer is hereby accepted." The OTP also details the amount to be paid and when, describes the property bought, and specifies for how long the offer was open. This was a firm offer, the acceptance of which bound Tobin to sell and McCarthy to buy the subject property. We conclude that the OTP reflects the parties' intention to be bound.

[The court found that Tobin had waived the August 16 deadline by words and conduct attributable to her, including her lawyer's failure to object to the passage of the deadline and his continued dealing with McCarthy's lawyer to craft an agreement.]

2. *Specific performance*.... McCarthy's right to specific performance is unaltered by Tobin's execution of a purchase and sale agreement with the DiMinicos. McCarthy filed this action prior to the execution of that agreement. The DiMinicos had actual notice of McCarthy's claim to the property and assumed the risk of a result favorable to McCarthy....

The judgment is vacated. The case is remanded to the Superior Court for the entry of a judgment in favor of McCarthy's claim for specific performance.

[Judgment for McCarthy]

Questions

1. State Tobin's position before the court.
2. Were there definite and certain terms agreed to by the parties regarding the purchase to Tobin's property?
3. Evaluate Ms. Tobin's strategy, after signing the OTP, of hiring an attorney to handle the purchase and sale agreement and closing.

The law does not favor the destruction of contracts because that would go against the social force of carrying out the intent of the parties.[8] Consequently, when it is claimed that a contract is too indefinite to be enforced, a court will do its best to find the intent of the parties and thereby reach the conclusion that the contract is not too indefinite. **For Example,** boxing promoter Don King had both a Promotional Agreement and a Bout Agreement with boxer Miguel Angel Gonzalez. The Bout Agreement for a boxing match held on March 7, 1998, with Julio Cesar Chavez gave King the option to promote the next four of Gonzalez's matches. The contract made clear that if Gonzalez won the Chavez match, he would receive at least $75,000 for the next fight unless the parties agreed otherwise, and if he lost, he would receive at least $25,000 for the subsequent fight unless otherwise agreed. The agreement did not explicitly state the purse for the subsequent match in the event of a draw. The Chavez match ended in a draw, and Gonzalez contended that this omission rendered the contract so indefinite that it was unenforceable. The court disagreed, stating that striking down a contract as indefinite and in essence

[8] *Mears v Nationwide Mut, Inc. Co.*, 91 F3d 1118 (8th Cir 1996).

THINKING THINGS THROUGH

THE RULES OF NEGOTIATIONS

Business agreements are often reached after much discussion, study, and posturing by both sides. Many statements may be made by both sides about the price or value placed on the subject of the transaction. Withholding information or presenting selective, self-serving information may be perceived by a party to the negotiations as protective self-interest. Does the law of contracts apply a duty of good faith and fair dealing in the negotiation of contracts? Does the Uniform Commercial Code provide for a general duty of good faith in the negotiation of contracts? Are lawyers under an ethical obligation to inform opposing counsel of relevant facts? The answer to all of these questions is no.

The Restatement (Second) of Contracts applies the duty of good faith and fair dealing to the performance and enforcement of contracts, not their negotiation* ; so also does the UCC.** The American Bar Association's Model Rules of Professional Conduct, Rule 4.1 Comment 1 requires a lawyer to be "truthful" when dealing with others on a client's behalf, but it also states that generally a lawyer has "no affirmative duty to inform an opposing party of relevant facts."*** Comment 2 to Rule 4.1 contains an example of a "nonmaterial" statement of a lawyer as "estimates of price or value placed on the subject of a transaction."

The legal rules of negotiations state that—in the absence of fraud, special relationships, or statutory or contractual duties—negotiators are not obligated to divulge pertinent information to the other party to the negotiations. The parties to negotiations themselves must demand and analyze pertinent information and ultimately assess the fairness of the proposed transaction. Should a party conclude that the elements of a final proposal or offer are excessive or dishonest, that party's legal option is to walk away from the deal. Generally, the party has no basis to bring a lawsuit for lack of good faith and fair dealing in negotiations.

However, thinking things through, the ethical standards for negotiations set forth in Chapter 2 indicate that establishing a reputation for trustworthiness, candor, and reliability oftens lead to commercial success for a company's continuing negotiations with its customers, suppliers, distributors, lenders, unions, and employees.

*Restatement (Second) of Contracts § 105, comment (c).

**Uniform Commercial Code § 1-203.

***American Bar Association Model Rule of Professional Conduct 4.1(a) Comment 1.

meaningless is at best a last resort. The court held that although the contract was poorly drafted, the Promotional Agreement contained explicit price terms for which a minimum purse for fights following a draw may be inferred.[9] A court may not rewrite the agreement of the parties in order to make it definite.

(a) Definite by Incorporation

An offer and the resulting contract that by themselves may appear "too indefinite" may be made definite by reference to another writing. **For Example,** a lease agreement that was too vague by itself was made definite because the parties agreed that the lease should follow the standard form with which both were familiar. An agreement may also be made definite by reference to the prior dealings of the parties and to trade practices.

(b) Implied Terms

Although an offer must be definite and certain, not all of its terms need to be expressed. Some omitted terms may be implied by law. **For Example,** an offer "to pay $400" for a certain Movado timepiece does

[9] *Gonzalez v Don King Productions, Inc.*, 17 F Supp 2d 313 (SDNY 1998); see also *Echols v Pelullo*, 377 F3d 272 (3rd Cir 2004).

FIGURE 13-1 Offer and Acceptance

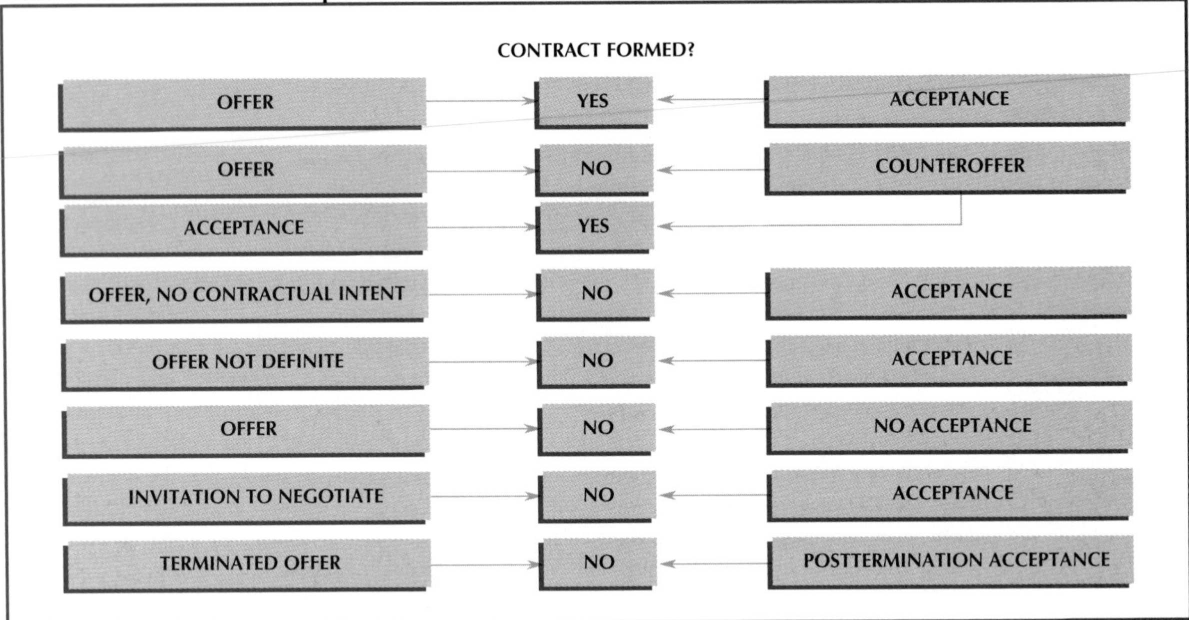

not state the terms of payment. A court, however, would not condemn this provision as too vague but would hold that it required that cash be paid and that the payment be made on delivery of the watch. Likewise, terms may be implied from conduct. As an illustration, when borrowed money was given to the borrower by a check on which the word *loan* was written, the act of the borrower in endorsing the check constituted an agreement to repay the amount of the check.

(c) "Best Efforts" Clauses

While decades ago it was generally accepted that a duty defined only in terms of "best efforts" was too indefinite to be enforced, such a view is no longer widely held. **For Example,** Thomas Hinc, an inventor, executed a contract with Lime-O-Sol Company (LOS) for LOS to produce and distribute Hinc's secret ingredient Stain Remover. Under the contract, Hinc was to receive $10 per gallon sold. The contract contained a clause obligating both parties to use their "best efforts" to market the product "in a manner that seems appropriate." Ultimately, LOS never produced, marketed, or sold Stain Remover for the duration of the contract. The court rejected the defense that the "best efforts" provision was vague and unenforceable stating "[b]est efforts, as commonly understood, means, at the very least *some* effort. It certainly does not mean *zero* effort—the construction LOS urges here to escape any obligation under its contract."[10]

(d) Divisible Contracts

When the agreement consists of two or more parts and calls for corresponding performances of each part by the parties, the agreement is a **divisible contract**. Thus, in a promise to buy several separate articles at different prices at the same time, the agreement may be regarded as separate or divisible promises for the articles. When a contract contains a number of provisions or performances to be rendered, the question arises as to whether the parties intended merely a group of separate, divisible contracts or whether it was to be a package deal so that complete performance by each party was essential.

(e) Exceptions to Definiteness

The law has come to recognize certain situations in which the practical necessity of doing business makes it desirable to have a contract, yet the situation is such that it is either impossible or undesirable to adopt definite terms in advance. In these cases, the indefinite term is often tied to the concept of good-faith performance or to some independent

[10] *Hinc v Lime-O-Sol Company*, 382 F3d 716 (7th Cir 2004).

factor that will be definitely ascertainable at some time in the future. The indefinite term might be tied to market price, cost to complete, production, or sales requirements. Thus, the law recognizes binding contracts in the case of a **requirements contract**—that is, a contract to buy all requirements of the buyer from the seller.[11] **For Example,** an agreement between Honeywell International Inc. and Air Products and Chemicals Inc. whereby Air Products would purchase its total requirements of wet process chemicals from Honeywell was held to be an enforceable requirements contract.[12] The law also recognizes as binding an **output contract**—that is, the contract of a producer to sell the entire production or output to a given buyer. These are binding contracts even though they do not state the exact quantity of goods that are to be bought or sold.

CPA 3. Communication of Offer to Offeree

An offer must be communicated to the offeree. Otherwise, the offeree cannot accept even though knowledge of the offer has been indirectly acquired. Internal management communications of an enterprise that are not intended for outsiders or employees do not constitute offers and cannot be accepted by them. Sometimes, particularly in the case of unilateral contracts, the offeree performs the act called for by the offeror without knowing of the offer's existence. Such performance does not constitute an acceptance. Thus, without knowing that a reward is offered for information leading to the arrest of a particular criminal, a person may provide information that leads to the arrest of the criminal. In most states, if that person subsequently learns of the reward, the reward cannot be recovered.[13]

Not only must the offer be communicated but also it must be communicated by the offeror or at the offeror's direction.

CPA B. Termination of Offer

An offeree cannot accept a terminated offer. Offers may be terminated by revocation, counteroffer, rejection, lapse of time, death or disability of a party, or subsequent illegality.

CPA 4. Revocation of Offer by Offeror

Ordinarily, an offeror can revoke the offer before it is accepted. If this is done, the offeree cannot create a contract by accepting the revoked offer. Thus, the bidder at an auction sale may withdraw (revoke) a bid (offer) before it is accepted, and the auctioneer cannot accept that bid later.

An ordinary offer may be revoked at any time before it is accepted even though the offeror has expressly promised that the offer will be good for a stated period and that period has not yet expired. It may also be revoked even though the offeror has expressly promised to the offeree that the offer would not be revoked before a specified later date.

The fact that the offeror expressly promised to keep the offer open has no effect when no consideration was given for that promise.

(a) What Constitutes a Revocation?

No particular form or words are required to constitute a revocation. Any words indicating the offeror's termination of the offer are sufficient. A notice sent to the offeree that the property that is the subject of the offer has been sold to a third person is a revocation of the offer. A customer's order for goods, which is an offer to purchase at certain prices, is revoked by a notice to the seller of the cancellation of the order, provided that such notice is communicated before the order is accepted.

(b) Communication of Revocation

A revocation of an offer is ordinarily effective only when it is made known to the offeree.[14] Until it is communicated to the offeree, directly or indirectly, the offeree has reason to believe that there is still an offer that may be accepted, and the offeree may rely on this belief. A letter revoking an offer made to a particular offeree is not effective until the offeree receives it. It is not a revocation when the offeror writes it or even when it is mailed or dispatched. A written revocation is effective, however, when it is

[11] *Simcala v American Coal Trade, Inc.*, 2001 WL 139 1992 (Nov 9, 2001).

[12] *Honeywell International Inc. v Air Products and Chemicals, Inc.*, 872 A2d 944 (Sup Ct Del 2005).

[13] With respect to the offeror, it should not make any difference, as a practical matter, whether the services were rendered with or without knowledge of the existence of the offer. Only a small number of states have adopted this view, however.

[14] *MD Drilling and Blasting, Inc. v MLS Construction, LLC*, 889 A2d 850 (Conn App 2006).

delivered to the offeree's agent or to the offeree's residence or place of business under such circumstances that the offeree may be reasonably expected to be aware of its receipt.

It is ordinarily held that there is a sufficient communication of the revocation when the offeree learns indirectly of the offeror's revocation. This is particularly true in a land sale when the seller-offeror, after making an offer to sell the land to the offeree, sells the land to a third person and the offeree indirectly learns of such sale. The offeree necessarily realizes that the seller cannot perform the original offer and therefore must be considered to have revoked it.

If the offeree accepts an offer before it is effectively revoked, a valid contract is created.

(c) Option Contracts

An *option contract* is a binding promise to keep an offer open for a stated period of time or until a specified date. An option contract requires that the promisor receive consideration—that is, something, such as a sum of money—as the price for the promise to keep the offer open. In other words, the option is a contract to refrain from revoking an offer.

(d) Firm Offers

As another exception to the rule that an offer can be revoked at any time before acceptance, statutes in some states provide that an offeror cannot revoke an offer prior to its expiration when the offeror makes a firm offer. A **firm offer** is an offer that states that it is to be irrevocable, or irrevocable for a stated period of time. Under the Uniform Commercial Code, this doctrine of firm offer applies to a merchant's signed, written offer to buy or sell goods but with a maximum of three months on its period of irrevocability.[15]

5. Counteroffer by Offeree

The offeree rejects the offer when she ignores the original offer and replies with a different offer.[16] If the offeree purports to accept an offer but in so doing makes any change to the terms of the offer, such action is a **counteroffer** that rejects the original offer. An "acceptance" that changes the terms of the offer or adds new terms is a rejection of the original offer and constitutes a counteroffer.[17]

Ordinarily, if *A* makes an offer, such as to sell a used automobile to *B* for $3,000, and *B* in reply makes an offer to buy at $2,500, the original offer is terminated. *B* is in effect indicating refusal of the original offer and in its place is making a different offer. Such an offer by the offeree is known as a *counteroffer*. No contract arises unless the original offeror accepts the counteroffer.

Counteroffers are not limited to offers that directly contradict the original offers. Any departure from or addition to the original offer is a counteroffer even though the original offer was silent on the point added by the counteroffer.

6. Rejection of Offer by Offeree

If the offeree rejects the offer and communicates this rejection to the offeror, the offer is terminated. Communication of a rejection terminates an offer even though the period for which the offeror agreed to keep the offer open has not yet expired. It may be that the offeror is willing to renew the offer, but unless this is done, there is no longer any offer for the offeree to accept.

7. Lapse of Time

When the offer states that it is open until a particular date, the offer terminates on that date if it has not yet been accepted. This is particularly so when the offeror declares that the offer shall be void after the expiration of the specified time. Such limitations are strictly construed.

If the offer contains a time limitation for acceptance, an attempted acceptance after the expiration of that time has no effect and does not give rise to a contract.[18] When a specified time limitation is imposed on an option, the option cannot be exercised after the expiration of that time, regardless of whether the option was exercised within what would have been held a reasonable time if no time period had been specified.

If the offer does not specify a time, it will terminate after the lapse of a reasonable time. What constitutes a reasonable time depends on the circumstances of each case—that is, on the nature of the

[15] UCC § 2-205.

[16] *Bourque v FDIC*, 42 F3d 704 (1st Cir 1994).

[17] *McLaughlin v Heikkila*, 697 NW2d 731 (Minn App 2005).

[18] *Century 21 Pinetree Properties, Inc. v Cason*, 469 SE2d 458 (Ga App 1996).

subject matter, the nature of the market in which it is sold, the time of year, and other factors of supply and demand. If a commodity is perishable or fluctuates greatly in value, the reasonable time will be much shorter than if the subject matter is of a stable value. An offer to sell a harvested crop of tomatoes would expire within a very short time. When a seller purports to accept an offer after it has lapsed by the expiration of time, the seller's acceptance is merely a counteroffer and does not create a contract unless the buyer accepts that counteroffer.

8. Death or Disability of Either Party

If either the offeror or offeree dies or becomes mentally incompetent before the offer is accepted, the offer is automatically terminated. **For Example,** Chet Wilson offers to sell his ranch to Interport, Inc., for $2.5 million. Five days later, Chet is killed in an aviation accident. Interport, Inc., subsequently writes to Chet Wilson Jr., an adult, that his father's offer is accepted. No contract is formed because the offer made by Chet died with him.

CPA 9. Subsequent Illegality

If the performance of the contract becomes illegal after the offer is made, the offer is terminated. **For Example,** if an offer is made to sell six semiautomatic handguns to a commercial firing range for $550 per weapon but a new law prohibiting such sales is enacted before the offer is accepted, the offer is terminated.

CPA C. Acceptance of Offer

An **acceptance** is the assent of the offeree to the terms of the offer. Objective standards determine whether there has been an agreement of the parties.

10. What Constitutes an Acceptance?

No particular form of words or mode of expression is required, but there must be a clear expression that the offeree agrees to be bound by the terms of the offer. If the offeree reserves the right to reject the offer, such action is not an acceptance.[19]

11. Privilege of Offeree

Ordinarily, the offeree may refuse to accept an offer. If there is no acceptance, by definition there is no contract. The fact that there had been a series of contracts between the parties and that one party's offer had always been accepted before by the other does not create any legal obligation to continue to accept subsequent offers.

CPA 12. Effect of Acceptance

The acceptance of an offer creates a binding agreement or contract,[20] assuming that all of the other elements of a contract are present. Neither party can subsequently withdraw from or cancel the contract without the consent of the other party.

CPA 13. Nature of Acceptance

An *acceptance* is the offeree's manifestation of intent to enter into a binding agreement on the terms stated in the offer. Whether there is an acceptance depends on whether the offeree has manifested an intent to accept. It is the objective or outward appearance that is controlling rather than the subjective or unexpressed intent of the offeree.[21]

In the absence of a contrary requirement in the offer, an acceptance may be indicated by an informal "okay," by a mere affirmative nod of the head, or in the case of an offer of a unilateral contract, by performance of the act called for.

The acceptance must be absolute and unconditional. It must accept just what is offered.[22] If the offeree changes any terms of the offer or adds any new term, there is no acceptance because the offeree does not agree to what was offered.

When the offeree does not accept the offer exactly as made, the addition of any qualification converts the "acceptance" into a counteroffer, and no contract arises unless the original offeror accepts such a counteroffer.

CPA 14. Who May Accept?

Only the person to whom an offer is directed may accept it. If anyone else attempts to accept it, no agreement or contract with that person arises.

If the offer is directed to a particular class rather than a specified individual, anyone within that class

[19] *Pantano v McGowan*, 530 NW2d 912 (Neb 1995).
[20] *Ochoa v Ford*, 641 NE2d 1042 (Ind App 1994).
[21] *Cowan v Mervin Mewes, Inc.*, 546 NW2d 104 (SD 1996).
[22] *Jones v Frickey*, 618 SE2d 29 (Ga App 2005).

E-COMMERCE AND CYBERLAW

CONTRACT FORMATION ON THE INTERNET

It is not possible for an online service provider or seller to individually bargain with each person who visits its Web site. The Web site owner, therefore, as offeror, places its proposed terms on its Web site and requires visitors to assent to these terms in order to access the site, download software, or purchase a product or service.

In a written contract, the parties sign a paper document indicating their intention to be bound by the terms of the contract. Online, however, an agreement may be accomplished by the visitor-offeree simply typing the words "I Accept" in an onscreen box and then clicking a "send" or similar button that indicates acceptance. Or the individual clicks an "I Agree" or "I Accept" icon or checkbox. Access to the site is commonly denied those who do not agree to the terms.

Such agreements have come to be called *clickon, clickthrough, or clickwrap* agreements. The agreements contain fee schedules and other financial terms and may contain terms such as a notice of the proprietary nature of the material contained on the site and of any limitations on the use of the site and the downloading of software. Moreover, the clickon agreements may contain limitations on liability, including losses associated with the use of downloaded software or products or services purchased from the site.

The use of clickon agreements has become standard practice for the sale of certain products and services online and the distribution of software. Although case law is scarce, where the agreements are not contrary to the basic principles of contract law, the contracts are legally enforceable.*

In Caspi v Microsoft Network,** the Superior Court of New Jersey Appellate Division upheld the enforcement of certain terms of Microsoft Network's (MSN) clickon membership agreement and dismissed a suit brought by subscribers on the basis of a forum selection clause contained in the membership agreement. The plaintiff-subscribers had argued in part that the forum selection clause did not apply to them because they did not receive adequate notice of the clause. The agreement formation process was explained by the trial court as follows:

> *Before becoming an MSN member, a prospective subscriber is prompted by MSN software to view multiple computer screens of information, including a membership agreement which contains the above clause. MSN's membership agreement appears on the computer screen in a scrollable window next to blocks providing the choices "I Agree" and "I Don't Agree." Prospective members assent to the terms of the agreement by clicking on "I Agree" using a computer mouse.*

The court stated that the plaintiffs were free to scroll through the various computer screens that presented the terms of their contracts before clicking their agreement. The court found that in any sense that matters, there is no significant distinction between the electronic form of this contract and a contract in printed form. Accordingly, the plaintiffs were forced to comply with the forum selection clause and bring their lawsuit challenging MSN's billing practices in the state of Washington rather than New Jersey.

In contrast, the U.S. Court of Appeals for the Second Circuit declined to enforce a clickthrough agreement in Specht v Netscape Communications Corp.*** in connection with Netscape's SmartDownload software. Users were able to download the program from Netscape's site simply by clicking a download icon. At the bottom of the download page, the text invited the user to review a licensing

E-COMMERCE AND CYBERLAW

continued

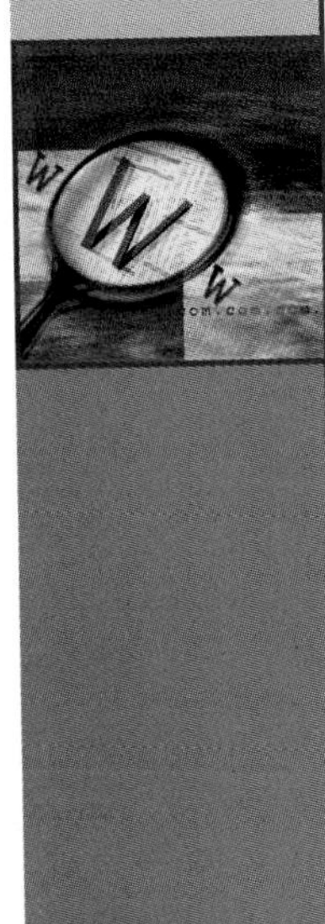

agreement before downloading and using the software, but the agreement itself was not available on the page. The court concluded that "a consumer's clicking on a download button does not communicate assent to contractual terms if the offer did not make clear to the consumer that clicking on the download button would signify assent to those terms."

*As will be seen in Chapter 23, Article Two of the Uniform Commercial Code deals with the sale of goods. It was adopted by most states in the 1960s, well before the contemplation and existence of the Internet and electronic contracting issues. The Uniform Computer Information Transactions Act (UCITA), a uniform law promulgated in July 1999 by the National Conference of Commissioners on Uniform State Laws, governs contracts involving the sale, licensing, maintenance, and support of computer software. The UCITA has been adopted by just two states, Virginia and Maryland. However, successful producers of software or financial institutions that license software to their customers may choose to locate or open an office in one of the UCITA states in order to obtain the coverage of UCITA rules. Choice-of-law rules under Section 109(b)(1) of the UCITA provide that the law of the UCITA state will govern each transaction as long as the software is delivered over the Internet. The UCITA is clear that clickon agreements allowing a user to convey consent through an onscreen click are legally enforceable as long as there has been an opportunity to review the terms before assenting. See UCITA § 112, Reporter Notes No. 5, Illustration 1. The UCITA is not applicable to electronically conducted transactions for the sale of goods that contain no embedded software.

**732 A2d 528 (NJ Super 1999).

***306 F3d 17, 29-30 (2d Cir 2002).

may accept it. If the offer is made to the public at large, any member of the public at large having knowledge of the existence of the offer may accept it.

When a person to whom an offer was not made attempts to accept it, the attempted acceptance has the effect of an offer. If the original offeror is willing to accept this offer, a binding contract arises. If the original offeror does not accept the new offer, there is no contract.

CPA 15. Manner and Time of Acceptance

The offeror may specify the manner and time for accepting the offer. When the offeror specifies that there must be a written acceptance, no contract arises when the offeree makes an oral acceptance. If the offeror calls for acceptance by a specified time and date, a late acceptance has no legal effect, and a contract is not formed. Where no time is specified in the offer, the offeree has a reasonable period of time to accept the offer. After the time specified in the offer or a reasonable period of time expires (when no time is specified in the offer), the offeree's power to make a contract by accepting the offer "lapses."

When the offeror calls for the performance of an act or of certain conduct, the performance thereof is an acceptance of the offer and creates a unilateral contract.

When the offeror has specified a particular manner and time of acceptance, generally, the offeree cannot accept in any other way. The basic rule applied by the courts is that the offeror is the master of the offer![23]

CPA (a) Silence as Acceptance

In most cases, the offeree's silence and failure to act cannot be regarded as an acceptance. Ordinarily, the offeror is not permitted to frame an offer in such a way as to make the silence and inaction of the offeree operate as an acceptance. Nor can a party to an existing contract effect a modification of that agreement without the other party's actual acceptance or approval. **For Example,** H. H. Taylor made a contract with Andy Stricker, a civil engineer, to design a small hotel. The parties agreed on an hourly rate with "total price not to exceed $7,200," and required that additional charges be presented to Taylor prior to proceeding with any changes. Andy was required to dedicate more hours to the project

23 See *1-800 Contacts, Inc v Weigner*, 127 P3d 1241 (Utah App 2005).

than anticipated but could not present the additional charges to Taylor because Taylor would not return his phone calls. He billed Taylor $9,035 for his services. Taylor's failure to act in not returning phone calls is not a substitute for the assent needed to modify a contract. Stricker is thus only entitled to $7,200.[24]

(b) Unordered Goods and Tickets

Sometimes a seller writes to a person with whom the seller has not had any prior dealings, stating that unless notified to the contrary, the seller will send specified merchandise and the recipient is obligated to pay for it at stated prices. There is no acceptance if the recipient of the letter ignores the offer and does nothing. The silence of the person receiving the letter is not an acceptance, and the sender, as a reasonable person, should recognize that none was intended.

This rule applies to all kinds of goods, books, magazines, and tickets sent through the mail when they have not been ordered. The fact that the items are not returned does not mean that they have been accepted; that is, the offeree is required neither to pay for nor to return the items. If desired, the recipient of the unordered goods may write "Return to Sender" on the unopened package and put the package back into the mail without any additional postage. The Postal Reorganization Act provides that the person who receives unordered mailed merchandise from a commercial sender has the right "to retain, use, discard, or dispose of it in any manner the recipient sees fit without any obligation whatsoever to the sender."[25] It provides further that any unordered merchandise that is mailed must have attached to it a clear and conspicuous statement of the recipient's right to treat the goods in this manner.

CPA 16. Communication of Acceptance

Acceptance by the offeree is the last step in the formation of a bilateral contract. Intuitively, the offeror's receipt of the acceptance should be the point in time when the contract is formed and its terms apply. When the parties are involved in face-to-face negotiations, a contract is formed upon the offeror's receipt of the acceptance. When the offeror hears the offeree's words of acceptance, the parties may then shake hands, signifying their understanding that the contract has been formed.

CPA (a) The Mailbox Rule

When the parties are negotiating at a distance from each other, special rules have developed as to when the acceptance takes effect based on the commercial expediency of creating a contract at the earliest period of time and the protection of the offeree. Under the so-called *mailbox rule*, a properly addressed, postage-paid mailed acceptance takes effect when the acceptance is placed into the control of the U.S. Postal Service[26] or, by judicial extension, is placed in the control of a private third-party carrier such as Federal Express or United Parcel Service. That is, the acceptance is effective upon dispatch even before it is received by the offeror.

The offeror may avoid the application of this rule by stating in the offer that acceptance shall take effect upon receipt by the offeror.

CPA (b) Determining the Applicable Means of Communication

The modern rule on the selection of the appropriate medium of communication of acceptance is that unless otherwise unambiguously indicated in the offer, it shall be construed as inviting acceptance in any manner and by any medium reasonable under the circumstances.[27] A medium of communication is normally reasonable if it is one used by the offeror or if it is customary in similar transactions at the time and place the offer is received. Thus, if the offeror uses the mail to extend an offer, the offeree may accept by using the mail. Indeed, acceptance by mail is ordinarily reasonable when the parties are negotiating at a distance even if the offer is not made by mail.

The *Cantu* case raises the question of whether a hand-delivered offer can be accepted by mail. In negotiations with respect to property with rapidly fluctuating value, such as corporate securities, an acceptance by mail may be too slow. It may be the custom of the parties to the negotiations to accept by telephone, e-mail, or fax.

24 *Stricker v Taylor*, 975 P2d 930 (Or App 1999).

25 Federal Postal Reorganization Act § 3009.

26 See *Adams v Lindsell*, 106 Eng Rep 250 (KB 1818). Common law jurisdictions have unanimously adopted the mailbox rule, as has the Restatement (Second) of Contracts § 63, and the UCC [see UCC § 1-201(26),(38)].

27 Restatement (Second) of Contracts § 30; UCC § 2-206(1)(a).

CANTU V CENTRAL EDUCATION AGENCY, 884 SW2D 563 (TEX APP 1994)

ACCEPTANCE BY MAIL MUST BE REASONABLE

Cantu had a teaching contract with the San Benito Consolidated Independent School District. She hand-delivered to her supervisor a written offer to resign. Three days later, the superintendent of schools mailed her a letter accepting the offer of resignation. Cantu then changed her mind, and the next day hand-delivered a letter withdrawing her resignation. The superintendent refused to recognize the attempted rescission of the resignation. Cantu appealed to the state district court. It decided against her, and she again appealed.

Judicial Opinion

SMITH, J. . . . On Saturday, August 18, 1990, shortly before the start of the school year, Cantu hand-delivered to her supervisor a letter of resignation, effective August 17, 1990. In this letter, Cantu requested that her final paycheck be forwarded to an address in McAllen, Texas, some fifty miles from the San Benito office where she tendered the resignation. The San Benito superintendent of schools, the only official authorized to accept resignations on behalf of the school district, received Cantu's resignation on Monday, August 20. The superintendent wrote a letter accepting Cantu's resignation the same day and deposited the letter, properly stamped and addressed, in the mail at approximately 5:15 P.M. that afternoon. At about 8:00 A.M. the next morning, August 21, Cantu hand-delivered to the superintendent's office a letter withdrawing her resignation. . . .

The aphorism "the offeror is the master of his offer" reflects the power of the offeror to impose conditions on acceptance of an offer, specify the manner of acceptance, or withdraw the offer before the offeree has effectively exercised the power of acceptance. However, more often than not, an offeror does not expressly authorize a particular mode, medium, or manner of acceptance. Consequently, particularly with parties communicating at a distance, a rule of law is needed to establish the point of contract formation and allocate the risk of loss and inconvenience that inevitably falls to one of the parties between the time that the offeree exercises, and the offeror receives, the acceptance. See I Arthur L. Corbin, *Contracts* § 78 (1963).

As Professor Corbin notes, courts could adopt a rule that no acceptance is effective until received, absent express authorization by the offeror; however, the mailbox rule, which makes acceptance effective on dispatch, closes the deal and enables performance more promptly, and places the risk of inconvenience on the party who originally has power to control the manner of acceptance. . . . "Even though the offer was not made by mail and there was no [express] authorization, the existing circumstances may be such as to make it reasonable for the offeree to accept by mail and to give the offeror reason to know that the acceptance will be so made." . . . In short, acceptance by mail is impliedly authorized if reasonable under the circumstances . . . .

We hold that it is proper to consider whether acceptance by mail is reasonably implied under the circumstances, whether or not the offer was delivered by mail.

. . . It was reasonable for the superintendent to accept Cantu's offer of resignation by mail. Cantu tendered her resignation shortly before the start of the school year—at a time when both parties could not fail to appreciate the need for immediate action by the district to locate a replacement. In fact, she delivered the letter on a Saturday, when the Superintendent could neither receive nor respond to her offer, further delaying matters by two days. Finally, Cantu's request that her final paycheck be forwarded to an address some fifty miles away indicated that she could no longer be reached in San Benito and that she did not intend to return to the school premises or school-district offices. The Commissioner of Education and district court properly considered that it was reasonable for the school district to accept Cantu's offer by mail. . . .

[Judgment affirmed]

Questions

1. At what point in time did the agreement to rescind Cantu's employment contract take effect?
2. Why did the court refer to the fact that Cantu's forwarding address was 50 miles away from the place where she delivered her offer to resign?
3. The *Cantu* case holds that a hand-delivered offer may always be accepted by a mailed acceptance. Appraise this statement.

CPA (c) Telephone and Electronic Communication of Acceptance

Although telephonic communication is very similar to face-to-face communication, most U.S. courts, nevertheless, have applied the mailbox rule, holding that telephoned acceptances are effective where and when dispatched.

The courts have yet to address the applicability of the mailbox rule to e-mail. However, when the offeree's server is under the control of an independent entity, such as an online service provider, and the offeree cannot withdraw the message, it is anticipated that the courts will apply the mailbox rule, and acceptance will take effect on proper dispatch. In the case of companies that operate their own servers, the acceptance will take effect when the message is passed onto the Internet.

Facsimile transmissions are substantially instantaneous and could be treated as face-to-face communications. However, it is anticipated that U.S. courts, when called upon to deal with this issue, will apply the mailbox acceptance-upon-dispatch rule as they do with telephoned acceptances.

(d) Effects of the Mailbox Rule

If an offer requires that acceptance be communicated by a specific date and the acceptance is properly dispatched by the offeree on the final date, the acceptance is timely and the contract is formed, even though the offeror actually receives the acceptance by well after the specified date has passed.

A situation may occur when a revocation and acceptance cross in the mail. As set forth previously, a revocation is effective only on the offeree's receipt. If an offeree dispatches an acceptance after the offeror has dispatched a revocation but before the revocation arrives, a contract is formed.

17. Auction Sales

At an auction sale, the statements made by the auctioneer to draw forth bids are merely invitations to negotiate. Each bid is an offer, which is not accepted

ETHICS & THE LAW

PepsiCo ran an ad and promotional campaign in 1996 called the "Drink Pepsi Get Stuff" campaign. The enormously successful campaign allowed customers to claim prizes in exchange for points on PepsiCo beverage containers, and the points could be combined with cash payments to obtain the prizes. The campaign was so successful that the second round of ads and promotions was not run because the prizes were nearly exhausted.

In one television ad, PepsiCo pictured a Harrier jet as a satirical spoof on the prizes available under the campaign. The jet was offered in the ad for 7 million beverage points. Harrier jets are made only for the Marine Corps and are not sold in the open market. They cost $33.8 million each and can be produced at a rate of only one dozen at a time.

John Leonard, a 21-year-old business student, called PepsiCo and was told he would need to drink 16.8 million cans of Pepsi in order to obtain the required points. He was also told that he had the option of buying PepsiCo points for 10¢ each. Leonard developed a pool of investors (Pepsi drinkers) and delivered 15 PepsiCo points and a check for $700,008.50 for the remaining 6,999,985 points plus shipping and handling.

PepsiCo refused to provide a Harrier jet to Leonard because it said the ad was not an offer but a joke. Leonard filed suit on August 6, 1996, but PepsiCo had already filed a preemptive suit on July 18, asking that Leonard's suit be dismissed and declared frivolous and that PepsiCo be reimbursed for its legal expenses.

Did PepsiCo make an offer? Did Leonard accept? What is the significance of Leonard's phone call and the verification of the PepsiCo points needed? Is there a contract? If you were a PepsiCo executive, what would you do? If there is a misunderstanding about the ad, is there an ethical obligation on the part of PepsiCo? Was Leonard taken advantage of, or is he taking advantage of PepsiCo? [*Leonard v PepsiCo, Inc.*, 210 F3d 88 (2d Cir 2000)]

until the auctioneer indicates that a particular offer or bid is accepted. Usually, this is done by the fall of the auctioneer's hammer, indicating that the highest bid made has been accepted.[28] Because a bid is merely an offer, the bidder may withdraw the bid at any time before it is accepted by the auctioneer.

Ordinarily, the auctioneer who is not satisfied with the amounts of the bids that are being made may withdraw any article or all of the property from the sale. Once a bid is accepted, however, the auctioneer cannot cancel the sale. In addition, if it had been announced that the sale was to be made "without reserve," the property must be sold to the person making the highest bid regardless of how low that bid may be.

In an auction "with reserve," the auctioneer takes bids as agent for the seller with the understanding that no contract is formed until the seller accepts the transaction.[29]

Funny Farm (1988) (PG)

Near the end of this Chevy Chase movie, two couples face a formation issue as one couple attempts to purchase a home. An offer, presented around a friendly kitchen table setting, is declined by the sellers. Do the buyers' threats to sue the sellers have any legal basis? While the buyers had made a special trip to see the land and felt that since they were offering more than the asking price that they had a contract, the sellers were free to reject the offer. Listing a house for a price is not an offer; it is an invitation for an offer.

For movie clips that illustrate business law concepts, see LawFlix at **http://wdvl.westbuslaw.com.**

[28] *Dry Creek Cattle Co. v Harriet Bros. Limited Partnership*, 908 P2d 399 (Wyo 1995).

[29] *Marten v Staab*, 543 NW2d 436 (Neb 1996). Statutes regulate auctions and auctioneers in all states. For example, state of Maine law prohibits an auctioneer from conducting an auction without first having a written contract with the consignor of any property to be sold, including (1) whether the auction is with reserve or without reserve, (2) the commission rate, and (3) a description of all items to be sold. See *Street v Board of Licensing of Auctioneers*, 889 A2d 319 (Me 2006).

Summary

Because a contract arises when an offer is accepted, it is necessary to find that there was an offer and that it was accepted. If either element is missing, there is no contract.

An offer does not exist unless the offeror has contractual intent. This intent is lacking if the statement of the person is merely an invitation to negotiate, a statement of intention, or an agreement to agree at a later date. Newspaper ads, price quotations, and catalog prices are ordinarily merely invitations to negotiate and cannot be accepted.

An offer must be definite. If an offer is indefinite, its acceptance will not create a contract because it will be held that the resulting agreement is too vague to enforce. In some cases, an offer that is by itself too indefinite is made definite because some writing or standard is incorporated by reference and made part of the offer. In some cases, the offer is made definite by implying terms that were not stated. In other cases, the indefinite part of the offer is ignored when that part can be divided or separated from the balance of the offer. In other cases, the requirement of definiteness is ignored either because the matter that is not definite is unimportant or because there is an exception to the rule requiring definiteness.

Assuming that there is in fact an offer that is made with contractual intent and that it is sufficiently definite, it still does not have the legal effect of an offer unless it is communicated to the offeree by or at the direction of the offeror.

In some cases, no contract arises because there is no offer that satisfies the requirements just stated. In other cases, there was an offer, but it was terminated before it was accepted. By definition, an attempted acceptance made after the offer has been terminated has no effect. The offeror may revoke the ordinary offer at any time. All that is required is the showing of intent to revoke and the communication of that intent to the offeree. The offeror's power to revoke is barred by the existence of an option contract under common law or a firm offer under the Uniform Commercial Code or local non-Code statute and by the application of the doctrine of detrimental reliance by the offeree. An offer is also terminated by the express rejection of the offer or by the making of a counteroffer, by the lapse of the time stated in the offer or of a reasonable time when none is stated, by the death or disability of either party, or by a change of law that makes illegal a contract based on the particular offer.

When the offer is accepted, a contract arises. Only the offeree can accept an offer, and the acceptance must be of the offer exactly as made without any qualification or change. Ordinarily, the offeree may accept or reject as the offeree chooses. Limitations on this freedom of action have been imposed by antidiscrimination and consumer protection laws.

The acceptance is any manifestation of intent to agree to the terms of the offer. Ordinarily, silence or failure to act does not constitute acceptance. The recipient of unordered goods and tickets may dispose of the goods or use the goods without such action constituting an acceptance. An acceptance does not exist until the words or conduct demonstrating assent to the offer is communicated to the offeror. Acceptance by mail takes effect at the time and place when and where the letter is mailed or the fax is transmitted. A telephoned acceptance is effective when and where dispatched.

In an auction sale, the auctioneer asking for bids makes an invitation to negotiate. A person making a bid is making an offer, and the acceptance of the highest bid by the auctioneer is an acceptance of that offer and gives rise to a contract. When the auction sale is without reserve, the auctioneer must accept the highest bid. If the auction is not expressly without reserve, the auctioner may refuse to accept any of the bids.

Questions and Case Problems

1. Bernie and Phil's Great American Surplus store placed an ad in the *Sunday Times* stating, "Next Saturday at 8:00 A.M. sharp, 3 brand new mink coats worth $5,000 each will be sold for $500 each! First come, First served." Marsha Lufklin was first in line when the store opened and went directly to the coat department, but the coats identified in the ad were not available for sale. She identified herself to the manager and pointed out that she was first in line in conformity with the store's advertised offer and that she was ready to pay the $500 price set forth in the store's offer. The manager responded that a newspaper ad is just an invitation to negotiate and that the store decided to withdraw "the mink coat promotion." Review the text on unilateral contracts in Section 12(b) of Chapter 12. Decide.
2. Brown made an offer to purchase Overman's house on a standard printed form. Underneath Brown's signature was the statement: "ACCEPTANCE ON REVERSE SIDE." Overman did not sign the offer on the back but sent Brown a letter accepting the offer. Later, Brown refused to perform the contract, and Overman sued him for breach of contract. Brown claimed there was no contract because the offer had not been accepted in the manner specified by the offer. Decide. [*Overman v Brown*, 372 NW2d 102 (Neb)]
3. Katherine mailed Paul an offer stating that it was good for 10 days. Two days later, she mailed Paul another letter stating that the original offer was revoked. That evening Paul phoned Katherine to say he accepted the offer. She said that he could not because she had mailed him a letter of revocation that he would undoubtedly receive in the next morning's mail. Was the offer revoked by Katherine?
4. Nelson wanted to sell his home. Baker sent him a written offer to purchase the home. Nelson made some changes to Baker's offer and wrote him that he, Nelson, was accepting the offer as amended. Baker notified Nelson that he was dropping out of the transaction. Nelson sued Baker for breach of contract. Decide. What social forces and ethical values are involved? [*Nelson v Baker*, 776 SW2d 52 (Mo App)]
5. Lessack Auctioneers advertised an auction sale that was open to the public and was to be conducted with reserve. Gordon attended the auction and bid $100 for a work of art that was worth much more. No higher bid, however, was made. Lessack refused to sell the item for $100 and withdrew the item from the sale. Gordon claimed that because he was the highest bidder, Lessack was required to sell the item to him. Was he correct?
6. Willis Music Co. advertised a television set at $22.50 in the Sunday newspaper. Ehrlich ordered a set, but the company refused to deliver it on the grounds that the price in the newspaper ad was a mistake. Ehrlich sued the company. Was it liable? Why or why not? [*Ehrlich v Willis Music Co.*, 113 NE2d 252 (Ohio App)]
7. When a movement was organized to build Charles City College, Hauser and others signed pledges to contribute to the college. At the time of signing, Hauser inquired what would happen if he should die or be unable to pay. The representative of the college stated that the pledge would then not be binding and that it was merely a statement of intent. The college failed financially, and Pappas was appointed receiver to collect and liquidate the assets of the college corporation. He sued Hauser for the amount due on his pledge. Hauser raised the defense that the pledge was not a binding contract. Decide. What ethical values are involved? [*Pappas v Hauser*, 197 NW2d 607 (Iowa)]
8. *A* signed a contract agreeing to sell land he owned but reserved the right to take the hay from the land until the following October. He gave the contract form to *B*, a broker. *C*, a prospective buyer, agreed to buy the land and

signed the contract but crossed out the provision regarding the hay crop. Was there a binding contract between *A* and *C*?

9. A. H. Zehmer discussed selling a farm to Lucy. After a 40-minute discussion of the first draft of a contract, Zehmer and his wife, Ida, signed a second draft stating: "We hereby agree to sell to W. O. Lucy the Ferguson farm complete for $50,000 title satisfactory to buyer." Lucy agreed to purchase the farm on these terms. Thereafter, the Zehmers refused to transfer title to Lucy and claimed they had made the contract for sale as a joke. Lucy brought an action to compel performance of the contract. The Zehmers claimed there was no contract. Were they correct? [*Lucy v Zehmer*, 84 SE2d 516 (Va App)]
10. Wheeler operated an automobile service station, which he leased from W. C. Cornitius, Inc. The lease ran for three years. Although the lease did not contain any provision for renewal, it was in fact renewed six times for successive three-year terms. The landlord refused to renew the lease for a seventh time. Wheeler brought suit to compel the landlord to accept his offer to renew the lease. Decide. [*William C. Cornitius, Inc. v Wheeler*, 556 P2d 666 (Or)]
11. Buster Cogdill, a real estate developer, made an offer to the Bank of Benton to have the bank provide construction financing for the development of an outlet mall, with funds to be provided at prime rate plus two percentage points. The bank's president Julio Plunkett thanked Buster for the proposal and said, "I will start the paperwork." Did Cogdill have a contract with the Bank of Benton? [*Bank of Benton v Cogdill*, 454 NE2d 1120 (Ill App)]
12. Ackerley Media Group, Inc., claimed to have a three-season advertising Team Sponsorship Agreement (TSA) with Sharp Electronics Corporation to promote Sharp products at all Seattle Supersonics NBA basketball home games. Sharp contended that a valid agreement did not exist for the third season (2000–2001) because a material price term was missing, thus resulting in an unenforceable "agreement to agree." The terms of the TSA for the 2000–2001 third season called for a base payment of $144,200 and an annual increase "not to exceed 6% [and] to be mutually agreed upon by the parties." No "mutually agreed" increase was negotiated by the parties. Ackerley seeks payment for the base price of $144,200 only. Sharp contends that since no price was agreed upon for the season, the entire TSA is un-enforceable, and it is not obligated to pay for the 2000–2001 season. Is Sharp correct? [*Ackerley Media Group, Inc. v Sharp Electronics Corp.*, 170 F Supp 2d 445 (SDNY)]
13. Calvin and Audrey Bones listed their ranch for sale with their real estate agent, Loren Johnson. On July 17, 1997, Dean Keller submitted an offer to buy the ranch for $490,000, with a deposit of $49,000 payable to the agent. The terms of the offer stated that it would be withdrawn if not accepted by July 21 at 5:00 P.M. At 4:53 P.M. on July 21, the Boneses faxed a signed copy of the offer to their agent. Paragraph 15 of the offer stated in part that "upon execution by seller this agreement shall become a binding contract." Loren Johnson, the sellers' real estate agent, did not telephone the buyer Keller to inform him of the acceptance until 5:12 P.M. on July 21, and then did so by leaving a message on Keller's answering machine. On July 22, the sellers had a change of heart and decided to sell to the current tenants of the ranch. Ms. Johnson called Keller to ask if he would be willing to allow the sellers to back out of the deal. Keller refused and brought suit to enforce "the contract." The Boneses contend that no valid contract was formed because the sellers' acceptance was not communicated to the buyer until after the deadline set forth in the offer had expired. Keller contends that as offeror he is the master of the offer, and the offer was silent with respect to the manner and time of acceptance. Thus, the manner and the time of acceptance must be rendered in a reasonable time and manner, where none is specified. The seller's agent left a message on the buyer's answering machine only 19 minutes after the seller signed the acceptance and 12 minutes after the 5:00 P.M. signing deadline, which according to Keller is a reasonable time and manner. Decide. [*Keller v Bones*, 615 NW2d 883 (Neb)]
14. On August 15, 2003, Wilbert Heikkila signed an agreement with Kangas Realty to sell eight parcels of Heikkila's property. On September 8, 2003, David McLaughlin met with a Kangas agent who drafted McLaughlin's offer to purchase three of the parcels. McLaughlin signed the offer and gave the agent checks for each parcel. On September 9 and 10, 2003, the agent for Heikkila prepared three printed purchase agreements, one for each parcel. On September 14, 2003, David's wife, Joanne McLaughlin, met with the agent and signed the agreements. On September 16, 2003, Heikkila met with his real estate agent. Writing on the printed agreements, Heikkila changed the price of one parcel from $145,000 to $150,000, the price of another parcel from $32,000 to $45,000, and the price of the third parcel from $175,000 to $179,000. Neither of the McLaughlins signed an acceptance of Heikkila's changes to the printed agreements before Heikkila withdrew his offer to sell. The McLaughlins learned that Heikkila had withdrawn his offer on January 1, 2004, when the real estate agent returned the checks to them. Totally shocked at Heikkila's conduct, the McLaughlins brought action to compel specific performance of the purchase agreement signed by Joanne McLaughlin on their behalf. Decide. [*McLaughlin v Heikkila*, 697 NW2d 231 (Minn App)]

CPA Questions

1. Able Sofa, Inc., sent Noll a letter offering to sell Noll a custom-made sofa for $5,000. Noll immediately sent a telegram to Able purporting to accept the offer. However, the telegraph company erroneously delivered the telegram to Abel Soda, Inc. Three days later, Able mailed a letter of revocation to Noll, which was received by Noll. Able refused to sell Noll the sofa. Noll sued Able for breach of contract. Able

   a. Would have been liable under the deposited acceptance rule only if Noll had accepted by mail

   b. Will avoid liability since it revoked its offer prior to receiving Noll's acceptance

   c. Will be liable for breach of contract

   d. Will avoid liability due to the telegraph company's error (Law, #2, 9911)

2. On September 27, Summers sent Fox a letter offering to sell Fox a vacation home for $150,000. On October 2, Fox replied by mail agreeing to buy the home for $145,000. Summers did not reply to Fox. Do Fox and Summers have a binding contract?

   a. No, because Fox failed to sign and return Summers's letter

   b. No, because Fox's letter was a counteroffer

   c. Yes, because Summers's offer was validly accepted

   d. Yes, because Summers's silence is an implied acceptance of Fox's letter (Law, #2, 0462)

3. On June 15, Peters orally offered to sell a used lawn mower to Mason for $125. Peters specified that Mason had until June 20 to accept the offer. On June 16, Peters received an offer to purchase the lawn mower for $150 from Bronson, Mason's neighbor. Peters accepted Bronson's offer. On June 17, Mason saw Bronson using the lawn mower and was told the mower had been sold to Bronson. Mason immediately wrote to Peters to accept the June 15 offer. Which of the following statements is correct?

   a. Mason's acceptance would be effective when received by Peters.

   b. Mason's acceptance would be effective when mailed.

   c. Peters's offer had been revoked and Mason's acceptance was ineffective.

   d. Peters was obligated to keep the June 15 offer open until June 20. (Law, #13, 3095)

CAPACITY AND GENUINE ASSENT

CHAPTER (14)

LEARNING OBJECTIVES

After studying this chapter, you should be able to

LO.1 Define *contractual capacity*

LO.2 State the extent and effect of avoidance of a contract by a minor

LO.3 Classify unilateral and bilateral mistakes

LO.4 Distinguish between innocent misrepresentation, fraud, and nondisclosure

LO.5 List those classes of persons who lack contractual capacity

LO.6 Distinguish between undue influence and duress

A *contract* is a binding agreement. This agreement must be made between parties who have the capacity to do so. They must also truly agree so that all parties have really consented to the contract. This chapter explores the elements of contractual capacity of the parties and the genuineness of their assent.

A. Contractual Capacity

Some persons lack contractual capacity, a lack that embraces both those who have a status incapacity, such as minors, and those who have a factual incapacity, such as persons who are insane.

1. Contractual Capacity Defined

Contractual capacity is the ability to understand that a contract is being made and to understand its general meaning. However, the fact that a person does not understand the full legal meaning of a contract does not mean that contractual capacity is lacking. Everyone is presumed to have capacity unless it is proven that capacity is lacking or there is status incapacity.[1] **For Example,** Jacqueline, aged 22, entered into a contract with Sunrise Storage Co. but later claimed it was not binding because she did not understand several clauses in the printed contract. The contract was binding. No evidence supported her claim that she lacked capacity to contract or to understand its subject. Contractual capacity can exist even though a party does not understand every provision of the contract.

(a) Status Incapacity

Over the centuries, the law has declared that some classes of persons lack contractual capacity. The purpose is to protect these classes by giving them the power to get out of unwise contracts. Of these classes, the most important today is the class identified as minors.

Until recent times, some other classes were held to lack contractual capacity in order to discriminate against them. Examples are married women and aliens. Still other classes, such as persons convicted of and sentenced for a felony, were held to lack contractual capacity in order to punish them. Today, these discriminatory and punitive incapacities have largely disappeared. Married women have the same contractual capacity as unmarried persons.[2]

By virtue of international treaties, the discrimination against aliens has been removed.

(b) Factual Incapacity

A *factual incapacity* contrasts with incapacity imposed because of the class or group to which a person belongs. A factual incapacity may exist when, because of a mental condition caused by medication, drugs, alcohol, illness, or age, a person does not understand that a contract is being made or understand its general nature. However, mere mental weakness does not incapacitate a person from contracting. It is sufficient if the individual has enough mental capacity to understand, to a reasonable extent, the nature and effect of what he is doing.[3]

2. Minors

Minors may make contracts.[4] To protect them, however, the law has always treated minors as a class lacking contractual capacity.

(a) Who Is a Minor?

At common law, any person, male or female, under 21 years of age was a minor. At common law, minority ended the day before the twenty-first birthday. The "day before the birthday" rule is still followed, but the age of majority has been reduced from 21 years to 18 years.

CPA (b) Minor's Power to Avoid Contracts

With exceptions that will be noted later, a contract made by a minor is voidable at the election of the minor. The minor may affirm or ratify the contract on attaining majority by performing the contract, by expressly approving the contract, or by allowing

[1] *In re Adoption of Smith*, 578 So 2d 988 (La App 1991).

[2] A few states have a limitation that a married woman cannot make a binding contract to pay the debt of her husband if he fails to.

[3] *Fisher v Schefers*, 656 NW2d 591 (Minn App 2003).

[4] *Buffington v State Automobile Mut. Ins. Co.*, 384 SE2d 873 (Ga App 1989).

a reasonable time to lapse without avoiding the contract.

CPA ***(1) What Constitutes Avoidance?*** A minor may avoid or *disaffirm* a contract by any expression of an intention to repudiate the contract. Any act inconsistent with the continuing validity of the contract is also an avoidance.

CPA ***(2) Time for Avoidance.*** A minor can disaffirm a contract only during minority and for a reasonable time after attaining majority. After the lapse of a reasonable time, the contract is deemed ratified and cannot be avoided by the minor.

CPA ***(3) Minor's Misrepresentation of Age.*** Generally, the fact that the minor has misrepresented his or her age does not affect the minor's power to disaffirm the contract. Some states hold that such fraud of a minor bars contract avoidance. Some states permit the minor to disaffirm the contract in such a case but require the minor to pay for any damage to the property received under the contract.

In any case, the other party to the contract may disaffirm it because of the minor's fraud.

CPA (c) Restitution by Minor after Avoidance

When a minor disaffirms a contract, the question arises as to what the minor must return to the other contracting party.

(1) Original Consideration Intact. When a minor still has what was received from the other party, the minor, on avoiding the contract, must return it to the other party or offer to do so. That is, the minor must put things back to the original position or, as it is called, restore the **status quo ante**.

(2) Original Consideration Damaged or Destroyed. What happens if the minor cannot return what has been received because it has been spent, used, damaged, or destroyed? The minor's right to disaffirm the contract is not affected. The minor can still disaffirm the contract and is required to return only what remains. The fact that nothing remains or that what remains is damaged does not bar the right to disaffirm the contract. In states that follow the common law rule, minors can thus refuse to pay for what has been received under a contract or can get back what had been paid or given even though they do not have anything to return or return property in a damaged condition. There is, however, a trend to limit this rule.

(d) Recovery of Property by Minor on Avoidance

When a minor disaffirms a contract, the other contracting party must return the money received. Any property received from the minor must also be returned. If the property has been sold to a third person who did not know of the original seller's minority, the minor cannot get the property back. In such cases, however, the minor is entitled to recover the property's monetary value or the money received by the other contracting party.

CPA (e) Contracts for Necessaries

A minor can disaffirm a contract for necessaries but must pay the reasonable value for furnished necessaries.

(1) What Constitutes Necessaries? Originally, **necessaries** were limited to those things absolutely necessary for the sustenance and shelter of the minor. Thus limited, the term would extend only to food, clothing, and lodging. In the course of time, the rule was relaxed to extend generally to things relating to the health, education, and comfort of the minor. Thus, the rental of a house used by a married minor is a necessary.

(2) Liability of Parent or Guardian. When a third person supplies the parents or guardian of a minor with goods or services that the minor needs, the minor is not liable for these necessaries because the third person's contract is with the parent or guardian, not with the minor.

When necessary medical care is provided a minor, a parent is liable at common law for the medical expenses provided the minor child. However, at common law, the child can be held contractually liable for her necessary medical expenses when the parent is unable or unwilling to pay.

In the *Schmidt* case, the court dealt with the public policy considerations behind this rule.

SCHMIDT V PRINCE GEORGE'S HOSPITAL, 784 A 2D 1112 (MD 2001)

THE CONCUSSION AND LEGAL REPERCUSSION

On March 7, 1997, sixteen-year-old Michelle Schmidt was involved in a two-vehicle auto collision. She was transported to the Shock Trauma Unit at Prince George's Hospital, where she was initially admitted as "Jane Doe," without an emergency contact person or telephone number, because she was unconscious at the time of arrival. Although the hospital later was able to identify her name and address, it was only able to determine that her father was "Mr. Schmidt," and it obtained a telephone number for him. Due to the severity of her injuries sustained in the collision, the hospital provided necessary emergency medical care for a brain concussion and an open scalp wound. As of her discharge on March 8, 1997, she had incurred hospital expenses in the amount of $1,756.24. Ms. Schmidt was insured with personal injury protection (PIP) benefits through her father's insurance company, Erie Insurance Group. Erie issued a check in the amount of $1,756.24 to "Lewis A. Schmidt for Minor, Michelle Schmidt" in reference to "Prince George's Hospital Center, Service Date 03-07-1997 to 03-08-1997." The check was negotiated, but the funds were not used to pay the hospital; rather, the funds apparently were used to purchase a replacement automobile for Ms. Schmidt. After Ms. Schmidt attained her eighteenth birthday and failed to pay the hospital, it brought suit against her. From a judgement for the hospital, she appealed to the seven justice Court of Appeals.

Judicial Opinion

HARRELL, J. . . .

[I]

A.

In the absence of a statute to the contrary, the prevailing modern rule is that a minor's contracts are voidable; nevertheless, it also is well established that a minor may be liable for the value of necessaries furnished to him or her. This doctrine, eponymously referred to as the doctrine of necessaries, is well recognized in Maryland law. In *Monumental Building Association v Herman*, 33 Md. 128, (1870), our venerable predecessor explained somewhat the breadth and application of this doctrine.

By the common law, persons, under the age of twenty-one years* are not bound by their contracts, *except for necessaries*, nor can they do any act, to the injury of their property, which they may not avoid, when arrived at full age. . . . Infants have this indulgence from their supposed want of judgment in their transactions with others, and the law takes this care of them to prevent them from being imposed upon, or overreached by persons of more years and experience.

They are allowed to contract for their benefit with power in most cases, to recede from their contract when it may prove prejudicial to them, *but in their contract for necessaries, such as board, apparel, medical aid, teaching and instruction, and other necessaries, they are absolutely bound, and may be sued and charged in execution;* but it must appear that the things were absolutely necessary, and suitable to their circumstances, and whoever trusts them does so at his peril, or as it is said, deals with them at arms' length.

Their power, thus to contract for necessaries, is for their benefit, because the procurement of these things is essential to their existence, and if they were not permitted so to bind themselves they might suffer.

Monumental, 33 Md. at 131–32 (emphasis added). . . .

The rationales underlying [named precedent cases] recognize that public policy and justice demand that an injured minor have the right to recover incurred medical expenses from a third-party tortfeasor, where the child's parents are unable or unwilling to pay for those expenses, *because the medical provider may sue to recover them*, either during the child's minority or within the statute of limitations after the child has reached the age of majority. By parity of reasoning, it would seem that such a child, upon attaining adulthood, may be liable in contract to pay for medical necessaries provided to him or her while a minor, if the parents were unable or unwilling to pay for such necessaries. Before we may reach such a holding, however, it seems prudent to examine how, if at all, our sister states

*Effective 1 July 1973, the age of majority in Maryland was reduced from 21 to 18 years of age. Maryland Code (1957, 1998 Repl. Vol.), Art. I § 24.

regard the unwillingness prong of this aspect of the doctrine of necessaries.

B.

There appears to be no case elsewhere that supplies a user-friendly, all-purpose definition or scope of the term "unwilling to pay" in connection with the doctrine of necessaries. The vast majority of these cases share two common traits; they are bereft of detailed or substantive analysis of the "unwillingness" standard, and the varying outcomes are largely fact-driven. . . .

Some states appear to hold that, in order to find a parent "unwilling," thus making a child liable for his or her necessaries, a court should require hard and fast proof of default by the parents. Those states note that in order to meet the requirement of "unwilling," it must be shown that a parent was billed and/or sued and still refused to pay. We shall not subscribe to that requirement as an essential prerequisite to a finding of unwillingness.

There are a significant number of states that interpret their version of the doctrine of necessaries as placing liability on a child *only* when his or her parents are financially unable to pay. . . .

. . . Overweighing the arguable unfairness to the minor in the balancing, at least in the present case, is the consideration of not placing hospitals and other emergency health care providers in a situation where apparently financially-able individuals may avoid paying for necessary medical treatment through a contrivance similar to that demonstrated on the record of this case.

. . . The doctrine of necessaries states that a minor may be held liable for the necessaries, including medical necessaries, which he or she is afforded when his or her parents are either unable or unwilling to pay. Consistent with this principle, Respondent, on the present facts, could have: (a) sued Petitioner, while she was still a minor, and her father; or, (b), as was done in the present case, sued Petitioner upon her reaching the age of majority.

. . . The father's refusal to apply the insurance proceeds to the debt owed Respondent—the existence of which he was well aware of as it was the facial premise for which he and Petitioner supplied to Erie in the first place—is a clear indication of his unwillingness to pay for Petitioner's medical expenses at a time fairly contemporaneous with the provision of the medical services, i.e., within 60 days. We agree with the Circuit Court, which found that, as an adult, Petitioner is liable for the medical treatment expenses which she incurred while a minor. We find no error in the Circuit Court's conclusions that Petitioner could be held liable for those medical expenditures provided for her benefit under the doctrine of necessaries, which trumps her defense that she was under the disability of minority when she entered into the implied promise to pay Respondent for the needed medical treatment. Lastly, we agree that the record supports that Petitioner's father was unwilling to pay for his then minor daughter's medical necessaries, which, in turn, left Petitioner primarily liable for the debt to Respondent.**

[Judgment affirmed]

Dissenting Opinion

RAKER, J., dissenting, joined by BELL, C.J., and ELDRIDGE, J.:

The majority finds petitioner liable to respondent because her father was *unwilling* to pay for petitioner's medical expenses, not because her father was *unable* to pay. . . . The majority believes that the father's failure to use insurance proceeds to pay the hospital for his daughter's medical bills is a "clear indication" of his unwillingness to pay for petitioner's medical expenses. There is little case law in this State, or any other state, to help us decide when a parent is unwilling to pay for his or her child's necessary medical costs. What little law there is, however, suggests that where a child is supported by his or her parents, the parents' failure or default on single necessary expense does not usually render the child liable for that expense.

Questions

1. What is the historical policy basis for the modern rule that minors' contracts are voidable; and what is the basis for the exception that minors may be liable for necessaries?
2. In layperson's terms, explain the public policy utilized to support the court's decision to hold Ms. Schmidt liable for the unpaid emergency care provided to her while she was a minor?
3. What is the dissent's view of the case?

** On this record, Petitioner may have been able to implead her father in this litigation, whose parental duties during Petitioner's minority included paying for her necessaries, such as the medical expenses in issue. If Petitioner's father was able, but merely unwilling, to pay for her medical necessaries, it would not violate public policy for Petitioner, as an adult, to sue her parent for failure to provide for her necessaries . . .

CPA (f) Ratification of Former Minor's Voidable Contract

A former minor cannot disaffirm a contract that has been ratified after reaching majority.[5]

CPA ***(1) What Constitutes Ratification?*** Ratification consists of any words or conduct of the former minor manifesting an intent to be bound by the terms of a contract made while a minor.

CPA ***(2) Form of Ratification.*** Generally, no special form is required for ratification of a minor's voidable contract, although in some states a written ratification or declaration of intention is required.

CPA ***(3) Time for Ratification.*** A person can disaffirm a contract any time during minority and for a reasonable time after that but, of necessity, can ratify a contract only after attaining majority. The minor must have attained majority, or the ratification would itself be regarded as voidable.

(g) Contracts That Minors Cannot Avoid

Statutes in many states deprive a minor of the right to avoid an educational loan[6]; a contract for medical care; a contract made while running a business; a contract approved by a court; a contract made in performance of a legal duty; and a contract relating to bank accounts, insurance policies, or corporate stock.

(h) Liability of Third Person for a Minor's Contract

The question arises as to whether parents are bound by the contract of their minor child. The question of whether a person cosigning a minor's contract is bound if the contract is avoided also arises.

(1) Liability of Parent. Ordinarily, a parent is not liable on a contract made by a minor child. The parent may be liable, however, if the child is acting as the agent of the parent in making the contract. Also, the parent is liable to a seller for the reasonable value of necessaries supplied by the seller to the child if the parent had deserted the child.

(2) Liability of Cosigner. When the minor makes a contract, another person, such as a parent or a friend, may sign along with the minor to make the contract more acceptable to the third person.

With respect to the other contracting party, the cosigner is bound independently of the minor. Consequently, if the minor disaffirms the contract, the cosigner remains bound by it. When the debt to the creditor is actually paid, the obligation of the cosigner is discharged.

If the minor disaffirms a sales contract but does not return the goods, the cosigner remains liable for the purchase price.

3. Mentally Incompetent Persons

A person with a mental disorder may be so disabled as to lack capacity to make a contract. If the person is so mentally incompetent as to be unable to understand that a contract is being made or the general nature of the contract, the person lacks contractual capacity.

(a) Effect of Incompetency

An incompetent person may ordinarily avoid a contract in the same manner as a minor. Upon the removal of the disability (that is, upon becoming competent), the formerly incompetent person can either ratify or disaffirm the contract.

A mentally incompetent person or his estate is liable for the reasonable value of all necessaries furnished that individual.

A current trend in the law is to treat an incompetent person's contract as binding when its terms and the surrounding circumstances are reasonable and the person is unable to restore the other contracting party to the status quo ante.

(b) Appointment of Guardian

If a court appoints a guardian for the incompetent person, a contract made by that person before the appointment may be ratified or, in some cases, disaffirmed by the guardian. If the incompetent person makes a contract after a guardian has been appointed, the contract is void and not merely voidable.

[5] *Fletcher v Marshall*, 632 NE2d 1105 (Ill App 1994).

[6] A Model Student Capacity to Borrow Act makes educational loans binding on minors in Arizona, Mississippi, New Mexico, North Dakota, Oklahoma, and Washington. This act was reclassified from a uniform act to a model act by the Commissioners on Uniform State Law, indicating that uniformity was viewed as unimportant and that the matter was primarily local in character.

ETHICS & THE LAW

Globe Life Insurance Company has undertaken a new sales program that targets neighborhoods in Los Angeles where drive-by shootings were a nightly occurrence. In two such shootings, children were killed as they sat in their living rooms.

Globe salespeople were instructed to "hit" the houses surrounding those where children were victims. They were also told to contact the parents of those children to sell policies for their other children.

Tom Raskin, an experienced Globe salesman, read of a drive-by shooting at Nancy Leonard's home, in which Leonard's five-year-old son was killed. The *Los Angeles Times* reported that Leonard was a single parent with four other children.

Raskin traveled to Leonard's home and described the benefits of a Globe policy for her other children. He offered her the $10,000 term life policy for each of the children for a total cost of $21 per month. Leonard was in the process of making funeral arrangements for her son, and Raskin noted, "See how much it costs for a funeral."

Leonard had been given several tranquilizers the night before by a physician at the hospital's emergency room. The physician had also given her 15 more tranquilizers to help her through the following week. She had taken one additional tranquilizer an hour before Raskin arrived, using a Coors Lite beer to take the pill.

Leonard signed the contract for the policy. After her son's funeral, she received the first month's bill for it and exclaimed, "I didn't buy any life insurance! Where did this come from?"

After you discuss Leonard's legal standing, discuss the ethical issues involved in Globe's sales program. Discuss the legal issues involved in Raskin's decision to target Leonard the day after her son's death.

FIGURE 14-1 Avoidance of Contract

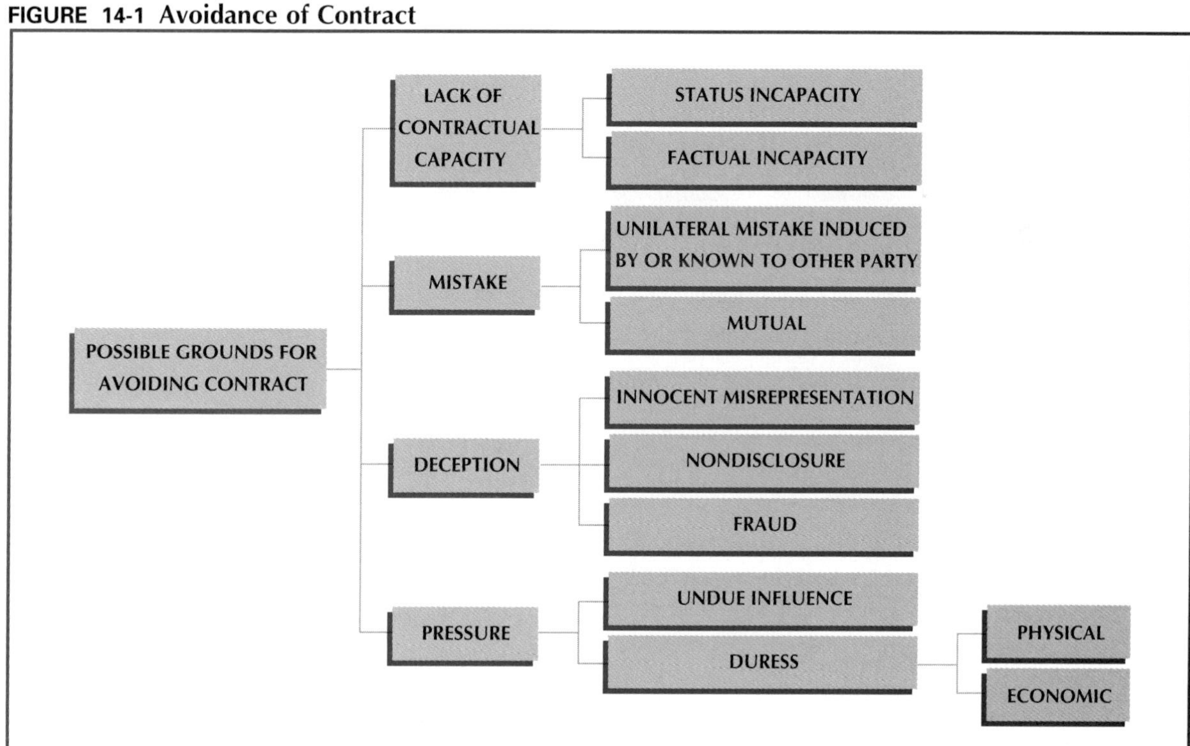

4. Intoxicated Persons

The capacity of a party to contract and the validity of the contract are not affected by the party's being impaired by alcohol at the time of making the contract so long as the party knew that a contract was being made.

If the degree of intoxication is such that a person does not know that a contract is being made, the contract is voidable by that person. The situation is the same as though the person were insane at the time and did not know what he or she was doing. On becoming sober, the individual may avoid or rescind the contract. However, an unreasonable delay in taking steps to set aside a known contract entered into while intoxicated may bar the intoxicated person from asserting this right.[7]

For Example, Edward made a contract while intoxicated. When he sobered up, he immediately disaffirmed the contract for lack of capacity as the result of his intoxication. The other contracting party claimed that voluntary intoxication cannot void a contract, but Edward could disaffirm the contract because he lacked the legal capacity to enter a contract.

The courts treat impairment caused by the use of drugs the same as impairment caused by the excessive use of alcohol.

CPA B. Mistake

The validity of a contract may be affected by the fact that one or both of the parties made a mistake. In some cases, the mistake may be caused by the misconduct of one of the parties.

5. Unilateral Mistake

A *unilateral mistake*—that is, a mistake by only one of the parties—as to a fact does not affect the contract when the mistake is unknown to the other contracting party.[8] When a contract is made on the basis of a quoted price, the validity of the contract is not affected by the fact that the party furnishing the quotation made a mathematical mistake in computing the price if there was no reason for the other party to recognize that there had been a mistake.[9] The party making the mistake may avoid the contract if the other contracting party knew or should have known of the mistake.

6. Mutual Mistake

When both parties enter into a contract under a mutually mistaken understanding concerning a basic assumption of fact or law on which the contract is made, the contract is voidable by the adversely affected party if the mistake has a material effect on the agreed exchange.[10]

In the *Mattson* case, both parties to the contract were mistaken in their belief that a lifetime agricultural leaseback was legal and a proper device to utilize in structuring their land contract, and the mistake had a material effect on the agreed exchange.

MATTSON V RACHETTO, 591 NW2D 814 (SD 1999)

IGNORANCE OF THE LAW IS AN EXCUSE IN THIS CASE

Jon and Barbara Mattson brought an action against Jerry and Joan Rachetto for rescission of a land contract after the contract's agricultural leaseback provision was found to be illegal. From a judgment for the Mattsons, the Rachettos appealed.

Judicial Opinion

GILBERTSON, J. . . . Jon and Barbara Mattson are husband and wife. Jerry and Joan Rachetto are husband and wife. Jerry Rachetto and Barbara Mattson are brother and sister. Additionally, Jon Mattson and Jerry Rachetto are both attorneys who shared a law office in Deadwood. . . .

In 1974 when Jerry Rachetto returned to Deadwood from law school, he went to work for Jon Mattson. He later

[7] *Diedrich v Diedrich*, 424 NW2d 580 (Minn App 1988).

[8] *Truck South Inc. v Patel*, 528 SE2d 424 (SC 2000).

[9] *Procan Construction Co. v Oceanside Development Corp.*, 539 NYS2d 437 (App Div 2d 1989).

[10] See *Browning v Howerton*, 966 P2d 367 (Wash App 1998).

expressed a desire to build a house on Tract A of the Mattson Ranch. The Mattsons deeded Tract A to Jerry and Joan Rachetto. Tract A consisted of 1.837 acres. No money was paid for this land. The Mattsons also gave the Rachettos an easement through their ranch property so the Rachettos could access their house from the highway. The easement passed through Tract C and the Ray Placer Sub-division.

In 1984, the Rachettos approached the Mattsons about buying Tract C so they could have a buffer zone between Rachettos' property and the Ray Placer Sub-division to ensure no future development adjacent to the Rachetto home. Tract C was composed of approximately eighteen (18) acres. The Mattsons were willing to sell Tract C but not without a specific leaseback provision that allowed them to cultivate hay and graze livestock on the tract for their lifetime. The Mattsons sold Tract C to the Rachettos for the consideration of $26,959.50 and the agricultural leaseback. The Mattsons also agreed to reimburse the Rachettos for the real property tax levied against the property for the term of the agricultural lease. The price charged was far less than the value of other lots on the ranch.

After several drafts of the agreement, the parties agreed to the terms for the sale. Neither party knew or realized the agricultural lease was void under SDCL 43–32–2.* In 1996, Jerry Rachetto came across the decision of *Commercial Trust & Sav. Bank v Christensen*, 535 N.W.2d 853 (S.D. 1995), in which we interpreted part of SDCL 43–32–2. The Rachettos, without informing the Mattsons of this discovery, erected an electric fence around Tract C. The Mattsons did not discover the mistake until the Rachettos put up the electric fence. Jerry Rachetto, when confronted, brought the *Christensen case* to the Mattsons' attention.

When the Mattsons learned the agricultural lease was invalid as a matter of law, they attempted to negotiate some type of compromise. All offers were rejected by the Rachettos, as they wanted to use the land for their own purposes.** The Mattsons attempted to tender rescission offering the purchase price plus interest. The Rachettos refused.

The Mattsons then filed a complaint for rescission of the land contract. . . .

The Rachettos claim the trial court erred or abused its discretion in allowing summary judgment on the Mattsons' count for rescission of the 1984 land sale. They claim the Mattsons do not need the land for agricultural use but instead want it back because of its significant increase in value and their desire to sub-divide the land.

The Mattsons . . . claim rescission is permissible due to a mistake of law. The Mattsons contend both parties made a mutual mistake of law—the lifetime agricultural leaseback in the contract. . . .

Mistake of Law.

The Mattsons claim that both parties made a mistake of law as defined in SDCL 53–4–10. This provision states:

A mistake of law in relation to consent to contract constitutes a mistake resulting in voidable consent only when it arises from:

(1) A misapprehension of the law by all parties, all supposing that they knew and understood it and all making substantially the same mistake as to the law[.]

"The equitable relief of rescission, being extraordinary, should never be granted, except where the evidence is clear and convincing." In an equity case, we are required to read all the evidence produced and give consideration to the facts and circumstances in the record.

The Mattsons had worked very hard over the years to build up their family ranch. They only acquired title to Tract C after a long struggle with the federal government. Tract C was the best hay and watering ground they had for their livestock. They sold Tract C to their relatives, the Rachettos, only because the Rachettos were close relatives, expressed their concerns over the encroaching sub-division and because they assured the Mattsons via the agricultural leaseback provision they could continue to graze cattle. It is quite clear that the Mattsons would not have sold Tract C at this price if they were not assured the use of the land via the agricultural leaseback. Tract C was the Mattsons' best grazing and hay land which is exhibited by the fact that after they were denied access to Tract C, the Mattsons were forced to purchase hay to feed their cattle.

Although there clearly was a mistake of law neither side took advantage of the other. Both parties admitted they did not know the agricultural leaseback was illegal. Mattson and Rachetto were licensed attorneys working in the same office who negotiated the terms of the agreement in good faith which went through several drafts before becoming acceptable to all parties.

The mere fact the statute is a public record is not the controlling factor in this case. It is a statutorily recognized exception to the old axiom "ignorance of the law is no excuse." Freedom from negligence is not a requirement to invoke the mistake of law claim provided by SDLC 53–4–10. . . .

The trial court restored the parties to where they were before they made their contractual mistake. The trial court

*SDCL 43–32–2 states:
"No lease or grant of agricultural land for a longer period than twenty years . . . shall be valid."

**Jerry Rachetto has built a golf course green and tee box on the property.

did not abuse its discretion in righting a wrong caused by a mutual mistake of law. As there is no genuine issue of material fact, we affirm. . . .

Following rescission of the contract the trial court ordered the Mattsons to repay Rachettos the purchase price of Tract C, $26,950.50 and pay an additional $24,212.69 in interest. . . .

[Judgment affirmed]

Questions

1. Is the ignorance of the applicable law a defense to a lawsuit based on mutual mistake of law?
2. Explain how the mutual mistake concerning a basic assumption of law on which the contract was made had a material effect on the agreed exchange between Mattson and Rachetto.

A contract based on *a mutual mistake in judgment* is not voidable by the adversely affected party. **For Example,** if both parties believe that a colt is not fast enough to develop into a competitive race horse and effect a sale accordingly, when the animal later develops into the winner of the Preakness as a three-year-old, the seller cannot rescind the contract based on mutual mistake because the mutual mistake was a mistake in judgment. In contrast, when two parties to a contract believe a cow to be barren at the time they contract for its sale, but before delivery of the animal to the buyer, it is discovered that the assumption was mistaken, such is a mutual mistake of fact making the contract void.[11]

7. Mistake in the Transcription or Printing of the Contract: Reformation

In some instances, the parties make an oral agreement, and in the process of committing it to writing or printing it from a manuscript, a phrase, term, or segment is inadvertently left out of the final, signed document. The aggrieved party may petition the court to **reform** the contract to reflect the actual agreement of the parties. However, the burden of proof is heightened to clear and convincing evidence that such a mistake was made. **For Example,** the Printers International Union reached agreement for a new three-year contract with a large regional printing company. As was their practice, the union negotiators then met with Sullivan Brothers Printers, Inc., a small specialty shop employing 10 union printers, and Sullivan Brothers and the union agreed to follow the contractual pattern set by the union and the large printer. That is, Sullivan Brothers agreed to give its workers all of the benefits negotiated for the employees of the large printing company. When the contract was typed, a new benefit of 75 percent employer-paid coverage for a dental plan was inadvertently omitted from the final contract that the parties signed. The mistake was not discovered until later, and Sullivan Brothers, Inc., is now reluctant to assume the additional expense. Based on the clear and convincing evidence of a practice of following the contractual pattern set by the large printer and Sullivan's assent to again follow the pattern, a court or arbitrator will reform the contract.

C. Deception

One of the parties may have been misled by a fraudulent statement. In such situations, there is no true or genuine assent to the contract, and it is voidable at the innocent party's option.

8. Intentional Misrepresentation

Fraud is a generic term embracing all multifarious means that human ingenuity can devise and that are resorted to by one individual to get advantage over another. It is classified in the law as a *tort.* However, where a party is induced into making a contract by a material misrepresentation of fact, this form of fraudulent activity adversely affects the genuineness of the assent of the innocent party, and this type of fraud is the focus of our discussion in the chapters on contracts.

9. Fraud

Fraud is the making of a material misrepresentation (or false statement) of fact with (1) knowledge of its falsity or reckless indifference to its truth, (2) the intent that the listener rely on it, (3) the result that the listener does so rely, and (4) the consequence that the listener is harmed.[12]

[11] See *Sherwood v Walker*, 66 Mich 568 (1887).

[12] *Maack v Resource Design & Construction, Inc.*, 875 P2d 570 (Utah 1994); *Bortz v Noon*, 729 A2d 555 (Pa 1999).

The *Tschira* case deals with the tort of fraudulent misrepresentation and is a clear example of how fraud impacts on the genuineness of the contractual assent of the affected party. Note that the Tschiras did not seek to *rescind* (cancel) the two contracts they entered as a result of the fraudulent misrepresentations, which ordinarily is the first remedy sought in fraud cases, because they canceled the management agreement upon discovery of the fraud, and they later sold at a loss the property that was the subject of the second contract. The remedies they sought were the actual damages they suffered as a result of the fraud and punitive damages to punish and make an example of the perpetrators of the wrongdoings.

TSCHIRA V WILLINGHAM, 135 F3D 1077 (6TH CIR 1998)

WATCH OUT! SOME PEOPLE HAVE A LOT OF NERVE

German citizens Klaus and Gerda Tschira brought suit against Corim, Inc., a U.S. real estate investment firm and its president Ben Willingham Jr. for fraudulent misrepresentation during a real estate transaction between the Tschiras and Corim. From a judgment for the Tschiras, Corim and Willingham appealed.

Judicial Opinion

GIBSON, J. . . . In 1988, Klaus Tschira benefitted financially when the company he helped to create, SAP AG ("SAP"), went public in Germany. In search of investment opportunities, Klaus learned through a German real estate broker, Claus Schenk, that Appellants were soliciting investors for commercial property in the southeastern United States. Intrigued by this information. Klaus, who was joined by other SAP founders, attended a meeting in Walldorf, Germany at which Willingham, who speaks fluent German, made a presentation. According to trial testimony, Willingham explained that Corim proposed to obtain buildings for purchase by investors at a "fair market price"; Corim then intended to enter into management contracts with the new owners. By the terms of the management contracts, Corim and Willingham would lease the buildings from the investors and, in return, would then pay the investors a contractually established rent amounting to approximately eight percent annually of the purchase price of the building. Klaus testified that he inquired as to how Willingham and Corim would earn a profit, and Willingham responded that Corim would receive revenue via the difference between the rents Corim would charge for its subleases and the rent Corim itself paid the investors.

The Tschiras found the investment attractive and initially agreed to buy four buildings in various southern cities and lease those properties back to Corim. The Tschiras did not procure independent American counsel for these transactions, as they claim to have regarded Willingham as their trusted agent. . . .

In late 1990, Schenk brought Klaus a Corim brochure about One Church Street, a Nashville, Tennessee property. The brochure advertised One Church Street as a five story commercial building erected in 1872, available for $1,985,000. The pamphlet described the property as having "a special architectural character" and said the building had been "recently renovated with substantial effort and expense." J.A. at 358. Corim guaranteed rent payments of $158,000 the first two years of the lease back, $165,000 the third and fourth years, and $171,000 the fifth year. The Tschiras expressed interest, and soon thereafter they received the Letter from Willingham. The document guaranteed that the building would be "insured sufficiently, so that it can be restored from the proceeds of the insurance in the event of destruction or damage." J.A. at 182. The final paragraph of the letter states that "[t]he powers of attorney given to us will only be used according to the forthcoming agreement." *Id.* Willingham had signed the copy of the Letter he mailed to the Tschiras. After reviewing the available materials, the Tschiras decided to invest in the property. They did not, however, secure independent counsel for the deal, visit One Church Street prior to the purchase, or obtain an appraisal from any source other than Corim.

The Tschiras and Corim subsequently entered into a Purchase Agreement for the Nashville property. They simultaneously executed a Management Agreement for the building. . . .

Several years later, the Tschiras discovered other details surrounding the sale of the Nashville building.

Namely, they learned that two closings occurred on December 14, 1990. In the first, One Church Street, Inc., shell corporation owned by Corim and Willingham, purchased the property from its owner, First Atlanta Services Corporation. The selling price in this deal was $774,000. In the second transaction, One Church Street, Inc. sold the building to the Tschiras for $1,985,000. Schenk, the German national who referred the Tschiras to Corim, received a $79,400 commission from Corim for his part in the sale. Willingham admitted at trial that the Tschiras were never advised that the shell company purchased the property and then resold it for an instant profit of $1,211,000. When the Tschiras became aware of these facts in the Spring of 1992, they canceled the Management Agreement with Corim and brought the instant lawsuit. In 1995, the Tschiras sold One Church Street for $665,000.

In their Complaint, the Tschiras claimed that Corim and Willingham. . . committed the tort of intentional misrepresentation. Two key pieces of evidence at trial were the title and liability insurance policies issued for One Church Street. The title insurance policy Willingham forwarded to the Tschiras indicated that the Ticor Title Insurance Company had provided protection up to $1,985,000. In actuality, Lisa Wilson, the local branch manager of Ticor, testified that the policy the company extended for the property was for only $774,000. Evidence also suggested that the liability insurance policy the Tschiras received, which purported to originate from Palmer Cay/Carswell and indicated coverage in the amount of $1,985,000, only provided protection up to $774,000. . . .

The jury awarded $1,420,000 in compensatory damages against Corim and Willingham, as well as $1,000,000 in punitive damages against Corim and $750,000 in punitive damages against Willingham. . . .

To establish a cause of action for fraudulent misrepresentation, a plaintiff must prove: (1) an intentional misrepresentation, (2) knowledge of the representation's falsity, (3) the plaintiff reasonably relied on the misrepresentation and suffered damages, and (4) the misrepresentation relates to an existing or past fact. See *Hill v John Banks Buick, Inc.*, 875 S.W.2d 667, 670 (Tenn.Ct.App.1993). The evidence presented at trial was sufficient to uphold the jury's finding of fraudulent misrepresentation. Willingham promised the Tschiras a fair market price for the property they were buying, as well as adequate title and property insurance to cover any losses. The evidence was sufficient to establish that, at the time Willingham promised this to the Tschiras, he knew the property's value was closer to $774,000, which is the price Corim paid for the property. The jury could have reasonably found that Willingham had knowledge of the false title and property insurance policies which only covered the property up to $774,000, while the Tschiras believed the property was covered up to $1,985,000—the price they paid for the property.

Appellants argue that the representations were not material because they provided a "guaranteed" return on the Tschiras' investment through the rental income. However, the jury could have reasonably found otherwise. The Tschiras believed they were paying "fair market price" for the purchase of the property, *in addition to* receiving a guaranteed return on their investment. The Tschiras believed, and the jury could have reasonably concluded, that the Tchiras actually paid $1,211,000 over the fair market price of the property and therefore lost that amount on their investment at the time of purchase. Finally, we conclude that the evidence was sufficient to support the jury's determination that the Tschiras reasonably relied on the representations and suffered damages as a result of that reliance. The Tschiras believed, based on the letter of November 26, 1990, that Willingham was their trusted agent and would not sell them property for above the "fair market value." As a result of that belief, the Tschiras paid well over the "fair market price" for the property, thereby losing a great deal of money on the "investment.". . .

For the reasons set forth in this opinion, we affirm the district court's judgment in all respects.

[Judgment affirmed]

Questions

1. Identify the material misrepresentations of fact evident in this case.
2. What was the measure of damages received by the Tschiras?
3. Assess Corim, Inc., and Willingham's argument on appeal that the representations made were not material because they provided a "guaranteed" return on the Tschiras' investment through rental income.

To prove fraud, there must be a material misrepresentation of fact. Such a misrepresentation is one that is likely to induce a reasonable person to assent to a contract. **For Example,** if a used car salesman says, "This Buick had but one owner, a retired teacher who kept it in mint condition," when in fact the auto had several owners, the last of which was an auto salvage company that rebuilt the car after a serious accident, the salesman's statement is a material misrepresentation of fact.

(a) Statement of Opinion or Value

Ordinarily, matters of opinion of value or opinions about future events are not regarded as fraudulent. Thus, statements that a building was "very good," it "required only normal maintenance," and the "deal was excellent" were merely matters of opinion. Therefore, a court considered the sophistication and expertise of the parties and the commercial setting of the transaction and enforced the contract "as is." The theory is that the person hearing the statement recognizes or should recognize that it is merely the speaker's personal opinion, not a statement of fact. A statement that is mere sales talk cannot be the basis of fraud liability. **For Example,** CEO Bernard Ellis sent a memo to shareholders of his Internet-related services business some four days before the expiration of a lockup period during which these shareholders had agreed not to sell their stock. In the memo, he urged shareholders not to sell their stock on the release date because in the event of a massive sell-off "our stock could plummet." He also stated, "I think our share price will start to stabilize and then rise as our company's strong performance continues." Based on Ellis's "strong performance" statement, a major corporate shareholder did not sell. The price of the stock fell from $40 a share to 29 cents a share over the subsequent nine-month period. The shareholder sued Ellis for fraud, seeking $27 million in damages. The court held that the first half of the sentence in question was framed as a mere opinion as to future events and thus was nonactionable; and as to the characterization of the company's performance as "strong," such a self-congratulatory comment constituted mere puffery on which no reasonable investor would rely.[13]

A statement of opinion may be fraudulent when the speaker knows of past or present facts that make the opinion false. **For Example,** Biff Williams, the sales manager of Abrasives International (AI), sold an exclusive dealership selling AI products to Fred Farkas for $100,000 down and a 3 percent royalty on all gross proceeds. Williams told Farkas, "You have the potential to earn $300,000 to $400,000 a year in this territory." He later added, "We have four dealerships making that kind of money today." Farkas was thus persuaded by the business potential of the territory and executed the purchase contract. He later found out AI had a total of just four distributorships at that time, and the actual earnings of the highest producer was $43,000. Assertions of opinions about the future profit potential alone may not amount to fraud, but the assertion of present fact—that four dealerships were presently earning $300,000 to $400,000 a year—was a material misstatement of fact that made the forecast sales potential for Farkas's territory a material misstatement of fact as well. Because there were reliance and damages, Farkas can rescind the contract based on fraud and recover all damages resulting from it.[14]

(b) Reliance on Statement

A fraudulent statement made by one party has no importance unless the other party relies on the statement's truth. **For Example,** after making thorough tests of Nagel Company's pump, Allstate Services Company ordered 100 pumps. It later sued Nagel on the ground that advertising statements made about the pumps were false. Allstate Services cannot impose fraud liability on Nagel for the advertisements, even if they were false, because it had not relied on them in making the purchase but had acted on the basis of its own tests.

If the alleged victim of the fraud knew that the statements were false because the truth was commonly known, the victim cannot rely on the false statements. When the statements of a seller are so "indefinite and extravagant" that reasonable persons would not rely on them, the statements cannot be the basis of a claim of fraud.[15]

(c) Proof of Harm

For an individual to recover damages for fraud, proof of harm to that individual is required. The injured party may recover the actual losses suffered as a result of the fraud as well as punitive damages when the fraud is gross or oppressive. The injured party has the right to have the court order the rescission or cancellation of the contract that has been induced by fraud.[16]

[13] *Next Century Communications v Ellis*, 318 F3d 1023 (11th Cir 2003).

[14] The Federal Trade Commission and state agencies have franchise disclosure rules that will penalize the franchisor in this case. See Chapter 41.

[15] *Eckert v Flair Agency, Inc.*, 909 P2d 1201 (Okla App 1995) (seller's statement that house would never be flooded again).

[16] *Paden v Murray*, 523 SE2d 75 (Ga App 2000).

10. Negligent Misrepresentation

While fraud requires the critical element of a known or recklessly made falsity, a claim of negligent misrepresentation contains similar elements except that it is predicated on a negligently made false statement. That is, the speaker failed to exercise due care regarding material information communicated to the listener but did not intend to deceive. When the negligent misrepresentation of a material fact that the listener relies on results in harm to the listener, the contract is voidable at the option of the injured party. If fraud is proven, as opposed to misrepresentation, recovery of punitive damages in addition to actual damages can occur. Because it may be difficult to prove the intentional falsity required for fraud, it is common for a lawsuit to allege both a claim of fraud and a claim of negligent misrepresentation. **For Example,** Marshall Armstrong worked for Fred Collins, the owner of Collins Entertainment, Inc., a conglomerate that owns and operates video games. Collins Entertainment's core product video poker was hurt by a court ruling that prohibited cash payouts, which adversely affected its business and resulted in a debt of $13 to $20 million to SouthTrust bank. Chief operating officer Armstrong, on his own time, came up with the idea of modifying bingo machines as a new venture. To exploit this idea, Collins agreed to form a corporation called Skillpins Inc., that was unencumbered by the SouthTrust debt and to give Armstrong a 10 percent ownership interest. After a period of time, with some 300 Skillpins machines producing income, Armstrong discovered the revenues from the new venture on the debt-laden Collins Entertainment profit and loss statement, not that of Skillpins, Inc. Armstrong's suit for both fraud and intentional misrepresentation was successful. In addition to actual damages, he received $1.8 million in punitive damages for fraud.[17]

11. Nondisclosure

Under certain circumstances, nondisclosure serves to make a contract voidable, especially when the nondisclosure consists of active concealment.

(a) General Rule of Nonliability

Ordinarily, a party to a contract has no duty to volunteer information to the other party. **For Example,** if Fox does not ask Tehan any questions, Tehan is not under any duty to make a full statement of material facts. Consequently, the nondisclosure of information that is not asked for does not impose fraud liability or impair the validity of a contract.

(b) Exceptions

The following exceptions to the general rule of nonliability for nondisclosure exist.

(1) Unknown Defect or Condition. A duty may exist in some states for a seller who knows of a serious defect or condition to disclose that information to the other party where the defect or condition is unknown to the other person and is of such a nature that it is unlikely that the other person would discover it. However, a defendant who had no knowledge of the defect cannot be held liable for failure to disclose it.[18]

(2) Confidential Relationship. If parties stand in a **confidential relationship,** failure to disclose information may be regarded as fraudulent. For example, in an attorney-client relationship,[19] the attorney has a duty to reveal anything that is material to the client's interest when dealing with the client. The attorney's silence has the same legal consequence as a knowingly made false statement that there was no material fact to be told the client.

(3) Active Concealment. Nondisclosure may be more than the passive failure to volunteer information. It may consist of a positive act of hiding information from the other party by physical concealment, or it may consist of knowingly or recklessly furnishing the wrong information. Such conduct constitutes fraud. **For Example,** when Nigel wanted to sell his house, he covered the wooden cellar beams with plywood to hide extensive termite damage. He sold the house to Kuehne, who sued Nigel for damages on later discovering the termite damage.

[17] 621 SE2d 368 (SC App 2005).

[18] *Nesbitt v Dunn*, 672 So 2d 226 (La App 1996).

[19] *In re Boss Trust*, 487 NW2d 256 (Minn App 1992).

Nigel claimed he had no duty to volunteer information about the termites, but by covering the damage with plywood, he committed active fraud as if he had made a false statement that there were no termites.

D. Pressure

What appears to be an agreement may not in fact be voluntary because one of the parties entered into it as the result of undue influence or physical or economic duress.

CPA 12. Undue Influence

An aged parent may entrust all business affairs to a trusted child; a disabled person may rely on a nurse; a client may follow implicitly whatever an attorney recommends. The relationship may be such that for practical purposes, one person is helpless in the hands of the other. When such a confidential relationship exists, it is apparent that the parent, the disabled person, or the client is not exercising free will in making a contract suggested by the child, nurse, or attorney but is merely following the will of the other person. Because of the great possibility of unfair advantage, the law presumes that the dominating person exerts **undue influence** on the other person whenever the dominating person obtains any benefit from a contract made with the dominated person. The contract is then voidable. It may be set aside by the dominated person unless the dominating person can prove that, at the time the contract was made, no unfair advantage had been taken.

The class of confidential relationships is not well defined. It ordinarily includes the relationships of parent and child, guardian and ward, physician and patient, and attorney and client, and any other relationship of trust and confidence in which one party exercises a control or influence over another.

Whether undue influence exists is a difficult question for courts (ordinarily juries) to determine. The law does not regard every influence as undue.

An essential element of undue influence is that the person making the contract does not exercise free will. In the absence of a recognized type of confidential relationship, such as that between parent and child, courts are likely to take the attitude that the person who claims to have been dominated was merely persuaded and there was therefore no undue influence.

CPA 13. Duress

A party may enter into a contract to avoid a threatened danger. The danger threatened may be a physical harm to person or property, called **physical duress,** or it may be a threat of financial loss, called **economic duress.**

(a) Physical Duress

A person makes a contract under **duress** when there is such violence or threat of violence that the person is deprived of free will and makes the contract to avoid harm. The threatened harm may be directed either at a near relative of the contracting party or against the contracting party. If a contract is made under duress, the resulting agreement is voidable at the victim's election.

Agreements made to bring an end to mass disorder or violence are ordinarily not binding contracts because they were obtained by duress.

One may not void a contract on grounds of duress merely because it was entered into with great reluctance and proves to be very disadvantageous to that individual.[20]

(b) Economic Duress

Economic duress is a condition in which one is induced by a wrongful act or threat of another to make a contract under circumstances that deprive one of the exercise of his own free will.[21] **For Example,** Richard Case, an importer of parts used to manufacture high-quality mountain bicycles, had a contractual duty to supply Katahdin Manufacturing Company's needs for specifically manufactured stainless steel brakes for the 2007 season. Katahdin's president, Bill Read, was in constant contact with Case about the delay in delivery of the parts and the adverse consequences it was having on Katahdin's relationship with its

[20] *Miller v Calhoun Johnson Co.*, 497 SE2d 397 (Ga App 1998).

[21] *Hurd v Wildman, Harrold, Allen, and Dixon*, 707 NE2d 609 (Ill App 1999).

retailers. Near the absolute deadline for meeting orders for the 2007 season, Case called Read and said, "I've got the parts in, but I'm not sure I'll be able to send them to you because I'm working on next year's contracts, and you haven't signed yours yet." Case's 2008 contract increased the cost of parts by 38 percent. Read signed the contract to obtain the delivery but later found a new supplier and gave notice to Case of this action. The defense of economic duress would apply in a breach of contract suit brought by Case on the 2008 contract because Case implicitly threatened to commit the wrongful act of not delivering parts due under the prior contract, and Katahdin Company had no means available to obtain parts elsewhere to prevent the economic loss that would occur if it did not receive those parts.

LAWFLIX

Jerry Maguire (1996) (R)

Consider the marriage proposal, its validity, and Dorothy's later statement, "I did this. I made this happen. And the thing is, I can do something about it." What was Maguire's state of mind at the time of the proposal? Consider its possible hypothetical nature and the issues of whether it was a joke and the possible presence of undue influence (the young boy).

For movie clips that illustrate business law concepts, see LawFlix at **http://wdvl.westbuslaw.com.**

Summary

An agreement that otherwise appears to be a contract may not be binding because one of the parties lacks contractual capacity. In such a case, the contract is ordinarily voidable at the election of the party who lacks contractual capacity. In some cases, the contract is void. Ordinarily, contractual incapacity is the inability, for mental or physical reasons, to understand that a contract is being made and to understand its general terms and nature. This is typically the case when it is claimed that incapacity exists because of insanity, intoxication, or drug use. The incapacity of minors arises because society discriminates in favor of that class to protect them from unwise contracts.

The age of majority is 18. Minors can disaffirm most contracts. If a minor received anything from the other party, the minor, on avoiding the contract, must return what had been received from the other party if the minor still has it.

When a minor disaffirms a contract for a necessary, the minor must pay the reasonable value of any benefit received.

Minors only are liable for their contracts. Parents of a minor are not liable on the minor's contracts merely because they are the parents. Frequently, an adult enters into the contract as a coparty of the minor and is then liable without regard to whether the minor has avoided the contract.

The contract of an insane person is voidable to much the same extent as the contract of a minor. An important distinction is that if a guardian has been appointed for the insane person, a contract made by the insane person is void, not merely voidable.

An intoxicated person lacks contractual capacity if the intoxication is such that the person does not understand that a contract is being made.

The consent of a party to an agreement is not genuine or voluntary in certain cases of mistake, deception, or pressure. When this occurs, what appears to be a contract can be avoided by the victim of such circumstances or conduct.

As to mistake, it is necessary to distinguish between unilateral mistakes that are unknown to the other contracting party and those that are known. Mistakes that are unknown to the other party usually do not affect the binding character of the agreement. A unilateral mistake of which the other contracting party has knowledge or has reason to know makes the contract avoidable by the victim of the mistake.

The deception situation may be one of innocent misrepresentation, nondisclosure, or fraud. A few courts allow recovery of damages. When one party to the contract knows of a fact that has a bearing on the transaction, the failure to volunteer information about that fact to the other contracting party is called *nondisclosure*. The law ordinarily does not attach any significance to nondisclosure. Contrary to this rule, there is a duty to volunteer information when a confidential relationship exists between the possessor of the knowledge and the other contracting party.

When concealment goes beyond mere silence and consists of actively taking steps to hide the truth, the conduct may be classified as fraud. A statement of opinion or value cannot ordinarily be the basis for fraud liability.

The free will of a person, essential to the voluntary character of a contract, may be lacking because the agreement had been obtained by pressure. This may range from undue influence through the array of threats of extreme economic loss (called *economic duress*) to the threat of physical force that would cause serious personal injury or damage to property (called *physical duress*).

When the voluntary character of an agreement has been destroyed by mistake, deception, or pressure, the victim may avoid or rescind the contract or may obtain money damages from the wrongdoer. When the mistake consists of an error in putting an oral contract in writing, either party may ask the court to reform the writing so that it states the parties' actual agreement.

Questions and Case Problems

1. Lester purchased a used automobile from MacKintosh Motors. He asked the seller if the car had ever been in a wreck. The MacKintosh salesperson had never seen the car before that morning and knew nothing of its history but quickly answered Lester's question by stating: "No. It has never been in a wreck." In fact, the auto had been seriously damaged in a wreck and, although repaired, was worth much less than the value it would have had if there had been no wreck. When Lester learned the truth, he sued MacKintosh Motors and the salesperson for damages for fraud. They raised the defense that the salesperson did not know the statement was false and had not intended to deceive Lester. Did the conduct of the salesperson constitute fraud?
2. Helen, age 17, wanted to buy a Harley-Davidson "Sportster" motorcycle. She did not have the funds to pay cash but persuaded the dealer to sell the cycle to her on credit. The dealer did so partly because Helen said that she was 22 and showed the dealer an identification card that falsely stated her age as 22. Helen drove the motorcycle away. A few days later, she damaged it and then returned it to the dealer and stated that she disaffirmed the contract because she was a minor. The dealer said that she could not because (1) she had misrepresented her age and (2) the motorcycle was damaged. Can she avoid the contract?
3. Paden signed an agreement dated May 28 to purchase the Murrays' home. The Murrays accepted Paden's offer the following day, and the sale closed on June 27. Paden and his family moved into the home on July 14, 1997. Paden had the home inspected prior to closing. The report listed four minor repairs needed by the home, the cost of which was less than $500. Although these repairs had not been completed at the time of closing, Paden decided to go through with the purchase. After moving into the home, Paden discovered a number of allegedly new defects, including a wooden foundation, electrical problems, and bat infestation. The sales agreement allowed extensive rights to inspect the property. The agreement provided:

   > *Buyer. . . shall have the right to enter the property at Buyer's expense and at reasonable times. . . to thoroughly inspect, examine, test, and survey the Property. . . . Buyer shall have the right to request that Seller repair defects in the Property by providing Seller within 12 days from Binding Agreement Date with a copy of inspection report(s) and a written amendment to this agreement setting forth the defects in the report which Buyer requests to be repaired and/or replaced. . . . If Buyer does not timely present the written amendment and inspection report, Buyer shall be deemed to have accepted the Property "as is."*

   Paden sued the Murrays for fraudulent concealment and breach of the sales agreement. If Mr. Murray told Paden on May 26 that the house had a concrete foundation, would this be fraud? Decide. [*Paden v Murray*, 523 SE2d 75 (Ga App)]
4. High-Tech Collieries borrowed money from Holland. High-Tech later refused to be bound by the loan contract, claiming the contract was not binding because it had been obtained by duress. The evidence showed that the offer to make the loan was made on a take-it-or-leave-it basis. Was the defense of duress valid? [*Holland v High-Tech Collieries, Inc.*, 911 F Supp 1021 (DC WA)]
5. Thomas Bell, a minor, went to work in the Pittsburgh beauty parlor of Sam Pankas and agreed that when he left the employment, he would not work in or run a beauty parlor business within a 10-mile radius of downtown Pittsburgh for a period of two years. Contrary to this provision, Bell and another employee of Pankas's opened a beauty shop three blocks from Pankas's shop and advertised themselves as Pankas's former employees. Pankas sued Bell to stop the breach of the noncompetition, or restrictive, covenant. Bell claimed that he was not bound because he was a minor when he had agreed to the covenant. Was he bound by the covenant? [*Pankas v Bell*, 198 A2d 312 (Pa)]

6. Aldrich and Co. sold goods to Donovan on credit. The amount owed grew steadily, and finally Aldrich refused to sell any more to Donovan unless Donovan signed a promissory note for the amount due. Donovan did not want to but signed the note because he had no money and needed more goods. When Aldrich brought an action to enforce the note, Donovan claimed that the note was not binding because it had been obtained by economic duress. Was he correct? [*Aldrich & Co. v Donovan*, 778 P2d 397 (Mont)]
7. James Fitl purchased a 1952 Mickey Mantle Topps baseball card from baseball card dealer Mark Strek for $17,750 and placed it in a safe deposit box. Two years later, he had the card appraised, and he was told that the card had been refinished and trimmed, which rendered it valueless. Fitl sued Strek and testified that he had relied on Strek's position as a sports card dealer and on his representations that the baseball card was authentic. Strek contends that Fitl waited too long to give him notice of the defects that would have enabled Strek to contact the person who sold him the card and obtain relief. Strek asserts that he therefore is not liable. Advise Fitl concerning possible legal theories that apply to his case. How would you decide the case? [See *Fitl v Strek*, 690 NW2d 605 (Neb)]
8. An agent of Thor Food Service Corp. was seeking to sell Makofske a combination refrigerator-freezer and food purchase plan. Makofske was married and had three children. After being informed of the eating habits of Makofske and his family, the agent stated that the cost of the freezer and food would be about $95 to $100 a month. Makofske carefully examined the agent's itemized estimate and made some changes to it. Makofske then signed the contract and purchased the refrigerator-freezer. The cost proved to be more than the estimated $95 to $100 a month, and Makofske claimed that the contract had been obtained by fraud. Decide. [*Thor Food Service Corp. v Makofske*, 218 NYS2d 93]
9. Blubaugh was a district manager of Schlumberger Well Services. Turner was an executive employee of Schlumberger. Blubaugh was told that he would be fired unless he chose to resign. He was also told that if he would resign and release the company and its employees from all claims for wrongful discharge, he would receive about $5,000 in addition to his regular severance pay of approximately $25,000 and would be given job-relocation counseling. He resigned, signed the release, and received about $40,000 and job counseling. Some time thereafter, he brought an action claiming that he had been wrongfully discharged. He claimed that the release did not protect the defendants because the release had been obtained by economic duress. Were the defendants protected by the release? [*Blubaugh v Turner*, 842 P2d 1072 (Wyo)]
10. Sippy was thinking of buying Christich's house. He noticed watermarks on the ceiling, but the agent showing the house stated that the roof had been repaired and was in good condition. Sippy was not told that the roof still leaked and that the repairs had not been able to stop the leaking. Sippy bought the house. Some time later, heavy rains caused water to leak into the house, and Sippy claimed that Christich was liable for damages. What theory would he rely on? Decide. [*Sippy v Christich*, 609 P2d 204 (Kan App)]
11. Pileggi owed Young money. Young threatened to bring suit against Pileggi for the amount due. Pileggi feared the embarrassment of being sued and the possibility that he might be thrown into bankruptcy. To avoid being sued, Pileggi executed a promissory note to pay Young the amount due. He later asserted that the note was not binding because he had executed it under duress. Is this defense valid? [*Young v Pileggi*, 455 A2d 1228 (Pa Super)]
12. Office Supply Outlet, Inc., a single-store office equipment and supply retailer, ordered 100 model RVX-414 computers from Compuserve, Inc. A new staff member made a clerical error on the order form and ordered a quantity that was far in excess of what Office Supply could sell in a year. Office Supply realized the mistake when the delivery trucks arrived at its warehouse. Its manager called Compuserve and explained that it had intended to order just 10 computers. Compuserve declined to accept the return of the extra machines. Is the contract enforceable? What additional facts would allow the store to avoid the contract for the additional machines?
13. C&J Publishing Co. told a computer salesman that it wanted a computer system that would operate its printing presses. C&J specified that it wanted only new equipment and no used equipment would be acceptable. The seller delivered a system to C&J that was a combination of new and secondhand parts because it did not have sufficient new parts to fill the order. When C&J later learned what had happened, it sued the seller for fraud. The seller contended that no statement or warranty had been made that all parts of the system were new and that it would not therefore be liable for fraud. Decide.
14. The city of Salinas entered into a contract with Souza & McCue Construction Co. to construct a sewer. City officials knew unusual subsoil conditions (including extensive quicksand) existed that would make performance of the contract unusually difficult. This information was not disclosed when city officials advertised for bids. The advertisement for bids directed bidders to examine carefully the site of the work and declared that the submission of a bid would constitute evidence that the bidder had made an examination. Souza & McCue was awarded the contract, but because of the subsoil conditions, it could not complete on time and was

sued by Salinas for breach of contract. Souza & McCue counterclaimed on the basis that the city had not revealed its information on the subsoil conditions and was thus liable for the loss. Was the city liable? [*City of Salinas v Souza & McCue Construction Co.*, 424 P2d 921 (Cal App 3d)]

15. Vern Westby inherited a "ticket" from Anna Sjoblom, a survivor of the sinking of the *Titanic*, which had been pinned to the inside of her coat. He also inherited an album of postcards, some of which related to the *Titanic*. The ticket was a one-of-a-kind item in good condition. Westby needed cash and went to the biggest antique dealer in Tacoma, operated by Alan Gorsuch and his family, doing business as Sanford and Sons, and asked about the value of these items. Westby testified that after Alan Gorsuch examined the ticket, he said, "It's not worth nothing." Westby then inquired about the value of the postcard album, and Gorsuch advised him to come back later. On Westby's return, Gorsuch told Westby, "It ain't worth nothing." Gorsuch added that he "couldn't fetch $500 for the ticket." Since he needed money, Westby asked if Gorsuch would give him $1,000 for both the ticket and the album, and Gorsuch did so.

    Six months later, Gorsuch sold the ticket at a nationally advertised auction for $110,000 and sold most of the postcards for $1,200. Westby sued Gorsuch for fraud. Testimony showed that Gorsuch was a major buyer in antiques and collectibles in the Puget Sound area and that he would have had an understanding of the value of the ticket. Gorsuch contends that all elements of fraud are not present since there was no evidence that Gorsuch intended that Westby rely on the alleged representations, nor did Westby rely on such. Rather, Gorsuch asserts, it was an arm's-length transaction and Westby had access to the same information as Gorsuch. Decide. [*Westby v Gorsuch*, 112 Wash App 558 (2002)]

CPA Questions

1. A building subcontractor submitted a bid for construction of a portion of a high-rise office building. The bid contained material computational errors. The general contractor accepted the bid with knowledge of the errors. Which of the following statements best represents the subcontractor's liability?
    a. Not liable, because the contractor knew of the errors
    b. Not liable, because the errors were a result of gross negligence
    c. Liable, because the errors were unilateral
    d. Liable, because the errors were material (5/95, Law, #17, 5351)

2. Egan, a minor, contracted with Baker to purchase Baker's used computer for $400. The computer was purchased for Egan's personal use. The agreement provided that Egan would pay $200 down on delivery and $200 thirty days later. Egan took delivery and paid the $200 down payment. Twenty days later, the computer was damaged seriously as a result of Egan's negligence. Five days after the damage occurred and one day after Egan reached the age of majority, Egan attempted to disaffirm the contract with Baker. Egan will
    a. Be able to disaffirm despite the fact that Egan was *not* a minor at the time of disaffirmance
    b. Be able to disaffirm only if Egan does so in writing
    c. Not be able to disaffirm because Egan had failed to pay the balance of the purchase price
    d. Not be able to disaffirm because the computer was damaged as a result of Egan's negligence (11/93, Law, #21, 4318)

CONSIDERATION

CHAPTER (15)

LEARNING OBJECTIVES

After studying this chapter, you should be able to

LO.1 Explain what constitutes consideration

LO.2 State the effect of the absence of consideration

LO.3 Identify promises that can serve as consideration

LO.4 Distinguish between present consideration and past consideration

LO.5 State when forbearance can be consideration

LO.6 Recognize situations in which adequacy of consideration has significance

LO.7 List the exceptions to the requirement of consideration

Will the law enforce every promise? Generally, a promise will not be enforced unless something is given or received for the promise.

A. General Principles

As a general rule, one of the elements needed to make an agreement binding is consideration.

1. Consideration Defined and Explained

Consideration is what each party to a contract gives up to the other in making their agreement.

(a) Bargained-for Exchange

Consideration is the bargained-for exchange between the parties to a contract. In order for consideration to exist, something of value must be given or promised in return for the performance or promise of performance of the other.[1] The value given or promised can be money, services, property, or the forbearance of a legal right.

For Example, Beth offers to pay Kerry $100 for her used skis, and Kerry accepts. Beth has promised something of value, $100, as consideration for Kerry's promise to sell the skis, and Kerry has promised Beth something of value, the skis, as consideration for the $100. If Kerry offered to *give* Beth the used skis and Beth accepted, these parties would have an agreement but not an enforceable contract because Beth did not provide any consideration in exchange for Kerry's promise of the skis. There was no *bargained-for exchange* because Kerry was not promised anything of value from Beth.

(b) Benefit-Detriment Approach

Some jurisdictions analyze consideration from the point of view of a *benefit-detriment approach*, defining *consideration* as a benefit received by the promisor or a detriment incurred by the promisee.

As an example of a unilateral contract analyzed from a benefit-detriment approach to consideration, Mr. Scully, a longtime summer resident of Falmouth, states to George Corfu, a college senior, "I will pay you $3,000 if you paint my summer home." George in fact paints the house. The work of painting the house by George, the promisee, was a legal detriment to him. Also, the painting of the house was a legal benefit to Scully, the promisor. There was consideration in this case, and the agreement is enforceable.

2. Gifts

Promises to make a gift are unenforceable promises under the law of contracts because of lack of consideration, as illustrated previously in the scenario of Kerry promising to give her used skis to Beth without charge. There was no bargained-for exchange because Kerry was not promised anything of value from Beth. A completed gift, however, cannot be rescinded for lack of consideration.[2]

Charitable subscriptions by which individuals make pledges to finance the construction of a college building, a church, or another structure for charitable purposes are binding to the extent that the donor (promisor) should have reasonably realized that the charity was relying on the promise in undertaking the building program. Some states require proof that the charity has relied on the subscription.[3]

3. Adequacy of Consideration

Ordinarily, courts do not consider the adequacy of the consideration given for a promise. The fact that the consideration supplied by one party is slight when compared with the burden undertaken by the other party is immaterial. It is a matter for the parties to decide when they make their contract whether each is getting a fair return. In the absence of fraud or other misconduct, courts usually will not interfere to make sure that each side is getting a fair return.

Because the adequacy of consideration is ignored, it is immaterial that consideration is so slight that the transaction is in part a "gift." However, the Internal Revenue Service may view a given transaction as part consideration, part gift, and assess a gift tax as appropriate.

The fact that the consideration turns out to be disappointing does not affect the binding character of the contract. Thus, the fact that a business purchased by a group of investors proves unprofitable does not constitute a failure of consideration that releases the buyers from their obligation to the seller.

[1] *Brooksbank v Anderson*, 586 NW2d 789 (Minn App 1998).
[2] *Homes v O'Bryant*, 741 So 2d 366 (Miss App 1999).
[3] *King v Trustees of Boston University*, 647 NE2d 1176 (Ma 1995).

4. Forbearance as Consideration

In most cases, consideration consists of the performance of an act such as providing a service, or the making of a promise to provide a service or goods, or paying money.[4] Consideration may also consist of **forbearance**, which is refraining from doing an act that an individual has a legal right to do, or it may consist of a promise of forbearance. In other words, the promisor may desire to buy the inaction or a promise of inaction of the other party.

The giving up of any legal right can be consideration for the promise of the other party to a contract. Thus, the relinquishment of a right to sue for damages will support a promise for the payment of money given in return for the promise to relinquish the right, if such is the agreement of the parties.

The promise of a creditor to forbear collecting a debt is consideration for the promise of the debtor to modify the terms of the transaction.

5. Illusory Promises

In a bilateral contract, each party makes a promise to the other. For a bilateral contract to be enforceable, there must be *mutuality of obligation*. That is, both parties must have created obligations to the other in their respective promises. If one party's promise contains either no obligation or only an apparent obligation to the other, this promise is an **illusory promise**. The party making such a promise is not bound because he or she has made no real promise. The effect is that the other party, who has made a real promise, is also not bound because he or she has received no consideration. It is said that the contract fails for lack of mutuality.

For Example, Mountain Coal Company promises to sell Midwest Power Company all the coal it may order for $48 per ton for the year 2007, and Midwest Power agrees to pay $48 for any coal it orders from Mountain Coal. Mountain Coal in its promise to Midwest Power has obligated itself to supply all coal ordered at a stated price. However, Midwest Power's promise did not obligate it to buy any coal whatsoever from Mountain Coal (note that it was not a requirements contract). Because Midwest has no obligation to Mountain Coal under its promise, there is no mutuality of obligation, and Midwest cannot enforce Mountain Coal's promise when the market price of coal goes to $55 a ton in the winter of 2007 as the result of severe weather conditions.

Consider as well the example of the Jacksonville Fire soccer team's contract with Brazilian soccer star Edmundo. Edmundo signed a contract to play for the Jacksonville franchise of the new International Soccer League for five years at $25 million. The extensive document signed by Edmundo set forth the details of the team's financial commitment and the details of Edmundo's obligations to the team and its fans. On page 4 of the document, the team inserted a clause reserving the right "to terminate the contract and team obligations at any time in its sole discretion." During the season, Edmundo received a $40 million five-year offer to play for Manchester United of the English Premier League, which he accepted. Because Jacksonville had a free way out of its obligation by the unrestricted cancellation provision in the contract, it thus made its promises to Edmundo illusory. Edmundo was not bound by the Jacksonville contract as a result of a lack of mutuality and was free to sign with Manchester United.

(a) Cancellation Provisions

Although a promise must impose a binding obligation, it may authorize a party to cancel the agreement under certain circumstances on giving notice by a certain date. Such a provision does not make this party's promise illusory, for the party does not have a free way out and is limited to living up to the terms of the **cancellation provision**. **For Example,** actress Zsa Zsa Gabor made a contract with Hollywood Fantasy Corporation to appear at a fantasy vacation in San Antonio, Texas, on May 2–4, for a $10,000 appearance fee plus itemized (extravagant) expenses. The last paragraph of the agreement stated: "It is agreed that if a significant acting opportunity in a film comes up, Ms. Gabor will have the right to cancel her appearance in San Antonio by advising Hollywood Fantasy in writing by April 15, 1991." Ms. Gabor sent a telegram on April 15, 1991, canceling her appearance. During the May 2 through 4 period, Ms. Gabor's only acting activity was a 14-second cameo role during the opening credits of *Naked Gun 2½*. In a lawsuit for breach of contract that followed, the jury saw this portion of the movie and

[4] *Prenger v Baumhoer*, 914 SW2d 413 (Mo App 1996).

concluded that Ms. Gabor had not canceled her obligation on the basis of a "significant acting opportunity," and she was held liable for breach of contract.[5]

(b) Conditional Promises

A *conditional promise* is a promise that depends on the occurrence of a specified condition in order for the promise to be binding. **For Example,** Mary Sparks, in contemplation of her signing a lease to take over a restaurant at Marina Bay, wanted to make certain that she had a highly qualified chef to run the restaurant's food service. She made a contract with John "Grumpy" White to serve as executive chef for a one-year period at a salary of $150,000. The contract set forth White's responsibilities and was conditioned on the successful negotiation of the restaurant lease with Marina Bay Management. Both parties signed it. Although the happening of the condition was within Mary's control because she could avoid the contract with Grumpy White by not acquiring the restaurant lease, she limited her future options by the contract with White. Her promise to White was not illusory because after signing the contract with him, if she acquired the restaurant lease, she was bound to hire White as her executive chef. Before signing the contract with White, she was free to sign any chef for the position. The contract was enforceable.

6. Third Parties

Because consideration is the price paid for each promise in a bilateral contract, it is unimportant who pays the price as long as it has been agreed that it should be paid in that manner. When a creditor releases a third person in consideration of the promise of another person to pay the debt of the released person, the fact that the promisor did not receive a direct benefit is immaterial. The obtaining of the release of the third person as desired was consideration for the promise to pay the debt.[6]

CPA B. Special Situations

The following sections analyze certain common situations in which a lawsuit turns on whether the promisor received consideration for the promise sued on.

7. Preexisting Legal Obligation

Ordinarily, doing or promising to do what one is already under a legal obligation to do is not consideration.[7] Similarly, a promise to refrain from doing what one has no legal right to do is not consideration. This preexisting duty or legal obligation can be based on statute, on general principles of law, on responsibilities of an office held, or on a preexisting contract.

For Example, Officer Mary Rodgers is an undercover police officer in the city of Pasadena, California. Officer Rodgers promised Elwood Farnsworth that she would diligently patrol the area of the Farnsworth estate on weekends to keep down the noise and drinking of rowdy young persons who gathered in this area, and Mr. Farnsworth promised to provide a $500 per month gratuity for this extra service. Farnsworth's promise is unenforceable because Officer Rodgers has a preexisting official duty as a police officer to protect citizens and enforce the antinoise and public drinking ordinances.

CPA (a) Completion of Contract

Suppose that a contractor refuses to complete a building unless the owner promises a payment or bonus in addition to the sum specified in the original contract, and the owner promises to make that payment. The question then arises as to whether the owner's promise is binding. Most courts hold that the second promise of the owner is without consideration.

If the promise of the contractor is to do something that is not part of the first contract, then the promise of the other party is binding. **For Example,** if a bonus of $5,000 is promised in return for the promise of a contractor to complete the building at a date earlier than that specified in the original agreement, the promise to pay the bonus is binding.

CPA ***(1) Good-Faith Adjustment.*** A current trend is to enforce a second promise to pay a contractor a higher amount for the performance of the original contract when there are extraordinary circumstances caused by unforeseeable difficulties and when the additional amount promised the contractor is reasonable under the circumstances. The classic *Angel v Murray,* decision involves a good-faith adjustment.

[5] *Hollywood Fantasy Corp. v Gabor*, 151 F2d 203 (5th Cir 1998).
[6] *First Union Bank of Georgia v Gurley*, 431 SE2d 379 (Ga App 1993).
[7] *Gardiner, Kamya & Associates v Jackson*, 369 F3d 1318 (Fed Cir 2004).

ANGEL V MURRAY, 113 RI 482, 322 A2D 630 (1974)

"YOU HAD A PREEXISTING LEGAL OBLIGATION," SAID THE PUBLIC GUARDIAN, MR. ANGEL.

John Murray was director of finance of the city of Newport. A contract was made with Alfred Maher to remove trash. Later, Maher requested that the city council increase his compensation. Maher's costs were greater than had been anticipated because 400 new dwelling units had been put into operation. The city council voted to pay Maher an additional $10,000 a year. After two such annual payments had been made, Angel and other citizens of the city sued Murray and Maher for a return of the $20,000. They said that Maher was already obligated by his contract to perform the work for the contract sum, and there was, accordingly, no consideration for the payment of the increased compensation. From a decision in favor of the plaintiffs, the city and Maher appealed.

Judicial Opinion

ROBERTS, C. J. . . . It is generally held that a modification of a contract is itself a contract, which is unenforceable unless supported by consideration. . . .

The preexisting duty rule is followed by most jurisdictions. . . .

The primary purpose of the preexisting duty rule is to prevent what has been referred to as the "hold-up game." . . . A classic example of the "hold-up game" is found in *Alaska Packers' Ass'n v Domenico*, 117 F 99 (9th Cir 1902). There 21 seamen entered into a written contract with Domenico to sail from San Francisco to Pyramid Harbor, Alaska. They were to work as sailors and fishermen out of Pyramid Harbor during the fishing season of 1900. The contract specified that each man would be paid $50 plus two cents for each red salmon he caught. Subsequent to their arrival at Pyramid Harbor, the men stopped work and demanded an additional $50. They threatened to return to San Francisco if Domenico did not agree to their demand. Since it was impossible for Domenico to find other men, he agreed to pay the men an additional $50. After they returned to San Francisco, Domenico refused to pay the men an additional $50. The court found that the subsequent agreement to pay the men an additional $50 was not supported by consideration because the men had a preexisting duty to work on the ship under the original contract, and thus the subsequent agreement was unenforceable.

Another example of the "hold-up game" is found in the area of construction contracts. Frequently, a contractor will refuse to complete work under an unprofitable contract unless he is awarded additional compensation. The courts have generally held that a subsequent agreement to award additional compensation is unenforceable if the contractor is only performing work which would have been required of him under the original contract. . . .

These examples clearly illustrate that the courts will not enforce an agreement that has been procured by coercion or duress and will hold the parties to their original contract regardless of whether it is profitable or unprofitable. However, the courts have been reluctant to apply the preexisting duty rule when a party to a contract encounters unanticipated difficulties and the other party, not influenced by coercion or duress, voluntarily agrees to pay additional compensation for work already required to be performed under the contract. For example, the courts have found that the original contract was rescinded, . . . abandoned, . . . or waived.

Although the preexisting duty rule has served a useful purpose insofar as it deters parties from using coercion and duress to obtain additional compensation, it has been widely criticized as a general rule of law. . . . The modern trend appears to recognize the necessity that courts should enforce agreements modifying contracts when unexpected or unanticipated difficulties arise during the course of the performance of a contract, even though there is no consideration for the modification, as long as the parties agree voluntarily.

Under the Uniform Commercial Code, §2-209(1), . . . "an agreement modifying a contract [for the sale of goods] needs no consideration to be binding." . . . Although at first blush this section appears to validate modifications obtained by coercion and duress, the comments to this section indicate that a modification under this section must meet the test of good faith imposed by the Code, and a modification obtained by extortion without a legitimate commercial reason is unenforceable.

The modern trend away from a rigid application of the preexisting duty rule is reflected by § 89D(a) of the American Law Institute's Restatement Second of the Law of Contracts, which provides: "A promise modifying a duty under a contract not fully performed on either side is binding (a) if the modification is fair and equitable in view of circumstances not anticipated by the parties when the contract was made. . . . "

We believe that § 89D(a) is the proper rule of law and find it applicable to the facts of this case. It not only prohibits modifications obtained by coercion, duress, or extortion but also fulfills society's expectation that agreements entered into voluntarily will be enforced by the courts. . . .

Section 89D(a), of course, does not compel a modification of an unprofitable or unfair contract; it only enforces a modification if the parties voluntarily agree and if (1) the promise modifying the original contract was made before the contract was fully performed on either side, (2) the underlying circumstances which prompted the modification were unanticipated by the parties, and (3) the modification is fair and equitable.

The evidence, which is uncontradicted, reveals that in June of 1968 Maher requested the city council to pay him an additional $10,000 for the year beginning on July 1, 1968, and ending on June 30, 1969. This request was made at a public meeting of the city council, where Maher explained in detail his reasons for making the request. Thereafter, the city council voted to authorize the Mayor to sign an amendment to the 1964 contract which provided that Maher would receive an additional $10,000 per year for the duration of the contract. Under such circumstances we have no doubt that the city voluntarily agreed to modify the 1964 contract.

Having determined the voluntariness of this agreement, we turn our attention to the three criteria delineated above. First, the modification was made in June of 1968 at a time when the five-year contract which was made in 1964 had not been fully performed by either party. Second, although the 1964 contract provided that Maher collect all refuse generated within the city, it appears this contract was premised on Maher's past experience that the number of refuse-generating units would increase at a rate of 20 to 25 per year. Furthermore, the evidence is uncontradicted that the 1967–1968 increase of 400 units "went beyond any previous expectation." Clearly, the circumstances which prompted the city council to modify the 1964 contract were unanticipated. Third, although the evidence does not indicate what proportion of the total this increase comprised, the evidence does indicate that it was a "substantial" increase. In light of this, we cannot say that the council's agreement to pay Maher the $10,000 increase was not fair and equitable in the circumstances.

[Judgment reversed and action remanded]

Questions

1. What was the basis for the plaintiff's suit?
2. How would the *Angel* case have been decided under the common law rule as to consideration?
3. Can an adversely affected contractor compell a modification of an unprofitable contract under the *Angel v Murray* decision?

(2) Contract for Sale of Goods. When the contract is for the sale of goods, any modification made in good faith by the parties to the contract is binding without regard to the existence of consideration for the modification.

CPA (b) Compromise and Release of Claims

The rule that doing or promising to do what one is already legally bound to do is not consideration applies to a part payment made in satisfaction of an admitted or *liquidated debt*. Thus, a promise to pay part of an amount that is admittedly owed is not consideration for a promise to discharge the balance. It will not prevent the creditor from demanding the remainder later. **For Example,** John owes Mark $100,000, which was due on March 1, 2006. On March 15, John offers to pay back $80,000 if Mark will agree to accept this amount as the discharge of the full amount owed. Mark agrees to this proposal, and it is set forth in writing signed by the parties. However, Mark later sues for the $20,000 balance. Mark will be successful in the lawsuit because John's payment of the $80,000 is not consideration for Mark's promise to discharge the full amount owed because John was doing only what he had a preexisting legal duty to do.

If the debtor pays the part payment before the debt is due, there is consideration because, on the day when the payment was made, the creditor was not entitled to demand any payment. Likewise, if the creditor accepts some article (even of slight value) in addition to the part payment, consideration exists.

A debtor and creditor may have a bona fide dispute over the amount owed or whether any amount is owed. Such is called an *unliquidated debt*. In this case, payment by the debtor of less than the amount claimed by the creditor is consideration for the latter's agreement to release or settle the claim. It is generally regarded as sufficient if the claimant believes in the merit of the claim.[8]

(c) Part-Payment Checks

When there is a good-faith dispute about the amount of a debt and the debtor tenders a check that states on its face "paid in full" and references the transaction in dispute, but the amount of the check is less than the full amount the creditor asserts is owed, the cashing of the check by the creditor discharges the entire debt.

(d) Composition of Creditors

In a **composition of creditors**, the various creditors of one debtor mutually agree to accept a fractional part of their claims in full satisfaction of the claims. Such agreements are binding and are supported by consideration. When creditors agree to extend the due date of their debts, the promise of each creditor to forbear is likewise consideration for the promise of other creditors to forbear.

8. Past Consideration

A promise based on a party's past performance lacks consideration.[9] It is said that **past consideration** is no consideration. **For Example,** Fred O'Neal came up with the idea for the formation of the new community bank of Villa Rica and was active in its formation. Just prior to the execution of the documents creating the bank, the organizers discussed that once the bank was formed, it would hire O'Neal, giving him a three-year contract at $65,000 the first year, $67,000 the second year, and $70,000 the third. In a lawsuit against the bank for breach of contract, O'Neal testified that the consideration he gave in exchange for the three-year contract was his past effort to organize the bank. The court stated that past consideration generally will not support a subsequent promise and that the purported consideration was not rendered to the bank, which had not yet been established when his promotion and organization work took place.[10] The presence of a bargained-for exchange is not present when a promise is made in exchange for a past benefit.

ETHICS & THE LAW

Alan Fulkins, who owns a construction company that specializes in single-family residences, is constructing a small subdivision with 23 homes. Tretorn Plumbing, owned by Jason Tretorn, was awarded the contract for the plumbing work on the homes at a price of $4,300 per home.

Plumbing contractors complete their residential projects in three phases. Phase one consists of digging the lines for the plumbing and installing the pipes that are placed in the foundation of the house. Phase two consists of installing the pipes within the walls of the home, and phase three is installing of the surface plumbing, such as sinks and tubs. However, industry practice dictates that the plumbing contractor receive one-half of the contract amount after completion of phase one.

Tretorn completed the digs of phase one for Fulkins and received payment of $2,150. Tretorn then went to Fulkins and demanded an additional $600 per house to complete the work. Fulkins said, "But you already have a contract for $4,300!" Tretorn responded, "I know, but the costs are killing me. I need the additional $600."

Fulkins explained the hardship of the demand, "Look, I've already paid you half. If I hire someone else, I'll have to pay them two-thirds for the work not done. It'll cost me $5,000 per house."

Tretorn responded, "Exactly. I'm a bargain because the additional $600 I want only puts you at $4,900. If you don't pay it, I'll just lien the houses and then you'll be stuck without a way to close the sales. I've got the contract all drawn up. Just sign it and everything goes smoothly."

Should Fulkins sign the agreement? Does Tretorn have the right to the additional $600? Was it ethical for Tretorn to demand the $600? Is there any legal advice you can offer Fulkins?

8 *F. H. Prince & Co. v Towers Financial Corp.*, 656 NE2d 142 (Ill App 1995).
9 *Smith v Locklear*, 906 So2d 1273 (Fla App 2005).
10 *O'Neal v Home Town Bank of Villa Rica*, 514 SE2d 669 (Ga App 1999).

FIGURE 15-1 Consideration and Promises

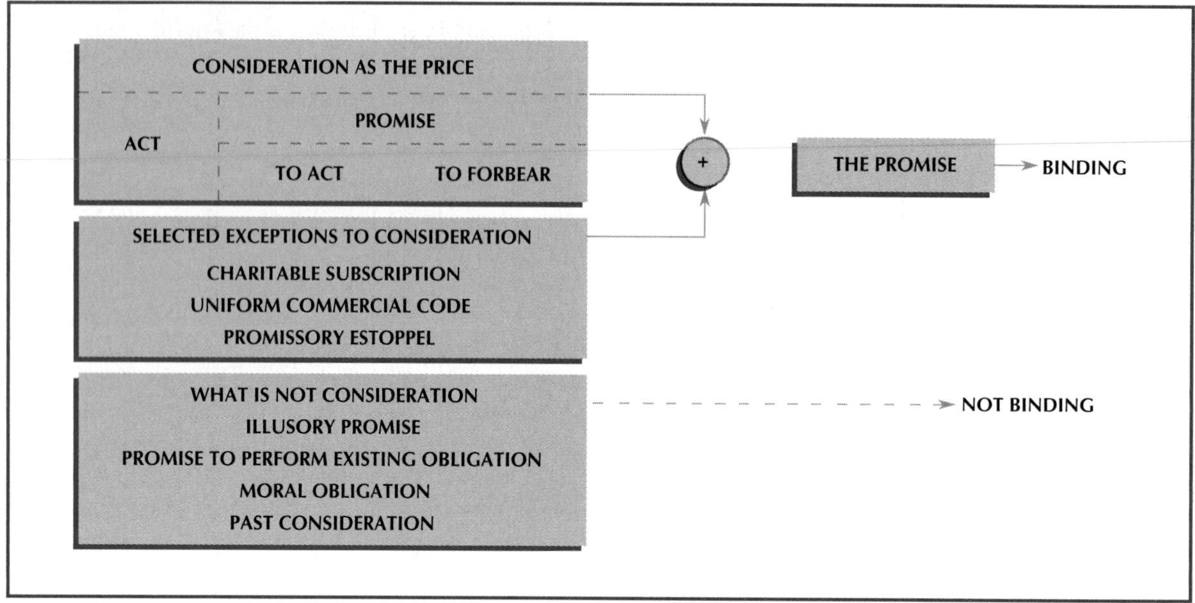

9. Moral Obligation

In most states, promises made to another based on "moral obligation" lack consideration and are not enforceable.[11] They are considered gratuitous promises and unenforceable. **For Example,** while on a fishing trip, Tom Snyder, a person of moderate means, met an elderly couple living in near-destitute conditions in a rural area of Texas. He returned to the area often, and he regularly purchased groceries for the couple and paid for their medical needs. Some two years later, the couple's son, David, discovered what Tom had been doing and promised to reimburse Snyder for what he had furnished his parents. This promise, based on a moral obligation, is unenforceable. A "past consideration" analysis also renders David's promise as unenforceable.

C. Exceptions to the Laws of Consideration

The ever-changing character of law clearly appears in the area of consideration as part of the developing law of contracts.

10. Exceptions to Consideration

By statute or decision, traditional consideration is not required in the following situations.

(a) Charitable Subscriptions

Where individuals made pledges to finance the construction of buildings for charitable purposes, consideration is lacking according to technical standards applied in ordinary contract cases. For public policy reasons, the reliance of the charity on the pledge in undertaking the project is deemed a substitute for consideration.

(b) Uniform Commercial Code

In a number of situations, the Uniform Commercial Code abolishes the requirement of consideration. **For Example,** under the Code, consideration is not required for (1) a merchant's written, firm offer for goods stated to be irrevocable, (2) a written discharge of a claim for an alleged breach of a commercial contract, or (3) an agreement to modify a contract for the sale of goods.[12]

[11] *Production Credit Ass'n of Manaan v Rub*, 475 NW2d 532 (ND 1991). As to the Louisiana rule of moral consideration, see *Thomas v Bryant*, 596 So 2d 1065 (La App 1992).

[12] UCC § 2-209(1).

(c) Promissory Estoppel

Under the doctrine of **promissory estoppel**, a promisor may be prevented from asserting that her promise is unenforceable because the promisee gave no consideration for the promise. This doctrine, sometimes called the *doctrine of detrimental reliance*, is applicable when (1) the promisor makes a promise that lacks consideration, (2) the promisor intends or should reasonably expect that the promisee will rely on the promise, (3) the promisee in fact relies on the promise in some definite and substantial manner, and (4) enforcement of the promise is the only way to avoid injustice.[13]

Legal difficulties often arise because parties take certain things for granted. Frequently, they will be sure that they have agreed to everything and that they have a valid contract. Sometimes, however, they do not. The courts are then faced with the problem of leaving them with their broken dreams or coming to their rescue when promissory estoppel can be established.

The *Chrysler* case is an example of the application of the doctrine of promissory estoppel.

CHRYSLER V CHAPLAKE HOLDINGS, LTD., 822 A2D 1024 (DEL 2003)

BRITS RESCUED BY PROMISSORY ESTOPPEL

Portman Lamborghini, Ltd. (Portman), was owned by Chaplake Holdings, Ltd/, a United Kingdom company, which was owned by David Jolliffe and David Lakeman as equal shareholders. Between 1984 and 1987, Portman sold approximately 30 new Lamborghinis each year through its exclusive concession contract with the car maker. It was then the largest Lamborghini dealer in the world, since Lamborghini's production was just 250 cars per year. These cars sold at a retail price between $200,000 and $300,000. In 1987, Chrysler Corporation bought Lamborghini; and its chairman, Lee Iacocca, presented a plan to escalate production to 5,000 units within five years. The plan included the introduction of a new model, the P140, with a retail price of $70,000. Between 1987 and 1991, all of the Chrysler/Lamborghini top executives with whom Jolliffe and Lakeman and their top advisors came in contact provided the same message to them—Chrysler was committed to the Expansion Plan, and in order for Portman to retain its exclusive UK market, it must expand its operational capacity from 35 cars in 1987 to 400 cars by 1992. Accordingly, Portman acquired additional financing, staff, and facilities and built a new distribution center. An economic downturn in the United States and major development and production problems at Lamborghini led Chrysler to reduce its expansion investment by two-thirds. Factory production delays eroded Portman's profitability and success, and it entered into receivership in April of 1992. Suit was brought on behalf of the Portman and Chaplake entities on a promissory estoppel theory against Chrysler, a Delaware corporation. The jury awarded £569,321 to Portman for costs incurred in implementing the Expansion Plan and awarded £462,686 to Chaplake for its investment in the plan. Chrysler appealed.

Judicial Opinion

WALSH, J. . . . Under the doctrine of promissory estoppel a plaintiff must demonstrate by clear and convincing evidence that:

(i) a promise was made;
(ii) it was the reasonable expectation of the promisor to induce action or forbearance on the part of the promisee;
(iii) the promisee reasonably relied on the promise and took action to his detriment; and
(iv) such promise is binding because injustice can be avoided only by enforcement of the promise.

There were a series of promises made by Chrysler and its various representatives to Portman, Chaplake and their representatives. First, the comments of then-chairman Iacocca upon the acquisition of Lamborghini made clear Chrysler's plans to expand production over a period of five

[13] *Neuhoff v Marvin Lumber and Cedar Co.*, 370 F3d 197 (1st Cir 2004).

to six years. More importantly, between 1987 and 1991 [Chrysler/Lamborghini executives] Novaro, Richards, Molaschi and Levy made similar statements promising that the Lamborghini line would expand ten-fold, and that Portman would retain its exclusivity deal *only* if it expanded its operational capacity. By making these promises. Chrysler should have expected that Portman and Chaplake would be induced to expand its operations in accordance with the promised expansion of the Lamborghini line of automobiles.

Portman and Chaplake reasonably relied upon the promises made by Chrysler, and took action to their detriment. Over a period of several years, Portman and Chaplake were regularly updated regarding the progress of the Expansion Plan. Portman would not have implemented the Portman Plan in the absence of these promises. The reasonableness of Portman and Chaplake's reliance is bolstered by the fact that the promises emanated from many of the most senior officers involved with the Expansion Plan.

Lakeman and Jolliffe were sophisticated businessmen in their own right, and in crafting the Portman Plan they employed the services of highly sophisticated advisors. Nevertheless, the record establishes that *all* of the Chrysler/Lamborghini executives with whom Lakeman, Jolliffe, and their advisors came in contact provided the same message: Chrysler is committed to the Expansion Plan, and in order for Portman to retain its exclusivity in the U.K. market, it must expand its operational capacity accordingly. Therefore, it was not unreasonable for Lakeman and Jolliffe to rely upon the promises made by these executives.

Chrysler also argues that the existing written contracts between the parties governed the relationship, and therefore promissory estoppel is inapplicable. Here, Portman and Chaplake relied on promises from Chrysler executives. Those promises induced them to increase operational capacity and investment to a degree that would have been unnecessary *but for* the Expansion Plan and the role they were promised therein. The contracts governing other aspects of the business relationship are of no consequence to this analysis because the promises made regarding Portman's role in the Expansion Plan were in addition to the existing relationship. Finally, Chrysler correctly points out that the trial court failed to address the fourth element—or the so-called "avoidance of injustice" element—of the *Lord* test. . . .

The prevention of injustice is the "fundamental idea" underlying the doctrine of promissory estoppel. *See Chrysler v Quimby*, 144 A.2d 123, 133 (Del.1958). Accordingly, the trial judge implicitly found that this element was satisfied, and the court did not err by failing to submit this element of the *Lord* test to the jury.

[Judgment affirmed] . . .

Case Questions

1. State the four elements of a promissory estoppel claim.
2. What is the significance of the fourth element of promissory estoppel, "avoidance of injustice"?
3. How did the court deal with Chrysler's assertion that existing written contracts between the parties preclude the application of promissory estoppel?

LAWFLIX

Baby Boom (1987) (PG)

Review the scene near the end of the movie when Diane Keaton is presented with an offer for the purchase of her company, Country Baby. List the elements of consideration that Food Giant is paying for the company. Explain what Ms. Keaton's consideration is in exchange.

For movie clips that illustrate business law concepts, see LawFlix at **http://wdvl.westbuslaw.com**.

Summary

A promise is not binding if there is no consideration for the promise. Consideration is what the promisor requires as the price for his promise. That price may be doing an act, refraining from the doing of an act, or merely promising to do or to refrain. In a bilateral contract, it is necessary to find that the promise of each party is supported by consideration. If either promise is not so supported, it is not binding, and the agreement of the parties is not a contract. Consequently, the agreement cannot be enforced. When a promise is the consideration, it must be a binding promise. The binding character of a promise is not affected by the circumstance that there is a condition precedent to the performance promised. Likewise, the binding character of the promise and of the contract is not affected by a provision in the contract for its cancellation by either one or both of the parties. A promise to do what one is already obligated to do is not consideration, although some exceptions are made. Such exceptions include the rendering of a partial performance or a modified performance accepted as a good-faith adjustment to a changed situation, a compromise and release of claims, a part-payment check, and a compromise of creditors. Because consideration is the price that is given to obtain the promise, past benefits conferred on the promisor cannot be consideration. In the case of a complex transaction, however, the past benefit and the subsequent transaction relating to the promise may have been intended by the parties as one transaction. In such a case, the earlier benefit is not past consideration but is the consideration contemplated by the promisor as the price for the promise subsequently made.

A promise to refrain from doing an act can be consideration. A promise to refrain from suing or asserting a particular claim can be consideration. Generally, the promise to forbear must be for a specified time, as distinguished from agreeing to forbear at will. When consideration is forbearance to assert a claim, it is immaterial whether the claim is valid as long as the claim has been asserted in the good-faith belief that it was valid.

When the promisor obtains the consideration specified for the promise, the law is not ordinarily concerned with the value or adequacy of that consideration. Exceptions are sometimes made in the case of fraud or unconscionability and under consumer protection statutes.

When the promisor does not actually receive the price promised for the promise, there is a failure of consideration, which constitutes a breach of the contract.

Questions and Case Problems

1. Sarah's house caught on fire. Through the prompt assistance of her neighbor Odessa, the fire was quickly extinguished. In gratitude, Sarah promised to pay Odessa $1,000. Can Odessa enforce this promise?
2. William E. Story agreed to pay his nephew, William E. Story II, a large sum of money (roughly equivalent to $50,000 in 2007 dollars) "if he would refrain from drinking liquor, using tobacco, swearing, and playing cards or billiards for money until he should come to be 21 years of age." William II had been using tobacco and occasionally drank liquor but refrained from using these stimulants over several years until he was 21 and also lived up to the other requirements of his uncle's offer. Just after William II's 21st birthday, Story acknowledged that William II had fulfilled his part of the bargain and advised that the money would be invested for him with interest. Story died, and his executor, Sidway, refused to pay William II because he believed the contract between Story and William II was without consideration. Sidway asserted that Story received no benefit from William II's performance and William II suffered no detriment (in fact, by his refraining from the use of liquor and tobacco, William II was not harmed but benefited, Sidway asserted). Is there any theory of consideration that William II can rely on? How would you decide this case? [*Hamer v Sidway*, 124 NY 538]
3. Dale Dyer, who was employed by National By-Products, Inc., was seriously injured at work as the result of a job-related accident. He agreed to give up his right to sue the employer for damages in consideration of the employer's giving him a lifetime job. The employer later claimed that this agreement was not binding because Dyer's promise not to sue could not be consideration for the promise to employ on the ground that Dyer in fact had no right to sue. Dyer's only remedy was to make a claim under workers' compensation. Was the agreement binding? [*Dyer v National By-Products, Inc.*, 380 NW2d 732 (Iowa)]
4. Charles Sanarwari retained Stan Gissel to prepare his income tax return for the year 2006. The parties agreed on a fee of $400. Charles had done a rough estimate based on last year's return and believed he would owe the IRS approximately $2,000. When Stan's work was completed, it turned out that Charles would receive a $2,321 tax refund. Stan explained how certain legitimate advantages were used to reduce Charles's tax obligation. Charles paid for Stan's services and was so pleased with the work that he promised to pay Stan an additional

$400 for the excellent job on the tax return when he received his tax refund. Thereafter, Stan and Charles had a falling out over a golf tournament where Charles was late for his tee time and Stan started without him, causing Charles to lose an opportunity to win the club championship. Stan was not paid the $400 promised for doing an excellent job on the tax return, and he sued Charles as a matter of principle. Decide.

5. Koedding hired West Roofers to put a roof on her house. She later claimed that the roofing job was defective, and she threatened to sue West. Both parties discussed the matter in good faith. Finally, West guaranteed that the roof would be free from leaks for 20 years in return for the guarantee by Koedding not to sue West for damages. The roof leaked the next year, and Koedding sued West on the guarantee. West claimed that the guarantee was not binding because there was no consideration for it. According to West, Koedding's promise not to sue had no value because Koedding did not have any valid claim against West; therefore, she was not entitled to sue. Was this defense valid?

6. Fedun rented a building to Gomer, who did business under the name of Mike's Cafe. Later, Gomer was about to sell the business to Brown and requested Fedun to release him from his liability under the lease. Fedun agreed to do so. Brown sold the business shortly thereafter. The balance of the rent due by Gomer under the original lease agreement was not paid, and Fedun sued Gomer on the rent claim. Could he collect after having released Gomer? [*Fedun v Mike's Cafe*, 204 A2d 776 (Pa Super)]

7. Alexander Proudfoot Co. was in the business of devising efficiency systems for industry. It told Sanitary Linen Service Co. that it could provide an improved system for Sanitary Linen that would save Sanitary Linen money. It made a contract with Sanitary Linen to provide a money-saving system. The system was put into operation, and Proudfoot was paid the amount due under the contract. The system failed to work and did not save money. Sanitary Linen sued to get the money back. Was it entitled to do so? [*Sanitary Linen Service Co. v Alexander Proudfoot Co.*, 435 F2d 292 (5th Cir)]

8. Sears, Roebuck and Co. promised to give Forrer permanent employment. Forrer sold his farm at a loss to take the job. Shortly after beginning work, he was discharged by Sears, which claimed that the contract could be terminated at will. Forrer claimed that promissory estoppel prevented Sears from terminating the contract. Was he correct? [*Forrer v Sears, Roebuck & Co.*, 153 NW2d 587 (Wis)]

9. Kemp leased a gas filling station from Baehr. Kemp, who was heavily indebted to Penn-O-Tex Oil Corp., transferred to it his right to receive payments on all claims. When Baehr complained that the rent was not paid, he was assured by the corporation that the rent would be paid to him. Baehr did not sue Kemp for the overdue rent but later sued the corporation. The defense was raised that there was no consideration for the promise of the corporation. Decide. [*Baehr v Penn-O-Tex Corp.*, 104 NW2d 661 (Minn)]

10. Bogart owed several debts to Security Bank & Trust Co. and applied to the bank for a loan to pay the debts. The bank's employee stated that he would take the application for the loan to the loan committee and "within two or three days, we ought to have something here, ready for you to go with." The loan was not made. The bank sued Bogart for his debts. He filed a counterclaim on the theory that the bank had broken its contract to make a loan to him and that promissory estoppel prevented the bank from going back on what the employee had said. Was this counterclaim valid?

11. Kelsoe worked for International Wood Products, Inc., for a number of years. One day Hernandez, a director and major stockholder of the company, promised Kelsoe that the corporation would give her 5 percent of the company's stock. This promise was never kept, and Kelsoe sued International for breach of contract. Had the company broken its contract? [*Kelsoe v International Wood Products, Inc.*, 588 So 2d 877 (Ala)]

12. Kathy left her classic 1978 Volkswagen convertible at Freddie's Service Station, requesting a "tune-up." When she returned that evening, Freddie's bill was $374. Kathy stated that Firestone and Sears advertise tune-ups for $70, and she asked Freddie, "How can you justify this bill?" Freddie responded, "Carburator work." Kathy refused to pay the bill and left. That evening, when the station closed, she took her other set of keys and removed her car, after placing a check in the station's mail slot. The check was made out to Freddie's Service Station for $200 and stated on its face: "This check is in full payment of my account with you regarding the tune-up today on my 1978 Volkswagen convertible." Freddie cashed the check in order to meet his business expenses and then sued Kathy for the difference owed. What result?

13. On the death of their mother, the children of Jane Smith gave their interests in their mother's estate to their father in consideration of his payment of $1 to each of them and his promise to leave them the property on his death. The father died without leaving them the property. The children sued their father's second wife to obtain the property in accordance with the agreement. The second wife claimed that the agreement was not a binding contract because the amount of $1 and future gifts given for the children's interests were so trivial and uncertain. Decide.

14. Radio Station KSCS broadcast a popular music program. It announced that it would pay $25,000 to any listener who detected that it did not play three consecutive songs. Steve Jennings listened to and heard a program in which two songs were followed by a commercial program. He

claimed the $25,000. The station refused to pay on the ground that there was no consideration for its promise to pay that amount. Was the station liable? [*Jennings v Radio Station KSCS*, 708 SW2d 60 (Tex App)]

15. Hoffman wanted to acquire a franchise for a Red Owl grocery store. (Red Owl was a corporation that maintained a system of chain stores.) An agent of Red Owl informed Hoffman and his wife that if they would sell their bakery in Wautoma, acquire a certain tract of land in Chilton (another Wisconsin city), and put up $6,000, they would be given a franchise. In reliance on the agent's promise, Hoffman sold his business and acquired the land in Chilton, but he was never granted a franchise. He and his wife sued Red Owl. Red Owl raised the defense that there had been only an assurance that Hoffman would receive a franchise, but because there was no promise supported by consideration, there was no binding contract to give him a franchise. Decide. [*Hoffman v Red Owl Stores, Inc.*, 133 NW2d 267 (Wis)]

LEGALITY AND PUBLIC POLICY

CHAPTER

(16)

LEARNING OBJECTIVES

After studying this chapter, you should be able to

LO.1 State the effect of illegality on a contract

LO.2 Compare illegality and unconscionability

LO.3 Distinguish between illegality in performing a legal contract and the illegality of a contract

LO.4 Recognize when a contract is invalid because it obstructs legal processes

LO.5 State the elements of a lottery

LO.6 State the extent to which agreements not to compete are lawful

A court will not enforce a contract if it is illegal, contrary to public policy, or unconscionable.

A. General Principles

An agreement is illegal either when its formation or performance is a crime or a tort or when it is contrary to public policy or unconscionable.

1. Effect of Illegality

Ordinarily, an illegal agreement is void. When an agreement is illegal, the parties are usually not entitled to the aid of the courts. Examples of illegal contracts where the courts have left the parties where they found them include a liquor store owner not being allowed to bring suit for money owed for goods (liquor) sold and delivered on credit in violation of statute and an unlicensed home improvement contractor not being allowed to enforce his contract for progress payments due him. If the illegal agreement has not been performed, neither party can sue the other to obtain performance or damages. If the agreement has been performed, neither party can sue the other to obtain damages or to set the agreement aside.[1]

Even if a contract appears to be legal on its face, it may be unenforceable if it was entered into for an illegal purpose. **For Example,** if zoning regulations in the special-purpose district of Washington, D.C., require that only a professional can lease space in a given building, and the rental agent suggests that two nonprofessionals take out the lease in their attorney's name, but all parties realize that the premises will be used only by the nonprofessionals, then the lease in question is illegal and unenforceable.[2]

2. Exceptions to Effect of Illegality

To avoid hardship, exceptions are made to the rules stated in Section 1.

(a) Protection of One Party

When the law that the agreement violates is intended to protect one of the parties, that party may seek relief. **For Example,** when, in order to protect the public, the law forbids the issuance of securities by certain classes of corporations, a person who has purchased them may recover the money paid.

(b) Unequal Guilt

When the parties are not ***in pari delicto***—equally guilty—the least guilty party is granted relief when public interest is advanced by doing so. **For Example,** when a statute is adopted to protect one of the parties to a transaction, such as a usury law adopted to protect borrowers, the person to be protected will not be deemed to be *in pari delicto* with the wrongdoer when entering into a transaction that the statute prohibits.

3. Partial Illegality

An agreement may involve the performance of several promises, some of which are illegal and some legal. The legal parts of the agreement may be enforced provided that they can be separated from the parts that are illegal.

When the illegal provision of a contract may be ignored without defeating the contract's basic purpose, a court will merely ignore the illegal provision and enforce the balance of the contract. Consequently, when a provision for the payment of an attorney's fee in a car rental agreement was illegal because a local statute prohibited it, the court would merely ignore the fee provision and enforce the balance of the contract.[3]

If a contract is susceptible to two interpretations, one legal and the other illegal, the court will assume that the legal meaning was intended unless the contrary is clearly indicated.

4. Crimes and Civil Wrongs

An agreement is illegal, and therefore void, when it calls for the commission of any act that constitutes a crime. To illustrate, one cannot enforce an agreement by which the other party is to commit an assault, steal property, burn a house, or kill a person. A contract to obtain equipment for committing a crime is illegal and cannot be enforced. Thus, a contract to manufacture and sell illegal slot machines is void.

An agreement that calls for the commission of a civil wrong is also illegal and void. Examples are agreements to slander a third person; defraud another; infringe another's patent, trademark, or copyright; or fix prices.

[1] *Sabia v Mattituck Inlet Marina, Inc.*, 805 NYS2d 346 (AD 2005).

[2] *McMahon v A, H, & B*, 728 A2d 656 (DC 1999).

[3] *Harbour v Arelco, Inc.*, 678 NE2d 381 (Ind 1997).

5. Good Faith and Fairness

Every contract has an implied obligation that neither party shall do anything that will have the effect of destroying or injuring the right of the other party to receive the fruits of the contract. This means that in every contract there exists an implied covenant of **good faith** and fair dealing. Thus, an owner of a large parcel of land on the Boston waterfront having the right under a contract with a real estate developer to approve or reject the plans submitted by the developer was guilty of a breach of the duty to act in good faith when it was shown that the owner refused to approve the developer's plans, not because the plans were "disapproved," but because the owner was trying to get more money from the developer.

6. Unconscionable Clauses

Ordinarily, a court will not consider whether a contract is fair or unfair, is wise or foolish, or operates unequally between the parties. **For Example,** the Kramper Family Farm sold 17.59 acres of land to Dakota Industrial Development, Inc. (DID), for $35,000 per acre if the buyer constructed a paved road along the property by December 31. The contract also provided that if the road was not completed by the date set forth in the contract, the price per acre would be $45,000. When the road was not completed by the December 31 date, Family Farm sued DID for the additional $10,000 per acre. DID defended that to apply the contract according to its plain language would create an unconscionable result and was an unenforceable penalty provision contrary to public policy. The court refused to allow DID to escape its contractual obligations on the pretext of unconscionability and public policy arguments. The parties are at liberty to contract as they see fit, the court concluded, and generally, a court will not inquire into the adequacy of consideration inasmuch as the value of property is a matter of personal judgment by the parties to the contract. In this case, the price consisted of either $45,000 per acre, or $35,000 per acre with the road by a certain date.[4]

However, in certain unusual situations, the law may hold a contract provision unenforceable because it is too harsh or oppressive to one of the parties. This principle may be applied to invalidate a clause providing for the payment by one party of an excessive penalty on the breaking of a contract or a provision inserted by the dominant party that it shall not be liable for the consequences of intentional torts, fraud, or gross negligence. This principle is extended in connection with the sale of goods to provide that "if the court . . . finds the contract or any clause of the contract to have been unconscionable at the time it was made, the court may refuse to enforce the contract, or it may enforce the remainder of the contract without the unconscionable clause, or it may so limit the application of any unconscionable clause as to avoid any unconscionable result."[5]

(a) What Constitutes Unconscionability?

A provision in a contract that gives what the court believes is too much of an advantage over a buyer may be held void as unconscionable.

(b) Determination of Unconscionability

Some jurisdictions analyze unconscionability as having two separate elements: procedural and substantive. Both elements must be present for a court to refuse to enforce a contract provision. Other jurisdictions analyze unconscionability by considering the doctrine of adhesion and whether the clause in question is unduly oppressive.

Procedural unconscionability has to do with matters of freedom of assent resulting from inequality of bargaining power and the absence of real negotiations and meaningful choice or a surprise resulting from hiding a disputed term in an unduly long document or fine print. Companywide standardized form contracts imposed on a take-it-or-leave-it basis by a party with superior bargaining strength are called **contracts of adhesion,** and they may sometimes be deemed procedurally unconscionable.

Substantive unconscionability focuses on the actual terms of the contract itself. Such unconscionability is indicated when the contract terms are so one-sided as to shock the conscience or are so extreme as to appear unconscionable according to the mores and business practices of the time and place.

The U.S. Supreme Court has made clear that arbitration is an acceptable forum for the resolution of employment disputes between employees and their employers, including employment-related

[4] *Kramper Family Farm v Dakota Industrial Development, Inc.*, 603 NW2d 463 (Neb App 1999).

[5] UCC § 2-302(1).

claims based on federal and state statutes.[6] The controlling arbitration agreement language is commonly devised and implemented by the employer. Under the Federal Arbitration Act (FAA), the employer can obtain a court order to stay court proceedings and compel arbitration according to the terms of the controlling arbitration agreement. The Supreme Court also made clear that in agreeing to arbitration of a statutory claim, a party does not forgo substantive rights afforded by the statute. In a growing number of court decisions, in effect employers are finding that courts will not enforce arbitration agreements in which the employer has devised an arbitration agreement that functions as a thumb on the employer's side of the scale.[7]

The *Circuit City II* decision on remand from the U.S. Supreme Court contains an example of an unenforceable arbitration clause.

CIRCUIT CITY STORES, INC. V ADAMS (CIRCUIT CITY II), 279 F3D 889 (9TH CIR 2002)

ARBITRATION AGREEMENT SHORT-CIRCUITED

Saint Clair Adams completed an application to work as a sales person at Circuit City. As part of the application, Adams signed the "Circuit City Dispute Resolution Agreement" (DRA). The DRA requires employees to submit all claims and disputes to binding arbitration. Incorporated into the DRA are a set of "Dispute Resolution Rules and Procedures" that define the claims subject to arbitration, discovery rules, allocation of fees, and available remedies. Under these rules, the amount of damages is restricted: Back pay is limited to one year, front pay to two years, and punitive damages to the greater of the amount of front and back pay awarded or $5,000. In addition, the employee is required to split the cost of the arbitration, including the daily fees of the arbitrator, the cost of a reporter to transcribe the proceedings, and the expense of renting the room in which the arbitration is held, unless the employee prevails and the arbitrator decides to order Circuit City to pay the employee's share of the costs. Circuit City is not required under the agreement to arbitrate any claims against the employee. An employee cannot work at Circuit City without signing the DRA. Adams filed a state court lawsuit against Circuit City and three co-workers alleging sexual harassment, retaliation, constructive discharge, and intentional infliction of emotional distress under the California Fair Employment and Housing Act (FEHA). Adams sought compensatory, punitive, and emotional distress damages for alleged repeated harassment during his entire term of employment. Circuit City responded by filing a petition in federal district court to compel arbitration pursuant to the FAA. The petition was granted by the trial court, reversed by the Ninth Circuit Court of Appeals, which court was reversed by the U.S. Supreme Court (*Circuit City I*) and the case remanded to the Ninth Circuit Court of Appeals.

Judicial Opinion

NELSON, C. J. . . . Circuit City has devised an arbitration agreement that functions as a thumb on Circuit City's side of the scale should an employment dispute ever arise between the company and one of its employees. We conclude that such an arrangement is unconscionable under California law.

A. Applicable Law

. . . Section 2 of the FAA provides that arbitration agreements "shall be valid, irrevocable, and enforceable, *save upon such grounds that exist at law or in equity for the revocation of any contract.*" 9 U.S.C. § 2 (emphasis added). In determining the validity of an agreement to arbitrate, federal courts "should apply ordinary state-law principles that govern the formation of contracts." *First Options of Chicago, Inc. v Kaplan*, 514 U.S. 938, 944, (1995) . . . . Thus general contact defenses such as fraud, duress, or unconscionability, grounded in state contract law, may operate to invalidate arbitration agreements . . . .

Under California law, a contract is unenforceable if it is both procedurally and substantively unconscionable.

[6] *Gilmer v Interstate/Johnson Lane Corp.*, 500 US 20 (1991); *Circuit City Stores, Inc. v Adams*, 121 S Ct 1301 (2001).
[7] See *Vassilkouska v Woodfield Nissan Inc.*, 830 NE2d 619 (Ill App 2005).

Arinendariz v Found. Health Pshychcare Svcs., Inc., 24 Cal.4th 83, 99 Cal.Rptr.2d 145, 6 P.3d 669, 690 (2000)...

B. The DRA and Unconscionability

The DRA is procedurally unconscionable because it is a contract of adhesion: a standard form contract, drafted by the party with superior bargaining power, which relegates to the other party the option of either adhering to its terms without modification or rejecting the contract entirely... Circuit City, which possesses considerably more bargaining power than nearly all of its employees or applicants, drafted the contract and uses it as its standard arbitration agreement for all of its new employees. The agreement is a prerequisite to employment, and job applicants are not permitted to modify the agreement's terms—they must take the contract or leave it....

The California Supreme Court's recent decision in *Armendariz* counsels in favor of finding that the Circuit City arbitration agreement is substantively unconscionable as well....

We find the arbitration agreement at issue here virtually indistinguishable from the agreement the California Supreme Court found unconscionable in *Armendariz.* Like the agreemerit in *Armendariz,* the DRA unilaterally forces employees to arbitrate claims against the employer. The claims subject to arbitration under the DRA include "any and all employment-related legal disputes, controversies or claims *of an Associate* arising out of, or relating to, an Associate's application or candidacy for employment, employment or cessation of employment with Circuit City." (emphasis added). The provision does not require Circuit City to arbitrate its claims against employees.... This unjustified onesidedness deprives the DRA of the "modicum of bilaterality" that the California Supreme Court requires for contracts to be enforceable under California law.

And again as in *Armendariz,* the asymmetry is compounded by the fact that the agreement limits the relief available to employees. Under the DRA, the remedies are limited to injunctive relief, up to one year of back pay and up to two years of front pay, compensatory damages, and punitive damages in an amount up to the greater of the amount of back pay and front pay awarded or $5,000. By contrast, a plaintiff in a civil suit for sexual harassment under the FEHA is eligible for all forms of relief that are generally available to civil litigants—including appropriate punitive damages and damages for emotional distress. The DRA also requires the employee to split the arbitrator's fees with Circuit City. This fee allocation scheme alone would render an arbitration agreement unenforceable.... In short, and just like the agreement invalidated by the California Supreme Court in *Armendariz,* the DRA forces Adams to arbitrate his statutory claims without affording him the benefit of the full range of statutory remedies.

In addition, our decision is entirely consistent with federal law concerning the enforceability of arbitration agreements. The Supreme Court, in *Gilmer v Interstate/Johnson Lane Corp.*, 500 U.S. 20, 26, 111 S.Ct. 1647, 114 L.Ed.2d 26(1991), held that "[b]y agreeing to arbitrate a statutory claim, [an employee] does not forgo the substantive rights afforded by the statute; [he] only submits to their resolution in an arbitral, rather than a judicial forum." While the Court in *Gilmer* affirmed that statutory rights can be resolved through arbitration, the decision also recognized that the arbitral forum must allow the employee to adequately pursue statutory rights. *Id.* at 28., 111 S. Ct. 1647

Courts have since interpreted *Gilmer* to require basic procedural and remedial protections so that claimants can effectively pursue their statutory rights.... We note that here, Circuit City's arbitration agreement... fails to provide for all of the types of relief that would otherwise be available in court, or to ensure that employees do not have to pay either unreasonable costs or... fees... as a condition of access to the arbitration forum....

C. Severability

Under California law, courts have discretion to sever an unconscionable provision or refuse to enforce the contract in its entirety....

In this case, as in *Armendariz,* the objectionable provisions pervade the entire contract. In addition to the damages limitation and the feesharing scheme, the unilateral aspect of the DRA runs throughout the agreement and defines the scope of the matters that are covered. Removing these provisions would go beyond mere excision to rewriting the contract, which is not the proper role of this Court. Therefore, we find the entire arbitration agreement unenforceable.

[Reversed]

Questions

1. What body of law may courts use to examine the validity of arbitration agreements?
2. What reason does the court of appeals give for its determination that Circuit City's DRA was procedurally unconscionable?
3. What reason(s) did the court of appeals give for its determination that Circuit City's DRA was substantively unconscionable?

B. Agreements Affecting Public Welfare

Agreements that may harm the public welfare are condemned as contrary to public policy and are not binding. Agreements that interfere with public service or the duties of public officials, obstruct legal process, or discriminate against classifications of individuals may be considered detrimental to public welfare and, as such, are not enforceable.

7. Agreements Contrary to Public Policy

A given agreement may not violate any statute but may still be so offensive to society that the courts feel that enforcing the contract would be contrary to public policy.

Public policy cannot be defined precisely but is loosely described as protection from that which tends to be injurious to the public or contrary to the public good or which violates any established interest of society. Contracts that may be unenforceable as contrary to public policy frequently relate to the protection of the public welfare, health, or safety; to the protection of the person; and to the protection of recognized social institutions. **For Example,** a woman entered into a services contract with a male in exchange for financial support. The record disclosed, however, that the association between the parties was one founded upon the exchange of money for sex. The court determined that the agreement for financial support in exchange for illicit sexual relations was violative of public policy and thus was unenforceable.[8] Courts are cautious in invalidating a contract on the ground that it is contrary to public policy because courts recognize that, on the one

THINKING THINGS THROUGH

FAIR ARBITRATION AGREEMENTS

An arbitration agreement that is fundamentally unfair will be subject to challenge by attorneys seeking to avoid arbitration. In cases when the arbitration agreement and employer actions "indicate a systematic effort to impose arbitration on an employee . . . as an inferior forum that works to the employer's advantage," the employer may well find that it will be unable to enforce the agreement to arbitrate under the FAA in federal court. Contrary to the perception that business may be attempting to "stack the deck" against claimant-employees, in reality most corporate boards and company executives devote significant human and economic resources to make sure that their companies are in full compliance with federal and state employment laws.

Thinking things through, a fair arbitration agreement will better serve the needs of employers than an unbalanced arbitration agreement that is unenforceable in court under the FAA. The advantages to arbitration for both the employer and employees are that the matters at issue are resolved in an expeditious, timely, and just manner, before an expert on employment law, with lower overall costs and in a shorter period of time than litigation. The decision is final and binding on the parties, with a very limited review of the decision under Section 10 of the FAA. Should the employee be successful and the actions of the employer's agents be found to be contrary to employment law, the employer is informed of the decision much sooner than in litigation, and the employer can take appropriate corrective action in a more expeditious fashion. The remedies for the employee are the same as provided in a court, and the process is a private one, not a source of adverse publicity with loss of goodwill. Should the employee be unsuccessful in her claims, the controversy is resolved in a shorter time than litigation, and the individual can move forward with her life, avoiding years of prolonged litigation.

[8] *Anonymous v Anonymous*, 740 NYS2d 341 (App Div 2002).

hand, they are applying a very vague standard and, on the other hand, they are restricting the freedom of the contracting parties to contract freely as they choose.[9]

8. Gambling, Wagers, and Lotteries

Gambling contracts are illegal. Largely as a result of the adoption of antigambling statutes, wagers or bets are generally illegal. Private **lotteries** involving the three elements of prize, chance, and consideration (or similar affairs of chance) are also generally held illegal. In many states, public lotteries (lotteries run by a state government) have been legalized by statute. Raffles are usually regarded as lotteries. In some states, bingo games, lotteries, and raffles are legalized by statute when the funds raised are used for a charitable purpose.

Sales promotion schemes calling for the distribution of property according to chance among the purchasers of goods are held illegal as lotteries without regard to whether the scheme is called a *guessing contest*, a *raffle*, or a *gift*.

Giveaway plans and games are lawful so long as it is not necessary to buy anything or give anything of value to participate. If participation is free, the element of consideration is lacking, and there is no lottery.

An activity is not gambling when the result is solely or predominantly a matter of skill. In contrast, it is gambling when the result is solely a matter of luck. Rarely is any activity 100 percent skill or 100 percent luck.

C. Regulation of Business

Local, state, and national laws regulate a wide variety of business activities and practices.

9. Effect of Violation

Whether an agreement made in connection with business conducted in violation of the law is binding or void depends on how strongly opposed the public policy is to the prohibited act. Some courts take the view that the agreement is not void unless the statute expressly specifies this. In some instances, a statute expressly preserves the validity of the contract. **For Example,** if someone fails to register a fictitious name under which a business is conducted, the violator, after registering the name as required by statute, is permitted to sue on a contract made while illegally conducting business.

10. Statutory Regulation of Contracts

To establish uniformity or to protect one of the parties to a contract, statutes frequently provide that contracts of a given class must follow a statutory model or must contain specified provisions. **For Example,** statutes commonly specify that particular clauses must be included in insurance policies to protect the persons insured and their beneficiaries. Other statutes require that contracts executed in connection with credit buying and loans contain particular provisions designed to protect the debtor.

Consumer protection legislation gives the consumer the right to rescind the contract in certain situations. Laws relating to truth in lending, installment sales, and home improvement contracts commonly require that an installment-sale contract specify the cash price, the down payment, the trade-in value (if any), the cash balance, the insurance costs, and the interest and finance charges.

CPA 11. Licensed Callings or Dealings

Statutes frequently require that a person obtain a license, certificate, or diploma before practicing certain professions, such as law and medicine. A license may also be required before carrying on a particular business or trade, such as that of a real estate broker, stockbroker, hotel keeper, or pawnbroker.

If a license is required to protect the public from unqualified persons, a contract made by an unlicensed person is unenforceable.[10] **For Example,** a corporation that does not hold a required real estate broker's license cannot sue to recover fees for services as a broker. An unlicensed insurance broker who cannot recover a fee because of the absence of a license cannot evade the statutory requirement by having a friend who is a licensed broker bill for the services and collect the payment for him.

[9] *Beacon Hill Civic Ass'n v Ristorante Toscano, Inc.*, 662 NE2d 1015 (Mass 1996).
[10] *Hancock Gannon Joint Venture II v McNuly*, 800 So 2d 294 (Fla App 2000).

CPA 12. Contracts in Restraint of Trade

An agreement that unreasonably restrains trade is illegal and void on the ground that it is contrary to public policy. Such agreements take many forms, such as a combination to create a monopoly or to obtain a corner on the market or an association of merchants to increase prices. In addition to the illegality of the agreement based on general principles of law, statutes frequently declare monopolies illegal and subject the parties to various civil and criminal penalties.[11]

CPA 13. Agreements Not to Compete

In the absence of a valid restrictive covenant, the seller of a business may compete with the buyer, or an ex-employee may solicit customers of the former employer.

A noncompetition covenant may be held invalid because of vagueness concerning the duration and geographic area of the restriction.[12] Moreover, if the agreement not to compete is not properly executed in accordance with state law, it will not be enforced. **For Example,** Holly Martinez worked for Avis Rent-A-Car at the New Bern, North Carolina, airport. When hired, she printed her name on the top of the form containing an agreement not to compete but did not sign it. On December 17, she resigned her position to return to school, saying that she planned to get a part-time job. The next day, she began working for Hertz Rent-A-Car at the counter adjacent to the Avis counter. Avis was unsuccessful in obtaining a restraining order to prevent Holly from working for its competitor because the agreement was not signed as required by state law.[13]

CPA (a) Sale of Business

When a going business is sold, it is commonly stated in the contract that the seller shall not go into the same or a similar business again within a certain geographic area or for a certain period of time, or both. In early times, such agreements were held void because they deprived the public of the service of the person who agreed not to compete, impaired the latter's means of earning a livelihood, reduced competition, and exposed the public to monopoly. To modern courts, the question is whether, under the circumstances, the restriction imposed on one party is reasonably necessary to protect the other party. If the restriction is reasonable, it is valid.

On the ground of reasonableness, a restriction has been sustained by which a business owner selling the business to a new owner agreed not to open a competing business within a 50-mile radius (where the business has a territorial range up to 100 miles) for five years.[14]

(b) Employment Contract

Restrictions to prevent competition by a former employee are held valid when reasonable and necessary to protect the interest of the former employer. **For Example,** a noncompete covenant executed by Dr. Samuel Keeley that prohibited his "establishing a competing cardiovascular surgery practice within a 75-mile radius of Albany, Georgia, for a period of two years following the date of termination" was upheld in court and did not include more territory than necessary to protect the professional corporation's business interests.[15]

Public policy requires that noncompetition covenants be strictly construed in favor of freedom of action of the employee.[16] A restrictive covenant is not binding when it places a restriction on the employee that is broader than reasonably necessary to protect the employer. **For Example,** Illinois manufacturer Arcor's noncompetition covenant, which had a restricted area of "the United States and Canada" precluding competition by a former employee for a one-year period, was found to be unenforceable as an industrywide ban that constituted a "blanket prohibition on competition."[17] In determining the validity of a restrictive covenant binding an employee, the court balances the aim of protecting the legitimate interests of the employer with the right of the employee to follow gainful employment and provide services required by the public and other employers.

[11] Sherman Antitrust Act, 15 USC §§ 1–7; Clayton Act, 15 USC §§ 12–27; Federal Trade Commission Act, 15 USC §§ 41–58.

[12] *Vukovich v Coleman*, 2003 WL 21290639 (Ind App).

[13] *New Hanover Rent-A-Car, Inc. v Martinez*, 525 SE2d 487 (NC App 2000).

[14] *Hicks v Doors By Mike, Inc.*, 579 SE2d 833 (Ga App 2003).

[15] *Keeley v CSA, P.C.*, 510 SE2d 880 (Ga App 1999).

[16] Noncompetition covenants are not valid in California. However, confidentiality agreements protecting trade secrets are enforceable in that state.

[17] *Arcor, Inc. v Haas*, 842 NE2d 265 (Ill App 2005).

As set forth in the *NIKE, Inc. v McCarthy* decision, presented in this section, these covenants will be enforced when they are (1) limited as to duration and geographic area, (2) based on some good consideration, and (3) reasonable, affording only fair protection to the employer in whose favor it is made and does not interfere with the interests of the public.

NIKE, INC. V MCCARTHY, 379 F3D 576 (9TH CIR 2004)

YOU MEAN TO SAY THAT CONFIDENTIALITY AGREEMENTS AND COVENANTS NOT TO COMPETE MEAN WHAT THEY SAY?

Eugene McCarthy left his position as director of sales for Nike's Brand Jordan division in June 2003 to become vice president of U.S. footwear sales and merchandising at Reebok, one of Nike's competitors. Nike sought a preliminary injunction to prevent McCarthy from working for Reebok for a year, invoking a noncompete agreement McCarthy had signed in 1997 when Nike had promoted him to his earlier position as a regional footwear sales manager. The agreement stated in pertinent part:

During EMPLOYEE'S employment by NIKE... and for one (1) year thereafter, (the "Restriction Period"), EMPLOYEE will not directly or indirectly... be employed by, consult for, or be connected in any manner with, any business engaged anywhere in the world in the athletic footwear, athletic apparel or sports equipment and accessories business, or any other business which directly competes with NIKE or any of its subsidiaries or affiliated corporations.

The U.S. District Court granted Nike's motion for a preliminary injunction, and McCarthy appealed.

Judicial Opinion

FISHER, C. J....

Protectible Interest

Even if the covenant not to compete is not void... it is a contract in restraint of trade that must meet three requirements under Oregon common law to be enforceable:

(1) it must be partial or restricted in its operation in respect either to time or place; (2) it must be on some good consideration; and (3) it must be reasonable, that is, it should afford only a fair protection to the interests of the party in whose favor it is made, and must not be so large in its operation as to interfere with the interests of the public.

Eldridge v Johnston, 245 P.2d 239, 250, (Or. 1952). To satisfy the reasonableness requirement, the employer must show as a predicate "that [it] has a 'legitimate interest' entitled to protection." *North Pac. Lumber Co. v Moore*, 551 P.2d 431, 434. McCarthy argues that Nike has failed to show such a legitimate interest in this case.*...

Nike has shown that McCarthy acquired information pertaining especially to Nike's business during the course of his employment with Nike. As Brand Jordan's director of sales, McCarthy obtained knowledge of Nike's product launch dates, product allocation strategies, new product development, product orders six months in advance and strategic sales plans up to three years in the future. This information was not general knowledge in the industry. For instance, McCarthy was privy to information about launch dates—the date Nike plans to introduce a product in the marketplace—for Brand Jordan shoes up through the spring of 2004. According to the undisputed testimony of one of Nike's executives, if a company knew its competitor's launch dates, it could time the launch dates of its own products to disrupt the sales of its competitor....

An employee's knowledge of confidential information is sufficient to justify enforcement of the noncompete if there is a "substantial risk" that the employee will be able to divert all or part of the employer's business given his knowledge. *See Volt Servs. Group v Adecco Employment Servs., Inc.*, 35 P.3d 329, 334 (Or. Ct. App. 2001).... Given the nature of the confidential information that McCarthy acquired at Nike and his new position with Reebok, there is a substantial risk that Reebok would be able to divert a significant part of Nike's business given McCarthy's knowledge. McCarthy had the highest access to confidential information concerning Nike's product allocation, product development and sales strategies. As vice president of U.S. footwear sales and merchandising

*McCarthy does not contest the geographic or temporal scope of the noncompete agreement, nor does he claim that it lacked consideration.

for Reebok, McCarthy would be responsible for developing strategic sales plans, providing overall direction for product allocation and shaping product lines, including how products are priced. Thus, McCarthy could help choose product allocation, sales and pricing strategies for Reebok that could divert a substantial part of Nike's footwear sales to Reebok based on his knowledge of information confidential to Nike without explicitly disclosing this information to any of Reebok's employees; Accordingly, the potential use of confidential information by McCarthy in his new position with Reebok is sufficient to justify enforcing the noncompete agreement. We conclude that Nike has demonstrated a likelihood of success as to the enforceability of its noncompete agreement with McCarthy.

Questions

1. Review the wording of the noncompete agreement as to duration and territory. Is it unreasonably restrictive on McCarthy?
2. Was the restraint reasonably necessary to protect Nike's business?

(c) Effect of Invalidity

When a restriction of competition agreed to by the parties is invalid because its scope as to time or geographic area is too great, how does this affect the contract? Some courts trim the restrictive covenant down to a scope they deem reasonable and require the parties to abide by that revision.[18] This rule is nicknamed the "blue-pencil rule." By applying this rule, one court has held that a covenant not to compete for three years was void because it was excessive but that it would be enforced for one year. In the *Arcor* case, with the restricted area encompassing the U.S. and Canada, the court refused to "blue pencil" the covenant because to render the clause reasonable, the court would in effect be writing a new agreement, which is inappropriate.[19]

Other courts refuse to apply the blue-pencil rule and hold that the restrictive covenant is void or that the entire contract is void.[20] There is also authority that a court should refuse to apply the blue-pencil

E-COMMERCE AND CYBERLAW

SPECIAL RULES FOR INTERNET E-COMMERCE EMPLOYEES?

Traditional noncompetition clauses are enforceable against former employees when the restrictions are reasonable and necessary to protect the interests of the employer who contracted for this protection. A one-year noncompetition clause is ordinarily a reasonable duration for such a restrictive covenant. However, a federal court has refused to issue a preliminary injunction against an Internet publishing business executive, Mark Schlack, who had signed a one-year noncompetition clause as part of his employment contract with EarthWeb, Inc., and thereafter left this company to start a competing Web site, **http://www.ITWorld.com,** for International Data Group, Inc. The court reasoned in part that "a one-year hiatus from the [Internet information technology] workforce is several generations, if not an eternity." The court ruled that EarthWeb's restrictive covenant "is too long... given the dynamic nature of this industry [and] its lack of geographical borders." This ruling may be the foundation on which special rules develop for Internet-related employment contracts.*

** Earthweb, Inc., v Schlack*, 71 F Supp 2d 299 (1999), aff'd in part, 205 F3d 1322 (2000).

18 *Unisource Worldwide, Inc. v Valenti*, 196 F Supp 2d 269 (EDNY 2002).

19 *Arcor Inc.*, 842 NE2d at 374.

20 *SWAT 24 v Bond*, 759 So 2d 1047 (La App 2000). Under California law, any "contract by which anyone is restrained from engaging in a lawful profession, trade or business is to that extent void." Cal B&P Code § 16600. A noncompete provision is permitted, however, when "necessary to protect the employer's trade secrets." See *Lotona v Aetna U.S. Healthcare Inc.*, 82 F Supp 2d 1089 (CD Cal 1999), where Aetna was liable for wrongful termination when it fired a California employee for refusing to sign a noncompete agreement.

ETHICS & THE LAW

William Stern and his wife were unable to have children because the wife suffered from multiple sclerosis and pregnancy posed a substantial health risk. Stern's family had been killed in the Holocaust, and he had a strong desire to continue his bloodline.

The Sterns entered into a surrogacy contract with Mary Beth Whitehead through the Infertility Center of New York (ICNY). William Stern and the Whiteheads (husband and wife) signed a contract for Mary Beth to be artificially inseminated and carry Stern's child to term, for which Stern was to pay Mary Beth $10,000 and ICNY $7,500.

Mary Beth was successfully artificially inseminated in 1985, and Baby M was born on March 27, 1986. To avoid publicity, the parents of Baby M were listed as "Mr. and Mrs. Whitehead," and the baby was called Sara Elizabeth Whitehead. On March 30, 1986, Mary Beth turned Baby M over to the Sterns at their home. They renamed the little girl Melissa.

Mary Beth became emotionally distraught and was unable to eat or sleep. The Sterns were so frightened by her behavior that they allowed her to take Baby M for one week to help her adjust. The Whiteheads took the baby and traveled throughout the East, staying in 20 different hotels and motels. Florida authorities found Baby M with Mary Beth's parents and returned her to the Sterns.

Mary Beth said the contract was one to buy a baby and was against public policy and therefore void. She also argued that the contract violated state laws on adoption and the severance of parental rights. The Sterns brought an action to have the contract declared valid and custody awarded to them.

Should the contract be valid or void? What types of behavior would be encouraged if the contract were declared valid? Is it ethical to "rent a womb"? Is it ethical to sell a child? See *In re Baby M,* 537 A2d 15 (NJ 1988).

THINKING THINGS THROUGH

LEGALITY AND PUBLIC POLICY

Karl Llewellyn, the principal drafter of the law that governs nearly all sales of goods in the United States—the Uniform Commercial Code (UCC)—once wrote, "Covert tools are never reliable tools." He was referring to unfairness in a contract or between the contracting parties.

The original intent of declaring certain types of contracts void because of issues of imbalance was based in equity. Courts stepped in to help parties who found themselves bound under agreements that were not fair and open in both their written terms and the communications between the parties. One contracts scholar wrote that the original intent could be described as courts stepping in to help "presumptive sillies like sailors and heirs . . ." and others who, if not crazy, are "pretty peculiar."

However, as the sophistication of contracts and commercial transactions increased, the importance of accuracy, honesty, and fairness increased. Unconscionability is a contracts defense that permits courts to intervene where contracts, if enforced, would "affront the sense of decency." UNCONSCIONABILITY is a term of ethics or moral philosophy used by courts to prevent exploitation and fraud.

rule when the restrictive covenant is manifestly unfair and would virtually keep the employee from earning a living.

14. Usurious Agreements

Usury is committed when money is loaned at a higher rate of interest than the law allows. Most states prohibit by statute charging more than a stated amount of interest. These statutes provide a maximum annual contract rate of interest that can be exacted under the law of a given state. In many states, the usury law does not apply to loans made to corporations.

When a lender incurs expenses in making a loan, such as the cost of appraising property or making a credit investigation of the borrower, the lender will require the borrower to pay the amount of such expenses. Any fee charged by a lender that goes beyond the reasonable expense of making the loan constitutes "interest" for the purposes of determining whether the transaction is usurious.[21]

Penalites for violating usury laws vary from state to state, with a number of states restricting the lender to the recovery of the loan but no interest whatsoever; other states allow recovery of the loan principal and interest up to the maximum contract rate. Some states also impose a penalty on the lender such as the payment of double the interest paid on a usurious loan.

As developed in the *Pinchuck* case, many states require forfeiture of the entire principal amount of the usurious loan.

PINCHUCK V CANZONERI, 920 SO2ND 713 (FLA APP 4, 2006)

A NEEDLE OF USURY IN A HAYSTACK OF SUBTERFUGE

Karen Canzoneri entered into two agreements with Howard Pinchuck. Under the first agreement Canzoneri advanced $50,000 to be repaid 12% per month for 12 consecutive months "as an investment profit." The second agreement required "$36,000 to be repaid on or before 6/1/01 with an investment profit of $36,000, total being $72,000." The annualized rate of return for the first transaction was 144%; and the annualized rate for the second transaction was 608%. The civil penalty for violating the state's maximum interest rate of 25% per annum is forfeiture of the entire principal amount. Canzoneri contends that the transactions were investments not subject to the usury law.

Judicial Opinion

HAZOURI, J. . . . In *Jersey Palm–Gross, Inc. v Paper*, 658 So.2d 531 (Fla. 1995), the supreme court stated:

> *The Florida Legislature enacted Chapter 687, Florida Statutes (1993), to protect borrowers from paying unfair and excessive interest to overreaching creditors. This chapter sets limits on interest rates and prescribes penalties for the violation of those limits. Section 687.071(2), Florida Statutes (1993), defines criminal usury as the willful and knowing charge or receipt of interest in excess of 25% per annum. Id. The civil penalty for violating this statute is forfeiture of the entire principal amount. § 687.071(7), Fla.Stat. (1993).*

Jersey Palm–Gross, Inc., 658 So.2d at 534.

The four requirements of a usurious transaction are:

(1) that such transaction must be a loan, expressed or implied; (2) that an understanding must exist between the parties that the money lent shall be returned; (3) that for such loan, a greater rate of interest than is allowed by law shall be paid or agreed to be paid as the case may be; and (4) that there must exist a corrupt intention to take more than the legal rate for the use of the money loaned.

Diversified Enters., Inc. v West, 141 So.2d 27, 29 (Fla. 2d DCA 1962).

The trial court found that the agreements included in counts I and V were valid and binding contracts. . . .

. . . Even though the agreements which were the subjects of counts I and V were put in terms of investment and the return is called profit, not interest, this does not change our conclusion that these were loans and the transactions were usurious.

It is well settled in Florida that the courts will look to the substance of the transaction rather than to the form to determine usury. See *Kay v Amendola*, 129 So.2d 170 (Fla. 2d DCA 1961).

[21] *Lentimo v Cullen Center Bank and Trust Co.*, 919 SW2d 743 (Tex App 1996).

Our usury statutes show a clear legislative intent to prevent accomplishment of a usurious scheme by indirection, and the concealment of the needle of usury in a haystack of subterfuge will not avail to prevent its pricking the body of the law into action.

[Reversed and Remanded]

Questions

1. State the four elements of a usurious transaction.
2. How did the court decide this case?
3. Did the court order the borrower, Pinchuck, to repay the principal amount owed the lender, Canzoneri?

LAWFLIX

Midnight Run (1988) (R)

Is the contract Robert DeNiro has for bringing in Charles Grodin, an embezzler, legal? Discuss the issues of consideration and ethics as the bail bondsman puts another bounty hunter on the case and DeNiro flees from law enforcement agents in order to collect his fee. And finally, discuss the legality of DeNiro's acceptance of money from Grodin and his release of Grodin at the end of the movie.

For movie clips that illustrate business law concepts, see LawFlix at **http://wdvl.westbuslaw.com.**

Summary

When an agreement is illegal, it is ordinarily void and no contract arises from it. Courts will not allow one party to an illegal agreement to bring suit against the other party. There are some exceptions to this, such as when the parties are not equally guilty or when the law's purpose in making the agreement illegal is to protect the person who is bringing suit. When possible, an agreement will be interpreted as being lawful. Even when a particular provision is held unlawful, the balance of the agreement will generally be saved so that the net result is a contract minus the clause that was held illegal.

The term *illegality* embraces situations in unconscionable contract clauses in which the courts hold that contract provisions are unenforceable because they are too harsh or oppressive to one of the parties to a transaction. If the clause is part of a standard form contract drafted by the party having superior bargaining power and is presented on a take-it-or-leave-it basis (a contract of adhesion) and the substantive terms of the clause itself are unduly oppressive, the clause will be found to be unconscionable and not enforced.

Whether a contract is contrary to public policy may be difficult to determine because public policy is not precisely defined. That which is harmful to the public welfare or general good is contrary to public policy. Contracts condemned as contrary to public policy include those designed to deprive the weaker party of a benefit that the lawmaker desired to provide, agreements injuring public service, and wagers and private lotteries. Statutes commonly make the wager illegal as a form of gambling. The lottery is any plan under which, for a consideration, a person has a chance to win a prize.

Illegality may consist of the violation of a statute or administrative regulation adopted to regulate business. An agreement not to compete is illegal as a restraint of trade except when reasonable in its terms and when it is incidental to the sale of a business or to a contract of employment.

The charging by a lender of a higher rate of interest than allowed by law is usury. Courts must examine transactions carefully to see whether a usurious loan is disguised as a legitimate transaction.

Questions and Case Problems

1. When are the parties to an illegal agreement *in pari delicto?*
2. John Iwen sued U.S. West Direct because of a negligently constructed yellow pages advertisement. U.S. West Direct moved to stay litigation and compel arbitration under the yellow pages order form, which required advertisers to resolve all controversies through arbitration, but allowed U.S. West (the publisher) to

pursue judicial remedies to collect amounts due it. Under the arbitration provision, Iwen's sole remedy was a pro rata reduction or refund of the cost of the advertisement. The order form language was drafted by U.S. West Direct on a take-it-or-leave-it basis and stated in part:

> *Any controversy or claim arising out of or relating to this Agreement, or breach thereof, other than an action by Publisher for the collection of amounts due under this Agreement, shall be settled by final, binding arbitration in accordance with the Commercial Arbitration rules of the American Arbitration Association.*

If forced to arbitration, Iwen would be unable to recover damages for the negligently constructed yellow pages ad, nor could he recover damages for infliction of emotional distress and punitive damages related to his many efforts to adjust the matter with the company, which were ignored or rejected. Must Iwen have his case resolved through arbitration rather than a court of law? [*Iwen v U.S. West Direct*, 977 P2d 989 (Mont)]

3. Alman made a contract to purchase an automobile from Crockett Motors on credit but failed to make payments on time. When Crockett sued to enforce the contract, Alman raised the defense that the price of the car had been increased because she was buying on credit and this increase was unconscionable. Crockett proved that the automobile was exactly what it was represented to be and that no fraud had been committed in selling the car to Alman. Does Crockett's evidence constitute a defense to Alman's claim of unconscionability?
4. The Civic Association of Plaineville raffled an automobile to raise funds to build a hospital. Lyons won the automobile, but the association refused to deliver it to her. She sued the association for the automobile. Can Lyons enforce the contract?
5. Ewing was employed by Presto-X-Co., a pest exterminator. His contract of employment specified that he would not solicit or attempt to solicit customers of Presto-X for two years after the termination of his employment. After working several years, his employment was terminated. Ewing then sent a letter to customers of Presto-X stating that he no longer worked for Presto-X and that he was still certified by the state. Ewing set forth his home address and phone number, which the customers did not previously have. The letter ended with the statement, "I thank you for your business throughout the past years." Presto-X brought an action to enjoin Ewing from sending such letters. He raised the defense that he was prohibited only from soliciting and there was nothing in the letters that constituted a seeking of customers. Decide. What ethical values are involved? [*Presto-X-Co. v Ewing*, 442 NW2d 85 (Iowa)]
6. The Minnesota adoption statute requires that any agency placing a child for adoption make a thorough investigation and not give a child to an applicant unless the placement is in the best interests of the child. Tibbetts applied to Crossroads, Inc., a private adoption agency, for a child to adopt. He later sued the agency for breach of contract, claiming that the agency was obligated by contract to supply a child for adoption. The agency claimed that it was required only to use its best efforts to locate a child and was not required to supply a child to Tibbetts unless it found him to be a suitable parent. Decide. [*Tibbetts v Crossroads, Inc.*, 411 NW2d 535 (Minn App)]
7. Siddle purchased a quantity of fireworks from Red Devil Fireworks Co. The sale was illegal, however, because Siddle did not have a license to make the purchase, which the seller knew because it had been so informed by the attorney general of the state. Siddle did not pay for the fireworks, and Red Devil sued him. He defended on the ground that the contract could not be enforced because it was illegal. Was the defense valid? [*Red Devil Fireworks Co. v Siddle*, 648 P2d 468 (Wash App)]
8. Onderdonk entered a retirement home operated by Presbyterian Homes. The contract between Onderdonk and the home required Onderdonk to make a specified monthly payment that could be increased by the home as the cost of operations increased. The contract and the payment plan were thoroughly explained to Onderdonk. As the cost of operations rose, the home continually raised the monthly payments to cover these costs. Onderdonk objected to the increases on the ground that the increases were far more than had been anticipated and that the contract was therefore unconscionable. Was his objection valid?
9. Smith was employed as a salesman for Borden, Inc., which sold food products in 63 counties in Arkansas, 2 counties in Missouri, 2 counties in Oklahoma, and 1 county in Texas. Smith's employment contract prohibited him from competing with Borden after leaving its employ. Smith left Borden and went to work for a competitor, Lady Baltimore Foods. Working for this second employer, Smith sold in 3 counties of Arkansas. He had sold in 2 of these counties while he worked for Borden. Borden brought an injunction action against Smith and Lady Baltimore to enforce the noncompete covenant in Smith's former contract. Was Borden entitled to the injunction? [*Borden, Inc. v Smith*, 478 SW2d 744 (Ark)]
10. Central Water Works Supply, a corporation, had a contract with its shareholders that they would not compete with it. There were only four shareholders, of whom William Fisher was one, but he was not an employee of the corporation. When he sold his shares in the corporation and began to compete with it, the corporation went to court to obtain an injunction to stop such competition. Fisher claimed that the corporation was not entitled to an injunction because he had not obtained any confidential information or made customer

contacts. The corporation claimed that such matters were relevant only when an employee had agreed not to compete but were not applicable when there was a noncompetitive covenant in the sale of a business and that the sale-of-a-business rule should be applied to a shareholder. Who was correct?

11. Vodra was employed as a salesperson and contracting agent for American Security Services. As part of his contract of employment, Vodra signed an agreement that for three years after leaving this employment, he would not solicit any customer of American. Vodra had no experience in the security field when he went to work for American. To the extent that he became known to American's customers, it was because of being American's representative rather than because of his own reputation in the security field. After some years, Vodra left American and organized a competing company that solicited American's customers. American sued him to enforce the restrictive covenant. Vodra claimed that the restrictive covenant was illegal and not binding. Was he correct? [*American Security Services, Inc. v Vodra*, 385 NW2d 73 (Neb)]
12. Potomac Leasing Co. leased an automatic telephone system to Vitality Centers. Claudene Cato signed the lease as guarantor of payments. When the rental was not paid, Potomac Leasing brought suit against Vitality and Cato. They raised the defense that the rented equipment was to be used for an illegal purpose—namely, the random sales solicitation by means of an automatic telephone in violation of state statute; that this purpose was known to Potomac Leasing; and that Potomac Leasing could therefore not enforce the lease. Was this defense valid? [*Potomac Leasing Co. v Vitality Centers, Inc.*,718 SW2d 928 (Ark)]
13. The English publisher of a book called *Cambridge* gave a New York publisher permission to sell that book any place in the world except in England. The New York publisher made several bulk sales of the book to buyers who sold the book throughout the world, including England. The English publisher sued the New York publisher and its customers for breach of the restriction prohibiting sales in England. Decide.
14. A state law required builders of homes to be licensed and declared that an unlicensed contractor could not recover compensation under a contract made for the construction of a residence. Although Annex Construction, Inc., did not have a license, it built a home for French. When he failed to pay what was owed, Annex sued him. He raised the defense that the unlicensed contractor could not recover for the contract price. Annex claimed that the lack of a license was not a bar because the president of the corporation was a licensed builder and the only shareholder of the corporation, and the construction had been properly performed. Was Annex entitled to recover?
15. Yarde Metals, Inc., owned six season tickets to New England Patriots football games. Gillette Stadium, where the games are played, had insufficient men's restrooms in use for football games at that time, which was the subject of numerous newspaper columns. On October 13, 2002, a guest of Yarde Metals, Mikel LaCroix, along with others, used available women's restrooms to answer the call of nature. As LaCroix left the restroom, however, he was arrested and charged with disorderly conduct. The Patriots organization terminated all six of Yarde's season ticket privileges, incorrectly giving as a reason that LaCroix was ejected "for throwing bottles in the seating section." Yarde sued, contending that "by terminating the plaintiff's season tickets for 2002 and for the future arbitrarily, without cause and based on false information," the Patriots had violated the implicit covenant of good faith and fair dealing of the season tickets contract. The back of each Patriots ticket states:

    This ticket and all season tickets are revocable licenses. The Patriots reserve the right to revoke such licenses, in their sole discretion, at any time and for any reason.

    How would you decide this case? [*Yarde Metals, Inc. v New England Patriots Ltd.*, 834 NE2d 1233 (Mass App Ct)]

CPA Questions

1. West, an Indiana real estate broker, misrepresented to Zimmer that West was licensed in Kansas under the Kansas statute that regulates real estate brokers and equires all brokers to be licensed. Zimmer signed a contract agreeing to pay West a 5 percent commission for selling Zimmer's home in Kansas. West did not sign the contract. West sold Zimmer's home. If West sued Zimmer for nonpayment of commission, Zimmer would be:
    a. Liable to West only for the value of services rendered
    b. Liable to West for the full commission
    c. Not liable to West for any amount because West did not sign the contract
    d. Not liable to West for any amount because West violated the Kansas licensing requirements (5/92, Law, #25)

2. Blue purchased a travel agency business from Drye. The purchase price included payment for Drye's goodwill. The agreement contained a covenant prohibiting Drye from competing with Blue in the travel agency business. Which of the following statements regarding the covenant is *not* correct?

   a. The restraint must be *no* more extensive than is reasonably necessary to protect the goodwill purchased by Blue.

   b. The geographic area to which it applies must be reasonable.

   c. The time period for which it is to be effective must be reasonable.

   d. The value to be assigned to it is the excess of the price paid over the seller's cost of all tangible assets. (11/87, Law, #2)

WRITING, ELECTRONIC FORMS, AND INTERPRETATION OF CONTRACTS

CHAPTER (17)

LEARNING OBJECTIVES

After studying this chapter, you should be able to

LO.1 State when a contract must be evidenced by a writing

LO.2 List the requirements of a writing that evidence a paper or electronic contract

LO.3 State the effects of the absence of a sufficient writing when a contract must be evidenced by a writing

LO.4 List the exceptions that have been made by the courts to the laws requiring written evidence of contracts

LO.5 Compare statute of frauds requirements with the parol evidence rule

LO.6 List exceptions to the parol evidence rule

LO.7 Compare the effects of objective and subjective intent of the parties to a contract

LO.8 State the rules for interpreting ambiguous terms in a contract

LO.9 State the effect of contradictory terms

When must a contract be written? What is the effect of a written contract? These questions lead to the statute of frauds and the parol evidence rule.

A. Statute of Frauds

A *contract* is a legally binding agreement. Must the agreement be evidenced by a writing?

1. Validity of Oral Contracts

In the absence of a statute requiring a writing, a contract may be oral or written. Managers and professionals should be more fully aware that their oral communications, including telephone conversations and dinner or breakfast discussions, may be deemed legally enforceable contracts. **For Example,** suppose that Mark Wahlberg, after reviewing a script tentatively entitled *The Bulger Boys*, meets with Steven Spielberg to discuss Mark's playing mobster James "Whitey" Bulger in the film. Steven states, "You *are* 'Whitey,' Marky! The nuns at Gate of Heaven Grammar School in South Boston—or maybe it was St. Augustine's—they don't send for the Boston Police when they are troubled about drug use in the schools; they send for you to talk to the kids. Nobody messes with you, and the kids know it. This is true stuff, I think, and this fugitive's brother Bill comes out of the Southie projects to be president of U Mass." Mark likes the script. Steven and Mark block out two months of time for shooting the film this fall. They agree on Mark's usual fee and a "piece of the action" based on a set percentage of the net income from the film. Thereafter, Mark's agent does not like the deal. He believes there are better scripts for Mark. Incredibly brutal things are coming out about "Whitey" that could severely tarnish the film. And with Hollywood accounting, a percentage of the "net" take is usually of little value. However, all of the essential terms of a contract have been agreed on, and such an oral agreement would be legally enforceable. As set forth in the following text, no writing is required for a services contract that can be performed within one year after the date of the agreement.

Certain contracts, on the other hand, must be evidenced by a writing to be legally enforceable. These contracts are covered by the **statute of frauds.**[1]

Because many oral contracts are legally enforceable, it is a good business practice in the preliminary stages of discussions to stipulate that no binding agreement is intended to be formed until a written contract is prepared and signed by the parties.

2. Contracts that Must Be Evidenced by a Writing

The statute of frauds requires that certain kinds of contracts be evidenced by a writing or they cannot be enforced. This means that either the contract itself must be in writing and signed by both parties or there must be a sufficient written memorandum of the oral contract signed by the person being sued for breach of contract. A *part performance* doctrine or exception to the statute of frauds may exist when the plaintiff's part performance is "unequivocally referable" to the oral agreement.[2]

(a) Agreement That Cannot Be Performed within One Year after the Contract Is Made

A writing is required when the contract, by its terms or subject matter, cannot be performed within one year after the date of the agreement. An oral agreement to supply a line of credit for two years cannot be enforced because of the statute of frauds. Likewise, a joint venture agreement to construct a condominium complex was subject to the one-year provision of the statute of frauds when the contract could not reasonably have been performed within one year. The plans of the parties projected a development over the course of three years.

The year runs from the time the oral contract is made rather than from the date when performance is to begin. In computing the year, the day on which the contract was made is excluded.

[1] The name is derived from the original English Statute of Frauds and Perjuries, which was adopted in 1677 and became the pattern for similar legislation in America. The 17th section of that statute governed the sale of goods, and its modern counterpart is § 2-201 of the UCC. The 4th section of the English statute provided the pattern for U.S. legislation with respect to contracts other than for the sale of goods described in this section of the chapter. The English statute was repealed in 1954 except as to land sale and guarantee contracts. The U.S. statutes remain in force, but the liberalization by UCC § 2-201 of the pre-Code requirements with respect to contracts for the sale of goods lessens the applicability of the writing requirement. Additional movement away from the writing requirement is seen in the 1994 Revision of Article 8, Securities, which abolishes the statute of frauds provision of the original UCC § 8-319 and goes beyond by declaring that the one-year performance provision of the statute of frauds is not applicable to contracts for securities. UCC § 8-113 [1994 Revision].

[2] *Carey & Associates v Ernst*, 802 NYS2d 160 (AD 2005).

No *part performance* exception exists to validate an oral agreement not performable within one year. **For Example,** Babyback's Foods negotiated a multi-year oral agreement to comarket its barbecue meat products with the Coca-Cola Co. nationwide and arranged to have several coolers installed at area grocery stores in Louisville under the agreement. Babyback's faxed to Coca-Cola a contract that summarized the oral agreement but Coca-Cola never signed it. Because Coca-Cola did not sign and no part performance exception exists for an oral agreement not performable within one year, Babyback's lawsuit was unsuccessful.[3]

When no time for performance is specified by the oral contract and complete performance could "conceivably occur" within one year, the statute of frauds is not applicable to the oral contract.[4]

When a contract may be terminated at will by either party, the statute of frauds is not applicable because the contract may be terminated within a year. **For Example,** David Ehrlich was hired as manager of Gravediggaz pursuant to an oral management agreement that was terminable at will by either Ehrlich or the group. He was entitled to receive 15 percent of the gross earnings of the group and each of its members, including rap artist Robert Diggs, professionally known as RZA, for all engagements entered into while he was manager under this oral agreement. Such an at-will contract is not barred by the statute of frauds.[5]

FIGURE 17-1 Hurdles in the Path of a Contract

WRITING REQUIRED	
STATUTE OF FRAUDS	EXCEPTIONS
MORE THAN ONE YEAR TO PERFORM SALE OF LAND ANSWER FOR ANOTHER'S DEBT OR DEFAULT PERSONAL REPRESENTATIVE TO PAY DEBT OF DECEDENT FROM PERSONAL FUNDS PROMISE IN CONSIDERATION OF MARRIAGE SALE OF GOODS FOR $500 OR MORE MISCELLANEOUS	PART PERFORMANCE PROMISOR BENEFIT DETRIMENTAL RELIANCE
PAROL EVIDENCE RULE	EXCEPTIONS
EVERY COMPLETE, FINAL WRITTEN CONTRACT	INCOMPLETE CONTRACT AMBIGUOUS TERMS FRAUD, ACCIDENT, OR MISTAKE TO PROVE EXISTENCE OR NONBINDING CHARACTER OF CONTRACT MODIFICATION OF CONTRACT ILLEGALITY

[3] *Coca-Cola Co. v Babyback's International Inc.*, 841 NE2d 557 (Ind 2006).

[4] *El Paso Healthcare System v Piping Rock Corp.*, 939 SW2d 695 (Tex App 1997).

[5] See *Ehrlich v Diggs*, 169 F Supp 2d 124 (EDNY 2001). See also *Sterling v Sterling*, 800 NYS2d 463 (AD 2005), in which the statute of frauds was no bar to an oral partnership agreement, deemed to be at will, that continued for an indefinite period of time.

(1) Oral Extension of a Contract. A contract in writing, but not required to be so by the statute of frauds because it is terminable at will, may be varied by a new oral contract, even if the original written contract provided that it should not be varied except by writing. However, the burden of proof on the party asserting the oral modification is a heavy one. The modification must be shown by "clear, unequivocal and convincing evidence, direct or implied." **For Example,** John Boyle is the sole shareholder of numerous entertainment-related companies called the Cellar Door Companies, valued at some $106,000,000. Through these companies, he controls much of the large concert business at outdoor amphitheaters in Virginia and North Carolina. Bill Reid worked for Boyle beginning in 1983 as president of one of Boyle's companies. Boyle conducted financial affairs with an "air of informality." Reid proposed to Boyle the need for an amphitheater in Virginia Beach, and Boyle promised him a "33 percent interest" "if he pulled it off." As a result of Reid's efforts, the 20,000-seat Virginia Beach Amphitheater opened in 1996. The Supreme Court of Virginia determined that clear and convincing evidence did support the oral modification of Reid's written contract, including the following excerpt from the Court's opinion:

> *Thomas J. Lyons, Jr., Boyle's friend for over 35 years, testified on behalf of Reid. Lyons and his wife attended a concert in July 1996 at the newly constructed Virginia Beach Amphitheater as guests of Boyle and his wife. Lyons complimented Boyle for the excellent work and effort that Reid had undertaken in making the amphitheater a reality. According to Lyons, Boyle stated: "Well that's why he's my partner... that's why he owns 35 percent in this—in the Amphitheater or this project." After Lyons finished his testimony, the chancellor remarked on the record that Boyle stood up from his seat and "hugged" Lyons, even though Lyons had just provided testimony detrimental to Boyle.*

Reid was thus entitled to a judgment equivalent to the value of his interest in the project, $3,566,343.[6]

(b) Agreement to Sell or a Sale of an Interest in Land

All contracts to sell land, buildings, or interests in land, such as mortgages, must be evidenced by a writing. Leases are also interests in land and must be in writing, except in some states where leases for one year or less do not have to be in writing.[7] **For Example,** if Mrs. O'Toole orally agrees to sell her house to the Gillespies for $250,000 and, thereafter, her children convince her that she could obtain $280,000 for the property if she is patient, Mrs. O'Toole can raise the defense of the statute of frauds should she be sued for breach of the oral agreement. Under the *part performance doctrine*, an exception exists by which an oral contract for the sale of land will be enforced by a court of equity in a suit for specific performance if the buyer has taken possession of the land under an oral contract and has made substantial improvements, the value of which cannot easily be ascertained, or has taken possession and paid part of the purchase price.

(c) Promise to Answer for the Debt or Default of Another

If an individual *I* promises a creditor *C* to pay the debt of *D* if *D* does not do so, *I* is promising to answer for the debt of another. Such a promise is sometimes called a **suretyship** contract, and it must be in writing to be enforceable. *I*, the promisor, is obligated to pay only if *D* does not pay. *I*'s promise is a *collateral* or *secondary* promise, and such promises must be in writing under the statute of frauds.[8]

(1) Main Purpose of Exception. When the main purpose of the promisor's promise to pay the debt of another is to benefit the promisor, the statute of

[6] *Reid v Boyle*, 527 SE2d 137 (Va 2000).

[7] See, however, *BBQ Blues Texas, Ltd. v Affiliated Business*, 183 SW3d 543 (Tex App 2006), in which Eddie Calagero of Affiliated Business and the owners of BBQ Blues Texas, Ltd. entered an oral commission agreement to pay Calagero a 10 percent commission if he found a buyer for the restaurant, and he did so. The oral agreement was held to be outside the statute of frauds because this activity of finding a willing buyer did not involve the transfer of real estate. The second contract between the buyer and seller of the restaurant, which involved the transfer of a lease agreement, was a separate and distinct agreement over which Calagero had no control.

[8] See *Martin Printing, Inc. v Sone*, 873 A2d 232 (Conn App 2005), in which James Kuhe in writing personally guaranteed Martin Printing, Inc, to pay for printing expenses of *Pub Links Golfer Magazine*, if his corporation, Abbey Inc., failed to do so. When Abbey, Inc., failed to pay, the court enforced Kuhe's promise to pay.

frauds is not applicable, and the oral promise to pay the debt is binding.

For Example, an individual *I* hires a contractor *C* to repair *I*'s building, and the supplier *S* is unwilling to extend credit to *C*. In an oral promise by *I* to pay *S* what is owed for the supplies in question if *C* does not pay, *I* is promising to pay for the debt of another, *C*. However, the *main purpose* of *I*'s promise was not to aid *C* but to get his own house repaired. This promise is not within the statute of frauds.

(d) Promise by the Executor or Administrator of a Decedent's Estate to Pay a Claim against the Estate from Personal Funds

The **personal representative** (**executor** or **administrator**) has the duty of handling the affairs of a deceased person, paying the debts from the proceeds of the estate and distributing any balance remaining. The executor or administrator is not personally liable for the claims against the estate of the **decedent.** If the personal representative promises to pay the decedent's debts with his or her own money, the promise cannot be enforced unless it is evidenced by a writing.

If the personal representative makes a contract on behalf of the estate in the course of administering the estate, a writing is not required. The representative is then contracting on behalf of the estate. Thus, if the personal representative employs an attorney to settle the estate or makes a burial contract with an undertaker, no writing is required.

(e) Promises Made in Consideration of Marriage

Promises to pay a sum of money or give property to another in consideration of marriage must be in writing under the statute of frauds.

For Example, if Mr. John Bradley orally promises to provide Karl Radford $20,000 on Karl's marriage to Mr. Bradley's daughter Michelle and Karl and Michelle marry, the agreement is not enforceable under the statute of frauds because it was not in writing.

Prenuptial or *antenuptial* agreements are entered into by the parties before their marriage. After full disclosure of each party's assets and liabilities, and in some states income,[9] the parties set forth the rights of each partner regarding the property and, among other things, set forth rights and obligations should the marriage end in a separation or divorce. Such a contract must be in writing.

For Example, when Susan DeMatteo married her husband M. J. DeMatteo in 1990, she had a 1977 Nova and $5,000 in the bank. M. Joseph DeMatteo was worth as much as $112 million at that time, and he insisted that she sign a prenuptial agreement before their marriage. After full disclosure of each party's assets, the prenuptial agreement was signed and videotaped some five days before their marriage ceremony. The agreement gave Susan $35,000 a year plus cost-of-living increases, as well as a car and a house, should the marriage dissolve. After the couple divorced, Susan argued before the state's highest court that the agreement was not "fair or reasonable" because it gave her less than 1 percent of her former husband's wealth. The court upheld the agreement, however, pointing out that Susan was fully informed about her fiancé's net worth and was represented by counsel.[10] When there is full disclosure and representation, prenuptial agreements, like other contracts, cannot be set aside unless they are unconscionable, which in a domestic relations setting means leaving a former spouse unable to support herself or himself.

(f) Sale of Goods

As will be developed in Chapter 23, Nature and Form of Sales, contracts for the sale of goods priced at $500 or more must ordinarily be in writing under UCC § 2-201.[11]

CPA 3. Note or Memorandum

The statute of frauds requires a writing to evidence those contracts that come within its scope. This writing may be a note or memorandum as distinguished from a contract.[12] The statutory requirement is,

[9] See FLA, STAT § 732 · 702 (2).

[10] *DeMatteo v DeMatteo*, 762 NE2d 797 (Mass 2002). See also *Waton v Waton*, 887 So2d 419 (Fla App 2004).

[11] As will be presented in Chapter 23, under Revised Article 2, § 2-201, the $500 amount is increased to $5,000. This revision has not yet been adopted by any states.

[12] *McLinden v Coco*, 765 NE2d 606 (Ind App 2002).

of course, satisfied if there is a complete written contract signed by both parties.

(a) Signing

The note or memorandum must be signed by the party sought to be bound by the contract. **For Example,** in the previous scenario involving Mark Wahlberg and Steven Spielberg, suppose the parties agreed to do the film according to the same terms but agreed to begin shooting the film a year from next April, and Mark wrote the essential terms on a napkin, dated it, and had Steven sign it "to make sure I got it right." Mark then placed the napkin in his wallet for his records. Because the contract could not be performed within one year after the date of the agreement, a writing would be required. If Steven thereafter decided not to pursue the film because of new murder indictments against Whitey Bulger, Mark could enforce the contract against him because the napkin-note had been signed by the party to be bound or "sought to be charged," Steven. However, if Mark later decided not to appear in the film, the agreement to do the film could not be enforced against Mark because no writing existed signed by Mark, the party sought to be charged.

Some states require that the authorization of an agent to execute a contract coming within the statute of frauds must also be in writing. In the case of an auction, it is usual practice for the auctioneer to be the agent of both parties for the purpose of signing the memorandum.

The signature may be an ordinary one or any symbol that is adopted by the party as a signature. It may consist of initials, figures, or a mark. In the absence of a local statute that provides otherwise, a signature may be made by pencil, pen, typewriter, print, or stamp. As will be discussed, electronic signatures have parity with on-paper signatures.

(b) Content

The note or memorandum must contain all of the essential terms of the contract so the court can determine just what was agreed. If any essential term is missing, the writing is not sufficient. A writing evidencing a sale of land that does not describe the land or identify the buyer does not satisfy the statute of frauds. The subject matter must be identified either within the writing itself or in other writings to which it refers. A deposit check given by the buyer to the seller does not take an oral land sales contract out of the statute of frauds. This is so because the check does not set forth the terms of the sale.

The note or memorandum may consist of one writing or of separate papers, such as letters, or a combination of such papers. Separate writings cannot be considered together unless they are linked. Linkage may be express reference in each writing to the other or by the fact that each writing clearly deals with the same subject matter.

4. Effect of Noncompliance

The majority of states hold that a contract that does not comply with the statute of frauds is **voidable.**[13] If an action is brought to enforce the contract, the defendant can raise the defense that the alleged contract is not enforceable because it is not evidenced by a writing, as required by the statute of frauds.

(a) Recovery of Value Conferred

In most instances, a person who is prevented from enforcing a contract because of the statute of frauds is nevertheless entitled to recover from the other party the value of any services or property furnished or money given under the oral contract. Recovery is not based on the terms of the contract but on a quasi-contractual obligation. The other party is to restore to the plaintiff what was received in order to prevent unjust enrichment at the plaintiff's expense. **For Example,** when an oral contract for services cannot be enforced because of the statute of frauds, the person performing the work may recover the reasonable value of the services rendered.

(b) Who May Raise the Defense of Noncompliance?

Only a party to the oral contract may raise a defense that it is not binding because there is no writing that satisfies the statute of frauds. Third persons, such as an insurance company or the Internal Revenue Service, cannot claim that a contract is void because the statute of frauds was not satisfied.

[13] The UCC creates several statutes of frauds of limited applicability, in which it uses the phrase "not enforceable": § 1-206 (sale of intangible personal property); § 2-201 (sale of goods); and § 8-319 (sale of securities). The Official Code Comment, point 4, to § 2-201 describes "not enforceable" as meaning what would ordinarily be called "voidable." Note that the 1994 Revision of Article 8 abolishes the statute of frauds with respect to securities. UCC § 8-113 [1994 Revision].

ELECTRONIC SIGNATURES IN THE INTERNET AGE

A SIGNATURE authenticates a writing by identifying the signers through their distinctive marks. The act of signing a document calls to the attention of the signing parties the legal significance of their act and expresses authorization and assent to the body of the signed writing. An ELECTRONIC SIGNATURE, including technology having digital or wireless capabilities, means any electronic sound, symbol, or process attached to, or logically associated with, a contract or other electronic record and executed with the intent to sign the record. An ELECTRONIC RECORD means any contract or other record created or stored in an electronic medium and retrievable in a perceivable form.

Conducting business electronically over the Internet has many advantages for consumers, businesses, and governments by allowing the instant purchase of goods, information, and services, and the reduction of sales, administrative, and overhead expenses. To facilitate the expansion of electronic commerce and place electronic signatures and electronic contracts on an equal footing with written signatures and paper contracts, Congress enacted a federal electronic signatures law.

Under the Electronic Signatures in Global and National Commerce Act (E-Sign),* electronically signed contracts cannot be denied legal effect because the signatures are in electronic form, nor can they be denied legal effect because they are delivered electronically. Contracts or documents requiring a notarized signature can be satisfied by the electronic signatures of the notaries coupled with the enclosure of all other required information as part of the record.

One of the goals of E-Sign is to spur states to enact the Uniform Electronic Transactions Act (UETA). Under E-Sign, a state may "modify, limit or supersede" the provisions of the federal act by enacting UETA "as approved and recommended for enactment in all the states" by the National Conference of Commissioners on Uniform State Laws or enacting a law that is consistent with E-Sign.** Thus, if a state enacts the official version of UETA or one consistent with E-Sign, the federal law is superseded by the state law. UETA is similar to E-Sign. It specifies that e-signatures and e-records can be used in contract formation, in audits, and as evidence. Selective differences between E-Sign and UETA are identified below. **For Example,** inventor Stewart Lamle sued toy maker Mattel, Inc., for breach of contract. The U.S. Court of Appeals for the Federal Circuit remanded the case for trial after resolving the motions before it. The facts reveal that after a June 11, 1997, meeting of the parties, Mattel employee Mike Bucher sent an e-mail dated June 26 to Lamle, which set forth the terms agreed to in principle at the meeting with the salutation "Best regards, Mike Bucher" appearing at the end of the e-mail. The court resolved the issue of whether an e-mail is a writing "subscribed by the party to be charged or the party's agent" in Lamle's favor. The court stated that under the UETA, the e-signature satisfies the state's (California's) Statute of Frauds. Because the e-mail was sent in 1997 prior to the effective date on the UETA, January 1, 2000, an evaluation of state common law was necessary. The court stated that it could see no meaningful difference between a typewritten signature on a telegram, which is sufficient to be a signature under state law, and the typed signature on the June 26 e-mail. It concluded that the e-mail satisfies the Statute of Frauds, assuming that there was a binding oral agreement on June 11.***

(a) General Rule of Parity. E-Sign provides for parity of electronic and paper signatures, contracts, and records. Electronic signatures and

*Pub L 106-229, 114 Stat 464, 15 USC § 7001.

**§ 102(a) and 102(a)(2). Forty-eight states and the District of Columbia have enacted the UETA in some form.

****Lamle v Mattel, Inc.*, 394 F3d 1355 (Fed Cir 2005).

E-COMMERCE AND CYBERLAW

continued

contracts satisfy the statute of frauds to the same extent they would if embodied as paper contracts with handwritten signatures. Internet contracts are neither more nor less valid, legal, and binding than are offline paper contracts. The rules are the same! The UETA is comparable to E-Sign in that it treats e-signatures and e-records as if they were handwritten.[†]

(b) Identity Verification. Neither E-Sign nor UETA is a digital signature law in that neither requires security procedures or a certification authority for the verification of electronic signatures. The parties themselves determine how they will verify each other's identity. Some options are a credit card, a password or PIN, public-key cryptographic exchange of digital signatures, or biometric signatures.

(c) Exceptions. The E-Sign Act exempts documents and records on trust and estate law so that it does not cover wills, codicils, and testamentary trusts or commercial law matters such as checks, negotiable instruments, and letters of credit. The act also does not cover court documents and cancellation of health and life insurance. Generally, the UETA also does not apply to these documents and records set forth previously.

(d) Consumer Protection and Notice and Consent Requirements. Consumer protection laws remain intact under E-Sign. Protections exist for consumers to consent to receiving electronic contracts, records, and documents; and businesses must tell consumers of their right to receive hard-copy documents.

Consumers must consent to receiving documents electronically or confirm consent electronically. For example, a consumer and a business may have negotiated terms of a contract by telephone and agreed to execute their agreement by e-mail. The consumer is then sent an e-mail that contains a consent disclosure, which contains a hypertext markup language (HTML) link the consumer can use to test her ability to view the contract in HTML. The consumer then returns the e-mail message to the business, thereby confirming electronically her consent to use this electronic means.

The UETA, like E-Sign, defers to existing substantive law regarding consumer protection.

(e) Time and Place of Sending and Receipt. E-Sign does not contain a provision addressing basic contract requirements such as sending and delivery, leaving such matters to existing contract law. However, the UETA provides that an electronic record is sent when it (1) is properly directed to an information processing system designated or used by the recipient to receive such records and from which the recipient may recover that record; (2) is in a form that the recipient's system is able to process; and (3) enters an information processing system that is in the control of the recipient but outside the control of the sender. An electronic record is received when (1) it enters an information processing system designated or used by the recipient to receive such records and from which the recipient is able to obtain the record and (2) it is in a form that the recipient's system can process.[††]

(f) Errors. Unlike E-Sign, which leaves matters relating to errors to be resolved by existing state contract law, UETA creates a system for dealing with errors. **For Example,** when Marv Hale clicks on "buy" to make an online purchase of 12 bottles of Napa Valley Supreme Chardonnay at $9.90 per bottle, the computer will produce the equivalent of an invoice that includes the product's name, description, quantity, and price to enable Marv to avoid possible error when forming the electronic contract. This procedure gives the buyer an opportunity to identify and immediately correct an error. When such a procedure is not in effect and an error is later discovered, prompt notice to the other party can cure the error under Section 10 of the UETA.[†††]

[†] UETA § 7(a) and 7(b).

[††] UETA § 15.

[†††] UETA § 10(2)(A)-(C).

B. Parol Evidence Rule

When the contract is evidenced by a writing, may the contract terms be changed by the testimony of witnesses?

5. Exclusion of Parol Evidence

The general rule is that parol or extrinsic evidence will not be allowed into evidence to add to, modify, or contradict the terms of a written contract that is fully integrated or complete on its face.[14] Evidence of an alleged earlier oral or written agreement within the scope of the fully integrated written contract or evidence of an alleged contemporaneous oral agreement within the scope of the fully integrated written contract is inadmissible as *parol evidence*.

Parol evidence is admissible, however, to show fraud, duress, or mistake and under certain other circumstances to be discussed in the following paragraphs.

The **parol evidence rule** is based on the theory that either there never was an oral agreement or, if there was, the parties abandoned it when they reached the stage in negotiations of executing their written contract. The social objective of the parol evidence rule is to give stability to contracts and to prevent the assertion of terms that did not exist or did not survive the bargaining of the parties so as to reach inclusion in the final written contract.

For Example, *L* (landlord), the owner of a new development containing a five-store mall, discusses leasing one of the stores to *T* (tenant), who is viewing the property with his sister *S*, a highly credible poverty worker on leave from her duties in Central America. *L*, in the presence of *S*, agrees to give *T* the exclusive right to sell coffee and soft drinks in the five-store mall. Soon *L* and *T* execute a detailed written lease for the store, which makes no provision for *T*'s exclusive right to sell soft drinks and coffee in the mall. Subsequently, when two of the mall's new tenants begin to sell soft drinks and coffee, *T* brings suit against *L* for the breach of the oral promise granting him exclusive rights to sell soft drinks and coffee. *T* calls *S* as his first witness to prove the existence of the oral promise. *L*, through his attorney, will object to the admission of any evidence of a prior oral agreement that would add to or amend the fully integrated written lease, which set forth all restrictions on the landlord and tenant as to uses of the premises. After study of the matter, the court, based on the parol evidence rule, will not hear testimony from either *S* or *T* about the oral promise *L* made to *T*. In order to preserve his exclusive right to sell the drinks in question, *T* should have made certain that this promise was made part of the lease. His lawsuit will not be successful.

6. When the Parol Evidence Rule Does Not Apply

The parol evidence rule will not apply in certain cases. The most common of these are discussed in the following paragraphs.

(a) Ambiguity

If a written contract is **ambiguous** or may have two or more different meanings, parol evidence may generally be admitted to clarify the meaning.[15]

Parol evidence may also be admitted to show that a word used in a contract has a special trade meaning or a meaning in the particular locality that differs from the common meaning of that word.

(b) Fraud, Duress, or Mistake

A contract apparently complete on its face may have omitted a provision that should have been included. Parol evidence may be admitted to show that a provision was omitted as the result of fraud, duress, or mistake and to further show what that provision stated. Parol evidence is admissible to show that a provision of the written contract was a mutual mistake even though the written provision is unambiguous.[16] When one party claims to have been fraudulently induced by the other to enter into a contract, the parol evidence rule does not bar proof that there was a fraud. **For Example,** the parol evidence rule does not bar proof that the seller of land intentionally misrepresented that the land was zoned to permit use as an industrial park. Such evidence does not contradict the terms of the contract but shows that the agreement is unenforceable.[17]

[14] *Speed v Muhana*, 619 SE2d 324 (Ga App 2005).

[15] *Berg v Hudesman*, 801 P2d 222 (Wash 1990). This is also the view followed by UCC § 2-202(a), which permits terms in a contract for the sale of goods to be "explained or supplemented by a course of dealing or usage of trade . . . or by course of performance." Such evidence is admissible not because there is an ambiguity but "in order that the true understanding of the parties as to the agreement may be reached." Official Code Comment to § 2-202.

[16] *Thompson v First Citizens Bank & Trust Co*, 151 NC App 704 (2002).

[17] *Edwards v Centrex Real Estate Corp.*, 61 Cal Rptr 518 (Cal App 1997).

(c) Modification of Contract

The parol evidence rule prohibits only the contradiction of a complete written contract. It does not prohibit proof that the contract was thereafter modified or terminated.

The *Bourg* case deals with an asserted oral modification of a written agreement.

BOURG V BRISTOL BOAT CO., 705 A2D 969 (RI 1998)

ALL SAIL AND NO ANCHOR

On April 2, 1990, Christian Bourg hired the Bristol Boat Co., Inc., and Bristol Marine Co. (defendants) to construct and deliver a yacht on July 1, 1990. However, the defendants did not live up to their promises and the contract was breached. On October 22, 1990, the defendants executed a written settlement agreement whereby Mr. Bourg agreed to pay an additional sum of $135,000 for the delivery of the yacht and to provide the defendants a loan of $80,000 to complete the construction of the vessel. Referencing the settlement agreement, the defendants at the same time executed a promissory note obliging them to repay the $80,000 loan plus interest in annual installments due on November 1 of each year, with the final payment due on November 1, 1994. The court stated in presenting the facts, "However, like the yacht itself, the settlement agreement soon proved to be just another hole in the water into which the plaintiff threw his money." Bourg sued the defendants after they failed to make certain payments on the note, and the trial court granted a motion for summary judgment in favor of Bourg for $59,081. The defendants appealed.

The defendants asserted that the trial court was in error because "at the time of the execution of the promissory note and settlement agreement upon which Plaintiff relies, it was understood and agreed that a substantial part of the note would be paid for by services rendered by the defendants. . . ."

Judicial Opinion

FLANDERS, J. . . . [T]he statement in defendants' affidavit that the alleged oral modification was agreed to "*[at] the time of* the execution of the promissory note and settlement agreement" (emphasis added) eviscierates defendants' contention on appeal that it was in fact a subsequent oral modification. Rather, because the affidavit recites that the alleged oral side agreement was entered into *at the time of* the settlement agreement and promissory note, it would have constituted a contemporaneous modification that would merge into the integrated promissory note and settlement agreement and thus be barred from admission into evidence under the parol evidence rule. In short, this alleged contemporaneous oral modification was legally "immaterial in ascertaining the terms of the transaction" between plaintiff and defendants. *Fram Corp.*, 121 R.I. at 587–88, 401 A.2d at 1272.

Finally, although parties to an integrated written contract—that is, "one where the parties adopt a writing or writings as a final and complete expression of [their] agreement," *id.* at 587, 401 A.2d at 1272—can modify their understanding by a subsequent oral pact, to be legally effective there must be evidence of mutual assent to the essential terms of the modification and adequate consideration. Here the defendants adduced no competent evidence of either mutual assent to particular terms or of a specific consideration that would be sufficiently definite to constitute an enforceable subsequent oral modification to the parties' earlier written agreements. Thus legally this alleged oral alteration was all sail and no anchor.

[Judgment affirmed]

Questions

1. Did the parties have a fully integrated written contract concerning the loan of $80,000 and the promissory note?
2. Can a contemporaneous oral agreement that "it was understood and agreed that a substantial part of the note would be paid for by services rendered by the defendants" be given weight as evidence to contradict the 1990 written settlement agreement and note that called for annual cash payments to repay the $80,000 loan?
3. Must a subsequent oral modification to a written agreement meet the essential elements for contract formation, including an agreement, and consideration?

C. Rules of Construction and Interpretation

In interpreting contracts, courts are aided by certain rules.

7. Intention of the Parties

When persons enter into an agreement, it is to be presumed that they intend for their agreement to have some effect. A court will strive to determine the intent of the parties and to give effect to it. A contract, therefore, is to be enforced according to its terms.[18] A court cannot remake or rewrite the contract of the parties under the pretense of interpreting.[19]

No particular form of words is required, and any words manifesting the intent of the parties are sufficient. In the absence of proof that a word has a peculiar meaning or that it was employed by the parties with a particular meaning, a common word is given its ordinary meaning.

(a) Meaning of Words

Ordinary words are to be interpreted according to their ordinary meaning.[20] **For Example,** when a contract requires the gasoline dealer to pay the supplier for "gallons" supplied, the term *gallons* is unambiguous and does not require that an adjustment of the gallonage be made for the temperature.[21] When a contract calls for a businessperson to pay a builder for the builder's "costs," the term *costs* is unambiguous, meaning actual costs, not a lesser amount based on the builder's bid.[22]

If there is a common meaning to a term, that meaning will be followed even though the dictionary may contain additional meanings. If technical or trade terms are used in a contract, they are to be interpreted according to the area of technical knowledge or trade from which the terms are taken.

(b) Incorporation by Reference

The contract may not cover all of the agreed terms. The missing terms may be found in another document. Frequently, the parties executing the contract

ETHICS & THE LAW

MARVIN WINDOWS CASES

Marvin Windows and Doors Company of Minnesota (Marvin Windows) is the largest custom window manufacturer in the world. The president of this privately held company, Bill Marvin, and his son Jake, the company's chief operating officer, met with PPG Industries' Bob Ponchot on Jake's front lawn on a summer morning in 1984 and listened to Ponchot sell PPG's new wood preservative PILT. Panchot allegedly said that products treated with PILT would last longer than the windows on Jake Marvin's home, which had been treated by a competitor's product "Penta" and had already lasted 26 years. Relying on Ponchot's promises made on behalf of PPG, Bill Marvin made a handshake deal to use the new product. The product was used by the company for four years and soon thereafter Marvin Windows started receiving complaints about premature wood rot from customers. Marvin Windows' study of the problem concluded that PILT was the culprit. PPG's analysis found PILT blameless, and it refused to help Marvin Windows cover the cost of replacing the defective windows. In 1994, Marvin Windows sued PPG for, *inter alia,* breach of contract, and four years of

[18] See *Greenwald v Kersh,* 621 SE2d 463 (Ga App 2005).

[19] *Abbot v Schnader, Harrison, Segal & Lewis, LLP,* 805 A2d 547 (Pa Super 2002).

[20] *Thorton v D.F.W. Christian Television, Inc.,* 925 SW2d 17 (Tex App 1995).

[21] *Hopkins v BP Oil, Inc.,* 81 F3d 1070 (11th Cir 1996).

[22] *Batzer Construction, Inc. v Boyer,* 125 P3d 773 (Or App 2006).

ETHICS & THE LAW

continued

discovery ensued. Bill Marvin stated that promises were made on Jake's lawn that summer morning, and he had a right to rely on them. "We never had a written contract, and I don't think that's naïve. They reneged on a handshake deal, and simply speaking, that's not right." PPG defended that there was no written agreement obliging PPG to pay for a portion of the cost of replacing the defective windows. PPG's attorney asserted that "Marvin Windows likes to tell you about a family-run business from a small town in Minnesota that does business on a handshake . . . but they are a $100 million international corporation with a long history of litigation." He further asserted that "experienced merchants ought to be smart enough to write a contract outlining who is responsible for what if the product they are buying doesn't work properly." Is Bill Marvin or PPG correct? Is it good business practice to have a written contract in effect for all company purchases, specifying the responsibilities of the parties if each product purchased does not work properly, or will this lead to a "battle of the forms" and increased expenses for both parties? Based on the assertions made by both Bill and Jake Marvin about the promises made by PPG, is it unethical for PPG to renege on the promises?

Assume that Marvin Windows prevails, asserting a warranty of future performance based on Panchot's statements. Acceptance of this theory allowed Marvin Windows to get around the statute of limitations issue raised by PPG and to obtain in excess of $100 million in damages, based in part on the position that it was incurring costs related to customer claims arising from the leaky and rotten windows. In *Kelleher v Marvin Lumber and Cedar Co.,** however, a homeowner who had purchased Marvin windows treated with PILT in 1986, discovered window rot problems in 17 of his windows in 1998. Litigation ensued, and Marvin Windows, seeking to avoid financial responsibility for the defective windows, produced a one-year limited warranty effective in 1986, which accompanied the windows that were delivered to the plaintiff. Marvin appealed a judgment for Kelleher, asserting the position that the one-year warranty applied, which position was directly contrary to the position it took in its litigation with PPG. Was it ethical for Marvin to take such a contradictory position in the lawsuit against it by the homeowner, after collecting more than $100 million in its successful lawsuit with PPG, in an attempt to avoid its liability for the homeowner's claim?

*891 A2d 477 (NH 2005); See *Marvin Lumber and Cedar Co. v PPG Industries*, 223 F3d 873 (8th Cir 2000).

for storage will simply state that a storage contract is entered into and that the contract applies to the goods listed in the schedule attached to and made part of the contract. Likewise, a contract for the construction of a building may involve plans and specifications on file in a named city office. The contract will simply state that the building is to be constructed according to those plans and specifications that are "incorporated herein and made part of this contract." When there is such an **incorporation by reference,** the contract consists of both the original document and the detailed statement that is incorporated in it.

When a contract refers to another document, however, the contract must sufficiently describe the document or so much of it as is to be interpreted as part of the contract.

8. Whole Contract

The provisions of a contract must be construed as a whole in such a way that every part is given effect.

Every word of a contract is to be given effect if reasonably possible. The contract is to be construed as a whole, and if the plain language of the contract thus viewed solves the dispute, the court is to make no further analysis.

9. Contradictory and Ambiguous Terms

One term in a contract may conflict with another term, or one term may have two different meanings. It is then necessary for the court to determine whether there is a contract and, if so, what the contract really means.

In the *Olander Contracting* case, the defendant City of Bismarck claimed that the contract was clear and unambiguous and that the trial judge, as a matter of law, should have decided in its favor. The contractor contended that the contract was ambiguous. It is the role of the judge—a question of law—to initially determine whether a contract is ambiguous. If the contract is ambiguous, it is the role of the jury—a question of fact—to determine which party's position is correct, with the aid of extrinsic evidence.

OLANDER CONTRACTING V WACHTER, 643 NW2D 29 (2002)

WHO PAYS THE PIPER?

Olander Contracting Co., developer Gail Wachter and the City of Bismarck, North Dakota, entered into a water and sewer construction contract including, among other things, connecting a 10-inch sewer line from Wachter's housing development to the city's existing 36-inch concrete sewer main and installing a manhole at the connection, to be paid for by Wachter. Olander installed the manhole, but it collapsed within a few days. Olander installed a second manhole, with a large base supported by pilings, but it too failed a few days after it was installed. Olander then placed a rock bedding under the city's sewer main, replaced 78 feet of the existing concrete pipe with PVC pipe, and installed a manhole a third time on a larger base. Olander sued Wachter and the City of Bismarck for damages of $456,536.25 for extra work it claims it was required to perform to complete its contract. Both defendants denied they were responsible for the amount sued under the contract. The jury returned a special verdict, finding Olander performed "extra work/unforeseen work...for which it is entitled to be compensated in excess of the contract price" in the amount of $220,849.67, to be paid by the City of Bismarck. Appeals were taken.

Judicial Opinion

SANDSTROM, J.... Bismarck contends it should have been granted summary judgment of dismissal, arguing (a) the trial court erred in refusing to interpret the contract and in "pass[ing] the task of interpreting the contract to the jury"; (b) Bismarck had no duty to pay for Olander's work, because the contract placed responsibility for payment for all work on Wachter,... and "[n]o language in the contract allowed extra payments to Olander for mere completion of the contract work."...

We recently addressed the construction of written agreements:

> *If the intent of the parties can be ascertained from the agreement alone, interpretation of the contract is a question of law. Thus, an unambiguous contract is particularly amenable to summary judgment. However, if the terms of the contract are ambiguous, extrinsic evidence regarding the parties' intent may be considered and the terms of the contract and parties' intent become questions of fact. When two good arguments can be made for either of two contrary positions as to the meaning of a term in a document, an ambiguity exists.*

Garofalao v Saint Joseph's Hosp., 2000 ND 149, ¶ 7, 615 N.W.2d 160 (citations omitted). "Whether or not a contract is ambiguous is a question of law." *Des Lacs Valley Land Corp. v Herzig*, 2001 ND 17, ¶ 9, 621 N.W.2d 860. "A determination of ambiguity is but the starting point in the search for the parties' ambiguously expressed intentions, which are questions of fact to be determined with the aid of extrinsic evidence." *Bohn v Johnson*, 371 N.W.2d 781, 788 (N.D. 1985).

Section (6) of the contract provides, in part:

> *The DEVELOPER [Wachter] will be responsible to pay the CONTRACTOR [Olander] for all of the contract work in accord with the plans, specifications, and proposal prepared by the DEVELOPER's Representative made a part of this contract.*

Section (9) of the contract provides, in part:

The CONTRACTOR shall guarantee all work against faulty materials and workmanship for a period of one year from the date of final payment. . . .

Section 126 of the General Provisions provides, in part:

EXTRA WORK. The Contractor shall perform unfor[e]seen work, for which there is no price included in the contract, whenever it is deemed necessary or desirable in order to complete fully the work as contemplated. Such work shall be performed in accordance with the specifications and as directed. When work not shown on the plans is to be performed by the Contractor the Engineer may order the work done on a force account basis when the measurement and pavement [sic] by unit prices becomes too cumbersome to be practicable, or when it is considered to be to the best interest of the City of Bismarck. Extra work will be paid for at the unit prices or lump sum stipulated in the order authorizing the work or the City of Bismarck may require the Contractor to do such work on a force account basis, to be compensated in the following manner. . . .

The contract requires Olander to "perform unfor[e]seen work, for which there is no price included in the contract, whenever it is deemed necessary or desirable in order to complete fully the work" and provides that "[e]xtra work will be paid for." The contract does not define unforeseen work or extra work, and does not specify which party is required to pay for such work. The parties have presented plausible arguments for contrary positions. The contract is, therefore, ambiguous, and there were genuine issues of material fact precluding summary judgment. We conclude the trial court properly received extrinsic evidence of the parties' ambiguously expressed intentions and properly submitted to the jury the factual questions of whether or not Olander performed extra work for which it was entitled to be paid and, if so, which party or parties were required to pay for it. . . .

Bismarck argues Olander failed to prove it had an enforceable agreement for payment for extra work, asserting "there is no language in the contract between the parties requiring Bismarck to pay anything for the work on this project." We have already determined the contract was ambiguous, and the trial court properly received extrinsic evidence about the parties' ambiguously expressed intentions and properly submitted to the jury the factual issue about extra work and which parties were to pay for it. . . .

Bismarck contends it should be granted a new trial because the trial court erred in conducting the trial by allowing the Jury to interpret the contract, and admitting evidence unfairly prejudicial to Bismarck. Bismarck's brief on these matters is very conclusory, with little or no supportive reasoning or citations to authorities. We have said that without supportive reasoning or citations to relevant authorities, an argument is without merit. . . .

We have already determined the trial court properly received extrinsic evidence of the parties' ambiguously expressed intentions, and properly submitted to the jury the factual questions of whether or not Olander performed extra work for which it was entitled to be paid and, if so, which party or parties were required to pay for it. In doing so, the trial court did not improperly allow the jury to interpret the contract. . . .

[Judgment affirmed]

Questions

1. State the City of Bismarck's position on the intention of the parties' contract regarding payment to the contractor.
2. State the position of Olander Contracting.
3. What is the role of judge and jury in interpreting ambiguous and unambiguous contract language? What is the significance of a "question of law" and a "question of fact"? What is "extrinsic evidence" regarding the contract between Wachter, Olander, and the City of Bismarck?

In some instances, apparent conflict between the terms of a contract is eliminated by the introduction of parol evidence or by the application of an appropriate rule of construction.[23]

(a) Nature of Writing

When a contract is partly a printed form or partly typewritten and partly handwritten and the written part conflicts with the printed or typewritten part, the written part prevails. When there is a conflict between a printed part and a typewritten part, the latter prevails. Consequently, when a clause typewritten on a printed form conflicts with what is stated by the print, the conflicting print is ignored and the typewritten clause controls. This rule is based on the belief that the parties had given greater

[23] *Lennox Lewis v Don King Productions*, 94 F Supp 2d 430 (SDNY 2000).

thought to what they typed or wrote for the particular contract as contrasted with printed words already in a form designed to cover many transactions. Thus, a typewritten provision to pay 90 cents per unit overrode a preprinted provision setting the price as 45 cents per unit.

When there is a conflict between an amount or quantity expressed both in words and figures, as on a check, the amount or quantity expressed in words prevails. Words control because there is less danger that a word will be wrong than a number.

(b) Ambiguity

A contract is *ambiguous* when the intent of the parties is uncertain and the contract is capable of more than one reasonable interpretation.[24] The background from which the contract and the dispute arose may help in determining the intention of the parties. **For Example,** when suit was brought in Minnesota on a Canadian insurance policy, the question arose whether the dollar limit of the policy referred to Canadian or U.S. dollars. The court concluded that Canadian dollars were intended. Both the insurer and the insured were Canadian corporations; the original policy, endorsements to the policy, and policy renewals were written in Canada; over the years, premiums had been paid in Canadian dollars; and a prior claim on the policy had been settled by the payment of an amount computed on the basis of Canadian dollars.

(c) Strict Construction against Drafting Party

An ambiguous contract is interpreted strictly against the party who drafted it.[25] **For Example,** an insurance policy containing ambiguous language regarding coverage or exclusions is interpreted against the insurer and in favor of the insured when two interpretations are reasonably possible. This rule is a secondary rule that may be invoked only after all of the ordinary interpretive guides have been exhausted. The rule basically assigns the risk of an unresolvable ambiguity to the party creating it.[26]

10. Implied Terms

In some cases, a court will imply a term to cover a situation for which the parties failed to provide or, when needed, to give the contract a construction or meaning that is reasonable.

The court often implies details of the performance of a contract not expressly stated in the contract. In a contract to perform work, there is an implied promise to use such skill as is necessary to properly perform the work. When a contract does not specify the time for performance, a reasonable time is implied.

In every contract, there is an implied obligation that neither party shall do anything that will have the effect of destroying or injuring the right of the other party to receive the fruits of the contract. This means that in every contract there exists an implied covenant of **good faith** and fair dealing. When a contract may reasonably be interpreted in different ways, a court should make the interpretation that is in harmony with good faith and fair dealing. **For Example,** when a contract is made subject to the condition that one of the parties obtain financing, that party must make reasonable, good-faith efforts to obtain financing. The party is not permitted to do nothing and then claim that the contract is not binding because the condition has not been satisfied. Likewise, when a contract requires a party to obtain government approval, the party must use all reasonable means to obtain it.[27]

The Uniform Commercial Code imposes an obligation of good faith in the performance or enforcement of every contract.[28]

11. Conduct and Custom

The conduct of the parties and the customs and usages of a particular trade may give meaning to the words of the parties and thus aid in the interpretation of their contract.

(a) Conduct of the Parties

The conduct of the parties in carrying out the terms of a contract is the best guide to determine the parties' intent. When performance has been repeatedly tendered and accepted without protest, neither party will be permitted to claim that the contract was too indefinite to be binding. **For Example,** a travel agent made a contract with a hotel to arrange for trips to the hotel. After some 80 trips had already been

[24] *Kaufman & Stewart v Weinbrenner Shoe Co.*, 589 NW2d 499 (Minn App 1999).

[25] *Idaho Migrant Council, Inc. v Warila*, 89 P2d 39 (Wyo 1995).

[26] *Premier Title Co. v Donahue*, 765 NE2d 513 (Ill App 2002).

[27] *Kroboth v Brent*, 625 NYS2d 748 (App Div 1995).

[28] UCC §§ 1-201(19), 1-203.

arranged and paid for by the hotel at the contract price without any dispute about whether the contract obligation was satisfied, any claim by the travel agent that it could charge additional fees must be rejected.

(b) Custom and Usage of Trade

The customs and **usages of trade** or commercial activity to which the contract relates may be used to interpret the terms of a contract.[29] **For Example,** when a contract for the construction of a building calls for a "turn-key construction," industry usage is admissible to show what this means: a construction in which all the owner needs to do is to turn the key in the lock to open the building for use and in which all construction risks are assumed by the contractor.[30]

Custom and usage, however, cannot override express provisions of a contract that are inconsistent with custom and usage.

12. Avoidance of Hardship

As a general rule, a party is bound by a contract even though it proves to be a bad bargain. If possible, a court will interpret a contract to avoid hardship. Courts will, if possible, interpret a vague contact in a way to avoid any forfeiture of a party's interest.

When hardship arises because the contract makes no provision for the situation that has occurred, the court will sometimes imply a term to avoid the hardship.

In the *Perkin case*, the weaker party claimed that the court should imply or read into the contract a protective term that was not expressed in the written terms of the contract.

PERKINS V STANDARD OIL CO., 383 P2D 107 (OR 1963)

COURT GLIDES WITH CLYDE

Standard Oil Co. made a jobbing, or wholesale, dealership contract with Clyde Perkins. The contract limited Perkins to selling Standard Oil's products and required him to maintain certain minimum prices. Standard Oil had the right to approve or disapprove Perkins' customers. In order to be able to perform under this contract, Perkins had to make a substantial monetary investment, and his only income was from commissions on sales of Standard Oil's products. Standard Oil made some sales directly to Perkins' customers. When Perkins protested, Standard Oil pointed out that the contract did not contain any provision making his rights exclusive. Perkins sued Standard Oil to compel it to stop dealing with his customers. From a decision in Standard Oil's favor, Perkins appealed.

Judicial Opinion

ROSSMAN, J.... The contract authorized the plaintiff [Perkins] to sell without Standard's written consent "on a nonexclusive basis" the products which Standard consigned to him but only to service stations or consuming accounts. Standard's written consent was required before the plaintiff could sell to any other account. The plaintiff promised in the contract to use his "best efforts to promote the sale of products consigned hereunder" and to sell a specified minimum amount during each year.... The plaintiff was required to deliver to Standard a complete list of the names and addresses of all his distributors and submit to it the names of any new potential distributors....

The plaintiff claims that the contract by its very nature contains an implied condition that Standard would not solicit business directly from his (plaintiff's) customers. Standard protests that such an implied condition would be contrary to the express terms of the contract since the latter (1) provides that the plaintiff was authorized to sell Standard's products only "on a nonexclusive basis" and (2) reserved to Standard the "right to select its own customers." Plaintiff proposes a more restricted interpretation.... He concedes that the contract reserved to Standard the right to sell to any new accounts which it found, and to accept or reject any new accounts which he (the plaintiff) might obtain, but he insists that it does not

[29] *Affiliated FM Ins. Co. v Constitution Reinsurance Corp.*, 626 NE2d 878 (Mass 1994).
[30] *Blue v R.L. Glossen Contracting, Inc.*, 327 SE2d 582 (Ga App 1985).

permit Standard to solicit accounts which it had approved as his customers. . . .

In order to be successful in his business and to comply with the terms of his contract, the plaintiff was obliged to make substantial investments in storage facilities, delivery trucks, and other equipment. He was also obliged to hire employees. He was required to use his "best efforts" to promote the sale of Standard's products. Only if he sold Standard's products exclusively could it be said that he was using his best efforts to promote their sale. It is clear, then, that the contract limited his dealership to Standard products. Plaintiff was also required to sell a minimum quantity of other designated Standard petroleum products. If he at any time failed to sell the minimum quantity, Standard was at liberty to terminate its contract with him. Plaintiff's compensation was based exclusively on the sales he made to customers, which he secured through his own efforts. No compensation was available for the plaintiff if he obtained customers for Standard who bought directly from it. Nor does the contract obligate Standard to compensate him for sales made directly by Standard to plaintiff's customers. . . .

. . . A condition must be implied that Standard would not solicit customers which had been obtained through plaintiff's efforts. The interpretation of the contract for which Standard contends would leave plaintiff and others in a position similar to his completely at the mercy of Standard. . . .

"We cannot accept [Standard's] construction of its meaning. An intention to make so one-sided an agreement is not readily to be inferred. . . .

"In every contract there is an implied covenant that neither party shall do anything that will have the effect of destroying or injuring the right of the other party to receive the fruits of the contract, which means that in every contract there exists a covenant of good faith and fair dealing." . . . 3 *Corbin* [*on Contracts* 278] 349–352 . . .

The implication of a condition finds support in many circumstances. . . . Plaintiff's only source of return on his substantial investments in the business was the sales he made to his customers. If Standard was at liberty to solicit his direct customers, as it contends. . . . plaintiff was in a state of economic servility; we do not believe that the parties intended such a result at the time the contract was signed. . . .

The contract before us is obviously a form contract prepared by Standard. It is a contract of "adhesion" in the sense that it is a take-it-or-leave-it whole. Such contracts are regarded by some authorities as anachronistic or inconsistent with real freedom of contract. At least they should be construed with an awareness of the inequality of the bargainers. . . .

[Judgment reversed]

Questions

1. What created the problem in the *Perkins* case?
2. Could the problem in the *Perkins* case have been avoided?

LAWFLIX

The Santa Clause (1996) (PG)

When Scott Calvin (Tim Allen) tries on a Santa suit, he discovers that he has assumed all of Santa's responsibility. Calvin tries to challenge his acceptance of the terms of the agreement. Analyze the problems with offer, acceptance, and terms in very fine print (a magnifying glass is required). Do the terms of the suit contract apply when Calvin did not know them at the time he put on the suit?

For movie clips that illustrate business law concepts, see LawFlix at **http://wdvl.westbuslaw.com.**

Summary

An oral agreement may be a contract unless it is the intention of the parties that they should not be bound by the agreement without a writing executed by them. Certain contracts must be evidenced by a writing, however, or else they cannot be enforced. The statutes that declare this exception are called *statutes of frauds.* Statutes of frauds commonly require that a contract be evidenced by writing in the case of (1) an agreement that cannot be performed within one year after the contract is made, (2) an agreement to sell any interest in land, (3) a promise to answer for the debt or default of another, (4) a promise by the executor or administrator of a decedent's estate to pay a claim against the estate from personal funds, (5) a promise made in consideration of marriage, and (6) a contract for the sale of goods for a purchase price of $500 or more.

To evidence a contract to satisfy a statute of frauds, there must be a writing of all essential terms. The writing must be signed by the defendant against whom suit is brought for enforcement of the contract.

If the applicable statute of frauds is not satisfied, the oral contract cannot be enforced. To avoid unjust enrichment, a plaintiff barred from enforcing an oral contract may recover from the other contracting party the reasonable value of the benefits conferred by the plaintiff on the defendant.

When there is a written contract, the question arises whether that writing is the exclusive statement of the parties' agreement. If the writing is the complete and final statement of the contract, parol evidence as to matters agreed to before or at the time the writing was signed is not admissible to contradict the writing. This is called the *parol evidence rule*. In any case, the parol evidence rule does not bar parol evidence when (1) the writing is ambiguous, (2) the writing is not a true statement of the agreement of the parties because of fraud, duress, or mistake, or (3) the existence, modification, or illegality of a contract is in controversy.

Because a contract is based on the agreement of the parties, courts must determine the intent of the parties manifested in the contract. The intent that is to be enforced is the intent as it reasonably appears to a third person. This objective intent is followed.

In interpreting a contract, ordinary words are to be given their ordinary meanings. If trade or technical terms have been used, they are interpreted according to their technical meanings. The court must consider the whole contract and not read a particular part out of context. When different writings are executed as part of the same transaction, or one writing refers to or incorporates another, all of the writings are to be read together as the contract of the parties.

When provisions of a contract are contradictory, the court will try to reconcile or eliminate the conflict. If this cannot be done, the conclusion may be that there is no contract because the conflict makes the agreement indefinite as to a material matter. In some cases, conflict is solved by considering the form of conflicting terms. Handwriting prevails over typing and a printed form, and typing prevails over a printed form. Ambiguity will be eliminated in some cases by the admission of parol evidence or by interpreting the provision strictly against the party preparing the contract, particularly when that party has significantly greater bargaining power.

In most cases, the parties are held to their contract exactly as it has been written. The law implies that performance is to be made within a reasonable time and that details of performance are reasonable when the contract fails to be specific on these points. Also, the law implies an obligation to act in good faith.

Questions and Case Problems

1. Kelly made a written contract to sell certain land to Brown and gave Brown a deed to the land. Thereafter, Kelly sued Brown to get back a 20-foot strip of the land. Kelly claimed that before making the written contract, it was agreed that Kelly would sell all of his land to Brown to make it easier for Brown to get a building permit, but after that was done, the 20-foot strip would be reconveyed to Kelly. Was Kelly entitled to the 20-foot strip? What ethical values are involved? [*Brown v Kelly*, 545 So 2d 518 (Fla App)]
2. Martin made an oral contract with Cresheim Garage to work as its manager for two years. Cresheim wrote Martin a letter stating that the oral contract had been made and setting forth all of its terms. Cresheim later refused to recognize the contract. Martin sued Cresheim for breach of the contract and offered Cresheim's letter in evidence as proof of the contract. Cresheim claimed that the oral contract was not binding because the contract was not in writing and the letter referring to the contract was not a contract but only a letter. Was the contract binding?
3. Lawrence loaned money to Moore, who died without repaying the loan. Lawrence claimed that when he mentioned the matter to Moore's widow, she promised to pay the debt. She did not pay it, and Lawrence sued her on her promise. Does she have any defense? [*Moore v Lawrence*, 480 SW2d 941 (Ark)]
4. Jackson signed an agreement to sell 79 acres of land to Devenyns. Jackson owned 80 acres and was apparently intending to keep for himself the acre on which his

home was located. The written agreement also stated that "Devenyns shall have the option to buy on property ____," but nothing was stated in the blank space. Devenyns sued to enforce the agreement. Was it binding? [*In re Jackson's Estate*, 892 P2d 786 (Wyo)]

5. Boeing Airplane Co. contracted with Pittsburgh–Des Moines Steel Co. for the latter to construct a supersonic wind tunnel. R.H. Freitag Manufacturing Co. sold materials to York-Gillespie Co., which subcontracted to do part of the work. To persuade Freitag to keep supplying materials on credit, Boeing and the principal contractor both assured Freitag that he would be paid. When Freitag was not paid by the subcontractor, he sued Boeing and the contractor. They defended on the ground that the assurances given Freitag were not written. Decide. What ethical values are involved? [*R.H. Freitag Mfg. Co. v Boeing Airplane Co.*, 347 P2d 1074 (Wash)]
6. Louise Pulsifer owned a farm that she wanted to sell and ran an ad in the local newspaper. After Russell Gillespie agreed to purchase the farm, Pulsifer wrote him a letter stating that she would not sell it. He sued her to enforce the contract, and she raised the defense of the statute of frauds. The letter she had signed did not contain any of the terms of the sale. Gillespie, however, claimed that the newspaper ad could be combined with her letter to satisfy the statute of frauds. Was he correct? [*Gillespie v Pulsifer*, 655 SW2d 123 (Mo)]
7. In February or March, Corning Glass Works orally agreed to retain Hanan as management consultant from May 1 of that year to April 30 of the next year for a present value fee of $200,000. Was this agreement binding? Is this decision ethical? [*Hanan v Corning Glass Works*, 314 NYS2d 804 (App Div)]
8. In letters between the two, Rita Borelli contracted to sell "my car" to Viola Smith for $2,000. It was later shown that Borelli owned two cars. She refused to deliver either car to Smith, and Smith sued Borelli for breach of contract. Borelli raised the defense that the contract was too indefinite to be enforced because it could not be determined from the writing which car was the subject matter of the contract. Is the contract too indefinite to be enforced?
9. Panasonic Industrial Co. (PIC) created a contract making Manchester Equipment Co., Inc. (MECI), a nonexclusive wholesale distributor of its products. The contract stated that PIC reserved the unrestricted right to solicit and make direct sales of the products to anyone, anywhere. The contract also stated that it contained the entire agreement of the parties and that any prior agreement or statement was superseded by the contract. PIC subsequently began to make direct sales to two of MECI's established customers. MECI claimed that this was a breach of the distribution contract and sued PIC for damages. Decide. What ethical values are involved? [*Manchester Equipment Co. Inc. v Panasonic Industrial Co.*, 529 NYS2d 532 (App Div)]
10. A contract made for the sale of a farm stated that the buyer's deposit would be returned "if for any reason the farm cannot be sold." The seller later stated that she had changed her mind and would not sell, and she offered to return the deposit. The buyer refused to take the deposit back and brought suit to enforce the contract. The seller contended that the "any reason" provision extended to anything, including the seller's changing her mind. Was the buyer entitled to recover? [*Phillips v Rogers*, 200 SE2d 676 (W Va)]
11. Integrated, Inc., entered into a contract with the state of California to construct a building. It then subcontracted the electrical work to Alec Fergusson Electrical Contractors. The subcontract was a printed form with blanks filled in by typewriting. The printed payment clause required Integrated to pay Fergusson on the 15th day of the month following the submission of invoices by Fergusson. The typewritten part of the contract required Integrated to pay Fergusson "immediately following payment" (by the state) to the general contractor. When was payment required? [*Integrated, Inc. v Alec Fergusson Electrical Contractors*, 58 Cal Rptr 503 (Cal App)]
12. Norwest Bank had been lending money to Tresch to run a dairy farm. The balance due the bank after several years was $147,000. The loan agreement stated that Tresch would not buy any new equipment in excess of $500 without the express consent of the bank. Some time later, Tresch applied to the bank for a loan of $3,100 to purchase some equipment. The bank refused to make the loan because it did not believe the new equipment would correct the condition for which it would be bought and would not result in significant additional income. Tresch then sued the bank, claiming that its refusal to make the loan was a breach of the implied covenant of good faith and fair dealing. Decide. [*Tresch v Norwest Bank of Lewistown*, 778 P2d 874 (Mont)]
13. Physicians Mutual Insurance Co. issued a policy covering Brown's life. The policy declared that it did not cover any deaths resulting from "mental disorder, alcoholism, or drug addiction." Brown was killed when she fell while intoxicated. The insurance company refused to pay because of the quoted provision. Her executor, Savage, sued the insurance company. Did the insurance company have a defense? [*Physicians Mutual Ins. Co. v Savage*, 296 NE2d 165 (Ind App)]
14. The Dickinson Elks Club conducted an annual Labor Day golf tournament. Charbonneau Buick-Pontiac offered to give a new car as a prize to anyone making "a hole in one on hole no. 8." The golf course of the club was only nine holes. To play 18 holes, the players would go around the course twice, although they would play from different tees or locations for the second nine holes.

On the second time around, what was originally the eighth hole became the seventeenth hole. Grove was a contestant in the tournament. He scored 3 on the no. 8 hole, but on approaching it for the second time as the seventeenth hole, he made a hole in one. He claimed the prize car from Charbonneau. The latter claimed that Grove had not won the prize because he did not make the hole in one on the eighth hole. Decide. [*Grove v Charbonneau Buick-Pontiac, Inc.*, 240 NW2d 8533 (ND)]

15. Beck and Co., a brewery, gave Gianelli Distributing Co. a franchise to distribute Beck's Beer. The franchise agreement specified that it would continue "unless and until terminated at any time by 30 days' written notice by either party to the other." Some time thereafter, Beck notified Gianelli that the franchise was terminated. Gianelli claimed that the franchise could be terminated only upon proof of reasonable cause. He offered evidence of trade usage to show that common practice required cause for termination and further claimed that such usage would be read into the franchise agreement with Beck. Is this evidence admissible?

CPA Questions

1. Which of the following statements is true with regard to the statute of frauds?

   a. All contracts involving consideration of more than $500 must be in writing.
   b. The written contract must be signed by all parties.
   c. The statute of frauds applies to contracts that can be fully performed within one year from the date they are made.
   d. The contract terms may be stated in more than one document.

2. With regard to an agreement for the sale of real estate, the statute of frauds

   a. Requires that the entire agreement be in a single writing
   b. Requires that the purchase price be fair and adequate in relation to the value of the real estate
   c. Does *not* require that the agreement be signed by all parties
   d. Does *not* apply if the value of the real estate is less than $500

3. In negotiations with Andrews for the lease of Kemp's warehouse, Kemp orally agreed to pay one-half of the cost of the utilities. The written lease, later prepared by Kemp's attorney, provided that Andrews pay all of the utilities. Andrews failed to carefully read the lease and signed it. When Kemp demanded that Andrews pay all of the utilities, Andrews refused, claiming that the lease did not accurately reflect the oral agreement. Andrews also learned that Kemp intentionally misrepresented the condition of the structure of the warehouse during the negotiations between the parties. Andrews sued to rescind the lease and intends to introduce evidence of the parties' oral agreement about sharing the utilities and the fraudulent statements made by Kemp. Will the parol evidence rule prevent the admission of evidence concerning each of the following?

	Oral agreement regarding who pays the utilities	*Fraudulent statements by Kemp*
a.	Yes	Yes
b.	No	Yes
c.	Yes	No
d.	No	No

THIRD PERSONS AND CONTRACTS

CHAPTER (18)

LEARNING OBJECTIVES

After studying this chapter, you should be able to

LO.1 Distinguish between a third-party beneficiary and an incidental beneficiary

LO.2 Define an assignment of contract rights

LO.3 State the limitations on assignability and right to performance

LO.4 Describe what constitutes a delegation of duties

LO.5 State the liability of the parties after a proper delegation of duties has been made

LO.6 Describe the status of an assignee with respect to defenses and setoffs available against the assignor

LO.7 State the significance of a notice of assignment

LO.8 State the liability of an assignor to an assignee

A. Third-Party Beneficiary Contracts

Generally, only the parties to a contract may sue on it. However, in some cases a third person who is not a party to the contract may sue on the contract.

CPA 1. Definition

When a contract is intended to benefit a third person, such a person is an **intended beneficiary** and may bring suit on and enforce the contract. In some states, the right of the intended **third-party beneficiary** to sue on the contract is declared by statute. **For Example,** Ibberson Co., the general contractor hired by AgGrow Oils, LLC to design and build an oilseed processing plant, contracted with subcontractor Anderson International Corp. to supply critical seed processing equipment for the project. Anderson's formal proposal to Ibberson identified the AgGrow Oils Project, and the proposal included drawings of the planned AgGrow plant. Under state law, this contract made between the contractor and subcontractor for the express benefit of the third party AgGrow Oils could be enforced by the intended third party beneficiary AgGrow Oils. The project was a failure. AgGrow was successful in the lawsuit against Anderson under the Anderson-Ibberson contract, having the standing to sue as an intended third-party beneficiary of that contract.[1]

(a) Creditor Beneficiary

The intended beneficiary is sometimes classified as a *creditor beneficiary* when the promisee's primary intent is to discharge a duty owed to the third party.[2] **For Example,** when Max Giordano sold his business, Sameway Laundry, to Harry Phinn, he had three years of payments totaling $14,500 owing to Davco, Inc., on a commercial Davco shirt drying and pressing machine purchased in 2006. Max (the promisee) made a contract with Harry to sell the business for a stipulated sum. A provision in this contract selling the business called for Harry (the promisor) to make the Davco machine payments when due over the next three years. Should Harry fail to make payments, Davco, Inc., as an intended creditor beneficiary under the contract between Max and Harry, would have standing to sue Harry for breach of the payment provision in the contract.

CPA (b) Donee Beneficiary

The second type of intended beneficiary is a *donee beneficiary* to whom the promisee's primary intent in contracting is to give a benefit. A life insurance contract is such an intended third-party beneficiary contract. The promisee-insured pays premiums to the insurer under the contract of insurance so that, upon the death of the insured, the promisor-insurer would pay the sum designated in the contract to the beneficiary. The beneficiary's rights vest upon the insured's death, and the beneficiary can sue the insurance company upon the insured's death even though the insurance company never made any agreement directly with the beneficiary.

(c) Necessity of Intent

A third person does not have the status of an intended third-party beneficiary unless it is clear at the time the contract was formed that the parties intended to impose a direct obligation with respect to the third person.[3] In determining whether there is intent to benefit a third party, the surrounding circumstances as well as the contract may be examined.[4] There is a strong presumption that the parties to a contract intend to benefit only themselves.[5]

(d) Description

It is not necessary that the intended third-party beneficiary be identified by name. The beneficiary may be identified by class, with the result that any member of that class is a third-party beneficiary. **For Example,** a contract between the promoter of an automobile stock car race and the owner of the racetrack contains a promise by the owner to pay specified sums of money to each driver racing a car in certain races. A person driving in one of the designated races is a third-party beneficiary and can sue the owner on the contract for the promised compensation.

[1] *AgGrow Oils, LLC v National Union Fire Ins.*, 420 F3d 751 (8th Cir 2005).

[2] The Restatement (Second) of Contracts § 302 substitutes "intended beneficiary" for the terms "creditor" and "donee" beneficiary. However, some courts continue to use the classifications of creditor and donee third-party beneficiaries. Regardless of the terminology, the law continues to be the same. See *Stein v Stewart*, 80 SW2d 586 (Tex 2002).

[3] *American United Logistics, Inc. v Catellus*, 319 F3d 921 (7th Cir 2003).

[4] *Gilliana v Paniaguas*, 708 NE2d 895 (Ind App 1999).

[5] *Barney v Unity Paving, Inc.*, 639 NE2d 592 (Ill App 1994).

2. Modification or Termination of Intended Third-Party Beneficiary Contract

Can the parties to the contract modify or terminate it so as to destroy the right of the intended third-party beneficiary? If the contract contains an express provision allowing a change of beneficiary or cancellation of the contract without the consent of the intended third-party beneficiary, the parties to the contract may destroy the rights of the intended beneficiary by acting in accordance with that contract provision.[6]

For Example, Roy obtained a life insurance policy from Phoenix Insurance Company that provided the beneficiary could be changed by the insured. Roy named his son, Harry, as the beneficiary. Later, Roy had a falling out with Harry and removed him as beneficiary. Roy could do this because the right to change the beneficiary was expressly reserved by the contract that created the status of the intended third-party beneficiary.

In addition, the rights of an intended third-party beneficiary are destroyed if the contract is discharged or ended by operation of law, for example, through bankruptcy proceedings.

3. Limitations on Intended Third-Party Beneficiary

Although the intended third-party beneficiary rule gives the third person the right to enforce the contract, it obviously gives no more rights than the contract provides. That is, the intended third-party beneficiary must take the contract as it is. If there is a time limitation or any other restriction in the contract, the intended beneficiary cannot ignore it but is bound by it.

If the contract is not binding for any reason, that defense may be raised against the intended third-party beneficiary suing on the contract.[7]

CPA 4. Incidental Beneficiaries

Not everyone who benefits from the performance of a contract between other persons is entitled to sue as a third-party beneficiary.[8] If the benefit was intended, the third person is an intended beneficiary with the rights described in the preceding sections. If the benefit was not intended, the third person is an *incidental beneficiary*.

Whether or not a third party is an *intended* or *incidental* beneficiary, therefore, comes down to determining whether or not a reasonable person would believe that the promisee intended to confer on the beneficiary an enforceable benefit under the contract in question. The intent must be clear and definite or expressed in the contract itself or in the circumstances surrounding the contract's execution.

B. Assignments

The parties to a contract have both rights and duties. Can rights be transferred or sold to another person or entity? Can duties be transferred to another person?

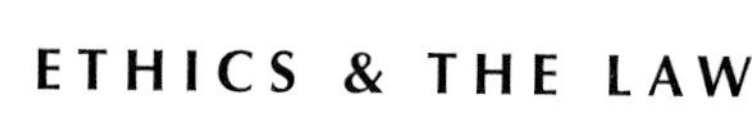

Ruth Bullis, 37, is a waitress at Stanford's Restaurant & Bar in Lake Oswego, Oregon. One evening, Bullis served a lumber broker who ordered a gin and tonic for $3.95. Before leaving, he put the tab for his drink on his American Express card and added a $1,000 tip for Bullis. Bullis verified with him that his intent was to give her the tip. Several other servers verified the tip and the fact that the lumber broker was not tipsy or addled.

After Bullis had spent the $1,000, American Express contacted Stanford's to reclaim the $1,000 because the customer had notified American Express that the tip was a mistake.

After you evaluate the legal positions of the four parties (Bullis, Stanford's, American Express, and the lumber broker), consider the ethical issues of giving a tip and then revoking it.

[6] A common form of reservation is the life insurance policy provision by which the insured reserves the right to change the beneficiary. Section 142 of the Restatement (Second) of Contracts provides that the promisor and the promisee may modify their contract and affect the right of the third-party beneficiary thereby unless the agreement expressly prohibits this or the third-party beneficiary has changed position in reliance on the promise or has manifested assent to it.

[7] *XL Disposal Corp. v John Sexton Contractors Co.*, 659 NE2d 1312 (Ill App 1995).

[8] *Jahannes v Mitchell*, 469 SE2d 255 (Ga App 1996).

FIGURE 18-1 Surfboard Transaction Diagram

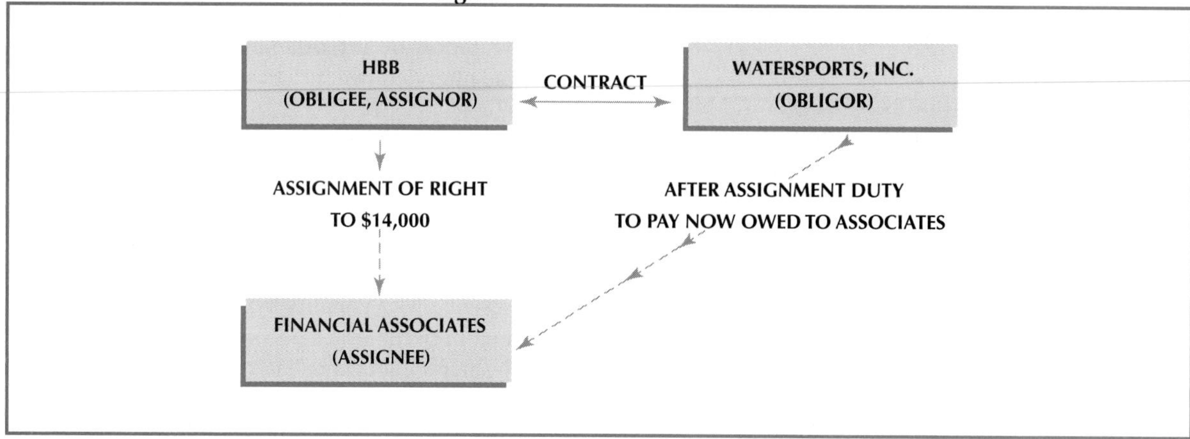

5. Definitions

Contracts create **rights** and **duties** between the parties to the contract. An **assignment** is a transfer of contractual rights to a third party. The party owing a duty or debt under the contract is the **obligor** or **debtor**, and the party to whom the obligation is owed is the **obligee**. The party making the assignment is the **assignor**. The third party to whom the assignment is made is the **assignee**. **For Example,** Randy Marshall and Marilee Menendez own Huntington Beach Board (HBB) Company, LLC, a five-employee start-up company making top-of-the line surfboards. Marilee was able to sell 100 Duke Kahanamoku–inspired "longboards" to Watersports, Inc., a large retail sporting goods chain, for $140 per board. However, the best payment terms she could obtain were payment in full in 90 days. A contract containing these terms was executed, and the goods were delivered. To meet internal cash flow needs, HBB assigned its right to receive the $14,000 payment from the buyer to West Coast Financial Associates (Associates) and received $12,800 cash from Associates on execution of the assignment documents. Notice was given at that time to Watersports, Inc., of the assignment. The right to receive the payment due in 90 days under the sales contract has thus been transferred by the seller HBB (assignor) to the third party, Associates (the assignee), to whom the buyer, Watersports, Inc. (obligor), now owes the duty of payment. Under the law of assignments, Associates, the assignee, now has direct rights against the obligor, Watersports, Inc. (See Figure 18-1.)

6. Form of Assignment

Generally, an assignment may be in any form. Statutes, however, may require that certain kinds of assignments be in writing or be executed in a particular form. Any words, whether written or spoken, that show an intention to transfer or assign will be given the effect of an assignment.[9]

7. Notice of Assignment

An assignment, if otherwise valid, takes effect the moment it is made. The assignee should give immediate notice of the assignment to the obligor, setting forth the obligor's duty to the assignee, in order to prevent improper payment.[10]

If the obligor is notified in any manner that there has been an assignment and that any money due must be paid to the assignee, the obligor's obligation can be discharged only by making payment to the assignee.

If the obligor is not notified that there has been an assignment and that the money due must be paid to the assignee, any payment made by the obligor to the assignor reduces or cancels that portion of the debt. The only remedy for the assignee is to sue the assignor to recover the payments that were made by the obligor.

[9] *Lone Mountain Production Co. v Natural Gas Pipeline Co. of America*, 984 F2d 1551 (10th Cir 1992).

[10] In some cases, an assignee will give notice of the assignment to the obligor in order to obtain priority over other persons who claim the same right or in order to limit the defenses that the obligor may raise against the assignee. UCC § 9-318.

The Uniform Consumer Credit Code (UCCC) protects consumer-debtors making payments to an assignor without knowledge of the assignment[11] and imposes a penalty for using a contract term that would destroy this protection of consumers.[12]

8. Assignment of Right to Money

Assignments of contracts are generally made to raise money. **For Example,** an automobile dealer assigns a customer's credit contract to a finance company and receives cash for it. Sometimes assignments are made when an enterprise closes and transfers its business to a new owner.

A person entitled to receive money, such as payment for goods sold to a buyer or for work done under a contract, may generally assign that right to another person.[13] A **claim** or **cause of action** against another person may be assigned. Isaac Hayes, an Academy Award®–winning composer, producer, and the voice of Chef in the television series South Park, assigned his copyright interests in several musical works in exchange for royalties from Stax Records.[14] A contractor entitled to receive payment from a building's owner can assign that right to a bank as security for a loan or can assign it to anyone else.

For Example, Celeste owed Roscoe Painters $5,000 for painting her house. Roscoe assigned this claim to the Main Street Bank. Celeste later refused to pay the bank because she had never consented to the assignment. The fact that Celeste had not consented is irrelevant. Roscoe was the owner of the claim and could transfer it to the bank. Celeste, therefore, is obligated to pay the assignee, Main Street Bank.

(a) Future Rights

By the modern rule, future and expected rights to money may be assigned. Thus, prior to the start of a building, a building contractor may assign its rights to money not yet due under an existing contract's payment on completion-phase schedule.

(b) Purpose of Assignment

The assignment of the right to money may be a complete transfer of the right that gives the assignee the right to collect and keep the money. In contrast, the assignment may be held for security. In this case, the assignee may hold the money only as a security for some specified obligation.

(c) Prohibition of Assignment of Rights

A clear and specific contractual prohibition against the assignment of rights is enforceable at common law. However, the UCC favors the assignment of contracts, and express contractual prohibitions on assignments are ineffective against (1) the assignment of rights to payment for goods or services, including accounts receivable,[15] and (2) the assignment of the rights to damages for breach of sales contracts.[16]

9. Nonassignable Rights

If the transfer of a right would materially affect or alter a duty or the rights of the obligor, an assignment is not permitted.[17]

(a) Assignment Increasing Burden of Performance

When the assignment of a right would increase the burden of the obligor in performing, an assignment is ordinarily not permitted. To illustrate, if the assignor has the right to buy a certain quantity of a stated article and to take such property from the seller's warehouse, this right can be assigned. However, if the sales contract stipulates that the seller should deliver to the buyer's premises and the assignee's premises are a substantial distance from the assignor's place of business, the assignment would not be given effect. In this case, the seller would be required to give a different performance by providing greater transportation if the assignment were permitted.

(b) Personal Services

Contracts for personal services are generally not assignable. **For Example,** were golf instructor David Ledbetter to sign a one-year contract to provide instruction for professional golfer Davis Love III, David Ledbetter could not assign his first assistant to

[11] UCCC § 2.412.

[12] UCCC § 5.202.

[13] *Pravin Banker Associates v Banco Popular del Peru*, 109 F3d 850 (2d Cir 1997).

[14] *Hayes v Carlin America, Inc.*, 168 F Supp 2d 154 (SDNY 2001).

[15] UCC § 9-318(4). This section of the UCC is applicable to most commercial assignments.

[16] UCC § 2-210(2).

[17] *Aslakson v Home Savings Ass'n*, 416 NW2d 786 (Minn App 1987) (increase of credit risk).

FIGURE 18-2 Limitations on Transfer of Rights and Duties

ASSIGNMENT OF RIGHT TO MONEY	ASSIGNMENT OF RIGHT TO PERFORMANCE	DELEGATION OF DUTIES
GENERALLY NO LIMITATION	INCREASE OF BURDEN PERSONAL SERVICES CREDIT TRANSACTION	PERSONAL OR NONSTANDARDIZED PERFORMANCE

provide the instruction, nor could Davis Love assign a protégé to receive instruction from Ledbetter. Professional athletes and their agents commonly deal with assignment or trading rights of the athletes in their contracts with professional sports franchises.

There is a split among jurisdictions regarding whether employee noncompetition covenants are assignable to the new owner of a business absent employee consent. That is, some courts permit a successor employer to enforce an employee's noncompetition agreement as an assignee of the original employer. However, a majority of states that have considered this issue have concluded that restrictive covenants are personal in nature and not assignable. **For Example,** in September 2000, Philip Burkhardt signed a noncompetition agreement with his employer, NES Trench Shoring. On June 30, 2002, United Rentals Purchased NES with all contracts being assigned to United Rentals. Burkhardt stayed on with the new owner for five weeks and thereafter went to work for Traffic Control Services, a direct competitor of United. United was unsuccessful in its action to enforce the noncompetition covenant Burkhardt had signed with NES. Burkhardt's covenant with NES did not contain a clause allowing the covenant to be assigned to a new owner, and the court refused to enforce it, absent an express clause permitting assignment.[18]

(c) Credit Transaction

When a transaction is based on extending credit, the person to whom credit is extended cannot assign any rights under the contract to another. **For Example,** Jack Aldrich contracted to sell his summer camp on Lake Sunapee to Pat Norton for $200,000, with $100,000 in cash due at the closing and the balance due on an installment basis secured by a mortgage on the property to be executed by Norton. Several days later, Norton found a more desirable property, and her sister Meg was very pleased to take over the Sunapee contract. Pat assigned her rights to Meg. Jack Aldrich, having received a better offer after contracting with Pat, refused to consent to the assignment. In this situation, the assignment to Meg is prohibited because the assignee, Meg, is a different credit risk even though the property to serve as security remained unchanged.

CPA 10. Rights of Assignee

Unless restricted by the terms of the assignment or applicable law, the assignee acquires all the rights of the assignor.[19]

An assignee stands exactly in the position of the assignor. The assignee's rights are no more or less than those of the assignor. If the assigned right to payment is subject to a condition precedent, that same condition exists for the assignee. **For Example,** when a contractor is not entitled to receive the balance of money due under the contract until all bills of suppliers of materials have been paid, the assignee to whom the contractor assigns the balance due under the contract is subject to the same condition. As set forth previously, in some states the assignee of a business purchasing all of the assets and rights of the business has the right to enforce a confidentiality and noncompetition agreement against a former employee of the assignor, just as though it were the assignor.[20]

[18] *Traffic Control Sources, Inc. v United Rentals Northwest, Inc.,* 87 P3d 1054 (Nov 2004).
[19] *Puget Sound National Bank v Washington Department of Revenue,* 868 P2d 127 (Wash 1994).
[20] *Artromick International, Inc. v Koch,* 759 NE2d 385 (Ohio App 2001).

11. Continuing Liability of Assignor

The making of an assignment does not relieve the assignor of any obligation of the contract. In the absence of a contrary agreement, an assignor continues to be bound by the obligations of the original contract. Thus, the fact that a buyer assigns the rights to goods under a contract does not terminate the buyer's liability to make payment to the seller. Similarly, when an independent contractor is hired to perform a party's obligations under a contract, that party is liable if the independent contractor does not properly perform the contract.

When a lease is assigned, the assignee becomes the principal obligor for rent payments, and the leasee becomes a surety toward the lessor for the assignee's performance. **For Example,** Tri-State Chiropractic (TSC) held a five-year lease on premises at 6010 East Main Street in Columbus, Ohio. Without the leasor's consent, TSC assigned that lease to Dr. T. Wilson and Buckeye Chiropractic, LLC, prior to the expiration of the lease. TSC continues to be liable for rent as surety during the term of the lease, even if the leasor (owner) had consented to the assignment or accepted payment from the assignee.[21] In order to avoid liability as a surety, TSC would have to obtain a discharge of the lease by **novation**, in which all three parties agree that the original contract (the lease) would be discharged and a new lease between Dr. Wilson and the owner would take effect. A novation allows for the discharge of a contractual obligation by the substitution of a new contract involving a new party.

12. Liability of Assignee

It is necessary to distinguish between the question of whether the obligor can assert a particular defense against the assignee and the question of whether any person can sue the assignee. Ordinarily, the assignee is not subject to suit by virtue of the fact that the assignment has been made.

(a) Consumer Protection Liability of Assignee

The assignee of the right to money may have no direct relationship to the original debtor except with respect to receiving payments. Consumer protection laws in most states, however, may subject the assignee to some liability for the assignor's misconduct. In the *Jackson v Dewitt* case, the court was faced with deciding whether a finance company had an obligation to return money already paid to it by a homeowner under a retail installment security agreement between the homeowner and a contractor, which agreement had been assigned to the finance company by the contractor.

JACKSON V DEWITT, 592 NW2D 262 (WIS APP 1999)

THE POOL AND THE AGREEMENT WILL NOT HOLD ANY WATER

Homeowner Michael Jackson entered into a contract for the construction of an in-ground lap pool with James DeWitt. The contract provided for a 12 ft. by 60 ft. pool at an estimated cost of $21,000. At the time the contract was signed, Jackson paid DeWitt $11,400 in cash and financed $7,500 through a Retail Installment Security Agreement (RISA). Associates Financial Services Co. (Associates) provided DeWitt with all the forms necessary to document the financing of the home improvements. Consumer requests for financing were subject to Associates' approval, which was given for Jackson's lap pool. When the RISA was completed, DeWitt assigned it to Associates. Jackson made two monthly payments of $202.90 and a final payment of $7,094.20 while the lap pool was still under construction. When the pool was filled, it failed to hold water, and Jackson had the pool and deck removed. Jackson sued DeWitt for breach of contract. He asserted that all valid claims and defenses he had against DeWitt were also valid against the assignee, Associates. Jackson sought the return of the $7,500 he had financed from Associates. The trial court held

[21] *Schottenstein Trustees v Carano,* 2000 Ohio App LEXIS 4493.

that because Jackson had paid the entire balance of the loan before Associates knew of Jackson's claim he could not obtain relief from Associates under the consumer protection law § ATCP 110.06. Jackson appealed this decision.

Judicial Opinion

ANDERSON, J. . . . WISCONSIN ADM.CODE § ATCP 110.06, governs home improvement contracts and provides:

1. *Every assignee of a home improvement contract takes subject to all claims and defenses of the buyer or successors in interest.*
2. *No seller shall enter into any home improvement contract wherein the buyer waives the right to assert against the seller or any assignee any claim or defense the buyer may have against the seller under the contract. . . .*

To subject all assignees or holders of "home improvement" contracts, including Associates, to the claims and defenses of the consumer, fulfills the intent of WIS. ADM. CODE ch. ATCP 110. As one commentator has noted, ch. ATCP 110 "deals with a virtual laundry list of unfair or deceptive home improvement practices that have resulted in substantial financial losses to home owners over the years." Jeffries 57 MARQ. L. REV. at 578. The Wisconsin Supreme Court has also noted, "[T]he home improvement trade is subject to comprehensive and stringent rules designed to protect the consumer." To protect the homeowner when the contractor or seller has failed to fulfill the obligations imposed by ch. ATCP 110, the homeowner must be able to seek restitutionary relief wherever it is available. [It] provide[s] relief from the assignee or holder on a "home improvement contract" by making the assignee or holder subject to the claims and defenses of the buyer. . . .

We conclude, from the statute and regulation, that a homeowner may proceed under § 100.20(5), STATS., when he or she has suffered pecuniary loss as a result of violations of WIS. ADM.CODE ch. ATCP 110. If the "home improvement contract" was financed with an "interlocking consumer loan," full payment before discovering the violations of the regulation does not eliminate the consumer's cause of action against the assignee or holder of the "home improvement contract."

Excel Management, like this case, involved contracts for the sale of swimming pools to consumers. *See Excel Management*, 111 Wis.2d at 483, 331 N.W.2d at 314. In *Excel Management*, like this case, the complaint alleged that the contracts were obtained in violation of WIS. ADM.CODE ch. ATCP 110. In *Excel Management*, like this case, the retailer used loan papers provided by the lender and assigned the completed contract to the lender. In *Excel Management*, like this case, the assigned contract contained a notice required by 16 C.F.R § 433.2, "Any holder of this consumer credit contract is subject to all claims and defenses which the debtor could assert against the seller of goods or services obtained pursuant hereto or with the proceeds hereof."

Considering these facts, the supreme court in *Excel Management*, readily concluded that although the contract was not a negotiable instrument, "[a]s an assignee of the contracts from Viking, First Savings takes each contract 'subject to all claims and defenses of the buyer of his successor in interest.'" . . . The supreme court commented that the warning language required by 16 C.F.R. § 433.2 clearly made the assignee of the contract aware that it took assignment of the contract subject to "any claims or defenses the buyer may assert." In *Excel Management*, the supreme court concluded that the consumers could bring actions against the assignees of their contracts for pecuniary losses stemming from the retailers' violations of the unfair trade statutes. *See id.* at 487, 331 N.W.2d at 316.

The factual similarity between this case and *Excel Management* requires us to reach a similar conclusion. Associates is an assignee of a "home improvement contract" that is governed by WIS. ADM.CODE § ATCP 110.06. The regulation provides, "Every assignee of a home improvement contract takes subject to all claims and defenses of the buyer or successors in interest." Section ATCP 110.06(1). Therefore, as the assignee of the RISA, Associates is subject to any claims Jackson may assert, without regard to the negotiability of the contract. . . .

[Reversed]

Questions

1. Identify the parties to the retail installment sales agreement (RISA), identify their obligations, explain how Associates became involved, and identify Associates' legal status.
2. Assess the validity of this statement: "The contractor botched the pool installation job. The finance company merely facilitated the transaction for the benefit of both parties and is innocent of wrongdoing. The homeowner therefore should obtain relief solely from the contractor."
3. What did Jackson claim he was due from Associates?

FIGURE 18-3 Can a Third Person Sue on a Contract?

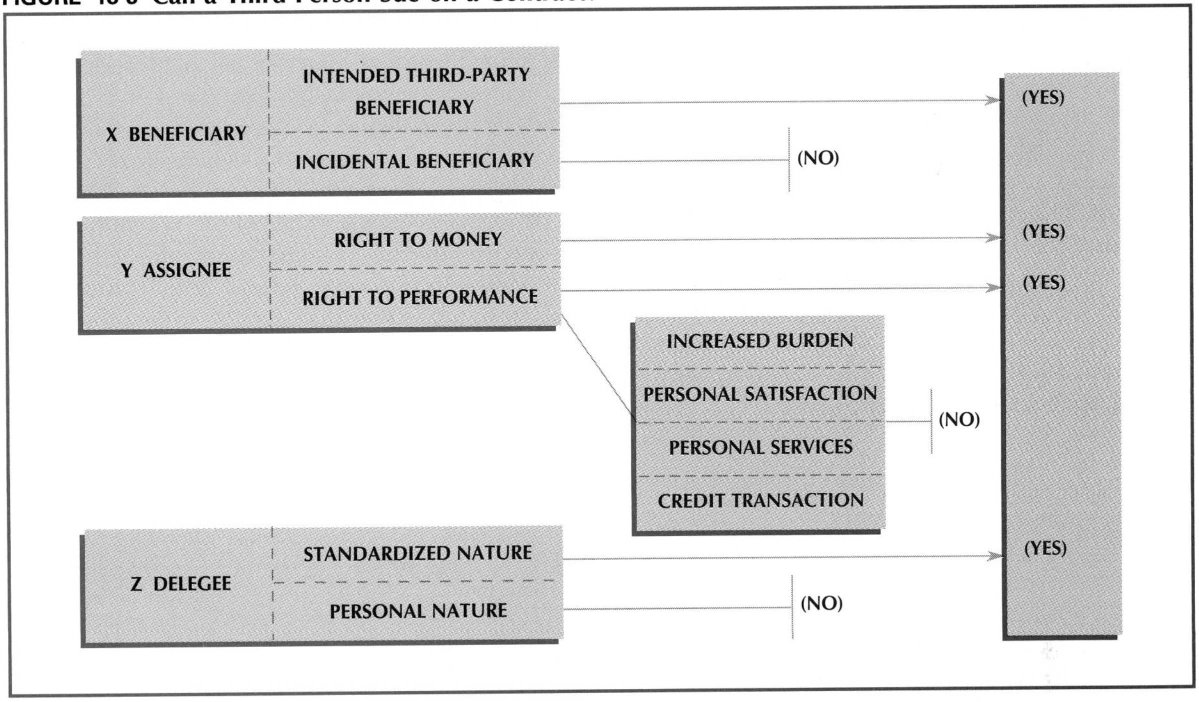

(b) Defenses and Setoffs

The assignee's rights are no greater than those of the assignor.[22] If the obligor could successfully defend against a suit brought by the assignor, the obligor will also prevail against the assignee.

The fact that the assignee has given value for the assignment does not give the assignee any immunity from defenses that the other party, the obligor, could have asserted against the assignor. The rights acquired by the assignee remain subject to any limitations imposed by the contract.

13. Warranties of Assignor

When the assignment is made for a consideration, the assignor is regarded as providing an **implied warranty** that the right assigned is valid. The assignor also warrants that the assignor is the owner of the claim or right assigned and that the assignor will not interfere with the assignee's enforcement of the obligation.

14. Delegation of Duties

A **delegation of duties** is a transfer of duties by a contracting party to another person who is to perform them. Under certain circumstances, a contracting party may obtain someone else to do the work. When the performance is standardized and nonpersonal, so that it is not material who performs, the law will permit the **delegation** of the performance of the contract. In such cases, however, the contracting party remains liable in the case of default of the person doing the work just as though no delegation had been made.[23]

A contract may prohibit a party owing a duty of performance under a contract from delegating that duty to another. **For Example,** Tom Joyce of Patriot Plumbing Co. contracts to install a new heating system for Mrs. Lawton. A notation on the sales contract that Tom Joyce will do the installation prohibits Patriot Plumbing from delegating the installation to another equally skilled plumber or to another company if a backlog of work occurs at Patriot Plumbing.

If the performance of a party to a contract involves personal skill, talents, judgment, or trust, the delegation of duties is barred unless consented to by the person entitled to the performance. Examples include performance by professionals such as physicians,

22 *Shoreline Communications, Inc. v Norwich Taxi, LCC,* 70 Conn App 60 (2002).

23 *Orange Bowl Corp. v Warren,* 386 SE2d 293 (SC App 1989).

dentists, lawyers, consultants, celebrities, artists, and craftpersons with unusual skills.

(a) Intention to Delegate Duties

An assignment of rights does not in itself delegate the performance of duties to the assignee. In the absence of clear language in the assignment stating that duties are or are not delegated, all circumstances must be examined to determine whether there is a delegation. When the total picture is viewed, it may become clear what was intended. The fact that an assignment is made for security of the assignee is a strong indication there was no intent to delegate to the assignee the performance of any duty resting on the assignor.[24]

(b) Delegation of Duties under the UCC

With respect to contracts for the sale of goods, "an assignment of 'the contract' or of 'all my rights under the contract' or an assignment in similar general terms is an assignment of rights and, unless the language or the circumstances (as in an assignment for security) indicate the contrary, it is a delegation of performance of the duties of the assignor, and its acceptance by the assignee constitutes a promise . . . to perform those duties. This promise is enforceable by either the assignor or the other party to the original contract."[25]

LAWFLIX

It Could Happen to You (1996) (PG)

Discuss the legal, ethical and contract issues involved in the first portion of the film in which a police officer (Nicholas Cage) promises to split a lottery ticket with a coffee shop waitress (Bridget Fonda) as her tip because he does not have enough money. The lottery ticket (purchased by Cage and his wife, Rosie Perez) is a winner, and Cage wrestles with his obligation to tell Fonda. You could discuss whether there was an assignment or whether Fonda was added as a third party beneficiary after the fact.

For movie clips that illustrate business law concepts, see LawFlix at **http://wdvl.westbuslaw.com.**

[24] *City National Bank of Fort Smith v First National Bank and Trust Co. of Rogers*, 732 SW2d 489 (Ark App 1987).

[25] UCC § 2-210(4).

Summary

Ordinarily, only the parties to contracts have rights and duties with respect to such contracts. Exceptions are made in the case of third-party beneficiary contracts and assignments.

When a contract shows a clear intent to benefit a third person or class of persons, those persons are called *intended third-party beneficiaries*, and they may sue for breach of the contract. A third-party beneficiary is subject to any limitation or restriction found in the contract. A third-party beneficiary loses all rights when the original contract is terminated by operation of law or if the contract reserves the right to change the beneficiary and such a change is made.

In contrast, an incidental beneficiary benefits from the performance of a contract, but the conferring of this benefit was not intended by the contracting parties. An incidental beneficiary cannot sue on the contract.

An assignment is a transfer of a right; the assignor transfers a right to the assignee. In the absence of a local statute, there are no formal requirements for an assignment. Any words manifesting the intent to transfer are sufficient to constitute an assignment. No consideration is required. Any right to money may be assigned, whether the assignor is entitled to the money at the time of the assignment or will be entitled or expects to be entitled at some time in the future.

A right to a performance may be assigned except when (1) it would increase the burden of performance, (2) the contract involves the performance of personal services, or (3) the transaction is based on extending credit.

When a valid assignment is made, the assignee has the same rights—and only the same rights—as the assignor. The assignee is also subject to the same defenses and setoffs as the assignor had been.

The performance of duties under a contract may be delegated to another person except when a personal element of skill or judgment of the original contracting party is involved. The intent to delegate duties may be expressly stated. The intent may also be found in an "assignment" of "the contract" unless the circumstances make it clear that only the right to money was intended to be transferred. The fact that there has been a delegation of duties does not release the assignor from responsibility for performance. The assignor is liable for breach of the contract if the assignee does not properly perform the delegated duties. In the absence of an effective delegation or the formation of a third-party beneficiary contract, an assignee of rights is not liable to the obligee of the contract for its performance by the assignor.

Notice is not required to effect an assignment. When notice of the assignment is given to the obligor together with a demand that future payments be made to the assignee, the obligor cannot discharge liability by payment to the assignor.

When an assignment is made for a consideration, the assignor makes implied warranties that the right assigned is valid and that the assignor owns that right and will not interfere with its enforcement by the assignee. The assignor does not warrant that the obligor on the assigned right will perform the obligation of the contract.

Questions and Case Problems

1. Give an example of a third-party beneficiary contract.
2. A court order required John Baldassari to make specified payments for the support of his wife and child. His wife needed more money and applied for Pennsylvania welfare payments. In accordance with the law, she assigned to Pennsylvania her right to the support payments from her husband. Pennsylvania then increased her payments. Pennsylvania obtained a court order directing John, in accordance with the terms of the assignment from his wife, to make the support-order payments directly to the Pennsylvania Department of Public Welfare. John refused to pay on the ground that he had not been notified of the assignment or the hearing directing him to make payment to the assignee. Was he correct? *Pennsylvania v Baldassari*, 421 A2d 306 (Pa Super)
3. Lee contracts to paint Sally's two-story house for $1,000. Sally realizes that she will not have sufficient money, so she transfers her rights under this agreement to her neighbor Karen, who has a three-story house. Karen notifies Lee that Sally's contract has been assigned to her and demands that Lee paint Karen's house for $1,000. Is Lee required to do so?
4. Assume that Lee agrees to the assignment of the house-painting contract to Karen as stated in question 3. Thereafter, Lee fails to perform the contract to paint Karen's house. Karen sues Sally for damages. Is Sally liable?
5. Jessie borrows $1,000 from Thomas and agrees to repay the money in 30 days. Thomas assigns the right to the $1,000 to Douglas Finance Co. Douglas sues Jessie. Jessie argues that she had agreed to pay the money only to Thomas and that when she and Thomas had entered into the transaction, there was no intention to benefit Douglas Finance Co. Are these objections valid?
6. Washington purchased an automobile from Smithville Motors. The contract called for payment of the purchase price in installments and contained the defense preservation notice required by the Federal Trade Commission regulation. Smithville assigned the contract to Rustic Finance Co. The car was always in need of repairs, and by the time it was half paid for, it would no longer run. Washington canceled the contract. Meanwhile, Smithville had gone out of business. Washington sued Rustic for the amount she had paid Smithville. Rustic refused to pay on the grounds that it had not been at fault. Decide.
7. Helen obtained an insurance policy insuring her life and naming her niece Julie as beneficiary. Helen died, and about a year later the policy was found in her house. When Julie claimed the insurance money, the insurer refused to pay on the ground that the policy required that notice of death be given to it promptly following the death. Julie claimed that she was not bound by the time limitation because she had never agreed to it, as she was not a party to the insurance contract. Is Julie entitled to recover?
8. Lone Star Life Insurance Co. agreed to make a long-term loan to Five Forty Three Land, Inc., whenever that corporation requested one. Five Forty Three wanted this loan to pay off its short-term debts. The loan was never made, as it was never requested by Five Forty Three, which owed the Exchange Bank & Trust Co. on a short-term debt. Exchange Bank then sued Lone Star for breach of its promise on the theory that the Exchange Bank was a third-party beneficiary of the contract to make the loan. Was the Exchange Bank correct? [*Exchange Bank & Trust Co. v Lone Star Life Ins. Co.*, 546 SW2d 948 (Tex App)]

9. The New Rochelle Humane Society made a contract with the city of New Rochelle to capture and impound all dogs running at large. Spiegler, a minor, was bitten by some dogs while in her schoolyard. She sued the school district of New Rochelle and the Humane Society. With respect to the Humane Society, she claimed that she was a third-party beneficiary of the contract that the Humane Society had made with the city. She claimed that she could therefore sue the Humane Society for its failure to capture the dogs that had bitten her. Was she entitled to recover? [*Spiegler v School District of the City of New Rochelle*, 242 NYS2d 430]
10. Zoya operated a store in premises rented from Peerless. The lease required Zoya to maintain liability insurance to protect Zoya and Peerless. Caswell entered the store, fell through a trap door, and was injured. She then sued Zoya and Peerless on the theory that she was a third-party beneficiary of the lease requirement to maintain liability insurance. Was she correct? [*Caswell v Zoya Int'l*, 654 NE2d 552 (Ill App)]
11. Henry was owed $10,000 by Jones Corp. In consideration of the many odd jobs performed for him over the years by his nephew, Henry assigned the $10,000 claim to his nephew Charles. Henry died, and his widow claimed that the assignment was ineffective so that the claim was part of Henry's estate. She based her assertion on the ground that the past performance rendered by the nephew was not consideration. Was the assignment effective?
12. Industrial Construction Co. wanted to raise money to construct a canning factory in Wisconsin. Various persons promised to subscribe the needed amount, which they agreed to pay when the construction was completed. The construction company assigned its rights and delegated its duties under the agreement to Johnson, who then built the cannery. Vickers, one of the subscribers, refused to pay the amount that he had subscribed on the ground that the contract could not be assigned. Was he correct?
13. The Ohio Department of Public Welfare made a contract with an accountant to audit the accounts of health care providers who were receiving funds under the Medicaid program. Windsor House, which operated six nursing homes, claimed that it was a third-party beneficiary of that contract and could sue for its breach. Was it correct? [*Thornton v Windsor House, Inc.*, 566 NE2d 1220 (Ohio)]

CPA Questions

1. On August 1, Neptune Fisheries contracted in writing with West Markets to deliver to West 3,000 pounds of lobster at $4.00 a pound. Delivery of the lobsters was due October 1, with payment due November 1. On August 4, Neptune entered into a contract with Deep Sea Lobster Farms that provided as follows: "Neptune Fisheries assigns all the rights under the contract with West Markets dated August 1 to Deep Sea Lobster Farms." The best interpretation of the August 4 contract would be that it was

   a. only an assignment of rights by Neptune.
   b. only a delegation of duties by Neptune.
   c. an assignment of rights and a delegation of duties by Neptune.
   d. an unenforceable third-party beneficiary contract.

2. Graham contracted with the city of Harris to train and employ high school dropouts residing in Harris. Graham breached the contract. Long, a resident of Harris and a high school dropout, sued Graham for damages. Under the circumstances, Long will

   a. win, because Long is a third-party beneficiary entitled to enforce the contract.
   b. win, because the intent of the contract was to confer a benefit on all high school dropouts residing in Harris.
   c. lose, because Long is merely an incidental beneficiary of the contract.
   d. lose, because Harris did not assign its contract rights to Long.

3. Union Bank lent $200,000 to Wagner. Union required Wagner to obtain a life insurance policy naming Union as beneficiary. While the loan was outstanding, Wagner stopped paying the premiums on the policy. Union paid the premiums, adding the amounts paid to Wagner's loan. Wagner died, and the insurance company refused to pay the policy proceeds to Union. Union may

   a. recover the policy proceeds because it is a creditor beneficiary.
   b. not recover the policy proceeds because it is a donee beneficiary.
   c. not recover the policy proceeds because it is not in privity of contract with the insurance company.
   d. not recover the policy proceeds because it is only an incidental beneficiary.

DISCHARGE OF CONTRACTS

CHAPTER (19)

LEARNING OBJECTIVES

After studying this chapter, you should be able to

LO.1 List the ways in which a contract can be discharged

LO.2 Distinguish between the effect of a rejected tender of payment and a rejected tender of performance

LO.3 Define when time is of the essence

LO.4 Compare performance to the satisfaction of the other contracting parties, performance to the satisfaction of a reasonable person, and substantial performance

LO.5 State when the consumer may rescind a consumer contract

LO.6 Compare the discharge of a contract by rescission, cancellation, substitution, and novation

LO.7 State the effect on a contract of the death or disability of one of the contracting parties

LO.8 Define the concept of *economic frustration*

In the preceding chapters, you studied how a contract is formed, what a contract means, and who has rights under a contract. In this chapter, attention is turned to how a contract is ended or discharged. In other words, what puts an end to the rights and duties created by a contract?

A. Conditions Relating to Performance

As developed in the body of this chapter, the ordinary method of discharging obligations under a contract is by performance. Certain promises may be less than absolute and instead come into effect only upon the occurrence of a specified event, or an existing obligation may be extinguished when an event happens. These are conditional promises.

1. Classifications of Conditions

When the occurrence or nonoccurrence of an event, as expressed in a contract, affects the duty of a party to the contract to perform, the event is called a **condition**. Terms such as *if, provided that, when, after, as soon as, subject to,* and *on the condition that* indicate the creation of a condition.[1] Conditions are classified as *conditions precedent, conditions subsequent,* and *concurrent conditions.*

(a) Condition Precedent

A **condition precedent** is a condition that must occur before a party to a contract has an obligation to perform under the contract. **For Example,** a condition precedent to a contractor's (MasTec's) obligation to pay a subcontractor (MidAmerica) under a "pay-if-paid" by the owner (PathNet) clause in their subcontract agreement is the receipt of payment by MasTec from PathNet. The condition precedent—payment by the owner—did not occur due to bankruptcy, and therefore MasTec did not have an obligation to pay MidAmerica.[2]

(b) Condition Subsequent

The parties to a contract may agree that a party is obligated to perform a certain act or pay a certain sum of money, but the contract contains a provision that relieves the obligation on the occurrence of a certain event. That is, on the happening of a **condition subsequent**, such an event extinguishes the duty to thereafter perform. **For Example,** Chad Newly served as the weekend anchor on *Channel 5 News* for several years. The station manager, Tom O'Brien, on reviewing tapes in connection with Newly's contract renewal, believed that Newly's speech on occasion was slightly slurred, and he suspected that it was from alcohol use. In the parties' contract discussions, O'Brien expressed his concerns about an alcohol problem and offered help. Newly denied there was a problem. O'Brien agreed to a new two-year contract with Newly at $167,000 for the first year and $175,000 for the second year with other benefits subject to "the condition" that the station reserved the right to make four unannounced drug-alcohol tests during the contract term; and should Newly test positive for drugs or alcohol under measurements set forth in the contract, then all of Channel 5's obligations to Newly under the contract would cease. When Newly subsequently failed a urinalysis test three months into the new contract, the happening of this event extinguished the station's obligation to employ and pay him under the contract.

SPORTS & ENTERTAINMENT LAW

ENDORSEMENT CONTRACTS

Sports marketing involves the use of famous athletes to promote the sale of products and services in our economy. Should an athlete's image be tarnished by allegations of immoral or illegal conduct, a company could be subject to financial losses and corporate embarrassment. Endorsement contracts may extend for multi-year periods, and should a "morals" issue arise,

[1] *Harmon Cable Communications v Scope Cable Television, Inc.,* 468 NW2d 350 (Neb 1990).

[2] *MidAmerica Construction Management, Inc. v MasTec North America, Inc.,* 436 F3d 1257 (10th Cir 2006).

SPORTS & ENTERTAINMENT LAW

continued

a company would be well served to have had a broad morals clause in its contract that would allow the company at its sole discretion to summarily terminate the endorsement contract. Representatives of athletes, on the other hand, seek narrow contractual language that allows for termination of endorsement contracts only upon the indictment for a crime, and they seek the right to have an arbitrator, as opposed to the employer, make the determination as to whether the morals clause was violated. NBA player Latrell Spreewell's endorsement contract with Converse Athletic Shoe Co. was terminated by the company following his altercation with his coach P.J. Carlisimo; John Daly's endorsement contract with Callaway Golf was terminated by the company when he violated his good conduct clause that restricted gambling and drinking activities.

Corporate sponsorship of the Olympics was recently subject to a "morals clause" by John Hancock Financial Services Co. in its sponsorship contract, allowing it the right to terminate its financial commitment to the International Olympic Committee (IOC) if the IOC became involved in improprieties. The Houston Astros did not have a morals clause in its $100 million, 30-year naming rights contract for its baseball stadium with the sponsoring Enron Corporation. When Enron refused to allow its name to be removed from the stadium, the Astros bought out the rights for $2.1 million.

Can the courts be utilized to resolve controversies over whether a "morals clause" has been violated? If so, is the occurrence of a morals clause violation a condition precedent or a condition subsequent?

(c) Concurrent Condition

In most bilateral contracts, the performances of the parties are *concurrent conditions*. That is, their mutual duties of performance under the contract are to take place simultaneously. **For Example,** concerning a contract for the sale and delivery of certain goods, the buyer must tender to the seller a certified check at the time of delivery as set forth in the contract, and the seller must tender the goods to the buyer at the same time.

B. Discharge by Performance

When it is claimed that a contract is discharged by performance, questions arise as to the nature, time, and sufficiency of the performance.

2. Normal Discharge of Contracts

A contract is usually discharged by the performance of the terms of the agreement. In most cases, the parties perform their promises and the contract ceases to exist or is thereby discharged. A contract is also discharged by the expiration of the time period specified in the contract.[3]

3. Nature of Performance

Performance may be the doing of an act or the making of payment.

(a) Tender

An offer to perform is known as a **tender**. If performance of the contract requires the doing of an act, the refusal of a tender discharges the party offering to perform and is a basis for that party to bring a lawsuit.

A valid tender of payment consists of an unconditional offer of the exact amount due on the date when due. A tender of payment is not just an expression of willingness to pay; it must be an actual offer to perform by making payment of the amount owed.

(b) Payment

When the contract requires payment, performance consists of the payment of money.

[3] *Washington National Ins. Co. v Sherwood Associates,* 795 P2d 665 (Utah App 1990).

E-COMMERCE AND CYBERLAW

CYBERSPACE PAYMENTS

The use of credit cards is the dominant form of payment for Internet transactions between businesses and consumers. Many businesses use Secure Sockets Layer (SSL) protocol to provide security for the transmission of customers' credit card information. SSL provides authentication of the merchant's server to the purchaser and encrypts the messages sent between the purchaser and the merchant. **For Example,** Amazon.com uses SSL.

New credit cards with built-in microprocessor chips plus hardware allowing cards to be read by home computers are now in use. Advantages include the ability to store account numbers and scramble them for safe e-mailing.

Credit cards offer consumers protection from losses from unauthorized transactions, international acceptance, and the ability to buy now and pay later.

(1) Application of Payments. If a debtor owes more than one debt to the creditor and pays money, a question may arise as to which debt has been paid. If the debtor specifies the debt to which the payment is to be applied and the creditor accepts the money, the creditor is bound to apply the money as specified.[4] Thus, if the debtor specifies that a payment is to be made for a current purchase, the creditor may not apply the payment to an older balance.

(2) Payment by Check. Payment by commercial paper, such as a check, is ordinarily a conditional payment. A check merely suspends the debt until the check is presented for payment. If payment is then made, the debt is discharged; if not paid, the suspension terminates, and suit may be brought on either the debt or the check. Frequently, payment must be made by a specified date. It is generally held that the payment is made on time if it is mailed on or before the final date for payment.

4. Time of Performance

When the date or period of time for performance is specified in the contract, performance should be made on that date or within that time period.

(a) No Time Specified

When the time for performance is not specified in the contract, an obligation to perform within a reasonable time is implied.[5] The fact that no time is specified neither impairs the contract on the ground that it is indefinite nor allows an endless time in which to perform. What constitutes a reasonable time is determined by the nature of the subject matter of the contract and the facts and circumstances surrounding the making of the contract.

(b) When Time Is Essential

If performance of the contract on or within the exact time specified is vital, it is said that "time is of the essence." Time is of the essence when the contract relates to property that is perishable or that is fluctuating rapidly in value. When a contract fixes by unambiguous language a time for performance and where there is no evidence showing that the parties did not intend that time should be of the essence, failure to perform within the specified time is a breach of contract entitling the innocent party to damages. **For Example,** Dixon and Gandhi agreed that Gandhi would close on the purchase of a motel as follows: "Closing Date. The closing shall be held . . . on the date which is within twenty (20) days after the closing of Nomura Financing." Gandhi did not close within the time period specified, and Dixon was allowed to retain $100,000 in prepaid closing costs and fees as liquidated damages for Gandhi's breach of contract.[6]

(c) When Time Is Not Essential

Unless a contract so provides, time is ordinarily not of the essence, and performance within a reasonable

[4] *Oakes Logging, Inc. v Green Crow, Inc.*, 832 P2d 894 (Wash App 1992).

[5] *First National Bank v Clark*, 447 SE2d 558 (W Va 1994).

[6] *Woodbull Corp. v Saibaba Corp.*, 507 SE2d 493 (Ga App 1998).

time is sufficient. In the case of the sale of property, time is not regarded as of the essence when there has not been any appreciable change in the market value or condition of the property and when the person who delayed does not appear to have done so for the purpose of speculating on a change in market price.

(d) Waiver of Essence of Time Limitation

A provision that time is of the essence may be waived. It is waived when the specified time has expired but the party who could complain requests the delaying party to take steps necessary to perform the contract.

5. Adequacy of Performance

When a party renders exactly the performance called for by the contract, no question arises as to whether the contract has been performed. In other cases, there may not have been a perfect performance, or a question arises as to whether the performance satisfies the standard set by the contract.

CPA (a) Substantial Performance

Perfect performance of a contract is not always possible when dealing with construction projects. A party who in good faith has provided **substantial performance** of the contract may sue to recover the payment specified in the contract. However, because the performance was not perfect, the performing party is subject to a counterclaim for the damages caused the other party. When a building contractor has substantially performed the contract to construct a building, the contractor is responsible for the cost of repairing or correcting the defects as an offset from the contract price.[7]

The measure of damages under these circumstances is known as "cost of completion" damages. If, however, the cost of completion would be unreasonably disproportionate to the importance of the defect, the measure of damages is the diminution in value of the building due to the defective performance.

Whether there is substantial performance is a question of degree to be determined by all of the facts, including the particular type of structure involved, its intended purpose, and the nature and relative expense of repairs.

For Example, a certain building contractor (BC) and a certain owner (O) made a contract to construct a home overlooking Vineyard Sound on Martha's Vineyard according to plans and specifications that clearly called for the use of General Plumbing Blue Star piping. The contract price was $1,100,000. Upon inspecting the work before making the final $400,000 payment and accepting the building, O discovered that BC had used Republic piping throughout the house. O explained to BC that his family had made its money by investing in General Plumbing, and he, therefore, would not make the final payment until the breach of contract was remedied. BC explained that Republic pipes were of the same industrial grade and quality as the Blue Star pipes. Moreover, BC estimated that it would cost nearly $300,000 to replace all of the pipes because of the destruction of walls and fixtures necessary to accomplish such a task. BC may sue O for $400,000 for breach of contract, claiming he had substantially performed the contract, and O may counterclaim for $300,000, seeking an offset for the cost of remedying the breach. The court will find in favor of the contractor and will not allow the $300,000 offset but will allow a "nominal" offset of perhaps $100 to $1,000 for the amount by which the Republic pipes diminished the value of the building.[8]

In most jurisdictions, the willfulness of the departure from the specifications of the contract does not by itself preclude some recovery for the contractor on the "cost of completion" basis but rather is a factor in consideration of whether there was substantial performance by the contractor.[9]

(b) Fault of Complaining Party

A party cannot complain that a performance was defective when the performance follows the terms of the contract required by the complaining party. Thus, a homeowner who supplied the specifications for poured cement walls could not hold a contractor liable for damages when the walls that were poured in exact compliance with those specifications proved defective.

[7] Substantial performance is not a defense to a breach of contract claim, however. See *Bentley Systems Inc. v Intergraph Corp.*, 922 So2d 61 (Ala 2005).

[8] See *Jacob & Youngs, Inc. v Kent*, 230 NY 239 (1921).

[9] But see *USX Corp. v M. DeMatteo Construction Co.*, 315 F3d 43 (1st Cir 2002), for application of a common law rule that prohibits a construction contractor guilty of a willful breach of contract from maintaining any suit on the contract against the other party.

FIGURE 19-1 Causes of Contract Discharge

- DISCHARGE OF CONTRACT
  - CONDITIONS
    - PRECEDENT
    - SUBSEQUENT
    - CONCURRENT
  - PERFORMANCE
  - UNILATERAL ACTION
    - CONSUMER PROTECTION RESCISSION
  - AGREEMENT
    - SUBSTITUTION
    - ACCORD AND SATISFACTION
  - IMPOSSIBILITY
    - DESTRUCTION OF PARTICULAR SUBJECT MATTER
    - CHANGE OF LAW
    - DEATH OR DISABILITY IN PERSONAL SERVICE CONTRACT
    - ACT OF OTHER PARTY
  - ECONOMIC DISAPPOINTMENT
    - COMMERCIAL IMPRACTICABILITY
    - FRUSTRATION OF PURPOSE
  - OPERATION OF LAW
    - BANKRUPTCY
    - STATUTE OF LIMITATIONS
    - CONTRACTUAL LIMITATIONS

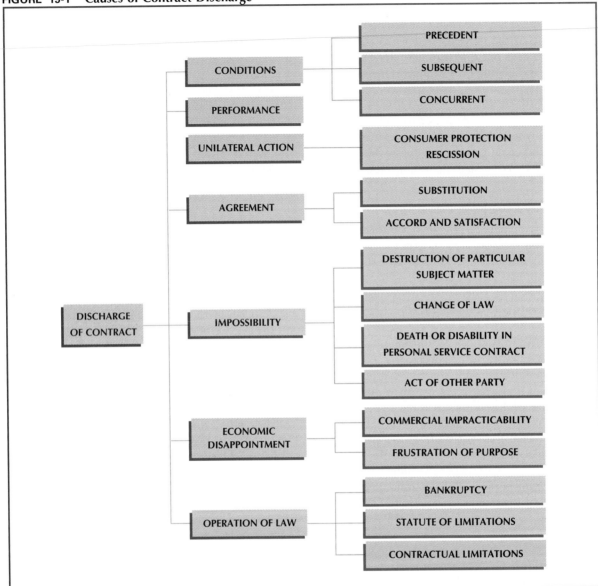

(c) Performance to the Satisfaction of the Contracting Party or a Third Party

Sometimes an agreement requires performance to the satisfaction, taste, or judgment of the other party to the contract. When the contract specifically stipulates that the performance must satisfy the contracting party, the courts will ordinarily enforce the plain meaning of the language of the parties and the work must satisfy the contracting party—subject, of course, to the requirement that dissatisfaction be made in good faith. **For Example,** the Perrones' written contract to purchase the Hills' residence contained a clause making performance subject to inspection to the Perrones' satisfaction. During the house inspection, the inspector found a piece of wood in a crawl space that appeared to have been damaged by termites and had possibly been treated some 18 years before with chlordane. At the end of the inspection Mr. Perrone indicated that he would perform on the contract. Thereafter, he went on the Internet and found that chlordane is a highly toxic pesticide now banned from use as a termite treatment. As a result, the Perrones rescinded the contract under the buyer satisfaction clause. The Hills sued, believing that speculation about a pesticide treatment 18 years ago was absurd. They contended that the Perrones had breached the contract without a valid reason. The court decided for the Perrones, since they exercised the "satisfaction clause" in good faith.[10] Good-faith personal satisfaction is generally required when the subject matter of the contract is personal, such as interior design work, tailoring, or the painting of a portrait.

With respect to things mechanical or routine performances, courts require that the performance be such as would satisfy a reasonable person under the circumstances.

When work is to be done subject to the approval of an architect, engineer, or another expert, most courts apply the reasonable person test of satisfaction.

C. Discharge by Action of Parties

Contracts may be discharged by the joint action of both contracting parties or, in some cases, by the action of one party alone.

6. Discharge by Unilateral Action

Ordinarily, a contract cannot be discharged by the action of either party alone. In some cases, however, the contract gives one of either party the right to cancel the contract by unilateral action, such as by notice to the other party. Insurance policies covering loss commonly provide that the insurer may cancel the policy upon giving a specified number of days' notice.

(a) Consumer Protection Rescission

A basic principle of contract law is that once made, a contract between competent persons is a binding obligation. Consumer protection legislation introduces into the law a contrary concept—that of giving the consumer a chance to think things over and to rescind the contract. Thus, the federal Consumer Credit Protection Act (CCPA) gives the debtor the right to rescind a credit transaction within three business days when the transaction would impose a lien on the debtor's home. **For Example,** a homeowner who mortgages his or her home to obtain a loan may cancel the transaction for any reason by notifying the lender before midnight of the third full business day after the loan is made.[11]

A Federal Trade Commission regulation gives the buyer three business days in which to cancel a home-solicited sale of goods or services costing more than $25.[12]

7. Discharge by Agreement

A contract may be discharged by the operation of one of its provisions or by a subsequent agreement. Thus, there may be a discharge by (1) the terms of the original contract, such as a provision that the contract should end on a specified date; (2) a mutual cancellation, in which the parties agree to end their contract; (3) a mutual **rescission**, in which the parties agree to annul the contract and return both parties to their original positions before the contract had been made; (4) the **substitution** of a new contract between the same parties; (5) a novation or substitution of a new contract involving a new party;[13] (6) an **accord and satisfaction**; (7) a release; or (8) a **waiver**.

(a) Substitution

The parties may decide that their contract is not the one they want. They may then replace it with another contract. If they do, the original contract is discharged by substitution.[14]

(b) Accord and Satisfaction

When the parties have differing views as to the performance required by the terms of a contract, they may agree to a different performance. Such an agreement is called an *accord*. When the accord is performed or executed, there is an accord and

10 *Hill v Perrones*, 42 P3d 210 (Kan App 2002).

11 If the owner is not informed of this right to cancel, the three-day period does not begin until that information is given. Consumer Credit Protection Act § 125, 15 USC § 1635(a), (e), (f).

12 CFR § 429.1. This displaces state laws making similar provisions for rescission, such as UCCC § 2.502.

13 *Eagle Industries, Inc. v Thompson*, 900 P2d 475 (Or 1995). In a few jurisdictions, the term *novation* is used to embrace the substitution of any new contract, whether between the original parties or not.

14 *Shawnee Hospital Authority v Dow Construction, Inc.*, 812 P2d 1351 (Okla 1990).

satisfaction, which discharges the original obligation. To constitute an accord and satisfaction, there must be a bona fide dispute, a proposal to settle the dispute, and performance of the agreement.

As seen in the *MKL Pre-Press* case, to constitute an accord and satisfaction, there must be a bona fide dispute, a proposal to settle the dispute, and performance of the agreement.

MKL PRE-PRESS ELECTRONICS V LA CROSSE LITHO SUPPLY, LLC, 840 NE2D 687 (ILL APP 2005)

A FULL COURT PRESS TO NO AVAIL

In September 2002 La Crosse Litho Supply, LLC (La Crosse) entered a distribution agreement with MKL Pre-Press Electronics (MKL) for the distribution of MKL printing systems. La Crosse purchased a 7000 System unit from MKL for its end user Printing Plus with MKL technicians providing service and training for the unit. The 7000 System at Printing Plus failed on three occasions and ultimately repairs were unsuccessful. On September 30, 2003 La Crosse cancelled the distribution agreement. On October 2, 2003 La Crosse sent a letter to MKL's Sales V.P. Bill Landwer setting forth an itemized accounting of what it owed MKL Pre-Press with deductions for the purchase price of the failed 7000 System and other offsets. MKL sent a subsequent bill for repairs and services, to which La Crosse objected and stated it would not pay them. MKL's attorney sent a demand letter for $26,453.31. La Crosse's president, Randall Peters, responded by letter dated December 30, 2003 explaining that with an offset for training and warranty work it performed, "we are sending you the final payment in the amount of $1696.47." He added, "[w]ith this correspondence, we consider all open issues between La Crosse Litho Supply and MKL Pre Press closed." Enclosed with the letter was a check for $1696.47 payable to MKL Pre-Press. In the remittance portion of the check, under the heading "Ref," was typed "FINAL PAYM." The check was endorsed and deposited on either January 26 or 27, 2004. MKL sued La Crosse for $24,756.84. La Crosse defended that the tender and subsequent deposit of the check for $1696.47 constituted an accord and satisfaction. Jill Fleming MKL's office manager, stated that it was her duty to process checks and that she did not read Peters' letter. From a judgment for La Crosse, MKL appealed.

Judicial Opinion

GREIMAN, J.... An accord and satisfaction is a contractual method of discharging debts or claims between the parties to such an agreement. In order for such an arrangement to exist, there must be: (1) a *bonafide* dispute as to the claims pending between the parties; (2) an unliquidated sum owed; (3) consideration, (4) a shared mutual intent to compromise the claims; and (5) execution of the agreement. The accord is the actual agreement between the parties, while the satisfaction is its execution or performance....

Where there is an honest dispute as to the amount owed and due between the parties and the debtor tenders an amount with the explicit understanding that it is full payment of all demands, the creditor's acceptance and negotiation of that amount constitutes an accord and satisfaction. *Koules v Euro–American Arbitrage, Inc.*, 689 N.E.2d 411 (1998). However, the partial payment of a fixed and certain demand due and not in dispute does not constitute satisfaction of the entire debt even where the creditor agrees to receive partial payment for the whole debt and gives a receipt for the whole demand. *Koules*, 689 N.E.2d 411.

As demonstrated by the October 2003 correspondence between Peters and Landwer concerning amounts still due and owing to plaintiff, plaintiff's subsequent invoices and Peters' objection there-to, and plaintiff's November 2003 demand letter, it is plainly apparent that a *bonafide* dispute existed as to the claims pending between the parties and an unliquidated sum was owed by defendant to plaintiff. The tender of the check by defendant and its deposit by plaintiff constituted consideration and execution. The only element remaining is a shared mutual intent by the parties to compromise the claims between them. Intent can be inferred from conduct; the act of knowingly accepting and depositing a check upon which conditional language has been added indicates the existence of an accord and satisfaction. Where creditor takes and keeps a debtor's reduced payment with actual or constructive knowledge of the condition, the creditor has accepted the debtor's offer, and the original debt is settled for the reduced amount....

Plaintiff additionally argues that the deposit of defendent's check by Fleming should not be imputed to it as an organization because Fleming had no responsibility to enter the organization into any sort of agreement like an accord and satisfaction and because the check contained no restrictive language indicating that it had been tendered in consideration of all claims pending between the parties. We disagree.

An organization's practice of authorizing its employee to endorse checks and deposit them into an account on its behalf cannot serve as a means of isolating the organization or its principals from the legal consequences that flow from the employee's actions in the scope of his or her duties. An employee whose authority includes depositing a check upon which restrictive language appeared will be presumed to have acted on behalf of the organization, and his or her acts will be imputed to the organization as a matter of law.

In this case, Fleming's affidavit clearly stated that it was within the scope of her duties to process and deposit checks on the plaintiff's behalf. She stated herself that she endorsed and deposited the check, the voucher portion of which clearly stated "FINAL PAYM." We cannot fathom what "FINAL PAYM" might mean, other than "final payment," meaning that defendant did not intend to send plaintiff any more money. Accordingly, we can only conclude that Fleming's conduct can and should be imputed to plaintiff and its principals, thereby constituting an accord and satisfaction....

[Affirmed]

Questions

1. What are the elements of an "accord and satisfaction"?
2. Was there a shared mutual intent to compromise the claims between the parties?
3. Is it fair to expect an office manager to know that by processing a check for $1,696.47 marked "final payment" that her company could lose the right to pursue its position that it was owed an additional $24,756.84?

D. Discharge by External Causes

Circumstances beyond the control of the contracting parties may discharge the contract.

8. Discharge by Impossibility

Impossibility of performance refers to external or extrinsic conditions. This is contrasted with an individual's personal inability to perform.[15] **For Example,** Pollard Excavating, Inc., made a contract with Comprehensive Builders, Inc., to install sewer piping from the foundation of a new home to the sewer main but withdrew from the job asserting impossibility because of problems arising from subsurface soil conditions and the fact that the sewer main was farther underground than the builder had stated. Pollard was held liable for "cost of completion" damages. The subsoil conditions and the location of the sewer main were discussed prior to making the contract and were not unanticipated events that made performance objectively impossible.[16]

Shortages of materials and similar factors, even though external, ordinarily do not excuse performance under a contract. However, a seller's duty may be excused by a failure of a particular source of supply that was specified by the parties to the contract. **For Example,** if a contractor's usual gravel source cannot be used (and it is necessary to transport gravel from a more distant source, making performance more costly), this by itself does not discharge the contractor from the obligation to construct a road. If there is nothing in the contract requiring that the gravel be obtained from the unavailable source, no question of impossibility of performance exists. A contract is not discharged merely because performance proves to be more burdensome or costly than was originally contemplated. However, if the parties specified the source of supply in their contract, that would constitute an impossibility that would excuse performance.

[15] *Haessly v Safeco Title Ins. Co.*, 825 P2d 1119 (Idaho 1992).

[16] *Comprehensive Bldg. v Pollard Excavating*, 674 NYS2d 869 (App Div 1998).

(a) Destruction of Particular Subject Matter

When parties contract expressly for, or with reference to, a particular subject matter, the contract is discharged if the subject matter is destroyed through no fault of either party. When a contract calls for the sale of a wheat crop growing on a specific parcel of land, the contract is discharged if that crop is destroyed by blight.

On the other hand, if there is merely a contract to sell a given quantity of a specified grade of wheat, the seller is not discharged when the seller's crop is destroyed by blight. The seller had made an unqualified undertaking to deliver wheat of a specified grade. No restrictions or qualifications were imposed as to the source. If the seller does not deliver the goods called for by the contract, the contract is broken, and the seller is liable for damages.

The parties may, by their contract, allocate the risk of loss. Thus, a contract for the sale of a building and land may specify that the seller should bear any loss from damage to the building.

(b) Change of Law

A contract is discharged when its performance is made illegal by a subsequent change in the law. Thus, a contract to construct a nonfireproof building at a particular place is discharged by the adoption of a zoning law prohibiting such a building within that area. Mere inconvenience or temporary delay caused by the new law, however, does not excuse performance.

(c) Death or Disability

When the contract obligates a party to render or receive personal services requiring peculiar skill, the death, incapacity, or illness of the party that was either to render or receive the personal services excuses both sides from a duty to perform. It is sometimes said that "the death of either party is the death of the contract."

The rule does not apply, however, when the acts called for by the contract are of such a character that (1) the acts may be as well performed by others, such as the promisor's personal representatives, or (2) the contract's terms contemplate continuance of the obligations after the death of one of the parties. **For Example,** Lynn Jones was under contract to investor Ed Jenkins to operate certain Subway sandwich shops and to acquire new franchises with funding provided by Jenkins. After Jenkins's death, Jones claimed he was no longer bound under the contract and was free to pursue franchise opportunities on his own. The contract between Jones and Jenkins expressed that it was binding on the parties' "heirs and assigns" and that the contract embodied property rights that passed to Jenkins's widow. The agreement's provisions thus established that the agreement survived the death of Jenkins, and Jones was therefore obligated to remit profits from the franchise he acquired for himself after Jenkins's death.[17]

(d) Act of Other Party

Every contract contains "an implied covenant of good faith and fair dealing." As a result of this covenant, a promisee is under an obligation to do nothing that would interfere with the promisor's performance. When the promisee prevents performance or otherwise makes performance impossible, the promisor is discharged from the contract. Thus, a subcontractor is discharged from any obligation when it is unable to do the work because the principal contractor refuses to deliver the material, equipment, or money required by the subcontract. When the default of the other party consists of failing to supply goods or services, the duty may rest on the party claiming a discharge of the contract to show that substitute goods or services could not be obtained elsewhere.

9. Developing Doctrines

Commercial impracticability and frustration of purpose may excuse performance.

(a) Commercial Impracticability

The doctrine of *commercial impracticability* (as opposed to *impossibility*) was developed to deal with the harsh rule that a party must perform its contracts unless it is absolutely impossible. However, not every type of impracticability is an excuse for nonperformance. **For Example,** I. Patel was bound by his franchise agreement with Days Inn, Inc., to maintain his 60-room inn on old Route 66 in Lincoln, Illinois, to at least minimum quality assurance standards. His inn failed five consecutive quality inspections over two years, with the inspector noting damaged guest rooms, burns in the bedding, and severely stained

[17] *Jenkins Subway, Inc. v Jones*, 990 SW2d 713 (Tenn App 1998).

carpets. Patel's defense when his franchise was cancelled after the fifth failed inspection was that bridge repairs on the road leading from I-55 to his inn had adversely affected his business and made it commercially impractical to live up to the franchise agreement. The court rejected his defense, determining that while the bridge work might have affected patronage, it had no effect on his duty to comply with the quality assurance standards of his franchise agreement.[18] Commercial impracticability is available only when the performance is made impractical by the subsequent occurrence of an event whose nonoccurrence was a basic assumption on which the contract was made.[19]

The *Specialty Tire* case deals with the application of the defense of impracticality.

SPECIALTY TIRES OF AMERICA, INC. V CIT, 82 F SUPP 2D 434 (WD PA 2000)

"WAIT A MINUTE. . . . THERE'S AN EXCEPTION TO THE 'A DEAL'S A DEAL' DOCTRINE!"

CIT, a major equipment leasing company, entered into a sale/leaseback contract with Condere Tire Corporation for 11 tire presses at Condere's tire plant in Natchez, Mississippi. Condere ceased making payments on these presses owned by CIT; and Condere filed for Chapter 11 bankruptcy. CIT thereafter contracted to sell the presses to Specialty Tires, Inc., for $250,000. When the contract was made, CIT, Condere, and Specialty Tires believed that CIT was the owner of the presses and was entitled to immediate possession. When CIT attempted to gain access to the presses to have them shipped, Condere changed its position and refused to allow the equipment to be removed from the plant. When the presses were not delivered, Specialty sued CIT for damages for nondelivery of the presses to date, and CIT asserted the defense of impracticability.

Judicial Opinion

SMITH, D. J. . . . In the overwhelming majority of circumstances, contractual promises are to be performed, not avoided: *pacta sunt servanda*, or, as the Seventh Circuit loosely translated it, "a deal's a deal." *Waukesha Foundary, Inc. v Industrial Engineering Inc.*, 91 F.3d 1002, 1010 (7th Cir. 1996). . . . This is an eminently sound doctrine, because typically

a court cannot improve matters by intervention after the fact. It can only destabilize the institution of contract, increase risk, and make parties worse off. . . . Parties to contracts are entitled to seek, and retain, personal advantage; striving for that advantage is the source of much economic progress. Contract law does not require parties to be fair, or kind, or reasonable, or to share gains or losses equally.

Industrial Representation, Inc. v CP Clare Corp., 74 F.3d 128, 131–32 (7th Cir. 1996). Promisors are free to assume risks, even huge ones, and promisees are entitled to rely on those voluntary assumptions. . . .

Even so, courts have recognized, in an evolving line of cases from the common law down to the present, that there are limited instances in which unexpectedly and radically changed conditions render the judicial enforcement of certain promises of little or no utility. This has come to be known, for our purposes, as the doctrines of impossibility and impracticability.* Because of the unexpected nature of such occurrences, litigated cases usually involve, not interpretation of a contractual term, but the judicial filling of a lacuna in the parties agreement. *See* 2 E. Allan Farnsworth, *Farnsworth on Contracts* § 9.5, at 603 (2d ed. 1998); Such "gapfilling," however, must be understood for

*The reported cases on this topic, unfortunately, are not characterized by either consistency or clarity of expression. As one respected treatise puts it, "Students who have concluded a first year contracts course in confusion about the doctrine of impossibility and have since . . . found that the cases somehow slip through their fingers when they try to apply them to new situations, may take some comfort in knowing that they are in good company." I White & Summers, *supra* § 3–10, at 164.

[18] *Days Inn of America, Inc. v Patel*, 88 F Supp 2d 928 (CD Ill 2000).

[19] See Restatement (Second) of Contracts § 261; UCC § 2-615.

what it is: a court-ordered, as opposed to bargained-for, allocation of risk between the parties....

Traditionally, there were three kinds of supervening events that would provide a legally cognizable excuse for failing to perform: death of the promisor (if the performance was personal), illegality of the performance, and destruction of the subject matter... beyond that the doctrine has grown to recognize that

relief is most justified if unexpected events inflict a loss on one party and provide a windfall gain for the other or where the excuse would save one party from an unexpected loss while leaving the other party in a position no worse than it would have without the contract.

Calamari & Perillo, *supra* § 13.1, at 496; *see also* 2 Farnsworth, *supra* § 9.6, at 612. Thus, the Second Restatement of Contracts expresses the doctrine of impracticability this way:

Where, after a contract is made, a party's performance is made impracticable without his fault by the occurrence of an event the non-occurrence of which was a basic assumption on which the contract was made, his duty to render that performance is discharged, unless the language or the circumstances indicate the contrary.

Restatement (Second) of Contracts § 261 (1981). Article 2 of the U.C.C., which applies to the sale of goods presented by the case *sub judice*, puts it similarly:

Delay in delivery or non-delivery in whole or in part by a seller... is not a breach of his duty under a contract for sale if performance as agreed has been made impracticable by the occurrence of a contingency the non-occurrence of which was a basic assumption on which the contract was made....

U.C.C. § 2–615(1)

The principal inquiry in an impracticability analysis, then, is whether there was a contingency the non-occurrence of which was a basic assumption underlying the contract. It is often said that this question turns on whether the contingency was "foreseeable." 2 Farnsworth, § 9.6, at 616,...

Generally speaking, while loss, destruction or a major price increase of fungible goods will not excuse the seller's duty to perform, the rule is different when the goods are unique, have been identified to the contract or are to be produced from a specific agreed-upon source. In such a case, the nonexistence or unavailability of a specific thing will establish a defense of impracticability. Murray, *supra*, § 113, at 649, 650;...

...CIT contracted to supply specific tire presses to Specialty. This was not a case of fungible goods; Specialty inspected, and bid for, certain identified, used presses located at the Natchez plant operated by Condere. All parties believed that CIT was the owner of the presses and was entitled to their immediate possession; Condere's representatives stated as much during the inspection visit. Neither Specialty nor CIT had any reason to believe that Condere would subsequently turn an about-face and assert a possessory interest in the presses....

Thus,... it is clear that this is not the sort of risk that CIT should have expected to either bear or contract against....

Plaintiff makes much of the argument that there was no "basic assumption" created by Condere upon which Specialty and CIT based their contract, stating that it relied upon CIT's representations alone. This is specious. As a matter of both law and logic, a basic assumption of any contract for the sale of specific, identified goods is that they are, in fact, available for sale. Accordingly, I reject this contention and conclude that the actions of Condere in detaining the presses presents sufficient grounds on which to base an impracticability defense....

...While CIT did assume the risk of its own inability to perform, it did not assume the risk of Condere making it unable to perform by detaining the presses, any more than CIT assumed the risk that thieves would steal the presses from Condere before the latter could deliver them. In sum, this risk was not "sufficiently within the control of [CIT] that [it should be inferred that it was] assumed by that party." 2 Fransworth, *supra* § 9.6, at 619–20. It was completely within the control of Condere.

Accordingly, I conclude on this record that CIT has made out its defense of impracticability.... CIT's performance is impracticable only in the temporary sense. Temporary impracticabilty only relieves the promisor of the obligation to perform as long as the impracticability lasts and for a reasonable time thereafter.... Once it receives possession of the presses, CIT asserts that it stands ready and willing to perform its contract with Specialty.... CIT is excused by the doctrine of impracticability and is entitled to full summary judgement.

[Judgment for CIT]

Questions

1. What is the rationale for the "a deal's a deal" doctrine; and what is its implication in the present case?
2. Summarize the Restatement (Second) Contracts expression of the defense of impracticality.
3. How did the court decide this case?

If a subsequent event occurs involving a severe shortage of raw materials or supplies that results in a marked increase in the cost of the materials or supplies and this event was foreseeable, the defense of commercial impracticability is not available.

(b) Frustration of Purpose Doctrine

Because of a change in circumstances, the purpose of the contract may have no value to the party entitled to receive performance. In such a case, performance may be excused if both parties were aware of the purpose and the event that frustrated the purpose was unforeseeable.[20]

For Example, National Southern Bank rents a home near Willowbend Country Club on the southeastern shore of North Carolina for $75,000 a week to entertain business guests at the Ryder Cup matches scheduled for the week in question. Storm damage from Hurricane David the week before the event caused the closing of the course and the transfer of the tournament to another venue in a different state. The bank's duty to pay for the house may be excused by the doctrine of *frustration of purpose*, because the transfer of the tournament fully destroyed the value of the home rental, both parties were aware of the purpose of the rental, and the cancellation of the golf tournament was unforeseeable.

(c) Comparison to Common Law Rule

The traditional common law rule refuses to recognize commercial impracticability or frustration of purpose. By the common law rule, the losses and disappointments against which commercial impracticability and frustration of purpose give protection are merely the risks that one takes in entering into a contract. Moreover, the situations could have been guarded against by including an appropriate condition subsequent in the contract. A condition subsequent declares that the contract will be void if a specified event occurs.[21] The contract also could have provided for a readjustment of compensation if there was a basic change of circumstances. The common law approach also rejects these developing concepts because they weaken the stability of a contract.

An indication of a wider recognition of the concept that "extreme" changes of circumstances can discharge a contract is found in the Uniform Commercial Code. The UCC provides for the discharge of a contract for the sale of goods when a condition that the parties assumed existed, or would continue, ceases to exist.[22]

10. Temporary Impossibility

Ordinarily, a temporary impossibility suspends the duty to perform. If the obligation to perform is suspended, it is revived on the termination of the impossibility. If, however, performance at that later date would impose a substantially greater burden on the party obligated to perform, some courts discharge the obligor from the contract.

After the September 11, 2001, terrorist attack on the World Trade Center, New York City courts followed wartime precedents that had developed the law of temporary impossibility. Such impossibility, when of brief duration, excuses performance until it subsequently becomes possible to perform rather than excusing performance altogether. Thus, an individual who was unable to communicate her cancellation of travel 60 days prior to her scheduled travel as required by her contract, which needed to occur on or before September 14, 2001, could expect relief from a cancellation penalty provision in the contract based on credible testimony of attempted phone calls to the travel agent on and after September 12, 2001, even though the calls did not get through due to communication problems in New York City.[23]

(a) Weather

Acts of God, such as tornadoes, lightning, and floods, usually do not terminate a contract even though they make performance difficult. Thus, weather conditions constitute a risk that is assumed by a contracting party in the absence of a contrary agreement. Consequently, extra expense sustained by a contractor because of weather conditions is a risk that the contractor assumes in the absence of an express provision for additional compensation in such a case. **For Example,** Danielo Contractors made a contract to

[20] The defense of frustration of purpose, or commercial frustration, is very difficult to invoke because the courts are extremely reluctant to allow parties to avoid obligations to which they have agreed. See *Wal-Mart Stores, Inc. v AIG Life Insurance Co.*, 872 A2d 611 (Del Ch 2005), denying application of the commercial frustration doctrine when the supervening event, the invalidation of hundreds of millions in tax deductions by the IRS, was reasonably foreseeable and could have been provided for in the contract.

[21] *Wermer v ABI*, 10 SW3d 575 (Mo App 2000).

[22] UCC § 2-615.

[23] See *Bugh v Protravel International, Inc.*, 746 NYS2d 290 (Civ Ct NYC 2002).

construct a shopping mall for the Rubicon Center, with construction to begin November 1. Because of abnormal cold and blizzard conditions, Danielo was not able to begin work until April 1 and was five months late in completing the construction of the project. Rubicon sued Danielo for breach of contract by failing to perform on schedule. Danielo is liable. Because the contract included no provision covering delay caused by weather, Danielo bore the risk of the delay and resulting loss.

Modern contracts commonly contain a "weather clause" and reflect the parties' agreement on this matter. When the parties take the time to discuss weather issues, purchasing insurance coverage is a common resolution.

11. Discharge by Operation of Law

A contract is discharged by **operation of law** by (1) an alteration or a material change made by a party, (2) the destruction of the written contract with intent to discharge it, (3) bankruptcy, (4) the operation of a statute of limitations, or (5) a contractual limitation.

(a) Bankruptcy

As set forth in the chapter on bankruptcy, even though all creditors have not been paid in full, a discharge in **bankruptcy** eliminates ordinary contract claims against the debtor.

CPA (b) Statute of Limitations

A **statute of limitations** provides that after a certain number of years have passed, a contract claim is barred. The time limitation provided by state statutes of limitations varies widely. The time period for bringing actions for breach of an oral contract is two to three years. The period may differ with the type of contract—ranging from a relatively short time for open accounts (ordinary customers' charge accounts) to four years for sales of goods.[24] A somewhat longer period exists for bringing actions for breach of written contracts (usually four to ten years). **For Example,** Prate Installations, Inc., sued homeowners Richard and Rebecca Thomas for failure to pay for a new roof installed by Prate. Prate had sent numerous invoices to the Thomases over a four-year period seeking payment to no avail. The Thomases moved to dismiss the case under a four-year limitation period. However, the court concluded that the state's ten-year limitations period on written contracts applied.[25] The maximum period for judgments of record is usually 10 to 20 years.

(c) Contractual Limitations

Some contracts, particularly insurance contracts, contain a time limitation within which suit must be brought. This is in effect a private statute of limitations created by the agreement of the parties.

A contract may also require that notice of any claim be given within a specified time. A party who fails to give notice within the time specified by the contract is barred from suing on the contract.

A contract provision requiring that suit be brought within one year does not violate public policy, although the statute of limitations would allow two years in the absence of such a contract limitation.[26]

LAWFLIX

Uncle Buck (1989) (PG-13)

John Candy plays ne'er-do-well Uncle Buck who promises to go to work at his girlfriend's tire store and marry her. When his brother calls in the middle of the night seeking help with his children, Buck tells his girlfriend (Chenise) that he can no longer honor his promise because he must go to the suburbs to care for his brother's children while his brother and sister-in-law travel to Indiana to be with his sister-in-law's very ill father.

Discuss Buck's excuse. Is it impossibility? Does the change in circumstances excuse Buck?

For movie clips that illustrate business law concepts, see LawFlix at **http://wdvl.westbuslaw.com.**

[24] UCC § 2-725(1).

[25] *Prate Installations, Inc. v Thomas,* 842 NE2d 1205 (Ill App 2006).

[26] *Keiting v Skauge,* 543 NW2d 565 (Wis App 1995).

Summary

A party's duty to perform under a contract can be affected by a condition precedent, which must occur before a party has an obligation to perform; a condition subsequent, that is, a condition or event that relieves the duty to thereafter perform; and concurrent conditions, which require mutual and often simultaneous performance.

Most contracts are discharged by performance. An offer to perform is called a *tender of performance*. If a tender of performance is wrongfully refused, the duty of the tenderer to perform is terminated. When the performance called for by the contract is the payment of money, it must be legal tender that is offered. In actual practice, it is common to pay and to accept payment by checks or other commercial paper.

When the debtor owes the creditor on several accounts and makes a payment, the debtor may specify which account is to be credited with the payment. If the debtor fails to specify, the creditor may choose which account to credit.

When a contract does not state when it is to be performed, it must be performed within a reasonable time. If time for performance is stated in the contract, the contract must be performed at the time specified if such time is essential (is of the essence). Performance within a reasonable time is sufficient if the specified time is not essential. Ordinarily, a contract must be performed exactly in the manner specified by the contract. A less-than-perfect performance is allowed if it is a substantial performance and if damages are allowed the other party. The other contracting party or a third person may guarantee a perfect performance. Such a guarantor is then liable if the performance is less than perfect.

A contract cannot be discharged by unilateral action unless authorized by the contract itself or by statute, as in the case of consumer protection rescission.

Because a contract arises from an agreement, it may also be terminated by an agreement. A contract may also be discharged by the substitution of a new contract for the original contract; by a novation, or making a new contract with a new party; by accord and satisfaction; by release; or by waiver.

A contract is discharged when it is impossible to perform. Impossibility may result from the destruction of the subject matter of the contract, the adoption of a new law that prohibits performance, the death or disability of a party whose personal action was required for performance of the contract, or the act of the other party to the contract. Some courts will also hold that a contract is discharged when its performance is commercially impracticable or there is frustration of purpose. Temporary impossibility, such as a labor strike or bad weather, has no effect on a contract. It is common, though, to include protective clauses that excuse delay caused by temporary impossibility.

A contract may be discharged by operation of law. This occurs when (1) the liability arising from the contract is discharged by bankruptcy, (2) suit on the contract is barred by the applicable statute of limitations, or (3) a time limitation stated in the contract is exceeded.

Questions and Case Problems

1. McMullen Contractors made a contract with Richardson to build an apartment house for a specific price. A number of serious apartment house fires broke out in the city, and the city council adopted an ordinance increasing the fire precautions that had to be taken in the construction of a new building. Compliance with these new requirements would make the construction of the apartment house for Richardson more expensive than McMullen had originally contemplated. Is McMullen discharged from the contract to build the apartment house?
2. Lymon Mitchell operated a Badcock Home Furnishings dealership, under which as dealer he was paid a commission on sales and Badcock retained title to merchandise on display. Mitchell sold his dealership to another and to facilitate the sale, Badcock prepared a summary of commissions owed with certain itemized offsets it claimed that Mitchell owed Badcock. Mitchell disagreed with the calculations, but he accepted them and signed the transfer documents closing the sale on the basis of the terms set forth in the summary and was paid accordingly. After pondering the offsets taken by Badcock and verifying the correctness of his position, he brought suit for the additional funds owed. What defense would you expect Badcock to raise? How would you decide the case? Explain fully. [*Mitchell v Badcock Corp.*, 496 SE2d 502 (Ga App)]
3. American Bank loaned Koplik $50,000 to buy equipment for a restaurant about to be opened by Casual Citchen Corp. The loan was not repaid, and Fast Foods, Inc., bought out the interest of Casual Citchen. As part of the transaction, Fast Foods agreed to pay the debt owed to American Bank, and the parties agreed to a new schedule of payments to be made by Fast Foods. Fast Foods did not make the payments, and American Bank sued Koplik. He contended that his obligation to repay $50,000 had been discharged by the execution of the agreement providing for the payment of the debt by Fast Foods. Was this defense valid? [*American Bank & Trust Co. v Koplik*, 451 NYS2d 426 (App Div)]
4. Metalcrafters made a contract to design a new earth-moving vehicle for Lamar Highway Construction Co.

Metalcrafters was depending on the genius of Samet, the head of its research department, to design a new product. Shortly after the contract was made between Metalcrafters and Lamar, Samet was killed in an automobile accident. Metalcrafters was not able to design the product without Samet. Lamar sued Metalcrafters for damages for breach of the contract. Metalcrafters claimed that the contract was discharged by Samet's death. Is it correct?

5. The Tinchers signed a contract to sell land to Creasy. The contract specified that the sales transaction was to be completed in 90 days. At the end of the 90 days, Creasy requested an extension of time. The Tinchers refused to grant an extension and stated that the contract was terminated. Creasy claimed that the 90-day clause was not binding because the contract did not state that time was of the essence. Was the contract terminated? [*Creasy v Tincher*, 173 SE2d 332 (W Va)]
6. Christopher Bloom received a medical school scholarship created by the U.S. Department of Health and Human Services to increase the number of doctors serving rural areas. In return for this assistance, Bloom agreed to practice four years in a region identified as being underserved by medical professionals. After some problem with his postgraduation assignment, Bloom requested a repayment schedule from the agency. Although no terms were offered, Bloom tendered to the agency two checks totaling $15,500 and marked "Final Payment." Neither check was cashed, and the government sued Bloom for $480,000, the value of the assistance provided. Bloom claimed that by tendering the checks to the agency, his liability had been discharged by an accord and satisfaction. Decide. [*United States v Bloom*, 112 F3d 200 (7th Cir)]
7. Dickson contracted to build a house for Moran. When it was approximately 25 percent to 40 percent completed, Moran would not let Dickson work any more because he was not following the building plans and specifications and there were many defects. Moran hired another contractor to correct the defects and finish the building. Dickson sued Moran for breach of contract, claiming that he had substantially performed the contract up to the point where he had been discharged. Was Dickson correct? [*Dickson v Moran*, 344 So 2d 102 (La App)]
8. A lessor leased a trailer park to a tenant. At the time, sewage was disposed of by a septic tank system that was not connected with the public sewage system. The tenant knew this, and the lease declared that the tenant had examined the premises and that the landlord made no representation or guarantee as to the condition of the premises. Some time thereafter, the septic tank system stopped working properly, and the county health department notified the tenant that he was required to connect the septic tank system with the public sewage system or else the department would close the trailer park. The tenant did not want to pay the additional cost involved in connecting with the public system. The tenant claimed that he was released from the lease and was entitled to a refund of the deposit that he had made. Was he correct? [*Glen R. Sewell Street Metal v Loverde*, 451 P2d 721 (Cal App)]
9. Oneal was a teacher employed by the Colton Consolidated School District. Because of a diabetic condition, his eyesight deteriorated so much that he offered to resign if he would be given pay for a specified number of "sick leave" days. The school district refused to do this and discharged Oneal for nonperformance of his contract. He appealed to remove the discharge from his record. Decide. What ethical values are involved? [*Oneal v Colton Consolidated School District*, 557 P2d 11 (Wash App)]
10. Northwest Construction, Inc., made a contract with the state of Washington for highway construction. Part of the work was turned over under a subcontract to Yakima Asphalt Paving Co. The contract required that any claim be asserted within 180 days. Yakima brought an action for damages after the expiration of 180 days. The defense was that the claim was too late. Yakima replied that the action was brought within the time allowed by the statute of limitations and that the contractual limitation of 180 days was therefore not binding. Was Yakima correct?
11. The Metropolitan Park District of Tacoma gave Griffith a concession to run the district's parks. The agreement gave the right to occupy the parks and use any improvements found therein. The district later wished to set this agreement aside because it was not making sufficient money from the transaction. While it was seeking to set the agreement aside, a boathouse and a gift shop in one of the parks were destroyed by fire. The district then claimed that the concession contract with Griffith was discharged by impossibility of performance. Was it correct? [*Metropolitan Park District of Tacoma v Griffith*, 723 P2d 1093 (Wash)]
12. Suburban Power Piping Corp., under contract to construct a building for LTV Steel Corp., made a subcontract with Power & Pollution Services, Inc., to do some of the work. The subcontract provided that the subcontractor would be paid when the owner (LTV) paid the contractor. LTV went into bankruptcy before making the full payment to the contractor, who then refused to pay the subcontractor on the ground that the "pay-when-paid" provision of the subcontract made payment by the owner a condition precedent to the obligation of the contractor to pay the subcontractor. Was the contractor correct? [*Power & Pollution Services, Inc. v Suburban Power Piping Corp.*, 598 NE2d 69 (Ohio App)]
13. Ellen borrowed money from Farmers' Bank. As evidence of the loan, she signed a promissory note by which she promised to pay to the bank in installments the amount of the loan together with interest and administrative costs. She was unable to make the payments on the scheduled dates. She and the bank then executed a new

agreement that gave her a longer period of time for making the payments. However, after two months, she was unable to pay on this new schedule. The bank then brought suit against her under the terms of the original agreement. She raised the defense that the original agreement had been discharged by the execution of the second agreement and could not be sued on. Decide.

14. Acme Hydraulic Press Co. manufactured large presses and sold them throughout the United States. The agreement-of-sale contract that Acme executed with its customers specified that they could make no claim for breach of contract unless notice of the breach was given within 10 days after the delivery of a press in question to the buyer and that no lawsuit could thereafter be brought if notice had not been given. Was this time limitation valid?

15. New Beginnings provides rehabilitation services for alcohol and drug abuse to both adults and adolescents. New Beginnings entered into negotiation with Adbar for the lease of a building in the city of St. Louis, and subsequently entered into a three-year lease. The total rent due for the three-year term was $273,000. After the lease was executed, the city denied an occupancy permit because Alderman Bosley and residents testified at a hearing in vigorous opposition to the presence of New Beginnings in the neighborhood. A court ordered the permit issued. Alderman Bosley thereafter contacted the chair of the state's appointment committee and asked her to pull the agency's funding. He received no commitment from her on this matter. After a meeting with the state director of Alcohol and Drug Abuse where it was asserted that the director said the funding would be pulled if New Beginnings moved into the Adbar location, New Beginnings's board decided not to occupy the building. Adbar brought suit for breach of the lease, and New Beginnings asserted it was excused from performance because of commercial impracticability and frustration of purpose. Do you believe the doctrine of commercial impracticability should be limited in its application so as to preserve the certainty of contracts? What rule of law applies to this case? Decide. [*Adbar v New Beginnings*, 103 SW2d 799 (Mo App)]

CPA Questions

1. Parc hired Glaze to remodel and furnish an office suite. Glaze submitted plans that Parc approved. After completing all the necessary construction and painting, Glaze purchased minor accessories that Parc rejected because they did not conform to the plans. Parc refused to allow Glaze to complete the project and refused to pay Glaze any part of the contract price. Glaze sued for the value of the work performed. Which of the following statements is correct?
   a. Glaze will lose because Glaze breached the contract by not completing performance.
   b. Glaze will win because Glaze substantially performed and Parc prevented complete performance.
   c. Glaze will lose because Glaze materially breached the contract by buying the accessories.
   d. Glaze will win because Parc committed anticipatory breach.

2. Ordinarily, in an action for breach of a construction contract, the statute of limitations time period would be computed from the date the:
   a. contract is negotiated.
   b. contract is breached.
   c. contract is begun.
   d. contract is signed.

3. Which of the following will release all original parties to a contract but will maintain a contractual relationship?

	Novation	*Substituted contract*
a.	Yes	Yes
b.	Yes	No
c.	No	Yes
d.	No	No

BREACH OF CONTRACT AND REMEDIES

CHAPTER (20)

LEARNING OBJECTIVES

After studying this chapter, you should be able to

LO.1 List and define the kinds of damages that may be recovered when a contract is broken

LO.2 Describe the requirement of mitigation of damages

LO.3 State when liquidated damages clauses are valid

LO.4 State when liability-limiting clauses are valid

LO.5 State when a breach of contract is waived

LO.6 List the steps that may be used to prevent a waiver of breach of contract

What can be done when a contract is broken?

A. What Constitutes a Breach of Contract?

The question of remedies does not become important until it is first determined that a contract has been violated or breached.

1. Definition of Breach

A **breach** is the failure to act or perform in the manner called for by the contract. When the contract calls for performance, such as painting an owner's home, the failure to paint or to paint properly is a *breach of contract*. If the contract calls for a creditor's forbearance, the creditor's action in bringing a lawsuit is a breach of the contract.

2. Anticipatory Breach

When the contract calls for performance, a party may make it clear before the time for performance arrives that the contract will not be performed. This is referred to as an **anticipatory breach**.

(a) Anticipatory Repudiation

When a party expressly declares that performance will not be made when required, this declaration is called an **anticipatory repudiation** of the contract. To constitute such a repudiation, there must be a clear, absolute, unequivocal refusal to perform the contract according to its terms. **For Example,** Procter & Gamble (P&G) sought payment on four letters of credit issued by a Serbian bank, Investbanka. P&G presented two letters by June 8, prior to their expiration dates, with the necessary documentation for payment to Beogradska Bank New York, Investbanka's New York agent. A June 11 letter from Beogradska Bank broadly and unequivocally stated that the bank would not pay the letters of credit. Two additional letters of credit totaling $20,000 issued by Investbanka that expired by June 30 were not thereafter submitted to the New York agent bank by P&G. However, a court found that the bank had anticipatorily breached its obligations under those letters of credit by its broad renouncements in the June 11 letter, and judgments were rendered in favor of P&G.[1]

The *Tips* case deals with the issue of anticipatory repudiation and damages.

TIPS V HARTLAND DEVELOPERS, INC., 961 SW2D 618 (TEX APP 1998)

SPLITTING TIPS—CONTRACT PRICE LESS COST OF COMPLETION

In 1985, Hartland Developers, Inc., agreed to build an airplane hangar for Robert Tips of San Antonio for $300,000, payable in three installments of $100,000, with the final payment due upon the completion of the building and the issuance of a certificate of completion by the engineer representing Tips. The evidence shows that Tips's representative Mr. Lavelle instructed Hartland to cease work on the building because Tips could no longer afford to make payments. Hartland ceased work as instructed before the completion of the building, having been paid $200,000 at that time. He sued Tips for breach of contract. On May 6, 1996, the trial court allowed Hartland the amount owing on the contract, $100,000, less the cost of completing the building according to the contract, $65,000, plus attorneys' fees and prejudgment and postjudgment interest. Tips appealed.

Judicial Opinion

HARDBERGER, C. J. . . .

Substantial Performance

Tips claims that the evidence is legally or factually insufficient to support the trial court's finding that Hartland had substantially performed under the agreement. . . .

We agree with Tips that Hartland had not substantially performed under the contract. However, we find this point irrelevant to the resolution of this case. Substantial performance is a doctrine that allows *breaching* parties who have substantially completed their obligations to recover on a contract. WHITE & SUMMERS, CONTRACTS § 11–18(b) (3rd ed 1987). Hartland was not a breaching party.

[1] *Procter & Gamble v Investbanka*, 2000 US Dist LEXIS 5636 (SDNY 2000).

A contractor can recover on a contract when the failure to substantially perform is the fault of the other party. A party injured by the anticipatory breach of another may elect to sue for damages under the contract, . . . (if owner repudiates construction contract, contractor may sue in damages or for restitution); *Taylor Pub. Co. v Systems Marketing Inc.* 686 S.W.2d 213, 217 (when party obligated to make fixed payment absolutely repudiates the agreement, the obligee is entitled to recover [in an] action for damages and receive the present value of the payments payable under the agreement).

The trial judge based his damage assessment on anticipatory repudiation of contract. The evidence that Tips's representative, Lavelle, instructed Hartland to cease work on the project because Tips no longer could afford to make payments was sufficient to support this finding. *See Tennessee Gas Pipeline Co. v Lenape Resources Corp.*, 870 S.W.2d 286, 302 (Tex App.—San Antonio 1993) (anticipatory repudiation occurs when a party repudiates a contract before time for performance), *aff'd in part, rev'd in part*, 925 S.W.2d 565 (Tex. 1996)

Offset Damages

Tips claims that the trial judge erred in not off-setting Hartland's award for its failure to provide electrical connections to the hangar. Tips also claims he should be compensated $11,000 for a temporary access ramp he was forced to construct in anticipation of a permanent ramp being installed. . . . [W]e find that the $65,000 offset for the construction of a permanent ramp is sufficient compensation for that deficiency. However, we agree with Tips that the damages award must be offset by the cost of providing electrical outlets to the hangar.

Tips is entitled to an offset for electrical connections under a breach of contract theory. Damages for breach of contract are the contract price, less, the cost of completion. *Sage Street Assoc. v Northdale Const. Co.*, 937 S.W.2d 425, 426 (Tex. 1996). The trial judge did not address in his findings of fact and conclusions of law whether the electrical connections were contemplated by the contract, but there was testimony at trial that they were, and electrical wiring is listed among Hartland's duties in the contract. A witness for Hartland admitted under cross examination that the work was part of the agreement and that it had not been completed. Tips testified that he had spent $23,000 to install connections. Hartland's damages should be further offset by this amount.

[Judgment affirmed as modified]

Questions

1. What facts did Hartland rely on to assert the anticipatory repudiation of the contract?
2. What is the measure of damages for a breach of a construction contract? Calculate what is owed Hartland excluding attorneys' fees and interest.
3. Why is prejudgment and postjudgment interest appropriate in a breach of contract lawsuit?

A refusal to perform a contract that is made before performance is required unless the other party to the contract does an act or makes a concession that is not required by the contract, is an anticipatory repudiation of the contract.[2]

A party making an anticipatory repudiation may retract or take back the repudiation if the other party has not changed position in reliance on the repudiation. However, if the other party has changed position, the party making the anticipatory repudiation

SPORTS & ENTERTAINMENT LAW

GET IT WHILE YOU CAN?

In 2000, the cast of *Friends*, one of the hottest shows on television, demanded a pay increase. The demand was made with a valid contract in place and near the time NBC was to announce its fall lineup. The six stars demanded $1,000,000 each per episode. NBC settled for $750,000 per star, up from the stars' $150,000 per episode figure renegotiated in 1998.

When stars seek to renegotiate contracts before their expiration, the network can replace

[2] *Chamberlain v Puckett Construction*, 921 P2d 1237 (Mont 1996).

SPORTS & ENTERTAINMENT LAW

continued

them if they fail to live up to their contracts, and it can enforce the standard contractual clause, which prohibits them from doing other television work until the expiration of their contracts. Recasting six stars for a highly successful show would not be feasible. To offset the stars' bargaining power, NBC prepared a television promotion that would relabel the last show for that season as the "series finale" and announce "See how it all ends on *Friends.*" The cast were informed of NBC's threat to end the series in this manner. Renegotiations quickly ensued and led to the $750,000 agreement. Two years later the six stars obtained their goal of $1 million per episode paychecks. Was it ethical for the stars to threaten to strike just before the fall lineup announcements? When Jay Leno was asked about the tactics of the *Friends* stars, he responded, "You have to get what you can while you can in this business." Is Mr. Leno right? Is such an attitude ethical? When the new agreement was reached, was there a mutual rescission of the existing contract and the substitution of a new contract, or did the new contract fail for lack of consideration?

cannot retract it. **For Example,** if a buyer makes another purchase when the seller declares that the seller will not perform the contract, the buyer has acted in reliance on the seller's repudiation. The seller will therefore not be allowed to retract the repudiation.

(b) Anticipatory Repudiation by Conduct

The anticipatory repudiation may be expressed by conduct that makes it impossible for the repudiating party to perform subsequently. To illustrate, there is a repudiation by conduct if a farmer makes a contract to sell an identified quantity of potatoes nearly equivalent to his entire crop and then sells and delivers them to another buyer before the date specified for the delivery to the first buyer.

B. Waiver of Breach

The breach of a contract may have no importance because the other party to the contract waives the breach.

3. Cure of Breach by Waiver

The fact that one party has broken a contract does not necessarily mean that there will be a lawsuit or a forfeiture of the contract. For practical business reasons, one party may be willing to ignore or waive the breach. When it is established that there has been a **waiver** of a breach, the party waiving the breach cannot take any action on the theory that the contract was broken. The waiver, in effect, erases the past breach. The contract continues as though the breach had not existed.

The waiver may be express or it may be implied from the continued recognition of the existence of the contract by the aggrieved party.[3] When the conduct of a party shows an intent to give up a right, it waives that right.[4]

4. Existence and Scope of Waiver

It is a question of fact whether there has been a waiver.

(a) Existence of Waiver

A party may express or declare that the breach of a contract is waived. A waiver of a breach is more often the result of an express forgiving of a breach. Thus, a party allowing the other party to continue performance without objecting that the performance is not satisfactory waives the right to raise that objection when sued for payment by the performing party.

For Example, a contract promising to sell back a parcel of commercial property to Jackson required Jackson to make a $500 payment to Massey's attorney on the first of the month for five months,

[3] *Huger v Morrison,* 2000 La App LEXIS 241.

[4] *Stronghaven Inc. v Ingram,* 555 SE2d 49 (Ga App 2001).

December through April. It was clearly understood that the payments would be "on time without fail." Jackson made the December payment on time. New Year's Day, a holiday, fell on a Friday, and Jackson made the second payment on January 4. He made $500 payments on February 1, March 1, and March 31, respectively, and the payments were accepted and a receipt issued on each occasion. However, Massey refused to convey title back to Jackson because "the January 4 payment was untimely and the parties' agreement had been breached." The court held that the doctrine of waiver applied due to Massey's acceptance of the late payment and the three subsequent payments without objection, and the court declared that Jackson was entitled to possession of the land.[5]

(b) Scope of Waiver

The waiver of a breach of contract extends only to the matter waived. It does not show any intent to ignore other provisions of the contract.

(c) Antimodification Clause

Modern contracts commonly specify that the terms of a contract shall not be deemed modified by waiver as to any breaches. This means that the original contract remains as agreed to. Either party may therefore return to, and insist on, compliance with the original contract.

In the example involving Jackson and Massey's contract, the trial court reviewed the contract to see whether the court was restricted by the contract from applying the waiver. It concluded: "In this case, the parties' contract did not contain any terms that could prevent the application of the doctrine of waiver to the acceptance of late payments."[6]

5. Reservation of Rights

It may be that a party is willing to accept a defective performance but does not wish to surrender any claim for damages for the breach. **For Example,** Midwest Utilities, Inc., accepted 20 carloads of Powder River Basin coal (sometimes called *Western coal*) from its supplier, Maney Enterprises, because its power plants were in short supply of coal. Midwest's requirements contract with Maney called for Appalachian coal, a low-sulfur, highly efficient fuel, which is sold at a premium price per ton. Midwest, in accepting the tendered performance with a **reservation of rights**, gave notice to Maney that it reserved all rights to pursue damages for the tender of a nonconforming shipment.

C. Remedies for Breach of Contract

One or more **remedies** may be available to the innocent party in the case of a breach of contract. There is also the possibility that arbitration or a streamlined out-of-court alternative dispute resolution procedure is available or required for determining the rights of the parties.

6. Remedies upon Anticipatory Repudiation

When an anticipatory repudiation of a contract occurs, the aggrieved person has several options. He may (1) do nothing beyond stating that performance at the proper time will be required, (2) regard the contract as having been definitively broken and bring a lawsuit against the repudiating party without waiting to see whether there will be proper performance when the performance date arrives, or (3) regard the repudiation as an offer to cancel the contract. This offer can be accepted or rejected. If accepted, there is a discharge of the original contract by the subsequent cancellation agreement of the parties.

7. Remedies in General and the Measure of Damages

Courts provide a *quasi-contractual* or *restitution* remedy in which a contract is unenforceable because it lacked definite and certain terms or was not in compliance with the statute of frauds, yet one of the parties performed services for the other. The measure of damages in these and other quasi-contract cases is the reasonable value of the services performed, not an amount derived from the defective contract.

In cases when a person retains money or when a contemplated contract is not properly formed and no work is performed, the party retaining the benefit is obligated to make restitution to the person conferring the benefit. **For Example,** Kramer Associates,

[5] *Massey v Jackson*, 726 So 2d 656 (Ala Civ App 1998).
[6] *Id.*, at 659.

FIGURE 20-1 What Follows the Breach

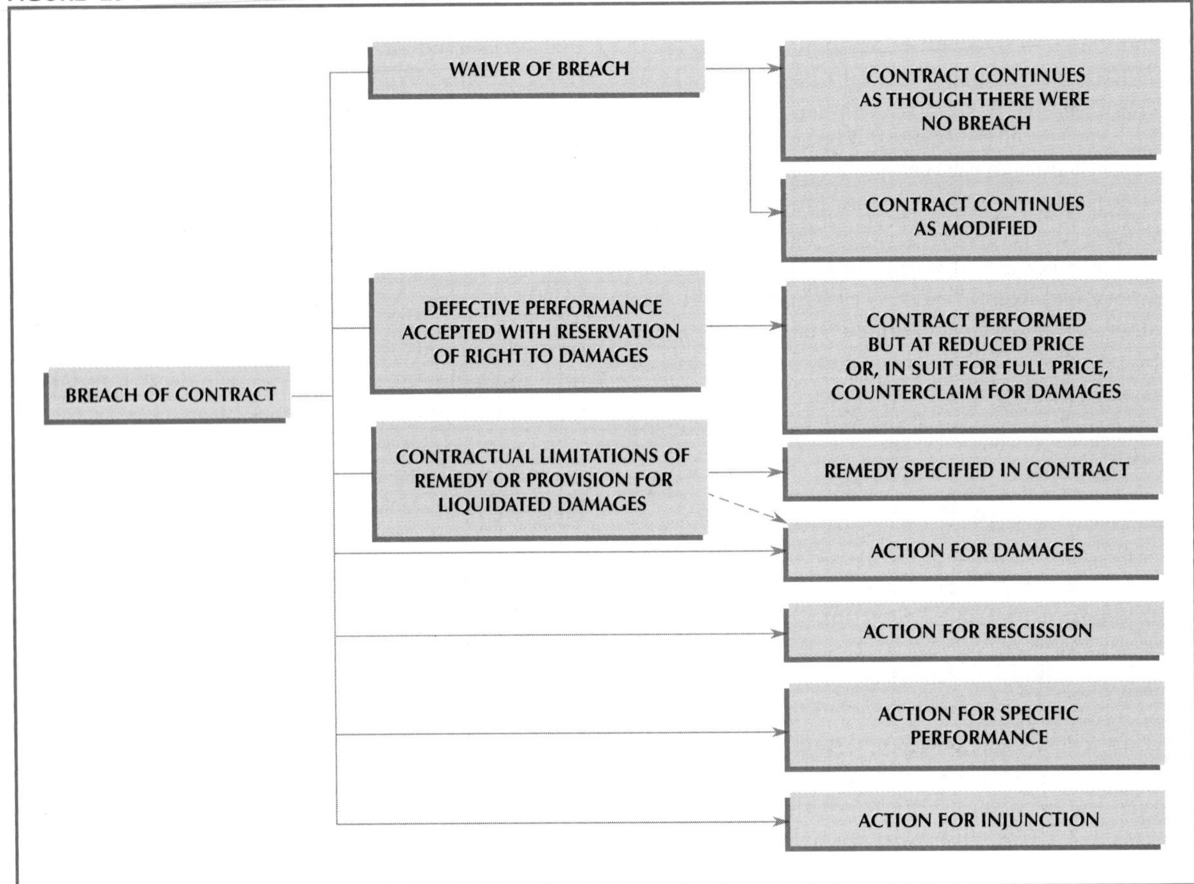

Inc. (KAI), a Washington D.C., consulting firm, accepted $75,000 from a Ghana-based corporation, Ikam, Ltd., to secure financing for a Ghana development project. No contract was ever executed, and KAI did virtually nothing to secure financing for the project. Restitution of the $75,000 was required.[7]

When there is a breach of contract, the regular remedy is an award of *monetary damages*. In unusual circumstances, when monetary damages are inadequate, the injured party may obtain **specific performance,** whereby the court will order that the contract terms be carried out.

The measure of monetary damages when there has been a breach of contract is the sum of money that will place the injured party in the same position that would have been attained if the contract had been performed.[8] That is, the injured party will be given the *benefit of the bargain* by the court. As seen in the *Tips v Hartland Developers* case, the nonbreaching party, Hartland, was awarded the contract price less the cost of completion of the project, which had the effect of giving the builder the benefit of the bargain.

8. Monetary Damages

Monetary damages are commonly classified as compensatory damages, nominal damages, and punitive damages. **Compensatory damages** compensate the injured party for the damages incurred as a result of the breach of contract. Compensatory damages have two branches, *direct damages* and *consequential* (or *special*) *damages.*

Injured parties that do not sustain an actual loss because of a breach of contract are entitled to a judgment of a small sum of money such as $1; these damages are called **nominal damages.**

[7] *Kramer Associates, Inc. v IKAM, Ltd.*, 888 A2d 247 (DC 2005).
[8] *Leingang v City of Mandan Weed Board*, 468 NW2d 397 (ND 1991).

Damages in excess of actual loss, imposed for the purpose of punishing or making an example of the defendant, are known as **punitive damages** or *exemplary damages*. In contract actions, punitive damages are not ordinarily awarded.[9]

(a) Direct and Consequential Damages

Direct damages (sometimes called *general damages*) are those that naturally flow from the given type of breach of contract involved and include *incidental damages*, which are extra expenditures made by the injured party to rectify the breach or mitigate damages. **Consequential damages** (sometimes called *special damages*) are those that do not necessarily flow from the type of breach of contract involved but happen to do so in a particular case as a result of the injured party's particular circumstances.

Consequential damages may be recovered only if it was reasonably foreseeable to the defendant that the kind of loss in question could be sustained by the nonbreaching party if the contract were broken.

For Example, in early August, Spencer Adams ordered a four-wheel-drive GMC truck with a rear-end hydraulic lift for use on his Aroostook County, Maine, potato farm. The contract price was $58,500. He told Brad Jones, the owner of the dealership, that he had to have the truck by Labor Day so he could use it to bring in his crop from the fields before the first frost, and Brad nodded that he understood. The truck did not arrive by Labor Day as promised in the written contract. After a two-week period of gradually escalating recriminations with the dealership, Adams obtained the same model GMC truck at a dealership 40 minutes away in Houlton but at the cost of $60,500. He was also able to rent a similar truck from the Houlton dealer for $250 for the day while the new truck was being prepared. Farmhands had used other means of harvesting, but because of the lack of the truck, their work was set back by five days. As a result of the delays, 30 percent of the crop was still in the fields when the first frost came, causing damages expertly estimated at $320,000. The *direct damages* for the breach of contract in this case would be the difference between the contract price for the truck of $58,500 and the market price of $60,500, or $2,000. These direct damages naturally flow from the breach of contract for the purchase of a truck. Also, the *incidental damages* of $250 for the truck rental are recoverable direct damages. The $320,000 loss of the potato crop was a consequence of not having the truck, and this sum is arguably recoverable by Spencer Adams as *consequential or special damages*. Adams notified Brad Jones of the reason he needed to have the truck by Labor Day, and it should have been reasonably foreseeable to Jones that loss of a portion of the crop could occur if the truck contract was breached. However, because of Spencer Adams's obligation to mitigate damages (as discussed below), it is unlikely that Adams will recover the full consequential damages. Truck rental availability or the lack of availability within the rural area, alternative tractor usage, and the actual harvesting methods used by Adams all relate to the mitigation issue to be resolved by the jury.

(b) Mitigation of Damages

The injured party is under the duty to mitigate damages if reasonably possible.[10] In other words, damages must not be permitted to increase if an increase can be prevented by reasonable efforts. This means that the injured party must generally stop any performance under the contract to avoid running up a larger bill. The duty to mitigate damages may require an injured party to buy or rent elsewhere the goods that the wrongdoer was obligated to deliver under the contract. In the case of breach of an employment contract by the employer, the employee is required to seek other similar employment. The wages earned from other employment must be deducted from the damages claimed. The discharged employee, however, is not required to take employment of less-than-comparable work.

(1) Effect of Failure to Mitigate Damages. The effect of the requirement of mitigating damages is to limit recovery by the nonbreaching party to the damages that would have been sustained had this party mitigated the damages where it was possible to do so. **For Example,** self-described "sports nut" Gary Baker signed up for a three-year club-seat "package" that entitled him and a companion to tickets for 41 Boston Bruins hockey games and 41 Boston Celtics basketball games at the New Boston Garden Corporation's Fleet Center for approximately $18,000 per year. After one year, Baker stopped

[9] A party who is not awarded actual damages but wins nominal damages can be considered a "prevailing party" for the purposes of a contractual attorney fee-shifting provision. *Brock v King*, 629 SE2d 829 (Ga App 2006).

[10] *West Pinal Family Health Center, Inc. v McBride*, 785 P2d 66 (Ariz 1989).

paying for the tickets, thinking that he would simply lose his $5,000 security deposit. Baker, a CPA, tried to work out a compromise settlement to no avail. New Boston sued Baker for breach of contract, seeking the balance due on the tickets of $34,866. At trial, Baker argued to the jury that although he had breached his contract, New Boston had an obligation to mitigate damages, for example, by treating his empty seats and those of others in the same situation as "rush seats" shortly before game time and selling them at a discount. New Boston argued that just as a used luxury car cannot be returned for a refund, a season ticket cannot be canceled without consequences. The jury accepted Baker's position on mitigation and reduced the amount owed New Boston by $21,176 to $13,690.[11]

9. Rescission

When one party commits a material breach of the contract, the other party may rescind the contract; if the party in default objects, the aggrieved party may bring an action for rescission. A breach is *material* when it is so substantial that it defeats the object of the parties in making the contract.[12]

An injured party who rescinds a contract after having performed services may recover the reasonable value of the performance rendered under restitutionary or quasi-contractual damages. Money paid by the injured party may also be recovered. The purpose is to restore the injured party to the position occupied before the contract was made. However, the party seeking restitutionary damages must also return what this party has received from the party in default.

For Example, Pedro Morena purchased real estate from Jason Alexander after Alexander had assured him that the property did not have a flooding problem. In fact, the property regularly flooded after ordinary rainstorms. Morena was entitled to the return of the purchase price and payment for the reasonable value of the improvements he made to the property. Alexander was entitled to a setoff for the reasonable rental value of the property during the time Morena was in possession of this property.

10. Action for Specific Performance

Under special circumstances, an injured party may obtain the equitable remedy of specific performance, which compels the other party to carry out the terms of a contract. Specific performance is ordinarily granted only if the subject matter of the contract is "unique," thereby making an award of money damages an inadequate remedy. Contracts for the purchase of land will be specifically enforced.[13]

Specific performance of a contract to sell personal property can be obtained only if the article is of unusual age, beauty, unique history, or other distinction. **For Example,** Maurice owned a rare Revolutionary War musket that he agreed to sell to Herb. Maurice then changed his mind because of the uniqueness of the musket. Herb can sue and win, requesting the remedy of specific performance of the contract because of the unique nature of the goods.

When the damages sustained by the plaintiff can be measured in monetary terms, specific performance will be refused. Consequently, a contract to sell a television station will not be specifically enforced when the buyer had made a contract to resell the station to a third person; the damages caused by the breach of the first contract would be the loss sustained by being unable to make the resale, and such damages would be adequate compensation to the original buyer.[14]

Ordinarily, contracts for the performance of personal services are not specifically ordered. This is because of the difficulty of supervision by the court and the restriction of the U.S. Constitution's Thirteenth Amendment prohibiting involuntary servitude except as criminal punishment.

11. Action for an Injunction

When a breach of contract consists of doing an act prohibited by the contract, a possible remedy is an **injunction** against doing the act. **For Example,** when the obligation in an employee's contract is to refrain from competing after resigning from the company and the obligation is broken by competing, a court may order or enjoin the former employee to stop competing. Similarly, when a vocalist breaks a contract to record exclusively for a particular label,

[11] Sacha Pfeiffer, "Disenchanted Fan Scores Win in Ticket Fight," *Boston Globe*, August 28, 1999, B-4.

[12] *Greentree Properties, Inc. v Kissee*, 92 SW3d 289 (Mo App 2003).

[13] *English v Muller*, 514 SE2d 195 (Ga 1999).

[14] *Miller v LeSea Broadcasting, Inc.*, 87 F3d 224 (7th Cir 1996).

she may be enjoined from recording for any other company. This may have the indirect effect of compelling the vocalist to record for the plaintiff.

12. Reformation of Contract by a Court

At times, a written contract does not correctly state the agreement already made by the parties. When this occurs, either party may seek to have the court reform or correct the writing to state the agreement actually made.

A party seeking reformation of a contract must clearly prove both the grounds for reformation and what the agreement actually was. This burden is particularly great when the contract to be reformed is written. This is so because the general rule is that parties are presumed to have read their written contracts and to have intended to be bound by them when they signed the contracts.

When a unilateral mistake is made and it is of such consequence that enforcing the contract according to its terms would be unreasonable, a court may reform the contract to correct the mistake.

D. Contract Provisions Affecting Remedies and Damages

The contract of the parties may contain provisions that affect the remedies available or the recovery of damages.

13. Limitation of Remedies

The contract of the parties may limit the remedies of the aggrieved parties. **For Example,** the contract may give one party the right to repair or replace a defective item sold or to refund the contract price. The contract may require both parties to submit any dispute to arbitration or another streamlined out-of-court dispute resolution procedure.

14. Liquidated Damages

The parties may stipulate in their contract that a certain amount should be paid in case of a breach. This amount is known as liquidated damages and may be variously measured by the parties. When delay is possible, **liquidated damages** may be a fixed sum, such as $1,000 for each day of delay. When there is a total default, damages may be a percentage of the contract price or the amount of the down payment.

(a) Validity

To be **valid,** a **liquidated damages clause** must satisfy two requirements: (1) The situation must be one in which it is difficult or impossible to determine the actual damages and (2) the amount specified must not be excessive when compared with the probable damages that would be sustained.[15] The validity of a liquidated damages clause is determined on the basis of the facts existing when the clause was agreed to.

(b) Effect

When a liquidated damages clause is held valid, the injured party cannot collect more than the amount specified by the clause. The defaulting party is bound to pay such damages once the fact is established that there has been a default. The injured party is not required to make any proof as to damages sustained, and the defendant is not permitted to show that the damages were not as great as the liquidated sum.

(c) Invalid Clauses

If the liquidated damages clause calls for the payment of a sum that is clearly unreasonably large and unrelated to the possible actual damages that might be sustained, the clause will be held to be void as a penalty. **For Example,** a settlement agreement between 27 plaintiffs seeking recovery for injuries resulting from faulty breast implants and the implants' manufacturer, Dow Corning Corp., called for seven $200,000 payments to each plaintiff. The agreement also called for a $100 per day payment to each plaintiff for any time when the payments were late as "liquidated damages." The court held that the $100 per day figure was not a reasonable estimate of anticipated damages. Rather, it was an unenforceable "penalty" provision.[16]

When a liquidated damages clause is held invalid, the effect is merely to erase the clause from the

[15] *Southeast Alaska Construction Co. v Alaska*, 791 P2d 339 (Alaska 1990).

[16] *Bear Stearns v Dow Corning Corp.*, 419 F3d 543 (6th Cir 2005).

contract, and the injured party may proceed to recover damages for breach of the contract. Instead of recovering the liquidated damages amount, the injured party will recover whatever actual damages he can prove. **For Example,** JRC Trading Corp (JRC) bought computer software and hardware from Progressive Data Systems (PDS) for $167,935, which it paid in full, to track the movement of its trucks with inventory and to process transactions. The purchase agreement also called for a $7,500 per year licensing fee for an 18-year period, and it stated that in the event of default, PDS could "accelerate and declare all obligations of Customer as a liquidated sum." A dispute arose between the parties, and when the case was litigated, the only actual contract charges owed PDS were license fees of $7,500 for two years. The application of the liquidated damages clause would yield an additional $120,000 cash for PDS for the future fees for 16 years without any reduction for expenses or the present cash value for the not-yet-earned fees. Actual damages were clearly ascertainable and not difficult to determine, and the amount sought was excessive. The court deemed the liquidated damages clause an unenforceable penalty and PDS was relegated to recovering its actual contractual damages.[17]

15. Limitation of Liability Clauses

A contract may contain a provision stating that one of the parties shall not be liable for damages in case of breach. Such a provision is called an **exculpatory clause,** or when a monetary limit to damages for breach of contract is set forth in the contract, it may be referred to as a **limitation-of-liability clause**.

(a) Content and Construction

If an exculpatory clause or a limitation-of-liability clause limits liability for damages caused only by negligent conduct, liability is neither excluded nor limited if the conduct alleged is found to be grossly negligent, willful, or wanton. **For Example,** Security Guards Inc. (SGI) provided services to Dana Corporation, a truck frame manufacturer under a contract that contained a limitation-of-liability clause capping losses at $50,000 per occurrence for damages "caused solely by the negligence" of SGI or its employees. When a critical alarm was activated by a fire in the paint shop at 5:39 P.M., the SGI guard on duty did not follow appropriate procedures, which delayed notification to the fire department for 15 minutes. Royal Indemnity Co., Dana's insurer, paid Dana $16,535,882 for the fire loss and sued SGI for $7 million, contending that the SGI guard's actions were grossly negligent and caused the plant to suffer increased damages. The court held that if SGI were to be found grossly negligent, the liability would not be limited to $50,000, and a jury could find damages far exceeding that amount.[18]

(b) Validity

As a general rule, experienced businesspersons are free to allocate liability in their contracts as they see fit. They have freedom to contract—even to make bad bargains or relinquish fundamental rights. However, courts in most states will not enforce a contract provision that *completely exonerates* a party from gross negligence or intentional acts.

(c) Releases

Release forms signed by participants in athletic and sporting events declaring that the sponsor, proprietor, or operator of the event shall not be liable for injuries sustained by participants because of its negligence are binding. **For Example,** when Merav Sharon sued the city of Newton for negligence as a result of an injury received while participating in a high school cheerleading practice, the city successfully raised a signed exculpatory release as a defense.[19] So also the exculpatory contract Nathan Henderson signed releasing a white-water rafting expedition operator from liability for its negligence barred Henderson's negligence claim against the operator for an injury suffered disembarking from the operator's bus.[20]

[17] *Jefferson Randolf Corporation v PDS*, 553 SE2d 304 (Ga App 2001).
[18] *Royal Indemnity Co. v Security Guards, Inc.*, 255 F Supp 2d 497 (ED Pa 2003).
[19] *Sharon v City of Newton*, 437 Mass 99 (2002).
[20] *Henderson v Quest Expeditions, Inc.*, 174 SW3d 730 (Tenn App 2005).

LAWFLIX

The Goodbye Girl (1977) (PG)

Richard Dreyfuss plays Elliott Garfield, a struggling Shakespearean actor who lands in New York with a sublease on an apartment still occupied by divorcee Marsha Mason and her daughter. The two work out living arrangements, split rent and food, and deal with the issue of whether Mason has any rights. Review all aspects of contracts as the characters discuss subleases, rent payment, living arrangements, and food costs.

For movie clips that illustrate business law concepts, see LawFlix at **http://wdvl.westbuslaw.com.**

Summary

When a party fails to perform a contract or performs improperly, the other contracting party may sue for damages caused by the breach. What may be recovered by the aggrieved person is stated in terms of being direct or consequential damages. Direct damages are those that ordinarily will result from the breach. Direct damages may be recovered on proof of causation and amount. Consequential damages can be recovered only if, in addition to proving causation and amount, it is shown that they were reasonably within the contemplation of the contracting parties as a probable result of a breach of the contract. The right to recover consequential damages is lost if the aggrieved party could reasonably have taken steps to avoid such damages. In other words, the aggrieved person has a duty to mitigate or reduce damages by reasonable means.

In any case, the damages recoverable for breach of contract may be limited to a specific amount by a liquidated damages clause. Damages may be canceled completely by a limitation-of-liability clause.

In a limited number of situations, an aggrieved party may bring an action for specific performance to compel the other contracting party to perform the acts called for by the contract. Specific performance by the seller is always obtainable for the breach of a contract to sell land or real estate on the theory that such property has a unique value. With respect to other contracts, specific performance will not be ordered unless it is shown that there was some unique element present so that the aggrieved person would suffer a damage that could not be compensated for by the payment of money damages.

The aggrieved person also has the option of rescinding the contract if (1) the breach has been made concerning a material term and (2) the aggrieved party returns everything to the way it was before the contract was made.

Although there has been a breach of the contract, the effect of this breach is nullified if the aggrieved person by word or conduct waives the right to object to the breach. Conversely, an aggrieved party may accept a defective performance without thereby waiving a claim for breach if the party makes a reservation of rights. A reservation of rights can be made by stating that the defective performance is accepted "without prejudice," "under protest," or "with reservation of rights."

Questions and Case Problems

1. The Forsyth School District contracted with Textor Construction, Inc., to build certain additions and alter school facilities, including the grading of a future softball field. Under the contract, the work was to be completed by August 1. Various delays occurred at the outset of the project attributable to the school district, and the architect's representative on the job, Mr. Hamilton, told Textor's vice president, William Textor, not to be concerned about a clause in the contract of $250 per day liquidated damages for failure to complete the job by August 1. Textor sued the school district for breach of contract regarding payment for the grading of the softball field, and the District counterclaimed for liquidated damages for 84 days at $250 per day for failure to complete the project by the August 1 date. What legal basis exists for Textor to defend against the counterclaim for failure to complete the job on time? Was it ethical for the school district to bring this counterclaim based on the facts before you? [*Textor Construction, Inc. v Forsyth R-III School District*, 60 SW3d 692 (Mo App)]
2. Anthony makes a contract to sell a rare painting to Laura for $100,000. The written contract specifies that if Anthony should fail to perform the contract, he will pay Laura $5,000 as liquidated damages. Anthony fails to deliver the painting and is sued by Laura for $5,000. Can she recover this amount?

3. Rogers made a contract with Salisbury Brick Corp. that allowed it to remove earth and sand from land he owned. The contract ran for four years with provision to renew it for additional four-year terms up to a total of 96 years. The contract provided for compensation to Rogers based on the amount of earth and sand removed. By an unintentional mistake, Salisbury underpaid Rogers the amount of $863 for the months of November and December 1986. Salisbury offered this amount to Rogers, but he refused to accept it and claimed that he had been underpaid in other months. Rogers claimed that he was entitled to rescind the contract. Was he correct? [*Rogers v Salisbury Brick Corp.*, 882 SE2d 915 (SC)]
4. A contractor departed from the specifications at a number of points in a contract to build a house. The cost to put the house in the condition called for by the contract was approximately $14,000. The contractor was sued for $50,000 for breach of contract and emotional disturbance caused by the breach. Decide.
5. Protein Blenders, Inc., made a contract with Gingerich to buy from him the shares of stock of a small corporation. When the buyer refused to take and pay for the stock, Gingerich sued for specific performance of the contract on the ground that the value of the stock was unknown and could not be readily ascertained because it was not sold on the general market. Was he entitled to specific performance? [*Gingerich v Protein Blenders, Inc.*, 95 NW2d 522 (Iowa)]
6. The buyer of real estate made a down payment. The contract stated that the buyer would be liable for damages in an amount equal to the down payment if the buyer broke the contract. The buyer refused to go through with the contract and demanded his down payment back. The seller refused to return it and claimed that he was entitled to additional damages from the buyer because the damages that he had suffered were more than the amount of the down payment. Decide. [*Waters v Key Colony East, Inc.*, 345 So 2d 367 (Fla App)]
7. Kuznicki made a contract for the installation of a fire detection system by Security Safety Corp. for $498. The contract was made one night and canceled at 9:00 the next morning. Security then claimed one-third of the purchase price from Kuznicki by virtue of a provision in the contract that "in the event of cancellation of this agreement . . . the owner agrees to pay 33⅓ percent of the contract price, as liquidated damages." Was Security Safety entitled to recover the amount claimed? [*Security Safety Corp. v Kuznicki*, 213 NE2d 866 (Mass)]
8. Health United Family Care, Inc., and its principals Maldonado, Romero, and Benitez entered into a five-year lease of office space with GFIC Management, Inc., to operate a medical facility. Rent was set at $4,041 per month. As part of the lease, GFIC agreed to expend $17,000 of its funds to renovate the leased space for use as a medical facility, to be finished by October 28 so that the medical facility could open on November 1. The parties agreed in the lease that if the construction was not finished on time, no rent would be due until actual possession. On October 26, Benitez called GFIC President Moses Grad and told him to stop construction. Grad met with Benitez and Romero soon thereafter, and they explained their problem as follows:

Grad: What happened?

Benitez and Romero [B+R]: The medical board came down hard on us O.K. The problem is that we have one doctor, one doctor, and he is covering (mumble) right now he is under investigation. As a matter of fact, they did investigate us, and right now they are coming down hard on us, and we are under a lawsuit. O.K., and he is ready to lose his license, and they will not give you another building to open O.K. I wish we could put this on hold, and right now if we get into this we cannot open.

[B+R]: We cannot open; we have no license to open.

Grad: What's the problem with getting another doctor? . . .

[B+R]: Right now no doctors want to touch us; we are under investigation.

Grad: I see.

[B+R]: Nobody wants to touch us at all, . . . but right now our attorney has instructed us to get out of it. You know he needs to get into it, but we don't want him because it's going to cost us more money, O.K. We would get some kind of agreement with you to see how we get out of it.

Grad: Is there anything I can do as the landlord of the premises to make you stay in the building?

[B+R]: No, because they won't give us permission to open.

Grad: Is there anything I can do for you? The only solution at this time that you see is to cancel the contract, this is the only. . . .

[B+R]: I think that's what our attorney instructed us to do, is to get out of it because right now our name is not the most popular name out there with the medical board, they will nail us, they are out to get us. . . . I think we should put a hold on the construction right now; that's what we should do.

Grad stopped the construction after this discourse on October 28. Subsequently, Ernesto Maldonado talked with Grad about settling obligations under the lease and stated that if the construction were completed by Grad, he would attempt to find a doctor. At that point, Grad was seeking one year's rent as damages for breach of the lease. Brad never restarted the construction, and Health United never took possession of the premises. GFIC sued Health United for breach of the lease contract. Health United denies the breach of the lease, contending that GFIC failed to perform a condition precedent by not completing the construction necessary to occupy the space. What legal theory would you rely on to respond to Health United's position that GFIC failed to perform the condition precedent? Do you believe Benitez and Romero were prudent in not utilizing their attorney to facilitate an amicable settlement of the contractual obligations? How would you decide this case? [*Health United Family Care, Inc. v GFIC Management, Inc.*, 2001 TexApp LEXIS]

9. Melodee Lane Lingerie Co. was a tenant in a building that was protected against fire by a sprinkler and alarm system maintained by the American District Telegraph Co. (ADT). Because of the latter's fault, the controls on the system were defective and allowed the discharge of water into the building, which damaged Melodee's property. When Melodee sued ADT, its defense was that its service contract limited its liability to 10 percent of the annual service charge made to the customer. Was this limitation valid? [*Melodee Lane Lingerie Co. v American District Telegraph Co.*, 218 NE2d 661 (NY)]

10. In May, a homeowner made a contract with a roofer to make repairs to her house by July 1. The roofer never came to repair the roof, and heavy rains in the fall damaged the interior of the house. The homeowner sued the roofer for breach of contract and claimed damages for the harm done to the interior of the house. Is the homeowner entitled to recover such damages?

11. Ken Sulejmanagic, aged 19, signed up for a course in scuba diving taught by Madison at the YMCA. Before the instruction began, Ken was required to sign a form releasing Madison and the YMCA from liability for any harm that might occur. At the end of the course, Madison, Ken, and another student went into deep water. After Ken made the final dive required by the course program, Madison left him alone in the water while he took the other student for a dive. When Madison returned, Ken could not be found, and it was later determined that he had drowned. Ken's parents sued Madison and the YMCA for negligence in the performance of the teaching contract. The defendants raised the defense that the release Ken signed shielded them from liability.
The plaintiffs claimed that the release was invalid. Who was correct? [*Madison v Superior Court*, 250 Cal Rptr 299 (Cal App)]

12. Wassenaar worked for Panos under a three-year contract stating that if the contract were terminated wrongfully by Panos before the end of the three years, he would pay as damages the salary for the remaining time that the contract had to run. After three months, Panos terminated the contract, and Wassenaar sued him for pay for the balance of the contract term. Panos claimed that this amount could not be recovered because the contract provision for the payment was a void penalty. Was this provision valid? [*Wassenaar v Panos*, 331 NW2d 357 (Wis)]

13. Soden, a contractor, made a contract to build a house for Clevert. The sales contract stated that "if either party defaults in the performance of this contract," that party would be liable to the other for attorney fees incurred in suing the defaulter. Soden was 61 days late in completing the contract, and some of the work was defective. In a suit by the buyer against the contractor, the contractor claimed that he was not liable for the buyer's attorney fees because he had made only a defective performance and because "default" in the phrase quoted meant "nonperformance of the contract." Was the contractor liable for the attorney fees? [*Clevert v Soden*, 400 SE2d 181 (Va)]

14. Protection Alarm Co. made a contract to provide burglar alarm security for Fretwell's home. The contract stated that the maximum liability of the alarm company was the actual loss sustained or $50, whichever was the lesser, and that this provision was agreed to "as liquidated damages and not as a penalty." When Fretwell's home was burglarized, he sued for the loss of approximately $12,000, claiming that the alarm company had been negligent. The alarm company asserted that its maximum liability was $50. Fretwell claimed that this was invalid because it bore no relationship to the loss that could have been foreseen when the contract was made or that in fact "had been sustained." Decide.

15. Shepherd-Will made a contract to sell Emma Cousar:

    5 acres of land adjoining property owned by the purchaser and this being formerly land of Shepherd-Will, Inc., located on north side of Highway 223. This 5 acres to be surveyed at earliest time possible at which time plat will be attached and serve as further description on property.

    Shepherd-Will owned only one 100-acre tract of land that adjoined Emma's property. This tract had a common boundary with her property of 1,140 feet. Shepherd-Will failed to perform this contract. Emma sued for specific performance of the contract. Decide. [*Cousar v Shepherd-Will, Inc.*, 387 SE2d 723 (SC App)]

CPA Questions

1. Master Mfg., Inc., contracted with Accur Computer Repair Corp. to maintain Master's computer system. Master's manufacturing process depends on its computer system operating properly at all times. A liquidated damages clause in the contract provided that Accur pay $1,000 to Master for each day that Accur was late responding to a service request. On January 12, Accur was notified that Master's computer system had failed.

Accur did not respond to Master's service request until January 15. If Master sues Accur under the liquidated damages provision of the contract, Master will

a. win, unless the liquidated damage provision is determined to be a penalty.

b. win, because under all circumstances liquidated damages provisions are enforceable.

c. lose, because Accur's breach was *not* material.

d. lose, because liquidated damage provisions violate public policy. (5/93, Law, #25)

2. Jones, CPA, entered into a signed contract with Foster Corp. to perform accounting and review services. If Jones repudiates the contract prior to the date performance is due to begin, which of the following is *not* correct?

a. Foster could successfully maintain an action for breach of contract after the date performance was due to begin.

b. Foster can obtain a judgment ordering Jones to perform.

c. Foster could successfully maintain an action for breach of contract prior to the date performance is due to begin.

d. Foster can obtain a judgment for the monetary damages it incurred as a result of the repudiation. (5/89, Law, #35)

3. Which of the following concepts affect(s) the amount of monetary damages recoverable by the nonbreaching party when a contract is breached?

	Forseeability of damages	*Mitigation of damages*
a.	Yes	Yes
b.	Yes	No
c.	No	Yes
d.	No	No

SALES AND LEASES OF GOODS

PERSONAL PROPERTY AND BAILMENTS

CHAPTER (21)

LEARNING OBJECTIVES

After studying this chapter, you should be able to

LO.1 Write a definition of personal property

LO.2 List and explain various types of gifts

LO.3 Identify the public policy reasons behind the law of escheat

LO.4 Identify the four forms of multiple ownership of personal property

LO.5 Describe how a bailment is created

LO.6 List and distinguish the various classifications of bailments

LO.7 Contrast the renting of space with the creation of a bailment

LO.8 Explain the standard of care a bailee is required to exercise over bailed property

LO.9 State the burden of proof when a bailor sues a bailee for damages to bailed property

What is personal property? Who owns it? How is it acquired? Think of personal property as all things of value other than real estate. Many instances arise in which the owner of personal property entrusts it to another—a person checks a coat at a restaurant or leaves a watch with a jeweler for repairs; or a company rents a car to a tourist for a weekend. The delivery of personal property to another under such circumstances is a bailment.

A. Personal Property

1. Personal Property in Context

In common usage, the term *property* refers to a piece of land or a thing or an object. As a legal concept, however, property also refers to the rights that an individual may possess in the piece of land or that thing or that object.[1] Property includes the rights of any person to possess, use, enjoy, and dispose of a thing or object of value. A right in a thing is property, without regard to whether this right is absolute or conditional, perfect or imperfect, legal or equitable.

Real property means land and things embedded in the land, such as oil tanks. It also includes things attached to the earth, such as buildings or trees, and rights in any of these things. **Personal property** is property that is movable or intangible, or rights in such things. As described in Chapter 10, rights in intellectual property, such as writings, computer programs, inventions, and trademarks, are valuable business properties that are protected by federal statutes.

Personal property then consists of (1) whole or fractional rights in things that are tangible and movable, such as furniture and books; (2) claims and debts, which are called **choses in action**; and (3) intangible property rights, such as trademarks, copyrights, and patents.

2. Title to Personal Property

Title to personal property may be acquired in different ways. For example, property is commonly purchased. The purchase and sale of goods is governed by the law of sales. In this chapter, the following methods of acquiring personal property will be discussed: gift, finding lost property, occupation, and escheat.

No title is acquired by theft. The thief acquires possession only, and if the thief makes a sale or gift of the property to another, the latter acquires only possession of the property. The true owner may reclaim the property from the thief or a thief's transferee. **For Example,** through a response to a classified ad, Ray purchased a Mongoose bicycle for his son from Kevin for $200, a favorable but fair price for this used bicycle. To protect himself, he obtained from Kevin a handwritten bill of sale that was notarized by a notary public. In fact, Kevin had stolen the bicycle. Its true owner, Juan, can reclaim the bike from Ray, even though Ray has a notarized bill of sale. Ray does not have legal title to the bicycle.

CPA 3. Gifts

Title to personal property may be transferred by the voluntary act of the owner without receiving anything in exchange—that is, by **gift.** The person making the gift, the **donor,** may do so because of things that the recipient of the gift, the **donee,** has done in the past or is expected to do in the future.

FIGURE 21-1 Inter Vivos Gift

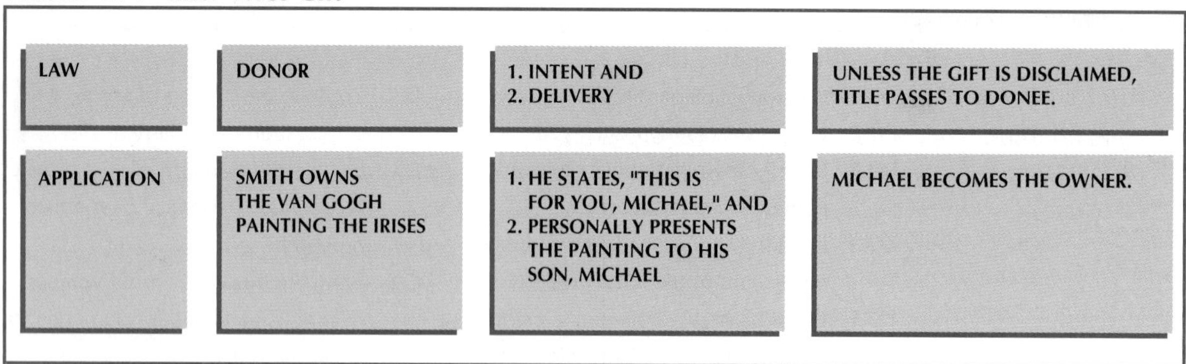

LAW
DONOR
1. INTENT AND
2. DELIVERY
UNLESS THE GIFT IS DISCLAIMED, TITLE PASSES TO DONEE.
APPLICATION
SMITH OWNS THE VAN GOGH PAINTING THE IRISES
1. HE STATES, "THIS IS FOR YOU, MICHAEL," AND
2. PERSONALLY PRESENTS THE PAINTING TO HIS SON, MICHAEL
MICHAEL BECOMES THE OWNER.

[1] *Presley Memorial Foundation v Crowell*, 733 SW2d 89 (Tenn App 1987).

However, such things are not deemed consideration and thus do not alter the "free" character of the gift. Five types of gifts are discussed below.

(a) Inter Vivos Gifts

The ordinary gift that is made between two living persons is an **inter vivos gift**. For practical purposes, such a gift takes effect when the donor (1) expresses an intent to transfer title and (2) makes delivery, subject to the right of the donee to disclaim the gift within a reasonable time after learning that it has been made.[2] Because there is no consideration for a gift, there is no enforceable contract, and an intended donee cannot sue for breach of contract if the donor fails to complete the gift.[3]

(1) Intent. The intent to make a gift requires an intent to transfer title at that time. **For Example,** former ballet star Rudolf Nureyev made a valid gift when he extended deeds of gift granting ownership of his New York City apartment and its $5 million artwork collection to a nonprofit dance foundation even though he retained the right to visit the apartment and pay for its maintenance. He gave up the right to live in the apartment and executed all documents necessary to divest his domain over it.[4] In contrast, an intent to confer a benefit at a future date is not a sufficient intent to create any right in the intended donee.

A delivery of property without the intent to make a gift does not transfer title. **For Example,** Mrs. Simpson's $80,000 check to her daughter and son-in-law, Shari and Karl Goodman, to help them buy a house was not a gift if the transaction was structured as a loan, notwithstanding Shari and Karl's assertion that it was structured as a loan simply to avoid gift taxes. The legal documents setting up the loan transaction indicated that no gift was intended.[5]

CPA ***(2) Delivery.*** Ordinarily, the delivery required to make a gift will be an actual handing over to the donee of the thing that is given.

The delivery of a gift may also be made by a **symbolic** or **constructive delivery**, such as by the delivery of means of control of property. Such means of control might be keys to a lock or keys to a garden tractor or papers that are essential to or closely associated with the ownership of the property, such as documents of title or a ship's papers.

The *Fontane* case deals with the question of constructive delivery.

FONTANE V COLT MANUFACTURING CO., 814 A2D 433 (CONN APP 2003)

BUT YOU GAVE IT TO ME IN FRONT OF ALL THOSE PEOPLE?

On March 6, 1999, Colt Manufacturing Co., a handgun manufacturer, sponsored a farewell dinner for one of its officers, Marc Fontane. At the dinner, two Colt officials presented Fontane with a single-action, .45 caliber Colt revolver. After the presentation, an agent of Colt's took possession of the revolver for the purpose of improving it by installing ivory grips and adding engraving. Fontane inquired over a period of months as to when he would receive the revolver and was ultimately told "the gun has been sold and there will be no replacement." Fontane sued Colt for the conversion of the gift with the promised improvements. For a judgment for Fontane for the value of the gun in an improved state, Colt appealed.

Judicial Opinion

PER CURIAM... Where actual delivery has not occurred, the resolution of the issue of whether a donor has made a constructive delivery depends on the circumstances of each case. "For a constructive delivery, the donor must do that which, under the circumstances, will in reason be

[2] *Bishop v Bishop*, 961 SW2d 770 (Ark 1998).

[3] *Dellagrotta v Dellagrotta*, 873 A2d 101 (RI 2005).

[4] *Rudolf Nureyev Dance Foundation v Noureeva-Francois*, 7 F Supp 2d 402 (SDNY 1998).

[5] *Simpson v Goodman*, 727 So 2d 555 (La App 1998). See also *Wright v Mallet*, 894 A2d 1016 (Conn App 2006) in which the evidence showed that a transfer in an interest in land was not intended to be a gift.

equivalent to an actual delivery. It must be as nearly perfect and complete as the nature of the property and the circumstances will permit." *Hebrew University Assn. v Nye* supra, 148 Conn. at 232–33, 169 A.2d 641.,

In the present case, there is no dispute that the defendant effectuated its donative intent of giving the plaintiff a gift of, at the very least, an unimproved revolver when it actually presented the same, along with a presentation case, to the plaintiff at the dinner. The evidence also supports the court's finding that the defendant intended, in accordance with its customary practice, to give the plaintiff the revolver with improvements to be made thereto. In the present case, the court found that the circumstances did not permit the defendant to deliver to the plaintiff at the retirement dinner a fully improved revolver; the defendant had not made the improvements to the revolver by that time. The evidence further supports the court's finding that the defendant did what was practicable under the circumstances: It publicly presented the defendant with the unimproved revolver and then immediately took possession of the revolver for the purpose of making the improvements that it intended to be part of the gift.

We agree with the court that the constructive, or symbolic, form of delivery employed by the defendant was sufficient to consummate the gift of an improved revolver.

We have concluded that the court properly found that the defendant's gift consisted of an improved revolver. Accordingly, that gift is what the defendant, almost immediately after having presented the gift to the plaintiff, converted. We therefore conclude that the court properly found that the value of the converted gift was $8155.

[Affirmed]

Questions

1. What test did the court use to determine whether a donor has made a constructive delivery of the revolver?
2. Did the court determine that a constructive delivery took place?

Failure to meet the "delivery" requirement will result in an ineffective gift. **For Example,** Walter Brownlee signed a bill of sale and attached a list of valuable construction equipment to it and left it with his attorney with instructions that it be passed to his son Randy after Walter's death. By leaving the bill of sale with his attorney, Walter retained control over the property, and therefore it was never effectively delivered to Randy, resulting in an ineffective gift.[6]

CPA ***(3) Donor's Death.*** If the donor dies before doing what is needed to make an effective gift, the gift fails.[7] An agent or the executor or administrator of the estate cannot thereafter perform the missing step on behalf of the decedent.

For Example, Mary Manning, who was in poor health, wanted to give her college-age granddaughter, Phyllis, her antique 1966 Ford Mustang convertible. She sent her daughter, Nel, to obtain the car's title from a file in the basement but was too tired to sign it on Nel's return. Mary passed away the next day without signing the document. Nel, the executrix under Mary's will, cannot complete the delivery of the gift by signing the title because it is beyond the authority of an executrix. Even though donative intent existed, no evidence of transfer of ownership and delivery to Phyllis occurred prior to Mary's death. Therefore, no valid gift was made.

(b) Gifts Causa Mortis

A **gift causa mortis** is made when the donor, contemplating imminent and impending death, delivers personal property to the donee with the intent that the donee shall own it if the donor dies. This is a conditional gift, and the donor is entitled to take the property back if (1) the donor does not die, (2) the donor revokes the gift before dying, or (3) the donee dies before the donor.

(c) Gifts and Transfers to Minors

Uniform acts provide for transferring property to a custodian to hold for the benefit of a minor.[8] When a custodian holds property for the benefit of a minor under one of the uniform acts, the custodian has

[6] *In re Estate of Walter Brownlee, Sr.*, 654 NW2d (SD 2002).

[7] *Laverman v Destocki*, 622 NE2d 1122 (Ohio App 1994).

[8] The Uniform Gifts to Minors Act (UGMA) was originally proposed in 1956. It was revised in 1965 and again in 1966. One of these versions is in effect in the following states: Delaware, New York, South Carolina, and Vermont. It has been adopted for the U.S. Virgin Islands.
The Uniform Transfers to Minors Act, which expands the type of property that can be made the subject of a gift, was originally proposed in 1983. It has been adopted, often with minor variations, in all states and the District of Columbia except South Carolina and Vermont.

discretionary power to use the property "for the support, maintenance, education, and benefit" of the minor, but the custodian may not use the custodial property for the custodian's own personal benefit. The gift is final and irrevocable for tax and all other purposes on complying with the procedures of the acts.

Under the uniform acts, custodianships terminate and the property is distributed when the minor reaches age 21.

(d) Conditional Gifts

A gift may be made subject to a condition, such as "This car is yours when you graduate" or "This car is yours unless you drop out of school." In the first example, the gift is subject to a condition precedent—graduation. A condition precedent must be satisfied before any gift or transfer takes place. In the second example, the gift is subject to a condition subsequent—dropping out of school.

Absent a finding of an intent to create a trust, a donative transaction will be analyzed as a gift subject to conditions. **For Example,** the gift by the Tennessee United Daughters of the Confederacy (UDC) to a building fund for Peabody College expressly reserved the right to recall the gift if the college failed to comply with the conditions of placing an inscription on the 1935 building naming it Confederate Memorial Hall. Peabody College for Teachers was merged into Vanderbilt University in 1979. In 2002, Vanderbilt decided to rename Confederate Memorial Hall. The Tennessee UDC's suit for the return of its gift was successful; the court decided it was not at liberty to relieve a party from its contractual obligations.[9]

Most courts regard an engagement ring as a conditional gift subject to the condition subsequent of a failure to marry. The inherent symbolism of the gift itself is deemed to foreclose the need to establish an express condition that there be a marriage.

Some jurisdictions require return of engagement rings only if the donor has not unjustifiably broken off the engagement. Most states now reject considerations of "fault" in the breaking of an engagement and always require the return of the ring to the donor when an engagement is broken. This "modern trend" is based on the theory that, in most cases, "fault" is impossible to determine as discussed in the *Meyer* case.

MEYER V MITNICK, 625 NW2D 136 (MICH APP 2001)

YOUR HONOR, MARRIAGES ARE NOT MADE IN HEAVEN, YOU SAY?

Dr. Barry Meyer and Robyn Mitnick became engaged on August 9, 1996, at which time Barry gave Robyn a custom-designed engagement ring that he purchased for $19,500. On November 8, 1996, Barry asked Robyn to sign a prenuptial agreement and Robyn refused. The engagement was broken during that meeting, with both Barry and Robyn contending the other party caused the breakup. Robyn did not return the ring, and Barry sued for its return. Robyn filed a counter-complaint, alleging that the ring was an unconditional gift and that because Barry broke the engagement, she was entitled to keep the ring.

Judicial Opinion

FITZGERALD, R. J. . . . Where a gift of personal property is made with the intent to take effect irrevocably, and is fully executed by unconditional delivery, it is a valid gift inter vivos. . . . Such a gift is absolute and, once made, cannot be revoked. . . . A gift, however, may be conditioned on the performance of some act by the donee, and if the condition is not fulfilled the donor may recover the gift. . . . We find the conditional gift theory particularly appropriate when the contested property is an engagement ring. The inherent symbolism of this gift forecloses the need to establish an express condition that marriage will ensue. Rather, the condition may be implied in fact or imposed by law in order to prevent unjust enrichment. . . .

Like the courts in other states . . . we find that engagement rings should be considered, by their very nature, conditional gifts given in contemplation of marriage. Once we recognize an engagement ring is a conditional gift, the question still remains: who gets the gift when the condition

[9] *Tennessee UDC v Vanderbilt University*, 174 SW3d 98 (Tenn Ct App 2005).

is not fulfilled? The general principles of law concerning a donor's right to the return of an engagement ring or its value when the marriage does not occur are contained in a collection of cases from multiple jurisdictions.... Generally, courts have taken two divergent paths. The older one rules that when an engagement has been unjustifiably broken by the donor, the donor shall not recover the ring. However, if the engagement is broken by mutual agreement, or unjustifiably by the donee, the ring should be returned to the donor. The critical inquiry in this fault-based line of cases is who was at "fault" for the termination of the relationship. The other rule, the so-called, "modern trend," holds that because an engagement ring is an inherently conditional gift, once the engagement has been broken the ring should be returned to the donor. Thus, the question of who broke the engagement and why, or who was "at fault," is irrelevant. This is the no-fault line of cases.

We find the reasoning of the no-fault cases persuasive. Because the engagement ring is a conditional gift, when the condition is not fulfilled the ring or its value should be returned to the donor no matter who broke the engagement or caused it to be broken. As stated by the court in *Aronow v Silver*, 223 N.J. Super. 344 (1987), in concluding that fault is irrelevant in an engagement setting:

What fact justifies the breaking of an engagement? The absence of a sense of humor? Differing musical tastes? Differing political views? The painfully-learned fact is that marriages are made on earth, not in heaven. They must be approached with intelligent care and should not happen without a decent assurance of success. When either party lacks that assurance, for whatever reason, the engagement should be broken. No justification is needed. Either party may act. Fault, impossible to fix, does not count.

In sum, we hold that an engagement ring given in contemplation of marriage is an impliedly conditional gift that is a completed gift only upon marriage. If the engagement is called off, for whatever reason, the gift is not capable of becoming a completed gift and must be returned to the donor.

[Judgment affirmed]

Questions

1. State the "older rule" regarding a donor's right to the return of an engagement ring.
2. What is the "modern trend" regarding return of engagement rings or their value to the donor after the breaking of an engagement?
3. Is fault a factor under the *Aronow v Silver* precedent case referred to by the court?

(e) Anatomical Gifts

Persons may make gifts of parts of their bodies, as in the case of kidney transplants. Persons may also make postdeath gifts. The Uniform Anatomical Gift Act[10] permits persons 18 years or older to make gifts of their bodies or any parts thereof. The gift takes effect on the death of the donor. The gift may be made to a school, a hospital, an organ bank, or a named patient. Such a gift may also be made, subject to certain restrictions, by the spouse, adult child, parent, adult brother or sister, or guardian of a deceased person. If a hospital misleads family members into consenting to tissue or organ donations that exceed their express wishes, such misconduct is sufficiently outrageous to support a claim for intentional infliction of emotional distress.[11]

CPA 4. Finding of Lost Property

Personal property is lost when the owner does not know where it is located but intends to retain title to or ownership of it. The person finding lost property does not acquire title but only possession. Ordinarily, the finder of lost property is required to surrender the property to the true owner when the latter establishes ownership. Meanwhile, the finder is entitled to retain possession as against everyone else.

Without a contract with the owner or a statute so providing, the finder of lost property usually is not entitled to a reward or to compensation for finding or caring for the property.

(a) Finding in Public Place

If the lost property is found in a public place, such as a hotel, under such circumstances that to a reasonable person it would appear the property had been intentionally placed there by the owner and the owner would be likely to recall where the property had been left and to return for it, the finder is not entitled to possession of the property. The finder must give it to the proprietor or manager of the public place to keep it for the owner. This exception does not apply if it appears that the property was not

[10] This act has been adopted in every state.

[11] See *Perry v Saint Francis Hospital*, 886 F Supp 1551 (D Kan 1995).

intentionally placed where it was found. In that case, it is not likely that the owner will recall having left it there.

(b) Statutory Change

Some states have adopted statutes permitting the finder to sell the property or keep it if the owner does not appear within a stated period of time. In this case, the finder is required to give notice—for example, by newspaper publication—to attempt to reach the owner.

5. Occupation of Personal Property

In some cases, title to personal property may be acquired by occupation—that is, by taking and retaining possession of the property.

(a) Wild Animals

Wild animals, living in a state of nature, are not owned by any individual. In the absence of restrictions imposed by game laws, the person who acquires dominion or control over a wild animal becomes its owner. What constitutes sufficient dominion or control varies with the nature of the animal and the surrounding circumstances. If the animal is killed, tied, imprisoned, or otherwise prevented from going at its will, the hunter exercises sufficient dominion or control over the animal and becomes its owner. If the wild animal, subsequent to its capture, should escape and return to its natural state, it resumes the status of a wild animal.

As a qualification to the ordinary rule, the following exception developed. If an animal is killed or captured on the land of another while the hunter is on the land without permission of the landowner, the animal, when killed or captured, belongs not to the hunter but to the landowner.

(b) Abandoned Personal Property

Personal property is deemed abandoned when the owner relinquishes possession of it with the intention to disclaim title to it. Yesterday's newspaper that is thrown out in the trash is abandoned personal property. Title to abandoned property may be acquired by the first person who obtains possession and control of it. A person becomes the owner at the moment of taking possession of the abandoned personal property. If, however, the owner of property flees in the face of an approaching peril, property left behind is not abandoned. An abandonment occurs only when the owner voluntarily leaves the property.

(c) Conversion

The tort of conversion has its origins in the ancient common law writ of trover, created "as a remedy against the finder of lost goods who refused to return them."[12] Because of that origin, the tort of conversion was limited to property that could be lost and found (i.e., tangible personalty as opposed to real property). As the nature of personal property evolved to the point that tangible documents represented highly valuable rights, such as promissory notes, stock certificates, insurance policies, and bank books, common law courts expanded the tort of conversion to include such documents within its definitional scope despite their intangible aspects, which, invariably, are primary components of the document's value. The concept of conversion today, which is the wrongful exclusionary retention of an owner's physical property, applies to an electronic record as much as it does to a paper record such as valuable stock certificates and bank books. **For Example,** a computerized client/investor list created by a real estate agent is "property" protected by the law of conversion.[13]

6. Escheat

Who owns unclaimed property? In the case of personal property, the practical answer is that the property will probably "disappear" after a period of time, or if in the possession of a carrier, hotel, or warehouse, it may be sold for unpaid storage charges. A growing problem arises with respect to unclaimed corporate dividends, bank deposits, insurance payments, and refunds. Most states have a statute providing for the transfer of such unclaimed property to the state government. This transfer to the government is often called by its feudal name of **escheat.** **For Example,** when James Canel's 280 shares of stock in Patrick Industries were turned over to the state treasurer's office by Harris Bank because his account at the bank had been inactive for more than five years, the property was presumed to be abandoned. Once Canel claimed the property, however, he was entitled to the return of the stock and the past dividends. The state was not entitled to retain the dividends under the court's reading of the state's

[12] Restatement, Second of Torts § 242, comment d.

[13] *Shmueli v Corcoran Group,* 802 NYS2d 871 (2005).

Unclaimed Property Act.[14] Funds held by stores for layaway items for customers who fail to complete the layaway purchases are subject to escheat to the state. To provide for unclaimed property, many states have adopted the Uniform Unclaimed Property Act (UUPA),[15] formerly called the Uniform Disposition of Unclaimed Property Act as referenced in the *Presley* case.

PRESLEY V CITY OF MEMPHIS, 769 SW2D 221 (TENN APP 1988)

THE KING IS DEAD! WHO GETS THE UNREFUNDED TICKET PROCEEDS?

Elvis Presley contracted with Mid-South Coliseum Board (City of Memphis) for the rental of the Coliseum and for personnel to sell tickets for concerts on August 27 and 28, 1977; $325,000 worth of tickets were sold. On August 16, 1977, Elvis Presley died. Refunds were given to those who returned their tickets to the Coliseum Board. Ten years after his death, however, $152,279 worth of ticket proceeds remained unclaimed in the custody of the Board. This fund had earned $223,760 in interest. Priscilla Presley and the coexecutors of the estate of Elvis Presley brought an action claiming the unrefunded ticket proceeds for the canceled concerts. The state of Tennessee claimed that it was entitled to the proceeds under the Uniform Disposition of Unclaimed Property Act. From a judgment for the coexecutors, the state appealed.

Judicial Opinion

HIGHERS, J. . . . Although the ticket may have some value as memorabilia apart from its intended function, such value was not the essence of the contract, had no bearing on the original proceeds, and has none now.

When Presley died, performance of the concert became impossible, and the contract was void. . . . The ticketholder was vested with a right to a refund of contract proceeds from the Coliseum as Presley's agent. . . .

Tennessee's version of the UDUPA is codified at T.C.A. § 66-29-101 et seq. . . . § 66-29-113 requires that the holder of the [abandoned] property report that property to the state treasurer. After notice is given . . . the property is to be delivered to the treasurer. . . .

The owner may recover at any time no matter how remote. . . .

The state has asserted that the definition in T.C.A. § 66-29-111 is applicable to the case at bar. That statute provides in pertinent part as follows:

66-29-111. Miscellaneous property held for another person.—All property, not otherwise covered by this chapter, including any income or increment thereon and deducting any lawful charges, that is held or owing in this state in the ordinary course of the holder's business and has remained unclaimed by the owner for more than seven (7) years after it became payable or distributable is presumed abandoned.

We agree with the state's assertion. The refunds in question have remained unclaimed in the more than seven years they have been held by the Coliseum in the ordinary course of its business. The ticketholder's right to a refund vested when the contract was voided. That right arose and the seven-year statutory period began when Elvis Presley died on August 16, 1977. Therefore, a presumption of abandonment as to unclaimed refunds matured on August 16, 1984. The present action . . . does not qualify as a claim under the statute because the plaintiffs have no legal right to the funds. Any right they might have had was lost when the contract was voided.

The presumption of abandonment under the UDUPA is statutory and therefore independent of common law principles of abandonment. . . . Intentional and voluntary relinquishment is not required under the statute. Statutory abandonment occurs when the conditions set out in the

[14] *Canel v Topinka*, 818 NE2d 311 (Ill 2004).

[15] The 1981 or 1995 version of the Act has been adopted in Alaska, Arizona, Arkansas, Colorado, Florida, Hawaii, Idaho, Illinois, Indiana, Kansas, Louisiana, Maine, Michigan, Montana, Nevada, New Hampshire, New Jersey, New Mexico, North Carolina, North Dakota, Oklahoma, Oregon, Rhode Island, South Carolina, South Dakota, U.S. Virgin Islands, Utah, Virginia, Washington, West Virginia, Wisconsin, and Wyoming.

UDUPA exist.... Only statutorily abandonment property is disposed of under the UDUPA....

We are well aware that this fund would not exist were it not for Elvis Presley's unique skills and talents while living and the legendary status he continues to hold in the years after his death.... These considerations might in the absence of the Tennessee statute merit granting the windfall to Presley's estate. But Presley's death voided the contract represented by each ticket sold... and Presley's estate [has] no legal claim to the ticket proceeds. Granting the proceeds to either of them or to the Coliseum constitutes the type of windfall the drafters of UDUPA sought to address.... We believe the drafters of the UDUPA and our legislature intended such windfalls to benefit the public rather than individuals in precisely the manner we hold here....

In summary, pursuant to the Tennessee UDUPA, we hold that the Coliseum must deliver all of the unclaimed ticket refunds and all of the accumulated interest thereon to the treasurer. Further, the treasurer shall publish the existence of the unclaimed funds and hold those amounts until such time as they are claimed by the rightful owners, the ticketholders.

[Judgment reversed and action remanded]

Questions

1. On what basis did the estate of Elvis Presley claim the unrefunded ticket proceeds and interest?
2. Present the state's legal position before the court.
3. Did the court think the intent of the drafters of the UDUPA would support the "windfall" in this case benefiting the estate of the individual whose legendary status generated the unclaimed funds? Explain.

CPA 7. Multiple Ownership of Personal Property

When all rights in a particular object of property are held by one person, that property is held in **severalty**. However, two or more persons may hold concurrent rights and interests in the same property. In that case, the property is said to be held in **cotenancy**. The various forms of cotenancy include (1) tenancy in common, (2) joint tenancy, (3) tenancy by entirety, and (4) community property.

(a) Tenancy in Common

A **tenancy in common** is a form of ownership by two or more persons. The interest of a tenant in common may be transferred or inherited, in which case the taker becomes a tenant in common with the others. **For Example,** Brandt and Vincent restored an 18-foot 1940 mahogany-hulled Chris Craft runabout and own it as tenants in common. If Brandt sold his interest in the boat to Andrea, then Vincent and Andrea would be co-owners as tenants in common. If Brandt died before Vincent, a one-half interest in the boat would become the property of Brandt's heirs.

CPA (b) Joint Tenancy

A **joint tenancy** is another form of ownership by two or more persons, but a joint tenancy has a *right of survivorship*.[16] On the death of a joint tenant, the remaining tenants take the share of the deceased tenant. The last surviving joint tenant takes the property as a holder in severalty. **For Example,** in Brandt and Vincent's Chris Craft case, if the boat were owned as joint tenants with a right of survivorship, Vincent would own the boat outright upon Brandt's death, and Brandt's heirs would obtain no interest in it.

A joint tenant's interest may be transferred to a third person, but this destroys the joint tenancy. If the interest of one of two joint tenants is transferred to a third person, the remaining joint tenant becomes a tenant in common with the third person. **For Example,** if Brandt sold his interest to Andrea, Vincent and Andrea would be co-owners as tenants in common.

Statutes in many states have modified the common law by adding a formal requirement to the creation of a joint tenancy with survivorship. At common law, such an estate would be created by a transfer of property to "*A* and *B* as joint tenants."[17]

[16] *Estate of Munier v Jacquemin*, 899 SW2d 114 (Mo App 1995).

[17] Some states have modified the common law by creating a condition that whenever two or more persons are listed as owners of a bank account or certificate of deposit, a presumption of joint tenancy with right of survivorship arises unless expressly negated by the signature card or another instrument or by extrinsic proof. Thus, when Herbert H. Herring had his bank change the designated owners of a certificate of deposit to read, "Herbert H. Herring or [his grandson] Robert J. Herring," and no words indicating survivorship upon the death of either were on the certificate, nevertheless under a 1992 Florida statute creating a presumption of survivorship, which presumption was not rebutted, grandson Robert was declared the owner of the certificate. *In re Estate of H. H. Herring*, 670 So 2d 145 (Fla App 1996).

Under these statutes, however, it is necessary to add the words "with right of survivorship" or other similar words if a right of survivorship is desired.

If no words of survivorship are used, the transfer of property to two or more persons will be construed as creating a tenancy in common. Under such a statute, a certificate of deposit issued only in the name of "*A* or *B*" does not create a joint tenancy because it does not contain words of survivorship.

(c) Tenancy by Entirety

At common law, a **tenancy by entirety** or **tenancy by the entireties** was created when property was transferred to both husband and wife. It differs from joint tenancy in that it exists only when the transfer is to husband and wife. Also, the right of survivorship cannot be extinguished, and one spouse's interest cannot be transferred to a third person. However, in some jurisdictions, a spouse's right to share the possession and the profits may be transferred. This form of property holding is popular in common law jurisdictions because creditors of only one of the spouses cannot reach the property while both are living. Only a creditor of both the husband and the wife under the same obligation can obtain execution against the property.

For Example, a husband and wife, Rui and Carla Canseco, purchased a 2007 Lexus LS 430 for cash. It was titled in the names of "Rui J. *and* Carla T. Canseco." Later that year, State National Bank obtained a money judgment against Rui for $200,000, and the bank claimed entitlement to half the value of the Cansecos' car, which it asserted was Rui's share as a joint tenant. A tenancy by entirety had been created, however, so the bank could not levy against the auto. If the car had been titled "Rui *or* Carla T. Canseco," in most states the use of the word "or" would indicate that the vehicle was held in joint tenancy even if the co-owners are husband and wife. As such, Rui's half interest could be reached by the bank.

The tenancy by entirety is, in effect, a substitute for a will because the surviving spouse acquires the complete property interest on the death of the other. There are usually other reasons, however, why each spouse should make a will.

In many states, the granting of an absolute divorce converts a tenancy by the entireties into a tenancy in common.

8. Community Property

In some states, property acquired during the period of marriage is the **community property** of the husband and wife. Some statutes provide for the right of survivorship; others provide that half of the property of the deceased husband or wife shall go to the heirs of that spouse or permit such half to be disposed of by will. It is commonly provided that property acquired by either spouse during the marriage is **prima facie** community property, even though title is taken in the spouse's individual name, unless it can be shown that it was obtained with property possessed by the spouse prior to the marriage.

B. Bailments

9. Definition

A **bailment** is the relationship that arises when one person delivers possession of personal property to another under an agreement, express or implied, by which the latter is under a duty to return the property or to deliver it or dispose of it as agreed. The person who turns over the possession of the property is the **bailor**. The person who accepts is the **bailee**. **For Example,** Arthur Grace, a world renowned photojournalist, had an agreement with Sygma-Paris and Sygma-New York whereby Grace turned over his photographs to Sygma, and Sygma agreed to act as Grace's agent to license the images and administer the fee-setting process and delivery and return of the images. The *bailor*, Grace, terminated its agreement with the *bailee*, Sygma, in 2001, and the *bailee* was unable to return all of the photographs to Grace as obligated under the agreement. Sygma's system of keeping track of images was "completely inadequate"; hence, it was liable for $472,000 in damages to the *bailor* for the failure to return some 40,000 images.[18]

10. Elements of Bailment

A bailment is created when the following elements are present.

(a) Agreement

The bailment is based on an *agreement*. This agreement may be express or implied. Generally, it contains all of the elements of a contract. The bailment transaction in fact consists of (1) a contract to bail

[18] *Grace v Corbis Sygma*, 403 F Supp2d 337 (SDNY 2005).

FIGURE 21-2 Bailment of Personal Property

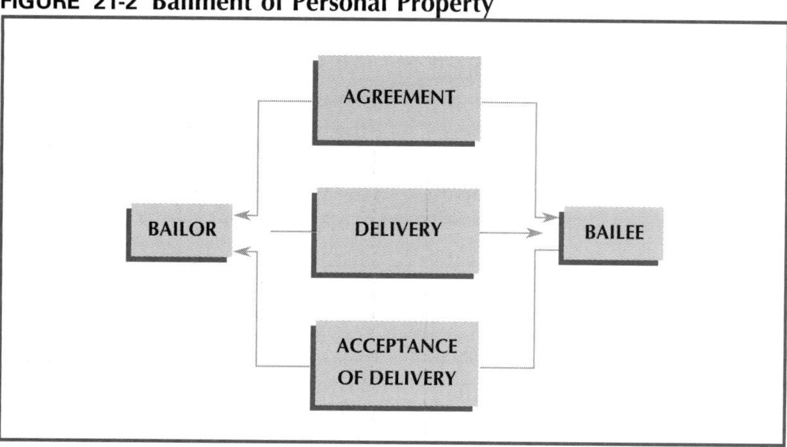

and (2) the actual bailing of the property. Ordinarily, there is no requirement that the contract of bailment be in writing. The subject of a bailment may be any personal property of which possession may be given.[19] Real property cannot be bailed.

(b) Delivery and Acceptance

The bailment arises when, pursuant to the agreement of the parties, the property is delivered to the bailee and accepted by the bailee as subject to the bailment agreement.

In the absence of a prior agreement to the contrary, a valid delivery and acceptance generally require that the bailee be aware that goods have been placed within the bailee's exclusive possession or control. **For Example,** photography equipment belonging to Bill Bergey, the photographer of Roosevelt University's student newspaper, was stolen from the newspaper's campus office. Bergey believes that the university breached its duty as bailee because records showed that no campus police officer checked the building on the night of the theft. Bergey's case against the university on this bailment theory will fail, however, because the university did not know the equipment was left in the office. Without this knowledge, there was neither a bailment agreement nor acceptance of delivery by the university as a bailee.

11. Nature of the Parties' Interests

The bailor and bailee have different legal interests in the bailed property.

(a) Bailor's Interest

The bailor is usually the owner, but ownership by the bailor is not required. It is sufficient that the bailor have physical possession. **For Example,** Crella Magee delivered a blue fox jacket for summer storage to Walbro, Inc. When it was not returned, she sued Walbro for the replacement cost of the jacket, $3,400. Walbro's defense that Magee was not entitled to recover the replacement cost of the lost jacket because she did not prove ownership was rejected as irrelevant by the court, and the case was decided in favor of Magee.[20]

(b) Bailee's Interest

The bailee has possession of the property only. Title to the property does not pass to the bailee, and the bailee cannot sell the property to a third person. If the bailee attempts to sell the property, such sale transfers only possession, and the owner may recover the property from the buyer.

12. Classification of Ordinary Bailments

Ordinary bailments are generally classified as being for (1) the sole benefit of the bailor, (2) the sole benefit of the bailee, or (3) the mutual benefit of both.

Bailments may or may not provide for compensation to the bailee. On the basis of compensation, bailments may be classified as (1) **bailments for mutual benefit** in which one party takes the personal property of another into her care or custody

[19] *Stone v CDI Corp.*, 9 SW3d 699 (Mo App 1999).
[20] *Magee v Walbro, Inc.*, 525 NE2d 975 (Ill App 1988).

in exchange for payment or other benefit and (2) **gratuitous bailments** in which the transfer of possession and use of the bailed property is without compensation. Bailments for the sole benefit of the bailor or for the sole benefit of the bailee are sometimes described as gratuitous. The fact that no charge is made by the bailor does not necessarily make the transaction a gratuitous bailment. If the bailment is made to further a business interest of the bailor, as when something is loaned free to a customer, the bailment is not gratuitous.

A **constructive bailment** arises when one person has lawfully acquired possession of another's personal property other than by virtue of a bailment contract and holds it under such circumstances that the law imposes on the recipient of the property the obligation to keep it safely and redeliver it to the owner. **For Example,** the City of Chicago is the constructive bailee of an automobile impounded by Chicago police at the time of a driver's arrest for drunk driving. It has a duty to keep the automobile safely and turn it over to the owner upon payment of towing and storage fees. When this duty is delegated to a private contractor to tow and store, a constructive bailment for the mutual benefit of the contractor and the owner exists.

13. Renting of Space Distinguished

When a person rents space in a locker or building under an agreement that gives the renter the exclusive right to use that space, the placing of goods by the renter in that space does not create a bailment, for it does not constitute a delivery of goods into the possession of the owner of the space. **For Example,** Winston Hutton entered into a rental agreement for a storage space at Public Storage Management's self-storage facility in New York City, and his stored property was stolen from the space. Hutton had procured his own lock for the storage space, and the rental agreement provided that management would not have a key. Hutton's lawsuit was unsuccessful because the defendant did not take possession of the property. The legal relationship was not a bailment.[21]

14. Duties and Rights of the Bailee

The bailee has certain duties concerning performance, care, and return of the bailed property. The bailee must perform his part of a contract and is liable for ordinary contract damages for failure to perform the contract.

The bailee is under a duty to care for the bailed property, and the duty of care owed differs according to classification, based in terms of "benefit." A bailment may be for the sole benefit of the bailor. **For Example,** when Fred allows Mary, a college classmate from out of state, to store her books and furniture in his basement over the summer, Fred, the bailee, is liable only for gross negligence relating to damage to these stored belongings. A bailment may be for the sole benefit of the bailee, as when Mary allows Fred to borrow her Les Paul Gibson guitar. Fred, the bailee, is liable even for slight negligence in the case of any damage to the guitar. Most bailments, however, are mutual benefit bailments. **For Example,** when Harry rents for a fee a trailer from U-Haul, Inc., to transport his son's belongings to college, Harry, the bailee, is responsible for using reasonable or ordinary care under the circumstances while possessing and using the trailer. U-Haul, the bailor, has a duty to warn Harry of any known defects or defects that could be discovered on reasonable inspection.

A bailee has a right to receive payment for charges due for storage or repairs. A **bailee's lien** gives the bailee the right to keep possession of the bailed property until charges are paid. A bailee who is authorized by statute to sell the bailed property to enforce a charge or claim against the bailor must give such notice as is required by the statute. A bailee who sells without giving the required notice is liable for conversion of the property.

15. Breach of Duty of Care: Burden of Proof

Although a bailment is contractual in nature, an action for breach of duty of care by a bailee "sounds in tort." That is, the true nature of the liability is not contractual at all but based on tort principles.

When the bailor sues the bailee for damages to the bailed property, the bailor has the burden of proving that the bailee was at fault and that such fault was the proximate cause of the loss. A prima facie right of the bailor to recover is established, however, by proof that the bailor delivered the property to the bailee in good condition and subsequently could not be returned by the bailee or was returned in a

[21] *Hutton v Public Storage Management, Inc.*, 676 NYS2d 887 (NY City Civ Ct 1998).

damaged condition. When this is done, the bailee has the burden of proving that the loss or damage was not caused by the bailee's failure to exercise the care required by law, which in the case of a mutual benefit bailment is that of an ordinary or due care, under all of the circumstances.

The *Hadfield* case involved a lawsuit where the bailee believed it was not responsible for damages to a bailed automobile, asserting that the bailment was for the sole benefit of the bailor, making it a gratuitous bailment in which the bailee can be held responsible only for gross negligence.

HADFIELD V GILCHRIST, 343 SC 88 (SC APP 2000)

TOWED INTO COURT

Mark Hadfield, a medical student in Charleston, South Carolina, went to retrieve his 1988 Lincoln Continental from a parking space on private property near the medical school where his wife had parked the car earlier that day without permission. The property owner called Gilchrist Towing Co. and had the auto removed. When Hadfield discovered that the car had been towed, he telephoned Gilchrist Towing and was told that he would have to wait until the next morning to retrieve the car after paying towing and storage fees. The next morning after paying the charges, he went to the storage lot and found that his car had been extensively vandalized along with a number of other vehicles. The owner of the company, S.A. Gilchrist, refused to pay the estimated cost of repairs, $4,021.43. Hadfield brought suit contending that a constructive bailment for the mutual benefit of Hadfield and Gilchrist had been created, and that Gilchrist breached his duty of care to Hadfield. Gilchrist contended that he towed the vehicle pursuant to Charleston Municipal Ordinances, which are for the sole benefit of the vehicle owners, intended to preserve their property. As such the relationship created was a gratuitous bailment, which limited his duty of care. Gilchrist contended he was not liable for the damages caused by unknown vandals.

Judicial Opinion

ANDERSON, J.... Although contractual in nature, and involving the conveyance of personal property, an action for breach of the duty of care owed by a bailee sounds in tort. See Kurt Philip Autor, Note, Bailment Liability: Toward a Standard of Reasonable Care, 61 S. Car. L. Rev. 2117, 2124 (Sept. 1998)....

The burden of proof in this case rests first upon the bailor, Hadfield, to prove *prima facie* case. He must show: 1) the goods were delivered to the bailee in good condition; and 2) they were lost or returned in a damaged condition. See *Fortner v Carnes*, 258 S.C. 455, 189 S. E. 2d 24 (1972) (burden is upon bailee to prove due or ordinary care on his part, to jury's satisfaction, if he is to relieve himself of liability for goods not returned in accordance with bailment contract; whether bailee has exercised due care with regard to stored goods has to be determined with reference to all circumstances of particular case); *Shoreland Freezers, Inc. v Textile Ice & Fuel Co.*, 241 S.C. 537, 129 S.E.2d 424 (1963). When the bailor, Hadfield, has so proven, the burden is then shifted to the bailee, Gilchrist, to show that he has used ordinary care in the good's storage and safekeeping.... Hadfield testified before the magistrate regarding the "nice" condition of the vehicle prior to being towed, and the damage to his vehicle, and the other vehicles on the lot. In addition, he introduced photographs depicting the damage. Thus, Hadfield made out his *prima facie* case. The burden then shifted to Gilchrist to show that he used ordinary care in protecting the vehicle while in his care.

Gilchrist impounded the cars in a storage lot surrounded by a chain link fence. There was an individual on the clock at all times. The person on duty spent time in the office and only visited the storage lot to check on it. The vandal cut a hole in the fence and broke into six to eight cars on the night in question. The fact the guard was not on duty at the impound lot and, considering the only other security for the vehicles was the chain link fence, the magistrate and Circuit Court judge could have concluded Gilchrist failed to exercise ordinary care. As explicated above, the decision of whether or not Gilchrist used ordinary care is a question of fact. Based on our standard of review, we must affirm the decision of the Circuit Court on the facts if it is supported by any evidence, and this Court finds no error of law. We find the facts support the finding that Gilchrist breached his duty as a bailee to Hadfield....

Damages

Gilchrist asserts the magistrate and the Circuit Court judge erred in the finding of damages. Yet, Gilchrist's own counsel stated: "And all they have proved is damages. There's no question that the plaintiffs were damaged."... Hadfield proffered the testimony of Rodney Smitz, an assistant manager at Rick Hendrick Collision Center, to explain the damages and the cost to repair the vehicle. Gilchrist's counsel did not cross-examine Smitz regarding the estimates. We find no merit in Gilchrist's argument that there was no evidence for the Circuit Court to calculate damages.

Conclusion

We rule that where a city ordinance is utilized as the legal justification for taking possession of a vehicle on private property the person or entity lawfully acquiring possession of the property under the ordinance becomes a constructive bailee as a matter of law. We find a constructive bailment, for the mutual benefit of Hadfield and Gilchrist, was created. Further, we hold an action for breach of the duty of care owed by a bailee, although contractual in nature, sounds in tort. We conclude the burden of proof in a constructive bailment case rests first upon a bailor to prove a prima facie case and, once so proven, the burden shifts to the bailee to show the use of ordinary care in the storage and safekeeping of the property.

[Judgment affirmed]

Questions

1. What type of bailment was created when Gilchrist took possession of Hadfield's car? Why is a determination about the type of bailment important?
2. Explain the burden of proof applicable in this case.
3. Explain the statement, "Although contractual in nature, and involving the conveyance of personal property, an action for breach of a duty of care owed by a bailee sounds in tort."

16. Liability for Defects in Bailed Property

In the case of a mutual benefit bailment, the bailor must not only inform the bailee of known defects but also make a reasonable investigation to discover defects. The bailor is liable for harm resulting from any such defects. If the bailment is for the sole benefit of the bailee, the bailor must inform the bailee of known defects.

In bailments for hire where the bailor is in the business of renting vehicles, machines, or equipment for use by bailees, such as Hertz or Avis car rental companies, Article 2A of the Uniform Commercial Code provides an implied warranty of merchantability and fitness for a particular purpose for the protection of bailee customers.[22]

17. Contract Modification of Liability

An ordinary bailee may limit liability (except for willful misconduct) by agreement or contract. If the bailee seeks to limit liability for its own negligence, the wording of the contract must clearly express this intention so that the other party will know what is being contracted away.[23] In some states, statutes prohibit certain kinds of paid bailees, such as automobile parking garages, from limiting their liability for negligence. Statutes in some states declare that a party cannot bar liability for negligent violations of common law standards of care where a public interest is involved. **For Example,** Bruce Gardner left his Porsche 911 automobile to be repaired at Downtown Porsche Auto, signing a repair order standardized adhesion contract that stated Downtown was "not responsible for loss of cars... in case of... theft." The car was stolen while in the garage for repairs due to Downtown's negligence. The California appeals court determined that because automobile repair contracts "affect the public interest," Downtown's exculpatory clause was invalid as to public policy.[24]

When a bailee attempts to limit liability by printing such a limitation on a claim check, the limitation must be called to the attention of the bailor in some reasonable fashion, such as a sign at the point of purchase, before it may become part of the bailment contract. **For Example,** a claim check for a coat that purports to limit liability is ineffective without a reasonably placed sign notifying customers of the limitation.

22 UCC §§ 2A-212, 2A-213.

23 *Hertz v Klein Mfg., Inc.*, 636 So 2d 189 (Fla App 1994).

24 *Gardner v Downtown Porsche Auto*, 225 Cal Rptr 757 (1986).

LAWFLIX

The Goonies (1985)(PG)

This story is about children finding a lost treasure they wish to claim as theirs and use to stop the condemnation of their parents' properties by developers. The issue of who owns the treasure is a fascinating one for discussion.

For movie clips that illustrate business law concepts, see LawFlix at **http://wdvl.westbuslaw.com.**

Summary

Personal property consists of whole or fractional ownership rights in things that are tangible and movable, as well as rights in things that are intangible.

Personal property may be acquired by purchase. Personal property may also be acquired by gift when the donor has present intent to make a gift and delivers possession to the donee or makes a constructive delivery. Personal property may be acquired by occupation and under some statutes may be acquired by finding. The state may acquire property by escheat.

All rights in a particular object of property can be held by one individual, in which case it is said to be held *in severalty*. Ownership rights may be held concurrently by two or more individuals, in which case it is said to be held in cotenancy. The major forms of cotenancy are (1) tenancy in common, (2) joint tenancy, (3) tenancy by entirety, and (4) community property.

A bailment is the relationship that exists when tangible personal property is delivered by the bailor into the possession of the bailee under an agreement, express or implied, that the identical property will be returned or delivered in accordance with the agreement. No title is transferred by a bailment. The bailee has the right of possession. When a person comes into the possession of the personal property of another without the owner's consent, the law classifies the relationship as a constructive bailment.

Bailments may be classified in terms of benefit—that is, for the (1) sole benefit of the bailor, (2) sole benefit of the bailee, or (3) benefit of both parties (mutual benefit bailment). Some courts state the standard of care required of a bailee in terms of the class of bailment. Thus, if the bailment is for the sole benefit of the bailor, the bailee is required to exercise only slight care and is liable for gross negligence only. When the bailment is for the sole benefit of the bailee, the bailee is liable for the slightest negligence. When the bailment is for the mutual benefit of the parties, as in a commercial bailment, the bailee is liable for ordinary negligence. An ordinary bailee may limit liability except for willful misconduct or where prohibited by law.

A bailee must perform the bailee's part of the contract. The bailee has a lien on the bailed property until they have paid for storage or repair charges.

In a mutual benefit bailment, the bailor is under a duty to furnish goods reasonably fit for the purposes contemplated by the parties. The bailor may be held liable for damages or injury caused by the defective condition of the bailed property.

Questions and Case Problems

1. Can a creditor of both the husband and wife under the same obligation obtain an execution against a Winnebago mobile home owned by the husband and wife in tenancy by entirety?
2. Joe obtained a box of antique Lenox china dishes that had been left at the Mashpee town dump. He supplemented the sizable but incomplete set of dishes with other Lenox pieces found at antique dealers. At dinner parties, he proudly told of the origin of his china. When Marlene discovered that Joe had taken her dishes from the dump, she hired an attorney to obtain their return. What result?
3. Joyce Clifford gave a check for $5,000 to her nephew Carl to help with living expenses for his last year of college. The face of the check stated, "As a loan." Years later, Carl wrote to his aunt asking what he should do about the loan. She responded on her Christmas card simply, "On money—keep it—no return." After Joyce's death, her administrator sued Carl after discovering the "As a loan" canceled check. Decide.

4. Ruth and Stella were sisters. They owned a house as joint tenants with right of survivorship. Ruth sold her half interest to Roy. Thereafter, Stella died, and Roy claimed the entire property by survivorship. Was he entitled to it?
5. Mona found a wallet on the floor of an elevator in the office building where she worked. She posted several notices in the building about finding the wallet, but no one appeared to claim it. She waited for six months and then spent the money in the wallet in the belief that she owned it. Jason, the person who lost the wallet, subsequently brought suit to recover the money. Mona's defense was that the money was hers because Jason did not claim it within a reasonable time after she posted the notices. Is she correct? (Assume that the common law applies.)
6. In 1971, Harry Gordon turned over $40,000 to his son, Murray Gordon. Murray opened two $20,000 custodial bank accounts under the Uniform Gifts to Minors Act for his minor children, Eden and Alexander. Murray was listed as the custodian of both accounts. On January 9, 1976, both accounts were closed, and a single bank check representing the principal of the accounts was drawn to the order of Harry Gordon. In April 1976, Murray and his wife, Joan, entered into a separation agreement and were later divorced. Thereafter, Joan, on behalf of her children, Eden and Alexander, brought suit against Murray to recover the funds withdrawn in January 1976, contending that the deposits in both accounts were irrevocable gifts. Murray contended that the money was his father's and that it was never intended as a gift but was merely a means of avoiding taxes. Decide. [*Gordon v Gordon*, 419 NYS2d 684 (App Div)]
7. New York's banking law provides that a presumption arises that a joint tenancy has been created when a bank account is opened in the names of two persons "payable to either or the survivor." While he was still single, Richard Coddington opened a savings account with his mother, Amelia. The signature card they signed stated that the account was owned by them as joint tenants with the right of survivorship. No statement as to survivorship was made on the passbook. Richard later married Margaret. On Richard's death, Margaret claimed a share of the account on the ground that it was not held in joint tenancy because the passbook did not contain words of survivorship and because the statutory presumption of a joint tenancy was overcome by the fact that Richard had withdrawn substantial sums from the account during his life. Decide. [*Coddington v Coddington*, 391 NYS2d 760 (Sup Ct App Div)]
8. Martin Acampora purchased a shotgun at a garage sale years ago, never used the weapon, and did not know of any defects in it. His 31-year-old son Marty borrowed the shotgun to go duck hunting. As Marty attempted to engage the safety mechanism, the shotgun fired. The force of the shotgun's firing caused it to fall to the ground and to discharge another shot, which struck Marty in the hand. Classify the bailment in this case. What duty of care was owed by the bailor in this case? Is Martin liable to his son for the injury?
9. Baena Brothers agreed to reupholster and reduce the size of the arms of Welge's sofa and chair. The work was not done according to the contract, and the furniture when finished had no value to Welge and was not accepted by him. Baena sued him for the contract price. Welge counterclaimed for the value of the furniture. Decide. [*Baena Brothers v Welge*, 3 Conn Cir 67, 207 A2d 749]
10. Schroeder parked his car in a parking lot operated by Allright, Inc. On the parking stub given him was printed in large, heavy type that the lot closed at 6:00 P.M. Under this information, printed in smaller, lighter type, was a provision limiting the liability of Allright for theft or loss. A large sign at the lot stated that after 6:00 P.M. patrons could obtain their car keys at another location. Schroeder's car was stolen from the lot sometime after the 6:00 P.M. closing, and he sued Allright for damages. Allright defended on the basis of the limitation-of-liability provision contained in the parking stub and the notice given Schroeder that the lot closed at 6:00 P.M. Decide. [*Allright, Inc. v Schroeder*, 551 SW2d 745 (Tex Civ App)]
11. John Hayes and Lynn Magosian, auditors for a public accounting firm, went to lunch at the Bay View Restaurant in San Francisco. John left his raincoat with a coatroom attendant, but Lynn took her new raincoat with her to the dining room, where she hung it on a coat hook near her booth. When leaving the restaurant, Lynn discovered that someone had taken her raincoat. When John sought to claim his raincoat at the coatroom, it could not be found. The attendant advised that it might have been taken while he was on his break. John and Lynn sued the restaurant, claiming that the restaurant was a bailee of the raincoats and had a duty to return them. Are both John and Lynn correct?
12. Rhodes parked his car in the self-service park-and-lock lot of Pioneer Parking Lot, Inc. The ticket that he received from the ticket meter stated the following: "NOTICE. THIS CONTRACT LIMITS OUR LIABILITY. READ IT. WE RENT SPACE ONLY. NO BAILMENT IS CREATED." Rhodes parked the car himself and kept the keys. There was no attendant at the lot. The car was stolen from the lot. Rhodes sued the parking lot on the theory that it had breached its duty as a bailee. Was there a bailment? [*Rhodes v Pioneer Parking Lot, Inc.*, 501 SW2d 569 (Tenn)]
13. Newman underwent physical therapy at Physical Therapy Associates of Rome, Inc. (PTAR), in Rome, Georgia, for injuries sustained in an auto accident. At a therapy session on February 6, it was necessary for Newman to take off two necklaces. She placed one of the necklaces on a peg on the wall in the therapy room, and

the therapist placed the other necklace on another peg. After the session, Newman forgot to retrieve her jewelry from the wall pegs. When she called the next day for the forgotten jewelry, it could not be found. She sued PTAR for the value of the jewelry on a bailment theory. PTAR raised the defense that there was no bailment because Newman retained the right to remove the jewelry from the wall pegs. Decide. [*Newman v Physical Therapy Associates of Rome, Inc.*, 375 SE2d 253 (Ga App)]

14. Contract Packers rented a truck from Hertz Truck Leasing. The brakes of the truck did not function properly. This resulted in injuring Packers' employee Cintrone while he was riding in the truck as it was driven by his helper. Cintrone sued Hertz for breach of the implied warranty that the truck was fit for normal use on public highways. Hertz contended that implied warranties apply only to sales, not to bailments for hire. Decide. [*Cintrone v Hertz Truck Leasing & Rental Service*, 212 A2d 769 (NJ)]

15. Charter Apparel, Inc., supplied fabric to Marco Apparel, Inc., in December to manufacture finished articles of clothing at its Walnut Grove, Mississippi, facilities. The fabric arrived just before the Christmas holiday shutdown and was stacked on cutting tables in the old building, which was known to have a roof that leaked. The evidence showed that no precautions were taken to cover the fabric and no guard was posted at the plant during the shutdown. Severe weather and freezing rain occurred during the shutdown, and it was discovered that the rain had leaked through the roof and destroyed more than $400,000 worth of the fabric. Marco denied that it was negligent and argued that it exercised ordinary care. It offered no evidence to rebut Charter's prima facie case or to rebut Charter's evidence of negligence. It asserted, however, that as a bailee it was not an insurer of goods against severe weather conditions. Decide. [*California Union Ins. v City of Walnut Grove*, 857 F Supp 515 (SD Miss)]

CPA Questions

1. Which of the following requirements must be met to create a bailment?

   I. Delivery of personal property to the intended bailee

   II. Possession by the intended bailee

   III. An absolute duty on the intended bailee to return or dispose of the property according to the bailor's directions

   a. I and II only

   b. I and III only

   c. II and III only

   d. I, II, and III.

LEGAL ASPECTS OF SUPPLY CHAIN MANAGEMENT

CHAPTER (22)

LEARNING OBJECTIVES

After studying this chapter, you should be able to

LO.1 Differentiate between negotiable and nonnegotiable warehouse receipts

LO.2 List the three types of carriers of goods

LO.3 State the common carrier's liability for loss or damage to goods

LO.4 Explain the effect of a sale on a consignment

LO.5 Describe a hotelkeeper's liability for loss of a guest's property

All bailments are not created equal. Because of the circumstances under which possession of the bailed property is transferred, the law imposes special duties in some cases on warehouses, common carriers, factors, and hotelkeepers. Documents of title facilitate the transportation, storage, and financing of goods in commerce.

A. Warehouses

The storage of goods in a warehouse is a special bailment.

1. Definitions

A **warehouse** is an entity engaged in the business of storing the goods of others for compensation. **Public warehouses** hold themselves out to serve the public generally, without discrimination.

A building is not essential to warehousing. Thus, an enterprise that stores boats outdoors on land is engaged in warehousing, for it is engaged in the business of storing goods for hire.

2. Rights and Duties of Warehouses

The rights and duties of a warehouse are for the most part the same as those of a bailee under a mutual benefit bailment.[1] A warehouse is not an insurer of goods. A warehouse is liable for loss or damage to goods stored in its warehouse when the warehouse is negligent.

(a) Statutory Regulation

The rights and duties of warehouses are regulated by the UCC, Article 7. Article 7 was revised in 2003 and 16 states have adopted the revised version.[2] The purpose of revision was to provide a framework for the future development of electronic documents of title and to update the article for modern times in light of state, federal, and international developments, including the need for medium and gender neutrality. For example, the term utilized to designate a person engaged in storing goods for hire under Article 7 is *warehouseman*.[3] The revised act uses the term *warehouse*.[4] In addition, most states have passed warehouse acts defining the rights and duties of warehouses and imposing regulations. Regulations govern charges and liens, bonds for the protection of patrons, maintenance of storage facilities in a suitable and safe condition, inspections, and general methods of transacting business.

(b) Lien of Warehouse

The public warehouse has a lien against the goods for reasonable storage charges.[5] It is a **specific lien** in

[1] UCC § 7-204.

[2] Revised Article 7 (2003) has been adopted by Alabama, Connecticut, Delaware, Hawaii, Idaho, Maryland, Minnesota, Montana, Nebraska, Nevada, New Jersey, New Mexico, North Dakota, Oklahoma, Texas, and Virginia. For more modern statutory drafting, the revised edition converts subparagraph designations from numbers to letters. For example, UCC § 7-307(1) is designated as Rev. UCC § 7-307(a).

[3] UCC § 7-102(1)(h).

[4] Rev. UCC § 7-102(a)(13).

[5] UCC § 7-209(1). The warehouse's lien provision of the UCC is constitutional as a continuation of the common law lien.

that it attaches only to the property on which the charges arose and cannot be asserted against any other property of the same owner in the possession of the warehouse. However, the warehouse may make a lien carry over to other goods by noting on the receipt for one lot of goods that a lien is also claimed for charges on the other goods. The warehouse's lien for storage charges may be enforced by sale after due notice has been given to all persons who claim any interest in the stored property.

3. Warehouse Receipts

A **warehouse receipt** is a written acknowledgment or record of an acknowledgment by a warehouse (bailee) that certain property has been received for storage from a named person called a **depositor** (bailor). The warehouse receipt is a memorandum of the contract between the **issuer**, the warehouse that prepares the receipt, and the depositor. No particular form is required, but usually the receipt (record) will provide:

> *(1) the location of the warehouse where the goods are stored, (2) the date of issuance of the receipt, (3) the consecutive number of the receipt, (4) information on the negotiability of the receipt, (5) the rate of storage and handling charges, (6) a description of the goods or the packages containing them, and (7) a statement of any liabilities incurred for which the warehouse claims a lien or security interest.*[6]

A warehouse receipt (as well as a bill of lading, discussed at a later point in this chapter) is considered a **document of title**—that is, a document that in the regular course of business or financing is treated as evidence that a person is entitled to receive, hold, and dispose of the document and the goods it covers.[7] Under revised Article 1 of the UCC, the term *record* is used in the definition of document of title, reflecting the present commercial reality of the use of electronic records as documents of title, in addition to traditional "written" documents of title inscribed on a tangible medium.[8] The person holding a warehouse receipt or the person specified in the receipt is entitled to the goods represented by the receipt. A warehouse receipt as a document of title can be bought or sold and can be used as security for a loan.

4. Rights of Holders of Warehouse Receipts

The rights of the holders of warehouse receipts differ depending on whether the receipts are nonnegotiable or negotiable.

CPA (a) Nonnegotiable Warehouse Receipts

A warehouse receipt in which it is stated that the goods received will be delivered to a specified person is a **nonnegotiable warehouse receipt.** A transferee of a nonnegotiable receipt acquires only the title and rights that the transferor had actual authority to transfer. Therefore, the transferee's rights may be defeated by a good-faith purchaser of the goods from the transferor of the receipt.

(b) Negotiable Warehouse Receipts

A warehouse receipt stating that the goods will be delivered "to the bearer" or "to the order of" any named person is a **negotiable warehouse receipt**.

(1) Negotiation. If the receipt provides for the delivery of the goods "to the bearer," the receipt may be negotiated by transfer of the document. If the receipt provides for delivery of the goods "to the order of" a named individual, the document must be indorsed[9] and delivered by that person in order for the document to be negotiated.

(2) Due Negotiation. If a receipt is duly negotiated, the person to whom it is negotiated may acquire rights superior to those of the transferor. A warehouse receipt is "duly negotiated" when the holder purchases the document in good faith without notice of any defense to it, for value, in an ordinary transaction in which nothing appears improper or irregular.[10] The holder of a duly negotiated document acquires title to the document and title to the

[6] UCC § 7-202(2)(a)–(i).

[7] UCC § 1-201(15).

[8] Rev. UCC § 1-201(b)(16). An "electronic" document of title is evidenced by a record consisting of information stored in an electronic medium. A "tangible" document of title is evidenced by a record consisting of information that is inscribed on a tangible medium.

[9] The spelling *endorse* is commonly used in business. The spelling *indorse* is used in the UCC.

[10] UCC § 7-501(4).

goods.[11] The holder also acquires the direct obligation of the issuer to hold or deliver the goods according to the terms of the warehouse receipt. The rights of a holder of a duly negotiated document cannot be defeated by the surrender of the goods by the warehouse to the depositor.[12]

It is the duty of the warehouse to deliver the goods only to the holder of the negotiable receipt and to cancel this receipt on surrendering the goods.[13]

The rights of a purchaser of a warehouse receipt by due negotiation are not cut off by the fact that (1) an original owner was deprived of the receipt in "bearer" form by misrepresentation, fraud, mistake, loss, theft, or conversion or (2) a bona fide purchaser bought the goods from the warehouse.

A purchaser of a warehouse receipt who takes by due negotiation does not cut off all prior rights. If the person who deposited the goods with the warehouse did not own the goods or did not have power to transfer title to them, the purchaser of the receipt is subject to the title of the true owner. Accordingly, when goods are stolen and delivered to a warehouse and a warehouse receipt is issued for them, the owner of the goods prevails over the due-negotiation purchaser of the warehouse receipt.

Study Figure 22.1, and note all of the features of a negotiable warehouse receipt in the context of the following. **For Example,** Latham and Loud (L&L) sporting goods manufacturers' representatives in Cleveland, Ohio, hijacked a truckload of ice skates from Bartlett Shoe and Skate Company of Bangor, Maine. L&L warehoused the skates at the Northern Transfer Company warehouse, and received a negotiable warehouse receipt. Jack Preston, a large sporting goods retailer who had had previous business dealings with L&L and believed it to be operated by honest individuals, made a bona fide purchase of the receipt. Bartlett, the true owner, discovered that the skates were at Northern's warehouse and informed Northern of the hijacking. Northern delivered the skates to Bartlett; Latham and Loud have fled the country. Preston believed he was entitled to delivery of the skates because he acquired the negotiable receipt by due negotiation and informed Northern of his status before delivery of the skates to Bartlett. He contemplated legal action against Northern. Preston, however, is not entitled to the skates. Ordinarily, a purchaser of a warehouse receipt obtained by due negotiation takes title to the document and title to the goods. However, an exception exists in the case of theft. Thus, because of the theft by L&L, Preston's rights have been cut off by the true owner in this case. When conflicting claims exist, the warehouse can protect itself by instituting proceedings under UCC § 7-603 to ascertain the validity of the conflicting claims.

CPA (c) Warranties

The transferor of a negotiable or nonnegotiable warehouse receipt makes certain implied warranties for the protection of the transferee. These warranties are that (1) the receipt is genuine, (2) its transfer is rightful and effective, and (3) the transferor has no

[11] UCC § 7-502(1).

[12] For electronic documents of title, Revised Article 7, Section 7-106, includes a list of how a party becomes a holder, and the result is that Article 7 creates a new concept of "control." That is, a holder who has control of a document of title (as evidenced by a record that may be electronic) has all the rights of a holder. The Revised Article states:

(a) A person has control of an electronic document of title if a system employed for evidencing the transfer of interests in the electronic document reliably establishes that person as the person to which the electronic document was issued or transferred,

(b) A system satisfies subsection (a) and a person is deemed to have control of an electronic document of title, if the electronic document is created, stored, and assigned in such a manner that:

(1) a single authoritative copy of the document exists which is unique, identifiable, and, except as otherwise provided in paragraphs (4), (5), and (6), unalterable.

(2) the authoritative copy identifies the person asserting control as:

(A) the person to which the document was issued; or

(B) if the authoritative copy indicates that the document has been transferred, the person to which the document was most recently transferred;

(3) the authoritative copy is communicated to and maintained by the person asserting control or its designated custodian;

(4) copies or amendments that add or change an identified assignee of the authoritative copy can be made only with the consent of the person asserting control;

(5) each copy of the authoritative copy and any copy of a copy is readily identifiable as a copy that is not the authoritative copy; and

(6) any amendment of the authoritative copy is readily identifiable as authorized or unauthorized.

[13] UCC § 7–403(3).

FIGURE 22-1 Negotiable Warehouse Receipt

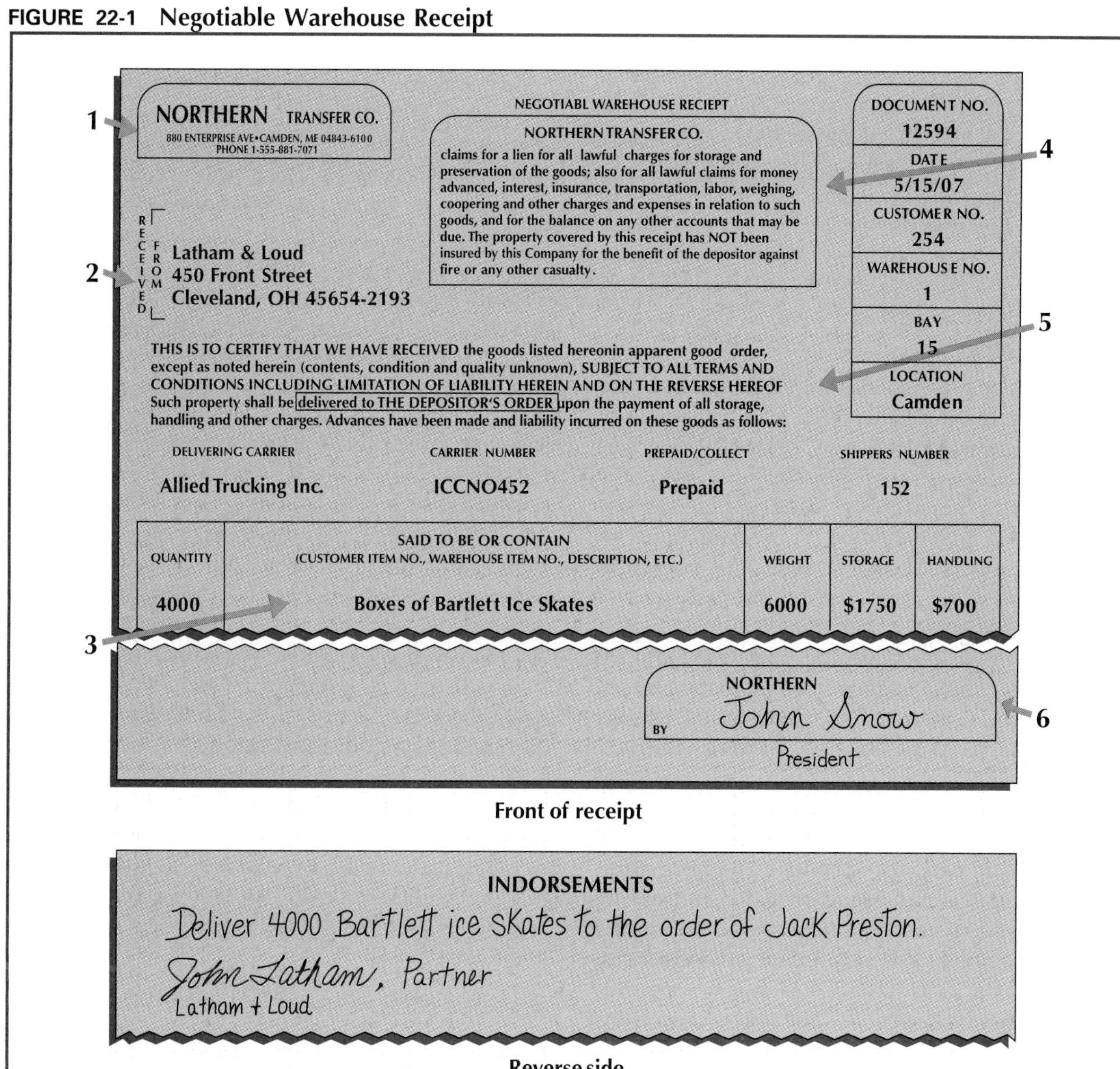
NORTHERN TRANSFER CO.
880 ENTERPRISE AVE•CAMDEN, ME 04843-6100
PHONE 1-555-881-7071

NEGOTIABL WAREHOUSE RECIEPT

NORTHERN TRANSFER CO.
claims for a lien for all lawful charges for storage and preservation of the goods; also for all lawful claims for money advanced, interest, insurance, transportation, labor, weighing, coopering and other charges and expenses in relation to such goods, and for the balance on any other accounts that may be due. The property covered by this receipt has NOT been insured by this Company for the benefit of the depositor against fire or any other casualty.

DOCUMENT NO.
12594
DATE
5/15/07
CUSTOMER NO.
254
WAREHOUSE NO.
1
BAY
15
LOCATION
Camden

RECEIVED FROM
Latham & Loud
450 Front Street
Cleveland, OH 45654-2193

THIS IS TO CERTIFY THAT WE HAVE RECEIVED the goods listed hereonin apparent good order, except as noted herein (contents, condition and quality unknown), SUBJECT TO ALL TERMS AND CONDITIONS INCLUDING LIMITATION OF LIABILITY HEREIN AND ON THE REVERSE HEREOF Such property shall be delivered to THE DEPOSITOR'S ORDER upon the payment of all storage, handling and other charges. Advances have been made and liability incurred on these goods as follows:

DELIVERING CARRIER	CARRIER NUMBER	PREPAID/COLLECT	SHIPPERS NUMBER
Allied Trucking Inc.	ICCNO452	Prepaid	152

QUANTITY	SAID TO BE OR CONTAIN (CUSTOMER ITEM NO., WAREHOUSE ITEM NO., DESCRIPTION, ETC.)	WEIGHT	STORAGE	HANDLING
4000	Boxes of Bartlett Ice Skates	6000	$1750	$700

NORTHERN
BY John Snow
President

Front of receipt

INDORSEMENTS
Deliver 4000 Bartlett ice skates to the order of Jack Preston.
John Latham, Partner
Latham + Loud

Reverse side

(1) Warehouse, (2) depositor, (3) goods, (4) warehouse's lien, (5) negotiable delivery terms, (6) warehouse's authorized agent. A negotiable warehouse receipt contains a promise to deliver the goods to the bearer or to the order of the depositor, unlike a nonnegotiable warehouse receipt, which promises only to deliver them to the depositor.

knowledge of any facts that impair the validity or worth of the receipt.[14]

5. Field Warehousing

Ordinarily, stored goods are placed in a warehouse belonging to the warehouse company. In other instances, the owner of goods, such as a manufacturer, keeps the goods in the owner's own storage area or building. The warehouse may then take exclusive control over the area in which the goods are stored and issue a receipt for the goods just as though they were in the warehouse. Such a transaction has the same legal effect with respect to other persons and purchasers of the warehouse receipts as though the

[14] UCC § 7-507. These warranties are in addition to any that may arise between the parties by virtue of the fact that the transferor is selling the goods represented by the receipt to the transferee. See Chapter 25 for a discussion of seller's warranties.

property were in fact in the warehouse. This practice is called **field warehousing** because the goods are not taken to the warehouse but remain "in the field."

The purpose of field warehousing is to create warehouse receipts that the owner of the goods may pledge as security for loans. The owner could, of course, have done this by actually placing the goods in a warehouse, but this would have involved the expense of transportation and storage.

CPA 6. Limitation of Liability of Warehouses

A warehouse may limit liability by a provision in the warehouse receipt specifying the maximum amount for which the warehouse can be held liable. This privilege is subject to two qualifications. First, the customer must be given the choice of storing the goods without such limitation if the customer pays a higher storage rate, and, second, the limitation must be stated for each item or for each unit of weight.[15] **For Example,** a limitation is proper when it states that the maximum liability for a piano is $5,000 or that the maximum liability per bushel of wheat is a stated amount. Conversely, there cannot be a blanket limitation of liability, such as "maximum liability $100," when the receipt covers more than one item.

General contract law determines whether a limitation clause is a part of the contract between the warehouse and the customer. **For Example,** warehouse Eastern Warehousing, Inc., and customer Delavau, Inc., executed a comprehensive contract for storage of a nutritional supplement after extensive negotiations between Eastern's chief operating officer and Delavau's president. The goods were damaged due to a leaking warehouse roof. Eastern was unsuccessful in its argument that the contract was formed when the goods were subsequently delivered to the warehouse and a preprinted warehouse receipt containing a limitation-of-liability provision was given to the customer's driver. The court ruled that the terms of the receipt were not part of the contract of the parties, and awarded Delavau $1,358,601 in damages.[16]

B. Common Carriers

The purpose of a bailment may be transportation. In this case, the bailee may be a common carrier.

7. Definitions

A **carrier** of goods is an individual or organization undertaking the transportation of goods regardless of the method of transportation or the distance covered. The **consignor** or shipper is the person who delivers goods to the carrier for shipment. The **consignee** is the person to whom the goods are shipped and to whom the carrier should deliver the goods.

A carrier may be classified as a common carrier, a contract carrier, or a private carrier. A **common carrier** holds itself out as willing to furnish transportation for compensation without discrimination to all members of the public who apply, assuming that the goods to be carried are proper and facilities of the carrier are available. A **contract carrier** transports goods under individual contracts, and a **private carrier** is owned and operated by the shipper. **For Example,** a truck fleet owned and operated by an industrial firm is a private carrier. Common carrier law or special bailment law applies to common carriers, ordinary bailment law to contract carriers, and the law of employment to private carriers.

The Federal Motor Carrier Safety Administration is the successor agency to the Interstate Commerce Commission and was created under the Interstate Commerce Commission Termination Act (ICCTA).[17] Under the ICCTA, Congress merged the separate classifications of common and contract carrier into one classification termed "motor carrier." However, as will be seen in the *Fortunoff* case, the fundamental distinction between the types of carriage remains explicit in the act.

8. Bills of Lading

When the carrier accepts goods for shipment or forwarding, the carrier ordinarily issues to the shipper a **bill of lading** in the case of land or water transportation or an **airbill** for air transportation. This instrument is a document of title and provides rights similar to those provided by a warehouse receipt. A bill of lading is both a receipt for the goods and a memorandum of a contract stating the terms of carriage. Title to the goods may be transferred by a transfer of the bill of lading made with that intention.

Bills of lading for intrastate shipments are governed by the Uniform Commercial Code. For interstate shipments, bills of lading are regulated by the Federal Bills of Lading Act (FBLA).[18]

[15] UCC § 7-204(2); *Lobel v Samson Moving & Storage, Inc.*, 737 NYS2d 24 (App Div 2002).

[16] *Delavau v Eastern American Trading & Warehousing, Inc.*, 810 A2d 672 (Pa Super 2002).

[17] 49 USC § 13906 (a)(3) (2000) (amended 2005).

[18] 49 USC § 81 *et seq.*

FORTUNOFF OF WESTBURY CORP. V PEERLESS INSURANCE CO., 432 F3D 127 (2ND CIR 2005)

THE LAW GETS TRICKY SOMETIMES. AN ABOLISHED DISTINCTION CONTINUES.

M. Fortunoff of Westbury operates a chain of department stores in New York and New Jersey. In March of 1997 it entered into a contract with Frederickson Motor Express, whereby the carrier agreed "as contract carrier and independent contractor...to transfer shipments...as authorized in Carrier's contract carrier permit...issued by the ICC." The contract further provided: "Although carrier is authorized to operate...as a common carrier, each and every shipment tendered to carrier by shipper...shall be deemed to be a tender to carrier as a motor contract carrier...". Fortunoff's goods were damaged in transit, prompting it to make a claim against Frederickson. When the carrier went out of business, Fortunoff asserted the same claim against the carrier's insurer, Peerless Insurance Co. for $13,249.42 under the BMC-32 endorsement (the mandatory attachment to all common carrier insurance policies) which was part of Frederickson's insurance policy. From a judgment for Fortunoff, on the ground that the ICCTA mandated the extension of BMC-32 endorsements to all motor carriers, Peerless appealed.

Judicial Opinion

CARDAMONE, C. J....[The] question is whether 49 U.S.C. § 13906(a)(3) (2000) (amended 2005), enacted as part of the Interstate Commerce Commission Termination Act of 1995 (ICCTA or Termination Act), to replace the Motor Carrier Act's insurance provisions, allowed the Federal Motor Carrier Safety Administration (agency or FMCSA)—the successor agency to the Interstate Commerce Commission (ICC) in this area of regulation—to continue to distinguish between types of motor carriage when requiring cargo liability insurance....

Although Congress' aim was to eliminate the separate registration requirements for common and contract carriers, we do not believe that fact is dispositive in this case. Rather, what is most important is the method by which Congress saw fit to implement the Termination Act. With respect to insurance, Congress left it to the Secretary of Transportation's discretion to require cargo liability insurance. As we have stated, § 13906(a)(3) replaced former § 10927(a)(3) and gave the Secretary discretion over whether "a registered motor carrier," including carriers once classified as common or contract, must insure cargo....

...Congress' creation of one type of motor carrier did not also create only one type of carriage. Indeed, common carriage services, that is, those services offered to the general public at fixed rates without negotiated bilateral contracts, continue to be different from contract carriage services, which are those services performed on an ongoing basis for a shipper pursuant to a contract individualy negotiated at arm's length. This fundamental distinction remains explicit in the terms of the Termination Act. *See* 49 U.S.C § 14101 (2000) (requiring motor carriers to perform common carrier services and permitting them to perform contract carrier services.)

...[R]equiring cargo liability insurance for common carriage but not contract carriage is not an arbitrary distinction. Instead, it makes economic sense because of the different types of services performed, and the customers served, by common carriage. Although the licensing distinction between common and contract carriers was abolished by the ICCTA, such occurred in large part because most carriers had a common carrier certificate and a contract carrier permit and provided both types of services anyway. But the functional distinction between the two types of carriage survives, and is still highly relevant to deciding which motor carriers must have cargo liability insurance....

In sum, we hold that the FMCSA's discretionary decision to require motor carriers to supply default cargo liability insurance only when performing common carriage services is consistent with the terms of the ICCTA, and the agency's decision is entitled to respect. As a consequence of this ruling we must reverse the district court's judgment in favor of plaintiff Fortunoff....

[Reversed and remanded]

Case Questions

1. State the issue in this case.
2. Can one trucking company engage in both common and contract carriage? What distinguishes a common motor carrier from a contract motor carrier?
3. Did the ICCTA abolish the distinction between the two types of carrier?

CPA (a) Contents of Bill of Lading

The form of the bill of lading is regulated in varying degrees by administrative agencies. Prior to the revisions to Article 7, negotiable bills of lading were printed on yellow paper, and nonnegotiable or straight bills of lading were printed on white paper. This color-coding may continue as commercial practice for those documents reduced to written form, but new commercial practices will evolve regarding the use of "records."[19]

As against the good faith transferee of the bill of lading, a carrier is bound by the recitals in the bill as to the contents, quantity, or weight of goods.[20] This means that the carrier must produce the goods that are described or pay damages for failing to do so. This rule is not applied if facts appear on the face of the bill that should keep the transferee from relying on the recital.

(b) Negotiation

A bill of lading is a **negotiable bill of lading** when by its terms the goods are to be delivered "to the bearer" or "to the order of" a named person.[21] Any other bill of lading, such as one that consigns the goods to a named person, is a **nonnegotiable** or **straight bill of lading**. Like transferees of warehouse receipts who take by due negotiation, holders of bills of lading who take by due negotiation ordinarily also acquire title to the bills and title to the goods represented by them.

Rights of a transferee are defeated by the true owner, however, when a thief delivers the goods to the carrier and then negotiates the bill of lading. The thief had no title to the goods at any time.

(c) Warranties

By transferring for value a bill of lading, whether negotiable or nonnegotiable, the transferor makes certain implied warranties to the transferee. The transferor impliedly warrants that (1) the bill of lading is genuine, (2) its transfer is rightful and is effective to transfer the goods represented by it, and (3) the transferor has no knowledge of facts that would impair the validity or worth of the bill of lading.[22]

9. Rights of Common Carrier

A common carrier of goods has the right to make reasonable and necessary rules for the conduct of its business. It has the right to charge such rates for its services to yield it a fair return on the property devoted to the business of transportation.

As security for unpaid transportation and service charges, a common carrier has a lien on goods that it transports. The carrier's lien also secures demurrage, the costs of preservation of the goods, and the costs of sale to enforce the lien.[23]

10. Duties of Common Carrier

A common carrier is required (1) to receive and carry proper and lawful goods of all persons who offer them for shipment as long as the carrier has space, (2) to furnish facilities that are adequate for the transportation of freight in the usual course of business and to furnish proper storage facilities for goods awaiting shipment or awaiting delivery after shipment, (3) to follow the directions given by the shipper, (4) to load and unload goods delivered to it for shipment, but the shipper or consignee may assume this duty by contract or custom, and (5) to deliver the goods in accordance with the shipment contract.

Goods must be delivered at the usual place of delivery at the specified destination. When goods are shipped under a negotiable bill of lading, the carrier must not deliver the goods without obtaining possession of the bill, properly indorsed. When goods are shipped under a straight bill of lading, the carrier may deliver the goods to the consignee or the consignee's agent without receiving the bill of lading unless notified by the shipper to deliver the goods to someone else. If the carrier delivers the goods to the wrong person, the carrier is liable for breach of contract and for the tort of conversion.

In the *Bottoms & Tops v UPS* case, the court deals with the issue of liability regarding a common carrier's delivery.

[19] The UCC contains no provision regulating the form of the bill of lading and the use of records, including electronic tracking, now covered under Revised Article 7. This means that new commercial practices will evolve.

[20] UCC § 7-301(1).

[21] UCC § 7-104(1)(a).

[22] UCC § 7-507; FBLA, 49 USC §§ 114, 116. When the transfer of the bill of lading is part of a transaction by which the transferor sells the goods represented thereby to the transferee, there will also arise the warranties that are found in other sales of goods.

[23] UCC § 7-307(1); FBLA, 49 USC § 105.

BOTTOMS & TOPS INT'L INC. V UPS, 610 NYS2D 439 (NY CITY CIV CT 1994)

MIAMI ICE

Bottoms & Tops International Inc. (plaintiff) (cross-movant) shipped a package containing jewelry via United Parcel Service (UPS) (defendant) (movant) to its salesman Ed Dwek at the Marco Polo Hotel in Miami Beach, Florida. The package was delivered to the hotel and signed for by the bell captain, who placed it in the package room and alerted Dwek by illuminating the call light in his room to contact the front desk. The bell captain released the package to an individual bearing a key to Dwek's room. Dwek did not receive the package, and Bottoms & Tops sued UPS for failure to deliver the package to Dwek.

Judicial Opinion

STEINHARDT, Judge . . . This is a motion brought on by the defendant, United Parcel Service, for an order dismissing the complaint of the plaintiff, or in the alternative, granting summary judgment against the plaintiff. Plaintiff cross-moves for an order granting summary judgment to it, as against defendant UPS.

It is the contention of the moving party that United Parcel Service fulfilled its obligation by delivering the package to the bell captain of the hotel. Cross-movant, on the other hand, maintains that delivery must be made not only to the correct address but to the correct addressee.

"The rule, doubtless, is that the common carrier of freight . . . must, in order to relieve himself from liability, deliver the goods at the place designated in good condition." It is equally well established that "[t]he common carrier also owes the duty of making delivery at a proper place where the consignee can, with convenience and safety to himself and his goods, take possession of the same."

. . . [W]hen a common carrier has transported the property to its destination, and done all of the acts pertaining to the carriage of the goods, his liability as such carrier ceases. There can, however, be no uniform rule as to what acts are necessary to be done to fulfill the carrier's contract. His duties must vary according to the nature of the consignment.

[G]enerally it is the duty of all common carriers to deliver goods carried to the consignee, unless otherwise directed in the bill of lading. But the necessities of trade and the usages and customs prevailing at the place of delivery may control, and frequently do control, the manner of discharging this duty.

The facts which form the subject matter of the above captioned action indicate to this court's satisfaction that the defendant UPS has fulfilled its duty to the plaintiff. Under the circumstances (shipment to a hotel guest) delivery to the bell captain obviated any possible liability on the part of the common carrier. "A usage, so long established, uniform and notorious, as to justify the presumption that both parties knew it, becomes a part of the contract, and may determine when the transit is over, and what is a sufficient delivery." By the terms of the contract between the plaintiff and defendant delivery only to Ed Dwek was not mandated. Delivery persons are, generally speaking, not permitted access to guest rooms in a hotel. Delivery "at a place safe and reasonable for the consignee [Dwek] to receive them" terminates the duty owed by United Parcel Service to the plaintiff.

As the issue of liability on the part of the hotel is not before this court there is no need to comment upon it. Plaintiff's cross motion for summary judgment is denied. Defendant's motion has been treated as a request for summary judgment and is granted in all respects.

Questions

1. To whom did UPS make its delivery?
2. What was the hotel procedure for packages?
3. Had UPS completed its duty as a common carrier?

CPA 11. Liabilities of Common Carrier

When goods are delivered to a common carrier for immediate shipment and while they are in transit, the carrier is absolutely liable for any loss or damage to the goods unless it can prove that the loss or damage was due solely to one or more of the following excepted causes: (1) an act of God, meaning a natural phenomenon that is not reasonably foreseeable, (2) an act of a public enemy, such as the military forces of an opposing government, as distinguished from ordinary robbers, (3) an act of a public authority, such as a health officer removing goods from the carrier, (4) an act of the shipper, such as fraudulent labeling or defective packing, or (5) the inherent nature of the goods, such as those naturally tending to spoil or deteriorate.

(a) Carrier's Liability for Delay

A carrier is liable for losses caused by its failure to deliver goods within a reasonable time. **For Example,** J.B. Hunt Transport, Inc., "lost" a shipment of boxed Christmas cards specially packaged for Target Stores, Inc., by the shipper, Paper Magic, Inc. The goods were shipped on October 16, 1998, and the invoice valued them at $130,080.48. Hunt located the shipment on February 5, 1999, and Target refused the goods because it was well after Christmas and the goods were worthless to Target. The cards were worthless to Paper Magic because they were packaged with Target's private label. The court found that awarding the shipper the invoice value was a permissible award under the Carmack Amendment to the Interstate Commerce Act.[24]

The carrier, however, is not liable for every delay. The shipper assumes the risk of ordinary delays incidental to transporting goods.

(b) Limitation of Liability of Carrier

In the absence of a constitutional or statutory prohibition, a common carrier generally has the right to limit its liability by contract.

Common carriers operating interstate may limit their liability for the negligent loss of consigned items to a stated dollar amount, such as $100 per package. Shippers, however, must be given a reasonable opportunity to select excess liability coverage for the higher value of their shipment, with payment of higher freight charges.[25]

The Carmack Amendment to the Interstate Commerce Act governs the liability of carriers for loss or damage in the interstate shipment of goods.[26] Shippers displeased with liability limitations permitted carriers under the Carmack Amendment may not sue a carrier under any state statute if the statute in any way enlarges the responsibility of a carrier for loss or damage to the goods.[27] The Carmack Amendment

ETHICS & THE LAW

The life of the long-haul trucker is grueling. Shippers impose deadlines that require round-the-clock time behind the wheel. The U.S. Department of Commerce regulates the maximum number of hours a trucker can log behind the wheel before a break is required. Enforcement of those maximums is difficult because the truckers themselves maintain the logs.

The investigation of an accident involving a semitrailer truck and several autos, in which there were fatalities, revealed that the driver of the truck had driven for 47 hours without sleep. The driver's logs showed that he was in compliance with U.S. mandates for breaks and sleep. A fellow trucker commented, "It's not us. To make a living, you have to meet their deadlines. They screw up and get behind on shipment dates and we're supposed to make up the time."

Who is responsible for violations of the break-and-sleep requirements? Is it just drivers, or do those paying for shipments share some responsibility? Do you think shippers should assume some responsibility for supervision of their drivers? Is it ethical for shippers to ask their drivers to make up the time they themselves have lost in fulfilling an order?

[24] *The Paper Magic Group, Inc. v J.B. Hunt Transport, Inc.*, 318 F3d 458 (3d Cir 2003). See also *National Hispanic Circus, Inc. v Rex Trucking*, 414 F3d 546 (5th Cir 2005).

[25] In *Sassy Doll Creations Inc. v Watkins Motor Lines Inc.*, 331 F3d 834 (11th Cir 2003), the carrier was held liable for the full value of a lost shipment of perfume, $28,273.60, rather than $10,000.00, the carrier's established limitation of its liability. The bill of lading prepared by the carrier contained a declared value box, which the shipper filled in. However, the document did not contain any space for requesting excess liability coverage and thus did not give the shipper a reasonable opportunity to select a higher level of coverage as required by the Carmack Amendment to the Interstate Commerce Act.

[26] 49 USC § 11707.

[27] *Dugan v FedEx Corp.*, 2002 WL 31305208 (CD Cal).

provides the exclusive remedy for loss or damage, and its purpose is to provide uniformity in the disposition of claims brought under a bill of lading or waybill.

(c) Notice of Claim

The bill of lading and applicable government regulations may require that a carrier be given notice of any claim for damages or loss of goods within a specified time, generally within nine months.

(d) COD Shipment

A common carrier transporting goods under a COD (cash on delivery) shipment may not make delivery of the goods without first receiving payment. If it does, it is liable to the shipper for any resulting loss. Thus, if a FedEx or UPS driver were to accept a bad check from a consignee on a COD shipment, the carrier would be liable to the shipper for the amount owed.

There are two forms of COD payments in addition to cash—certified and cashier's checks.

(e) Rejected Shipments

When a common carrier tenders delivery of consigned goods to a consignee that refuses to accept the delivery, the carrier is no longer a common carrier but becomes a warehouse. When the carrier-turned-warehouse receives new shipping instructions from the owner, its status again changes to that of a common carrier.

C. Factors and Consignments

A **factor** is a special type of bailee who sells consigned goods as though the factor were the owner of those goods.

12. Definitions

Entrusting a person with the possession of property for the purpose of sale is commonly called **selling on consignment**.[28] The owner who consigns the goods for sale is the *consignor*. The person or agent to whom they are consigned is the factor or *consignee*; this individual may also be known as a **commission merchant**. A consignee's compensation is known as a **commission** or **factorage**. **For Example,** *consignor* Rolly Tasker Sails Co., Ltd. (RTS) would ship sails from Thailand to the *consignee*, Bacon & Associates of Annapolis, Maryland, with a bill of lading and an "invoice price" for each sail. Mrs. Bacon would then set her "retail fair market value price." Once a set of sails was sold, Mrs. Bacon would deposit a check to the consignor's account at Alex Brown Co. at the invoice price. Her *commission* was the difference between the retail price and the invoice price. This arrangement began in 1971, but began to unravel 27 years later. RTS was successful in its breach of *consignment agreement* lawsuit against Bacon for $345,327 in damages and $78,660 in interest.[29]

13. Effect of Factor Transaction

In a sale on consignment, the property remains the property of the owner-consignor, and the consignee acts as the agent of the owner to pass the owner's title to the buyer. A consignment sale is treated as a sale or return under Article 2 of the Uniform Commercial Code (UCC), and the factor-consignee has full authority to sell the goods for the consignor and can pass title to those goods. For this reason, creditors of the consignee can obtain possession of the goods and have a superior right to them over the consignor. If, however, the owner-consignor complies with the security interest and perfection provisions of Article 9 of the UCC (Chapter 34), there is public notice of the consignment, and the goods will be subject to the claims of the owner's creditors, but not to those of the factor-consignee.[30]

If the consignor is not the owner, as when a thief delivers stolen goods to the factor, a sale by the factor passes no title and is an unlawful **conversion**.

28 *Amoco Oil Co. v DZ Enterprises, Inc.*, 607 F Supp 595 (SDNY 1985).

29 *Bacon & Associates, Inc. v Rolly Tasker Sails Co. Ltd. (Thailand)*, 841 A2d 53 (Md App 2004).

30 Revised Article 2 (1999) modifies the rules on consignments slightly in that all transactions are treated as sales or return or sales on approval unless steps are taken to identify a transaction as a consignment and to comply with state laws on consignment. The new UCC § 2-326(a), (b), and (c) provides as follows:

> The provisions of this subsection are applicable even though an agreement purports to reserve title to the person making delivery until payment or resale or uses such words as "on consignment" or "on memorandum." However, this subsection is not applicable if the person making delivery
>
> (a) complies with an applicable law providing for a consignor's interest or the like to be evidenced by a sign, or
>
> (b) establishes that the person conducting the business is generally known by his creditors to be substantially engaged in selling the goods of others, or
>
> (c) complies with the filing provisions of the Article on Second Transactions (Article 9).

D. Hotelkeepers

A hotelkeeper has a bailee's liability with respect to property specifically entrusted to the hotelkeeper's care. In addition, the hotelkeeper has special duties with respect to a guest's property brought into the hotel. The rules governing the special relationship between a hotelkeeper and a guest arose because of the special needs of travelers.

14. Definitions

The definitions of *hotelkeeper* and *guest* exclude lodging of a more permanent character, such as that provided by boardinghouse keepers to boarders.

(a) Hotelkeeper

A **hotelkeeper** is an operator of a hotel, motel, or tourist home or anyone who is regularly engaged in the business of offering living accommodations to transient persons. In the early law, the hotelkeeper was called an *innkeeper* or a *tavernkeeper*.

(b) Guest

A **guest** is a transient. The guest need not be a traveler or come from a distance. A person living within a short distance of a hotel who engages a room at the hotel and remains there overnight is a guest.

In contrast, a person who enters a hotel at the invitation of a guest or attends a dance or a banquet given at the hotel is not a guest. Similarly, the guest of a registered occupant of a motel room who shares the room with the occupant without the knowledge or consent of the management is not a guest of the motel because there is no relationship between that person and the motel.

15. Duration of Guest Relationship

The relationship of guest and hotelkeeper does not begin until a person is received as a guest by the hotelkeeper. The guest–hotelkeeper relationship does not automatically end when the hotel bill is paid.[31]

The relationship terminates when the guest leaves or ceases to be a transient, as when the guest arranges for a more or less permanent residence at the hotel. The transition from the status of guest to the status of boarder or lodger must be clearly indicated. It is not established by the mere fact that one remains at the hotel for a long period, even though it runs into months.

Circumstances arise when a hotel assumes an obligation to deliver packages to a guest from a person who is not a guest of the hotel. The hotelkeeper has a bailee's liability for the care of such packages. **For Example,** Richard St. Angelo, vice president of sales for jewelry manufacturer Don-Linn Inc., left two boxes of jewelry prototypes at the front desk of the Westin Hotel with instructions to deliver the boxes to the hotel's guest from Dillard's Inc., a national department store. This delivery took place. Thereafter, a Dillard's representative notified St. Angelo that Dillard's review of the products was complete and he could pick up the boxes at the hotel but specified no location. St. Angelo and the Westin staff later searched for the boxes, but they were never found. The manufacturer's lawsuit against the Westin asserting a breach of bailment was not successful. St. Angelo was not a guest at the Westin, thus the obligation assumed for the care of the packages initially left at the Westin was not as a hotelkeeper but a bailee. When the Westin surrendered the packages to Dillard's group, it completed its bailment agreement. No bailment or any other legal obligation between Don-Linn and the Westin was shown to exist with regard to the return of the jewelry prototypes.[32]

16. Hotelkeeper's Liability for Guest's Property

With respect to property expressly entrusted to the hotelkeeper's care, the hotelkeeper has a bailee's liability. At common law, the hotelkeeper was absolutely liable for damage to, or loss of, a guest's property unless the hotelkeeper could show that the damage or loss was caused solely by an act of God, a public enemy, an act of a public authority, the inherent nature of the property, or the fault of the guest.[33]

In most states, statutes limit or provide a method of limiting the common law liability of a hotelkeeper. The statutes may limit the extent of liability, reduce the liability of a hotelkeeper to that of an ordinary bailee, or permit the hotelkeeper to limit liability by contract or by posting a notice of the limitation. Some statutes relieve the hotelkeeper from liability

[31] *Garrett v Impac Hotels, LLC*, 87 SW3d 870 (Mo App 2002).

[32] *Don-Linn Jewelry Co. v The Westin Hotel Co.*, 877 A2d 621 (RI 2005).

[33] *Cook v Columbia Sussex Corp.*, 807 SW2d 567 (Tenn App 1991).

when the guest has not complied with directions for depositing valuables with the hotelkeeper.[34] A hotelkeeper must substantially comply with such statutes in order to obtain their protection.

The *Paraskevaides* case involves the application of a statute allowing hotels to limit common law liability for the loss of guests' property.

PARASKEVAIDES V FOUR SEASONS WASHINGTON, 148 F SUPP 2D 20 (D DC 2002)

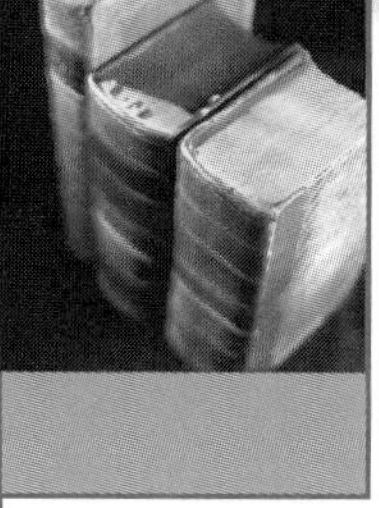

THE CASE ABOUT PROBLEMS FACED BY THE RICH AND FAMOUS AT A FIVE STAR HOTEL

Thlema Paraskevaides and others were guests at the Four Seasons Hotel in Washington, D.C. Upon arrival, they placed and locked their valuables in their room safe and left the room for the day. Upon their return, they found the room ransacked and the safe opened, and their valuables worth at $1.2 million missing. Thlema theorized that the hotel's master key to the room safes had been missing, and she believed she should have been informed of this by the hotel. The hotel contends that it satisfied the conditions for the statutory bar to strict liability for the loss under District of Columbia law.

Judicial Opinion

LAMBERTH, D. J. . . .

Statutory and Common Law Scheme

There are two aspects of law at issue here, one common law, and one statutory. Under the common law doctrine of infra hospitium, an innkeeper is strictly liable for loss or damage to a guest's property. But, in the District of Columbia (hereinafter "DC"), as in many other jurisdictions, this common law doctrine has been limited and qualified by statutory enactment. In DC, the statutory limitation exists in the provision codified at D.C.Code Ann. §§ 34–101. In pertinent part, that statute reads that:

(a) If a hotel, motel, or similar establishment in the District of Columbia which provides lodging to transient guests: (1) provides a suitable depository (other than a checkroom) for the safekeeping of personal property (other than a motor vehicle); and (2) displays conspicuously in the guest and public rooms of that establishment a printed copy of this section (or summary thereof); that establishment shall not be liable for the loss or destruction of, or damage to, any personal property of a guest or patron not deposited for safekeeping. . . .

Disposition

. . . The common law rule of infra hospitium, to the extent that it exists in DC, has been limited and qualified by § 34–101 of the DC Code, which contains an affirmative defense that the defendant can avail itself of in the instant case for the following reasons.

The bar on hotel liability of a guest's property loss is extinguished, under the statute, if the hotel a) fails to display a copy of the statute, and b) fails to post the notice conspicuously, or c) the property is that which a prudent guest would usually or commonly keep in their room with the reasonable expectation that the hotel would guard against its loss. Contrary to the plaintiffs' contentions none of these factors is fatal to the defendant's affirmative defense on the facts of this case, and no reasonable jury, based on the evidence proffered by the plaintiffs, could make a finding to the contrary.

First, § 34–101 applies when the host hotel has either posted a "printed copy of § 34–101 (or summary thereof)." As maintained by the defendant and admitted by the plaintiffs, the hotel did post a summary of § 34–101 next to the safe in which the plaintiffs placed their valuables. This was sufficient to place the plaintiffs on notice and satisfy the defendant's obligation under the statute to do such. Second, the posting was "conspicuous" enough to put the plaintiffs on notice as evidenced by the fact that the notice is placed right next to the in-room convenience depository box, as well as the fact that the plaintiffs admit to having seen the notice during various prior stays at the hotel. Third, the plaintiffs' decision to place $1.2 million dollars worth of jewelry in their hotel room safe, which was noticed with the warning that more suitable safety deposit boxes were

[34] *Chappone v First Florence Corp.*, 504 SE2d 761 (Ga App 1998). But see *World Diamond Inc. v Hyatt Corp.*, 699 NE2d 980 (Ohio App 1997), where the court held that when special arrangements have been made between the innkeeper and the guest, the innkeeper is liable for the loss of any property so received when the loss is caused by the innkeeper's negligence.

maintained at the front desk of the hotel, was not "usual, common, or prudent" as evinced by the plaintiffs' own statement that they had never brought property of that much value to the hotel before, and that they usually do not travel with property of that much value....

Conclusion

The defendant [is] not liable for the plaintiffs' property loss.

Questions

1. What is the common law doctrine of *infra hospitium* (within the inn)?
2. Does a District of Columbia statute limit the hotel's common law strict liability for the loss of a guest's valuables?
3. How did the court decide this case?

17. Hotelkeeper's Lien

The hotelkeeper has a lien on the baggage of guests for the agreed charges or, if no express agreement was made, for the reasonable value of the accommodations furnished. Statutes permit the hotelkeeper to enforce this lien by selling the goods of the guests at a public sale. The lien of the hotelkeeper is terminated by (1) the guest's payment of the hotel charges, (2) any conversion of the guest's goods by the hotelkeeper, or (3) final return of the goods to the guest.

18. Boarders or Lodgers

The hotelkeeper owes only the duty of an ordinary bailee of personal property under a mutual benefit bailment to those persons who are permanent boarders or lodgers rather than transient guests.

A hotelkeeper has no lien on property of boarders or lodgers, as distinguished from guests, in the absence of an express agreement creating such a lien. A number of states, however, have adopted legislation giving a lien to keepers of boardinghouses or lodging houses.

LAWFLIX

Nine to Five (1980) (PG)

At the heart of the twists and turns in this boss/secretary caper are the warehouse receipts an executive is using to embezzle from his company. Analyze what the executive was doing with the documents.

For movie clips that illustrate business law concepts, see LawFlix at **http://wdvl.westbuslaw.com.**

Summary

A warehouse stores the goods of others for compensation and has the rights and duties of a bailee in an ordinary mutual benefit bailment. A warehouse issues a warehouse receipt to the depositor of the goods. This receipt is a document of title that ordinarily entitles the person in possession of the receipt to receive the goods. The warehouse receipt can be bought, sold, or used as security to obtain a loan. A nonnegotiable warehouse receipt states that the goods received will be delivered to a specified person. A negotiable warehouse receipt states that the goods will be delivered "to the bearer" or "to the order of" a named person. If a negotiable warehouse receipt is duly negotiated, the transferee may acquire rights superior to those of the transferor. A warehouse may limit its liability for loss or damage to goods resulting from its own negligence to an agreed valuation of the property stated in the warehouse receipt, provided the depositor is given the right to store the goods without the limitation at a higher storage rate.

A common carrier of goods is in the business of transporting goods received from the general public. It issues to the shipper a bill of lading or an airbill. Both of these are documents of title and provide rights similar to those provided by a warehouse receipt. A common carrier is absolutely liable for any loss or damage to the goods unless the carrier can show that the loss was caused solely by an act of God, an act of a public enemy, an act of a public authority, an act of the shipper, or the inherent nature of the goods. The carrier may limit its liability in the same manner as a warehouse.

A factor is a special type of bailee who has possession of the owner's property for the purpose of sale. The factor, or consignee, receives a commission on the sale.

A hotelkeeper is in the business of providing living accommodations to transient persons called guests. Subject to exceptions, at common law, hotelkeepers were absolutely liable for loss or damage to their guests' property. Most states, however, provide a method of limiting this liability. A hotelkeeper has a lien on the property of the guest for the agreed charges.

Questions and Case Problems

1. What social forces are involved in the rule of law governing the liability of a common carrier for loss of freight?
2. American Cyanamid shipped 7,000 vials of DPT—a vaccine for immunization of infants and children against diphtheria, pertussis, and tetanus—from its Pearl River, New York, facility to the U.S. Defense Department depot in Mechanicsburg, Pennsylvania, by New Penn Motor Express, a common carrier. Cyanamid's bill of lading included a "release value," which stated the value of the property was declared as not exceeding $1.65 per pound. Cyanamid's shipment weighed 1,260 pounds. The bill of lading accepted by New Penn on picking up the DPT vaccine on February 6 also clearly stated that the shipment contained drugs and clearly warned to "protect from freezing." The bill further recited "rush . . . must be delivered by February 8, 1989." New Penn permitted the vaccine to sit in an unheated uninsulated trailer while it gathered enough other merchandise to justify sending a truck to Mechanicsburg. The DPT vaccine was delivered on February 10 in worthless condition, having been destroyed by the cold. New Penn admitted it owed $2,079 in damages pursuant to the bill of lading ($1.65 × 1,260 lbs.). Cyanamid claimed that the actual loss was much greater, $53,936.75. It stated that because New Penn breached its contract with Cyanamid, it could not invoke the benefits of that same contract, namely, the release value clause.

   Was it ethical for New Penn to hold the vaccine while waiting for enough merchandise to justify the trip? How would you decide the case? [*American Cyanamid Co. v New Penn Motor Express, Inc.*, 979 F2d 301 (3d Cir)]
3. Compare the liens of carriers, warehouses, and hotels in terms of being specific.
4. Compare the limitations of the liability of a warehouse and of a hotelkeeper.
5. Compare warehouse receipts and bills of lading as to negotiability.
6. Doyle Harms applied to his state's Public Utilities Commission for a Class B permit authorizing performance as a common carrier. Doyle testified that it was not his intention to haul in a different direction than he was already going, stating in part:

   No way, that's not what I'm asking for. I've got enough business of my own, it's just the times when you get done with a sale at the end of the day and you've got a half load and somebody else has a half load, then you'd be able to help each other out. It's kind of the name of the game in my mind.

   He also testified that the application was so he could haul cattle for his own customers. State law defines a common carrier as "a motor carrier which holds itself out to the general public as engaged in the business of transporting persons or property in intrastate commerce which it is accustomed to and is capable of transporting from place to place in this state, for hire." Its property is "devoted to the public service." Should Doyle Harms be issued a common carrier permit? [*In re Harms*, 491 NW2d 760 (SD)]
7. Welch Brothers Trucking, Inc., a common carrier, made an agreement with B&L Export and Import Co. of San Francisco to transport a shipment of freshly harvested bluefin tuna from Calais, Maine, to the Japan Air Lines freight terminal at New York's Kennedy Airport. The bluefin tuna had been packed in ice and were to be shipped by Japan Air Lines to Tokyo. Fresh bluefin are used in the traditional Japanese raw fish dish sashimi and command very high prices. When transportation charges were not paid by B&L's representative in New York, Welch Brothers refused to release the shipment to Japan Air Lines. B&L's representative in New York explained that he had no check-writing authority but assured Welch that it would be paid and pleaded for the release of the cargo because of its perishable nature. Transportation charges were not paid in the next 12-hour period because the principals of B&L were on a business trip to the Far East and could not be contacted. After waiting the 12-hour period, Welch sent a telegram to B&L's offices in San Francisco, stating the amount due and that it intended to auction the cargo in 24 hours if transportation charges were not paid. Welch also sent telegrams seeking bidders to all fish wholesalers listed in the New York City Yellow Pages. In the telegrams, Welch advised

that the cargo would be sold at auction in 24 hours if the charges were not paid. Welch sold the shipment to the highest bidder at the appointed time for an amount just in excess of the transportation charges plus a demurrage charge for the 36-hour waiting period. When the principals of B&L were later informed of what happened, they sued Welch for the profits they would have earned if the cargo had been shipped and sold in Japan. Decide.

8. Richard Schewe and others placed personal property in a building occupied by Winnebago County Fair Association, Inc. Prior to placing their property in the building, they signed a "Storage Rental Agreement" prepared by the County Fair Association, which stated: "No liability exists for damage or loss to the stored equipment from the perils of fire. . . ." The property was destroyed by fire. Suit was brought against the County Fair Association to recover damages for the losses on the theory of negligence of a warehouse. The County Fair Association claimed that the language in the storage agreement relieved it of all liability. [*Allstate Ins. Co. v Winnebago County Fair Ass'n, Inc.*,475 NE2d 230 (Ill App)]
9. Buffett sent a violin to Strotokowsky by International Parcel Service (IPS), a common carrier. Buffett declared the value of the parcel at $500 on the pick-up receipt given him by the IPS driver. The receipt also stated: "Unless a greater value is declared in writing on this receipt, the shipper hereby declares and agrees that the released value of each package covered by this receipt is $100.00, which is a reasonable value under the circumstance surrounding the transportation." When Strotokowsky did not receive the parcel, Buffett sued IPS for the full retail value of the violin—$2,000. IPS's defense was that it was liable for just $100. Decide.
10. Glen Smith contracted with Dave Watson, a common carrier, to transport 720 hives of live bees along with associated equipment from Idabel, Oklahoma, to Mandan, North Dakota. At 9:00 A.M. on May 24, 1984, while en route, Watson's truck skidded off the road and tipped over, severely damaging the cargo. Watson notified Smith what had happened, and Smith immediately set out for the scene of the accident. He arrived at 6:00 P.M. with two bee experts and a Bobcat loader. They were hindered by the turned-over truck on top of the cargo, and they determined that they could not safely salvage the cargo that evening. The next day, an insurance adjuster determined that the cargo was a total loss. The adjuster directed a bee expert, Dr. Moffat, to conduct the cleanup; Moffat was allowed to keep the salvageable cargo, valued at $12,326, as compensation. Smith sued Watson for damages. Watson denied liability and further contended that Smith failed to mitigate damages. Decide. [*Smith v Watson*, 406 NW2d 685 (ND)]
11. A guest in a motel opened the bedroom window at night and went to sleep. During the night, a prowler pried open the screen, entered the room, and stole property of the guest. The guest sued the motel. The motel asserted that it was not responsible for property in the possession of the guest and that the guest had been contributorily negligent in opening the window. Could the guest recover damages? [*Buck v Hankin*, 269 A2d 344 (Pa Super)]
12. On March 30, Emery Air Freight Corp. picked up a shipment of furs from Hopper Furs, Inc. Hopper's chief of security filled in certain items in the airbill. In the box entitled ZIP Code, he mistakenly placed the figure "61,045," which was the value of the furs. The ZIP Code box was immediately above the Declared Value box. The airbill contained a clause limiting liability to $10 per pound of cargo lost or damaged unless the shipper makes a declaration of value in excess of the amount and pays a higher fee. A higher fee was not charged in this case, and Gerald Doane signed the airbill for the carrier and took possession of the furs. The furs were lost in transit by Emery, and Hopper sued for the value of the furs, $61,045. Emery's offer to pay $2,150, the $10-per-pound rate set forth in the airbill, was rejected. Hopper claimed that the amount of $61,045, which was mistakenly placed in the ZIP Code box, was in fact part of the contract set forth in the airbill and that Emery, on reviewing the contract, must have realized a mistake was made. Decide. [*Hopper Furs, Inc., v Emery Air Freight Corp.*, 749 F2d 1261 (8th Cir)]
13. When de Lema, a Brazilian resident, arrived in New York City, his luggage consisted of three suitcases, an attaché case, and a cylindrical bag. The attaché case and the cylindrical bag contained jewels valued at $300,000. De Lema went from JFK Airport to the Waldorf Astoria Hotel, where he gave the three suitcases to hotel staff in the garage, and then he went to the lobby to register. The assistant manager, Baez, summoned room clerk Tamburino to assist him. De Lema stated, "The room clerk asked me if I had a reservation. I said, 'Yes. The name is José Berga de Lema.' And I said, 'I want a safety deposit box.' He said, 'Please fill out your registration.'" While de Lema was filling out the registration form, paying $300 in cash as an advance, and Tamburino was filling out a receipt for that amount, de Lema had placed the attaché case and the cylindrical bag on the floor. A woman jostled de Lema, apparently creating a diversion, and when he next looked down, he discovered that the attaché case was gone. De Lema brought suit against the hotel for the value of the jewels stolen in the hotel's lobby. The hotel maintained a safe for valuables and posted notices in the lobby, garage, and rooms as required by the New York law that modifies a hotelkeeper's common law liability. The notices stated in part that the hotel was not liable for the loss of valuables that a guest neglected to deliver to the hotel for safekeeping. The hotel's defense was that de Lema neglected to inform it of the presence of the jewels and to deliver the jewels to the

hotel. Is the hotel liable for the value of the stolen jewels? [*De Lema v Waldorf Astoria Hotel, Inc.*, 588 F Supp 19 (SDNY)]

14. Frosty Land Foods shipped a load of beef from its plant in Montgomery, Alabama, to Scott Meat Co. in Los Angeles via Refrigerated Transport Co. (RTC), a common carrier. Early Wednesday morning, December 7, at 12:55 A.M., two of RTC's drivers left the Frosty Land plant with the load of beef. The bill of lading called for delivery at Scott Meat on Friday, December 9, at 6:00 A.M. The RTC drivers arrived in Los Angeles at approximately 3:30 P.M. on Friday, December 9. Scott notified the drivers that it could not process the meat at that time. The drivers checked into a motel for the weekend, and the load was delivered to Scott on Monday, December 12. After inspecting 65 of the 308 carcasses, Scott determined that the meat was in off condition and refused the shipment. On Tuesday, December 13, Frosty Land sold the meat, after extensive trimming, at a loss of $13,529. Frosty Land brought suit against RTC for its loss. Decide. [*Frosty Land Foods v Refrigerated Transport Co.*, 613 F2d 1344 (5th Cir)]

15. Tate hired Action-Mayflower Moving & Storage to ship his belongings. Action prepared a detailed inventory of Tate's belongings, loaded them on its truck, and received the belongings at its warehouse, where they would be stored until Tate asked that they be moved. Months later, a dispute arose, and Tate asked Action to release his property to a different mover. Tate had prepaid more than enough to cover all charges to this point. Action refused to release the goods and held them in storage. After allowing storage charges to build up for 15 months, Action sold Tate's property under the warehouser's public sale law. Tate sued Action for damages. Decide. [*Tate v Action-Mayflower Moving & Storage, Inc.*, 383 SE2d 229 (NC App)]

CPA Questions

1. A common carrier bailee generally would avoid liability for loss of goods entrusted to its care if the goods are
   a. Stolen by an unknown person
   b. Negligently destroyed by an employee
   c. Destroyed by the derailment of the train carrying them due to railroad employee negligence
   d. Improperly packed by the party shipping them

2. Under a nonnegotiable bill of lading, a carrier who accepts goods for shipment must deliver the goods to
   a. Any holder of the bill of lading
   b. Any party subsequently named by the seller
   c. The seller who was issued the bill of lading
   d. The consignee of the bill of lading

3. Under the UCC, a warehouse receipt
   a. Is negotiable if, by its terms, the goods are to be delivered to bearer or to the order of a named person
   b. Will not be negotiable if it contains a contractual limitation on the warehouse's liability
   c. May qualify as both a negotiable warehouse receipt and negotiable commercial paper if the instrument is payable either in cash or by the delivery of goods
   d. May be issued only by a bonded and licensed warehouser

4. Under the Documents of Title Article of the UCC, which of the following acts may limit a common carrier's liability for damages to the goods in transit?
   a. Vandalism
   b. Power outage
   c. Willful acts of third person
   d. Providing for a contractual dollar liability limitation

NATURE AND FORM OF SALES

CHAPTER (23)

LEARNING OBJECTIVES

After studying this chapter, you should be able to

LO.1 Define a sale of goods and explain when UCC Article 2 applies to contracts

LO.2 Distinguish between an actual sale of goods and other types of transactions in goods

LO.3 Describe how contracts are formed under Article 2, and list the differences in formation standards between the UCC and common law

LO.4 Explain when a contract for the sale of goods must be in writing

LO.5 List and explain the exceptions to the requirement that certain contracts be in writing

LO.6 Discuss the purpose of the United Nations Convention on Contracts for the International Sale of Goods

LO.7 Discuss the distinguishing features of a consumer lease and a finance lease

Chapters 12 through 20 examined the common law of contracts. That source of contract law applies to contracts whose subject matter is land or services. However, there is another source of contract law, **Article 2** of the Uniform Commercial Code (UCC).

Article 2 was revised substantially by the National Conference of Commissioners on Uniform State Laws (NCCUSL) and the American Law Institute (ALI) in August 2003. As of June 2006, Revised Article 2 had not been adopted in any states.[1] The changes to Article 2 that have been adopted but not yet fully legislated are covered in this chapter and Chapters 24–27.

Article 2 governs the sale of everything from boats to televisions to compact discs. The UCC is a source of contract law derived from the law merchant, a body of contract law that began in common law England to facilitate transactions in goods. Today's UCC Article 2, which applies to contracts for the sale of goods, exists as a result of the work of businesspeople, commercial transactions lawyers, and legal experts who together have developed a body of contract law suitable for the fast pace of business. Article 2 continues to be refined and modified to ensure seamless laws for transactions in goods across the country.[2]

A. Nature and Legality

A *sale of goods* is defined under Article 2 as transfer of title to tangible personal property for a price.[3] This price may be a payment of money, an exchange of other property, or the performance of services.

The parties to a sale are the person who owns the goods, the seller or vendor, and the person to whom the title is transferred, the buyer or vendee.

CPA 1. Subject Matter of Sales

Goods, as defined under the UCC, consist of all forms of tangible personal property, including specially manufactured goods—everything from a fan to

[1] Kansas had introduced Article 2 for passage in 2005 but did not adopt it. The reluctance of states to adopt the revised version may have its roots in the disagreement that existed during the revision process.

[2] The UCC Article 2 (prior to the 2003 revisions) has been adopted in 49 states plus the Virgin Islands and the District of Columbia. Louisiana adopted only Article 1; 1990 Revision of Article 3; 1990 Amendments to Article 4; Article 4A (Funds Transfers); 1995 Revision of Articles 5 and 7; 1994 Revision of Article 8; and 2000 Revision of Article 9. The newest revisions of Article 2 were reconciled in July, 2003. The changes in Revised Article 2 are noted throughout this chapter and Chapters 24–27.

[3] UCC § 2-105(1).

a painting to a yacht.[4] Not covered under Article 2 are (1) investment securities, such as stocks and bonds, the sale of which is regulated by Article 8 of the UCC; (2) insurance policies, commercial paper, such as checks, and promissory notes because they are regulated under Articles 3 and 4 of the UCC; and (3) real estate, such as houses, factories, farms, and land itself.

(a) Nature of Goods

Article 2 applies not only to contracts for the sale of familiar items of personal property, such as automobiles or chairs, but also to the transfer of commodities, such as oil, gasoline, milk, and grain.[5]

(b) Existing and Future Goods

Goods that are already manufactured or crops already grown and owned by the seller at the time of the transaction are called **existing goods.** All other goods are called **future goods,** which include both goods that physically exist but are not owned by the seller and goods that have not yet been produced, as when a buyer contracts to purchase custom-made office furniture.

2. Sale Distinguished from Other Transactions

Other types of transactions in goods are not covered by Article 2 because they are not transfers of title to the goods.

(a) Bailment

A **bailment** is not a sale because only possession is transferred to a **bailee.** Title to the property is not transferred. (For more information on bailments, their nature, and the rights of the parties, see Chapter 21.) A lease of goods, such as an automobile, is governed by Article 2A of the UCC, which is covered later in Section D of this chapter.

(b) Gift

A **gift** is a gratuitous (free) transfer of the title to property. The Article 2 definition of a sale requires that the transfer of title be made for a price. Gifts are not covered under Article 2.

(c) Contract for Services

A contract for services, such as a contract for painting a home, is not a sale of goods and is not covered under Article 2 of the UCC. Contracts for services are governed by common law principles.

(d) Contract for Goods and Services

If a contract calls for both rendering services and supplying materials to be used in performing the services, the contract is classified according to its dominant element. **For Example,** a homeowner may purchase a security system. The homeowner is paying for the equipment that is used in the system as well as for the seller's expertise and installation of that system. Is the homeowner's contract governed by Article 2, or is it a contract for services and covered under the common law of contracts?

If the service element dominates, the contract is a service contract and is governed by common law rather than Article 2. If the goods make up the dominant element of the contract, then the parties' rights are determined under Article 2. In the home security system contract example, the question requires comparing the costs of the system's parts versus the costs of its installation. In some contracts, the equipment costs are minimal, and installation is key for the customer. In more sophisticated security systems, the installation is a small portion of the overall contract price, and the contract would be governed by the UCC.[6]

One of the critical issues under Article 2 that has resulted from the new high-tech environment is whether Article 2 covers computer software

[4] *State v Cardwell*, 718 A2d 594 (Conn 1998) (concert tickets are goods); *Leal v Holtvogh*, 702 NE2d 1246 (Ohio App 1998) (transfer of part interest in a horse is a good); *Bergeron v Aero Sales*, 134 P3d 964 (Or App 2006) (jet fuel is a good); *Rite Aid Corp. v Levy-Gray*, 894A 2d 563 (Md 2006) (prescription drug is a good); *Willis Mining v Noggle*, 509 SE2d 731 (Ga App 1998) (granite blocks are goods); *Sterling Power Partners, L.P. v Niagra Mohawk Power Corp.*, 657 NYS2d 407 (1997) (electricity is a good); *Gladhart v Oregon Vineyard Supply Co.*, 994 P2d 134 (Or App 1999) (grape plants bought from nursery are goods); *Dantzler v S.P. Parks, Inc.*, 1988 WL 131428 (ED Pa 1988) (purchase of ticket to amusement ride is not transaction in goods); *Rossetti v Busch Entm't Corp.*, 87 F Supp 2d 415 (ED Pa 2000) (computer software programs are goods); and *Saxton v Pets Warehouse, Inc.*, 691 NYS2d 872 (1999) (dog is goods).

[5] UCC § 2-105(1)–(2).Goods include minerals, some fixtures (or personal property attached to the land), growing crops, the unborn young of animals, and building materials to be removed by the seller. UCC § 2-105 (1990); *Koch Oil Co. v Wilber*, 895 SW2d 85 (Tex App 1995).

[6] *TK Power, Inc. v Textron, Inc.*, 433 F Supp 2d 1058 (ND Cal 2006); see also *J. O. Hooker's Sons v Roberts Cabinet*, 683 So 2d 396 (Miss 1996), in which a subcontractor's agreement to dispose of cabinets it removed from a public housing redevelopment project was held to be a service contract not governed by the UCC.

included with the sale of a computer, thus subjecting software manufacturers to warranty liability and the damage provisions of the UCC.[7] Whether software would be covered under Article 2 was the most spirited debate in the 2003 revision process.[8] Under the final draft, Article 2 does not cover "information," but information is not defined. Comments on this issue (comments are insights into the UCC sections, but they are not part of the code) indicate that Article 2 does not cover the sale of "information" not associated with goods. If this interpretation in the comment is applied, courts will be required to apply the test of whether a contract is primarily for the goods or the "information."[9]

COOK V DOWNING, 891 P2D 611 (OKLA APP 1995)

THE DECAYING RELATIONSHIP BETWEEN THE DENTIST AND HIS PATIENT: WHEN THE DENTURES DO NOT FIT, DOES THE UCC APPLY?

Mrs. Downing (appellee) was fitted for dentures by a dentist, Dr. Cook (appellant). After she received her dentures, Mrs. Downing began experiencing mouth pain she attributed to Dr. Cook's manufacture of dentures that did not fit her properly. Mrs. Downing filed suit against Dr. Cook for breach of warranty under Article 2 of the UCC. Dr. Cook defended on the grounds that his denture work was a service and, therefore, not covered under Article 2 warranties. The trial court found for Mrs. Downing, and Dr. Cook appealed.

Judicial Opinion

HUNTER, J.... 12A O.S.1991 § 2-104(1) defines *merchant* as "a person who deals in the goods of the kind or otherwise by his occupation holds himself out as having knowledge or skill peculiar to the practices or goods involved in the transaction or to whom such knowledge or skill may be attributed by his employment of an agent or broker or other intermediary who by his occupation holds himself out as having such knowledge or skill." The law of implied warranty in the commercial code is found in § 2-315 which states:

"Where the seller at the time of contracting has reason to know any particular purpose for which the goods are required and that the buyer is relying on the seller's skill or judgment to select or furnish suitable goods, there is unless excluded or modified under the next section an implied warranty that the goods shall be fit for such purpose."

We agree with Appellant's position that any claim Appellee might have sounds in tort. In Oklahoma, dentists, professionals who are regulated by the state, furnish dentures. In general, dentists must use ordinary skill in treating their patients. A patient does not establish the elements of legal detriment by only showing nonsuccess or unsatisfactory results.

A dentist is not a merchant and the Uniform Commercial Code is not the law to apply to these facts. Finding no Oklahoma law on point. we align ourselves with the reasoning stated by the Court of Appeals of North Carolina in *Preston v Thompson*, 53 N.C.App. 290, 280 S.E.2d 780 [31 UCC Rep Serv 1592] (1981). In the *Preston* case, the patient determined through her research in the yellow pages that the dentist was a specialist in dentures. The patient claimed the doctor made oral assurances that the dentures would fit satisfactorily. The dentures did not fit well and subsequent attempts at correcting the problem were not successful.

[7] *Multi-Tech Systems, Inc. v Floreat, Inc.*, 47 UCC Rep Serv 2d 924 (D Minn 2002).

[8] Section 2-103(1)(k) of Revised Article 2 defines goods as follows:
all things movable at the time of identification to a contract for sale. The term includes future goods, specially manufactured goods, the unborn young of animals, growing crops, and other identified things attached to realty as described in § 2-107. The term does not include information, the money in which the price is to be paid, investment securities under Article 8, the subject matter of foreign exchange transactions and choses in action.

[9] Section 2-102(4)–(5) provides:

(4) A transaction in a product consisting of computer information and goods that are solely the medium containing the computer information is not a transaction in goods, but a court is not precluded from applying provisions in this article to a dispute concerning whether the goods conform to the contract.

(5) Nothing in this article alters, creates, or diminishes rights in intellectual property.

The patient sued the dentist on an implied warranty theory pursuant to the Uniform Commercial Code. The court held that the transaction was not of "goods" and that a dentist was not a "merchant" under the UCC. We adopt the rule as enunciated by the North Carolina court, that "those who, for a fee, furnish their professional medical services for the guidance and assistance of others are not liable in the absence of negligence or intentional misconduct." [citation omitted] The court further held that "the fact that defendant holds himself out as specializing in the preparing and fitting of dentures does not remove him from the practice of dentistry and transform him into a merchant." We hold that under the laws of Oklahoma, a dentist is not a merchant and dentures, furnished by a dentist, are not goods under the UCC.

A dentist could be sued for breach of contract, if such contract were alleged to exist, but that is not the fact as revealed in the record in our case. Appellee presented evidence of an advertisement guaranteeing dentures to fit, but testified that she did not see this ad until after she had begun her treatment with Appellant. The evidence does not support any breach of contract action.

As a matter of law, Appellee erroneously based her cause of action on the Uniform Commercial Code rather than negligence. The court erred in entering judgment in favor of Appellee based on this law. For this reason, we reverse the judgment of the trial court and remand the matter with directions to enter judgment in favor of Appellant.

[Reversed and remanded with directions]

Dissenting Opinion

JONES, J., dissenting. As is typical of small claims . . . [t]he transaction of a patient being fitted for and purchasing dentures from a dentist is actually a hybrid. It is not purely a sale of goods by a merchant, nor is it purely the providing of a service by a health care professional. Whether implied warranties under Article 2 of the U.C.C. apply to such a transaction should depend on whether the predominant element of the transaction is the sale of goods or the rendering of services. If the sale of goods predominates, it would be within the scope of Article 2 and the implied warranties contained therein. However, if the service aspect predominates, there would be no implied warranties.

Although the record contains no specific findings of fact, the record does contain evidence from which it could be concluded that this transaction was principally a sale of goods and that the implied warranty of merchantability applies thereto. The evidence was also sufficient that the trier of fact could have concluded that the dentures were not fit for their ordinary purpose as required to establish a prima facie case for breach of the implied warranty of merchantability. We must affirm a law action tried to the court if there is any competent evidence to support the judgment. *United Engines, Inc. v McConnell Const. Inc.*, 641 P.2d 1101 (Okla. 1980).

In contemporary society the old distinctions separating health care professionals from other businessmen are blurring in many respects. This court's holding that a dentist is *not* a merchant, and dentures, furnished by a dentist, are *not* goods ignores the fact that nothing excludes them from the statutory definitions of merchant and goods. It also ignores the fact that health care professionals in some instances *are* selling goods to their "patients", with the providing of professional services being secondary to the sale. To such transactions there is no reason Article 2 of the UCC should not apply.

I respectfully dissent.

Questions

1. What policy issues would arise if dentures were treated as sale of goods?
2. Is Mrs. Downing left without a remedy or does she have alternatives?
3. Is Dr. Cook a merchant? Why or why not?

CPA 3. Formation of Sales Contracts

(a) Necessary Detail for Formation

To streamline business transactions, Article 2 of the UCC does not have standards as rigid as the formation standards of common law contracts.

Under the UCC, the formation of a contract can be recognized even though one or more terms are left open so long as the parties clearly intend to contract.[10] The minimum terms required for formation of an agreement under the UCC are the subject matter and quantity (if there is more than

10 5 UCC § 2-204(3); *Cargill v Jorgenson Farms*, 719 NW 2d 226 (Minn App 2006). This provision on formation assumes that the agreement the parties do have provides "a reasonably certain basis for giving an appropriate remedy." Revised § 2-204 provides for electronic communication.

one).[11] **For Example,** an agreement that described "the sale of my white Ford Taurus" would be sufficient, but an agreement to purchase "some Ford Tauruses" would require a quantity in order to qualify for formation.[12] Other provisions under Article 2 can cover any missing terms so long as the parties are clear on their intent to contract. Article 2 contains provisions covering price, delivery, time for performance, payment, and other details of performance in the event the parties agree to a sale but have not discussed or reduced to writing their desires in these areas.[13]

(b) The Merchant versus Nonmerchant Parties

Because Article 2 applies to all transactions in goods, it is applicable to sales by both **merchants** and nonmerchants,[14] including consumers. In most instances, the UCC treats all buyers and sellers alike. However, some sections in Article 2 are applicable only to merchants, and as a result, there are circumstances in which merchants are subject to different standards and rules. Generally, these areas of different treatment constitute the UCC's recognition that merchants are experienced, have special knowledge of the relevant commercial practices, and often need to have greater flexibility and speed in their transactions. The sections that have different rules for merchants and nonmerchants are noted throughout Chapters 24–27.

CPA (c) Offer

Just as in common law, the **offer** is the first step in formation of a sales contract under Article 2.[15] The common law contract rules on offers are generally applicable in sales contract formation with the exception of the **firm offer**[16] provision, which is a special rule on offers applicable only to merchants: An offer by a merchant cannot be revoked if the offer (1) expresses an intention that it will be kept open, (2) is in a writing, and (3) is signed by the merchant.[17]

The period of irrevocability in a merchant's offer cannot exceed three months. If no specific time is given in the merchant's firm offer for its duration, it remains irrevocable only for a reasonable time. A firm offer for the three months' maximum time is effective regardless of whether the merchant received any consideration to keep the offer open. **For Example,** a rain check given by a store on advertised merchandise is a merchant's firm offer. The rain check guarantees that you will be able to purchase two bottles of Windex at $1.99 each for a period specified in the rain check.

For nonmerchants and contracts in which the parties want periods in excess of three months, there must be consideration because to be enforceable, there must be an option contract just like those used in common law contracts (see Chapters 12 and 13).

(d) Acceptance—Manner

Unlike the common law rules on acceptance, which control with great detail the method of **acceptance,** the UCC rules on acceptance are much more flexible. Under Article 2, an acceptance of an offer may be in any manner and by any medium that is reasonable under the circumstances.[18] Acceptance can occur through written communication or through performance as when a seller accepts an offer for prompt shipment of goods by simply shipping the

11 Although, see *A. M. Capern's Co. Inc. v American Trading & Production Corp.*, 973 F Supp 247 (DPR 1997), in which the court held that the absence of quantity was not fatal to the formation of a contract.

12 *Syrovy v Alpine Resources, Inc.*, 859 P2d 51 (Wash 1993).

13 For information on terms, see UCC §§ 2-305 (price), 2-307 to 2-308 (delivery), 2-310 (payment), and 2-311 (performance).

14 *Merchant* is defined in UCC § 2-104(1). An operator of a turkey farm is not a merchant with regard to heaters used on turkey farms, only for the turkeys themselves. *Jennie-O-Foods, Inc. v Safe-Glo Prods. Corp.*, 582 NW2d 576 (Minn App 1998).

15 A purchase order is generally considered an offer, but it must have enough information to meet the minimum standards for an offer. *Biotech Pharmacal, Inc. v International Business Connections*, LLC184 SW3d 447, 53 UCC Rep Serv 2d 476 (Ark Ct App 2004).

16 Firm offers are found in UCC § 2-205.

17 A *quotation* is a firm offer. *Rich Products Corp. v Kemutec, Inc.*, 66 F Supp 2d 937 (ED Wis 1999).

18 UCC § 2-206(1). UCC § 2-206 governs acceptance methods and provides:

(1) Unless otherwise unambiguously indicated by the language or circumstances (a) an offer to make a contract shall be construed as inviting acceptance in any manner and by any medium reasonable in the circumstances; (b) an order or other offer to buy goods for prompt or current shipment shall be construed as inviting acceptance either by a prompt promise to ship or by the prompt . . . shipment of . . . [goods].

see Gulf States Utilities Co. v NEI Peebles Elec. Products, Inc., 819 F Supp 538 (MD La 1993).

goods.[19] However, just as under common law, Article 2 requires that if the offer specifies the manner or medium of acceptance, the offer can be accepted only in that manner.

CPA (e) Acceptance—Timing

The timing rules of the common law for determining when a contract has been formed are used to determine the formation of a contract under Article 2 with one slight modification. The **mailbox rule** applies under the UCC not just for the use of the same method of communication as that used by the offeror, but so long as the acceptance is communicated using any reasonable method of communication. Under the common law, the same method of communication used by the offeror had to be used by the offeree in order to have the mailbox rule of acceptance be effective upon mailing or dispatch. A UCC offeree can use a reasonable method and still obtain the priority timing so that his acceptance is effective when it is sent. For example, suppose that Feather-Light Brownies sent a letter offer to Cane Sugar Suppliers offering to buy 500 pounds of confectioner's sugar at $1 per pound. Cane Sugar Suppliers faxes back an acceptance of the letter offer. Cane Sugar Suppliers' acceptance is effective when it sends the fax.

CPA (f) Acceptance—Language

Under the common law, the **mirror image rule** applies to acceptances. To be valid acceptances under common law, the language of the acceptance must be absolute, unconditional, and unequivocal; that is, the acceptance under common law must be the mirror image of the offer in order for a contract to be formed. However, the UCC has liberalized this rigid rule and permits formation even in circumstances when the acceptance includes terms that vary from the offer. The following sections explain the old UCC rules on differing terms in acceptances. These rules for additional terms in acceptance will be eliminated under Revised Article 2 (discussed later).

(1) Additional Terms in Acceptance—Nonmerchants. Under Article 2, unless an offer expressly specifies that an offer to buy or sell goods must be accepted exactly as made, the offeree may accept an offer and at the same time propose an additional term or terms. The additional term or terms in the acceptance does not result in a rejection as it would under common law. A contract is formed with the terms of the original offer. The additional terms are proposals for addition to the contract and may or may not be accepted by the other party.[20] **For Example,** Joe tells Susan, "I'll sell you my X-box for $150," and Susan responds, "I'll take it. The Halo game is included." Susan has added an additional term in her acceptance. At this point, Joe and Susan have a contract for the sale of the X-box for $150. Whether the Halo game is included is up to Joe; Joe is free to accept Susan's proposal or reject it, but his decision does not control whether he has a contract. There is a contract because Susan has made a definite statement of acceptance. To avoid being bound by a contract before she is clear on the terms, Susan should make an inquiry before using the language of acceptance, such as "Would you include the Halo game as part of the sale?" Susan's inquiry is not an acceptance and leaves the original offer still outstanding, which she is free to accept or reject.

(2) Additional Terms in Acceptance—Merchants. Under Article 2, the use of additional terms in acceptances by merchants is treated slightly differently. The different treatment of merchants in acceptances is the result of a commercial practice known as the **battle of the forms,** which results because a buyer sends a seller a purchase order for the purchase of goods. The seller sends back an invoice to the buyer. Although the buyer and seller may agree on the front of their documents that the subject matter of their contracts is 500 treadmills, the backs of their forms have details on the contracts, often called *boilerplate language,* that will never match. Suppose, for example, that the seller's invoice adds a payment term of "10 days same as cash." Is the payment term now a part of the parties' agreement? The parties have a meeting of the minds on the subject matter of the contract but now have a slight difference in performance terms.

Under Article 2, in a transaction between merchants, the additional term or terms sent back in an acceptance become part of the contract if the additional term or terms do not materially alter the offer

[19] UCC § 2-206(1)(b). Shipment of coal in response to an offer is acceptance. *Central Illinois Public Service Co. v Atlas Minerals, Inc.,* 146 F3d 448 (7th Cir 1998).

[20] Revised Article 2 provides protections for consumers on terms they would not expect, that were not negotiated, or of which they had no knowledge. Rev UCC § 2-206.

FIGURE 23-1 Terms in Contracts under UCC Article § 2-207

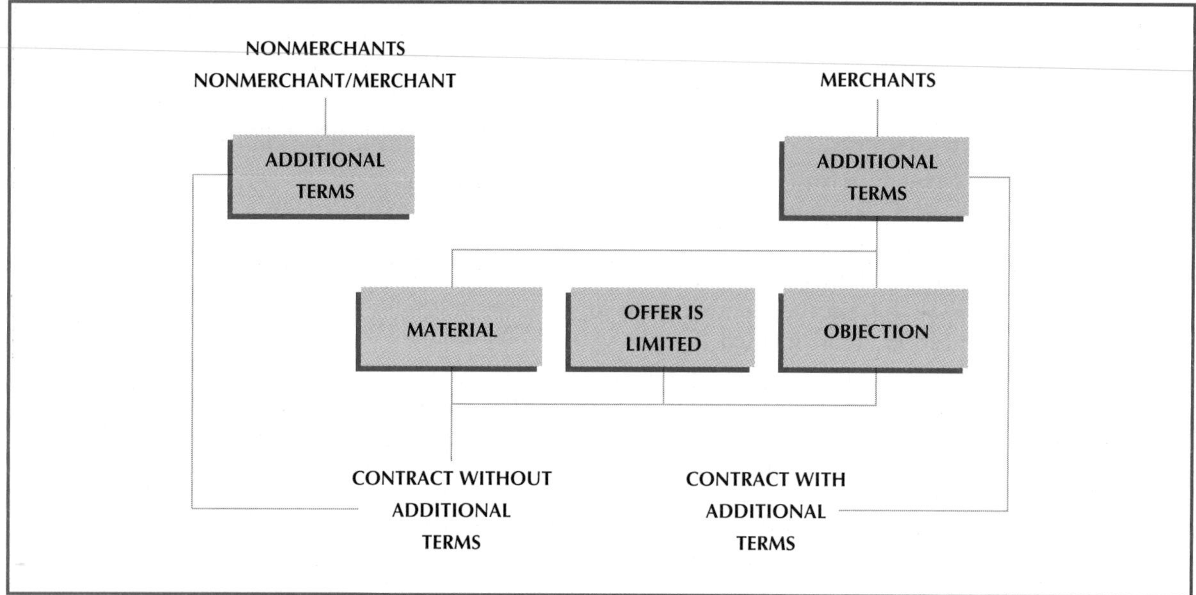

and the offeror does not object in a timely fashion.[21] **For Example,** returning to the Joe and Susan example, suppose that they are both now secondary market video game merchants negotiating for the sale and purchase of a used X-box. They would have a contract, and the Halo game would be included as part of the sale. Joe could, however, avoid the problem by adding a limitation to his offer, such as "This offer is limited to these terms." With that limitation, Susan would have a contract, but the contract would not include the Halo game. Joe could also object immediately to Susan's proposal for the Halo game and still have a contract without this additional term.[22]

If the proposed additional term in the acceptance is material, a contract is formed, but the material additional term does not become a part of the contract.[23] **For Example,** if Susan added to her acceptance the statement, "Game system carries one-year warranty," she has probably added a material term because the one-year warranty for a used game system would be unusual in the secondary market and costly for Joe.[24] Again, Joe can avoid this problem by limiting his offer so as to strike any additional terms, whether material or immaterial.

The most significant changes under Revised Article 2 deal with § 2-207. Because there were so many confusing circumstances with additional terms, the effect of the new § 2-207 is to leave the issues of what is or is not included in a contract to the courts. The courts will determine, on a case-by-case basis, what is included as part of the contract, in some cases regardless of what the "record" provides. Revised § 2-207 applies to merchants and nonmerchants alike and regardless of whether the parties use forms.

Figure 23-1 is a graphic picture of the rules on acceptance and contract terms under current Article 2 when additional terms are proposed. Figure 23-2 provides a diagram of Revised § 2-207.

Even without all the UCC provisions on contract terms, an offeror may expressly or by conduct agree to a term added by the offeree to its acceptance of the offer. The offeror may agree orally or in writing to the additional term. There can be acceptance by

21 UCC § 2-207(2).

22 *Transwestern Pipeline Co. v Monsanto Co.*, 53 Cal Rptr 2d 887 (Ct App 1996). Revised UCC Article 2 makes changes in the way these additional terms operate. When there is a record of an agreement, with no objection, the terms in the record are the terms of the contract.

23 Damage limitations clauses are considered material. *Jom, Inc. v Adell Plastics, Inc.*, 193 F3d 47 (1st Cir 1999).

24 A statute of limitations of one year added to the acceptance of an offer is considered a material change because it limits so severely the amount of time for bringing suit on the contract. *American Tempering, Inc. v Craft Architectural Metals Corp.*, 483 NYS2d 304 (1985).

FIGURE 23-2 Terms in Contracts under UCC Revised Article § 2-207

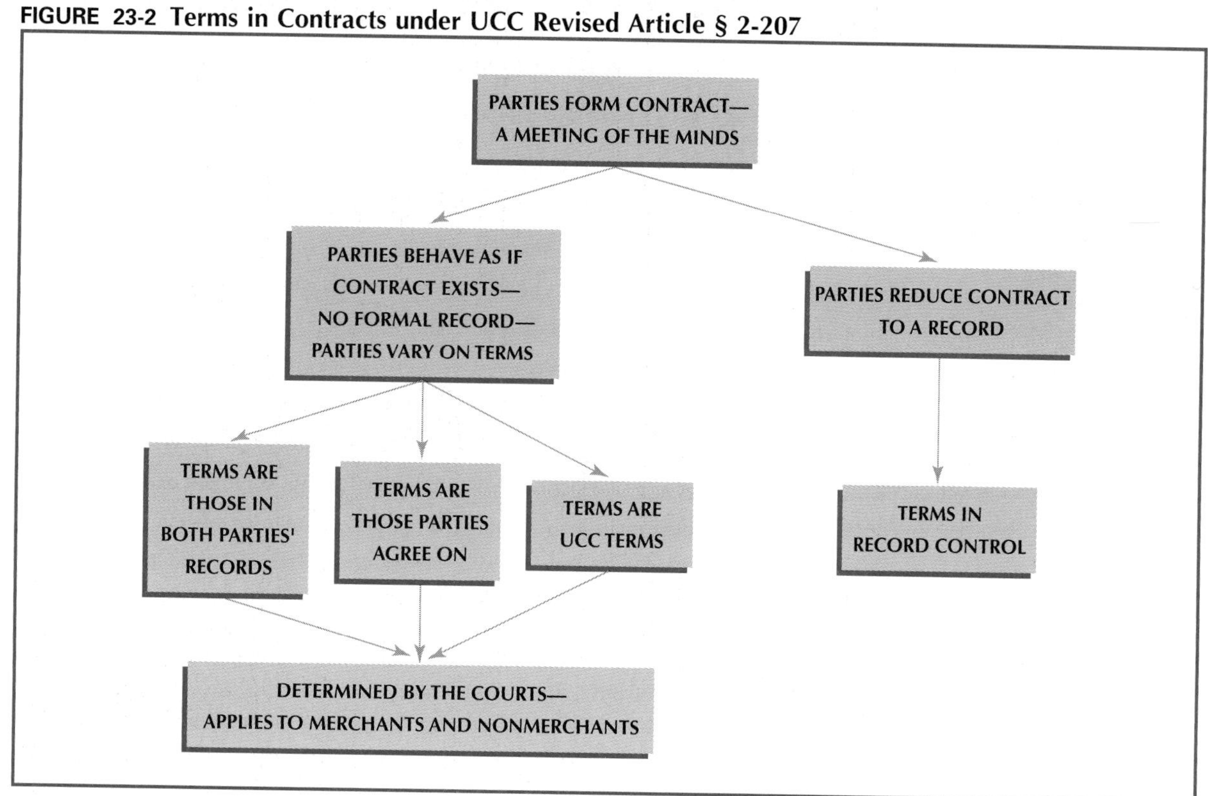

conduct of the additional term if the parties just perform their obligations under the contract with knowledge that the term has been added by the offeree.[25]

(3) Conflicting Terms in Acceptance. In some situations, the offeree has not added a different term from the original offer but has instead proposed terms that contradict the terms of the offer. **For Example,** a buyer's purchase order may require the seller to offer full warranty protection, whereas the seller's invoice may include a disclaimer of all warranties. The buyer's purchase order may include a clause that provides "payment in 30 days same as cash," whereas the seller's invoice may include a term that has "10 days same as cash." Once again, it is clear that the parties intended to enter into a contract, and the subject matter is also clear. The task for Article 2 becomes one of establishing the rules that determine the terms of a contract when both sides have used different forms. However, if there are conflicting terms on the basic requirements (such as price) for formation, the courts may conclude that the parties have not met minds.[26]

When a term of an acceptance conflicts with a term of an offer but it is clear that the parties intended to be bound by a contract, the UCC still recognizes the formation of a contract. The terms that are conflicting cancel each other and are ignored. The contract then consists of the terms of the offer and acceptance that agree. **For Example,** if one party's contract form provided for full warranty protection and the other party's form provided for no warranty protection, the terms cancel each other out, and the parties' contract includes only those warranties provided under Article 2 (see Chapter 25 for a discussion of those warranties).

[25] Revised UCC §2-207 provides: (3) Conduct by both parties which recognizes the existence of a contract is sufficient to establish a contract for sale although the writings of the parties do not otherwise establish a contract. In such case the terms of the particular contract consist of those terms on which the writings of the parties agree, together with any supplementary terms incorporated under any other provisions of this Act.

[26] *Howard Const. Co. v Jeff-Cole Quarries, Inc.*, App, 669 SW2d 221(1984), where the acceptance changed the price there was not an acceptance but a counteroffer.

UNITED STATES SURGICAL CORP. V ORRIS, INC., 5 F SUPP 2D 1201 (D KAN 1998); AFFIRMED 185 F3D 885 (10TH CIR 1999) AND 230 F3D 1382 (FED CIR 2000)

CUTS LIKE A KNIFE AND MORE THAN ONCE

U.S. Surgical manufactures medical surgical instruments and markets the instruments to hospitals. U.S. Surgical registered trademarks on its own name and its products' names and registered patents on its products. The corporation has expended substantial time, effort, and money to develop and promote customer recognition of its trademarks and exercises stringent quality control methods to assure that its customers receive a superior quality product.

U.S. Surgical enters into contracts with its customers for the sale of its disposable instruments. It also enters into contracts with distributors who in turn sell its disposable instruments. The customers submit individual orders by telephone, fax, mail, or electronic data interchange for the purchase of products. The orders are received in Connecticut and entered into U.S. Surgical's computer system in Connecticut. Within 24 hours of shipment of each order, U.S. Surgical sends the customer an invoice, which includes Standard Terms and Conditions of Sale, including specific modifications of terms as negotiated between U.S. Surgical and the customer. The invoice states that the contract shall be governed by and construed under the laws of the state of Connecticut. Each product shipment also includes a shipping document.

The packaging for U.S. Surgical's disposable medical instruments is labeled "for single use only." As an example, one label contains the following language: "Unless opened or damaged, contents of package are sterile. DO NOT RESTERILIZE. For multiple use during a SINGLE surgical procedure. DISCARD AFTER USE." The instruction booklets contain similar language in the "Cautions" section: "These devices are provided STERILE and are intended for use during a SINGLE procedure only. DISCARD AFTER USE. DO NOT RESTERILIZE."

Orris provides a service to the hospitals that purchase U.S. Surgical's disposable instruments. After the hospitals use or open the instruments, Orris cleans, resterilizes, and/or resharpens the instruments for future use and returns them to the hospitals from which they came. In the past, Orris marketed its service by indicating that the reprocessed instruments have "restored original quality" and are "as good as new." Presently, Orris only suggests that the instruments will function as the manufacturer intended.

U.S. Surgical admits that Orris may resterilize opened but unused instruments notwithstanding the "do not resterilize" language. The Food and Drug Administration requires the "single use only" or similar language on the labels of instruments that U.S. Surgical designates as disposable. Beginning in November 1995, U.S. Surgical began asserting that reprocessing, repackaging, and reuse of its disposable instruments constituted a breach of contract by the hospitals. The lower court found the "single use" term was an additional one not accepted by the hospitals. U.S. surgical appealed.

Judicial Opinion

VAN BEBBER, C. J.... U.S. Surgical contends that the "single use only" labels created a contractually enforceable restriction on the implied license limiting the hospitals' use of the instruments to a single surgical procedure. Such a limitation on the implied license could arise if the "single use only" language was a valid condition of the sale, or if the language was a limitation on the implied license independent of the sales contract.

The sale of medical instruments is governed by Article 2 of the Uniform Commercial Code. U.S. Surgical argues, and the court agrees, that each sales contract was concluded when U.S. Surgical received customer orders in Connecticut. Thus, the single use only language that appeared on the product label and instructions was a proposed post-sale modification of the agreement under U.C.C. 2-209.

Section 2-209 allows a modification to an existing agreement without independent consideration. Nonetheless, the post-sale proposed "single use only" restriction required assent by the customers to become a binding term of the sales agreement. "[A] writing will be a final expression of, or a binding modification to, an earlier agreement only if the parties so intend." "[T]he assent must be express and cannot be inferred merely from a party's conduct in continuing with the agreement."

Even if the product label is considered a written confirmation of the order under U.C.C. § 2-207, the "single use only" term is not binding on the customer if the additional term materially alters the agreement and the customer does not confirm the seller's expressly conditional acceptance requiring the additional term or otherwise expressly assent to the additional term. Any reasonable trier of fact would conclude that, in a product sales context, a term that reduces the customer's right to use the product from unlimited use to a single use materially alters the contract. Moreover, the label did not expressly condition the seller's acceptance of the customer's offer on the customer's allowance of the additional term. The label stated only, "for single use only."

The express assent analysis is the same under § 2-207 and § 2-209. Neither U.S. Surgical nor the court's own exhaustive search of the record produces evidence of any express assent to the subsequent modification to the agreement. A hospital's mere compliance with the previously entered agreement did not constitute assent or indicate any intent to adopt the single use only language as a modification to the agreement. Accordingly, under either § 2-207 or § 2-209, the "single use only" term was not a binding term of the sales agreement.

[Affirmed]

Questions

1. What provision appeared on U.S. Surgical's products?
2. Is the provision material?
3. Will U.S. Surgical be permitted to enforce the provision?

(g) Defenses to Formation

Article 2 incorporates the common law defenses to formation of contracts by reference to the common law defenses in § 1-103 (see Chapter 14 for a full discussion of those defenses). **For Example,** a party to a contract who can establish that the other party engaged in fraud to get the contract formed may cancel the contract and recover for losses that result from any damages for goods already delivered or payment already made.

(1) Unconscionability. The UCC includes an additional contract defense for parties to a sale contract called *unconscionability*.[27] This section permits a court to refuse to enforce a sales contract that it finds to be **unconscionable,** which is generally defined as grossly unfair.[28] A court may also find a clause or portions of a contract to be unconscionable and refuse to enforce those clauses or sections.[29]

(2) Illegality. At common law, a contract is void if its subject matter itself is illegal, such as a contract for hire to murder someone. Under the UCC, a contract for the sale of heroin would be void. Likewise, a contract for the sale of a recalled or banned toy would be void.

(3) The Effect of Illegal Sale. An illegal sale or contract to sell cannot be enforced. As a general rule, courts will not aid either party in recovering money or property transferred under an illegal agreement.

4. Terms in the Formed Contract

As noted earlier, contracts can be formed under Article 2 with terms of performance still missing or open. A contract is formed with just the quantity agreed on, but there are issues that must be resolved if the contract is to be completed. Article 2 has provisions for such missing terms.

CPA (a) Price

If the price for the goods is not expressly fixed by the contract, the price may be an open term, whereby the parties merely indicate how the price should be determined at a later time. In the absence of any reference to price, the price will be a reasonable price at the time of the delivery of the goods, which is generally the market price.[30]

[27] UCC § 2-302. *El Paso Natural Gas Co. v Minco Oil & Gas Co., Inc.*, 8 SW3d 309 (Tex 1999).

[28] Disparity in bargaining power is an issue but is not controlling. In *Intrastate Piping & Controls, Inc. v Robert-James Sales, Inc.*, 39 UCC Rep Serv 2d 347 (Ill Cir Ct 1999), a clause limiting remedies to replacement of defective pipe with no additional damages was upheld because while the seller was a large, national business and the buyer a small, local business, the contract merely incorporated industry practice in terms of remedies.

[29] An example would be voiding exorbitant interest charges but enforcing the underlying sale.

[30] UCC § 2-305(1) provides, "the price is a reasonable price at the time for delivery."

Parties often use formulas for determining price in sales of goods. The price itself is missing from the contract until the formula is applied at some future time. The so-called **cost plus** formula for determining price has been used a great deal, particularly in commercial contracts. Under this formula, the buyer pays the seller the seller's costs for manufacture or obtaining the goods plus a specified percentage as profit.

The UCC allows contracts that expressly provide that one of the parties may determine the price. In such a case, that party must act in good faith, another requirement under the UCC that applies to merchants and nonmerchants in the formation and performance of their contracts.[31]

CPA (b) Output and Requirements Contracts

The **output contract** and the **requirements contract**[32] do not specify the quantity to be sold or purchased. Instead, the contract amount is what the seller produces or the buyer requires. **For Example,** a homeowner may contract to purchase propane fuel for her winter heating needs. The propane company agrees to sell her the amount of propane she needs, which will vary from year to year according to the winter weather, her time at home, and other factors. Although the open quantity in contracts such as these introduces an element of uncertainty, such sales contracts are valid but subject to two limitations: (1) The parties must act in good faith and (2) the quantity offered or demanded must not be unreasonably disproportionate to prior output or requirements or to a stated estimate. With these restrictions, the homeowner will obtain all of the propane she needs for heating but could not use her particularly beneficial price under her open-quantity contract to purchase additional propane to sell to others.

(c) Indefinite Duration Term

When the sales contract is a continuing contract, such as one calling for periodic delivery of coal, but no time is set for the life of the contract, the contract runs for a reasonable time. It may be terminated by notice from either party to the other party.

CPA (d) Changes in Terms: Modification of Contract

An agreement to modify a contract for the sale of goods is binding even though the modification is not supported by consideration.[33] The modification is valid so long as the agreement is voluntary. **For Example,** suppose that Chester's Drug Store has agreed to purchase 300 bottles of vitamins from Pro-Life, Inc., at a price of $3.71 per bottle. Pro-Life has experienced substantial cost increases from its suppliers and asks Chester to pay $3.74 per bottle. Chester is not required to agree to such a price increase because it has a valid contract for the lower price. If Chester agrees to the price increase, however, the agreement for the higher price is valid despite the lack of additional consideration on the part of Pro-Life. Chester may agree to the higher price because Pro-Life's price is still much lower than its competitors and Chester has a longstanding relationship with Pro-Life and values its customer service. However, Pro-Life could not threaten to cut off Chester's supply in order to obtain the price increase because that would be a breach of contract and would also be duress that would invalidate Chester's consent to the higher price. (See Chapter 14 for a discussion of duress.)

CPA (e) Contradicting Terms: Parol Evidence Rule

The **parol evidence rule** (see Chapter 17 for a complete discussion) applies to the sale of goods, with the slight modification that a writing is not presumed to represent the entire contract of the parties unless the court specifically decides that it does.[34] If the court so decides, parol evidence is not admissible to add to or contradict the terms of the writing. **For Example,** suppose that Ralph Rhodes and Tana Preuss negotiate the sale of Ralph's 1965 Mustang to Tana. During their discussions, Ralph agrees to pay for an inspection and for new upholstery for the car. However, Tana and Ralph sign a simple sales contract that includes only a description of the Mustang and the price. Tana cannot enforce the two provisions because she failed to have them written into their final

[31] Good faith requires that the party act honestly and, in the case of a merchant, also requires that the party follow reasonable commercial standards of fair dealing that are recognized in the trade. UCC §§ 1-201(1)(a), 2-103(1)(b); *Uptown Heights Associates, Ltd., Partnership v Seafirst Corp.*, 891 P2d 693 (Or 1995).

[32] UCC § 2-306; *Lenape Resources Corp. v Tennessee Gas Pipeline Co.*, 925 SW2d 565 (Tex 1996).

[33] UCC § 2-209(1); *Horbach v Kacz Marek*, 934 F Supp 981 (ND Ill 1996), aff'd, 388 F3d 969 (7th Cir 2002).

[34] UCC § 2-202.

agreement. The parol evidence rule requires the parties to be certain that everything they want is in their agreement before they sign. The courts cannot referee disputes over collateral agreements the parties fail to put in writing.

If the court decides that the writing was not intended to represent the entire contract, the writing may be supplemented by additional extrinsic evidence, including the proof of additional terms as long as these terms are not inconsistent with the written terms. Parol evidence may also be admitted to interpret contract terms or show what the parties meant by their words. The parol evidence rule also does not prohibit the proof of fraud, misrepresentation, and any other defenses in formation.

(f) Interpreting Contract Terms: Course of Dealing and Usage of Trade

The patterns of doing business the parties develop through their prior contractual transactions, or **course of dealing,** become part of their contract.[35] These patterns may be used to find what was intended by the express provisions in their contract and to supply otherwise missing terms. **For Example,** if the parties had 10 previous agreements and payment was always made on the 30th day following delivery, that conduct could be used to interpret the meaning of a clause "payment due in 30 days" when the start of the 30 days is not specifically agreed to in the contract.

In addition, the customs of the industry, or **usage of trade,** are adopted by courts in their interpretation of contract terms. **For Example,** suppose that a contract provides for the sale of mohair. There are two types of mohair: adult and kid. Because adult mohair is cheaper and easier to find, industry custom provides that unless the parties specifically place the term *kid* with the term *mohair* in the contract, the contract is one for the sale of adult mohair. Under Article 2, the court need not find that a contract is ambiguous or incomplete in order to examine the parties' pattern of previous conduct as well as industry custom.[36]

5. Bulk Transfers

Bulk transfer law, Article 6 of the UCC, was created to deal with situations in which sellers of businesses fail to pay the creditors of the business and instead use the proceeds of the sale for their own use.

ETHICS & THE LAW

Triple Crown America, Inc., said that it had been involved in extensive discussions with Biosynth AG, a German company, to be Biosynth's exclusive distributor for melotonin to the U.S. "natural food" market. The companies, in fact, began performance of a distribution contract with Biosynth sending melotonin to Triple Crown. Triple Crown, however, said that the amount sent was insufficient for national distribution. Biosynth was, in fact, sending melotonin to other distributors and not honoring what Triple Crown maintained was an exclusive sales arrangement. In addition, an article in the *Chemical Marketing Reporter* quoted a "spokeswoman" for Biosynth as saying that it had an exclusive distributorship arrangement with Triple Crown.

Biosynth said that it never formalized its arrangements with Triple Crown and was free to deal with others. Should Biosynth be held to its publicly reported statements, or should it be able to rely on contract formation issues and the lack of specifics as a defense to the agreement? Do you think the article is an admission of the contract?*

* *Triple Crown America, Inc. v Biosynth AG,* 38 UCC Rep Serv 2d 746 (1999).

[35] UCC § 2-208. Under Revised Article 2, § 2-208 is eliminated for those states that have adopted Revised Article 1 because Revised Article 1 contains the definition for course of performance.

[36] Revised § 2-202 provides different rules for the use of extrinsic evidence but still includes "course of performance, course of dealing, or usage of trade" as sources for interpretation of contract terms.

In 1989, the NCCUSL recommended that UCC Article 6 be repealed because it was obsolete and had little value in the modern business world. At the same time, the commissioners adopted a revised version of Article 6 (Alternative B) for adoption by those states that desired to retain the concept for bulk sales. Rather than relying on the bulk sales law, the trend is for suppliers to use UCC Article 9, Secured Transactions, for protection (See Chapter 34).

B. Form of Sales Contract

A contract for the sale of goods may be oral or written. However, under the UCC, certain types of contracts must be in writing or they cannot be enforced in court.

CPA 6. Amount

Whenever the sales price of goods is $500 or more, the sales contract must be in writing to be enforceable. Under Revised Article 2, this amount has been increased to $5,000.[37] The section of the UCC that establishes this requirement is known as the **statute of frauds.** (For more detail on the statute of frauds and its role in common law contracts, see Chapter 17.)

7. Nature of the Writing Required

The requirement for a written contract may be satisfied by a complete written contract signed by both parties. Under Article 2, so that the state laws will be consistent with federal laws on electronic signatures (see Chapter 11), the requirement of a writing has been changed to the requirement of a "record." Under Article 2, two merchants can reduce their agreement to a record in much simpler fashion because the detail required under common law is not required to satisfy the UCC standards.

ROSENFELD V BASQUIAT, 78 F3D 84 (2ND CIR 1996)

IS A CRAYON-SCRAWLED CONTRACT GOOD ENOUGH FOR THE STATUTE OF FRAUDS?

Michelle Rosenfeld, an art dealer, alleges she contracted with artist Jean-Michel Basquiat to buy three of his paintings. The works that she claims she contracted to buy were entitled *Separation of the K, Atlas,* and *Untitled Head.* Rosenfeld testified that she went to Basquiat's apartment on October 25, 1982; while she was there, he agreed to sell her three paintings for $4,000 each, and she picked out three. Basquiat asked for a cash deposit of 10 percent; she left his loft and later returned with $1,000 in cash, which she paid him. When she asked for a receipt, he insisted on drawing up a contract and got down on the floor and wrote it out in crayon on a large piece of paper, remarking that some day this contract would be worth money. The handwritten document listed the three paintings, bore Rosenfeld's signature and Basquiat's signature, and stated: "$12,000—$1,000 DEPOSIT = Oct 25 82." Rosenfeld later returned to Basquiat's loft to discuss delivery, but Basquiat convinced her to wait for at least two years so that he could show the paintings at exhibitions. After Basquiat's death, the estate argued that there was no contract because the statute of frauds made the agreement unenforceable. The estate contended that a written contract for the sale of goods must include the date of delivery. From a judgment in favor of the estate, the plaintiff appealed.

Judicial Opinion

CARDAMONE, J. . . . Because this case involves an alleged contract for the sale of three paintings, any question regarding the Statute of Frauds is governed by the U.C.C. (applicability to "transactions in goods") (contract for $500 or more is unenforceable "unless there is some writing sufficient to indicate that a contract for sale has been made between the parties and signed by the party [charged]"). Under the U.C.C., the only term that *must* appear in the writing is the quantity. See U.C.C. § 2-201.

Beyond that, "[a]ll that is required is that the writing afford a basis for believing that the offered oral evidence

[37] Under Revised Article 2, the new amount of $5,000 is found at UCC Rev. Art. 2, § 2-201.

rests on a real transaction." The writing supplied by the plaintiff indicated the price, the date, the specific paintings involved, and that Rosenfeld paid a deposit. It also bore the signatures of the buyer and seller. Therefore, the writing satisfied the requirements of § 2-201.

Citing *Berman Stores Co. v Hirsch*, 240 N.Y. 209 (1925), the estate claims that a specific delivery date, if agreed upon, must be in the writing. *Berman Stores* was decided before the enactment of the U.C.C., and was based on the principle that "the note or memorandum . . . should completely evidence the contract which the parties made." The rule that a specific delivery date is "an essential part of the contract and must be embodied in the memorandum" was rejected by the legislature—at least for sale-of-goods cases—when it enacted the U.C.C. That rule and the statute upon which it was based were repealed to make way for the U.C.C. The U.C.C. "[c]ompletely re-phrased" the provisions of prior legislation and "intended to make it clear that . . . [t]he required writing need not contain all the material terms."

. . . Because the writing, allegedly scrawled in crayon by Jean-Michel Basquiat on a large piece of paper, easily satisfied the requirements of § 2-201 of the U.C.C., the estate is not entitled to judgment as a matter of law. It is of no real significance that the jury found Rosenfeld and Basquiat settled on a particular time for delivery and did not commit it to writing. . . . As a consequence, . . . the alleged contract is not invalid on Statute of Frauds grounds. . . .

[Judgment reversed]

Questions

1. Why was the contract required to be in writing?
2. Did the contract comply with the statute of frauds?
3. Does a writing that does not comply with the statute of frauds make the alleged contract void?

(a) Terms

To satisfy the UCC statute of frauds, the record must indicate that there has been a completed transaction covering certain goods. Specifically, the record must (1) indicate that a sale or contract to sell has been made and (2) state the quantity of goods involved.[38] Any other missing terms may be supplied by reference to Code sections (discussed earlier) or shown by parol evidence.

CPA (b) Signature

The record must be signed or authenticated by the person who is being held to the contract or by the authorized agent of that person. Whatever form of authentication is being used must be put in place in the record with the intention of authenticating the record. The authentication may consist of initials or may be a printed, stamped, electronic, or typewritten signature placed with the intent to authenticate.[39] **For Example,** when you enter into a contract as part of an online transaction, you are generally asked to check a box that states that you understand you are entering into a contract. Once you check that box, a pop-up appears that explains that you are about to charge your credit card or account and that you have agreed to the purchase. These steps are used to authenticate your electronic version of a signature.

The UCC statute of frauds does provide an important exception to the signature requirement for merchants that enables merchants to expedite their transactions. This exception allows merchants to create a confirmation memorandum of their oral agreement as evidence of an agreement. A merchant's *confirmation memorandum* is a letter, memo, or electronic document signed or authenticated by one of the two merchant parties to an oral agreement.[40] This memorandum can be used by either party to enforce the contract. **For Example,** suppose that Ralph has orally agreed to purchase 1,000 pounds of T-bone steak from Jane for $5.79 per pound. Jane sends Ralph a signed memo that reads, "This is to confirm our telephone conversation earlier today. I will sell you 1,000 pounds of T-bone @ $5.79 per pound." Either Ralph or Jane can use the memo to enforce the contract.

[38] *Kelly-Stehney & Assoc., Inc. v McDonald's Indus.* Products, Inc. 893 NW 2d 394 (Mich 2005).

[39] UCC §§ 1-201(39), 2-201; *Nebraska Builders Products Co. v Industrial Erectors, Inc.*, 478 NW2d 257 (Neb 1992). Revised Article 2 permits electronic forms and signature and "record" includes e-mail, EDI transmissions, faxes, and printouts of screen pages reflecting transactions.

[40] *GPL Treatment, Ltd. v Louisiana-Pacific Corp.*, 914 P2d 682 (Ore 1996). A farmer was held not to be a merchant because of his lack of experience in selling his crops and a confirmation memo could not be used to enforce a contract against him. *Harvest State Co-op v Anderson*, 577 NW2d 381 (Wis App 1998), review denied, 584 NW2d 124 (Wis 1998).

HOME BASKET CO., LLC V PAMPERED CHEF, LTD., 55 UCC REP SERV 2D 792 (D KAN 2005)

A REAL BASKET CASE

The Greenbrier Basket Company (GBC) (plaintiff) (seller), a goods distributor, entered into a business relationship in October 2003 to sell woven baskets to The Pampered Chef (TPC) (defendant) (buyer). On October 28, 2003, an executive sales agreement was drafted but never signed by the parties. Prior to the October 28, 2003 aborted sales agreement, GBC had accepted purchase orders from TPC.

The ordering process would begin with TPC e-mailing GBC regarding an offer to fill an order. GBC would then go to TPC's website and fill out the purchase order using TPC's purchase order management system and would click on the 'Accept P.O.' button at the end of the terms and conditions field.

Cyndee Pollock (a manager at GBC) would receive offers to purchase goods via e-mail from TPC and would tell an employee, Mark Beal, to accept these purchase orders via TPC's internet site. GBC denies knowing that there were terms and conditions, including a forum selection clause, on the TPC's internet acceptance site. TPC sent Mark Beal an e-mail with an attachment showing him how to use TPC's purchase order management system. The attachment included instructions regarding the use of the purchase order management system, including, in section four, three paragraphs under the title 'Accepting and Rejecting Purchase Orders'. The relevant portion of which states:

Clicking on the Accept P.O. button will cause the terms and conditions of the purchase order to pop-up. The user should review these terms and conditions and click the Accept P.O. button at the bottom of the pop-up screen.... If the purchase order is not acceptable in it's [sic] current form, the user may click on the Reject and Request Changes button. This causes a pop-up window to appear where the user may enter a free-form text describing the reason for rejecting the purchase order and request changes that would make the purchase order acceptable.

Clause 17 of the Terms and Conditions in TPC's purchase management order system states:

This Purchase Order shall be deemed to have been made in Addison, Illinois USA and shall be governed by and construed in accordance with the laws of State of Illinois [sic]. The sole and exclusive jurisdiction for the purpose of resolving any dispute shall be the United States District Court, Northern District of Illinois, Eastern Division.

When disputes over orders and payments arose, GBC filed suit against TPC in Kansas for breach of contract. TPC moved to dismiss the suit for improper venue.

Judicial Opinion

BROWN, Senior J.... Defendant alleges improper venue because of an allegedly agreed upon forum selection clause. Plaintiff does not dispute that the forum selection clause is valid. Plaintiff instead argues that the forum selection clause was never part of the parties' contract.

TPC's e-mails containing purchase order information constituted an offer to buy baskets. The e-mails consisted of information about the quantity of baskets to be bought, price, shipment information and delivery dates. None of the e-mails had any forum selection clause; however, they did state a specific manner of acceptance:

1. Upon receipt of order, please acknowledge via internet at [website]. By acknowledging this P.O. [purchase order], you also acknowledge the terms and conditions of this P.O.
2. To accept this P.O. via internet, visit [website].

The evidence shows at least nine such e-mail offers. GBC consistently went to the TPC website to accept these offers.

Plaintiff first argues that the e-mail offers are ambiguous because it did not alert GBC to the forum selection clause that had to be accepted on the website. The TPC e-mails state that the way to acknowledge (i.e. accept) the purchase order was to go to the website. The e-mail is not ambiguous as it also alerted GBC that there were terms and conditions associated with acknowledging the P.O. on the website.

GBC next argues that it should not be held to the terms and conditions accepted on the website because plaintiff thought that the e-mails' terms and conditions were all inclusive.

It is a well-established rule of law that contracting parties have a duty to learn the contents of a written contract before signing it, and such duty includes reading the contract and obtaining an explanation of its terms. Therefore, a party who signs a written contract is bound by its provisions regardless of the failure to read or understand the terms, unless the contract was entered into through fraud, undue influence, or mutual mistake.

In determining intent to form a contract, the test is objective, rather than subjective, meaning that the relevant inquiry is the 'manifestation of a party's intention, rather than the actual or real intention.

This was a website that required action on the part of GBC. Plaintiff objectively agreed to the forum selection clause by scrolling through the terms and conditions and clicking on the 'Accept P.O.' button. Plaintiff's subjective beliefs that it was the e-mail and not the website terms and conditions that governed the contract are both misplaced and irrelevant. Plaintiff was under a duty to read and understand the terms and conditions prior to clicking the 'Accept P.O.' button as this was the formal acceptance required by TPC's offer to purchase baskets. Failure to read or understand the terms and conditions is not a valid reason to render those provisions nugatory.

Plaintiff next argues that the forum selection clause should not be read into the contract because GBC rejected an Exclusive Sales Agreement containing such a clause. Plaintiff claims that the failure to sign this agreement shows that they did not intend that a forum selection clause be part of the contract. The evidence shows that the Exclusive Sales Agreement was discussed on October 28, 2003. The date of the first e-mail inviting GBC to accept a purchase order was October 7, 2003. Plaintiff's subjective reasons for refusing to sign the Exclusive Sales Agreement are irrelevant as GBC consistently agreed, in an objective manner prior to the Exclusive Sales Agreement, to contracts with the terms and conditions on TPC's website. The Court will not alter the plain terms in the parties' contract because GBC refused to sign the Exclusive Sales Agreement.

Plaintiff also argues that there was no meeting of the minds regarding the forum selection clause on the website. A meeting of the minds requirement is proved when the evidence shows with reasonable definiteness that the minds of the parties met upon the same matter and agreed upon the terms of the contract. Part of clause 17 states 'each shipment received by Buyer from Seller shall be deemed to be only upon the terms and conditions as set forth in this Purchase Order. . . .' GBC agreed upon these terms and conditions published on TPC's website by clicking the 'Accept P.O.' button and this satisfied the meeting of the minds standard.

The Court holds that the forum selection clause in the terms and conditions on TPC's website are a part of the parties' contract.

The Defendant's Motion to Dismiss due to improper venue is denied. The case is transferred to the United States District Court for Northern District of Illinois, Eastern Division.

Questions

1. Describe the ordering process between the two parties.
2. Does it matter to the court that neither side ever signed a written agreement?
3. What responsibility does the court impose on those who use websites for contracting purposes?

A confirming memo, in various forms of communication, sent by one merchant to another results in a binding and enforceable contract that satisfies the statute of frauds. Such a confirmation binds the nonsigning or nonauthenticating merchant, just as if he had signed the letter or a contract. A merchant can object when he receives the confirmation memo, but he must do so immediately because the confirming memo takes effect in 10 days if there is no objection.[41] This confirmation procedure makes it necessary for merchants to watch their communications and all forms of correspondence and to act within 10 days of receiving a confirmation.

(c) Purpose of Execution

A writing or record can satisfy a statute of frauds even though it was not made for that purpose. For example, if a buyer writes to the seller to complain that the goods have not been delivered, there is proof of the contract because the buyer's complaint indicates that there was some kind of understanding or an acknowledgment that there was a sale of those goods.

[41] A confirmation memo is not effective when there is no underlying agreement or the parties did not agree on the terms. *Precise-Marketing Corp. v Simpson Paper Co.*, 38 UCC Rep Serv 2d 717, 1999 WL 259518 (SDNY 1999).

(d) Particular Writings

Formal contracts, bills of sale, letters, and telegrams are common forms of writings that satisfy the recorder writing requirement.[42] E-mails, faxes, EDI communications, and verifications through screen printouts will generally satisfy the requirement as to record and authentication so long as they meet minimum formation standards and comply with the requirement of the UCC to specify any quantity. Two or more writings grouped together may constitute a record that will be sufficient to satisfy the UCC statute of frauds.[43]

8. Effect of Noncompliance

A sales agreement that does not satisfy the statute of frauds cannot be enforced. However, the oral contract itself is not unlawful and may be voluntarily performed by the parties.

9. Exceptions to Requirement of a Writing

The absence of a writing does not always mean that a sales contract is unenforceable. Article 2 provides some exceptions for the enforceability of certain oral contracts.

CPA (a) Specially Manufactured Goods

No writing is required when the goods are specially made for the buyer and are of such an unusual nature that they are not suitable for sale in the ordinary course of the seller's business. **For Example,** a manufacturer who builds a stair lift for a two-story home cannot resell the $8,000 device to someone else because it is specially built for the stairs in the buyer's home. The manufacturer could enforce the oral contract against the buyer despite the price being in excess of $500 ($5,000 under Revised Article 2).

For this nonresellable goods exception to apply, the seller must have made a substantial beginning in manufacturing the goods or, if a distributor is the seller, in procuring them before the buyer indicates she will not honor the oral contract.[44] The stair lift manufacturer, for example, must have progressed to a point beyond simply ordering materials for construction of the lift because those materials could be used for any lift.

CPA (b) Receipt and Acceptance

An oral sales contract may be enforced if it can be shown that the goods were delivered by the seller and were both received and accepted by the buyer even if the amount involved is over $500 ($5,000 Revised) and there is no writing. The receipt and acceptance of the goods by the buyer makes the contract enforceable despite the statute of frauds issue. Both receipt and acceptance of the goods by the buyer must be shown. If only part of the goods have been received and accepted, the contract may be enforced only insofar as it relates to those goods received and accepted.[45] **For Example,** suppose that Wayne ordered 700 baseball jackets at a price of $72 each from Pamela. The order was taken over the telephone, and Wayne emphasized urgency. Pamela immediately shipped the 320 jackets she had on hand and assured Wayne the remainder would be finished during the next two weeks. Wayne received the 320 jackets and sold them to a golf tournament sponsor. Wayne refused to pay Pamela because the contract was oral. Wayne must pay for the 320 jackets, but Pamela will not be able to recover for the remaining 380 jackets she manufactured.

CPA (c) Payment

An oral contract may be enforced if the buyer has made full payment. In the case of partial payment for divisible units of goods, a contract may be enforced only with respect to the goods for which payment has been made and accepted. In the Pamela and Wayne example, if the circumstances were changed so that Pamela agreed to ship only if Wayne sent payment, then Pamela, upon accepting the payment, would be required to perform the contract for the amount of payment received. If partial payment is made for indivisible goods, such as an automobile, a partial

42 Contract terms can be pieced together from invoices sent over the period of the agreement and that the buyer paid. *Fleming Companies, Inc. v. Krist Oil Co.*, 324 F Supp 2d 933, 54 UCC Rep Serv 2d 120 (WD Wi 2004).

43 *American Dredging Co. v Plaza Petroleum, Inc.*, 799 F Supp 1335 (EDNY 1993), vacated in part on issues related to negligence and seaworthiness, 845 F Supp 91 (EDNY 1993). Letters grouped together satisfy UCC § 2-201. *Pepsi-Cola Co. v Steak 'N Shake, Inc.*, 981 F Supp 1149 (SD Ind 1997). Letters and faxes also satisfy the writing requirement. *Den Norske Stats Oljeselskap*, 992 F Supp 913 (SD Tex 1998), aff'd, 161 F3d 8 (5th Cir 1998).

44 *Golden State Porcelain Inc. v Swid Powell Design Inc.*, 37 UCC Rep Serv 2d 928 (NY 1999). Where manufacture has not begun, this exception to the statute of frauds does not apply. *EMSG Sys. Div., Inc. v Miltope Corp.*, 37 UCC Rep Serv 2d 39 (EDNC 1998).

45 *Allied Grape Growers v Bronco Wine Co.*, 249 Cal Rptr 872 (Ct App 1988).

THINKING THINGS THROUGH

STOP THE PRESSES! OR AT LEAST STOP PRINTING!

Clinton Press of Tolland operated a printing press and, for several decades, provided written materials, including books and pamphlets for Adelma G. Simmons, a woman who operated a farm known as Caprilands Herb Farm, an attraction for tourists. The books and pamphlets contained informational articles as well as collections of recipes. They were clearly identified as Caprilands Herb Farm materials.

Due to limited storage space at Caprilands, Clinton and Simmons agreed that the written materials would remain stored at the print shop until Simmons decided that delivery was necessary. The materials were delivered either routinely, based on Simmons' ordinary need for materials, or upon her request for a special delivery. After each delivery, Clinton sent an invoice requesting payment by Simmons, who honored these invoices.

In 1991, the town of Tolland acquired the land on which Simmons resided. In early 1997, Simmons was notified that she would have to leave the property by the end of the year. She closed Caprilands Herb Farm as a result. Clinton and Simmons agreed that the materials printed for Caprilands and stored at the print shop would be delivered on an accelerated basis. Simmons directed an employee, Jack Lee, to begin to transport the stored materials to Caprilands, and he made occasional trips to the print shop to do so.

On December 3, 1997, after several months of deterioration of her physical health, Simmons died. Simmons' will was admitted to probate, and Mr. Edward Cook was appointed executor of her estate. Clinton submitted a claim against the estate for $24,599.38 for unpaid deliveries to Caprilands. These deliveries took place from February 12, 1997, to December 11, 1997, with the last two deliveries occurring after Simmons' death. The court denied the claim.*

Why would the court deny the claim? Think through the UCC Article 2 issues you see in the situation. Should the decision be reversed?

**Kalas v Cook*, 800 A2d 553 (Conn. 2002).

payment avoids the statute of frauds and is sufficient proof to permit enforcement of the entire oral contract.

(d) Admission

An oral contract may be enforced against a party if that party admits in pleadings, testimony, or otherwise in court that a contract for sale was made. The contract, however, is not enforceable beyond the quantity of goods admitted.[46]

10. Noncode Requirements

In addition to the UCC requirements for contracts that must be evidenced by a record, other statutes may impose requirements. **For Example,** state consumer protection legislation commonly requires that there be a detailed contract and that a copy of it be given to the consumer.

[46] *Harvey v McKinney*, 581 NE2d 786 (Ill App 1991).

11. Bill of Sale

Regardless of the requirement of the statute of frauds, the parties may wish to execute a writing as evidence or proof of the sale. Through custom, this writing has become known as a **bill of sale,** but it is neither a bill nor a contract. It is merely a receipt or writing signed by the seller reciting the transfer to the buyer of the title to the described property. A bill of sale can be used as proof of an otherwise oral agreement.

C. Uniform Law for International Sales

The United Nations Convention on **Contracts for the International Sale of Goods (CISG)** applies to contracts between parties in the United States and parties in the other nations that have ratified the convention.[47] The provisions of this convention or international agreement have been strongly influenced by Article 2 of the UCC. The international rules of the convention automatically apply to contracts for the sale of goods if the buyer and seller have places of business in different countries that have ratified the convention. The parties may, however, choose to exclude the convention provisions in their sales contract.

12. Scope of the CISG

The CISG does not govern all contracts between parties in the countries that have ratified it. The CISG does not apply to goods bought for personal, family, or household use. The CISG also does not apply to contracts in which the predominant part of the obligations of the party who furnishes the goods consists of the supply of labor or other services. In addition, the CISG does not apply the seller's liability to any person for death or personal injury caused by the goods.

The CISG governs the formation of the contract of sale and the rights and obligations of the seller and the buyer arising from such a contract. The CISG provides a basis for answering questions and settling issues the parties failed to cover in their contract. The CISG has five chapters and 101 articles, and the articles have no titles to them. There is a limited body of case law interpreting the CISG because so many of the decisions under the CISG come through arbitration and other forms of dispute resolution, typical of international commercial arrangements.

13. Irrevocable Offers

An offer under the CISG is irrevocable if it states that it is irrevocable or if the offeree reasonably relies on it as being irrevocable. Such a CISG offer is irrevocable even if there is no writing and no consideration. This provision differs from the common law, which requires consideration for an offer to be irrevocable, and from the UCC's merchant's firm offer, which must be in writing to be irrevocable.

14. Statute of Frauds

Under the CISG, a contract for the sale of goods need not be in any particular form and can be proven by any means. The convention, by this provision, has abolished the statute of frauds' requirement of a writing. Article 11 of the CISG provides, "A contract of sale need not be concluded in or evidenced by writing and is not subject to any other requirement as to form. It may be proved by any means, including witnesses." Countries may, however, retain the UCC requirements of the statute of frauds by requiring certain contracts to be in writing.

15. The Mirror-Image Rule Returns under CISG

Under Article 19 of the CISG, the rules of common law acceptance with regard to additional terms in acceptance are the dominating theme for acceptance. The UCC provisions on additional terms are recognized in part, but the parties cannot vary certain aspects of the offer if they wish to form a contract. If one party objects or the provision is material, then such additional terms and provisions are eliminated from the parties' agreement.

D. Leases of Goods

Leases of goods represent a significant part of both contract law and the economy. There are more than $240 billion worth of lease transactions in the United States, each year an amount equal to roughly one-third of all capital investment each year in the United States.[48] One-fourth of all vehicles in the United States are leased. Article 2A of the UCC codifies the law of leases for tangible movable goods. Article 2A applies to any transaction, regardless of form, that creates a lease of personal property or fixtures. Many of the provisions of Article 2 were carried over but changed to reflect differences in style, leasing terminology, or leasing practices.[49] As a practical matter, leases will be of durable goods, such as equipment and vehicles of any kind, computers, boats, airplanes, and household goods and appliances. A **lease** is "a transfer

[47] 52 Fed Reg 6262 (1987). While the list of adopting countries is always increasing, those countries involved in NAFTA, GATT, and the European Union (EU) (see Chapter 7) have adopted the CISG. For complete text, commentary, and case law on CISG, go to **http://www.cisg.law.pace.edu.**

[48] U.S. Department of Commerce, Bureau of Economic Analysis, International Trade Administration and Equipment Leasing Association of America, Trends and Forecasts for Equipment Leasing in the United States (2002).

[49] Forty-nine states (Louisiana has not adopted Article 2A), the District of Columbia, and the Virgin Islands have adopted all or some portions of Article 2A. Not all states have adopted the 1997 version of Article 2A, and some have adopted only selected portions of the 1997 version.

of the right to possession and use of goods for a term in return for consideration."[50]

16. Types of Leases

Article 2A regulates consumer leases, commercial leases, finance leases, nonfinance leases, and subleases. These categories may overlap in some cases, such as when there is a commercial finance lease.

(a) Consumer Lease

A **consumer lease** is made by a merchant lessor regularly engaged in the business of leasing or selling the kinds of goods involved. A consumer lease is made to a natural person (not a corporation) who takes possession of the goods primarily for personal, family, or household use. Each state places a cap on the amount that will be considered a consumer lease. Section 2A-103(f) simply provides that the state should place its own amount in this section with the admonition to place the cap at a level that ensures that vehicle leases will be covered under the law.

(b) Commercial Lease

When a lease does not satisfy the definition of a consumer lease, it may be called a **nonconsumer** or a **commercial lease. For Example,** a contractor's one-year rental of a truck to haul building materials is a commercial lease.

(c) Finance Lease

A **finance lease** is a three-party transaction involving a lessor, a lessee, and a supplier. Instead of going directly to a supplier for goods, the customer goes to a financier and tells the financier where to obtain the goods and what to obtain. The financier then acquires the goods and either leases or subleases the goods to its customer. The financier-lessor is in effect a paper channel, or conduit, between the supplier and the customer-lessee. The customer-lessee must approve the terms of the transaction between the supplier and the financier-lessor.[51]

17. Form of Lease Contract

The lease must be evidenced by a record if the total of the payments under the lease will be $1,000 or more. The record must be authenticated by the party against whom enforcement is sought. The record must describe the leased goods, state the term of the lease, and indicate that a lease contract has been made between the parties.[52]

18. Warranties

Under Article 2A, the lessor, except in the case of finance leases, makes all usual warranties that are made by a seller in a sale of goods. In a finance lease, however, the real parties in interest are the supplier, who supplies the lessor with the goods, and the lessee, who leases the goods. The supplier and the lessee stand in a position similar to that of seller and buyer. The lessee looks to the supplier of the goods for warranties. Any warranties, express or implied, made by the supplier to the lessor are passed on to the lessee, who has a direct cause of action on them against the supplier regardless of the lack of privity.[53] **For Example,** if a consumer leased an auto and the auto had a defective steering mechanism that resulted in injury to the consumer, the consumer would have a cause of action against the auto manufacturer. The financier-lessor does not make any implied warranty, but does have liability for any express warranties it makes.

One area of lessor liability that has been evolving is that of the liability of the lessor to those who are injured by the lessee. In New York alone, there were almost $7 billion in vicarious liability claims against automobile lessors in 2004. Vicarious liability suits result, for example, when the lessee of an auto is in an accident. A third party is injured as a result of the lessee's accident. The injured party can recover from the lessee, but increasingly, third parties have been turning to the lessor for recovery.[54] Twenty-one states have vicarious liability statutes. Other states

[50] UCC § 2A-103(1)(j). The definition of what constitutes a lease is the subject of continuing examination by the UCC Article 2A drafters and the American Law Institute. The questions being examined are installment contracts, rent-to-own contracts, and other such arrangements to determine whether these are leases, secured transactions, or sales of goods.

[51] UCC § 2A-103(1)(g). One of the evolving issues in lease financing is the relationship of the parties, the use of liens, and the role of Article 9 security interests (see Chapter 34). The NCCUSL has appointed a drafting committee to create a new uniform state Certificate of Title Act (COTA) so that the interrelationships of lien laws, Article 2, and Article 9 are clear.

[52] UCC § 2-201(b).

[53] UCC § 2A-209.

[54] *Andreozzi v Brownell* Not Reported in A2d, 2004 WL 1542228 (RI Super)

E-COMMERCE AND CYBERLAW

LOL AT WAX SEALS: THE ELECTRONIC CONTRACT

The federal Electronic Signatures in Global and National Commerce Act (E-Sign) took effect October 1, 2000. The NATIONAL LAW JOURNAL stated: "Not since notarized written signatures replaced wax and signet rings has history seen such a fundamental change in contract law."*

The states can now use the Uniform Electronic Transactions Act (UETA) for meeting the new federal mandates on E-sign. The UETA was passed as a uniform law in July 1999, and 43 states plus the District of Columbia and the Virgin Islands have adopted it in some form.**

Issues that remain unresolved in this new era of electronic contracting are security and verification. Businesses must be able to verify that the electronic signatures are authentic and that orders from their stated origins are authentic. Furthermore, companies must be able to provide some form of record for auditors to verify transactions.

Consumer signatures will remain a different issue because the problems of security and authenticity are exacerbated when there are not ongoing relationships as there are in business-to-business transactions.

*Mark Ballard, "E-Sign a Nudge, Not a Revolution," *NATIONAL LAW JOURNAL*, September 25, 2000, B1, B4.

**UETA states are Alabama, Arizona, Arkansas, California, Colorado, Connecticut, Delaware, District of Columbia, Florida, Hawaii, Idaho, Indiana, Iowa, Kansas, Kentucky, Louisiana, Maine, Maryland, Massachusetts, Michigan, Minnesota, Mississippi, Montana, Nebraska, Nevada, New Hampshire, New Jersey, New Mexico, North Carolina, North Dakota, Ohio, Oklahoma, Oregon, Pennsylvania, Rhode Island, South Carolina, South Dakota, Tennessee, Texas, Utah, Virginia, West Virginia, Wisconsin, and Wyoming. State legislatures will continue to consider passage of both of UETA and other uniform acts such as the Uniform Computer Information Transactions Act (UCITA).

have no statutes, and some states have vicarious liability by case law.[55] Congress has legislation pending to limit the vicarious liability of lessors to third parties for injuries caused by the lessees.[56] Many financing companies and leasing firms have stopped doing business in states in which they have exposure for the injuries caused by their lessees.[57]

19. Irrevocable Promises: Commercial Finance Leases

Under ordinary contract law, the obligations of the lessee and lessor are mutually dependent. In contrast, upon a commercial finance lessee's acceptance of the goods, the lessee's promises to the lessor become irrevocable and independent from the obligations of the lessor. This irrevocability and independence require the lessee to perform even if the lessor's performance after the lessee's acceptance is not in accordance with the lease contract. The lessee must make payment to the lessor no matter how badly the leased goods perform. This is known as a **"hell or high water" clause.** It does not apply to consumer leases.[58] In some cases, the lessor assigns the lease contract to a third party, and that third party collects

55 Alabama, Alaska, District of Columbia, Georgia, Idaho, Iowa, Kansas, Kentucky, Louisiana, Michigan, Minnesota, Mississippi, Montana, Nebraska, Nevada, New Mexico, North Dakota, Ohio, Oregon, South Dakota, and Utah. The 17 states with no vicarious liability and no vicarious liability statutes or case law include Arizona, Arkansas, Colorado, Hawaii, Indiana, Missouri, New Hampshire, North Carolina, Pennsylvania, South Carolina, Tennessee, Texas, Vermont, Virginia, Washington, West Virginia, and Wyoming.

56 The Small Business Liability Reform Act of 2001, H.R. 1805, S. 865, 107th Cong. § 204(c)(2) (2001).

57 In New York, Connecticut, Rhode Island, Maine, and the District of Columbia, a vehicle owner/lessor's vicarious liability is potentially unlimited; in California, Florida, Idaho, Michigan, and Minnesota, a vehicle owner/lessor's vicarious liability is "capped" at the statutory minimum for mandatory auto insurance. Treatise on Leasing, UCC Transaction Guide § 11:17; Equipment Leasing-Leveraged Leasing § 10:5.1 (2001). Prosser & Keeton, *On the Law of Torts* §§ 69–73 (W. Page Keeton ed., 5th ed. 1984). In some states, banks will no longer finance auto loans due to liability as owners.

58 UCC § 2A-407; *Wells Fargo Bank Northwest, N.A. v TACA International Airlines, S.A.*, 247 F Supp 2d 352 (SDNY 2002).

payment from the lessee. Some courts are requiring that the assignee of the lease contract take the lease assignment in good faith and without knowledge of problems with the lease or leased goods.

In a finance lease, the only remedy of the lessee for nonconformity of the goods is from the supplier. That is, the lessee can recover from the lessor only if the lease is not a finance lease or if the lessor has made an express warranty or promise.

20. Default

The lease agreement and provisions of Article 2A determine whether the lessor or lessee is in default. If either the lessor or the lessee is in default under the lease contract, the party seeking enforcement may obtain a judgment or otherwise enforce the lease contract by any available judicial or nonjudicial procedure. Neither the lessor nor the lessee is entitled to notice of default or notice of enforcement from the other party. Both the lessor and the lessee have rights and remedies similar to those given to a seller in a sales contract.[59] If the lessee defaults, the lessor is entitled to recover any rent due, future rent, and incidental damages.[60] (See Chapter 27 for more information on remedies.)

[59] UCC §§ 2A-501, 2A-503; *Torres v Banc One Leasing Corp*, 226 F Supp 2d 1345 (ND Ga 2002).
[60] UCC § 2A-529.

Summary

Contracts for services and real estate are governed by the common law. Contracts for the sale of goods are governed by Article 2 of the UCC. *Goods* are defined as anything movable at the time they are identified as the subject of the transaction. Goods physically existing and owned by the seller at the time of the transaction are *existing goods*.

A *sale of goods* is the transfer of title to tangible personal property for a price. A *bailment* is a transfer of possession but not title and is therefore not a sale. A *gift* is not a sale because no price is paid for the gift. A contract for services is an ordinary contract and is not governed by the UCC. If a contract calls for both the rendering of services and the supplying of goods, the contract is classified according to its dominant element.

The common law contract rules for intent to contract apply to the formation of contracts under the UCC. However, several formation rules under the UCC differ from common law contract rules. A merchant's firm offer is irrevocable without the payment of consideration. The UCC rules on additional terms in an acceptance permit the formation of a contract despite the changes. These proposals for new terms are not considered counteroffers under the UCC. The terms that are included are determined by detailed rules under both the current and Revised UCC. If the transaction is between nonmerchants, a contract is formed without the additional terms, which the original offeror is free to accept or reject. If the transaction is between merchants, the additional terms become part of the contract if those terms do not materially alter the offer and no objection is made to them. Under Revised Article 2, terms that are in both parties' records, that the parties agree on, that are part of the Code terms or that are part of their ongoing performance become part of the contract. There is no distinction between merchant and nonmerchant for additional terms under Revised Article 2.

The same defenses available to formation under common law are incorporated in Article 2. In addition, the UCC recognizes unconscionability as a defense to formation.

The UCC does not require the parties to agree on every aspect of contract performance for the contract to be valid. Provisions in Article 2 will govern the parties' relationship in the event their agreement does not cover all terms. The price term may be expressly fixed by the parties. The parties may make no provision as to price, or they may indicate how the price should be determined later. In output or requirements contracts, the quantity that is to be sold or purchased is not specified, but such contracts are nevertheless valid. A contract relating to a sale of goods may be modified even though the modification is not supported by consideration. The parol evidence rule applies to a sale of goods in much the same manner as to ordinary contracts. However, the UCC permits the introduction of course of dealing and usage of trade as evidence for clarification of contract terms and performance.

The UCC's statute of frauds provides that a sales contract for $500 (now $5,000 under Revised Article 2) or more must be evidenced by a writing (Revised Article 2 requires only a "record" in order to allow for e-commerce transactions). The UCC's merchant's confirmation memorandum allows two merchants to be bound to an otherwise oral agreement by a memo or letter signed by only one party that stands without objection for 10 days. Several exceptions to the UCC statute of frauds exist: when the goods are specially made or procured for the buyer and are nonresellable in the seller's ordinary market;

when the buyer has received and accepted the goods; when the buyer has made either full or partial payment; and when the party against whom enforcement is sought admits in court pleadings or testimony that a contract for sale was made.

Uniform rules for international sales are applicable to contracts for sales between parties in countries that have ratified the CISG. Under the CISG, a contract for the sale of goods need not be in any particular form and can be proven by any means.

Article 2A of the UCC regulates consumer leases, commercial leases, finance leases, nonfinance leases, and subleases of tangible movable goods. A lease subject to Article 2A must be in writing if the lease payments will total $1,000 or more.

Questions and Case Problems

1. Triple H Construction Co. contracted with Hunter's Run Stables, Inc., to erect a horse barn and riding arena on Hunter's Run's property in Big Flats, New York. Hunter's Run got a guarantee in its contract with Triple H that "such design with the span so shown will support its weight and will withstand natural forces including but not limited to snow load and wind." Hunter's Run also got the following guarantee from Rigidply, the manufacturer of the rafters: "Rigidply . . . hereby guarantees that the design to be used for the construction of a horse barn by Triple H . . . will support the weight of such barn and to snow load and wind as per drawings." The barn was completed in 1983 and collapsed under the weight of snow in 1994. Hunter's Run has sued Triple H for UCC Article 2 remedies. Does Article 2 apply? [*Hunter's Run Stables, Inc. v Triple H, Inc.*, 938 F Supp 166 (WDNY)]
2. R-P Packaging manufactured cellophane wrapping material that was used by Kern's Bakery in packaging its product. Kern's decided to change its system for packaging cookies from a tied bread bag to a tray covered with printed cellophane wrapping. R-P took measurements to determine the appropriate size for the cellophane wrapping and designed the artwork to be printed on the wrapping. After agreeing that the artwork was satisfactory, Kern placed a verbal order for the cellophane at a total cost of $13,000. When the printed wrapping material was received, Kern complained that it was too short for the trays and the artwork was not centered. The material, however, conformed exactly to the order placed by Kern. Kern returned the material to R-P by overnight express. R-P sued Kern. Kern claimed that because there was no written contract, the suit was barred by the statute of frauds. What resulted? [*Flowers Baking Co. v R-P Packaging, Inc.*, 329 SE2d 462 (Va)]
3. Smythe wrote to Lasco Dealers inquiring about the price of a certain freezer. Lasco wrote her a letter, signed by its credit manager, stating that Smythe could purchase the freezer in question during the next 30 days for $400. Smythe wrote back the next day ordering a freezer at that price. Lasco received Smythe's letter the following day, but Lasco wrote a response letter stating that it had changed the price to $450. Smythe claims that Lasco could not change its price. Is she correct?
4. Would silicone breast implants be covered by the UCC Article 2 warranties? Does implantation of silicone gel implants constitute a sale of goods by the surgeon? [*In re Breast Implant Product Liability Litigation*, 503 SE2d 445 (SC)]
5. Meyers was under contract with Henderson to install overhead doors in a factory that Henderson was building. Meyers obtained the disassembled doors from the manufacturer. His contract with Henderson required Meyers to furnish all labor, materials, tools, and equipment to satisfactorily complete the installation of all overhead doors. Henderson felt the doors were not installed properly and paid less than one-half of the contract price after subtracting his costs for correcting the installation. Because of a business sale and other complications, Meyers did not sue Henderson for the difference in payment until five years later. Henderson raised the defense that because the contract was for the sale of goods, it was barred by the Code's four-year statute of limitations. Meyers claimed that it was a contract for services and that suit could be brought within six years. Decide. [*Meyers v Henderson Construction Co.*, 370 A2d 547 (NJ Super)]
6. Valley Trout Farms ordered fish food from Rangen. Both parties were merchants. The invoice that was sent with the order stated that a specified charge—a percentage common in the industry—would be added to any unpaid bills. Valley Trout Farms did not pay for the food and did not make any objection to the late charge stated in the invoice. When sued by Rangen, Valley Trout Farms claimed that it had never agreed to the late charge and therefore was not required to pay it. Is Valley Trout Farms correct? [*Rangen, Inc. v Valley Trout Farms, Inc.*, 658 P2d 955 (Idaho)]
7. On August 14, 1998, Justin Wyman was driving a vehicle leased by his mother (Maureen Wyman) with her permission. While Justin was driving the car in Cranston, Rhode Island, the vehicle left the roadway and struck a tree, injuring Michael Regan, who was a passenger in the car. Michael Regan filed suit against both Wymans and the leasing company, Nissan North America, Inc. Regan alleges that Wyman was either vicariously liable for the negligence of her son or was negligent in entrusting her

vehicle to her son. Regan alleges that Nissan is liable to him for his injuries because it is the owner of property that caused physical injury and damages. Is Regan correct? [*Regan v Nissan North America, Inc.*, 810 A2d 255 (RI)]

8. LTV Aerospace Corp. manufactured all-terrain vehicles for use in Southeast Asia. LTV made an oral contract with Bateman under which Bateman would supply the packing cases needed for the vehicles' overseas shipment. Bateman made substantial beginnings in the production of packing cases following LTV's specifications. LTV thereafter stopped production of its vehicles and refused to take delivery of any cases. When Bateman sued for breach of contract, LTV argued that the contract could not be enforced because there was no writing that satisfied the statute of frauds. Was this a valid defense? [*LTV Aerospace Corp. v Bateman*, 492 SW2d 703 (Tex App)]

9. Syrovy and Alpine Resources, Inc., entered into a "Timber Purchase Agreement." Syrovy agreed to sell and Alpine agreed to buy all of the timber produced during a two-year period. The timber to be sold, purchased, and delivered was to be produced by Alpine from timber on Syrovy's land. Alpine continued harvesting for one year and then stopped after making an initial payment. Syrovy sued Alpine. Alpine alleged there was no contract because the writing to satisfy the statute of frauds must contain a quantity term. Decide. [*Syrovy v Alpine Resources, Inc.*, 841 P2d 1279 (Wash App)]

10. Ray Thomaier placed an order with Hoffman Chevrolet, Inc., for a specifically optioned 1978 Limited Edition Corvette Coupe. The order form described the automobile and the options Mr. Thomaier wanted, included the purchase price, and provided for delivery to the purchaser "A.S.A.P." Thomaier signed the order form in the place designated for his signature and gave the dealer a $1,000 check as a deposit. This check was deposited into the account of Hoffman Chevrolet and cleared. On the same day that Thomaier gave Hoffman the check, Hoffman placed a written order with defendant General Motors Corporation, Chevrolet Motor Division, for the 1978 Limited Edition Corvette Coupe. The order was placed on a form supplied by General Motors, was signed by the dealer and listed Thomaier as the "customer." About a month later, Hoffman sent Thomaier a letter that explained that "market conditions" had made his "offer" unacceptable and that his deposit of $1,000 was being refunded. The vehicle was ultimately manufactured by Chevrolet and delivered to Hoffman. Hoffman sold this specific vehicle to a third party.

    Thomaier filed suit, but Hoffman responded that because it had never signed the order, it was not binding. Hoffman argues there was no acceptance and therefore no binding contract. Is Hoffman correct? [*Thomaier v. Hoffman Chevrolet, Inc.*, 410 NYS2d 645 (Supreme Court NY)]

11. Fastener Corp. sent a letter to Renzo Box Co. that was signed by Ronald Lee, Fastener's sales manager, and read as follows: "We hereby offer you 200 type #14 Fastener bolts at $5 per bolt. This offer will be irrevocable for ten days." On the fifth day, Fastener informed Renzo it was revoking the offer, alleging that there was no consideration for the offer. Could Fastener revoke? Explain.

12. Richard, a retailer of video equipment, telephoned Craft Appliances and ordered a $1,000 videotape recorder for his business. Craft accepted Richard's order and sent him a copy of the purchase memorandum that stated the price, quantity, and model ordered and that was stamped "order accepted by Craft." Richard, however, did not sign or return the purchase memorandum and refused to accept delivery of the recorder when Craft delivered it to him three weeks later. Craft sued Richard, who raised the statute of frauds as a defense. Will Richard prevail? Why or why not?

13. REMC furnished electricity to Helvey's home. The voltage furnished was in excess of 135 volts and caused extensive damage to his 110-volt household appliances. Helvey sued REMC for breach of warranty. Helvey argued that providing electrical energy is not a transaction in goods but a furnishing of services, so that he had six years to sue REMC rather than the UCC's four-year statute of limitations, which had expired. Was it a sale of goods or a sale of services? Identify the ethical principles involved in this case. [*Helvey v Wabash County REMC*, 278 NE2d 608 (Ind App)]

14. Curtis Moeller is a crop and dairy farmer. Huntting Elevator Company sells and applies herbicides and fertilizers in addition to its other grain and crop-related businesses. In the spring of 1995, Moeller met with Huntting's manager, Paul Steier, who suggested fertilizers and herbicides that Moeller should use on his fields. Moeller agreed to notify the elevator when his fields were ready to be sprayed with herbicide. Between May 5 and May 18, 1995, Moeller planted corn. On May 20, 1995, he told the secretary at Huntting that he had finished planting and that his fields were ready for spraying. After waiting 10 days for the sprayers, Moeller returned to Huntting and again notified the company that his fields were ready for spraying.

    On June 13, 1995, after considerable complaining from Moeller about the height of the foxtail and other weeds in his field, Huntting's staff sprayed 119 acres of Moeller's fields and, three days later, sprayed the remaining 34 acres.

    The spray was not as effective as promised, and Moeller, who lost substantial portions of his crops, filed suit under UCC Article 2 for breach of express warranty, warranty for a particular purpose, and the warranty of merchantability. Huntting maintains the contract is not covered under the UCC and that Moeller's only remedy must be to show that Huntting was somehow negligent in its work. Who is correct? Is the contract governed by UCC or common law? [*Moeller v Huntting Elevator Co.*, 1999 WL 387320 (Minn App 1999)]

15. Flora Hall went to Rent-A-Center in Milwaukee and signed an agreement to make monthly payments of $77.96 for 19 months in exchange for Rent-A-Center's allowing her to have a Rent-A-Center washer and dryer in her home. In addition, the agreement required Hall to pay tax and a liability waiver fee on the washer and dryer. The total amount she would pay under the agreement was $1,643.15. The agreement provided that Hall would return the washer and dryer at the end of the 19 months, or she could, at that time, pay $161.91 and own the washer and dryer as her own. Is this a sales contract? Is this a consumer lease? At the time Hall leased her washer and dryer, she could have purchased a set for about $600. What do you think about the cost of her agreement with Rent-A-Center? Is it unconscionable? Refer to Chapter 33, and determine whether any other consumer laws apply. Must this contract be in writing? [*Rent-A-Center, Inc. v Hall*, 510 NW2d 789 (Wis)]

CPA Questions

1. Webstar Corp. orally agreed to sell Northco, Inc., a computer for $20,000. Northco sent a signed purchase order to Webstar confirming the agreement. Webstar received the purchase order and did not respond. Webstar refused to deliver the computer to Northco, claiming that the purchase order did not satisfy the UCC statute of frauds because it was not signed by Webstar. Northco sells computers to the general public, and Webstar is a computer wholesaler. Under the UCC Sales Article, Webstar's position is:

   a. Incorrect, because it failed to object to Northco's purchase order
   b. Incorrect, because only the buyer in a sale-of-goods transaction must sign the contract
   c. Correct, because it was the party against whom enforcement of the contract is being sought
   d. Correct, because the purchase price of the computer exceeded $500

2. On May 2, Lace Corp., an appliance wholesaler, offered to sell appliances worth $3,000 to Parco, Inc., a household appliances retailer. The offer was signed by Lace's president and provided that it would not be withdrawn before June 1. It also included the shipping terms: "F.O.B.—Parco's warehouse." On May 29, Parco mailed an acceptance of Lace's offer. Lace received the acceptance June 2. Which of the following is correct if Lace sent Parco a telegram revoking its offer and Parco received the telegram on May 25?

   a. A contract was formed on May 2.
   b. Lace's revocation effectively terminated its offer on May 25.
   c. Lace's revocation was ineffective because the offer could not be revoked before June 1.
   d. No contract was formed because Lace received Parco's acceptance after June 1.

3. Bond and Spear orally agreed that Bond would buy a car from Spear for $475. Bond paid Spear a $100 deposit. The next day, Spear received an offer of $575, the car's fair market value. Spear immediately notified Bond that Spear would not sell the car to Bond and returned Bond's $100. If Bond sues Spear and Spear defends on the basis of the statute of frauds, Bond will probably:

   a. Lose, because the agreement was for less than the fair market value of the car
   b. Win, because the agreement was for less than $500
   c. Lose, because the agreement was not in writing and signed by Spear
   d. Win, because Bond paid a deposit

4. Cookie Co. offered to sell Distrib Markets 20,000 pounds of cookies at $1.00 per pound, subject to certain specified terms for delivery. Distrib replied in writing as follows: "We accept your offer for 20,000 pounds of cookies at $1.00 per pound, weighing scale to have valid city certificate." Under the UCC:

   a. A contract was formed between the parties.
   b. A contract will be formed only if Cookie agrees to the weighing scale requirement.
   c. No contract was formed because Distrib included the weighing scale requirement in its reply.
   d. No contract was formed because Distrib's reply was a counteroffer.

TITLE AND RISK OF LOSS

CHAPTER (24)

LEARNING OBJECTIVES

After studying this chapter, you should be able to

LO.1 Explain when title and risk of loss pass with respect to goods

LO.2 Determine who bears the risk of loss when goods are damaged or destroyed

LO.3 Discuss carrier liability and risk of loss

LO.4 Explain why it is important to know when risk of loss and title pass in transactions for the sale of goods

LO.5 Describe the passage of title and risk in special situations, such as a sale or return or a sale on approval

LO.6 Classify the various circumstances in which title can be passed to a bona fide purchaser

LO.7 Discuss risk of loss and title in special situations, such as bailments, consignments, factors, sales on approval, and sales or returns

In most sales, the buyer receives the proper goods and makes payment, and the transaction is completed. However, problems may arise during performance that can result in issues of liability. For example, what if the goods are lost in transit? Must the buyer still pay for those lost goods? Can the seller's creditors take goods from the seller's warehouse when they are packed for shipment to buyers? The parties can include provisions in their contract to address these types of problems. If their contract does not cover these types of problems, however, then specific rules under Uniform Commercial Code (UCC) Article 2 apply. These rules are covered in this chapter.

In businesses today, the management of issues of risk and title as goods flow through commerce is called *supply chain management*. Effective managers know the law and the rules of risk of loss and title so that they can negotiate risk-reducing contracts and be certain that they have all necessary arrangements and paperwork to move goods through streams of commerce.

A. Identifying Types of Potential Problems and Transactions

The types of problems that can arise in supply chain management include damage to the goods in transit, claims by creditors of buyers and sellers while the goods are in transit, and questions relating to whose insurance will cover what damage and when such coverage applies.

1. Damage to Goods

One potential problem occurs if the goods are damaged or totally destroyed without any fault of either the buyer or the seller. With no goods and a contract performance still required, the parties have questions: Must the seller bear the loss and supply new goods to the buyer? Or is it the buyer's loss so that the buyer must pay the seller the purchase price even though the goods are damaged or destroyed?[1] What liability does a carrier have when goods in its possession are damaged? The fact that there may be insurance does not avoid this question because the questions of whose insurer is liable and the extent of liability still remain.

CPA 2. Creditors' Claims

Another potential problem that can arise affecting the buyer's and seller's rights occurs when creditors of the seller or buyer seize the goods under the belief that their debtor has title. The buyer's creditors may seize them because they believe them to be the buyer's. The seller's creditors may step in and take goods because they believe the goods still belong to the seller, and the buyer is left with the dilemma of whether it can get the goods back from the creditors.

[1] UCC § 2-509 provides for the allocation of the risk of loss in those situations where the goods are destroyed and neither party has breached the contract.

The question of title or ownership is also important in connection with a resale of the goods by the buyer and in determining the parties' liability for, or the computation of, inventory or personal property taxes.

CPA 3. Insurance

Until the buyer has received the goods and the seller has been paid, both the seller and the buyer have an economic interest in the sales transaction. A question that can arise is whether either or both have enough of an interest in the goods to allow them to insure them, in other words, do they have an **insurable interest?** There are certain steps that must take place and timing requirements that must be met before that insurable interest can arise. Once buyers have an insurable interest in goods that are the subject matter of their contracts, they have the right to obtain insurance and can submit claims for losses on the goods.

B. Determining Rights: Identification of Goods

The **identification** of the goods to the contract is a necessary step to provide the buyer an insurable interest. How goods that are the subject matter of a contract are identified depends on the nature of both the contract and the goods themselves.[2]

CPA 4. Existing Goods

Existing goods are goods physically in existence at the time of the contract and owned by the seller. When particular goods have been selected by either the buyer or the seller, or both, as being the goods called for by the sales contract, the goods are **identified.** **For Example,** when you go into a store, point to a particular item, and tell the clerk, "I'll take that one," your sales transaction relates to existing goods that are now identified by you. This step of identification provides you with certain rights in those goods because of your contract as well as Article 2 protections for buyers when goods are identified.

CPA 5. Future Goods

Future goods are those not yet owned by the seller or not yet in existence. **For Example,** suppose that your company is sponsoring a 10-K run and will furnish the t-shirts for the 10,000 runners expected to participate in the race. You have contacted Sporting Tees, Inc., to produce the t-shirts with the name of the race and your company logo on the shirts. The shirts are future goods because you are contracting for goods that will be produced.

Future goods are identified when they are shipped, marked, or otherwise designated by the seller as goods to which the contract refers.[3] The t-shirts cannot be identified until Sporting Tees has manufactured them and designated them for your company. The earliest that the shirts can be identified is when they come off the production line and are designated for your company. Prior to identification of these goods, the buyer has only a future interest at the time of the contract and has few rights with respect to them.[4]

CPA 6. Fungible Goods

Fungible goods are goods that, when mixed together, are indistinguishable. **For Example,** crops such as soybeans and dairy products such as milk are fungible goods. A seller who has 10,000 cases of cling peaches has fungible, unidentified goods. Like future goods, these fungible goods are identified when they are shipped, marked, or otherwise designated for the buyer.[5] The seller's act of tagging, marking, labeling, or in some way indicating to those responsible for shipping the goods that certain goods are associated with a particular contract or order means that identification has occurred.

CPA 7. Effect of Identification

Once goods that are the subject matter of a contract have been identified, the buyer holds an *insurable interest* in them. Once the buyer's economic interest in and the identity of the goods are clear, the buyer's insurance company has an obligation to provide coverage for any mishaps that could occur until the contract is performed completely.

Identification is also significant because the questions surrounding passage of title and risk of loss

[2] UCC § 2-501(1)(a).

[3] UCC § 2-501(1)(b). Specially manufactured goods are fully identified when the goods are made. *Colonel's Inc. v Cincinnati Milacron Marketing Co.*, 149 F3d 1182 (6th Cir 1998).

[4] *In re Quality Processing, Inc.*, 9 F3d 1360 (8th Cir 1993).

[5] Farm products, such as corn, are fungible goods. However, contracts for future crops are not contracts for the sale of goods because there are no goods identified as yet for such contracts. *Top of Iowa Co-Op v Sime Farms, Inc.*, 608 NW2d 454 (Iowa 2000).

cannot be resolved until the goods have been identified. Identification is the first step in resolving questions about liability for damaged goods and rights of the parties and third parties, including creditors, in the goods. UCC § 2-401(1) provides, "Title to goods cannot pass under a contract for sale prior to their identification to the contract."

C. Determining Rights: Passage of Title

When title to goods passes to the buyer (following identification) depends on whether there is a document of title, whether the seller is required to ship the goods, and what the terms of that shipping agreement are. In the absence of an agreement by the parties as to when title will pass, several Article 2 rules govern the timing for passage of title.

8. Passage of Title Using Documents of Title

A **document of title** is a means whereby the parties can faciliate the transfer of title to the goods without actually moving them or provide a means for a creditor to take an interest in the goods. The use of a document of title also provides a simple answer to the question of when title to the goods passes from seller to buyer in a sales transaction. Title to the goods passes when the document of title is transferred from the seller to the buyer.[6]

Documents of title are governed under Article 7 of the UCC, the final section of the UCC to undergo major revisions in the last decade of the 20th century. The purpose of the 2003 revisions to Article 7 was to address the issues that have arisen because of electronic filing of documents of title. Article 7 adoptions have just begun with seven states passing the new Article 7 by 2006.[7]

Article 7 now addresses the commercial reality of electronic tracking and the use of electronic records as documents of title. Under Article 7, the definition of a document of title now includes electronic documents of title.

The discussion of documents of title here is limited to commercial transactions, transport, and storage. Many forms of documents of title are not covered under Article 7. For example, all states have some form of title system required for the transfer of title to motor vehicles.[8] Those systems govern title passage for automobiles. The two primary forms of documents of title under Article 7 used to pass title to goods are **bills of lading** (issued by a carrier) and **warehouse receipts**.[9] Details on these documents and the rights of the parties are found in Chapter 22.

CPA 9. Passage of Title in Nonshipment Contracts

Unless the parties to the contract agree otherwise, UCC Article 2 does not require that the seller deliver the contracted-for goods to the buyer. In the absence of a provision in the contract, the place of delivery is the seller's place of business or the seller's residence if the seller is not a merchant. When there is no specific agreement for shipment or delivery of the goods and there is no document of title and the goods to the contract have been identified, title passes to the buyer at the time the contract is entered into by the buyer and seller.

10. Passage of Title in Warehouse Arrangements

When the goods to a contract are in a warehouse or the possession of a third party (not the seller), the title to the goods passes from the seller to the buyer when the buyer receives the document of title or, if there is no document of title, any other paperwork required for the third party or warehouse to turn over the goods and the goods are available for the buyer to take. When goods are in the possession of a warehouse, the parties have certain duties and rights. Those rights and duties were covered in Chapter 22.

11. Passage of Title in Bailments and Other Forms of Possession

As a general rule, a seller can sell only what the seller owns. However, some issues of passage of title can

[6] UCC § 2-401(3).

[7] The revisions to Article 7 and their history can be found at **http://www.nccusl.org.** The seven states that had adopted Revised Article 7 as of July 2006 were New Hampshire, Utah, West Virginia, Mississippi, Colorado, Arizona, and Rhode Island. States where Article 7 is under legislative review are Massachusetts, California, and North Carolina.

[8] Other types of transportation, such as a boat, may not require a title document to be transferred, and title passes at the time of contracting. However, where there are title statutes, they preempt UCC provisions. *Ladd v NBD Bank*, 550 NW2d 826 (Mich App 1996). See also *Pierce v First Nat'l Bank*, 899 SW2d 365 (Tex App 1995).

[9] UCC § 7-202(1) provides, "A warehouse receipt need not be in any particular form. Under Revised Article 7, it can be in electronic form."

arise in specific circumstances. Those circumstances are covered in the following sections.

CPA (a) Stolen Property

Neither those who find stolen property nor thieves can pass title to goods. A thief simply cannot pass good title to even a good-faith purchaser. Anyone who has purchased stolen goods must surrender them to the true owner. The fact that the negligence of the owner made the theft possible or contributed to losing the goods does not bar the owner from recovering the goods or money damages from the thief, the finder, or a good-faith purchaser. It does not matter that the thief may have passed the goods along through several purchasers. Title cannot be cleansed by distance between the thief and the good-faith purchaser. The good-faith purchaser always takes the goods subject to the claim by the owner. The public policy reason for this protection of true owners is to deter theft. Knowing there is no way to sell the goods should deter those who steal and caution those who buy goods to check title and sources.

ALAMO RENT-A-CAR V MENDENHALL, 937 P2D 69 (NEV 1997)

THE DOWNSIDE OF BUYING A LEXUS CURBSIDE

John C. Clark, using the alias Thomas Pecora, rented a 1994 Lexus from Alamo Rent-A-Car on December 21, 1994. Clark did not return the car and, using falsified signatures, obtained a so-called California quick title. Clark advertised the car for sale in the *Las Vegas Review Journal.* Terry and Vyonne Mendenhall called the phone number in the ad and reached Clark. He told them that he lived at a country club and could not have people coming to his house to look at the car. He instead drove the car to their house for their inspection the next morning. The car title was in the name of J. C. Clark Enterprises. The Mendenhalls bought the car for $34,000 in cash. They made some improvements on the car and registered it in Utah. On February 24, 1995, Alamo reported the car stolen. On March 21, 1995, the Nevada Department of Motor Vehicles seized the car from the Mendenhalls. The car was returned to Alamo, and the Mendenhalls filed suit. The lower court found for the Mendenhalls and Alamo appealed.

Judicial Opinion

PER CURIAM:...The district court erred in awarding ownership and possession of the 1994 Lexus to the Mendenhalls instead of Alamo.

On appeal, the primary questions raised are whether Clark had voidable title to the Lexus when he sold it to the Mendenhalls, and whether the Mendenhalls were, in fact, good faith or *bona fide* purchasers of the car. If either of these questions is answered in the negative, the transfer was void. As a fallback position, the Mendenhalls argue that even if the transfer was void, Alamo should be estopped from asserting ownership of the Lexus because of its delay in reporting the Lexus as stolen.

We need not reach the issue of the Mendenhalls' status as bona fide purchasers because we conclude that Clark did not have voidable title. Therefore, even if we assume that the district court properly found the Mendenhalls to be bona fide purchasers, the transfer was void.

Clark did not have voidable title to transfer to the Mendenhalls.

Other jurisdictions have considered the effect of a sale by a thief:

The owner of stolen goods is not divested of title therein by the theft, and even though an innocent subsequent purchaser may be treated as having title as against everyone but the rightful owner, a sale by the thief... does not vest title on the purchaser as against the owner....

The true owner may recover a stolen motor vehicle... from a good-faith [(*bona fide*)] purchaser even though the thief had also stolen, or forged a title certificate, or obtained a title certificate in another state and delivered it to the purchaser.

The fact that the negligence of the owner contributed to or facilitated the theft does not estop the true owner from asserting title.

Because Alamo still had possession of the Lexus' title, Clark could not have had voidable title simply by fraudulently obtaining a facially valid California title. Accordingly, the Mendenhalls, even if found to be *bona fide* purchasers, could not have taken ownership superior to

Alamo's. However, because the Mendenhalls were found to be *bona fide* purchasers, Alamo must be ordered to reimburse the Mendenhalls for any improvements made to the Lexus while in their possession.

Alamo is not equitably estopped from contesting the Mendenhalls' ownership of the 1994 Lexus.

The Mendenhalls argued and the lower court, quoting *Godfrey v Gilsdorf*, 86 Nev. 714, 718, 476 P.2d 3, 5-6 (1970), concluded that although both parties were innocent, "ALAMO, due to its inaction in reporting the car stolen '... set in motion the chain of events which led to the sale of the car and should bear the loss incurred'" and that "the principle of estoppel precludes ALAMO from asserting its title against MENDENHALL who purchased the vehicle in good faith, for value and without notice of the interest of ALAMO."

In *Gilsdorf*, a seller was estopped to assert title as against a bona fide purchaser where the seller had placed his car with a used car dealer with the intent that the dealer would sell his car to a third party. *Gilsdorf* is inapposite here because Alamo did not entrust its car to Clark for the express purpose of having it sold to a third party. Moreover, to invoke the doctrine of estoppel, a party must prove four elements:

[T]he party to be estopped must have been aware of the facts; it must have intended that its act or omission be acted upon, or act in such a manner that the party asserting estoppel had a right to believe that it so intended; the party asserting estoppel must have been unaware of the true facts; and it must have relied upon the other party's conduct to its detriment.

In the instant case, all four elements of estoppel have not been established. First of all, on January 9, 1995, the date that the Mendenhalls purchased the Lexus from Clark, Alamo did not know that its property had been stolen. Moreover, even if it did know, the San Diego police required that Alamo send a certified demand letter to Clark, and wait ten days before filing a stolen vehicle report. Secondly, Alamo did not, merely by renting a car to Clark, act in such a manner as to induce the Mendenhalls to buy the car. Finally, assuming that the third element of estoppel (the Mendenhalls had no knowledge of the true facts) has been satisfied, the Mendenhalls could not show detrimental reliance on Alamo's conduct (i.e., failing to report the vehicle stolen before February 24, 1995).

Although the Mendenhalls made some inquiry before purchasing the car (e.g., calling Lexus Financial Services to inquire as to the appearance of a valid California title, comparing signatures on Clark's Nevada driver's license with that on the title, verifying that license plate and VIN were consistent with title), none of these inquiries could have yielded any information which would have been available from a timely filed stolen vehicle report. Thus, even if Alamo had filed a stolen vehicle report by January 9, 1995, the Mendenhalls would not have found out about it, and would have still given $34,000.00 to Clark in exchange for the Lexus.

[T]he district court erroneously determined that Clark had voidable title. Therefore, ownership remained in Alamo, and Alamo was not estopped from asserting its rightful ownership. Accordingly, we reverse the district court's judgment and remand with instructions to award ownership and possession to Alamo and order Alamo to reimburse the Mendenhalls for improvements made to the Lexus while it was in their possession.

Questions

1. Give a history of how the parties came to be involved in a dispute over the Lexus.
2. Why does it make no difference to the appellate court whether the Mendenhalls were good faith purchasers?
3. Who gets the Lexus?

(b) Estoppel

If an owner has acted in a way that misleads others, the owner of personal property may be prevented, or **estopped,** from asserting ownership. The owner would be barred from denying the right of another person to sell the property. **For Example,** a minor buys a car and puts it in his father's name so that he can obtain lower insurance rates. If the father then sells the car to a good-faith purchaser, the son would be estopped from claiming ownership.

CPA (c) Authorization

In certain circumstances, persons who just possess someone else's property may sell the property and pass title. Lienholders can sell property if there is a default on the money owed to them. **For Example,** if you store your personal property in a storage locker and fail to pay rent, the owner of the storage locker holds a lien on your personal property and could sell it to pay the rent due on your storage unit. Good title passes to the buyer from such a sale. All states have

THINKING THINGS THROUGH

EVEN THE BEST JEWELER IN ORANGE COUNTY CAN'T ALWAYS SPOT A PHONY

Scott Wayne Simmons purchased a 15.05-carat heart-shaped diamond from Angel Archer Estate Jewelers. Simmons gave a check for $70,000 for the diamond and was given a certificate of authenticity from the European Gemological Laboratory (EGL). Simmons then sold the diamond to Glenn Verdult, d/b/a Winston's Newport Jewelers, a jewelry store named the best in Orange County with an impeccable reputation. Verdult paid $40,000 for the diamond and the certificate from EGL. The Simmons check was fictitious; there was no money in the account. Simmons was charged with writing a fictitious check by Riverside County, and the Riverside County Sheriff's Office took the diamond back to Angel Archer as its rightful owner. Verdult filed suit, claiming that he was the rightful owner of the diamond. What could Verdult argue to convince the court that he is entitled to the diamond? People v Simmons, 2003 WL 21350737 (Cal App 4 Dist, unpublished opinion)

some form of statute giving those who find property the authority to sell the property after certain time periods have passed or when the owner cannot be found.

(d) Voidable Title

If the buyer has a **voidable title**—for example, when the goods were obtained by fraud—the seller can rescind the sale. However, if the buyer resells the property to a good-faith purchaser before the seller has rescinded the transaction, the subsequent purchaser acquires valid title. It is immaterial whether the buyer with the voidable title had obtained title by criminal fraud.[10]

(e) Bailments or Sale by an Entrustee

A bailee can pass good title to a good-faith purchaser even when the sale was not authorized by the owner and the bailee has no title to the goods but is in the business of selling those particular types of goods.[11] **For Example,** if Gunnell's Jewelry sells and repairs watches and Julie has left her watch with Gunnell's for repair, she has created a bailment. If Gunnell's Jewelry sells Julie's watch by mistake because it is both a new and old watch dealer to David, a good-faith purchaser, David has valid title to the watch. Julie will have a cause of action against Gunnell's for conversion, and in some states, if Gunnell's sold the watch knowing that it belonged to Julie, the sale could constitute a crime, such as larceny. However, all of these legal proceedings will involve Gunnell's, Julie, and possibly a government prosecution, but not David who will take good title to the watch.

In the case of an entrustee who is not a merchant, such as a prospective customer trying out an automobile, there is no transfer of title to the buyer from the entrustee. Similarly, there is no transfer of title when a mere bailee, such as a repairer who is not a seller of goods of that kind, sells the property of a customer.

12. Delivery and Shipment Terms

If delivery is required under the terms of the parties' agreement, the seller is normally required only to make shipment, and the seller's part of the contract is completed by placing the goods in the possession of a carrier for shipment. However, the parties may agree to various shipping provisions that do affect the

[10] "Criminal fraud" is the language of Revised Article 2, adopted to increase the scope of the original term *larceny* and intended to encompass all forms of criminal activity that might lead to the possession or entrustment of goods. Revised Article 2 also covers all conduct punishable under criminal law.

[11] *Beall Transport Equipment Co. v Southern Pacific Transportation*, 13 P3d 130 (Or App 2000), affirmed, 60 P2d 530 (Or 2002), with decision clarified, 68 P3d 259 (Or App 2003); see also, *Abrams v General Start Indemnity*, 67 P3d 931 (Or 2003).

FIGURE 24-1 Delivery and Shipping Terms

COD	CASH ON DELIVERY (PAYMENT TERM, NOT SHIPMENT TERM)
CF	COST PLUS FREIGHT LUMP SUM; PRICE INCLUDES COST AND FREIGHT RISK: BUYER ON DELIVERY TO CARRIER TITLE: BUYER ON DELIVERY TO CARRIER COST, INSURANCE AND FREIGHT EXPENSES: SELLER PAYS; INCLUDES COST OF FREIGHT IN CONTRACT PRICE
CIF	LUMP SUM; PRICE INCLUDES COST, INSURANCE, AND FREIGHT RISK: BUYER ON DELIVERY TO CARRIER TITLE: BUYER ON DELIVERY TO CARRIER EXPENSES: INCLUDED IN CONTRACT PRICE (SELLER BUYS INSURANCE IN BUYER'S NAME AND PAYS FREIGHT)
FOB	FREE ON BOARD
FAS	FREE ALONGSIDE SHIP (FOB FOR BOATS)

passage of title under Article 2.[12] With the 2003 changes to Article 2, the statutory definitions of terms such as *FOB*, *FAS*, *CF*, and *CIF* were eliminated. The elimination occurred because the nature of contracts and shipping has changed substantially and continues to do so at such a rapid pace that it is difficult to have any generic and statutory definitions that will have universal application.[13] The parties can still use such terms, but Article 2 no longer controls their intent and interpretation. Because the terms are still used, Figure 24-1 summarizes the shipping terms the parties can use in their sales contracts and the liabilities and responsibilities under each.

(a) FOB Place of Shipment

FOB is a shipping term that is an acronym for free on board.[14] If a contract contains a delivery term of **FOB place of shipment,** then the seller's obligation under the contract is to deliver the goods to a carrier for shipment. **For Example,** if the contract between a New York buyer and a Los Angeles seller provides for delivery as FOB Los Angeles, then the seller's responsibility is to place the goods in the possession of a Los Angeles carrier and enter into a contract to have the goods shipped to New York.

CPA (b) FOB Place of Destination

If a contract contains a delivery term of **FOB place of destination,** then the seller's responsibility is to get the goods to the buyer. **For Example,** if the contract between the New York buyer and the Los Angeles seller is FOB New York, then the seller is responsible for getting the goods to New York. An FOB destination contract holds the seller accountable throughout the journey of the goods across the country.

CPA (c) FAS

FAS is a shipping term that means free alongside ship; it is the equivalent of FOB for boat transportation.[15] **For Example,** a contract between a London buyer and a Norfolk, Virginia, seller that is FAS Norfolk requires only that the seller deliver the goods to a ship in Norfolk.

CPA (d) CF, CIF, and COD

CF is an acronym for cost and freight, and **CIF** is an acronym for cost, insurance, and freight.[16] Under a

12 UCC § 2-401(2). When a seller simply ships goods in response to a telephone order and there is no paperwork to indicate shipping terms, the contract is one of shipment (FOB place of shipment). *California State Electronics Ass'n v Zeos Int'l Ltd.*, 49 Cal Rptr 2d 127 (1996).

13 Under Revised Article 2, §§ 2-319 through 2-324 are deleted. The comment to the section indicates that Article 2 will no longer contain "terms that amount to commercial shorthand."

14 UCC § 2-319.

15 UCC § 2-319.

16 UCC §§ 2-320 and 2-321.

FIGURE 24-2 Passage of Title under Article 2 and Revised Article 2

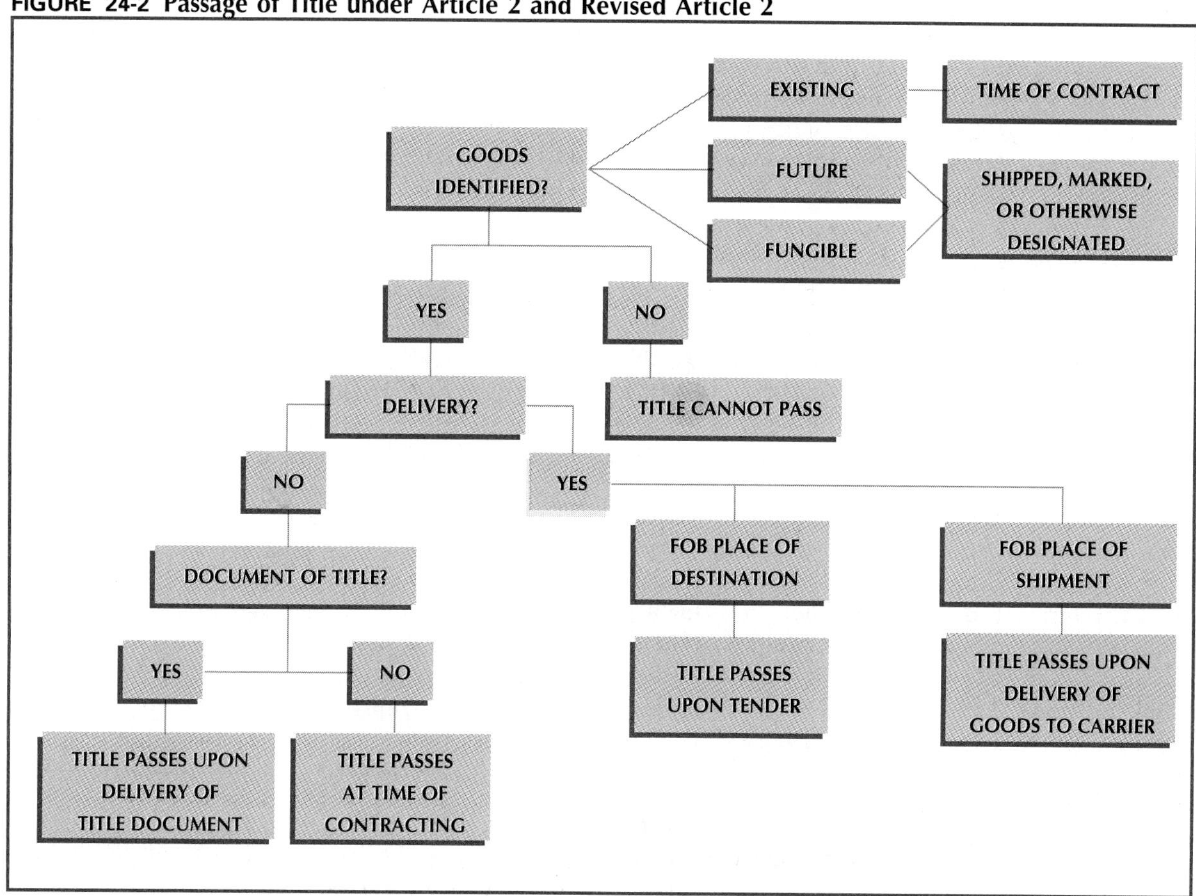

CF contract, the seller gets the goods to a carrier, and the cost of shipping the goods is included in the contract price. Under a CIF contract, the seller must get the goods to a carrier and buy an insurance policy in the buyer's name to cover the goods while in transit. The costs of the freight and the insurance policy are included in the contract price.

Often contracts for the sale of goods provide for **COD.** The acronym stands for cash on delivery. Even though the term includes the word *delivery*, COD is not a shipping term but a payment term that requires the buyer to pay in order to gain physical possession of the goods.

13. Passage of Title in Shipment Contracts

When the parties have shipment and delivery terms in their contract, the type of shipment contract the parties have agreed to controls when title to the goods has passed and, as a result, the rights of creditors of the buyer and seller in those goods.

Revised Article 2 provides for the same results on passage of title in shipment contracts as under Article 2, but the FOB terms are not specifically delineated under the Revised Article 2. (See Figure 24-2.) Revised Article 2 simply uses the generic language of shipment contracts and those shipment contracts in which the seller is required to get the goods to a particular destination.

CPA (a) Passage of Title in a Shipment Only Contract (FOB Shipment)

Title to the goods passes from the seller to the buyer in an FOB shipment contract or under a shipment contract for Revised Article 2 when the seller delivers the goods to the carrier.[17] The title to the goods no longer rests with the Los Angeles seller once the goods are delivered to the carrier if the contract is just

[17] UCC § 2-401(2).

a shipment contract only (an FOB Los Angeles contract). **For Example,** if the Internal Revenue Service received authorization to collect taxes by seizing the seller's property, it could not take those goods once they were delivered to the carrier. Under a shipment contract (an FOB shipment contract), the buyer owns the goods once they are in the hands of the carrier.

CPA (b) Passage of Title in a Destination Contract (FOB Place of Destination)

Title to the goods passes from the seller to the buyer in an FOB destination contract when the goods are tendered to the buyer at the destination. **Tender** occurs when the goods have arrived and are available for the buyer to pick up and the buyer has been notified of their availability. **For Example,** when the contract contains an FOB destination provision requiring the seller to deliver to New York, title to the goods passes to the New York buyer when the goods have arrived in New York, they are available for pickup, and the buyer has been notified of their arrival. Thus, the IRS could seize the goods during shipment if the contract is FOB New York because title remains with the seller until actual tender. In the preceding example, the seller's obligation is complete when the goods are at the rail station in New York and the buyer has been notified that she may pick them up at any time during working hours.

D. Determining Rights: Risk of Loss

Identification determines insurability, and title determines rights of such third parties as creditors. **Risk of loss** determines who must pay under a contract in the event the goods that are the subject of the contract are damaged or destroyed during the course of performance.

14. Risk of Loss in Nonshipment Contracts

As noted earlier, Article 2 has no provision for delivery in the absence of an agreement. The rules for passage of risk of loss from the seller to the buyer in a nonshipment contract make a distinction between a merchant seller and a nonmerchant seller. If the seller is a merchant, the risk of loss passes to the buyer on actual receipt of the goods from the merchant.[18] If the seller is a nonmerchant, the risk of loss passes when the seller makes the goods available to the buyer or upon tender.

The highly technical aspect of the nonshipment rule was modified under Revised Article 2, which has a uniform rule on nonshipment contracts with the risk of loss passing upon receipt of the goods, whether a merchant or nonmerchant seller is involved.[19] **For Example,** if John buys a refrigerator at Kelvinator Appliances or at his neighbor's garage sale and then leaves it there while he goes to borrow a pickup truck, the risk of loss has not yet passed to John under Revised Article 2. He may have had title at the time he entered into the contract for the existing goods, and the goods are identified, but the risk of loss will not pass to John until he has actually receives the refrigerator. His receipt will not occur until the refrigerator is placed in the back of his pickup truck. John is fully protected if anything happens to the refrigerator until then.

E-COMMERCE AND CYBERLAW

SUPPLY CHAIN AND RISK MANAGEMENT

In today's sophisticated supplier and transportation relationships, buyers, sellers, and carriers can pinpoint exactly where goods are and when they have been delivered, and all parties have access to that information online. In many contracts, the parties can avert problems or breaches by monitoring closely the progress of the shipment. The computer interconnection of the supply chain permits faster and better communication among the parties when problems under the contract or in shipment arise. The shipment can be tracked from the time of delivery to the carrier through its route to final signature upon its arrival.

[18] UCC § 2-509; *Charia v Cigarette Racing Tea, Inc.*, 583 F2d 184 (5th Cir 1978).
[19] UCC § 2-509(3).

15. Risk of Loss in Shipment Contracts

If the parties have agreed to delivery or shipment terms as part of their contract, the rules for risk of loss are different.[20]

CPA (a) Contract for Shipment to Buyer (FOB Place of Shipment)

In a contract for shipment only, or FOB place of shipment, the risk of loss passes to the buyer at the same time as title does: when the goods are delivered to the carrier, that is, at the time and place of shipment. After the goods have been delivered to the carrier, the seller has no liability for, or insurable interest in, the goods unless the seller has reserved a security interest in them. **For Example,** if the Los Angeles seller has a shipment contract (an FOB Los Angeles contract), once the goods are in the hands of the carrier, the risk belongs to the buyer or the buyer's insurer. If the goods are hijacked outside Kansas City, the New York buyer must still pay the Los Angeles seller for the goods according to the contract price and terms.

CPA (b) Contract for Delivery at Destination (FOB Place of Destination)

When the contract requires the seller to deliver the contract goods at a particular destination (FOB place of destination), the risk of loss does not pass to the buyer until the carrier tenders the goods at the destination. **For Example,** if the contract is FOB New York and the goods are hijacked in Kansas City, the seller is required to find substitute goods and perform under the contract because the risk of loss does not pass to the buyer until the goods arrive in New York and are available to the notified buyer.

16. Damage to or Destruction of Goods

In the absence of a contract provision, Article 2 provides for certain rights for the parties in the event of damage to or destruction of goods that are the subject matter in a contract.

(a) Damage to Identified Goods before Risk of Loss Passes

Goods that were identified at the time the contract was made may be damaged or destroyed without the fault of either party before the risk of loss has passed. If so, the UCC provides, "if the loss is total the contract is avoided."[21] The loss may be partial, or the goods may have so deteriorated that they do not conform to the contract. In this case, the buyer has the option, after inspecting the goods, to either avoid the contract or accept the goods subject to an allowance or a deduction from the contract price. There is no breach by the seller, so the purpose of the law is simply to eliminate the legal remedies, allow the buyer to choose to take the goods, and have the insurers involved cover the losses.[22]

GRAFF V BAKKER BROTHERS OF IDAHO, INC., 934 P2D 1228 (WASH APP 1997)

PEELING BACK THE LAYERS IN THE GREAT ONION CONTRACT BREACH

Bakker Brothers of Idaho agreed to buy Charles E. Graff's 1989 onion seed crop. The contract required that the onion seeds have an 85 percent germination rate. Despite careful testing and advice from experts, Bakker Brothers could not get a germination rate on the seed that tested higher than 62 to 69 percent. Bakker Brothers rejected the seed, notified Graff, and awaited instructions. Graff gave no instructions and the seed spoiled. Graff sought to recover the contract price from Bakker Brothers because the risk of loss had passed. The trial court granted summary judgment for Bakker Brothers, and Graff appealed.

20 UCC § 2-509. Revised UCC § 2-612 retains the rules for risk of loss in shipment contracts. See Patricia A., Tauchert, "Symposium on Revised Article 1 and Proposed Revised Article 2 of the Uniform Commercial Code Article," *54 Southern Methodist Law Review* 971 (2001).

21 UCC § 613(a).

22 *Design Data Corp. v Maryland Casualty Co.*, 503 NW2d 552 (Neb 1993).

Judicial Opinion

SWEENEY, Chief Judge. . . . Mr. Graaff argues that application of trade usage here effectively nullifies the contract's risk of loss provision. He claims that since the contract required him to "deliver all the seed F.O.B. as directed" he transported the seed at his own risk and upon delivery to Bakker the risk of loss passed to Bakker. He is mistaken.

"Where a tender or delivery of goods so fails to conform to the contract as to give a right of rejection the risk of their loss remains on the seller until cure or acceptance." "[T]he seller by his individual action cannot shift the risk of loss to the buyer unless his action conforms with all the conditions resting on him under the contract." Therefore, even if we assume that the contract's use of F.O.B. passed the risk of loss, the term only became operative when Mr. Graaff tendered conforming goods. The post-germination rate of Mr. Graaff's onion seed was below the contract's requirements. The goods were, therefore, nonconforming.

We affirm the trial court's grant of summary judgment in favor of Bakker.

Questions

1. What types of goods were involved and what went wrong?
2. Did the buyer act properly under the circumstances?
3. Did the risk of loss pass to the buyer?

(b) Damage to Identified Goods after Risk of Loss Passes

If partial damage or total destruction occurs after the risk of loss has passed to the buyer, it is the buyer's loss. The buyer may be able to recover the amount of the damages from the carrier, an insurer, the person in possession of the goods (such as a warehouse), or any third person causing the loss.[23]

(c) Damage to Unidentified Goods

As long as the goods are unidentified, no risk of loss passes to the buyer. If any goods are damaged or destroyed during this period, the loss is the seller's. The buyer is still entitled to receive the goods described by the contract. The seller is therefore liable for breach of contract if the proper goods are not delivered.

The only exceptions to these general rules on damage or destruction arise when the parties have expressly provided in the contract that the destruction of the seller's inventory, crop, or source of supply releases the seller from liability, or when it is clear that the parties contracted for the purchase and sale of part of the seller's supply to the exclusion of any other possible source of such goods. In these cases, destruction of, or damage to, the seller's supply is a condition subsequent that discharges the contract.

17. Effect of Seller's Breach in Risk of Loss

When the seller breaches the contract by sending the buyer goods that do not conform to the contract and the buyer rejects them, the risk of loss does not pass to the buyer. If there has been a breach, the risk of loss remains with the seller even though the risk, according to the contract terms or the Article 2 rules discussed earlier, would ordinarily have passed to the buyer.

Figures 24-3 and 24-4 provide a summary of all the risk provisions for parties in a sales transaction.

E. Determining Rights: Special Situations

18. Returnable Goods Transactions

The parties may agree that the goods to be transferred under the contract can be returned to the seller. This type of arrangement in which goods may be returned is classified as one of the following: (1) a sale on approval, (2) a sale or return, or (3) a consignment sale. In the first two types of transactions, the buyer is allowed to return the goods as an added inducement to purchase. The consignment sale is used when the seller is actually the owner's agent for the purpose of selling goods.[24]

[23] For a discussion of parties rights, see *Learning Links, Inc. v United Parcel Services of America, Inc.* 2006 WL 785274 (SDNY).
[24] *In re Thomas*, 182 BR 347, 26 UCC2d 774 (Bankr SD Fla 1995).

FIGURE 24-3 Risk of Loss

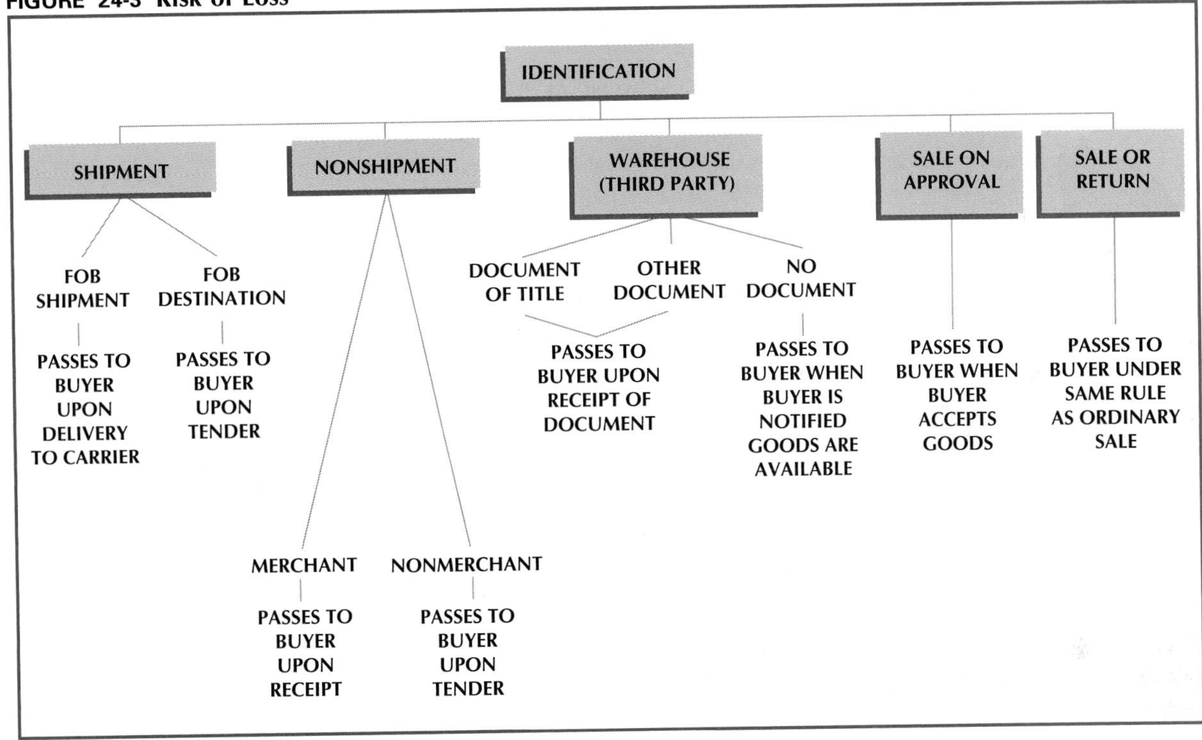

FIGURE 24-4 Risk of Loss—Revised Article 2

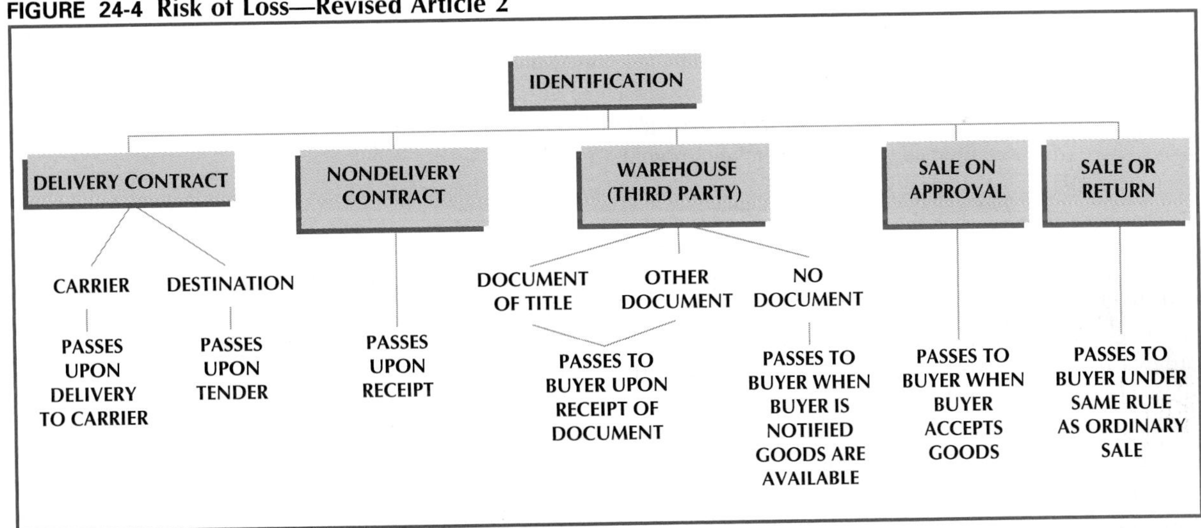

CPA (a) Sale on Approval

In a **sale on approval,** no sale takes place (meaning there is no transfer of title) until the buyer approves, or accepts, the goods. Title and risk of loss remain with the seller until there is an approval. Because the buyer is not the "owner" of the goods before approval, the buyer's creditors cannot attach or take the goods before the buyer's approval of the goods.

The buyer's approval may be shown by (1) express words, (2) conduct, or (3) lapse of time. Trying out or testing the goods does not constitute approval or acceptance. Any use that goes beyond trying out or testing, such as repairing the goods or giving them

ETHICS & THE LAW

HIGH-FALUTIN' MERCHANDISE AND HIGH CHARGE BACKS

Some vendors are going to court to challenge the deductions retailers take before paying their vendors' bills. In May 2005, Ben Elias Industries, a family-owned clothing manufacturer, located in the garment district of New York City, and that holds the license of making the Mary McFadden line of clothing, filed suit against Dillard's, the third-largest department store in the United States. In the suit, Elias offered the following information about the scope of the markdowns:

Dillard's took a 36.1% discount on $842,621 invoiced amount when the maximum discount the contract provided for was 10%. The discounts are taken for a variety of reasons that range from merchandise defects and quality to the inability to sell the line of clothing. Candie's filed suit against Saks for taking $176,016 in deductions on $200,000 in merchandise.

No one is quite sure how this practice of charge backs became so entrenched. However, there was at least some reciprocity in the 1980s when the practice began. Manufacturers wanted their clothing lines in stores such as Saks, Bloomingdale's, and others. When a store agreed to sell a line, it would order, for example, $100,000 in inventory. The manufacturers would encourage the retailer to take $150,000 (pitching the idea that the retailer could sell more). The manufacturer agreed to take a discount or "markdown" on what actually sold so that the retailer would still have a profit on the $150,000 in merchandise. The retailers began deducting other amounts from invoices, and the phenomenon of charge backs began. Manufacturers were charged for goods that did not arrive on time, failure to sell, mislabeling, and mispackaging. Some retailers were so finely attuned to this process that they drafted unduly complex contracts for charge backs, right down to allow certain types of hangers to be used. The following have been the results of these systems:

- Increasingly complex and increasing amount of charge backs and markdowns
- Difficulties with accounting to reflect the practices

How would the risk of loss rules apply to these situations?

Source: Tracie Rozhon, "Stores and Vendors Take Their Haggling over Payments to Court," *New York Times*, May 17, 2005, C1, C3.

away as a present, is inconsistent with the seller's continued ownership. These types of uses show approval by the buyer. **For Example,** a buyer may order a home gym through a television ad. The ad allows buyers to try the room full of equipment for 30 days and then promises, "If you are not completely satisfied, return the home gym and we'll refund your money." The offer is one for a sale on approval. If the buyer does not return the home gym equipment or contact the seller within 30 days, the sale is complete.

The contract may give the buyer a fixed number of days for approval. The expiration of that period of time, without any action by the buyer, constitutes an approval. Also during this time, the buyer's creditors cannot take the goods pursuant to a judgment or lien. If no time is stated in the contract, the lapse of a reasonable time without action by the buyer constitutes an approval. If the buyer gives the seller notice of disapproval, the lapse of time thereafter has no effect.

If the buyer does not approve the goods, the seller bears the risk of and expense for their return.

(b) Sale or Return

A **sale or return** is a completed sale with an option for the buyer to return the goods. Revised Article 2 provides a new distinction between sale on approval and sale or return but with the same basic rules on title and risk of loss:

> *Unless otherwise agreed, if delivered goods may be returned by the buyer even though they conform to the contract, the transaction is:*

(a) a "sale on approval" if the goods are delivered primarily for use, and
(b) a "sale or return" if the goods are delivered primarily for resale.[25]

In a sale or return transaction, title and risk of loss pass to the buyer as in the case of the ordinary or absolute sale. Until the actual return of the goods is made, title and risk of loss remain with the buyer. The buyer bears the expense for and risk of return of the goods. In a sale or return, so long as the goods remain in the buyer's possession, the buyer's creditors may treat the goods as belonging to the buyer.

19. Consignments and Factors

Under a **consignment,** the owner of the goods entrusts them to a dealer for the purpose of selling them. The seller is the **consignor,** and the dealer is the **consignee.** The dealer-consignee is often referred to as a **factor,** a special type of bailee (see Chapter 22) who sells consigned goods just as if the goods were her own. The dealer-consignee is paid a fee for selling the goods on behalf of the seller-consignor. A consignment sale is treated as a sale or return under Article 2, and the dealer-consignee has full authority to sell the goods for the consignor and can pass title to those goods. While the goods are in the possession of the consignee, they are subject to the claims of the seller's creditors.[26]

20. Self-Service Stores

In the case of goods in a self-service store, the reasonable interpretation of the circumstances is that the store, by its act of putting the goods on display on its shelves, makes an offer to sell such goods for cash and confers on a prospective customer a license to carry the goods to the cashier to make payment. Most courts hold that there is no transfer of title until the buyer makes payment to the cashier. Under this view, the store does not have warranty liability until the buyer pays. For example, if a customer is injured because a light bulb in his cart explodes as he is shopping, the remedy is against the manufacturer, not the store, unless the shopper could show that the store was storing the bulbs in a manner that would cause their sudden explosion.

A contrary rule adopts the view that a contract to sell is formed when the customer accepts the seller's offer by taking the item from the shelf. In other words, a sale actually occurs when the buyer takes the item from the shelf. Title passes at that moment to the buyer even though the goods have not yet been paid for. Under this view, the buyer would have a right of recovery for injury resulting from goods in the cart.

CPA 21. Auction Sales

When goods are sold at an auction in separate lots, each lot is a separate transaction, and title to each passes independently of the other lots. Title to each lot passes when the auctioneer announces by the fall of the hammer or in any other customary manner that the lot in question has been sold to the bidder. Under Revised Article 2, a bid that is made while the auctioneer is in the process of accepting a bid can be honored or not honored at the discretion of the auctioneer. It is the auctioneer's choice whether to end the bidding or reopen the process to allow the new bid and any others that might follow.

"With reserve" auctions are those that give the auctioneer the right to withdraw the goods from the sale process if the bids are not high enough. If an auction is held "without reserve," the goods must be sold regardless of whether the auctioneer is satisfied with the levels of the bids.

[25] For a discussion of the distinctions between sale on approval and sale or return, see 1 Hawkland UCC Series § 2-326:2 (2006).

[26] This clarification of creditors' rights in consignments came from Revised Article 9 (see Chapter 34). Revised Article 2 was changed to make the sale or return rights of creditors consistent with Revised Article 9. Prior to these changes, and under current Article 2, whether the seller's creditor could seize the goods depended upon the filing of an Article 9 security interest.

Summary

All along the supply chain of a business are issues of risk and title that are often complicated by additional questions about damage to goods in transit, the claims of creditors to goods that are in process under a contract, and insurance. Unless the parties specifically agree otherwise, the solution to these problems depends on the nature of the transaction between the seller and the buyer.

The first issue to be addressed in answering questions of risk, title, and loss is whether the goods are identified. Existing goods are identified at the time the contract is entered into.

Future goods, or goods not yet owned by the seller or not yet in existence (as in goods to be manufactured by the seller), are identified when they are shipped, marked, or otherwise designated for the buyer. Without identification, title and risk of loss cannot pass from buyer to seller, nor can the buyer hold an insurable interest.

Once identification has occurred, the issue of title, and hence creditor's rights, can be addressed. If there are identified goods but there is no document of title associated with the goods, then title to the goods passes from the seller to the buyer at the time of the contract.

Sellers can have their goods covered by a document of title. The most common types of documents of title are bills of lading and warehouse receipts. These documents of title, if properly transferred, transfer title to both the document and the underlying goods.

While the seller has no obligation under UCC Article 2 to deliver the goods to the buyer, the parties can agree on delivery as part of their contract. Several common delivery terms are used in supply chain management. *FOB* is "free on board," and its meaning depends on the location that follows the term. *FOB place of shipment* requires the seller to deliver the goods to the carrier. In an FOB place of shipment contract, title to the goods passes from the seller to the buyer when the goods are delivered to the carrier. *FOB place of destination* requires the seller to get the goods to the buyer or a location specified by the buyer and tender the goods there. *FAS* is "free alongside ship," which means free on board for shipment by sea. *CF* is "cost and freight" and requires the seller to deliver the goods to the carrier and make a contract for their shipment. *CIF* is "cost, insurance, and freight" and requires the seller to deliver the goods to the carrier, make a contract for shipment, and purchase insurance for the goods in transit. *COD* means "cash on delivery" and requires the buyer to pay for the goods before taking possession of them.

Revised Article 2 no longer uses these commercial shipping terms. It simply makes a distinction between those types of contracts in which the seller agrees to ship the goods only and those in which the seller agrees to deliver the goods to a particular destination. For delivery to a particular destination (FOB place of destination), the time for passage of risk of loss and title is upon tender. *Tender* means that the goods are available for the buyer to pick up, the buyer is aware that the goods are available, and the buyer has the necessary documentation to pick up the goods.

Ordinarily, sellers cannot pass any title greater than that which they possess. In some cases, however, the law permits a greater title to be transferred even though the transferor may hold voidable title or be in possession of the goods only as in a bailment. These exceptions protect good-faith purchasers.

Risk of loss is an issue for buyers, sellers, and insurers. When risk of loss passes from seller to buyer is controlled, again, by the terms of the contract. In a contract in which there is no agreement on delivery, the risk of loss passes to the buyer upon receipt of the goods if the seller is a merchant and upon tender if the seller is a nonmerchant. Under Revised Article 2, the risk of loss in nonshipment contracts always passes upon receipt, regardless of whether the contract involves a merchant or nonmerchant. If there is an agreement for delivery and the contract provides for shipment only, or FOB place of shipment, then risk of loss passes from seller to buyer when the goods are delivered to the carrier. If the contract provides for delivery to a particular location, or FOB place of destination, then the risk of loss passes from the seller to the buyer when the goods are tendered to the buyer.

Some types of arrangements, such as sales on approval, sales or returns, and consignments or factor arrangements, have specific rules for passage of title and risk of loss. Also, if there is a breach of the contract and the seller ships goods different from those ordered, the breach prevents the risk of loss from passing from the seller to the buyer.

Questions and Case Problems

1. Schock, the buyer, negotiated to purchase a mobile home that was owned by and located on the sellers' property. On April 15, 1985, Schock appeared at the Ronderos' (the sellers') home and paid them the agreed-on purchase price of $3,900. Shock received a bill of sale and an assurance from the Ronderos that the title certificate to the mobile home would be delivered soon. Also on April 15 and with the permission of the sellers, Schock prepared the mobile home for removal. His preparations included the removal of skirting around the mobile home's foundation, the tie-downs, and the foundation blocks, leaving the mobile home to rest on the wheels of its chassis. Schock intended to remove the mobile home from the Ronderos' property a week later, and the Ronderos had no objection to having the mobile home remain on their premises until that time. The Ronderos also promised to have the electricity and natural gas disconnected by that time. Two days later, the mobile home was destroyed by high winds as it sat on the Ronderos' property. Schock received a clear certificate of title to the mobile home in the mail. Thereafter, Schock sued the Ronderos for return of his money on the ground that when the mobile home was destroyed, the risk of loss remained with the Ronderos. Who should win the lawsuit? [*Schock v Ronderos*, 394 NW2d 697 (ND)]
2. In 1989, Michael Heinrich wanted to buy a particular model of a new Ford pickup truck. James Wilson represented himself to Heinrich as a dealer-broker who was licensed to buy and sell vehicles. Because he did not know that Wilson had lost his Washington vehicle

dealer's license a year earlier, Heinrich retained Wilson to make the truck purchase but did not direct Wilson to any particular dealer.

Wilson negotiated with Titus-Will Sales for a pickup truck with the options Heinrich had specified. Wilson had completed hundreds of transactions over the years with Titus-Will, which also was unaware that Wilson had lost his license. Heinrich made two initial payments to Wilson: an $1,800 down payment and a $3,000 payment when Titus-Will ordered the truck. Wilson gave Heinrich a receipt with his vehicle dealer's license number and then ordered the truck from Titus-Will, using his own check to provide a $7,000 down payment. Wilson told the Titus-Will salesman with whom he placed the order that he was buying the truck for resale.

When the truck arrived, Titus-Will issued a dealer-to-dealer title to it after Heinrich had paid the remaining $15,549.55 due on the sale. However, Wilson's original check for $7,000 failed to clear, and Titus-Will refused to issue the title and took the truck back from Heinrich. Seeking to have his truck returned, Heinrich sued Titus-Will and Wilson. Can Heinrich get his truck back? [*Heinrich v Titus-Will Sales, Inc.*, 868 P2d 169 (Wash App)]

3. Felix DeWeldon is a well-known sculptor and art collector. He owned three paintings valued at $26,000 that he displayed in his home in Newport, Rhode Island. In 1991, he declared bankruptcy and DeWeldon, Ltd., purchased all of DeWeldon's personal property from the bankruptcy trustee. Nancy Wardell, the sole shareholder of DeWeldon, Ltd., sold her stock to Byron Preservation Trust, which then sold Felix an option to repurchase the paintings. At all times, the paintings were on display in DeWeldon's home.

   In 1994, DeWeldon's son Byron told Robert McKean that his father was interested in selling the paintings. After viewing them, McKean then purchased the paintings for $50,000. DeWeldon, Ltd., brought suit to have the paintings returned, claiming McKean did not have title because Byron did not have the authority to sell the paintings. Will McKean get the paintings? [*DeWeldon, Ltd. v McKean*, 125 F3d 24 (1st Cir)]

4. Helen Thomas contracted to purchase a pool heater from Sunkissed Pools. As part of the $4,000 contract, Sunkissed agreed to install the pool heater, which was delivered to Thomas's home and left in the driveway. The heater was too heavy for Thomas to lift, and she was forced to leave it in the driveway because no one from Sunkissed responded to her calls about its installation. Subsequently, the heater disappeared from the driveway. Sunkissed maintained the risk of loss had passed to Thomas. Thomas maintained that the failure to install the heater as promised is a breach of contract. Who should bear the risk for the stolen pool heater? [*In re Thomas*, 182 BR 774 (Bankr SD Fla)]

5. Petrosol, a wholesale marketer and distributor of petroleum products, acts as an agent between gas line producers and gas distributors. Because it immediately resells the propane that it purchases, Petrosol does not have its own storage facilities. Commonwealth, also a marketer and distributor, does have such storage facilities and reserves much of the liquid propane gas it purchases for resale on a later date.

   On November 5, 1982, Cal Gas Corporation, a propane supplier, entered into a contract with Petrosol for the sale and delivery of 10,000 barrels of propane stored at Lake Underground Storage, a storage facility in Painesville, Ohio. Petrosol agreed to pay $0.57 per gallon for the propane. Petrosol entered into a contract with Commonwealth on the same day for the sale and delivery of 10,000 barrels of propane at a price of $0.58 per gallon. Commonwealth paid Petrosol for the propane two days later. Sales Acknowledgements indicated that the "delivery point" was "Painesville, Ohio" and that the stated price was "$0.58 USF/USG F.O.B. Lake Underground Storage." In addition, beside the "to be delivered in" caption on the front of the Sales Acknowledgments, there were five boxes indicating different types of delivery methods (buyer's tank trucks or cars, seller's tank trucks or cars, or pipeline PTO). None of these boxes was checked on either form.

   In February 1983, a wall in the cavern of Lake Underground collapsed. As a result, the propane was apparently either lost or destroyed before Commonwealth was able to remove it from the storage facility. Commonwealth subsequently sued both Petrosol and Cal Gas for the lack of sufficient propane to fill the agreements. Had the risk of loss passed to Commonwealth, or was Petrosol still responsible for the loss of the propane? [*Commonwealth Petroleum Co. v Petrosol Intern., Inc.*, 901 F2d 1314 (6th Cir)]

6. A thief stole a car and sold it to a good-faith purchaser for value. This person resold the car to another buyer, who also purchased in good faith and for value. The original owner of the car sued the second purchaser for the car. The defendant argued that he had purchased the car in good faith from a seller who had sold in good faith. Was this defense valid? [*Johnny Dell, Inc. v New York State Police*, 375 NYS2d 545 (Misc)]

7. Using a bad check, B purchased a used automobile from a dealer. B then took the automobile to an auction at which the automobile was sold to a party who had no knowledge of its history. When B's check was dishonored, the dealer brought suit against the party who purchased the automobile at the auction. Was the dealer entitled to reclaim the automobile? [*Greater Louisville Auto Auction, Inc. v Ogle Buick, Inc.*, 387 SW2d 17 (Ky)]

8. Coppola, who collected coins, joined a coin club, First Coinvestors, Inc. The club would send coins to its members, who were to pay for them or return them

within 10 days. What was the nature of the transaction? [*First Coinvestors, Inc. v Coppola*, 388 NYS2d 833 (Misc)]

9. Would buying a car from a mechanic who works at a car dealership qualify as purchasing a car in the ordinary course of business? [*Steele v Ellis*, 961 F Supp 1458 (D Kan)]

10. Does a pawnbroker who purchases property in good faith acquire good title to that property? Can the pawnbroker pass good title? [*Fly v Cannon*, 813 SW2d 458 (Tenn App)]

11. Larsen Jewelers sold a necklace to Conway on a layaway plan. Conway paid a portion of the price and made additional payments from time to time. The necklace was to remain in the possession of Larsen until payment was fully made. The Larsen jewelry store was burglarized, and Conway's necklace and other items were taken. Larsen argued that Conway must bear the risk of loss. Conway sought recovery of the full value of the necklace. Decide. [*Conway v Larsen Jewelry*, 429 NYS2d 378 (Misc)]

12. Future Tech International, Inc., is a buyer and distributor of Samsung monitors and other computer products. In 1993, Future Tech determined that brand loyalty was important to customers, and it sought to market its own brand of computer products. Future Tech, a Florida firm, developed its own brand name of MarkVision and entered into a contract in 1994 with Tae II Media, a Korean firm. The contract provided that Tae II Media would be the sole source and manufacturer for the MarkVision line of computer products.

    The course of performance on the contract did not go well. Future Tech alleged that from the time the ink was dry on the contract, Tae II Media had no intention of honoring its commitment to supply computers and computer products to Future Tech. Future Tech alleged that Tae II Media entered into the contract with the purpose of limiting Future Tech's competitive ability because Tae II Media had its own Tech Media brand of computers and computer products.

    Future Tech, through threats and demands, was able to have the first line of MarkVision products completed. Tae II Media delivered the computers to a boat but, while in transit, ordered the shipping line (Maersk Lines) to return the computers. The terms of their contract provided for delivery "FOB Pusan Korea." Future Tech filed suit, claiming that Tae II Media could not take the computer products because title had already passed to Future Tech. Is this interpretation of who has title correct? [*Future Tech Int'l, Inc. v Tae II Media, Ltd.*, 944 F Supp 1538 (SD Fla 1996)]

13. Smith operated a marina and sold and repaired boats. Gallagher rented a stall at the marina, where he kept his vessel, the *River Queen*. Without any authorization, Smith sold the vessel to Courtesy Ford. Gallagher sued Courtesy Ford for the vessel. What was the result? [*Gallagher v Unenrolled Motor Vessel River Queen*, 475 F2d 117 (5th Cir)]

14. Without permission, Grissom entered onto land owned by another and then proceeded to cut and sell the timber from the land. On learning that the timber had been sold, the owner of the land brought an action to recover the timber from the purchaser. The purchaser argued that he was a good-faith purchaser who had paid value and therefore was entitled to keep the timber. Decide. [*Baysprings Forest Products, Inc. v Wade*, 435 So 2d 690 (Miss)]

15. Brown Sales ordered goods from Eberhard Manufacturing Co. The contract contained no agreement about who would bear the risk of loss. There were no shipping terms. The seller placed the goods on board a common carrier with instructions to deliver the goods to Brown. While in transit, the goods were lost. Which party will bear the loss? Explain. [*Eberhard Manufacturing Co. v Brown*, 232 NW2d 378 (Mich App)]

CPA Questions

1. Bond purchased a painting from Wool, who is not in the business of selling art. Wool tendered delivery of the painting after receiving payment in full from Bond. Bond informed Wool that Bond would be unable to take possession of the painting until later that day. Thieves stole the painting before Bond returned. The risk of loss
    a. Passed to Bond at Wool's tender of delivery
    b. Passed to Bond at the time the contract was formed and payment was made
    c. Remained with Wool, because the parties agreed on a later time of delivery
    d. Remained with Wool, because Bond had not yet received the painting

2. Which of the following statements applies to a sale on approval under the UCC Sales Article?
    a. Both the buyer and seller must be merchants.
    b. The buyer must be purchasing the goods for resale.
    c. Risk of loss for the goods passes to the buyer when the goods are accepted after the trial period.
    d. Title to the goods passes to the buyer on delivery of the goods to the buyer.

3. If goods have been delivered to a buyer pursuant to a sale or return contract, the
   a. Buyer may use the goods but not resell them
   b. Seller is liable for the expenses incurred by the buyer in returning the goods to the seller
   c. Title to the goods remains with the seller
   d. Risk of loss for the goods passed to the buyer

4. Cey Corp. entered into a contract to sell parts to Deck, Ltd. The contract provided that the goods would be shipped "FOB Cey's warehouse." Cey shipped parts different from those specified in the contract. Deck rejected the parts. A few hours after Deck informed Cey that the parts were rejected, they were destroyed by fire in Deck's warehouse. Cey believed that the parts were conforming to the contract. Which of the following statements is correct?
   a. Regardless of whether the parts were conforming, Deck will bear the loss because the contract was a shipment contract.
   b. If the parts were nonconforming, Deck had the right to reject them, but the risk of loss remains with Deck until Cey takes possession of the parts.
   c. If the parts were conforming, risk of loss does not pass to Deck until a reasonable period of time after they are delivered to Deck.
   d. If the parts were nonconforming, Cey will bear the risk of loss, even though the contract was a shipment contract.

5. Under the Sales Articles of the UCC, when a contract for the sale of goods stipulates that the seller ship the goods by common carrier "FOB purchaser's loading dock," which of the parties bears the risk of loss during shipment?
   a. The purchaser, because risk of loss passes when the goods are delivered to the carrier
   b. The purchaser, because title to the goods passes at the time of shipment
   c. The seller, because risk of loss passes only when the goods reach the purchaser's loading dock
   d. The seller, because risk of loss remains with the seller until the goods are accepted by the purchaser

PRODUCT LIABILITY: WARRANTIES AND TORTS

CHAPTER (25)

LEARNING OBJECTIVES

After studying this chapter, you should be able to

LO.1 List the theories of product liability

LO.2 Identify who may sue and who may be sued when a defective product causes harm

LO.3 List and define the implied warranties and distinguish them from express warranties

LO.4 Explain and distinguish between full warranties and limited warranties under federal law

LO.5 State what constitutes a breach of warranty

LO.6 Describe the extent and manner in which implied warranties may be disclaimed under the UCC and the CISG

What happens when goods do not work? Who can recover for injury caused by defective goods? What can you do when the goods are not as promised or pictured?

A. General Principles

When defective goods result in damages or injury to the buyer or other parties, the UCC and tort law provide remedies.

1. Theories of Liability

Two centuries ago, a buyer was limited to recovery from a seller for breach of an express guarantee or for negligence or fraud. After the onset of mass production and distribution, however, these remedies had little value. A guarantee was good, but in the ordinary sales transaction no one stopped to get a guarantee. Few customers remembered to ask the manager of the supermarket to give a guarantee that the loaf of bread purchased was fit to eat. Further, negligence and fraud have become difficult to prove in a mass production world. How can one prove there was a problem in the production process for a can of soup prepared months earlier?

To give buyers protection from economic loss and personal injuries, the concept of warranty liability developed. **Warranties** are either express or implied and can be found in the UCC. As with other UCC areas, there have been changes in warranty liability under the Revised UCC, and those areas of change are discussed in the sections that follow. Many courts have decided that still broader protection beyond the UCC contract remedies is required and have created the additional concept of **strict tort liability** for defective goods.

There are five theories in law for what is often called *product liability*, or the protection of buyers for injury and economic loss: express warranty, implied warranty, negligence, fraud, and strict tort liability. Any statutory remedies under consumer law or employment law are additional means of recovery. The plaintiff does not have a choice of all theories in every case; the facts of the case dictate the choices the plaintiff has available for possible theories of recovery.

2. Nature of Harm

A defective product can cause harm to person, property, or economic interests. **For Example,** the buyer of a truck may be injured when, through a defect, the truck goes out of control and plunges down the side of a hill. Passengers in the truck, bystanders, or the driver of a car hit by the truck may also be injured. The defective truck may cause injury to a total stranger who seeks to rescue one of the victims. Property damage could occur if the buyer's truck careens off the road into a fence or even a house and causes damages. Another driver's car may be damaged. Commercial and economic interests of the buyer are affected by the fact that the truck is defective. Even if there is no physical harm, the defective truck is not as valuable as it would have been. The buyer who has paid for the truck on the basis of its value as it should have been has sustained an economic loss. If the buyer is required to rent a truck from someone else or loses an opportunity to haul freight for compensation, the fact that the truck was defective also causes economic or commercial loss.

CPA 3. Who Is Liable in Product Liability

Until the early part of the 20th century, only the parties to a sales contract could recover from each other on product liability issues. A seller was liable to the buyer, but the seller was not liable to others because they were not in **privity of contract** with the seller or in a direct contract relationship with the seller.

This requirement of privity of contract has now been widely rejected.[1] The law has moved toward the notion that persons harmed because of a defective product may recover from anyone who is in any way responsible.

(a) Who Can Recover Under UCC Warranties

Today, not only the buyer but also customers and employees of the buyer and even third persons or bystanders may recover because of harm caused by a defective product. Most states have abolished the requirement of **privity** when the person injured by a product is a member of the buyer's family or household or is a guest of the buyer and has sustained personal injury because of the product.[2] A few states require privity of contract, particularly when the plaintiff does not sustain personal injury or property damage and seeks to recover only economic loss.[3]

Revised section 2-318 provides alternatives for who can recover for breach of warranty (and these protections cannot be excluded or limited by the seller under Alternatives A and B and cannot be excluded or limited for personal injury under Alternative C). Revised section 2-318 now includes definitions of those covered by the warranties. Under Revised Article 2, the following alternatives are available for state adoption for determining who has rights of recovery:

- Alternative A extends warranty protection to "any natural person who is in the family or household . . . of the remote purchaser or who is a guest in the home [of the remote purchaser] . . . if it is reasonable to expect that the person may use, consume or be affected by the goods" and is "injured in person" by breach of remedial promise, warranty, or obligation.
- Alternative B extends warranty protection to "any natural person who may reasonably be expected to use, consume or be affected by the goods" and is "injured in person" by the breach of the remedial promise, warranty, or obligation.
- Alternative C extends warranty protection to "any person that may reasonably be expected to use, consume or be affected by the goods" and is injured by the breach of the remedial promise, warranty, or obligation.

(b) Who Is Liable under UCC Warranties

Someone who is injured by a defective product can recover from the seller, a remote seller, the manufacturer of the product, and generally even the manufacturer of the component part of the product that caused the harm.[4] **For Example,** when a person is struck by an automobile because the driver has lost control because of the car's defective brakes, the

[1] UCC § 2-318, Alternative A. The Code gives the states the option of adopting the provision summarized in this chapter or of making a wide abolition of the requirement of privity by adopting Alternative B or C of § 2-318. As of March 2004, these states/areas had adopted the versions of § 2-318 (not Revised Article 2) as follows: Alternative A adopted in Alaska, Arizona, Arkansas, Connecticut, District of Columbia, Florida, Georgia, Idaho, Illinois, Indiana, Kentucky, Maryland, Michigan, Mississippi, Missouri, Montana, Nebraska, Nevada (has adopted Revised Article 2), New Jersey, New Mexico, North Carolina, Ohio, Oklahoma, Oregon, Pennsylvania, Tennessee, Virgin Islands, Washington, West Virginia, and Wisconsin. Alternative B adopted in Alabama, Colorado, Delaware, Kansas (has adopted Revised Article 2), New York, South Carolina, South Dakota, Vermont, and Wyoming. Alternative C adopted in Hawaii, Iowa, Minnesota, North Dakota, and Utah.

[2] Lack of privity is not a defense in a suit for breach of warranty. *Williams v Gradall Co.*, 990 F Supp 442 (D Va 1998). Revised Article 2 extends warranty protection (§§ 2-408 and 2-409) to immediate buyers, remote buyers, or transferees who use or are affected by the product.

[3] *Barnett v Leiserv, Inc.*, 137 F3d 1356 (11th Cir 1998).

[4] However, see *Barnett v Leiserv*, 968 F Supp 690 (ND Ga 1997), where the child of the person who bought coffee for a friend could not sue to recover for burns from coffee spilled on her by the friend. The court also noted that a child who spills coffee on himself could not recover either.

person who was struck and injured may seek recovery from the seller and the manufacturer of the car. The maker of the brake assembly or system that the car manufacturer installed in the car may also be liable. The concepts of remote purchasers and immediate buyers have been defined and incorporated into Revised Article 2 and are defined in a new subsection added to section 2-313.[5]

B. Express Warranties

A warranty may be express or implied. Both express and implied warranties operate as though the defendant had made an express promise or statement of fact. Both express and implied warranties are governed primarily by the UCC.

CPA 4. Definition of Express Warranty

An **express warranty** is a statement by the defendant relating to the goods; the statement is part of the basis of the bargain.[6]

"Basis of the bargain" means that the buyer has purchased the goods because of what the seller has stated about those goods. A statement by the seller regarding the quality, capacity, or other characteristic of the goods is an express warranty. **For Example,** express warranties in sellers' statements are "This cloth is all wool," "This paint is for household woodwork," and "This engine can produce 50 horsepower." A representation that an airplane is a 2007 model is an express warranty. "This computer monitor has a glare-proof screen" is another example of an express warranty.

The changes in Revised Article 2 in the express warranty section deal with promises made by parties in direct contract and the validity of those promises to "remote buyers"—that is, those buyers who purchase farther down the chain of distribution from the manufacturer who is selling to the wholesaler under a direct contract. The revisions to section 2-313 change the language to "the immediate buyer" when an express warranty is defined. Section 2-313 applies only in situations in which there is privity of contract between the parties. Section 2-313(1)(a) and (b) outlines the responsibilities of sellers to "remote purchasers"—that is, those who buy from the immediate buyer or others in the chain of distribution.[7] **For Example,** WorldWide Wholesalers could purchase Pop-Tarts from Kellogg's. Kellogg's makes warranties to WorldWide Wholesalers directly through their contract relationship, one of privity. WorldWide Wholesalers then sells those Pop-Tarts to grocery stores, convenience stores, and perhaps even to commercial food distributors who then sell them to cafeterias in schools and nursing homes. WorldWide's buyers are remote purchasers. Only WorldWide (and any other companies who buy from Kellogg's directly) is an immediate buyer.

Under Revised UCC, the seller's obligations and promises to remote buyers are the same as the seller's obligations and promises to immediate buyers if the seller "makes an affirmation of fact or promise that relates to the goods, provides a description that relates to the goods, or makes a remedial promise"; and that affirmation, promise, description, or remedial promise is "in a record packaged with or accompanying the goods"; and the seller "reasonably expects the record to be, and the record is, furnished to the remote purchaser."[8]

5. Form of Express Warranty

No particular group of words is necessary to constitute an express warranty. A seller need not state that a warranty is being made or that one is intended. It is sufficient that the seller asserts a fact that becomes a basis of the bargain or transaction between the parties. UCC § 2-313(2) provides, "It is not necessary to the creation of an express warranty that the seller use formal words such as 'warrant' or 'guarantee' or that the seller have a specific intention to make a warranty."[9]

An express warranty can be written or printed as well as oral. The words on the label of a can and in a newspaper ad for "boned chicken" constitute an express warranty that the can contains chicken that is free of bones.

[5] Revised UCC § 2-313(1)(a) and (b).

[6] UCC § 2-313; *Valleyside Dairy Farms, Inc. v A. O. Smith Corp.*, 944 F Supp 612 (WD Mich 1995); *Smith v Bearfield*, 950 SW2d 39 (Tenn App 1997). In the UCC Revised Article 2, the "basis of the bargain" requirement is changed to "become part of the agreement." UCC § 2-313(1)(a). Also, § 2-404 is the new express warranty section.

[7] Revised UCC § 2-313(1)(a) and (b).

[8] Revised UCC § 2-313(2)(a).

[9] UCC § 2-313(2).

Descriptions of goods, such as the illustrations in a seller's catalog, are express warranties. The express warranty given is that the goods will conform to the catalog illustrations.

6. Time of Making Express Warranty

It is immaterial whether the express warranty is made at the time of or after the sale. No separate consideration is required for the warranty when it is part of a sale. If a warranty is made after the sale, no consideration is required because it is regarded as a modification of the sales contract.

7. Seller's Opinion or Statement of Value

A statement about the value of goods or the seller's opinion or commendation of the goods does not create a warranty.[10] Section 2-313(1)(b) provides, "an affirmation merely of the value of the goods or a statement purporting to be merely the seller's opinion or commendation of goods does not create a warranty."[11] A buyer cannot hold a seller liable for sales talk. **For Example,** sales talk or puffery by a seller that his cloth is "the best piece of cloth on the market" or that her glassware is "as good as anyone else's" is merely an opinion that the buyer cannot ordinarily treat as a warranty. Statements made by a cosmetics seller that its products are "the future of beauty" and are "just the product for [the plaintiff]" are sales talk arising in the ordinary course of merchandising. They do not constitute warranties.

The UCC does permit an exception to the sales talk liability exemption when the circumstances are such that a reasonable person would rely on such a statement. If the buyer has reason to believe that the seller has expert knowledge of the conditions of the market, and the buyer requests the seller's opinion as an expert, the buyer is entitled to accept as a fact the seller's statement of whether a particular good is the best obtainable. The opinion statement could be reasonably regarded as forming part of the basis of the bargain. A statement by a florist that bulbs are of first-grade quality may be a warranty.[12]

8. Warranty of Conformity to Description, Sample, or Model

When the contract is based in part on the understanding that the seller will supply goods according to a particular description or that the goods will be the same as the sample or a model, the seller is bound by an express warranty that the goods conform to the description, sample, or model.[13] Section 2-313 of the UCC provides, "Any sample or model which is made part of the basis of the bargain creates an express warranty that the whole of the goods shall conform to the sample or model."[14] **For Example,** a blender sitting out in a store is a warranty that the blenders in the boxes below are the same. A model of a mobile home is an express warranty that the mobile home being sold contains the same features.

9. Federal Regulation of Express Warranties

A seller who makes a written express warranty for a consumer product costing more than $10 must conform to certain standards imposed by federal statute[15] and by regulations of the Federal Trade Commission (FTC).[16] The seller is not required to make any express warranty. However, if the seller does make an express warranty in a consumer sale, it must be stated in ordinary, understandable language and must be made available for inspection before purchasing so that the consumer may comparison shop.[17]

(a) Full Warranties

If the seller or the label states that a full warranty is made, the seller is obligated to fix or replace a defective product within a reasonable time without

[10] Id.; *Jordan v Paccar, Inc.*, 37 F3d 1181 (6th Cir 1994).

[11] UCC § 2-313(1)(b).

[12] Likewise, a statement by an art gallery owner that a "painting is by Francis Bacon" is an express warranty. *Rogath v Siebenmann*, 129 F3d 902 (7th Cir 1997).

[13] *Poly Products Corp. v AT&T Nassau Metals, Inc.*, 839 F Supp 1238 (ED Tex 1993).

[14] UCC § 2-313(1)(c).

[15] The Magnuson-Moss Act, or Federal Consumer Product Warranty Law, can be found at 15 USC § 2301 *et seq.*

[16] 16 CFR § 700.1 *et seq.*

[17] Federal warranty language rules apply only in consumer sales, or sales for personal or home use, not in business purchases. *Weaver v Dan Jones Ford, Inc.*, 679 So 2d 1105 (Ala 1996).

cost to the buyer. If the product cannot be fixed or if a reasonable number of repair attempts are unsuccessful, the buyer has the choice of a cash refund or a free replacement. No unreasonable burden may be placed on a buyer seeking to obtain warranty service. **For Example,** a manufacturer offering a full warranty cannot require that the buyer pay the cost of sending the product to or from a warranty service point. A warrantor making a full warranty cannot require the buyer to return the product to a warranty service point if the product weighs over 35 pounds, to return a part for service unless it can be easily removed, or to fill out and return a warranty registration card shortly after purchase to make the warranty effective. If the manufacturer imposes any of these requirements, the warranty is not a "full warranty" under federal law and must be labeled a *limited warranty*. A **full warranty** runs with the product and lasts for its full term regardless of who owns the product.

(b) Limited Warranties

A **limited warranty** is any warranty that does not meet the requirements for a full warranty. **For Example,** a warranty is limited if the buyer must pay any cost for repair or replacement of a defective product, if only the first buyer is covered by the warranty, or if the warranty covers only part of the product. A limited warranty must be conspicuously described as such by the seller.[18]

10. Effect of Breach of Express Warranty

If an express warranty is false, there is a breach of warranty. The warrantor is then liable. It is no defense that the seller or manufacturer who made the express warranty honestly believed that the warranty was true, had exercised due care in manufacturing or handling the product, or had no reason to believe that the warranty was false.[19]

FORBES V GENERAL MOTORS CORP., 2006 WL 1431228 (MISS)

AN INFLATED AIR BAG WARRANTY?

FACTS: On December 15, 1997, Hilda Forbes and her three grandchildren were traveling to Columbia, Mississippi, in her 1992 Oldsmobile Delta 88. Mrs. Forbes was driving behind a 1981 Chevrolet Chevette, which suddenly stopped and attempted to turn into a private driveway. Mrs. Forbes struck the Chevette from the rear. Both automobiles were damaged. The air bag in Mrs. Forbes' automobile did not inflate.

As a result of the impact, Mrs. Forbes was propelled forward into the windshield. She suffered a subdural hematoma. Dr. Howard Katz, a specialist in physical medicine, rehabilitation, and spinal cord injuries, testified by deposition that Mrs. Forbes suffered significant cognitive dysfunction and never completely recovered from the injury to her brain.

The air bag system and Mrs. Forbes' automobile were manufactured by GM. The owner's manual contains the following statement, "The 'air bag' part of the SIR [Supplemental Inflatable Restraint] system is in the middle of the steering wheel. The SIR system is only for crashes where the front area of your vehicle hits something. If the collision is hard enough, the 'air bag' inflates in a fraction of a second." Mr. Forbes asked the salesman about the air bag and was assured that the car had an effective one.

The Forbeses purchased their car from Mike Smith Motors, which subsequently was purchased by Mack Grubbs Motors, Inc. Angela Coleman was the driver of the 1981 Chevrolet Chevette.

18 The federal regulations here do not preempt Article 2 warranty coverage. *Mitchell v Collagen Corp.*, 126 F3d 902 (7th Cir 1997).

19 The failure to disclose, however, is not covered—that is, there is no warranty of omission. *Witherspoon v Philip Morris, Inc.*, 964 F Supp 455 (DDC 1997).

On December 7, 2000, Hilda and Hoyt Forbes filed suit against Coleman and later added GM as a defendant. Following their case, the Forbeses voluntarily dismissed Angela Coleman from the suit. Mack Grubbs Motors, Inc. moved for a directed verdict, which was granted. GM moved for a directed verdict, which the judge also granted. The Forbeses appealed on the grounds that GM had breached an express warranty.

Judicial Opinion

CARLSON, Justice. . . . The essence of the Forbeses' argument is that GM sold its product with the express warranty that the air bag would deploy in the event of a front-end collision when the impact was "hard enough." The Forbeses claim that the amount of force sustained by their car in this accident was certainly hard enough according to their experts' testimony, and that therefore the express warranty was breached. The express warranty referred to is a portion of the owner's manual for their automobile which states that if a front-end collision "is hard enough, the 'air bag' inflates in a fraction of a second."

As the Court of Appeals stated, because the salesman who sold Mr. Forbes the Delta 88 stressed the importance of an air bag and explained that the car was equipped with one, the Forbeses claim to have been given a factual representation on which they relied. As both the trial court and the Court of Appeals correctly pointed out, the salesman was a representative of Mike Smith Motors or Mack Grubbs Motors, not GM. However, GM is the only remaining party to this case, and no representative from GM actually made any statement to the Forbeses regarding the air bag in their car, outside of the owner's manual. In any case, the Forbeses never once claimed in their brief or in their petition that the oral statement made by the salesman was the express warranty upon which they relied.

They instead focus wholly on the owner's manual, as we will as well.

The Court of Appeals also pointed out that the Forbeses do not deny that they never read the alleged warranty in the owner's manual and that they thus fail to show sufficient reliance on the owner's manual. The Court of Appeals relied on *Palmer v Volkswagen of America, Inc.*, 904 So.2d 1077, 1084 (Miss.2005), where we stated, "[t]he presence or absence of anything in an unread owner's manual simply cannot proximately cause a plaintiff's damages." In *Palmer* we noted that, with regard to proximate cause, a plaintiff who has not read an owner's manual at all cannot claim to have been misled by it. However, Palmer is not applicable to the issue before us. In *Palmer*, we were confronted with the issue of a failure to warn being the proximate cause; however, the issue today is a "failure to perform in accordance with a factual representation," in the words of the Court of Appeals, or rather a failure to conform to a factual representation upon which the claimant justifiably relied. In any case, that the Forbeses never read their owner's manual is not fatal to their case. It is still possible to rely on assertions therein without having actually read them. It would be quite unusual for a consumer to read an owner's manual before buying a car. Even more unusual would be for a consumer to insist upon reading the manual before buying the automobile and requiring that an understanding of the manual be a condition precedent to purchasing the car. The fact remains that Mr. Forbes did make his purchase conditional on one factor, the presence of a functional driver's side air bag. Forbes inquired about the presence of an air bag from the salesman and ensured that the vehicle he was purchasing was equipped with one as a specific feature. More importantly, he paid a higher price to have an air bag included. While the salesman himself may not substantively assert facts making GM liable, here he was doing nothing more that conveying the express warranty to Forbes. The salesman was merely relaying a fact GM represented in their owner's manual, that the car he was buying had a working air bag. Relying on that fact, Mr. Forbes decided to purchase this particular car. To meet the first part of the statutory claim, the Forbeses must show that the product either "breached an express warranty or failed to conform to other express factual representations" upon which he justifiably relied in electing to use the product. In this case, there is both an express warranty, the promise of a functional driver's side air bag, and justifiable reliance, the fact that, but for the promise of the air bag, Forbes would not have purchased the vehicle. The statutory requirements are thus met.

Remanded for trial on the issue of the breach of an express warranty.

Questions

1. Where and when was the express warranty made?
2. Does it make any differences that the Forbeses had not read the owner's manual prior to their purchase?
3. Did the car fail to conform to an express factual representation?

C. Implied Warranties

Whenever a sale of goods is made, certain warranties are implied unless they are expressly excluded. Implied warranties differ depending on whether the seller is a merchant.

11. Definition of Implied Warranty

An **implied warranty** is one that was not expressly made by the seller but that is implied in certain circumstances by law. An implied warranty arises automatically from the fact that a sale has been made regardless of the seller's conduct.

Express warranties arise because they form part of the basis on which the sale has been made. Implied warranties can exist independent of express warranties. When both express and implied warranties exist, they are interpreted as consistent, if possible. If the warranties cannot be applied together, then the express warranty prevails over any implied warranty except that an implied warranty of fitness for a particular purpose prevails over an express warranty.

12. Implied Warranties of Sellers

Sellers give different types of implied warranties.

CPA (a) Warranty of Title

Every seller, by the mere act of selling, makes an implied warranty that the seller's title to the goods is good and that the seller has the right to transfer title to the goods.[20]

The **warranty of title** may be disclaimed either by using the words, "There is no warranty of title," or by certain circumstances.[21] If a buyer has reason to know that the seller does not claim to hold the title or that the seller is limited in what can be promised, the warranty of title is disclaimed. **For Example,** no warranty of title arises when the seller makes the sale in a representative capacity, such as a sheriff, an auctioneer, or an administrator of a decedent's estate. Similarly, no warranty arises when the seller makes the sale as a creditor disposing of a debtor's collateral (security). The damages for warranty of title are often the purchase price because the buyer may have to surrender the goods to their rightful owner.[22]

(b) Warranty against Encumbrances

Every seller makes an implied **warranty against encumbrances**, that is, that the goods will be delivered free from any security interest or any other lien or encumbrance of which the buyer at the time of the sales transaction had no knowledge. If the seller sells an automobile to the buyer and then delivers a car with an outstanding lien on it that was unknown to the buyer at the time of the sale, there is a breach of the warranty against encumbrances.

CPA (c) Warranty of Fitness for a Particular Purpose[23]

A buyer may intend to use the goods for a particular or unusual purpose, as contrasted with the ordinary use for which they are customarily sold. If the seller states that the goods will be fit for the buyer's purpose with the buyer relying on the seller's skill or judgment to select or furnish suitable goods, and the seller, at the time of contracting, knows or has reason to know of both the buyer's particular purpose and the buyer's reliance on the seller's judgment, then the seller has created an implied warranty of fitness for a particular purpose.[24] **For Example,** when the seller represents to a buyer that the two hamsters being sold are of the same gender and can safely occupy the same cage with no offspring, an implied warranty of fitness has been given. When the buyer makes the purchase without relying on the seller's skill and judgment, no warranty of fitness for a particular purpose arises.[25]

13. Additional Implied Warranties of Merchant Sellers

A seller who deals in goods of the kind in question is classified as a merchant by the UCC and is held to a higher degree of responsibility for the product than one who is merely making a casual sale.

[20] UCC § 2-312. The key change in the language in Revised Article 2 is that the seller warrants that the buyer will not be subjected to unreasonable litigation.

[21] *Quality Components Corp. v Kel-Keef Enterprises, Inc.*, 738 NE2d 524 (Ill App 2000).

[22] *Curran v Ciaramelli*, 37 UCC Rep Serv 2d 94 (NY 1998).

[23] UCC § 2-315. The warranty does not apply when the injury is not caused by any function represented for the product. For example, a buyer could not recover when she hit her head on a wall-mounted fire extinguisher, for the representations were that it would work for home fires, not about mounting it in the home. *Hayes v Larsen Mfg. Co., Inc.*, 871 F Supp 56 (D Me 1996).

[24] UCC § 2-315. This warranty applies to every seller, but ordinarily it is merchant sellers who have such skill and judgment that the UCC provision will apply.

[25] *Potomac Plaza Terraces, Inc. v QSC Products, Inc.*, 868 F Supp 346 (DDC 1994). Manufacturing to buyer's specifications precludes recovery for breach of the warranty of fitness for a particular purpose. *Saratoga Spa & Bath, Inc. v Beeche Systems Corp.*, 656 NYS2d 787 (1997).

E-COMMERCE AND CYBERLAW

The warranty against infringement has become a critical one because of issues relating to software as well as the downloading of copyrighted music from the Internet. Those who are selling software warrant that they have the rights to do so and would be liable for infringement themselves, as well as the costs their buyers incur in defending themselves against charges of infringement.

Even those who provide the servers for the downloading of music or films can be held liable for infringement if they are aware of the downloading of copyrighted music or copyrighted films and take no steps to stop or prevent it. In fact, those who operate servers must be able to show that they took appropriate precautions to prevent such downloading and warn users against doing it.

(a) Warranty against Infringement

Unless otherwise agreed, every merchant seller warrants that the goods will be delivered free of the rightful claim of any third person by way of patent, copyright, or trademark infringement.

For Example, if a buyer purchases videos from a seller who is later discovered to be a bootlegger of the films on the videos, the buyer has a cause of action against the seller for any damages he experiences for perhaps renting out the bootlegged videos. Under Revised Article 2, the seller can disclaim the warranty against infringement.

(b) Warranty of Merchantability or Fitness for Normal Use

A merchant seller makes an **implied warranty of the merchantability** of the goods sold.[26] This warranty is a group of promises, the most important of which is that the goods are fit for the ordinary purposes for which they are sold. This warranty, unless disclaimed, is given in every sale of goods by a merchant. Section 2-314 provides, "Unless excluded or modified, a warranty that the goods shall be merchantable is implied in a contract for their sale if the seller is a merchant with respect to goods of that kind."[27]

VILLETTE V SHELDORADO ALUMINUM PRODUCTS, INC., 2001 WL 881055 (NY SUP) 45 UCC REP SERV 2D 470 (NY CIV CT 2001)

THE SNOW JOB ON THE AWNINGS

On July 27, 2000, Sheldorado Aluminum Products, Inc. (defendant), installed an aluminum awning on the back of Marie Villette's (claimant's) home for use as a carport. On January 11, 2001, the awning collapsed on top of Ms. Villette's new Mercedes automobile. Ms. Villette brought suit against Sheldorado seeking recovery of the $3,000 she had paid to them for the awning.

A trial was held on April 23, 2001. Ms. Villette appeared without counsel and testified, as did her husband, Dr. Max Samuel. Sheldorado appeared without counsel by its manager, Daniel Rabinowitz, who testified, as did its salesman Jack Finklestein.

There was no formal written contract between the parties; the only writing is a one-page order/bill designated a "contract," dated July 11, 2000, and signed by Ms. Villette and apparently by Mr. Finklestein. No advertising or promotional material was presented by either party. Ms. Villette testified to no express warranty or representation on

[26] UCC § 2-314; *Ford v Starr Fireworks, Inc.*, 874 P2d 230 (Wyo 1994); *Williams v Gradall Co.*, 990 F Supp 442 (ED Va 1998).

[27] UCC § 2-314. Revised Article 2 makes only one change as follows: "(c) are fit for the ordinary purposes for which [deleted word *such* here] goods [added following phrase] *of that description* are used. . . ." The comment explains the change: "The phrase 'goods of that description' rather than 'for which such goods are used' is used in subsection (2)(c). This emphasizes the importance of the agreed description in determining fitness for ordinary purposes."

the transaction, and none appears in the writing. Sheldorado acknowledges that no instructions or warnings were given to Ms. Villette as to care, maintenance or use of the awning.

Ms. Villette and Dr. Samuel testified to a leak from the awning the day after it was installed. Sheldorado attempted to repair the leak without success three weeks later.

When the awning collapsed, Sheldorado took the position that the cause was an accumulation of snow and high winds and that it bore no responsibility for the loss. It did not inspect the collapsed awning, contending at trial it was intimidated by Dr. Samuel. Its only response to the incident was to refer Ms. Villette and Dr. Samuel to the insurer on their homeowner's policy.

Judicial Opinion

BATTAGLIA, J.... The Code implies a warranty of "merchantability" in sales of goods by a merchant, and that includes a warranty that the goods are "fit for the ordinary purposes for which such goods are used." U.C.C. § 2-314(2)(c). This warranty applies as well to "specifically manufactured goods." U.C.C. § 2-105(1). A "hybrid service-sale transaction," like our case, "can give rise to a cause of action for breach of warranty... if the sales aspect of the transaction predominates and the service aspect is merely incidental." Services have been found to predominate in a contract for a sprinkler system, for a swimming pool, and "to furnish and erect the structural steel" for a bridge. *Schenectady Steel Co., Inc. v Bruno Trimpoli Const. Co., Inc.*, 43 AD2d 234, 237 [3d Dept 1974]. There are similarities between those types of transactions and the one involved here.

On the other hand, where the services are comprised of merely installing the goods, and making them operational, the contract has been considered a sale of goods. (voice and data communications equipment); *Back O'Beyond, Inc. v Telephonic Enterprises, Inc.*, 76 *AD2d 897* [2d Dept 1980] (security fire alarm system). And there are similarities between those types of transactions and that involved here.

Since there was no formal written contract between the parties, only the order/bill is available to indicate how the parties saw their transaction. First, the full name of the defendant on the writing is Sheldorado Aluminum Products, Inc. The top of the writing lists the following products: awnings (circled on this one), windows, doors, mirrors, window treatments, storefronts and siding. The body contains the handwritten description, "Supply and install one alum roof," and adds dimensions, materials ("white posts steel"), design characteristics ("Flat roof with pitch"), and colors for the roof, stripes and fringe.

As noted, the total price was $3,000.00. A line for sales tax shows a handwritten line above it, and a line for installation says "included." It is not clear whether both the sales tax and installation were included in the price, or whether no sales tax was considered due on the transaction....

Finally, there are several sentences printed above the signatures of the parties. The one relevant here reads: "The legal title of the above [language] installed properties remains vested in Sheldorado Aluminum Products, Inc. with the right of removal, unless full payment as per this agreement has been made in legal tender."

In short, there is nothing in this writing that suggests that the parties understood their transaction to be predominantly for services. Rather, everything suggests a sale of goods, with the incidental service of installation. Since the predominant purpose of the transaction is a sale of goods, Article 2 of the Code, including the implied warranty of merchantability of §2-314, applies to claimant's benefit.

As noted, the implied warranty of merchantability assures the buyer that the goods "are fit for the ordinary purposes for which such goods are used." U.C.C. §2-314(2)(c).

The claimant's case is quite simple: the ordinary purposes of an awning are to provide shade and other protection from the elements; an awning that leaks and then collapses is clearly not fit for those purposes. Sheldorado's defense is likewise simple: the claimant was putting the awning to an extraordinary purpose and misusing the product, because weather conditions were not ordinary and claimant failed to keep the awning from an accumulation of snow that it could not hold.

Looking first at claimant's case, the Court of Appeals of Maryland addressed very similar facts in *Little v Woodall*, 224 A2d 852 [1966]. The plaintiffs sued for "breach of warranty in a contract for the sale and installation of an aluminum awning carport for the [plaintiffs'] home." There was testimony that, "It always leaked between the house and the carport." During a snow storm, the awning collapsed onto the plaintiffs' car. Unlike this case, however, the defendant "did not know why the awning fell. In his opinion, the snow was not heavy enough to collapse the carport, and he did not contend it came down because of a gust of wind."

Also unlike our case, there was an express warranty that the court found to mean "that the carport will stay up, as far as the materials and workmanship are concerned.... [T]he guarantee was not intended to be unconditional, but was limited to the durability of the material and the quality of the workmanship." Although the case was ultimately decided on the quality of the workmanship, i.e. a tort-like ground that is not the basis of this claim, the court's opinion is helpful in resolving this claim.

The court found, based on the testimony about constant leakage that "[i]t was a permissible inference...that this flow of water during any kind of precipitation would weaken the supports by which the aluminum carport was attached, thereby increasing the risk that the carport would collapse under the weight of snow." Although the doctrine of ***res ipsa loquitor*** was not strictly applicable, it was applied by analogy.

While the carport passed from the [defendant's] control, it was he who had the peculiar knowledge of how it had been installed, and what precautions should have been taken to prevent the defect which resulted. The foreseeability of the risk of the weight of snow operating upon a defective installation may reasonably be charged to the seller. Under the circumstances, the purchaser does not have the burden of establishing that the defective installation was the sole probable cause of the collapse.

That "defense" is that claimant put the awning to an extraordinary purpose and misused it. There was no evidence introduced as to the exact weather conditions before the collapse of the awning, or as to how those weather conditions compared to those that might have been expected. In other words, except for Sheldorado's vague and indefinite importuning about the bad weather, there was no evidence of an "extraordinary" purpose. Moreover, there was no evidence that it was the "extraordinary" purpose, rather than some defect in the awning, that caused it to fall. Sheldorado refused to investigate, and simply referred claimant and her husband to their insurer. As for the claim of intimidation by Dr. Samuels, the Court agrees that he is someone who is likely to get attention when he is angry; but will not accept that arrangements could not have been made to inspect the damage, particularly since Dr. Samuel's anger was the result of defendant's refusal to even consider that it might be responsible.

As to the alleged misuse in that claimant failed to keep the awning free from an accumulation of snow, the short answer is that there is no evidence that it was so. Since the defendant failed to investigate, it cannot say what accumulation there might have been. In any event, "[a]ny issue concerning the [claimant's] alleged misuse...was relevant only to the issue of intervening or superseding cause and the apportionment of fault.... [C]ulpability on the part of a [claimant] in mishandling the product...will not bar recovery unless that conduct is found to be the sole cause of the [claimant's] injury."

Sheldorado does, indeed, claim that, "as a matter of common sense," the claimant should have kept the awning free from accumulation of snow; and there was no evidence that any failure to do so was "reasonably foreseeable." However, since it was clearly Sheldorado's burden to prove its defense, and since it acknowledged having given the claimant no warnings or instructions whatsoever as to the use of the awning, the Court finds that it cannot shift any of the responsibility of the loss onto the claimant.

Judgment is awarded to the claimant for $3,000.00, with interest.

Questions

1. What happened to the awning and why?
2. How does the court determine that the transaction is governed by the UCC?
3. What damages are awarded and why?

14. Implied Warranties in Particular Sales

Particular types of sales may involve special considerations in terms of the seller's liability and the buyer's rights.

(a) Sale on Buyer's Specifications

When the buyer furnishes the seller with exact specifications for the preparation or manufacture of goods, the same warranties arise as in the case of any other sale of such goods by the particular seller. No warranty of fitness for a particular purpose can arise, however. It is clear that the buyer is purchasing on the basis of the buyer's own decision and is not relying on the seller's skill and judgment. Similarly, the manufacturer is not liable for loss caused by a design defect.[28]

[28] *Hallday v Sturm, Ruger, & Co., Inc.*, 792 A2d 1145 (CA MD 2002).

(b) Sale of Secondhand or Used Goods

Under the UCC, there is a warranty of merchantability in the sale of both new and used goods unless it is specifically disclaimed. However, with respect to used goods, what is considered "fit for normal use" under the warranty of merchantability will be a lower standard. Some courts still follow their pre-Code law under which no warranties of fitness arise in the sale of used goods.

CPA (c) Sale of Food or Drink

The implied warranty of merchantability also applies to the purchase of food in grocery stores and restaurants. The food sold must be of average quality and fit for its ordinary purpose, which is consumption by humans.[29] The types of restaurant and grocery store cases brought under the warranty of merchantability include those in which the buyer or customer finds foreign substances such as grasshoppers in a can of baked beans.[30]

The application of this warranty to food cases becomes more complex when it is not a nail in a can of crabmeat, but crab shell in a can of crabmeat, or a cherry pit in the cherries of a McDonald's cherry pie. Some courts refuse to impose warranty liability if the thing in the food that caused the harm was naturally present, such as crab shell in crabmeat, prune stones in stewed prunes, or bones in canned fish. Other courts reject this foreign substance/natural substance liability test. They hold that there is liability if the seller does not deliver to the buyer goods of the character that the buyer reasonably expected. Under this view, there is a breach of the implied warranty of fitness for normal use if the buyer reasonably expected the food to be free of harm-causing natural things, such as shells and bones that could cause harm.[31]

MITCHELL V T.G.I. FRIDAY'S, 748 NE2D 89 (OHIO APP 2000)

DIGGING FOR TEETH AMONG THE CLAMS

On April 11, 1996, Sandra Mitchell (appellant) was having dinner at T.G.I. Friday's restaurant (hereinafter "Friday's" or appellee). Ms. Mitchell was eating a fried clam strip when she bit into a hard substance that she believed to be a piece of a clam shell. She experienced immediate pain and later sought dental treatment. Some time later, the crown of a tooth came loose. It was determined that the crown could not be reattached and the remaining root of the tooth was extracted.

Ms. Mitchell filed a product liability action against Friday's, which served the meal, and Pro Source Distributing (hereinafter "Pro Source" or appellee), the supplier of the fried clams. Both Friday's and Pro Source filed motions for summary judgment, which the trial court granted without explanation.

Ms. Mitchell appealed.

Judicial Opinion

WAITE, Judge. . . . Appellant argues that in light of Ohio's product liability legislation, the trial court should have applied the "reasonable-expectation test" to her claim and in doing so the court should not have granted appellees' motions for summary judgment. R. C. 2307.74 provides that "[a] product is defective [if] . . . [i]t deviated in a material way from the design specifications, formula, or performance standards of the manufacturer . . . ." R.C. 2307.75(A)(2) provides that a product is defective in design or formulation if "[i]t is more dangerous than an ordinary consumer would expect when used in an intended or reasonably foreseeable manner." According to appellant, by the enactment of

29 *Goldman v Food Lion, Inc.*, 879 F Supp 33 (ED Va 1995).

30 *Metty v Shurfine Central Corporation*, 736 SW2d 527 (Mo 1987).

31 A new type of test for the food cases is called the "duty risk analysis" rule, in which the court examines the injury in light of the risk that comes from the failure to process the items out of the food and weighs that risk with the cost of the processing. *Porteous v St. Ann's Café & Deli*, 713 So 2d 454 (La 1998). Note that the case is from Louisiana, the nation's non-UCC state.

these statutes the "reasonable-expectation" test supersedes the traditional "foreign-natural test" applied in cases where injury is caused by substances in food. Appellant asserts that there is a reasonable expectation that clams are completely cleaned of their shells and free of foreign materials.

In the present case, Friday's set forth in its motion for summary judgment appellant's deposition testimony to the effect that while eating a clam strip, she bit down on "a hard, foreign substance." Appellant stated that she assumed it was a piece of a clam shell. Appellant described the size of the object as about a quarter of the size of a small fingernail or about a quarter of an inch or smaller and irregular in shape. Moreover, Friday's attached an affidavit from its manager, Eric Hicks, who immediately responded to appellant's report of the incident. In that affidavit, Hicks confirmed that the object appellant presented to him was indeed a piece of clam shell and that it was approximately one-quarter inch in length and irregularly shaped. In its motion for summary judgment, Pro Source adopted and incorporated the statement of Friday's, appellant's deposition testimony, and the affidavit of Eric Hicks. In her response, appellant set forth no facts to dispute that the object in the clam strip was in fact a piece of clam shell.

There being no factual dispute here, we must decide whether appellees are entitled to judgment as a matter of law. Both Friday's and Pro Source presented essentially the same argument, that regardless of whether the foreign-natural test or reasonable expectation test was applied, appellant has no claim against appellees. Appellant, however, has argued for the application only of the reasonable-expectation test. She argues that Ohio's product liability statute supersedes cases employing the foreign-natural test where deleterious substances are found in food. Appellant contends that what a consumer should reasonably expect to be present in food is a question for the jury to decide.

The basis of appellant's argument for application of the reasonable-expectation test is found in R.C. 2307.75, which provides that a product is defective if it is more dangerous than an ordinary consumer would reasonably suspect. However, appellant has not set forth any case law or analysis that would suggest that food products fall under the purview of the statute. We can find no case that has analyzed a food item in that context. Indeed, the weight of product liability cases deal with synthetic products, for example, a cargo door hinge, a glass bottle, or a prosthetic hip joint. Thus, we see no compelling reason to abandon any established test due to the enactment of Ohio's product liability legislation.

Under the foreign-natural test:

"'Bones which are natural to the type of meat served cannot legitimately be called a foreign substance, and a consumer who eats meat dishes ought to anticipate and be on his guard against the presence of such bones.'"

The reasonable-expectation test states:

"'The test should be what is "reasonably expected" by the consumer in the food as served, not what might be natural to the ingredients of that food prior to preparation.... As applied to the action for common-law negligence, the test is related to the foreseeability of harm on the part of the defendant. The defendant is not an insurer but has the duty of ordinary care to eliminate or remove in the preparation of the food he serves such harmful substances as the consumer of the food, as served, would not ordinarily anticipate and guard against.'"

Most courts have adopted the foreign-natural test. However, other courts endorse the reasonable-expectation test. One such case is *Thompson v Lawson Milk Co.*, on which appellant relies for her proposition that what should be reasonably expected is a question for the jury to decide.

"Courts cannot and must not ignore the common experience of life and allow rules to develop that would make sellers of food or other consumer goods insurers of the products they sell."

In the present case, it cannot be disputed that the piece of clam shell that caused appellant's injury was natural to the clam strip she consumed. Turning to the question of whether appellant should have reasonably anticipated the presence of the clam shell, we are reminded that "the possible presence of a piece of oyster shell in or attached to an oyster is so well known to anyone who eats oysters that we can say as a matter of law that one who eats oysters can reasonably anticipate and guard against eating such a piece of shell...." We therefore hold that, as a matter of law, one who eats clams can reasonably anticipate and guard against eating a piece of shell.

As appellant's claim fails under both tests, we overrule her assignment of error and affirm the judgment of the trial court.

[Judgment affirmed]

Questions

1. What did Ms. Mitchell eat and what were her resulting injuries?
2. What did the lower court do in the case that caused an admonition from the appellate court?
3. What test does Ohio follow—the foreign-natural or the reasonable expectation test?

THINKING THINGS THROUGH

WHAT'S FOREIGN TO YOU . . .

Based on the discussion and the *T. G. I. Friday's* case, decide which of the following would be considered a breach of the implied warranty of merchantability:

Customer suffered an injury to the throat as a result of a bone in a chicken sandwich getting stuck in his throat. RUVOLO V HOMOVICH 778 NE2d 661 (Ohio App 2002).

Customer bit into a Baby Ruth candy bar, manufactured by Standard Brands, that contained a "snake bone (vertebrae)" and the customer experienced severe psychological difficulty. GATES V STANDARD BRANDS INC., 719 P2d 130 (Wash App 1986).

Customer experienced tooth and jaw damage after she bit into a pistachio nut while eating an ice cream cone with pistachio nut ice cream. LEWIS V HANDEL'S HOMEMADE ICE CREAM AND YOGURT 2003 WL 21509258 (Ohio App).

15. Necessity of Defect

To impose liability for breach of the implied warranty of merchantability, it is ordinarily necessary to show that there was a defect in the product, that this defect made the product unfit for its normal use, and that this caused the buyer's harm. A product may be defective because there is (1) a manufacturing defect, (2) a design defect, (3) inadequate instruction on how to use the product, or (4) inadequate warning against dangers involved in using the product.

For Example, if the manufacturer's blueprint shows that there should be two bolts at a particular place and the factory puts in only one bolt, there is a manufacturing defect. If the two bolts are put in but the product breaks because four bolts are required to provide sufficient strength, there is no manufacturing defect, but there is a design defect. A product that is properly designed and properly manufactured may be dangerous because the user is not given sufficient instructions on how to use the product. Also, a product is defective if there is a danger that is not obvious and there is no warning at all or a warning that does not describe the full danger.[32]

Many courts impose liability when the goods are in fact not fit for their normal purpose. These courts allow the buyer to prove that the goods are not fit for their normal purpose with evidence that the goods do not function properly even though the buyer does not establish the specific defect.

In contrast with a breach of the implied warranty of merchantability, it is not necessary under the breach of the implied warranty of fitness for a particular purpose or of an express warranty or a guarantee to show that there was a defect that caused the breach. It is sufficient to show that the goods did not perform to meet the particular purpose or did not conform to the express warranty or to the guarantee. Why they did or did not so conform is immaterial.

16. Warranties in the International Sale of Goods

The warranties of both merchantability and fitness for a particular purpose exist under the Convention on Contracts for the International Sale of Goods (CISG). In most cases, the provisions are identical to those of the UCC. Sellers, however, can expressly disclaim the convention's warranties without mentioning merchantability or making the disclaimer conspicuous.

D. Disclaimer of Warranties

The seller and the buyer may ordinarily agree that there will be no warranties. In some states, disclaimers of warranties are prohibited for reasons of public policy or consumer protection.

17. Validity of Disclaimer

Warranties may be disclaimed by agreement of the parties, subject to the limitation that such a provision must not be unconscionable, must be conspicuous, and in certain cases must use certain language.[33]

[32] *Red Hill Hosiery Mill, Inc. v Magnetek, Inc.* 582 SE2d 632 (NC Ct App 2003). Following government standards does not mean a product is without defect.

[33] UCC § 2-316; *Safadi v Thompson*, 487 SE2d 457 (Ga App 1997). The revised UCC section is now § 2-406.

(a) Conspicuousness

A disclaimer provision is made conspicuous when it appears in a record under a conspicuous heading that indicates there is an exclusion or modification of warranties. A heading cannot be relied on to make such a provision conspicuous when the heading is misleading and wrongfully gives the impression there is a warranty. **For Example,** the heading "Vehicle Warranty" is misleading if the provision that follows contains a limitation of warranties. A disclaimer that is hidden in a mass of materials or records handed to the buyer is not conspicuous and is not effective to exclude warranties. Similarly, an inconspicuous disclaimer of warranties under a posted notice of "Notice to Retail Buyers" has no effect.

When a disclaimer of warranties fails because it is not conspicuous, the implied warranties apply to the buyer.[34]

(b) Unconscionability and Public Policy

An exclusion of warranties made in the manner specified by the UCC is not unconscionable. In some states, warranty disclaimers are invalid because they are contrary to public policy or because they are prohibited by consumer protection laws.

When a breach of warranty is the result of negligence of the seller, a disclaimer of warranty liability and a limitation of remedies to a refund of the purchase price are not binding. Such limitations are unreasonable, unconscionable, and against public policy.

ANTZ V GAF MATERIALS CORP., 719 A2D 758 (PA SUPER 1998); APPEAL DENIED 739 A2D 1054 (PA 1999)

GETTING THE SHAFT ON THE SHINGLES

In August 1989, GAF, a manufacturer of shingles, shipped 48 squares of its Timberline shingles to Mr. Antz for purposes of installation at his newly constructed home. The package in which the shingles were shipped contained a label stating the shingles were covered by a 30-year limited warranty and a copy of the warranty was available from the distributor of the shingles or directly from GAF. No other language appeared on the label to clarify the express limited warranty, and no other warranty language was included with the shingles when they were delivered to Mr. Antz. The express limited warranty contained a disclaimer of the implied warranties of merchantability and fitness for a particular purpose. In addition, it contained language limiting replacement labor costs to within the first year following installation.

After approximately 48 months of use, the shingles showed signs of defects, and Mr. Antz made a claim to GAF pursuant to the 30-year warranty. After investigation, it was determined the shingles contained manufacturing defects. GAF sent Mr. Antz a letter dated December 29, 1994, informing him that his claim was being approved for settlement. GAF thereafter sent Mr. Antz a roofing materials certificate for Timberline shingles. Mr. Antz refused to redeem the certificate and instead retained a roofer to install another brand of shingles on his house.

Mr. Antz commenced an action against GAF asserting breaches of express warranty, warranty of merchantability, and warranty of fitness for a particular purpose. He sought to recover the labor costs involved in replacing the Timberline shingles and the value of the new shingles. GAF filed a motion for partial summary judgment because Mr. Antz's claims for replacement labor costs in connection with the defective shingles, were time barred under 13 Pa.C.S.A. § 2725 and were precluded based on GAF's disclaimer of implied warranties and its express limited warranty's limitation of damages provisions.

[34] A warranty disclaimer written in all caps just below the signature line is conspicuous. *Gooch v E. I. DuPont de Nemours & Co.*, 40 F Supp 3d 863 (WD Ky 1999).

Both parties agreed to submit the matter for the trial court's decision based on stipulated facts. The trial court issued an opinion and order awarding Mr. Antz damages in the amount of $11,745.00 for replacement labor costs and the replacement shingles. By order, the trial court denied GAF's motion for judgment n.o.v. and granted its motion for a molded verdict, reducing the award of damages to $9,349.73 to reflect the value of the replacement shingles tendered by GAF but refused by Mr. Antz. Mr. Antz appealed.

Judicial Opinion

ORIE MELVIN, Judge. . . . Chris Antz's claims were not time-barred. We find Mr. Antz's claims based on the express warranty were not time barred under 13 Pa.C.S.A. § 2725 because the complaint was filed within four years after discovery of defects in the shingles. Furthermore, we find the limitation of damages provisions contained in GAF's express limited warranty are unconscionable and unenforceable.

In the instant case, Mr. Antz's claims for breach of the implied warranties of merchantability and fitness for a particular purpose are time barred. Such claims were not filed within four years after tender of delivery of the shingles and do not meet the exception under § 2725(b) as they cannot relate to future performance. However, the express warranty provided a thirty year limited warranty. Such a warranty explicitly extends to future performance of the shingles up to thirty years. Mr. Antz initially discovered the defects in the shingles four years after they were delivered in August 1989. GAF acknowledged the shingles were defective by letter dated December 29, 1994. The complaint, filed on December 18, 1995, was well within the four year period of limitations if the discovery of the defect occurred when either Mr. Antz initially noticed the defects or GAF acknowledged the defects in December 1994.

Whether the language of the express warranty limits Mr. Antz's recovery is another issue.

The limitation of damages provisions in question set forth in the express limited warranty read as follows:

2. REMEDIES AND LIMITATION OF LIABILITY. To remedy breach of the above warranties, GAF will:

a. replace professionally installed Shingles containing manufacturing defects within one year of completion of installation with an equivalent amount of Shingles and will pay 100 percent of the reasonable labor cost for replacing these Shingles, provided, however, that GAF's maximum liability will not exceed the original purchase price of the Shingles and the reasonable original installation costs. During the remaining warranty period, GAF will adjust valid claims for professionally installed Shingles containing manufacturing defects by an amount determined by decreasing annually the original purchase price of the Shingles divided by the remaining warranty period, less any costs incurred by GAF for replacement during previous years.

2. LIMITATIONS ON COVERAGE. GAF will not be liable for and this warranty does not apply to:

a. labor costs incurred for the application of the Shingles except as provided herein, tear-off, metal work, flashing or other related work . . .

We must consider whether GAF succeeded in limiting its liability for replacement labor costs.

A provision is unconscionable if 1) one of the parties had no meaningful choice with respect to the provision, and 2) the provision unreasonably favors the other party. *Borden, Inc. v Advent Ink Company*, 701 A.2d 255, 264 (Pa.Super.1997). "In determining whether a clause is unconscionable, the court should consider whether, in light of the general commercial background and the commercial needs of a particular trade, the clause is so one-sided that it is unconscionable under the circumstances." The question before us is whether Mr. Antz had a meaningful choice regarding the provisions limiting damages for replacement labor costs and whether those particular provisions unreasonably favored GAF. We find the provisions unconscionable and therefore unenforceable for the following reasons.

The limitation of remedies provisions were not provided to Mr. Antz at the time of purchase and delivery. The only information Mr. Antz was provided when the shingles were shipped was a label which included language stating "30-Year LIMITED WARRANTY only" and "[t]his product is sold with an express LIMITED WARRANTY only. A copy of the LIMITED WARRANTY stating its terms and restrictions may be obtained from the distributor of this product or directly from GAF Building Materials Corporation. . . . " The language explaining the terms and conditions of the limitations was not given to Mr. Antz.

In consumer cases, the conspicuousness of a limitation of damages provision is a factor in considering whether a provision is unconscionable.

In the present case, the language limiting Mr. Antz's damages was well beyond merely inconspicuous.The provisions were not even in his possession but in the possession of GAF. If Mr. Antz was not provided with the limitations, then it cannot be said that he had any meaningful choice with regard to those limitations. Furthermore, Mr. Antz ordered the shingles for installation on his new home. He did not install them himself but hired a roofer. He was clearly not a commercial customer. As an individual buying roofing material for his home, Mr. Antz was certainly not in a position to expect that if the shingles were defective he would not be reimbursed for the cost of replacing them beyond one year after their installation, especially in light of the label he received which indicated the shingles were covered by a thirty year warranty.

A term or clause is conspicuous when it is so written that a reasonable person against whom it is to operate ought to have noticed it. 13 Pa.C.S.A. § 1201. The provisions in issue were clearly not conspicuous.

We find such provisions unreasonably favor GAF because the cost of installing the shingles far exceeds the cost of the materials. The thirty-year warranty on the shingles loses much of its allure when the limitation of damages provisions are made apparent. In the instant case, the provisions were not made apparent to Mr. Antz. Accordingly, we find the limitation of damages provisions contained in the warranty are unconscionable and unenforceable. Therefore, the provisions cannot prohibit Mr. Antz's claim for replacement labor costs or the trial court's award of damages for such costs.

We believe the trial court should have refused to enforce the disclaimer of implied warranties rather than find the express warranty unenforceable as a whole. Therefore, Mr. Antz's recovery of damages for replacement labor costs would be based on breach of the express warranty instead of breach of implied warranties as the trial court found.

We may affirm for reasons other than those relied upon by the trial court. As long as the result is correct, the decision will be affirmed.

Questions

1. When did the shingles go bad?
2. Give the times for the warranty, the disclaimer, and the statute of limitations.
3. Is the warranty disclaimer enforceable?

18. Particular Language for Disclaimers

The disclaimer requirements under Revised Article 2 have been changed in a way that makes disclaimers for consumer contracts different from disclaimers for contracts between merchants. The rules for disclaimer of warranties for merchants remain the same as they were under previous Article 2. Language such as "as is," "with all faults," "as they stand," or "There are no warranties that extend beyond the description on the face hereof," serve to exclude the implied warranty of merchantability as well as the implied warranty of fitness for a particular purpose. Such disclaimers are valid between merchants even if they are oral.

Under Revised Article 2, any warranty disclaimers for consumer buyers must be placed in a record (*record* includes written agreements but, as noted in Chapter 23, also includes e-mail and electronic exchanges), must be conspicuous, and must use statutory language now provided. To waive the warranty of merchantability, the record must contain the following language: "The seller undertakes no responsibility for the quality of the goods except as otherwise provided in this contract."[35] The required language for waiving the warranty of fitness for a particular purpose is as follows: "The seller assumes no responsibility that the goods will be fit for any particular purpose for which you may be buying these goods, except as otherwise provided in the contract."[36]

In consumer contracts, the use of terms such as "as is" can also disclaim the warranties, as it does for merchant transactions, but the disclaimers must be in the record and must be conspicuously set forth in that record.

Figure 25-1 provides a summary of the warranties under Article 2 and the methods for making disclaimers.

19. Exclusion of Warranties by Examination of Goods

Revised Article 2 modifies the requirements for inspections as a waiver of warranty. For an inspection of goods by the buyer to constitute a waiver, the seller must demand that the buyer inspect the goods as part of the contracting process. The seller may not use inspection as a defense to warranty issues if

[35] Revised UCC § 2-316(2).

[36] *Id.*

FIGURE 25-1 UCC Warranties

NAME OF WARRANTY	CREATION	RESTRICTION	DISCLAIMER
EXPRESS	AFFIRMATION OF FACT, PROMISE OF PERFORMANCE (INCLUDES SAMPLES, MODELS, DESCRIPTIONS)	MUST BE PART OF THE BASIS OF THE BARGAIN	CANNOT MAKE A DISCLAIMER INCONSISTENT WITH AN EXPRESS WARRANTY
IMPLIED WARRANTY OF MERCHANTABILITY	GIVEN IN EVERY SALE OF GOODS BY A MERCHANT ("FIT FOR ORDINARY PURPOSES")	ONLY GIVEN BY MERCHANTS	MUST USE STATUTORY LANGUAGE DISCLAIMER OF "AS IS" OR "WITH ALL FAULTS"; MUST BE CONSPICUOUS IN THE RECORD
IMPLIED WARRANTY OF FITNESS FOR A PARTICULAR PURPOSE	SELLER KNOWS OF BUYER'S RELIANCE FOR A PARTICULAR USE (BUYER IS IGNORANT)	SELLER MUST HAVE KNOWLEDGE; BUYER MUST RELY ON SELLER	(1) MUST HAVE A RECORD (2) MUST BE CONSPICUOUS (3) ALSO DISCLAIMED WITH "AS IS" OR "WITH ALL FAULTS"
TITLE	GIVEN IN EVERY SALE	DOES NOT APPLY IN CIRCUMSTANCES WHERE APPARENT WARRANTY IS NOT GIVEN	MUST SAY "THERE IS NO WARRANTY OF TITLE"
MAGNUSON-MOSS (FEDERAL CONSUMER PRODUCT WARRANTY LAW)	ONLY CONSUMER PRODUCTS OF $10 OR MORE	MUST LABEL "FULL" OR "LIMITED"	

that demand was not made at the time the parties contracted.[37]

20. Postsale Disclaimer

Frequently, a statement purporting to exclude or modify warranties appears for the first time in a written contract sent to confirm or memorialize an oral contract made earlier. The exclusion or modification may likewise appear in an invoice, a bill, or an instruction manual delivered to the buyer at or after the time the goods are received. Such postsale disclaimers have no effect on warranties that arose at the time of the sale.

E. Other Theories of Product Liability

In addition to recovery for breach of an express guarantee, an express warranty, or an implied warranty, a plaintiff in a given product liability case may be able to recover for negligence, fraud, or strict tort liability.

[37] Revised UCC § 2-316(3)(b).

21. Negligence

A person injured because of the defective condition of a product may be entitled to recover from the seller or manufacturer for the damages for **negligence**. The injured person must be able to show that the seller was negligent in the preparation or manufacture of the article or failed to provide proper instructions and warnings of dangers. An action for negligence rests on common law tort principles. Negligence does not require privity of contract.

22. Fraud

The UCC expressly preserves the pre-Code law governing fraud. A person defrauded by a distributor's or manufacturer's false statements about a product generally will be able to recover damages for the harm sustained because of such misrepresentations. False statements are fraudulent if the party who made them did so with knowledge that they were false or with reckless indifference to their truthfulness.

CPA 23. Strict Tort Liability

Independently of the UCC, a manufacturer or distributor of a defective product is liable under strict tort liability to a person who is injured by the product. Strict tort liability exists without regard to whether the person injured is a purchaser, a consumer, or a third person, such as a bystander.[38] It is no defense that privity of contract does not exist between the injured party and the defendant. Likewise, it is no defense that the defect was found in a component part purchased from another manufacturer.[39] **For Example,** defective tires sold on a new car were probably purchased from a tire supplier by the auto manufacturer. However, the manufacturer is not excused from liability.

Strict tort liability requires that the defect in the product exist at the time it left the control of the manufacturer or distributor. The defective condition is defined in the same way as under negligence: defective by manufacturing error or oversight, defective by design, or defective by the failure to warn.[40] There is liability if the product is defective and unreasonably dangerous and has caused harm. It is immaterial whether the seller was negligent or whether the user was contributorily negligent. Knowledge of the defect is not a requirement for liability. Assumption of risk by the injured party, on the other hand, is a defense available to the seller.[41]

24. Cumulative Theories of Liability

The theories of product liability are not mutually exclusive. A given set of facts may give rise to two or more theories of liability. **For Example,** suppose that a manufacturer advertises, "Coaches! Protect your players' eyes! Shatterproof sunglasses for baseball." If the glasses shattered and injured a player, an express warranty, implied warranty, implied warranty for a particular purpose, and strict tort liability could apply for recovery.

AUSTIN V WILL-BURT COMPANY, 232 F SUPP 2D 682 (D MISS 2002) AFFIRMED 361 F3D 862 (5TH CIR 2004)

SHOCKING WARRANTY ISSUES

FACTS: Will-Burt builds steel masts used by the military, border control, firefighters, and the television broadcast industry. Will-Burt built one such mast in 1982 for use in the television broadcast industry on an electronic news-gathering van (ENG van). Will-Burt sold the mast in 1982 to Quality Coach of Elkhart, Indiana. In 1989, this mast resurfaced by reference in an invoice from a business called Alan W. Haines, Custom Construction (Haines). The invoice indicates that the mast had been "completely rebuilt." Mississippi Telecasting Company d/b/a WABG-TV purchased the mast from Haines along with several other component parts from Mobile Manufacturers and others who previously settled their cases with Barksdale Austin, a 24-year-old college graduate employed as a production manager by

[38] The concept of strict tort liability was judicially declared in *Greenman v Yuba Power Products*, 377 P2d 897 (Cal 1963). This concept has been incorporated in the Restatement (Second) and (Third) of Torts as § 402A.

[39] *Guiffrida v Panasonic Industrial Co., Inc.*, 607 NYS2d 72 (Sup Ct App Div 1994); *Ford v Beam Radiator, Inc.*, 708 So 2d 1158 (La App 1998).

[40] *Lewis v Ariens*, 751 NE 2d 862 (Mass 2001).

[41] *Clark v Mazda Motor Corp.* 68 P3d 207 (OK 2003).

WABG-TV in Greenville, Mississippi. One of his duties at WABG was to set up the TV station's ENG van for remote broadcasts. This duty entailed operating the telescoping mast on the van. Austin received safety training that included checking for obstructions before raising the mast, to ensure that the ENG van was on level ground and, pursuant to station policy, keeping a clearance of at least 20 feet from any power line if the mast was to be raised.

On June 17, 1997, Austin was assigned to a live shot at Greenville City Hall, three blocks from the WABG-TV station and within the direct line of sight of the station's antenna. The van was parked underneath visible transformers and power lines by someone other than Austin. The Will-Burt mast, which was attached to the van, contacted an 8,000-volt power line while being raised. The voltage went down the mast and into the van, energizing the van and its extending cables. Austin walked to the van, touched it, and was electrically shocked to death.

The mast still had the following warnings on its base: "DANGER! PLEASE READ INSTRUCTIONS BEFORE RAISING!" and "DANGER. WATCH FOR WIRES. YOU CAN BE KILLED IF THIS PRODUCT COMES NEAR ELECTRICAL POWER LINES." The labels were located on the base of the mast inside the van in bright yellow with red and black lettering. The instructions in the product manual also warned operators to never to raise the mast under or near power lines and to check for obstructions within the proximity to the maximum height of the mast.

Austin's family (the appellants) filed suit for breach of warranty and negligence.

Judicial Opinion

GARWOOD, Circuit Judge. . . . The appellants claim that the mast at issue was defectively designed and unreasonably dangerous when it left Will-Burt's control in May 1982 because of inadequate warnings. The district court dismissed this claim, noting that the warning labels that were placed on the mast specifically cautioned the operator that he or she could be killed if the mast were raised "near" power lines. In Mississippi, a warning may be held adequate as a matter of law where the adverse effect was one that the manufacturer specifically warned against.

There were also warnings in product manuals which Will-Burt supplied with its masts not to raise the mast under or near power lines and to check for overhead obstructions in proximity to the mast's line of extension and maximum height.

The warnings on the mast clearly connected contact with power lines and risk of death. Moreover, to the extent this danger was not already obvious, we refer to the testimony of Donnie Reid, the operations manager at WABG who conducted Austin's safety training and trained him in setting up the "live truck." Reid warned Austin that before raising the mast he should check that the truck was on level ground, check for obstacles overhead such as trees and power lines, never raise the mast if there were overhead obstacles, and maintain a twenty-foot clearance from any power lines. Furthermore, on the day in question Reid specifically told Austin that he did not need to raise the mast to do the shot from the City Hall location.

The warnings on the mast seem clearly adequate, particularly "taking into account . . . the ordinary knowledge common to an ordinary consumer who purchases the product.

Appellants claim that the Will-Burt mast was defectively designed in two respects, namely that it did not have a proximity warning device (PWD) and that it was not insulated. Appellants claim that the mast should have had a PWD which would have either given a warning sound or signal, or stopped the mast from continuing to rise, when the mast came within a certain distance of a power line. Will-Burt has manufactured and sold such a device, called a D-Tec, starting in 1998; it commenced attempting to develop the D-Tec in 1996 and produced a prototype which it exhibited at the April 1997 National Association of Broadcasters convention. Thereafter, it made some improvements to the D-Tec and began selling it in September 1998. The only other PWD referenced in the evidence is the Sigalarm, manufactured by another company. It was first used in the broadcast industry in 1995 or 1996. PWDs used in the broadcast industry or in ENG vans are and were sold by the manufacturer either to van assembling companies, which then sell the van with mast, payload, and PWD to broadcasters, or are sold directly to the station, which does its own integration. The PWD is a separate item, not a part of the mast itself, and is affixed on top of the mast payload (the pan-and-tilt and antenna) which itself sits on the top of the mast. The pan-and-tilt and antenna are likewise items separate from the mast itself and are manufactured by companies other than mast manufacturers. The cost of a PWD is and has been approximately 28 to 30 percent of the cost of the mast.

The summary judgment evidence showed without contradiction that neither telescoping masts used in the broadcast industry or in ENG vans, nor pan-and-tilt devices, nor their cameras or antennas, were or had ever been insulated.

We conclude that the MPLA, in section 11-1-63(f), unambiguously precludes recovery against the manufacturer on the basis of design defect unless the product "failed to function as expected." Under the undisputed facts here, the relevant time is accordingly May 1982, when Will-Burt sold the elevating mast to Quality Coach.

The "failed to function as expected" requirement of section 11-1-63(f) appears to largely reinstate for design defect cases a frequently expressed requirement of the "consumer expectations test."

Here, the evidence is that at the relevant time—May 1982, when the mast left Will-Burt's control—no telescoping masts (or their "payloads"), whether in the broadcast industry or any other, were insulated so as not to conduct electricity or were either equipped or used with any sort of PWD, and the danger of electrocution if the mast was raised so that it or its "payload" came into contact with an overhead power line was well recognized. There is no contrary evidence. This not only continued to be the case in the broadcast industry until the tragic 1997 accident in question but apparently still continues to be the case. There is no evidence that anyone in the industry ever—in 1982 or 1997 or at any other time–did not realize that a telescoping mast such as this, if raised when under a power line, would not extend to the height of the power line so that the "payload" on top of the mast (or even the mast itself) would come into contact with the power line with serious resultant electric shock, or that any device on or used with the mast, or any characteristic of the mast or of any such device, would prevent such a result or give a prior warning signal of it. The evidence is that Austin had been made aware of these dangers, and there is no contrary evidence. There is simply no evidence that the mast "failed to function as expected." That a truly tragic accident occurred in using the mast does not mean that the mast failed to function as expected. The mast did nothing unusual or unexpected. An ordinary revolver functions as expected if, when loaded and off-safety, the trigger is normally pulled and a bullet is expelled, and this is no less so because, quite unintentionally, someone is struck by the bullet. So also with a cigarette lighter normally ignited and applied to flammable material, notwithstanding that a tragic fire results, or an intact hatchet which strikes a hand placed or left on the target wood.

Because there is no evidence that the mast "failed to function as expected," recovery against Will-Burt for design defect is precluded . . .

The judgment of the district court is

[Affirmed]

Questions

1. What were the theories of product liability that were used to try and recover for the death?
2. What was missing in those claims?
3. Does a tragic accident always mean there is a defect in the product?

ETHICS & THE LAW

THE HEART OF THE MERCK CASES

The first of the Merck product liability cases for its drug Vioxx (now withdrawn from the market) began in late July 2005. The first case was brought by Carol Ernst, 59, the widow of Robert Ernst, a man who died of arrhythmia, an irregular interruption of the heart rhythm. Mr. Ernst was also 59 and was an accomplished triathlete. He was taking Vioxx at the time of his arrhythmia and resulting death. Mrs. Ernst alleged that Vioxx, an antiarthritic drug manufactured by Merck, was placed on the market despite the company's knowledge of its risks and evidence of harm in patients with heart problems. The company estimates that 20 million people in the United States have taken Vioxx, and between 4,000 and 7,000 product liability suits are

ETHICS & THE LAW

continued

pending (there are differing reports on the total).

In his 2.5-hour opening statement, Mark Lanier, the lawyer for Mrs. Ernst, told the jury to be "detectives." "If we were going to put it into a TV show, this would be 'CSI Angleton.' "* The first witness in the case Mrs. Ernst's lawyer presented was Dr. Nancy Santanello, a physician employed by Merck as its head of epidemiology, and an adverse or hostile witness. Dr. Santanello's job at Merck is to study data results from tests involving Merck drugs. Dr. Santanello took Vioxx herself.

Critical elements that came out during the trial:

- Merck had evidence from a study in 2000 that 14.6 percent of 4,000 Vioxx patients studied (590 people) had cardiovascular problems while taking the drug.
- In a letter to physicians once it had the 14.6 percent number, Merck said the percentage was 0.5, or a total of 20 people.
- The study showed that only 0.5 percent had heart attacks while on Vioxx. The 14.6 percent did indeed have less severe cardiovascular problems. The letter from Merck reads "the rate of cardiovascular events was 0.5 percent among patients taking VIOXX."
- Merck also sent the study along to the *New England Journal of Medicine* and suggested in the letter to doctors that they consult that report for more details on the study.
- A training document for sales representatives compared answering questions about Vioxx safety to a game of dodge ball.
- Dr. James F. Fries, a professor at Stanford University, criticized Vioxx and then sent a letter to Merck complaining that he was threatened by Dr. Louis Sherwood, a senior scientist at Merck. Dr. Fries wrote that Sherwood threatened to destroy his career.
- Merck did no follow-up studies after the 2000 study.
- Dr. Santanello removed the name of one of her subordinates from authorship on a research paper that reached negative conclusions about Vioxx. The study was published in *Circulation* and had been a joint study by Harvard Medical School and Merck.

List the possible theories that Mrs. Ernst could use for recovery.

Sources: Alex Berenson, *"Merck's Case Withstands First Week of Punches," New York Times*, July 25, 2005, C1–C7; and Alex Berenson, *"At Vioxx Trial, a Discrepancy Appears to Undercut Merck's Defense," New York Times*, July 20, 2005, C1–C8.

*Barbara Martinez, "*Merck Doctor Likely to Testify In Vioxx Trial*," *Wall Street Journal*, July 18, 2005, B1–B6.

LAWFLIX

The Incredible Shrinking Woman (1981) (PG)

Lily Tomlin's exposure to various combinations of products causes her to shrink. Which companies would be liable and how could one go about proving joint and several liability? Discuss privity of contract and whether the interaction with other products would be covered.

For movie clips that illustrate business law concepts, see LawFlix at **http://wdvl.westbuslaw.com.**

Summary

Five theories protect parties from loss caused by nonconforming goods: (1) express warranty, (2) implied warranty, (3) negligence, (4) fraud, and (5) strict tort liability.

Theories of product liability are not mutually exclusive. A given set of facts may give rise to liability under two or more theories.

The requirement of privity of contract (that is, the parties to the sales contract for warranty liability) has been widely rejected. The law is moving toward the conclusion that persons harmed because of an improper product may recover from anyone who is in any way responsible. The requirement of privity has been abolished by most states, and remote buyers as well as their families, members of their households, and guests are covered under the UCC warranties.

Warranties may be express or implied. The types of implied warranties are the warranty of title, the implied warranty of merchantability, and the implied warranty of fitness for a particular purpose. The warranty of title provides that the transfer is lawful, the title is good, and there are no infringement issues. Under Revised Article 2, the warranty of title also protects the buyer against unreasonable litigation. The warranty of merchantability is given by merchants and warrants that the goods are of average quality and will do what those types of goods commonly can do. The implied warranty of fitness for a particular purpose is given in those circumstances in which the buyer relies on the seller's expertise and the seller is aware of that reliance and offers a recommendation on the types of goods.

Express warranties arise from statements of fact and promises of performance made by the seller to the buyer that become a part of the basis for the buyer contracting. Express warranties arise from samples, models, and descriptions.

Warranties may be disclaimed by agreement of the parties provided the disclaimer is not unconscionable. Merchants can have oral disclaimers, but for consumers, warranty disclaimers must be in a record and must be conspicuous. Also for consumers, certain language must be used to disclaim each type of warranty. However, for both merchants and nonmerchants, the use of terms such as "as is" or "with all faults" can disclaim both the warranty of merchantability and the implied warranty of fitness for a particular purpose (although for consumers, there must still be a record and the language must be conspicuous).

The warranties of merchantability and fitness exist under the CISG. However, disclaimers under the CISG need not mention merchantability, nor must such disclaimers be conspicuous.

The strict tort liability plaintiff must show that there was a defect in the product at the time it left the control of the defendant. No negligence need be established on the part of the defendant, nor is the plaintiff's contributory negligence a defense. If negligence is established, however, knowledge by the seller can result in punitive damages. The defendant may show that the injured party assumed the risk.

Questions and Case Problems

1. Maria Gonzalez lived in a rental unit with her sons in Queens, New York. The hot water supplied to their apartment was heated by a Morflo water heater, which had a temperature control device on its exterior manufactured by Robertshaw and sold to Morflo. Maria Garcia, the owner of the Gonzalezes' apartment, had purchased and installed the water heater. The Morflo heater was located in the basement of the apartment house, which was locked and inaccessible to tenants.

   Extensive warnings were on the water heater itself and in the manual given to Garcia at the time of her purchase. The warning on the Robertshaw temperature device read: "CAUTION: Hotter water increases the risk of scald injury." The heater itself contained a picture of hot water coming from a faucet with the word "DANGER" printed above it. In addition, the water heater had a statement on it: "Water temperature over 120 degrees Fahrenheit can cause severe burns instantly or death from scalds. Children, disabled, and elderly are at highest risk of being scalded. Feel water before bathing or showering. Temperature limiting valves are available, see manual."

   In the Morflo manual, the following warning appeared:

   > *DANGER! The thermostat is adjusted to its lowest temperature position when shipped from the factory. Adjusting the thermostat past the 120 degree Fahrenheit bar on the temperature dial will increase the risk of scald injury. The normal position is approximately 120 degrees Fahrenheit.*
   >
   > *DANGER: WARNING: Hot water can produce first degree burns in 3 seconds at 140 degrees Fahrenheit (60 degrees Celsius), in 20 seconds at 130 degrees Fahrenheit (54 degrees Celsius), in 8 minutes at 120 degrees Fahrenheit (49 degrees Celsius).*

   On October 1, 1992, 15-month-old Angel Gonzalez was being bathed by his 15-year-old brother, Daniel. When the telephone rang, Daniel left Angel alone in the bathtub. No one else was at home with the boys, and Daniel left the water running. Angel was scalded by the water that came from the tap. Angel and his mother brought suit against Morflo and Robertshaw, alleging defects in the design of the water heater and the failure to warn. Should they recover? [Gonzalez v Marflo Industries, Inc., 931 F Supp 159 (EDNY)]

2. Paul Parrino purchased from Dave's Professional Wheelchair Service a wheelchair manufactured by 21st Century Scientific, Inc. The sales brochure from 21st Century Scientific stated that the wheelchair would "serve [the buyer] well for many years to come." Parrino had problems with the wheelchair within a few years and filed suit against Dave's and 21st Century for breach of express warranty. Both defended on the grounds that the statement on years of service was puffery, not an express warranty. Are they right? [Parrino v Sperling, 648 NYS2d 702]
3. Jane Jackson purchased a sealed can of Katydids, chocolate-covered pecan caramel candies manufactured by NestlT. Shortly after, Jackson bit into one of the candies and allegedly broke a tooth on a pecan shell embedded in the candy. She filed a complaint, asserting breach of implied warranty. How would you argue on behalf of the company? How would you argue on behalf of Jackson? In your answer, discuss both the reasonable expectation test and the foreign substance/natural substance test. [Jackson v NestlT-Beich, Inc., 589 NE2d 547 (Ill App)]
4. Webster ordered a bowl of fish chowder at the Blue Ship Tea Room. She was injured by a fish bone in the chowder, and she sued the tea room for breach of the implied warranty of merchantability. The evidence at trial showed that when chowder is made, the entire unboned fish is cooked. Should she recover? [Webster v Blue Ship Tea Room, 198 NE2d 309]
5. Andy's Sales (owned by Andy Adams) sold a well-built trampoline to Carl and Shirley Wickers. The Wickerses later sold the trampoline to Herbert Bryant. While using the trampoline, Herbert's 14-year-old nephew, Rex, sustained injuries that left him a quadriplegic. Rex's guardian filed suit for breach of express warranty and merchantability. The sales brochure for the round trampoline described it as "safe" because it had a "uniform bounce" and "natural tendency to work the jumper toward the center." The Wickerses had purchased an oval-shaped trampoline. Discuss Rex's ability to recover. Is privity an issue? [Bryant v Adams, 448 SE2d 832 (NC App)]
6. Advent purchased ink from Borden. On the labels of the ink drums delivered to Advent, Borden had imprinted in one-sixteenth-inch type in all caps:

   SELLER MAKES NO WARRANTY, EXPRESS OR IMPLIED, CONCERNING THE PRODUCT OR THE MERCHANTABILITY OR FITNESS THEREOF FOR ANY PURPOSE CONCERNING THE ACCURACY OF ANY INFORMATION PROVIDED BY BORDEN.

   This language was printed beneath the following:

   BORDEN PRINTING INKS—"ZERO DEFECTS: THAT'S OUR GOAL"

   All of the printing was in boldface type. The disclaimer was also printed on the sales invoice and on the reverse side of the Borden form, but there was nothing on the front to call attention to the critical nature of the terms on the back because there were simply capital letters reading "SEE REVERSE SIDE." All of the terms on the back were in boldface and although the disclaimer was the first of 19 paragraphs, nothing distinguished it from the other 18 paragraphs of detailed contract terms.

   Advent said that Borden failed to age the black ink that it purchased with the result that the ink separated in Advent's printing machines. Advent refused to pay for the ink and wrote to Borden explaining that it would not tender payment because the ink was defective and demanding that Borden reimburse it for its lost profits from the downtime of printing machines. The trial court held that Borden had disclaimed any and all warranties on the ink and Advent appealed. What would you decide about the disclaimer and why? [Borden, Inc. v Advent Ink Co., 701 A2d 255 (Pa Sup)]
7. Avery purchased a refrigerator from a retail store. The written contract stated that the refrigerator was sold "as is" and that the warranty of merchantability and all warranties of fitness were excluded. This was stated in large capital letters printed just above the line on which Avery signed her name. The refrigerator worked properly for a few weeks and then stopped. The store refused to do anything about it because of the exclusion of the warranties made by the contract. Avery claimed that this exclusion was not binding because it was unconscionable. Was Avery correct? [Avery v Aladdin Products Div., Nat'l Service Industries, Inc., 196 SE2d 357 (Ga App)]
8. The 1143 East Jersey Avenue Associates, Inc., owned a 10-story building. The Associates hired Duall Building Restoration, Inc., to restore the surface of its building. The contract between the Associates and Duall specified that Duall would use Modac, a waterproof paint manufactured by Monsey Products, to cover the three brick sides of the building.

   Shortly after the Modac paint was applied to the three sides of the building, it began to peel disastrously. One of the principals in the Associates described the situation as follows: "The entire building is peeling. It's . . . going wild. I mean . . . the surface is a whole bunch of spaghetti. Maybe noodles, I should say. It's curlicues of surface coming off all over the place." The Associates sued both Duall and Monsey Products. Monsey Products claimed that the Associates were remote purchasers and it was not liable to the Associates because of lack of privity. It would cost $185,000 for a new paint job. Can there be recovery? As you answer, be sure to discuss which warranty theory you would use and whether the issue of privity prevents recovery. [Duall Bldg. Restoration, Inc. v 1143 East Jersey Avenue Associates, Inc., 652 A2d 1225 (NJ Super)]

9. In April 1990, Herbert S. Garten went to Valley Motors to purchase a new 1990 Mercedes-Benz Model 300E. Robert Bell, a Mercedes salesman, told Garten that except for some cosmetic changes, the 1990 300E was "identical" to the 1986 300E.

   On April 9, 1990, Garten brought in his 1986 car and asked Bell to describe the exact differences between the 1986 model and the new 1990 model of the 300E. Bell explained the changes as only cosmetic; he gave Garten a $17,500 trade-in allowance for his 1986 300E and sold him a 1990 300E for $42,500.

   The following morning, Garten had trouble shifting from second to third gear in his new car and called to complain to Bell. Bell convinced him to wait until the 1,000-mile check to see if the problem worked itself out.

   On May 3, 1990, Garten brought the 1990 300E to Valley Motors for the 1,000-mile checkup and presented a memorandum describing the problems he was having with the car, focusing on the automobile's delayed upshift from second to third gear. (The delayed upshift was the result of an emissions control system designed to bring the catalytic converter quickly to operating temperature from a cold start.) Garten returned the 1990 300E to Valley Motors on May 9, 1990, and on the same day, Garten delivered two letters to Valley Motors stating that the 1990 300E was defective and he was revoking his acceptance and rescinding the sale. Garten left the keys to the 1990 300E, requested the return of his 1986 300E, and asked Valley Motors how it could retransfer titles to the two cars. Finally, Garten informed Valley Motors that he would be renting a car until this matter was resolved.

   The 1990 300E sat parked in the lot at Valley Motors for approximately seven months until December 1990, when Garten retrieved the car. He subsequently traded in the 1990 300E for a new 1991 300E that he purchased from another Mercedes-Benz dealer. The total purchase price of the 1991 300E was $43,123.50; he also traded in the 1990 300E for $31,500. Garten says the salesman's statement was an express warranty that he relied on in buying the car. Can he recover? [Mercedes-Benz of North America, Inc. v Garten, 618 A2d 233 (Md App)]

10. Zogarts manufactured and sold a practice device for beginning golfers. According to the statements on the package, the device was completely safe, and a player could never be struck by the device's golf ball. Hauter was hit by the ball while practicing with the device. He sued Zogarts, which denied liability on the ground that the statements were merely matters of opinion, so liability could not be based on them. Was this a valid defense? [Hauter v Zogarts, 534 P2d 377 (Cal)]

11. A buyer purchased an engine to operate an irrigation pump. The buyer selected the engine from a large number that were standing on the floor of the seller's stockroom. A label on the engine stated that it would produce 100 horsepower. The buyer needed an engine that would generate at least 80 horsepower. In actual use in the buyer's irrigation system, the engine generated only 60 horsepower. The buyer sued the seller for damages. The seller raised the defense that no warranty of fitness for the buyer's particular purpose of operating an irrigation pump had arisen because the seller did not know of the use to which the buyer intended to put the engine. Also, the buyer had not relied on the seller's skill and judgment in selecting the particular engine. Did the seller have any liability based on warranties? [Potter v Tyndall, 207 SE2d 762 (NC)]

12. After watching a male horse owned by Terry and Manita Darby perform at a horse show, Ashley Sheffield contacted the Darbys about buying him. The Darbys assured her that the horse had no problems and would make a good show horse for use in competition. In the presence of and in consultation with her father (who raised horses for a business), Sheffield rode the horse and decided to purchase him for $8,500. Within three weeks, Sheffield and her trainer discerned that the horse was lame. Sheffield sued the Darbys for fraud and for breach of express and implied warranties, and the court entered summary judgment in favor of the Darbys on all claims. Sheffield appealed. Was the court correct in granting summary judgment? Was there a breach of an express warranty? [Sheffield v Darby, 535 SE2d 776 (Ga App)]

13. Drehman Paving & Flooring Co. installed a brick floor at Cumberland Farms that its salesman promised would be "just like" another floor Cumberland had installed several years earlier. The bricks in the new floor came loose because Drehman had failed to install expansion joints. Expansion joints were not included in the second floor contract but were part of the first. Can Cumberland recover? What theory? [Cumberland Farms, Inc. v Drehman Paving & Flooring Co., 520 NE2d 1321 (Mass Ct App)]

14. Brian Felley went to the home of Tom and Cheryl Singleton on June 8 to look at a used car that the Singletons had advertised for sale in the local paper. The car was a 1991 Ford with 126,000 miles on it. Following a test drive and the Singletons' representation that the car was "in good mechanical condition," Felley purchased the car for $5,800. By June 18, 1997, Felley had the car in the shop and paid $942.76 to have its clutch fixed. By July 9, 1997, Felley also had paid $971.18 for a new brake job. By September 16, 1997, Felley had paid another $429.09 for further brake work.

Felley brought suit for breach of express warranty. An auto expert testified that the clutch and brakes were defective when Felley bought the car. Was an express warranty breached? Why or why not? [Felley v Singleton, 705 NE2d 930 (Ill App)]

15. Lewis and Sims, a contracting corporation, was installing a water and sewer system in the town of North Pole, Alaska. The order for the pipe stated the size and quantity and specified that the pipe had to be "coal tar enamel lined." The pipe could not withstand the intense cold, and before the pipelines could be constructed, the enamel lining had pulled away from the pipe. Lewis and Sims then sued the suppliers of the original pipe for damages for breach of warranty of fitness for a particular purpose. Can it recover? [Lewis and Sims, Inc. v Key Industries, Inc., 557 P2d 1318]

CPA Questions

1. Under the UCC Sales Article, the warranty of title may be excluded by
   a. Merchants or nonmerchants, provided the exclusion is in writing
   b. Nonmerchant sellers only
   c. The seller's statement that it is selling only such right or title that it has
   d. Use of an "as is" disclaimer

2. Which of the following factors result(s) in an express warranty with respect to a sale of goods?
   I. The seller's description of the goods is part of the basis of the bargain.
   II. The seller selects goods knowing the buyer's intended use.
   a. I only
   b. II only
   c. Both I and II
   d. Neither I nor II

3. Morgan is suing the manufacturer, wholesaler, and retailer for bodily injuries caused by a power saw Morgan purchased. Which of the following statements is correct under the theory of strict liability?
   a. The manufacturer will avoid liability if it can show it followed the custom of the industry.
   b. Morgan may recover even if he cannot show any negligence was involved.
   c. Contributory negligence on Morgan's part will always be a bar to recovery.
   d. Privity will be a bar to recovery insofar as the wholesaler is concerned if the wholesaler did not have a reasonable opportunity to inspect.

4. On May 2, Handy Hardware sent Ram Industries a signed purchase order that stated, in part: "Ship for May 8 delivery 300 Model A-X socket sets at current dealer price. Terms 2/10/net 30." Ram received Handy's purchase order on May 4. On May 5, Ram discovered that it had only 200 Model A-X socket sets and 100 Model W-Z socket sets in stock. Ram shipped the Model A-X and Model W-Z sets to Handy without any explanation concerning the shipment. The socket sets were received by Handy on May 8. Assuming a contract exists between Handy and Ram, which of the following implied warranties would result?
   I. Implied warranty of merchantability
   II. Implied warranty of fitness for a particular purpose
   III. Implied warranty of title
   a. I only
   b. III only
   c. I and III only
   d. I, II, and III

OBLIGATIONS AND PERFORMANCE

CHAPTER (26)

A. General Principles

1. Obligation of Good Faith
2. Time Requirements of Obligations
3. Repudiation of the Contract
4. Adequate Assurance of Performance

B. Duties of the Parties

5. Seller's Duty to Deliver
6. Buyer's Duty upon Receipt of Goods
7. Buyer's Duty to Accept Goods
8. Buyer's Duty to Pay
9. When Duties Are Excused

LEARNING OBJECTIVES

After studying this chapter, you should be able to

LO.1 Define the obligation of good faith as applied to merchants and nonmerchants

LO.2 List the steps that can be taken when a party to a sales contract feels insecure about the other party's performance

LO.3 Explain the obligations of the seller and the buyer in a sales contract

LO.4 Identify the types of actions and conduct that constitute acceptance

Contracts for the sale of goods impose both obligations and requirements for performance on the parties.

A. General Principles

Each party to a sales contract is bound to perform according to the terms of the contract. Each is likewise under a duty to exercise **good faith** in the contract's performance and to do nothing that would impair the other party's expectation that the contract will be performed.

1. Obligation of Good Faith

Every contract or duty within the Uniform Commercial Code (UCC) imposes an obligation of good faith in its performance or enforcement.[1] The UCC defines good faith as "honesty in fact in the conduct or transaction concerned."[2] In the case of a merchant seller or buyer of goods, the UCC carries the concept of good faith further. The UCC imposes the additional requirement that merchants observe "reasonable commercial standards of fair dealing in the trade."[3] Section 1-203 of the UCC provides, "Every contract or duty within this Act imposes an obligation of good faith in its performance or enforcement."[4]

2. Time Requirements of Obligations

In a cash sale that does not require delivery of the goods, the duties of the seller and buyer are concurrent. Each one has the right to demand that the other perform at the same time. That is, as the seller hands over the goods, the buyer hands over the purchase money. If either party refuses to act, the other party has the right to withhold performance. In self-service stores, the performance occurs simultaneously—the buyer pays as the items are bagged at checkout.

In other types of contracts, there may be blocks of time between when the parties enter into an agreement and when performance, either delivery or payment, is due. During those time periods, buyers may become concerned about the ability of a seller experiencing a labor strike to complete production of the goods ordered in the contract. A seller may feel that a buyer who is experiencing credit difficulties may not be able to pay for the goods. Article 2 covers these periods of time and the conduct of the parties after the contract is entered into but before performance is due.

3. Repudiation of the Contract

If the seller or the buyer refuses to perform the contract when the time for performance arises, a **repudiation** of the contract results. Often, before the time for performance arrives, a party to the contract may inform the other that she will not perform the terms of the contract. This repudiation made in advance of the time for performance is called an **anticipatory repudiation.**[5] Under Revised Article 2, repudiation occurs when the party furnishes a *record* (as noted in other chapters, a term that allows for e-mails) including "language that a reasonable party would interpret to mean that the other party will not or cannot make a performance still due under the contract" or when the party exhibits "voluntary, affirmative conduct that would appear to a reasonable party to make a future performance by the other party impossible."[6]

4. Adequate Assurance of Performance

This time between contracting and actual performance may see some developing events that cause the parties concern about the ability of each to perform.[7] **For Example,** if the seller's warehouse is destroyed by fire, the buyer might conclude that the seller might not be able to make a delivery scheduled for the following month. Whenever a party to a sales contract has reasonable grounds to be concerned about the future performance of the other party, a demand may be made in a record for *assurance* that the contract will be performed.[8] **For Example,** a seller who

[1] UCC § 1-203; *Potomac Plaza Terraces, Inc. v QSC Products, Inc.*, 868 F Supp 346 (DDC 1994).

[2] UCC § 1-201(19); *Kotis v Nowlin Jewelry, Inc.*, 844 SW2d 920 (Tex App 1992). Revised UCC adds "observance of reasonable commercial standards of fair dealing" as part of good faith.

[3] UCC § 2-103(1)(b); *Amoco Oil Co. v Ervin*, 908 P2d 493 (Colo 1995); *El Paso Natural Gas Co. v Minco Oil & Gas Co.*, 964 SW2d 54 (Tex App 1998); *General Electric Co. v Compagnie Euralair*, 945 F Supp 527 (SDNY 1996).

[4] UCC § 1-203.

[5] UCC § 2-610; *Aero Consulting Corp. v Cessna Aircraft Co.*, 867 F Supp 1480 (D Kan 1994).

[6] Revised UCC § 2-610. This change incorporates the definition of repudiation from both the existing comments to § 2-610 as well as the language from the Restatement of Contracts § 250.

[7] UCC § 2-609.

[8] *S & S, Inc. v Meyer*, 478 NW2d 857 (Iowa App 1991).

is concerned about a buyer's ability to pay for goods could demand an updated credit report, financial statement, or even additional security or payment.

(a) Form of Assurance

The person on whom demand for assurance is made must give "such assurance of due performance as is adequate under the circumstances of the particular case."[9] The UCC does not specify the exact form of assurance. If the party on whom demand is made has an established reputation, a reaffirmation of the contract obligation and a statement that it will be performed may be sufficient to assure a reasonable person that it will be performed. In contrast, if the party's reputation or economic position at the time is such that mere words and promises would not give any real assurance, it may be necessary to have a third person (or an insurance company) guarantee performance or to put up property as security for performance.

(b) Failure to Give Assurance

If adequate assurance is not given within 30 days from the time of demand, the demanding party may treat the contract as repudiated. The party demanding assurances may then proceed as if there were a breach and may pursue damage remedies. The nonbreaching party also has the right to enter into a substitute contract with a third person to obtain goods contracted for under the now-broken contract.

HORNELL BREWING CO., INC., V SPRY, 664 NYS2D 698 (SUP CT 1997)

THE EVAPORATING LINES OF CREDIT FOR THE BEVERAGE DISTRIBUTOR

Hornell Brewing Company, Inc. (plaintiff or Hornell), is a supplier and marketer of alcoholic and nonalcoholic beverages, including the popular iced tea drink "Arizona." In 1992, Stephen A. Spry approached Don Vultaggio, Hornell's chairman of the board, about becoming a distributor for Hornell's beverages. In January 1993, Spry presented Vultaggio with a most ambitious plan for distributing Hornell beverages in Canada. Based on the proposed plan and Vultaggio's understanding of Spry's stellar reputation as a distributor, Hornell granted Spry the exclusive rights to distribute Arizona products in Canada. Spry formed a Canadian corporation, Arizona Iced Tea, Ltd. (defendants), for the sole purpose of distributing these products.

The initial arrangement was an oral agreement, and in response to Spry's request for a letter he needed in order to secure financing, Hornell provided a letter that confirmed the distributorship arrangement but which contained no other details. Hornell had agreements with its other distributors, but this arrangement was unique in its lack of paperwork.

During 1993 and 1994, Hornell shipped beverages on 10-day credit terms, but between December of 1993 and February of 1994, Spry's credit balances grew from $20,000 to $100,000, and a $31,000 check from Spry was returned for insufficient funds.

In March 1994, Hornell demanded that Spry obtain a line and/or letter of credit to pay for the beverages in order to place their relationship on more secure footing. Vanguard Financial did send a letter to Spry confirming a "$1,500,000 revolving credit facility," but it never evolved into an actual line of credit. Following a meeting with Spry, during which a factor (Metro Factors, Inc.) was brought in by telephone, Vultaggio demanded that Spry pay all of his arrears and then obtain a $300,000 line of credit or the shipments of the products would not be continued. Vultaggio confirmed these terms in a letter. The deadline for the payment of arrears (April 19, 1994) passed with no payment and no response until April 25, 1994, when Spry proposed that a company named "Metro" pay the amount due of $79,316.24 by May 2, 1994.

[9] UCC § 2-609(4).

Hornell received no payment on May 2, 1994. It did receive a wire transfer from Metro of the full amount on May 9, 1994. Upon immediate confirmation of that payment, Spry ordered 30 trailer loads of "product" from Hornell, at a total purchase price of $390,000 to $450,000. In the interim between April 25, 1994, and May 9, 1994, Hornell learned from several sources, including its regional sales manager Baumkel, that Spry's warehouse was empty, that he had no managerial, sales, or office staff, that he had no trucks, and that in effect his operation was a sham.

On May 10, 1994, Hornell wrote to Spry, acknowledging receipt of payment and confirming that they would extend up to $300,000 of credit to him, net 14 days cash "based on your prior representation that you have secured a $1,500,000 U.S. line of credit."

Spry did not respond to this letter. Spry never sent Hornell a copy of his agreement with Metro Factors, Inc., which Spry had signed on March 24, 1994, and which was fully executed on March 30, 1994. On May 26, 1994, Vultaggio met with Spry to discuss termination of their business relationship. Vultaggio presented Spry with a letter of agreement as to the termination, which Spry took with him but did not sign. After some months of futile negotiations by counsel, Hornell filed suit.

Judicial Opinion

LOUISE GRUNER GANS, J. . . . At the outset, the court determines that an enforceable contract existed between plaintiff and defendants based on the uncontroverted facts of their conduct. Under Article 2 of the Uniform Commercial Code, parties can form a contract through their conduct rather than merely through the exchange of communications constituting an offer and acceptance.

Both parties' undisputed actions over a period of many months clearly manifested mutual recognition that a binding obligation was undertaken.

Notwithstanding the parties' conflicting contentions concerning the duration and termination of defendants' distributorship, plaintiff has demonstrated a basis for lawfully terminating its contract with defendants in accordance with section 2-609 of the Uniform Commercial Code. Section 2-609 authorizes one party upon "reasonable grounds for insecurity" to "demand adequate assurance of due performance and until he receive such assurance . . . , if commercially reasonable, suspend performance for which he has not already received the agreed return."

Whether a seller, as the plaintiff in this case, has reasonable grounds for insecurity is an issue of fact that depends upon various factors, including the buyer's exact words or actions, the course of dealing or performance between the parties, and the nature of the sales contract and the industry.

Once the seller correctly determines that it has reasonable grounds for insecurity, it must properly request assurances from the buyer. Although the Code requires that the request be made in writing, UCC § 2-609(1), courts have not strictly adhered to this formality as long as an unequivocal demand is made. After demanding assurance, the seller must determine the proper "adequate assurance." What constitutes "adequate" assurance of due performance is subject to the same test of commercial reasonableness and factual conditions.

Applying these principles to the case at bar, the overwhelming weight of the evidence establishes that at the latest by the beginning of 1994, plaintiff had reasonable grounds to be insecure about defendants' ability to perform in the future. Defendants were substantially in arrears almost from the outset of their relationship with plaintiff, had no financing in place, bounced checks, and had failed to sell even a small fraction of the product defendant Spry originally projected.

Reasonable grounds for insecurity can arise from the sole fact that a buyer has fallen behind in his account with the seller, even where the items involved have to do with separate and legally distinct contracts, because this "impairs the seller's expectation of due performance."

Here, defendants do not dispute their poor payment history, plaintiff's right to demand adequate assurances from them and that plaintiff made such demands. Rather, defendants claim that they satisfied those demands by the April 15, 1994 telephone conversation between Vultaggio and Richard Worthy of Metro Factors, Inc., followed by Vultaggio's April 18, 1994 letter to Metro, and Metro's payment of $79,316.24 to Hornell, and that thereafter plaintiff had no right to demand further assurance. The court disagrees with both plaintiff and defendants in their insistence that only one demand for adequate assurance was made in this case to which there was and could be only a single response. Even accepting defendants' argument that payment by Metro was the sole condition Vultaggio required when he spoke and wrote to Metro, and that such condition was met by Metro's actual payment, the court is persuaded that on May 9, 1994, Hornell had further reasonable grounds for insecurity and a new basis for seeking further adequate assurances.

Here, there was a further change of circumstances. Vultaggio's reported conversation with Worthy on April 15 and his April 25 letter to Metro, both anticipate that once payment of defendants' arrears was made, Hornell would release ***up to*** $300,000 worth of product on the further condition that defendants met the 14 day payment terms. The arrangement, by its terms, clearly contemplated an opportunity for Hornell to test out defendants' ability to make payment within 14-day periods.

By placing a single order worth $390,000 to $450,000 immediately after receipt of Metro's payment, Spry not only demanded a shipment of product which exceeded the proposed limit, but placed Hornell in a position where it would have ***no*** opportunity to learn whether Spry would meet the 14-day payment terms, before Spry again became indebted to Hornell for a very large sum of money. These circumstances, coupled with information received in early May (on which it reasonably relied) that Spry had mislead Hornell about the scope of his operation, created new and more acute grounds for Hornell's insecurity and entitled Hornell to seek further adequate assurance from defendants in the form of a documented line of credit or other guarantee. Defendants' failure to respond constituted a repudiation of the distributorship agreement, which entitled plaintiff to suspend performance and terminate the agreement.

The court notes in conclusion that its evaluation of the evidence in this case was significantly influenced by Mr. Spry's regrettable lack of credibility. The court agrees with plaintiff, that to an extent far greater than was known to Hornell in May 1994, Mr. Spry was not truthful, failed to pay countless other creditors almost as a matter of course, and otherwise engaged in improper and deceptive business practices.

For the foregoing reasons, it is hereby ORDERED and ADJUDGED that plaintiff Hornell Brewing Co., Inc. have a declaratory judgment that defendants Stephen A. Spry and Arizona Tea Products, Ltd. were duly terminated and have no continuing rights with respect to plaintiff Hornell Brewing Co.'s beverage products in Canada or elsewhere.

Questions

1. What type of assurances did Hornell want?
2. Do you think Hornell was reasonable in its time demands and types of assurances?
3. Was there a breach of contract?

B. Duties of the Parties

The obligations of the parties to a sales contract include (1) the seller's duty to deliver the goods, (2) the buyer's duty to accept the goods, and (3) the buyer's duty to pay for the goods.

5. Seller's Duty to Deliver

The seller has the duty to deliver the goods according to the terms of the contract.

(a) Place, Time, and Manner of Delivery

The terms of the contract determine whether the seller is to send the goods or the buyer is to call for them and whether the goods are to be transported from the seller to the buyer or the transaction is to be completed by the delivery of documents without the movement of the goods. In the absence of a provision in the contract or a contrary course of performance or usage of trade, the place of delivery is the seller's place of business if the seller has one; otherwise, it is the seller's residence. (See Chapter 24 for more details on delivery and shipping terms.)[10] However, if the subject matter of the contract consists of identified goods that are known by the parties to be in some other place, that place is the place of delivery. If no time for shipment or delivery is stated, delivery or shipment is required within a reasonable time.

When a method of transportation called for by the contract becomes unavailable or commercially unreasonable, the seller must make delivery by means of a commercially reasonable substitute if available.

(b) Quantity Delivered

The buyer has the right to insist that all the goods be delivered at one time. If the seller delivers a smaller

[10] UCC § 2-308.

or larger quantity than what is stipulated in the contract, the buyer may refuse to accept the goods.[11]

6. Buyer's Duty upon Receipt of Goods

The buyer must accept goods that conform to the contract, and the refusal to do so is a breach of the contract. However, the buyer has certain rights prior to acceptance.

CPA (a) Right to Examine Goods—The Buyer's Right of Inspection[12]

To determine whether the goods in fact conform to the contract, the buyer has the right to examine the goods when tendered by the seller. An exception to this rule occurs when goods are sent COD. In a COD shipment, the buyer has no right to examine the goods until payment is made.

The buyer's right of inspection includes the right to remove goods from cartons and to conduct tests. **For Example,** a buyer who is purchasing potatoes for use in making potato chips has the right to peel and test a portion of the potatoes to determine whether they are the appropriate type for "chipping."

(b) Right to Refuse or Return the Goods—The Buyer's Right of Rejection[13]

If the goods the seller has tendered do not conform to the contract in any way, the buyer can *reject* the goods. **For Example,** the buyer may reject a mobile home when it does not contain an air conditioner with the capacity specified by the contract. The buyer may reject the goods if they are not perfect.[14] The standard for rejection does not require that the defect in the goods or the breach be material. **For Example,** a small pressure mark on an ottoman is not material; the ottoman will function just as well. However, the buyer still has the right to reject the ottoman because it has a defect.

The buyer has the right to reject the full shipment, accept the full shipment and seek damages for the goods' diminished value (see Chapter 27), or accept any commercial units and reject the remainder. Commercial units are defined by trade and industry according to the customary size of cartons or containers for the goods shipped. Envelopes come in **commercial units** of boxes of 500. Computer disks often come in packages of 20 or 50. Rejection by a buyer would be not of individual envelopes or disks but of boxes. **For Example,** if Donna purchased a package of 20 disks and 4 of the 20 disks were defective, Donna would return the box of 20 disks for a new box. Rejection and acceptance in commercial units prevent the problems created when a seller has to open other units and mix and match goods in each.

After rejecting the goods, the buyer may not exercise any right of ownership over the goods.

The buyer's rejection must be made within a reasonable time after the delivery or tender of the goods. The buyer must notify the seller of the rejection and, in transactions with merchants particularly, provide the seller with the reason for the rejection.[15]

CPA (c) Cure of Defective Tender or Delivery

The reason for the notification of rejection to the seller by the buyer is that the UCC gives a right of cure to the seller if the seller tenders or delivers nonconforming goods. The buyer's rejection is not an end to the transaction. The seller is given a second chance, or a **right to cure,** to make a proper tender of conforming goods.[16]

This right of cure means that the buyer must give notice of rejection and the reason for that rejection, if the seller has the right, but not necessarily the intent, to cure. That is, the seller has the right to cure if the seller is able to make the cure within the time remaining under the contract. If the time for making delivery under the contract has not expired, the seller

11 UCC § 2-307; Seller must not cause damage during delivery. *Kaghann's Korner, Inc. v Brown & Sons Fuel Co., Inc.*, 706 NE 2d 556 (Ind App 1999).

12 UCC § 2-601.

13 UCC § 2-602; *In re S.M. Acquisition Co.*, 319 BR 553 (ND Ill 2005).

14 Revised UCC eliminates the word "rightful" from the title of § 2-601, clarifying a point the drafters thought important: A buyer has the right of rejection even if it is wrongful and a breach of contract. The title "Manner and Effect of Rightful Rejection" has now been changed to "Manner and Effect of Rejection." *Precision Mirror & Glass v Nelms*, 797 NYS 2d 720 (2005).

15 UCC § 2-602(1); *Loden v Drake*, 881 P2d 467 (Colo App 1994). Revised UCC makes significant changes for rejection and buyers' rights regarding notifying or the failure to notify the seller of the rejection and the reasons for that rejection. *Adams v Wacaster Oil Co., Inc.*, 98 SW 3d 832, 50 UCC Rep Serv 2d (West) 774 (Ark Ct App 2003).

16 *Allied Semi-Conductors Int'l v Pulsar Components Int'l, Inc.*, 907 F Supp 618 (EDNY 1995). The seller's right to cure is expanded under Revised Article 2 (§ 2-709) in that the seller can cure whether there is acceptance or rejection by the buyer.

WEIL V MURRAY, 161 F SUPP 2D 250 (SDNY 2001)

LEAVING THE SELLERS HANGING ON A PAINTING: BRUSHING OFF REJECTION

Mark Murray and Ian Peck are art dealers who own separate art galleries located at 980 Madison Avenue, New York, New York. Robert and Jean Weil (plaintiffs) reside in Montgomery, Alabama, and are art collectors. Murray and Sam Lehr, a business acquaintance of his, traveled to Montgomery to see the various paintings in the Weils' collection, including a painting by Edgar Degas titled "Aux Courses" (the "Degas"), which Murray examined under ultraviolet light.

Murray telephoned Weil and told him that he had spoken with someone who might be interested in purchasing the Degas. On November 3, 1997, the director of Murray's gallery, Stephanie Calman, traveled to Weil's home in Alabama. Calman, on behalf of Murray, and Weil executed an agreement that provided for consignment of the Degas to Murray's gallery "for a private inspection in New York for a period of a week" from November 3, "to be extended only with the express permission of the consignor." Calman returned to New York with the painting the same day.

Murray then showed the Degas to Peck. Peck acknowledges only that he expressed an interest in purchasing the Degas after seeing it and that the price of $1,125,000 was discussed. Murray asserts that on or before November 8, 1997, he agreed with Peck that Peck would purchase the painting for $1,125,000 with Murray "acting as a broker."

On November 8, 1997, Murray called Weil to inform him that he had a buyer for the Degas, and the two orally agreed to the sale. The agreement subsequently was confirmed in writing. Peck's attorney wrote the first draft. Murray retyped that draft, changing the references to the buyer from Peck to Murray and changing the purchase price from $1,125,000 to $1 million. Murray then forwarded the draft to Weil. Weil responded with an alternative version. Murray retyped Weil's version on Mark Murray Fine Paintings letterhead. On November 26, 1997, Murray signed the agreement drafted by Weil and retyped on Murray's letterhead. Weil signed the agreement on December 1, 1997.

The signed agreement defines the "buyer" as Mark Murray; the "sellers" are defined as Jean K. Weil and Robert S. Weil, Partners Weil Brothers.

Neither Murray nor anyone else ever paid Weil the $1 million. Nonetheless, Murray maintained possession of the Degas from November 3, 1997, through March 25, 1998, when Weil requested its return.

At some point before its return to Weil, the Degas was sent to Juan Perdiguero, an art conservator. Although Murray claims the painting was sent at Peck's request, Peck asserts that he and Murray "collectively" went to Perdiguero. A "condition report" prepared by Perdiguero and dated December 3, 1997, showed that Perdiguero sought to correct the alleged deterioration of the painting. Peck paid for Perdiguero's work. Weil first become aware of this work in March 1998. The Weils filed suit seeking the price for the painting via summary judgment.

Judicial Opinion

II. MUKASEY, District Judge.... To recover on an action for the price pursuant to Section 2-709(1)(a) of the New York Uniform Commercial Code, plaintiffs must show that 1) they had a contract; 2) the buyer failed to pay the purchase price; and 3) the buyer accepted the goods.

Although plaintiffs and Murray do not dispute the existence of an agreement, they do dispute the extent of Murray's obligations pursuant to it.

Plaintiffs have established also the remaining elements of their action for the price pursuant to Section 2-709(1)(a) of the New York Uniform Commercial Code. Section 2-709(1)(a) provides that "[w]hen the buyer fails to pay the price as it becomes due the seller may recover, together with any incidental damages under the next section, the price of goods accepted...." N.Y. U.C.C. § 2-709(1)(a) (McKinney 1993).

The undisputed facts establish also that Murray accepted the Degas. As noted above, Murray first inspected the Degas under an ultraviolet light when he viewed it at the Weils' home in late October. Murray had the opportunity to further examine the Degas at his gallery in New York pursuant to the consignment agreement and his continued possession of the painting following the expiration of the consignment agreement. It is also undisputed that Murray was present when Simon Parkes assessed the condition of the painting sometime between November 3 and November 19, 1997. Not only did Murray have a reasonable time to inspect the goods, but also it is undisputed that he actually did inspect the Degas. There is no evidence that Murray found the painting unsatisfactory or non-conforming. Although the question of whether the buyer has had a reasonable time to inspect is generally a question for the trier of fact, no reasonable jury could find that Murray did not accept the Degas in light of the undisputed facts that he inspected the Degas on at least two occasions, signed the written agreement, and continued to retain possession of the Degas.

Moreover, it is undisputed that, without Weil's consent, Murray, at a minimum, permitted the painting to be cleaned and restored in late November or early December. Murray's participation in the alteration of the painting, regardless of whether such alteration increased its value, was an act inconsistent with plaintiffs' ownership. Plaintiffs have established that Murray agreed to purchase the Degas, accepted it, and nonetheless failed to pay the purchase price.

The return of the painting to Weil and his current possession of the Degas do not preclude a finding that plaintiffs are entitled to the contract price. Section 2-709(2) of the New York Uniform Commercial Code provides for a seller's retention of goods. The statute requires only that "the net proceeds of any... resale must be credited to the buyer and payment of the judgment entitles [the buyer] to any goods not resold."

Plaintiffs are entitled to the contract price of $1 million and any incidental damages. Incidental damages include prejudgment interest, which, in a diversity case, is controlled by the rule of the jurisdiction whose law controls liability. Plaintiffs are entitled to a judgment of $1,298,849.31. Upon payment of the judgment, Murray is entitled to the Degas. Summary judgment for the Weils.

Questions

1. Describe how long the buyers had the painting and what they did with it.
2. Why is sending the painting back to the Weils not enough to remedy the situation?
3. What acts are inconsistent with rejection?

E-COMMERCE AND CYBERLAW

REJECTION IN CYBERSPACE

Rejection of computers and software present novel issues for the UCC provisions on rejection because use of the goods is not so easily defined or distinguished by a bright line. With software, for example, the buyer can use the software as a means of conducting an inspection of the goods. However, fully loading the software constitutes acceptance, and the buyer would then step into the UCC provisions on revocation of acceptance, as opposed to rejection. If the software causes the buyer's computer to "crash" every 10 minutes, the buyer has grounds for either rejection or revocation of acceptance. The buyer could also agree to allow the seller to modify the software to prevent the "crashing" problems. Once the buyer decides to reject the software or revoke acceptance of it, he or she cannot continue to use the software, for such use is inconsistent with the claim that the goods (the software) fail to conform to the contract.*

A buyer is also permitted to test a computer for purposes of inspection and rejection. If, however, the buyer rejects the computer system, it cannot continue to use the system, and allowing third parties to make alterations to the system to help it function better constitutes acceptance.**

* *Cooperative Resources, Inc. v Dynasty Software, Inc.*, 39 UCC Rep Serv 2d 101 (NH Dist Ct 1998).

** *Softa Group, Inc. v Scarsdale Development*, 632 NE2d 13 (Ill App 1993) (using a computer the buyer claims was "defective from inception" is inconsistent with rejection and the required basis for a rejection). *Licitra v Gateway, Inc.*, 189 Misc2d 721, 734 NYS2d 389, 47 UCC Rep Serv 2d 59 (2001).

need only give the buyer **seasonable** (timely) notice of the intention to make a proper delivery within the time allowed by the contract. Under Revised Article 2, the seller also has the right of cure if the time for making the delivery has expired through the allowance of additional reasonable time in which to make a substitute conforming tender. Such additional time is allowed if (1) the seller so notifies the buyer and (2) the seller had acted reasonably in making the original tender, believing that it would be acceptable to the buyer.[17] Under Revised UCC, installment contracts are also governed under this rule.

7. Buyer's Duty to Accept Goods

Assuming that the buyer has no grounds to reject the goods after inspection, the next step in the performance of the contract is the buyer's **acceptance** of the goods.

CPA (a) What Constitutes Acceptance of Goods[18]

Acceptance of goods means that the buyer, pursuant to a contract, has, either expressly or by implication, taken the goods permanently. The buyer's statement of acceptance is an express acceptance. A buyer can accept goods by implication if there is no rejection after a reasonable opportunity to inspect them or within a reasonable time after the buyer has inspected them. Another form of acceptance by implication is conduct by the buyer that is inconsistent with rejection, as when a buyer uses or sells the delivered goods.[19]

A buyer accepts goods by making continued use of them and by not attempting to return them. A buyer also accepts goods by modifying them because such action is inconsistent with a rejection or with the continued ownership of the goods by the seller.[20]

CPA (b) Revocation of Acceptance

Even after acceptance of the goods, the performance under the contract may not be finished if the buyer exercises the right to revoke acceptance of the goods.[21] The buyer may revoke acceptance of the goods when they do not conform to the contract, the defect is such that it substantially impairs the value of the contract to the buyer, and either the defect is such that the buyer could not discover the problem or the seller has promised to correct a problem the buyer was aware of and pointed out to the seller prior to acceptance.[22] **For Example,** a buyer who purchased an emergency electric power generator found that the generator produced only about 65 percent of the power called for by the contract. This amount of power was insufficient for the operation of the buyer's electrical equipment. The seller's repeated attempts to improve the generator's output failed. The buyer, despite having used the generator for three months, could revoke his acceptance of it because its value was substantially impaired and he continued to keep it and use it only because of the seller's assurances that it would be repaired.

Substantial impairment is a higher standard than the one of "fails to conform in any respect" for rejection. Substantial impairment requires proof of more than the mere fact that the goods do not conform to the contract. The buyer is not required to show that the goods are worthless but must prove that their use to the buyer is substantially different from what the contract promised.

A revocation of acceptance is not a cancellation of the contract with the seller. After revocation of acceptance, the buyer can choose from the remedies available for breach of contract or demand that the seller deliver conforming goods. (See Chapter 27 for more information on remedies for breach.)

(c) Notification of Revocation of Acceptance

To revoke acceptance properly, the buyer must take certain steps. The buyer must give the seller notice of revocation. The revocation of acceptance is effective when the buyer notifies the seller. The buyer need not actually return the goods to make the notification or the revocation effective.

The notice of revocation of acceptance must be given within a reasonable time after the buyer discovers

[17] This right to cure after the time for performance has expired exists in nonconsumer contracts only.

[18] UCC § 2-606; *Stenzel; Dell, Inc.*, 870 A2d 133 (ME 2005).

[19] *Fabrica de Tejidos Imperial v Brandon Apparel Group, Inc.*, 218 F Supp 2d 974 (ND Ill 2002).

[20] Under Revised Article 2 (§ 2-706), the buyer is deemed to have accepted goods even if the buyer communicates acceptance to the seller before inspection. UCC § 2-606(1)(a), (b), and (c).

[21] UCC § 2-608; *Fode v Capital RV Center, Inc.*, 575 NW2d 682 (ND 1998).

[22] Repeated requests for service satisfy the requirement for notifying the seller. *Cliffstar Corp. v Elmar Industries, Inc.*, 678 NYS2d 222 (1998).

or should have discovered the problems with the goods. The right of revocation is not lost if the buyer gives the seller a longer period of time to correct the defects in the goods.[23] Even the lapse of a year will not cost the buyer the right of revocation of acceptance if the seller has been experimenting during that time trying to correct the problems with the goods.

JACKSON HOLE TRADERS, INC., V JOSEPH, 931 P2D 244 (WYO 1997)

JACKSON HOLE TRADERS: THE RETAILER LOOKING FOR A LOOP HOLE

Catherine Joseph, who does business as Metro Classics (appellee), sold clothing to Jackson Hole Traders, Inc., a corporation owned by David and Elizabeth Speaks (appellants). Jackson Hole Traders is located in Jackson, Wyoming, and sells clothing for men and women through a retail store and mail-order catalog business. The clothing Joseph sold was specially manufactured for Jackson Hole Traders and had a total contract price of $50,000, with terms being net 30.

When the clothing items were shipped between July and September 1994, approximately 900 items were sent. Elizabeth Speaks complained about the quality on some of the clothing items when they arrived and was given a credit of $1,096 for returned merchandise. However, Jackson Hole Traders did not pay $32,000 of the total Joseph bill despite it being well past the net-30-day period for payment. When Joseph demanded payment, Elizabeth Speaks boxed up approximately 350 items of the clothing and sent them back, demanding a credit for revocation of acceptance. Joseph filed suit for payment alleging that it was too late for revocation of acceptance. The trial court found for Joseph, and the Speakses appealed.

Judicial Opinion

MACY, J. . . . Appellants claim that the trial court improperly concluded that the Uniform Commercial Code governed the parties' transaction, arguing that this transaction was principally one for labor and services. Appellee counters that the trial court appropriately applied the Uniform Commercial Code to this transaction because it was for the sale of goods.

For support of their proposition that this transaction was one for services rather than for goods, Appellants rely on *Wells v 10-X Manufacturing Company*, 609 F.2d 248 (6th Cir.1979). That case, however, differs from the case at bar because the buyer in ***Wells*** furnished the manufacturer with virtually everything but the labor.

Although Appellants purchased and supplied the outer fabric for some of the garments produced by Appellee, Appellee supplied all the other materials which were used to manufacture the garments; i.e., buttons, linings, interfacing, special care labels, as well as the outer fabric for the remaining garments. Some garments were patterned from Appellee's own designs. Even for those styles which utilized a design provided by Appellants, Appellee and her pattern maker had to restyle them because of various changes which were requested by Appellants. Each pattern was then graded into the particular sizes to be used for that garment. Under the facts of this case, the trial court correctly applied the Uniform Commercial Code as this transaction was one for the sale of goods even though labor was involved in producing the goods.

David Speaks gave the following testimony:

[APPELLEE'S ATTORNEY:] Now, I sent you a letter dated December 9 asking for thirty-two thousand dollars for [Appellee], did I not?

A. Yes, you did.

Q. And your response was to pack up 350 garments that she had manufactured at your request and ship them back in bulk to her, wasn't it?

A. That's what we did, yes.

. . . .

[Q.] Now, the goods that you shipped back to [Appellee], you instructed—either you or Ms. Speaks instructed someone working for you to take the goods off of the showroom floor and box

23 A buyer who took her pop-up camper in for repairs but was then given a different camper without being told about it was entitled to revoke her acceptance. *Head v Phillips Camper Sales & Rental, Inc.*, 593 NW2d 595 (Mich Ct App 1999).

them up and send them back. Some of the goods that were returned to [Appellee] were pulled off the showroom floor, weren't they?

A. Most likely, yes. I'm almost positive, yeah.

Q. And some of those items were pulled off the shelves where they had been stored for several months, weren't they?

A. You're talking about in the warehouse?

Q. Yes.

A. Yes, they were.

. . . .

Q. If you don't think the goods got there on time and you think that you have been put in a bad way as a result of that, you can refuse the shipment, can't you?

A. You can refuse the shipment, yes, you can. That is one option.

Q. And you could have done that, couldn't you?

A. That's an option, yes.

Q. But you didn't refuse the shipment, did you?

A. No, we did not.

Q. And you put the goods in your warehouse, didn't you?

A. Yes, they were in the warehouse.

Q. And put them on your showroom floor, didn't you?

A. Yes, we did.

Q. And you sold them through your catalog; is that right?

A. Yes, we did.

Q. And you sold many of them in your store, didn't you?

A. Yes, we did.

. . . .

[Q.] When I sent you the letter on December 9th asking for payment of the thirty-two thousand plus dollars owed to [Appellee], your response within 72 hours was to take everything and ship it back to [Appellee]; is that correct?

A. Yes, it was.

Appellants breached the contract when they failed to pay for the garments which had been sent to them and which they had accepted for resale. The trial court properly awarded damages in an amount which would place Appellee in the same position that she would have occupied had the contract been performed.

[Affirmed]

Questions

1. How long had the goods been with the buyer?
2. Where were the goods when they were packaged to be sent back?
3. Will the seller get her money?

THINKING THINGS THROUGH

WHAT TO DO WHEN YOU WANTED FLAKES AND GOT CHUNKS INSTEAD

Scotwood, a wholesaler, sells calcium chloride flake to suppliers, including Miller and Sons, for use in ice melt products. In 2004, Miller and Sons ordered from Scotwood a large number of bags of 74–75 percent calcium chloride flake. From July 19, 2004, until September 3, 2004, Scotwood delivered 37 shipments of calcium chloride flake to Miller and Sons' warehouse. Following each delivery, Scotwood forwarded to Miller and Sons an invoice listing numerous "Terms and Conditions," including paragraph 8(a), which limited the time for bringing any claims against Scotwood.

Although it paid 35 of the 37 invoices for the 37 shipments it received, Miller and Sons was not happy with the deliveries because the calcium chloride flake was substantially defective. The bags it was delivered in were ripped and the calcium chloride flake in the bags was chunked. Miller and Sons was forced to conduct the labor-intensive process of sorting the chunked calcium chloride from the usable flakes in the shipments it received from Scotwood.

What did they do that constituted rejection? What did they do that constituted acceptance? What should Miller and Sons have done? [Scotwood Industries, Inc. v Frank Miller & Sons, Inc., 453 F Supp 2d 1160 (D Kan 2006)]

ETHICS & THE LAW

At Saks Fifth Avenue, they call it the "return season." Return season occurs within the week following a major fund-raising formal dance. Women who have purchased formal evening wear return the dresses after the dance. The dresses have been worn, and the tags have been cut, but the women return the dresses with requests for a full refund. Neiman Marcus also experiences the same phenomenon of returns.

Some stores have implemented a policy that formal evening wear may not be returned if the tags are cut from it. Others require a return within a limited period of seven days. Others offer an exchange only after five days.

Are the women covered by a right of rejection under Article 2? What do you think of the conduct of the women? Is it simply revocation of acceptance? Is there good faith on the part of the women?

(d) Buyer's Responsibilities upon Revocation of Acceptance

After a revocation of acceptance, the buyer must hold the goods and await instructions from the seller. If the buyer revokes acceptance after having paid the seller in advance, the buyer may retain possession of the goods as security for the refund of the money that has been paid.

8. Buyer's Duty to Pay

The buyer must pay the amount stated in the sales contract for accepted goods.

(a) Time of Payment

The sales contract may require payment in advance or may give the buyer credit by postponing the time for payment.[24]

(b) Form of Payment

Unless otherwise agreed, payment by the buyer requires payment in cash. The seller may accept a check or a promissory note from the buyer. If the check is not paid by the bank, the purchase price remains unpaid. A promissory note payable at a future date gives the buyer credit by postponing the time for payment.

The seller can refuse to accept a check or a promissory note as payment for goods but must give the buyer reasonable time in which to obtain legal tender with which to make payment.

CPA 9. When Duties Are Excused

Under Article 2, the doctrine of commercial impracticability is available as a defense to performance of a contract. The doctrine of **commercial impracticability** is the modern commercial law version of the common law doctrine of impossibility. If a party to a contract can establish that there has been an occurrence or a contingency not anticipated by the parties and not a basic assumption in their entering into a contract, the party can be excused from performance.

The standard for commercial impracticability is objective, not subjective. Additional cost alone is not grounds for application of commercial impracticability.[25]

For Example, if a farmer has contracted to sell 2 tons of peanuts to an airline and the crop fails, the farmer is not excused on the grounds of commercial impracticability. So long as peanuts are available for the farmer to buy, even at a higher price, and then sell to the buyer to satisfy their contract terms, the farmer is not excused. Commercial impracticability refers to those circumstances in which peanuts are not available anywhere because the entire peanut harvest was destroyed rather than just the individual farmer's crop.

[24] UCC § 2-310.

[25] UCC § 2-615(a). The key change in Revised Article 2 for this section is that "delivery" is changed to "performance" because the issues may relate to other aspects of performance beyond just delivery of the goods.

LEANIN' TREE, INC. V THIELE TECHNOLOGIES, INC.,
48 UCC REP SERV 2D 991 (CA COLO 2002)

WHEN THE CARTONS CANNOT BE CONTAINED

FACTS: Leanin' Tree manufactures, distributes, and sells greeting cards and other miscellaneous gift products. Leanin' Tree has regularly hired seasonal personnel to assist in the process of packaging greeting cards in clear plastic cartons for retail display and sale. In 1995, Leanin' Tree began exploring the possibility of automating its process of packaging cards. Leanin' Tree entered into a written agreement with Thiele in Spring of 1998 whereby Thiele agreed to design and manufacture a "cartoner" (i.e., an automated carton-packing machine). Thiele had considerable experience in designing and manufacturing equipment that utilized cardboard cartons, but very little experience in designing and manufacturing equipment that utilized plastic cartons, such as those used by Leanin' Tree.

Prior to entering into the agreement, Leanin' Tree provided Thiele with samples of the plastic cartons it normally used for packaging cards. Thiele expressed confidence that it could design and produce such a machine. On September 11, 1998, Thiele wrote to Leanin' Tree setting forth various "specifications concerning the manufacture of [the] cartons." The letter stated that if Leanin' Tree's "suppliers w[ould] follow the enclosed specifications, then Thiele w[ould] be able to successfully erect, fill and close the carton."

The parties revised their agreement on several occasions between late 1998 and May 1999 to allow for various design changes. According to the final revised agreement, the machine was to be completed and shipped to Leanin' Tree on June 30, 1999, at a total price of $468,682. Thiele was unable to get the cartoner to operate properly. Thiele did not meet the agreed shipping date and, in July 1999, informed Leanin' Tree of the problems. Although they later agreed to modify the design, those modifications did not solve the problem.

In late November or early December 1999, Thiele decided to stop working on the cartoner. Even though the carton set-up portion of the machine was still not functioning properly, Thiele informed Leanin' Tree that, in its opinion, the cartoner was finished and its obligations under the agreement were fulfilled. Thiele further informed Leanin' Tree that any problems with the cartoner were the result of Leanin' Tree's failure to provide an acceptable carton design and were Leanin' Tree's responsibility. At the time of its decision, Thiele's costs in designing and producing the machine were in the neighborhood of $750,000, more than $250,000 above the contract price, and more than $350,000 above Thiele's anticipated costs of design and production.

On December 17, 1999, after sending a representative to observe the cartoner at Thiele's facility (and confirming that the cartoner was not working properly), Leanin' Tree formally rejected the cartoner "based on its failure to conform to the [parties'] agreement." Leanin' Tree filed suit for breach of contract. The district court found in favor of Leanin' Tree on its breach of contract claim. The district court awarded Leanin' Tree: (1) $283,669, an amount equal to the payments it had made to Thiele under the written agreement, plus prejudgment interest; and (2) consequential damages in the amount of $146,508.22 (to cover costs incurred by Leanin' Tree on the cartoner project). The district court rejected Leanin' Tree's request for damages to cover the extra labor costs it incurred in 1999 and 2000 for hand-packing its greeting cards.

Thiele appealed.

Judicial Opinion

BRISCOE, Circuit Judge. . . . Thiele asserts that § 4-2-615 of the Colorado Uniform Commercial Code "excuses a seller whose performance has been rendered impracticable by the failure of a contingency that both parties expected to be satisfied." According to Thiele, such a contingency occurred here when the manufacturer hired by Leanin' Tree to produce the plastic cartons failed to "supply production cartons equal in quality to the samples it supplied [to Leanin' Tree and Thiele] in August 1998." Thiele contends the cartons did not contain score lines running to the ends of the cartons, which made it difficult for the cartoner to erect them properly (Thiele also suggested in the district court that the production cartons were not properly glued). Thiele suggests these carton problems made performance under the agreement impracticable.

"The rationale for the defense of commercial impracticability is that the circumstance causing the breach has rendered performance so vitally different from what was anticipated that the contract cannot be reasonably thought to govern." *Waldinger Corp. v CRS Group Engineers, Inc.*, 775 F.2d 781, 786 (7th Cir.1985).

Generally speaking, three conditions must be satisfied before a seller's performance under a commercial contract is excused as commercially impracticable: "(1) a contingency has occurred; (2) the contingency has made performance impracticable; and (3) the nonoccurrence of that contingency was a basic assumption upon which the contract was made." The establishment of each factor is a question of fact, subject to review by this court for clear error.

In rejecting Thiele's § 4-2-615 defense, the district court found that neither the second nor third factors had been established by Thiele. More specifically, the district court stated:

They [Leanin' Tree] were given [carton] specs [by Thiele] which they tried their best to follow; and, indeed, as pointed out by counsel, there were no specifications about full scoring or full gluing . . . and the Court thinks this is a red herring anyway. I don't think the full scoring and the full gluing would have made this machine work. I think [Leanin' Tree's expert witness] Mr. Luciano has it right that it takes a lot more than that. You would have to have this overbreak with the pressure on them to work.

Well, as far as Leanin' Tree was concerned, there wasn't any contingency. They had been using these plastic cartons for years, hand-packing them. They were willing to do whatever Thiele wanted them to do, but they certainly weren't told about scoring to the very edge or gluing to the very edge as a spec that they had to meet in order to make this work as a contingency. And, indeed, that didn't come in till later. And, indeed, the Court is convinced that that wouldn't have made any difference in making this machine work.

[The scoring and gluing specifications] certainly should have been within the contemplation of the expert in the machinery, Thiele. Leanin' Tree didn't even think about whether you needed scoring all the way or gluing all the way and really didn't have to. They weren't experts in cartoning machinery or in the requirements for what it needed, what was needed to erect or fill or close these.

So 615 really doesn't help the defendant. Thiele knew that they had to try to make a machine to work with the cartons of Leanin' Tree. They did not do the investigation, the homework, that they should have done before entering into this contract. Probably making the scores up to the edge may very well result in tearing, which is not going to make these cartons work. As Mr. Luciano indicated, making the scores better or making the glue better may not be possible, and Thiele should have found out about these problems at the very beginning.

The district court's findings are not, in our view, clearly erroneous. Leanin' Tree's expert witness, consulting engineer Robert Luciano, opined that the alleged carton scoring problems pointed to by Thiele as a contingency could not have been corrected by the carton manufacturer and, even if capable of correction, would not have resulted in the cartoner working properly. Instead, Luciano opined, the plastic cartons needed a 180-degree "overbreak" to allow them to work properly in the cartoner. Leanin' Tree also presented the testimony of Greg Fulkerson, Thiele's director of applications engineering, who admitted that: (a) the sample cartons provided by Leanin' Tree were not run through any test machines, but instead were examined by hand by Thiele personnel and deemed to be "machineable"; (b) Thiele had no significant experience in designing and manufacturing machines that worked with plastic cartons, and had little understanding of the unique properties of plastic (as compared to the cardboard cartons with which it typically worked) when it agreed on an initial carton design and confirmed machinability; (c) prior to actual production of the cartoner, Thiele did not direct Leanin' Tree to have the cartons scored or glued to any specific lengths; and (d) by producing the cartoner without successful pre-production tests, and without an adequate understanding of plastics, Thiele severely limited the options available for making the machine work (effectively limiting the available options to changing the cartons themselves). In light of this testimony, we conclude the district court's rulings were well within the evidence when it found that the alleged problems with the cartons did not render Thiele's performance under the agreement impracticable, the parties' agreement contained no basic assumptions regarding the design of the cartons, and Thiele should have foreseen the carton problems identified.

Questions

1. How much extra over the contract amount had Thiele expended in developing the cartoner?
2. Why does Thiele believe commercial impracticability applies here?
3. Why does the court believe commercial impracticability does not apply?

Summary

Every sales contract imposes an obligation of good faith in its performance. Good faith means honesty in fact in the conduct or transaction concerned. For merchants, the UCC imposes the additional requirement of observing "reasonable commercial standards of fair dealing in the trade."

In the case of a cash sale where no transportation of the goods is required, both the buyer and the seller may demand concurrent performance.

A buyer's or a seller's refusal to perform a contract is called a *repudiation*. A repudiation made in advance of the time for performance is called an *anticipatory repudiation* and is a breach of the contract. If either party to a contract feels insecure about the performance of the other, that party may demand by a record adequate assurance of performance. If that assurance is not given, the demanding party may treat the contract as repudiated.

The seller has a duty to deliver the goods in accordance with the terms of the contract. This duty does not require physical transportation; it requires that the seller permit the transfer of possession of the goods to the buyer.

With the exception of COD contracts, the buyer has the right to inspect the goods upon tender or delivery. Inspection includes the right to open cartons and conduct tests. If the buyer's inspection reveals that the seller has tendered nonconforming goods, the buyer may reject them. Subject to certain limitations, the seller may then offer to replace the goods or cure the problems the buyer has noted.

The buyer has a duty to accept goods that conform to the contract, and refusal to do so is a breach of contract. The buyer is deemed to have accepted goods either expressly or by implication through conduct inconsistent with rejection or by lapse of time. The buyer must pay for accepted goods in accordance with the terms of the contract. The buyer can reject goods in commercial units, accept the goods and collect damages for their problems, or reject the full contract shipment. The buyer must give notice of rejection to the seller and cannot do anything with the goods that would be inconsistent with the seller's ownership rights. The buyer should await instructions from the seller on what to do with the goods.

Even following acceptance, the buyer may revoke that acceptance if the problems with the goods substantially impair their value and the problems were either not easily discoverable or the buyer kept the goods based on the seller's promises to repair them and make them whole. Upon revocation of acceptance, the buyer should await instructions from the seller on what steps to take.

Performance can be excused on the grounds of commercial impracticability, but the seller must show objective difficulties that have created more than cost increases.

Questions and Case Problems

1. In 1992, Donna Smith telephoned Clark, the manager of Penbridge Farms, in response to an advertisement Clark had placed in the July issue of the *Emu Finder* about the availability for sale of proven breeder pairs. Clark told Smith he had a breeder pair available for purchase. Clark sold the pair to Smith for $16,500. Some months later, after Smith had had a chance to inspect the pair, she discovered that Clark had sold her two male emus. Smith immediately notified Clark and revoked her acceptance of the animals. Clark said the revocation was too late. Was it? [*Smith v Penbridge Associates, Inc.*, 655 A2d 1015 (Pa Super)]
2. On January 3, 1991, Central District Alarm (CDA) and Hal-Tuc entered into a written sales agreement providing that CDA would sell and install new security equipment described on an equipment list attached to the contract. This list included a Javelin VCR. When the system was installed, CDA installed a used JVC VCR instead of a new Javelin VCR. Hal-Tuc called CDA the day after the installation and complained that the equipment was not the Javelin brand, and that the VCR was a used JVC VCR. CDA told Hal-Tuc that the equipment was not used and that a JVC VCR was better than a Javelin. Hal-Tuc telephoned CDA personnel over a two-week period during which they denied that the equipment was used.

   After two weeks of calls, CDA's installation manager went to the store to see the equipment and admitted that it was used. No one from CDA advised Hal-Tuc in advance that it was installing used equipment temporarily until the right equipment arrived. CDA offered to replace it with a new Javelin VCR as soon as one arrived, which would take one or two months. Hal-Tuc asked CDA to return its deposit and take the equipment back, but CDA refused. Hal-Tuc put all the equipment in boxes and stored it. CDA filed a petition against Hal-Tuc for damages for breach of contract. Hal-Tuc filed a counterclaim, alleging fraud. CDA asserted it had the right to cure by tendering conforming goods after Hal-Tuc rejected the nonconforming goods. Was CDA correct? [*Central District Alarm, Inc. v Hal-Tuc, Inc.*, 866 SW2d 210 (Mo App)]
3. Bobby Murray Chevrolet, Inc., submitted a bid to the Alamance County Board of Education to supply 1,200 school bus chassis to the district. Bobby Murray was awarded the contract and contracted with General

Motors (GM) to purchase the chassis for the school board.

Between the time of Bobby Murray's contract with GM and the delivery date, the Environmental Protection Agency (EPA) enacted new emission standards for diesel vehicles, such as school buses. Under the new law, the buses Bobby Murray ordered from GM would be out of compliance, as would the buses Bobby Murray specified in its bid to the school board.

GM asked for several extensions to manufacture the buses within the new EPA guidelines. The school board was patient and gave several extensions, but then, because of its need for buses, purchased them from another supplier after notifying Bobby Murray of its intent to do so. The school board had to pay an additional $150,152.94 for the buses from its alternative source and sued Bobby Murray for that amount. Bobby Murray claimed it was excused from performance on the grounds of commercial impracticability. Is Bobby Murray correct? Does the defense of commercial impracticability apply in this situation? Be sure to compare this case with other cases and examples in the chapter. [*Alamance County Board of Education v Bobby Murray Chevrolet, Inc.*, 465 SE2d 306 (NC App); rev. denied, 467 SE2d 899 (NC)]

4. The Home Shopping Club ordered 12,000 Care Bear lamps from Ohio International, Ltd. When the lamps arrived, they had poor painting and staining, certain elements were improperly glued and could come loose (a danger to the children likely to have the lamps in their rooms), and they overheated very easily (another danger for children as well as a fire hazard). Home Shopping Network notified International and gave it three months to remedy the problems and provide different lamps. After three months, Home Shopping Network returned all lamps and notified International that it was pulling out of the contract. Could they do so, or had too much time passed? [*Home Shopping Club, Inc. v Ohio International, Ltd.*, 27 UCC Rep Serv 2d 433 (Fla Cir Ct)]

5. Lafer Enterprises sold Christmas decorations to B. P. Development & Management Corp., the owners and operators of the Osceola Square Mall. The package of decorations was delivered to Osceola Square Mall prior to Thanksgiving 1986 for a total cost of $48,775, which B. P. would pay in three installments. Cathy Trivigno, a manager at B. P. who supervised the installation of the decorations, indicated that she and the Osceola Square Mall merchants were not satisfied with the quality of the decorations, but they needed to be in place for the day after Thanksgiving (the start of the holiday shopping season). B. P. complained to Lafer about the quality of the decorations but had the decorations installed. B. P. paid the first installment to Lafer but then stopped payment on the last two checks. B. P. claimed it had rejected the decorations. Lafer claimed breach for nonpayment because B. P. used the decorations. Did B. P. accept the decorations? [*B. P. Dev. & Management Corp. v Lafer Enterprises, Inc.*, 538 So 2d 1379 (Fla App)]

6. Westinghouse Electric Corporation entered into uranium supply contracts with 22 electric utilities during the late 1960s. The contract prices ranged from $7 to $10 per pound. The Arab oil embargo and other changes in energy resources caused the price of uranium to climb to between $45 and $75 per pound. Supply tightened because of increased demand.

In 1973, Westinghouse wrote to the utilities and explained that it was unable to perform on its uranium sales contracts. The utilities needed uranium. Westinghouse did not have sufficient funds to buy the uranium it had agreed to supply, assuming that it could find a supply. One utility executive commented, after totaling up all 22 supply contracts, that Westinghouse could not have supplied the uranium even under the original contract terms. He said, "Westinghouse oversubscribed itself on these contracts. They hoped that not all the utilities would take the full contract amount."

Westinghouse says it is impossible for it to perform. The utilities say they are owed damages because they must still find uranium somewhere. What damages would the law allow? What ethical issues do you see in the original contracts and in Westinghouse's refusal to deliver? Should we excuse parties from contracts because it is so expensive for them to perform? [*In re Westinghouse Uranium Litigation*, 436 F Supp 990 (ED Va)]

7. Steel Industries, Inc., ordered steel from Interlink Metals & Chemicals. The steel was to be delivered from a Russian mill. There were political and other issues in Russia, and the mill was shut down. Interlink did not deliver the steel to Steel Industries, claiming that it was excused from performance because it could not get the steel from the Russian mill. What would Interlink have to establish to show that it was excused from performing under the doctrine of commercial impracticability? [*Steel Industries, Inc. v Interlink Metals & Chemicals, Inc.*, 969 F Supp 1046 (ED Mich)]

8. Spaulding & Kimball Co. ordered from Aetna Chemical Co. 75 cartons of window washers. The buyer received them and sold about a third to its customers but later refused to pay for them, claiming that the quality was poor. The seller sued for the price. Would the seller be entitled to the contract price? Refer to the case in this chapter regarding the Degas painting for some insight. [*Aetna Chemical Co. v Spaulding & Kimball Co.*, 126 A 582 (Vt)]

9. A computer manufacturer promoted the sale of a digital computer as a "revolutionary breakthrough." The manufacturer made a contract to deliver one of these computers to a buyer. The seller failed to deliver the computer and explained that its failure was caused by unanticipated technological difficulties. Was this an

excuse for nonperformance by the seller? [*United States v Wegematic Corp.*, 360 F2d 674 (2d Cir)]

10. Economy Forms Corp. sold concrete-forming equipment to Kandy. After using the equipment for more than six months, Kandy notified Economy that the equipment was inadequate. Economy Forms alleged that Kandy had accepted the goods. Kandy denied liability. Was there an acceptance? Why or why not? [*Economy Forms Corp. v Kandy, Inc.*, 391 F Supp 944 (ND Ga)]

11. Michael Smyers operates his business, Engineered Specialty Products (ESP), in Olathe, Kansas. ESP manufactures and sells resistance welders and quartz crystal X-ray machines called *goniometers*. Quartz Works is a Massachusetts corporation in the business of purchasing welders, goniometers, and other related equipment and reselling the equipment as a package to businesses that wish to operate quartz crystal manufacturing facilities.

    Quartz Works and ESP began negotiations for Quartz Works to purchase two welders from ESP, and they also explored the possibility of ESP manufacturing two goniometers for Quartz Works. On September 21, 1992, Quartz Works offered to purchase two welders from ESP at a total price of $88,825. At the time of its offer, Quartz Works also sent ESP a check for $66,618.75, representing a 75 percent down payment. Upon receiving Quartz Works' order, ESP sent back a counteroffer reflecting price adjustments for some of the related parts and a total purchase price of $89,125 for the welders. The invoice that ESP sent back to Quartz Works credited the payment Quartz Works had made and indicated that the total amount due was now $22,506.25. ESP began work on the goniometers, but after nine months, Quartz Works still owed money on the welders and had not paid 90 percent of what was due on the contract for the goniometers. ESP demanded full payment on the welders or it would not continue work on the goniometers. Quartz Works said that ESP could not demand assurances related to nonperformance on another contract. Was Quartz Works correct? Could ESP stop work on the goniometers if the welder contract was not performed? Why or why not? [*Smyers v Quartz Works Corp.*, 880 F Supp 1425 (D Kan)]

12. Rockland Industries is a Maryland corporation that manufactures drapery lining fabrics. Rockland uses approximately 500,000 pounds per year of antimony oxide, a fire retardant, on its fabrics. Manley-Regan is a Pennsylvania chemical distribution company. Rockland usually purchased its antimony oxide from HoltraChem on an "as-needed" basis, where HoltraChem had quoted a price based on the understanding that Rockland required approximately 500,000 pounds per year of antimony oxide. HoltraChem charged about $0.86 per pound during its last year as Rockland's supplier.

    Due to a serious worldwide crisis in the supply of this chemical in the spring of 1994, HoltraChem could no longer maintain its existing supply relationship with Rockland. Rockland, in exploring other suppliers, found that the antimony oxide market was extremely tight, with rising prices and no known recovery period.

    Rockland contracted with Manley-Regan for delivery of antimony oxide (114,000 pounds total) at $1.80 per pound. That supply fell through because of the nature of the market and Rockville contracted with another supplier for 44,092 pounds of antimony oxide at $2.65 per pound and with still another supplier for 88,184 pounds at $2.54 per pound.

    Rockland filed suit seeking as damages the difference between the price of $1.80 per pound and the various other prices it had paid. Manley-Regan used UCC § 2-615 as its defense claiming commercial impracticability. Does Manley-Regan have a good case using this defense? [*Rockland Industries, Inc. v E+E (US) Inc.*, 991 F Supp 468 (D Md)]

13. Trefalcon (a commercial arm of the government of Ghana) entered into a contract with Supply Commission as a purchaser of residual fuel oil (RFO). Supply Commission agreed, among other things, to supply Trefalcon with RFO at competitive prices as reserves permitted. Approximately six weeks into the agreement, on May 3, 1974, Supply Commission wrote a letter to Trefalcon proposing a method for pricing the refined fuel it would sell to Trefalcon.

    A dispute arose six months later when Supply Commission first began to raise the price of RFO to account for escalations. In an effort to continue the contract, the parties orally agreed to a so-called Standstill Agreement, pursuant to which Ghana temporarily would forgo payment of escalations. By May 12, 1975, Trefalcon had paid only the base price for each of the 26 residual fuel cargoes it had received.

    On May 26, 1975, J.V.L. Mensah, a representative of Supply Commission, sent a letter to Trefalcon demanding payment of $7,885,523.12 for escalation charges and declaring that no further oil would be sold until payment in full was made. After receiving the Mensah letter, Trefalcon tendered two payments to the Bank of Ghana—one in the amount of $1,617,682.29 (tendered June 10, 1975), and the other in the amount of $1,185,000 (tendered June 27, 1975).

    With full payment still outstanding in July 1975, Supply Commission canceled the contract and sought damages for breach following the failure to provide assurances. Will Supply Commission recover? [*Reich v Republic of Ghana*, 2002 WL 142610 (SDNY 2002)]

14. Harry Ulmas made a contract to buy a new car from Acey Oldsmobile. He was allowed to keep his old car until the new car was delivered. The sales contract gave him a trade-in value of $650 on the old car but specified that the

car would be reappraised when it was actually brought to the dealer. When Ulmas brought the trade-in to the dealer, an Acey employee took it for a test drive and said that the car was worth between $300 and $400. Acey offered Ulmas only $50 for his trade-in. Ulmas refused to buy from Acey and purchased from another dealer, who appraised the trade-in at $400. Ulmas sued for breach of contract on the grounds of violation of good faith. Was he right? [*Ulmas v Acey Oldsmobile, Inc.*, 310 NYS2d 147 (NY Civ)]

15. Cornelia and Ed Kornfeld contracted to sell a signed Picasso print to David Tunick, Inc. The print, entitled *Le Minotauromachie*, was signed "Pablo Picasso." The signature on the print was discovered to be a forgery, and the Kornfelds offered Tunick a substitute Picasso print. Tunick refused the Kornfelds' substituted performance and demanded a return of the contract price. The Kornfelds refused on the grounds that their cure had been refused. Was the substitute print an adequate cure? [*David Tunick, Inc. v Kornfeld*, 838 F Supp 848 (SDNY)]

CPA Questions

1. Under the sales article of the UCC, which of the following statements is correct?
   a. The obligations of the parties to the contract must be performed in good faith.
   b. Merchants and nonmerchants are treated alike.
   c. The contract must involve the sale of goods for a price of more than $500.
   d. None of the provisions of the UCC may be disclaimed by agreement.
2. Rowe Corp. purchased goods from Stair Co. that were shipped COD. Under the sales article of the UCC, which of the following rights does Rowe have?
   a. The right to inspect the goods before paying
   b. The right to possession of the goods before paying
   c. The right to reject nonconforming goods
   d. The right to delay payment for a reasonable period of time
3. Bibbeon Manufacturing shipped 300 designer navy blue blazers to Custom Clothing Emporium. The blazers arrived on Friday, earlier than Custom had anticipated and on an exceptionally busy day for its receiving department. They were perfunctorily examined and sent to a nearby warehouse for storage until needed. On Monday of the following week, upon closer examination, it was discovered that the quality of the blazer linings was inferior to that specified in the sales contract. Which of the following is correct insofar as Custom's rights are concerned?
   a. Custom can reject the blazers upon subsequent discovery of the defects.
   b. Custom must retain the blazers since it accepted them and had an opportunity to inspect them upon delivery.
   c. Custom's only course of action is rescission.
   d. Custom had no rights if the linings were merchantable quality.
4. Parker ordered 50 cartons of soap from Riddle Wholesale Company. Each carton contains 12 packages of soap. The terms were: $8.00 per carton 2/10, net/30, FOB buyer's delivery platform, delivery June 1. During transit approximately one-half the packages were damaged by the carrier. The delivery was made on May 28. Answer the following with "Yes" or "No."
   a. Riddle had the risk of loss during transit.
   b. If Parker elects to accept the undamaged part of the shipment, he will be deemed to have accepted the entire shipment.
   c. To validly reject the goods, Parker must give timely notice of rejection to Riddle within a reasonable time after delivery.
   d. If Riddle were notified of the rejection on May 28, Riddle could cure the defect by promptly notifying Parker of intention to do so and making a second delivery to Parker of conforming goods by June 1.
   e. The statute of frauds is inapplicable to the transaction in the facts given.

REMEDIES FOR BREACH OF SALES CONTRACTS

CHAPTER (27)

A. Statute of Limitations

1. Time Limits for Suits under the UCC
2. Time Limits for Other Suits

B. Remedies of the Seller

3. Seller's Lien
4. Seller's Remedy of Stopping Shipment
5. Resale by Seller
6. Cancellation by Seller
7. Seller's Action for Damages under the Market Price Formula
8. Seller's Action for Lost Profits
9. Other Types of Damages
10. Seller's Action for the Purchase Price
11. Seller's Nonsale Remedies

C. Remedies of the Buyer

12. Rejection of Improper Tender
13. Revocation of Acceptance
14. Buyer's Action for Damages for Nondelivery—Market Price Recovery
15. Buyer's Action for Damages for Nondelivery—Cover Price Recovery
16. Other Types of Damages
17. Action for Breach of Warranty
18. Cancellation by Buyer
19. Buyer's Resale of Goods
20. Action for Specific Performance
21. Nonsale Remedies of the Buyer

D. Contract Provisions on Remedies

22. Limitation of Damages
23. Down Payments and Deposits

LEARNING OBJECTIVES

After studying this chapter, you should be able to

LO.1 List the remedies of the seller when the buyer breaches a sales contract

LO.2 List the remedies of the buyer when the seller breaches a sales contract

LO.3 Determine the validity of clauses limiting damages

LO.4 Discuss the waiver of and preservation of defenses of a buyer

If one of the parties to a sale fails to perform the contract, the nonbreaching party has remedies under Article 2 of the Uniform Commercial Code (UCC). In addition, the parties may have included provisions on remedies in their contract.

A. Statute of Limitations

Judicial remedies have time limitations. After the expiration of a particular period of time, the party seeking a remedy can no longer resort to the courts. The UCC **statute of limitations** applies to actions brought for remedies on the breach of a sales contract.[1] When a suit is brought on the basis of a tort theory, such as negligence, fraud, or strict tort liability, other general statutes of limitations apply.

CPA 1. Time Limits for Suits under the UCC

An action for breach of a sales contract must be commenced within four years after the time of the **breach.**[2] Revised UCC § 2-725(1) extends the statute of limitations to a maximum of five years to cover those cases in which the breach is discovered in year four.[3] The statute of limitations can be reduced as between merchants to as little as one year but cannot be reduced in consumer contracts.

When a cause of action arises depends on the nature of the breach. The previous UCC had three measurements for determining when a breach occurs. Revised Article 2 has eight accrual rules for the timing of a breach and the resulting statute of limitations. The basic rule is that the time begins to run when the breach occurs, but that rule has seven exceptions that include special timing rules for repudiation, infringement, breach of warranty, and future performance.

A buyer seeking damages because of a breach of the sales contract must give the seller notice of the breach within a reasonable time after the buyer discovers or should have discovered it.[4]

2. Time Limits for Other Suits

When a party seeks recovery on a non-Code theory, such as on the basis of strict tort liability, fraud, or negligence, the UCC statute of limitations does not apply. The action is subject to each state's tort statute of limitations. Tort statutes of limitations are found in individual state statutes, and the time limitations

[1] UCC § 2-703.

[2] The cause of action arises as soon as the breach occurs even if the party is unaware of the breach at that time. This unfairness is remedied under Revised Article 2 with a statute of limitations of the latter of four years after the breach or one year after the breach was or should have been discovered (no longer than five years total).

[3] Revised UCC § 2-725(1).

[4] UCC § 2-607(3)(a).

vary by state. However, the tort statutes of limitations tend to be shorter than the UCC statute of limitations.

B. Remedies of the Seller

When the buyer breaches a sales contract, the seller has different remedies available that are designed to afford the seller compensation for the losses caused by the buyer's breach.[5] Revised Article 2 allows the remedies provided to be used together, and although the various remedies may be called out in separate sections, there is no requirement that a party elect only one of the remedies. In many cases of breach, only a combination of the various remedies can make the nonbreaching party whole again.

3. Seller's Lien

In the absence of an agreement for the extension of credit to the buyer for the purchase of goods, and until the buyer pays for the goods or performs whatever actions the contract requires, the seller has the right to retain possession of the goods.[6]

CPA 4. Seller's Remedy of Stopping Shipment

When the buyer has breached the contract prior to the time the goods have arrived at their destination, the seller can stop the goods from coming into the buyer's possession. This remedy is important to sellers because it eliminates the need for sellers to try to recover goods from buyers who have indicated they cannot or will not pay.

A seller has the right to stop shipment if the buyer has received goods on credit and the seller learns that the buyer is insolvent, the buyer has not provided assurances as requested, or the seller has grounds to believe performance by the buyer will not occur.[7] Also, the right to retrieve the goods in the case of a credit buyer's insolvency continues for "a reasonable time after the buyer's receipt of the goods."

Revised UCC eliminates the time limit of 10 days after the buyer actually has received the goods. Revised UCC also eliminates the distinctions on sizes of shipments and rights because of the ease with which all types and sizes of shipments can now be tracked.[8]

CPA 5. Resale by Seller

When the buyer has breached the contract, the seller may resell any of the goods the seller still holds. After the resale, the seller is not liable to the original buyer on the contract and does not have to surrender any profit obtained on the resale. On the other hand, if the proceeds are less than the contract price, the seller may recover the loss from the original buyer.[9] Under Revised UCC, the failure of the seller to resell the goods does not mean the seller cannot recover under the other remedies available under Article 2.

The seller must give reasonable notice to the breaching buyer of the intention to resell the goods. Such notice need not be given if the goods are perishable or could decline rapidly in value. The seller must conduct any method of resale under standards of commercial reasonableness.[10] The formula for damages under resale provided in Revised § 2-706(1) is substantially similar.[11]

6. Cancellation by Seller

When the buyer materially breaches the contract, the seller may cancel the contract. Such a cancellation ends the contract and discharges all unperformed obligations on both sides. Following cancellation, the seller has any remedy with respect to the breach by the buyer that is still available.

CPA 7. Seller's Action for Damages under the Market Price Formula

When the buyer fails to pay for accepted goods, the seller may resell the goods, as discussed earlier, or bring a contract action to recover damages. One formula for a seller's damages is the difference

[5] Under Revised Article 2 (§ 2-803), the overall policy change on remedies relates to the parties' expectations. The revision allows courts to deny a remedy if one party thereby benefits to more than a full performance position.

[6] UCC § 2-703.

[7] Revised UCC § 2-705. Under Revised UCC, the right of the seller has been broadened. Because shipments are tracked so easily now with technology, the seller can stop a shipment of any size for any of the reasons given, regardless of shipment size.

[8] Revised UCC § 2-705(1).

[9] Revised UCC § 2-706(1), (6); *Cook Composites, Inc. v Westlake Styrene Corp.*, 155 W3d 124 (CA Tex 2000).

[10] *Plano Lincoln Mercury, Inc. v Roberts*, 167 SW3d 616 (CA Tex 2005).

[11] Revised UCC § 2-706(1).

between the market price at the time and place of the tender of the goods and the contract price.[12] Under Revised Article 2, in the case of an anticipatory repudiation, the measurement of damages is the difference between the contract price and the market price "at the expiration of a commercially reasonable time after the seller learned of the repudiation" but not later than the time of tender. Whether the seller chooses to resell or recover the difference between the contract price and the market price is the seller's decision. The flexibility in the remedies under the UCC is provided because certain goods have very high market fluctuations. **For Example,** suppose that Sears has agreed to purchase 10 refrigerators from Whirlpool at a price of $1,000 each, but then Sears notifies Whirlpool that it will not be buying the refrigerators after all. Whirlpool determines the market price at the time of tender to be $850 per refrigerator. The best Whirlpool can find from an alternate buyer after a search is $800. Whirlpool can select the resale remedy ($1,000 – $800, or $200 in damages) to adequately compensate for the change in the market price between the time of tender and the time damages are sought.

CPA 8. Seller's Action for Lost Profits

If the market and resale price measures of damages do not place the seller in the same position in which the seller would have been had the buyer performed, the seller is permitted to recover lost profits.[13] The recovery of lost profits reimburses the seller for costs incurred in gearing up for contract performance.[14] **For Example,** suppose that a buyer has ordered 200 wooden rocking horses from a seller-manufacturer. Before production on the horses begins, the buyer breaches. The seller has nothing to resell, and the goods have not been identified to even permit a market value assessment. Nonetheless, the seller has geared up for production, counted on the contract, and perhaps bypassed other contracts in order to perform. An appropriate remedy for the seller of the rocking horses would be the profits it would have made had the buyer performed.

Some courts also follow the lost volume doctrine that allows sellers to recover for the profits they would have made if the buyer had completed the transaction.[15] For example, suppose that Maytag has a contract to sell 10 washing machines for $600 each to Lakewood Apartment Managers. Lakewood breaches the agreement and refuses to take or pay for the washing machines. Maytag is able to resell them to Suds 'n Duds Laundromat for $600 each. The price is the same, but the theory of lost volume profits is that Maytag could have sold 20 washers, not just 10, if Lakewood had not breached. Maytag's profit on each machine is $200. Lost volume profits in this situation would be 10 times the $200, or $2,000.

THINKING THINGS THROUGH

In 1996, Collins Entertainment Corporation contracted to lease video poker machines to two bingo hall operations known as Ponderosa Bingo and Shipwatch Bingo. The six-year lease required that any purchaser of the premises assume the lease. In 1997, American Bingo and Gaming Corporation purchased the assets of the bingo parlors. American failed to assume the lease and removed Collins' machines from the premises. Collins had $1.5 million in profits remaining on the lease at the time its machines were removed. However, Collins was able to place the video poker machines in other casinos. Collins filed suit against American Bingo. American Bingo says that Collins has no damages because the machines were already earning money for it. Is American Bingo correct? [COLLINS ENTERTAINMENT CORP. v COATS AND COATS RENTAL AMUSEMENT, 629 SE2d 635 (SC 2006)]

[12] Revised UCC § 2-708.

[13] Note that this is a change under Revised Article 2. Prior to this change, the remedy of lost profits was available only under the market price remedy. Now it is available under market price and resale remedies.

[14] Revised UCC § 2-709.

[15] *Sunrich v Pacific Foods of Oregon*, 2004 WL 1124495 (D Or 2004).

CPA 9. Other Types of Damages

So far, the discussion of remedies has focused on the damages that result because the seller did not sell the goods. However, the seller may incur additional expenses because of the breach. Some of those expenses can be recovered as damages. UCC § 2-710 provides that the seller can also recover, as **incidental damages,** any commercially reasonable charges, expenses, or commissions incurred[16] in recovering damages.[17] **For Example,** the seller may recover expenses for the transportation, care, and storage of the goods after the buyer's breach, as well as any costs incurred in the return or resale of the goods. Such damages are in addition to any others that may be recovered by the seller.

CPA 10. Seller's Action for the Purchase Price

If goods are specially manufactured and the buyer refuses to take them, it is possible for the seller to recover as damages the full purchase price and keep the goods.[18] **For Example,** a printing company that has printed catalogs for a retail mail-order merchant will not be able to sell the catalogs to anyone else. The remedy for the seller is recovery of the purchase price.[19]

11. Seller's Nonsale Remedies

In addition to the seller's traditional sales remedies, many sellers enter into other transactions that provide protection from buyer breaches. One such protection is afforded when the seller obtains a security interest from the buyer under UCC Article 9. A **secured transaction** is a pledge of property by the buyer-debtor that enables the seller to take possession of the goods if the buyer fails to pay the amount owed. (See Chapter 34.)

Figure 27-1 is a summary of the remedies available to the seller under Article 2.

FIGURE 27-1 Seller's Remedies under Article 2

REMEDY	STOP DELIVERY	RESALE PRICE	MARKET PRICE	ACTION FOR PRICE	LOST PROFIT
SECTION NUMBER	2–703	2–706 2–710	2–708 2–710	2–709 2–708	2–708(2)
WHEN AVAILABLE	Insolvency Advance breach by buyer	Buyer fails to take goods	Buyer fails to take goods	Specially manufactured goods	Anticipatory repudiation Breach
NATURE OF REMEDY	Stop delivery of any size shipment or recover goods if buyer insolvent (Revised UCC)	Contract price – Resale price + Incidental damages – Expenses saved + Consequential damages	Contract price – Market price + Incidental damages – Expenses saved + Consequential damages	Contract price + Incidental damages – Expenses saved + Consequential damages	Profits + Incidental damages – Salvage value + Consequential damages

[16] Revised UCC § 2-710.

[17] Revised UCC § 2-710; *Purina Mills, L.L.C. v Less*, 295 F Supp 2d 1017 (ND Iowa 2003).

[18] *In re Moltech Power Systems, Inc.*, 326 BR 178 (ND Fla 2005).

[19] UCC § 2-709(1)(a) and (b).

C. Remedies of the Buyer

When the seller breaches a sales contract, the buyer has a number of remedies under Article 2 of the UCC. Additional remedies based on contract or tort theories of product liability may also be available. (See Chapter 25.)

12. Rejection of Improper Tender

As discussed in Chapter 26, if the goods tendered by the seller do not conform to the contract in some way, the buyer may reject them. However, the rejection is the beginning of the buyer's remedies. Following rejection, the buyer can proceed to recover under the various formulas provided for buyers under the UCC.

13. Revocation of Acceptance

The buyer may revoke acceptance of the goods when they do not conform to the contract, the defect substantially impairs the value of the contract to the buyer, and the buyer either could not discover the problem or kept the goods because of a seller's promise of repair (see Chapter 26). Again, following revocation of acceptance, the buyer has various remedies available under the UCC.

CPA 14. Buyer's Action for Damages for Nondelivery—Market Price Recovery

If the seller fails to deliver the goods as required by the contract or repudiates the contract, the buyer is entitled to collect from the seller damages for breach of contract. Under Revised Article 2, the buyer is entitled to recover the difference between the market price at the time of tender and the contract price; this is a change from the previous Article 2 that measured damages at the time the buyer learned of the breach.[20]

CPA 15. Buyer's Action for Damages for Nondelivery—Cover Price Recovery

A buyer may also choose, as a remedy for the seller's nondelivery of goods that conform to the contract, to purchase substitute goods or cover.[21] If the buyer acts in good faith, the measure of damages for the seller's nondelivery or repudiation is then the difference between the cost of cover and the contract price.[22]

The buyer need only make a reasonable cover purchase as a substitute for the contract goods. The goods purchased need not be identical to the contract goods. **For Example,** if the buyer could secure only 350 five-speed blenders when the contract called for 350 three-speed blenders, the buyer's cover would be reasonable despite the additional expense of the five-speed blenders.

CPA 16. Other Types of Damages

The buyer is also entitled to collect incidental damages in situations in which he must find substitute goods. Those incidental damages could include additional shipping expenses or perhaps commissions paid to find the goods and purchase them. Buyers often also experience **consequential damages**, which are those damages the buyer experiences with respect to a third party as a result of the seller's breach. Revised UCC provides consequential damages for sellers and buyers. The seller's section provides, "Consequential damages resulting from the buyer's breach include any loss resulting from general or particular requirements and needs of which the buyer at the time of contracting had reason to know and which could not reasonably be prevented by resale or otherwise."[23] **For Example,** a seller's failure to deliver the goods may cause the buyer's production line to come to a halt. The buyer might then breach on its sales and delivery contracts with its buyers. In the case of a government contract, the buyer may have to pay a penalty for being late. These types of damages are consequential ones and can be recovered if the seller knew about the consequences or they were foreseeable. Under Revised Article 2, consequential damages cannot be recovered from a consumer.

17. Action for Breach of Warranty

A remedy available to a buyer when goods are delivered but fail to conform to warranties is an action for breach of warranty.

[20] Revised UCC § 2-713.

[21] Revised UCC § 2-712; *Conagra, Inc. v Nierenberg*, 7 P3d 369 (Mont 2000). Buyers are also entitled to recover any deposits paid [*Selectouch Corp. v Perfect Starch, Inc.*, 111 SW3d 830, 51 UCC Rep Serv 2d 1070 (Tex App 2004)].

[22] Revised UCC § 2-712(1) and (2). See *Conductores Monterrey, S.A. de C.V. v Remee Products Corp.*, 45 UCC Rep Serv 2d 111 (SDNY 2000).

[23] Revised UCC § 2-710. Revised Article 2 redefines and broadens the availability of consequential damages. The revisions are expected to increase both the amounts and the recoverability of consequential damages.

(a) Notice of Breach

If the buyer has accepted goods that do not conform to the contract or there has been a breach of any warranties given, the buyer must notify the seller of the breach within a reasonable time after the breach is discovered or should have been discovered.[24]

(b) Measure of Damages

If the buyer has given the necessary notice of breach, the buyer may recover damages measured by the loss resulting in the normal course of events from the breach. If suit is brought for breach of warranty, the measure of damages is the difference between the value of the goods as they were at the time of tender and the value that they would have had if they had been as warranted. Under Revised Article 2, the buyer is also entitled to any of the other damage remedies necessary to make the buyer whole.

(c) Notice of Third-Party Action against Buyer

When a buyer elects the remedy of resale and sells the contract goods to a third party, that third party has the right of suit against the buyer for breach of warranty. In such a case, it is the buyer's option whether to give the seller notice of the action and request that the seller defend that action.

18. Cancellation by Buyer

The buyer may cancel or rescind the contract if the seller fails to deliver the goods, if the seller has repudiated the contract, or if the goods have been rightfully rejected or their acceptance revoked.[25] A buyer who cancels the contract is entitled to recover as much of the purchase price as has been paid, including the value of any property given as a trade-in as part of the purchase price. The fact that the buyer cancels the contract does not destroy the buyer's cause of action against the seller for breach of that contract. The buyer may recover from the seller not only any payment made on the purchase price but also damages for the breach of the contract. The damages represent the difference between the contract price and the cost of cover.[26]

The right of the buyer to cancel or rescind the sales contract may be lost by a delay in exercising the right. A buyer who, with full knowledge of the defects in the goods, makes partial payments or performs acts of ownership of the goods inconsistent with the decision to cancel may lose certain remedy provisions or be limited in recovery under Article 2.

FURLONG V ALPHA CHI OMEGA SORORITY, 657 NE 2D 866 (OHIO MUN CT 1993)

THE ALPHA CHI OMEGA BATTLE OF THE SWEATERS

Emily Lieberman and Amy Altomondo were members of the Alpha Chi Omega (defendant) sorority at Bowling Green State University. Lieberman and Altomondo negotiated with Johnathan James Furlong (plaintiff) for the purchase of custom-designed sweaters for them and their sorority sisters for a total price of $3,612. Lieberman and Altomondo paid Furlong a $2,000 deposit.

Lieberman and Altomondo had a friend pick up the sweaters in Columbus and deliver them to Bowling Green. Upon opening the boxes, they discovered that Furlong had made color and design alterations in the lettering imprinted on the sweaters as part of their custom design. Altomondo, as president of AXO, called Furlong and told him that the sweaters were unacceptable and offered to return them. Furlong refused, stating that any changes were immaterial. Altomondo refused to pay the balance due and demanded the return of the $2,000 deposit. Furlong filed suit for breach of contract.

Judicial Opinion

BACHMAN, J. . . . Defendant rejected the sweaters, rather than accepted them, as those terms (*"reject"* and *"accept"*) are defined by the law. Defendant's rejection was done within a reasonable time after delivery and was effective because of seasonable notice to plaintiff.

---

24 *Dunleavey v Paris Ceramics, USA, Inc.*, 819 A2d 945 (Super Ct 2002); *Muehlbauer v General Motors Corp.*, 431 F Supp 2d 847 (ND Ill 2006).
25 Revised UCC § 2-720.
26 Revised UCC § 2-712(1), (2); *Valley Timber Sales, Inc. v Midway Forest Products, Inc.*, 563 So 2d 612 (Ala App 1990).

Therefore, plaintiff has breached the contract; defendant has not. Defendant is entitled to cancel the contract, recover so much of the price as has been paid, and hold the sweaters until recovery of that payment. Plaintiff is not entitled to recover the balance of the purchase price, but is entitled to the return of the sweaters upon return of the down payment to defendant.

Furlong was a jobber for Argento Bros., Inc. ("Argento") and had Argento print the sweaters. In doing so, Furlong worked with Argento's artists. Early in the morning of Thursday (October 22, 1992), the artist(s) began to prepare the art work and recommended changes to the design. Furlong authorized the artist(s) to change the design without the knowledge or consent of AXO. Argento spent about eight hours printing the sweaters all day Thursday. Furlong did not phone AXO about the changes until the next day, Friday (October 23), after the sweaters were printed with those changes. Here are the five design changes that he made:

- The ***first change*** was to delete the agreed-upon outline for the letters (namely, the navy blue outline).
- The ***second change*** was to reduce the agreed-upon number of colors for the fronts and the backs (from three colors per side to two colors per side).
- The ***third change*** was to alter one of the agreed-upon colors (from maroon to red).
- The ***fourth change*** was to alter the agreed-upon scheme of colors for the letters on the fronts and the backs (namely, both sides were to have the same two colors of maroon and hunter green; whereas in fact the backs had neither of those colors, and instead had a navy blue color for the letters).
- The ***fifth change*** was to alter the agreed-upon color of the masks (from hunter green to maroon—actually red).

The court specifically finds that the color was *red* (actually, scarlet) and was *not maroon* (like the maroon-colored letters on the Ohio Wesleyan sweater).

Conclusions of law: The sweaters did not conform to the contract (specifically, the express warranty in the contract). Thus (in the words of the statute), the sweaters did "fail in any respect to conform to the contract." Actually, the sweaters failed in at least five respects. Further, not only did they "fail in any respect," they failed in a substantial respect. In either event, they were a nonconforming tender of goods.

As concluded above, the sweaters were nonconforming goods because they "failed in any respect"—actually in many material respects—to conform to the contract (namely, to the express warranty in the contract).

The court rejects Furlong's assertion that he did all that he could do under the circumstances. The obvious answer is that he did not do enough. He should have gotten AXO's prior consent to the changes. He could have done this by providing for more lead time—between the time that Argento prepared the art work and the time that it printed the sweaters. Instead, he had both done at the same time (Thursday morning).

Further, he should have not entered into the contract until Argento had completed the art work and AXO had consented to it. Then, he would not have had to make "an immediate decision" at a time when it "would be difficult if not impossible, to contact [Emily]"—a day before the delivery due date.

Finally, and alternatively, plaintiff should have entered into a contract that gave him discretion to make design changes without AXO's consent. We must remember that "these sweaters," as Furlong himself admits (and describes), were to be "custom-designed" for AXO. Thus, they were to be printed according to AXO's specifications, and not according to Furlong's discretion.

Next, Furlong asserts that AXO—after learning of the changes—should have agreed to his offer of compromise: namely, that he would reduce the unit price of the sweaters in exchange for AXO's keeping them and paying the reduced price. Also, Furlong asserts that AXO should have communicated his compromise offer to AXO's members and pledges. In both respects, the court disagrees: Although the law allowed AXO to do so, it did not require AXO to do so. Instead, AXO did exactly what the law allowed: AXO rejected the nonconforming goods in whole.

In regard to the following four types of seller's remedies, Furlong has no legal remedies because AXO did not breach the contract. Thus, he is not entitled to an award for the $1,612 balance that he claims is due on the contract price.

AXO has the following buyer's remedies:

a. Buyer's remedies in general; buyer's security interest in rejected goods (R.C. 1302.85 [UCC § 2-711]).

   - As concluded above, AXO rightfully rejected the sweaters, after having paid part of the purchase price: namely, $2,000. AXO is entitled to cancel the contract and to recover the partial payment of the purchase price (R.C. 1302.85[A] [UCC § 2-711(1)]).

- Also, as concluded above, AXO still has rightful possession or control of the sweaters. AXO has a security interest in the sweaters in its possession or control for the part payment made on the purchase price—but when reimbursed for that part payment AXO must return the sweaters to Furlong.
- There is no evidence that AXO has incurred any expenses for their inspection, receipt, transportation, care, and custody. Further, AXO does not claim any such expenses. AXO is not entitled to recover for any such type of expenses.

b. Buyer's damages for breach in regard to accepted goods. As concluded above, AXO never accepted the sweaters, in the legal sense of the word "*acceptance.*" Therefore, AXO is not entitled to any damages under this statute.

c. Buyer's incidental and consequential damages. AXO does not claim any of these types of damages, and there was no evidence to justify an award for them. AXO is not entitled to any damages under this statute.

Questions

1. What was wrong with the sweaters?
2. Did AXO have to accept the sweaters at a reduced price?
3. What are AXO's damages?

19. Buyer's Resale of Goods

When the buyer has possession of the goods after rightfully rejecting them or after rightfully revoking acceptance, the buyer is treated as a seller in possession of goods after default by a buyer. When the seller has breached, the buyer has a security interest in the goods to protect the claim against the seller for breach and may proceed to resell the goods. From the proceeds of the sale, the aggrieved buyer is entitled to deduct any payments made to the seller and any expenses reasonably incurred in the inspection, receipt, transportation, care and custody, and resale of the goods.[27]

CPA 20. Action for Specific Performance

Specific performance is available under both existing and Revised UCC. Revised UCC expands this remedy a bit.[28] Revised Article 2 does not limit specific performance to the buyer. Specific performance is available to both sellers and buyers, and it is enforceable as a contract provision in nonconsumer contracts.

Under Article 2, specific performance is a remedy available only to buyers in those circumstances in which the goods are specially manufactured, unique, or rare, such as antiques or goods with sentimental value for the buyer. For example, a buyer with a contract to buy a chair from Elvis Presley's home would be entitled to a specific performance remedy of delivery of the chair. Distributors have been granted specific performance against suppliers to deliver goods covered by supply contracts because of the unique dependence of the supply chain and the assumed continuous feeding of that chain.

Specific performance will not be granted, however, merely because the price of the goods purchased from the seller has gone up. In such a case, the buyer can still purchase the goods in the open market. The fact that it will cost more to cover can be compensated for by allowing the buyer to recover the cost increase from the seller.

21. Nonsale Remedies of the Buyer

In addition to the remedies given the buyer under UCC Article 2, the buyer may have remedies based on contract or tort theories of liability.

The pre-Code law on torts still applies in UCC Article 2 transactions. The seller may therefore be held liable to the buyer for any negligence, fraud, or strict tort liability that occurred in the transaction. (See Chapter 25.)

A defrauded buyer may both avoid the contract and recover damages. The buyer also has the choice of retaining the contract and recovering damages for the losses caused by the fraud.[29]

Figure 27-2 provides a summary of the remedies available to buyers under Article 2.

[27] Revised UCC § 2-715(1); *Gordon v Gordon*, 929 So 2d 981 (Miss App 2006).
[28] Revised UCC § 2-716(1).
[29] *Baker v Wade*, 949 SW2d 199 (Mo App 1997).

FIGURE 27-2 Buyer's Remedies under Article 2

REMEDY	SPECIFIC PERFORMANCE (REPLEVIN IDENTIFICATION)	COVER	MARKET PRICE
SECTION NUMBER	2–711	2–712 2–715	2–708 2–710
WHEN AVAILABLE	Rare or unique goods	Seller fails to deliver or goods are defective (rejection) or revocation of acceptance	Seller fails to deliver or goods are defective (rejection or revocation of acceptance)
NATURE OF REMEDY	Buyer gets goods + incidental damages + consequential damages	Cover price – Contract price + Incidental damages + Consequential damages – Expenses saved	Market price – Contract price + Incidental damages + Consequential damages – Expenses saved

D. Contract Provisions on Remedies

The parties to a sales contract may modify the remedies provided under Article 2 or limit those remedies.

22. Limitation of Damages

CPA (a) Liquidated Damages

The parties may specify the exact amount of damages that may be recovered in case of breach. A **liquidated damages** clause in a contract can be valid if it meets the standards of Article 2. Under Revised Article 2, the enforceability of a liquidated damages clause in a consumer contract is determined by comparing the amount of the liquidated damages specified with the anticipated or actual harm, the difficulties of proof of loss, and the availability of an otherwise adequate remedy. For nonconsumer contracts, the enforceability of a liquidated damages clause depends on whether the amount is reasonable in light of the anticipated or actual harm.

(b) Exclusion of Damages

The sales contract may provide that in case of breach, no damages may be recovered or no consequential damages may be recovered. When goods are sold for consumer use and personal injuries are sustained, such total exclusions are unconscionable and unenforceable. Such a contract limitation is not enforceable in other types of contracts (nonconsumer) unless the party seeking to enforce it is able to prove that the limitation of liability was commercially reasonable and fair rather than oppressive and surprising. As discussed in Chapter 25, limitations on damages for personal injuries resulting from breaches of warranty are not enforceable.

CPA 23. Down Payments and Deposits

A buyer can make a deposit with the seller or an initial or down payment at the time of making the contract. If the contract contains a valid provision for liquidation of damages and the buyer defaults, the seller must return any part of the down payment or

RODRIGUEZ V LEARJET, INC., 946 P2D 1010 (KAN APP 1997)

THE COST OF BREACHING A JET-SET CONTRACT

On August 21, 1992, Miguel A. Diaz Rodriguez (Diaz) entered into a contract with Learjet to buy a model 60 jet aircraft for $3,000,000 with a $250,000 deposit made upon execution of the contract; a $750,000 payment on September 18, 1992; $1,000,000 180 days before delivery of the aircraft; and the balance due upon delivery of the aircraft. Diaz paid the $250,000 deposit but made no other payments. In fact, near the end of September 1992, Diaz told Alberto Castaneda of Learjet that he was purchasing the aircraft for Alejandro Burillo, his supervisor at Televisa, and that Burillo no longer wanted the aircraft. Diaz asked for the deposit to be returned.

On September 30, 1992, Castaneda sent Diaz a fax requesting payment. Then on October 6, 1992, Castaneda sent Diaz a letter with the following language: "Unless we receive payment from you or your company by October 9, 1992, [Learjet, Inc.,] will consider this agreement terminated and will retain all payments as liquidation damages in accordance with Paragraph C... of Section VII... of said agreement." By letter dated October 20, 1992, Learjet informed Diaz that it considered their contract terminated and that the $250,000 deposit was being retained as liquidated damages.

The contract provides, in part:

Learjet may terminate this Agreement as a result of the Buyer's failure to make any progress payment when due. If this Agreement is terminated by Learjet for any reason stipulated in the previous sentence Learjet shall retain all payments theretofore made by the Buyer as liquidated damages and not as a penalty and the parties shall thenceforth be released from all further obligations hereunder. Such damages include, but are not limited to, loss of profit on this sale, direct and indirect costs incurred as a result of disruption in production, training expense advance and selling expenses in effecting resale of the Airplane.

After Diaz breached the contract, Circus Circus Enterprises, Inc., purchased the Learjet Diaz had ordered with some changes that cost $1,326. Learjet realized a $1,887,464 profit on the sale of the aircraft to Circus Circus, which was a larger profit than Learjet had originally budgeted for the sale to Diaz.

Diaz filed suit seeking to recover the $250,000 deposit. The district court granted summary judgment to Learjet, and Diaz appealed. The case was remanded for a determination of the reasonableness of the liquidated damages. The district court upheld the $250,000 as reasonable damages, and Diaz appealed.

Judicial Opinion

MARQUARDT, Presiding J.... Diaz argues that the district court erred in holding that the liquidated damages clause was reasonable and enforceable. Diaz reasons that the liquidated damages clause was unreasonably large and, therefore, void as a penalty.

A determination concerning the reasonableness and enforceability of a liquidated damages clause is a question of law subject to unlimited review by this court. *Kvassay v Murray*, 15 Kan.App.2d 426, 429, 808 P.2d 896, *rev. denied* 248 Kan. 996 (1991).

K.S.A. 84-2-718 governs liquidated damages in contracts for the sale of goods and provides, in part:

(1) Damages for breach by either party may be liquidated in the agreement but only at an amount which is reasonable in the light of the anticipated or actual harm caused by the breach, the difficulties of proof of loss, and the inconvenience or nonfeasibility of otherwise obtaining an adequate remedy. A term fixing unreasonably large liquidated damages is void as a penalty.

In *Kvassay*, 15 Kan.App.2d at 430, 808 P.2d 896, this court noted that "reasonableness is the only test" for liquidated damages under the Uniform Commercial Code. This court paraphrased the three criteria for measuring the reasonableness of a liquidated damages clause provided in K.S.A. 84-2-718: "(1) anticipated or actual harm caused by breach; (2) difficulty of proving loss; and (3) difficulty of obtaining an adequate remedy." 15 Kan.App.2d at 430, 808 P.2d 896.

A liquidated damages clause that "'fixes damages in an amount grossly disproportionate to the harm actually sustained or likely to be sustained' " is considered a penalty and will not be enforced by the courts. If a liquidated damages clause is invalidated as a penalty, then the nonbreaching party may recover actual damages instead. The burden of proving that a liquidated damages clause is unenforceable rests with the party challenging its enforcement.

Diaz' challenge to the reasonableness of the liquidated damages clause focuses on the first factor of K.S.A. 84-2-718—the anticipated or actual harm caused by the breach. The question of whether a seller qualifies as a lost volume seller is relevant when evaluating whether a liquidated damages clause is reasonable in light of the anticipated or actual harm caused by the breach.

Diaz argues that the district court erred in concluding that Learjet qualifies as a lost volume seller. As a lost volume seller, Learjet's actual damages would include lost profits, notwithstanding that Circus purchased the aircraft which Diaz had contracted to buy and that Learjet made a profit on the Circus sale. The two contracts contained identical base prices, and both contracts had escalation clauses. The evidence indicates that the lost profit from the Diaz contract would have been approximately $1.8 million.

Whether a seller is a lost volume seller is a question of fact. Awarding lost profits to a lost volume seller serves the general principle that the purpose of awarding damages is to make a party whole by restoring the nonbreaching party to the position that the party occupied prior to the breach—to place a seller in as good a position as if a buyer had performed.

In *Diasonics*, 826 F.2d at 685, the court held that in order to qualify as a lost volume seller and recover for lost profits, a seller must establish three factors: (1) that it possessed the capacity to make an additional sale, (2) that it would have been profitable for it to make an additional sale, and (3) that it probably would have made an additional sale absent the buyer's breach. See also *R.E. Davis Chemical Corp. v Diasonics*, 924 F.2d 709, 711 (7th Cir.1991) (restating rule formulated in prior appeal of case);

Applying the more specific criteria established in *Diasonics*, there is adequate evidence to support the district court's finding. The master scheduler for Learjet testified that Learjet was operating at 60 percent capacity during the relevant time period and that Learjet was able to accelerate its production schedule to produce more of the model 60 planes in any given year. Learjet also presented testimony about its accounting system which indicated that an additional sale would have been profitable to Learjet. Learjet's profit from the Circus transaction and the similarity between the Diaz contract price and the Circus contract price also indicate that the additional sale would have been profitable.

We agree with the district court that Learjet qualifies as a lost volume seller and that the $250,000 in liquidated damages was reasonable in light of the anticipated or actual harm caused by the breach.

Even if we were to conclude that Learjet was not a lost volume seller, there is authority to support the holding that the liquidated damages clause was reasonable. In *Aero Consulting Corp. v Cessna Aircraft Co.*, 867 F.Supp. 1480, 1493–94 (D.Kan, 1994), the court held that a liquidated damages clause in an aircraft purchase agreement was reasonable under Kansas law. The *Aero* court did not consider the lost volume theory. The base price of the aircraft was $3,995,000. The liquidated damages, which were in the form of a deposit that was retained by Cessna after Aero breached, equaled $425,000. The court found that the liquidated damages clause "was reasonable in light of the damages that Cessna could reasonably anticipate would flow from such a cancellation of the contract." The court also noted that "in light of the nature of the production of aircraft and the costs associated with maintaining production, it would not be feasible for Cessna to otherwise obtain an adequate remedy for breach." Under both analyses, the liquidated damages claimed by Learjet were reasonable.

[Affirmed]

Questions

1. Does it matter that Learjet resold the Diaz plane?
2. Is the $250,000 reasonable?
3. Of what relevance is the fact that Learjet is a volume seller of goods?

deposit in excess of the amount specified by the liquidated damages clause. In the absence of such a liquidated damages clause and in the absence of proof of greater damages, the seller's damages are computed as 20 percent of the purchase price or $500, whichever is smaller. Offsetting the $500 against actual damages has been eliminated under Revised Article 2.

ETHICS & THE LAW

THE PHOTO FINISH ON A CONTRACT

Stock Solution is a "stock photo agency" that leases photographic transparencies produced by professional photographers for use in media advertising. Between October 1, 1994, and May 31, 1995, Stock Solution entered into four separate contracts with Axiom. Stock Solution delivered to Axiom, and Axiom took possession of 107 color transparencies to be used in Axiom's advertising. Each of the contracts between Stock Solution and Axiom contained identical provisions concerning the use and return of the leased transparencies. The contracts provided that in the event the transparencies were not returned by the specified "return date," Axiom would pay the following fees: (1) an initial "service charge" of $30; (2) "holding fee[s]" in the amount of "$5.00 per week per transparency"; (3) "service fees" at a rate of "one and one-half percent per month" on unpaid balances of invoices beginning 30 days after invoice; and (4) reimbursement for loss or damage of each "original transparency" in the amount of $1,500. Additionally, the contracts provided that if Stock Solution undertook the enforcement of the contracts, Axiom would "pay a reasonable attorney's fee . . . together with all costs of court."

Axiom failed to return 37 of the 107 transparencies in breach of the contracts. Of the 37 missing transparencies, 36 were original color transparencies and 1 was a duplicate color transparency. Stock Solution filed suit seeking damages (1) for the 36 missing original transparencies, the agreed liquidated value of $54,000 plus sales tax of $3,294; (2) for the 1 missing duplicate color transparency, $1 plus sales tax of $0.06; (3) holding fees on the 37 missing transparencies in the amount of $23,914.83; (4) service fees and charges as provided for in the contracts; and (5) attorney fees.

Discuss whether the liquidated damage clause was enforceable under the law. Discuss the ethical issues in the collection of such large sums for damages on contracts with relatively low fees. Do you think this contract is governed by UCC or common law? [*Bair v Axiom Design, L.L.C.*, 20 P3d 388 (Utah 2001)]

24. Limitation of Remedies

The parties may limit the remedies that are provided by the Code in the case of breach of contract. A seller may specify that the only remedy of the buyer for breach of warranty will be the repair or replacement of the goods or that the buyer will be limited to returning the goods and obtaining a refund of the purchase price, subject to the restrictions discussed in Chapter 25.

25. Waiver of Defenses

A buyer can be barred from claiming a breach of the contract by the seller if the sales contract expressly states that the buyer will not assert any defenses against the seller.

26. Preservation of Defenses

Consumer protection law prohibits the waiver of defenses in consumer contracts.

(a) Preservation Notice

Consumer defenses are preserved by a Federal Trade Commission (FTC) regulation. This regulation requires that the papers signed by a consumer contain a provision that expressly states that the consumer reserves any defense arising from the transaction.[30] A defense of the consumer arising from the original transaction may be asserted against any third person who acquires rights by assignment in the contract (see Chapter 33).

[30] 316 CFR § 433.1: It is an unfair or deceptive trade practice to take or receive a consumer credit contract that fails to contain such a preservation notice.

THINKING THINGS THROUGH

SOFTWARE AND CONSEQUENTIAL DAMAGES

The courts have been nearly universal in permitting software manufacturers to limit damages recoverable by buyers of software to replacement, return, or refund. Consequential damages have not been permitted as a part of a software purchaser's breach of contract against a manufacturer. Discuss the reasons the courts are willing to enforce these limitations that are limited to the price of software. [TAYLOR INVESTMENT CORP. v WEIL, 169 F Supp 2d 1046 (D Minn 2001)]

(b) Prohibition of Waiver

When the FTC preservation notice is included in the contract that is obtained by, or transferred to, a third party, a waiver of defenses cannot be made. If the preservation notice is not included, the seller has committed an unfair trade practice.

E. Remedies in the International Sale of Goods

The United Nations Convention on Contracts for the International Sale of Goods (CISG) provides remedies for breach of a sales contract between parties from nations that have approved the CISG.

27. Remedies of the Seller

Under the CISG, if the buyer fails to perform any obligations under the contract, the seller may require the buyer to pay the price, take delivery, and perform other obligations under the contract. The seller may also declare the contract void if the failure of the buyer to perform obligations under the contract amounts to a fundamental breach of contract.

28. Remedies of the Buyer

Under the CISG, a buyer may reject goods only if the tender is a fundamental breach of the contract. This standard of materiality of rejection is in contrast to the UCC requirement of perfect tender. Under the CISG, a buyer may also reduce the price when nonconforming goods are delivered even though no notice of nonconformity is given. However, the buyer must have a reasonable cause for failure to give notice about the nonconformity.

E-COMMERCE AND CYBERLAW

CONSEQUENTIAL DAMAGES AND SOFTWARE

Computer systems and software often do not function as intended or have some glitches when installed at a company. For example, suppose that a software company sold to a utility a software package that was represented as one that would simplify the utility's billing processes. The program is installed and tested, and some changes are made as a result of trial runs. When the program was fully implemented and all customers and bills were run through the new system, there was a complete breakdown. The bills could not be produced or sent to customers, and the utility company was without cash flow. Without bills going out, no payments are coming in, and the utility must borrow from a high-interest line of credit at an interest cost of $400,000 per month. What damages could the utility collect? Could the software manufacturer limit its liability?

Summary

The law provides a number of remedies for the breach of a sales contract. Remedies based on UCC theories generally are subject to a four-year statute of limitations, with Revised UCC adding an extension of one additional year (making it five years) in cases in which the breach is discovered in year four. If the remedy sought is based on a non-UCC theory, a tort or contract statute of limitations established by state statute will apply.

Remedies of the seller may include (1) a lien on the goods until the seller is paid, (2) the right to resell the goods, (3) the right to cancel the sales contract, (4) the right to recover the goods from the carrier and the buyer, and (5) the right to bring an action for damages or, in some cases, for the purchase price. The seller may also have remedies because of secured transactions.

Remedies of the buyer may include (1) the rejection of nonconforming goods, (2) the revocation of acceptance, (3) an action for damages for nondelivery of conforming goods, (4) an action for breach of warranty, (5) the cancellation of the sales contract, (6) the right to resell the goods, (7) the right to bring an action for conversion, recovery of goods, or specific performance, and (8) the right to sue for damages and cancel if the seller has made a material breach of the contract.

The parties may modify their remedies by a contractual provision for liquidated damages, for limitations on statutory remedies, or for waiver of defenses. When consumers are involved, this freedom of contract is to some extent limited for their protection.

Under the CISG, the seller may require the buyer to pay the price, take delivery, and perform obligations under the contract, or the seller may avoid the contract if there is a fundamental breach.

A buyer may reject goods under the CISG only if there is a fundamental breach of contract. The buyer may also reduce the price of nonconforming goods.

Questions and Case Problems

1. Firwood Manufacturing Co. had a contract to sell General Tire 55 model 1225 postcure inflators (PCIs). PCIs are $30,000 machines used by General Tire in its manufacturing process. The contract was entered into in 1989, and by April 1990 General Tire had purchased 22 PCIs from Firwood. However, General Tire then closed its Barrie, Michigan, plant. Firwood reminded General Tire that it still had the obligation to purchase the 33 remaining PCIs. General Tire communicated to Firwood that it would not be purchasing the remaining ones. Firwood then was able, over a period of three years, to sell the remaining PCIs. Some of the PCIs were sold as units, and others were broken down and sold to buyers who needed parts. Firwood's sales of the remaining 33 units brought in $187,513 less than the General Tire contract provided, and Firwood filed suit to collect the resale price difference plus interest. Can Firwood recover? Why or why not? [*Firwood Manufacturing Co., Inc. v General Tire, Inc.*, 96 F3d 163 (6th Cir)]
2. Soon after Gast purchased a used auto from a Chevrolet dealer, he experienced a series of mechanical problems with the car. Gast refused to make further payments on the bank note that had financed the purchase. The bank took possession of the automobile and sold it. Gast then brought an action against the dealer, alleging that he had revoked his acceptance. Was Gast correct? Explain your answer. [*Gast v Rodgers-Dingus Chevrolet*, 585 So 2d 725 (Miss)]
3. Formetal Engineering submitted to Presto a sample and specifications for precut polyurethane pads to be used in making air-conditioning units. Formetal paid for the goods as soon as they were delivered but subsequently discovered that the pads did not conform to the sample and specifications in that there were incomplete cuts, color variances, and faulty adherence to the pad's paper backing. Formetal then informed Presto of the defects and notified Presto that it would reject the pads and return them to Presto, but they were not returned for 125 days. Presto argued that it was denied the right to cure because the goods were not returned until some 125 days after Formetal promised to do so. Was there a breach of the contract? Did the buyer (Formetal) do anything wrong in seeking its remedies? [*Presto Mfg. Co. v Formetal Engineering Co.*, 360 NE2d 510 (Ill App)]
4. Lam entered into contracts with Dallas Semiconductor to build six machines, referred to in its contracts as Tools A-F. The price and status of the tools were as follows:

   Tool A priced at $3,629,298.10 had been tested, crated, and was ready to be shipped.

   Tool B priced at $4,121,049.30 had been tested and was ready to be shipped.

   Tool C priced at $3,435,835.50—construction of the machine had begun but was not finished.

   Tool D priced at $3,065,071.50—construction of the machine had never been started but materials had been ordered.

   Tool E priced at $1,027,805—construction of the machine had never been started but materials had been ordered.

Tool F priced at $4,107,522.85—construction of the machine had never been started but materials had been ordered.

The contracts were entered into in 2000 and in 2001, but Maxim Integrated acquired Dallas Semiconductor in 2001. The employees at Dallas who were in charge of the contracts continued to assure Lam that everything was on track. Lam representatives also had meetings with Maxim representatives. However, those discussions broke down and after Lam issued a demand letter for which there was no response, he filed suit for breach of contract. Lam was able to sell the machines to other customers for an equal or greater price. Lam asked for total damages in the amount of $13,860,847, representing lost profits on all six tools, plus lost profits on the extended warranties and training packages for the tools. Is Lam entitled to such recovery? [*Lam Research Corp. v. Dallas Semiconductor Corp.*, Excerpt from 2006 WL 1000573 (Cal.App)]

5. McNeely entered into a contract with Wagner to pay $250,000 as a lump sum for all timber present in a given area that Wagner would remove for McNeely. The contract estimated that the volume in the area would be 780,000 board feet. Wagner also had provisions in the contract that made no warranties as to the amount of lumber and that he would keep whatever timber was not harvested if McNeely ended the contract before the harvesting was complete. The $250,000 was to be paid in three advances. McNeely paid two of the three advances but withheld the third payment and ended the contract because he said there was not enough timber. Wagner filed suit for the remaining one-third of the payment. McNeely said Wagner could not have the remaining one-third of the payment as well as the transfer; he had to choose between the two remedies. Is he correct? [*Wagner v McNeely*, 38 UCC2d 1176 (Or)]

6. Brown Machine Company, a division of Kvaerner U.S., Inc., entered into a contract to supply a machine and tools to Hakim Plast, a food container–producing company based in Cairo, Egypt, to enable Hakim to meet its growing demand for plastic containers. The plastic containers were for customers to use in the ice cream distribution industry. It was understood that the equipment would be ready for delivery before the busy summer ice cream season. Brown Machine was not able to meet the twice extended deadline. It attempted to obtain another extension, but Hakim Plast refused without additional consideration. Brown refused to provide the requested consideration. Hakim Plast declared the contract breached on September 25, 1994. Brown then sold the equipment and brought suit for breach of contract, requesting damages for the loss of the sale. Hakim Plast countersued for Brown's breach seeking out-of-pocket expenses and consequential damages for loss of business. Discuss who breached the contract and determine what possible damages might be recovered. [*Kvaerner U.S., Inc. v Hakim Plast Co.*, 74 F Supp 2d 709 (ED Mich)]

7. When she was 17 years old, Cathy Bishop's parents signed a purchase contract for a new Hyundai automobile on which she made all payments. She was the primary driver of the vehicle, and while it was still under warranty, a manufacturing defect resulted in a fire that damaged it beyond reasonable repair. Although Hyundai was promptly notified and soon acknowledged responsibility for the fire, offers of replacement vehicles were rejected because they were not equivalent to the one destroyed, and monetary offers were rejected as being below its actual value. After Hyundai stated its final offer would expire on June 3, 1992 (some six months after negotiations began), Bishop sued for reimbursement of the vehicle's purchase price, as well as incidental and general damages, asking they be trebled by way of penalty for Hyundai's willful violation of the California "lemon law."

   At trial, Bishop testified at length to her emotional distress resulting from the unavailability of her car upon which she had relied to attend college classes and from her inability to procure new transportation, due in part because of her obligation to make the car payments to the lender. The jury awarded Bishop the value of her car, or $8,312.18, plus damages for "loss of use" in the amount of $17,223, incidental damages of $1,444, and emotional distress damages of $5,000. The jury found Hyundai's lemon law violation to be willful, making its total award $95,937.54. Bishop was awarded more than $50,000 in costs and attorney fees. Discuss all of the damage awards other than the lemon law awards and determine whether they are proper damages under the UCC. [*Bishop v Hyundai Motor America*, 44 Cal App 4th 750, 52 Cal Rptr 2d 134]

8. Mrs. Kirby purchased a wheelchair from NMC/Continue Care. The wheelchair was customized for her and her home. When the wheelchair arrived, it was too wide to fit through the doorways in her home. What options does Mrs. Kirby have? [*Kirby v NMC Continue Care*, 993 P2d 951 (Wyo)]

9. Wolosin purchased a vegetable and dairy refrigerator case from Evans Manufacturing Corp. When Evans sued Wolosin for the purchase price, Wolosin claimed damages for breach of warranty. The sales contract provided that Evans would replace defective parts free of charge for one year; it also stated, "This warranty is in lieu of any and all other warranties stated or inferred, and of all other obligations on the part of the manufacturer, which neither assumes nor authorizes anyone to assume for it any other obligations or liability in connection with the sale of its products." Evans claimed that it was liable only for replacement of parts. Wolosin claimed that the quoted clause was not sufficiently specific to satisfy the limitation-of-remedies requirement of UCC § 2-719. Provide some insight on this issue for the parties by

discussing damage limitation clauses under the UCC. [*Evans Mfg. Corp. v Wolosin*, 47 Luzerne County Leg Reg 238 (Pa)]

10. McInnis purchased a tractor and scraper as new equipment of the current model year from Western Tractor & Equipment Co. The written contract stated that the seller disclaimed all warranties and that no warranties existed except those stated in the contract. Actually, the equipment was not the current model but that of the prior year. The equipment was not new but had been used for 68 hours as a demonstrator model, after which the hour meter had been reset to zero. The buyer sued the seller for damages. The seller's defense was based on the ground that all liability for warranties had been disclaimed. Was this defense valid? [*McInnis v Western Tractor & Equipment Co.*, 388 P2d 562 (Wash)]
11. Elmore purchased a car from Doenges Brothers Ford. The car had been placed with the dealership by a dealership employee as part of a consignment arrangement. Elmore was unable to obtain title to the car because the Environmental Protection Agency had issues with the car's compliance with emissions equipment requirements. Elmore was unable to drive the car. He brought suit because he was forced to sell the car for $10,300 less than he paid because of the title defect, and the fact that only a salvage dealer would purchase it. Because he lost his transportation, he was out of work for eight months and experienced a $20,000 decline in income. What damages could Elmore recover under the UCC? [*Elmore v Doenges Bros. Ford, Inc.*, 21 P3d 65 (Okla App)]
12. The day after Adventists Living Center declared bankruptcy, one of its creditors, who had sold food for the home, demanded the return of the food. Can you provide a legal right that the food vendor might have to reclaim the food? [*In re Adventist Living Centers, Inc.*, 52 F3d 159 (7th Cir)]
13. Ramtreat Metal Technology provided for a "double your money back" remedy in its contracts for the sale of its metal drilling assemblies. A buyer filed suit seeking consequential damages and cost of replacement. Ramtreat said that its clause was a limitation of remedies. Could Ramtreat limit its remedies to "double your money back"? [*Adcock v Ramtreat Metal Technology, Inc.*, 44 UCC Rep Serv 2d 1026 (Wash App)]
14. Joseph Perna purchased a 1981 Oldsmobile at a traffic auction conducted by Locascio. The car had been seized pursuant to action taken by the New York City Parking Violation Bureau against Jose Cruz. Perna purchased the car for $1,800 plus tax and towing fees "subject to the terms and conditions of any and all chattel mortgages, rental agreements, liens, conditional bills of sale, and encumbrances that may be on the motor vehicle of the above judgment debtor." The Olds had 58,103 miles on it at the time of Perna's purchase. On May 7, 1993, Perna sold the car to Elio Marino, a coworker, for $1,200. The vehicle had about 65,000 miles on it at the time of this sale.

    During his period of ownership, Marino replaced the radiator ($270), repaired the power steering and valve cover gasket ($117), and replaced a door lock ($97.45). He registered and insured the vehicle. In February 1994, Marino's son was stopped by the police and arrested for driving a stolen vehicle. The son was kept in jail until his arraignment, but the charges were eventually dropped. The Oldsmobile was never returned to Marino, who filed suit for breach of contract because he had been given a car with a defective title. He asked for damages that included the costs of getting his son out of jail and having the theft charges dropped. Is he entitled to those damages? [*Marino v Perna*, 629 NYS2d 669 (NY Cir)]
15. Stephan's Machine & Tool, Inc., purchased a boring mill from D&H Machinery Consultants. The mill was a specialized type of equipment and was essential to the operation of Stephan's plant. The purchase price was $96,000, and Stephan's had to borrow this amount from a bank to finance the sale. The loan exhausted Stephan's borrowing capacity. The mill was unfit, and D&H agreed to replace it with another one. D&H did not keep its promise, and Stephan's sued it for specific performance of the contract as modified by the replacement agreement. Is specific performance an appropriate remedy? Discuss. [*Stephan's Machine & Tool, Inc. v D&H Machinery Consultants, Inc.*, 417 NE2d 579 (Ohio App)]

CPA Questions

1. On April 5, 1987, Anker, Inc., furnished Bold Corp. with Anker's financial statements dated March 31, 1987. The financial statements contained misrepresentations that indicated that Anker was solvent when in fact it was insolvent. Based on Anker's financial statements, Bold agreed to sell Anker 90 computers, "F.O.B.—Bold's loading dock." On April 14, Anker received 60 of the computers. The remaining 30 computers are in the possession of the common carrier and in transit to Anker. If, on April 28, Bold discovered that Anker was insolvent, then with respect to the computers delivered to Anker on April 14, Bold may

    a. Reclaim the computers upon making a demand
    b. Reclaim the computers irrespective of the rights of any third party

c. Not reclaim the computers since 10 days have elapsed from their delivery
d. Not reclaim the computers since it is entitled to recover the price of the computers

2. February 15, Mazur Corp. contracted to sell 1,000 bushels of wheat to Good Bread, Inc., at $6.00 per bushel with delivery to be made on June 23. On June 1, Good advised Mazur that it would not accept or pay for the wheat. On June 2, Mazur sold the wheat to another customer at the market price of $5.00 per bushel. Mazur had advised Good that it intended to resell the wheat. Which of the following statements is correct?
   a. Mazur can successfully sue Good for the difference between the resale price and the contract price.
   b. Mazur can resell the wheat only after June 23.
   c. Good can retract its anticipatory breach at any time before June 23.
   d. Good can successfully sue Mazur for specific performance.

3. Lazur Corp. entered into a contract with Baker Suppliers, Inc., to purchase a used word processor from Baker. Lazur is engaged in the business of selling new and used word processors to the general public. The contract required Baker to ship the goods to Lazur by common carrier pursuant to the following provision in the contract: "FOB Baker Suppliers, Inc., loading dock." Baker also represented in the contract that the word processor had been used for only 10 hours by its previous owner. The contract included the provision that the word processor was being sold "as is," and this provision was in a larger and different type style than the remainder of the contract. Assume that Lazur refused to accept the word processor even though it was in all respects conforming to the contract and that the contract is otherwise silent. Under the UCC Sales Article:
   a. Baker can successfully sue for specific performance and make Lazur accept and pay for the word processor.
   b. Baker may resell the word processor to another buyer.
   c. Baker must sue for the difference between the market value of the word processor and the contract price plus its incidental damages.
   d. Baker cannot successfully sue for consequential damages unless it attempts to resell the word processor.

PART (4)

NEGOTIABLE INSTRUMENTS

KINDS OF INSTRUMENTS, PARTIES, AND NEGOTIABILITY

CHAPTER (28)

LEARNING OBJECTIVES

After studying this chapter, you should be able to

LO.1 Explain the importance and function of negotiable instruments

LO.2 Name the parties to negotiable instruments

LO.3 Describe the concept of negotiability and distinguish it from assignability

LO.4 List the essential elements of a negotiable instrument

For convenience and as a way to facilitate transactions, businesses began to accept certain kinds of paper called **commercial paper** or negotiable instruments as substitutes for money or as a means of offering credit. Negotiable commercial paper is special paper created for the special purpose of facilitating transfer of funds and payment. In addition, the use of this special paper for special purposes can create additional rights in a special person status known as a *holder in due course.* Although the details on holders in due course are covered in Chapters 29 and 30, it is important to understand that one of the purposes of the use of special paper is to allow parties to achieve the special status of holder in due course and its protections and rights. Taking each component of negotiable instruments in step-by-step sequences, from their creation to the rights associated with each, and to their transfer, helps in understanding how commercial paper is used for special purposes in order to create rights for special persons.

A. Types of Negotiable Instruments and Parties

Article 3 of the Uniform Commercial Code (UCC) defines the types of negotiable instruments and the parties for each.[1] Article 3 of the UCC was last amended in 2002 with those reforms adopted in some states and under consideration in others.[2] Those changes are explained in each of the relevant sections.

CPA 1. Definition

Section 3-104(a)(1) and (2) of the UCC defines a **negotiable instrument** as "an unconditional promise or order to pay a fixed amount of money, . . . if it (1) is payable to bearer or order . . . ; (2) is payable on demand or at a definite time; and (3) does not state any other undertaking or instruction . . . to do any act in addition to the payment of money. . . ."[3] A *negotiable instrument* is a record of a signed promise or order to pay a specified sum of money.[4] The former requirement that the instrument be in writing to be valid has been changed to incorporate requirements of UETA (Uniform Electronic Transactions Act) and E-Sign (Electronic Signatures in Global and National Commerce Act of 2000). Many lenders now use electronic promissory notes.[5] In addition, we now have telephonic checks, or those withdrawals from your account that you authorize over the phone.

Instruments are negotiable when they contain certain elements required by the UCC. These elements are listed and explained in Section 5 of this chapter. However, even those instruments that do not meet the requirements for negotiability may still be referred to by their UCC names or classifications.

CPA 2. Kinds of Instruments

There are two categories of negotiable instruments: (1) promises to pay, which include promissory notes and certificates of deposit,[6] and (2) orders to pay, including drafts and checks.

(a) Promissory Notes

A **promissory note** is a written promise made and signed by the maker to pay a *sum certain* in money to the holder of the instrument.[7] (See Figure 28-1.)

CPA (b) Certificates of Deposit

A **certificate of deposit (CD)** is a promise to pay issued by a bank.[8] Through a CD, a bank acknowledges the customer's deposit of a specific sum of money and promises to pay the customer that amount plus interest when the certificate is surrendered.

[1] The law covering negotiable instruments has been evolving and changing. The latest version of Article 3 was adopted in 1990. The 1990 version of Article 3 had been adopted in all 50 states by August 1999. States with variations are Alabama, Georgia, Montana, Ohio, South Dakota, and Wisconsin.

[2] As of June 2006, Arkansas, Minnesota, Nevada, and Texas had adopted the amendments to Article 3.

[3] UCC § 3-104(a)(1) and (2).

[4] See UCC § 3-104. Article 3 has also been adopted in the District of Columbia, Puerto Rico, and the Virgin Islands. The earlier version was called UCC-Commercial Paper, and the 1990 version is called UCC-Negotiable Instruments.

[5] Electronic Signatures in Global and National Commerce Act, 15 USCS § 7001 (Supp 2001); James A. Newell, and Michael R. Gordon, "Electronic Commerce and Negotiable Instruments (Electronic Promissory Notes)," 31 *Idaho L. Rev.* 819, 826–834 (1995) (discussing the conversion of paper-based documentation to electronic form in commercial transactions).

[6] UCC § 3-104(j).

[7] *Apartment Inv. and Management Co. v National Loan Investors, L.P.* 518 SE2d 627 (Va 1999).

[8] UCC § 3-104(j).

FIGURE 28-1 Promissory Note

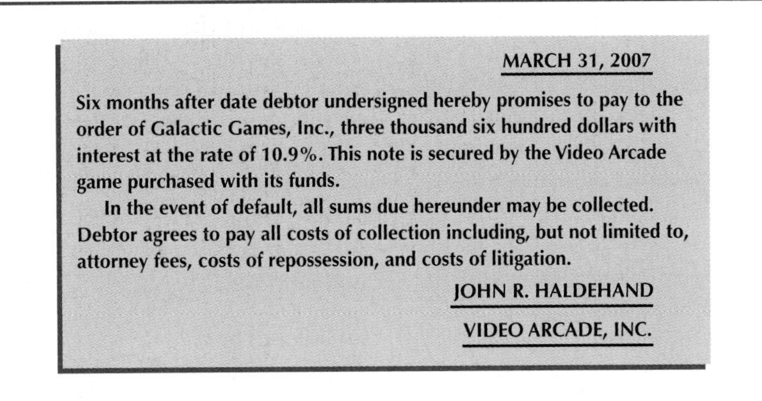

MARCH 31, 2007

Six months after date debtor undersigned hereby promises to pay to the order of Galactic Games, Inc., three thousand six hundred dollars with interest at the rate of 10.9%. This note is secured by the Video Arcade game purchased with its funds.

In the event of default, all sums due hereunder may be collected. Debtor agrees to pay all costs of collection including, but not limited to, attorney fees, costs of repossession, and costs of litigation.

JOHN R. HALDEHAND

VIDEO ARCADE, INC.

(c) Drafts

A **draft,** or **bill of exchange,** is an order by one party to pay a sum of money to a second party. (See Figure 28-2.) The party who gives the order is called the *drawer*, and the party on whom the order to pay is drawn is the *drawee.*[9] The party to whom payment is to be made is the *payee.* The drawer may also be named as the payee, as when a seller draws a draft naming a buyer as the drawee. The draft is then used as a means to obtain payment for goods delivered to that buyer. A drawee is not bound to pay a draft simply because the drawer has placed his name on it. However, the drawee may agree to pay the draft by accepting it, which then attaches the drawee's liability for payment.

CPA (d) Checks

Under UCC § 3-104(f), *check* means "a draft, other than a documentary draft, payable on demand and drawn on a bank."[10] A **check** is an order by a depositor (the drawer) on a bank or credit union (the drawee) to pay a sum of money to the order of another party (the payee).[11]

In addition to the ordinary checks just described, there are also cashier's checks, teller's checks, traveler's checks, and bank money orders. A **cashier's check** is a draft drawn by a bank on itself. UCC § 3-104(g) defines a cashier's check as "a draft with respect to which the drawer and drawee are the same bank or branches of the same bank."[12] A **teller's**

FIGURE 28-2 Draft

TO: Topa Fabrics, Inc.
1700 W. Lincoln
Marina Del Rey, CA

March 17, 20 07

Thirty days from date PAY TO THE ORDER OF
Malden Mills, Inc.
THE SUM OF sixteen thousand and no/100 DOLLARS

ACCEPTED BY:

DATE

Aaron Johnson
Malden Mills, Inc.

[9] UCC § 3-103(a)(2)–(3).

[10] UCC § 3-104(f).

[11] *Id.*

[12] UCC § 3-104(g).

check is a draft drawn by a bank on another bank in which it has an account.[13] A **traveler's check** is a check that is payable on demand, provided it is countersigned by the person whose signature was placed on the check at the time the check was purchased.[14] Money orders are issued by both banks and nonbanks. A **money order** drawn by a bank is also a check.[15]

3. Parties to Instruments

A note has two original parties: the *maker* and the *payee*.[16] A draft or a check has three original parties: the *drawer*, the *drawee*, and the *payee*. The names given to the parties to these instruments are important because the liability of the parties varies depending on the parties' roles. The rights and liabilities of the various parties to negotiable instruments are covered in Chapters 29 and 30.

A **party** to an instrument may be a natural person, an artificial person such as a corporation, or an unincorporated enterprise such as a government agency.

CPA (a) Maker

The **maker** is the party who writes or creates a promissory note, thereby promising to pay the amount specified in the note.

CPA (b) Drawer

The **drawer** is the party who writes or creates a draft or check.

CPA (c) Drawee

The **drawee** is the party to whom the draft is addressed and who is ordered to pay the amount of money specified in the draft. The bank is the drawee on a check, and the credit union is the drawee on a share draft. Again, a drawee on a draft has no responsibility under the draft until it has accepted that instrument.

CPA (d) Payee

The **payee** is the person named in the instrument to receive payment. **For Example,** on a check with the words "Pay to the order of John Jones," the named person, John Jones, is the payee.

The payee has no rights in the instrument until the drawer or the maker has delivered it to the payee. Likewise, the payee is not liable on the instrument in any way until the payee transfers the instrument to someone else.

(e) Acceptor

When the drawee of a draft has indicated by writing or record, a willingness to pay the amount specified in the draft, the drawee has accepted liability and is called the **acceptor.**[17]

(f) Secondary Obligor (Accommodation Party)

When a party who is not originally named in an instrument allows her name to be added to it for the benefit of another party in order to add strength to the collectability of the instrument, that party becomes a secondary obligor (formerly called an **accommodation party**) and assumes a liability role.[18] Revised Article 3 now refers to drawer, indorsers, and accommodation parties as "secondary obligors."[19]

B. Negotiability

An instrument is a form of contract that, if negotiable, affords certain rights and protections for the parties. **Negotiability** is the characteristic that distinguishes commercial paper and instruments from ordinary contracts or what makes such paper and instruments special paper.[20] That an instrument is negotiable means that certain rights and protections may be available to the parties to the instrument under Article 3. A **nonnegotiable instrument's**

[13] UCC § 3-104(h).

[14] UCC § 3-104(i).

[15] Some items are held to be checks for purposes other than Article 3 negotiability. For example, in *In re Armstrong* 291 F3d 517 (CA 8 2002), the court held that gambling markers were checks for purposes of the state's "bad check" law.

[16] UCC § 3-103(a)(5).

[17] UCC § 3-103(a)(1).

[18] UCC § 3-419; *In re TML, Inc.*, 291 BR 400, 50 UCC Rep Serv 2d 511 (WD Mich 2003); *Interbank of New York v Markou*, 649 NY Supp 2d 462 (1996).

[19] Revised Article 3, § 3-103(12), has the following definition of a secondary obligor on an instrument: "an indorser, a drawer, an accommodation party, or any other party to the instrument that has a right of recourse against another party to the instrument. . . ." This definition was changed to make the language of Revised Article 3 consistent with the Restatement of Surety.

[20] UCC § 3-104.

E-COMMERCE AND CYBERLAW

THE CHECK IS IN THE INTERNET

The Check Clearing for the 21st Century Act ("Check 21") allows banks to use electronic images of checks as full and complete records of transactions, the same status formerly used only for paper checks that had been canceled.

terms are enforceable, but the instrument is treated simply as a contract governed by contract law.[21]

4. Definition of Negotiability

If an instrument is negotiable, it is governed by Article 3 of the UCC, and it may be transferred by negotiation. This form of transfer permits the transferee to acquire rights greater than those afforded assignees of contracts under contract law. The quality of negotiability in instruments creates opportunities for transfers and financings that streamline payments in commerce. Transfers can be made with assurance of payment without the need for investigation of the underlying contract. The process of negotiation is covered in Chapter 29. For more information on the rights of assignees of contracts, refer to Chapter 18.

CPA 5. Requirements of Negotiability

To be negotiable, an instrument (1) must be evidenced by a record[22] and (2) must be signed (authenticated under Revised Article 3) by the maker or the drawer, (3) must contain an unconditional promise or order to pay, (4) must pay a sum certain, (5) must be payable in money, (6) must be payable on demand or at a definite time, and (7) must be payable to order or bearer, using what are known as words of negotiability.[23]

(a) A Record (Writing)

A negotiable instrument must be evidenced by a record. The requirement of a *record*, under Revised Article 3, is satisfied by handwriting, typing, printing, electronic record, and any other method of making a record. A negotiable instrument may be partly printed and partly typewritten. No particular form is required for an instrument to satisfy the record requirement, although customers of banks may agree to use the banks' forms as part of their contractual agreement with their banks. The telephonic check has become a widely used tool for consumers to pay bills. They simply contact their creditor, give the creditor the routing and account numbers for their checking accounts, and the creditor receives the payment electronically. At least one court has held that the telephonic check is a check, complete with a record, for purposes of Article 3 rights and obligations.

(b) Authenticated (Signed) by the Maker or Drawer

The instrument must be authenticated (signed under old Article 3) by the maker or the drawer. When a signature is used as authentication, it usually appears at the lower right-hand corner of the face of the instrument, but there is no requirement for where the signature must be placed on the instrument.[24]

The authentication may consist of the full name or of any symbol placed with the intent to authenticate

21 A note payable when "lessee is granted possession of the premises" is not a negotiable instrument, but it is an enforceable contract. *Schiffer v United Grocers, Inc.*, 989 P2d 10 (Or 1999).

22 This refers to Revised Article 3. Existing Article 3 requires a writing, but the revisions reflect electronic transactions and the federal mandate for recognizing electronic transactions as valid and on equal footing with paper transactions. The definition of a record is found in Revised UCC § 3-103(a)(14), which provides that *record* "means information that is inscribed on a tangible medium or which is stored in an electronic or other medium and is retrievable in perceivable form."

23 UCC § 3-104.

24 According to Revised UCC § 3-103, *authenticate* means (a) to sign or (b) to execute or otherwise adopt a symbol, or encrypt or similarly process a record in whole or in part, with the present intent of the authenticating person to identify the person and adopt or accept a record.

the instrument. Other means of authentication that are valid as signatures include initials, figures, and marks. Electronic security devices can be used as a means of authentication for electronic records. A person signing a trade name or an assumed name is liable just as if the signer's own name had been used.

(1) Agent. An authentication may be made by the drawer or the maker or by his or her authorized agent. **For Example,** Eileen Smith, the treasurer of Mills Company, could sign a note for her company as an agent. No particular form of authorization for an agent to authenticate an instrument is required. An authenticating agent should disclose on the instrument (1) the identity of the principal and (2) the fact that the authentication was done in a representative capacity. When this information appears on the face of the instrument, an authorized agent is not liable on it.

The representative capacity of an officer of an organization can be shown by the authentication of the officer along with the title of the office and the organization's name.[25] **For Example,** a signature of "James Shelton, Treasurer, NorWest Utilities, Inc.," or "NorWest Utilities, Inc., by James Shelton, Treasurer," on a note is enough to show Shelton's representative capacity. NorWest Utilities, not Shelton, would be liable on the note.

(2) Absence of Representative Capacity or Identification of Principal. If an instrument fails to show the **representative capacity** of the person who is authenticating or fails to identify the person, then the individual who authenticates the instrument is personally liable on the instrument to anyone who acquires superior rights, such as the rights of a holder in due course (see Chapter 30). Because the instrument is a final agreement, the parol evidence rule applies, and the party who authenticated is not permitted to introduce extrinsic evidence that might clarify his or her representative capacity. The party who authenticated, in order to avoid personal liability, must indicate on the face of the instrument his or her role in the principal, such as president or vice president. (For more information about the parol evidence rule, see Chapter 17.)

However, an agent is not personally liable on a check that is drawn on the bank account of the principal and authenticated by him or her, even though the agent failed to disclose his or her representative capacity on the check. **For Example,** a check that is already imprinted with the employer's name is not the check of the employee, regardless of whether the employee only authenticates with his or her name or also adds a title such as "Payroll Clerk" or "Treasurer" near the signature.

MAJOR PRODUCTS CO., INC. V NORTHWEST HARVEST PRODUCTS, INC.,

979 P2D 905 (WASH APP 1999)

THE STICKY NOTE THAT WAS A REMINDER OF PERSONAL LIABILITY

FACTS: Northwest Harvest Products, Inc. fell behind on payments on its account with Major Products Company, Inc. Major requested a note for the debt, and Northwest sent a $79,000 corporate note. The balance on the note was incorrect, and Northwest sent a second corporate note for $79,361.89. After further discussion, Major sent yet another note for $78,445.24. The Chief Executive Officer of Northwest at that time signed the note "Donald H Eoll CEO," attached a Post-It™ fax transmittal memo indicating that the note came from Donald Eoll at Northwest, and sent the note via facsimile. The note was not paid, and Major sued both Eoll and Northwest for the debt. Only the facsimile copy of the note was presented at trial, and the trial court found that the writing on the Post-It note, coupled with the signature, identified Northwest as the principal on the note. The trial court held that Eoll was not personally liable for the debt because he signed the note as an agent for Northwest. Major appealed.

25 UCC § 3-402.

Judicial Opinion

BAKER, J.... Major appeals, contending that the Post-It brand fax transmittal memo served as a mere convenience for Eoll's transmission of the note and thus Eoll's signature did not identify Northwest as the principal on the note. We agree with Major that the writing on a Post-It brand fax transmittal memo is independent of an underlying document. Thus Eoll's signature did not identify Northwest as the principal on the note and it is not apparent from the body of the note that he signed as an agent for Northwest. Eoll bore the burden of rebutting a presumption of personal liability. Because Eoll did not provide evidence or testimony that rebutted that presumption, he is personally liable on the note.

Unless the instrument clearly indicates that a signature is made in some other capacity it is an indorsement.

Major contends that the Post-It brand memo was merely a convenience for Eoll to facilitate the transmission of the agreement from one facsimile machine to another and did not form an integral part of the parties' agreement. The legal effect of such a memo presents an issue of first impression in this state. In *Birenbaum v Option Care, Inc.*, 971 S.W.2d 497 (Tex.App.1997), a Post-It brand fax transmittal memo with writing and a signature was attached to a document prior to its transmission. The court found that a signature on a Post-It brand memo is not evidence from which the trial court could infer an intent to sign the underlying document. Instead, the information and signature on the Post-It brand memo were independent of the underlying document and were not operative on that document in the same manner as a signature on the underlying document would have been.

We think that *Birenbaum* sets forth a sound approach for dealing with Post-It brand fax transmittal memos and the like. We hold that such writings are independent of an underlying document and do not have the same legal effect as writing on the face of a document. Although extrinsic evidence may sometimes show that such writings form an integral part of an agreement, our holding furthers contract law's objective of protecting the justified expectations of parties by promoting certainty in business dealings. The transmission of documents via facsimile is a technological advance that should reinforce the justified expectations of parties by improving transactional communications, and we reject Eoll's arguments that attempt to introduce legal uncertainty into business dealings that are assisted by such advances. If a party wishes to include information or make a modification on the face of a document transmitted via facsimile, such information or modification should be made in writing on the document directly, not by means of a writing that is easily detached or separated from the original.

Because the Post-It brand fax transmittal memo here is independent of the note, the signature on the parties' agreement reads only "Donald H Eoll CEO." Thus for purposes of former RCW 62A.3-403(2)(b), the note does not name the person represented (Northwest), but does show that Eoll signed in a representative capacity. That signature might indicate that the parties intended Eoll would be personally bound by the note or that Eoll would not be personally bound by the note, and thus further inquiry into the parties' intent is warranted.

The indication that the signature is made in another capacity must be clear without reference to anything but the instrument. It may be found in the language used. Thus if John Doe signs after "I, John Doe, promise to pay," he is clearly a maker; and "John Doe, witness" is not liable at all. The capacity may be found in any clearly evidenced purpose of the signature, as where a drawee signing in an unusual place on the paper has no visible reason to sign at all unless he is an acceptor. It may be found in usage or custom. Thus by long established practice judicially noticed or otherwise established a signature in the lower right hand corner of an instrument indicates an intent to sign as the maker of a note or the drawer of a draft. Any similar clear indication of an intent to sign in some other capacity may be enough to remove the signature from the application of this section.

Although extrinsic evidence was admissible as an aid to show these parties' intent, ... Eoll failed to present extrinsic evidence which would rebut a presumption of personal liability. Eoll is personally liable on this note.

Reversed Questions

1. Without the Post-it, what information was on the promissory note?
2. Why does the court believe that we should not include what is written on Post-it notes as part of a document?
3. Would the court have allowed extrinsic evidence to show who was liable?

CPA (c) Promise or Order to Pay

A promissory note must contain a promise to pay money. A mere acknowledgment of a debt, such as a record stating "I.O.U.," is not a promise. A draft or check must contain an order or command to pay money.

(d) Unconditional Promise or Order

For an instrument to be negotiable, the promise or order to pay must be unconditional.[26]

For Example, when an instrument makes the duty to pay dependent on the completion of the construction of a building, the promise is conditional and the instrument is nonnegotiable. The instrument is enforceable as a contract, but it is not a negotiable instrument given all the rights and protections afforded under Article 3.

An order for the payment of money out of a particular fund is negotiable. The instrument can refer to a particular account or merely indicate a source of reimbursement for the drawee, such as "Charge my expense account." Nor is an instrument conditional when payment is to be made only from an identified fund if the issuer is a government or government unit or agency, or when payment is to be made from the assets of a partnership, unincorporated association, trust, or estate.[27] However, the fund noted must in fact exist because payment from a fund to be created by a future event would be conditional. **For Example,** making an instrument "payable from the account I'll establish when the sale of my house occurs" is conditional because the fund's creation is tied to an event whose time of occurrence is unknown.

THINKING THINGS THROUGH

Work through the following examples of signatures on negotiable instruments, capacity, and personal liability.

1. George S. Avery signed a letter regarding the unpaid balance on a $20,000 promissory note owed to Jim Whitworth in the form of a letter addressed to Whitworth stating: "This is your note for $45,000.00, secured individually and by our Company for your security, due February 7, 1984." The letter was signed: "Your friend, George S. Avery." It was typed on stationery with the name of Avery's employer, V & L Manufacturing Co., Inc., printed at the bottom and the words "George Avery, President" printed at the top. Avery says he is not personally liable on the note. The court granted summary judgment for Whitworth and Avery appealed. Who is liable? AVERY V WHITWORTH, 414 SE2d 725 (Ga App 1992)
2. A corporate guaranty was signed contemporaneously with the promissory note. The guaranty reads, "[f]or good and valuable consideration, The Producers Group of Florida, Inc. hereby guarantees the Tampa Bay Economic Development Corporation prompt and full payment of the following debt." The corporate guaranty was signed as follows:

   THE PRODUCERS GROUP OF FLA., INC. a Florida corporation, by the following officers solely on behalf of the corporation:

   /s/ Eddie Beverly, as its President
   CORPORATE PRESIDENT Eddie Beverly

   /s/ Stephen Edman, as its Secretary
   CORPORATE SECRETARY Steve Edman

   /s/ John Bauder, as its Treasurer
   CORPORATE TREASURER John Bauder

   Are the officers personally liable on the guaranty? TAMPA BAY ECONOMIC DEVELOPMENT CORP. V EDMAN, 598 So 2d 172 (Fla App 1992)

[26] UCC § 3-109(c).

[27] *De Bry v Cascade Enterprises*, 879 P2d 1353 (Utah 1994).

ETHICS & THE LAW

HOT DOG! HE HAS LIABILITY!

Fred Dowie was the president and sole shareholder of Fred Dowie Enterprises, a catering business. Dowie learned that the Pope was coming to visit Des Moines, Iowa, and decided to operate a hot dog concession stand near the site of the Pope's speech. Dowie ordered 325,000 hot dog buns from Colonial Baking Company of Des Moines. He paid for them with a postdated check that had the name "Dowie Enterprises, Inc.," imprinted on it. Dowie signed the check "Frederick J. Dowie" in the appropriate place.

The demand for hot dogs during the Pope's visit to Des Moines was not what Dowie had anticipated. As a result, there was nothing left financially to Fred Dowie Enterprises. The check to Colonial did not clear the catering business account. Colonial then presented the check to Dowie for payment. Dowie has told Colonial he was not liable for the amount. Is he correct? What ethical issues do you see in one person running an undercapitalized corporation but enjoying the legal protection afforded this business entity? Apart from his legal obligation, does Dowie have an ethical obligation to pay for the buns? [*Colonial Baking Co. of Des Moines v Dowie,* 330 NW2d 279 (Iowa 1983)]

The standards for negotiability do not require that the issuer of the instrument be personally obligated to pay it.[28] An instrument's negotiability is not destroyed by a reference to a related document. Section 3-106(b) provides, "A promise or order is not made conditional (i) by a reference to another writing for a statement of rights with respect to collateral, prepayment, or acceleration."[29] **For Example,** if a note includes the following phrase, "This note is secured by a mortgage on the property located at Hilding Lane," the note is still negotiable.[30]

(e) Payment in Money

A negotiable instrument must be payable in money. **Money** is defined to include any medium of exchange adopted or authorized by the United States, a foreign government, or an intergovernmental organization. The parties to an instrument are free to decide which currency will be used for payment even though their transaction may occur in a different country.[31] **For Example,** two parties in the United States are free to agree that their note will be paid in pesos.

If the order or promise is not for money, the instrument is not negotiable. **For Example,** an instrument that requires the holder to take stock or goods in place of money is nonnegotiable. The instrument is enforceable as a contract, but it cannot qualify as a negotiable instrument for purposes of Article 3 rights.

CPA (f) Sum Certain

Negotiable instruments must include a statement of a **sum certain,** or an exact amount of money. Without a definite statement as to how much is to be paid under the terms of the instrument, there is no way to determine how much the instrument is worth.

There are some minor variations from sum certain requirement. **For Example,** an instrument is not nonnegotiable because its interest rate provisions include changes in the rate at maturity or because it provides for certain costs and attorney fees to be recovered by the holder in the event of enforcement action or litigation.[32]

In most states, the sum payable under an instrument is certain even though it calls for the payment

[28] UCC § 3-110(c)(1)–(2) (1990); and *DH Cattle Holdings Co. v Smith,* 607 NYS2d 227 (1994).
[29] UCC § 3-106(b).
[30] Reference to a bill of lading does not affect negotiability. *Regent Corp., U.S.A. v Azmat Bangladesh, Ltd.,* 686 NYS2d 24 (1999).
[31] UCC § 3-107.
[32] UCC § 3-106.

of a floating or variable interest rate.[33] An instrument is negotiable even though it provides for an interest rate of 1 percent above the prime rate of a named bank. It is immaterial that the exact amount of interest that will be paid cannot be determined at the time the paper is issued because the rate may later change. It is also immaterial that the amount due on the instrument cannot be determined without looking at records outside of the face of the instrument.[34]

CPA (g) Time of Payment

A negotiable instrument must be payable on demand or at a definite time.[35] If an instrument is payable "when convenient," it is nonnegotiable because the day of payment may never arrive. An instrument payable only upon the happening of a particular event that may or may not happen is not negotiable. **For Example,** a provision in a note to pay the sum certain when a person marries is not payable at a definite time because that particular event may never occur. It is immaterial whether the contingency in fact has happened because from an examination of the instrument alone, it still appears to be subject to a condition that might not occur.

(1) Demand. An instrument is *payable on demand* when it expressly states that it is payable "on demand," at sight, or on presentation. UCC § 3-108(a) provides "A promise or order is 'payable on demand' if (i) it states that it is payable on demand or at sight, or otherwise indicates that it is payable at the will of the holder, or (ii) it does not state any time of payment."[36] Presentation occurs when a holder demands payment. Commercial paper is deemed to be payable on demand when no time for payment is stated in the instrument.[37]

(2) Definite Time. The time of payment is a **definite time** if an exact time or times are specified or if the instrument is payable at a fixed time after sight or acceptance or at a time that is readily ascertainable. The time of payment is definite even though the instrument provides for prepayment, for acceleration, or for extensions at the option of a party or automatically on the occurrence of a specified contingency.

(3) Missing Date. An instrument that is not dated is deemed dated on the day it is issued to the payee. Any holder may add the correct date to the instrument.

(4) Effect of Date on a Demand Instrument. The date on a demand instrument controls the time of payment, and the paper is not due before its date. Consequently, a check that is postdated ceases to be demand paper and is not properly payable before the date on the check. A bank making earlier payment does not incur any liability for doing so unless the drawer has given the bank a postdated check notice.

NORTHERN BANK V PEFFERONI PIZZA CO., 562 NW2D 374 (NEB 1997)

THE PIZZA NOTE WITH NO DEFINITE TIME FOR DELIVERY

On September 30, 1987, Pefferoni Pizza (defendant-appellant) agreed to purchase certain businesses from W. E. Peffer Enterprises, Inc. Duane J. Dowd, president of Pefferoni Pizza, signed a $125,000 promissory note payable to Peffer Enterprises. The note (referred to as the collateral note) included the following provision:

The Maker hereof has certain rights under Purchase Agreement dated September 30, 1987, to negotiate a new loan for [Peffer Enterprises] to replace the Underlying Notes in an amount up to $125,000.00 at a lower rate of interest and for a term extending up to 84 months from and after the closing on the purchase. In the event that

[33] *Means v Clardy*, 735 SW2d 6 (Mo App 1987); while revised Article 3 permits variable and market rates, notes entered into before the revised act was adopted will be governed under old Article 3; *YYY Corp. v Gazda*, 761 A2d 395 (NH 2000), *Barnsley v Empire Mortgage, Ltd. Partnership*, 720 A2d 63 (NH 1998).

[34] *SCADIF, S.A. v First Union Nat. Bank*, 208 F Supp 2d 1352 (SD Fla 2002), aff'd, 344 F3d 1123 (CA 11 2003). See also *Bankers Trust v 236 Beltway Investment*, 865 F Supp 1186 (ED Va 1994).

[35] UCC § 3-108.

[36] UCC § 3-108(a).

[37] UCC § 3-112; *Universal Premium Acceptance Corp. v York Bank's Trust Co.*, 69 F3d 695 (3d Cir 1995).

the Maker hereof negotiates such a loan, then as of the date that the Underlying Notes are paid in full or reduced with the proceeds of the new loan, the remaining principal balance due and owing under this Note shall be re-amortized over such term and at such rate of interest as may be negotiated for [Peffer Enterprises] by the Maker hereof on the new loan. When and if such events occurs [sic], a written amendment evidencing such modification shall be executed by the Maker and Holder hereof.

On January 14, 1988, Northern Bank (plaintiff-appellee) loaned Walter Peffer Jr. $35,000, which was evidenced by a promissory note (called the Peffer note). As security for this $35,000 loan, Walter Peffer assigned the collateral note to Northern. On July 25, 1988, Northern advised Pefferoni of the assignment and that all payments should be made directly to Northern. Pefferoni had made all regular payments to Walter Peffer through July 1, 1988. However, Walter Peffer defaulted on his note and a judgment was entered against him on September 1, 1989.

Northern's position is that the collateral note is a negotiable instrument and that it holds the instrument as a holder in due course (see Chapter 29) and is entitled to payment free and clear of any defenses in the Peffer/Pefferoni Pizza contract. Northern filed suit, and the district court granted summary judgment. The court of appeals held the note to be nonnegotiable, and Northern appealed.

Judicial Opinion

CAPORALE, J.... For a writing to be a negotiable instrument, it must, among other things, be payable on demand or at a definite time. Instruments payable on demand include those payable at sight or on presentation and those in which no time for payment is stated. The instant writing is not payable at sight or on presentation; thus, it is not payable on demand.

An instrument is payable at a definite time if by its terms it is payable (a) on or before a stated date or at a fix period after a stated date, or (b) at a fixed period after sight, or (c) at a definite time subject to any acceleration, or (d) at a definite time subject to extension at the option of the holder, or to extension to a further definite time at the option of the maker or acceptor or automatically upon or after a specified act or event. The time for payment is definite if it can be determined from the face of the instrument. If an extension is to be at the option of the maker, a definite time limit must be stated or the time of payment remains uncertain and the instrument is not negotiable.

The collateral note recites that it was made "in conjunction with a certain Purchase Agreement dated September 30, 1987," and stipulated it be paid in 60 equal monthly installments of $2,748.75 commencing on the first day of November 1987, and on the first of every month thereafter, subject to the extension described in the provision set forth previously. Therefore, if Pefferoni Pizza were to negotiate a new loan for the underlying notes, the repayment schedule of the collateral note would be altered to match the repayment schedule of the renegotiated underlying notes. Although the renegotiation clause in the collateral note declares that the extension cannot exceed 84 months from and after the closing on the purchase, the note does not state the date of closing.

Northern recognizes that in order to be definite, the time for payment must be determinable from the face of the collateral note, and contends that by the references made in the note to other documents, it becomes clear that any extension could not exceed 84 months from and after September 30, 1987. More specifically, Northern argues:

A promissory note made at the same time and in conjunction with a purchase agreement, secured by a security agreement also made and given at the same time and as part of the same transaction and which specifies that interest accrues from its date and that the first payment of principal and interest will be due one month from its date can only lead to the conclusion that the purchase was closed at the same time and on the same date that the purchase agreement, note and security agreement were signed. If the purchase contemplated by the Purchase Agreement was to be closed at some date after the date of the Collateral Note and the Purchase Agreement, then the Collateral Note would not have specified that interest was to accrue from the date of the Collateral Note. Rather, it would have specified that the interest was to accrue only upon the later closing date.

Although Northern's argument is a plausible interpretation of the various provisions of the note, it is equally plausible to suggest that if the closing was in fact held on September 30, 1987, contemporaneously with the execution of the collateral note, there would have been no reason for the note to refer to an unspecified closing date; rather, the note would simply have recited that the extension could not be longer than 84 months thereafter, or through September 30, 1994. In short, the inferences to be drawn from the recitations in the note are far too ambiguous to permit us to conclude that the closing of the purchase necessarily took place on September 30, 1987. That being so, we must conclude that the collateral note is not on its face payable at a definite time and that it is therefore not negotiable.

The judgment of the Court of Appeals being correct, it is, as noted in the first paragraph hereof, affirmed.

[Affirmed]

Questions

1. What is the problem with the note?
2. Why is it important for Northern to have a negotiable note?
3. How could the parties have made the note negotiable?

CPA (h) Words of Negotiability: Payable to Order or Bearer

An instrument that is not a check must be **payable to order** or **bearer.**[38] This requirement is met by such phrases as "Pay to the order of John Jones," "Pay to John Jones or order," "Pay to bearer," and "Pay to John Jones or bearer." The use of the phrase "to the order of John Jones" or "to John Jones or order" shows that the person executing the instrument had no intention of restricting payment of the instrument to John Jones. These phrases indicate that there is no objection to paying anyone to whom John Jones orders the paper to be paid. Similarly, if the person executing the instrument originally wrote that it will be paid "to bearer" or "to John Jones or bearer," there is no restriction on the payment of the paper to the original payee. However, if the instrument is not a check and it is payable on its face "to John Jones," the instrument is not negotiable.[39] Whether an instrument is bearer or order paper is important because the two instruments are transferred in different ways and because the liability of the transferors can be different.

CPA *(1) Order Paper.* An instrument is payable to order, or **order paper,** when by its terms it is payable to the order of any person described in it ("Pay to the order of K. Read") or to a person or order ("Pay to K. Read or order").

CPA *(2) Bearer Paper.* An instrument is payable to bearer, or **bearer paper,** when it is payable (1) to bearer or the order of bearer, (2) to a specified person or bearer, or (3) to "cash," "the order of cash," or any other designation that does not purport to identify a person or when (4) the last or only indorsement is a blank indorsement (an indorsement that does not name the person to whom the instrument is negotiated). An instrument that does not identify any payee is payable to bearer.[40]

Whether an instrument is bearer or order paper is important for determining how the instrument is transferred (see Chapter 28) and what the liability of the parties under the instrument is. Review Figure 28-3 for more background.

CPA 6. Factors not Affecting Negotiability

Omitting a date of execution or antedating or **postdating** an instrument has no effect on its negotiability.

Provisions relating to **collateral,** such as specifying the collateral as security for the debt or a promise to maintain, protect, or give additional collateral, do not affect negotiability. **For Example,** the phrase "This note is secured by a first mortgage" does not affect negotiability.

CPA 7. Ambiguous Language

The following rules are applied when **ambiguous** language exists in words or descriptions:

1. Words control figures where conflict exists.
2. Handwriting supersedes conflicting typewritten and printed terms.
3. Typewritten terms supersede preprinted terms.
4. If there is a failure to provide for the payment of interest or if there is a provision for the payment of interest but no rate is mentioned, the judgment rate at the place of payment applies from the date of the instrument.

[38] *Smith v Haran,* 652 NE2d 1167 (Ill App 1995).
[39] UCC § 3-108.
[40] UCC § 3-104(d).

FIGURE 28-3 Bearer versus Order Paper

"Pay to the order of ABC Corp."	ORDER
"Pay to the order of Bearer."	BEARER
"Pay to the order of ABC Corp. or Bearer"	BEARER
"Pay to the order of ABC Corp., Bearer"	ORDER
"Pay to the order of John Jones" (note)	NONNEGOTIABLE
"Pay to the order of John Jones" (check)	ORDER
"Pay to John Jones" (note)	NONNEGOTIABLE
"Pay to John Jones" (check)	NEGOTIABLE
"Pay to the order of John Jones or Bearer"	BEARER
"Pay to cash"	BEARER
"Pay to the order of cash"	BEARER

NEW MEXICO V HERRERA, 20 P3D 810 (NM APP 2001)

I MAY BE A THIEF, BUT UNDER ARTICLE 3 BEARER PAPER RULES, I AM NOT A FORGER

FACTS: Joshua Herrera (defendant) found a purse in a dumpster near San Pedro and Kathryn Streets in Albuquerque. Herrera took the purse with him to a friend's house. Either Herrera or his friend called the owner of the purse and the owner retrieved the purse at some point. After the purse was returned to the owner, he returned to the dumpster where he found a check and some other items. The check Herrera found was written out to "Cash" and that he thought this meant that he "could get money for [the] check."

When he presented the check to the teller at a credit union to cash it, the teller instructed him to put his name on the payee line next to "Cash." Herrera added "to Joshua Herrera" next to the word "Cash" on the payee line of the check and indorsed the check.

Herrera had pleaded guilty to one count of forgery in violation of NMSA 1978, § 30-16-10 (1963) but moved to have the indictment dismissed on the grounds that adding his name to a bearer instrument was not forgery. He appealed the denial of the motion to dismiss the indictment.

Judicial Opinion

WECHSLER, Judge.... Under Section 30-16-10(B) the State must prove that the defendant gave or delivered a document to a victim with the intent to injure, deceive or cheat the victim or another, knowing that the document (1) was a false document; (2) contained a false signature; (3) had a false indorsement; or (4) was changed so that its effect was different from the original.

Defendant did not make a false signature or offer a false indorsement. Defendant could only have committed forgery by changing the legal effect of the check. If Defendant did change the legal effect of the check, he could have committed forgery under Section 30-16-10(A) and if he transferred the forged check he could have committed forgery under Section 30-16-10(B). Under either subsection of Section 30-16-10, the State must prove that Defendant changed the legal effect of the check. Therefore, whether Defendant changed the legal effect of the check is the dispositive question in this case. Defendant argues that the act of adding his name to the payee line next to the word "Cash" failed to alter the legal effect of the check. We look to the Uniform Commercial Code to determine whether Defendant is correct.

When a negotiable instrument is made payable to "Cash," it is a bearer instrument. A bearer instrument refers to an instrument that is payable to anyone possessing the instrument and is negotiable by transfer alone.

In contrast, an instrument payable to an identified person is considered an order instrument. An order instrument requires the indorsement of the identified person before it can be negotiated. See 55-3- 201(b). The legal effect of an order instrument is different from a bearer instrument because each type of instrument has different negotiability requirements:

[W]hether an instrument is an order instrument or a bearer instrument is important in determining how an instrument is negotiated. If the instrument is payable to bearer, it can be negotiated by delivery alone. If it is payable to the order of an identified person it cannot be negotiated without the indorsement of that person.

At the time Defendant presented the check to the credit union teller, he possessed a bearer instrument because the check was written out to "Cash." At the direction of the teller, however, Defendant added the words "to Joshua Herrera" to the payee line after the word "Cash." By doing so, Defendant added a specific payee to what was otherwise a bearer instrument. We analyze whether Defendant changed the legal effect of the check by adding his name on the payee line of the check.

The words "Cash" and "Bearer" have distinct legal meanings. Their presence upon the face of an instrument signifies the particular legal status of that instrument; namely, that the instrument is payable to anyone bearing it. Similarly, the presence of an identified payee such as "Joshua Herrera" on the face of an instrument signifies that the instrument is payable only to Joshua Herrera.

In this circumstance, with the check payable "to the order of Cash to Joshua Herrera," one who received it could reasonably be confused because it contains both bearer and order instructions. The Uniform Commercial Code resolves such confusion by making the bearer term prevail. We do not view the conjunction "to" in this case as sufficient to avoid confusion from the conflicting terms so as to preclude application of the principles of the commentary.

Indeed, under specific circumstances, a bearer instrument can be transformed to an order instrument. Section 55-3-109(c) provides that when a bearer instrument is specially indorsed, it can be transformed to an order instrument. A special indorsement is one that "identifies a person to whom it makes the instrument payable." Defendant's indorsement in this case included only his name and did not include language making the check payable to an identified person. See § 55-3- 205(c). Thus, the indorsement was not a special indorsement and was not sufficient to transform the legal effect of the check from bearer to order. Instead, because Defendant's indorsement included only his signature, the indorsement qualified as an indorsement in blank. See § 55-3-205(b). Section 55-3-205(b) states that when an instrument is indorsed in blank, "the instrument 'becomes payable to bearer and may be negotiated by transfer of possession alone.'" Consequently, Defendant's indorsement did not change the legal effect of the check from a bearer instrument into an order instrument under Section 55-3-109.

Because Defendant did not change the legal effect of the check when he added his name to the payee line or when he indorsed it, Defendant did not commit the crime of forgery.

Defendant did not commit the crime of forgery. We reverse the district court's denial of Defendant's motion to dismiss the indictment.

[Reversed and remanded]

Questions

1. What type of instrument was the check when Herrera found it?
2. What type of instrument was the check when Herrera added his name to the "Pay to" line?
3. Could Herrera be charged with forgery?

8. Statute of Limitations

Article 3 of the UCC establishes a three-year statute of limitations for most actions involving negotiable instruments. This limitation also applies to actions for the conversion of such instruments and for breach of warranty. There is a six-year statute of limitations for suits on certificates of deposit and accepted drafts.

Summary

An instrument or piece of commercial paper is a transferable, signed promise or order to pay a specified sum of money that is evidenced by a record. An instrument is negotiable when it contains the terms required by the UCC.

Negotiable instruments have two categories: (1) promises to pay and (2) orders to pay. Checks and drafts are orders to pay. Notes and certificates of deposits are promises to pay. In addition to ordinary checks, there are cashier's checks and teller's checks. A bank money order is a check even though it bears the words *money order*.

The original parties to a note are the maker and the payee. The original parties to a draft are the drawer, the drawee, and the payee. The term *party* may refer to a natural person or to an artificial person, such as a corporation. Indorsers and accommodation parties are considered secondary obligors.

The requirements of negotiability are that the instrument (1) be evidenced by a record, (2) be signed (authenticated) by the maker or the drawer, and (3) contain a promise or order (4) of an unconditional character (5) to pay in money (6) a sum certain (7) on demand or at a definite time (8) to order or bearer. A check may be negotiable without being payable to order or bearer.

If an instrument meets the requirements of negotiability, the parties have the rights and protections of Article 3. If it does not meet the requirements of negotiability, the rights of the parties are governed under contract law.

Questions and Case Problems

1. Harold H. Heidingsfelder signed a credit agreement as vice president of J. O. H. Construction Co. for a line of credit with Pelican Plumbing Co. The credit agreement contained the following language:

   > *In consideration of an open account privilege, I hereby understand and agree to the above terms. Should it become necessary to place this account for collection I shall personally obligate myself and my corporation, if any, to pay the entire amount due including service charges (as outlined above terms) thirty-three and one-third (33⅓%) attorney's fees, and all costs of collection, including court costs.*
   >
   > *Signed [Harold H. Heidingsfelder]*
   >
   > *Company J. O. H. Construction Co., Inc.*

   When J. O. H. Construction failed to make payment, Pelican, claiming it was a holder of a negotiable instrument, sued Heidingsfelder to hold him personally liable for his failure to indicate a representative capacity on the credit agreement. He claims that a credit application is not a negotiable instrument and that he could not be held personally liable. Is he right? [*Pelican Plumbing Supply, Inc. v J. O. H. Construction Co., Inc.*, 653 So 2d 699 (La)]

2. East Penn Broadcasting Co. borrowed money from Hershey National Bank. The promissory note representing the loan was made payable "to the Hershey National Bank." It also contained a provision authorizing confession of judgment against the borrower at any time. This provision allowed a judgment to be entered against East Penn without giving the defendant the opportunity to make a defense or to oppose the entry of such judgment. The note was signed with the typewritten name of the borrowing corporation and the handwritten signature of three individuals including the defendant, Frank. The loan was not paid. The bank sued Frank and the others on the note; they raised defenses under the UCC. Who is liable on the note? [*Frank v Hershey National Bank*, 306 A2d 207 (Md Ct Spec App)]

3. Charter Bank of Gainesville had in its possession a note containing the following provision: "This note with interest is secured by a mortgage on real estate, of even date herewith, made by the maker hereof in favor of said payee. . . . The terms of said mortgage are by this reference made a part hereof." When the bank sued on the note, it said it was a holder of a negotiable instrument. Is this instrument negotiable? [*Holly Hill Acres, Ltd. v Charter Bank of Gainesville*, 314 So 2d 209 (Fla App)]

4. On October 14, 1980, United American Bank of Knoxville made a $1,700,000 loan to Frederic B. Ingram. William F. Earthman, the president of the bank and a beneficiary of the loan, had arranged for the loan and prepared the loan documents. Mr. Ingram and Mr. Earthman were old friends, and Mr. Ingram had loaned Mr. Earthman money in the past. Mr. Ingram was in jail at the time of this loan and was unable to complete the documents for the loan. Mr. Earthman says that Mr. Ingram authorized him to do the loan so long as it did not cost him anything to do it.

   Also on October 14, 1980, Mr. Earthman prepared and executed a personal $1,700,000 note to Mr. Ingram, using a standard Commerce Union Bank note form. Mr. Earthman wrote "Frederic B. Ingram" in the space for identifying the lending bank and also filled in another blank stating that the note would be due "Eighteen Months after Date." With regard to the interest, Mr. Earthman checked a box signifying that the interest would be "At the Bank's 'Prime Rate' plus % per year." The standard form note defined the term "prime rate" as follows:

   > *Prime Rate means the Bank's rate for loans to its most credit worthy customers for 90-day unsecured loans. At the time of this agreement, that rate is ______ % per year, although it will change from time to time. If a change in the Prime Rate occurs, the interest on my loan may be adjusted upward or downward.*

   Mr. Earthman then sold both of the notes, which ended up in the hands of third parties (holders in due course) who demanded payment. Mr. Ingram raised the defense that he had not authorized Mr. Earthman to handle the transactions. The third parties said the notes were negotiable instruments and they were entitled to payment without listening to Mr. Ingram's defenses. Mr. Earthman says his note to Mr. Ingram as well as the bank note from Mr. Ingram are not negotiable and that they can both raise defenses to the third parties seeking payment.

Who is correct? What do you think of Mr. Earthman's banking processes and procedures? What ethical issues do you see in these loan transactions? [*Ingram v Earthman*, 993 SW2d 611 (Tenn)]

5. The state of Alaska was a tenant in a large office building owned by Univentures, a partnership. The state made a lease payment of $28,143.47 to Univentures with state treasury warrant No. 21045102. Charles LeViege, the managing partner of Univentures, assigned the warrant to Lee Garcia. A dispute then arose among the Univentures partners, and the company notified the state that it should no longer pay LeViege the rent. The state placed a stop payment order on the warrant. Garcia claimed that he was a holder of a negotiable instrument and that the state owed him the money. The state claimed that a warrant did not qualify as a negotiable instrument. The warrant is in writing, is signed by the governor of the state, provides a definite sum of $28,143.47, and states that "it will be deemed paid unless redeemed within two years after the date of issue." The warrant states that it is "payable to the order of Univentures." Does the warrant meet the requirements for a negotiable instrument? [*National Bank v Univentures*, 824 P2d 1377 (Alaska)]
6. Nation-Wide Check Corp. sold money orders through local agents. A customer would purchase a money order by paying an agent the amount of the desired money order plus a fee. The customer would then sign the money order as the remitter or sender and would fill in the name of the person who was to receive the money following the printed words "Payable to." In a lawsuit between Nation-Wide and Banks, a payee on some of these orders, the question was raised whether these money orders were checks and could be negotiable even though not payable to order or to bearer. Are the money orders negotiable instruments? [*Nation-Wide Check Corp. v Banks*, 260 A2d 367 (DC)]
7. Nelson gave Buchert the following instrument, dated July 6, 1988:

   One year after date I promise to pay to the order of Dale Buchert one thousand dollars in United States Savings Bonds payable at Last Mortgage Bank. (signed) Ronald K. Nelson

   Does this instrument qualify as a negotiable instrument?
8. Bellino made a promissory note that was payable in installments and contained the provision that on default of the payment of any installment, the holder had the option to declare the entire balance due and payable on demand. The note was negotiated to Cassiani, who sued Bellino for the full debt when there was a default on the installment. Is a note with an acceleration clause still negotiable? [*Cassiani v Bellino*, 157 NE2d 409 (Mass)]
9. A corporation borrowed money from a bank after the president negotiated the loan and signed the promissory note. On the first blank signature line of the note, the president wrote the name of the corporation. On the second such line, he signed his own name. The note was negotiated by the lending bank to the Federal Reserve Bank. The note was not paid when due, and the Federal Reserve Bank sued the corporation and its president. The president claimed that he was not bound on the note because he did not intend to bind himself and because the money obtained by the loan was used by the corporation. Is the president liable on the note? [*Talley v Blake*, 322 So 2d 877 (La App) (non-Code); *Geer v Farquhar*, 528 P2d 1335 (Or)]
10. Lloyd and Mario Spaulding entered into a contract to purchase property from Richard and Robert Krajcir. The two Spaulding brothers signed a promissory note to the Krajcir brothers with the following language: "The amount of $10,000 [is] to be paid sellers at the time of the initial closing [delivery of the deed]; plus, the principal amount payable to sellers at the time of the final indorsement of the subject H.U.D. loan." In litigation over the note, the Spauldings said it was not a negotiable instrument. The lower court found it to be a negotiable promissory note and the Spaulding partners appealed. Is the note negotiable? [*Krajcir v Egid*, 712 NE2d 917 (Ill App)]
11. Is the following instrument negotiable?

    I, Richard Bell, hereby promise to pay to the order of Lorry Motors Ten Thousand Dollars ($10,000) upon the receipt of the final distribution from the estate of my deceased aunt, Rita Dorn. This negotiable instrument is given by me as the down payment on my purchase of a 1986 Buick to be delivered in three weeks.

    Richard Bell (signature).
12. Smith has in his possession the following instrument:

    September 1, 2003

    I, Selma Ray, hereby promise to pay Helen Savit One Thousand Dollars ($1,000) one year after date. This instrument was given for the purchase of Two Hundred (200) shares of Redding Mining Corporation, Interest 6%.

    Selma Ray (signature).

    What is this instrument? Is it negotiable?

13. Master Homecraft Co. received a promissory note with a stated face value from Sally and Tom Zimmerman. The note was payment for remodeling their home and contained unused blanks for installment payments but contained no maturity date. When Master Homecraft sued the Zimmermans on the note, the couple argued that they should not be liable on the note because it is impossible to determine from its face the amount due or the date of maturity. Decide. [*Master Homecraft Co. v Zimmerman*, 22 A2d 440 (Pa)]

14. A note from Mark Johnson with HealthCo International as payee for $28,979.15 included the following language:

    [p]ayable in __________, Successive Monthly Installments of $ Each, and in 11 Successive Monthly Installments of $2,414.92 Each thereafter, and in a final payment of $2,415.03 thereafter. The first installment being payable on the ________ day of ________ 20________, and the remaining installments on the same date of each month thereafter until paid.

    Johnson signed the note. Is it negotiable? [*Barclays Bank, P.L.C. v Johnson*, 499 SE2d 769 (NC App)]

15. The text of text of a handwritten note stated simply that "'I Robert Harrison owe Peter Jacob $25,000 . . . ,' /s/ Robert Harrison." Peter Jacob sought to use the handwritten note as a negotiable promissory note. Can he? [*Jacob v Harrison*, 49 UCC Rep Serv 2d 554 (Del Super 2002)]

CPA Questions

1. A company has in its possession the following instrument:

$500.00 **Dayton, Ohio**
October 2, 1987

Sixty days after the date I promise to pay to the order of

Cash

Five Hundred **Dollars**

at Miami, Florida

Value received with interest at the rate of nine percent. This instrument is secured by a conditional sales contract.

No. 11 **Due** Dec. 1, 1987 Craig Burk
Craig Burk

This instrument is

a. Not negotiable until December 1, 1987
b. A negotiable bearer note
c. A negotiable time draft
d. A nonnegotiable note because it states that it is secured by a conditional sales contract

2. The instrument below is a

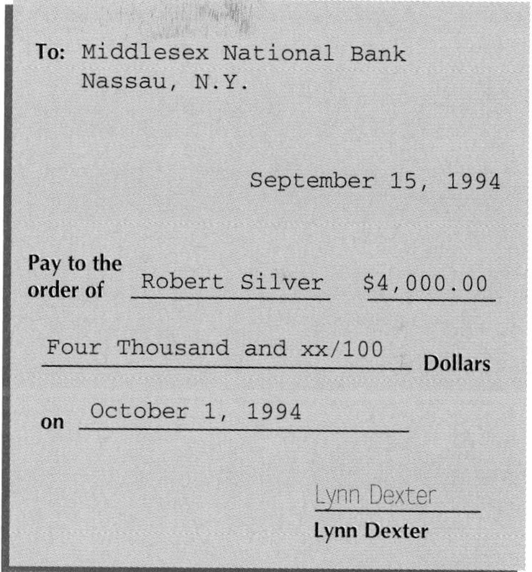

To: Middlesex National Bank
Nassau, N.Y.

September 15, 1994

Pay to the order of Robert Silver $4,000.00

Four Thousand and xx/100 **Dollars**

on October 1, 1994

Lynn Dexter
Lynn Dexter

a. Draft
b. Postdated check
c. Trade acceptance
d. Promissory note

3. Under the commercial paper article of the UCC, for an instrument to be negotiable, it must

a. Be payable to order or to bearer
b. Be signed to the payee

c. Contain references to all agreements between the parties
d. Contain necessary conditions of payment

4. An instrument reads as follows:

> **$10,000** **Ludlow, Vermont**
> **February 1, 1993**
>
> **I promise to pay to the order of Custer Corp. $10,000 within 10 days after the sale of my two-carat diamond ring. I pledge the sale proceeds to secure my obligation hereunder.**
>
> R.Harris
> **R. Harris**

Which of the following statements correctly describes this instrument?

a. The instrument is nonnegotiable because it is not payable at a definite time.
b. The instrument is nonnegotiable because it is secured by the proceeds of the sale of the ring.
c. The instrument is a negotiable promissory note.
d. The instrument is a negotiable sight draft payable on demand.

5. Which of the following instruments is subject to the provisions of the Negotiable Instruments Article of the UCC?

a. A bill of lading
b. A warehouse receipt
c. A certificate of deposit
d. An investment security

TRANSFERS OF NEGOTIABLE INSTRUMENTS AND WARRANTIES OF PARTIES

CHAPTER (29)

LEARNING OBJECTIVES

After studying this chapter, you should be able to

LO.1 Distinguish between an assignment and a negotiation

LO.2 Explain the difference between negotiation of order paper and negotiation of bearer paper

LO.3 List the types of indorsements and describe their uses

LO.4 Determine the legal effect of forged and unauthorized indorsements

LO.5 Be familiar with the forged payee impostor exceptions

LO.6 List the indorser's warranties and describe their significance

Much of the commercial importance of negotiable instruments lies in the ease with which they can be transferred. This chapter covers the requirements for, and issues in, the transfer or negotiation of negotiable instruments.

A. Transfer of Negotiable Instruments

Negotiable instruments are transferred by a process known as *negotiation.*

1. Effect of Transfer

When a contract is assigned, the transferee has the rights of the transferor. The transferee is entitled to enforce the contract but, as assignee, has no greater rights than the assignor. The assignee is in the same position as the original party to the contract and is subject to any defense that could be raised in a suit on an assigned contract.

When a negotiable instrument is transferred by negotiation, the transferee becomes the *holder of the paper*. A holder who meets certain additional requirements may also be a **holder in due course.** The status of holder in due course gives immunity from certain defenses that might have been asserted against the transferor (see Chapter 30 for a discussion of the rights and role of a holder in due course).

2. Definition of Negotiation

Under UCC § 3-201(a), **negotiation** means "a transfer of possession . . . of an instrument by a person other than the issuer to a person who thereby becomes a holder."[1] Negotiation, then, is simply the transfer of a negotiable instrument in such a way that the transferee becomes a holder.[2] A **holder** is different from a possessor or an assignee of the paper. A holder is a transferee in possession of an instrument that runs to her. An instrument runs to a party if it is payable to her order, is indorsed to her, or is bearer paper.

CPA 3. How Negotiation Occurs: The Order or Bearer Character of an Instrument

The order or bearer character of the paper determines how it may be negotiated. The order or bearer character of an instrument is determined according to the words of negotiability used (see Chapter 28 for a complete discussion of order and bearer words of negotiation and more examples of bearer versus order instruments). The types of instruments that qualify as bearer paper include those payable to bearer as well as those payable to the order of "Cash" or payable in blank. The character of an instrument is determined as of the time negotiation takes place even though its character originally or at the time of prior transfers may have been different.

[1] Revised UCC § 3-201(a).

[2] Revised UCC § 3-201; *Mandolfo v Chudy*, 564 NW2d 266 (Neb App 1997).

CPA B. How Negotiation Occurs: Bearer Instruments

UCC § 3-201(b) provides, "If an instrument is payable to bearer, it may be negotiated by transfer of possession alone."[3] If an instrument qualifies for bearer status, then it is negotiated by **delivery** to another.[4] Delivery can be accomplished by actual transfer of possession wherein the transferee has possession of the instrument, or constructive transfer, whereby the transferee has exclusive access. Bearer paper is negotiated to a person taking possession of it without regard to whether such possession is lawful. Because delivery of a bearer instrument is effective negotiation, it is possible for a thief or an embezzling officer to transfer title to an instrument. Such a person's presence in the chain of transfer does not affect the rights of those who have taken the bearer instrument in good faith.[5]

Even though a bearer instrument may be negotiated by a mere transfer of possession, the one to whom the instrument is delivered may require the bearer to indorse the instrument. This situation most commonly arises when a check payable to "Cash" is presented to a bank for payment. The reason a transferee of bearer paper would want an indorsement is to obtain the protection of an indorser's warranties from the bearer.[6] The bank wants an indorsement on a check made payable to "Cash" so that it can turn to the check casher in the event payment issues arise.

C. How Negotiation Occurs: Order Instruments

UCC § 3-201(b) provides, "if an instrument is payable to an identified person, negotiation requires transfer of possession of the instrument and its indorsement by the holder."[7] A negotiable instrument that is payable to the order of a specific party is *order paper*, which can be negotiated only through indorsement and transfer of possession of the paper.[8] **Indorsement** and transfer of possession can be made by the person to whom the instrument is then payable or by an authorized agent of that person.[9]

TOWN OF FREEPORT V RING, 727 A2D 901 (ME 1999)

THE TAX MAN COMETH, BUT HE CAN'T PROVIDE YOUR INDORSEMENT

Thorton Ring was behind on his property taxes for his property in Freeport, Maine. When he received a check payable to his order from Advest, Inc., in the amount of $11,347.09, he wrote the following on the back of the check: "Payable to Town of Freeport Property Taxes 2 Main St."; he sent it along with a letter to the town offices. The letter included the following: "I have paid $11,347.09 of real estate taxes and request the appropriate action to redeem the corresponding property." Ring did nothing further and his property was then liened by the tax clerk. Ring objected because he had paid the taxes. The town argued that the check was not indorsed, and Ring thus had not paid the taxes in time to avoid the lien. The lower court found for the town and Ring appealed.

3 Revised UCC § 3-201(b).

4 If no payee is named, the instrument is bearer paper and is negotiated by delivery. *Waldron v Delffs*, 998 SW2d 132 (Tenn App 1999).

5 Revised UCC §§ 3-202 and 3-204; *Midfirst Bank, SSB v C.W. Hayndi Co., Inc.*, 893 F Supp 1304 (DSC 1994).

6 The Uniform Electronic Transactions Act (UETA), promulgated by the National Conference of Commissioners on Uniform State Laws in July 1999 and enacted in 38 states, provides that the transfer of a note by electronic record affords the transferee the same rights as a holder or holder in due course would have with regard to a tangible written note.

7 Revised UCC § 3-201(b). Although the modern spelling is "endorsement," the UCC has retained the British spelling of "indorsement."

8 Revised UCC § 3-204; *Knight Publishing Co., Inc. v Chase Manhattan Bank*, 479 SE2d 478 (NC App 1997).

9 Revised UCC § 3-204.

Judicial Opinion

CLIFFORD, J.... The filing of a tax lien certificate with a registry of deeds by a town creates a tax lien mortgage to secure the payment of outstanding taxes. The tax lien mortgage continues to exist until the taxes are paid or until the lien is terminated by operation of law. A taxpayer has an eighteen month period following the filing of the tax lien certificate to redeem the property by paying the outstanding taxes, plus interest and fees. If the taxes, interest, and fees are not paid within eighteen months after the date of filing, the tax lien mortgage is deemed to have been foreclosed. Because the Town filed the tax lien certificate with the registry of deeds on September 7, 1995, Ring had to redeem his property by March 7, 1997. Ring delivered a check to the Town in January of 1997. The Superior Court, however, concluded that the check did not constitute payment of the outstanding taxes:

> *With an endorsement, Freeport would have been able to cash the check; without the endorsement, it is doubtful that Freeport could have cashed it. The Court concludes that the unendorsed check delivered by Thornton Ring to Freeport was not a tender of payment, and Freeport was not required to accept it as payment of any of the outstanding taxes.*

With respect to a check that is made payable to the order of a specific person, negotiation occurs, and the person receiving the check becomes a holder of a negotiable instrument, if possession of the check is transferred and the check is indorsed by the transferor.

An indorsement is a signature of someone other than the maker, or some other designation identifying the indorser, that is made on an instrument for the purpose of negotiating the instrument.

The check Ring sent to the Town was issued by Advest, Inc., payable to the order of Thornton D. Ring. Because it was payable to Ring's order, the check could only be negotiated by Ring through indorsement and transfer of possession. Ring's signature, however, does not appear on the back of the check. The words that do appear on the back of the check—"Payable To Town of Freeport[/] Property Taxes[/]2 Main st[.]"—do not identify Ring. The words only indicate to whom the instrument should have been payable had the check been properly indorsed. Thus, the writing is an incomplete attempt to create a special indorsement. A special indorsement is an indorsement that identifies a person to whom the indorser is making the check payable. See *id.* The special indorsement still must be signed or otherwise indorsed by the person to whom the check was originally payable. Although Ring could attempt to prove that the words were intended to indorse the instrument in a judicial proceeding brought by the Town to gain payment of the check, payment for purposes of redemption in tax lien cases cannot be contingent upon proof at a judicial proceeding.

Ring contends that the signature of Advest, Inc. is a signature that constitutes a proper indorsement of the check. The statute explicitly states, however, that an indorsement is a signature of anyone other than the maker or issuer of the instrument. Advest, Inc. is the issuer of the check. Alternatively, Ring cites to section 3-1401's description of a signature in support of its position that the check was properly indorsed. That section, however, refers to the means through which indorsers can become liable on the instrument, so-called indorser's liability. That section is not applicable in the determination of whether an instrument is properly indorsed for purposes of receiving payment.

The statement included within the letter accompanying the check does not serve as a valid indorsement either. In determining whether an instrument is properly indorsed, any papers affixed to the instrument are considered part of the instrument. This language specifically references only "affixed" documents. Courts interpreting this language have concluded that a signature on a separate, unattached piece of paper is not an indorsement of the instrument. Ring does not dispute that there is no evidence on record to suggest that the letter was physically attached to the check. (An indorsement on a separate sheet of paper is technically called an allonge.) Many courts have held that signatures included on an allonge are only effective as an indorsement of an instrument if there is no room on the instrument itself for an indorsement.

Ring also contends that even in the absence of an indorsement, the check should have been accepted as payment of his outstanding taxes because the Town (1) had a statutory right to demand an indorsement of the check, or (2) was entitled to enforce the instrument without the indorsement. Title 11 M.R.S.A. § 3-1203(3) provides that "if an instrument is transferred for value and the transferee does not become a holder because of lack of indorsement by the transferor, the transferee has a specifically enforceable right to the unqualified indorsement of the transferor...." Section 3-1203(2) provides, "Transfer of an instrument, whether or not the transfer is a negotiation, vests in the transferee any right of the transferor to enforce the instrument...."

Even if the Town could demand an indorsement pursuant to § 3-1203(3), negotiation does not occur until the indorsement is made. Thus, at the time the check was received, the Town had a right to demand an indorsement, but could not go to the bank to demand payment of the check. Pursuant to 11 M.R.S.A. § 3-1203(2), the bank also had the right to enforce the instrument as the transferee of an instrument from a holder. That right, however, could be enforced only through a judicial proceeding. Such contingent rights to receive payment are not sufficient to redeem property subject to a municipal tax lien. Checks are meant to be the functional equivalent of cash when they are properly issued and negotiated. If the Town has to institute a judicial proceeding to receive the cash equivalent of the check, the check has not served its purpose. The unindorsed check presented to the Town is not the type of payment the redemption option of the tax lien statute contemplates.

Because there is no genuine issue of material fact and the $11,347.09 check Ring sent to the Town does not constitute payment of the outstanding taxes as a matter of law, the tax lien certificate for the 1995 real estate taxes is deemed to have foreclosed on March 7, 1997 and the entry of the summary judgment in favor of the Town was proper.

[Judgment affirmed]

Questions

1. Why did Ring need to have the check delivered to the town within a certain time frame?
2. Was the signature of the issuer enough for the transfer of the check?
3. Was the check indorsed and payment made to the town?

CPA 4. Blank Indorsement

When the indorser merely signs a negotiable instrument, the indorsement is called a **blank indorsement** (see Figure 29-1). A blank indorsement does not indicate the person to whom the instrument is to be paid, that is, the transferee. A blank indorsement turns an order instrument into a bearer instrument. A person who possesses an instrument on which the last indorsement is blank is the holder.[10] **For Example,** if a check is payable to the order of Jill Barnes and Ms. Barnes indorses the check on the back "Jill Barnes," then the check that was originally an order instrument is now a bearer instrument. The check can now be transferred as bearer paper, which requires only delivery of possession. Once Jill Barnes's signature appears as a blank indorsement on the back, the check becomes transferrable simply by delivery of possession to another party.

FIGURE 29-1 Blank Indorsement

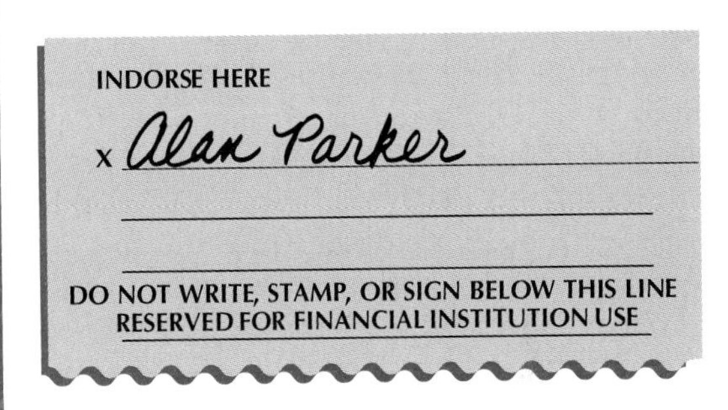

INDORSE HERE
x Alan Parker
DO NOT WRITE, STAMP, OR SIGN BELOW THIS LINE
RESERVED FOR FINANCIAL INSTITUTION USE

E-COMMERCE AND CYBERLAW

NEW FLEXIBILITY FOR CYBERSPACE COMMERCIAL PAPER

The Check Clearing for the 21st Century Act (sometimes called "Check 21") allows banks to use images of checks as a substitute for paper checks. The substitute check is the legal equivalent of the paper check that has, for so long, dominated U.S. commerce. Federal Reserve Board regulations define the substitute check as follows: "A substitute check is a paper reproduction of an original check that contains an image of the front and back of the original check and is suitable for automated processing in the same manner as the original check." With Check 21, banks can sort items electronically and use images from automatic teller machine (ATM) transactions. All the new regulations on check substitutes are known as Regulation CC and can be found at Regulation CC, 12 CFR § 229.2(zz)(2).

[10] *Golden Years Nursing Home, Inc. v Gabbard,* 682 NE2d 731 (Ohio 1996).

FIGURE 29-2 Special Indorsement

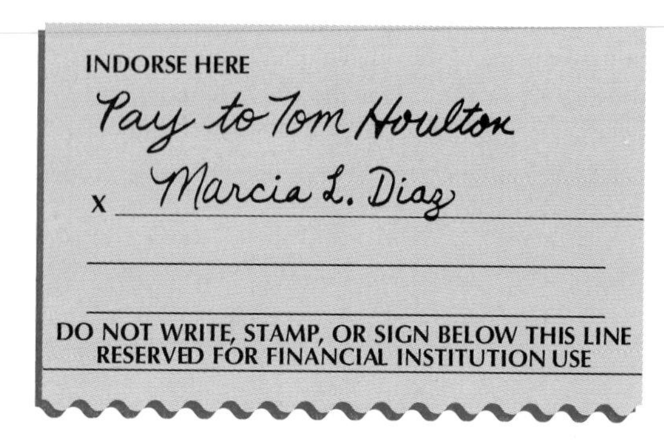

FIGURE 29-3 Qualified Indorsement

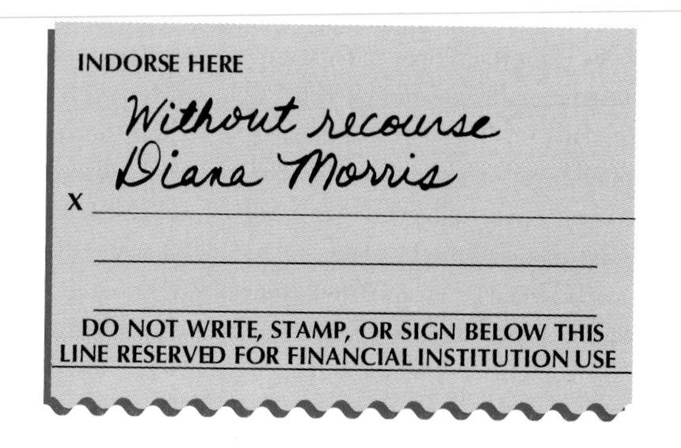

CPA 5. Special Indorsement

A **special indorsement** consists of the signature of the indorser and words specifying the person to whom the indorser makes the instrument payable, that is, the **indorsee** (see Figure 29-2).[11] **For Example,** if Jill Barnes wrote on the back of the check payable to her "Pay to Jack Barnes, /s/ Jill Barnes," the check could be negotiated further only through the signature and possession of Jack Barnes. A special indorsement in this case continues an order instrument as an order instrument. If, after receiving the check, Jack Barnes simply signed it on the back, the check would become bearer paper and could be transferred through possession only.

Although words of negotiability are required on the front of negotiable instruments, it is not necessary that indorsements contain the word *order* or *bearer*. Consequently, the paper indorsed as shown in Figure 29-2 continues to be negotiable and may be negotiated further.[12]

An indorsement of "Pay to account [number]" is a special indorsement. In contrast, the inclusion of a notation indicating the debt to be paid is not a special indorsement.

CPA 6. Qualified Indorsement

A **qualified indorsement** is one that qualifies the effect of a blank or a special indorsement by disclaiming certain liability of the indorser to a maker or a drawee. This disclaimer is given by using the phrase "Without recourse" as part of the indorsement (see Figure 29-3). Any other words that indicate an intent to limit the indorser's secondary liability in the event the maker or the drawee does not pay on the instrument can also be used.[13]

The qualification of an indorsement does not affect the passage of title or the negotiable character of the instrument. It merely disclaims certain of the indorser's secondary liabilities for payment of the instrument in the event the original parties do not pay as the instrument provides.

This qualified form of indorsement is most commonly used when the indorser is a person who has no personal interest in the transaction. **For Example,** an agent or an attorney who is merely indorsing a check of a third person to a client might make a qualified indorsement because he is not actually a party to the transaction.

CPA 7. Restrictive Indorsement

A **restrictive indorsement** specifies the purpose of the indorsement or the use to be made of the instrument (see Figure 29-4).[14] An indorsement is restrictive when it includes words showing that the instrument is to be deposited (such as "For deposit only"), when it is negotiated for collection or to an agent or a trustee, or when the negotiation is conditional.[15]

A restrictive indorsement does not prevent transfer or negotiation of the instrument even when it expressly states that transfer or negotiation is prohibited.

[11] Revised UCC § 3-205; *Bolduc v Beal Bank*, 994 F Supp 2d 82 (DNH 1998).

[12] Only a check may use the phrase "Pay to" on its face and remain negotiable. All other instruments require words of negotiability on their face. Indorsements, however, are sufficient on all instruments with simply "Pay to." UCC § 3-110.

[13] *Florida Coast Bank v Monarch Dodge*, 430 So 2d 607 (Fla App 1983).

[14] Revised UCC § 3-206.

[15] *Id.*

FIGURE 29-4 Restrictive Indorsement

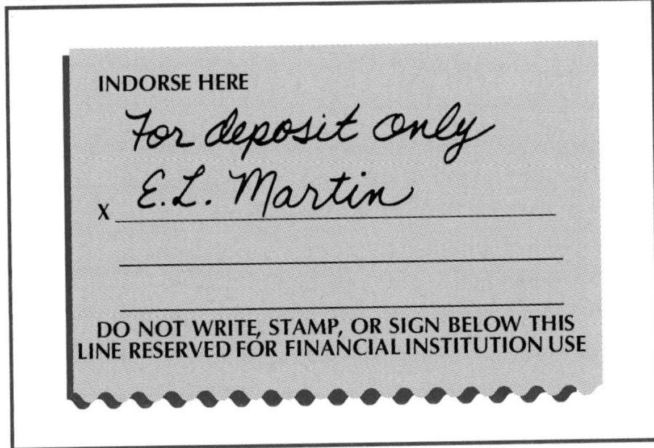

The indorsement "For deposit only" requires that the first party who receives the instrument after the restriction is placed on it comply with that restriction. The indorsement "For deposit only" makes an instrument a bearer instrument for any bank. If the indorser's account number is added to a "For deposit only" indorsement, then the only party who can take the instrument after this restrictive indorsement is a bank with that account number. A restrictive indorsement reduces the risk of theft or unauthorized transfer by eliminating the bearer quality of a blank indorsement.

8. Correction of Name by Indorsement

Sometimes the name of the payee or the indorsee of an instrument is spelled improperly. **For Example,** H. A. Price may receive a paycheck that is payable to the order of "H. O. Price." If this error in Price's name was a clerical one and the check is indeed intended for H. A. Price, the employee may ask the employer to write a new check payable to the proper name. However, under Article 3, a much simpler solution allows the payee or indorsee whose name is misspelled to indorse the wrong name, the correct name, or both. The person giving or paying value or taking it for collection for the instrument may require both forms of the signature.[16]

This correction of name by indorsement may be used only when it was intended that the instrument should be payable to the person making the corrective indorsement. If there were in fact two employees, one named H. A. Price and the other H. O. Price, it would be forgery for one to take the check intended for the other and, by indorsing it, obtain the benefit of the proceeds of the check.[17]

A fictitious, assumed, or trade name is treated the same as a wrong name. The same procedure for correction of a misspelled name with indorsement of both names applies to these forms of payee identification as well.[18]

9. Bank Indorsement

To simplify the transfer and collection of negotiable instruments from one bank to another, "any agreed method which identifies the transferor bank is sufficient for the item's further transfer to another bank."[19] A bank could simply indorse with its Federal Reserve System number instead of using its name.

Likewise, when a customer has deposited an instrument with a bank but has failed to indorse it, the bank may make an indorsement for the customer unless the instrument expressly requires the payee's personal indorsement. Furthermore, the mere stamping or marking on the item of any notation showing that it was deposited by the customer or

THINKING THINGS THROUGH

Dana Kaskel, a widow with five children, invested $250,000 of the proceeds of her late husband's life insurance policy with Martin, Livingston & Sterling, Ltd. (MLS) in the form of a loan that MLS was to repay at the end of six weeks with interest at an annual rate of 8 percent. She wrote a check for $250,000 to MLS, and an agent of MLS named Forrester mailed the check to a Dr. Steven Shook. He was supposed to use it to obtain a $25 million loan from a

[16] Revised UCC § 3-204(d).

[17] If a check is made payable to an individual "as guardian" for another, it cannot be negotiated until that individual is actually appointed as guardian. *Citibank v Bank of Salem*, 35 UCC2d 173 (WDNY 1998).

[18] Revised UCC § 3-204(d).

[19] Revised UCC § 4-103.

THINKING THINGS THROUGH

continued

company of which he was a principal and to invest the proceeds of the loan, generating profits in which MLS would share over and above the amount necessary to repay Mrs. Kaskel's $250,000 loan with the agreed-upon interest. Shook deposited the check in his personal account at the Bank of America, which presented the check for payment to Northern Trust Company, that being the bank in which the insurance company had deposited the proceeds of Mr. Kaskel's life insurance policy in an account of which she was the beneficiary. Although MLS had not endorsed the check, Northern paid it and so the $250,000 went into Shook's account. No one knows what happened to the money and Forrester remains a shadowy character, but he was authorized to send the check to Shook.

Mrs. Kaskel's loan to MLS has never been repaid, although over a period of slightly less than two years she did receive some $40,000 in dribs and drabs from Shook, MLS, and others. MLS still exists, and it acknowledges the debt, but whether the remaining balance of the loan will ever be repaid, with or without the mounting interest due on it, is uncertain. Mrs. Kaskel brought suit against Northern Trust because when Northern paid $250,000 from Mrs. Kaskel's account to Shook, it violated the terms of its contract with her by not requiring an indorsement. She was not aware there was no indorsement until she requested copies of the check from Northern. As permitted by law, Northern was not required to send copies of checks each month.

Is Mrs. Kaskel correct? Is Northern Trust responsible for her loss? KASKEL v NORTHERN TRUST CO., 328 F3d 358 (CA 7 2003)

ETHICS & THE LAW

Does it make a difference to you that Mrs. Kaskel accepted the loan payments? Is she raising the issue of the lack of indorsement too late? Is it fair to Northern Trust because it went on for two years without any objection? Why do you think Mrs. Kaskel was so taken in by MLS and Shook?

credited to the customer's account is effective as an indorsement by the customer.

10. Multiple Payees and Indorsements

Ordinarily, one person is named as the payee in the instrument, but two or more payees may be named. In that case, the instrument may specify that it is payable to any one or more of them or that it is payable to all jointly. **For Example,** if the instrument is made payable "to the order of Ferns and Piercy," then Ferns and Piercy are joint payees. The indorsements of both Ferns and Piercy are required to negotiate the instrument.

If the instrument is payable to **alternative payees** or if it has been negotiated to alternative indorsees, such as "Stahl or Glass" or "Stahl/Glass," it may be indorsed and delivered by either of them.

Under old Article 3, if the instrument was not clear on the relationship or types of multiple payees or indorsees, they were to be considered joint, and the signatures of all parties were required. Under Revised Article 3, when a court is faced with two or more payees who are separated by a comma or other symbol, for example, "Pay to the order of Jeff Bridges–Susan Sarandon," the court must first determine whether the symbols or separating marks are sufficiently clear to make the instrument payable jointly. If the court concludes that the instrument is ambiguous, then the preference is for alternative payees, which means that either Jeff or Susan could negotiate the instrument with one signature; they would not have to have the other's indorsement for negotiation. Under Revised Article 3, if the instrument is ambiguous, the payees or indorsees are considered payees in the alternative.

HYATT CORP. V PALM BEACH NAT. BANK, 840 SO2D 300 (FLA APP 2003)

BEAUTIFUL PALM BEACH, A MESS OF AN INDORSEMENT ISSUE

FACTS: J & D Financial Corporation is a factoring company. Skyscraper Building Maintenance, LLC, had a contract with Hyatt Corporation (Appellant/defendant) to perform maintenance work for various Hyatt hotels in South Florida. Skyscraper entered into a factoring agreement with J & D. As part of the factoring agreement, J & D requested Hyatt to make checks payable for maintenance services to Skyscraper and J & D. Of the many checks issued by Hyatt to Skyscraper and J & D, two were negotiated by the bank but endorsed only by Skyscraper. They were made payable as follows:

1. Check No. 1-78671 for $22,531 payable to:
   J & D Financial Corp. Skyscraper Building Maint P.O. Box 610250 North Miami, Florida 33261-0250
2. Check No. 1-75723 for $21,107 payable to:
   Skyscraper Building Maint J & D Financial Corp. P.O. Box 610250 North Miami, Florida 33261-0250

Only one of the payees, Skyscraper, endorsed these two checks. The bank cashed the checks. According to J & D, it did not receive the benefit of these two payments.

J & D filed a complaint against Skyscraper and Hyatt and the bank. J & D sought damages against Skyscraper under the factoring agreement and separately against Hyatt and the bank for negotiation of the two checks. Hyatt raised the bank's "fault" as an affirmative defense. The bank raised proper payment as an affirmative defense. The bank, Hyatt and J & D then moved for summary judgment on the issue of whether the bank properly negotiated the checks.

The bank argued that the checks were payable to J & D and Skyscraper alternatively, and thus the bank could properly negotiate the checks based upon the endorsement of either of the two payees. The bank further argued that the checks were drafted ambiguously as to whether they were payable alternatively or jointly, and thus under Section 673.1101(4), Florida Statutes, the checks would be construed as a matter of law to be payable alternatively.

Hyatt's position was that the checks were not ambiguous, were payable jointly and not alternatively, and thus under Section 673.1101, the checks could only be negotiated by endorsement of both of the payees. J & D similarly argued that the checks were payable jointly. The trial court granted Summary Judgment in favor of the bank, finding that Section 673.1101(4) precluded the bank's liability. Hyatt appealed. J & D filed a cross-appeal.

Judicial Opinion

LEVY, Judge. . . . The issue on appeal is whether or not a check payable to J & D Financial Corporation Skyscraper Building Maintenance (stacked payees) is payable jointly to both payees requiring the endorsement of both, or whether it is ambiguous regarding whether the check was drafted payable alternatively, so that the bank could negotiate the check when it was endorsed by only one of the two payees.

In 1990, Article 3 of the UCC was revised, and the language of UCC Section 3-116 was added to UCC section 3-110 and became subsection (d). Revised UCC Section 3-110(d), which added language to follow former 3-116(a) and (b), states, "If an instrument payable to two or more persons is ambiguous as to whether it is payable to the persons alternatively, the instrument is payable to the persons alternatively." The net effect of the amendment was to change the presumption. What was unambiguous before is now ambiguous.

Turning to our jurisdiction, Florida has adopted the statutory revision to UCC 3-110, with its enactment of Section 673.1101, Florida Statutes (1992). Section 673.1101(4) now provides the following:

(4) If an instrument is payable to two or more persons alternatively, it is payable to any of them and may be negotiated, discharged, or enforced by any or all of them in possession of the instrument. If an instrument is payable to two or more persons not alternatively, it is payable to all of them and may be negotiated, discharged, or enforced only by all of them. If an instrument payable to

two or more persons is ambiguous as to whether it is payable to the persons alternatively, the instrument is payable to the persons alternatively.

§ 673.1101(4), Fla. Stat.

The issue under review has not reached Florida's appellate courts. Although Florida appellate courts have not yet considered the issue at hand, other courts in the country have. For example, a case which has addressed this particular issue with almost identical facts to those before us is Allied Capital Partners, L.P. v Bank One, Texas, N.A., 68 S.W.3d 51 (Tx.Ct.App.2001). In Allied, the checks were made payable to:

Complete Design Allied Capital Partners, LLP. 2340 E. Trinity Mills St. 300 Carrollton, Texas 75006

The debtor endorsed the checks and deposited them into a corporate bank account. The factor then sued the bank for conversion for payment on the debtor's endorsement.

On appeal from the adverse summary judgment, the factor cited pre-revision law. The Texas appellate court affirmed the summary judgment, stating:

While it does appear that former section 3.116 would have required the checks in this case to be payable to and negotiable only by all of the payees listed, this is no longer the case . . .

Allied Capital Partners, L.P. v Bank One, 68 S.W.3d at 54.

Under these facts, the court found that the check was unambiguous. We conclude that based on the 1990 amendment to the Uniform Commercial Code, when a check lists two payees without the use of the word "and" or "or", the nature of the payee is ambiguous as to whether they are alternative payees or joint payees. Therefore, the UCC amendment prevails and they are to be treated as alternative payees, thus requiring only one of the payees' signatures. Consequently, the bank could negotiate the check when it was endorsed by only one of the two payees, thereby escaping liability.

Hyatt's position, in sum, is that if a stacked payee designation was considered unambiguous and payable jointly before the amendment of the applicable statute, that same payee designation is unambiguous after the amendment of the statute. However, based on the foregoing case law, we find this position untenable because it ignores the shift in presumption brought about by the UCC revision. With the statutory presumption removed, the same stacked payee designation that was unambiguous and payable jointly pre-1992 is now ambiguous and payable in the alternative. Thus, we hold that the trial court was correct in granting the Summary Final Judgment.

[Affirmed]

Questions

1. What was the standard before the 1990 UCC amendments when there was more than one payee?
2. What is the standard now?
3. How does the change in standard affect Hyatt?

11. Agent or Officer Indorsement

An instrument may be made payable to the order of an officeholder. **For Example,** a check may read "Pay to the order of Receiver of Taxes." Such a check may be received and negotiated by the person who at the time is the receiver of taxes. This general identification of a payee is a matter of convenience, and the drawer of the check is not required to find out the actual name of the receiver of taxes at that time.

If an instrument is drawn in favor of an officer of a named corporation, the instrument is payable to the corporation, the officer, or any successor to such officer. Any of these parties in possession of the instrument is the holder and may negotiate the instrument.[20]

12. Missing Indorsement

When the parties intend to negotiate an order instrument but for some reason the holder fails to indorse it, there is no negotiation. The transfer without indorsement has only the effect of a contract assignment.[21] If the transferee gave value for the instrument (see Chapter 30 for more information on what constitutes giving value), the transferee has the right to require that the transferor indorse the instrument unqualifiedly and thereby negotiate the instrument.

20 Revised UCC § 3-110(cc)(2)(li).

21 Revised UCC § 3-204(d).

D. Problems in Negotiation of Instruments

The issues of signatures and requirements for negotiation can become quite complex when issues such as forgery, employee misconduct, and embezzlement arise.

CPA 13. Forged and Unauthorized Indorsements

A **forged** or **unauthorized indorsement** is not a valid indorsement.[22] Accordingly, anyone who has possession of a forged instrument is not a holder because the indorsement of the person whose signature was forged was necessary for effective negotiation of the instrument to the possessor. However, proof of forgery requires expert testimony and a split from a pattern of payments is helpful.[23]

If payment of an instrument is made to one claiming under or through a forged indorsement, the payor ordinarily remains liable to the person who is the rightful owner of the paper. However, if the rightful owner has been negligent and contributed to the forgery or unauthorized signature problem, there are exceptions to these general rules on liability for forged indorsements (see Chapter 30 for more information on the rights and liabilities of the parties).

CPA 14. Quasi Forgeries: The Impostor Rule

The **impostor rule** provides three exceptions to the rule that a forged indorsement is not effective to validly negotiate an instrument. If one of the three impostor exceptions applies, the instrument is still effectively negotiated, even though there may have been a forgery of an indorsement.

(a) When the Impostor Rule Applies

The impostor rule applies in cases where an indorser is impersonating a payee and in two cases where the indorser is a dummy payee.[24]

(1) Impersonating Payee. The impersonation of a payee in the impostor rule exception includes impersonation of the agent of the person who is named as payee. **For Example,** if Jones pretends to be the agent of Brown Corporation and thereby obtains a check payable to the order of the corporation, the impostor exception applies.

(2) Dummy Payee. Another impostor scenario arises when the preparer of the instrument intends that the named payee will never benefit from the instrument. Such a "dummy" payee may be an actual or a fictitious person. This situation arises when the owner of a checking account wishes to conceal the true purpose of taking money from the account at the bank. The account owner makes out a check purportedly in payment of a debt that in fact does not exist.[25]

(3) Dummy Payee Supplied by Employee. The third impostor situation arises when an agent or employee of the maker or the drawer has supplied the name to be used for the payee, intending that the payee should not have any interest in the paper.[26] This last situation occurs when an employee fraudulently causes an employer to sign a check made to a customer or another person, whether existing or not. The employee does not intend to send it to that person but rather intends to forge the latter's indorsement, cash the check, and keep the money. This exception to the impostor rule imposes responsibility on employers to have adequate internal controls to prevent employees from taking advantage of an accounting system with loopholes so that others are not required to bear the cost of the employer's lack of appropriate precautions.

(b) Effect of Impostor Rule

When the impostor rule is applicable, any person may indorse the name of the payee. This indorsement is treated as a genuine indorsement by the payee and cannot be attacked on the ground that it is a forgery. This recognition of the fictitious payee's signature as valid applies even though the dummy payee of the paper is a fictitious person.[27]

(c) Limitations on Impostor Rule

The impostor rule does not apply when there is a valid check to an actual creditor for a correct amount

22 Revised UCC § 3-403(2); *Bloom v G.P.F.*, 588 So 2d 607 (Fla App 1991).

23 *Wagner v Bank of America*, 51 UCC Rep Serv 2d (West) 781 (Cal App 2003).

24 Revised UCC § 3-405; *Shearson Lehman Brothers, Inc. v Wasatch Bank*, 788 F Supp 1184 (D Utah 1992).

25 *Texas Stadium Corp. v Savings of America*, 933 SW2d 616 (Tex 1996).

26 *Guardian Life Ins. Co. of America v Weisman*, 30 F Supp 3d 730 (DNJ 1998).

27 *Bank of Glen Burnie v Elkridge Bank*, 707 A2d 438 (Md App 1988).

owed by the drawer and someone later forges the payee's name. The impostor rule does not apply in this situation even if the forger is an employee of the drawer.

Even when the unauthorized indorsement of the payee's name is effective by virtue of the impostor rule, a person forging the payee's name is subject to civil and criminal liability for making such an indorsement.

For the impostor rule to apply, the holders or the takers of the instrument must show that they took the instrument (1) in good faith and (2) for payment or collection.

(d) Negligence of Drawee Not Required

The impostor rule applies without regard to whether the drawee bank acted with reasonable care.

GETTY PETROLEUM CORP. V AMERICAN EXPRESS TRAVEL RELATED SERVICES COMPANY, INC., 683 NE2D 311 (NY 1997)

THE SLICK OIL COMPANY EMPLOYEE

Getty Petroleum (respondent) distributes gasoline through dealer-owned stations. Customers who buy gas at a Getty station can pay by cash or credit card. When a customer uses a credit card, Getty processes the transactions, receives payment from the credit card company, and then issues computer-generated checks payable to dealers to reimburse them for their credit card sales. Many checks, however, are not intended for negotiation and are never delivered to the payees. Instead, Getty uses these checks for bookkeeping purposes, voiding them and then crediting the check amount toward the dealer's future purchases of gasoline from Getty.

Lorna Lewis, a supervisor in Getty's credit processing department, was given full responsibility for voiding the checks. From April 1991 to October 1992, Lewis stole over 130 checks, forged the indorsements of the payees by hand or rubber stamp, and then submitted the checks to American Express (appellant) and other credit card companies in order to pay her own debts. The credit card companies then forwarded the checks through ordinary banking channels to Chemical Bank where Getty had its checking account. Chemical Bank honored the checks Lewis had forged.

Getty, upon discovering the larceny of Lewis, sought recovery of the amounts from the credit card companies. Getty sought payment on 31 of the checks from American Express. At trial, a judge held American Express liable to Getty for $58,841.60. The appeals court found that American Express was grossly negligent in taking and cashing the checks and also held it liable. American Express appealed.

Judicial Opinion

KAYE, C. J.... The provisions of article 3 of the Uniform Commercial Code relating to check fraud have as their purpose ensuring the ready negotiability of commercial paper and advancing the important policy of assigning loss based upon the relative responsibility of the parties. Article 3 accomplishes these ends by establishing commercially sound rules designed to place the risk of loss attributable to fraud such as forged indorsements with the party best able to prevent.

Losses caused by a forged instrument are in the first instance allocated to the drawee bank because, as between that bank and its drawer, the drawee bank is in the better position to detect the forgery before payment. Consistent with this premise, the Code deems a forged indorsement "wholly inoperative" and upon improper payment by the drawee bank over a forged indorsement, the drawee bank must recredit the drawer's account.

Article 3, however, shifts the risk of loss to the drawer in situations where the drawer is the party best able to prevent the loss. In particular, UCC 3-405(1)(b)—the fictitious payee rule—provides that "[a]n indorsement by any person in the name of a named payee is effective if... a person signing as or on behalf of a maker or drawer intends the payee to have no interest in the instrument."

The situation presented here is precisely that contemplated by UCC 3-405(1)(b). Getty drew more than 4,000 checks to the order of payees with no intention that they would be delivered or negotiated. Rather, it was Getty's intention to void the checks and use them to create a paper trail of gasoline credits. Of these, over 130 were misappropriated by Lewis, who then forged the indorsement of the dealers. In short, the drawer (Getty) made checks payable to a payee (a dealer), intending the payee to have no interest in the instruments, thus rendering the forged indorsement by Lewis on the checks "effective."

As the record demonstrates, Getty was in the best position to prevent the losses by its book-keeping practices, by supervising its employees, by enforcing its rules and by examining records relating to a fraud that had been in progress for a considerable time. Under UCC 3-405(1)(b), the loss brought about by Lewis's misconduct should therefore fall to her employer, not the depositary party (bank).

That conclusion does not end the analysis. Getty claims that even though the fictitious payee rule applies, American Express should be denied the benefit of the rule because of its own gross negligence.

As an initial matter Getty misstates the exception to UCC 3-405. UCC 3-405 does not require that a transferee demonstrate due care in order to enjoy its protection, unlike other risk-shifting provisions which permit a drawer to defeat a transferee's defenses by demonstrating the transferee's failure to observe "reasonable commercial standards" or to use ordinary care. Thus, while a drawer can defeat a defense to forgery by showing that the transferee acted negligently under these two sections of the Code, there is no similar qualifying language incorporated in UCC 3-405. In short, UCC 3-405 does not invite courts to balance the relative culpability of the parties.

[W]hile "the Legislature might have opted for a statutory standard that apportioned liability according to each party's actual fault in a particular transaction—as it did elsewhere in the Code—it chose instead in UCC 3-405(1)(c), as a policy matter, to allocate the loss to the drawer-employer because it perceived that party was in a better position to prevent such loss from occurring in the first instance."

Consequently, a transferee's lapse of wary vigilance, and disregard of suspicious circumstances which might have well induced a prudent banker to investigate and other permutations of negligence, are not relevant considerations under section 3-405. Rather, there is a "commercial bad faith" exception to UCC 3-405, applicable when the transferee "acts dishonestly—where it has actual knowledge of facts and circumstances that amount to bad faith, thus itself becoming a participant in a fraudulent scheme."

Getty therefore had the heavy burden of demonstrating that American Express's conduct amounted to dishonesty or complicity in Lewis's plans. Both Supreme Court and the Appellate Division found that American Express accepted 31 checks on behalf of Lewis even though neither her name nor the name of American Express appeared on these checks. Those courts also determined that American Express routinely processed stale checks, checks payable to neither American Express nor the customer, checks where neither American Express nor the customer was listed on the check, checks from unrelated third parties, and multiple checks from multiple third parties with different addresses in different States for a single transaction. Such conduct was surely lamentable, likely even grossly negligent. There is no evidence, however, that American Express had actual knowledge of Lewis's wrongdoing or was somehow a participant in Lewis's fraudulent scheme. Getty thus failed to meet its burden of proving commercial bad faith as a matter of law.

Accordingly, the order of the Appellate Division should be reversed, with costs, and the complaint dismissed.

[Reversed]

Questions

1. What impostor scenario did Lewis fit into?
2. Why is American Express's conduct and whether it was grossly negligent important in the case?
3. Can Getty recover from American Express? Why or why not?

15. Effect of Incapacity or Misconduct on Negotiation

A negotiation is effective even though (1) it was made by a minor or any other person lacking capacity; (2) it was an act beyond the powers of a corporation; (3) it was obtained by fraud, duress, or a mistake of any kind; or (4) the negotiation was part of an illegal transaction or was made in breach of duty. Under general principles of law apart from the UCC, the transferor in such cases may be able to set aside the negotiation or obtain some other form of legal relief.

However, rights of certain parties (holders in due course) may limit the ability to set aside the negotiation because of incapacity and other contract defenses (see Chapter 30).

16. Lost Instruments

The liability on lost instruments depends on who is demanding payment from whom and on whether the instrument was order or bearer paper when it was lost.

(a) Order Instruments

If the lost instrument is order paper, the finder does not become the holder because the instrument has not been indorsed and delivered by the person to whom it was then payable. The former holder who lost it is still the rightful owner of the instrument.

(b) Bearer Instruments

If the lost instrument is in bearer form when it is lost, the finder, as the possessor of a bearer instrument, is the holder and is entitled to enforce payment.

E. Warranties in Negotiation

When a negotiable instrument is transferred by negotiation, the transferors give certain implied warranties.

17. Warranties of Unqualified Indorser

When the transferor receives consideration for the indorsement and makes an unqualified indorsement, the warranties stated in this section are given by the transferor by implication. No distinction is made between an unqualified blank indorsement and an unqualified special indorsement.

(a) Scope of Warranties

The warranties of the unqualified indorser are found in § 3-416 of the Revised UCC as follows:

(1) *the warrantor is a person entitled to enforce the instrument;*
(2) *all signatures on the instrument are authentic and authorized;*
(3) *the instrument has not been altered;*
(4) *the instrument is not subject to a defense or claim in recoupment of any party which can be asserted against the warrantor;*
(4A) *with respect to any item drawn on a consumer account, which does not bear a handwritten signature purporting to be the signature of the drawer, that the purported drawer of the draft has authorized the issuance of the item in the amount for which the item is drawn; and*
(5) *the warrantor has no knowledge of any insolvency proceeding commenced with respect to the maker or acceptor or, in the case of an unaccepted draft, the drawer.*[28]

Those who present an instrument for payment (see Chapter 30), or the last party in line before the payor, make three warranties:

(1) *the warrantor is, or was, at the time the warrantor transferred the draft, a person entitled to enforce the draft or authorized to obtain payment or acceptance of the draft on behalf of a person entitled to enforce the draft;*
(2) *the draft has not been altered; and*
(3) *the warrantor has no knowledge that the signature of the drawer of the draft is unauthorized.*[29]

If a forged indorsement has appeared during the transfer of the instrument, and there is a refusal to pay because of that problem, the last party who is a holder may turn to her transferor to recover on the basis of these implied warranties. These warranties give those who have transferred and held the instrument recourse against those parties who were involved in the transfer of the instrument, although they were not parties to the original instrument. This warranty section of Article 3 of the UCC attaches liability to those who transfer instruments.

(b) What Is Not Warranted

The implied warranties stated here do not guarantee that payment of the instrument will be made. Similarly, the holder's indorsement of a check does not give any warranty that the account of the drawer in the drawee bank contains funds sufficient to cover the check. However, implied warranties do, for example, promise that the signatures on the instrument are not forged. Likewise, they promise that no one has altered the amount on the instrument. The warranties are not warranties of payment or solvency. They are simply warranties about the nature of the instrument. A holder may not be paid the amount due on the instrument, but if the lack of payment results from a forgery, the holder has rights against those who transferred the instrument with a forged signature.

[28] Revised UCC § 3-416 (1990).

[29] Revised UCC § 3-417. These warranties are limited to consumer accounts and do not apply to commercial accounts.

(c) Beneficiary of Implied Warranties

The implied warranties of the unqualified indorser pass to the transferee and any subsequent transferees. There is no requirement that subsequent transferees take the instrument in good faith to be entitled to the warranties. Likewise, the transferee need not be a holder to enjoy warranty protections.

(d) Disclaimer of Warranties

The unqualified indorser cannot disclaim any warranty when the instrument is a check. Warranties may be disclaimed when the instrument is not a check.

A disclaimer of warranties is ordinarily made by adding "Without warranties" to the indorsement.

(e) Notice of Breach of Warranty

To enforce an implied warranty of an indorser, the party claiming under the warranty must give the indorser notice of the breach. This notice must be given within 30 days after the claimant learns or has reason to know of the breach and the identity of the indorser. If proper notice is not given, the warranty claim is reduced by the amount of the loss that could have been avoided had timely notice been given.

18. Warranties of Other Parties

Warranties are also made by the indorser who indorses "Without recourse" and by one who transfers by delivery only.

(a) Qualified Indorser

The warranty liability of a qualified indorser is the same as that of an unqualified indorser.[30] A qualified indorsement means that the indorser does not assume liability for the payment of the instrument as written. (See § 3-416(4).) However, a qualified indorsement does not eliminate the implied warranties an indorser makes as a transferor of an instrument. The implied warranty that is waived by a qualified indorsement is the fourth warranty on defenses. A qualified indorser still makes the other warranties on signatures and alteration but waives the warranty on defenses.

(b) Transfer by Delivery

When the negotiable instrument is negotiated by delivery without indorsement, the warranty liability of the transferor runs only to the immediate transferee. In all other respects, the warranty liability is the same as in the case of the unqualified indorser. **For Example,** Thomas, a minor, gives Craig his note payable to bearer. Craig transfers the note for value and by delivery only to Walsh, who negotiates it to Hall. Payment was refused by Thomas, who chose to disaffirm his contract. Hall cannot hold Craig liable. Craig, having negotiated the instrument by delivery only, is liable on his implied warranties only to his immediate transferee, Walsh. Likewise, because Craig did not indorse the note, he is not secondarily liable for payment of the note.

[30] Revised UCC § 3-416(a).

Summary

Negotiation is the transferring of a negotiable instrument in such a way as to make the transferee the holder. When a negotiable instrument is transferred by negotiation, the transferee becomes the holder of the instrument. If such a holder becomes a holder in due course, the holder will be immune to certain defenses.

An *order instrument* is negotiated by an indorsement and delivery by the person to whom it is then payable. A bearer instrument is negotiated by delivery alone. The order or bearer character of an instrument is determined by the face of the instrument as long as the instrument is not indorsed. If the instrument has been indorsed, the character is determined by the last indorsement.

A number of different kinds of indorsements can be made on negotiable instruments. When an indorser merely authenticates the instrument, the indorsement is called a *blank indorsement*. If the last indorsement is a blank indorsement, the instrument is bearer paper, which may be negotiated by change of possession alone. A special indorsement consists of the authentication by the indorser and words specifying the person to whom the indorser makes the instrument payable. If the last indorsement is a special indorsement, the instrument is order paper and may be negotiated only by an indorsement and delivery. A qualified indorsement eliminates the liability of the indorser to answer for dishonor of the paper by the maker or the drawee. A restrictive indorsement specifies the purpose of the instrument or its use.

A forged or unauthorized indorsement is no indorsement, and the possessor of the instrument cannot be a holder. The impostor rule makes three exceptions to this rule:

dummy payee; employee fraud; and impersonating a payee.

A negotiation is effective even though (1) it is made by a minor, (2) it is an act beyond the powers of a corporation, (3) it is obtained by fraud, or (4) the negotiation is part of an illegal transaction. However, the transferor may be able to set aside the negotiation under general legal principles apart from the UCC. The negotiation cannot be set aside if the instrument is held by a person paying it in good faith and without knowledge of the facts on which the rescission claim is based.

The warranties of the unqualified indorser are as follows: (1) the warrantor is a person entitled to enforce the instrument; (2) all signatures on the instrument are authentic and authorized; (3) the instrument has not been altered; (4) the instrument is not subject to a defense or claim in recoupment of any party that can be asserted against the warrantor; with respect to any item drawn on a consumer account, which does not bear a handwritten signature purporting to be the signature of the drawer, that the purported drawer of the draft has authorized the issuance of the item in the amount for which the item is drawn; and (5) the warrantor has no knowledge of any insolvency proceeding commenced with respect to the maker or acceptor or, in the case of an unaccepted draft, the drawer.

Questions and Case Problems

1. C&N and Alabama Siding perform construction work at job sites throughout the southeastern United States. On Wednesday of each week, the foreman at each job site telephoned Bivens and gave her the names of the employees working on the job and the number of hours they had worked. Bivens then conveyed this information to Automatic Data Processing (ADP). Under a contract with C&N and Alabama Siding, ADP prepared payroll checks for the two companies. After preparing the payroll checks based on the information given to it by Bivens, ADP sent the checks to the offices of C&N and Alabama Siding for authorized signatures. Bivens was not an authorized signer. After the checks were signed, Bivens sent the checks to the job site foreman to deliver to the employees.

   Bivens soon began conveying false information and hours worked. On the basis of this false information, ADP prepared payroll checks payable to persons who were actually employees but had not worked the hours Bivens had indicated. After obtaining authorized signatures, Bivens intercepted the checks, forged the indorsements of the payees, and either cashed them at Community Bancshares or deposited them into her checking account at Community, often presenting numerous checks at one time. Bivens continued this practice for over a year, forging more than 100 indorsements.

   The vice president of C&N discovered the embezzlement after noticing payroll checks payable to employees who had not recently performed services for the corporations. Bivens later admitted to forging the indorsements. C&N brought suit against the bank for paying on forged indorsements. Can C&N recover? [*C&N Contractors, Inc. v Community Bancshares, Inc.*, 646 So 2d 1357 (Ala)]
2. How could a check made out to "Joseph Klimas and his Attorney Fritzshall & Gleason & Blue Cross Blue Shield Company and Carpenters Welfare Fund" be negotiated further? What would be required? [*Chicago District Council of Carpenters Welfare Fund v Gleason's Fritzshall*, 693 NE2d 412 (Ill App)]
3. An insurer issued a settlement check on a claim brought by an injured minor that was payable to "Trudy Avants attorney for minor child Joseph Walton, mother Dolores Carpenter 11762 S. Harrells Ferry Road #E Baton Rouge LA 70816." The lawyer indorsed the check. Two unknown individuals forged indorsements for the other two names and obtained payment of the check. The insurer sued the payor bank claiming the instruments were not properly payable because of the forged indorsements. The court is unclear whether the indorsement required is one for an either/or payee or joint payee. What advice can you offer the court as it faces this issue? [*Coregis Insurance Co. v Fleet National Bank*, 793 A2d 254 (Conn App 2002)]
4. Higgins owes the Packard Appliance store $100. He mails a check to Packard. The check is drawn on First National Bank and states "Pay to the order of cash $100." This check is stapled to a letter stating that the $100 is in payment of the debt owed by Higgins. Edwards, who is employed by Packard in the mailroom, removes the letter from its envelope, detaches the check, and disappears. No one knows what has become of the check until a person identifying himself as Gene Howard presents it at First National Bank. The bank pays this person $100 and debits that amount against the account of Higgins. Higgins protests that this cannot be done because the check was lost and never belonged to Howard. Is Higgins correct?
5. Jerry O. Peavy, Jr., who did not have a bank account of his own, received a draft from CNL Insurance America in the amount of $5,323.60. The draft was drawn on CNL's account at Bank South, N.A., and was "payable to the order of Jerry Peavy and Trust Company Bank." Jerry O. Peavy, Sr., allowed his son Peavy, Jr., to deposit the draft in his account at Bank South, N.A. Bank South accepted the draft and deposited it on December 29,

1992, with only the signature of Jerry Peavy, Jr. Both Mr. and Mrs. Peavy, Sr., then wrote checks on the amount of the draft using the full amount to benefit their son.

On March 30, 1993, Bank South realized that it had improperly deposited the draft because it was lacking an indorsement from Trust Company Bank and reversed the transaction by debiting Mr. and Mrs. Peavy's account for the full amount of the draft. A bank officer then called Mr. and Mrs. Peavy, told them what had happened with the draft, and "threatened to send them to jail if they did not immediately deposit the sum of $5,323.60." The Peavys deposited that amount from the sale of some stock they owned and then filed suit against Bank South for its conversion of their son's draft and funds. Do the Peavys have a case? [*Peavy v Bank South*, 474 SE2d 690 (Ga App)]

6. The Gasts owned a building that they contracted to sell to the Hannas. The building was insured against fire with American Casualty Co. Thereafter, when the building was damaged by fire, a settlement was reached with the insurance company through Sidney Rosenbaum, a public fire adjuster. In order to make payment for the loss, the insurance company drew a draft on itself payable to the Hannas, the Gasts, and Sidney Rosenbaum. Apparently the Hannas indorsed the draft, forged the names of the other payees as indorsers, cashed the draft by presenting it to American Casualty Co., and disappeared. Thereafter, the Gasts sued American Casualty. Decide. [*Gast v American Casualty Co.*, 240 A2d 682 (NJ Super)]

7. Snug Harbor Realty Co. had a checking account in First National Bank. When construction work was obtained by Snug Harbor, its superintendent, Magee, would examine the bills submitted for labor and materials. He would instruct the bookkeeper which bills were approved, and the bookkeeper then prepared the checks in accordance with his instructions. After the checks were signed by the proper official of Snug Harbor, Magee picked them up for delivery. Instead of delivering certain checks, he forged the signatures of the respective payees as indorsers and cashed the checks. The drawee bank then debited the Snug Harbor account with the amount of the checks. Snug Harbor claimed this was improper and sued the bank for the amount of the checks. The bank claimed it was protected by the impostor rule. Will the bank be successful? Explain. [*Snug Harbor Realty Co. v First National Bank*, 253 A2d 581 (NJ Super)]

8. Benton, as agent for Savidge, received an insurance settlement check from Metropolitan Life Insurance Co. He indorsed it "For deposit" and deposited it in Bryn Mawr Trust Co. in Savidge's account. What were the nature and effect of this indorsement? [*Savidge v Metropolitan Life Ins. Co.*, 110 A2d 730 (Pa)]

9. Allstate Insurance Company issued a check payable to "Chuk N. Tang & Rosa C. Tang HWJT" with "Bank of America" on the second line and the following explanation on the front of the check: "Settlement of our rental dwelling loss caused by fire on 11/21/93." The Tangs indorsed the check and forged the indorsement of Bank of America. When Bank of America objected, the Tangs claimed that only they needed to sign the instrument for further negotiations. The check was intended as a joint payment for Bank of America as the mortgagee on the Tangs' rental property because the insurance policy required that the mortgagee be paid first before any proceeds went to the property owners. Bank of America sued Allstate. Is Bank of America entitled to recover for the lack of its indorsement? Was its indorsement necessary for further negotiation? [*Bank of America Nat'l Trust & Savings Ass'n v Allstate Insurance Co.*, 29 F Supp 2d 1129 (CD Cal)]

10. When claims filed with an insurance company were approved for payment, they were given to the claims clerk, who would prepare checks to pay those claims and then give the checks to the treasurer to sign. The claims clerk of the insurance company made a number of checks payable to persons who did not have any claims and gave them to the treasurer with the checks for valid claims, and the treasurer signed all of the checks. The claims clerk then removed the false checks, indorsed them with the names of their respective payees, and cashed them at the bank where the insurance company had its account. The bank debited the account of the insurance company with the amount of these checks. The insurance company claimed that the bank could not do this because the indorsements on the checks were forgeries. Was the insurance company correct? [*General Accident Fire & Life Assur. Corp. v Citizens Fidelity Bank & Trust Co.*, 519 SW2d 817 (Ky)]

11. Eutsler forged his brother Richard's indorsement on certified checks and cashed them at First National Bank. When Richard sought to recover the funds from the bank, the bank stated that it would press criminal charges against Eutsler. Richard asked the bank to delay prosecution to give him time to collect directly from his brother. His brother promised to repay him the money but vanished some six months later without having paid any money. Richard sued the bank. What was the result? [*Eutsler v First Nat'l Bank, Pawhuska*, 639 P2d 1245 (Okla)]

12. Michael Sykes, the president of Sykes Corp., hired Richard Amelung to handle the company's bookkeeping and deal with all of its vendors. Amelung entered into an agreement with Eastern Metal Supply to help reduce Sykes's debt to Eastern. Whenever Sykes received a check, Amelung would sign it over to Eastern and allow it to keep 30 percent of the check amount. On 28 checks that totaled $200,000, Amelung indorsed the back as follows: "Sykes & Associates or Sykes Corporation, Richard Amelung." Amelung then turned the checks over

to Eastern, and Eastern deposited them into its account at Barnett Bank. Eastern would then write one of its checks to Sykes Corp. for the 70 percent remaining from the checks. When Michael Sykes learned of the arrangement, he demanded the return of the 30 percent from Barnett Bank, claiming that it had paid over an unauthorized signature and that the indorsement was restricted and had been violated by the deposit into Eastern's account. What type of indorsement did Amelung make? Did he have the authority to do so? Should Sykes be reimbursed by Barnett? [*Sykes Corp. v Eastern Metal Supply, Inc.*, 659 So 2d 475 (Fla App)]

13. In January 1998, Allied Capital Partners, L.P., and American Factors Corporation were in the business of factoring accounts receivable for third-party clients. Allied assigned its factoring contract with Complete Design, Inc., to American but retained an interest in the factoring of Complete Design's invoices. On January 25, 1998, in payment of invoices issued by Complete Design, Clark Wilson Homes, Inc., issued a check for $6,823.15. The check was payable to:

    Complete Design
    Allied Capital Partners, L.P.
    2340 E. Trinity Mills Ste. 300
    Carrollton, Texas 75006

    On February 10, 1998, Clark Wilson issued another check for $26,329.32 made payable to:

    Complete Design
    Allied Capital Partners, L.P.
    2340 E. Trinity Mills Ste. 300
    Carrollton, Texas 75006

    Complete Design deposited both checks in its account at Bank One. However, Allied and American received none of the proceeds of the checks.

    Complete Design subsequently declared bankruptcy, and Allied and American made demand on Bank One for damages resulting from Bank One's conversion of the two checks. Bank One denied all liability for conversion of the checks. Allied and American subsequently sued Bank One, asserting conversion. Bank One filed a motion for summary judgment asserting that, because it was ambiguous to whom the checks at issue were payable, they were payable upon a single endorsement. The trial court granted Bank One's motion. Allied and American appealed. Who is correct here? Were both signatures necessary for a proper indorsement, or will one do? [*Allied Capital Partners, L.P. v Bank One, Texas, N.A.*, 68 SW3d 51 (Tex App)]

14. Would a bank be liable to a customer who indorsed a check "For deposit only into account #071698570" if that check were deposited into the wrong account? What if the customer's indorsement was "For deposit only"? Would any account qualify? Would any bank qualify? [*Qatar v First American Bank of Virginia*, 885 F Supp 849 (ED Va)]

15. Two employees of the state of New Mexico fraudulently procured and indorsed a warrant (a draft drawn against funds of the state) made out to the Greater Mesilla Valley Sanitation District. There was no such sanitation district. The employees obtained payment from Citizens Bank. Western Casualty, the state's insurer, reimbursed the state for its loss and then brought suit against the bank for negligently paying the warrant. Is the bank liable for its payment? Discuss your answer. [*Western Casualty & Surety Co. v Citizens Bank of Las Cruces*, 676 F2d 1344 (10th Cir)]

CPA Questions

1. Hand executed and delivered to Rex a $1,000 negotiable note payable to Rex or bearer. Rex then negotiated it to Ford and endorsed it on the back by merely signing his name. Which of the following is a correct statement?
    a. Rex's endorsement was a special endorsement.
    b. Rex's endorsement was necessary to Ford's qualification as a holder.
    c. The instrument initially being bearer paper cannot be converted to order paper.
    d. The instrument is bearer paper, and Ford can convert it to order paper by writing "pay to the order of Ford" above Rex's signature.

2. Jane Lane, a sole proprietor, has in her possession several checks that she received from her customers. Lane is concerned about the safety of the checks since she believes that many of them are bearer paper which may be cashed without endorsement. The checks in Lane's possession will be considered order paper rather than bearer paper if they were made payable (in the drawer's handwriting) to the order of
    a. Cash
    b. Ted Tint, and endorsed by Ted Tint in blank
    c. Bearer, and endorsed by Ken Kent making them payable to Jane Lane
    d. Bearer, and endorsed by Sam Sole in blank

3. West Corp. received a check that was originally made payable to the order of one of its customers, Ted Burns.

The following endorsement was written on the back of the check:

Ted Burns, without recourse, for collection only

Which of the following describes the endorsement?

	Special	*Restrictive*
a.	Yes	Yes
b.	No	No
c.	No	Yes
d.	Yes	No

4. An instrument reads as follows:

$250.00 Chicago, Illinois April 1, 1992
Thirty days after date I promise to pay to the order of Cash
Two hundred and fifty Dollars at
New York City

Value received with interest at the rate of six percent per annum. This agreement arises out of a separate agreement.

No. 20 Due May 1, 1992 Robert Smith

Answer "Yes" or "No" for the following questions about the previous item.

a. The instrument is a draft.
b. The instrument is order paper.
c. This is a negotiable instrument.
d. Robert Smith is the maker.
e. The instrument may be negotiated without indorsement.

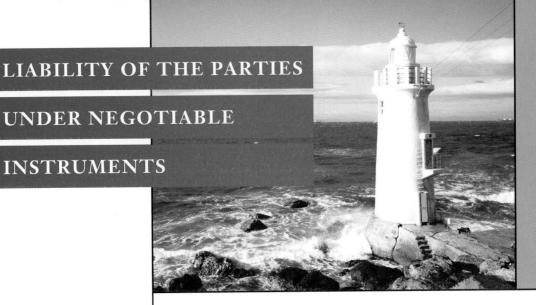

LIABILITY OF THE PARTIES UNDER NEGOTIABLE INSTRUMENTS

CHAPTER (30)

LEARNING OBJECTIVES

After studying this chapter, you should be able to

LO.1 Distinguish between an ordinary holder and a holder in due course

LO.2 List the requirements for becoming a holder in due course

LO.3 Explain the rights of a holder through a holder in due course

LO.4 List and explain the limited defenses not available against a holder in due course

LO.5 List and explain the universal defenses available against all holders

LO.6 Describe how the rights of a holder in due course have been limited by the Federal Trade Commission

Chapters 28 and 29 introduced the requirements for negotiable instruments and the methods for transfer of those instruments. However, the requirements of negotiability and transfer are simply preliminary steps for the discovery of the real benefit of using negotiable instruments in commerce, which is to streamline payment in commercial transactions. This chapter explains the streamlining special status and rights of the special parties to negotiable instruments. These special parties are protected from many underlying contract defenses that can arise between the original parties. The extent of the parties' rights and protections is covered in this chapter.

A. Parties to Negotiable Instruments: Rights and Liabilities

The rights and defenses of the parties to negotiable instruments are determined by the types of parties involved.

1. Types of Parties

Parties with rights in a negotiable instrument can be **assignees** or **holders**. A holder may be an ordinary holder or a **holder in due course**. As noted in Chapter 28, a holder in due course is a special party to an instrument with special rights beyond those of the ordinary holder.

CPA 2. Ordinary Holders and Assignees

A holder is a party in possession of an instrument that runs to him. An instrument "runs" to a party if it is payable to his order, is bearer paper, or is indorsed to him (see Chapter 29). Any holder has all of the rights given through and under the negotiable instrument. The holder may demand payment or bring suit for collection on the instrument. A holder can give a discharge or release from liability on the instrument.

A holder who seeks payment of the instrument is required only to produce the instrument and show that the signature of the maker, drawer, or indorser is genuine. If the party obligated to pay under the instrument has no valid defense (such as forgery, which was discussed in Chapter 29), the holder is entitled to payment of the instrument.

The holder can recover from any of the parties who are liable on the instrument, regardless of the order of the signatures on the instrument. A holder could recover from the first indorser on an instrument or from the last party to indorse the instrument.

The rights of a holder are no different from the rights of a contract assignee (see Chapter 18). The assignee of a contract is in the same position and has the same rights as an ordinary holder. **For Example,** if a farmer who signed a note to pay for his tractor has a warranty problem with the tractor, he has a defense to payment on the note. Anyone who is assigned that note as an assignee or holder is also subject to the farmer's defense. (See Figure 30-1 and also the provisions on consumer credit protection under the discussion of the Federal Trade Commission rule in Chapter 33 and later in this chapter.)

3. The Holder-in-Due-Course Protections

The law gives certain holders of negotiable instruments special rights by protecting them from certain defenses. This protection makes negotiable instruments more attractive and allows greater ease of transfer. Holders in due course have an immunity from contract assignment defenses not enjoyed by ordinary holders or assignees. Figure 30-1 shows the different statuses of the parties as holders, assignees, and holders in due course.

(a) Holder in Due Course

To obtain the preferred status of a holder in due course,[1] a person must first be a holder. However, the preferred status of holder in due course requires these types of holder to meet additional standards. Those holders who do not meet the standards for holder in due course have all the rights of a holder. However, holders in due course enjoy additional protections beyond those basic holder rights. Under Uniform Commercial Code (UCC) § 3-302(a), there are four requirements for becoming a holder in due course.[2]

CPA ***(1) Value.*** **Value** is similar to consideration (see Chapter 15). **For Example,** a person who receives

[1] Revised UCC § 3-302; *Bolduc v Beal Bank, SSB*, 994 F Supp 82 (DNH 1998) aff'd and remanded on other grounds, 167 F3d 667 (1st Cir 1999).

[2] Revised UCC § 3-302(a).

FIGURE 30-1 Assignee, Holder, and Holder-in-Due-Course Rights

Suppose that Farmer Fred signs an installment contract to purchase a tractor from John Deere for $153,000. John Deere assigns the contract to Finance Co.

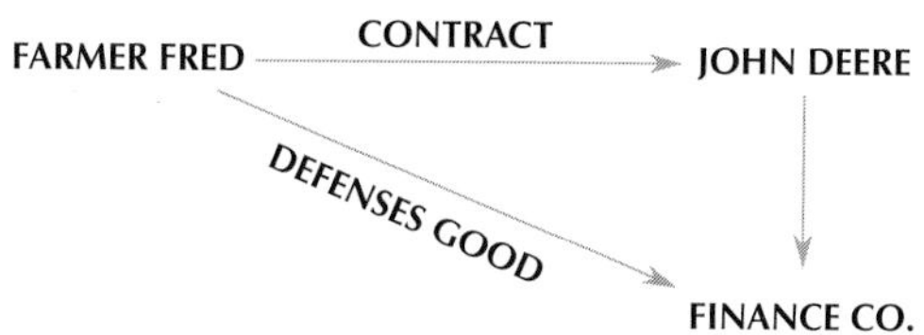

Suppose that Farmer Fred signs a negotiable promissory note for $153,000 and John Deere then transfers it to Finance Co., a holder in due course.

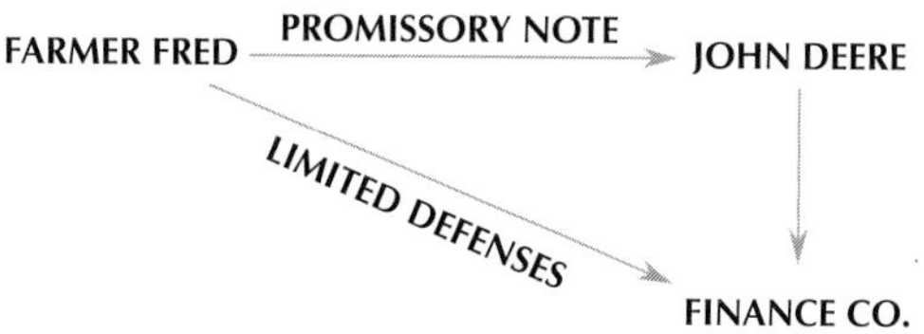

Suppose that Farmer Fred has a roofing company replace the roof on his home, and he signs a negotiable promissory note for $5,000. Roofing Co. transfers the note to Finance Co.

CONTRACTS/CONSUMER (FTC RULE)

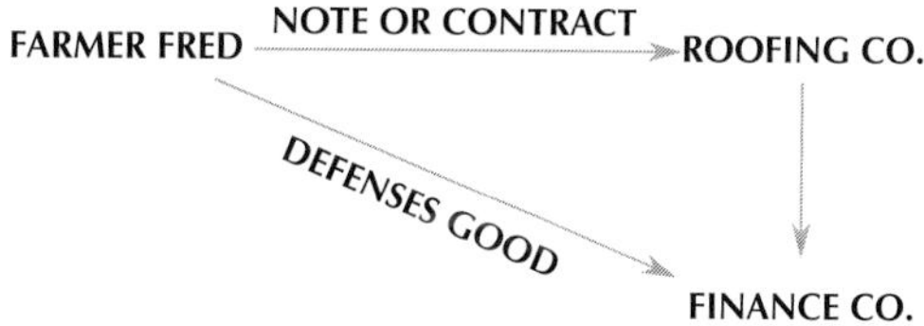

a negotiable note under a will does not give value because the note is a gift. An heir who receives her non–holder-in-due-course uncle's promissory notes under the provisions in his will is not a holder in due course because the notes were a gift, and she gave no value for the notes.[3]

A person takes an instrument for value when (1) the instrument is issued or transferred for a promised undertaking of performance, to the extent the promised undertaking has been performed; (2) the transferee acquires a security interest or other lien in the instrument, other than a lien obtained by judicial proceeding; (3) the instrument is issued or transferred as payment of, or as security for, an antecedent claim against any person, whether or not the claim is due; (4) the instrument is issued or transferred in exchange for a negotiable instrument; or (5) the instrument is issued or transferred in exchange for the incurring of an irrevocable obligation to a third party by the person taking the instrument.[4] As with consideration,

[3] However, if the uncle were a holder in due course, it might be possible under a special Article 3 protection for the heir to also be a holder in due course despite the gift acquisition. UCC § 3-302(c)(iii). This protection for gift transfers by holders in due course is called the *shelter provision* (and is covered later in this chapter).

[4] Revised UCC § 3-303.

the courts do not consider whether the value is enough; they determine only whether some value has been given.[5]

Under Revised Article 3, the original payee of a note is not a holder in due course unless that note is transferred to others and then back to the payee.[6]

A bank does not give value for a deposited check when it credits the depositor's account with the amount of the deposit. The bank gives value to the extent that the depositor is permitted to withdraw funds against that deposit.[7] **For Example,** if Janice deposits a $300 check into her account, which already has $400 in it, Janice's bank does not give value until Janice has written checks or withdrawn funds beyond the existing $400. The code follows FIFO (first in, first out) for drawing on funds. A bank that lets the customer draw on the funds deposited gives value.[8]

In a few special cases, a purchaser of a negotiable instrument is not considered a holder in due course. A holder who acquires a negotiable instrument by legal process or by purchase in an execution, bankruptcy, or creditor's sale or similar proceeding cannot be a holder in due course. A holder who acquires a negotiable instrument as part of a bulk transaction or as the successor in interest to an estate or other organization is also not a holder in due course.[9]

CARTER & GRIMSLEY V OMNI TRADING, INC., 716 NE2D 320 (ILL APP 1999)

THE GRAIN CHECKS AS A RETAINER: PLANTING THE SEEDS OF LITIGATION

Omni Trading issued two checks totaling $75,000 to Country Grain Elevators for grain it had purchased. Country Grain indorsed the checks over to the law firm of Carter & Grimsley as a retainer. Country Grain then collapsed as a business, and Omni stopped payment on the checks because all of its grain had not been delivered. Carter & Grimsley claimed it was a holder in due course and entitled to payment. However, the Department of Agriculture claimed its interest in the checks for liens and maintained Carter & Grimsley was not a holder in due course because it had not given value. The trial court granted summary judgment for the Department of Agriculture because the checks were indorsed as a retainer for future legal work and Carter & Grimsley had not given value. Carter and Grimsley appealed.

Judicial Opinion

LYTTON, Justice.... Carter argues that its motion for summary judgment should have been granted because, as a holder in due course, it has the right to recover on the checks from the drawer, Omni.

Section 3-303(a) of the UCC... states that: (a) "An instrument is issued or transferred for value if: (1) the instrument is issued or transferred for a promise of performance, to the extent that the promise has been performed.... Carter contends that in Illinois a contract for future legal services should be treated differently than other executory contracts. It contends that when the attorney-client relationship is created by payment of a fee or retainer, the contract is no longer executory. Thus, Carter would achieve holder in due course status. We are not persuaded.

A retainer is the act of a client employing an attorney; it also denotes the fee paid by the client when he retains the

[5] Revised UCC § 3-303; *United Catholic Parish Schools of Beaver Dam Educational Ass'n v Card Services Center*, 636 NW2d 206 (Wis App 2001). *Agriliance, L.L.C. v Farmpro Services, Inc.*, 328 F Supp 2d 958 (SD Iowa 2003).

[6] Revised UCC § 3-302(c) provides "(c) A person does not become a holder in due course in a transaction in which the obligor issues or transfers the instrument directly to that party without the participation of a remitter or other intermediary."

[7] Revised UCC § 4-211 (1990).

[8] Allowing a deposit of a check with provisional credit does not make a bank a holder in due course, but on a cashier's check, when the bank becomes both the drawer and the drawee, the bank is obligated to pay on the instrument. *Flatiron Linen, Inc. v First American State Bank*, 23 P3d 1209 (Colo 2001). If the bank does not impose provisional credit and makes the funds available immediately for the customer, it gives value and qualifies as a holder in due course. *Maine Family Federal Credit Union v Sun Life Assur. Co. of Canada*, 727 A2d 335, 37 UCC2d 875 (Me 1999) but see *Travelers Cas. and Sur. Co. of America v Wells Fargo Bank N.A.*, 374 F3d 521, 53 UCC Rep Serv 2d 695 (CA 7 2004).

[9] Revised UCC § 3-302(c).

attorney to act for him. We have found no Illinois cases construing section 3-303(a) as it relates to a promise to perform future legal services under a retainer. The general rule, however, is that "an executory promise is not value." "[T]he promise does not rise to the level of 'value' in the commercial paper market until it is actually performed."

The UCC comment to section 303 gives the following example:

"Case # 2. X issues a check to Y in consideration of Y's promise to perform services in the future. Although the executory promise is consideration for issuance of the check it is value only to the extent the promise is performed. Subsection (a)(1)." We have found no exceptions to these principles for retainers. Indeed, courts in other jurisdictions interpreting similar language under section 3-303 have held that attorneys may be holders in due course only to the extent that they have actually performed legal services prior to acquiring a negotiable instrument. We agree.

This retainer was a contract for future legal services. Under section 3-303(a)(1), it was a "promise of performance," not yet performed. Thus, no value was received, and Carter is not a holder in due course.

Furthermore, in this case, no evidence was presented in the trial court that Carter performed any legal services for Country Grain prior to receiving the checks. Without an evidentiary basis for finding that Carter received the checks for services performed, the trial court correctly found that Carter failed to prove that it was a holder in due course. The trial court properly granted the Department's motion for summary judgment.

[Affirmed]

Presiding Justice HOLDRIDGE, dissenting:

I respectfully dissent. In a contractual relationship between attorney and client, the payment of a fee or retainer creates the relationship, and once that relationship is created the contract is no longer executory... Carter's agreement to enter into an attorney-client relationship with Country Grain was the value exchanged for the checks indorsed over to the firm. Thus, the general rule cited by the majority that "an executory promise is not value" does not apply to the case at bar. On that basis I would hold that the trial court erred in determining that Carter was not entitled to the check proceeds and I therefore dissent.

Questions

1. Why is it important that the retainer contract is executory for purposes of the court's decision?
2. How could the law firm have given value?
3. What is the dissent's argument and position?

CPA ***(2) Good Faith.*** The element of **good faith** for becoming a holder in due course requires that a holder of a negotiable instrument act honestly in acquiring the instrument. In addition, the taker must have observed reasonable standards of fair dealing.[10] Karl Llewellyn, one of the key drafters of the UCC, said that to comply with reasonable standards and good faith, the party must act with a "pure heart and an empty head."

Bad faith can sometimes exist just because the holder has given such a small amount as value. The transferee need not give value equal to the face of the negotiable instrument; however, a gross disparity between the value given and the value of the instrument may be evidence of bad faith. A steep discount on an instrument just before its due date should have been a signal that perhaps there were problems with the instrument. **For Example,** if a holder acquires a note at a 75 percent discount on the day before it is due, there is some indication that the note may have some issues because that close to its due date it should command a price close to its value.

The **close-connection doctrine** applies in circumstances that indicate a problem with the instrument and put the party on notice. Under this doctrine, the holder has taken so many instruments from its transferor or is so closely connected with the transferor that any knowledge the transferor has is deemed transferred to the holder, preventing holder-in-due-course status. Examples include consumer transactions where the holder in due course is a company that regularly does business with a company that has continual problems with consumer complaints.[11]

[10] Revised UCC § 3-103(a)(4); *Choo Choo Tire Service, Inc. v Union Planters National Bank*, 498 SE2d 799 (Ga App 1998); issue of whether a party is a holder in due course is always an issue of fact, *In re SGE Mortgage Funding Corp.*, 278 BR 653 (MD Ga 2001).

[11] *Associates Home Equity Services, Inc. v Troup*, 778 A2d 529 (NJ Super AD 2001); *Gonzalez v Old Kent Mortgage Co.*, 2000 WL 1469313 (ED Pa 2000).

(3) Ignorance of the Instrument's Being Overdue or Dishonored. An instrument can be negotiated even though it has been dishonored, it is overdue,[12] or it is demand paper, such as a check, that has been outstanding for more than a reasonable time.[13] These instruments can still be transferred and the transferee is still a holder. However, the fact that the instrument is circulating at a late date or after it has been dishonored is a suspicious circumstance is notice that there may be some adverse claim or defense. A person who acquires title to the instrument under such circumstances can be a holder but cannot be a holder in due course. **For Example,** buying a discounted note after its due date is notice that something may be wrong with the instrument.

(4) Ignorance of Defenses and Adverse Claims. Prior parties on an instrument may have defenses that entitle them to withhold payment from a holder of an instrument. **For Example,** the drawer of a check, upon demand for payment by the payee, could assert as a defense to payment that the merchandise the payee delivered under the terms of their underlying contract was defective. A person who acquires an instrument with notice or knowledge that there is a defense that a party may have or that there is any adverse claim of ownership of the instrument cannot be a holder in due course. In general, transferees who are aware of facts that would make a reasonable person ask questions are deemed to know what they would have learned if they had asked questions.[14] Such knowledge and the failure to ask questions will cost them their special status of holder in due course; they remain simply holders.

Knowledge acquired by a holder after the instrument was acquired does not prevent the holder from being a holder in due course. Consequently, the fact that a holder, after acquiring the instrument, learns of a defense does not work retroactively to destroy the holder's character as a holder in due course.

ANY KIND CHECKS CASHED, INC. V TALCOTT, 830 SO 2D 160 (FLA APP 2002)

ANY KIND OF CHECK WON'T DO

FACTS: In the 1990s, John G. Talcott, Jr., a 93-year-old Massachusetts resident, was sold an investment of $75,000 by D. J. Rivera, a "financial advisor" to Talcott, and Salvatore Guarino, a cohort of Rivera. The investment produced no returns.

On December 7, 1999, Guarino established check cashing privileges at Any Kind Checks Cashed, Inc. (Any Kind) by filling out a customer card. On the card, Guarino listed himself as a broker.

On January 10, 2000, Rivera telephoned Talcott and talked him into sending him a check for $10,000 made out to Guarino, which was to be used for travel expenses to obtain a return on the original $75,000 investment. Rivera received the check on January 11.

Talcott spoke to Rivera on the morning of January 11. Rivera indicated that $10,000 was more than what was needed for travel. He said that $5,700 would meet the travel costs. Talcott called his bank and stopped payment on the $10,000 check.

Guarino went to Any Kind's Stuart, Florida, office on January 11 and presented the $10,000 check to Nancy Michael. She was a supervisor with the company with the authority to approve checks over $2,000. Guarino showed Michael his driver's license and the Federal Express envelope from Talcott in which he received the check. She was unable to contact the maker of the check by telephone. Based on her experience, Michael believed the check was good; the Federal Express envelope was "very crucial" to her decision because it indicated that the maker of the check had sent it

[12] *St. Bernard Savings & Loan Ass'n v Cella*, 826 F Supp 985 (ED La 1993); *Cadle Co. v DeVincent*, 57 Mass App Ct 13, 781 NE2d 817, 49 UCC Rep Serv 2d 1261 (Mass App 2003); *Federal Financial Co. v Gerard*, 949 P2d 412 (Wash App 1998).

[13] Revised UCC § 3-304.

[14] *Unr-Rohn, Inc. v Summit Bank*, 687 NE2d 235 (Ind App 1997); but see contra view, *Pero's Steak and Spaghetti House v Lee*, 90 SW3d 614 (Tenn 2002).

to the payee trying to cash the check. After deducting the 5 percent check cashing fee, Michael cashed the check and gave Guarino $9,500. The next day she deposited the check in the company's bank.

On January 15, 2000, Rivera called Talcott and asked about the $5,700, again promising to send him a return on his investment. The same day, Talcott sent a check for $5,700. On January 17, 2000, Guarino went into the Stuart Any Kind store and presented the $5,700 check to the teller, Joanne Kochakian. He showed her the Federal Express envelope in which the check had come. Kochakian noticed that Michael had previously approved the $10,000 check. She called Michael and told her about Guarino's check. Michael instructed the cashier not to cash the check until she contacted the maker, Talcott, to obtain approval. On her first attempt, using the number on the back of Guarino's check cashing card, Kochakian received no answer. When she told Guarino that she would not cash his check, he gave her another number to call, which was the same as the first number except that two numbers were reversed. On the second call, Talcott approved cashing the $5,700 check. There was no discussion of the $10,000 check. Any Kind cashed the second check for Guarino, from which it deducted a 3 percent fee.

On January 19, Rivera called Talcott to warn him that Guarino was a cheat and a thief. Talcott immediately called his bank and stopped payment on the $5,700 check. Talcott's daughter called Any Kind and told it of the stop payment on the $5,700 check.

Any Kind filed suit against Guarino and Talcott, claiming that it was a holder in due course. Talcott's defense was that Any Kind was not a holder in due course. The trial court entered for Any Kind for only the $5,700 check. The court found that the circumstances surrounding the cashing of the $10,000 check were suspicious and should have put Any Kind on notice of a problem.

Judicial Opinion

GROSS, Judge. . . . The issue in this case is whether a check cashing store qualifies as a holder in due course so that it can collect on a $10,000 check written by an elderly man who was fraudulently induced to issue the check by the person who cashed it.

We hold that the check cashing store was not a holder in due course, because the procedures it followed with the $10,000 check did not comport with reasonable commercial standards of fair dealing.

Unless Any Kind is a holder in due course, its right to enforce Talcott's obligation to pay the draft is subject to (1) all defenses Talcott could raise "if the person entitled to enforce the instrument were enforcing a right to payment under a simple contract," and (2) a claim of "recoupment" Talcott could raise against Guarino. Because Talcott was fraudulently induced to issue the checks, this case turns on Any Kind's entitlement to holder in due course status.

A "holder in due course" is a holder who takes an instrument without "apparent evidence of forgery or alteration" for value, in good faith, and without notice of certain claims and defenses.

The question for this court is whether the trial court erred in finding that Any Kind was not a holder in due course of the $10,000 check based on the findings of fact made at trial, keeping in mind that Any Kind bore the burden of proof. That question turns on whether Any Kind acted "[i]n good faith."

The good faith requirement of the holder in due course doctrine "has been the source of an ancient and continuing dispute." On the one hand, [s]hould the courts apply a so-called objective test, and ask whether a reasonably prudent person, behaving the way the alleged holder in due course behaved, would have been acting in good faith? Or should the courts instead apply a subjective test and examine the person's actual behavior, however stupid and irrespective of the reaction a reasonably prudent person would have had in the same circumstance? The legal establishment has steered a crooked course through this debate.

Application of [the] "honesty in fact" standard to Any Kind's conduct in this case would clothe it with holder in due course status. It is undisputed that Any Kind's employees were pure of heart, that they acted without knowledge of Guarino's wrongdoing. However, in 1992, the legislature adopted a new definition of "good faith" that applies . . . '[g]ood faith' means honesty in fact and the observance of reasonable commercial standards of fair dealing." To the old, subjective good faith, "honesty in fact" standard, the legislature added an objective component—the "pure heart of the holder must now be accompanied by reasoning that assures conduct comporting with reasonable commercial standards of fair dealing." No longer may a holder of an instrument act with "a pure heart and an empty head and still obtain holder in due course status."

A holder "must act in a way that is fair according to commercial standards that are themselves reasonable." Even assuming that Any Kind's procedures for checks over $2,000 met the industry's gold standard, we hold that in this case the procedures followed were not reasonably related to achieve fair dealing with respect to the $10,000 check, taking into consideration all of the participants in the transaction, Talcott, Guarino, and Any Kind.

Check cashing businesses occupy a special niche in the financial industry. They are part of the "alternative financial services" or "fringe banking" sector, a part of the market that "has become a major source of traditional banking services for low-income and working poor consumers, residents of minority neighborhoods, and people with blemished credit histories." Check cashing stores are often in locations where traditional banks fear to tread. [They] are usually located in lower income neighborhoods:

Attractions of check cashing outlets are convenience and speed. As the amicus points out, many check cashing businesses are open twenty-four hours a day, seven days a week. Unlike banks, check cashing stores cannot place a hold on a check before releasing funds.

Against this backdrop, we cannot say that the trial court erred in finding that the $10,000 check was a red flag. The $10,000 personal check was not the typical check cashed at a check cashing outlet. The size of the check, in the context of the check cashing business, was a proper factor to consider under the objective standard of good faith in deciding whether Any Kind was a holder in due course. Guarino was not the typical customer of a check cashing outlet. As the trial judge observed, because of the 5% fee charged, it is unusual for a small businessman such as a broker to conduct business through a check cashing store instead of through a traditional bank. Guarino did not have a history with Any Kind of cashing checks of similar size without incident. The need for speed in a business transaction is usually less acute than for someone cashing a paycheck or welfare check to pay for life's necessities. The need for speed in cashing a large business check is consistent with a drawer who, for whatever reason, might stop payment. Fair dealing in this case required that the $10,000 check be approached with a degree of caution.

If a drawer has a right to stop payment of a check, and a traditional bank usually places a hold on uncollected funds after a payee deposits a check into an account, then the legal dispute after a stop payment will usually be between the drawer of the check and the payee, the two parties that had the dealings leading to the payment. Thus, where a check is cashed at a bank or savings and loan, the law will often place the loss on the wrongdoer in the underlying transaction. This is a desirable goal.

Where a check cashing store releases funds immediately, the holder in due course doctrine steps in, frequently putting the loss on a wronged maker, in furtherance of the policy that facilitating the transfer of checks benefits the economy. In this case, the policy reasons behind easy negotiability do not outweigh the reasons for caution. Very loose application of the objective component of "good faith" would make check cashing outlets the easy refuge of scam artists who want to take the money and run. The concept of "fair dealing" includes not being an easy, safe harbor for the dishonest.

To affirm the trial court is not to wreak havoc with the check cashing industry. Verification with the maker of a check will not be necessary to preserve holder in due course status in the vast majority of cases arising from check cashing outlets. This was neither the typical customer, nor the typical transaction of a check cashing outlet.

In this case, reasonable commercial fairness required Any Kind to approach the $10,000 check with some caution and to verify it with the maker if it wanted to preserve its holder in due course status.

[Affirmed]

Discussion Questions

1. What is the purpose of check cashing stores?
2. Why does this purpose put the owners and operators on notice when a $10,000 check comes through?
3. What do commercial reasonableness standards require?

CPA (b) Holder Through a Holder in Due Course

Those persons who become holders of the instrument after a holder in due course has held it are given the same protection as the holder in due course, provided they are not parties to any fraud or illegality that affects the instrument. This status of **holder through a holder in due course** is given in these circumstances even if the transferee from a holder in due course does not satisfy the requirements for

ETHICS & THE LAW

THE CORNER CHECK CASHING COMPANY AND GOOD FAITH

Some public policy experts have argued that no check cashing company, defined as one that takes a portion of the amount of the check as a fee for cashing checks for individuals who cannot get them cashed at banks and credit unions, should ever be allowed holder in due course status. Do you agree with this argument? Are check cashing companies ethical in their behavior?

holder-in-due-course status. This elevated or protected status is called Article 3's "shelter rule," and it allows a person who is not a holder in due course to hide under the "umbrella" with a holder in due course and be sheltered from claims and defenses as if actually being a holder in due course. **For Example,** a person who acquires an instrument as an inheritance from an estate does not give value and is missing one of the requirements for being a holder in due course. However, if the estate was a holder in due course, that status does transfer to the heir. Furthermore, suppose that Avery is a holder in due course of a $5,000 promissory note due May 31, 2007. Avery gives the note to his nephew Aaron for Aaron's birthday on June 1, 2007. Aaron did not give value because the note was a gift, and he has taken the note as a holder after it has already become due. Nonetheless, because Avery was a holder in due course, Aaron assumes that status under Article 3's shelter provision.

B. Defenses to Payment of a Negotiable Instrument

One of the key reasons for attaining holder-in-due-course status is to be able to obtain payment on the negotiable instrument free of any underlying problems between the original parties to the instrument. A holder in due course takes an instrument free from certain types of defenses to payment. Whether a defense may be raised against a holder in due course claiming under a negotiable instrument depends on the nature of the defense.

CPA 4. Classification of Defenses

The importance of being a holder in due course or a holder through a holder in due course is that such holders are not subject to certain defenses called *limited defenses.* Another class of defenses, *universal defenses,* may be asserted against any party, whether an assignee, an ordinary holder, a holder in due course, or a holder through a holder in due course.[15]

5. Defenses against Assignee or Ordinary Holder

Assignees of negotiable instruments are subject to every defense raised. Similarly, a holder who does not become a holder in due course is subject to every payment defense just as though the instrument were not negotiable.

6. Limited Defenses not Available against a Holder in Due Course

Holders in due course are not subject to any of the following defenses.

CPA (a) Ordinary Contract Defenses

In general terms, the defenses that could be raised in a breach of contract claim cannot be raised against a holder in due course. The defenses of lack, failure, or illegality of consideration with respect to the instrument's underlying transaction cannot be asserted against the holder in due course. Misrepresentation about the goods underlying the contract is also not a defense. **For Example,** a businessperson cannot refuse to pay a holder in due course on the note used to pay for her copy machine just because her copy machine does not have the speed she was promised.

[15] Under the pre-Code law and under the 1952 Code, the universal defense was called a *real defense,* and the limited defense was called a *personal defense.* These terms have now been abandoned, but some licensing and CPA examinations may continue to use these pre-Code terms.

(b) Incapacity of Maker or Drawer

Ordinarily, the maker's or drawer's lack of capacity (except minors) may not be raised as a defense to payment to a holder in due course. Such incapacity is a defense, however, if the incapacity is at a legal level that makes the instrument a nullity. **For Example,** a promissory note made by an insane person for whom a court has appointed a guardian is void. In the case of a claim on the note by a holder in due course, the incapacity of the maker would be a defense.

CPA (c) Fraud in the Inducement

If a person is persuaded or induced to execute the instrument because of fraudulent statements, such **fraud in the inducement** cannot be raised against a party with holder-in-due-course status. **For Example,** suppose Mills is persuaded to purchase an automobile because of Pagan's statements that the car was a demonstrator for the dealership and in good mechanical condition with a certification from the dealership's head mechanic. Mills, a car dealer, gives Pagan a note, which is negotiated until it reaches Han, who is a holder in due course. Mills meanwhile learns that the car has been in an accident and has a cracked engine block, that the head mechanic was paid to sign the certification, and that Pagan's statements were fraudulent. When Han demands payment of the note, Mills cannot refuse to pay on the ground of Pagan's fraud. Mills must pay the note because Han, as a holder in due course, does not take the note subject to any fraud or misrepresentation in the underlying transaction. Mills is left with the remedy of recovering from Pagan for misrepresentation or fraud.

(d) Miscellaneous Defenses[16]

The limited defenses listed in the preceding three subsections are those most commonly raised against demands by holders in due course for payment. In addition, the following limited defenses may be asserted: (1) prior payment or cancellation of the instrument, (2) nondelivery, (3) conditional or special-purpose delivery, (4) breach of warranty, (5) duress consisting of threats, (6) unauthorized completion, and (7) theft of a bearer instrument. These defenses, however, have a very limited effect in terms of defending against a holder in due course's demand for payment.

7. Universal Defenses Available against All Holders

Certain defenses are regarded as so basic that the social interest in preserving them outweighs the social interest of giving negotiable instruments the freely transferable qualities of money. Accordingly, such defenses are given universal effect and may be raised against all holders, whether ordinary holders, holders in due course, or holders through a holder in due course. These defenses are called **universal defenses.**[17]

CPA (a) Fraud as to the Nature or Essential Terms of the Instrument

The fact that a person signs an instrument because the person is fraudulently deceived as to its nature or essential terms is a defense available against all holders.[18] When one person induces another to sign a note by falsely representing that, for example, it is a contract for repairs or that it is a character reference, the note is invalid, and the defense of the misrepresentation of the character of the instrument can be used against a holder in due course. This defense, however, cannot be raised when the defending party was negligent in examining and questioning the true nature and terms of the instrument. **For Example,** suppose that two homeowners are asked to sign a statement for a salesperson that he was in their home and did a demonstration of a new solar water heater. Just as the homeowners are about to sign the verification statement, the salesman distracts them and then switches the verification for a purchase contract and promissory note for a $5,000 solar water heating system that the owners declined to purchase. The owners would have a defense of fraud in factum against a holder in due course of this note. The difference between fraud in the inducement—a personal defense—and fraud in factum—a real defense—is that fraud in factum involves deception as to the documents themselves, not as to the underlying goods, services, or property.

CPA (b) Forgery or Lack of Authority

The defense that a signature was forged or signed without authority can be raised by a drawer or maker against any holder unless the drawer or maker whose

[16] Revised UCC § 3-305.

[17] In previous versions of the Code, the universal defenses were referred to as *real* defenses.

[18] Revised UCC § 3-305(a)(1)(iii).

name was signed has ratified it or is estopped by conduct or negligence from denying it.[19] The fact that the negligence of the drawer helped the wrongdoer does not prevent the drawee from raising the defense of forgery. (See Chapters 29 and 31 for more discussion of the impact of forgery on liability.)

(c) Duress Depriving Control

A party may execute or indorse a negotiable instrument in response to a force of such a nature that, under general principles of law, duress makes the transaction void rather than merely voidable. Duress of this type and level may be raised as a defense against any holder. Economic duress, in the form of a reluctance to enter into a financially demanding instrument, is not a universal defense.[20] Duress that is attempted murder is a universal defense.

(d) Incapacity

The fact that the defendant is a minor who under general principles of contract law may avoid the obligation is a matter that may be raised against any kind of holder. Other kinds of incapacity may be raised as a defense if the effect of the incapacity is to make the instrument void, as when there has been a formal declaration of insanity.[21]

(e) Illegality

If an instrument is void by law when executed in connection with certain conduct, such as a note for gambling or one that involves usury, such defenses may be raised against any holder.

CPA (f) Alteration

An **alteration** is an unauthorized change or completion of a negotiable instrument designed to modify the obligation of a party to the instrument.[22] **For Example,** changing the amount of an instrument from $150 to $450 is an alteration.[23]

(1) Person Making Alteration. By definition, an alteration is a change made by a party to the instrument. A change of the instrument made by a nonparty has no effect. Recovery on the instrument is still possible under the terms of the instrument as though the change had not been made, provided it can be proven how the instrument existed in its original form.

(2) Effect of Alteration. If the alteration to the instrument was made fraudulently, the person whose obligations under the instrument are affected by that alteration is discharged from liability on the instrument. The instrument, however, can be enforced according to its original terms or its terms as completed. This right of enforcement is given to holders in due course who had no notice of such alteration.[24] While a holder in due course would come within the protected class on alteration, such status is not required for this recovery provision in the event of alteration. **For Example,** Ryan signed a negotiable demand note for $100 made payable to Long. A subsequent holder changed the amount from $100 to $700. A later holder in due course presented the note to Ryan for payment. Ryan would still be liable for the original amount of $100.

A summary of the universal and limited defenses is presented in Figure 30-2.

8. Denial of Holder-in-Due-Course Protection

In certain situations, the taker of a negotiable instrument is denied the status of a holder in due course or is denied the protection of a holder in due course.

(a) Participating Transferee

The seller of goods on credit frequently assigns the sales contract and buyer's promissory note to the manufacturer who made the goods, to a finance company, or to a bank. In such a case, the assignee of the seller will be a holder in due course of the buyer's

[19] *Bank of Hoven v Rausch*, 382 NW2d 39 (SD 1986); for general discussion of estoppel and ratification, see *Ziegler Furniture and Funeral Home, Inc. v Cicmanec*, 709 NW2d 350, 2006 (SD 2006).

[20] *Miller v Calhoun/Johnson Co.*, 497 SE2d 397 (Ga App 1998); *Smith v Gordon*, 598 SE2d 92 (Ga App 2004).

[21] Revised UCC § 3-305(a)(1)(ii).

[22] Revised UCC § 3-407(a); *Stahl v St. Elizabeth Medical Center*, 948 SW2d 419 (Ky App 1997). A material alteration made based on the parties' negotiations (a 13 percent versus an 18 percent interest rate) is not fraudulent. *Darnall v Petersen*, 592 NW2d 505 (Neb App 1999); *Knoefler v Wojtalewicz*, 2003 WL 21496933 (Neb App 2003) (difference between bank interest rate and judgment interest rate is not material).

[23] However, if an instrument, such as a note, has been altered and the maker continues to pay without objection to the alteration, the alteration does not discharge the maker's liability. *Stahl v St. Elizabeth Medical Center*, 948 SW2d 419 (Ky App 1997); again, for a general discussion of continuing payment as estoppel, see *Ziegler Furniture and Funeral Home, Inc. v Cicmanec*, 709 NW2d 350, 2006 (SD 2006).

[24] Revised UCC § 3-407(b), (c).

FIGURE 30-2 Defenses to Payment of Negotiable Instrument

UNIVERSAL (AVAILABLE AGAINST ASSIGNEES, HOLDERS, AND HOLDERS IN DUE COURSE) (REAL)	LIMITED (AVAILABLE AGAINST ASSIGNEES AND HOLDERS BUT NOT AGAINST HOLDERS IN DUE COURSE) (PERSONAL)	MIXED (CIRCUMSTANCES VARY THE AVAILABILITY OF THESE DEFENSES)
FRAUD AS TO THE NATURE OF THE INSTRUMENT (FRAUD IN FACTUM)	FRAUD IN THE INDUCEMENT	DURESS
FORGERY	MISREPRESENTATION	INCAPACITY
UNAUTHORIZED SIGNATURE	LACK OF CONSIDERATION	
INCAPACITY (DECLARATION)	BREACH OF WARRANTY	
ILLEGALITY	CANCELLATION	
ALTERATION	FAILURE OF DELIVERY	
CONSUMER CREDIT CONTRACTS WITH FTC NOTICE	UNAUTHORIZED COMPLETION	
	ALL ORDINARY CONTRACT DEFENSES	

note if the note is properly negotiated and the transferee satisfies all of the elements of being a holder in due course. The transferee, however, may take such an active part in the sale to the seller's customer or may be so related to the seller that it is possible to conclude that the transferee was in fact a party to the original transaction. This close-connection doctrine (discussed earlier in this chapter as an issue in the good-faith requirement for becoming a holder in due course) prevents a transferee with intimate knowledge of the transferor's business practices from becoming a holder in due course.[25]

(b) The Federal Trade Commission Rule

In 1976, the Federal Trade Commission (FTC) adopted a rule that limits the rights of a holder in due course in a consumer credit transaction. The rule protects consumers who purchase goods or services for personal, family, or household use on credit.[26] When the note the buyer gave the seller as payment for the consumer goods is transferred to even a holder in due course, the consumer buyer may raise any defense that could have been raised against the seller. The FTC regulation requires that the following notice be included in boldface type at least 10 points in size in consumer credit contracts covered under the rule:

Notice
Any holder of this consumer credit contract is subject to all claims and defenses which the debtor could assert against the seller of goods or services obtained with the proceeds hereof. Recovery hereunder by the debtor shall not exceed amounts paid by the debtor hereunder.[27]

When a notice preserving consumer defenses is included in a negotiable instrument, no subsequent

25 *Midfirst Bank v C. W. Haynes & Co.*, 893 F Supp 1304 (DSC 1994), aff'd 87 F3d 1308 (4th Cir 1998); *AIG Global Securities Lending Corp. v Banc of America Securities LLC Slip Copy*, 2006 WL 1206333 (SDNY 2006).

26 The regulation does not cover purchases of real estate, securities, or consumer goods or services for which the purchase price is more than $25,000. *Roosevelt Federal Savings & Loan Ass'n v Crider*, 722 SW2d 325 (Mo App 1986).

27 One of the controversial changes to Article 3 is found in subsections 3-305(e) and (f). This change provides that if the Federal Trade Commission requires a notice to be included, but it is not, the instrument is deemed to have included it implicitly.

THINKING THINGS THROUGH

THE CORNER CHECK-CASHING COMPANY AND THIEVES—WHO WINS?

Now is an ideal time to bring together all of the concepts you have learned in Chapters 27, 28, and 29. Analyzing this problem will help you integrate your knowledge about negotiable instruments. Sid's Salmon has purchased salmon from Fred's Fisheries. Sid wrote a check for $22,000 to Fred's. A thief broke into Fred's offices and took the cash on hand as well as the unindorsed check from Sid's. The thief took the check to the Corner Check Cashing Company (CCCC) and received $22,000 less the cashing fee of $2,000. Fred notified Sid who then notified First Commerce Bank, the drawee of the check of the theft. CCCC has presented the check for payment, and First Commerce refuses to pay. CCCC says it is a holder in due course. Are you able to help First Commerce Bank develop its response to CCCC?

Suppose that Fred had already indorsed the check when the thief stole it. Would CCCC be a holder in due course?

person can be a holder in due course of the instrument.[28]

C. Liability Issues: How Payment Rights Arise and Defenses Are Used

In this chapter and in Chapters 28 and 29, issues surrounding the types of instruments, transfers, holders, and holders in due course have been covered. However, there are procedures under Article 3 for bringing together all of the parties, instruments, and defenses so that ultimate liability and, hopefully, payment can be determined and achieved.

CPA 9. The Roles of Parties and Liability

Every instrument has primary and secondary parties. The **primary party** is the party to whom the holder or holder in due course must turn first to obtain payment. The primary party on a note or certificate of deposit is the **maker.** The primary party on a draft is the **drawee,** assuming that the drawee has accepted the draft. Although a check must first be presented to the drawee bank for payment, the bank is not primarily liable on the instrument because the bank has the right to refuse to pay the check (see following and Chapter 31). The drawee bank on a check is the party to whom a holder or holder in due course turns first for payment despite the lack of primary-party status on the part of that drawee bank. The maker of a note is the party to whom holders and holders in due course must turn first for payment.

The **secondary parties** (or *secondary obligors,* as they are now called under Revised Article 3) to an instrument are those to whom holders turn when the primary party, for whatever reason, fails to pay the instrument. Secondary parties on notes are **indorsers,** and secondary parties on checks and drafts are **drawers** and *indorsers.*

CPA 10. Attaching Liability of the Primary Parties: Presentment

Presentment occurs when the holder or holder in due course of an instrument orally, in writing, or by electronic communication to the primary party requests that the instrument be paid according to its terms. The primary party has the right to require that

[28] Revised UCC § 3-106(d). This goes beyond the scope of the FTC regulation. The latter merely preserves the defenses of the consumer but does not bar holder-in-due-course protection for other parties, such as an accommodation party to a consumer's note. Also, the FTC regulation does not change the common law and permits the maker to bring contract actions against the holder of the note for contract breaches committed by the maker's original contract party. The rule changes the status of the parties as holders in due course. It does not change contract rights. *LaBarre v Credit Acceptance Corp.*, 11 F Supp 2d 1071 (D Minn 1998); aff'd in part, reversed in part, 175 F3d 640 (8th Cir 1999).

E-COMMERCE AND CYBERLAW

ELECTRONIC PRESENTMENT: ONE FELL SWOOP

The presentment of checks has evolved from the formal presentation of an original document to electronic check conversion (ECC), which Wal-Mart and other retailers used as a system of payment prior to the availability of debit cards. Under ECC, the check was run through an electronic system that read the magnetic encoding on the check and the check was presented to the bank for payment at the point of sale. The UCC permitted such electronic presentment. Now presentment occurs entirely electronically, and the only paper the consumer has at the point of sale is the receipt. The account is debited automatically at the time the transaction occurs. Likewise, the notion of electronic presentment allows electronic dishonor. The debit is honored only if the account has sufficient funds that are available at the time of the transaction. Some of the UCC Article 3 provisions are now unnecessary in these types of transactions, and the rights of the merchants and the buyers are covered under various federal and state laws on electronic funds transfers (covered in Chapter 31). Issues continue to evolve, such as what laws govern the popular PayPal system so closely affiliated with the millions of consumer transactions on eBay. Electronic technology requires that we change laws and grow into the new systems for commercial transactions and payments.

the presentment be made in a "commercially reasonable manner," which would include reasonable times for presentment, such as during business hours. The primary party can also require identification, authorization, and even a signature of receipt of the funds due under the instrument. In addition, the primary party can demand a valid indorsement on the instrument prior to making payment. Upon presentment, the primary party is required to pay according to the terms of the instrument unless there are defenses such as forgery, any of the other universal defenses for holders in due course, or any defenses for holders.

If the primary party refuses to pay the instrument according to its terms, there has been a *dishonor*, and the holder is then left to turn to the secondary parties.

CPA 11. Dishonor and Notice of Dishonor

Dishonor occurs when the primary party refuses to pay the instrument according to its terms. The primary party is required to give **notice of dishonor.** The notice that the instrument has been dishonored can be oral, written, or electronic. That notice is subject to time limitations. **For Example,** a bank must give notice of dishonor by midnight of the next banking day. Nonbank primary parties must give notice of dishonor within 30 days following their receipt of notice of dishonor. Returning the dishonored check is sufficient notice of dishonor. (See Chapter 31 for more discussion of liability issues on dishonor of checks.) Upon dishonor, the holder must then turn to the secondary parties for payment.

The obligation of the secondary parties in these situations is to pay according to the terms of the instrument. These secondary parties will have **limited defenses** if the presenting party is a holder in due course. **For Example,** suppose that a check drawn on First Interstate Bank is written by Ben Paltrow to Julia Sutherland as payment for Julia's Bentley auto that Ben purchased. Julia deposits Ben's check into her account at AmeriBank, and AmeriBank sends the check to First Interstate to present it for payment. First Interstate finds that Ben's account has insufficient funds and dishonors the check. AmeriBank must notify First Interstate by midnight of the next banking day that the check has been dishonored, and then First Interstate must notify Julia by midnight of the next banking day that Ben's check was dishonored. Julia then has 30 days to notify Ben and turn to him as a drawer, or secondary party, for payment on the check.

Summary

A holder of a negotiable instrument can be either an ordinary holder or a holder in due course. The ordinary holder has the same rights that an assignee would have. Holders in due course and holders through a holder in due course are protected from certain defenses. To be a holder in due course, a person must first be a holder—that is, the person must have acquired the instrument by a proper negotiation. The holder must then also take for value, in good faith, without notice that the paper is overdue or dishonored, and without notice of defenses and adverse claims. Those persons who become holders of the instrument after a holder in due course are given the same protection as the holder in due course through the shelter provision, provided they are not parties to any fraud or illegality affecting the instrument.

The importance of being a holder in due course or a holder through a holder in due course is that those holders are not subject to certain defenses when they demand payment or bring suit on the instrument. These defenses are limited defenses and include ordinary contract defenses, incapacity unless it makes the instrument void, fraud in the inducement, prior payment or cancellation, nondelivery of an instrument, conditional delivery, duress consisting of threats, unauthorized completion, and theft of a bearer instrument. Universal defenses may be asserted against any plaintiff whether that party is an assignee, an ordinary holder, a holder in due course, or a holder through a holder in due course. Universal defenses include fraud as to the nature or essential terms of the paper, forgery or lack of authority, duress depriving control, incapacity, illegality that makes the instrument void, and alteration. Alteration is only a partial defense; the favored holder may enforce the instrument according to its original terms.

The Federal Trade Commission rule on consumer credit contracts limits the immunity of a holder in due course from defenses of consumer buyers against their sellers. Immunity is limited in consumer credit transactions if the notice specified by the FTC regulation is included in the sales contract. When a notice preserving consumer defenses is stated in a negotiable instrument, no subsequent person can be a holder in due course.

Holders and holders in due course are required to present instruments for payment to primary parties. Primary parties are makers and drawees. If the primary party refuses to pay, or dishonors, the instrument, it must give notice of dishonor in a timely fashion. The holder can then turn to secondary parties, drawers, and indorsers (secondary obligors) for payment.

Questions and Case Problems

1. Randy Bocian had a bank account with First of America-Bank (FAB). On October 8, Bocian received a check for $28,800 from Eric Christenson as payment for constructing a pole barn on Christenson's property. Bocian deposited the check at FAB on October 9 and was permitted to draw on the funds through October 12. Bocian wrote checks totaling $12,334.21, which FAB cleared. On October 12, Christenson stopped payment on the check as the result of a contract dispute over the pole barn. Bocian's account was then overdrawn once the check was denied clearance by Christenson's bank. FAB brought suit against both Bocian and Christenson to collect its loss. Christenson counterclaimed against Bocian for his contract breach claims on the pole barn construction. FAB maintained that it had given value and was a holder in due course and that, as such, it was not required to be subject to the pole barn issues or the stop payment order. Is FAB right? [*First of America-Bank Northeast Illinois v Bocian*, 614 NE2d 890 (Ill App)]
2. Cronin, an employee of Epicycle, cashed his final paycheck at Money Mart Check Cashing Center. Epicycle had issued a stop payment order on the check. Money Mart deposited the check through normal banking channels. The check was returned to Money Mart marked "Payment Stopped." Money Mart brought an action against Epicycle, claiming that, as a holder in due course, it was entitled to recover against Epicycle. Epicycle argued that Money Mart could not be a holder in due course because it failed to verify the check as good prior to cashing it. Is Money Mart a holder in due course? [*Money Mart Check Cashing Center, Inc. v Epicycle Corp.*, 667 P2d 1372 (Colo)]
3. Halleck executed a promissory note payable to the order of Leopold. Halleck did not pay the note when due, and Leopold brought suit on the note, producing it in court. Halleck admitted that he had signed the note but claimed plaintiff Leopold was required to prove that the note had been issued for consideration and that the plaintiff was in fact the holder. Are these elements of proof required as part of the case? [*Leopold v Halleck*, 436 NE2d 29 (Ill App)]
4. Calhoun/Johnson Company d/b/a Williams Lumber Company (Williams) sold building materials to Donald Miller d/b/a Millercraft Construction Company (Millercraft) on credit. Miller had signed a personal guaranty for the materials. Miller requested lien waivers from Williams for four of his projects and asked for them from Fabian Boudreau, Williams's credit manager. Fabian refused to grant the waivers because Miller was $28,000 delinquent on his account. Miller agreed to

bring his account current with the exception of $11,000 for which he signed a no-interest promissory note. Miller obtained the lien waivers and then defaulted on the note. Williams brought suit for payment, and Williams said there was lack of consideration and that the note was not valid. He said he must give value to be able to recover on the note. Was he correct? [*Miller v Calhoun/Johnson Co.*, 497 SE2d 397 (Ga App)]

5. Statham drew a check. The payee indorsed it to Kemp Motor Sales. Statham then stopped payment on the check on the grounds that there was a failure of consideration for the check. Kemp sued Statham on the check. When Statham raised the defense of failure of consideration, Kemp replied that he was a holder in due course. Statham claimed that Kemp could not recover because Statham learned of his defense before Kemp deposited the check in its bank account. Discuss the parties' arguments and rights in this situation. [*Kemp Motor Sales v Statham*, 171 SE2d 389 (Ga App)]
6. Can check cashing companies be holders in due course? What arguments can you make for and against their holder-in-due-course status? [*Dal-Tile Corp. v Cash N' Go*, 487 SE2d 529 (Ga App)]
7. Jones, wishing to retire from a business enterprise that he had been conducting for a number of years, sold all of the assets of the business to Jackson Corp. Included in the assets were a number of promissory notes payable to the order of Jones that he had taken from his customers. Upon the maturity of one of the notes, the maker refused to pay because there was a failure of consideration. Jackson Corp. sued the maker of the note. Who should succeed? Explain.
8. Elliot, an officer of Impact Marketing, drew six postdated checks on Impact's account. The checks were payable to Bell for legal services to be subsequently performed for Impact. Financial Associates purchased them from Bell and collected on four of the checks. Payment was stopped on the last two when Bell's services were terminated. Financial argued that it was a holder in due course and had the right to collect on the checks. Impact claimed that because the checks were postdated and issued for an executory promise, Financial could not be a holder in due course. Who was correct? Why? [*Financial Associates v Impact Marketing*, 394 NYS2d 814 (Misc)]
9. *D* drew a check to the order of *P*. *P* took the check postdated. *P* knew that *D* was having financial difficulties and that the particular checking account on which this check was drawn had been frequently overdrawn. Do these circumstances prevent *P* from being a holder in due course? [*Citizens Bank, Booneville v National Bank of Commerce*, 334 F2d 257 (10th Cir); *Franklin National Bank v Sidney Gotowner*, 4 UCC Rep Serv 953 (NY Supp)]
10. Daniel, Joel, and Claire Guerrette are the adult children of Elden Guerrette, who died on September 24, 1995. Before his death, Elden purchased a life insurance policy from Sun Life Assurance Company of Canada through a Sun Life agent, Steven Hall, and named his children as his beneficiaries. Upon his death, Sun Life issued three checks, each in the amount of $40,759.35, to each of Elden's children. The checks were drawn on Sun Life's account at Chase Manhattan Bank in Syracuse, New York. The checks were given to Hall for delivery to the Guerrettes. Hall and an associate, Paul Richard, then fraudulently induced the Guerrettes to indorse the checks in blank and to transfer them to Hall and Richard, purportedly to be invested in HER, Inc., a corporation formed by Hall and Richard. Hall took the checks from the Guerrettes and turned them over to Richard, who deposited them in his account at the Credit Union on October 26, 1995. The Credit Union immediately made the funds available to Richard.

    The Guerrettes quickly regretted having negotiated their checks to Hall and Richard, and they contacted Sun Life the next day to request that Sun Life stop payment on the checks. Sun Life immediately ordered Chase Manhattan to stop payment on the checks.

    When the checks were ultimately presented to Chase Manhattan for payment, Chase refused to pay the checks, and they were returned to the Credit Union. The Credit Union received notice that the checks had been dishonored on November 3, 1995, the sixth business day following their deposit. By the time the Credit Union received notice, however, Richard had withdrawn from his account all of the funds represented by the three checks. The Credit Union was able to recover almost $80,000 from Richard, but there remained an unpaid balance of $42,366.56.

    The Credit Union filed suit against Sun Life, and all of the parties became engulfed in litigation. The Credit Union indicated it was a holder in due course and was entitled to payment on the instrument. Sun Life alleged fraud. Is the Credit Union a holder in due course? Can the parties allege the fraud defense against it? [*Maine Family Federal Credit Union v Sun Life Assur. Co. of Canada*, 727 A2d 335 (Me)]
11. A bank customer purchased a bank money order and paid for it with a forged check. The money order was negotiable and was acquired by *N*, who was a holder in due course. When *N* sued the bank on the money order, the bank raised the defense that its customer had paid with a bad check. Could this defense be raised against *N*? Why or why not? [*Bank of Niles v American State Bank*, 303 NE2d 186 (Ill App)]
12. Sanders gave Clary a check but left the amount incomplete. The check was given as advance payment on the purchase of 100 LT speakers. The amount was left blank because Clary had the right to substitute other LT speakers if they became available and the substitution

would change the price. It was agreed that in no event would the purchase price exceed $5,000. Desperate for cash, Clary wrongfully substituted much more expensive LT speakers, thereby increasing the price to $5,700. Clary then negotiated the check to Lawrence, one of his suppliers. Clary filled in the $5,700 in Lawrence's presence, showing him the shipping order and the invoice applicable to the sale to Sanders. Lawrence accepted the check in payment of $5,000 worth of overdue debts and $700 in cash. Can Lawrence recover the full amount? Why or why not?

13. GRAS is a Michigan corporation engaged in the business of buying and selling cars. Between 1997 and 2000, Katrina Stewart was employed as a manager by GRAS. During that period, Stewart wrote checks, without authority, on GRAS's corporate account payable to MBNA and sent them to MBNA for payment of her husband's MBNA credit card account. MBNA accepted the checks and credited the proceeds to Stewart's husband's credit card debt. MBNA accepted and processed the GRAS checks in its normal manner through electronic processing. When MBNA receives a check for a credit card payment, the envelope containing the check and the payment slip is opened by machine and the check and the payment slip are electronically processed and credited to the cardholder's account balance. MBNA does not normally review checks for credit card payments. After crediting a payment check to the card holder's account, MBNA transfers it to the bank on which it is written for collection. Pursuant to its standard practice, MBNA did not review the checks it received from Stewart. GRAS did not have a customer relationship with MBNA during the relevant time period.

    GRAS sought a refund of the amounts Stewart embezzled via the MBNA application of the checks to Stewart's husband's credit card account. MBNA said it was a holder in due course. Was MBNA a holder in due course? Was MBNA subject to GRAS's defense of unauthorized instruments? [*Grand Rapids Auto Sales, Inc. v MBNA America Bank*, 227 F Supp 2d 721 (WD Mich)]

14. Shade asked Dow to give him a check for $100 in return for Shade's delivery the next day of a television set. Dow gave the check, but Shade never delivered the television set. Does Dow have a defense if sued on the instrument (a) by Shade; (b) by Shade's brother, to whom Shade gave the unindorsed check as a gift; and (c) by a grocer to whom Shade's brother gave the instrument for value in the ordinary course of business the next day? (The grocer took the check without knowledge of the defense and while acting in good faith.) Explain your answers.

15. Dorsey was negligent in not determining that the paper he was signing was actually a promissory note. The note was negotiated by proper indorsement and delivery to New Jersey Mortgage & Investment Co., a holder in due course. Dorsey refused to pay, alleging fraud in the nature of essential terms. Decide. [*New Jersey Mortgage & Investment Co. v Dorsey*, 165 A2d 297 (NJ)]

CPA Questions

1. Under the Commercial Paper Article of the UCC, which of the following requirements must be met for a person to be a holder in due course of a promissory note?

    a. The note must be payable to bearer.
    b. The note must be negotiable.
    c. All prior holders must have been holders in due course.
    d. The holder must be the payee of the note.

2. A maker of a note will have a real defense against a holder in due course as a result of any of the following conditions except

    a. Discharge in bankruptcy
    b. Forgery
    c. Fraud in the execution
    d. Lack of consideration

3. Under the commercial paper article of the UCC, in a nonconsumer transaction, which of the following are real (universal) defenses available against a holder in due course?

	Material Alteration	*Discharge in Bankruptcy*	*Breach of Contract*
a.	No	Yes	Yes
b.	Yes	Yes	No
c.	No	No	Yes
d.	Yes	No	No

4. A holder in due course will take free of which of the following defenses?

    a. Infancy, to the extent that it is a defense to a simple contract
    b. Discharge of the maker in bankruptcy
    c. A wrongful filling-in of the amount payable that was omitted from the instrument
    d. Duress of a nature that renders the obligation of the party a nullity

5. Mask stole one of Bloom's checks. The check was already signed by Bloom and made payable to Duval. The check was drawn on United Trust Company. Mask forged Duval's signature on the back of the check at the Corner Check Cashing Company, which in turn deposited it with its bank, Town National Bank of Toka. Town National proceeded to collect on the check from United. None of the parties mentioned were negligent. Who will bear the loss, assuming the amount cannot be recovered from Mask?

   a. Bloom
   b. Duval
   c. United Trust Company
   d. Corner Check Cashing Company

6. Robb stole one of Markum's blank checks, made it payable to himself, and forged Markum's signature to it. The check was drawn on the Unity Trust Company. Robb cashed the check at the Friendly Check Cashing Company, which in turn deposited it with its bank, Farmer's National. Farmer's National proceeded to collect on the check from Unity Trust. The theft and forgery were quickly discovered by Markum, who promptly notified Unity. None of the parties mentioned were negligent. Who will bear the loss, assuming the amount cannot be recovered from Robb?

   a. Markum
   b. Unity Trust Company
   c. Friendly Check Cashing Company
   d. Farmer's National

CHECKS AND FUNDS TRANSFERS

CHAPTER (31)

LEARNING OBJECTIVES

After studying this chapter, you should be able to

LO.1 Discuss the significance of certification

LO.2 List and explain the duties of the drawee bank

LO.3 Explain the methods for, and legal effect of, stopping payment

LO.4 State when a check must be presented for payment to charge secondary parties

LO.5 Describe the liability of a bank for improper payment and collection

LO.6 Discuss the legal effect of forgeries and material alterations

LO.7 Specify the time limitations for reporting forgeries and alterations

LO.8 Describe the electronic transfer of funds and laws governing it

The three previous chapters have focused on the characteristics, parties, and transfer of all negotiable instruments. This chapter covers checks as negotiable instruments, the issues related to their transfer and payment because of the involvement of banks, and special rules applicable to banks as drawees. New technology has also enhanced the ability of banks and consumers to make rapid commercial transactions through the use of electronic funds transfers. Special rules and rights have been developed to govern these forms of payment that serve to facilitate everything from a consumer's withdrawing money from an automated teller machine to a buyer's wiring money to a seller whose business is located continents away.

CPA A. Checks

As discussed in Chapter 28, a **check** is a draft payable on demand that is drawn on a bank. Uniform Commercial Code (UCC) § 3-104(f) defines a check as "(i) a draft . . . payable on demand and drawn on a bank or (ii) a cashier's check or teller's check. An instrument may be a check even though it is described on its face by another term, such as 'money order.'"[1] Under Revised Article 4, the change in consumer payment patterns away from formal, signed checks is reflected with the addition of "remotely-created consumer item," which are items directing payment that are drawn on a consumer account but do not carry a handwritten signature of the drawer.[2] These types of payments include PayPal authorizations to pay from consumer checking accounts and automatic bill payments that consumers direct remotely.

Consumer account is defined as a bank account used for household, family, or personal purposes.[3]

The distinguishing characteristics of checks[4] and drafts are summarized in Figure 31-1.

[1] Revised UCC § 3-104(f).

[2] Revised UCC § 3-104(16).

[3] Revised UCC § 3-104(2).

[4] Checks are governed by both Article 3 of the UCC and Article 4 governing bank deposits and collections. The 2001 and 2002 versions of Article 4 are covered in this chapter, along with notations of the changes since the 1990 version. The new versions of Article 4 incorporate provisions in the American Bankers Association Bank Collection Code, enacted in 18 states, and followed in many other states. The purpose of the code was to introduce clarity into the processing of millions of electronic and paper transactions that banks must handle and to recognize the reality of electronic payments. The following states have adopted some of the 2001 version of Article 4 (including the definition changes in Article 1 of the UCC): Alabama, Arkansas, Connecticut, Delaware, Hawaii, Idaho, Minnesota, Montana, Nebraska, Nevada, New Mexico, Oklahoma, Texas, Virgin Islands, and Virginia. The following jurisdictions have adopted the 2002 amendments conforming to Revised Article 3 of the Code: Arkansas has adopted some portions; Minnesota with variations; Nevada with variations; and Texas with variations. There are significant state variations in the Articles 3 and 4 adoptions.

FIGURE 31-1 Differences between a Check and a Draft

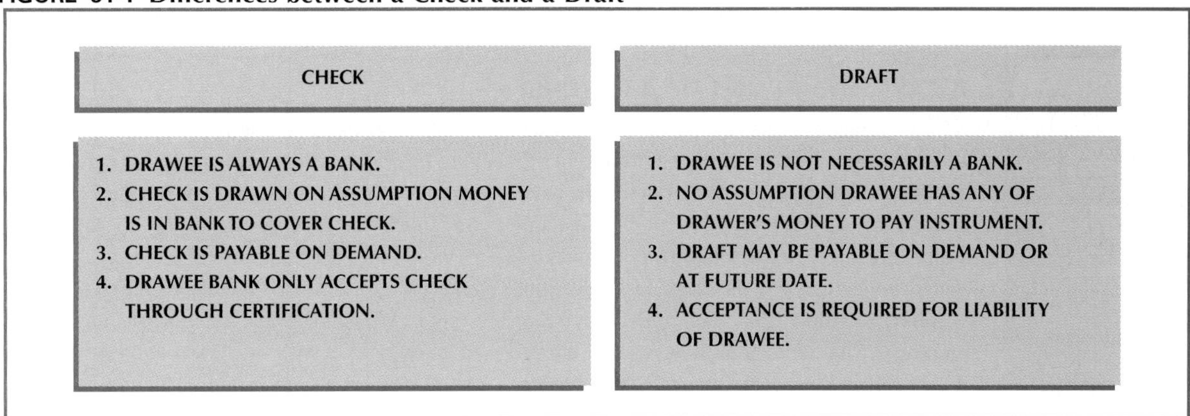

CHECK	DRAFT
1. DRAWEE IS ALWAYS A BANK. 2. CHECK IS DRAWN ON ASSUMPTION MONEY IS IN BANK TO COVER CHECK. 3. CHECK IS PAYABLE ON DEMAND. 4. DRAWEE BANK ONLY ACCEPTS CHECK THROUGH CERTIFICATION.	1. DRAWEE IS NOT NECESSARILY A BANK. 2. NO ASSUMPTION DRAWEE HAS ANY OF DRAWER'S MONEY TO PAY INSTRUMENT. 3. DRAFT MAY BE PAYABLE ON DEMAND OR AT FUTURE DATE. 4. ACCEPTANCE IS REQUIRED FOR LIABILITY OF DRAWEE.

1. Nature of a Check

(a) Sufficient Funds on Deposit

As a practical matter, a check is drawn on the assumption that the bank has on deposit in the drawer's account an amount sufficient to pay the check. In the case of other drafts, there is no assumption that the drawee has any of the drawer's money with which to pay the instrument. In international transactions, sellers may require buyers not only to accept a draft agreeing to pay but also to back up that draft with a line of credit from the buyer's bank. That line of credit is the backup should the funds for the draft not be forthcoming from the buyer.

If a draft is dishonored, the drawer is civilly liable. If a check is drawn with intent to defraud the person to whom it is delivered, the drawer is also subject to criminal prosecution in most states. The laws under which such drawers are prosecuted are known as **bad check laws.** Most states provide that if the check is not made good within a stated period, such as 10 days, there is a presumption that the drawer originally issued the check with the intent to defraud.

CPA (b) Demand Paper

A draft may be payable either on demand or at a future date. A check is a form of **demand draft.** The standard form of check does not specify when it is payable, and it is therefore automatically payable on demand.

One exception arises when a check is **postdated**—that is, when the check shows a date later than the actual date of execution. Postdating a check means that the check is not payable until the date arrives, and it changes the check from a demand draft to a **time draft.**[5] However, banks are not obligated to hold a postdated check until the time used on the check unless the drawer has filed the appropriate paperwork with the bank for such a delay. Because of electronic processing, banks are not required to examine each instrument and honor postdated instrument requests unless the hold is placed into the bank's processing system by the customer.

(c) Form of the Check

A check can be in any form of writing.[6] However, a bank customer may agree, as part of the contract with her bank, to use certain forms for check writing. A remotely created consumer item need only be evidenced by a *record*, not by a written document. Under Revised UCC § 3-104(a)(14), a *record* is defined as "information that is inscribed on a tangible medium or which is stored in an electronic or other medium and is retrievable in perceivable form."[7]

(d) Delivery not Assignment

The delivery of a check is not an assignment of the money on deposit, so it does not automatically transfer the rights of the depositor against the bank to the holder of the check. A check written by a

[5] *In re Channel Home Centers, Inc.*, 989 F2d 682 (3d Cir 1993), cert. denied, 510 U.S. 865 (1993). A bank is required to comply with a postdate on a check only if it is notified of the postdate in the same way the customer issues a stop payment order.

[6] Although not required for negotiation or presentment, a printed bank check, when the customer is using a written form, is preferable because it generally carries magnetic ink figures that facilitate sorting and posting.

[7] Revised UCC § 3-104(a)(14).

E-COMMERCE AND CYBERLAW

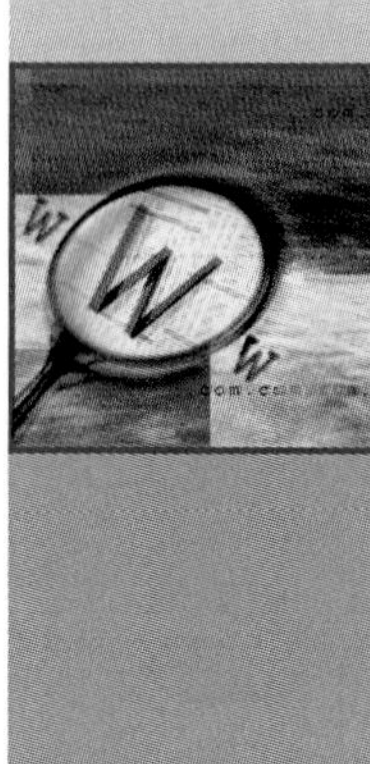

A PAY CARD IN LIEU OF A PAYCHECK

Some employees are using a new device known as the *payroll card.* Rather than issuing checks and running the risk of fictitious payees and other payroll scandals, employees are simply given a card that allows them access to their pay by using a personal identification number at the bank designated by the employer. The benefits of the system are that it is subject to greater controls and easier audits. The downside is that no one is quite sure how to handle the transactions under the law. Are they consumer electronic funds transfers? Are they governed by federal law, or would they be taken care of under state law and UCC provisions on electronic or substitute checks? The law once again has not quite caught up with the new means we have developed for commercial transactions.

drawer on his drawee bank does not result in a duty on the part of the drawee bank to the holder to pay the holder the amount of the check.[8] An ordinary check drawn on a customer's account is direction from a customer to the bank for payment, but it does not impose absolute primary liability on the bank at the time the check is written.

Banks assume more responsibility for some types of checks than for the ordinary customer's check. **For Example,** a bank **money order** payable to John Jones is a check and has the bank as both the drawer and the drawee.[9] UCC § 3-104(g) defines a cashier's check as "a draft with respect to which the drawer and drawee are the same bank or branches of the same bank."[10] In other words, a **cashier's check** is a check or draft drawn by a bank again on itself. If a cashier's check is drawn on another bank in which the drawer bank has an account, it is a **teller's check.** Although the drawer and drawee may be the same on a money order or a cashier's check, the instrument does not lose its three-party character or its status as a check.

Under new federal laws that Revised Article 4 recognizes, there is the new term **substitute check,** which is an electronic image or paper printout of an electronic image of a check. A substitute check has the same legal effect as a paper check. The bank that converts the paper check into electronic form, called the *reconverting bank*, has certain duties imposed by federal regulations to be certain that the electronic version or substitute check has all of the necessary legal information such as visible indorsements, magnetic bank code strip, payee, and signature of drawer.

2. Certified Checks

The drawee bank may *certify* or accept a check drawn on it. Under UCC § 3-409(d), a certified check is "a check accepted by the bank on which it is drawn."[11] While a bank is under no obligation to certify a check, if it does so, the certification has the effect of the bank accepting primary liability on the instrument. Check certification requires that the actual certification be written on the check and authenticated by the signature of an authorized representative of the bank.[12] Upon certification, the bank must set aside, in a special account maintained by the bank, the amount of the certified check taken from the drawer's account. The certification is a promise by the bank that when the check is presented for payment, the bank will make payment according to the terms of the check. Payment is made regardless of the status of the drawer's account at that time.

[8] *Roy Supply, Inc. v Wells Fargo Bank*, 46 Cal Rptr 2d 309 (1995); distinguished in an unpublished opinion, *Citibank v Shen*, 2003 WL 253962 (Cal App 2003).

[9] Revised UCC § 3-104(f) (2002).

[10] Revised UCC § 3-104(g).

[11] Revised UCC § 3-409(d).

[12] Many courts treat cashier's checks and certified checks as the same because of their uniform commercial acceptability. See *Weldon v Trust Co. Bank of Columbus*, 499 SE2d 393 (Ga App 1998) (found later in the chapter). However, the rights of the parties are different because certification discharges all other parties to the instrument. A cashier's check does not result in the discharge of other parties on the instrument.

THINKING THINGS THROUGH

WRITING CERTIFIED CHECKS FOR PSYCHICS MEANS TROUBLE IN THE FUTURE

Benito Dalessio was dating Jennifer Lopez. Ms. Lopez (no relation to Ben Affleck or Marc Anthony) introduced Dalessio to Linda Kressler, psychic. Kressler told Dalessio that Lopez would marry him if—and the future was contingent here—Dalessio gave Kressler money to pay her debts. Sadly, Dalessio believed Kressler and issued a check to her in the amount of $107,000, which Republic National Bank of New York certified at his request.

When Dalessio appeared at the bank the next day with another odd request, that of receiving $15,000 in cash, the teller asked the branch manager to step in. Dalessio then explained that Kressler and Lopez, unsatisfied, had been to his house and demanded the cash.

The branch manager then called Dalessio's sister, a co-signer on the bank account that had become the source of largesse for the psychic and her friend. The manager suggested legal help. The sister's lawyer went to court claiming fraud and naming the bank as a defendant in relation to the certified check. The judge entered a temporary restraining order (TRO) stopping payment on the check. The TRO was served on the bank's assistant treasurer the next day. The same day, the bank paid the check, but no one was sure whether the bank paid the check before or after it received service of the TRO. There was also some confusion at the lower court on whether Kressler, as a psychic, could be a holder in due course.

The bank argued that it was powerless to stop payment on a certified check. Kressler argued that there was only fraud in the inducement and that she was still entitled to payment. UCC § 4-303 provides that knowledge, notice or stop orders, legal process served, or setoff exercised after certification of a check are too late to stop payment—but can a court injunction stop the payment of a certified check? What would happen if the payment of the check were permitted to stand as valid? What would happen if the payment on the certified check was set aside and the bank was held liable to Dalessio for its failure to honor the court order? [Dalessio v Kressler, 773 NYS2D 434 (NY App Div 2004)]

A holder or drawer may request that a check be certified by a bank. When certification is at the request of the holder, all prior indorsers and the drawer are released from liability. When certification is at the request of the drawer, the indorsers and drawer, as secondary parties, are not released. Unless otherwise agreed, the delivery of a certified check, a cashier's check, or a teller's check discharges the debt for which the check is given, up to the amount of that check.[13]

CPA 3. Presentment for Obtaining Payment on a Check

A holder of a check must take required steps to obtain payment. As discussed in Chapter 30, there are primary and secondary parties for every negotiable instrument. Primary parties are makers and drawees. Under Revised Article 3, secondary parties are referred to as *secondary obligors* and are defined to include "an indorser, a drawer, an accommodation party, or any other party to the instrument that has a right of recourse against another party to the instrument."[14]

The process for a holder to be paid on an instrument involves mandatory steps with time limitations. The holder must first seek payment from the drawee through **presentment.** No secondary obligor is liable on an instrument until presentment has been made. Presentment is required for checks, and presentment is made first to the drawee bank.[15]

[13] Revised UCC § 3-104(h) defines a traveler's check as "a draft drawn by a bank (i) on another bank, or (ii) payable at or through a bank."

[14] Revised UCC § 3-104(12).

[15] It is important to note that the bank is unique as a drawee because its contract as a primary party is limited by its right to dishonor a check and its right to give only provisional credit.

(a) Presentment Requirements

Presentment occurs when the holder of a check or other consumer transaction authorization demands payment.[16] Under Revised Article 3, the party presents either the check or a record for payment. If the presentment is done in person, the party to whom presentment is made can require that the presenter exhibit identification. The holder who is presenting the instrument must present the check or record for payment in a commercially reasonable manner; banks can treat the transaction as having occurred the following day when presentment is made after *the close of the business day.*[17] In the case of electronic banking, banks are permitted to impose times after which posting will occur the next day. If a check is presented to the drawee bank for payment and paid, the drawer has no liability because payment has been made. (For more details on presentment, generally, of instruments, see Chapter 30.)

CPA (b) Time for Presentment of a Check for Payment[18]

Under the UCC, presentment must be made within a reasonable time after the drawers and indorsers have signed the check. What constitutes a reasonable time is determined by the nature of the instrument, by commercial usage, and by the facts of the particular case.

Failure to make timely presentment discharges all secondary obligors (prior indorsers) of the instrument. It also discharges the drawer to the extent that the drawer has lost, through the bank's failure, money that was on deposit at the bank to make the payment due under the check.[19]

The UCC establishes two presumptions as to what is a reasonable time for presentment of checks. If the check is not certified and is both drawn and payable within the United States, it is presumed that 90 days after the date of the check or the date of its issuance, whichever is later, is the reasonable period in which to make presentment for payment in order to attach secondary liability to the drawer.[20] With respect to attachment of the liability of an indorser, 30 days after indorsement is presumed to be a reasonable time.[21]

If a check is dated with the date of issue, it may be presented immediately for payment. If it is postdated, ordinarily it may not be presented until that date arrives. However, as noted earlier, the bank need not honor the date on the postdated instrument. If the holder delays in making presentment, the delay discharges the drawer if the bank itself fails during such delay.[22] If the holder of the check does not present it for payment or collection within 90 days after an indorsement was made, the secondary obligors (indorsers) are discharged from liability to the extent that the drawer has lost, through the bank's failure, money that was on deposit at the bank to meet the payment under the check.

Under Revised Articles 3 and 4, agreeing to honor an instrument beyond this time limit changes the obligation of the primary obligor and, as a result, changes the obligation of the secondary obligors. Such changes in the terms and conditions of payment serve to discharge the secondary obligors, a change that brings UCC Articles 3 and 4 in line with the principles of surety law (see Chapter 33).

A bank may continue to honor checks presented for payment after the 90-day period, but it does so with understanding of the discharge of liability for the primary and secondary obligors. A bank honoring a check that is overdue subjects the bank to questions about whether it exercised good faith and reasonable care in honoring it.[23]

4. Dishonor of a Check

If the bank refuses to make payment, the drawer is then subject to the same secondary liability as the

[16] In addition to the UCC restrictions on times for presentment, banks must comply with federally imposed time constraints. Under the Expedited Funds Availability Act, USC § 401 *et seq.*, banks are required to lift provisional credits on customer accounts.

[17] Revised UCC § 4-107(1).

[18] Revised UCC § 3-501.

[19] Revised UCC § 3-605.

[20] Under the previous versions of Articles 3 and 4, the time was six months.

[21] Revised UCC § 3-304.

[22] Revised UCC § 4-208(c).

[23] Revised Article 3 changed the "negligence" of the bank to the "failure to exercise ordinary care" in § 3-406. A bank need not pay a check that is presented to it after six months from the date of issue (except for certified checks), but it can honor such a check and charge the customer's account if it does so in good faith.

drawer of an ordinary draft.[24] To be able to attach that secondary liability, the holder of the instrument must notify the drawer of the dishonor by the drawee. The notice of dishonor may be oral, written, or electronic.

CPA (a) Time for Notice of Dishonor

Banks in the chain of collection for a check must give notice of dishonor by midnight of the next banking day. Others, including the payee or holder of the check, must give notice of dishonor within 30 days after learning that the instrument has been dishonored.[25] If proper notice of dishonor is not given to the drawer of the check, the drawer will be discharged from liability to the same extent as the drawer of an ordinary draft.[26]

CPA (b) Overdraft

If the bank pays the check but the funds in the account are not sufficient to cover the amount, the excess of the payment over the amount on deposit is an **overdraft.** This overdraft is treated as a loan from the bank to the customer, and the customer must repay that amount to the bank.

If the bank account from which the check is drawn is one held by two or more persons, the joint account holder who does not sign the check that creates an overdraft is not liable for the amount of the overdraft if she received no benefit from the proceeds of that check.[27] Additional issues on overdrafts and dishonor of checks are covered in Section 5.

5. The Customer-Bank Relationship

The relationship between banks and customers is governed by Articles 3 and 4 of the UCC as well as by several federal statutes. These laws impose duties and liabilities on both banks and customers.

(a) Privacy

The bank owes its customer the duty of maintaining the privacy of the information that the bank acquires in connection with its relationship with the customer. Law enforcement officers and administrative agencies cannot require the disclosure of information relating to a customer's account without first obtaining the customer's consent or a search warrant or without following the statutory procedures designed to protect customers from unreasonable invasions of privacy.[28] The **USA Patriot Act** does impose certain reporting requirements on banks, financial institutions, and businesses with regard to deposits of cash and large cash payments. These reporting requirements were imposed to be able to track money laundering efforts as well as possible funding of terrorist activities.[29] For example, checks that involve amounts of more than $10,000 generally trigger the bank reporting systems under the USA Patriot Act.

With the advent of the Internet and other electronic exchanges of information, it has become much easier for businesses, including banks, to exchange information about customers. All businesses are subject to federal constraints on the use of customer information. (See Chapter 33 for more information.)

(b) Payment

A bank is under a general contractual duty to its customers to pay on demand all checks to the extent of the funds in a depositor's account.

CPA ***(1) Stale Checks.*** A bank acting in good faith may pay a check presented more than six months after its date (commonly known as a **stale check**), but unless the check is certified, the bank is not required to do so.[30] The fact that a bank may refuse to pay a check that is more than six months old does not mean that it must pay a check that is less than six months old or that it is not required to exercise reasonable care in making payment on any check.

(2) Payment after Depositor's Death. From the time of death, the bank can continue paying items

24 Revised UCC § 3-414.

25 The former time frame for nonbanks was midnight of the third business day.

26 Revised UCC § 4-213. Under Federal Reserve regulations, notice of dishonor may be given by telephone. *Security Bank and Trust Co. v Federal Nat'l Bank*, 554 P2d 119 (Okla Ct App 1976). But see *General Motors Acceptance Corp. v Bank of Richmondville*, 611 NYS2d 338 (App Div 1994) and *City Check Cashing, Inc. v Manufacturers Hanover Trust Co.*, 764 A2d 411, 43 UCC Rep Serv2d 768 (NJ 2001).

27 Revised UCC §§ 4-214 and 4-401(b).

28 Right to Financial Privacy Act of 1978, 12 USC § 3401 *et seq.*

29 USC §§ 5311 *et seq.* 2001.

30 Revised UCC §§ 3-304 and 4-404; *Leibling, P.C. v Mellon, PSFS (NJ) N.A.*, 710 A2d 1067, 35 UCC2d 590 (NJ 1998).

until it actually knows of the customer's death.[31] The bank has the right to continue to pay items for 10 days unless, for example, an heir or a government tax agency steps in to stop the payments.[32]

CPA 6. Stopping Payment of a Check

A drawer may stop payment of a check by notifying the drawee bank in the required manner.[33] **Stop payment orders** are often used when a check is lost or mislaid. The drawer can always write a duplicate check but wants assurance that the original lost or misplaced check will not then also be presented for payment. The drawer can stop payment on the first check to prevent double-dipping. A drawer can also use a stop payment order on a check if the payee has not kept his end of the contract or has failed to provide assurances (see Chapter 26). However, the drawer must keep in mind that if a holder in due course has the check, the holder in due course can demand payment because she would not be subject to the personal defenses of breach of contract or nonperformance of contract. (See Chapter 30 and the rights of holders in due course.)

Stop payment orders are invalid for some forms of checks even when properly executed. Neither the drawer nor a bank customer can stop payment of a **certified check.** A bank customer cannot stop payment of a cashier's check.

CPA (a) Form of Stop Payment Order

The stop payment order may be either oral or by record (written or evidence of electronic order). If oral, however, the order is binding on the bank for only 14 calendar days unless confirmed in writing within that time. A record of the stop payment order or confirmation is effective for six months. A stop payment order can be renewed for an additional six months if the customer provides the bank a written extension.

(b) Liability to Holder for Stopping Payment

The act of stopping payment may in some cases make the drawer liable to the holder of the check. If the drawer has no proper ground for stopping payment, the drawer is liable to the holder of the check. In any case, the drawer is liable for stopping payment with respect to any holder in due course or any other party having the rights of a holder in due course unless payment was stopped for a reason that may be asserted as a defense against a holder in due course (see Chapter 30). The fact that payment of a check has been stopped does not affect its negotiable character.[34]

7. Wrongful Dishonor of a Check

A check is **wrongfully dishonored** by the drawee bank if the bank refuses to pay the amount of the check although (1) it is properly payable and (2) the account on which it is drawn is sufficient to pay the item.

Dishonor for lack of funds can be a breach of contract if the customer has an agreement with the bank that it will pay overdraft items.

CPA (a) Bank's Liability to Drawer of Check

The contract between the customer (drawer) and the bank (drawee) obligates the drawee bank to pay in accordance with the orders of its customer as long as sufficient money is on deposit to make such payment. If the bank improperly refuses to make payment, it is liable to the drawer for damages sustained by the drawer as a consequence of such dishonor.

(b) Bank's Liability to Holder

If a check has not been certified, the holder has no claim against the bank for the dishonor of the check regardless of the fact that the bank acted in breach of its contract with its customer. The bank that certifies a check is liable to the holder when it dishonors the check. The certification imposes primary liability on the bank and requires it to pay the face amount of the check.

(c) Holder's Notice of Dishonor of Check

When a check is dishonored by nonpayment, the holder must follow the procedure for notice to the secondary parties discussed earlier. Notice of dishonor need not be given to the drawer who has stopped payment on a check or to drawers and indorsers who are aware that there are insufficient funds on deposit to cover the check. In those circumstances, no party

[31] Revised UCC § 4-405(2).

[32] Revised UCC § 4-405(b); *Hieber v Uptown Nat'l Bank of Chicago*, 557 NE2d 408 (Ill App 1990).

[33] Revised UCC § 4-403.

[34] *Perini Corp. v First Nat'l Bank*, 553 F2d 398 (5th Cir 1977).

has reason to expect that the check will be paid by the bank.

8. Agency Status of Collecting Bank

When a customer deposits negotiable instruments in a bank, the bank is regarded as being merely an **agent,** even though the customer may be given the right to make immediate withdrawals against the deposited item. Because of the bank's **agency** status, the customer remains the owner of the item and is subject to the risks of ownership involved in its collection.

When a bank cashes a check deposited by its customer or cashes a check drawn by its customer based on an amount from a deposited check, it is a holder of the check deposited by its customer. The bank may still collect from the parties on the check even though the bank is an agent for collection and has the right to charge back the amount of the deposited check if it cannot be collected.

9. Bank's Duty of Care

A bank is required to exercise ordinary care in the handling of items. The liability of a bank is determined by the law of the state where the bank, branch, or separate office involved is located.

CPA (a) Modification of Bank Duties

The parties in the bank collection process may modify their rights and duties by agreement. However, a bank cannot disclaim liability for lack of good faith or failure to exercise ordinary care, nor can it limit the measure of damages for such lack of care.

When a bank handles checks by automated processes, the standard of ordinary care does not require the bank to make a physical examination of each item unless the bank's own procedures require such examination or general banking usage regards the absence of physical examination of the items as a lack of ordinary care.

(b) Encoding Warranty and Electronic Presentment

In addition to transfer and presentment warranties, an **encoding warranty** is also given by those who transfer instruments. Under this warranty, anyone placing information on an item or transmitting the information electronically warrants that the information is correct. When there is an agreement for electronic presentment, the presenter warrants that the transfer is made in accordance with the terms of the agreement for such transmissions.[35]

B. Liability of a Bank

Banks can make mistakes in the payment and collection of items presented to them by their customers. **For Example,** a check may slip through and be cashed over a customer's properly executed stop payment order. The bank would be liable for this improper payment and may also be liable for improperly collecting, paying, or refusing to pay a check.

10. Premature Payment of a Postdated Check

A check may be postdated, but the bank is not liable for making payments on the check before the date stated unless the drawer has given the bank prior notice. Such a notice is similar to a stop payment order; it must provide sufficient information so that the bank is moved to action by the trigger of the order the check as it flows through its electronic processing system.[36]

11. Payment over a Stop Payment Order

A bank must be given a reasonable time in which to put a stop payment order into effect. However, if the bank makes payment of a check after it has been properly notified to stop payment, and there has been sufficient time for the order to be put into the system, the bank is liable to the drawer (customer) for the loss the drawer sustains in the absence of a valid limitation of the bank's liability.[37] The burden of establishing losses that result from the bank's failure to stop payment rests with the customer. The bank must have complete information on a stop payment order, such as the payee, check number, and amount, to be held responsible for the failure to stop payment.

[35] Revised UCC §§ 4-207 to 4-209.

[36] Note that a "postdated check" is not a check but a time draft. UCC §§ 4-401 to 4-402.

[37] Revised UCC § 4-403(c); *Gornicki v M & T Bank*, 617 NYS2d 448 (1994).

ROVELL V AMERICAN NATIONAL BANK, 194 F3D 867 (7TH CIR 1999)

THE DOUBLE-DIPPING DETECTIVE AGENCY: NO STOPPING PAYMENT WITHOUT DETAILS

Michael Rovell, a lawyer (Rovell or Debtor), practiced law in his own firm in Chicago, but his work took him on occasion to Arizona and California, where he engaged the services of an Arizona private investigator, Patricia O'Connor, and her firm, Pretty Eyes Detective Agency. On August 30, 1994, pursuant to a fee agreement between Rovell and O'Connor, Rovell's firm wrote a check to O'Connor for her services. The check in the amount of $38,250 was not immediately cashed. About three weeks later on September 19, Rovell discovered that the firm had overpaid O'Connor by more than $10,000. Wishing to correct the mistake, Rovell directed his associate, attorney Lisa I. Fair, to contact their banker, ANB in Chicago, and inquire whether the check had been cashed. Fair called the firm's account representative at ANB, Linda Williams, to request a stop-payment order.

Fair asserted that she called Williams and asked if the check had been cashed. Because she did not know the check number, she could only supply the account number, check amount, and payee. Fair added that it might be in the range of six checks beginning with number 1084, but that she could not be sure because no record had been kept of the check number. Fair said that Williams put her on hold and then returned to report that the check had not cleared. Fair testified that she then asked for a stop-payment order to be issued and contended that Williams never told her that the bank could not stop payment without a check number. Fair also denied that Williams advised her to wait before writing a replacement check. The correct number for the first check written to Pretty Eyes turned out to be 1105.

Williams recalled the conversation differently. She remembered Fair calling and not knowing the check number, but requesting a stop payment on checks numbered 1084 and 1086, neither of which had cleared the bank yet. Williams processed the stop-payment order on those two checks and said she cautioned Fair to wait a few days before writing the replacement. Williams, who had 26 years of banking experience, said she routinely cautioned customers not to write checks immediately after a stop-payment order had been issued but did not recall specifically telling Fair that a check number was necessary for a stop-payment order.

Williams processed the stop-payment order that day for checks 1084 and 1086, and the order took effect at the start of business the next day. Between the time Williams ended her conversation with Fair and the close of business that day, the check for $38,250 was presented for payment and cashed. Two days later, without waiting for the stop-payment confirmation order to arrive and without calling back to check on the status of the account, Fair wrote a replacement check for $27,284.50 and mailed it by overnight express mail to Arizona. That check also was cashed, causing Rovell to overdraw his account the following December. Despite the uncertainty surrounding the stop-payment order, Rovell never read or responded to the stop-payment confirmation orders and failed to open his monthly account statements for many weeks. Only when he realized that he had overdrawn his account and incurred penalties did Rovell become a dutiful and prolific correspondent with the bank.

In October 1995, Rovell initiated a voluntary bankruptcy under Chapter 11 of the Bankruptcy Code. ANB presented a claim on a secured line of credit for $50,081.25, the validity of which is undisputed.

Rovell, however, filed an objection seeking to reduce the claim by the amount he lost due to the overpayment to Pretty Eyes. He asserted claims under Illinois law for breach of contract on the ground that ANB had promised to stop payment on the first check and negligent misrepresentation based on the bank's alleged "assurance that the check had not cleared and could be stopped."

The bankruptcy court denied both claims. The district court, based on the bankruptcy court's findings of fact, agreed that Rovell's reliance on the alleged misrepresentation was unreasonable and therefore not compensable. Rovell appealed.

Judicial Opinion

KANNE, Circuit Judge.... When a law firm plagued by sloppy bookkeeping mistakenly writes a check that results in an overpayment to a private investigator who then decides to pocket the money, should the law firm's bank ultimately bear the loss?

We cannot say that the bankruptcy court's determination that Rovell could not reasonably rely on Williams' advice that a check could be stopped immediately, even without a check number, constituted clear error. Accepting, as we must, the bankruptcy judge's finding that both Fair and Williams presented credible testimony, we are faced with a probability that the conversation between Fair and Williams occurred as Fair recalled it equal to the probability that it occurred as Williams recalled it.

According to Fair's recollection, Fair gave Williams the amount of the check, Rovell's account number and the name of the payee. She could not tell her the check number, but instead provided her with a general range of possible check numbers, which it turned out, was far from the actual check number. Fair then testified that based on this sketchy information, Williams definitively told her the check had not been presented for payment but failed to warn her that she should wait until the stop-payment order could be processed before writing a replacement check.

Williams then remembered Fair saying she wanted to send a replacement check to Pretty Eyes, to which she responded, "Well, Lisa, you should wait a few days." When Fair said she would send a letter explaining that the first check was for the wrong amount, Williams questioned whether the payee could be trusted not to cash both checks.

Taking both memories of the conversation as credible, it appears therefore that this is a case of two honestly held, but differing, memories of a conversation. The question, however, is whether a reasonable person would rely on either version of this exchange, and it seemed clear to both the bankruptcy judge and district judge that they would not.

A reasonable person certainly would not immediately send a replacement check based on the conversation remembered by Williams with an explicit warning to wait a few days. Furthermore, the fact that Williams remembered expressing concerns to Fair about whether the payee was "reputable," would have put a reasonable person on notice that the situation presented a potential for danger.

Even accepting Fair's recollection of the conversation, it seems unreasonable to issue a replacement check before receiving any written confirmation that the check had been effectively stopped. Fair knew that the information she provided Williams for the stop-payment order was incomplete at best, lacking a vital piece of identifying information—the exact check number. One does not need to be a banker or versed in banking law to know that this is a vital piece of information for locating or stopping a check. It is, as the courts below noted, a matter of common sense.

Had Rovell waited until he received the confirmation orders, he would have seen that the stop-payment order covered specific check numbers, alerting him to the strong possibility that the order would not be effective for other check numbers. In fact, Rovell, who often failed to review his monthly bank statements, cannot recall receiving the confirmation orders and apparently did not know they were in his own files until ANB asked for them during discovery. This hardly suggests reasonableness. Finally, we cannot say why Rovell was so anxious to resend a check to a payee who apparently had not been anxious to cash the much larger check sent three weeks earlier, but there certainly seems to be no evidence of a need so pressing that would make Rovell's unexplained haste more reasonable under the circumstances.

Because the record supports the finding of no reasonable reliance, we cannot find that the bankruptcy court committed clear error in denying Rovell's negligent misrepresentation claim. The decision of the district court is

[Affirmed]

Questions

1. Make a list of the things Mr. Rovell did that the court labels unreasonable.
2. What does a bank need for a valid stop payment order?
3. What does the court say about the differing recollections of the conversation about the stop order?

CPA 12. Payment on a Forged Signature of Drawer

A forgery of the signature of the drawer occurs when the name of the drawer has been signed by another person without authority to do so with the intent to defraud by making it appear that the drawer signed the check. The bank is liable to the drawer if it pays a check on which the drawer's signature has been forged because a forgery ordinarily has no effect as a signature. The risk of loss caused by the forged signature of the drawer is placed on the bank without regard to whether the bank could have detected the forgery.[38] The reasoning behind the bank's liability for a forged drawer's signature is that the bank is presumed to know its own customers' signatures even if it does not regularly review checks for authenticity of the signature.

A bank's customer whose signature has been forged may be barred from holding the bank liable if the customer's negligence substantially contributed to the making of the forgery. This preclusion rule prevents or precludes the customer from making a forgery claim against the bank. However, to enjoy the protection of the preclusion rule, the bank, if negligent in its failure to detect the forgery or alteration, must have cashed the check in good faith or have taken it for value or collection.[39]

Article 4 of the UCC extends forgery protections and rights to alterations and unauthorized signings (those made with no fraudulent intent). When an officer with authority limited to signing $5,000 checks signs a check for $7,500, the signature is unauthorized. If the principal for the drawer account is an organization and has a requirement that two or more designated persons sign negotiable instruments on its behalf, signatures by fewer than the specified number are also classified as unauthorized signatures.

CPA 13. Payment on a Forged or Missing Indorsement

A drawee bank that honors a customer's check bearing a forged indorsement must recredit the customer's account upon the drawer's discovery of the forgery and notification to the bank. A drawee bank is liable for the loss when it pays a check that lacks an essential indorsement.[40] In such a case, the instrument is not properly payable. Without proper indorsements for an order instrument and special indorsements, the person presenting the check for payment is not the holder of the instrument and is not entitled to demand or receive payment. However, the bank can then turn to the indorsers and transferors of the instrument for breach of warranty liability in that all signatures were not genuine or authorized and they did not have title. All transferors can turn to their previous transferor until liability ultimately rests with the party who first accepted the forged indorsement. This party had face-to-face contact and could have verified signatures.

When a customer deposits a check but does not indorse it, the customer's bank may make an indorsement on behalf of the depositor unless the check expressly requires the customer's indorsement. A bank cannot add the missing indorsement of a person who is not its customer when an item payable is deposited in a customer's bank account.[41]

14. Alteration of a Check

If the face of a check has been altered so that the amount to be paid has been increased, the bank is liable to the drawer for the amount of the increase when it makes payment of the greater amount.

The drawer may be barred from claiming that there was an alteration if there was negligence in writing the check or reporting its alteration. A drawer is barred from claiming alteration if the check was written negligently, the negligence substantially contributed to the making of the material alteration, and the bank honored the check in good faith and observed reasonable commercial standards in doing so. **For Example,** the drawer is barred from claiming alteration when the check was written with blank spaces that readily permitted a change of "four" to "four hundred" and the drawee bank paid out the latter sum because the alteration was not obvious. A careful drawer will write figures and words close together and run a line through or cross out any blank spaces.

[38] *Sun Bank v Merrill Lynch, Pierce, Fenner & Smith, Inc.*, 637 So 2d 279 (Fla App 1994).

[39] Revised UCC § 4-406(e); *Knight Pub. Co., Inc. v Chase Manhattan Bank, N.A.*, 479 SE2d 478 (NC App 1997), but see *American Airlines Employees Federal Credit Union v Martin*, 29 SW3d 86, 42 UCC Rep Serv 2d 359 (Tex 2000). For review (May 11, 1999).

[40] *First Guaranty Bank v Northwest Georgia Bank*, 417 SE2d 348 (Ga App 1992).

[41] *Bursey v CFX Bank*, 756 A2d 1001, (NH 2000).

15. Unauthorized Collection of a Check

Although a bank acts as agent for its customer in obtaining payment of a check deposited with it by its customer, the bank may be liable to a third person when its customer's action toward that third person is unauthorized or unlawful. If a customer has no authority to deposit the check, some banks, in obtaining payment from the drawee of the check and later depositing the proceeds of the check in its customer's account, may be liable for conversion of the check to the person lawfully entitled to the check and its proceeds.

A collecting bank, or a bank simply collecting an item for a customer, is protected from liability when it follows its customer's instructions. It is not required to inquire or verify that the customer had the authority to give such instructions. In contrast, instructions do not protect a payor bank. It has an absolute duty to make proper payment. If it does not do so, it is liable unless it is protected by estoppel or by the preclusion rule. The person giving wrongful instructions is liable for the loss caused by those instructions.

16. Time Limitations

The liability of the bank to its depositor is subject to certain time limitations.

CPA (a) Forgery and Alteration Reporting Time

A customer must examine with reasonable care and promptness a bank statement and relevant checks that are paid in good faith and sent to the customer by the bank and must try to discover any unauthorized signature or alteration on the checks. The customer must notify the bank promptly after discovering either a forgery or an alteration. If the bank exercises ordinary care in paying a forged or an altered check and suffers a loss because the customer fails to discover and notify the bank of the forgery or alteration, the customer cannot assert the unauthorized signature or alteration against the bank.[42]

Under the Check Truncation Act (which is part of the Check 21 statute covered in Chapter 28), banks now have the right to substitute electronic images of checks for customer billing statements. The Check Truncation Act (CTA) became effective October 8, 2004. The CTA is largely implemented through Federal Reserve Board regulations found at 12 CFR § 229.2. Banks do not need to provide the original check to their customers and can simply send copies of electronic images so long as the image provides enough clarity for the customer to see payee, encoding, indorsements, and so on.

With the use of substituted checks and online banking, consumers now have additional rights and time limits with substituted checks. Under the Check 21 statute, consumers have a new right to an expedited recredit to their account if a substitute check was charged improperly to their account. They have the right to see the original check if they can explain why it is necessary and that they are suffering a loss as a result of the improper charge of a substitute check to their account. Consumers have 40 calendar days from whichever of the following is later: (1) the delivery of their monthly bank statements or (2) that date on which the substitute check was made available to them for examination and/or review. If a consumer has been traveling or been ill, the rules permit the extension of the deadline for purposes of challenging a substitute check. Consumers can even call their bank and challenge a payment, but they will not then get the benefit of all the rights and protections under Check 21 and its regulations if they choose to proceed without a written demand on a substitute check.[43] Once the demand is made, the bank must either recredit the consumer's account within one business day or explain why it believes the substitute check was charged properly to the consumer's account. The oral demand does not start this clock running for the consumer's protection. There are also fines and overdraft protections provided while the substitute check issue is in the dispute/investigation stage.

Some cases of forgery are the result of a customer's lack of care, such as when an employee is given too much authority and internal controls are lacking with the result that the employee is able to forge checks on a regular basis not easily detected by the bank. Referred to as the *fictitious payee and impostor exceptions*, this issue was covered in Chapter 29.

Customers are precluded from asserting unauthorized signatures or alterations if they do not report them within one year from the time the bank statement is received.[44] A forged indorsement must be reported within three years.

42 *Quilling v National City Bank of Michigan/Illinois*. Not Reported in F Supp 2d, 2001 WL 1516732 (ND Ill), 46 UCC Rep Serv 2d 207 (ND Ill 2001).

43 12 CFR § 229.54(b)(1)(iii).

44 Revised UCC § 4-406.

(b) Unauthorized Signature or Alteration by Same Wrongdoer

If there is a series of improperly paid items and the same wrongdoer is involved, the customer is protected only as to those items that were paid by the bank before it received notification from the customer and during that reasonable amount of time that the customer has to examine items or statements and to notify the bank. The time limit on the customer's duty to examine the bank statement and report forgeries is 30 days. If the customer failed to exercise reasonable promptness and failed to notify the bank but the customer can show that the bank failed to exercise ordinary care in paying the items, the loss will be allocated between the customer and the bank.[45]

(c) Statute of Limitations

An action to enforce a liability imposed by Article 4 must be commenced within three years after the cause of action accrued.

MERCANTILE BANK OF ARKANSAS V VOWELL, 117 S.W.3D 603 (CT. APP. ARK. 2003)

STEALING EVERYTHING FROM MOM, INCLUDING WHAT'S BENEATH THE KITCKEN SINK

John G. Vowell (appellee) and his wife, now deceased, had a checking account and a savings/money-market account with Mercantile Bank of Arkansas. They signed account agreements with a requirement that they examine them within 60 days.

In June 1997, Dr. Vowell and his wife allowed their daughter, Suzan Vowell, now also deceased, and her boyfriend to move in with them at their home. At that time, they knew that Suzan and her boyfriend had been involved with drugs, alcohol, writing bad checks, and stealing. They also knew that Suzan had stolen checks from them in the past and forged either Dr. Vowell's or his wife's signatures. They took precautions against future theft and forgeries by Suzan by hiding Mrs. Vowell's purse, which contained their checkbook, under the kitchen sink. Mrs. Vowell suffered from diabetes mellitus and alcoholism, conditions that forced her to stay in bed either all or most of the time. It was Mrs. Vowell's assignment to review the bank statements and to balance the checkbooks.

Beginning in June 1997 and continuing into September 1997, Suzan forged Mrs. Vowell's signature on 42 checks, drawn on both accounts, and committed nine unauthorized ATM withdrawals in the aggregate amount of $12,028.75. Suzan found her mother's purse hidden under the kitchen sink and stole the checkbooks and ATM card from the purse. She apparently had access to, or figured out, the personal identification number (PIN) for the accounts because the number was identical to the home security system code.

The Vowells received the following statements from the bank for the checking and savings accounts.

Statement Sent	*Amount of Forgery or ATM Withdrawal*	*Dates of Transactions*
July 9, 1997	$230.00	June 6–July 7, 1997
August 8, 1997	$1,235.25	July 8–August 6, 1997
August 23, 1997	$5,140.00	July 23–Aug 21, 1997
September 9, 1997	$1,423.50	Aug 7–Sept 7, 1997
September 26, 1997	$4,000.00	Aug 22–Sept 22, 1997

[45] Revised UCC § 4-406 (1990); but see *Tumlinson v First Victoria Nat'l Bank*, 865 SW2d 176 (Tex App 1993) and *Community Bank & Trust, S.S.B. v Fleck*, 21 SW3d 923 (Tex App 2000).

On September 15, 1997, Dr. Vowell discovered a receipt for an unauthorized credit-card transaction and notified Mercantile Bank about his discovery. Mercantile froze their accounts, alerted its tellers and computer system, and began investigating the alleged forgeries and other unauthorized transactions pursuant to its policy.

As a result of the alert on the account, Suzan was arrested on September 16, 1997, after she attempted to obtain an unauthorized cash advance at another branch. No more unauthorized transactions occurred after the alert was issued. There were 42 forged checks and nine unauthorized ATM withdrawals.

The bank refused to credit the Vowells' account because it maintained that their negligence in handling their daughter caused the losses. The trial court found that the Vowells were not negligent, but they had failed to exercise reasonable promptness in the examination and reporting of the forged checks on the June checking account statement and the July checking account statement. Therefore, the court found that the bank was liable for only $6,014.38, one-half of the entire sum of Suzan Vowell's unauthorized bank transactions and forgeries.

The bank appealed.

Judicial Opinion

STROUD, Chief Judge.... Our state uses a version of the applicable Uniform Commercial Code section 3-406, as provided in Arkansas Code Annotated section 4-3-406 (Repl.2001).

Here, the trial court concluded that appellee attempted to take proper precautions to safeguard the checkbooks, ATM cards, and PIN from their daughter, Suzan Vowell. We find no clear error in that factual determination. Consequently, we also find that the trial court did not err in concluding that appellee was not precluded from asserting the forgeries and unauthorized transactions against appellant pursuant to section 4-3-406 because the preclusion would only apply if appellee failed to exercise ordinary care that substantially contributed to the loss. Moreover, there could be no allocation of loss in this case under section 4-3-406 because it requires a lack of ordinary care by the customer and the bank, neither of which occurred here.

Appellee is precluded from recovering on any of the items contained in the June and July checking account statements because of the thirty-day time limit contained in the customer-account agreement, which was quoted previously. According to the agreement, if the customer fails to examine his or her statement and notify the bank of any unauthorized transactions within thirty days of the date that the statement is deemed to be received, and the bank is not at fault, then the customer is precluded from recovery.

The terms of the customer-account agreement do not preclude appellee from recovering on the items contained in the three bank statements, i.e., the July savings, the August checking, and the August savings statements, because the bank was notified before thirty days had elapsed following the deemed-receipt dates of those statements, to wit September 24, October 11, and October 26, 1997.

However, the preclusion provision of Arkansas Code Annotated section 4-4-406(d)(2) does affect the July savings, the August checking, and the August savings statements because "the same wrongdoer," Suzan Vowell, was involved in all of the unauthorized transactions contained in these statements. This section precludes appellee from recovering on any unauthorized transactions that occurred after August 10, 1997, which is thirty days from the deemed receipt-date of the first statement, i.e., the June checking account statement. This totally precludes appellee's recovery under the August checking and the August savings statements. However, the July savings account statement contains seventeen items, some of which are precluded and some of which are not. The last ten items have transaction dates after August 10, 1997, and are therefore precluded.

These seven transactions total $1,725. Allowing recovery for the items that the bank paid before August 10, 1997, but precluding recovery for those items that were paid after August 10 is in keeping with the purpose of section 4-4-406.

Affirmed in part and reversed and remanded in part for entry of a judgment in the amount of $1,725.

ANDREE LAYTON ROAF, Judge, concurring in part and dissenting in part.

I would reverse this case because I do not believe that the appellee, John G. Vowell, is entitled to recover any of his losses from appellant Mercantile Bank of Arkansas with regard to the forged checks, and would I reverse and remand with respect to the unauthorized cash withdrawals.

First, regarding the checks, I agree with the concurring judge that the trial court erred in finding, pursuant to Ark.Code Ann. § 4-3-406(a) (Repl.2001), that the Vowells exercised ordinary care in safeguarding their checks from their daughter and her companion while they resided in their home. It is not necessary to reiterate the sad circumstances this family found itself in during the time that the check forgeries took place, for they are set out in the majority opinion. However, I do not believe that simply placing a purse under a kitchen sink, in light of the daughter's history, Ms. Vowell's incapacities, and Dr. Vowell's inattention to family banking matters, constitutes the exercise of ordinary care.

Accordingly, Vowell should be precluded from asserting his losses regarding any of the forged instruments against Mercantile Bank pursuant to § 4-3-406(a).

It is clear to me that the Vowells' conduct before the forgery played a "substantial part" in making the deception possible. Consequently, Mercantile Bank should be absolved from any liability with regard to the forged checks, and I dissent from the majority's decision to the contrary.

Neither Vowell nor Mercantile Bank raised to the trial court the applicability of the federal statute to the cash withdrawals, and the trial court's judgment treats the forged checks and cash withdrawals alike in its analysis of Vowells's right to recover from the bank pursuant to Ark.Code Ann. §§ 4-3-406 and 4-4-406. Clearly, section 4-3-406 pertains to forged instruments and alteration of instruments only, and has no application to cash withdrawals, and section 4-4-406, contained in Chapter 4, excludes funds transfers from its purview.

The statute generally limits a customer's liability for unauthorized electronic-fund transfers to the lesser of $50 or the amount of money obtained prior to the time the financial institution was notified of such unauthorized transfer. 15 U.S.C. § 1693(g) (2001). Neither Vowell nor the bank raised this law to the trial court, so it was not a "reason" that the trial court was given the opportunity to consider.

Nevertheless, I cannot conclude that the finding with regard to the cash withdrawals from Vowell's account should be affirmed based upon the trial court reaching the right result for the wrong reason. Moreover, bank customers receive notification of ATM withdrawals on their bank statements, and appear to have an obligation pursuant to federal regulation to notify the bank of unauthorized transactions appearing on the statements to avoid further liability. Consequently, I concur in the majority's analysis of Vowell's entitlement to allocation pursuant to Ark.Code Ann. § 4-4-406, only as to the cash withdrawals, and only as to those items paid prior to August 10, 1997, and appearing on the July statements.

Questions

1. Why would lack of ordinary care on either side be important in this case?
2. What does the dissenting judge say about the case that is critical to the differing view?
3. Where did the $1,725 come from as the final amount due according to the court of appeals?

C. Consumer Funds Transfers

Consumers are using electronic methods of payment at an increasing rate. From the swipe of the card at the grocery store checkout to the retrieval of funds from the local automated teller machine, *electronic funds transfers* represent a way of life for many consumers. A federal statute protects consumers making electronic funds transfers.

17. Electronic Funds Transfer Act

Congress passed the **Electronic Funds Transfer Act (EFTA)** to protect consumers making electronic transfers of funds.[46] **Electronic funds transfer (EFT)** means any transfer of funds (other than a transaction originated by check, draft, or similar paper instrument) that is initiated through an electronic terminal, telephone, computer, or magnetic tape that authorizes a financial institution to debit or credit an account. The service available from an automated teller machine is a common form of EFT.

18. Types of Electronic Funds Transfer Systems

Currently, five common types of EFT systems are in use. In some of these systems, the consumer has a card to access a machine. The consumer usually has a private code that prevents others who wrongfully obtain the card from using it.

[46] 15 USC § 1693 *et seq.*

ETHICS & THE LAW

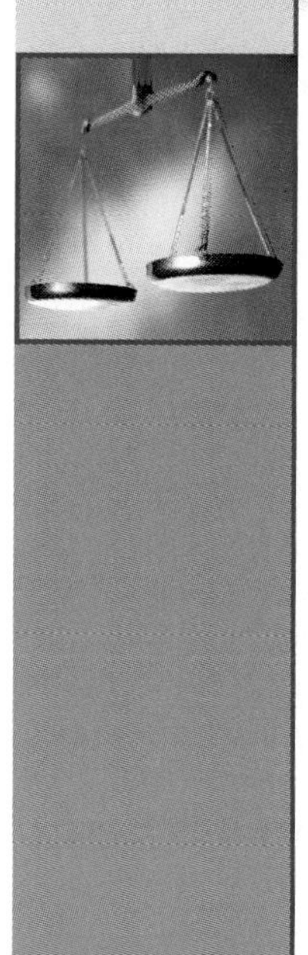

Electronic funds transfer technology has made life very convenient. We can withdraw cash from teller machines at the bank, the university, the airport, or the mall. We can use our debit cards to pay for our groceries just by swiping our card through a machine at the checkout counter. The ease of credit card use finds us using such cards even for our fast-food purchases.

However, these electronic devices keep perfect records. Every cash withdrawal amount and location is recorded. Every grocery purchase can be traced. Your location can be determined by the last business where you used your credit card. The electronic age brings convenience, but it also brings a loss of privacy. With the information gained about you through the use of electronic funds transfers, a firm can put together a profile that estimates your income, outlines your budget and expenditures, specifies your shopping preferences, and provides an itemized list of grocery store purchases.

This extensive information is invaluable for effective marketing. Knowing when, where, and how much households and individual consumers spend can help companies target customers. Metromail is a consumer information firm that sells lists of customers to businesses. The lists are customized and are developed from Metromail's consumer database (which it says covers 90 percent of all U.S. households) following criteria established by the buyer. For example, Metromail sold a *Los Angeles Times* reporter a mailing list for children with 5,000 names. The reporter used the name of Richard Allen Davis, the convicted murderer of 12-year-old Polly Klaas, a young girl snatched from the bedroom of her home during a slumber party with her friends. Should there be restrictions on the use of EFT information? Do you think its use should be regulated? What policies would you implement to prevent misuse of information about customers?

(a) Automated Teller Machine

The *automated teller machine (ATM)* performs many of the tasks once performed exclusively by bank employees. Once a user activates an ATM, he can deposit and withdraw funds from his account, transfer funds between accounts, make payments on loan accounts, and obtain cash advances from bank credit cards.[47]

(b) Pay-by-Phone System

This system facilitates paying telephone, mortgage, utility, and other bills without writing checks. The consumer calls the bank and directs the transfer of funds to a designated third party.

(c) Direct Deposit and Withdrawal

Employees may authorize their employers to deposit wages directly to their accounts. A consumer who has just purchased an automobile on credit may elect to have monthly payments withdrawn from a bank account to be paid directly to the seller.

(d) Point-of-Sale Terminal

The *point-of-sale terminal* allows a business with such a terminal to transfer funds from a consumer's account to the store's account. The consumer must be furnished in advance with the terms and conditions of all EFT services and must be given periodic statements covering account activity. Any automatic EFT from an individual's account must be authorized in writing in advance.

Financial institutions are liable to consumers for all damages proximately caused by the failure to make an EFT in accordance with the terms and conditions of an account. Exceptions exist if the consumer's

[47] *Curde v Tri-City Bank & Trust Co.*, 826 SW2d 911 (Tenn App 1992).

account has insufficient funds, the funds are subject to legal process, the transfer would exceed an established credit limit, or insufficient cash is available in an ATM.

(e) Internet Banking

Internet banking is the customer use of computer access to bank systems to pay bills, balance accounts, transfer funds, and even obtain loans. Increasing in popularity, this form of banking still suffers from concerns about privacy and security. However, the revisions to Articles 3 and 4 recognize electronic records as valid proof of payment.

CPA 19. Consumer Liability

A consumer who notifies the issuer of an EFT card within two days after learning of a loss or theft of the card can be held to a maximum liability of $50 for unauthorized use of the card. Failure to notify within this time will increase the consumer's liability for losses to a maximum of $500.

Consumers have the responsibility to examine periodic statements provided by their financial institution. If a loss would not have occurred but for the failure of a consumer to report within 60 days of the transmittal of the statement any unauthorized transfer, then the loss is borne by the consumer.

CPA D. Funds Transfers

The funds transfers made by businesses are governed by the UCC and Federal Reserve regulations.

20. What Law Governs?

In states that have adopted Article 4A of the Uniform Commercial Code, that article governs funds transfers.[48] In addition, whenever a Federal Reserve Bank is involved, the provisions of Article 4A apply by virtue of Federal Reserve regulations.

21. Characteristics of Funds Transfers

The transfers regulated by Article 4A are characteristically made between highly sophisticated parties dealing with large sums of money. Speed of transfer is often an essential ingredient. An individual transfer may involve many millions of dollars, and the national total of such transfers on a business day can amount to trillions of dollars.

22. Pattern of Funds Transfers

In the simplest form of funds transfer, both the debtor and the creditor have separate accounts in the same bank.[49] In this situation, the debtor can instruct the bank to pay the creditor a specified sum of money by subtracting that amount from the debtor's account and adding it to the creditor's account. As a practical matter, the debtor merely instructs the bank to make the transfer, and the bank, upon making the transfer, debits the debtor's account.

A more complex situation is involved if each party has an account in a different bank. In that case, the funds transfer could involve only these two banks and no clearinghouse. The buyer can instruct the buyer's bank to direct the seller's bank to make payment to the seller. There is direct communication between the two banks. In a more complex situation, the buyer's bank may relay the payment order to another bank, called an **intermediary bank,** and that bank, in turn, transmits the payment order to the seller's bank. Such transactions become even more complex when two or more intermediary banks or a clearinghouse is involved.

23. Scope of UCC Article 4A

Article 4A applies to all funds transfers except as expressly excluded by its own terms, by federal preemption, or by agreement of the parties or clearinghouse rules. Some funds transfers are excluded from Article 4A because of their nature or because of the parties involved.

[48] The following states have adopted the 1990 version of Article 4A: Alabama, Arizona, Arkansas, California, Colorado, Connecticut, Delaware, District of Columbia, Florida, Georgia, Hawaii, Idaho, Illinois, Indiana, Iowa, Kansas, Kentucky, Louisiana, Maine, Maryland, Massachusetts, Michigan, Minnesota, Mississippi, Missouri, Montana, Nebraska, Nevada, New Hampshire, New Jersey, New Mexico, New York, North Carolina, North Dakota, Ohio, Oklahoma, Oregon, Pennsylvania, Rhode Island, South Carolina, South Dakota, Tennessee, Texas, Utah, Vermont, Virginia, Washington, West Virginia, Wisconsin, and Wyoming. Article 4A has also been adopted in Puerto Rico.

[49] The text refers to *debtor* and *creditor* in the interest of simplicity and because that situation is the most common in the business world. However, a gift may be made by a funds transfer. Likewise, a person having separate accounts in two different banks may transfer funds from one bank to another.

(a) EFTA and Consumer Transactions

Article 4A does not apply to consumer transaction payments to which the EFTA applies. If any part of the funds transfer is subject to the EFTA, the entire transfer is expressly excluded from the scope of UCC Article 4A.[50]

(b) Credit and Debit Transfers

When the person making payment, such as the buyer, requests that payment be made to the beneficiary's bank, the transaction is called a **credit transfer.** If the beneficiary entitled to money goes to the bank according to a prior agreement and requests payment, the transaction is called a **debit transfer.** The latter transfer type is not regulated by Article 4A. Article 4A applies only to transfers begun by the person authorizing payment to another.

(c) Nonbank Transfers

For Article 4A to apply to a money transfer, it is necessary that once the transfer has begun, all communication be between banks. Thus, sending money by Western Union does not come under Article 4A because there is no bank-to-bank communication. Payment by check is also not covered because the drawer of the check sends the check directly to the payee. Banks have no involvement until the payee deposits the check or presents it for payment. Likewise, payment by credit card is excluded under Article 4A even when the transaction does not come within the scope of the EFTA.

24. Definitions

Article 4A employs terms that are peculiar to that article or are used in a very different context from the contexts in which they appear elsewhere.

(a) Funds Transfer

A **funds transfer** is more accurately described as a communication of instructions or a request to pay a specific sum of money to, or to the credit of, a specified account or person. There is no actual physical transfer or passing of money.

(b) Originator

The person starting the funds transfer is called the **originator** of the funds transfer.[51]

(c) Beneficiary

The **beneficiary** is the ultimate recipient of the benefit of the funds transfer. Whether the recipient is the beneficiary personally, an account owned by the beneficiary, or a third person to whom the beneficiary owes money is determined by the payment order.

(d) Beneficiary's Bank

The **beneficiary's bank** is the final bank in the chain of transfer that carries out the transfer by making payment or application as directed by the payment order.

(e) Payment Order

The **payment order** is the direction the originator gives to the originator's bank or by any bank to a subsequent bank to make the specified funds transfer. Although called a *payment order*, it is in fact a request. No bank is required or obligated to accept a payment order unless it is so bound by a contract or a clearinghouse rule that operates independently of Article 4A.

(f) Acceptance of Payment Order

When a receiving bank other than the beneficiary's bank receives a payment order, it accepts or executes that order by issuing a payment order to the next bank in the transfer chain. When the beneficiary's bank agrees to, or actually makes, the application of funds as directed by the payment order, the order has been accepted by that bank.

25. Form of Payment Order

The form of the payment order has no specific legal requirements. Funds transfer orders or documents are not required to be in writing. As a practical matter, there probably will be a written contract between an originator and the originator's bank. In addition, agreements between parties and banks as well as clearinghouse and funds transfer system rules may mandate a writing.

26. Manner of Transmitting Payment Order

Article 4A makes no provisions for the manner of transmitting a payment order. As a practical matter,

50 UCC § 4A-108 (1990). This exclusion applies when any part of the transaction is subject to Regulation E adopted under the authority of that statute.

51 UCC § 4A-201.

most funds transfers under Article 4A are controlled by computers, and payment orders are electronically transmitted. Article 4A, however, applies to any funds transfer payment order even if made orally, such as by telephone, or in writing. Also, the agreement of the parties or the clearinghouse and funds transfer system rules may impose some restrictions on the methods for communicating orders.

27. Security Procedure

Because the typical electronic funds transfer involves no writing and no face-to-face contact, Article 4A contemplates that the banks in the transfer chain will agree on a commercially reasonable security procedure. Reasonable commercial practice requires that a bank receiving a payment order be able to verify that the payment order was authorized by the purported sender and that it is free from error.[52] When a bank receives a payment order that passes the security procedure, it may act on the basis of the order. It is immaterial that the order was not authorized or was fraudulent.

28. Regulation by Agreement and Funds Transfer System Rules

Article 4A, with minor limitations, permits the parties to make agreements that modify or change the provisions of Article 4A that would otherwise govern. Likewise, the rules of a clearinghouse or a funds transfer system through which the banks operate may change the provisions of the Code.

(a) Choice of Law

When the parties enter into an agreement for a funds transfer, they may designate the law that is to apply in interpreting the agreement. The parties are given a free hand to select a jurisdiction. Contrary to the rule applicable in other Code transactions, there is no requirement that the jurisdiction selected bear any relationship to the transaction.

(b) Clearinghouse Rules

The banks involved in a particular funds transfer may be members of the same clearinghouse. In such a case, they will be bound by the lawful rules and regulations of the house. The rights of the parties involved in a funds transfer may be determined by the rules of FedWire, a clearinghouse system operated by the Federal Reserve System, or by CHIPS, which is a similar system operated by the New York clearinghouse.

29. Acceptance of Payment Order

A bank receiving a payment order accepts the order when it complies with the order's terms. What acceptance means depends on whether the receiving bank is an intermediary bank or the beneficiary's bank.

(a) Intermediary Bank

An intermediary bank accepts a payment order when it carries out or executes the order by transmitting a similar payment order to the next bank in the transfer chain. Unlike a check sent through bank collection channels, the original payment order is not transferred, but a new payment order by the intermediary bank is dispatched.

(b) Beneficiary's Bank

The beneficiary's bank accepts a payment order when it notifies the beneficiary that it holds the amount of the payment order at the disposal of the beneficiary. The payment order may require the beneficiary's bank to credit the amount to an account or to a named person. The person so named may be the beneficiary, as when a buyer uses a funds transfer to pay the purchase price to the seller. A beneficiary can also be a designated third person. **For Example,** a buyer could direct the crediting of the bank account of a manufacturer to discharge or reduce the debt of the seller to the manufacturer. The transfer to the manufacturer would reduce or discharge the debt of the buyer to the seller by the amount transferred.

When the beneficiary's bank complies with the payment order, it accepts the order. When the bank does so, it takes the place of the originator as the debtor owing the beneficiary. In such a case, the originator no longer owes the beneficiary, and the debt to the beneficiary is discharged or reduced by the amount of the payment order.[53]

30. Reimbursement of the Bank

After the beneficiary's bank accepts the payment order, it and every bank ahead of it in the funds

[52] UCC § 4A-201. But see *Credit Lyonnais–New York v Washington Strategic Consulting Group*, 886 F Supp 92 (DDC 1995). See also *Hedged Investment Partners, L.P. v Norwest Bank Minnesota*, 578 NW2d 765 (Minn 1998).

[53] UCC § 4A-406.

transfer chain is entitled to reimbursement of the amount paid to or for the beneficiary. This reimbursement is due from the preceding bank. By going back along the funds transfer chain, the originator's bank, and ultimately the originator, makes payment of this reimbursement amount.

31. Refund on Noncompletion of Transfer

If the funds transfer is not completed for any reason, the sender or originator is entitled to a refund of any payment that has been made in advance to the originator's bank. The sender or originator is not required to reimburse any bank for payment made by it.

32. Error in Funds Transfer

There may be an error in a payment order. The effect of an error depends on its nature.

(a) Type of Error

The error in a payment order may consist of a wrong identification or a wrong amount.

(1) Wrong Beneficiary or Account Number. The payment order received by the beneficiary's bank may contain an error in the designation of the beneficiary or in the account number. This error may result in payment being made to or for the wrong person or account.

(2) Excessive Amount. The payment order may call for the payment of an amount that is larger than it should be. For example, the order may wrongly add an additional zero to the specified amount.

(3) Duplicating Amount. The payment order may be issued after a similar payment order has already been transferred, so that the second order duplicates the first. This duplication would result in doubling the proper amount paid by the beneficiary's bank.

(4) Underpayment. The payment order may call for the payment of a smaller sum than was ordered. For example, the order may drop off one of the zeros from the amount ordered by the originator.

(b) Effect of Error

When the error falls under one of the first three classes just discussed, the bank committing the error bears the loss because it will not be reimbursed for any amount that it caused to be wrongfully paid. In contrast, when the error is merely underpayment, the bank making the mistake can cure the fault by making a supplementary order for the amount of the underpayment. If verification by the agreed-upon security procedure would disclose an error in the payment order, a bank is liable for any loss caused by the error if it failed to verify the payment order by such a procedure. In contrast, if the security procedure followed did not reveal any error, there is no liability for accepting the payment order.

When an error of any kind is made, there may be liability under a collateral agreement of the parties, a clearinghouse or funds transfer system rule, or general principles of contract law. However, the right of the originator to complain that there is an error may be lost in certain cases by failure to notify the involved bank that the mistake has been made.

33. Liability for Loss

Unless otherwise regulated by agreement or clearinghouse rule, very slight liability is imposed on a bank in the funds transfer chain that has followed the agreed-upon security procedure.

(a) Unauthorized Order

If a bank executes or accepts an unauthorized payment order, it is liable to any prior party in the transfer chain for the loss caused. However, as a practical matter, such loss will rarely be imposed because the transfer is typically made under an agreement establishing a security procedure. If a bank acts on the basis of an unauthorized order that nevertheless is verified by the security procedure, the bank is not liable for the loss that is caused.

The customer, however, can avoid this effect of security procedure verification by proving that the security procedure was not commercially reasonable or that a total stranger initiated the payment order. The latter requires the customer to show that the initiator was not the customer's employee or agent having access to confidential security information or a person who obtained that information from a source controlled by the customer. However, it is immaterial whether the customer was at fault.

(b) Failure to Act

A bank that fails to carry out a payment order is usually liable at the most for interest loss and expenses. There is no liability for the loss sustained by the originator or for consequential damages suffered because payment was not made to satisfy the originator's obligation to the beneficiary. A person seeking to exercise an option by forwarding money to the optionor cannot recover for the loss of the option when the failure of a bank to act results in the optionor's not receiving the money in time.

Summary

A *check* is a particular kind of draft; it is drawn on a bank and is payable on demand. A delivery of a check is not an assignment of money on deposit with the bank on which it is drawn. A check does not automatically transfer the rights of the depositor against the bank to the holder of the check, and there is no duty on the part of the drawee bank to the holder to pay the holder the amount of the check.

A check may be an *ordinary check*, *a cashier's check*, or a *teller's check*. The name on the paper is not controlling. Unless otherwise agreed, the delivery of a certified check, a cashier's check, or a teller's check discharges the debt for which it is given, up to the amount of the check.

Certification of a check by the bank is the acceptance of the check—the bank becomes the primary party. Certification may be at the request of the drawee or the holder. Certification by the holder releases all prior indorsers and the drawer from liability.

Notice of nonpayment of a check must be given to the drawer of a check. If no notice is given, the drawer is discharged from liability to the same extent as the drawer of an ordinary draft.

A depositor may stop payment on a check. However, the depositor is liable to a holder in due course unless the stop payment order was for a reason that may be raised against a holder in due course. The stop payment order may be made orally (binding for 14 calendar days) or with a record (effective for six months).

The depository bank is the agent of the depositor for the purpose of collecting a deposited item. The bank may become liable when it pays a check contrary to a stop payment order or when there has been a forgery or an alteration. The bank is not liable, however, if the drawer's negligence has substantially contributed to the forgery. A bank that pays on a forged instrument must recredit the drawer's account. A depositor is subject to certain time limitations to enforce liability of the bank. Banks are subject to reporting requirements under the Patriot Act.

A customer and a bank may agree that the bank should retain canceled checks and simply provide the customer with a list of paid items. The customer must examine canceled checks (or their electronic images) or paid items to see whether any were improperly paid.

An *electronic funds transfer (EFT)* is a transfer of funds (other than a transaction originated by check, draft, or other commercial paper) that is initiated through an electronic terminal, telephone, computer, or magnetic tape to authorize a financial institution to debit or credit an account. The Electronic Funds Transfer Act requires that a financial institution furnish consumers with specific information containing all the terms and conditions of all EFT services. Under certain conditions, the financial institution will bear the loss for unauthorized transfers. Under other circumstances, the consumer will bear the loss.

Funds transfers regulated by UCC Article 4A are those made between highly sophisticated parties that deal with large sums of money. If any part of the funds transfer is subject to the EFTA, such as consumer transactions, the entire transfer is expressly excluded from the scope of Article 4A. A funds transfer is simply a request or an instruction to pay a specific sum of money to, or to the credit of, a specified person. The person who originates the funds transfer is called the *funds transfer originator*. The beneficiary is the ultimate recipient of the funds transfer.

Questions and Case Problems

1. On August 24, 1989, Karrer and her son opened a joint checking account with Georgia State Bank. The signature card agreement contained a provision that Karrer should report any account problem to the bank within 60 days of her statement or lose her rights to assert the problem against the bank. On August 15, 1990, Karrer tendered a check signed by her in the amount of $1,510 to Casey Construction. At the time the check was tendered, Karrer knew there were insufficient funds in her account to cover the check. Casey, who had an account at the same bank, deposited the check to its account along with another check and received $965 in cash.

   On Saturday, August 18, 1990, Karrer went to the main office of the bank and for the first time notified it that she wanted to stop payment on the check because of

Casey's defective work. Her account did not have sufficient funds to honor the check, so the bank assured her that it would do everything to stop payment. The stop payment order was not implemented before the check was returned to Casey for insufficient funds. Casey's attorney notified Karrer on August 24 by registered mail that the check was dishonored and that if she failed to pay the full amount of the check, both civil and criminal actions would be filed against her. The letter was returned "Unclaimed." The letter was sent to the same address that Karrer and her son used when they opened the account.

Karrer was arrested on October 9 for the issuance of a bad check. She never tried to make the check good prior to her arrest or communicate to the bank any problems she had with the requested stop payment order or the return of the check for insufficient funds until June 4, 1991, almost eight months after her arrest. Even on closing her account in February 1991, she said nothing to the bank about its handling of the check or the stop payment order. In August 1991, Karrer filed suit against the bank, alleging that its return of the check for insufficient funds was wrongful, unlawful, and improper. She also alleged a breach of the agreement between herself and the bank and demanded damages for her arrest, imprisonment, and indictment on charges of issuing a bad check. Is she entitled to collect? [*Karrer v Georgia State Bank of Rome*, 452 SE2d 120 (Ga App)]

2. Helen was a very forgetful person, so she had placed her bank code (PIN number) on the back of her debit card. A thief stole Helen's card and was able to take $100 from an ATM on the day of the theft. That same day, Helen realized that the card was gone and phoned her bank. The following morning, the thief withdrew another $100. For how much, if anything, is Helen responsible? Why?
3. Shirley drew a check on her account at First Central Bank. She later telephoned the bank to stop payment on the check, and the bank agreed to do so. Sixteen days later, the check was presented to the bank for payment, and the bank paid it. Shirley sued the bank for violating the stop payment order. The bank claimed it was not liable. Is Shirley entitled to recover?
4. Arthur Odgers died, and his widow, Elizabeth Odgers (Elizabeth Salsman by remarriage), retained Breslow as the attorney for her husband's estate. She received a check payable to her drawn on First National City Bank. Breslow told her to deposit it in her husband's estate. She signed an indorsement "Pay to the order of Estate of Arthur J. Odgers." Breslow deposited this check in his trustee account in National Community Bank, which collected the amount of the check from the drawee, First City National Bank. Thereafter, Elizabeth, as administratrix of the estate of Arthur J. Odgers, sued National Community Bank for collecting this check and crediting Breslow's trustee account with the proceeds. Was National Community Bank liable? Explain. [*Salsman v National Community Bank*, 246 A2d 162 (NJ Super)]
5. Shipper was ill for 14 months. His wife did not take care of his affairs carefully, nor did she examine his bank statements as they arrived each month. One of Shipper's acquaintances had forged his name to a check in favor of himself for $10,000. The drawee bank paid the check and charged Shipper's account. Shipper's wife did not notify the bank for 13 months after she received the statement and the forged check. Can she compel the bank to reverse the charge? Why or why not?
6. Gloria maintains a checking account at First Bank. On the third day of January, the bank sent her a statement of her account for December accompanied by the checks that the bank had paid. One of the checks had her forged signature, which Gloria discovered on the 25th of the month when she prepared a bank reconciliation. On discovering this, Gloria immediately notified the bank. On January 21, the bank had paid another check forged by the same party who had forged the December item. Who must bear the loss on the forged January check?
7. Dean bought a car from Cannon. As payment, Dean gave him a check drawn on South Dorchester Bank of Eastern Shore Trust Co. Cannon cashed the check at the Cambridge Bank of Eastern Shore Trust Co. The drawee bank refused payment when the check was presented on the ground that Dean had stopped payment because of certain misrepresentations made by Cannon. Will Eastern Shore Trust Co. succeed in an action against Dean for payment? [*Dean v Eastern Shore Trust Co.*, 150 A 797 (Md)]
8. A depositor drew a check and delivered it to the payee. Fourteen months later, the check was presented to the drawee bank for payment. The bank had no knowledge that anything was wrong and paid the check. The depositor then sued the person receiving the money and the bank. The depositor claimed that the bank could not pay a stale check without asking the depositor whether payment should be made. Was the depositor correct? [*Advanced Alloys, Inc. v Sergeant Steel Corp.*, 340 NYS2d 266 (Queens Co Civ Ct)]
9. Siniscalchi drew a check on his account in Valley Bank of New York. About a week later, the holder cashed the check at the bank on a Saturday morning. The following Monday morning, Siniscalchi gave the bank a stop payment order on the check. The Saturday morning transaction had not yet been recorded, and neither the bank nor Siniscalchi knew that the check had been cashed. When that fact was learned, the bank debited Siniscalchi's account for the amount of the check. He claimed that the bank was liable because the stop payment order had been violated. Was the bank liable? [*Siniscalchi v Valley Bank of New York*, 359 NYS2d 173 (Nassau Co Dist Ct)]

10. Bogash drew a check on National Safety Bank and Trust Co. payable to the order of Fiss Corp. At the request of Fiss Corp., the bank certified the check. The bank later refused to make payment on the check because of a dispute between Bogash and the corporation over the amount due the corporation. The corporation sued the bank on the check. Can Fiss recover? [*Fiss Corp. v National Safety Bank and Trust Co.*, 77 So 2d 293 (NY City Ct)]
11. David Marx was a gentleman in his 90s and a longtime customer of Whitney National Bank. His account had been in his name only until April 24, 1995, when he added his son, Stanley Marx, and his daughter, Maxine Marx Goodman, as joint owners and signatories on the account. The account names read: "David Marx or Maxine M. Goodman or Stanley B. Marx." At that time, the bank began sending the statements to Stanley Marx.

    Joel Goodman, David Marx's grandson, visited his grandfather often and had access to his grandfather's checkbook. Joel forged 22 checks on his grandfather's account for a total of $22,834. The first ten checks went unnoticed because they were cleared and the bank statement David Marx received during this time was never reviewed. The last five checks, which appeared on the May 16, 1995, bank statement, were discovered when Stanley Marx reviewed the statement. David and Stanley notified the bank and completed the appropriate forms for the five checks, which totaled $10,000. Whitney National Bank refused to pay the $10,000, and David and Stanley filed suit. The trial court granted summary judgment for David and Stanley, and Whitney appealed. Who is liable on the checks? Did David and Stanley wait too long or are they protected by letting the bank know when they did?
12. Norris, who was ill in the hospital, was visited by his sister during his last days. Norris was very fond of his sister and wrote a check to her that she deposited in her bank account. Before the check cleared, Norris died. Could the sister collect on the check even though the bank knew of the depositor's death? Explain. [*In re Estate of Norris*, 532 P2d 981 (Colo)]
13. Scott D. Leibling gave his bank, Mellon Bank, an oral stop payment order. Nineteen months later, the check emerged and Mellon Bank honored it. Leibling has filed suit against Mellon Bank for acting unreasonably under the circumstances. Is Mellon Bank liable to Leibling for paying the 19-month-old check when there was an oral stop payment order? Discuss your reasons for your answer. [*Leibling, P.C. v Mellon, PSFS (NJ) NA*, 311 NJ Super 651, 710 A2d 1067, 35 UCC2d 590]
14. Hixson paid Galyen Petroleum Co. money he owed by issuing three checks to Galyen. The bank refused to cash the three checks because of insufficient funds in the Hixson account to pay all three. Galyen sued the bank. What was the result? Why? [*Galyen Petroleum Co. v Hixson*, 331 NW2d 1 (Neb)]
15. What is the maximum liability of a consumer who fails to notify the issuer of an EFT card after learning of the loss or theft of the card?

CPA Questions

1. A check has the following endorsements on the back:

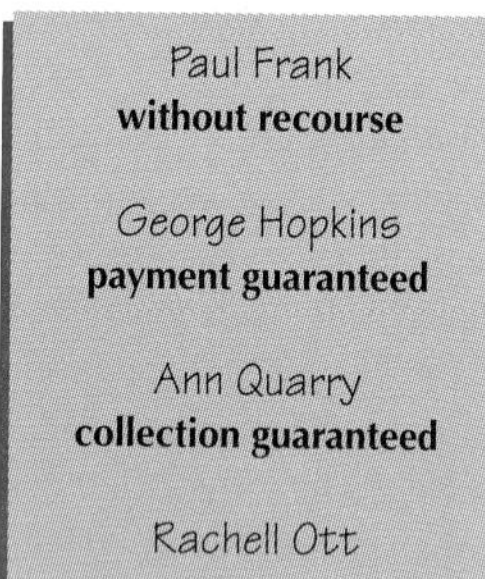

Paul Frank
without recourse
George Hopkins
payment guaranteed
Ann Quarry
collection guaranteed
Rachell Ott

Which of the following conditions occurring subsequent to the endorsements would discharge all of the endorsers?

    a. Lack of notice of dishonor
    b. Late presentment
    c. Insolvency of the maker
    d. Certification of the check

2. Blare bought a house and provided the required funds in the form of a certified check from a bank. Which of the following statements correctly describes the legal liability of Blare and the bank?

    a. The bank has accepted; therefore, Blare is without liability.
    b. The bank has not accepted; therefore, Blare has primary liability.
    c. The bank has accepted, but Blare has secondary liability.
    d. The bank has not accepted, but Blare has secondary liability.

3. In general, which of the following statements is correct concerning the priority among checks drawn on a particular account and presented to the drawee bank on a particular day?

   a. The checks may be charged to the account in any order convenient to the bank.

   b. The checks may be charged to the account in any order provided no charge creates an overdraft.

   c. The checks must be charged to the account in the order in which the checks were dated.

   d. The checks must be charged to the account in the order of lowest amount to highest amount to minimize the number of dishonored checks.

PART (5)

DEBTOR-CREDITOR RELATIONSHIPS

NATURE OF THE DEBTOR-CREDITOR RELATIONSHIP

CHAPTER (32)

A. Creation of the Credit Relationship

B. Suretyship and Guaranty

1. Definitions
2. Indemnity Contract Distinguished
3. Creation of the Relationship
4. Rights of Sureties
5. Defenses of Sureties

C. Letters of Credit

6. Definition
7. Parties
8. Duration
9. Form
10. Duty of Issuer
11. Reimbursement of Issuer

LEARNING OBJECTIVES

After studying this chapter, you should be able to

LO.1 Distinguish a contract of suretyship from a contract of guaranty

LO.2 Define the parties to a contract of suretyship and a contract of guaranty

LO.3 List and explain the rights of sureties to protect themselves from loss

LO.4 Explain the defenses available to sureties

LO.5 Explain the nature of a letter of credit and the liabilities of the various parties to a letter of credit

LO.6 List the exceptions to the requirement of consideration

This section of the book deals with all aspects of debt: the creation of the debtor-creditor relationship, the statutory requirements for disclosure in those credit contracts, the means by which creditors can secure repayment of debt, and finally, what happens when debtors are unable to repay their debts. This chapter covers the creation of the debtor-creditor relationship, as well as two means of ensuring payment: the use of a surety or guarantor and the creation of a line of credit.

A. Creation of the Credit Relationship

A debtor-creditor relationship arises when the parties enter into a contract that provides for the creditor to advance funds to the debtor and requires the debtor to repay that principal amount with specified interest over an agreed-upon time. The credit contract, so long as it complies with all the requirements for formation and validity covered in Chapters 12 through 17, is enforceable just like any other contract. However, credit contracts often have additional statutory obligations and relationships that provide assurances on rights and collection for both the debtor and the creditor. Chapter 33 covers the rights of both debtors and creditors in consumer credit relationships. Chapter 34 covers the additional protection that creditors enjoy when debtors offer security interests in collateral. This chapter covers the additional relationships for securing repayment of debt known as *suretyships* and *lines of credit*.

CPA B. Suretyship and Guaranty

A debtor can make a separate contract with a third party that requires the third party to pay the debtor's creditor if the debtor does not pay or defaults in the performance of an obligation. This relationship, in which a third party agrees to be responsible for the debt or other obligation, is used most commonly to ensure that a debt will be paid or that a contractor will perform the work called for by a contract. **For Example,** a third-party arrangement occurs when a corporate officer agrees to be personally liable if his corporation does not repay funds received through a corporate note. Contractors are generally required to obtain a surety bond in which a third party agrees to pay damages or complete performance of the construction project in the event the contractor fails to perform in a timely manner or according to the contract terms.

CPA 1. Definitions

One type of agreement to answer for the debt or default of another is called a **suretyship.** The **obligor** or third party who makes good on a debtor's obligation is called a **surety.** The other kind of agreement is called a **guaranty,** and the obligor is called a **guarantor.** In both cases, the person who owes the money or is under the original obligation to pay or perform is called the **principal, principal debtor,** or **debtor.**[1] The person to whom the debt or obligation is owed is the **obligee** or **creditor.**

As discussed in Chapters 28 and 31, the revisions to Articles 3 and 4 put accommodation parties (now secondary obligors) in the same legal status as those in a surety/guarantor relationship. The revisions place secondary obligors in the position of a surety.

Suretyship and guaranty undertakings have the common feature of a promise to answer for the debt or default of another. The terms are often used interchangeably. However, certain forms of guaranty are qualified by one distinction. A surety is liable from the moment the principal is in default. The creditor or obligee can demand performance or payment from the surety without first proceeding against the principal debtor. A **guaranty of collection** is one in which the creditor generally cannot proceed directly against the guarantor and must first attempt to collect from the principal debtor. An exception is an **absolute guaranty,** which creates the same obligation as a suretyship. A **guaranty of payment** creates an absolute guaranty and requires the guarantor to pay upon default by the principal debtor.

CPA 2. Indemnity Contract Distinguished

Both suretyship and guaranty differ from an **indemnity contract.** An indemnity contract is an undertaking by one person, for a consideration, to pay another person a sum of money in the event that the other person sustains a specified loss. **For Example,**

[1] Unless otherwise stated, *surety* as used in the text includes guarantor as well as surety. Often, the term *guarantee* is used for guaranty. In law, guarantee is actually one who benefits from the guaranty.

a fire insurance policy is an indemnity contract. The insurance you obtain when you use a rental car is also an example of an indemnity contract.

3. Creation of the Relationship

Suretyship, guaranty, and indemnity relationships are based on contract. The principles relating to capacity, formation, validity, and interpretation of contracts are applicable. Generally, the ordinary rules of offer and acceptance apply. Notice of acceptance usually must be given by the obligee to the guarantor.

In most states, the statute of frauds requires that contracts of suretyship and guaranty be in writing to be enforceable. No writing is required when the promise is made primarily for the promisor's benefit.

When the suretyship or guaranty is created at the same time as the original transaction, the consideration for the original promise that is covered by the guaranty is also consideration for the promise of the guarantor. When the suretyship or guaranty contract is entered into after and separate from the original transaction, there must be new consideration for the promise of the guarantor.

FONTAINE V GORDON CONTRACTORS BUILDING SUPPLY, INC.,
567 SE2D 324 (GA APP 2002)

I'M SURE I'M NOT A SURETY!

Charles Fontaine (defendant) completed a form for Gordon Contractors (plaintiff) in which he signed that portion of the form labeled, "NAME OF GUARANTOR." His signature followed immediately after a paragraph beginning, "[I]n consideration of the extension of credit by Gordon Building Supply Inc. the undersigned customer hereby agrees that the terms and conditions of all sales are as follows." There is also a blank following this paragraph for "Customer Name," and it is signed by a Robert Schlaefli, although it is unclear whether he signed it individually or as an agent. At the beginning of the application, the blank for "Name of INDIVIDUAL APPLYING" is filled in with both Fontaine's and Schlaefli's names, and the blank for "Name of COMPANY OR BUSINESS" bears the words "McIntyre Development, Inc." Finally, the blank for "NAMES OF PEOPLE AUTHORIZED TO PURCHASE" is filled in with Schlaefli's name and that of a Glen Bush.

Upon default of the debtor (never clearly identified in the agreement), Gordon Contractors filed suit to collect from Fontaine as a guarantor. Fontaine moved for summary judgment because he was not identified on the contract as a guarantor. The trial court granted Gordon Contractors a summary judgment against Fontaine and Fontaine appealed.

Judicial Opinion

MILLER, Judge.... Fontaine claims that the credit application violates the applicable portion of the Statute of Frauds, requiring a signed writing for enforceability of a promise to answer for the debt or default of another. He contends that this is so because it fails to identify the principal debtor. If he is correct that the principal debtor is unidentified, that omission mandates reversal under a line of cases going back to 1982. *Roden Elec. Supply, Inc. v Faulkner*, 240 Ga.App. 556(1), 524 S.E.2d 247 (1999); *Workman v Sysco Food Svcs. of Atlanta*, 236 Ga.App. 784, 784-785, 513 S.E.2d 523 (1999).

Gordon points out that the credit application "identifies the name of the company or business as 'McIntyre Development, Inc.'" In *Roden*, however, the controlling document consisted of a credit application portion and a guaranty portion, neither of which stated the identity of the principal debtor, although the credit application portion showed a corporation as the "billable party" and the guaranty portion referred to "the above business." In appealing from the grant of summary judgment to the purported guarantor, the *Roden* creditor argued that the guaranty sufficiently identified the principal debtor for purposes of the statute of frauds. We affirmed, however, pointing out the necessity of explicit identification of the principal debtor.

Where a guaranty omits the name of the principal debtor, it is unenforceable as a matter of law. This is true even where the intent of the parties is manifestly obvious. Further, this Court is not authorized to determine the identity of the principal debtor by inference as this would entail consideration of impermissible parol evidence. Neither may we construe the defect *sub judice* as in the nature of contractual ambiguity. Parol evidence is inadmissible to provide a description of that which is wholly omitted... [h]ere there is no clear identification of the principal debtor.

[W]here the name of the principal debtor is omitted from the document, the agreement is not enforceable because it fails to satisfy the statute of frauds.... [T]he contemporaneous writing rule, even if applicable, would not authorize a different result. Although the "Terms Agreement" and "Individual Personal Guaranty" appear on the same paper, the two sections do not incorporate each other by reference or use the same terms. The terms agreement refers to "seller"... and "purchaser."... In contrast, the individual personal guaranty refers to "company" (unidentified, unnamed) and seller.... The trial court correctly found that in order to determine the identity of the "company" debtor, it would have to make inferences and consider impermissible parol evidence.... Judicial construction of the contract of guaranty at issue is improper because this defect cannot be treated as an ambiguity.

We also noted "the statutory bar precluding the extension of a contract of guaranty by interpretation or implication." Here there is no other writing that could arguably invoke the contemporaneous writing rule. Finally, Gordon points to Fontaine's admission in his deposition that he signed this document as a guarantor "on behalf of McIntyre Development." A similar situation was presented in *Workman*, however, and there this Court held it was irrelevant that the purported guarantor testified that it was her intent to guarantee the debt.

[Judgment reversed]

Questions

1. Who is the principal debtor under the terms of the agreement?
2. Does it matter that Fontaine stated in a deposition that he was acting as a guarantor?
3. Is the guarantor liable for the amount of the default debt?

4. Rights of Sureties

Sureties have a number of rights to protect them from loss, to obtain their discharge because of the conduct of others that would be harmful to them, or to recover money that they were required to pay because of the debtor's breach.

CPA (a) Exoneration

A surety can be exonerated from liability, a means of discharging or relieving liability, if the creditor could have taken steps to stop or limit the surety's exposure for the debt. For example, suppose that the surety learns that a debtor is about to leave the state, an act that makes it more difficult to collect debts. The surety may call on the creditor to take action against the debtor to provide a literal and figurative roadblock to the debtor's planned departure. If the creditor could proceed against the debtor who is about to leave and thereby protect the repayment and fails to do so, the surety is released or **exonerated** from liability to the extent that the surety has been harmed by such failure.

CPA (b) Subrogation

When a surety pays a claim that it is obligated to pay, it automatically acquires the claim and the rights of the creditor. This stepping into the shoes or position of another is known as **subrogation.**[2] That is, once the creditor is paid in full, the surety stands in the same position as the creditor and may collect from the debtor or enforce any rights the creditor had against the debtor to recover the amount it has paid. The effect is the same as if the creditor, on being paid, made an express assignment of all rights to the surety. Likewise, the surety acquires any rights the debtor has against the creditor. **For Example,** if the creditor has not complied with statutory requirements, the surety can enforce those rights against the creditor just as the original debtor could.

[2] *Middlesex Mut. Assur. Co. v Vaszil*, 873 A2d 1030 (Conn App 2005); insurer had right of subrogration where guarantor had signed for tenant's liability for causing damage to the landlord's property once the insurer had paid the landlord.

CPA (c) Indemnity

A surety that has made payment of a claim for which it was liable as surety is entitled to **indemnity** from the principal debtor; that is, it is entitled to demand from the principal reimbursement of the amount that it has paid.

CPA (d) Contribution

If there are two or more sureties (known as co-sureties), each is liable to the creditor or claimant for the full amount of the debt until the claim or debt has been paid in full. Between themselves, however, each co-surety is liable only for a proportionate share of the debt. Accordingly, if a surety has paid more than its share of the debt, it is entitled to demand **contribution** from its **co-sureties.** In the absence of a contrary agreement, co-sureties must share the debt repayment on a *pro rata* basis. **For Example,** Aaron and Bobette are co-sureties of $40,000 and $60,000, respectively, for Christi's $60,000 loan. If Christi defaults, Aaron owes $24,000 and Bobette owes $36,000.

5. Defenses of Sureties

The surety's defenses include those that may be raised by a party to any contract and special defenses that are peculiar to the suretyship relation.

CPA (a) Ordinary Contract Defenses

Because the relationship of suretyship is based on a contract, the surety may raise any defense that a party to an ordinary contract may raise. For example, a surety may raise the defense of lack of capacity of parties, absence of consideration, fraud, or mistake.

Fraud and concealment are common defenses. Fraud on the part of the principal that is unknown to the creditor and in which the creditor has not taken part does not ordinarily release the surety.

Because the risk of the principal debtor's default is thrown on the surety, it is unfair for a creditor to conceal from the surety facts that are material to the surety's risk. Under common law, the creditor was not required to volunteer information to the surety and was not required to disclose that the principal was insolvent. A modern view that is receiving increased support is that the creditor should be required to inform the surety of matters material to the risk when the creditor has reason to believe that the surety does not possess such information.

CPA (b) Suretyship Defenses

Perhaps the most important thing for a surety to understand is the type of defense that does not result in a discharge of her obligation in the suretyship. The insolvency or bankruptcy of the principal debtor does not discharge the surety. The financial risk of the principal debtor is the reason that a surety was obtained from the outset. The lack of enforcement of the debt by the creditor is not a defense to the surety's obligation or a discharge. The creditor's failure to give the surety notice of default is not a defense. The creditor's right, without a specific guarantee of collection, is simply to turn to the surety for payment.[3]

In some cases, the creditor may have also taken a **pledge** of collateral for the debt in addition to the commitment of a surety. It is the creditor's choice as to whether to proceed against the collateral or the surety. If, however, the creditor proceeds first against the surety, the surety then has the right of exoneration and can step into the shoes of the creditor and repossess that collateral.

Changes in the terms of the loan agreement do not discharge a compensated surety. A surety who is

THINKING THINGS THROUGH

PRO RATA SHARES FOR CO-SURETIES

AFC Corporation borrowed $90,000 from First Bank and demanded three sureties for the loan. Anna Flynn agreed to be a surety for $45,000 for AFC's debt. Frank Conlan agreed to be a surety for $60,000, and Charles Aspen agreed to be a surety for $75,000. When AFC owed $64,000, it defaulted on the loan and demanded payment from the co-sureties. However, Frank Conlan was in bankruptcy. How much would Anna and Charles have to pay to First Bank?

[3] *Fleet National Bank v Phillips*, 2006 WL 2044655 (Mass App Div).

acting gratuitously, however, would be discharged in the event of such changes. Changes in the loan terms that would discharge a gratuitous surety's obligation include extension of the loan terms and acceptance of late payments.

A surety is discharged when the principal debtor performs his obligations under the original debt contract. If a creditor refuses to accept payment from a debtor, a surety is discharged.

A surety is also discharged, to the extent of the value of the collateral, if a creditor releases back to the debtor any collateral in the creditor's possession. **For Example,** suppose that Bank One has in its possession $10,000 in gold coins as collateral for a loan to Janice in the amount of $25,000. Albert has agreed to serve as a surety for the loan to Janice in the amount of $25,000. If a Bank One manager returns the $10,000 in coins to Janice, then Albert is discharged on his suretyship obligation to the extent of that $10,000. Following the release of the collateral, the most that Albert could be held liable for in the event of Janice's default is $15,000.

A surety is also discharged from her obligation if the creditor substitutes a different debtor. A surety and a guarantor make a promise that is personal to a specific debtor and do not agree to assume the risk of an assignment or a delegation of that responsibility to another debtor. A surety also enjoys the discharge rights afforded all parties to contracts, such as the statute of limitations. If the creditor does not enforce the suretyship agreement within the time limits provided for such contract enforcement in the surety's jurisdiction, the obligation is forever discharged.[4]

Figures 32-1and 32-2 provide summaries of the defenses and release issues surrounding suretyship and guaranty relationships.

FIGURE 32-1 No Release of Surety

1. FRAUD BY DEBTOR
2. MISREPRESENTATION BY DEBTOR
3. CHANGES IN LOAN TERMS (E.G., EXTENSION OF PAYMENT)—COMPENSATED SURETY ONLY
4. RELEASE OF PRINCIPAL DEBTOR
5. BANKRUPTCY OF PRINCIPAL DEBTOR
6. INSOLVENCY OF PRINCIPAL DEBTOR
7. DEATH OF PRINCIPAL DEBTOR
8. INCAPACITY OF PRINCIPAL DEBTOR
9. LACK OF ENFORCEMENT BY CREDITOR
10. CREDITOR'S FAILURE TO GIVE NOTICE OF DEFAULT
11. FAILURE OF CREDITOR TO RESORT TO COLLATERAL

FIGURE 32-2 Release of Surety

1. PROPER PERFORMANCE BY DEBTOR
2. RELEASE, SURRENDER, OR DESTRUCTION OF COLLATERAL (TO EXTENT OF VALUE OF COLLATERAL)
3. SUBSTITUTION OF DEBTOR
4. FRAUD/MISREPRESENTATION BY CREDITOR
5. REFUSAL BY CREDITOR TO ACCEPT PAYMENT FROM DEBTOR
6. CHANGE IN LOAN TERMS—UNCOMPENSATED SURETY ONLY
7. STATUTE OF FRAUDS
8. STATUTE OF LIMITATIONS

[4] *The Clark Const. Group, Inc. v Wentworth Plastering of Boca Raton, Inc.*, 840 So2d 357 (Fla App 2002).

CONTINENTAL AIRLINES, INC., V LELAKIS, 943 F SUPP 300 (SDNY 1996)

IT WAS GREEK TO ME, BUT THE CONTRACT WAS IN ENGLISH

Continental Airlines (plaintiff) is an airline operating in the United States and around the world. In 1989, Continental established an "Air Travel Plan Account" that permitted Regency Cruises to purchase air travel and other related services from Continental and charge those services to the Air Travel Plan Account. Regency Cruises is an owner and operator of a fleet of pleasure ships and a wholly owned subsidiary of Regency Holdings, Inc., which is incorporated in the Cayman Islands. Antonios Lelakis (defendant) is the chairman of the board of Regency Holdings.

To establish the account, Regency signed a contract with Continental providing that Regency would be billed on a monthly basis and would be required to make payments on the account. From July 1994 through October 1994, Regency fell behind on its payments to Continental. Officials of Continental and Regency Holdings signed an addendum to the travel account agreement in which it agreed to be jointly and severally liable for any existing and future Regency Cruises debt on the account. Regency Holdings also executed a promissory note payable to Continental in the amount of $10,476,992.23 to be paid by June 30, 1995. Mr. Lelakis signed an individual guarantee to Continental for the $10,476,992.23 note.

During 1995, Continental renegotiated the payment schedule for the note with Regency Holdings. However, by March 2, 1995, Regency Holdings had made only two payments on the note, and Continental declared Regency Holdings in default, accelerated the amount due, and demanded full payment of the note. Both Regency Holdings and Regency Cruises filed for Chapter 11 bankruptcy in November 1995. Continental demanded payment of the note from Mr. Lelakis as a surety. Mr. Lelakis refused on the grounds of misrepresentation, duress, and changes in the surety's obligations under the original agreement.

Judicial Opinion

SCHEINDLIN, D. J. . . . Defendant alleges that his spoken and written English skills are limited, and as such, he did not understand all that transpired at the October 5, 1994 meeting at which the guaranty was negotiated. Defendant further contends that Continental represented that the guaranty was only an "assurance" that Regency Cruises would meet its obligations under the UATP [the air travel plan account] that he was asked to sign as chairman of Regency Holdings, and not a personal guaranty that defendant himself would pay if Regency Cruises did not. Under Greek law, defendant contends, such an assurance only exposes the signer to liability after corporate assets are exhausted.

Drawing all inferences in favor of the defendant, Lelakis has presented facts sufficient to support two of the three essential elements of his fraudulent inducement claim: that he does not understand English and that Continental misrepresented the nature of the guaranty to him. Lelakis has not, however, presented facts sufficient to support the third element of his fraudulent inducement defense, namely that he was not negligent in signing the guaranty.

Lelakis alleges that when he attended the October 5, 1994 meeting, he believed he did so in his corporate and not his individual capacity. After the meeting, at the request of Regency Holdings' Chief Financial Officer, David Groelinger, Regency Holdings' counsel, Robert Shaw, drafted the guaranty. Defendant alleges that he was unaware of Shaw's involvement at the time. Although Shaw is fluent in both English and Greek, Lelakis alleges that he and Shaw neither discussed the guaranty, nor did Shaw translate the guaranty into Greek for defendant then or at any time after the meeting.

Defendant admits that his usual practice is to consult with counsel or to have legal documents translated into Greek before affixing his signature. Yet when he received the final draft guaranty at a later date, he departed from his usual practice and did neither because he believed that Continental had already explained its meaning to him. In fact, Lelakis failed to take any of these steps despite his admission that he had encountered and signed personal guaranties in a corporate setting in past transactions.

Defendant argues that he was not negligent because he was unrepresented by counsel in his individual capacity at the time when the guaranty was negotiated, and therefore was entitled to rely on Continental's representations. Lelakis, however, had a minimal duty to inquire of Robert

Shaw, the corporation's bilingual attorney, about the nature of a document he was signing on the corporation's behalf. Had he inquired of Shaw in his corporate capacity, he would have learned the nature of the guaranty.

Thus, for Lelakis to claim that he was not negligent, he must succeed in shifting the burden of his failure to communicate about the guaranty with his own counsel and organization—the very people who drafted, negotiated, and arranged for his execution of the guaranty—onto Continental.

Finally, defendant's alleged inability to speak English does not obliterate the overarching requirement of a fraudulent inducement defense that his reliance on Continental's representatives be justified and reasonable.

Here, Lelakis has not alleged, nor can he allege that the nature of the guaranty was peculiarly within Continental's knowledge, when he had ample opportunity to have the guaranty either explained to him or translated before he actually signed it. This is particularly true when Lelakis acknowledges that his failure to do so departed from his normal course of action. Moreover, Lelakis' own team negotiated with Continental for the guaranty with Lelakis present. Even if he did not understand all that transpired, he unjustifiably credited Continental's explanation without so much as asking for an explanation from his own team.

Under the circumstances, defendant was negligent as a matter of law in failing to take any steps either at the October 5, 1995 meeting, or in the intervening days before he signed the guaranty on October 21, 1995 to ascertain the nature of the guaranty, as was his custom in business transactions. In addition, defendant's reliance on Continental's alleged misrepresentation was not justified under the circumstances. Because Lelakis has failed to raise sufficient facts to support an essential element of his fraudulent inducement defense, Continental is entitled to summary judgment on this defense.

A guarantor's obligations must be strictly construed according to the terms of the guaranty and cannot be "altered, extended or enlarged" by either creditor or debtor without the guarantor's consent. See *Fehr Bros., Inc. v. Scheinman*, 121 A.D.2d 13, 509 N.Y.S.2d 304, 306 (1st Dep't 1986). The guarantor cannot be held responsible to guarantee a performance different from that identified in the guaranty. However, a guarantor-defendant

cannot escape liability by relying on changes he initiated for his own benefit, which changes did not, in any case, have the effect of creating a new corporate identity or materially altering the relationship between the principal-debtor and the creditor or the obligations defendant freely chose to assume under the guaranty.

As noted above, a defendant cannot rely on the defense of change of risk if the change was initiated for the defendant's benefit and was within the defendant's control. See *Fehr Bros.*, 509 N.Y.S.2d at 310; *Caldor*, 817 F.Supp. at 412. In *Caldor*, defendant Caldor had guaranteed payment to Mattel, Inc. of the present and future debts of Caldor's wholly owned subsidiary, Leisure Line Toys, Inc. Over ten years later and after being acquired itself by another store, Caldor divested itself of assets including those related to Leisure Line. Leisure Line was not successful on its own and fell behind in its payments to Mattel. Mattel demanded that Caldor honor the guaranty, and Caldor countered, *inter alia*, that its loss of control over Leisure Line constituted a material alteration of Caldor's assumed risks and voided the guaranty. The court disagreed, finding that Caldor's loss of control over Leisure Line changed the nature of the risk, but that "standing alone, loss of control is not enough to discharge the duties of the Guarantor." In addition, the court noted that Caldor had itself created the conditions that caused the change in risk and could be considered to have consented to it.

Here, unlike in *Caldor*, Lelakis had control over Regency Holdings when the ships were sold and the change of risk allegedly occurred. Lelakis himself consented to the sale of the vessels to Kawasaki. Although this sale may have changed the personal risk to Lelakis in that it liquidated allegedly valuable assets of the company whose debt he guaranteed, Lelakis initiated this change of risk himself. He consented to the Kawasaki sale after the in-court announcement that the broader deal with Summer Breeze had fallen through. Even if Lelakis believed Summer Breeze would follow through on the portion of the deal discharging the guaranty, he sold the ships with knowledge that the Summer Breeze deal was dead. As a result, any change of risk Lelakis assumed, he assumed voluntarily. The change of risk to Lelakis was initiated by Lelakis and entirely within his control.

Defendant has failed to satisfy an essential element of his change of risk defense, namely that the change of risk was beyond his control. Continental is entitled to summary judgment on this defense as well.

[Judgment for Continental]

Questions

1. Why did Continental want a guaranty from the chairman of the board of the holding company?
2. Did the renegotiation of the note's terms discharge Lelakis?
3. What does the court find regarding Lelakis and his lack of English skills?

FIGURE 32-3 Letter of Credit

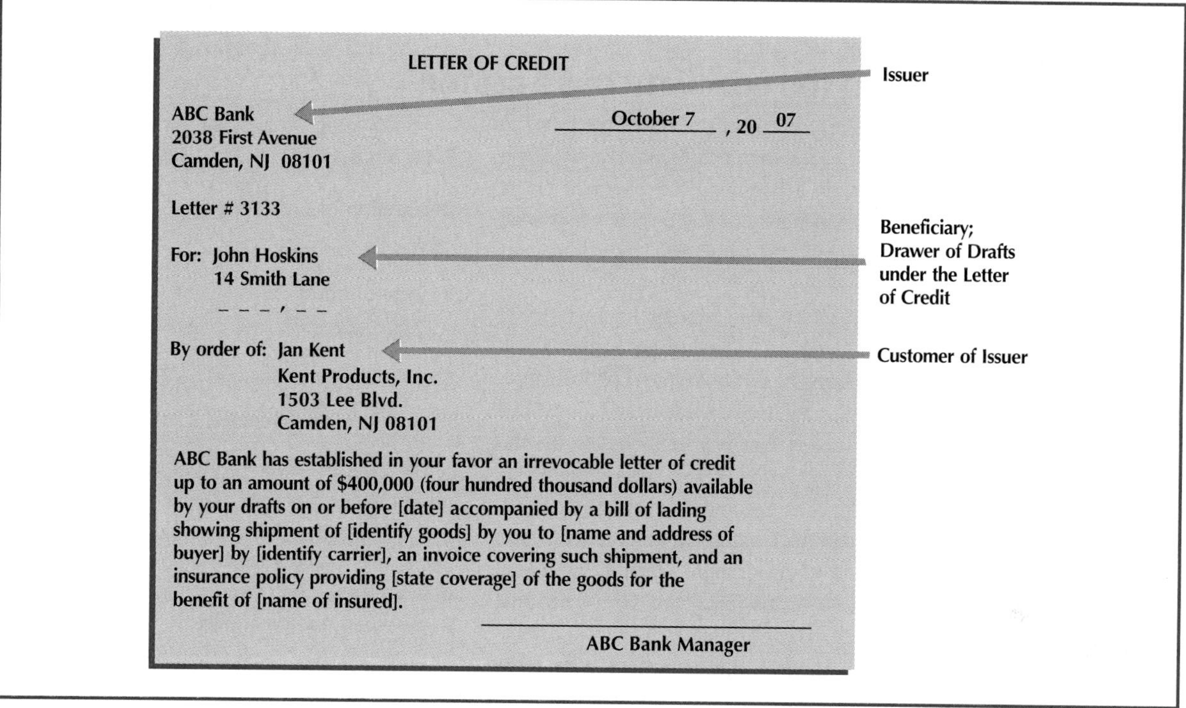

LETTER OF CREDIT

ABC Bank
2038 First Avenue
Camden, NJ 08101

October 7, 20 07

Letter # 3133

For: John Hoskins
14 Smith Lane
_ _ _ , _ _

By order of: Jan Kent
Kent Products, Inc.
1503 Lee Blvd.
Camden, NJ 08101

ABC Bank has established in your favor an irrevocable letter of credit up to an amount of $400,000 (four hundred thousand dollars) available by your drafts on or before [date] accompanied by a bill of lading showing shipment of [identify goods] by you to [name and address of buyer] by [identify carrier], an invoice covering such shipment, and an insurance policy providing [state coverage] of the goods for the benefit of [name of insured].

ABC Bank Manager

C. Letters of Credit

A **letter of credit** is a three-party arrangement with a payor, a beneficiary, and a party on whom the letter of credit is drawn, or **issuer.** A letter of credit is an agreement that the issuer of the letter will pay drafts drawn by the beneficiary of the letter. Letters of credit are a form of advance arrangement for financing. Sellers of goods, for example, know in advance how much money may be obtained from the issuer of the letter. A letter of credit may also be used by a creditor as a security device because the creditor knows that the drafts that the creditor draws will be accepted or paid by the issuer of the letter.[5]

The use of letters of credit arose in international trade. While international trade continues to be the primary area of use, there is a growing use of letters in domestic sales and in transactions in which the letter of credit takes the place of a surety bond. A letter of credit has been used to ensure that a borrower would repay a loan, that a tenant would pay the rent due under a lease, and that a contractor would properly perform a construction contract. This kind of letter of credit is known as a **standby letter.**

There are few formal requirements for creating a letter of credit. Although banks often use a standardized form for convenience, they may draw up individualized letters of credit for particular situations (see Figure 32-3).

In international letters of credit, there are several sources of recognized standards that businesses use for the creation and execution of letters of credit. Along with the UCC, there is the Uniform Customs and Practice for Documentary Credits (or UCP), something that reflects ordinary international banking operational practices on letters of credit. The UCP is revised, generally, about every ten years by the International Chamber of Commerce (ICC; see Chapter 7).

6. Definition

A letter of credit is an engagement by its issuer that it will pay or accept drafts when the conditions specified in the letter are satisfied. The issuer is usually a bank.

Three contracts are involved in letter-of-credit transactions: (1) the contract between the issuer and the customer of the issuer, (2) the letter of credit itself,

[5] *U.S. Material Supply, Inc. v Korea Exchange Bank*, 417 F Supp 2d 652 (DNJ 2006), discussing the character and purpose of letters of credit.

ETHICS & THE LAW

GETTING TOO COZY WITH ONE'S DEBTOR

Very often the creditors of a business can exercise a great deal of authority over the operation of the business when it has missed a payment on its debt or has experienced some business or market setbacks. Without owning any stock in a corporation, creditors will, in more than 50 percent of all cases in which they express concern about repayment, succeed in having both boards and officers replaced in part or in toto. **For Example,** Worlds of Wonder, Inc., a creative and innovative toy manufacturer that was responsible for the first talking toy, Teddy Ruxpin, was required by demands from its secured and unsecured creditors to obtain the resignation of its founder and CEO, Donald Kingsborough. Kingsborough was paid $212,500 at his departure for "emotional distress."*

Studies show** that creditors also have input on the following corporate actions:

Type of Decision	*Percentage of Creditors with Vote*
Declaration of dividends	48
Increased security	73
Restructuring of debt	55
Cap on borrowing	50
Cap on capital expenses	25
Restrictions on investment	23

Is it fair to have creditors control corporate governance? Will they always make the choices that are best for the shareholders? Is it unconscionable to have these control covenants in loan agreements? Why do creditors need them in their loan agreements?

* "Toymaker Has Financing Pact," *New York Times*, April 2, 1988, C1 (Reuters item).

** See Tim Reason, "Keeping Skin in the Game," *CFO Magazine*, February 1, 2005, **http://www.cfo.com**, for a discussion of why creditors are involved and what they can do to help manage a debtor.

and (3) the underlying agreement, often a contract of sale, between the beneficiary and the customer of the issuer of the letter of credit (see Figure 32-4). The letter of credit is completely independent from the other two contracts. Consideration is not required to establish or modify a letter of credit.

The issuer of the letter of credit is in effect the obligor on a third-party-beneficiary contract made for the benefit of the beneficiary of the letter. The key to the commercial success of letters of credit is their independence. **For Example,** a bank obligated to issue payment under a letter of credit "when the

FIGURE 32-4 The Contracts Involved in Letter-of-Credit Transactions

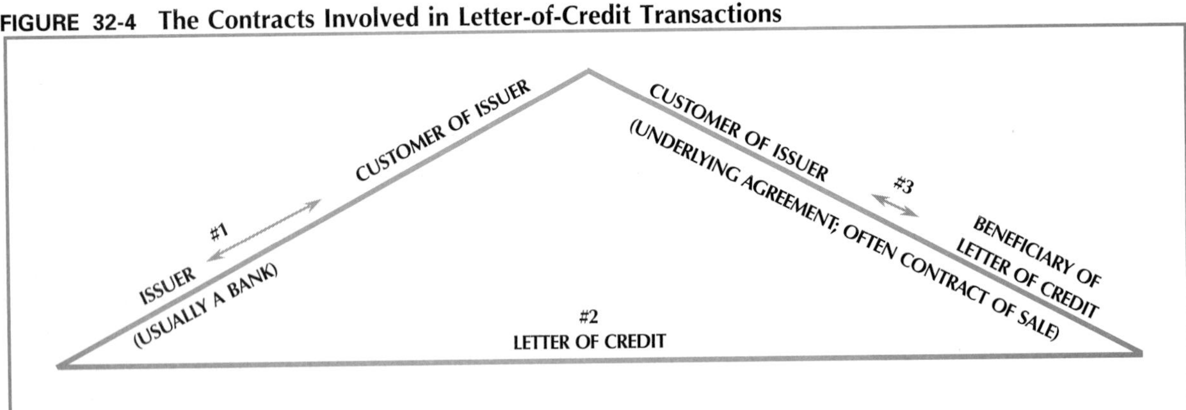

goods are delivered" must honor that obligation even if the buyer has complaints about the goods. It is the terms of the letter of credit that control the payment, not the relationship, contract, or problems of the beneficiary or issuer of the letter of credit.

The key to the commercial vitality and function of a letter of credit is that the issuing bank's promise is independent of the underlying contracts and the bank should not resort to them in interpreting a letter of credit. Sometimes called *the strict compliance rule*, banks must honor the letter of credit terms using strict interpretation. The respective parties are protected by a careful description of the documents that will trigger payment. The claim of a beneficiary of a letter of credit is not subject to defenses normally applicable to third-party contracts. Known as the *independence rule*, banks cannot, except in limited circumstances, delve into the underlying contract issues; the focus of the bank is only on the terms of the letter of credit.

SOUTHTRUST BANK OF ALABAMA, N.A. V WEBB-STILES CO., INC., 2005, WL 2692482 (ALA.), 58 UCC REP SERV 2D 60 (ALA 2005)

GIVE ME A LITTLE CREDIT, NOT TEMPORARY RESTRAINT

FACTS: In 1995, the Airport Authority of India (AAI) retained Transact International, Inc. (Transact), to build a cargo-handling facility at the Indira Gandhi International Airport in New Delhi, India. Webb-Stiles Company, Inc., a manufacturer of conveyor systems, was one of Transact's subcontractors on the airport project.

State Bank of India (SBI) agreed to guarantee Transact's performance to AAI. In return, SBI required that Transact obtain an irrevocable standby letter of credit in favor of SBI. Webb-Stiles helped Transact obtain the letter of credit from SouthTrust. On November 13, 1996, SouthTrust issued its letter of credit for $175,661. Transact signed the letter of credit as applicant, and Webb-Stiles signed as surety for Transact's obligation to reimburse SouthTrust for any payment made under the letter of credit. Although the letter of credit was originally to expire on September 30, 1998, the parties extended it to January 31, 2005.

Between 1999 and 2004, AAI and Transact had numerous disputes about their obligations under the contract. By late 2004, the parties were still unable to resolve their differences. On December 10, 2004, SBI notified SouthTrust that AAI had made a demand for the full amount of the performance guarantee ($175,661). In turn, SBI immediately made a demand on the letter of credit in the same amount. Under its terms, the letter of credit is payable by SouthTrust upon SouthTrust's receipt of a proper demand from SBI. SBI's demand conformed to the requirements of the letter of credit.

Webb-Stiles sued for an injunction to stop SouthTrust from honoring the letter of credit, claiming that AAI had fraudulently misrepresented its right to make demand against the SBI performance guarantee. The trial court granted Webb-Stiles a preliminary injunction preventing payment on the letter of credit. AAI appealed.

Judicial Opinion

NABERS, Chief Justice... As enacted in Alabama, the Uniform Commercial Code grants a trial court the power to enjoin payment of a letter of credit to prevent fraud:

"If an applicant claims that a required document is forged or materially fraudulent or that honor of the presentation would facilitate a material fraud by the beneficiary on the issuer or applicant, a court of competent jurisdiction may temporarily or permanently enjoin the issuer from honoring a presentation...."

The commercial importance of letters of credit allows courts to enjoin payment only in extraordinary circumstances. In *Southern Energy Homes, Inc. v AmSouth Bank of Alabama*, 709 So.2d 1180 (Ala.1998), a case that was factually similar to this case, this Court thoroughly analyzed an effort to enjoin payment of a letter of credit issued by an Alabama bank in connection with a foreign construction contract.

In *Southern Energy*, this Court clearly set forth the principles governing international letters of credit:

"Parties that enter into a credit arrangement do so to avail themselves of the benefits of that arrangement. Shifting litigation costs is one of the functions of a standby credit. In this situation, the parties negotiate their relationship while bearing in mind that litigation may occur. This cost-shifting function gives one party the benefit of the money in hand pending the outcome of any litigation. It is important to understand the functions of letters of credit in order to fully understand the consequences the fraud exception has on this commercial device. A demand for payment made upon a standby credit usually indicates that something has gone wrong in the contract. Indeed, this is the nature of the standby letter of credit. In contrast to the commercial credit, nonperformance that triggers payment in a standby credit situation usually indicates some form of financial weakness by the applicant. For this reason, parties choose this security arrangement over another so that they may have the benefit of prompt payment before any litigation occurs. We recognize that, as a general rule, letters of credit cannot exist without independence from the underlying transaction. Thus, when courts begin 'delving into the underlying contract, they are impeding the swift completion of the credit transaction.' 'The certainty of payment is the most important aspect of a letter of credit transaction, and this certainty encourages hesitant parties to enter into transactions, by providing them with a secure source of credit'."

In *Southern Energy*, this Court went on to say that the parties to a letter-of-credit transaction "bargain for the advantages and disadvantages of credit" and "recognize its functions and negotiate its terms." The Court concluded that "to invoke the fraud exception [to payment of the letter of credit] would require an inquiry into the underlying contract" and that "'[f]raud claims should not become surrogates for breach of contract claims.'" The Court's analysis was based on the danger of "disrupting the important commercial functions of credit law."

After setting forth these principles, and in light of the Court's reluctance to disrupt "the important commercial functions" of the letter of credit, the Court held that it would not address the merits of a claim of fraud in a letter-of-credit transaction when the plaintiff has an adequate remedy at law and will not suffer irreparable harm upon payment of the letter of credit.

Applying the same analysis to the instant case, the Court concludes that Webb-Stiles has likewise failed to satisfy the elements necessary for injunctive relief.

If Transact were the plaintiff in the action underlying this appeal, the case would be essentially identical to *Southern Energy*. The Court's inquiry would then focus first on whether Transact had an adequate remedy at law in an Indian court. Although in this case it is a surety that is seeking the injunction, our analysis is the same. Webb-Stiles's only alleged loss is monetary. Because it has an adequate remedy at law, Webb-Stiles has not established that it is entitled to a preliminary injunction.

Webb-Stiles's duty to reimburse SouthTrust arises solely out of Webb-Stiles's position as surety for Transact. If Webb-Stiles must pay that obligation, it has the remedy against Transact that it accepted when it became Transact's surety. Webb-Stiles can sue Transact in an American court to recover any money it must pay on Transact's behalf.

Like the plaintiff in *Southern Energy*, Webb-Stiles has failed to show that it lacks an adequate remedy at law. Webb-Stiles can sue Transact for damages for any loss it suffers as a result of its obligation to reimburse SouthTrust. The trial court therefore exceeded its discretion by enjoining payment of the letter of credit.

The order of the trial court is reversed, and the case is remanded with instructions to dissolve the preliminary injunction.

[Reversed and remanded]

Questions

1. What are the requirements for stopping payment under a letter of credit?
2. Why is the court hesitant to grant an injunction to stop the payment under a letter of credit?
3. What would happen if the court upheld the injunction?

7. Parties

The parties to a letter of credit are (1) the issuer; (2) the customer who makes the arrangements with the issuer; and (3) the beneficiary, who will be the drawer of the drafts that will be drawn under the letter of credit. There may also be (4) an **advising bank**[6] if the local issuer of the letter of credit requests its **correspondent bank,** where the beneficiary is located, to notify or advise the beneficiary that the letter has been issued. **For Example,** a U.S. merchant may want to buy goods from a Spanish merchant. There may have been prior dealings

[6] See UCC § 5-107; *Sun Marine Terminals, Inc. v Artoc Bank and Trust, Ltd.*, 797 SW2d 7 (Tex 1990).

E-COMMERCE AND CYBERLAW

THE E-COMMERCE WALLET

Internet transactions have provided new ways to guarantee payments. For example, there is now "digital cash," which is a virtual currency on the Web. Customers and retailers each have the software that permits them to transfer the digital cash and have it accepted. The Internet currency is purchased using real currency or a credit card. The software program simply dictates, as do letters of credit, when that Internet currency can be released to the retailer by the consumer.

Some Web customers are also setting up "digital wallets," which is a way of paying Web retailers through one source. Customers simply refer retailers to their digital wallet, set up through software programs, and provide the authorization necessary for the retailer to use the credit card(s) set up in the digital wallet for ease of payment.

between the parties so that the seller is willing to take the buyer's commercial paper as payment or to take trade acceptances drawn on the buyer. If the foreign seller is not willing to do this, the U.S. buyer, as customer, may go to a bank, the issuer, and obtain a letter of credit naming the Spanish seller as beneficiary. The U.S. bank's correspondent or advising bank in Spain will notify the Spanish seller that this has been done. The Spanish seller will then draw drafts on the U.S. buyer. Under the letter of credit, the issuer is required to accept or pay these drafts.

8. Duration

A letter of credit continues for any length of time it specifies. Generally, a maximum money amount is stated in the letter, so that the letter is exhausted or used up when the issuer has accepted or paid drafts aggregating that maximum. A letter of credit may be used in installments as the beneficiary chooses. The issuer or the customer cannot revoke or modify a letter of credit without the consent of the beneficiary unless that right is expressly reserved in the letter.

9. Form

A letter of credit must be in writing and signed by the issuer. If the credit is issued by a bank and requires a documentary draft or a documentary demand for payment[7] or if the credit is issued by a nonbank and requires that the draft or demand for payment be accompanied by a document of title, the instrument is presumed to be a letter of credit (rather than a contract of guarantee). Otherwise, the instrument must conspicuously state that it is a letter of credit.

10. Duty of Issuer

The issuer is obligated to honor drafts drawn under the letter of credit if the conditions specified in the letter have been satisfied. The issuer takes the risk that the papers submitted are the ones required by the letter. If they are not, the issuer cannot obtain reimbursement for payment made in reliance on such documents. The issuer has no duty to verify that the papers are properly supported by facts or that the underlying transaction has been performed. It is immaterial that the goods sold by the seller in fact do not conform to the contract so long as the seller tenders the documents specified by the letter of credit. If the issuer dishonors a draft without justification, it is liable to its customer for breach of contract.[8]

11. Reimbursement of Issuer

When the issuer of a letter of credit makes proper payment of drafts drawn under the letter of credit, it may obtain reimbursement from its customer for such payment. No reimbursement can be obtained if

[7] A *documentary draft* or a *documentary demand for payment* is one for which honor is conditioned on the presentation of one or more documents. A document could be a document of title, security, invoice, certificate, notice of default, or other similar paper. UCC § 5-103(1)(b).

[8] *Amwest Sur. Ins. Co. v Concord Bank*, 248 F Supp 2d 867 (ED Mo 2003). In some cases, letters of credit are so poorly drafted that payment must be made despite evolving concerns by the parties. *Nissho Iwai Europe PLC v Korea First Bank*, 99 NY2d 115, 782 NE2d 55, 752 NYS2d 259, 49 UCC Rep Serv 2d 259 (NY 2002).

per. This will be the case ter the letter has expired or n amount exceeding that Reimbursement cannot be obtained if the payment is made without the proper presentation of required documents or if the payment is made in violation of a court injunction against payment.

guaranty undertakings have the common feature of a promise to answer for the debt or default of another. The terms are used interchangeably, but a guarantor of collection is ordinarily only secondarily liable, which means that the guarantor does not pay until the creditor has exhausted all avenues of recovery. If the guarantor has made an absolute guarantee, then its status is the same as that of a surety, which means that both are liable for the debt in the event the debtor defaults, regardless of what avenues of collection, if any, the creditor has pursued.

Surety and guaranty relationships are based on contract. Sureties have a number of rights to protect them. They are exoneration, subrogation, indemnity, and contribution. In addition to those rights, sureties also have certain defenses. They include ordinary contract defenses as well as some defenses peculiar to the suretyship relationship, such as release of collateral, change in loan terms, substitution of debtor, and fraud by the creditor.

A letter of credit is an agreement that the issuer of the letter will pay drafts drawn on the issuer by the beneficiary of the letter. The issuer of the letter of credit is usually a bank. There are three contracts involved in letter-of-credit transactions: (1) the contract between the issuer and the customer of the issuer, (2) the letter of credit itself, and (3) the underlying agreement between the beneficiary and the customer of the issuer of the letter of credit.

The parties to a letter of credit are the issuer, the customer who makes the arrangement with the issuer, and the beneficiary who will be the drawer of the drafts to be drawn under the letter of credit. The letter of credit continues for any time it specifies. The letter of credit must be in writing and signed by the issuer. Consideration is not required to establish or modify a letter of credit. If the conditions in the letter of credit have been complied with, the issuer is obligated to honor drafts drawn under the letter of credit.

Questions and Case Problems

1. First Interstate Bank issued a letter of credit in favor of Comdata Network. Comdata is engaged in money transfer services. It provides money to truckers on the road by way of cash advances through form checks written by truckers. When Comdata enters into a business relationship with a trucking company, it requires a letter of credit. This requirement is to secure advances made on behalf of the trucking company. One of the trucking companies defrauded the bank that issued the letter of credit. Comdata demanded that the bank make payment to it under the letter of credit for cash advances that the trucking company had not repaid. The bank, alleging fraud by the trucking company, refused. Comdata filed suit. Can Comdata force payment? [*Comdata Network, Inc. v First Interstate Bank of Fort Dodge*, 497 NW2d 807 (Iowa App)]
2. Kiernan Construction Co. entered into a contract with Jackson to build a house for Jackson. Century Surety Co. executed a bond to protect Jackson from loss if Kiernan failed to construct the house or pay labor and materials bills. Kiernan failed to build the house, and Jackson sued Century Surety, which claims that Jackson must first sue Kiernan. Is it correct?
3. On August 1, 1987, Dori Leeds signed a "guarantee of credit" with Sun Control Systems, which guaranteed "the prompt payment, when due, of every claim of [Sun Control Systems] against [Dori Leeds dba 'Blind Ambitions']." At the time she signed the guarantee of credit, Blind Ambitions was in the business of installing window treatments and installed only Faber brand blinds, which were purchased from Sun Control Systems. In 1991, Sun Control Systems sold and assigned all of its assets to Faber. Shortly thereafter, Dori assigned her interest in Blind Ambitions to David and Judith Leeds, who continued to do business as Blind Ambitions. In 1994 and 1995, Blind Ambitions made credit purchases from Faber and did not pay under the terms of those contracts. Faber brought suit against Dori Leeds as the guarantor of credit for Blind Ambitions. Dori refused to pay on the grounds that she was acting as a personal guarantor for her business, not for Blind Ambitions. Is she correct? [*Faber Industries, Ltd. v Dori Leeds Witek*, 483 SE2d 443 (NC App)]
4. Fern Schimke's husband, Norbert, was obligated on two promissory notes in favor of Union National Bank. Some time prior to his death, Union National Bank prepared a guarantee contract that was given to Norbert for his wife to sign. She signed the guarantee at the request of her husband without any discussion with him about the provisions of the document she was signing.

On Norbert's death, the bank brought suit against Fern on the basis of the guarantee. Fern argued that because there was no consideration for the guarantee, she could not be liable. Is Fern correct? Must there be consideration for a guarantor to be responsible for payment? [*Union Nat'l Bank v Fern Schimke*, 210 NW2d 176 (ND)]

5. In May 1989, Alma Equities Corp., owned by its sole shareholder and president, Lewis Futterman, purchased a hotel and restaurant in Vail, Colorado, from Alien for $3,900,000. Alma paid $600,000 in cash to Alien, and Alien provided a purchase money loan to Alma for the remaining amount of the sale price, with the loan secured by a deed of trust on the hotel and restaurant. The hotel and restaurant did not do well, and Futterman negotiated a friendly foreclosure on the property in 1991, whereby Alma would continue to operate the hotel and restaurant on a lease basis, with Futterman providing a personal guarantee for the lease. Alma failed to make the lease payments for the months of November and December 1991 and, following an unlawful detainer action filed by Alien for possession of the hotel and restaurant, was forced into bankruptcy. Alien turned to Futterman for satisfaction on the lease payments. Futterman said he should not have been forced to pay because Alien's unlawful detainer forced Alma into bankruptcy. Was Futterman correct? Did he have a defense? [*Alien, Inc. v Futterman*, 924 P2d 1063 (Colo)]
6. Eberstadt owed Terence $500 and gave his note for that amount to Terence. At the same time, an agreement signed by Reid and given to Terence was as follows: "I agree to be surety for the payment of Eberstadt's note for $500." On maturity of the note, Eberstadt paid $200 on account and gave a new note for $300 due in three months. Reid was not informed of this transaction. The new note was not paid at maturity. Terence sued Reid. Does Reid have any defense?
7. Gilbert signed a guarantee for the benefit of his son with Cobb Exchange Bank. The guarantee included all extensions and renewals of the son's obligation. Subsequently, a renewal of the note added an additional $600 to the original obligation. On the son's default, Cobb Bank brought suit on the guarantee. Who should win? Why? [*Gilbert v Cobb Exchange Bank*, 231 SE2d 508 (Ga App)]
8. In June 1995, Southern Energy and Gesellschaft Fur Bauen Und Wohnen Hannover (GBH) entered into a construction contract for the second of two housing projects known as "socialized housing" to be built in Hannover, Germany. The socialized housing contract called for a bank guarantee issued by a European bank as security for Southern Energy's performance of the contract. GBH wired to Southern Energy 555,117 deutsche marks, representing the first 30 percent due on the contract, less the 15 percent value-added tax. Deutsche Bank issued the performance guarantee to GBH on the condition that the guarantee would be secured by a standby letter of credit. To facilitate the performance guarantee in favor of GBH, AmSouth issued a letter of credit to Deutsche Bank for an amount not to exceed 1,276,770 deutsche marks relating to Southern Energy's performance under the socialized housing contract. The letter of credit served as Deutsche Bank's security for issuing the performance guarantee.

   In January 1996, Southern Energy informed GBH that it would be unable to perform the contract at the agreed price without suffering a substantial financial loss. In February 1996, GBH responded by letter, stating that it would hold Southern Energy in default if Southern Energy failed to complete the project at the agreed time. GBH extended the deadline for performance from March 1, 1996, to March 15, 1996. GBH began rebidding the socialized housing project to other contractors. Southern Energy submitted another quote on the project, but GBH rejected its offer and awarded the contract to another builder. Meanwhile, the date of performance had passed on the initial contract. In June 1996, GBH requested that the advanced installment money on the contract, DM 555,117.39, be refunded. Southern Energy complied and transferred the money to GBH's account. Southern Energy asserted that because all of GBH's advanced monies had been returned, GBH no longer had any basis in fact to demand payment on the bank guarantee, and that Deutsche Bank had no legitimate basis to demand payment on the letter of credit. GBH, quoting the terms of the letter of credit itself, decided to "exercise its rights under the performance guarantee" by asserting its right to damages. The next day, Deutsche Bank presented a draft for payment. After AmSouth informed Southern Energy that it would honor the draft but before payment had been made, the Jefferson County Circuit Court granted Southern Energy's request for a temporary restraining order but later reversed itself. Southern Energy appealed. Should the temporary restraining order be reversed? Can a court halt the payment on a letter of credit? [*Southern Energy Homes, Inc. v AmSouth Bank of Alabama*, 709 So 2d 1180 (Ala)]
9. Ribaldgo Argo Consultores entered into a contract with R. M. Wade & Co. for the purchase of irrigation equipment. Ribaldgo obtained a letter of credit from Banco General, a bank with its principal place of business in Quito, Ecuador. The letter of credit required that Wade submit certain documents to obtain payment. The documents were submitted through Citibank as correspondent bank for Banco General. However, the documents were incomplete, and Citibank demanded additional information as required under the letter of credit. By the time Wade got the documents to Citibank, more than 15 days had expired, and the letter of credit required that Wade submit all documentation within

15 days of shipping the goods to obtain payment. Citibank refused to authorize the payment. Wade filed suit. Must Citibank pay? Why or why not? [*Banco General Runinahui, S.A. v Citibank International*, 97 F3d 480 (11th Cir)]

10. Hugill agreed to deliver shingles to W. I. Carpenter Lumber Co. and furnished a surety bond to secure the faithful performance of the contract on his part. After a breach of the contract by Hugill, the lumber company brought an action to recover its loss from the surety, Fidelity & Deposit Co. of Maryland. The surety denied liability on the grounds that there was concealment of (a) the price to be paid for the shingles and (b) the fact that a material advance had been made to the contractor equal to the amount of the profit that he would make by performing the contract. Decide. [*W. I. Carpenter Lumber Co. v Hugill*, 270 P 94 (Wash)]
11. Donaldson sold plumbing supplies. The St. Paul-Mercury Indemnity Co., as surety for him, executed and delivered a bond to the state of California for the payment of all sales taxes. Donaldson failed to pay, and the surety paid the taxes that he owed and then sued him for the taxes. What was the result? [*St. Paul-Mercury Indemnity Co. v Donaldson*, 83 SE2d 159 (SC)]
12. Paul owed Charles a $1,000 debt due September 1. On August 15, George, for consideration, orally promised Charles to pay the debt if Paul did not. On September 1, Paul did not pay, so Charles demanded $1,000 from George. Is George liable? Why or why not?
13. First National Bank hired Longdon as a secretary and obtained a surety bond from Belton covering the bank against losses up to $100,000 resulting from Longdon's improper conduct in the performance of his duties. Both Longdon and the bank signed the application for the bond. After one year of service, Longdon was promoted to teller, and the original bond remained in effect. Shortly after Longdon's promotion, examination showed that Longdon had taken advantage of his new position and stolen $50,000. He was arrested and charged with embezzlement. Longdon had only $5,000 in assets at the time of his arrest. (a) If the bank demands a payment of $50,000 from Belton, what defense, if any, might Belton raise to deny any obligation to the bank? (b) If Belton fully reimburses the bank for its loss, under what theory or theories, if any, may Belton attempt to recover from Longdon?
14. Jack Smith was required by his bank to obtain two sureties for his line of credit of $100,000. Ellen Weiss has agreed to act as a surety for $50,000, and Allen Fox has agreed to act as a surety for $75,000. Smith has used the full $100,000 in the line of credit and is now in bankruptcy. What is the maximum liability of Weiss and Fox if the bank chooses to collect from them for Smith's default? How should the $100,000 be allocated between Weiss and Fox?
15. Industrial Mechanical had a contract with Free Flow Cooling, Ltd., a British company. Free Flow owed Industrial $171,974.44 for work Industrial had performed on a construction project in Texas. Free Flow did not pay Industrial, and Industrial filed suit against Siemens Energy & Automation as a guarantor or surety on the debt. Industrial alleges that Siemens is a surety based on a fax it received from Siemens on January 27, 1994. The fax is handwritten and states: "We have received preliminary notices and we like [*sic*] to point out that the contract we have signed does not allow for such action to recourse [*sic*] with the customer. Please advise all subcontractors and suppliers that the only recourse that they will have is against Siemens." The fax was signed "kind regards" by Arnold Schultz, Siemens's senior project manager for the Texas construction project. Nowhere in the fax did Siemens guarantee the debt of any specified entity or state that Siemens was agreeing to indemnify anyone or pay the obligations on behalf of anyone else. The fax failed to identify the principal debtor whom Siemens purportedly agreed to indemnify and failed to state that Siemens agreed to answer for that entity's debt. Can Industrial collect the amount of Free Flow's debt from Siemens? Why or why not? [*Industrial Mechanical, Inc. v Siemens Energy & Automation, Inc.*, 495 SE2d 103 (Ga App)]

CPA Questions

1. Marbury Surety, Inc., agreed to act as a guarantor of collection of Madison's trade accounts for one year beginning on April 30, 1980, and was compensated for same. Madison's trade debtors are in default in payment of $3,853 as of May 1, 1981. As a result,
   a. Marbury is liable to Madison without any action on Madison's part to collect the amounts due.
   b. Madison can enforce the guarantee even if it is not in writing because Marbury is a del credere agent.
   c. The relationship between the parties must be filed in the appropriate county office because it is a continuing security transaction.
   d. Marbury is liable for those debts for which a judgment is obtained and returned unsatisfied.
2. Queen paid Pax and Co. to become the surety on a loan that Queen obtained from Squire. The loan is due, and Pax wishes to compel Queen to pay Squire. Pax has not made any payments to Squire in its capacity as Queen's

surety. Pax will be most successful if it exercises its right to

a. Reimbursement (indemnification)
b. Contribution
c. Exoneration
d. Subrogation

3. Which of the following defenses by a surety will be effective to avoid liability?

a. Lack of consideration to support the surety undertaking
b. Insolvency in the bankruptcy sense of the debtor
c. Incompetency of the debtor to make the contract in question
d. Fraudulent statements by the principal debtor that induced the surety to assume the obligation and that were unknown to the creditor

4. For each of the numbered words or phrases, select the one best phrase from the list a through j. Each response may be used only once.

(1) Indemnity contract
(2) Suretyship contract
(3) Surety
(4) Third-party beneficiary
(5) Co-surety
(6) Statute of Frauds
(7) Right of contribution
(8) Reimbursement
(9) Subrogation
(10) Exoneration

a. Relationship whereby one person agrees to answer for the debt or default of another
b. Requires certain contracts to be in writing to be enforceable
c. Jointly and severally liable to creditor
d. Promises to pay debt on default of principal debtor
e. One party promises to reimburse debtor for payment of debt or loss if it arises
f. Receives intended benefits of a contract
g. Right of surety to require the debtor to pay before surety pays
h. Upon payment of more than his/her proportionate share, each co-surety may compel other co-sureties to pay their shares
i. Upon payment of debt, surety may recover payment from debtor
j. Upon payment, surety obtains same rights against debtor that creditor had

CONSUMER PROTECTION

CHAPTER (33)

A. General Principles

1. Expansion of Consumer Protection
2. Who Is a Consumer?
3. Who Is Liable under Consumer Protection Statutes?
4. When Is There Liability under Consumer Protection Statutes?
5. What Remedies Do Consumers Have?
6. What Are the Civil and Criminal Penalties under Consumer Protection Statutes?

B. Areas of Consumer Protection

7. Advertising
8. Labeling
9. Selling Methods
10. The Consumer Contract
11. Credit Disclosures
12. Credit Cards
13. Payments
14. Preservation of Consumer Defenses
15. Product Safety
16. Credit, Collection, and Billing Methods
17. Protection of Credit Standing and Reputation
18. Other Consumer Protections

LEARNING OBJECTIVES

After studying this chapter, you should be able to

LO.1 Discuss the purpose of consumer protection statutes

LO.2 Explain the areas of concern and regulation in consumer protection

LO.3 List the rights and protections that are available for consumer debtors under federal law

LO.4 Describe the role of the Federal Trade Commission in protecting consumer rights

LO.5 Give a description of the protections for consumers under the Truth-in-Lending laws, the Fair Credit Reporting Act, and the Fair Debt Collections Practices Act.

LO.6 Explain the remedies available for consumers under protection laws

The consumer protection movement, which began in the 1960s, continues to expand with rights for consumers in everything from ads to credit collection. These statutory protections exist at both the state and federal level.

A. General Principles

Consumer protection began with the goal of protecting persons of limited means and limited knowledge. One writer described consumer protection statutes as laws that protect "the little guy."[1] Over the past 20 years, however, that protection has expanded considerably in both who is protected and the types of activities that are regulated or provide consumers with statutory remedies.

1. Expansion of Consumer Protection

Some statutes are worded so that consumer protections apply only to natural persons. Some statutes are interpreted to apply only to consumer transactions, not to commercial transactions. However, many consumer protection statutes, once limited to individuals, now include partnerships, corporations, banks, or government entities that use goods or services as consumers. The statutes thus go beyond providing protection only for the unsophisticated and uneducated.[2] **For Example,** in defining **consumer,** courts have held that a collector paying nearly $100,000 for jade art objects, a glass manufacturer purchasing 3 million gallons of diesel oil fuel, and the city of Boston purchasing insurance are all consumers for purposes of statutory protections. Some states, such as Arizona, Arkansas, Delaware, Illinois, Iowa, Missouri, and New Jersey, even have two separate statutes, one for the protection of individual consumers and another for the protection of businesses. In addition, the protected consumer may be a firm of attorneys.[3]

Today, all 50 states and the District of Columbia have some version of what are called "Little FTC Acts" (the Federal Trade Commission [FTC] discussed later in the chapter is the federal consumer protection statute that prohibits unfair or deceptive practices) or "unfair or deceptive acts or practices" ("UDAP") statutes. Although there are 51 versions of consumer protection statutes, they have several common threads. First, consumer protection statutes provide faster remedies for consumers. Statutory

[1] Olha N. M. Rybakoff, "An Overview of Consumer Protection and Fair Trade Regulation in Delaware," 8 *Delaware Law Review* 63 (2005). This article provides a good history and summary of consumer protection laws.

[2] *Boubelik v Liberty State Bank*, 527 NW2d 589 (Minn App 1995).

[3] *Catallo Associates, Inc. v MacDonald & Goren*, 465 NW2d 28 (Mich App 1990). Statutes that broaden the protected group to protect buyers of goods and services are often called *deceptive trade practices statutes* instead of being referred to by the earlier term, *consumer protection statutes*.

remedies under consumer protection statutes often mean that consumers need not establish that a tort has been committed or establish actual damage levels because the statute provides for both the elements for recovery and perhaps even a formula for recovery of damages. Second, the harms addressed by consumer statutes tend to affect the public generally and involve more than just one contract or even one seller. **For Example,** one area of consumer protection provides consumers control over both the release and content of their credit report information. The use of credit information, the granting of credit, and the use of credit to make purchases all have a profound impact on buyers, sellers, and national, state, and local economies. These protections provide a statutory formula for consumer damages when credit information is misused or is incorrect. Credit information on consumers is regulated because many consumers were affected by less-than-accurate information and unauthorized disclosures of their private credit information.

2. Who Is a Consumer?

A consumer claiming a violation of the consumer protection statute has the burden of proving that the statutory definition of consumer has been satisfied. The business accused of unfair or deceptive trade practices then has the burden of showing that the statute does *not* apply, as well as establishing exceptions and exemptions. **For Example,** some consumer protection statutes do not apply when a buyer is purchasing goods for resale.

3. Who Is Liable under Consumer Protection Statutes?

Those who are liable for violations of consumer protection situations are persons or enterprises that regularly enter into the type of transaction in which the injured consumer was involved. **For Example,** the merchant seller, the finance company, the bank, the leasing company, the home contractor, and any others who regularly enter into transactions with consumers are subject to the statutes. Some consumer protection statutes apply only to specific types of merchants and service providers such as auto repair and sale statutes, funeral home disclosure statutes and regulations, and swimming pool contractors.

CROWE V TULL, 126 P3D 196 (COLO 2006)

THE CLIENT WHO WAS A WRECK BECAUSE OF HIS ACCIDENT LAWYERS

FACTS: Azar & Associates is a law firm specializing in personal injury lawsuits. In television advertisements that air throughout Colorado, the Azar firm represents itself as a firm that can recover money for its clients that other attorneys cannot. The commercials claim that the Azar firm will always "obtain as much as we can, as fast as we can" for its clients. One of the firm's commercials employs the slogan "In a wreck, get a check" while another portrays Franklin D. Azar, the President of the Azar firm, as the "strong arm" who muscles insurance adjusters into paying up.

Richard E. Crowe (petitioner) claims that he saw the Azar firm's television commercials before and after he was injured in an accident in Colorado Springs. He suffered numerous physical injuries, including mild traumatic brain injury with speech impairment, and his vehicle sustained heavy damages. According to the police report, a seventeen year old driving a Dodge Ram truck caused the accident when he ran a stop sign and collided with Crowe's two-door Honda with an estimated impact speed of 45 mph. The seventeen year old was charged with a traffic offense for failing to obey the stop sign.

Crowe retained Marc B. Tull and Franklin D. Azar (respondents), to represent him in his personal injury claim. Crowe was offered $4,000 by the truck driver's insurer to settle the claim and Tull advised him to accept the offer. Crowe relied on Tull's advice and accepted the $4,000 settlement offer.

Crowe later filed suit against Tull and Azar, claiming that the settlement was far below the real value of his claim given that he had already accumulated over $17,000 in medical and rehabilitation costs and lost over $7,000 in wages at the time Tull advised him to settle the case for $4,000. Crowe based his suit on professional negligence (legal malpractice), violation of the Colorado Consumer Protection Act (CCPA), and breach of fiduciary obligation. Crowe's CCPA and breach of fiduciary obligation claims were dismissed by the trial court, which found that those two claims duplicated Crowe's legal malpractice claim. The court stated that the "actual practice of law" was not a commercial activity regulated by the CCPA and that the focus of Crowe's claims was the allegation of poor legal work. The court also reasoned that while the Azar firm's commercials may have lured Crowe to retain them, the commercials did not cause Crowe's alleged financial injuries.

Crowe appealed to the Colorado Supreme Court.

Judicial Opinion

MULLARKEY, Chief Justice.... The CCPA was enacted to provide "prompt, economical, and readily available remedies against consumer fraud." This court has taken "[a]n expansive approach... in interpreting the CCPA by reading and considering the CCPA in its entirety and interpreting the meaning of any one section by considering the overall legislative purpose."

These purposes must be applied to an ever-evolving commercial marketplace. The change has been especially dramatic for attorney advertising which was once strictly forbidden by ethical codes. [A]ttorney advertising has become ubiquitous. It appears in print media including telephone directories, newspapers, and billboards. In addition, the electronic media of radio, television, and the Internet are widely used by attorneys advertising their services to the public.

Deceptive marketing practices are not the sole domain of the bait-and-switch retailer or the purveyor of phony price comparisons. Since the CCPA was enacted, the role and reach of advertising has expanded and with it the potential for fraud. Our cases have consistently applied the CCPA to advertising and marketing practices that fit within its tenets based on the applicability of the Act to the actions alleged and without regard to the occupational status of the defendant.

The CCPA applies to any "person [who] engages in a deceptive trade practice... in the course of such person's business, vocation, or occupation." The statute applies to representations related to "services" throughout. There is no specific mention of professional services. Consequently, the plain language of the CCPA is silent on whether it applies to lawyers.

Furthermore, we have found that the omission of a specific mention of a particular industry in the CCPA was not determinative of whether that industry was covered by the Act. Since the CCPA was enacted in 1969, the legislature has had ample opportunity to exclude attorneys from liability under the Act, and the "omission of an exemption... strongly indicates that the General Assembly did not intend such an exemption."

The proper test for CCPA liability under our law is whether or not an attorney's conduct constitutes a deceptive trade practice with the requisite intent and meets the elements of public impact and causation.

Therefore, we conclude that attorneys may be found liable for CCPA violations under the best interpretation of the Act's plain language and consistent with its legislative intent. Attorney conduct that constitutes deceptive or unfair trade practices is not "in compliance" with the rules of professional conduct and is not exempted from CCPA liability. The consumer act's prohibitions against misleading statements and misrepresentations of the quality of services echo the disciplinary rules. There is no conflict between the CCPA and the professional rules in the types of conduct proscribed.

The CCPA's purpose is to remedy consumer fraud. An injured party who prevails under the CCPA may recover treble damages and attorney's fees. Awarding treble damages serves to deter fraudulent practices, to punish those who engage in those practices, and to encourage private enforcement of the statute. These remedies provide redress to private citizens affected by deceptive trade practices and promote the CCPA's function as a general deterrent, discouraging fraud on the public through the large potential damage exposure.

Contemporary advertising and marketing practices for attorney services more closely reflect the commercial marketplace as a whole and do not reflect the traditional image of the small-town practitioner hanging up a shingle and relying on personal contacts to create business. Marketing consultants and branding advisors are common tools in legal circles now. Many law firms resemble mid-size corporations rather than the image of small groups of like-minded professionals that still retains some hold on the popular consciousness. Lawyer advertising today potentially affects a large swath of the public via television, print media, radio, and the Internet. It is reasonable that special protections exist for those instances in which attorney marketing representations are falsely conveyed. Such protections are all the more necessary because the practice of law is complicated and information that allows the average consumer to discriminate among different legal service providers is limited. In many cases, the unsophisticated consumer will have only an attorney's or law firm's own representations of the quality of services with which to decide whether or not to retain that attorney or firm. Frequently, that decision must be made under the added pressure of a fast-running statute of limitations.

Attorney advertising is likely to have the most impact on the unsophisticated and the underprivileged segments of the public that are most in need of safeguards. Lawyers may target these communities because of their susceptibility to advertising. Due to the disparity in sophistication and expertise between an attorney and the typical consumer of legal services, "misstatements that might be overlooked or deemed unimportant in other advertising may be found quite inappropriate in legal advertising." This potential for consumer targeting demonstrates the need for the same protections against deceptive legal advertising as exist for other purveyors of goods and services. The CCPA was enacted for this very purpose, to protect vulnerable consumers and the consuming public as a whole. There is ample justification in the realities of modern legal practice and its effects on the public for application of the CCPA to the deceptive trade practices of attorneys and law firms. Application of the CCPA to attorneys is consistent with the Act's broad intent and fulfills its purpose of protecting the public from fraud. We hold, therefore, that the CCPA applies to protect the vulnerable consumer of legal services and the consumer public as a whole in the situation in which the purveyor of those services knowingly misrepresents the quality and likely benefit of those services.

[Reversed and remanded]

Questions

1. What misrepresentation does Crowe say the law firm made?
2. Why does the court feel that regulating attorney advertising is an important consumer protection?
3. Whom does the court feel is most likely to be misled by attorney advertising?

4. When Is There Liability under Consumer Protection Statutes?

Consumer protection laws typically list the types of conduct or failures to act properly that are prohibited as harmful to consumers. For example, the failure to disclose all of the charges related to a consumer loan or a credit purchase made by a consumer would be an omission that carries rights for the consumers and penalties for the business. *Deceptive advertising* is an act that is prohibited by consumer protection statutes that provide remedies for consumers who were deceived or misled by the ads. Proof of these acts or omissions that are listed and described in detail in the consumer protection statutes is often easier for consumers to prove than a common law case of fraud. Consumer protection statutes do not require proof of intent. An ad might not have seemed deceptive to the merchant selling computers when he reviewed the ad copy for the newspaper. However, a consumer without the merchant's sophistication could be misled. **For Example,** suppose that a consumer sees the ad for a 19-inch flat-screen computer monitor for $158 after rebate that reads, "Compare this price with any 19-inch flat-screen monitor, and you will see we cannot be matched." The average consumer might not understand that speakers are not included with such monitors. The computer store, on the other hand, might have assumed that everyone understands that flat-screen monitors with speakers are in a different price category. Adding "no speakers" or "speakers not included" would have allowed the consumer the information needed to shop and compare.

Consumers enjoy a great deal of protection when there are omissions or misleading information is given, but consumer protection does not protect consumers from their own negligence. If a consumer signs a contract without reading or understanding what it means, she is bound. Moreover, when the contract signed by the consumer clearly states one thing, the consumer cannot introduce evidence about statements the merchant made when the contract that was signed is clear. Consumers must exercise reasonable care and cannot blindly trust consumer protection law to rescue them from their own blunders.

5. What Remedies Do Consumers Have?

Although consumers have the theoretical right to bring suit for defenses to contracts or enforcement when the other party does not perform, the right to prove fraud, misrepresentation, duress, or breach is often of little practical value to consumers because both the costs of litigation and the burden of proof are high. The amount that the consumer has lost may be too small to be worth pursuing when compared with the cost of litigation. Consumer protection legislation provides special remedies for consumers so that pursuing their rights in court is cost beneficial. For example, some federal statutes permit debtors to bring class action suits, and their recovery is a statutory percentage of the net worth of the company that has violated their rights.

In addition, consumer statutes often provide initial or alternative means for consumers to enforce their rights. Consumer statutes provide procedural steps for consumers to use to try to resolve their problem and to document what has happened in their contract or relationship with a business. **For Example,** some statutes require consumers to give the business involved written notice of the consumer's complaint. Having this notice then provides the business an opportunity to examine the consumer's complaint or concerns and possibly work out a solution.[4]

In addition to procedural remedies other than litigation, consumer protection statutes provide other ways for consumers to seek their remedies, sometimes with the help of others who are more experienced in resolving consumer protection statutory violations.

(a) Government Agency Action

At both the federal and state levels, administrative agencies that are responsible for the enforcement of laws and regulations also have the power to take steps to obtain relief for consumers. For example, the Federal Trade Commission (FTC) can file a complaint against a company for false advertising. In settling the complaint with the company that advertised, the FTC could require the company to refund to the consumers involved the money they spent on the product based on the ad claims.

(b) Action by Attorney General

A number of states allow their state attorneys general to bring actions on behalf of consumers who are victims of fraud or other unfair conduct. In these actions, the attorney general can request that consumers' contracts be canceled and that they be given restitution of whatever they paid. These suits by attorneys general are not criminal actions; they are civil suits in which the standard of proof is a preponderance of the evidence, not proof beyond a reasonable doubt. For example, the litigation brought by state attorneys general for alleged deception by tobacco companies on the health harms of using tobacco resulted in settlements by those companies. The funds were used to compensate the states for health care costs for individuals with tobacco-related illnesses for whom the state was caring. The funds were also used to pay for educational programs and ads that caution young people not to smoke and warn them about the health hazards of using tobacco.

Many states also permit their attorneys general to bring actions for an injunction against violations of the consumer protection statute. These statutes commonly give the attorney general the authority to obtain a voluntary cease-and-desist consent decree (see Chapter 6) for improper practices before seeking an injunction from a court. The attorney general, like the agency, can impose a penalty for a violation.

(c) Action by Consumer

Consumer protection statutes can also provide that a consumer who has been harmed by a violation of the statutes may recover by his own suit against the business that acted improperly.[5] The consumer may either seek to recover a penalty provided for in the consumer protection statute or bring an action on behalf of consumers as a class. Consumer protection statutes are often designed to rely on private litigation as an aid to enforcement of the statutory provisions. The Consumer Product Safety Act of 1972 authorizes "any interested person" to bring a civil action to enforce a consumer product safety rule and certain orders of the Consumer Product Safety Commission.[6]

[4] *Fredericks v Rosenblatt*, 667 NE2d 287 (Mass App 1996).

[5] *Provident American Ins. Co. v Castaneda*, 914 SW2d 273 (Tex App 1996).

[6] 15 USC § 2051 *et seq.*

In other cases, however, the individual consumer cannot bring any action, and enforcement of the law is given exclusively to an administrative agency. However, consumer protection statutes are liberally construed to provide consumers with the maximum protection.[7]

(d) Replacement or Refund

Some state consumer protection statutes require that the consumer be made whole by the replacement of the good, the refund of the purchase price, or the repair of the item within a reasonable time.[8]

(e) Invalidation of Consumer's Contract

Other consumer protection statutes provide that when the contract made by a consumer violates the statute, the consumer's contract is void. In such a case, the seller cannot recover from the consumer buyer for any unpaid balance. Likewise, the seller cannot repossess the goods for nonpayment. The consumer keeps the goods without making any further payment.[9]

6. What Are the Civil and Criminal Penalties under Consumer Protection Statutes?

Only certain government agencies and attorneys general can seek criminal and civil penalties against those who violate consumer protection statutes. The agency or attorney general may use those penalties to provide compensation to consumers who have been victims of the violations. When consumers successfully bring individual or class action suits against those who violate their rights as consumers, they recover damages. Some consumer protection statutes authorize the recovery of **compensatory damages** to compensate the consumer for the loss. These types of statutes are designed to put the customer in as good a position as he would have been in had there not been a deception, breach, or violation of other requirements under the consumer protection statute. Other statutes authorize the recovery of **punitive damages,**[10] which are additional damages beyond compensatory damages and may be a percentage of the company's net worth. In the case of antitrust statutes that prohibit anticompetitive behavior, consumers could collect treble punitive damages for the violation. Although consumer protection statutes are interpreted in favor of the consumer, a consumer cannot claim both treble damages authorized by such a statute and punitive damages under the common law. Such double recovery would give the consumer duplicative remedies for the same wrong.

B. Areas of Consumer Protection

The following sections discuss important areas of consumer protection. Figure 33-1 provides an overview of these areas.

7. Advertising

Statutes commonly prohibit fraudulent advertising. Most advertising regulations are entrusted to an administrative agency, such as the FTC, which is authorized to issue orders to stop false or misleading advertising. Statutes prohibiting false advertising are liberally interpreted.

A store is liable for false advertising when it advertises a reduced price sale of a particular item that is out of stock when the sale begins. It is no defense that the presale demand was greater than usual.

(a) Deception

Under consumer protection statutes, *deception* rather than *fraud* is the significant element.[11] A breach of these statutes occurs even without proof that the wrongdoer intended to defraud or deceive anyone.

The deception statutes and regulations represent a shift in the law and public policy. These regulations are not laws based on fault; rather, they concern the problem of the buyer who is likely to be misled. The good faith of an advertiser or the absence of intent to deceive is immaterial. The purpose of false advertising regulation is to protect the *consumer* regardless of the advertiser's motives.

[7] *Equity Plus Consumer Finance & Mortgage Co. v Howes*, 861 P2d 214 (NM 1993).

[8] *Buford v General Motors Corp.*, 435 SE2d 782 (NC App 1993). Note that apart from these statutes, the buyer may have protection under a warranty to repair or replace. Likewise, a revocation of acceptance under the UCC would give the right to a refund of the purchase price.

[9] *Glouster Community Bank v Winchell*, 659 NE2d 330 (Ohio App 1995).

[10] *Maberry v Said*, 927 F Supp 1456 (D Kan 1996).

[11] *Rucker v Huffman*, 392 SE2d 419 (NC App 1990).

FIGURE 33-1 The Legal Environment of the Consumer

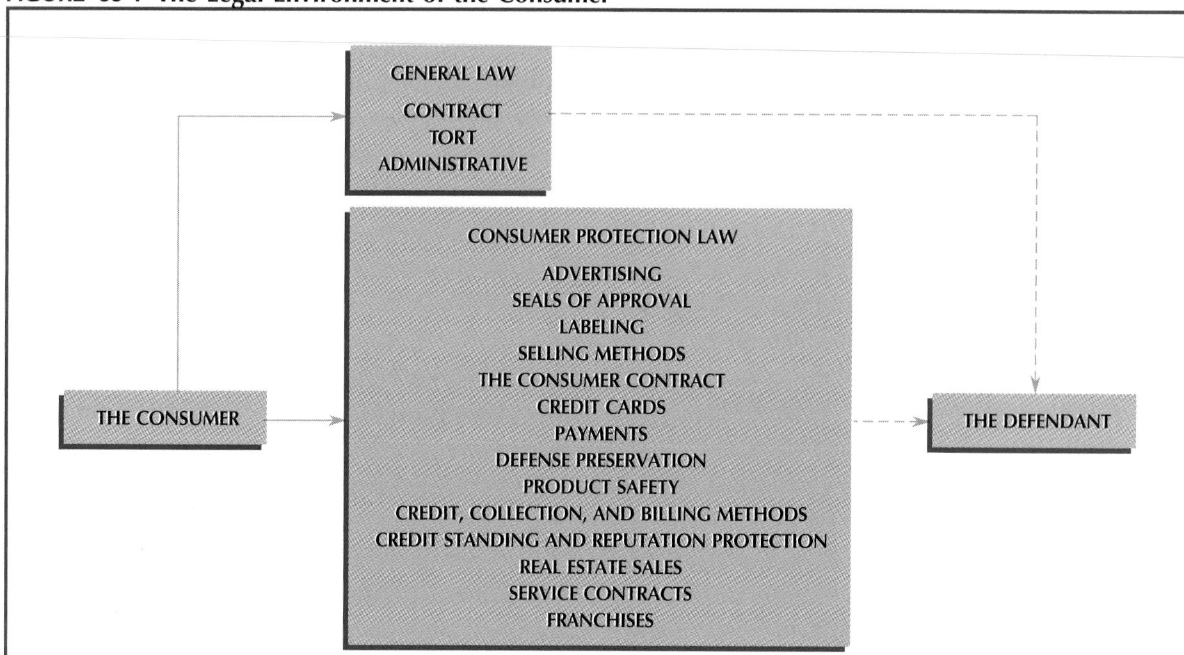

The FTC requires advertisers to maintain records of the data used as support for statements made in ads that deal with the safety, performance, efficacy, quality, or comparative price of an advertised product. The FTC can require the advertiser to produce these data and backup material. If it is in the interest of the consumer, the FTC can make this information public except to the extent that it contains trade secrets or privileged material.

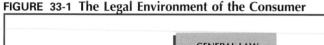

PELMAN V MCDONALD'S CORP., 237 F SUPP 2D 512 (SDNY 2003) PELMAN EX REL. PELMAN V MCDONALD'S CORP., 396 F3D 508 (CA 2 2005)

ATTACKING THE MAKER OF THE BIG MAC

Ashley Pelman, Roberta Pelman, Jazlen Bradley, and Israel Bradley (plaintiffs) brought suit against McDonald's Corporation and several of its franchisees (defendants) alleging that in making and selling their products they have engaged in deception and that this deception has caused the minors who have consumed McDonald's products to injure their health because they have become overweight and have developed diabetes, coronary heart disease, high blood pressure, elevated cholesterol intake, and/or other detrimental and adverse health effects.

The following is an excerpt from the district court decision that dismissed the complaint.

Judicial Opinion

SWEET, District Judge.... Questions of personal responsibility, common knowledge and public health are presented, and the role of society and the courts in addressing such issues.

Laws are created in those situations where individuals are somehow unable to protect themselves and where society needs to provide a buffer between the individual and some other entity—whether herself, another individual or a behemoth corporation that spans the globe.

This opinion is guided by the principle that legal consequences should not attach to the consumption of hamburgers and other fast food fare unless consumers are unaware of the dangers of eating such food. As Sir Francis

Bacon noted, "Nam et ipsa scientia potestas est," or knowledge is power. Following from this aphorism, one important principle in assigning legal responsibility is the common knowledge of consumers. If consumers know (or reasonably should know) the potential ill health effects of eating at McDonalds, they cannot blame McDonald's if they, nonetheless, choose to satiate their appetite with a surfeit of supersized McDonald's products. On the other hand, consumers cannot be expected to protect against a danger that was solely within McDonald's knowledge. Thus, one necessary element of any potentially viable claim must be that McDonald's products involve a danger that is not within the common knowledge of consumers.

McDonald's has also, rightfully, pointed out that this case, the first of its kind to progress far enough along to reach the stage of a dispositive motion, could spawn thousands of similar "McLawsuits" against restaurants. Even if limited to that ilk of fare dubbed "fast food," the potential for lawsuits is great: Americans now spend more than $110 billion on fast food each year, and on any given day in the United States, almost one in four adults visits a fast food restaurant. Eric Schlosser, *Fast Food Nation* 3 (2002). The potential for lawsuits is even greater given the numbers of persons who eat food prepared at other restaurants in addition to those serving fast food.

First, with regard to the Consumer Protection Act, there is no allegation of any specific advertisements or public statements arising from McDonald's of New York. Further, there is no allegation that McDonald's of New York had in its possession any particular knowledge that consumers did not have that would require it to promulgate information about the nutritional contents of the products. Therefore, the deceptive practices claim cannot stand against McDonald's of New York.

Counts I and II allege that McDonald's violated the New York Consumer Protection Act, N.Y. Gen. Bus. Law §§ 349 and 350, by (1) deceptively advertising their food as not unhealthful and failing to provide consumers with nutritional information (Count I) and (2) inducing minors to eat at McDonald's through deceptive marketing ploys (Count II). The standard for whether an act or practice is misleading is objective, requiring a showing that a reasonable consumer would have been misled by the defendant's conduct.

The plaintiffs only cite to two advertising campaigns ("McChicken Everyday!" and "Big N' Tasty Everyday") and to a statement on the McDonald's website that "McDonald's can be part of any balanced diet and lifestyle." These are specific examples of practices, act or advertisements and would survive a motion to dismiss based on lack of specificity. Whether they would survive a motion to dismiss on the substantive issue of whether such practices, act and advertisements are deceptive is less clear. The two campaigns encouraging daily forays to McDonald's and the statement regarding making McDonald's a part of a balanced diet, if read together, may be seen as contradictory—a balanced diet likely does not permit eating at McDonald's everyday. However, the advertisements encouraging persons to eat at McDonald's "everyday!" do not include any indication that doing so is part of a well-balanced diet, and the plaintiffs fail to cite any advertisement where McDonald's asserts that its products may be eaten for every meal of every day without any ill consequences. Merely encouraging consumers to eat its products "everyday" is mere puffery, at most, in the absence of a claim that to do so will result in a specific effect on health. As a result, the claims likely would not be actionable if alleged.

[P]laintiffs clearly have outlined the allegedly deceptive practice: the fact that McDonald's failed to post nutritional labeling on the products and at points of purchase. However, because this is a purportedly deceptive act based on an omission, it is not sufficient for the plaintiffs to point to the omission alone. They must also show why the omission was deceptive—a duty they have shunned.

The plaintiffs fail to allege that the information with regard to the nutritional content of McDonald's products was solely within McDonald's possession or that a consumer could not reasonably obtain such information. It cannot be assumed that the nutritional content of McDonald's products and their usage was solely within the possession of McDonald's.

The Complaint does not identify a single specific advertisement, promotion or statement directed at infant (minors) consumers, and Count II must be dismissed in the absence of such specificity.

They focus on two specific promotions geared toward minors: (1) a plastic beef steak figure named "Slugger," accompanied by a nutritional pamphlet encouraging children to eat two servings a day in the meat group to "make it easier to do things like climb higher and ride your bike farther," and (2) promotions of the "Mighty Kids Meal," a souped-up Happy Meal, that equate eating the larger-portioned meal with being more grown-up. With regard to the latter, plaintiffs still fail to identify specific exhortations or promises associated with the Mightier Kids Meals, and such bare allegations would also be dismissed for lack of specificity were they included in an amended complaint. In any case, if plaintiffs are only concerned about the appellation "Mightier Kids Meal," such name is seemingly mere puffery, rather than any claim that children who eat a

"Mightier Kids Meal" will become mightier. The former is sufficiently specific, were it included in the Complaint, to survive a motion to dismiss for failure to state a claim with sufficient specificity. Of course, plaintiffs would still have to set forth grounds to establish that the promotion was deceptive and that they suffered some injury as a result of that particular promotion.

For the foregoing reasons, the Complaint is dismissed in its entirety.

THE FOLLOWING IS FROM THE APPELLATE COURT DECISION

RAKOFF, District Judge (sitting on the appellate panel by designation)

Plaintiffs' appellate brief does, however, challenge the district court's dismissal of the claims under § 349 of the New York General Business Law, which makes unlawful "[d]eceptive acts or practices in the conduct of any business, trade or commerce or in the furnishing of any service in this state." Unlike a private action brought under § 350, a private action brought under § 349 does not require proof of actual reliance.

Although the district court recognized that § 349 does not require proof of reliance, the district court nonetheless dismissed the claims under § 349 because it concluded that "[p]laintiffs have failed, however, to draw an adequate causal connection between their consumption of McDonald's food and their alleged injuries." Thus, the district court found it fatal that the complaint did not answer such questions as:

What else did the plaintiffs eat? How much did they exercise? Is there a family history of the diseases which are alleged to have been caused by McDonald's products? Without this additional information, McDonald's does not have sufficient information to determine if its foods are the cause of plaintiffs' obesity, or if instead McDonald's foods are only a contributing factor.

This, however, is the sort of information that is appropriately the subject of discovery, rather than what is required to satisfy the limited pleading requirements.

Although the district court also dismissed the § 349 claims on the ground that plaintiffs' allegations of a generalized campaign to create a false impression were vague and conclusory, the cure for such deficiencies, in a claim not required to be plead with particularity, is a motion for a more definite statement under Rule 12(e), Fed.R.Civ.P., rather than dismissal. As for the district court's finding that McDonald's representations regarding its French fries and hash browns were objectively nonmisleading, the § 349 claims are not subject to dismissal on that basis given that the amended complaint alleges the deceptiveness of many other representations.

Accordingly, the district court's dismissal is VACATED, and the case is REMANDED.

Questions

1. What does the district court say is missing from the complaint?
2. What does the district court give as an example of puffery?
3. Why does the appellate court allow the portions of the suit that allege violations of New York consumer protection statutes to stand?

(b) Corrective Advertising

When an enterprise has made false and deceptive statements in advertising, the FTC may require new advertising to correct the former statements so that consumers are aware of the truth. This corrective advertising required by the FTC is also called *retractive advertising*.

SPORTS & ENTERTAINMENT LAW

NO DESSERT UNTIL YOU SIGN A WAIVER

Seattle's Queen Ann Hill area has a popular restaurant, the 5 Spot, which features a dessert called The Bulge, a calorie-laden sugar-coated fried banana with ice cream, macadamia nuts, whipped cream, and two kinds of syrup. Before customers are permitted to have this dessert, they must first sign a liability waiver that states in part, "I release the 5 Spot from all liability of

SPORTS & ENTERTAINMENT LAW

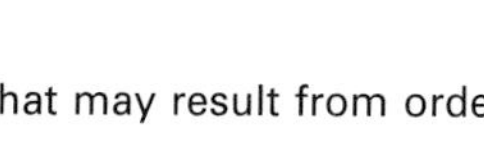

continued

any weight gain that may result from ordering and devouring this sinfully fattening treat."* Is this waiver a response to cases such as the McDonald's case? Do you think the waiver would be legally binding?

*Sandy Coleman, "Drafting Manager's Duties," *Boston Globe*, September 25, 2003, 2; Shirleen Holt, "Go Ahead, Splurge on the Bulge, But Any Resulting Fat Is on You," *Seattle Times*, September 6, 2003, A1.

E-COMMERCE AND CYBERLAW

UNDERCOVER BUZZ

Undercover marketing is all over the Internet. Sometimes called *buzz marketing* or *guerilla marketing,* this form of marketing on the Internet gets products and services noticed by Internet users because many of them are not aware that the companies are behind the informational type of approaches used. Sometimes also called *viral marketing,* this tactic uses a link, some news item, or an activity that makes the Internet consumers believe that they have come across a product or service as a function of serendipity from Internet surfing. They are not aware that the news, information, activity, or really cool Web page was created by the company in a stealth way (yet another name for this is *stealth marketing*) to grab their interest and sell a product or service. Lee Jeans used grainy video clips to attract attention on the Internet and from there built a campaign tied to a video game and secret codes found only on Lee products.

Buzz campaigns begin in chat rooms where experts in undercover marketing pretend to be chat room users who begin a conversation that leads to the company's product or service. They get the buzz going without identifying themselves as being associated with or working for the company. Personal blogs are also used for stealth marketing because the blogger does not always disclose affiliation with the company.

Internet users have objected to these practices, but others point out that companies have used "fake consumers" in coffee shops and as tourists to introduce products to consumers who believe they are simply talking with another patron or tourist about a camera or a car. While there is concern about the level of stealth marketing on the Internet, the ability to find out who and what is real can be difficult. State deceptive ad statutes may not cover these types of specific ad approaches, and the FTC faces the same investigative issues of finding out who is at the heart of the ads.

THINKING THINGS THROUGH

FRUITY SUIT

On May 16, 2003, Sari Smith filed a class action lawsuit in Cook County, Illinois, against J.M. Smucker Co. on behalf of "[a]ll purchasers in the United States of America of spreadable fruit products labeled "Simply 100% Fruit" manufactured, produced, and sold by J.M. Smucker

THINKING THINGS THROUGH

continued

Co. excluding its directors, officers and employees" for consumer fraud, deceptive business practices, unjust enrichment, and breach of warranty, alleging that Smucker's Simply 100% Fruit products do not contain 100% fruit. The premium jam's label indicates that, for example, its Strawberry jam also contains "fruit syrup, lemon juice concentrate, fruit pectin, red grape juice concentrate and natural flavors."

Is the label a form of deceptive advertising? If you were a Smuckers executive, what would you argue in the case on deceptive ads? [J.M. Smucker Co. v Rudge, 877 So 2d 820 (Fla App 2004)]

8. Labeling

Closely related to the regulation of advertising is the regulation of labeling and marking products. Various federal statutes are designed to give consumers accurate information about a product, whereas others require warnings about dangers of use or misuse. Consumer protection regulations prohibit labeling or marking products with such terms as *jumbo*, *giant*, and *full*, which tend to exaggerate and mislead. **For Example,** the health foods store Eating Well sold a number of foods with the label "Fat Free." This label was false, and Eating Well knew that the foods so labeled were ordinary foods not free of fat. Eating Well violated consumer protection statutes prohibiting false labeling. As for sales made with the false label, it also committed the tort of fraud and the crime of obtaining money by false pretenses.

9. Selling Methods

In addition to regulating ads, consumer protection statutes regulate the methods used to sell goods and services.

(a) Home-Solicited Sales

A sale of goods or services for $25 or more made to a buyer at home may be set aside within three business days. This right of rescission may be exercised merely because the buyer does not want to go through with the contract. There is no requirement of proving any misconduct of the seller or any defect in the goods or services.[12]

When the buyer has made an oral agreement to purchase and the seller comes to the buyer's home to work out the details, the transaction is not a home-solicited sale and cannot be avoided under the federal regulation.[13] A sale was also not home-solicited when the seller phoned the consumer at his or her home for permission to mail the consumer a promotional brochure, and thereafter the consumer went to the seller's place of business where the contract was made.[14]

(b) Referral Sales

The technique of giving the buyer a price reduction for referring customers to the seller is theoretically lawful. In effect, the seller is merely paying the buyer a commission for the promotion of other sales. In actual practice, however, this referral sales technique is often accompanied by fraud or exorbitant pricing, so consumer protection laws variously condemn referral selling. As a result, the referral system of selling has been condemned as unconscionable under the Uniforma Commercial Code (UCC) and is expressly prohibited by the UCC.

(c) Telemarketing Fraud

In recent years, high-pressure selling by telephone has produced a new kind of fraud that is estimated to rob U.S. citizens of some $40 billion a year. Following passage by Congress of a mandate on control of telemarketing, the Telephone Consumer Protection Act (TCPA), the FTC developed a series of rules on telemarketing restrictions.[15] The federal statute

[12] Federal Trade Commission Regulation, 16 CFR § 429:1.

[13] *Cooper v Crow*, 574 So 2d 438 (La App 1991).

[14] *United Consumers Club v Griffin*, 619 NE2d 489 (Ohio App 1993).

[15] 47 USCA § 227.

makes it unlawful for telemarketers to "make any call (other than a call made for emergency purposes or made with the prior express consent of the called party) using any automatic telephone dialing system or an artificial or prerecorded voice"; to "make any call to an emergency telephone line . . . the telephone line of any guest room or patient room of a hospital, health care facility, elderly home"; to "use any telephone facsimile machine, computer, or other device to send an unsolicited advertisement to a telephone facsimile machine"; or to make any calls "before 8 A.M. or after 9 P.M." There are additional state regulations on telemarketing, with some states requiring sellers who solicit orders by telephone to register with a particular government agency.[16]

In 2003, the FTC promulgated its rules for a National Do Not Call Registry.[17] Adding to its already extensive regulations on telemarketing, the FTC created a means whereby consumers could register to not be called as part of telephone solicitation campaigns by merchants and service providers.[18] As of the end of 2005, 100 million consumers had signed up for the Do Not Call Registry.

When a consumer registers with the do not call list, merchants and service providers cannot contact the consumer by telephone. Exceptions apply when the consumer has voluntarily given her telephone number to a company. Charitable organizations are also exempt from the rule. The constitutionality of the Do Not Call Registry was challenged in court but upheld.

10. The Consumer Contract

Consumer contracts are regulated in different ways.

(a) Form of Contract

Consumer protection laws commonly regulate the form of the contract, requiring that certain items be specifically listed, that payments under the contract be itemized, and that the allocation to such items as principal, interest, and insurance be indicated. Generally, certain portions of the contract or all of it must be printed in type of a certain size, and a copy must be furnished to the buyer. Such statutory requirements are more demanding than the statute of frauds section of the UCC. Often, the copy of the contract furnished to the consumer must be completely filled in. Back-page disclaimers are void if the front page of the contract does not call attention to the presence of such terms.

(b) Contracts Printed on Two Sides

To be sure that consumers see disclosures required by federal law, special provision is made when the terms of a transaction are printed on both the front and the back of a sheet or contract. In this case, (1) both sides of the sheet must carry the warning "NOTICE: see other side for important information," and (2) the page must be signed at the end of the second side. Conversely, the requirements of federal law are not satisfied if there is no warning of "see other side" and the parties sign the contract only on the face, or the first side, of the paper.

(c) Particular Sales and Leases

The Motor Vehicle Information and Cost Savings Act requires a dealer to disclose to the buyer various elements in the cost of an automobile. The act prohibits selling an automobile without informing the buyer that the odometer has been reset below the true mileage. A buyer who is caused actual loss by odometer fraud may recover from the seller three times the actual loss or $1,500, whichever amount is higher.[19] The federal statute is breached when the seller knows that the odometer has turned over at 100,000 miles but the seller states that the mileage is 20,073 miles instead of 120,073. The Consumer Leasing Act of 1976 requires that persons leasing automobiles and other durable goods make a full disclosure to consumers of the details of a transaction.[20]

Although the federal statute imposes liability only when the seller "knowingly" violates the statute, it is not necessary to prove actual knowledge. An experienced auto dealer cannot claim lack of knowledge that the odometer was false when that conclusion was reasonably apparent from the condition of the car.[21]

[16] *Distributel, Inc. v Alaska*, 933 P2d 1137 (Alaska 1997).

[17] 16 CFR § 310.8.

[18] The national list supplements the law in 28 states that already had some form of do-not-call registers. However, constitutional issues (see Chapter 5) limited those protections across state lines so that the national regulation was necessary.

[19] 15 USC § 1901 *et seq.*, as amended; recodified as 49 USC §§ 32701–32711.

[20] 15 USC § 1667.

[21] *Denmon v Nicks Auto Sales*, 537 So 2d 796 (La App 1989).

(d) Contract Terms

Consumer protection legislation does not ordinarily affect the right of the parties to make a contract on whatever terms they choose. It is customary, however, to prohibit the use of certain clauses that are harsh on the debtor or that have too great a potential for exploitive abuse by a creditor, such as the UCCC prohibition against creditors entering a judgment against a debtor without giving the debtor any chance to make a defense.[22]

The federal Warranty Disclosure Act of 1974 establishes disclosure standards for consumer goods warranties to help consumers understand them.[23]

The parties to a credit transaction may agree that payment can be made in installments but that if there is a default on any installment, the creditor may accelerate the due date or declare the entire balance due at once. Such acceleration of the debt can cause the debtor great hardship. Some state statutes limit or prohibit the use of **acceleration clauses.**

(e) Limitations on Credit

Various laws may limit the ability to borrow money or purchase on credit. Some states prohibit **open-end mortgages** that secure a specified debt as well as additional loans that may be made later. Federal laws and regulations impose disclosure requirements on home equity loans.

An FTC regulation makes requiring a consumer borrowing or buying on credit to give the lender or seller a security interest in all of the consumer's household goods as collateral an unfair trade practice.[24]

Consumer debt in the United States had grown to more than $2 trillion dollars as of the end of 2005. Credit is available even to those who have bad credit histories through what has been called the **subprime lending market.** This credit market makes loans to consumers who have bankruptcies, no credit history, or a poor credit history. A subprime lender is one who offers credit to a high-risk consumer, often loaning money to pay off other debts the consumer is facing as due. The subprime market tripled in size, to $330 billion between 1997 and 2003. In addition to higher risk, the characteristics of a subprime market loan are lower loan amounts, higher origination costs, brokers' fees, credit insurance fees, high interest rates, significant collateral pledges, large prepayment penalties so that the consumer debtor is locked into the high interest rate, faster repayment, and difficulty in determining all of the charges and fees from the documentation. The types of loans include title loans (when the loan is made in exchange for the title to the consumer's car or house, which will turn over to the lender upon default). Not all loans in the subprime market are unfair to consumers. Many of the terms of the loan are high to compensate the lender for the risk in loaning to a consumer with a poor credit history. However, part of the subprime lending market includes lenders who take advantage of less sophisticated consumers or even consumers who are just desperate for funds. These lenders use their superior bargaining positions to obtain credit terms that go well beyond compensating them for their risk. Sometimes called **predatory lending,** both states and the federal government have begun passing new statutes and regulations to cover predatory lending.[25] One of the issues in the regulation is defining what constitutes predatory lending that can be regulated and what may be ethical issues about lending practices to consumers in difficult financial situations.

(f) Unconscionability

To some extent, consumer protection has been provided under the UCC by those courts that hold that the "unconscionability" provision protects from "excessive" or "exorbitant" prices when goods are sold on credit.[26]

Some statutes are aimed at preventing price gouging on consumer goods or services for which the demand is abnormally greater than the supply. **For Example,** New York's statute provides: "During any abnormal disruption of the market for consumer goods and services vital and necessary for the health, safety, and welfare of consumers, resulting from stress of weather, convulsion of nature, failure

22 UCCC §§ 2.415, 3.407.

23 The act known as the *Magnuson Moss Act* is found at 15 USC § 2301.

24 16 CFR § 444.2(4)(1999).

25 NJ Stat Ann § 46:10B-22 (West 2006); 2003 Ark Acts 2598; Cal Fin Code §§ 4970-4979.7 (West 2006); Ga Code Ann § 7-6A-1-13 (2006); 2003 Ill Laws 93-561; 2003 NM Laws 436; 2001 NY Laws 11856; NC Gen Stat § 24-1.1e (2006); 2003 SC Acts 42; 2003 NC Sess Laws 24-10.2.

26 UCC § 2-302(1).

or shortage of electric power or other source of energy . . . no merchant shall sell or offer to sell any such consumer goods or services for an amount which represents an unconscionably excessive price." *Consumer goods and services* are defined as "those used, bought, or rendered primarily for personal, family, or household purposes." Such a statute protects, for example, purchasers of electric generators for home use during a hurricane-caused blackout. During 2006, with the rise in gas prices, many attorneys general conducted investigations into price gouging on gas prices at the pump.

11. Credit Disclosures

While general consumer statutes prohibit deception in ads and sales practices, specific federal laws require the disclosure of all interest charges, points, and fees for all types of loans and credit contracts. These laws require disclosure of an annual percentage rate (APR) so that the consumer can see just how much the transaction costs per year and can compare alternatives.[27] The Truth in Lending Act (TILA) provides the requirements for disclosures in credit contracts and consumer rights when full disclosure is not made. When a consumer sale or contract provides for payment in more than four installments, it is subject to the TILA. The application of the TILA is required even when there is no service or finance charge for the installment payments. There are additional obligations of disclosure under the Fair Credit and Charge Card Disclosure Act[28] and by the Home Equity Loan Consumer Protection Act.[29]

When consumer credit is advertised as repayable in more than four installments and no finance charge is expressly imposed, the advertisement must "clearly and conspicuously" state that "the cost of credit is included in the price" quoted for the goods and services.

If sellers advertise that they will sell or lease on credit, they cannot state merely the monthly installments that will be due. They must give the consumer additional information: (1) the total cash price, (2) the amount of the down payment required, (3) the

E-COMMERCE AND CYBERLAW

ID THEFT

The largest identity theft ring in the history of the United States was broken up in December 2002 when federal authorities arrested those responsible for stealing the credit identities of at least 30,000 people. The total amount obtained through the identity theft is believed to have been about $3 million. In one example, the identity thieves opened a line of credit in another's name, using another's good credit. When the line of credit was funded for $35,000, the thief wrote a check for $34,000.

Ford Motor Credit was a key player in the arrests when it noticed that it was being billed for credit reports it did not order. The thieves used access codes to obtain credit reports and then had the companies billed. Other companies are now checking their bills and notifying those whose reports were ordered so that they can check for possible fraudulent charges and uses of their credit ratings to obtain credit cards and lines of credit.

USA Today offers the following insights on what identity thieves do:

- Change the mailing address on credit cards so cardholders do not notice the lack of bills or the charges.
- Purchase cell phones in another's name so they can give creditors a phone number.
- Open bank accounts with a line of credit, and write checks on the accounts.

The Department of Justice has information on its Web site for avoiding identity theft at **http://www.usdoj.gov/**.

[27] Consumer Credit Protection Act (CCPA), 15 USC §§ 1605, 1606, 1636; Regulation Z adopted by the Federal Reserve, 12 CFR § 226.5.
[28] 15 USC § 1601, note, *et seq.*
[29] *Id.*

number, amounts, and due dates of payments, and (4) the annual percentage rate of the credit charges.[30]

12. Credit Cards

Credit cards permit cardholders to buy on credit. Credit cards and credit arrangements are so readily available that consumers tell of receiving credit cards when they apply in the name of their Labrador retrievers. Because of the extensive availability of credit cards and the ease with which they are issued, there are extensive federal regulations of credit card use and the rights of consumers with credit cards.[31]

(a) Unsolicited Credit Cards

Federal regulations prohibit the unsolicited distribution of credit cards to persons who have not applied for them. The practice of simply sending credit cards through the mail to consumers is now illegal. The problems with rising identity theft have made this protection especially important to consumers because identity thieves were able to intercept the mail and seize the unsolicited credit cards.

(b) Surcharge Prohibited

Under some statutes, a seller cannot add any charge to the purchase price because the buyer uses a credit card instead of paying with cash or a check.[32]

(c) Unauthorized Use

A cardholder is not liable for more than $50 for the unauthorized use of a credit card. To even recover the $50 amount, the credit card issuer must show that (1) the credit card was an accepted card,[33] (2) the issuer gave the holder adequate notice of possible liability in such a case, (3) the issuer furnished the holder with notification means in the event of loss or theft of the credit card, (4) the issuer provided a method by which the user of the card could be identified as the person authorized to use it,[34] and (5) unauthorized use of the card had occurred or might occur as a result of loss, theft, or some other event.

The burden of proof is on the card issuer to show that the use of the card was authorized or that the holder is liable for its unauthorized use.[35]

(d) Unauthorized Purpose Distinguished

Unauthorized use of a credit card occurs only when it is used without the permission or approval of the cardholder. In contrast, the holder may authorize another person to use the card but only for a particular purpose, such as to buy a certain item. If the person uses the card for other than the purpose specified by the holder, this is still an authorized use of the card even though it is for an unauthorized purpose.[36] In such a case, the cardholder is liable for all charges made on the card even though they were not intended by the cardholder when the card was loaned. The same rule is applied when an employer has cards issued to employees for making employment-related purchases but an employee uses the card for personal purposes.

(e) Late Payment Fee

The contract between a credit card issuer and a holder may require the holder to pay a late payment fee computed as the rate of interest allowed by the law of the state where the bank is located. The federal Banking Deregulation Act cancels out any state consumer protection law that prohibits such a charge on bank credit cards.[37]

13. Payments

Consumer legislation may provide that when a consumer makes a payment on an open charge account, the payment must be applied toward payment of the earliest charges. The result is that, should there be a default at a later date, any right of repossession of the creditor is limited to the later, unpaid items. This first-charged, first-payment-applied method outlaws contract provisions by which, on the default of the

[30] Regulation Z, § 1210; Consumer Leasing Act of 1976, 15 USC § 1667.

[31] Heidi Mandanis Schooner, "Consuming Debt: Structuring the Federal Response to Abuses in Consumer Credit," 18 *Loyola Consumer Law Review* 43 (2005).

[32] In contrast, the Truth in Lending Act Amendment of 1976, 15 USC § 1666f, permits a merchant to offer a discount to cash-paying customers but not to customers using a credit card.

[33] A credit card is accepted when the cardholder has requested and received or has signed, used, or authorized another to use the card for the purpose of obtaining money, property, labor, or services on credit.

[34] Regulation Z of the Board of Governors of the Federal Reserve, 12 CFR § 226.13(d), as amended, provides that the identification may be by signature, photograph, or fingerprint on the credit card or by electronic or mechanical confirmation.

[35] *Band v First Bankcard Center*, 644 So 2d 211 (La App 1994).

[36] *American Express Travel Related Services Co. v Web, Inc.*, 405 SE2d 652 (Ga 1991).

[37] *Stoorman v Greenwood Trust Co.*, 908 P2d 133 (Colo 1995).

buyer, sellers could repossess all purchases that had been made at any prior time. Such a provision is outlawed by the UCCC and probably would be found unconscionable under the UCC. **For Example,** over the years, Jilda purchased many household articles from the Montparnasse Department Store by using her charge account. When Jilda made a payment on her account, Montparnasse applied a fraction of it to each item Jilda had purchased so that no item was ever paid for in full. Montparnasse claimed that it could do this because a creditor can decide how to apply payments when a debtor does not make any specification. Under the ordinary contract law rule, Montparnasse is correct, but consumer protection statutes in many states require the creditor to apply a payment to the oldest debt so that it is paid off in full and only the most recent remain unpaid. This means that Montparnasse would have no claim on Jilda's earlier purchases even though Jilda had not paid in full for the more recent ones.

14. Preservation of Consumer Defenses

Consumer protection laws generally prohibit a consumer from waiving or giving up any defense provided by law. In the ordinary contract situation, when goods or services purchased or leased by a consumer are not proper or are defective, the consumer is not required to pay the seller or lessor or is required to pay only a reduced amount. With the modern expansion of credit transactions, sellers and lessors have used several techniques for getting paid without regard to whether the consumer had any complaint against them. To prevent this, the FTC has adopted a regulation requiring that in every sale or lease of goods or services to a consumer, the contract contain a clause giving the consumer the right to assert defenses. This notice can be found in the discussion of negotiable instruments and the rights of the parties in Chapter 29.

15. Product Safety

A variety of statutes and rules of law, some of which antedate the modern consumer protection era, protects the health and well-being of consumers. Most states have laws governing the manufacture of various products and establishing product safety standards. The federal Consumer Product Safety Act provides for research and setting uniform standards for products to reduce health hazards. This act also establishes civil and criminal penalties for the distribution of unsafe products, recognizes the right of an aggrieved person to recover damages and to obtain an injunction against the distribution of unsafe products, and creates a Consumer Product Safety Commission to administer the act.[38]

A consumer, as well as various nonconsumers, may hold a seller or manufacturer liable for damages when a product causes harm. Liability may be based on guarantees, warranties, negligence, fraud, or strict tort liability (see Chapters 9 and 24).

16. Credit, Collection, and Billing Methods

Various laws and regulations protect consumers from discriminatory and improper credit and collection practices.

CPA (a) Equal Credit Opportunity Act: Credit Discrimination

Under the Equal Credit Opportunity Act (ECOA), it is unlawful to discriminate against an applicant for credit on the basis of race, color, religion, national origin, gender, marital status, or age; because all or part of the applicant's income is obtained from a public assistance program; or because the applicant has in good faith exercised any right under the Consumer Credit Protection Act (CCPA). When a credit application is refused, the applicant must be furnished a written explanation. **For Example,** when Eloise applied for a loan from Tradesman Bank, she was told on the phone that the loan would not be made to her unless her husband, Robert, signed as cosigner. The bank violated antidiscrimination laws in two respects: (1) The bank was required to give Eloise a written explanation of why it would not make the loan to her and (2) it is unlawful to refuse to make a loan to a woman merely because she is married and her husband is not a cosigner.[39]

(b) Fair Credit Billing Act: Correction of Errors

When a consumer believes that a credit card issuer has made a billing error, the consumer should send

38 15 USC §§ 2051–2081.

39 Richard A. Oppel, Jr., and Patrick McGeehan, "Citigroup Revamps Lending Unit to Avoid Abusive Practices," *New York Times*, November 6, 2000, C1, C2.

the creditor a written statement and explanation of the error. The creditor or card issuer must investigate and make a prompt written reply to the consumer.[40]

(c) Improper Collection Methods

Unreasonable methods of debt collection are often expressly prohibited by statute or are held by courts to constitute an unreasonable invasion of privacy.[41] The Consumer Credit Protection Act (CCPA) prohibits the use of extortionate methods of loan collection. A creditor may be prohibited from informing a debtor's employer that the employee owes money.

A creditor is liable for unreasonably attempting to collect a bill that in fact has been paid. This liability can arise under general principles of tort law as well as under special consumer protection legislation.

(1) Fault of Agent or Employee. When improper collection methods are used, it is no defense to the creditor that the improper acts were performed by an agent, an employee, or any other person acting on behalf of the creditor. Under general principles of agency law, a creditor hiring an individual or an agency to collect a debt is liable to the debtor for damages for unlawful conduct by the collector. It is no defense that the creditor did not intend, or have any knowledge of, this conduct.

CPA ***(2) Fair Debt Collection Practices Act (FDCPA).*** The federal FDCPA prohibits improper practices in the collection of debts incurred primarily for personal, family, or household purpose.[42]

(i) Collection Letters. The act requires that the notice to a debtor state that the debtor has 30 days in which to dispute all or part of the debt.[43]

A debt collector who sends a form letter to debtors that uses the letterhead and the facsimile signature of a lawyer who is not actually representing the collector violates the FDCPA.[44] A letter from a collection agency to a consumer that gives the impression a lawsuit is about to be brought against the consumer when in fact it will not be brought is a violation of the FDCPA.[45]

A debt collection letter sent to the debtor's place of employment was a violation of the FDCPA when the words "final demand for payment" could be read through the envelope. The fact that it was likely that the debtor would be embarrassed by the delivery of such a letter to the employer's address affected the outcome of the case. In another case, a bank's threat to prosecute depositors if they did not return money that had been paid to them by mistake violated a state debt collection law. No criminal statute prohibited the depositors' conduct.

(ii) What Is Not a Defense. When a collection agency violates the FDCPA, it is liable to the debtor for damages. It is no defense that the debtor owed the money that the agency was seeking to collect. When a creditor uses improper collection methods, it is no defense that the improper acts were performed by an agent, employee, or any other person acting on behalf of the creditor.

(iii) Applicability of Fair Debt Collection Practices Act. The FDCPA applies not to original creditors but to third parties collecting for creditors. Lawyers who regularly engage in debt collection are also covered under the FDCPA.[46]

The FDCPA applies only to those who regularly engage in the business of collecting debts for others—primarily to collection agencies. The act does not apply when a bank attempts to collect debts owed to it by directly contacting the debtors.

(iv) Federal Preemption. In a conflict between collection practices under federal law and a state consumer protection statute, federal law preempts or displaces state law.[47]

(d) Consumer Leases

In some states, the lease of goods to a consumer is treated as a consumer credit sale and is given the same statutory protection as transactions in which

[40] Fair Credit Billing Act, 15 USC § 1601.

[41] Fair Debt Collection Practices Act, 15 USC § 1692 *et seq.*; Federal Trade Commission Regulation, 16 CFR pt. 237.

[42] *Bloom v I.C. System, Inc.*, 972 F2d 1067 (9th Cir 1992).

[43] *Avila v Rubin*, 84 F3d 222 (7th Cir 1996).

[44] *Taylor v Perrin, Landry, duLauney & Durand*, 103 F3d 1232 (5th Cir 1996).

[45] *Bentley v Great Lakes Collection Bureau*, 6 F3d 60 (2d Cir 1993).

[46] *Jenkins v Heintz*, 25 F3d 536 (7th Cir 1994), aff'd, 514 US 291 (1995).

[47] *Fischer v Unipac Service Corp.*, 519 NW2d 793 (Iowa 1994).

ETHICS & THE LAW

WIDOWED, BROKE, SICK, AND IN DEBT TO A HOSPITAL WITH NO CASH

Jeanette White was treated at Yale-New Haven Hospital for cancer. She died there in 1993 after almost 20 years of treatment. The hospital added interest of 10% per annum to the bill and the amount ultimately due was about $40,000. The hospital tried to collect the bill from her husband Quinton White, who was 77 and suffering from heart and kidney ailments.

Mr. White became a cause célèbre when the *Wall Street Journal* ran a top-fold B1 color-picture story on his plight. Yale-New Haven explained that while it was operating in the black, it had $52 million in bad debt and uncompensated care for 2002. The hospital itself does not charge interest, but when the debts are assigned to third parties, such as lawyers, for collection, they are permitted to charge interest.

Mr. White missed only 17 payments to the hospital since he began making payments for his wife's treatment in almost 20 years. However, the hospital was aggressive through its law firm in pursuing the Whites' assets whenever a payment was missed. The first suit resulted in a judgment for the hospital that was reduced to a lien on the White's house in 1982. If and when the house were sold, proceeds would go first to the mortgage company and then to the hospital. The Whites had offered to pay $25 per month on the bill, but the hospital declined and used the court proceedings. The judge ordered payments of $5 per week, which was tripled to $15 per week after Mrs. White died. Most of the 17 missed payments occurred during 2002 when Mr. White began experiencing his health problems. The hospital's law firm went back to court and received a judgment for Mr. White's bank account, a judgment that was halted when Mr. White established that all of the funds in the account were his Social Security payments.

When Mr. White's story was published, students at the free clinic at Yale Law School undertook representation of Mr. White. A plethora of stories about hospital bills, hospital collections, and excessive charges have followed along with class action suits challenging everything from hospital billing policies to collection practices.

What ethical issues arise for the hospitals on uncompensated care? What property does a judgment cover? Who has priority on the Whites' house? Why does a judgment last nearly 20 years?

Source: Lucette Lagnado, "Twenty Years and Still Paying," *Wall Street Journal*, March 13, 2003, B1, B2; "Dunned for Old Bills, Poor Find Some Hospitals Never Forget," *Wall Street Journal*, June 8, 2004, A1, A6; and "Anatomy of a Hospital Bill," *Wall Street Journal*, Sept. 21, 2004, B1, B4.

the consumer has the option to purchase at the end of the lease or becomes the owner after renting for a specified period of time.[48]

CPA 17. Protection of Credit Standing and Reputation

When a person purchases on credit or applies for a loan, a job, or an insurance policy, those who will extend these benefits often wish to know more about the applicant. Credit reporting agencies gather such information on borrowers, buyers, and applicants and sell the information to interested persons.

The Fair Credit Reporting Act (FCRA)[49] protects consumers from various abuses that may arise as this information is recorded and revealed. This statute governs credit reporting agencies, sometimes called *credit bureaus.*

The FCRA applies only to **consumer credit,** which is defined as credit for "personal, family, and household" use; it does not apply to business or commercial transactions. The act does not apply to

[48] *Muller v Colortyme, Inc.*, 518 NW2d 544 (Minn 1994); and *Rent-A-Center, Inc. v Hall*, 510 NW2d 789 (Wis App 1993), reh'g denied, 515 NW2d 715 (Wis 1994).

[49] 15 USC § 1681 *et seq.*

the investigation report made by an insurance company of a policy claim.[50]

(a) Privacy

A report on a person based on personal investigation and interviews is called an **investigative consumer report** and cannot be made without informing the subject of the right to discover the results of the investigation. Credit reporting agencies are not permitted to disclose information to persons not having a legitimate use for it. It is a federal crime to obtain or to furnish a credit report for an improper purpose.

On request, a credit reporting agency must tell a consumer the names and addresses of persons to whom it has made a credit report during the previous six months. It must also tell, when requested, which employers were given such a report during the previous two years.

A store may not publicly display a list of named customers from whom it will not accept checks; such action is an invasion of the privacy of those persons.

(b) Protection from False Information

Much of the information obtained by credit bureaus is based on statements made by persons, such as neighbors, when interviewed by the bureau's investigator. Sometimes the statements are incorrect. Quite often they are **hearsay evidence** and would not be admissible in a legal proceeding. Nevertheless, such statements may go on credit records without further verification and be furnished to a client of the agency, who will tend to regard them as accurate and true.

A person has a limited right to request that a credit bureau disclose the nature and substance of the information it possesses. The right to know, however, does not extend to medical information. The bureau is not required to identify the persons giving information to its investigators, nor is it required to give the applicant a copy of, or to permit the applicant to see, any file.

When a person claims that report information is erroneous, the credit bureau must take steps within a reasonable time to determine the accuracy of the disputed item.

Adverse information obtained by investigation cannot be given to a client after three months unless it is verified to determine that it is still valid. Most legal proceedings cannot be reported by a bureau after seven years, although a bankruptcy proceeding can be reported for ten years.

PHILLIPS V GRENDAHL, 312 F3D 357 (8TH CIR 2002)

TROUBLE WITH THE FUTURE IN-LAWS AND THE FCRA

FACTS: Mary Grendahl's daughter Sarah became engaged to marry Lavon Phillips and moved in with him. Mary Grendahl (defendant) became suspicious that Phillips was not telling the truth about his past, particularly about whether he was an attorney and whether he had done legal work in Washington, D.C. She also was confused about who his ex-wives and girlfriends were and where they lived. She contacted Kevin Fitzgerald (defendant), a family friend who worked for McDowell (defendant), a private investigation agency. She asked Fitzgerald to do a "background check" on Phillips, and she gave him the name of the woman Phillips had lived with before he began living with Sarah Grendahl.

Fitzgerald began his search by obtaining Phillips's Social Security number from a computer database. He searched public records in Minnesota and Alabama, where Phillips had lived earlier. He discovered one suit against Phillips for delinquent child support in Alabama, a suit to establish child support for two children in Minnesota, and one misdemeanor conviction for writing dishonored checks.

[50] *Reynolds v Hartford Financial Services Group, Inc.*, 416 F3d 1097 (CA 9 2005). The FCRA does apply, however, to insurers using credit reports to determine policy rates.

Fitzgerald then supplied the Social Security information to Econ Control and asked for "Finder's Reports" on Phillips and the former girlfriend. Econ Control was in the business of furnishing credit reports, Finder's Reports, and credit scoring for credit grantors and for private investigators. Robert McDowell, on behalf of McDowell Agency, had signed an Econ Control registration agreement, titled "Agreement for Consumer Credit Services." One clause of the registration agreement stated:

3. I certify that I will order consumer reports, as defined by the Fair Credit Reporting Act, only when they are intended to be used as a factor in establishing a consumer's eligibility for new or continued credit, collections of an account, insurance, licensing, employment purposes, or otherwise in connection with a legitimate business transaction involving the consumer. Such reports will be used for no other purpose. Each time I request a report I intend to use for employment purposes, I will specifically identify it to [Econ Control] at the time I request the report.

Econ Control did not ask why McDowell wanted the report, and McDowell did not tell them. Econ Control obtained a report from Computer Science Corporation on Phillips and passed it onto McDowell.

Fitzgerald met with Mary Grendahl and gave her the results of his investigation, including the Finder's Report. Phillips eventually found out about the background check and became angry, as did Sarah. Mary Grendahl then telephoned and left the following voicemail for Sarah: "Sarah, this is Mom. I didn't directly do a credit report. I hired a PI, and they have every right to do that." Phillips brought suit against Mary Grendahl, McDowell Agency, and Econ Control, alleging violations of the Fair Credit Reporting Act. Phillips appealed the lower court's summary judgment for Grendahl and the others on the grounds that what they had obtained was not a consumer report in violation of the FCRA.

Judicial Opinion

GIBSON, Circuit Judge.... The first step in establishing liability under section 1681n(a) or section 1681o for obtaining a consumer report without a permissible purpose is to show that the document at issue was a "consumer report." The statutory definition is complex. Section 1681a(d) defines a consumer report as (1) any written, oral, or other communication of information (2) by a consumer reporting agency (3) bearing on a consumer's credit worthiness, credit standing, credit capacity, character, general reputation, personal characteristics, or mode of living (4) which is used or expected to be used or collected in whole or in part for the purpose of serving as a factor in establishing the consumer's eligibility for (A) credit or insurance to be used primarily for personal, family, or household purposes; (B) employment purposes; or (C) any other purposes authorized under section 1681b.

In this case, there is no dispute that the Finder's Report was (1) a written communication (2) by a consumer reporting agency, Computer Science Corporation. The two issues in dispute pertaining to whether the Finder's Report is a consumer report are (3) whether it contained the sort of personal information that would bring it within the definition and (4) whether anyone "expected" the Finder's Report or the information in it to be used for one of the purposes listed in the definition or "collected" the information in it for that purpose.

A consumer report must contain information "bearing on a consumer's credit worthiness, credit standing, credit capacity, character, general reputation, personal characteristics, or mode of living." 15 U.S.C. § 1681a(d). The Finder's Report listed "Trade line Information," consisting of the names of several creditors with whom Phillips had credit accounts and the existence of a child support obligation, with dates for "last activity," but no other details such as amount of obligation or payment history. The Finder's Report also lists Phillips's former employers, which also would bear on his mode of living by showing that he has been employed. We conclude that the Finder's Report contains the kind of personal information required by the definition of consumer report.

The second question, whether the putative consumer report or the information in it was "used or expected to be used" or "collected for" one of the listed purposes, such as use in a credit or employment decision, § 1681a(d), is more difficult. Three statutory ambiguities in this clause could affect what communications are covered by the clause: the statutory language does not specify who must do the using, collecting or expecting; whether those verbs describe a specific or habitual action; or whether those actions must be done with regard to "information" or with regard to the consumer report itself. McDowell Agency essentially argues the clause requires that either the credit agency prepared the Finder's Report in the expectation that it would be used for a statutory purpose or that the requestors did so use it. McDowell Agency contends that the Finder's Report was too incomplete to enable anyone to base a credit decision on it, so neither the requestors nor the credit agency could have expected the report to be used in a credit decision. Phillips, on the other hand, focuses on the information in the report, rather than the report itself. He argues that some of the information was of a type habitually "used" by people within the credit industry for the purposes covered by the statute and that therefore no showing about anyone's actual intent with regard to the Finder's Report was necessary to make it a consumer report.

The record demonstrates that the Finder's Report, not just the information in it, was actually intended by the credit reporting agency that prepared it to be used for a statutory purpose. The sample Finder's Report supplied by Econ Control to McDowell Agency states: "FINDERS delivers skip-locate power in a cost-effective, easy-to-use format. This remarkable product was designed by and for collections professionals who need timely debt-recovery support at an economical price." It therefore appears that the Finder's Report was prepared by Computer Science Corporation with the expectation that it would be used for a statutory purpose. That being the case, the Finder's Report is a consumer report even though the requestor never used or intended to use it for a statutory purpose.

We next determine whether each of the defendants "obtained or used" the consumer report. There is no dispute that McDowell Agency and Econ Control obtained a consumer report, for each of them requested a Finder's Report.

Mary Grendahl, on the other hand, testified that she did not request the release of any credit information on Phillips. Mere passive receipt of the report would not be enough to satisfy the statutory element that she "use or obtain" a consumer report. However, Phillips argues that the phone machine message Grendahl left for Sarah is evidence that she asked Fitzgerald to obtain credit information: "Sarah, this is mom. I didn't directly do a credit report. I hired a PI and they have every right to do that." This evidence is ambiguous. On the one hand, it could mean that Grendahl hired a private investigator because she thought he was entitled to do a credit report. On the other hand, it could mean that she simply hired a private investigator who ordered a credit report on his own initiative, which she now understood he was entitled to do. Because this case was disposed of on summary judgment, we must resolve any ambiguities in the evidence in favor of Phillips. In this procedural posture, the ambiguous telephone message is sufficient to create a genuine issue of fact as to whether Mary Grendahl asked Fitzgerald to obtain a consumer report on Phillips.

The next inquiry is whether any of the defendants had a permissible statutory purpose for obtaining the consumer report. The only purpose for obtaining the report was to obtain information on Mary Grendahl's prospective son-in-law. Investigating a person because he wants to marry one's daughter is not a statutory consumer purpose under section 1681b(a). Even if getting married can be characterized as a consumer transaction under section 1681b(a)(3), it was not Mary Grendahl, but her daughter, whom Phillips was engaged to marry. He had no business transaction pending with Mary Grendahl. There was no permissible purpose for obtaining or using a consumer report.

The element of culpability varies according to whether the cause arises under section 1681n generally, section 1681n(a), or section 1681o. Section 1681n(a) provides civil liability for willful noncompliance with any requirement of the Fair Credit Reporting Act.

Fitzgerald testified, "To the best of my knowledge, a finder's report is not considered a credit history." He also testified: "I did not do anything that I know to be illegal, unethical, or outside the standard practice of private investigators." Mary Grendahl testified that she only asked Fitzgerald to look into Phillips's background and that she gave him no instructions on how to do the investigation. She stated: "At no time did I ask Mr. Fitzgerald to try to obtain credit information or a 'credit report,' and it is my understanding that he did not do so."

On the other hand, there is also evidence that each defendant had some experience in dealing with credit reports and either knew of the Fair Credit Reporting Act or at least knew that such reports can only be obtained legally under certain circumstances. This kind of experience can support an inference that the defendants knew that their actions were impermissible. There is also the telephone message that could be interpreted to mean that Mary Grendahl directed Fitzgerald to obtain a credit report. Additionally, someone wrote on the Phillips Finder's Report: "Credit Inquiry Report & Employment Trace." These facts are sufficient to create a genuine issue of material fact as to whether defendants acted knowingly and with conscious disregard for Phillips's legal rights.

Section 1681o provides a private cause of action for negligent failure to comply with the Fair Credit Reporting

Act. Since Phillips has raised factual issues sufficient to require trial on whether defendants willfully violated his rights under the Act, it follows that he has also made a submissible case as to negligent violation of those same rights.

We reverse the entry of summary judgment on Phillips's Fair Credit Reporting Act. We remand for further proceedings in accordance with this opinion.

Questions

1. What evidence does the court point to to show that the defendants knew they might be violating the FCRA?
2. What evidence does the court use to show that when the report was prepared there was an awareness that it was going to be used for purpose that made its use covered by the statutory requirements?
3. What kind of personal information was in the report?

18. Other Consumer Protections

Various laws aimed at protecting purchasers of real estate, buyers of services, and prospective franchisees have been adopted in the states and at the federal level.

(a) Real Estate Development Sales: Interstate Land Sales Full Disclosure Act

Anyone promoting the sale of a real estate development that is divided into 50 or more parcels of less than 5 acres each must file a **development statement** with the secretary of Housing and Urban Development (HUD). This statement must set forth significant details of the development as required by the federal Interstate Land Sales Full Disclosure Act (ILSFDA).[51]

Anyone buying or renting one of the parcels in the subdivision must be given a **property report,** which is a condensed version of the development statement filed with the secretary of HUD. This report must be given to the prospective customer at least 48 hours before the signing of the contract to buy or lease.

If the development statement is not filed with HUD, the sale or rental of the real estate development may not be promoted through interstate commerce (telephones) or by the use of the mail.

If the property report is given to the prospective buyer or tenant less than 48 hours before the signing of a contract to buy or lease, or after it has been signed, the contract may be voided within 48 hours. If the property report is never received, the contract may be voided, and there is no statutory limitation on the time in which this may be done.

State statutes complement the ILSFDA and frequently require that particular enterprises selling property disclose certain information to prospective buyers. Some state statutes provide protection for sales of real property interests such as time-sharing condominiums that are not covered under the ILSFDA.[52]

(b) Service Contracts

The UCCC treats a consumer service contract the same as a consumer sale of goods if (1) payment is made in installments or a credit charge is made and (2) the amount financed does not exceed $25,000. The UCCC defines *services* broadly as embracing work, specified privileges, and insurance provided by a noninsurer. The inclusion of these privileges in service contracts makes the UCCC apply to contracts calling for payment on the installment plan or including a financing charge for transportation, hotel and restaurant accommodations, education, entertainment, recreation, physical culture (such as athletic clubs or bodybuilding schools), hospital accomodations, funerals, and cemetery accommodations.

In some states, it is unlawful for a repair shop to make unauthorized repairs to an automobile and then refuse to return the automobile to the customer until the customer has paid for the repairs. In some states, a consumer protection statute imposes multiple damages on a repair shop that delays unreasonably in performing a contract to repair property of the consumer.[53]

(c) Franchises

To protect prospective **franchisees** from deception by **franchisors** that seek to sell interests, an FTC regulation requires that the franchisor give a prospective franchisee a disclosure statement 10 days before the franchisee signs a contract or pays any money for a **franchise.** The disclosure statement

[51] 15 USC § 1701 *et seq.*

[52] *Becherer v Merrill Lynch, Pierce, Fenner & Smith, Inc.*, 127 F3d 479 (6th Cir 1997) (condominium units sold for 14-day time-sharing rights not covered under ILSFDA).

[53] *Crye v Smolak*, 674 NE2d 779 (Ohio App 1996).

provides detailed information relating to the franchisor's finances, experience, size of operation, and involvement in litigation. The statement must set forth any restrictions imposed on the franchisee; any costs that must be paid initially or in the future; and the provisions for termination, cancellation, and renewal of the franchise. False statements regarding sales, income, or profits are prohibited. Violators of the regulation are subject to a fine of $10,000.

(d) Automobile Lemon Laws

All states have adopted special laws for the protection of consumers buying automobiles that develop numerous defects or defects that cannot be corrected. These statutes protect only persons buying automobiles for personal, family, or household use. They generally classify an automobile as a *lemon* if it cannot be put in proper or warranted condition within a specified period of time or after a specified number of repair attempts. In general, they give the buyer greater protection than is given to other buyers by the UCC or other consumer protection statutes (see Chapter 24). In some states, the seller of a car that turns out to be a lemon is required to give the buyer a brand-new replacement car. In some states, certain agencies may also bring an action to collect civil penalties from the seller of a lemon car.

Lemon laws in most states are designed to increase the prelitigation bargaining power of consumers and reduce the greater power of manufacturers to resist complaints or suits by consumers.[54] **For Example,** Abdul, who owned a paint store, purchased two automobiles from Prime Motors, one for delivering paint to his customers and the second for his wife to use for shopping and taking their children to school. Both cars were defective and in need of constant repair. Abdul claimed that he was entitled to remedies provided by the local automobile lemon law. He was wrong with respect to the store's delivery car because lemon laws do not cover cars purchased for commercial use, but the other car was protected by the lemon law because it was clearly a family car.

LAWFLIX

Matilda (1997) (PG)

This is a story of a brilliant little girl living with some unethical parents. Several scenes show Danny DeVito (the father and used car dealer) cheating. In one scene, he shows Matilda how to roll back odometers.

For movie clips that illustrate business law concepts, see LawFlix at **http://wdvl.westbuslaw.com.**

54 *Church v Chrysler Corp.*, 585 NW2d 685 (Wis App 1998).

Summary

Modern methods of marketing, packaging, and financing have reduced the ordinary consumer to a subordinate position. To protect the consumer from the hardship, fraud, and oppression that could result from being in such an inferior position, consumer protection laws, at both the state and federal levels, afford rights to consumers and impose requirements on those who deal with consumers.

When a consumer protection statute is violated, an action may sometimes be brought by the consumer against the wrongdoer. More commonly, an action is brought by an administrative agency or by the state attorney general.

Consumer protection laws are directed at false and misleading advertising; misleading or false use of labels; the methods of selling, with specific requirements on the disclosure of terms, permitting consumer cancellation of home-solicited sales, and types of credit arrangements. The consumer is protected in a contract agreement by regulation of its form, prohibition of unconscionable terms, and limitation of the credit that can be extended to a consumer. Credit card protections include prohibition of the unauthorized distribution of credit cards and limited liability of the cardholder for the unauthorized use of a credit card. Included in consumer protection laws are the application of payments; the preservation of consumer defenses as against a transferee of the consumer's contract; product safety; the protection of credit standing and reputation; and (to some extent) real estate development sales, franchises, and service contracts. Lemon laws provide special protection to buyers of automobiles for personal, household, or family use.

Questions and Case Problems

1. The San Antonio Retail Merchants Association (SARMA) was a credit reporting agency. It was asked by one of its members to furnish information on William Douglas Thompson III. It supplied information from a file that contained data on William III and on William Daniel Thompson Jr. The agency had incorporated information related to William Jr. into the file relating to William III so that all information appeared to relate to William III. This was a negligent mistake because each William had a different Social Security number, which should have raised a suspicion that there was a mistake. In addition, SARMA should have used a number of checkpoints to ensure that incoming information would be put into the proper file. William Jr. had bad credit standing. Because of its mistake, SARMA gave a bad report on William III, who was denied credit by several enterprises. The federal Fair Credit Reporting Act makes a credit reporting agency liable to any consumer about whom it furnishes a consumer report without following reasonable procedures to ensure maximum possible accuracy of information. William III sued SARMA for its negligence in confusing him with William Jr. Is SARMA liable? [*Thompson v San Antonio Retail Merchants Ass'n*, 682 F2d 509 (5th Cir Tex)]
2. Colgate-Palmolive Co. ran a television commercial to show that its shaving cream, Rapid Shave, could soften even the toughness of sandpaper. The commercial showed what was described as the sandpaper test. Actually, what was used was a sheet of Plexiglas on which sand had been sprinkled. The FTC claimed that this was a deceptive practice. The advertiser contended that actual sandpaper would merely look like ordinary colored paper and that Plexiglas had been used to give the viewer an accurate visual representation of the test. Could the FTC prohibit the use of this commercial? [*Federal Trade Commission v Colgate-Palmolive Co.*, 380 US 374]
3. Sharolyn Charles wrote a check for $17.93 to a Poncho's Restaurant on July 4, 1996, as payment for a meal she had there. The check was returned for insufficient funds. Poncho's forwarded the check to Check Rite for collection.

   On July 19, Check Rite sent a letter to Charles, stating that "[t]his is an attempt to collect a debt" and requesting total payment of $42.93—the amount of the check plus a service charge of $25. On August 7, Check Rite sent a second letter, requesting payment of $42.93 and advising Charles that failure to pay the total amount due might result in additional liability for damages and attorneys' fees, estimated at $242.93.

   Check Rite subsequently referred the matter to the law firm of Lundgren & Associates for collection. On September 8, Lundgren sent a letter to Charles offering to settle within 10 days for a total amount of $127.93—the amount of the check plus a settlement amount of $110. Lundgren further advised that it had made no decision to file suit, that it could later decide to do so, and that Charles's potential liability was $317.93. Charles immediately sent to Lundgren a money order in the amount of $17.93. On September 13, Lundgren sent a second letter, repeating the settlement offer made in the September 8 letter. Lundgren then returned Charles's payment on September 14, declining to accept it as payment in full and repeating the settlement offer. On September 19, Lundgren sent a fourth letter to Charles, repeating the settlement offer.

   On October 15, 1996, Charles filed suit in federal district court alleging violations of the Fair Debt Collections Practices Act (FDCPA). Lundgren & Associates moved to dismiss the case on the grounds that an attempt to collect on a check is not a "debt" governed by the FDCPA. The district court dismissed the case, and Charles appealed. Should Charles win? Is she protected under the FDCPA? [*Charles v Lundgren & Associates, P.C.*, 119 F3d 739 (9th Cir)]
4. On November 3, 1989, John York purchased a 1988 truck from Conway Ford for $5,350. York purchased the truck in reliance on representations from the Conway Ford sales staff that the truck was a "like-new" demonstrator and that it had never been titled to anyone other than the dealership. From the outset, the truck had problems that required its return to Conway for service. During one of his numerous visits to Conway, York was told by a mechanic that the truck had been in an accident and had a bent frame. York then returned the truck and asked for his money back. Conway refused. Conway stored the truck for a time and then sold it to satisfy storage fees. York brought suit against Conway for breach of contract, fraud, and violation of South Carolina's Unfair Trade Practices Act (UTPA). Who wins? Why? [*York v Conway Ford, Inc.*, 480 SE2d 726 (SC)]

5. Thomas was sent a credit card through the mail by a company that had taken his name and address from the telephone book. Because he never requested the card, Thomas left the card lying on his desk. A thief stole the card and used it to purchase merchandise in several stores in Thomas's name. The issuer of the credit card claimed that Thomas was liable for the total amount of the purchases made by the thief. Thomas claimed that he was not liable for any amount. The court decided that Thomas was liable for $50. Who is correct? Why?
6. Wilke was contemplating retiring. In response to an advertisement, he purchased from Coinway 30 coin-operated testing machines because Coinway's representative stated that by placing these machines at different public places, Wilke could obtain supplemental income. This statement was made by the representative, although he had no experience with the cost of servicing the machines or their income-producing potential. Wilke's operational costs for the machines exceeded the income. Wilke sued Coinway to rescind the contract, alleging that it was fraudulent. Coinway argued that the statements made were merely matters of opinion and did not constitute deception. Does Wilke have any consumer protection remedies? [*Wilke v Coinway, Inc.*, 64 Cal Rptr 845 (Cal App)]
7. Iberlin and others subscribed to the services of TCI Cablevision of Wyoming, which imposed a $2 late charge on any bill not paid when due. Iberlin brought suit against the cable company, claiming that the late charge was for extending credit and thus did not comply with state and federal laws governing credit charges. Was Iberlin correct? [*Iberlin v TCI Cablevision of Wyoming*, 855 P2d 716 (Wyo)]
8. International Yogurt Co. (IYC) developed a unique mix for making frozen yogurt and related products. Morris and his wife purchased a franchise from the company but were not told that a franchise was not a requirement for obtaining the mix—that the company would sell its yogurt mix to anyone. The Morrises' franchise business was a failure, and they sold it at a loss after three years. They then sued the company for fraud and for violation of the state Franchise Investment Protection Act and the state Consumer Protection Act for failing to inform them that the mix could be obtained without a franchise. IYC claimed that no liability could be imposed for failing to make the disclosure. Was it correct? [*Morris v International Yogurt Co.*, 729 P2d 33 (Wash)]
9. Lutz Appellate Services received unsolicited faxed messages from Curry & Taylor. The first of these messages read as follows:

   CURRY & TAYLOR
   IS NOW HIRING
   ALL POSITIONS
   CALL TODAY 1-800-222-8738

   The second stated:

   CURRY & TAYLOR
   —APPELLATE SPECIALISTS NEEDED
   —GENEROUS PAY STRUCTURE
   —EXPERIENCE WELCOME BUT NOT NECESSARY
   —CALL 1-800-409-0060 TODAY, ASK FOR BILL

   Curry was a competitor of Lutz and was seeking to hire away employees. Lutz filed suit alleging that the unsolicited faxes were advertisements prohibited by the Telephone Consumer Protection Act. What do you think? Does the TCPA prohibit these faxes?
10. A suit was brought against General Foods on the grounds that it was violating the state law prohibiting false and deceptive advertising. Its defense was that the plaintiffs had failed to show that the public had been deceived by the advertising, that the public in fact had not relied on the advertising, and that there was no proof that anyone had sustained any damage because of the advertising. Were these valid defenses? [*Committee on Children's Television, Inc. v General Foods Corp.*, 673 P2d 660 (Cal)]
11. The town of Newport obtained a corporate MasterCard that was given to the town clerk for purchasing fuel for the town hall. The town clerk used the card for personal restaurant, hotel, and gift shop debts. The town refused to pay the card charges on the grounds that they were unauthorized. Was the town correct? [*MasterCard v Town of Newport*, 396 NW2d 345 (Wis App)]
12. Donnelly purchased a television set on credit from D.W.N. Advertising, Inc. He also contracted for service on the set. D.W.N. assigned the sales contract to Fairfield Credit Corp., D.W.N. went out of existence, and the service contract was never performed. Fairfield sued Donnelly for the balance due on the purchase price. Donnelly raised the defense that the service contract had never been performed. Fairfield claimed that this defense could not be asserted against it because the sales contract contained a waiver of defenses. Was Fairfield right? [*Fairfield Credit Corp. v Donnelly*, 264 A2d 547 (Conn)]
13. Stevens purchased a pair of softball shoes manufactured by Hyde Athletic Industries. Because of a defect in the shoes, she fell and broke an ankle. She sued Hyde under the state consumer protection act, which provided that "any person who is injured in . . . business or property . . . could sue for damages sustained." Hyde claimed that the act did not cover personal injuries. Stevens claimed that she was injured in her "property" because of the money that she had to spend for medical treatment and subsequent care. Decide. [*Stevens v Hyde Athletic Industries, Inc.*, 773 P2d 87 (Wash App)]
14. A consumer made a purchase on a credit card. The card issuer refused to accept the charge, and an attorney then sued the consumer for the amount due. In the complaint filed in the lawsuit, the attorney wrongly stated that

interest was owed at 18 percent per annum. This statement was later corrected by an amendment of the complaint to 5 percent. The case against the consumer was ultimately settled, but the consumer then sued the attorney for penalties under the Fair Debt Collection Practices Act, claiming that the overstatement of the interest due in the original complaint was a violation of that act. The attorney defended on the ground that the act did not apply. Did it? [*Green v Hocking*, 9 F3d 18 (6th Cir)]

15. Classify each of the following activities as proper or prohibited under the various consumer statutes you have studied.

    a. Calling a hospital room to talk to a debtor who is a patient there.
    b. Calling a hospital room to sell surgical stockings.
    c. Rolling back the odometer on one's car before selling it privately.
    d. No TILA disclosures on an instant tax refund program in which the lender takes 40 percent of the tax refund as a fee for advancing the money when the taxpayer files the tax return.

SECURED TRANSACTIONS IN PERSONAL PROPERTY

CHAPTER (34)

LEARNING OBJECTIVES

After studying this chapter, you should be able to

LO.1 Describe a secured transaction in personal property

LO.2 Explain the requirements for creating a valid security interest

LO.3 List the major types of collateral

LO.4 Define perfection and explain its significance in secured transactions

LO.5 Discuss the priorities of parties with conflicting interests in collateral when default occurs

LO.6 State the rights of the parties on the debtor's default

To provide creditors additional assurance that money will be repaid, legal rights in property can be assigned to creditors so that if the person obligated to pay does not pay, the creditor can turn to the property as a means of satisfying the obligation.

A. Creation of Secured Transactions

A *secured transaction* is one means by which personal property is used to provide a backup plan or security for the creditor in the event the borrower does not pay. Secured transactions are governed by Article 9 of the Uniform Commercial Code (UCC). Article 9 was revised in 2000, and the revisions to it have been adopted in all states and the District of Columbia.[1]

1. Definitions

A **secured transaction** in personal property is created by giving the creditor a security interest in that property. A **security interest** is like a lien in personal property; it is a property right that enables the creditor to take possession of the property if the debtor does not pay the amount owed. **For Example,** if you borrow money from a bank to buy a car, the bank takes a security interest in the car. If you do not repay the loan, the bank can repossess the car and sell it to recover the money the bank has loaned you. If you purchase a side-by-side refrigerator from Kelvin's Appliances on credit, Kelvin's takes a security interest in the refrigerator. If you do not repay Kelvin's, Kelvin's can repossess the refrigerator and sell it to cover the amount you still owe.

The property that is subject to the security interest is called **collateral.** In the preceding examples, the car was the bank's collateral for the loan, and the refrigerator was Kelvin's collateral.

(a) Parties

The person to whom the money is owed, whether a seller or a lender, is called the **creditor** or **secured party.** The buyer on credit or the borrower is called the **debtor.**

(b) Nature of Creditor's Interest

The creditor does not own the collateral, but the security interest is a property right. That property

[1] All 50 states, including Louisiana, have some version of Article 9 as law. The latest version of Article 9 (Revised Article 9) was adopted in 1999 and took effect on July 1, 2001. This newest version, adopted as modified in 2000, is referred to as either "New Article 9" or "Revised Article 9." Contrasts between the previous Article 9 and Revised Article 9 are noted in footnotes throughout the chapter. Not all states, however, have adopted verbatim versions. For example, the application of Article 9 to governmental units varies significantly among the states.

right can ripen into possession and the right to transfer title by sale as the section on default in this chapter discusses. However, the creditor also has certain present property interests and rights even prior to default. **For Example,** having a security interest gives the creditor standing to sue a third person who damages, destroys, or improperly repossesses the collateral.

If the creditor has possession of the collateral, the UCC imposes a duty of care on the creditor. The UCC provides that reasonable care must be exercised in preserving the property. The creditor is liable for damage that results from failing to do so.

(c) Nature of Debtor's Interest

A debtor who is a borrower ordinarily owns the collateral[2]; see Section 2(c) of this chapter. As such, the debtor has all rights of any property owner to recover damages for the loss or improper seizure of, or damage to, the collateral.[3]

CPA 2. Creation of a Security Interest

An attachment, or the creation of a valid security interest, occurs when the following three conditions are satisfied: There is (1) a security agreement, (2) value has been given, and (3) the debtor has rights in the collateral. These three conditions can occur in any order. A security interest will attach when the last of these conditions has been met.[4] When the security interest attaches, it is then enforceable against the debtor and the collateral.

CPA (a) Agreement

The **security agreement** is the agreement of the creditor and the debtor that the creditor will have a security interest. This required agreement must identify the parties, contain a reasonable description of the collateral,[5] indicate the parties' intent that the creditor have a security interest in it, describe the debt or the performance that is secured thereby, and be authenticated by the debtor.

Revised Article 9 eliminated the signature requirement to permit electronic means of entering into security agreements. The standard is now not a signature but an authenticated document; authentication can come from the debtor's actions that indicate an understanding of a credit and secured debt agreement.[6] Also under Revised Article 9, a description is valid if it "reasonably identifies what is described."[7] Examples of reasonable identification include a specific listing, category,[8] quantity, and computational or allocational formula. "Supergeneric descriptions"[9] such as "all the debtor's personal property" are insufficient,[10] but "livestock" is a sufficient description.[11] The requirement for description of consumer goods as collateral is more stringent than for other types of collateral.[12]

2 *Gibson County Farm Bureau Co-op Ass'n v Greer*, 643 NE2d 313 (Ind App 1994); *Belke v M&I First Nat'l Bank*, 525 NW2d 737 (Wis App 1994).

3 Article 9 does cover consignment arrangements. The consignor continues to own the goods, and the consignee is treated as a secured creditor with a purchase money security interest in the consigned goods.

4 UCC § 9-203 (Revised Article 9, § 9-203); *Farm Credit Services of Midlands, PCA v First State Park of Newcastle, Wyoming*, 575 NW2d 250 (SD 1998). Because Revised Article 9 now includes bank accounts as a form of security, the security interest attaches when the creditor has "control" of the account (Revised Article 9, § 9-104) and there is a security agreement. *Control* is defined later in the chapter under *perfection by control.*

5 UCC §§ 9-201 (Revised Article 9, § 9-203), 9-110 (Revised Article 9, § 9-108); *Color Leasing 3, L. P. v FDIC*, 975 F Supp 177 (D RI 1997). In *In re Cottage Grove Hospital*, 38 UCC2d 683 (Bankr Ct D Or 1999), the court held that "All Debtor's Income" was an insufficient description.

6 Revised Article 9, § 9-102(a)(69) defines *record*, the new substitute for *signed agreement* of old Article 9, as "information that is inscribed on a tangible medium and is retrievable in perceivable form." Authentication need not be a signature. One court held that a debtor using the proceeds from the loan that was the basis for the security interest constituted authentication, *Barlow Lane Holdings Ltd. v Applied Carbon Technology (America), Inc.*, 2004 WL 1792456 (WDNY 2004); see also 2004 WL 2110733 (WDNY 2004).

7 UCC § 9-110.

8 Commercial tort claims and consumer transactions cannot be sufficiently described by type of collateral. The security agreement must give more specifics. § 9-108(e)(1) and (2).

9 UCC § 9-108(c).

10 The comments to § 9-108 indicate that serial numbers are not necessarily required, but an outsider must be able to tell from the description what property is or is not included under the security agreement. Official Comment, § 9-108, 2.

11 *Baldwin v. Castro County Feeders I, Ltd.*, 678 NW2d 796 (SD 2004).

12 Under § 9-108, in consumer transactions and goods, description by "type of collateral" is insufficient.

MCLEOD V SEARS, ROEBUCK & CO., 41 UCC2D 302 (BANKR ED MICH 2000)

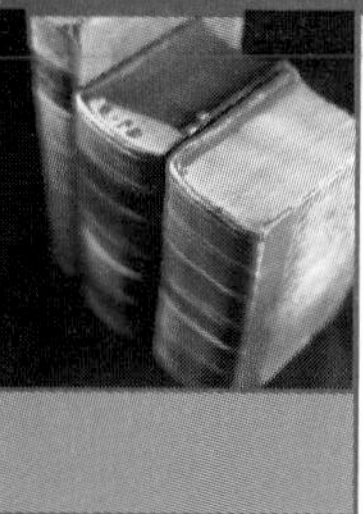

THE UMBRELLA, THE SAW, THE BRACELET, THE CD, THE TV, THE LUGGAGE, AND THE EARRINGS AS COLLATERAL

Donald and Jill McLeod (Donald is referred to as "Debtor") purchased several items from Sears, Roebuck (Defendant) on credit. The description of the items, in which Sears took a purchase money security interest, was as follows: "MITER SAW; LXITVRACDC [a television, video cassette recorder, and compact disk spinner]; 25″ UPRIGHT, 28″ UPRIGHT [two pieces of luggage]; BRACELET, DIA STUDS, RING; 14K EARR, P, EARRINGS, P [diamond bracelet, ring, and earrings]; and 9-INCH E-Z-LIFT [an outdoor umbrella]."

In a dispute over creditors' priorities in McLeods' bankruptcy, one creditor argued that the description of the goods was insufficient to give Sears a security interest.

Judicial Opinion

SHAPERO, Bankruptcy Judge.... Attachment of a security interest occurs when (1) "debtor has signed a security agreement which contains a description of the collateral"; (2) "Value has been given"; and (3) "The debtor has rights in the collateral." "'Security agreement' means an agreement which creates or provides for a security interest.'" The description of the collateral is sufficient "if it reasonably identifies what is described." A security interest holder need not file a financing statement in order to perfect a purchase money security interest in consumer goods. Because filing is not required, a security interest is perfected at attachment. The filing of a financial statement is only required to protect against a subsequent sale to a buyer for value and without knowledge, an exception that is not applicable in this case.

As to the first requirement of attachment, the stipulated facts show that Debtor entered into a revolving charge account with Defendant in 1990, received regular updates of the Agreement, and added his wife as an authorized buyer on February 6, 1997. Although Debtors did not sign the SearsCharge Agreement, § 445.862 of the Michigan Retail Installment Sales Act provides that "[a] retail charge agreement shall be considered signed and accepted by the buyer... if the retail charge account is used by the buyer." The record further shows that Debtor or his wife signed the sales slips for each purchase at issue. The items for which Debtor's wife signed were purchased after she became an authorized buyer. The sales slips identified the item(s) purchased, incorporated the SearsCharge Agreement, and granted Defendant a security interest. Debtor challenges the adequacy of the description, stating that the items must be "specifically identified" when there could be "more than one [item] in [the] household." The miter saw is identified as "MITER SAW"; the televison, video cassette recorder and compact disk spinner as "LXITV-RACDC, CD SPIN"; the luggage as "25″ UPRIGHT, 28″ UPRIGHT"; the jewelry as "BRACELET, DIA STUDS, RING" and "14K EARR, P, EARRINGS, P"; and the outdoor "Easy-Lift" umbrella as "9″ E-Z LIFT."

Debtor cites *In re Carlos*, 215 B.R. 52 (Bankr. C.D.Cal.1997). Decided under the California commercial code, the court held that the sufficiency of the description of individual items depended on what it termed "a two-part test," which is really a test in the alternative. ...

First, if the collateral is such that the debtor may own other similar items (regardless of whether the debtor in fact has more than one), the description must enable a third party to distinguish the collateral from other property. Alternatively, if the debtor is not likely to own more than one such item, a more general description is sufficient. The court went on to apply a "community standard in determining whether a debtor may own other similar items," and found that the description of a washing machine was sufficient because a debtor was only likely to own one, but insufficient for a television or video cassette recorder.

Although this case does support Debtor's argument, *Carlos* was decided under California law. Defendant's security interest is governed by Michigan law, and Debtor does not cite nor can the Court find a case adopting this rule and standard in Michigan. To the contrary, the Official Comment to the pertinent Michigan statute rejects strict tests:

The test of sufficiency of a description laid down by this section is that the description do the job assigned to it—that it make possible the identification of the thing described. Under this rule courts should refuse to follow the holdings... that descriptions are insufficient unless they are of the most exact and detailed nature, the so-called "serial number" test.

In this case, given the fact that the security interest is a purchase money security interest in consumer goods purchased by Debtors, the "job assigned" to the description is that it be sufficient for Debtors and Defendant to identify the goods at issue. *Carlos* has been criticized for misapplying the description standard for financing statements, where third parties dealing with a debtor must be given adequate notice, to a purchase money security interest where no financing statement is required. The Court agrees that this third party standard is not appropriate under the facts in this case, and even if it were, that the descriptions were sufficient to put third parties on notice that "'further inquiry... will be necessary to disclose the complete state of affairs.'"

As to the remaining elements of perfection, the sales slips also stated that the items were "purchased under my SearsCharge Agreement, incorporated by reference, I grant Sears a security interest in this merchandise until paid, unless prohibited by law." Further, the parties stipulated that Debtors agreed to the terms of the charge account and security agreement, which also expressly stated that Defendant retained a security interest in all items purchased until paid in full. The agreement, taken with the signed sales slips, is sufficient to meet the statutory requirements for a valid grant of a security interest to Defendant. The other requirements of attachment are met because Defendant gave value by providing the items to Debtors, and Debtors took possession of the merchandise. Because the security interest secured the purchase price of consumer goods, the Court concludes that Defendant held a perfected security interest as of the time Debtors purchased the items.

For the above reasons, the Court concludes that Defendant is entitled to judgment as a matter of law that it had a perfected security interest in the goods at issue, that this security interest survived Debtors' bankruptcy as a valid lien on the goods at issue

Questions

1. How were the goods described?
2. What case does the debtor use to support his position?
3. What does the court decide about the description of the goods and the security interest and why?

If the creditor has possession of the collateral, the security agreement may be oral regardless of the amount involved.[13] **For Example,** if you pledge your stereo system to a friend as security for the loan and the friend will keep it at his home until you have repaid him, your friend has possession of the collateral, and your oral security agreement is valid and enforceable by your friend. If the creditor does not have possession of the collateral, as in the case of credit sales and most secured loans, the security agreement must be evidenced by a record and meet the other requirements stated earlier.

Field warehousing, covered in Chapter 22, is another form of possession of goods that permits an oral security agreement. Credit unions and banks can possess an account pledged as security if the funds cannot be used by the account holder without permission and clearance from a bank officer.

(b) Value

The creditor gives **value** either by lending money to the debtor or by delivering goods on credit. The value may be part of a contemporaneous exchange or given previously as a loan. **For Example,** a debtor who already owes a creditor $5,000 could later pledge a water scooter as collateral for that loan and give the debtor a security interest in the scooter. In fact, creditors who become nervous about repayment often request collateral later during the course of performance of a previously unsecured loan.

(c) Rights in the Collateral

The debtor must have rights in the collateral for a security interest to attach. These rights can include everything from title to the right to possession.[14]

CPA 3. Purchase Money Security Interest

When a seller sells on credit and is given a security interest in the goods sold, that interest is called a **purchase money security interest (PMSI).** If the buyer borrows money from a third person so that the purchase can be made for cash, a security interest

[13] UCC § 9-207 (Revised Article 9, § 9-207); *Myers v Fifth Third Bank*, 624 NE2d 748 (Ohio App 1993). If there is no written security agreement (*record* under Revised Article 9), the security interest itself is destroyed when the collateral is surrendered.

[14] UCC § 9-112 (Revised Article 9, § 9-202).

given the lender in the goods is also called a purchase money security interest.[15] Certain special priority rights are given in some circumstances to creditors who hold a PMSI.

CPA 4. The Nature and Classification of Collateral

The nature of the collateral in a credit transaction, as well as its classification under Article 9, affects the procedural obligations and rights of creditors. Revised Article 9 contains an extensive list of the types of collateral, including the traditional types such as consumer goods, equipment, inventory, general intangibles, farm products, and fixtures,[16] but also accounts, accounts receivable, accounts receivable held because of credit card transactions or license fees, energy contracts, insurance policy proceeds, amounts due for services rendered, amounts earned from chartering a vessel, winnings in the state lottery, and health care insurance receivables. The general category of "account" does not include commercial tort claims, deposit accounts,[17] investment property, or letters of credit but does include insurance claims, lottery winnings, and property proceeds.[18] New Article 9 has also dropped prejudices against some potential forms of collateral. The result is that other issues with respect to these general categories of collateral arise, such as whether the security interest covers the collateral when it changes form—for example, when the inventory is sold in exchange for a promissory note.

(a) Consumer Goods

Collateral that is classified as **consumer goods** can result in different rights and obligations under Article 9, regardless of the type of property it is. Collateral is considered consumer goods if it is "used or bought for use primarily for personal, family, or household purposes."[19] The use of the good, and not its properties, controls its classification. **For Example,** a computer purchased by an architect for her office is not a consumer good. That same computer purchased by the same architect for use by her children at their home is a consumer good. A refrigerator purchased for the kitchen near an office conference center is not a consumer good. That same model refrigerator purchased for a home is a consumer good. The use of the goods controls the label that is applied to the collateral.

CPA (b) After-Acquired Collateral and Ongoing Credit

A creditor's rights can be expanded to include coverage of all future loans and funds advances as well as future acquisitions of collateral. If the security agreement so provides, the security interest attaches to **after-acquired goods** and applies to all loans to the debtor.[20] **For Example,** a security interest can cover the current inventory of the debtor and any future replenishments if a clause in the security agreement adds "after-acquired property" to the description of the inventory. Referred to in lay terms as a **floating lien,** the creditor's interest attaches to the inventory regardless of its form or time of arrival in terms of the attached security interest.

There are restrictions on after-acquired clauses in consumer credit contracts. An after-acquired property clause in a consumer security agreement can cover only goods acquired by the debtor within 10 days after the creditor gave value to the debtor.

(c) Proceeds

The UCC defines proceeds as "whatever is received upon the sale, exchange, collection, or other disposition of collateral."[21] Collateral may change its form and character during the course of the security agreement. **For Example,** a debtor who has pledged its inventory of cars as collateral will be selling those cars. However, the buyers will sign credit contracts for the purchase of those cars. Article 9 considers the credit contracts and the right to payment under those contracts as proceeds. If the collateral has been insured and is damaged or destroyed, the debtor will receive money from the insurance company. Proceeds are

15 UCC § 9-107 (Revised Article 9, § 9-103); *First Nat'l Bank v Erb Equipment Co.*, 921 SW2d 57 (Mo App 1996).

16 UCC §§ 9-106, 9-109. See Revised Article 9, § 9-102.

17 Deposit accounts are not considered "general intangibles" under new Article 9 because of new, specific provisions on accounts. UCC §§ 9-102(a)(29), 9-104, 9-109(d)(13), 9-312(b)(1), and 9-314.

18 UCC §§ 9-102(2)(a)(5), 9-102(72), and 9-109(a)(2).

19 UCC § 9-109(1).

20 UCC § 9-109 (Revised Article 9, § 9-204).

21 UCC § 9-306(1).

automatically subject to the creditor's security interest unless the contrary was stated in the security agreement. The proceeds may be in any form, such as cash, checks, promissory notes, or other property.

(d) Electronic Chattel Paper

"Electronic chattel paper" is a record of a right to funds, payment, or property that is stored in an electronic medium. **For Example,** it is possible to pledge the funds you have available in your Internet shopping account as an Article 9 security interest.[22]

CPA B. Perfection of Secured Transactions

The attachment of a security interest gives the creditor the important rights of enforcement of the debt through repossession of the collateral (see Section 25 for more discussion of enforcement and repossession). *Attachment* allows the secured party to resort to the collateral to collect the debt when the debtor defaults. However, more than one creditor may hold an attached security interest in the same collateral. A creditor who obtains a **perfected security interest** enjoys priority over unperfected interests and may in some cases enjoy priority over other perfected interests. A security interest is valid against the debtor even though it is not perfected. However, perfection provides creditors with rights superior to those of other creditors with unperfected interests. Attachment provides creditors with rights; perfection gives them priority.

A creditor can obtain perfection in collateral in several ways.

CPA 5. Perfection by Creditor's Possession

If the collateral is in the possession of the creditor, the security interest in the possessed goods is perfected.[23] It remains perfected until that possession is surrendered. **For Example,** when a creditor has taken a security interest in 50 gold coins and has those gold coins in his vault, his possession of the coins is perfection.

A more complex example of possession as a means of perfection is found in the commercial tool of **field warehousing.** (See Chapter 22.) In this arrangement, a creditor actually has an agent on site at a buyer's place of business, and the creditor's agent controls the buyer's access to, use of, and transfer of the collateral. **For Example,** an aircraft manufacturer may have an agent on site at an aircraft dealership. That agent decides when the planes can be released to buyers and who will receive the buyers' payments or notes.[24]

CPA 6. Perfection for Consumer Goods

A purchase money security interest in consumer goods is perfected from the moment it attaches.[25] Known as **automatic perfection,** no other action is required for perfection as against other creditors. Because so many consumer purchases are made on credit, the UCC simplifies perfection so that creditors who are merchant sellers are not overly burdened with paperwork. However, as discussed later in this chapter in the section on priorities, the automatic perfection of a PMSI in consumer goods has some limitations. It may be destroyed by the debtor consumer's resale of the goods to a consumer who does not know of the security interest.

7. Perfection for Health Care Insurance Receivables

Revised Article 9 created a new form of collateral known as *health care insurance receivables.* This form of collateral has a unique method of perfection. When a consumer gives a creditor a security interest in health insurance proceeds that are forthcoming, the creditor need not make any filing or take any further steps to have a perfected security interest in those proceeds. The perfection is automatic.[26]

8. Automatic Perfection

A creditor attains automatic perfection in certain circumstances under Article 9. **For Example,** a creditor has an automatic PMSI in software that is sold with a computer that is subject to a creditor's PMSI.

22 UCC § 9-105.

23 UCC § 9-305; *Shurlow v Bonthuis,* 576 NW2d 159 (Mich 1998).

24 Revised Article 9, § 9-312.

25 UCC § 9-302 (Revised Article 9, §§ 9-301 and 9-304); *Heidelberg Eastern, Inc. v Weber Lithography, Inc.,* 631 NYS2d 370 (NY 1995).

26 Revised Article 9, § 9-309.

If you buy an IBM ThinkPad® from CompUSA on credit and get Microsoft Office software as part of your package deal, CompUSA has an automatically perfected security interest not only in the consumer goods (your new computer) but also in the software sold with it.[27] The perfection for consumer purchase money security interests that occurs when the security interest attaches is also a form of automatic perfection.

CPA 9. Temporary Perfection

Some creditors are given **temporary perfection** for the collateral.[28] **For Example,** a creditor is generally given four months to refile its financing statement in a state to which a debtor has relocated. During that four-month period, the interest of the creditor is temporarily perfected in the new state despite no filing of a financing statement in that state's public records. Most creditors' agreements provide that the failure of the debtor to notify the creditor of a move constitutes a default under the credit agreement. Creditors need to know of the move so that they can refile in the debtor's new state.[29] Creditors enjoy a 20-day temporary perfection in negotiable instruments taken as collateral. Following the expiration of the 20-day period, measured from the time their security interest attaches, creditors must perfect in another way, such as by filing a financing statement or by possession.

CPA 10. Perfection by Control

Control is a form of possession under Article 9;[30] it occurs when a bank or creditor is able to require the debtor account holder to clear all transactions in that account with the bank or creditor. The debtor cannot use the funds that have been pledged as collateral without permission from the party holding the control. **For Example,** a credit union member could secure a loan with the credit union by giving the credit union a security interest in her savings account. The credit union then has control of the account and is perfected by the ability to dictate what the credit union member can do with those funds.

11. Perfection for Motor Vehicles

In most states, a non-Code statute provides that a security interest in a noninventory motor vehicle must be noted on the vehicle title registration. When so noted, the interest is perfected.[31] In states that do not have a separate motor vehicle perfection system, there must be a filing of a financing statement, as described in the next section.

CPA 12. Perfection by Filing a Financing Statement

The **financing statement** (known as a *UCC-1*) is an authenticated record statement that gives sufficient information to alert third persons that a particular creditor may have a security interest in the collateral described (see Figure 34-1). Under previous Article 9, the financing statement had to be in writing and signed by the debtor. Under Revised Article 9, the creditor must simply be able to show that the documents filed were "authorized" and an "authenticated record."[32] In other words, the debtor's signature is not required for the financing statement to be valid. The notion of authorization by a debtor for financing statements is a critical one under Revised Article 9. Revised Article 9 gives three ways for the debtor to authorize a financing statement:

1. By authenticating a security agreement.[33]
2. By becoming bound under a security agreement, the debtor agrees to allow financing statements to be filed on the collateral in the security agreement.
3. By acquiring collateral subject to a security agreement.

An unauthorized financing statement filed without meeting one of these requirements does not provide the creditor perfected creditor status.[34]

27 Revised Article 9, §§ 9-102 and 9-103.

28 UCC § 9-304 (Revised Article 9, § 9-312).

29 UCC § 9-316(a).

30 UCC § 9-104.

31 Revised Article 9 does not change this principle.

32 The sample financing form included with Revised Article 9, § 9-521 does not even have a place for the debtor's signature. While a signed security agreement and signed financing statement are valid for both the security agreement and financing statement, the revisions also make it clear that such formalities are no longer necessary.

33 Revised Article 9, § 9-509 permits the debtor and creditor to agree otherwise. For example, a debtor can place a requirement in the security agreement that the creditor obtain his or her signature before filing a financing statement.

34 Revised Article 9, § 9-510.

FIGURE 34-1 Sample Financial Statement

UCC FINANCING STATEMENT

FOLLOW INSTRUCTIONS (front and back) CAREFULLY

A. NAME & PHONE OF CONTACT AT FILER [optional]

B. SEND ACKNOWLEDGEMENT TO: (Name and Address)

THE ABOVE SPACE IS FOR FILING OFFICE USE ONLY

1. DEBTOR'S EXACT FULL LEGAL NAME—Insert only one debtor name (1a or 1b)—do not abbreviate or combine

1a. ORGANIZATION'S NAME			
OR 1b. INDIVIDUAL'S LAST NAME	FIRST NAME	MIDDLE NAME	SUFFIX

1c. MAILING ADDRESS	CITY	STATE	POSTAL CODE	COUNTRY

1d. TAX ID#: SSN OR EIN	ADD'L INFO RE ORGANIZATION DEBTOR	1e. TYPE OF ORGANIZATION	1f. JURISDICTION OF ORGANIZATION	1g. ORGANIZATION ID #, if any ☐ NONE

2. ADDITIONAL DEBTOR'S EXACT FULL LEGAL NAME—Insert only one debtor name (2a or 2b)—do not abbreviate or combine names

2a. ORGANIZATION'S NAME			
OR 2b. INDIVIDUAL'S LAST NAME	FIRST NAME	MIDDLE NAME	SUFFIX

2c. MAILING ADDRESS	CITY	STATE	POSTAL CODE	COUNTRY

2d. TAX ID#: SSN OR EIN	ADD'L INFO RE ORGANIZATION DEBTOR	2e. TYPE OF ORGANIZATION	2f. JURISDICTION OF ORGANIZATION	2g. ORGANIZATION ID #, If any ☐ NONE

3. SECURED PARTY'S NAME (or NAME of TOTAL ASSIGNEE of ASSIGNOR S/P)—Insert only one secured party name (3a or 3b)

3a. ORGANIZATION'S NAME			
OR 3b. INDIVIDUAL'S LAST NAME	FIRST NAME	MIDDLE NAME	SUFFIX

3c. MAILING ADDRESS	CITY	STATE	POSTAL CODE	COUNTRY

4. This FINANCING STATEMENT covers the following collateral:

5. ALTERNATIVE DESIGNATION (if applicable) ☐ LESSEE/LEASOR ☐ CONSIGNEE/CONSIGNOR ☐ BAILEE/BAILOR ☐ SELLER/BUYER ☐ AG. LIEN ☐ NON-UCC FILING

6. ☐ This FINANCING STATEMENT is to be filed [for record](or recorded)in the REAL ESTATE RECORDS. Attach Addendum [if applicable]	7. Check to REQUEST SEARCH REPORT(s) on DEBTOR(s) [ADDITIONAL FEE] [optional]	☐ All Debtors ☐ Debtor 1 ☐ Debtor 2

8. OPTIONAL FILER REFERENCE DATA

NATIONAL UCC FINANCING STATEMENT (FORM UCC 1) (REV. 07/29/98)

CPA (a) The Content of the Financing Statement

A financing statement must provide "the name of the debtor . . . the name of the secured party or representative of the secured party . . . [and an indication of] the collateral covered by the financing statement."[35] The form provided by Revised Article 9 drafters (see Figure 34-1) includes much more information. Under § 9-516, additional requirements are imposed for initial financing statements that include "a mailing address for the debtor [and] . . . whether the debtor is an individual or organization."[36] Furthermore, § 9-511 requires that the secured party of record provide an address so that there is an address for mailing notices required under other sections. So, while a financing statement with simply the debtor's and secured party's name and a description of the collateral is sufficient for perfection, it may not provide all the rights and protections the parties need. The requirements are simply listed in different sections in revised Article 9 as opposed to a listing in one section in former Article 9.

Because the filings for Article 9 perfection became electronic in 2006, the precise identification of the debtor has become critical. With electronic filings, those who will be doing searches on debtors will not find matches when the name of the debtor has not been properly entered on the financing statement. Prior to the Article 9 revisions, the courts had some tolerance for human error in determining whether a financing statement identified the debtor sufficiently to provide notice of the security interest in the debtor's property. However, with computer technology, additional precision is necessary or the search is thwarted. The effect under the Revised Article 9 is to increase the consequences for misspelling a consumer's name, which will be a loss of priority by perfection because the electronic search in the state did not uncover prior interests. Courts will be finding more variations in names to be "seriously misleading" because the nature of electronic filings has increased the need for precision.[37]

RECEIVABLES PURCHASING CO., INC. V R & R DIRECTIONAL DRILLING, L.L.C., 588 SE2D 831 (GA APP 2003)

"NET WORK" VS. "NETWORK": JUST ONE SPACE EQUALS A WORLD OF DIFFERENCE UNDER ARTICLE 9

Dillard Smith hired Network Solutions, Inc. as a subcontractor on several projects. Network later assigned all rights that it had to payment for this work to Receivables Purchasing Company (Receivables) and R & R Drilling LLC (R & R). On April 2, 2001, Receivables filed a UCC-1 financing statement in Bartow County to perfect Reçeivables' security interest in these payments. The financing statement listed the debtor as "Net work Solutions, Inc." rather than the correct name "Network Solutions, Inc." R & R subsequently performed drilling services for Network, for which R & R was not paid. On May 23, 2002, R & R obtained a judgment against Network in the amount of $40,993.74. According to R & R's counsel, R & R performed a UCC search under the name "Network Solutions, Inc." to determine if any individual or entity held a superior claim to the funds. When the search failed to reveal any debtor named Network Solutions, Inc., R & R filed a summons and affidavit of garnishment on July 12, 2002, against Network and Dillard Smith for the amount owed to R & R. Dillard Smith answered the summons, stating that it was holding a sum of $32,136.84 which was owed to Network, but that these funds were also being claimed by Receivables. Dillard Smith requested the court to allow the $32,136.84 to be deposited with it. Receivables then filed a motion for withdrawal of the $32,136.84, contending that Receivables had a superior right to these funds by virtue of the UCC-1 financing statement it filed on

35 UCC § 9-502(a).
36 UCC § 9-516(b)(5).
37 UCC § 9-506(a) (2000).

April 2, 2001. R & R responded, arguing that Receivables' UCC-1 statement was not a perfected security interest that could defeat R & R's lien on the proceeds because Receivables failed to properly name Network Solutions, Inc. as the debtor on the financing statement.

The trial court found in favor of R & R. Receivables appealed.

Judicial Opinion

RUFFIN, Presiding Judge.... R & R requested that the Georgia Superior Court Clerks Cooperative Authority (GSCCCA) perform a UCC search pursuant to OCGA § 11-9-523(c). The GSCCCA did a certified search under the correct name Network Solutions, Inc. The search did not reveal Receivables' financing statement, which, as noted above, was filed incorrectly under "Net work Solutions, Inc."

This case turns on whether Receivables has a perfected security interest by virtue of its financing statement. If the security interest is not perfected, R & R is entitled to the funds pursuant to its lien on the proceeds, which dates from the service of the summons and garnishment. Following a hearing on October 10, 2002, the trial court entered a lengthy findings of fact and conclusions of law. The trial court concluded that the incorrect name made the financing statement "seriously misleading" pursuant to OCGA § 11-9-506(b) and thus the statement was not sufficient to perfect Receivables' security interest. Accordingly, the court found in favor of R & R and ordered that R & R could withdraw the $32,136.84 deposited with the court.

Receivables appeals, contending that the trial court erred in making a factual determination that R & R conducted a diligent search. Receivables also contends that the trial court erred in finding that "Net work Solutions, Inc." is seriously misleading pursuant to OCGA § 11-9-506(b).

The trial court's order does not make a finding that R & R's search was "diligent," and Receivables does not cite to any such finding in the record. Accordingly, we do not specifically address this argument. However, we note that the provisions of OCGA § 11-9-506 set forth what type of search is required to determine whether a financing statement is sufficient to perfect a security interest, and the remainder of this opinion addresses that issue.

Under Georgia law, a financing statement is sufficient to perfect a security interest only if it provides the name of the debtor. With respect to a registered organization, as in the present case, the debtor's name is deemed sufficient if the financing statement provides the name of the debtor indicated on the public record of the debtor's jurisdiction of organization which shows the debtor to have been organized.

Accordingly, to be sufficient under the statute, Receivables needed to correctly identify Network Solutions, Inc. on the financing statement. As we have noted, however, Network is incorrectly listed as "Net work Solutions, Inc." OCGA § 11-9-506 defines the effects of such an error:

(a) Minor errors and omissions. A financing statement substantially satisfying the requirements of this part is effective, even if it has minor errors or omissions, unless the errors or omissions make the financing statement seriously misleading. (b) Financing statement seriously misleading. Except as otherwise provided in subsection (c) of this Code section, a financing statement that fails sufficiently to provide the name of the debtor in accordance with subsection (a) of Code Section 11-9-503 is seriously misleading. (c) Financing statement not seriously misleading. If a search of the records of the filing office under the debtor's correct name, using the filing office's standard search logic, if any, would disclose a financing statement that fails sufficiently to provide the name of the debtor in accordance with subsection (a) of Code Section 11-9-503, the name provided does not make the financing statement seriously misleading.

Receivables contends that in finding "Network Solutions, Inc." seriously misleading pursuant to OCGA § 11-9-506(b), the trial court relied too heavily on *Citizens Bank v Ansley*. 467 F.Supp. 51 (M.D.Ga.1979). Receivables also contends that a subsequent Georgia case, *Lehigh Press v Nat. Bank of Ga.*, 193 Ga.App. 888, 389 S.E.2d 376 (1989) compels a different result here. We disagree on both counts.

First, the trial court, although discussing *Citizens Bank* (and several other cases dealing with various errors in a debtor's name on a financing statement), specifically stated that the question in this case is answered by OCGA § 11-9-506, not *Citizens Bank*. Second, both *Citizens Bank* and Lehigh were decided prior to the enactment of OCGA § 11-9-506(b) and (c) and thus neither case refers to these sections. As set forth above, however, these sections specifically define what makes an error or omission in a financing statement seriously misleading. Accordingly, a party filing a financing statement now acts at his peril if he files the statement under an incorrect name.

In the present case, it is undisputed that a search through the Bartow County Superior Court Clerk's Office using the correct name did not reveal the financing statement. Thus, the plain language of OCGA § 11-9-506(b) and (c) mandates the result reached by the trial court. Because the name of the debtor on the financing statement is seriously misleading, Receivables does not have a perfected security interest. Accordingly, we find that the trial court ruled correctly in favor of R & R.

[Judgment affirmed]

Questions

1. What happened when the officials in charge of records ran a search under the name Network Solutions, Inc.?
2. Why does the court not deal with the case law in the cases cited by Receivables?
3. Is "Net work" vs. "Network" seriously misleading, and if so, why?

E-COMMERCE AND CYBERLAW

ENGINES ARE FROM MARS; PRIORITIES ARE FROM FINANCING STATEMENTS

In 2001, the International Association of Corporate Administrators promulgated Model Administrative Rules (MARS), a set of rules for the standards for search engines for court system, land, tax, and lien records. State and local governments will have different technology and standards that range from a liberal search engine to a strict search engine. A *liberal search engine* is similar to Google, which kicks back a corrected term and says, "Did you mean____?" when you type in a name or word that is misspelled. A *strict search engine*, such as the simple one in Microsoft Word, will not find a word or phrase in a document unless you have spelled the search item exactly the way it appears in the document.

The MARS standards migrate toward the strict search engine. However, states have adopted different standards, and the result is that the electronic searches for debtors in various states can be very different. If there is a strict search engine in a state and the person doing the search types in "Ann Smythe," the correct spelling of the debtor's name, the financing statement against "Smythe" that was filed as "Ann Smith" will not be a match and the electronic system will kick out a "NO MATCH FOUND." Likewise, a creditor who files under the name "House, Roger" when the debtor's actual name is "Rodger House" has not perfected.* The same would be true of a financing statement filed under "Terry J. Kinderknecht" when the debtor's actual legal name is "Terrance Joseph Kinderknecht."**

Revised Article 9 created a standard rules for search logic that tend toward the "strict" end of the spectrum. The majority of states have now adopted some version of MARS, although many states have modified the rules in some respect (which has resulted in a great deal of inconsistency; furthermore, some states have not adopted any rule on search logic at all). In general, when a debtor's name has been modified by the applicable search logic, the search will produce a financing statement only if the names "exactly match." if there is no match, the security interest will be "seriously misleading," and therefore unperfected and susceptible to a "strong-arm" attack by a bankruptcy trustee or debtor-in-possession (see the following bankruptcy discussion).

* *Pankratz Implement Company v Citizens National Bank* 004 Kan App LEXIS 1173 (Nov. 19, 2004).

** These examples would result in a "NO MATCH FOUND" and emphasize the importance of using both the debtor's legal name and correct spelling. Furthermore, the courts in all three cases, which are Revised Article 9 cases, did not honor the financing statement as perfection because the names were misleading. The person doing the search is permitted to assume that the debtor has no other secured creditors. *In re Kinderknecht (Clark v Deere & Co.)*, 2004 Bankr LEXIS 477 (10th Cir BAP 2004).

THINKING THINGS THROUGH

YOU SAY "SANG WOO GU," I PUT DOWN "GU, SANG WOO"—WHO WINS?

Creditor ABC filed a financing statement to protect its interest in the assets of debtor, Gu, who owed it $235,000. The financing statement filed in Dekalb County Superior Court listed the debtor's name as "Gu, Sang Woo" and stated the name of the business as "CCO Check Cashing-Buford." The debtor's name is actually "Sang Woo Gu," and the correct name of the business is "CCO Check Cashing." Gu sold his business (that included the assets described in the financing statement) to another party whose lawyer, Jim Choi, conducted a search to determine whether there were any liens or security interests in the property. When Choi ran the search on the correct name of Gu's business, the perfected security interests arose. Choi's client paid $197,000 for the business and ABC sought to foreclose on its interest in the assets so that it could sell them to satisfy the debt Gu owed. Choi claims his client is not subject to the security interest because the financing statement was seriously misleading. Who has priority here? Is the financing statement misleading? [ALL BUSINESS CORP. v CHOI, 2006 WL 1550710 (Ga App)]

Like the security agreement changes under Revised Article 9, the requirements for description of the collateral in the financing statements are now more general.[38] The financing statement need not include the terms of the agreement between the parties. However, a security agreement can be filed as a financing statement if it contains all of the aforementioned required information.

Because the financing statement is intended as notice to third parties, it must be filed in a public place.[39] Revised Article 9 simplifies the formerly complex issues of filing location as a means of encouraging electronic systems that will be statewide, accessible across state lines, and organized simply by name in any index. Revised Article 9's general rule is central filing for financing statements for all types of collateral. Filings for fixtures and other property-related interests have also been simplified with Revised Article 9, deferring to state laws on the proper filing location.[40]

Revised Article 9 also includes an option for filing financing statements for fixtures in the same way as for other forms of collateral. A typical central filing location in many states, both before and after Revised Article 9, is the office of the secretary of state.

CPA (b) Defective Filing

When the filing of the financing statement is defective either because the statement is so erroneous or incomplete that it is seriously misleading or the filing is made in a wrong county or office, the filing fails to perfect the security interest. The idea of perfection by filing is to give public notice of a creditor's interest. To the extent that the notice cannot be located or does not give sufficient information, the creditor then cannot rely on it to obtain the superior position of perfection.

Revised Article 9 has been referred to by commentators as "medium-neutral," which is their way of saying that the means the parties choose for filing, whether by fax or electronically, are to be treated as equals with formal writings for purposes of both the creation of a security interest and its perfection. A comment to Revised Article 9 reads, "data transmitted electronically to the filing office and reduced to tangible form constitute a financing statement or other filing under Article 9 if they provide all the information required under the applicable provision of Article 9." This sanctioning of electronic filing follows the Canadian lead where electronic filing was in place prior to the Article 9 changes here. Because of Revised Article 9, each state has developed its own system for such electronic filing (effective during 2006). While the electronic systems have created some additional issues that still require resolution, many of the issues and exceptions that caused confusion and complexity under old Article 9 have been eliminated

38 However, the sample financing form included with Revised Article 9, § 9-521 includes boxes for all of the same information required under existing Article 9. The sample form in Figure 34-1 would meet the requirements for Revised Article 9.

39 UCC § 9-401; *In re Pacific/West Communications Group, Inc.*, 301 F3d 1150, 48 UCC Rep Serv 2d 462 (9th Cir 2002).

40 Revised Article 9, § 9-501.

with the fast, central, and efficient form of electronic filing.[41]

13. Loss of Perfection

The perfection of the security interest can be lost if the creditor does not comply with the Article 9 requirements for continuing perfection.

(a) Possession of Collateral

When perfection is obtained because the creditor takes possession of the collateral, that perfection is lost if the creditor voluntarily surrenders the collateral to the debtor without any restrictions.

(b) Consumer Goods

The perfection obtained by the automatic status of a PMSI is lost in some cases by removal of the goods to another state. The security interest may also be destroyed by resale of the goods to a consumer. To protect against these types of losses of protection, the creditor needs to file a financing statement. In the case of a PMSI, the perfection is good against other creditors but is not superior when it comes to buyers of the goods.

(c) Lapse of Time

The perfection obtained by filing a financing statement lasts five years. The perfection may be continued for successive five-year periods by filing a continuation statement within six months before the end of each five-year period.[42] Revised Article 9 permits a "manufactured home" exception allowing financing statements on mobile homes to be effective for 30 years.[43]

(d) Removal from State

In most cases, the perfection of a security interest lapses when the collateral is taken by the debtor to another state unless, as noted earlier, the creditor makes a filing in that second state within the four-month period of temporary perfection.

(e) Motor Vehicles

If the security interest is governed by a non-Code statute creating perfection by title certificate notation, the interest, if so noted, remains perfected without regard to lapse of time or removal to another state. The perfection is lost only if a state issues a new title without the security interest notation.

C. Rights of Parties Before Default

The rights of parties to a secured transaction are different in the time preceding the debtor's default from those in the time following the default.

14. Status of Creditor Before Default

The status of a creditor who has loaned money to a debtor is determined by ordinary principles of contract law. A creditor who is a seller of goods has the rights granted by Article 2, Sales, of the UCC. If the creditor is the lessor of goods, that status is determined by Article 2A, Leases, of the UCC.

15. Status of Debtor Before Default

The status of the debtor before default depends on whether there is a loan, a sale, or a lease. The status of a debtor who has borrowed money from a creditor is determined by ordinary principles of contract law. If the debtor is a buyer or lessee of goods, the debtor's status is determined by Article 9, Secured Transactions, and by either Article 2 or 2A of the UCC.

16. Statement of Account

To keep the record straight, the debtor may send the creditor a written statement of the amount the debtor thinks is due and an itemization of the collateral together with a request that the creditor approve the statement as submitted or correct and return the statement. Within two weeks after receiving the debtor's statement, the creditor must send the debtor a written approval or correction. If the secured creditor has assigned the secured claim, the creditor's reply must state the name and address of the assignee.

[41] For a discussion of the legal issues that have arisen in electronic filing, see Meghan M. Sercombe, "Good Technology and Bad Law: How Computerization Threatens Notice Filing Under Revised Article 9," *84 Tex. L. Rev.*1065 (2006).

[42] UCC § 9-403 (Revised Article 9, § 9-516). Failure to file with the secretary of state was fatal for a priority of secured creditor when a central filing was required, despite the filing at the county level. *In re Ferro*, 37 UCC2d 1175 (Bankr WD Mo 1999).

[43] Revised Article 9, § 9-515.

17. Termination Statements

A debtor who has paid his debt in full may make a written demand on the secured creditor, or the latter's assignee if the security interest has been assigned, to send the debtor a **termination statement,**[44] which states that a security interest is no longer claimed under the specified financing statement. The debtor may present this statement to the filing officer, who marks the record terminated and returns the various papers that were filed to the secured party. The termination statement clears the debtor's record so subsequent buyers or lenders will not be subject to the now-satisfied security interest. The creditor has 20 days from receipt of a demand for a termination statement from a debtor to file a termination statement (one month for consumer goods).[45]

18. Correction Statements

Because Revised Article 9 permits creditors and others to simply file "authorized" financing statements, debtors are given protection for abusive filings of Article 9 interests. Under Revised Article 9, debtors are permitted to protest filed financing statements with a filing of their own correction statements. While the security interest is not abolished by such a filing, its content does provide public notice of an underlying dispute. A debtor can also file a correction statement when a creditor fails to provide a termination statement.[46]

D. Priorities

Two or more parties may have conflicting interests in the same collateral. This section discusses the rights of creditors and buyers with respect to each other and to collateral that carries a secured interest or perfected secured interest.

CPA 19. Unsecured Party Versus Unsecured Party

When creditors are unsecured, they have equal priority. In the event of insolvency or bankruptcy of the debtor, all the unsecured creditors stand at the end of the line in terms of repayment of their debts (see Chapter 35 for more details on bankruptcy priorities). If the assets of the debtor are insufficient to satisfy all unsecured debtors, the unsecured debtors simply receive a **pro rata** share of their debts.

CPA 20. Secured Party Versus Unsecured Party

A secured creditor has a right superior to that of an unsecured creditor because the secured creditor can take back the collateral from the debtor's assets, while an unsecured creditor simply waits for the leftovers once all secured creditors have taken back their collateral. If the collateral is insufficient to satisfy the secured creditor's debt, the secured debtor can still stand in line with the unsecured creditors and collect any additional amount not satisfied by the collateral or a pro rata share. **For Example,** suppose that Linens Galore has a security interest in Linens R Us's inventory. Linens Galore has the right to repossess the inventory and sell it to satisfy the debt Linens R Us owes. Suppose that Linens R Us owes Linens Galore $22,000, and the sale of the inventory brings $15,000. Linens Galore still has a claim as an unsecured creditor for the remaining $7,000 due.

CPA 21. Secured Party Versus Secured Party

If two creditors have a security interest in the same collateral, their priority is determined according to the **first-in-time provision;** that is, the creditor whose interest attached first has priority in the collateral.[47] The secured party whose interest was last to attach must then proceed against the debtor as an unsecured creditor because the collateral was given to the creditor whose interest attached first. **For Example,** if Bob pledged his antique sign collection to Bill on January 15, 2007, with a signed security agreement in exchange for a $5,000 loan, and then pledged the same collection to Jane on February 20, 2007, with a signed security agreement, Bill has priority because his security agreement attached first.

[44] UCC § 9-404 (Revised Article 9, § 9-513); *Kultura, Inc. v Southern Leasing Corp.*, 923 SW2d 536 (Tenn 1996), but see but see *Mac'Kie v. Wal-Mart Stores, Inc.*, 127 F3d 1102 (6th Cir 1997).

[45] UCC § 9-513(b) and (c).

[46] Revised Article 9, § 9-518.

[47] UCC § 9-312 (Revised Article 9, § 9-313); *Melcher v Bank of Madison, Nebraska*, 529 NW2d 814 (Neb App 1995) and *Maryott v Oconto Cattle Co.*, 259 Neb 41, 607 NW2d 820, 41 UCC Rep Serv 2d 279 (Neb 2000).

CPA 22. Perfected Secured Party Versus Secured Party

The perfected secured creditor takes priority over the unperfected secured creditor and is entitled to take the collateral. The unperfected secured party is then left to seek remedies as an unsecured creditor because the collateral has been given to the perfected creditor. **For Example,** with respect to Bob's sign collection, if Jane filed a financing statement on February 21, 2007, she would have priority over Bill because her perfected interest would be superior to Bill's unperfected interest even though Bill's interest attached before Jane's.

The perfected secured party's interest as against other types of creditors, such as lienors, mortgagees, and judgment creditors, is also determined on a **first-to-perfect basis.** If the secured party perfects before a judgment lien or mortgage is recorded, the perfected secured creditor has priority.[48] The perfected party takes priority over the secured party even when the perfected secured party is aware of the security interest prior to perfection.[49]

GENERAL MOTORS ACCEPTANCE CORP. V LINCOLN NATIONAL BANK, 18 SW3D 337, 40 UCC REP SERV 2D 610, 42 UCC REP SERV 2D 834 (KY 2000)

THE BANK DOESN'T WIN: WHEN SECURED PARTIES TAKE PRIORITY OVER OVERDRAFTS

General Motors Acceptance Corporation (GMAC) financed the inventory of Donohue Ferrill Motor Company, Inc., which gave GMAC a security interest in its vehicle inventory and all the proceeds of that inventory. The security agreement and financing statements were executed, and GMAC properly filed the financing statements.

Shortly before Donohue Ferrill's business failed, it sold six trucks and then deposited the proceeds of $124,610.80 from the sale of those trucks into its account at Lincoln National Bank. Lincoln took the deposited funds and applied them to account overdrafts that Donohue Ferrill had. For 38 of the 62 business days of September, October, and November 1991, Donohue Ferrill's account was overdrawn. Lincoln National honored 133 overdrafts during these three months and charged Donohue Ferrill a total of $1,995 in fees. The total amount of the overdrawn balances for those 38 days was $1,943,306.25.

GMAC objected, saying that it had priority in those funds. The trial court and court of appeals found for the bank and GMAC appealed.

Judicial Opinion

LAMBERT, Chief Justice. . . . The issue presented is whether a bank may apply the cash proceeds of collateral to overdrafts allowed a depositor, thereby defeating established priorities.

GMAC based its claim upon KRS 355.9-306(2), which states

Except where this article otherwise provides, a security interest continues in collateral notwithstanding sale, exchange or other disposition thereof unless the disposition was authorized by the secured party in the security agreement or otherwise, and also continues in any identifiable proceeds including collections received by the debtor.

Where cash proceeds are covered into the debtor's checking account and paid out in the operation of the debtor's business, recipients of the funds of course take free of any claim which the secured party may have in them as proceeds. What has been said relates to payments and transfers in ordinary course. The law of fraudulent conveyances would no doubt in appropriate cases support recovery of proceeds by a secured party from a transferee out of ordinary course or otherwise in collusion with the debtor to defraud the secured party.

Payment of an overdraft by a bank is of the nature of a loan to the account owner and is premised upon the condition of repayment. Thus, Lincoln National made loans

48 *General Elec. Capital Corp. v Union Planters Bank,* N.A., 290 BR 676, 49 UCC Rep Serv 2d 1298 (ED Mo 2003)

49 *St. Paul Mercury Insurance Company v Merchants & Marine Bank,* 882 So 2d 766 (Miss 2004).

to Donohue Ferrill in the amount of the overdrafts paid. Since the bank had no security for such loans, it was an unsecured creditor of Donohue Ferrill. Thus, as an unsecured creditor, Lincoln National was without any right to take or retain assets of Donohue Ferrill that were subject to the perfected security interest of other secured creditors.

The trial court and the Court of Appeals found such an exception in Official Comment 2(c) to the UCC § 9-306 (KRS 355.9-306), holding that the proceeds of the collateral used to cover prior overdrafts were transferred out of Donohue Ferrill's account in the ordinary course of business. We disagree with this interpretation. Although the commentary provides an exception for proceeds from the debtor's checking account and paid in the ordinary course of the operation of the debtor's business, this exception does not apply when a bank seizes funds deposited in a customer's account and applies such funds to payment of overdrafts or antecedent debts. Such an interpretation would eviscerate the security interest in proceeds of collateral contrary to KRS 355.9-306(2) and permit a bank that had made an unsecured loan to leapfrog secured creditors.

Our conclusion here . . . is that a secured party's right to proceeds of collateral deposited to the debtor's bank account is superior to the bank's right to a setoff of the same proceeds against amounts the debtor owes the bank.

For the foregoing reasons, the decision of the Court of Appeals is reversed, and this cause is remanded to the trial court for entry of judgment consistent herewith.

Questions

1. What did the bank do to the debtor's account?
2. What would happen if banks were permitted to take proceeds deposited by creditors into their accounts?
3. Who has priority in the funds, the bank or GMAC?

CPA 23. Perfected Secured Party Versus Perfected Secured Party

The general rule for priority among two perfected secured creditors in the same collateral is also a first-in-time rule: The creditor who perfected first is given priority. **For Example,** again with respect to Bob's sign collection, if Bill filed a financing statement on February 22, 2007, Jane would still have priority because she perfected her interest first. If, however, Bill filed a financing statement on January 31, 2007, he would have priority over Jane. There are, however, three exceptions to this rule of first-in-time, first-in-right for perfected secured creditors.

CPA (a) The Purchase Money Security Interest in Inventory[50]

If the collateral is inventory, the purchase money secured creditor must do two things to prevail even over prior perfected secured creditors. The creditor must (1) perfect before the debtor receives possession of the goods that will be inventory and (2) give notice to any other secured party who has previously filed a financing statement with respect to that inventory.[51] The other secured parties must receive this notice before the debtor receives possession of the goods covered by the purchase money security interest. Compliance with these notice requirements gives the last creditor to extend credit for the inventory the priority position, which is a rule of law based on the practical notion that a debtor must be able to replenish its inventory to stay in business and keep creditors paid in a timely fashion. With this priority for subsequently perfected creditors, debtors have the opportunity to replenish inventory. **For Example,** suppose that First Bank has financed the inventory for Roberta's Exotic Pets, taken a security interest in the inventory, and filed a financing statement covering Roberta's inventory. Two months later, Animal Producers sells reptiles on credit to Roberta, taking a security interest in Roberta's inventory. To take priority over First Bank, Animal Producers would have to file the financing statement on the inventory before Roberta receives the reptiles and notify First Bank at the same time. The commercial rationale for this priority exception is to permit businesses to replenish their inventories by giving new suppliers a higher priority.

(b) Purchase Money Security Interest—Noninventory Collateral

If the collateral is *noninventory collateral,* such as equipment, the purchase money secured creditor prevails over all others as to the same collateral if that

[50] Revised Article 9, § 9-103 expands the definition of a PMSI in inventory. Consignments are treated as PMSIs in inventory.

[51] Revised Article 9, § 9-324.

creditor files a financing statement within 20 days after the debtor takes possession of the collateral. **For Example,** First Bank loans money to debtor Kwik Copy and properly files a financing statement covering all of Kwik Copy's present and subsequently acquired copying equipment. Second Bank then loans money to Kwik Copy for the purchase of a new copier. Second Bank's interest in the copier will be superior to First Bank's interest if Second Bank perfects its interest by filing either before the debtor receives the copier or within 20 days thereafter.

(c) Status of Repair or Storage Lien

What happens when the debtor does not pay for the repair or storage of the collateral? In most states, a person repairing or storing goods has a lien or right to keep possession of the goods until paid for such services. The repairer or storer also has the right to sell the goods to obtain payment if the customer fails to pay and if proper notice is given.[52]

Article 9 makes a lien for repairs or storage superior to the perfected security interest in the collateral. The only exception to this rule makes the perfected security interest superior if the lien was created by statute rather than by common law and that statute expressly states that the lien is subordinate to a perfected security interest in the collateral.

Figure 34-2, on page 692, provides a summary of the priorities of various parties with respect to secured and unsecured creditor interests.

24. Secured Party Versus Buyer of Collateral from Debtor

The debtor may sell the collateral to a third person. How does this sale affect the secured creditor?

CPA (a) Sales in the Ordinary Course of Business

A buyer who buys goods from the debtor in the ordinary course of business is not subject to any creditor's security interest regardless of whether the interest was perfected or unperfected and regardless of whether the buyer had actual knowledge of the security interest. The reason for this protection of buyers in the ordinary course of business is that subjecting buyers to a creditor's reclaim of goods would cause great delay and hesitation in commercial and consumer sales transactions.[53]

SCHULTZ V BANK OF THE WEST, C.B.C., 934 P2D 421 (ORE 1997)

THE MOTOR HOME THAT TRAVELED FROM CREDITORS TO DEBTORS TO BUYERS IN ORDINARY COURSE

In 1987, the Muirs (defendants) bought a motor home. In 1988, the Muirs created and Bank of the West (defendant/the Bank) acquired and perfected a security interest in the motor home. In 1992, the Muirs entered into an agreement with Gateleys' Fairway Motors (Gateleys) by which Gateleys would sell the motor home by consignment. Gateleys was a motor home dealer. Gateleys sold the motor home to Howard and Ann Schultz (plaintiffs). The Schultzes did not know of the consignment arrangement or of the security interest of the Bank. Gateleys failed to give the sales money to the Muirs and then filed for bankruptcy.

The Schultzes brought suit seeking a declaration that they owned the motor home free of the Bank's security interest. The trial court granted the Schultzes summary judgment, and the Court of Appeals reversed.

Judicial Opinion

GILLETTE, J. . . . " 'Buyer in ordinary course of business' means a person who in good faith and without knowledge that the sale to the person is in violation of the ownership rights or security interest of a third party in the goods buys in ordinary course from a person in the business of selling goods of that kind but does not include a pawnbroker."

If plaintiffs can show that they come within the terms of ORS 79.3070(1), they own the motor home free of the Bank's security interest.

52 UCC § 9-310 (Revised Article 9, § 9-333); *In re Northrup*, 220 BR 855, 35 UCCRS2d 711 (Bankr CED Pa 1998).

53 Revised Article 9, § 9-320 covers the rights of buyers of goods.

This case brings to mind the military adage that all battles are fought at the corner of two maps.

Were plaintiffs buyers in the ordinary course of business?

As always, in construing an Oregon statute, this court's task is to discern the intent of the legislature. In doing so, this court looks first to the text and context of the statute.

Here, the relevant text from ORS 71.2010(9) states that a buyer in ordinary course "buys . . . from a person in the business of selling goods of that kind." Clearly, the plaintiffs bought from Gateleys, which was in the business of selling goods of that kind. But does the text require that the "person in the business of selling goods" have title to the specific goods that the buyer buys, i.e., be the "seller" of the goods. This inquiry is important, because Gateleys disposed of the Muirs' motor home on consignment—it did not have title.

The text does not require that the "person" from whom the goods are purchased have title. This is clear, first, from the text itself. Use of the word, "person," instead of "seller" in a law as carefully crafted as the UCC is a conscious choice. That choice recognizes that there will be those who hold out goods for sale who do not have title, e.g., consignees such as Gateleys, in circumstances in which the stability of the marketplace would be undermined if good faith purchases from those parties were not valid. This point is made even more clear by the textual exclusion of "pawnbroker"—a special kind of consignee—from the definition. Finally, the text of ORS 71.2010(9) recognizes that a sale to a buyer in ordinary course may be "in violation of the ownership rights . . . of a third party." Any ownership rights in a third party would mean that the "person in the business" did not have title to the goods. Thus, the text of ORS 71.2010(9) indicates that "person" does not mean "seller."

If there were any doubt about the foregoing conclusion, the UCC provides other contextual clues to flesh out the concept of a buyer in ordinary course for the purposes of ORS 71.2010(9). ORS 72.4030(3), which is a part of the "sales" chapter of the UCC, [and] provides that "[a]ny entrusting of possession of goods to a merchant who deals in goods of that kind gives the merchant power to transfer all rights of the entruster to a buyer in ordinary course of business." And, as already noted, another section in that chapter, ORS 72.1060(1), defines a "sale" as "the passing of title from the seller to the buyer for a price." When those two sections are read together, it becomes clear that the UCC presumes that a buyer can qualify as a buyer in the ordinary course when the buyer purchases goods from a dealer who only possesses, but does not have legal title to, those goods.

Moreover, in examining context, we also look to the UCC commentary and to the decisions of other jurisdictions. The UCC commentary does not address explicitly the question whether a buyer who buys from a consignment dealer qualifies as a buyer in the ordinary course. However, the commentary apparently presumes that such a buyer can so qualify. Most jurisdictions similarly have presumed that buyers who buy from consignment dealers can qualify as buyers in the ordinary course.

The text and context of ORS 71.2010(9) demonstrate that a buyer of consignment goods who buys from a consignment dealer can be a buyer in ordinary course for the purposes of that statute. There is no dispute here that plaintiffs meet the other requirements for being buyers in ordinary course. Consequently, we conclude that plaintiffs were buyers in ordinary course when they bought the consigned motor home at Gateleys.

We hold that plaintiffs are entitled to the protection of ORS 79.3070(1), because they were buyers in the ordinary course of business and the seller created the security interest. The Court of Appeals erred in reaching a contrary result.

The decision of the Court of Appeals is reversed, and the judgment of the circuit court is affirmed.

[Reversed]

Questions

1. Were the Schultzes buyers in the ordinary course of business?
2. Does it make any difference that the motor home was there on consignment?
3. Who has priority in the motor home?

CPA (b) Sales Not in the Ordinary Course of Business: The Unperfected Security Interest

A sale not in the ordinary course of business is one in which the seller is not usually a seller of such merchandise. **For Example,** if a buyer purchases a computer desk from an office supply store, the sale is in the ordinary course of business. If that same buyer purchases that same computer desk from a law firm that is going out of business, that buyer is not purchasing in the ordinary course of business. If a buyer is purchasing the collateral and the purchase is not in

FIGURE 34-2 Priority of Secured Interest Under Article 9

CONFLICT	PRIORITY
SECURED PARTY VERSUS SECURED PARTY	FIRST TO ATTACH
UNSECURED PARTY VERSUS SECURED PARTY	SECURED PARTY
PERFECTED SECURED PARTY VERSUS SECURED PARTY	PERFECTED SECURED PARTY
PERFECTED SECURED PARTY VERSUS PERFECTED SECURED PARTY	PARTY WHO IS FIRST TO PERFECT
PERFECTED SECURED PARTY VERSUS LIENOR	PARTY WHO FILED (FINANCING STATEMENT OR LIEN) FIRST [§ 9-307(2)] (REV. § 9-317)
EXCEPTIONS	
PMSI IN FIXTURES VERSUS PERFECTED SECURED PARTY	PMSI CREDITOR IF PERFECTED BEFORE ANNEXATION OR WITHIN 20 DAYS AFTER ANNEXATION (PMSI WILL HAVE PRIORITY EVEN OVER PRIOR PERFECTED SECURED PARTY) (§ 9-313, § 9-314) (REV. § 9-317)
PMSI IN EQUIPMENT VERSUS PERFECTED SECURED PARTY	PMSI IS PERFECTED WITHIN 20 DAYS AFTER DELIVERY [§ 9-301(2), § 9-312(4)] (REV. § 9-317)
PMSI IN INVENTORY VERSUS PERFECTED SECURED PARTY	PMSI IS PERFECTED BEFORE DELIVERY AND IF PERFECTED SECURED PARTY GIVEN NOTICE BEFORE DELIVERY [§ 9-312(3)] (REV. § 9-317)
PMSI IN CONSUMER GOODS VERSUS BUYER	BUYER UNLESS PERFECTION IS BY FILING BEFORE PURCHASE [§ 9-302(1)(D)] (REV. § 9-317)
PERFECTED SECURED PARTY VERSUS BUYER	BUYER IN ORDINARY COURSE WINS EVEN WITH KNOWLEDGE [§ 9-306(1)(D)] (REV. § 9-320)

the ordinary course of business but the security interest is unperfected, such a security interest has no effect against a buyer who gives value and buys in good faith, that is, not knowing of the security interest. A buyer who does not satisfy these conditions is subject to the security interest.

CPA (c) Sales Not in the Ordinary Course of Business: The Perfected Security Interest

If the security interest was perfected, the buyer of the collateral is ordinarily subject to the security interest unless the creditor consented to the sale.[54]

[54] In Revised Article 9, § 1-201(9) adds that a purchase from a pawnbroker will not be considered a sale in the ordinary course of business.

FIGURE 34-3 Priorities in Transfer of Collateral by Sale

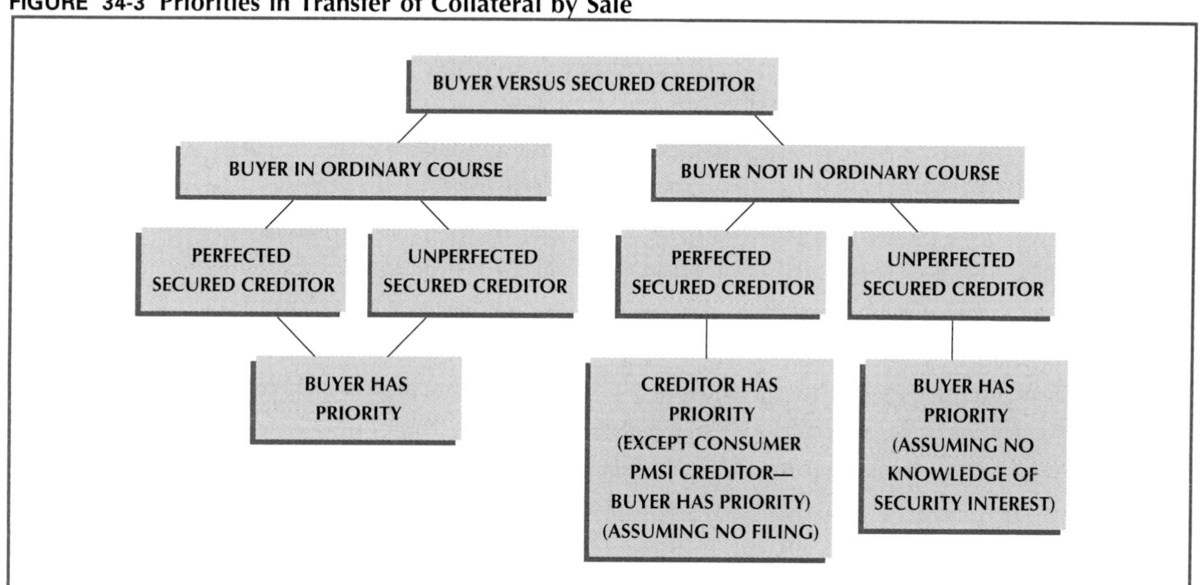

CPA (d) Sales Not in the Ordinary Course of Business: The Consumer Debtor's Resale of Consumer Goods

When the collateral constitutes consumer goods in the hands of the debtor, a resale of the goods to another consumer destroys the automatically perfected PMSI of the consumer debtor's creditor. Assuming that the buyer from the consumer debtor has no knowledge of a security interest, she will take the collateral free and clear from the creditor's security interest even though there was perfection by that creditor. Thus, the perfection without filing option afforded consumer PMSI creditors has a flaw in its coverage when it comes to a consumer debtor selling his refrigerator to a neighbor. Without a filed financing statement, the neighbor buyer takes the refrigerator free and clear of the creditor's security interest in it. However, consumer creditors can avoid the loss of this perfected interest by perfecting through filing. With filing, consumer PMSI creditors enjoy continuation of their interests even when the neighbor has paid the consumer debtor for the refrigerator.

Figure 34-3 offers a summary of the rights of buyers of collateral with respect to the creditors who hold security interests in that collateral.

E. Rights of Parties After Default

When a debtor defaults on an obligation in a secured transaction, the secured creditor has the option to sue the debtor to enforce the debt or of proceeding against the collateral.

CPA 25. Creditor's Possession and Disposition of Collateral

Upon the debtor's default, the secured party is entitled to take the collateral from the debtor.[55] **Self-help repossession** is allowed if this can be done without causing a **breach of the peace.** If a breach of the peace might occur, the seller must use court action to obtain the collateral.

The secured creditor may sell, lease, or otherwise dispose of the collateral to pay the defaulted debt.[56]

[55] UCC § 9-503 (Revised Article 9, § 9-607). Repossession on private property where a creditor cut a lock was not a breach of the peace when security agreement authorized such trespass for repossession. *Wombles Charters, Inc. v Orix Credit Alliance, Inc.*, 39 UCC2d 599 (SDNY 1999).

[56] Revised Article 9, § 9-611 requires the secured party to notify all other secured parties and lienholders who have filed or recorded interests in the collateral of its intent to sell the collateral. This requirement was eliminated in the 1972 version of Article 9, but it is now once again a requirement.

CHRYSLER CREDIT V KOONTZ, 661 NE2D 1171 (ILL APP CT 1996)

I WAS IN MY DRIVEWAY IN MY UNDERWEAR WHEN THEY REPOSSESSED MY CAR!

Koontz entered into an agreement with Chrysler to purchase a 1988 Sundance in exchange for 60 monthly payments of $185.92. When Koontz defaulted on the contract in early 1991, Chrysler notified him that it would repossess the vehicle if he did not make up the missed payments. Koontz notified Chrysler that he would make every effort to catch up on the payments, that he did not want the vehicle to be repossessed, and that Chrysler was not to enter his private property to repossess the car. Chrysler repossessed the car, however, according to the self-help repossession statute of the UCC.

When Koontz heard the repossession in progress, he rushed outside in his underwear and hollered, "Don't take it," to the repossessor. The repossessor did not respond and proceeded to take the vehicle. Chrysler sold the car and filed a complaint against Koontz seeking a deficiency judgment for the balance due on the loan. Koontz alleged that the repossession was a breach of the peace. From a judgment in favor of Chrysler, Koontz appealed.

Judicial Opinion

KUEHN, J. . . . Koontz raises only a single issue on appeal. He contends that the trial court erred in finding that Chrysler's repossession did not breach the peace because there was evidence that Koontz made an unequivocal oral protest to the repossession of his vehicle at the time of repossession. Koontz argues that when the vehicle was taken despite his protest, "Don't take it," a breach of the peace occurred, citing *Dixon v Ford Motor Credit Co.* (1979), 72 Ill. App.3d 983, 391 N.E.2d 493. In *Dixon*, the court, relying upon White and Summers, Uniform Commercial Code § 26-6, at 972, stated that "[w]hen a creditor repossesses in disregard of the debtor's unequivocal oral protest, the repossession may be found to be in breach of the peace."

Chrysler contends that Koontz's oral protest did not breach the peace because "none of the elements of violence indicated in the decisions cited by the Defendant exists [*sic*] in this case." Chrysler argues by implication that without an element of violence there can be no breach of the peace. Chrysler also argues that if we find that an oral protest without an element of violence constitutes a breach of the peace, then we would be narrowing the self-help repossession statute to the point that it would be useless to a secured creditor.

We recognize that the self-help repossession statute extends a conditional self-help privilege to secured parties; however, we must apply the statute in a way that reduces the risk to the public associated with extrajudicial conflict resolution. It is apparent that the self-help remedy is efficient for secured creditors and results in reduced costs for both creditors and debtors. Efficiency and reduced litigation costs are desirable. Still, a debtor's private property interests and society's interest in tranquility must also be protected.

Because self-help repossession is statutory, we look to the language of § 9-503 to establish the parameters of the remedy that the statute offers to secured parties who seek to repossess collateral without judicial process. The statute provides in pertinent part: "Unless otherwise agreed a secured party has on default the right to take possession of the collateral. In taking possession a secured party may proceed without judicial process if this can be done without breach of the peace or may proceed by action." . . . The key to whether a self-help repossession is permissible depends on whether the peace has been or is likely to be breached.

Section 9-503 does not define breach of the peace, and the phrase "breach of the peace" has never had a precise meaning in relation to specific conduct. The phrase has been construed on several occasions. In *Cantwell v State of Connecticut* (1940), 310 U.S. 296, 308, 84 L. Ed. 1213, 60 S. Ct. 900, 905, the court stated: "The offense known as breach of the public peace embraces a great variety of conduct destroying or menacing public order and tranquility. It includes not only violent acts but acts and words likely to produce violence in others." In *Leavitt v Charles R. Hearn, Inc.* (1974), 19 Ill. App. 3d 980, 312 N.E.2d 806, we noted that implied force may also constitute a breach of the peace. Threats and epithets directed at another may or may not constitute a breach of the peace, depending upon the likelihood that a disturbance will follow.

We therefore conclude that the term "breach of the peace" connotes conduct which incites or is likely to incite immediate public turbulence, or which leads to or is likely to lead to an immediate loss of public order and tranquility. Violent conduct is not a necessary element. The probability of violence at the time of or immediately prior to the repossession is sufficient.

After a thorough examination of the record, we find no abuse of discretion on the part of the trial court in ruling that Chrysler's repossession did not breach the peace. Whether a given act provokes a breach of the peace depends upon the accompanying circumstances of each particular case. In this case, Koontz testified that he only yelled, "Don't take it," and that the repossessor made no verbal or physical response. He also testified that although he was close enough to the repossessor to run over and get into a fight, he elected not to because he was in his underwear. Furthermore, there was no evidence in the record that Koontz implied violence at the time of or immediately prior to the repossession by holding a weapon, clenching a fist, or even vehemently arguing toe-to-toe with the repossessor so that a reasonable repossessor would understand that violence was likely to ensue if he continued with the vehicle repossession. We think that the evidence, viewed as a whole, could lead a reasonable fact finder to determine that the circumstances of the repossession did not amount to a breach of the peace.

We note that to rule otherwise would be to invite the ridiculous situation whereby a debtor could avoid a deficiency judgment by merely stepping out of his house and yelling once at a nonresponsive repossessor. Such a narrow definition of the conduct necessary to breach the peace would, we think, render the self-help repossession statute useless. Therefore, we reject Koontz's invitation to define "an unequivocal oral protest," without more, as a breach of the peace. . . .

In this case, Koontz testified that he notified Chrysler prior to the repossession that it was not permitted to enter onto his property. He also testified that he pulled his vehicle into his front yard so that he could see it by the light of the front porch. This testimony was uncontroverted. There was no testimony, however, that Chrysler entered through any barricade or did anything other than simply enter onto the property and drive the car away. Viewing this evidence in the light most favorable to the prevailing party, we believe that Chrysler's entry upon the private real property of Koontz and taking possession of the secured collateral, without more, did not constitute a breach of the peace. Chrysler enjoyed a limited privilege to enter Koontz's property for the sole and exclusive purpose of effecting the repossession. So long as the entry was limited in purpose (repossession), and so long as no gates, barricades, doors, enclosures, buildings, or chains were breached or cut, no breach of the peace occurred by virtue of the entry onto his property. . . .

[Affirmed]

Questions

1. What was the basis for Koontz arguing that there was a breach of the peace?
2. Did Chrysler have a right to repossess the car?
3. What determines the rights of the parties after default?
4. How did the court define a breach of the peace?

THINKING THINGS THROUGH

BREAKING, ENTERING, AND DRAGGING TO REPOSSESS

Christopher and Joy Callaway had purchased a 1993 Geo Tracker sport utility vehicle from Summerdale Budget Auto & Truck, Inc. Baldwin Finance, Inc., which financed the Callaways' purchase of the Tracker, held a lien on it. The Callaways fell behind on their payments, and the Tracker was repossessed once, but it was redeemed when the Callaways paid what was due. The Callaways fell behind in their payments again, and Baldwin sent Michael Whittenton to repossess the Tracker again. Joy heard noises outside their residence, and when she went outside to see what was happening, she saw Whittenton, who was repossessing the Tracker. Joy asked Whittenton to leave the property, but Whittenton continued with the repossession. Joy went back inside the house and told Christopher that Whittenton was taking the Tracker. Christopher told Whittenton to stop and told Whittenton that he needed to get some

THINKING THINGS THROUGH

continued

things out of the Tracker before Whittenton took it. Joy telephoned Budget to make sure that the due date for the October payment had been extended and, while she was on the telephone with Budget, she heard Christopher talking to Whittenton. Then she heard her husband scream.

The following events apparently preceded his scream. Whittenton had secured the Tracker to his truck, and Christopher saw Whittenton walk around to the driver's side of his truck and get in. Whittenton was not looking in Christopher's direction when Christopher walked outside. Christopher grabbed the roll bar on the Tracker as Whittenton began to drive away. Christopher banged on Whittenton's truck and yelled to get Whittenton's attention. Then, as Whittenton was driving down the driveway, the Tracker hit a pothole, and Christopher lost his balance. While he was trying to regain his balance, the rear tire on the driver's side of the Tracker ran over his foot. He then grabbed the roll bar on the Tracker again so that it would not run over him. Whittenton continued driving, dragging Christopher down the driveway and 60 to 100 feet down Highway 10. One of the vehicles ran over the family's cat.

Whittenton said that he did not have a conversation with Joy as he was hooking up the Tracker to tow it, and that he saw Christopher run through a ditch, run beside the Tracker, and jump onto the vehicle. Whittenton testified that he stopped his truck after turning onto Highway 10 because he saw Christopher jump between the truck towing the Tracker and the Tracker. Another witness, Ronnie Black, testified that he saw Christopher run through a ditch and jump onto the Tracker while it was on Highway 10.

The Callaways sued Whittenton, Budget, and Baldwin Finance, alleging assault and battery, negligence, wantonness, trespass, civil conspiracy, and wrongful repossession. Is this wrongful repossession? [CALLAWAY V WHITTENTON, 892 So 2d 852 (Ala 2003)]

The sale may be private or public, at any time and place, and on any terms provided that the sale is done in a manner that is commercially reasonable. The creditor's sale eliminates all of the debtor's interest in the collateral.

26. Creditor's Retention of Collateral

Instead of selling the collateral, the creditor may wish to keep it and cancel the debt owed.[57]

(a) Notice of Intention

To retain the collateral in satisfaction of the debt, the creditor must send the debtor written notice of this intent.[58]

CPA (b) Compulsory Disposition of Collateral

In two situations, the creditor must dispose of the collateral. A creditor must sell the collateral if the debtor makes a written objection to retention within 21 days after the retention notice was sent. The creditor must also dispose of the collateral if it consists of consumer goods and the debtor has paid 60 percent or more of the cash price or of the loan secured by the security interest. The sale must be held within 90 days of the repossession. However, the debtor, after default, surrenders the right to require the resale.[59]

A creditor who fails to dispose of the collateral when required to do so is liable to the debtor for conversion of the collateral or for the penalty imposed by the Code for violation of Article 9.[60]

57 UCC § 9-505 (Revised Article 9, §§ 9-620, 9-621, 9-624).

58 Revised Article 9, §§ 9-620 through 9-622.

59 Revised Article 9, § 9-620.

60 UCC § 9-507 (Revised Article 9, §§ 9-625 through 9-627).

ETHICS & THE LAW

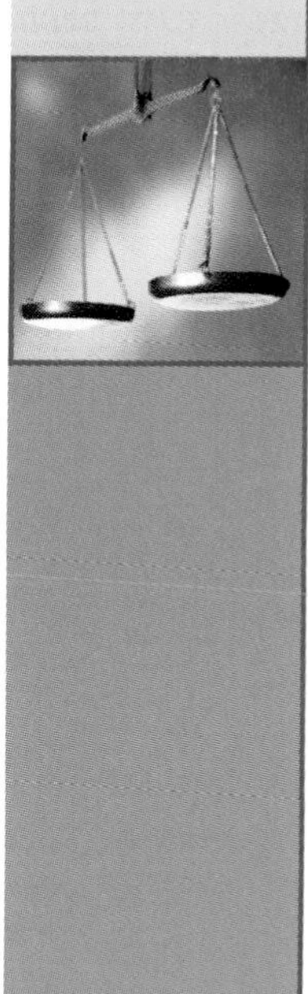

WOMEN, CHILDREN, AND THE REPO GUYS

Repossessions of autos financed on credit are at an all-time high. Lenders explain that the growth period of the 1990s inspired many to overextend themselves with credit purchases, and now the repossessions are taking place.

According to the "repo industry," about 15 percent of debtors surrender their cars voluntarily. Confrontations occur about 10 percent of the time during repossession. Many debtors change the color of their cars, change the tires and rims, or cover the vehicle identification number to foil repossession companies' efforts. One auto dealer, trying to repossess a woman's car, had two male employees scale the fence of the Murfeesboro, Tennessee Domestic Violence Program Shelter. The shelter's security cameras spotted the men and after police were notified, they were ordered off the premises. The woman who owned the car left the shelter to make the necessary payments to bring her obligations current. The shelter director said that if the men had come through the proper administrative channels at the shelter, the shelter would have cooperated with them. The shelter director called the men's scaling of the fence at a shelter for women and children "irresponsible." Do you think it is ethical for the debtors to do these things? Should debtors surrender their cars voluntarily?

In two incidents in 2006, cars that were repossessed had children sleeping in them. The cars were hooked to the tow vehicle and the children were transported to the tow yards. An industry spokesman said that "repo guys" have to get in and hook the cars up as quickly as possible; they do not have time to check the inside of the vehicle.

Source: Rich Beattie, "Boom Times for Repo Guys," *New York Times*, April 18, 2003, D1, D8.

27. Debtor's Right of Redemption

The debtor may redeem the collateral at any time prior to the time the secured party has disposed of the collateral or entered into a binding contract for resale. To redeem, the debtor must tender the entire obligation that is owed plus any legal costs and expenses incurred by the secured party.[61]

28. Disposition of Collateral

Upon the debtor's default, the creditor may sell the collateral at a public or private sale or may lease it to a third party. The creditor must give any required notice and act in a commercially reasonable manner. Revised Article 9 imposes specific notice requirements and provides a form that, if used by the creditor, is deemed adequate notice of sale. There are different notice forms for consumer and other transactions, but the basic information required is the day, time, location for the sale, and a contact number for questions the debtor and other secured parties might have. The notice must be sent to the debtor and any other creditors with an interest in the property.[62]

CPA 29. Postdisposition Accounting

When the creditor disposes of the collateral, the proceeds are applied in the following order. Proceeds are first used to pay the expenses of disposing of the collateral. Next, proceeds are applied to the debt owed the secured creditor making the disposition. Remaining proceeds are applied to any debts owed other creditors holding security interests in the same collateral that are subordinate to the interest of the disposing creditor.[63]

(a) Distribution of Surplus

If there is any money remaining, the surplus is paid to the debtor.[64]

[61] UCC § 9-506 (Revised Article 9, § 9-623).

[62] UCC §§ 9-613 and 9-614.

[63] Revised Article 9, § 9-615.

[64] Revised Article 9, § 9-616. The distribution of proceeds remains substantially unchanged under Revised Article 9.

(b) Liability for Deficit

If the proceeds of the disposition are not sufficient to pay the costs and the debt of the disposing creditor, the debtor is liable for the deficiency. However, the disposition of the collateral must have been conducted in the manner required by the Code. This means that proper notice must have been given, if required, and that the disposition must have been made in a commercially reasonable manner.

LAWFLIX

Fun with Dick and Jane (1977) (PG); remake (2005) (PG13)

Jane Fonda and George Segal play a married couple in financial distress. When Segal loses his job, creditors appear to reclaim purchases, including landscapers who repossess the lawn by rolling up the sod. What form of collateral is the sod? Is the repossession appropriate?

For movie clips that illustrate business law concepts, see LawFlix at **http://wdvl.westbuslaw.com.**

Summary

A security interest is an interest in personal property or fixtures that secures payment or performance of an obligation. The property that is subject to the interest is called the *collateral*, and the party holding the interest is called the *secured party*. *Attachment* is the creation of a security interest. To secure protection against third parties' claims to the collateral, the secured party must perfect the security interest. *Tangible collateral* is divided into classes: consumer goods, equipment, inventory, general intangibles, farm products, and fixtures. Under Revised Article 9, intangibles have been expanded to include bank accounts, checks, notes, and health care insurance receivables.

Perfection of a security interest is not required for its validity, but it does provide the creditor certain superior rights and priorities over other types of creditors and creditors with an interest in the same collateral. Perfection can be obtained through possession, filing, automatically (as in the case of a PMSI in consumer goods), by control for accounts under Revised Article 9, or temporarily when statutory protections are provided for creditors for limited periods of time.

Priority among creditors is determined according to their status. Unperfected, unsecured creditors simply wait to see whether there will be sufficient assets remaining after priority creditors are paid. Secured creditors have the right to take the collateral on a priority basis. As between secured creditors, the first creditor's interest to attach takes priority in the event the creditors hold security interests in the same collateral. A perfected secured creditor takes priority over an unperfected secured creditor. Perfected secured creditors with interests in the same collateral take priority generally on a first-to-perfect basis. Exceptions include PMSI inventory creditors who file a financing statement before delivery and notify all existing creditors, and equipment creditors who perfect within 20 days of attachment of their interests.

A buyer in the ordinary course of business always takes priority, even over perfected secured creditors who have knowledge of the creditor's interest. A buyer not in the ordinary course of business loses out to a perfected secured creditor but extinguishes the rights of a secured creditor unless the buyer had knowledge of the security interest. A buyer from a consumer debtor takes free and clear of the debtor's creditor's perfected security interest unless the creditor has filed a financing statement and perfected beyond just the automatic PMSI consumer goods perfection.

Upon default, a secured party may repossess the collateral from the buyer if this can be done without a breach of the peace. If a breach of the peace could occur, the secured party must use court action to regain the collateral. If the buyer has paid 60 percent or more of the cash price of the consumer goods, the seller must resell them within 90 days after repossession unless the buyer, after default, has waived this right in writing. Notice to the debtor of the sale of the collateral is usually required. A debtor may redeem the collateral prior to the time the secured party disposes of it or contracts to resell it.

Questions and Case Problems

1. Charles Lakin, who did business as Sun Country Citrus, owned a citrus-packing plant in Yuma, Arizona. In 1985, the packing plant was leased to Sunco Partners. Under the terms of the lease, Sunco had the right to replace existing packing, sizing, and grading equipment with "state-of-the-art" equipment.

   In 1986, PKD, Inc., purchased Sunco. Sunco signed a bill of sale for all of its "personal property, including, but not limited to, packing equipment, boilers, compressors, and packinghouse-related supplies." The bill of sale was secured by an Article 9 security interest executed by PKD as the debtor and Lakin/Sunco as the creditors.

   In February 1987, PKD changed its name to Amcico and negotiated for the purchase and lease of citrus-sorting equipment from Pennwalt Corp., now Elf Atochem. The documents for the transaction specifically provided that title to the equipment would remain with Elf Atochem until all payments were made under the terms of the sale and lease agreement.

   In December 1987, Amcico defaulted on its payments to Lakin and Sunco. Lakin and Sunco took possession of all of the equipment in the Yuma plant. Elf Atochem objected, claiming its title to the citrus-sorting equipment. Lakin and Sunco produced the security agreement giving them such equipment as collateral. Elf Atochem claimed that because it retained title in the citrus-sorting equipment, there was no interest in it on the part of Amcico, and the security interest of Sunco and Lakin never attached. Was Elf Atochem correct? [*Elf Atochem North America, Inc. v Celco, Inc.*, 927 P2d 355 (Ariz App)]

2. In 1983, Carpet Contracts owned a commercial lot and building, which it operated as a retail carpet outlet. In April of that year, Carpet Contracts entered into a credit sales agreement with Young Electric Sign Corp. (Yesco) for the purchase of a large electronic sign for the store. The total cost of the sign was $113,000, with a down payment of $25,000 and 60 monthly payments of $2,100 each.

   In August 1985, Carpet Contracts agreed to sell the property to Interstate. As part of the sale, Carpet Contracts gave Interstate an itemized list showing that $64,522 of the proceeds from the sale would be used to pay for the"Electronic Sign." The property was transferred to Interstate, and the Carpet Contracts store continued to operate there, but now it paid rent to Interstate. In June 1986, Carpet Contracts asked Yesco to renegotiate the terms of the sign contract. Yesco reduced Carpet Contracts' monthly payments and filed a financing statement on the sign at the Utah Division of Corporations and Commercial Code.

   In December 1986, Interstate agreed to sell the property and the sign to the Webbs, who conducted a title search on the property, which revealed no interest with respect to the electronic sign. Interstate conveyed the property to the Webbs. Carpet Contracts continued its operation but was struggling financially and had not made its payments to Yesco for some time. By 1989, Yesco declared the sign contract in default and contacted the Webbs, demanding the balance due of $26,100. The Webbs then filed suit, claiming Yesco had no priority as a creditor because its financing statement was not filed in the real property records where the Webbs had done their title search before purchasing the land. Was the financing statement filed properly for perfection? [*Webb v Interstate Land Corp.*, 920 P2d 1187 (Utah)]

3. Wayne Smith purchased a computer from Lee Sounds for personal use. Smith signed an installment purchase note and a security agreement. Under the terms of the note, Smith was to pay $100 down and $50 a month for 20 months. The security agreement included a description of the computer; however, Lee did not file a financing statement. Did Lee fulfill the requirements necessary for the attachment and perfection of its security interest in the computer? Why or why not?

4. When Johnson Hardware Shop borrowed $20,000 from First Bank, it used its inventory as collateral for the loan. First Bank perfected its security interest by filing a financing statement. The inventory was subsequently damaged by fire, and Flanders Insurance Co. paid Johnson Hardware $5,000 for the loss, but First Bank claimed the proceeds of the insurance. Was First Bank correct? Why or why not?

5. Consider the following cases and determine whether the financing statements as filed would be valid under Article 9. Be sure to consider the standard of "seriously misleading" under Revised Article 9.

   a. *In re Thriftway Auto Supply, Inc.*, 159 BR 948, 22 UCC Rep Serv 2d 605 (WD Okla). The creditor used the debtor's corporate trade name, "Thriftway Auto Stores," not its legal name, "Thriftway Auto Supply, Inc."

   b. *In re Mines Tire Co., Inc.*, 194 BR 23, 29 UCC2d 617 (Bankr WDNY). The creditor used the name "Mines Company Inc." instead of "Mines Tire Company, Inc."

   c. *Mountain Farm Credit Service, ACA v Purina Mills, Inc.*, 119 NC App 508, 459 SE2d 75, 27 UCC2d 1441. The creditor filed the financing statement under "Warren Killian and Robert Hetherington dba Grey Daw Farms" in a situation in which the two individuals were partners running Grey Daw Farms as a partnership.

   d. *B.T. Lazarus & Co. v Christofides*, 104 Ohio App 3d 335, 662 NE2d 41, 29 UCC2d 627. The creditor filed a financing statement in the debtor's old name when, prior to filing, the debtor had changed its name from B.T.L., Inc., to Alma Manufacturing, Inc.

e. *In re SpecialCare, Inc.*, 209 BR 13, 34 UCC2d 857 (Bankr ND Ga). The creditor failed to refile an amended financing statement to reflect debtor's name change from "Davidson Therapeutic Services, Inc." to "SpecialCare, Inc."

f. *Industrial Machinery & Equipment Co. Inc. v Lapeer County Bank & Trust Co.*, 213 Mich App 676, 540 NW2d 781, 28 UCC2d 1033. The creditor filed the financing statement under the company's trade name, KMI, Inc., instead of its legal name, Koehler Machine, Inc.

g. *First Nat'l Bank of Lacon v Strong*, 278 Ill App 3d 762, 215 Ill Dec 421, 663 NE2d 432, 29 UCC2d 622. Creditor filed the financing statement using the trade name "Strong Oil Co." instead of the legal name "E. Strong Oil Company."

6. First Union Bank of Florida loaned money to Dale and Lynn Rix for their purchase of Ann's Hallmark, a Florida corporation. First Union took a security interest in the store's equipment, fixtures, and inventory and filed the financing statement under the names of Dale and Lynn Rix. Subsequently, the Rixes incorporated their newly acquired business as Michelle's Hallmark Cards & Gifts, Inc. When Michelle's went into bankruptcy, First Union claimed it had priority as a secured creditor because it had filed its financing statement first. Other creditors said First Union had priority against the Rixes but not against the corporation. Who was correct? What was the correct name for filing the financing statement? [*In re Michelle's Hallmark Cards & Gifts, Inc.*,36 UCC2d 225 (Bankr MD Fla)]

7. Rawlings purchased a typewriter from Kroll Typewriter Co. for $600. At the time of the purchase, he made an initial payment of $75 and agreed to pay the balance in monthly installments. A security agreement that complied with the UCC was prepared, but no financing statement was ever filed for the transaction. Rawlings, at a time when he still owed a balance on the typewriter and without the consent of Kroll, sold the typewriter to a neighbor. The neighbor, who had no knowledge of the security interest, used the typewriter in her home. Could Kroll repossess the typewriter from the neighbor?

8. Kim purchased on credit a $1,000 freezer from Silas Household Appliance Store. After she had paid approximately $700, Kim missed the next monthly installment payment. Silas repossessed the freezer and billed Kim for the balance of the purchase price, $300. Kim claimed that the freezer, now in the possession of Silas, was worth much more than the balance due and requested that Silas sell the freezer to wipe out the balance of the debt and to leave something for her. Silas claimed that because Kim had broken her contract to pay the purchase price, she had no right to say what should be done with the freezer. Was Silas correct? Explain.

9. Benson purchased a new Ford Thunderbird automobile. She traded in her old car and used the Magnavox Employees Credit Union to finance the balance. The credit union took a security interest in the Ford. Subsequently, the Ford was involved in a number of accidents and was taken to a dealer for repairs. Benson was unable to pay for the work done. The dealer claimed a lien on the car for services and materials furnished. The Magnavox Employees Credit Union claimed priority. Which claim had priority? [*Magnavox Employees Credit Union v Benson*, 331 NE2d 46 (Ind App)]

10. Lockovich borrowed money from a bank to purchase a motorboat. The bank took a security interest in it but never filed a financing statement. A subsequent default on the loan occurred, and the debtor was declared bankrupt. The bank claimed priority in the boat, alleging that no financing statement had to be filed. Do you agree? Why? [*In re Lockovich*, 124 BR 660 (Bankr WD Pa)]

11. Hull-Dobbs sold an automobile to Mallicoat and then assigned the sales contract to Volunteer Finance & Loan Corp. Later Volunteer repossessed the automobile and sold it. When Volunteer sued Mallicoat for the deficiency between the contract price and the proceeds on resale, Mallicoat argued that he had not been properly notified of the resale. The loan manager of the finance company testified that Mallicoat had been sent a registered letter stating that the car would be sold. He did not state, however, whether the letter merely declared in general terms that the car would be sold or specified a date for its resale. He admitted that the letter never was delivered to Mallicoat and was returned to the finance company "unclaimed." The loan manager also testified that the sale was advertised by posters, but on cross-examination, he admitted that he was not able to state when or where it was advertised. It was shown that Volunteer knew where Mallicoat and his father lived and where Mallicoat was employed. Mallicoat claimed that he had not been properly notified. Volunteer asserted that sufficient notice had been given. Was the notice of the resale sufficient? [*Mallicoat v Volunteer Finance & Loan Corp.*, 415 SW2d 347 (Tenn App)]

12. On April 18, 2000, Philip Purkett parked his car, on which he owed $213 in payments, in his garage and locked the garage. Later that night, TWAS, Inc., a vehicle repossession company, broke into the garage and repossessed the car without notice to Purkett. To get the car back, Purkett paid a $140 storage fee and signed a document stating that he would not hold TWAS liable for any damages. Did TWAS and Key Bank violate Article 9 requirements on repossession? [*Purkett v Key Bank USA, Inc.*, 2001 WL 503050, 45 UCC Rep Serv 2d 1201 (ND Ill)]

13. *A* borrowed money from *B* and orally agreed that *B* had a security interest in certain equipment that was standing in *A*'s yard. Nothing was in writing, and no filing of any kind was made. Nine days later, *B* took possession of the equipment. What kind of interest did *B* have in the equipment after taking possession of it? [*Transport Equipment Co. v Guaranty State Bank*, 518 F2d 373 (10th Cir)]
14. Cook sold Martin a new tractor truck for approximately $13,000, with a down payment of approximately $3,000 and the balance to be paid in 30 monthly installments. The sales agreement provided that "on default in any payment, Cook [could] take immediate possession of the property . . . without notice or demand. For this purpose vendor may enter upon any premises on which the property may be." Martin failed to pay the installments when due, and Cook notified him that the truck would be repossessed. Martin left the tractor truck attached to a loaded trailer and locked on the premises of a company in Memphis. Martin intended to drive to the West Coast with the trailer. When Cook located the tractor truck, no one was around. To disconnect the trailer from the truck (because he had no right to the trailer), Cook removed the wire screen over a ventilator hole by unscrewing it from the outside with his penknife. He next reached through the ventilator hole with a stick and unlocked the door of the tractor truck. He then disconnected the trailer and had the truck towed away. Martin sued Cook for unlawfully repossessing the truck by committing a breach of the peace. Decide. [*Martin v Cook*, 114 So 2d 669 (Miss)]
15. Muska borrowed money from the Bank of California and secured the loan by giving the bank a security interest in equipment and machinery at his place of business. To perfect the interest, the bank filed a financing statement that did not contain Muska's address. Muska later filed for bankruptcy. The trustee in bankruptcy claimed that the security interest of the bank was not perfected because the omission of the residence address from the financing statement made it defective. Was the financing statement valid? [*Lines v Bank of California*, 467 F2d 1274 (9th Cir)]
16. Kimbrell's Furniture Co. sold a new television set and tape player to Charlie O'Neil and his wife. Each purchase was on credit, and in each instance, a security agreement was executed. Later on the same day of purchase, O'Neil carried the items to Bonded Loan, a pawnbroker, and pledged the television and tape deck as security for a loan. Bonded Loan held possession of the television set and tape player as security for its loan and contended that its lien had priority over the unrecorded security interest of Kimbrell. Who had priority? [*Kimbrell's Furniture Co. v Sig Friedman, d/b/a Bonded Loan*, 198 SE2d 803 (SC)]

CPA Questions

1. On March 1, Green went to Easy Car Sales to buy a car. Green spoke to a salesperson and agreed to buy a car that Easy had in its showroom. On March 5, Green made a $500 down payment and signed a security agreement to secure the payment of the balance of the purchase price. On March 10, Green picked up the car. On March 15, Easy filed the security agreement. On what date did Easy's security interest attach?

   a. March 1
   b. March 5
   c. March 10
   d. March 15

2. Carr Corp. sells VCRs and videotapes to the public. Carr sold and delivered a VCR to Sutter on credit. Sutter executed and delivered to Carr a promissory note for the purchase price and a security agreement covering the VCR. Sutter purchased the VCR for personal use. Carr did not file a financing statement. Is Carr's security interest perfected?

   a. No, because the VCR was a consumer good
   b. No, because Carr failed to file a financing statement
   c. Yes, because Carr retained ownership of the VCR
   d. Yes, because it was perfected at the time of attachment

3. On July 8, Ace, a refrigerator wholesaler, purchased 50 refrigerators. This comprised Ace's entire inventory and was financed under an agreement with Rome Bank that gave Rome a security interest in all refrigerators on Ace's premises, all future-acquired refrigerators, and the proceeds of sales. On July 12, Rome filed a financing statement that adequately identified the collateral. On August 15, Ace sold one refrigerator to Cray for personal use and four refrigerators to Zone Co. for its business. Which of the following statements is correct?

   a. The refrigerators sold to Zone will be subject to Rome's security interest.
   b. The refrigerators sold to Zone will not be subject to Rome's security interest.
   c. The security interest does not include the proceeds from the sale of the refrigerators to Zone.
   d. The security interest may not cover after-acquired property even if the parties agree.

4. Fogel purchased a television set for $900 from Hamilton Appliance Store. Hamilton took a promissory note signed by Fogel and a security interest for the $800 balance due on the set. It was Hamilton's policy not to file a financing statement until the purchaser defaulted. Fogel obtained a loan of $500 from Reliable Finance, which took and recorded a security interest in the set. A month later, Fogel defaulted on several loans outstanding and one of his creditors, Harp, obtained a judgment against Fogel, which was properly recorded. After making several payments, Fogel defaulted on a payment due to Hamilton, who then recorded a financing statement subsequent to Reliable's filing and the entry of the Harp judgment. Subsequently, at a garage sale, Fogel sold the set for $300 to Mobray. Which of the parties has the priority claim to the set?

   a. Reliable
   b. Hamilton
   c. Harp
   d. Mobray

BANKRUPTCY

CHAPTER (35)

LEARNING OBJECTIVES

After studying this chapter, you should be able to

LO.1 List the requirements for the commencement of a voluntary bankruptcy case and an involuntary bankruptcy case

LO.2 Describe the rights of a trustee in bankruptcy

LO.3 Explain the procedure for the administration of a debtor's estate

LO.4 List a debtor's duties and exemptions

LO.5 Explain the significance of a discharge in bankruptcy

LO.6 Explain when a business reorganization and an extended-time payment plan might be used

What can a person or business do when overwhelmed by debts? Bankruptcy proceedings can provide temporary and sometimes permanent relief from those debts.

A. Bankruptcy Law

Bankruptcy is a statutory proceeding with detailed procedures and requirements.

1. The Federal Law

Bankruptcy law is based on federal statutes that have been refined over the years. In October 2005, the Bankruptcy Abuse Prevention and Consumer Protection Act of 2005 (BAPCPA) took effect.[1] The BAPCPA was passed more than 10 years after the Bankruptcy Reform Commission was created, and the changes in bankruptcy law reflect an expressed congressional desire to curb a 15-year trend of increases in the number of bankruptcies.

Jurisdiction over bankruptcy proceedings is vested in the federal district courts. The district courts have the authority to transfer such matters to courts of special jurisdiction called **bankruptcy courts.**

2. Types of Bankruptcy Proceedings

The three types of bankruptcy proceedings that existed before the 2005 reforms are still available to individuals and businesses.

CPA (a) Liquidation or Chapter 7 Bankruptcy

A **Chapter 7 bankruptcy** is one in which all of the debtor's assets (with some exemptions) will be **liquidated** to pay debts. Those debts that remain unpaid or are paid only partially are discharged, with some exceptions. The debtor who declares Chapter 7 bankruptcy begins again with a nearly clean slate.

Chapter 7 bankruptcy is available to individuals, partnerships, and corporations. However, farmers, insurance companies, savings and loans, municipalities, Small Business Administration companies, and railroads are not entitled to declare Chapter 7 bankruptcy because they are specifically governed by other statutes or specialized sections of the Bankruptcy Code.[2]

Under the BAPCPA, consumers will have difficulty filing immediately for Chapter 7 liquidation bankruptcy because the reforms require that the consumers demonstrate that they do not have the means to repay the debts before they are permitted a Chapter 7 liquidation.[3] The means test, which is discussed later, considers the disposable income that is available after the bankruptcy court has deducted allowable expenses that are listed as part of the means section of the BAPCPA, including items such as health insurance and child support.

CPA (b) Reorganization or Chapter 11 Bankruptcy

Chapter 11 bankruptcy is a way for a debtor to reorganize and continue a business with protection

[1] Pub. L. No. 109-8, 119 Stat. 23 (2005); the act is codified at 11 USC § 101 *et. seq.*

[2] For example, the Small Business Investment Act governs the insolvency of small business investment companies, 11 USC § 109(b). Municipalities' bankruptcies are governed by Chapter 9 of the Bankruptcy Code, and farmers' bankruptcies are covered under Chapter 12.

[3] 11 USC §707(C)(2)(a). There are exceptions to the requirements of establishing no means, such as those who incurred their debts while on active military service.

ETHICS & THE LAW

BANKRUPTCY RECORDS

According to **http://www.bankruptcydata.com**, the total bankruptcy filings in the United States from 2000 to 2005 were as follows:

Year	*Total Business*	*Total Nonbusiness*
2005	39,201	2,039,214
2004	34,317	1,563,145
2003	35,037	1,660,245
2002	38,540	1,566,358
2001	40,099	1,492,129
2000	35,472	1,217,972

According to **http://www.bankruptcydata.com**, the following are the largest bankruptcies in the history of the United States:

Company	*Bankruptcy Date*	*Total Assets Prebankruptcy*	*Filing Court District*
WorldCom, Inc.	7/21/2002	$103,914,000,000	NY-S
Enron Corp.	12/2/2001	63,392,000,000	NY-S
Conseco, Inc.	12/18/2002	61,392,000,000	IL-N
Texaco, Inc.	4/12/1987	35,892,000,000	NY-S
Financial Corp. of America	9/9/1988	33,864,000,000	CA-C
Refco	10/17/2005	33,333,172,000	NY-S
Global Crossing Ltd.	1/28/2002	30,185,000,000	NY-S
Pacific Gas and Electric Co.	4/6/2001	29,770,000,000	CA-N
Calpine	12/20/2005	27,216,088,000	NY-S
UAL Corp	12/9/2002	25,197,000,000	IL-N
Delta Air Lines	9/14/2005	21,801,000,000	NY-S
Adelphia Communications	6/25/2002	21,499,000,000	NY-S

Do you think, as many federal regulators and representatives and senators did in enacting the reforms, that the bankruptcy laws were being abused and that too many people were declaring bankruptcy just to avoid paying obligations? Is there an ethical component to declaring bankruptcy?

from overwhelming debts and without the requirement of liquidation. Because the same credit counseling requirements apply to individuals who file for Chapter 7 liquidation and Chapter 11 protection, anyone who qualifies for one qualifies for the other. The same exemptions also apply with the exception of railroads, which may declare Chapter 11 bankruptcy. Stockbrokers, however, are not eligible for Chapter 11 bankruptcy.

CPA (c) Chapter 13 Bankruptcy or Payment Plans or Consumer Debt Adjustment Plans

Chapter 13 of the federal Bankruptcy Code provides consumers an individual form of reorganization.

Chapter 13 works with consumer debtors to develop a plan to repay debt. To be eligible for **Chapter 13 bankruptcy,** the individual must owe unsecured debts of less than $307,675 and secured debts of less than $922,975 and have regular income.[4] Under proposed reforms, Chapter 13 would play an expanded role in bankruptcy because reforms require debtors with the means to pay their debts to go first into Chapter 13 bankruptcy rather than automatically declaring Chapter 7 bankruptcy.

B. How Bankruptcy Is Declared

Bankruptcy can be declared in different ways. The federal Bankruptcy Code spells out in detail the exact requirements and process for declaration.

CPA 3. Declaration of Voluntary Bankruptcy

A **voluntary bankruptcy** is begun when the debtor files a petition with the bankruptcy court. A joint petition may be filed by a husband and wife. When a voluntary case is begun, the debtor must file a schedule of current income and current expenditures unless the court excuses this filing.

Under the 2005 reforms, a court can dismiss an individual debtor's (consumer's) petition for abuse if the debtor does not satisfy the **means test,** which measures the debtor's ability to pay by computing the debtor's disposable income. Only those debtors who fall below their state's median disposable income will be able to continue in a Chapter 7 proceeding. Individual debtors who meet the means test are required to go into Chapter 13 bankruptcy because they have not qualified for Chapter 7 bankruptcy. The formula for applying the means test is as follows:

Debtor's current monthly income less
Allowable expenses under the Bankruptcy Code
= Disposable income
Disposable income × 60

The debtor is guilty of bankruptcy abuse if this number is not less than the lower of the following:

- 25 percent of the debtor's unsecured claims or $6,000, whichever is greater
- $10,000

A finding of abuse means that the debtor's Chapter 7 voluntary petition is dismissed. Previously, the law required the judge to find "substantial abuse" before dismissing the petition; now the standard reads only "abuse."[5]

Under the Reform Act, the bankruptcy judge also has the discretion to order the debtor's lawyer to reimburse the trustee for costs and attorney's fees and to assess a civil penalty against the lawyer if the court finds that the lawyer has not acted in good faith in filing the debtor's bankruptcy petition.[6] As part of this change, lawyers must declare themselves (in public ads as well as in an individual) to be "debt relief agencies" or state that they "help people file for relief under the Bankruptcy Code." The Code now requires those who help consumers deal with creditors to disclose that part of that assistance may include filing for bankruptcy. Lawyers who advertise their credit/bankruptcy expertise are subject to the laws and regulations that apply to debt relief agencies. If the agency/lawyer advises them to do something that causes the court to declare that there has been bankruptcy abuse, the lawyer/debt relief agency is responsible as well. As part of their role as a debt counselor, lawyers are prohibited under the changes in the law from advising clients to undertake more debt in contemplation of filing bankruptcy.[7]

Debtors are required to undergo credit counseling (from an approved nonprofit credit counseling agency) within the 180 days prior to declaring a bankruptcy. In addition, the court applies the means test described earlier to determine whether the debtor qualifies for bankruptcy.[8]

[4] 11 USC §109(e).
[5] 11 USC § 707(b).
[6] 11 USC § 707(b)(4).
[7] 11 USC §§ 526–528.
[8] 11 USC § 109(h)(2) provides that "an individual may not be a debtor under this title unless such individual has, during the 180-day period preceding the date of filing the petition by such individual, received from an approved nonprofit budget and credit counseling agency . . . an individual or group briefing (including a briefing conducted by telephone or on the Internet) that outlined the opportunities for available credit counseling and assisted such individual in performing a related budget analysis." 11 USC § 106(e) lists the requirements for a counseling agency that are necessary before it can gain court approval for debtor counseling. There are exceptions to the counseling requirements such as active military duty, disability, and emergencies.

SPORTS & ENTERTAINMENT LAW

HIP-HOP TO THE TOP: BANKRUPTCY TO THE BOTTOM

TLC was an Atlanta rhythm, blues, and hip-hop band that performed at clubs in 1991. The three-woman group signed a recording contract with LaFace Records. The group's first album that LaFace produced, *Ooooooohhh on the TLC Tip,* sold almost 3 million albums in 1992. The group's second album, *Crazysexycool,* also produced by LaFace, sold 5 million albums through June 1996. The two albums together had six top-of-the-chart singles.

LaFace had the right to renew TLC's contract in 1996 following renegotiation of the contract terms. In the industry, royalty rates for unknown groups, as TLC was in 1991, are generally 7 percent of the revenues for the first 500,000 albums and 8 percent for sales on platinum albums (albums that sell over 1 million copies). The royalty rate increases to 9.5 percent for all sales on an eighth album. Established artists in the industry who renegotiate often have royalty rates of 13 percent, and artists with two platinum albums can command an even higher royalty.

The three women in TLC—Tionne Watkins (T-Boz), Lisa Lopes (Left-Eye, who has since died), and Romanda Thomas (Chili)—declared bankruptcy in July 1995. All three listed debts that exceeded their assets, which included sums owed to creditors for their cars and to Zale's and The Limited for credit purchases. Lopes was being sued by Lloyd's of London, which claimed she owed it $1.3 million it had paid on a policy held by her boyfriend on his home that was destroyed by fire. Lopes pleaded guilty to one count of arson in the destruction of the home but denied that she intended to destroy it. She was sentenced to five years probation and treatment at a halfway house.

Lopes asked that the Lloyd's claim be discharged in her bankruptcy. All three members of TLC asked that their contract with LaFace be discharged in bankruptcy because being bound to their old contract could impede their fresh financial starts.

Did the three women meet the standards for declaring bankruptcy? Evaluate whether Lopes's Lloyd's claim should be discharged. Determine whether the record contract should be discharged.

During 1996, the members of three music groups declared bankruptcy just before their contracts were due for renegotiation. One record company executive has noted that record company owners are frightened by the trend: "You invest all the money and time in making them stars. Then they leave for the bigger companies and a higher take on sales. It has all of us scared."

Is declaring bankruptcy by the members of these musical groups legal? Is it ethical? Are the musicians using bankruptcy as a way to avoid contract obligations? Are the musicians using bankruptcy as a way to maximize their income?

Pop singer Billy Joel also had a record contract with a small company during the initial stages of his career. When the company refused, during renegotiations, to increase his royalty rate, Joel did not produce another album during the period of the contract renewal option. Instead, he used a clause in the contract that limited him to nightclub and piano bar appearances in the event another album was not produced. For three years, Joel played small clubs and restaurants and did not produce an album. At the end of that period when his contract had expired, he negotiated a contract with Columbia. His first album with Columbia was *Piano Man,* a multiplatinum album. Did Joel take an ethical route? Is his solution more ethical than bankruptcy?

IN RE JASS, 340 BR 411 (UTAH 2006)

DISPOSABLE INCOME AND PREDISPOSED NOT TO PAY

The Jasses filed for chapter 13 bankruptcy relief. Their Form B22C indicated that their yearly household aggregate income was $143,403.96 based on income they received during the six-month period before filing. After deducting allowed expenses and deductions from their income, the Jasses' Statement of Current Monthly Income shows a "disposable income" of $3,625.63 per month.

The Jasses filed a chapter 13 plan which proposed to return $790.00 to unsecured creditors. At the hearing, the Trustee objected to confirmation because the Jasses' "disposable income," as calculated on their Form B22C, is $3,625.63, and they proposed to pay only $790.00 to unsecured creditors. The Trustee argued that because the Jasses were not proposing to pay their full disposable income of $3,625.63 to unsecured creditors, their plan did not comply with this "disposable income test."

The Jasses argued that the word "projected" modifies the definition of "disposable income." Mrs. Jass testified that beginning in December, 2005 her husband experienced serious medical problems involving injuries to his intestines. She testified that her family incurred $12,000 in medical expenses. In light of these expenses, the Jasses argued that their income in the future will not be commensurate with the "disposable income" shown on Form B22C. They argued that the changes under the BAPCPA do not require them to pay unsecured creditors the amount resulting from their Form B22C, so long as they can show that the income and expenses reported on the Form are inadequate representations of their future budget.

Judicial Opinion

THURMAN, Bankruptcy Judge.... [t]he Court is called upon to determine whether the Jasses' "disposable income" as determined by their Form B22C is the same as "projected disposable income." This matter presents an issue of first impression in light of the Bankruptcy Abuse Prevention and Consumer Protection Act ("BAPCPA"). The Court determines that "disposable income" as calculated by Form B22C is not the same as "projected disposable income."

"Current monthly income" is defined in § 101(10A) as the debtor's income for the six-month period preceding bankruptcy.

The Court believes that the language of § 1325(b)(1)(B) [of the bankruptcy code] is clear and unambiguous—section 1325(b)(1)(B)'s requirement that a plan propose to pay "projected disposable income" means that the number resulting from Form B22C is a starting point for the Court's inquiry only. Section 1325(b)(2) defines "disposable income" but § 1325(b)(1)(B) requires that a debtor propose a plan paying "projected disposable income." The Court must give meaning to the word "projected," as it obviously has independent significance. The word "projected" means "[t]o calculate, estimate, or predict (something in the future), based on present data or trends." Thus, the word "projected" is future-oriented. By definition under § 1325(b)(2), the term "disposable income" is oriented in historical numbers. By placing the word "projected" next to "disposable income" in § 1325(b)(1)(B), Congress modified the import of "disposable income." The significance of the word "projected" is that it requires the Court to consider both future and historical finances of a debtor.

To require all debtors to propose plans paying the number resulting from Form B22C would essentially ignore the word "projected" and give meaning only to the term "disposable income." The only way for the word "projected" to have independent significance is if the word modifies the term "disposable income."

Under the clear meaning of the statute, a debtor must propose to pay unsecured creditors the number resulting from Form B22C, unless the debtor can show that this number does not adequately represent the debtor's budget projected into the future.

The changes under the BAPCPA merely served to change the definition of "disposable income." Pre-BAPCPA cases interpreting the dichotomy between "projected disposable income" and "disposable income" held as the Court does today—that the definition of "disposable income" under § 1325(b)(2) was merely a starting point for the Court's inquiry into whether the debtor was proposing to pay "projected disposable income."

The overarching policy of the Bankruptcy Code is to afford a debtor a "fresh start." Although the changes to the Code under the BAPCPA serve to benefit creditors, the changes are not so broad as to undermine the "fresh start" policy of the Code.

If § 1325(b)(1)(B) required a debtor to always pay the calculated disposable income amount resulting from Form B22C, the Court would essentially foreclose the potential for bankruptcy relief from a group of chapter 13 debtors who are otherwise eligible for relief.

The facts of this case serve as a good example. The Jasses argue that they have recently experienced a change in circumstances, such that their future income will not be commensurate with the income they received six months before filing. If the Court were to require the Jasses to pay the disposable income amount resulting from Form B22C, any plan they propose would not be feasible. Because people are frequently forced to file for bankruptcy relief as a result of sudden life-altering events, the Jasses are exemplary of numerous debtors who would be foreclosed from seeking bankruptcy protections. This result is clearly at odds with the overarching policy that debtors who are eligible for bankruptcy relief be afforded an opportunity for a "fresh start."

The Statement of Current Monthly Income filed by the Jasses would require them to propose a plan paying unsecured creditors $3,625.63 per month. The Court presumes that this number is the "projected disposable income" required in the Jasses' case unless they can present evidence to show a substantial change in circumstances. Because the Jasses have not yet presented evidence addressing the inadequacy of figures contained in their Statement of Current Monthly Income, the Court finds that the Jasses have not carried their burden to rebut the presumption that their "projected disposable income" is the number resulting from Form B22C. The Court may reevaluate this determination if the Jasses present additional evidence at the continued hearing on this matter.

The hearing on confirmation of the Jasses' proposed chapter 13 plan is CONTINUED to address remaining issues in the Jasses' case.

Questions

1. What interpretation has this court given to the disposable income test that will be used for the means test in bankruptcy?
2. Why does the court make this interpretation?
3. What evidence will now be part of the determination of disposable income?

CPA 4. Declaration of Involuntary Bankruptcy

(a) Eligibility

An **involuntary bankruptcy** is begun when creditors file a petition with the bankruptcy court. An involuntary case may be commenced against any individual, partnership, or corporation, except those excluded from filing voluntary petitions. Nonprofit corporations are also exempt from involuntary proceedings.[9]

CPA (b) Number and Claims of Petitioning Creditors

If there are 12 or more creditors, at least 3 of those creditors whose unsecured and undisputed claims total $12,300 or more must sign the involuntary petition.[10] If there are fewer than 12 creditors, excluding employees or insiders (that is, the debtor's relatives, partners, directors, and controlling persons), any creditor whose unsecured claim is at least $12,300 may sign the petition. In the case of involuntary consumer petitions, there is disagreement as to whether the debtor will still be required to complete the credit counseling requirement prior to the granting of the automatic stay.

If a creditor holds security for a claim, only the amount of the claim in excess of the value of the security is counted. The holder of a claim that is the subject of a **bona fide** dispute may not be counted as a petitioning creditor.[11] **For Example,** David, a CPA, is an unsecured creditor of Arco

[9] 11 USC § 303(a).

[10] 11 U.S.C. § 303. The term "undisputed" was added to this section and commentators are unclear as to whether this addition will make it easier for debtors to challenge involuntary bankruptcies.

[11] 11 USC § 303(b)(1).

THINKING THINGS THROUGH

MEANS TEST JUSTIFYING THE END OF DEBT

The following excerpt is a hypothetical case an experienced bankruptcy attorney worked through to illustrate the application of the means test because no bankruptcy means cases have made their way through to appellate decision.

The Brokes, a married couple in their early 40s, have two children in private schools. They are residents of Memphis, Shelby County, Tennessee; their annual gross income is $86,496. Like many debtors, the Brokes lost their home following an unsuccessful Chapter 13 case three years ago. They now rent a house for $2,000 a month. They owe back federal taxes in the amount of $9,000. They have secured debt on two cars with remaining balances of $10,000 and $6,000 and unsecured, consumer debt totaling $28,000. They desire to seek relief under Chapter 7 of the Bankruptcy Code.

The Brokes' gross monthly income is $7,208. After deducting taxes and other mandatory payroll deductions of $1,509, the couple has $5,699 in monthly income. The means test requires several additional deductions from the Brokes' gross monthly income. Section 707(b)(A)(2)(ii) provides a deduction for living and housing expenses using National Standards and Local Standards and additional Internal Revenue Service (IRS) figures. Allowable living expenses for a family of four in Ura and Ima Brokes' income bracket, based on national standards, total $1,564, while housing and utility figures for Shelby County, Tennessee, allow $1,354. In addition, there are allowable expenses for transportation. Based on IRS figures, the Brokes can subtract national ownership costs of $475 for the first car and $338 for the second, as well as regional operating and public transportation costs of $242 and $336, respectively. They can also deduct their reasonably necessary health insurance costs, here the sum of $600, and $250 a month for private school tuition. Subtracting all of these figures from the Brokes' monthly income leaves $540.

Under § 707(b)(2)(A)(iii), the Brokes can subtract payments on secured debt. The amount contractually due on their two automobiles over the next 60 months is $16,000. After dividing this total by 60 and rounding to the nearest dollar, the monthly allowable deduction for secured debt is $267. Subtracting this amount from $540 leaves $273.

Next come priority claim deductions. The Brokes are not subject to any child support or alimony claims, but they do owe $9,000 in back taxes. Again, dividing this amount by 60 yields a deductible amount of $150. Subtracting this from $273 leaves $123 in disposable monthly income. This figure would be multiplied by 60, amounting to a total of $7,380 in disposable income over the five-year period. Abuse is thus statutorily presumed because the debtors' current monthly income reduced by allowable amounts is not less than either $7,000 (25 percent of their nonpriority unsecured claims of $28,000) or $6,000. The Brokes' Chapter 7 case will therefore be dismissed (or they will be allowed voluntarily to convert their Chapter 7 case to a case under Chapter 13).

Do you think that the use of the means test will make it more difficult for debtors to declare bankruptcy?*

*Robert J. Landry III, and Nancy Hisey Mardis, "Consumer Bankruptcy Reform: Debtors' Prison without Bars or 'Just Desserts' for Deadbeats?" 36 *Golden Gate U. L. Rev.* 91 (2006).

Company for $13,000. Arco has a total of 10 creditors, all of whom are unsecured. Arco has not paid any of the creditors for three months. The debtor has fewer than 12 creditors. Any one of the creditors may file the petition if the unsecured portion of the amount due that creditor is at least $12,300.[12] Because David is owed $13,000 in unsecured debts, he may file the petition alone.

[12] The amount was $10,000 originally, but the bankruptcy reforms had a built-in clause for increases in this figure. The amount $12,300 took effect on October 17, 2005.

ETHICS & THE LAW

THE NONPROFIT CREDIT COUNSELORS WITH TIES TO PROFITS

The credit counseling business is funded in one of two ways, the most common of which is that the agency works with debtors to develop a debt management plan (DMP) and then receives from the creditor a percentage of any payments the debtor makes to the creditor as part of the plan. A second way is that the debtor pays a fee to the agency for the service. For the most part, debtors had not been counseled on creditor relationships but had been convinced to develop a DMP. Under a DMP, the debtor pays one monthly payment to the credit counseling agency, the agency negotiates payments with the debtor's creditors (generally a reduced amount), and the agency keeps a percentage (generally 12 to 15 percent) of each payment made to each creditor.

The Federal Trade Commission (FTC) cited a third possible funding arrangement: Although it can collect a donation from the debtor, the agency is primarily funded through for-profit collection agencies that earn a percentage fee of the total amount collected from the debtor. In late 2003, the FTC had filed a complaint against AmeriDebt, alleging that the credit counseling agency duped new clients into making a "voluntary contribution" to enroll in the program, which allowed AmeriDebt to keep these "contributions" as fees without consumers' knowledge. Furthermore, the FTC alleged that AmeriDebt was not a charitable organization as it had advertised but was really a front organization for two for-profit agencies, DebtWorks and Andris Pukke, to which AmeriDebt funneled profits of approximately $170 million. By mid-2004, AmeriDebt had declared bankruptcy, and the FTC case was settled.

Discuss the ethics of AmeriDebt's operations. Was it fair to make these arrangements without telling the debtors of its ties to profit agencies? Do you think that the mandatory counseling requirement for bankruptcy will cause more problems such as AmeriDebt?*

* *In re AmeriDebt Inc.*, Case No. 04-23649-PM (D Md); *Federal Trade Commission v AmeriDebt, Inc., DebtWorks, Inc., Andris Pukke, and Pamela Pukke,* also known as Pamela Shuster, File No. 0223171 (D Md 2003); *In re AmeriDebt Inc.*, Case No. 04-23649-PM (D Md 2005).

CPA (c) Grounds For Relief For Involuntary Case

The mere filing of an involuntary case petition does not result in an order of relief. The debtor may contest the bankruptcy petition. If the debtor does not contest the petition, the court will enter an order of relief if at least one of the following grounds exists: (1) The debtor is generally not paying debts as they become due or (2) within 120 days before the filing of the petition, a custodian has been appointed for the debtor's property.

CPA 5. Automatic Stay

Just the filing of either a voluntary or an involuntary petition operates as an **automatic stay,** which prevents creditors from taking action, such as filing suits or foreclosure actions, against the debtor.[13] The stay freezes all creditors in their filing date positions so that no one creditor gains an advantage over other creditors. This automatic stay ends when the bankruptcy case is closed or dismissed (for example, on a finding of abuse by the debtor who has failed to survive the means-to-pay test) or when the debtor is granted a discharge. An automatic stay means that all activity by creditors with respect to collection must stop, with some exceptions incorporated for child support and other family support issues under the 2005 reforms. All litigation with the debtor is halted, and any judgments in place cannot be executed.[14]

[13] 11 USC § 362.

[14] The reforms exempt dissolution, custody, child support, and other related litigation from the stay.

FIGURE 35-1 Declaration of Bankruptcy

	CHAPTER 7	CHAPTER 11	CHAPTER 13
TRUSTEE	YES	NO	YES
ELIGIBLE PERSONS:			
INDIVIDUALS	YES (CONSUMER RESTRICTIONS)	YES (INDIVIDUAL RESTRICTIONS)	YES (CONSUMER RESTRICTIONS)
PARTNERSHIPS	YES	YES	NO
CORPORATIONS	YES	YES	NO
VOLUNTARY	YES	YES	YES
INVOLUNTARY	YES, EXCEPT FOR FARMERS AND NONPROFITS**	YES, EXCEPT FOR FARMERS AND NONPROFITS	NO
EXEMPTIONS	S & L's, CREDIT UNIONS, SBA, RAILROADS, MUNICIPALITIES	SAME AS CHAPTER 7 PLUS STOCKBROKERS*	ONLY INDIVIDUALS ALLOWED
REQUIREMENTS-VOLUNTARY	DEBTS; MEANS TEST APPLIES TO CONSUMERS	DEBTS; MEANS TEST APPLIES TO CONSUMERS	INCOME: <$307,675 UNSECURED; <$922,975 SECURED
REQUIREMENTS-INVOLUNTARY	<12 = 1/$12,300 ≥12 = 3/$12,300	<12 = 1/$12,300 ≥12 = 3/$12,300	N/A

*RAILROADS ARE ELIGIBLE
**CHAPTER 9 — MUNICIPALITIES; CHAPTER 12 — FARMERS

6. If the Creditors Are Wrong: Rights of Debtor in an Involuntary Bankruptcy

If an involuntary petition is dismissed other than by consent of all petitioning creditors and the debtor, the court may award costs, reasonable attorney fees, or damages to the debtor. The damages are those that were caused by taking possession of the debtor's property. The debtor may also recover damages against any creditor who filed the petition in bad faith.[15]

Figure 35-1 provides a summary of the requirements for declaration of bankruptcy and the standards for relief.

C. Administration of the Bankruptcy Estate

The administration of the bankruptcy estate varies according to the type of bankruptcy declared. This section of the chapter focuses on the process for liquidation or Chapter 7 bankruptcy. Figure 35-2 provides a flowchart view of the Chapter 7 liquidation process.

7. The Order of Relief

The **order of relief** is granted by the bankruptcy court and is the procedural step required for the case to proceed in bankruptcy court.[16] An order of relief is entered automatically in a voluntary case and in an involuntary case when those filing the petition have established that the debtor is unable to pay his, her, or its debts as they become due. In consumer cases and Chapter 11 cases that involve an individual, the bankruptcy court must apply the means test to determine whether the individual is eligible for declaring bankruptcy or whether there has been an abuse of the bankruptcy court and system.

8. List of Creditors

It is the debtor's responsibility to furnish the bankruptcy court a list of creditors. Although imposing the responsibility for disclosing debts on the debtor may not seem to be effective, the debtor has an incentive

[15] *Arizona Public Service v Apache County*, 847 P2d 1339 (Ariz App 1993).
[16] USC § 301.

FIGURE 35-2 Anatomy of Bankruptcy Case

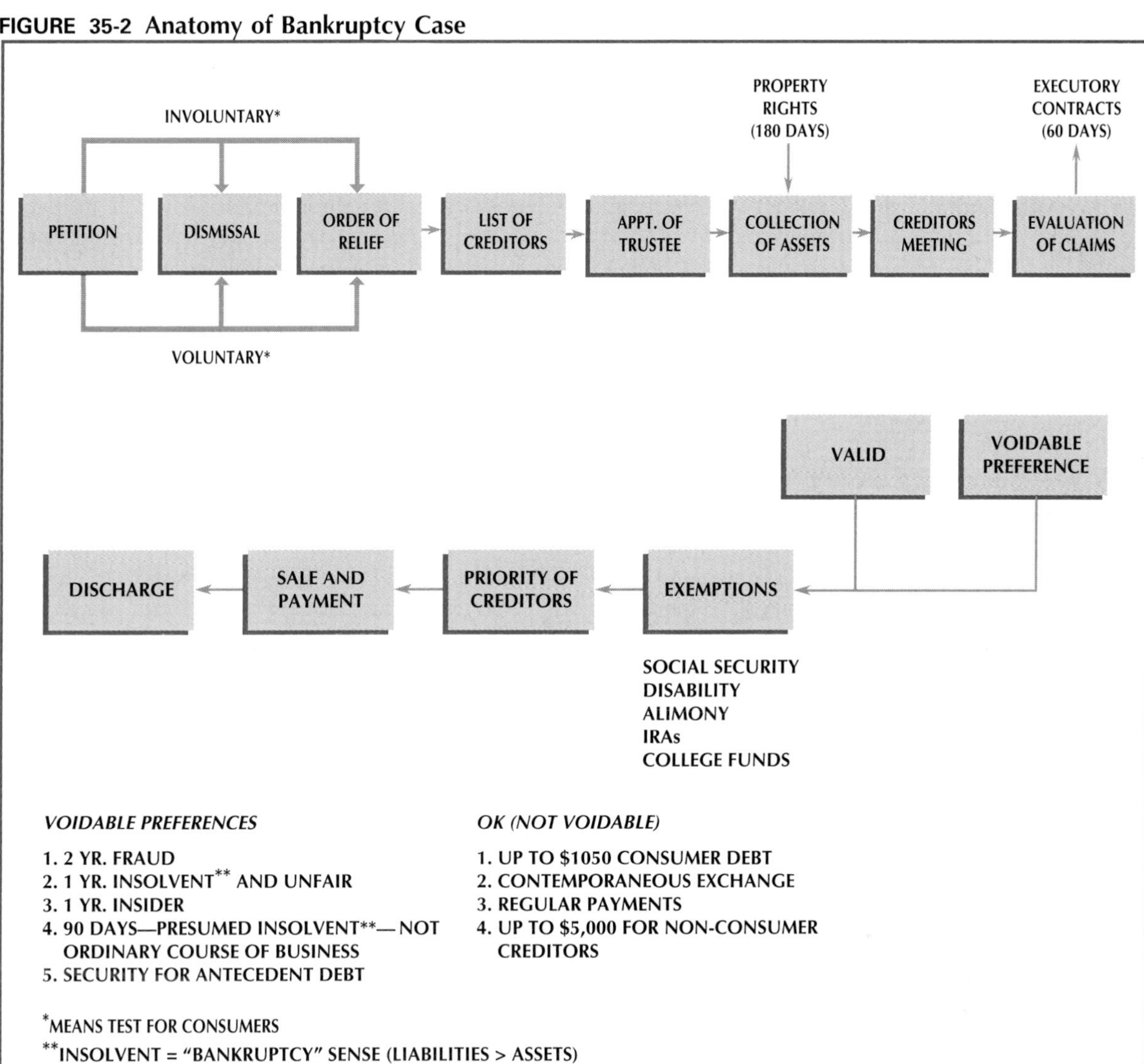

for full disclosure. Those debts not disclosed by the debtor will not be discharged in bankruptcy.

9. Trustee in Bankruptcy

The **trustee in bankruptcy** is elected by the creditors. The court or the U.S. trustee will appoint an interim trustee if the creditors do not elect a trustee.

The trustee is the successor to the property rights of the debtor. By operation of law, the trustee automatically becomes the owner of all of the debtor's property in excess of the property to which the debtor is entitled under exemption laws. The trustee holds all of the rights formerly owned by the debtor.

CPA 10. The Bankrupt's Estate

All of the debtor's property, with certain exceptions discussed later, is included in the *bankrupt's estate.* Property inherited by the debtor within six months after the filing of the petition also passes to the trustee.

In many cases, when a debtor knows that insolvency is a problem and bankruptcy is imminent, the debtor attempts to hang onto property or reputation by making transfers of assets to friends, relatives, and creditors. However, trustees have the authority to set aside or void (1) transfers by the debtor that a creditor holding a valid claim under state law could have avoided at the commencement of the bankruptcy case, (2) **preferences,** that is, transfers of property by the debtor to a creditor, the effect of which is to enable the creditor to obtain payment of a higher percentage of the creditor's claim than the creditor would have received if the debtor's assets had been liquidated in bankruptcy, and (3) statutory liens that became effective against the debtor at the commencement of the bankruptcy.

CPA 11. Voidable Preferences

A debtor may not transfer property to prevent creditors from satisfying their legal claims. The trustee may void any such transfer, known as a *fraudulent transfer*, made or obligation incurred by the debtor within two years of bankruptcy when the debtor's actual intent was to hinder, delay, or defraud creditors by doing so.[17]

The trustee may also void certain transfers of property made by a debtor merely because their effect is to make the debtor insolvent or to reduce the debtor's assets to an unreasonably low amount.[18]

(a) The Insolvent Debtor

A debtor is insolvent for purposes of determining voidable transfers when the total fair value of all of the debtor's assets does not exceed the debts owed by the debtor. This test for **insolvency** under voidable transfers is commonly called the **balance sheet test** because it is merely a comparison of assets to liabilities without considering whether the debtor will be able to meet future obligations as they become due. The debtor is presumed to be insolvent in the 90 days prior to declaration of bankruptcy.

(b) Preferential Transfers

A transfer of property by the debtor to a creditor may be set aside as **preferential transfers** and the property recovered by the debtor's trustee in bankruptcy if (1) the transfer was made to pay a debt incurred at some earlier time, (2) the transfer was made when the debtor was insolvent and within 90 days before the filing of the bankruptcy petition, and (3) the transfer resulted in the creditor receiving more than the creditor would have received in a liquidation of the debtor's estate. A debtor is presumed to be insolvent on and during the 90 days immediately preceding the date of the filing of the bankruptcy petition.[19]

Transfers made to **insiders** within the 12 months prior to the filing of the petition may be set aside.[20] **For Example,** if a building contractor transferred title to one of his model homes to the company accountant just six months before declaring bankruptcy, the transfer would be a preferential one that would be set aside. However, a transfer by an insider to a non-insider is not subject to recovery by the trustee. The sale of that same model home to a good faith buyer just three days before bankruptcy would be valid.

The trustee may not set aside certain transfers by a debtor as preferences. A transaction for a present consideration, such as a cash sale, is not set aside.[21] A payment by a debtor in the ordinary course of business, such as the payment of a utility bill, will not be set aside. Under the prior bankruptcy law, a payment was not a voidable preference if it was made in the ordinary course of business and it was made according to industry terms and practices. Under the 2005 reforms, the *and* is changed to *or*, and it is now easier for creditors to show that they were not the recipients of a voidable preference. Also under the 2005 reforms, nonconsumer debt payments that have a value of less than $5,000 are not subject to the voidable preference standards. The expectation is that the time and effort spent by bankruptcy trustees and courts will be reduced because of the minimum amount required before a challenge can be made. In nonconsumer debts, transfers of less than $5,000 within the voidable preference period are not considered voidable preferences.

On consumer debts, a payment by an individual debtor is not subject to being set aside if the aggregate value of the transfer is less than $1,050. Child support and alimony payments are also not subject to

[17] Prior to the reforms, the time period for fraudulent transfers was one year. However, the new two-year expanded scope takes effect only one year after the effective date of the 2005 amendments (October 2005).

[18] 11 USC § 548.

[19] 11 USC § 547(f).

[20] 11 USC § 547(b)(4)(B).

[21] *In re A. W. & Associates, Inc.*, 136 F3d 1439 (11th Cir 1998).

the preferential provisions with some exceptions now provided for in the Reform Act.

(c) Self-Settled Trust

Under the Reform Act, the trustee has the ability to set aside the transfer of property into a "self-settled" (a self-created personal trust) any time within the past ten years if the trustee can establish that the trust was created with actual intent to hinder, delay, or defraud existing or future creditors.[22] This section was added to address the problem of the many assets of individuals being in personal trusts for which those individuals serve as trustees.

12. Proof of Claim

Bankruptcy law regulates the manner in which creditors present their claims and the way in which the debtor's assets are distributed in payment of these claims.

After the debtor has filed a list of creditors, the court then sends a notice of the bankruptcy proceedings to listed creditors. The creditors who wish to participate in the distribution of the proceeds of the liquidation of the debtor's estate must file a proof of claim. A **claim** is a right to payment, whether liquidated (certain and not disputed), unliquidated, contingent, unmatured, disputed, legal, or equitable. A **proof of claim** is a written statement, signed by the creditor or an authorized representative, setting forth any claim made against the debtor and the basis for it. It must ordinarily be filed within 90 days after the first meeting of creditors.[23] A creditor must file within that time even though the trustee in bankruptcy in fact knows of the existence of the creditor's claim.

CPA 13. Priority of Claims

Creditors who hold security for payment, such as a lien or a mortgage on the debtor's property, are not affected by the debtor's bankruptcy. Secured creditors may enforce their security interest to obtain payment of their claims up to the value of their security, the collateral in which they hold an interest. **For Example,** suppose that First Bank holds a mortgage on a company's office building. The mortgage amount is $750,000. The building is sold for $700,000. First Bank is entitled to the $700,000 from the sale. For the remaining portion of the debt, First Bank drops down in priority to wait with the other unsecured creditors for its remaining $50,000. Unsecured creditors with unsecured debts that have priority and their order of priority following the secured creditors' rights in their collateral are covered in the following list.[24] Once the bottom of the priority list is reached, any remaining unsecured creditors share on a pro rata basis any remaining assets of the debtor. Any balance remaining after all creditors have been paid goes to the debtor. However, in 98 to 99 percent of all bankruptcies, no unsecured creditors receive any payments, so it is highly unlikely that the debtor would ever receive anything from the bankruptcy litigation of the debtor's property and funds.

The following is a list of the priorities for unsecured creditors following the payment to any secured creditors from the debtors' pledged property:[25]

1. Allowed claims for debts to a spouse, former spouse, or child of the debtor and for alimony to, maintenance for, or support of such spouse or child (that were obligations at the time of the filing of the bankruptcy petition).
2. Costs and expenses of administration of the bankruptcy case, including fees to trustees, attorneys, and accountants, and the reasonable expenses of creditors in recovering property transferred or concealed by the debtor.
3. Claims arising in the ordinary course of a debtor's business or financial affairs after the commencement of the case but before the order of relief (involuntary).
4. Claims for wages, salaries, or commissions, including vacation, severance, or sick leave pay earned within 180 days before the filing of the petition or the date of cessation of the debtor's business, whichever occurred first, limited, however, to $10,000 for each person.[26]
5. Claims arising for contributions to employee benefit plans, based on services rendered within 180 days before the filing of the petition or when the debtor ceased doing business, whichever occurred first; the maximum amount is

[22] 11 USC § 548(e).
[23] 11 USC § 302(c).
[24] 11 USC § 507(1)–(6).
[25] 11 USCA § 507.
[26] Prior to the 2005 reforms, the amount limit was $4,650 and the time period was 90 days.

$4,650. Under the 2005 reforms (especially in Chapter 11 reorganizations), payments of key-employee retention plans are not permitted unless the plans are "essential" to keeping the key employee at the company that is in bankruptcy. Proving that they are essential requires the key employee actually to have a "bona fide" offer of employment from another company. In addition, there are limits on how much can be paid under a key employee retention plan.

6. Farm producers (up to $10,000) and fishers against debtors who operate grain storage facilities or fish produce storage or processing facilities, up to $4,925 per claim.
7. Claims by consumer creditors, not to exceed $2,225 for each claimant, arising for the purchase of consumer goods or services when such property or services were not delivered or provided.
8. Certain taxes and penalties due government units, such as income and property taxes.
9. All other unsecured creditors.
10. Remainder (if any) to debtor.

Each claim must be paid in full before any lower claim is paid anything. If a class of claims cannot be paid in full, the claims in that case are paid on a pro rata basis. **For Example,** suppose that following the payment of all secured creditors, $10,000 is left to be distributed. The accountants who performed work on the bankruptcy are owed $15,000, and the lawyers who worked on it are owed $10,000. Because there is not enough to pay two parties in the same priority ranking, the $10,000 is split proportionately. The accountants will receive 15/25, or 3/5, of the $10,000, or $6,000, and the lawyers will receive 10/25, or 2/5, of the $10,000, or $4,000.

D. Debtor's Duties and Exemptions

Bankruptcy law imposes certain duties on the debtor and provides for specific exemptions of some of the debtor's estate from the claims of creditors.

14. Debtor's Duties

A debtor must file with the court a list of creditors, a schedule of assets and liabilities, and a statement of her financial affairs. The debtor must also appear for examination under oath at the first meeting of creditors.

CPA 15. Debtor's Exemptions

A debtor is permitted to claim certain property of the estate in the trustee's possession and keep it free from claims of creditors. Exemptions are provided under federal law, but state laws also provide for exemptions. In 14 states (examples are Massachusetts, New Jersey, Pennsylvania, and Connecticut), debtors can elect either federal or state exemption. In the other states (New York, California, Florida, and Delaware are examples), debtors are permitted to use only the state exemptions.[27] Examples of exempt property from the federal code include wedding rings, property used to earn a living, one VCR, and one car. New York exemptions include "all stoves in the home, one sewing machine, the family Bible, a pew in a public house of worship, enough food for sixty days, a wedding ring, and a watch not exceeding thirty-five dollars in value."[28] California exempts tools of the trade and the family cemetery plot.[29]

The principal exemptions provided by the Bankruptcy Code are the debtor's interest in real or personal property used as a residence. The Reform Act has greatly limited the homestead exemption and, in effect, preempts state law on this debtor exemption. Debtors are required to live in the home for two years prior to bankruptcy, and the amount of the homestead exemption would be limited to $125,000.[30] To be able to use a higher state homestead exemption, the debtor must have lived in the home for 1215 days (40 months).[31] Labeled as the most flagrant abuse of the existing bankruptcy system, debtors have used the homestead exemption to shift their assets into expensive homes to shield everything from bankruptcy. Known as the "mansion loophole," the changes in the reform act related to the homestead exemption were among the most debated and the most dramatic.[32] Florida's full

[27] 11 USC § 522.
[28] NY CPLR § 5205 (McKinney 1997).
[29] Cal Civ Proc Code § 704.010-704.210 (West 1987).
[30] The time requirement is at 11 USC § 522(b)(3)(A), and the amount limitation is at 11 USC § 522(o)(1).
[31] 11 USC § 522(b)(2).
[32] 11 USC § 522(p).

ETHICS & THE LAW

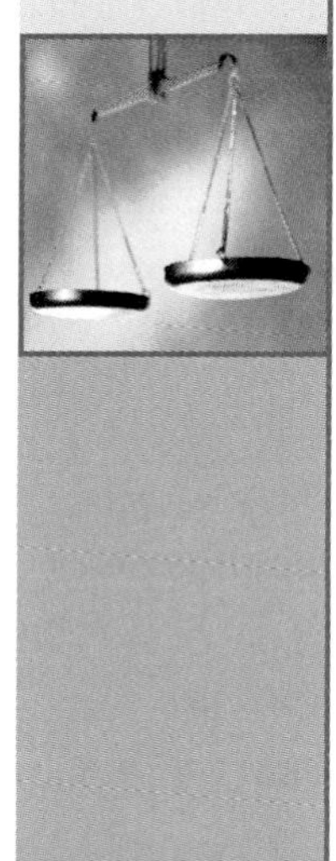

THE SKIES ARE NOT SO FRIENDLY TO EMPLOYEE PENSIONS

As part of its Chapter 11 bankruptcy, United Airlines was relieved of its pension liabilities. Employees and unions wonder how a company can be permitted to renege on those benefits when so many protections were built into the law under ERISA. Congressional hearings now reveal that there were loopholes in the accounting processes for pension fund reporting that permitted United, and many others, to report pension numbers that made the pension funds look healthy when they really were not. The loopholes were Enronesque in nature. Companies could spin the pension obligations off the books so that the existing levels of obligations of the plan looked small and the assets very rich. Because of United's pension bailout, Congress will be examining and changing the accounting for pension plans to avoid the problem of the rosy picture when the funds really need further funding. One interesting approach to protecting pension plans is to require companies to fund the pension plans according to the numbers they have reported to the SEC in their financials. The numbers reported to the SEC for company pensions are accurate whereas the numbers reported for ERISA purposes are inflated. If United had funded its plans when its SEC numbers indicated it needed to (e.g., in 1998), the plan would have been sufficiently funded. Under ERISA guidelines, it was not required to kick in funds until 2002 when it was grossly underfunded.

Were companies acting ethically on their pension accounting? Were they acting legally?*

*Marry Williams Walsh, "Pension Law Loopholes Helped United Hide Its Troubles," *New York Times*, June 7, 2005, C1.

exemption allows those declaring bankruptcy to shield an unlimited amount in their residences. **For Example,** actor Burt Reynolds declared bankruptcy in Florida and was relieved of millions in debt, but he was able to keep his $2.5 million Valhalla estate there. Corporate raider Paul Bilzerian, who was convicted of securities fraud, also declared bankruptcy in Florida but kept his mansion, the largest home in Hillsborough County, Florida. Wendy Gramm, who sat on Enron's board, purchased 200 acres of land in Texas and is constructing a large home with her husband, former senator Phil Gramm, to take advantage of homestead exemptions available in Texas. Former WorldCom CFO Scott Sullivan (who entered a guilty plea to fraud and other charges and is serving a five-year sentence) built a multimillion-dollar home in Florida to take advantage of Florida's protections for homeowners who declare bankruptcy. However, the Reform Act closed this corporate executive loophole by requiring that the $125,000 exemption apply to debtors who are convicted of securities fraud or bankruptcy fraud. These debtors cannot use the larger state exemptions.[33]

Other exemptions include payments under a life insurance contract, alimony and child support payments, and awards from personal injury litigation.[34] Under the Reform Act, college savings accounts and IRAs are exempt property under the federal exemptions and can be used even by those debtors who are using state exemptions. The IRA exemption is limited to $1,000,000.[35]

Businesses that declare bankruptcy would not have included in their bankruptcy estates employee pension plan contributions. Those contributions would be returned to the employees. The proposed changes are the result of the numerous large corporate bankruptcies, such as the one involving United Airlines and the pensions of its employees.[36]

[33] 11 USC § 522(q).

[34] 11 USC § 522(d) (including automatic adjustments effective April 1, 1998); *Jost v Key Bank of Maine*, 136 F3d 1455 (11th Cir 1998).

[35] 11 USC § 522(n).

[36] 11 USC § 541(b).

IN RE JENNIFER L.L. MURPHY, DEBTOR, 305 BR 780 (ED VA 2004)

80 GRAND IS QUITE ENOUGH FOR MAKING GOOD ON STUDENT LOANS

Jennifer Murphy (Murphy) filed an individual Chapter 7 petition. To finance her education at Virginia Polytechnic Institute and two years of medical school at Eastern Virginia Medical School, Murphy had taken out loans under various programs, including loans guaranteed by the United States through its Department of Education.

Murphy's oldest child, Kayla Murphy, was afflicted with Pfeiffer Syndrome. Because of her daughter's medical condition, Murphy discontinued medical school and is unable to work due to the daily requirements involved in caring for her daughter. Murphy requests a discharge due to the undue hardship associated with the repayment of her student loans.

Murphy is indebted for approximately $58,000.00. Murphy last worked full-time from June to August 1991 as a laboratory intern at Virginia Polytechnic Institute. Murphy testified that she worked for Wal-Mart for a brief time after the birth of her daughter but was unable to continue working due to scheduling difficulties.

Mr. Murphy is a computer programmer and has been employed at BMH since December 1, 2003. Mr. Murphy's annual salary at BMH is $82,000. Prior to his employment at BMH, Mr. Murphy was a computer programmer for Net Decisions JAVA Business Solutions for four to five years. He earned $84,000 in 2001 and $83,500 in 2002.

The family expenses follow:

First mortgage	$891.00
Second mortgage	25.00
Utilities	125.00
Gas	80.00
Phone	40.00
Car payment	291.00
Groceries	700.00
Car repairs	150.00
Water	45.00
Sewer	15.00
Storm Water Management fee	5.00
AAA	5.83
Insect control	34.00
Tuition for daughter	507.00
Recreation	135.00
Sports fee	128.00
Insurance	363.00
Total	$3,539.83

These specific expenses, when deducted from her net family income, produce a monthly surplus of $1,360.17 available for student loan repayment. Murphy asked that her loans be discharged in bankruptcy.

Judicial Opinion

ST. JOHN, Bankruptcy Judge.... Student loans generally are nondischargeable debts and pass through the bankruptcy process unaffected. Congress has provided that government-guaranteed student loans are nondischargeable in bankruptcy unless the debtor can demonstrate that the repayment of such student loans would constitute an "undue hardship." 11 U.S.C. § 523(a)(8) This exception from discharge of student loans "was enacted to prevent indebted students or graduate students from filing for bankruptcy immediately upon graduation, thereby absolving themselves of the obligation to repay their student loans."

The term "undue hardship" is undefined in the Bankruptcy Code. The Fourth Circuit Court of Appeals has adopted the three-part test articulated in the decision of *Brunner v. New York State Higher Educ. Servs. Corp.*, 831 F2d 395, 396 (2nd Cir1987). Thus, in order to discharge a government-guaranteed student loan, a debtor "must establish (1) that he cannot maintain a minimal standard of living for himself and his dependents, based on his current income and expenses, if he is required to repay the student loans; (2) that additional circumstances indicate that his inability to do so is likely to exist for a significant portion of the repayment period of the student loans; and (3) that he has made good faith efforts to repay the loans."

The initial prong of the *Brunner* inquiry requires this Court to assess whether the debtor has proven she cannot maintain, based on current income and expenses, a minimal standard of living for herself and her dependents if forced to repay the student loans.

Taking as reasonable and necessary all of Murphy's specified expenses, and without consideration of whether Murphy's declination of any working opportunities inside or outside the home or part-time is mandated in perpetuity by her daughter's condition, Murphy still has substantial monthly income available to repay her remaining student loans.

The second *Brunner* prong requires a student loan debtor to establish that additional circumstances indicate a debtor's inability to maintain a minimal standard of living for herself and her dependents if required to repay the student loans is likely to exist for a significant portion of the repayment period of the student loans. Undue hardship is not based on a present inability to pay but rather upon a "certainty of hopelessness that future payments cannot be made." Here Murphy has testified that her daughter's disability is permanent and she will require a high level of care indefinitely. Having not demonstrated any inability to repay her student loans and maintain a minimal standard of living, and in fact conceding her family income of in excess of $80,000.00 annually is expected to continue, the Court must conclude there is a failure to establish the second Brunner prong.

The third prong of the *Brunner* test requires a court to measure whether a debtor has made a good faith effort to repay the outstanding student loans.

In determining whether a debtor has made a good faith effort to repay a student loan obligation, a primary consideration is whether the debtor actually made any payments on the obligation, and if so, the total amount of payments. Murphy has not convinced the Court that she has made a good faith effort to make payments on the... loans. By her admission, Murphy has never made any payments on these student loans. This absence of payments is despite what by any reasonable measure appears to be substantial monthly family income available to make payments on these loans. By her own admission, the sole purpose of Murphy's [bankruptcy] filing was to relieve herself of her student loans.

It is doubtless that Murphy's burden of caring for her disabled daughter is immeasurable and her disappointment in her inability to complete her medical education immense. But discharge of a student loan must be founded on more than notions of sympathy or fairness. While rearing her daughter is consumptive of Murphy, nonetheless Murphy and her family fortuitously do not also share the additional burden of an insubstantial family income. Rather, because of her husband's successful employment, Murphy and her dependents enjoy an income well in excess of nearly all who seek an undue hardship discharge and a substantially more comfortable lifestyle than the minimal one contemplated by the Brunner criterion. While perhaps not entirely painless, Murphy can repay the remaining student loans... without inflicting serious financial burden upon herself or her family.

For the reasons expressed herein, the Court finds the ECMC loans are not discharged.

Questions

1. What does the court say about the role of tragic personal circumstances in determining the discharge of student loans?
2. What is the effect of making no payments on student loans?
3. What does the court do with the income of the spouse's debtor for purposes of determining whether the student loans can be repaid?

16. Debtor's Protection against Discrimination

Federal, state, and local law may not discriminate against anyone on the basis of a discharge in bankruptcy. For example, a state cannot refuse to issue a new license to an individual if the license fees on a previous one have been discharged as a debt in the individual's declaration of bankruptcy.

E. Discharge in Bankruptcy

The main objectives of a bankruptcy proceeding are to collect and distribute the debtor's assets and the subsequent **discharge in bankruptcy** of the debtor from obligations. The decree terminating the bankruptcy proceeding is generally a discharge that releases the debtor from most debts. Under the proposed reforms, a discharge would be available only once every eight years.

17. Denial of Discharge

The court will refuse to grant a discharge if the debtor has (1) within one year of the filing of the petition fraudulently transferred or concealed property with intent to hinder, delay, or defraud creditors, (2) failed to keep proper financial records, (3) made a false oath or account,[37] (4) failed to explain satisfactorily any loss of assets, (5) refused to obey any lawful order of the court or refused to testify after having been granted immunity, (6) obtained a discharge within the last eight years,[38] (7) filed a written waiver of discharge that is approved by the court,[39] or (8) in the case of a consumer debtor, has failed to complete a personal financial management instructional course.[40]

A discharge releases the debtor from the unpaid balance of most debts except for taxes, customs duties, child support obligations, and tax penalties.[41] Student loan obligations are not discharged in bankruptcy unless the loan first became due more than seven years before bankruptcy or unless not allowing a discharge would impose undue hardship on the debtor.

In addition, the following debts are not discharged by bankruptcy: (1) loans obtained by use of a false financial statement made with intent to deceive and on which the creditor reasonably relied, (2) debts not scheduled or listed with the court in time for allowance, (3) debts arising from fraud while the debtor was acting in a fiduciary capacity or by reason of embezzlement or larceny, (4) alimony and child support, (5) a judgment for willful and malicious injury, (6) a consumer debt to a single creditor totaling more than $500 for luxury goods or services (within 90 days of the order of relief) and cash advances exceeding $750 based on consumer open-end credit, such as a credit card (within 70 days of the order of relief),[42] (7) damages arising from drunk driving or the operation of vessels and aircrafts by people who are inebriated,[43] (8) loans used to pay taxes (including credit cards),[44] (9) taxes not paid as a result of a fraudulent return, although other unpaid taxes beyond the past three years can be discharged,[45] (10) prebankruptcy fees and assessments owed to homeowners associations, and (11) debts owed to tax-qualified retirement plans. **For Example,** in regard to (5), the finding of malice in *Goldman v O. J. Simpson* precluded the discharge by bankruptcy of the $8.5 million damage award from Simpson to the Goldmans and Browns. See Figure 35-3 for a listing of nondischargeable debts.

F. Reorganization Plans under Chapter 11

In addition to liquidation under Chapter 7, the Bankruptcy Code permits debtors to restructure the organization and finances of their businesses so that

[37] The debtor must actually make a false statement. In *In re Mercer*, 211 F3d 214 (5th Cir 2000), the debtor ran up $3,186.82 on a credit card she was given by AT&T with a $3,000 credit limit. The credit card was issued to the debtor on a preapproved basis, so there was no fraud, just a great deal of spending.

[38] 11 USC § 727(a)(8).

[39] 11 USC § 523; *Barax v Barax*, 667 NYS2d 733 (1998).

[40] 11 USC § 727(a)(11). The financial management course requirement applies to both Chapter 7 and Chapter 13 consumer bankruptcies.

[41] Child support obligations enjoy additional protections and priorities in bankruptcy. 11 USC § 507(a).

[42] 11 USC § 523(a)(2)(c)(i).

[43] 11 USC § 523(a)(9).

[44] 11 USC § 523(a)(14A),(14B).

[45] 11 USC §§ 1129(a)(9)(c), (D), 1129(b)(2)(B), 1141(d)(6)(B).

FIGURE 35-3 Nondischargeable Debts in Bankruptcy

1. TAXES WITHIN THREE YEARS OF FILING BANKRUPTCY PETITION
2. LIABILITY FOR OBTAINING MONEY OR PROPERTY BY FALSE PRETENSES
3. WILLFUL AND MALICIOUS INJURIES
4. DEBTS INCURRED BY DRIVING DWI*
5. ALIMONY, MAINTENANCE, OR CHILD SUPPORT
6. UNSCHEDULED DEBTS (UNLESS ACTUAL NOTICE)
7. DEBTS RESULTING FROM FRAUD AS A FIDUCIARY (EMBEZZLEMENT)
8. GOVERNMENT FINES OR PENALTIES IMPOSED WITHIN THREE YEARS PRIOR
9. EDUCATIONAL LOANS DUE WITHIN SEVEN PRIOR YEARS (UNLESS HARDSHIP)
10. PRIOR BANKRUPTCY DEBTS IN WHICH DEBTOR WAIVED DISCHARGE
11. PRESUMPTION ON LUXURY GOODS: $1,150 GOODS; $1,150 CASH
12. REAFFIRMATION AGREEMENTS — WRITING; FILED WITH COURT; NOT RESCINDED PRIOR TO DISCHARGE

*INCLUDES VESSELS AND AIRCRAFT

they may continue to operate. In these rehabilitation plans, the debtor keeps all of the assets (exempt and nonexempt), continues to operate the business, and makes a settlement that is acceptable to the majority of the creditors. This settlement is binding on the minority creditors.

Individuals, partnerships, and corporations in business may all be reorganized under the Bankruptcy Code. The first step is to file a plan for the debtor's reorganization. This plan may be filed by the debtor, any party in interest, or a committee of creditors. If the debtor wishes to move from a Chapter 11 proceeding (in the case of an individual debtor), the debtor must survive the means test that is now a requirement for determining eligibility for bankruptcy.

18. Contents of the Plan

The plan divides ownership interests and debts into those that will be affected by the adoption of the plan and those that will not be. It then specifies what will be done to those interests and claims that are affected. **For Example,** when mortgage payments are too high for the income of a corporation, a possible plan would be to reduce the mortgage payments and give the mortgage holder preferred stock to compensate for the loss sustained.

All creditors, shareholders, and other interest holders within a particular class must be treated the same way. **For Example,** the holders of first mortgage bonds must all be treated similarly.

A plan can also provide for the assumption, rejection, or assignment of executory contracts. The trustee or debtor can, under certain circumstances, suspend performance of a contract not yet fully performed. **For Example,** collective bargaining agreements may be rejected with the approval of the bankruptcy court.[46]

19. Confirmation of the Plan

After the plan is prepared, the court must approve or confirm it. A plan will be confirmed if it has been submitted in good faith and if its provisions are reasonable.[47] After the plan is confirmed, the owners and creditors of the enterprise have only the rights that are specified in the plan. They cannot go back to their original contract positions.

[46] 11 USC § 1113.
[47] 11 USC § 1129.

CPA G. Payment Plans under Chapter 13

The Bankruptcy Code also provides for the adoption of extended-time payment plans for individual debtors who have regular income. These debtors must owe unsecured debts of less than $307,675 and secured debts of less than $922,975.

An individual debtor who has a regular income may submit a plan for the installment payment of outstanding debts. If the court approves it, the debtor may then pay the debts in the installments specified by the plan even if the creditors had not originally agreed to such installment payments.

20. Contents of the Plan

The individual debtor plan is, in effect, a budget of the debtor's future income with respect to outstanding debts. The plan must provide for the eventual payment in full of all claims entitled to priority under the Bankruptcy Code. All creditors holding the same kind or class of claim must be treated the same way.

21. Confirmation of the Plan

The plan has no effect until the court approves or confirms it. A plan will be confirmed if it was submitted in good faith and is in the best interests of the creditors.[48] When the plan is confirmed, debts are payable in the manner specified in the plan.

22. Discharge of the Debtor

After all of the payments called for by the plan have been made, the debtor is given a discharge. The discharge releases the debtor from liability for all debts except those that would not be discharged by an ordinary bankruptcy discharge.[49] Under the bankruptcy reforms, the court cannot grant a discharge until the debtor has completed an instructional course concerning personal financial management.[50] If the debtor does not perform under the plan, the creditors can move to transfer the debtor's case to a Chapter 7 proceeding, but they would still face the means test in qualifying for Chapter 7.

48 11 USC § 1325.
49 11 USC § 1328.
50 11 U.S.C. § 1328(g)(1).

Summary

Jurisdiction over bankruptcy cases is in U.S. district courts, which may refer all cases and related proceedings to adjunct bankruptcy courts.

Three bankruptcy proceedings are available: liquidation (Chapter 7), reorganization (Chapter 11), and extended-time payment (Chapter 13). A liquidation proceeding under Chapter 7 may be either voluntary or involuntary. A *voluntary case* is commenced by the debtor's filing a petition with the bankruptcy court. A voluntary petition is subject to the means test to determine if the debtor meets the standard for declaring bankruptcy. An involuntary case is commenced by the creditors' filing a petition with the bankruptcy court. If there are 12 or more creditors, at least 3 whose unsecured claims total $12,300 or more must sign the involuntary petition. If there are fewer than 12 creditors, any creditor whose unsecured claim is at least $12,300 may sign the petition. If the debtor contests the bankruptcy petition, it must be shown that the debtor is not paying debts as they become due. Eligibility for Chapters 7 and 11 bankruptcy excludes railroads, municipalities, and Small Business Administration companies. Individual debtors are restricted on Chapter 7 and 11 filings by their ability to repay. If found to have the means to pay, they go into a Chapter 13 proceeding. Chapter 13 eligibility is limited to consumers with $307,675 in unsecured debt and $922,975 in secured debt.

An automatic stay prevents creditors from taking legal action against the debtor after a bankruptcy petition is filed. The trustee in bankruptcy is elected by the creditors and is the successor to, and acquires the rights of, the debtor. In certain cases, the trustee can avoid transfers of property to prevent creditors from satisfying their claims. Preferential transfers may be set aside. A transfer for a present consideration, such as a cash sale, is not a preference.

Bankruptcy law regulates the way creditors present their claims and how the assets of the debtor are to be distributed in payment of the claims. Some assets of the debtor are exempt from the bankruptcy estate, such as a portion of the value of the debtor's home.

Secured claims are not affected by the debtor's bankruptcy. Unsecured claims are paid in the following order of priority:

1. Support or maintenance for a spouse, former spouse, or child.

2. Costs and expenses of administration of the bankruptcy case.
3. Claims arising in the ordinary course of a debtor's business or financial affairs after the commencement of the case but before the order of relief (involuntary).
4. Claims for wages, salaries, or commissions, including vacation, severance, or sick leave pay earned within 180 days before the filing of the petition or the date of cessation of the debtor's business, limited to $10,000 for each person.
5. Claims arising for contributions (up to $4,650) to employee benefit plans based on services rendered within 180 days before the filing of the petition or when the debtor ceased doing business.
6. Farm producers (up to $10,000) and fishers against debtors who operate grain storage facilities or fish produce storage or processing facilities, up to $4,925 per claim.
7. Claims by consumer creditors, not to exceed $2,225 for each claimant.
8. Certain taxes and penalties due government units, such as income and property taxes.
9. All other unsecured creditors.
10. Remainder (if any) to debtor.

The decree terminating bankruptcy proceedings is generally a discharge that releases the debtor from most debts. Certain debts, such as income taxes, student loans, loans obtained by use of a false financial statement, alimony, and debts not listed by the debtor, are not discharged.

Under Chapter 11 bankruptcy, individuals, partnerships, and corporations in business may be reorganized so that the business can continue to operate. A plan for reorganization must be approved by the court. Under a Chapter 13 bankruptcy proceeding, individual debtors with a regular income may adopt extended-time payment plans for the payment of debts. A plan for extended-time payment must also be confirmed by the court. Federal, state, and local law may not discriminate against anyone on the basis of a discharge in bankruptcy.

Questions and Case Problems

1. Hall-Mark regularly supplied electronic parts to Peter Lee. On September 11, 1992, Lee gave Hall-Mark a $100,000 check for parts it had received. Hall-Mark continued to ship parts to Lee. On September 23, 1992, Lee's check was dishonored by the bank. On September 25, 1992, Lee delivered to Hall-Mark a cashier's check for $100,000. Hall-Mark shipped nothing more to Lee after receipt of the cashier's check. On December 24, 1992, Lee filed a voluntary petition for bankruptcy. The trustee filed a complaint to have the $100,000 payment to Hall-Mark set aside as a voidable preference. Hall-Mark said it was entitled to the payment because it gave value to Lee. The trustee said that the payment was not actually made until the cashier's check was delivered on September 25, 1992, and that Hall-Mark gave no further value to Lee after that check was paid. Who was correct? [*In re Lee*, 108 F3d 239 (9th Cir)]
2. Orso, who had declared bankruptcy, received a structured tort settlement in a personal injury claim he had pending. The settlement would pay him an annuity each year for 30 years because the claim was the result of an auto accident that left him permanently and severely brain damaged with an IQ of about 70. His wife had a pending claim for $48,000 in arrearages on Orso's $1,000 per month child support payments. His wife wanted the annuity included in the bankruptcy estate. Would this property have been included in Orso's bankruptcy estate? [*In re Orso*, 214 F3d 637 (5th Cir)]
3. Harold McClellan sold ice-making machinery to Bobbie Cantrell's brother for $200,000 to be paid in installment payments. McClellan took a security interest in the ice machine but did not perfect it by filing a financing statement. The brother defaulted when he owed $100,000, and McClellan brought suit. With the suit pending, the brother "sold" the ice machine to Bobbie Cantrell for $10. Bobbie then sold the machine to someone for $160,000 and refused to explain what happened to that money. McClellan added Bobbie as a defendant in his suit against her brother. Bobbie then declared bankruptcy. McClellan sought to have the various transfers set aside. The trial court refused to do so, and McClellan appealed. Should the transfers be set aside? Why or why not? [*McClellan v Cantrell*, 217 F3d 890 (7th Cir)]
4. Okamoto owed money to Hornblower &Weeks-Hemphill, Noyes (a law firm and hereafter Hornblower). Hornblower filed an involuntary bankruptcy petition against Okamoto, who moved to dismiss the petition on the ground that he had more than 12 creditors and the petition could not be filed by only one creditor. Hornblower replied that the other creditors' claims were too small to count and, therefore, the petition could be filed by one creditor. Decide. [*In re Okamoto*, 491 F2d 496 (9th Cir)]
5. Jane Leeves declared voluntary Chapter 7 bankruptcy. The trustee included the following property in her bankruptcy estate:

   - Jane's wedding ring
   - Jane's computer for her consulting business that she operated from her home

- Jane's car
- Payment from a client in the amount of $5,000 that was received 91 days after Jane filed bankruptcy

After collecting all of Jane's assets, the bankruptcy trustee was trying to decide how to distribute the assets. Jane had the following creditors:

- Mortgage company—owed $187,000 (the trustee sold Jane's house for $190,000)
- Expenses of the bankruptcy—$3,000
- Federal income taxes—$11,000
- Utility bills—$1,000
- Office supply store open account—$1,000

The trustee had $11,500 in cash, including the $3,000 additional cash left from the sale of the house after the mortgage company was paid. How should the trustee distribute this money? What if the amount were $14,500; how should that be distributed?

6. Kentile sold goods over an extended period of time to Winham. The credit relationship began without Winham's being required to furnish a financial statement. After some time, payments were not made regularly, and Kentile requested a financial statement. Winham submitted a statement for the year that had just ended. After that, Kentile requested a second statement. The second statement was false. Kentile objected to Winham's discharge in bankruptcy because of the false financial statement. Should the discharge be granted? Why or why not?
7. Essex is in serious financial difficulty and is unable to meet current unsecured obligations of $40,000 to some 20 creditors, who are demanding immediate payment. Essex owes Stevens $5,000, and Stevens has decided to file an involuntary petition against Essex. Can Stevens file the petition?
8. Sonia, a retailer, has the following assets: a factory worth $1 million; accounts receivable amounting to $750,000, which fall due in four to six months; and $20,000 cash in the bank. Sonia's sole liability is a $200,000 note falling due today, which she is unable to pay. Can Sonia be forced into involuntary bankruptcy under the Bankruptcy Code?
9. Samson Industries ceased doing business and is in bankruptcy proceedings. Among the creditors are five employees seeking unpaid wages. Three of the employees are owed $3,500 each, and two are owed $1,500 each. These amounts became due within 90 days preceding the filing of the petition. Where, in the priority of claims, will the employees' wage claims fall?
10. Carol Cott, doing business as Carol Cott Fashions, is worried about an involuntary bankruptcy proceeding being filed by her creditors. Her net worth, using a balance sheet approach, is $8,000 ($108,000 in assets minus $100,000 in liabilities). However, her cash flow is negative, and she has been hard pressed to meet current obligations as they mature. She is in fact some $12,500 in arrears in payments to her creditors on bills submitted during the past two months. Will the fact that Cott is solvent in the balance sheet sense result in the court's dismissing the creditors' petition if Cott objects to the petition? Explain.
11. On July 1, Roger Walsh, a sole proprietor operating a grocery, was involuntarily petitioned into bankruptcy by his creditors. At that time, and for at least 90 days prior to that time, Walsh was unable to pay current obligations. On June 16, Walsh paid the May electric bill for his business. The trustee in bankruptcy claimed that this payment was a voidable preference. Was the trustee correct? Explain.
12. Steven and Teresa Hornsby are married and have three young children. On May 25, 1993, the Hornsbys filed a voluntary Chapter 7 petition. They had by that date accumulated more than $30,000 in debt, stemming almost entirely from student loans. They wanted a discharge of their student loans on grounds of undue hardship. The Hornsbys attended a succession of small Tennessee state colleges. Both studied business and computers, but neither graduated. Although they received several deferments and forbearances on the loans, they ultimately defaulted before making any payments. Interest had accumulated on the loans to the extent that Steven was indebted to the Tennessee Student Assistance Corporation (TSAC) for $15,058.52, and Teresa was indebted to TSAC for $18,329.15.

    Steven was working for AT&T in Dallas, Texas; he made $6.53 per hour, occasionally working limited overtime hours. Teresa was employed by KinderCare Learning Center. Although she had begun work in Tennessee, she had transferred to become the director of a child care facility in Dallas. Teresa was earning $17,500 per year with medical benefits at the time of the hearing. In monthly net income, Steven earned approximately $1,083.33, and Teresa earned $1,473.33, amounting to $2,556.66 of disposable income per month. The Hornsbys' reported monthly expenses came to $2,364.90. They operated with a monthly surplus of $191.76 to $280.43, depending on whether Steven earned overtime for a particular month. Under the federal bankruptcy laws, are the Hornsbys entitled to a discharge on their student loans? Explain your answer. [*In re Hornsby*, 144 F3d 433 (6th Cir)]
13. On March 19, 1997, Jairath, as seller, and Bletnitsky, as buyer, entered into a real estate contract for sale of an apartment building located at 930 Ontario in Oak Park, Illinois, for a price of $3.1 million. The contract closed on June 4, 1997. Jairath represented to Bletnitsky that the building contained 21 apartments. Jairath's real estate broker had told Bletnitsky that the building contained

21 units, and the real estate broker's package also stated that the building contained 21 units.

While neither Jairath nor his realtor were shown to have stated expressly that all 21 units in the building were legally available to be converted to condos, Jairath's real estate broker represented that the building was suitable for conversion into condominiums. Also, the real estate broker's package provided "for condo developer, this opportunity provides an opportunity with substantial returns. See Real Estate Broker Package, Investment Property Description."

The contract did not state the number of units in the building or warrant that the building was suitable for condominium use. In fact, the contract stated:

It is understood and agreed that the Property is being sold as is; that Buyer has or will have prior to the closing date inspected the Property; and that neither the Seller nor Agent makes any representation or warranty as to the physical condition or value of the Property or its suitability for the Buyer's intended use.

Prior to the closing on June 4, 1997, Bletnitsky received a copy of an inspection report prepared by an agency of the Village of Oak Park. The report stated that an inspection had taken place May 27, 1997, and that the apartment building contained only 20 units. On May 30, 1999, Bletnitsky wrote a letter to Jairath and indicated that he had received and read the Oak Park inspection report. In this letter, Bletnitsky stated that the inspection uncovered several violations, listed each violation, and estimated the repair costs at $88,595.

In September 1997, Bletnitsky sought approval of Oak Park to convert all 21 units of the apartment building into condominiums. Oak Park informed Bletnitsky that 20 units could be converted but that unit 1E was an illegal apartment and must be demolished. Bletnitsky was unable to sell that unit as a condominium. Bletnitsky claims that he would not have paid $3.1 million dollars for the building had he known that it only contained 20 legal units. Bletnitsky claims that as a result of Jairath's representation that the building contained 21 units, he sustained a loss of $100,000. An arbitration proceeding awarded Bletnitsky damages for misrepresentation.

Jairath then filed for Chapter 7 bankruptcy. Bletnisky has filed to have the obligation on the damages from the arbitration not be discharged in the bankruptcy because there was fraud involved. Does Beltnisky have grounds for the obligation surviving Jairath's bankruptcy? [*In re Jairath*, 259 BR 308 (ND Ill)]

14. Place the following in order for a bankruptcy proceeding:

    a. Order of relief
    b. Collection of bankrupt's estate
    c. List of creditors
    d. Petition
    e. Evaluation of claims
    f. Voidable preferences
    g. Discharge

15. Three general unsecured creditors are owed $45,000 as follows: *A*, $15,000; *B*, $5,000; and *C*, $25,000. After all other creditors were paid, the amount left for distribution to general unsecured creditors was $9,000. How will the $9,000 be distributed?

CPA Questions

1. Which of the following statements is correct concerning the voluntary filing of a petition of bankruptcy?

    a. If the debtor has 12 or more creditors, the unsecured claims must total at least $12,300.
    b. The debtor must be solvent.
    c. If the debtor has less than 12 creditors, the unsecured claims must total at least $12,300.
    d. The petition may be filed jointly by spouses. (AICPA adapted)

2. On February 28, Master, Inc., had total assets with a fair market value of $1,200,000 and total liabilities of $990,000. On January 15, Master made a monthly installment note payment to Acme Distributors Corp., a creditor holding a properly perfected security interest in equipment having a fair market value greater than the balance due on the note. On March 15, Master voluntarily filed a petition in bankruptcy under the liquidation provisions of Chapter 7 of the federal Bankruptcy Code. One year later, the equipment was sold for less than the balance due on the note to Acme.

    If a creditor challenged Master's right to file, the petition would be dismissed

    a. If Master had less than 12 creditors at the time of filing
    b. Unless Master can show that a reorganization under Chapter 11 of the federal Bankruptcy Code would have been unsuccessful
    c. Unless Master can show that it is unable to pay its debts in the ordinary course of business or as they come due
    d. If Master is an insurance company

3. A voluntary petition filed under the liquidation provisions of Chapter 7 of the federal Bankruptcy Code

   a. Is not available to a corporation unless it has previously filed a petition under the reorganization provisions of Chapter 11 of the federal Bankruptcy Code
   b. Automatically stays collection actions against the debtor except by secured creditors for collateral only
   c. Will be dismissed unless the debtor has 12 or more unsecured creditors whose claims total at least $12,300
   d. Does not require the debtor to show that the debtor's liabilities exceed the fair market value of assets

4. Which of the following conditions, if any, must a debtor meet to file a voluntary bankruptcy petition under Chapter 7 of the federal Bankruptcy Code?

	Insolvency	*Three or More Creditors*
a.	Yes	Yes
b.	Yes	No
c.	No	Yes
d.	No	No

5. On July 15, 1988, White, a sole proprietor, was involuntarily petitioned into bankruptcy under the liquidation provisions of the Bankruptcy Code. White's nonexempt property has been converted to $13,000 cash, which is available to satisfy the following claims:

Unsecured claim for 1986 state income tax	$10,000
Fee owed to Best & Co., CPAs, for services rendered from April 1, 1988, through June 30, 1988	$6,000
Unsecured claim by Stieb for wages earned as an employee of White during March 1988	$3,000

There are no other claims.

What is the maximum amount that will be distributed for the payment of the 1986 state income tax?

   a. $4,000
   b. $5,000
   c. $7,000
   d. $10,000

6. On May 1, 1997, two months after becoming insolvent, Quick Corp., an appliance wholesaler, filed a voluntary petition for bankruptcy under the provisions of Chapter 7 of the federal Bankruptcy Code. On October 15, 1996, Quick's board of directors had authorized and paid Erly $50,000 to repay Erly's April 1, 1996, loan to the corporation. Erly is a sibling of Quick's president. On March 15, 1996, Quick paid Kray $100,000 for inventory delivered that day. Which of the following is not relevant in determining whether the repayment of Erly's loan is a voidable preferential transfer?

   a. Erly is an insider.
   b. Quick's payment to Erly was made on account of an antecedent debt.
   c. Quick's solvency when the loan was made by Erly.
   d. Quick's payment to Erly was made within one year of the filing of the bankruptcy petition.

INSURANCE

CHAPTER

(36)

LEARNING OBJECTIVES

After studying this chapter, you should be able to

LO.1 Define *insurable interest*

LO.2 Compare contracts of insurance with ordinary contracts

LO.3 Explain the purpose of business liability insurance, marine insurance, fire and homeowners insurance, automobile insurance, and life insurance

LO.4 Explain the effect of an incontestability clause

By means of insurance, protection from loss and liability may be obtained.

A. The Insurance Contract

Insurance is a contract by which one party for a stipulated consideration promises to pay another party a sum of money on the destruction of, loss of, or injury to something in which the other party has an interest or to indemnify that party for any loss or liability to which that party is subjected.

1. The Parties

The promisor in an insurance contract is called the **insurer** or **underwriter.** The person to whom the promise is made is the **insured** or the policyholder. The promise of the insurer is generally set forth in a written contract called a **policy.**

Insurance contracts are ordinarily made through an agent or broker. The **insurance agent** is an agent of the insurance company, often working exclusively for one company. For the most part, the ordinary rules of agency law govern the dealings between this agent and the applicant for insurance.[1]

An **insurance broker** is generally an independent contractor who is not employed by any one insurance company. When a broker obtains a policy for a customer, the broker is the agent of the customer for the purpose of that transaction. Under some statutes, the broker is made an agent of the insurer with respect to transmitting the applicant's payments to the insurer.

2. Insurable Interest

A person obtaining insurance must have an insurable interest in the subject matter insured. If not, the insurance contract cannot be enforced.

CPA (a) Insurable Interest in Property

A person has an insurable interest in property whenever the destruction of the property will cause a direct pecuniary loss to that person.

It is immaterial whether the insured is the owner of the legal or equitable title, a lienholder, or merely a person in possession of the property.[2] **For Example,** Vin Harrington, a builder, maintained fire insurance on a building he was remodeling under a contract with its owner, Chestnut Hill Properties. The building was destroyed by fire before renovations were completed. Harrington had an insurable interest in the property to the extent of the amount owed him under the renovation contract.

To collect on property insurance, the insured must have an insurable interest at the time the loss occurs.

(b) Insurable Interest in Life

A person who obtains life insurance can name anyone as beneficiary regardless of whether that beneficiary has an insurable interest in the life of the insured. A beneficiary who obtains a policy, however, must have an insurable interest in the life of the insured. Such an interest exists if the beneficiary can reasonably expect to receive pecuniary gain from the continued life of the other person and, conversely, would suffer financial loss from the latter's death. Thus, a creditor has an insurable interest in the life of the debtor because he may not be paid the amount owed upon the death of the debtor.

A partner or partnership has an insurable interest in the life of each of the partners because the death of any one of them will dissolve the firm and cause some degree of loss to the partnership. A business enterprise has an insurable interest in the life of an executive or a key employee because that person's death would inflict a financial loss on the business to the extent that a replacement might not be readily available or could not be found.

In the case of life insurance, the insurable interest must exist at the time the policy is obtained. It is immaterial that the interest no longer exists when the loss is actually sustained. Thus, the fact that a husband (insured) and wife (beneficiary) are divorced after the life insurance policy was procured does not affect the validity of the policy. Also, the fact that a partnership is terminated after a life insurance policy is obtained by one partner on another does not invalidate the policy.

In the *Graves* case, the court was faced with two questions: (1) Does a partner have an insurable interest in the life of another partner? (2) Was the surviving partner required to remit the insurance proceeds to the estate of the deceased partner?

[1] *Tidelands Life Ins. Co. v France*, 711 So 2d 728 (Tex App 1986).

[2] *Gorman v Farm Bureau Town & Country Insurance Co.*, 977 SW2d 519 (Mo App 1998).

GRAVES V NORRED, 510 SO 2D 816 (ALA 1987)

PROCEEDS TO THE SURVIVING PARTNER OR THE DECEASED PARTNER'S WIFE?

Jewell Norred's husband, James Norred, was the business partner of Clyde Graves for about 10 years. On May 7, 1979, Graves and Norred took out term life insurance policies, with Graves being the beneficiary of Norred's policy and Norred being the beneficiary of Graves's policy. Premiums were paid out of partnership funds. On February 28, 1983, Graves and Norred divided the partnership assets but did not perform the customary steps of dissolving the partnership. Graves became the sole owner of the business and continued to pay the premiums on both insurance policies until James Norred died on December 5, 1983. Jewell Norred sued Graves to obtain the proceeds of the insurance policy for herself, alleging that Graves had no insurable interest in the life of James Norred at the time of his death. She also contended that the proceeds should go to the estate as a payment for Norred's interest in the partnership. From a judgment on behalf of the estate, Graves appealed.

Judicial Opinion

ADAMS, J. . . . Jewell Norred argues that she should receive the benefits of the insurance policy because she alone had an insurable interest in the insurance contract. . . . The prevailing rule among the states is that a partner or partnership has an insurable interest in the life of one of the partners. . . . It is not the mere existence of the partnership which provides the basis for the insurable interest. It is the insuring partner's "reasonable expectation of pecuniary benefit from the continuance of the insured's life." . . . This interest continues even if the partnership is discontinued prior to death of one of the partners. . . .

In the instant case each partner took out a life insurance policy on the other. Both sides testified that the purpose was to provide for one partner at the other partner's death. . . . There is not legal uncertainty that both partners had an insurable interest in the life of the other partner.

We next turn our analysis to the designation of the beneficiary in order to determine who should be entitled to the proceeds of the life insurance policy. In the case of *Williams v Williams*, 438 So. 2d 735 (Ala. 1983), a partner designated the other partners (his brothers) as the beneficiaries of his life insurance policy. Pursuant to the partnership's dissolution agreement, the surviving partners were to receive the insurance proceeds and then use those proceeds to purchase the deceased partner's interest. . . . Unlike the present case, in *Williams* a written partnership agreement and a dissolution agreement existed. However, both agreements involved the designation of the partners as beneficiaries instead of the spouse or estate. As stated by Chief Justice Torbert, "The fact that the decedent selected his partners, as opposed to his spouse or estate, as beneficiaries of the life insurance . . . is unquestionably permissible. Partners continue to be free to select whomever they wish to benefit from insurance on their lives." *Williams*, 438 So. 2d at 739. In this case, the plaintiff's evidence that the decedent intended for the proceeds to go to his estate consisted solely of oral testimony from the plaintiff's brother (the insurance agent) and an ambiguous statement from a mutual friend of both partners. No ambiguity existed in the designation of the beneficiary. There was no written agreement like the dissolution agreement in *Williams*, supra, which provided that the surviving partners were to use the proceeds to purchase the deceased partner's interest. We require more than oral testimony, like the testimony presented here, in order to show that it was not the intention of the decedent that the designated beneficiary retain the proceeds. Therefore, we reverse the trial court's judgment designating Norred's estate as the rightful recipient of the proceeds instead of the designated beneficiary.

[Reversed and remanded]

Questions

1. Did Graves have an insurable interest in the life of Norred following the discontinuance of the partnership?
2. Was Graves required to remit the proceeds of the insurance to Norred's estate?
3. Can an individual select his or her business partner, as opposed to his or her spouse or estate, as beneficiary under a life insurance policy?

E-COMMERCE AND CYBERLAW

INSURANCE CONTRACTS AND E-SIGN

The Electronic Signatures in Global and National Commerce Act (E-Sign) applies broadly to the insurance business.* Thus, with consent of the consumer, contracts may be executed with electronic signatures and documents may be delivered by electronic means. E-Sign also provides protections for insurance agents against liability resulting from any deficiencies in the electronic procedures set forth in an electronic contract, provided the agent did not engage in tortious conduct and was not involved in the establishment of the electronic procedures.

Insurance providers are precluded from canceling health insurance or life insurance protection by means of electronic notices.

*15 USC § 7001(i).

3. The Contract

The formation of a contract of insurance is governed by the general principles applicable to contracts. By statute, it is now commonly provided that an insurance policy must be written. To avoid deception, many statutes also specify the content of certain policies, in whole or in part. Some statutes specify the size and style of type to be used in printing the policies. Provisions in a policy that conflict with statutory requirements are generally void.

(a) The Application as Part of the Contract

The application for insurance is generally attached to the policy when issued and is made part of the contract of insurance by express stipulation of the policy.

The insured is bound by all statements in the attached application.

(b) Statutory Provisions as Part of the Contract

When a statute requires that insurance contracts contain certain provisions or cover certain specified losses, a contract of insurance that does not comply with the statute will be interpreted as though it contained all the provisions required by the statute. When a statute requires that all terms of the insurance contract be included in the written contract, the insurer cannot claim that a provision not stated in the written contract was binding on the insured.

4. Antilapse and Cancellation Statutes and Provisions

If the premiums are not paid on time, the policy under ordinary contract law would lapse because of nonpayment. However, with life insurance policies, by either policy provision or statute, the insured is allowed a grace period of 30 or 31 days in which to make payment of the premium due. When there is a default in the payment of a premium by the insured, the insurer may be required by statute to (1) issue a paid-up policy in a smaller amount, (2) provide extended insurance for a period of time, or (3) pay the cash surrender value of the policy.

The contract of insurance may expressly declare that it may or may not be canceled by the insurer's unilateral act. By statute or policy provision, the insurer is commonly required to give a specific number of days' written notice of cancellation.[3]

5. Modification of Contract

As is the case with most contracts, a contract of insurance can be modified if both insurer and insured agree to the change. The insurer cannot modify the contract without the consent of the insured when the right to do so is not reserved in the insurance contract.

To make changes or corrections to the policy, it is not necessary to issue a new policy. An endorsement on the policy or the execution of a separate rider is

[3] *Transamerican Ins. Co. v Tab Transportation*, 48 Cal Rptr 2d 159 (Sup Ct 1995).

effective for the purpose of changing the policy. When a provision of an endorsement conflicts with a provision of the policy, the endorsement controls because it is the later document.

6. Interpretation of Contract

A contract of insurance is interpreted by the same rules that govern the interpretation of ordinary contracts. Words are to be given their plain and ordinary meaning and interpreted in light of the nature of the coverage intended. However, an insurance policy is construed strictly against the insurer, who chooses the language of the policy, and if a reasonable construction may be given that would justify recovery, a court will do so. **For Example,** Dr. Kolb consented to an elective surgical procedure on his right eye after which "something happened that caused the wound to start leaking" and resulted in loss of vision in his eye. This forced him to retire as an orthopedic surgeon. His Paul Revere Life Insurance disability income insurance policy provided income for life for a disability due to "accidental bodily injury." The policy provided benefits for a shorter duration if the disability was caused by "sickness." Dr. Kolb's vision loss was not expected and proceeded from an unidentified postsurgical cause. Applying the plain and ordinary meaning of "accidental" and "injury," the court decided that Dr. Kolb was entitled to income for life under the "injury" provision of the policy.[4]

The courts are increasingly recognizing the fact that most persons obtaining insurance are not specially trained. Therefore, the contract of insurance is to be read as it would be understood by the average person or by the average person in business rather than by one with technical knowledge of the law or of insurance.[5]

If there is an ambiguity in the policy, the provision is interpreted against the insurer. **For Example,** on August 29, 2005, the Buentes' residence in Gulfport, Mississippi, was damaged during Hurricane Katrina. Allstate tendered a check for $2,600.35 net after the deductible, under its Deluxe Homeowner's Policy. The Buentes contend their covered losses are between $50,000 and $100,000. They brought suit against Allstate. The trial judge denied Allstate's motion to dismiss, finding the two provisions of the policy that purport to exclude coverage for wind and rain damage were ambiguous in light of other policy provisions granting coverage for wind and rain damage and in light of the inclusion of a "hurricane deductible" as part of the policy. The court found that because the policy was ambiguous, its weather exclusion was unenforceable in the context of losses attributable to wind and rain that occur in a hurricane.[6]

7. Burden of Proof

When an insurance claim is disputed by the insurer, the person bringing suit has the burden of proving that there was a loss, that it occurred while the policy was in force, and that the loss was of a kind that was within the coverage or scope of the policy.[7]

A policy will contain exceptions to the coverage. This means that the policy is not applicable when an exception applies to the situation. Exceptions to coverage are generally strictly interpreted against the insurer. The insurer has the burden of proving that the facts were such that there was no coverage because an exception applied.

Under state cancellation statutes, insurers must produce proof that each cancellation notice was mailed to the address of record.[8]

8. Insurer Bad Faith

As is required in the case of all contracts, an insurer must act in good faith in processing and paying claims under its policy. In some states, laws have been enacted making an insurer liable for a statutory penalty and attorney fees in case of a bad-faith failure or delay in paying a valid claim within a specified period of time. A bad-faith refusal is generally considered to be any frivolous or unfounded refusal to comply with the demand of a policyholder to pay according to the policy.[9]

When it is a liability insurer's duty to defend the insured and the insurer wrongfully refuses to do so, the insurer is guilty of breach of contract and is liable for all consequential damages resulting from the

[4] *Kolb v Paul Revere Life Insurance Co.*, 355 F3d 1132 (8th Cir 2004).
[5] *Bering Strait School District v RLT Ins. Co.*, 872 P2d 1292 (Alaska 1994).
[6] *Buente v Allstate Ins. Co.*, 422 F Supp 2d 690 (SD Miss 2006).
[7] *Koslik v Gulf Insurance Co.*, 673 NW2d 343 (Wis App 2003).
[8] *Ragan v Columbia Mutual Ins. Co.*, 701 NE2d 493 (Ill 1998).
[9] *Uberti v Lincoln National Life Ins. Co.*, 144 F Supp 2d 90 (D Conn 2001).

breach. In some jurisdictions, an insured can recover for an excess judgment rendered against the insured when it is proven that the insurer was guilty of negligence or bad faith in failing to defend the action or settle the matter within policy limits.

If there is a reasonable basis for the insurer's belief that a claim is not covered by its policy, its refusal to pay the claim does not subject it to liability for a breach of good faith or for a statutory penalty.[10] This is so even though the court holds that the insurer is liable for the claim.

For Example, the following illustrates an insurer's bad-faith failure to pay a claim, as opposed to an insurer's reasonable basis for failure to pay. Carmela Garza's home and possessions were destroyed in a fire set by an arsonist on August 19. Carmela's husband, Raul, who was no longer living at the home, had a criminal record. An investigator for the insurer stated that while he had no specific information to implicate the Garzas in the arson, Carmela may have wanted the proceeds to finance relocation to another city. By October, however, Aetna's investigators ruled out the possibility that Garza had the motive or the opportunity to set the fire. The insurer thus no longer had a reasonable basis to refuse to pay the claim after this date. Yet it took over a year and a half and court intervention for Aetna to allow Carmela to see a copy of her policy, which had been destroyed in the fire. Two years after the fire, Aetna paid only $28,624.55 for structural damage to the fire-gutted home, which was insured for $111,000. The court held that Aetna's actions constituted a bad-faith failure to pay by the insurer.[11]

In the case of a bad-faith breach of an insurance claim, the insurer not only is exposed to compensatory damages but also may be liable for exemplary or punitive damages. **For Example,** when State Farm intentionally and unreasonably denied payment on Cindy Robinson's personal injury auto accident claim and State Farm's position was found not to be "fairly debatable," the jury awarded $9.5 million in punitive damages. The state supreme court reviewing the case noted that the evidence showed that the insurer's claims-handling procedures were designed to increase profits by reducing costs using biased paper reviews and by inducing lower settlements through denial or delay of claims. Given State Farm's billions in profits, the court determined that the $9.5 million punitive damages award was not excessive and had a reasonable relation to an amount needed to stop similar conduct in the future.[12]

9. Time Limitations on Insured

The insured must comply with a number of time limitations in making a claim. For example, the insured must promptly notify the insurer of any claim that may arise, submit a proof-of-loss statement within the time set forth in the policy, and bring any court action based on the policy within a specified time period.[13]

10. Subrogation of Insurer

In some instances, the insured has a claim against a third person for the harm covered by the insurance policy. **For Example,** *A* sells an automobile insurance policy that provides collision coverage to *B*. *C* "rear-ends" *B*'s car at a traffic rotary in the city. *A* pays *B* the full amount of the property damage repair costs. *A* is then **subrogated** to *B*'s claim against *C*, the person who caused the harm. See Figure 36-1. When the insurer is subrogated to the insured's claim, the insurer may enforce that claim against the third person.[14]

B. Kinds of Insurance

Businesses today have specialized **risk** managers who identify the risks to which individual businesses are exposed, measure those risks, and purchase insurance to cover those risks (or decide to self-insure in whole or in part).

[10] *Shipes v Hanover Ins. Co.*, 884 F2d 1357 (11th Cir 1989).

[11] See *Aetna Casualty & Surety Co. v Garza*, 906 SW2d 543 (Tex App 1995).

[12] *Robinson v State Farm Mutual Automobile Ins. Co.*, 2000 Ida LEXIS 144. See *State Farm Mutual Automobile Co. v Campbell*, 123 S Ct 1513 (2003), where the U.S. Supreme Court set aside an award of $145 million in punitive damages against State Farm for its bad-faith failure to settle for the insured's policy limits; the compensatory damages were $1 million. The Court held that the due process clause of the Fourteenth Amendment prohibits the imposition of grossly excessive punitive damages.

[13] But see *Seeman v Sterling Ins. Co.*, 699 NYS2d 542 (App Div 1999), where the insured's four-month delay in notifying the insuer was excused because of his belief that only on-premises injuries were covered by his homeowners insurance policy and thus the policy would not cover an injury in which a paintball he fired at work struck his coworker in the eye.

[14] *Julson v Federated Mutual Ins. Co.*, 562 NW2d 117 (SD 1997).

FIGURE 36-1 Subrogation

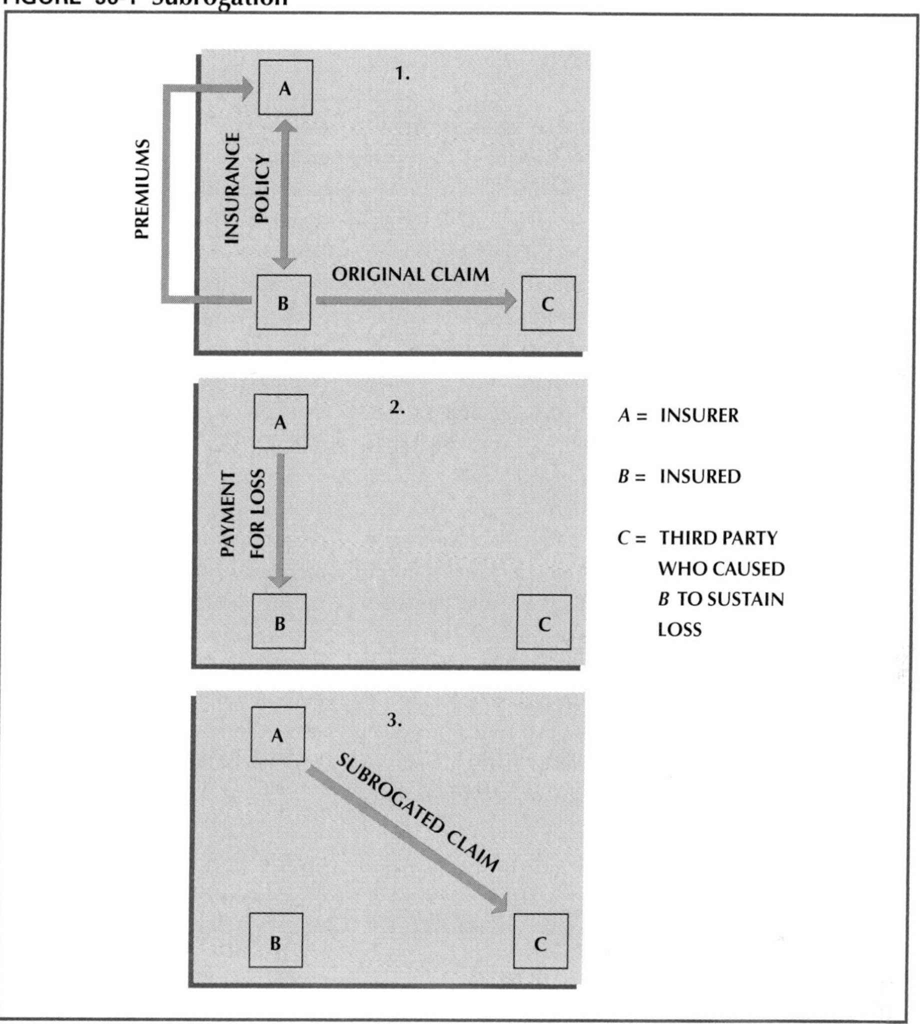

ETHICS & THE LAW

On September 11, 2001, terrorist attacks killed 3,119 persons, devastated the U.S. airline industry, and had a severe impact on the U.S. insurance industry. In New York City, several office buildings, including One and Two World Trade Center, were destroyed, and other businesses in lower Manhattan were forced to shut down.

Business interruption insurance coverage is usually written as part of a company's commercial property insurance package. It not only covers policyholders for their lost profits and fixed charges and expenses for interruption to their business caused by physical damage or destruction to the insured's own property, but it may also cover "contingent business interruption" resulting from suspension of operations caused by damages to the property of a key supplier, distributor, or manufacturer. Such coverage, however, contains an exclusion for "war or military action." Are the September 11, 2001, terrorist attacks an "act of war" such that

ETHICS & THE LAW

continued

insurers are not responsible for business interruption claims? Can the president's words regarding war with al Qaeda be used to prove an "act of war" exclusion?

A court called upon to interpret an "act of war" exclusion will apply the plain and ordinary meaning of the policy's terms, and any ambiguity will be construed against the insurer. In *Pan American World Airways, Inc., v Aetna Casualty & Surety Co.,** the Second Circuit Court of Appeals held that an air carrier was entitled to recover for the destruction of its plane by terrorists in Cairo, Egypt, and the damage was not excluded under the policy's "act of war" exclusion. The court reasoned in part that there was no existing "war" between recognized sovereign states.

Pressured by historic losses, insurance companies in certain areas excluded perils resulting from "terrorism" in new commercial property insurance policies. The industry's framework for a definition of *terrorism* as a policy exclusion is an incident in which insured property damage exceeds $25 million and 50 or more individuals are seriously injured or die. Also excluded from coverage under the definition are losses due to nuclear, biological, or chemical weapons. Is it fair for insurers to exclude coverage altogether for losses due to acts of terrorism? Is it best to have the community absorb the losses? Is it best to have individuals and individual businesses cover the losses? See the Terrorism Risk Insurance Extension Act of 2005, by which Congress extended its temporary terrorism insurance program though December 31, 2007, providing a system of shared public private compensation for insured losses resulting from acts of terrorism. The Secretary of State in concurrence with the Attorney General of the United States has authority to certify an event as an act of terrorism, thereby initiating the provisions and benefits of the act.

*See *Pan American World Airways, Inc. v Aetna Casualty & Surety Co.*, 505 F2d 989 (2d Cir 1974).

Insurance policies can be grouped into certain categories. Five major categories of insurance are considered here: (1) business liability insurance, (2) marine and inland marine insurance, (3) fire and homeowners insurance, (4) automobile insurance, and (5) life insurance.

11. Business Liability Insurance

Businesses may purchase Commercial General Liability (CGL) policies. This insurance is a broad, "all-risk" form of insurance providing coverage for all sums that the insured may become legally obligated to pay as damages because of "bodily injury" or "property damage" caused by an "occurrence." The insurer is obligated to defend the insured business and pay damages under CGL policies for product liability cases, actions for wrongful termination of employees, sexual harassment cases, damages caused by business advertising or employee dishonesty, and trademark infringement suits.[15] The insurer may also be obligated to pay for damages in the form of cleanup costs imposed for contamination of land, water, and air under environmental statutes.[16]

In the *Anderson Development Co.* case, the insurer was obligated to pay for cleanup costs and the cost of the insured's defense.

The insurer must defend when coverage is a "close issue" regarding whether the policy would provide indemnity. It is common for the insurer to seek a declaratory judgment if it believes the policy

[15] *Charter Oak Fire Ins. Co. v Heedon & Cos.*, 280 F3d 730 (7th Cir 2002).

[16] *Chemical Leaman Tank Lines, Inc. v Aetna Casualty Co.*, 788 F Supp 846 (DNJ 1992); and *United States v Pepper's Steel, Inc.*, 823 F Supp 1574 (SD Fla 1993). But see *Northville Industries v National Union Fire and Ins. Co.*, 636 NYS2d 359 (Sup Ct App Div 1995); and *Aydin Corp. v First State Ins. Co.*, 62 Cal Rptr 2d 825 (Cal App 1997).

ANDERSON DEVELOPMENT CO. V TRAVELERS INDEMNITY CO., 49 F3D 1128 (6TH CIR 1995)

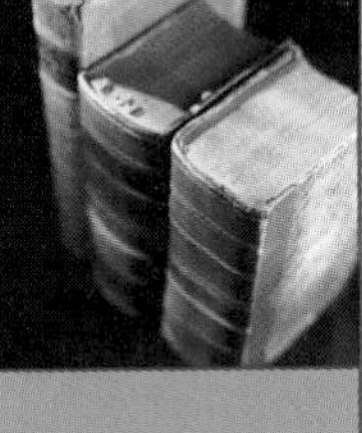

EPA'S PRP SUITS THE COURT JUST FINE

Anderson Development Co. (ADC) manufactures and sells specialty organic materials in Adrian, Michigan. It built a lagoon to handle the occasional accidental discharge of Curene 442 process water, believing it to be insoluble in water. Curene 442, which it manufactured between 1970 and 1979, was a known animal carcinogen, and it turned out to be soluble. The lagoon's discharge piping was connected to the sewer system and found its way to the city's sewage treatment plant. In 1985, the Environmental Protection Agency (EPA) sent ADC a formal notification that it was considered a "potentially responsible party" (PRP) for the release of hazardous substances into the soil and groundwater. This notice was called a "PRP" letter. ADC notified Travelers Indemnity Co., its insurer, of the letter, and Travelers contended that it was not prepared to defend or cover ADC in the matter. ADC did a study that revealed contamination on its property. The EPA and ADC entered a consent decree wherein ADC agreed to the cleanup activities required by the EPA, spending over $6 million on the cleanup. ADC brought an action against its insurer seeking coverage under its general liability insurance policies for the cost of its defense and the cost of the cleanup. Travelers alleged that it was not liable under the policies.

Judicial Opinion

BROWN, C.J. . . . Travelers and ADC entered into a series of general liability and umbrella insurance contracts spanning a period of 1974 to 1980. The contracts covering the Adrian facility provided in pertinent part that:

The Travelers will pay on behalf of the Insured all sums which the Insured shall become legally obligated to pay as damages because of body injury or property damage to which this insurance applies, caused by an occurrence.

As to Travelers' duty to defend, the policies further provided that:

Travelers shall have the right and duty to defend any suit against the Insured seeking damages on account of such bodily injury or property damage. . . .

. . . The district court determined that the issuance of the PRP letter and other actions taken by the EPA did not constitute a "suit" triggering Travelers' duty to defend ADC. . . .

The Michigan Supreme Court, however, recently having had the opportunity to rule on this exact issue, . . . held that a PRP letter issued by the EPA is the functional equivalent of a "suit" brought in a court of law. *Michigan Miller Mut. Ins. Co. v Bronson Plating Co.*, 445 Mich. 558, 519 N.W.2d 864, 870 (1994). Factually, *Bronson Plating* is also substantially similar to our case: The insurer brought an action against its insured seeking a declaration that it had no duty to defend or indemnify the insured with respect to EPA administrative actions (PRP letter) regarding environmental contamination of the insured's operation site. Moreover, the insurance policy provisions with respect to the insurer's duty to defend and indemnify, as well as the relevant portions of the PRP letter, were essentially identical to those in our case. The court first noted that the term "suit" is ambiguous and capable of application to nontraditional legal actions that are the functional equivalent of a suit brought in a court of law. Under this definition, the court concluded, a PRP letter constitutes the initiation of a suit that the insurers are obligated to defend. The court reasoned that "[t]he significant authority given to the EPA in such matters allows it essentially to usurp the traditional role of a court in determining and apportioning liability," and may be viewed as "coercing the voluntary participation of PRP's." *Id.* 519 N.W.2d at 871–72.

In light of the *Bronson Plating* decision, we reverse the district court as to the first issue and hold that the PRP letter received by ADC constituted the initiation of a suit triggering Travelers' duty to defend.

We now turn to the issue of whether environmental response and clean-up costs mandated by the EPA are "damages" within the meaning of the insurance contract, thereby triggering Travelers' duty to indemnify. Travelers notes that these costs are equitable in nature. Likewise, Travelers contends that the word "damages" is clear and unambiguous, and that it refers to legal and not equitable relief. Hence, Travelers maintains that the district court correctly held that the term "damages" does not contemplate the relief sought here. . . .

In *United States Aviex Co. v Travelers Ins. Co.*, 125 Mich. App. 579, 336 N.W.2d 838 (1983), the Michigan Court of Appeals specifically addressed the question whether environmental clean-up costs constituted damages under the insurance policies at issue. In that case, the Michigan Department of Natural Resources notified the insured that the insured had the obligation to conduct an investigation regarding the extent of on-site contamination and to correct the same. The Department threatened legal action if the insured did not comply. The insured later brought an action against its insurer, Travelers, for a declaratory judgment seeking coverage under the insurance contract for costs incurred in determining and correcting the contamination....

...We construe the Michigan appellate court cases to hold that response and environmental clean-up costs mandated by the EPA constitute damages. The fact that the insured cooperates and assumes the obligation to conduct the clean-up, rather than forcing the EPA to incur the expenses of a clean-up and then bring a coercive suit, does not change the bottom line that a legal obligation exists. Accordingly, we reverse the district court as to the second issue and hold that, under Michigan law, government imposed environmental clean-up costs constitute "damages." ...

We therefore reverse the district court's grant of summary judgment for the Defendant/Appellee, Travelers, affirm the grant of summary judgment on behalf of the Plaintiff/Appellant, ADC, and remand to the district court for further proceedings in accordance with this opinion.

Questions

1. Was Travelers obligated under its insurance policies with ADC to defend ADC in its dealings with the EPA?
2. Was Travelers obligated to pay for the clean-up costs under the insurance policies with ADC?
3. Assess the business judgment of Travelers in refusing to defend ADC and refusing to pay the cleanup costs.

does not call for either a defense or indemnity. **For Example,** Capital Associates sent unsolicited advertisements to the fax machines of a number of businesses that objected to them under the Telephone Consumer Protection Act, which resulted in a class action lawsuit on behalf of all recipients of those junk faxes. Capital Associates tendered the defense of the lawsuit to American States Insurance Co., its CGL insurer. In the declaratory judgment action brought by the insurer, the court determined that the CGL policy's intentional tort exclusion relieved the insurer of a need to defend or indemnify because Capital intended to send the faxes in violation of federal law.[17]

Businesses may purchase policies providing liability insurance for their directors and officers. Manufacturers and sellers may purchase product liability insurance. Professional persons, such as accountants, physicians, lawyers, architects, and engineers, may obtain liability insurance protection against malpractice suits. **For Example,** the architects of the MCI Center, a sports arena in Washington, D.C., were entitled under their professional liability insurance coverage to be defended by their insurer in a lawsuit seeking only injunctive relief for the firm's alleged failure to comply with the Americans with Disabilities Act's enhanced sightline requirements.[18]

12. Marine Insurance

Marine insurance policies cover perils relating to the transportation of goods. **Ocean marine** insurance policies cover the transportation of goods in vessels in international and coastal trade. **Inland marine** insurance principally covers domestic shipments of goods over land and inland waterways.

(a) Ocean Marine

Ocean marine insurance is a form of insurance that covers ships and their cargoes against "perils of the sea." Four classes of ocean marine insurance are generally available: (1) hull, (2) cargo, (3) liability, and (4) freight. **Hull insurance** covers physical damage to the vessel.[19] **Cargo insurance** protects the cargo owner against financial loss if the goods being shipped are lost or damaged at sea.[20]

In the *Commodities Reserve Co.* case, a cargo owner sued the insurer for breach of an ocean marine cargo policy.

[17] *American States Insurance Co. v Capital Associates of Jackson County Inc.*, 392 F3d 939 (7th Cir 2004).
[18] *Washington Sports and Entertainment, Inc. v United Coastal Ins.*, 7 F Supp 2d 1 (DDC 1998).
[19] *Lloyd's v Labarca*, 260 F3d 3 (1st Cir 2001).
[20] *Kimta, A. S. v Royal Insurance Co., Inc.*, 9 P3d 239 (Wash App 2001).

COMMODITIES RESERVE CO. V ST. PAUL FIRE & MARINE INS. CO., 879 F2D 640 (9TH CIR 1989)

THIS COVERAGE IS WORTH A HILL OF BEANS

Commodities Reserve Co. (CRC) contracted to sell 1,008 tons of beans and 50 tons of seeds to purchasers in Venezuela. CRC purchased the beans and seeds in Turkey and chartered space on the ship *MV West Lion.* The cargo was insured under an ocean marine policy issued by St. Paul Fire & Marine Insurance Co. (St. Paul). While the ship was sailing through Greek waters, Greek authorities seized the vessel for carrying munitions. CRC had to go to the expense of obtaining an order from a court in Crete to release the cargo. When St. Paul refused to pay the costs of the Cretan litigation, CRC brought suit against St. Paul. Judgment was entered for St. Paul. CRC appealed.

Judicial Opinion

FARRIS, C. J.... Commodities Reserve primarily seeks recovery under the Sue & Labor Clause of its insurance contract with St. Paul, which provides:

In case of any loss or misfortune, it shall be lawful and necessary to and for the Assured... to sue, labor and travel for, in and about the defense, safeguard and recovery of the said goods and merchandise... to the charges whereof, the [insurer] will contribute according to the rate and quantity of the sum hereby insured.

This standard provision requires the insurer to reimburse the assured for expenses incurred in preventing a loss for which, if it had occurred, the insurer would be liable....

The Average Clause is the general basis for liability. It provides that the policy covers "all risks of physical loss or damage from any external cause excepting those risks excluded by the F.C. & S. [Free of Capture & Seizure] and S.R. & C.C. [Strikes, Riots & Civil Commotions] Clauses...."

The F.C. & S. Clause, one of the Paramount Warranties, declares that:

Notwithstanding anything herein contained to the contrary, this insurance is warranted free from: (a) capture, seizure, arrest, restraint, detainment, confiscation, preemption, requisition or nationalization, and the consequences thereof or any attempt thereat, whether in time of peace or war and whether lawful or otherwise....

St. Paul argues that the F.C. & S. Clause... excuses it from liability....

When the Greek authorities detained the ship, they did not claim jurisdiction over Commodities Reserve's cargo.... Instead, the captain refused to release the cargo. Due to the captain's conduct, Commodities Reserve had to secure a court order compelling the release of its cargo. The litigation expenses incurred to release the cargo are recoverable under the Average Clause, which covers "all risks of physical loss or damage from any external cause." See *Champion Int'l Corp. v Arkwright-Boston Mfr. Mutual Ins. Co.*, 1982 AMC 2496 (S.D.N.Y.), aff'd, 714 F.2d 112 (2d Cir. 1982) (insured entitled to recover for expenses, including litigation, incurred to recover cargo after carrier converted it under policy insuring plaintiff against "all risk of physical loss or damage to its cargo from an external source"). The Sue and Labor Clause required Commodities Reserve to "sue... for . . recovery of said goods and merchandise" in case of loss or misfortune, and mandates payment of the charges by the insurer.

The detention by Greek authorities was not the proximate cause of the litigation expenses. The detention did not necessitate the suit in Crete. The litigation expenses were incurred solely because of the captain's refusal to release the cargo. Consequently, the Free of Capture and Seizure Clause does not preclude recovery of these expenses.

The district court erred in granting St. Paul summary judgment on this issue. Summary judgment for the litigation expenses should be awarded to Commodities Reserve on its crossmotion for summary judgment.

[Reversed and remanded]

Questions

1. What defense did the insurer raise?
2. Were the litigation expenses incurred because of the seizure of the vessel by Greek authorities?
3. Under the ocean marine policy in effect, was the insurer held liable for the litigation expenses?

Cargo insurance does not cover risks prior to the loading of the insured cargo on board the vessel. An additional warehouse coverage endorsement is needed to insure merchandise held in a warehouse prior to import or export voyages.

Liability insurance covers the shipowner's liability if the ship causes damage to another ship or its cargo. **Freight insurance** ensures that the shipowner will receive payment for the transportation charges. "All-risk" policies consolidate coverage of all four classes of ocean marine insurance into one policy.[21]

(b) Inland Marine

Inland marine insurance evolved from marine insurance. It protects goods in transit over land; by air; or on rivers, lakes, and coastal waters. Inland marine insurance can be used to insure property held by a bailee. Moreover, it is common for institutions financing automobile dealers' new car inventories to purchase inland marine insurance policies to insure against damage to the automobiles while in inventory.

13. Fire and Homeowners Insurance

A **fire insurance policy** is a contract to indemnify the insured for property destruction or damage caused by fire. In almost every state, the New York standard fire insurance form is the standard policy. A **homeowners insurance policy** is a combination of the standard fire insurance policy and comprehensive personal liability insurance. It thus provides fire, theft, and certain liability protection in a single insurance contract.

(a) Fire Insurance

For fire insurance to cover fire loss, there must be an actual hostile fire that is the immediate cause of the loss. A *hostile fire* is one that becomes uncontrollable, burns with excessive heat, or escapes from the place where it is intended to be. To illustrate, when soot is ignited and causes a fire in the chimney, the fire is hostile. On the other hand, if a loss is caused by the smoke or heat of a fire that has not broken out of its ordinary container or become uncontrollable, the loss results from a friendly fire. The policy does not cover damage from a friendly fire.

By policy endorsement, however, the coverage may be extended to include loss by a friendly fire.

CPA ***(1) Coinsurance.*** The insurer is liable for the actual amount of the loss sustained up to the maximum amount stated in the policy. An exception exists when the policy contains a coinsurance clause. A **coinsurance clause** requires the insured to maintain insurance on the covered property up to a certain amount or a certain percentage of the value (generally 80 percent). Under such a provision, if the policyholder insures the property for less than the required amount, the insurer is liable only for the proportionate share of the amount of insurance required to be carried. **For Example,** suppose that the owner of a building with a value of $400,000 insures it against loss to the extent of $240,000. The policy contains a coinsurance clause requiring that insurance of 80 percent of the value of the property be carried (in this case, $320,000). Assume that a $160,000 loss is then sustained. The insured would receive not $160,000 from the insurer but only three-fourths of that amount, which is $120,000, because the amount of the insurance carried ($240,000) is only three-fourths of the amount required ($360,000).

Some states prohibit the use of a coinsurance clause.

CPA ***(2) Assignment.*** Fire insurance is a personal contract, and in the absence of statute or contractual authorization, it cannot be assigned without the consent of the insurer.

CPA ***(3) Occupancy.*** Provisions in a policy of fire insurance relating to the use and occupancy of the property are generally strictly construed because they relate to the hazards involved.

(b) Homeowners Insurance

In addition to providing protection against losses resulting from fire, the homeowners policy provides liability coverage for accidents or injuries that occur on the premises of the insured. Moreover, the liability provisions provide coverage for unintentional injuries to others away from home for which the insured or any member of the resident family is held responsible, such as injuries caused to others by golfing, hunting, or fishing accidents.[22] Generally, motor vehicles, including mopeds and recreational vehicles, are excluded from such personal liability coverage.

[21] *Transamerican Leasing, Inc. v Institute of London Underwriters*, 7 F Supp 2d 1340 (SD Fla 1998).

[22] *American Concept Ins. Co. v Lloyds of London*, 467 NW2d 480 (SD 1991).

A homeowners policy also provides protection from losses caused by theft. In addition, it provides protection for all permanent residents of the household, including all family members living with the insured. Thus, a child of the insured who lives at home is protected under the homeowners policy for the value of personal property lost when the home is destroyed by fire.

14. Automobile Insurance

Associations of insurers, such as the National Bureau of Casualty Underwriters and the National Automobile Underwriters Association, have proposed standard forms of automobile insurance policies. These forms have been approved by the association members in virtually all states. The form used today by most insurers is the Personal Auto Policy (PAP).

(a) Perils Covered

Part A of the policy provides liability coverage that protects the insured driver or owner from the claims of others for bodily injuries or damage to their property. Part B of the policy provides coverage for medical expenses sustained by a covered person or persons in an accident. Part C of the PAP provides coverage for damages the insured is entitled to recover from an *uninsured motorist.*[23] Part D provides coverage for loss or damage to the covered automobile. Coverage under Part D includes collision coverage and coverage of "other than collision" losses, such as fire and theft.

(b) Covered Persons

Covered persons include the named insured or any family member (a person related by blood, marriage, or adoption or a ward or foster child who is a resident of the household). If an individual is driving with the permission of the insured, that individual is also covered.

(c) Use and Operation

The coverage of the PAP policy is limited to claims arising from the "use and operation" of an automobile. The term *use and operation* does not require that the automobile be in motion. Thus, the term embraces loading and unloading as well as actual travel.[24]

(d) Notice and Cooperation

The insured is under a duty to give notice of claims, to inform, and to cooperate with the insurer. Notice and cooperation are conditions precedent to the liability of the insurer.

(e) No-Fault Insurance

Traditional tort law (negligence law) placed the economic losses resulting from an automobile accident on the one at fault. The purpose of automobile liability insurance is to relieve the wrongdoer from the consequences of a negligent act by paying defense costs and the damages assessed. Under no-fault laws, injured persons are barred from suing the party at fault for ordinary claims. When the insured is injured while using the insured automobile, the insurer will make a payment without regard to whose fault caused the harm. However, if the automobile collision results in a permanent serious disablement or disfigurement, or death, or if the medical bills and lost wages of the plaintiff exceed a specified amount, suit may be brought against the party who was at fault.

15. Life Insurance

There are three basic types of life insurance: term insurance, whole life insurance, and endowment insurance.

Term insurance is written for a specified number of years and terminates at the end of that period. If the insured dies within the time period covered by the policy, the face amount is paid to the beneficiary. If the insured is still alive at the end of the time period, the contract expires, and the insurer has no further obligation. Term policies have little or no cash surrender value.

Whole life insurance (or ordinary life insurance) provides lifetime insurance protection. It also has an investment element.

Part of every premium covers the cost of insurance, and the remainder of the premium builds up a **cash surrender value** of the policy.

An **endowment insurance** policy is one that pays the face amount of the policy if the insured dies within the policy period. If the insured lives to the end of the policy period, the face amount is paid to the insured at the end of the period.

Many life insurance companies pay double the amount of the policy, called **double indemnity,** if

[23] *Montano v Allstate Indemnity,* 2000 US App LEXIS (10th Cir 2002).

[24] *State Farm Ins. v Whitehead,* 711 SW2d 198 (Mo App 1986).

death is caused by an accident and death occurs within 90 days afterward. A comparatively small additional premium is charged for this special protection.

In consideration of an additional premium, many life insurance companies also provide insurance against total permanent disability of the insured. **Disability** is usually defined in a life insurance policy as any "incapacity resulting from bodily injury or disease to engage in any occupation for remuneration or profit."

(a) Exclusions

Life insurance policies frequently provide that death is not within the protection of the policy and that a double indemnity provision is not applicable when death is caused by (1) suicide,[25] (2) narcotics, (3) the intentional act of another, (4) execution for a crime, (5) war activities, or (6) operation of aircraft.

(b) The Beneficiary

The recipient of life insurance policy proceeds that are payable upon the death of the insured is called the **beneficiary.** The beneficiary may be a third person or the estate of the insured, and there may be more than one beneficiary.

The beneficiary named in a policy may be barred from claiming the proceeds of the policy. It is generally provided by statute or stated by court decision that a beneficiary who has feloniously killed the insured is not entitled to receive the proceeds of the policy.

The customary policy provides that the insured reserves the right to change the beneficiary without the latter's consent. When the policy contains such a provision, the beneficiary cannot object to a change that destroys all of that beneficiary's rights under the policy and that names another person as beneficiary.

An insurance policy will ordinarily state that to change the beneficiary, the insurer must be so instructed in writing by the insured and the policy must then be endorsed by the company with the change of the beneficiary. These provisions are construed liberally. If the insured has notified the insurer but dies before the endorsement of the change by the company, the change of beneficiary is effective.[26] However, if the insured has not taken any steps to comply with the policy requirements, a change of beneficiary is not effective even though a change was intended.

(c) Incontestability Clause

Statutes commonly require the inclusion of an **incontestability clause** in life insurance policies. Ordinarily, this clause states that after the lapse of two years, the policy cannot be contested by the insurance company. The insurer is free to contest the validity of the policy at any time during the contestability period. Once the period has expired, the insurer must pay the stipulated sum upon the death of the insured and cannot claim that in obtaining the policy, the insured had been guilty of misrepresentation, fraud, or any other conduct that would entitle it to avoid the contract of insurance.[27]

Courts and legislatures have addressed the issue of "imposter fraud." In *Amex Life Assurance Co. v Superior Court*, the California Supreme Court concluded that after the contestability period had expired, an insurer may not assert the defense that an imposter took the medical examination. Jose Morales had applied for a life insurance policy from Amex. A paramedic working for Amex met a man claiming to be Morales and took blood and urine samples, listing him as 5′10″ and weighing 172 pounds. His blood sample was HIV negative. The individual did not provide identification. Some two years later, Morales died of AIDS–related causes. Morales had listed his height as 5′6″ and his weight as 142 on his insurance application. The California Supreme Court stated that Amex, which had done nothing to protect its interest but collect premiums, could not challenge coverage based on the imposter defense.[28] Subsequent to the court's decision, the California legislature amended state insurance law to provide for an "imposter defense" in that state. As set forth in the *Miller* case, Florida does not recognize an imposter defense to incontestability. The legislative purpose of such clauses is to protect beneficiaries from an insurer's refusal to honor policies by asserting preexisting conditions, leaving beneficiaries in the untenable position of having to battle with powerful insurance companies in court.

[25] *Mirza v Maccabees Life and Annuity Co.*, 466 NW2d 340 (Mich App 1991).

[26] *Zeigler v Cardona*, 830 F Supp 1395 (MD Ala 1993).

[27] *Standard Insurance Co. v Carls*, 2000 U.S. Dist LEXIS 8401.

[28] *Amex Life Assurance Co. v Superior Court*, 60 Cal Rptr 2d 898 (Sup Ct 1997).

ALLSTATE LIFE INS. CO. V MILLER, 424 F3D 1113 (11TH CIR 2005)

The Allstate life insurance policy on which this case centers went into effect on September 20, 2000, insuring the life of John Miller. The policy stated that if the insured died while the policy was in force, Allstate would pay a death benefit to the policy beneficiaries upon receiving proof of death. As required by Fla. Stat. § 627.455, the policy further provided that it would become incontestable after remaining in force during the lifetime of the insured for a period of two years from its effective date. John Miller died on April 20, 2003—more than two years after the policy went into effect. The beneficiaries accordingly filed statements seeking to collect benefits under the policy. Rather than disburse the benefits, Allstate sought a declaratory judgment that the policy was void alleging that the application was completed using fraudulent information and that an imposter had appeared at the medical exam in place of John Miller. The beneficiaries counter-claimed, alleging breach of contract based on Allstate's failure to pay benefits upon proof of death in accordance with the insurance policy's terms. From a judgment in favor of the beneficiaries Allstate appealed.

Judicial Opinion

BARKETT, C. J.... Florida law requires that "[e]very insurance contract shall provide that the policy shall be incontestable after it has been in force during the lifetime of the insured for a period of 2 years from its date of issue...." Fla. Stat. § 627.455....

The Florida Supreme Court has explained that incontestability clauses, such as the one contained in § 627.455, are "in the nature of, and serve[ ] a similar purpose as, a statute of limitations." *Prudential Ins. Co. of Am. v Prescott,* 130 Fla. 11, 176 So. 875, 878 (1937). As such, while incontestability clauses "recognize[ ] fraud and all other defenses, [they] provide[ ] a reasonable time in which they may be, but beyond which they cannot be, established." *Id.* The incontestability clause thus works to the mutual advantage of the insurer and the insured, "giv[ing] the insured a guaranty against expensive litigation to defeat his policy after the lapse of the time specified, and at the same time giv[ing] the company a reasonable time and opportunity to ascertain whether the [insurance] contract should remain in force." *Id.*

Accordingly, just as Florida courts would dismiss an otherwise-valid action once the statute of limitations on that claim had run, Florida's appellate courts have uniformly held that once the incontestability clause becomes effective, insurers are barred from attempting to rescind or cancel the insurance policy based on allegations that the insured engaged in fraud or misrepresentation....

...Allstate relies on the "weight of authority in other jurisdictions" to argue that we should recognize an imposter exception to the incontestability period....

As discussed above, the Florida appellate courts have uniformly and expressly held that the § 627.455 incontestability clause bars an insurer from rescinding or contesting the policy based on alleged fraudulent misrepresentations the insured made in the policy application. We can discern no indication that the Florida Supreme Court would disagree. While Allstate argues that its so-called "imposter defense" is different in kind from the sorts of fraud and misrepresentation that Florida's appellate courts have rejected as a basis for obviating the statutory incontestability clause, we agree with the district court that the "imposter defense" is merely a species of fraud, indistinguishable from the use of an imposter for incontestability purposes.

[Affirmed]

Questions

1. Why are incontestability clauses placed in life insurance contracts?
2. Do incontestability clauses work to the mutual advantage of the insurer and the insured?
3. Express your opinion on whether or not there should be an imposter defense to incontestability clauses.

LAWFLIX

Double Indemnity (1944)

In this Billy Wilder film, Fred MacMurray is an insurance salesman coerced into a murder plot. The movie provides good coverage of insurable interest in life.

For movie clips that illustrate business law concepts, see LawFlix at **http://wdvl.westbuslaw.com.**

Summary

Insurance is a contract called a *policy*. Under an insurance policy, the insurer provides in consideration of premium payments, to pay the insured or beneficiary a sum of money if the insured sustains a specified loss or is subjected to a specified liability. These contracts are made through an insurance agent, who is an agent for the insurance company, or through an insurance broker, who is the agent of the insured when obtaining a policy for the latter.

The person purchasing an insurance contract must have an insurable interest in the insured's life or property. An insurable interest in property exists when the damage or destruction of the property will cause a direct monetary loss to the insured. In the case of property insurance, the insured must have an insurable interest at the time of loss. An insurable interest in the life of the insured exists if the purchaser would suffer a financial loss from the insured's death. This interest must exist as of the time the policy is obtained.

Ocean marine policies insure ships and their cargoes against the perils of the sea. Inland marine policies insure goods being transported by land, by air, or on inland and coastal waterways.

For fire insurance to cover a fire loss, there must be an actual hostile fire that is the immediate cause of the loss. The insurer is liable for the actual amount of the loss sustained up to the maximum amount stated in the policy. An exception exists when the policy contains a coinsurance clause requiring the insured to maintain insurance up to a certain percentage of the value of the property. To the extent this is not done, the insured is deemed a coinsurer with the insurer, and the insurer is liable for only its proportional share of the amount of insurance required to be carried. A homeowners insurance policy provides fire, theft, and liability protection in a single contract.

Automobile insurance may provide protection for collision damage to the insured's property and injury to persons. It may also cover liability to third persons for injury and property damage as well as loss by fire or theft.

A life insurance policy requires the insurer to pay a stated sum of money to a named beneficiary upon the death of the insured. It may be a term insurance policy, a whole life policy, or an endowment policy. State law commonly requires the inclusion of an incontestability clause, whereby at the conclusion of the contestability period, the insurer cannot contest the validity of the policy.

Questions and Case Problems

1. Cecil Usher owned Belize NY, Inc. (Belize), a small construction company doing business in New York City. Belize purchased a commercial general liability insurance policy from Mount Vernon Fire Insurance Co. The policy's first page, entitled "Policy Declarations," describes the insured as "Belize N.Y., Inc.;" it classifies the "Form of Business" as "Corporation," the "Business Description" as "Carpentry," and indicates that Belize was afforded commercial liability insurance in the amount of $1,000,000 per occurrence and $2,000,000 in the aggregate for the period June 1, 1995, to June 1, 1996. Two classifications are listed under "Premium Computation" on the Declarations page: "Carpentry—Interior—001" and "Carpentry—001." The policy makes no further mention of these two terms. Belize performed some $60,000 of demolition work on the United House of Prayer's renovation project on 272 West 125th Street in New York City. Belize was thereafter hired to supervise subcontractors working on the job. During that period of time, a person entered the building, shot several people with a firearm, and started a fire. Seven people died and several others were injured.

The estates of the victims sued Belize, Inc., for "negligence, carelessness and recklessness" regarding the fire, and Belize notified Mount Vernon of the lawsuit. Mount Vernon refused to defend or indemnify Belize because Belize was not engaging in its carpentry operations in the building at the time of the incident. It asserted that its risk is limited to carpentry operations in accordance with the classifications set forth in the policy. Belize contended that the language of the policy did not provide that the classification "Carpentry" defined covered risks, and exclusions should have been stated in the contract. Decide. [*Mount Vernon Fire Insurance Co. v Belize NY, Inc.*, 227 F3d 232 (2d Cir)]

2. Martin Carls, a San Francisco teacher and counselor, applied for disability insurance from Standard Insurance Co. on April 4, 1996. On the application and supplement, Carls ticked "no" in response to whether he suffered recurring headaches, heart disease, skin problems, a spinal condition, or immune system disorder. He also denied taking any prescription medicine, stated that he had visited doctors only for general checkups in the past five years, and stated that he was covered under one additional disability insurance policy. Standard issued a disability policy with an effective date of June 12, 1996. On February 2, 1999, Carls filed a claim for benefits under the policy, stating that he had become totally disabled by symptoms of AIDS. After investigating the claim, Standard denied coverage and filed a lawsuit seeking rescission of the insurance policy based on fraud. According to Standard, at the time Carls submitted his insurance application, he suffered from a variety of serious ailments, including recurrent migraines, heart disease, chronic back pain, and HIV-positive status. Also, Standard asserts that Carls willfully failed to disclose extensive medical treatments, prescription drugs, and four additional disability insurance policies. What defense will be raised on behalf of Carls? How would you decide this case? [*Standard Insurance Co. v Carls*, 2000 U.S. Dist LEXIS 8401]
3. On April 6, 1988, Luis Serrano purchased for $75,000 a 26′8″–long Carrera speedboat named *Hot Shot.* First Federal Savings Bank provided $65,000 financing for this purchase. Serrano obtained a marine yacht policy for hull insurance on the boat for $75,000 from El Fenix, with First Federal being named as payee under the policy.

   On May 2, 1988, Serrano sold the boat to Reinaldo Polito, and Serrano furnished First Federal with documents evidencing the sale. Polito assumed the obligation to pay off the balance due First Federal. On October 6, 1989, Serrano again applied to El Fenix for a new yacht policy, covering the period from October 6, 1989, through October 6, 1990, and the coverage extended to peril of confiscation by a governmental agency. Serrano did not have ownership or possession of the boat on October 6, 1989. First Federal, the named payee, had not perfected or recorded a mortgage on *Hot Shot* until July 5, 1990.

   On November 13, 1989, in the waters off Cooper Island in the British Virgin Islands (BVI), *Hot Shot* was found abandoned after a chase by governmental officials. A large shipment of cocaine was recovered, although no one was arrested. When Serrano and First Federal were informed that *Hot Shot* was subject to mandatory forfeiture under BVI law, they both filed claims under the October 6, 1989, insurance policy. What defenses would you raise on behalf of the insurer in this case? Decide. [*El Fenix v Serrano Gutierrez*, 786 F Supp 1065 (DPR)]
4. From the United Insurance Co., Rebecca Foster obtained a policy insuring the life of Lucille McClurkin and naming herself as beneficiary. McClurkin did not live with Foster, and Foster did not inform McClurkin of the existence of the policy. Foster paid the premiums on the policy and upon the death of McClurkin sued the United Insurance Co. for the amount of the insurance. At the trial, Foster testified vaguely that her father had told her that McClurkin was her second cousin on his side of the family. Was Foster entitled to recover on the policy? [*Foster v United Ins. Co.*, 158 SE2d 201 (SC)]
5. Dr. George Allard and his brother-in-law, Tom Rowland, did not get along after family land that was once used solely by Rowland was partitioned among family members after the death of Rowland's father. Rowland had a reputation in the community as a bully and a violent person. On December 17, Allard was moving cattle down a dirt road by "trolling" (leading the cattle with a bucket of feed, causing them to follow him). When he saw a forestry truck coming along the road, he led the cattle off the road onto Rowland's land to prevent frightening the cattle. When Rowland saw Allard, Rowland ran toward him screaming at him for being on his land. Allard, a small older man, retreated to his truck and obtained a 12-gauge shotgun. He pointed the gun toward the ground about an inch in front of Rowland's left foot and fired it. He stated that he fired the shot in this fashion to bring Rowland to his senses and that Rowland stepped forward into the line of fire. Allard claimed that if Rowland had not stepped forward, he would not have been hit and injured. Allard was insured by Farm Bureau homeowners and general liability policies, which did not cover liability resulting from intentional acts by the insured. Applying the policy exclusion to the facts of this case, was Farm Bureau obligated to pay the $100,000 judgment against Allard? [*Southern Farm Bureau Casualty Co. v Allard*, 611 So 2d 966 (Miss)]
6. Arthur Katz testified for the U.S. government in a stock manipulation case. He also pled guilty and testified against three of his law partners in an insurance fraud case. He received a six-month sentence in a halfway house and a $5,000 fine. Katz was placed in the Federal

Witness Protection Program. He and his wife changed their names to Kane and moved to Florida under the program. Both he and his wife obtained new driver's licenses and Social Security numbers. Using his new identity, "Kane" obtained two life insurance policies totaling $1.5 million. He named his wife beneficiary. A routine criminal background check on Kane found no criminal history.

From 1984 to 1987, Kane invested heavily in the stock market. On October 17, 1987, the day the stock market crashed, Kane shot and wounded his stockbroker, shot and killed the office manager, and then committed suicide. The insurers refused to pay on the policies, claiming that they never insure persons with criminal records. Mrs. Kane contended that the policies were incontestable after they had been in effect for two years. Decide. [*Bankers Security Life Ins. Society v Kane*, 885 F2d 820 (11th Cir)]

7. Linda Filasky held policies issued by Preferred Risk Mutual Insurance Co. Following an injury in an automobile accident and storm damage to the roof of her home, Filasky sustained loss of income, theft of property, and water damage to her home. These three kinds of losses were covered by the policies with Preferred, but the insurer delayed unreasonably in processing her claims and raised numerous groundless objections to them. Finally, the insurer paid the claims in full. Filasky then sued the insurer for the emotional distress caused by the bad-faith delay and obstructive tactics of the insurer. The insurer defended that it had paid the claims in full and that nothing was owed Filasky. Decide. [*Filasky v Preferred Risk Mut. Ins. Co.*, 734 P2d 76 (Ariz)]
8. Baurer purchased a White Freightliner tractor and agreed that his son-in-law, Britton, could use it in the trucking business. In return, Britton agreed to haul Baurer's hay and cattle, thus saving Baurer approximately $30,000 per year. Baurer insured the vehicle with Mountain West Farm Bureau Insurance Company. The policy contained an exclusionary clause that provided: "We don't insure your [truck] while it is rented or leased to others.... This does not apply to the use of your [truck] on a share expense basis." When the vehicle was destroyed, Mountain West refused to pay on the policy, contending that the arrangement between Baurer and Britton was a lease of the vehicle, which was excluded under the policy. Baurer sued, contending that it was a "share expense basis" allowed under the policy. Is the insurance policy ambiguous? What rule of contract construction applies in this case? Decide. [*Baurer v Mountain West Farm Bureau Ins.*, 695 P2d 1307 (Mont)]
9. Collins obtained from South Carolina Insurance Co. a liability policy covering a Piper Colt airplane he owned. The policy provided that it did not cover loss sustained while the plane was being piloted by a person who did not have a valid pilot's certificate and a valid medical examination certificate. Collins held a valid pilot's certificate, but his medical examination certificate had expired three months before. Collins was piloting the plane when it crashed, and he was killed. The insurer denied liability because Collins did not have a valid medical certificate. It was stipulated by both parties that the crash was in no way caused by the absence of the medical certificate. Decide. [*South Carolina Ins. Co. v Collins*, 237 SE2d 358 (SC)]
10. Marshall Produce Co. had insured its milk- and egg-processing plant against fire. When smoke from a fire near its plant permeated the environment and was absorbed into the company's egg powder products, cans of powder delivered to the U.S. government were rejected as contaminated. Marshall Produce sued the insurance company for a total loss, but the insurer contended there had been no fire involving the insured property and no total loss. Decide. [*Marshall Produce Co. v St. Paul Fire & Marine Ins. Co.*, 98 NW2d 280 (Minn)]
11. Amador Pena, who had three insurance policies on his life, wrote a will in which he specified that the proceeds from the insurance policies should go to his children instead of to Leticia Pena Salinas and other beneficiaries named in the policies. He died the day after writing the will. The insurance companies paid the proceeds of the policies to the named beneficiaries. The executor of Pena's estate sued Salinas and the other beneficiaries for the insurance money. Decide. [*Pena v Salinas*, 536 SW2d 671 (Tex App)]
12. Spector owned a small automobile repair garage in rural Kansas that was valued at $40,000. He purchased fire insurance coverage against loss to the extent of $24,000. The policy contained an 80 percent coinsurance clause. A fire destroyed a portion of his parts room, causing a loss of $16,000. Spector believes he is entitled to be fully compensated for this loss, as it is less than the $24,000 of fire protection that he purchased and paid for. Is Spector correct?
13. Carman Tool & Abrasives, Inc., purchased two milling machines, FOB Taiwan, from the Dah Lih Machinery Co. Carman obtained ocean marine cargo insurance on the machines from St. Paul Fire and Marine Insurance Co. and authorized Dah Lih to arrange for the shipment of the two machines to Los Angeles, using the services of Evergreen Lines. Dah Lih booked the machinery for shipment on board Evergreen's container ship, the *M/V Ever Giant;* arranged for the delivery of the cargo to the ship; provided all of the shipping information for the bill of lading; and was the party to whom the bill was issued. Dah Lih then delivered the bill of lading to its bank, which in turn negotiated it to Carman's bank to authorize payment to Dah Lih. After the cargo was removed from the vessel in Los Angeles but before it was delivered to Carman, the milling machines were damaged to the extent of $115,000. Is the insurer liable to Carman? Can

the insurer recover from Evergreen? [*Carman Tool & Abrasives, Inc. v Evergreen Lines*, 871 F2d 897 (9th Cir)]

14. Vallot was driving his farm tractor on the highway. It was struck from the rear by a truck, overturned, exploded, and burned. Vallot was killed, and a death claim was made against All American Insurance Co. The death of Vallot was covered by the company's policy if Vallot had died from "being struck or run over by" the truck. The insurance company claimed that the policy was not applicable because Vallot had not been struck; the farm tractor had been struck, and Vallot's death occurred when the overturned tractor exploded and burned. The insurance company also claimed that it was necessary that the insured be both struck and run over by another vehicle. Decide. [*Vallot v All American Ins. Co.*, 302 So 2d 625 (La App)]
15. When Jorge de Guerrero applied for a $200,000 life insurance policy with John Hancock Mutual Life Insurance Co., he stated on the insurance application that he had not seen a physician within the past five years. In fact, he had had several consultations with his physician, who three weeks prior to the application had diagnosed him as overweight and suffering from goiter. His response to the question on drug and alcohol use was that he was not an alcoholic or user of drugs. In fact, he had been an active alcoholic since age 16 and was a marijuana user. De Guerrero died within the two-year contestability period included in the policy, and John Hancock refused to pay. The beneficiary contended that all premiums were fully paid on the policy and that any misstatements in the application were unintentional. John Hancock contended that if the deceased had given the facts, the policy would not have been issued. Decide. [*de Guerrero v John Hancock Mutual Life Ins. Co.*, 522 So 2d 1032 (Fla App)]

CPA Questions

1. Beal occupies an office building as a tenant under a 25-year lease. Beal also has a mortgagee's (lender's) interest in an office building owned by Hill Corp. In which capacity does Beal have an insurable interest?

	Tenant	*Mortgagee*
a.	Yes	Yes
b.	Yes	No
c.	No	Yes
d.	No	No

2. With respect to property insurance, the insurable interest requirement
   a. Need only be satisfied at the time the policy is issued
   b. Must be satisfied both at the time the policy is issued and at the time of the loss
   c. Will be satisfied only if the insured owns the property in fee simple absolute
   d. Will be satisfied by an insured who possesses a leasehold interest in the property
3. Lawfo Corp. maintains a $200,000 standard fire insurance policy on one of its warehouses. The policy includes an 80 percent coinsurance clause. At the time the warehouse was originally insured, its value was $250,000. The warehouse now has a value of $300,000. If the warehouse sustains $30,000 of fire damage, Lawfo's insurance recovery will be a maximum of
   a. $20,000
   b. $24,000
   c. $25,000
   d. $30,000
4. In 1992, King bought a building for $250,000. At that time, King took out a $200,000 fire insurance policy with Omni Insurance Co. and a $50,000 fire insurance policy with Safe Insurance Corp. Each policy contained a standard 80 percent coinsurance clause. In 1996, when the building had a fair market value of $300,000, a fire caused $200,000 in damage. What dollar amount would King recover from Omni?
   a. $100,000
   b. $150,000
   c. $160,000
   d. $200,000

PART (6)

AGENCY AND EMPLOYMENT

AGENCY

CHAPTER

(37)

LEARNING OBJECTIVES

After studying this chapter, you should be able to

LO.1 Differentiate between an agent and an independent contractor

LO.2 Explain and illustrate who may be a principal and who may be an agent

LO.3 State the three classifications of agents

LO.4 Differentiate between express authority, incidental authority, customary authority, and apparent authority

LO.5 Explain the effect of the proper exercise of authority by an agent

LO.6 Describe the duty of a third person to determine the extent of an agent's authority

LO.7 List the four ways an agency relationship may be created

LO.8 List six ways an agency may be terminated by an act of one or both of the parties to the agency agreement

LO.9 List five ways an agency may be terminated by operation of law

One of the most common business relationships is that of agency.

By virtue of the agency device, one person can make contracts at numerous places with many different parties at the same time.

A. Nature of the Agency Relationship

Agency is ordinarily based on the consent of the parties, and for that reason is called a *consensual relationship*. However, the law sometimes imposes an agency relationship. If consideration is present, the agency relationship is contractual.

1. Definitions and Distinctions

Agency is a relationship based on an express or implied agreement by which one person, the **agent**, is authorized to act under the control of and for another, the **principal**, in negotiating and making contracts with third persons.[1] The acts of the agent obligate the principal to third persons and give the principal rights against third persons. (See Figure 37-1.)

The term *agency* is frequently used with other meanings. It is sometimes used to denote the fact that one has the right to sell certain products, such as when a dealer is said to possess an automobile agency. In other instances, the term is used to mean an exclusive right to sell certain articles within a given territory. In these cases, however, the dealer is not an agent in the sense of representing the manufacturer.

It is important to be able to distinguish agencies from other relationships because certain rights and duties in agencies are not present in other relationships.

(a) Employees and Independent Contractors

Control and authority are characteristics that distinguish ordinary employees and independent contractors from agents.

(1) Employees. An agent is distinguished from an ordinary employee who is not hired to represent the employer in making contracts with third persons. It is possible, however, for the same person to be both an agent and an employee. **For Example,** the driver for a spring water delivery service is an agent in making contracts between the company and its customers but is an employee with respect to the work of delivering products.

(2) Independent Contractors. An **independent contractor** is bound by a contract to produce a

[1] Restatement (Second) of Agency § 1; *Union Miniere, S.A. v Parday Corp.*, 521 NE2d 700 (Ind App 1988).

FIGURE 37-1 Agency Relationships

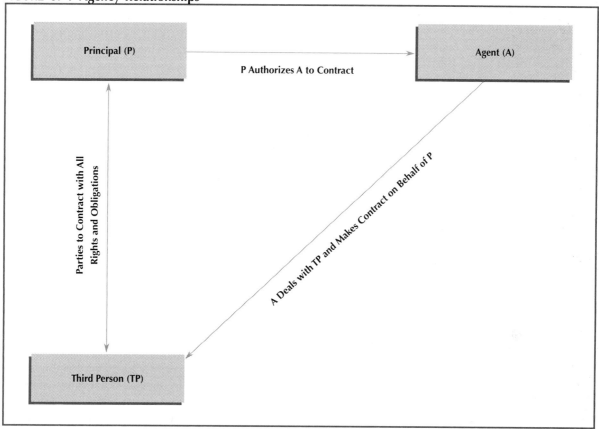

certain result—for example, to build a house. The actual performance of the work is controlled by the contractor, not the owner. An agent or employee differs from an independent contractor in that the principal or employer has the right to control the agent or employee, but not the contractor, in the performance of the work. **For Example,** Ned and Tracy Seizer contract with Fox Building Company to build a new home on Hilton Head Island, South Carolina, according to referenced plans and specifications. Individuals hired by Fox to work on the home are subject to the authority and control of Fox, the independent contractor, not the Seizers. However, Ned and Tracy could decide to build the home themselves, hiring two individuals from nearby Beaufort, Ted Chase and Marty Bromley, to do the work the Seizers will direct each day. Because Ted and Marty would be employees of the Seizers, the Seizers would be held responsible for any wrongs committed by these employees within the scope of their employment. As a general rule, on the other hand, the Seizers are not responsible for the torts of Fox, the independent contractor, and the contractor's employees. A "right to control" test determines whether an individual is an agent, an employee, or an independent contractor.[2]

A person who appears to be an independent contractor may in fact be so controlled by the other party that the contractor is regarded as an agent of, or employee of, the controlling person. **For Example,** Pierce, who was under contract to Brookville Carriers, Inc., was involved in a tractor-trailer/car collision with Rich and others. Pierce owned the tractor involved in the accident on a lease from Brookville but could use it only to haul freight for Brookville; he had no authority to carry freight on his own, and all of his operating authority belonged to Brookville. The "owner/operator" was deemed an employee

[2] *NE Ohio College of Massotherapy v Burek*, 759 NE2d 869 (Ohio App 2001).

rather than independent contractor for purposes of assessing the liability of the employer.[3] The separate identity of an independent contractor may be concealed so that the public believes that it is dealing with the principal. When this situation occurs, the principal is liable as though the contractor were an agent or employee.

2. Classification of Agents

A **special agent** is authorized by the principal to handle a definite business transaction or to do a specific act. One who is authorized by another to purchase a particular house is a special agent.

A **general agent** is authorized by the principal to transact all affairs in connection with a particular type of business or trade or to transact all business at a certain place. To illustrate, a person who is appointed as manager by the owner of a store is a general agent.

A **universal agent** is authorized by the principal to do all acts that can be delegated lawfully to a representative. This form of agency arises when a person absent because of being in the military service gives another person a blanket power of attorney to do anything that must be done during such absence.

CPA 3. Agency Coupled with an Interest

An agent has an **interest in the authority** when consideration has been given or paid for the right to exercise the authority. To illustrate, when a lender, in return for making a loan of money, is given, as security, authority to collect rents due the borrower and to apply those rents to the payment of the debt, the lender becomes the borrower's agent with an interest in the authority given to collect the rents.

An agent has an **interest in the subject matter** when, for a consideration, she is given an interest in the property with which she is dealing. Hence, when the agent is authorized to sell property of the principal and is given a lien on such property as security for a debt owed to her by the principal, she has an interest in the subject matter.

B. Creating the Agency

An agency may arise by appointment, conduct, ratification, or operation of law.

4. Authorization by Appointment

The usual method of creating an agency is by **express authorization;** that is, a person is appointed to act for, or on behalf of, another.

In most instances, the authorization of the agent may be oral. However, some appointments must be made in a particular way. A majority of the states, by statute, require the appointment of an agent to be in writing when the agency is created to acquire or dispose of any interest in land. A written authorization of agency is called a **power of attorney.** An agent acting under a power of attorney is referred to as an **attorney in fact.**[4]

5. Authorization by Conduct

Conduct consistent with the existence of an agency relationship may be sufficient to show authorization. The principal may have such dealing with third persons as to cause them to believe that the "agent" has authority. Thus, if the owner of a store places another person in charge, third persons may assume that the person in charge is the agent for the owner in that respect. The "agent" then appears to be authorized and is said to have *apparent authority*, and the principal is estopped from contradicting the appearance that has been created.[5]

The term *apparent authority* is used when there is only the appearance of authority but no actual authority, and that appearance of authority was created by the principal. The test for the existence of apparent authority is an objective test determined by the principal's outward manifestations through words or conduct that lead a third person reasonably to believe that the "agent" has authority. A principal's express restriction on authority not made known to a third person is no defense.

Apparent authority extends to all acts that a person of ordinary prudence, familiar with business usages and the particular business, would be justified in believing that the agent has authority to perform. It is essential to the concept of apparent authority that the third person reasonably believe that the agent has authority. The mere placing of property in the possession of another does not give that person either actual or apparent authority to sell the property.

[3] *Rich v Brookville Carriers, Inc.*, 256 F Supp 2d 26 (D Me 2003).
[4] *Lamb v Scott*, 643 So 2d 972 (Ala 1994).
[5] *Intersparex Leddin KG v AL-Haddad*, 852 SW2d 245 (Tenn App 1992).

CPA 6. Agency by Ratification

An agent may attempt, on behalf of the principal, to do an act that was not authorized, or a person who is not the agent of another may attempt to act as such an agent. Generally, in such cases, the principal for whom the agent claimed to act has the choice of ignoring the transaction or of ratifying it. Ordinarily, any unauthorized act may be ratified.

(a) Intention to Ratify

Initially, ratification is a question of intention. Just as in the case of authorization, when there is a question of whether the principal authorized the agent, there is a question of whether the principal intended to approve or ratify the action of the unauthorized agent.

The intention to ratify may be expressed in words, or it may be found in conduct indicating an intention to ratify.[6] **For Example,** James Reiner signed a five-year lease of commercial space on 320 West Main Street in Avon, Connecticut, because his father Calvin was away on vacation, and the owner, Robert Udolf, told James that if he did not come in and sign the lease, his father would lose the opportunity to rent the space in question. James was aware that his father had an interest in the space, and while telling Robert several times that he had no authority, James did sign his name to the lease. In fact, his father took occupancy of the space and paid rent for three years and then abandoned the space. James is not liable on the remainder of the lease because the owner knew at the time of signing that James did not have authority to act. Although he did not sign the lease, Calvin ratified the lease signed by James by his conduct of moving into the space and doing business there for three years with full knowledge of all material facts relating to the transaction. The owner, therefore, had to bring suit against Calvin, not James.[7]

CPA (b) Conditions for Ratification

In addition to the intent to ratify, expressed in some instances with a certain formality, the following conditions must be satisfied for the intention to take effect as a ratification:

1. The agent must have purported to act on behalf of or as agent for the identified principal.
2. The principal must have been capable of authorizing the act both at the time of the act and at the time it was ratified.
3. The principal must have full knowledge of all material facts.

It is not always necessary, however, to show that the principal had actual knowledge. Knowledge will be imputed if a principal knows of other facts that would lead a prudent person to make inquiries or if that knowledge can be inferred from the knowledge of other facts or from a course of business. **For Example,** Stacey, without authorization but knowing that William needed money, contracted to sell one of William's paintings to Courtney for $298. Stacey told William about the contract that evening; William said nothing and helped her wrap the painting in a protective plastic wrap for delivery. A favorable newspaper article about William's art appeared the following morning and dramatically increased the value of all of his paintings. William cannot recover the painting from Courtney on the theory that he never authorized the sale because he ratified the unauthorized contract made by Stacey by his conduct in helping her wrap the painting with full knowledge of the terms of the sale. The effect is a legally binding contract between William and Courtney.

(c) Effect of Ratification

When an unauthorized act is ratified, the effect is the same as though the act had been originally authorized. Ordinarily, this means that the principal and the third party are bound by the contract made by the agent.[8] When the principal ratifies the act of the unauthorized person, such ratification releases that person from the liability that would otherwise be imposed for having acted without authority.

CPA 7. Proving the Agency Relationship

The burden of proving the existence of an agency relationship rests on the person who seeks to benefit by such proof. The third person who desires to bind the principal because of the act of an alleged agent has the burden of proving that the latter person was in

[6] *Streetscenes, LLC v ITC Entertainment Group, Inc.*, 126 Cal Rptr 2d 754 (Cal App 2002).

[7] *Udolf v Reiner*, 2000 Conn Super LEXIS 1252.

[8] *Bill McCurley Chevrolet v Rutz*, 808 P2d 1167 (Wash App 1991).

fact the authorized agent of the principal and possessed the authority to do the act in question.[9]

C. Agent's Authority

When there is an agent, it is necessary to determine the scope of the agent's authority.

8. Scope of Agent's Authority

The scope of an agent's authority may be determined from the express words of the principal to the agent or it may be implied from the principal's words or conduct or from the customs of the trade or business.

(a) Express Authority

If the principal tells the agent to perform a certain act, the agent has express authority to do so. Express authority can be given orally or in writing.

(b) Incidental Authority

An agent has implied **incidental authority** to perform any act reasonably necessary to execute the express authority given to the agent. **For Example,** if the principal authorizes the agent to purchase goods without furnishing funds to the agent to pay for them, the agent has the implied incidental authority to purchase the goods on credit.[10]

(c) Customary Authority

An agent has implied **customary authority** to do any act that, according to the custom of the community, usually accompanies the transaction for which the agent is authorized to act. An agent who has express authority to receive payments from third persons, for example, has the implied customary authority to issue receipts.

(d) Apparent Authority

A person has **apparent authority** as an agent when the principal's words or conduct leads a third person to reasonably believe that the person has that authority and the third person relies on that appearance.[11]

In the *CSX* case, the court considered whether a business clothed an individual with apparent authority solely by allowing him to use its e-mail domain name.

CSX TRANSPORTATION, INC. V RECOVERY EXPRESS, INC., 415 F SUPP 2D 6 (D MASS 2006)

CSX GETS RAILROADED BY ALBERT ARILLOTTA

Recovery Express and Interstate Demolition (IDEC) are two separate corporations located at the same business address in Boston. On August 22, 2003 Albert Arillotta, a "partner" at IDEC sent an e-mail to Len Whitehead Jr. of CSX Transportation expressing an interest in buying "rail cars as scrap." Arillotta represented himself to be "from interstate demolition and recovery express" in the e-mail. And the e-mail address from which he sent his inquiry was "albert@recoveryexpress.com." Arillotta went to the CSX rail yard, disassembled the cars and transported them away. Thereafter CSX sent invoices for payment for the scrap railcars totaling $115,757.36 addressed to IDEC at its Boston office shared with Recovery Express. Whitehead believed Arillotta was authorized to act for Recovery Express, based on the e-mail's domain name—"recoveryexpress.com." Recovery claims that Arillotta never worked for it. Recovery's president Thomas Trafton allowed the "fledgling" company to use telephone, fax and e-mail services at its offices, but never shared anything with IDEC—assets, funds, books of business, or financials. CSX sued Recovery for the invoice amount on the doctrine of "apparent authority." IDEC is now defunct. Recovery claims that Arillotta never worked for it, and it is not liable.

Judicial Opinion

YOUNG, D. J. . . . The case, then, rests on the doctrine of apparent authority. "Apparent authority is the power held by an agent or other actor to affect a principal's legal relations with third parties when a third party reasonably believes the actor has authority to act on behalf of the principal and that belief is traceable to the principal's manifestations." Restatement at § 2.03. It "is not

[9] *Cummings, Inc. v Nelson*, 115 P3d 536 (Alaska 2005).
[10] *Badger v Paulson Investment Co.*, 803 P2d 1178 (Ore 1991).
[11] *Alexander v Chandler*, 179 SW2d 385 (Mo App 2005).

established by the putative agent's words or conduct, but by those of the principal." . . . Moreover, apparent authority "may exist only when the plaintiff *reasonably* may believe as a result of the principal's words or conduct that the agent is authorized to act on its behalf." . . .

In what looks to be an issue of first impression, the facts of this case set up the question whether an e-mail domain name, by itself, cloaks a purported agent with authority sufficient as matter of law to be called "apparent." Because apparent authority depends on that knowledge held by Whitehead and CSX of Arillotta's authority, which knowledge was derived from actions of Recovery, the only relevant conduct by Recovery is that it issued Arillotta an e-mail address with its domain name. Such associations as Recovery having the same offices, mailing address, phone number, or fax number are red herrings; these facts—if Whitehead even possessed them prior to entering the contract—emanated from Arillotta by way of his e-mail signature or telephone representations. There is no evidence of the manifestation of those facts by Recovery to Whitehead and CSX (i.e., by way of its website, as CSX asserted at oral argument) until after the contract was entered and collection efforts had begun.

The only act taken by Recovery known to Whitehead and CSX prior to entering the contract and upon which Whitehead could rely, was its issuance to Arillotta of an e-mail address sporting Recovery's domain name (@recoveryexpress.com). The Court holds that Whitehead and CSX were unreasonable, as matter of law, in their reliance solely on an e-mail domain name. Such a manifestation by Recovery cannot be sufficient to sustain a claim of apparent authority. Granting an e-mail domain name, by itself, does not cloak the recipient with carte blanche authority to act on behalf the grantee. Were this so, every subordinate employee with a company e-mail address—down to the night watchman—could bind a company to the same contracts as the president. This is not the law.

Though e-mail communication may be relatively new to staid legal institutions, the results in analogous low-tech situations confirm this conclusion. The Court could find no cases where, for example, giving someone a business card with the company name or logo, access to a company car, or company stationery, *by themselves*, created sufficient indicia of apparent authority. . . .

An e-mail domain name is sufficiently analogous to business cards, company vehicles, and letterhead for these cases to be persuasive. Those indicia of apparent authority all convey some degree of association between the purported principal and agent. By themselves, however, no reasonable person could conclude that apparent authority was present. The same is true with e-mail domain names.

In the end, CSX and Whitehead should have been more suspicious of an unsolicited, poorly written e-mail that arrived late one Friday afternoon. There are means by which CSX could have protected itself (e.g., requiring a purchase order form from IDEC or Recovery).* Before delivering goods worth over $115,000 to a stranger, one reasonably should be expected to inquire as to the authority of that person to have made such a deal. Given the anonymity of the Internet, this case illustrates the potential consequences of operating—even in today's fast-paced business world—as did CSX.

[Judgment for Recovery]

Questions

1. Appraise the correctness of the following statement: "Apparent authority comes from the actions of a principal, not the statements of an individual who claims to be an agent.
2. Is Recovery liable as a principal because it issued Arillotta an e-mail address with its domain name?
3. What means should CSX have taken to protect itself against the actions of Arillotta?

* "Parties can feel confident that they have formed binding contracts while communicating over open networks only if they use reliable authentication procedures." Jane Kaufman Winn, *Open System, Free Markets, and Regulation of Internet Commerce*, 72 Tulane L. Rev 1177, 1180 (1998) (discussing potential legal problems and technical solutions in Internet commerce).

9. Effect of Proper Exercise of Authority

When an agent with authority properly makes a contract with a third person that purports to bind the principal, there is by definition a binding contract between the principal and the third person. The agent is not a party to this contract. Consequently, when the owner of goods is the principal, the owner's agent is not liable for breach of warranty with respect to the goods "sold" by the agent. The owner-principal, not the agent, was the "seller" in the sales transaction.

E-COMMERCE AND CYBERLAW

AGENCY LAW IN CYBERSPACE

An *electronic agent* is a computer program or an electronic or other automated means used independently to initiate an action or respond to electronic records or performances in whole or in part without review or action by an individual at the time of the action or response.* An automated teller machine (ATM) is such an agent for the bank that owns the ATM, and the bank is the principal. Electronic agents are fabricated and do not have the human qualities attributable to human agents. Under the law of agency, agents themselves may be liable for their torts or for breach of contract when they exceed their authority. Of course, electronic agents, being nonhuman, are never liable for any action. It is the electronic agent's principal that may be liable. The law governing electronic agents is just beginning to develop because such agents are now an important part of e-commerce. Basic principles of agency, contract, and tort law along with judicial common sense will form the basis for the resolution of developing controversies.

Litigation has often arisen over the scope of a human agent's authority. The scope of an electronic agent's authority may well be an issue. Julie Frisoli placed an online order for a Taylor Made golf club with an Internet sporting goods supply company that serves both retail and wholesale customers. Because of a computer glitch that picked her up as a wholesale customer, the electronic agent listed the price for Julie as "$300 less a 20 percent discount," making the amount owed $240 plus shipping costs and tax, COD. Julie clicked her acceptance of the purchase online and was delighted that she had purchased it on sale. A half hour later, a supervisor discovered and "corrected" the mistaken discount intended for wholesale buyers only, raising the COD bill to the $300 retail price plus shipping and taxes. Julie insists she is legally entitled to the $240 price. Her position is correct. From an agency law perspective, electronic agents have authority to make contracts.** As to the third person, Julie, the principal sporting goods supply company held out the electronic agent as having authority to make the contract. Under contract law, the unilateral mistake of the agent is not a basis to set aside the contract when Julie did not know that a mistake was made.

*Electronic Signatures in Global and National Commerce Act, 15 USC § 7006(3).

**Uniform Electronic Transactions Act, § 14(1).

CPA 10. Duty to Ascertain Extent of Agent's Authority

A third person who deals with a person claiming to be an agent cannot rely on the statements made by the agent concerning the extent of authority.[12] If the agent is not authorized to perform the act or is not even the agent of the principal, the transaction between the alleged agent and the third person will have no legal effect between the principal and the third person.

Third persons who deal with an agent whose authority is limited to a special purpose are bound at their peril to find out the extent of the agent's authority. An attorney is such an agent. Unless the client holds the attorney out as having greater authority than usual, the attorney has no authority to settle a claim without approval from the client.

(a) Agent's Acts Adverse to Principal

The third person who deals with an agent is required to take notice of any acts that are clearly adverse to the interest of the principal. Thus, if the agent is obviously using funds of the principal for the agent's personal benefit, persons dealing with the agent

[12] *Breed v Hughes Aircraft Col.*, 35 Fed App 864 (Fed Cir 2002).

should recognize that the agent may be acting without authority and that they are dealing with the agent at their peril.

The only certain way that third persons can protect themselves is to inquire of the principal whether the agent is in fact the agent of the principal and has the necessary authority. If the principal states that the agent has the authority, the principal cannot later deny this authorization unless the subject matter is such that an authorization must be in writing to be binding.

11. Limitations on Agent's Authority

A person who has knowledge of a limitation on the agent's authority cannot ignore that limitation. When the third person knows that the authority of the agent depends on whether financing has been obtained, the principal is not bound by the act of the agent if the financing in fact was not obtained. If the authority of the agent is based on a writing and the third person knows that there is such a writing, the third person is charged with knowledge of limitations contained in it.

(a) "Obvious" Limitations

In some situations, it may be obvious to third persons that they are dealing with an agent whose authority is limited. When third persons know that they are dealing with a representative of a government agency, they should recognize that such a person will ordinarily have limited authority. Third persons should recognize that a contract made with such an officer or representative may not be binding unless ratified by the principal.

The federal government places the risk on any individual making arrangements with the government to accurately ascertain that the government agent is within the bounds of his or her authority, as set forth in the *Humlen* case.

HUMLEN V UNITED STATES, 49 FED CL 497 (2001)

HUMLEN WAS HAD?

In 1993, the U.S. Customs Service contacted Peder Humlen on numerous occasions regarding an ongoing investigation of Columbian cartel leader John Jairo Montoya's drug trafficking activities. In early 1994, FBI Special Agents Craig Howland and Ralph Hope sought Humlen's assistance in an FBI attempt to secure Montoya's conviction. Humlen was formally "opened" as an FBI cooperative witness and agreed to wear equipment to record conversations with the subjects of an FBI criminal investigation known as Steelwind. He alleges that Special Agents Hope and Howland promised to reimburse him for his reasonable expenses and compensate him up to $2,000 per month. In addition, Humlen claims that the FBI, through Special Agents Hope and Howland, promised to pay him 25 percent of any monies recovered from property or money forfeiture, $500 for every kilogram of cocaine seized, and a lump-sum award of up to $250,000 at the conclusion of the investigation.

On January 20, 1994, Humlen executed a "Non-Personal Services Agreement" with the FBI to formalize his status as a confidential informant. This agreement was reviewed by the FBI Contracts Unit at FBI Headquarters and signed by the FBI Supervisory Special Agent James Dietz. Under the terms of the agreement, Humlen would provide the FBI with information regarding Montoya's drug trafficking activities in exchange for a monthly compensation of, at most, $2,000. In addition,

The FBI may, at its sole option and choice, elect to furnish Humlen with an award of money upon the completion of the investigation. The amount of any award is at the complete and total discretion *of the FBI and/or the Attorney General of the United States and, as stated in* 28 U.S.C. § 524 *[(1994)], any award for information or assistance leading to a civil or criminal forfeiture is at the complete and full discretion of the Attorney General and shall not exceed the lesser of $250,000 or one-fourth of the amount realized by the United States from the property forfeited.*

In addressing the scope of the agreement, the document expressly stated:

This document constitutes the full and complete agreement between Humlen and the FBI. Modifications to this agreement will have no force and effect unless and until such modifications are reduced to writing and signed by all parties thereto.

The agreement also provided that Special Agent Hope is the "designated representative for the FBI Contracting Officer."

Humlen asserts that when FBI Special Agents Howland and/or Hope presented the agreement for his signature, he asked the agents why the written contract differed from the oral promises they had made to him regarding the 25 percent reward, the $500 per kilogram of cocaine seized, and the "up to $250,000 lump-sum." In response, the agents allegedly explained that the agreement had to be "couched" in that way because it was a discoverable document in any future criminal prosecution and thus could be used to discredit the plaintiff's reliability and credibility. The plaintiff maintains that the agents assured him that despite the wording of the contract, he would receive 25 percent of all forfeited money and property, as well as $500 per kilogram of cocaine seized.

Based in part on information provided by the plaintiff, Montoya was arrested and pleaded guilty on November 27, 1995, to Interstate Travel and Transportation in Aid of a Racketeering Enterprise, among other charges. In addition, Humlen claims his information led to the arrest of three of Montoya's colleagues, the seizure of 428 kilograms of cocaine, the seizure and eventual forfeiture of $754,000, a residence on Allesandro Street in Los Angeles, a Nissan pickup truck, two Ford Aerostar vans, and a 1990 Blue Camaro. The government, on the other hand, maintains that the plaintiff's information supplied to the FBI in the Steelwind Investigation led to the arrest of Montoya's colleagues, and the seizure of over 230 kilograms of cocaine, and approximately $50,000.

During the course of the FBI Steelwind Investigation, Humlen's handling agents changed due to transfer assignments. Humlen maintains that throughout the investigations, FBI Special Agents Howland, Hope, Embry and Sierra, and USCS Agent O'Shaughnessy repeatedly assured him that he would receive his anticipated remuneration for continued cooperation in the investigative effort as Special Agents Hope and Howland originally promised.

From the time Humlen executed the agreement through the prosecutoral phase of the FBI Steelwind Investigation, the FBI remitted to the plaintiff monthly payments of up to $2,000. Also in accordance with the agreement, he was reimbursed for the reasonable expenses he incurred in furtherance of the criminal investigation and offered sponsorship into the Federal Witness Protection Program. The DEA also remitted to him a one-time lump sum $5,000 payment to relocate himself and his family. A final $2,000 payment request was made on January 1996, and when no additional payment was forthcoming, Humlen sued the U.S. Government in the Court of Federal Claims.

Judicial Opinion

MARGOLIS, S. J. . . . On January 25, 1996, Agent Sierra prepared a request for a final $2,000 payment to plaintiff and noted that "this will be the final payment to the source from case funds; however, 'Sara 5' is preparing a request for lump sum payment which will be forwarded via separate cover *for approval.*". . . On or about March 27,1996, Agent Sierra prepared a formal request for a $50,000 one-time lump-sum award payment for plaintiff's "services" as a cooperative witness during the FBI Steelwind Investigation. Ultimately intended for review and possible approval by FBI Headquarters, Agent Sierra's request was forwarded to her immediate supervisor [Linas] Danilevicius and then to his immediate supervisor, Steinhauser. On April 10, 1996, Steinhauser returned the awarded request to Danilevicius with a note stating:

Linas—the [cooperative witness] is credited with 232 kilos of coke, $50K cash sized, 3 arrests and convictions. For this, he has been paid $50,000 on a personal services agreement during 1/20/94 to 2/12/96. We are now asking for a lump sum of $50,000 for the same information and accomplishments for the same period of time! I must be missing something here!

Please shed some light and provide justification; I have reviewed the file and I don't see it.

No further action was taken on this request. Agent Sierra informed [Peder Humlen] that the requested $50,000 had been denied. On May 23, 1996, the FBI officially "closed" plaintiff as a cooperative witness.

Discussion

...The Government, unlike private parties, cannot be bound by the apparent authority of its agents. See *Roy v United States, 38 Fed. Cl. 184, 187 (1997)*. Thus, the Court must determine "whether plaintiff has submitted sufficient evidence to establish a disputed issue of fact as to whether the FBI [Special Agents] with whom he allegedly dealt had [actual] authority contractually to obligate the Government." The general rule regarding the authority of government agents to bind the government is set forth in *Federal Crop Insurance Corp. v Merrill, 332 U.S. 380, 92 L. Ed. 10, 68 S. Ct. 1 (1947)*: "Anyone entering into an arrangement with the Government takes the risk of having accurately ascertained that he who purports to act for the Government stays within the bounds of his authority...this is so even though...the agent may have been unaware of the limitations upon his authority." *Federal Crop Insurance, 332 U.S. at 384*. When an agent exceeds his authority, the government can "disavow the [agent's] words and is not bound by an implied contract."

Implied actual authority, like express actual authority, also can bind the Government for the acts of its agents. See *H. Landau & Co., 886 F.2d at 324*. Authority is "generally implied when such authority is considered to be an integral part of the duties assigned to that Government employee." As a general rule, DEA Field Agents and FBI Special Agents lack the requisite actual authority—either expressed or implied—to contractually bind the United States to remit rewards to confidential informants/cooperative witnesses. This is so because contractual duty is not considered to be an integral part of their duties. See *Roy, 38 Fed. Cl. at 188-91* (contracting authority is not essential or necessary for FBI Special Agents to effectively perform their tasks of developing, controlling and supervising confidential informants);...In *Roy* the court held that the doctrine of implied actual authority was inapplicable because "contracting authority is not integral to FBI [Special Agents'] informant responsibilities." Accordingly, this Court holds that any promises that Special Agents Howland, Hope, Embry and Sierra might have made to the plaintiff cannot bind the government because the Special Agents lack the requisite authority.

Plaintiff attempts to circumvent this principle by maintaining that, at the very least, Special Agent Hope, in his capacity as the "designated representative of the contracting officer," had both express and implied actual authority to bind the government. Plaintiff argues that Hope, acting as the designated representative of the contracting officer, made oral compensation promises that were incidental and integral to his specific assigned duties as the "designated representative," and thus he possessed the requisite authority to bind the Government.

Contrary to what plaintiff claims, FBI Contracting Officer Dietz did not formally delegate the authority to bind the Government to Special Agent Hope. The agreement merely labeled Special Agent Hope as the "designated representative for the FBI contracting officer." Without a formal delegation of contacting authority, such designation is not enough to give a contracting officer authority....

Preclusive Effects of the Integration Clause

Even if the Special Agents did have the requisite authority to contractually bind the Government, plaintiff's claims are barred by the Agreement's Integration Clause. The Integration Clause provides:

This document constitutes the full and complete agreement between HUMLEN and the FBI. Modifications to this agreement will have no force and effect unless and until such modifications are reduced to writing and signed by all parties thereto.

It is undisputed that the alleged compensation promises were not contained in the parties' written agreement, nor the subject of a written modification. Therefore, plaintiff's claims to enforce additional oral compensation terms directly collides with the plain language of the agreement.

Conclusion

...Defendant's motion for summary judgment is granted.

Questions

1. State the rule of law applicable to third persons dealing with representatives of the U.S. government. Does an apparent authority rule bind the government? May the government "disavow" the promises made by their agents beyond their authority?
2. Was it "okay" for the government agents to explain away the terms of the written agreement as being "couched" for discovery purposes, and to assure Humlen that he would get the anticipated remuneration promised?

(b) Secret Limitations

If the principal has clothed an agent with authority to perform certain acts but the principal gives secret instructions that limit the agent's authority, the third person is allowed to take the authority of the agent at its face value. The third person is not bound by the secret limitations of which the third person has no knowledge.

D. Duties and Liabilities of Principal and Agent

The creation of the principal-agent relationship gives rise to duties and liabilities.

12. Duties and Liabilities of Agent during Agency

While the agency relationship exists, the agent owes certain duties to the principal.

(a) Loyalty

An agent must be loyal or faithful to the principal. The agent must not obtain any secret benefit from the agency. If the principal is seeking to buy or rent property, the agent cannot secretly obtain the property and then sell or lease it to the principal at a profit.

An agent who owns property cannot sell it to the principal without disclosing that ownership to the principal. If disclosure is not made, the principal may avoid the contract even if the agent's conduct did not cause the principal any financial loss. Alternatively, the principal can approve the transaction and sue the agent for any secret profit obtained by the agent.

A contract is voidable by the principal if the agent who was employed to sell the property purchases the property, either directly or indirectly, without full disclosure to the principal.

An agent cannot act as agent for both parties to a transaction unless both know of the dual capacity and agree to it. If the agent does act in this capacity without the consent of both parties, any principal who did not know of the agent's double status can avoid the transaction.

An agent must not accept secret gifts or commissions from third persons in connection with the agency. If the agent does so, the principal may sue the agent for those gifts or commissions. Such practices are condemned because the judgment of the agent may be influenced by the receipt of gifts or commissions.

It is a violation of an agent's duty of loyalty to make and retain secret profits.

In the *Ellison* case, the agent took additional secret compensation for himself.

ELLISON V ALLEY, 842 SW2D 605 (TENN 1992)

THIS "OPTION" QUARTERBACK IS OUT OF BOUNDS!

Real estate broker Donald Alley Sr. had a listing contract that gave him the exclusive right to sell Wayman Ellison's farm for at least $200,000. Ellison was told that a buyer was found. The buyer, Cora Myers, who had been paid $585,000 for her small farm because the land was needed for a commercial development, agreed to pay $380,000 for the large Ellison farm. Alley told Ellison that the sale price was $200,000. The buyer paid $380,000, however, and Alley kept the difference. When Ellison later learned of these details, he sued Alley for the $180,000. From a judgment for Ellison, Alley appealed, seeking at least his commission on the sale.

Judicial Opinion

O'BRIEN, J. . . . We are in agreement with the finding of breach of fiduciary duty and the award to the plaintiff of the defendant's profits. But, on the narrow issue upon which this appeal was granted, we find that the defendant [is] not entitled to a commission on the sale of the Ellison property. It is apparent that the defendant manipulated [the] transactions in such a manner as to willfully, and wrongfully, conceal [his] true role and [his] intention to reap a $180,000 ill-gained profit from the sale of the property.

It is well settled that the real estate agent acts as a fiduciary to the client. In any transaction or dealing related to such relationship, "the agent can in no way and under no circumstances act for himself or for any other than the principal without first making full and complete disclosure of the facts to the principal. He cannot profit by his failure to make such disclosure." . . . When a broker procures legal title to property, in violation of a fiduciary duty owed to the owner, equity constructs a trust out of the transaction. In such a case, the property owner is entitled to the profits wrongfully received by the broker in the transaction. . . . The construction of such a trust is without regard to whether the principal received a fair price for the conveyance of the property. . . .

Likewise, "where a broker's actions in a sale transaction amounts to bad faith or misconduct, the broker is not entitled to a commission on the sale." . . . It is undeniable that the defendant acted in these transactions with bad faith and beyond the bounds of ethical conduct. To permit the defendant credit for a reasonable commission on the sale of the Ellison property would be no more than offering an undeserved reward for avarice. . . .

[Judgment affirmed]

Questions

1. Is the seller's right to a remedy not defeated by the fact that the seller received the net price he sought?
2. May an agent ever buy a principal's property?
3. Did Alley act contrary to any ethical principles?
4. Since Alley did find a ready, willing, and able buyer, is he not at least entitled to his commission?

An agent is, of course, prohibited from aiding the competitors of a principal or disclosing to them information relating to the business of the principal. It is also a breach of duty for the agent to knowingly deceive a principal.[13]

(b) Obedience and Performance

An agent is under a duty to obey all lawful instructions.[14] The agent is required to perform the services specified for the period and in the way specified. An agent who does not do so is liable to the principal for any harm caused. For example, if an agent is instructed to take cash payments only but accepts a check in payment, the agent is liable for the loss caused the principal if a check is dishonored by nonpayment.

(c) Reasonable Care

It is the duty of an agent to act with the care that a reasonable person would exercise under the circumstances. **For Example,** Ethel Wilson applied for fire insurance for her house with St. Paul Reinsurance Co., Ltd., through her agent Club Services Corp. She thought she was fully covered. Unbeknown to her, however, St. Paul had refused coverage and returned her premium to Club Services, who did not refund it to Ms. Wilson or inform her that coverage had been denied. Fire destroyed her garage and St. Paul denied coverage. Litigation resulted, and St. Paul ended up expending $305,406 to settle the Wilson matter. Thereafter, St. Paul successfully sued Club Services Corp. under basic agency law principles that an agent (Club Services) is liable to its principal for all damages resulting from the agent's failure to discharge its duties.[15] In addition, if the agent possesses a special skill, as in the case of a broker or an attorney, the agent must exercise that skill.

(d) Accounting

An agent must account to the principal for all property or money belonging to the principal that comes into the agent's possession. The agent must, within a reasonable time, give notice of collections made and render an accurate account of all receipts and expenditures. The agency agreement may state at what intervals or on what dates such accountings are to be made. An agent must keep the principal's property and money separate and distinct from that of the agent.

(e) Information

It is the duty of an agent to keep the principal informed of all facts relating to the agency that are relevant to protecting the principal's interests.[16]

13. Duties and Liabilities of Agent after Termination of Agency

When the agency relationship ends, the duties of the agent continue only to the extent necessary to perform prior obligations. For example, the agent

13 *Koontz v Rosener*, 787 P2d 192 (Colo App 1990).

14 *Stanford v Neiderer*, 341 SE2d 892 (Ga App 1986).

15 *St. Paul Reinsurance Co., Ltd. v Club Services Corp.*, 2002 US App LEXIS 2277.

16 Restatement (Second) of Agency § 381; *Lumberman's Mutual Ins. Co. v Franey Muha Alliant Ins.*, 388 F Supp 2d 292 (SDNY 2005).

must return to the former principal any property that had been entrusted to the agent for the purpose of the agency. With the exception of such "winding-up" duties, the agency relationship is terminated, and the former agent can deal with the principal as freely as with a stranger.[17]

14. Duties and Liabilities of Principal to Agent

The principal must perform the contract, compensate the agent for services, make reimbursement for proper expenditures and, under certain circumstances, must indemnify the agent for loss.

(a) Employment According to Terms of Contract

When the contract is for a specified time, the principal is obligated to permit the agent to act as agent for the term of the contract. Exceptions are made for just cause or contract provisions that permit the principal to terminate the agency sooner. If the principal gives the agent an exclusive right to act in that capacity, the principal cannot give anyone else the authority to act as agent, nor may the principal do the act to which the exclusive agent's authority relates. **For Example,** if Jill Baker gives Brett Stamos the exclusive right for six months to sell her house, she cannot give another real estate agent the right to sell it during the six-month period or undertake to sell the house herself. If the principal or another agent sells the house, the exclusive agent is entitled to full compensation just as though the act had been performed by the exclusive agent.

In the *Holzman* case, the court was faced with deciding whether the exclusive agent was entitled to a commission where the sale was not completed.

HOLZMAN V BLUM, 726 A2D 818 (MD APP 1999)

WOULD YOU EVER SIGN AN EXCLUSIVE LISTING AGREEMENT AFTER READING THIS CASE?

The Holzmans signed an Exclusive Listing Agreement with the Blum real estate brokerage firm. The contract provided that the Holzmans had an obligation to pay a commission "... if they enter into a written agreement to sell the property to any person during the term of this exclusive listing agreement." The Holzmans entered into a written agreement to sell their three-story brick house containing eight bedrooms and nine full baths located on several acres of land in Baltimore County for $715,000 to the Noravians. On the advice of their attorney, the Holzmans included a default provision in this contract that stated in the event of default by the Holzmans, the Noravians' only remedy would be a refund of their deposit. The contract also called for the Noravians to pay the real estate commission. Soon thereafter, Gil and Ellen Stern offered $850,000 for the property, and the Holzmans canceled their contract with the Noravians and returned the deposit. After the exclusive listing period expired, the Holzmans executed a contract to sell their property to the Sterns at the offered price of $850,000 with the contract calling for the Holzmans to pay half of the real estate fee to Blum and half to a cooperating broker. Blum was in fact paid this fee. Thereafter, Blum brought suit against Holzman seeking the full commission for the Noravian contract under the Exclusive Listing Agreement. From a judgment for Blum for the full amount of the commission, less an offset for the commission paid Blum in the subsequent sale to the Sterns, plus attorney's fees, both parties appealed.

Judicial Opinion

HOLLANDER, J.... The matter proceeded to trial on February 10, 1998. At the proceeding, [Blum, Inc.,] presented testimony from... Mr. Blum.

In his testimony, Mr. Blum acknowledged:

I had a fiduciary relationship to the Holzmans, my listing contract until that time ran out, I was working for them. We would

[17] *Corron & Black of Illinois, Inc. v Magner*, 494 NE2d 785 (Ill App 1986).

bring all the offers regardless of whether there was a contract in force or not, we would bring all letters of intent regardless of whether there is a contract or not. That's our job. And my relationship was to do the best that we could for Mr. and Mrs. Holzman.

[Emphasis added.] Nevertheless, Mr. Blum acknowledged that, when the Holzmans decided to pursue the Sterns' offer, he did not advise them about their obligation to pay the commission under the Noravian contract. Indeed, Mr. Blum testified that he was "advised by . . . [counsel] not to say anything to the Holzmans." . . .

At the conclusion of the trial, the court stated:

. . . Apparently, [appellants] took the time to consult with a lawyer prior to signing this contract [of sale]. And unfortunately they didn't take the time, or there has been no testimony that they took the time to consult with a lawyer prior to signing the exclusive right to sell listing contract, which they signed. Had they consulted with a lawyer the lawyer would have told them that it's unambiguous, that this exclusive right to sell listing contract . . . which by the way this court recognizes, quite frankly, as the standard listing contract if you deal with a multiple listing agent.

* * *

The lawyer would have told [appellants] that if you enter into a contract during the term of this listing agreement you are obligated to pay a commission. . . .

I am not reducing the judgment. I think the judgment I imposed—I've not been convinced that I made a mistake in ordering the judgment that I ordered. I think it was correct. I do think that . . . [appellant] gets credit towards that judgment of $21,500 that has been paid as commission to [appellee] for the sale of this property.

We shall include additional facts in our discussion of the issues.

Appellants contend that settlement on the Noravian contract was a condition precedent to appellee's entitlement to a commission. . . .

Maryland law requires that we give legal effect to the unambiguous provisions of a contract. . . .

The trial court determined that the Agreement was unambiguous, and that it obligated the Holzmans to pay the fee because they entered into a written agreement to sell the Property during the term of the Agreement.

In this case, the Agreement did not state that the commission was to be paid from the "proceeds of the sale." Rather, it required payment of the fee if the Sellers executed "a written agreement to sell" the Property. . . .

Appellants claim that appellee breached its fiduciary duty to them because, when the Sellers sought to cancel the Noravian contract of sale, the Broker failed to advise them that the Agreement obligated them to pay the commission, even if the sale was not consummated, or that they would expose themselves to liability for more than one commission if they sold the Property to another party. . . .

It is certainly unfortunate that the Broker did not opt to remind the Holzmans of the terms of the Agreement, with which the Broker undoubtedly had far more familiarity. Nevertheless, under the circumstances of this case, we perceive no breach by appellee of its fiduciary duty to appellants.*

The Agreement clearly addressed the terms and conditions under which appellants would owe the Broker a fee, and appellee had no legal duty to remind appellants of the terms of the Agreement that appellants had signed. To the contrary, the Holzmans had a duty to ascertain their obligations under the Agreement.

One is under a duty to learn the contents of a contract before signing it; if, in the absence of fraud, duress, undue influence, and the like he fails to do so, he is presumed to know the contents, signs at his peril, suffers the consequences of his negligence, and is estopped to deny his obligation under the contract.

17 C. J. S. Contracts § 137(b) (1963). . . .

Moreover, this is not a case in which the Sellers lacked any experience as to real estate transactions. Rather, the testimony clearly indicated that the Holzmans had experience with listing contracts, as they had previously listed the subject property with another agent. Indeed, Mr. Holzman testified that the parties decided to use the "same pattern" for calculating the commission here as appellants had employed previously with another agent.

It is also noteworthy that there is no contention that appellee induced appellants to default on the Noravian contract. To the contrary, the evidence suggests that the Holzmans never endeavored to discuss with the Broker their intention to cancel the Noravian contract. Nonetheless, they knew enough to seek the advice of their counsel.

*Mr. Blum's description at trial of his "fiduciary relationship" with the Holzmans does not create a fiduciary duty under the law. Nevertheless, given Mr. Blum's testimony as to his "fiduciary relationship" and his desire "to do the best" for the clients, it is somewhat surprising that the Broker, in effect, opposed its client's desire to obtain the highest possible purchase price for the Property. Similarly, in pursuing its contract claim against the Sellers, we assume the Broker fully considered the impact such a suit might have on its reputation as an advocate for its customers. Moreover, but for the involvement of a cooperating broker on behalf of the Sterns, who was to share the commission for the Sterns contract, we presume that appellee, like appellants, would have preferred the Sterns contract, because the purchase price was substantially higher.

We are amply satisfied that the evidence shows neither fraud in the procurement of the Agreement, nor deception preventing appellants from reading its provisions. As a consequence, we find no merit to appellants' claims that appellee breached its fiduciary duty.

The trial court determined that, under the terms of the Agreement, appellee earned a commission when appellants executed the Noravian contract. Later, the court reduced the commission by $21,500. The amount of the reduction was equal to the fee recovered by appellee as the commission for the Stern contract. In its cross-appeal, the Broker challenges the trial court's decision to reduce the judgment by the amount of the commission it subsequently earned. Appellee argues that the Stern contract was a separate contract of sale.... Therefore, it contends that, under the Agreement, it was entitled to commissions for both the Noravian contract and the Stern contract....

We are satisfied that the trial court properly reduced the judgment by the amount of the commission appellee received from the subsequent sale of the Property to the Sterns.

[Judgment affirmed]

Questions

1. Does a court have discretion to rewrite a contract clause when the result of the plain and unambiguous language of the clause leads to a harsh or unfair result?
2. Did Blum have a legal obligation to remind Holzman that the commission provision of the Exclusive Listing Agreement obligated him to pay the full commission if Holzman canceled the contract with the first buyer?
3. Does the court imply in its footnote that it was not good for the business reputation of the Blum Real Estate Agency to seek to collect a commission under the facts before it?
4. What could the Holzmans have done to avoid this litigation?

(b) Compensation

The principal must pay the agent the agreed compensation.[18] If the parties have not fixed the amount of the compensation by their agreement but intended that the agent should be paid, the agent may recover the customary compensation for such services. If there is no established compensation, the agent may recover the reasonable value of the services rendered.

(1) Repeating Transactions. In certain industries, third persons make repeated transactions with the principal. In these cases, the agent who made the original contract with the third person commonly receives a certain compensation or percentage of commissions on all subsequent renewal or additional contracts. In the insurance business, for example, the insurance agent obtaining the policyholder for the insurer receives a substantial portion of the first year's premiums and then receives a smaller percentage of the premiums paid by the policyholder in subsequent years.

(2) Postagency Transactions. An agent is not ordinarily entitled to compensation in connection with transactions, such as sales or renewals of insurance policies, occurring after the termination of the agency even if the postagency transactions are the result of the agent's former activities. However, if the parties' employment contract calls for such compensation, it must be paid. **For Example,** real estate agent Laura McLane's contract called for her to receive $1.50 for every square foot the Atlanta Committee for the Olympic Games, Inc. (ACOG), leased at an Atlanta building; and even though she had been terminated at the time ACOG executed a lease amendment for 164,412 additional square feet, she was contractually entitled to a $246,618 commission.[19]

E. Termination of Agency

An agency may be terminated by the act of one or both of the parties to the agency agreement or by operation of law. When the authority of an agent is terminated, the agent loses all right to act for the principal.

15. Termination by Act of Parties

The duration of the agency relationship is commonly stated in the contract creating the relationship. In most cases, either party has the power to terminate the agency relationship at any time. However, the terminating party may be liable for damages to the other if the termination is in violation of the agency contract.

When a principal terminates an agent's authority, it is not effective until the agent receives the notice.

[18] *American Chocolates, Inc. v Mascot Pecan Co., Inc.*, 592 So 2d 93 (Miss 1992).

[19] *McLane v Atlanta Market Center Management Co.*, 486 SE2d 30 (Ga App 1997).

Because a known agent will have the appearance of still being an agent, notice must be given to third persons of the termination, and the agent may have the power to bind the principal and third persons until this notice is given.

16. Termination by Operation of Law

The agency relationship is a personal one, and anything that renders one of the parties incapable of performing will result in the termination of the relationship by operation of law. The death of either the principal or the agent ordinarily terminates the authority of an agent automatically even if the death is unknown to the other.[20]

An agency is also terminated by operation of law on the (1) insanity of the principal or agent, (2) bankruptcy of the principal or agent, (3) impossibility of performance, such as the destruction of the subject matter, or (4) when the country of the principal is at war with that of the agent.

17. Disability of the Principal under the UDPAA

The Uniform Durable Power of Attorney Act (UDPAA) permits the creation of an agency by specifying that "this power of attorney shall not be affected by subsequent disability or incapacity of the principal." Alternatively, the UDPAA permits the agency to come into existence upon the disability or incapacity of the principal. For this to be effective, the principal must designate the attorney in fact in writing. The writing must contain words showing the intent of the principal that the authority conferred shall continue notwithstanding the disability or incapacity of the principal. The UDPAA, which has been adopted by most states,[21] changes the common law and the general rule that insanity of the principal terminates the agent's authority to act for the principal. Society today recognizes that it may be in the best interest of a principal and good for the business environment for a principal to designate another as an attorney in fact to act for the principal when the principal becomes incapacitated.[22] It may be prudent to grant durable powers of attorney to different persons for property matters and for health care decisions.

Durable powers of attorney grant only those powers that are specified in the instrument. A durable power of attorney may be terminated by revocation by a competent principal and by the death of the principal.

The *Estate of Graham* case deals with issues related to the utilization of a durable power of attorney.

ESTATE OF GRAHAM V MORRISON, 607 SE2D 295 (NC APP 2005)

BROAD POWERS . . . BUT THERE IS A LIMIT, LUCILLE

On May 31, 2001 Thomas Graham made his niece Lucille Morrison his attorney-in-fact by executing a durable power of attorney. It was notarized and filed at the Registry of Deeds. The power of attorney granted Lucille broad powers and discretion in Graham's affairs. However, it did not contain express authority to make gifts. On October 26, 2000 Lucille conveyed 11.92 acres of property valued at between $400,000 and $700,000 to herself based upon consideration of services rendered to the principal, Thomas Graham. On June 5, 2001 Lucille, as attorney-in-fact for Graham, conveyed Graham's house in Charlotte to her son Ladd Morrison. And, on June 20, 2001 she conveyed Graham's Oakview Terrace property to her brother John Hallman for $3,000 to pay for an attorney to defend Graham in a competency proceeding. Graham died on August 7, 2001 and the estate of Thomas Graham sued to set aside the deeds, alleging Lucille's breach of fiduciary duties. After a judgment for the defendants, the estate appealed.

[20] *New York Life Ins. Co. v Estate of Haelen*, 521 NYS2d 970 (Sup Ct AD 1987).

[21] The Uniform Durable Power of Attorney Act has been adopted in some fashion in all states except Connecticut, Florida, Georgia, Illinois, Indiana, Louisiana, and Missouri.

[22] The Uniform Probate Code and the Uniform Durable Power of Attorney Act provide for the coexistence of durable powers and guardians or conservators. These acts allow the attorney in fact to continue to manage the principal's financial affairs while the court-appointed fiduciary takes the place of the principal in overseeing the actions of the attorney in fact. See *Rice v Flood*, 768 SW2d 57 (Ky 1989).

Judicial Opinion

HUNTER, J.... [W]e hold that in situations where an attorney-in-fact conveys the principal's property to herself based upon a consideration of alleged services rendered to the principal, the valuable consideration must reflect a fair and reasonable price when compared to the fair market value of the property....

Although Lucille took care of Graham and his wife during their illnesses and helped handle their business affairs,... Graham did not execute the deed to Lucille. Rather, Lucille utilized her power of attorney to execute the deed to herself. Given that during the time the deed was drafted, Graham was trying to sell the property, and that Lucille testified the deed was drafted to help finalize the sale of Graham's property, the testimony tends to indicate that the land was not conveyed to Lucille as compensation for her past services. Moreover, there was no testimony indicating the value of Lucille's services were comparable to the value of the real property, between $400,000.00 and $700,000.00. Accordingly, we conclude the trial court erroneously denied plaintiffs' motion for judgment notwithstanding the verdict.

Plaintiff has also challenged a conveyance of Graham's home on Coronet Way in Charlotte, North Carolina, to Ladd Morrison, the son of Lucille Morrison.... Lucille testified that Ladd had spent over $12,000.00 to improve the condition of the house so Graham could live in it. Ladd paid for windows, paint, supplies, a furnace, and labor. Ladd testified, however, that "[he] was just taking care of [his] family" and that he never expected to get the money back. According to Lucille, Graham told her to give Ladd the property on Coronet Way and she indicated that she was following his instructions. However, there was no indication in the testimony that the conveyance was intended to be payment for services. Thus, this deed must be set aside because this Court has already determined that the power of attorney held by Lucille over Graham's affairs did not give her the power to make gifts....

Plaintiffs contend Lucille sold property owned by Graham to her brother, John to secure an attorney for herself. However, Lucille testified that the money was used to retain an attorney to represent Graham in an incompetency proceeding. According to the testimony, on 6 June 2001, Graham was admitted to the hospital. The next day, on 7 June 2001, his daughter filed a petition to have Graham declared incompetent. Upon learning of the petition, Lucille testified she sold the property and retained an attorney to represent herself and Graham at the hearing. The power of attorney granted Lucille the power to sell Graham's real estate and to "perform all and every act or thing, whatsoever requisite or necessary to be done for [Graham's] upkeep, care, and maintenance, and for the management of any property owned by me, as fully, and to all intents and purposes as I might or could do if I were personally present and acting...." The power of attorney also granted Lucille the authority to make contracts, including selling real property for adequate consideration, on Graham's behalf. As Lucille testified that she hired the attorney to represent Graham in the competency hearing, and the power of attorney granted Lucille the authority to take such actions, we conclude the trial court properly denied plaintiff's motion for judgment notwithstanding the verdict on this particular conversion allegation....

...Lucille did not have authority under the power of attorney to give Graham's property to herself or her son. Therefore, she breached the fiduciary duty owed to Graham....

[Affirmed in part, reversed and remanded in part]

Judges WYNN and THORNBURG concur.

Judge THORNBURG concurred in this opinion prior to 31 December 2004.

Questions

1. Can an attorney in fact convey property to herself based on consideration of services rendered to the principal?
2. Can an attorney in fact sell a principal's property to obtain funds to pay an attorney to represent the principal?
3. Was the conveyance of the home in Charlotte to Ladd Morrison allowable under the power of attorney?

18. Termination of Agency Coupled with an Interest

An agency coupled with an interest is an exception to the general rule as to the termination of an agency. Such an agency cannot be revoked by the principal before the expiration of the interest. It is not terminated by the death or insanity of either the principal or the agent.

19. Protection of Agent from Termination of Authority

The modern world of business has developed several methods of protecting an agent from the termination of authority for any reason.[23]

These methods include the use of an exclusive agency contract, a secured transaction, an escrow deposit, a standby letter of agreement, or a guarantee agreement.

20. Effect of Termination of Authority

If the principal revokes the agency, the authority to act for the principal is not terminated until the agent receives notice of revocation. As between the principal and the agent, the right of the agent to bind the principal to third persons generally ends immediately upon the termination of the agent's authority. This termination is effective without giving notice to third persons.

When the agency is terminated by the act of the principal, notice must be given to third persons. If this notice is not given, the agent may have the power to make contracts that will bind the principal and third persons. This rule is predicated on the theory that a known agent will have the appearance of still being the agent unless notice to the contrary is given to third persons. **For Example,** Seltzer owns property in Boca Raton that he uses for the month of February and leases the remainder of the year. O'Neil has been Seltzer's rental agent for the past seven years, renting to individuals like Ed Tucker under a power of attorney that gives him authority to lease the property for set seasonal and off-season rates. O'Neil's right to bind Seltzer on a rental agreement ended when Seltzer faxed O'Neil a revocation of the power of attorney on March 1. A rental contract with Ed Tucker signed by O'Neil on behalf of Seltzer on March 2 will bind Seltzer, however, because O'Neil still appeared to be Seltzer's agent and Tucker had no notice to the contrary.

When the law requires giving notice in order to end the power of the agent to bind the principal, individual notice must be given or mailed to all persons who had prior dealings with the agent. In addition, notice to the general public can be given by publishing in a newspaper of general circulation in the affected geographic area a statement that the agency has been terminated.

If a notice is actually received, the power of the agent is terminated without regard to whether the method of giving notice was proper. Conversely, if proper notice is given, it is immaterial that it does not actually come to the attention of the party notified. Thus, a member of the general public cannot claim that the principal is bound on the ground that the third person did not see the newspaper notice stating that the agent's authority had been terminated.

[23] These methods generally replace the concept of an agency coupled with an interest because of the greater protection given to the agent. Typically, the rights of the agent under these modern devices cannot be defeated by the principal, by operation of law, or by claims of other creditors.

Summary

An agency relationship is created by an express or implied agreement by which one person, the agent, is authorized to make contracts with third persons on behalf of, and subject to, the control of another person, the principal. An agent differs from an independent contractor in that the principal, who controls the acts of an agent, does not have control over the details of performance of work by the independent contractor. Likewise, an independent contractor does not have authority to act on behalf of the other contracting party.

A special agent is authorized by the principal to handle a specific business transaction. A general agent is authorized by the principal to transact all business affairs of the principal at a certain place. A universal agent is authorized to perform all acts that can be lawfully delegated to a representative.

The usual method of creating an agency is by express authorization. However, an agency relationship may be found to exist when the principal causes or permits a third person to reasonably believe that an agency relationship exists. In such a case, the "agent" appears to be authorized and is said to have apparent authority.

An unauthorized transaction by an agent for a principal may be ratified by the principal.

An agent acting with authority has the power to bind the principal. The scope of an agent's authority may be determined from the express words of the principal to the agent; this is called *express authority*. An agent has incidental authority to perform any act reasonably necessary to execute the authority given the agent. An agent's authority may be implied so as to enable the agent to perform any act in accordance with the general customs or usages in a business or an industry. This authority is often referred to as customary authority.

The effect of a proper exercise of authority by an agent is to bind the principal and third person to a contract. The agent, not being a party to the contract, is not liable in any respect under the contract. A third person dealing with a person claiming to be an agent has a duty to ascertain the extent of the agent's authority and a duty to take notice of any acts that are clearly adverse to the principal's interests. The third person cannot claim that apparent authority existed when that person has notice that the agent's conduct is adverse to the interests of the principal. A third person who has knowledge of limitations on an agent's authority is bound by those limitations. A third person is not bound by secret limitations.

While the agency relationship exists, the agent owes the principal the duties of (1) being loyal, (2) obeying all lawful instructions, (3) exercising reasonable care, (4) accounting for all property or money belonging to the principal, and (5) informing the principal of all facts relating to the agency that are relevant to the principal's interests. An agency relationship can be terminated by act of either the principal or the agent. However, the terminating party may be liable for damages to the other if the termination is in violation of the agency contract.

Because a known agent will have the appearance of still being an agent, notice must be given to third persons of the termination, and the agent may have the power to bind the principal and third persons until this notice is given.

An agency is terminated by operation of law upon (1) the death of the principal or agent, (2) insanity of the principal or agent, (3) bankruptcy of the principal or agent, (4) impossibility of performance, caused, for example, by the destruction of the subject matter, or (5) war.

In states that have adopted the Uniform Durable Power of Attorney Act (UDPAA), an agency may be created that is not affected by subsequent disability or incapacity of the principal. In UDPAA states, the agency may also come into existence upon the "disability or incapacity of the principal." The designation of an attorney in fact under the UDPAA must be in writing.

Questions and Case Problems

1. How does an agent differ from an independent contractor?
2. Compare authorization of an agent by (a) appointment and (b) ratification.
3. Ernest A. Kotsch executed a durable power of attorney when he was 85 years old, giving his son, Ernie, the power to manage and sell his real estate and personal property "and to do all acts necessary for maintaining and caring for [the father] during his lifetime." Thereafter, Kotsch began "keeping company" with a widow, Margaret Gradl. Ernie believed that the widow was attempting to alienate his father from him, and he observed that she was exerting a great deal of influence over his father. Acting under the durable power of attorney and without informing his father, Ernie created the "Kotsch Family Irrevocable Trust," to which he transferred $700,000, the bulk of his father's liquid assets, with the father as grantor and initial beneficiary and Ernie's three children as additional beneficiaries. Ernie named himself trustee. His father sued to avoid the trust. Ernie defended his action on the ground that he had authority to create the trust under the durable power of attorney. Decide. [*Kotsch v Kotsch*, 608 So 2d 879 (Fla App)]
4. Ken Jones, the number-one-ranked prizefighter in his weight class, signed a two-year contract with Howard Stayword. The contract obligated Stayword to represent and promote Jones in all business and professional matters, including the arrangement of fights. For these services, Jones was to pay Stayword 10 percent of gross earnings. After a year, when Stayword proved unsuccessful in arranging a title match with the champion, Jones fired Stayword. During the following year, Jones earned $4 million. Stayword sued Jones for $400,000. Jones defended himself on the basis that a principal has the absolute power at any time to terminate an agency relationship by discharging the agent, so he was not liable to Stayword. Was Jones correct?
5. Paul Strich did business as an optician in Duluth, Minnesota. Paul used only the products of the Plymouth Optical Co., a national manufacturer of optical products and supplies with numerous retail outlets and some franchise arrangements in areas other than Duluth. To increase business, Paul renovated his office and changed the sign on it to read "Plymouth Optical Co." Paul did business this way for more than three years—advertised under that name, paid bills with checks bearing the name of Plymouth Optical Co., and listed himself in the telephone and city directories by that name. Plymouth immediately became aware of what Paul was doing. However, because Paul used only Plymouth products and Plymouth did not have a franchise in Duluth, it saw no advantage at that time in prohibiting Paul from using the name and losing him as a customer. Paul contracted with the *Duluth Tribune* for advertising, making the contract in the name of Plymouth Optical Co. When the advertising bill was not paid, the *Duluth Tribune* sued Plymouth Optical Co. for payment. Plymouth's defense was that it had never authorized Paul to do business under the name, nor had it authorized him to make a contract with the newspaper. Decide.

6. Record owned a farm that was managed by his agent, Berry, who lived on the farm. Berry hired Wagner to bale the hay and told him to bill Record for this work. Wagner did so and was paid by Record. By the summer of the following year, the agency had been terminated by Record, but Berry remained in possession as tenant of the farm and nothing appeared changed. Late in the summer, Berry asked Wagner to bale the hay as he had done the previous year and bill Record for the work. He did so, but Record refused to pay on the ground that Berry was not then his agent. Wagner sued him. Decide. [*Record v Wagner*, 100 NH 419]
7. Gilbert Church owned Church Farms, Inc., in Manteno, Illinois. Church advertised its well-bred stallion Imperial Guard for breeding rights at $50,000, directing all inquiries to "Herb Bagley, Manager." Herb Bagley lived at Church Farms and was the only person available to visitors. Vern Lundberg answered the ad, and after discussions in which Bagley stated that Imperial Guard would remain in Illinois for at least a two-year period, Lundberg and Bagley executed a two-year breeding rights contract. The contract was signed by Lundberg and by Bagley as "Church Farms, Inc., H. Bagley, Mgr." When Gil Church moved Imperial Guard to Oklahoma prior to the second year of the contract, Lundberg brought suit for breach of contract. Church testified that Bagley had no authority to sign contracts for Church Farms. Decide. [*Lundberg v Church Farms, Inc.*, 502 NE2d 806 (Ill)]
8. Although a woman of means, Bird was living in deplorable conditions. Neighbors contacted her cousin, Logan Ledbetter, who, in turn, had Bird examined by Dr. Phillips, a psychiatrist. Dr. Phillips determined that Bird was suffering from "an organic brain syndrome, chronic," that "her mental function was very impaired," and that, in his opinion, Bird was "mentally incompetent at the time of the examination." Ledbetter planned to deal with the situation by selling off a number of valuable real estate holdings owned by Bird and using the proceeds to pay for proper care for her.

   Soon thereafter, Bird executed a power of attorney designating Logan Ledbetter as her attorney in fact, and Ledbetter entered into a contract to sell a large parcel of Bird's land to Andleman Associates. Bird's niece, Barbara, who disliked Ledbetter, filed a petition to have Bird declared incompetent and herself named guardian of her estate. The court appointed Barbara as guardian, and Barbara refused to allow the sale of the land to Andleman. In the lawsuit that resulted, Ledbetter and Andleman contended that Ledbetter acted in good faith and had a properly executed power of attorney; therefore, his signing the sales contract with Andleman was binding on Bird (the principal). Atkins (the real estate agent who had produced the ready, willing, and able buyer) sought his 10 percent commission under the listing agreement signed by Ledbetter as agent for Bird. Barbara contended that the power of attorney was void and that Ledbetter owed the real estate commission because he breached his implied warranty that he had a principal with capacity. Decide.
9. Tillie Flinn properly executed a durable power of attorney designating her nephew James C. Flanders and/or Martha E. Flanders, his wife, as her attorney in fact. Seven months later, Martha Flanders went to the Capitol Federal Savings and Loan Association office. She had the durable power of attorney instrument, five certificates of deposit, and a hand-printed letter identifying Martha as an attorney in fact and stating that Tillie wished to cash her five CDs that Martha had with her. At approximately 10:31 A.M., five checks were given to Martha in the aggregate amount of $135,791.34, representing the funds in the five CDs less penalties for early withdrawal. Some of the checks were drawn to the order of Martha individually and some to the order of James and Martha, as individuals. Tillie was found dead of heart disease later that day. The time of death stated on her death certificate was 11:30 A.M. The Flanderses spent the money on themselves. Bank IV, as administrator of Tillie's estate, sued Capitol Federal to recover the amount of the funds paid to the Flanderses. It contended that Capitol Federal breached its duty to investigate before issuing the checks. Capitol Federal contended that it did all that it had a duty to do. Decide. [*Bank IV v Capitol Federal Savings and Loan Ass'n*, 828 P2d 355 (Kan)]
10. Lew owns a store on Canal Street in New Orleans. He paid a person named Mike and other individuals commissions for customers brought into the store. Lew testified that he had known Mike for less than a week. Boulos and Durso, partners in a wholesale jewelry business, were visiting New Orleans on a business trip when Mike brought them into the store to buy a stereo. While Durso finalized the stereo transaction with the store's manager, Boulos and Mike negotiated to buy 2 cameras, 3 videos, and 20 gold Dupont lighters. Unknown to the store's manager, Mike was given $8,250 in cash and was to deliver the merchandise later that evening to the Marriott Hotel, where Boulos and Durso were staying. Mike gave a receipt for the cash, but it showed no sales tax or indication that the goods were to be delivered. Boulos testified that he believed Mike was the store owner. Mike never delivered the merchandise and disappeared. Boulos and Durso contended that Lew is liable for the acts of his agent, Mike. Lew denied that Mike was his agent, and the testimony showed that Mike had no actual authority to make a sale, to use a cash register, or even to go behind a sales counter. What ethical principle applies to the conduct of Boulos and Durso? Decide. [*Boulos v Morrison*, 503 So 2d 1(La)]
11. Martha Christiansen owns women's apparel stores bearing her name in New Seabury, Massachusetts; Lake

Placid, New York; Palm Beach, Florida; and Palm Springs, California. At a meeting with her four store managers, she discussed styles she thought appropriate for the forthcoming season, advised them as always to use their best judgment in the goods they purchased for each of their respective stores, and cautioned "but no blue jeans." Later, Jane Farley, the manager of the Lake Placid store, purchased a line of high-quality blue denim outfits (designer jeans with jacket and vest options) from Women's Wear, Inc., for the summer season. The outfits did not sell. Martha refused to pay for them, contending that she told all of her managers "no blue jeans" and that if it came to a lawsuit, she would fly in three managers to testify that Jane Farley had absolutely no authority to purchase denim outfits and was, in fact, expressly forbidden to do so. Women's Wear sued Martha, and the three managers testified for her. Is the fact that Martha had explicitly forbidden Farley to purchase the outfits in question sufficient to protect her from liability for the purchases made by Farley?

12. Fred Schilling, the president and administrator of Florence General Hospital, made a contract, dated August 16, 1989, on behalf of the hospital with CMK Associates to transfer the capacity to utilize 25 beds from the hospital to the Faith Nursing Home. Schilling, on behalf of the hospital, had previously made a contract with CMK Associates on May 4, 1987. Schilling had been specifically authorized by the hospital board to make the 1987 contract. The hospital refused to honor the 1989 contract because the board had not authorized it. CMK contended that Schilling had apparent authority to bind the hospital because he was president and administrator of the hospital and he had been the person who negotiated and signed a contract with CMK in 1987. Thus, according to CMK, the hospital had held out Schilling as having apparent authority to make the contract. The hospital disagreed. Decide. [*Pee Dee Nursing Home v Florence General Hospital*, 419 SE2d 843 (SC Ct App)]

13. Barbara Fox was the agent of Burt Hollander, a well-known athlete. She discovered that Tom Lanceford owned a 1957 Chevrolet convertible, which had been stored in a garage for the past 15 years. After demonstrating to Lanceford that she was the authorized agent of Hollander, she made a contract with Lanceford on behalf of Hollander to purchase the Chevrolet. Lanceford later discovered that the car was much more valuable than he originally believed, and he refused to deliver the car to Fox. Fox sued Lanceford for breach of contract. Can she recover?

14. Francis Gagnon, an elderly gentleman, signed a power of attorney authorizing his daughter, Joan, "to sell any of my real estate and to execute any document needed to carry out the sale... and to add property to a trust of which I am grantor or beneficiary." This power was given in case Gagnon was not available to take care of matters personally because he was traveling. When Joan learned that Gagnon intended to sell his Shelburne property to Cosby for $750,000, she created an irrevocable trust naming Gagnon as beneficiary and herself as trustee. Acting then on the basis of the authority set forth in the power of attorney, she conveyed the Shelburne property to herself as trustee of the irrevocable trust, thus blocking the sale to Cosby. When Gagnon learned of this, he demanded that Joan return the Shelburne property to him, but she refused, saying she had acted within the authority set forth in the power of attorney. Did Joan violate any duty owed to Gagnon? Must she reconvey the property to Gagnon? [*Gagnon v Coombs*, 654 NE2d 54 (Mass App)]

15. Daniels and Julian were employed by the Marriott Hotel in New Orleans and were close personal friends. One day after work, Daniels and Julian went to Werlein's music store to open a credit account. Julian, with Daniels's authorization and in her presence, applied for credit using Daniels's name and credit history. Later, Julian went to Werlein's without Daniels and charged the purchase of a television set to Daniels's account, executing a retail installment contract by signing Daniels's name. Daniels saw the new television in Julian's home and was informed that it was charged to the Werlein's account. Daniels told Julian to continue making payments. When Werlein's credit manager first contacted Daniels and informed her that her account was delinquent, she claimed that a money order for the television was in the mail. On the second call, she asked for a "payment balance." Some four months after the purchase, she informed Werlein's that she had not authorized the purchase of the television nor had she ratified the purchase. Werlein's sued Daniels for the unpaid balance. Decide. [*Philip Werlein, Ltd. v Daniels*, 536 So 2d 722 (La App)]

CPA Questions

1. Generally, an agency relationship is terminated by operation of law in all of the following situations except the

   a. Principal's death
   b. Principal's incapacity
   c. Agent's renunciation of the agency
   d. Agent's failure to acquire a necessary business license

2. Able, on behalf of Pix Corp., entered into a contract with Sky Corp., by which Sky agreed to sell computer

equipment to Pix. Able disclosed to Sky that she was acting on behalf of Pix. However, Able had exceeded her actual authority by entering into the contract with Sky. If Pix wishes to ratify the contract with Sky, which of the following statements is correct?

a. Pix must notify Sky that Pix intends to ratify the contract.
b. Able must have acted reasonably and in Pix's best interest.
c. Able must be a general agent of Pix.
d. Pix must have knowledge of all material facts relating to the contract at the time it is ratified.

3. Which of the following actions requires an agent for a corporation to have a written agency agreement?

a. Purchasing office supplies for the principal's business
b. Purchasing an interest in undeveloped land for the principal
c. Hiring an independent general contractor to renovate the principal's office building
d. Retaining an attorney to collect a business debt owed the principal

4. Simmons, an agent for Jensen, has the express authority to sell Jensen's goods. Simmons also has the express authority to grant discounts of up to 5 percent of list price. Simmons sold Hemple a 10 percent discount. Hemple had not previously dealt with either Simmons or Jensen. Which of the following courses of action may Jensen properly take?

a. Seek to void the sale to Hemple
b. Seek recovery of $50 from Hemple only
c. Seek recovery of $50 from Simmons only
d. Seek recovery of $50 from either Hemple or Simmons

5. Ogden Corp. hired Thorp as a sales representative for nine months at a salary of $3,000 per month plus 4 percent of sales. Which of the following statements is correct?

a. Thorp is obligated to act solely in Ogden's interest in matters concerning Ogden's business.
b. The agreement between Ogden and Thorp formed an agency coupled with an interest.
c. Ogden does not have the power to dismiss Thorp during the nine-month period without cause.
d. The agreement between Ogden and Thorp is not enforceable unless it is in writing and signed by Thorp.

6. Frost's accountant and business manager has the authority to

a. Mortgage Frost's business property
b. Obtain bank loans for Frost
c. Insure Frost's property against fire loss
d. Sell Frost's business

THIRD PERSONS IN AGENCY

CHAPTER (38)

LEARNING OBJECTIVES

After studying this chapter, you should be able to

LO.1 Describe how to execute a contract as an agent on behalf of a principal

LO.2 Identify when an agent is liable to a third person on a contract

LO.3 State the effect of a payment made by a third person to an authorized agent

LO.4 Explain and illustrate the doctrine of *respondeat superior*

LO.5 Contrast the liability of an owner for a tort committed by an independent contractor with the liability of an employer for a tort committed by an employee

LO.6 Distinguish between the authority of a soliciting agent and that of a contracting agent

The rights and liabilities of the principal, the agent, and the third person with whom the agent deals are generally determined by contract law. In some cases, tort or criminal law may be applicable.

A. Liability of Agent to Third Person

The liability of the agent to the third person depends on the existence of authority and the manner of executing the contract.

1. Action of Authorized Agent of Disclosed Principal

If an agent makes a contract with a third person on behalf of a disclosed principal and has proper authority to do so and if the contract is executed properly, the agent has no personal liability on the contract. Whether the principal performs the contract or not, the agent cannot be held liable by the third party.

In speaking of an agent's **action** as authorized or unauthorized, it must be remembered that *authorized* includes action that, though originally *unauthorized*, was subsequently ratified by the principal. Once there is an effective ratification, the original action of the agent is no longer treated as unauthorized.

2. Unauthorized Action

If a person makes a contract as agent for another but lacks authority to do so, the contract does not bind the principal. When a person purports to act as agent for a principal, an implied warranty arises that that person has authority to do so.[1] If the agent lacks authority, there is a breach of this warranty.

If the agent's act causes loss to the third person, that third person may generally hold the agent liable for the loss.

It is no defense for the agent in such a case that she acted in good faith or misunderstood the scope of authority. The purported agent is not liable for conduct in excess of authority when the third person knows that she is acting beyond the authority given by the principal.

An agent with a written authorization may avoid liability on the implied warranty of authority by showing the written authorization to the third person and permitting the third person to determine the scope of the agent's authority.

3. Disclosure of Principal

There are three degrees to which the existence and identity of the principal may be disclosed or not disclosed. An agent's liability as a party to a contract with a third person is affected by the degree of disclosure.

[1] *Walz v Todd & Honeywell, Inc.*, 599 NYS2d 638 (App Div 1993).

(a) Disclosed Principal

When the agent makes known the identity of the principal and the fact that the agent is acting on behalf of that principal, the principal is called a **disclosed principal.** The third person dealing with an agent of a disclosed principal ordinarily intends to make a contract with the principal, not the agent. Consequently, the agent is not a party to, and is not bound by, the contract that is made.[2]

(b) Partially Disclosed Principal

When the agent makes known the existence of a principal but not the principal's identity, the principal is a **partially disclosed principal.** Because the third party does not know the identity of the principal, the third person is making the contract with the agent, and the agent is therefore a party to the contract.

(c) Undisclosed Principal

When the third person is not told or does not know that the agent is acting as an agent for anyone else, the unknown principal is called an **undisclosed principal.**[3] In this case, the third person is making the contract with the agent, and the agent is a party to that contract.

In the *Burch case*, the court was faced with deciding whether an agent was liable under a contract made on behalf of a principal.

BURCH V HANCOCK, 56 SW3D 257 (2001)

YOU'VE GOT TO TELL THEM YOU'RE CONTRACTING ON BEHALF OF THE CORPORATION, SILLY

Duncan Burch is the president of Deja Vu, Inc., which operates a 3,400-acre ranch in Emory, Texas. It does business under the assumed name of Rocking D Ranch. Mr. Hancock went out to the Rocking D Ranch to meet with Duncan Burch about grinding stumps at the ranch. Approximately six acres of land containing timber had been cleared and the stumps had to be removed so that the land could be planted for cattle grazing. The record reflects that Hancock and Burch met alone and agreed that Hancock would grind stumps on the ranch and would be paid five dollars for each stump ground, regardless of size. Hancock testified that, at the time he entered into the agreement, he knew nothing about Deja Vu and thought that Burch owned the ranch. The evidence is undisputed that, during this meeting, Burch never stated to Hancock that he was acting as agent of Rocking D Ranch, Deja Vu, or anyone else. Hancock was paid for two invoices submitted to the ranch. His third invoice was not paid, and he eventually brought suit against Burch. From a judgment for Hancock, Burch appealed.

Judicial Opinion

GRIFFITH, J. . . .

Individual Liability of Agent on Contract

Appellants contend that the trial court erred in finding Burch individually liable on the contract. We disagree. Regarding the liability on corporate contracts, officers of corporations are in the same position as agents of private individuals. In order for an agent to avoid personal liability on a contract, he has the duty to disclose not only that he is acting in a representative capacity but also the identity of his principal. The party with whom the agent deals has no duty to discover the principal. The inference that the agent is a party to the contract exists until the agent gives such complete information concerning the principal's identity that the principal can be readily distinguished. If the other party has no reasonable means of ascertaining the principal, the inference prevails unless the parties have agreed otherwise. . . .

In the case at hand, the record reflects that Hancock and Burch met alone and agreed that Hancock would grind stumps on the ranch and would be paid five dollars for each stump ground, regardless of size. Hancock testified that, at the time he entered into the agreement, he knew nothing about Deja Vu and thought that Burch owned the ranch. The evidence is undisputed that, during this meeting,

[2] *Stinchfield v Weinreb*, 797 NYS2d 521 (App Div 2005).

[3] *Brunswick Leasing Corp. v Wisconsin Central, Ltd.*, 136 F3d 521 (7th Cir 1998).

Burch never stated to Hancock that he was acting as agent of Rocking D Ranch, Deja Vu, or anyone else. However, Appellants, relying heaviliy on *Armstrong*, contend that other circumstances existed sufficient to put Hancock on notice that he was dealing with Burch in his capacity as officer of Deja Vu. . . .

Although Appellants briefly acknowledge the authority on agency . . . Appellants ask that we disregard such authority and consider their contention that:

> *Additionally, public policy concerns in this area exist. The law in Texas in the new millennium cannot allow people dealing with large businesses with assumed names, multiple employees, etc. to feign ignorance of corporate existence. If everyone who has a corporation must, from the top officer down, always remind those they are dealing with that "you are ordering your hamburger and french fries from the McDonalds Corporation or from Joe's Hamburgers[,] Inc. or "your dry cleaning will be done by XYZ(,) Inc. d.b.a. Main Cleaners," to guarantee that if something goes wrong with the transaction personal liability doesn't exist, business and commerce will be disrupted. Any principle of general agency to the contrary is far outdated and the law "must be consistent with the conditions and circumstances of our people."*

We do not agree with the supposition that large businesses with assumed names, multiple employees and the like invariably adopt the corporate form. Texas has a variety of legal protections for entities, which vary from the traditional corporate model, and which, like the corporate model, are available for entities both large and small. Furthermore, agency law is alive and well in Texas and is an important part of our jurisprudence. Appellant's contention that disclosure of the corporate form has become impractical and antiquated in the modern age is not supported by relevant authority and is insufficient to discharge Appellants' burden.

Having reviewed the record, we conclude that there was legally sufficient evidence that Hancock lacked actual knowledge that Burch was contracting as a representative of Deja Vu. Further, given the fact that it is undisputed that only Burch and Hancock were present during the negotiations of the stump-grinding agreement, and given the fact that Burch offered no testimony indicating that he represented to Hancock that he was acting on behalf of Deja Vu, we conclude that the record does not uncover any great weight of evidence contradicting the finding made by the trial court in this case, nor does the verdict otherwise shock the conscience of this Court. Appellants' issues one, two and three are overruled.

[Judgment affirmed]

Questions

1. Was Deja Vu, Inc. a partially disclosed principal?
2. Did Burch have an obligation to notify Hancock that he was acting in a representative capacity and identify the name of the principal?
3. Is the defendant correct in asserting that in this day and age state law cannot allow people like Mr. Hancock, dealing with large businesses with assumed names and multiple employees, to feign ignorance of corporate existence?

4. Assumption of Liability

Agents may intentionally make themselves liable on contracts with third persons.[4] This situation frequently occurs when the agent is a well-established local brokerage house or other agency and when the principal is located out of town and is not known locally.

In some situations, the agent makes a contract that will be personally binding. If the principal is not disclosed, the agent is necessarily the other contracting party and is bound by the contract. Even when the principal is disclosed, the agent may be personally bound if it was the intention of the parties that the agent assume a personal obligation even though this was done to further the principal's business. To illustrate, an attorney who hires an expert witness to testify on behalf of a client is an agent acting on behalf of a disclosed principal and is not personally liable for an expert witness fee.

However, when an expert witness asks the attorney about payment and the attorney states, "Don't worry, I will take care of it," the attorney (agent) has assumed a personal obligation and is liable for the fee.[5]

5. Execution of Contract

A simple contract that would appear to be the contract of the agent can be shown by other evidence, if believed, to have been intended as a contract between the principal and the third party.

[4] *Fairchild Publications v Rosston*, 584 NYS2d 389 (NY County Sup 1992).

[5] *Boros v Carter*, 537 So 2d 1134 (Fla App 1989).

The *Walton* case raised the question of whether a daughter was responsible for her mother's unpaid medical bills because she had signed nursing home admission papers.

To avoid any question of interpretation, an agent should execute an instrument by signing the principal's name and either *by* or *per* and the agent's name. **For Example,** if Jane R. Craig is an agent for B. G. Gray,

WALTON V MARINER HEALTH, 894 A2D 584 (MD 2006)

IF YOU SIGN AS AN AGENT, YOU DON'T HAVE TO PAY

Audrey Walton was transferred from a hospital to Mariner Health Nursing Home on January 26, 2001. Her daughter, Patricia Walton signed a thirty page document entitled "Resident's Agent Financial Agreement." Patricia indicated in that agreement that the only method of payment would be Medicare or Medical Assistance. Medicare assistance stopped in February 2001. On January 10, 2003 Mariner Health sued both Audrey and Patricia for unpaid monthly bills amounting to $86,235. From a judgment for Mariner Health against both the patient and her daughter, Patricia appealed.

Judicial Opinion

GREENE, J. . . If the contract is to benefit the principal only, the agent is immune from personal liability for breach of that contract. ("It is also a universal principle of the law of agency that the powers of the agent are to be exercised for the benefit of the principal only, and not for the agent or third parties."); ("It is a well settled principle of agency law that an agent acting within the scope of his authority for a disclosed principal is not bound on a contract made in the principal's name."). . . .

Patricia, as an agent, had a primary duty to Audrey, the principal, and Patricia's duty to Mariner Health, a third party, was limited. Agency law precludes a finding against Patricia for damages. As an agent, Patricia entered into the contract only for the benefit of Audrey and is personally insulated from liability by virtue of her station as an agent. . . .

In 1988, the General Assembly passed House Bill 683 which amended § 19–344 of the Health–General Article and prescribed in subsection 19–344(c) the rights and responsibilities of an "agent." The legislature intended to limit an agent's personal liability. That intent was evidenced by the bill summary, which states: ". . . the legislative rationale for the amendment was that the circumstances surrounding admission to a nursing home are highly stressful for applicants and their families. Most people are not in a position to carefully read and negotiate a contract at this time. It is vital that the contracts be screened to assure that they conform to existing law and are clear and understandable. . . ."

Supra at 2.

In summary, an agent's responsibility is limited to the administration and management of the resident's funds. An agent is not personally liable for the resident's nursing home care costs, unless the agent, voluntarily and knowingly agrees to pay for the resident's care with the agent's own funds. . . .

Questions

1. What defense did Patricia Walton raise in the lawsuit against her by the nursing home for payment of her mother's nursing home bills?
2. How did the court decide this case?
3. Speculate on why the state enacted a Nursing Home Bill of Rights Law.

ETHICS & THE LAW

Some time ago, dairy farmers owned large tracts of land in south Tempe, Arizona. The farmers used the land for grazing animals. Economic growth in this suburb of Phoenix was limited because of the state's inability at that time to attract large businesses to the area for relocation or location of new facilities.

In 1973, three farmers who owned adjoining parcels of land in the south Tempe area were approached by a local real estate agent with an

ETHICS & THE LAW

continued

offer for the purchase of their property. The amount of the offer was approximately 10 percent above the property's appraised value. The three farmers discussed the offer and concluded that with their need to retire, it was best to accept the offer and sell the land. All three signed contracts for the sale of their land.

After the contracts were entered into but before the transactions had closed, the three farmers learned that the land was being purchased by a real estate development firm from southern California. The development firm had planned, and would be proposing to the Tempe City Council, a residential community, the Lakes. The Lakes would consist of upper-end homes in a community laced with parks, lakes, and ponds, with each house in the developed area backing up to its own dock and water recreation. The development firm had begun the project because it had learned of the plans of American Express, Rubbermaid, and Dial to locate major facilities in the Phoenix area.

The three farmers objected to the sale of their land when they learned the identity of the buyer. "If we had known who was coming in here and why, we never would have sold for such a low price." Were the farmers' contracts binding?

Is it ethical to use the strategy of an undisclosed principal? What is the role of an agent in a situation in which the third party is making a decision not as beneficial to him or her as it could or should be? Can the agent say anything?

Craig should execute instruments by signing either "B. G. Gray, by Jane R. Craig" or "B. G. Gray, per Jane R. Craig." Such a signing is in law a signing by Gray, and the agent is therefore not a party to the contract. The signing of the principal's name by an authorized agent without indicating the agent's name or identity is likewise in law the signature of the principal.

If the instrument is ambiguous as to whether the agent has signed in a representative or an individual capacity, parol evidence is admissible as between the original parties to the transaction for establishing the character in which the agent was acting.

6. Torts and Crimes

Agents are liable for harm caused third persons by the agents' fraudulent, intentional, or negligent acts.[6] The fact that persons were acting as agents at the time or that they acted in good faith under the directions of a principal does not relieve them of liability if their conduct would impose liability on them when acting for themselves.

If an agent commits a crime, such as stealing from a third person or shooting a third person, the agent is liable for the crime without regard to the fact of acting as an agent. The agent is liable without regard to whether the agent acted in self-interest or sought to advance the interest of the principal.

B. Liability of Principal to Third Person

The principal is liable to the third person for the properly authorized and executed contracts of the agent and, in certain circumstances, for the agent's unauthorized contracts.

7. Agent's Contracts

The liability of a principal to a third person on a contract made by an agent depends on the extent of disclosure of the principal and the form of the contract that is executed.

CPA (a) Simple Contract with Principal Disclosed

When a disclosed principal with contractual capacity authorizes or ratifies an agent's transaction with a third person and when the agent properly executes a contract with the third person, a binding contract exists between the principal and the third person. The principal and the third person may each sue the other in the event of a breach of the contract. The

[6] *Mannish v Lacayo*, 496 So 2d 242 (Fla App 1986).

agent is not a party to the contract, is not liable for its performance, and cannot sue for its breach.[7]

The liability of a disclosed principal to a third person is not discharged by the fact that the principal gives the agent money with which to pay the third person. Consequently, the liability of a buyer for the purchase price of goods is not terminated by the fact that the buyer gave the buyer's agent the purchase price to remit to the seller.

(b) Simple Contract with Principal Partially Disclosed

A partially disclosed principal is liable for a simple contract made by an authorized agent. The third person may recover from either the agent or the principal.

(c) Simple Contract with Principal Undisclosed

An undisclosed principal is liable for a simple contract made by an authorized agent. Although the third person initially contracted with the agent alone, the third person, on learning of the existence of the undisclosed principal, may sue that principal.[8] In most jurisdictions, third persons can sue and collect judgments from the agent, the principal, or both until the judgment is fully satisfied (joint and several liability).[9]

8. Payment to Agent

When the third person makes payment to an authorized agent, the payment is deemed made to the principal. Even if the agent never remits or delivers the payment to the principal, the principal must give the third person full credit for the payment so long as the third person made the payment in good faith and had no reason to know that the agent would be guilty of misconduct.[10]

Because apparent authority has the same legal effect as actual authority, a payment made to a person with apparent authority to receive the payment is deemed a payment to the apparent principal.

When a debtor makes payment to a person who is not the actual or apparent agent of the creditor, such a payment does not discharge the debt unless that person in fact pays the money to the creditor.

9. Agent's Statements

A principal is bound by a statement made by an agent while transacting business within the scope of authority. This means that the principal cannot later contradict the statement of the agent and show that it is not true. Statements or declarations of an agent, in order to bind the principal, must be made at the time of performing the act to which they relate or shortly thereafter.

10. Agent's Knowledge

The principal is bound by knowledge or notice of any fact that is acquired by an agent while acting within the scope of actual or apparent authority. When a fact is known to the agent of the seller, the sale is deemed made by the seller with knowledge of that fact.

The rule that the agent's knowledge is imputed to the principal is extended in some cases to knowledge gained prior to the creation of the agency relationship. The notice and knowledge in any case must be based on reliable information. Thus, when the agent hears only rumors, the principal is not charged with notice.

If the subject matter is outside the scope of the agent's authority, the agent is under no duty to inform the principal of the knowledge, and the principal is not bound by it. The principal is not charged with knowledge of an agent when (1) the agent is acting adversely to the principal's interest or (2) the third party acts in collusion with the agent for the purpose of cheating the principal.

C. Liability of Principal for Torts and Crimes of Agent

Under certain circumstances, the principal may be liable for the torts or crimes of the agent or the employee.

CPA 11. Vicarious Liability for Torts and Crimes

Assume that an agent or an employee causes harm to a third person. Is the principal or the employer liable for this conduct? If the conduct constitutes a crime, can the principal or the employer be criminally prosecuted? The answer is that in many instances, the principal or the employer is liable civilly and may

[7] *Levy v Gold & Co., Inc.*, 529 NYS2d 133 (App Div 1988).

[8] *McDaniel v Hensons, Inc.*, 493 SE2d 529 (Ga App 1997).

[9] *Crown Controls, Inc. v Smiley*, 756 P2d 717 (Wash 1988).

[10] This general rule of law is restated in some states by Section 2 of the Uniform Fiduciaries Act, which is expressly extended by Section 1 of the act to agents, partners, and corporate officers. Similar statutory provisions are found in a number of other states.

also be prosecuted criminally. That is, the principal or the employer is liable although personally free from fault and not guilty of any wrong. This concept of imposing liability for the fault of another is known as **vicarious liability.**

This situation arises both when an employer's employee or a principal's agent commits the wrong. The rules of law governing the vicarious liability of the principal and the employer are the same. In the interest of simplicity, this section is stated in terms of employees acting in the course of employment. Remember that these rules are equally applicable to agents acting within the scope of their authority. As a practical matter, some situations will arise only with agents. **For Example,** the vicarious liability of a seller for the misrepresentations made by a salesperson arise only when the seller appointed an agent to sell. In contrast, both the employee hired to drive a truck and an agent driving to visit a customer could negligently injure a third person with their vehicles. In many situations, a person employed by another is both an employee and an agent, and the tort is committed within the phase of "employee work."

The rule of law imposing vicarious liability on an innocent employer for the wrong of an employee is also known as the doctrine of ***respondeat superior***. In modern times, this doctrine can be justified on the grounds that the business should pay for the harm caused in the doing of the business, that the employer will be more careful in the selection of employees if made responsible for their actions, and that the employer may obtain liability insurance to protect against claims of third persons.

(a) Nature of Act

The wrongful act committed by an employee may be a negligent act, an intentional act, a fraudulent act, or a violation of a government regulation. It may give rise only to civil liability of the employer, or it may also subject the employer to prosecution for crime.

(1) Negligent Act. Historically, the act for which liability would be imposed under the doctrine of *respondeat superior* was a negligent act committed within the scope of employment.

(2) Intentional Act. Under the common law, a master was not liable for an intentional tort committed by a servant. The modern law holds that an employer is liable for an intentional tort committed by an employee for the purpose of furthering the employer's business.[11] **For Example,** Crane Brothers, Inc., drilled a well for Stephen May. When May did not pay his bill, two Crane Brothers' employees went to May's workplace, and an altercation ensued in which May was injured. Crane Brothers, Inc., was held vicariously liable for the torts of the employees, not because the employer itself committed the wrongful acts but because it was answerable for the manner in which its agents, the two employees, conducted themselves in doing the business of the employer.[12]

(3) Fraud. Modern decisions hold the employer liable for fraudulent acts or misrepresentations. The rule is commonly applied to a principal-agent relationship. To illustrate, when an agent makes fraudulent statements in selling stock, the principal is liable for the buyer's loss. In states that follow the common law rule of no liability for intentional torts, the principal is not liable for the agent's fraud when the principal did not authorize or know of the agent's fraud.

(4) Government Regulation. The employer may be liable because of the employee's violation of a government regulation. These regulations are most common in the areas of business and of protection of the environment. In such cases, the employer may be held liable for a penalty imposed by the government. In some cases, the breach of the regulation will impose liability on the employer in favor of a third person who is injured as a consequence of the violation.

(b) Course of Employment

The mere fact that a tort or crime is committed by an employee does not necessarily impose vicarious liability on the employer. It must also be shown that the individual was acting within the scope of authority if an agent or in the course of employment if an employee. If an employee was not acting within the scope of employment, there is no vicarious liability.[13] **For Example,** after Rev. Joel Thomford accidentally shot and killed his parishioner during a deer hunting trip, the parishioner's wife brought a wrongful death action against the pastor and the church. Because the

[11] *Restatement (Second) of Agency* § 231.

[12] *Crane Brothers, Inc. v May*, 556 SE2d 865 (Ga App 2001).

[13] *Young v Taylor-White LLC*, 181 SW2d 324 (Tenn 2005).

accident occurred on the pastor's day off and the trip was not sponsored by the church, the pastor was not acting within the course of his employment at the time of the accident, and the church was not liable.[14]

The *Studebaker* case raised questions of whether the tortfeasor was an employee of the defendant and had acted in furthering the employer's business.

STUDEBAKER V NETTIE'S FLOWER GARDEN, 842 SW2D 227 (MO CT APP 1992)

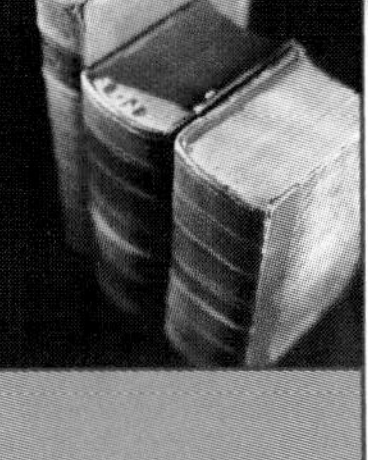

HE WAS BACK TO NETTIE'S BUSINESS WHEN HE HIT THE STUDEBAKER

Judith Studebaker was injured when a van driven by James Ferry collided with her vehicle. She brought an action against Nettie's Flower Garden, Inc. (Nettie's), under a *respondeat superior* theory in the belief that Ferry was Nettie's employee at the time of the accident. Nettie's maintained that Ferry was an independent contractor, not an employee. From a judgment in favor of Studebaker for $125,000, Nettie's appealed.

Judicial Opinion

CRANDALL, P. J. . . . Ferry delivered flowers for Nettie's from its main shop on Grand Avenue in the City of St. Louis. Ferry was paid, not by the hour, but at a rate of $2.50 to $3.00 per delivery. If there were no deliveries, he was not paid. He delivered only in an area of St. Louis which Nettie's designated as his territory. Nettie's required him to make two runs each day: one in the morning at 9:30 A.M.; one in the afternoon at 1:30 P.M. When he arrived at the shop, he set up his own route based upon the location of the deliveries in his area. He generally got to work at 8:00 A.M. to prepare for the morning run and at 12:00 P.M. to prepare for the afternoon run. Nettie's also required Ferry to stop by its shop in downtown St. Louis at St. Louis Centre before noon each day to pick up items which needed to be transported to the Grand Avenue shop. After this stop, Ferry proceeded to the Grand Avenue shop for his afternoon run. Nettie's paid Ferry $5.00 for this stop, whether or not there was anything for him to take to the Grand Avenue shop.

Ferry used his own van for the deliveries; Nettie's required that it be heated and airconditioned to protect the flowers and plants. Although he did not wear a uniform, Nettie's directed that Ferry be neat in appearance and that he conduct himself in a certain manner when on the job. If his behavior or appearance fell below its standards, Nettie's reprimanded Ferry. Ferry paid his own expenses and received no fringe benefits from Nettie's.

On August 9, 1989, the date of the accident in question, Ferry made his morning run and then his mid-day stop at the downtown shop at about 11:00 A.M. There was nothing for him to transport to the Grand Avenue shop. After Ferry left the downtown shop, he stopped at a pawn shop to conduct personal business. He then proceeded to the Grand Avenue shop to prepare for his afternoon run. On the way to the Grand Avenue shop, at approximately 11:45 A.M., Ferry's van collided with plaintiff's automobile. . . .

Under the doctrine of respondeat superior an employer is liable for those negligent acts or omissions of his employee which are committed within the scope of his employment. . . . Liability based on respondeat superior requires some evidence that a master-servant relationship existed between the parties. . . . The test to determine if respondeat superior applies to a tort is whether the person sought to be charged as master had the right or power to control and direct the physical conduct of the other in the performance of the act. . . . If there was no right to control there is no liability; for those rendering services but retaining control over their own movements are not servants. . . . The master-servant relationship arises when the person charged as master has the right to direct the method by which the master's service is performed. . . . An additional inquiry is whether the person sought to be charged as the servant was engaged in the prosecution of his master's business and not simply whether the accident occurred during the time of employment. . . . Whether a party is liable under the doctrine of respondeat superior depends on the facts and circumstances in evidence in each particular case and no single test is conclusive of the issue of the party's interest in the activity and his right of control. . . .

Nettie's first asserts that, when the accident in question occurred, Ferry was not driving his vehicle to serve Nettie's business interests. It argues that Ferry was on his own time, conducting his own business. . . .

[14] *Hentges v Thomford*, 569 NW2d 424 (Minn App 1997).

Ferry's slight detour prior to the accident to conduct personal business did not mean that he was using his van exclusively for his independent purposes.... The object of Ferry's trip was not just to go to the pawn shop. At the time of the accident, Ferry was doing Nettie's business because he was returning to the Grand Avenue shop after making his routine mid-day stop at the downtown shop. This stop was so encompassed within his daily routine that it would be difficult to segregate it from his morning and afternoon runs.

There was sufficient evidence for the jury to determine that at the time of the accident, Ferry was engaged primarily in advancing the business interests of Nettie's and thus was acting within the scope of his employment. Nettie's first point is denied.

Nettie's further contends that there was no substantial evidence that Nettie's controlled or had the right to control Ferry at the time of the collision. Whether or not the right of control existed in a particular case is ordinarily a question of fact for the jury....

In the instant action, Ferry furnished his own means of transportation; but it was mandatory that he have a vehicle to carry out his job responsibilities. Nettie's required that his vehicle be equipped with heating and airconditioning systems. Nettie's also set standards for Ferry's dress and conduct while he was on the job, and monitored his compliance with these standards. In addition, although Ferry mapped out his own route to deliver the flowers, Nettie's gave him the list of customers and determined his territory. Nettie's directed Ferry to make the mid-day stop at its downtown shop on a daily basis and paid him for that stop. Ferry incorporated that stop into his route. The stop usually occurred after his morning run and prior to his return trip to the Grand Avenue shop for his afternoon run. In addition, Nettie's always paid him for this stop, whether or not he transported anything. There was substantial evidence from which a jury reasonably could have found that, at the time of the accident in question, Nettie's either controlled or had the right to control the manner in which Ferry performed the duties for which he was employed. Nettie's second point is denied.

[Judgment affirmed]

Questions

1. Did Nettie's control or have the right to control Ferry at the time of the collision?
2. Is not the fact that Ferry, just prior to the accident, had gone to a pawn shop compelling evidence he was using his van exclusively for his independent purposes and was not acting within the course of his employer's business?
3. Review the ethical principles set forth in Chapter 3 and give your opinion of the ethics of businesses converting employees to independent contractors to reduce or eliminate costs, such as health and retirement benefits, overtime, and maintenance and proper insurance of motor vehicles.

(c) Employee of the United States

The Federal Tort Claims Act (FTCA) declares that the United States shall be liable vicariously whenever a federal employee driving a motor vehicle in the course of employment causes harm under such circumstances that a private employer would be liable. Contrary to the general rule, the statute exempts the employee driver from liability.[15]

12. Negligent Hiring and Retention of Employees

In addition to a complaint against the employer based on the doctrine of *respondeat superior*, a lawsuit may often raise a second theory, that of negligent hiring or retention of an employee.[16] Unlike the *respondeat superior* theory by which the employer may be vicariously liable for the tort of an employee, the negligent hiring theory is based on the negligence of the employer in the hiring process. Under the *respondeat superior* rule, the employer is liable only for those torts committed within the scope of employment or in the furtherance of the employer's interests. The negligent hiring theory has been used to impose liability in cases when an employee commits an intentional tort, almost invariably outside the scope of employment, against a customer or the general public, and the employer knew or should have known that the employee was incompetent, violent, dangerous, or criminal.[17]

(a) Need for Due Care in Hiring

An employer may be liable on a theory of negligent hiring when it is shown that the employer knew, or in the exercise of ordinary care should have known, that the job applicant would create an undue risk of harm to others in carrying out job responsibilities. Moreover, it

[15] Claims of negligent hiring are not permissible under the FTCA. See *Tonelli v United States*, 60 F3d 492 (8th Cir 1995).
[16] *Medina v Graham's Cowboys, Inc.*, 827 P2d 859 (NM App 1992).
[17] *Rockwell v Sun Harbor Budget Suites*, 925 P2d 1175 (Nev 1996).

FIGURE 38-1 Liability for Torts of Agent or Employee

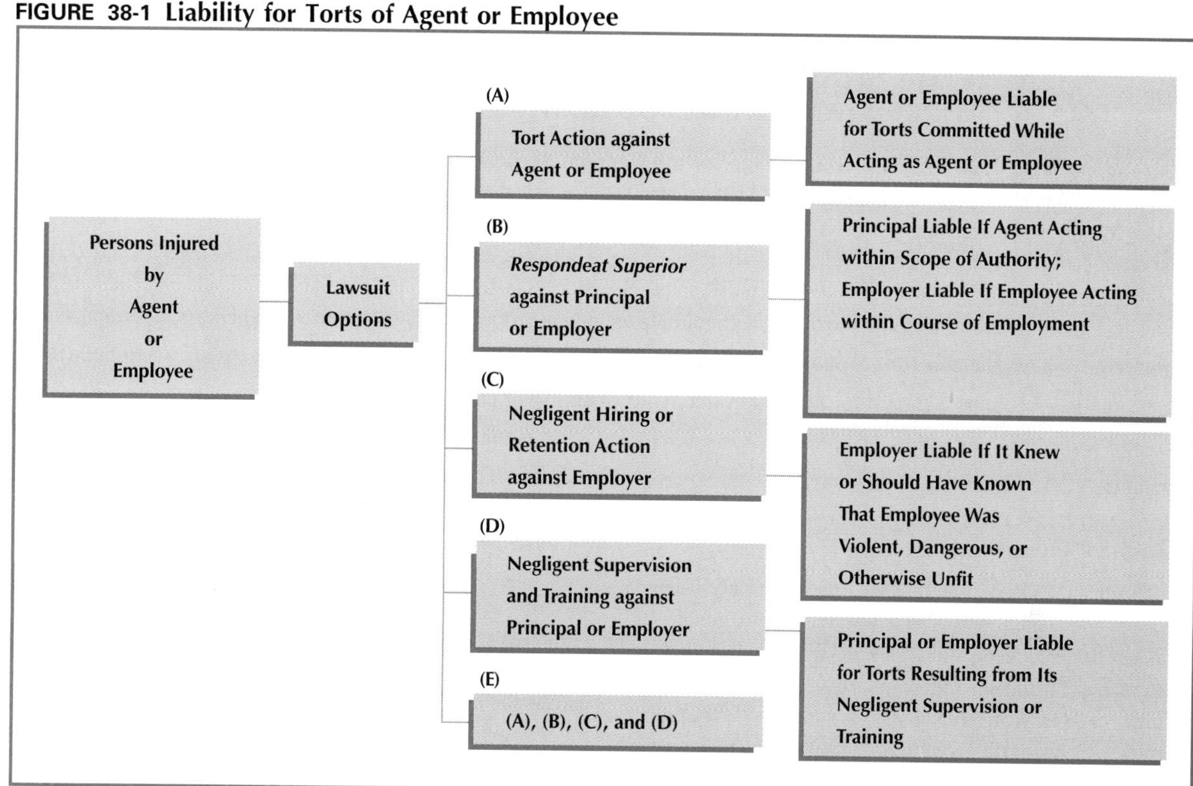

must also be shown that the employer could have reasonably foreseen injury to the third party. Thus, an employer who knows of an employee's preemployment drinking problems and violent behavior may be liable to customers assaulted by that employee.

Employers might protect themselves from liability in a negligent hiring case by having each prospective employee fill out an employment application form and then checking into the applicant's work experience, background, character, and qualifications. This would be evidence of due care in hiring. Generally, the scope of a preemployment investigation should correlate to the degree of opportunity the prospective employee would have to do harm to third persons. A minimum investigation consisting of filling out an application form and conducting a personal interview would be satisfactory for hiring an outside maintenance person, but a full background inquiry would be necessary for hiring a security guard. However, such inquiry does not bar *respondeat superior* liability.

(b) Employees with Criminal Records

The hiring of an individual with a criminal record does not by itself establish the tort of negligent hiring.[18] An employer who knows that an applicant has a criminal record has a duty to investigate to determine whether the nature of the conviction in relationship to the job to be performed creates an unacceptable risk to third persons.

(c) Negligent Retention

Courts assign liability under negligent retention on a basis similar to that of negligent hiring. That is, the employer knew, or should have known, that the employee would create an undue risk of harm to others in carrying out job responsibilities.

A hospital is liable for negligent retention when it continues the staff privileges of a physician that it knew or should have known had sexually assaulted a female patient in the past.[19]

The *Bryant v Livigni* case involves *respondeat superior* liability as well as negligent retention liability.

[18] *Connes v Molalla Transportation Systems*, 831 P2d 1316 (Colo 1992).

[19] *Capithorne v Framingham Union Hospital*, 520 NE2d 139 (Mass 1988); see also *Sparks Regional Medical Center v Smith*, 976 SW2d 396 (Ark App 1998), in which the hospital was found negligent in supervising an employee following a report that the employee had abused other psychiatric patients.

BRYANT V LIVIGNI, 619 NE2D 550 (ILL APP CT 1993)

(1) ALCOHOL, (2) BATTERY, AND (3) NEGLIGENT RETENTION: THREE STRIKES AND YOU'RE OUT!

Mark Livigni was manager of the National Super Markets, Inc., store in Cahokia, Illinois. After drinking alcoholic beverages one evening, he stopped by the store to check the premises when he observed a 10-year-old boy's unacceptable behavior outside the store. Livigni chased the boy to a car, where he pulled another child, a four-year-old named Farris Bryant, from the car and threw him through the air. A multicount lawsuit was brought against National and Livigni. A verdict was rendered against National for $20,000 under a *respondeat superior* theory of the battery of Farris Bryant. A verdict was also rendered against National for $15,000 in negligent retention of Livigni and for $115,000 punitive damages for willful and wanton retention. National appealed the trial court's denial of its motions for directed verdicts on these counts.

Judicial Opinion

MAAG, J.... On March 18, 1987, while off duty, Livigni stopped by the Cahokia National store. As manager, he was authorized to check and supervise the operation of the store even during off-duty hours. He was intoxicated at the time of this visit, which was a violation of National rules.... Livigni observed a young man urinating on the store wall outside the east exit doors. He hollered at the young man and followed the fleeing youth to the parked vehicle of Diana Bryant.

Livigni pulled four-year-old Farris Bryant from the automobile,... throwing the child through the air.

Farris was taken to Centreville Township Hospital's emergency room for medical treatment. Farris was admitted to the hospital and was released after four days. He was released from all medical treatment approximately one month after the battery....

At trial, Livigni's supervisor testified that during Livigni's 17-year tenure with National, Livigni had been a good employee. This supervisor never received any reports from customers or employees that Livigni had "violent-related" problems, although he was aware of a report that Livigni threw an empty milk crate which struck a coworker.

Evidence was offered of two batteries committed by Livigni prior to his attack of Farris. In 1980, Livigni had a disagreement with a subordinate employee resulting in Livigni throwing an empty milk crate at the employee striking him on the arm and necessitating medical treatment. At the time of this battery, Livigni was an assistant store manager. A workers' compensation claim was filed against National by the injured employee. A short time after the workers' compensation claim was resolved, Livigni was promoted to store manager by National in spite of this incident.

The second battery occurred in 1985 when Livigni, while disciplining his 13-year-old son, threw the boy into a bed causing the boy to sustain a broken collar bone. In June 1986 Livigni pleaded guilty to aggravated battery to a child and was sentenced to two years' probation. He was still on probation at the time he attacked Farris.

Livigni testified at trial that he had not told any of his supervisors at National about the battery of his son. He admitted to telling employees of equal or lesser positions than himself about the battery. He considered these people to be his friends....

According to National, there was no evidence that it knew or had reason to know that Livigni was anything other than "an excellent store manager, fit for his position." To support this argument, National claims that there was conflicting evidence regarding the 1980 incident where Livigni threw a milk crate at a coworker causing injury. It argues that the 1980 incident was of uncertain origin since differing versions of the incident and its cause were presented in the evidence. It asserts that due to this conflicting evidence the incident could not form the basis for a negligent retention claim....

Rather than disciplining Livigni after he injured a subordinate employee in an unprovoked attack, National promoted him following the resolution of the injured employee's workers' compensation claim.

National further argues that it had no knowledge of the incident involving Livigni's son that resulted in Livigni's felony conviction for aggravated battery of a child. Relying upon *Campen v Executive House Hotel, Inc.* (1982), 105 Ill. App.3d 576, 61 Ill.Dec. 358, National points to the general rule which states that to impute knowledge of this occurrence to National a showing was required that an agent or employee of National had notice or knowledge of the incident and that the knowledge concerned a matter within the scope of the agent's authority. According to National, evidence of such knowledge was lacking. . . .

National first admits that Livigni told employees of equal or lesser rank within the corporation about the battery involving his son. However, it claims that this is insufficient notice to the corporation. It argues that the people Livigni told were his "friends" and that as mere "coworkers" of equal or subordinate position no notice could legally be imputed to National. We disagree. . . .

. . . Viewing the evidence in the light most favorable to the plaintiff (Pedrick), we believe that a reasonable jury could have concluded that the information concerning the battery of Livigni's son, learned by these coworkers, was within the scope of their authority to act upon. Whether reported to higher authorities or not, the information still constitutes "corporate knowledge." (*Campen*, 105 Ill. App.3d at 586.) In such a case, their knowledge is chargeable to National. . . .

We conclude that the circuit court did not err in denying National's motion for a directed verdict, nor did it err in refusing to grant a judgment *n.o.v.* on plaintiff's claim of negligent retention. Viewing the evidence in the light most favorable to the plaintiff, we cannot state that the evidence so overwhelmingly favored National that this verdict cannot stand.

National next claims that the circuit court should have directed a verdict in its favor or granted a judgment *n.o.v.* on the plaintiff's punitive damages claim. This count alleged that National's retention of Mark Livigni as a management employee constituted willful and wanton misconduct. . . .

The Restatement (Second) of Torts, section 909, at 467 (1977) provides:

"*Punitive damages can properly be awarded against a master or other principal because of an act by an agent if, but only if,*

* * * * * *

*(b) the agent was unfit and the principal or a managerial agent was reckless in * * * retaining him.*"

This count did not seek to impose liability upon the defendant vicariously. Rather, the plaintiff's cause of action alleged wrongful conduct on the part of National itself. Section 909(b) of the Restatement (Second) of Torts speaks directly to the issue under discussion. So too does the case of *Easley v Apollo Detective Agency, Inc.* (1979), 69 Ill.App.3d 920.

Easley recognized that it is settled law that a cause of action exists in Illinois for negligent hiring of an employee, and that if the defendant's conduct could properly be characterized as willful and wanton then punitive damages are recoverable. We see little difference between a punitive damages claim for willfully and wantonly hiring an employee in the first instance and a claim for willfully and wantonly retaining an unfit employee after hiring. In both instances, the interest to be protected is the same. Employers that wrongfully (whether negligently or willfully and wantonly) hire or retain unfit employees expose the public to the acts of these employees. In such cases it is not unreasonable to hold the employer accountable when the employee causes injury or damage to another. The principle at issue is not *respondeat superior*, although that may also be implicated. Rather, the cause of action is premised upon the wrongful conduct of the employer itself. . . .

The jury heard evidence that Livigni attacked a fellow employee in 1980 and was then promoted. He injured his own son, he was convicted of aggravated battery in a criminal proceeding, and members of National's management admittedly knew of that incident. National took no action. Then while a store manager, in an intoxicated state, he attacked a four-year-old child and threw him through the air, resulting in hospitalization. National itself characterizes this attack on young Farris as outrageous. We cannot say the jury was unjustified in concluding the same and also concluding that retaining this man as a managerial employee constituted willful and wanton misconduct. . . .

Finally, National asks that a judgment *n.o.v.* be entered in its favor on the plaintiffs' *respondeat superior* claims. . . .

In order to impose liability upon National, it was not necessary that Livigni be motivated *solely* by a desire to further National's interest. It is sufficient if his actions were prompted only *in part* by a purpose to protect store property or further the employers' business. (*Wilson v Clark Oil & Refining Corp.* (1985), 134 Ill.App.3d 1084, 1089.) The evidence was sufficient to justify such a conclusion by the jury.

Finally, the actions of Livigni in attacking Farris were committed within the constraints of the authorized time and location of his employment, thus bolstering a finding that the battery occurred within the course and scope of his employment. *Sunseri v Puccia* (1981), 97 Ill. App.3d 488. . . .

[Judgment affirmed]

J. WELCH, concurring in part and dissenting in part . . . I concur with the majority's opinion with respect to, and would affirm the judgment of the circuit court on the jury verdict against National Food Stores on, the *respondeat superior* counts of plaintiffs' complaint. With respect to the majority's opinion concerning the judgment against National on the negligent and willful and wanton retention counts of plaintiffs' complaint, however, I must respectfully dissent....

From a practical standpoint, the majority's opinion sends a message to all employers that in order to insulate themselves from liability for negligent or willful and wanton retention any employee who has ever had an altercation on or off the workplace premises must be fired. Moreover, the majority opinion places an unreasonable investigative burden upon the employer by forcing the employer to discover, retain, and analyze the criminal records of its employees. Is not the majority's opinion then at cross-purposes with the established public policy and laws of Illinois protecting the privacy of citizens and promoting the education and rehabilitation of criminal offenders? See Ill.Rev.Stat.1991, ch. 68, par. 2-103 (making it a civil rights violation to ask a job applicant about an arrest record); see also Ill.Rev.Stat.1991, ch. 38, par. 1003-12-1 *et seq.* (concerning correctional employment programs whose function is to teach marketable skills and work habits and responsibility to Illinois prisoners).

I would have granted defendant National Food Stores' motion for judgment *non obstante veredicto*....

Questions

1. Was there *respondeat superior* liability in this case?
2. Should National have reasonably known about Livigni's violence-related problems? If so, did it act negligently in retaining him as an employee?
3. From Judge Welch's dissent, will the *Livigni* case hurt the employment prospects of other individuals who have criminal records involving violence?

13. Negligent Supervision and Training

A separate theory of liability in addition to the doctrine of *respondeat superior* is that of negligent supervision and training, that holds the principal directly liable for its negligence in regard to training and supervision of its employees and agents. **For Example,** Monadnock Training Council, Inc., certified Robert Hebert as an "authorized Monadnock instructor" and granted him actual authority to market and promote its PR-24 police baton. In a training session run by Hebert at the Chesire County House of Corrections in New Hampshire, Charles Herman suffered severe head trauma when training with Hebert without protective headgear in a room with unpadded cement walls. Monadnock was held directly liable for Herman's injuries based on its negligent supervision and training of Hebert.[20]

14. Agent's Crimes

A principal is liable for the crimes of an agent committed at the principal's direction. When not authorized, however, the principal is ordinarily not liable for an agent's crime merely because it was committed while the agent was otherwise acting within the scope of the latter's authority or employment. **For Example,** the owner of the Main Tower Cafe in Hartford, Connecticut, was not vicariously liable for injuries sustained by a patron who was shot by a bouncer while attempting to enter the bar because the bouncer's intentional and willful act was motivated by his own spleen and malevolence against the victim in clear departure from his employment.[21] As an exception to the rule of nonliability just stated, courts now hold an employer criminally liable when the employee has in the course of employment violated environmental protection laws, liquor sales laws, pure food laws, or laws regulating prices or prohibiting false weights. **For Example,** an employer may be held criminally responsible for an employee's sale of liquor to a minor in violation of the liquor law even though the sale was not known to the employer and violated instructions given to the employee.

15. Owner's Liability for Acts of an Independent Contractor

If work is done by an independent contractor rather than by an employee, the owner is not liable for harm caused by the contractor to third persons or their property. Likewise, the owner is not bound by the contracts made by the independent contractor. The owner is ordinarily not liable for harm caused to third persons by the negligence of the employees of the independent contractor.[22]

20 *Herman v Monadnock PR-24 Training Council, Inc.*, 2002 NH LEXIS 78.

21 *Pruitt v Main & Tower, Inc.*, 2002 WL 532467 (Conn Super 2002); see also *Tanks v Lockheed Martin Corp.*, 417 F3d 456 (5th Cir 2005).

22 *King v Lens Creek, Ltd., Partnership*, 483 SE2d 265 (W Va 1996).

(a) Exceptions to Owner's Immunity

There is a trend toward imposing liability on the owner when work undertaken by an independent contractor is inherently dangerous.[23] That is, the law is taking the position that if the owner wishes to engage in a particular activity, the owner must be responsible for the harm it causes. The owner cannot be insulated from such liability by the device of hiring an independent contractor to do the work.

Regardless of the nature of the activity, the owner may be liable for the torts and contracts of the independent contractor when the owner controls the conduct of the independent contractor.

In the *Haag* case, the owners believed that they should not be held liable for the injury of an attendee at an auction because the auctioneers were independent contractors and the assistants were servants of the auctioneers.

HAAG V BONGERS, 589 NW2D 318 (NEB 1999)

RETAINING CONTROL LED TO LIABILITY

Leo Bongers died intestate on October 8, 1992. Alfred Bongers and Delores Kuhl, Leo's nephew and niece, were appointed personal representatives of his estate. Leo left substantial real and personal property, including farms and more than 120 antique cars, trucks, and motorcycles. The Estate hired Bauer-Moravec to sell the vehicles at auction. Auctioneer Russ Moravec suggested that the vehicles be sold at an airstrip at an auction in May, June, or July 1993. The Estate rejected this recommendation and insisted that the sale be conducted on a farm owned by the Estate in January 1993. On January 30, 1993, the auction took place beginning at 9:30 A.M., with temperatures below freezing and some 800 people jammed into the bid barn. One auctioneer had purchased Putnam hitch balls to be used with mylar-type ropes so that small farm tractors could tow vehicles into and out of the bid barn. Doug Reznicek assisted the auctioneer in making arrangements to move vehicles. One hour into the auction, an attendee, Joseph Haag, was seriously injured when the hitch ball came loose from the drawbar of the tractor towing an antique Studebaker truck. Haag brought a multiple-count suit including an action against the Estate claiming that Baurer-Moravec was acting as an agent for the Estate and that its negligence in not properly attaching the hitch ball as well as using Mylar-type tow rope rather than chains should be imputed to the Estate under the doctrine of *respondent superior*. From a judgment for Haag, the Estate appealed.

Judicial Opinion

MILLER-LERMAN, J. . . . Generally, the employer of an independent contractor is not liable for physical harm caused to another by the acts or omissions of the contractor or his servants. *Kime v Hobbs*, 252 Neb. 407, 562 N.W.2d 705 (1997). There are two recognized exceptions to the general rule. The employer of an independent contractor may be vicariously liable to a third party (1) if the employer retains control over the contractor's work or (2) if, by rule of law or statute, the employer has a nondelegable duty to protect another from harm caused by the contractor. . . .

Based on the facts of this case, we conclude that the auctioneers served as independent contractors. However, the Estate exercised sufficient control over the auction to subject it to liability, notwithstanding the participation of the auctioneers as independent contractors. The factors which demonstrate the Estate's control include, but are not limited to, the following facts: The auction was held on the Estate's property, and the Estate insisted that the auction be conducted in winter rather than in summer in a more expansive setting. The Estate was responsible for putting the vehicles in running order but failed to do so, resulting in the necessity of towing the vehicles at the auction. The Estate approved the use of tractors to tow the vehicles at the auction. The Estate approved the use of assistants. The Estate paid the assistants. The Estate insisted that the auction be heavily advertised, resulting in a shoulder-to-shoulder crowd through which the vehicles were to be towed. The Estate and the auctioneers decided to extend the bid barn and charge a $25 fee. Bongers was present at the auction at the time of the accident.

[23] *Hinger v Parker & Parsley Petroleum Co.*, 902 P2d 1033 (NM App 1995).

Although actual performance of the task of towing the vehicles was to be performed by the independent contractor auctioneers, the facts in this case as to the Estate's active and considerable control over the activities that led to the accident are sufficient to subject the Estate to liability. In this regard, we note that the Restatement (Second) of Torts § 414 at 387 (1965) provides:

One who entrusts work to an independent contractor, but who retains the control of any part of the work, is subject to liability for physical harm to others for whose safety the employer owes a duty to exercise reasonable care, which is caused by his failure to exercise his control with reasonable care.

See, *Kime v Hobbs, supra; Parrish v Omaha Pub. Power Dist.*, 242 Neb. 783, 496 N.W.2d 902 (1993). We conclude that because the Estate retained considerable control over the relevant work, it is therefore liable for a failure to exercise reasonable care in the use of that control. Accordingly, imputing the negligence of the assistants to the Estate was justified by the facts.

[Affirmed]

Questions

1. Was the auctioneer an independent contractor under the facts of this case?
2. As a general rule, is an owner held legally responsible for injuries caused by the negligence of an independent contractor's employee?
3. By utilizing an independent contractor to perform the tasks involved in the selling of 120 antique vehicles at auction, did the Estate avoid liability for the plaintiff's injuries?

In certain circumstances, such as providing security for a business, collecting bills, and repossessing collateral, there is an increased risk that torts may be committed by the individuals performing such duties. The trend of the law is to refuse to allow the use of an independent contractor for such work to insulate the employer.

(b) Undisclosed Independent Contractor

In some situations, the owner appears to be doing the act in question because the existence of the independent contractor is not disclosed or apparent. This situation occurs most commonly when a franchisee does business under the name of the franchisor; when a concessionaire, such as a restaurant in a hotel, appears to be the hotel restaurant, although in fact it is operated by an independent concessionaire; or when the buyer of a business continues to run the business in the seller's name. In such cases of an undisclosed independent contractor, it is generally held that the apparent owner (that is, the franchisor, the grantor of the concession, or the seller) is liable for the torts and contracts of the undisclosed independent contractor.

16. Enforcement of Claim by Third Person

A lawsuit may be brought by a third person against the agent or the principal if each is liable. In most states and in the federal courts, the plaintiff may sue either or both in one action when both are liable. If both are sued, the plaintiff may obtain a judgment against both, although the plaintiff is allowed to collect the full amount of the judgment only once.

D. Transactions with Sales Personnel

Many transactions with sales personnel do not result in a contract with the third person with whom the salesperson deals.

17. Soliciting and Contracting Agents

Giving an order to a salesperson often does not give rise to a contract. Ordinarily, a salesperson is a **soliciting agent,** whose authority is limited to soliciting offers from third persons and transmitting them to the principal for acceptance or rejection. Such an agent does not have authority to make a contract that will bind the principal to the third person. The employer of the salesperson is not bound by a contract until the employer accepts the order, and the third person (customer) may withdraw the offer at any time prior to acceptance.

In contrast, if the person with whom the buyer deals is a **contracting agent** with authority to make contracts, by definition a binding contract exists between the principal and the customer from the moment that the agent agrees with the customer. In other words, the contract arises when the agent accepts the customer's order.

Summary

An agent of a disclosed principal who makes a contract with a third person within the scope of authority has no personal liability on the contract. It is the principal and the third person who may each sue the other in the event of a breach. A person purporting to act as an agent for a principal warrants by implication that there is an existing principal with legal capacity and that the principal has authorized the agent to act. The person acting as an agent is liable for any loss caused the third person for breach of these warranties. An agent of a partially disclosed or an undisclosed principal is a party to the contract with the third person. The agent may enforce the contract against the third person and is liable for its breach. To avoid problems of interpretation, an agent should execute a contract "Principal, by Agent." Agents are liable for harm caused third persons by their fraudulent, malicious, or negligent acts.

An undisclosed or a partially disclosed principal is liable to a third person on a simple contract made by an authorized agent. When a third person makes payment to an authorized agent, it is deemed paid to the principal.

A principal or an employer is vicariously liable under the doctrine of *respondeat superior* for the torts of an agent or an employee committed within the scope of authority or the course of employment. The principal or the employer may also be liable for some crimes committed in the course of employment. An owner is not liable for torts caused by an independent contractor to third persons or their property unless the work given to the independent contractor is inherently hazardous.

A salesperson is ordinarily an agent whose authority is limited to soliciting offers (orders) from third persons and transmitting them to the principal. The principal is not bound until he or she accepts the order. The customer may withdraw an offer at any time prior to acceptance.

Questions and Case Problems

1. Richard Pawlus was an owner of Dutch City Wood Products, Inc., which did business as "Dutch City Marketing." Pawlus purchased merchandise from Rothschild Sunsystems from April 24 to June 24 using the designation "Richard Pawlus Dutch City Marketing" on orders and correspondence. In October, Rothschild was notified that Pawlus was acting on behalf of the corporation when the merchandise was purchased. Rothschild sued Pawlus for payment for the merchandise. Pawlus contended that he was an agent of the corporation and was thus not personally liable. Decide. [*Rothschild Sunsystems, Inc. v Pawlus*, 514 NYS2d 572 (App Div)]
2. Myles Murphy was appointed by Cy Sinden, a famous developer, to purchase land for a shopping center near the intersection of I-95 and Route 1. Mary Mason, the property owner, contracted with Murphy for the sale of the property. Because of an economic downturn, Sinden was unable to provide the planned behind-the-scenes financing for the venture, and the contract was not performed. Mason's real estate experts determined that she lost $2 million because of the breach of contract. Mason also discovered that Sinden was "behind the deal." If Mason elects to sue Sinden, who turns out to be unable to pay the judgment because of the collapse of his business "empire," can she later bring suit against Murphy?
3. What is the justification for the doctrine of *respondeat superior?*
4. Beverly Baumann accompanied her mother to Memorial Hospital, where her mother was placed in intensive care for heart problems. A nurse asked Baumann to sign various documents, including one that authorized the hospital to release medical information and to receive the mother's insurance benefits directly. This form stated: "I understand I am financially responsible to the hospital for charges not covered by this authorization." Baumann's mother died during the course of her hospitalization. The hospital later sued Baumann to recover $19,013.42 in unpaid hospital charges based on the form she signed, which the hospital called a "guarantee of payment." Baumann contended that she signed the document as an agent for her mother and was thus not personally liable. Decide. [*Memorial Hospital v Baumann*, 474 NYS2d 636]
5. Mills Electric Co. signed a contract with S&S Horticulture Architects, a two-person landscaping partnership operated by Sullivan and Smyth, to maintain the grounds and flowers at the Mills Electric Co. plant in Jacksonville, Florida. Mills checked references of S&S and found the company to be highly reputable. The contract set forth that S&S would select the flowers for each season and would determine when to maintain the lawns so long as they were properly maintained. The contract called for payments to be made to S&S on the first workday of each month, and the contract stipulated that "nothing herein shall make S&S an agent of the company." The contract also required that S&S personnel wear uniforms identifying them as employees of S&S. S&S had other accounts, but the large Mills Electric plant took up most of its time. While working on a terraced area near the visitors' entrance to the plant, Sullivan lost control of his

large commercial mower, and the mower struck Gillespie, a plant visitor, causing her serious injury. A witness heard Sullivan apologizing to Gillespie and saying that "running that mower on the terrace is a two-person job." Gillespie brought suit against Mills Electric Co., contending Mills should be held vicariously liable. Decide.

6. A. D. McLeod contacted Thompson's agent and agreed that certain property would be leased for a period of two years at a rental rate of $700 per month for the first year and $800 per month for the second year. McLeod's personal check paid the first month's rent. McLeod and his associates manufactured mattresses on the premises under the trademark Sleep, and the business was incorporated as Sleep System, Inc. After some six months of operation during which the rent was paid by the corporation, McLeod informed Thompson that he had been "kicked out" of the company. When the subsequent rent was not paid, Thompson sued McLeod for the back rent. McLeod alleged that Thompson knew or should have known that McLeod was acting as an agent of Sleep System, Inc., and that after he was "kicked out" of the company, it should have been very clear that he would no longer be responsible for rent. Thompson responded that if McLeod were an agent, he had an obligation to disclose that he was acting in a representative capacity when the lease was made, not six months later. Decide. [*McLeod v Thompson*, 615 So 2d 90 (Ala Civ App)]
7. On July 11, 1984, José Padilla was working as a vacation-relief route salesperson for Frito-Lay. He testified that he made a route stop at Sal's Beverage Shop, where he was told by Mrs. Ramos that she was dissatisfied with Frito-Lay service and no longer wanted its products in the store. He asked if there was anything he could do to change her mind. She said no and told him to pick up his merchandise. He took one company-owned merchandise rack to his van and was about to pick up another rack when Mr. Ramos said that the rack had been given to him by the regular route salesperson. Padilla said the route salesperson had no authority to give away Frito-Lay racks. A confrontation occurred over the rack, and Padilla pushed Mr. Ramos against the cash register, injuring Ramos's back. Frito-Lay has a company policy, clearly communicated to all employees, that prohibits them from getting involved in any type of physical confrontation with a customer. Frito-Lay contended that Padilla was not acting within the course and scope of his employment when the pushing incident took place and that the company was therefore not liable to Ramos. Ramos contended that Frito-Lay was responsible for the acts of its employee Padilla. [*Frito-Lay, Inc. v Ramos*, 770 SW2d 887 (Tex App)]
8. Jason Lasseigne, a Little League baseball player, was seriously injured at a practice session when he was struck on the head by a poorly thrown baseball from a team member, Todd Landry. The league was organized by American Legion Post 38. Claude Cassel and Billy Johnson were the volunteer coaches of the practice session. The Lasseignes brought suit on behalf of Jason against Post 38, claiming that the coaching was negligent and that Post 38 was vicariously liable for the harm caused by such negligence. Post 38 contended that it had no right to control the work of the volunteer coaches or the manner in which practices were conducted and as a result should not be held vicariously liable for the actions of the coaches. Decide. [*Lasseigne v American Legion Post 38*, 543 So 2d 1111 (La App)]
9. Moritz, a guest at Pines Hotel, was sitting in the lobby when Brown, a hotel employee, dropped a heavy vacuum cleaner on her knee. When Moritz complained, the employee insulted her and hit her with his fist, knocking her unconscious. She sued the hotel for damages. Was the hotel liable? [*Moritz v Pines Hotel, Inc.*, 383 NYS2d 704 (App Div)]
10. Steve Diezel, an employee of Island City Flying Service in Key West, Florida, stole a General Electric Credit Corp. (GECC) aircraft and crashed the plane while attempting to take off. GECC brought suit against Island City on the theory that it had negligently hired Diezel as an employee and was therefore legally responsible for Diezel's act of theft. Diezel had a military prison record as a result of a drug offense and had been fired by Island City twice previously but had been immediately reinstated each time. Island City claimed that the evidence was insufficient to establish that it had been negligent in employing Diezel. Decide. [*Island City Flying Service v General Electric*, 585 So 2d 274 (Fla)]
11. The Bay State Harness Horse Racing and Breeding Association conducted horse races at a track where music for patrons was supplied by an independent contractor hired by the association. Some of the music played was subject to a copyright held by Famous Music Corp. The playing of that music was a violation of the copyright unless royalties were paid to Famous Music. No royalties were paid, and Famous Music sued the association, which raised the defense that the violation had been committed by an independent contractor specifically instructed not to play Famous Music's copyrighted material. Decide. [*Famous Music Corp. v Bay State Harness Horse Racing and Breeding Association, Inc.*, 554 F2d 1213 (1st Cir)]
12. Steven Trujillo, told by the assistant door manager of Cowboys Bar "to show up to work tonight in case we need you as a doorman," came to the bar that evening wearing a jacket with the bar logo on it. Trujillo "attacked" Rocky Medina in the parking lot of the bar, causing him serious injury. Prior to working for Cowboys, Trujillo was involved in several fights at that bar and in its parking lot, and Cowboys knew of these matters. Medina sued Cowboys on two theories of liability: (1) *respondeat superior* and (2) negligent hiring

of Trujillo. Cowboys's defense was that *respondeat superior* theory should be dismissed because the assault was clearly not within the course of Trujillo's employment. Concerning the negligent hiring theory, Cowboys asserted that Trujillo was not on duty that night as a doorman. Decide. [*Medina v Graham's Cowboys, Inc.*, 827 P2d 859 (NM App)]

13. Neal Rubin, while driving his car in Chicago, inadvertently blocked the path of a Yellow Cab Co. taxi driven by Robert Ball, causing the taxi to swerve and hit Rubin's car. Angered by Rubin's driving, Ball got out of his cab and hit Rubin on the head and shoulders with a metal pipe. Rubin sued Yellow Cab Co. for the damages caused by this beating, contending that the employer was vicariously liable for the beating under the doctrine of *respondeat superior* because the beating occurred in furtherance of the employer's business, which was to obtain fares without delay. The company argued that Ball's beating of Rubin was not an act undertaken to further the employer's business. Is the employer liable under *respondeat superior*? [*Rubin v Yellow Cab Co.*, 507 NE2d 114 (Ill App)]

14. Brazilian & Colombian Co. (B&C), a food broker, ordered 40 barrels of olives from Mawer-Gulden-Annis (MGA). MGA's shipping clerk was later told to make out the bill of lading to B&C's customer Pantry Queen; the olives were shipped directly to Pantry Queen. Eight days after delivery, the president of B&C wrote MGA to give it the name of its principal, Pantry Queen, and advised MGA to bill the principal directly. Pantry Queen was unable to pay for the olives, and MGA sued B&C for payment. B&C contended that it was well known to MGA that B&C was a food broker (agent) and the olives were shipped directly to the principal by MGA. It stated that as an agent, it was not a party to the contract and was thus not liable. Decide. [*Mawer-Gulden-Annis, Inc. v Brazilian & Colombian Coffee Co.*, 199 NE2d 222 (Ill App)]

CPA Questions

1. Frey entered into a contract with Cara Corp. to purchase televisions on behalf of Lux, Inc. Lux authorized Frey to enter into the contract in Frey's name without disclosing that Frey was acting on behalf of Lux. If Cara repudiates the contract, which of the following statements concerning liability on the contract is *not* correct?
   a. Frey may not hold Cara liable and obtain money damages.
   b. Frey may hold Cara liable and obtain specific performance.
   c. Lux may hold Cara liable upon disclosing the agency relationship with Frey.
   d. Cara will be free from liability to Lux if Frey fraudulently stated that he was acting on his own behalf.

2. A principal will *not* be liable to a third party for a tort committed by an agent
   a. Unless the principal instructed the agent to commit the tort
   b. Unless the tort was committed within the scope of the agency relationship
   c. If the agency agreement limits the principal's liability for the agent's tort
   d. If the tort is also regarded as a criminal act

3. Cox engaged Datz as her agent. It was mutually agreed that Datz would *not* disclose that he was acting as Cox's agent. Instead, he was to deal with prospective customers as if he were a principal acting on his own behalf. This he did and made several contracts for Cox. Assuming Cox, Datz, or the customer seeks to avoid liability on one of the contracts involved, which of the following statements is correct?
   a. Cox must ratify the Datz contracts in order to be held liable.
   b. Datz has *no* liability once he discloses that Cox was the real principal.
   c. The third party can avoid liability because he believed he was dealing with Datz as a principal.
   d. The third party may choose to hold either Datz or Cox liable.

4. Which of the following statements is (are) correct regarding the relationship between an agent and a nondisclosed principal?
   I. The principal is required to indemnify the agent for any contract entered into by the agent within the scope of the agency agreement.
   II. The agent has the same actual authority as if the principal had been disclosed.
   a. I only
   b. II only
   c. Both I and II
   d. Neither I nor II

REGULATION OF EMPLOYMENT

CHAPTER (39)

LEARNING OBJECTIVES

After studying this chapter, you should be able to

LO.1 Explain the contractual nature of the employment relationship

LO.2 Identify the five employer unfair labor practices

LO.3 Identify the nine union unfair labor practices

LO.4 State the four ways in which ERISA provides protection for the pension interests of employees

LO.5 Set forth the eligibility requirements for unemployment compensation

LO.6 Explain how the Occupational Safety and Health Act is designed to reach the goal of ensuring safe and healthful working conditions

LO.7 List the three types of benefits provided by workers' compensation statutes

Employment law involves the law of contracts and the law established by lawmakers, courts, and administrative agencies.

A. The Employment Relationship

The relationship of an employer and an employee exists when, pursuant to an express or implied agreement of the parties, one person, the employee, undertakes to perform services or to do work under the direction and control of another, the employer, for compensation. In older cases, this relationship was called the *master-servant relationship*.

1. Characteristics of Relationship

An employee is hired to work under the control of the employer. An employee differs from an agent, who is to negotiate or make contracts with third persons on behalf of, and under the control of, a principal. However, a person may be both an employee and an agent for the other party. An employee also differs from an independent contractor, who is to perform a contract independent of, or free from, control by the other party.[1]

[1] *Ost v West Suburban Travelers Limousine, Inc.*, 88 F3d 435 (7th Cir 1996).

2. Creation of Employment Relationship

The relationship of employer and employee can be created only with the consent of both parties. Generally, the agreement of the parties is a contract. It is therefore subject to all of the principles applicable to contracts. The contract will ordinarily be express, but it may be implied, such as when the employer accepts the rendering of services that a reasonable person would recognize as being rendered with the expectation of receiving compensation.

(a) Individual Employment Contracts

As in contracts generally, both parties must assent to the terms of an employment contract. Subject to statutory restrictions, the parties are free to make a contract on any terms they wish.

(b) Collective Bargaining Contracts

Collective bargaining contracts govern the rights and obligations of employers and employees in many private and public areas of employment. Under collective bargaining, representatives of the employees bargain with a single employer or a group of employers for an agreement on wages, hours, and working conditions. The agreement worked out by the representatives of the employees, usually union officials, is generally subject to a ratification vote by the employees. Terms usually found in collective bargaining contracts are (1) identification of the work belonging exclusively to designated classes of employees, (2) wage and benefits clauses, (3) promotion and layoff clauses, which are generally tied in part to seniority, (4) a management's rights clause, and (5) a grievance procedure. A grievance procedure provides a means by which persons claiming that the contract was violated or that they were disciplined or discharged without just cause may have their cases decided by impartial labor arbitrators.

3. Duration and Termination of Employment Contract

In many instances, the employment contract does not state any time or duration. In such a case, it may be terminated at any time by either party. In contrast, the employment contract may expressly state that it shall last for a specified period of time; an example would be an individual's contract to work as general manager for five years. In some instances, a definite duration may be implied by the circumstances.

(a) Employment-at-Will Doctrine and Developing Exceptions

Ordinarily, a contract of employment may be terminated in the same manner as any other contract. If it is to run for a definite period of time, the employer cannot terminate the contract at an earlier date without justification. If the employment contract does not have a definite duration, it is terminable at will. Under the **employment-at-will doctrine,** the employer has historically been allowed to terminate the employment contract at any time for any reason or for no reason.[2] Recent court decisions—and in some instances, statutes—have changed the rule in most states by limiting the power of the employer to discharge the employee. Some courts have carved out exceptions to the employment-at-will doctrine when the discharge violated an established public policy.

Public policy exceptions are often made to the employment-at-will doctrine when an employee is discharged in retaliation for insisting that the employer comply with the state's food and drug act or for filing a workers' compensation claim.[3] In some states, so-called whistleblower laws have been enacted to protect employees who disclose employer practices that endanger public health or safety. Also, a statutory right exists for at-will employees who are terminated in retaliation for cooperating with a federal criminal prosecution or are terminated in violation of the public policy to provide truthful testimony.[4]

The *Adams* case involves the application of a state whistleblower law.

[2] *Brown v Hammond,* 810 F Supp 644 (ED Pa 1993).

[3] *Brigham v Dillon Companies, Inc.,* 935 P2d 1054 (Kan 1997).

[4] *Fitzgerald v Salsbury Chemical, Inc.,* 613 NW2d 275 (Iowa 2000). In *Garcetti v Ceballos,* 126 SCt 1951 (2006), the U.S. Supreme Court held that when public employees make statements pursuant to their official duties, the First Amendment of the Constitution does not insulate their communications from employer discipline because the employees are not speaking as citizens for First Amendment purposes. In his dissent, Justice Souter argued that a public employee should have constitutional protection when the employee acts as a whistleblower, pointing out the limitations of protections afforded public employee whistleblowers (at pages 1970 and 1971).

ADAMS V UNO RESTAURANTS, INC., 18 IER CASES, 998 (RI 2002)

PRETEXT AT THE PIZZERIA

After a jury returned a verdict in favor of the plaintiff, Gerald K. Adams, finding that his employer, the Warwick Rhode Island Pizzaria Uno had wrongfully terminated Adams in violation of the state's Whistleblowers Act,* the trial court set aside the jury's award of $7,500 in damages, and Adams appealed to the state's Supreme Court.

Judicial Opinion

PER CURIAM: On May 20, 1996, the plaintiff, who had been employed by the defendant for several years, arrived for his nighttime line cooking shift at the defendant's Warwick restaurant. Shortly after his shift began, the plaintiff noticed that the kitchen floor was saturated with a foulsmelling liquid coming from drains and backing up water onto the floor. He complained of illness and went home, at which time he contacted the Department of Health about the drainage problem in the restaurant's kitchen. A Department of Health representative visited the restaurant that evening and noticed that the floor drains were backed up and that the floor was wet and slippery. She ordered the kitchen staff to dispose of all the food they had touched with their bare hands and closed the restaurant for the night, leaving instructions to sanitize the kitchen area and clear all the drains. She also inquired about which employee went home sick. The restaurant reopened the next day after sanitizing the kitchen.

On May 22, 1996, two days after the incident, the plaintiff, who was not scheduled to work that day, returned to the restaurant curious to determine whether there was any hostility toward him resulting from his having called the Department of Health. The plaintiff testified that he was summarily ordered by David Badot, the restaurant's manager, to come into his office and that Badot proceeded to shout at him while inquiring whether he had contacted the Department of Health. The plaintiff testified that he shouted back at Badot and acknowledged that he had indeed called the Department of Health. Badot then accused the plaintiff of stealing one of the defendant's softball team shirts and of taking a work schedule home. Badot then left his office, and the plaintiff followed him out into the general cooking area, where other employees were present. The shouting match between Badot and the plaintiff continued and in the course thereof, the plaintiff told Badot that he "was going to follow him back to Massachusetts on this, and [he] was going to blow the intelligence out of his head." The plaintiff then left the restaurant. Badot claimed to have perceived the plaintiff's words as threatening and instructed an employee to call the police. When the plaintiff later heard that the police were looking for him, he voluntarily went to the Warwick police station, whereupon he was then charged with disorderly conduct, arraigned, and pled not guilty. No trial on the charge ensued. The charge was later filed. One year later his record of arrest and charge automatically was expunged pursuant to the case filing statute.

Shortly thereafter, the plaintiff commenced this civil action against the defendant alleging therein that he had been unlawfully terminated only because he had notified the Department of Health regarding the unsanitary kitchen conditions existing at the defendant's Warwick Pizzeria Uno Restaurant & Bar. . . .

After examining the evidence in the light most favorable to the plaintiff, the trial justice decided that a reasonable jury could have found that Badot's actions in badgering the plaintiff and then having him arrested were a pretext for retaliating against the plaintiff for having called in the Department of Health. The trial justice concluded that a reasonable jury certainly could have found that the confrontation between Badot and the plaintiff was designed by Badot to provoke a reaction from the plaintiff that would serve as Badot's excuse to fire him, even though that was merely a pretext for the real reason—the plaintiff's call to the Department of Health. . . .

Although the plaintiff at trial did not specifically quantify his damages, he did testify that it took him eleven days to find employment after his being terminated by the defendant. In addition to his economic damages, he claimed and testified that he suffered emotional distress and humiliation as a result of the defendant's wrongful conduct in initiating criminal proceedings against him that resulted in the loss of his National Guard security clearance and disqualification from an overseas National Guard

*The Rhode Island Whistleblowers' Protection Act, G.L. 1956 28-50-4(a) provides that "A person who alleges a violation of this act may bring a civil action for appropriate injunctive relief, or actual damages, or both within three (3) years after the occurrence of the alleged violation of this chapter."

mission. He offered no expert medical testimony in support of his claim for emotional distress. . . .

On the particular case facts before us, we do not find the absence of expert medical testimony to support the plaintiff's claim for damages resulting from his alleged emotional distress and humiliation to be fatal to that portion of his claim for damages. Unlike the usual case where a claim for emotional distress and humiliation is oftentimes made without objective facts to substantiate such a claim, expert medical testimony is deemed necessary to assist the fact-finder in determining not only the validity but also the casual relationship of any emotional distress. In this case, the trial jury had before it clear objective and uncontroverted evidence concerning the complaint to the Warwick police; his arrest by the Warwick police; the criminal charge for disorderly conduct made against him; his arraignment on that charge; the revocation of his military security clearance and the resulting loss of his opportunity to accompany his National Guard unit in an overseas mission to Germany.** From such objective and uncontradicted evidence, we believe that an ordinary lay person or trial juror would be capable of determining without the aid of expert medical testimony whether emotional distress and humiliation could ordinarily and naturally follow from such events. Trial jurors, we are satisfied, do not leave their common sense in the cloakroom when they come to sit in the courtroom. . . .

In this case, the trial evidence clearly reveals that the plaintiff Adams was particularly troubled over his being arrested for disorderly conduct and the resulting loss of his security clearance as a National Guard reservist. That loss of security clearance subsequently prevented him from participating with his National Guard unit in an overseas mission to Germany. The trial justice apparently noted the significance of those matters upon the plaintiff's emotional well-being, when in overruling defense counsel's objection to the plaintiff's testimony concerning those matters he noted: "I'll allow it. To him it's very important. Whether it is to you or the jury remains to be seen."

In passing upon and granting the defendant's motion to set aside the jury's damages award to the plaintiff, the trial justice pondered whether the proximate cause for any damages the plaintiff would otherwise have been entitled to recover had been interrupted when the plaintiff threatened Badot. However, he later acknowledged that the jury could have reasonably concluded from the plaintiff's testimony that he did suffer actual economic losses and mental anguish from his having been terminated and humiliated by Badot in the presence of the plaintiff's fellow employees as well as from embarrassment stemming from the police visit to his second employer inquiring about the threat made against Badot. He observed also that the jury could reasonably have concluded that the plaintiff's loss of his National Guard security clearance and subsequent inability to participate in overseas missions caused him emotional distress. . . .

Conclusion

For the reasons set out above, the case papers are remanded to the court for entry of an amended final judgment that will include the trial jury's award of damages to the plaintiff in the amount of $7,500.

Questions

1. Is it illegal under state law for an employer to retaliate against an employee for calling the state Health Department about an unsafe or unsanitary kitchen condition?
2. What is a pretext? How did the pretext apply in this case?
3. Was Adams entitled to damages for emotional distress without supportive expert medical testimony?

**The plaintiff aptly summarized the scope of his damages at trial: "So now I'm still fighting through the momentum that they caused on me affecting my civil life, my military career, my standing in the job market."

The contract of employment may be construed to bar a discharge of the employee except for cause. If so construed, good cause would then be required for the discharge of an at-will employee. Written personnel policies used as guidelines for supervisors have also been interpreted as being part of the employment contract. These policies have thus been held to restrict the employer's right to discharge at-will employees without proof of good or just cause. Moreover, employee handbooks that provide for "proper notice and investigation" before termination may bar employers from terminating employees without providing such notice and an investigation.[5]

Other courts still follow the common law at-will rule because they believe that a court should not rewrite the contract of the parties to provide employee protection that was never intended.[6]

[5] *Carlson v Lake Chelan Community Hospital*, 66 P3d 1080 (Wash App 2003); but see *Trabing v Kinko's, Inc.*, 57 P3d 1248 (Wyo 2002) and *Williams v First Tennessee National Corp.*, 97 SW3d 798 (Tex App 2003).

[6] See *Texas Farm Bureau Mutual Insurance Co. v Sears*, 84 SW3d 604 (Tex 2002).

(b) Justifiable Discharge

An employer may be justified in discharging an employee because of the employee's (1) nonperformance of duties, (2) misrepresentation or fraud in obtaining the employment, (3) disobedience of proper directions, (4) disloyalty, (5) theft or other dishonesty, (6) possession or use of drugs or intoxicants, (7) misconduct, or (8) incompetence.

Employers generally have the right to lay off employees because of economic conditions, including a lack of work. Such actions are sometimes referred to as *reductions in force (RIFs)*.

Employers, however, must be very careful not to make layoffs based on age, for that is a violation of the Age Discrimination in Employment Act.

In some states, a "service letter" statute requires an employer on request to furnish to a discharged employee a letter stating the reason for the discharge.

4. Whistleblower Protection Under The Sarbanes-Oxley Act

The Sarbanes-Oxley Act (SOA or SOX Act) of 2002 was enacted to restore investor confidence in financial markets following the exposure in 2001–2002 of widespread misconduct by directors and officers of publicly held companies. The SOA contains reforms regarding corporate accountability, enhanced disclosure requirements, and enforcement and liability provisions. Title VIII of the act contains protections for corporate whistleblowers.[7]

(a) Protection Provided

The SOA prohibits a publicly traded company or any agent of it from taking an adverse employment action against an employee who provides information, testifies, or "otherwise assists" in proceedings regarding (1) mail, wire, bank, or securities fraud, (2) any violation of an SEC rule or regulation, or (3) any federal law protecting shareholders against fraud. The act sets forth the types of adverse employment actions that qualify for protection, specifically protecting employees from discharge, demotion, suspension, threats, harassment, failure to hire or rehire, blacklisting, or action otherwise discriminatory against employees in their terms and conditions of employment.

An employee who provides information to the SEC may be incorrect in the belief that an activity is illegal. Nevertheless, the employee is considered involved in a protected activity so long as the employee had an objectively "reasonable belief" that the reported activity was in violation of a federal law protecting shareholders from fraud. **For Example,** when an employee reported to the SEC what he believed to be a financial impropriety regarding delays in payments owed by the company to a subsequent quarter and an SEC investigation exonerated the employer, an administrative law judge found the whistleblower to have been engaged in "protected activities" because he had a reasonable belief that the company action was illegal.[8]

(b) Procedures

An individual who believes that she has been subject to an adverse employment action because of whistleblowing activities must file a complaint with the Department of Labor's Occupational Safety and Health Administration (OSHA) within 90 days after the asserted adverse employment action. OSHA administers 13 other federal whistleblower laws and has experienced investigators to facilitate its responsibilities under the SOA.[9]

The burden of proof is on the complainant to demonstrate that the complainant's protected activity was a "contributing factor" in the adverse employment action. If this is established, the burden shifts to the employer to prove by "clear and convincing evidence"—a heavy burden of proof—that it would have taken the same adverse action in the absence of the protected activity.[10]

Whistleblowers are entitled to make whole relief including reinstatement with all rights unimpaired and compensatory damages, including back pay with interest, and "special damages" such as reasonable attorneys' fees and expert witness fees.

The *Welch* case deals with reinstatement and backpay issues.

[7] 18 USC § 1514A (2005).

[8] *Halloum v Intel Corp.*, 2003-SOX-7 (ALJ Mar. 4, 2004).

[9] An investigator has authority to order reinstatement of an employee claiming protection of the SOA at the investigatory stage. See *Bechtel v Competitive Technologies, Inc.*, 205-SOX-33 (Oct. 5, 2005).

[10] 18 USC § 1514A(b)(2)(C), and 29 CFR § 1980.104.

WELCH V CARDINAL BANKSHARES CORP., 2003-SOX-15 (ALJ FEB 15, 2005)

WELCH LIKES THE SOX — SARBANES-OXLEY

On January 28, 2004, the first recommended decision by an ALJ that an employer, a rural Virginia bank, Cardinal Bankshares Corp., had violated the SOA was issued. The ALJ found that the bank's chief financial officer (CFO) David Welch had been terminated for engaging in protected whistleblower activity under the SOA. Welch sought to be reinstated to his CFO position with back pay. The bank contends that Welch is unfit to be CFO because of all of the hostility engendered by the litigation, leaving Welch to work closely with employees, officers and directors who have critized him since the litigation began.

Judicial Opinion

PURCELL, ALJ . . . Reinstatement is a drastic remedy and will frequently pose difficulties, but reinstatement as a remedy is generally appropriate to further the stated remedial goal of Sarbanes-Oxley, i.e. to make complainants whole. *Id.* Indeed, despite the inherent problems posed by reinstatement, it is the default or presumptive remedy in wrongful termination cases. . . .

Cardinal is, as Respondent's counsel notes, a small employer, and upon reinstatement Welch will be required to work closely with other employees, officers, and directors who have criticized him since this litigation commenced. Indeed, there is little doubt that hostility continues to exist at Cardinal which will make reinstatement difficult. One of the clearest examples of this hostility may be garnered from a review of the declarations of the board and CEO, and the pleadings filed by Respondent's counsel, parts of which I find are patently inconsistent with other record evidence. . . .

. . . I find that reinstatement, while it will be difficult, is appropriate. Welch clearly seeks reinstatement, and he has professed a willingness to work with Respondent's employees, officers, and directors if his request is granted. As a prevailing complainant in this matter, Welch is presumptively entitled to reinstatement absent unusual circumstances, . . . and Cardinal should not be allowed to profit from its unlawful conduct by preventing Welch from returning to his former position as CFO. . . . Any hostility which has developed since his discharge is no different in kind or degree from that which, regrettably, occurs all too frequently following litigation of this sort. Furthermore, although Welch will be required to report to a CEO and board of directors who have been openly critical of Welch since this litigation was initiated, that circumstance is not sufficiently unusual in the context of a Sarbanes-Oxley whistleblower case to warrant denying him reinstatement. Indeed, doing so would send a clear message to other corporate officers that the Act, which was passed by Congress for the express purpose of encouraging employees to disclose conduct which they reasonably believe to be unlawful, does not apply to them.

Under the Act and its implementing regulations, Welch is entitled to be made whole, and the only reasonable alternative to reinstatement would be front pay, a remedy which the parties have neither sought nor addressed in their post-hearing briefs. I find that ordering Welch's reinstatement as CFO under the facts of this case is both reasonable and necessary to make Welch whole and to further the ends of Sarbanes-Oxley. . . .

Recommended Order

Based on the foregoing findings of fact and conclusions of law, it is HEREBY RECOMMENDED that Respondent, Cardinal Bankshares Corporation, be ORDERED to:

Reinstate Complainant David Welch as the Chief Financial Officer of Cardinal Bankshares Corporation with the same seniority, status, and benefits he would have had but for Respondent's unlawful discrimination.

Pay Complainant $38,327.76 in back wages for the period October 1, 2002 through December 31, 2004.

Pay Complainant $26,505.58 in special damages, exclusive of attorney's fees.

Pay Complainant's counsel, D. Bruce Shine, $108,006.37 in attorney's fees and expenses.

Pay Complainant back wages for the period January 1, 2005 to the date of his reinstatement calculated in the manner set forth above.

Pay Complainant prejudgment interest on all back wages owed for the period October 1, 2002 to the date of his reinstatement calculated in the manner set forth above.

Questions

1. Did the ALJ determine that Welch was not entitled to reinstatement to his CFO position because hostility existed between Welch and the board of directors and the bank's CEO?
2. What other remedy option is available to the parties and the agency in resolving a SOA controversy where the return of the protected employee would lead to a disruption of the employer's operations?

Criminal penalties may be imposed against the employer or its agents for retaliating against an informant who has provided truthful information relating to a federal offense.[11]

5. Duties of the Employee

The duties of an employee are determined primarily by the contract of employment with the employer. The law also implies certain obligations.

(a) Services

Employees are under the duty to perform such services as may be required by the contract of employment.

(b) Trade Secrets

An employee may be given confidential trade secrets by the employer but must not disclose this knowledge to others. An agreement by the employee to refrain from disclosing trade secrets is binding. If the employee violates this obligation, the employer may enjoin the use of the information by the employee and by any person to whom it has been disclosed by the employee.

Former employees who are competing with their former employer may be enjoined from using information about suppliers and customers that they obtained while employees when this information is of vital importance to the employer's business. Injunctive relief is denied, however, if the information is not important or not secret.

(c) Inventions

Employment contracts commonly provide that an employer will own any invention or discovery made by an employee, whether during work hours, after work hours, or for a period of one or two years after leaving the employment. In the absence of an express or implied agreement to the contrary, the inventions of an employee usually belong to the employee. This is true even though the employee used the time and property of the employer in the discovery. In this case, however, the employer has what is known as a **shop right** to use the invention without cost in its operations.

6. Rights of the Employee

The rights of an employee are determined by the contract of employment and by the law as declared by courts, lawmakers, and administrative agencies.

(a) Compensation

The rights of an employee with respect to compensation are governed in general by the same principles that apply to the compensation of an agent. In the absence of an agreement to the contrary, when an employee is discharged, whether for cause or not, the employer must pay wages to the expiration of the last pay period. State statutes commonly authorize employees to sue employers for wages improperly withheld and to recover penalties and attorney fees. In addition to hourly wages, payments due for vacations and certain bonuses are considered "wages" under state statutes.[12] **For Example,** Diane Beard worked for Summit Institute as a licensed practical nurse for 13 months when she walked off the job and terminated her employment. She requested her accrued vacation pay of $432, but Summit refused to pay her, claiming she had abandoned her job and thus forfeited her right to vacation pay under company policy. Accrued vacation qualifies as "wages," and she was entitled to the $432 vacation pay plus a penalty equal to 90 days' wages at the employee's rate of pay or $9,720, plus $2,400 in attorneys' fees for the trial and an additional $2,600 in attorneys' fees for the appeal. These statutes with their penalty provisions are designed as a coercive means to compel employers to promptly pay their employees.[13]

CPA (b) Federal Wage and Hour Law

Workers at enterprises engaged in interstate commerce are covered by the Fair Labor Standards Act (FLSA),[14] popularly known as the Wage and Hour Act. These workers cannot be paid less than a specified minimum wage.

The FLSA has been amended to cover domestic service workers, including housekeepers, cooks, and full-time babysitters. Executive, administrative, and professional employees and outside salespersons are exempt from both the minimum wage and overtime provisions of the law.

[11] 18 USC § 1513(e) (2005).

[12] *Knutson v Snyder Industries, Inc.*, 436 NW2d 496 (Neb 1989).

[13] *Beard v Summit Institute of Pulmonary Medicine and Rehabilitation, Inc.*, 707 So 2d 1233 (La 1998); see also *Beckman v Kansas Dep't. of Human Resources*, 43 P3d 891 (Kan App 2002).

[14] PL 75-718, 52 Stat 1060, 29 USC § 201 *et seq.*

(1) Subminimum Wage Provisions. The FLSA allows for the employment of full-time students at institutions of higher education at wage rates below the statutory minimum. Also, individuals whose productive capacity is impaired by age, physical or mental deficiency, or injury may be employed at less than the minimum wage to prevent the curtailment of work opportunities for these individuals. In these cases, however, a special certificate is needed by the employer from the Department of Labor's (DOL's) Wage and Hour Division, which has offices throughout the United States.

(2) Wage Issues. Deductions made from wages as a result of cash or merchandise shortages and deductions for tools of the trade are not legal if they reduce wages below the minimum wage. An employer's requirement that employees provide uniforms or tools of their own is a violation of the law to the extent that the expenses for these items reduce wages below the minimum wage.

Job-related training generally is compensable under the FLSA. However, an exception exists for voluntary training not directly related to an employee's job when the employee does not perform productive work. **For Example,** Hogar, Inc., operates a nursing home and required new employees to undergo two days of unpaid training before assuming paid duties as nurses' aides, maintenance/laundry workers, and kitchen workers. Little or no instruction was offered to these "trainees," and each individual would perform the regular duties of the position for the two-day period. Hogar's practices did not fall within the training exception because the trainees performed productive work with little or no actual training during a regular shift. In a lawsuit brought by the Secretary of Labor, Hogar was ordered by the court to pay 14 hours' pay (two days' pay) for each employee so "trained," plus liquidated damages of an additional 14 hours pay.[15]

(3) Overtime Pay. Overtime must be paid at a rate of one and a half times the employee's regular rate of pay for each hour worked in excess of 40 hours in a workweek.[16]

(4) Child Labor Provisions. The FLSA child labor provisions are designed to protect educational opportunities for minors and prohibit their employment in occupations detrimental to their health and well-being. The FLSA restricts hours of work for minors under 16 and lists hazardous occupations too dangerous for minors to perform.

B. Labor Relations Laws

Even if employers are not presently unionized, they are subject to certain obligations under federal labor relations law. It is important to both unionized and nonunionized employers to know their rights and obligations under the National Labor Relations Act (NLRA).[17] Employee rights and obligations are also set forth in this act. The Labor-Management Reporting and Disclosure Act regulates internal union affairs.[18]

7. The National Labor Relations Act

The National Labor Relations Act (NLRA), passed in 1935, was based on the federal government's power to regulate interstate commerce granted in Article 1, Section 8, of the Constitution. Congress, in enacting this law, explained that its purpose was to remove obstructions to commerce caused by employers who denied their employees the right to join unions and refused to accept collective bargaining.[19] Congress stated that these obstructions resulted in depression of wages, poor working conditions, and diminution of purchasing power.

Section 7 of the amended NLRA is the heart of the act, stating in part that "[e]mployees shall have the right to self-organization . . . to bargain collectively through representatives of their own choosing and to engage in other concerted activities for the purpose of collective bargaining or other mutual aid

[15] *Herman v Hogar Praderas De Amor, Inc.*, 130 F Supp 2d 257 (SD PR 2001).

[16] New DOL regulations, referred to as the *white collar exemptions* from the overtime requirements of the FLSA took effect on August 23, 2004. Generally, executive, administrative, professional, outside sales, computer professional, and certain "highly compensated employees" are exempt from the overtime requirements if they meet the "tests" set forth in the new regulations. The U.S. Department of Labor's fact sheets on the new rule are available at **http://www.dol.gov/regs/compliance/whd/fairpay/main.htm**.

[17] 29 USC §§ 141–169. Note that in the *Lechmere* and *Transportation Management* cases presented in this section, the employers were not unionized.

[18] 29 USC §§ 401–531.

[19] NLRA § 1; 29 USC § 141.

or protection . . . and shall have the right to refrain from such activities. . . ."

Section 8 of the NLRA contains employer and union unfair labor practices, set forth in Figure 39-1, and authorizes the National Labor Relations Board to conduct proceedings to stop such practices.

The act applies to private-sector employers with gross incomes of $500,000 or more. The Railway Labor Act applies to employees of railroad and air carriers.

8. National Labor Relations Board

Administration of the NLRA is entrusted to the five-member National Labor Relations Board (NLRB, or Board) and the general counsel of the Board. The general counsel is responsible for investigating and prosecuting all unfair labor practice cases. The five-member Board's major function is to decide unfair labor practice cases brought before it by the general counsel.

The Board is also responsible for conducting representation and decertification elections. This responsibility is delegated to the regional directors of the 32 regional offices located throughout the United States who (1) determine the appropriateness of each proposed bargaining unit for the purpose of collective bargaining, (2) investigate petitions for the certification or decertification of unions, and (3) conduct elections to determine the choice of the majority of those employees voting in the election. Should a majority of the employees voting select a union, the NLRB will certify that union as the exclusive representative of all employees within the unit for the purpose of bargaining with the employer to obtain a contract with respect to wages, hours, and other conditions of employment.

9. Election Conduct

The Board of the NLRB has promulgated preelection rules restricting electioneering activities so that the election will express the true desire of employees. The NLRA prohibits employer interference or coercion during the preelection period. The act also prohibits during this period employer statements that contain threats of reprisal or promises of benefits. **For Example,** it is a violation of section 8(c) of the NLRA for a Southern California manufacturer to make implied threats to relocate its plant to Mexico if the employees choose union representation. Furthermore, when the company announced its intent to move to Mexico one day after the union won a representation election, the Labor Board obtained an injunction against the move.[20]

The Board prohibits all electioneering activities at polling places and has formulated a "24-hour rule," which prohibits both unions and employers from making speeches to captive audiences within 24 hours of an election. The rationale is to preserve free elections and prevent any party from obtaining undue advantage.

10. Union Activity on Private Property

Although section 7 of the NLRA gives employees the statutory right to self-organization, employers have the undisputed right to make rules to maintain discipline in their establishments. Generally speaking, employers may prohibit union solicitation by employees during work periods. During nonworking time, employers may prohibit activity and communications only for legitimate efficiency and safety reasons and only if the prohibitions are not manifestly intended to impede employees' exercise of their rights under the law. Nonunion employers, moreover, may not refuse to interview or retain union members because of their union membership. And even if a union pays an individual working for a nonunion employer to help organize the company, that individual is still protected under the NLRA.[21]

An employer may validly post its property against all nonemployee solicitations, including distribution of union literature, if reasonable efforts by the union through other available channels of communication would enable it to reach the employees with its message.

11. Firing Employees for Union Activity

Although employers and supervisors often feel betrayed by individual employees who take leadership roles in forming organizations, the NLRA prohibits discrimination against such employees because of their union activity.

[20] See *Quadrtech Corp.*, NLRB, No 21–CA–33997 (settlement Dec. 11, 2000).

[21] *NLRB v Town & Country Electric, Inc.*, 516 US 85 (1995).

FIGURE 39-1 Employer and Union Unfair Labor Practices Charge

UNFAIR LABOR PRACTICES CHARGES AGAINST EMPLOYERS	SECTION OF THE NLRA*
1. Restrain or coerce employees in the exercise of their rights under section 7; threat of reprisals or promise of benefits	8(a)(1); 8(c)
2. Dominate or interfere with the formation or administration of a labor organization or contribute financial or other support to it	8(a)(2)
3. Discriminate in regard to hire or tenure of employment or any term or condition of employment in order to encourage or discourage membership in any labor organization	8(a)(3)
4. Discharge or otherwise discriminate against employees because they have given testimony under the act	8(a)(4)
5. Refuse to bargain collectively with representatives of its employees	8(a)(5)

UNFAIR LABOR PRACTICES CHARGES AGAINST UNIONS	SECTION OF THE NLRA
1. Restrain or coerce employees in the exercise of their rights under section 7	8(b)(1)(A)
2. Restrain or coerce an employer in the selection of its representatives	8(b)(1)(B)
3. Cause or attempt to cause an employer to discriminate against an employee	8(b)(2)
4. Refuse to bargain collectively with the employer	8(b)(3)
5. Require employees to pay excessive fees for membership	8(b)(5)
6. Engage in "featherbed practices" of seeking pay for services not performed	8(b)(6)
7. Use secondary boycotts (banned, except for publicity proviso)	8(b)(4)
8. Allow recognitional and organizational picketing by an uncertified union	8(b)(7)
9. Enter into "hot cargo" agreements, except for construction and garment industries	8(e)

* 29 USC § 151.

The NLRB has found evidence of discrimination against active union supporters when the employer

1. Discharges on the strength of past misdeeds that were condoned;
2. Neglects to give customary warnings prior to discharge;
3. Discharges for a rule generally unenforced;
4. Applies disproportionately severe punishment to union supporters; or
5. Effects layoffs in violation of seniority status with disproportionate impact on union supporters.

The NLRA preserves the right of the employer to maintain control over the workforce in the interest of discipline, efficiency, and pleasant and safe customer

ETHICS & THE LAW

MAY A "SALT" LIE HIS WAY INTO A JOB?

"Salting" is a practice whereby a union inserts paid organizers into a workforce in the hope of organizing it. Starnes stated on his job application for work at Hartman Brothers, Inc., that he had been "laid off" by a previous employer from a job paying $11 an hour when in truth he had taken a leave of absence to participate in a union's organizing efforts at Hartman Brothers. Hartman Brothers paid $8.50 per hour, so had Starnes disclosed that he had taken a leave of absence from a higher-paying job, Hartman might have "smelled a rat," for why would someone take a leave of absence to earn less pay unless he were a "salt"? When Mr. Hartman was informed Starnes was a union organizer, Starnes was sent home. State law makes it a crime for a person to "knowingly or intentionally make a false or misleading written statement with the intent to obtain . . . employment." A lie related solely to one's union affiliation or unionizing intentions, rather than one's fitness for the job, cannot be material to a hiring decision under the U.S. Supreme Court's *Town & Country* decision. Can an employer turn down an applicant for a job on the basis of a lie about salt status? Will state law prevail over the *Town & Country* precedent? Is an employer entitled to infer that a salt will not be a bona fide employee? Is it ethical for an employee to lie about salt status when he knows that if he tells the truth, he will not be hired? [See *Hartman Brothers Heating & Air Conditioning, Inc. v NLRB,* 280 F3d 1110 (7th Cir 2002); and *Fluor Daniel Inc., v NLRB,* 332 F3d 961 (6th Cir 2003), *cert denied* 125 SCt 964 (2005)]

E-COMMERCE AND CYBERLAW

UNION ORGANIZING AND OTHER MANAGEMENT CHALLENGES THROUGH ELECTRONIC COMMUNICATIONS

E-mail and the Internet are efficient and effective means of communicating information about employment-related matters. Section 7 of the National Labor Relations Act permits "employees" to engage in "concerted activities for the purposes of collective bargaining or other mutual aid or protection." The term *employee* is broadly defined to include job applicants and all current nonsupervisory employees, either union or nonunion. Many labor unions maintain Web sites that assist individuals in forming labor unions.* And many employees with access to computers at work can readily communicate with one

*For example, the United Auto Workers's Web site is **http://www.uaw.org;** the United Food and Commercial Workers's Web site is **http://www.ufcw.org;** and the Teamsters Union's Web site is **http://www.teamsters.org.**

E-COMMERCE AND CYBERLAW

continued

another about the benefits of unionization or otherwise challenge certain management policies.

In the National Labor Relations Board's TIMEKEEPING SYSTEMS INC.** decision, the Board ordered the reinstatement with back pay of a nonunion software employee, Lawrence Leinweber, who was fired for sending an e-mail to fellow employees critical of the company's new mandatory vacation policy that would close the business December 23 and reopen it on January 2 each year. The company memo announcing the policy asserted that employees would "actually get more days off each year." Leinweber demonstrated in his e-mail that the company's assertion was false. The Board found that the e-mail message to other employees in opposition to the company's proposal was "concerted activity" protected under section 7 of the NLRA even though the company was a nonunion employer.

The TIMEKEEPING SYSTEMS case indicates that the NLRB will apply traditional labor law precedents to electronic communications.

** 323 NLRB No. 30 (1997).

relations. Employees, on the other hand, have the right to be free from coercive discrimination resulting from union activity.

At times these two rights may collide. For example, an employee may be discharged for apparently two reasons: (1) violation of a valid company rule and (2) union activity. The employer gives the former as the reason for termination; the latter remains unstated on the employer's part, causing the filing of a section 8(a)(3) unfair labor practice charge against the employer. These are known as *dual motive cases.* The general counsel must present on behalf of the dismissed employee a prima facie case that such protected conduct as union activity was a motivating factor in the dismissal. After this showing, the burden shifts to the employer, who must prove that the employee would have been dismissed for legitimate business reasons even absent the protected conduct.

The *Transportation Management* case is a dual motive case.

NLRB V TRANSPORTATION MANAGEMENT CORP., 462 US 393 (1983)

THE SAM SANTILLO STORY

Prior to his discharge, Sam Santillo was a bus driver for Transportation Management Corp. On March 19, 1979, Santillo talked to officials of the Teamster's Union about organizing the drivers who worked with him. Over the next four days, Santillo discussed with his fellow drivers the possibility of joining the Teamsters and distributed authorization cards. On the night of March 23, George Patterson, who supervised Santillo and the other drivers, told one of the drivers that he had heard of Santillo's activities. Patterson referred to Santillo as two-faced and promised to get even with him. Later that evening, Patterson talked to Ed West, who was also a bus driver for Transportation Management. Patterson asked, "What's with Sam and the Union?" Patterson said that he took Santillo's actions personally, recounted several favors he had done for Santillo, and added that he would remember Santillo's activities when Santillo again asked for a favor. On Monday, March 26, Santillo was discharged. Patterson told Santillo that he was being fired for leaving his keys in the bus and taking unauthorized breaks. Santillo filed charges with the Board, and the General Counsel issued a complaint alleging that Santillo was discharged because of his union activities in distributing authorization cards to fellow employees. The administrative law judge (ALJ) determined that Patterson's disapproval of Santillo's practice of leaving his keys in the bus was clearly a pretext because this practice was commonplace among company employees. The company identified two types of unauthorized breaks: coffee breaks and stops at home. With respect to both coffee breaks and stopping at home, the ALJ found that Santillo was never cautioned or admonished about such behavior and that the employer had not followed its customary practice of issuing three written warnings before discharging a driver. The ALJ also found that taking coffee breaks during work hours was normal practice and that the company tolerated the practice unless the breaks interfered with the driver's duties. The ALJ found that the company had never taken any adverse personnel action against an employee because of such behavior. The Board adopted the ALJ's findings. The U.S. Court of Appeals for the First Circuit refused to enforce the Board's order, and an appeal was taken to the Supreme Court.

Judicial Opinion

WHITE, J. . . . The Court of Appeals erred in holding that § 10 (c) forbids placing the burden on the employer to prove that absent the improper motivation he would have acted in the same manner for wholly legitimate reasons. . . .

The employer is a wrongdoer; he has acted out of a motive that is declared illegitimate by the statute. It is fair that he bear the risk that the influence of legal and illegal motives cannot be separated, because he knowingly created the risk and because the risk was created not by innocent activity but by his own wrongdoing. . . .

The Board was justified in this case in concluding that Santillo would not have been discharged had the employer not considered his efforts to establish a union. At least two of the transgressions that purportedly would have in any event prompted Santillo's discharge were commonplace, and yet no transgressor had ever before received any kind of discipline. Moreover, the employer departed from its usual practice in dealing with rules infractions; indeed, not only did the employer not warn Santillo that his actions would result in being subjected to discipline, it never even expressed its disapproval of his conduct. In addition, Patterson, the person who made the initial decision to discharge Santillo, was obviously upset with Santillo for engaging in such protected activity. It is thus clear that the Board's finding that Santillo would not have been fired if the employer had not had an anti-union animus was "supported by substantial evidence on the record considered as a whole." . . .

[Judgment reversed]

Questions

1. According to the General Counsel, why was Santillo fired by his employer?
2. According to the company, why was Santillo fired?
3. Did the Supreme Court find that the Board was justified in concluding that Santillo would not have been discharged had the employer not considered his efforts to establish a union?

12. Duty of Employer to Bargain Collectively

Once a union wins a representative election, the Board certifies the union as the exclusive bargaining representative of the employees. The employer then has the obligation under the NLRA to bargain with the union in good faith over wages, hours, and working conditions. These matters are *mandatory subjects of bargaining* and include seniority provisions, promotions, layoff and recall provisions, no-strike no-lockout clauses, and grievance procedures. Employers also have an obligation to bargain about the "effects" of the shutdown of a part of a business[22] and may have an obligation to bargain over the decision to relocate bargaining unit work to other plants.[23]

Permissive subjects of bargaining are those over which an employer's refusal to bargain is not a section 8(a)(5) unfair labor practice. Examples are the required use of union labels, internal union affairs, union recognition clauses, and benefits for already retired workers.

[22] *First National Maintenance v NLRB*, 452 US 666 (1981).

[23] *Dubuque Packing Co. and UFCWIU, Local 150A*, 303 NLRB 66 (1991).

13. Right to Work

The NLRA allows states to enact **right-to-work laws.** These laws restrict unions and employers from negotiating clauses in their collective bargaining agreements that make union membership compulsory.[24]

Advocates of such laws contend that compulsory union membership is contrary to the First Amendment right of freedom of association. Unions have attacked these laws as unfair because unions must represent all employees, and in right-to-work states where a majority of employees vote for union representation, nonunion employees receive all of the benefits of collective bargaining contracts without paying union dues.

14. Strike and Picketing Activity

If the parties reach an impasse in the negotiation process for a collective bargaining agreement, a union may call a strike and undertake picketing activity to enforce its bargaining demands. Strikers in such a situation are called **economic strikers.** Although the strike activity is legal, the employers may respond by hiring temporary or permanent replacement workers.

(a) Rights of Strikers

Economic strikers who unconditionally apply for reinstatement when their positions are filled by permanent replacements are not entitled to return to work at the end of the economic strike. They are, however, entitled to full reinstatement when positions become available.

Strikers responsible for misconduct while out on strike may be refused reemployment by the employer.

When employees strike to protest an employer's unfair labor practice, such as firing an employee for union-organizing activity, these unfair labor practice strikers have a right to return to their jobs immediately at the end of the strike. This right exists even if the employer has hired permanent replacements.[25]

(b) Picketing

Placing persons outside a business at the site of a labor dispute so that they may, by signs or banners, inform the public of the existence of a labor dispute is called **primary picketing** and is legal. Should the picketing employees mass together in great numbers in front of the gates of the employer's facility to effectively shut down the entrances, such coercion is called **mass picketing**; it is illegal. **Secondary picketing** is picketing an employer with whom a union has no dispute to persuade the employer to stop doing business with a party to the dispute. Secondary picketing is generally illegal under the NLRA. An exception exists for certain product picketing at supermarkets or other multiproduct retail stores provided that it is limited to asking customers not to purchase the struck product at the neutral employer's store.[26]

15. Regulation of Internal Union Affairs

To ensure the honest and democratic administration of unions, Congress passed the Labor-Management Reporting and Disclosure Act (LMRDA).[27] Title IV of the LMRDA establishes democratic standards for all elections for union offices, including

1. Secret ballots in local union elections;
2. Opportunity for members to nominate candidates;
3. Advance notice of elections;
4. Observers at polling and at ballot-counting stations for all candidates;
5. Publication of results and preservation of records for one year;
6. Prohibition of any income from dues or assessments to support candidates for union office; and
7. Advance opportunity for each candidate to inspect the membership name and address lists.

[24] Right-to-work statutes declare unlawful any agreement that denies persons the right to work because of nonmembership in a union or the failure to pay dues to a union as a condition of employment. These laws have been adopted in Alabama, Arizona, Arkansas, Florida, Georgia, Idaho, Iowa, Kansas, Louisiana, Mississippi, Nebraska, Nevada, North Carolina, North Dakota, Oklahoma, South Carolina, South Dakota, Tennessee, Texas, Utah, Virginia, and Wyoming.

[25] *Poly America, Inc. v NLRB,* 260 F3d 465 (5th Cir 2001).

[26] *NLRB v Fruit and Vegetable Packers, Local 760 (Tree Fruits, Inc.),* 377 US 58 (1964); but see *NLRB v Retail Clerks, Local 1001 (Safeco Title Ins. Co.),* 477 US 607 (1980).

[27] 29 USC §§ 401–531.

C. Pension Plans and Federal Regulation

The Employee Retirement Income Security Act (ERISA)[28] was adopted in 1974 to protect employee pensions.

CPA 16. ERISA

The act sets forth fiduciary standards and requirements for administration, vesting, funding, and termination insurance.

(a) Administration

Commonly a "benefits claims committee" is set up under the plan to make determinations about coverage issues, and courts will not disturb the finding of a benefits committee unless the determinations are "arbitrary and capricious." **For Example,** Joe Gustafson, who provided chauffeur services for senior executives at NYNEX for a number of years while classified as an independent contractor, sought benefits under ERISA because he asserted he was a common law employee of NYNEX. While the court determined he was in fact an employee entitled to overtime compensation under the Fair Labor Standards Act, the court was compelled to defer to the benefits committee's determination that Gustafson was not an employee under the NYNEX plan because he was not "on the payroll" as required by the plan guidelines. The court found that such a determination was not arbitrary or capricious.[29]

CPA (b) Fiduciary Standards and Reporting

Persons administering a pension fund must handle it to protect the interest of employees.[30]

The fact that an employer contributed all or part of the money to the pension fund does not entitle it to use the fund as though the employer still owned it. Persons administering pension plans must make detailed reports to the Secretary of Labor.

CPA (c) Vesting

Vesting is the right of an employee to pension benefits paid into a pension plan in the employee's name by the employer. Prior to ERISA, many pension plans did not vest accrued benefits until an employee had 20 to 25 years of service. Thus, an employee who was forced to terminate service after 18 years would have no pension rights or benefits. Under ERISA, employees' rights must be fully vested within five or seven years in accordance with the two vesting options available under the law.

In the past, it had been common for pension plans to contain break-in-service clauses, whereby employees who left their employment for a period longer than one year for any reason other than an on-the-job injury lost pension eligibility rights. Under the Retirement Equity Act of 1984,[31] an individual can leave the workforce for up to five consecutive years and still retain eligibility for pension benefits.

CPA (d) Funding

ERISA requires that employers make contributions to their pension funds on a basis that is actuarially determined so that the pension fund will be large enough to make the payments that will be required of it.

(e) Termination Insurance

ERISA established an insurance plan to protect employees when an employer goes out of business. To provide this protection, the statute created a Pension Benefit Guaranty Corporation (PBGC). In effect, this corporation guarantees that employees will receive benefits in much the same way as the Federal Deposit Insurance Corporation protects bank depositors. The PBGC is financed by small payments made by employers for every employee covered by a pension plan.

(f) Enforcement

ERISA authorizes the Secretary of Labor and employees to bring court actions to compel the observance of statutory requirements.

D. Unemployment Benefits, Family Leaves, and Social Security

Generally, when employees are without work through no fault of their own, they are eligible for unemployment compensation benefits. Twelve-week

[28] PL 93-406, 88 Stat 829, 29 USC §§ 1001–1381.

[29] *Gustafson v Bell Atlantic Corp.*, 171 F Supp 2d 311 (SDNY 2001).

[30] *John Hancock Mutual Life Ins. Co. v Harris Trust*, 510 US 86 (1993).

[31] PL 98-397, 29 USC § 1001.

maternity, paternity, or adoption leaves and family and medical leaves are available for qualifying employees. Social Security provides certain benefits, including retirement and disability benefits.

17. Unemployment Compensation

Unemployment compensation today is provided primarily through a federal-state system under the unemployment insurance provisions of the Social Security Act of 1935.[32] All states have laws that provide similar benefits, and the state agencies are loosely coordinated under the federal act. Agricultural employees, domestic employees, and state and local government employees are not covered by this federal-state system. Federal programs of unemployment compensation exist for federal civilian workers and former military service personnel. A separate federal unemployment program applies to railroad workers.

(a) Eligibility

In most states, an unemployed person must be available for placement in a similar job and willing to take such employment at a comparable rate of pay. Full-time students generally have difficulty proving that they are available for work while they are still going to school.

If an employee quits a job without cause or is fired for misconduct, the employee is ordinarily disqualified from receiving unemployment compensation benefits. **For Example,** stealing property from an employer constitutes misconduct for which benefits will be denied. Moreover, an employee's refusal to complete the aftercare portion of an alcohol treatment program has been found to be misconduct connected with work, disqualifying the employee from receiving benefits.

(b) Funding

Employers are taxed for unemployment benefits based on each employer's "experience rating" account. Thus, employers with a stable workforce with no layoffs, who therefore do not draw on the state unemployment insurance fund, pay lower tax rates. Employers whose experience ratings are higher pay higher rates. Motivated by the desire to avoid higher unemployment taxes, employers commonly challenge the state's payment of unemployment benefits to individuals who they believe are not properly entitled to benefits.

18. Family and Medical Leaves of Absence

The Family and Medical Leave Act of 1993 (FMLA)[33] entitles an eligible employee, whether male or female, to a total of 12 workweeks of unpaid leave during any 12-month period (1) because of the birth or adoption of the employee's son or daughter, (2) to care for the employee's spouse, son, daughter, or parent with a serious health condition, or (3) because of a serious health condition that makes the employee unable to perform the functions of his or her position. Notice should be given by the employer to an employee that the leave he or she is taking will count against FMLA entitlement in order to comply with the Secretary of Labor's regulations.[34] In the case of an employee's serious health condition or that of a covered family member, an employer may require the employee to use any accrued paid vacation, personal, medical, or sick leave toward any part of the 12-week leave provided by the act. When an employee requests leave because of the birth or adoption of a child, the employer may require the employee to use all available paid personal, vacation, and medical leave, but not sick leave, toward any FMLA leave.

To be eligible for FMLA leave, an employee must have been employed by a covered employer for at least 12 months and have worked at least 1,250 hours during the 12-month period preceding the leave. Covered employers are those that employ 50 or more employees.[35] Upon return from FMLA leave, the employee is entitled to be restored to the same or an equivalent position with equivalent pay and benefits. **For Example,** when Magda Brenlla returned to her position at LaSorsa Buick in the Bronx, New York, after quadruple bypass surgery, she was terminated by the owner who told her he had decided to consolidate the positions of office manager and controller, even though he had no business plan for restructuring, and soon thereafter had to hire additional help in the office. The judge upheld a jury verdict of $320,000, finding that the jury had ample

[32] 42 USC §§ 301–1397e.

[33] 29 USC §§ 2601–2654.

[34] See *Ragsdale v Volverine World Wide, Inc.*, 122 S Ct 1155 (2002).

[35] *Bellum v PCE Constructors Inc.*, 407 F3d 734 (5th Cir 2005).

evidence to conclude that the real reason for her termination was her FMLA leave.[36]

The FMLA provides specific statutory relief for violations of the provisions of the act, including pay to the employee for damages equal to lost wages and benefits or any actual monetary losses, plus interest, plus an equal amount in liquidated damages.[37]

19. Leaves for Military Service Under USERRA

The Uniformed Services Employment and Re-Employment Rights Act (USERRA) was enacted in 1994 to encourage noncareer service in the armed services, minimize the disruption experienced in the civilian careers of reservists, and promote prompt reemployment of reservists upon return from military leave.[38] In the context of mobilizing more than 500,000 reservists between September 11, 2001, and the summer of 2006, the USERRA has and will have a broad impact on U.S. employers as it provides reemployment and benefit protection rights for returning military personnel and prohibits discrimination against individuals because of their application for or performance of military service.[39]

(a) Protections

Section 4312 of the USERRA generally requires returning reservists to be "promptly reemployed" and returned to the same or comparable positions of like seniority, status, and pay they would have had if they had not been activated. Moreover, Section 4316(c) provides that persons reemployed under the act shall not be discharged from employment within a year of their reemployment if their period of service was more than 180 days. For service of more than 30 days, the protective period is 180 days. However, the employer may terminate an individual for cause regardless of the duration of service.

Sections 4312(a)(3) and (4) provide protection for those disabled while in the service and requires employers to make reasonable efforts to accommodate each employee's disability so that each individual may return to the same or comparable positions or, if no longer qualified for the position, allow for the transfer to a position the disabled individual can perform closest to the prior position in terms of seniority, status, and pay.

Section 4323 of the act provides a full range of remedies, including back pay for loss of wages and benefits as well as liquidated damages in an amount equal to the actual damages when the employer's failure to comply with the act was willful. The Department of Labor has issued USERRA regulations.[40] The act's enforcement is performed by the U.S. Justice Department's Division of Civil Rights.

(b) Defenses

In addition to an employer's right to terminate a reemployed serviceperson for cause, employers may be excused from reemploying or continuing employment of persons under § 4312(d)(1) of the act when the employer's circumstances have so changed as to make reemployment impossible, unreasonable, or an undue hardship. The burden of proof on the matter is on the employer. **For Example,** Joseph Duarte was called to active duty in the Marine Corps Reserve from November 2002 to July 2003. On his return, he was given his same pay but diminished status by being assigned a temporary assignment rather than acting as a primary consultant to one of the employer's business groups. Faced with financial need to reduce its payroll, the employer eliminated Duarte's temporary assignment and terminated him in November 2003 for what it believed was economic "cause." Duarte believed that his termination violated the USERRA. The court disagreed with the employer and determined that Duarte was within the act's one-year protective period and had been returned to work in the diminished status of a temporary assignment that was a direct result of his military service. Duarte was awarded back pay of $114,500 and front pay of $324,000, less $55,000 in severance benefits already paid him, for a total of $384,000 in damages.[41] Liquidated damages equal to $384,000 were declined because the employer's actions were not deemed willful.

[36] *Brenlla v LaSorsa Buick*, 2002 WL 1059117 (SDNY 2002).

[37] See *Arban v West Publishing Co.*, 345 F3d 390 (6th Cir 2003), in which the U.S. Court of Appeals required the doubling of a jury verdict of $130,000 under the FMLA provision providing for liquidated damages unless the employer is able to prove that it acted "in good faith..." and had reasonable grounds to believe it was not in violation of the FMLA. 29 USC § 2617(a)(iii).

[38] 38 USC § 4301 (2005).

[39] 38 USC § 4312, 4316, and 4317 (2005).

[40] 30 Federal Register Vol. 70 No. 242 (Dec. 19, 2005).

[41] *Duarte v Agilent Technologies, Inc.*, 366 F Supp 2d 1039 (D Colo 2005).

(c) Discrimination and Retaliation Protection

As opposed to the protections contained in Section 4312, the act's Section 4311 provides separate and distinct statutory protection against discrimination of employees on the basis of military service and retaliation against individuals, whether military or not, who give testimony or statements on behalf of a USERRA claimant. **For Example,** a Section 4311 descrimination violation is made out that bakery driver Robert Mills was terminated by Multigrain Baking Co. because of his need to have time off for reserve duty training after the personnel director, Marsha Coyle, testified on cross-examination, "If we knew Bobby Mills was in the Guard, we would not have hired him. These drivers have to be available to protect their territories or we lose business."

20. Social Security

Employees and employers are required to pay Social Security taxes, which provide employees with four types of insurance protection: retirement benefits, disability benefits, life insurance benefits, and health insurance (Medicare). The federal Social Security Act established a federal program of aid for the aged, the blind, and the disabled. This is called the Supplemental Security Income (SSI) program. Payments are administered directly by the Social Security Administration, which became an independent government agency in 1995.

E. Employees' Health and Safety

The Occupational Safety and Health Act of 1970 (OSHA) was passed to assure every worker, so far as possible, safe and healthful working conditions and to preserve the country's human resources.[42] OSHA provides for (1) the establishment of safety and health standards and (2) effective enforcement of these standards and the other employer duties required by OSHA.

21. Standards

The Secretary of Labor has broad authority under OSHA to promulgate occupational safety and health standards.[43] Except in emergency situations, public hearings and publication in the *Federal Register* are required before the secretary can issue a new standard. Any person adversely affected may then challenge the validity of the standard in a U.S. court of appeals. The secretary's standards will be upheld if they are reasonable and supported by substantial evidence. The secretary must demonstrate a need for a new standard by showing that it is reasonably necessary to protect employees against a "significant risk" of material health impairment. The cost of compliance with new standards may run into billions of dollars. The secretary is not required to do a cost-benefit analysis for a new standard but must show that the standard is economically feasible.

22. Employer Duties

Employers have a "general duty" to furnish each employee a place of employment that is free from hazards that are likely to cause death or serious physical injuries.

OSHA requires employers to maintain records of occupational illness and injuries if they result in death, loss of consciousness, or one or more lost workdays or if they require medical treatment other than first aid. Such records have proven to be a valuable aid in recognizing areas of risk. They have been especially helpful in identifying the presence of occupational illnesses.

23. Enforcement

The Occupational Safety and Health Administration (also identified as OSHA) is the agency within the Department of Labor that administers the act. OSHA has authority to conduct inspections and to seek enforcement action when noncompliance has occurred. Worksite inspections are conducted when employer records indicate incidents involving fatalities or serious injuries.[44] These inspections may also result from employee complaints. The act protects employees making complaints from employer retaliation. Employers have the right to require an OSHA inspector to secure a warrant before inspecting the employer's plant.

If OSHA issues a citation for a violation of workplace health or safety standards, the employer may challenge the citation before the Occupational Safety and Health Review Commission (OSHRC). Judicial review of a commission ruling is obtained

[42] 29 USC § 651 *et seq.*

[43] *Martin v OSHRC*, 499 US 144 (1991).

[44] *Chao v Mallard Bay Drilling Co.*, 122 S Ct 738 (2002).

before a U.S. court of appeals. **For Example,** after an accident at Staley Manufacturing Company's Decatur, Illinois, plant in which an employee was fatally asphyxiated, OSHA inspectors issued citations for multiple violations of the OSH Act. The employer challenged the citations before the OSHRC. Upon review by the U.S. Court of Appeals, the court affirmed OSHRC's decision, finding that the company's "plain indifference" to act on the hazards at the workplace and train employees how to handle the hazards was a willful violation of the act, allowing for civil penalty of no more than $70,000 for each violation.[45]

The Occupational Safety and Health Act provides that no employer shall discharge or in any manner discriminate against employees because they filed a complaint with OSHA, testified in any OSHA proceeding, or exercised any right afforded by the act. A regulation issued by the Secretary of Labor under the act provides that if employees with no reasonable alternative refuse in good faith to expose themselves to a dangerous condition, they will be protected against subsequent discrimination. The Secretary of Labor may obtain injunctive and other appropriate relief in a U.S. district court against an employer who discriminates against employees for testifying or exercising any right under the act.

24. State "Right-to-Know" Legislation

Laws that guarantee individual workers the "right to know" if there are hazardous substances in their workplaces have been enacted by many states in recent years. These laws commonly require an employer to make known to an employee's physician the chemical composition of certain workplace substances in connection with the employee's diagnosis and treatment by the physician. Furthermore, local fire and public health officials, as well as local neighborhood residents, are given the right to know if local employers are working with hazardous substances that could pose health or safety problems.

F. Compensation for Employees' Injuries

For most kinds of employment, workers' compensation statutes govern compensation for injuries. These statutes provide that an injured employee is entitled to compensation for accidents occurring in the course of employment from a risk involved in that employment.

CPA 25. Common Law Status of Employer

In some employment situations, common law principles apply. Workers' compensation statutes commonly do not apply to employers with fewer than a prescribed minimum number of employees or to agricultural, domestic, or casual employment. When an exempted area of employment is involved, it is necessary to consider the duties and defenses of employers apart from workers' compensation statutes.

(a) Duties

The employer is under the common law duty to furnish an employee with a reasonably safe place in which to work, reasonably safe tools and appliances, and a sufficient number of competent fellow employees for the work involved. The employer is also under the common law duty to warn the employee of any unusual dangers particular to the employer's business.

(b) Defenses

At common law, the employer is not liable to an injured employee if the employee is harmed by the act of a fellow employee. Similarly, an employer is not liable at common law to an employee harmed by an ordinary hazard of the work because the employee assumed such risks. If the employee is guilty of contributory negligence, regardless of the employer's negligence, the employer is not liable at common law to an injured employee.

26. Statutory Changes

The rising incidence of industrial accidents resulting from the increasing use of more powerful machinery and the growth of the industrial labor population led to a demand for statutory modification of common law rules relating to the liability of employers for industrial accidents.

(a) Modification of Employer's Common Law Defenses

One type of change by statute was to modify the defenses that an employer could assert when sued by an

[45] *A. E. Staley Manufacturing Co. v Chao*, 295 F3d 1341 (DC Cir 2002).

employee for damages. **For Example,** under the Federal Employer's Liability Act (FELA), which covers railroad workers, the injured employee must still bring an action in court and prove the negligence of the employer or other employees. However, the burden of proving the case is made lighter by limitations on employers' defenses. Under FELA, contributory negligence is a defense only in mitigation of damages; assumption of the risk is not a defense.[46]

(b) Workers' Compensation

A more sweeping development was made by the adoption of workers' compensation statutes in every state. In addition, civil employees of the U.S. government are covered by the Federal Employees' Compensation Act. When an employee is covered by a workers' compensation statute and the injury is job connected, the employee's remedy is limited to that provided in the workers' compensation statute.[47]

Workers' compensation proceedings are brought before a special administrative agency or workers' compensation board. In contrast, a common law action for damages or an action for damages under an employer's liability statute is brought in a court of law.

The *Wal-Mart Stores* case illustrates the exclusivity of workers' compensation acts.

BRYANT V WAL-MART STORES, INC., 417 SE2D 688 (GA CT APP 1922)

LOCKED IN

Bryant was the administrator of the estate of a deceased employee and the guardian of the deceased's minor child. He sued Wal-Mart for damages following the death of the employee on the theory of unlawful false imprisonment. While working on the night restocking crew, the employee suffered a stroke. Medical personnel arrived six minutes later but could not enter the store because management had locked all the doors, and no manager was present to open one. By the time the medical crew entered the store to assist the employee, it was unable to revive her and she died 15 minutes later. Bryant contends that false imprisonment occurred between the time the employee became ill until the time the medical team was able to enter the store. Wal-Mart claimed that Bryant's exclusive remedy was under Georgia's Workers' Compensation Act. From a judgment for Wal-Mart, Bryant appealed.

Judicial Opinion

COOPER, J.... Even if appellant established a claim of false imprisonment, "it is well settled in this state that a claim under the workers' compensation act is the employee's sole and exclusive remedy for injury or occupational disease incurred *in the course of employment.* This edict is statutory... as well as judicial, and its policy reasons are well understood.... The Act precludes recovery "for willful or intentional acts of the employer so long as the injury arises out of and in the course of employment...." It is undisputed that the deceased was locked in the store for business purposes, that she was engaged in the performance of her work duties at the time she suffered the stroke and that the emergency medical crew was unable to render immediate assistance to the deceased due to the delay in gaining entrance to the store. Therefore, insofar as appellant seeks to recover for the death of the deceased, that claim is barred by the exclusivity provisions of the Act.

Appellant contends however, that in certain counts of his complaint, he seeks to recover for injuries to the deceased's peace, happiness, and feelings and that these "nonphysical" injuries are not included within the definition of injury found in the Act.... "That an injury is not *compensable* under the act does not necessarily mean it is not within the *purview* of the act.... 'In exchange for the right to recover scheduled compensation without proof of negligence on the part of the employer in those cases in which a right of recovery is granted, the employee forgoes other rights and remedies which he might otherwise have had, but if he accepts the terms of the Act he as well as the employer is limited to those things for which the Act makes provision.'"... Appellant argues that the deceased's

[46] 45 USC § 1 *et seq.*

[47] Immunity from a tort action based on workers' compensation law applies only to the injured employee's employer, not the owner of the work location. See *Peronto v Case Corp.*, 693 NW2d 133 (Wisc App 2005).

nonphysical injuries and subsequent death occurred due to the inability of the emergency medical personnel to render prompt medical attention. That injuries to the deceased's peace, happiness, and feelings may not be compensable under the Act does not take those injuries out of the purview of the Act.... Accordingly, we hold that under the facts of this case, the Workers' Compensation Act provides the exclusive remedy and precludes appellant's common law tort action.

[Judgment affirmed]

Questions

1. State the issue before the court.
2. Why did Bryant bring an action for damages in a court of law when the deceased was covered by the workers' compensation law?
3. When nonphysical injuries are not compensable under the Workers' Compensation Act, may the victim sue under a common law tort theory such as false imprisonment?

For injuries arising within the course of the employee's work from a risk involved in that work, workers' compensation statutes usually provide (1) immediate medical benefits, (2) prompt periodic wage replacement, often computed as a percentage of weekly wages (ranging from 50 percent to 80 percent of the injured employee's wage) for a specified number of weeks, and (3) a death benefit of a limited amount.[48] In such cases, compensation is paid without regard to whether the employer or the employee was negligent. However, no compensation is generally allowed for a willful, self-inflicted injury or one sustained while intoxicated.

There has been a gradual widening of the workers' compensation statutes, so compensation today is generally recoverable for both accident-inflicted injuries and occupational diseases.

G. Employee Privacy

Employers may want to monitor employee telephone conversations in the ordinary course of their business to evaluate employee performance and customer service; to document business transactions between employees and customers; or to meet special security, efficiency, or other needs. Employers may likewise want to monitor e-mail for what they perceive to be sound business reasons. Employers also may seek to test employees for drug use or search employee lockers for illicit drugs. Litigation may result because employees may believe that such activities violate their right to privacy.

27. Source of Privacy Rights

The Bill of Rights contained in the U.S. Constitution, including the Fourth Amendment, which protects against unreasonable search and seizure, provides a philosophical and legal basis for individual privacy rights for federal employees. The Fourteenth Amendment applies this privacy protection to actions taken by state and local governments that affect their employees. The privacy rights of individuals working in the private sector are not directly controlled by the Bill of Rights, however, because challenged employer actions are not government actions. Limited employee privacy rights in the private sector are provided by statute, case law, and collective bargaining agreements.

28. Monitoring Employee Telephone Conversations

The Federal Wiretapping Act[49] makes it unlawful to intercept oral and electronic communications and provides for both criminal liability and civil damages against the violator. There are two major exceptions, however. The first allows an employer to monitor a firm's telephones in the "ordinary course of business" through the use of extension telephones; a second exception applies when there is prior employee consent to the interception. If employer monitoring results in the interception of a business call, it is within the ordinary-course-of-business exception. Personal calls can be monitored, however, only to the extent necessary to determine that the call is personal, and the employer must then cease listening. **For Example,** Newell Spears taped all phone conversations at his store in trying to find out if an employee was connected to a store theft. He listened to virtually all 22 hours of intercepted and recorded telephone conversations between his employee Sibbie Deal and her boyfriend Calvin Lucas without regard to the conversations' relation to Spears's

[48] *Union Light & Power Co. v DC Department of Employment Services,* 796 A2d 665 (DC App 2002).

[49] Title III of the Omnibus Crime Control and Safe Streets Act of 1968, 28 USC §§ 2510–2520.

business interest. While Spears might well have legitimately monitored Deal's calls to the extent necessary to determine that the calls were personal and made or received in violation of store policy, the scope of the interception in this case was well beyond the boundaries of the ordinary-course-of-business exception and in violation of the act.[50]

Employer monitoring of employee phone calls can be accomplished without fear of violating the act if consent is established. Consent may be established by prior written notice to employees of the employer's monitoring policy. It is prudent, as well, for the employer to give customers notice of the policy through a recorded message as part of the employer's phone-answering system.

29. E-Mail Monitoring

Electronic mail (e-mail) is a primary means of communication in many of today's businesses, serving for some employers as an alternative to faxes, telephones, or the U.S. Postal Service. Employers may want to monitor employees' e-mail messages to evaluate the efficiency and effectiveness of their employees or for corporate security purposes, including the protection of trade secrets and other intangible property interests. When employees are disciplined or terminated for alleged wrongful activities discovered as a result of e-mail searches, however, the issue of privacy may be raised. (See Chapter 2 for a discussion of use of e-mail in litigation and discovery.)

The Electronic Communications Privacy Act of 1986 (ECPA)[51] amended the federal wiretap statute and was intended in part to apply to e-mail. However, ordinary-course-of-business and consent exceptions apply to e-mail, and it would appear that employers have broad latitude to monitor employee e-mail use. **For Example,** Alana Shoars, an e-mail administrator for Epson America, was fired after complaining about her supervisor's reading of employee e-mail messages. Her state court invasion of privacy case was unsuccessful.[52] Very few cases involving e-mail and Web site issues have been adjudicated so far under the ECPA. It has been held that for an employee's secure Web site to be "intercepted" in violation of the wiretap act, the electronic documents acquired must be acquired during transmission, not while in electronic storage.[53]

An employer can place itself within the consent exception of the act by issuing a policy statement to all employees that informs them of the monitoring program and its purposes and justification.

30. Property Searches

Protected by the Fourth Amendment, public-sector employees have a reasonable expectation of privacy with respect to their desks and file cabinets. However, depending on the fact-specific purpose, justification, and scope of the search, the balance of interest should favor the public employer because its interests in supervision, control, and the efficient operation of the workplace outweigh a public employee's privacy interests.[54] Search of a postal service employee's locker was held not to be a Fourth Amendment violation because well-publicized regulations informed employees that their lockers were subject to search to combat pilferage and stealing. However, the warrantless search of the desk and files of a psychiatrist employed by a state hospital was found to be a Fourth Amendment violation, exceeding the scope of a reasonable work-related search when the search examined his private possessions, including purely personal belongings, and management sought to justify the search on false grounds.[55]

In the private sector, employers may create a reasonable expectation of privacy by providing an employee a locker and allowing the employee to provide his or her own lock. A search of that locker could be an invasion of privacy.[56] If, however, the employer provides a locker and lock but retains a master key and this is known to employees, the lockers may be subject to legitimate reasonable searches by the employer. If a private-sector employer notifies all employees of its policy on lockers, desks,

[50] *Deal v Spears*, 580 F2d 1153 (8th Cir 1992); *Arias v Mutual Central Alarm Services, Inc.*, 182 FRD 407 (SDNY 1998).

[51] 18 USC §§ 2510–2520.

[52] See *Shoars v Epson America, Inc.*, 1994 Cal LEXIS 3670 (June 29, 1994).

[53] *Konop v Hawaiian Airlines, Inc.*, 302 F3d 868 (9th Cir 2002); *Fraser v Nationwide Mutual Insurance Co.*, 352 F3d 107 (3rd Cir 2003) (court held that the wiretaps act was not violated because the employer did not "intercept" the e-mail but retrieved it after it had been sent and received).

[54] *O'Connor v Ortega*, 480 US 709 (1987).

[55] *Ortega v O'Connor*, 146 F3d 1149 (9th Cir 1998).

[56] *Kmart Corp. v Trotti*, 677 SW2d 632 (Tex App 1984).

and office searches and the employer complies with its own policy, employees will have no actionable invasion of privacy case.

Many businesses use overt or hidden video cameras as a security method in the workplace to enhance worker safety and to prevent and/or detect theft or other criminal conduct. To avoid state constitutional or statutory claims for invasion of privacy, employers should not set up video cameras in areas where employees have a reasonable expectation of privacy.[57] Utilizing signs to notify employees and members of the public that certain areas are under video surveillance is a common business practice not likely to initiate privacy claims. Additionally, employers should disseminate their written policy on surveillance and obtain a consent form from employees acknowledging that they received this notice to preserve their consent defense.

31. Drug and Alcohol Testing

Drug and alcohol testing is an additional source of privacy concerns for employees. Public-sector employees may see drug and alcohol testing as potentially infringing on their Fourth and Fifth Amendment rights, although they may be subject to this testing on the basis of reasonable suspicion. In ordinary circumstances, however, random drug testing is not permissible in the public sector except for mass transit workers and some safety-sensitive positions. The Federal Omnibus Transportation Employee Testing Act,[58] which covers certain classes of employees working in the airline, railroad, and trucking industries, makes covered employees subject to random drug and alcohol testing. Random drug and alcohol testing of employees working in safety-sensitive positions in the private sector also is permissible, as is the testing of private-sector employees on the basis of reasonable suspicion.

H. Employer-Related Immigration Laws

The Immigration and Naturalization Act (INA), the Immigration Reform and Control Act of 1986 (IRCA), and the Immigration Act of 1990[59] are the principal employer-related immigration laws.

32. Employer Liability

The IRCA sets criminal and civil penalties against employers who knowingly hire aliens who have illegally entered the United States. The IRCA was designed to stop illegal immigration by eliminating job opportunities for these aliens.

33. Employer Verification and Special Hiring Programs

Upon hiring a new employee, an employer must verify that the employee is legally entitled to work in the United States. Both the employer and the employee must fill out portions of Form I-9. Verification documents include a U.S. passport, a certificate of U.S. citizenship, or an Alien Registration Card ("green card"). In lieu of these documents, a state driver's license and a Social Security card are sufficient to prove eligibility to work. The 1990 act prohibits employers from demanding other documentation. Thus, if a prospective employee with a "foreign accent" offers a driver's license and Social Security card and the employer seeks a certificate of U.S. citizenship or a green card, the employer has committed an unfair immigration practice. The employer will be ordered to hire the individual and provide back pay.

H-1 classification visas allow aliens of "distinguished merit and ability" to enter and work in the United States on a temporary basis. These persons include architects, engineers, lawyers, physicians, and teachers. Temporary, foreign, high-tech, "highly skilled" workers are classified as H-1B visa employees. The H-1B Visa Reform Act of 2004 exempts 20,000 individuals from the annual cap applied to the H-1B visa classification of 65,000 visas if the applicants involved have a master's or doctoral degree from a U.S. college or university.[60]

The hiring employer must attest that it will not lay off a U.S. employee 90 days before or after filing a petition to employ a foreign worker regarding any

[57] *See Kline v Security Guards, Inc.*, 386 F3d 246 (3rd Cir 2004). Some 370 employees of Dana Corporation's Reading, Pennsylvania, facility sued the corporation and its security guard company after employees learned that a new audio and video surveillance system at the entrance of the facility allowed what was said in the area where employees "punch in" for work to be observed and heard in the guard booth. The Third Circuit Court of Appeals rejected the employer's preemption claims and remanded the matter to the state court to handle the invasion of privacy and other tort claims.

[58] PL 102-143, 105 Stat 952, 49 USC § 1301 nt.

[59] PL 101-649, 8 USC § 1101.

[60] PL 108-447, 8 USC § 1101 (2005).

THINKING THINGS THROUGH

Unemployed U.S. information technology workers are upset that U.S. high-tech companies are utilizing the H-1B visa program to hire foreign workers in a period of economic decline; they are also upset that U.S. companies are moving computer jobs overseas to countries where labor costs are a fraction of the living wages paid in the United States. For example, General Electric has its computer programming work performed for its worldwide operations in India, employing some 10,000 workers there. Are H-1B foreign professionals taking jobs from qualified U.S. workers? What is the rationale for the H1-B program? Should laws exist restricting the transfer of U.S. technology jobs to countries paying very low wages?

position to be filled by the foreign worker. H-1B professionals must be paid the higher of the actual or prevailing wage for each position to eliminate economic incentives to use this foreign workers program. H-1B professionals may work in the United States for up to six years.

Summary

The relationship of employer and employee is created by the agreement of the parties and is subject to the principles applicable to contracts. If the employment contract sets forth a specific duration, the employer cannot terminate the contract at an earlier date unless just cause exists. If no definite time period is set forth, the individual is an at-will employee. Under the employment-at-will doctrine, an employer can terminate the contract of an at-will employee at any time for any reason or for no reason. Courts in many jurisdictions, however, have carved out exceptions to this doctrine when the discharge violates public policy or is contrary to good faith and fair dealing in the employment relationship. The Fair Labor Standards Act regulates minimum wages, overtime hours, and child labor.

Under the National Labor Relations Act, employees have the right to form a union to obtain a collective bargaining contract or to refrain from organizational activities. The National Labor Relations Board conducts elections to determine whether employees in an appropriate bargaining unit desire to be represented by a union. The NLRA prohibits employers' and unions' unfair labor practices and authorizes the NLRB to conduct proceedings to stop such practices. Economic strikes have limited reinstatement rights. Federal law sets forth democratic standards for the election of union offices.

The Employees Retirement Income Security Act (ERISA) protects employees' pensions by requiring (1) high standards of those administering the funds, (2) reasonable vesting of benefits, (3) adequate funding, and (4) an insurance program to guarantee payments of earned benefits.

Unemployment compensation benefits are paid to persons for a limited period of time if they are out of work through no fault of their own. Persons receiving unemployment compensation must be available for placement in a job similar in duties and comparable in rate of pay to the job they lost. Twelve-week maternity, paternity, and adoption leaves are available under the Family and Medical Leave Act. Employers and employees pay Social Security taxes to provide retirement benefits, disability benefits, life insurance benefits, and Medicare.

The Occupational Safety and Health Act provides for the (1) establishment of safety and health standards and (2) effective enforcement of these standards. Many states have enacted "right-to-know" laws, which require employers to inform their employees of any hazardous substances present in the workplace.

Workers' compensation laws provide for the prompt payment of compensation and medical benefits to persons injured in the course of employment without regard to fault. An injured employee's remedy is generally limited to the remedy provided by the workers' compensation statute. Most states also provide compensation to workers for occupational diseases.

The Bill of Rights is the source of public-sector employees' privacy rights. Private-sector employees may obtain limited privacy rights from statutes, case law, and collective bargaining agreements. Employers may monitor employee telephone calls, although once it is determined that the call is personal, the employer must stop listening or be in violation of the federal wiretap statute. The ordinary-course-of-business and consent exceptions to the Electronic Communications Privacy Act of 1986 (ECPA) give private employers a great deal of latitude to monitor employee e-mail. Notification to employees of employers' policies on searching lockers, desks, and offices reduces employees' expectations of privacy, and a search conducted in conformity with a known policy is generally not an invasion of privacy. Drug and alcohol testing is generally permissible if it is based on reasonable suspicion; random drug and alcohol testing may also be permissible in safety-sensitive positions.

Immigration laws prohibit the employment of aliens who have illegally entered the United States.

Questions and Case Problems

1. What remedies does an employee who has been wrongfully discharged have against an employer?
2. Michael Smyth was an operations manager at Pillsbury Co., and his employment status was that of an employee at will. Smyth received certain e-mail messages at home, and he replied to his supervisor by e-mail. His messages contained some provocative language including the phrase "kill the backstabbing bastards" and a reference to an upcoming company party as the "Jim Jones Koolaid affair." Later, Smyth was given two weeks' notice of his termination, and he was told that his e-mail remarks were inappropriate and unprofessional. Smyth believes that he is the victim of invasion of privacy because the e-mail messages caused his termination, and the company had promised that e-mail communications would not be intercepted and used as a basis for discipline or discharge. The company denies that it intercepted the e-mail messages and points out that Smyth himself sent the unprofessional comments to his supervisor. Is Smyth entitled to reinstatement and back pay because of the invasion of privacy? [*Smyth v Pillsbury Co.*, 914 F Supp 97 (ED Pa)]
3. Michael Hauck claimed that he was discharged by his employer, Sabine Pilot Service, because he refused its direction to perform the illegal act of pumping the bilges of the employer's vessel into the waterways. Hauck was an employee at will, and Sabine contends that it therefore had the right to discharge him without having to show cause. Hauck brought a wrongful discharge action against Sabine. Decide. [*Sabine Pilot Service, Inc., v Hauck*, 687 SW2d 733 (Tex)]
4. Jeanne Eenkhoorn worked as a supervisor at a business office for the New York Telephone Co. While at work, she invented a process for terminating the telephone services of delinquent subscribers. The telephone company used the process but refused to compensate her for it, claiming a shop right. Eenkhoorn then sued for damages on a quasi-contract theory. Decide. [*Eenkhoorn v New York Telephone Co.*,568 NYS2d 677]
5. One Monday, a labor organization affiliated with the International Ladies Garment Workers Union began an organizational drive among the employees of Whittal & Son. On the following Monday, six of the employees who were participating in the union drive were discharged. Immediately after the firings, the head of the company gave a speech to the remaining workers in which he made a variety of antiunion statements and threats. The union filed a complaint with the NLRB, alleging that the six employees were fired because they were engaging in organizational activity and were thus discharged in violation of the NLRA. The employer defended its position, arguing that it had a business to run and that it was barely able to survive in the global economy against cheap labor from third-world countries. It asserted that the last thing it needed was "union baloney." Was the NLRA violated?
6. David Stark submitted an application to the maintenance department of Wyman-Gordon Co. Stark was a journeyman millwright with nine years' experience at a neighboring company at the time of his application to Wyman-Gordon. Stark was vice president of the local industrial workers' union. In his preliminary interview with the company, Ms. Peevler asked if Stark was involved in union activity, and Stark detailed his involvement to her. She informed Stark that Wyman-Gordon was a nonunion shop and asked how he felt about this. Peevler's notes from the interview characterize Stark's response to this question as "seems to lean toward third-party intervention." Company officials testified that Stark's qualifications were "exactly what we were looking for," but he was not hired. Stark claimed that he was discriminated against. Wyman-Gordon denied that any discrimination had occurred. Is a job applicant (as opposed to an employee) entitled to protection from antiunion discrimination? On the facts of this case, has any discrimination taken place? [*Wyman-Gordon Co. v NLRB*, 108 LRRM 2085 (1st Cir)]
7. Michael Paolella was employed as sales manager for Browning-Ferris, Inc. (BFI), with responsibility for a district in Delaware. When the state's Solid Waste Authority announced plans to raise disposal rates 25 percent, the district manager, Ronald Hanley, devised a scheme to increase BFI's revenues by leading customers to believe that increased fees were the result of the 25 percent increase in disposal rates when, in fact, a significant portion of the increased charges to customers was based on an artificially inflated average weight per cubic yard. Paolella admitted that he did not object to the plan when it was proposed by Hanley. He testified that

later he raised concern with Hanley at least twice weekly but nevertheless complied with instructions to send a letter to customers advising them of the 25 percent increase in June 1992. He also negotiated contracts with customers based on these rates.

In late 1993, Paolella sent BFI a letter warning BFI to "cease all illegal activities." He was fired at 51 years of age, on January 17, 1994, for "poor performance." He sued BFI for wrongful discharge under the public policy exception to the employment-at-will doctrine based on the public policy set forth in the state law against theft by false pretenses. The jury returned a verdict of $732,000, representing $135,000 of back pay and $597,000 in front pay. The judge reduced the damages by $132,000 because of Paolella's participation. BFI appealed, contending that Paolella's participation should preclude him from relying on the public policy exception, and it contended that the front pay was excessive. Is BFI correct? Decide. [*Paolella v Browning-Ferris, Inc.*, 158 F3d 195 (3d Cir)]

8. Armenda Malone and Stephen Krantz were induced to leave other employment and join ABI's CD-Rom division as national account managers in part because of a favorable commission agreement at ABI. Their employment relationship with ABI had no set duration, and as such they were employees at will. For the first two quarters of their employment, their commission reports were approved by the president of the division and paid without incident. Thereafter, a new management team took over the division. When the mid-level manager presented third quarter commission reports based on the prior practice to the new vice president, Bruce Lowry, for approval, he was told, "You got to learn how to f— these people." Lowry then utilized severable variables—some of which the mid-level manager found "ridiculous"—to reduce the commission figures. After much discourse that carried on well into the fourth quarter, Lowry announced that a new model for determining commissions would be implemented. Commissions for both the third and fourth quarters, ending in December, were then calculated based on this model. ABI asserts that because Malone and Krantz were employees at will, the employer had the right to interpret or alter how it pays employees as it sees fit. Krantz and Malone left ABI and have sued for what they believe are the full commissions earned in the third and fourth quarters. Present a legal theory on behalf of Malone and Krantz for the payment of back commissions. Assess the strengths and weaknesses of Lowry's approach to employee relations. How would you decide this case? [*Malone v American Business Information, Inc.*, 647 NW2d 569 (Neb)]

9. Jane Richards was employed as the sole crane operator of Gale Corp. and held the part-time union position of shop steward for the plant. On May 15, Richards complained to OSHA concerning what she contended were seven existing violations of the Occupational Safety and Health Act that were brought to her attention by members of the bargaining unit. On May 21, she stated to the company's general manager at a negotiating session: "If we don't have a new contract by the time the present one expires on June 15, we will strike." On May 22, an OSHA inspector arrived at the plant, and Richards told her supervisor, "I blew the whistle." On May 23, the company rented and later purchased two large electric forklifts that were used to do the work previously performed by the crane, and the crane operator's job was abolished. Under the existing collective bargaining contract, the company had the right to lay off for lack of work. The contract also provided for arbitration, and it prohibited discipline or discharge without "just cause." On May 23, Richards was notified that she was being laid off "for lack of work" within her classification of crane operator. She was also advised that the company was not planning on using the crane in the future and that, if she were smart, she would get another job. Richards claimed that her layoff violated the National Labor Relations Act, the Occupational Safety and Health Act, and the collective bargaining agreement. Was she correct?

10. Samuel Sullivan, president of the Truck Drivers and Helpers International Union, also holds the position of president of the union's pension fund. The fund consists of both employer and employee contributions, which are forwarded quarterly to the fund's offices in New York City. Sullivan ordered Mark Gilbert, the treasurer of the fund, not to give out any information to anyone at any time concerning the fund because it was union money and because the union was entitled to take care of its own internal affairs. Was Sullivan correct?

11. In May, the nurses union at Waterbury Hospital went on strike, and the hospital was shut down. In mid-June, the hospital began hiring replacements and gradually opened many units. To induce nurses to take employment during the strike, the hospital guaranteed replacement nurses their choice of positions and shifts. If a preferred position was in a unit that was not open at that time, the hospital guaranteed that the individual would be placed in that position at the end of the strike. The strike ended in October and as the striking workers returned to work, the hospital began opening units that had been closed during the strike. It staffed many of these positions with replacement nurses. The nurses who had the positions prior to the strike and were waiting to return to work believed that they should have been called to fill these positions rather than the junior replacements who had held other positions during the strike. Decide. [*Waterbury Hospital v NLRB*, 950 F2d 849 (2d Cir)]

12. Buffo was employed by the Baltimore & Ohio Railroad. Along with a number of other workers, he was removing old brakes from railroad cars and replacing them with new brakes. In the course of the work, rivet heads and

scrap from the brakes accumulated on the tracks under the cars. This debris was removed only occasionally when the workers had time. Buffo, while holding an air hammer in both arms, was crawling under a car when his foot slipped on scrap on the ground, causing him to strike and injure his knee. He sued the railroad for damages under the Federal Employers Liability Act. Decide. [*Buffo v Baltimore & Ohio Railroad Co.*, 72 A2d 593 (Pa)]

13. Mark Phipps was employed as a cashier at a Clark gas station. A customer drove into the station and asked him to pump leaded gasoline into her 1976 Chevrolet, an automobile equipped to receive only unleaded gasoline. The station manager told Phipps to comply with the request, but he refused, believing that his dispensing leaded gasoline into the gas tank was a violation of law. Phipps stated that he was willing to pump unleaded gas into the tank, but the manager immediately fired him. Phipps sued Clark for wrongful termination. Clark contended that it was free to terminate Phipps, an employee at will, for any reason or no reason. Decide. [*Phipps v Clark Oil & Refining Corp.*, 396 NW2d 588 (Minn App)]

14. Reno, Nevada, police officers John Bohach and Jon Catalano communicated with each other on the Alphapage computer system, typing messages on a keyboard and sending them to each other by use of a "send" key. The computer dials a commercial paging company, which receives the message by modem, and the message is then sent to the person paged by radio broadcast. When the system was installed, the police chief warned that every Alphapage message was logged on the network, and he barred messages that were critical of department policy or discriminatory. The two police officers sought to block a department investigation into their messages and prevent disclosure of the messages' content. They claimed that the messages should be treated the same as telephone calls under federal wiretap law. The department contended that the system was essentially a form of e-mail whose messages are by definition stored in a computer, and the storage was itself not part of the communication. Was the federal wiretap law violated? [*Bohach v City of Reno*, No. 96-403-ECR (DC Nev)]

15. Michael Kittell was employed at Vermont Weatherboard. While operating a saw at the plant, Kittell was seriously injured when a splinter flew into his eye and penetrated his head. Kittell sued Vermont Weatherboard, seeking damages under a common law theory. His complaint alleged that he suffered severe injuries solely because of the employer's wanton and willful acts and omissions. The complaint stated that he was an inexperienced worker, put to work without instructions or warning on a saw from which the employer had stripped away all safety devices. Vermont Weatherboard made a motion to dismiss the complaint on the ground that the Workers' Compensation Act provided the exclusive remedy for his injury. Decide. [*Kittell v Vermont Weatherboard, Inc.*, 417 A2d 926 (Vt)]

EQUAL EMPLOYMENT OPPORTUNITY LAW

CHAPTER (40)

LEARNING OBJECTIVES

After studying this chapter, you should be able to

LO.1 Explain and illustrate the difference between disparate treatment employment discrimination and disparate impact employment discrimination

LO.2 Recognize and remedy sexual harassment problems in the workplace

LO.3 Evaluate the legality of voluntary affirmative action programs by applying five court-approved principles

LO.4 State the consequences of discriminating against employees and job applicants because of their age

LO.5 State and illustrate an employer's legal obligation to make reasonable accommodations for individuals with disabilities

Laws of the United States reflect our society's concern that all Americans, including minorities, women, and persons with disabilities, have equal employment opportunities and that the workplace is free from discrimination and harassment. Title VII of the Civil Rights Act of 1964, as amended in 1972, 1978, and 1991, is the principal law regulating equal employment opportunities in the United States. Other federal laws require equal pay for men and women doing substantially the same work and forbid discrimination because of age or disability.

CPA A. Title VII of the Civil Rights Act of 1964, as Amended

Title VII of the Civil Rights Act of 1964[1] seeks to eliminate employer and union practices that discriminate against employees and job applicants on the basis of race, color, religion, sex, or national origin. The law applies to the hiring process and to discipline, discharge, promotion, and benefits.

1. Theories of Discrimination

The Supreme Court has created, and the Civil Rights Act of 1991 has codified, two principal legal theories under which a plaintiff may prove a case of unlawful employment discrimination: disparate treatment and disparate impact.

A *disparate treatment* claim exists where an employer treats some individuals less favorably than others because of their race, color, religion, sex, or national origin. Proof of the employer's discriminatory motive is essential in a disparate treatment case.[2]

Disparate impact exists when an employer's facially neutral employment practices, such as hiring or promotion examinations, although neutrally applied and making no adverse reference to race, color, religion, sex, or national origin, have a significantly adverse or disparate impact on a protected group. In addition, the employment practice in question is not shown by the employer to be job related and consistent with business necessity. Under the disparate impact theory, it is not a defense for an employer to demonstrate that it did not intend to discriminate.

For Example, if plant manager Jones is heard telling the personnel director that the vacant welder's position should be filled by a male because "this is man's work," a qualified female applicant turned down for the job would prevail in a *disparate treatment* theory case against the employer because she was not hired because of her gender. Necessary evidence of the employer's discriminatory motive would be satisfied by testimony about the manager's "this is man's work" statement.

If the policy for hiring new pilots at Generic Airlines, Inc., required a minimum height of 5 feet 7 inches, and no adverse reference to gender was stated in this employment policy, nevertheless, the 5-feet-7-inch minimum height policy has an adverse or disparate impact on women because far fewer women than men reach this height. Such an employment policy would be set aside on a *disparate impact* theory, and a minimum height for the position would be established by the court based on evidence of job-relatedness and business necessity. One court set a 5-feet-5-inch height requirement for pilots.

The *Griggs v Duke Power Co.* case is a disparate impact case.

GRIGGS V DUKE POWER CO., 401 US 424 (1971)

NUMBER 1 ON THE CHARTS! THE CASE THAT CREATED THE DISPARATE IMPACT THEORY

Griggs and other black employees at Duke Power Company's Dan River Station challenged Duke Power's requirements of a high school diploma and passing standardized general intelligence tests in order to transfer to more desirable "inside jobs." The district court and court of appeals found no violation of Title VII because Duke Power did not adopt the diploma and test requirements with the purpose of intentionally discriminating against black employees. The case was appealed to the Supreme Court.

[1] 42 USC § 2000(e) *et seq.*

[2] *Woodson v Scott Paper Co.*, 109 F3d 913 (3d Cir 1997).

Judicial Opinion

BURGER, C. J. . . . The objective of Congress in the enactment of Title VII is plain from the language of the statute. It was to achieve equality of employment opportunities and remove barriers that have operated in the past to favor an identifiable group of white employees over other employees. Under the Act, practices, procedures, or tests neutral on their face, and even neutral in terms of intent, cannot be maintained if they operate to "freeze" the status quo of prior discriminatory employment practices.

. . . In short, the Act does not command that any person be hired simply because he was formerly the subject of discrimination, or because he is a member of a minority group. Discriminatory preference for any group, minority or majority, is precisely and only what Congress has proscribed. What is required by Congress is the removal of artificial, arbitrary, and unnecessary barriers to employment when the barriers operate invidiously to discriminate on the basis of racial or other impermissible classification.

Congress has now provided that tests or criteria for employment or promotion may not provide equality of opportunity merely in the sense of the fabled offer of milk to the stork and the fox. On the contrary, Congress has now required that the posture and condition of the job-seeker be taken into account. It has—to resort again to the fable—provided that the vessel in which the milk is proffered be one all seekers can use. The Act proscribes not only overt discrimination but also practices that are fair in form, but discriminatory in operation. The touch-stone is business necessity. If an employment practice which operates to exclude Negroes cannot be shown to be related to job performance, the practice is prohibited.

On the record before us, neither the high school completion requirement nor the general intelligence test is shown to bear a demonstrable relationship to successful performance of the jobs for which it was used. Both were adopted, as the Court of Appeals noted, without meaningful study of their relationship to job-performance ability. Rather, a vice president of the Company testified, the requirements were instituted on the Company's judgment that they generally would improve the overall quality of the work force.

The evidence, however, shows that employees who have not completed high school or taken the tests have continued to perform satisfactorily and make progress in departments for which the high school and test criteria are now used. . . .

The Court of Appeals held that the Company had adopted the diploma and test requirements without any "intention to discriminate against Negro employees." We do not suggest that either the District Court or the Court of Appeals erred in examining the employer's intent; but good intent or absence of discriminatory intent does not redeem employment procedures or testing mechanisms that operate as "built-in headwinds" for minority groups and are unrelated to measuring job capability.

The Company's lack of discriminatory intent is suggested by special efforts to help the undereducated employees through Company financing of two-thirds the cost of tuition for high school training. But Congress directed the thrust of the Act to the *consequences* of employment practices, not simply the motivation. More than that, Congress has placed on the employer the burden of showing that any given requirement must have a manifest relationship to the employer in question.

The facts of this case demonstrate the inadequacy of broad and general testing devices as well as the infirmity of using diplomas or degrees as fixed measures of capability. History is filled with examples of men and women who rendered highly effective performance without the conventional badges of accomplishment in terms of certificates, diplomas, or degrees. Diplomas and tests are useful servants, but Congress has mandated the common sense proposition that they are not to become masters of reality.

The Company contends that its general intelligence tests are specifically permitted by Section 703(h) of the Act. That section authorizes the use of "any professionally developed ability test" that is not "designed, intended or *used* to discriminate because of race. . . ." [Emphasis added.]

The Equal Employment Opportunity Commission, having enforcement responsibility, has issued guidelines interpreting Section 703(h) to permit only the use of job-related tests. The administrative interpretation of the Act by the enforcing agency is entitled to great deference. . . . Since the Act and its legislative history support the Commission's construction, this affords good reason to treat the guidelines as expressing the will of Congress. . . .

Nothing in the Act precludes the use of testing or measuring procedures; obviously they are useful. What Congress has forbidden is giving these devices and mechanisms controlling force unless they are demonstrably a reasonable measure of job performance. Congress has not commanded that the less qualified be preferred over the better qualified simply because of minority origins. Far from disparaging job qualifications as such, Congress has made such qualifications the controlling factor, so that race, religion, nationality, and sex become irrelevant. What Congress has commanded is that any tests used must measure the person for the job and not the person in the abstract. . . .

[Judgment reversed]

Questions

1. What is the question before the Supreme Court?
2. What was the objective of Congress in the enactment of Title VII?
3. Would the Court order the case against the employer to be dismissed if it found that the employer had adopted the diploma and test requirements without any intention to discriminate against minority employees?
4. As a result of the *Griggs* decision, may employers insist that both minority and white job applicants meet the applicable job qualifications as determined through the use of testing or measuring procedures?

2. The Equal Employment Opportunity Commission

The Equal Employment Opportunity Commission (EEOC) is a five-member body appointed by the president to establish equal employment opportunity policy under the laws it administers. The EEOC supervises the agency's conciliation and enforcement efforts.

The EEOC administers Title VII of the Civil Rights Act, the Equal Pay Act (EPA), the Age Discrimination in Employment Act (ADEA), section 501 of the Rehabilitation Act (which prohibits federal-sector discrimination against persons with disabilities), and Title I (the employment provisions) of the Americans with Disabilities Act (ADA).

(a) Procedure

Where a state or local EEO agency with the power to act on claims of discriminatory practices exists, the charging party must file a complaint with that agency. The charging party must wait 60 days or until the termination of the state proceedings, whichever occurs first, before filing a charge with the EEOC. If no state or local agency exists, a charge may be filed directly with the EEOC so long as it is filed within 180 days of the occurrence of the discriminatory act. The commission conducts an investigation to determine whether reasonable cause exists to believe that the charge is true. If such cause is found to exist, the EEOC attempts to remedy the unlawful practice through conciliation. If the EEOC does not resolve the matter to the satisfaction of the parties, it may decide to litigate the case when unusual circumstances exist, including a "pattern or practice of discrimination." In most instances, however, the EEOC issues the charging party a *right-to-sue letter*. Thereafter, the individual claiming a violation of EEO law has 90 days to file a lawsuit in a federal district court.[3]

(b) Damages

Title VII sets damages available to victims of discrimination (see Figure 40-1).

The *Pollard* case deals with whether "front pay" damages are compensatory damages, subject to a statutory cap.

POLLARD V E. I. DUPONT DE NEMOURS & CO., 121 SCT 1946 (2001)

UP FRONT WITH VICTIMS OF SEX DISCRIMINATION

Sharon Pollard sued her former employer, E. I. du Pont de Nemours and Company (DuPont), alleging that she had been subjected to a hostile work environment based on her sex, in violation of Title VII. After a trial, the District Court found that Pollard was subjected to co-worker sexual harassment of which her supervisors were aware. The District Court further found that the harassment resulted in a medical leave of absence from her job for psychological assistance and her eventual dismissal for refusing to return to the same hostile work environment. The court awarded Pollard $107,364 in backpay and benefits, $252,997 in attorney's fees, and $300,000 in compensatory damages—the maximum permitted under the statutory cap for such damages in 42 U. S. C. § 1981a(b)(3). The court observed that the award was

[3] An individual who misses the filing deadline of Title VII may be able to bring a race discrimination case under the two-year time limit allowed under section 1981 of the Civil Rights Act of 1964, codified at 42 USC § 1981, and sometimes called a *section 1981 lawsuit.* In the *Edelman v Lynchburg College decision*, 152 L Ed 2d 188 (2002), the U.S. Supreme Court approved an EEOC regulation that allows certain defective charges to be cured, with the cured charge relating back to the date the EEOC first received the initial charge, which was within the 300-day filing period.

insufficient to compensate Pollard, but that it was bound by an earlier Sixth Circuit holding that front pay—money awarded for lost compensation during the period between judgment and reinstatement or in lieu of reinstatement—was subject to the damages cap of § 1981a(b)(3). The Sixth Circuit affirmed.

Judicial Opinion

THOMAS, J.... The issue presented for review here is whether front pay constitutes an element of "compensatory damages" under 42 U.S.C. § 1981a and thus is subject to the statutory damages cap imposed by that section. Although courts have defined "front pay" in numerous ways, front pay is simply money awarded for lost compensation during the period between judgment and reinstatement or in lieu of reinstatement. For instance, when an appropriate position for the plaintiff is not immediately available without displacing an incumbent employee, courts have ordered reinstatement upon the opening of such a position and have ordered front pay to be paid until reinstatement occurs. In cases in which reinstatement is not viable because of continuing hostility between the plaintiff and the employer or its workers, or because of psychological injuries suffered by the plaintiff as a result of the discrimination, courts have ordered front pay as a substitute for reinstatement. See, *e.g., Gotthardt v National R. R. Passenger Corp.*, 191 F. 3d 1148, 1156 (CA9 1999). For the purposes of this opinion, it is not necessary for us to explain when front pay is an appropriate remedy. The question before us is only whether front pay, if found to be appropriate, is an element of compensatory damages under the Civil Rights Act of 1991 and thus subject to the Act's statutory cap on such damages.

Here, the District Court observed that "the $300,000.00 award is, in fact, insufficient to compensate plaintiff," 16 F. Supp. 2d 913, 924, n. 19, but it stated that it was bound by the Sixth Circuit's decision in *Hudson v Reno*, 130 F. 3d 1193 (1997), which held that front pay was subject to the cap....

Plaintiffs who allege employment discrimination on the basis of sex traditionally have been entitled to such remedies as injunctions, reinstatement, back pay, lost benefits, and attorney's fees under § 706(g) of the Civil Rights Act of 1964. In the Civil Rights Act of 1991, Congress expanded the remedies available to these plaintiffs by permitting, for the first time, the recovery of compensatory and punitive damages. 42 U.S.C. § 1981a(a)(1) ("[T]he complaining party may recover compensatory and punitive damages as allowed in subsection (b) of this section, in addition to any relief authorized by section 706(g) of the Civil Rights Act of 1964"). The amount of compensatory damages awarded under § 1981a for "future pecuniary losses, emotional pain, suffering, inconvenience, mental anguish, loss of enjoyment of life, and other nonpecuniary losses," and the amount of punitive damages awarded under § 1981a, however, may not exceed the statutory cap set forth in § 1981a(b)(3). The statutory cap is based on the number of people employed by the respondent. In this case, the cap is $300,000 because DuPont has more than 500 employees.

The Sixth Circuit has concluded that front pay constitutes compensatory damages awarded for future pecuniary losses and thus is subject to the statutory cap of § 1981a(b) (3). 213 F. 3d, at 945; *Hudson, supra*, at 1203. For the reasons discussed below, we conclude that front pay is not an element of compensatory damages within the meaning of § 1981a, and, therefore, we hold that the statutory cap of § 1981a(b)(3) is inapplicable to front pay....

Congress... made clear through the plain language of the statute that the remedies newly authorized under § 1981a were in *addition to* the relief authorized by § 706(g). Section 1981a(a)(1) provides that, in intentional discrimination cases brought under Title VII, "the complaining party may recover compensatory and punitive damages as allowed in subjection (b) of [§ 1981a], *in addition to any relief authorized by section 706(g) of the Civil Rights Act of 1964*, from the respondent." (Emphasis added.) And § 1981a(b) (2) states that "[c]ompensatory damages awarded under [§1981a] shall not include backpay, interest on backpay, *or any other type of relief authorized under section 706(g) of the Civil Rights Act of 1964*." (Emphasis added.) According to these statutory provisions, if front pay was a type of relief authorized under §706(g), it is excluded from the meaning of compensatory damages under § 1981a.

The original language of § 706(g) authorizing backpay awards was modeled after the same language in the NLRA. This provision in the NLRA had been construed to allow awards of backpay up to the date of reinstatement, even if reinstatement occurred after judgment. Accordingly, backpay awards made for the period between the date of judgment and the date of reinstatement, which today are called front pay awards under Title VII, were authorized under § 706(g).

As to front pay awards that are made in lieu of reinstatement, we construe § 706(g) as authorizing these awards as well. We see no logical difference between front pay awards made when there eventually is reinstatement and those made when there is not. Moreover, to distinguish between the two cases would lead to the strange result that employees could receive front pay when reinstatement eventually is available but not when reinstatement is not an option—whether because of continuing hostility between the plaintiff and the employer or its workers, or because of psychological injuries that the discrimination has caused the plaintiff. Thus, the most egregious offenders could be subject to the least sanctions. Had Congress drawn such a line in the statute and foreclosed front pay awards in lieu of reinstatement, we certainly would honor that line. But, as written, the text of the statute does not lend itself to such a distinction, and we will not create one. The statute authorized courts to "order such affirmative action as may be appropriate." 42 U.S.C. § 2000e–5(g)(1). We conclude that front pay awards in lieu of reinstatement fit within this statutory term.

Because front pay is a remedy authorized under § 706(g), Congress did not limit the availability of such awards in § 1981a. Instead, Congress sought to expand the available remedies by permitting the recovery of compensatory and punitive damages in addition to previously available remedies, such as front pay.

* * *

The judgment of the Court of Appeals is reversed, and the case is remanded for further proceedings consistent with this opinion.

It is so ordered.

Questions

1. What are the traditional remedies available to victims of employment discrimination under § 706(g) of the Civil Rights Act of 1964?
2. Did Congress in the Civil Rights act of 1991 expand the remedies available to plaintiffs? Explain.
3. What are the two types of front pay? Is front pay an element of compensatory damages subject to the cap for sex and religious discrimination?

(c) The Arbitration Option

With the exception of transportation employees, employers can craft arbitration agreements that require employees to arbitrate any employment dispute, including statutory discrimination claims, and these mandatory arbitration clauses can be enforced in federal courts under the Federal Arbitration Act.[4] Courts do, however, require that the arbitration clauses be "fair." Moreover, a party agreeing to arbitration does not forgo substantive rights afforded by Title VII or alter federal antidiscrimination statutes. A fair arbitration clause requires adequate discovery, mandates that the arbitrator have authority to apply the same types of relief available from a court, and should not preclude an employee from vindicating statutory rights because of arbitration costs.[5]

B. Protected Classes and Exceptions

To successfully pursue a Title VII lawsuit, an individual must belong to a protected class and meet the appropriate burden of proof. Exceptions exist for certain employment practices.

3. Race and Color

The legislative history of Title VII of the Civil Rights Act demonstrates that a primary purpose of the act is to provide fair employment opportunities for black Americans. The protections of the act are applied to blacks based on race or color.

The word *race* as used in the act applies to all members of the four major racial groupings: white, black, Native American, and Asian-Pacific. Native Americans can file charges and receive the protection of the act on the basis of national origin, race, or, in some instances, color. Individuals of Asian-Pacific origin may file discrimination charges based on race, color, or, in some instances, national origin. Whites are also protected against discrimination because of race and color.

For Example, two white professors at a predominately black university were successful in discrimination suits against the university when it was held that the university had discriminated against them on the basis of race and color in tenure decisions.[6]

4. Religion

Title VII requires employers to accommodate their employees' or prospective employees' religious

[4] *Circuit City Stores, Inc. v Adams,* 121 S Ct 1302 (2001).

[5] See *Circuit City II,* 279 F3d 889 (9th Cir 2002).

[6] *Turgeon v Howard University,* 571 F Supp 679 (DDC 1983).

FIGURE 40-1 Unlawful Discrimination under Title VII of the Civil Rights Act of 1964 as Amended by the Civil Rights Act of 1991

DISCRIMINATORY TREATMENT IN EMPLOYMENT DECISIONS ON THE BASIS OF RACE, COLOR, RELIGION, SEX, OR NATIONAL ORIGIN

DISPARATE TREATMENT THEORY	DISPARATE IMPACT THEORY
NONNEUTRAL PRACTICE OR NONNEUTRAL APPLICATION	FACIALLY NEUTRAL PRACTICE AND NEUTRAL APPLICATION
REQUIRES PROOF OF DISCRIMINATORY INTENT	DOES NOT REQUIRE PROOF OF DISCRIMINATORY INTENT REQUIRES PROOF OF ADVERSE EFFECT ON PROTECTED GROUP AND EMPLOYER IS UNABLE TO SHOW THAT THE CHALLENGED PRACTICE IS JOB-RELATED FOR THE POSITION IN QUESTION AND IS CONSISTENT WITH BUSINESS NECESSITY
EITHER PARTY HAS A RIGHT TO REQUIRE A JURY TRIAL WHEN SEEKING COMPENSATORY OR PUNITIVE DAMAGES	NO RIGHT TO A JURY TRIAL
REMEDY REINSTATEMENT, HIRING, OR PROMOTION BACK PAY LESS INTERIM EARNINGS RETROACTIVE SENIORITY ATTORNEY AND EXPERT WITNESS FEES PLUS COMPENSATORY* AND PUNITIVE DAMAGES DAMAGES CAPPED FOR CASES OF SEX AND RELIGIOUS DISCRIMINATION DEPENDING ON SIZE OF EMPLOYER: NUMBER OF EMPLOYEES — DAMAGES CAP 100 OR FEWER — $ 50,000 101 TO 200 — 100,000 201 TO 500 — 200,000 OVER 500 — 300,000 NO CAP ON DAMAGES FOR RACE CASES	**REMEDY** REINSTATEMENT, HIRING, OR PROMOTION BACK PAY LESS INTERIM EARNINGS RETROACTIVE SENIORITY ATTORNEY AND EXPERT WITNESS FEES

* COMPENSATORY DAMAGES INCLUDE FUTURE PECUNIARY LOSSES AND NONPECUNIARY LOSSES SUCH AS EMOTIONAL PAIN AND SUFFERING.

practices. Most cases involving allegations of religious discrimination revolve around the determination of whether an employer has made reasonable efforts to accommodate religious beliefs.

If an employee's religious beliefs prohibit working on Saturday, an employer's obligation under Title VII is to try to find a volunteer to cover for the employee on Saturdays. The employer would not have an obligation to violate a seniority provision of a collective bargaining agreement or call in a substitute worker if such accommodation would require more than a *de minimis* or very small cost.

Many employers have work rules or grooming policies for employees who provide service to customers on behalf of the employers. Employees have challenged employer bans on body art as religious discrimination, asserting that the employers have not made reasonable efforts to accommodate religious beliefs. EEOC's 1980 Guidelines broadly define religion "to include moral or ethical beliefs as to what is right and wrong which are sincerely held with the strength of traditional religious views."[7] The Guidelines do not limit religion to theistic practices or to beliefs professed by organized religions. **For Example,** Kimberly Cloutier was a member of the Church of Body Modification. Costco's grooming policy prohibited any "visible facial or tongue jewelry" in order to present a professional image to its customers. Ms. Cloutier wore an eyebrow ring as a religious practice. Ms. Cloutier rejected Costco's offer to return her to work if she wore a band-aid or plastic retainer over the jewelry because it would violate her religious beliefs. The U.S. Court of Appeals determined that her refusal to accept an accommodation short of an exemption was an undue hardship for the employer because an exemption would negatively impact the company's policy of professionalism.[8]

Some courts, however, look for actual proof of harm to the employer in assessing whether undue hardship exists for an employer. **For Example,** the EEOC brought an action against Red Robin Gourmet Burgers, Inc., for failure to provide an exemption from its grooming policy for an employee's religious tattoos surrounding his wrists. The federal district court looked for actual proof of the restaurant's assertion that the tattoos contravened the company's "family-oriented image," such as customer complaints or other evidence, as opposed to the mere assertion. The court concluded that the employer failed to provide sufficient evidence of undue hardship in accommodating an exemption for the employee.[9]

Title VII permits religious societies to grant hiring preferences in favor of members of their religion. It also provides an exemption for educational institutions to hire employees of a particular religion if the institution is owned, controlled, or managed by a particular religious society. The exemption is a broad one and is not restricted to the religious activities of the institution.

5. Sex

Employers who discriminate against female or male employees because of their sex are held to be in violation of Title VII. The EEOC and the courts have determined that the word *sex* as used in Title VII means a person's gender, not the person's sexual orientation. State and local legislation, however, may provide specific protection against discrimination based on sexual orientation.

(a) Height, Weight, and Physical Ability Requirements

Under the *Griggs v Duke Power* precedent, an employer must be able to show that criteria used to make an employment decision that has a disparate impact on women, such as minimum height and weight requirements, are in fact job related. All candidates for a position requiring physical strength must be given an opportunity to demonstrate their capability to perform the work. Women cannot be precluded from consideration just because they have not traditionally performed such work.

(b) Pregnancy-Related Benefits

Title VII was amended by the Pregnancy Discrimination Act (PDA) in 1978. The amendment prevents employers from treating pregnancy, childbirth, and related medical conditions in a manner different from the manner in which other medical conditions are treated. Thus, women unable to work

[7] 29 CFR § 1605.1 (1980). The EEOC's definition of religion was derived from early Selective Service cases that moved beyond institutional religions and theistic belief structures in handling exemptions to the draft and military service. See *Welsh v U.S.*, 398 U.S. 333, 343-44 (1970), which allows for expansion of belief systems to include nonreligious ethical or moral codes.

[8] *Cloutier v Costco*, 390 F3d 126 (1st Cir 2004).

[9] *EEOC v Red Robin Gourmet Burger, Inc.*, 2005 US Dist LEXIS 36219.

as a result of pregnancy, childbirth, or related medical conditions must be provided the same benefits as all other workers. These include temporary and long-term disability insurance, sick leave, and other forms of employee benefit programs. An employer who does not provide disability benefits or paid sick leave to other employees is not required to provide them for pregnant workers.

6. Sexual Harassment

Tangible employment action and hostile work environment are two classifications of sexual harassment.

(a) Tangible Employment Action

Sexual harassment classified as *tangible employment action* involves situations in which a supervisor performs an "official act" of the enterprise, such as discharge, demotion, or undesirable reassignment against a subordinate employee because of the employee's refusal to submit to the supervisor's demand for sexual favors. The employer is always vicariously liable for this harassment by a supervisor under the so-called aided-in-the-agency-relation standard. That is, the supervisor is aided in accomplishing the wrongful objective by the existence of the agency relationship. The employer empowered the supervisor as a distinct class of agent to make economic decisions affecting other employees under the supervisor's control. The employer can raise no affirmative defense based on the presence of an employer's antiharassment policy in such a case.

(b) Hostile Work Environment

A second type of sexual harassment classified as *hostile work environment* occurs when a supervisor's conduct does not affect an employee's economic benefits but causes anxiety and "poisons" the work environment for the employee. Such conduct may include unwelcome sexual flirtation, propositions, or other abuses of a sexual nature, including the use of degrading words or the display of sexually explicit pictures.[10] This type of sexual harassment applies to all cases involving supervisors in which the enterprise takes no official act, including constructive discharge cases. The plaintiff must prove severe and pervasive conduct on the supervisor's part to meet the plaintiff's burden of proof.[11] The employer may raise an affirmative defense to liability for damages by proving that (1) it exercised reasonable care to prevent and promptly correct any sexually harassing behavior at its workplace and (2) the plaintiff employee unreasonably failed to take advantage of corrective opportunities provided by the employer. The existence of an employer's sexual harassment policy and notification procedures (see Figure 40-2) will aid the employer in proving the affirmative defense in hostile working environment cases.

(c) Rationale

The "primary objective of Title VII, like that of any statute meant to influence primary conduct, is not to provide redress but to avoid harm."[12] When there is no "official act" of the employer, the employer may raise an affirmative defense. This approach fosters the preventative aspect of Title VII, encouraging employers to exercise reasonable care to prevent and correct sexual harassment while providing damages only when the conduct is clearly attributed to an official action of the enterprise or when the employer has not exercised reasonable care to prevent and correct misconduct. **For Example,** Kim Ellerth alleged that she was subject to constant sexual harassment by her supervisor, Ted Slowik, at Burlington Industries. Slowik made comments about her breasts, told her to "loosen up," and warned, "You know, Kim, I could make your life very hard or very easy at Burlington." When Kim was being considered for promotion, Slowik expressed reservations that she was not "loose enough" and then reached over and rubbed her knee. She received the promotion, however. After other such incidents, she quit and filed charges alleging that she was constructively discharged because of the unendurable working conditions resulting from the hostile work environment created by Slowik. She did not use Burlington's sexual harassment internal complaint procedures.

[10] According to EEOC Guidelines § 1604.11(f), unwelcome sexual advances, requests for sexual favors, and other verbal or physical conduct of a sexual nature constitute sexual harassment when (1) submission to or rejection of such conduct has the purpose or effect of unreasonably interfering with an individual's work performance or creating an intimidating, hostile, or offensive working environment.

[11] *Oncale v Sundowner Offshore Services, Inc.*, 523 US 75 (1998). The Supreme Court stated in *Oncale* that it did not intend to turn Title VII into a civility code, and the Court set forth the standard for judging whether the conduct in question amounted to sexual harassment requiring that the conduct be judged from the perspective of a reasonable person in the plaintiff's position, considering all circumstances. The Court warned that "common sense" and "context" must apply in determining whether the conduct was hostile or abusive.

[12] *Faragher v City of Boca Raton*, 524 US 775 at 805, citing *Albemale Paper Co. v Moody*, 422 US 405, 418 (1975).

FIGURE 40-2 Employer Procedure—Sexual Harassment

A. DEVELOP AND IMPLEMENT AN EQUAL EMPLOYMENT POLICY THAT SPECIFICALLY PROHIBITS SEXUAL HARASSMENT AND IMPOSES DISCIPLINE UP TO AND INCLUDING DISCHARGE. SET FORTH SPECIFIC EXAMPLES OF CONDUCT THAT WILL NOT BE TOLERATED SUCH AS

- UNWELCOME SEXUAL ADVANCES, WHETHER OR NOT THEY INVOLVE PHYSICAL TOUCHING
- SEXUAL EPITHETS AND JOKES; WRITTEN OR ORAL REFERENCES TO SEXUAL CONDUCT; GOSSIP REGARDING ONE'S SEX LIFE; COMMENTS ON AN INDIVIDUAL'S BODY; AND COMMENTS ABOUT AN INDIVIDUAL'S SEXUAL ACTIVITY, DEFICIENCIES, OR PROWESS
- DISPLAY OF SEXUALLY SUGGESTIVE OBJECTS, PICTURES, AND CARTOONS
- UNWELCOME LEERING, WHISTLING, BRUSHING AGAINST THE BODY, SEXUAL GESTURES, AND SUGGESTIVE OR INSULTING COMMENTS
- INQUIRIES INTO ONE'S SEXUAL EXPERIENCES
- DISCUSSION OF ONE'S SEXUAL ACTIVITIES

B. ESTABLISH ONGOING EDUCATIONAL PROGRAMS, INCLUDING ROLE PLAYING AND FILMS TO DEMONSTRATE UNACCEPTABLE BEHAVIOR.

C. DESIGNATE A RESPONSIBLE SENIOR OFFICIAL TO WHOM COMPLAINTS OF SEXUAL HARASSMENT CAN BE MADE. AVOID ANY PROCEDURE THAT REQUIRES AN EMPLOYEE TO FIRST COMPLAIN TO THE EMPLOYEE'S SUPERVISOR, BECAUSE THAT INDIVIDUAL MAY BE THE OFFENDING PERSON. MAKE CERTAIN COMPLAINANTS KNOW THAT THERE WILL BE NO RETALIATION FOR FILING A COMPLAINT.

D. INVESTIGATE ALL COMPLAINTS PROMPTLY AND THOROUGHLY.

E. KEEP COMPLAINTS AND INVESTIGATIONS AS CONFIDENTIAL AS POSSIBLE AND LIMIT ALL INFORMATION TO ONLY THOSE WHO NEED TO KNOW.

F. IF A COMPLAINT HAS MERIT, IMPOSE APPROPRIATE AND CONSISTENT DISCIPLINE.

Because she was not a victim of a tangible employment action involving an official act of the enterprise, because she received the promotion sought, the employer will be able to raise an affirmative defense. Kim will be able to prove severe and pervasive conduct on the part of a supervisor under a hostile work environment theory. However, the employer may defeat liability by proving both that it exercised reasonable care to prevent and correct sexual harassing behavior through its internal company complaint policies and that Kim unreasonably failed to take advantage of the company procedures.[13]

(d) Nonsupervisors

An employer is liable for the sexual harassment caused its employees by coworkers or customers only when it knew or should have known of the misconduct and failed to take prompt remedial action.

7. Protection Against Retaliation

Section 704(a) of Title VII prohibits retaliation against an employee "because he [or she] has made a charge, testified, assisted or participated in any manner in an investigation, proceeding hearing

[13] *Burlington Industries, Inc. v Ellerth*, 524 US 742 (1998); see also *Faragher v City of Boca Raton*, 524 US 775 (1998). In *Pennsylvania v Suders*, 542 U.S. 129 (2004), the U.S. Supreme Court reviewed a decision of the Third Circuit Court of Appeals that held that a "constructive discharge," if proved, constituted a "tangible employment action" that renders the employer liable for damages and precludes an affirmative defense. The Supreme Court disagreed with the Third Circuit's reading of its *Ellerth/Faragher* decisions, and made it very clear that "an official act of the enterprise" is necessary for the plaintiff to defeat the employer's right to raise an affirmative defense.

under this subchapter." This antiretaliation provision prohibits employer actions that are "materially adverse" to a reasonable employee or applicant. The reference to "material adversity" is to separate significant harms that are prohibited by the act as opposed to trivial harms that are not actionable. A retaliation plaintiff must show that the challenged employer action "well might have dissuaded a reasonable worker from making or supporting a charge of discrimination."[14]

BURLINGTON NORTHERN SANTA FE RAILWAY CO. V WHITE, 126 SCT 2405 (2006)

NEW TRACTION FOR THE ANTIRETALIATION PROVISIONS THANKS TO TRACK LABORER WHITE

Shelia White was hired by the BNSF Railway as a track laborer at the Carrier's Tennessee Yard. She was the only woman in the track department. When hired she was given the job of forklift operator, as opposed to the ordinary track labor tasks. Three months after being hired she complained to the Roadmaster that her foreman treated her differently than male employees, and twice made inappropriate remarks. The foreman was suspended without pay for ten days and ordered to attend sexual harassment training. Also at that time the Roadmaster reassigned the forklift duties to the former operator who was "senior" to White, and assigned White to track labor duties. Six months into her employment White refused to ride in a truck as directed by a different foreman, and she was suspended for insubordination. Some thirty seven days later she was reinstated with full backpay and the discipline was removed from her record. She filed a complaint with the EEOC claiming the reassignment to track laborer duties was unlawful gender discrimination and retaliation for her complaint about her treatment by the foreman. The 37 days suspension led to a second retaliation charge. A jury rejected her gender discrimination claim and awarded her compensatory damages for her retaliation claims. BNSF appealed contending that Ms. White was hired as a track laborer and it was not retaliatory to assign her to do the work she was hired to do. And, it asserts that the suspension of 37 days was corrected and she was made whole for her loss.

Judicial Opinion

BREYER, J. . . . To be sure, reassignment of job duties is not automatically actionable. Whether a particular reassignment is materially adverse depends upon the circumstances of the particular case, and "should be judged from the perspective of a reasonable person in the plaintiff's position, considering 'all the circumstances.'" *Oncale*, 523 U.S., at 81, 118 S.Ct. 998. But here, the jury had before it considerable evidence that the track labor duties were "by all accounts more arduous and dirtier"; that the "forklift operator position required more qualifications, which is an indication of prestige"; and that "the forklift operator position was objectively considered a better job and the male employees resented White for occupying it." 364 F. 3d, at 803 (internal quotation marks omitted). Based on this record, a jury could reasonably conclude that the reassignment of responsibilities would have been materially adverse to a reasonable employee.

Second, Burlington argues that the 37–day suspension without pay lacked statutory significance because Burlington ultimately reinstated White with backpay. Burlington says that "it defies reason to believe that Congress would have considered a rescinded investigatory suspension with full back pay" to be unlawful. . . .

. . . White did receive backpay. But White and her family had to live for 37 days without income. They did not know during that time whether or when White could return to work. Many reasonable employees would find a month without a paycheck to be a serious hardship. And White described to the jury the physical and emotional hardship that 37 days of having "no income, no money" in fact caused. 1 Tr. 154 ("That was the worst Christmas I had out of my life. No income, no money, and that made all of us feel bad. . . . I got very depressed"). Indeed, she obtained medical treatment for her emotional distress. A reasonable employee facing the choice between retaining

[14] *Burlington Northern Santa Fe Railway Co. v White*, 126 SCt 2405 (2006).

her job (and paycheck) and filling a discrimination complaint might well choose the former. That is to say, an indefinite suspension without pay could well act as a deterrent, even if the suspended employee eventually received backpay. Cf. *Mitchell*, 361 U.S., at 292, 80 S.Ct, 332 ("[I]t needs no argument to show that fear of economic retaliation might often operate to induce aggrieved employees quietly to accept substandard conditions"). Thus, the jury's conclusion that the 37–day suspension without pay was materially adverse was a reasonable one.

[Affirmed]

It is so ordered.

Questions

1. Was the reassignment of Sheila White from forklift operator duties to track laborer duties unlawful gender discrimination and retaliation for her complaint about her treatment by the first foreman?
2. Can a rescinded disciplinary suspension with full back pay, be considered a materially adverse employer action in violation of Title VII's prohibition against retaliation?

The EEOC takes the position that claims can be filed for retaliation not only under Title VII but also under the Americans with Disabilities Act, the Age Discrimination in Employment Act, and the Equal Pay Act.

8. National Origin

Title VII protects members of all nationalities from discrimination. The judicial principles that have emerged from cases involving race, color, and gender employment discrimination are generally applicable to cases involving allegations of discrimination related to national origin. Thus, physical standards, such as minimum height requirements, that tend to exclude persons of a particular national origin because of the physical stature of the group have been found unlawful when these standards cannot be justified by business necessity.

Adverse employment action based on an individual's lack of English language skills violates Title VII when the language requirement bears no demonstrable relationship to the successful performance of the job to which it is applied.

In the *Fragante* case, the court considered whether there was unlawful national origin discrimination when a job applicant with a heavy Filipino accent was not selected for employment.

FRAGANTE V CITY AND COUNTY OF HONOLULU, 888 F2D 591 (9TH CIR 1989)

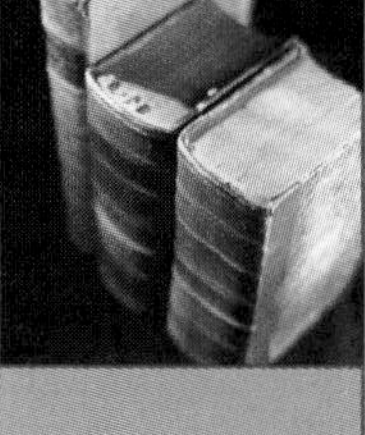

A CLOSE CALL

Manuel Fragante applied for a clerk's job with the city and county of Honolulu. Although he placed high enough on a civil service eligibility list to be chosen for the position, he was not selected because of a deficiency in oral communication skill caused by his "heavy Filipino accent." Fragante brought suit, alleging that the defendants discriminated against him on the basis of his national origin in violation of Title VII of the Civil Rights Act. The district court held that the ability to communicate orally and clearly was a legitimate occupational qualification for the job in question. There was no proof of a discriminatory intent or motive by the defendant. The court dismissed Fragante's complaint. Fragante appealed to the court of appeals.

Judicial Opinion

TROTT, C. J. ... Preliminarily, we do well to remember that this country was founded and has been built in large measure by people from other lands, many of whom came here—especially after our early beginnings—with a limited knowledge of English. This flow of immigrants has continued and has been encouraged over the years. From its inception, the United States of America has been a dream to many around the world. We hold out promises of freedom, equality, and economic opportunity to many who only know these words as concepts. It would be more than ironic if we followed up our invitation to people such as

Manuel Fragante with a closed economic door based on national origin discrimination. It is no surprise that Title VII speaks to this issue and clearly articulates the policy of our nation: unlawful discrimination based on national origin shall not be permitted to exist in the workplace. But, it is also true that there is another important aspect of Title VII: the "preservation of an employer's remaining freedom of choice."...

Accent and national origin are obviously inextricably intertwined in many cases. It would therefore be an easy refuge in this context for an employer unlawfully discriminating against someone based on national origin to state falsely that it was not the person's national origin that caused the employment or promotion problem, but the candidate's inability to measure up to the communication skills demanded by the job. We encourage a very searching look by the district courts at such a claim.

An adverse employment decision may be predicated upon an individual's accent when—but only when—it interferes materially with job performance. There is nothing improper about an employer making an *honest* assessment of the oral communication skills of a candidate for a job when such skills are reasonably related to job performance. EEOC Compliance Manual (CCH) 4035 at 3877-78 (1986); *see also Mejia v New York Sheraton Hotel*, 459 F. Supp. 375, 377 (S.D.N.Y. 1978) (Dominican chambermaid properly denied promotion to front desk because of her "inability to articulate clearly or coherently and to make herself adequately understood in... English"); *Carino v University of Oklahoma Board of Regents*, 750 F.2d 815, 819 (10th Cir. 1984) (plaintiff with a "noticeable" Filipino accent was improperly denied a position as supervisor of a dental laboratory where his accent did not interfere with his ability to perform supervisory tasks); *Berke*, 628 F.2d at 981 (employee with "pronounced" Polish accent whose command of English was "well above that of the average adult American" was improperly denied two positions because of her accent)....

... In a letter, dated June 28, 1982, the reasons why [Fragante] was not selected were [stated] as follows:

As to the reason for your non-selection we felt the two selected applicants were both superior in their verbal communication ability. As we indicated in your interview, our clerks are constantly dealing with the public and the ability to speak clearly is one of the most important skills required for the position. Therefore, while we were impressed with your educational and employment history, we felt the applicants selected would be better able to work in our office because of their communication skills.

The interviewers' record discloses Fragante's third place ranking was based on his "pronounced accent which is difficult to understand." Indeed, Fragante can point to no facts which indicate that his ranking was based on factors other than his inability to communicate effectively with the public. This view was shared by the district court....

Fragante argues the district court erred in considering "listener prejudice" as a legitimate, nondiscriminatory reason for failure to hire. We find, however, that the district court did not determine defendants refused to hire Fragante on the basis that some listeners would "turn off" a Filipino accent. The district court after trial noted that: "Fragante, in fact, has a difficult manner of pronunciation and the Court further finds as a fact from his general testimony that he would often not respond directly to the questions as propounded."...

In sum, the record conclusively shows that Fragante was passed over because of the deleterious *effect* of his Filipino accent on his ability to communicate orally, not merely because he had such an accent.

[Judgment affirmed]

Questions

1. Why do courts take a very careful look at nonselection decisions based on foreign accents?
2. Why was Fragante not selected for the clerk's position when he had higher test scores than the two successful candidates?
3. Is it ethical for employers to hire "Americans" over individuals with heavy foreign accents who have the legal credentials to work in the United States?

9. Title VII Exceptions

Section 703 of Title VII defines which employment activities are unlawful. This same section, however, also exempts several key practices from the scope of Title VII enforcement. The most important are the bona fide occupational qualification exception, the testing and educational requirement exception, and the seniority system exception.

(a) Bona Fide Occupational Qualification Exception

It is not an unlawful employment practice for an employer to hire employees on the basis of religion, sex, or national origin in those certain instances where religion, sex, or national origin is a bona fide occupational qualification (BFOQ) reasonably necessary to the normal operation of a particular enterprise. **For Example,** a valid BFOQ is a men's clothing store's policy of hiring only males to do measurements for suit alterations. An airline's policy of hiring only female flight attendants is not a valid BFOQ because such a policy is not reasonably necessary to safely operate an airline. Note that there is no BFOQ for race or color.

The Supreme Court in the *Johnson Controls* case considered the employer's BFOQ defense to its "fetal-protection policy" to be discriminatory against women.

UAW V JOHNSON CONTROLS, 499 US 187 (1991)

IT'S A WOMAN'S CHOICE

Johnson Controls, Inc. (JCI), manufactures batteries. A primary ingredient in the battery manufacturing process is lead. Occupational exposure to lead entails health risks, including the risk of harm to any fetus carried by a female employee.

After eight of its employees became pregnant while maintaining blood lead levels exceeding those set by the Centers for Disease Control (CDC) as dangerous for a worker planning to have a family, JCI announced a new personnel policy. This policy barred all women, except those whose infertility was medically documented, from jobs involving actual or potential lead exposure exceeding OSHA standards. Petitioners brought a class action in the district court, claiming that the policy constituted sex discrimination violative of Title VII of the Civil Rights Act of 1964, as amended. The court granted summary judgment for JCI, and the court of appeals affirmed. The case was appealed to Supreme Court.

Judicial Opinion

BLACKMUN, J. . . . The bias in Johnson Controls' policy is obvious. Fertile men, but not fertile women, are given a choice as to whether they wish to risk their reproductive health for a particular job. Section 703(a) of the Civil Rights Act of 1964, 78 Stat. 255, as amended, 42 U.S.C. § 2000e-2-(a), prohibits sex-biased classifications in terms and conditions of employment, in hiring and discharging decisions, and in other employment decisions that adversely affect an employee's status. Respondent's fetal-protection policy explicitly discriminates against women on the basis of their sex. The policy excludes women with childbearing capacity from lead-exposed jobs and so creates a facial classification based on gender. . . .

First, Johnson Controls' policy classifies on the basis of gender and childbearing capacity, rather than fertility alone. Respondent does not seek to protect the unconceived children of all its employees. Despite evidence in the record about the debilitating effect of lead exposure on the male reproductive system, Johnson Controls is concerned only with the harms that may befall the unborn offspring of its female employees. . . .

. . . We hold that Johnson Controls' fetal-protection policy is sex discrimination forbidden under Title VII unless respondent can establish that sex is a "bona fide occupational qualification."

Under § 703(e)(1) of Title VII, an employer may discriminate on the basis of "religion, sex, or national origin in those certain instances where religion, sex, or national origin is a bona fide occupational qualification reasonably necessary to the normal operation of that particular business or enterprise." We therefore turn to the question whether Johnson Controls' fetal-protection policy is one of those "certain instances" that come within the BFOQ exception.

The BFOQ defense is written narrowly, and this Court has read it narrowly. . . . Our emphasis on the restrictive scope of the BFOQ defense is grounded on both the language and the legislative history of 703.

The wording of the BFOQ defense contains several terms of restriction that indicate that the exception reaches only special situations. The statute thus limits the situations in which discrimination is permissible to "certain instances" where sex discrimination is "reasonably necessary" to the "normal operation" of the "particular" business. Each one of these terms—certain, normal, particular—prevents the use of general subjective standards and favors an objective, verifiable requirement. But the most telling term is "occupational"; this indicates that these objective, verifiable requirements must concern job-related skills and aptitudes.

Johnson Controls argues that its fetal-protection policy falls within the so-called safety exception to the BFOQ. Our cases have stressed that discrimination on the basis of sex because of safety concerns is allowed only in narrow circumstances. In *Dothard v Rawlinson*, this Court indicated that danger to a woman herself does not justify discrimination. 433 U.S., at 335, 97 S. Ct. at 2729–2730. We there allowed the employer to hire only male guards in contact areas of maximum-security male penitentiaries only because more was at stake than the "individual woman's decision to weigh and accept the risks of employment." *Ibid.* We found sex to be a BFOQ inasmuch as the employment of a female guard would create real risks of safety to others if violence broke out because the guard was a woman. Sex discrimination was tolerated because sex was related to the guard's ability to do the job—maintaining prison security. We also required in *Dothard* a high correlation between sex and ability to perform job functions and refused to allow employers to use sex as a proxy for strength although it might be a fairly accurate one....

Our case law, therefore, makes clear that the safety exception is limited to instances in which sex or pregnancy actually interferes with the employee's ability to perform the job. This approach is consistent with the language of the BFOQ provision itself, for it suggests that permissible distinctions based on sex must relate to ability to perform the duties of the job. Johnson Controls suggests, however, that we expand the exception to allow fetal-protection policies that mandate particular standards for pregnant or fertile women. We decline to do so. Such an expansion contradicts not only the language of the BFOQ and the narrowness of its exception but the plain language and history of the Pregnancy Discrimination Act....

We have no difficulty concluding that Johnson Controls cannot establish a BFOQ. Fertile women, as far as appears in the record, participate in the manufacture of batteries as efficiently as anyone else. Johnson Controls' professed moral and ethical concern about the welfare of the next generation do not suffice to establish a BFOQ of female sterility. Decisions about the welfare of future children must be left to the parents who conceive, bear, support, and raise them rather than to the employers who hire those parents....

A word about tort liability and the increased cost of fertile women in the workplace is perhaps necessary....

More than 40 states currently recognize a right to recover for a prenatal injury based either on negligence or on wrongful death. According to Johnson Controls, however, the company complies with the lead standard developed by OSHA and warns its female employees about the damaging effects of lead. It is worth noting that OSHA gave the problem of lead lengthy consideration and concluded that "there is no basis whatsoever for the claim that women of childbearing age should be excluded from the workplace in order to protect the fetus or the course of pregnancy." Instead, OSHA established a series of mandatory protections which, taken together, "should effectively minimize any risk to the fetus and newborn child." ... Without negligence, it would be difficult for a court to find liability on the part of the employer. If, under general tort principles, Title VII bans sex-specific fetal-protection policies, the employer fully informs the woman of the risk, and the employer has not acted negligently; the basis for holding an employer liable seems remote at best....

[Judgment reversed and action remanded]

Questions

1. Did Johnson Controls' "fetal-protection policy" discriminate against women?
2. JCI's policy was adopted only after eight employees became pregnant but maintained blood lead levels exceeding those set by the CDC as critical. Considering JCI's moral and ethical obligations to the unborn fetuses and its possible extensive liability in future lawsuits, should not the BFOQ defense be available to it?
3. Was JCI's policy within the so-called safety exception to the BFOQ?

(b) Testing and Educational Requirements

Section 703(h) of the act authorizes the use of "any professionally developed ability test [that is not] designed, intended, or used to discriminate." Employment testing and educational requirements must be "job related"; that is, the employers must prove that the tests and educational requirements bear a relationship to job performance.

Courts will accept prior court-approved validation studies developed for a different employer in a different state or region so long as it is demonstrated that the job for which the test was initially validated is essentially the same job function for which the test is currently being used. **For Example,** a firefighters' test that has been validated in a study in California will be accepted as valid when later used in Virginia. Such application is called *validity generalization.*

The Civil Rights Act of 1991 makes it an unlawful employment practice for an employer to adjust scores or use different cutoff scores or otherwise alter the results of employment tests to favor any race, color, religion, sex, or national origin. This provision addresses the so-called race-norming issue, whereby the results of hiring and promotion tests are adjusted to ensure that a minimum number of minorities are included in application pools.

(c) Seniority System

Section 703(h) provides that differences in employment terms based on a bona fide seniority system are sanctioned so long as the differences do not stem from an intention to discriminate. The term *seniority system is* generally understood to mean a set of rules that ensures that workers with longer years of continuous service for an employer will have a priority claim to a job over others with fewer years of service. Because such rules provide workers with considerable job security, organized labor has continually and successfully fought to secure seniority provisions in collective bargaining agreements.

10. Affirmative Action and Reverse Discrimination

Employers have an interest in *affirmative action* because it is fundamentally fair to have a diverse and representative workforce. Employers, under **affirmative action plans** (AAPs), may undertake special recruiting and other efforts to hire and train minorities and women and help them advance within the company. The plan may also provide job preferences for minorities and women. Such aspects of affirmative action plans have resulted in numerous lawsuits contending that Title VII, the Fifth and Fourteenth Amendments, or collective bargaining contracts have been violated.[15]

(a) Permissible AAPs

A permissible AAP should conform to the following criteria:

1. The affirmative action must be in connection with a "plan."
2. There must be a showing that affirmative action is justified as a remedial measure.
3. The plan must be voluntary.
4. The plan must not unnecessarily trammel the interests of whites.
5. The plan must be temporary.[16]

(b) Reverse Discrimination

When an employer's AAP is not shown to be justified or "unnecessarily trammels" the interests of nonminority employees, it is often called *reverse discrimination.* **For Example,** a city's decision to rescore police promotional tests to achieve specific racial and gender percentages unnecessarily trammeled the interests of nonminority police officers.[17]

(c) Executive Order

Presidential Executive Order 11246 regulates contractors and subcontractors doing business with the federal government. This order forbids discrimination against minorities and women and in certain situations requires affirmative action to be taken to offer better employment opportunities to minorities and women. The Secretary of Labor has established the Office of Federal Contract Compliance Programs (OFCCP) to administer the order.

[15] In *Adarand Constructors, Inc. v Pena,* 115 S Ct 2097 (1995), the U.S. Supreme Court held that a subcontractor had standing to receive relief where a federal program provided financial incentives to prime contractors to hire "disadvantaged" subcontractors, and race-based presumptions were used to identify such individuals. The program was found to violate the equal protection component of the Fifth Amendment's due process clause. After this decision, the EEOC issued a statement on affirmative action, stating in part, "Affirmative action is lawful only when it is designed to respond to a demonstrated and serious imbalance in the workforce, is flexible, time-limited, applies only to qualified workers, and respects the rights of non-minorities and men." Daily Lab Rep (BNA) No. 147, at S-47 (August 1, 1995).

[16] *Steelworkers v Weber,* 443 US 193 (1979); *Johnson v Santa Clara County Transportation Agency,* 480 US 616 (1987).

[17] *San Francisco Police Officers Ass'n v San Francisco,* 812 F2d 1125 (9th Cir 1987).

ETHICS & THE LAW

T. J. Rodgers was the founder and CEO of Cypress Semiconductors. Some time ago, Mr. Rodgers received a letter from Sister Doris Gromley, the director of corporate social responsibility for the Sisters of St. Francis of Philadelphia, stating that her order would use its shareholder votes against the Cypress board (including Mr. Rodgers) to attempt to remove them because of a lack of women and minorities on the Cypress board. Mr. Rodgers responded with a detailed letter to Sister Gromley. Part of the letter follows:

> *Thank you for your letter criticizing the lack of racial and gender diversity of Cypress's Board of Directors. I received the same letter from you last year. I will reiterate the management arguments opposing your position. Then I will provide the philosophical basis behind our rejection of the operating principles espoused in your letter, which we believe to be not only unsound, but even immoral. . . .*
>
> *The semiconductor business is a tough one with significant competition from the Japanese, Taiwanese, and Koreans. There have been more corporate casualties than survivors. For that reason, our Board of Directors is not a ceremonial watchdog, but a critical management function. The essential criteria for Cypress board membership are as follows:*
>
> — Experience as a CEO of an important technology company
>
> — Direct expertise in the semiconductor business based on education and management experience
>
> — Direct experience in the management of a company that buys from the semiconductor industry
>
> *A search based on these criteria usually yields a male who is 50-plus years old, has a Master's degree in engineering science, and has moved up the managerial ladder to the top spot in one or more corporations. Unfortunately, there are currently few minorities and almost no women who chose to be engineering graduate students 30 years ago (this picture will be dramatically different in 10 years, due to the greater diversification of graduate students in the 80s). Bluntly stated, a "woman's view" on how to run our semiconductor company does not help us, unless that woman has an advanced technical degree and experience as a CEO. I do realize there are other industries in which the last statement does not hold true. We would quickly embrace the opportunity to include any woman or minority person who could help us as a director, because we pursue talent and we don't care in what package that talent comes.*
>
> *I believe that placing arbitrary racial or gender quotas on corporate boards is fundamentally wrong.*

Explain to Mr. Rodgers the advantages of having women and minorities on the board. Do you believe that Cypress, if it wanted to, could find highly qualified women and minorities who could help it as directors? Suggest such a person or persons (for example, Anne Mulcahy, CEO of Xerox, or Patricia Russo, CEO of Lucent Technologies). Has Mr. Rodgers violated any laws with his posture? Is the board an appropriate place for affirmative action?

C. Other Equal Employment Opportunity (EEO) Laws

Major federal laws require equal pay for men and women doing equal work and forbid discrimination against older people and those with disabilities.

11. Equal Pay

The Equal Pay Act prohibits employers from paying employees of one gender a lower wage rate than the rate paid employees of the other gender for equal work, or substantially equal work, in the same establishment for jobs that require substantially equal skill, effort, and responsibility and that are performed under similar working conditions.[18] The Equal Pay Act does not prohibit all variations in wage rates paid men and women but only those variations based solely on gender. The act sets forth four exceptions. Variances in wages are allowed where there is (1) a seniority system, (2) a merit system, (3) a system that measures earnings by quantity or quality of production, or (4) a differential based on any factor other than gender.

12. Age Discrimination

The Age Discrimination in Employment Act (ADEA) forbids discrimination by employers, unions, and employment agencies against persons over 40 years of age.[19] Section 4(a) of the ADEA sets forth the employment practices that are unlawful under the act, including the failure to hire because of age and the discharge of employees because of age. Section 7(b) of the ADEA allows for doubling the damages in cases of willful violations of the act. Consequently, an employer who willfully violates the ADEA is liable not only for back wages and benefits but also for an additional amount as liquidated damages.[20]

The *Rhodes* case deals with an ADEA claim by a discharged employee who was qualified for the job and was within the protected class but was replaced by a younger individual. The employer gave its reasons for the termination, and the jury believed the true reason for the termination was age discrimination.

RHODES V GUIBERSON OIL TOOLS, 75 F3D 989 (5TH CIR 1996)

MIFFED AT BEING RIF'D

Calvin Rhodes began his employment with Dresser Industries in 1955 as an oil industry salesman. In the throes of a severe economic downturn, Rhodes took a job selling oil field equipment at another Dresser company that became Guiberson Oil Tools. After seven months, he was discharged and told the reason was a reduction in force but that he would be eligible for rehiring. At that time, he was 56 years old. Within two months, Guiberson hired a 42-year-old salesperson to do the same job. Rhodes sued Guiberson for violating the ADEA. A jury found for plaintiff Rhodes, but a divided panel of the U.S. Court of Appeals for the Fifth Circuit rendered judgment for the employer. The matter was reheard *en banc* before the court of appeals.

Judicial Opinion

DAVIS, C. J. . . . Lee Snyder terminated Rhodes on October 31, 1986. Mr. Snyder told Rhodes he was part of a reduction in force (RIF) because of adverse economic conditions that persisted in the oil field. Snyder told Rhodes, however, that Guiberson would consider him for reemployment. Rhodes' personnel file reflected this same reason for the discharge. It was uncontradicted that Rhodes' position remained unfilled for only 6 weeks and that Guiberson knew at the time of termination or soon after that Rhodes would be replaced. . . .

Lee Snyder, Rhodes' supervisor, testified via deposition that more than one salesman was clearly needed for the territory. Jack Givens, who had been Snyder's supervisor,

[18] 29 USC § 206 (d)(1).
[19] 29 USC § 623.
[20] In *Reeves v Sanderson Plumbing Products Co., Inc.*, 120 S Ct 2097 (2000), the Supreme Court reinstated a $98,490 judgment for Roger Reeves, which included $35,000 in back pay, $35,000 in liquidated damages, and $28,490.80 in front pay, and held that the plaintiff's evidence establishing a prima facie case and showing that the employer's stated reason for the termination was false was sufficient to prove that age was the motivation for the discharge.

testified that he told Snyder to replace Rhodes. Givens also testified that the business required more than one salesman, and that Rick Attaway had been hired to replace Rhodes. James Sewell, Snyder's other supervisor, testified that Rhodes was told that his position was being eliminated and that this statement was not true. The evidence supports a finding that Guiberson did not tell Rhodes the truth about why it was discharging him.

Guiberson Oil's defense at trial was not that Rhodes was RIF'd, but that he was discharged because of his poor work performance. Here, too, Rhodes presented evidence to counter Guiberson's assertion. . . .

Guiberson officials' testimony . . . provided support for Rhodes' contention that Guiberson's "productivity" justification of his termination was a pretext for age discrimination. Lee Snyder testified that the memo placed in Rhodes' file explaining that Rhodes lacked technical expertise in downhole operations was substantially true but noted that it was also a "CYA . . .(cover your _ss)" letter. Snyder testified that Rhodes was a good salesman with strong customer contacts and noted that Jack Givens—Snyder's boss who instructed Snyder to fire Rhodes—once said that he could hire two young salesmen for what some of the older salesmen were costing. Snyder quickly backed away from this statement and said that Givens had said he could hire two *new* salesmen for what some of the *others* were costing him. Givens said he was not aware of telling Snyder this. He also admitted that he had never talked to any of Rhodes' customers about Rhodes' performance as a salesman.

James Sewell, Snyder's other supervisor, testified that he had been very impressed with Rhodes' sales plans and that technical ability was not necessary to sell the product. He also testified that Rhodes had a poor customer base, but admitted that he did not know who Rhodes' customers were, had not talked to any of Rhodes' customers, and had no documentation to support his testimony about Rhodes' poor performance.

Lloyd Allen, the other salesman in the New Orleans office with whom Rhodes was compared, at first testified that his sales were much higher than Rhodes' but clarified on cross-examination that Rhodes' sales during the period in question nearly matched his own. Allen also admitted that the records supporting his testimony may have been incomplete, that Rhodes may have made another sale for which Allen had not credited him, and that another salesman may have been responsible for one of the sales Allen credited to himself. . . .

Based on this evidence, the jury was entitled to find that the reasons given for Rhodes' discharge were pretexts for age discrimination. The jury was entitled to find that Guiberson's stated reason for discharging Rhodes—RIF—was false. Additionally, the reason for discharge that Guiberson Oil proffered in court to meet Rhodes' prima facie case was countered with evidence from which the jury could have found that Rhodes was an excellent salesman who met Guiberson Oil's legitimate productivity expectations. Viewing this evidence in the light most favorable to Rhodes, a reasonable jury could have found that Guiberson Oil discriminated against Rhodes on the basis of his age.

Conclusion

After considering all of the evidence in the record under the standard set forth in *Boeing Co. v Shipman*, we are convinced that the district court properly accepted the jury's verdict on liability and willfulness. Guiberson Oil's motion for JNOV was properly denied. . . .

[Judgment affirmed]

Questions

1. Why did his employer tell Rhodes that he was being terminated because of a RIF, and why did the supervisor Snyder place a memo in Rhodes's file about lacking expertise in downhole operations?
2. Evaluate the statement attributed to Jack Givens, the person who directed that Rhodes be fired, that "I could hire two young salesmen for what some of the older salesmen are costing."
3. Was the jury "entitled" to find that the reasons given by the employer for Rhodes's discharge were merely pretexts for age discrimination?

The Older Workers Benefit Protection Act (OWBPA) of 1990[21] amends the ADEA by prohibiting age discrimination in employee benefits and establishing minimum standards for determining the validity of waivers of age claims. The OWBPA amends the ADEA by adopting an "equal benefit or equal cost" standard, providing that older workers must be given benefits at least equal to those provided for younger workers unless the employer can prove that the cost of providing an equal benefit would be more for an older worker than for a younger one.

[21] 29 USC § 623. This law reverses the Supreme Court's 1989 ruling in *Public Employees Retirement System of Ohio v Betts*, 492 US 158 (1989), which had the effect of exempting employee benefit programs from the ADEA.

Employers commonly require that employees electing to take early retirement packages waive all claims against their employers, including their rights or claims under the ADEA. The OWBPA requires that employees be given a specific period of time to evaluate a proposed package.

Enforcement of the ADEA is the responsibility of the EEOC. Procedures and time limitations for filing and processing ADEA charges are the same as those under Title VII.[22]

13. Discrimination against Persons with Disabilities

The right of persons with disabilities to enjoy equal employment opportunities was established on the federal level with the enactment of the Rehabilitation Act of 1973.[23]

Although not specifically designed as an employment discrimination measure but as a comprehensive plan to meet many of the needs of persons with disabilities, the act contains three sections that provide guarantees against discrimination in employment. Section 501 is applicable to the federal government itself, section 503 applies to federal contractors, and section 504 applies to the recipients of federal funds.

Title I of the Americans with Disabilities Act[24] extends protection in employment-related cases beyond the federal level. This complex statute prohibits all private employers with 15 or more employees from discriminating against individuals with disabilities who, with or without reasonable accommodations, are qualified to perform the essential functions of the job. Enforcement of Title I of the ADA is the responsibility of the EEOC.

Title III of the ADA forbids discrimination against disabled "clients and customers" in areas of "public accommodation," and its application may have employment implications. **For Example,** professional golfer Casey Martin, who paid the Professional Golf Association $3,000 for an opportunity to compete in qualifying tournaments, was thus a "client or customer" of the PGA and because of his circulatory disorder that makes walking an 18-hole golf course painfully difficult, using a golf cart was found to be a "reasonable accommodation" to the PGA rule requiring golfers to walk the course during professional rounds. The court determined that the accommodation did not fundamentally alter the nature of the golf competition.[25]

Under Title I of the ADA, an employer may make preemployment inquiries into the ability of a job applicant to perform job-related functions. Under new "user-friendly" EEOC guidelines on preemployment inquiries under the ADA, an employer may ask applicants whether they will need reasonable accommodations for the hiring process. If the answer is yes, the employer may ask for reasonable documentation of the disability. In general, the employer may not ask questions about whether an applicant will need reasonable accommodations to do the job. However, the employer may make preemployment inquiries regarding job applicant's ability to perform job-related functions.

After making a job offer contingent on passing a medical examination, an offer may be rescinded when the position in question poses a direct threat to the worker's health or safety. **For Example,** Mario Echazabal was initially offered a job at Chevron's El Segundo, California, oil refinery, but the offer was rescinded when company doctors determined that exposure to chemicals on the job would further damage his already reduced liver functions due to his hepatitis C and might potentially kill him. An affirmative defense then exists for employers not only when hiring an individual poses a direct threat to the health or safety of other employees in the workplace but also when there is a direct threat to self. However,

[22] In *Smith v City of Jackson, Mississippi,* 544 US 228 (2005), the U.S. Supreme Court determined that disparate impact claims of age discrimination are permitted under the ADEA. The Court relied on its Title VII *Griggs v Duke Power Co.* precedent, which interpreted text identical to that in the ADEA, with the substitution of the word "age" for the words "race, color, religion, sex or national origin," the narrowing of the coverage of the ADEA, which permits employers to take actions that would otherwise be prohibited based on "reasonable factors other than age" (called the *RFOA provision*) and the EEOC regulations permitting disparate impact claims. The dissenting justices asserted that in the nearly four decades since the law's enactment, the Court had never read it to impose liability on an employer without proof of discriminatory intent. The *Smith v City of Jackson* court decided the disparate impact case before it against the petitioning police officers, finding that the City's larger pay raises to younger employees were based on a RFOA that responded to the City's legitimate goal of retaining its new police officers.

[23] 42 USC §§ 701–794.

[24] Id. §§ 12101–12117.

[25] *PGA Tour, Inc. v Martin,* 121 S Ct 1879 (2001).

the employer must make an individualized medical risk assessment of the employee's condition.[26]

(a) Proving a Case

The plaintiff must prove that she or he is "disabled," which ordinarily involves proving that she or he suffers from a physical or mental impairment that substantially limits a major life activity.[27] The focus is not solely on workplace limitations. When addressing each major life activity, the central inquiry must be whether the individual is substantially limited or unable to perform the tasks central to most people's daily lives, not just the tasks of a particular job.[28] Major life activities include seeing, hearing, speaking, walking, breathing, performing manual tasks, learning, and working.

Impairments are evaluated in their corrected state to determine whether they are disabilities covered under Title I of the ADA.

(b) Individualized Assessments

The assessment of a disability must be made on a case-by-case basis. **For Example,** persons with monocular vision "ordinarily" will meet the ADA's definition of disabled, but they must prove their disability by offering evidence in terms of their own experience concerning loss of depth perception and visual field, thus showing that their major life activity of seeing is substantially limited.[29] Concerning individuals with contagious diseases protected under the ADA, individualized medical judgments are utilized in each case to determine whether such an individual can work. This approach reconciles competing interests in prohibiting discrimination and preventing the spread of disease. Persons with an HIV infection, even when the disease has not progressed to the symptomatic phase, are protected under the ADA.[30]

(c) Reasonable Accommodations under the ADA

Section 101(9) of the ADA defines an employer's obligation to make "reasonable accommodations" for individuals with disabilities to include (1) making existing facilities accessible to and usable by individuals with disabilities and (2) restructuring jobs, providing modified work schedules, and acquiring or modifying equipment or devices. An employer is not obligated under the ADA to make accommodations that would be an "undue hardship" on the employer.

For Example, before passage of the ADA, a supermarket meatcutter unable to carry meat from a refrigerator to a processing area might have been refused clearance to return to work after a back injury until he was able to perform all job functions. Today, under the ADA, it would be the employer's obligation to provide that worker with a cart to assist him in performing the job even if the cart cost $500. However, if the meatcutter was employed by a small business with limited financial resources, an "accommodation" costing $500 might be an undue hardship that the employer could lawfully refuse to make.

Seniority systems provide for a fair and uniform method of treating employees whereby employees with more years of service have a priority over employees with less years of service when it comes to layoffs, job selection, and other benefits such as days off and vacation periods. Seniority rules apply not only under collective bargaining agreements but also to many nonunion job classifications and to nonunion settings. An employer's showing that a requested accommodation conflicts with seniority rules is ordinarily sufficient to show that the requested "accommodation" is not "reasonable." **For Example,** Robert Barnett, a cargo handler for U.S. Airways, Inc., sought a less physically demanding job in the mailroom due to a back injury. Because a senior employee bid the job, U.S. Airways refused Barnett's request to accommodate his disability by allowing him to work the mailroom position. Barnett filed suit under the ADA, and the case progressed to the U.S. Supreme Court, which determined that ordinarily such a requested accommodation is not "reasonable." On remand to the trial court, Barnett was given the opportunity to show that the company allowed exceptions to the seniority rules and he fit within such exceptions.[31]

[26] *Chevron v Echazabal,* 122 S Ct 2045 (2002).
[27] 42 USC § 12111(8).
[28] *Toyota Motor Manufacturing, Inc., v Williams,* 122 S Ct 681 (2002).
[29] See *Albertson, Inc., v Kirkingburg,* 119 S Ct 2162 (1999).
[30] *Bragdon v Abbott,* 118 S Ct 2196 (1998).
[31] *U.S. Airways v Barnett,* 122 S Ct 1516 (2002).

(d) Exclusions from Coverage of the ADA

The act excludes from its coverage employees or applicants who are "currently engaging in the illegal use of drugs." The exclusion does not include an individual who has been successfully rehabilitated from such use or is participating in or has completed supervised drug rehabilitation and is no longer engaging in the illegal use of drugs.

Title V of the act states that behaviors such as transvestitism, transsexualism, pedophilia, exhibitionism, compulsive gambling, kleptomania, pyromania, and psychoactive substance use disorders resulting from current illegal use of drugs are not in and of themselves considered disabilities.

D. Extraterritorial Employment

The Civil Rights Act of 1991 amended both Title VII and the ADA to protect U.S. citizens employed in foreign countries by American-owned or American-controlled companies against discrimination based on race, color, religion, national origin, sex, or disability.[32] The 1991 act contains an exemption if compliance with Title VII or the ADA would cause a company to violate the law of the foreign country in which it is located.

LAWFLIX

Disclosure (1996) (R)

Michael Douglas and Demi Moore portray corporate climbers involved in a power struggle. The movie also depicts the sticky issue of sexual harassment. Several scenes during the course of the arbitration hearing offer definitions of sexual harassment and background as to why this problem exists and is prohibited in the workplace.

For movie clips that illustrate business law concepts, see LawFlix at **http://www.westbuslaw.com.**

[32] Section 109 of the Civil Rights Act of 1991, PL 102-166, 105 Stat 1071.

Summary

Title VII of the Civil Rights Act of 1964, as amended, forbids discrimination on the basis of race, color, religion, sex, or national origin. The EEOC administers the act. Intentional discrimination is unlawful when there is disparate treatment of individuals because of their race, color, religion, gender, or national origin. Also, employment practices that make no reference to race, color, religion, sex, or national origin, but that nevertheless have an adverse or disparate impact on the protected group, are unlawful. In disparate impact cases, the fact that an employer did not intend to discriminate is no defense. The employer must show that there is a job-related business necessity for the disparate impact practice in question. Employers have several defenses they may raise in a Title VII case to explain differences in employment conditions: (1) bona fide occupational qualifications reasonably necessary to the normal operation of the business, (2) job-related professionally developed ability tests, and (3) bona fide seniority systems. If a state EEO agency or the EEOC is not able to resolve the case, the EEOC issues a right-to-sue letter that enables the person claiming a Title VII violation to sue in a federal district court. An affirmative action plan is legal under Title VII provided there is a voluntary "plan" justified as a remedial measure and provided it does not unnecessarily trammel the interests of whites.

Under the Equal Pay Act (EPA), employers must not pay employees of one gender a lower wage rate than the rate paid to employees of the other gender for substantially equal work. Workers over 40 years old are protected from discrimination by the Age Discrimination in Employment Act (ADEA). Employment discrimination against persons with disabilities is prohibited by the Americans with Disabilities Act (ADA). Under the ADA, employers must make reasonable accommodations without undue hardship on them to enable individuals with disabilities to work.

Questions and Case Problems

1. List the major federal statutes dealing with the regulation of equal rights in employment.
2. Casey Martin, a professional golfer with a circulatory disorder that makes walking an 18-hole golf course painfully difficult, was successful in his Title III of the Americans with Disabilities Act lawsuit against the PGA, and he was allowed to use a golf cart as a reasonable accommodation to the PGA rule requiring golfers on the professional tour to walk the course during professional rounds. Subsequently, Stephan Kuketz, a world-class wheelchair racquetball player, sued the Brockton Athletic Club under the ADA when the club refused to allow him to participate in nonhandicapped tournaments, with the only adjustment to the rules being that he be allowed two bounces rather than one, before he hit the ball from his wheelchair. Did the Casey Martin accommondation fundamentally alter the golf competition? Did the Kuketz proposed accommondation fundamentally alter the racquetball competition? Decide. [*Kuketz v Brockton Athletic Club*, *Boston Globe*, August 30, 2001, B-1]
3. Dial Corp. implemented a "work tolerance test," which all new employees were required to pass to obtain employment in its Armour Star brand sausage-making department. Of the applicants who passed the test, 97 percent were male and 38 percent were female. The EEOC "demonstrated" that the facially neutral work tolerance test "caused" a disparate impact on women. The defending employer did not deny that the employment practice in question caused the disparate impact. Rather, the employer responded that the test was "job related" and "necessary" to reduce job-related injuries at the plant and submitted evidence that the number of job injuries had been reduced after implementation of the testing program. The evidence showed that the company had initiated numerous other safety initiatives that had an impact on reducing injuries at the plant. After they failed the test, 52 women were denied jobs. Decide this case. [*EEOC v Dial Corp.*, 2005 WL 2839977]
4. Continental Photo, Inc., is a portrait photography company. Alex Riley, a black man, applied for a position as a photographer with Continental. Riley submitted an application and was interviewed. In response to a question on a written application, Riley indicated that he had been convicted for forgery (a felony) six years before the interview, had received a suspended sentence, and was placed on five-year probation. He also stated that he would discuss the matter with his interviewer if necessary. The subject of the forgery conviction was subsequently not mentioned by Continental's personnel director in his interview with Riley. Riley's application for employment was eventually rejected. Riley inquired about the reason for his rejection. The personnel director, Geuther, explained to him that the prior felony conviction on his application was a reason for his rejection. Riley contended that the refusal to hire him because of his conviction record was actually discrimination against him because of his race in violation of Title VII. Riley felt that his successful completion of a five-year probation without incident and his steady work over the years qualified him for the job. Continental maintained that because its photographers handle approximately $10,000 in cash per year, its policy of not hiring applicants whose honesty was questionable was justified. Continental's policy excluded all applicants with felony convictions. Decide. Would the result have been different if Riley had been a convicted murderer? [*Continental Photo, Inc.*, 26 Fair Empl Prac Cas (BNA) 1799 (EEOC)]
5. Beth Faragher worked part-time and summers as an ocean lifeguard for the Marine Safety Section of the city of Boca Raton, Florida. Bill Terry and David Silverman were her supervisors over the five-year period of her employment. During this period, Terry repeatedly touched the bodies of female employees without invitation and would put his arm around Faragher, with his hand on her buttocks. He made crudely demeaning references to women generally. Silverman once told Faragher, "Date me or clean the toilets for a year." She was not so assigned, however. The city adopted a sexual harassment policy addressed to all employees. The policy was not disseminated to the Marine Safety Section at the beach, however. Faragher resigned and later brought action against the city, claiming a violation of Title VII and seeking nominal damages, costs, and attorney fees. The city defended that Terry and Silverman were not acting within the scope of their employment when they engaged in harassing conduct, and the city should not be held liable for their actions. Are part-time employees covered by Title VII? Was Silverman's threat, "Date me or clean toilets for a year," a basis for *quid pro quo* vicarious liability against the city? Decide this case. [*Faragher v City of Boca Raton*, 118 S Ct 2275]
6. Mohen is a member of the Sikh religion whose practice forbids cutting or shaving facial hair and requires wearing a turban that covers the head. In accordance with the dictates of his religion, Mohen wore a long beard. He applied for a position as breakfast cook at the Island Manor Restaurant. He was told that the restaurant's policy was to forbid cooks to wear facial hair for sanitary and good grooming reasons and that he would have to shave his beard or be denied a position. Mohen contended that the restaurant had an obligation to make a reasonable accommodation to his religious beliefs and let him keep his beard. Is he correct?
7. Sylvia Hayes worked as a staff technician in the radiology department of Shelby Memorial Hospital. On October 1, Hayes was told by her physician that she was pregnant.

When Hayes informed the doctor of her occupation as an X-ray technician, the doctor advised Hayes that she could continue working until the end of April so long as she followed standard safety precautions. On October 8, Hayes told Gail Nell, the director of radiology at Shelby, that she had discovered she was two months pregnant. On October 14, Hayes was discharged by the hospital. The hospital's reason for terminating Hayes was its concern for the safety of her fetus given the X-ray exposure that occurs during employment as an X-ray technician. Hayes brought an action under Title VII, claiming that her discharge was unlawfully based on her condition of pregnancy. She cited scientific evidence and the practice of other hospitals where pregnant women were allowed to remain in their jobs as X-ray technicians. The hospital claimed that Hayes's discharge was based on business necessity. Moreover, the hospital claimed that the potential for future liability existed if an employee's fetus was damaged by radiation encountered at the workplace. Decide. [*Hayes v Shelby Memorial Hospital*, 546 F Supp 259 (ND Ala)]

8. Overton suffered from depression and was made sleepy at work by medication taken for this condition. Also, because of his medical condition, Overton needed a work area away from public access and substantial supervision to complete his tasks. His employer terminated him because of his routinely sleeping on the job, his inability to maintain contact with the public, and his need for supervision. Overton argued that he is a person with a disability under the ADA and the Rehabilitation Act, fully qualified to perform the essential functions of the job, and that the employer had an obligation to make reasonable accommodations, such as allowing some catnaps as needed and providing some extra supervision. Decide. [*Overton v Reilly*, 977 F2d 1190 (7th Cir)]

9. A teenage female high school student named Salazar was employed part-time at Church's Fried Chicken Restaurant. Salazar was hired and supervised by Simon Garza, the assistant manager of the restaurant. Garza had complete supervisory powers when the restaurant's manager, Garza's roommate, was absent. Salazar claimed that while she worked at the restaurant, Garza would refer to her and all other females by a Spanish term that she found objectionable. According to Salazar, Garza once made an offensive comment about her body and repeatedly asked her about her personal life. On another occasion, Garza allegedly physically removed eye shadow from Salazar's face because he claimed it was unattractive. Salazar also claimed that one night she was restrained in a back room of the restaurant while Garza and another employee fondled her. Later that night, when Salazar told a customer what had happened, she was fired. Salazar brought suit under Title VII against Garza and Church's Fried Chicken, alleging sexual harassment. Church's, the corporate defendant, maintained that it should not be held liable under Title VII for Garza's harassment. Church's based its argument on the existence of a published fair treatment policy. Decide. [*Salazar v Church's Fried Chicken, Inc.*, 44 Fair Empl Prac Cas (BNA) 472 (SD Tex)]

10. John Chadbourne was hired by Raytheon on February 4, 1980. His job performance reviews were uniformly high. In December 1983, Chadbourne was hospitalized and diagnosed with AIDS. In January 1984, his physician informed Raytheon that Chadbourne was able to return to work. On January 20, 1984, Chadbourne took a return-to-work physical examination required by Raytheon. The company's doctor wrote the County Communicable Disease Control Director, Dr. Juels, seeking a determination of the appropriateness of Chadbourne's returning to work. Dr. Juels informed the company that "contact of employees to an AIDS patient appears to pose no risk from all evidence accumulated to date." Dr. Juels also visited the plant and advised the company doctor that there was no medical risk to other employees at the plant if Chadbourne returned to work. Raytheon refused to reinstate Chadbourne to his position until July 19, 1984. Its basis for denying reinstatement was that coworkers might be at risk of contracting AIDS. Was Raytheon entitled to bar Chadbourne from work during the six-month period of January through July? [*Raytheon v Fair Employment and Housing Commission*, 261 Cal Rptr 197 (Ct App)]

11. Connie Cunico, a white woman, was employed by the Pueblo, Colorado, School District as a social worker. She and other social workers were laid off in seniority order because of the district's poor financial situation. However, the school board thereafter decided to retain Wayne Hunter, a black social worker with less seniority than Cunico because he was the only black on the administrative staff. No racial imbalance existed in the relevant workforce with black persons constituting 2 percent. Cunico, who was rehired over two years later, claimed that she was the victim of reverse discrimination. She stated that she lost $110,361 in back wages plus $76,000 in attorney fees and costs. The school district replied that it was correct in protecting with special consideration the only black administrator in the district under the general principles it set forth in its AAP. Did the employer show that its affirmative action in retaining Hunter was justified as a remedial measure? Decide. [*Cunico v Pueblo School District No. 6*, 917 F2d 431 (10th Cir)]

12. Della Janich was employed as a matron at the Yellowstone County Jail in Montana. The duties of the position of matron resemble those of a parallel male position of jailer. Both employees have the responsibility for booking prisoners, showering and dressing them, and placing them in the appropriate section of the jail depending on the offender's sex. Because 95 percent of the prisoners at the jail were men and 5 percent were women, the matron was

assigned more bookkeeping duties than the jailer. At all times during Janich's employment at the jail, her male counterparts received $125 more per month as jailers. Janich brought an action under the Equal Pay Act, alleging discrimination against her in her wages because of her sex. The county sheriff denied the charge. Decide. [*Janich v Sheriff,* 29 Fair Empl Prac Cas (BNA) 1195 (D Mont)]

13. Following a decline in cigarette sales, L & M, Inc., hired J. Gfeller as vice president of sales and charged him to turn around the sales decline. After receiving an analysis of the ages of sales personnel and first-line management, Gfeller and his assistant, T. McMorrow, instituted an intensive program of personnel changes that led to the termination of many older managers and sales representatives. A top manager who sought to justify keeping an older manager was informed that he was "not getting the message." Gfeller and McMorrow emphasized that they wanted young and aggressive people and that the older people were not able to conform or adapt to new procedures. R. E. Moran, who had been rated a first-rate division manager, was terminated and replaced by a 27-year-old employee. Gfeller and McMorrow made statements about employees with many years' experience: "It was not 20 years' experience, but rather 1 year's experience 20 times." The EEOC brought suit on behalf of the terminated managers and sales representatives. The company vigorously denied any discriminatory attitude in regard to age. Decide. [*EEOC v Liggett and Meyers, Inc.*, 29 FEP 1611 (EDNC)]
14. Mazir Coleman had driven a school bus for the Casey County, Kentucky, Board of Education for four years. After that time, Coleman's left leg had to be amputated. Coleman was fitted with an artificial leg and underwent extensive rehabilitation to relearn driving skills. When his driving skills had been sufficiently relearned over the course of four years, Coleman applied to the county board of education for a job as a school bus driver. The board refused to accept Coleman's application, saying that it had no alternative but to deny Coleman a bus-driving job because of a Kentucky administrative regulation. That regulation stated in part: "No person shall drive a school bus who does not possess both of these natural bodily parts: feet, legs, hands, arms, eyes, and ears. The driver shall have normal use of the above named body parts." Coleman brought an action under the Rehabilitation act, claiming discrimination based on his physical handicap. The county board of education denied this charge, claiming that the reason they rejected Coleman was because of the requirement of the state regulation. Could Coleman have maintained an action for employment discrimination in light of the state regulation on natural body parts? Decide. [*Coleman v Casey County Board of Education,* 510 F Supp 301 (ND Ky)]
15. Marcia Saxton worked for Jerry Richardson, a supervisor at AT&T's International Division. Richardson made advances to Saxton on two occasions over a three-week period. Each time Saxton told him she did not appreciate his advances. No further advances were made, but thereafter Saxton felt that Richardson treated her condescendingly and stopped speaking to her on a social basis at work. Four months later, Saxton filed a formal internal complaint, asserting sexual harassment, and went on "paid leave." AT&T found inconclusive evidence of sexual harassment but determined that the two employees should be separated. Saxton declined a transfer to another department, so AT&T transferred Richardson instead. Saxton still refused to return to work. Thereafter, AT&T terminated Saxton for refusal to return to work. Saxton contended she was a victim of hostile working environment sexual harassment. AT&T argued that while the supervisor's conduct was inappropriate and unprofessional, it fell short of the type of action necessary for sexual harassment under federal law (the *Harris* case). Decide. [*Saxton v AT&T Co.*, 10 F3d 526 (7th Cir)]

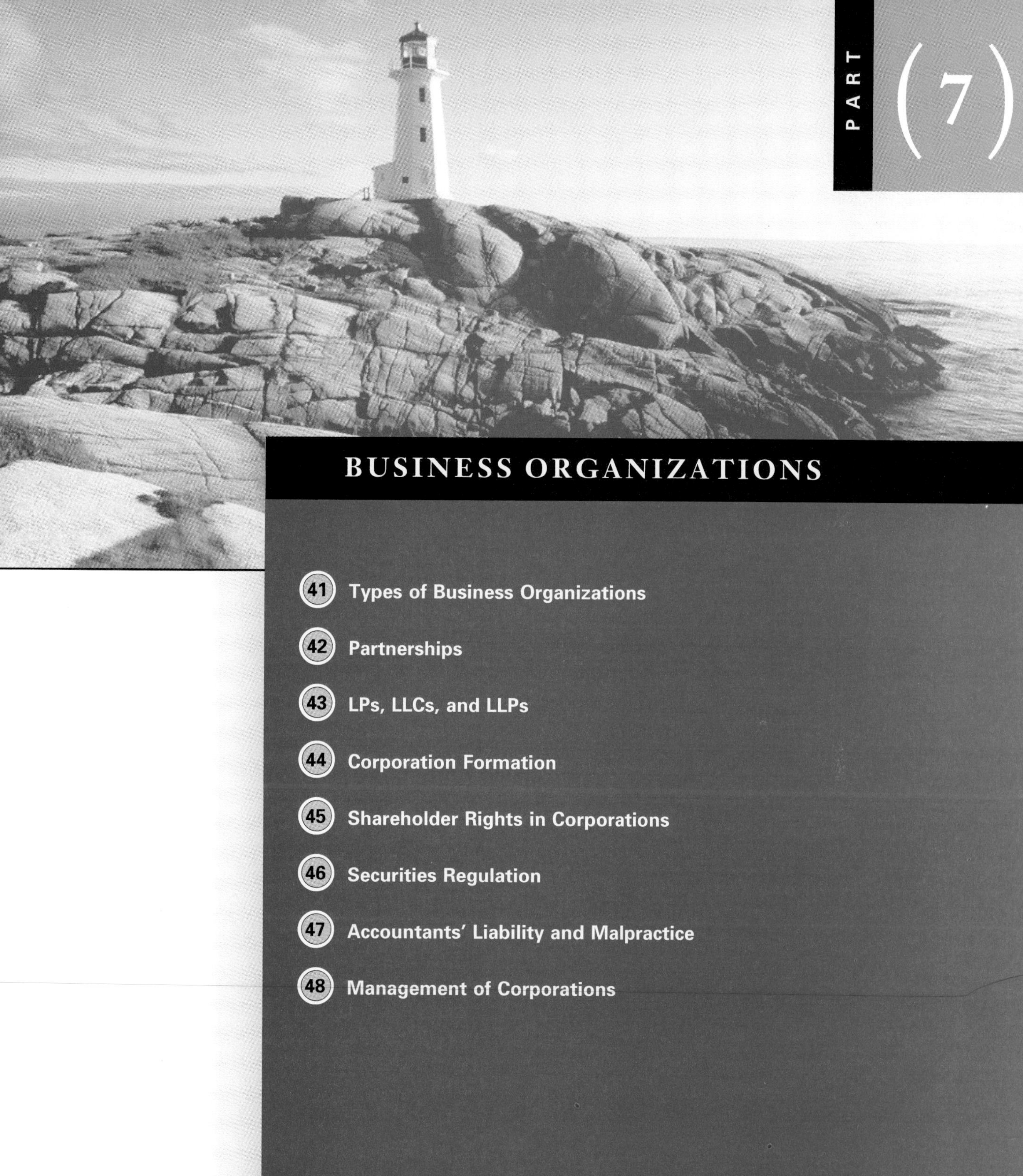

PART (7)

BUSINESS ORGANIZATIONS

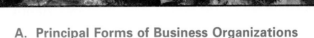

TYPES OF BUSINESS ORGANIZATIONS

CHAPTER (41)

LEARNING OBJECTIVES

After studying this chapter, you should be able to

LO.1 List the advantages and disadvantages of the three principal forms of business

LO.2 Determine whether a business arrangement is a franchise

LO.3 State the reasons for FTC disclosure requirements

LO.4 Distinguish a joint venture from a partnership

LO.5 Compare an unincorporated association with a cooperative

What form of legal organization should you have for your business? The answer will be found in your needs for money, personnel, control, tax and estate planning, and protection from liability.

A. Principal Forms of Business Organizations

The law of business organizations may be better understood if the advantages and disadvantages of proprietorships, partnerships, and corporations are first considered.

1. Individual Proprietorships

A **sole or individual proprietorship** is a form of business ownership in which one individual owns the business. The owner may be the sole worker of the business or employ as many others as needed to run the concern. Individual proprietorships are commonly used in retail stores, service businesses, and agriculture.

(a) Advantages

The proprietor or owner is not required to expend resources on organizational fees. The proprietor, as the sole owner, controls all decisions and receives all profits. The net earnings of the business are not subject to corporate income taxes but are taxed only as personal income.

(b) Disadvantages

The proprietor is subject to unlimited personal liability for the debts of the business and cannot limit this risk. The investment capital in the business is limited by the resources of the sole proprietor. Because all contracts of the business are made by the owner or in the owner's name by agents of the owner, the authority to make contracts terminates on the death of the owner, and the business is subject to disintegration.

2. Partnerships, LLPs, and LLCs

A **partnership** involves the pooling of capital resources and the business or professional talents of two or more individuals whose goal is making a profit. Law firms, medical associations, and architectural and engineering firms may operate under the partnership form. Today, however, these firms may convert to a **limited liability partnership (LLP).** A wide range of small manufacturing, retail, and service businesses operate as partnerships. These businesses may operate under the form of organization called **limited liability company (LLC),** which allows tax treatment as a partnership with limited liability for the owners.

(a) Advantages

The partnership form of business organization allows individuals to pool resources and then initiate and conduct their business without the requirement of a formal organizational structure.

(b) Disadvantages

Major disadvantages of a partnership are the unlimited personal liability of each partner and the uncertain duration of the business because the partnership is dissolved by the death of one partner. Unlimited personal liability is remedied by the LLC form of business organization. Professional partnerships that convert to an LLP shield innocent partners from personal liability beyond their investment in the firm.

3. Corporations

Business **corporations** exist to make a profit and are created by government grant. State statutes regulating the creation of corporations require a corporate structure consisting of shareholders, directors, and officers. The shareholders, as the owners of the business, elect a board of directors, which is responsible for managing the business. The directors employ officers, who serve as the agents of the business and run day-to-day operations. Corporations range in size from incorporated one-owner enterprises to large multinational concerns.

(a) Advantages

The major advantage to the shareholder, or investor, is that the shareholder's risk of loss from the business is limited to the amount of capital she invested in the business or paid for shares. This factor, coupled with the free transferability of corporate shares, makes the corporate form of business organization attractive to investors.

By purchasing shares, a large number of investors may contribute the capital assets needed to finance large business enterprises. As the capital needs of a business expand, the corporate form becomes more attractive.

A corporation is a separate legal entity capable of owning property, contracting, suing, and being sued in its own name. It has perpetual life. In other words, a corporation is not affected by the death of any of its shareholders or the transfer of their shares. In contrast to the case of a partnership or proprietorship, the death of an owner has no legal effect on the corporate entity.

(b) Disadvantages

A corporation is required to pay corporate income taxes. Shareholders are required to pay personal income taxes on the amount received when they receive a distribution of profits from the corporation. This is a form of double taxation.

Incorporation involves the expenditure of funds for organizational expenses. Documents necessary for the formation of a corporation, which are required by state law, must be prepared, and certain filing fees must be paid. State corporation laws may also require filing an annual report and other reports.

B. Specialized Forms of Organizations

CPA 4. Joint Ventures

A **joint venture,** or joint adventure, is a relationship in which two or more persons combine their labor or property for a single business undertaking and share profits and losses equally or as otherwise agreed.[1] When several contractors pool all their assets to construct one tunnel, the relationship is a joint venture.

A joint venture is similar in many respects to a partnership. It differs primarily in that the joint venture typically involves the pursuit of a single enterprise or transaction, although its accomplishment may require several years. A partnership is generally a continuing business or activity but may be expressly created for a single transaction. Because the distinction is so insubstantial, most courts hold that joint ventures are subject to the same principles of law as partnerships. **For Example,** the Virginia Uniform Partnership Act was utilized to enable PGI, Inc., to sue Rathe Productions, Inc., for conversion of its share of a settlement agreement with the Smithsonian Institute because PGI/Rathe was involved in a joint venture and the "rules of law governing the rights, duties and liabilities of joint ventures are substantially the same as those which govern partnerships."[2]

It is essential that the venturers have a common purpose and that each has an equal right to control the operations or activities of the undertaking.[3] The actual control of the operations may be entrusted to one of the joint venturers. Thus, the fact that one joint venturer is placed in control of the farming and livestock operations of an undertaking, for example, and appears to be the owner of the land does not destroy the joint venture relationship.

(a) Duration of Joint Venture

A joint venture continues for the time specified in the agreement of the parties. In the absence of a fixed-duration provision, a joint venture is ordinarily terminable at the will of any participant. When the joint venture clearly relates to a particular transaction, such as the construction of a specified bridge, the joint venture ordinarily lasts until the particular transaction or project is completed or becomes impossible to complete.

(b) Liability to Third Persons

The conclusion that persons are joint venturers is important when a suit is brought by or against a third person for personal injuries or property damage. If there is a joint venture, the fault or negligence of one venturer will be imputed to the other venturers.[4]

5. Unincorporated Associations

An **unincorporated association** is a combination of two or more persons for the furtherance of a common purpose.[5] No particular form of organization is required. Any conduct or agreement indicating an attempt to associate or work together for a common purpose is sufficient.

[1] See *Latiolais v BFI of Louisiana, Inc.*, 567 So 2d 1159 (La App 1990).

[2] *PGI, Inc. v Rathe Productions, Inc.*, 576 SE2d 438 (Va 2003).

[3] *Dunbar v RKG Engineering, Inc.*, 746 SW2d 314 (Tex App 1988).

[4] *Kim v Chamberlain*, 504 So 2d 1213 (Ala App 1987).

[5] The National Conference of Commissioners on Uniform State Laws has adopted a Uniform Unincorporated Nonprofit Association Act. In addition, community associations are being widely formed, primarily for the purpose of community planning and environmental protection.

The authority of an unincorporated association over its members is governed by ordinary contract law. Except when otherwise provided by statute, an unincorporated association does not have any legal existence apart from its members. Thus, an unincorporated association cannot sue or be sued in its own name.

Generally, the members of an unincorporated association are not liable for the debts or liabilities of the association by the mere fact that they are members. It must usually be shown that they authorized or ratified the act in question. If either authorization or ratification by a particular member can be shown, that member has unlimited liability for the act.

6. Cooperatives

A **cooperative** consists of a group of two or more independent persons or enterprises that cooperate for a common objective or function. Thus, farmers may pool their farm products and sell them. Consumers may likewise pool their orders and purchase goods in bulk.

(a) Incorporated Cooperatives

Statutes commonly provide for the special incorporation of cooperative enterprises. Such statutes often provide that any excess of payments over the cost of operation shall be refunded to each participant member in direct proportion to the volume of business that the member has done with the cooperative. This contrasts with the payment of a dividend by an ordinary business corporation in which the payment of dividends is proportional to the number of shares held by the shareholder and is unrelated to the extent of the shareholder's business activities with the enterprise.

(b) Antitrust Law Exemption

The agreement by the members of sellers' cooperatives that all products shall be sold at a common price is an agreement to fix prices. Therefore, the sellers' cooperative is basically an agreement in restraint of trade and a violation of antitrust laws. The Capper-Volstead Act of 1922 expressly exempts normal selling activities of farmers' and dairy farmers' cooperatives from the operation of the federal Sherman Antitrust Act so long as the cooperatives do not conspire with outsiders to fix prices.

C. The Franchise Business Format

In individual situations, *franchising* is a *method* of doing business, not a *form* of business organization. A franchisor or franchisee could be a sole proprietor, a partnership, a limited liability company, or a corporation. It is a *business format*, as opposed to a business organization. Franchising relies on contract law to set forth the rights and obligations of the parties. However, the Federal Trade Commission Act and certain state laws require disclosure. Any federal and/or state laws regulating securities, intellectual property, antitrust violations, sales, agency, and tort law apply to franchises.

Section 5 of the Federal Trade Commission Act prohibits deceptive, manipulative, or unfair business practices,[6] and state deceptive trade practices acts similarly prohibit such practice.

7. Definition and Types of Franchises

The Federal Trade Commission (FTC) has defined a **franchise** as "an arrangement in which the owner of a trademark, trade name, or copyright licenses others, under specified conditions or limitations, to use the trademark, trade name, or copyright in purveying goods or services." The **franchisor** is the party granting the franchise, and the **franchisee** is the person to whom the franchise is granted. There are three principal types of franchises. The first is a *manufacturing* or *processing franchise*, in which the franchisor grants the franchisee authority to manufacture and sell products under the trademark(s) of the franchisor. The franchisor may supply an essential ingredient in a processing franchise, such as the syrup for an independent regional Coca-Cola bottling company. The second type of franchise is a *service franchise*, whereby the franchisee renders a service to customers under the terms of a franchise agreement. The drain-cleaning service provided by Roto-Rooter is an example of a service franchise. The third type is a *distribution franchise*, in which the franchisor's products are sold to a franchisee, who then resells to customers in a geographical area. Exxon Mobil Oil Company's products are often sold to retail customers through independent distribution franchises.

[6] 15 USC § 45.

A common issue in litigation under state laws protecting franchisees is whether the business arrangement of the parties is a franchise or a businessperson is a franchisee under the applicable state law.[7]

8. The Franchise Agreement

The relationship between the franchisor and the franchisee is ordinarily an arm's-length relationship between two independent contractors. Their respective rights are determined by the contract existing between them, called the **franchise agreement.** The agreement sets forth the rights of the franchisee to use the **trademarks, trade name, trade dress,** and **trade secrets** of the franchisor. **For Example,** Burger King Corporation licenses franchisees to use the trademarks Burger King, Whopper, Croissanwich, and Whopper Jr.[8] The franchise agreement commonly requires the franchisor to provide training for the franchisee's employees, including processing or repair training. Thus, a new Chili's Bar and Grill franchise can expect to have its employees taught how to prepare and serve the food on its menu. In a distribution franchise, an Acura dealer can expect the franchisor to train its mechanics to repair the automobiles it sells. The franchise agreement also deals with terms for payment of various fees by the franchisee and sets forth compliance requirements for quality control set by the franchisor.

The duration of a franchise is a critical element of the franchise agreement. The franchise may last for as long as the parties agree. The laws in some states may require advance written notice of cancellation.[9] Franchise contracts generally specify the causes for which the franchisor may terminate the franchise, such as the franchisee's death, bankruptcy, failure to make payments, or failure to meet sales quotas. Implied obligations of good faith and fair dealing apply to these contracts.[10]

The *McDonald's Corp.* case is an example of the basic contractual nature of franchising.

MCDONALD'S CORP. V CB MANAGEMENT CO., INC., 13 F SUPP 3D 705 (ND ILL 1998)

BIG MAC WINS

McDonald's Corp. leased two restaurants in Cleveland, Ohio, to CB Management and gave CB franchises to run the restaurants. Caesar Burkes is the president of CB. The franchise agreements between the parties required CB to make monthly payments of license and lease fees to McDonald's as well as real estate taxes, and the agreements provided for the termination of the franchises if CB should fail to make monthly payments. The agreements also provided that upon termination CB was required to discontinue the use of all McDonald's service marks and trademarks and immediately deliver the premises to McDonald's. On July 25, 1997, McDonald's sent a notice of default to CB for failure to pay $223,576.88 in rent, service fees, and real estate taxes; and it gave CB an opportunity to cure all defaults by August 25, 1997. CB did not make the required payments, and McDonald's terminated the franchises. On August 29, 1997, McDonald's brought an action requiring CB to vacate the restaurants and comply with the contractual provision regarding termination and demanded that it make all payments due. On September 5, 1997, CB attempted to pay McDonald's $200,000, but all checks were returned by McDonald's.

Judicial Opinion

MORAN, S. D. J.... Under Illinois law the starting point of any contractual analysis is the language of the contract itself. In interpreting a contract our overriding concern is to give effect to the intent of the parties. *Church v. General Motors Corp.*, 74 F.3d 795, 799 (7th Cir.1996). If a contract

[7] *Morrison v Chilton Professional Automotive, Inc.*, 984 F Supp 1018 (WD Tex 1997).

[8] *Burger King Corp. v Hinton, Inc.*, 2002 US Dist LEXIS 9020.

[9] See, for example, Mo Rev Stat § 407.405; *Ridings v Thoele*, 739 SW2d 547 (Mo 1987).

[10] *Dunkin Donuts, Inc., v Gav-Stra Donuts, Inc.*, 139 F Supp 2d 147 (D Ma 2002).

is clear and unambiguous we must determine the intention of the parties "solely from the plain language of the contract" and may not consider extrinsic evidence outside the "four corners" of the document itself. . . .

CB does not dispute that it failed to timely pay amounts due under the franchise agreements, nor does it dispute that the termination provisions described above were in effect at the time of its delinquency. . . . CB argues that, although there is no explicit duty to subordinate or defer termination pending a franchisee's loan application, the contract terms confer discretion on McDonald's to subordinate, as it has done in the past with CB and other franchisees. McDonald's failure to exercise that discretion in good faith constituted a breach of the franchise agreement.

. . . The fact that McDonald's may have declined to exercise its contractual right to terminate in the past does not somehow transform that *right* into a *discretionary decision* governed by the standard of good faith and fair dealing. McDonald's right to terminate was not modified by its past leniency, and there is no evidence indicating that McDonald's was not justified in exercising that right on August 25, 1997, after CB had failed to pay its outstanding contractual obligations.

Neither does the fact that McDonald's may have acted with improper motive in retaliation for Burkes' previously filed lawsuit, render the franchise termination a bad faith exercise of discretion. CB attempts to establish improper motive. . . . However, it is well established that where there is good cause for a franchise termination, there can be no bad faith. *See Dayan*, 81 Ill.Dec. 156, 466 N.E.2d at 974 (quoting Corbin on Contracts, § 1266 at 368 (Supp.1982)). Nowhere does CB dispute that it had violated the terms of the franchise agreements by failing to make timely payments, and that this violation constituted a material breach. *Dayan* controls this point: "Where the franchisee is in substantial breach of the franchising agreement . . . no legitimate expectations of the franchisee are violated by termination regardless of what other motives the franchisor might have." 81 Ill.Dec. 156, 466 N.E.2d at 974 . . .

Next, CB contends that its claim against McDonald's under the Illinois Franchise Disclosure Act (IFDA) precludes McDonald's summary judgment motion. . . .

Since the St. Clair and Carnegie McDonald's are located in Cleveland, Ohio, McDonald's contends that they do not fall within the ambit of the IFDA under the statute's explicit terms. . . .

We follow the weight of authority in finding that the IFDA does not apply to non-Illinois franchisees. . . .

. . . McDonald's is entitled to immediate possession of the St. Clair and Carnegie McDonald's and CB is to comply with the terms of the agreements regarding surrender of possession. McDonald's is entitled to damages for CB's unlawful post-termination use of its trade names, service marks and trademarks under the Lanham Act and for pretermination payments due and unpaid under the franchise agreements.

[Judgment affirmed]

Questions

1. On what legal basis did McDonald's contend that it had a right to terminate the franchise and take possession of the restaurants?
2. Did the fact that McDonald's was aware that CB was pursuing a loan to pay its delinquency indicate that McDonald's failed to apply the franchise agreement in good faith?
3. Is an improper motive a valid defense where there is good cause for a franchise termination?

Franchise agreements frequently contain an arbitration provision under which a neutral party is to make a final and binding determination whether there has been a breach of the contract sufficient to justify cancellation of the franchise.[11] The arbitration provision may provide that the franchisor can appoint a trustee to run the business of the franchisee while arbitration proceedings are pending.

9. Special Protections Under Federal Laws

Holders of automobile dealership franchises are protected from bad-faith termination of their dealerships by the federal Automobile Dealers' Day in Court Act (ADDCA).[12] **For Example,** Anthony Arciniaga was allowed to proceed with his ADDCA lawsuit against

[11] *Central New Jersey Freightliner, Inc., v Freightliner Corp.*, 987 F Supp 289 (DNJ 1998).
[12] 15 USC §§ 1221–1225.

General Motors. The court refused to allow GM to create and apply a corporate structure that evades the ADDCA. Collectively, the court looked to the Dealer Sales and Service Agreement, the Shareholders' Agreement, and other documents that together made up the understanding between Arciniaga and GM, which made it possible for Arciniaga to become an automobile dealer. The court concluded that all of the agreements viewed together constituted a "motor vehicle franchise contract." The court refused to focus on just one document as asserted by GM because doing so would negate the protective features of the ADDCA.[13]

When an automobile manufacturer makes arbitrary and unreasonable demands and then terminates a dealer's franchise for failure to comply with the demands, the manufacturer is liable for the damages caused. The right of a franchisee to transfer its contractual rights in the franchise is protected by the state law subject to notice and approval by the franchisor.[14]

In the *VW Credit, Inc.*, case, the court was faced with a question of whether or not the franchisor unreasonably withheld approval of a transfer, and if so, what should be the remedy.

VW CREDIT, INC. V COAST AUTOMOBILE GROUP, LTD., 787 A2D 951 (NJ SUPER 2002)

AN ASSOCIATE OF TONY AND CARMELLA SOPRANO? PROVE IT

After a fire at its Volkswagen-Audi dealership in Tom's River, New Jersey, the owner, Coast Automotive Group, Ltd., agreed to transfer all assets to Aspen Knolls, Ltd., in order to salvage its franchise investment. Volkswagen of America (VOA) and Audi of America (AOA) brought suit to terminate Coast's franchise. Aspen Knolls meanwhile proceeded with the formality of submitting applications to VOA and AOA to transfer the Coast dealership, which were rejected by VOA and AOA. The trial court determined that VOA and AOA unreasonably withheld approval of the transfer and ordered specific performance of the transfer. VOA and AOA appealed.

Judicial Opinion

NEWMAN, J.... VWOA and AOA assert that the Act does not authorize the relief granted by the trial court. WVOA and AOA argue that the court erred in determining that the consent was unreasonably withheld and, even if it was, the court was limited to awarding damages under *N.J.S.A.* 56:10–10 for a violation of the Act, and only to a franchisee, not to a potential transferee who is not covered by the Act....

The pivotal provision of the Act in terms of the transfer or sale of a franchise is *N.J.S.A.* 56:10–6, which provides:

It shall be a violation of this act for any franchisee to transfer, assign or sell a franchise or interest therein to another person unless the franchisee shall first notify the franchisor of such intention by written notice setting forth in the notice of intent the prospective transferee's name, address, statement of financial qualification and business experience during the previous 5 years. The franchisor shall within 60 days after receipt of such notice either approve in writing to the franchisee such sale to proposed transferee or by written notice advise the franchisee of the unacceptability of the proposed transferee setting forth material reasons relating to the character, financial ability or business experience of the proposed transferee. If the franchisor does not reply within the specified 60 days, his approval is deemed granted. No such transfer, assignment or sale hereunder shall be valid unless the transferee agrees in writing to comply with all the requirements of the franchise then in effect.

We have previously interpreted *N.J.S.A.* 56:10–6 to impose a requirement of reasonableness on a franchisor's decision to disapprove a transfer. *Simmons, supra,* 180 *N.J.Super.* at 539, 435 A.2d 1167. The standard of review to determine the reasonableness of withholding consent to transfer of a franchise is an objective test that requires that the decision be supported by substantial evidence showing that the proposed franchisee is materially deficient. *In re Van Ness Auto Plaza, Inc.* 120 *B.R.* 545, 549

[13] *Arciniaga v General Motors Corp.*, 418 FSupp 2d 374 (SDNY 2005).

[14] *KMS Restaurant Corp. v Wendy's International*, 361 F3d 1321 (11th Cir 2004).

(Bankr.N.D.Cal.1990). The burden of presenting credible reasons for the refusal to consent rests on the franchisor. *Ibid.* We agree with the trial judge that VWOA and AOA did not meet this burden.

In support of their determination to withhold consent, VWOA and AOA asserted that Aspen Knolls submitted a deficient application and that there were concerns related to the character of Mazzuoccola, the majority member of Aspen Knolls. The trial court made the following findings regarding the reasons asserted by VWOA and AOA for withholding consent to assignment of the franchise.

As to the issue of business experience, the court found that Reynolds and Rutigliano, both of whom are principals of Aspen Knolls, began to operate an Audi Dealership in Bernardsville in 1995, and within the first year of operation, the dealership was ranked third in the nation in volume and sales. Since its inception, that dealership has maintained a high ranking among the 365 Audi dealerships in the country in terms of sales and volume. There was also testimony that the Bernardsville dealership ranked in the top ten percentiles in customer satisfaction in both the regional area and the nation. The judge also noted that Reynolds and Rutigliano had extensive prior experience as automobile dealers.

Mazzuoccola's experience was not as extensive. However, the judge noted that Mazzuoccola, a race car enthusiast who sponsored a professional racing team, did own a Jeep dealership in Essex County. The judge found that Aspen Knolls, an entity comprising Reynolds, Rutigliano, and Mazzuoccola, demonstrated an ability to operate the Coast dealership.

As to the issue of VWOA and *[sic.]* AOA's concerns regarding Mazzuoccola's character, the judge noted that VWOA and AOA based those concerns upon certain allegations raised in an affidavit filed by Shansab in the litigation between Coast and Aspen Knolls. The affidavit, which had been withdrawn by Shansab, raised issues of whether Mazzuoccola had affiliated or associated with known organized crime figures as well as the propriety of his business practices. The underlying litigation in which the affidavit had been submitted settled.... In this regard, the judge noted that

> *no testimony was produced by either side to address the allegations that related to the character allegations involving Mr. Mazzuoccola. And that Mr. Mazzuoccola, in fact, took the stand and exposed himself to the opportunity for cross examination by the . . . franchisor's representatives. That the issue of his involvement with any unsavory business activities, or association with undesirable individuals, or people of known criminal connections or histories or even personalities, was just not raised.*
>
> . . .
>
> *[T]he hearing was . . . scheduled primarily to address these issues of character. . . . I continue to be fully satisfied that any purported deficiencies in terms of character have not been proved. And even if raised . . . [the allegations] have been effectively dispelled through the testimony of the parties. . . . Character, then, cannot form a basis for the rejection of the proposed franchisees under . . . these circumstances. . . .*

We are satisfied that Judge Ford's findings that VWOA and AOA unreasonably withheld their consent to the proposed transfer are supported by adequate, substantial, and credible evidence. *Rova Farms Resort, Inc. v. Investors Ins. Co. of Am.*, 65 *N.J.* 474, 484, 323 A.2d 495 (1974).

VWOA and AOA's contention that the relief granted by the trial court is not authorized, amounts to a claim that under *N.J.S.A.* 56:10–6, the franchisor has a right to reject a proposed transferee and once it does, regardless of the reasonableness of its disapproval, the remedy of specific performance is unavailable. We disagree....

Section six entitles a franchisee to specific performance if the franchisor fails to approve or disapprove of the transfer, in writing, within the sixty day period. *N.J.S.A.* 56:10–6. That section restricts a franchisee's ability to assign a franchise without the franchisor's consent. Section six also restricts a franchisor's ability to reject a proposed transferee.

When a franchisor receives notice that a franchisee intends to transfer a franchise, section six mandates that the franchisor shall, in writing, inform the franchisee either of its approval of the transfer or "of the unacceptability of the proposed transferee, setting forth the material reasons relating to the character, financial ability or business experience of the proposed transferee" to support the rejection. *N.J.S.A.* 56:10–6. Thus, the franchisor's rejection must be based on a bona fide business decision. In addition, if the franchisor chooses to not respond to the notice within sixty days of that notice, the franchisor's "approval is deemed granted" and the franchise agreement between the franchisee and the franchisor is automatically deemed amended to incorporate such transfer.

The provisions, read together, evidence that the statute contemplates the remedy of specific performance where the franchisor severs the franchise relationship without good cause subject to the proposed transferee's written assurance that it will comply with the existing franchise agreement....

The franchisor should not be able to circumvent the automatic approval contemplated by the Legislature by giving notice of disapproval within the time period and facially complying with section six. We agree with the trial judge that it would be nonsensical for the Legislature to allow for specific performance if the franchisor did nothing, but if the franchisor timely rejected the proposed transfer in bad faith, the franchisee is limited to damages . . .

Other courts have also recognized these benefits and granted the remedy of specific performance to franchisees and proposed transferees. *Bayview Buick–GMC Truck, Inc. v Gen. Motors Corp.*, 597 *So.*2d 887 (Fla.Dist. Ct.App. 1992)(holding refusal to consent presumptively unreasonable where proposed transferee is already a franchisee of the franchisor); *Culligan Soft Water Serv. of Inglewood, Inc. v Culligan Int'l Co.*, 288 *N.W.*2d 213 (Minn.1979) (holding refusal to consent unreasonable where proposed transferee is qualified to assume franchise); *DeBauge Bros., Inc. v Whitsitt*, 212 *Kan.* 758, 512 *P.*2d 487 (1973) (contract for the sale or transfer of franchise, along with real property necessary to operate the business, is a proper subject for specific performance); and *Bidwell v Long*, 14 *A.D.*2d 168, 218 *N.Y.S.*2d 108 (App.Div.1961) (specific performance granted where the franchise was the prime consideration for the sale, notwithstanding the parent corporation's lack of approval as required by the agreement. . . .

Accordingly we hold that specific performance is an appropriate remedy under section six of the Act where a franchisor unreasonably withholds consent to a transfer. We note for completeness, that while the relief granted by the trial judge benefited Aspen Knolls, the court did not grant relief to Aspen Knolls. Instead, Judge Ford granted relief to the franchisee, Coast. The fact that enforcement of section six results in benefits to a proposed transferee does not render the relief inappropriate.

The order approving Aspen Knolls as the franchise transferee of Coast's Volkswagen and Audi franchises is affirmed. . . .

[Judgement affirmed]

Questions

1. Under Section 6 of the state Franchise Practices Act, on what statutory basis may a franchisor reject a proposed transferee? Which party has the burden of proof?
2. May a franchisor reject a transferee on character grounds because the transferee is a race car enthusiast, sponsors a professional racing team, and is suspected of associating with organized crime figures?
3. Is there an indication to be found in the court's opinion that the decision is in line with other courts' handling of similar situations throughout the country?

The Petroleum Marketing Practices Act (PMPA) gives gas station franchisees the opportunity to continue in business by purchasing the entire premises used in selling motor fuel when the franchisor decides to sell the property and not renew a lease. In some instances, the franchisor's intentions are unclear and its actions may be perceived as contrary to the PMPA. Litigation may be necessary to resolve the matter. **For Example,** eight independent gas station operators who leased stations from Shell Oil Co. and sold Shell products were successful in their PMPA lawsuit against Shell when Shell phased out rental subsidies provided franchisees under the parties' lease agreements and set the wholesale prices it charged dealers for gasoline so high that the increase would squeeze dealers' profits or force them to raise prices that competition could undercut. The dealers argued this was done to reduce the number of independent gas stations in the region. A jury awarded $3.3 million in compensatory damages.[15]

The PMPA prohibits early termination of a franchise, but only when the franchisee's failure to comply with a provision of the franchise is so serious as to undermine the entire relationship.[16]

10. Disclosure

The FTC has adopted a franchise disclosure rule that requires franchisors to give prospective franchisees a full disclosure statement 10 days before a franchisee signs a contract or pays any money for a franchise.

[15] Kimberly Blanton, "Jury Rules for Franchisees in Shell Trial," *Boston Globe*, December 9, 2004, C-3.

[16] In *Chevron v El-Khoury*, 285 F3d 1159 (9th Cir. 2002), the Court of Appeals remanded a franchise termination case for trial on the materiality of a franchisee's failure to pay $15,000 in California sales taxes when the oil company had unsuccessfully attempted to buy out the dealer and, when the last buyout offer was rejected, had selected him to be audited. The dealer eventually paid all taxes due. One of Chevron's executives testified the failure to pay taxes was between "the dealer and the state" rather than the dealer and Chevron. However, Chevron contended that the failure to pay all taxes when due was a violation of the franchise agreement and tarnished the company's image.

Fourteen states also have protective regulations requiring disclosure in the sale of franchises. Effective on and after December 21, 1995, all 14 states and the FTC accepted the 1993 revised version of the Uniform Franchise Offering Circular as being in full compliance with state and FTC disclosure rules.

The disclosure statement must include (1) the business experience of the franchisor and its brokers, (2) any current and past litigation against the franchisor, (3) any previous bankruptcy, (4) the material terms of the franchise agreement, (5) initial and recurring payments, (6) restrictions on territories, (7) grounds for termination of the franchise, and (8) actual, average, or projected sales, profits, or earnings.

Under the FTC disclosure rule, a franchisor must pay a civil penalty of as much as $10,000 for each violation when it is shown that a sale of a franchise subject to the FTC rule was made, the franchisor knew or should have known of the disclosure rule, and no disclosure statement was given to the buyer. Also, the franchisor may be required to make the buyer whole for any losses suffered.

11. Vicarious Liability Claims Against Franchisors

In theory, a franchisor is not liable to a third person dealing with or affected by the franchise holder. This freedom from liability is one of the main reasons franchisors use franchises. If the negligence of the franchisee causes harm to a third person, the franchisor is not liable because the franchisee is an independent contractor. However, franchisors continue to be subject to lawsuits based on the wrongful conduct of their franchisees under the theory of either actual authority or apparent authority.

The *D.L.S. v Maybin* decision presents both the plaintiffs' and franchisor's views on liability.

D.L.S. V MAYBIN, 121 P3D 1210 (WASH APP 2005)

BIG MAC WINS AGAIN. WHY FRANCHISORS USE FRANCHISES!

[William Roberts operated a McDonald's restaurant in Newcastle, Washington under a franchise agreement with McDonald's Corporation. A thriving drug scene existed among employees and assistant managers at the restaurant. In May of 2000, fifteen year old D.L.S. was hired by the restaurant and within weeks she was part of the drug scene there, and thereafter she left home to live with an assistant manager and use drugs. Her father, Clifford Street, and D.L.S. sued McDonald's Corp. and Roberts for introducing D.L.S. to drugs and sex. The trial court dismissed the claims against McDonald's Corp. and D.L.S. and her father appealed. Mr. Street testified that "no person in their right mind would believe that McDonald's did not control what happened at the individual restaurants."]

Judicial Opinion

KENNEDY, J. . . .

Discussion

The only question before us is whether McDonald's Corporation has liability as Roberts' principal. The parties' franchise agreement clearly provided that Roberts was not an agent of McDonald's, and the evidence established no control over daily operations. Under these circumstances, McDonald's has no liability as Roberts' actual principal.

Rather, the issue is whether Roberts was McDonald's ostensible agent. Apparent agency occurs, and vicarious liability for the principal follows, where a principal makes objective manifestations leading a third person to believe the wrongdoer is an agent of the principal. Restatement, (Second) of Agency § 267 (1957). The doctrine is intended to protect third parties who justifiably rely upon the belief that another is the agent of a principal.

D.L.S. appears to argue that her parents' permission for her to work was given in reliance upon their belief that she would be working for McDonald's Corporation. We thus turn to her father's claims.

Apparent authority can be inferred only from acts of the principal which cause the third party to "actually, or subjectively, believe that the agent has authority to act for the principal."

Mr. Street and D.L.S.'s stepmother testified that they gave permission for D.L.S. to work at the Newcastle McDonald's in the belief that "a McDonald's is a McDonald's" and would offer a safe, wholesome environment for teenage workers.

They contend this belief came from McDonald's marketing and advertising.

Mr. Street described McDonald's ads portraying McDonald's as a "very positive, safe environment with young children getting 'Happy Meals' and playing in McDonald's play areas." He also points to ads emphasizing McDonald's support for the Olympics, successful young athletes, and the Ronald McDonald House. This marketing made McDonald's appear to be a highly organized, well-run corporation that values "good citizenship and youth," in "a uniform, quality, wholesome environment." He points out that McDonald's advertising emphasizes "youth-related themes" and shows "smiling, happy, and friendly young people as their employees." He testified that "[b]ased [on] McDonald's targeting of minors as employees, I believed that McDonald's would take at least ordinary precautions in the hiring and supervising of its employees, especially the teenagers." He declared that McDonald's marketing of its wholesome image "deliberately misleads parents such as myself to think a McDonald's restaurant is a good, safe working environment for our teenage children to try out their first jobs."

D.L.S.'s parents denied any knowledge that the Newcastle McDonald's was a franchise, or that most McDonald's are franchises, and alleged they allowed D.L.S. to work there believing that McDonald's "stands for a uniform, quality, wholesome environment[.]" *Id.* at 309. Mr. Street contended that "[n]o person in their right mind would believe that McDonald's did not control what happened at the individual restaurants." He thus contends a question of fact exists as to whether the Corporation, through its intentional creation of a wholesome image, held out its franchisees as its agents.

More is required of the principal before its acts can create liability under the apparent authority doctrine....

Beyond the general impression created by its advertising that McDonald's restaurants offer a wholesome environment, D.L.S.'s father points to no representations or acts by McDonald's upon which he relied in believing that D.L.S. worked for the Corporation or that McDonald's would ensure a safe working environment in its franchise restaurants. Using young people in advertisements, serving Happy Meals, sponsoring the Ronald McDonald house, and supporting Olympic athletes are not enough to create an apparent employment relationship between McDonald's Corporation and its franchisees' employees.

The circumstances of D.L.S.'s employment at the Newcastle McDonald's franchise are deeply regrettable. But the trial court did not err in concluding the theory of liability advanced against McDonald's is unsupported. D.L.S. and her parents must pursue their claims against the tortfeasor and the franchisee.

[Affirmed]

Questions

1. Was Roberts an actual agent of McDonald's Corporation?
2. Did McDonald's Corporation make objective manifestations leading Mr. Street to reasonably believe that his daughter worked for McDonald's Corporation?
3. Speculate on why the Streets were so intent on suing the corporation because they had the clear right to sue the tortfeasor assistant manager and the franchisee Roberts.

THINKING THINGS THROUGH

Ken Miyamoto was president and a shareholder of Bixby's Food Systems, Inc. (Bixby's), a franchisor of bagel restaurants. The business is incorporated and provides limited liability to Miyamoto and its other corporate investors. Bixby's hired a lawyer familiar with franchise disclosure laws in Illinois and drafted a franchise offering circular (FOC) in accordance with state laws. Jan and Phillip McKay attended a meeting of existing and prospective franchisees where Miyamoto spoke and said that prospective franchisees had signed and paid for 340 development agreements; a similar statement also appeared in a Bixby's newsletter. The McKays soon thereafter executed a franchise agreement. Based on Miyamoto's view that a lease of larger retail space than recommended in Bixby's circular

THINKING THINGS THROUGH

continued

would bring in larger revenues, the McKays executed the larger-than-recommended lease and spent $400,000 making their restaurant operational, which was a much higher investment than projected in the FOC. When the restaurant opened, sales did not come close to the figures estimated in the FOC. After eight months of operations, Bixby's terminated the McKays' franchise for their inability to pay Bixby's franchise royalty fees. Bixby's sued the McKays for continuing to use its trademark, and the McKays counterclaimed against Bixby's, Inc. and Miyamoto as an individual for violation of the state Franchise Disclosure Act and the state Deceptive Business Practices Act.

Bixby's FOC was not shown to contain material misstatements of fact. However, the McKays listed a number of statements made by Miyamoto that were untrue concerning future events regarding costs, profitability, and financial success, like his encouraging them to rent larger than recommended retail space to bring in larger revenues, which did not materialize. The court held that such statements about future events, costs, and profitability are not actionable misrepresentations under the state Franchise Disclosure Act. Corporate executives selling franchises have latitude to take the facts set forth in franchise offering circulars and project a bright future in most respects. That is, they have a legal right to put their "spin" on the facts, just as society does in governmental and personal affairs. Of course, buyers must beware and view assertions about future events, costs, and profitability with critical analysis and informed skepticism.

With his business incorporated and his circulars drafted by competent counsel, was Miyamoto immune from personal liability in this case? The answer is no. When Miyamoto told the group of prospective franchisees that some 340 development agreements had been signed and paid for and later repeated this statement in a newsletter, he was not thinking things through. Through the discovery process that preceded a trial, the McKays' attorney "discovered" that Bixby's had just 15 agreements executed and paid for at the time of Miyamoto's assertion that 340 agreements were executed and paid for. Such a material misstatement of fact was a violation of the state franchising and deceptive practices laws.

The economic resources expended by Bixby's, Inc., to provide limited liability could not shield its shareholder-president from the consequences of his enormous lie. Along with Bixby's, Inc., Miyamoto was held personally liable to the McKays under the state statutes.*

*Bixby's Food Systems, Inc. v McKay, 2002 US Dist LEXIS 5243.

To maintain uniform systems for processing or distributing goods or rendering services, franchisors often place significant controls on their franchisees' businesses. These controls are set forth in franchise agreements and operating manuals. In a lawsuit brought against a franchisor for the wrongful conduct of its franchisee, the franchise agreement and operations manuals may be used as evidence of the franchisor's right to control the franchisee and the existence of an agency relationship rather than an independent contractor relationship.[17]

To avoid negating its franchisees' independent contractor status and being liable for the wrongful conduct of a franchisee, the franchisor should make certain that the franchise agreement minimizes the number and kind of provisions that authorize the

[17] *J. M. v Shell Oil Co.*, 1996 Bus. Franchise Guide (CCH) ¶ 10,817 (Mo App).

franchisor to control the "means" of operating the business. **For Example,** the franchisor should not exercise control over employment-related matters.[18]

Franchisors may also insulate themselves from liability by requiring individual franchisees to take steps to publicly maintain their own individual business identities.

For Example, a gas station may post a sign stating that it is "dealer owned and operated," or a real estate franchise may list on its business sign the franchise name and the name of the local owner, such as Century 21, L & K Realty Co. All invoices, purchase orders, paychecks, and notices to employees should contain notice of the independent ownership and operation of the business. Finally, franchisors should require their franchisees to maintain appropriate comprehensive general liability insurance, workers' compensation insurance, and other appropriate insurance.

LAWFLIX

Good Burger (1997)

This film is a story of the competition, mass marketing, and secret sauce issues in franchising. The movie provides a look at liability, product quality, and espionage.

For movie clips that illustrate business law concepts, see LawFlix at **http://www.westbuslaw.com.**

[18] Consider the degree of control exercised by McDonald's Corp. over its franchises. Only designated food and beverages may be served, and franchisees are required to use prescribed buildings and equipment. The franchisor dictates the level of quality, service, and cleanliness. All franchisees' employees must wear the uniforms designated by the franchisor with McDonald's logos. McDonald's dictates management, advertising, and personnel policies and requires that managers be trained at its "Hamburger University." The Illinois Court of Appeals held that the question of whether a franchise was an apparent agent of McDonald's was an issue of material fact that should go to a jury in a lawsuit involving a customer's slip and fall on ice in the franchised restaurant's bathroom. The court stated that the employees responsible for maintaining the bathroom wore "McDonald's uniforms" and were required to follow McDonald's standards of "quality, service, and cleanliness." *O'Banner v McDonald's Corp.*, 653 NE2d 1267 (Ill App 1995). On further appeal to the Supreme Court of Illinois, the court of appeals was reversed because in order to recover on an apparent agency theory, the customer had to show that he actually relied on the apparent agency in going to the restaurant where he was injured. The customer failed to do so, thus losing the right to hold McDonald's Corp. liable for his injuries. *O'Banner v McDonald's Corp.*, 670 NE2d 632 (Ill 1996).

Summary

The three principal forms of business organizations are sole proprietorships, partnerships, and corporations. A *sole proprietorship* is a form of business organization in which one person owns the business, controls all decisions, receives all profits, and has unlimited liability for all obligations and liabilities. A *partnership* involves the pooling of capital resources and talents of two or more persons whose goal is making a profit; the partners are subject to unlimited personal liability. However, newly created forms of business organizations—the limited liability company and the limited liability partnership—allow for tax treatment as a partnership with certain limited liability for the owners.

A business *corporation* exists to make a profit. It is created by government grant, and its shareholders elect a board of directors whose members are responsible for managing the business. A shareholder's liability is limited to the capital the shareholder invested in the business or paid for shares. Corporate existence continues without regard to the death of shareholders or the transfer of stock by them.

The selection of the form of organization is determined by the nature of the business, tax considerations, the financial risk involved, the importance of limited liability, and the extent of management control desired.

A joint venture exists when two or more persons combine their labor or property for a single business undertaking and share profits and losses as agreed. An unincorporated association is a combination of two or more persons for the pursuit of a common purpose.

A cooperative consists of two or more persons or enterprises, such as farmers, who cooperate to achieve a common objective, such as the distribution of farm products.

By a franchise, the owner of a trademark, trade name, or copyright licenses others to use the mark or copyright in selling goods or services. To protect against fraud, the FTC requires that franchisors provide prospective franchisees with a disclosure statement 10 days prior to any transaction. The Automobile Dealers' Day in Court Act and the Petroleum Marketing Practices Act are federal laws that provide covered franchisees with protection from bad-faith terminations. State laws also protect franchisees in a wide range of businesses. A franchisor is not liable to third persons dealing with its franchisees. Liability of the franchisor may, however, be imposed on the ground of the apparent authority of the franchisee or the latter's control by the franchisor. Liability of the franchisor may also arise in cases of product liability.

Questions and Case Problems

1. When is a franchisor held liable to a third person dealing with or affected by the franchisee?
2. Jerome, Sheila, Gary, and Ella agreed to purchase a tract of land and make it available for use as a free playground for neighborhood children. They called the enterprise Meadowbrook Playground. Jerome and Gary improperly hung one of the playground swings, and a child was injured. Suit was brought against Meadowbrook Playground. Can damages be recovered?
3. Morris Friedman was president of Tiny Doubles International, Inc. He sold business opportunities for Tiny Doubles Studios, which made small photographic statues of people for customers. Friedman was the primary negotiator with prospective buyers of these studio business opportunities. He advised buyers up front that the opportunities were not franchises, and accordingly, he did not provide all of the information set forth in the disclosure rule on franchising, although he did provide full answers to all questions asked. Many businesses closed, however, because of lack of success. The FTC claims Friedman violated its disclosure rule. Friedman disagrees. Decide. [*FTC v Tiny Doubles Int'l, Inc.*, 1996 Bus. Franchise Guide (CCH) ¶ 10,831]
4. Wolf, King, and others sold business "opportunities" in vending machines by taking out ads in newspapers throughout the country. When individuals responded, telemarketers called "fronters" would tell them of false earnings estimates, and those who could afford $16,000 to $25,000 for vending machines were turned over to "closers" who promised wonderful results. References were provided who were "shills"—they did not own vending machines but were paid to tell "stories" that were monitored by Wolf, King, and other supervisors. None of the individuals was given franchise disclosure documents. King induced one investor to mortgage her house so that she could pay $70,000 for a number of vending machines. In three years Wolf, King, and others took in some $31.3 million. The FTC alleged that the defendants violated the FTC franchise disclosure rule.

   Is there a franchise disclosure rule violation if Wolf and King were merely selling vending machines? What if Wolf and King promised exclusive territories for the machines? Why would a franchise disclosure rule be necessary in this case? Decide. [*FTC v Wolf*, Bus. Franchise Guide ¶ 27,655 (CCH D Fla)]
5. Katherine Apostoleres owned the rights to Dunkin Donuts franchises in Brandon and Temple Terrace, Florida. The franchisor offered all its franchisees the right to renew their existing franchise agreements if they agreed to abide by advertising decisions favored by two-thirds of the local franchise owners in a given television market. Apostoleres refused the offer because she did not want to be bound by the two-thirds clause. Soon thereafter, Dunkin Donuts audited her two stores, and using a "yield and usage" analysis, it concluded that gross sales were being underreported. Based on these audits and a subsequent audit, Dunkin Donuts gave notice of immediate termination of Apostoleres's franchises, contending that the franchise agreement had been violated. Apostoleres stated that an implied obligation of good faith exists by operation of law in every contract, and she asserted that the audits were in retaliation for her refusal to accept the renewal agreement. The yield and usage test used in the audit was not specified in the franchise agreement as a measure to be used to enforce the franchisor's rights, and certain accounting experts testified as to the unreliability of this test. Was Dunkin Donuts liable for breach of its implied obligation of good faith in this case? [*Dunkin Donuts of America v Minerva, Inc.*, 956 F2d 1566 (11th Cir)]
6. If a group of farmers agrees among themselves to pool their products and set a common price for the sale of these products, would this be price fixing in violation of federal antitrust laws?
7. For a five-year period, Laurie Henry worked for James Doull, the owner of four Taco Bell franchises. During that time, she had an affair with Doull. He was the father of her two illegitimate children. Enraged over a domestic matter, Doull physically assaulted her at the Taco Bell Restaurant and then fired her and ordered her off the premises. Later, on Doull's recommendation, she was hired by a "company store" in an adjoining state. Henry brought suit against Doull, his corporate entity Taco Tia, Inc., and the Taco Bell Corporation (TBC). She did not characterize her suit as a case of sexual harassment. Rather, she contended that TBC was responsible for

Doull's actions because he was TBC's agent. She sought damages for the loss of romantic and material satisfactions a person might expect from a traditional courtship and wedding. TBC denied that Doull was its employee or agent. The evidence showed that Henry knew that Doull's stores differed from TBC "company" stores. She insisted, having worked for four years for Doull at stores adorned with Taco-Bell signs, that Taco Bell was responsible for Doull's actions. Decide. [*Henry v Taco Tia, Inc.*, 606 So 2d 1376 (La App)]

8. The Armory Committee was composed of officers from various National Guard units. It organized a New Year's Eve dance at a charge of $2 per person to defray costs. Perry, along with others, was a member of the Armory Committee. Libby was a paying guest at the dance who was injured by slipping on frozen ruts in the immediate approaches to the steps leading to the armory building where the dance was held. He sued Perry, Turner, and the other committee members. The evidence showed that every member of the committee had taken some part in planning or running the dance with the exception of Turner. Was the Armory Committee an unincorporated association or a joint venture? Decide. [*Libby v Perry*, 311 A2d 527 (Me)]

9. The Kawasaki Shop of Aurora, Illinois (dealer), advised Kawasaki Motors Corp. (manufacturer) that it intended to move its Kawasaki franchise from New York Street to Hill Avenue, which was in the same market area. The Hill Avenue location was also the site of a Honda franchise. The manufacturer's sales manager advised the dealer that he did not want the dealer to move in with Honda at the Hill Avenue site. In February, the dealer moved to the Hill Avenue location. Effective May 1, the manufacturer terminated the dealer's franchise. The dealer brought suit against the manufacturer under the state's Motor Vehicle Franchise Act, which made it unlawful to terminate franchises for site control (requiring that the dealer's site be used exclusively as a Kawasaki dealership). The manufacturer argued that it had a right to have its products sold by a dealer who was not affiliated with a competitor. Decide. [*Kawasaki Shop v Kawasaki Motors Corp.*, 544 NE2d 457 (Ill App)]

10. Goodward, a newly hired newspaper reporter for the *Cape Cod News*, learned that the local cranberry growers had made an agreement under which they pooled their cranberry crops each year and sold them at what they determined to be a fair price. Goodward believes that such an agreement is in restraint of trade and a violation of the antitrust laws. Is he correct?

11. Food Caterers of East Hartford, Connecticut, obtained a franchise from Chicken Delight to use that name at its store. Food Caterers agreed to the product standards and controls specified by the franchisor. The franchise contract required the franchisee to maintain a free delivery service to deliver hot, freshly prepared food to customers. The franchisee used a delivery truck that bore no sign or name. Its employee Carfiro was driving the truck in making a food delivery when he negligently struck and killed McLaughlin. The victim's estate sued Chicken Delight on the theory that Carfiro was its agent because he was doing work that Chicken Delight required and that benefited Chicken Delight. Was Carfiro the agent of Chicken Delight? [*McLaughlin's Estate v Chicken Delight, Inc.*, 321 A2d 456 (Conn)]

12. Groseth had the International Harvester (IH) truck franchise in Yankton, South Dakota. The franchise agreement Groseth signed required dealers to "cooperate with the Company by placing orders for goods in accordance with advance ordering programs announced by the Company." IH wanted to terminate Groseth's franchise because he refused to comply with IH's requirement that a computerized "dealer communication network" (DCN) be set up. Under the DCN, each dealer was required to obtain a computer terminal, display screen, and software. The DCN was initially used for ordering parts and allowed IH to reduce the number of employees needed for manual processing of "parts" orders. Groseth refused to set up the DCN because of the expense. Moreover, he contended that the task of ordering parts was easily accomplished by telephone or written orders. Did IH have good cause to terminate Groseth's franchise? [*Groseth International Harvester, Inc. v International Harvester*, 442 NW2d 229 (SD)]

13. Brenner was in the scrap iron business. Almost daily, Plitt lent Brenner money with which to purchase scrap iron. The agreement of the parties was that when the scrap was sold, Plitt would be repaid and would receive an additional sum as compensation for making the loans. The loans were to be repaid in any case without regard to whether Brenner made a profit. A dispute arose over the nature of the relationship between the two men. Plitt claimed that it was a joint venture. Decide. [*Brenner v Plitt*, 34 A2d 853 (Md)]

14. Donald Salisbury, William Roberts, and others purchased property from Laurel Chapman, a partner of Chapman Realty, a franchisee of Realty World. The purchasers made payments directly to Laurel Chapman at the Realty World office, and Chapman was to make payments on the property's mortgage. However, Chapman did not make the payments and absconded with the funds. Salisbury and Roberts sued the franchisor, Realty World, claiming that Realty World was liable for the wrongful acts of the apparent agent, Chapman. Realty World and Chapman Realty were parties to a franchise agreement stating that the parties were franchisor and franchisee. The agreement contained a clause that required Chapman to prominently display a certificate in the office setting forth her status as an independent

franchisee. Chapman displayed such a sign, but the plaintiffs did not recall seeing it. Chapman Realty hires, supervises, and sets the compensation for all of its employees. The plaintiffs pointed out that Chapman Realty used the service mark Realty World on its signs, both outside and inside its offices. They pointed out that a Realty World manual sets forth the general standards by which franchisees must run their businesses and that this represents clear control over the franchise. They contended that, all things considered, Realty World held out Chapman Realty as having authority to bind Realty World. Realty World disagreed, stating that both were independent businesses. Decide. [*Salisbury v Chapman and Realty World, Inc.*,65 NE2d 127 (Ill App)]

15. H.C. Blackwell Co. held a franchise from Kenworth Truck Co. to sell its trucks. After 12 years, the franchise was nearing expiration. Kenworth notified Blackwell that the franchise would not be renewed unless Blackwell sold more trucks and improved its building and bookkeeping systems within the next 90 days. Blackwell spent $90,000 attempting to meet the demands of Kenworth but could not do so because a year was required to make the specified changes. Kenworth refused to renew the franchise. Blackwell sued Kenworth for damages under the federal Automobile Dealers' Day in Court Act. Blackwell claimed that Kenworth had refused to renew in bad faith. Decide. [*Blackwell v Kenworth Truck Co.*, 620 F2d 104 (5th Cir)]

CPA Questions

1. A joint venture is a(an)

   a. Association limited to no more than two persons in business for profit
   b. Enterprise of numerous co-owners in a nonprofit undertaking
   c. Corporate enterprise for a single undertaking of limited duration
   d. Association of persons engaged as co-owners in a single undertaking for profit

PARTNERSHIPS

CHAPTER (42)

LEARNING OBJECTIVES

After studying this chapter, you should be able to

LO.1 Describe the characteristics of a partnership

LO.2 Distinguish between a partner and an employee

LO.3 List the seven rules that aid in determining whether the parties have created a partnership

LO.4 Explain the effect of a dissolution of a partnership

LO.5 Describe how a partnership may be dissolved by the acts of partners, by operation of law, and by order of the court

LO.6 Describe the extent of a partner's authority during the winding up of a partnership's business

LO.7 Distinguish between express authority and customary authority of a partner to act for the partnership

LO.8 Identify the situations that indicate the existence of limitations on a partner's authority

LO.9 Name six transactions that a partner cannot undertake unless expressly authorized to do so

LO.10 List the duties of partners to one another

Partnerships may be created without the formality of even a written partnership agreement when two or more individuals simply operate a business for a profit as co-owners. In the 1970s, David Silvernail, Sr. operated a welding business out of a shop adjacent to his residence. Years later, his son Paul joined him in the business. In 1999, David withdrew (dis-associated) from the business, and Paul continued to operate it. When the parties could not agree on a division of assets in 2002, a court reverted to partnership law to resolve the controversy.[1] Partnership relations are not narrowly governed by partnership law but are governed by the partners' partnership agreement. Only when the partnership agreement does not resolve an issue does partnership law apply. In many instances, individuals do not obtain legal advice in choosing the partnership form of business organization. Properly informed individuals today will probably not choose the partnership form of organization because partners are open to unlimited personal liability; they may choose a limited liability company to insulate the members from personal liability.

A. Nature and Creation

Partnerships are created by agreement. A codification of general partnership law is found in the Uniform Partnership Act (UPA), which has been revised (Revised Uniform Partnership Act, or RUPA). Together, the UPA and the RUPA are in effect in 49 states.[2] Limited partnerships (LPs) and limited liability partnerships (LLPs) differ significantly from general partnerships and are discussed in the next chapter. The 1994 version of the Revised Uniform Partnership Act is being phased in or already applies in 33 states.[3] Like the UPA, most of the provisions of

[1] *Silvernail v Silvernail*, 804 NYS2d 116 (App Div 2005).

[2] The UPA or the RUPA is in effect in all states except Louisiana.

[3] The RUPA or versions of it have been adopted by Alabama, Alaska, Arizona, Arkansas, California, Colorado, Connecticut, Delaware, District of Columbia, Florida, Hawaii, Idaho, Illinois, Iowa, Kansas, Maryland, Minnesota, Mississppi, Montana, Nebraska, New Jersey, New Mexico, North Dakota, Oklahoma, Oregon, South Dakota, Tennessee, Texas, Vermont, Virginia, Washington, West Virginia, and Wyoming. The RUPA was approved in 1992 and amended in 1993, 1994, and 1997. It provides for a transition period after passage, during which only newly created partnerships come under the new law, with all partnerships in the state eventually being governed by the RUPA (see RUPA § 1206(a)).

the RUPA apply only when the partners do not have partnership agreement language that deals with the matter at issue.[4] Certain features of the RUPA that differ from those of the UPA are identified in the text.

1. Definition

A **partnership** (also called a **general partnership**) is a relationship created by the voluntary "association of two or more persons to carry on as co-owners a business for profit."[5] The persons so associated are called **partners** or **general partners.** A partner is the agent of the partnership and of each partner with respect to partnership matters. A partner is not an employee of the partnership even when doing work that would ordinarily be done by an employee.

2. Characteristics of a Partnership

A partnership has distinguishing characteristics:

1. A partnership is a voluntary, consensual relationship.
2. A partnership involves partners' contributions of capital, services, or a combination of these.
3. The partners are associated as co-owners to transact the business of the firm for profit.

If profit is not the object, the group will commonly be an **unincorporated association.**

The UPA does not make the partnership a separate entity, and, therefore, suit cannot be brought by the firm in its name in the absence of a special statute or procedural rule so providing. However, in RUPA states, partnerships are recognized as "entities."

3. Rights of Partners

The rights of partners are determined by the partnership agreement. If written, this agreement is interpreted by the same rules that govern the interpretation of any other written document. Any matter not covered by the partnership agreement may be covered by a provision of the applicable UPA or RUPA.

4. Partnership Agreement

Because of the complexity of the problems involved, *partnership agreements* are typically written. However, there is no requirement that they be in writing unless compliance with a statute of frauds is required. **For Example,** the world's highest-paid performers in the early 1990s, the New Kids on the Block, who grossed $74.1 million in one year, were a group started by promoter Maurice Starr. He obtained $60,000 from James Martorano, who was connected with organized crime, and $50,000 from businessman Jeffrey Furst to finance the initial recording and promotion of the group. Martorano and Furst testified that ultimately all three agreed with a handshake that 50 percent of the profits from the group would be shared between Martorano as a silent partner and Furst, who would also provide limousine service and security. They testified that Starr would keep half of the profits. Starr denied that a partnership existed because he believed that such an alleged business arrangement would have had to be reduced to writing with great detail. However, based on the evidence, which included damaging testimony that Starr tried to buy some witnesses' silence, a jury decided that a binding oral partnership agreement existed.[6]

ETHICS & THE LAW

Gin Miller, a nationally known fitness instructor, tore a knee ligament. During her recovery, a physical therapist suggested that she step up and down on a wooden step to strengthen her knee. Miller discovered that there was an aerobic component to this physical therapy, and she

[4] See *Mission West v Republic,* 873 A2d 372 (Md App 2005).

[5] UPA § 6(1).

[6] *Boston Globe,* November 13, 1995, 13. For an example of a situation in which no oral partnership was found to exist, see *Prince v O'Brien,* 683 NYS2d 504 (App Div 1998). Marvin Prince and Darren O'Brien met and became friends while living in Toronto. Prince, a Jamaican native, helped O'Brien refine his reggae-singing ability and knowledge of Jamaican dialect, and participated in the coining of O'Brien's stage name "Snow." Before O'Brien became a success with his debut reggae album *12 Inches of Snow,* the friends may have casually discussed splitting their hypothetical profits equally but never agreed to share losses. Later, when Marvin Prince toured with O'Brien, he was designated and paid as an employee of O'Brien's corporation. The court found that Prince failed to prove the existence of an oral partnership agreement.

ETHICS & THE LAW

continued

began using the wooden step-up in teaching her aerobic classes. Using music and choreographed routines, Miller began an aerobic trend with what she called the "Bench Blast."

Richard Boggs, the owner of seven Atlanta health clubs, noticed the "Bench Blast" and formed a partnership with several Atlanta businessmen to market The Step, a plastic platform that was marketed to health clubs. The Step was available in three versions, ranging in price from $59 to $199, and included a videotape.

Reebok noticed The Step and formed a joint venture with Boggs to market the product nationally. The Step carried Reebok's name and was included in Reebok's national marketing plan. Sales of The Step went from $7.8 million annually to $40 million annually within two years.

As his health club sales dropped off, Boggs wanted to sell directly to the in-home market, but Reebok wanted that market for itself. Boggs began marketing The Step through television infomercials, but his product did not have the Reebok name and thus was offered at a lower price than the Reebok in-home model.

Was it proper for Boggs to sell The Step in the home market without Reebok? Was it proper for Reebok to sell to the in-home market without Boggs? Both sides argued that they did not contemplate the in-home market when they formed their partnership. How would you respond to that point? What about Boggs's initial partnership without Miller? Did he steal her idea?

To reduce or avoid disputes and litigation, partnership agreements should be in writing.

The formal document that is prepared to evidence the contract of the parties is termed a **partnership agreement, articles of partnership,** or **articles of copartnership.** The partnership agreement governs the partnership during its existence and may contain provisions relating to dissolution. (See Figure 42-1.)

The *Smith* case illustrates the importance of having a written partnership agreement. The case sets forth factors considered by courts in determining whether a partnership exists.

SMITH V REDD, 593 SO 2D 989 (MISS 1991)

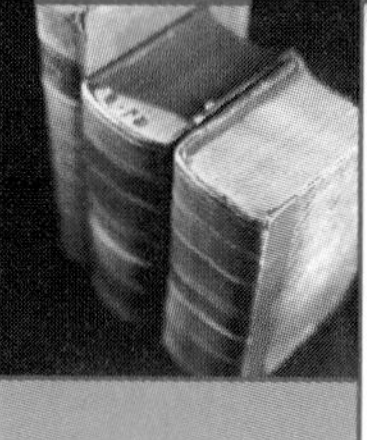

THE ORAL PARTNERSHIP AGREEMENT MUDDIED WITH THE PASSAGE OF TIME

Thomas Smith and Jackie Lea were partners in a logging business. In 1981, they joined Gordon Redd and went into business running a sawmill, calling the business Industrial Hardwood Products (IHP). Smith and Lea used their logging equipment at the mill site. Smith hauled 400 loads of gravel, worth some $26,000, from his father's land for the mill yard in the process of getting the mill operational. Smith and Lea received $300 a week compensation, which was reported on federal W-2 forms. They worked up to 65 hours per week and were not paid overtime. All three discussed business decisions. Smith and Lea had check-writing authority and the authority to hire and fire employees. Lea left the business in 1983 and was paid $20,000. The testimony indicated that the three individuals agreed in January 1981 that as soon as the bank loan was paid off and Redd was paid his investment, Lea and Smith would be given an interest in the mill, but no written agreement existed. Redd invested $410,452 in the business and had withdrawn $500,575 from it. As of December 31, 1986, IHP had sufficient retained earnings to pay off the bank loan. In April 1987, Smith petitioned the chancery court for the dissolution of the "partnership" and an accounting. Redd denied that any partnership was formed and asserted that Smith was an employee. The chancery court awarded Smith $50,000 for the gravel and use of equipment but held that no partnership existed. Smith appealed.

Judicial Opinion

PRATHER, J. . . . Smith asserts that the trial court erred in finding that no partnership existed between himself and Redd. A partnership as defined by statute is "an association of two (2) or more persons to carry on as co-owners a business for profit." [UPA § 6(1)]. The determination of whether a partnership exists is governed by statute. . . .

These statutes codified the common-law rules of partnership. . . . However, the common law is still used to supplement the statute in determining when a partnership exists. Generally, a partnership exists when two or more persons join together with their money, goods, labor, or skill for purposes of carrying on a trade, profession or business with a community interest in the profits and losses. . . . The three main questions that are considered in partnership determination are (1) the intent of the parties, (2) the control question, and (3) profit sharing. . . .

A. Intent

Intent of the parties to form a partnership must be established by the proof. In this case this Court does not have to look to circumstances to infer such an intent. The parties—Lea, Smith, and Redd—all agree that there was an express intent to form a partnership. Additionally, the surrounding circumstances bear out that express intent; Lea and Smith brought assets of L & S Logging into the IHP business, prepared the plant site without remuneration, and ran the sawmill business.

The issue here, then, is not whether the parties intended to become partners. The issue is whether the condition precedent occurred to seal that partnership contract. Those expressed conditions precedent to the partnership's formation were two:

1. the payment of the bank debt; and
2. the repayment of Redd of his initial investment. . . .

B. Control

The undisputed arrangement for operating IHP was for Redd to handle the financial matters, being his expertise, and for Lea and Smith to direct the sawmill operations, being their expertise. All parties made business decisions; all parties hired and fired employees and supervised them. All three entered into management decisions, such as building an office building and constructing a mill to build pallets. The facts shown support the conclusion that control over the business was exercised by Smith, not just as a manager or supervisor, but as one with ownership interest.

C. Profit Sharing

Admittedly, there was no profit-sharing evidenced by the testimony except as to splitting cash on occasions. But that division evidences the position of Smith. Additionally, Lea received $20,000 from Redd at his departure from the business evidencing more than an ordinary employer-employee relationship.

Lea and Smith were paid as employees with withholdings of income tax and social security tax. Benefits from workers' compensation were claimed by Smith. On the other hand, Smith and Lea worked approximately sixty-five (65) hours a week in 1981 without overtime pay.

Recognizing that Smith was working toward the retirement of debts of IHP to Redd and the bank so that the partnership could come to fruition, the receipt of wages during this preliminary period does not per se defeat the existence of a partnership.

Smith was working long hours for little remuneration to establish the business and to pay off the debts. It was for this reason that the chancellor awarded Smith the amount of $50,000 to be equitable for his labor.

D. Chancellor's Finding

The chancellor found that Smith and Lea were employees drawing a regular salary and that there was an agreement to enter into a partnership as soon as the bank and Redd were repaid. Since the bank, not Redd, had not been paid, the chancellor found there was no partnership and Smith was owed nothing. These findings overlook important testimony. Redd admitted to Smith in a tape-recorded statement that a partnership existed:

SMITH: O.K. Gordon, I want to ask you, do you remember what all you told me whenever we went to logging?

. . . .

REDD: I called ya' ll to come up here and we went right in there and sit down, and I asked ya' ll if you want to do it? Said yes. Alright, I said when we get the debt paid down, when we get me paid, that's the words I said, I said you get a percentage in it, you can get a third, a half, a quarter or all of whatever you want. Ya' ll spoke up and said no we want you to have controlling interest. I said well whatever, we'll do it.

SMITH: Right, right.

REDD: That's the words I said.

SMITH: Well, I don't remember about when we get the debt paid and paying you, I mean that part.

REDD: I said that at least a dozen times.

SMITH: Well, I'm being honest now with what I said, I don't remember you saying that part. O.K. Me and you set over there in the office before Christmas and talked about it and what all you told me, I mean how come you never did do nothing about it.

REDD: Because I got tied up on some more business and I just hadn't had a chance. I've had my nose to the grindstone.

. . . .

SMITH: Well, I mean what I'm talking about it's been going on 6 years, I mean. Alright, now, after Jackie got out of it, what did you feel like, Gordon, I mean when Jackie got out of it, being honest between me and you?

. . . .

SMITH: Well, do you remember telling me that when Jackie got out of it that it would mean more to me and you?

REDD: That's right, that's exactly right.

SMITH: That maybe, the way it sounded to me that I would have a little bit more in it and you would have a little bit more in it.

. . . .

REDD:. . . . that's what I said, it just mean more to you.

SMITH: Well as of last week, if you were going to draw it up and everything what percentage would you base your figures on over there?

REDD: I'd base the figures on about a third for you and two-thirds for me.

SMITH: On it?

REDD: That's what I base it on.

SMITH: In other words if Jackie had stayed on, it a been a third for him, say, and a third, you know, for me, and then, you know, a third for you?

REDD: No, if Jackie had stayed in, it been about 20/20 and 60. Cause the words ya' ll said, no, I said, I said a quarter, a third, a half or all of whatever and that, you know, that even. . . .

SMITH: A third, or a quarter or half or whatever we wanted?

REDD:. . . . that's right. And then ya' ll both spoke up and said naugh we wanted you to have control of the thing, naugh and that's the same words that you told me over there when we sit. . . .

SMITH: In other words, what you saying you figure my percentage is a, is a third. . . .

REDD: Yes, sir.

SMITH: A third? In other words, whatever the sawmill is worth and whatever it's all valued at and the cash and what on the books add up, I should get a third?

REDD: And whatever, and less whatever's owed.

SMITH: Ya, and what's ever less is owed, I should get a third of it?

REDD: In other words, the net that's what I feel like.

. . . In sum, the partnership should have come into existence according to Redd and Smith's agreement no later than December 31, 1986. This Court reverses the chancellor on these two findings and renders judgment on the issue of whether a partnership existed between Smith and Redd as of December 31, 1986. That is, this Court holds that a partnership did indeed exist.

. . . The cause is remanded for a determination by the chancellor of the partnership interests of Redd and Smith. . . . Upon that determination, the chancery court will be in a position to determine the value of Smith's interest as of December 31, 1986, for dissolution of the partnership.

[Reversed in part and remanded]

Questions

1. Does the fact that Smith received wages defeat his claim that he was a partner?
2. What were Smith's contributions to the partnership?
3. Assess the ethics of the parties, applying the ethical principles set forth in the preface. Should persons form a partnership without setting forth their underlying agreement in writing concerning such matters as contributions, control, and profits and losses?

FIGURE 42-1 Partnership Agreement

PARTNERSHIP AGREEMENT

THIS IS A PARTNERSHIP AGREEMENT EXECUTED AT CINCINNATI, OHIO, THIS 9TH DAY OF SEPTEMBER, 1998, BY AND AMONG LOUIS K. HALL, SHARON B. YOUNG, AND C. LYNN MUELLER, INDIVIDUALS RESIDING IN CINCINNATI, OHIO, HEREINAFTER SOMETIMES REFERRED TO INDIVIDUALLY AS "PARTNER" AND COLLECTIVELY AS "PARTNERS."

RECITALS

THE PARTNERS TO THIS AGREEMENT DESIRE TO ACQUIRE A CERTAIN PARCEL OF REAL ESTATE AND TO DEVELOP SUCH REAL ESTATE FOR LEASE OR SALE, ALL FOR INVESTMENT PURPOSES. THIS AGREEMENT IS BEING EXECUTED TO DELINEATE THE BASIS OF THEIR RELATIONSHIP.

PROVISIONS

1. NAME; AND PRINCIPAL OFFICES. THE NAME OF THE PARTNERSHIP SHALL BE: HALL, YOUNG AND MUELLER, ASSOCIATES. ITS PRINCIPAL PLACE OF BUSINESS SHALL BE AT: 201 RIVER ROAD, CINCINNATI, OHIO 45238.

2. PURPOSE. THE PURPOSE OF THE PARTNERSHIP SHALL BE TO PURCHASE AND OWN FOR INVESTMENT PURPOSES, A CERTAIN PARCEL OF REAL ESTATE LOCATED AT 602 SIXTH STREET, CINCINNATI, OHIO, AND TO ENGAGE IN ANY OTHER TYPE OF INVESTMENT ACTIVITIES THAT THE PARTNERSHIP MAY FROM TIME TO TIME HEREINAFTER UNANIMOUSLY AGREE UPON.

3. CAPITAL CONTRIBUTIONS. THE CAPITAL OF THE PARTNERSHIP SHALL BE THE AGGREGATE AMOUNT OF CASH AND PROPERTY CONTRIBUTED BY THE PARTNERS. A CAPITAL ACCOUNT SHALL BE MAINTAINED FOR EACH PARTNER.

A. CAPITAL CONTRIBUTIONS. ANY ADDITIONAL CAPITAL WHICH MAY BE REQUIRED BY THE PARTNERSHIP SHALL BE CONTRIBUTED TO THE PARTNERSHIP BY THE PARTNERS IN THE SAME RATIO AS THAT PARTNER'S ORIGINAL CONTRIBUTION TO CAPITAL AS TO THE TOTAL OF ALL ORIGINAL CAPITAL CONTRIBUTIONS TO THE PARTNERSHIP UNLESS OTHERWISE AGREED BY THE PARTNERS.

CPA 5. Determining the Existence of a Partnership

If the parties agree that the legal relationship between them shall be such that they in fact operate a business for profit as co-owners, a partnership is created even though the parties may not have labeled their new relationship as such.[7] The law is concerned with the substance of what is done rather than the name. Conversely, a partnership does not arise if the parties do not agree to the elements of a partnership even though they call it one.[8]

The *Byker v Mannes* decision deals with the question of whether individuals have to be aware of their status as "partners" in order to have a legal partnership.

BYKER V MANNES, 641 NW2D 210 (MICH 2002)

THE CASE OF THE ABSOLUTELY DUMBFOUNDED INVESTOR (PARTNER)

David Byker an accountant and Tom Mannes an individual with a real estate background stipulated to the following facts in a lawsuit brought by Byker against Mannes:

[T]he Plaintiff . . . and Defendant . . . agreed to engage in an ongoing business enterprise, to furnish capital, labor and/or skill to such enterprise, to raise investment funds and to share equally in the profits, losses and expenses of such enterprise. . . . In order to facilitate investment of limited partners, Byker and Mannes created separate entities wherein they were general partners or shareholders for the purposes of operating each separate entity.

[7] *In re Estate of Bolinger*, 921 P2d 767 (Mont 1998).

[8] See *Cleland v Thirion*, 704 NYS2d 316 (App Div 2000).

Over the years, the parties pursued various business enterprises, including five limited partnerships, where they served as general partners or shareholders in order to operate each separate entity. With regard to these entities, they shared equally in commissions, financing fees, and termination costs, and they personally guaranteed loans from financial lenders. A subsequent entity, Pier 1000, Ltd., created by Byker and Mannes to own and manage a marina, was not successful, and they took profits from a prior entity and borrowed money from financial institutions to continue its operations. Mannes subsequently refused to make any additional contributions. Thereafter, the unsuccessful marina venture was returned to its previous owners in exchange for assumption of Bykes' and Mannes' direct obligations to that business. The nine-year business relations between Byker and Mannes ceased. Subsequently, Byker approached Mannes for him to share equally in the payments resulting from losses incurred from their various entities. Mannes was in his words "absolutely dumbfounded" by Byker's request for money, and he refused payment. Byker sued, contending that the obligations between him and Mannes were not limited to their formal business relationships established by the individual partnerships and corporate entities, but that there was a "general" partnership underlying all their business affairs. In response, Mannes asserted that he merely invested in separate business ventures with Byker and that there were no other understandings between them.

The trial court decided in favor of Byker as follows:

Having weighed the credibility of the witnesses, principally plaintiff and defendant, we conclude that they began their relationship with a general agreement that they were partners and would share profits and losses equally. Whether understood or not they had a general or super partnership. The evidence supports that both understood it.

The court of appeals reversed, finding that no underlying partnership existed because the parties did not intend to form a partnership. The case was thereafter heard by the state supreme court.

Judicial Opinion

MARKMAN, J. . . .

Discussion

A. Uniform Partnership Acts

In 1917, the Michigan Legislature drafted the Michigan Uniform Partnership Act. 1917 PA 72. In this act, a partnership was defined as "an association of two [2] or more persons to carry on as co-owners a business for profit. . . ." at § 6, codified in 1929 CL 9846. Over the years, the definition has remained essentially constant. At present, partnership is defined as "an association of 2 or more persons, which may consist of husband and wife, to carry on as co-owners a business for profit. . . ." M.C.L. § 449.6(1). This definition, as well as its predecessors, was modeled after the definition of partnership set forth in the 1914 UPA. In 1914, the UPA had defined a partnership as "an association of two or more persons to carry on as owners a business for profit." Uniform Partnership Act of 1914, § 6. In construing § 6, courts had "universal[ly]" determined that a partnership was formed by "the association of persons whose intent is to carry on as co-owners a business for profit, regardless of their subjective intention to be 'partners.' "

In 1994, however, the UPA definition of partnership was amended by the National Conference of Commissioners. The amended definition stated that "the association of two or more persons to carry on as co-owners a business for profit forms a partnership, *whether or not the persons intend to form a partnership*." Section 202 (emphasis added). Although the commissioners were apparently satisfied with the existing judicial construction of the definition of partnership, the commissioners added the new language "whether or not the persons intend to form a partnership" in order to "codif[y] the universal judicial construction of UPA Section 6(1) that a partnership is created by the association of persons whose intent is to carry on as co-owners a business for profit, regardless of their subjective intention to be 'partners.' " Section 202 (Comment 1). The commissioners emphasized that "[n]o substantive change in the law" was intended by the amendment of § 6. To date, Michigan has not adopted the amended definition of partnership.

B. MCL 449.6(1)

Although Michigan has not adopted the amended definition of partnership as set forth in § 202 of the Uniform Partnership Act of 1994, we believe nonetheless that M.C.L. § 449.6 is consistent with the amendment. . . .

As already noted, a partnership in Michigan is statutorily defined as "an association of 2 or more persons, which may consist of husband and wife, to carry on as co-owners a business for profit. . . ." M.C.L. § 449.6(1). That is, if the parties associate themselves to "carry on" as co-owners a business for profit, they will be deemed to have formed a partnership relationship regardless of their subjective intent to form such a legal relationship. The statutory language is devoid of any requirement that the individuals have the subjective intent to create a partnership. Stated more plainly, the statute does not require partners to be aware of their status as "partners" in order to have a legal partnership. . . .

When the Legislature initially drafted M.C.L. § 449.6(1) the definition of partnership was well established in our common law, and is consistent with the interpretation that we give it today. See *Beecher v Bush* 45 Mich. 188, 193–194, 7 N.W. 785 (1881). . . .

Conclusion

With the language of the statute as our focal point, we conclude that the intent to create a partnership is not required if the acts and conduct of the parties otherwise evidence that the parties carried on as co-owners a business for profit. MCL 449.6, 449.7. Thus, we believe that, to the extent that the Court of Appeals regarded the absence of subjective intent to create a partnership as dispositive regarding whether the parties carried on as co-owners a business for profit, it incorrectly interpreted the statutory (and the common) law of partnership in Michigan.

Pursuant to M.C.L. § 449.6(1), in ascertaining the existence of a partnership, the proper focus is on whether the parties intended to, and in fact did, "carry on as co-owners a business for profit" and not on whether the parties subjectively intended to form a partnership. . . .

Accordingly, we remand this matter to the Court of Appeals for analysis under the proper test for determining the existence of a partnership under the Michigan Uniform Partnership Act.

[Reversed and remanded]

Questions

1. Is it the law that individuals must be aware of their status as "partners" in order to have a legal partnership?
2. In a footnote to the state supreme court's decision, the court reported that the parties stipulated that the alleged partnership was never memorialized in a written partnership agreement, had no formal name, no tax identification number, and no income tax filings. Based on these facts and the other facts of record, is it nevertheless possible for a partnership to exist?
3. Assess the fairness of Mannes's contention that he merely invested in separate business ventures and that no other understanding existed.

A partnership is shown to exist when it is established that the parties have agreed to the formation of a business organization that has the characteristics of a partnership. The burden of proving the existence of a partnership is on the person who claims that one exists.[9]

When the nature of the relationship is not clear, the following rules aid in determining whether the parties have created a partnership.

CPA (a) Control

The presence or absence of control of a business enterprise is significant in determining whether there is a partnership and whether a particular person is a partner.

CPA (b) Sharing Profits and Losses

The fact that the parties share profits and losses is strong evidence of a partnership.

CPA (c) Sharing Profits

An agreement that does not provide for sharing losses but does provide for sharing profits is evidence that the parties are partners. If the partners share profits, it is assumed that they will also share losses. Sharing profits is prima facie evidence of a partnership. However, a partnership is not to be inferred when profits are received in payment (1) of a debt, (2) of wages, (3) of an annuity to a deceased partner's surviving spouse or representative, (4) of interest, or (5) for the goodwill of the business.[10] **For Example,**

[9] *MacArthur v Stein*, 934 P2d 214 (Mont 1997).
[10] UPA § 7(4).

the fact that one doctor receives one-half of the net income does not establish that doctor as a partner of another doctor when the former was guaranteed a minimum annual amount. Also, federal income tax and Social Security contributions were deducted from the payments to the doctor, thus indicating that the relationship was employer and employee. If there is no evidence of the reason for receiving the profits, a partnership of the parties involved exists.

CPA (d) Gross Returns

The sharing of gross returns is itself very slight, if any, evidence of partnership. **For Example,** in a case in which one party owned a show that was exhibited on land owned by another under an agreement to divide the gross proceeds, no partnership was proven. There was no co-ownership or community of interest in the business.

CPA (e) Contribution of Skill or Labor

The fact that all persons have not contributed capital to an enterprise does not establish that the enterprise is not a partnership. A partnership may be formed even though some of its members furnish only skill or labor.

In the *Pettes* case, the individual asserting the existence of a partnership did not contribute any of the capital used to start the business but brought expertise to the business and worked many hours longer than an ordinary employee.

PETTES V YUKON, 912 SW2D 709 (TENN APP 1995)

CAN YOU FIRE YOUR PARTNER?

On graduating from Vanderbilt University with a degree in economics, James Pettes began working for Video Magic, a video rental business. In 1987, Dr. Gordon Yukon, a pediatrician, wanted to invest in a two-store video business called "Rent-a-Flick"; one of his stores was located on Quince Road and the other in Germantown. Pettes testified that Dr. Yukon paid $42,000 for the business. Yukon and Pettes agreed that they would be partners, with Pettes managing the two stores and earning the same amount he earned at Video Magic. Pettes testified that he worked 70 to 80 hours a week and his capital contribution was "sweat equity." He also testified that many times Yukon told him and others that Pettes and Yukon were partners. In December 1992, Pettes made a written demand for an accounting. On January 5, 1993, Yukon "fired" Pettes. Pettes sued for breach of an oral partnership agreement and an accounting.

Judicial Opinion

CRAWFORD, J.... "A partnership is an association of two (2) or more persons to carry on as co-owners of a business for profit." The sharing of gross returns does not of itself establish a partnership, but "the receipt by a person of a share of the profits is *prima facie* evidence that he is a partner in the business." However, no inference is drawn if the profits are received as wages of an employee. [UPA 7(4)(6)] ...

The burden of proof on the existence of a partnership is upon the one who alleges the partnership. *Mullins v Evans,* 43 Tenn. App. 330, 308 (Tenn.App.1957).

In the case at bar, Pettes contends that the parties entered into an oral agreement of partnership from the beginning of their relationship. Conversely, Yukon denies this. However, Yukon does admit that at some point he discussed with Pettes that the future held the possibility of a partnership or co-ownership. It appears from the evidence that Yukon held Pettes out as his partner to the public at large, while at the same time operating the business as a sole proprietorship by controlling the financing, business papers, and tax returns. The chancellor made no specific finding concerning credibility, but his statement that Dr. Yukon "strung the plaintiff along," indicates that he accredits Pettes's testimony to that effect. Findings of fact by the trial court involving the credibility of witnesses are entitled to great weight on appeal.

Pettes asserts that in the middle of 1992, the parties agreed to work toward dividing the business so that the Germantown store would go to Yukon and the Quince store would go to Pettes. Yukon denies that there was any such arrangement. Yukon does admit, however, that after the time that this agreement was allegedly made, he removed videos from the Quince store to the Germantown store. An independent witness, Sutherland, an employee of the Quince store, corroborated the fact that he took the films from the Quince store to the Germantown store. Significantly, she testified that before Yukon did this he told her that he was "washing his hands" of the Quince store and would have nothing else to do with it. It is also significant that notwithstanding Yukon's denials of a partnership arrangement, Sutherland testified that when he advised her that he was firing Pettes, she questioned this action since Pettes was a partner. Yukon's reply was not a denial of partnership, but rather a claim that in the absence of written proof Pettes could not prove such an arrangement.

We believe from a review of the totality of the proof in this case that at least as of the middle of 1992, the parties intended a partnership and co-ownership to the extent that a dissolution agreement of the arrangement would result in Yukon acquiring solely the Germantown store and Pettes acquiring solely the Quince store. This is consistent with the chancellor's findings concerning Dr. Yukon's leading Pettes on, and we differ with the chancellor only with respect to his finding that the proof was inconclusive as to the extent of Yukon's commitment.

Accordingly, we find . . . that there was an implied partnership and agreed dissolution thereof upon the terms that Yukon would acquire solely the Germantown store and Pettes would acquire solely the Quince store. The. . . . case is remanded to the trial court for further proceedings to determine the value of the Quince store as of January 3, 1993, for which judgment shall be entered for Pettes. Costs of the appeal are assessed against appellee.

[Judgment vacated and case remanded]

Questions

1. Does the fact that Pettes received wages preclude him from asserting the existence of a partnership?
2. Does the fact that there was no written proof that a partnership agreement existed preclude the legal existence of a partnership?
3. Can one partner "fire" another partner?

CPA (f) Fixed Payment

When a person who performs continuing services for another receives a fixed payment that does not depend on the existence of profit and is not affected by losses, that person is not a partner.

CPA 6. Partners as to Third Persons

In some instances, persons who are in fact not partners may be held liable to third persons as though they were partners. This liability arises when they conduct themselves in such a manner that others are reasonably led to believe that they are partners and to act in reliance on that belief to their injury.[11] A person who is held liable as a partner under such circumstances is termed a *nominal partner*, a *partner by estoppel*, or an *ostensible partner*.

Partnership liability may arise by estoppel when a person who in fact is not a partner is described as a partner in a document filed with the government provided the person so described has in some way participated in the filing of the document and the person claiming the benefit of the estoppel had knowledge of that document and relied on the statement. **For Example,** Jean Collins allowed the partnership of Holt and Schwark to use her name to help the partnership get started. A business name registration certificate filed at city hall and signed by all of the individuals specifies Holt, Schwark, and Collins as partners. If a creditor who sees this registration statement extends credit to the firm in reliance in part on the fact that Collins is a partner, Collins is estopped from denying that she is a partner. She has a partner's liability along with the other partners insofar as that creditor is concerned.

Under the RUPA, an apparent partnership or partnership by estoppel is called a *purported* partnership, and a third person who relies on the partnership's representations that the purported partner had authority to bind the partnership can hold it liable as if the purported partner were an actual partner with authority.[12] Under the RUPA, a partnership can limit potential liability with a publicly recorded statement of partnership authority or limitation on partner authority.[13]

CPA 7. Partnership Property

In general, partnership property consists of all property contributed by the partners or acquired for the firm or with its funds.

[11] UPA § 16(1); *Andrews v Elwell*, 367 F Supp 2d 35 (D Mass 2005).

[12] RUPA § 308.

[13] RUPA § 303.

There is usually no limitation on the type and amount of property that a partnership may acquire. The firm may own real as well as personal property unless it is prohibited from doing so by statute or by the partnership agreement.

The parties may agree that real estate owned by one of the partners should become partnership property. When this intent exists, the particular property constitutes partnership property even if it is still in the name of the original owner.

Article 2 of the RUPA recognizes that partnerships are "entities" that can acquire and own property in the partnership's name. If a partner desires to retain an interest in property contributed to the partnership in RUPA states, the partner must condition the transfer of the property to the partnership to reflect this interest or set forth the condition in the partnership agreement. Otherwise, the property becomes partnership property under the entity theory, and the contributing partner has no right to get it back, even in liquidation.[14]

CPA 8. Tenancy in Partnership

Under the UPA, partners hold title to firm property by **tenancy in partnership.**[15] The characteristics of such a tenancy are as follows:

1. Each partner has an equal right to use firm property for partnership purposes in the absence of a contrary agreement.
2. A partner possesses no divisible interest in any specific item of partnership property that can be voluntarily sold, assigned, or mortgaged by a partner.
3. A creditor of a partner cannot proceed against any specific items of partnership property. The creditor can proceed only against the partner's interest in the partnership. This is done by applying to a court for a **charging order.** By this procedure, the share of any profits that would be paid to the debtor-partner is paid to a receiver on behalf of the creditor, or the court may direct the sale of the interest of the debtor-partner in the partnership.
4. Upon the death of a partner, the partnership property vests in the surviving partners for partnership purposes and is not subject to the rights of the surviving spouse of the deceased partner.

CPA 9. Assignment of a Partner's Interest

Although a partner cannot transfer specific items of partnership property in the absence of authority to so act on behalf of the partnership, a partner's interest in the partnership may be voluntarily assigned by the partner. The assignee does not become a partner without the consent of the other partners. Without this consent, the assignee is entitled to receive only the assignor's share of the profits during the continuance of the partnership and the assignor's interest upon the dissolution of the firm. The assignee has no right to participate in the management of the partnership or to inspect the books of the partnership.

B. Authority of Partners

The scope of a partner's authority is determined by the partnership agreement and by the nature of the partnership.

10. Authority of Majority of Partners

When there are more than two partners in a firm, the decision of the majority prevails in matters involving how the ordinary functions of the business will be conducted. To illustrate, a majority of the partners of a firm decide to increase the firm's advertising. They subsequently enter into a contract for that purpose. The transaction is valid and binds the firm and all of the partners.

Majority action is not binding if it contravenes the partnership agreement. For such matters, unanimous action is required.[16] Thus, the majority of the members cannot change the nature of the business against the protests of the minority.

When there are an even number of partners, an even division on a matter that requires majority approval is always a possibility. In such a case, the partnership is deadlocked. When the partners are evenly divided on any question, one partner has no authority to act.

If the division is over a basic issue and the partners persist in the deadlock so that it is impossible to continue the business, any one of the partners may petition the court to order the dissolution of the firm.

[14] RUPA § 204.

[15] UPA § 25(1); *Krause v Vollmar*, 614 NE2d 1136 (Ohio App 1992).

[16] UPA § 18(h).

11. Express Authority of Individual Partners

An individual partner may have **express authority** to perform certain acts either because the partnership agreement provides for this or because a sufficient number of partners have agreed to it.

A partner's authority to act for the firm is similar to that of an agent to act for a principal. Thus, in addition to express authority, a partner has the authority to do those acts that are customary for a member of a partnership conducting the particular business of that partnership.[17] As in the case of an agent, the acts of a partner in excess of authority do not ordinarily bind the partnership.

12. Customary Authority of Individual Partners

A partner, by virtue of being a comanager of the business, customarily has certain powers necessary and proper for carrying out that business. The scope of such powers varies with the nature of the partnership and with the business customs and usages of the area in which the partnership operates.

A partner may make any contract necessary to transact the firm's business.

A partner can sell the firm's goods in the regular course of business, make purchases within the scope of the business, and borrow money for firm purposes. When borrowing money, a partner may execute commercial paper in the firm's name or give security such as a mortgage.[18] A partner may purchase insurance, hire employees, and adjust claims for or against the firm. Notice given to a partner is effective notice to the partnership.[19]

13. Limitations on Authority

The partners may agree to limit the powers of each partner. When a partner, contrary to such an agreement, executes a contract on behalf of the firm with a third person, the firm is bound if the third person was unaware of the limitation. In this case, the partner violating the agreement is liable to the other partners for any loss caused by the breach of the limitation. Under the UPA, if the third person knew of the limitation, the firm would not be bound.[20] Under the RUPA, the term *knew* is confined to actual knowledge,[21] which is cognitive awareness. Under the RUPA, a partnership may file a statement of partnership authority setting forth any restrictions on a general partner's authority.[22] **For Example,** Bernard Roeger was general partner of RNR, with three limited partners. Restrictions were clearly set forth in the partnership agreement limiting Roeger's borrowing authority to no more than $650,000 for the construction of a building on partnership property. Roeger on behalf of RNR entered a construction loan agreement with People's Bank with a note and mortgage in the amount of $990,000, and over an 18-month period, the bank disbursed an aggregate sum of $952,699. The bank did not request a written consent from any of the other partners or review the partnership agreement. When the loan was not paid, the bank foreclosed on the property. RNR defended on behalf of the partnership that the bank negligently failed to investigate and discover the limitation on Roeger's authority to borrow. The case was decided for the bank because it had no actual knowledge or notice of the restriction on the general partner's authority. The court also pointed out that the partnership could have protected itself by filing a statement of partnership authority setting forth the restrictions on the general partner under RUPA section 303.[23]

A third person must not assume that a partner has all of the authority that the partner purports to have. If there is anything that would put a reasonable person on notice that the partner's powers are limited, the third person is bound by that limitation.

The third person must be on the alert for the following prohibited transactions because they warn that the partner with whom the third person deals has either restricted authority or no authority at all. (See Figure 42-2.)

[17] *Ball v Carlson*, 641 P2d 303 (Colo App 1981).

[18] *U.S. Leather v H&W Partnership*, 60 F3d 222 (5th Cir 1995).

[19] *Cham, Hill, Inc., v Block & Veatch*, 557 NW2d 829 (Wis App 1996).

[20] UPA § 9(4).

[21] RUPA § 102(a).

[22] RUPA § 303.

[23] *RNR Investments, Ltd. v People's First Community Bank*, 2002 Fla App LEXIS 4061.

FIGURE 42-2 Limitations on Authority of Individual Partner to Bind Partnership

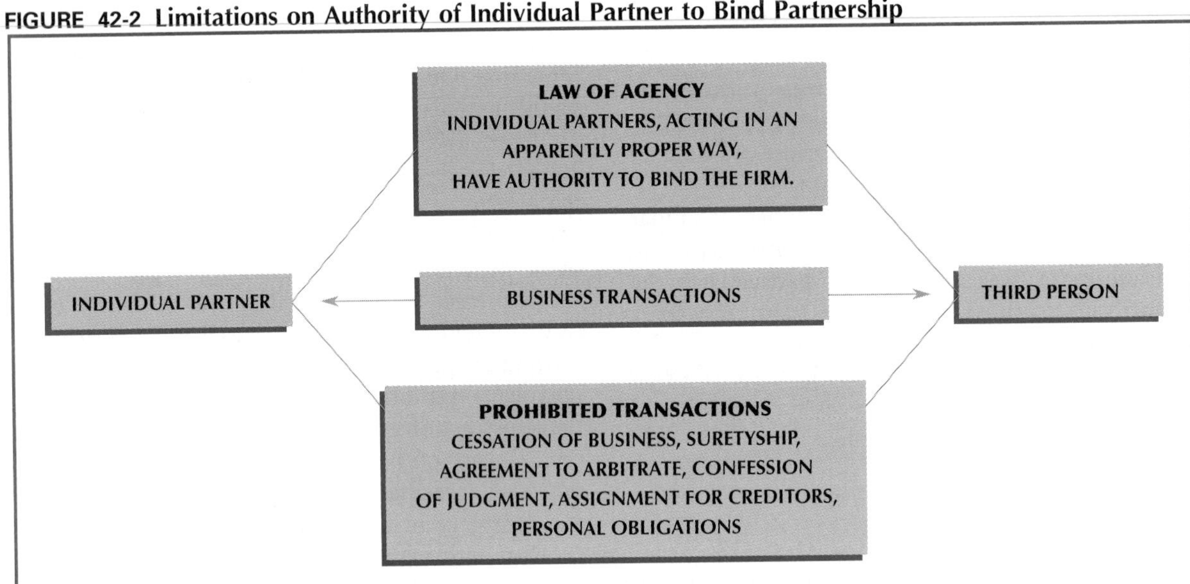

14. Prohibited Transactions

A partner cannot enter into certain transactions on behalf of the partnership unless expressly authorized to do so. A third person entering into such a transaction does so at the risk that the partner has not been authorized. The following are prohibited transactions.

(a) Cessation of Business

A partner cannot bind the firm by a contract that would make it impossible for the firm to conduct its usual business.[24]

(b) Suretyship

A partner has no implied authority to bind the firm by contracts of surety, guarantee, or indemnity for purposes other than firm business.[25]

(c) Arbitration

A partner cannot submit controversies of the firm to arbitration "unless authorized by the other partners or unless they have abandoned the business."[26]

(d) Confession of Judgment

All partners should have an opportunity to defend in court. Because of this, a partner cannot confess judgment against the firm on one of its obligations. Exceptions exist when the other partners consent or when they have abandoned the business.

(e) Assignment for Creditors

A partner cannot make a general assignment of firm property for the benefit of creditors unless authorized by the other partners or unless they have abandoned the business.

(f) Personal Obligations

A partner cannot discharge personal obligations or claims of the firm by interchanging them in any way.

C. Duties, Rights, and Liabilities of Partners

The rights and duties of partners are based on their dual capacity of agent and co-owner.

15. Duties of Partners

In many respects, the duties of a partner are the same as those of an agent.

(a) Loyalty and Good Faith

Each partner must act in good faith toward the partnership. One partner must not take any advantage

[24] *Wales v Roll*, 769 P2d 899 (Wyo 1989).
[25] *First Interstate Bank of Oregon v Bergendahl*, 723 P2d 1005 (Or App 1986).
[26] UPA § 9(3)(e).

over the other(s) by the slightest misrepresentation or concealment.[27] Each partner owes a duty of loyalty to the firm. This duty requires a partner's devotion to the firm's business and bars making any secret profit at the expense of the firm.[28]

Moreover, the duty of loyalty bars the use of the firm's property for personal benefit or the exploitation of a business opportunity of the partnership for personal gain. **For Example,** when one partner renewed the lease of the building occupied by the firm but the lease was renewed in the name of that partner alone, that partner was compelled to hold the lease for the firm. The failure to renew the lease in the name of the firm was a breach of the duties of good faith and loyalty owed to the firm.

A partner cannot promote a competing business. A partner who does so is liable for damages sustained by the partnership.

Each partner also owes a fiduciary duty of good faith to all other partners. This duty extends to any transaction connected with the formation, conduct, or liquidation of the partnership.

A breach of fiduciary duty requires the complete forfeiture of all compensation during the period of the breach. **For Example,** general partners Michael Morton and Scott DeGraff breached their fiduciary duty to their partners when they did not disclose the parts of a deal they were keeping for themselves relating to a proposed relocation of the partnership's Las Vegas nightclub, Drink. Morton and DeGraff had been paid $833,190 in management fees during the period of time they were found to be in breach of their fiduciary duty to the partnership, and the court ordered them to return these funds to the partnership.[29]

(b) Obedience

Each partner is obligated to perform all duties and to obey all restrictions imposed by the partnership agreement or by the vote of the required number of partners.[30] **For Example,** when the partnership agreement required that each partner in an insurance sales firm give his "entire time" to the business and "not engage in any other business that would work to the disadvantage of the partnership," Richard Levatino's engaging in an insurance-related business outside the firm was a breach of the partnership agreement and was a proper basis for the assessment of punitive damages.[31]

(c) Other Duties

A partner must refrain from engaging in grossly negligent or intentional misconduct in transacting firm business under the RUPA.[32] Partners are accountable as a fiduciary and must hold as trustee for the firm any profits derived by a partner without the consent of the other partners.[33]

CPA 16. Rights of Partners as Owners

Each partner, in the absence of a contrary agreement, has the following rights. These rights stem from the fact that the partner is a co-owner of the partnership business.

CPA (a) Management

Each partner has a right to take an equal part in transacting the business of the firm. It is immaterial that one partner contributed more than another or that one contributed only services.

Incidental to the right to manage the partnership, each partner has the right to possession of the partnership property for the purposes of the partnership.

CPA (b) Inspection of Books

All partners are equally entitled to inspect the books of the firm. "The partnership books shall be kept, subject to any agreement between the partners, at the principal place of business of the partnership, and every partner shall at all times have access to and may inspect and copy any of them."[34]

CPA (c) Share of Profits

Each partner is entitled to a share of the profits. The partners may provide, if they so wish, that profits

[27] *Brosseau v Ranzau*, 81 SW3d 381 (Tex App 2002).

[28] Under RUPA 404(e), partners may pursue their own interests without automatically violating their fiduciary duties to the firm.

[29] *Caparos v Morton*, 845 NE2d 773 (Ill App 2006).

[30] *Cobin v Rice*, 823 F Supp 1419 (D Ind 1993).

[31] *Gates, Duncan, and VanCamp v Levatino*, 962 SW2d 21 (Tenn App 1997).

[32] RUPA § 404(c).

[33] UPA § 21; RUPA § 404(b)(1).

[34] UPA § 19. See *Smith v Brown & Jones*, 633 NYS2d 436 (Sup Ct 1995).

shall be shared in unequal proportions. In the absence of such a provision in the partnership agreement, each partner is entitled to an equal share of the profits without regard to the amount of capital contributed or services performed for the partnership.

CPA (d) Compensation

In the absence of a contrary agreement, a partner is not entitled to compensation for services performed for the partnership. There is no right to compensation even if the services are unusual or more extensive than the services rendered by other partners. Consequently, when one partner becomes seriously ill and the other partners transact all of the firm's business, they are not entitled to compensation for those services. The sickness of a partner is considered a risk assumed in the relationship. No agreement can be inferred that the active partners are to be compensated even though the services rendered by them are such that they would ordinarily be rendered in the expectation of receiving compensation. As an exception, "a surviving partner is entitled to reasonable compensation for services performed in winding up the partnership affairs."[35]

Contrary to the preceding, the partners may agree that one of the partners will devote full time as manager of the business and receive for such services a salary in addition to the managing partner's share of the profits.

(e) Repayment of Loans

A partner is entitled to the return of any money advanced to or for the firm. Such amounts must be separate and distinct from original or additional contributions to the capital of the firm.

CPA (f) Payment of Interest

In the absence of an agreement to the contrary, contributions to capital do not draw interest. The theory is that the profits constitute sufficient compensation. Advances by a partner in the form of loans are treated as if they were made by a stranger and bear interest from the date the advance is made. When the partnership business continues after dissolution, a retiring partner is entitled to interest on the value of her interest in the partnership.[36]

CPA (g) Contribution and Indemnity

A partner who pays more than a proportionate share of the debts of the firm has a right to contribution from the other partners. Under this principle, if an employee of a partnership negligently injures a third person while acting within the scope of employment and if the injured party collects damages from one partner, the latter may enforce contribution from the other partners to divide the loss proportionately among them.

The partnership must indemnify every partner for payments made and personal liabilities reasonably incurred in the ordinary and proper conduct of its business or for the preservation of its business or property. A partner has no right, however, to indemnity or reimbursement if the partner has (1) acted in bad faith, (2) negligently caused the necessity for payment, or (3) previously agreed to assume the expense alone.[37]

CPA (h) Distribution of Capital

After the payment of all creditors and the repayment of loans made to the firm by partners, every partner is entitled to receive a share of the firm property upon dissolution. Unless otherwise stated in the partnership agreement, all partners are entitled to the return of their capital contributions.

After such distribution is made, each partner is the sole owner of the fractional part distributed to that partner rather than a co-owner of all the property as during the existence of the partnership.

CPA 17. Liability of Partners and Partnership

The liability of a partnership and of the partners for the acts of individual partners and of employees is governed by the same principles that apply to the liability of an employer or a principal for the acts of an employee or agent.

CPA (a) Nature and Extent of Partner's Liability

Partners are jointly liable on all firm contracts. They are jointly and severally liable for all torts committed by an employee or one of the partners in the scope of the partnership business. When partners are liable for the wrongful injury caused a third person, the latter may sue all or any of the members of the firm.

[35] UPA § 18(f).

[36] *Lewis v Edwards*, 554 SE2d 17 (NC App 2001).

[37] *Gramacy Equities Corp. v DuMont*, 531 NE2d 629 (NY App Div 1988).

Partners who have satisfied a claim against the partnership have the right to contribution from the other partners, whereby the liability is apportioned among all partners. Unlike the UPA, partners under the Revised Uniform Partnership Act (RUPA) are jointly and severally liable for both tort and contract obligations of the firm.[38] However, the RUPA alters the traditional application of "joint and several" liability by requiring that the creditors and tort victims satisfy their claims against the partnership before pursuing the personal assets of a partner.

CPA (b) Liability of New Partners

A person admitted as a partner into an existing partnership has *limited liability* for all obligations of the partnership arising before such admission. This is a limited liability in that the preadmission claim may be satisfied only out of partnership property and does not extend to the individual property of the newly admitted partner.[39] **For Example,** Citizens Bank was unsuccessful in its attempt to satisfy part of a $1.2 million deficiency judgment against the Parkham-Woodman Medical partnership from the individual property of Dr. Hunley, who had joined the practice after the underlying obligation leading to the deficiency judgment was assumed.[40]

(c) Effect of Dissolution on Partner's Liability

A partner remains liable after dissolution of the partnership unless expressly released by the creditors or unless all claims against the partnership have been satisfied. The dissolution of the partnership does not of itself discharge the existing liability of any partner. The individual property of a deceased partner is liable for the obligations of the partnership that were incurred while the deceased partner was alive. However, the individual creditors of the deceased partner have priority over the partnership creditors with respect to such property.[41]

18. Enforcement and Satisfaction of Creditors' Claims

The firm may have been sued in the name of all individual partners doing business as the partnership, as in the case of "*Plaintiff v A, B, C, doing business as the Ajax Warehouse.*" The partners named are bound by the judgment against the firm if they have been properly served in the suit.

If a debt is contractual in origin, common law requires that the partnership's assets be resorted to and exhausted before partnership creditors can reach a partner's individual assets.[42]

Personal creditors of a partner must first pursue the assets of that partner for satisfaction of their claims. After a partner's personal assets are exhausted, the creditor may enforce the unpaid portion of a judgment by obtaining a charging order against the partner's interest in the partnership. Under such an order, a court requires that the partner's share of the profits be paid to the creditor until the debt is discharged.

D. Dissolution and Termination

The end of a partnership's existence is marked by dissolution and termination.

CPA 19. Effect of Dissolution

Dissolution is the "change in the relationship of the partners caused by any partner ceasing to be associated in the carrying on as distinguished from the winding-up of the business."[43] Dissolution does not necessarily mean that the business has ended. If the partnership agreement provides that the business is to be continued by the remaining partner(s), it will continue without a winding up, and the former partner's interest will be bought out according to the partnership agreement. Also, when breach of the partnership agreement causes dissolution, innocent partners may continue the business, provided they pay the breaching partner the value of his or her interest.[44]

[38] RUPA § 307(d).
[39] UPA § 17; see also UPA § 41(1), (7).
[40] *Citizens Bank v Parkman Woodman Medical Associates,* 874 F Supp 705 (D Mass 1995).
[41] UPA § 36.
[42] *McCune & McCune v Mountain Bell Tel. Co.,* 758 P2d 914 (Utah 1988).
[43] UPA § 29.
[44] UPA § 38 (2)(b).

If no legal basis exists to continue the business, dissolution ends the right of the partnership to exist as a going concern, but it does not end the existence of the partnership.[45] Dissolution is followed by a winding-up period at the conclusion of which the partnership's legal existence terminates.

Dissolution reduces the authority of the partners. From the moment of dissolution, the partners lose authority to act for the firm "except so far as may be necessary to wind up partnership affairs or to complete transactions begun but not then finished."[46] The vested rights of the partners are not extinguished by dissolving the firm, and the existing liabilities remain.

20. Dissolution by Act of the Parties

A partnership may be dissolved by action of the parties. However, certain acts of the parties do not cause a dissolution.

(a) Agreement

A partnership may be dissolved in accordance with the terms of the original agreement of the parties. This may be by the expiration of the period for which the relationship was to continue or by the performance of the object for which the partnership was organized.[47] The relationship may also be dissolved by subsequent agreement. The partners may agree to dissolve the firm before the lapse of the time specified in the articles of partnership or before the attainment of the object for which the firm was created.

(b) Expulsion

A partnership is dissolved by the expulsion of any partner from the business, whether or not authorized by the partnership agreement.[48]

(c) Alienation of Interest

Neither a voluntary sale of a partner's interest nor an involuntary sale for the benefit of creditors works a dissolution of the partnership.

(d) Withdrawal

A partner has the power to withdraw from the partnership at any time. However, if the withdrawal violates the partnership agreement, the withdrawing partner becomes liable to the copartners for damages for breach of contract. When the relationship is for no definite purpose or time, a partner may withdraw without liability at any time. **For Example,** a partner, Mary Harshman, was able to bring about the dissolution of a family partnership that held and managed 1,879 acres of land in New York state and force the distribution of the partnership assets because it was an at-will partnership with no definite term or particular objective to be achieved.[49] Restrictive provisions on later employment are commonly found in professional and marketing partnership agreements.

21. Dissolution by Operation of Law

A partnership is dissolved by **operation of law** in the following instances.

(a) Death

A partnership is dissolved immediately upon the death of any partner. Thus, when the executor of a deceased partner carries on the business with the remaining partner, there is legally a new firm.

(b) Bankruptcy

Bankruptcy of the firm or of one of the partners causes the dissolution of the firm; insolvency alone does not.

(c) Illegality

A partnership is dissolved by an event that makes it unlawful for the business of the partnership to be carried on or for the members to carry it on in partnership. To illustrate, when it is made unlawful by statute for judges to engage in the practice of law, a law firm is dissolved when one of its members becomes a judge.

22. Dissolution by Decree of Court

A court may decree the dissolution of a partnership for proper cause. A court will not order the dissolution for trifling causes or temporary grievances that do not involve a permanent harm or injury to the partnership.

[45] *Sheppard v Griffin*, 776 SW2d 119 (Tenn App 1989).

[46] UPA § 33.

[47] UPA § 31(1)(a).

[48] *Susman v Cypress Venture*, 543 NE2d 184 (Ill App 1989).

[49] *Harshman v Pantaleoni*, 741 NYS2d 348 (App Div 2002).

The filing of a complaint seeking a judicial dissolution does not in itself cause a dissolution of the partnership; it is the decree of the court that has that effect.

A partner may obtain a decree of dissolution for any of the following reasons.

(a) Insanity

A partner has been judicially declared insane or of unsound mind.

(b) Incapacity

One of the partners has become incapable of performing the terms of the partnership agreement.

(c) Misconduct

One of the partners has been guilty of conduct that substantially prejudices the continuance of the business. The habitual drunkenness of a partner is a sufficient cause for judicial dissolution.

(d) Impracticability

One of the partners persistently or willfully acts in such a way that it is not reasonably practicable to carry on the partnership business. Dissolution will be granted when dissensions are so serious and persistent that continuance is impracticable or when all confidence and cooperation between the partners have been destroyed.

(e) Lack of Success

The partnership cannot continue in business except at a loss.

(f) Equitable Circumstances

A decree of dissolution will be granted under any other circumstances that equitably call for a dissolution. Such a situation exists when one partner was induced by fraud to enter into the partnership.

CPA 23. Dissociation Under the RUPA

Under the RUPA and its "entity" concept, a partner can leave the firm and not disrupt the partnership's legal existence. The RUPA uses the term *dissociation* for the departure of a partner[50] and reserves the term *dissolution* for those instances when a partner's departure results in the winding up and termination of the business.[51]

A partner has the absolute power to dissociate at will, just as a partner has the power to withdraw under the UPA, even if it is wrongful.[52] If wrongful, the partner is liable for damages for breach of contract.

A partner's dissociation from a firm ends the individual's right to participate in the management of the business. It also ends the duty of loyalty owed the firm, and the individual may compete with the firm once dissociated.[53] If the partnership business continues after a partner dissociates from a firm, the partnership must buy out the dissociated partner's interest based on his share of the higher of the liquidation value of the firm or the value of the firm's business as a going concern on the date of dissociation, with interest.[54]

The RUPA created "notices" to deal with lingering authority of a dissociated partner based on apparent authority. To avoid liability, notice of lack of authority or liability should be given to customers and creditors regarding the dissociation of a partner. A filing with the Secretary of State limits liability and authority to 90 days after filing.[55] If no notice is given or filed, the partnership may be bound by the acts of a dissociated partner for up to two years after dissociation based on apparent authority.[56]

CPA 24. Notice of Dissolution

Under some circumstances, one partner may continue to possess the power to make a contract that binds the partnership even though the partnership has been dissolved.

(a) Notice to Partners

When the firm is dissolved by the act of a partner, notice must be given to the other partners unless that partner's act clearly shows an intent to withdraw from or to dissolve the firm. If the withdrawing partner acts without notice to the other partners,

[50] RUPA § 601 cmt 1.

[51] RUPA § 801.

[52] RUPA § 601(1), 602(a).

[53] RUPA § 404(2).

[54] RUPA § 701(b).

[55] RUPA § 704.

[56] RUPA § 702.

that partner is bound by contracts created for the firm.

When the dissolution is caused by the act, death, or bankruptcy of a partner, each partner is liable to the copartners for a share of any liability created by any other partner acting for the partnership without knowledge or notice of the act, death, or bankruptcy of the partner who caused the dissolution.

CPA (b) Notice to Third Persons

When dissolution is caused by the act of a partner or of the partners, notice must be given to third parties. A notice should expressly state that the partnership has been dissolved. Circumstances from which a termination may be inferred are generally not sufficient notice.

Thus, the fact that the partnership checks added the abbreviation *Inc.* after the partnership name was not sufficient notice that the partnership did not exist and that the business had been incorporated.

Actual notice of dissolution must be given to persons who have dealt with the firm.

For persons who have had no dealings with the firm, a publication of the fact of dissolution is sufficient. Such notice may be by newspaper publication, by posting a placard in a public place, or by any similar method. Failure to give proper notice continues the power of each partner to bind the others with respect to third persons on contracts within the scope of the business.

When dissolution has been caused by operation of law, notice to third persons is not required. As between the partners, however, the UPA requires knowledge or notice of dissolution by death and bankruptcy.

25. Winding Up Partnership Affairs

Most established partnerships deal with the question of how to proceed with the business upon the death of a partner in the written partnership agreement. The agreement may set forth a method for establishing the value of the deceased partner's interest as of the date of death or allow for the remaining partners to purchase the deceased partner's interest. The agreement may also allow for the continuation of the business as usual while the valuation process is completed. However, in the absence of an agreement, either express or implied, permitting the surviving partners to continue the business, the partners must wind up the business and account for the share of the deceased partner.[57]

When dissolution is obtained by court decree, the court may appoint a receiver to conduct the winding up of the partnership business. This may be done in the usual manner, or the receiver may sell the business as a going concern to those partners who wish to continue its operation.

With a few exceptions, all partners have the right to participate in the winding up of the business.[58]

CPA 26. Distribution of Assets

Creditors of the firm have first claim on the assets of the partnership.[59] Difficulty arises when there is a contest between the creditors of the firm and the creditors of the individual partners. The general rule is that firm creditors have first claim on assets of the firm. The individual creditors share in the remaining assets, if any.

After the firm's liabilities to nonpartners have been paid, the assets of the partnership are distributed as follows: (1) each partner is entitled to a refund of advances made to or for the firm, (2) contributions to the capital of the firm are then returned, and (3) the remaining assets, if any, are divided equally as profits among the partners unless there is some other agreement. A partner who contributes only services to the partnership is not considered to have made a capital contribution, absent an agreement to the contrary.

If the partnership has sustained a loss, the partners assume it equally in the absence of a contrary agreement. Distribution of partnership assets must be made on the basis of actual value when it is clear that the book values are merely nominal or arbitrary amounts.

A provision in a partnership agreement that upon the death of a partner the interest of the partner shall pass to that partner's surviving spouse is valid. Such a provision takes effect against the contention that it is not valid because it does not satisfy the requirements applicable to wills.

27. Continuation of Partnership Business

As a practical matter, the business of the partnership is commonly continued after dissolution and winding

[57] *Chaney v Burdett*, 560 SE2d 21 (Ga 2002); *King v Stoddard*, 104 Cal Rptr 903 (Cal App 1972).

[58] UPA § 37.

[59] *Holmes v Holmes*, 849 P2d 1140 (Or App 1993).

up. In all cases, however, there is a technical dissolution, winding up, and termination of the life of the original partnership.

If the business continues, either with the surviving partners or with them and additional partners, it is a new partnership. Again, as a practical matter, the liquidation of the old partnership may in effect be merely a matter of bookkeeping entries, with all partners contributing again or relending to the new business any payment to which they would be entitled from the liquidation of the original partnership.

Summary

A *partnership* is a relationship created by the voluntary association of two or more persons to carry on as co-owners a business for profit.

A partnership agreement governs the partnership during its existence and may also contain provisions relating to dissolution. The partnership agreement will generally be in writing, and this may be required by the statute of frauds. The existence of a partnership may be found from the existence of shared control in the running of the business and the fact that the parties share profits and losses. The sharing of gross returns, as opposed to profits, is slight evidence of a partnership.

Partners hold title to firm property by tenancy in partnership. A creditor of a partner cannot proceed against any specific item of partnership property but must obtain a charging order to seize the debtor-partner's share of the profits. An assignee of a partner's interest does not become a partner without the consent of the other partners and is entitled only to a share of the profits and the assignor's interest upon dissolution.

When there are more than two partners in a firm, the decisions of the majority prevail on ordinary matters relating to the firm's business unless the decisions are contrary to the partnership agreement. A partner's authority to act for the firm is similar to that of an agent to act for a principal. A partner may not bind the firm by a contract that makes it impossible for the firm to conduct its business.

A partner's duties are the same as those of an agent. If there is no contrary agreement, each partner has the right to take an equal part in the management of the business, to inspect the books, to share in the profits, and after payment of all of the firm's debts and the return of capital, to share in the firm's property or surplus upon dissolution.

Partners have unlimited personal liability for partnership liabilities. Partners are jointly liable on all firm contracts. They are jointly and severally liable for all torts committed by one of the partners or by a firm employee within the scope of the partnership's business. A partner remains liable after dissolution unless expressly released by creditors. An incoming partner is not liable for the existing debts of the partnership unless the new partner expressly assumes those debts.

Dissolution ends the right of the partnership to exist as a going concern. Dissolution is followed by a winding-up period and the distribution of assets. A partnership may be dissolved by the parties themselves in accordance with the terms of the partnership agreement, by the expulsion of a partner, by the withdrawal of a partner, or by the bankruptcy of the firm or one of the partners. A court may order dissolution of a partnership upon the petition of a partner because of the insanity, incapacity, or major misconduct of a partner. Dissolution may be decreed because of lack of success, impracticability, or other circumstances that equitably call for dissolution. Notice of dissolution, except dissolution by operation of law, must be given. Actual notice must be given to those who have dealt with the firm as a partnership.

All partners generally have a right to participate in the winding up of the business. After the firm's liabilities to nonpartners have been paid, the assets are distributed among the partners as follows: (1) refund of advances, (2) return of contributions to capital, and (3) division of remaining assets in accordance with the partnership agreement or, if no agreement is stated, division of net assets equally among the partners.

Questions and Case Problems

1. Ray, Linda, and Nancy form a partnership. Ray and Linda contribute property and cash. Nancy contributes only services. Linda dies, and the partnership is liquidated. After all debts are paid, the surplus is not sufficient to pay back Linda's estate and Ray for the property and cash originally contributed by Linda and Ray. Nancy claims that the balance should be divided equally among Ray, Linda's estate, and Nancy. Is she correct?
2. Baxter, Bigelow, Owens, and Dailey were partners in a New York City advertising agency. Owens, who was in poor health and wanted to retire, advised the partners that she had assigned her full and complete interest in the partnership to her son, Bartholomew, a highly qualified person with 10 years of experience in the advertising business. Baxter, Bigelow, and Dailey refused to allow Bartholomew to attend management meetings and refused his request to inspect the books. Bartholomew pointed out that his mother had invested as much in the firm as any other partner. He believed, as assignee of his mother's full and complete partnership interest, that he is

entitled to (a) inspect the books as he sees fit and (b) participate fully in the management of the firm. Was Bartholomew correct?

3. Amy Gargulo and Paula Frisken operated as a partnership Kiddies Korner, an infants' and children's clothing store. They operated the business very successfully for three years, with both Paula and Amy doing the buying and Paula keeping the books and paying the bills. Amy and Paula decided to expand the business when an adjoining store became vacant. At the same time, they incorporated the business. Children's Apparel, Inc., was a major supplier to the business before the expansion. After the expansion, business did not increase as anticipated, and when a nationally known manufacturer of children's apparel opened a factory outlet nearby, the business could no longer pay its bills. Children's Apparel, which had supplied most of the store's stock after expansion, sued Amy and Paula as partners for bills due for expansion stock. Children's Apparel did not know that Amy and Paula had incorporated. Amy and Paula contended that the business was incorporated and that they therefore were not liable for business debts occurring after incorporation. Were Amy and Paula correct?
4. Calvin Johnson and Rudi Basecke did business as the Stockton Cheese Co., a partnership, which owned a building and equipment. The partners agreed to dissolve the partnership but never got around to completing the winding-up process. Calvin continued to use the building and to pay insurance on it but removed Rudi's name as an insured on the policy. When the building was later destroyed by fire, Calvin claimed the proceeds of the fire insurance policy because he and his wife were the named insureds on the policy and they had paid the premiums. Rudi claimed that although the partnership was dissolved before the fire, the winding up of the partnership was not completed at the time of the fire. He therefore claimed that he was entitled to half of the net proceeds of the policy. Decide. [*State Casualty v Johnson*, 766 SW2d 113 (Mo App)]
5. Samuel Shaw purchased a ticket through Delta Airlines to fly a "Delta Connection" flight on SkyWest Airlines to Elko, Nevada. He was seriously injured when the SkyWest plane crashed near Elko. SkyWest's relationship with Delta was a contractual business referral arrangement, whereby Delta benefits through its charges for issuing tickets to connecting passengers to and from smaller communities, and SkyWest benefits from revenue generated by passengers sent to it by Delta. Both firms make a profit from this arrangement. SkyWest and Delta are often mentioned together by Delta in national print advertisements. Shaw believed that regardless of how the airlines characterize themselves, these airlines are in fact partners because they share profits from their combined efforts. Delta contended that it had no control over SkyWest's airplane operations and that sharing profits as compensation for services does not create a partnership. Decide. [*Shaw v Delta Airlines, Inc.*, 798 F Supp 1453 (D Nev)]
6. Larson entered into a Special Manager Incentive Agreement (SMIA) with Tandy Corp. He agreed to manage a Radio Shack store for compensation equal to one-half of the adjusted gross profit of the store as computed by a specific formula and to provide the company with a $20,000 "security deposit" on equipment used to set up the store. The agreement was for a period of two years, automatically renewable annually until either party gave notice of termination 30 days prior to the end of a fiscal year. After some eight and one-half years of operating under renewed agreements, Tandy gave Larson notice of his termination. Larson sued Tandy, claiming that the SMIA was a partnership agreement because there were shared risks, expenses, profits, and losses. He sought an accounting for his reasonable share in the value of the store. Tandy argued that under the SMIA, Larson was an employee-manager, not a partner, and that the ultimate decision making on all matters was Tandy's. Decide. [*Larson v Tandy Corp*, 371 SE2d 663 (Ga App)]
7. Two brothers, Eugene and Marlowe Mehl, formed a partnership to operate the family farm. One year, Eugene Mehl withdrew $7,200 from the partnership account and bought the Dagmar Bar. The warranty deed and the liquor license to the bar were obtained in the names of Eugene Mehl and his wife, Bonnie. In a subsequent lawsuit, Marlowe claimed that the bar was a partnership asset. Decide. [*Mehl v Mehl*, 786 P2d 1173 (Mont)]
8. Chaiken and two others ran a barbershop. The Delaware Employment Security Commission claimed that the other two persons were employees of Chaiken and that Chaiken had failed to pay the unemployment compensation tax assessed against employers. His defense was on the ground that he had not "employed" the other two and that all three were partners. The evidence showed that Chaiken owned the barbershop; he continued to do business under the same trade name as he had before he was joined by the two additional barbers; and he had a separate contract with each of the two, which specified the days for work and the days off. It was also shown that Chaiken had registered the partnership name and the names of the three partners and that federal tax returns used for partnerships had been filed. Decide. [*Chaiken v Employment Security Comm'n*, 274 A2d 707 (Del Sup Ct)]
9. Thomas Bartomeli decided to leave his employment to join his brother Raymond full-time in a small construction company. The brothers each contributed individual assets to the company and worked together to acquire equipment with both signing notes jointly to acquire certain equipment. Thomas considered himself a partner in the company; Raymond often referred to Thomas as his partner. It was the practice of the company to garage the equipment at Thomas's house. In 1983, the company was incorporated, but Thomas never held any shares in the company. On several occasions, Thomas's careless

operation of equipment resulted in loss or damage to the company. Raymond became dissatisfied with Thomas's work performance, and on January 17, 1991, Thomas was removed as secretary of the corporation.

On April 19, 1991, Thomas went to the company office and demanded a blank check from the secretary. Raymond found out about this demand and fired him. On April 20, 1991, Thomas demanded from Raymond either 50 percent of the company or certain equipment owned by the company. On April 22, 1991, Thomas was removed as vice president of the company. Raymond attempted to reach an agreement with Thomas on a division of company assets at that point but was not successful. Thereafter, Thomas sued his brother, alleging that Raymond breached the brothers' contract of partnership. Because the company was a corporation, is it legally inconsistent for Thomas to contend that there was a contract for partnership in the company? How would you decide this case? [*Bartomeli v Bartomeli*, 783 A2d 1050 (Ct App)]

10. Friedman, the "O" Street Carpet Shop, Inc., and Langness formed a partnership known as NFL Associates. "O" Street Carpet's net contribution to capital was $5,004; Langness contributed $14,000 in cash; and Friedman contributed his legal services, on which no value was placed by the articles of partnership. The articles stated that Friedman was entitled to 10 percent of the profits and that Langness was to receive payments of $116.66 per month. The partnership's accountant treated the payments to Langness as a return of her capital. Years later, the partnership sold the rental property owned by the partnership, and the partnership was wound up. Friedman claimed that he was entitled to 10 percent of the partnership capital upon dissolution. Langness claimed that Friedman was not entitled to a capital distribution and that the monthly payments to her should not have been treated as a return of capital. Decide. [*Langness v "O" Street Carpet, Inc.*, 353 NW2d 709 (Neb)]
11. Ross, Marcos, and Albert are partners. Ross and Marcos each contributed $60,000 to the partnership; Albert contributed $30,000. At the end of the fiscal year, distributable profits total $150,000. Ross claims $60,000 as his share of the profits. Is he entitled to this sum?
12. Leland McElmurry was one of three partners of MHS Enterprises, a Michigan partnership. Commonwealth Capital Investment Corp. sued the partnership and obtained a judgment of $1,137,285 against it, but the partnership could not pay the judgment. Commonwealth then sued McElmurry for the entire debt on the theory that, as a partner of MHS, he was liable for its debts. What, if any, is McElmurry's liability? [*Commonwealth Capital Investment Corp. v McElmurry*, 302 NW2d 222 (Mich App)]
13. George and James McCune did business as McCune & McCune, a general law partnership. Mountain Bell provided telephone service to McCune & McCune through November 1983, when the partnership dissolved and its telephone service was discontinued. Mountain Bell transferred the unpaid balance of the partnership's account to the individual business account of George McCune. George brought suit against Mountain Bell to enjoin it from suspending his service when this transferred bill was not paid. He contended that partnership law requires that partnership assets be marshaled and exhausted before a partnership creditor can reach a partner's individual assets. Mountain Bell contended that it had the right to cross-bill customers' accounts for unpaid bills, and if the bill remained unpaid, it had a right to suspend service on the account to which the debt had been transferred. Decide. [*McCune & McCune v Mountain Bell Tel. Co.*, 758 P2d 914 (Utah)]
14. Mason and Phyllis Ledbetter operated a business in Northbrook, Illinois, as a partnership called Ledbetters' Nurseries that specialized in the sale of garden lilies. The grounds of the nurseries were planted with numerous species of garden lilies, and hundreds of people toured the Ledbetters' gardens every day. After a tour, Sheila Clark offered to buy the facilities at a "top-notch price." Mason felt he could not refuse the high offer, and he signed a contract to sell all the facilities, including all flowers and the business name. When Phyllis refused to go along with the contract, Clark sued the Ledbetters' Nurseries partnership, seeking to obtain specific performance of the sales contract. Decide.
15. St. John Transportation Co., a corporation, made a contract with the partnership of Bilyeu and Herstel, contractors, by which the latter was to construct a ferryboat. Herstel, a member of the firm of contractors, executed a contract in the firm name with Benbow for certain materials and labor in connection with the construction of the ferryboat. In an action brought by Benbow to enforce a lien against the ferryboat, the *James Johns*, it was contended that all members of the firm were bound by the contract made by Herstel. Do you agree? [*Benbow v The Ferryboat James Johns*, 108 P 634 (Or)]

CPA Questions

1. Acorn and Bean were general partners in a farm machinery business. Acorn contracted, on behalf of the partnership, to purchase 10 tractors from Cobb Corp. Unknown to Cobb, Acorn was not authorized by the partnership to make such contracts. Bean refused to allow the partnership to accept delivery of the tractors, and Cobb sought to enforce the contract. Cobb will

a. Lose, because Acorn's action was beyond the scope of Acorn's implied authority
b. Prevail, because Acorn had implied authority to bind the partnership
c. Prevail, because Acorn had apparent authority to bind the partnership
d. Lose, because Acorn's express authority was restricted, in writing, by the partnership agreement

2. Upon dissolution of a general partnership, distributions will be made on account of

I. Partners' capital accounts,
II. Amounts owed partners with respect to profits, and
III. Amounts owed partners for loans to the partnership in the following order:

a. III, I, II
b. I, II, III
c. II, III, I
d. III, II, I

3. Which of the following statements is correct with respect to a limited partnership?

a. A limited partner may *not* be an unsecured creditor of the limited partnership.
b. A general partner may *not* also be a limited partner at the same time.
c. A general partner may be a secured creditor of the limited partnership.
d. A limited partnership can be formed with limited liability for all partners.

4. When a partner in a general partnership lacks actual or apparent authority to contract on behalf of the partnership, and the party contracted with is aware of this fact, the partnership will be bound by the contract if the other partners:

	Ratify the Contract	*Amend the Partnership Agreement*
a.	Yes	Yes
b.	Yes	No
c.	No	Yes
d.	No	No

LPs, LLCs, AND LLPs

CHAPTER (43)

LEARNING OBJECTIVES

After studying this chapter, you should be able to

LO.1 Distinguish between a general partner and a limited partner

LO.2 List the factors that aid in determining whether to use the LLC or LLP form of business organization

LO.3 Explain the nature and extent of a limited partner's liability for the debts of the firm

LO.4 Recognize what actions of a limited partner will cause the loss of protection from limited liability

LO.5 Explain the advantages of a limited liability company

A. The Arrival of Partnership Limited Liability

Individuals owning businesses or professional firms are concerned about exposing their personal wealth to liability beyond that invested in their businesses or firms. As discussed previously, limited liability is not a feature of general partnership law. The concept of making limited liability available to general partnerships was considered by the RUPA Drafting Committee when it began its work to revise the Uniform Partnership Act in 1987, but the concept was rejected. A limited partnership form of business organization had existed since 1916 under the Uniform Limited Partnership Act with limited partners (investors) having limited liability, but the firms' general partners were exposed to personal liability for firm debts under this act. The concept of full limited liability for partnerships began to take hold in 1986 when businesses forming limited partnerships under the Revised Uniform Limited Partnership Act utilized corporate general partners, with the general partners avoiding limited liability by the simple expedient of incorporating.

An IRS ruling classifying a Wyoming limited liability company (LLC) as a partnership for tax purposes led to the rapid spread of LLC statutes to every state within six years of the IRS ruling.[1] As part of the limited liability trend established by the swift enactment of LLC laws throughout the country, most states have also enacted limited liability partnership (LLP) acts. Like LLCs, they provide businesses and those offering professional services the benefit of single taxation as a partnership as well as limited liability.

B. Limited Partnership

A limited partnership is a special kind of partnership.

1. Formation of Limited Partnerships

The Uniform Limited Partnership Act (ULPA) was approved by the National Conference of Commissioners on Uniform State Law in 1916. It was revised in 1976 (RULPA), and this RULPA was amended in 1985. All states except Louisiana have adopted a version of the RULPA.

CPA (a) Members of a Limited Partnership

In a **limited partnership,** certain members contribute capital but have limited liability for firm debts. The most these members can lose is their investment. These members are known as **limited partners.** The partners who manage the business and are personally liable for the firm debts are **general partners.**[2] A limited partnership can be formed by "one or more general partners and one or more limited partners."[3]

CPA (b) Certificate of Limited Partnership

Unlike a general partnership, a limited partnership can be created only by executing a certificate of limited partnership.

Under the 1985 amendments to the RULPA, the certificate requires the following information: (1) the limited partnership's name, (2) the address of the partnership's registered office and the name and business address of its agent for service of process, (3) the name and business address of each general partner, (4) the partnership's mailing address, and (5) the latest date on which the limited partnership is to dissolve. The names of the limited partners (the investors) are not required. This allows for the preservation of the confidentiality of the investors' names from competitors. Moreover, new investors may be admitted as limited partners without the significant administrative burden involved in amending the certificate, as was required under the ULPA. The RULPA provides for filing the certificate with the office of the secretary of state, as opposed to the local filing required under the ULPA.

When there is no filing of the limited partnership certificate, all participants have the status and liability of general partners in a general partnership. However, technical defects in the certificate do not prevent formation of a limited partnership if there has been substantial, good-faith compliance with the filing requirements.[4]

[1] Rev. Rul 88-76, 1988—2 CB 360.

[2] *Brooke v Mt. Hood Meadows, Ltd.*, 725 P2d 925 (Or App 1986).

[3] RULPA § 101(7).

[4] RULPA § 201(b); *Fabry Partnership v Christensan*, 794 P2d 719 (Nev 1990).

CPA (c) Limited Partnership Agreement

The RULPA embodies the policy of freedom of contract and maximum flexibility regarding the limited partnership agreement.[5] Most limited partnership agreements are drafted almost exclusively by their founding general partners, and courts resolve ambiguities against the drafting general partners and in favor of the reasonable expectations of the limited partners. **For Example,** when the general partners of the Nantucket Island Associates Limited Partnership unilaterally amended the limited partnership agreement to add a new class of preferred limited partnership units with superior rights to existing unit holders, ambiguous agreement language was construed against the general partners by the court, and the general partners were found to be in breach of the agreement by adding the new class of units.[6]

2. Characteristics of Limited Partnerships

A limited partnership has the following characteristics.

CPA (a) Capital Contributions

Under the ULPA, a limited partner contributed either cash or property but not services. Under the RULPA, however, a limited partner may contribute services.

CPA (b) Firm Name

With certain exceptions, a limited partner's name cannot appear in the firm name. Under the RULPA, the words *limited partnership* must appear without abbreviation in the firm name.

CPA (c) Management and Control of the Firm

The general partners manage the business and are personally liable for firm debts. However, general partners may avoid personal liability by incorporating. Limited partners (the investors) have the right to a share of the profits and a return of capital upon dissolution and have limited liability.

The limitation of liability is lost, however, if they participate in the control of the business as seen in the *Gilroy, Sims & Associates, Ltd.* case.

AMERICAN NATIONALS INS. CO. V GILROY, SIMS & ASSOCIATES, LTD.,
847 F SUPP 971 (ED MO 1995)

THE PROBLEM OF LIMITED PARTNERS IN CONTROL

Gilroy, Sims & Associates, Ltd. (Gilroy, Sims), was a limited partnership engaged in real estate development whose original general partners were Richard Gilroy and William Sims. Thomas Green and John Murphy Jr. were listed as limited partners along with certain other individuals on the certificate of limited partnership. Green and Murphy took an active role in the day-to-day operations of the real estate developed by the limited partnership. Financing was obtained to construct the venture's building in St. Louis in 1968, and a mortgage was payable to American National Insurance Co. over 27 years. In 1976, the partnership executed a Restated Agreement, and Green and Murphy became general partners of Gilroy, Sims, agreeing to "unlimited liability for the debts of the partnership." In the fall of 1990, the partnership stopped making mortgage payments. After foreclosure by American National, a deficiency of $1,437,840 was outstanding. Green and Murphy believed that as limited partners when the debt was incurred in 1968, they were absolved from any personal liability beyond the assets of the firm. American National disagreed.

Judicial Opinion

GUNN, D. J. . . . With respect to defendants Green and Murphy's motion for summary judgment for the remaining deficiency, the Court finds that defendants are liable for the remaining deficiency pursuant to the terms of the Restated Agreement.

[5] See *Gotham Partners, L.P. v Hallowood Realty Partners, L.P.*, 817 A2d 160 (Del 2002).
[6] *In re Nantucket Island Associates Limited Partnership Unit Holders Litigation*, 810 A2d 351 (Del Ch 2002).

Even though the Restated Agreement signed by Green and Murphy provides that "the partners shall have unlimited liability for the debts of the partnership," Green and Murphy contend that as incoming partners they are liable for prior debts only to the extent of partnership property and are absolved of personal liability under § 17 of the Uniform Partnership Act. An incoming partner, however, may by agreement bind himself to personal liability for past debts. See *Resolution Trust Corp v Teem Partnership*, 835 F. Supp. 563, 570 (D.Colo. 1993) (some jurisdictions interpreting parallel statutes have held that UPA § 17 does not apply to incoming partner who expressly assumes pre-existing obligation).

The dispositive issue before the Court is whether Green and Murphy assumed personal liability for the pre-existing debts and, if so, to what extent. In executing the Restated Agreement, defendants failed to limit the debts or time period of the debts for which they assumed unlimited liability, but instead assumed liability as general partners for all of the debts of the partnership in section 10. Defendants expressly adopted the partnership obligation incurred prior to their execution of the Restated Agreement by their words as well as their actions. Moreover, section 5 of the Restated Agreement describing the duration of the partnership specifically provides that the partnership commenced on November 1, 1968.

Under Missouri law, limited partners are not liable as general partners if they do not take part in the control of the day-to-day business operations of the partnership. *First Wisconsin Nat'l Bank v Towboat Partners, Ltd.*, 630 F. Supp. 171, 176 (E.D.Mo.1986) (limited partners not liable if only possible control was over expenditure of funds from extended line of credit agreed to by limited partners under restructuring agreement to keep partnership afloat). Although Green and Murphy's limited partner status would ordinarily limit their potential liability to creditors, their active roles in taking part in the control of the business subjected them to potential general partner liability.

[Judgment against Green and Murphy]

Questions

1. Were the incoming general partners, Green and Murphy, personally liable for the pre-existing partnership obligations in this case?
2. Under what circumstances may limited partners be subjected to general partner liability?
3. Were Green and Murphy subject to unlimited personal liability as general partners for the indebtedness that arose while they were limited partners?

The RULPA lists a number of "safe harbor" activities in which limited partners may engage without losing their protection from liability. These activities include

1. Being a contractor for, or an agent or employee of, the limited partnership or of a general partner;
2. Consulting with and advising a general partner regarding the partnership business;
3. Acting as a surety for the limited partnership; and
4. Voting on partnership matters, such as dissolving and winding up the limited partnership or removing a general partner.

(d) Right to Sue

A limited partner may bring a derivative action on behalf of the limited partnership to enforce a claim that the limited partnership possesses against others but that the partnership refuses to enforce. This derivative suit is filed in the name of the limited partner, and the partnership is named as a defendant, with the limited partnership deriving the benefits of the action.

Limited partners may sue their partnership's general partner to protect the limited partners' interest. General partners today are commonly corporations with their own boards of directors and management teams, with the limited partnership format providing investment and tax incentives for investor–limited partners and the general partners reserving to themselves broad authority to act in the general partners' sole discretion and often in the general partners' own best interest. **For Example,** Donald Weedon and others formed a limited partnership under Delaware law to raise capital for the securities broker–dealer business. The partnership agreement, as allowed by Delaware law, gave the corporate general partners and its directors the right to restrict their fiduciary duties in managing the partnership and gave the general partner broad power to act, even in conflicted situations, subject only to very loose constraints of a subjective bad-faith standard. Nonemployee limited partners referred to by the court as the "outside investors" brought suit against the corporate general partners and members of the general partner's board of directors and top management for squeezing out all nonemployee limited partners and paying less than the fair value for their units in violation of fiduciary duties and the partnership agreement. The trial court decided in favor of the plaintiffs, stating in part:

> *. . . Even given the wide discretion the partnership agreement gives to the defendants to issue new units without fear of liability, the defendants managed to step out of bounds in one important respect. By deciding to permit the general partner's outside directors to acquire new units at a favorable price and by denying the same opportunity to Outside Investors, the defendants breached their contractual duties. This decision, I find, was not undertaken in good faith but instead as quid pro quo for the outside directors' willing assent to the issuance of a large number of new units to management and employees. . . .*

The plaintiffs received a make-whole remedy from the court with monetary damages tied to fair market values.[7]

(e) Dissolution

The dissolution and winding up of limited partnerships is governed by the same principles applicable to general partnerships.

C. Limited Liability Companies

Limited liability company (LLC) acts were rapidly adopted by state legislatures throughout the country following a favorable tax ruling on this form of organization by the Internal Revenue Service.[8] This corporate-sounding entity is considered in this chapter because it is a form of limited partnership.

CPA 3. Characteristics of LLCs

The IRS has determined that an LLC may qualify for partnership federal tax treatment. Unlike a corporation, an LLC pays no federal taxes on its income as an entity. Instead, the income (or losses, deductions, and credits) flows through to the LLC's owners (called *members*) based on their proportionate interest in the company. The members report the income on their personal tax returns. The LLC combines this tax advantage with the limited liability feature of the corporate form of business organization. The owners and managers are not personally liable for the debts and obligations of the entity, provided that these individuals fulfill their common law duty to disclose that they are acting as agents for the limited liability company.

CPA (a) Formation

As set forth previously, general partnerships may be created without the formality of even a written partnership agreement when two individuals simply operate a business for profit as co-owners. LLCs, however, require a formal filing of articles of organization with the secretary of state in a manner similar to a filing of articles of incorporation by a corporation or a certificate of limited partnership for a limited partnership.

The articles for an LLC must contain the name, purpose, duration, registered agent, and principal office of the LLC. An LLC must use the words *limited liability company* or *LLC* in the company's name. The LLC is a legal entity with authority to conduct business in its own name.[9] LLC acts are characterized as "flexible statutes" because they generally permit owners to engage in the private ordering of relationships, with broad freedom of contract to govern these relationships or set forth in their operating agreements.[10]

CPA (b) Capital Contributions

An ownership interest in an LLC may be issued for cash, property, or services. The owners of the entity are known as *members*.

[7] *Gelfman v Weeden Investors, L.P.*, 859 A2d 89 (Del Ch 2004).

[8] IRS Rev Rul 88-76. LLCs have been adopted by every state and the District of Columbia. A Uniform Limited Liability Company Act was approved by the National Conference of Commissioners on Uniform State Law.

[9] An individual has a right to appear before a court and represent himself or herself. However, a member of an LLC who as such is not personally liable for the LLC's actions cannot appear before a court on behalf of the LLC entity. The LLC may appear in court only through counsel. Thus, a nonattorney member of an LLC was not allowed to represent the LLC in a court case. *Collier v Cobalt, LLC*, 2002 US Dist LEXIS 7892.

[10] *Elf Atochem N. America, Inc. v Jaffari*, 727 A2d 286 (Del Super Ct 1999).

Capital contributions must comply with the "operating agreement" as discussed in the following paragraph. **For Example,** William Eichengrun claims his capital contribution to the LLC was in services not cash because he was the LLC's managing member. However, in proceedings to dissolve the LLC and distribute its assets, Eichengrun was not allowed to participate in the distribution because the operating agreement required that "initial capital contributions" of members be in cash or the fair market value of property.[11]

CPA (c) Management

Management of an LLC is vested in its members. An *operating agreement*, equivalent to the bylaws of a corporation or a partnership agreement, sets forth the specific management authority of members and managers.

The operating agreement need not be in writing. All amendments must be unanimous unless otherwise agreed to by the members. Oral amendments may modify written terms unless otherwise set forth in the operating agreement. To promote certainty in management, it is recommended that the operating agreement be in writing and that it be changed only by written amendments adopted by a specified percentage or number of members.

The management structure created in the operating agreement may provide for the company to be member managed. However, members commonly delegate authority to run the entity to managers who may or may not be required to be members of the LLC. A member is not entitled to compensation for services performed by an LLC unless it is stipulated in the operating agreement. (Members receive profits and losses according to the terms of the operating agreement.)

In a member-managed company, each member has equal rights in management, with decisions made by a majority vote of the members.[12] In a manager-managed company, nonmanager members have no rights in management except for extraordinary matters, such as amending the operating agreement or consenting to merge with another entity.

Managers have the same fiduciary duties to the entity as corporate officers have to a corporation. In many states, members of manager-managed LLCs owe no fiduciary duty to the LCC unless a member exercises some or all of the authority of a manager pursuant to the operating agreement.[13]

The basic rule on fiduciary duties of members is set forth in the *Katris* case.

KATRIS V CARROLL, 842 NE2D 221 (IND APP 2005)

WHY YOU NEED TO MAKE SURE BUSINESS RELATIONSHIP OBLIGATIONS OF MEMBERS ARE SET FORTH IN THE OPERATING AGREEMENT

Stephen Doherty wrote a software program called "Viper" for Lester Szlendak. Peter Katris and William Hamburg joined Szlendak and Doherty in forming an LLC to exploit the capabilities of the software. Katris and Hamburg were elected the "sole managers" of the LLC and Szlendak and Doherty were members with marketing and technical responsibilities. Prior to and at the time of the LLC's formation, Doherty worked as an independent contractor for Patrick Carroll, an Ernst & Co. employee. Thereafter Ernst & Co. hired Doherty to work for Carroll. As part of his duties he developed a software program ultimately called "WorldWideOptions Web" (WWOW). Katris and the LLC sued Carroll, Ernst & Co. and Doherty alleging that Doherty breached his fiduciary duty to the LLC, and charging collusion by Carroll and Ernst in developing WWOW, which was functionally similar to Viper. From a judgment against Katris and the LLC, they appealed.

11 *KSI Rockville, LLC v Eichengrun*, 760 NYS2d 520 (App Div 2003).
12 *IIC Holdings, LLC v HR Software Acquisition Group, Inc.*, 750 NYS2d 425 (Sup Ct 2002).
13 But see *Melcher v Apollo Medical Fund Management*, 808 NYS2d 207 (App Div 2006), referencing Delaware Code, Title 6, § 18-1101(c).

Judicial Opinion

McNulty, P. J.... In this appeal, Katris contends that summary judgment was improper because Doherty owed Katris and the LLC such a fiduciary duty.

We look to the applicable provisions of the Act in determining the fiduciary duties owed by the managers and members of the LLC. ("Like corporations and limited partnerships, limited liability companies are creatures of statute"). The parties here agree that section 15–3(g) of the Act applies to determine Doherty's fiduciary duties.

Katris acknowledges that theirs was a manager-managed LLC and that, pursuant to the Act, a member of a manager-managed LLC "who is not also a manager owes no duties to the company or to the other members solely by reason of being a member." Katris thus concedes that Doherty did not owe any fiduciary duties solely by reason of being a member of the LLC.

Katris contends, however, that Doherty owed fiduciary duties to the LLC pursuant to section 15–3(g)(3) of the Act. Section 15–3(g)(3) provides:

> *"[A] member who pursuant to the operating agreement exercises some or all of the authority of a manager in the management and conduct of the company's business is held to the standards of conduct in subsections (b), (c), (d), and (e) of this Section to the extent that the member exercises the managerial authority vested in a manager by this Act[.]" 805 ILCS 180/15–3(g)(3) (West 2002).*

Katris contends that Doherty exercised some of the authority of a manager in his capacity as director of technology for the LLC and thus falls within the ambit of this section. Carroll and Ernst disagree, contending that pursuant to the plain terms of the statute, Doherty was only subject to fiduciary duties if he exercised managerial authority pursuant to the operating agreement. They maintain that Doherty did not have any such managerial authority under the operating agreement. We agree.

The plain meaning of the language used by the legislature is the best indication of legislative intent, and when the language is clear, this court should not look to extrinsic aids for construction.

Looking at the plain language of section 15–3(g)(3) of the Act, Doherty was subject to fiduciary duties if he exercised some or all of the authority of a manager pursuant to the LLC's operating agreement. The Act provides for the creation of an operating agreement, stating that "[a]ll members of a limited liability company may enter into an operating agreement to regulate the affairs of the company and the conduct of its business and to govern relations among the members, managers, and company." The four members of the LLC here entered into such an operating agreement on February 14, 1997.

Looking to that operating agreement, it specifically provides that the business and affairs of the LLC "shall be managed by its [m]anagers," provides for the election of Katris and Hamburg as the "sole [m]anagers" of the LLC, and sets forth the powers of the managers of the LLC. Although the operating agreement also sets forth the rights and obligations of the members, these provisions do not provide for any managerial authority. Accordingly, Doherty did not exercise any managerial authority pursuant to the LLC's operating agreement.

The undisputed facts of this case show that Doherty was a member of a manager-managed LLC and exercised no managerial authority pursuant to the LLC's operating agreement. Accordingly, the undisputed facts show that Doherty owed no fiduciary duties to Katris or the LLC pursuant to the Act and Katris' collusion claim against Carroll and Ernst fails as a matter of law. We therefore conclude that the circuit court properly granted the motion for summary judgment.

[Affirmed]

Questions

1. Did Doherty owe a fiduciary duty to the LLC solely by reason of being a member of the LLC?
2. Did another basis exist under the LLC statute to establish in Doherty a fiduciary duty to the LLC?
3. What could the managers of the LCC have done to protect against a member developing competing software?

CPA (d) Distributions

Profits and losses are shared according to the terms of the operating agreement.

Liquidating distributions must first be applied to return all contributions not previously returned, and the remainder is distributed per capita to members unless members alter these rules in the operating agreement.

Any distribution made when the company is insolvent is unlawful. Each member or manager who votes to make an unlawful distribution is in violation of his or her fiduciary duty to the firm and is personally liable for the amount of distribution improperly paid. However, the individual may compel contribution from all other responsible members and managers.

FIGURE 43-1 Comparison of General Partnership, Limited Partnership, Limited Liability Company, and Limited Liability Partnership

	GENERAL PARTNERSHIP	LIMITED PARTNERSHIP	LIMITED LIABILITY COMPANY (LLC)	LIMITED LIABILITY PARTNERSHIP (LLP)
CREATION	NO FORMALITY REQUIRED.	FILING A CERTIFICATE OF LIMITED PARTNERSHIP WITH APPROPRIATE STATE OFFICE.	FILING ARTICLES OF ORGANIZATION WITH SECRETARY OF STATE.	REGISTRATION OF LLP FILED WITH STATE GOVERNMENT.
LIABILITY	UNLIMITED LIABILITY OF EACH PARTNER FOR FIRM DEBTS.	GENERAL PARTNERS: UNLIMITED LIABILITY FOR FIRM DEBTS. LIMITED PARTNERS: NO LIABILITY BEYOND LOSS OF INVESTMENT.	ALL MEMBERS ARE LIABLE FOR LLC DEBTS TO THE EXTENT OF THEIR CAPITAL CONTRIBUTIONS AND EQUITY IN FIRM. NO PERSONAL LIABILITY BEYOND THIS.	NO LIABILITY FOR PARTNERS BEYOND THEIR CONTRIBUTIONS AND EQUITY IN FIRM, EXCEPT UNLIMITED PERSONAL LIABILITY FOR THEIR OWN WRONGFUL ACTS AND THOSE OF PERSONS WHOM THEY SUPERVISE.
MANAGEMENT	ALL PARTNERS ACCORDING TO THEIR PARTNERSHIP AGREEMENT OR THE UPA OR RUPA.	GENERAL PARTNERS ACCORDING TO THEIR PARTNERSHIP AGREEMENT OR THE UPA OR RUPA. LIMITED PARTNERS EXCLUDED.	BY MEMBERS OF FIRM, WHO MAY DELEGATE AUTHORITY TO MANAGERS.	ALL PARTNERS ACCORDING TO PARTNERSHIP AGREEMENT OR THE UPA.
DISSOLUTION	AS SET FORTH IN THE PARTNERSHIP AGREEMENT OR THE UPA OR RUPA.	AS SET FORTH IN THE PARTNERSHIP AGREEMENT OR THE ULPA OR RULPA.	AS SET FORTH IN LLC STATUTE OR ARTICLES OF ORGANIZATION.	AS SET FORTH IN PARTNERSHIP AGREEMENT OR THE UPA OR RUPA.

(e) LLC Property

The LLC is an independent entity separate and distinct from the members. The LLC owns and holds property in its own name.[14]

(f) Assignment

An interest in an LLC is personal property and is generally assignable. However, LLC members cannot transfer the right to participate in management without the consent of the other members of the LLC. A creditor's right against a member's interest in an LLC is limited to a *charging order*. The creditor with such an order has only the rights of an assignee of an interest in an LLC.

(g) Dissolution

Most LLC statutes provide that an LLC will dissolve by the consent of the members or upon the death, retirement, resignation, expulsion, or bankruptcy of a member. Statutes also provide, however, that the business of the LLC may be continued with the consent of all of the remaining members. With a change in IRS regulations away from its four-factor corporate characteristics test, discussed in the following section, some states have begun to amend LLC laws to give limited liability companies the option of perpetual existence.

Situations in which it is not reasonably practicable to carry on the business in conformity with the operating agreement may arise. The LLC statute commonly permits a court to decree dissolution of the LLC when such a situation occurs. **For Example,** Haley and Talcott each had a 50 percent interest in a real estate LLC. They had a falling out. The operating agreement contained an exit mechanism to buy out Haley's share, but the mechanism could not relieve Haley of his obligation as a personal guarantor for the LLC's mortgage. Because the LLC was deadlocked and the exit mechanism was not an adequate remedy, the court ordered the dissolution of the LLC and the sale of its property.[15]

Upon the winding up of an LLC, the assets are distributed according to the operating agreement. Should the agreement fail to provide for this event, the assets will be distributed according to the state's LLC statute.

(h) Tax Classification

The IRS applied a four-factor corporate characteristics test in determining whether an LLC would be taxed as a partnership or a corporation, allowing no more than two characteristics to exist to qualify for taxation as a partnership. The factors were continuity of life, centralized management, limited liability, and free transferability of interest. The four-factor test became obsolete on the implementation by the IRS of its so-called check-the-box entity classification election procedure available to unincorporated associations that are not publicly traded.[16] Now, if an LLC wants to be classified as a partnership, all it needs to do is make that election by checking the box on the appropriate IRS form.

(i) Disregarding the LLC Entity

Some LLC statutes provide that courts may disregard the LLC entirely and hold the owners personally liable beyond their investments to the same extent as done in corporate law when exceptional circumstances demand.[17]

The *Kaycee Land and Livestock* case involves the issue of LLC piercing.

KAYCEE LAND AND LIVESTOCK V FLAHIVE, 46 P3D 323 (WYO 2002)

PIERCING THE LLC VEIL

Flahive Oil & Gas is a Wyoming Limited Liability Company with no assets at this time. Kaycee Land and Livestock (Kaycee) entered into a contract with Flahive Oil & Gas LLC allowing Flahive Oil & Gas to use the surface of its real property. Roger Flahive is and was the managing member of Flahive Oil & Gas at all relevant times. Kaycee alleges that Flahive Oil & Gas caused environmental contamination to its real property. Kaycee seeks to pierce the LLC veil and disregard the LLC entity

[14] *Northeast Realty, LLC v Misty Bayou, LLC,* 920 So2d 938 (La App 2006).

[15] *Haley v Talcott,* 864 A2d 86 (Del Ch 2004).

[16] Treas Reg 301.7701 *et seq.*

[17] *Milstar (NY) Inc., v Natasha Diamond Jewelry, LLC,* 797 NYS2d 10 (AD 2005).

of Flahive Oil & Gas and hold Roger Flahive individually liable for the contamination. There is no allegation of fraud. The question presented to the Wyoming Supreme Court is whether, in the absence of fraud, the remedy of piercing the veil is available against a company formed under the Wyoming Limited Liability Company Act?

Wyoming courts, as well as courts across the country, have typically utilized a fact driven inquiry to determine whether circumstances justify a decision to pierce a corporate veil. This case comes to us as a certified question in the abstract with little factual context, and we are asked to broadly pronounce that there are no circumstances under which this court will look through a failed attempt to create a separate LLC entity and prevent injustice. We simply cannot reach that conclusion and believe it is improvident for this court to prohibit this remedy from applying to any unforeseen circumstance that may exist in the future....

We note that Wyoming was the first state to enact LLC statutes. Many years passed before the Internal Revenue Service's approval of taxation of LLCs as partnerships led to other states adopting LLC legislation and the broad usage of this form for business organizations. William D. Bagley, *The History of the LLC in the USA*, Limited Liability Company Reporter 94–302 (May/June 1994); *see also* Karin Schwindt, *Limited Liability Companies: Issues in Member Liability*, 44 UCLA L. Rev. 1541, 1543 (1997). Wyoming's statute is very short and establishes only minimal requirements for creating and operating LLCs. It seems highly unlikely that the Wyoming legislature gave any consideration to whether the common law doctrine of piercing the veil should apply to the liability limitation granted by that fledgling statute. It is true that some other states have adopted specific legislation extending the doctrine to LLCs while Wyoming has not. However, that situation seems more attributable to the fact that Wyoming was a pioneer in the LLC arena and states which adopted LLC statutes much later had the benefit of years of practical experience during which this issue was likely raised.

Mr. Flahive insists that, if the legislature intended for liability to be asserted against the members of an LLC, it could have added similar language to the LLC chapter at the same time it adopted provisions of the revised Model Business Corporation Act. However, adoption of those amendments in 1989, twelve years after the enactment of the LLC statutes, while remaining silent on the issue of piercing the veil in the LLC statutes, is far too attenuated to indicate a clear legislative intent to restrict application of the common law to LLCs. It stands to reason that, because it is an equitable doctrine, "the paucity of statutory authority for LCC piercing should not be considered a barrier to its application." Schwindt, *supra* at 1552. Lack of explicit statutory language should not be considered an indication of the legislature's desire to make LLC members impermeable....

With the dearth of legislative consideration on this issue in Wyoming, we are left to determine whether applying the well established common law to LLCs somehow runs counter to what the legislature would have intended had it considered the issue. In that regard, it is instructive that: "Every state that has enacted LLC piercing legislation has chosen to follow corporate law standards and not develop a separate LLC standard." Philip P. Whynott, *The Limited Liability Company* § 11:140 at 11-5 (3d ed. 1999). Statutes which create corporations and LLCs have the same basic purpose-to limit the liability of individual investors with a corresponding benefit to economic development. Statutes created the legal fiction of the corporation being a completely separate entity which could act independently from individual persons. If the corporation were created and operated in conformance with the statutory requirements, the law would treat it as a separate entity and shelter the individual shareholders from any liability caused by corporate action, thereby encouraging investment. However, courts throughout the country have consistently recognized certain unjust circumstances can arise if immunity from liability shelters those who have failed to operate a corporation as a separate entity. Consequently, when corporations fail to follow the statutorily mandated formalities, co-mingle funds, or ignore the restrictions in their articles of incorporation regarding separate treatment of corporate property, the courts deem it appropriate to disregard the separate identity and do not permit shareholders to be sheltered from liability to third parties for damages caused by the corporations' acts.

We can discern no reason, in either law or policy, to treat LLC's differently than we treat corporations. If the members and officers of an LLC fail to treat it as a separate entity as contemplated by statute, they should not enjoy immunity from individual liability for the LLC's acts that cause damage to third parties. Most, if not all, of the expert LLC commentators have concluded the doctrine of piercing the veil should apply to LLCs. Stephen B. Presser, *Piercing the Corporate Veil* § 4.01[2] (2002); Ann M. Seward & Laura Stubberud, *The Limits of Limited*

Liability-Part Two, Limited Liability Company Reporter 94–109 (January/February 1994); Schwindt, *supra*. It also appears that most courts faced with a similar situation—LLC statutes which are silent and facts which suggest the LLC veil should be pierced—have had little trouble concluding the common law should be applied and the factors weighed accordingly.

Certainly, the various factors which would justify piercing an LLC veil would not be identical to the corporate situation for the obvious reason that many of the organizational formalities applicable to corporations do not apply to LLCs. The LLC's operation is intended to be much more flexible than a corporation's. Factors relevant to determining when to pierce the corporate veil have developed over time in a multitude of cases. It would be inadvisable in this case, which lacks a complete factual context, to attempt to articulate all the possible factors to be applied to LLCs in Wyoming in the future. For guidance, we direct attention to commentators who have opined on the appropriate factors to be applied in the LLC context.

Conclusion

No reason exists in law or equity for treating an LLC differently than a corporation is treated when considering whether to disregard the legal entity. We conclude the equitable remedy of piercing the veil is an available remedy under the Wyoming Limited Liability Company Act.

Questions

1. How did this case happen to come to be heard before the state's Supreme Court?
2. How have the legislative bodies in other states dealt with the question of LLC veil piercing?
3. What public policy reason(s), if any, exists to create separate standards for LLC veil piercing versus corporate veil piercing?

4. LLCs and Other Entities

LLCs are distinguishable from Subchapter S corporations and limited partnerships.

(a) LLC Distinguished from a Subchapter S Corporation

Under a Subchapter S corporation (so named from Subchapter S of the Internal Revenue Code), shareholders of a close corporation may be treated as partners for tax purposes and retain the benefit of limited liability under the corporate form. An S corporation is limited to 75 shareholders who must be U.S. citizens or resident aliens. Although partnerships and corporations may generally not be shareholders, employee stock ownership plans (ESOPs) and nonprofit entities may be. In contrast, an LLC has no limit on the number of owners, and there is no restriction on the types of entities or persons that may own an LLC. Thus, partnerships, corporations, and foreign investors may be owners of an LLC. Because substantial taxes on appreciated assets are payable on the liquidation of an S corporation, it is generally not feasible to convert an existing S corporation to an LLC.

CPA (b) LLC Distinguished from a Limited Partnership

Limited partners in a limited partnership have the advantage of limited liability. However, every limited partnership must have a general partner who manages the business, and this partner can be subject to unlimited liability. This structural feature is a major disadvantage of the limited partnership form that does not exist in a limited liability company (LLC). Also, individual limited partners may lose their limited liability if they participate in the control of the business. Under an LLC, the members may actively participate in the control of the business and still receive limited liability protection. As stated previously in this chapter, a general partner may avoid unlimited liability on a sizeable limited partnership project by incorporating.

(c) Usage

It is expected that the LLC will in many instances replace general and limited partnerships as well as close corporations and S corporations. The LLC will not replace the publicly traded corporation, however, because publicly traded partnerships and LLCs must be classified as corporations for tax purposes.[18]

[18] See IRS Notice 88-75, 1988, 1988-2 CB 386. The traditional corporation retains many advantages, such as the low corporate income tax on corporate profits, which allows accumulation of capital for expansion or the distribution of all corporate earnings as compensation as well as providing fringe benefits for employee-owners with pretax dollars (IRC §§ 79, 119, 162).

D. Limited Liability Partnerships

As part of the limited liability trend established by the swift enactment of LLC laws throughout the country, most states have recently enacted limited liability partnership (LLP) acts. Like LLCs, they provide businesses and those offering professional services the benefit of single taxation as a partnership as well as limited liability.[19]

CPA 5. Extent of Limited Liability

In a general partnership, partners are jointly liable for partnership debts and jointly and severally liable for partnership torts. LLP statutes were initially drafted to shield innocent partners from vicarious negligence or malpractice liability of their partners. Some states now provide "full shields" for innocent partners that eliminate the vicarious personal liability of these partners for the obligations of the partnership and free them from any obligation to contribute personal assets beyond their investments in the partnership. In every state, however, LLP partners remain fully liable for their own negligence and continue to have unlimited liability for the wrongful acts of those whom they directly supervise and control.

Professional LLPs continue to be subject to professional regulations, and the appropriate regulating boards set the amount and type of malpractice insurance firms must carry to operate as an LLP.

For Example, to illustrate the effects of a change from a general partnership to an LLP, surgeons Jones, Smith, and Gray are partners. Jones inadvertently removed Miller's healthy kidney rather than his diseased kidney, and a jury returned a verdict of $2 million. Smith and Gray, although innocent partners, are jointly and severally liable along with Jones under general partnership law, and their personal assets can be reached to pay the judgment if necessary. Under an LLP, only partnership assets and the personal assets of Jones are available to pay the judgment. Smith's and Gray's personal assets cannot be reached.

CPA 6. Registration and Usage

LLP statutes are designed to permit the conversion of existing general partnerships into limited liability

ETHICS & THE LAW

When the Office of the Special Counsel concluded its work in both civil and criminal litigation against officers, directors, and consultants involved with failed savings and loan institutions in the late 1980s, it released a report on its work. On the civil side, the Office of the Special Counsel had obtained settlements from defendants in civil suits of $2.9 billion in restitution. Accounting firms, along with lawyers and consultants, comprised 71 percent of the defendants.

Because most accounting firms were organized as partnerships, the result was that many partners were required to dig into their personal assets to meet the restitution requirements imposed by the federal government. Since the creation of LLPs, all of the largest accounting firms in the United States have restructured, with most choosing the LLP for conducting business. All forms of restructuring will ensure limited personal liability for their principals.

Was the restructuring undertaken to avoid liability? Does limited liability insulate those who make decisions from liability for those decisions? Financiers attempt to determine what stake the officers in a corporation have in the corporation. Stock ownership and exposure to losses through the value of those shares are seen as a positive influence. Do liability limitations reduce the stake a principal has? Is it good to have decision makers separated from the costs of those decisions?

[19] The 1994 Revised Uniform Partnership Act (RUPA) was amended in 1996 to include two new articles: Article 10, dealing with limited liability partnerships, and Article 11, dealing with foreign limited liability partnerships. Articles 1 through 11 constitute the Uniform Limited Liability Partnership Act.

partnerships. The statutes require registration with the secretary of state, and the name of the partnership must contain the term *limited liability partnership* or *LLP*.

Traditional partnership agreements, like those used by many accounting and law firms and other professional partnerships, can be converted into limited liability partnership agreements without major redrafting or renegotiating of the underlying agreements. It is thus expected that many of these professional firms will organize under this new form of partnership.

Summary

A limited partnership consists of one or more limited partners who contribute cash, property, or services without liability for losses beyond their investment, and one or more general partners, who manage the business and have unlimited personal liability. A limited partner's protection from unlimited liability may be lost if the partner participates in the control of the business. "Safe harbor" activities for limited partners are set forth in the RULPA. General partners may avoid personal liability by incorporating. A certificate of limited partnership must be filed when the partnership is formed for the law to apply. Otherwise, general partnership law applies.

A limited liability company is a hybrid form of business organization that combines the tax advantages of a partnership with the limited liability feature of the corporation. It must be formed in accordance with state law in order to have effect, and the designation LLC must appear with the company's name. Management of an LLC is vested in its members, and members can delegate authority to run the entity to managers, the terms of which are set forth in the company's operating agreement. Members receive profits and losses according to the operating agreement. A member's interest in an LLC is assignable, but consent of the other members is needed for the assignee to participate in the firm's management.

A limited liability partnership is a new form of business organization that allows existing partnerships to convert to this form without major renegotiation of the underlying partnership agreement. Innocent partners in a limited liability partnership are not personally liable for the torts of other partners beyond their investment in the firm.

Questions and Case Problems

1. What is the principal advantage of an LLP over an LLC?
2. Alan Waung, a Hong Kong businessperson, purchased a golf course in Saginaw, Michigan, as an investment. As an avid golfer, Alan anticipates spending several weeks during the year at his "Northern Pines" course. He has been informed that a Subchapter S corporation would allow him and his family-member shareholders to be treated as partners for U.S. tax purposes while retaining the limited liability of the corporate form. Advise Mr. Waung on this matter. What form of business organization would you recommend?
3. Kate Haley, an experienced builder, formed a limited partnership in August 2003, along with two limited partners, Drs. Growbioski and Gailen, who each provided $100,000 to the partnership for initial capital for the construction of a medical office building near Stowe, Vermont. With the bustle of getting building and environmental permits and placating abutters to the property, as well as lining up suppliers and subcontractors and getting the job started, Kate simply did not find an opportunity to take the long drive to file the certificate of limited partnership with the secretary of state's office in Montpelier. A confluence of bad weather, an accident causing serious personal injury, financing disappointments, labor difficulties, design problems, and some personal problems resulted in the project being stopped before completion with some $550,000 in overdue bills. Dr. Growbioski has been approached by several suppliers and craftsmen seeking payment for supplies and work performed. As a limited partner, he believes that he is not liable for firm debts beyond his investment, which was $100,000. Explain to Dr. Growbioski his obligations at this point.
4. Alice Meyers, Monroe Moylan, and Bart Means practice medicine as Bay Area Anesthetics Associates (BAAA), a limited liability partnership. A newly certified nurse anesthesiologist, Mary Noyes, working with Dr. Means and not realizing a patient's allergy condition set forth on her chart, inadvertently administered the wrong anesthesia, which resulted in the patient's death. In a malpractice suit against Bay Area Anesthetics Associates, LLP, is the partnership liable for Mary Noyes's actions if she was employed by the hospital? What if she was employed by the partnership? Explain in detail.
5. Sebastian Hafner joined a start-up business with a business plan focused on making breads without common food allergens, such as wheat, yeast, dairy, and gluten, to be marketed in a major metropolitan area. The five founders of the business, including Sebastian, selected the limited liability company (LLC) as their form of business organization. The Articles of Organization for the limited liability company were duly filed with the secretary

of state. The Operating Agreement simply provided that founding member Jillian Lopez would be the sole manager of the firm, and it set a salary for her at $40,000 per year. She hired employees to perform production, delivery, and sales work. Sebastian and the other three members spent time nights and early mornings "pitching in" at the bakery. After two months of diligent work, Sabastian, a second-year MBA student, sought back pay for the 40 hours each week he spent at the bakery during the previous eight weeks. He pointed out to the other members of the LLC that state law authorizes employees to sue for their wages. What are Sabastian's rights regarding pay for the service he performed for the LLC?

6. Hurwitz and Padden practiced law as equal partners for a short period of time before converting to an LLC. Some three years later, Padden informed Hurwitz that he intended to leave the firm. When they could not agree on how to divide $200,000 in fees relating to work acquired before the dissolution of the LLC, Hurwitz filed suit seeking an equal division of the fees under partnership principles. Padden contended that partnership principles should not apply to the dissolution of an LLC even though the state's LLC law incorporated the definition and use of the term *dissolution* from the UPA. Decide. [*Hurwitz v Padden*, 581 NW2d 359 (Minn App)]
7. Don Mason and Beth Daley were managers and members of Pacific Beach Developers, LLC (PBD), a start-up real estate development company focusing on rehabilitating older properties for increased rental values and possible resale. Daley made a contract with San Diego Architects Associates (SDAA) to provide plans for the rehabilitation of a 60-unit building on Ingraham Street for $97,000, signing the contract "Beth Daley, manager P.B.D. LLC." Financing for the Ingraham Street property fell through, and PBD's option on the property expired. Although Daley notified SDAA that the "Ingraham Street deal was off," SDAA had nearly completed its work, and SDAA brought suit for the contract price against both the LLC and Beth Daley. At the point the lawsuit was initiated, PBD had no working capital remaining, and Don and Beth had "moved on," having taken jobs as mutual fund salespersons. Advise Beth of her legal obligations to SDAA.
8. John and Amelia have general commitments from a number of individuals to invest in their Sproondrift Cove Club golf course and distinctive residential community in Duval County. John wants to form a limited partnership. He realizes that every limited partnership must have a general partner who manages the business and is subject to unlimited liability for all debts and liabilities of the limited partnership. But he says that is no problem because the general partner can be a corporation and can limit its liability exposure by simply creating a "shell" corporation. John stated to Amelia, "As officers of the corporate general partner, you and I can operate the business without the limited partners interfering... we run the show!" Amelia responded, "John, what you propose seems so very complicated, risky, and expensive. A number of our investors are relatives who may want to be listened to, and some of our investors are professionals who could give us some valuable advice. Maybe a limited liability company would be a better entity for us." Compare the advantages and disadvantages of an LLC with a limited partnership and recommend the most appropriate form of business organization for this venture.
9. Hacienda Farms, Ltd., was organized as a limited partnership with Ricardo de Escamilla as the general partner and James L. Russell and H. W. Andrews as limited partners. The partnership raised vegetables and truck crops that were marketed principally through a produce concern controlled by Andrews. All three individuals decided which crops were to be planted. The general partner had no power to withdraw money from the partnership's two bank accounts without the signature of one of the limited partners. After operating for some seven and one-half months under these procedures, the limited partners demanded that the general partner resign as farm manager, which he did. Six weeks later, the partnership went into bankruptcy. Laurance Holzman, as trustee in bankruptcy, brought an action against Russell and Andrews, claiming that they had become liable to the creditors of the partnership as general partners because they had taken part in the control of the partnership business. How would you decide the case under the ULPA? Would the outcome be different under the RULPA? [*Holzman v de Escamilla*, 195 P2d 833 (Cal App)]
10. Jerome Micco was a major shareholder and corporate officer of Micco and Co., Inc., which was a limited partner in Harbor Creek, Ltd., a limited partnership formed to build a condominium complex. Hommel, an electrical contractor, was the successful bidder on certain electrical work for the project. For several months, Hommel worked under the direction of the construction supervisor and was paid by the limited partnership for his work. Because of financial difficulties, the supervisor was released. Thereafter, Jerome Micco played a major role in the building of the project, directing what work was to be performed. Hommel submitted payment invoices directly to Micco. When Hommel was not paid, he sued Micco, contending that Micco was a limited partner who ran the operation personally and was personally responsible for the debt. Micco argued that he was an employee or agent of a corporation (Micco and Co., Inc.) and thus could not be held liable for the debt. The evidence reveals that Micco had no occasion to tell Hommel that he was acting as a corporate officer. Is it ethical for a corporate officer and shareholder to seek to avoid individual liability in this

case? How would you decide the case? [*Hommel v Micco*, 602 NE2d 1259 (Ohio App)]

11. Ralph and Maureen K. Hagan (collectively "Hagan") owned the Stuart Court Apartments in Richmond, Virginia. On April 30, 1994, Hagan executed an agreement with Adams Property Associates, Inc. (Adams), giving Adams the exclusive right to sell the property for $1,600,000. The agreement provided that if the property was "sold or exchanged" within one year, with or without Adams's assistance, Hagan would pay Adams a fee of 6 percent of the "gross sales amount." Seven days before the year expired, Hagan, Roy T. Tepper, and Lynn Parsons formed a limited liability company, Hagan, Parsons, & Tepper, LLC (HPT). By deed dated April 23, 1995, Hagan transferred the property to HPT. Adams contends it is entitled to a commission from Hagan pursuant to the April 1994 agreement. Hagan contends the transaction was just a contribution of capital to a new company, not a sale. Decide. [*Hagan v Adams Property Associates, Inc.*, 482 SE2d 805 (Va 1997)]

CPA Questions

1. Which of the following statements is correct with respect to a limited partnership?

   a. A limited partner may *not* be an unsecured creditor of the limited partnership.

   b. A general partner may *not* also be a limited partner at the same time.

   c. A general partner may be a secured creditor of the limited partnership.

   d. A limited partnership can be formed with limited liability for all partners.

CORPORATION FORMATION

CHAPTER

(44)

LEARNING OBJECTIVES

After studying this chapter, you should be able to

LO.1 Classify corporations according to their nature, state of incorporation, and functions performed

LO.2 State why/when the corporate entity will be ignored

LO.3 List the steps to be taken in forming a corporation

LO.4 Compare corporations de jure, de facto, and by estoppel

LO.5 List and describe the ways in which corporate existence may be terminated

LO.6 Compare consolidations, mergers, and conglomerates

The corporation is one of the most important forms of business organization.

A. Nature and Classes

A *corporation* is an artificial person that is created by government action.

1. The Corporation as a Person

A **corporation** is an artificial person created by government action and granted certain powers. It exists in the eyes of the law as a person, separate and distinct from the persons who own the corporation.

The concept that the corporation is a distinct legal person means that the corporation's property is owned not by the persons who own shares in the corporation but by the corporation. Debts of the corporation are debts of this artificial person, not of the persons running the corporation or owning shares of stock in it.[1] The corporation can sue and be sued in its own name, but shareholders cannot be sued or held liable for corporate actions or obligations.

The *Hayes v Collins* case addresses the issue of personal liability of the sole owner of a corporation for a corporate debt.

HAYES V COLLINS, 538 SE2D 785 (GA APP 2000)

COLLINS CLAIMS CARDINAL RULE

Lisa Hayes sued Jennifer Collins seeking repayment of a loan. Ms. Hayes's late husband, Tony Hayes, loaned Corporate Staffing Solutions, Inc. (the "Corporation"), a total of $33,500 by writing three checks from his home equity line of credit. Mr. Hayes made two of the checks payable to the Corporation and the third payable to himself. The third check was deposited into the Corporation's account. The terms of the loan were not reduced to writing, and Mr. Hayes did not establish any deadlines for repayment. Mr. Hayes died in February 1998. On May 28, 1998, Ms. Hayes and Ms. Collins held a meeting with the executor of the estate. Collins, who is the Corporation's president and sole shareholder, stated that she would attempt to repay the loan made to the Corporation. Ms. Hayes testified that she subsequently discovered that her late husband and Ms. Collins had been engaged in an affair prior to his death. Ms. Hayes filed suit against Collins individually. The complaint alleged that Collins had failed to repay the loan made to the Corporation and sought judgment in the amount of the outstanding corporate debt. Collins filed an answer in which she denied individual liability for the corporate debt. The court entered judgment in favor of Collins and Hayes appealed.

Judicial Opinion

MIKELL, J. . . . We conclude that the trial court properly entered summary judgment in favor of Collins. It is an undisputed fact that Mr. Hayes made the loan at issue to the Corporation. It is also undisputed that the Corporation has not repaid the loan; however, Collins cannot be held personally liable for corporate debts absent evidence to warrant piercing the corporate veil. "Because the cardinal rule of corporate law is that a corporation possesses a legal existence separate and apart from that of its officers and shareholders, the mere operation of a corporate business does not render one personally liable for corporate acts."

Whether to pierce the corporate veil is normally a question for jury determination. However, in order for the trial court to submit the issue to a jury, the plaintiff must introduce evidence "that the corporate arrangement was a sham, used to defeat justice, to perpetrate fraud, or to evade statutory, contractual or tort responsibility." There is no such evidence in the record. Contrary to the argument of Ms. Hayes, "[s]ole ownership of a corporation by one person . . . is not a factor, and neither is the fact that the sole owner uses and controls it to promote [her] own ends. . . ."

"One who deals with a corporation as such an entity cannot, in the absence of fraud, deny the legality of the corporate existence for the purpose of holding the owner liable." Because the record is devoid of evidence to warrant piercing the corporate veil, Ms. Hayes cannot recover from Collins individually for repayment of the corporate loan. The trial court properly granted summary judgment to Collins.

[Judgment affirmed]

[1] *American Truck Lines, Inc. v Albino*, 424 SE2d 367 (Ga App 1992).

Questions

1. Should Ms. Collins as sole owner of Corporate Staffing Solutions, Inc. (CSS, Inc.), be legally obligated to repay a loan to the estate of a friend who loaned money to CSS, Inc., from his home equity line of credit?
2. State the cardinal rule of corporate law set forth in the court's opinion.

A corporation is formed by obtaining approval of a **certificate of incorporation, articles of incorporation**, or a **charter** from the state or national government.[2]

2. Classifications of Corporations

Corporations may be classified in terms of their relationship to the public, the source of their authority, and the nature of their activities.

(a) Public, Private, and Quasi-Public Corporations

A **public corporation** is one established for governmental purposes and for the administration of public affairs. A city is a public or municipal corporation acting under authority granted to it by the state.

A **private corporation** is one organized for charitable and benevolent purposes or for purposes of finance, industry, and commerce. Private corporations are often called *public* in business circles when their stock is sold to the public.

A **quasi-public corporation**, sometimes known as a public service corporation or a public utility, is a private corporation furnishing services on which the public is particularly dependent. An example of a quasi-public corporation is a gas and electric company.

(b) Public Authorities

The public increasingly demands that government perform services. Some of these are performed directly by government. Others are performed by separate corporations or **authorities** created by government. **For Example,** a city parking facility may be organized as a separate municipal parking authority, or a public housing project may be operated as an independent housing authority.

(c) Domestic and Foreign Corporations

A corporation is called a **domestic corporation** with respect to the state under whose law it has been incorporated. Any other corporation going into that state is called a **foreign corporation**. Thus, a corporation holding a Texas charter is a domestic corporation in Texas but a foreign corporation in all other states.

(d) Special Service Corporations

Corporations formed for transportation, banking, insurance, and savings and loan operations and similar specialized functions are subject to separate codes or statutes with regard to their organization. In addition, federal and state laws and administrative agencies regulate in detail the way these businesses are conducted.

(e) Close Corporations

A corporation whose shares are held by a single shareholder or a small group of shareholders is known as a **close corporation**. Its shares are not traded publicly. Many such corporations are small firms that are incorporated to obtain either the advantage of limited liability or a tax benefit, or both.

Many states have statutes that have liberalized corporation law as it applies to close corporations. **For Example,** Nancy Davis Judson and Hall Davis IV are siblings who inherited their parents' stock in a domestic close corporation, Hall's Mortuary, Inc., a prominent and successful funeral home in Port Allen, Louisiana. Nancy was the secretary-treasurer, a director, and shareholder of fifty percent of the corporation's stock. Hall was president, a director, and the shareholder of the other fifty percent of the corporation's stock. The siblings had a falling out. Nancy filed a court action to compel Hall to comply with the bylaws regarding her participation in the

[2] *Charter, certificate of incorporation,* and *articles of incorporation* are all terms used to refer to the documents that serve as evidence of a government's grant of corporate existence and powers. Most state incorporation statutes now provide for a certificate of incorporation issued by the secretary of state, but a Revised Model Business Corporation Act (RMBCA) has done away with the certificate of incorporation. Under the RMBCA, corporate existence begins when articles of incorporation are filed with the secretary of state. An endorsed copy of the articles together with a fee, receipt, or acknowledgment replaces the certificate of incorporation. See RMBCA §§ 1.25 and 2.03 and footnote 6 in this chapter.

management of the business and to allow her access to all corporate records. Hall responded with accusations of his own. Thereafter, Hall alleged that he and Nancy were deadlocked in the management of corporate affairs and petitioned the court for involuntary dissolution and the appointment of a liquidator. Nancy objected and wanted a jury trial on a number of issues. The court applied a statute, nearly identical to a Delaware statute, "designed to obviate a deadlocked vote of two equal shareholders" of a close corporation and ordered the dissolution of the corporation.[3]

CPA (f) Subchapter S Corporations

Subchapter S is a subdivision of the Internal Revenue Code. If corporate shareholders meet the requirements of this subdivision, they may elect Subchapter S status, which allows the shareholders to be treated as partners for tax purposes and retain the benefit of limited liability under the corporate form. A Subchapter S corporation is limited to 75 shareholders.

Under the Small Business Job Protection Act of 1996, employee stock ownership plans (ESOPs) and tax-exempt entities may be shareholders subject to certain special taxation rules.[4] Other reforms in this act make it easier for small businesses to comply with S corporation rules.

(g) Professional Corporations

A corporation may be organized for the purpose of conducting a profession. Each officer, director, and shareholder of a professional corporation must be licensed to practice the profession. Professional incorporation does not shield a practitioner from personal liability relating to the professional services rendered.

(h) Nonprofit Corporations

A *nonprofit corporation* (or an **eleemosynary corporation**), is one that is organized for charitable or benevolent purposes. Nonprofit corporations include hospitals, nursing homes, and universities.[5] Special procedures for incorporation are prescribed, and provision is made for a detailed examination of and hearing regarding the purpose, function, and methods of raising money for the enterprise.

3. Corporations and Governments

Problems arise about the power of governments to create and regulate corporations.

(a) Power to Create

Because by definition a corporation is created by government, the right to be a corporation must be obtained from the proper governmental agency. The federal government may create corporations whenever appropriate to carry out the powers granted to it.

Generally, a state by virtue of its **police power** may create any kind of corporation for any purpose. Most states have a **general corporation code**, which lists certain requirements, and anyone who satisfies the requirements and files the necessary papers with the government may automatically become a corporation. In 1950, the American Bar Association (ABA) published a Model Business Corporation Act (MBCA) to assist legislative bodies in the modernization of state corporation laws. An updated version was published in 1969. Statutory language similar to that contained in the 1969 version of the MBCA has been adopted in whole or in part by 35 states. A complete revision of the model act was approved in 1984 (RMBCA).[6] Updates to the model act have been approved subsequent to the scandals involving public corporations in recent years.[7] Jurisdictions following the model act have made numerous modifications to reflect their differing views about balancing the interests of public corporations, shareholders, and management. Caution must therefore be exercised in making generalizations about model act jurisdictions. There is no *uniform* corporation act.

[3] *Judson v Davis*, 916 So2d 1106 (La App 2005).

[4] Pub L No 104-188 (August 20, 1996).

[5] The Committee on Corporate Laws of the American Bar Association has prepared a Model Nonprofit Corporation Act. A revised Model Nonprofit Corporation Act was approved in 1986.

[6] The Revised Model Business Corporation Act (1984) was approved by the Committee on Corporate Laws Section of Business Law of the American Bar Association. The committee approved revisions to sections 6.40 and 8.33 on March 27, 1987, and to section 7.08 on June 16, 1996; changes to Subchapters B and D of Chapter 1 of the model act, which accommodate the use of electronic means for transmitting and filing required corporate documents with the secretary of state, were approved on September 20, 1997. Model act citations are to the 1984 Revised Model Business Corporation Act (RMBCA) unless designated otherwise.

[7] Revisions included in the 2005 edition of the act apply to directors' conflicting interest transactions, provisions relating to directors' involvement with corporate opportunities, and updates on the role and responsibilities of corporate directors and officers.

(b) Power to Regulate

Subject to constitutional limitations, corporations may be regulated by statutes.

(1) Protection of the Corporation as a Person. The Constitution of the United States prohibits the national government and state governments from depriving any person of life, liberty, or property without due process of law. Many state constitutions contain a similar limitation on their respective state governments. A corporation is regarded as a "person" within the meaning of such provisions.

The federal Constitution prohibits a state from denying to any person within its jurisdiction the equal protection of the laws. No such express limitation is placed on the federal government, although the due process clause binding the federal government is liberally interpreted so that it prohibits substantial inequality of treatment.

(2) Protection of the Corporation as a Citizen. For certain purposes, such as determining the right to bring a lawsuit in a federal court, a corporation is a citizen of any state in which it has been incorporated and of the state where it has its principal place of business.

B. Corporate Powers

Except for limitations in the federal Constitution or the state's own constitution, a state legislature may give corporations any lawful powers. The RMBCA contains a general provision on corporate powers granting a corporation "the same powers as an individual to do all things necessary or convenient to carry out its business and affairs."[8]

4. Particular Powers

Modern corporation codes give corporations a wide range of powers.

(a) Perpetual Life

One of the distinctive features of a corporation is its perpetual or continuous life—the power to continue as an entity forever or for a stated period of time regardless of changes in stock ownership or the death of any shareholders.

(b) Corporate Name

A corporation must have a name to identify it. As a general rule, it may select any name for this purpose. Most states require that the corporate name contain some word indicating the corporate character[9] and that the name not be the same as, or deceptively similar to, the name of any other corporation. Some statutes prohibit the use of a name that is likely to mislead the public.

(c) Corporate Seal

A corporation may have a distinctive seal. However, a corporation need not use a seal in the transaction of business unless this is required by statute or a natural person in transacting that business would be required to use a seal.

CPA (d) Bylaws

Bylaws are the rules and regulations enacted by a corporation to govern the affairs of the corporation and its shareholders, directors, and officers.

Bylaws are adopted by shareholders, although in some states they may be adopted by the directors of the corporation. Approval by the state or an amendment of the corporate charter is not required to make the bylaws effective.

The bylaws are subordinate to the general law of the state, the statute under which the corporation is formed, and the charter of the corporation.[10] Bylaws that conflict with such superior authority or that are in themselves unreasonable are invalid. Bylaws that are valid are binding on all shareholders regardless of whether they know of the existence of those bylaws or were among the majority that consented to their adoption. Bylaws are not binding on third persons, however, unless they have notice or knowledge of them.

(e) Stock

A corporation may issue certificates representing corporate stock. Under the RMBCA, authorized, but unissued, shares may be issued at the price set by the board of directors. Under UCC Article 8 (1978 and

[8] RMBCA § 3.02. State statutes generally contain similar broad catchall grants of powers.

[9] RMBCA § 4.01(a) declares that the corporate name must contain the word *corporation, company, incorporated, or limited* or an abbreviation of one of these words.

[10] *Roach v Bynum*, 403 So 2d 187 (Ala 1981).

1994 versions), securities may be "uncertificated," or not represented by an instrument.

(f) Making Contracts

Corporation codes give corporations the power to make contracts.

(g) Borrowing Money

Corporations have the implied power to borrow money in carrying out their authorized business purposes.

(h) Executing Negotiable Instruments

Corporations have the power to issue or indorse negotiable instruments and to accept drafts.

(i) Issuing Bonds

A corporation may exercise its power to borrow money by issuing bonds.

(j) Transferring Property

The corporate property may be leased, assigned for the benefit of creditors, or sold. In many states, however, a solvent corporation may not transfer all of its property without the consent of all or a substantial majority of its shareholders.

A corporation, having power to incur debts, may mortgage or pledge its property as security for those debts. This rule does not apply to public service companies, such as street transit systems and gas and electric companies.

(k) Acquiring Property

A corporation has the power to acquire and hold such property as is reasonably necessary for carrying out its express powers.

(l) Buying Back Stock

Generally, a corporation may purchase its own stock if it is solvent at the time and the purchase does not impair capital. Stock that is reacquired by the corporation that issued it is commonly called **treasury stock**.

Although treasury stock retains the character of outstanding stock, it has an inactive status while it is held by the corporation.[11] Thus, the treasury shares cannot be voted, nor can dividends be declared on them.

(m) Doing Business in Another State

A corporation has the power to engage in business in other states. However, this does not exempt the corporation from satisfying valid restrictions imposed by the foreign state in which it seeks to do business.

(n) Participating in an Enterprise

Corporations may generally participate in an enterprise to the same extent as individuals. Not only may they enter into joint ventures, but also the modern statutory trend is to permit a corporation to be a member of a partnership, and a corporation may be a limited partner. The RMBCA authorizes a corporation "to be a promoter, partner, member, associate, or manager of any partnership, joint venture, trust, or other entity."[12]

(o) Paying Employee Benefits

The RMBCA empowers a corporation "to pay pensions and establish pension plans, pension trusts, profit-sharing plans, share bonus plans, share option plans, and benefit or incentive plans for any or all of its current or former directors, officers, employees, and agents."[13]

(p) Charitable Contributions

The RMBCA authorizes a corporation, without any limitation, "to make donations for the public welfare or for charitable, scientific, or educational purposes."[14] In some states, a limitation is imposed on the amount that can be donated for charitable purposes.

5. *Ultra Vires* Acts

When a corporation acts in excess of or beyond the scope of its powers, the corporation's act is described as ***ultra vires***. Such an action is improper in the same way that it is improper for an agent to act beyond the scope of the authority given by the principal. It is also improper with respect to shareholders and creditors of the corporation because corporate funds have been diverted to unauthorized uses.

[11] When a corporation reacquires its own shares, it has the choice of retiring them and thus restoring them to the status of authorized, but unissued, shares or of treating them as still issued and available for transfer. The latter are described as treasury shares.

[12] RMBCA § 3.02(9).

[13] RMBCA § 3.02(12).

[14] RMBCA § 3.02(13).

The modern corporation statute will state that every corporation formed under it will have certain powers unless the articles of incorporation expressly exclude some of the listed powers, and then the statute will list every possible power that is needed to run a business. In some states, the legislature makes a blanket grant of all power that a natural person running the business would possess.[15] The net result is that the modern corporation possesses such a broad scope of powers that it is difficult to find an action that is *ultra vires*. If a mining corporation should begin to manufacture television sets, that might be an *ultra vires* transaction, but such an extreme departure rarely happens.

Because nonprofit corporations have a more restricted range of powers than business corporations, actions not authorized by the charters of nonprofit corporations are more likely to be found *ultra vires*.[16]

C. Creation and Termination of the Corporation

All states have general laws governing the creation of corporations.

CPA 6. Promoters

Corporations come into existence as the result of the activities of one or more persons known as **promoters** who bring together persons interested in the enterprise, aid in obtaining subscriptions to stock, and set in motion the machinery that leads to the formation of the corporation itself.

A corporation is not liable on a contract made by its promoter for its benefit unless the corporation takes some affirmative action to adopt such a contract. This action may be express words of adoption, or it may be acceptance of the contract's benefits. A corporation may also become bound by such contracts through assignment or novation.

The promoter is personally liable for all contracts made on behalf of the corporation before its existence unless the promoter is exempted by the terms of the agreement or by the circumstances surrounding it.

In *Clinton Investors*, a person executing a preincorporation lease in the name of a proposed corporation did not believe himself to be a promoter, nor did he think that he could be personally liable for obligations incurred under the lease.

CLINTON INVESTORS CO. V WATKINS, 536 NYS2D 270 (APP DIV 1989)

THE PROMOTER IS PERSONALLY LIABLE

Clinton Investors Co. (Clinton), as landlord, entered into a three-year lease with "The Clifton Park Learning Center" (learning center) as tenant. The lease was signed by Berne Watkins as treasurer of the learning center. On May 31, 1984, the day before the lease's term commenced, Watkins signed a rider to the lease. He again signed as treasurer of the tenant but identified the tenant as "the Clifton Park Learning Center, Inc." Watkins had not consulted an attorney regarding the formation of the corporation. He mistook reserving the business name with the secretary of state as a filing of a certificate of incorporation. On February 11, 1985, a certificate of incorporation was filed. By March 1986, the learning center had become delinquent in rental payments and other fees in the amount of $18,103. Clinton sued Watkins and the learning center for the amounts due. The court dismissed the complaint, and Clinton appealed.

Judicial Opinion

VESAWICH, J.... Because no corporation existed when Watkins signed the lease with plaintiff, his legal status was that of a promoter of the learning center.... Generally, a promoter who executes a preincorporation contract in the name of a proposed corporation is himself personally liable on the contract unless the parties have otherwise agreed. Watkins asserts that because the learning center corporation subsequently adopted the lease, he is therefore no longer liable on the lease. However, corporate adoption of a contract "gives rise to corporate liability in addition to any individual liability" (*Universal Inds. Corp. v Lindstrom*,

[15] Note the broad powers granted under RMBCA § 3.02; see also Cal Corp Code §§ 202(b), 207, 208 for an all-purpose clause granting all of the powers of a natural person in carrying out business activities. See *MIC v Battle Mountain Corp.*, 70 P3d 1176 (Colo 2003), where Colorado's *ultra vires* statute prohibits claims that a corporation is acting beyond the scope of its powers.

[16] *Lovering v Seabrook Island Property Owners Ass'n*, 344 SE2d 862 (SC App 1986). But see *St. Louis v Institute of Med. Ed. & Res.*, 786 SW2d 885 (Mo App 1990).

92 A.D. 2d 150, 152, 459, N.Y.S.2d 492) so that the promoter nevertheless remains obligated unless there has been a novation between the corporation and the plaintiff, which is not the situation here. Nor does the record disclose any explicit or implicit agreement by plaintiff not to hold Watkins personally liable on the lease. . . .

[Judgment reversed and summary judgment entered against Watkins]

Questions

1. What was Watkins's status when he signed the lease?
2. Is it true that because the learning center corporation subsequently adopted the lease, Watkins was no longer liable on the lease?

A promoter is liable for all torts committed in connection with the promoter's activities. The corporation is not ordinarily liable for the torts of the promoter, but it may become liable by its conduct after incorporation. If a promoter induces making a contract by fraud, the corporation is liable for the fraud if it assumes or ratifies the contract with knowledge or notice of such fraud.

A promoter stands in a fiduciary relation to the corporation and to stock subscribers and cannot make secret profits at their expense. Accordingly, if a promoter makes a secret profit on a sale of land to the corporation, the promoter must surrender the profit to the corporation.

The corporation is not liable in most states for the expenses and services of the promoter unless it subsequently promises to pay for them, or the corporation's charter or a statute imposes such liability on it.

7. Incorporation

One or more natural persons or corporations may act as **incorporators** of a corporation by signing and filing appropriate forms with a designated government official.[17] These papers are filed in duplicate, and a filing fee must be paid. The designated official (usually the secretary of state), after being satisfied that the forms conform to statutory requirements, stamps "Filed" and the date on each copy. The official then retains one copy and returns the other copy, along with a filing fee receipt, to the corporation.[18]

Statutes may require incorporators to give some form of public notice, such as by advertising in a newspaper, of their intention to form a corporation, stating its name, address, and general purpose.

8. Application for Incorporation

In most states, the process of forming a corporation is begun by filing an application for a certificate of incorporation. This application contains or is accompanied by articles of incorporation. The instrument is filed with the secretary of state and sets forth certain information about the new corporation. The articles of incorporation must contain (1) the name of the corporation, (2) the number of shares of stock the corporation is authorized to issue, (3) the street address of the corporation's initial registered office and the name of its initial registered agent, and (4) the name and address of each incorporator.[19] The articles of incorporation may also state the purpose or purposes for which the corporation is organized. If there is no "purpose clause," the corporation automatically has the purpose of engaging in any lawful business.[20] Also, if no reference is made to the duration of the corporation in the articles of incorporation, it will automatically have perpetual duration.[21]

9. The Certificate of Incorporation

Most state incorporation statutes now provide for a certificate of incorporation to be issued by the secretary of state after articles of incorporation that conform to state requirements have been filed. The Revised Model Business Corporation Act (RMBCA) has eliminated the certificate of incorporation in an effort to reduce the volume of paperwork handled by the secretary of state.

Under the RMBCA, corporate existence begins when the articles are filed with the secretary of state.[22] In some states, corporate existence begins when the proper government official issues a certificate of

[17] RMBCA § 2.01.
[18] RMBCA § 1.25.
[19] RMBCA § 2.02.
[20] RMBCA § 3.01.
[21] RMBCA § 3.02.
[22] RMBCA § 2.03(a).

incorporation. In other states, it does not begin until an organizational meeting is held by the new corporation.

10. Proper and Defective Incorporation

If the procedure for incorporation has been followed, the corporation has a legal right to exist. It is then called a **corporation de jure**, meaning that it is a corporation by virtue of law.

Assume that there is some defect in the corporation that is formed. If the defect is not a material one, the law usually overlooks the defect and holds that the corporation is a corporation de jure.

The RMBCA abolishes objections to irregularities and defects in incorporating. It provides that the

> *secretary of state's filing of the articles of incorporation is conclusive proof that the incorporators satisfied all conditions precedent to incorporation. . . .*[23]

Many state statutes follow this pattern. Such an approach is based on the practical consideration that when countless persons are purchasing shares of stock and entering into business transactions with thousands of corporations, it becomes an absurdity to expect that anyone is going to make the detailed search that would be required to determine whether a given corporation is a corporation de jure.[24]

(a) De Facto Corporation

The defect in the incorporation may be so substantial that it cannot be ignored, and the corporation will not be accepted as a corporation de jure, yet compliance may be sufficient for recognizing that there is a corporation. When this occurs, the association is called a **de facto** corporation.

Although conflict exists among authorities, the traditional elements of a de facto corporation are that (1) a valid law exists under which the corporation could have been properly incorporated, (2) an attempt to organize the corporation has been made in good faith, (3) a genuine attempt to organize in compliance with statutory requirements has been made, and (4) corporate powers have been used.

(b) Corporation by Estoppel

The defect in incorporation may be so great that by law the association cannot be accepted as a de facto corporation. In such a case then, there is no corporation. If the individuals involved proceed to run the business in spite of such irregularity, they may be held personally liable as partners for the business's debts.[25] This rule is sometimes not applied when a third person has dealt with the business as though it were a corporation.[26] In such instances, the third person is estopped from denying that the "corporation" had legal existence. In effect, there is **corporation by estoppel** with respect to that person.

Several jurisdictions that follow the 1969 MBCA have expressly retained the doctrines of corporation by estoppel and de facto corporations.[27] Numerous courts interpreting the language of the 1969 MBCA, however, have held that the doctrines of de facto corporation and corporation by estoppel no longer exist.

The court in the *American Vending Services, Inc.*, case dealt with both of these doctrines.

AMERICAN VENDING SERVICES, INC. V MORSE, 88 P2D 917 (UTAH 1994)

NO ESTOPPEL HERE

Wayne and Dianne Morse built a car wash in 1984 and operated it for approximately 11 months. Thereafter, they entered into a contract with Douglas Durbano and Kevin Garn, both licensed attorneys acting as officers of American Vending Services, Inc. (AVSI), to purchase the car wash for $65,000—$20,000 down and the remainder to be paid off monthly. Durbano and Garn claimed that they represented to the Morses that the corporate entity, AVSI, would purchase and operate the

[23] RMBCA § 2.03(b).

[24] This trend and the reasons for it may be compared to those involved in the concept of the negotiability of commercial paper. Note the similar protection from defenses given to the person purchasing shares of stock for value and without notice. UCC § 8-202.

[25] In a minority of states, a court will not hold individuals liable as partners but will hold liable the person who committed the act on behalf of the business on the theory that that person was an agent who acted without authority and is therefore liable for breach of the implied warranties of the existence of a principal possessing capacity and of proper authorization.

[26] *Am South Bank v Holland*, 669 So 2d 151 (Ala Civ App 1994).

[27] See Ga Bus Corp Code § 22-5103; Minn Bus Corp Act § 301:08. See also *H. Rich Corp. v Feinberg*, 518 So 2d 377 (Fla App 1987).

car wash. At the time the parties executed the contract on July 10, 1985, Durbano had not filed articles of incorporation for AVSI, although he had received permission from the Utah Division of Corporations to use the name American Vending Services, Inc. Durbano claimed a delay in filing the articles occurred because of a name conflict. The articles of incorporation for AVSI were finally executed on August 1, 1985, and subsequently filed on August 19, 1985. Durbano's explanation for not filing them before the parties executed the contract on July 10, 1985, was that he was "moving offices and was too busy and distracted to file the articles." AVSI operated the car wash for three years but never made any monthly payments to the Morses because of financial difficulties. The Morses sued AVSI as well as Durbano and Garn individually. The Morses asserted the personal liability of Durbano and Garn because the corporation did not legally exist when the parties executed the contract. The trial court dismissed the Morses' claims against Durbano and Garn, finding that Durbano's efforts to file articles of incorporation "constitute[d] a bona fide attempt to organize the corporation." A judgment was issued against AVSI for $76,832, but AVSI had no assets or income to satisfy the judgment. The court's decision was appealed by both parties.

Judicial Opinion

GREENWOOD, J.... The MBCA strove to codify a uniform set of laws regarding corporations and to provide some clarity and brightline tests to previously clouded areas. Many states, including Utah, adopted the MBCA in whole or in part. Each of the MBCA's sections has comments indicating the purpose and intent of that section. MBCA sections 56 and 146 (corresponding to Utah's sections 51 and 139 respectively) contain an express intent to abolish the concept of de facto corporations. The comment to section 56 states:

Under the Model Act, de jure incorporation is complete upon the issuance of the certification of incorporation.... Under the unequivocal provisions of the Model Act, any steps short of securing a certificate of incorporation would not constitute apparent compliance. Therefore a de facto corporation cannot exist under the Model Act....

...We are convinced that more recent case law in Utah, supported by the comments to the MBCA, ... supports our conclusion today that Utah's adoption of the Business Corporation Act extinguished the doctrine of de facto corporations.

...We believe that the Legislature intended to extinguish the doctrine of de facto corporations when it adopted the Business Corporation Act because the relevant portions of the Act, sections 51 and 139, were taken verbatim from the MBCA....

Accordingly, the trial court erred when it concluded as a matter of law that AVSI was a de facto corporation when the car wash was purchased.... [1969 MBCA § 1 & 6] imposes joint and several liability on Mr. Durbano and Mr. Garn for all the debts and liabilities that they incurred or that arose as a result of their actions before the corporation legally existed. In the present case, that liability is for the judgment amount entered against AVSI by the trial court.

AVSI argues next that the Morses are estopped from arguing that it was not a corporation because the Morses knew all along that Mr. Durbano and Mr. Garn intended to have AVSI purchase and run the car wash. The question of whether the doctrine of corporation by estoppel remains viable in this State after adoption of the Business Corporation Act is an issue of first impression....

...A review of jurisdictions that have addressed this issue reveals a divergence of views. For example, Oklahoma, and apparently Georgia, have adopted the position that the doctrine of corporation by estoppel cannot be invoked to deny corporate existence unless the corporation has at least a de facto existence. *Don Swann Sales Corp. v Echols*, 160 Ga.App. 539, 287 S.E.2d 577, 579–80 (1981); *James v Unknown Trustees*, 203 Okla. 312, 220 P.2d 831, 835 (1950). The District of Columbia and Tennessee have taken the position that the MBCA eliminated estoppel corporations altogether. *Robertson v Levy*, 197 A2d 443, 446 (D.C.App.1964); *Thompson & Green Mach. v Music City Lumber Co.*, 683 S.W.2d 340, 344–45 (Tenn. App. 1984). Another view, taken by Alaska, allows corporations by estoppel even when the corporation has not achieved de facto existence. *Willis v City of Valdez*, 546 P.2d 570, 574 (Alaska 1976). Still another jurisdiction, Arkansas, has stated that corporation by estoppel rests "wholly upon equitable principles ... and should be applied only where there are equitable grounds for doing so." *Childs v Philpot*, 253 Ark. 589, 487 S.W.2d 637, 641 (1972). Finally, Florida has adopted the position that the doctrine of corporation by estoppel cannot be invoked where the individual seeking to avoid liability had constructive or actual knowledge that the corporation did not exist. *Harry Rich Corp. v Feinberg*, 518 So.2d 377, 381 (Fla. App. 1987).

I am unpersuaded by the argument that the adoption of the Utah Business Corporation Act extinguished the doctrine of corporation by estoppel in addition to de facto corporations. While some jurisdictions have adopted this position, I find no basis in the comments to the MBCA for such a stance....

The fact that directors, officers, and shareholders in Utah generally enjoy limited liability is a benefit conferred by the Legislature and is the result of a public policy decision aimed at encouraging Utah's citizens to engage in private enterprise with all its attendant risks. To make this limited liability available with relative ease, the Business Corporation Act, and its successor, the Revised Business Corporation Act, make the act of incorporation fairly painless—both in terms of the financial cost and effort required to incorporate. Given the ease of incorporating, I am hesitant to carve out exceptions to the general rule found in section [1969 MBCA § 146] that individuals who assume to act as a corporation before that corporation exists are jointly and severally liable.

Notwithstanding my reluctance to make an exception, I am persuaded by the reasoning of the Florida Court of Appeals that the doctrine of corporation by estoppel should be viable in the narrow situation when those individuals acting on behalf of the corporation have no actual or constructive knowledge that the corporation does not exist....

...I would hold that the doctrine of corporation by estoppel, because it coexists with section [§ 146], can be invoked only where both parties reasonably believe they are dealing with a corporation and neither party has actual or constructive knowledge that the corporation does not exist.

In the present case, the parties dispute whether both sides knew that a corporation was involved. Mr. Garn and Mr. Durbano claim that the Morses knew from the beginning that AVSI was to purchase the car wash. Conversely, the Morses claim that they only discovered the involvement of AVSI when they signed the papers at closing. Despite the parties' conflicting accounts, it is undisputed that at the time the Morses signed the contract, Mr. Durbano and Mr. Garn had actual or constructive knowledge that AVSI did not legally exist under the laws of Utah. Accordingly, neither Mr. Durbano nor Mr. Garn can invoke the doctrine of corporation by estoppel to shield them from personal liability for the debts that they incurred while assuming to act on behalf of the nonexistent corporation.

Conclusion

We reverse the trial court's conclusions that AVSI was a de facto corporation and a corporation by estoppel at the time the car wash sale was consummated and hold that Mr. Durbano and Mr. Garn are personally liable, pursuant to Utah Code Ann. § 16-10-139 (1991), for the judgment entered by the trial court against AVSI....

[Judgment affirmed]

REGNAL W. GARFF, concurring...I concur with the reasoning of Judge Greenwood in all but that part of the opinion dealing with corporation by estoppel, wherein I concur in the result only.

I do not believe corporation by estoppel exists in Utah because [1969 MBCA § 56] clearly states that corporate existence does not begin until the certificate of incorporation is issued. Because this wording is unambiguous, there is no justifiable reason to conclude that the legislative intent was otherwise....

I agree with the courts of appeal of the District of Columbia and Tennessee, whose statutes are substantially similar to those of Utah and the Model Act. Those courts rejected the concept of corporation by estoppel.

> *No longer must the courts inquire into the equities of a case to determine whether there has been "colorable compliance" with the statute. The corporation comes into existence only when the certificate has been issued. Before the certificate issues, there is no corporation de jure, de facto or by estoppel.*
>
> ....
>
> *It is immaterial whether the third person believed he was dealing with a corporation or whether he intended to deal with a corporation. The certificate of incorporation provides the cut off point; before it is issued, the individuals, and not the corporation, are liable.*
>
> *Robertson v Levy*, 197 A.2d 443, 446–47 (D.C.App.1964).

> *The General Assembly ... saw fit to place statutory liability upon those who assume to act as a corporation without authority.... No exceptions are contained in [the statute]. For this Court to hold that under the circumstances here Mr. Walker is not liable, it would be necessary that this Court rewrite the Tennessee General Corporations Act and hold that the Act does not mean what it says....*
>
> *We are of the opinion that the doctrine of corporation by estoppel met its demise by the enactment of the [Act].*
>
> *Thompson & Green Mach. v Music City Lumber Co.*, 683 S.W.2d 340, 345 (Tenn.App. 1984)....

BENCH, concurring...I concur in the concurring opinion of Judge GARFF.

Note: The three-judge panel that heard the appeal in this case—Judges Greenwood, Garff, and Bench—disagreed about the existence of the doctrine of corporation by estoppel. Judge Greenwood believed a narrow exception existed that would allow the doctrine to be invoked where all parties reasonably believe they are dealing with a corporation and no party has actual or constructive knowledge that the corporation does not exist. Judges Garff and Bench believed that corporation by estoppel does not exist in the state, and their majority view on this point is now the controlling law in this state.

Questions

1. Would Durbano and Garn avoid personal liability under Judge Greenwood's reading of the state's Business Corporation Act?
2. Read the divergence of views by courts on the applicability of corporation by estoppel as set forth in Judge Greenwood's opinion. Express your opinion about the fairness of the drafters of the MBCA adopting a "bright-line" test for when a corporation exists.
3. Would Durbano and Garn be personally liable under the 1984 RMBCA?

With respect to preincorporation debts, the 1984 act imposes liability only on persons who act as, or on behalf of, a corporation while knowing that no corporation exists.[28]

11. Insolvency, Bankruptcy, and Reorganization

When a corporation has financial troubles so serious that it is insolvent, the best thing may be to go through bankruptcy or reorganization proceedings. The law with respect to bankruptcy and reorganizations is discussed in Chapter 35.

12. Forfeiture of Charter

In states that have adopted the RMBCA, the secretary of state may commence proceedings to administratively dissolve a corporation if (1) the corporation does not pay franchise taxes within 60 days after they are due, (2) the corporation does not file its annual report within 60 days after it is due, or (3) the corporation is without a registered agent or registered office for 60 days or more.[29] In other states, judicial proceedings may be brought to forfeit a corporate charter when the corporation repeatedly acts beyond the powers granted it or engages in illegal activity. After a corporate charter has been forfeited, the owners and officers of the dissolved corporation are not shielded from personal liability by using the corporate name when making contracts. **For Example,** Todd Crosland was president, director, and principal shareholder of Crosland Industries. Even though Crosland's corporate status was suspended and subsequently discontinued, Todd authorized a guarantee on a note in the name of the corporation. A default occurred and Crosland failed to honor its guarantee. Todd was personally liable on the guarantee.[30]

After a corporation is dissolved, a contract made by an officer of the dissolved corporation cannot be enforced against the other party to the contract. **For Example,** a lucrative contract with Florio Entertainment, Inc., was signed "Louis Lofredo, LL Associates as company president" using a letterhead "LL Associates, Inc." In fact, the corporation "LL Associates, Inc." had been dissolved years before the contract was negotiated and signed, and Lofredo had made no effort to reinstate the corporation. LL Associates, Inc., had no legal existence and thus could not be a party to the contract and could not enforce the contract.[31]

A corporation whose powers are suspended for nonpayment of taxes cannot sue or defend a lawsuit while its taxes remain unpaid.[32]

13. Judicial Dissolution

Judicial dissolution of a corporation may be decreed when its management is deadlocked and the deadlock cannot be broken by the shareholders.[33] In

[28] RMBCA § 2.04.

[29] RMBCA § 14.20.

[30] *Murphy v Crosland*, 915 P2d 491 (Utah 1996). But see *L-Tec Electronics Corp. v Cougar Electronic Org. Inc.*, 198 F3d 85 (2d Cir 1999), where it was held that reinstatement of corporation relieved officers of any potential personal liability for actions taken in the corporation's name during a period when its corporate status had lapsed.

[31] *Animazing Entertainment, Inc. v Louis Lofredo Associates, Inc.*, 88 F Supp 2d 265 (SDNY 2000).

[32] *Kaufman, Inc. v Performance Plastering, Inc.*, 39 Cal Rptr 3d 33 (Cal App 2006).

[33] *In re 212 East 52nd Street Corp.*, 712 NYS2d 777 (NY Sup 2000).

FIGURE 44-1 Consolidation

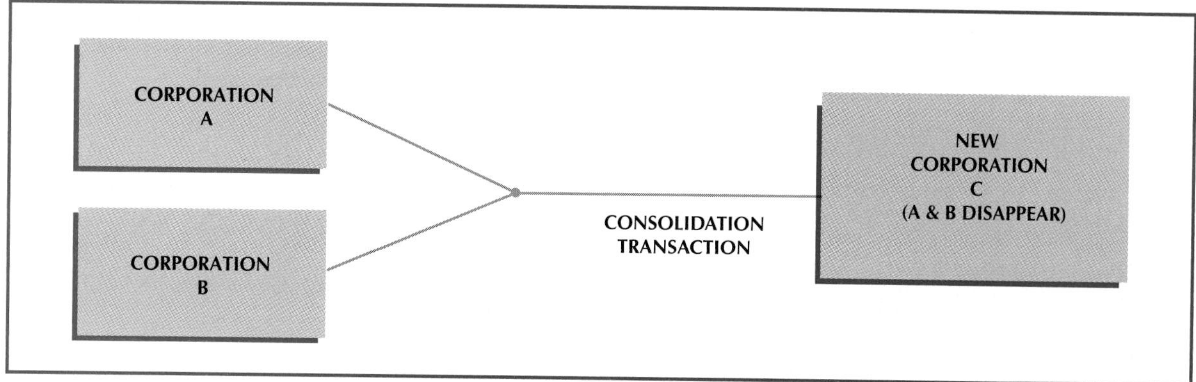

FIGURE 44-2 Merger

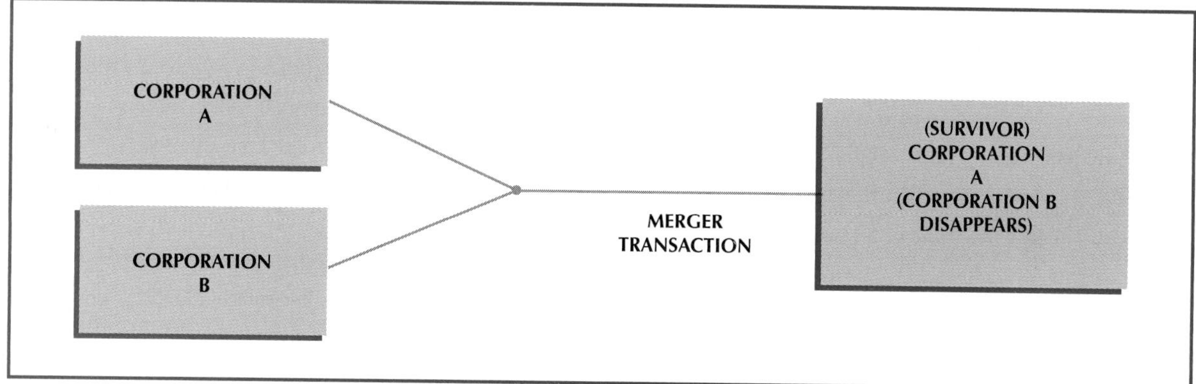

some states, a "custodian" may be appointed for a corporation when the shareholders are unable to break a deadlock in the board of directors and irreparable harm is threatened to, or sustained by, the corporation because of the deadlock.

D. Consolidations, Mergers, and Conglomerates

Two or more corporations may be combined to form a new structure or enterprise.

CPA 14. Definitions

Enterprises may be combined by a consolidation or merger of corporations or by the formation of a conglomerate.

CPA (a) Consolidation

In a **consolidation** of two or more corporations, their separate existences cease, and a new corporation with the property and assets of the old corporations comes into being (see Figure 44-1).

When a consolidation occurs, the new corporation ordinarily succeeds to the rights, powers, and immunities of its component parts. However, limitations may be imposed by constitution, statute, or certificate of incorporation.

CPA (b) Merger

When two corporations **merge**, one absorbs the other. One corporation retains its original charter and identity and continues to exist; the other disappears, and its corporate existence terminates (see Figure 44-2).

CPA ***(1) Objection of Shareholder.*** A stockholder who objects to a proposed consolidation or merger or who fails to convert existing shares into stock of the new or continuing corporation may apply to a court to appraise the value of the stock that she holds.[34] Should either party act arbitrarily,

[34] *Delaware Open MRI Radiology v Kessler*, 898 A2d 290 (Del Ch 2006).

vexatiously, or not in good faith in the appraisal process, the courts have the right to assess court costs and attorney fees. The new or continuing corporation is then required to pay the fair value of the stock to the stockholder.[35]

In the *Trapp Family Lodge, Inc.*, case, the court was called upon to decide what *fair value* means and how it applied to dissenting shareholders who objected to a merger into a new corporation.

IN RE 75,629 SHARES OF COMMON STOCK OF TRAPP FAMILY LODGE, INC., 725 A 2D 927 (VT 1999)

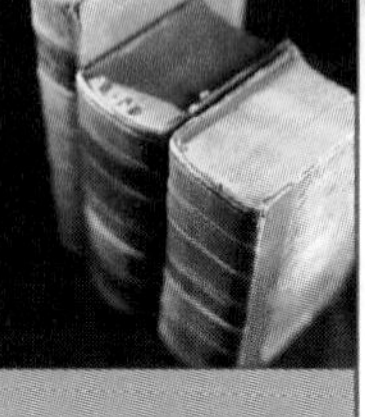

THE SOUND OF MUSIC: $63.44 PER SHARE

The Trapp Family Lodge, Inc. (TFL), was incorporated in 1962 as a holding company for certain assets of the Von Trapp family, including the Trapp Family Lodge, a resort hotel complex located in Stowe, Vermont, and other assets including certain royalty rights related to the family's story as portrayed in a Broadway musical and movie. A majority of TFL shareholders approved a merger with a new corporation in 1994, and the merger took place on January 28, 1995. The dissenting shareholders, holding 75,629 of the corporation's 198,000 outstanding shares, were paid $33.84 per share as fair value by the TFL board of directors. The dissenting shareholders brought suit seeking a higher price as fair value. After the trial court set the fair value of $63.44, TFL appealed.

Judicial Opinion

JOHNSON, J. . . . Under the statute, a shareholder of a Vermont corporation who dissents from certain enumerated corporate actions, including consummation of a plan of merger, is entitled to obtain from the corporation payment of the "fair value" of his or her shares. Section 13.01(3) defines "fair value" to mean "the value of the shares immediately before the effectuation of the corporate action to which the dissenter objects, excluding any appreciation or depreciation in anticipation of the corporate action unless exclusion would be inequitable." This definition mirrors the definition of "fair value" in the Model Business Corporation Act. See Model Bus. Corp. Act § 13.01 (1978). The official comment to the Model Act indicates that this broad definition "leaves untouched the accumulated case law" on the various methods of determining fair value.

Dissenters' rights statutes were enacted in response to the common-law rule that required unanimous consent from shareholders to make fundamental changes in a corporation. See *Hansen v 75 Ranch Co.*, 957 P.2d 32, 37 (Mont.1998). Under this rule, minority shareholders could block corporate change by refusing to cooperate in hopes of establishing a nuisance value for their shares. In response, legislatures enacted statutes authorizing corporate changes by majority vote. See *Hansen*, 957 P.2d at 37. To protect the interests of minority shareholders, the statutes generally permitted a dissenting minority to recover the appraised value of its shares. Most recent statutes allow dissenting shareholders to demand that the corporation buy back shares at fair value.

The basic concept of fair value under a dissenters' rights statute is that the stockholder is entitled to be paid for his or her "proportionate interest in a going concern." *Weinberger v UOP, Inc.*, 457 A.2d 701, 713 (Del.1983); accord *In re Valuation of Common Stock of McLoon Oil Co.*, 565 A.2d 997, 1004 (Me.1989); *Friedman v Beway Realty Corp.*, 87 N.Y.2d 161, 638 N.Y.S.2d 399, 661 N.E.2d 972, 976 (1995). The focus of the valuation "is not the stock as a commodity, but rather the stock only as it represents a proportionate part of the enterprise as a whole." *McLoon Oil*, 565 A.2d at 1004. Thus, to find fair value, the trial court must determine the best price a single buyer could reasonably be expected to pay for the corporation as an entirety and prorate this value equally among all shares of its common stock. See *id.* Under this method, all shares of the corporation have the same fair value. See *id.*

[35] *Martin v Martin Brothers Container Corp.*, 241 F Supp 2d 815 (ND Ohio 2003).

A dissenting shareholder is not in the position of a willing seller, however, and thus, courts have held that fair value cannot be equated with "fair market value." See, e.g., *McLoon Oil*, 565 A.2d at 1005; *Hansen*, 957 P.2d at 41. Accordingly, methods of stock valuation used in tax, probate or divorce cases to determine fair market value are inapposite to the determination of "fair value" under the dissenters' rights statute. A shareholder who disapproves of a proposed merger gives up the right of veto in exchange for the right to be bought out at "fair value," not at market value. See *Hansen*, 957 P.2d at 41.

Finally, a fair-value determination is "necessarily a fact-specific process."...

...The dissenters' expert, Gordon, a certified financial analyst, conducted his appraisal using a net-asset-value approach; he used different methods to arrive at the values for individual assets, which were the lodge, the guest house option, the other guest house subsidiary assets, the royalties, and the excess land. Gordon used two methods to determine the value of the lodge. First, he used a discounted-cashflow method; the value of the lodge added to the value of TFL's other assets resulted in a share value of $64.00. Second, Gordon recalculated the net assets value using a prior real estate appraisal by Frank Bredice for the lodge; the Bredice value of the lodge added to the other TFL assets resulted in a share value of $62.67. Averaging these results, Gordon determined that the fair value of TFL was $63.44 per share.

TFL's expert, Haut, a certified public accountant, separated TFL's assets into three separate groups: the lodge facility and related operations, the excess land, and the guest house option...Haut valued TFL in its entirety at $6,700,000, which yields a per share value of $33.84.

The trial court held that the fair value of TFL was $63.44 per share, as established by Gordon. The court rejected Haut's appraisal for several reasons, including (1) Haut's valuation lacked the thoroughness and credibility of Gordon's valuation and the Bredice appraisal, (2) Haut unreasonably assumed TFL's earnings would not grow, (3) Haut valued the lodge operations at $7,300,000 in 1992, $7,000,000 in 1993, but then at only $4,748,000 for 1994, and (4) Haut overstated income taxes reducing after-tax cashflows.

We conclude...that the trial court's finding setting the fair value of TFL's stock at $63.44 is supported by the evidence and is not clearly erroneous....

TFL next contends that the trial court erred as a matter of law by refusing to consider certain "agreed values" determined pursuant to a shareholders' restriction agreement. Under the agreement, a shareholder who desired to transfer shares to anyone other than ascendants or lineal descendants was required to offer the shares first to TFL. If TFL declined to purchase them, then the shareholder was required to offer the shares to the remaining shareholders. The purchase price for the shares was determined by an "agreed value" established by the stockholders of at least seventy-five percent of the outstanding shares. In the absence of an "agreed value," the stock price was set by "book value" calculated pursuant to the procedures in the agreement. The agreed value under the stock restriction agreement for 1992 was $28.78 and for 1993 was $30.92. The trial court found that the agreed values were based upon the fair market value for minority interest shares and were not timely representations of the "fair value" of the shares in January 1995. TFL claims it was reversible error to accord no weight to the "agreed values."

In close corporations, "shareholders' agreements restricting the manner in which shareholders may dispose of their shares are quite common." *Hansen*, 957 P.2d at 37. Such an agreement does not apply, however, to a fair value determination pursuant to the dissenters' rights statute unless the agreement so provides....The shareholders' objective in establishing an agreed value for voluntary sale of shares may be very different than the court's objective in determining fair value in a dissenters' rights case.

Similarly, the restriction agreement here is not applicable because it did not contemplate establishing share values for a corporate merger. Moreover, the agreed values for 1992 and 1993 were not indicative of the fair value in January 1995 because they were untimely in the sense that they were no longer in effect, and because they were based on fair market value of a minority interest. The court weighed these factors and was not persuaded that the agreed values provided any basis for the fair value in January 1995. It was within the court's discretion to determine the weight to be given any particular evidence....

[Affirmed]

Questions

1. Why were dissenters' rights statutes enacted?
2. What does "fair value" mean, and how is it determined?
3. Do you believe that TFL's expert attempted to fairly value the stock, or did he simply draft figures to support what the corporation asserted was fair value, $33.84? Is this ethical? How does it square with his oath as a witness to "tell the whole truth"?

(2) Origin of Plan. In some cases, the plan to merge or consolidate originates within the corporations involved. In other cases, it originates with an outside investor. In that situation, the transaction is frequently called a *two-step merger*. First, an outside investor purchases control of the majority shares of the target corporation. Then this newly acquired control is used to arrange for the target and a second corporation controlled by the outside investor to merge.

Statutes commonly regulate mergers and consolidations by requiring disclosure of the details a stated number of days before any action can be taken. The purpose of these statutes is not to prohibit or restrain mergers and consolidations but only to make certain that all stockholders are fully informed about the nature and effect of the proposed action.

(c) Conglomerate

Conglomerate describes the relationship of a parent corporation to subsidiary corporations engaged in diversified fields of activity unrelated to the parent corporation's field of activity. **For Example,** a wire-manufacturing corporation that owns all stock of a newspaper corporation and of a drug-manufacturing corporation would be described as a conglomerate. In contrast, if the wire-manufacturing company owned a mill that produced the metal used in making the wire and a mine that produced the ore that was used by the mill, the relationship would probably be described as an *integrated industry* rather than as a conglomerate. This term is merely a matter of usage rather than of legal definition. Likewise, when the parent company is not engaged in production or the rendering of services, it is customary to call it a *holding company*.

Without regard to whether the enterprise is a holding company or whether the group of corporations constitutes a conglomerate or an integrated industry, each part is a distinct corporation to which ordinary corporation law applies. In some instances, additional principles apply because of the nature of the relationships existing among the several corporations involved.

15. Legality

Consolidations, mergers, and asset acquisitions between enterprises are prohibited by federal antitrust legislation when the effect is to lessen competition in interstate commerce. A business corporation may not merge with a charitable corporation because this combination would divert the assets of the respective corporations to purposes not intended by their shareholders.

16. Liability of Successor Corporations

When corporations are combined in any way, the question of who is liable for the debts and obligations of the predecessor corporation arises.

(a) Mergers and Consolidations

Generally, the enterprise engaging in or continuing the business after a merger or consolidation succeeds to all of the rights and property of the predecessor, or disappearing, corporation.[36] The enterprise continuing the business is also subject to all of the debts and liabilities of the predecessor corporation.[37]

ETHICS & THE LAW

Mo Siegel founded Celestial Seasonings Tea Company in the late 1960s. Mr. Siegel gathered herbs from around Aspen and put together a line of herbal teas that were sold only in health food stores initially. The teas grew in popularity, and by 1982, Celestial enjoyed a dominant position in the international market. Celestial was known for its freewheeling approach in managing employees, and Mr. Siegel was famous for developing new ideas and products while lunching with employees, who were given free hot lunches as part of their jobs.

In 1984, Kraft Foods approached Mr. Siegel about purchasing the privately held Celestial for

[36] *Corporate Express Office Products, Inc. v Phillips*, 847 So 2d 406 (Fla 2003).

[37] *Beck v Roper Whitney, Inc.*, 190 F Supp 2d 524 (WDNY 2001).

ETHICS & THE LAW

continued

$40 million. Mr. Siegel accepted the offer and retired as president of Celestial. The new Kraft management team ended the Rocky Mountain casual approach to corporate management and terminated birthday bonuses, required drug testing of all employees, and assigned parking spaces. Barney Feinblum, Siegel's vice president of finance and president of Celestial under Kraft, was unhappy with the changes Kraft implemented and the "big-time corporate structure" Kraft demanded. The disagreements in philosophies resulted in new products that flopped and problems with sales and marketing of the original herbal teas.

Feinblum made an offer to Kraft to buy back Celestial. Kraft refused, and Thomas J. Lipton made an offer to purchase the company. A competitor stopped the combination of the Lipton tea giant with the giant of herbal teas. Feinblum made another offer to Kraft, and Kraft accepted Feinblum's $60 million offer. Siegel returned as president, and the company was forced to "go public" with two stock offerings in 1993 and 1994 totaling $38 million to pay back the debt to Kraft. Today, Celestial holds about 54 percent of the herbal tea market but has had trouble breaking into the bottled iced tea market, the industry's growth area.

Trace the history of Celestial's ownership. Explain the takeovers and relationships among Kraft, Lipton, and Celestial. What are the ethical issues in taking over a company like Celestial? What are the management problems in taking over a company like Celestial?

Liabilities of predecessor corporations can be imposed on a successor corporation when the transaction is a de facto merger[38] or the successor is a mere continuation of the predecessor. **For Example,** Steven Stepp manufactured pleasure boats through Thoroughbred Power Boats, Inc., until August 1996 at which time Thoroughbred, Inc., ceased manufacturing and selling boats. In August 1996, Velocity Power Boats, Inc., began manufacturing and selling pleasure boats at the same location. Stephen Stepp and his wife were the only officers and board members of both corporations. Finding that Velocity is merely a "new hat" for Thoroughbred, Inc., with the same or similar management and ownership, Velocity Boats, Inc., was held liable as a successor corporation for damages for a May 6, 1995, boating accident caused by a defective Thoroughbred, Inc., manufactured boat.[39]

(b) Asset Sales

In contrast with a merger or consolidation, a corporation may merely purchase the assets of another business. In that case, the purchaser does not become liable for the obligations of the predecessor business. **For Example,** Hull Corporation sold one of its operating divisions to SP Industries, Inc. (SPI) for $6 million under an asset purchase agreement (APA) that stated that the buyer SPI assumed no liability for preclosing claims against Hull. In fact as Hull and SPI were negotiating the APA, Hull was having difficulties regarding engineering and installation work the division had performed in China for Berg Chilling Systems, Inc. Berg Chilling sued SPI under the doctrine of successor liability for the payment of a $1,650,000 arbitration award because of the defective work done by Hull in China. The court held that SPI did not assume Hull's contractual liability to Berg Chilling under any exception to the traditional corporate rule of successor nonliability.[40]

Corporations may seek to avoid liability for the obligations of a predecessor corporation by attempting to disguise a consolidation or merger as being merely a sale of assets. Courts will not recognize such a sham and will impose a successor's liability on the successor corporation.[41]

[38] *Ulanet v D'Artagnan, Inc.*, 170 F Supp 2d 356 (EDNY 2001); see *Callahan & Sons, Inc. v Dykeman Electric Co. Inc.*, 2003 WL 21356450 (D Mass).

[39] *Paten v Thoroughbred Power Boats, Inc.*, 2002 US App LEXIS 11382 (5th Cir 2002).

[40] *Berg Chilling Systems Inc. v Hull Corp.*, 435 F3d 455 (3rd Cir 2006).

[41] *State v Westwood Squibb Pharmaceutical Co., Inc.*, 981 F Supp 760 (WDNY 1997).

LAWFLIX

Barbarians at the Gate (1996) (R)

In this movie that focuses on the law and ethics of takeovers, you can see the manipulation that occurs and the impact greed has on the companies themselves.

For movie clips that illustrate business law concepts, see LawFlix at **http://www.westbuslaw.com.**

Summary

A *corporation* is an artificial person created by government action. It exists as a separate and distinct entity possessing certain powers. In most states, the corporation comes into existence when the secretary of state issues a certificate of incorporation. The most common forms of corporations are private business corporations whose stock is sold to the public (publicly held) and close corporations, which are business firms whose shares are not traded publicly. Corporations may be formed for purposes other than conducting a business. For example, there are nonprofit corporations, municipal corporations, and public authorities for governmental purposes.

An *ultra vires* act occurs when a corporation acts beyond the scope of the powers given it. Because states now grant broad powers to corporations, it is unlikely that a modern corporation would act beyond the scope of its powers.

A *promoter* is a person who brings together the persons interested in the enterprise and sets in motion all that must be done to form a corporation. A corporation is not liable on contracts made by its promoter for the corporation unless it adopts the contracts. The promoter is personally liable for contracts made for the corporation before its existence. A promoter stands in a fiduciary relation to the corporation and stockholders.

The procedures for incorporation are set forth in the statutes of each state. In most states, the corporation comes into existence on issuance of the certificate of incorporation. When all requirements have been satisfied, the corporation is a corporation de jure. When there has not been full compliance with all requirements for incorporation, a de facto corporation may be found to exist. Or when sufficient compliance for a de facto corporation does not exist, in some jurisdictions a third person may be estopped from denying the legal existence of the "corporation" with which it did business (corporation by estoppel).

A corporation has the power to continue as an entity forever or for a stated period of time regardless of changes in the ownership of the stock or the death of a shareholder. It may make contracts, issue stocks and bonds, borrow money, execute commercial paper, transfer and acquire property, acquire its own stock if it is solvent and the purchase does not impair capital, and make charitable contributions. Subject to limitations, a corporation has the power to do business in other states. A corporation may also participate in a business enterprise to the same extent as an individual; that is, it may be a partner in a partnership, or it may enter a joint venture or other enterprise. Special service corporations, such as banks, insurance companies, and railroads, are subject to separate statutes governing their organization and powers.

Two or more corporations may be combined to form a new enterprise. This combination may be a consolidation, with a new corporation coming into existence, or a merger, in which one corporation absorbs the other.

Questions and Case Problems

1. Edwin Edwards and Karen Davis owned EEE, Inc., which owned three convenience stores, all of which sold gasoline. Reid Ellis delivered to the three convenience stores $26,675.02 worth of gasoline for which he was not paid. Ellis proved that Edwards and Davis owned the business, ran it, and in fact personally ordered the gasoline. He claimed that they were personally liable for the debt owed him by EEE, Inc. Decide. [*Ellis v Edwards*, 348 SE2d 764 (Ga App)]
2. Graham and Black were each 50 percent shareholders of a building supply business. When Graham filed a petition to dissolve the corporation under RMBCA § 14.30, the court appointed a custodian with full powers to run the corporation's day-to-day operations. Subsequently, the

court concluded that Black and Graham functioned as directors, they were deadlocked within the meaning of RMBCA § 14.30(2)(1), and adequate grounds existed to dissolve the corporation because of the lack of cooperation between Black and Graham and its probable irreparable harm to the business. The court entered an order directing that within one week of receiving an expected appraisal, each would submit a sealed bid in writing for the other's stock. The custodian was to accept the high bid, and the purchaser was to immediately tender the purchase price. In the event that neither stockholder made a bona fide offer, the custodian would be redesignated the receiver and proceed to dissolve the corporation (RMBCA § 14.32 [c]-[e]). The sale was unsuccessful, and by subsequent order, the court converted the custodianship into a receivership, directing that the receiver wind up and liquidate the business affairs of the corporation. Black did not believe that the successful business should be liquidated, and he directed his attorney to appeal. Decide. [*Black v Graham*, 464 SE2d 814 (Ga)]

3. Compare and contrast consolidations, mergers, and conglomerates.
4. On January 27, 1982, Joe Walker purchased a wheel-loader machine from Thompson & Green Machinery Co. (T&G). Walker signed a promissory note for $37,886.30 on behalf of "Music City Sawmill, Inc., by Joe Walker, President." When Sawmill was unable to make payments on the loader, the machine was returned to T&G. T&G brought suit against Sawmill and subsequently discovered that Sawmill had not been incorporated on January 27, 1982, when the machine was purchased but had been incorporated the next day. T&G then sued Walker individually. The lawsuit was Walker's first notice that Sawmill was not incorporated on the date of the sale. Walker's defense was that T&G dealt with Sawmill as a corporation and did not intend to bind him personally on the note and therefore was estopped to deny Sawmill's corporate existence. Decide based on the 1969 MBCA. What would be the result if the RMBCA applied? [*Thompson & Green Machinery Co. v Music City Lumber Co., Inc., Music City Sawmill Co., Inc.*, 683 SW2d 340 (Tenn App)]
5. North Pole, Inc., approved a plan to merge with its subsidiary, Santa's Workshop, Inc. The merger plan provided that certain of Workshop's shareholders would receive $3.50 per share. The highest independent appraisal of the stock was $4.04 per share. Hirschfeld, Inc., a shareholder, claimed the fair value was $16.80 per share. Workshop offered to make its corporate books and records available to Hirschfeld to assess the validity of the $16.80 demand. This offer was declined. Hirschfeld did not attempt to base the $16.80 demand on any recognizable method of stock valuation. Hirschfeld contended it had a right to get the asking price. Refer to RMBCA §§ 13.02, 13.28, and 13.31. Could Hirschfeld have blocked the merger until Workshop paid the $16.80? Decide. [*Santa's Workshop v Hirschfeld, Inc.*, 851 P2d 264 (Colo App)]
6. Norman was organizing a new corporation: Collins Home Construction Co. Fairchild knew the corporation was not yet formed but made a contract by which he agreed to sell certain goods to Collins. The corporation was later organized and ratified the contract that Norman had made with Fairchild. Fairchild, however, did not perform the contract and was sued by Collins. Fairchild raised the defense that he had never made any contract with Collins and that a corporation that did not exist could not have made a contract. Were these defenses valid?
7. Morris Gray leased waterfront property on the Ross Barnett Reservoir to a restaurant, Edgewater Landing, Inc., for a ten-year term. After a year and a half, Edgewater's original shareholder, Billy Stegall, sold all of his shares in the corporation to Tom Bradley and Bradley's bookkeeper, Sandra Martin. Gray visited the property in the ninth year of the lease and found many problems with the condition of the property. He claimed that the lease required the tenant to make necessary repairs. Gray sued Edgewater Landing, Inc., and Tom Bradley and Sandra Martin individually for breach of the lease. Bradley and Martin replied that they were not liable for the debt of the corporation. Decide. [*Gray v Edgewater Landing, Inc.*, 541 So 2d 1044 (Miss)]
8. Emick was a director and shareholder of Colonial Manors, Inc. (CM). He organized another corporation named Oahe Enterprises, Inc. To obtain shares of the Oahe stock, Emmick transferred CM shares arbitrarily valued by him at $19 per share to Oahe. The CM shares had a book value of $.47 per share, but Emmick believed that the stock would increase to a value of $19. The directors of Oahe approved Emmick's payment with the valuation of $19 per share. Golden sued Emmick on the ground that he had fraudulently deceived Oahe Corp. about the value of the CM shares and thus had made a secret profit when he received the Oahe shares that had a much greater value than the CM shares he gave in exchange. Emmick contended that his firm opinion was that the future potential value of CM shares would surely reach $19 per share. Decide. [*Golden v Oahe Enterprises, Inc.*, 295 NW2d 160 (SD)]
9. Madison Associates purchased control of the majority of shares of 79 Realty Corp. from the Kimmelmans and the Zauders, who then resigned as directors. The Alpert group, which owned the remaining 26 percent of 79 Realty refused to sell their shares. Partners of Madison Associates replaced the Kimmelmans and Zauders as directors of 79 Realty Corp., and as controlling directors, they approved a plan to merge 79 Realty Corp. with the Williams Street Corp., which was owned by Madison

Associates. A shareholders' meeting was called, and the merger was approved by two-thirds of the shareholders. The Alpert group's shares were then forcibly canceled, with the price paid for these shares determined at their fair market value. The Alpert group brought suit contending the merger was unlawful because the sole purpose was to benefit the Madison Associates. Decide. [*Alpert v 28 Williams Street Corp.*, 473 NE2d 19 (NY)]

10. The Seabrook Island Property Owners Association, Inc., is a nonprofit corporation organized under state law to maintain streets and open spaces owned by property owners of Seabrook Island. Seabrook Island Co. is the developer of Seabrook Island and has majority control of the board of directors of the association. The association's bylaws empower the board of directors to levy an annual maintenance charge. Neither the association's charter nor its bylaws authorize the board to assess any other charges. When the board levied, in addition to the annual maintenance charge, an emergency budget assessment on all members to rebuild certain bridges and to revitalize the beach, the Loverings and other property owners challenged in court the association's power to impose the assessment. Decide. [*Lovering v Seabrook Island Property Owners Ass'n*, 344 SE2d 862 (SC App)]

11. Adams and two other persons were promoters for a new corporation, Aldrehn Theaters Co. The promoters retained Kridelbaugh to perform legal services in connection with the incorporation of the new business and promised to pay him $1,500. Aldrehn was incorporated through Kridelbaugh's services, and the promoters became its only directors. Kridelbaugh attended a meeting of the board of directors at which he was told that he should obtain a permit for the corporation to sell stock because the directors wished to pay him for his previous services. The promoters failed to pay Kridelbaugh, and he sued the corporation. Was the corporation liable? [*Kridelbaugh v Aldrehn Theaters Co.*, 191 NW 803 (Iowa)]

12. On August 19, 1980, Joan Ioviero injured her hand when she slipped and fell while leaving the dining room at the Hotel Excelsior in Venice, Italy. This hotel was owned by an Italian corporation, Cigahotels, S.p.A. (The designation *S.p.A.* stands for *Societa per Azionean*, the Italian term for *corporation*.) In 1973, a firm called Ciga Hotels, Inc., was incorporated in New York. Its certificate of incorporation was amended in 1979, changing the name of the firm to Landia International Services, Inc. This New York corporation was employed by the Italian corporation Cigahotels, S.p.A., to provide sales and promotional services in the United States and Canada. Ioviero sought to hold the New York corporation liable for her hand injury at the Venice hotel. She pointed to the similarity of the first corporate name used by the New York firm to the name Cigahotels, S.p.A., and the fact that the New York firm represented the interests of the Italian firm in the United States as clear evidence that the two firms were the same single legal entity. She asked that the court disregard the separate corporate entities. The New York corporation moved that the case be dismissed because it was duly incorporated in New York and did not own the Excelsior Hotel in which Ioviero was injured. Decide. [*Ioviero v CigaHotel, Inc., aka Landia I.S., Inc.*, 475 NYS2d 880 (App Div)]

13. William Sullivan was ousted from the presidency of the New England Patriots Football Club, Inc. Later, he borrowed $5,348,000 to buy 100 percent control of the voting shares of the corporation. A condition of the loan was that he reorganize the Patriots so that the income from the corporation could be devoted to repayment of the personal loan and the team's assets could be used as collateral. Sullivan, therefore, arranged for a cash freeze-out merger of the holders of the 120,000 shares of nonvoting stock. David Coggins, who owned 10 shares of nonvoting stock and took special pride in the fact that he was an owner of the team, refused the $15-a-share buyout and challenged the merger in court. He contended that the merger was not for a legitimate corporate purpose but to enable Sullivan to satisfy his personal loan. Sullivan contended that legitimate business purposes were given in the merger proxy statement, such as the National Football League's policy of discouraging public ownership of teams. Coggins responded that before the merger, Sullivan had 100 percent control of the voting stock and thus control of the franchise, and that no legal basis existed to eliminate public ownership. Decide. [*Coggins v New England Patriots Football Club*, 492 NE2d 1112 (Mass)]

CPA Questions

1. Which of the following statements is correct concerning the similarities between a limited partnership and a corporation?

   a. Each is created under a statute and must file a copy of its certificate with the proper state authorities.

   b. All corporate stockholders and all partners in a limited partnership have limited liability.

   c. Both are recognized for federal income tax purposes as taxable entities.

   d. Both are allowed statutorily to have perpetual existence.

2. Rice is a promoter of a corporation to be known as Dex Corp. On January 1, 1985, Rice signed a nine-month contract with Roe, a CPA, which provided that Roe would perform certain accounting services for Dex. Rice did not disclose to Roe that Dex had not been formed. Prior to the incorporation of Dex on February 1, 1985, Roe rendered accounting services pursuant to the contract. After rendering accounting services for an additional period of six months pursuant to the contract, Roe was discharged without cause by the board of directors of Dex. In the absence of any agreements to the contrary, who will be liable to Roe for breach of contract?

   a. Both Rice and Dex
   b. Rice only
   c. Dex only
   d. Neither Rice nor Dex

3. In general, which of the following must be contained in articles of incorporation?

   a. The names of the states in which the corporation will be doing business
   b. The name of the state in which the corporation will maintain its principal place of business
   c. The names of the initial officers and their terms of office
   d. The classes of stock authorized for issuance

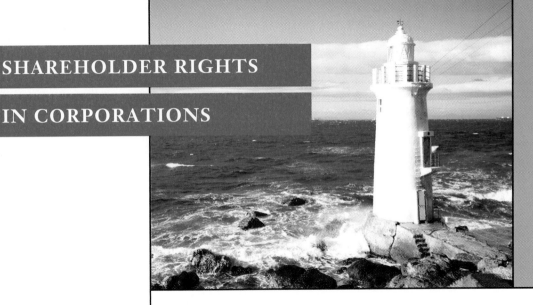

SHAREHOLDER RIGHTS IN CORPORATIONS

CHAPTER (45)

LEARNING OBJECTIVES

After studying this chapter, you should be able to

LO.1 Distinguish between subscriptions for stock and transfers of stock

LO.2 Describe the mechanics of transferring stock

LO.3 Describe the rights of shareholders

LO.4 State the exceptions to the limited liability of shareholders

LO.5 Distinguish between stocks and bonds

The two most common instruments used to provide funds for a corporation are stocks and bonds.

A. Corporate Stocks and Bonds

Ownership of a corporation is represented by stock. A *bond* is a corporate debt.

1. Nature of Stock

An interest in a corporation is based on ownership of one or more shares of stock of the corporation. Each share represents a fractional interest in the total property of the corporation. The shareholder does not own or have an interest in any specific property of the corporation; the corporation is the owner of all of its property. The terms *share*, *stock*, and *share of stock* mean the same thing.

(a) Capital and Capital Stock

Capital refers to the net assets of the corporation. Shares that have been issued to holders are said to be **outstanding. Capital stock** refers to the value received by the corporation for its outstanding stock.

(b) Valuation of Stock

Corporate stock may have a specified **par value.** This means that the person subscribing to the stock and acquiring it from the corporation must pay that amount.

Shares may be issued with no par value. In that case, no amount is stated in the certificate, and the amount that the subscriber pays the corporation is determined by the board of directors. The Revised Model Business Corporation Act (RMBCA) eliminates the concept of par value, so stock issued by corporations in states following the RMBCA is always no par.

The value found by dividing the value of the net corporate assets by the number of shares outstanding is the **book value** of the shares. **For Example,** Roger Eggett entered a Shareholder Agreement in 1995 with Todd Cusick and Curtis Chisholm, forming the Wasatch Energy Corporation. The terms of the Shareholder Agreement provided that should a shareholder separate from the corporation, the remaining shareholders would have the option to purchase that shareholder's corporate stock. The remaining shareholders, as per the Shareholder Agreement, would either purchase the stock for book value, if the separating shareholder voluntarily left the corporation, or for par value if the shareholder was terminated for cause. The Shareholder Agreement defined *book value* as the shareholder's net equity in the corporation, which would be determined by Wasatch's certified year-end financial statements. The Shareholder Agreement defined *par value* as the original price the shareholder paid for the stock. Egget tendered his resignation two years later, and offered to sell his stock according to the Shareholder Agreement "for the audited book value of the corporation as of June 30, 1997 divided by the number of shares he owned." Wasatch Corp. responded by firing Egget, wrongly asserting the firing was for cause, and tendered him a check for the par value of his stock, \$1,217, Eggett's original investment. Eggett sued and was awarded the book value of his shares, \$135,671, plus \$60,000 in attorney fees.[1] The **market value** of a share of stock is the

[1] *Eggett v Wasatch Energy Corp.*, 29 P3d 668 (Utah App 2001).

price at which that stock can be voluntarily bought or sold in the open market.

2. Certificates of Stock and Uncertificated Shares

A corporation ordinarily issues a **certificate of stock** or *share certificate* as evidence of the shareholder's ownership of stock. The issuance of such certificates is not essential either to the existence of a corporation or to the ownership of its stock.

In states that have adopted the 1978 and 1994 amendments to Article 8 of the UCC, uncertificated shares may be issued. Uncertificated shares are not represented by instruments. Their ownership and transfer are registered on the books maintained by, or on behalf of, the issuer corporation.[2]

3. Kinds of Stock

The stock of a corporation may be divided into two or more classes.

CPA (a) Classification by Preferences

Common stock is ordinary stock that has no preferences. Each share usually entitles the holder to have one vote, to receive a share of the profits in the form of dividends when declared, and to participate in the distribution of capital upon dissolution of the corporation. **Preferred stock** has a priority over common stock. The priority may be with respect to either dividends or the distribution of capital upon dissolution of the corporation, or both. Preferred stock is ordinarily nonvoting.

CPA ***(1) Cumulative Preferred Stock.*** The right to receive dividends depends on the declaration of dividends by the board of directors for a particular period of time. If there is no fund from which the dividends may be declared or if the directors do not declare them from an available fund, the shareholder has no right to dividends. The fact that a shareholder has not received dividends for the current year does not in itself give the right to accumulate or carry over into the next year a claim for those dividends. However, in the absence of a statement that the right to dividends is noncumulative, courts frequently hold that preferred stock has the right to accumulate dividends for each year in which there was a surplus available for dividend payment but dividends were not declared.

CPA ***(2) Participating Preferred Stock.*** Sometimes the preferred stock is given the right of participation. If it is, then after the common shares receive dividends or a capital distribution is made equal to that first received by the preferred stock, both kinds participate or share equally in the balance.

(b) Duration of Shares

Ordinarily, shares continue to exist for the life of the corporation. However, any kind of share, whether common or preferred, may be made terminable at an earlier date.

(c) Fractional Shares

A corporation may issue fractional shares or scrip or certificates representing fractional shares. These can be sold or combined for the acquisition of whole shares.

4. Characteristics of Bonds

A **bond** is an instrument promising to repay a loan of money to a corporation. Typically, the loan is for a relatively long period of time, generally five years or longer. A bond obligates the corporation to pay the bondholder the amount of the loan, called the *principal,* at a stated time, called the **maturity date,** and to pay a fixed amount of *interest at* regular intervals, commonly every six months. The relationship between the bondholder and the issuing corporation is that of creditor and debtor. Unlike dividends, which are discretionary, bond interest must be paid. A bond may be secured by a mortgage or lien on corporate property. A **debenture** is an unsecured bond of the corporation with no specific corporate assets pledged as security for payment.

Bonds are negotiable securities.[3] Bonds held by owners whose names and addresses are registered on the books of the corporation are called **registered bonds.**

5. Terms and Control

The contractual terms of a particular bond issue are set forth in an agreement called a **bond indenture** or **deed.** An **indenture trustee,** usually a commercial

[2] UCC § 8-102(1)(b). The 1978 and 1994 amendments to Article 8 of the UCC have been adopted in all of the states except Alabama.
[3] UCC § 8-105.

banking institution, represents the interests of the bondholders in making sure that the corporation meets the terms and covenants of the bond issue.[4] For example, the terms of the bond indenture may require a **sinking fund,** by which the borrowing corporation is required to set aside a fixed amount of money each year toward the ultimate payment of the bonds. The indenture trustee makes certain that such terms are complied with in accordance with its responsibilities set forth in the bond indenture.

Bondholders do not vote for directors or have the right to vote on matters on which shareholders vote. However, when the debt is risky, it is highly likely that significant restraints on the corporation's freedom of action will be imposed by the terms of the indenture.

B. Acquisition of Shares

Shares may be acquired from the corporation or from an existing shareholder.

6. Nature of Acquisition

Shares of stock may be acquired (1) from the corporation by subscription, either before or after the corporation is organized, or (2) by transfer of existing shares from a shareholder or from the corporation. The transfer may be voluntary, as by a sale, gift, or bequest by will, or involuntary, as by an execution sale to pay the judgment of a creditor. The transfer may also take place by operation of law—as when the stock of a shareholder passes to the shareholder's trustee in bankruptcy.

7. Statute of Frauds

Under the 1978 version of Article 8, a contract for the sale of corporate shares must be evidenced by a writing, or it cannot be enforced.[5] The writing must show that there has been a contract for the sale of a stated quantity of described securities at a defined or stated price. The writing must be signed in the manner required by the statute of frauds for the sale of goods. The 1994 version of Article 8 renders the statute of frauds inapplicable to contracts for the sale or purchase of securities.[6] The commentary notes explain that the 1978 statute's potential for filtering out fraudulent claims is outweighed by the obstacles the statute presents to the development of modern commercial practices in the securities business.

No writing is required for a contract by which a broker agrees with a customer to buy or sell securities for the customer. That is an agency agreement, not a sale made between the customer and the broker.

8. Subscription

A **stock subscription** is a contract or an agreement to buy a specific number and kind of shares when the corporation issues them. As in the case of any other contract, the agreement to subscribe to shares of a corporation may be avoided for fraud.

(a) Subscription before Incorporation

In many states, a preincorporation subscription of shares is an offer to the corporation. According to this view, it is necessary for the corporation to accept the subscription offer either expressly or by conduct. A few states hold that subscriptions automatically become binding contracts when the organization of the corporation has been completed. In some states, the preincorporation subscription is irrevocable for a stated period. The RMBCA provides that "a subscription for shares entered into before incorporation is irrevocable for six months unless the subscription agreement provides a longer or shorter period or all the subscribers agree to revocation."[7]

(b) Subscription after Incorporation

Subscriptions may be made after incorporation. In that event, the transaction is like any other contract with the corporation. The offer of the subscription may come from the subscriber or from the corporation. In either case, there must be an **acceptance.** Upon acceptance, the subscriber immediately becomes a shareholder with all the rights, privileges, and liabilities of a shareholder even though she has not paid any of the purchase price. Moreover, the subscriber is a shareholder even though no share certificate has been issued. In contrast with a contract for immediate subscription to shares, the contract may be one for the future issue of shares. In that case,

[4] *Lorenc v CSX Corp.*, CCH Sec L Rep 95298 (WD Pa 1990).

[5] UCC § 8-319(a); *Goldfinger v Brown*, 564 NYS2d 461 (App Div 1991).

[6] UCC § 8-113.

[7] RMBCA § 6.20(a).

the contracting party has only a contract and is not a shareholder as of the formation of the contract.

9. Transfer of Shares

In the absence of a valid restriction, a shareholder may transfer shares to anyone.

(a) Restrictions on Transfer

Restrictions on the transfer of stock are valid if they are not unreasonable. It is lawful to require that the corporation or other stockholders be given the first right to purchase stock before a shareholder may sell stock to an outsider.

A provision giving a corporation the right to purchase a shareholder's shares on the death of the shareholder is valid.

A restriction on the right of a certificate's purchaser to transfer his stock is not valid unless the restriction is conspicuously noted on the certificate or the transferee had actual knowledge of the restriction. A restriction on the transfer of stock is strictly interpreted.[8]

When no restrictions exist, the issuer has a duty to register the transfer. **For Example,** Richard Jones purchased 1,000 certificated shares of International Generic Corporation (IGC) from Madison Tucker on March 30, 2007, at fair market value. Tucker properly indorsed the certificates to Jones on that date, and her signatures were duly notarized. On September 15, 2007, Jones presented the securities to IGC to register the transfer of shares and to collect dividends for the second quarter (April 1 through June 30) and the third quarter (July 1 through September 30). IGC refused to register the shares in Jones's name, believing him to be a person of questionable integrity that it did not want as an "owner" of IGC. Under either the 1978 or 1994 version of Article 8 of the UCC, it was improper for IGC to fail to register the stock that had been transferred to a bona fide purchaser, Jones.[9] No restrictions existed on the certificate, and IGC had a duty to register the transfer and was liable for its failure to do so. Jones was entitled to the dividends from the date of presentation of the stock for transfer. Prior to that date, the issuer, IGC, was entitled to treat the registered owner, Madison Tucker, as exclusively entitled to exercise the rights of ownership, including the right to dividends.[10] Thus, IGC was not liable to Jones for the second-quarter dividends. However, dividends declared after the date of presentment, which included the third-quarter dividend declared in October 2007 with a record date in October, must be paid to Jones by IGC.

(b) Interest Transferred

The transfer of shares may be absolute; that is, it may divest all ownership and make the transferee the full owner. The transfer may be of only a partial interest in the stock, or the transfer may be for security, such as when stock is pledged to secure the repayment of a loan.

10. Mechanics of Transfer

When stock is represented by a certificate, the ownership of shares is transferred by the delivery of the certificate of stock, indorsed by its owner in blank or to a specified person. Ownership may also be transferred by the delivery of the certificate accompanied by a separate assignment or power of attorney executed by the owner.[11]

A delivery from the owner of the shares directly to the transferee is not required. It can be made to an intermediary. When there is no delivery of the share certificate to anyone, however, there is no transfer of ownership of the shares.

A physical transfer of the certificate without a necessary indorsement is effective as between the parties. Thus, a gift of shares is binding even though no indorsement has been made. An indorsement is required to make the transferee a bona fide purchaser.

11. Effect of Transfer

The transfer of existing shares of stock may raise questions between the parties to the transfer and between them and the corporation.

(a) Validity of Transfer

Because a transfer of shares is a transfer of ownership, the transfer must satisfy the requirements governing any other transfer of property or agreement to transfer

[8] *Capano v Wilmington Country Club, Inc.*, 2000 Del Ch LEXIS 127.

[9] UCC § 8-401 (1978); UCC § 8-401 (1994).

[10] UCC § 8-207(1) (1978); UCC § 8-207(a) (1994).

[11] UCC § 8-309. The second alternative of a delivery of an unindorsed certificate is designed to keep the certificate clean—for example, when the transfer is for a temporary or special purpose, as in the case of a pledge of the certificate as security for a loan.

property.[12] As between the parties, a transfer may be set aside for any ground that would warrant similar relief under property law. If the transfer has been obtained by duress, the transferor may obtain a rescission of the transfer.

(b) Negotiability

Under common law, the transferee of shares of stock had no greater right than the transferor because the certificate and the shares represented by the certificate were nonnegotiable. By statute, the common law rule has been changed by imparting negotiability to certificated stock. Just as various defenses cannot be asserted against the holder in due course of a commercial paper, statutory law provides that similar defenses cannot be raised against the person acquiring the certificate in good faith and for value. Against such a person, the defense cannot be raised that the transferor did not own the shares or did not have authority to deliver the certificate or that the transfer was made in violation of a restriction on transfer not known to the person and not noted conspicuously on the certificate.

Statements sent by the issuer identifying the ownership of uncertificated securities are neither certificated securities nor negotiable instruments. Although certificated securities have the quality of negotiability, they are not commercial paper within Article 3 of the UCC.

(c) Secured Transaction

Corporate stock is frequently delivered to a creditor as security for a debt owed by the shareholder. Thus, a debtor borrowing money from a bank may deliver shares of stock to the bank as collateral security for the repayment of the loan. A broker's customer purchasing stock on margin may leave the stock in the possession of the broker as security for the payment of any balance due. The delivery of the security to the creditor is a pledge. This gives rise to a perfected security interest without any filing by the creditor. In itself, the pledge does not make the pledgee of the corporate stock the owner of the stock.

(d) Effect of Transfer on Corporation

The corporation is entitled to treat as the owner of shares the person whose name is on the corporation's books as the owner. Therefore, until there is a transfer on its books, the corporation may still treat a transferor of shares as the owner. The corporation may properly refuse to recognize a transferee when the corporation is given notice or has knowledge that the transfer is void or in breach of trust. In such a case, the corporation properly refuses to register a transfer until the rights of the parties have been determined. The corporation may also refuse to register the transfer of shares when the outstanding certificate is not surrendered to it or there is a lack of satisfactory proof that the certificate has been lost, destroyed, or stolen.

12. Lost, Destroyed, and Stolen Share Certificates

The owner of a lost, destroyed, or stolen share certificate is entitled to a replacement if the owner files a sufficient indemnity bond and requests the new certificate within a reasonable time before the issuer has notice that the original certificate has been acquired by a bona fide purchaser. **For Example,** if established by clear and convincing evidence, Linda Rosso would be entitled to the replacement of damaged jointly held stock certificates that her late husband Richard disposed of and never replaced. The court pointed out that there is a distinction between certificates issued a shareholder and the "shares" issued the shareholder. A *share* is the actual property of the shareholder while the *certificate* is merely the authentic evidence of the stockholder's ownership of shares.[13] If, after the new security is issued, a bona fide purchaser appears with the original certificate, the corporation must register a transfer of the security to that person and accept that person as the owner of the shares.

CPA C. Rights of Shareholders

The rights of shareholders stem from their status as owners.

CPA 13. Ownership Rights

Shareholder control over the corporation is indirect. Periodically (ordinarily once a year), the shareholders elect directors and by this means control the corporation. At other times, however, the shareholders have no right or power to control corporate activity so long as it is conducted within lawful channels.

[12] *Gallant v Kanterman*, 671 NYS2d 50 (App Div 1998).

[13] *Rosso v Rosso*, 701 NW2d 355 (Neb 2005).

CPA (a) Certificates of Stock

A shareholder has the right to have a properly executed certificate as evidence of ownership of shares. An exception is made when the corporation is authorized to issue uncertificated securities.

CPA (b) Transfer of Shares

Unless limited by a valid restriction, a shareholder has the right to transfer her shares. The shareholder may sell the shares at any price or transfer them as a gift. The fact that the seller sells at a price higher than the market price is not unlawful even if the seller is a director or an officer.

In the *Shoaf* case, the court considered whether a shareholder who controlled a majority of the corporation's shares had a duty to refrain from making a profit by selling his controlling stock above the market price.

SHOAF V WARLICK, 380 SE2D 865 (SC CT APP 1989)

CONTROL OF COKE-ANDERSON, S.C.: IT'S THE REAL THING, ENTITLED TO A PREMIUM

Paul Warlick Jr. was the president, chief executive officer, and a stockholder of Coca-Cola Bottling Co. of Anderson, South Carolina (Coke-Anderson). He controlled 273.5 shares of stock of the total of 480 shares of stock outstanding, including the stock of his mother, uncle, and aunt. Warlick agreed to sell this controlling interest in Coke-Anderson to Coke-Ashville for $4 million, which included a premium (difference between market and sale price) to be paid him for his controlling interest. Wayne Shoaf, a minority shareholder, brought suit against Warlick, contending that Warlick had violated his fiduciary duty to the corporation and had received an unlawful premium for the sale of the majority interest in Coke-Anderson. From a judgment for Warlick, Shoaf appealed.

Judicial Opinion

SHAW, J. . . . The issues we are asked to consider are whether Warlick had a fiduciary duty owed to the other stockholders and whether he breached this duty, and whether Warlick has a basis to claim appellants are equitably estopped from attacking his premium received for his stock.

South Carolina has long followed the general rule that corporate stock is personal property which the owner may "dispose of . . . as he sees fit." . . . Concomitantly, when selling stock, stockholders must "necessarily act for themselves, and not as trustees for other stockholders." . . . This general rule applies as well to majority shareholders:

"A dominant or majority shareholder is generally under no duty to the minority stockholders to refrain from receiving a premium upon the sale of his controlling stock."

"The law of the marketplace dictates that a shareholder who has a controlling interest in a corporation will likely be able to receive a higher price per share than a minority shareholder. *'As a general rule, nothing in the law of the courthouse prevents a majority shareholder from retaining this 'control premium.' . . . This is so even if, as is so frequently the case, the controlling shareholder is an officer or director of the corporation. . . . A shareholder, irrespective of whether he is also a director, officer, or both, may sell his shares, just as he may sell other kinds of personal property, for whatever price he can obtain, even if his shares constitute a controlling block and the price per share is enhanced by that fact.'* Further, the courts generally hold that neither the selling shareholder nor his purchaser is under an obligation to see that other shareholders are provided opportunities to sell their shares on the same favorable terms as the controlling shareholder or even to inform minority shareholders of the price and other terms of the sale of the controlling interest."

Martin v Martin, 529 So. 2d 1174 (Fla. 3d Dist. Ct. App. 1988)

[Judgment affirmed]

Questions

1. What did the plaintiff contend?
2. Can a shareholder who is also an officer and director of a corporation lawfully obtain a premium for selling controlling interest in a corporation?
3. State the general rule of law applicable to this case.

CPA 14. Right to Vote

The right to vote means the right to vote at shareholders' meetings for the election of directors and on other special matters that shareholders must vote on. **For Example,** a proposal to change the capital structure of the corporation or a proposal to sell all or substantially all assets of the corporation must be approved by the shareholders.

CPA (a) Who May Vote

Ordinarily, only shareholders of record—those common shareholders in whose name the stock appears on the books of the corporation—are entitled to vote. The board of directors may fix a date for closing the corporate books for this purpose.

CPA (b) Number of Votes

Unless there is a provision to the contrary, for each share owned, each shareholder is entitled to one vote on each matter to be voted. This procedure is called *straight voting,* and it is the normal method for shareholder voting on corporate matters. However, in the case of voting to elect directors only, **cumulative voting** is mandatory in nearly half of the states. This requirement is imposed by either state constitution or state statute. Cumulative voting is permitted by law in other states when provided for in the articles of incorporation or bylaws.

Cumulative voting is a form of voting that is designed to give proportional representation on the board of directors to minority shareholders. Under a cumulative voting plan, each shareholder has as many votes as the number of shares owned multiplied by the number of directors to be elected. A shareholder may cast all of these votes for one candidate or may divide the votes between two or more candidates. This system enables minority shareholders to cast all of their votes for a candidate who will represent their interests on the board of directors.

Under straight voting, minority shareholders would always be outvoted. **For Example,** assume that minority shareholder Susan Jones owned 400 shares of stock and majority shareholder C. J. Katz controlled the remaining 600 shares. Also assume that five directors are to be elected to the board. If straight voting were used for the election of directors, C. J., with 600 shares, would always outvote Susan's 400 shares. However, under cumulative voting, Susan would be allowed 2,000 votes (400 shares times five directors), and C. J. would be allowed 3,000 votes (600 shares times five directors). The five candidates with the highest number of votes will be elected. If Susan casts 1,000 votes for each of two directors and C. J. casts 1,000 votes for each of three directors, Susan, who owns 40 percent of the stock, is able to elect two-fifths of the board to represent her interests.

(c) Voting by Proxy

A shareholder has the right to authorize another to vote the shares owned by the shareholder. This procedure is known as **voting by proxy.** In the absence of restrictions to the contrary, any person, even someone who is not a shareholder, may act as a proxy. The authorization from the shareholder may be made by any writing.[14] The authorization is also commonly called a **proxy**.

(d) Voting Agreements and Trusts

Shareholders, as a general rule, are allowed to enter into an agreement by which they concentrate their voting strength for the purpose of electing directors or voting on any other matter.

A **voting trust** is created when by agreement a group of shareholders or all of the shareholders transfer their shares in trust to one or more persons as trustees. The trustees are authorized to vote the stock during the life of the trust agreement.[15] In general, such agreements are upheld if their object is lawful. In some jurisdictions, such trusts cannot run beyond a stated number of years. There are some signs of a relaxation as to time. Several states have abandoned all time limitations, several have extended the time limitation, and many provide for an extension or renewal of the agreement.

CPA 15. Preemptive Offer of Shares

If the capital stock of a corporation is increased, shareholders ordinarily have the **preemptive right** to subscribe to the same percentage of the new shares that their old shares represented of the former total of capital stock. This right is given to enable shareholders to maintain their relative interests in the corporation.

The existence of a preemptive right may make it impossible to conclude a transaction in which the corporation is to transfer a block of stock as consideration. Moreover, practical difficulties arise as to how stock

[14] RMBCA § 7.07.

[15] *Bettner Trust v Bettner,* 495 NE2d 194 (Ind App 1986).

should be allocated among shareholders of different classes.

The RMBCA provides that shareholders do not have preemptive rights unless the articles of incorporation provide for them.

CPA 16. Inspection of Books

A shareholder has the right to inspect the books of the shareholder's corporation. In some states, there are no limitations on this right. In most states, the inspection must be made in good faith, for proper motives, and at a reasonable time and place.[16] In many states, a shareholder must own a certain percentage of the outstanding stock of a corporation (commonly 5 percent) or must own at least one share of stock for a minimum amount of time (commonly six months) to have the right to inspect the books. A shareholder is not relegated to accepting opinions and numbers offered by a company's auditor and may employ an expert accountant of his own to review and analyze the books and records of the corporation.[17]

The purpose of inspection must be reasonably related to the shareholder's interest as a shareholder.[18] A shareholder is entitled to inspect the records to determine the financial condition of the corporation, the quality of its management, and any matters relating to rights or interests in the corporate business, such as the value of stock.[19]

The *Security First* case deals with a stockholder's right to inspect books and records when there is some credible basis to believe there is mismanagement, versus management's right to protect the corporation from indiscriminate "fishing expeditions."

SECURITY FIRST V U.S. DIE CASTING, INC., 687 A 2D 563 (DEL SUPR 1997)

. . . NO FURY LIKE A STOCKHOLDER SCORNED

U.S. Die Casting, Inc., is a closely held Ohio corporation that owns 5 percent of Security First Corporation, a Delaware Corporation, which owns an Ohio savings and loan bank. David Slyman is the president of U.S. Die and its sole stockholder. The defendant, Security First, entered into a merger agreement with Mid Am, Inc., a large regional bank holding company; and after the announcement of the merger, Security First's stock increased significantly. The merger agreement required Security First to pay a termination fee of $2 million plus third-party expenses not to exceed $250,000 contingent on the occurrence of certain events within one year after termination, should Security First pull out of the merger. The merger did not go through, and the market price for Security First stock dropped significantly. Security First gave as a reason for failing to go through with the merger "the realization that Mid Am's management philosophy and direction were fundamentally different from its own." Security First paid Mid Am $275,000 and agreed to pay an additional $2 million if a certain event occurred within a year and one-half after termination. U.S. Die submitted a written demand to Security First persuant to Section 220 to inspect all of its books and records related to the Mid Am merger and its termination. Security First refused to comply. The Court of Chancery granted U.S. Die's demand, and Security First appealed.

Judicial Opinion

VEASEY, C. J. . . . Concerning the purpose for the inspection, Slyman testified:

I would like to make my own decision as to why the merger was not completed. Telling me that it was a difference of philosophies didn't get me to understand why it was not completed. The philosophy was there prior to it. . . .

Defendant argues that the purpose which Slyman articulated at trial was insufficient and that this insufficiency is fatal. This argument must fail. Slyman's testimony

[16] RMBCA § 16.02(c); *Leary v Foley*, 884 So2d 655 (La App 2004).
[17] *Missouri v III Investments, Inc.*, 80 SW3d 855 (Mo App 2002).
[18] *Hess v Reg-Ellen Machine Tool Corp.*, 423 F3d 653 (7th Cir 2005).
[19] *Ihrig v Frontier Equity Exchange*, 128 P3d 993 (Kan App 2006).

does call into question defendant's purported reason for abrogating the Merger Agreement—namely, that "the realization that Mid Am's management philosophy and direction were fundamentally different from its own." The Court of Chancery found defendant's reason suspect. The Court stated that "[a] reasonable stockholder could conclude prudent management would have researched 'fundamental' similarities and dissimilarities of the merging company before entering the Merger Agreement."...

Defendant maintains that plaintiff failed to produce any evidence of mismanagement. This argument misses the point. In a Section 220 action, a stockholder has the burden of proof to demonstrate a proper purpose, but a stockholder is "not required to prove by a preponderance of the evidence that waste and [mis]management are actually occurring." The threshold for a plaintiff in a Section 220 case is not insubstantial. Mere curiosity or a desire for a fishing expedition will not suffice. But the threshold may be satisfied by a credible showing, through documents, logic, testimony or otherwise, that there are legitimate issues of wrongdoing.

As specific instances of misconduct, plaintiff questions defendant's payment of $275,000 to Mid Am "when Defendant never broke the Merger Agreement." Plaintiff also questions defendant's failure to request documentation from Mid Am of its expenses to justify defendant's expenditure of $275,000, which was $25,000 more than the Merger Agreement stipulated for expenses. On their face, these issues raise questions. The effect of the Vice Chancellor's conclusion after trial is that the questions remain.

Defendant also agreed to pay Mid Am $2 million contingent on the occurrences of certain events of the Termination Agreement. Pursuant to the Merger Agreement, defendant previously had agreed to pay Mid Am $2 million contingent on the same occurrences within one year. As plaintiff's counsel, in a letter dated 1/19/95 to Security First's Chairman and CEO Charles Valentine, stated "This either takes the company 'out of play' or diminishes the amount payable to the stockholders if it is sold. In either event, the agreement seems inappropriate and destructive to stockholder values.

Section 220(c) provides that "[t]he Court may, in its discretion, prescribe any limitations or conditions with reference to the inspection." While the trial court has wide latitude in determining the proper scope of inspection, it is the responsibility of the trial court to tailor the inspection to the stockholder's stated purpose. "Undergirding this discretion is a recognition that the interests of the corporation must be harmonized with those of the inspecting stockholder."...

Section 220 proceedings are an important part of the corporate governance landscape in Delaware. Stockholders have a right to at least a limited inquiry into books and records when they have established some credible basis to believe that there has been wrongdoing. In fact, a Section 220 proceeding may serve a salutary mission as a prelude to a derivative suit. Yet it would invite mischief to open corporate management to indiscriminate fishing expeditions. The trial court must assure that a proper balance is struck.

The judgment of the Court of Chancery granting U.S. Die's entitlement to inspect books and records is **AFFIRMED**. The breadth of the order is **REVERSED** on this record, however. This case is **REMANDED** to the Court of Chancery to open the record and to consider whether the plaintiff has carried its burden of proving that each category of books and records is essential to the accomplishment of the stockholder's articulated purpose for the inspection.

Questions

1. Why did the president of U.S. Die seek to inspect the books and records?
2. Does a stockholder have the right to demand to review books and records at his or her discretion or must the stockholder prove waste and mismanagement are occurring? Or, is there a different standard for the stockholder?
3. Did U.S. Die make a credible showing that there was a legitimate issue of wrongdoing? Explain.

A shareholder is entitled to inspect the books to obtain information needed for a lawsuit against the corporation or its directors or officers, to organize the other shareholders into an "opposition" party to remove the board of directors at the next election, or to buy the shares of other shareholders.

Inspection has frequently been refused when it was sought merely from idle curiosity or for "speculative purposes." Inspection has sometimes been denied on the ground that it was sought merely to obtain a mailing list of persons who would be solicited to buy products of another enterprise.

Inspection has also been refused when the object of the shareholder was to advance political or social beliefs without regard to the welfare of the corporation. Cases that deny the right of inspection do so when it would be harmful to the corporation[20] or is sought only for the purpose of annoying, harassing, or causing vexation or of aiding competitors of the corporation.

(a) Form of Books

There are generally no requirements regarding the form of corporate books and records. The RMBCA recognizes that corporate books and records may be stored in modern data storage systems. "A corporation shall maintain its records in written form or in any other form capable of conversion into written form within a reasonable time."[21]

(b) Financial Statements

The RMBCA requires a corporation to furnish annual financial statements. These statements include a balance sheet as of the end of the fiscal year, an income statement for that year, and a statement of changes in shareholders' equity for that year.[22] A number of state statutes contain similar provisions and set forth a statutory penalty for any officer responsible for providing the financial statements who fails to perform such duties after written request.

CPA 17. Dividends

A shareholder has the right to receive a proportion of dividends as they are declared, subject to the relative rights of other shareholders to preferences, accumulation of dividends, and participation. There is no absolute right that dividends be declared, but dividends, when declared, must be paid in the manner indicated.

CPA (a) Funds Available for Declaration of Dividends

Statutes commonly provide that no dividends may be declared unless there is an "earned surplus" for their payment. Earned surplus, also known as *retained earnings*, consists of the accumulated profits earned by the corporation since its formation less prior dividend distributions. Dividend payments are prohibited if the corporation is insolvent or would be rendered insolvent by the payment of the dividend.

As an exception to these rules, a wasting assets corporation may pay dividends out of current net profits without regard to the preservation of the corporate assets. **Wasting assets corporations** are those designed to exhaust or use up the assets of the corporation (for example, by extracting oil, coal, iron, and other ores) as compared with manufacturing plants whose object is to preserve the plant as well as to continue to manufacture. A wasting assets corporation may also be formed for the purpose of buying and liquidating a stock of merchandise from a company that has received a discharge in bankruptcy court.

In some states, statutes provide that dividends may be declared from earned surplus or from current net profits without regard to the existence of a deficit from former years.

CPA (b) Discretion of Directors

Assuming that a fund is available for the declaration of dividends, it is then a matter primarily within the discretion of the board of directors whether a dividend shall be declared. The fact that there is an earned surplus that could be used for dividends does not mean that they must be declared. This rule is not affected by the nature of the shares. Thus, the fact that the shareholders hold cumulative preferred shares does not give them any right to demand a declaration of dividends or to interfere with an honest exercise of discretion by the directors.

Maintaining an adequate cash and working capital position is an important practical consideration in determining whether to declare a cash dividend. In general, courts refuse to substitute their judgment for the judgment of the directors of the corporation and interfere with their decision on dividend declaration only when it is shown that their conduct is harmful to the welfare of the corporation or its shareholders.[23]

(c) Form of Dividends

Customarily, a dividend is paid in money. However, it may be paid in property, such as a product manufactured by the corporation; in shares of other corporations held by the corporation; or in shares of the corporation itself.

[20] *Retail Property Investors, Inc., v Skeens*, 471 SE2d 181 (Va 1996).

[21] RMBCA § 16.01(d).

[22] RMBCA § 16.20. See *Troccoli v Lab Contract Industries, Inc.*, 687 NYS2d 400 (App Div 1999).

[23] *Gabelli & Co. v Liggett Group, Inc.*, 479 A2d 276 (Del Super 1984).

(d) Effect of Transfer of Shares

When a corporation declares a cash or property dividend, the usual practice is for the board of directors to declare a dividend as of a certain date—the *declaration date*—payable to shareholders of record on a stated future date—the *record date*—with a *payment date* following the record date, usually by some 30 days. The person who is the owner of the shares on the record date is entitled to the dividend even if the shares are transferred prior to the payment date.

If the dividend consists of shares in the corporation declaring the dividend, ownership of the dividend is determined by the date of distribution. Whoever is the owner of the shares when the stock dividend is distributed is entitled to the stock dividend. The reason for this variation from the cash dividend rule is that the declaration of a stock dividend has the effect of diluting the existing corporate assets among a larger number of shares. The value of the holding represented by each share is diminished as a result. Unless the person who owns the stock on the distribution date receives a proportionate share of the stock dividend, the net effect will be to lessen that person's holding.

18. Capital Distribution

Upon dissolution of the corporation, shareholders are entitled to receive any balance of the corporate assets that remains after the payment of all creditors. Certain classes of stock may have a preference or priority in this distribution.

CPA 19. Shareholders' Actions

When the corporation has the right to sue its directors, officers, or third persons for damages caused by them to the corporation or for breach of contract, one or more shareholders may bring such action if the corporation refuses to do so. This is a **derivative (secondary) action** in that the shareholder enforces only the cause of action of the corporation and any money recovery is paid into the corporate treasury.

In a derivative action, when a corporation has failed to enforce a right, a shareholder bringing such a suit must show that a demand was made on the directors to enforce the right in question. The shareholder must show (1) that the directors refused to enforce the right[24] or (2) such a demand that the directors enforce the right is excused because the directors are deemed incapable of making an impartial decision regarding the pursuit of the litigation. Mere allegations that a director and other directors move in the same social circles or are characterized as close friends is not enough to negate a director's independence for presuit demand excusal purposes. **For Example,** Monica Bean, a shareholder of Martha Stewart Living Omnimedia, Inc. (MSO), filed a derivative action against Martha Stewart and the other MSO board of directors alleging that Stewart breached her duties to MSO by illegally selling ImClone stock and mishandling media attention jeopardizing the financial future of MSO. The case was dismissed because Beam failed to plead particularized facts demonstrating presuit demand futility raising reasonable doubt that a majority of the outside directors were not independent of Stewart. Allegations that Director Darla Moore attended a wedding reception hosted by Stewart's personal lawyer for his daughter and was a friend of a longtime friend of Stewart did not create a reasonable doubt about her independence, nor did the allegation that Director Naomi Seligman made a phone call to publisher John Wiley Inc. to express concern over a planned book critical of Stewart. The Supreme Court of Delaware noted that had Beam brought an action to inspect MSO's books and records, she might have uncovered facts that would have created a reasonable doubt, enabling the case to go to trial.[25]

THINKING THINGS THROUGH

Shareholders brought a derivative action on behalf of Oracle Corporation alleging inside trading by CEO L. Ellison, CFO J. Henley, and Directors D. Lucas and M. Boskin while in possession of material, nonpublic information showing that Oracle would not meet earnings

[24] *Marx v Akers*, 666 NE2d 1034 (NY 1996).
[25] *Beam v Stewart*, 845 A2d 1040, 1056 (Del 2004).

THINKING THINGS THROUGH

continued

guidance for the third quarter of 2001. Oracle's board of directors formed a special litigation committee (SLC) to investigate the derivative action and determine whether Oracle should go forward with the claims raised by the plaintiffs, settle them, or terminate the action. The SLC brought a motion to terminate the derivative action before the court, and the plaintiffs contend the motion should be denied because of ties among the two SLC members to three of the four named Trading Defendants.

The two Oracle board members named to the SLC joined the Oracle board on October 15, 2001, well after the third quarter of 2001 closed. Their investigation was extensive, including interviews of 70 witnesses. The SLC wrote a 1,110-page report on the matter and concluded that the claims were without merit and that Oracle should not pursue the plaintiffs' claims against the Trading Defendants.

Professors Garcia-Molina, chair of the Computer Science Department at Stanford University, and Joseph Grundfest, Franke Professor of Law and Business at Stanford University, served as the two directors on the SLC. Defendant director Boskin is also a chaired professor at Stanford and taught Grundfest as a Ph.D candidate there. Defendant Lucas is a Stanford alumnus with both undergraduate and graduate degrees and is a generous Stanford benefactor. Defendant Ellison, Oracle's CEO, is one of the wealthiest men in America and a Stanford benefactor. He had been discussing with Stanford an Ellison Scholars Program funded at $170 million, modeled after Oxford's Rhodes Scholarship, just prior to the appointment of the SLC.

The burden of persuasion is on the SLC to show that no material issues of fact exist to call into doubt its independence.* The question of independence turns on whether there is any substantial reason to believe that the two SLC directors were incapable of making a decision with only the best interests of the corporation in mind. Do professors of Stanford University regularly make independent judgments resulting in the granting or denial of tenure of fellow faculty members without the specter of charges of lack of independence? Is there a substantial or rational basis to reject the SLC's determination based merely on the Stanford connections? Assess the fairness of this statement: "A purpose for forming an SLC committee is to promote confidence in the integrity of the corporate decision making by vesting the company's power to respond to accusations of serious misconduct by directors and officers in an impartial group of independent directors." Was the social atmosphere involving the defendants and the SLC members "painted in too much vivid Stanford Cardinal red" to meet the SLC's burden of persuasion or was the independent judgment of two distinguished academics from one of the nation's most prestigious universities after extensive study a compelling basis to dismiss the plaintiffs' claims? [In Re Oracle Corp.-Derivative Litigation, 824 A2d 917 (Del Ch 2003)]

*Unlike the presuit demand excusal context discussed in the Martha Stewart Living example, when the board of directors is presumed to be independent, the SLC has the burden of establishing its own independence because SLC members are vested with enormous power in the SLC's business judgment to pursue the corporate claim or seek dismissal of a derivative suit. This power is exercised in a setting in which presuit demand is already excused.

Shareholders may also intervene or join in an action brought against the corporation when the corporation refuses to defend the action against it or is not doing so in good faith. Otherwise, the shareholders may take no part in an action by or against the corporation.

Lawsuits may be brought by minority shareholders against majority shareholders who are oppressive toward minority shareholders. Oppressive conduct may include payment of grossly excessive salaries and fringe benefits to the majority stockholders who are also officers of the corporation.

Shareholders may bring a derivative action to obtain a dissolution of the corporation by judicial decree.[26]

D. Liability of Shareholders

A shareholder is ordinarily protected from the liabilities of the corporation. Some exceptions exist, however.

20. Limited Liability

The liability of a shareholder is generally limited. This means that the shareholder is not personally liable for the debts and liabilities of the corporation. The capital contributed by shareholders may be exhausted by the claims of creditors, but there is no personal liability for any unpaid balance.

21. Ignoring the Corporate Entity

Ordinarily a corporation is regarded and treated as a separate legal entity, and the law does not look behind a corporation to see who owns or controls it.

The fact that two corporations have identical shareholders does not justify a court's regarding the two corporations as one. Similarly, the fact that there is a close working relationship between two corporations does not in itself constitute any basis for ignoring their separate corporate entities when they in fact are separately run enterprises.

(a) "Piercing the Corporate Veil"

A court may disregard the corporate entity, or figuratively "pierce the corporate veil," when exceptional circumstances warrant. The decision whether to disregard the corporate entity is made on a case-by-case basis, weighing all factors before the court. Factors that may lead to piercing the corporate veil and imposing liability on its owners (the shareholders) are (1) the failure to maintain adequate corporate records and the commingling of corporate and other funds,[27] (2) grossly inadequate capitalization,[28] (3) the diversion by shareholders of corporate funds or assets,[29] (4) the formation of the corporation to evade an existing obligation, (5) the formation of the corporation to perpetrate a fraud or conceal illegality, and (6) a determination that injustice and inequitable consequences would result if the corporate entity were recognized.[30]

In the *Boles* case, the plaintiffs claimed that the corporate entities should be ignored.

BOLES V NATIONAL DEVELOPMENT CO. INC., 175 SW3D 226 (TENN APP 2005)

WHEN THE LAKE WOULD HOLD NO WATER COULD A STREAM OF ASSETS BE DIVERTED TO "THE MAN"?

Gladys Boles and twenty eight other owners of property at Hidden Valley Lakes Development sued the corporate developer, National Development Co. Inc. (NDC), NDC's parent Sunstates Corporation and the individual behind both corporations Clyde Engle, for breach of contract and fraud. The centerpiece of this development, a recreational thirty acre lake, named Crystal Lake, failed to hold water; and it was determined that it would never hold water. Instead of having a thirty-acre lake as the centerpiece, the plaintiffs had a thirty acre hole in the ground. While the controversy over the breach of contract by NDC was pending, Clyde Engle made a "proposal" to the CEO of Sunstates to transfer

[26] *Lasday v Weiner*, 652 NE2d 1198 (Ill App 1996).

[27] *East Market v Tycorp Pizza IV, Inc.*, 625 SE2d 191, 198 (NC App 2006).

[28] An example of grossly inadequate capitalization is found in *Klokke Corp. v Classic Exposition, Inc.*, 912 P2d 929 (Or App 1996), in which Classic's two shareholders invested $1,000 of capital to start a business and immediately took out a $200,000 loan. The business remained undercapitalized until part of it was sold. However, the two shareholders effectively withdrew all of the proceeds of the sale in October 1991, and the business was again without sufficient capital, leaving it unable to meet its financial obligations. The court held that the shareholders were personally liable up to the amount withdrawn in October 1991 after the partial sale of the business.

[29] See *Trustees of the National Elevator Industry Pension Fund v Lutyk*, 332 F3d 188 (3d Cir 2003), in which the court of appeals found the equitable remedy of piercing the corporate veil justified. The sole shareholder, Andrew Lutyk, siphoned funds over the final months of the corporation's operations while it was known to be deeply insolvent, used corporate funds to pay entertainment expenses without an identifiable business purpose, and commingled corporate assets with his own. Personal liability was imposed on Lutyk to make unpaid payments to a union's benefit plans.

[30] *Barton v Moore*, 558 NW2d 746 (Minn 1997).

$2.4 million in NDC's receivables to Sunstates in exchange for an unsecured promissory note to NDC. Evidence showed that all of Sunstates' assets were transferred to Engle making the note NDC held from Sunstates worthless. Sunstates purchased approximately $1.9 million dollars of oriental art, antique jewelry, rare books and other collectibles which were maintained in Clyde Engle's home in Illinois. Likewise Sunstates purchased a Rolls Royce from Libco, a corporation in which Engle was the majority shareholder. This automobile also appears to be in the possession or control of Mr. Engle. The trial court awarded the plaintiffs $2,540,867 in compensatory damages, and pierced the corporate veils of NDC and Sunstates and held Engle personally liable for the judgment. Engle appealed, contending that the corporations were separate legal entities with limited liability.

Judicial Opinion

CLEMENT, J.... It is evident to [the trial court] that Mr. Engle exercised complete dominion over Sunstates, National Development Corporation, and all of the other... companies.... There was evidence of Mr. Engle's dominion not only over the transfers of funds which were funneled to him up the corporate chain through the Bank of Lincolnwood, but also over the particular business decision in this case i.e. the transfer of N.D.C.'s assets to Sunstates Corporation. All of the corporations under Engle's control are now insolvent, and it would be an injustice to allow Mr. Engle to use the corporate entity as a shield to thwart the satisfaction of the judgment obtained in this case. The evidence supports the conclusion that NDC, Sunstates and the other companies were mere instrumentalities for Mr. Engle and therefore the corporate entity will be disregarded in order to accomplish justice in this case.

Therefore, the Court finds plaintiffs prior judgment against National Development Corporation, Inc. shall likewise be a judgment against Sunstates Corporation and Clyde Engle, individually....

Our [the court of appeals] review of the record not only leads us to the conclusion that the evidence does not preponderate against the specific findings of the trial court, the record fully supports those findings.... Thus, the issue is whether the facts as found by the trial court are sufficient to sustain, as a matter of law, the trial court's conclusion that Clyde Engle was the alter ego of National....

Since the piercing of the corporate veil is a "matter particularly within the province of the trial court," *Electric Power Bd.*, 691 S.W.2d at 526, we conclude that there is no basis for disagreeing with the trial court's explicit finding that the piercing of the corporate veil was "necessary to accomplish justice."

[Affirmed]

Questions

1. Why do you suppose piercing the corporate veil is particularly within the province of the trial court?
2. Can a court disregard the corporation as a separate entity because it is "necessary to accomplish justice"?

(b) "Alter Ego" Theory

Some courts express their reasons for disregarding the corporate entity by stating that the corporation is the "*alter ego*" of the wrongdoer. A corporation is a separate and distinct person from the person or persons who own the corporation. However, when a corporation is so dominated and controlled by a shareholder(s), officer(s), or director(s) that the separate personalities of the individual and the corporation no longer exist and there is a wrongful use of that control, the courts will disregard the corporate entity so as not to sanction a fraud or injustice.[31] **For Example,** V&M Industries, Inc., owned land on which some 40,000 plus used tires caught fire. It took nearly a week to extinguish the fire and caused severe air pollution in the St. Louis area. Vernon Leirer originally owned 99 percent of V&M corporate stock; all corporate officers other than Leirer were nonfunctioning; the corporation was inadequately capitalized; no stock certificates were issued; and corporate records were generally not kept. At a time just before the fire, when Leirer was no longer a shareholder or officer, he exercised total direction and control over the corporation and

[31] *Dishon v Ponthie*, 918 So2d 1132 (La App 2005).

"ran the show." The court held that to adhere to the fiction of separate corporate existence would sanction fraud. It concluded that V&M, Inc., was the *alter ego* for Leirer, and Leirer was personally responsible for civil penalties under the Environmental Protection Act.[32]

Limited liability is important to our economy by encouraging investors to make investments in high-risk ventures. It should be disregarded only in exceptional circumstances. When fraud or deceit is absent, other circumstances for piercing the corporate veil must be so strong as to clearly indicate that the corporation is the alter ego of the controlling person.

(c) Obtaining Advantages of Corporate Existence

Courts will not go behind the corporate identity merely because the corporation has been formed to obtain tax savings or to obtain limited liability for its shareholders. Similarly, the corporate entity will not be ignored merely because the corporation does not have sufficient assets to pay the claims against it.

One-person, family, and other closely held corporations are permissible and entitled to all of the advantages of corporate existence. The fact that the principal shareholder runs or oversees the day-to-day operations does not justify ignoring the corporate entity.

22. Other Exceptions to Limited Liability

Liability may be imposed on a shareholder as though there were no corporation when the court ignores the corporate entity either because of the particular circumstances of the case or because the corporation is so defectively organized that it is deemed not to exist.

(a) Wage Claims

Statutes sometimes provide that the shareholders shall have unlimited liability for the wage claims of corporate employees. This exception has been abandoned in some states in recent years or has been confined to corporate officers who are active in corporate decision making.[33]

(b) Unpaid Subscriptions

Most states prohibit the issuance of par value shares for less than par or except for "money, labor done, or property actually received." Whenever shares issued by a corporation are not fully paid for, the original subscriber receiving the shares, or any transferee who does not give value or who knows that the shares were not fully paid for, is liable for the unpaid balance if the corporation is insolvent and the money is required to pay its creditors.[34]

If the corporation has issued the shares as fully paid for, has given them as a bonus, or has agreed to release the subscriber for the unpaid balance, the corporation cannot recover that balance. The fact that the corporation is thus barred does not prevent creditors of the corporation from bringing an action to compel payment of the balance. The same rules are applied when stock is issued as fully paid for in return for property or services that were overvalued so that the stock is not actually paid for in full. A conflict of authority exists, however, as to whether the shareholder is liable from the mere fact that the property or service given for the shares was in fact overvalued by the directors or whether it must also be shown that the directors acted in bad faith in making the erroneous valuation. The trend of modern statutes is, in the absence of proof of fraud, to prohibit disputing the valuation placed by the corporation on services or property.

(c) Unauthorized Dividends

If dividends are improperly paid out of capital, shareholders are generally liable to creditors to the extent of such depletion of capital. In some states, the liability of a shareholder depends on whether the corporation was insolvent at the time and whether debts were existing at the time.

23. The Professional Corporation

The extent to which incorporation limits the liability of shareholders of a professional corporation depends on the interpretation of the statute under which the corporation was formed.

(a) Act of Shareholder in Creating Liability

The statutes that authorize the formation of professional corporations usually require that share

[32] *Illinois v V&M Industries*, 700 NE2d 746 (Ill App 1998).

[33] *Cusimano v Metro Auto, Inc.*, 860 P2d 532 (Colo App 1993).

[34] *Frasier v Trans-western Land Corp.*, 316 NW2d 612 (Neb 1982). But *see Brunfield v Horn*, 547 So 2d 415 (Ala 1989).

ownership be limited to duly licensed professionals. If a shareholder in a professional corporation, such as a corporation of physicians, negligently drives the professional corporation's automobile in going to attend a patient or is personally obligated on a contract made for the corporation or is guilty of malpractice, the physician-shareholder is liable without limit for the liability that has been created. This is the same rule of law that applies in the case of the ordinary business corporation.

Professional corporation statutes generally repeat the rule governing malpractice liability by stating that the liability of a shareholder for malpractice is not affected by the fact of incorporation.

(b) Malpractice Liability of an Associate

The liability of a shareholder in a professional corporation for the malpractice of an associate varies from state to state depending on the language of the professional corporation statute in effect and on the court decisions under the statute.[35]

If the statute provides for limited liability, as in a business corporation, then where doctors *A*, *B*, and *C* are a professional corporation, *A* and *B* will not be liable for the malpractice of *C* beyond the extent of corporate assets. If the statute provides for vicarious personal liability, as in a partnership, and doctors *A*, *B*, and *C* are a professional corporation, each will have unlimited liability for any malpractice liability incurred by the others. Often the statutory reference to malpractice liability is not very clear, and the courts are called on to resolve the question of the liability of a professional shareholder for the malpractice of an associate.

LAWFLIX

Meet Joe Black (1998) (PG-13)

A transfer of corporate control and the role of shareholder control is at the heart of this film about a corporation under takeover fire.

For movie clips that illustrate business law concepts, see LawFlix at **http://www.westbuslaw.com.**

[35] ABA Model Professional Corporation Act Amendments (1984), § 34, offers three alternative positions regarding the liability of shareholders: (1) limited liability, as in a business corporation, (2) vicarious personal liability, as in a partnership, and (3) personal liability limited in amount and conditioned on financial responsibility in the form of insurance or a surety bond.

Summary

The ownership of a corporation is evidenced by a holder's shares of stock that have been issued by the corporation. Common stock is ordinary stock that has no preferences but entitles the holder to (1) participate in the control of the corporation by exercising one vote per share of record, (2) share in the profits in the form of dividends, and (3) participate, upon dissolution, in the distribution of net assets after the satisfaction of all creditors (including bondholders). Other classes of stock exist, such as preferred stock, that have priority over common stock with regard to distribution of dividends and/or assets upon liquidation. Shares may be acquired by subscription of an original issue or by transfer of existing shares.

Bonds are debt securities, and a bondholder is a creditor rather than an owner of the corporation. Bondholders' interests are represented by an indenture trustee who is responsible for ensuring that the corporation complies with the terms of the bond indenture.

Shareholders control the corporation, but this control is indirect. Through their voting rights, they elect directors, and by this means, they can control the corporation. *Preemptive rights*, if they exist, allow shareholders to maintain their voting percentages when the corporation issues additional shares of stock. Shareholders have the right to inspect the books of the corporation unless it would be harmful to the corporation. Shareholders also have the right to receive dividends when declared at the discretion of the directors. Shareholders may bring a derivative action on behalf of the corporation for damages to the corporation. Shareholders are ordinarily protected from liability for the acts of the corporation.

Ordinarily, each corporation is treated as a separate person, and the law does not look beyond the corporate identity merely because the corporation was formed to obtain tax savings or limited liability. The fact that two corporations have the same shareholders does not justify disregarding the separate corporate entities. However, when a corporation is formed to perpetrate a fraud, a court ignores the corporate form, or "pierces the corporate veil." The corporate form is also ignored to prevent injustice or because of the functional reality that the two corporations in question are one.

Questions and Case Problems

1. Six members of the Weston family, who owned 6.8 percent of the stock of Weston Paper and Manufacturing Company, brought suit against three corporate directors and CFIS, a firm hired by the company to make the annual evaluation of the company's stock for allocating stock options to its employees. The Westons stated that their claims against the defendants were personal claims, alleging that they were injured by CFIS and the three directors who kept the price of the stock low to obtain more shares of stock through the stock option plan. From an adverse ruling on their right to maintain a direct action against the directors, the Westons appealed. How would you decide this case? [*Weston v Weston Paper and Manufacturing Co.*, 74 Ohio St 377]
2. Tomlinson and Hubbard were two of five shareholders in Multimedia Software Distributors, a corporation. The corporation was formed in 1992 and filed for bankruptcy in 1994. In 1996, Tomlinson filed a claim in his own name, alleging that Hubbard had breached his fiduciary duties to Tomlinson by diverting proceeds owned by Multimedia to another business owned by Hubbard. Hubbard contends that Tomlinson is an improper plaintiff. Decide. [*Hubbard v Tomlinson*, 747 NE2d 69 (Ind App)]
3. Barbara, Joel, and Edna each own less than 5 percent of the stock of Enrico Storm Door Corp. Individually, their holdings are too small to be significant in any shareholder's election. Barbara suggests that they and other small shareholders combine their votes by transferring their shares to trustees, who will vote the aggregate of their shares as a block. Joel agrees with the idea but says he is afraid this is an illegal conspiracy. Is he correct?
4. Russell Nugent was involved in the roofing business in Kansas City, incorporating his business as Russell Nugent Roofing, Inc. In 1985, the name was changed to On Top Roofing, Incorporated. On August 27, 1987, On Top, Inc., ceased to exist, and RNR, Inc., was incorporated. RNR, Inc., went out of business in 1988, and RLN Construction, Inc., was incorporated. In 1989, the business was organized as Russell Nugent, Inc. Nugent and his wife had been sole shareholders, officers, and directors of each corporation. When one roofing company was incorporated, the prior roofing company ceased doing business. All of the companies were located at the same business address and used the same telephone number. Nugent paid himself and his wife more than $100,000 in salaries in 1986. In 1986, the corporation paid $99,290 in rent for property that the Nugents owned. Nugent testified that he changed to a new corporation every time he needed to get a "fresh start." The evidence showed that he used the On Top Roofing logo on his trucks and Yellow Pages advertisements throughout the period of the successive corporations. Suppliers who were not paid for materials in 1986 and 1987 by the insolvent corporations sought to pierce the corporate veils and hold Nugent personally liable. Nugent defended that as a shareholder, he had no personal liability. Decide. [*K.C. Roofing Center v On Top Roofing, Inc.*, 807 SW2d 545 (Mo App)]
5. The stock of West End Development Co. was subject to a transfer restriction. This restriction required that any shareholder selling shares first offer every other shareholder the right to purchase a proportion of the shares being sold. The proportions were to be the same as the percentages of the outstanding shares that the other shareholders already owned. This restriction was stated in the articles of incorporation but was not stated on the stock certificate of the corporation. The Taylors owned stock in the company and sold their stock to Vroom, an officer of the corporation, without first offering any stock to the other shareholders, as required by the restriction. The other shareholders brought an action against Vroom to recover from him the percentages of the shares they would have been entitled to if the Taylors had followed the transfer restriction. Decide. [*Irwin v West End Development Co.*, 481 F2d 34 (10th Cir)]
6. Siebrecht organized Siebrecht Realty Co., a corporation, and then transferred his building to the corporation in exchange for its stock. The corporation rented different parts of the building to different tenants. Elenkrieg, an employee of one of the tenants, fell and was injured because of the defective condition of a stairway. She sued Siebrecht individually on the ground that the corporation had been formed by him for the purpose of securing limited liability. Decide. [*Elenkrieg v Siebrecht*, 144 NE 519 (NY)]

7. William Carter, a former officer and employee of Wilson Construction Co., Inc., owned 317 shares of stock in Wilson. Carter left Wilson to become part owner and employee of C&L Contracting Co., which was a direct competitor of Wilson. Carter requested access to Wilson's corporate books to determine the value of his shares. Wilson refused, not wanting to divulge its business practices to a direct competitor. Decide. [*Carter v Wilson Construction Co., Inc.*, 348 SE2d 830 (NC App)]
8. Ken and Charlotte Maschmeier were the majority shareholders of Southside Press; each owned 1,300 shares. Marty and Larry Maschmeier, who each owned 1,200 shares of the corporation, had a falling out with Ken and Charlotte and were terminated as employees of the business. Ken and Charlotte started a new corporation, which employed most of the employees of the old corporation and which took most of its former customers. Gross receipts of Southside Press went from $613,258 down to $18,172 two years later. The $18,172 figure was from the lease of equipment. Ken and Charlotte continued to draw from Southside annual salaries of $20,000, which were in excess of the gross receipts of the business. Marty and Larry brought suit against Ken and Charlotte, alleging "oppressive" conduct. Ken and Charlotte stated that they paid Marty and Larry excellent salaries when they were employed by the corporation. Ken and Charlotte contended they had a right to start a new corporation as they saw fit. Decide. [*Maschmeier v Southside Press, Inc.*,435 NW2d 377 (Iowa App)]
9. Harper owned corporate stock, and telling O'Brien that he was going to give the stock to O'Brien, he handed the stock certificate to O'Brien. O'Brien requested Harper to indorse the certificate. Harper refused. Who was the owner of the stock? [*Smith v Augustine*, 368 NYS2d 675]
10. Ed Klein was the sole shareholder, director, and chief executive officer of The Gun Exchange, Inc., a retail firearms dealership. The inventory of The Gun Exchange had been pledged as security for a $622,500 debt owed to InterFirst Bank. It also owed $231,484.60 to Sporting Goods, Inc.; this debt was unsecured. On May 20, InterFirst Bank notified Klein of its intention to foreclose on the inventory and sell it at public auction. InterFirst Bank further advised Klein that, pursuant to his personal guarantee, he would be responsible for any deficiency following the sale. Klein immediately incorporated The Gun Store, Inc., for the purpose of purchasing the assets of The Gun Exchange at the foreclosure sale. Before the foreclosure sale, Klein obtained a $650,000 line of credit from CharterBank on behalf of The Gun Store. At the sale, Klein purchased the assets of The Gun Exchange for $650,000 even though the highest prior bid was $175,000. (Had the $175,000 bid been accepted, Klein would have been personally liable for the deficiency to InterFirst Bank.)

    After the foreclosure sale, no funds existed to pay the unsecured creditors of The Gun Exchange. Following the sale, The Gun Store began operating as a retail firearms dealer with the inventory purchased from the foreclosure sale. It operated in the same location and with the same personnel as The Gun Exchange. Sporting Goods, Inc., sued Klein individually for the $231,484.60. Klein contended that the corporate form under which he did business insulated him as a shareholder from liability for corporate obligations. Decide. Is it ethical to seek limited liability under the corporate form, as Klein did in this case? [*Klein v Sporting Goods, Inc.*, 772 SW2d 173 (Tex Civ App)]
11. Ibanez owned shares of stock in Farmers Underwriters. He left the stock certificate lying on top of his desk in his office. Many persons continually passed through the office, and one day Ibanez realized that someone had taken the certificate from the top of his desk. Ibanez applied to Farmers Underwriters for a duplicate stock certificate. The corporation refused to issue a duplicate on the ground that it was Ibanez's own fault that the original certificate had been stolen. Ibanez claimed that he was entitled to a new certificate even though he had been at fault. Was he correct? [*Ibanez v Farmers Underwriters Ass'n*, 534 P2d 1336 (Cal)]
12. On March 3, 2002, pursuant to a public offering, First All State Trucking Corp. (FAST) issued securities to investors in denominations of $1,000. The interest rate was 7 percent per year payable semiannually, and the maturity date was March 3, 2010. The rights and obligations of the issuer, FAST, and the holders of the securities were set forth in an indenture agreement. Because the securities were not secured by a mortgage or lien on corporate property, Alec believes they are shares of preferred stock. Is Alec correct? Fully explain the type of security involved, and discuss the extent of the holders' voting rights.
13. Linhart owned shares of stock in First National Bank. She borrowed money from the bank and pledged the stock as security. She later decided to transfer 70 head of cattle and the shares of stock to her son, but she could not deliver the share certificate to him because it was held by the bank. She therefore executed a bill of sale reciting the transfer of the cattle and the stock to the son. She gave him the bill of sale, and he had the bill recorded. After her death, the son brought an action to determine the ownership of the stock. Was the son the owner of the shares?
14. Birt was a hospital patient. The doctor who treated him was a shareholder of a professional corporation organized under the Indiana Medical Professional Corporation Act. Birt claimed that the doctor who treated him was guilty of malpractice, and he sued the doctor. He also sued the professional corporation and all of its officers,

directors, and shareholders. These other defendants asserted that they were not liable because the corporate entity shielded them. The plaintiff claimed that the corporation was not a shield because in fact all of the persons were rendering medical services and should be held liable as in a partnership. The statute did not expressly regulate the matter of limited liability beyond declaring that it did not change the law between a person supplying medical services and the patient. Decide. [*Birt v St. Mary Mercy Hospital*, 370 NE2d 379 (Ind App)]

15. Ronald Naquin, an employee of Air Engineered Systems & Services, Inc., owned one-third of its outstanding shares. After six years, he was fired and an offer was made to buy out his interest in Air Engineered at a price that Naquin thought inadequate. He then formed a competing business and made a written request to examine the corporate records of Air Engineered. This request was denied. Naquin filed suit to require Air Engineered to allow him to examine the books. Air Engineered raised the defense that he was a competitor seeking to gain unfair competitive advantage. Decide. [*Naquin v Air Engineered Systems & Services, Inc.*, 463 So 2d 992 (La App)]

CPA Questions

1. A stockholder's right to inspect books and records of a corporation will be properly denied if the stockholder
   a. Wants to use corporate stockholder records for a personal business
   b. Employs an agent to inspect the books and records
   c. Intends to commence a stockholder's derivative suit
   d. Is investigating management misconduct

2. The limited liability of a stockholder in a closely held corporation may be challenged successfully if the stockholder
   a. Undercapitalized the corporation when it was formed
   b. Formed the corporation solely to have limited personal liability
   c. Sold property to the corporation
   d. Was a corporate officer, director, or employee

3. Price owns 2,000 shares of Universal Corp.'s $10 cumulative preferred stock. During its first year of operations, cash dividends of $5 per share were declared on the preferred stock but were never paid. In the second year, dividends on the preferred stock were neither declared nor paid. If Universal is dissolved, which of the following statements is correct?
   a. Universal will be liable to Price as an unsecured creditor for $10,000.
   b. Universal will be liable to Price as a secured creditor for $20,000.
   c. Price will have priority over the claims of Universal's bond owners.
   d. Price will have priority over the claims of Universal's unsecured judgment creditors.

4. Under the Revised Model Business Corporation Act, a dissenting stockholder's appraisal right generally applies to which of the following corporate actions?

	Consolidations	*Shares from mergers*
a.	Yes	Yes
b.	Yes	No
c.	No	Yes
d.	No	No

SECURITIES REGULATION

CHAPTER

(46)

LEARNING OBJECTIVES

After studying this chapter, you should be able to

LO.1 Determine whether state or federal securities laws apply to a transaction

LO.2 Define *security*

LO.3 Compare and distinguish between the Securities Act of 1933 and the Securities Exchange Act of 1934

LO.4 Discuss the factors that subject an individual to liability for insider trading

LO.5 List the reasons for the regulation of cash tender offers

LO.6 Identify the sections of the federal securities laws under which accountants may be subject to liability

Is there anything that protects you when you buy corporate securities?

A. State Regulation

To protect the public from the sale of fraudulent securities, many states have adopted statutes regulating the intrastate sale of securities.

CPA 1. State Blue Sky Laws

State laws regulating securities are called **blue sky laws.** The term *blue sky* is derived from the purpose of such laws, which is to prevent the sale of speculative schemes that have no more value than the blue sky. The state statutes vary in detail. They commonly contain (1) an antifraud provision prohibiting fraudulent practices and imposing criminal penalties for violations, (2) broker-dealer licensing provisions regulating the persons engaged in the securities business, and (3) provisions for the registration of securities, including disclosure requirements, with a designated government official.

A Uniform Securities Act, covering the foregoing three categories of regulations, exists to provide guidance to states in updating their securities laws. This act also contains alternative regulations that can be adopted by states with different regulatory philosophies.

2. National Securities Markets Improvement Act

Congress reallocated responsibility between state and federal security regulators in the National Securities Markets Improvement Act (NSMIA) of 1996,[1] recognizing that the dual system of state and federal regulation of securities resulted in duplicative regulation and expenses. Title I of the act exempts from state review and registration securities offered by mutual funds and stocks listed on the New York Stock Exchange, the American Stock Exchange, the NASDAQ National Market system, and other stock exchanges identified by the Securities and Exchange Commission (SEC). The act preserves the states' authority to investigate and bring enforcement actions for fraud or deceit or for unlawful conduct by a broker or dealer in connection with securities transactions.[2] Also, the states may continue to collect filing fees for securities in effect as of October 25, 1996. The act also eliminates duplicative registration requirements for investment advisors by dividing regulatory authority between the SEC, which exclusively regulates investment advisors with assets under management of $25 million or more, and the states, which have the responsibility to regulate all investment advisors managing lower sums of money.[3]

B. Federal Regulation

The stock market crash of 1929 and the Great Depression that followed led to the enactment of federal legislation to regulate the securities industry.

3. Federal Laws Regulating the Securities Industry

Six federal securities regulation laws were passed between 1933 and 1940. The two principal laws that provide the basic framework for the federal regulation of the sale of securities in interstate commerce are the Securities Act of 1933 and the Securities Exchange Act of 1934.

The 1933 act deals with the original distribution of securities by the issuing corporations. It is a disclosure statute designed to secure essential facts for the investor. The 1934 act is concerned with the secondary distribution of securities in the national securities exchanges and in the over-the-counter markets. That is, the 1933 act regulates the issuance of securities by a corporation to the first owner. The 1934 act regulates the sale of securities from one owner to another. Four other federal laws deal with specific aspects of the securities industry.[4] These aspects include holding companies in utility

[1] PL 104-290, 110 Stat 3416, 15 USC § 78a nt.

[2] The 1996 act amends § 18(c) of the 1933 Securities Act to accomplish this result.

[3] NSMIA § 303(a), which adds a new § 203A to the Investment Advisors Act of 1940.

[4] The Public Utility Holding Company Act of 1935 (15 USC § 79 *et seq.*) provides comprehensive regulation of holding companies and their subsidiaries in interstate gas and electric utilities businesses. The Trust Indenture Act of 1939 (15 USC §§ 77aaa to 77bbb) was enacted to protect the interests of the holders of bonds and other debt securities offered to the public in interstate commerce by requiring the appointment of independent institutional trustees. The Investment Company Act of 1940 (15 USC §§ 80a-1 to 80a-52) provides for the registration and comprehensive regulation of mutual funds and all other investment companies. The Investment Advisors Act of 1940 (15 USC §§ 80b-1 to 80b-21) requires registration with the Securities and Exchange Commission of all persons engaged in the business of providing investment advice in interstate commerce. In 1970, the Securities Investors Protection Act was enacted to protect investors from the business failures of brokers and dealers.

E-COMMERCE AND CYBERLAW

FACILITATION OF THE USE OF ELECTRONIC RECORD-KEEPING

Under the Electronic Signatures in Global and National Commerce Act of 2000 (E-Sign), brokerage firms and mutual funds may avoid the expense of paper mailings of legally required documents, such as monthly statements, trade confirmations, prospectuses, and financial reports, and deliver these documents or "records" by electronic means. The consumer must, however, consent to receiving these electronic records, and the consumer must consent electronically or confirm the consent electronically. Moreover, firms must inform consumers of their right to receive hard copy documents.

businesses, trustees for debt securities, mutual funds, and investment advisors.

The Securities Enforcement Remedies and Penny Stock Reform Act of 1990[5] (Remedies Act) expands the enforcement remedies of the SEC to reduce fraudulent financial reporting and financial fraud. Under the Remedies Act, the SEC may start administrative proceedings against any person or entity, whether regulated by the SEC or not, and may issue a temporary cease-and-desist order prior to notice and a hearing. The SEC may also order an accounting and disgorgement of ill-gotten gains. In addition, the Remedies Act authorizes courts to bar individuals who have engaged in fraudulent activities from serving as officers and directors of public corporations.

The Securities Acts Amendments of 1990[6] authorize sanctions against SEC-regulated persons for violation of foreign laws. The amendments facilitate the ability of the SEC and foreign regulators to exchange information and cooperate in international securities law enforcement.

The Market Reform Act of 1990[7] was enacted to provide the SEC with powers to deal with market volatility. Under the law, the SEC has the power to suspend all trading when markets are excessively volatile. Also, the SEC may require "large traders" to identify themselves and provide information concerning their trading.

The Private Securities Litigation Reform Act (PSLRA) of 1995[8] was passed to alleviate abuses in private securities litigation. The intent of the act is to reduce the number of lawsuits brought against issuers of securities and accounting firms. This law applies only to private securities litigation, and the SEC's enforcement activities are not affected by the act.

The NSMIA, previously referred to in regard to the allocation of responsibility for securities regulation between the states and the federal government, also provides for national standards allowing brokers and dealers to improve their ability to borrow funds to finance market-making and underwriting activities.[9] This act also provides new national standards regulating margin restriction.

The Sarbanes-Oxley Act of 2002[10] contains numerous reforms regarding corporate accountability, enhanced disclosure requirements, auditor- and accounting-related provisions, and enforcement and liability provisions, which will be discussed in this chapter and the subsequent chapter on accountants' liability.

CPA 4. Definition of Security

For the securities acts to apply, the transaction must involve a "security" within the meaning of the acts.[11] Congress adopted a definition of **security** sufficiently broad to encompass virtually any instrument that might be sold as an investment.

The definition of *security* includes not only investment instruments such as stocks and bonds but

[5] PL 101-429, 104 Stat 931, 15 USC § 77g.

[6] PL 101-550, 104 Stat 2713, 15 USC § 78a.

[7] PL 101-432, 104 Stat 963, 15 USC § 78a.

[8] PL 104-67, 109 Stat 737, 15 USC § 78a nt.

[9] NSMIA § 104, PL 104-290, 110 Stat 3416, 15 USC § 776.

[10] PL 107-204, 116 Stat 745.

[11] The Supreme Court has consistently held that the definition of a security set forth in § 3(a)(10) of the 1934 act is identical to the definition set forth in § 2(1) of the 1933 act. The definition of security under these acts is not to be confused with the narrower definition in Article 8 of the Uniform Commercial Code. See *SEC v Infinity Group Co.*, 993 F Supp 321 (ED Pa 1998).

also "investment contracts." The definition of an *investment contract*, developed by the Supreme Court, is sufficiently broad to allow the securities acts to apply to a wide range of investment transactions or schemes, including the sale of bottled whiskey, cattle-breeding programs, and a limited liability partnership to operate local telephone companies.[12] Under the Supreme Court's definition, an investment contract exists if the following elements are present: (1) an investment of money, (2) a common enterprise, and (3) an expectation of future profits from the efforts of others. **For Example,** the sale of citrus groves to investors, coupled with the execution of service contracts to plant, harvest, and sell the fruit and the distribution of the profits of the venture to the investors, is an investment contract. An instrument denominated as a "note" may in fact be a "security" subject to regulation under the 1934 act.[13]

In the *Edwards* case, the Supreme Court considered whether a commercial equipment lease can be an "investment contract" subject to the securities laws.

SEC V EDWARDS, 124 SCT 892 (2004)

10,000 INVESTORS WISH THEY MISSED THIS OPPORTUNITY

"Opportunity doesn't always knock...sometimes it rings." (ETS Payphones promotional brochure). And sometimes it hangs up. So it did for the 10,000 people who invested a total of $300 million in the payphone sale-and-leaseback arrangements touted by ETS under that slogan. Charles Edwards was the chairman, chief executive officer, and sole shareholder of ETS Payphones, Inc. ETS, acting partly through a subsidiary sold payphones to the public via independent distributors. The payphones were offered packaged with a site lease, a 5-year leaseback and management agreement, and a buyback agreement. The purchase price for the payphone packages was approximately $7,000. Under the leaseback and management agreement, purchasers received $82 per month, a 14% annual return. Purchasers were not involved in the day-to-day operation of the payphones they owned. ETS selected the site for the phone, installed the equipment, arranged for connection and long distance service, collected coin revenues, and maintained and repaired the phones. Under the buyback agreement, ETS promised to refund the full purchase price of the package at the end of the lease or within 180 days of the purchaser's request. The payphones did not generate enough revenue for ETS to make the payments required by the leaseback agreements, so the company depended on funds from new investors to meet its obligations. In September 2000, ETS filed for bankruptcy protection. The SEC brought this civil enforcement action alleging that Edwards and ETS had violated the registration requirements and antifraud provisions of the 1933 Act. The district court concluded the arrangement was an "investment contract" subject to the securities laws. The Eleventh Circuit Court of Appeals reversed the lower court because the scheme offered a contractual entitlement to a fixed rather than a variable return.

Judicial Opinion

O'CONNOR, J...."Congress' purpose in enacting the securities laws was to regulate *investments*, in whatever form they are made and by whatever name they are called." *Reves v. Ernst & Young*, 494 U.S. 56, 61, 110 S.Ct. 945, 108 L.Ed.2d 47 (1990). To that end, it enacted a broad definition of "security," sufficient "to emcompass virtually any instrument that might be sold as an investment." *Ibid.*...

The test for whether a particular scheme is an investment contract was established in our decision in *SEC v W.J. Howey Co.*, 328 U.S. 293, (1946). We look to "whether the scheme involves an investment of money in a common enterprise with profits to come solely from the efforts of others." *Id.*, at 301. This definition "embodies a flexible rather than a static principle, one that is capable of adaptation to meet the countless and variable schemes

[12] *SEC v Shiner*, 2003 WL 2146302 (SD Fla).
[13] *SEC v Wallenbrock*, 313 F3d 532 (9th Cir 2002).

devised by those who seek the use of the money of others on the promise of profits." *Id.*, at 299. . . .

. . . [W]hen we held that "profits" must "come solely from the efforts of others," we were speaking of the profits that investors seek on their investment, not the profits of the scheme in which they invest. We used "profits" in the sense of income or return, to include, for example, dividends, other periodic payments, or the increased value of the investment.

There is no reason to distinguish between promises of fixed returns and promises of variable returns for purposes of the test, so understood. In both cases, the investing public is attracted by representations of investment income, as purchasers were in this case by ETS' invitation to " 'watch the profits add up.' " Moreover, investments pitched as low-risk (such as those offering a "guaranteed" fixed return) are particularly attractive to individuals more vulnerable to investment fraud, including older and less sophisticated investors. Under the reading respondent advances, unscrupulous marketers of investments could evade the securities laws by picking a rate of return to promise. We will not read into the securities laws a limitation not compelled by the language that would so undermine the laws' purposes. . . .

The Eleventh Circuit's perfunctory alternative holding, that respondent's scheme falls outside the definition because purchasers had a contractual entitlement to a return, is incorrect and inconsistent with our precedent. We are considering investment *contracts*. The fact that investors have bargained for a return on their investment does not mean that the return is not also expected to come solely from the efforts of others. Any other conclusion would conflict with our holding that an investment contract was offered in *Howey* itself. 328 U.S., at 295-296, 66 S.Ct. 1100 (service contract entitled investors to allocation of net profits).

We hold that an investment scheme promising a fixed rate of return can be an "investment contract" and thus a "security" subject to the federal securities laws. The judgment of the United States Court of Appeals for the Eleventh Circuit is reversed, and the case is remanded for further proceedings consistent with this opinion.

It is so ordered.

Questions

1. ETS argued that the arrangement involved commercial equipment leases, not securities. Did Congress intend to cover the leases under the securities laws?
2. Is it fair to say that investments promising a fixed return are attractive to individuals more vulnerable to investment fraud?
3. State the *Hovey* test for determining whether a particular scheme is an investment contract.

THINKING THINGS THROUGH

PROBLEM: CONFLICTS OF INTEREST—REMEDY: COMMONSENSE RULES

Full-service brokerage firms serve both retail and corporate clients. On the retail side, brokers buy and sell stocks and bonds for retail clients from all walks of life. The firms' research analysts perform the very important function of studying the performance of companies listed on the major stock exchanges, and the analysts make recommendations on these companies' securities, such as "buy," "hold," or "sell," for the benefit of their brokers and clients. Brokerage firms also serve corporate clients by underwriting and distributing new issues of stocks and bonds. This is called the INVESTMENT BANKING function of the firm. When a manufacturing or service company issues securities for the first time, the transaction is called an INITIAL PUBLIC OFFERING or IPO. Lucrative fees are earned by brokerage firms from the successful placement of such issues and subsequent new equity issues for established publicly held companies. These securities are sold to retail clients and the public by the brokerage firms, with firm analysts' recommendations being an important element in the success of the placements and the overall profitability of the brokerage firms.

An investigation into Merrill Lynch by the New York Attorney General's Office revealed that while certain Merrill analysts were publicly

THINKING THINGS THROUGH

continued

recommending certain dot-coms that were investment banking clients of the firm, internal e-mails indicated that these analysts believed the same dot-coms were "crap" and "junk." One wrote to a colleague questioning his "positive" recommendation of a dot-com company whose numbers seemed weak to her, and his response was he had written "pos," as in piece of [expletive deleted].

The public and retail clients believed that the firm's analysts were independent of the investment banking function of the firm and that the recommendations were made solely with retail clients' interests in mind. The New York Attorney General's Office concluded, however, that analysts and investment bankers were closely involved in each other's work and were not independent; that the analyst department's compensation was tied to the results of the investment banking department's results; and that analysts were negotiating with investment banking clients for ratings. This blatant conflict of interest not only had and will continue to have an adverse impact on Merrill Lynch's retail client business, but it also demoralized Merrill Lynch's brokers who were uninformed of the practices. Moreover, it will lead to years of litigation.

The SEC has initiated new rules to eliminate conflicts of interests at full-service brokerage firms. These rules are based on management common sense. The rules include these: (1) Investment banking divisions may not supervise firms' analysts, (2) compensation for analysts may not be linked to specific investment banking transactions, (3) analysts must disclose whether they own shares in a company they recommend and certify that their recommendations are their true opinions, (4) analysts appearing in public forums before the media must disclose whether they have an interest in the company being discussed, and (5) firms must make comprehensive disclosures about their rating systems and the firms they represent as investment banking clients.*

*Section 501(a) of the Sarbanes-Oxley Act requires the SEC to adopt rules that address potential conflicts of interest in securities research. Regulation Analyst Certification ("Regulation AC") requires certification of any research report by an analyst that the views expressed accurately reflect the analyst's personal views. Moreover, the written certification requires disclosure of any compensation received by the analyst that was either directly or indirectly paid in relation to the views or recommendations expressed in the report or the views expressed in any public appearance. The SEC has approved National Association of Securities Dealers (NASD) and New York Stock Exchange (NYSE) rule changes relating to research analyst conflicts of interest.

CPA 5. Securities Act of 1933

The 1933 act deals with the original issue of securities. It prohibits the offer or sale of securities to the public in interstate commerce before a registration statement is filed with the SEC. A **registration statement** is a document disclosing specific financial information regarding the security, the issuer, and the underwriter. The seller must also provide a prospectus to each potential purchaser of the securities. The **prospectus** sets forth the key information contained in the registration statement. The object is to provide the interested investor detailed information about the security and the enterprise. The SEC does not approve or disapprove the securities as being good or bad investments but only reviews the form and content of the registration statement and the prospectus to ensure full disclosure. The requirements of advance disclosure to the public through the filing of the registration statement with the SEC and the sending of a prospectus to each potential purchaser are commonly referred to as the **registration requirements** of the 1933 act.

CPA (a) Applicability

The 1933 act applies to (1) stocks, (2) corporate bonds, and (3) any conceivable type of corporate interest or instrument that has the characteristics of an investment security, including convertible securities and variable annuities. The act applies to all such instruments that have investment characteristics.

CPA (b) The Registration Process

Section 5 of the 1933 act provides for the division of the registration process into three time periods: (1) the prefiling period, (2) the waiting period, from the date of filing with the SEC to the date the registration statement becomes effective (a minimum of 20 days but commonly extended for additional 20-day periods after each amendment by the issuer in compliance with SEC requirements for additional information), and (3) the posteffective period. The time divisions allow the public an opportunity to study the information disclosed in the registration process before a sale can be made. Permissible, required, and prohibited activities during these time periods are set forth in Figure 46-1.

CPA (c) Regulation A Offerings

Regulation A provides a simplified registration process for small issues of securities by small businesses. Although technically exempt from the 1933 act registration requirements, a Regulation A offering involves a "mini-registration" with the SEC. Under the SEC's Small Business Initiative, Regulation A applies to the offerings of securities up to $5 million in a 12-month period. Disclosure requirements are simplified by the use of the small corporate offerings registration (SCOR) form, with its question-and-answer, "fill-in-the-blank" format. Also, the financial statements required in a Regulation A offering are less extensive than those required for a registered public offering.

FIGURE 46-1 Registration Periods

	PROHIBITED OR REQUIRED ACTIVITIES	PERMITTED ACTIVITIES
PREFILING PERIOD	ISSUER MUST NOT SELL OR OFFER FOR SALE A SECURITY BEFORE REGISTRATION STATEMENT IS FILED.	ISSUER MAY PLAN WITH UNDERWRITERS THE DISTRIBUTION OF THE SECURITY.
WAITING PERIOD	NO FINAL SALE OF A SECURITY PERMITTED DURING THIS PERIOD.	PRELIMINARY PROSPECTUS* CONTAINING INFORMATION FROM THE REGISTRATION STATEMENT BEING REVIEWED BY THE SEC MAY BE DISTRIBUTED TO INVESTORS, WHO MAY MAKE OFFERS. ADVERTISEMENTS MAY BE PLACED IN FINANCIAL PUBLICATIONS, IDENTIFYING PARTICULARS OF THE SECURITY, FROM WHOM A PROSPECTUS CAN BE OBTAINED, AND BY WHOM ORDERS WILL BE EXECUTED.**
POSTEFFECTIVE PERIOD	MUST PROVIDE A COPY OF FINAL PROSPECTUS WITH EVERY WRITTEN OFFER, CONFIRMATION OF SALE, OR DELIVERY OF SECURITY. MUST UPDATE PROSPECTUS WHENEVER IMPORTANT NEW DEVELOPMENTS OCCUR OR AFTER NINE MONTHS.	SALES OF THE SECURITY MAY BE COMPLETED.

*The preliminary prospectus is commonly called the *red herring* prospectus because of the red ink caption required by the SEC, informing the public that a registration statement has been filed but is not yet effective and that no final sale can be made until after the effective date.

**These advertisements are sometimes called *tombstone ads* because they are commonly framed by a black ink border.

Issuers may broadly solicit indications of interest from prospective investors before filing an *offering statement* with the SEC. This allows the issuer to "test the waters" and explore investor interest before incurring the expenses associated with a Regulation A offering. Solicitation-of-interest documents must be factual and comply with the antifraud provisions of the securities acts. No sales may be made until the SEC qualifies the offering statement and the seller delivers the final-offering circular, including the offering price, to the investor.

CPA (d) Registration Exemptions

Certain private and limited offerings of securities are exempt from the registration requirements of the act under SEC Regulation D.

Offerings of securities restricted to residents of the state in which the issuing corporation is organized and doing business are exempt from federal regulation. This intrastate offering exemption is applied very narrowly by the SEC and the courts, and such offerings are subject to state laws.

CPA ***(1) Rule 506 Exemption.*** The most important exemption under Regulation D is SEC Rule 506. This rule provides general permission to offer and sell to a potentially indefinite number of individuals who meet the definition of *accredited investor.*[14] It is commonly referred to as the *private placement exemption*. There is no limitation on the amount of money that can be raised by the offering.[15] Specific information must be provided to all buyers if any buyers are nonaccredited investors; the number of nonaccredited investors is limited to no more than 35.

CPA ***(2) Rule 505 Exemption.*** SEC Rule 505 of Regulation D exempts from registration offerings of less than $5 million to no more than 35 nonaccredited purchasers over a 12-month period. No limit exists on the number of accredited investors who may participate. No general solicitation or general advertising is permitted under Rule 505. If any prospective investors are nonaccredited, the issuer must furnish all investors specific information on the issuer, its business, and the securities offered for sale.

CPA ***(3) Rule 504 Exemption.*** Under SEC Rule 504 of Regulation D, as amended in 1999, an issuer can offer and sell securities up to $1 million within a 12-month period without registration and without most of the restrictions contained in Rules 505 and 506.

CPA ***(4) Restrictions.*** Securities acquired under Rules 506, 505, and 504 exemptions from registration are considered restricted securities. Their resale may require registration. Rules requiring registration of these Regulation D securities prior to resale ensure that investors purchase these securities as an investment rather than for public distribution. When there is no attempt to make public distributions, investors ordinarily fit within one of several exemptions to registration upon resale. Generally, all restrictions expire after two years.

CPA (e) Liability

Issuers, sellers, and "aiders and abettors" may be subject to civil and criminal liability under the 1933 act.

CPA ***(1) Issuer's Civil Liability for False or Misleading Statements.*** The Securities Act of 1933 imposes civil liability under section 11 for making materially false or misleading statements in a registration statement and for omitting any required material fact. An issuing company has virtually no defense if there has been a false statement and a loss.

CPA ***(2) Civil Liability of Sellers of Securities.*** Section 12 of the 1933 act applies to those who "offer or sell" securities and employ any device or scheme to defraud or obtain money by means of untrue statements of material facts. This section makes such persons or firms liable to purchasers for damages sustained.

CPA ***(3) Criminal Liability.*** Section 24 of the 1933 act imposes criminal penalties on anyone who willfully makes untrue statements of material facts or omits required material facts from a registration statement. Section 17 of the act makes it unlawful for any person to employ any device, scheme, or artifice to defraud in the offer or sale of securities.

[14] The term *accredited investor* is defined to include virtually every type of institution that participates in the private placement market such as banks, stock brokerage firms, insurance companies, mutual fund companies, retirement plans with assets in excess of $5 million, and so on as well as individual investors with substantial income or large net worth.

[15] *Kunz v SEC*, 2003 WL 1605865 (10th Cir).

6. Securities Exchange Act of 1934

The 1934 act deals with the secondary distribution of securities. It was designed to prevent fraudulent and manipulative practices on the security exchanges and in over-the-counter markets. The act requires the disclosure of information to buyers and sellers of the securities. Furthermore, the act controls credit in these markets.

CPA (a) Registration and Reporting Requirements

Exchanges, brokers, and dealers who deal in securities traded in interstate commerce or on any national security exchange must register with the SEC unless exempted by it.

Companies whose securities are listed on a national securities exchange and unlisted companies with assets in excess of $10 million and 500 or more shareholders are subject to the reporting requirements of the act.[16]

CPA ***(1) Principal Reports.*** *Form 10-K* is the principal annual report form used by commercial and industrial companies required to file under the 1934 act. The reports require nonfinancial information about the registrant's activities during the year, such as the nature of the firm's business, the property or businesses it owns, and a statement concerning legal proceedings by or against the company. The report requires the submission of financial statements with management's analysis of the financial condition of the company as well as a report and analysis of the performance of corporate shares. It requires a listing of all directors and executive officers and disclosure of executive compensation information.

Registrants who are required to file 10-K reports must also file quarterly reports, called *10-Q reports*. The 10-Q reports are principally concerned with financial information relevant to the quarterly period.

The SEC requires that annual shareholder reports be submitted to shareholders in any proxy solicitation on behalf of management. These reports contain essentially the same information as the 10-K.

CPA ***(2) Certifications and Disclosure Controls.*** The Sarbanes-Oxley Act of 2002 requires written certification of the 10-K and 10-Q reports by each company's CEO and CFO, as set forth in section 302(a) of the act and shown in the following excerpt. A "knowing" misrepresentation in connection with the certification process is punishable by fine up to $1 million and imprisonment of up to 10 years. A "willful" misrepresentation in connection with the certification process is punishable by fine up to $5 million and imprisonment of up to 20 years.[17]

Section 302(a) of the act requires CEOs and CFOs to certify that:

(1) the signing officer has reviewed the report;
(2) based on the officer's knowledge, the report does not contain any untrue statement of a material fact or omit to state a material fact necessary in order to make the statements made, in light of the circumstances under which such statements were made, not misleading;
(3) based on such officer's knowledge, the financial statements, and other financial information included in the report, fairly present in all material respects the financial condition and results of operations of the issuer as of, and for, the periods presented in the report;
(4) the signing officers—
(A) are responsible for establishing and maintaining internal controls. . . .

The SEC considers information "material" if there is a substantial likelihood that it would have been viewed by a reasonable investor as having significantly altered the total mix of information made available and if a reasonable investor would have considered the fact important in making an investment decision. The SEC has recommended that each company organize key employees into a "disclosure committee" responsible for considering the "materiality" of information and the company's disclosure obligations. For example, any transactions with insiders should be carefully considered for SEC filings.

Before Sarbanes-Oxley, many public companies published pro forma (provided in advance) financial results in press releases before filing their official quarterly reports with the SEC. This approach allowed these companies to cast their "financials" in a favorable light. The SEC financial statements are prepared under a set of accounting conventions called *generally accepted accounting principles*, or GAAP. Pro forma financial results are not prepared using GAAP, and they may not provide a true and accurate picture of a company's financial status. Section 401 of the Sarbanes-Oxley Act instructed the SEC to issue rules requiring the presentation of pro forma financial

[16] 61 FR 21354, 21356 (May 9, 1996).
[17] 18 USC § 1350(c).

statements in a manner that does not contain material misstatements or omit material facts and can be reconciled with financial results using GAAP. SEC Regulation G imposes a broad range of limitations on the use of pro forma results. If a company issues a press release saying that its pro forma earnings will be $5 million for the quarter when its official GAAP earnings will be just $4 million, the company will have to disclose both figures and explain what expenses were excluded from the pro forma figures and why.

CPA (b) Antifraud Provision

Section 10(b) of the 1934 act makes it unlawful for any person to use any manipulative or deceptive device in contravention of SEC rules. Under the authority of Section 10(b) of the 1934 act, the SEC has promulgated *Rule 10b-5*. This rule is the principal antifraud rule relating to the secondary distribution of securities. The rule states:

> *It shall be unlawful for any person, directly or indirectly, by use of any means or instrumentality of interstate commerce, or of the mails or of any facility of any national securities exchange,*
>
> *(a) To employ any device, scheme, or artifice to defraud,*
>
> *(b) To make any untrue statement of a material fact or to omit to state a material fact necessary in order to make the statements made, in the light of the circumstances under which they were made, not misleading, or*
>
> *(c) To engage in any act, practice, or course of business that operates or would operate as a fraud or deceit upon any person, in connection with the purchase or sale of any security.*[18]

CPA ***(1) Private Actions.*** Rule 10b-5 applies to all securities, whether registered or not, as long as use is made of the mail, interstate commerce, or a national stock exchange. Subject to the safe harbor provisions of the Private Securities Litigation Reform Act as discussed in the following section, under Rule 10b-5, a civil action for damages may be brought by any private investor who purchased or sold a security and was injured because of false, misleading, or undisclosed information.[19]

CPA ***(2) Liability for "Material Misstatements or Omissions of Fact."*** Rule 10b-5 prohibits the making of any untrue statement of a "material" fact or the omission of a material fact necessary to render statements made not misleading. In every Rule 10b-5 case, the plaintiff must show "reliance" on the misrepresentation and resulting injury.

In a merger context, "materiality" depends on the probability that the transaction will be consummated and on the significance to the issuer of the securities.[20] That is, "materiality" depends on the facts and must be determined on a case-by-case basis. **For Example,** assume that Corporation *A* was involved in merger discussions with Corporation *B*. During this time, Corporation *A* made public statements denying that any merger negotiations were taking place or that it knew of any corporate developments that would account for heavy trading activity in its stock. Corporation *A* may be held liable for damages to its shareholders who sold their stock after the public denial of merger activity and before a later merger announcement.

In *Basic, Inc., v Levinson*, the Supreme Court dealt with the question of what should be the standard of "materiality" in merger cases.

BASIC INC., V LEVINSON, 485 US 224 (1988)

WHY SILENCE IS GOLDEN

In December 1978, Combustion Engineering, Inc., and Basic, Inc., agreed to merge. During the preceding two years, representatives of the two companies had held meetings regarding the possibility of a merger. During this time, Basic made three public statements denying that any merger negotiations were taking place or that it knew of any corporate developments that would account for the heavy trading activity in its stock. Some time later, it was publicly announced that

[18] 17 CFR § 240.10b-5.

[19] *Carley Capital Group v Deloitte Touche, LLP*, 27 F Supp 2d 1324 (ND Ga 1998).

[20] See *Rizzo v The MacManus Group, Inc.*, 158 F Supp 2d 297 (SDNY 2001).

there would be a merger. Certain former shareholders who had sold their Basic stock between Basic's first public denial of merger activity and the public announcement of the merger brought a Section 10(b) and Rule 10b-5 action against Basic and some of its directors, contending that material misrepresentation had been made by Basic in its public statements denying merger activity. Basic raised the defense that the alleged misrepresentations were not material and that there was no showing of reliance by the shareholders on Basic's statements. The court of appeals reversed the district court's summary judgment for Basic that preliminary merger discussions are not material information. Basic appealed to the U.S. Supreme Court.

Judicial Opinion

BLACKMUN, J.... The 1934 Act was designed to protect investors against manipulation of stock prices.... Underlying the adoption of extensive disclosure requirements was a legislative philosophy: "There cannot be honest markets without honest publicity. Manipulation and dishonest practices of the market place thrive upon mystery and secrecy." H. R. Rep. No. 1383, 73d Cong. 2d Sess., 11 (1934). This Court "repeatedly has described the 'fundamental purpose' of the Act as implementing a 'philosophy of full disclosure.'"...

Pursuant to its authority under § 10(b) of the 1934 Act, 15 U.S.C. § 78j, the Securities and Exchange Commission promulgated Rule 10b-5. Judicial interpretation and application, legislative acquiescence, and the passage of time have removed any doubt that a private cause of action exists for a violation of § 10(b) and Rule 10b-5, and constitutes an essential tool for enforcement of the 1934 Act's requirements....

The Court previously has addressed various positive and common-law requirements for a violation of § 10(b) or of Rule 10b-5.... The Court also explicitly has defined a standard of materiality under the securities laws; see *TSC Industries, Inc., v Northway, Inc.*, 426 U.S. 438, 96 S. Ct. 2126, 48 L. Ed. 2d 757 (1976), concluding in the proxy-solicitation context that "an omitted fact is material if there is a substantial likelihood that a reasonable shareholder would consider it important in deciding how to vote."... Acknowledging that certain information concerning corporate developments could well be of "dubious significance,"... the Court was careful not to set too low a standard of materiality; it was concerned that a minimal standard might bring an overabundance of information within its reach, and lead management "simply to bury the shareholders in an avalanche of trivial information—a result that is hardly conducive to informed decision making."... It further explained that to fulfill the materiality requirement "there must be a substantial likelihood that the disclosure of the omitted fact would have been viewed by the reasonable investor as having significantly altered the 'total mix' of information made available."... We now expressly adopt the *TSC Industries* standard of materiality for the § 10(b) and Rule 10b-5 context....

As we clarify today, materiality depends on the significance the reasonable investor would place on the withheld or misrepresented information.... Because the standard of materiality we have adopted differs from that used by both courts below, we remand the case for reconsideration of the question whether a grant of summary judgment is appropriate on this record.

We turn to the question of reliance and the fraud-on-the-market theory. Succinctly put:

The fraud-on-the-market theory is based on the hypothesis that, in an open and developed securities market, the price of a company's stock is determined by the available material information regarding the company and its business.... Misleading statements will therefore defraud purchasers of stock even if the purchasers do not directly rely on the misstatements.... The causal connection between the defendants' fraud and the plaintiffs' purchase of stock in such a case is no less significant than in a case of direct reliance on misrepresentations. Peil v Speiser, 806 F.2d 1154, 160-1161 (CA3 1986)....

Requiring proof of individualized reliance from each member of the proposed plaintiff class effectively would have prevented respondents from proceeding with a class action, since individual issues then would have overwhelmed the common ones....

We agree that reliance is an element of a Rule 10b-5 cause of action.... Reliance provides the requisite causal connection between a defendant's misrepresentation and a plaintiff's injury.... Commentators generally have applauded the adoption of one variation or another of the fraud-on-the-market theory. An investor who buys or sells stock at the price set by the market does so in reliance on the integrity of that price. Because most publicly available information is reflected in market price, an investor's reliance on any public material misrepresentations, therefore, may be presumed for purposes of a Rule 10b-5 action....

In summary:

We specifically adopt, for the § 10(b) and Rule 10b-5 context, the standard of materiality set forth in *TSC Industries, Inc., v Northway, Inc.*, 426 U.S., at 449....

Materiality in the merger context depends on the probability that the transaction will be consummated, and its significance to the issuer of the securities. Materiality depends on the facts and thus is to be determined on a case-by-case basis.

It is not inappropriate to apply a presumption of reliance supported by the fraud-on-the-market theory.

That presumption, however, is rebuttable.

[Judgment vacated and action remanded]

Questions

1. What was the legislative philosophy underlying the adoption of the extensive disclosure requirements of the 1934 act?
2. What is the standard of materiality to be applied in a merger-related context?
3. What is the "fraud-on-the-market theory"?

CPA ***(3) SEC Actions.*** Overturning 30 years of court precedent, the Supreme Court has ruled that private investors may not bring action under section 10(b) of the 1934 securities act against aiders or abettors, such as accountants, lawyers, and investment bankers, who provide assistance to the primary violator.[21] However, the SEC itself has authority to bring civil and criminal enforcement actions against aiders and abettors who knowingly provide substantial assistance to the primary violator.[22]

CPA (c) Litigation Reform Act

The Private Securities Litigation Reform Act (PSLRA, or the Litigation Reform Act) of 1995 was passed because of (1) congressional concern over an excess of frivolous private securities lawsuits, (2) the financial burdens placed on accountants and other professional advisors by such litigation, and (3) concern that the investors in a class-action lawsuit have their interests fairly represented. Important features of the act are as follows.

CPA ***(1) Safe Harbor Rules.*** Issuers of securities frequently believed that lawsuits against them under Rule 10b-5 occurred simply because the corporation made a projection that failed to materialize. The Litigation Reform Act provides shelter for issuers from private liability for forward-looking statements that were not known to be false when made and that were accompanied by meaningful cautionary statements informing investors of contingencies that could cause results to differ from projected results.

To preserve the protections of the PSLRA, quarterly and annual reports to the SEC (Forms 10-Q and 10-K) and quarterly and annual reports to stockholders, as well as corporate press releases on financial matters, now commonly utilize the expression *forward-looking statements* regarding corporate statements that estimate or project the short-term and long-term outlook for a business. Moreover, these reports typically include a section entitled "Cautionary Statements" or "Risk Factors," and contain a statement such as:

> *Forward-looking statements as contained in this report involve a number of risks, including but not limited to product demand, pricing, market acceptance, supply problems, intellectual property rights and litigation, and risks in product and technology development.*

Corporations do not have to caution against every conceivable factor that may cause results to differ from the issuer's forward-looking statements. **For Example,** Ivax Corporation, a drug company, issued a press release including optimistic assumptions about future events. Attached to the release was an italicized warning that stated in specific detail the kinds of misfortunes that could befall Ivax and could cause results to differ from its forward-looking statements. This cautionary statement did not mention that a large goodwill writedown could occur; and when a writedown did occur, Ivax stock declined sharply. Harris, Wolpin, and others brought a Rule 10b-5 fraud suit against Ivax based on the omission of a warning about the writedown risk. The court held that the cautionary statements were sufficient to warn an investor of risks similar to that actually realized and the statements satisfied Ivax's burden to warn under the statute. Ivax was not required to list

[21] *Central Bank of Denver v First Interstate Bank of Denver*, 511 US 164 (1994). See, however, *McGann v Ernst & Young*, 95 F3d 821 (9th Cir 1996), in which the Ninth Circuit Court of Appeals held that an accounting firm could be subject to "primary liability" under § 10(b) for preparing a fraudulent audit report that it knew its client would include in a Form 10-K annual report.

[22] Civil actions may be brought by the SEC under § 20(f) of the 1934 act. Criminal prosecution may be pursued under 18 USC § 2 (1994).

all risk factors, and the failure to mention one risk that in fact occurred did not "blow Ivax out of the safe harbor."[23]

CPA ***(2) Litigation Reform.*** The Litigation Reform Act places a heightened pleading requirement on plaintiffs attempting to plead fraud in securities cases, and requires not only that the plaintiffs specify each statement alleged to have been false or misleading and the reason for the belief but also that the plaintiffs plead "scienter"—the mental state embracing intent to deceive, manipulate, or defraud.[24]

The Litigation Reform Act also provides for *proportionate liability*, as opposed to joint and several liability, for defendants who are found not to have knowingly committed a violation of the security laws. In addition, securities fraud is eliminated as a predicate for private RICO actions absent a prior criminal conviction. Under the act, frivolous private securities lawsuits require payment of the defendant's reasonable attorney fees.

CPA ***(3) Class-Action Reforms.*** Reforms were necessary to protect against "lawyer-driven lawsuits" in which a class-action counsel would direct a "professional" plaintiff to buy a security to have standing to bring a class-action lawsuit. Thereafter, the class-action counsel would race to the courthouse to file before any other plaintiff and thus be able to claim enhanced standing to represent the class. The Litigation Reform Act provides that the status of lead plaintiff is offered to the person with the largest financial interest in the case, who then selects the lead counsel.

CPA ***(4) Auditor Disclosure.*** The Litigation Reform Act amends the 1934 act by requiring auditors who discover illegal acts to notify management and the board of directors and, in some cases, to notify the SEC if the issuer does not.[25] Auditors are relieved from liability for any such disclosure to the SEC.

CPA ***(5) Lawyer Reporting of Wrongdoing.*** The ABA Model Rules of Professional Conduct, which serve as a basis for most states' ethics rules for lawyers, were revised in 2003 to free lawyers from their duty of confidentiality to those clients who use the lawyers' advice to commit a crime or fraud.[26] The ABA also revised its Model Rules to allow a lawyer who knows that an officer or employee of a corporation will likely harm the company to refer the matter to higher-up officials of the organization.[27]

7. Trading on Insider Information

Section 10(b) and Rule 10b-5 form a basis for imposing sanctions for trading on **insider information.** The Insider Trading and Securities Fraud Enforcement Act of 1988, which amended the 1934 act, gave the SEC authority to bring an action against an individual purchasing or selling a security while in possession of material inside information. The court may impose a civil penalty of up to three times the profit gained or loss avoided as a result of the unlawful sale. Persons who "aid or abet" in the violation may also be held liable under the act.

Under the 1988 insider trading act, "controlling persons," including employers whose lax supervision may allow employees to commit insider trading violations, are subject to civil penalties.[28] The SEC must prove "knowing" or "reckless" behavior by the controlling person. The 1988 law establishes bounty programs that allow the SEC to reward informants giving information on insider trading activity. The reward is up to 10 percent of any penalty imposed.

(a) Trading by Insiders and Tippees

An **insider** may be a director or corporate employee. A **temporary insider** is someone retained by the corporation for professional services, such as an attorney, accountant, or investment banker. Insiders and temporary insiders are liable for inside trading when they fail to disclose material nonpublic information before trading on it and thus make a secret profit. A **tippee** is an individual who receives

23 *Harris v Ivax Corp.*, 182 F3d 799 (11th Cir 1999).

24 *In re Honeywell International, Inc. v Securities Litigation*, 182 F Supp 2d 414 (DNJ 2001).

25 PL 104-671, 109 Stat 763, 15 USC § 78j-l nt.

26 Model Rule 1·6, "Confidentiality of Information."

27 Model Rule 1·13, "Organization as Client."

28 PL 100-704, 102 Stat 4677, 15 USC § 78u-1(a)(2).

information from an insider or a temporary insider. A tippee is subject to the insider's fiduciary duty to shareholders when the insider has breached the fiduciary duty to shareholders by improperly disclosing the information to the tippee and when the tippee knows or should know there has been a breach.[29] Such a breach occurs when an insider benefits personally from her disclosure. When the insider does not breach a fiduciary duty, a tippee does not violate the securities laws.

In the *Dirks* case, the Supreme Court discussed the factors that subject a tippee to liability.

DIRKS V SEC, 463 US 646 (1983)

NO SECRETS FROM SECRIST!

On March 6, 1973, Raymond Dirks, an investment analyst, received information from Ronald Secrist, a former officer of Equity Funding of America, alleging that the assets of Equity Funding were vastly overstated as the result of fraudulent corporate practices. Upon investigation, Dirks received only denials from senior management, but certain corporation employees corroborated the charges of fraud. Neither Dirks nor his firm owned or traded any Equity Funding stock, but throughout his investigation, he openly discussed the information he had obtained with a number of clients and investors, causing liquidation of Equity Funding stock in excess of $16 million. Dirks urged the *Wall Street Journal* to publish a story on the fraud allegations. However, it declined because it feared that publishing damaging hearsay might be libelous. Dirks continued his investigation and spread word of Secrist's charges over the next two weeks. During this time, Equity Funding stock fell from $26 per share to less than $15 per share. On March 27, the NYSE halted trading of Equity Funding stock, and a subsequent investigation revealed the vast fraud that had taken place. The SEC, investigating Dirks's role in the exposure of the fraud, found that Dirks had aided and abetted violations of the Securities Act of 1933, the Securities Exchange Act of 1934, and SEC Rule 10b-5 by publicly repeating the allegations of fraud. Upon appeal by Dirks, the decision of the lower court was upheld by the court of appeals. An appeal was taken to the Supreme Court.

Judicial Opinion

POWELL, J. . . . In the seminal case of *In re Cady, Roberts & Co.*, 40 S.E.C. 907 (1961), the SEC recognized that the common law in some jurisdictions imposes on "corporate 'insiders', particularly officers, directors, or controlling stockholders" an "affirmative duty of disclosure . . . when dealing in securities." The SEC found that not only did breach of this common-law duty also establish the elements of a Rule 10b-5 violation, but that individuals other than corporate insiders could be obligated either to disclose material nonpublic information before trading or to abstain from trading altogether. In *Chiarella* [445 U.S. 222 (1980)], we accepted the two elements set out in *Cady, Roberts* for establishing a Rule 10b-5 violation: "(i) the existence of a relationship affording access to inside information intended to be available only for a corporate purpose, and (ii) the unfairness of allowing a corporate insider to take advantage of that information by trading without disclosure." In examining whether Chiarella had an obligation to disclose or abstain, the Court found that there is no general duty to disclose before trading on material nonpublic information, and held that "a duty to disclose under § 10(b) does not arise from the mere possession of nonpublic market information." Such a duty arises rather from the existence of a fiduciary relationship.

Not "all breaches of fiduciary duty in connection with a securities transaction," however, come within the ambit of Rule 10b-5. There must also be "manipulation or deception." In an inside-trading case this fraud derives from the "inherent unfairness involved where one takes advantage" of "information intended to be available only for a corporate purpose and not for the personal benefit of anyone." Thus, an insider will be liable under Rule 10b-5 for inside trading only where he fails to disclose material nonpublic information before trading on it and thus makes "secret profits."

[29] *United States v Chestman*, 974 F2d 564 (2d Cir 1991).

We were explicit in *Chiarella* in saying that there can be no duty to disclose where the person who has traded on inside information "was not [the corporation's] agent, . . . was not a fiduciary, [or] was not a person in whom the sellers [of the securities] had placed their trust and confidence." Not to require such a fiduciary relationship, we recognized, would "depart radically from the established doctrine that duty arises from as specific relationship between two parties" and would amount to "recognizing a general duty between all participants in market transactions to forgo actions based on material nonpublic information." This requirement of a specific relationship between the shareholders and the individual trading on inside information has created analytical difficulties for the SEC and courts in policing tippees who trade on inside information. Unlike insiders who have independent fiduciary duties to both the corporation and its shareholders, the typical tippee has no such relationships.* In view of this absence, it has been unclear how a tippee acquires the *Cady, Roberts* duty to refrain from trading on inside information.

The SEC's position, as stated in its opinion in this case, is that a tippee "inherits" the *Cady, Roberts* obligation to shareholders whenever he receives inside information from an insider. . . .

In effect, the SEC's theory of tippee liability . . . appears rooted in the idea that the antifraud provisions required equal information among all traders. This conflicts with the principle set forth in *Chiarella* that only some persons, under some circumstances, will be bared from trading while in possession of material nonpublic information. . . .

Imposing a duty to disclose or abstain solely because a person knowingly receives material nonpublic information from an insider and trades on it could have an inhibiting influence on the role of market analysts, which the SEC itself recognizes is necessary to the preservation of a healthy market. It is commonplace for analysts to "ferret out and analyze information," and this often is done by meeting with and questioning corporate officers and others who are insiders. And information that the analysts obtain normally may be the basis for judgments as to the market worth of a corporation's securities. The analyst's judgment in this respect is made available in market letters or otherwise to clients of the firm. It is the nature of this type of information, and indeed of the markets themselves, that such information cannot be made simultaneously available to all of the corporation's stockholders or the public generally.

The conclusion that recipients of inside information do not invariably acquire a duty to disclose or abstain does not mean that such tippees always are free to trade on the information. The need for a ban on some tippee trading is clear. Not only are insiders forbidden by their fiduciary relationship from personally using undisclosed corporate information to their advantage, but they may not give such information to an outsider for the same improper purpose of exploiting the information for their personal gain. See 15 USC § 78t(b) (making it unlawful to do indirectly "by means of any other person" any act made unlawful by the federal securities laws). Similarly, the transactions of those who knowingly participate with the fiduciary in such a breach are "as forbidden" as transactions "on behalf of the trustee himself." . . .

Thus, some tippees must assume an insider's duty to the shareholders not because they receive inside information, but rather because it has been made available to them *improperly*. And for Rule 10b-5 purposes, the insider's disclosure is improper only where it would violate his *Cady, Roberts* duty. Thus, a tippee assumes a fiduciary duty to the shareholders of a corporation not to trade on material nonpublic information only when the insider has breached his fiduciary duty to the shareholders by disclosing the information to the tippee and the tippee knows or should know that there has been a breach.

In determining whether a tippee is under an obligation to disclose or abstain, it thus is necessary to determine whether the insider's "tip" constituted a breach of the insider's fiduciary duty. All disclosures of confidential corporate information are not inconsistent with the duty insiders owe to shareholders. . . . Thus, the test is whether the insider personally will benefit, directly or indirectly, from his disclosure. Absent some personal gain, there has been no breach of duty to stockholders. And absent a breach by the insider, there is no derivative breach. . . .

Under the inside-trading and tipping rules set forth above, we find that there was no actionable violation by Dirks. It is undisputed that Dirks himself was a stranger to Equity Funding, with no pre-existing fiduciary duty to its shareholders. He took no action, directly or indirectly, that

*Under certain circumstances, such as where corporate information is revealed legitimately to an underwriter, accountant, lawyer, or consultant working for the corporation, these outsiders may become fiduciaries of the shareholders. The basis for recognizing this fiduciary duty is not simply that such persons acquired nonpublic corporate information, but rather that they have entered into a special confidential relationship in the conduct of the business of the enterprise and are given access to information solely for corporate purposes. . . . When such a person breaches his fiduciary relationship, he may be treated more properly as a tipper than a tippee. . . . For such a duty to be imposed, however, the corporation must expect the outsider to keep the disclosed nonpublic information confidential, and the relationship at least must imply such a duty.

induced the shareholders or officers of Equity Funding to repose trust or confidence in him. There was no expectation by Dirks' sources that he would keep their information in confidence. Nor did Dirks misappropriate or illegally obtain the information about Equity Funding. Unless the insiders breached their *Cady, Roberts* duty to shareholders in disclosing the nonpublic information to Dirks, he breached no duty when he passed it on to investors as well as to the *Wall Street Journal*.

It is clear that neither Secrist nor the other Equity Funding employees violated their *Cady, Roberts* duty to the corporation's shareholders by providing information to Dirks. The tippers received no monetary or personal benefit for revealing Equity Funding's secrets, nor was their purpose to make a gift of valuable information to Dirks. As the facts of this case clearly indicate, the tippers were motivated by a desire to expose the fraud.

[Judgment reversed]

BLACKMUN, J., dissenting.... The Court today takes still another step to limit the protections provided investors by § 10(b) of the Securities Exchange Act of 1934.... The device employed in this case engrafts a special motivational requirement on the fiduciary duty doctrine. This innovation excuses a knowing and intentional violation of an insider's duty to shareholders if the insider does not act from a motive of personal gain. Even on the extraordinary facts of this case, such an innovation is not justified....

In my view, Secrist violated his duty to Equity Funding shareholders by transmitting material nonpublic information to Dirks with the intention that Dirks would cause his clients to trade on that information. Dirks, therefore, was under a duty to make the information publicly available or to refrain from actions that he knew would lead to trading. Because Dirks caused his clients to trade, he violated 10(b) and Rule 10b-5. Any other result is a disservice to this country's attempt to provide fair and efficient capital markets.

Questions

1. State the SEC's theory of tippee liability. Would such a theory have an inhibiting influence on the role of market analysts?
2. When is a tippee subject to a fiduciary duty to the shareholders not to trade on material nonpublic information?
3. Does the court establish a "constructive insider" rule in its footnote?

(b) Misappropriators

Individuals who misappropriate or steal valuable nonpublic information in breach of a fiduciary duty to their employer and trade in securities on that information are guilty of insider trading as "misappropriators." **For Example,** an employee working for a financial printing firm was found guilty of insider trading under section 10(b) and Rule 10b-5.[30] While proofreading a financial document being prepared for a client firm, he figured out the identity of tender offer targets. Soon after that, he traded on this valuable nonpublic information to his advantage.

It is no defense to a section 10(b) and Rule 10b-5 criminal charge of participating in a "scheme to defraud" that the victim of the fraud (an employer) had no economic interest in the securities traded. The convictions of a stockbroker and a columnist for the *Wall Street Journal* were upheld under section 10(b) of the 1934 act. The columnist violated his fiduciary duty to his employer by revealing prepublication information about his column to the stockbroker. The stockbroker then used the information to trade in the securities identified in the column.[31]

Where an individual misappropriates confidential information for security trading purposes in breach of a fiduciary duty owed to the source of the information rather than to the shareholders who sold securities to the individual, that individual may be convicted of security fraud in violation of section 10(b) and Rule 10b-5.

The *O'Hagan* case involves the propriety of criminal liability under Rule 10b-5 under a misappropriation theory.

30 *SEC v Materia*, 745 F2d 197 (2d Cir 1984).

31 *Carpenter v United States*, 484 US 19 (1987).

UNITED STATES V O'HAGAN, 117 S CT 2199 (1997)

THE CASE OF THE DASTARDLY MISAPPROPRIATOR

James O'Hagan was a partner in the law firm of Dorsey & Whitney in Minneapolis, Minnesota. In July 1988, Grand Metropolitan PLC, a company based in London, England, retained Dorsey & Whitney as local counsel to represent Grand Met regarding a potential tender offer for the common stock of the Pillsbury Company headquartered in Minneapolis. O'Hagan did no work on the Grand Met representation. Dorsey & Whitney withdrew from representing Grand Met on September 9, 1988. Less than a month later, on October 4, 1988, Grand Met publicly announced its tender offer for Pillsbury stock. Previously, on August 18, 1988, while Dorsey & Whitney was still representing Grand Met, O'Hagan began purchasing call options for Pillsbury stock. Each option gave him the right to purchase 100 shares of Pillsbury stock by a specified date in September. Later, in August and September, O'Hagan purchased additional Pillsbury call options. By the end of September, he owned 2,500 unexpired Pillsbury options, apparently more than any other individual investor. O'Hagan also purchased, in September 1988, some 5,000 shares of Pillsbury common stock at a price just under $39 per share. When Grand Met announced its tender offer in October, the price of Pillsbury stock rose to nearly $60 per share. O'Hagan then sold his Pillsbury call options and common stock, making a profit of more than $4.3 million. O'Hagan was charged and convicted of securities fraud in violation of Section 10(b) and Rule 10b-5. On appeal, he claimed that he was not a "misappropriator," for he had no fiduciary duty to the Pillsbury shareholders from whom he purchased calls and stock; in fact, he had not even worked on the transaction at the law firm. From the reversal of the conviction by the Eighth Circuit Court of Appeals, the U.S. Supreme Court granted *certiorari.*

Judicial Opinion

GINSBURG, J.... Under the "traditional" or "classical theory" of insider trading liability, § 10(b) and Rule 10b-5 are violated when a corporate insider trades in the securities of his corporation on the basis of material, nonpublic information. Trading on such information qualifies as a "deceptive device" under § 10(b), we have affirmed, because "a relationship of trust and confidence [exists] between the shareholders of a corporation and those insiders who have obtained confidential information by reason of their position with that corporation." *Chiarella v United States,* 445 U.S. 222, 228, (1980). That relationship, we recognized, "gives rise to a duty to disclose [or to abstain from trading] because of the 'necessity of preventing a corporate insider from... tak[ing] unfair advantage of... uninformed... stockholders.'" *Id.,* at 228–229, (citation omitted). The classical theory applies not only to officers, directors, and other permanent insiders of a corporation, but also to attorneys, accountants, consultants, and others who temporarily become fiduciaries of a corporation. See *Dirks v. SEC,* 463 U.S. 646, 655, n. 14, 103 S.Ct. 3255, 3262, 77 L.Ed.2d 911 (1983).

The "misappropriation theory" holds that a person commits fraud "in connection with" a securities transaction, and thereby violates § 10(b) and Rule 10b-5, when he misappropriates confidential information for securities trading purposes, in breach of a duty owed to the source of the information. Under this theory, a fiduciary's undisclosed, self-serving use of a principal's information to purchase or sell securities, in breach of a duty of loyalty and confidentiality, defrauds the principal of the exclusive use of that information. In lieu of premising liability on a fiduciary relationship between company insider and purchaser or seller of the company's stock, the misappropriation theory premises liability on a fiduciary-turned-trader's deception of those who entrusted him with access to confidential information.

The two theories are complementary, each addressing efforts to capitalize on nonpublic information through the purchase or sale of securities. The classical theory targets a corporate insider's breach of duty to shareholders with whom the insider transacts; the misappropriation theory outlaws trading on the basis of nonpublic information by a corporate "outsider" in breach of a duty owed not to a trading party, but to the source of the information. The misappropriation theory is thus designed to "protec[t] the integrity of the securities markets against abuses by 'outsiders' to a corporation who have access to confidential information that will affect th[e] corporation's security price when revealed, but who owe no fiduciary or other duty to that corporation's shareholders." *Ibid.*

In this case, the indictment alleged that O'Hagan, in breach of a duty of trust and confidence he owed to his law firm, Dorsey & Whitney, and to its client, Grand Met, traded on the basis of nonpublic information regarding Grand Met's planned tender offer for Pillsbury common stock. This conduct, the Government charged, constituted a fraudulent device in connection with the purchase and sale of securities.

We agree with the Government that misappropriation, as just defined, satisfies § 10(b)'s requirement that chargeable conduct involve a "deceptive device or contrivance" used "in connection with" the purchase or sale of securities. We observe, first, that misappropriators, as the Government describes them, deal in deception. A fiduciary who "[pretends] loyalty to the principal while secretly converting the principal's information for personal gain," Brief for United States 17, "dupes" or defrauds the principal....

....Because the deception essential to the misappropriation theory involves feigning fidelity to the source of information, if the fiduciary discloses to the source that he plans to trade on the nonpublic information, there is no "deceptive device" and thus no § 10(b) violation—although the fiduciary-turned-trader may remain liable under state law for breach of a duty of loyalty.

We turn next to the § 10(b) requirement that the misappropriator's deceptive use of information be "in connection with the purchase or sale of [a] security." This element is satisfied because the fiduciary's fraud is consummated, not when the fiduciary gains the confidential information, but when, without disclosure to his principal, he uses the information to purchase or sell securities. The securities transaction and the breach of duty thus coincide. This is so even though the person or entity defrauded is not the other party to the trade, but is, instead, the source of the nonpublic information....A misappropriator who trades on the basis of material, nonpublic information, in short, gains his advantageous market position through deception; he deceives the source of the information and simultaneously harms members of the investing public....

The misappropriation theory comports with § 10(b)'s language, which requires deception "in connection with the purchase or sale of any security," not deception of an identifiable purchaser or seller. The theory is also well-tuned to an animating purpose of the Exchange Act: to insure honest securities markets and thereby promote investor confidence....

....The misappropriation at issue here was properly made the subject of a § 10(b) charge because it meets the statutory requirement that there be "deceptive" conduct "in connection with" securities transactions.

In sum, the misappropriation theory, as we have examined and explained it in this opinion, is both consistent with the statute and with our precedent....

[Reversed and remanded]

Justices SCALIA and THOMAS and the Chief Justice concurred in part and dissented in part.

Questions

1. Identify and explain the two types of insider training liability under Rule 10b-5.
2. Explain how O'Hagen violated Rule 10b-5.
3. What is the purpose behind the "misappropriation theory" of insider trading?

(c) Regulation FD

Effective October 23, 2000, the SEC adopted a new rule, Regulation FD (Fair Disclosure), to end the practice of selective disclosure by issuers of securities to security analysts and selected institutional investors of important nonpublic information, such as advance warnings of negative or positive earnings results, before disclosing the information to the general public. Those privy to the early release of the information had been able to make a profit or avoid a loss at the expense of the uninformed general public. For example, uninformed investors may have watched the price of XYZ Corporation fall from $47 a share to $32 a share over two days only to find out later in a subsequently disseminated general press release by the corporation that "earnings will not meet street estimates." Analysts with prior knowledge of the negative earnings reports were able to take action before the public was informed. Regulation FD requires that any disclosure be a public disclosure by filing Form 8-K or other disclosures to the public, including use of the Internet to broadly disseminate information.[32] **For Example,** when Kenneth Lewis, CEO of Bank of America, speaks to

[32] 17 CFR § 240.10b5-1.

a group of investment analysts about his company at a Wall Street meeting, Bank of America may broadcast the talk over the Web and issue a press release summarizing Lewis' comments to comply with Regulation FD.

(d) Remedy for Investors

Investors who lack the inside information possessed by the insider and sell their stock during the relevant time period may recover damages from any insider who made use of undisclosed information. Recovery is by a civil action based on Rule 10b-5.

8. Disclosure of Ownership and Short-Swing Profits

Corporate directors and officers owning equity securities in their corporation and any shareholder owning more than 10 percent of any class of the corporation's equity securities are statutorily defined as insiders and must file with the SEC a disclosure statement regarding such ownership and all related transactions. This is required under section 16(a) of the 1934 act. Under section 403(a) of the Sarbanes-Oxley Act of 2002 and effective July 30, 2003, by SEC rule, these individuals must electronically report transactions in company stock to the SEC by the second business day after the transaction. Moreover, the transaction must be posted on the SEC's and the company's Web sites within one day after the filing date.

Section 16 is designed to prevent the unfair use of information available to these corporate insiders. This section prevents insiders from participating in short-term trading in their corporation's securities.

If such a person sells at a profit any of these securities less than six months after their purchase, the profit is called a **short-swing profit.** Under section 16(b), the corporation may sue a director, officer, or major stockholder for a short-swing profit.[33] The corporation may recover that profit even without a fraudulent intent in acquiring and selling the securities.

9. Tender Offers

A corporation or group of investors may seek to acquire control of another corporation by making a general offer to all shareholders of the target corporation to purchase their shares for cash at a specified price. This is called a **cash tender offer.** The offer to purchase is usually contingent on the tender of a fixed number of shares sufficient to ensure takeover. The bid price is ordinarily higher than the prevailing market price. Should more shares be tendered than the offeror is willing to purchase, the tender offeror must purchase shares from each shareholder on a pro rata basis.

The Williams Act, which amended the 1934 act,[34] was passed to ensure that public shareholders who are confronted with a cash tender offer will not be required to act without adequate information. Under section 14(d) of the Williams Act, a person making a tender offer must file appropriate SEC forms. These forms provide information about the background and identity of the person filing, the source of funds used to make stock purchases, the amount of stock beneficially owned, the purpose of the purchases, any plan the purchaser proposes to follow if it gains control over the target corporation, and any contracts or understandings that it has with other persons concerning the target corporation.[35]

Section 14(e) of the Williams Act is the antifraud section. It prohibits fraudulent, deceptive, or manipulative practices. SEC Rule 14e-1 requires any tender offer to remain open for a minimum of 20 business days from the date it is first published or given to security holders. Federal and state legislation, as well as administrative regulation, is aimed at requiring disclosure of information and allowance of a reasonable length of time for consideration of the facts. These requirements are designed to make agreement to takeovers the result of voluntary action based on full knowledge of material facts.

As far as the courts are concerned, takeovers must be regarded with a neutral eye. If there is misrepresentation or other misconduct, the law will interfere.

33 *Levy v Southbrook International Investments, Ltd.*, 263 F3d 10 (2d Cir 2001); *Donaghue v Natural Microsystems Corp.*, 198 F Supp 2d 487 (SDNY 2002).

34 PL 90-439, 82 Stat 454, 15 USC § 78m(d), (e).

35 Section 14(d) requires a filing by any person making a tender offer that, if successful, would result in the acquisition of 5 percent of any class of an equity security required to be registered under the 1934 act. Section 13(d) of the act requires disclosure to the issuer, the SEC, and the appropriate stock exchange when a person acquires 5 percent of a class of equity security through stock purchases on exchanges or through private purchases. The person may have acquired the stock for investment purposes, not for control but must still file disclosure forms under §13(d). See *SEC v Bilzerian*, 814 F Supp 116 (DDC 1993). Section 14(d) applies only to shares to be acquired by tender offer.

Otherwise, freedom of contract requires that courts not interfere with the judgment of the contracting parties.

10. Regulation of Accountants and Attorneys by the SEC

Accountants play a vital role in financial reporting under the federal securities laws administered by the SEC. Sections 1, 12, 17, and 24 of the 1933 act and section 10(b) of the 1934 act are the sections under which accountants may be subject to liability.

An accountant who prepares any statement, opinion, or other legal paper filed with the SEC with the preparer's consent is deemed to be practicing before the SEC. Because it relies so heavily on accountants, the SEC has promulgated Rule 2(e), which regulates and provides the basis for discipline of accountants, attorneys, and consultants who practice before the SEC.[36] Under Rule 2(e), the SEC may suspend or disbar from practice before it those who are unqualified or unethical or who have violated federal securities laws or SEC rules.[37]

E-COMMERCE AND CYBERLAW

Douglas Colt was a second-year law student who developed a way to make money from the Internet. He set up a free Web site promising folks hot tips on stocks. However, Colt bought the stocks himself at low prices before pumping them up at his Web site. Once the shares were pumped up to a high enough price from the users of his Web site buying the shares, he would then sell all of his shares (i.e., dump them). Colt made more than $345,000 using the old tool of "pump-and-dump" in the new technology, the Internet.

Colt had attracted 9,000 investors to his Web site (Fast-Trades.com). One of his shares, American Education Corporation, climbed 700 percent before he sold his holdings.

Those who participated in the pump-and-dump scam, including Colt's mother, a councilwoman from Colorado, agreed to a consent decree settlement. None will pay a fine and none will repay their profits. They have simply agreed not to violate federal securities laws in the future. Georgetown University, Colt's law school, said there will be no disciplinary action.

Did Colt violate insider trading laws or any federal securities laws?

Was Colt's conduct ethical?

Enforcement on insider trading has been on the increase. The SEC has created a new group, called its Cyberforce, to deal specifically with insider trading over the Internet.

John J. Freeman, clerk at Goldman Sachs and Credit Suisse First Boston, devised a plan with two investors. Their Internet chat room expanded with information from Freeman and eventually came to be a group of 19 trading on inside information. The group made a total of $8.4 million on tips from Freeman, a part-time graphics clerk who moved through several firms during that time. Freeman entered a guilty plea for sharing inside information on pending mergers in exchange for $70,000 to $110,000 in kickbacks from the investment group's trading profits.

The difference between this trading and the 1980s Boesky scandals is the type of investor. The trading group indicted included insurance salespeople, waiters, a dentist, and a schoolteacher. But the indictment represents the largest insider trading case ever brought in terms of the number of people indicted and the number of transactions. They were discovered quite simply because the records showed the same people doing their trading in advance of mergers.

[36] 17 CFR § 201.2e.

[37] Rule 2(e) provides: "Suspension and disbarment. (1) The Commission may deny, temporarily or permanently, the privilege of appearing or practicing before it in any way to any person who is found by the Commission after notice of an opportunity for hearing in the matter (i) not to possess the requisite qualifications to represent others, or (ii) to be lacking in character or integrity or to have engaged in unethical or improper professional conduct, or (iii) to have willfully violated, or willfully aided and abetted, the violation of any provision of the federal securities laws (15 USC §§ 77a to 80B-20), or the rules and regulations thereunder." 17 CFR § 201.2e.

Section 307 of the Sarbanes-Oxley Act explicitly requires the SEC to establish minimum standards of professional conduct for attorneys practicing before the SEC in the representation of publicly held companies. The act and SEC rules require that attorneys report evidence of material violations of securities laws, up the chain of command, to the companies' general counsel, CEO, audit committees, or the full board of directors.

C. Industry Self-Regulation

To protect the public from unprofessional or negligent conduct of securities salespersons, the securities industry itself has provided means to resolve controversies relating to the sale of securities.

11. Arbitration of Securities Disputes

Member firms of the National Association of Securities Dealers (NASD), a self-regulatory organization, have adopted a code of arbitration that allows customers of NASD members to submit disputes to arbitration. The arbitration rights are contractual and are set forth in writing on opening an account with a dealer.

Securities firms with seats on the New York Stock Exchange have a similar arbitration code. Parties who have agreed to arbitrate their securities disputes can be compelled to arbitrate rather than sue in courts.[38] Courts are very reluctant to vacate an arbitration award.

LAWFLIX

Wall Street (1987) (R)

This movie will walk you through not just the evolution of greed but the evolution of a young broker moving from gathering information to stealing it to obtaining it through insiders. The movie chronicles the market's regulations as well as an individual's loss of values.

For movie clips that illustrate business law concepts, see LawFlix at **http://wdvl.westbuslaw.com.**

[38] *99 Commercial Street, Inc. v Goldberg*, 811 F Supp 900 (SDNY 1992).

Summary

State blue sky laws, which apply only to intrastate transactions, protect the public from the sale of fraudulent securities. The term *security* is defined sufficiently broadly to encompass not only stocks and bonds but also any conceivable type of corporate interest that has investment characteristics.

Two principal laws provide the basic framework for federal regulation of the sale of securities in interstate commerce. The Securities Act of 1933 deals with the issue or original distribution of securities by issuing corporations. The Securities Exchange Act of 1934 regulates the secondary distribution or sale of securities on exchanges. These acts are administered by the Securities and Exchange Commission. Except for certain private and limited offerings, the 1933 act requires that a registration statement be filed with the SEC and that a prospectus be provided to each potential purchaser. Criminal and civil penalties exist for fraudulent statements made in this process. The 1934 act provides reporting requirements for companies whose securities are listed on a national exchange and unlisted companies that have assets in excess of $10 million and 500 or more shareholders.

Rule 10b-5 is the principal antifraud rule under the 1934 act. Trading on "inside information" is unlawful and may subject those involved to a civil penalty of three times the profit made on the improperly disclosed information. Cash tender offers are regulated by the SEC under authority of the Williams Act. The securities industry provides arbitration procedures to resolve disputes between customers and firms.

Questions and Case Problems

1. What is the major distinction between the Securities Act of 1933 and the Securities Exchange Act of 1934?
2. On what rationale does the SEC allow the private placement of securities with accredited investors without any limitation on the amount that may be raised?
3. *Business Week* magazine is sent to a national distributor of magazines, Curtis Circulations Co., which sells the magazines to various wholesalers, including Hudson News. *Business Week* publishes a column entitled "Inside Wall Street," and the evidence shows that stocks discussed favorably in the column tend to increase in value after release to the public. *Business Week* has a strict confidentiality policy prior to release of the magazine to the public applicable to all employees involved in production and distribution. This policy also applies to Hudson News. Gregory Savage, an employee of Hudson News, and the "top person" in the delivery room area, arranged to have the "Inside Wall Street" column faxed to his neighbor, a stockbroker named Larry Strath, prior to the close of the market on Thursday and prior to release to the public that evening. Strath traded on the information and passed it on to Joseph Falcone, who likewise traded on the basis of this information. While Falcone paid Strath $200 for a copy of the column each week, he contends that the information he received was too remote from the *Business Week* confidentiality policy to be actionable by the SEC. What theory do you believe the SEC pursued against Falcone? What are the elements of the theory? How would you decide this case? [*United States v Falcone*, 257 F3d 226 (2d Cir)]
4. Minnesota Prostate Research Labs, Inc. (MPRL), made an inital public offering of its shares in August 1998. It stated in its prospectus that research on laboratory animals indicated that the lab may have discovered a cure for prostate cancer in humans. MPRL pointed out as well that results in animal testing did not necessarily mean that the same positive result would occur in humans. MPRL shares initially traded at $10 per share in 1999 and rose to $18 in August 2001, when the MPRL prostate cancer drug was finally approved for sale to the public. Tuttle reviewed the initial prospectus and analysts' reports on the drug and purchased 10,000 shares at $18 per share on August 18, 2001. In September of 2002, an independent study of the four leading prostate medicines indicated that MPRL's product was as effective as sugar pills in curing prostate cancer and other prostate symptoms. The price of MPRL shares plummeted to $6 per share. Tuttle is contemplating a Rule 10b-5 securities fraud class-action lawsuit against MPRL. Advise him of his chances of success in this lawsuit and any expenses that he would be exposed to other than the cost of his attorney.
5. The following transactions in Heritage Cosmetics Co., Inc., stock took place: On January 21, Jones, the corporation's vice president of marketing, purchased 1,000 shares of stock at $25 per share. On January 24, Sylvan, a local banker and director of Heritage, purchased 500 shares of stock at $26 per share. On January 30, McCarthy, a secretary at Heritage, purchased 300 shares of stock at $26.50. On February 12, Winfried, a rich investor from New England, purchased 25,000 shares at an average price of $26 per share. At that time, Heritage had a total of 200,000 shares of stock outstanding. On June 14, Winfried sold his entire holding in Heritage at an average price of $35 per share. In a local newspaper interview, Winfried was quoted regarding his reasons for selling the stock: "I have not had the pleasure of meeting any person from Heritage, but I have the highest regard for the Heritage Company,... I sold my stock simply because the market has gone too high and in my view is due for a correction." After independently reading Winfried's prediction on the stock market, Jones, Sylvan, and McCarthy sold their shares on June 15 for $33 per share. On June 20, Heritage Co. demanded that Jones, Sylvan, McCarthy, and Winfried pay the corporation the profits made on the sale of the stock. Was the corporation correct in making such a demand on each of these people?
6. The plaintiffs Lindelow and others filed a class-action suit on behalf of all persons who purchased Sabratek stock between July 6, 1999, and October 6, 1999, alleging fraud violations under section 10(b) of the 1934 act. The litigation arose out of a July 6, 1999, press release. The press release announcing Sabratek's acquisition of Moon Communications Co. stated, "Sabratek acquires Moon Communications, Internet Portal/ASP Company." The portions of the press release that were at issue stated:

   With Sabratek's involvement and guidance since the execution of a product licensing agreement, Moon has been evolving into a vertical healthcare portal with characteristics of an Application Service Provider (ASP).

   The press release also quoted defendant Hill, Moon's CEO, as stating:

   We are very excited about, and are getting ready for, our controlled market launch of OneMedPlace.com, Moon's Internet portal,' said Jay Hill, Moon's CEO. 'We have until now remained very much in stealth mode, as we incorporated knowledge gained from trial sites to make our system as robust as it could be. Over the course of 1999, we look forward to systematic implementation of our product and rollout strategy. Our goal is to make OneMedPlace.com the de facto web based network of choice for physicians, patients, providers and payers.

The press release concluded with the following statement:

> *This press release contains forward-looking statements. The actual results may differ materially from those projected in the forward-looking statements.*

The press release went on to advise investors that additional information concerning factors that could cause the actual results to differ from those contained in the forward-looking statements could be found in Sabratek's publicly filed periodic reports.

Plaintiffs allege that these statements were false and misleading at the time they were made because (1) there were no OneMedPlace.com trial sites; (2) there was no OneMedPlace.com "system," but merely a dummy demo version with woefully minimal content; (3) given the lack of any kind of operational system and the enormous hurdles involved in creating one, there was no reasonable possibility of a "product rollout" or "market launch" of OneMedPlace.com in 1999 (as Moon's own technical personnel had advised defendant Hill); (4) no material steps had been taken to evolve Moon into a "vertical healthcare portal"; and (5) Moon had no near-term ability to assist in the creation of an "all-encompassing, interactive, web-enabled, on-line medical network" linking multiple constituents in the health care arena. The defendants filed motions to dismiss because of the safe harbor protection by the PSLRA's provision for forward-looking statements. Assuming the plaintiffs' version of the facts can be proven, is Sabratek protected under the safe harbor provisions of the Litigation Reform Act? Decide. [*Lindelow v Hill*, 2001 US Dist LEXIS 10301]

7. Mary Dale worked in the law office of Emory Stone, an attorney practicing securities law. While proofreading Mary's keying of a document relating to the merger of two computer software companies, Emory joked to her, "If I weren't so ethical, I could make a few bucks on this info. Nomac Software stock prices are going to take off when this news hits 'The Street.'" That evening, Mary told her friend Rick Needleworth, a stockbroker, what her boss had said. Needleworth bought 500 shares of Nomac Software stock the next day and sold it three days later when the news of the merger was made public. He made a profit of $3,500. Did Dale, Stone, or Needleworth violate any securities law(s) or ethical principles with respect to the profit made by Needleworth?
8. International Advertising, Inc. (IA), would like to raise $10 million in new capital to open new offices in eastern Europe. It believes it could raise the capital by selling shares of stock to its directors and executive officers as well as to its bank and a large insurance company whose home office is located near IA's headquarters. Opposition to the financing plan exists because of the trouble, time, and cost involved with registering with the SEC. Advise IA how best to proceed with the registration of the new issue of stock.
9. Dubois sold Hocking a condominium that included an option to participate in a rental pool arrangement. Hocking elected to participate in the arrangement. Under it, the rental pool's agent rented condominiums, pooled the income, and after deducting a management fee, distributed the income to the owners on a pro rata basis. Hocking brought a Rule 10b-5 fraud action against Dubois. Dubois contended that the sale of the condominium was not a security under the securities acts, so Hocking could not bring a securities suit against her. Was Dubois correct? [*Hocking v Dubois*, 839 F2d 290 (9th Cir)]
10. William Rubin, president of Tri-State Mining Co., sought a loan from Bankers Trust Co. To secure the loan, he pledged worthless stock in six companies and represented that the stock was worth $1.7 million. He also arranged for fictitious quotations to appear in an investment reporting service used by the bank to value the pledged securities. The bank loaned Rubin $475,000 and took the securities as pledged collateral. In a criminal action against Rubin under section 17(a) of the 1933 act, Rubin's defense was that the pledging of securities did not constitute an offer or sale of securities under the act. Was Rubin correct? [*Rubin v United States*, 449 US 424]
11. J. C. Cowdin, a director of Curtis-Wright Co., phoned Robert Gintel, a partner of Cady, Roberts & Co., a stock brokerage house, and advised him that Curtis-Wright's quarterly dividend had been cut. Gintel immediately entered orders selling Curtis-Wright shares for his customers' accounts. The stock was selling at over $40 a share when the orders were executed but fell to $30 soon after the dividend cut was announced to the public. The SEC contended that the firm, Cady, Roberts & Co., and Gintel violated section 10(b) of the 1934 act, Rule 10b-5, and section 17(a) of the 1933 act. Gintel and Cady, Roberts & Co. disagreed. Decide. [*In re Cady, Roberts & Co.*,40 SEC 907]
12. In a January 2000 prospectus for its initial public offering of shares, Apex Oil Discovery Co. (AODC) estimated a sizable volume of oil production based on the studies of two geologists and a test well at one of its Oklahoma properties. A cautionary statement advised that the projections were only estimates based on the opinion of the two experts and a test well, and that actual production could vary significantly. Lutz bought 10,000 shares of Apex in May 2000 for $20 per share. By October 2000, 12 of its 15 drilling operations under way that year turned out to be dry holes. On October 18, 2000, AODC stock fell to $6 per share. Lutz brought a private securities civil action under SEC Rule 10b-5 against AODC, alleging that the AODC oil production estimates that induced

him to buy the stock were fraudulent as evidenced by the 80 percent failure rate of its drilling operations. What defense, if any, does AODC have in this case? Decide.

13. Douglas Hansen, Leo Borrell, and Bobby Lawrence were three psychiatrists who recognized the need for an inpatient treatment facility for adolescents and children in their community. They became limited partners in building a for-profit psychiatric facility. Each had a 6.25 percent interest in the partnership. Healthcare International, Inc., the general partner with a 75 percent interest, had expertise in hospital construction, management, and operation. Hansen, Borrell, and Lawrence asserted that the managerial control of the partnership was undertaken and operated by the general partner to the exclusion of the limited partners. The doctors claimed that their interest was a security—"an investment contract"—that gave them status to file a securities suit against the general partner under the 1934 act. The general partner disagreed. Decide. [*L & B Hospital Ventures, Inc. v Healthcare International, Inc.*, 894 F2d 150 (5th Cir)]

14. Texas International Speedway, Inc. (TIS), filed a registration statement and prospectus with the Securities and Exchange Commission offering a total of $4,398,900 in securities to the public. The proceeds of the sale were to be used to finance the construction of an automobile speedway. The entire issue was sold on the offering date. TIS did not meet with success, and the corporation filed a petition for bankruptcy. Huddleston and Bradley instituted a class-action suit in U.S. distri... of themselves and other ... Their complain... 1934 act. The p... the offering, incl... MacLean. Herma... concerning certain ... balance sheet that ... statement and prosp... defendants had engaged in a fraudulent scheme to misrepresent or conceal material facts regarding the financial condition of TIS, including the costs incurred in building the speedway. Herman & MacLean contended that the case should be dismissed because section 11 of the 1933 act provides an express remedy for a misrepresentation in a registration statement, so an action under section 10(b) of the 1934 act is precluded. Decide. [*Herman & MacLean v Huddleston*, 459 US 375]

15. Melvin J. Ford, president of International Loan Network, Inc. (ILN), promoted ILN's financial enrichment programs to ILN members and prospective members with evangelical fervor at revival-style "President's Night" gatherings. His basic philosophy was this:

> *The movement of money creates wealth. What we believe is that if you organize people and get money moving, it can actually create wealth.*

One ILN program was the Maximum Consideration Program, which, somewhat like a chain letter, provided $5,000 awards to members who sold $3,000 worth of new memberships called PRAs and made a deposit on the purchases of nonresidential real estate. According to Ford, an individual purchasing $16,000 worth of PRAs could receive an award of up to $80,000 because "all of a sudden the velocity of money increases to such a point, the ability to create wealth expands to such a degree, that ... d come back and give somebody an award for up ...00." The SEC contended that ILN was selling ...red investment contracts in violation of the ... ILN disagreed, contending that the program ...anteed a return and was thus not an investment ...ecide. Could ILN have provided full dis... ...vestors concerning the program in a ... required by the 1933 act? [*SEC v ILN, Inc.*, ... (DC Cir)]

Chapter 10
SQ 10-2, 4, 9, 10
SP 10-1, 10-5, 10-7

CPA Questio...

1. Which of the following ... security under the Secur...

   a. Stock options
   b. Warrants
   c. General partnership int...
   d. Limited partnership inte...

... ld act unlawfully if it were to sell the ... without providing the investor with a ...

... termine the investment value of the ... mon stock before approving the offering.

d. The issuer may make sales 10 days after filing the registration statement.

2. When a common stock offering requires registration under the Securities Act of 1933,

   a. The registration statement is automatically effective when filed with the SEC.

3. Hamilton Corp. is making a $4,500,000 securities offering under Rule 505 of Regulation D of the Securities Act of 1933. Under this regulation, Hamilton is

   a. Required to provide full financial information to accredited investors only

b. Allowed to make the offering through a general solicitation
c. Limited to selling to no more than 35 nonaccredited investors
d. Allowed to sell to an unlimited number of investors both accredited and nonaccredited.

4. Under the liability provisions of Section 11 of the Securities Act of 1933, an auditor may help to establish the defense of due diligence if

   I. The auditor performed an additional review of the audited statements to ensure that the statements were accurate as of the effective date of a registration statement.

   II. The auditor complied with GAAS

a. I only
b. II only
c. Both I and II
d. Neither I nor II

5. Under the Securities Exchange Act of 1934, which of the following conditions generally will allow an issuer of securities to terminate the registration of a class of securities and suspend the duty to file periodic reports?

	The corporation has fewer than 300 shareholders	*The securities are listed on a national securities exchange*
a.	Yes	Yes
b.	Yes	No
c.	No	Yes
d.	No	No

ACCOUNTANTS' LIABILITY AND MALPRACTICE

CHAPTER (47)

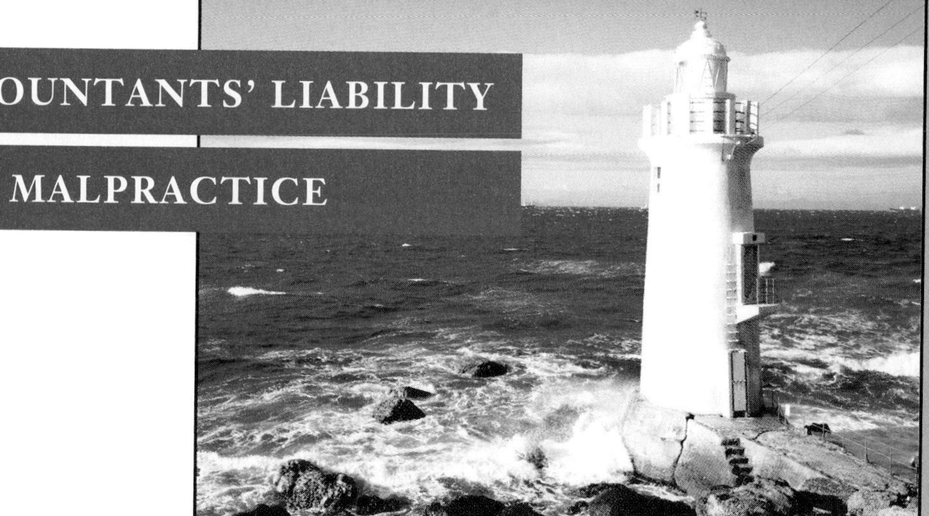

LEARNING OBJECTIVES

After studying this chapter, you should be able to

LO.1 Define *malpractice*

LO.2 Distinguish malpractice liability from breach of contract liability

LO.3 Explain the effect of contributory negligence in malpractice liability cases

LO.4 List which third parties may recover for the malpractice liability of accountants and when they may do so

LO.5 Discuss the extent to which statutes have regulated the malpractice liability of accountants

LO.6 Explain how Sarbanes-Oxley has affected the accounting profession and accountants' liability

When is a professional, such as an accountant, liable for harm caused by improper performance?

A. General Principles of Accountants' Liability

The liability of an accountant for malpractice raises questions of what constitutes malpractice, what remedies are available to enforce liability for malpractice, the effect of the others' conduct on liability, and what limitations of liability exist.

1. What Constitutes Malpractice?

An accountant who makes a contract to perform services has a duty to exercise the skill and care that are common for the accounting profession.[1] If the services are not rendered in accordance with those standards, the result is **malpractice,** as it is commonly called, which is a form of negligence and constitutes a tort.

Accountants are not insurers for the content of financial statements and are not normally liable for detecting fraud, unless they agree to do so. Also, under Sarbanes-Oxley (covered later in the chapter), accountants who perform audit work do undertake the role of certifying the internal controls of companies. Such certification is done with the hope that adequate internal controls can prevent fraud.[2] An accountant must also investigate suspicious issues and items.[3]

The standards of professional performance to which an accountant is held are found in state and federal statutes (See Chapter 46 for a discussion of federal securities issues, liabilities, and standards), court decisions, the actual contract with the client, and professional standards as established by generally accepted auditing standards (GAAS) and generally accepted accounting practices (GAAP).[4] Following GAAP and GAAS is persuasive but not conclusive evidence of meeting standards for the profession. Likewise, customs in the profession are persuasive in terms of professional performance but not conclusive.

Recovery from an accountant for malpractice requires proof of the elements of negligence (See Chapter 9 for more information). The duty and breach of duty elements are determined by the professional performance standards. The breach of professional standards must have caused the losses or damages, which must also be established.

Certified public accountants are liable for damages proximately caused by their negligence just like other skilled professions. Accountants owe their clients a duty to exercise the degree of care, skill, and competence that reasonably competent members of their profession would exercise under similar circumstances.[5]

Accountants are liable for losses they caused their clients by their failure to observe sound accounting practices.[6] Accountants are also liable if they fail to call attention to a condition that causes losses if the client could have taken preventive steps following the accountant's warning.[7]

An accountant is liable to the client if the accountant negligently fails to detect or fraudulently conceals signs that an employee of the client is embezzling or the internal audit controls of the client's business are not being observed or are lax. An accountant who prepares tax returns and acts as tax manager for the client will be liable when additional taxes or penalties are assessed against the client as a result of the accountant's negligent advice. For example, a client may recover damages from the accountant when the accountant negligently fails to inform the client of the tax consequences of selling the business.[8]

1 *Aetna Casualty & Surety Co. v Leahey Const. Co., Inc.*, 22 F Supp 2d 695 (ND Ohio 1998).

2 Section 404 of Sarbanes-Oxley has become a day-to-day term in business language as companies work to obtain their "404 certifications" from auditors. Securities and Exchange Commission, MANAGEMENT'S REPORTS ON INTERNAL CONTROLS OVER FINANCIAL REPORTING AND CERTIFICATION IN EXCHANGE ACT PERIODIC REPORTS, Securities Act Release No. 33-8283 (June 5, 2003).

3 *AUSA Life Ins. Co. v Ernst & Young*, 991 F Supp 234 (SDNY 1997).

4 *SEC v Chester Holdings, Ltd.*, 41 F Supp 2d 505 (DNJ 1999).

5 *Greenstein, Logan & Co. v Burgess Marketing, Inc.* 744 SW2d 170 (Tex 1987).

6 However, clients seeking recovery must show that their losses were the accountant's fault, not the result of their own poor business practices. *D. D. Hamilton Textiles, Inc. v Mate*, 703 NYS2d 451 (2000).

7 *Ronson v David S. Talesnick, CPA*, 33 F Supp 2d 347 (DNJ 1999).

8 *Deloitte, Haskins, & Sells v Green*, 403 SE2d 818 (Ga 1991).

O'BRYAN V. ASHLAND 717 SW2D 832 (SD 2006)

THIS IS INTERESTING—YOU OWE ME

FACTS: Bruce Ashland is a certified public accountant. He began providing services for Doug O'Bryan Contracting in 1987–1988. From 1979 through the first quarter of 1995, O'Bryan operated as a sole proprietorship. On several occasions over the years, Ashland recommended to O'Bryan that he incorporate. O'Bryan ultimately followed Ashland's advice and incorporated effective April 1, 1995.

For taxation purposes, incorporating in April meant that O'Bryan remained a cash basis taxpayer for the first quarter of the year, January 1, 1995 through March 31, 1995. Then, on incorporation, the business changed to accrual basis accounting for the last three quarters, April 1, 1995 through December 31, 1995. But, when Ashland prepared O'Bryan's 1995 tax return in October 1996, he mistakenly calculated O'Bryan's income for the first quarter using accrual based figures. As a result, Ashland understated, and consequently underreported, the income O'Bryan realized for the first quarter.

Ashland's mistake was discovered by another accountant during O'Bryan's divorce proceedings in 1997. After the accountant informed Ashland, he wrote a letter to O'Bryan disclosing the mistake and the need to correct the tax return. O'Bryan's divorce attorney hired a different accountant to review and amend the mistaken return, and, as of June 28, 1998, O'Bryan had $239,933 in additional tax liability for 1995, together with approximately $50,000 in interest. O'Bryan brought suit against Ashland for malpractice, seeking recovery for the additional expenses he incurred in correcting the erroneous tax returns. He also sought the interest the IRS charged on his unpaid tax liability.

At trial, Ashland admitted negligence and left for the jury the question of damages. The jury held Ashland liable for, among other things, the interest the IRS assessed against O'Bryan.

Based on the jury verdict the court awarded $39,038.83 in interest charges as damages. Ashland appealed.

Judicial Opinion

KONENKAMP, Justice.... In ordinary circumstances, when a tax advisor's negligence leads to an underpayment of tax, the taxpayer cannot recover as damages the tax deficiency itself because the tax liability arose not from the negligent advice, but from the ongoing obligation to pay the tax. An issue never before decided in South Dakota, however, is whether the taxpayer can recover from the negligent advisor the accrued interest the IRS charged on the delinquent tax.

Ashland urges us to follow a line of authority generally holding that recovery of interest payable to the IRS is not allowed because taxpayers have the interim use of the taxes, and therefore they are not damaged by later having to pay interest for the period of that use.

As a matter of settled law, the circuit court ruled that O'Bryan's delinquent tax debt ($239,933) could not be included in his measure of damages because it was solely O'Bryan's obligation, which he would have owed regardless of his accountant's negligence.

While Ashland conceded that under certain situations a negligent accountant should pay interest assessed against the taxpayer, such requirement would apply only to situations where the client had "the money just sitting in their one percent savings account...." Here, Ashland argued, the situation was distinguishable because O'Bryan did not have the cash readily available when his 1995 tax return was originally filed in October 1996, and if it would have been correctly filed, O'Bryan would have had to borrow the money to pay the tax at a higher interest rate than the IRS charged. As a result, Ashland contended that the loss O'Bryan sustained should not include the interest assessed by the IRS.

O'Bryan, on the other hand, maintained that he would have been able to fully pay his 1995 tax obligation had it been properly calculated, and thus he would have incurred no interest. Ashland asks us to adopt a categorical rule that interest payable to the IRS is not recoverable as a measure of damages. O'Bryan, on the other hand, asserts that he was damaged by the interest charged against him, and he should be allowed to recover it. These conflicting arguments have divided the courts around the country. Some jurisdictions hold that interest is never recoverable because delinquent taxpayers will have had the interim use of the funds owed to the IRS, and thus they are not damaged by having to pay interest for the period of that use. Other jurisdictions conclude that taxpayers would not have had to pay interest if they had received competent advice, and therefore awarding interest allows them to be restored to the situation they would have been in had they not received the faulty advice.

But what if taxpayers can prove they were truly damaged? Acknowledging this possibility, several courts refuse to adopt an absolute rule barring recovery: whether a taxpayer has been damaged is left to the finder of fact, with the burden of proof on the taxpayer. The courts taking this approach recognize that, under traditional damage principles, if the taxpayer has been injured, recovery should be allowed. These decisions focus on the position the parties would have been in had they not received the negligent advice.

Our own precedent supports the rule that "[i]n a professional negligence action, the appropriate measure of damages is the difference between what the taxpayer would have owed absent the negligence, and what [the taxpayer] paid because of [the] accountant's negligence, plus incidental damages." While this standard does not expressly include interest payable to the IRS, it does lay the foundation for such an award.

Having concluded that interest charged by the IRS may be recoverable in the proper circumstance, we now examine the facts of this case. Confronted with O'Bryan's and Ashland's conflicting theories, the trial court allowed them to be evaluated by the jury, and, through special interrogatories, the jury found that O'Bryan was damaged by the interest assessed. There was evidence to support this verdict. He said that he would not have necessarily had to borrow the money from a bank; he may have been able to borrow money from his family as he had done before. Only a trier of fact could adequately assess these claims. We conclude that there was sufficient evidence in the record to support the jury's determination that the interest charged by the IRS was directly related to Ashland's negligence and that O'Bryan suffered a loss as a result. Therefore, the circuit court did not err when it allowed the issue to go to the jury.

[Affirmed]

Questions

1. What was the malpractice by the accountant?
2. What were the financial consequences to the client?
3. What argument does the accountant make against having to pay the interest charges?

2. Choice of Remedy

In addition to liability under tort law for malpractice, accountants may be held liable for breach of contract for their failure to meet professional standards.

(a) Breach of Contract

A breach of an accountant's contract occurs if the audit work, for example, was not completed. In such a situation, the client need not pay the accountant's fee. If the work was complete, but there were minor errors, the client can seek to have the fee adjusted for the damages caused by the error.

Remedies for breach of contract are not available to third parties against accountants because they are not ordinarily considered third-party beneficiaries of contracts with accountants.

(b) Tort Liability

A client or third party may be able to recover from an accountant on the basis of negligence, gross negligence, or fraud. These theories are covered in the remaining sections of the chapter.

Because malpractice is both a breach of contract and an independent tort, the client who is harmed has the choice of recovering for breach of contract or for the particular tort that is involved. Generally, the client will bring a tort action when justified by the facts because torts provide for higher damages than those afforded for a breach of contract. The statute of limitations on torts versus contracts may also influence the theory for liability. The statute of limitations begins to run on the tort of malpractice from the date the harm was discovered. The contract statute of limitations runs from the date the contract is breached. This time differential may be very important because in some cases, the client may not realize that there has been any harm until some time after a breach of the contract occurred.

3. The Environment of Accountants' Malpractice Liability

Accountants have moved from being primarily clerical business participants to being essential players in business strategies. In addition, accountants have moved from being employees of one employer to being independent contractors performing accounting services for many clients. Accountants are now employed to produce data that third parties use and rely on in making decisions about loans or investments. **For Example,** accountants prepare statements submitted to banks that will use those statements to determine whether to make a loan or extend a line of credit. Auditors' certifications of financial statements become part of the documents given to potential investors in companies. As these changes in the role of accountants took place, it became natural for courts to allow third parties relying on accountants' work and certifications to recover from the accountants when the accountants' and auditors' malpractice caused damages to them.

At the same time that these changes were taking place in the nature and role of accountants, changes were also taking place in other areas of the law. Manufacturers and parts suppliers were held liable to those who purchased the final products and were injured by defects in them. The rising tide of liability to third parties has naturally influenced the law regulating accountants.[9]

4. Limitation of Liability

Can accountants protect themselves from liability for malpractice claims of clients and third parties? Because the law generally permits any contracting party to limit or disclaim liability for negligence, an accountant may exclude liability for malpractice on a theory of negligence. Influenced by the consumer protection movement and by the law governing product liability, courts will require such disclaimers to be (1) clear and unambiguous and (2) conspicuous. If these requirements are not met, the disclaimers will not be held effective.

(a) Scope of Limitation

Disclaimers are valid when the circumstances are such that it is not reasonable to expect the accountant to stand behind particular data. **For Example,** when a client owns land in a foreign country, it is reasonable for the accountant to accept the valuation placed on the land by someone in that foreign country. If the accountant includes in the financial statement prepared for the client a statement that the valuation of that land was obtained from an identified person in the foreign country and that the accountant assumes no responsibility for the accuracy of that valuation, the accountant is protected if that information proves to be false. If the accountant's examination has been restricted, the accountant is protected from claims of third parties when the accountant makes a certification or statement that certain assets were not examined and that the figures relating to them have not been verified. **For Example,** when the accountant is restricted from examining accounts receivable and the accountant's certification states that no opinion was expressed as to accounts receivable, the accountant cannot be held liable if the information relating to accounts receivable was not accurate.[10]

(b) Limitations on Exculpatory Provisions

A disclaimer based on lack of knowledge does not protect the accountant from liability if the accountant knew or had reason to know that the statements made were false. If the accountant states that he had no personal knowledge, he impliedly represents that he did not have any knowledge or reason to know that the statements were not correct. If the accountant attempted a disclaimer with such knowledge, the result would be **misrepresentation** and liability for such.[11]

In some states, a **limitation-of-liability** or **exculpatory clause** protects the accountant from a malpractice suit brought by a client only, not from a suit brought by a third party. In such cases, courts apply the general rule of contract law that only a party to a contract is bound by an exculpatory or limitation-of-liability clause.

When the malpractice liability of accountants is based on intentional falsification of data, a limitation of liability will not be binding. It is against public

[9] The interplay between the various areas of malpractice liability and those of accountants is seen further in the fact that the Restatement (Second) of Torts does not contain a separate provision applicable only to accountants but deals with the subject of malpractice liability of accountants to third parties in a general section (§ 552). Section 552 provides that

> *[O]ne who in the course of his business, profession or employment, or in any other transaction in which he has a pecuniary interest, supplies false information for the guidance of others in their business transactions, is subject to liability for pecuniary loss caused to them by their justifiable reliance on the information, if he fails to exercise reasonable care or competence in obtaining or communicating the information.*

The section then defines which parties can enforce this liability.

[10] *Stephans Industries, Inc. v Haskins & Sells*, 438 F2d 357 (10th Cir 1971).

[11] However, an accountant can provide financial information on an employee's severance package and disclaim liability by advising the employee to obtain independent tax advice. *Buehner v IBM Corp.*, 704 NYS2d 303 (2000).

policy to permit a limitation of liability when an intentional tort has been committed.

B. Accountants' Liability to Third Parties: Beyond Privity

Most accountants' malpractice litigation involves the question of whether third parties may recover from the accountants, not on what standards of conduct accountants should observe. Various issues and factors determine whether accountants will be held liable to various third parties. Judicial decisions and statutes control liability issues.[12]

5. Status of the Accountant

An accountant may be a full-time employee of a company, an independent contractor doing regular work for a client, or an independent outside auditor. What constitutes negligence is the same for all three types of accountants. When a third party seeks recovery from the accountant, it is immaterial that there is no fiduciary relationship between them. The liability of the accountant to the third party, when recognized, is based on the reliance of the third party on the work of the accountant.[13]

6. Conflicting Theories of Accountants' Third-Party Liability

A number of theories have been developed to determine whether a third party sustaining a loss because of an accountant's negligence can recover from the accountant for loss or whether the third party is an interloper who has no cause of action. These views may be identified as (1) the privity rule, (2) the contact rule, (3) the known user rule, (4) the foreseeable user rule, and (5) the intended user rule. In addition, some courts follow (6) a flexible rule, deciding each case as it arises. Each of these views is an attempt to draw a boundary line between the interloper and the "proper" plaintiff. In some states, statutes have been adopted defining when nonprivity plaintiffs may sue an accountant for negligence.[14]

(a) The Privity Rule

The **privity rule** precludes a negligence malpractice suit by a third party. This rule holds that only the party in privity with the accountant—that is, the accountant's client—may recover from the accountant.[15] When the privity rule is applied, a bank lending money to the accountant's client cannot recover from the accountant for malpractice.

AUSA LIFE INSURANCE CO. V ERNST & YOUNG, 206 F3D 202 (2D CIR 2000) AND 119 F SUPP 2D 394 (SDNY 2000), AFF'D IN UNPUBLISHED OPINION

WHEN THE COMPANY GOES BELLY UP, MUST THE ACCOUNTANT ANTE UP?

AUSA Life Insurance Company and others (plaintiffs/appellants) were institutional investors in the securities of JWP, Inc., a company that went belly-up, resulting in nearly a 100 percent loss of their investments. Ernst & Young (appellee) served as auditor for JWP from 1985 to 1992. During most of that period, JWP was in a period of rapid expansion financed by private placements of debt securities, and it became increasingly leveraged. By 1991, it was losing an average of $10 million per month. Ernst & Young knew of "accounting irregularities" from at least 1988 through 1991 but did not insist on their correction. Ernst & Young issued unqualified financial opinions for all of those years. One of the irregularities was recording anticipated future tax benefits of net operating losses forward in violation of GAAP.

AUSA and its fellow investors sued Ernst & Young for their losses. The federal district court dismissed the case and AUSA appealed.

[12] *Chestnut Corp. v Pestine, Brinati, Gamer, Ltd.*, 667 NE2d 543 (Ill 1996).

[13] *Brown v KPMG Peat Marwick*, 756 SW2d 742 (Tex 1993).

[14] See, e.g., Ark Code Ann § 16-114-302; Ill Stat Ann § 225/450/30.1; Kan Stat Ann § 1-402; NJ Stat Ann § 2A:53A-25; Utah Code Ann § 58-26-12; and Wyo Stat § 33-3-201.

[15] This rule was originally known as the New York rule, *Ultramares Corp. v Touche*, 174 NE 441 (NY 1931). Although it has been replaced in New York by the contact rule, the privity rule is still the law in many jurisdictions.

Judicial Opinion

OAKES, Senior Circuit Judge.... E & Y's statements about JWP's financial health were less than accurate and were not always in accordance with GAAP or GAAS ("generally accepted auditing standards"). However, E & Y did not fail to notice that often JWP's financial representations about itself were not in accordance with GAAP; rather, E & Y consistently noticed, protested, and then acquiesced in these misrepresentations: E & Y's failure lay in the seeming spinelessness of John LaBarca [the partner in charge of the JWP audit] and the other E & Y accountants in their dealings with JWP, and particularly with its CEO, Ernest Grendi.... Grendi almost invariably succeeded in either persuading or bullying them to agree that JWP's books required no adjustment. Part of the problem was undoubtedly the close personal relationship between Grendi and LaBarca. Grendi had been a partner of LaBarca in E & Y's predecessor firm and they continued to be good friends, regularly jogging together in preparation for the New York City Marathon.

"It became a well-worn inside joke to refer to the lax accounting standards at JWP as 'EGAAP,' an acronym for Ernest Grendi's Accepted Accounting Practices." In August of 1992, JWP retained Deloitte & Touche ("D & T"), another major accounting firm, to review thoroughly JWP's books and E & Y's audits. D & T concluded that JWP's annual reports for 1990–1992 should be restated to reduce the 1990 after-tax net income by 15% (from $59 million to $50 million), that the 1991 after-tax income should be reduced by 52% from $60 million to $29 million, and that 1992 loss of $612 million with a corresponding net worth of negative $176 million should be reflected. E & Y concurred.

The appellants appeal on... [t]hese bases: (1) the district court's refusal to find causation between E & Y's actions or inactions and the appellants' losses; (2) the district court's standards for assessing the transaction causation and scienter elements of the appellants' federal securities claims and the appellants' common law fraud claims; and (3) the district court's finding that there was not a near-privity relationship between the investors and E & Y.

We agree with the district court that E & Y did not perform the most efficacious accounting in this situation. However, we part company with the district court on its determination that it was "unforeseeable post-audit developments [that] caused JWP's insolvency and default even if its financial condition had been fully as healthy as was represented in those reports."

Causation in this context has two elements: transaction causation and loss causation. Loss causation is causation in the traditional "proximate cause" sense—the allegedly unlawful conduct caused the economic harm. Transaction causation means that "the violations in question caused the appellant to engage in the transaction in question."

There is ample evidence in the record that the appellants relied on E & Y's certifications of the financial soundness of JWP both in making their note purchases and in continuing to hold the notes. This was not a situation where the notes were marketed en masse, and E & Y had a barely tangential role in the transaction. Rather, the purchasers of these private placement notes specifically required the audits of E & Y before purchasing the notes and as a condition of their purchase. Applying to these facts the legal definition of transaction causation, we find that transaction causation was established.

Addressing loss causation is a more difficult endeavor. How far back should the line be drawn in the causal chain, before which, "because of convenience, of public policy, of a rough sense of justice," proximate cause cannot be found? *Palsgraf v Long Island R. Co.*, 248 N.Y. 339, 352, 162 N.E. 99, 103 (1928). In the vernacular, where does the buck stop?

The appellee maintains—and the district court agreed—that the events leading to the demise of JWP and the loss of appellants' investments were due to external events for which appellee cannot be held accountable, and therefore loss causation was not established. The district court said specifically that JWP's insolvency and resulting default on its note obligations were caused not by the differences between its actual financial condition and that reflected in its audited annual reports, but by much more significant factors, including JWP's disastrous acquisition of the failing. We disagree, however, with this conclusion of the district court to the extent that the district court did not fully consider the legal definition of "loss causation" and the requisite factual points in determining whether loss causation was established.

The test should not be whether the defrauded party might conceivably still have lost, had the fraud not been practiced, but whether there was a reasonable probability that the fraud actually accomplished the result it was intended to bring about.

When a significant period of time has elapsed between the defendant's actions and the plaintiff's injury, there is a greater likelihood that the loss is attributable to events occurring in the interim. Similarly, when the plaintiff's loss coincides with a marketwide phenomenon causing comparable losses to other investors, the prospect that the plaintiff's loss was caused by the fraud decreases.

The purpose of the proximate cause requirement is to fix a legal limit on a person's responsibility, even for wrongful acts. Central to the notion of proximate cause is the idea that a person is not liable to all those who may have been injured by his conduct, but only to those with respect to whom his acts were "a substantial factor in the sequence of responsible causation," and whose injury was "reasonably foreseeable or anticipated as a natural consequence."...Many considerations enter into the proximate cause inquiry including "the foreseeability of the particular injury, the intervention of other independent causes, and the factual directness of the causal connection."

It would be manifestly unfair, as well as contrary to law, to hold E & Y jointly and severally liable to reimburse in full losses that JWP's noteholders sustained as a result of unforeseeable and independent post-audit events and not because of fiscal infirmities which were concealed by JWP's misleading financial statements.

The story in this complaint is familiar in securities litigation. At one time the firm bathes itself in a favorable light. Later the firm discloses that things are less rosy. The plaintiff contends that the difference must be attributable to fraud. "Must be" is the critical phrase, for the complaint offers no information other than the differences between the two statements of the firm's condition.... Investors must point to some facts suggesting that the difference is attributable to fraud....That ingredient is missing in the [plaintiffs'] complaint.

The foreseeability query is whether E & Y could have reasonably foreseen that their certification of false financial information could lead to the demise of JWP, by enabling JWP to make an acquisition that otherwise would have been subjected to higher scrutiny, which led to harm to the investors.

By way of offering a tow rope to assist the district court through this Serbonian Bog, we note the following: A foreseeability finding turns on fairness, policy, and, as before, "a rough sense of justice." "A 'reasonably foreseeable act' might well be regarded as an act that a reasonable person who knew everything that the defendant knew at the time would have been able to know in advance with a fair degree of probability." Where foreseeability is less than immediately obvious, it is appropriate to make a judgment based on "some social idea of justice or policy." These considerations should be coupled with the recognition that proximate cause is a common law concept, and such concepts evolve in a manner that reflects "economic, social, and political developments."

We reverse the district court's determination that there was no privity.

We hold that transaction causation was established. We vacate and remand the loss causation determination. We hold that scienter was established. We reverse the privity determination

Questions

1. What is the difference between causation and forseeability?
2. Why does the court remand the case?
3. What does the court say about Ernst & Young's work in the audits?

(b) The Contact Rule

In relaxing the privity requirement, New York now allows a third party to recover from a negligent accountant if there was some contact between the third party and the accountant. **For Example,** an accountant may go to a bank to see what information the bank requires for the accountant's client to obtain a loan. In this case, there is a sufficient "link" or "contact" between the bank and the accountant to allow the bank to recover from the accountant if it sustains a loss because of the accountant's negligence.[16] The New York *contact rule* requires that the accountant meet or communicate with the nonprivity party to establish a relationship equivalent to privity. The accountant must also know the purpose of the accounting work and foresee the nonprivity party's reliance on that work.[17]

There must be enough contact with, or dealings between, the third party and the accountant to give the accountant reason to know that the third party

16 *Credit Alliance Corp. v Arthur Andersen & Co.*, 483 NE2d 110 (NY 1985). Some courts are strict on the contact rule describing the contact rule not as a different rule but as requiring "a relationship sufficiently intimate to be equated with privity." *Empire of American v Arthur Andersen & Co.*, 514 NYS2d 578 (NY 1987). The contact rule has been adopted by a minority of states. *Idaho Bank & Trust Co. v First Bankcorp of Idaho*, 772 P2d 720 (Idaho 1989).

17 *Security Pacific Business Credit, Inc. v Peat Marwick Main & Co.*, 597 NE2d 1080 (NY 1992).

was relying for a particular purpose on the financial statements prepared by the accountant.[18]

(c) The Known User Rule

Under this rule for nonprivity parties, the accountant is liable to third parties who experience a loss as a result of the accountant's negligence when the accountant knew that the third party would be using the accountant's work product. **For Example,** a shareholder may recover from an accountant for negligently preparing and certifying an annual financial report that was prepared for distribution to shareholders.[19]

Under the known user rule, the fact that the nonprivity party's reliance on a financial statement was foreseeable does not entitle the third party to recover from the accountant for negligent preparation of the statement. The third party must show that the accountant knew the statement would be furnished to that plaintiff. Thus, under this rule, the plaintiff's reliance must thus be actually foreseen and not merely reasonably foreseeable.[20]

Under the known user rule, it is sufficient if the user or third party is a member of a known class even though the identity of the particular user is not known to the accountant. However, some states hold that when the identity of the intended user is known to the accountant, another party coming within the same class cannot recover from the accountant.[21] **For Example,** an accountant prepares a financial statement for a client with the knowledge that the client will take it to First National Bank to obtain a loan. First National Bank may recover from the accountant for negligent loss even though the bank never had any direct contact or dealings (that is, was never in privity) with the accountant. However, no one other than First National may seek recovery from the accountant for negligence.

The fact that the third party was a foreseeable user does not afford a basis for recovery in a "known user" state. When an accountant prepares a financial statement for the client and nothing is said about what further use of the statement will be made, creditors of the client cannot recover from the accountant for negligent preparation of the statement. The client would be the only known user.

If the court follows the privity rule or the contact rule described in the two preceding sections, the known user cannot seek recovery from the accountant for negligent malpractice. Moreover, some courts that follow the known user rule apply it so strictly that a substitute foreseeable user is not permitted to recover. To illustrate, assume that in the example just given, the client was refused the loan by First National Bank. The client might then make an application for a loan to Second National Bank. It has been held that Second National Bank could not recover from the accountant because it was not a known user. However, Second National Bank might be permitted to recover under the rules discussed in the following section.

(d) The Foreseeable User Rule

The accountant may foresee that a particular class of unknown parties will rely on her work. **For Example,** when the accountant prepares a financial statement knowing that the client is going to use it to borrow money from some bank or finance company, the accountant foresees a class of lenders. Similarly, the accountant may know that the financial statement will be used to sell the stock of the client corporation. Here again, there is a foreseeable class consisting of unknown parties.

The *foreseeable user rule* imposes liability on the accountant for negligent malpractice when he can foresee the parties who will rely on his work in the financial statements. The foreseeable user rule allows these third parties to recover for their losses without regard to the lack of privity of contract between them and the accountant.[22]

(e) The Intended User Rule

Fear that the foreseeability rule does not sufficiently restrict the number of potential claimants has led some courts to limit recovery to those nonprivity

[18] The contact rule applies to malpractice defendants generally. It is not limited to suits against accountants. *Ossining Union Free School District v Anderson*, 539 NE2d 91 (NY 1989).

[19] *Boykin v Arthur Andersen & Co.*, 639 So 2d 504 (Ala 1994).

[20] *Lindner Fund v Abney*, 770 SW2d 437 (Mo App 1989). The rule that the nonprivity plaintiff may recover from the accountant for malpractice negligence only if the accountant's statement was furnished to that plaintiff, or the accountant knew that the client who was given the statement would in turn give the statement to the plaintiff, is often identified as "the Restatement rule." This rule is based on Restatement (Second) Torts § 522(2) (1977). There is, however, some uncertainty as to the exact boundaries of the Restatement rule. See *Selden v Burnett*, 754 P2d 256 (Alaska 1988); *Raritan River Steel Co. v Cherry, Bekaert & Holland*, 867 SE2d 609 (NC 1988).

[21] *Blue Bell, Inc. v Peat, Marwick, Mitchell & Co.*, 715 SW2d 408 (Tex App 1986).

[22] *Bily v Arthur Young & Co.*, 834 P2d 745 (Cal 1992). See also *Nycal Corp. v KPMG Peat Marwick LLP*, 688 NE2d 1368 (Mass 1998).

users who were not merely foreseeable but also expected or intended to rely on the work of the accountant in a particular transaction or another similar transaction.[23] In this view, the accountant must have furnished the information directly to the nonprivity user or to the client, knowing that the client would transmit the information to the nonprivity plaintiff.

(f) The Flexible Rule

Some courts have rejected the requirement of privity for malpractice against accountants but have not adopted any of the rules discussed in the preceding sections. These courts prefer to keep the question open and to decide each case as it arises.

(g) Unknown User

When the accountant has no knowledge of, or reason to know of, any third party's use of the accountant's work, the third party is not able to come within any exception to the requirement of privity. Consequently, a nonprivity party cannot recover for the accountant's negligence when the accountant had no knowledge of any use that could affect the party.[24]

7. Nonliability Parties

There are some third parties to whom accountants do not have liability.

(a) Interlopers

No court imposes liability on the accountant to a total stranger who gets possession of the accountant's work and then sustains a loss because of a false statement in the work. This applies regardless of whether the statement was negligent or intentional. **For Example,** assume that a negligently prepared financial statement of a corporation is thrown in the wastepaper basket and is then retrieved by a security guard. If the guard thinks that the statement is a "hot tip" and invests in the stock of the corporation on the basis of the statement, the guard cannot recover from the accountant for negligence in preparing the

THINKING THINGS THROUGH

HOW MANY PLAINTIFFS CAN THERE BE IN A CLASS-ACTION SECURITIES LITIGATION? HOW MANY DEFENDANTS?

With the collapse of Enron and WorldCom, numerous civil suits were filed against Arthur Andersen, the auditor for both companies. The following is a list of all of the types of plaintiffs who have brought suit against Arthur Andersen:

- Shareholders who purchased Enron stock.
- State pension funds with Enron stock in their portfolios.
- Banks and other institutions that lent money to Enron.
- Banks and other institutions that accepted Enron stock as collateral for loans to institutions and individuals who owned Enron stock.
- Universities that received Enron stock as endowment gifts.
- Companies that contracted with Enron after having requested financial statements from Enron.
- Dynegy, a company that was in negotiations for the purchase of Enron but discovered accounting issues and had to terminate the acquisition and experienced litigation and damages over the termination of the acquisition.
- Brokers who valued clients' accounts and margins based on the values of their Enron stock.

Applying the various standards for accountant liability you have learned, discuss whether each of these groups will be able to recover from Andersen, and why or why not.

[23] Some courts regard this rule as representing the majority view. The foreseeable user rule brings the law with respect to accountants into harmony with the tort law relating to other parties and activities.

[24] *Sundamerican Bank & Trust Co. v Harrison*, 851 SW2d 563 (Mo App 1993).

statement. Accountants are not liable to interlopers, but courts continue to struggle with drawing the line between interlopers and rightful third parties.

(b) Parties Affected by the Decision of Accountant's Client

On the basis of information furnished by the accountant to a client, the client may make a decision that affects a third party. **For Example,** a report by an independent auditor may indicate that a fiscal officer of the client has not handled funds properly. The report may indicate that it is economically unsound to enter into a contract with a third party. Assume that the client relies on the accountant's report and fires the employee or refuses to make a contract with the third party. If the report of the accountant was negligently made and the true facts would not have justified the action taken by the client, most courts hold that third parties harmed in this indirect way may not recover.[25]

8. Defenses to Accountants' Liability: Contributory and Comparative Negligence of the Client or Third Party

(a) Contributory Negligence

When an accountant has been negligent, the client's comparative negligence may reduce the accountant's liability. To establish client **contributory negligence,** the accountant must show that the client contributed to the accountant's failure or that the client ignored the accountant's instructions.

When suit is brought by a third party for malpractice, the accountant may raise the defense of the third party's contributory negligence. If the third party acted negligently in relying on a financial statement, the third party cannot recover from the accountant for negligently preparing the statement. **For Example,** when the financial statement indicates that it is merely a working examination and is not certified by the accountant, the third party is negligent in relying on the statement and has been contributorily negligent.

In some cases, it may be apparent on the face of the financial statement that the business is in poor financial condition. When a prudent party would see danger in the financial statement, recovery from the accountant on the ground that the statement was negligently prepared is limited.

If the user of a financial statement is highly sophisticated and a shareholder of the corporate client and has been warned by its own advisors that the corporate assets have been overvalued, the user cannot hold the accountant liable for negligence in overstating the value of the corporate assets. In such a case, the user is not entitled to rely on the audit made by the accountant and is contributorily negligent in so doing. Such negligence bars recovery from the accountant.[26]

Some states ignore the negligence of the client unless it actually contributed to the accountant's negligence or interfered with the accountant's audit. The negligence of the accountant's client in keeping records is not a bar to the accountants' liability to the client for the accountant's failure to discover the true facts.[27] The issue in these circumstances becomes not whether the accountant knew, but whether she should have known. Client interference with the accountant's work will excuse the accountant's liability.

(b) Comparative Negligence

Can an accountant reduce liability for negligence by proving that the client was also negligent? Some states apply the **comparative negligence** concept and permit proof of the client's negligence.[28] The result is that the accountant and the client are assessed a percentage of blame for their respective levels of negligence in the use and preparation of the financial statements, and the client's recovery is reduced by its percentage of fault. For example, if a jury finds that the client was responsible for 30 percent of the resulting loss, recovery from the accountant is reduced by 30 percent.

9. Accountants' Fraud Malpractice Liability to Third Parties

Society in general condemns fraud more strongly than it does negligence. There is greater liability of accountants for fraudulent malpractice.

[25] *Harper v Inkster Public Schools*, 404 NW2D 776 (Mich App 1987).

[26] *Scottish Heritable Trust v Peat Marwick Main & Co.*, 81 F3d 606 (5th Cir 1996).

[27] *World Radio Laboratories, Inc. v Coopers & Lybrand*, 538 NW2d 501 (Neb App 1995).

[28] *American Nat'l Bank v Touche Ross & Co.*, 659 NE2d 1276 (Ohio 1996).

FIGURE 47-1 Theories of Accountants' Liability to Third Parties

THEORY	TYPE OF LIABILITY	THIRD PARTY LIABILITY	CLIENT LIABILITY
STATUTORY	1933 SECURITIES ACT—OMISSION OR MISSTATEMENT IN REGISTRATION STATEMENT 1934 SECURITIES EXCHANGE ACT—10b (SEE CHAPTER 48)	PURCHASERS OF SHARES SHAREHOLDERS; PURCHASER OF SHARES	COMPANY
CONTRACT	BREACH OF CONTRACT	NO—NOT CONSIDERED THIRD PARTY BENEFICIARIES	MATERIAL BREACH; MINOR BREACH DAMAGES
TORT	PRIVITY REQUIRED	NO RECOVERY	RECOVERY ALLOWED UNLESS DEFENSES APPLY
	CONTACT RULE REQUIRED	CAN RECOVER IF ACTUAL CONTACT WITH ACCOUNTANT	
	KNOWN USER RULE	CAN RECOVER IF ACCOUNTANT KNOWS THIRD PARTY WILL USE FINANCIALS/WORK	
	FORESEEABLE USER RULE	CAN RECOVER IF ACCOUNTANT CAN FORESEE UNKNOWN PERSONS RELYING ON FINANCIALS	
	INTENDED USER RULE	CAN RECOVER IF ACCOUNTANT KNOWS CLIENT WILL GIVE IT TO ANOTHER	
	UNKNOWN USER	NO RECOVERY	
FRAUD	KNOWN AND UNKNOWN	RECOVERY	RECOVERY

(a) What Constitutes Fraud by Accountants

Fraud is defined as a false statement made with knowledge that it was false or with reckless indifference as to whether it was true[29] with the intent that the listener rely on it. In the field of accounting, the false statement typically is a statement of accounting in such a way as to make the client appear to be in a better financial position than is actually the case. **For Example,**

[29] *Perlberger v Perlberger*, 32 F Supp 2d 197 (ED Pa 1998), vacated in part, modified in part, 34 F Supp 2d 282.

the client may own assets that are worthless, but the accountant retains them in the financial statement at cost or some other unreasonable value.

At times, the falsification of the financial statement may be designed to downgrade the financial condition of a corporation. Such undervaluation is done to induce shareholders to sell their stock to a dominant group of shareholders. The false financial statement purposely undervalues the corporation's assets to make the shareholders believe their stock has little value and that sale at the low price offered by the dominant group is a good buy.

(b) Accountants' Fraud Liability to Intended Victims

When an accountant commits fraud, it typically misleads a third party or a class of parties whose identity is known to the accountant. Any such victim, whether an identified party or member of a contemplated class of potential victims, may recover from the accountant for loss caused by fraud. The problem of privity (relating to liability for negligence) is ignored when the basis of the malpractice suit is fraud. The social force of preventing fraud overrides concern for creating a hardship on the accountant by allowing third parties to bring suit.

An accountant might make a false financial statement for a corporate client with knowledge that it will be used in selling the corporation's securities to third parties. If so, the third parties may recover from the accountant for the damages sustained. **For Example,** an accountant has been held liable for disguising the true character of a hoped-for profit from the sale and resale of real estate. The accountant described the sale and resale as "deferred income," although there was little reason to believe that the transaction could ever be completed because, the buyer, who was obligated to pay $5 million for the property, had assets of only $100,000. The financial statement would have shown a loss instead of a substantial profit if the true character of this risky transaction had been disclosed.

CARLSON V XEROX CORP. 392 F SUPP 2D 267 (D CONN 2005)

WHEN THE AUDITOR JUST DUPLICATES WHAT MANAGEMENT WANTS

FACTS: Throughout the early and mid-1990s, Xerox financial reports reflected a financially healthy company with revenues rising at a double-digit rate. By the late 1990s, however, Xerox faced increasing competition from Japanese competitors in the digital copier market and it was able to meet Wall Street's earning expectations only by engaging in massive accounting fraud.

An SEC complaint alleged that Xerox reallocated revenues from service to the equipment portion of sales-type leases by assuming an artificial gross margin differential between the two lease components (or an assumed profit margin) that had no basis in economic reality. Equipment margins were in fact falling. Xerox used this method to pull forward $617 million of equipment revenues from 1997–2000. Internally, KPMG referred to this method as "half-baked revenue recognition." By relying on this methodology, from 1997 to 1999, Xerox inflated its pre-tax earnings by a net of $43 million. According to the SEC, in 1996, KPMG objected to this practice as violating GAAP but, after arguments with Xerox senior management, approved its implementation in 1998, while continuing to criticize its use.

In 1999, KPMG informed Xerox that this practice violated GAAP, but Xerox refused to follow this advice. Nevertheless, KPMG certified Xerox's 1999 and 2000 financial statements.

In November of 1999, Xerox senior managers discussed the fact that without their accounting actions, Xerox had essentially no growth through the late 1990s. In 2001, Xerox began issuing a series of earnings restatements that would total $11 billion. In late 2001, Xerox announced that PriceWaterhouse Coopers, LLP ("PwC") was replacing KPMG as the company's new auditor for the 2001 fiscal year. Xerox paid a $10 million fine to the SEC to settle civil charges and also agreed to complete its restatement of earnings for 1997 through 2001.

Investors such as the Florida State pension plan and other individual investors (plaintiffs) brought suit against the executive officers of Xerox as well as KPMG for fraud.

KPMG moved to have the complaint against it dismissed because of its lack of scienter.

Judicial Opinion

THOMPSON, District Judge. . . . It is not hard to visualize a slippery slope where accounting integrity is degraded in tiny increments in the pursuit of earnings consistency. In the case of Xerox, it is troubling that the company could become so financially distressed in such a short period of time.

The $10 million fine was the largest ever paid by a public company to settle a case brought by the SEC. The SEC stated that the "largest fine ever obtained by the SEC against a public company in a financial fraud case" was called for "because of the fact that Xerox's senior management orchestrated a four-year scheme to disguise the company's true operating performance" and that the size of the fine also reflected, in part, a sanction "for the company's lack of full cooperation in the investigation."

To satisfy the requirement for pleading scienter, as set forth in 15 U.S.C. § 78u-4(b)(2), "a complaint may (1) allege facts that constitute strong circumstantial evidence of conscious misbehavior or recklessness, or (2) allege facts to show that defendants had both motive and opportunity to commit fraud."

[A]llegations of GAAP violations or accounting irregularities, standing alone, are insufficient to state a securities fraud claim.

KPMG contends that the plaintiffs have failed to allege scienter as to it under either the motive and opportunity prong or the conscious misbehavior or recklessness prong of scienter. When the factual allegations in the Complaint are viewed as a whole, the plaintiffs have at a minimum alleged facts constituting strong circumstantial evidence of recklessness on the part of KPMG. The plaintiffs have alleged inter alia,

(i) that Xerox used artificially low interest rate assumptions to artificially inflate the recognized present value of long-term leases, and KPMG expressly approved Xerox's use of such artificially depressed interest rates in countries with extremely high interest rates, such as Mexico and Brazil, for purposes of calculating revenues from leases; and that ROE was a series of top-side adjustments, and KPMG never tested Xerox's claim that the top-side adjustments were necessary, notwithstanding the fact that in 1998 the American Institute of Certified Public Accountants issued an Audit Risk Alert pointing out the increased risk associated with such;

(ii) that KPMG knew that Xerox engaged in "margin normalization," knew this practice violated GAAP, and internally referred to the practice as "half-baked revenue recognition"; and that KPMG expressed concern to Xerox about the frequency with which Xerox's long-term leasing revenue recognition methodology was changing, but took no corrective action and permitted Xerox to recognize the revenue in violation of GAAP;

(iii) that although GAAP prohibits increasing the estimated residual value of leased equipment for any reason after it is first established, Xerox recorded adjustments of at least $95 million as a result of retroactive revisions to residual values, and while KPMG initially objected to this practice as being in violation of GAAP, after "heated debates with Xerox management, KPMG approved its implementation in 1997 and allowed the practice to continue through 1998"

* * *

(iv) that after KPMG informed Xerox in 1999 that Xerox's practice of immediately recognizing revenue from price increases and extensions on leases with existing lease customers violated GAAP, Xerox did not cease this practice but merely reduced the amount of revenue it recognized, and KPMG nonetheless signed off on Xerox's 1999 and 2000 financial statements;

(v) that after the 1999 audit, Xerox "approached KPMG with a plan dubbed 'Project Mozart,' that would have shifted Xerox's big losses from selling copiers to homes and small businesses to an off-balance sheet vehicle," but the plan was scrapped after Ronald Safran, the senior audit engagement partner at KPMG, refused to sign off on the plan, after which Xerox insisted that KPMG replace Safran as the engagement partner and KPMG did so, replacing him with Michael Conway.

In March 2001, Safran was subpoenaed to appear before the SEC and was confronted with evidence of "numerous accounting irregularities engaged in by Xerox" that in March 2001, KPMG and its attorneys confronted Xerox officials with some of the documents shown to KPMG by the SEC, including an anonymous note to Xerox executives alleging "fake transactions" and "illegal revenue recognition," and KPMG interpreted the executive's response as a signal that Xerox had "a culture that didn't recognize that it was not a good thing to be getting anonymous letters about fraud"; that KPMG knew prior to the First Restatement "that the SEC already suspected the massive overstatement of profit from 1997 to 2000 that it detailed in its consent decree with Xerox"; and that it was in the context of all of the foregoing that KPMG required the First Restatement, which represented "only minor restatements of [Xerox's] past financials", and "[i]n fact . . . Romeril intimidated KPMG into signing off on the Xerox audit despite the improper accounting devices by threatening KPMG that any refusal to sign could trigger debt default and throw [Xerox] into bankruptcy"

Thus, the factual allegations in the Complaint do, in fact, portray KPMG as a "virtual pushover" in its dealings with the Xerox Defendants, which at a minimum went along with accounting practices it knew to be clear violations of GAAP, and which, even after it was clear early in 2001 that there were very serious concerns about Xerox's accounting practices and it was apparent that it was questionable–at best–whether Xerox took seriously its obligation to comply with applicable accounting rules, was intimidated into signing off on a minimal restatement of Xerox's financial statements that accounted for only a small portion of Xerox's overstatements of revenues and pre-tax earnings. The court concludes that the allegations of the Complaint describe conduct on the part of a non-fiduciary accountant that is highly unreasonable and represents an extreme departure from the standards of ordinary care. The court denied KPMG's motion to dismiss after concluding that there was enough in the pleadings to give rise to scienter.

Questions

1. Give some examples of "turning points" or events when KPMG should have acted differently.
2. Describe the level of accounting errors at Xerox from 1997 through 2001.
3. Why do you think the officers and KPMG auditors acted as they did?

ETHICS & THE LAW

THE ACCOUNTING FIRM THAT SAID "NO!"

Johns Manville, Inc., had been a producer of asbestos since the nineteenth century. Since 1936, health issues involving asbestos workers had been developing and included breathing difficulties as well as a cancer linked to asbestos fibers in the lungs. With each passing year, Manville and other producers experienced more litigation and liability.

Prior to 1982, the disclosures in Manville's financial statements had explained the pending and resolved liability suits but concluded that it was impossible, under Financial Accounting Standards Board Directive #5 (FASB-5), to quantify the potential liability: "The company is unable to predict at this time the outcome or liability in these cases." In 1982, Coopers & Lybrand, the auditors for Manville, were given a report from Manville's Litigation Analysis Group that the cost of disposition of all the asbestos suits would be $1.9 billion. Because of this expert opinion, Coopers & Lybrand told Manville that it was now possible to "reasonably estimate" the liability costs and refused to issue a clean audit report unless some form of financial disclosure regarding the asbestos liability was made. Coopers & Lybrand felt that, based on its expert analysis, the liability was quantifiable. Manville fired Coopers & Lybrand and filed appropriate notices with the Securities and Exchange Commission that it was changing audit firms. Manville then hired Price Waterhouse as its new audit firm. After examining the records and the status of litigation as well as the expert opinions, Price Waterhouse also refused to issue a clean audit statement without the disclosure.

The effect of the refusals of both audit firms to issue clean financial opinions was that Manville declared bankruptcy on August 26, 1982, and was required to sign over $2.5 billion of its assets (mostly stock) and contribute 20 percent of its annual net income to a trust for asbestos workers. The result of the bankruptcy for Manville shareholders was the loss of their investment in the company.

Did the auditors do the right thing? Were their decisions ethical? Didn't their decisions in effect destroy the value of the shareholders' investment? Would you have done the same thing?

C. Sarbanes-Oxley Auditor and Accounting-Related Provisions

Following the collapses of Enron and WorldCom during 2001–2002, Congress quickly passed sweeping legislation (see Chapters 8 and 46) designed to increase the liability for securities violations, financial fraud, and obstruction of justice and to impose new responsibility and accountability with regard to financial reporting by companies. Called the *Sarbanes-Oxley Act* (SOX), this legislation imposes substantial requirements on auditors and the standards and practices of the audit profession.

10. Auditor Independence

One of the concerns reflected in Sarbanes-Oxley's provisions was that auditors were not exercising sufficient discretion and independence in conducting audits of their clients. The act takes several steps to increase the auditor's independence as it conducts its audits of company financial records.

(a) Public Company Accounting Oversight Board

The first section of Sarbanes-Oxley created a new Public Company Accounting Oversight Board (PCAOB, often referred to as *Peekaboo*) that is responsible for promoting high professional standards among auditors.[30] The board, which consists of five presidential appointees, is not a governmental body but a nonprofit organization with its own budgeting and staffing authority. No more than two members of the board can be CPAs, and members of the board operate on a full-time basis. The board has the following responsibilities:

- Operating a registration system for public accounting firms that prepare audit reports for companies that issue securities.
- Enforcing and refining rules to ensure audit quality, ethics, and independence by auditors.
- Conducting inspections of public accounting firms to determine their compliance with Sarbanes-Oxley requirements.
- Investigating violations and imposing disciplinary sanctions where necessary for members of the profession.
- Encouraging the highest professional standards among public accounting firms and auditors.

(b) Registration with the Board

Any public accounting firm that conducts audits for companies that issue securities must register with the board. That registration requires the accounting firm to disclose all companies for which it has done audits and the fees paid by those companies—both audit fees and nonaudit fees for services commonly referred to as *consulting services.* The accounting firm is also required to disclose any sanctions and pending civil or criminal proceedings against it, along with its policies and procedures for quality control in audits. The board then approves the accounting firm for continued work in the audit of issuers of securities. That approval or denial must be made within 45 days following the accounting firm's filing of its annual registration statement.

(c) Maintaining Auditor Independence

In many of the companies that experienced financial collapse prior to Sarbanes-Oxley, there was a clear pattern of a lack of independence by the auditors issuing the certified financial statements. In other words, the auditors had conflicts that may have tainted their independent judgment on accounting issues with the company or even whether the company was a viable entity. **For Example,** many of the audit firms received substantial fees from companies for management consulting services for which they were providing certified statements. Arthur Andersen received $21 million annually for its audit work with Enron and another $29 million for its consulting services. The consulting contract created a conflict that interfered with the audit firm's ability to make honest decisions in its audit work.

To help eliminate conflicts of interest, Sarbanes-Oxley now prohibits certain activities by audit firms for their audit clients. The specific section of Sarbanes-Oxley prohibits:

1. Bookkeeping and other services related to the accounting records or financial statements of the audit client.
2. Design and implementation of financial information systems.
3. Appraisal and valuation services, fairness opinions, and contribution-in-kind reports.

[30] In the financial industry, professionals have translated the acronym for the new board, PCAOB, as Peekaboo because of the board's role in shedding light on financial systems and reporting.

ETHICS & THE LAW

SELF-CORRECTION IS ALIVE AND WELL

The earnings restatements for the first 10 months of 2004 numbered 619. For the first 10 months of 2005, that number was at 971 and was estimated to reach a total of 1,200 for 2005. Totals for 2003 were 514, for 2002 were 330, and for 2001 were 270 restatements. The reasons for the increase in restatements follow:

- Sarbanes-Oxley Section 404 requires intense review of internal controls and the processes for reaching the numbers. Companies have uncovered flaws in their accounting systems and have made the necessary changes.
- In this post-SOX world, what was once considered immaterial (5% or less) is no longer so, and companies are opting for disclosure and correction rather than risking some misinterpretation.
- Audit firms are now more aggressive and willing to tell clients "no" because they know that liability is on the line if they say nothing.

Why do you think Sarbanes-Oxley had an effect on financial reporting and restatements?

Source: Greg Farrell, "Restatements of Earnings in 2005 to Break Record," *USA Today*, December 30, 2005, 3B.

4. Actuarial services.
5. Internal audit outsourcing services.
6. Management functions and human resources.
7. Broker or dealer, investment adviser, and investment banking services.
8. Legal services and expert services unrelated to the audit.
9. Any other service that the board determines, by regulation, is impermissible.[31]

All nonaudit services to be conducted by the auditor for its audit client (except those listed above as expressly prohibited) require prior approval by the board.

In addition, to ensure that audit partners do not become entrenched, Sarbanes-Oxley requires audit firms to change audit partners at least once every five years.[32] The rotation of the audit partner in charge of a company account brings a new perspective to the issues in the financial systems and reports and helps to eliminate the bias of close, personal relationships that develop over longstanding working relationships.

Sarbanes-Oxley also requires accounting firms to set up internal systems for developing and monitoring professional ethics and for the discussion of ethical issues that arise during the course of the audits of clients.

11. Audit Committees

Sarbanes-Oxley does not address only issues involving auditors, their firms, and their roles in financial reporting but also issues on the corporate side of the interaction between auditors and companies—the audit committee of the company's board. Under the statute, audit committees must be composed of board members who are independent, defined in the statute as directors who do not accept consulting or other fees from the company and who are not affiliated with the company certain of its employees, or any of its subsidiaries.[33]

Members of audit committees must also be allowed to interact with auditors without management being present and also permitted to hire independent advisors. At least one member of the audit committee must be a financial expert or someone who understands financial reporting and audit work. Although SOX provides for exceptions to these standards, the audit committee is now the central point for ensuring that SOX standards are being followed.

[31] 15 USC § 78j-1.

[32] *Id.*

[33] 15 USC § 1741.

Audit committees are required to establish procedures whereby they can be notified of problems with the company's internal controls and by which auditors can raise issues. These procedures include, but are not limited to, holding meetings apart from the company's management team. Audit committees need to establish the means and mechanisms for monitoring the company's internal control systems so they can verify that financial reports are based on data generated by effective company reporting systems.

12. Records Retention

One of the first convictions of the post-Enron era was of the accounting firm Arthur Andersen on one count of obstruction of justice. This conviction was related to Andersen's destruction of documents during the months Enron was under investigation by the SEC. The conviction was later reversed because the court held that although there may have been sufficient evidence about individual Andersen employees' knowing destruction of documents, the jury instructions were flawed in attributing that knowledge to the full Andersen firm automatically without proof of actual knowledge (an element required in all criminal cases; see Chapter 8[34]). The statute used for prosecution in that case was not specific enough, and both the charges and the verdict were difficult to achieve in cases such as Andersen's that were tied exclusively to financial reporting. Furthermore, the penalties, even with such a conviction, were minimal, and as discussed in Chapter 8, Sarbanes-Oxley substantially increased both the scope of and penalties for the obstruction of justice through accountants' and auditors' destruction of records. Under Sarbanes-Oxley, those who destroy, conceal, alter, or mutilate documents when either a civil or criminal investigation is pending are subject to up to 20 years' imprisonment as well as fines.[35]

E-COMMERCE AND CYBERLAW

DESTRUCTION OF DOCUMENTS, DESTRUCTION OF A CAREER, DESTRUCTION OF A FIRM

The congressional investigation into the Enron collapse uncovered the following e-mails:

- A May 28, 1999, e-mail to David Duncan from Benjamin Neuhausen, a member of Andersen's Professional Standards Group at its Chicago main office, evaluated the wisdom of having Enron's CFO Andrew Fastow as the principal in a company that was off the books and doing trades with Enron: "Setting aside the accounting, the idea of a venture entity managed by CFO is terrible from a business point of view. Conflicts galore. Why would any director in his or her right mind ever approve such a scheme?"
- A June 1, 1999, e-mail from David Duncan responded: "[O]n your point 1 (i.e., the whole thing is a bad idea), I really couldn't agree more. Rest assured that I have already communicated and it has been agreed to by Andy that CEO, General [Counsel], and Board discussion and approval will be a requirement, on our part, for acceptance of a venture similar to what we have been discussing."

These e-mails are admissible as evidence in Congress and in both civil and criminal proceedings in the case. All e-mail is discoverable when litigation results from an auditor's work. The only protections are the privilege between lawyer and client, but these e-mails were between auditors who worked for the same audit firm.

[34] *Andersen, LLP v U.S.*, 544 US 696 (2005). David Duncan, the partner in charge of the Enron account, withdrew his guilty plea on obstruction when the court reversed the firm's verdict.

[35] 15 USC § 1512.

LAWFLIX

Midnight Run (1988)(R)

Charles Grodin plays an accountant who embezzles from his mafia boss but gives the money to charity.

For movie clips that illustrate business law concepts, see LawFlix at **http://wdvl.westbuslaw.com.**

Summary

Professionals who agree to perform services for others must perform those services according to the standards of the profession. Accountants, as professionals, must perform their audit work at the levels and standards of competency and thoroughness established for their profession. If an accountant negligently fails to observe those standards, both a breach of contract and a tort occur. This tort of negligent breach of contract constitutes malpractice, and the other party to the contract can sue the wrongdoer either for breach of contract or for the negligence involved.

In some circumstances, not only is the accountant liable to its client, but it may also be liable for malpractice to certain categories of third parties who have used or relied on the financial statement. States and courts differ as to when an accountant is liable to third parties. Some courts do not recognize accountant liability to third parties; these courts require privity between the parties. Most courts hold accountants liable to some third parties but differ as to which third parties and how far to extend the accountant's liability. The various rules that determine accountant liability to third parties are the contact rule, which requires that the third party must have had some contact with the accountant before there can be liability; the known user rule in which the accountant is aware of the third party who will use the accountant's information; the foreseeability rule in which the accountant is held liable if it was possible to foresee that the third party would use the accountant's information; the intended user rule in which the client tells the accountant of the intended use of the audit work; the unknown user rule in which the accountant is not liable to third parties it could not have known would use the information or audit work; and the flexible rule that decides on a case-by-case basis.

Accountants guilty of fraud have liability to all third parties, even those not in privity of contract with the accountant.

To a limited degree, an accountant is protected from malpractice liability by a disclaimer of liability or by the contributory negligence of the plaintiff.

Following the collapses of Enron and WorldCom, Congress passed the Sarbanes-Oxley reform legislation. This federal law increases the penalties for accountants who destroy documents when civil or criminal investigations are pending. The act also prohibits conduct by accountants that creates a conflict of interest and requires audit firms to register for authorization to do audit work on public companies. Audit committees of boards are now required to work closely with auditors to make sure that the financial systems in the company and its reports are sound. A new federal oversight board reviews the work of audit firms and is authorized to discipline audit firms and accountants for their failure to honor standards or comply with the law.

Questions and Case Problems

1. The auditing firm of Timm, Schmidt & Co. prepared annual financial statements for Clintonville Fire Apparatus, Inc. (CFA). CFA showed these statements to Citizens State Bank and asked for loans. On the basis of the financial statements, Citizens loaned CFA approximately $380,000. Timm later discovered that the financial statements overvalued CFA by more than $400,000. Citizens demanded repayment of the loans. CFA could not pay the balance, and Citizens sued Timm and its malpractice liability insurer. They raised the defense that the suit was barred by lack of privity and the fact that no one in the Timm firm knew that CFA intended to use the financial statements to obtain loans from anyone. Is the lack of privity a defense? [*Citizens State Bank v Timm, Schmidt & Co.*, 335 NW2d 361 (Wis)]
2. The president of Jones Corp. wondered whether it would be necessary to borrow money to pay taxes. The corporation employed Roanne to prepare a financial statement

of the corporation. When the president saw this statement, he decided that money should be borrowed. The lending bank required the corporation to submit a financial statement, and the statement prepared by Roanne was submitted. It contained a number of negligent mistakes that misled the bank into lending the money to Jones. Jones went into bankruptcy shortly afterward, and the bank recovered only a small percentage of the loan. The bank sued Roanne for the amount it could not collect. Was she liable in a state that followed the known user rule?

3. David S. Talesnick served as the accountant for Kenneth Ronson and his wife as well as for Ronson's company, performing accounting and tax services for all. From 1980 to 1983, Ronson, his wife, and his company invested in the White Rim Oil & Gas, Pine Coal, and Winchester Coal limited partnerships. During those years, the Ronsons and his company were able to report losses on their income tax returns because of these investments. However, the IRS determined that the limited partnerships were not qualified investments under the tax code and disallowed the loss deductions. The Ronsons and his company all owed back taxes, interest, and penalties as a result. The Ronsons disputed the finding and asked Talesnick how they might appeal the ruling and not have the interest clock ticking on what they owed. Talesnick wrote a letter and advised them to post a bond of $91,300, the amount then due. Talesnick was incorrect in his advice on payment and accrual of interest, and by the time the final determination was made against the Ronsons and Ronson's company, they owed $235,063 with interest. The Ronsons sued Talesnick for malpractice. Could they recover? How much? [*Ronson v Talesnick*, 33 F Supp 2d 347 (DNJ)]
4. The certified public accounting partnership of James, Guinn, and Head prepared a certified audit report of four corporations, known as the Paschal Enterprises, with knowledge that their report would be used to induce Shatterproof Glass Corp. to lend money to those corporations. The report showed the corporations to be solvent when in fact they were insolvent. Shatterproof relied on the audit report, loaned approximately $500,000 to the four corporations, and lost almost all of it because the liabilities of the companies were in excess of their assets. Shatterproof claimed that James and other accountants had been negligent in preparing the report and sued them to recover the loss on the loan. The accountants raised the defense that they had been retained not by Shatterproof but by Paschal. Was this defense valid? [*Shatterproof Glass Corp. v James*, 466 SW2d 873 (Tex App)]
5. Landau made an audit and a financial report of Suits Galore, a clothing manufacturer. The statement prepared by Landau was not certified. It stated that it was a review report only and that no opinion was expressly stated by the accountant. On the basis of this report, William Iselin & Co. extended credit to Suits Galore. Shortly after, Suits Galore went into bankruptcy, and Iselin was not repaid the money it had loaned. Iselin sued Landau on the ground that the financial report had been negligently prepared and that Iselin could recover from Landau for the loss sustained. Was it correct? [*William Iselin & Co. v Landau*, 513 NYS2d 3]
6. For almost 13 years, Touche Ross had prepared the annual audit of Buttes Gas and Oil Co. Buttes wanted to obtain a loan from Dimensional Credit Corp. (DCC) and showed DCC its most recent annual audit. DCC made the loan on the basis of what it learned from the audit. The loan was not repaid, and DCC then realized that it had been misled by negligent statements about Buttes's financial condition that appeared in the annual statement prepared by Touche Ross. Would DCC be able to recover against Touche Ross for its negligence in preparing this report?
7. Henry Hatfield, CPA, was hired to prepare audited financial statements for Happy Campers, a nonprofit organization providing summer camp scholarships for inner-city, low-income children. The executive director of Happy Campers was embezzling but falsified records that Hatfield used in his audit. First Bank gave Happy Campers a $100,000 loan based on Hatfield's certified financials. The embezzlement was discovered, and Happy Campers defaulted on the loan. Can First Bank recover its loss from Hatfield?
8. Ernst & Whinney made an audit report for W. L. Jackson Mfg. Co. On the basis of this report, Bethlehem Steel sold on credit to Jackson Mfg. The report had been negligently prepared, and Jackson went broke shortly afterward. Bethlehem Steel did not get paid and then sued Ernst & Whinney for negligent malpractice. Ernst & Whinney raised the defense that it was not liable because it was not in privity with Bethlehem and did not know the name of Bethlehem in connection with its audit statements. Was this a valid defense? [*Bethlehem Steel Corp. v Ernst & Whinney*, 822 SW2d 592 (Tenn)]
9. Hicks, the president and manager of Intermountain Merchandising, wanted to sell the business to Montana Merchandising, Inc. To provide a basis for the transaction, he retained Bloomgren, an accountant, to make an audit of Intermountain. Bloomgren knew that Montana would use the audit report in making the purchase of the business from Intermountain. Bloomgren's audit report showed the Intermountain business as profitable. Thayer, Montana's president, relied on this report in agreeing to purchase the business of Intermountain and in agreeing to the terms of the purchase. Some time later, it was discovered that the accountant had made a number of mistakes and that the business that was sold was actually insolvent. Thayer and Montana Merchandising sued Hicks and Bloomgren for damages. The suit claimed that

the accountant had negligently misrepresented the facts. The accountant defended on the basis that Thayer was not in privity of contract with him and therefore could not sue him. Was he right? [*Thayer v Hicks*, 793 P2d 784 (Mont)]

10. Seven shareholders of HM, a home furnishings retailer, filed suit for securities fraud and common law fraud arising from misrepresentations and omissions they alleged were made by HM's outside auditor, Deloitte & Touche, in connection with HM's annual report issued on May 30, 2000. Deloitte performed an audit of the financial statements of HM as of the fiscal year ending on February 29, 2000. The audit report was incorporated in full in HM's annual report (Form 10-K) for that fiscal year issued on May 30, 2000.

    On March 22, 2000, Deloitte presented its unqualified audit report to the HM board of directors. On May 29, 2000, the HM board of directors approved the annual report, and it was filed with the Securities and Exchange Commission (SEC) on May 30, 2000.

    Deloitte represented in the financial statement materials included in these reports that (1) Deloitte had audited the balance sheets, consolidated statements of operations, and stockholders' equity of HM, (2) HM's financial statements "present fairly, in all material respects, the financial position" of HM as of February 29, 2000, and (3) the audit was in conformity with accounting principles generally accepted in the United States. Deloitte's unqualified audit opinion also represented that, as of February 29, 2000, and May 30, 2000, HM was solvent; that it had almost $535 million in shareholder equity; and that its book value was $8.81 per share.

    In fact, Deloitte was aware that the board of HM had instructed management to prepare for a bankruptcy filing and seek possible suitors for purchasing the company's assets. This information was not disclosed in the reports. By November 2003, HM issued a report with the following information:

    - HM's assets had shrunk over $611,474,000.
    - Total revenues for the quarter decreased 7.8 percent.
    - Operating expenses exceeded revenue by more than $48 million.
    - The net loss increased $536,835,000.
    - Accounts payable increased by $27,313,000.
    - The loss per share was $9.71.
    - Total shareholder equity went from $534,748,000 in May 2000 to ($75,057), a decrease of $609,805,000.

    That quarterly report also stated that more than $142.9 million in goodwill and all of the previously stated book value was gone. Can Deloitte & Touche be held liable? What would be the basis for such liability? [*Arnlund v Deloitte & Touche LLP*, 199 F Supp 2d 461 (ED Va)]

11. Equisure, Inc., was required to file audited financial statements when it applied for a listing on the American Stock Exchange (AMEX). Stirtz, Equisure's auditor, issued a favorable audit opinion used for the AMEX application. Stirtz also issued "clean" opinions on Equisure's required SEC filings, such as its 10k.

    Noram, a securities broker, loaned $900,000 in margin credit to purchasers of Equisure's stock based on the firm's audited financials. AMEX stopped trading on Equisure's stock because of allegations of insider trading and stock manipulation, and Noram was left without collateral for $2.5 million in loans. Stirtz resigned as Equisure's auditor, and Noram filed suit against Stirtz. The trial court granted Stirtz summary judgment. Noram appealed. Who is liable here? Was the court's decision correct? [*Noram Investment Services, Inc. v Stirtz Bernards Boyden*, 611 NW2d 372 (Minn App)]

CPA Questions

1. In general, the third-party (primary) beneficiary rule as applied to a CPA's legal liability in conducting an audit is relevant to which of the following causes of action against a CPA?

	Fraud	*Constructive Fraud*	*Negligence*
a.	Yes	Yes	No
b.	Yes	No	No
c.	No	Yes	Yes
d.	No	No	Yes

2. Beckler & Associates, CPAs, audited and gave an unqualified opinion on the financial statements of Queen Co. The financial statements contained misstatements that resulted in a material overstatement of Queen's net worth. Queen provided the audited financial statements to Mac Bank in connection with a loan made by Mac to Queen. Beckler knew that the financial statements would be provided to Mac. Queen defaulted on the loan. Mac sued Beckler to recover for its losses associated with Queen's default. Which of the following must Mac prove in order to recover?

    I. Beckler was negligent in conducting the audit.

    II. Mac relied on the financial statements.

    a. I only
    b. II only
    c. Both I and II
    d. Neither I nor II

3. In a common law action against an accountant, lack of privity is a viable defense if the plaintiff

   a. Is the client's creditor who sues the accountant for negligence
   b. Can prove the presence of gross negligence that amounts to a reckless disregard for the truth
   c. Is the accountant's client
   d. Bases the action upon fraud

4. Cable Corp. orally engaged Drake & Co., CPAs, to audit its financial statements. Cable's management informed Drake that it suspected the accounts receivable were materially overstated. Though the financial statements Drake audited included a materially overstated accounts receivable balance, Drake issued an unqualified opinion. Cable used the financial statements to obtain a loan to expand its operations. Cable defaulted on the loan and incurred a substantial loss.

   If Cable sues Drake for negligence in failing to discover the overstatement, Drake's best defense would be that Drake did *not*

   a. Have privity of contract with Cable
   b. Sign an engagement letter
   c. Perform the audit recklessly or with an intent to deceive
   d. Violate generally accepted auditing standards in performing the audit

5. Which of the following services is a CPA generally required to perform when conducting a personal financial planning engagement?

   a. Assisting the client to identify tasks that are essential in order to take action on planning decisions
   b. Assisting the client to take action on planning decisions
   c. Monitoring progress in achieving goals
   d. Updating recommendations and revising planning decisions

6. Which of the following statements is (are) correct regarding the common law elements that must be proven to support a finding of constructive fraud against a CPA misrepresentation?

   I. The plaintiff has justifiably relied on the CPA's misrepresentation.
   II. The CPA has acted in a grossly negligent manner.

   a. I only
   b. II only
   c. Both I and II
   d. Neither I nor II

MANAGEMENT OF CORPORATIONS

CHAPTER (48)

LEARNING OBJECTIVES

After studying this chapter, you should be able to

LO.1 State the requirements for meetings of shareholders and directors

LO.2 Define and illustrate the liability of corporate officers and directors to the corporation

LO.3 Define and illustrate the liability of corporate officers and directors to third persons

LO.4 State the criminal liability of officers and directors of a corporation

LO.5 State when an officer, director, or employee of a corporation may obtain indemnification from the corporation

A corporation is managed, directly or indirectly, by its shareholders, board of directors, and officers.

A. Shareholders

As owners, the shareholders have the right to control the corporation.

1. Extent of Management Control by Shareholders

As a practical matter, control of the shareholders is generally limited to voting at shareholders' meetings to elect directors. In this sense, shareholders indirectly determine the management policies of the business. At shareholders' meetings, they may also vote to amend bylaws, approve shareholder resolutions, or vote on so-called extraordinary corporate matters. *Extraordinary matters* include the sale of corporate assets outside the regular course of the corporation's business or the merger or dissolution of the corporation.

2. Meetings of Shareholders

To have legal effect, action by the shareholders must ordinarily be taken at a regular or special meeting.

(a) Regular Meetings

The time and place of regular or stated meetings are usually prescribed by the articles of incorporation or the bylaws. Notice to shareholders of such meetings is ordinarily not required, but it is usually given as a matter of good business practice. Some statutes require that notice of all meetings be given.

(b) Special Meetings

Generally, notice must be given specifying the subject matter of special meetings. Unless otherwise prescribed, special meetings are called by the directors. It is sometimes provided that a special meeting may be called by a certain percentage of shareholders.[1] Notice of the day, hour, and place of a special meeting must be given to all shareholders. The notice must include a statement of the nature of the business to be transacted, and no other business may be transacted at this meeting.

(c) Quorum

A valid meeting requires the presence of a quorum of the voting shareholders. A **quorum** is the minimum number of persons (shareholders or persons authorized to vote a stated proportion of the voting stock) required to transact business. If a quorum is present, a majority of those present may act on any matter unless there is an express requirement of a higher affirmative vote.

When a meeting opens with a quorum, the quorum is generally not broken if shareholders leave the meeting and those remaining are not sufficient to constitute a quorum.

[1] NY Bus Corp Law § 603.

3. Action Without Meeting

A number of statutes provide for corporate action by shareholders without holding a meeting. The Revised Model Business Corporation Act (RMBCA) provides that "action required or permitted by this Act to be taken at a shareholders' meeting may be taken without a meeting if the action is taken by all shareholders entitled to vote on the action."[2] The action must be evidenced by a written consent describing the action taken, signed by all shareholders entitled to vote on the action, and delivered to the corporation for inclusion in the minutes.

B. Directors

The board of directors has oversight responsibility for a company's business affairs, including (1) approving strategic plans, (2) reviewing operating and financial results, (3) approving SEC filings, (4) approving the hiring of executives, (5) evaluating management's performance and approving executive compensation packages, (6) appointing and meeting with auditors, and (7) evaluating and acting on extraordinary matters, such as the merger, acquisition, or sale of the business.

Most states now permit the number of directors to be fixed by the bylaws. Many specify that the board of directors shall consist of not less than three directors; a few authorize one or more.[3] Professional corporation legislation often authorizes or is interpreted as authorizing a one- or two-person board of directors.

4. Qualifications

Eligibility for membership on a board of directors is determined by statute, articles of incorporation, or bylaws.[4] In the absence of a contrary provision, any person (including a nonresident, a minor, or a person who is not a shareholder) is eligible for membership. Bylaws may require that a director own stock in the corporation although this requirement is not ordinarily imposed.

CPA 5. Powers of Directors

The board of directors has authority to manage the corporation. Courts will not interfere with the board's discretion in the absence of (1) illegal conduct or (2) fraud harming the rights of creditors, shareholders, or the corporation.

The board of directors may enter into any contract or transaction necessary to carry out the business for which the corporation was formed. The board may appoint officers and other agents to act for the company, or it may appoint several of its own members as an executive committee to act for the board between board meetings. (See Figure 48-1.) Broad delegation of authority, however, may involve the risk of being treated as an unlawful abdication of the board's management power.

CPA 6. Conflict of Interest

A director is disqualified from taking part in corporate action involving a matter in which the director has an undisclosed conflicting interest. Because it cannot be known how the other directors would have acted if they had known of the conflict of interest, the corporation generally may avoid any transaction because of a director's secret disqualification.

A number of states provide by statute that a director's conflict of interest does not impair the transaction or contract entered into or authorized by the board of directors if the disqualified director disclosed the interest and if the contract or transaction is fair and reasonable with respect to the corporation. Thus, a director may lend money to a corporation if the board of directors is informed of the transaction and the terms approximate the market rate for businesses with similar credit ratings. Some states simply require notice of the conflicting interests and abstaining from all participation in the transaction. **For Example,** Delos Yancey, Jr. and Delos Yancey III were directors of State Mutual Insurance Co. Subsequently, they formed North American Services, Inc., and served as directors of both companies. State Mutual decided to sell one of its companies, Atlas Life Insurance, Inc. North

[2] RMBCA § 7.04(a).

[3] Del Code § 141(b). See also RMBCA § 8.03.

[4] In family-owned businesses, shareholder agreements are often utilized to impose restrictions on the voting of shares and eligibility standards for membership on the board of directors to maintain continuity of management, ownership, and control of a corporation. See *Miniat v EMI*, 315 F3d 712 (7th Cir 2002).

FIGURE 48-1 Powers of Directors

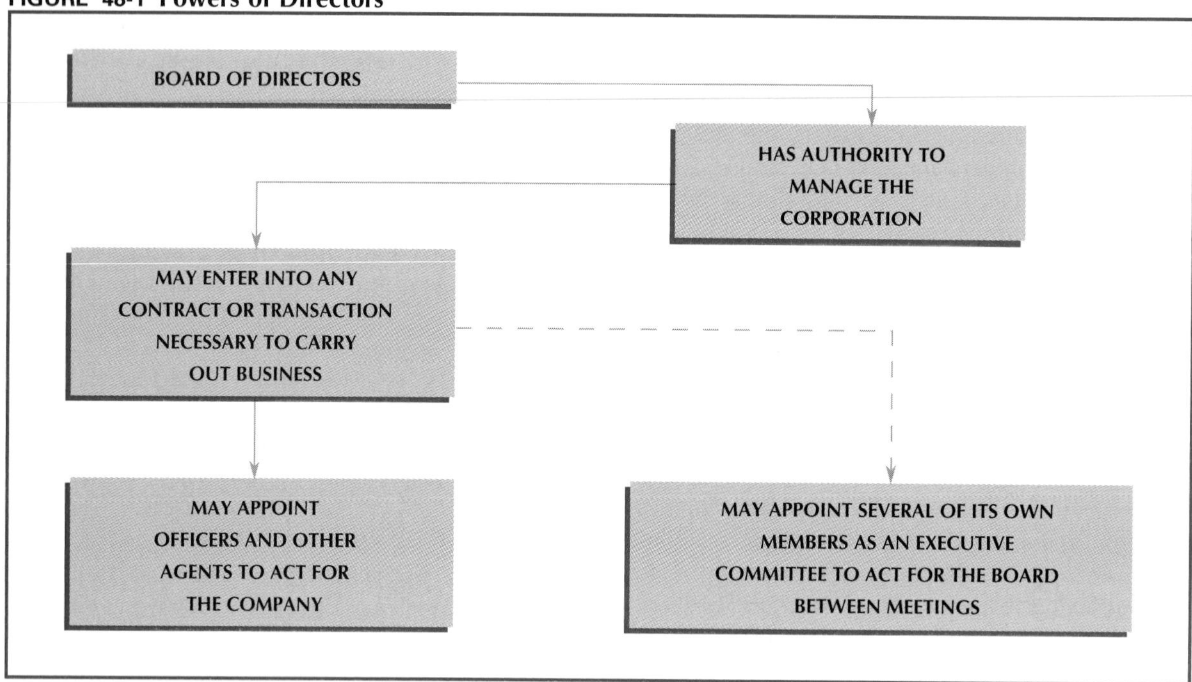

American expressed an interest in purchasing Atlas, and thereafter the Yanceys recused themselves from State Mutual's decision-making process in selling the company. State Mutual sold Atlas to North American at a $5.2 million loss. Some two years later, North American resold Atlas for a $22.6 million gain, and a shareholder derivative suit was brought against the Yanceys. The court decided the case in favor of the Yanceys, holding that they complied with the state's "safe harbor" law by giving notice of their conflicting interest to State Mutual and thereafter abstaining from all participation in the corporate transaction.[5]

To prevent conflicts of interest and covert compensation schemes, section 402(a) of the federal Sarbanes-Oxley Act[6] prohibits all loans either directly or indirectly to directors and executive officers by their corporations, with an exception for companies in the consumer credit business, who may make loans to directors and officers on terms no more favorable than those offered to the general public.

Prior to Sarbanes-Oxley, it was a common practice for publicly traded companies to provide low-interest loans to company officers. **For Example,** Bernard Ebbers, while CEO of WorldCom, Inc., used company stock as collateral for bank loans used to buy additional shares of WorldCom stock. When WorldCom's share prices weakened in late 2000 and Ebbers needed to put up additional collateral to cover his loans, WorldCom's board of directors decided to lend him more than $400 million dollars at just over 2 percent interest with no fixed due date. The company rate was far below the personal loan rate at banks near company headquarters of between 9.75 percent and 16.67 percent, and well below margin loan rates at 5 percent. Business conglomerate Tyco International Ltd. maintained a "key employee loan fund" that was used like a revolving line of credit by Tyco executives Dennis Kozlowski and Martin Swartz to fund their lavish lifestyles. The language of Sarbanes-Oxley is broad and far reaching and prohibits all direct personal loans by public companies, such as relocation loans, tax loans, and loans to purchase securities.

The *Dunbar* case involved a conflict of interest.

[5] *Fisher v State Mutual Insurance Co.*, 290 F3d 1256 (11th Cir 2002).
[6] PL 107-204, 116 Stat 745.

DUNBAR V WILLIAMS, 554 SO 2D 56 (LA CT APP 1989)

"I'M THE PRESIDENT AND I'M ENTITLED TO A FEW PERKS, RIGHT?"

Childs E. Dunbar Jr., a minority shareholder of Algiers Ironworks and Dry Dock Co., Inc. (AIW), brought a shareholder's derivative action against the majority shareholders to recover damages on behalf of the corporation, AIW. Thomas S. Williams was the president and director of AIW; his wife was also a director. The Williamses also owned Tower Crane Co. Tower used AIW's phones, address, land for storing cranes, and some personnel, but Tower did not pay for any of these. Tower sold two cranes to AIW, and AIW's board did not consider or approve these transactions. Williams personally bought a yacht, *Patty Jean*, and testified that work valued at $43,303 was expended on the vessel by AIW and over $50,000 worth of business entertaining on behalf of AIW was conducted on the vessel. When the Williamses charged $17,583 on an AIW credit card, Williams admitted that $4,571.45 was not business related. Williams also admitted that $4,590.56 in gasoline charges to AIW were not business related. The trial court issued a judgment against Williams for $9,162.01, reflecting these two admissions, and the minority shareholders appealed.

Judicial Opinion

BARRY, J. . . . [A Louisiana statute provides that]

No contract or transaction between a corporation and one or more of its directors or officers, or between a corporation and any other business . . . in which one or more of its directors or officers are directors or officers or have a financial interest, shall be void or voidable solely for this reason . . . or solely because his or their votes were counted for such purpose, if:

1. *The material facts as to his interest and as to the contract or transaction were disclosed or known to the board of directors or the committee, and the board or committee in good faith authorized the contract or transaction by a vote sufficient for such purpose without counting the vote of the interested director or directors; or*
2. *The material facts as to his interest and as to the contract or transaction were disclosed or known to the shareholders entitled to vote thereon, and the contract or transaction was approved in good faith by vote of the shareholders; or*
3. *The contract or transaction was fair as to the corporation as of the time it was authorized, approved or ratified by the board of directors, committee, or shareholders.*

The questioned officer or director has the burden to establish that the transaction was fair and in good faith, essentially that it was at arm's length. . . . *Noe v Roussel,* 310 So. 2d 806, 818–19 (La. 1975). The Noe court explained: "[T]he agent or fiduciary may not take even the slightest advantage, but must zealously, diligently and honestly guard and champion the rights of his principal. . . ."

. . . The two crane purchases by Williams (as president of AIW) from his company (Tower) were not authorized by AIW's Board, hence, both purchases fail the test of [the statute]. . . . [On rehearing, May 9, 1989, on the issue of the Tower crane transactions, the district court was reversed. On second rehearing on the crane transactions held on November 16, 1989, the amount owed AIW was set at $15,000, which represented the profit gained by Tower from the sale to AIW.]

The use of AIW's premises, services, and personnel by Tower was clearly improper. AIW received no payment or discernible benefit and Williams' actions on behalf of Tower violated his fiduciary duty to AIW. . . .

We therefore remand for the trial court to conduct a hearing to determine the value of the various benefits and to enter a judgment in favor of AIW and against Williams. . . .

Williams personally bought the PATTY JEAN for $5,000 in August or September, 1977, apparently in very poor condition. Williams testified that he informally told [members of the board of directors] Dr. and Mrs. Grundmeyer and Edgar Williams that he intended to use the yacht to entertain customers and they approved. Williams did not discuss the matter with Dunbar, the other Board member. . . .

The trial court adjusted all of Williams' estimated amounts spent to refurbish, repair, and maintain the yacht to reflect the costs of a regular customer and concluded the work should be valued at $43,303. We have no basis to find manifest error in that valuation.

As for the alleged benefits AIW received from the PATTY JEAN, twenty-one fishing trips were made entertaining approximately 152 people. Plaintiffs complain that not all of those trips were business related. Dunbar acknowledged the necessity for AIW to entertain, but maintained it would have been cheaper to charter a boat.

Jack Faulkner, an expert on overnight charters in the Gulf Coast area, testified that the standard charter fee for a vessel similar to the PATTY JEAN for a three-day fishing trip would be $125 per person per day with a four person minimum (not including alcohol) or $1,500. According to Williams, a trip cost approximately $600 to $800 and he computed the value of all the trips at over $50,000.

We disagree that a promotional trip is not business related, or that a guest unrelated to the shipping industry constitutes nonbusiness usage. It appears that the value of the trips fairly approximates the expense incurred by AIW to repair the vessel.

We conclude there was no fiduciary breach by Williams or manifest error in the trial court's finding that use of the PATTY JEAN by AIW in exchange for repairs, maintenance and refurbishing was reasonable and carried out in good faith. . . .

Plaintiffs claim the defendants breached their fiduciary duties by giving themselves unearned compensation in the form of. . . . fringe benefits. . . .

The questioned benefits are (a) American Express charges, (b) gas charges, (c) charges at service stations, restaurants and food stores, (d) company cars, (e) home phone bills, (f) Grundmeyer's country club bills, and Williams' carnival club dues.

Plaintiffs contend those personal expenses were paid by AIW and are not business related, and the failure to keep records as to the business purpose constitutes a fiduciary breach. There is no question that AIW paid the expenses and the defendants must show their connection to AIW's business.

Mr. and Mrs. Williams, according to two ledger sheets in evidence, charged $17,583.97 on an AIW American Express account from February 1980 through August 1985. Of that amount Williams admitted $4,571.45 was not business related. As to gasoline charges from 1980 to 1984, Williams admitted that he or his family charged $4,590.56 which was not business related. The trial court judgment against Williams for $9,162.01, [the total of these] two sums, was not appealed and is final.

As for Williams' carnival club dues. . . a local businessman testified for the defense that he considered them to be legitimate business expenses. . . .

Carnival dues are not, ipso facto, business related. Nor is there proof that Williams' membership in a carnival organization produced any revenue to AIW. The record and briefs are unclear as to which organizations Williams belonged to and at what costs to AIW.

We remand to the trial court to determine the amounts paid by AIW for carnival club dues and to enter the appropriate judgment in favor of AIW and against Williams.

[Judgment affirmed in part; reversed and action remanded in part]

Questions

1. Did a state law set guidelines to validate a corporate transaction in which an officer or director had a personal interest?
2. Was the board of directors required to approve the crane purchases in order to satisfy the state conflict of interest law?
3. Review the ethical principles set forth in Chapter 3 and express an opinion on the ethics of the following conduct: (1) sale of the cranes to AIW; (2) use of AIW facilities and personnel by Tower Crane Co.; (3) AIW's payment to refurbish the yacht *Patty Jean;* and (4) AIW's payment of fringe benefits, including carnival club dues.

7. Meetings of Directors

Action by directors is ordinarily taken at a meeting of the board of directors. Bylaws sometimes require the meeting to be held at a particular place. Generally, a director is not allowed to vote by proxy.

Most states permit action to be taken by the board of directors without holding an actual meeting. It is required when such action is taken that it be set forth in writing and signed by all directors.

8. Liability of Directors

In dealing with the corporation, the directors act in a fiduciary capacity. It is into their care that the stockholders have entrusted the control of the corporate property and the management of the business.

CPA (a) The Business Judgment Rule

Courts recognize that the decisions of corporate directors often involve weighing and balancing legal, ethical, commercial, promotional, public relations, and other factors. Accordingly, courts will not sit in judgment on the wisdom of decisions made by directors. If the directors have acted in good faith on the basis of adequate information, courts will not enjoin the course of action taken by the directors.[7] Moreover, even though such action causes loss to the corporation, the directors will not be held personally liable for it. This principle is called the **business judgment rule**.

CPA ***(1) The Traditional Rule.*** Courts apply the business judgment rule as a presumption that in making a business decision, the directors acted (1) on an informed basis, (2) in good faith, and (3) in the honest belief that the action taken was in the best interest of the corporation. The party challenging the directors' actions has the burden of proving that they did not act on an informed basis or in good faith or in the best interest of the corporation.[8] The *Disney* case illustrates an application of the business judgment rule.

IN RE WALT DISNEY CO. DERIVITIVE LITIGATION, 2005 WL 2056651 (DEL CH)

PROBLEM: "A MISMATCH OF CULTURES AND STYLES" SOLUTION: $140 MILLION SEVERANCE PAYMENT SHAREHOLDERS: NOT HAPPY

[Michael Ovitz was a founder of Creative Artists Agency (CAA), an agency in 1995 with 1400 of Hollywood's top actors, directors, writers and musicians. Ovitz was considered one of the most powerful figures in Hollywood at that time. Because of the untimely death of Disney's prior president in a helicopter crash, Disney CEO Michael Eisner focused on hiring Ovitz as president. The Chairman of Disney's Compensation Committee, Irwin Russell, in consultation with Eisner negotiated the Ovitz employment agreement (OEA). As part of the OEA, if Disney fired Ovitz for any reason other than gross negligence or malfeasance Ovitz would be entitled to a Non-Fault Termination (NFT) package consisting of his remaining salary for the five year period, bonuses and the immediate vesting of stock options. Russell met with a compensation expert for advice on the contract, and had telephone conversations with two compensation committee members, Sidney Poitier and Ignatio Lozano. CEO Eisner telephoned each member of the board of directors to inform them of his plan to hire Ovitz. On September 26, 1995 the Compensation Committee had a one hour meeting to discuss several topics, including the Ovitz employment contract. Thereafter, the full board of directors met and elected Ovitz president of Disney. After joining Disney it soon became apparent that a "mismatch of cultures and styles" ensued and Ovitz was not succeeding as president. The trial court gave an example as follows:

In January 1996, a corporate retreat was held at Walt Disney World in Orlando, Florida. At that retreat, Ovitz failed to integrate himself in the group of executives by declining to participate in group activities, insisting on a limousine, when the other executives, including Eisner, were taking a bus, and making inappropriate demands of the park employees. In short, Ovitz "was a little elitist for the egalitarian Walt Disney World cast members [employees]," and a poor fit with his fellow executives.

When it became clear that Ovitz was not working out, Eisner considered his options. Sanford Litvak, Disney's General Counsel advised Eisner and other directors that Ovitz had not been shown to have been grossly negligent or malfeasant in his year at Disney, and no cause existed to avoid the NFT payments. Eisner decided it was necessary to terminate Ovitz on a non-fault basis, and notified the board members. The board members supported this decision under the non-fault termination agreement. Ovitz was ultimately paid $140 million in severance pay. Stockholders

[7] In discharging their duties, directors are not individually liable if acting in good faith they rely on "the opinion of counsel for the corporation" or "upon written reports setting forth financial data concerning the corporation and prepared by an independent public accountant or certified public accountant or firm of such accountants" which opinions or statements turn out to be flawed. *Casey v Brennan*, 344 NJ Super 83 (2002).

[8] *Huang Group v LTI*, 760 NE2d 14 (Ohio App 2002).

brought a derivative suit asserting that Eisner and the board of directors had breached their fiduciary duties in connection with the hiring and termination of Ovitz. Years of litigation cumulated in a thirty seven day trial that ended on January 19, 2005.]

Judicial Opinion

CHANDLER, Ch.... Unlike ideals of corporate governance, a fiduciary's duties do not change over time. How we understand those duties may evolve and become refined, but the duties themselves have not changed, except to the extent that fulfilling a fiduciary duty requires obedience to other positive law. This Court strongly encourages directors and officers to employ best practices, as those practices are understood at the time a corporate decision is taken. But Delaware law does not—indeed, the common law cannot—hold fiduciaries liable for a failure to comply with the aspirational ideal of best practices, any more than a common-law court deciding a medical malpractice dispute can impose a standard of liability based on ideal—rather than competent or standard—medical treatment practices, lest the average medical practitioner be found inevitably derelict.

...Fiduciaries who act faithfully and honestly on behalf of those whose interests they represent are indeed granted wide latitude in their efforts to maximize shareholders' investment. Times may change, but fiduciary duties do not. Indeed, other institutions may develop, pronounce and urge adherence to ideals of corporate best practices. But the development of aspirational ideals, however worthy as goals for human behavior, should not work to distort the legal requirements by which human behavior is actually measured.

Because this matter, by its very nature, has become something of a public spectacle—commencing as it did with the spectacular hiring of one of the entertainment industry's best-known personalities to help run one of its iconic businesses, and ending with a spectacular failure of that union, with breathtaking amounts of severance pay the consequence—it is, I think, worth noting what the role of this Court must be in evaluating decision-makers' performance with respect to decisions gone awry, spectacularly or otherwise. It is easy, of course, to fault a decision that ends in a failure, once handsight makes the result of that decision plain to see. But the essence of business is risk—the application of informed belief to contingencies whose outcomes can sometimes be predicted, but never known. The decision-makers entrusted by shareholders must act out of loyalty to those shareholders. They must in good faith act to make informed decisions on behalf of the shareholders, untainted by self-interest. Where they fail to do so, this Court stands ready to remedy breaches of fiduciary duty.

Even where decision-makers act as faithful servants, however, their ability and the wisdom of their judgments will vary. The redress for failures that arise from faithful management must come from the markets, through the action of shareholders and the free flow of capital, and not from this Court. Should the Court apportion liability based on the ultimate outcome of decisions taken in good faith by faithful directors or officers, those decision-makers would necessarily take decisions that minimize risk, not maximize value. The entire advantage of the risk-taking, innovative, wealth-creating engine that is the Delaware corporation would cease to exist, with disastrous results for shareholders and society alike. That is why, under our corporate law, corporate decision-makers are held strictly to their fiduciary duties, but within the boundaries of those duties are free to act as their judgment and abilities dictate, free of *post hoc* penalties from a reviewing court using perfect hindsight. Corporate decisions are made, risks are taken, the results become apparent, capital flows accordingly, and shareholder value is increased....

The Business Judgment Rule...

Delaware law is clear that the business and affairs of a corporation are managed by or under the direction of its board of directors. The business judgment rule serves to protect and promote the role of the board as the ultimate manager of the corporation. Because courts are ill equipped to engage in *post hoc* substantive review of business decisions, the business judgment rule "operates to preclude a court from imposing itself unreasonably on the business and affairs of a corporation."

The business judgment rule is not actually a substantive rule of law, but instead it is a presumption that "in making a business decision the directors of a corporation acted on an informed basis,...and in the honest belief that the action taken was in the best interests of the company [and its shareholders]." This presumption applies when there is no evidence of "fraud, bad faith, or self-dealing in the usual sense of personal profit or betterment" on the part of the directors. In the absence of this evidence, the board's decision will be upheld unless it cannot be "attributed to any rational business purpose."...

Upon long and careful consideration, I am of the opinion that the concept of *intentional dereliction of duty*, a *conscious disregard for one's responsibilities*, is an appropriate (although not the only) standard for determining whether fiduciaries have acted in good faith. Deliberate indifference and inaction *in the face of a duty to act* is, in my mind, conduct that is clearly disloyal to the corporation. It is the epitome of faithless conduct. . . .

. . . . [P]laintiffs must prove by a preponderance of the evidence that the presumption of the business judgment rule does not apply either because the directors breached their fiduciary duties, acted in bad faith or that the directors made an "unintelligent or unadvised judgment," by failing to inform themselves of all material information reasonably available to them before making a business decision.

If plaintiffs cannot rebut the presumption of the business judgment rule, the defendants will prevail. . . .

By virtue of his Machiavellian (and imperial) nature as CEO, and his control over Ovitz's hiring in particular, Eisner to a large extent is responsible for the failings in process that infected and handicapped the board's decision-making abilities. Eisner stacked his (and I intentionally write "his" as opposed to "the Company's") board of directors with friends and other acquaintances who, though not necessarily beholden to him in a legal sense, were certainly more willing to accede to his wishes and support him unconditionally than truly independent directors. On the other hand, I do not believe that the evidence, considered fairly, demonstrates that Eisner actively took steps to defeat or short-circuit a decisionmaking process that would otherwise have occurred. . . .

. . . [T]he decision to hire Ovitz and enter into the OEA is one of business judgment, to which the presumptions of the business judgment rule apply. In order to prevail, therefore, plaintiffs must demonstrate by a preponderance of the evidence that Eisner was either grossly negligent or acted in bad faith in connection with Ovitz's hiring and the approval of the OEA.

As I mentioned earlier, Eisner was very much aware of what was going on as the situation developed. In the limited instances where he was not the primary source of information relating to Ovitz, Russell kept Eisner informed of negotiations with Ovitz. Eisner knew Ovitz; he was familiar with the career Ovitz had built at CAA and he knew that the Company was in need of a senior executive. . . . In light of this knowledge, I cannot find that plaintiffs have demonstrated by a preponderance of the evidence that Eisner failed to inform himself of all material information reasonably available or that he acted in a grossly negligent manner.

Notwithstanding the foregoing, Eisner's actions in connection with Ovitz's hiring should not serve as a model for fellow executives and fiduciaries to follow. His lapses were many. He failed to keep the board as informed as he should have. He stretched the outer boundaries of his authority as CEO by acting without specific board direction or involvement. He prematurely issued a press release that placed significant pressure on the board to accept Ovitz and approve his compensation package in accordance with the press release. To my mind, these actions fall far short of what shareholders expect and demand from those entrusted with a fiduciary position. Eisner's failure to better involve the board in the process of Ovitz's hiring, usurping that role for himself, although not in violation of law, does not comport with how fiduciaries of Delaware corporations are expected to act.

Despite all of the legitimate criticisms that may be leveled at Eisner, especially at having enthroned himself as the omnipotent and infallible *monarch* of his *personal Magic Kingdom*, I nonetheless conclude, after carefully considering and weighing all the evidence, that Eisner's actions were taken in good faith. That is, Eisner's actions were taken with the subjective belief that those actions were in the best interests of the Company—he believed that his taking charge and acting swiftly and decisively to hire Ovitz would serve the best interests of the Company notwithstanding the high cost of Ovitz's hiring and notwithstanding that two experienced executives who had arguably been passed over for the position (Litvack and Bollenbach) were not completely supportive. Those actions do not represent a knowing violation of law or evidence a conscious and intentional disregard of duty. In conclusion, Eisner acted in good faith and did not breach his fiduciary duty of care because he was not grossly negligent.

[The court found that CEO Eisner acted in accordance with his fiduciary duties and in good faith when he terminated Ovitz. It determined that the chairman of the Compensation Committee and the general counsel acted in good faith in the respective hiring and termination of Ovitz, and that no director had breached a fiduciary duty.]

Questions

1. Explain the business judgment rule.
2. Did the court approve of CEO Eisner's management practices?
3. When it becomes evident to shareholders that the directors approved the hiring of a president who turned out to be a spectacular failure with the consequence being the payment of a breathtaking amount of severance pay to the failed president, should the directors not be held liable under corporate law for such an error in judgment?

CPA ***(2) Application in Corporate Control Transactions.*** When a corporation receives a takeover bid, the target board of directors may tend to take actions that are in their own interest and not in the interest of the shareholders. Courts have recognized the potential for director self-interest in this situation. (See the *Van Gorkom* case.)

In *Smith v Van Gorkom*, the directors relied on the business judgment rule to shield themselves from individual liability in a lawsuit charging that the directors did not act on an "informed basis" in accepting and recommending a merger.

SMITH V VAN GORKOM, 488 A2D 858 (DEL 1985)

DIRECTORS—INDEPENDENT EVALUATORS, NOT PAWNS

On September 13, 1980, Jerome Van Gorkom as chairman and chief executive officer of Trans Union, Inc., a holding company in the railcar leasing business, arranged a meeting with Jay Pritzker, a well-known takeover specialist and social acquaintance, to determine his interest in acquiring Trans Union. On Thursday, September 18, Pritzker made an offer of $55 per share (a price suggested by Van Gorkom) with a decision to be made by the board no later than Sunday, September 21. On Friday, Van Gorkom called a special meeting of the board of directors for noon the following day; no agenda was announced. At the directors' meeting, Van Gorkom made a 20-minute oral analysis of the merger transaction, showed that the company was having difficulty generating sufficient income, and discussed his meeting with Pritzker and the reasons for the meeting. Copies of the proposed merger agreement were delivered too late to be studied before or during the meeting. No consultants or investment advisers were called upon to support the merger price of $55 per share. The merger was approved at the end of the two-hour meeting. Certain shareholders brought a class action suit against the directors, contending that the board's decision was not the product of informed business judgment. The directors replied that their good-faith decision was shielded by the business judgment rule. From a decision for the directors, the shareholders appealed.

Judicial Opinion

HORSEY, J. . . . Under Delaware law, the business judgment rule is the offspring of the fundamental principle, codified in 8 *Del. C.* § 141(a), that the business and affairs of a Delaware corporation are managed by or under its board of directors. In carrying out their managerial roles, directors are charged with an unyielding fiduciary duty to the corporation and its shareholders. The business judgment rule exists to protect and promote the full and free exercise of the managerial power granted to Delaware directors. The rule itself "is a presumption that in making a business decision, the directors of a corporation acted on an informed basis, in good faith and in the honest belief that the action taken was in the best interests of the company." [*Aronson v Lewis*, Del. Supr., 473 A2d 805, 812]. Thus, the party attacking a board decision as uninformed must rebut the presumption that its business judgment was an informed one.

The determination of whether a business judgment is an informed one turns on whether the directors have informed themselves "prior to making a business decision, of all material information reasonably available to them." . . .

A director's duty to exercise an informed business judgment is in the nature of a duty of care, as distinguished from a duty of loyalty. . . .

The standard of care applicable to a director's duty of care has also been recently restated by this Court. In *Aronson, supra*, we stated:

> *While the Delaware cases use a variety of terms to describe the applicable standard of care, our analysis satisfies us that under the business judgment rule director liability is predicated upon concepts of gross negligence.*

473 A2d at 812.

We again confirm that view. We think the concept of gross negligence is also the proper standard for determining whether a business judgment reached by a board of directors was an informed one.

In the specific context of a proposed merger of domestic corporations, a director has a duty under 8 *Del. C.* 251(b), along with his fellow directors, to act in an informed and deliberate manner in determining whether to approve an agreement of merger before submitting the proposal to the stockholders. Certainly in the merger context, a director may not abdicate that duty by leaving to the shareholders alone the decision to approve or disapprove the agreement. . . .

It is against those standards that the conduct of the directors of Trans Union must be tested . . . regarding their exercise of an informed business judgment in voting to approve the Pritzker merger proposal.

. . . The issue of whether the directors reached an informed decision to "sell" the Company on September 20, 1980 must be determined only upon the basis of the information then reasonably available to the directors and relevant to their decision to accept the Pritzker merger proposal. . . .

On the record before us, we must conclude that the Board of Directors did not reach an informed business judgment on September 20, 1980 in voting to "sell" the Company for $55 per share pursuant to the Pritzker cash-out merger proposal. Our reasons, in summary, are as follows:

The directors (1) did not adequately inform themselves as to Van Gorkom's role in forcing the "sale" of the Company and in establishing the per share purchase price; (2) were uninformed as to the intrinsic value of the Company; and (3) given these circumstances, at a minimum, were grossly negligent in approving the "sale" of the Company upon two hours' consideration, without prior notice, and without the exigency of a crisis or emergency.

As has been noted, the Board based its September 20 decision to approve the cash-out merger primarily on Van Gorkom's representations. None of the directors, other than Van Gorkom and Chelberg, had any prior knowledge that the purpose of the meeting was to propose a cash-out merger of Trans Union. No members of Senior Management were present, other than Chelberg, Romans and Peterson; and the latter two had only learned of the proposed sale an hour earlier. Both general counsel Moore and former general counsel Browder attended the meeting, but were equally uninformed as to the purpose of the meeting and the documents to be acted upon.

Without any documents before them concerning the proposed transaction, the members of the Board were required to rely entirely upon Van Gorkom's 20-minute oral presentation of the proposal. No written summary of the terms of the merger was presented; the directors were given no documentation to support the adequacy of $55 price per share for sale of the Company; and the Board had before it nothing more than Van Gorkom's statement of his understanding of the substance of an agreement which he admittedly had never read, nor which any member of the Board had ever seen. . . .

We hold, therefore, that the Trial Court committed reversible error in applying the business judgment rule in favor of the director defendants in this case.

On remand, the Court of Chancery shall conduct an evidentiary hearing to determine the fair value of the shares represented by the plaintiffs' class, based on the intrinsic value of Trans Union on September 20, 1980. . . . Thereafter, an award of damages may be entered to the extent that the fair value of Trans Union exceeds $55 per share.

[Judgment reversed and action remanded]

Questions

1. Did the court hold that the business judgment rule shielded the directors from personal liability in this case?
2. Upon what facts did the court rely in reaching its decision in this case?
3. State the applicable standard of care for determining whether a board of directors' decision was an informed one.

(3) Protection of Directors. In the wake of court decisions holding directors personally liable for damages for gross negligence and in the wake of the resulting general reluctance of individuals to serve as directors, states have passed statutes to protect directors. The aim of the various state laws is essentially the same: to reduce the risk of personal liability for directors who act in good faith when their decisions are challenged. The laws permit a corporation, by a stockholder-approved amendment to its charter or certificate of incorporation, to protect its directors from monetary liability for duty-of-care violations (gross negligence) provided they have not acted in bad faith, breached their duty of loyalty, or gained an improper personal benefit.[9] The laws provide for indemnification and advancement of expenses.

For Example, to avoid supervision by the Office of Thrift Supervision (OTS), the directors of Oak Tree Savings Bank, a subsidiary of Landmark Land Company, Inc., which had loaned subsidiary land

[9] See Del Code § 102(b)(7); NY Bus Corp Law §§ 721–723; Ohio Gen Corp Law § 1701.59; Ind Bus Corp Law, ch 35, § 1(e); Mo Gen Bus Corp Law 351.355 §§ 2, 7.

development companies $986 million, placed the bank in bankruptcy. Because of this, director Bernard Ille resigned. In civil proceedings brought against all of the bank directors, Ille successfully defended himself against the OTS charges. He thus would be entitled to mandatory indemnification from the bank. In addition, employees Trapani and Braun, who were subpoenaed and deposed under adversarial circumstances but were not charged, were deemed to have succeeded on the merits in their defense and were entitled to mandatory indemnification for legal expenses under state law. The other directors and employees charged were found not to have acted in good faith and were not entitled to indemnification.[10]

(b) Actions against Directors

Actions against directors should be brought by the corporation. If the corporation fails to act, as is the case when the directors alleged to be liable control the corporation, shareholders may bring the action in a representative capacity for the corporation.[11]

(c) Removal of Director

Ordinarily, directors are removed by vote of the shareholders. In some states, the board of directors may remove a director and elect a successor on the ground that the removed director (1) did not accept office, (2) failed to satisfy the qualifications for office, (3) was continually absent from the state without a leave of absence granted by the board, generally for a period of six months or more, (4) was discharged in bankruptcy, (5) was convicted of a felony, (6) was unable to perform the duties of director because of any illness or disability, generally for a period of six months or more, or (7) had been judicially declared of unsound mind.[12]

The RMBCA provides for removal of directors "with or without cause" by a majority vote of the shareholders unless the articles of incorporation provide that directors may be removed only for cause.[13] **For Example,** former Conseco, Inc., director Dennis Murray, Sr., was unsuccessful in his action against the board of directors challenging his removal from the board. The court held that the directors had unlimited authority to remove a fellow director without regard for the reasons why the other directors wished to remove him.[14] Directors may always be voted out of office at a regular meeting of shareholders held for the election of directors.

THINKING THINGS THROUGH

ARE THE DAYS OF THE IMPERIAL CEO OVER?

Many changes clarifying the role of corporate directors have occurred since the Enron and WorldCom debacles that came to light in 2001. Federal regulations under the Sarbanes-Oxley Act now apply to directors and officers, and a Corporate Director's Guidebook* was revised and published in 2004 by the American Bar Association's Committee on Corporate Laws, explaining the general legal concepts that apply to directors of public companies. However, the core values associated with the corporate directors' role—good faith, general oversight, informed judgment, and dedication to the corporation's best interests—continue to be the touchstone for evaluating directors' conduct.**

Michael Eisner, considered by many as the Imperial CEO, stacked the board with his friends and expected and received loyalty from them regarding all important corporate decisions. Is it critical for a board's nominating/corporate

* "Corporate Director's Guidebook," *The Business Lawyer*, Vol. 59, pp. 1059–1116 (May 2004).
** *Id.* at 1115.

[10] *In re Landmark Land Co. of California*, 76 F3d 553 (4th Cir 1996).

[11] *In re Abbott Laboratories Derivative Shareholder Litigation*, 325 F3d 795 (7th Cir 2003).

[12] See California Corp Code § 807, recognizing grounds (1), (2), (5), and (7).

[13] RMBCA § 8.08(a).

[14] *Murray v Conseco, Inc.*, 766 NE2d 38 (Ind App 2002).

THINKING THINGS THROUGH

continued

governance committee to receive nominations from not only other directors but also institutional investors and shareholders rather than just the CEO as was the case at Disney with CEO Eisner?***

The chairman of Disney's Compensation Committee hired a highly regarded consultant regarding Ovitz's employment contract and telephoned two members of the committee to inform them of progress. A vote was taken on September 26, after less than an hour of discussion by the committee, and thereafter Ovitz was elected president. As a best practice, should the entire compensation committee have been kept in the loop on this significant matter during negotiations by e-mail, executive summaries, and backup documentation? Should the Disney board have been given meaningful documentation on this appointment to study a week before the board meeting? Do you think it would have been good form for a Disney director in 1995 to question Mr. Eisner, regarding the Ovitz appointment: "I don't think we are ready to vote . . . give us some more supporting documents"? Do you believe that members of a board of directors today feel much more entitled to have adequate and timely information and to ask the tough questions?

***See for example, Boston Scientific's Corporate Governance Manual, Standing Committees and Code of Conduct available at **www.bostonscientifc.com** under Investor Relations. Boston Scientific's 2006 proxy statement reports that 10 of its 14 directors are "independent from management" under NYSE rules. Company bylaws invite shareholders to nominate individuals as directors along with nominations from the Nominating and Governance Committee and the CEO.

C. Officers, Agents, and Employees

Corporations generally have a president, at least one vice president, a secretary, a treasurer, and frequently a chief executive officer (CEO). The duties of these officers are generally set forth in the corporation's bylaws. The duty of the secretary to keep minutes of the proceedings of shareholders and directors is commonly included. Corporation codes generally expressly permit the same person to be both secretary and treasurer. In large corporations, there is often a recording secretary and a corresponding secretary.

Sometimes the officers are elected by the shareholders, but usually they are appointed by the board of directors. The RMBCA follows the general pattern of providing for the appointment of officers by the board of directors.[15] Ordinarily, no particular formality is required to make such appointments. Unless prohibited, a director may hold an executive office.

Officers ordinarily hire the employees and agents of the corporation.

9. Powers of Officers

The officers of a corporation are its agents. Consequently, their powers are controlled by the laws of agency.[16] As in the case of any other agency, a third person has the burden of proving that a particular officer had the authority he or she purported to have.

The fact that the officer or employee acting on behalf of the corporation is a major shareholder does not give either any greater agency powers. Moreover, the person dealing with the officer or employee is charged with knowledge of any limitation on authority contained in the recorded corporate charter or articles of incorporation.

When the nature of the transaction is unusual, that unusual nature should alert a third person to the necessity of specific authorization from the corporation.

(a) President

It is sometimes held that, in the absence of some limitation on authority, the president of a corporation has by virtue of that office the authority to act as

[15] RMBCA § 8.40(a).

[16] *IFC Credit Corp. v Nuova Pasta Co.*, 815 F Supp 268 (ND Ill 1993).

agent on behalf of the corporation within the scope of the business in which the corporation is empowered to engage. It has also been held, however, that the president has such broad powers only when the president is the general manager of the corporation. In instances in which a corporation has a president and chief executive officer, the CEO has authority to exercise personal judgment and discretion in the administrative and executive functions of the corporation as endowed by its bylaws and the resolutions of the board of directors. When a corporation has both a CEO and a president, the CEO is ordinarily the officer entrusted with the broader decisional powers, whereas the president is the executing officer. The president does not have authority by virtue of that office to make a contract that, because of its unusual character, would require action by the board of directors or shareholders.[17]

The president cannot make a contract to fix long-term or unusual contracts of employment, release a claim of the corporation, promise that the corporation will later repurchase shares issued to a subscriber, or mortgage a corporate property.[18]

It is ordinarily held that the president of a business corporation is not authorized to execute commercial paper in the name of the corporation. However, the president may do so when authorized by the board of directors to borrow money for the corporation.

(b) Other Officers and Employees

The authority of corporate employees and other officers, such as the secretary or treasurer, is generally limited to the duties of their office. However, the authority may be extended by the conduct of the corporation in accordance with the general principles governing apparent authority based on the conduct of the principal. An unauthorized act may, of course, be ratified. The authority of the general manager of the corporation is determined by principles of ordinary agency law.

10. Liability Relating to Fiduciary Duties

The relationship of officers to the corporation, like that of directors, is a fiduciary one. Because corporate officers devote all or most of their time to a corporation's business and receive a salary as officers, their fiduciary duties are more extensive than those of directors, who do not work for the corporation on a daily basis and receive little or no salary.[19] Officers, because of their access to corporate information developed in the pursuit of their daily duties on behalf of the corporation, have an obligation to inform the directors of material information relating to the business. Officers have an obligation not to make any secret financial gain at the expense of the corporation. Because of their level of knowledge of the business, officer-directors have a high fiduciary duty to the corporation.

(a) Corporate Opportunities

If an officer diverts a corporate opportunity, the corporation may recover from the officer the profits of which the corporation has been deprived.

In the *Demoulas* case, the court was faced with multiple issues relating to corporate opportunities.

DEMOULAS V DEMOULAS SUPER MARKETS, INC., 677 NE2D 159 (MASS 1997)

RULING WISELY AND DECENTLY?

Demoulas Super Markets, Inc. (DSM), was owned by brothers George and Telemachus Demoulas, each owning an equal number of shares of stock. From 1964 through May 1971, the company grew from 5 stores to a chain of 14 supermarkets, including 2 stores in New Hampshire. George died suddenly on June 27, 1971, and at his death, Telemachus assumed control of DSM under the terms of a voting trust. Valley Properties, Inc. (Valley), was set up in 1974 to provide real estate for DSM. In 1990, George's son Arthur, age 22 and a shareholder of DSM and Valley, brought shareholder derivative actions on behalf of DSM and Valley, contending that since George's death Telemachus had diverted business opportunities away from DSM into other businesses that were solely owned by Telemachus's branch of the family. The evidence

[17] *French v Chosin Few, Inc.*, 173 F Supp 2d (WDNY 2001).

[18] *Schmidt v Farm Credit Services*, 977 F2d 511 (10th Cir 1992).

[19] *Fletcher Cyc. Corp.* § 991 (perm ed 1986). See also *Geller v Allied-Lyons PLC*, 674 NE2d 1334 (Mass App 1997).

showed that in the 1970s two new corporations were formed and operated supermarkets in New Hampshire; DSM supplied the financing and management, but ownership was held in Telemachus's sister's and daughter's names. By 1986, these stores grew into a single supermarket chain operating under the Market Basket name and entirely owned by members of Telemachus's branch of the family. The trial court judge determined that Telemachus diverted these corporate opportunities from DSM, and the court ordered the transfer back to DSM of the assets and liabilities of the new corporations. In her decision, the judge cited lines from *Ulysses,* by Alfred Lord Tennyson, in which Ulysses speaks lovingly of his son Telemachus, expressing the belief that he would rule wisely and decently after his death. Telemachus denied that any acts were improper or gave rise to liability and charged that the judge was not impartial, as evidenced by her quotation from Tennyson's poem.

Judicial Opinion

GREANEY, J. . . . *Alleged bias of the judge.* We reject the various arguments that a new trial is required because the judge was not impartial. . . .

The judge's use of a literary reference from Tennyson's "Ulysses" to begin her findings of fact and rulings of law and the few sharp remarks alluded to by the defendants make no case for bias. The literary reference was the judge's stylistic way of stating the theme of her decision, based on the facts she had found. The trial was long, arduous, and, at times, very bitter. "There might have been, from time to time, a momentary lapse—but, especially in a case as acrimonious as this one proved to be, 'appellate courts must grant the presider some margin of humanity.'" *Fashion House, Inc. v. K mart Corp.*, 892 F.2d 1076, 1096 (1st Cir.1989), quoting *United States v. Polito*, 856 F.2d 414, 418 (1st Cir.1988). . . .

Diversion of Corporate Opportunities and Assets

The judge found that DSM and Valley had been injured when "corporate opportunities," namely, potential business ventures that should rightfully have been offered to those corporations, were instead pursued either by the individual defendants or by other companies in which those defendants held ownership interests. The judge found as well that "self-dealing" transactions had occurred in which defendants who had fiduciary duties to DSM and Valley transferred assets from these corporations to other defendant-owned companies, for less than fair value. The requirements that determine the propriety of pursuing corporate opportunities and engaging in self-dealing transactions are similar, and will be referred to here as the "corporate opportunity doctrine." In applying the doctrine to the facts of this case, we agree with the judge's conclusions that the defendants participated in, or benefited from, improper diversions of corporate opportunities and self-dealing transactions, to the detriment of DSM and Valley. . . .

. . . In the case of a close corporation, which resembles a partnership, duties of loyalty extend to shareholders, who owe one another substantially the same duty of utmost good faith and loyalty in the operation of the enterprise that partners owe to one another, a duty that is even stricter than that required of directors and shareholders in corporations generally. . . . In the often repeated words of then Chief Judge Cardozo of the New York Court of Appeals, "[n]ot honesty alone, but the punctilio of an honor the most sensitive, is then the standard of behavior" that describes this more rigorous duty. *Id.* at 594, 328 N.E.2d 505. . . .

A director or officer is not entirely barred from pursuing a corporate opportunity, but a person holding either position cannot do so unless the opportunity is first offered to the corporation and rejected by it. In this aspect, the corporate opportunity doctrine may be considered to be a rule of disclosure. . . . To satisfy the principle of fairness to the corporation and to meet his duty of loyalty, the fiduciary must fully disclose to the corporation, all material facts concerning the opportunity. . . .

In short, to meet a fiduciary's duty of loyalty, a director or officer who wishes to take advantage of a corporate opportunity or engage in self-dealing must first disclose material details of the venture to the corporation, and then either receive the assent of disinterested directors or shareholders, or otherwise prove that the decision is fair to the corporation. Otherwise, the officer or director acts in violation of his fiduciary duties, and whatever gain or advantage that he acquires may be held for the benefit of the corporation so as to deny him any benefit or profit. *Durfee, supra* at 198, 80 N.E.2d 522, citing *Guth v. Loft, Inc.*, 23 Del. Ch. 255, 270, 5 A.2d 503 (1939).

With these principles in mind, we next examine the ventures and transactions that the judge found to have been conducted in violation of the fiduciary duties of DSM's and Valley's directors and officers. . . .

Market Basket. The judge concluded that Market Basket represents a corporate opportunity that rightfully belonged to DSM and was diverted from it in a breach of fiduciary duty, and that its assets are derived from that diversion or from additional wrongful self-dealing transactions. She therefore ordered the return of Market Basket's assets and liabilities to DSM. We conclude that the result reached by the judge is supported by her extensive factual findings (which in turn have support in the evidence).

Market Basket's status as a diverted corporate opportunity is based on the history of its predecessor corporations, Seabrook Sales and P & P Foods.... Both were corporate opportunities of DSM that were never made available to the corporation, and both were diverted in a breach of fiduciary duty by a director-officer (Telemachus). The defendants argue that Seabrook Sales and P & P Foods were not corporate opportunities for DSM, because New Hampshire liquor laws restricted the number of licenses for beer sales available to a person or entity, and thus DSM could not have opened additional supermarkets in that State (except by forgoing beer and wine sales). However, as we have just indicated, the existence of a legal or other impediment is a matter for a corporation's board to consider when deciding whether to accept or decline an opportunity that has been disclosed to it, and the existence of any impediment does not excuse the failure of a fiduciary to present the opportunity to the board and to disclose all material details before pursuing it himself. If these opportunities had been disclosed to the board of DSM and rejected, then, given the absence of a disinterested and independent board, the fiduciary would have had to show that the rejection was fair to the corporation, and the existence of legal impediments would have been relevant to determining the fairness of the fiducary's action. However, because full disclosure did not occur here, we do not need to address whether DSM could have feasibly pursued these opportunities. The nondisclosure of a corporate opportunity is, in itself, unfair to a corporation and a breach of fiduciary duty.

The creation of Seabrook Sales and P & P Foods was a breach of Telemachus's fiduciary duty of loyalty, notwithstanding the fact that the companies were initially owned by persons who were not themselves directors or officers of DSM. (As has been mentioned, Telemachus's sister Ann Burliss owned Seabrook, and his daughter Frances owned P & P Foods. In 1981, Frances exercised an option that had been arranged by Telemachus and purchased Seabrook from Burliss.) A fiduciary is liable either where he benefits directly or where profits flow instead to a third party or to another company under the fiduciary's control. See Principles of Corporate Governance, *supra* at §§ 1.03, 5.08 (fiduciary violates duty of loyalty by advancing pecuniary interests of associate, such as a child or sibling, in manner that would constitute a breach if he had acted for himself). It is clear from the judge's findings that these companies were set up at Telemachus's direction and were independent in name only. DSM, which Telemachus fully controlled, managed and financed the operations of these companies. The use of DSM's corporate resources to support these companies indicates that they were wrongfully diverted corporate opportunities. See 1 J.D. Cox & T.L. Hazen, Corporations § 11.7, at 11.33, 11.39 (1995) (fiduciary's use of corporate assets or personnel to acquire or nurture opportunity indicates breach of duty of loyalty).

Seabrook Sales opened its second store in 1975 under the Market Basket name (which had previously been registered by DSM in both Massachusetts and New Hampshire), and changed its corporate name to Market Basket, Inc., in 1979 (with DSM's permission). In 1981, P & P Foods exercised Frances's option and acquired Market Basket, Inc. The latter was a subsidiary of P & P Foods until the two were merged in December, 1983; the next month, P & P changed its name to Market Basket. By this time, the company owned seven stores: six in New Hampshire, and one in Chelsea, Massachusetts (a store whose ownership by Market Basket instead of DSM belies the defendants' argument that Seabrook Sales and P & P Foods were created simply to overcome New Hampshire liquor law restrictions).

Because the entity that is now Market Basket arose from the merger of two diverted corporate opportunities that rightfully belonged to DSM, the relief ordered with respect to the current assets and liabilities of Market Basket could rest on that fact alone....

[With certain technical adjustments, the Supreme Judicial Court of Massachusetts upheld the trial court's order to the Telemachus Branch to transfer back to the original corporations the assets and liabilities of the entities that benefited from the improper diversion of corporate opportunities and resources]

Questions

1. Is a director or officer of a corporation totally barred from pursuing corporate opportunities?
2. What, if anything, is wrong with Telemachus setting up his sister Ann as owner of the Seabrook Corporation and his daughter Frances as owner of the P & P Foods Corporation in order to avoid the appearance of violating his fiduciary duty to DSM? Surely family members have a right to start their own businesses.
3. What is the remedy in this case?

An opportunity that would be advantageous to the corporation must first be offered to the corporation before an officer or a director, who owes a fiduciary duty to the corporation, can take advantage of the opportunity. Full disclosure is required. Only if the opportunity is rejected by a majority of disinterested directors may the officer then take advantage of the opportunity. **For Example,** Nancy Harris was president of the Northeast Harbor Golf Club, Inc. In her capacity as club president, she learned of an opportunity to purchase the Gilpin property, which adjoined the golf club. Her private purchase of the property constituted the taking of a corporate opportunity and resulted in her liability to the club. Harris believed that her purchase, in a separate transaction, of the Smallidge land, which was adjacent to three of the golf club's holes and could be developed, was not usurpation of a corporate opportunity because she learned of the availability independently of the club. However, this also was a corporate opportunity because it was so closely related to the club's business. She was obligated to disclose the opportunity to the corporation and let it decide whether to pursue it.[20]

Officers may avail themselves of all opportunities lying outside the field of their duties as officers when business opportunities come to them in an individual capacity.[21]

(b) Secret Profits

Officers are liable to the corporation for secret profits made in connection with, or at the expense of, the business of the corporation.

11. Agents and Employees

The authority, rights, and liabilities of an agent or employee of a corporation are governed by the same rules as those applicable when the principal or employer is a natural person. The authority of corporate employees is also governed by general agency principles. **For Example,** when Juantai Li signed a promissory note in his own name and did not indicate that he was an agent of a corporation, he was held personally liable for $523,823 under the note he signed.[22]

The fact that a person is acting on behalf of a corporation does not serve as a shield from the liability that would be imposed for acts done on behalf of a natural person.

D. Liability

Limited liability is a major reason for incorporating. Management, however, is not free from all civil and criminal liability simply because the corporate form is used.

12. Liability of Management to Third Persons

Officers and managers of a corporation are not liable to third parties for the economic consequences of their advice so long as they acted in good faith to advance the interests of the corporation, even if they cause the corporation to refuse to deal with or break its contract with these third persons.

Ordinarily, the management of a corporation (its directors, officers, and executive employees) is not liable to third persons for the effect of its management or advice. The liability of a director or an officer for misconduct may usually be enforced only by the corporation or by shareholders bringing a derivative action on behalf of the corporation. Ordinarily, directors or officers are not liable to a third person for loss caused by the negligent performance of their duties as directors or officers even if, because of such negligence, the corporation is in turn liable to the third person to whom the corporation owed the duty to use care or was under a contract obligation to render a particular service.

However, in those rare cases when a director or an officer has in some way participated in or directed the tortious act, personal liability will attach. For example, a corporate officer and director may be held personally liable for the tort of fraud in the inducement regarding a false promise to grant an insurance agency an exclusive territory selling viatical settlements, by which life insurance policies of terminally ill people are purchased at a discount in exchange for an immediate cash settlement.[23]

[20] *Northeast Harbor Golf Club v Harris*, 725 A2d 1018 (Me 1999); see *Anderson v Bellino*, 658 NW2d 645 (Neb 2003).

[21] *Hill v Southeastern Floor Covering Co.*, 596 So 2d 874 (Miss 1992).

[22] *Wujin Nanxiashu v Ti-Well International*, 807 NYS2d 47 (App Div 2005.)

[23] *First Financial USA, Inc. v Steinger*, 760 So 2d 996 (Fla App 2000).

ETHICS & THE LAW

For the past five years, one of the concerns shareholders and others have raised about corporate officers is their level of compensation. The following figures are some examples of CEO total annual compensation packages for 2006.*

Company	*CEO*	*Amount*
Capital One Financial	Richard D. Fairbank	$249,420,000
Yahoo	Terry S. Semel	230,550,000
Cendant	Henry R. Silverman	139,960,000
KB Home	Bruce Karatz	135,530,000
Lehman Bros. Holdings	Richard S. Fuld, Jr	122,670,000
Occidental Petroleum	Ray R. Irani	80,730,000
Oracle	Lawrence J. Ellison	75,330,000
Symantec	John W. Thompson	71,840,000
Caremark Rx	Edwin M. Crawford	69,660,000**

On gross sales of $2 billion, is $5 million for a CEO's salary out of line? Is it troublesome to shareholders and perhaps employees that downsizing and cost cutting occur but CEO salaries remain at the same levels or higher? If the board members approve the salaries, aren't they accountable to the shareholders?

**Source:* Forbes.com: Forbes Best Paid CEOs 2006.

**On July 27, 2006, the SEC issued revised rules requiring more disclosure on executive pay and benefits and the disclosure of a single number for total compensation for each top executive. Moreover, companies will have to explain themselves on the timing of stock option awards.

13. Criminal Liability

Officers and directors, as well as the corporation itself, may be criminally accountable for business regulatory offenses.

(a) Active Participation

Officers and directors, as in the case of agents, are personally responsible for any crimes committed by them even when they act on behalf of the corporation.[24] At the local level, they may be criminally responsible for violation of ordinances relating to sanitation, safety, and hours of closing.

At the state level, they may be criminally liable for conducting a business without obtaining necessary licenses or after the corporate certificate of incorporation has been forfeited.

At the federal level, officers and directors may be criminally liable for tax and securities law violations as well as egregious environmental protection law and worker safety law violations. International transactions may lead to potential criminal exposure. Under the Foreign Corrupt Practices Act, it is a crime for a U.S. firm to make payments or gifts to a foreign officer to obtain business. Not only is the U.S. corporation subject to a fine but also the officers and individuals involved are subject to fine and imprisonment.

(b) Responsible Corporate Officer Doctrine

Officers and directors may be criminally liable under a number of federal and state statutes for failure to prevent the commission of a crime if they are found to be the "responsible corporate officers." These

[24] *Joy Management Co. v City of Detroit*, 455 NW2d 55 (Mich App 1990).

statutes include the Food, Drug and Cosmetic Act, the Federal Hazardous Substances Act, the Occupational Safety and Health Act, the Federal Water Pollution Act, and, at the state level, the California Corporate Criminal Liability Act. **For Example,** Gary Lundgren was a shareholder and officer of KIE, Inc., which owned and operated a sewage treatment plant on Ketron Island. He knew of the facility's discharge of pollutants into Puget Sound without a permit. As the "responsible corporate officer," he was held personally liable for a $250,000 penalty because he controlled the facility with knowledge of the violations.[25] The California Corporate Criminal Liability Act requires managers in control of corporate operations who have knowledge of "serious concealed dangers" to employees or customers to notify the appropriate regulatory authority or be subject to criminal liability.[26]

(c) Liability of the Corporation Itself

A corporation itself may be convicted of a criminal offense if its agent committed the offense acting within the scope of the agent's authority.

(d) Punishment of Corporations

Under the Organizational Federal Sentencing Guidelines, organizations, including corporations, trusts, pension funds, unions, and nonprofit organizations, are subject to greatly increased fines for criminal convictions. However, corporations and other covered organizations that implement an effective compliance program designed to prevent and detect corporate crimes and voluntarily disclose such crimes to the government will be subject to much lower fines under the guidelines.[27]

14. Indemnification of Officers, Directors, Employees, and Agents

While performing what they believe to be their duty, officers, directors, employees, and agents of corporations may commit acts for which they are later sued or criminally prosecuted. The RMBCA broadly authorizes the corporation to indemnify these persons if they acted in good faith and in a manner reasonably believed to be in, or not opposed to, the interests of the corporation and had no reason to believe that their conduct was unlawful.[28] In some states, statutory provision is made requiring the corporation to indemnify directors and officers for reasonable expenses incurred by them in defending unwarranted suits brought against them by shareholders.

15. Liability for Corporate Debts

Because the corporation is a separate legal person, debts that it owes are ordinarily the obligations of the corporation only. Consequently, neither directors nor officers are individually liable for corporate debts, even though it may have been their acts that gave rise to the debts.

In some states, liability for corporate debts is imposed on the corporation's officers and directors when the corporation improperly engages in business.

16. Protection of Shareholders

Shareholders may obtain protection from misconduct by management and by the majority of the shareholders. Shareholders may protect themselves by voting at the next annual election for new directors and for new officers if the latter are elected. Shareholders may take remedial action at a special meeting called for that purpose. Objecting shareholders may bring a legal action when the management misconduct complained of constitutes a legal wrong.[29]

17. Civil Liability of the Corporation

A corporation is liable to third persons for the acts of its officers, employees, and agents to the same extent that a natural person is liable for the acts of agents and employees. This means that the ordinary rules of agency law determine the extent to which the corporation is liable to a third person for a contract made or a tort committed by management personnel, employees, and agents.

[25] *State Department of Ecology v Lundgren*, 971 P2d 948 (Wash App 1999).

[26] Cal Penal Code § 387 (West 2006).

[27] U.S. Sentencing Commission Guidelines Manual §§ 8C2.5(f), 8C2.6. On April 8, 2004, the Commission adopted amendments to the Guidelines and requires a periodic assessment of the "risk of criminal conduct" by the corporation or organization.

[28] Subchapter 8E, added in 1980 and revised in 1994.

[29] *Christner v Anderson, Nietzke & Co.*, 444 NW2d 779 (Mich 1989).

Summary

Ordinarily, stockholder action is taken at a regular or special meeting of the stockholders. The presence of a quorum of the voting shareholders is required.

Management of a corporation is under the control of a board of directors elected by the shareholders. Courts will not interfere with the board's judgment in the absence of unusual conduct such as fraud. A director is disqualified from taking part in corporate action when the director has a conflict of interest. Action by directors is usually taken at a properly called meeting of the board. Directors act in a fiduciary capacity in dealing with the corporation. Directors who act in good faith and have exercised reasonable care are not liable for losses resulting from their management decisions. Ordinarily, directors are removed by shareholders.

Officers of a corporation, including a CEO, president, vice president, secretary, and treasurer, are usually selected and removed by the board of directors. Officers are agents of the corporation, and their powers are governed by the law of agency. Their relations with the corporation are fiduciary in nature, and they are liable for any secret profits and for diverting corporate opportunities to their own advantage.

Directors and officers, as in the case of agents generally, are personally responsible for any torts or crimes they commit even if they act on behalf of the corporation. The corporation itself may be prosecuted for crimes and is subject to fines if convicted. The ordinary rules of agency law determine the extent to which a corporation is liable for a contract made or tort committed by a director, officer, corporate agent, or employee.

Questions and Case Problems

1. What constitutes a quorum at a meeting of shareholders?
2. In 1996, Congress offered national banks the opportunity to become Subchapter S entities. Amboy Bancorporation was a small, highly profitable New Jersey Bank that was overcapitalized. Amboy's president and CEO utilized Bank Advisory Group, Inc. (BAG), to calculate the fair value of individual shares of Amboy stock. The board of directors approved a merger cash buy-out program designed to reduce the shareholder base to below the 75 qualified shareholders necessary to obtain Subchapter S status. BAG incorrectly applied a minority and marketability discount to its evaluation of the fair value of the stock, bringing it down from $110 per share to $70.13 per share. Casey and other shareholders who cashed out under the plan at $73 per share sued the board of directors individually for damages for approving such a flawed plan. Are directors personally liable when they act in reliance on a report by an outside expert whose advice is flawed? If a public accounting firm or an attorney gave the flawed advice, would the directors be personally liable? [*Casey v Brennan*, 344 NJ Super 83]
3. The majority shareholder and president of Dunaway Drug Stores, Inc., William B. Dunaway, was structuring and executing the sale of virtually all of the corporation's assets to Eckerd Drug Co. While doing this, he negotiated a side noncompete agreement with Eckerd, giving Dunaway $300,000 plus a company car in exchange for a covenant not to compete for three years. He simultaneously amended two corporate leases with Eckerd, thereby decreasing the value of the corporation's leasehold estates. The board of directors approved the asset sale. Minority shareholders brought a derivative action against William Dunaway, claiming breach of his fiduciary duty in negotiating the undisclosed noncompete agreement, which did not require him to perform any service for buyer Eckerd Drug. Did William Dunaway make sufficient disclosure about all of the negotiations of the asset sale to Eckerd Drug? Did William Dunaway violate any fiduciary duty to the corporation? Decide. [*Dunaway v Parker*, 453 SE2d 43 (Ga App)]
4. Larry Phillips was hired for a two-year period as executive secretary of the Montana Education Association (MEA). Six months later, he was fired. He then sued MEA for breach of contract and sued the directors and some of the other employees of MEA on the theory that they had caused MEA to break the contract with him and were therefore guilty of the tort of maliciously interfering with his contract with MEA. The evidence showed that the individual defendants, without malice, had induced the corporation to break the contract with Phillips but that this had been done to further the welfare of the corporation. Was MEA liable for breach of contract? Were the individual defendants shielded from personal liability? [*Phillips v Montana Education Ass'n*, 610 P2d 154 (Mont)]
5. Christy Pontiac, a corporation, was indicted for theft by swindle and forgery involving a GM cash rebate program. Hesli, a middle-management employee of Christy Pontiac, had forged the cash rebate applications for two cars so that the rebate money was paid to Christy Pontiac instead of its customers. When confronted by a customer who should have received a rebate, the president of the dealership attempted to negotiate a settlement. The president did not contact GM headquarters until after an

investigation was begun by the state attorney general. Christy Pontiac argued that it could not be held responsible for a crime involving specific intent because only natural persons, as opposed to corporations, can form such intent. Decide. [*State v Christy Pontiac-GMC, Inc.*, 354 NW2d 17 (Minn)]

6. Directors must always own stock of the corporation to ensure they will be attentive to their duties. Appraise this statement.
7. Discuss the power of a corporation president to employ a sales manager and to agree that the manager should be paid a stated amount per year plus a percentage of any increase in the dollar volume of sales that might take place.
8. Richard Grassgreen was executive vice president and then president and chief operating officer of Kinder-Care, Inc., the largest proprietary provider of child care in the country. The company was restructured in 1989 and changed its name to the Enstar Group, Inc. Between 1985 and 1990, while Grassgreen served as the corporation's investment manager, he invested millions of dollars of company money in junk bond deals with Michael Milken, and he secretly retained some $355,000 in commitment fees. When the corporation discovered this, Grassgreen repaid the corporation. It sued him to recover any compensation paid him over the five-year period during which the secret payments were made, some $5,197,663. Grassgreen defended that his conduct caused little, if any, damage to the corporation because the corporation did not lose any money on any of the investments for which he received personal fees. Decide. [*Enstar Group, Inc., v Grassgreen*, 812 F Supp 1562 (MD Ala)]
9. Danny Hill, the general manager of Southeastern Floor Covering Co., Inc. (SE), had full authority to run the business. His responsibilities included preparing and submitting bid proposals to general contractors for floor coverings and ceilings on construction projects. Hill prepared and submitted a bid for a job for Chata Construction Co. for asbestos encapsulation, ceramic tile, ceilings, carpets, and vinyl tile flooring. However, because SE was not licensed by the EPA, the asbestos work was withdrawn. In the past, SE had used Larry Barnes's company, which was EPA licensed, to do asbestos work under a subcontract agreement. Hill did not pursue a subcontract with Barnes for the Chata job. Rather, Hill and Barnes worked up a bid together and submitted it to Chata for the asbestos work. The bid was accepted, and Hill made $90,000 from the Chata job. Two years later, SE found out about Hill's role in the asbestos work done for Chata, and the corporation sued him for the lost profits. Hill argued that SE was not licensed by the EPA to do asbestos work and thus could not claim a lost corporate opportunity when it was not qualified to do the work. Decide. Are any ethical principles applicable to this case? [*Hill v Southeastern Floor Covering Co.*, 596 So 2d 874 (Miss)]
10. A director of a corporation cannot lend money to the corporation because that would create the danger of a conflict of interest between the director's status as a director and as a creditor. Appraise this statement.
11. Hamway and other minority shareholders brought an action against majority shareholders of Libbie Rehabilitation Center, Inc., including Frank Giannotti, CEO–director; Alex Grossman, president–director; Henry Miller, vice president–director; Ernest Dervishian, secretary and corporate attorney; and Lewis Cowardin, treasurer–director. The minority shareholders contended that the corporation paid excessive salaries to these director-officers and was wasting corporate assets. Prior to coming to Libbie, Giannotti had been a carpet and tile retailer, Grossman a pharmacist, Miller a real estate developer, Dervishian a lawyer, and Cowardin a jeweler. The evidence showed that the extent of their work for the corporation was very limited. For example, Cowardin, Libbie's finance officer, who was paid $78,121 in 1985, demonstrated no knowledge of the Medicare and Medicaid programs, the principal source of Libbie's income. Although he claimed to have spent 20 to 25 hours a week on corporate duties, he reported on the tax return for his jewelry business that he spent 75 percent of his working time in that business in 1984. One expert witness of the plaintiff testified that the five men were performing the management functions of one individual. The director-officers contended that the business was making a profit and that all salaries were approved by a board of directors that had extensive business experience. Were the directors within their rights to elect themselves officers and set pay for themselves as they saw fit? Did they violate any legal or ethical duty to their shareholders?
12. Anthony Yee was the president of Waipahu Auto Exchange, a corporation. As part of his corporate duties, he arranged financing for the company. Federal Services Finance Corp. drew 12 checks payable to the order of Waipahu Auto Exchange. These were then indorsed by its president, "Waipahu Auto Exchange, Limited, by Anthony Yee, President," and were cashed at two different banks. Bishop National Bank of Hawaii, on which the checks were drawn, charged its depositor, Federal Services, with the amount of the checks. Federal Services then sued Bishop National Bank to restore to its account the amount of the 12 checks on the ground that Bishop National Bank had improperly made payment on the checks because Anthony Yee had no authority to cash them. Did Yee have authority to indorse and cash the checks? [*Federal Services Finance Corp. v Bishop Nat'l Bank of Hawaii*, 190 F2d 442 (9th Cir)]
13. Klinicki and Lundgren incorporated Berlinair, Inc., a closely held Oregon corporation. Lundgren was president and responsible for developing business. Klinicki

served as vice president and director responsible for operations and maintenance. Klinicki owned one-third of the stock, and Lundgren controlled the rest. They both met with BFR, a consortium of Berlin travel agents, about contracting to operate some charter flights. After the initial meeting, all contracts with BFR were made by Lundgren, who learned that there was a good chance that the BFR contract would be available. He incorporated Air Berlin Charter Co. (ABC) and was its sole owner. He presented BFR with a contract proposal, and it awarded the contract to ABC. Although Lundgren was using Berlinair's working time and facilities, he managed to keep the negotiations a secret from Klinicki. When Klinicki discovered Lundgren's actions, he sued him for usurping a corporate opportunity for Berlinair. Lundgren contended that it was not a usurpation of corporate opportunity because Berlinair did not have the financial ability to undertake the contract with BFR. Decide. Are any ethical principles applicable to this case? Consider the applicability of Chief Justice Cardozo's statement in *Meinhard v Salmon*, 164 NE 545 (NY 1928), concerning the level of conduct for fiduciaries: "A trustee is held to something stricter than the morals of the marketplace. Not honesty alone, but the punctillo of an honor the most sensitive, is then the standard of behavior. . . ." [*Klinicki v Lundgren*, 695 P2d 906 (Or)]

14. Rudolph Redmont, the president of Abbott Thinlite Corp., left Abbott to run Circle Corp. in competition with his former employer. It was claimed that he diverted contracts from his former employer to his new one, having gained the advantage of specific information about the deals in progress while employed by Abbott. Abbott sued Redmont and Circle Corp. to recover lost profits. Redmont contended that all of the contracts in question were made after he left Abbott, at which time his fiduciary duty to Abbott had ceased. Decide. [*Abbott Thinlite Corp. v Redmont*, 475 F2d 85 (2d Cir)]

15. William Gurtler was president and a board member of Unichem Corp., which produced and sold chemical laundry products. While president of Unichem, he encouraged his plant manager to leave to join a rival business, which Gurtler was going to join in the near future. Moreover, Gurtler sold Unichem products to his son, G. B. Gurtler, in January 1982 at a figure substantially below their normal price and on credit even though G. B. had no credit history. Gurtler made the sales with full knowledge that G. B. was going to start a rival business. Also at that time, Gurtler was aware that his wife was soliciting Unichem employees to join the new Gurtler Chemical Co., and he helped her design Gurtler's label so that it would look like Unichem's. On February 9, 1982, Gurtler guaranteed a $100,000 loan for Gurtler Chemical Co. with funds to be disbursed after he left Unichem, which occurred on March 12, 1982. On March 15, 1982, he became president of Gurtler Chemical Co. Unichem sued Gurtler for breach of fiduciary duty and for the loss of profits that resulted. Gurtler contended that his sales to G. B. guaranteed needed revenue to Unichem and constituted a sound business decision that should be applauded and that was protected under the business judgment rule. Decide. Are any ethical principles applicable to this case? [*Unichem Corp. v Gurtler*, 498 NE2d 724 (Ill App)]

CPA Questions

1. Davis, a director of Active Corp., is entitled to
   a. Serve on the board of a competing business
   b. Take sole advantage of a business opportunity that would benefit Active
   c. Rely on information provided by a corporate officer
   d. Unilaterally grant a corporate loan to one of Active's shareholders

2. Absent a specific provision in its articles of incorporation, a corporation's board of directors has the power to do all of the following *except*
   a. Repeal the bylaws
   b. Declare dividends
   c. Fix compensation of directors
   d. Amend the articles of incorporation

3. Which of the following statements is correct regarding fiduciary duty?
   a. A director's fiduciary duty to the corporation may be discharged by merely disclosing his or her self-interest.
   b. A director owes a fiduciary duty to the shareholders but *not* to the corporation.
   c. A promoter of a corporation to be formed owes no fiduciary duty to anyone, unless the contract engaging the promoter so provides.
   d. A majority shareholder as such may owe a fiduciary duty to fellow shareholders.

PART (8)

REAL PROPERTY AND ESTATES

REAL PROPERTY

CHAPTER (49)

LEARNING OBJECTIVES

After studying this chapter, you should be able to

LO.1 List the types of real property interests

LO.2 Distinguish between liens, licenses, and easements

LO.3 List and illustrate the forms of co-ownership of real property

LO.4 Define *deed* and describe how it works to convey title to land

LO.5 Describe and illustrate the warranties of the grantor and the grantee of real property

LO.6 Describe the characteristics and effect of a mortgage

The law of real property can be highly technical and still relies on vocabulary drawn from the days of feudal lords and castles. This chapter presents a simplified look at the law of real property.

A. Nature of Real Property

Real property has special characteristics of permanence and uniqueness. These characteristics have strongly influenced the rules that society has developed to resolve disputes concerning real property.

1. Land

Land means more than the surface of the earth. It is composed of the soil and all things of a permanent nature affixed to the ground, such as herbs, grass, trees, and other growing, natural products. The word also includes the waters on the ground and things that are embedded beneath the surface.

Technically, land extends downward to the earth's center and upward indefinitely. The general view is that the owner of the land owns the space above that land subject to the right of flying aircraft that do not interfere with the use of the land and are not dangerous to persons or property on the land.

CPA 2. Easements

An **easement** is the right to use another's property, such as the right to cross another's land. Rights in another person's land also include profits. The easement belongs to the land that is benefited. The benefited land is called the **dominant tenement**, and the land that is subject to the easement is called the **servient tenement**.[1]

(a) Creation of Easement

Because an easement is an interest in land, an oral promise to create an easement is not binding because of the statute of frauds. An oral grant of an easement would be a license (see Section 4). An easement created by agreement is transferred by deed. However, an easement may also be created by implication. An **easement by implication** arises when one conveys part of the land that has been used as a dominant

[1] *Tipperman v Tsiatos*, 915 P2d 446 (Or App 1996).

estate in relation to the part retained. **For Example,** if water pipes or drain pipes run from the part of the land conveyed through the part retained, there is an implied right to continue using the pipes. For an easement to be implied, the use, as in this case with the pipes, must be apparent, continuous, and reasonably necessary.

Easements may also be created by implication when necessary for the use of the land that is conveyed. An easement by implication arises when one subdivides land and sells a portion to which no entry can be made except over the land retained or over the land of a stranger. The grantee's right to use the land retained by the grantor for the purpose of going to and from the land conveyed is known as a **way of necessity**.

An easement may be created by **estoppel**, such as when the grantor conveys a plot of land bounded by what the deed describes as a street. In such a case, if the grantor owns the adjoining land, the public cannot be denied the right to use the area for access to the street.

An easement may be created by **prescription**. Under prescription, a person acquires an easement by adverse use, or use contrary to the landowner's use, for a statutory period. No easement is acquired by prescription if the use of the land is with the permission of the owner.

(b) Termination of Easement

Once an easement has been granted, it cannot be destroyed by the act of the grantor. A "revocation" attempted without the easement owner's consent has no effect.

An easement may be lost by nonuse when surrounding circumstances show an intent to abandon the easement.[2] **For Example,** when a surface transit system had an easement to maintain trolley tracks but abandoned the easement when the tracks were removed and all surface transportation was discontinued, the easement was lost through abandonment. Likewise, when the owner of the easement planted a flower bed on the land across the end of the path of the easement, the intent to abandon the easement was evident.

CPA 3. Profits

Profits are rights to take part of the soil or produce of the land belonging to another. **For Example,** profits include the right to remove coal from the land of another and the right to use the water from another's land.

CPA 4. Licenses

A **license** is a personal, revocable privilege to perform an act or series of acts on the land of another. Unlike an easement, a license is not an interest in land. **For Example,** the person allowed to come into the house to use the telephone has a license. The advertising company that has permission to paint a sign on the side of a building also has a license.

A license may be terminated at the will of the licensor. It continues only as long as the licensor is the owner of the land.

THINKING THINGS THROUGH

CAN THERE BE ADVERSE POSSESSION OF A LAKE USING JET SKIS?

In 1972, Donald and Joyce Carnahan purchased a one-acre lot located on a 22-acre lake. The purchase included a portion of the lake bed. The Carnahans used the lake for recreational activity in both winter and summer, and their activities included motorboats, jet skis, and wave runners. In 1991, the Moriah Property Owners Association, Inc., acquired title to the majority of the lots along the lake and imposed restrictive covenants on the use of the lake, including one that prohibited all motors on the lake except for those powered by 12-volt batteries. The Carnahans filed suit to establish a prescriptive easement in their right to use the lake for all their activities. Do you think the Carnahans acquired an easement by prescription? [CARNAHAN V MORIAH PROPERTY OWNERS ASS'N, INC., 716 NE2d 437 (Ind 1999)]

[2] *Louis W. Epstein Family Partnership v Kmart Corp.*, 13 F3d 762 (3d Cir 1993).

CPA 5. Liens

Real property may be subject to **liens** that arise by the voluntary act of the owner of the land. **For Example,** the lien of a mortgage is created when the owner borrows money and uses the land as security for repayment of the debt.

Liens may also arise involuntarily, as in the case of **tax liens**, **judgment liens**, and **mechanics' liens**. In the case of taxes and judgments, the liens provide a means for enforcing the obligations of the owner of the land to pay the taxes or the judgment. Mechanics' liens give persons furnishing labor and materials in the improvement of real estate the right to proceed against the real estate for the collection of the amounts due them.

6. Fixtures

Under the laws relating to fixtures, personal property becomes real property.

CPA (a) Definition

A **fixture** is personal property that is attached to the earth or placed in a building in such a way or under such circumstances that it is considered part of the real property.

A person may buy a refrigerator, an air conditioner, a furnace, or some other item that is used in a building and then have the item installed. The question of whether such an item is a fixture, and therefore part of a building, can arise in a variety of situations: (1) The real estate tax assessor assesses the building and adds in the value of the item on the theory that it is part of the building, (2) the buyer of the item owns and then sells the building, and the new owner of the building claims that the item stays with the building, (3) the buyer places a mortgage on the building, and the mortgagee claims that the item is bound by the mortgage, (4) the buyer is a tenant in the building in which the item is installed, and the landlord claims that the item must stay in the building when the tenant leaves, and (5) the buyer does not pay in full for the item, and the seller of the item has a security interest that the seller wishes to enforce against the buyer or against the landlord of the building in which the buyer installs the item. The seller of the item may also assert a claim against the mortgagee of the building or against the buyer of the building. The determination of the rights of these parties depends on the common law of fixtures, as occasionally modified by statute.

CPA (b) Tests of a Fixture

In the absence of an agreement between the parties, the courts apply three tests to determine whether personal property has become a fixture.

(1) Annexation. Generally, personal property becomes a fixture if it is so attached to the realty that it cannot be removed without materially damaging the real property or destroying the personal property itself. If the property is so affixed as to lose its specific identity, such as bricks in a wall, it becomes part of the realty. When railroad tracks are so placed as to be immovable, they are fixtures.

(2) Adaptation. Personal property especially adapted or suited to the use made of the building may constitute a fixture.

SPORTS & ENTERTAINMENT LAW

USING A VIEW AS EASEMENT OR A LICENSE IN LIEU OF A TICKET

There are 13 rooftops on buildings that surround Wrigley Field. When the Chicago Cubs play at Wrigley, the rooftops are packed with folks who, with coolers full of drinks and plenty of food stacked on tables, are watching the games. Kayakers pack McCovey's Cove near San Francisco's SBC Park's right field to watch the Giants. Hot tubs and roofs overlook the Arizona Diamondback's games in Chase Ballpark (once BankOne Ballpark or BOB).

Do the folks using these areas need a license? An easement? If they own the property or are there with the owner's permission, are they permitted to watch the games?*

*Lee Jenkins, "The Best Seats in the House Are Just Outside Wrigley," *New York Times*, June 12, 2005, 8–1 (Sports 1).

(3) Intent. The true test is the intention of the person affixing the property.[3] Intent is considered as of the time the property was affixed. In the absence of direct proof of such intent, courts resort to the nature of the property, the method of its attachment, and all the surrounding circumstances to determine intent.

The fact that machinery installed in a plant would be very difficult and expensive to move or is so delicate that the moving would cause damage and unbalancing is significant in reaching the conclusion that the owner of the plant had installed the equipment as a permanent addition and thus had the intent to make the equipment fixtures. **For Example,** when the floors in a large apartment house are made of concrete and covered with a thin sheet of plywood to which wall-to-wall carpeting is stapled, the carpeting constitutes a fixture that cannot be removed from the building. Removal would probably destroy the carpeting because it was cut to size. In addition, the carpeting is necessary to make the building livable as an apartment.

CPA (c) Movable Machinery and Equipment

Machinery and equipment that are movable are ordinarily held not to be fixtures even though, in order to move them, it is necessary to unbolt them from the floor or to disconnect electrical wires or water pipes. **For Example,** refrigerators, freezers, and gas and electric ranges are not fixtures. They do not lose their character as personal property when they are readily removable after disconnecting pipes or unplugging wires. A portable window air conditioner that rests on a rack that is affixed to the windowsill by screws and is connected directly to the building only by an electric cord plug is not a fixture.

The mere fact that an item may be unplugged, however, does not establish that it is not a fixture. **For Example,** a computer and its related hardware constitute fixtures when there is such a mass of wires and cables under the floor that the installation gives the impression of permanence.

CPA (d) Trade Fixtures

Equipment that a tenant attaches to a rented building and uses in a trade or business is ordinarily removable by the tenant when the tenant permanently leaves the premises. Such equipment is commonly called a *trade fixture.*[4]

[3] *Hubbard v Hardeman County Bank*, 868 SW2d 656 (Tenn 1993).
[4] *Bence v Sanato*, 538 NW2d 614 (Wis App 1995).

CPA B. Nature and Form of Real Property Ownership

A person's interest in real property may be defined in terms of the period of time for which the person will remain the owner as (1) a **fee simple estate** or (2) a **life estate**. These estates are termed *freehold estates*, which are interests of uncertain duration. At the time of creation of a freehold estate, a termination date is not known. When a person owns property for a specified period of time, this interest is not regarded as a freehold estate; it is a **leasehold estate**, subject to special rules of law.

CPA 7. Fee Simple Estate

An **estate in fee**, a fee simple, or a fee simple absolute lasts forever. The owner of such a land interest held in fee simple has the absolute and entire interest in the land. The important characteristics of this estate are that (1) it is alienable, or transferable, during life, (2) it is alienable by will, (3) it passes to heirs of the owner if it is not specifically devised (transferred by will), (4) it is subject to rights of the owner's surviving spouse, and (5) it can be attached or used to satisfy debts of the owner before or after death.

There are other forms of the fee simple estate generally used for control of land use. **Fee simple defeasibles** are interests that give the grantee all the rights of a fee simple holder provided that the grantee complies with certain restrictions. **For Example,** the grant "To Ralph Watkins so long as he uses the property for school purposes" is an example of a fee simple defeasible. Watkins will have all the rights of a fee simple holder provided that he uses the property for school purposes. If Watkins ever stops using the property for school purposes, the property reverts back to the grantor.

CPA 8. Life Estate

A *life estate* (or life tenancy), as its name indicates, lasts only during the life of a person (ordinarily its owner). Upon the death of the person by whose life the estate was measured, the owner of the life estate has no interest remaining to pass to heirs or by will. **For Example,** a grant of a life estate would be "To my husband, Nathan Jones, for life, and then to my children." Jones would hold title to the property only for the time he is alive. When Jones dies, he cannot give the property away by will. If Jones conveys the property while he is alive, the grantee for the property holds title to the land only until Jones's death.

CPA 9. Future Interests

In several of the examples given to illustrate fee simple and life estates, an interest has been created in more than one person. **For Example,** in the preceding life estate example, the children of the grantor are given an interest in the land at the same time that Jones is. However, the interests of the children will not take effect until Jones dies. The children have a future interest in the land. Their interest is referred to as a **remainder interest** because they have the remaining interest in the land once the life estate ends.

In the Watkins fee simple defeasible example, the grantor has a future interest if Watkins violates the restriction. The grantor's interest is called a **possibility of reverter**. It is a future interest because it cannot exist unless Watkins violates the use restriction placed on his present interest.

C. Liability to Third Persons for Condition of Real Property

A person entering the land of another may be injured by the condition of the land. Who is liable for such harm?

CPA 10. Common Law Rule

Under the common law, liability to a person entering onto land was controlled by the status of the injured person—that is, whether the person injured was a **trespasser**, a **licensee**, or an **invitee**. A different duty was owed by the owner (or occupier, as when a tenant is leasing property) of land to persons in each of these three categories.

(a) Trespassers

For a trespasser, the landowner ordinarily owes the duty of refraining from causing intentional harm only once the presence of the trespasser is known. The landowner is not under any duty to warn of dangers or to make the premises safe to protect the trespasser from harm. The most significant exception to this rule arises in the case of small children. Even when children are trespassers, they are generally afforded greater protection through the **attractive nuisance doctrine**. **For Example,** the owner of a tract of land was held liable for the death of a seven-year-old child who drowned in a creek on that land. Snow had covered the ice on the creek, and children running across the land did not know of the creek's location or the danger of the ice. The landowner had a duty to fence the creek, put up warnings, or control the children's access.[5]

(b) Licensees

Licensees are on the premises with the permission of the landowner, who owes the duty of warning of nonobvious dangers that are known to the owner. A host must warn a guest of such dangers. **For Example,** when a sliding glass door is "invisible" if the patio lights are on and the house lights are off, the owner must warn guests of the presence of the glass. The owner is liable if he has not warned guests of the danger and a guest is injured in shattering the glass. An owner, however, owes no duty to a licensee to take any steps to learn of the presence of dangers that are unknown to the owner.

(c) Invitees

Invitees are persons who enter another's land by invitation. The entry is connected with the owner's business or with an activity the occupier conducts on the land. Business customers, for example, are invitees.

Owners have a duty to take reasonable steps to discover any danger and a duty to warn the invitee or to correct the danger. **For Example,** a store must make a reasonable inspection of the premises to determine that there is nothing on the floor that would be dangerous, such as a slippery substance that might cause a patron to fall. The store must correct the condition, appropriately rope off the danger area, or give suitable warning. If the owner of the premises fails to conform to the degree of care described and if harm results to an invitee on the premises, the owner is liable for such harm.

In most states, the courts have expanded the concept of invitees beyond the category of those persons whose presence will economically benefit the occupier. Invitees now usually include members of

[5] *Pasierb v Hanover Park Park District*, 431 NE2d 1218 (Ill App 1981); see also *Carson v Kosinski*, 801 F Supp 75 (ND Ill 1992).

the public who are invited when it is apparent that such persons cannot be reasonably expected to make an inspection of the premises before using them and who would not be able to make repairs to correct any dangerous condition. Some courts have also made inroads into the prior law by treating a recurring licensee, such as a letter carrier, as an invitee. For more information on landowner liability, refer to Chapter 9 on torts.

11. Modern Changes

A number of courts have begun ignoring the common law distinctions between trespassers, licensees, and invitees. These courts hold the owner liable according to ordinary negligence standards. That is, when the owner as a reasonable person should foresee from the circumstances that harm would be caused to a third person, the owner has the duty to

DELTA TAU DELTA V JOHNSON, 712 NE2D 968 (IND 1999)

THE DRUNK ALUM WHO CRASHED THE FRAT PARTY AND INJURED AN INVITEE

Delta Tau Delta (DTD) is a fraternity house located on the campus of Indiana University. Tracey Johnson attended a party at DTD by invitation, where she met Joseph Motz, an alumnus of Indiana and DTD who had driven to Bloomington for the football game. Both drank beer and Motz offered Johnson a ride home. She refused and Motz locked them in a room together where he sexually assaulted her. Johnson brought suit against DTD and the national organization. The trial court denied the national organization's motion for summary judgment and it appealed. The court of appeals reversed and the parties appealed.

Judicial Opinion

SELBY, J.... In *Burrell v Meads*, this Court held that a social guest who has been invited by a landowner onto the landowner's land is to be treated as an invitee. 569 N.E.2d 637, 643 (Ind.1991). Thus, a social host owes his guests the duty to exercise reasonable care for their protection. The issue in this case is whether a landowner may have a duty to take reasonable care to protect an invitee from the criminal acts of a third party.

The question of whether and to what extent landowners owe any duty to protect their invitees from the criminal acts of third parties has been the subject of substantial debate among the courts and legal scholars in the past decade. See, e.g., *McClung v Delta Square Ltd. Partnership*, 937 S.W.2d 891, 897 (Tenn.1996) (noting that the debate caused the court to reconsider its law in this area). The majority of courts that have addressed this issue agree that, while landowners are not to be made the insurers of their invitees' safety, landowners do have a duty to take reasonable precautions to protect their invitees from foreseeable criminal attacks.

A further question arises, however, in that courts employ different approaches to determine whether a criminal act was foreseeable such that a landowner owed a duty to take reasonable care to protect an invitee from the criminal act. There are four basic approaches that courts use to determine foreseeability in this context: (1) the specific harm test, (2) the prior similar incidents test, (3) the totality of the circumstances test, and (4) the balancing test.

Under the specific harm test, a landowner owes no duty unless the owner knew or should have known that the specific harm was occurring or was about to occur. Most courts are unwilling to hold that a criminal act is foreseeable only in these situations.

Under the prior similar incidents (PSI) test, a landowner may owe a duty of reasonable care if evidence of prior similar incidents of crime on or near the landowner's property shows that the crime in question was foreseeable. Although courts differ in the application of this rule, all agree that the important factors to consider are the number of prior incidents, their proximity in time and location to the present crime, and the similarity of the crimes. Courts differ in terms of how proximate and similar the prior crimes are required to be as compared to the current crime.

The public policy considerations are that under the PSI test the first victim in all instances is not entitled to recover, landowners have no incentive to implement even nominal security measures, the test incorrectly focuses on the specific crime and not the general risk of foreseeable harm, and the lack of prior similar incidents relieves a defendant of liability when the criminal act was, in fact, foreseeable. *Id.*

Under the totality of the circumstances test, a court considers all of the circumstances surrounding an event, including the nature, condition, and location of the land, as well as prior similar incidents, to determine whether a criminal act was foreseeable. The most frequently cited limitation of this test is that it tends to make the foreseeability question too broad and unpredictable, effectively requiring that landowners anticipate crime.

Under the final approach, the balancing test, a court balances "the degree of foreseeability of harm against the burden of the duty to be imposed." In other words, as the foreseeability and degree of potential harm increase, so, too, does the duty to prevent against it. *Id.* This test still relies largely on prior similar incidents in order to ensure that an undue burden is not placed upon landowners.

We agree with those courts that decline to employ the specific harm test and prior similar incidents test. We find that the specific harm test is too limited in its determination of when a criminal act is foreseeable. While the prior similar incidents test has certain appeal, we find that this test has the potential to unfairly relieve landowners of liability in some circumstances when the criminal act was reasonably foreseeable.

As between the totality of the circumstances and balancing tests, we find that the totality of the circumstances test is the more appropriate.

Applying the totality of the circumstances test to the facts of this case, we hold that DTD owed Johnson a duty of reasonable care. Within two years of this case, two specific incidents occurred which warrant consideration. First, in March 1988, a student was assaulted by a fraternity member during an alcohol party at DTD. Second, in April 1989 at DTD, a blindfolded female was made, against her will, to drink alcohol until she was sick and was pulled up out of the chair and spanked when she refused to drink. In addition, the month before this sexual assault occurred, DTD was provided with information from National concerning rape and sexual assault on college campuses. Amongst other information, DTD was made aware that "1 in 4 college women have either been raped or suffered attempted rape," that "75% of male students and 55% of female students involved in date rape had been drinking or using drugs," that "the group most likely to commit gang rape on the college campus was the fraternity," and that fraternities at seven universities had "recently experienced legal action taken against them for rape and/or sexual assault." We believe that to hold that a sexual assault in this situation was not foreseeable, as a matter of law, would ignore the facts and allow DTD to flaunt the warning signs at the risk of all of its guests.

As a landowner under these facts, DTD owed Johnson a duty to take reasonable care to protect her from a foreseeable sexual assault. It is now for the jury to decide whether DTD breached this duty, and, if so, whether the breach proximately caused Johnson's injury. While this may be the exceptional case wherein a landowner in a social host situation is held to have a duty to take reasonable care to protect an invitee from the criminal acts of another, when the landowner is in a position to take reasonable precautions to protect his guest from a foreseeable criminal act, courts should not hesitate to hold that a duty exists.

We vacate the Court of Appeals' decision and affirm the trial court in part and reverse the trial court in part.

Questions

1. What are the four tests courts employ to determine liability of landowners for the criminal acts of others committed on their property?
2. Explain the totality of circumstances test.

take reasonable steps to prevent such harm. This duty exists regardless of whether the potential victim would be traditionally classified as a trespasser, a licensee, or an invitee.

Some courts have taken an intermediate position. They have merely abolished the distinction between licensees and invitees so that the owner owes the same duty of care to all lawful visitors. Whether one is a licensee or an invitee is merely a circumstance to be considered by the jury in applying the ordinary rule of negligence.

D. Co-Ownership of Real Property

Real property may be owned by one or several persons, and the method of co-ownership determines the extent of the owners' rights.

12. Multiple Ownership

Several persons may have *concurrent interests* (or interests that exist at the same time) in the same real

E-COMMERCE AND CYBERLAW

WEB LISTINGS

The Internet has proven to be a help in selling real property. Real estate agents use the Web to post listings and provide potential buyers with virtual tours of properties that interest them. Visit the National Association of Realtors Web site at **http://www.nar.com** and view its materials related to selling real property.

property. The forms of multiple ownership for real property are the same as those for personal property. Real property can be held by tenants in common, by joint tenants with right of survivorship, by tenants by the entirety, or under community property rights. When co-owners sell property, they hold the proceeds of sale by the same kind of tenancy as that in which they held the original property.

13. Condominiums

A **condominium** is a combination of co-ownership and individual ownership. **For Example,** persons owning an office building or an apartment house by condominium are co-owners of the land and of the halls, lobby, elevators, stairways, exits, surrounding land, incinerator, laundry rooms, and other areas used in common. Each apartment or office in the building, however, is individually owned and is transferred in the same way as other forms of real property.

(a) Control and Expense

In some states, owners of the various units in the condominium have equal voice in its management and share an equal part of its expenses. In others, control and liability for expenses are shared by a unit owner in the same ratio that the value of the unit bears to the value of the entire condominium project. In all states, unit owners have equal rights to use the common areas. An owners' association is created by the condominium owners to operate the common areas of the condominium property and resolve any disputes among owners.

The owner of each condominium unit makes the repairs required by the owner's deed or contract of ownership. The owner is prohibited from making any major change that would impair or damage the safety or value of an adjoining unit.

(b) Collection of Expenses from Unit Owner

When a unit owner fails to pay the owner's share of taxes, operating expenses, and repairs, the owners' association generally has the right to a lien against that owner's unit for the amount due.

(c) Tort Liability

Most condominium projects fail to make provision for the liability of unit owners for a tort occurring in the common areas. A few states expressly provide that when a third person is injured in a common area, a suit may be brought only against the condominium association. Any judgment recovered is a charge against the association to be paid off as a common expense. When the condominium association is incorporated, the same result should be obtained by applying ordinary principles of corporation law. Under principles of corporation law, liability for torts occurring on the premises of the corporation would not be the liability of individual shareholders.

(d) Cooperatives Distinguished

Ownership in a condominium is to be distinguished from ownership in a **cooperative**. An apartment cooperative is typically a corporation that owns an apartment complex. The "ownership" interests of the apartment occupants are as stockholders of the corporation.

E. Transfer of Real Property by Deed

Although many of the technical limitations of the feudal system and earlier common law on transfer of land have disappeared, much of the law relating to the modern deed originated in those days.

CPA 14. Definitions

A **deed** is an instrument or writing by which an owner or **grantor** transfers or conveys an interest in land to a new owner. The new owner is called a **grantee** or **transferee**.

FIGURE 49-1 Form of Warranty Deed

THIS DEED, made the twentieth day of November, two thousand and . . . between James K. Damron, residing at 132 Spring Street in the Borough of Manhattan, City and State of New York, party of the first part, and Terrence S. Bloemker, residing at 14 Steinway Street in the Borough of Queens, City and State of New York, party of the second part,

WITNESSETH, that the party of the first part, in consideration of the sum of one dollar ($1), lawful money of the United States, and other good and valuable consideration paid by the party of the second part, does hereby grant and release unto the party of the second part, his heirs and assigns forever,

ALL that certain lot, piece, and parcel of land situated in the Borough of Manhattan, City and County of New York, and State of New York, and bounded and described as follows:

Beginning at a point on the northerly side of Spring Street, distant two hundred (200) feet westerly from the corner formed by the intersection of the northerly side of Spring Street with the westerly side of 6th Avenue, running thence northerly parallel with 6th Avenue one hundred (100) feet, thence westerly and parallel with said Spring Street one hundred (100) feet; thence southerly, again parallel with said 6th Avenue one hundred (100) feet to the northerly side of Spring Street, and thence easterly along the said northerly side of Spring Street one hundred (100) feet to the point or place of beginning.

Together with the appurtenances and all the estate and rights of the party of the first part in and to said premises.

TO HAVE AND TO HOLD the premises herein granted unto the party of the second part, his heirs and assigns forever.

AND the party of the first part covenants as follows:

First. That the party of the first part is seised of the said premises in fee simple, and has good right to convey the same;

Second. That the party of the second part shall quietly enjoy the said premises;

Third. That the said premises are free from encumbrances except as expressly stated;

Fourth. That the party of the first part will execute or procure any further necessary assurance of the title to said premises;

IN WITNESS WHEREOF, the party of the first part has hereunto set his hand and seal the day and year first above written.

JAMES K. DAMRON

(L.S.)

In presence of:

DIANA L. REILMAN

State of New York
County of New York } s.s.:*

On the twentieth day of November in the year two thousand and . . . , before me personally came James K. Damron, to me known and known to me to be the individual described in, and who executed, the foregoing instrument, and he acknowledged that he executed the same.

DIANA L. REILMAN
Notary Public, New York County

*Note: Acknowledgment before a notary public is not essential to the effectiveness of a deed, but it is typically required to qualify the deed for recording.

In contrast to the situation with a contract, no consideration is required to make a deed effective. Although consideration is not required to make a deed valid or to transfer title by deed, the absence of consideration may show that the owner makes the transfer to defraud creditors. The creditors may then be able to set aside the fraudulent transfer.

Real property may be either sold or given as a gift. A deed, however, is necessary to transfer title to land, even if it is a gift.

CPA 15. Classification of Deeds

Deeds may be classified according to the interest conveyed as **quitclaim deeds** or **warranty deeds**. A quitclaim deed merely transfers whatever interest, if any, the grantor may have in the property without specifying that interest in any way. A warranty deed transfers a specified interest and warrants or guarantees that such interest is transferred. Figure 49-1 is a sample warranty deed.

CPA 16. Execution of Deeds

Ordinarily, the grantor must sign, by signature or mark, a deed. To have the deed recorded, statutes generally require that two or more witnesses sign the deed and that the grantor then acknowledge the deed before a notary public or other officer. In the interest of legibility, the signatures of the parties are followed by their printed or typewritten names. The deed remains binding between the grantor and the grantee even if it has not been acknowledged or recorded.

A deed must be executed and delivered by a person having capacity. It may be set aside by the grantor on the ground of the fraud of the grantee provided that innocent third persons have not acquired rights in the land.

17. Delivery and Acceptance of Deeds

A deed has no effect and title does not pass until the deed has been delivered. Delivery is a matter of intent as shown by words and conduct; no particular form of ceremony is required. The essential intent in delivering a deed is not merely that the grantor intends to hand over physical control and possession of the paper on which the deed is written but also that the grantor intends thereby to transfer the ownership of the property described in the deed. That is, the grantor must deliver the deed with the intent that it should take effect as a deed and convey an interest in the property.

A deed is ordinarily made effective by handing it to the grantee with the intention that the grantee should then be the owner of the property described in the deed. A delivery may also be made by placing the deed, addressed to the grantee, in the mail or by giving it to a third person with directions to hand it to the grantee.

An effective delivery of a deed may be made symbolically, or constructively, such as by delivering to the grantee the key to a locked box and informing the grantee that the deed to the property is in the box. **For Example,** the delivery of a safe deposit box key has been held to constitute delivery of a deed that was in the box.

When a deed is delivered to a third person for the purpose of delivery to the grantee on the happening of some event or contingency, the transaction is called a **delivery in escrow**. No title passes until the fulfillment of the condition or the happening of the event or contingency.

Generally, there must be an **acceptance** by the grantee. In all cases, an acceptance is presumed. However, the grantee may disclaim the transfer if the grantee acts within a reasonable time after learning that the transfer has been made.

SARGENT V BAXTER, 673 SO 2D 979 (FLA APP 1996)

FOR THE RECORD: WAS THE DEED DELIVERED?

The decedent, John Smith, executed a quitclaim deed in favor of his daughter, Connie Sargent. He instructed his attorney, Freedman, not to record the deed, saying he would be back in touch regarding recording. Freedman testified that he would not record the deed without further instructions from Smith. Before his death, Smith asked his nephew Gerald Buscemi to have Freedman record the deed. However, Buscemi did not contact Freedman before Smith's death. Freedman's office mailed the unrecorded deed to Sargent, who recorded it. Later, the personal representative of Smith's estate executed a quitclaim deed to the same property to himself, individually, and recorded it. The trial court ruled that the Smith deed to Sargent failed for lack of delivery. Both deeds were declared void, and the court left title to be determined in pending probate proceedings. Sargent appealed the decision, finding both deeds void and alleged that she was the rightful owner of the property.

Judicial Opinion

STONE, J. . . . Delivery of a deed is essential to its effectiveness; "[w]ithout delivery, nothing passes to the grantee." A deed is essentially worthless as an instrument of title without delivery, even if delivery may have been intended but failed due to an accident.

A critical factor in determining whether delivery has been accomplished is whether the grantor retained the "locus poenitentiae," or opportunity to change his or her mind:

The test of delivery of a conveyance is whether the grantor intended to reserve to himself the locus poenitentiae, and, if he did, there is no delivery; but if he parts with the control of the deed, or evinces an intention to do so, and to pass it to the grantee, though he may retain the custody or turn it over to another, or place it upon record, the delivery is complete.

Smith v Owens, 91 Fla. 995, 1002, 108 So. 891, 893 (1926).

A grantor's recording of a deed, in the absence of fraud on the grantor, is generally presumed equivalent to delivery. But in this case, Smith did not record the deed, or cause it to be recorded, during his life. What Smith intended to do cannot be inferred on the basis of what Sargent did after Smith's death. Delivery is not effective when made to a third person pending further instructions from the grantor. In such circumstances, obviously, the deed remains subject to the grantor's control and the grantor can revoke or annul it at will.

We recognize that there may be constructive delivery of a deed. In *Smith*, the court noted that actual manual delivery is not always required, and the intention of the grantor is the determining factor. However, in *Smith* the deed had actually been recorded by the grantor, who had returned the recorded deed to his son and instructed his housekeeper to deliver the deed, which she did about an hour after his death. The court found the circumstances were equivalent to this manual delivery.

In *Howarth v Moreau*, 430 So 2d 576 (Fla. 5th DCA 1983), the grantor had her attorney prepare a deed, but asked that it not be delivered until the conclusion of some litigation. The grantor died before the conclusion of the litigation, having previously asked the attorney to destroy the deed. The trial court validated the deed, granting a directed verdict to the grantee, but the appellate court reversed, concluding there was no evidence in the record from which a jury could have determined that there had been unconditional delivery, applying the test of whether the grantor had intended to reserve the opportunity to change her mind. In the instant case, even if Smith ultimately intended to make the deed effective by having it recorded, that intention was not fulfilled. Sargent's subsequent possession of the deed does not alone evidence delivery to her.

We need not consider whether, under the totality of the circumstances, a delivery would have occurred had Buscemi advised Freedman of Smith's desire that the deed be recorded, as this did not occur. There is no indication that Buscemi had any authority other than as a simple messenger. Here, Freedman, as Smith's agent, was bound to follow Smith's instructions. When Smith died, that agency relationship terminated. There was no evidence that Smith had relinquished, as between himself and Freedman, the opportunity to change his mind concerning delivery of the deed to Sargent at any time before his death.

[Judgment affirmed]

Questions

1. What is most important in determining whether delivery has occurred?
2. What is the legal effect of a grantor recording a deed?
3. Is actual delivery of the deed to the grantee always required?

CPA 18. Recording of Deeds

The owner of land may record the deed in the office of a public official, sometimes called a **recorder** or *commissioner of deeds*. The recording is not required to make the deed effective to pass title, but it is done so that the public will know that the grantee is the present owner and thereby prevent the former owner from making any future transfer or transaction relating to the property. The recording statutes provide that a person purchasing land from the last holder of record will take title free of any unrecorded claim to the land of which the purchaser does not have notice or knowledge.

When no document is recorded, states have statutes for determining who obtains title and who will be left to take action against the party that has conveyed the property to more than one person. **For Example,** suppose that Grant conveys a tract of land to Dee. Dee does not record her deed. Grant then conveys the same tract of land to Joe, who also does not record his deed, but Joe is unaware of Dee's acquisition. Then Grant conveys the same property to Larry who knows about Dee and Joe but records his deed. Who will hold title, and who will be left to pursue Grant for remedies? Under **race statutes**, the first party to record the deed holds title, so Larry holds title. Under **notice statutes**, the last good-faith or bona fide purchaser (BFP), someone who does not know about the previous conveyances, takes title. Under notice, Joe holds title because he is the last BFP. Larry knows about the prior transactions and that fact controls title, not the recording of his deed under notice statutes. Under **notice-race** or **race-notice statutes**, the first BFP to record the deed holds title. So, if Dee records first, she holds title. If Joe records first, he will. Larry has recorded but does not meet the second requirement of race-notice, which is that one must be the first BFP to record to take title in a race-notice state. Suppose that Larry is a BFP, but Joe is not because he is aware of the conveyance to Dee. Under race, Larry holds title. Under notice, Larry holds title. Under race-notice, Larry wins again. If Dee records her deed, all of these issues are moot because recording the deed is complete notice for all subsequent purchasers.

The fact that a deed is recorded charges everyone with knowledge of its existence even if they in fact do not know of it because they have neglected to examine the record. The recording of a deed, however, is only such notice if the deed was properly executed. Likewise, the grantee of land cannot claim any protection by virtue of the recording of a deed when (1) a claim is made by one whose title is superior to that of the owner of record, (2) the grantee had notice or knowledge of the adverse claim when title was acquired, (3) a person acting under a hostile claim was then in possession of the land, (4) the grantee received the land as a gift, or (5) the transfer to the grantee was fraudulent.

19. Additional Protection of Buyers

In addition to the protection given to buyers and third persons by the recorded title to property, a buyer is generally protected by procuring title insurance or an abstract of title. An **abstract of title** is a summarized report of the title to the property as shown by the records, together with a report of all judgments, mortgages, and similar recorded claims against the property.

20. Grantor's Warranties

The warranties of the grantor relate to the title transferred by the grantor and to the fitness of the property for use.

CPA (a) Warranties of Title

In the common law deed, the grantor may expressly warrant or make certain *covenants* as to the title conveyed. The statutes authorizing a short form of deed provide that, unless otherwise stated in the deed, the grantor is presumed to have made certain **warranties of title**.

The more important of the **covenants (or warranties) of title** that the grantor may make are (1) **covenant of seisin**, or guarantee that the grantor owns the estate conveyed, (2) **covenant of right to convey**, or guarantee that the grantor, if not the owner as in the case of an agent, has the right or authority to make the conveyance, (3) **covenant against encumbrances**, or guarantee that the land is not subject to any right or interest of a third person, such as a lien or an easement, (4) **covenant of quiet enjoyment**, or guarantee by the grantor that the grantee's possession of the land will not be disturbed either by the grantor, in the case of a **limited covenant**, or by the grantor or any person claiming title under the grantor, in the case of a general covenant, and (5) **covenant of further assurances**, or guarantee that the grantor will execute any additional documents that may be required to perfect the title of the grantee.

(b) Fitness for Use

Courts in most states hold that when a builder or real estate developer sells a new house to a home buyer, an implied warranty that the house and foundation are fit for occupancy or use arises. This warranty arises regardless of whether the house was purchased before, during, or after completion of construction.[6] This warranty will not be implied against the first buyer when the house is resold. However, there is authority that the second buyer may recover from the

[6] *Richards v Powercraft Homes, Inc.*, 678 P2d 427 (Ariz 1984).

original contractor for breach of the implied warranty even though there is no privity of contract.[7]

21. Grantee's Covenants

In a deed, the grantee may agree to do or to refrain from doing certain acts. Such an agreement becomes a binding contract between the grantor and the grantee. The grantor may recover from the grantee for its breach.

The right to enforce the covenant also **runs with the land** owned by the grantor to whom the promise was made. **For Example,** a promise not to use a tract of land for a parking lot between two adjoining landowners would pass to any buyers who subsequently acquire these tracts. For more information on covenants, see Chapter 50, Environmental Law and Land Use Controls.

F. Other Methods of Transferring Real Property

Title to real property can also be acquired by eminent domain and by adverse possession.

CPA 22. Eminent Domain

Under **eminent domain**, property is taken from its private owner for a public purpose. The title is then taken by a government or public authority. There are constitutionally protected rights of property owners under eminent domain. Known as the "takings clause," this portion of the Fifth Amendment to the U.S. Constitution requires compensation when private property is taken for public use. Two important issues arise under the takings clause: (1) whether there is a taking of property and (2) whether the property is taken for a public use. With respect to whether a taking has occurred, it is not necessary that the owner be physically deprived of the property but that normal use of the property has been impaired or lost. Whether there is a public use for the taking is a question that continues to be challenged in court because the definition of public purpose is so broad. **For Example,** property can be taken to build a freeway as well as for the preservation of a historic site. In the eminent domain cases after 2000, much of the litigation concerned whether revitalization of areas with urban blight were permissible takings. Eminent domain has activated the public as state and local governments take more and more houses and land for purposes of economic development.

KELO V CITY OF NEW LONDON, 545 U.S. 469 (2005)

FACTS: In 1978, the city of New London, Connecticut undertook a redevelopment plan for purposes of creating a redeveloped area in and around the existing park at Fort Trumball. The plan had the goals of achieving all the related ambience a state park should have, including the absence of pink cottages and other architecturally eclectic homes. Part of the redevelopment plan was the city's deal with Pfizer Corporation for the location of its research facility in the area. The preface to the city's development plan stated that the plan would *"create jobs, increase tax and other revenues, encourage public access to and use of the city's waterfront, and eventually "build momentum" for the revitalization of the rest of the city, including its downtown area."*

Susette Kelo, and other property owners whose homes would be razed and whose land would be taken to allow for the park, Pfizer, and redevelopment (15 total), asked to be permitted to stay in the area. The city refused their request. Kelo and the other landowners filed suit challenging New London's legal authority to take their homes. The trial court issued an injunction preventing New London from taking certain of the properties but allowing others to be taken. Those property owners who were held subject to eminent domain appealed.

The appellate court found for New London on all the claims, and the landowners (petitioners) appealed.

[7] Many states have passed statutes that govern the extent of the implied warranty of habitability. Although the statutes vary, the types of defects covered include defects in construction, design, and appearance.

Judicial Opinion

STEVENS, Justice* .... [i]t has long been accepted that the sovereign may not take the property of A for the sole purpose of transferring it to another private party B, even though A is paid just compensation. On the other hand, it is equally clear that a State may transfer property from one private party to another if future "use by the public" is the purpose of the taking; the condemnation of land for a railroad with common-carrier duties is a familiar example. Neither of these propositions, however, determines the disposition of this case.

As for the first proposition, the City would no doubt be forbidden from taking petitioners' land for the purpose of conferring a private benefit on a particular private party. Nor would the City be allowed to take property under the mere pretext of a public purpose, when its actual purpose was to bestow a private benefit. The takings before us, however, would be executed pursuant to a"carefully considered" development plan.

The disposition of this case therefore turns on the question whether the City's development plan serves a "public purpose." Without exception, our cases have defined that concept broadly, reflecting our longstanding policy of deference to legislative judgments in this field.

In *Berman v. Parker*, 348 U.S. 26, 75 S.Ct. 98, 99 L.Ed. 27 (1954), this Court upheld a redevelopment plan targeting a blighted area of Washington, D. C., in which most of the housing for the area's 5,000 inhabitants was beyond repair. Under the plan, the area would be condemned and part of it utilized for the construction of streets, schools, and other public facilities. The remainder of the land would be leased or sold to private parties for the purpose of redevelopment, including the construction of low-cost housing.

Writing for a unanimous Court, Justice Douglas refused to evaluate this claim in isolation, deferring instead to the legislative and agency judgment that the area "must be planned as a whole" for the plan to be successful.

Those who govern the City were not confronted with the need to remove blight in the Fort Trumbull area, but their determination that the area was sufficiently distressed to justify a program of economic rejuvenation is entitled to our deference. The City has carefully formulated an economic development plan that it believes will provide appreciable benefits to the community, including—but by no means limited to—new jobs and increased tax revenue. As with other exercises in urban planning and development, the City is endeavoring to coordinate a variety of commercial, residential, and recreational uses of land, with the hope that they will form a whole greater than the sum of its parts. Given the comprehensive character of the plan, the thorough deliberation that preceded its adoption, and the limited scope of our review, it is appropriate for us, as it was in *Berman*, to resolve the challenges of the individual owners, not on a piecemeal basis, but rather in light of the entire plan. Because that plan unquestionably serves a public purpose, the takings challenged here satisfy the public use requirement of the Fifth Amendment.

[P]etitioners urge us to adopt a new bright-line rule that economic development does not qualify as a public use. Promoting economic development is a traditional and long accepted function of government. There is, moreover, no principled way of distinguishing economic development from the other public purposes that we have recognized. [I]n *Berman*, we endorsed the purpose of transforming a blighted area into a"well-balanced" community through redevelopment. Clearly, there is no basis for exempting economic development from our traditionally broad understanding of public purpose.

Just as we decline to second-guess the City's considered judgments about the efficacy of its development plan, we also decline to second-guess the City's determinations as to what lands it needs to acquire in order to effectuate the project. "It is not for the courts to oversee the choice of the boundary line nor to sit in review on the size of a particular project area. Once the question of the public purpose has been decided, the amount and character of land to be taken for the project and the need for a particular tract to complete the integrated plan rests in the discretion of the legislative branch."

The judgment of the Supreme Court of Connecticut is affirmed.

It is so ordered.

Dissenting Opinion

O'CONNOR, Justice, joined by Justices SCALIA, THOMAS and REHNQUIST

Under the banner of economic development, all private property is now vulnerable to being taken and transferred to another private owner, so long as it might be upgraded—i.e., given to an owner who will use it in a way that the legislature deems more beneficial to the public—in the process. To reason, as the Court does, that the incidental public benefits resulting from the subsequent ordinary use of private

*The decision in this case was 5-4 with each justice filing either a concurring or dissenting opinion. Justice Rehnquist, in one of his last acts on the bench before his passing, said when he announced the decision and individual opinions on this case, "I didn't know we had that many people on our court." Joan Biskupic, *Rehnquist Leaves Them Laughing—and Guessing,*" USA TODAY, June 28, 2005, p. 2A.

property render economic development takings "for public use" is to wash out any distinction between private and public use of property—and thereby effectively to delete the words "for public use" from the Takings Clause of the Fifth Amendment. Accordingly I respectfully dissent.

Where is the line between "public" and "private" property use? We give considerable deference to legislatures' determinations about what governmental activities will advantage the public. But were the political branches the sole arbiters of the public-private distinction, the Public Use Clause would amount to little more than hortatory fluff. An external, judicial check on how the public use requirement is interpreted, however limited, is necessary if this constraint on government power is to retain any meaning.

If it is true that incidental public benefits from new private use are enough to ensure the "public purpose" in a taking, why should it matter, as far as the Fifth Amendment is concerned, what inspired the taking in the first place? How much the government does or does not desire to benefit a favored private party has no bearing on whether an economic development taking will or will not generate secondary benefit for the public. And whatever the reason for a given condemnation, the effect is the same from the constitutional perspective—private property is forcibly relinquished to new private ownership.

Questions

1. What is different from this case and a case in which property is taken for a freeway?
2. What is the concern of the dissent about the decision?
3. Why does the majority state that the courts should be reluctant to get involved in local government eminent domain activities?

ETHICS & THE LAW

HELL HATH NO FURY LIKE A NOWMP

The NIMBYs (Not In My Backyard) challenge the placement of everything from power plants to refineries to Wal-Marts. There are also the BANANAs (Build Absolutely Nothing Anywhere Near Anything). Finally, the NOWMPs (Not With My Property) are opposed to eminent domain, the taking of their property for a public use.

Think back to your readings on ethics in Chapter 3. What ethical principles could you apply in favor of the NIMBYs, the BANANAs, and the NOWMPs? What ethical principles could you apply that find that the NIMBYs, the BANANAs and the NOWMPs are acting unethically?

Source: For more information, see Marianne M. Jennings, "NIMBYs, BANANAs, LULUs, NOPEs, and NOWMPs: The Percolating World of Eminent Domain (The Par Boil Stage or Part I)," *Real Estate Law Journal* 33(4): 445-457 (2005).

THINKING THINGS THROUGH

PUTTING THE BRAKES ON EMINENT DOMAIN

Bailey's Brake Service, a bit of an eyesore at a main intersection near a failing downtown area of Mesa, Arizona, was a family-founded, owned, and operated business that had been open in its existing location since 1970. Lenhart's True Value Hardware store was also a longstanding Mesa business with a location south and east of Bailey's and a desire for a better location. The Lenharts had purchased the property abutting Bailey's but felt that the street-facing Bailey's property was necessary for its location.

The city did a taking by eminent domain and then "reissued" the property to Lenhart's for its store. The Baileys challenged the city's taking in the Superior Court as unconstitutional, but the court held that the taking was constitutional as part of the city's plan for redevelopment and revitalization of the area. The Baileys appealed the trial court decision. Should the Baileys get their property back? Was this a proper eminent domain taking? [BAILEY V MYERS, 76 P3d 398 (Az Ct App 2003)]

23. Adverse Possession

Title to land may be acquired by possessing it adversely for a statutorily prescribed period of time. A possessor who complies with the physical and time requirements gains title by **adverse possession**. If such possession is maintained, the possessor automatically becomes the owner of the property, even though the possessor admittedly had no lawful claim to the land.

To acquire title in this manner, possession must be (1) actual, (2) visible and notorious, (3) exclusive, (4) hostile, and (5) continuous for a required period of time.

Commonly, the period of time is 21 years, but state statutes may provide 10 to 20 years. Occupation of land in the mistaken belief that one is the owner is a "hostile" possession.[8]

G. Mortgages

An agreement that creates an interest in real property as security for an obligation but an interest that is to cease upon the performance of the obligation is a **mortgage**. The property owner, whose interest in the property is given as security, is the *mortgagor*. The person who receives the security is the *mortgagee*.

CPA 24. Characteristics of a Mortgage

A mortgage has three characteristics: (1) the termination of the mortgagee's interest on the performance of the obligation secured by the mortgage, (2) the right of the mortgagee to enforce the mortgage by foreclosure on the mortgagor's failure to perform, and (3) the mortgagor's right to redeem or regain the property.

25. Property Subject to Mortgage

In general, any form of property that may be sold or conveyed may be mortgaged. It is immaterial whether the right is a present right, a future interest, or merely a right in the land of another. It is not necessary that the mortgagor have complete or absolute ownership in the property. Mortgagors may mortgage any type of land interest they own.

26. Form of Mortgage

Because a mortgage of real property transfers an interest in the property, it must be in writing by virtue of the statute of frauds. As a general rule, no particular form of language is required if the language used expresses the intent of the parties to create a mortgage. Many state statutes provide a standardized form of mortgage that may be used.

27. Creative Forms of Financing

In many situations in which a buyer seeks to purchase property, the conventional methods for obtaining a mortgage are not available because of affordability or qualifications required for a loan. Many creative forms of financing have been developed to help buyers purchase property. **For Example,** residential land buyers often use an **adjustable rate mortgage (ARM)**, in which the lower interest rates applied at the beginning of the mortgage help the buyer qualify for the loan. The ARM changes interest rates along with the market, going up and down, unless the ARM has a fixed minimum rate. Other buyers may have the seller finance their purchase through the use of a land or an installment contract. Some new forms of financing, such as the **reverse mortgage**, permit those who have paid off their mortgages on their property to get the value out of their property by having a mortgage company take a mortgage out on the property and pay them money over time. Many senior citizens are able to obtain the additional monthly income they may need by this form of financing, which permits them to draw on their equity in their land.

28. Recording or Filing of Mortgage

An unrecorded mortgage is valid and binding between/among the parties to it. The heirs or donees of a mortgagor cannot defend against the mortgage on the ground that it has not been recorded. The recording statutes discussed earlier also apply to mortgages.

29. Responsibilities of the Parties

The mortgagor and mortgagee have the following duties and liabilities when a mortgage is placed on real property.

CPA (a) Repairs and Improvements

In the absence of an agreement to the contrary, a mortgagor is under no duty to make improvements or to restore or repair parts of the premises that are

[8] The state with the shortest period for adverse possession is Texas, whose adverse possession period can be as short as 3 years. The state with the longest adverse possession period is Wyoming, with 40 years.

destroyed or damaged through no fault of the mortgagor.

CPA (b) Taxes, Assessments, and Insurance

The duty to pay taxes and assessments rests with the mortgagor. In the absence of an agreement, neither party is under a duty to insure the mortgaged property. Both parties, however, may insure their respective interests. It is common practice for the mortgagor to obtain a single policy of insurance on the property payable to the mortgagee and the mortgagor generally according to the standard mortgagee clause that pays the outstanding loan balance first.

(c) Impairment of Security

The mortgagor is liable to the mortgagee for any damage to the property caused by the mortgagor that impairs the security of the mortgage by materially reducing the value of the property. Both the mortgagor and the mortgagee have a right of action against a third person who wrongfully injures the property.

30. Transfer of Interest

Questions arise as to transfers by the mortgagor and the mortgagee of their respective interests and of the liability of a transferee of the mortgagor.

CPA (a) Transfer by Mortgagor

The mortgagor may ordinarily transfer the property without the consent of the mortgagee. Such a transfer passes only the interest of the mortgagor and does not divest or impair a properly recorded mortgage.

The transfer of the property by the mortgagor does not affect the liability of the mortgagor to the mortgagee. Unless the mortgagee has agreed to substitute the mortgagor's grantee for the mortgagor, the mortgagor remains liable for the mortgage debt as though no transfer had been made.[9]

CPA (b) Liability of the Parties in a Transfer by a Mortgagor

There are two ways to transfer mortgaged property, and each way has different results in terms of personal liability for the transferee. In the assumption of a mortgage, the transferee agrees to assume liability. In an **assumption**, the mortgagor remains liable, the transferee is liable, and the property is subject to foreclosure by the mortgagee in the event the payments are not made. **For Example,** if Bob sold his house with a $175,000 mortgage for $200,000 to Jane, Jane could pay Bob $25,000 cash and then agree to assume Bob's mortgage. Jane may get the benefit of a lower interest rate by assuming Bob's mortgage. Both Bob and Jane are personally liable, and the mortgagee may foreclose on the property if the payments are not made.

The second method of transfer is called a "subject to" transfer. In this type of transfer, the property is subject to foreclosure, but the transferee does not agree to assume the mortgage personally. The mortgagor remains liable in this type of transfer, too.

(c) Transfer by Mortgagee

In most states, a mortgage may be transferred or assigned by the mortgagee.

31. Rights of Mortgagee After Default

Upon the mortgagor's default, the mortgagee in some states is entitled to obtain possession of the property and collect the rents or to have a receiver appointed for that purpose. In all states, the mortgagee may enforce the mortgage by **foreclosure**, a judicial procedure resulting in sale of the mortgaged property.

Generally, upon any default under the terms of the mortgage agreement, the mortgagee has the right to accelerate the debt or declare that the entire mortgage debt is due. The mortgagee generally has this right even though the default related only to paying an installment or to doing some act, such as maintaining insurance on the property or producing receipts for taxes.

A sale resulting from the foreclosure of the mortgage destroys the mortgage, and the property passes free of the mortgage to the buyer at the sale. However, the extinction of the mortgage by foreclosure does not destroy the debt that was secured by the mortgage. The mortgagor remains liable for any unpaid balance or deficiency. By statute, the mortgagor is generally given credit for the fair value of the property if it was purchased by the mortgagee.[10]

[9] *In re Argianis*, 156 BR 683 (MD Fla 1993); see also *Comerica Bank-Illinois v Ham's Bank Hinsdale*, 673 NE2d 388 (Ill App 1996).
[10] *San Paolo U.S. Holding Co., Inc. v 816 South Figueroa Co.*, 73 Cal Rptr 2d 272 (1998).

32. Rights of Mortgagor After Default

After default, the mortgagor may seek to stop or stay foreclosure or to redeem the mortgaged land.

(a) Stay of Foreclosure

In certain cases authorized by statute, a **stay** (or delay) **of foreclosure** may be obtained by the mortgagor to prevent undue hardship.

CPA (b) Redemption

The right of **redemption** is the right of the mortgagor to free the property of the mortgage lien after default. By statute in many states, the right may be exercised during a certain time following foreclosure and sale of the mortgaged land.

Summary

Real property includes land, buildings, fixtures, and rights in the land of another. Some land interests include the right to use the land, such as easements. Easements can be granted or arise by implication or prescription.

The interest held by a person in real property may be defined in terms of the period of time for which the person will remain the owner. The interest may be a fee simple estate, which lasts forever, or a life estate, which lasts for the life of a person. These estates are known as *freehold estates*. If the ownership interest exists for a specified number of days, months, or years, the interest is a leasehold estate.

Personal property may be attached to, or associated with, real property in such a way that it becomes real property. In such a case, it is called a *fixture*. To determine whether property has in fact become a fixture, the courts look to the method of attachment, to how the property is adapted to the realty, and to the intent of the person originally owning the personal property.

Under common law, the liability of an occupier of land for injury to third persons on the premises depends on the status of the third persons as trespassers, licensees, or invitees. Many jurisdictions, however, are ignoring these common law distinctions in favor of an ordinary negligence standard or are giving licensees the same protection as invitees.

Real property may be the subject of multiple ownership. The forms of multiple ownership are the same as those for personal property. In addition, there are special forms of co-ownership for real property, such as condominiums and cooperatives.

A *deed* is an instrument by which a grantor transfers an interest in land to a grantee. A deed can be a quitclaim deed or a warranty deed. To be effective, a deed must be signed or sealed by the grantor and delivered to the grantee. Recording the deed is not required to make the deed effective to pass title, but recording provides notice to the public that the grantee is the present owner. The warranties of the grantor relate to the title transferred by the grantor and to the fitness of the property for use. In the absence of any express warranty in the deed, no warranty of fitness arises under the common law in the sale or the conveyance of real estate. Most states today hold that when a builder or real estate developer sells a new home to a buyer, an implied warranty of habitability arises. Title to real estate may also be acquired by eminent domain and adverse possession.

An agreement that creates an interest in real property as security for an obligation and that ends upon the performance of the obligation is a mortgage. A mortgage must be in writing under the statute of frauds. If the mortgage is unrecorded, it is valid between the parties. The mortgage should be recorded to put good-faith purchasers on notice of the mortgage. A purchaser of the mortgaged property does not become liable for the mortgage debt unless the purchaser assumes the mortgage. The mortgagor still remains liable unless the mortgagee agrees to a substitution of parties. If the mortgagor defaults, the mortgagee may enforce the mortgage by foreclosure. Such foreclosure may be delayed because of undue hardship.

Questions and Case Problems

1. The federal government was taking property near Roanoke, Virginia, for public purposes. The government proposed to pay the Tobiases for the property because they were the title holders of record. However, the Johnsons had been using the land and claimed they were the actual title holders. Are the Johnsons entitled to compensation under eminent domain? Why or why not? [*United States v 369.31 Acres of Land in Roanoke County, VA*, 696 F Supp 185 (WD Va)]
2. Bunn and his wife claimed that they had an easement to enter and use the swimming pool on neighboring land. A contract between the former owners of the Bunns' property and the adjacent apartment complex contained a provision that the use of the apartment complex's

swimming pool would be available to the purchaser and his family. No reference to the pool was made in the contract between the former owners and the Bunns, nor was there any reference to it in the deed conveying the property to the Bunns. Decide. [*Bunn v Offutt*, 222 SE2d 522 (Va)]

3. After executing the various deeds, J. M. Fernandez Jr. placed them in a closet (with other valuable papers) for safekeeping until they could be physically delivered to the various grantees, including Sylvia Sheppard, when she returned to Key West. This closet was in the home that Fernandez shared with Betty DeMerritt. They were not married but lived together the final 15 years of Fernandez's life. Shortly thereafter, Fernandez was debilitated by a stroke and became a total invalid. He never regained his health and died before Sylvia Sheppard could return to Key West to receive physical delivery of the deed personally from him. When Sylvia Sheppard did arrive in Key West, Betty DeMerritt gave her the deed. This took place two or three days after the death of Fernandez. When questioned as to why she turned the deed over to Sylvia, Betty DeMerritt stated, "I knew he wanted me to do it . . . because he couldn't do it." She was speaking of Fernandez's physical disability. Does Sylvia have title to the property? Was there delivery? [*Kerr v Fernandez*, 792 So 2d 685 (Fla)]
4. Kenneth Corson, 10, lived with his mother, Lynda Lontz, in an apartment building owned by Bruno and Carolyn Kosinski. While playing with other children who lived in the same building, Corson was drawn to a stairwell that provided access to the building's laundry room and roof. Corson and the other children climbed to the roof and discovered an area where they could jump from the roof of their building to that of the building next door. The children engaged in roof hopping for several days. On the last day, Corson misjudged his jump and fell the three stories to the ground below. Corson and his mother filed suit against the Kosinskis to collect damages for Corson's injuries. What theory might be used to hold the Kosinskis liable? [*Corson by Lontz v Kosinski*, 801 F Supp 75 (ND Ill)]
5. Determine whether the following would be fixtures or personal property.
    a. Refrigerator in a home
    b. Refrigerators in an apartment complex with furnished units
    c. Refrigerators in a restaurant kitchen
    d. Refrigeration/freezer units in a grocery store
    e. Mini-refrigerator in a student dorm
6. What is the relationship between trespass and adverse possession?
7. Bradham and other members and trustees of the Mount Olivet Church brought an action to cancel a mortgage on the church property. The mortgage had been executed previously by Davis and other former trustees of the church and given to Robinson as mortgagee. The court found that the church was not indebted to the mortgagee for any amount. Should the mortgage be canceled? [*Bradham v Robinson*, 73 SE2d 555 (NC)]
8. Miller executed a deed to real estate, naming Zieg as grantee. He placed the deed in an envelope on which was written "To be filed at my death" and put the envelope and deed in a safe deposit box in the National Bank that had been rented in the names of Miller and Zieg. After Miller's death, Zieg removed the deed from the safe deposit box. Moseley, as executor under Miller's will, brought an action against Zieg to declare the deed void. Decide. [*Moseley v Zieg*, 146 NW2d 72 (Neb)]
9. Henry Lile owned a house. When the land on which it was situated was condemned for a highway, he moved the house to the land of his daughter, Sarah Crick. In the course of construction work, blasting damaged the house. Sarah Crick sued the contractors, Terry & Wright, who claimed that Lile should be joined in the action as a plaintiff and that Sarah could not sue by herself because it was Lile's house. Were the defendants correct? [*Terry & Wright v Crick*, 418 SW2d 217 (Ky)]
10. Bradt believed his backyard ran all the way to a fence. Actually, a strip on Bradt's side of the fence belonged to his neighbor Giovannone, but Bradt never intended to take land away from anyone. Bradt later brought an action against Giovannone to determine who owned the strip on Bradt's side of the fence. Who is the owner? Why? [*Bradt v Giovannone*, 315 NYS2d 96]
11. Robert E. Long owned land in the City of Hampton that he leased to Adams Outdoor Advertising Limited Partnership. Adams had an advertising billboard placed on the property. On October 6, 1993, Long notified Adams that he was terminating the lease. Adams accepted the termination and told Long that it would have the electrical service disconnected and would schedule demolition of the billboard for the first week in November. Long wanted to use the billboard to advertise his own business and filed suit to enjoin Adams from destroying the billboard. Long maintained the billboard was part of the land and belonged to him. Adams asserted that it owned the billboard as a lessee. The trial court found for Long, and Adams appealed. Decide. [*Adams Outdoor Adv., Ltd., Part. v Long*, 483 SE2d 224 (Va)]
12. Smikahl sold Hansen a tract of land on which were two houses and four trailer lots equipped with concrete patios and necessary connections for utility lines. The tract Hansen purchased was completely surrounded by the land owned by Smikahl and third persons. To get onto the highway, it was necessary to cross the Smikahl tract. Several years after the sale, Smikahl put a barbed wire fence around his land. Hansen sued to prevent obstruction to travel between his land and the highway over the

Smikahl land. Smikahl's defense was that no such right of travel had been given to Hansen. Was he correct? [*Hansen v Smikahl*, 113 NW2d 210 (Neb)]

13. Martin Manufacturing decided to raise additional long-term capital by mortgaging an industrial park it owned. First National Loan Co. agreed to lend Martin $1 million and to take a note and first mortgage on the land and building. The mortgage was duly recorded. Martin sold the property to Marshall, who took the property and assumed the mortgage debt. Does Marshall have any personal liability on the mortgage debt? Is Martin still liable on the mortgage debt? Explain.
14. Christine and Steve Mallock buried their son in a burial plot purchased at Southern Memorial Park, Inc. Each year the Mallocks conducted a memorial service for their son at his burial plot. On the seventh anniversary of their son's death, the Mallocks went to their son's grave at 11:00 A.M. for the annual service, which generally took 30 minutes. When they arrived, they discovered that a tent and chairs set up for funeral services on the plot next to their son's grave were actually resting on his gravesite. The Mallocks asked Southern's management if the tent and chairs could be moved until they could conduct their service. The managers refused, and the Mallocks went ahead with their ceremony, cutting it to five minutes, after they moved the chairs and tents by themselves.

    Southern's managers called the police and had the Mallocks evicted. Southern claimed the Mallocks had no rights on the property except for the grave and that their deed for the plot did not award an easement for access. Did the Mallocks have the right to access to the gravesite? [*Mallock v Southern Memorial Park, Inc.*, 561 So 2d 330 (Fla Ct App)]
15. *O* conveys property to *A* on December 1, 2006. *O* conveys the same property to *B* who does not know about *A* and who records his deed on December 2, 2006. *O* then conveys the same property to *C*. Who has title to the property?

CPA Questions

1. Which of the following statements is correct with respect to a real estate mortgage?

    a. It must be signed only by the mortgagor (borrower).
    b. It must be recorded in order to be effective between the mortgagor and the mortgagee.
    c. It does *not* have to be recorded to be effective against third parties without notice if it is a purchase money mortgage.
    d. It is effective even if *not* delivered to the mortgagee.

2. To be enforceable against the mortgagor, a mortgage must meet all the following requirements *except*

    a. Be delivered to the mortgagee
    b. Be in writing and signed by the mortgagor
    c. Be recorded by the mortgagee
    d. Include a description of the debt and land involved

3. Ritz owned a building in which there was a duly recorded first mortgage held by Lyn and a recorded second mortgage held by Jay. Ritz sold the building to Nunn. Nunn assumed the Jay mortgage and had no actual knowledge of the Lyn mortgage. Nunn defaulted on the payments to Jay. If both Lyn and Jay foreclosed and the proceeds of the sale were insufficient to pay both Lyn and Jay,

    a. Jay would be paid after Lyn was fully paid.
    b. Jay and Lyn would be paid proportionately.
    c. Nunn would be personally liable to Lyn but not to Jay.
    d. Nunn would be personally liable to Lyn and Jay.

4. Which of the following deeds will give a real property purchaser the greatest protection?

    a. Quitclaim
    b. Bargain and sale
    c. Special warranty
    d. General warranty

ENVIRONMENTAL LAW AND LAND USE CONTROLS

CHAPTER (50)

LEARNING OBJECTIVES

After studying this chapter, you should be able to

LO.1 List and describe the federal statutes that regulate various aspects of the environment

LO.2 Explain how environmental laws are enforced

LO.3 Describe the criminal penalties for violation of environmental laws

LO.4 Define *nuisance* and list the remedies available

LO.5 Distinguish between restrictive covenants and zoning

LO.6 Explain the role and application of zoning laws

LO.7 Discuss how businesses and regulators recognize that resources should be conserved and the environment protected from pollution

A. Statutory Environmental Law

As the United States changed from a rural, agricultural society to an urban, industrial one, new laws were needed to prevent the pollution of the environment.

1. Air Pollution Regulation

(a) Legislative History of Air Pollution Regulation

The first legislation that dealt with air pollution, passed in 1955, was the Air Pollution Control Act, which was simply a statutory recognition of a concern about air quality. Even the first statute regulating air pollution, the **Clean Air Act,** passed in 1963, produced no response from the states, which were charged with the responsibility of developing pollution standards and enforcement mechanisms. It was not until the 1970 amendments to the Clean Air Act that the federal law on air pollution got some teeth, for it was in those amendments that Congress established the federal agency responsible for enforcing the law, the Environmental Protection Agency (EPA). The EPA was authorized to establish national air quality standards and see that the states developed plans for the implementation of those standards.

CPA (b) Modern Legislation and Requirements

Under the 1970 Clean Air Act,[1] as well as the 1977 and 1990 amendments to it, states must measure their air content of sulfur dioxide, carbon monoxide, and hydrocarbons and then take appropriate steps to bring their air quality within the federal limits established for each of these. States that do not meet federal standards are called **nonattainment areas,** or *dirty areas*, and their plans for implementation are strictly reviewed by the EPA, which can halt federal highway funding in the event the implementation plan is not followed. Those states that do meet the federal standards must still have a plan to remain at that level.

For nonattainment areas, the EPA developed an **emissions offset policy,** which controls whether new factories can be built. For a new plant to obtain a permit to begin operations in a nonattainment area, the business proposing the new plant must be able to show that (1) the plant will have the greatest possible emissions controls, which means better than existing emissions standards, (2) the business has all of its other plants and operations in compliance with federal emissions standards, and (3) the new plant's emissions will be offset by reductions in emissions in other facilities in the area. This last requirement is often referred to as the **bubble concept,** which requires an examination of all emissions from all sources in an area. Before any new operations with emissions can be permitted, the business seeking approval must be able to show that overall emissions in the area will not increase.

The 1990 amendments to the Clean Air Act increased the role of the bubble concept with the ability of businesses to transfer their emissions permits. Those businesses that can reduce their emissions below their allowable amounts or that can eliminate their emissions are free to transfer their permit rights to emit to someone else who can then use them without affecting total emissions in the bubble area. There is a market exchange for emissions permits because the EPA will not, under the 1990 act, issue any additional permits beyond the rights to emission that already exist. Today, approximately 10 percent of all the emissions permit rights are owned by environmental groups.

(c) The Kyoto Protocol

At the Kyoto meeting of the United Nations Framework Convention for Climate Change (UNFCCC), the delegates adopted the *Kyoto Protocol,* a plan for reducing six greenhouse gases, with the primary goal being to reduce carbon dioxide in the United States and other industrial nations. Under the Protocol, signatory countries agree to reduce their carbon dioxide levels to less than their 1990 levels of emission, which would mean a halt in further industrial development in the countries to which the Protocol applies. The Protocol took effect in 2005 and as of July 2006, had 164 signatory countries. The United States has not adopted the Kyoto Protocol as a treaty, and there is strong opposition to it from businesses that believe the goal is the transfer of wealth from developed nations to undeveloped nations. Nonetheless, environmental groups are very active in seeking its adoption by the United States, and they have staged protests at meetings of the World Trade Organization.

[1] 42 USC § 1857 *et seq.*

CPA 2. Water Pollution Regulation

The first meaningful regulation in water pollution began at about the same time as effective air pollution regulation. The first legislation with enforcement power was passed in 1972 as the Federal Water Pollution Control Act and then amended and renamed in 1977 as the **Clean Water Act.**[2] Under the Clean Water Act, the EPA has developed **effluent guidelines,** which are ranges for discharges organized according to industrial groups and for specific plants in each of these groups. The guidelines establish the maximum amounts that can be discharged, and those maximums are coupled with a permit system that requires each plant to obtain a permit from the EPA before discharging anything into any type of pool, pond, river, lake, stream, or ocean. **For Example,** a plant that releases hot water from a steam generator must still have a permit just to release hot water into the stream near the plant. The EPA also has standards for the treatment of water that is used in a plant's production process before that water can be discharged. The treatment and permit regulations apply to all plants.[3] **For Example,** a plant must still have a permit to discharge water even though that water is cleaner as it is discharged from the plant than it was when it was brought in to be used in production or manufacturing.

CPA 3. Solid Waste Disposal Regulation

The disposal of solid waste (garbage) has also been regulated since the 1960s, but the initial legislation simply provided money for research by state and local governments on how to dispose of solid waste.[4] In 1970, the **Resource Recovery Act** provided federal money for cities and states with recycling programs.

After several major open-dumping problems that produced community-wide illnesses, including those in the Love Canal area near Buffalo, New York, Congress passed the **Toxic Substances Control Act (TOSCA),** which controls the manufacture, use, and disposal of toxic substances, a list of which the EPA developed. Along with TOSCA, Congress passed the **Resource Conservation and Recovery Act (RCRA),** which regulates the disposal of potentially harmful substances through a permit system and uses federal grants to encourage the restoration of damaged resources.[5] **For Example,** many strip mine locations were restored due to the RCRA.

In 1980, Congress passed the **Comprehensive Environmental Response, Compensation, and Liability Act (CERCLA),**[6] which authorizes the U.S. president to issue funds to be used for the cleanup of areas that were once disposal sites for hazardous wastes. The act set up a trust fund for cleanups, to be reimbursed by the company responsible for such hazardous wastes. The funds in the trust are available for government use but are not subject to attachment by private citizens who seek to get an area cleaned up by removing the hazardous waste. Under CERCLA, the EPA has the authority to designate **Superfund sites,** or parcels of land that are deemed to have, or potentially have, hazardous wastes that require cleanup.

The **Superfund Amendment and Reauthorization Act,** passed in 1986, authorizes the EPA to bring suit for the purpose of collecting the costs of cleanup from those who are responsible for the hazardous wastes on the site. The act and its judicial interpretations provide a very broad definition of who is responsible under CERCLA for the costs of cleanup. Four classes of parties can be held liable under CERCLA. "Owners and operators" of contaminated property are liable under the statute. *Owners* include present owners as well as past owners, whether or not they are responsible for the hazardous wastes being dumped on the property. *Operators* include those who are leasing the property, again whether or not they are responsible for the hazardous waste being dumped. **For Example,** many gas stations have been designated as Superfund sites because the underground tanks have leaks, causing gas to seep into the soil. Current and past owners of

[2] 33 USC § 1251 *et seq.* The pollution of navigable waters had been regulated by the Rivers and Harbors Act of 1899, which required a permit for discharging into navigable rivers, streams, and lakes, but which was limited in its effect because only the permit was required—there were no limits on the amount or type of discharge into the waters. The act remains in effect today, although other, more recent federal laws are utilized for preventing unauthorized discharges.

[3] The best conventional treatment (BCT) is required for conventional pollutants. The best available treatment (BAT) is required for toxic pollutants.

[4] See the Solid Waste Disposal Act, 42 USC § 3251 *et seq.*, and the Resource Recovery and Policy Act of 1970, 42 USC § 3251 *et seq.*

[5] 42 USC § 6901 *et seq.*

[6] 42 USC § 9601 *et seq.*

such a station are responsible under CERCLA, as well as an owner who has converted the station into some other use.[7]

Other responsible parties under CERCLA include anyone who transported hazardous waste to a site and anyone who hired another or arranged to transport hazardous waste to the site. Lenders were, at one time, also held liable for cleanup costs in the event they took back property from a debtor. However, the Asset Conservation, Lender Liability, and Deposit Insurance Protection Act of 1996 provides an exclusion for lenders provided the lender does not actually participate in the management or operational affairs of the facility of the debtor.[8]

CERCLA liability has been extended to those who merge or buy corporations; these parties also buy into CERCLA liability, and liability under CERCLA cannot be avoided by a transfer of ownership. The U.S. Supreme Court has ruled in *United States v Bestfoods*, 525 US 51 (1998), that a parent corporation is not automatically liable under CERCLA for a subsidiary corporation's conduct but may be responsible if the subsidiary is simply a shell. In other words, CERCLA liability of parent corporations for the actions of their subsidiaries is governed by corporate law on piercing the corporate veil (see Chapter 45 for more information).

One of the new key areas for minimizing CERCLA liability is that of the self-audit, a company's internal investigation of its operations and lands to determine whether any environmental hazards are on its properties. Many companies wanted to know, for the sake of financial planning and minimizing harm, whether they had any Superfund issues. However, they did not want their voluntary investigations and cleanups to work against them. To encourage these types of internal investigations and self-reporting, the EPA developed its Incentives for Self-Policing, Disclosure, Correction, and Prevention of Violations. Under this EPA program, companies can have their penalties reduced and not waive any rights if they follow the procedures and meet the following requirements: (1) the violations were uncovered as part of a self-audit, (2) the violations were uncovered voluntarily, (3) the violations were reported to the EPA within 10 days, (4) the discovery was made independently and disclosed independently, and no one was threatening disclosure, (5) the violations are corrected within 60 days, (6) there is a written agreement that the conduct will not happen again, (7) there is no history of repeat violations, (8) no serious harm came to anyone as a result of the conduct, and (9) the company cooperates completely with the EPA. If these requirements are met, the company is eligible for reductions in fines and penalties of up to 75 percent.

CPA 4. Environmental Quality Regulation

The federal statutes on air, water, and solid waste pollution are directed at private parties in their use of land. However, the federal government also regulates itself in terms of its operations and impact on the environment. The **National Environmental Policy Act (NEPA)** requires federal agencies to consider the impact on the environment of their proposed projects.[9] An agency must prepare a report, called an **environmental impact statement (EIS),** that documents the impact of the proposed federal project on the environment and covers consideration of practical and feasible alternatives with a lesser impact.[10] **For Example,** the federal government has been required to file an EIS for the Alaska oil pipeline, the extermination of wild horses, the construction of a post office, the implementation of a change in national park airport procedures that would permit jets to land, and highway construction.

CPA 5. Other Environmental Regulations

In addition to the major categories of environmental laws just covered, several other important statutes regulate specific areas of the environment. The **Noise Control Act** sets standards for noise from low-flying aircraft for the protection of landowners

[7] However, in *Acushnet Company v Mohasco*, 191 F3d 69 (1st Cir 1999), the court held that there must be some proof of causation between a company's conduct and the resulting toxic contamination.

[8] "Participating" does not include monitoring or enforcing the security agreement, monitoring or inspecting the premises, providing financial advice, mandating cleanup of hazardous materials, restructuring the loan, foreclosing, or selling or leasing the property. However, a parent corporation can be held liable for the conduct of a subsidiary if there is sufficient knowledge and control. *United States v Best Foods, Inc.*, 524 US 51 (1998).

[9] 42 USC § 4321 *et seq.*

[10] An EIS "functions as an environmental 'alarm bell' whose purpose it is to alert the public and its responsible officials to environmental changes before they have reached ecological points of no return . . . and to demonstrate to an apprehensive citizenry that the agency has in fact analyzed and considered ecological implications of its action." *Silveira v Las Gallina Valley Sanitary District*, 63 Cal Rptr 244 (1997).

who are in flight paths.[11] The **Endangered Species Act (ESA)** gives the secretary of the interior the responsibility of identifying and protecting endangered terrestrial species, while the secretary of commerce is responsible for endangered marine species.[12] These cabinet-level federal officers have the authority to curtail any development, noise, or other act that threatens those species on their endangered lists.[13]

BABBITT V SWEET HOME CHAPTER OF COMMUNITIES FOR A GREAT OREGON, 515 US 687 (1995)

THE LOGGERS AND THE NATURALISTS CAN'T BE FRIENDS: OREGON—WHERE THE SPOTTED OWL COMES FLYING IN THE TREES

Two U.S. agencies halted logging in the Pacific Northwest because it endangered the habitat of the northern spotted owl and the red-cockaded woodpecker, both endangered species. Sweet Home Chapter (respondents) is a group of landowners, logging companies, and families dependent on the forest products industries in the Pacific Northwest. They brought suit seeking clarification of the authority of the secretary of the interior and the director of the Fish and Wildlife Service (petitioners) to include habitation modification as a harm covered by the Endangered Species Act (ESA).

The federal district court found for the secretary and director and held that they had the authority to protect the northern spotted owl through a halt to logging. The court of appeals reversed. Babbitt, the secretary of the interior, appealed.

Judicial Opinion

STEVENS, J. . . . Section 9(a)(1) of the Endangered Species Act provides the following protection for endangered species:

Except as provided in sections 1535(g)(2) and 1539 of this title, with respect to any endangered species of fish or wildlife listed pursuant to section 1533 of this title it is unlawful for any person subject to the jurisdiction of the United States to—(B) take any such species within the United States or the territorial sea of the United States[.] 16 U.S.C. § 1538(a)(I).

Section 3(19) of the Act defines the statutory term "take":

The term 'take' means to harass, harm, pursue, hunt, shoot, wound, kill, trap, capture, or collect, or to attempt to engage in any such conduct. 16 U.S.C. § 1532(19).

The Act does not further define the terms it uses to define "take." The Interior Department regulations that implement the statute, however, define the statutory term "harm":

Harm in the definition of 'take' in the Act means an act which actually kills or injures wildlife. Such act may include significant habitat modification or degradation where it actually kills or injures wildlife by significantly impairing essential behavioral patterns, including breeding, feeding, or sheltering. 50 CFR § 17.3 (1994).

We assume respondents have no desire to harm either the red-cockaded woodpecker or the spotted owl; they merely wish to continue logging activities that would be entirely proper if not prohibited by the ESA. On the other hand, we must assume *arguendo* that those activities will have the effect, even though unintended, of detrimentally changing the natural habitat of both listed species and that, as a consequence, members of those species will be killed or injured. Under respondents' view of the law, the Secretary's only means of forestalling that grave result—even when the actor knows it is certain to occur—is to use his § 5 authority to purchase the lands on which the survival of the species depends. The Secretary, on the other hand, submits that the § 9 prohibition on takings, which

[11] 42 USC § 4901.
[12] 16 USC § 1530 *et seq.*
[13] The authority to bring suit rests with both landowners and environmentalists. *Bennett v Spear*, 520 US 154 (1997).

Congress defined to include "harm," places on respondents a duty to avoid harm that habitat alteration will cause the birds unless respondents first obtain a permit pursuant to § 10.

The text of the Act provides three reasons for concluding that the Secretary's interpretation is reasonable. First, an ordinary understanding of the word "harm" supports it. The dictionary definition of the verb form of "harm" is "to cause hurt or damage to: injure." Webster's Third New International Dictionary 1034 (1966). In the context of the ESA, that definition naturally encompasses habitat modification that results in actual injury or death to members of an endangered or threatened species.

Respondents argue that the Secretary should have limited the purview of "harm" to direct applications of force against protected species, but the dictionary definition does not include the word "directly" or suggest in any way that only direct or willful action that leads to injury constitutes "harm." Moreover, unless the statutory term "harm" encompasses indirect as well as direct injuries, the word has no meaning that does not duplicate the meaning of other words that § 3 uses to define "take." A reluctance to treat statutory terms as surplusage supports the reasonableness of the Secretary's interpretation.

Second, the broad purpose of the ESA supports the Secretary's decision to extend protection against activities that cause the precise harms Congress enacted the statute to avoid. As stated in § 2 of the Act, among its central purposes is "to provide a means whereby the ecosystems upon which endangered species and threatened species depend may be conserved."

Third, the fact that Congress in 1982 authorized the Secretary to issue permits for takings that § 9(a)(1)(B) would otherwise prohibit, "if such taking is incidental to, and not the purpose of, the carrying out of an otherwise lawful activity," 16 U.S.C. § 1539(a)(1)(B), strongly suggests that Congress understood § 9(a)(1)(B) to prohibit indirect as well as deliberate takings. The permit process requires the applicant to prepare a "conservation plan" that specifies how he intends to "minimize and mitigate" the "impact" of his activity on endangered and threatened species, 16 U.S.C. § 1539(a)(2)(A), making clear that Congress had in mind foreseeable rather than merely accidental effects on listed species.

The Court of Appeals made three errors in asserting that "harm" must refer to a direct application of force because the words around it do. First, the court's premise was flawed. Several of the words that accompany "harm" in the § 3 definition of "take," especially "harass," "pursue," "wound," and "kill," refer to actions or effects that do not require direct applications of force. Second, to the extent the court read a requirement of intent or purpose into the words used to define "take," it ignored § 9's express provision that a "knowing" action is enough to violate the Act. Third, the court employed *noscitur a sociis* to give "harm" essentially the same function as other words in the definition, thereby denying it independent meaning. The canon, to the contrary, counsels that a word "gathers meaning from the words around it." The statutory context of "harm" suggests that Congress meant that term to serve a particular function in the ESA, consistent with but distinct from the functions of the other verbs used to define "take." The Secretary's interpretation of "harm" to include indirectly injuring endangered animals through habitat modification permissibly interprets "harm" to have "a character of its own not to be submerged by its association."

The proper interpretation of a term such as "harm" involves a complex policy choice. When Congress has entrusted the Secretary with broad discretion, we are especially reluctant to substitute our views of wise policy for his. In this case, that reluctance accords with our conclusion, based on the text, structure, and legislative history of the ESA, that the Secretary reasonably construed the intent of Congress when he defined "harm" to include "significant habitat modification or degradation that actually kills or injures wildlife."

In the elaboration and enforcement of the ESA, the Secretary and all persons who must comply with the law will confront difficult questions of proximity and degree; for, as all recognize, the Act encompasses a vast range of economic and social enterprises and endeavors. These questions must be addressed in the usual course of the law, through case-by-case resolution and adjudication.

The judgment of the Court of Appeals is reversed.

Questions

1. Is habitat modification harming endangered species?
2. Does the Court's interpretation mean no intent is required to violate ESA?
3. Did Congress intend to give the secretary authority to shut down an industry?
4. Is logging prevented now?
5. What ethical issues arise from this case?*

*Following this decision, Congress passed a rider to a budget-reduction bill that suspended environmental laws in many national forests in Washington and Oregon. The logging industry, paper products processors, and environmentalists have since worked together to find mutually acceptable solutions to logging and the protection of endangered species. Known as the "Sustainable Forestry Initiative," the goal is ecofriendly logging.

THINKING THINGS THROUGH

THE RANCHERS AND THE SUCKERS: COMPETING FOR WATER

The Fish and Wildlife Service issued an opinion on the Klamath Irrigation Project in southern Oregon and northern California. The opinion concluded that the project must be halted because it could affect the Lost River Sucker and the Shortnose Sucker, two species of fish listed as endangered species as of 1988.

Halting the project meant that ranchers, such as Brad Bennett, would not be able to get the water they needed for their operations. Bennett and the other ranchers filed suit alleging that the report had factual errors and was incorrect in its conclusion. They asked that the court intervene and prohibit Fish and Wildlife from halting the project. Environmental groups said that the ranchers could not bring suit under the Endangered Species Act (ESA) because they were not suing to obtain protection for the two species. Does the ESA permit the ranchers' suit? [Bennett v Spear, 520 US 154 (1997)]

ETHICS & THE LAW

HITTING A JAM ON LOGGING

Asia Pacific Resources International Holdings, Ltd. (called April) is about to sign what many are calling a landmark agreement with the World Wildlife Fund, an environmental activist group. The agreement will curb April's timber-cutting areas to preserve a natural rainforest with great diversity of species in Sumatra, Indonesia. Over the past 20 years, more than half of the forest has been cut down for lumber.

These agreements are becoming more common because, for example, April's customers, such as Procter & Gamble (maker of Charmin and Bounty paper towels), were shunning the company because of its notorious reputation in damaging biodiverse areas in Indonesia. While April complied with Indonesian law (leaving 20 percent of the forest untouched), it did so in long ribbon strips that were insufficient to support the many species of wildlife located there.

Terms of the deal include the following:

- April will not allow other loggers to use its transportation system (barges and roads).
- April will verify the source of all logs it purchases.
- April will plant tree plantations and expects to be able to sell only plantation-grown wood by 2009.

Local residents are not fond of the agreements because their livelihoods have been blocked as April closes its road and prohibits use by illegal loggers.

What advantages do you see in allowing nongovernmental groups to obtain private contract promises on environmental policy? What disadvantages do you see? What ethical issues exist for April?*

* Steve Stecklow, "Environmentalists, Loggers Near Deal on Asian Rainforest," *Wall Street Journal*, February 23, 2006, A1, A14.

The **Safe Drinking Water Act** requires the EPA to establish national standards for contaminants in drinking water. The **Oil Pollution Act** is a federal law that came about following the oil spill from the *Exxon Valdez* off the coast of Alaska, which resulted in damage to the waters, fish, and birds in that area. Under this law, companies are financially responsible for the cleanup of their spills that occur in U.S.

waters. The act also provides for substantial penalties for failure to take action to clean up a spill, and those penalties can be as high as $25,000 per day or $3,000 per barrel if the spill is the result of negligence or willful misconduct.[14] Failure to report a spill carries penalties of up to five years in prison and/or $250,000 per individual and $500,000 for corporations. In addition, civil penalties for the failure to clean up an oil spill can cost the company up to $50,000,000 in penalties.

6. State Environmental Regulation

All states have some form of environmental regulation, and their environmental agencies work closely with the EPA on enforcement and standards. All states have some form of hazardous waste controls that define hazardous waste differently and carry a range of penalties for violations. **For Example,** Oregon imposes a fine of $3,500 per animal killed as a result of hazardous waste dumping. Other states mandate disclosure of the history of property use before that property can be sold, transferred, or mortgaged.

B. Enforcement of Environmental Laws

Federal environmental laws can be enforced through criminal sanctions, penalties, injunctions, and suits by private citizens. In addition to federal enforcement rights, certain common law remedies exist for the protection of property rights, such as the remedies for nuisance.

7. Parties Responsible for Enforcement

The EPA is the primary federal agency responsible for the enforcement of federal environmental laws, including those on air and water pollution, solid waste disposal, toxic substance control, and noise pollution. The EPA establishes emissions standards through regulation and then enforces them with a system of permits and sanctions for violations. The EPA works closely with state environmental agencies in enforcement.

The **Council on Environmental Quality (CEQ)** was established in 1966 as a part of the executive branch to establish national policy on environmental quality and then make recommendations for legislation for the implementation of that policy. Other federal agencies with responsibility for enforcement of federal environmental laws include the Department of Commerce, the Department of the Interior, the U.S. Forest Service, the Bureau of Land Management, and the Federal Power Commission.

Private citizens also have the right to enforce federal environmental laws through private litigation. **For Example,** a private citizen can bring a suit to halt the construction of a dam by the federal government if the agency responsible failed to conduct an environmental impact study or if the EIS is inadequate.

8. Criminal Penalties

Most of the federal environmental laws carry criminal penalties for violations. Figure 50-1 provides a summary of those penalties to which both companies and their employees are subject.

CPA 9. Civil Remedies

Although criminal remedies are costly to businesses, the EPA also has the authority to have the polluting activity halted through the use of **injunctions.** The EPA simply brings suit against a business and shows that it is engaged in unauthorized dumping, the release of emissions in excess of a permit, or discharge without a permit. A court can then order the business to halt the activity that is resulting in the violation. In some cases, the effect of the injunction is to shut down the business. The business is then required to negotiate with the EPA to meet certain standards before the EPA will agree to have the injunction lifted.

Private citizens can also bring suit for injunctions against companies that are in violation of federal law or not in compliance with statutory procedures. **For Example,** private citizens have filed suit against developers to stop construction when there is an issue of possible violation of the Endangered Species Act.

[14] 33 USC § 2701 *et seq.* The act establishes a cleanup fund for those spills in which the party to blame is unknown or is financially unable to pay the cost of cleanup. The act also requires that boats be double-hulled. Exxon still has cases pending on the $4.5 billion punitive damage awards made against it. The settlement with government authorities allowed them to request additional damages up to $100 million. The federal and state governments made a request of an additional $92 million in 2006.

FIGURE 50-1 Penalties for Violations of Federal Environmental Laws

ACT	PENALTIES	PRIVATE SUIT
CLEAN AIR ACT	$25,000 PER DAY; UP TO 1 YEAR OF IMPRISONMENT; 15 YEARS FOR WILLFUL OR REPEAT VIOLATIONS; $10,000 REWARDS	CITIZEN SUITS; AUTHORIZED EPA SUIT FOR INJUNCTIVE RELIEF
CLEAN WATER ACT	$25,000 PER DAY, UP TO 1 YEAR; $50,000 AND/OR 3 YEARS FOR VIOLATIONS WITH KNOWLEDGE; $100,000 AND/OR 6 YEARS FOR SUBSEQUENT VIOLATIONS	CITIZEN SUITS; AUTHORIZED EPA SUIT FOR INJUNCTIVE RELIEF
RESOURCE CONSERVATION RECOVERY ACT (SOLID WASTE DISPOSAL ACT)	$250,000 AND/OR 15 YEARS' IMPRISONMENT FOR INTENTIONAL VIOLATIONS; $1,000,000 FOR CORPORATIONS, $50,000 AND/OR 5 YEARS FOR OTHERS	CITIZEN AND NEGLIGENCE SUITS (AFTER EPA REFUSES TO HANDLE)
HAZARDOUS SUBSTANCE/ RESPONSE TRUST	FUND FOR CLEANUP	EPA SUIT FOR INJUNCTIVE RELIEF AND REIMBURSEMENT OF TRUST FUNDS
OIL POLLUTION ACT	$25,000 PER DAY, OR $1,000 PER BARREL; $3,000 PER BARREL IF WILLFUL OR NEGLIGENT; $250,000 AND/OR 5 YEARS FOR FAILURE TO REPORT	PRIVATE SUITS

CPA 10. Private Remedies: Nuisance

Conduct that unreasonably interferes with the enjoyment or use of land is a **nuisance,**[15] which may be smoke from a chemical plant that damages the paint on neighboring houses. It may be noise, dirt, or vibration from passing heavy trucks. Some conduct is clearly so great an interference that it is easy to conclude that it constitutes a nuisance, but not every interference is a nuisance. Furthermore, determining whether the interference is sufficiently great to be halted as unreasonable is frequently difficult. The fact that the activity or business is lawful and is conducted in a lawful manner does not mean that it is not a nuisance. The effect on others determines whether there is a nuisance.[16] A landfill may be a nuisance even though it is operated by a city in a non-negligent manner and in accordance with the state's solid waste disposal statutes.[17]

The courts attempt to balance the social utility of the activity with the resulting harm. The mere fact that there is harm does not establish that there is a nuisance. When community welfare outweighs the harm to land and owners, the activity is not a nuisance.[18] **For Example,** courts have held that smoke, fumes, and noise from public utilities and power plants were not nuisances, although they did create harm. The interests of the community in the activity of the public utilities outweighed the interests of those affected.

The proper use of land does not constitute a nuisance to a neighbor even though the neighbor does not like the use. The fact that neighbors do not approve of the aesthetics of a building or fence does not make that structure a nuisance.[19]

15 *Ardis Mobile Home Park v Tennessee,* 910 SW2d 863 (Tenn App 1995).
16 *Kolstad v Rankin,* 534 NE2d 1373 (Ill 1989).
17 *Williams v Great Falls,* 732 P2d 1315 (Mont 1987).
18 *Kopecky v National Farms, Inc.,* 510 NW2d 41 (Neb 1994).
19 *Indiana State Board of Registration v Norde,* 600 NE2d 124 (Ind App 1992).

If conduct is held to constitute a nuisance, the persons affected may be awarded money damages for the loss of the use of the land caused by the conduct and may obtain an injunction or court order to stop the offending conduct. If the nuisance is permanent, the measure of damages is the reduction in the fair market value of the affected property. If the nuisance can be stopped, the measure of damages is the reduction in rental value of the property during the time that the nuisance was allowed to continue.[20]

CPA (a) Private and Public Nuisances

When a nuisance affects only one or a few persons, it is called a **private nuisance.** When it affects the community or public at large, it is called a **public nuisance.** Planting trees or erecting a fence, although otherwise lawful, constitutes a public nuisance when it creates a traffic hazard by obscuring an intersection. However, a landowner did not create a public nuisance by allowing trees to grow tall even though the height of the trees required the neighboring county airport to alter its approach patterns, which, in turn, triggered the Federal Aviation Administration to order the airport to shorten the usable portion of its runways.[21] The existence of a statutory environmental protection procedure may bar or supersede the common law of nuisance.

(b) Permanent and Continuing Nuisances

If the interference is caused by a construction or a method of operation that can be remedied at a reasonable expense, it is classified as a **temporary nuisance.** If it cannot be so remedied, it is a **permanent nuisance,**[22] which consists of a single act that has caused permanent harm. A **continuing nuisance** is a series of related acts or a continuation of an activity, such as the emission of smoke from a factory. **For Example,** the Devon Gun and Skeet Club owned a tract of land on which it maintained rifle and skeet ranges. Bullets from the rifles and shot from the skeet guns repeatedly went beyond the boundaries of the Devon land and onto land owned by Sergio. Sergio sought an injunction to prevent bullets from straying onto his land. The action of the Devon Club is a continuing nuisance because it unreasonably interferes with the use and enjoyment of the neighboring land. It is probable that a court would not enjoin all shooting on the Devon land but would require that the direction of shooting be changed or that a barricade be erected on the boundary line of Sergio's property so that bullets would not cross the boundary line.

(c) Remedy for Nuisance

A criminal nuisance may be terminated by abatement or closure by government authority. A civil nuisance may be stopped by an injunction, and the injured person may sue for money damages for the harm caused.

When an injunction is issued, the court must exercise great care to halt the nuisance while avoiding going too far by enjoining conduct that is otherwise lawful.[23]

(d) The Technological Environment of the Law of Nuisance

As technology changes, new ways of manufacturing, new methods of transportation, and new ways of living develop. As the environment changes, corresponding changes are reflected in the law.

JORDAN V GEORGIA POWER CO., 466 SE2D 601 (GA APP 1995)

TANGLED IN THE NUISANCE OF OVERHEAD WIRES

Larry Jordan purchased property in Douglas County, Georgia, in 1972. At the time of the purchase, Jordan was aware of an easement Georgia Power held in the property. Power lines were built on the property in 1973. Mr. Jordan married Nancy in 1983, and she then moved into his home. In 1985, Nancy Jordan was diagnosed with breast cancer, and in 1989, she was diagnosed with non-Hodgkin's lymphoma. In 1990, the Jordans moved from the property but had a difficult time selling the house. The bank foreclosed on the property because it did not sell, and Larry Jordan could no longer continue to make double payments on their new house and the old one.

[20] *City of Warner Robins v Holt,* 470 SE2d 238 (Ga App 1996).
[21] *County of Westchester v Town of Greenwich, Connecticut,* 76 F3d 42 (2d Cir 1996).
[22] *Huffman v United States,* 82 F3d 703 (6th Cir 1996).
[23] *Fowler v First Federal Savings & Loan Ass'n of Defuniak Springs,* 643 So 2d 30 (Fla App 1994).

The Jordans filed suit in 1991 against Georgia Power Company and Oglethorpe Power Corporation, alleging that electromagnetic radiation from the electromagnetic fields (EMFs) created by the presence of the power lines on their property caused Mrs. Jordan's breast cancer and lymphoma. Their suit alleged both trespass and nuisance. The trial court found for the power company, and the Jordans appealed.

Judicial Opinion

POPE, Presiding J. . . . The Jordans claim that the court erred in granting summary judgment on their trespass claim. They argue that the court invaded the province of the jury.

In their motion for summary judgment, Oglethorpe and Georgia Power argued that EMFs are not tangible matter and that their alleged presence on the Jordans' property could not constitute a trespass. In response, the Jordans filed the affidavit of Roy Martin, a licensed professional electrical engineer, in which he stated that electromagnetic radiation from high power lines is tangible. Martin further stated that a magnetic field could be detected and measured by appropriate measuring devices and that such fields obeyed physical laws.

In its order granting the motion, the court concluded that although the Jordans claimed that there was a detectable entry on their property by the EMFs, these fields were not tangible as defined by law for purpose of trespass determinations. The court stated: "[I]n Georgia a physical invasion of some kind is required in order to state a cause of action for trespass. There has been no physical injury to the real estate alleged. There has been no physical entry alleged. The plaintiffs allege there is a detectable entry by non-tangible, magnetic fields. However, such fields are not tangible as that term is defined by law for purpose of trespass determination."

OCGA Section 1-3-3(20) provides: "'[T]respass' means any misfeasance, transgression, or offense which damages another's health, reputation or property." With respect to injuries to real estate, OCGA Section 51-9-1 defines the cause of action for interference with enjoyment of property, stating: "[T]he right of enjoyment of private property being an absolute right of every citizen, every act of another which unlawfully interferes with such enjoyment is a tort for which an action shall lie."

Although arguably the Jordans' trespass action could present a jury question, we conclude that for policy reasons, the trial court's grant of summary judgment was proper. The scientific evidence regarding whether EMFs cause harm of any kind is inconclusive; the invasive quality of these electric fields cannot generally constitute a trespass. In reaching this conclusion, we do not close the door on the possibility that science may advance to a point at which damage from EMFs is legally cognizable and a trespass action may lie.

The Jordans claim that the court erred by granting a directed verdict on the nuisance and property damage claims. In directing the verdict, the court concluded that there were no measurable damages or injury and that there was no nuisance.

Here, the Jordans argue that the court's conclusion that there was no evidence of property damage ignored the fact that the trial was bifurcated as to damages and causation. They contend that because of the bifurcation, evidence of nominal damages was sufficient to prove this claim.

OCGA Section 41-1-1 defines a nuisance as "anything that causes hurt, inconvenience, or damage to another and the fact that the act done may otherwise be lawful shall not keep it from being a nuisance. The inconvenience complained of shall not be fanciful, or such as would affect only one of fastidious taste, but it shall be such as would affect an ordinary, reasonable man." Moreover, "while a physical invasion is generally necessary, noise, odors and smoke which impair the landowners' enjoyment of his [*sic*] property are also actionable nuisances, if, and only if, a partial condemnation of the property results."

Here, the trial court properly directed a verdict on the nuisance claim. . . . [T]he present state of science does not authorize recovery based on these facts.

[While the court found there was no cause of action for trespass or nuisance, it did reverse the case for error on evidence admissibility and for retrial on the other grounds the Jordans alleged for liability including negligence.]

[Reversed on other grounds]

Questions

1. What do the Jordans allege occurred as a result of the power lines being located on their property?
2. Is it important that the Jordans could not sell their house?
3. What is missing that is needed to establish nuisance?
4. What is missing that is needed to establish a trespass?

E-COMMERCE AND CYBERLAW

Because any electrical current sets up a magnetic field, computers and wire transmissions to and from computers set up magnetic fields that might affect electrical equipment in buildings on neighboring land. The stronger the current, the greater the magnetic field.

For example, Meridian Data Processing Center is an independent contractor that performed all of the data processing for many banks and stockbrokers. Because of the large number of computers and direct wire lines to its customers, the Center's operation set up a substantial magnetic field that interfered with some of the electronic display equipment in several neighboring stores. The stores sued to obtain an injunction against the Center for creating a nuisance. However, unless the stores can show some negligence in the maintenance of the Center's equipment that produced unnecessary sparking or a similar cause of electrical disturbance, they have not established a nuisance. Because of the social utility of the Center's business, a court would not condemn this necessary activity as a nuisance. If, however, the stores could suggest a reasonable method of shielding the equipment, it is possible that the court would order the Center to take such protective measures.

CPA 11. Private Remedies: Due Diligence

Another method by which problems with land are remedied is through sales transactions in which the buyer demands that a situation or problem on the land be fixed before signing a contract for purchase. **Due diligence** is the process by which the buyer conducts a thorough investigation of the property and its current and former uses to determine whether any problems with respect to environmental law or nuisance exist. Due diligence is conducted through a search of public records, an inspection of the land, and often, when problems appear in these first two steps, some soil testing. This advance determination of problems is a civil means for land cleanup because sellers will be unable to transfer their properties until they meet the buyers' standards, determined by a close examination of the property for violations.

C. Land Use Controls

In addition to environmental laws, other restrictions, both private and public, place controls and limits on how land can be used.

12. Restrictive Covenants in Private Contracts

In the case of private planning, a real estate developer takes an undeveloped tract or area of land, maps out on paper an ideal community, and then constructs the buildings shown on the plan. These buildings are then sold to private purchasers. The buyers' deeds contain **restrictive covenants** that obligate the buyers to observe certain limitations in the use of their property, the nature of buildings that will be maintained or constructed on the land, and so on. If a restrictive covenant is valid, it binds any prospective buyer of the land who had actual notice or knowledge of the restriction from the previous owner or the restriction was recorded with the deed. Consequently, the owner of any one of the tracts may stop another owner from violating the covenant even though there is no contract between the property owners. If a restrictive covenant violates a statute, rule of law, or public policy, it is not valid and will not be enforced.

A restrictive covenant is to be construed by the same rules of construction that are applied in interpreting contracts. A restrictive covenant is given its ordinary meaning, and it is given effect according to its terms but is not extended beyond them.

A restrictive covenant must be clearly stated to be effective. If any uncertainty exists, the covenant will be construed strictly in favor of the free use of the land. When there is no uncertainty and no reason to depart from the meaning of the words of the covenant, a court will enforce those words.

The social forces favoring freedom of action and the free use of property cause courts to interpret restrictive covenants narrowly to permit the greatest possible use of the land. However, courts often disagree as to what is permitted by a restrictive covenant. **For Example,** a conflict of authority results as to whether the use of a home for the day care of children violates a restrictive covenant prohibiting any but a residential use.[24]

A restrictive covenant that violates any statute or administrative regulation is void. A restrictive covenant that discriminates against persons with disabilities is void because it violates the Fair Housing Act.[25]

A restrictive covenant may also be ignored when it has not been observed. A requirement that no house can be built without first obtaining the approval of the architectural control committee will be ignored if the committee has never had any meetings and houses have been built on other lots of the subdivision without any committee approval.[26]

13. Public Zoning

By **zoning,** a governmental unit such as a city adopts an ordinance imposing restrictions on the use of the land. The object of zoning is to ensure an orderly physical development of the regulated area. In effect, zoning is the same as restrictive covenants; the difference is in the source of authority. In most cases, zoning is based on an ordinance of a local political subdivision, such as a municipality or a county. Restrictive covenants, on the other hand, are created by agreement of the parties.

The zoning power permits any regulation that is conducive to advancing public health, welfare, and safety. The object of a particular zoning regulation may be to prevent high-density population.

Some zoning ordinances may be conservation inspired. An ordinance may prohibit or regulate the extraction of natural resources from any land within the zoned area. The fact that a zoning restriction limits the owner in the use of a property does not amount to a "taking" of property for which compensation must be made.[27] A zoning ordinance may make it impossible for landowners to make any economically feasible use of their land. As long as that restriction advances the health, safety, or welfare of the community, it is valid. If it does not advance the community interest,

SPORTS & ENTERTAINMENT LAW

HELL HATH NO FURY LIKE A STAR WHO LOSES GARDEN SPACE

Ralph Horowitz owned land located in the Los Angeles area that had been zoned for manufacturing and warehousing. When he acquired the land, it had not been used for those purposes since 1992 when about 350 local residents had begun a communal garden there. The garden included trees and had even been praised by the Los Angeles mayor as a lovely respite among the industrial plants and warehouses. Mr. Horowitz had difficulty getting the gardeners to leave the property. He agreed to allow them to harvest their gardens and then leave, but they refused to leave. Among the gardeners and their supporters were Danny Glover, Laura Dern, Joan Baez, and Daryl Hannah. After several days of lofty protest, Ms. Hannah had to be removed from a tree by police who were using a fire truck ladder. She stated, "I'm very confident this is the morally right thing to do, to take a principled stand in solidarity with the farmers." Some violence broke out as police removed other protestors who had chained themselves to a walnut tree in the garden. The gardeners said they wanted Mr. Horowitz to commit the land to an urban garden.*

What are their rights? What are Mr. Horowitz's rights?

*http://www.bbc.com, accessed June 14, 2006.

[24] *Stewart v Jackson*, 635 NE2d 186 (Ind App 1994).

[25] *Hill v Community of Damien of Molokai*, 911 P2d 861 (NM 1996).

[26] *Stuart v Chawney*, 560 NW2d 336 (Mich App 1997).

[27] *Longview of St. Joseph, Inc. v City of St. Joseph*, 918 SW2d 364 (Mo App 1996).

the zoning restriction is unconstitutional.[28] For example, the issue of single-family housing use restrictions has resulted in differing decisions among courts about whether cities can have zoning laws that require only a family to live in a single-family residence.[29]

(a) Nonconforming Use

When the use of land is in conflict with a zoning ordinance at the time the ordinance goes into effect, such use is described as a **nonconforming use. For Example,** when a zoning ordinance that requires a setback of 25 feet from the boundary line is adopted, an existing building that has a 10-foot setback is a nonconforming use.

A nonconforming use has a constitutionally protected right to continue, but if the nonconforming use is discontinued, it cannot be resumed.[30] The right to a nonconforming use may be lost by abandonment. If a garage is a nonconforming use and its owner stops using it as a garage and uses it for storing goods, a return to the use of the property as a garage will be barred by abandonment.

At times, a real estate development or building construction is only partly completed when a zoning ordinance that would prohibit such development or building is adopted. To avoid hardship for the persons involved, it is customary to exempt such partly finished projects from the zoning ordinance just as though they were existing nonconforming uses.[31]

(b) Variance

The administrative agency charged with the enforcement of a zoning ordinance may grant a **variance.** This permits the owner of the land to use it in a specified manner that is inconsistent with the zoning ordinance.

Agencies ordinarily are reluctant to permit a variance when neighboring property owners object because, to the extent that variation is permitted, the basic plan of the zoning ordinance is defeated. Likewise, the allowance of an individual variation, or **spot zoning,** may result in such inequality as to be condemned by the courts.[32] In addition, there is a consideration of practical expediency. If variances are readily granted, every property owner will request a variance and flood the agency with these requests.

When the desired use of land is in harmony with the general nature of surrounding areas, a zoning variance is usually granted. A zoning variance is not granted on the ground of hardship, however, when the landowner created the hardship by purchasing land that was subject to a zoning ordinance.

CROWN COMMUNICATION OF NEW YORK V DEPARTMENT OF TRANSPORTATION

824 NE2D 934 (CA NY 2005)

DO ZONING LAWS TRUMP CELL PHONE TOWERS?

FACTS: In 1997, the New York State Police and the Department of Transportation (DOT or collectively the State), entered into an agreement with Crown Communication to construct and operate telecommunications towers on state-owned lands and rights-of-way. Under the agreement, Crown could license space on the towers to localities and commercial wireless providers, and the State could co-locate its own communications equipment on the towers.

After Crown identified two potential locations for towers on state-owned property within the City of New Rochelle (the City), the State approved construction of both towers.

[28] *W. O. Brisben Co. v City of Montgomery*, 837 NE2d 347 (Ohio App 1994).

[29] See, for example, Ark Code Ann § 20-48-603(4)(A) (Michie 1991) (setting cap at eight for a "Family Home I"); Colo Rev Stat Ann § 31-23-303(2)(a) (West 1997) (setting cap at eight); Ind Code Ann § 12-11-1-1(b)(1) (Michie 1997) (setting cap at eight for "supervised group living programs").

[30] *Hansen Brothers Enterprises v Board of Supervisors*, 907 P2d 1325 (Cal 1996).

[31] See, for example, *Cuseo v Horry County Planning Commission*, 445 SE2d 644 (SC App 1994).

[32] *Gullickson v Stark County Board*, 474 NW2d 890 (ND 1991).

In June 2000, Crown and the State gave a public presentation to the Mayor and City Council regarding the purpose and use of the two proposed towers. At this meeting, the City voiced no objection to the siting or construction of the towers and Crown offered space for use by its public safety agencies. DOT's environmental review found that neither the replacement tower nor the maintenance yard tower would result in any significant adverse environmental or aesthetic impact.

Crown proceeded with the construction of the towers and entered into license agreements with a number of telecommunications providers to lease space on the towers. During construction, the City issued a stop work order, contending that the towers were subject to the City's zoning laws and that Crown must apply for a special permit from the City's Planning Board.

The Supreme Court (a trial court in New York state) determined that Crown need not comply with local zoning requirements. The Appellate Division also determined that the wireless telecommunications providers are not subject to local zoning regulation and affirmed. The parties appealed.

Judicial Opinion

GRAFFEO, Justice.... In this case we are asked whether the installation of private antennae on two state-owned telecommunications towers is exempt from local zoning regulation.

The City argues that, although the towers themselves are exempt from regulation, no justification exists to extend such immunity to the installation of commercial equipment on the towers. Specifically, the City asserts that it has the right pursuant to its zoning authority to evaluate whether private antennae are necessary to close cellular telecommunications coverage gaps or should be placed elsewhere, and to require some form of aesthetic camouflaging of equipment. In response, Crown and the State contend that the private carriers are entitled to share in the immunity already enjoyed by the state-owned towers. They claim that the State's plan envisions a public-private partnership and that the joint use of its towers facilitates the State's public safety and environmental goals.

[T]he State submitted evidence of numerous benefits the government's use of the towers would afford the public, which the Supreme Court took into account in finding the towers immune from local regulation under the balancing test. For example, the State is currently in the process of developing its telecommunications infrastructure in anticipation of establishing a Statewide Wireless Network (SWN), which will replace outdated systems with a state-of-the-art digital land mobile radio network designed to permit interagency and intergovernmental communications across the state in emergency situations. Consultants retained by the State Police have indicated that in order to operate in the higher frequency range, it will be necessary to construct three to four times the approximately 150 existing state-maintained radio sites. The State has therefore reserved space on the replacement and maintenance yard towers for anticipated SWN use when the network becomes operational.

Additionally, DOT has developed an Intelligent Transportation System (ITS), which monitors traffic flow, weather and road conditions. DOT's Director of Traffic Engineering and Safety stated that the collection of such data aids DOT and public safety entities in being able to "respond to emergency situations, manage and divert traffic, and provide real-time traffic information to motorists," thereby improving the safety of the traveling public and reducing travel times.

Finally, the State has followed a policy of offering space on its towers to local public safety authorities and offered such space on the two towers to the City in this case. Currently, Westchester County has placed antennae on the replacement tower for use by its Department of Public Safety.

[We] agree with the Appellate Division that the installation of licensed commercial antennae on the towers should also be accorded immunity because co-location serves a number of significant public interests that are advanced by the State's overall telecommunications plan. At this time, there are apparently more private than public antennae on the towers, but the presence of commercial equipment does not exclusively serve private interests. The private antennae will improve the availability of 911 emergency cellular calls made by the public, thereby promoting the public safety interest central to construction of the State's towers. Significantly, the co-location of public and private equipment also eliminates the need for the proliferation of telecommunications towers, an important environmental and aesthetic public concern. Furthermore, profits derived from licensing space to wireless providers will ultimately aid in financing the construction of the State's telecommunications infrastructure plan.

The fact that the wireless providers will also realize profit from their services does not undermine the public interests served by co-location. In sum, the public and private uses of the towers are sufficiently intertwined to justify exemption of the wireless providers from local zoning regulations.

The order of the Appellate Division should be affirmed, with costs.

CIPARICK, J. (dissenting).

Because I do not believe the exemption from local zoning regulation accorded to the state-owned telecommunications towers should be applied to the private telecommunications providers here, I respectfully dissent.

Placement of private wireless service facilities is ordinarily subject to local zoning requirements. This case differs from the typical scenario because the private providers locate their antennae on a state tower that is immune from local regulation. The issue before this Court is whether that immunity should be extended to benefit the private providers—allowing them immunity from local zoning simply because they opt to co-locate on a state, rather than a private, tower.

The State's immunity from local zoning requirements should not be extended to the private providers. The State has not preempted this area and there is no indication that the local zoning regulations would conflict with the State's purposes. Thus, I would reverse the order of the Appellate Division and reinstate the order of Supreme Court.

Questions

1. Why is the presence of private users an issue in the case?
2. What test does the court apply in determining whether the towers are exempt from local ordinances?
3. What is the focus of the dissenting justice's opinion?

LAWFLIX

Erin Brockovich (2000) (R)

The movie is the story of ground water pollution and private litigation for recovery.

For movie clips that illustrate business law concepts, see LawFlix at **http://www.westbuslaw.com.**

Summary

Public and private regulations apply to land use. The public regulations consist of environmental laws and zoning. Environmental laws exist at both the state and the federal levels. At the federal level, regulations govern air pollution through limits on emissions and permits for discharges; water pollution with permit requirements, discharge prohibitions, and treatment standards; solid waste disposal with limitations on dumping and liability for cleanup when hazardous materials are found on property; and environmental quality through the use of advance studies on projects and their impact on the environment. Other federal regulations on the environment protect endangered species, set standards for drinking water, and impose liability for oil spills as well as safety standards for oil tankers.

Environmental laws are primarily enforced at the federal level by the Environmental Protection Agency (EPA), but other federal agencies as well as state agencies work together to enforce these laws, using criminal and civil penalties and injunctions to halt pollution. Private citizens also have the right to bring suit under federal statutes to enforce the requirements imposed.

A *nuisance* is a public or private interference with the use and enjoyment of land, and individuals can bring suit to halt nuisances. Courts perform a balancing test in deciding how to handle concerns about nuisances. They seek to balance the use and enjoyment of land with the economic interests of all involved parties.

Restrictive covenants in deeds are valid land use restrictions that pass from owner to owner and are enforceable as long as they do not violate any constitutional rights. *Zoning* is a public means of regulating land use. Zoning laws are part of an overall plan for development adopted by a governmental entity. Some landowners can obtain variances from zoning laws, and some preexisting uses are permitted to continue with the protection of a nonconforming use.

Questions and Case Problems

1. Union Electric wishes to construct a new coal-fired plant in the northeastern corner of Arizona. Union plans to use the maximum achievement technology for the scrubbers on the plant to reduce emissions. Will Union be able to obtain a permit from the EPA to build and operate the new power plant? Discuss the issues that Union faces.
2. Federal Oil Co. was loading a tanker with fuel oil when the loading hose snapped for some unknown reason and about 1,000 gallons of oil poured into the ocean. Federal Oil was prosecuted for this water pollution. It raised the defense that it had exercised due care, was not at fault in any way, and had not intended to pollute the water. What statutes could be used to prosecute Federal Oil? What are the potential penalties?
3. Philip Carey Co. owned a tract of land in Plymouth Township, Pennsylvania, on which it deposited a large pile of manufacturing waste containing asbestos. Carey sold the land to Celotex, and Celotex sold the land to Smith Land & Improvement Corp. The EPA notified Smith that unless it took steps to eliminate the asbestos hazard, the EPA would do the work and pursue reimbursement. Smith cleaned up the land to the EPA's satisfaction at a cost of $218,945.44. Smith asked Celotex and Carey for reimbursement. Which firms have liability for the cleanup costs? [*Smith Land & Improvement Corp. v Celotex*, 851 F2d 86 (3d Cir)]
4. The McConnells bought a home in Sherwood Estates. The land was subject to a restrictive covenant that "no building, fence, or other structure" could be built on the land without the approval of the developer of the property. The McConnells built a dog pen in their yard that consisted of a cement base with fencing surrounding the base. They claimed that approval was not required on the theory that the restrictive covenant did not apply because it showed an intent to restrict only major construction, not minor additions to the landscape. A lawsuit was brought to compel the McConnells to remove the dog pen because prior approval had not been obtained. Are restrictive covenants applied this expansively to homeowners? Must the McConnells have prior approval? [*Sherwood Estates Homes Ass'n, Inc. v McConnell*, 714 SW2d 848 (Mo App)]
5. General Automotive operates Grand Auto Parts Stores, which receive used automotive batteries from customers as trade-ins. General's policy in disposing of these batteries had been to drive a screwdriver through each spent battery and then sell them to a battery-cracking plant operated by Morris P. Kirk & Sons, Inc., which extracted and smelted the lead. After the lead was extracted from the batteries, Kirk washed and crushed the battery casings, loaded them into a dump truck, and then dumped them. Tons of pieces of crushed batteries were dumped onto Catellus Development Corp.'s property. Under CERCLA, Catellus sought to recover from General the costs of cleaning up the hazardous battery parts from its property. General maintained that it was not liable because it sold the batteries to Kirk, and Kirk did the dumping. Was General correct? [*Catellus Development Corp. v United States*, 34 F3d 748 (9th Cir)]
6. A zoning ordinance of the city of Dallas, Texas, prohibited the use of property in a residential district for gasoline filling stations. Lombardo brought an action against the city to test the validity of the ordinance. He contended that the ordinance violated the rights of the owners of property in such districts. Do you agree with this contention? [*Lombardo v City of Dallas*, 73 SW2d 475 (Tex)]
7. Taback began building a vacation home on a parcel of wooded land. It was to be a three-story house, 31 feet high. This height violated the local zoning ordinance that limited residential homes to two and one-half stories, not exceeding 35 feet. When Taback learned of this violation, he applied for a zoning variance. Because of the delay of the zoning board and because winter was approaching, Taback finished the construction of the building as a three-story house. At a later hearing before the zoning board, he showed that it would be necessary for him to rebuild the third floor to convert the house into a two and one-half story house. The zoning board recognized that Taback's violation could not be seen from neighboring properties. Was Taback entitled to a zoning variance? [*Taback v Town of Woodstock Zoning Board of Appeals*, 521 NYS2d 838 (App Div)]
8. Bermuda Run Country Club, Inc., developed a tract of land, formed a country club, and sold some of the lots to individual buyers. Following various sales and litigation, an agreement was executed giving the board of governors power to veto club members' assessments. The agreement declared that this was a restrictive covenant that would run with the land and bind subsequent owners. The corporation that later purchased the country club claimed it did not have that effect. Was the provision in question a restrictive covenant that ran with the land? [*Bermuda Run Country Club, Inc. v Atwell*, 465 SE2d 9 (NC App)]
9. The Stallcups lived in a rural section of the state. In front of their house ran a relatively unused, unimproved public county road. Wales Trucking Co. transported concrete pipe from the plant where it was made to a lake where the pipe was used to construct a water line to bring water to a nearby city. In the course of four months, Wales made 825 trips over the road, carrying from 58,000 to 72,000 pounds of pipe per trip and making the same number of empty return trips. Because the heavy use of the road by

Wales cut up the dirt and made it like ashes, the Stallcups sued Wales for damages caused by the deposit of dust on their house and for the physical annoyance and discomfort it caused. Wales defended its position on the ground that it had not been negligent and that its use of the road was not unlawful. Decide. [*Wales Trucking Co. v Stallcup*, 465 SE2d 44 (Tex Civ App)]

10. Some sections of the city of Manitou Springs have hills of varying degrees of slope. To protect against water drainage and erosion, the city adopted a hillside zoning ordinance that required homes on hillsides to be surrounded by more open land than in the balance of the city. Sellon owned land on a hillside and claimed that the hillside ordinance was unconstitutional because it did not treat all homeowners equally. Was the ordinance valid? [*Sellon v City of Manitou Springs*, 745 P2d 229 (Colo)]
11. Patrick Bossenberry owned a house in a planned community area. Each lot in the area was limited by a restrictive covenant to use for a single-family dwelling. The covenant defined *family* as a blood or marital relationship between most of the occupants. Bossenberry rented his building to Kay-Jan, Inc., which wanted to use the building as a care home for not more than six adult mentally retarded persons. The neighbors sought to enjoin this use as a breach of the covenant. A number of Michigan statutes had been adopted that advanced the public policy of providing care for mentally retarded persons. Could the neighbors prevent the use of the property as a care home for mentally retarded adults? [*Craig v Bossenberry*, 351 NW2d 596 (Mich App)]
12. Kenneth and Mary Norpel purchased a house, and Kenneth attached a 35-foot flagpole to it. He did not obtain the permission of the architectural committee of the Stone Hill Community Association. This consent was required by a restrictive covenant to which the Norpel house was subject. The association objected to the flagpole from which Norpel then flew the American flag. The association brought an action to compel the removal of the pole. Norpel claimed that as a combat veteran of World War II, he had a constitutionally protected right to fly the American flag. Can he be compelled to remove the flagpole?
13. In 1997, Isbell purchased a building in San Diego with the intent to open an adult entertainment establishment there. Because this building was located within 1,000 feet of a residential area, however, a San Diego zoning ordinance precluded him from operating there. Isbell applied for a variance but was unsuccessful. He then filed suit, arguing that the city's ordinance violates the First Amendment, and that its standards for variances violate the equal protection clause. Can the city restrict the operation of this business? What must the city be able to establish? [*Isbell v City of San Diego*, 258 F3d 1108 (9th Cir)]
14. Explain why a company would want to perform a self-audit to determine whether it has any environmental violations.
15. Manufacturer's National Bank of Detroit had extended credit to Z&Z Leasing and had taken a mortgage on Z&Z's property as security for the line of credit. Z&Z defaulted on its payments, and Manufacturer's took possession of the property. The EPA then notified the bank that underground storage tanks on the property were leaking hazardous materials and that the cleanup would be in the $10,000,000 range. Is Manufacturer's liable for the cleanup costs? Are there other parties the EPA could pursue for the costs? [*Z & Z Leasing, Inc. v Graying Reel, Inc.*, 760 F2d 549 (DC)]

CPA Questions

1. Which of the following remedies is available against a real property owner to enforce the provisions of federal acts regulating air and water pollution?

	Citizen Suits Against the Environmental Protection Agency to Enforce Compliance	*State Suits to Enforce the Laws Against Violators*	*Citizen Suits Against Violators to Enforce the Laws*
a.	Yes	Yes	Yes
b.	Yes	Yes	No
c.	No	Yes	Yes
d.	Yes	No	Yes

2. Under the Comprehensive Environmental Response, Compensation, and Liability Act (CERCLA), commonly known as Superfund, which of the following parties would be liable to the Environmental Protection Agency (EPA) for the expense of cleaning up a hazardous waste disposal site?

   I. The current owner or operator of the site
   II. The person who transported the wastes to the site
   III. The person who owned or operated the site at the time of the disposal

   a. I and II
   b. I and III
   c. II and III
   d. I, II, and III

3. The National Environment Policy Act was passed to enhance and preserve the environment. Which of the following is not true?

   a. The act applies to all federal agencies.
   b. The act requires that an environmental impact statement be provided if any proposed federal legislation may significantly affect the environment.
   c. Enforcement of the act is primarily accomplished by litigation of persons who decide to challenge federal government decisions.
   d. The act provides generous tax breaks to those companies that help accomplish national environmental policy.

4. Which of the following actions should a business take to qualify for leniency if an environmental violation has been committed?

	Conduct Environmental Audits	*Report Environmental Violations to the Government*
a.	Yes	Yes
b.	Yes	No
c.	No	Yes
d.	No	No

LEASES

CHAPTER

(51)

LEARNING OBJECTIVES

After studying this chapter, you should be able to

LO.1 Define *lease* and list its essential elements

LO.2 List the ways in which a lease may be terminated

LO.3 List and explain the rights and duties of the parties to a lease

LO.4 Describe the remedies of a landlord for breach by the tenant

LO.5 Describe a landlord's liability for a tenant's and a third person's injuries sustained on the premises

LO.6 Define *sublease* and *assignment of a lease* and distinguish between them

If you cannot buy a house or piece of business property, leasing such a property from someone who does own it may be the answer.

A. Creation and Termination

Leases are governed by the common law of property as modified by judicial decisions and statutes.[1]

1. Definition and Nature

A **lease** is the relationship in which one person is in lawful possession of real property owned by another. In common speech, *lease* also refers to the agreement that creates that relationship.

The person who owns the real property and permits the occupation of the premises is known as the **lessor,** or **landlord.** The **lessee,** or **tenant,** is the one who occupies the property. A lease establishes the relationship of landlord and tenant.

Basically, a lease is much like a **bailment** in personal property, in which there is an agreement to make the bailment and a subsequent transfer of possession to carry out that agreement. In the case of a lease, there is the lease contract and the interest thereafter acquired by the tenant when possession is delivered under the lease contract. Common law looked at the transfer of possession and regarded the lease as merely the creation of an interest in land. Modern law regards the lease to be the same as renting an automobile. With this new approach, typical contract law concepts of unconscionability, mitigation of damages, and warranties are brought into the law on leases of real property.

2. Creation of the Lease Relationship

The relationship of landlord and tenant is created by an express or implied contract. An oral lease is valid at common law, but statutes in most states require written leases for certain tenancies. Many states provide that a lease for a term exceeding three years must be in writing. Statutes in other states require written leases when the term exceeds one year.

(a) Antidiscrimination

Statutes in many states prohibit an owner who rents property for profit from discriminating against prospective tenants on the basis of race, color, religion, or national origin. Also, the federal *Fair Housing Act* prohibits such discrimination. In addition, landlords are subject to the Americans with Disabilities Act (ADA) and must make reasonable accommodations for tenants with disabilities.[2]

[1] A uniform act, the Uniform Residential Landlord and Tenant Act (URLTA), has been adopted in some form in twenty states. The twenty states are: Alaska, Arizona, Connecticut, Florida, Hawaii, Iowa, Kansas, Kentucky, Michigan, Mississippi, Montana, Nebraska, New Mexico, Oklahoma, Oregon, Rhode Island, South Carolina, Tennessee, Virginia, and Washington. URLTA does not apply to dorm rooms, fraternities or halfway houses. *Burke v Oxford House of Oregon Chapter V*, 103 P3d 1184 (Or App 2004).

[2] *Salute v Stratford Green Apartments*, 136 F3d 293 (2d Cir 1998) and see *Giebeler v M & B Associates*, 343 F3d 1143 (9th Cir 2003) for an even broader interpretation of the protections of ADA.

(b) Unconscionability

At common law, the parties to a lease had freedom to include such terms as they chose. However, that freedom has been curbed in some states that require that leases follow the pattern of UCC section 2-302 and not include terms and conditions that are unconscionable.[3] **For Example,** a provision in a residential lease stating that the landlord cutting off heat or water will not constitute an eviction is unconscionable. Such a clause does not prevent the tenant from recovering on the grounds of unconscionability or for breach of the implied warranty of habitability when there has been no heat or water.

3. Classification of Tenancies

Tenancies are classified by duration as tenancies for years, from year to year, at will, and by sufferance.

CPA (a) Tenancy for Years

A **tenancy for years** is one under which the tenant has a lease that runs for a definite duration. The expression "for years" is used to describe such a tenancy whether the duration of the tenancy is for only six months or as long as ten years.

(b) Periodic Tenancy

A **periodic tenancy** is one under which a tenant has a lease that has an indefinite duration and under which the tenant pays annual, monthly, or weekly rent. This tenancy does not terminate at the end of a year, month, or week except with proper notice. Proper notice, in most states, means giving notice for at least one period before ending the lease. **For Example,** on a month-to-month tenancy, the notice must be at least one month prior to ending the lease.

In almost all states, a periodic tenancy is implied if the tenant, with the consent of the landlord, stays in possession of property after a tenancy for years. Consent exists when there is an express statement or by conduct, such as when a landlord continues to accept rent.[4]

CPA (c) Tenancy at Will

When a lease runs for an indefinite period, which may be terminated at any time by the landlord or the tenant, a **tenancy at will** exists. A person who enters into possession of land for an indefinite period with the owner's permission but without any agreement as to rent is a tenant at will. Statutes in some states and decisions in others require advance notice of termination of this kind of tenancy.

CPA (d) Tenancy at Sufferance

When a tenant remains in possession after the termination of the lease without permission of the landlord, the landlord may treat the tenant as either a trespasser or a tenant. Until the landlord elects to do one or the other, a **tenancy at sufferance** exists. **For Example,** if John's one-year lease expired on January 31, 2006, and John remained in the apartment for a week, he would be a tenant at sufferance during that week. If John's landlord accepted a rental payment at the end of the first week, John would be a *periodic* or *month-to-month tenant*. In this situation, John was a tenant for years, a tenant at sufferance, and then a periodic tenant.

4. Termination of Lease

A lease is generally not terminated by the death, insanity, or bankruptcy of either party except in the case of a tenancy at will. Leases may be terminated in the following ways.

(a) Termination by Notice

A lease may give the landlord the power to terminate it by giving notice to the tenant. In states that follow the common law on termination by notice, it is immaterial why the landlord terminates. A provision giving the landlord the right to terminate the lease by notice if specified conditions exist is strictly construed against the landlord.

(b) Expiration of Term in a Tenancy for Years

When a tenancy for years exists, the relation of landlord and tenant ceases on the expiration of the term. There is no requirement that one party give the other any notice of termination. Express notice to end the term may be required of either or both parties by provisions of the lease except when a statute prohibits the landlord from imposing such a requirement.

(c) Notice in a Periodic Tenancy

In the absence of an agreement of the parties, notice for termination of a periodic tenancy is now usually

[3] *35 Park Ave. Corp. v Campagna* 48 NY2d 813, 399 NE2d 1144, 424 NYS2d 123 (1979); URLTA § 1.303.

[4] *Roosen v Schaffer*, 621 P2d 33 (Ariz App 1980) and *Weingarten/Arkansas, Inc. v ABC Interstate Theatres, Inc.*, 31 Ark App 109, 789 SW2d 1 (Ark App 1990).

governed by statute. It is common practice for the parties to require 30 or 60 days' notice to end a tenancy from year to year. As to tenancies for periods of less than a year, statutory provisions commonly require notice of only one week.

(d) Forfeiture

The landlord may terminate the lease because of the tenant's misconduct or breach if the lease or a statute so provides. In the absence of such a provision, the landlord may claim damages only for the breach. The courts do not favor terminating leases by forfeiture.

(e) Destruction of Property

If a lot and a building on it are leased, either an express provision in the lease or a statute generally releases the tenant from liability to pay rent if the building is destroyed. Alternatively, the amount of rent may be reduced in proportion to the loss sustained. Such statutes do not require the landlord to repair or restore the property to its former condition.

When the lease covers rooms or an apartment in a building, a destruction of the leased premises terminates the lease.

(f) Fraud

Because a lease is based on a contract, a lease agreement is subject to the contract defense of fraud. (See Chapter 14.)

(g) Transfer of the Tenant

Residential leases may contain a provision for termination on the tenant's being transferred by an employer to another city or on the tenant's being called into military service. Such provisions are strictly construed against the tenant. Therefore, when entering into a lease, the tenant should be certain that the provision is broad enough to cover personal situations that may arise.

5. Notice of Termination

When notice of termination is required, no particular words are necessary to constitute a sufficient notice so long as the words used clearly indicate the intention of the party. The notice, whether given by the landlord or the tenant, must be definite. Statutes sometimes require that the notice be in writing. In the absence of such a provision, however, oral notice is generally sufficient.

6. Renewal of Lease

When a lease terminates for any reason, the landlord and the tenant ordinarily enter into a new agreement if they wish to extend or renew the lease. The power to renew the lease may be stated in the original lease by declaring that the lease runs indefinitely, as from year to year, subject to being terminated by either party's giving written notice of a specified number of days or months before the termination date. Renewal provisions are strictly construed against the tenant.

The lease may require the tenant to give written notice of intention to renew the lease. In such a case, there is no renewal if the tenant does not give the required notice but merely remains on the premises after the expiration of the original term.[5]

B. Rights and Duties of Parties

The rights and duties of the landlord and tenant are based on principles of real estate law and contract law. There is an increasing tendency to treat the residential lease like any other type of consumer contract and to govern the rights and duties of the parties by general principles of contract law.

7. Possession

The tenant has the right to acquire **possession** of the property and to remain in possession of that property until the term of the lease has expired or he or she is removed according to legal proceedings provided to landlords for removal of tenants in breach of the lease.

(a) Tenant's Right to Acquire Possession

By making a lease, the lessor or landlord agrees to give possession of the premises to the tenant at the time specified in the lease. If the landlord rents a building that is being constructed, there is an implied promise in the contract that the leased premises will be ready for occupancy on the date specified in the lease for the beginning of the lease term.

(b) Tenant's Right to Retain Possession

After the lease begins and the tenant takes possession, that possession and control of the premises are the exclusive right of the tenant for the duration of

[5] *Garrido v Empty Nester Homes, Ltd.*, not reported in NE2d, 2004 WL 51791 (Ohio App 2004).

the lease. This right of possession ends with the lease or if the tenant is in breach and the landlord had taken the proper steps provided by law to have the tenant removed. Under the exclusive right of possession, a tenant can refuse the landlord access, even for reasonable requests. Some leases specify that the landlord can show the property to prospective tenants.

If the landlord interferes with the tenant's possession, the landlord has breached the lease agreement, and legal remedies are available to the tenant. *Interference* is generally defined to be an eviction that occurs by judicial proceedings or when the landlord prevents access by the tenant, as when the locks are changed and the tenant does not have a key. If the landlord wrongfully deprives the tenant of the use of one room when the tenant is entitled to use an entire apartment or building, there is a partial eviction. An eviction in violation of the lease or law entitles the tenant to collect damages from the landlord for interference with possession of the leased premises.

(c) Covenant of Quiet Enjoyment

Most written leases today contain an express promise by the landlord called a **covenant of quiet enjoyment.** Such a provision protects the tenant from interference with possession by the landlord or the landlord's agent, but it does not impose liability on the landlord for the unlawful acts of third persons.[6]

(d) Constructive Eviction

A **constructive eviction** occurs when some act or omission of the landlord substantially deprives the tenant of the use and enjoyment of the premises.

To establish a constructive eviction, the tenant must show that the condition of the property is such that it is impossible for the tenant to remain in possession. In addition, constructive eviction is not established unless the tenant actually leaves the premises. If the tenant continues to occupy the premises for more than a reasonable time after what is claimed to be a constructive eviction, the tenant waives or loses the right to object to the landlord's conduct. The definition of *constructive eviction* requires the establishment of conditions so awful that a tenant is forced to leave. The tenant's remaining behind in the leased premises contradicts one of the elements required for establishing constructive eviction.[7] **For Example,** a condition of constructive eviction would be sewage backing up through the bathtub. The tenant could claim the sewage in the apartment constituted constructive eviction, but the tenant would also need to move out of the apartment.

8. Use of Premises

The lease generally specifies those uses authorized for the tenant. In the absence of express or implied restrictions, a tenant is entitled to use the premises for any lawful purpose for which they are adapted or for which they are ordinarily employed or in a manner contemplated by the parties in executing the lease. A provision specifying the use to be made of the property is strictly construed against the tenant.

(a) Change of Use

If the tenant uses the property for any purpose other than the one specified, the landlord has the option to declare the lease terminated.

(b) Continued Use of Property

A tenant is ordinarily required to give the landlord notice of nonuse or vacancy of the premises. This notice is a practical issue; landlords need to be aware when premises are vacant because there is an increased danger of damage to the premises by vandalism or fire. Also, there is commonly a provision in the landlord's fire insurance policy making it void if a vacancy continues for a specified time.

(c) Rules

The modern lease generally contains a blanket agreement by the tenant to abide by the provisions of rules and regulations adopted by the landlord. These rules are generally binding on the tenant whether they exist at the time the lease was made or are adopted afterward.

(d) Prohibition of Pets

A lease restriction prohibiting pet ownership is valid, as are cleaning fees for violations of the restriction.

[6] *Bown v Hamilton*, 601 A2d 1074 (DC 1992).

[7] Some states prohibit a landlord of residential property from willfully turning off the utilities of a tenant for the purpose of evicting the tenant. *City and County of San Francisco v Sainez*, 77 Cal App 4th 1302, 92 Cal Rptr 2d 418, (Cal App 2000) (imposing civil penalty of $663,000 for shutting off utilities for 530 days). Such conduct is also a violation of ULTRA §§ 2.104 and 4.105.

9. Rent

The tenant is under a duty to pay rent as compensation to the landlord. The amount of rent agreed to by the parties may be subject to government regulation, as when a city or county has enacted rent control laws.[8]

(a) Time of Payment

The time of payment of rent is ordinarily fixed by the lease. When the lease does not specify the time of payment, rent generally is not due until the end of the term. However, statutes or custom may require rent to be paid monthly or may require a substantial deposit before the lease begins.

CPA (b) Assignment

If the lease is assigned (the tenant's entire interest is transferred to a third person), the assignee is liable to the landlord for the rent. However, the assignment does not in itself discharge the tenant from the duty to pay the rent. If the assignee of the lease does not make the lease payments, the landlord may bring an action for the rent against either the original tenant or the assignee, or both, but is entitled to payment of only what is due under the lease, not a double amount as collected from each party. A **sublessee** (a person to whom part of a tenant's interest is transferred) ordinarily is not liable to the original lessor for rent unless that liability has been expressly assumed or is imposed by statute.

(c) Rent Escalation

When property is rented for a long term, it is common to include some provision for the automatic increase of the rent at periodic intervals. Such a provision is often tied to increases in the cost of living or in the landlord's operating costs and is called an **escalation clause.** There may, however, also be rent controls that would prohibit such rent increases.[9]

10. Repairs and Condition of Premises

In the absence of an agreement to the contrary, the tenant has no duty to make repairs. When the landlord makes repairs, reasonable care must be exercised to make them in a proper manner. The tenant is liable for any damage to the premises caused by his or her willful or negligent acts.

(a) Inspection of Premises

Under the URLTA, the landlord has the right to enter the leased premises for emergency purposes or with notice to the tenant for repairs, evaluations, and estimates.

(b) Housing Laws

Various laws protect tenants by requiring landlords to observe specified safety, health, and fire prevention standards. Some statutes require a landlord who leases a building for dwelling purposes to keep it in a condition fit for habitation. Leases commonly require the tenant to obey local ordinances and laws relating to the care and use of the premises.

Landlords must comply with the ADA. Compliance means that landlords cannot discriminate on the basis of disability in deciding whether to rent to a particular tenant. Also, landlords are required to make reasonable modifications to accommodate tenants with disabilities, which can include everything from making sure that sidewalks on the property are smooth enough for operation of wheelchairs to permitting guide dogs to live with their sight-impaired owners.[10]

One of the developing areas of landlord-tenant law involves landlords' rights with regard to leasing to convicts and those who are registered as sex offenders. About 600,000 inmates are released from prisons each year, and their housing choices generally involve leasing.[11] The federal government requires public housing authorities to screen and evict tenants for drug-related or "safety-threatening" behavior. Public housing authorities that receive federal funds must include a lease clause that requires automatic lease termination for any drug or violent criminal activity, even if the activity does not occur on the landlord's property.

[8] *Fisher v City of Berkeley, California*, 475 US 260 (1986).

[9] *Id.*

[10] *Crowder v Kitagawa*, 81 F3d 1480 (9th Cir 1996); *Kinney v Yerusalim*, 9 F3d 1067 (3d Cir 1993); cert. denied, 511 US 1033 (1996).

[11] Heidi Lee Cain, "Housing Our Criminals: Finding Housing for the Ex-Offender in the Twenty-First Century," 33 *Golden Gate U. L. Rev.* 131 (2003).

DEPARTMENT OF HOUSING AND URBAN DEVELOPMENT V RUCKER 535 U.S. 125 (2002)

BUT I'M INNOCENT!!!

FACTS: Several young men, grandsons of William Lee and Barbara Hill, both of whom were residents on leases of the Oakland Housing Authority (OHA), were caught in the apartment complex parking lot smoking marijuana. The daughter of Pearlie Rucker, who resided with her and was listed on the OHA lease as a resident, was found with cocaine and a crack cocaine pipe three blocks from Rucker's apartment. On three instances within a two-month period, Herman Walker's, another OHA resident, caregiver and two others were found with cocaine in Walker's apartment.

After OHA initiated the eviction proceedings in state court against the Hills, Rucker, and Walker (respondents), they commenced actions against OHA in federal district court, challenging the Department of Housing and Urban Development's (HUD's) interpretation of the federal statute requiring eviction of tenants for criminal activity or the failure to control criminal activity in their apartments. The tenants of OHA argued that the federal statute and HUD regulations result in the eviction of "innocent" tenants and are unconstitutional.

The district court issued a preliminary injunction, enjoining OHA from terminating the leases of the tenants. A panel of the court of appeals reversed, and the full court of appeals reversed the panel and reinstated the district court's injunction. HUD appealed to the U.S. Supreme Court.

Judicial Opinion

REHNQUIST, Chief Justice... With drug dealers "increasingly imposing a reign of terror on public and other federally assisted low-income housing tenants," Congress passed the Anti-Drug Abuse Act of 1988. § 5122, 102 Stat. 4301, 42 U.S.C. § 11901(3) (1994 ed.). The Act, as later amended, provides that each "public housing agency shall utilize leases which... provide that any criminal activity that threatens the health, safety, or right to peaceful enjoyment of the premises by other tenants or any drug-related criminal activity on or off such premises, engaged in by a public housing tenant, any member of the tenant's household, or any guest or other person under the tenant's control, shall be cause for termination of tenancy."

42 U.S.C. § 1437d(l)(6) unambiguously requires lease terms that vest local public housing authorities with the discretion to evict tenants for the drug-related activity of household members and guests whether or not the tenant knew, or should have known, about the activity.

That this is so seems evident from the plain language of the statute. It provides that "[e]ach public housing agency shall utilize leases which... provide that... any drug-related criminal activity on or off such premises, engaged in by a public housing tenant, any member of the tenant's household, or any guest or other person under the tenant's control, shall be cause for termination of tenancy." Thus, any drug-related activity engaged in by the specified persons is grounds for termination, not just drug-related activity that the tenant knew, or should have known, about.

The *en banc* Court of Appeals also thought it possible that "under the tenant's control" modifies not just "other person," but also "member of the tenant's household" and "guest. The court ultimately adopted this reading, concluding that the statute prohibits eviction where the tenant, "for a lack of knowledge or other reason, could not realistically exercise control over the conduct of a household member or guest." But this interpretation runs counter to basic rules of grammar. The disjunctive "or" means that the qualification applies only to "other person." Indeed, the view that "under the tenant's control" modifies everything coming before it in the sentence would result in the nonsensical reading that the statute applies to "a public housing tenant... under the tenant's control." HUD offers a convincing explanation for the grammatical imperative that "under the tenant's control" modifies only "other person": "by 'control,' the statute means control in the sense that the tenant has permitted access to the premises." Implicit in the terms "household member" or "guest" is that access to the premises has been granted by the tenant. Thus, the plain language of § 1437d(l)(6) requires leases that grant public housing authorities the discretion to terminate tenancy without regard to the tenant's knowledge of the drug-related criminal activity.

And, of course, there is an obvious reason why Congress would have permitted local public housing authorities to conduct no-fault evictions: Regardless of knowledge, a tenant who "cannot control drug crime, or other criminal activities by a household member which threaten health or safety of other residents, is a threat to other residents and the project." With drugs leading to "murders, muggings, and other forms of violence against tenants," and to the "deterioration of the physical environment that requires substantial government expenditures," it was reasonable for Congress to permit no-fault evictions in order to "provide public and other federally assisted low-income housing that is decent, safe, and free from illegal drugs,"

There are, moreover, no "serious constitutional doubts" about Congress' affording local public housing authorities the discretion to conduct no-fault evictions for drug-related crime. *Reno v. Flores,* 507 U.S. 292, 314, n. 9, 113 S.Ct. 1439, 123 L.Ed.2d 1 (1993).

The en banc Court of Appeals held that HUD's interpretation "raise[s] serious questions under the Due Process Clause of the Fourteenth Amendment," because it permits "tenants to be deprived of their property interest without any relationship to individual wrongdoing." The government is not attempting to criminally punish or civilly regulate respondents as members of the general populace. It is instead acting as a landlord of property that it owns, invoking a clause in a lease to which respondents have agreed and which Congress has expressly required.

The Court of Appeals sought to bolster its discussion of constitutional doubt by pointing to the fact that respondents have a property interest in their leasehold interest, citing *Greene v. Lindsey,* 456 U.S. 444, 102 S.Ct. 1874, 72 L.Ed.2d 249 (1982). This is undoubtedly true, and *Greene* held that an effort to deprive a tenant of such a right without proper notice violated the Due Process Clause of the Fourteenth Amendment. But, in the present cases, such deprivation will occur in the state court where OHA brought the unlawful detainer action against respondents. There is no indication that notice has not been given by OHA in the past, or that it will not be given in the future. Any individual factual disputes about whether the lease provision was actually violated can, of course, be resolved in these proceedings.

Accordingly, the judgment of the Court of Appeals is reversed, and the cases are remanded for further proceedings consistent with this opinion.

Questions

1. Why was it important to have landlord eviction rights in public housing regardless of the tenant's knowledge?
2. Why is drug dealing targeted by the statute for automatic eviction?
3. Why are there no constitutional issues here in the automatic eviction?

THINKING THINGS THROUGH

WITH FRIENDS AND RELATIVES LIKE THESE . . .

Applying the *Rucker* case, determine whether eviction of tenants would be allowed in the following circumstances.

1. Marilyn Murphy lived in a subsidized federal housing apartment of the Wellston Housing Authority. The terms of her lease provided that it could be terminated for criminal activity by the tenant, any household member, a guest, or other person under the tenant's control. Wellstone did not allow leases with tenants who had criminal records.

   Morris Lockett, who had felony convictions and had been released from prison recently, visited Murphy and stayed with her in her apartment. When Murphy inquired about adding him to the lease, however, she was informed of his criminal record and told he could not live there. Murphy continued to allow Lockett to live at her apartment. The Housing Authority arrested Lockett for trespassing and evicted Murphy. Murphy challenged the eviction. Will she win? [Wellston Housing Authority v Murphy, 131 SW3d 378 (Mo App 2004)]
2. Santosha Scarborough was a resident of a public housing apartment building. The lease prohibited the possession of guns and any criminal activity by the tenant or

THINKING THINGS THROUGH

continued

tenants' guests. Her cousin, Delante Simmons, entered her apartment after he had been drinking and began an altercation with her. Scarborough's boyfriend, Desmond Barr, who was also present, withdrew a shotgun and fatally shot Simmons. Executing a search warrant for the apartment the next day, the police found a loaded 12-gauge semiautomatic shotgun next to the water heater in the furnace room, a loaded semiautomatic pistol under the seat cushion of a couch, a box of Remington shotgun ammunition containing 23 shotgun shells, and a box of cartridges for the semiautomatic pistol. Barr was later acquitted of second-degree murder (the jury apparently accepting his claim of self-defense) but convicted of possession of an unregistered firearm and ammunition.

Santosha was evicted from her apartment the day after the shotgun was found pursuant to the warrant. Ms. Scarborough objected because she had not been involved in any criminal activity. Could she still be evicted? [Scarborough v Winn Residential L.L.P./Atlantic Terrace Apartments, 890 A2d 249 (DC 2006)]

CPA (c) Warranty of Habitability

At common law, a landlord was not bound by any obligation that the premises be fit for use unless the lease contained an express warranty to that effect. Most jurisdictions now reject this view and have created a **warranty of habitability** to protect tenants. The warranty of habitability requires, in most states, that the premises have running water, have heat in winter, and be free from structural defects and infestation. If the landlord breaches a warranty of habitability, the tenant is entitled to damages. These damages may be set off against the rent that is due, or if no rent is due, the tenant may bring an independent lawsuit to recover damages from the landlord.[12]

(d) Abatement and Escrow Payment of Rent

To protect tenants from unsound living conditions, statutes sometimes provide that a tenant is not required to pay rent as long as the premises are not fit to live in. As a compromise, some statutes require the tenant to continue to pay the rent but require that it be paid into an escrow or agency account. The money in the escrow account is paid to the landlord only upon proof that the necessary repairs have been made to the premises.

11. Improvements

In the absence of a special agreement, neither the tenant nor the landlord is under a duty to make improvements, as contrasted with repairs.[13] Either party may, as a term of the original lease, agree to make improvements, in which case a failure to perform will result in liability in an action for damages for breach of contract brought by the other party. In the absence of an agreement to the contrary, improvements become part of the realty and belong to the landlord.

12. Taxes and Assessments

In the absence of an agreement to the contrary, the landlord, not the tenant, is usually under a duty to pay taxes and/or assessments. The lease may provide for an increase in rent if taxes on the rented property are increased.[14]

If taxes or assessments are increased because of improvements made by the tenant, the landlord is liable for such increases if the improvements remain

[12] *In re Cassell*, 13 Fed Appx 298 (6th Cir 2001).

[13] The Americans with Disabilities Act requires commercial landlords and tenants to comply with legal requirements for access by the disabled. Shopping centers, medical offices, banks, and professional buildings must be in compliance. See *Pinnock v International House of Pancakes*, 844 F Supp 574 (SD Cal 1993); *Anderson v Little League Baseball, Inc.*, 794 F Supp 342 (D Ariz 1992).

[14] *Brazelton v Jackson Drug Co., Inc.*, 796 P2d 808 (Wyo 1990).

with the property. If the improvements can be removed by the tenant, the amount of the increase must be paid by the tenant.

13. Tenant's Deposit

A landlord may require a tenant to make a deposit to protect the landlord from any default on the part of the tenant.[15] There may be statutory limits on the amount of the deposit. Some states provide tenants with protections on these deposits. For example, the landlord may have to hold the deposits in a trust fund or be responsible for paying interest for the period the deposit is held. The landlord may be subject to a penalty if the money is used before the lease would allow for its use.

14. Protection from Retaliation

The URLTA and most state laws protect tenants from retaliation by the landlord for the tenants' exercise of their lawful rights or reporting the landlord for violations of housing and sanitation codes. The types of retaliation from which reporting tenants are protected include refusing to renew a lease and evicting the tenant.

15. Remedies of Landlord

If a tenant fails to pay rent, the landlord may bring an ordinary lawsuit to collect the amount due and in some states may seize and hold the property of the tenant.

(a) Landlord's Lien

In the absence of an agreement or a statute, the landlord does not have a lien on the personal property or crops of the tenant for money due for rent. The parties may create, by express or implied contract, a lien in favor of the landlord for rent and also for advances, taxes, or damages for failure to make repairs. In the absence of a statutory provision, the lien of the landlord is superior to the claims of all other persons except prior lienors and good-faith purchasers.

(b) Suit for Rent

Whether or not the landlord has a lien for unpaid rent, the landlord may collect rent from the tenant as specified in the lease. In some jurisdictions, the landlord is permitted to bring a combined action against the tenant to recover the possession of the land and the overdue rent at the same time.

(c) Recovery of Possession

A lease commonly provides that on the breach of any of its provisions by the tenant, such as the failure to pay rent, the lease terminates or the landlord may exercise the option to declare the lease terminated. When the lease is terminated for any reason, the landlord then has the right to evict the tenant and retake possession of the property.

Modern cases hold that a landlord cannot lock out a tenant for overdue rent. The landlord must employ legal process to regain possession even if the lease expressly gives the landlord the right to self-help.

The landlord may resort to legal process to evict the tenant to enforce the right to possession of the premises. Statutes in many states provide a summary remedy to recover possession that is much more efficient than the slow common law remedies. Often referred to as a **forcible entry and detainer,** this action restores the property to the landlord's possession unless the tenant complies with payment requirements.

(d) Landlord's Duty to Mitigate Damages

If the tenant leaves the premises before the expiration of the lease, is the landlord under any duty to rent the premises again to reduce the rent or damages for which the departing tenant will be liable? By common law and majority rule, a tenant owns an estate in land, and if the tenant abandons it, there is no duty on the landlord to find a new tenant for the premises. But a growing minority view places greater emphasis on the contractual aspects of a lease. Under this view, when the tenant abandons the property, thereby defaulting on the contract, the landlord has a duty to seek to mitigate the damages caused by the tenant's breach and make a reasonable effort to rent the abandoned property.

C. Liability for Injury on Premises

When the tenant, a member of the tenant's family, or a third person is injured because of the condition of the premises, the question of who is liable for the damages sustained by the injured person arises.

[15] URLTA § 2.101(a).

16. Landlord's Liability to Tenant

At common law, in the absence of a covenant to keep the premises in repair, the landlord was not liable for the tenant's personal injuries caused by the defective condition of the premises that, by the lease, are placed under the control of the tenant. Likewise, the landlord was not liable for the harm caused by an obvious condition that was known to the tenant at the time the lease was made.[16] However, recent cases have imposed liability on landlords for their failure to keep leased premises in repair, even when there is no covenant of repair.

ERRICO V LAMOUNTAIN, 713 A2D 791 (RI 1998)

PLEASE HELP ME, I'VE FALLEN

Kimberly Errico, a senior at Providence College, leased a three-bedroom apartment with two friends. The apartment was located on the second floor of a house owned by the LaMountains (defendants). Errico went out onto the balcony of the second-floor apartment and leaned on the railing to speak to a friend below. The railing collapsed and Errico fell 15 feet to the ground, sustaining head lacerations and multiple fractures, including a fractured pelvis. She filed suit against the LaMountains. The jury awarded Errico $100,000, and the LaMountains appealed.

Judicial Opinion

FLANDERS, Justice. . . . At common law a landlord was not liable for injuries sustained by a tenant or a guest on the leased premises unless the injuries resulted either from a latent defect known to the landlord but not to the tenant or from the landlord's breach of a covenant to repair in the lease. The defendants urge that their conduct in this case was "clearly governed" by this line of authority and that application of the common-law rule should have shielded them from any liability. They further claim that their lease agreement with Errico contained no express covenant to repair, that there was insufficient evidence of a defect in the balcony railing or, if the railing was defective, the defect was latent and they were unaware of any railing problem when they entered into the lease with Errico. For the reasons explained below, defendants' reliance on the common-law rule is misplaced because it no longer serves to immunize residential landlords from liability for their failure to put and keep the leased premises in a fit and habitable condition.

The defendants' duties to Errico were defined and governed by the act, which took effect on January 1, 1987, and applies to rental agreements for residential dwelling units entered into, extended, or renewed after that date. The LaMountains' 1989 lease with Errico was such a rental agreement. In passing the act the Legislature hoped to "[s]implify, clarify, modernize and revise the law governing the rental of dwelling units and the rights and obligations of landlords and tenants." Thus the act's intended and actual effect is to supersede any common-law rules relating to residential tenants and landlords in conflict with its provisions. Among those obligations that the act imposes on landlords is the duty to "[m]ake all repairs and do whatever is necessary to put and keep the premises in a fit and habitable condition." This duty, one of several set forth in the act as part of a landlord's ongoing responsibility to maintain the leased premises, is a continuing one, and the act does not provide that it ceases when the tenant takes possession of the leased premises.

We agree with the trial justice that the evidence introduced at trial was sufficient to justify a finding that the wooden railing had deteriorated "well, well before the events of the Fall of 1989." Testimony established that just after the accident the ends of the railing's wooden spindles appeared to be rotten at the very point where they became detached during Errico's fall. Photographs introduced at trial further substantiated the railing's visible deterioration. And the unobjected-to evidence that defendants replaced the entire railing with new wood several months after the accident (and then reinforced the new railing by installing metal corner brackets) was also corroborative of the railing's unfit condition at the time of the fall.

To buttress their position that the railing had not been defective and that in any event they made reasonable inspections thereof, defendants rely in part upon the trial testimony of Mrs. LaMountain. She testified that "every year" she inspected the balcony, making a visual and tactile check of the railing ("I would just give it a good shake and

[16] *Carey v Bradford*, 486 SE2d 623 (Ga App 1997).

test it"). She further testified that as a result of her inspection she believed the railing to be "perfectly safe." However, we note that the trial justice concluded that Mrs. LaMountain "was not a credible witness" and that "[h]er testimony in particular about her inspections and testing of the porch rail were not credible." The defendants also point to the testimony of Mr. LaMountain, whom the trial justice acknowledged was a "somewhat more credible" witness than his wife. He had inspected the railing during the course of painting it. Indeed he said he had given it a "good hard brush." But Mr. LaMountain, who knew the house was sixty years old when he purchased it, only painted the railing twice while he owned the structure, never leaned against it to test a person's weight, and never had the toe rail checked by a carpenter before the accident. We conclude that the observable evidence of the railing's physical deterioration, in conjunction with defendants' admission that they had inspected the railing at various times before the accident occurred, supports the conclusion of the jury and the trial justice that the railing was structurally unsound when Errico fell and that defendants either knew of this condition or failed to inspect the railing properly to detect this structural problem, thereby breaching their statutory duty to Errico.

Questions

1. Describe the tenant's injuries and how she was injured.
2. What is the rule of law on the landlord's liability once the tenant takes possession of the property?
3. Is the landlord liable for the tenant's injuries and resulting damages?

SPORTS & ENTERTAINMENT LAW

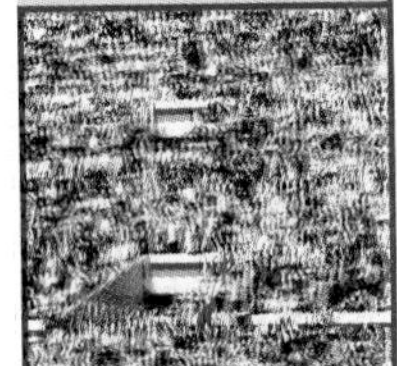

THE QUARTER PIPE 360 LIABILITY ISSUE

Timothy Lucier, two days shy of his thirteenth birthday, went with his father and several of his friends to Impact (a commercial skate park located in East Providence, Rhode Island) to skateboard to celebrate his birthday. At the skate park, Timothy's father signed the waiver that was required of all who used the park. Timothy donned a helmet, kneepads, and elbow pads, and then he and his friends used the skate park half pipes and quarter pipes. At one point, Timothy climbed on top of the quarter pipe, and as he pushed forward to go down the ramp, the front wheel of his skateboard caught inside a "nub" or "little tiny hole" in the ramp, causing the tail of his skateboard to swing around in a clockwise direction. Timothy twisted off the skateboard and fell on his right leg causing a spiral fracture in his right leg. Timothy said that after he fell, he looked back at the ramp and saw that there was a split in the wood covering the ramp.

Timothy's parents filed suit against Impact Recreation, Ltd., the operator of the skateboard facility, and Eugene Voll, Impact's landlord. They alleged that there had been a failure by the landlord to ensure that the commercial tenant was not engaging in an activity that was inherently dangerous to the public at large.

Voll required Impact to have insurance, obtain signed waivers from all participants, and obtain his approval prior to the installation of any equipment. Do you believe the landlord is liable to the Luciers? Why or why not? [Lucier v Impact Recreation, Ltd., 864 A2d 635 (RI 2005)]

(a) Crimes of Third Persons

Ordinarily, the landlord is not liable to the tenant for crimes committed on the premises by third persons, such as when a third person enters the premises and commits larceny or murder. The landlord is not required to establish a security system to protect the tenant from crimes of third persons.

In contrast, when the criminal acts of third persons are reasonably foreseeable, the landlord may be held liable for the harm caused a tenant. **For Example,** when a tenant has repeatedly reported that the deadbolt on the apartment door is broken, the landlord is liable for the tenant's loss when a thief enters through the door because such criminal conduct was foreseeable. Likewise, when the landlord of a large apartment complex does not take reasonable steps to prevent repeated criminal acts, the landlord is liable to the tenant for the harm caused by the foreseeable criminal act of a third person.[17]

SHARON P. V ARMAN, LTD., 989 P2D 121 (CAL 1999) *CERT DEN* 530 US 1243

THE LIGHTS WERE OUT, THE SECURITY CAMERAS WERE DOWN, AND CRIME WAS UP

Sharon P. (plaintiff) was an employee at a business located in the Coast Savings building located at 1180 South Beverly Drive, Los Angeles. On Thursday, April 8, 1993, Sharon P. entered the underground parking garage of the building at 11:00 a.m. and parked in her assigned space. While she was leaning back into her car to remove some items from her back seat, a man with a gun who was wearing a ski mask approached her. She was forced back into her car and sexually assaulted.

In the months preceding her attack, the condition of the parking garage had deteriorated. Lights were out (the lights were out in the immediate area of her attack that day), areas of the garage smelled of urine, and security cameras in the garage had not worked for months. In some places, there were cots set up where apparently the homeless had moved into the garage.

Sharon P. brought suit against Arman, Ltd. (defendant), the owner of the building and garage, and APCOA (defendant), the manager of the parking garage. APCOA's responsibilities were collection of revenues from those using the garage. The trial court entered summary judgment for Arman and APCOA. Sharon P. appealed. The Court of Appeal reversed, but then vacated its decision and remanded the case for a jury determination on causation. The parties appealed the remand to the California Supreme Court.

Judicial Opinion

BAXTER, J. . . . The critical issue in this case is whether a sexual assault by a third party in the tenant garage was sufficiently foreseeable to support a requirement that defendants secure that area against such crime.

Plaintiff contends that, because underground commercial parking structures are inherently dangerous, they carry with them a higher foreseeability of violent criminal attacks with a corresponding obligation to provide more than just minimal security measures. Although plaintiff claims she "is not asking for security guards," she asserts that requiring security guards "is justified, should the court so find." Second, she argues that, even if the hiring of security guards was not required, the violent attack upon her was sufficiently foreseeable—due to the inherently dangerous nature of the parking garage, the prior bank robberies elsewhere on the premises and the statistical crime rate of the surrounding area—to impose upon defendants a minimal duty of protection. In plaintiff's words, "[s]imple things like a clean, brightly lit garage, with working security cameras, and periodic walk throughs [by existing personnel], all give the appearance that someone cares about this garage and sends a message to any potential criminal to go elsewhere."

By now it is well established that landowners must maintain their premises in a reasonably safe condition, and that in the case of a landlord, the general duty of maintenance includes "the duty to take reasonable steps to secure common areas against foreseeable criminal acts of third parties that are likely to occur in the absence of such precautionary measures."

To resolve whether the sexual attack upon plaintiff was sufficiently foreseeable to require the hiring of security guards, we consider first *Ann M.* 863 P2d 307. In *Ann M.*, the plaintiff was raped while working at a photo store in a secluded area of the defendants' shopping center. In opposition to the defendants' motion for summary judgment, the plaintiff presented evidence that, in the year

[17] *Harrison v Housing Resources Management, Inc.*, 588 So 2d 64 (Fla App 1991).

preceding the attack, violent crimes had occurred in the census tract in which the shopping center was located. Transients loitering in the common areas had caused tenants and employees of the shopping center to be concerned about their safety. There also was evidence that the defendants failed to provide security patrols despite a request by the merchants' association and that assaults, purse snatchings and bank robberies may have occurred in the shopping center.

Emphasizing foreseeability as a "crucial factor" in determining the existence of duty, *Ann M.* determined that "a duty to take affirmative action to control the wrongful acts of a third party will be imposed only where such conduct can be reasonably anticipated."

Ann M. concluded that, in light of the vagueness of the obligation to provide patrols adequate to deter crime and the significant monetary and social costs that are implicated in imposing such an obligation, a "high degree of foreseeability" is required in order to find that the scope of a landowner's duty of care includes the hiring of security guards to protect against violent crime by third parties. *Ann M.* cautioned that the requisite degree of foreseeability "rarely, if ever, can be proven in the absence of prior similar incidents of violent crime on the landowner's premises." "To hold otherwise," *Ann M.* emphasized, "would be to impose an unfair burden upon landlords and, in effect, would force landlords to become the insurers of public safety, contrary to well-established policy in this state."

Upon careful deliberation, we reject the view that underground parking structures are "so inherently dangerous that, even in the absence of prior similar incidents, providing security guards will fall within the scope of a landowner's duty of care." Several considerations factor into our decision.

First, we are not directed to any evidence or authorities from which we might confidently conclude that all underground parking structures, regardless of their individual physical characteristics and locations, are prone to violence and therefore are inherently dangerous in nature. Moreover, a survey of the decisions cited to us by the parties and *amici curiae* indicates that aboveground commercial and residential buildings are just as prone to violent sex crimes by unknown third parties. In the absence of solid support for the categorical conclusion that all parking garages are inherently dangerous, and are distinctly so in comparison to other types of premises, we are reluctant to single out garage owners for imposition of the substantial monetary and social costs associated with the hiring of security guards.

The mere fact that a crime has occurred almost always allows one to draw the conclusion, after the fact, that the premises were inherently dangerous. Moreover, any duty premised on the idea that the business attracts crime ignores the fact that many such businesses are economically viable precisely because they do not require any on-site labor. Once proprietors are forced to provide security guards at all-night laundromats or at bank teller machines, those operations cease to become profitable. "It serves no one to impose a duty which, rather than protecting customers, forces the businesses which they frequent to close." Were we to find that the occurrence of violent crime in commercial underground parking structures is highly foreseeable as a matter of law, we would be opening the door to virtually limitless litigation over what other types of property could also be characterized as "inherently dangerous."

Finally, adoption of the view that violent crime in underground parking structures is highly foreseeable as a matter of law would lead to incongruous results. In the present case, for instance, the record reflects that the underground tenant garage had no reported incidents of crime for 10 years prior to the assault upon plaintiff. The only evidence of prior criminal acts on the premises consisted of the seven bank robberies on the street level of the office building located above the parking structure. As already discussed, application of *Ann M.'s* analysis to this record leads to the conclusion that defendants' duty of care did not include the hiring of security guards for the garage because the bank robberies were not sufficiently similar to the sexual assault crime to establish a high degree of foreseeability. Nor would such a duty be found if the assault on plaintiff had occurred in other areas of the office building instead of the garage (e.g., in a common hallway or at plaintiff's place of business).

In *Ann M.*, we reaffirmed our commitment to the principle that the scope of a landowner's duty to provide protection against third party crime is determined in part by balancing the foreseeability of the harm against the burden to be imposed.

Viewing the record in the light most favorable to plaintiff, it shows that robbers repeatedly targeted a bank on the ground floor of the subject premises in the 27-month period preceding the sexual assault. Apart from those incidents, there is no evidence of other prior crimes against property or persons on the premises, either in the office building or in the underground parking garage. Since sexual assault is not a reasonably foreseeable risk associated with bank robberies (see *People v Nguyen* (1993) 21 Cal.App.4th 518, 533, 26 Cal.Rptr.2d 323 [observing that rapes consummated during the robbery of a bank appear to be a rarity]), the bank robberies did not portend the vicious assault committed upon plaintiff.

Finally, the police department records of crimes occurring in the 50 square blocks surrounding the parking garage do not aid plaintiff's case.

It is difficult to quarrel with the abstract proposition that the provision of improved lighting and maintenance, operational surveillance cameras and periodic walk-throughs of the tenant garage owned and operated by defendants might have diminished the risk of criminal attacks occurring in the garage. But absent any prior similar incidents or other indications of a reasonably foreseeable risk of violent criminal assaults in that location, we cannot conclude defendants were required to secure the area against such crime.

The contrary judgment of the Court of Appeal is reversed and the matter is remanded to that court with directions to enter judgment in favor of defendants.

Questions

1. What is the relevance of crime in the area and the types of crime on the property?
2. Are parking garages inherently dangerous?
3. Was Sharon P.'s assault foreseeable?
4. Who is liable to Sharon P.?

(b) Limitation of Liability

A provision in a lease excusing or exonerating the landlord from liability is generally valid regardless of the cause of the tenant's loss. A number of courts, however, have restricted the landlord's power to limit liability in the case of residential, as distinguished from commercial, leasing. A provision in a residential lease excusing a landlord from liability for damage caused by water, snow, or ice is void.

Third persons on the premises, even with the consent of the tenant, are generally not bound by a clause exonerating the landlord. Such third persons may generally recover from the landlord when they sustain injuries.

(c) Indemnification of Landlord

The modern lease commonly contains a provision declaring that the tenant will indemnify the landlord for any liability of the landlord to a third person that arises from the tenant's use of the rented premises.

17. Landlord's Liability to Third Persons

A landlord is ordinarily not liable to third persons injured because of the condition of any part of the rented premises that is in the possession of a tenant by virtue of a lease. If the landlord retains control over a portion of the premises, such as hallways or stairways, however, a landlord's liability exists for injuries to third persons caused by failure to exercise proper care in connection with that part of the premises. Most courts impose liability on the landlord for harm caused to a third person when the landlord was obligated, under a contract with the tenant, to correct the condition that caused the harm or to keep the premises in repair.

CPA 18. Tenant's Liability to Third Persons

A tenant in possession has control of the property and is liable when his or her failure to use due care under the circumstances causes harm to (1) licensees, such as a person allowed to use a telephone, and (2) invitees, such as customers entering a store. For both classes, the liability is the same as that of an owner in possession of property. It is likewise immaterial whether the property is used for residential or business purposes.

The liability of the tenant to third persons is not affected by the fact that the landlord may have contracted in the lease to make repairs that, if made, would have avoided the injury. The tenant can be protected, however, in the same manner that the landlord can be protected: by procuring liability insurance for indemnity against loss from claims of third persons.

D. Transfer of Rights

Both the landlord and the tenant have property and contract rights with respect to the lease. Can they be transferred or assigned?

19. Transfer of Landlord's Reversionary Interest

The **reversionary interest** of the landlord may be transferred voluntarily by the landlord or involuntarily by a **judicial** or an **execution sale.** The tenant then becomes the tenant of the new owner of the reversionary interest, and the new owner is bound by the terms of the lease.

CPA 20. Tenant's Assignment of Lease and Sublease

An **assignment** of a lease is a transfer by the tenant of the tenant's entire interest in the premises to a third person. A tenancy for years may be assigned by the tenant unless the tenant is restricted from making such an assignment by the terms of the lease or by a statute. A **sublease** is a transfer to a third person, the *sublessee*, of less than the tenant's entire interest, or full lease term.

(a) Limitations on Rights

The lease may contain provisions denying or limiting the right to assign or sublet. Such restrictions protect the landlord from new tenants who might damage the property or be financially irresponsible.

Restrictions in the lease are construed liberally in favor of the tenant. No violation of a provision prohibiting assignment or subleasing occurs when the tenant merely permits someone else to use the premises.

(b) Effect of Assignment or Sublease

An assignee or a sublessee has no greater rights than the original lessee.[18] An assignee becomes bound by the obligations of the lease by the act of taking possession of the premises.

Neither the act of subletting nor the landlord's agreement to it releases the original tenant from liability under the terms of the original lease. When a lease is assigned, the original tenant remains liable for the rent that becomes due thereafter.

The tenant should require the sublessee to perform all obligations under the original lease and to indemnify the tenant for any loss caused if the sublessee defaults. Such liability on the part of the sublessee requires an express covenant. The fact that the sublease is made "subject to" the terms of the original lease merely recognizes the superiority of the original lease but does not impose any duty on the sublessee to perform the tenant's obligation under the original lease. If the sublessee promises to assume the obligations of the original lease, the landlord, as a third-party beneficiary, may recover from the sublessee for breach of the provisions of the original lease.

LAWFLIX

Barefoot in the Park (1967) (PG)

The movie is a study about Manhattan newlyweds in which you can see many issues about habitability and constructive eviction. Discuss the options the couple has for remedies.

For movie clips that illustrate business law concepts, see LawFlix at **http://wdvl.westbuslaw.com.**

[18] *Gulden v Newberry Wrecker Service, Inc.*, 267 SE2d 763 (Ga App 1980).

Summary

The agreement between a lessor and a lessee by which the latter holds possession of real property owned by the former is a lease. Statutes in many states prohibit discrimination by an owner who rents property. Statutes in some states require that the lease not be unconscionable. Tenancies are classified according to duration as tenancies for years, from year to year, at will, and at sufferance.

A lease is generally not terminated by the death, insanity, or bankruptcy of either party except for a tenancy at will. Leases are usually terminated by the expiration of the specified term, notice, surrender, forfeiture, or destruction of the property or because of fraud. A tenant has the right to acquire possession at the beginning of the lease and has the right to retain possession until the lease is ended. Evictions may be either actual or constructive. The tenant is under a duty to pay rent as compensation to the landlord.

An assignment of a lease by the tenant is a transfer of the tenant's entire interest in the property to a third person; a sublease is a transfer of less than an entire interest—in either space or time. A lease may prohibit both an assignment and a sublease. If the lease is assigned, the assignee is liable to the landlord for the rent. Such an assignment, however, does not discharge the tenant from the duty to pay rent. In a sublease, the sublessee is not liable to the original lessor for rent unless that liability has been assumed or is imposed by statute.

The tenant need not make repairs to the premises, absent an agreement to the contrary. A warranty of habitability was not implied at common law, but most states now reject this view and imply in residential leases a warranty that the premises are fit for habitation.

A landlord is usually liable to the tenant only for injuries caused by latent defects or by defects that are not apparent but of which the landlord had knowledge. The landlord is not liable to the tenant for crimes of third persons unless they are reasonably foreseeable.

Questions and Case Problems

1. Johnny C. Carpenter and Harvey E. Hill died of asphyxiation when a fire broke out in their Hattiesburg, Mississippi, apartment on the morning of February 20, 1983. There were no smoke detectors in the apartment at the time of the fire, as required under Hattiesburg City Ordinance 2021. The administrators of the estates of Carpenter and Hill filed suit against London, Stetelman, and Kirkwood, the owners and managers of the apartment complex. Who is liable? [*Hill v London, Stetelman, and Kirkwood, Inc.*, 906 F2d 204 (5th Cir)]
2. King leased a single dwelling to Moorehead. King brought an action against Moorehead to recover the premises because of nonpayment of rent and to collect the unpaid rent. Moorehead raised the defense that the house was not habitable and that it violated the housing code. Is this defense valid? Explain. [*King v Moorehead*, 495 SW2d 65 (Mo App)]
3. Rod had a five-year lease in a building owned by Darwood and had agreed to pay $800 a month rent. After two years, Rod assigned his rights under the lease to Kelly. Kelly moved in and paid the rent for a year and then, owing two months' rent, moved out without Darwood's knowledge or consent. Darwood demanded that Rod pay him the past-due rent. Must Rod do so? Why or why not?
4. Sue A. Merrill injured her right shoulder when she fell as she was ascending the front steps leading to the porch and front door of the mobile home that her daughter, Sherri Pritchard, rented from Alvina Jansma. The step became loose during the time Ms. Pritchard rented the home. Prior to the fall, Ms. Pritchard attempted to repair the step by securing it with nails. When that failed, she informed the manager of the property that the step was loose. The manager suggested Ms. Pritchard try using screws to secure the step. Ms. Pritchard told the manager she did not have a screw gun. The manager had one and said she would screw the step into place. Subsequently, and without Ms. Pritchard's knowledge, the manager attempted to repair the step. Apparently, that effort was unsuccessful and Ms. Merrill fell when the step separated from the porch as she stepped on it. Ms. Merrill filed a negligence claim against Ms. Jansma to recover for her medical expenses, lost wages, and damages for emotional distress and pain and suffering. Could Ms. Merrill recover? [*Merrill v Jansma*, 86 P3d 270 (Wyo 2004)]
5. Alexis Gale was shot and killed while working in the rented business offices of her employer, Mon Ami International. Gale's husband sued the property owners and managers of the office complex where Mon Ami's rented offices were located, claiming the landlord breached a duty to provide adequate security at the complex. The lease provided that the landlord would provide security services in the common areas of the complex and that the lessee was given exclusive control of the portion of the premises rented as office space. Gale was shot and killed by a coworker, not in a common area over which the landlord had control but in the Mon Ami office space over which the lessee had exclusive control and in which the landlord had no duty to provide security. Gale's husband also alleged that the landlord knew an attack was about to take place because of some strange happenings that had taken place earlier that day. That morning, a maintenance worker noticed a man opening the back door of the Mon Ami office from the inside. This man appeared to be acting strangely: he took a handkerchief out of his suit pocket and picked up a briefcase sitting outside the door. He was wearing what the worker described as a costume-type wig on his head but looked vaguely familiar. Later that day, Gale's body was discovered. The maintenance worker reported what he had seen to the landlord and to the police. It was eventually determined that this was the coworker who had shot Gale, and it was also determined that the landlord knew of numerous arguments between Gale and the coworker. Gale's spouse alleged that the landlord had a duty to prevent the shooting. Did such a duty exist? [*Gale v North Meadow Associates*, 466 SE2d 648 (Ga App)]
6. On June 21, 1997, Julio Ramos was helping his cousin move out of a second-floor apartment. He positioned

himself on the outer side of the second-floor balcony railing, his feet between its spindles, to pass furniture to a friend on the ground below. While perched in this precarious position, Ramos held onto the railing with one hand and used his other hand to move the furniture. The reason for this method of removing the furniture was that many pieces were too large to be taken down the stairs. After approximately an hour of moving furniture in this manner, Ramos heard some cracking and felt the railing giving way. He released the furniture and attempted to grab onto the railing with both hands, but the spindles broke, and Ramos fell to the ground.

Ramos brought suit against the landlord to recover for his injuries. How does this case differ from the *Errico* case? (See the *Errico* case in the chapter.) Should the landlord in this case be held liable? [*Ramos v Granajo*,822 A2d 936 (RI 2003)]

7. A tenant leased an apartment in which so much noise emanated from surrounding apartments late at night and in the wee hours of the morning that he could not get much sleep. The tenant brought suit against the landlord, alleging that the landlord had breached the implied warranty of habitability. Is the tenant correct? Can noise be a breach of the warranty of habitability? [*Nostrand Gardens Co-op v Howard*, 634 NYS2d 505]
8. Morgan, who rented an apartment in the Melrose Apartments, wanted Melrose to hire additional security guards to protect the lessees from possible crimes. Was Melrose required to do so when crimes by third persons were not reasonably foreseeable?
9. During the remodeling of an apartment building, tenants had so much dust from the construction settle in their apartment that they experienced damage to their expensive sound and recording equipment. They had rented the very specialized and large apartment because it was suitable to use as a recording studio. Would the presence of the dust be grounds for constructive eviction? Would it be a breach of the warranty of habitability? The construction workers wore masks during the time they were working on the building. [*Minjak Co. v Rudolph*, 528 NYS2d 554]
10. Cantanese leased a building for the operation of his drugstore from Saputa. He moved his drugstore from Saputa's building to another location but continued to pay rent to Saputa. Saputa, fearing that he was losing his tenant, entered the premises without Cantanese's permission and made extensive alterations to the premises to suit two physicians who had agreed to rent the premises from Saputa. Cantanese informed Saputa that he regarded the making of the unauthorized repairs as grounds for canceling the lease. Saputa then claimed that Cantanese was liable for the difference between the rent that Cantanese had agreed to pay and the rent that the doctors would pay for the remainder of the term of the Cantanese lease. Was Cantanese liable for such rent? [*Saputa v Cantanese*, 182 So 2d 826 (La App)]
11. Sargent rented a second-floor apartment in a building owned by Ross. Anna, Sargent's four-year-old daughter, fell from an outdoor stairway and was killed. Suit was brought against Ross for her death. Ross contended that she did not have control over the stairway and therefore was not liable for its condition. Was this defense valid? [*Sargent v Ross*,308 A2d 528 (NH)]
12. Charles leased a house from Donald for four years. The rent agreed on was $850 per month. After two years, Charles assigned his rights under the lease to Smith, who moved in and paid rent regularly for a year. Owing rent, Smith moved out sometime later without Donald's knowledge or consent. Donald demanded that Charles pay the rent. Is Charles liable?
13. Green rented an apartment from Stockton Realty. The three-story building had a washroom and clothesline on the roof for use by the tenants. The clothesline ran very near the skylight, and there was no guard rail between the clothesline and the skylight. Green's friend, who was 14 years old, was helping Green remove clothes from the line when she tripped on an object and fell against the skylight. The glass was too weak to support her weight, and she fell to the floor below, sustaining serious injuries. Is the landlord responsible for damages for the injury sustained? Decide. [*Reiman v Moore*, 180 P2d 452 (Cal)]
14. Suzanne Andres was injured when she fell from the balcony of her second-floor apartment in the Roswell-Windsor Village Apartments. Andres was leaning against the railing on the balcony when it gave out, and she and the railing fell to the ground. Andres filed suit against Roswell-Windsor for its failure to maintain the railing. Roswell-Windsor maintains that the railing was not in a common area and was in Andres's exclusive possession and that she was responsible for its maintenance or at least letting the manager know the railing needed repairs. Should Andres recover from the landlord for her injuries? [*Andres v Roswell-Windsor Village Apartments*, 777 F2d 671 (11th Cir)]
15. Williams, an elderly man who was sensitive to heat, rented an apartment in the Parker House. His apartment was fully air-conditioned, which enabled him to stand the otherwise unbearable heat of the summer. The landlord was dissatisfied with the current rent, and although the lease had a year to run, insisted that Williams agree to an increase. Williams refused. The landlord attempted to force Williams to pay the increase by turning off the electricity and thereby stopping the apartment's air conditioners. He also sent up heat on the hot days. After one week of such treatment, Williams, claiming that he had been evicted, moved out. Has there been an eviction? Explain.

CPA Questions

1. Which of the following provisions must be included to have an enforceable written residential lease?

	A Description of the Leased Premises	*A Due Date for the Payment of Rent*
a.	Yes	Yes
b.	Yes	No
c.	No	Yes
d.	No	No

2. Bronson is a residential tenant with a 10-year written lease. In the absence of specific provisions in the lease to the contrary, which of the following statements is correct?

   a. The premises may not be sublet for less than the full remaining term.
   b. Bronson may not assign the lease.
   c. The landlord's death will automatically terminate the lease.
   d. Bronson's purchase of the property will terminate the lease.

3. Which of the following provisions must be included in a residential lease agreement?

   a. A description of the leased premises.
   b. The due date for payment of rent.
   c. A requirement that the tenant have public liability insurance.
   d. A requirement that the landlord will perform all structural repairs to the property.

DECEDENTS' ESTATES AND TRUSTS

CHAPTER (52)

LEARNING OBJECTIVES

After studying this chapter, you should be able to

LO.1 Define *testamentary capacity* and *testamentary intent*

LO.2 Distinguish among signing, attesting, and publishing a will

LO.3 Explain how a will may be modified or revoked

LO.4 Describe briefly the probate and contest of a will

LO.5 Describe the ordinary pattern of distribution by intestacy

LO.6 Explain the nature of a trust

What happens to your property after you die? Public policy dictates that your debts be settled, that property owned at the time of your death be applied to the payment of estate administration expenses and your debts, and that any remainder be distributed among those entitled to receive it.

The law of decedents' estates is governed by state statutes and court decisions. The general principles and the procedures discussed in this chapter may be considered typical, but state variations exist. The American Bar Association and the National Conference of Commissioners on Uniform State Law have taken a step toward national uniformity by approving a **Uniform Probate Code (UPC)** and submitting it to the states for adoption.[1]

A. Wills

If a **decedent** made a valid will, described as having died **testate,** the will determines which persons are entitled to receive the estate property following payment of obligations. If the decedent did not make a valid will, laws for **intestate distribution** determine the distribution.

1. Definitions

Testate distribution describes the distribution that is made when the decedent leaves a valid will. A **will** is ordinarily a writing that provides for a distribution of property upon death but that confers no rights prior to that time. A man who makes a will is called a **testator;** a woman, a **testatrix.**

A gift of personal property by will is a **legacy** or **bequest,** in which case the beneficiary may also be called a **legatee.** A gift of real property by will is a **devise,** and the beneficiary may be called a **devisee.**

2. Parties to Will

Each state has variations on the qualifications of persons who wish to make a will. The following requirements are typical.

(a) Testator

Generally, the right to make a will is limited to persons 18 or older. The testator must have **testamentary capacity,**[2] which means that a person must have sufficient mental capacity to understand that the writing that is being executed is a will—that is, that it disposes of the person's property after death. The testator must also have a reasonable appreciation of the identity of relatives and friends and of the nature and extent of the property that may exist at death.

The excessive and continued use of alcohol or multiple medications, producing mental deterioration, may be sufficient to justify the conclusion that the decedent lacked testamentary capacity.

[1] The Uniform Probate Code has been adopted in Alaska, Arizona, Colorado, Florida, Hawaii, Idaho, Maine, Michigan, Minnesota, Montana, Nebraska, New Mexico, North Dakota, South Carolina, South Dakota, and Utah. Twenty other states have adopted portions of the UPC: Arkansas, California, Georgia, Illinois, Indiana, Kansas, Kentucky, Maryland, Missouri, New Jersey, Ohio, Oklahoma, Oregon, Pennsylvania, Texas, Virginia, Washington, West Virginia, Wisconsin, and Wyoming. The predominant form of the UPC continues to be the 1969 version, but the 1990 version is gaining in popularity, with some states adopting various sections from it and integrating it with the 1969 version.

[2] *In re Estate of Herbert,* 935 P2d 130 (Hawaii 1997).

BRACEWELL V BRACEWELL, 20 SW2D 14 (TEX APP 2000)

THE WILL OF THE WALKING WOUNDED: WHEN DOES ILLNESS EQUAL INCAPACITY?

Irene Bracewell was married to W. T. Bracewell and they had a son, Charles. Although Irene loved both her husband and her son, it was clear to everyone that her husband and her son did not get along. Often, Irene did not get along with W. T., and she spent a great deal of time living on Charles's ranch. Charles had named a lake on his property Lake Irene and paid considerable attention to his mother when she lived with him. Irene suffered from Parkinson's disease, hypertension, hyperthyroidism, anxiety, and degenerative bone disease. She had a long list of medications including tranquilizers. Irene and W. T. executed wills in 1975 that left their property to each other. In 1989, while living with Charles, Irene was taking so much medication that doctors said she suffered from dementia, delusions, hallucinations, paranoia, and incoherence. Charles took her to have a new will executed that left all of her property to him. When she died in 1995, W. T. wanted the 1975 will probated because he said Irene lacked capacity to make the 1989 will valid. The probate court refused to admit the 1989 will and Charles appealed.

Judicial Opinion

FOWLER, Justice.... As proponent of the 1989 will, Charles had the burden to show that Irene had the requisite testamentary capacity on the day that she signed it.

The Texas Probate Code requires proof that the will's testator had a "sound mind" before probate will be allowed. Courts in Texas have defined the term "sound mind" to mean "testamentary capacity." Thus, to form a valid will, in Texas, the testatrix must have had "testamentary capacity" when the will was executed. Testamentary capacity has been defined by Texas courts to mean "sufficient mental ability, at the time of the execution of the will, to understand the business in which the testatrix is engaged, the effect of her act in making the will, and the general nature and extent of her property." The testatrix must also know her next of kin and the natural objects of her bounty, and she must have "sufficient memory to assimilate the elements of the business to be transacted, to hold those elements long enough to perceive their obvious relation to each other, and to form a reasonable judgment as to them."

In his brief, W. T. contends that the trial record shows that Irene lacked testamentary capacity on the day the 1989 will was executed. At trial, W. T. testified that Irene was hospitalized in 1984. According to W. T., Irene was "sick a lot" from that time on, and that she was a different woman. W. T. stated that, following her diagnosis with Parkinson's Disease, Irene quit driving a car, quit going to church, and "didn't want no company." W. T. concluded that, in 1989, "Irene was in pretty bad shape."

Bobbie Bracewell Rigby

W. T. and Irene's daughter, Bobbie Bracewell Rigby, testified on W. T.'s behalf. According to Bobbie, Irene's health "got bad in 1984." She added that, although Irene had been a devout woman previously, her mother quit going to church because of her condition. Bobbie stated further that, after 1984, Irene socialized with other people less frequently. Bobbie reported that, during 1987, and most of 1988, she visited Irene every day so that she could bathe her mother, brush her teeth, and fix her hair. Bobbie added that Irene "acted like a little child" while her daughter brushed her teeth for her. During the summer of 1989, Bobbie and her husband traveled to Pennsylvania to pursue his work in the oil pipeline industry. Bobbie noted that she "didn't think" that Irene was "of sound mind" during the 1989 time period "because the way she was about church and everything." In 1991, Bobbie wrote a letter to Charles and expressed her concern that something was wrong with Irene, who did not appear to realize that Bobbie had moved away.

Dr. Luke Scamardo is a physician specializing in internal medicine at the Navasota Medical Center in Navasota, Texas. Dr. Scamardo treated Irene from November of 1980, until her death in 1995, for a number of ailments, including Parkinson's Disease, hypothyroidism, anxiety, and degenerative joint disease. Dr. Scamardo noted that Irene was taking "multiple medication[s]" for these maladies. Dr. Scamardo testified that he prescribed the "minor tranquilizer" Librium to treat Irene's anxiety and, later, Diazepam, which is a relative of Valium. In addition, Dr. Scamardo prescribed Sinequan, which he described as a "major tranquilizer," for Irene's anxiety. Dr. Scamardo also prescribed Valium to treat Irene's anxiety disorder. During the course of her treatment for anxiety, Irene was also taking pain killers for degenerative joint disease in addition to thyroid medication. After she was diagnosed with Parkinson's Disease, Dr. Scamardo prescribed Sinemet and a number of other medications to treat symptoms related to that condition.

Dr. Scamardo testified that he was informed by Charles, in 1987, that Irene was experiencing "periods of incoherence" at home. Dr. Scamardo added that Irene's family had to supply information for her when she came in for treatment because she was incoherent "ninety-nine percent" of the time. Medical records admitted at trial show that, in May of 1987, Irene was admitted to the hospital for problems related to Parkinson's Disease, degenerative joint disease, and dehydration.

Dr. Scamardo testified that, in his opinion, Irene would not have had testamentary capacity on the day she executed the 1989 will.

Dr. Gary Newsome

In 1992, Dr. Scamardo referred Irene to Dr. Gary Newsome. Dr. Newsome is a medical doctor and a licensed psychiatrist at the Columbia Hospital in Bryan, Texas, where he is certified in "Geriatric Psychiatry." Dr. Newsome first examined Irene on April 14, 1992. Dr. Newsome testified that, on that date, Irene was "extremely confused," and suffering from "delirium." Dr. Newsome described Irene's "confused state" as both "acute" and "chronic." Dr. Newsome added that Parkinson's Disease causes a "degeneration of the brain" which affects patients' ability to "think clearly and put their proper processes together and be able to function, even in the most simple way."

In Dr. Newsome's opinion, Irene's lack of competency wasn't even a "close" question. Dr. Newsome added that, given the medications described in the Clouser Pharmacy records, he was "not sure if [he] would know what planet [he] was on if [he] took these medicines." Dr. Newsome commented further that Irene's decision to lock herself in the bathroom for the purpose of executing her will could be considered an indication of the level of her paranoia at the time. Dr. Newsome also noted that Irene's decision to leave the bulk of her estate to Charles showed that she was unaware of her "bounty" and unaware that she had any children "other than Charles Bracewell."

Charles complains that the testimony presented by Drs. Scamardo and Newsome is "no evidence to support a finding that Irene lacked testamentary capacity on the day she executed the will" because each concedes that he did not examine Irene on August 17, 1989.

We disagree with Charles that Dr. Scamardo and Dr. Newsome's testimony was no evidence of incapacity. In fact, we find their testimony the most compelling. This constitutes some evidence, in conjunction with the medical testimony, from which the jury could have logically inferred that Irene lacked testamentary capacity to execute a will on August 17, 1989.

In conclusion, we overrule the issue challenging the jury's finding that Irene lacked testamentary capacity to execute a valid will on August 17, 1989. We also overrule the issue regarding the trial court's decision to grant W. T.'s application to probate the 1975 will.

Questions

1. Describe the two wills and their intended beneficiaries.
2. What do the doctors believe caused the lack of testamentary capacity?
3. If Irene lacked capacity to make the 1989 will, and the court has refused the probate of the 1975 will, what happens to Irene's property?

(b) Beneficiary

Generally, the capacity of the **beneficiary** is not an issue. However, when part of a decedent's estate passes to a minor, a guardian may be appointed to administer that interest for the minor. If a will directs that any share payable to a minor be held by a particular person as trustee for the minor, the minor's interest will be so held, and a guardian is not required. Statutes often provide that if the estate or interest of the minor is not large, it may be paid directly to the minor or to the parent or person by whom the minor is maintained.

3. Testamentary Intent

There cannot be a will unless the testator manifests an intention to make a provision that will be effective only upon death. This is called **testamentary intent.**[3] Ordinarily, this is an intention that certain persons become the owners of certain property upon the death of the testator. However, a writing also manifests a testamentary intent when the testator designates an executor only and does not make any disposition of property.

[3] *Burns v Adamson*, 854 SW2d 723 (Ark 1993).

4. Form

Because the privilege of disposing of property by will is purely statutory, the will must be executed in the manner required by state statutes. Unless statutory requirements are met, the will is invalid, and the testator is considered to have died intestate. In such a case, the decedent's property will be distributed according to the laws of intestacy of the particular state.

(a) Writing

Ordinarily, a will must be in writing. Some state statutes, however, permit oral wills in limited circumstances, and the use of videotaped wills is gaining some legal ground.

(b) Signature

A written will must be signed by the testator. In case of physical incapacity, the testator may be assisted in signing the will. Witnesses to the will can then verify that simple marks were indeed made by the testator while experiencing a physically debilitating condition.

Generally, a will must be signed at the bottom or end. The purpose of this requirement is to prevent unscrupulous persons from taking a will that has been validly signed and writing or typing additional provisions in the space below the signature.

(c) Attestation

Attestation is the act of witnessing the execution of a will. Generally, it includes signing the will as a witness after a clause that recites that the witness has observed either the execution of the will or the testator's acknowledgment of the writing as the testator's will. This clause is commonly called an **attestation clause.** Statutes often require that attestation be made by the witnesses in the presence of the testator and in the presence of each other. Most states and the Uniform Probate Code (UPC) require two witnesses; a few states require three.

E-COMMERCE AND CYBERLAW

With technology, wills are no longer always just written but may be supplemented with electronic verification. The American Bar Association's Web site (**www.abanet.org**) offers the following thoughts on the new trend in video wills:

More and more people are preparing a video in which they read the will and explain why certain gifts were made and others not made. The video recording might also show the execution of the will. Should a disgruntled relative decide to challenge the will, the video can provide compelling proof that the person making the will was mentally competent and observed the formalities of execution.

Keep in mind that videos do not last forever and are subject to damage. You should consult a lawyer before making such a video to find out about your state's laws on video wills. Generally, such a video would supplement.

SPORTS & ENTERTAINMENT LAW

The following are provisions from the wills of famous people:

- Malcolm Forbes left $1,000 each to owners of nine New York restaurants, including Lutece, the Four Seasons, and Mortimer's; and $1,000 each to 30 motorcycle clubs.
- Bob Fosse left $25,000 to be divided among 66 friends including Dustin Hoffman, Lisa Minelli, and Neil Simon "to go out and have dinner on me."
- Cole Porter left his clothes to the Salvation Army.

SPORTS & ENTERTAINMENT LAW

continued

- Lillian Hellman gave her Toulouse-Lautrec poster to Mike Nichols.
- Jim Morrison left everything to his wife, who died three years later, so Morrison's estate went to his father-in-law.
- Alan Jay Lerner, among other bequests in his will, left $1,000 to two friends: "The purpose of this modest remembrance is to defray the cost of one evening's merriment to be devoted to cheerful recollections of their departed friend."
- Philip, fifth Earl of Pembroke, used his will to get back at a friend: "I give to the Lieutenant-General Cromwell one of my words...which he must want, seeing that he hath never kept any of his own."
- John Lennon's will disinherited anyone who contested it.
- Judy Garland left $250,000 to each child to be paid twice at ages 25 and 35, but the probate located only $40,000 in assets and $1,000,000 in debts.*

*Marianne M. Jennings, *Real Estate Law*, 7th ed. (Cincinnati, OH: Thomson, 2005). Reprinted with permission.

Self-proved wills are wills that eliminate some formalities of proof by being executed in the way set forth by statute. Self-proved wills are recognized in those states following the UPC. A will may be simultaneously executed, attested, and made self-proving by acknowledgment by the testator and by affidavits of the witnesses. The **acknowledgment** and **affidavits** must each be made before an officer authorized to administer oaths under the laws of the state in which execution occurs. They must be evidenced by the officer's certificate under official seal.

The self-proving provisions attached to the will are not a part of the will. The only purpose served by self-proving provisions is to admit a will to probate without requiring the testimony of the witnesses to the will. It was not the purpose of legislatures, on enacting the statute permitting self-proving wills, to amend or repeal the requirement that the will itself meet the requirements of the law. The execution of a valid will is a condition precedent to use of the self-proving provisions.

In some jurisdictions, a witness cannot be a beneficiary under the will. Use of a beneficiary as a witness will not affect the will, but the witness's share is limited to whatever would have been received if there had been no will. Under the UPC, a will or any provision therein is not invalid because the will is signed by an interested person.

(d) Date

There is generally no requirement that a testator must date a will, but it is advisable to do so. When there are several wills, the most recent prevails with respect to conflicting provisions.

5. Modification of Will

A will may be modified by executing a *codicil*, a separate writing that amends a will. The will, except as changed by the codicil, remains the same. The result is as though the testator rewrote the will, substituting the provisions of the codicil for those provisions of the will that are inconsistent with the codicil. A codicil must be executed with all the formality of a will and is treated in all other respects the same as a will.

A will cannot be modified merely by crossing out a clause and writing in what the testator wishes. Such an **interlineation** is not operative unless it is executed with the same formality required of a will or, in some states, unless the will is republished in its interlineated form.

6. Revocation of Will

At any time during the testator's life, the testator may **revoke** the will made or make changes in its terms. It may be revoked by act of the testator or by operation of law. A testator must have the same degree of mental capacity to revoke a will as is required to make one.

(a) Revocation by Act of Testator

A will or a codicil is revoked when the testator destroys, burns, or tears it or crosses out the provisions of the will or codicil with the intention to revoke them. The revocation may be in whole or in part.[4]

(b) Revocation by Operation of Law

In certain instances, statutes provide that a change of circumstances has the effect of a revocation. **For Example,** when a person marries after executing a will, the will is revoked or is presumed revoked unless it was made in contemplation of marriage or unless it provided for the future spouse. In some states, the revocation is not total but is effective only to the extent of allowing the spouse to take such share of the estate as that to which the spouse would have been entitled had there been no will.

The birth or adoption of a child after the execution of a will commonly works a revocation or partial revocation of the will as to that child. In the case of a partial revocation, the child is entitled to receive the same share as if the testator had died intestate.

The divorce of the testator does not in itself work a revocation. However, the majority of courts hold that if a property settlement is carried out on the basis of the divorce, a prior will of the testator is revoked, at least to the extent of the legacy given to the divorced spouse.

7. Election to Take against the Will

To protect the husband or wife of a testator, the surviving spouse may generally ignore the provisions of a will and elect to take against the will. In such a case, the surviving spouse receives the share of the estate he or she would have received had the testator died without leaving a will or receives a fractional share specified by statute.

The right to take against the will is generally barred by certain kinds of misconduct by the surviving spouse. If a spouse is guilty of desertion or nonsupport that would have justified the decedent's obtaining a divorce, the surviving spouse usually cannot elect to take against the will.

8. Disinheritance

With some exceptions, any person may be **disinherited** or excluded from sharing in the estate of a decedent.[5] A person who would inherit if there were no will is excluded from receiving any part of a decedent's estate if the decedent has left a will giving everything to other persons.

9. Special Types of Wills

In certain situations, special types of wills are used.

(a) Holographic Wills

A **holographic will** is an unwitnessed will that is written by the testator entirely by hand. In some states, no distinction is made between holographic and other wills. In other states, the general body of the law of wills applies, but certain variations are established. Some states require that a holographic will be dated. Under the UPC, a holographic will is valid, whether witnessed or not, if the signatures and the material provisions are in the handwriting of the testator.[6]

(b) Living Wills

Living wills are documents by which individuals may indicate that if they become unable to express their wishes and they are in an irreversible, incurable condition, they do not want life-sustaining medical treatments (see Figure 52-1). Living wills are legal in most states. Such personal wishes are entitled to constitutional protection as long as they are expressed clearly.

B. Administration of Decedents' Estates

A decedent's estate consists of the assets the decedent owned at death, and it must be determined who is entitled to receive that property. If the decedent owed debts, those debts must be paid first. After that, any balance is to be distributed according to the terms of the will or by the intestate law if the decedent did not leave a valid will.

10. Definitions

The decedent has the privilege of naming in the will the person who will administer the estate. A man named in a will to administer the estate of the decedent is an **executor;** a woman, an **executrix.** If the decedent failed to name an executor or

[4] *In re Estate of Foxley*, 568 NW2d 912 (Neb App 1997).

[5] One exception, for example, is a surviving spouse. A surviving spouse has marital property rights and cannot be disinherited completely.

[6] However, a photocopy of a holographic will may not be admitted to probate. *In re Estate of Foxley*, 575 NW2d 150 (Neb 1998).

FIGURE 52-1 Living Will

Living Will

INSTRUCTIONS:

This is an important legal document It sets forth your directions regarding medical treatment. You have the right to refuse treatment you do not want. You may make changes in any of these directions, or add to them, to conform them to your personal wishes.

I, John Jones, being of sound mind, make this statement as a directive to be followed if I become permanently unable to participate in decisions regarding my medical care. These instructions reflect my firm and settled commitment to decline medical treatment under the circumstances indicated below:

I direct my attending physician to withhold or withdraw treatment that serves only to prolong the process of my dying, if I should be in an incurable or irreversible mental or physical condition with no reasonable expectation of recovery.

These instructions apply if I am (a) in a terminal condition; (b) permanently unconscious; or (c) if I am conscious but have irreversible brain damage and will never regain the ability to make decisions and express my wishes.

I direct that treatment be limited to measures to keep me comfortable and to relieve pain, including any pain that might occur by withholding or withdrawing treatment.

While I understand that I am not legally required to be specific about future treatments, if I am in the condition(s) described above I feel especially strongly about the following forms of treatment:

I do not want cardiac resuscitation.
I do not want mechanical respiration.
I do not want tube feeding.
I do not want antibiotics.
I do want maximum pain relief.

Other directions (insert personal instructions): NONE

Sign and date here in the presence of two adult witnesses, who should also sign.

These directions express my legal right to refuse treatment, under the law of [name of state]. I intend my instructions to be carried out, unless I have rescinded them in a new writing or by clearly indicating that I have changed my mind.

Signed: John Jones

Witness: Earl Hummel

Address: 7852 Bailey Avenue
Buffalo, New York

Witness: Ramona Valey

Address: 8921 Clinton Street
Buffalo, New York

Keep the signed original with your personal papers at home. Give copies of the signed original to your doctor, family, lawyer, and others who might be involved in your care.

executrix or did not leave a will, the law permits another person, usually a close relative, to obtain the appointment of someone to wind up the estate. This person is an **administrator** or **administratrix.** Administrators and executors are referred to generally under the UPC as **personal representatives** of the decedents because they represent the decedents or stand in their place.

11. Probate of Will

Probate is the act by which the proper court or official accepts a will and declares that the instrument satisfies the statutory requirements as the will of the testator. Until a will is probated, it has no legal effect.

When witnesses have signed a will, generally they must appear and state that they saw the testator sign the will (unless the will is self-proving). If those witnesses cannot be found, have died, or are outside the jurisdiction, the will may be probated nevertheless. When no witnesses are required, it is customary to require two or more persons to identify the signature of the testator at the time of probate.

After the probate witnesses have made their statements under oath, the official or court will ordinarily admit the will to probate in the absence of any particular circumstances indicating that the writing should not be probated. A certificate or decree that officially declares that the will is the will of the testator and has been admitted to probate is then issued.

Any qualified person wishing to object to the probate of the will on the ground that it is not a proper will may appear before the official or court prior to the entry of the decree of probate. A person may petition after probate to have the probate of the will set aside.

12. Will Contest

The probate of a will may be refused or set aside on the ground that the will is not the free expression of the intention of the testator. It may be attacked on the ground of (1) a lack of mental capacity to execute a will, (2) undue influence, duress, fraud, or mistake existing at the time of the execution of the will that induced or led to its execution, or (3) forgery. With the exception of mental capacity, these terms mean the same as they do in contract law.

If any one of these problems exists, the probate court can refuse to admit the will for probate. The decedent's estate is then distributed as if there had been no will unless an earlier will can be probated.

RAMSEY V TAYLOR, 999 P2D 1178 (OR APP 2000)

THERE'S A MELODY IN THE HEIRS

John C. Ramsey Sr. (Senior) executed a will in the last months of his life that left the bulk of his estate to Melody Taylor, his paramour. Senior's relationships with his son and grandsons were strained, and his will included the following clause:

I have intentionally provided significant, yet smaller amounts for my son and grandsons because they have for several years alienated my affections by being irresponsible, contentious, and constantly seeking financial support from me rather than providing for themselves.

I have made provisions for MELODY J. TAYLOR because MELODY J. TAYLOR provides me care and support.

Senior was suffering from cancer and renal failure, and his pain was extraordinary. His doctors prescribed high doses of morphine that Melody administered. Senior died from an overdose of morphine.

John Ramsey Jr. (Junior), Senior's son, challenged the validity of the will on the grounds of undue influence, as well as felonious killing of a testator by a beneficiary. The trial court found there was undue influence and refused to admit the will to probate. Melody appealed.

Judicial Opinion

MUNZ, Presiding Judge.... The issue is whether Taylor exercised undue influence over Senior in the payment of her mortgage, the assignment of a right of survivorship in his checking account, and the disposition of his estate under his final will and trust.

We agree with the trial court that a confidential relationship existed between Senior and Taylor. Evidence in the record establishes not only that Taylor and Senior spent most of their time together in the last few months of his life but also establishes that Taylor took increasing responsibility over that time in managing all aspects of Senior's day-to-day life, including procuring and administering his medications, arranging and driving him to medical and business appointments, caring for his house and clothes, providing his food, and managing his checkbook.

The evidence also amply demonstrates that Senior made numerous financial decisions in the final months of his life that provided monetary benefits to Taylor. Moreover, evidence that Senior was strong-minded does not directly bear on the question of whether he had a confidential relationship with Taylor; that evidence is more properly considered in conjunction with the "susceptibility to influence" factor discussed below. Given the circumstances, we conclude that a confidential relationship existed between Senior and Taylor.

It is undisputed that the documents that Senior actually signed on August 10 did not reflect the same changes in the disposition of his estate as did the changes that Taylor assisted in preparing. However, it also is undisputed that the documents actually executed on August 10 did, in fact, give a greater amount of Senior's estate to Taylor than did the revision that Taylor helped to prepare.

This factor concerns whether Senior "had the benefit of the independent advice of his own attorney in drawing up the new will" that benefitted Taylor. Also relevant to this factor is whether the beneficiary was present during the meeting with the attorneys. That a beneficiary made the appointment and escorted a testator to an attorney's office do not, in themselves, support an inference of undue influence. Evidence in the record establishes that Senior met with his attorneys on two occasions to prepare his final will and trust and that Taylor was not present at those meetings. Although we have found it to be a suspicious circumstance where a testator is taken to a beneficiary's attorney rather than his or her own attorney to prepare a will, it is undisputed that Senior consulted his own attorneys, who had previously prepared a will and trust for him. Moreover, one of the attorneys testified that Senior told him that Taylor had been of no help to him in deciding how to dispose of his estate. Also, the attorneys discussed with Senior his intent to benefit Taylor and the reasons why he was benefitting Taylor to a greater extent than he was benefitting his family. We conclude that no "suspicious circumstance" was present regarding whether Senior received independent advice concerning his last will and trust.

Over the last decade of his life, Senior's various wills and trusts did not reveal any settled intent as to the disposition of his estate. Although all of them, including the last, benefitted family members to some extent, which family members were benefitted varied greatly, apparently based on Senior's most recent dealings with them.

On this record, we feel compelled to honor Senior's wishes as to the disposition of his estate. Although Taylor was on the scene only for a short time, she provided Senior the care and comfort that he wanted and needed during the final stages of a very painful illness.

We therefore conclude that the trial court erred in setting aside the portions of Senior's final will and trust that benefitted Taylor. For essentially the same reasons set forth above, we also conclude that the trial court erred in setting aside Senior's inter vivos gifts to Taylor.

Taylor did not feloniously kill Senior by administering the prescribed morphine, John II argues that, as a matter of "equity and good conscience," Taylor should not be entitled to keep any money that she received from Senior because she "was the person who administered or directed the administration of the morphine." We reject John II's argument. We agree with the trial court's conclusion that Taylor administered the morphine in the amounts prescribed by Senior's physicians. We also agree with its conclusion that that amount of morphine was required to control the excruciating pain that Senior was experiencing during the last days of his life. The record shows that, although it was common medical knowledge that administering such an amount of morphine to a terminal cancer patient suffering from renal failure could lead to the result seen here, physicians are known to use morphine in these circumstances anyway, in order to ease the suffering of dying patients.

We have concluded that Taylor did not exercise undue influence over Senior when she received *inter vivos* gifts from him or when he made her a major beneficiary of his final will and trust. Reversed and remanded on appeal with instructions to administer John C. Ramsey Sr.'s estate in accordance with his final will and trust.

Questions

1. What was the relationship of the testator to Taylor? What were his family relationships like?
2. What factors are considered when determining whether there was undue influence?
3. What does the court see as the evidence that overcomes the findings of some of the factors of undue influence?

ETHICS & THE LAW

JOSEPHINE'S KEEPER AND PRIMARY BENEFICIARY

Josephine Kapp was the aunt of William Kapp and the great-aunt of Keith Kapp, William's son. William lived approximately one and one-half miles from Josephine, and he farmed a 71-acre tract of land owned by Josephine. William advised Josephine on such matters as whether to take a penalty on a certificate of deposit in order to reinvest it at a higher rate and whether to take advantage of stock options.

Josephine spoke with a lawyer in July 1980 to inquire how to make a will. Based on the lawyer's advice, Josephine drew up her own holographic will on August 13, 1980, in which she stated, "William H. Kapp and Michael Keith Kapp to buy the land (the 71-acre tract) at a reasonable price and to pay it to my estate."

William took Josephine to her lawyer's office four times between September 1980 and January 1981. Sometimes William was present for part of these discussions, and at other times he left. Josephine's will was executed on January 21, 1981. The will directed that William and Keith were to be able to purchase the 71-acre tract of land even if they were acting as the executors of her estate. She also executed an option that permitted William to purchase the tract at $500 per acre or for $35,705 during her lifetime and for six months after her death.

Josephine died on March 11, 1986. William exercised his option within six months after her death and then sold the property in 1988 for $1,423,000. Josephine's remaining heirs challenged the will on the grounds of undue influence and the purchase of the property by William as executor as a breach of his fiduciary duty.

Do you think the court should allow William to keep the property? Would you allow him to keep the property? What things would the heirs point to in order to raise issues of impropriety? Could William and Josephine have done anything differently to prevent the challenge by the heirs? [*Kapp v Kapp*, 442 SE2d 499 (NC 1994)]

13. When Administration Is Not Necessary

No administration is required when the decedent did not own any property at the time of death. In some states, special statutes provide for a simplified administration when the decedent leaves only a small estate. Likewise, when all property owned by the decedent was jointly owned with another person who acquired the decedent's interest by right of survivorship, no administration is required.

14. Appointment of Personal Representative

Both executors and administrators must be appointed to act as such by a court or an officer designated by law. The appointment is made by granting to the personal representative **letters testamentary**, in the case of an executor, or **letters of administration**, in the case of an administrator.

15. Proof of Claims against the Estate

Statutes vary widely with respect to the presentation of **claims** against a decedent's estate. In very general terms, statutes provide for some form of public notice of the grant of letters testamentary or letters of administration, as by advertisement. Creditors are then required to give notice of their claims within a period specified by either statute or a court order (for example, within six months). In most states, failure to present a claim within the specified time bars the claim.

16. Construction of a Will

The will of a decedent is to be interpreted according to the ordinary or plain meaning evidenced by its words. The court will strive to give effect to every provision of the will to avoid concluding that any part of the decedent's estate was not disposed of by the will.[7]

[7] *In re Estate of Lubins*, 656 NYS2d 851 (1997).

THINKING THINGS THROUGH

NOT QUITE "LAYED" TO REST

Ken Lay, the former CEO of Enron, a company that collapsed after accounting fraud was discovered, died shortly after being found guilty on all counts of bank and securities fraud. Legal experts noted that his criminal conviction no longer has any effect because he did not have a chance to appeal the verdict before his death. However, civil suits by shareholders and pension plans were pending against Mr. Lay. Will the assets of his estate still be subject to claim in the event these plaintiffs win their suits? Will the suits continue?

17. Testate Distribution of an Estate

If the decedent died leaving a valid will, the last phase of the administration of the estate by the decedent's personal representative is the distribution of property remaining after the payment of all debts and taxes in accordance with the provisions of the will.

The testator ordinarily bequeaths to named persons certain sums of money called **general legacies** because no particular money is specified. The testator may bequeath identified property called **specific legacies** or **specific devises. For Example,** a testator may give "$1,000 to *A;* $1,000 to *B;* my automobile to *C.*" The first two bequests are general; the third is specific. After such bequests, the testator may make a bequest of everything remaining, called a *residuary bequest,* such as "the balance of my estate to *D.*"

(a) Abatement of Legacies

Assume in the preceding example that after all debts are paid, only $1,500 and the automobile remain. What disposition is to be made? Legacies **abate** or bear loss in the following order: (1) residuary, (2) general, (3) specific. The law also holds that legacies of the same class abate proportionately. **For Example,** in the hypothetical case, *C,* the specific legatee, would receive the automobile; *A* and *B,* the general legatees, would each receive $750; and *D,* the residuary legatee, would receive nothing.

(b) Ademption of Property

When specifically bequeathed property is sold or given away by the testator prior to death, the bequest is considered **adeemed,** or canceled. The specific legatee in this instance is not entitled to receive any property or money. *Ademption* has the same consequence as though the testator had formally canceled the bequest. **For Example,** if Aunt Claire left her 2003 Honda Accord to her niece, Helen, but Aunt Claire sold the Honda Accord in 2005 and died in 2007, Helen receives nothing from Aunt Claire's estate because the bequest of the Honda is adeemed or canceled.

(c) Antilapse Statutes

If the beneficiary named in the testator's will died before the testator and the testator did not make any alternate provision applicable in such a case, the gift ordinarily does not lapse. **Antilapse statutes** commonly provide that the gift to the deceased beneficiary shall not lapse but that the children or heirs of that beneficiary may take the legacy in the place of the deceased beneficiary. An antilapse statute does not apply if the testator specified a disposition that should be made of the gift if the original legatee had died.

18. Intestate Distribution of an Estate

If the decedent does not effectively dispose of all property by will or does not have a will, the decedent's property is distributed to certain relatives. Because such persons acquire or succeed to the rights of the decedent and because the circumstances under which they do so is the absence of an effective will, it is said that they acquire title by **intestate succession.**

The right of intestate succession or inheritance is not a basic right of the citizen or an inalienable right. It exists only because the state legislature so provides. It is within the power of the state legislature to modify or destroy the right to inherit property.

Although wide variations exist among the statutory provisions of the states, a common pattern of intestate distribution exists.

(a) Spouses

The surviving spouse of the decedent, whether husband or wife, shares in the estate. Generally, the amount received is a fraction that varies with the number of children. If no children survive, the spouse is generally entitled to take the entire estate. Otherwise, the surviving spouse ordinarily receives a one-half or one-third share of the estate.

(b) Lineals

Lineals or **lineal descendants** are blood descendants of the decedent. Lineal descendants include children and grandchildren. That portion of the estate that is not distributed to the surviving spouse is generally distributed to lineals.

(c) Parents

If the estate has not been fully distributed by this time, the remainder is commonly distributed to the decedent's parents.

(d) Collateral Heirs

These are persons who are not descendants of the decedent but are related through a common ancestor. Generally, brothers and sisters and their descendants share any part of the estate that has not already been distributed. Statutes vary as to how far distribution will be made to the descendants of brothers and sisters. Under some statutes, a degree of relationship is specified, such as first cousins, and no person more remotely related to the decedent is permitted to share in the estate.

If the entire estate is not distributed within the permitted degree of relationship, the property that has not been distributed is given to the state government. This right of the state to take the property is the **right of escheat.** Under some statutes, the right of escheat arises only when there is no relative of the decedent, however remotely related.

(e) Distribution per Capita and per Stirpes

The fact that different generations of distributees may be entitled to receive the estate creates a problem of determining the proportions in which distribution is to be made (see Figure 52-2). When all the distributees stand in the same degree of relationship to the decedent, distribution is made **per capita,** each receiving the same share. **For Example,** if the decedent is survived by three children—*A*, *B*, and *C*—each of them is entitled to receive one-third of the estate.

If the distributees stand in different degrees of relationship, distribution is made in as many equal parts as there are family lines, or **stirpes,** represented in the nearest generation. Parents take to the exclusion of their children or subsequent descendants, and

FIGURE 52-2 Distribution per Capita and per Stirpes

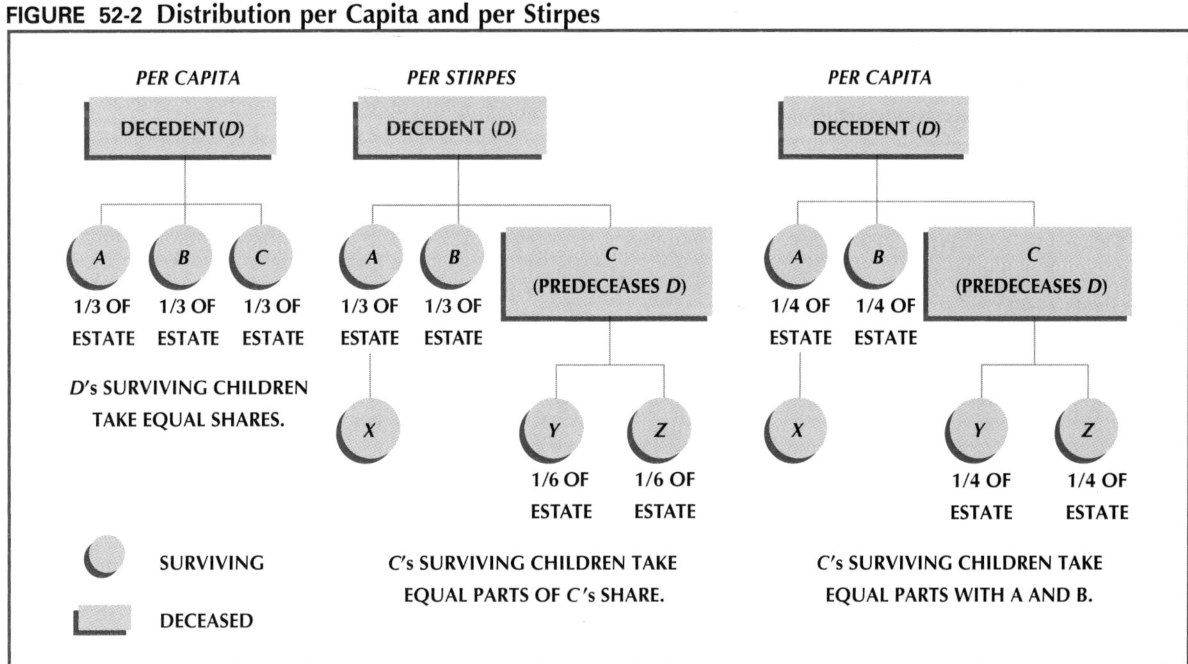

when members of the nearest generation have died, their descendants take by way of representation. This is called **distribution per stirpes** or **stirpital distribution.** **For Example,** Thomas dies leaving two living children, *A* and *B*, and one child, *C*, who predeceased him but left two children (Thomas's grandchildren, *D* and *E*). *A* and *B* would each take one-third of Thomas's estate, and *D* and *E* would, under a **per stirpes** distribution, split a one-third interest, each receiving one-sixth of the estate.

(f) Murder of Decedent

Statutes generally provide that a person who murders the decedent cannot inherit from the victim by intestacy. In the absence of such a statute, courts are divided over whether the heir may inherit.

IN RE ESTATE OF MORRIS P. VAN DER VEEN, 935 P2D 1042 (KAN 1997)

GUILTY FATHER; INNOCENT CHILD: DOES THE CHILD INHERIT AS A GRANDCHILD?

On or about April 30, 1993, Kent Van Der Veen murdered his parents, Morris and Deanne Van Der Veen. Kent was 19 years old at the time and had fathered a child two years earlier who had been legally adopted by persons not identified in the court proceedings. Morris and Deanne were not aware of the existence of Kent's child prior to their deaths.

The 1989 joint will of Morris and Deanne Van Der Veen provides for the following distribution of their estate after debts and obligations are paid:

Upon the death of the survivor of us, each of us hereby gives, devises, and bequeaths all of the rest, residue, and remainder of our property of every kind, character, and description, and wherever located, unto our children, Laura Ann Van Der Veen (appellee) and Kent Phillip Van Der Veen, equally and per stirpes.

Kent Van Der Veen was disqualified from inheriting any portion of his parents' estate under Kansas's slayer statute. Kent's child, the biological grandchild of Morris and Deanne, petitioned to inherit one-half of her biological grandparents' estate. The grandchild is identified in the case only as D.B.B. The trial court denied the grandchild any interest in the estate, and the grandchild appealed.

Judicial Opinion

ALLEGRUCCCI, J. . . . In their will, the Van Der Veens bequeathed one-half of their estate to each of their children, Laura and Kent. It is agreed that Kent is statutorily disqualified from inheriting property from his parents.

This appeal challenges the district court's determination that the statute prevails over the express terms of the Van Der Veens' will, resulting in D.B.B.'s being disinherited. The argument made on behalf of D.B.B. by her guardian *ad litem* is that the language of her grandparents' bequest to their children, "equally and per stirpes," must be construed to give what would have been Kent's share, if he had not been disqualified, to his heir, D.B.B. D.B.B.'s guardian *ad litem* further argues that D.B.B.'s adoptive status is irrelevant because K.S.A. 59-2118(b) provides that "[a]n adoption shall not terminate the right of the child to inherit . . . through the birth parent."

Appellee Laura Van Der Veen counters that the language of 59-2118(b), on which D.B.B. relies, was added in 1993 and became effective after the Van Der Veens' deaths. If the effective date of the amendment does not prevent it from applying in the present case, appellee further argues, the statute should be construed to restrict inheritance "through the birth parent" to instances where the birth parent has died. In other words, it should be interpreted so as to exclude inheritance through a birth parent who is alive but disqualified. In appellee's words, the statute should be interpreted so that the disqualified killer is treated as if he never existed rather than as if he had died.

We first address whether D.B.B.'s adoption affects her right to inherit from her biological grandparents. There is no doubt that the legislature intended that 59-2118(b), at all pertinent times, permitted an adoptee to inherit from and through his or her biological parents.

We find the Court of Appeals' rationale persuasive and conclude that D.B.B.'s adoption would not bar her from inheriting from or through her biological parent.

We next consider whether Kent's being barred from inheriting from his parents prevents the inheritance from passing through him to his child. This was the basis for the trial court's decision and has not been decided by the appellate courts of this state. The question has arisen in other jurisdictions, however, and has been pondered by commentators, scholars, and the National Conference of Commissioners on Uniform State Laws.

In *In re Estate of Benson*, 548 So.2d 775 (Fla.App. 1989), a murderer's minor children were allowed to inherit his share of intestate and testate estates. Margaret Benson, the deceased testator, was the mother of Carol Benson Kendall, Steven Benson, and Scott Benson. Steven had minor children; Scott had no heirs. Steven killed Margaret and Scott. Margaret's will devised her property to her three children in equal shares and per stirpes. Scott died intestate. An intestacy section of Florida's probate code provides that the property of a decedent such as Scott, without parents or lineal descendants, passes to the decedent's siblings and the descendants of deceased siblings. Florida's "slayer statute" provides that "the estate of the decedent passes as if the killer had predeceased the decedent." 548 So.2d at 777. The trial judge applied Florida's anti-lapse statute in concluding that Steven's minor children inherited through him.

With regard to the UPC, the Tennessee Court of Appeals, in *Carter v Hutchison*, 707 S.W.2d 533, 537 n. 10 (Tenn.App. 1985), noted:

"A vast majority of states enacting the forfeiture statutes have patterned them after the model statute proposed by Dean Wade in 1936, see J. Wade, [Acquisition of Property by Willfully Killing Another—A Statutory Solution, 49 Harv. L.Rev. 715, 753–55 (1936)], or the Uniform Probate Code. Thus, in twenty-nine states there is a statutory presumption that the victim's property passes to his estate as if the slayer had predeceased the decedent. Four states provide for forfeiture but are silent as to distribution. Tennessee is among ten states that provide for forfeiture and for distribution to the decedent's heirs through the laws of intestate succession. The eight remaining states without statutes have forfeiture provisions by court decision."

It appears that Kansas is one of the few states that does not expressly provide for distribution of the forfeited share.

Turning to the present case, it is clear that under either version of the UPC, appellee would take one-half of the estate of her parents. The other half would be taken by her disqualified brother's minor child.

Kansas' anti-lapse statute, K.S.A. 59-615(a), provides, in part:

"If a devise or bequest is made to . . . any relative by lineal descent . . . and such . . . relative dies before the testator, leaving issue who survive the testator, such issue shall take the same estate which said devisee or legatee would have taken if he or she had survived, unless a different disposition is made or required by the will."

The anti-lapse provision is not applicable in the present case. The possibility that one or both of their children would predecease them was taken into account in the Van Der Veens' will by the inclusion of the phrase "per stirpes."

[J]ust treatment of the other beneficiaries does not demand that the slayer's heirs be disqualified or penalized. To illustrate this proposition in the circumstances of the present case, we need only look at appellee's situation. She would take one-half of her parents' estate if they had died from natural causes, and she would take the same if Kent is disqualified for killing their parents and his share passes as if he predeceased them. In contrast, if Kent's child were disqualified because Kent killed his parents, the innocent child would be penalized, and appellee would take twice what the testators intended and what she expected.

We conclude that the better rule where the slayer's heir or heirs are wholly innocent would be to dispose of the disqualified slayer's share as if the slayer predeceased the victim(s).

The Van Der Veens intended for their daughter to take one-half of their estate. Their knowledge of Kent's troubled nature is reflected in a provision of the Van Der Veens' will that nominates Laura to serve as Kent's guardian and conservator. Nonetheless, they bequeathed one-half of their estate to him There is nothing in the instrument from which the court could conclude that the Van Der Veens intended for Laura to receive the entire estate in the event of Kent's incapacity or disqualification. By extension, it may reasonably be inferred that they would not have intended for Kent's innocent child to be disqualified in order for Laura to receive the entire estate.

Appellee invites the court to speculate that the Van Der Veens would not have intended for their unknown, illegitimate grandchild to share in their estate. We decline the invitation and note there is no factual support in the record for such a speculation.

[The judgment of the district court is reversed]

Questions

1. What is a "slayer statute"?
2. What does the court find about adopted children inheriting from their biological parents?
3. What does the court find about grandchildren of murderers inheriting the barred murderer's share of an estate?
4. Is Laura's position different from what it would have been if the inheritance by the grandchild were disallowed?

(g) Death of Distributee after Decedent

The persons entitled to distribution of a decedent's estate are determined as of the date of death. If a distributee dies after that, the rights of the distributee are not lost but pass from the original decedent's estate to the deceased distributee's estate.

(h) Simultaneous Death

The **Uniform Simultaneous Death Act**[8] provides that when survivorship cannot be established, the property of each person shall be disposed of as if he or she had survived the other.

C. Trusts

A **trust** is a legal device by which property, real or personal, is held by one person for the benefit of another. Legal problems in the area of trusts invariably require a determination of the nature of the relationship created by the trust and the rights and obligations of the parties with respect to that relationship.

19. Definitions

The property owner who creates the trust is the **settlor.** (The word *settlor* is taken from the old legal language of "settling the property in trust.") The settlor is sometimes called the **donor** or **trustor.** The person to whom the property is transferred in trust is the **trustee.** The person for whose benefit the trustee holds the property is the beneficiary (or ***cestui que trust***).

Property held in trust is sometimes called the **trust corpus, trust fund, trust estate,** or **trust res.** A distinction is made between the **principal,** or the property in trust, and the **income** that is earned by the principal and distributed by the trustee.

If the trust is created to take effect within the lifetime of the settlor, it is a **living trust,** or an ***inter vivos* trust.** If the trust is provided for in the settlor's will and is to become effective only when the will takes effect after death, the trust is called a **testamentary trust.**

20. Creation of Trusts

The requirements to create a trust are not uniform, but there are certain typical requirements.

(a) Capacity of Beneficiary

The capacity of the beneficiary of the trust to hold property or to contract is immaterial. Many trusts are created because the beneficiary lacks legal or actual capacity to manage the property. The trustee, as the holder of legal title, must have capacity.

(b) Formality

In creating a trust, it is common practice to execute a writing, called a **trust agreement** or **deed of trust.** No particular form of language is necessary to create a trust as long as the property, the trust purpose, and the beneficiaries are designated. If an *inter vivos* trust relates to an interest in land, the statute of frauds requires that the trust be in writing with the details of the trust included. A writing signed by the trustee and referring to a deed from the trustor can satisfy this requirement. When the trust depends on a transfer of title to land, there must be a valid transfer of the title to the trustee.

A trust in personal property may be declared orally without any writing. If a trust is created by the will of the settlor, there must be a writing that meets the requirements of a will. The same is true when the trust is not intended to come into existence until the death of the settlor.

In the absence of a specific requirement of the statute of frauds as to land or of the statutes setting forth the formal requirements for wills, any conduct or writing that shows an intent to create a trust will be given effect.

(c) Intention

The settler must express some intention to place property in trust. It is not necessary, however, that the word *trust* or *trustee* be used. The settlor will ordinarily name a trustee, but failure to do so is not fatal to the trust because a trustee will be appointed by the court.

(d) Identity of Beneficiary

Every trust must have a beneficiary. In a private trust, the beneficiaries must be identified by name, description, or designation of the class to which the beneficiaries belong. In a charitable trust, it is sufficient that the beneficiaries be members of the public at large or a general class of the public.

[8] The 1940 version of this act has been adopted in all states except Louisiana and Ohio. The newest version of the act (1993) has been adopted in Arizona, Colorado, Hawaii, Kansas, Montana, New Mexico, North Dakota, South Dakota, and Virginia.

(e) Acceptance of Trust

Because the performance of a trust imposes duties on the trustee, a trustee may renounce or reject the trust. Acceptance will be presumed in the absence of a disclaimer. A renunciation does not affect the validity of the trust because a court will appoint a substitute trustee if the settlor does not do so.

21. Nature of Beneficiary's Interest

When property is transferred to a trust, the trustee has **legal title** and the beneficiary has **equitable title.** The beneficiary may transfer or assign such interest in the trust. The beneficiary's creditors may reach that interest in satisfaction of their claims. However, the trustor can protect beneficiaries from creditors by creating a **spendthrift trust,** which does not allow creditors of the beneficiary to attach the beneficial interest, nor is the beneficiary permitted to assign or pledge that interest.[9]

22. Powers of Trustee

A trustee can exercise only those powers that are given by law or the trust instrument or those that the court will construe as being given by implication. Modern trusts commonly give the trustee discretion to make decisions on matters that could not be foreseen by the settlor. **For Example,** the trustee may be authorized to expend principal as well as income when, in the trustee's opinion, it is necessary for the education or medical care of a beneficiary. The trustee must exercise discretion in a reasonable manner.

23. Duties of Trustee

The duty of a trustee is to administer the trust. The trustee who accepts the appointment must take all necessary steps to carry out the trust in a proper manner.

(a) Performance

A trustee is under a duty to carry out the trust according to its terms and is personally liable for any loss sustained from an unjustified failure to perform such duties. A trustee cannot delegate the performance of personal duties.

(b) Due Care

The trustee is under a duty to use reasonable skill, prudence, and diligence in the performance of trust duties. More simply stated, the trustee must use the care that would be exercised by a reasonable person under the circumstances.

(c) Loyalty

A trustee is not permitted to profit personally from the position of trustee other than to receive the compensation allowed by contract or law.[10]

(d) Possession and Preservation of Trust Property

The trustee has a duty to take possession of trust property and to preserve it from loss or damage. If the property includes accounts receivable or outstanding debts, the trustee is responsible for collecting them.

(e) Production of Income

By either express or implied direction, the trustee is required to invest the money or property in enterprises or transactions that will yield an income to the estate.

In the absence of specific investment instructions, a trustee must invest the trust property as a reasonable and prudent investor would.

(f) Accounting and Information

A trustee must keep accurate records so that it can be determined whether the trust has been properly administered. On request by a beneficiary, the trustee must furnish information about the trust. Periodically or at certain times, as determined by the law in each state, a trustee must file an account in court. At such time, the court examines the stewardship of the trust.

In some trusts, the trustee must balance the interests of the life beneficiary (the party entitled to the income from the trust while he or she is alive) with those of the eventual recipients of the trust res. **For Example,** a testator might put this provision in her will: "To my husband in trust for his life, and upon his death in fee simple to my children." How does the trustee account for rental income? What if

[9] However, in *In re Marriage of Chapman*, 697 NE2d 365 (Ill App 1998), the court did permit invasion of an ex-husband's spendthrift trust for purposes of collecting back child support.

[10] *Moretz v Miller*, 486 SE2d 85 (NC App 1997).

FIGURE 52-3 Trust Principal/Income Allocation

PRINCIPAL	PAYABLE FROM PRINCIPAL	INCOME	PAYABLE FROM INCOME
ORIGINAL TRUST PROPERTY	LOANS (PRINCIPAL)	RENT	LOANS (INTEREST)
PROCEEDS AND GAINS FROM SALE	LITIGATION EXPENSES	INTEREST	TAXES
INSURANCE PAYMENTS	PERMANENT IMPROVEMENTS	CASH	INSURANCE PREMIUMS
NEW PROPERTY PURCHASED WITH PRINCIPAL	COSTS OF PURCHASE	DIVIDENDS	REPAIRS
STOCK DIVIDENDS		ROYALTIES	
STOCK SPLITS			

the rental properties need repairs? Do the repairs come from the income, or are they taken from principal? There are clear rules for the allocation of income and principal and the expenses of operation of the trust and the trust properties. These rules are summarized in Figure 52-3.

24. Remedies for Breach of Trust

A breach of trust may occur in a variety of ways. The manner in which a trust is breached affects the remedies available. These remedies include the following:

1. A money judgment against the trustee for the loss caused by him or her.
2. An injunction or order to compel the trustee to do or refrain from doing an act.
3. Criminal prosecution of the trustee for misconduct.
4. Tracing and recovery of trust property that has been converted by the trustee unless the property was acquired by a bona fide purchaser who gave value and purchased without notice of the breach of trust
5. Removal of the trustee for misconduct
6. A suit against third persons who participated in a breach of trust

25. Termination of Trust

A trust may be terminated (1) by its own terms—for example, the trust is an education fund that has a termination date of college graduation, (2) because of the impossibility of attaining the object of the trust—for example, the trust is for the trustor's grandchild and his only child has died before having any children, (3) via revocation by the settlor when allowed by the terms of the trust, but trusts are presumed irrevocable unless the trust document permits revocation, (4) by merger of all interests in the same person (as when there is only one trustee and one beneficiary and they are the same person), or (5) upon the request of all the beneficiaries, as approved by a court, when there is no express purpose that requires continuation of the trust.

LAWFLIX

***Melvin and Howard* (1980) (PG)**

An interesting look at the difficulty of establishing the validity of an eccentric's will, particularly when the provisions of that will defy conventional notions of proper distribution of one's largesse upon death.

For movie clips that illustrate business law concepts, see LawFlix at **http://wdvl.westbuslaw.com.**

Summary

A *will* is a writing that provides for a disposition of property to take effect upon death. A man who makes a will is called a *testator*; a woman, a *testatrix*. The person to whom property is left by will is a *beneficiary*. A *legacy* is a gift of personal property by will; a gift of real property by will is a *devise*. A testator must have testamentary capacity to make a will and must manifest some intention that the will is to be effective only upon death. The will must be signed by the testator and be witnessed.

A will may be modified by a codicil or revoked either by the act of the testator or by operation of law.

Probate is the process by which a proper court official accepts a will. Probate may be refused or set aside on grounds that the will is not the free expression of the testator.

A *holographic* will is an unwitnessed will written entirely in the handwriting of the testator. A *self-proved will* may be admitted to probate without the testimony of subscribing witnesses. A *living will* allows a person to make wishes known regarding life-sustaining medical treatment.

If there is a valid will, the last phase of administration of the estate is the distribution of property after the payment of all debts and taxes. *General legacies* are bequests of money, whereas *specific legacies* or *specific devises* are gifts of identified personal or real property. Legacies abate in the following order: residuary, general, and specific. If a beneficiary named in the will has died before the testator and no alternate provision has been made for that beneficiary, antilapse statutes provide that the gift will not lapse. In that event, the children or heirs of the beneficiary may take the legacy in the place of the deceased beneficiary.

If the decedent does not dispose of all property by will or does not have a will, the property will be distributed according to state intestacy statutes. A surviving spouse may generally elect to take the statutory allocation instead of that provided in the will.

The estate of the testator will be administered by the person appointed in the will (the *executor*) or, if there is no will, by a person appointed by the court (an *administrator*). Creditors who have claims against the estate are required to give notice of their claims to the personal representative; otherwise, the claims will be barred.

A *trust* is a legal device by which property is held by one person for the benefit of another. The settlor creates the trust, and the person for whose benefit the trustee holds the property is the beneficiary. Property held in trust is called the *trust corpus*, *trust fund*, *trust estate*, or *trust res*.

A trust is usually created by a trust agreement or deed of trust. No particular form or language is required. A trust is not created unless an active duty is placed on the trustee to manage the property in some manner. A trustee's acceptance of duties is presumed.

Legal title to trust property is given to the trustee, and the beneficiary holds equitable title. A beneficiary may transfer an interest in the trust except in the case of a spendthrift trust.

The trustee can exercise only those powers that are given by law or the trust instrument. The trustee must administer the trust and carry out the trust in a proper manner. A trustee is liable for breach of the terms of the trust agreement. A trust comes to an end when its terms so provide or when it becomes impossible to attain the object of the trust.

Questions and Case Problems

1. Joseph McKinley Bryan was an elderly, wealthy, and eccentric man. Before his death, he had made provisions for a testamentary trust for his grandchildren and great-grandchildren. Under the terms of the trust, each grandchild who survived him was to receive $500,000, and each great-grandchild who survived him was to receive $100,000. By the time of Bryan's death on April 26, 1995, there had been at least five versions of the trust's provisions. His will was originally dated June 29, 1990, but the trust agreement was originally made in 1985, with two changes in 1988, one in 1990, and another in 1992. In May 1995, NationsBank Corp., the trustee, notified Bryan's grandchildren by letter that they would be receiving only $100,000. Because the grandchildren had understood that they were to receive $500,000, they asked to see the trust agreements. The trustee refused, contending that there was no duty to share the agreement with the trust beneficiaries. Was the trustee right? [*Taylor v NationsBank Corp.*, 481 SE2d 358 (NC App)]
2. Rose Lakatosh was a woman in her early to mid-70s in March 1988 when she hired Roger Jacobs to do odd jobs for her around her home in Northampton, Pennsylvania. Rose, who had no contact with her family except for an occasional visit from her sister Margaret, became very dependent on Jacobs for her physical care, and he began to assist her with her financial affairs. In late 1988, at Jacobs's suggestion, Rose executed a power of attorney making Roger her attorney in fact. At the same time that she executed the power of attorney, Rose executed a will leaving all of her property, with the exception of $10,000 to her church, to Roger.

   Rose was, at the time of Jacobs's involvement with her, also the defendant in a slander lawsuit brought against her by her nephew. Three days after Rose had executed her will leaving her property to Jacobs, her attorney in the slander lawsuit petitioned the court to have her evaluated for competency. Her lawyer said she could not provide information for discovery in the case, did not remember things, and could not seem to grasp how much property she owned. While the lawsuit progressed and the competency issue remained unresolved by the court, Rose died, with the will leaving her property to Jacobs still valid. Rose's relative, Donald Spry, challenged the will on the grounds of mental incapacity and undue influence by Jacobs. Did Rose lack the mental capacity necessary to make a will? [*In re Estate of Lakatosh*, 656 A2d 1378 (Pa Super)]

3. Iona wrote her will. The following year, she wrote another will that expressly revoked the earlier will. Later, while cleaning house, she came across the second will. She mistakenly thought that it was the first will and tore it up because the first will had been revoked. Iona died shortly thereafter. The beneficiaries named in the second will claimed that the second will should be probated. The beneficiaries named in the first will claimed that the second will had been revoked when it was torn up. Had the second will been revoked?
4. Logsdon, who had three children, disliked one of them without any reason. In his will, he left only a small amount to the child he disliked and gave the bulk of his estate to the remaining two. On his death, the disliked child claimed that the will was void and had been obtained by undue influence. Do you agree? [*Logsdon v Logsdon*, 104 NE2d 622 (Ill)]
5. Field executed a will. On her death, the will was found in her safe deposit box, but the part of it containing the fifth bequest had been torn from the will. This torn fragment was also found in the box. There was no evidence that anyone other than Field had ever opened the box. A proceeding was brought to determine whether the will was entitled to be probated. Had the will been revoked? Was the will still valid with a portion torn from it? [*Flora v Hughes*, 228 SW2d 27 (Ky)]
6. Miller wrote a will that was 11 pages long and enclosed it in an envelope, which she sealed. She then wrote on the envelope "My last will & testament" and signed her name below this statement. This was the only place where she signed her name on any of the papers. Was this signature sufficient to allow this writing to be admitted to probate as her will? [*Miller's Executor v Shannon*, 299 SW2d 103 (Ky)]
7. Lingenfelter's will was offered for probate and was opposed. The testatrix was sick, highly nervous, and extremely jealous; and she committed suicide a week after executing the will. She had, however, seemed to understand the will when she discussed it with an attorney. The will disinherited her husband because she feared he was not faithful to her despite the fact that he was seriously ill when she wrote the will. He died the day after she executed the will, and she grieved his death terribly for one week before committing suicide. Did she have the capacity to make a will? Should it be admitted to probate? [*In re Lingenfelter's Estate*, 241 P2d 990 (Cal)]
8. Copenhaver wrote a will in ink, which was found with her other papers in her bedroom at her death. Pencil lines had been drawn through every provision of the will and the signature. There was no evidence as to the circumstances under which this had been done. Was the will revoked? Why or why not? [*Franklin v Maclean*, 66 SE2d 504 (Va)]
9. George Baxter executed a will that left the bulk of his estate to the Church of Christ in New Boston, Texas. Two members of the church served as the witnesses for the will. Is the will valid? [*In re Estate of Gordon*, 519 SW2d 902 (Tex)]
10. Jeanette Wall worked for D. J. Sharron for many years. Sharron executed a will leaving his entire estate to Jeanette. He reexecuted the same will sometime thereafter with the same provisions. Sharron's children contested the will, offering evidence that Sharron was a very sick man, physically as well as mentally, and that Wall was active in Sharron's business as well as his personal life. They offered no evidence that Wall had any involvement in the procurement of the original or the reexecuted will. Who is entitled to the estate? Why? [*Wall v Hodges*, 465 So 2d 359 (Ala App)]
11. Bill Cruxton, single and 80 years old, left the bulk of his $500,000 estate to a waitress at Dink's Restaurant in Chagrin Falls, Ohio. He had lunch and dinner there every day and was grateful for the fellowship and service. His relatives challenged the will with the provision on the grounds of capacity. Could they have the will set aside?
12. Valerie and Flora are the beneficiaries of a trust left to them by their mother upon her death. Their mother named Art Casanelli, a family friend, as the trustee. Flora has seen Art driving a new car and has learned that he just purchased a new and rather large home. She is concerned about the trust funds and Art's unfettered access to them. How can she determine whether Art is using trust funds? What happens if she finds that he is?
13. Can a murderer inherit property from his victim? Why or why not?
14. James Horne's will provides that his estate is to be distributed to his heirs per capita. Upon his death, two of his three children are surviving and his deceased child left two children (James's grandchildren). His will provides that all his property is to be distributed per capita to these children and grandchildren. How will the property be distributed? How would it be distributed if he had provided for a per stirpes distribution?
15. Craig delivers bonds in the amount of $100,000 to White in trust to hold and to pay over the income in quarterly payments to Craig's niece, Helen, during her minority. Who is the settlor or creator of the trust? Who is the trustee? Who is the beneficiary?

CPA Questions

1. A decedent's will provided that the estate was to be divided among the decedent's issue, per capita and not per stirpes. If there are two surviving children and three grandchildren who are children of a predeceased child at the time the will is probated, how will the estate be divided?
   a. One-half to each surviving child
   b. One-third to each surviving child and one-ninth to each grandchild
   c. One-fourth to each surviving child and one-sixth to each grandchild
   d. One-fifth to each surviving child and grandchild

APPENDIX (1)

HOW TO FIND THE LAW

In order to determine what the law on a particular question or issue is, it may be necessary to examine (1) compilations of constitutions, treaties, statutes, executive orders, proclamations, and administrative regulations; (2) reports of state and federal court decisions; (3) digests of opinions; (4) treatises on the law; and (5) loose-leaf services. These sources can be either researched traditionally or using fee- and/or non-fee-based computerized legal research accessed through the World Wide Web.

Compilations

In the consideration of a legal problem in business it is necessary to determine whether the matter is affected or controlled by a constitution, national or state; by a national treaty; by an Act of Congress or a state legislature, or by a city ordinance; by a decree or proclamation of the President of the United States, a governor, or a mayor; or by a regulation of a federal, state, or local administrative agency.

Each body or person that makes laws, regulations, or ordinances usually compiles and publishes at the end of each year or session all of the matter that it has adopted. In addition to the periodical or annual volumes, it is common to compile all the treaties, statutes, regulations, or ordinances in separate volumes. To illustrate, the federal Anti-Injunction Act may be cited as the Act of March 23, 1932, 47 Stat 70, 29 USC Sections 101 et seq. This means that this law was enacted on March 23, 1932, and that it can be found at page 70 in Volume 47 of the reports that contain all of the statutes adopted by the Congress.

The second part of the citation, 29 USC Sections 101 et seq., means that in the collection of all of the federal statutes, which is known as the United States Code, the full text of the statute can be found in the sections of the 29th title beginning with Section 101.

Court Decisions

For complicated or important legal cases or when an appeal is to be taken, a court will generally write an opinion, which explains why the court made the decision. Appellate courts as a rule write opinions. The great majority of these decisions, particularly in the case of the appellate courts, are collected and printed. In order to avoid confusion, the opinions of each court are ordinarily printed in a separate set of reports, either by official reporters or private publishers.

In the reference "Pennoyer v Neff, 95 US 714, 24 LEd 565," the first part states the names of the parties. It does not necessarily tell who was the plaintiff and who was the defendant. When an action is begun in a lower court, the first name is that of the plaintiff and the second name that of the defendant. When the case is appealed, generally the name of the person taking the appeal appears on the records of the higher court as the first one and that of the adverse party as the second. Sometimes, therefore, the original order of the names of the parties is reversed.

The balance of the reference consists of two citations. The first citation, 95 US 714, means that the opinion which the court filed in the case of Pennoyer v Neff may be found on page 714 of the 95th volume of a series of books in which are printed officially the opinions of the United States Supreme Court. Sometimes the same opinion is printed in two different sets of volumes. In the example, 24 LEd 565 means that in the 24th volume of another set of books, called Lawyer's Edition, of the United States Supreme Court Reports, the same opinion begins on page 565.

In opinions by a state court there may also be two citations, as in the case of "Morrow v Corbin, 122 Tex 553, 62 SW2d 641." This means that the opinion in the lawsuit between Morrow and Corbin may be found in the 122d volume of the reports of the highest court of Texas, beginning on page 553; and also in Volume 62 of the Southwestern Reporter, Second Series, at page 641.

The West Publishing Company publishes a set of sectional reporters covering the entire United States. They are called "sectional" because each reporter, instead of being limited to a particular court or a particular state, covers the decisions of the courts of a particular section of the country. Thus the decisions of the courts of Arkansas, Kentucky, Missouri, Tennessee, and Texas are printed by the West Publishing company as a group in a sectional reporter called the Southwestern Reporter.[1] Because of the large number of decisions involved, generally only the opinions of the state appellate courts are printed. A number of states[2] have discontinued publication of the opinions of their courts, and those opinions are now found only in the West reporters.

The reason for the "Second Series" in the Southwestern citation is that when there were 300 volumes in the original series, instead of calling the next volume 301, the publisher called it Volume 1, Second Series. Thus 62 SW2d Series really means the 362d volume of the Southwestern Reporter. Six to eight volumes appear in a year for each geographic section.

In addition to these state reporters, the West Publishing Company publishes a Federal Supplement, which primarily reports the opinions of the Federal District Courts; the Federal Reporter, which primarily reports the decisions of the United States Courts of Appeals; and the Supreme Court Reporter, which reports the decisions of the United States Supreme Court. The Supreme Court decisions are also reported in a separate set called the Lawyers' Edition, published by the Lawyers Cooperative Publishing Company.

The reports published by the West Publishing Company and Lawyers Cooperative Publishing Company are unofficial reports, while those bearing the name or abbreviation of the United States or of a state, such as "95 US 714" or "122 Tex 553" are official reports. This means that in the case of the latter, the particular court, such as the United States Supreme Court, has officially authorized that its decisions be printed and that by federal statute such official printing is made. In the case of the unofficial reporters, the publisher prints the decisions of a court on its own initiative. Such opinions are part of the public domain and not subject to any copyright or similar restriction.

Digests of Opinions

The reports of court decisions are useful only if one has the citation, that is, the name and volume number of the book and the page number of the opinion one is seeking. For this reason, digests of the decisions have been prepared. These digests organize the entire field of law under major headings, which are then arranged in alphabetical order. Under each heading, such as "Contracts," the subject is divided into the different questions that can arise with respect to that field. A master outline is thus created on the subject. This outline includes short paragraphs describing what each case holds and giving its citation.

Treatises and Restatements

Very helpful in finding a case or a statute are the treatises on the law. These may be special books, each written by an author on a particular subject, such as Williston on Contracts, Bogert on Trusts, Fletcher on Corporations, or they may be general encyclopedias, as in the case of American Jurisprudence, American Jurisprudence, Second, and Corpus Juris Secundum.

Another type of treatise is found in the restatements of the law prepared by the American Law Institute. Each restatement consists of one or more volumes devoted to a particular phase of the law, such as the Restatement of the Law of Contracts, Restatement of the Law of Agency, and Restatement of the Law of Property. In each restatement, the American Law Institute, acting through special committees of judges, lawyers, and professors of law, has set forth what the law is; and in many areas where there is no law or the present rule is regarded as unsatisfactory, the restatement specifies what the Institute deems to be the desirable rule.

Loose-Leaf Services

A number of private publishers, notably Commerce Clearing House and Prentice-Hall, publish loose-leaf books devoted to particular branches of the law. Periodically, the publisher sends to the purchaser a number of pages that set forth any decision, regulation, or statute made or adopted since the prior set of pages was prepared. Such services are unofficial.

Computerized Legal Research

National and local computer services are providing constantly widening assistance for legal research. The database in such a system may be opinions, statutes, or administrative regulations stored word for word; or the later history of a particular case giving its full citation and showing whether the case has been followed by other courts; or the text of forms and documents. By means of a terminal connected to the system, the user can retrieve the above information at a great saving of time and with the assurance that it is up-to-date.

[1] The sectional reporters are: Atlantic—A. (Connecticut, Delaware, District of Columbia, Maine, Maryland, New Hampshire, New Jersey, Pennsylvania, Rhode Island, Vermont); Northeastern—N.E. (Illinois, Indiana, Massachusetts, New York, Ohio); N.W. (Iowa, Michigan, Minnesota, Nebraska, North Dakota, South Dakota, Wisconsin); Pacific—P. (Alaska, Arizona, California, Colorado, Hawaii, Idaho, Kansas, Montana, Nevada, New Mexico, Oklahoma, Oregon, Utah, Washington, Wyoming); Southeastern—S.E. (Georgia, North Carolina, South Carolina, Virginia, West Virginia); Southwestern—S.W. (Arkansas, Kentucky, Missouri, Tennessee, Texas); and Southern—So. (Alabama, Florida, Louisiana, Mississippi). There is also a special New York State reporter known as the New York Supplement and a special California State reporter known as the California Reporter.

[2] See, for example, Alaska, Florida, Iowa, Kentucky, Louisiana, Maine, Mississippi, Missouri, North Dakota, Oklahoma, Texas, and Wyoming.

There are two leading, fee-based systems for computer-aided research. Listed alphabetically, they are LEXIS and WESTLAW.

A specialized service of legal forms for business is provided by Shepard's BUSINESS LAW CASE MANAGEMENT SYSTEM. A monthly fee is required for usage.

Numerous free, private sites offer a lot of legal resources. The federal government offers a variety of case law, regulations, and code enactments, either pending or newly promulgated. To find the most comprehensive source of government-maintained legal information, go to **http://www.law.house.gov/**.

Increasingly, some states offer their regulations and codes online. As an example, go to the State of California's site, **http://www.leginfo.ca.gov/**, as an example of a government-based legal information provider. For a complete listing of state homepages, go to **http://www.law.house.gov/17.htm**.

For sources of all types of law, and legal resources, a new internet site, Hieros Gamos, **http://www.hg.org** claims that "virtually all online and offline (published) legal information is accessible within three levels." It is important to note, however, that non-fee-based services do not guarantee the integrity of the information provided. Therefore, when accessing free information over the Internet, one should be careful to double-check the authority of the provider and the accuracy of the data obtained. This caution extends to sites maintained by federal and state governments as well.

The computer field has expanded to such an extent that there is now a Legal Software Review of over 500 pages prepared by Lawyers Library, 12761 New Hall Ferry, Florissant, MO 63033.

APPENDIX (2)

THE CONSTITUTION ON THE UNITED STATES

We the people of the United States of America, in order to form a more perfect union, establish justice, insure domestic tranquility, provide for the common defense, promote the general welfare, and secure the blessings of liberty to ourselves and our posterity, do ordain and establish this Constitution for the United States of America.

ARTICLE I

Section 1. All legislative powers herein granted shall be vested in a Congress of the United States, which shall consist of a Senate and House of Representatives.

Section 2. 1. The House of Representatives shall be composed of members chosen every second year by the people of the several States, and the electors in each State shall have the qualifications requisite for electors of the most numerous branch of the State legislature.

2. No person shall be a representative who shall not have attained to the age of twenty-five years, and been seven years a citizen of the United States, and who shall not, when elected, be an inhabitant of that State in which he shall be chosen.

3. Representatives and direct taxes shall be apportioned among the several States which may be included within this Union, according to their respective numbers, which shall be determined by adding to the whole number of free persons, including those bound to service for a term of years, and excluding Indians not taxed, three fifths of all other persons.[1] The actual enumeration shall be made within three years after the first meeting of the Congress of the United States, and within every subsequent term of ten years, in such manner as they shall by law direct. The number of representatives shall not exceed one for every thirty thousand, but each State shall have at least one representative; and until such enumeration shall be made, the State of New Hampshire shall be entitled to choose three, Massachusetts eight, Rhode Island and Providence Plantations one, Connecticut five, New York six, New Jersey four, Pennsylvania eight, Delaware one, Maryland six, Virginia ten, North Carolina five, South Carolina five, and Georgia three.

4. When vacancies happen in the representation from any State, the executive authority thereof shall issue writs of election to fill such vacancies.

5. The House of Representatives shall choose their speaker and other officers; and shall have the sole power of impeachment.

Section 3. 1. The Senate of the United States shall be composed of two senators from each State, chosen by the legislature thereof, for six years; and each senator shall have one vote.

2. Immediately after they shall be assembled in consequence of the first election, they shall be divided as equally as may be into three classes. The seats of the senators of the first class shall be vacated at the expiration of the second year, of the second class at the expiration of the fourth year, and of the third class at the expiration of the sixth year, so that one third may be chosen every second year; and if vacancies happen by resignation, or otherwise, during the recess of the legislature of any State, the executive thereof may make temporary appointments until the next meeting of the legislature, which shall then fill such vacancies.[2]

3. No person shall be a senator who shall not have attained to the age of thirty years, and been nine years a citizen of the United States, and who shall not, when elected, be an inhabitant of that State for which he shall be chosen.

4. The Vice President of the United States shall be President of the Senate, but shall have no vote, unless they be equally divided.

5. The Senate shall choose their other officers, and also a president pro tempore, in the absence of the Vice President, or when he shall exercise the office of the President of the United States.

[1]See the 14th Amendment.

[2]See the 17th Amendment.

6. The Senate shall have the sole power to try all impeachments. When sitting for that purpose, they shall be on oath or affirmation. When the President of the United States is tried, the chief justice shall preside: and no person shall be convicted without the concurrence of two thirds of the members present.

7. Judgment in cases of impeachment shall not extend further than to removal from office, and disqualification to hold and enjoy any office of honor, trust or profit under the United States: but the party convicted shall nevertheless be liable and subject to indictment, trial, judgment and punishment, according to law.

Section 4. 1. The times, places, and manner of holding elections for senators and representatives, shall be prescribed in each State by the legislature thereof; but the Congress may at any time by law make or alter such regulations, except as to the places of choosing senators.

2. The Congress shall assemble at least once in every year, and such meeting shall be on the first Monday in December, unless they shall by law appoint a different day.

Section 5. 1. Each House shall be the judge of the elections, returns and qualifications of its own members, and a majority of each shall constitute a quorum to do business; but a smaller number may adjourn from day to day, and may be authorized to compel the attendance of absent members, in such manner, and under such penalties as each House may provide.

2. Each House may determine the rules of its proceedings, punish its members for disorderly behavior, and, with the concurrence of two thirds, expel a member.

3. Each House shall keep a journal of its proceedings, and from time to time publish the same, excepting such parts as may in their judgment require secrecy; and the yeas and nays of the members of either House on any question shall, at the desire of one fifth of those present, be entered on the journal.

4. Neither House, during the session of Congress, shall, without the consent of the other, adjourn for more than three days, nor to any other place than that in which the two Houses shall be sitting.

Section 6. 1. The senators and representatives shall receive a compensation for their services, to be ascertained by law, and paid out of the Treasury of the United States. They shall in all cases, except treason, felony, and breach of the peace, be privileged from arrest during their attendance at the session of their respective Houses, and in going to and returning from the same; and for any speech or debate in either House, they shall not be questioned in any other place.

2. No senator or representative shall, during the time for which he was elected, be appointed to any civil office under the authority of the United States, which shall have been created, or the emoluments whereof shall have been increased during such time; and no person holding any office under the United States shall be a member of either House during his continuance in office.

Section 7. 1. All bills for raising revenue shall originate in the House of Representatives; but the Senate may propose or concur with amendments as on other bills.

2. Every bill which shall have passed the House of Representatives and the Senate, shall, before it becomes a law, be presented to the President of the United States; if he approves he shall sign it, but if not he shall return it, with his objections to that House in which it shall have originated, who shall enter the objections at large on their journal, and proceed to reconsider it. If after such reconsideration two thirds of that House shall agree to pass the bill, it shall be sent, together with the objections, to the other House, by which it shall likewise be reconsidered, and if approved by two thirds of that House, it shall become a law. But in all such cases the votes of both Houses shall be determined by yeas and nays, and the names of the persons voting for and against the bill shall be entered on the journal of each House respectively. If any bill shall not be returned by the President within ten days (Sundays excepted) after it shall have been presented to him, the same shall be a law, in like manner as if he had signed it, unless the Congress by their adjournment prevent its return, in which case it shall not be a law.

3. Every order, resolution, or vote to which the concurrence of the Senate and the House of Representatives may be necessary (except on a question of adjournment) shall be presented to the President of the United States; and before the same shall take effect, shall be approved by him, or being disapproved by him, shall be repassed by two thirds of the Senate and House of Representatives, according to the rules and limitations prescribed in the case of a bill.

Section 8. The Congress shall have the power

1. To lay and collect taxes, duties, imposts, and excises, to pay the debts and provide for the common defense and general welfare of the United States; but all duties, imposts, and excises shall be uniform throughout the United States;

2. To borrow money on the credit of the United States;

3. To regulate commerce with foreign nations, and among the several States, and with the Indian tribes;

4. To establish a uniform rule of naturalization, and uniform laws on the subject of bankruptcies throughout the United States;

5. To coin money, regulate the value thereof, and of foreign coin, and fix the standard of weights and measures;

6. To provide for the punishment of counterfeiting the securities and current coin of the United States;

7. To establish post offices and post roads;

8. To promote the progress of science and useful arts, by securing for limited times to authors and inventors the exclusive rights to their respective writings and discoveries;

9. To constitute tribunals inferior to the Supreme Court;

10. To define and punish piracies and felonies committed on the high seas, and offenses against the law of nations;

11. To declare war, grant letters of marque and reprisal, and make rules concerning captures on land and water;

12. To raise and support armies, but no appropriation of money to that use shall be for a longer term than two years;

13. To provide and maintain a navy;

14. To make rules for the government and regulation of the land and naval forces;

15. To provide for calling forth the militia to execute the laws of the Union, suppress insurrections and repel invasions;

16. To provide for organizing, arming, and disciplining the militia, and for governing such part of them as may be employed in the service of the United States, reserving to the States respectively, the appointment of the officers, and the authority of training the militia according to the discipline prescribed by Congress;

17. To exercise exclusive legislation in all cases whatsoever, over such district (not exceeding ten miles square) as may, by cession of particular States, and the acceptance of Congress, become the seat of the government of the United States, and to exercise like authority over all places purchased by the consent of the legislature of the State in which the same shall be, for the erection of forts, magazines, arsenals, dockyards, and other needful buildings; and

18. To make all laws which shall be necessary and proper for carrying into execution the foregoing powers, and all other powers vested by this Constitution in the government of the United States, or in any department or officer thereof.

Section 9. 1. The migration or importation of such persons as any of the States now existing shall think proper to admit, shall not be prohibited by the Congress prior to the year one thousand eight hundred and eight, but a tax or duty may be imposed on such importation, not exceeding ten dollars for each person.

2. The privilege of the writ of habeas corpus shall not be suspended, unless when in cases of rebellion or invasion the public safety may require it.

3. No bill of attainder or ex post facto law shall be passed.

4. No capitation, or other direct, tax shall be laid, unless in proportion to the census or enumeration hereinbefore directed to be taken.[3]

5. No tax or duty shall be laid on articles exported from any State.

6. No preference shall be given by any regulation of commerce or revenue to the ports of one State over those of another: nor shall vessels bound to, or from, one State be obliged to enter, clear, or pay duties in another.

7. No money shall be drawn from the treasury, but in consequence of appropriations made by law; and a regular statement and account of the receipts and expenditures of all public money shall be published from time to time.

8. No title of nobility shall be granted by the United States: and no person holding any office of profit or trust under them, shall, without the consent of the Congress, accept of any present, emolument, office, or title, of any kind whatever, from any king, prince, or foreign State.

Section 10. 1. No State shall enter into any treaty, alliance, or confederation; grant letters of marque and reprisal; coin money; emit bills of credit; make anything but gold and silver coin a tender in payment of debts; pass any bill of attainder, ex post facto law, or law impairing the obligation of contracts, or grant any title of nobility.

2. No State shall, without the consent of the Congress, lay any imposts or duties on imports or exports, except what may be absolutely necessary for executing its inspection laws: and the net produce of all duties and imposts laid by any State on imports or exports, shall be for the use of the treasury of the United States; and all such laws shall be subject to the revision and control of the Congress.

3. No State shall, without the consent of the Congress, lay any duty of tonnage, keep troops, or ships of war in time of peace, enter into any agreement or compact with another State, or with a foreign power, or engage in war, unless actually invaded, or in such imminent danger as will not admit of delay.

ARTICLE II

Section 1. 1. The executive power shall be vested in a President of the United States of America. He shall hold his office during the term of four years, and, together with the Vice President, chosen for the same term, be elected as follows:

2. Each State shall appoint, in such manner as the legislature thereof may direct, a number of electors, equal to the whole number of senators and representatives to which the State may be entitled in the Congress: but no senator or representative, or person holding an office of trust or profit under the United States, shall be appointed an elector.

The electors shall meet in their respective States, and vote by ballot for two persons, of whom one at least shall not be an inhabitant of the same State with themselves. And they shall make a list of all the persons voted for, and of the number of votes for each; which list they shall sign and certify, and transmit sealed to the seat of the government of the United States, directed to the president of the Senate. The president of the Senate shall, in the presence of the Senate and House of Representatives, open all the certificates, and the votes shall then be counted. The person having the greatest number of votes shall be the President, if such number be a majority of the whole number of electors appointed; and if there be more than one who have such majority, and have an equal number of votes, then the House of Representatives shall immediately choose by ballot one of them for President; and if no person have a majority, then from the five highest on the list the said House shall in like manner choose the

[3]See the 16th Amendment.

President. But in choosing the President, the votes shall be taken by States, the representation from each State having one vote; a quorum for this purpose shall consist of a member or members from two thirds of the States, and a majority of all the States shall be necessary to a choice. In every case, after the choice of the President, the person having the greatest number of votes of the electors shall be the Vice President. But if there should remain two or more who have equal votes, the Senate shall choose from them by ballot the Vice President.[4]

3. The Congress may determine the time of choosing the electors, and the day on which they shall give their votes; which day shall be the same throughout the United States.

4. No person except a natural born citizen, or a citizen of the United States, at the time of the adoption of this Constitution, shall be eligible to the office of President; neither shall any person be eligible to that office who shall not have attained to the age of thirty-five years, and been fourteen years a resident within the United States.

5. In the case of removal of the President from office, or of his death, resignation, or inability to discharge the powers and duties of the said office, the same shall devolve on the Vice President, and the Congress may by law provide for the case of removal, death, resignation, or inability, both of the President and Vice President, declaring what officer shall then act as President, and such officer shall act accordingly, until the disability be removed, or a President shall be elected.

6. The President shall, at stated times, receive for his services a compensation, which shall neither be increased nor diminished during the period for which he shall have been elected, and he shall not receive within that period any other emolument from the United States, or any of them.

7. Before he enter on the execution of his office, he shall take the following oath or affirmation:—"I do solemnly swear (or affirm) that I will faithfully execute the office of President of the United States, and will to the best of my ability, preserve, protect and defend the Constitution of the United States."

Section 2. 1. The President shall be commander in chief of the army and navy of the United States, and of the militia of the several States, when called into the actual service of the United States; he may require the opinion, in writing, of the principal officer in each of the executive departments, upon any subject relating to the duties of their respective office, and he shall have power to grant reprieves and pardons for offenses against the United States, except in cases of impeachment.

2. He shall have power, by and with the advice and consent of the Senate, to make treaties, provided two thirds of the senators present concur; and he shall nominate, and by and with the advice and consent of the Senate, shall appoint ambassadors, other public ministers and consuls, judges of the Supreme Court, and all other officers of the United States, whose appointments are not herein otherwise provided for, and which shall be established by law: but the Congress may by law vest the appointment of such inferior officers, as they think proper, in the President alone, in the courts of law, or in the heads of departments.

3. The President shall have power to fill up all vacancies that may happen during the recess of the Senate, by granting commissions which shall expire at the end of their next session.

Section 3. He shall from time to time give to the Congress information of the state of the Union, and recommend to their consideration such measures as he shall judge necessary and expedient; he may, on extraordinary occasions, convene both Houses, or either of them, and in case of disagreement between them with respect to the time of adjournment, he may adjourn them to such time as he shall think proper; he shall receive ambassadors and other public ministers; he shall take care that the laws be faithfully executed, and shall commission all the officers of the United States.

Section 4. The President, Vice President, and all civil officers of the United States, shall be removed from office on impeachment for, and conviction of, treason, bribery, or other high crimes and misdemeanors.

ARTICLE III

Section 1. The judicial power of the United States shall be vested in one Supreme Court, and in such inferior courts as the Congress may from time to time ordain and establish. The judges, both of the Supreme and inferior courts, shall hold their offices during good behavior, and shall, at stated times, receive for their services, a compensation, which shall not be diminished during their continuance in office.

Section 2. 1. The judicial power shall extend to all cases, in law and equity, arising under this Constitution, the laws of the United States, and treaties made, or which shall be made, under their authority;—to all cases affecting ambassadors, other public ministers and consuls;—to all cases of admiralty and maritime jurisdiction;—to controversies to which the United States shall be a party;—to controversies between two or more States; between a State and citizens of another State;[5]—between citizens of different States;—between citizens of the same State claiming lands under grants of different States, and between a State, or the citizens thereof, and foreign States, citizens or subjects.

2. In all cases affecting ambassadors, other public ministers and consuls, and those in which a State shall be party, the Supreme Court shall have original jurisdiction. In all the other cases before mentioned, the Supreme Court shall have appellate jurisdiction, both as to law and to fact, with such exceptions, and under such regulations as the Congress shall make.

[4]Superseded by the 12th Amendment.

[5]See the 11th Amendment.

3. The trial of all crimes, except in cases of impeachment, shall be by jury; and such trial shall be held in the State where the said crimes shall have been committed; but when not committed within any State, the trial shall be at such place or places as the Congress may by law have directed.

Section 3. 1. Treason against the United States shall consist only in levying war against them, or in adhering to their enemies, giving them aid and comfort. No person shall be convicted of treason unless on the testimony of two witnesses to the same overt act, or on confession in open court.

2. The Congress shall have power to declare the punishment of treason, but no attainder of treason shall work corruption of blood, or forfeiture except during the life of the person attainted.

ARTICLE IV

Section 1. Full faith and credit shall be given in each State to the public acts, records, and judicial proceedings of every other State. And the Congress may by general laws prescribe the manner in which such acts, records and proceedings shall be proved, and the effect thereof.

Section 2. 1. The citizens of each State shall be entitled to all privileges and immunities of citizens in the several States.[6]

2. A person charged in any State with treason, felony, or other crime, who shall flee from justice, and be found in another State, shall on demand of the executive authority of the State from which he fled, be delivered up to be removed to the State having jurisdiction of the crime.

3. No person held to service or labor in one State under the laws thereof, escaping into another, shall in consequence of any law or regulation therein, be discharged from such service or labor, but shall be delivered up on claim of the party to whom such service or labor may be due.[7]

Section 3. 1. New States may be admitted by the Congress into this Union; but no new State shall be formed or erected within the jurisdiction of any other State, nor any State be formed by the junction of two or more States, or parts of States, without the consent of the legislatures of the States concerned as well as of the Congress.

2. The Congress shall have power to dispose of and make all needful rules and regulations respecting the territory or other property belonging to the United States; and nothing in this Constitution shall be so construed as to prejudice any claims of the United States, or of any particular State.

Section 4. The United States shall guarantee to every State in this Union a republican form of government, and shall protect each of them against invasion; and on application of the legislature, or of the executive (when the legislature cannot be convened) against domestic violence.

[6]See the 14th Amendment, Sec. 1.

[7]See the 13th Amendment.

ARTICLE V

The Congress, whenever two thirds of both Houses shall deem it necessary, shall propose amendments to this Constitution, or, on the application of the legislature of two thirds of the several States, shall call a convention for proposing amendments, which in either case, shall be valid to all intents and purposes, as part of this Constitution when ratified by the legislatures of three fourths of the several States, or by conventions in three fourths thereof, as the one or the other mode of ratification may be proposed by the Congress; provided that no amendment which may be made prior to the year one thousand eight hundred and eight shall in any manner affect the first and fourth clauses in the ninth section of the first article; and that no State, without its consent, shall be deprived of its equal suffrage in the Senate.

ARTICLE VI

1. All debts contracted and engagements entered into, before the adoption of this Constitution, shall be as valid against the United States under this Constitution, as under the Confederation.[8]

2. This Constitution, and the laws of the United States which shall be made in pursuance thereof; and all treaties made, or which shall be made, under the authority of the United States, shall be the supreme law of the land; and the judges in every State shall be bound thereby, anything in the Constitution or laws of any State to the contrary notwithstanding.

3. The senators and representatives before mentioned, and the members of the several State legislatures, and all executive and judicial officers, both of the United States and of the several States, shall be bound by oath or affirmation to support this Constitution; but no religious test shall ever be required as a qualification to any office or public trust under the United States.

ARTICLE VII

The ratification of the conventions of nine States shall be sufficient for the establishment of this Constitution between the States so ratifying the same.

Done in Convention by the unanimous consent of the States present the seventeenth day of September in the year of our Lord one thousand seven hundred and eighty-seven, and of the independence of the United States of America the twelfth. In witness whereof we have hereunto subscribed our names.

Amendments

First Ten Amendments passed by Congress Sept. 25, 1789.

Ratified by three-fourths of the States December 15, 1791.

[8]See the 14th Amendment, Sec. 4.

AMENDMENT I

Congress shall make no law respecting an establishment of religion, or prohibiting the free exercise thereof; or abridging the freedom of speech, or of the press; or the right of the people peaceably to assemble, and to petition the government for a redress of grievances.

AMENDMENT II

A well regulated militia, being necessary to the security of a free State, the right of the people to keep and bear arms, shall not be infringed.

AMENDMENT III

No soldier shall, in time of peace be quartered in any house, without the consent of the owner, nor in time of war, but in a manner to be prescribed by law.

AMENDMENT IV

The right of the people to be secure in their persons, houses, papers, and effects, against unreasonable searches and seizures, shall not be violated, and no warrants shall issue, but upon probable cause, supported by oath or affirmation, and particularly describing the place to be searched, and the person or things to be seized.

AMENDMENT V

No person shall be held to answer for a capital, or otherwise infamous crime, unless on a presentment or indictment of a grand jury, except in cases arising in the land or naval forces, or in the militia, when in actual service in time of war or public danger; nor shall any person be subject for the same offense to be twice put in jeopardy of life or limb; nor shall be compelled in any criminal case to be a witness against himself, nor be deprived of life, liberty, or property, without due process of law; nor shall private property be taken for public use without just compensation.

AMENDMENT VI

In all criminal prosecutions, the accused shall enjoy the right to a speedy and public trial, by an impartial jury of the State and district wherein the crime shall have been committed, which district shall have been previously ascertained by law, and to be informed of the nature and cause of the accusation; to be confronted with the witnesses against him; to have compulsory process for obtaining witnesses in his favor, and to have the assistance of counsel for his defense.

AMENDMENT VII

In suits at common law, where the value in controversy shall exceed twenty dollars, the right of trial by jury shall be preserved, and no fact tried by a jury shall be otherwise reexamined in any court of the United States, then according to the rules of the common law.

AMENDMENT VIII

Excessive bail shall not be required, nor excessive fines imposed, nor cruel and unusual punishments inflicted.

AMENDMENT IX

The enumeration in the Constitution of certain rights shall not be construed to deny or disparage others retained by the people.

AMENDMENT X

The powers not delegated to the United States by the Constitution, nor prohibited by it to the States, are reserved to the States respectively, or to the people.

AMENDMENT XI

Passed by Congress March 5, 1794. Ratified January 8, 1798.

The judicial power of the United States shall not be construed to extend to any suit in law or equity, commenced or prosecuted against one of the United States by citizens of another State, or by citizens or subjects of any foreign State.

AMENDMENT XII

Passed by Congress December 12, 1803. Ratified September 25, 1804.

The electors shall meet in their respective States, and vote by ballot for President and Vice President, one of whom, at least, shall not be an inhabitant of the same State with themselves; they shall name in their ballots the person voted for as President, and in distinct ballots, the person voted for as Vice President, and they shall make distinct lists of all persons voted for as President and of all persons voted for as Vice President, and of the number of votes for each, which lists they shall sign and certify, and transmit sealed to the seat of the government of the United States, directed to the President of the Senate;—The President of the Senate shall, in the presence of the Senate and House of Representatives, open all the certificates and the votes shall then be counted;—The person having the greatest number of votes for President, shall be the President, if such number be a majority of the whole number of electors appointed; and if no person have such majority, then from the persons having the highest numbers not exceeding three on the list of those voted for as President, the House of Representatives shall choose immediately, by ballot, the President. But in choosing the President, the votes shall be taken by States, the representation from each State having one vote; a quorum for this purpose shall consist of a member or members from two thirds of the States, and a majority of all the States shall be necessary to a choice. And if the House of Representatives shall not choose a President whenever the right of choice shall devolve upon them, before the fourth day of March next following, then the Vice President shall act as President, as in the case of the death or other constitutional disability of the President. The person having the greatest number of votes as Vice President shall be the Vice President, if such number be a majority of the whole number of electors appointed, and if no person have a majority, then from the two highest numbers on the list, the Senate shall choose the Vice President; a quorum for the purpose shall consist of two thirds of the whole number of Senators, and a majority of the whole number shall be necessary to a choice. But no person constitutionally ineligible to the office of President shall be eligible to that of Vice President of the United States.

AMENDMENT XIII

Passed by Congress February 1, 1865. Ratified December 18, 1865.

Section 1. Neither slavery nor involuntary servitude, except as punishment for crime whereof the party shall have been duly convicted, shall exist within the United States, or any place subject to their jurisdiction.

Section 2. Congress shall have power to enforce this article by appropriate legislation.

AMENDMENT XIV

Passed by Congress June 16, 1866. Ratified July 23, 1868.

Section 1. All persons born or naturalized in the United States, and subject to the jurisdiction thereof, are citizens of the United States and of the State wherein they reside. No State shall make or enforce any law which shall abridge the privileges or immunities of citizens of the United States; nor shall any State deprive any person of life, liberty, or property, without due process of law; nor deny to any person within its jurisdiction the equal protection of the laws.

Section 2. Representatives shall be apportioned among the several States according to their respective numbers, counting the whole number of persons in each State, excluding Indians not taxed. But when the right to vote at any election for the choice of electors for President and Vice President of the United States, representatives in Congress, the executive and judicial officers of a State, or the members of the legislature thereof, is denied to any of the male inhabitants of such State, being twenty-one years of age, and citizens of the United States, or in any way abridged, except for participation in rebellion, or other crime, the basis of representation therein shall be reduced in the proportion which the number of such male citizens shall bear to the whole number of male citizens twenty-one years of age in such State.

Section 3. No person shall be a senator or representative in Congress, or elector of President and Vice President, or hold any office, civil or military, under the United States, or under any State, who having previously taken an oath, as a member of Congress, or as an officer of the United States, or as a member of any State legislature, or as an executive or judicial officer of any State, to support the Constitution of the United States, shall have engaged in insurrection or rebellion against the same, or given aid or comfort to the enemies thereof. But Congress may by a vote of two thirds of each House, remove such disability.

Section 4. The validity of the public debt of the United States, authorized by law, including debts incurred for payment of pensions and bounties for services in suppressing insurrection or rebellion, shall not be questioned. But neither the United States nor any State shall assume or pay any debt or obligation incurred in aid of insurrection or rebellion against the United States, or any claim for the loss or emancipation of any slave; but all such debts, obligations, and claims shall be held illegal and void.

Section 5. The Congress shall have power to enforce, by appropriate legislation, the provisions of this article.

AMENDMENT XV

Passed by Congress February 27, 1869. Ratified March 30, 1870.

Section 1. The right of citizens of the United States to vote shall not be denied or abridged by the United States or by any State on account of race, color, or previous condition of servitude.

Section 2. The Congress shall have power to enforce this article by appropriate legislation.

AMENDMENT XVI

Passed by Congress July 12, 1909. Ratified February 25, 1913.

The Congress shall have power to lay and collect taxes on incomes, from whatever source derived, without apportionment among the several States, and without regard to any census or enumeration.

AMENDMENT XVII

Passed by Congress May 16, 1912. Ratified May 31, 1913.

The Senate of the United States shall be composed of two senators from each State, elected by the people thereof, for six years; and each senator shall have one vote. The electors in each State shall have the qualifications requisite for electors of the most numerous branch of the State legislature.

When vacancies happen in the representation of any State in the Senate, the executive authority of such State shall issue writs of election to fill such vacancies: Provided, That the legislature of any State may empower the executive thereof to make temporary appointments until the people fill the vacancies by election as the legislature may direct.

This amendment shall not be so construed as to affect the election or term of any senator chosen before it becomes valid as part of the Constitution.

AMENDMENT XVIII

Passed by Congress December 17, 1917. Ratified January 29, 1919.

After one year from the ratification of this article, the manufacture, sale, or transportation of intoxicating liquors within, the importation thereof into, or the exportation thereof from the United States and all territory subject to the jurisdiction thereof for beverage purposes is hereby prohibited.

The Congress and the several States shall have concurrent power to enforce this article by appropriate legislation.

This article shall be inoperative unless it shall have been ratified as an amendment to the Constitution by the legislatures of the several States, as provided in the Constitution, within seven years from the date of the submission hereof to the States by Congress.

AMENDMENT XIX

Passed by Congress June 5, 1919. Ratified August 26, 1920.

The right of citizens of the United States to vote shall not be denied or abridged by the United States or by any State on account of sex.

The Congress shall have power by appropriate legislation to enforce the provisions of this article.

AMENDMENT XX

Passed by Congress March 3, 1932. Ratified January 23, 1933.

Section 1. The terms of the President and Vice President shall end at noon on the 20th day of January, and the terms of Senators and Representatives at noon on the 3d day of January, of the years in which such terms would have ended if this article had not been ratified; and the terms of their successors shall then begin.

Section 2. The Congress shall assemble at least once in every year, and such meeting shall begin at noon on the 3d day of January, unless they shall by law appoint a different day.

Section 3. If, at the time fixed for the beginning of the term of the President, the President-elect shall have died, the Vice President-elect shall become President. If a President shall not have been chosen before the time fixed for the beginning of his term, or if the President-elect shall have failed to qualify, then the Vice President-elect shall act as President until a President shall have qualified; and the Congress may by law provide for the case wherein neither a President-elect nor a Vice President-elect shall have qualified, declaring who shall then act as President, or the manner in which one who is to act shall be selected, and such person shall act accordingly until a President or Vice President shall have qualified.

Section 4. The Congress may by law provide for the case of the death of any of the persons from whom the House of Representatives may choose a President whenever the right of choice shall have devolved upon them, and for the case of the death of any of the persons from whom the Senate may choose a Vice President whenever the right of choice shall have devolved upon them.

Section 5. Sections 1 and 2 shall take effect on the 15th day of October following the ratification of this article.

Section 6. This article shall be inoperative unless it shall have been ratified as an amendment to the Constitution by the legislatures of three-fourths of the several States within seven years from the date of its submission.

AMENDMENT XXI

Passed by Congress February 20, 1933. Ratified December 5, 1933.

Section 1. The eighteenth article of amendment to the Constitution of the United States is hereby repealed.

Section 2. The transportation or importation into any State, Territory, or possession of the United States for delivery or use therein of intoxicating liquors in violation of the laws thereof, is hereby prohibited.

Section 3. This article shall be inoperative unless it shall have been ratified as an amendment to the Constitution by conventions in the several States, as provided in the Constitution, within seven years from the date of the submission thereof to the States by the Congress.

AMENDMENT XXII

Passed by Congress March 24, 1947. Ratified February 26, 1951.

Section 1. No person shall be elected to the office of the President more than twice, and no person who has held the office of President, or acted as President, for more than two years of a term to which some other person was elected President shall be elected to the office of the President more than once. But this article shall not apply to any person holding the office of President when this article was proposed by the Congress, and shall not prevent any person who may be holding the office of President, or acting as President, during the term within which this article becomes operative from holding the office of President or acting as President during the remainder of such term.

Section 2. This article shall be inoperative unless it shall have been ratified as an amendment to the Constitution by the legislatures of three-fourths of the several States within seven years from the date of its submission to the States by the Congress.

AMENDMENT XXIII

Passed by Congress June 16, 1960. Ratified April 3, 1961.

Section 1. The District constituting the seat of Government of the United States shall appoint in such manner as the Congress may direct:

A number of electors of President and Vice President equal to the whole number of Senators and Representatives in Congress to which the District would be entitled if it were a State, but in no event more than the least populous State; they shall be in addition to those appointed by the States, but they shall be considered, for the purposes of the election of President and Vice President, to be electors appointed by a State; and they shall meet in the District and perform such duties as provided by the twelfth article of amendment.

Section 2. The Congress shall have power to enforce this article by appropriate legislation.

AMENDMENT XXIV

Passed by Congress August 27, 1962. Ratified February 4, 1964.

Section 1. The right of citizens of the United States to vote in any primary or other election for President or Vice President, for electors for President or Vice President, or for Senator or Representative in Congress, shall not be denied or abridged by the United States or any State by reason of failure to pay any poll tax or other tax.

Section 2. The Congress shall have power to enforce this article by appropriate legislation.

AMENDMENT XXV

Passed by Congress July 6, 1965. Ratified February 23, 1967.

Section 1. In case of the removal of the President from office or of his death or resignation, the Vice President shall become President.

Section 2. Whenever there is a vacancy in the office of the Vice President, the President shall nominate a Vice President who shall take office upon confirmation by a majority vote of both Houses of Congress.

Section 3. Whenever the President transmits to the President pro tempore of the Senate and the Speaker of the House of Representatives his written declaration that he is unable to discharge the powers and duties of his office, and until he transmits to them a written declaration to the contrary, such powers and duties shall be discharged by the Vice President as Acting President.

Section 4. Whenever the Vice President and a majority of either the principal officers of the executive departments or of such other body as Congress may by law provide, transmit to the President pro tempore of the Senate and the Speaker of the House of Representatives their written declaration that the President is unable to discharge the powers and duties of his office, the Vice President shall immediately assume the powers and duties of the office as Acting President.

Thereafter, when the President transmits to the President pro tempore of the Senate and the Speaker of the House of Representatives his written declaration that no inability exists, he shall resume the powers and duties of his office unless the Vice President and a majority of either the principal officers of the executive department or of such other body as Congress may by law provide, transmit within four days to the President pro tempore of the Senate and the Speaker of the House of Representatives their written declaration that the President is unable to discharge the powers and duties of his office. Thereupon Congress shall decide the issue, assembling within forty-eight hours for that purpose if not in session. If the Congress, within twenty-one days after receipt of the latter written declaration, or, if Congress is not in session, within twenty-one days after Congress is required to assemble, determines by two-thirds vote of both Houses that the President is unable to discharge the powers and duties of his office, the Vice President shall continue to discharge the same as Acting President; otherwise, the President shall resume the powers and duties of his office.

AMENDMENT XXVI

Passed by Congress March 23, 1971. Ratified July 5, 1971.

Section 1. The right of citizens of the United States, who are eighteen years of age or older, to vote shall not be denied or abridged by the United States or by any State on account of age.

AMENDMENT XXVII

Passed by Congress September 25, 1789. Ratified May 18, 1992.

No law, varying the compensation for the services of the Senators and Representatives, shall take effect, until an election of Representatives shall have intervened.

GLOSSARY

A

abate—put a stop to a nuisance; reduce or cancel a legacy because the estate of the decedent is insufficient to make payment in full.

absolute guaranty—agreement that creates the same obligation for the guarantor as a suretyship does for the surety; a guaranty of payment creates an absolute guaranty.

absolute privilege—complete defense against the tort of defamation, as in the speeches of members of Congress on the floor and witnesses in a trial.

abstract of title—history of the transfers of title to a given piece of land, briefly stating the parties to and the effect of all deeds, wills, and judicial proceedings relating to the land.

acceleration clause—provision in a contract or any legal instrument that advances the time for the performance of specified obligations; for example, a provision making the balance due upon debtor's default.

acceptance—unqualified assent to the act or proposal of another; as the acceptance of a draft (bill of exchange), of an offer to make a contract, of goods delivered by the seller, or of a gift or deed.

acceptor—drawee who has accepted the liability of paying the amount of money specified in a draft.

accommodation party—person who signs an instrument to lend credit to another party to the paper.

accord and satisfaction—agreement to substitute for an existing debt some alternative form of discharging that debt, coupled with the actual discharge of the debt by the substituted performance.

acknowledgment—admission or confirmation, generally of an instrument and usually made before a person authorized to administer oaths, such as a notary public; used to establish that the instrument was executed by the person making the instrument, that it was a voluntary act, or that the instrument is recorded.

act-of-state doctrine—doctrine whereby every sovereign state is bound to respect the independence of every other sovereign state, and the courts of one country will not sit in judgment of another government's acts done within its own territory.

adeemed—canceled; as in a specifically bequeathed property being sold or given away by the testator prior to death, thus canceling the bequest.

adjustable rate mortgage (ARM)—mortgage with variable financing charges over the life of the loan.

administrative agency—government body charged with administering and implementing legislation.

administrative law—law governing administrative agencies.

Administrative Procedure Act—federal law that establishes the operating rules for administrative agencies.

administrative regulations—rules made by state and federal administrative agencies.

administrator, administratrix—person (man, woman) appointed to wind up and settle the estate of a person who has died without a will.

admissibility—the quality of the evidence in a case that allows it to be presented to the jury.

adverse possession—hostile possession of real estate, which when actual, visible, notorious, exclusive, and continued for the required time, will vest the title to the land in the person in such adverse possession.

advising bank—bank that tells beneficiary that letter of credit has been issued.

affidavit—statement of facts set forth in written form and supported by the oath or affirmation of the person making the statement setting forth that such facts are true on the basis of actual knowledge or on information and belief. The affidavit is executed before a notary public or other person authorized to administer oaths.

affirm—action taken by an appellate court that approves the decision of the court below.

affirmative action plan (AAP)—plan to have a diverse and representative workforce.

after-acquired goods—goods acquired after a security interest has attached.

agency—the relationship that exists between a person identified as a principal and another by virtue of which the latter may make contracts with third persons on behalf of the principal. (Parties–principal, agent, third person)

agent—person or firm who is authorized by the principal or by operation of law to make contracts with third persons on behalf of the principal.

airbill—document of title issued to a shipper whose goods are being sent via air.

alteration—unauthorized change or completion of a negotiable instrument designed to modify the obligation of a party to the instrument.

alternative payees—those persons to whom a negotiable instrument is made payable, any one of whom may indorse and take delivery of it.

ambiguous—having more than one reasonable interpretation.

answer—what a defendant must file to admit or deny facts asserted by the plaintiff.

anticipatory breach—promisor's repudiation of the contract prior to the time that performance is required when such repudiation is accepted by the promisee as a breach of the contract.

anticipatory repudiation—repudiation made in advance of the time for performance of the contract obligations.

antilapse statutes—statutes providing that the children or heirs of a deceased beneficiary may take the legacy in the place of the deceased beneficiary.

apparent authority—appearance of authority created by the principal's words or conduct.

appeal—taking a case to a reviewing court to determine whether the judgment of the lower court or administrative agency was correct. (Parties–appellant, appellee)

appellate jurisdiction—the power of a court to hear and decide a given class of cases on appeal from another court or administrative agency.

appropriation—taking of an image, likeness, or name for commercial advantage.

arbitration—the settlement of disputed questions, whether of law or fact, by one or more arbitrators by whose decision the parties agree to be bound.

Article 2—section of Uniform Commercial Code that governs contracts for the sale of goods.

articles of copartnership—See *Partnership Agreement*

articles of incorporation—document filed to create a corporation; the basic structure of a company and the rights of its owners.

articles of partnership—See *Partnership Agreement*

assignee—third party to whom contract benefits are transferred.

assignment—transfer of a right. Generally used in connection with personal property rights, as rights under a contract, commercial paper, an insurance policy, a mortgage, or a lease. (Parties–assignor, assignee)

assignor—party who assigns contract rights to a third party.

association tribunal—a court created by a trade association or group for the resolution of disputes among its members.

assumption—mortgage transfers in which the transferee and mortgagor are liable and the property is subject to foreclosure by the mortgagee if payments are not made.

attestation clause—clause that indicates a witness has observed either the execution of the will or the testator's acknowledgment of the writing as the testator's will.

attorney in fact—agent authorized to act for another under a power of attorney.

attractive nuisance doctrine—a rule imposing liability upon a landowner for injuries sustained by small children playing on the land when the landowner permits a condition to exist or maintains equipment that a reasonable person should realize would attract small children who could not realize the danger. The rule does not apply if an unreasonable burden would be imposed upon the landowner in taking steps to protect the children.

authorities—corporations formed by government that perform public service.

automatic perfection—perfection given by statute without specific filing or possession requirements on the part of the creditor.

automatic stay—order to prevent creditors from taking action such as filing suits or seeking foreclosure against the debtor.

B

bad check laws—laws making it a criminal offense to issue a bad check with intent to defraud.

bailee—person who accepts possession of a property.

bailee's lien—specific, possessory lien of the bailee upon the goods for work done to them. Commonly extended by statute to any bailee's claim for compensation, eliminating the necessity of retention of possession.

bailment—relationship that exists when personal property is delivered into the possession of another under an agreement, express or implied, that the identical property will be returned or will be delivered in accordance with the agreement. (Parties–bailor, bailee)

bailment for mutual benefit—bailment in which the bailor and bailee derive a benefit from the bailment.

bailor—person who turns over the possession of a property.

balance sheet test—comparison of assets to liabilities made to determine solvency.

bankruptcy—procedure by which one unable to pay debts may surrender all assets in excess of any exemption claim to the court for administration and distribution to creditors, and the debtor is given a discharge that releases him from the unpaid balance due on most debts.

bankruptcy courts—court of special jurisdiction to determine bankruptcy issues.

battle of the forms—merchants' exchanges of invoices and purchase orders with differing boilerplate terms.

bearer—person in physical possession of commercial paper payable to bearer, a document of title directing delivery to bearer, or an investment security in bearer form.

bearer paper—instrument with no payee, payable to cash or payable to bearer.

bedrock view—a strict constructionist interpretation of a constitution.

beneficiary—person to whom the proceeds of a life insurance policy are payable, a person for whose benefit property is held in trust, or a person given property by a will; the ultimate recipient of the benefit of a funds transfer.

beneficiary's bank—the final bank, which carries out the payment order, in the chain of a transfer of funds.

bequest—gift of personal property by will.

bicameral—a two-house form of the legislative branch of government.

bilateral contract—agreement under which one promise is given in exchange for another.

bill of lading—document issued by a carrier acknowledging the receipt of goods and the terms of the contract of transportation.

bill of sale—writing signed by the seller reciting that the personal property therein described has been sold to the buyer.

blackmail—extortion demands made by a nonpublic official.

blank indorsement—an indorsement that does not name the person to whom the paper, document of title, or investment security is negotiated.

blocking laws—laws that prohibit the disclosure, copying, inspection, or removal of documents located in the enacting country in compliance with orders from foreign authorities.

blue sky laws—state statutes designed to protect the public from the sale of worthless stocks and bonds.

bona fide—in good faith; without any fraud or deceit.

bond—obligation or promise in writing and sealed, generally of corporations, personal representatives, and trustees; fidelity bonds.

bond indenture—agreement setting forth the contractual terms of a particular bond issue.

book value—value found by dividing the value of the corporate assets by the number of shares outstanding.

breach—failure to act or perform in the manner called for in a contract.

breach of the peace—violation of the law in the repossession of the collateral.

bubble concept—method for determining total emissions in one area; all sources are considered in an area.

business ethics—balancing the goal of profits with values of individuals and society.

business judgment rule—rule that allows management immunity from liability for corporate acts where there is a reasonable indication that the acts were made in good faith with due care.

bylaws—rules and regulations enacted by a corporation to govern the affairs of the corporation and its shareholders, directors, and officers.

C

cancellation provision—crossing out of a part of an instrument or a destruction of all legal effect of the instrument, whether by act of party, upon breach by the other party, or pursuant to agreement or decree of court.

capital stock—declared money value of the outstanding stock of the corporation.

cargo insurance—insurance that protects a cargo owner against financial loss if goods being shipped are lost or damaged at sea.

carrier—individual or organization undertaking the transportation of goods.

case law—law that includes principles that are expressed for the first time in court decisions.

cash surrender value—sum paid the insured upon the surrender of a policy to the insurer.

cash tender offer—general offer to all shareholders of a target corporation to purchase their shares for cash at a specified price.

cashier's check— draft drawn by a bank on itself.

cause of action—right to damages or other judicial relief when a legally protected right of the plaintiff is violated by an unlawful act of the defendant.

cease-and-desist order—order issued by a court or administrative agency to stop a practice that it decides is improper.

certificate of deposit (CD)—promise-to-pay instrument issued by a bank.

certificate of incorporation—written approval from the state or national government for a corporation to be formed.

certificate of stock—document evidencing a shareholder's ownership of stock issued by a corporation.

certified check—check for which the bank has set aside in a special account sufficient funds to pay it; payment is made when check is presented regardless of amount in drawer's account at that time; discharges all parties except certifying bank when holder requests certification.

cestui que trust—beneficiary or person for whose benefit the property is held in trust.

CF—cost and freight.

Chapter 11 bankruptcy—reorganization form of bankruptcy under federal law.

Chapter 7 bankruptcy—liquidation form of bankruptcy under federal law.

Chapter 13 bankruptcy—proceeding of consumer debt readjustment plan bankruptcy.

charging order—order by a court, after a business partner's personal assets are exhausted, requiring that the partner's share of the profits be paid to a creditor until the debt is discharged.

charter—grant of authority from a government to exist as a corporation. Generally replaced today by a certificate of incorporation approving the articles of incorporation.

check—order by a depositor on a bank to pay a sum of money to a payee; a bill of exchange drawn on a bank and payable on demand.

choice-of-law clause—clause in an agreement that specifies which law will govern should a dispute arise.

chose in action—intangible personal property in the nature of claims against another, such as a claim for accounts receivable or wages.

CIF—cost, insurance, and freight.

civil disobedience—the term used when natural law proponents violate positive law.

claim—creditor's right to payment.

Clayton Act—a federal law that prohibits price discrimination.

Clean Air Act—federal legislation that establishes standards for air pollution levels and prevents further deterioration of air quality.

Clean Water Act—federal legislation that regulates water pollution through a control system.

close corporation—corporation whose shares are held by a single shareholder or a small group of shareholders.

close-connection doctrine—circumstantial evidence, such as an ongoing or a close relationship, that can serve as notice of a problem with an instrument.

COD—cash on delivery.

coinsurance clause—clause requiring the insured to maintain insurance on property up to a stated amount and providing that to the extent that this is not done, the insured is to be deemed a coinsurer with the insurer, so that the latter is liable only for its proportionate share of the amount of insurance required to be carried.

collateral—property pledged by a borrower as security for a debt.

comity—principle of international and national law that the laws of all nations and states deserve the respect legitimately demanded by equal participants.

commerce clause—that section of the U.S. Constitution allocating business regulation.

commercial impracticability—situation that occurs when costs of performance rise suddenly and performance of a contract will result in a substantial loss.

commercial lease—any nonconsumer lease.

commercial paper—written, transferable, signed promise or order to pay a specified sum of money; a negotiable instrument.

commercial unit—standard of the trade for shipment or packaging of a good.

commission merchant—bailee to whom goods are consigned for sale.

commission or factorage—consignee's compensation.

common carrier—carrier that holds out its facilities to serve the general public for compensation without discrimination.

common law—the body of unwritten principles originally based upon the usages and customs of the community that were recognized and enforced by the courts.

common stock—stock that has no right or priority over any other stock of the corporation as to dividends or distribution of assets upon dissolution.

community property—cotenancy held by husband and wife in property acquired during their marriage under the law of some of the states, principally in the southwestern United States.

comparative negligence—defense to negligence that allows plaintiff to recover reduced damages based on his level of fault.

compensatory damages—sum of money that will compensate an injured plaintiff for actual loss.

complaint—the initial pleading filed by the plaintiff in many actions, which in many states may be served as original process to acquire jurisdiction over the defendant.

composition of creditors—agreement among creditors that each shall accept a partial payment as full payment in consideration of the other creditors doing the same.

Comprehensive Environmental Response, Compensation, and Liability Act (CERCLA)—federal law that authorizes the president to issue funds for the cleanup of areas that were once disposal sites for hazardous wastes.

computer crimes—wrongs committed using a computer or with knowledge of computers.

concealment—failure to volunteer information not requested.

condition—stipulation or prerequisite in a contract, will, or other instrument.

condition precedent—event that if unsatisfied would mean that no rights would arise under a contract.

condition subsequent—event whose occurrence or lack thereof terminates a contract.

condominium—combination of co-ownership and individual ownership.

confidential relationship—relationship in which, because of the legal status of the parties or their respective physical or mental conditions or knowledge, one party places full confidence and trust in the other.

conflict of interest—conduct that compromises an employee's allegiance to that company.

conglomerate—relationship of a parent corporation to subsidiary corporations engaged in diversified fields of activity unrelated to the field of activity of the parent corporation.

consent decrees—informal settlements of enforcement actions brought by agencies.

consequential damages—damages the buyer experiences as a result of the seller's breach with respect to a third party; also called *special damages.*

consideration—promise or performance that the promisor demands as the price of the promise.

consignee—(1) person to whom goods are shipped, (2) dealer who sells goods for others.

consignment—bailment made for the purpose of sale by the bailee. (Parties–consignor, consignee)

consignor—(1) person who delivers goods to the carrier for shipment, (2) party with title who turns goods over to another for sale.

consolidation (of corporations)—combining of two or more corporations in which the corporate existence of each one ceases and a new corporation is created.

conspiracy—agreement between two or more persons to commit an unlawful act.

constitution—a body of principles that establishes the structure of a government and the relationship of the government to the people who are governed.

constructive bailment—bailment imposed by law as opposed to one created by contract, whereby the bailee must preserve the property and redeliver it to the owner.

constructive delivery—see "symbolic delivery."

constructive eviction—act or omission of the landlord that substantially deprives the tenant of the use and enjoyment of the premises.

consumer—any buyer afforded special protections by statute or regulation.

consumer credit—credit for personal, family, and household use.

consumer goods—goods used or bought primarily for personal, family, or household use.

consumer lease—lease of goods by a natural person for personal, family, or household use.

continuing nuisance—series of related acts or a continuation of an activity.

contract—a binding agreement based on the genuine assent of the parties, made for a lawful object, between competent parties, in the form required by law, and generally supported by consideration.

contract carrier—carrier that transports on the basis of individual contracts that it makes with each shipper.

contract interference—tort in which a third party interferes with others' freedom to contract.

contract of adhesion—contract offered by a dominant party to a party with inferior bargaining power on a take-it-or-leave-it basis.

contract under seal—contract executed by affixing a seal or making an impression on the paper or on some adhering substance such as wax attached to the document.

contracting agent—agent with authority to make contracts; person with whom the buyer deals.

Contracts for the International Sale of Goods (CISG)—uniform international contract code contracts for international sale of goods.

contractual capacity—ability to understand that a contract is being made and to understand its general meaning.

contribution—right of a co-obligor who has paid more than a proportionate share to demand that the other obligor pay the amount of the excess payment made.

contributory negligence—negligence of the plaintiff that contributes to injury and at common law bars recovery from the defendant although the defendant may have been more negligent than the plaintiff.

conversion—act of taking personal property by a person not entitled to it and keeping it from its true owner or prior possessor without consent.

cooperative—group of two or more persons or enterprises that acts through a common agent with respect to a common objective, such as buying or selling.

copyright—exclusive right given by federal statute to the creator of a literary or an artistic work to use, reproduce, and display the work.

corporation—artificial being created by government grant, which for many purposes is treated as a natural person.

corporation by estoppel—corporation that comes about when parties estop themselves from denying that the corporation exists.

corporation de jure—corporation with a legal right to exist by virtue of law.

correspondent bank—will honor the letter of credit from the domestic bank of the buyer.

cost plus—method of determining the purchase price or contract price equal to the seller's or contractor's costs plus a stated percentage as the profit.

co-sureties—sureties for the same debtor and obligor.

cotenancy—when two or more persons hold concurrent rights and interests in the same property.

Council on Environmental Quality (CEQ)—federal agency that establishes national policies on environmental quality and then recommends legislation to implement these policies.

counterclaim—a claim that the defendant in an action may make against the plaintiff.

counteroffer—proposal by an offeree to the offeror that changes the terms of, and thus rejects, the original offer.

course of dealing—pattern of performance between two parties to a contract.

court—a tribunal established by government to hear and decide matters properly brought to it.

covenant against encumbrances—guarantee that conveyed land is not subject to any right or interest of a third person.

covenant of further assurances—promise that the grantor of an interest in land will execute any additional documents required to perfect the title of the grantee.

covenant of quiet enjoyment—covenant by the grantor of an interest in land to not disturb the grantee's possession of the land.

covenant of right to convey—guarantee that the grantor of an interest in land, if not the owner, has the right or authority to make the conveyance to a new owner.

covenant of seisin—guarantee that the grantor of an interest in land owns the estate conveyed to a new owner.

covenants of title—grantor's covenants of a deed that guarantee such matters as the right to make the conveyance, to ownership of the property, to freedom of the property from encumbrances, or that the grantee will not be disturbed in the quiet enjoyment of the land.

credit transfer—transaction in which a person making payment, such as a buyer, requests payment be made to the beneficiary's bank.

creditor—person (seller or lender) who is owed money; also may be a secured party.

crime—violation of the law that is punished as an offense against the state or government.

cross-examination—the examination made of a witness by the attorney for the adverse party.

cumulative voting—system of voting for directors in which each shareholder has as many votes as the number of voting shares owned multiplied by the number of directors to be elected, and such votes can be distributed for the various candidates as desired.

customary authority—authority of an agent to do any act that, according to the custom of the community, usually accompanies the transaction for which the agent is authorized to act.

cybercrime—crimes committed via the Internet.

cyberlaw—laws and precedent applicable to Internet transactions and communications.

cyberspace—World Wide Web and Internet communication.

cybersquatters—term for those who register and set up domain names on the Internet for resale to the famous users of the names in question.

D

de facto—existing in fact as distinguished from as of right, as in the case of an officer or a corporation purporting to act as such without being elected to the office or having been properly incorporated.

debenture—unsecured bond of a corporation, with no specific corporate assets pledged as security for payment.

debit transfer—transaction in which a beneficiary entitled to money requests payment from a bank according to a prior agreement.

debtor—buyer on credit (i.e., a borrower).

decedent—person whose estate is being administered.

deed—instrument by which the grantor (owner of land) conveys or transfers the title to a grantee.

defamation—untrue statement by one party about another to a third party.

defendant—party charged with a violation of civil or criminal law in a proceeding.

definite time—time of payment computable from the face of the instrument.

delegated powers—powers expressly granted the national government by the Constitution.

delegation—transfer to another of the right and power to do an act.

delegation of duties—transfer of duties by a contracting party to another person who is to perform them.

delivery—constructive or actual possession.

delivery in escrow—transaction in which a deed is delivered to a third person for the purpose of delivery to the grantee upon the happening of some event or contingency.

demand draft—draft that is payable upon presentment.

demurrer—a pleading to dismiss the adverse party's pleading for not stating a cause of action or a defense.

deposition—the testimony of a witness taken out of court before a person authorized to administer oaths.

depositor—person, or bailor, who gives property for storage.

derivative action—secondary action for damages or breach of contract brought by one or more corporate shareholders against directors, officers, or third persons.

development statement—statement that sets forth significant details of a real estate or property development as required by the federal Land Sales Act.

devise—gift of real estate made by will.

devisee—beneficiary of a devise.

direct damages—losses that are caused by breach of a contract.

direct examination—examination of a witness by his or her attorney.

directed verdict—a direction by the trial judge to the jury to return a verdict in favor of a specified party to the action.

disability—any incapacity resulting from bodily injury or disease to engage in any occupation for remuneration or profit.

discharge in bankruptcy—order of the bankruptcy court relieving the debtor from obligation to pay the unpaid balance of most claims.

disclosed principal—principal whose identity is made known by the agent as well as the fact that the agent is acting on the principal's behalf.

discovery—procedures for ascertaining facts prior to the time of trial in order to eliminate the element of surprise in litigation.

dishonor—status when the primary party refuses to pay the instrument according to its terms.

disinherited—excluded from sharing in the estate of a decedent.

Dispute Settlement Body—means, provided by the World Trade Organization, for member countries to resolve trade disputes rather than engage in unilateral trade sanctions or a trade war.

distribution per stirpes—distribution of an estate made in as many equal parts as there are family lines represented in the nearest generation; also known as *stirpital distribution.*

distributor—entity that takes title to goods and bears the financial and commercial risks for the subsequent sale of the goods.

divestiture order—a court order to dispose of interests that could lead to a monopoly.

divisible contract—agreement consisting of two or more parts, each calling for corresponding performances of each part by the parties.

document of title—document treated as evidence that a person is entitled to receive, hold, and dispose of the document and the goods it covers.

domestic corporation—corporation that has been incorporated by the state in question as opposed to incorporation by another state.

dominant tenement—land that is benefited by an easement.

donee—recipient of a gift.

donor—person making a gift.

double indemnity—provision for payment of double the amount specified by the insurance contract if death is caused by an accident and occurs under specified circumstances.

downsizing—a reduction in workforce.

draft or bill of exchange—an unconditional order in writing by one person upon another, signed by the person giving it, and ordering the person to whom it is directed to pay upon demand or at a definite time a sum certain in money to order or to bearer.

drawee—person to whom the draft is addressed and who is ordered to pay the amount of money specified in the draft.

drawer—person who writes out and creates a draft or bill of exchange, including a check.

due diligence—process of checking the environmental history and nature of land prior to purchase.

due process—the constitutional right to be heard, question witnesses, and present evidence.

due process clause—in the Fifth and Fourteenth Amendments, a guarantee of protection from unreasonable procedures and unreasonable laws.

dumping—selling goods in another country at less than their fair value.

duress—conduct that deprives the victim of free will and that generally gives the victim the right to set aside any transaction entered into under such circumstances.

duty—an obligation of law imposed on a person to perform or refrain from performing a certain act.

E

easement—permanent right that one has in the land of another, as the right to cross another's land or an easement of way.

easement by implication—easement not specifically created by deed that arises from the circumstances of the parties and the land location and access.

economic duress—threat of financial loss.

Economic Espionage Act (EEA)—federal law that makes it a felony to copy, download, transmit, or in any way transfer proprietary files, documents, and information from a computer to an unauthorized person.

economic strikers—union strikers trying to enforce bargaining demands when an impasse has been reached in the negotiation process for a collective bargaining agreement.

effects doctrine—doctrine that states that U.S. courts will assume jurisdiction and will apply antitrust laws to conduct outside of the United States when the activity of business firms has direct and substantial effect on U.S. commerce; the rule has been modified to require that the effect on U.S. commerce also be foreseeable.

effluent guidelines—EPA standards for maximum ranges of discharge into water.

electronic funds transfer (EFT)—any transfer of funds (other than a transaction originated by a check, draft, or similar paper instrument) that is initiated through an electronic terminal, telephone, computer, or magnetic tape so as to authorize a financial institution to debit or credit an account.

Electronic Funds Transfer Act (EFTA)—federal law that provides consumers with rights and protections in electronic funds transfers.

eleemosynary corporation—corporation organized for a charitable or benevolent purpose.

embezzlement—statutory offense consisting of the unlawful conversion of property entrusted to the wrongdoer.

eminent domain—power of government and certain kinds of corporations to take private property against the objection of the owner, provided the taking is for a public purpose and just compensation is made for it.

emissions offset policy—controls whether new factories can be built in a nonattainment area.

employment-at-will doctrine—doctrine in which the employer has historically been allowed to terminate the employment contract at any time for any reason or for no reason.

en banc—the term used when the full panel of judges on the appellate court hears a case.

encoding warranty—warranty made by any party who encodes electronic information on an instrument; a warranty of accuracy.

Endangered Species Act (ESA)—federal law that identifies and protects species that are endangered from development or other acts that threaten their existence.

endowment insurance—insurance that pays the face amount of the policy if the insured dies within the policy period.

environmental impact statement (EIS)—formal report prepared under NEPA to document findings on the impact of a federal project on the environment.

equitable title—beneficial interest in a trust.

equity—the body of principles that originally developed because of the inadequacy of the rules then applied by the common law courts of England.

escalation clause—provision for the automatic increase of the rent at periodic intervals.

escheat—transfer to the state of the title to a decedent's property when the owner of the property dies intestate and is not survived by anyone capable of taking the property as heir.

E-sign—signature over the Internet.

estate in fee—largest estate possible, in which the owner has absolute and entire interest in the land.

estoppel—principle by which a person is barred from pursuing a certain course of action or of disputing the truth of certain matters.

ethics—a branch of philosophy dealing with values that relate to the nature of human conduct and values associated with that conduct.

***ex post facto* law**—a law making criminal an act that was lawful when done or that increases the penalty when done. Such laws are generally prohibited by constitutional provisions.

exculpatory clause—provision in a contract stating that one of the parties is not liable for damages in case of breach; also called *limitation-of-liability clause.*

executed contract—agreement that has been completely performed.

execution—the carrying out of a judgment of a court, generally directing that property owned by the defendant be sold and the proceeds first be used to pay the execution or judgment creditor.

executive branch—the branch of government (e.g., the president) formed to execute the laws.

executor, executrix—person (man, woman) named in a will to administer the estate of the decedent.

executory contract—agreement by which something remains to be done by one or both parties.

exhaustion of administrative remedies—requirement that an agency make its final decision before the parties can go to court.

existing goods—goods that physically exist and are owned by the seller at the time of a transaction.

exoneration—agreement or provision in an agreement that one party shall not be held liable for loss; the right of the surety to demand that those primarily liable pay the claim for which the surety is secondarily liable.

expert witness—one who has acquired special knowledge in a particular field as through practical experience or study, or both, whose opinion is admissible as an aid to the trier of fact.

export sale—direct sale to customers in a foreign country.

express authorization—authorization of an agent to perform a certain act.

express contract—agreement of the parties manifested by their words, whether spoken or written.

express warranty—statement by the defendant relating to the goods, which statement is part of the basis of the bargain.

extortion—illegal demand by a public officer acting with apparent authority.

F

facilitation payments—(grease payments) legal payments to speed up or ensure performance of normal government duties.

factor—bailee to whom goods are consigned for sale.

fair use—principle that allows the limited use of copyrighted material for teaching, research, and news reporting.

false imprisonment—intentional detention of a person without that person's consent; called the *shopkeeper's tort when shoplifters are unlawfully detained.*

FAS—free alongside the named vessel.

federal district court—a general trial court of the federal system.

Federal Register—government publication issued five days a week that lists all administrative regulations, all presidential proclamations and executive orders, and other documents and classes of documents that the president or Congress direct to be published.

Federal Register Act—federal law requiring agencies to make public disclosure of proposed rules, passed rules, and activities.

Federal Sentencing Guidelines—federal standards used by judges in determining mandatory sentence terms for those convicted of federal crimes.

federal system—the system of government in which a central government is given power to administer to national concerns while individual states retain the power to administer to local concerns.

fee simple defeasibles—fee simple interest can be lost if restrictions on its use are violated.

fee simple estate—highest level of land ownership; full interest of unlimited duration.

felony—criminal offense that is punishable by confinement in prison for more than one year or by death, or that is expressly stated by statute to be a felony.

field warehousing—stored goods under the exclusive control of a warehouse but kept on the owner's premises rather than in a warehouse.

Fifth Amendment—constitutional protection against self-incrimination; also guarantees due process.

finance lease—three-party lease agreement in which there is a lessor, a lessee, and a financier.

financing statement—brief statement (record) that gives sufficient information to alert third persons that a particular creditor may have a security interest in the collateral described.

fire insurance policy—a contract that indemnifies the insured for property destruction or damage caused by fire.

firm offer—offer stated to be held open for a specified time, which must be so held in some states even in the absence of an option contract, or under the UCC, with respect to merchants.

first-in-time provision—creditor whose interest attached first has priority in the collateral when two creditors have a secured interest.

first-to-perfect basis—rule of priorities that holds that first in time in perfecting a security interest, mortgage, judgment, lien, or other property attachment right should have priority.

fixture—personal property that has become so attached to or adapted to real estate that it has lost its character as personal property and is part of the real estate.

floating lien—claim in a changing or shifting stock of goods of the buyer.

FOB place of destination—general commercial language for delivery to the buyer.

FOB place of shipment—"ship to" contract.

forbearance—refraining from doing an act.

forcible entry and detainer—action by the landlord to have the tenant removed for nonpayment of rent.

foreclosure—procedure for enforcing a mortgage resulting in the public sale of the mortgaged property and, less commonly, in merely barring the right of the mortgagor to redeem the property from the mortgage.

foreign corporation—corporation incorporated under the laws of another state.

Foreign Corrupt Practices Act (FCPA)—federal law that makes it a felony to influence decision makers in other countries for the purpose of obtaining business, such as contracts for sales and services; also imposes financial reporting requirements on certain U.S. corporations.

forged or unauthorized indorsement—instrument indorsed by an agent for a principal without authorization or authority.

forgery—fraudulently making or altering an instrument that apparently creates or alters a legal liability of another.

formal contracts—written contracts or agreements whose formality signifies the parties' intention to abide by the terms.

Fourth Amendment—privacy protection in the U.S. Constitution; prohibits unauthorized searches and seizures.

franchise—(1) privilege or authorization, generally exclusive, to engage in a particular activity within a particular geographic area, such as a government franchise to operate a taxi company within a specified city, or a private franchise as the grant by a manufacturer of a right to sell products within a particular territory or for a particular number of years; (2) right to vote.

franchise agreement—sets forth rights of franchisee to use trademarks, etc., of franchisor.

franchisee—person to whom franchise is granted.

franchising—granting of permission to use a trademark, trade name, or copyright under specified conditions; a form of licensing.

franchisor—party granting the franchise.

fraud—making of a false statement of a past or existing fact, with knowledge of its falsity or with reckless indifference as to its truth, with the intent to cause another to rely thereon, and such person does rely thereon and is harmed thereby.

fraud in factum—fraud committed through deception on documents or the nature of the transaction as opposed to the subject matter or parties in the transaction (fraud in the inducement).

fraud in the inducement—fraud that occurs when a person is persuaded or induced to execute an instrument because of fraudulent statements.

Freedom of Information Act—federal law permitting citizens to request documents and records from administrative agencies.

freight forwarder—one who contracts to have goods transported and, in turn, contracts with carriers for such transportation.

freight insurance—insures that shipowner will receive payment for transportation charges.

full warranty—obligation of a seller to fix or replace a defective product within a reasonable time without cost to the buyer.

funds transfer—communication of instructions or requests to pay a specific sum of money to the credit of a specified account or person without an actual physical passing of money.

fungible goods—homogeneous goods of which any unit is the equivalent of any other unit.

future goods—goods that exist physically but are not owned by the seller and goods that have not yet been produced.

G

garnishment—the name given in some states to attachment proceedings.

general agent—agent authorized by the principal to transact all affairs in connection with a particular type of business or trade or to transact all business at a certain place.

general corporation code—state's code listing certain requirements for creation of a corporation.

general jurisdiction—the power to hear and decide most controversies involving legal rights and duties.

general legacies—certain sums of money bequeathed to named persons by the testator; to be paid out of the decedent's assets generally without specifying any particular fund or source from which the payment is to be made.

general partnership—partnership in which the partners conduct as co-owners a business for profit, and each partner has a right to take part in the management of the business and has unlimited liability.

general partners—partners who publicly and actively engage in the transaction of firm business.

gift—title to an owner's personal property voluntarily transferred by a party not receiving anything in exchange.

gift causa mortis—gift, made by the donor in the belief that death was immediate and impending, that is revoked or is revocable under certain circumstances.

good faith—absence of knowledge of any defects in or problems; "pure heart and an empty head."

goods—anything movable at the time it is identified as the subject of a transaction.

grantee—new owner of a land conveyance.

grantor—owner who transfers or conveys an interest in land to a new owner.

gratuitous bailment—bailment in which the bailee does not receive any compensation or advantage.

gray market goods—foreign-made goods with U.S. trademarks brought into the United States by a third party without the consent of the trademark owners to compete with these owners.

grease payments—(facilitation payments) legal payments to speed up or ensure performance of normal government duties.

guarantor—one who undertakes the obligation of guaranty.

guaranty—agreement or promise to answer for a debt; an undertaking to pay the debt of another if the creditor first sues the debtor.

guaranty of collection—form of guaranty in which creditor cannot proceed against guarantor until after proceeding against debtor.

guaranty of payment—absolute promise to pay when a debtor defaults.

guest—transient who contracts for a room or site at a hotel.

H

hearsay evidence—statements made out of court that are offered in court as proof of the information contained in the statements and that, subject to many exceptions, are not admissible in evidence.

"hell or high water" clause—lease agreement clause that requires the lessee to continue paying regardless of any problems with the lease.

holder—someone in possession of an instrument that runs to that person (i.e., is made payable to that person, is indorsed to that person, or is bearer paper).

holder in due course—a holder who has given value, taken in good faith without notice of dishonor, defenses, or that instrument is overdue, and who is afforded special rights or status.

holder through a holder in due course—holder of an instrument who attains holder-in-due-course status because a holder in due course has held it previous to him or her.

holographic will—unwitnessed will written by hand.

homeowners insurance policy—combination of standard fire insurance and comprehensive personal liability insurance.

hotelkeeper—one regularly engaged in the business of offering living accommodations to all transient persons.

hull insurance—insurance that covers physical damage on a freight-moving vessel.

I

identification—point in the transaction when the buyer acquires an interest in the goods subject to the contract.

identified—term applied to particular goods selected by either the buyer or the seller as the goods called for by the sales contract.

identity theft—use of another's credit tools, social security number, or other IDs to obtain cash, goods, or credit without permission.

illusory promise—promise that in fact does not impose any obligation on the promisor.

impeach—using prior inconsistent evidence to challenge the credibility of a witness.

implied contract—contract expressed by conduct or implied or deduced from the facts.

implied warranty—warranty that was not made but is implied by law.

implied warranty of merchantability—group of promises made by the seller, the most important of which is that the goods are fit for the ordinary purposes for which they are sold.

impostor rule—an exception to the rules on liability for forgery that covers situations such as the embezzling payroll clerk.

in pari delicto—equally guilty; used in reference to a transaction as to which relief will not be granted to either party because both are equally guilty of wrongdoing.

incidental authority—authority of an agent that is reasonably necessary to execute express authority.

incidental damages—incurred by the nonbreaching party as part of the process of trying to cover (buy substitute goods) or sell (selling subject matter of contract to another); includes storage fees, commissions, and the like.

income—money earned by the principal, or property in trust, and distributed by the trustee.

incontestability clause—provision that after the lapse of a specified time the insurer cannot dispute the policy on the ground of misrepresentation or fraud of the insured or similar wrongful conduct.

incorporation by reference—contract consisting of both the original or skeleton document and the detailed statement that is incorporated in it.

incorporator—one or more natural persons or corporations who sign and file appropriate incorporation forms with a designated government official.

indemnity—right of a person secondarily liable to require that a person primarily liable pay for loss sustained when the secondary party discharges the obligation that the primary party should have discharged; the right of an agent to be paid the amount of any loss or damage sustained without fault because of obedience to the principal's instructions; an undertaking by one person for a consideration to pay another person a sum of money to indemnify that person when a specified loss is incurred.

indemnity contract—agreement by one person, for consideration, to pay another person a sum of money in the event that the other person sustains a specified loss.

indenture trustee—usually a commercial banking institution, to represent the interests of the bondholders and ensure that the terms and covenants of the bond issue are met by the corporation.

independent contractor—contractor who undertakes to perform a specified task according to the terms of a contract but over whom the other contracting party has no control except as provided for by the contract.

indorsee—party to whom special indorsement is made.

indorsement—signature of the payee on an instrument.

indorser—secondary party (or obligor) on a note.

informal contract—simple oral or written contract.

informal settlements—negotiated disposition of a matter before an administrative agency, generally without public sanctions.

infringement—violation of trademarks, patents, or copyrights by copying or using material without permission.

injunction—order of a court of equity to refrain from doing (negative injunction) or to do (affirmative or mandatory injunction) a specified act.

inland marine—insurance that covers domestic shipments of goods over land and inland waterways.

insider—full-time corporate employee or a director or their relatives.

insider information—privileged information on company business only known to employees.

insolvency—excess of debts and liabilities over assets, or inability to pay debts as they mature.

instruction—summary of the law given to jurors by the judge before deliberation begins.

insurable interest—the right to hold a valid insurance policy on a person or property.

insurance—a plan of security against risks by charging the loss against a fund created by the payments made by policyholders.

insurance agent—agent of an insurance company.

insurance broker—independent contractor who is not employed by any one insurance company.

insured—person to whom the promise in an insurance contract is made.

insurer—promisor in an insurance contract.

integrity—the adherence to one's values and principles despite the costs and consequences.

intellectual property rights—trademark, copyright, and patent rights protected by law.

intended beneficiary—third person of a contract whom the contract is intended to benefit.

intentional infliction of emotional distress—tort that produces mental anguish caused by conduct that exceeds all bounds of decency.

intentional torts—civil wrong that results from intentional conduct.

inter vivos gift—any transaction that takes place between living persons and creates rights prior to the death of any of them.

interest in the authority—form of agency in which an agent has been given or paid for the right to exercise authority.

interest in the subject matter—form of agency in which an agent is given an interest in the property with which that agent is dealing.

interlineation—writing between the lines or adding to the provisions of a document, the effect thereof depending upon the nature of the document.

intermediary bank—bank between the originator and the beneficiary bank in the transfer of funds.

interrogatories—written questions used as a discovery tool that must be answered under oath.

intestate—condition of dying without a will as to any property.

intestate succession—distribution, made as directed by statute, of a decedent's property not effectively disposed of by will.

invasion of privacy—tort of intentional intrusion into the private affairs of another.

investigative consumer report—report on a person based on personal investigation and interviews.

invitee—person who enters another's land by invitation.

involuntary bankruptcy—proceeding in which a creditor or creditors file the petition for relief with the bankruptcy court.

issuer—party who issues a document such as a letter of credit or a document of title such as a warehouse receipt or bill of lading.

J

joint tenancy—estate held jointly by two or more with the right of survivorship as between them, unless modified by statute.

joint venture—relationship in which two or more persons or firms combine their labor or property for a single undertaking and share profits and losses equally unless otherwise agreed.

judge—primary officer of the court.

judgment lien—lien by a creditor who has won a verdict against the landowner in court.

judgment n.o.v.,—or *non obstante veredicto* (notwithstanding the verdict), a judgment entered after verdict upon the motion of the losing party on the ground that the verdict is so wrong that a judgment should be entered the opposite of the verdict.

judicial branch—the branch of government (courts) formed to interpret the laws.

judicial or execution sale—sale made under order of court by an officer appointed to make the sale or by an officer having such authority as incident to the office. The sale may have the effect of divesting liens on the property.

judicial triage—court management tool used by judges to expedite certain cases in which time is of the essence, such as asbestos cases in which the plaintiffs are gravely ill.

jurisdiction—the power of a court to hear and determine a given class of cases; the power to act over a particular defendant.

jurisdictional rule of reason—rule that balances the vital interests, including laws and policies, of the United States with those of a foreign country.

jury—a body of citizens sworn by a court to determine by verdict the issues of fact submitted to them.

land—earth, including all things embedded in or attached thereto, whether naturally or by the act of humans.

landlord—one who leases real property to another.

law—the order or pattern of rules that society establishes to govern the conduct of individuals and the relationships among them.

lease—agreement between the owner of property and a tenant by which the former agrees to give possession of the property to the latter in consideration of the payment of rent. (Parties–landlord or lessor, tenant or lessee)

leasehold estate—interest of a tenant in rented land.

legacy—gift of money made by will.

legal title—title held by the trustee in a trust situation.

legatee—beneficiary who receives a gift of personal property by will.

legislative branch—the branch of government (e.g., Congress) formed to make the laws.

lessee—one who has a possessory interest in real or personal property under a lease; a tenant.

lessor—one who conveys real or personal property by a lease; a landlord.

letter of credit—commercial device used to guarantee payment to a seller, primarily in an international business transaction.

letters of administration—written authorization given to an administrator of an estate as evidence of appointment and authority.

letters testamentary—written authorization given to an executor of an estate as evidence of appointment and authority.

liability insurance—covers the shipowner's liability if the ship causes damage to another ship or its cargo.

libel—written or visual defamation without legal justification.

license—personal privilege to do some act or series of acts upon the land of another, as the placing of a sign thereon, not amounting to an easement or a right of possession.

licensee—someone on another's premises with the permission of the occupier, whose duty is to warn the licensee of nonobvious dangers.

licensing—transfer of technology rights to a product so that it may be produced by a different business organization in a foreign country in exchange for royalties and other payments as agreed.

lien—claim or right, against property, existing by virtue of the entry of a judgment against its owner or by the entry of a judgment and a levy thereunder on the property, or because of the relationship of the claimant to the particular property, such as an unpaid seller.

life estate—an estate for the duration of a life.

limitation-of-liability clause—provision in a contract stating that one of the parties shall not be liable for damages in case of breach; also called an *exculpatory clause.*

limited covenant—any covenant that does not provide the complete protection of a full covenant.

limited defenses—defenses available to secondary parties if the presenting party is a holder in due course.

limited liability partnership (LLP)—partnership in which at least one partner has a liability limited to the loss of the capital contribution made to the partnership.

limited partner—partner who neither takes part in the management of the partnership nor appears to the public to be a general partner.

limited partnership—partnership that can be formed by "one or more general partners and one or more limited partners."

limited (special) jurisdiction—the authority to hear only particular kinds of cases.

limited warranty—any warranty that does not provide the complete protection of a full warranty.

lineals—relationship that exists when one person is a direct descendant of the other; also called *lineal descendants.*

liquidated damages—damages established in advance of breach as an alternative to establishing compensatory damages at the time of the breach.

liquidated damages clause—specification of exact compensation in case of a breach of contract.

liquidation—process of converting property into money whether of particular items of property or of all the assets of a business or an estate.

living trust—trust created to take effect within the lifetime of the settlor; also called *inter vivos trust.*

living will—document by which individuals may indicate that if they become unable to express their wishes and are in an irreversible, incurable condition, they do not want life-sustaining medical treatments.

living-document view—the term used when a constitution is interpreted according to changes in conditions.

lottery—any plan by which a consideration is given for a chance to win a prize; it consists of three elements: (1) there must be a payment of money or something of value for an opportunity to win, (2) a prize must be available, and (3) the prize must be offered by lot or chance.

mailbox rule—timing for acceptance tied to proper acceptance.

maker—party who writes or creates a promissory note.

malpractice—when services are not properly rendered in accordance with commonly accepted standards; negligence by a professional in performing his or her skill.

marine insurance—policies that cover perils relating to the transportation of goods.

market power—the ability to control price and exclude competitors.

market value—price at which a share of stock can be voluntarily bought or sold in the open market.

mask work—specific form of expression embodied in a chip design, including the stencils used in manufacturing semiconductor chip products.

mass picketing—illegal tactic of employees massing together in great numbers to effectively shut down entrances of the employer's facility.

maturity date—date that a corporation is required to repay a loan to a bondholder.

means test—new standard under the Reform Act that requires the court to find that the debtor does not have the means to repay creditors; goes beyond the past requirement of petitions being granted on the simple assertion of the debtor saying, "I have debts."

mechanic's lien—protection afforded by statute to various kinds of laborers and persons supplying materials, by giving them a lien on the building and land that has been improved or added to by them.

mediation—the settlement of a dispute through the use of a messenger who carries to each side of the dispute the issues and offers in the case.

merchant—seller who deals in specific goods classified by the UCC.

merger (of corporations)—combining of corporations by which one absorbs the other and continues to exist, preserving its original charter and identity while the other corporation ceases to exist.

minitrial—a trial held on portions of the case or certain issues in the case.

***Miranda* warnings**—warnings required to prevent self-incrimination in a criminal matter.

mirror image rule—common law contract rule on acceptance that requires language to be absolutely the same as the offer, unequivocal and unconditional.

misdemeanor—criminal offense with a sentence of less than one year that is neither treason nor a felony.

misrepresentation—false statement of fact made innocently without any intent to deceive.

mistrial—a court's declaration that terminates a trial and postpones it to a later date; commonly entered when evidence has been of a highly prejudicial character or when a juror has been guilty of misconduct.

money—medium of exchange.

money order—draft issued by a bank or a nonbank.

moral relativism—takes into account motivation and circumstance to determine whether an act was ethical.

mortgage—interest in land given by the owner to a creditor as security for the payment of the creditor for a debt, the nature of the interest depending upon the law of the state where the land is located. (Parties—mortgagor, mortgagee)

most-favored-nation clause—clause in treaties between countries whereby any privilege subsequently granted to a third country in relation to a given treaty subject is extended to the other party to the treaty.

motion for summary judgment—request that the court decide a case on basis of law only because there are no material issues disputed by the parties.

motion to dismiss—a pleading that may be filed to attack the adverse party's pleading as not stating a cause of action or a defense.

National Environmental Policy Act (NEPA)—federal law that mandates study of a project's impact on the environment before it can be undertaken by any federal agency.

natural law—a system of principles to guide human conduct independent of, and sometimes contrary to, enacted law and discovered by man's rational intelligence.

necessaries—things indispensable or absolutely necessary for the sustenance of human life.

negligence—failure to exercise due care under the circumstances in consequence of which harm is proximately caused to one to whom the defendant owed a duty to exercise due care.

negotiability—quality of an instrument that affords special rights and standing.

negotiable bill of lading—document of title that by its terms calls for goods to be delivered "to the bearer" or "to the order of" a named person.

negotiable instruments—drafts, promissory notes, checks, and certificates of deposit that, in proper form, give special rights as "negotiable commercial paper."

negotiable warehouse receipt—receipt that states the covered goods will be delivered "to the bearer" or "to the order of."

negotiation—the transfer of commercial paper by indorsement and delivery by the person to whom it is then payable in the case of order paper and by physical transfer in the case of bearer paper.

Noise Control Act—federal law that controls noise emissions from low-flying aircraft.

nominal damages—nominal sum awarded the plaintiff in order to establish that legal rights have been violated although the plaintiff in fact has not sustained any actual loss or damages.

nonattainment areas—"dirty" areas that do not meet federal standards under the Clean Air Act.

nonconforming use—use of land that conflicts with a zoning ordinance at the time the ordinance goes into effect.

nonconsumer lease—lease that does not satisfy the definition of a consumer lease; also known as a *commercial lease.*

nonnegotiable bill of lading—see *straight bill of lading.*

nonnegotiable instrument—contract, note, or draft that does not meet negotiability requirements of Article 3.

nonnegotiable warehouse receipt—receipt that states the covered goods received will be delivered to a specific person.

notice of dishonor—notice that an instrument has been dishonored; such notice can be oral, written, or electronic but is subject to time limitations.

notice statute—statute under which the last good faith or bona fide purchaser holds the title.

notice-race statute—statute under which the first bona fide purchaser to record the deed holds the title.

novation—substitution for an old contract with a new one that either replaces an existing obligation with a new obligation or replaces an original party with a new party.

nuisance—conduct that harms or prejudices another in the use of land or which harms or prejudices the public.

O

obligee—promisee who can claim the benefit of the obligation.

obligor—promisor.

ocean marine—policies that cover transportation of goods in vessels in international and coastal trade.

offer—expression of an offeror's willingness to enter into a contractual agreement.

offeree—person to whom an offer is made.

offeror—person who makes an offer.

Oil Pollution Act—federal law that assigns cleanup liability for oil spills in U.S. waters.

ombudsman—a government official designated by a statute to examine citizen complaints.

open meeting law—law that requires advance notice of agency meeting and public access.

open-end mortgage—mortgage given to secure additional loans to be made in the future as well as to secure the original loan.

opening statements—statements by opposing attorneys that tell the jury what their cases will prove.

operation of law—attaching of certain consequences to certain facts because of legal principles that operate automatically as contrasted with consequences that arise because of the voluntary action of a party designed to create those consequences.

option contract—contract to hold an offer to make a contract open for a fixed period of time.

order of relief—The order from the bankruptcy judge that starts the protection for the debtor; when the order of relief is entered by the court, the debtor's creditors must stop all proceedings and work through the bankruptcy court to recover debts (if possible). Court finding that creditors have met the standards for bankruptcy petitions.

order paper—instrument payable to the order of a party.

original jurisdiction—the authority to hear a controversy when it is first brought to court.

originator—party who originates the funds transfer.

output contract—contract of a producer to sell its entire production or output to a buyer.

outstanding—name for shares of a company that have been issued to stockholders.

overdraft—negative balance in a drawer's account.

holder of such a written authorization.

public corporation—corporation that has been established for governmental purposes and for the administration of public affairs.

public nuisance—nuisance that affects the community or public at large.

public policy—certain objectives relating to health, morals, and integrity of government that the law seeks to advance by declaring invalid any contract that conflicts with those objectives even though there is no statute expressly declaring such a contract illegal.

public warehouses—entities that serve the public generally without discrimination.

pump-and-dump—self-touting a stock to drive its price up and then selling it.

punitive damages—damages, in excess of those required to compensate the plaintiff for the wrong done, that are imposed in order to punish the defendant because of the particularly wanton or willful character of wrongdoing; also called *exemplary damages.*

purchase money security interest (PMSI)—the security interest in the goods a seller sells on credit that become the collateral for the creditor/seller.

Q

qualified indorsement—an indorsement that includes words such as "without recourse" that disclaims certain liability of the indorser to a maker or a drawee.

qualified privilege—media privilege to print inaccurate information without liability for defamation, so long as a retraction is printed and there was no malice.

quantum meruit—as much as deserved; an action brought for the value of the services rendered the defendant when there was no express contract as to the purchase price.

quasi contract—court-imposed obligation to prevent unjust enrichment in the absence of a contract.

quasi-judicial proceedings—forms of hearings in which the rules of evidence and procedure are more relaxed but each side still has a chance to be heard.

quasi-public corporation—private corporation furnishing services on which the public is particularly dependent, for example, a gas and electric company.

quitclaim deed—deed by which the grantor purports to give up only whatever right or title the grantor may have in the property without specifying or warranting transfer of any particular interest.

quorum—minimum number of persons, shares represented, or directors who must be present at a meeting in order to lawfully transact business.

R

race statute—statute under which the first party to record the deed holds the title.

race-notice statute—see *notice-race statute.*

Racketeer Influenced and Corrupt Organizations (RICO) Act—federal law, initially targeting organized crime, that has expanded in scope and provides penalties and civil recovery for multiple criminal offenses, or a pattern of racketeering.

real property—land and all rights in land.

recognizance—obligation entered into before a court to do some act, such as to appear at a later date for a hearing. Also called a *contract of record.*

recorder—public official in charge of deeds.

recross-examination—an examination by the other side's attorney that follows the redirect examination.

redemption—buying back of one's property, which has been sold because of a default, upon paying the amount that had been originally due together with interest and costs.

redirect examination—questioning after cross-examination, in which the attorney for the witness testifying may ask the same witness other questions to overcome effects of the cross-examination.

reference to a third person—settlement that allows a nonparty to resolve the dispute.

reformation—remedy by which a written instrument is corrected when it fails to express the actual intent of both parties because of fraud, accident, or mistake.

registered bonds—bonds held by owners whose names and addresses are registered on the books of the corporation.

registration requirements—provisions of the Securities Act of 1933 requiring advance disclosure to the public of a new securities issue through filing a statement with the SEC and sending a prospectus to each potential purchaser.

registration statement—document disclosing specific financial information regarding the security, the issuer, and the underwriter.

remainder interest—land interest that follows a life estate.

remand—term used when an appellate court sends a case back to trial court for additional hearings or a new trial.

remedy—action or procedure that is followed in order to enforce a right or to obtain damages for injury to a right.

rent-a-judge plan—dispute resolution through private courts with judges paid to be referees for the cases.

representative capacity—action taken by one on behalf of another, as the act of a personal representative on behalf of a decedent's estate, or action taken both on one's behalf and on behalf of others, as a shareholder bringing a representative action.

repudiation—result of a buyer or seller refusing to perform the contract as stated.

request for production of documents—discovery tool for uncovering paper evidence in a case.

requirements contract—contract in which the buyer buys its needs (requirements) from the seller.

rescission—action of one party to a contract to set the contract aside when the other party is guilty of a breach of the contract.

reservation of rights—assertion by a party to a contract that even though a tendered performance (e.g., a defective product) is accepted, the right to damages for nonconformity to the contract is reserved.

Resource Conservation and Recovery Act (RCRA)—federal law that regulates the disposal of potentially harmful substances and encourages resource conservation and recovery.

Resource Recovery Act—early federal solid waste disposal legislation that provided funding for states and local governments with recycling programs.

respondeat superior—doctrine that the principal or employer is vicariously liable for the unauthorized torts committed by an agent or employee while acting within the scope of the agency or the course of the employment, respectively.

restrictive covenants—covenants in a deed by which the grantee agrees to refrain from doing specified acts.

restrictive indorsement—an indorsement that restricts further transfer, such as in trust for or to the use of some other person, is conditional, or for collection or deposit.

reverse—the term used when the appellate court sets aside the verdict or judgment of a lower court.

reverse mortgage—mortgage in which the owners get their equity out of their home over a period of time and return the house to the lender upon their deaths.

reversible error—an error or defect in court proceedings of so serious a nature that on appeal the appellate court will set aside the proceedings of the lower court.

reversionary interest—interest that a lessor has in property that is subject to an outstanding lease.

revoke—testator's act of taking back his or her will and its provisions.

right—legal capacity to require another person to perform or refrain from an action.

right of escheat—right of the state to take the property of a decedent that has not been distributed.

right of first refusal—right of a party to meet the terms of a proposed contract before it is executed, such as a real estate purchase agreement.

right of privacy—the right to be free from unreasonable intrusion by others.

right to cure—second chance for a seller to make a proper tender of conforming goods.

right-to-work laws—laws restricting unions and employees from negotiating clauses in their collective bargaining agreements that make union membership compulsory.

risk—peril or contingency against which the insured is protected by the contract of insurance.

risk of loss—in contract performance, the cost of damage or injury to the goods contracted for.

Robinson-Patman Act—a federal statute designed to eliminate price discrimination in interstate commerce.

run with the land—concept that certain covenants in a deed to land are deemed to run or pass with the land so that whoever owns the land is bound by or entitled to the benefit of the covenants.

S

Safe Drinking Water Act—a federal law that establishes national standards for contaminants in drinking water.

sale on approval—term indicating that no sale takes place until the buyer approves or accepts the goods.

sale or return—sale in which the title to the property passes to the buyer at the time of the transaction but the buyer is given the option of returning the property and restoring the title to the seller.

search engine—Internet service used to locate Web sites.

search warrant—judicial authorization for a search of property where there is the expectation of privacy.

seasonable—timely.

secondary parties—called *secondary obligors* under Revised Article 3; parties to an instrument to whom holders turn when the primary party, for whatever reason, fails to pay the instrument.

secondary picketing—picketing an employer with which a union has no dispute to persuade the employer to stop doing business with a party to the dispute; generally illegal under the NLRA.

secrecy laws—confidentiality laws applied to home-country banks.

secured party—person owed the money, whether as a seller or a lender, in a secured transaction in personal property.

secured transaction—credit sale of goods or a secured loan that provides special protection for the creditor.

securities—stocks and bonds issued by a corporation. Under some investor protection laws, the term includes any interest in an enterprise that provides unearned income to its owner.

security agreement—agreement of the creditor and the debtor that the creditor will have a security interest.

security interest—property right that enables the creditor to take possession of the property if the debtor does not pay the amount owed.

self-help repossession—creditor's right to repossess the collateral without judicial proceedings.

self-proved wills—wills that eliminate some formalities of proof by being executed according to statutory requirements.

selling on consignment—entrusting a person with possession of property for the purpose of sale.

semiconductor chip product—product placed on a piece of semiconductor material in accordance with a predetermined pattern that is intended to perform electronic circuitry functions.

service mark—mark that identifies a service.

servient tenement—land that is subject to an easement.

settlor—one who settles property in trust or creates a trust estate.

severalty—ownership of property by one person.

shared powers—powers that are held by both state and national governments.

Sherman Antitrust Act—a federal statute prohibiting combinations and contracts in restraint of interstate trade, now generally inapplicable to labor union activity.

shop right—right of an employer to use in business without charge an invention discovered by an employee during working hours and with the employer's material and equipment.

shopkeeper's privilege—right of a store owner to detain a suspected shoplifter based on reasonable cause and for a reasonable time without resulting liability for false imprisonment.

short-swing profit—profit realized by a corporate insider from selling securities less than six months after purchase.

sinking fund—fixed amount of money set aside each year by the borrowing corporation toward the ultimate payment of bonds.

situational ethics—a flexible standard of ethics that permits an examination of circumstances and motivation before attaching the label of right or wrong to conduct.

Sixth Amendment—the U.S. constitutional amendment that guarantees a speedy trial.

slander—defamation of character by spoken words or gestures.

slander of title—malicious making of false statements as to a seller's title.

small claims courts—courts that resolve disputes between parties when those disputes do not exceed a minimal level; no lawyers are permitted; the parties represent themselves.

sole or individual proprietorship—form of business ownership in which one individual owns the business.

soliciting agent—salesperson.

sovereign compliance doctrine—doctrine that allows a defendant to raise as an affirmative defense to an antitrust action the fact that the defendant's actions were compelled by a foreign state.

sovereign immunity doctrine—doctrine that states that a foreign sovereign generally cannot be sued unless an exception to the Foreign Sovereign Immunities Act of 1976 applies.

special agent—agent authorized to transact a specific transaction or to do a specific act.

special drawing rights (SDRs)—rights that allow a country to borrow enough money from other International Money Fund (IMF) members to permit that country to maintain the stability of its currency's relationship to other world currencies.

special indorsement—an indorsement that specifies the person to whom the instrument is indorsed.

specific legacies—identified property bequeathed by a testator; also called *specific devises.*

specific lien—right of a creditor to hold particular property or assert a lien on particular property of the debtor because of the creditor's having done work on or having some other association with the property, as distinguished from having a lien generally against the assets of the debtor merely because the debtor is indebted to the lien holder.

specific performance—action brought to compel the adverse party to perform a contract on the theory that merely suing for damages for its breach will not be an adequate remedy.

spendthrift trust—a trust that, to varying degrees, provides that creditors of the beneficiary shall not be able to reach the principal or income held by the trustee and that the beneficiary shall not be able to assign any interest in the trust.

spot zoning—allowing individual variation in zoning.

stakeholder analysis—the term used when a decision maker views a problem from different perspectives and measures the impact of a decision on various groups.

stakeholders—those who have a stake, or interest, in the activities of a corporation; stakeholders include employees, members of the community in which the corporation operates, vendors, customers, and any others who are affected by the actions and decisions of the corporation.

stale check—a check whose date is longer than six months ago.

standby letter—letter of credit for a contractor ensuring he will complete the project as contracted.

stare decisis—"let the decision stand"; the principle that the decision of a court should serve as a guide or precedent and control the decision of a similar case in the future.

status quo ante—original positions of the parties.

statute of frauds—statute that, in order to prevent fraud through the use of perjured testimony, requires that certain kinds of transactions be evidenced in writing in order to be binding or enforceable.

statute of limitations—statute that restricts the period of time within which an action may be brought.

statutory law—legislative acts declaring, commanding, or prohibiting something.

stay of foreclosure—delay of foreclosure obtained by the mortgagor to prevent undue hardship.

stirpes—family lines; distribution per stirpes refers to the manner in which descendants take property by right of representation.

stock subscription—contract or agreement to buy a specific number and kind of shares when they are issued by the corporation.

stop payment order—order by a depositor to the bank to refuse to make payment of a check when presented for payment.

straight (or nonnegotiable) bill of lading—document of title that consigns transported goods to a named person.

strict liability—civil wrong for which there is absolute liability because of the inherent danger in the underlying activity, for example, the use of explosives.

strict tort liability—product liability theory that imposes liability upon the manufacturer, seller, or distributor of goods for harm caused by defective goods.

subject matter jurisdiction—judicial authority to hear a particular type of case.

sublease—a transfer of the premises by the lessee to a third person, the sublessee or subtenant, for a period of less than the term of the original lease.

sublessee—person with lease rights for a period of less than the term of the original lease; also known as *subtenant.*

subprime lending market—a credit market that makes loans to high-risk consumers (those who have bankruptcies, no credit history, or a poor credit history), often loaning money to pay off other debts the consumer has due.

subrogation—right of a party secondarily liable to stand in the place of the creditor after making payment to the creditor and to enforce the creditor's right against the party primarily liable in order to obtain indemnity from such primary party.

substantial impairment—material defect in a good.

substantial performance—equitable rule that if a good-faith attempt to perform does not precisely meet the terms of the agreement, the agreement will still be considered complete if the essential purpose of the contract is accomplished.

substantive law—the law that defines rights and liabilities.

substitute check—electronic image of a paper check that a bank can create and that has the same legal effect as the original instrument.

substitution—substitution of a new contract between the same parties.

sum certain—amount due under an instrument that can be computed from its face with only reference to interest rates.

summary jury trial—a mock or dry-run trial for parties to get a feel for how their cases will play to a jury.

summation—the attorney address that follows all the evidence presented in court and sums up a case and recommends a particular verdict be returned by the jury.

Superfund Amendment and Reauthorization Act—federal law that authorizes the EPA to collect cleanup costs from those responsible for the ownership, leasing, dumping, or security of hazardous waste sites.

Superfund sites—areas designated by the EPA for cleanup of hazardous waste.

surety—obligor of a suretyship; primarily liable for the debt or obligation of the principal debtor.

suretyship—undertaking to pay the debt or be liable for the default of another.

symbolic delivery—delivery of goods by delivery of the means of control, such as a key or a relevant document of title, such as a negotiable bill of lading; also called *constructive delivery.*

T

takeover laws—laws that guard against unfairness in corporate takeover situations.

tariff—(1) domestically—government-approved schedule of charges that may be made by a regulated business, such as a common carrier or warehouser; (2) internationally—tax imposed by a country on goods crossing its borders, without regard to whether the purpose is to raise revenue or to discourage the traffic in the taxed goods.

tax lien—lien on property by a government agency for nonpayment of taxes.

teller's check—draft drawn by a bank on another bank in which it has an account.

temporary insider—someone retained by a corporation for professional services on an as-needed basis, such as an attorney, accountant, or investment banker.

temporary nuisance—interference caused by a construction or a method of operation that can be remedied at a reasonable expense.

temporary perfection—perfection given for a limited period of time to creditors.

tenancy at sufferance—lease arrangement in which the tenant occupies the property at the discretion of the landlord.

tenancy at will—holding of land for an indefinite period that may be terminated at any time by the landlord or by the landlord and tenant acting together.

tenancy by entirety or tenancy by entireties—transfer of property to both husband and wife.

tenancy for years—tenancy for a fixed period of time, even though the time is less than a year.

tenancy in common—relationship that exists when two or more persons own undivided interests in property.

tenancy in partnership—ownership relationship that exists between partners under the Uniform Partnership Act.

tenant—one who holds or possesses real property by any kind of right or title; one who pays rent for the temporary use and occupation of another's real property under a lease.

tender—goods have arrived, are available for pickup, and buyer is notified.

term insurance—policy written for a specified number of years that terminates at the end of that period.

termination statement—document (record), which may be requested by a paid-up debtor, stating that a security interest is no longer claimed under the specified financing statement.

testamentary capacity—sufficient mental capacity to understand that a writing being executed is a will and what that entails.

testamentary intent—designed to take effect at death, as by disposing of property or appointing a personal representative.

testamentary trust—trust that becomes effective only when the settlor's will takes effect after death.

testate—condition of leaving a will upon death.

testate distribution—distribution of an estate in accordance with the will of the decedent.

testator, testatrix—man, woman who makes a will.

third-party beneficiary—third person whom the parties to a contract intend to benefit by the making of the contract and to confer upon such person the right to sue for breach of contract.

time draft—bill of exchange payable at a stated time after sight or at a definite time.

tippee—individual who receives information about a corporation from an insider or temporary insider.

tort—civil wrong that interferes with one's property or person.

Toxic Substances Control Act (TOSCA)—first federal law to control the manufacture, use, and disposal of toxic substances.

trade dress—product's total image including its overall packaging look.

trade libel—written defamation about a product or service.

trade name—name under which a business is carried on and, if fictitious, must be registered.

trade secret—any formula, device, or compilation of information that is used in one's business and is of such a nature that it provides an advantage over competitors who do not have the information.

trademark—mark that identifies a product.

transferee—buyer or vendee.

traveler's check—check that is payable on demand provided it is countersigned by the person whose specimen signature appears on the check.

treasury stock—corporate stock that the corporation has reacquired.

treble damages—three times the damages actually sustained.

trespass—an unauthorized action with respect to person or property.

trial *de novo*—a trial required to preserve the constitutional right to a jury trial by allowing an appeal to proceed as though there never had been any prior hearing or decision.

tripartite—three-part division (of government).

trust—transfer of property by one person to another with the understanding or declaration that such property be held for the benefit of another; the holding of property by the owner in trust for another, upon a declaration of trust, without a transfer to another person. (Parties—settlor, trustee, beneficiary)

trust agreement—instrument creating a trust; also called *deed of trust.*

trust corpus—fund or property that is transferred to the trustee or held by the settlor as the body or subject matter of the trust; also called *trust fund, trust estate, and trust res.*

trustee—party who has legal title to estate and manages it.

trustee in bankruptcy—impartial person elected to administer the debtor's estate.

trustor—donor or settlor who is the owner of property and creates a trust in the property.

tying—the anticompetitive practice of requiring buyers to purchase one product in order to get another.

U

ultra vires—act or contract that the corporation does not have authority to do or make.

unconscionable—unreasonable, not guided or restrained by conscience and often referring to a contract grossly unfair to one party because of the superior bargaining powers of the other party.

underwriter—insurer.

undisclosed principal—principal on whose behalf an agent acts without disclosing to the third person the fact of agency or the identity of the principal.

undue influence—influence that is asserted upon another person by one who dominates that person.

Uniform Probate Code (UPC)—uniform statute on wills and administration of estates.

Uniform Simultaneous Death Act—law providing that when survivorship cannot be established, the property of each person shall be disposed of as though he or she had survived the other.

unilateral contract—contract under which only one party makes a promise.

unincorporated association—combination of two or more persons for the furtherance of a common nonprofit purpose.

universal agent—agent authorized by the principal to do all acts that can lawfully be delegated to a representative.

universal defenses—defenses that are regarded as so basic that the social interest in preserving them outweighs the social interest of giving negotiable instruments the freely transferable qualities of money; accordingly, such defenses are given universal effect and may be raised against all holders.

USA Patriot Act—federal law that, among other things, imposes reporting requirements on banks.

usage of trade—language and customs of an industry.

usury—lending money at an interest rate that is higher than the maximum rate allowed by law.

uttering—crime of issuing or delivering a forged instrument to another person.

valid—legal.

valid contract—agreement that is binding and enforceable.

value—consideration or antecedent debt or security given in exchange for the transfer of a negotiable instrument or creation of a security interest.

variance—permission of a landowner to use the land in a specified manner that is inconsistent with the zoning ordinance.

vicarious liability—imposing liability for the fault of another.

void agreement—agreement that cannot be enforced.

voidable contract—agreement that is otherwise binding and enforceable but may be rejected at the option of one of the parties as the result of specific circumstances.

voidable title—title of goods that carries with it the contingency of an underlying problem.

***voir dire* examination**—the preliminary examination of a juror or a witness to ascertain fitness to act as such.

voluntary bankruptcy—proceeding in which the debtor files the petition for relief.

voting by proxy—authorizing someone else to vote the shares owned by the shareholder.

voting trust—transfer by two or more persons of their shares of stock of a corporation to a trustee who is to vote the shares and act for such shareholders.

waiver—release or relinquishment of a known right or objection.

warehouse—entity engaged in the business of storing the goods of others for compensation.

warehouse receipt—receipt issued by the warehouse for stored goods. Regulated by the UCC, which clothes the receipt with some degree of negotiability.

warrant—authorization via court order to search private property for tools or evidence of a crime.

warranty—promise either express or implied about the nature, quality, or performance of the goods.

warranty against encumbrances—warranty that there are no liens or other encumbrances to goods except those noted by seller.

warranty deed—deed by which the grantor conveys a specific estate or interest to the grantee and makes one or more of the covenants of title.

warranty of habitability—implied warranty that the leased property is fit for dwelling by tenants.

warranty of title—implied warranty that title to the goods is good and transfer is proper.

wasting assets corporation—corporation designed to exhaust or use up the assets of the corporation, such as by extracting oil, coal, iron, and other ores.

way of necessity—grantee's right to use land retained by the grantor for going to and from the conveyed land.

White-Collar Crime Penalty Enhancement Act of 2002—federal reforms passed as a result of the collapses of companies such as Enron; provides for longer sentences and higher fines for both executives and companies.

white-collar crimes—crimes that do not use nor threaten to use force or violence or do not cause injury to persons or property.

whole life insurance—ordinary life insurance providing lifetime insurance protection.

will—instrument executed with the formality required by law by which a person makes a disposition of his or her property to take effect upon death.

writ of *certiorari*—order by the U.S. Supreme Court granting a right of review by the court of a lower court decision.

wrongfully dishonored—error by a bank in refusing to pay a check.

zoning—restrictions imposed by government on the use of designated land to ensure an orderly physical development of the regulated area.

CASE INDEX

New cases to this edition are in cyan boldface. Opinion cases are in boldface type: cited cases are in Roman type.

(A)

B

(C)

(D)

G

(H)

(I)

(J)

(K)

(L)

(M)

(N)

(Q)

(R)

(S)

(T)

(U)

(V)

(W)

(Y)

(Z)

SUBJECT INDEX

A

(B)

D

(E)

F

G

H

(N)

Q

R

(S)

(U)

V

(W)

(X)

(Z)